TWENT
ED

KOVELS'
Antiques &
Collectibles
PRICE LIST

For the 1990 Market

ILLUSTRATED

Crown Publishers, Inc.
New York

BOOKS BY RALPH AND TERRY KOVEL

American Country Furniture 1780–1875
Dictionary of Marks — Pottery & Porcelain
Kovels' Advertising Collectibles Price List
Kovels' American Silver Marks
Kovels' Antiques & Collectibles Price List
Kovels' Book of Antique Labels
Kovels' Bottles Price List
Kovels' Collector's Guide to American Art Pottery
Kovels' Collectors' Source Book
Kovels' Depression Glass & American Dinnerware Price List
Kovels' Guide to Selling Your Antiques & Collectibles
Kovels' Illustrated Price Guide to Royal Doulton
Kovels' Know Your Antiques
Kovels' Know Your Collectibles
Kovels' New Dictionary of Marks — Pottery & Porcelain
Kovels' Organizer for Collectors
Kovels' Price Guide for Collector Plates, Figurines, Paperweights,
     and Other Limited Editions

Published by Crown Publishers, Inc., 201 East 50th Street,
New York, New York 10022
CROWN is a trademark of Crown Publishers, Inc.
Manufactured in the U.S.A.
Library of Congress Catalog Card Number: 83-643618

ISBN: 0-517-57331-8
10 9 8 7 6 5 4 3 2 1
First Edition

Dear Reader,

American furniture gained new status in 1989. Although prices for eighteenth-century furniture have been rising for many years, there were always pieces of European furniture that were more important and, therefore, more expensive. In June 1989, a six-shell desk and bookcase made about 1760 in Newport, Rhode Island, by John Goddard was sold at auction for the astounding price of $12.1 million. It broke the previous record of $2.7 million for an American piece and the $2.97 million record for any piece of furniture, a French table that had belonged to Marie Antoinette.

Once again "investment potential" is making headlines. Record prices are reported in newspapers and on TV because they are surprising to the non-collector. Those who follow the antiques market know dozens of records are set each year as collectors find new interests and as changing values of money, silver, and stocks influence prices.

Over the years we have read millions of prices and used thousands of pictures in *Kovels' Antiques & Collectibles Price List*. Prices listed here include a random selection of pieces offered for sale *this* year. We report on everyday antiques like pressed glass and oak furniture, exotic Tiffany and Lalique, and uncommon skorps and roemers. The smallest item is probably an earring, the largest a 10-foot-long seed counter. The least expensive is a 50-cent Strohs beer can; the most expensive a mahogany chest, made about 1775, for $9,900.

The book is changed slightly each year. Categories are added or omitted to make it easier for you to find your antiques. The book is kept about 800 pages long because it is written to go with you to sales. We try to have a balanced format--not too much glass, pottery, or collectibles, not too many items that sell for over $5,000. The prices are *from* the American market *for* the American market. No European sales are reported. We take the editorial privilege of not including any prices that seem to result from "auction fever."

Old *Kovels'* price books should be saved for reference, tax, and appraisal information. The index is so complete it amazes us. Use it often. An internal alphabetical index is also included. For example, there is a category for "celluloid." Most items will be found there, but if there is a toy made of celluloid, it will be listed under "toy" and also indexed under "celluloid."

All pictures and prices are new every year, except pictures that are pattern examples shown in "Depression glass" and "pressed glass." Pictured antiques are not museum pieces but items offered for sale.

The hints are set in easy-to-notice special type. Leaf through the book and learn how to wash porcelains, store textiles, guard against theft, and much more.

RECORD PRICES

The $12.1 million desk bookcase was not the only newsworthy piece of furniture. Mission style pieces, especially by Gustav Stickley, set record after record all year long. An oak and wrought iron sideboard, c. 1903, made for Stickley's own home, sold for $363,000; a Harvey Ellis-designed music cabinet for $46,750; an even-armed spindled settle for $49,500; a spindled cube settee for $27,500; a Harvey Ellis-designed high back inlaid armchair for $25,300; a Stickley Morris chair for $7,250; and a stool for $9,075. Other Mission pieces were also record-priced. An L. & J. G. spindle prairie settle, c. 1912, brought $93,500; a book table was $9,900, and a Limbert cut-out armchair sold at $3,520.

Shaker furniture also set records. A marked Shaker cherry stand, made in New Lebanon, New York, in 1837, sold for $154,000; a mustard-colored poplar tall chest, made about 1840 to 1850, sold for $99,000; and a maple production chair, Number 7, with walnut stain and taped seat from Mt. Lebanon, brought $4,675. Victorian was also popular. An armchair by John Henry Belter brought $28,600 and a carved rosewood and marble center table, made about 1850, brought $71,500. Another famous Victorian maker, Herter Brothers, also set records. An 1877 ebonized cherry library table that had been sold for $500 in 1942 sold in 1989 for $280,500. A Windsor settee, low back, brought $82,500.

For eight months the world record for a piece of furniture sold at auction was $2.97 million for Marie Antoinette's console table made in 1781. But the French lost the title to the $12.1 million American desk and bookcase in June. An English Queen Anne armchair also sold for $209,000 and a pair of George III library armchairs for $495,000. Furniture of the 1920s by name designers is still rising in price. A Pierre Legrain banquette of limed African oak and ebony brought $275,000; a cubist center table by Eyre de Lanux brought $71,500; and an Eileen Gray black lacquer screen set the record at $374,000.

Ceramics, espcially art pottery, continued to rise. A 17½-in. Teco vase made in 1903 auctioned for $34,100; two-color Grueby vase for $22,000; Rookwood iris glaze 14-inch vase decorated with flying geese, $23,000; Ohr red-glazed vase, $17,600; Fulper Vase-kraft black, blue, and green floor vase, $12,100; Newcomb vase with oaks and moon, $5,225; Van Briggle green matte vase with poppyseed pods, $4,180. Lesser known art potteries also did well. A Merrimac vase brought $4,675; North Dakota School of Mines, $2750; Walrath, $2,475; Walley, $1,670; Denver Denaura, $1,430; Wheatley, $2,200.

Other ceramic records include an English Liverpool jug decorated with the three-masted ship "Roxana of Boston" that sold for $18,700; Ming vase with copper-red decoration for $2,183,099; and a 1935 Hummel figurine, "Silent Night with Black Child," for $20,000.

Handel peacock lamps sold at several auctions this year--the record price: $22,550. A Limbert Mission-style lamp of copper with a scene of a Dutch boy in colored glass inserts brought a record $5,750.

Silver is always valuable. A lighthouse-shaped coffeepot and tray by Charles le Roux of New York, c. 1730, was auctioned for $308,000; a tankard by Jeremiah Dummer of Boston, c. 1690, for $137,000. But an inkstand made in 1729 by the English silversmith Paul de Lamerie was auctioned in London for $1,432,000. A pair of 1905 candlesticks by Jarvie of Chicago went for $31,900.

Collectors are interested in collectibles as well as decorative arts. A Wallace Nutting picture of fifteen cows by a stream brought $1,430, while a Currier print of "The Road-Winter" sold for $35,200. A sketch of Mickey Mouse by Walt Disney sold at a private sale for $110,000, while an animation cel of Donald Duck from a 1924 cartoon auctioned for $286,000. Elvis Presley's white one-piece stage suit, worn in 1972, auctioned at $47,762; and a dust pan made by the Shakers in 1860 was $4,180. A leather fire bucket picturing Mercury was $29,700, while a carousel animal, shaped like a rooster, brought $148,500.

If the $12.1 million desk and bookcase had not been the star of last year, it would have been toys. Several large, important collections were sold at sales and at auction; and prices skyrocketed for rarities. Records included a Freedman's mechanical bank for $250,000; Darky Watermelon bank, $245,000; Kenton cast iron horse-drawn double eagle chariot nodder for $45,000; Punch and Judy bell toy, $28,000; tin paddlewheel boat, "Niagara," $40,000; The Game of the Man in the Moon, a board game by McLoughlin Brothers, c. 1901, $5,060. Collectors also bid record highs and bought a celluloid key-wind Mickey and Pluto toy for $6,600, a 1930s Buck Rogers rocket ship toy for $2,500, and a Kammer & Reinhardt bisque character doll from Germany, circa 1909, $169,576.

Outdoor games also interest collectors today. A Philbrook and Paine trout reel sold for $20,900; an H. S. Gillum trout rod, $19,250; and a Lake Chautauqua, New York, fishing decoy, $6,325.

The prices in this book are reports of the general antiques market, not the record-setting examples. Each year every price in the book is new. We do *not* estimate or "update" prices. Prices are the actual asking price, although the buyer may have negotiated to a lower figure. No price is an estimate. *We do not ask dealers and writers to estimate prices.* Experience has shown that a collector of one type of antique is prejudiced in favor of that item, and prices are usually high or low, but rarely a true report. If a price range is given, it is because at least two identical items were offered for sale at different times. The computer records prices and prints the high and low figures. Price ranges are found only in categories like "pressed glass," where identical items can be identified. Some prices in *Kovels' Antiques & Collectibles Price List* may seem high and some may seem low because of regional variations. But each price is one you could have paid for the object.

If you are selling your collection, do *not* expect to get retail value unless you are a dealer. Wholesale prices for antiques are from 20 to 50 percent less than retail. Remember, the antiques dealer must make a profit or go out of business.

HOW TO USE THIS BOOK

There are a few rules for using this book. Each listing is arranged in the following manner: CATEGORY (such as pressed glass or furniture), OBJECT (such as vase), DESCRIPTION (as much information as possible about size, age, color, and pattern). Some types of glass are exceptions to this rule. These are listed CATEGORY, PATTERN, OBJECT, DESCRIPTION. All items are presumed to be in good condition, undamaged, unless otherwise noted.

Several special categories were formed to make a more sensible listing possible. "Kitchen" and "Tool" include special equipment. The casual collector might not know the proper name for an "adze" or "trephine," so we have created special categories. Masonic has been put into the larger category "Fraternal." New categories are "Head Vases" and "Salt & Pepper." The index can help you locate items.

Several idiosyncrasies of style appear because the book is printed by computer. Everything is listed according to the computer alphabetizing system. This means words such as "Mt." are alphabetized as "M-T," not as "M-O-U-N-T." All numerals are before all letters, thus 2 comes before Z. A quick glance will make this clear, as it is consistent throughout the book.

We made several editorial decisions. A bowl is a "bowl" and not a dish unless it is a special dish, such as a pickle dish. A butter dish is a "butter." A salt dish is called a "salt" to differentiate it from a saltshaker. It is always "sugar and creamer," never "creamer and sugar." Where one dimension is given, it is the height; or if the object is round, the dimension is the diameter. Height of a picture is listed before width. Glass is clear unless a color is indicated.

Every entry is listed alphabetically. The problem of language remains. Some antiques terms, like "Sheffield" or "snow baby," have two meanings. Be sure to read the paragraph headings to know the meaning used. All category headings are based on the language of the average person at an average show, and we use terms like "mud figures" even if not technically correct.

This book does not include price listings of fine art paintings, books, comic books, stamps, coins, and a few other special categories.

All pictures in *Kovels' Antiques & Collectibles Price List* are listed with the prices asked by the seller. "Illus" (illustrated on the page) is part of the description if a picture is shown.

There have been misinformed comments about how this book is written. We *do* use the computer. It alphabetizes, ranges prices, sets type, and does other time-consuming jobs. Because of the computer, the book can be produced quickly. The last entries are added in June; the book is available in October. This is six months faster than would be possible any other way. But it is human help that finds prices and checks accuracy. We read everything at least twice, sometimes more. We edit from 100,000 entries to the 50,000 entries found here. We correct spelling, remove incorrect data, write category headings, and decide on new categories. We sometimes make errors.

Prices are reports from all parts of the United States and Canada (translated to U.S. dollars) between June 1988 and June 1989. A few prices are from auctions, most are from shops and shows. Every price is checked for accuracy, but we are not responsible for errors.

It is unprofessional for an appraiser to set a value for an unseen item. Because of this we cannot answer your letters asking for specific price information. But please write if you have any requests for categories to be included in future editions.

When you see us at the shows, stop and say hello. Since our television show has been on stations in all parts of the country, we find we can no longer be anonymous buyers. It may mean the dealers know us before we ask a price, but it has been wonderful to meet all of you. Don't be surprised if we ask for your suggestions for the next edition of *Kovels' Antiques & Collectibles Price List*. Or you can write us at P.O. Box 22200, Beachwood, Ohio 44122.

Ralph & Terry Kovel
Senior Members, American Society of Appraisers
June 1989

ACKNOWLEDGMENTS

Special thanks should go to those who helped us with pictures and deeds: Della Graham (Neal Alford), David & Linda Arman, Noel Barrett, B. O'Rourke (Belleek, Ireland), Bill Bertoia, Claudia Bourne (Richard A. Bourne Co. Inc.), Lynn Geyer (The Brewery), Alexandra Destler (Butterfield & Butterfield), Roberta Maneker (Christie's), Bethe Goldberg (Christie's East), Michael DeFina, Garth Auctions, Barbara Mintz (Guernseys), Jim Hagenbuch (The Glassworks), Morton M. Goldberg Auction Gallery, Gene Harris, Inc., Hart Galleries, Willis Henry Auctions, Leslie Hindman, Tony Hyman, Michael Ivankovich, James D. Julia, Richard W. Oliver, Richard Opfer, Phillips, David Rago, Lloyd Ralston, Brian Riba, Alicia Gordon and Sarah Hamill (Skinner, Inc.), Wolfgang Schmidt, Sotheby's, Theriault's, Don Treadway, Rachel Davis (Wolf's), and Woody Auction Company. Lee Markley has once again made suggestions for the carnival glass problems.

To the others in the antiques trade who knowingly or unknowingly contributed prices or pictures to this book, we say "Thank You!" We cannot do it without you. Some of you are: The Ahlfelds, American Clay Exchange, American Pin Collection, Americana, Antique Bottle

& Glass Collector, M. A. Arnold Collectibles, Art 'N' Things, The Autograph Alcove, Robin Bellamy, Benedict J. Blachowicz, Mary Brougham, Caddo Trading Company, Inc., Steven and Kathy Chittick, Cibola Traders, Pat & Ed Coggins, Country Accessories, Robert Crooker (Mouse Man Ink), D & M Collectibles, Darbys, Craig Dinner (Antique Search & Research, Inc.), Jeannine Dobbs, The Duke, DuMouchelles Art Galleries Co., Robert C. Eldred Co., Inc., Fenner's Antiques, Madeleine Fortunoff Fine Prints, Garth's Auctions, Inc., Leigh R. Giarde (Time Travelers), Robert P. Hanafee, Katherine Hansard, Stan & Peggy Hecker, Gary Hendershott, Holiday Antiques, Stephanie Horvath, Judith A. Huber, Norman Huczek, Timothy Hughes (Rare & Early Newspapers), Intercol London Limited, International Petroliana Collectors Association, Klingenberg's, Robert Laferriere, William Linehan Autographs, Lithophane Collectors' Club, Lyons Ltd. Antique Prints, The Manion's International Auction House Inc., M. Margulies, Mike's General Store, Miscellaneous Man, Eileen Mosteller (Dollworks), The Mystic Light of the Aladdin Knights, National Toothpick Holder Collectors Society, Scott H. Nelson, Old Glory Antiques and Objets D'Art, Old Storefront Antiques, Marion L. Paltz, Pen Fancier's Magazine, Betty Petzoldt, Phoenix Bird Discoveries, The Political Bandwagon, Postcard Collector, Powder Puff, Q's Country Shoppe, R. Neil Reynolds (Vintage Posters & Graphics), Riba Auctions Inc., Kenneth E. Schneringer, Ruth B. Schowalter, Jack Seiderman, George Shaw, Shawnee Pottery, The Snoopy Trader, Something to Appreciate, Stebbins Antiques, Collectibles & Crafts, Jim Swank, Team Antiques, Eva G. Thompson, Tool Ads, The Union, Leni Vargo, Charlie Weatherbee, Mary and Palmer Welch, Larry D. Wells, Whirligig Antiques, Wicker Basket, Willow Hollow, Tom Witte's Antiques, J.L. Young.

MORE ANTIQUE PRICE NEWS

Each year *Kovels' Antiques & Collectibles Price List* is completely rewritten. Every entry is new because of the changing antiques market. Many collectors need more current information about prices, trends, and sales. We have been writing a monthly newsletter, *Kovels on Antiques and Collectibles* for the collector and investor for fifteen years. Our newsletter includes reviews of price books, information about what to buy and sell, tips on refinishing, and articles on marks, fakes, and more. It is a 12-page, picture-filled newsletter about antiques that interest the collector and dealer. For more information about *Kovels on Antiques and Collectibles*, send a stamped, self-addressed envelope to Kovels, P.O. Box 22200-K, Beachwood, Ohio 44122.

Our new TV series, "The Collectors Journal," will start in January on the Discovery Channel. The show includes news, prices, and information. Watch us to see collectors and collections.

Almaric Walter made pate–de–verre glass under contract at the
Daum glassworks from 1908 to 1914. He started his own firm in
Nancy, France, in 1919. Pieces made before 1914 are signed "Daum,
Nancy" with a cross. After 1919 the signature is "A. Walter Nancy."

A.WALTER, Bowl, Berry–Laden Branches, Signed, C.1925, 4 3/4 In.	3850.00
Dish, Arrowroot Blossoms, Snail End, C.1925, 6 1/4 In.	3850.00
Dish, Bumblebee, Signed, C.1925, 6 5/8 In.	3025.00
Dish, Face of Bacchus, Center, Yellow, Pate–De–Verre, 6 1/2 In.	2650.00
Dish, Flying Fish, Seaweed Ground, Signed, C.1925, 6 3/8 In.	4500.00
Dish, Green & Black Reptile On Side, Signed, C.1925, 4 1/2 In.	7150.00
Paperweight, Reptile, Streaked Ground, Signed, C.1920, 1 3/4 In.	2200.00
Paperweight, Snail, Dragging Shell, Signed, C.1920, 3 In.	3575.00

ABC plates, or children's alphabet plates, were most popular from
1780 to 1860, but are still being made. The letters on the plate were
meant as teaching aids for children learning to read. The plates were
made of pottery, porcelain, metal, or glass.

ABC, Dish, Baby Feeder, Hungry Piggy	26.00
Dish, Divided, Pink, Hankscraft	10.00
Mug, Little Jack Horner, Brown Transfer, Staffordshire, 2 3/4 In.	80.00
Mush Set, Border of Cobalt Blue Letters, Animals, Germany	70.00
Plate & Mug, Nursery Rhymes, Humpty Dumpty, Sectioned Plate	85.00
Plate, Alphabet, Months of Year, Days of Week, 7 In.	40.00
Plate, Boy, Girl, Campbell Kids	47.00
Plate, Boys Playing Baseball, Multicolored	42.00
Plate, Boys Playing Cricket, Embossed Letters, 7 In.	55.00
Plate, Brownie Copyright, 1906, 5 1/4 In.	95.00
Plate, Campbell Kids, Drayton	75.00
Plate, Chickens, No Easter Without Us, Milk Glass, 6 1/4 In.	55.00
Plate, Cricket Game, Staffordshire, 7 1/2 In.	125.00
Plate, Crying Girl With Dog, Holdfast	78.00
Plate, Desert Scene, Arabs, Horses, 6 3/4 In.	35.00
Plate, Dogs, Glass	15.00
Plate, Evening Bathing Scene At Manhattan Beach, Polychrome, 7 1/2 In.	85.00
Plate, Gathering Cotton, Black Family Center, Staffordshire, 5 1/2 In.	195.00
Plate, Girl On Swing, Alphabet Around Rim, Painted Tin, 3 In.	25.00
Plate, Hickory Dickory Dock, Rolled Edge, Tin	80.00
Plate, Humorous, Man Sliding Down A Hill, Staffordshire	55.00
Plate, Independence Hall, Alphabet Border, Dated 1776–1876	125.00
Plate, Indian Center, Wagons & Cavalcade, 7 1/2 In.	55.00
Plate, Little Boy Blue, With Horn & Sheep, Staffordshire, 7 1/4 In.	35.00
Plate, Little Girl Holding Doll & Crying, Adults, 5 3/8 In.	130.00
Plate, Little Girl On Tiptoes To Reach Piano, 7 In.	125.00
Plate, Man On Horse Center, Sir Colin Campbell, Tin, 4 1/4 In.	195.00
Plate, Milkmaid With Cows, Raised Alphabet, Staffordshire, 5 In.	110.00
Plate, Mother, Baby In Cradle, Angels, Staffordshire, 5 In.	125.00
Plate, Mr.& Mrs. Rabbit, Wreath of Hand Signals, Aynsley, 6 1/4 In.	150.00
Plate, Niagara Falls Scene, 7 1/2 In.	85.00
Plate, Punch & Judy, Allerton, 5 1/2 In.	30.00
Plate, Raggedy Ann, 1941	32.50
Plate, Riddle, Black People, Answer On Back, Staffordshire, 5 In.	225.00
Plate, Robinson Crusoe On Raft	140.00
Plate, Robinson Crusoe Scenes, England, 7 1/4 In. ....*Illus*	165.00
Plate, Seated Women With Pottery, Alphabet Border, Staffordshire, 7 In.	125.00
Plate, Sign Language, Dutch Children & Goose, 6 1/4 In.	95.00
Plate, Silks & Satins, Put Out Kitchen Fire, Staffordshire, 7 In.	125.00
Plate, Sioux Indian Chief, Brown Transfer, England, 6 3/4 In.	85.00
Plate, Stable Yard, Pony, Horse & Barn, 8 In.	135.00
Plate, Their First Day, Hotel China	50.00
Plate, Thousand Eye, Clock Center, Glass	50.00
Plate, Train Center, Coal Burning	125.00
Plate, Uncle Tom's Cabin, Pottery, 8 In. ....*Illus*	77.00
Plate, Wild Animals, Elephant, Pottery, 7 1/4 In. ....*Illus*	110.00

ABC, Plate, Uncle Tom's Cabin, Pottery, 8 In.   ABC, Plate, Wild Animals, Elephant, Pottery, 7 1/4 In.   ABC, Plate, Robinson Crusoe Scenes, England, 7 1/4 In.

Plate, Woman & Man, Strolling Through Park, Sayings 200.00

Abingdon Pottery was established in 1934 by Raymond E. Bidwell as the Abingdon Sanitary Manufacturing Company. The company made art pottery and other wares. Sixteen varieties of cookie jars are known. The factory ceased production of art pottery in 1950.

ABINGDON, Bookends, Horsehead, White 40.00
Cookie Jar, 3 Bears 40.00
Cookie Jar, Clock 45.00
Cookie Jar, Granny 90.00
Cookie Jar, Mammy 110.00
Cookie Jar, Mary Had A Little Lamb 170.00
Cookie Jar, Money Bag, White, Pink Knob, Cover 45.00
Cookie Jar, Pineapple .... 45.00 To 65.00
Cookie Jar, Train .... 55.00 To 65.00
Figurine, Duck, Pink, 4 In. 25.00
Figurine, Heron, White 25.00
Figurine, Kneeling Nude, Yellow, Gold Trim, Decal 195.00
Figurine, Peacock 18.50
Flowerpot, Cattail 10.00
Lamp, Carriage, Green 60.00
Planter, Bow, White 9.50
Planter, Mexican Boy 15.50
Planter, Star, White 6.00
Salt & Pepper, Figural, Elsie & Elmer 45.00
Salt & Pepper, Humpty Dumpty 45.00
Salt & Pepper, Raggedy Ann & Andy, Large 18.00
Tile, Coolie & Geisha, Glossy Blue, Paper Label, Pair 70.00
Vase, Blue, White, Label, No.517, 8 In. 25.00
Vase, Cornucopia, White Underglaze Flowers, Blue 9.00
Vase, Daisies, 9 In. 26.50
Vase, Fish, Pink, 5 In. 14.00
Vase, Morning Glory, 8 In. 17.00
Vase, Raised Blue Flying Bird, White Ground, 7 In. 20.00
Vase, Silver Deposit Design, Deer, Trees, Silver Handles, 8 3/4 In. 100.00
Wall Pocket, Lily 28.00

Adams china was made by William Adams and Sons of Staffordshire, England. The firm was founded in 1769 and is still working. All types of tablewares and useful wares have been made through the years. Other pieces of Adams will be found listed under Flow Blue.

ADAMS, Hatpin Holder, Grecian Figures, Blue 175.00
Plate, Mt. Washington Steamer, Blue & White, 8 In. 30.00
Teapot, Walrus Design 75.00
Tray, Art Deco, 8 X 20 In. 165.00

The old country store with the crackers in a barrel and a potbellied stove is a symbol of an earlier, less hectic time. The advertisements, containers, and products sold in these stores are now all collectibles. We have tried to list items in the logical places, so large store fixtures will be found under the Architectural category, enameled tin dishes under Graniteware, etc. Listed here are many of the advertising items. Other similar pieces may be found under the product name such as Planters Peanuts.

ADVERTISING, see also Paper

ADVERTISING, Album, Card Set, 50 Hollywood Stars, Player's Cigarettes, 1933	78.00
Apron, Carpenter's, White Canvas, Rubberoid Roofing–Shingles	50.00
Ashtray, A.Coors Co., Golden Colo., Ceramic, Holder, 6 In.	27.00
Ashtray, Atlas Beer, Shape of Monkey, White Porcelain	20.00
Ashtray, Buick Car, Metal, 1943	10.00
Ashtray, Firestone Tire, Amber Glass, 1936 Texas Centennial	75.00
Ashtray, Firestone Transport Tire, Glass Insert	10.00
Ashtray, Goodrich Rubber Tire, Silvertown, Green Glass Insert	10.00
Ashtray, Goodyear Rubber Tire, Glass Insert, Richmond, Ind.	7.00
Ashtray, Kelly Heavy–Duty Tire, Glass Insert	25.00
Ashtray, LaFendrich, Bronze, 100th Anniversary, 1850–1950	18.00
Ashtray, Lowell Cold Cream, Cobalt Blue Glass	15.00
Ashtray, Michelin Man, Bakelite	65.00 To 75.00
Ashtray, Michelin Tire	25.00
Ashtray, Miller's Mutual, Brass, 75th Anniversary, 1877–1952	9.00
Ashtray, Mohawk Tire Co., Glass Insert	18.00
Ashtray, Mountain States Telephone, Porcelain	85.00
Ashtray, Paperweight, Security Nat'l Bank, Brown, 5 X 3 In.	15.00
Ashtray, U.S.Tires Are Good Tires, Different Styles of Tread	35.00
Ashtray, Winston Cigarettes, Tin	1.00
Badge, Tony The Tiger, Astronaut Figure, 1960s, 1 1/4 In.	4.00
Bag, Arthur Godfrey, 1940s, Radio Show Souvenir	20.00
Bag, Feed Sack, Old Black Joe	15.00
Bag, Franklin Cane Sugar, Contents, Paper, 10 Lbs.	22.00
Bag, Moxie, Paper, Frank Archer, Copyright 1932	25.00
Bag, Purina, Clothespin	20.00
Banner, Cow–Ease, Allen's Foot Ease, Cloth, 20 X 32 In.	70.00
Banner, Dr. A.C. Daniels Horse Renovator, Cloth, 24 X 12 In.	75.00
Banner, I'd Walk A Mile For A Camel, 94 X 44 In.	125.00
Banner, Prince Albert Tobacco, Cloth–Like, 96 X 44 In.	100.00
Banner, Remington, Silk, Fringe, 20 X 30 In.	88.00
Banner, Sweet Caporal, Canvas, 3 X 5 Ft.	22.00
Banner, Winchester Ammunition, Cloth, 21 X 29 In.	95.00
Barrel, Coffee, Our Breakfast, Factory On Lid, 34 X 22 In.	75.00
Barrel, Gun Powder, E.I.Dupont DeNemours, Dogs On Lid	140.00
Baseball Bat, Mages Sport Store, Grand Opening, C.1930, 19 In.	40.00
Baseball Bat, Mountain Dew	45.00
Beaker, Nestle, Etched	20.00
Beanie, I Can Yo–Yo, Can You?, Duncan, White, Triangles	35.00
Beer Foam Scraper, Pickwick Ale, White Plastic, 8 3/4 In.	12.00
Belt, Hamm's, Leather, Stamped Bear & Hamm's Scenes, Size 34–36	35.00
Bill Hook, Red Goose Shoes, Dated 1949	8.50
Bin, A & P Coffee, No.10, Red, Slant Top	495.00
Bin, A & P Coffee, Original Decals, 8 X 10 In.	375.00
Bin, Beechnut Tobacco, Slant Front, Green	110.00 To 195.00
Bin, Cadillac Tobacco	750.00
Bin, Dunham's Coconut, Monkeys In Trees, Countertop, Rolltop	725.00
Bin, Ginger, Far Eastern Lady, Gina, 1900, 10 X 7 X 6 In.	120.00
Bin, Grain, Neal's, Corn & Oats, Blue–Green	1350.00
Bin, Parke–Davis Botanic Drug	40.00
Bin, Perfection Java Coffee, Lift Top, Whitehead & Turner, 1900	130.00
Bin, Plow Boy Tobacco	1100.00
Bin, Red Band Tobacco	475.00
Bin, Tiger Tobacco, Cylinder	1150.00

Advertising, Box, Cigar, Dark Horse,
Wooden Cigar, With Prizes

Advertising, Tin,
Japanese, Potpourri,
Somers, 4 1/2 In.

Advertising, Toy, Pop, Kelloggs,
Rubber, 7 1/2 In.

Bin, Uncle Sam's Coffee, Thomas Wood & Co., 50 Lb.	190.00
Blotter, Bovinine, Prepared By Cold Process, 1902–03	8.00
Blotter, Burroughs Typewriters, Adding Machine, 1930, 3 X 6 In.	4.50
Blotter, Coolerator Ice Box, Wisconsin Ice, 1930, 3 1/2 X 6 In.	4.50
Blotter, Duffy's Pure Malt Whiskey, Unused	3.50
Blotter, DuPont, Blue, Shows Blasting Powder	10.00
Blotter, Goodrich Rubber Tennis Shoe, Kids Playing Ball, 1920s	9.00
Blotter, Green River Whiskey	28.00
Blotter, Smith Brothers, 1905	10.00
Blotter, Texaco, Rectangular Green Oil Can Picture	2.25
Blotter, Turck's Compound Emulsion, Early 1900s	15.00
Blotter, Vitale Fireworks Mfg. Co.	35.00
Blotter, Wilsom Hammell, Flappers Picture, 1920s, 4 X 9 In.	6.50
ADVERTISING, BOOK, see Paper, Book	
Booklet, Alka–Seltzer, Our Presidents, To FDR, 1933, 5 X 6 In.	6.00
Booklet, Arm & Hammer, 1939	3.50
Booklet, Carters Little Liver Pills, Early 1900s	12.00
Booklet, Chase & Sanborn, History of Our American Flags, 1898	7.50
Booklet, Comic, Schwinn Bicycles, 1958	10.00
Booklet, Jello, Parrish, 1924	40.00
Booklet, Kellogg Company, Kinkey Dog, Cloth Cutout	35.00
Bookmark, Anglus Marshmallow	18.00
Bootjack, Mussleman's Plug Tobacco, Cast Iron	145.00
ADVERTISING, BOTTLE, see Bottle	
ADVERTISING, BOTTLE OPENER, see Bottle Opener	
Bowl, Ralston Purina, Find The Bottom, Rabbit, Blue, 6·1/8 In.	45.00
ADVERTISING, BOX, see also Box	
Box, Aunt Sally Brand Oats, 9 1/2 X 5 In.	10.00
Box, Bing Crosby Ice Cream, Dated 1953	2.25
Box, Bobby Pin, Gayla	3.00
Box, Boston Cigarette Tobacco, Quebec, 1936, Cardboard, 1/2 Lb.	5.00
Box, Cigar, Dark Horse, Wooden Cigar, With Prizes ....*Illus*	85.00

Box, Cigar, Golden Brown Panatelas, Wood, Hinged, 6 X 6 In. 40.00
Box, Clark Candy Bar, Holds 24 Bars, 1950s, 9 1/2 X 8 1/2 In. 12.00
Box, Codfish, Dovetailed Wood, Slide Cover, Letters, 6 X 4 In. 3.25
Box, Cracker, National Biscuit Co., Tin, Hinged, 7 X 10 In. 40.00
Box, Delivery, General Baking Co., Wooden, Handles, 18 X 26 In. 50.00
Box, Display, Hop Plaster, Soothing, Pain Killing, 6 X 9 In. 25.00
Box, Draft Cream Cheese, Open Top, Wooden, 3 Lb. 2.00
Box, DuPont Dynamite, Dovetailed Wood 5.00
Box, Eatmore Cranberry, Wooden 15.00
Box, El Verso Cigars, 39 In Box 30.00
Box, Enzo Gelantine, Picture Glider Plane, Contents, 26 In. 10.00
Box, Fairy Christmas Box, Fairbank's Fairy Soap, 16 X 17 In. 115.00
Box, Gold Dust Twins, 1930s, Contents, 5 Oz. 12.50
Box, Heinz Ketchup 13.00
Box, Hills Bros.Candied Peels, Wooden, 10 Lb. 30.00
Box, Jell–O, Wooden, 14 X 7 3/4 X 8 In. 45.00
Box, Kotex Sanitary Napkin 7.50
Box, Kraft Pimento, Green Design, Wood, Red Ends, 5 Lbs. 5.00
Box, Kraft Swiss Process Cheese, 9 X 3 X 2 1/2 In. 2.00
Box, Little Fairies' Baking Powder, Cardboard, Round, 15 Oz. 20.00
Box, Log, Chocolate, Redwood Bear, Carved, Slide Top, 19 In. 495.00
Box, Marsh Wheeling Mountaineers Cigars, 83 In Box 55.00
Box, Matches, Hamm's Beer, Wooden, 1930s, 1/2 X 1/2 X 2 In. 2.50
Box, Murad 20's 15.00
Box, National Biscuit Co., Brass, Glass Door, 1920s, 10 1/2 In. 30.00
Box, Norwine Coffee, Wooden, Round, 100 Lbs. 200.00
Box, Our Mother's Cocoa, 2 Lb. 37.50
Box, Patent Polish, Wm.F.Pratt, Bentwood, 1860, 2 1/2 In. 4.00
Box, Penn's Spells Quality, Pencil Tip Wide Hole Side, 6 In. 25.00
Box, Philips Choice Vegetable Seeds, Pa., 4 X 19 X 9 In. 300.00
Box, Seed, Hiram Sibley 275.00
Box, Seed, Printed Labels, Lewis Atwood & Son., Pine, 9 X 21 In. 175.00
Box, Smokey, The Bear Animal Cookies, Figural Fire Truck 50.00
Bracelet, Columbia Records, 1940 .... 15.00
Bracelet, Red Comet Fire Extinguisher 27.50
Brooch, Cameo, Scarlett, Lux Soap, Sept.1940, With Ad 200.00
Cabinet, Beech–Nut Gum, Stand–Up, Flip Cover, 4 Shelves, Tin 550.00
Cabinet, Diamond Dye, Children Jumping Rope, 25 X 15 In. 975.00
Cabinet, Diamond Dye, Court Jester, 1905, 30 X 21 X 8 3/4 In. 650.00
Cabinet, Diamond Dye, Girls In A Yard With Ribbons 1650.00
Cabinet, Diamond Dye, Governess, Tin, Wood, 1905, 30 X 21 In. 400.00
Cabinet, Diamond Dye, Mansion, 1905, 24 X 15 X 8 In. 500.00
Cabinet, Diamond Dye, Petal Picture Sign Front, Wooden, 27 In. 650.00
Cabinet, Dr. Claris Veterinary, Oak, Glass Door, 1900 .... 160.00
Cabinet, Dr.Daniel's Veterinary, Tin Front 1150.00
Cabinet, Drake's Cakes & Pastry, 15 X 13 X 15 In. 225.00
Cabinet, P. Lorillar & Co., Tobacco, 2 Glass Doors, 4 Panels 3300.00
Cabinet, Putnam Dye, Men On Horseback, Metal 125.00
Cabinet, Rainbow Dye, Double Sided, Domed Top, 19 X 12 X 6 In. 225.00
Cabinet, Rainbow Dyes, Dome Top, 1915, 19 X 12 X 6 In. 225.00
Cabinet, Rit Dye, Double Slant Top, 6 Wooden Drawers In Back 295.00
Cabinet, Rit Dye, Metal, Concave, 18 X 21 In. 150.00
Cabinet, Sauer's Extracts, Wooden, 1910, 25 X 11 X 7 In. 150.00
Cabinet, Spool, Brainard & Armstrong, 36 Drawers 1000.00
Cabinet, Spool, Glass Lift Top, Stenciled Spencerian, 2 Drawers 160.00
Cabinet, Spool, J & P Coats, Etched Spools 2000.00
Cabinet, Spool, J & P Coats, Oak, Roll Up, 25 X 31 X 11 In. 750.00
Cabinet, Spool, J & P Coats, Wooden 1200.00
Cabinet, Spool, Richardson Silk, 6 Drawers, Glass Fronts, Oak 495.00
Cabinet, Spool, Richardson Silk, 6 Drawers, Oak, Brass Hardware 495.00
Can Opener, Pet Milk, Chromed Tin, 2 Spikes In Round Lid 3.25
Can, Mona Motor Oil, 1/2 Gal. 200.00
Can, United Airlines Pennzoil Oil, Airplane, 1940–41, 1 Qt. 14.00
Candy Dish, Pickering's Furniture, Carpets, Glass, Handle 35.00

Candy Jar, Antoine Drops 35.00
ADVERTISING, CANISTER, see Advertising, Tin
Case, California Fruit & Pepsin Chewing Gum, Counter 450.00
Case, Display, Eveready–Mazda Light Bulbs, 3 Drawers, 1920s 65.00
Case, Display, Howard Cutlery, Glass Sides, 3 Round Shelves 375.00
Chair, Coors Beer 155.00
Chalkboard, 7–Up, Tin 30.00
ADVERTISING, CHANGE RECEIVER, see also Advertising, Tip Tray
Change Receiver, Cuticura, Glass 35.00
Change Receiver, Kool Cigarettes, Rubber, Green 5.50
Charm, Setter, Off–White, Schenley's, Old Quaker, 3/4 In. 8.00
Cigarette Case, Camel, Enameled 185.00
Clicker, Real–Kill Bug Killer 18.00
Clip, Pencil, Borden's, Drive Carefully 3.00
Clipboard, Monsanto Chemical Co., Brass, Small 8.00
Clothespin Bag, Big Jo Flour 7.00
Clothespin Bag, Purina 12.00
Clothespin, Wooden, Diamond Match Co., Box, 24 Piece 15.00
Coaster, Beer, Drewey, Shield Shape, Canadian Mountie 2.00
Coaster, Malt City, Red, Blue, 4 1/4 In., Pair 16.00
Coaster, Trommer's Beer, Square, Set of 10 .... 28.00
ADVERTISING, COFFEE GRINDER, see Coffee Grinder
Coin Purse, Schlitz Bar 25.00
Cookie Cutter, Robin Hood Flour, Characters From Movie 5.00
Cooler, Ice Cold Moxie, Moxie Nerve Food, 35 In. 250.00
Cooler, Moxie Bottle, Ice Cold Moxie, Boston & New York, 35 In. 250.00
Crate, DeLaval Separator 5.00
Cream Separator, DeLaval, With Shipping Case 80.00
Creamer, Child's, Pressed Glass, Post Cereals, 2 3/4 In. 24.00
Creamer, Meadow Gold 9.00
Creamer, Sanitary Milk Company, Canton 12.00
Creamer, Union Leader 175.00
Cup & Saucer, Greyhound, Syracuse China 5.00
Cup & Saucer, Kent Cigarettes, Royal Crown China, Demitasse 35.00
Cup, Figural Man, Quaker Oats 14.00
Cup, Folding, Big Jo Flour 10.00
Cup, Measuring, Kelloggs, 3 Spout, Green 16.50
Cup, Measuring, Maytag, Metal .... 15.00 To 17.00
Cup, Paper, Heinz, Pickle Picture, Salesman's 15.00
Cup, Pillsbury Doughboy 10.50
Custard Cup, Atlas, Clear 2.00
Dish, Baker, Tuna, Chicken of The Sea, Pottery, Cover 12.00
Dish, Elsie, Ice Cream 8.00
Dish, Sundae, Fountain, House of David, Benton Harbor, 6 Piece 49.00
Dispenser, 5–Cent Safe–T–Cone, Plastic 35.00
Dispenser, Cherry Cheer, 5 Cent, Patent 1886 .... 375.00
Dispenser, Cherry Fizz 9000.00
Dispenser, Cherry Smash, 5 Cent Glass, Porcelain Pump, 11 In. 2600.00
Dispenser, Christo Ginger Ale, Barrel Shape 1250.00
Dispenser, Citro, The Thirst Quencher, Barrel Shape 950.00
Dispenser, Cold Fudge, Stoneware, Johnson 150.00
Dispenser, Dad's Old Fashioned Root Beer, Bronze Feet 250.00
Dispenser, Dr Pepper's Phos–Ferrates, White Ceramic Tank 9900.00
Dispenser, Fan–Jaz Drink 5 Cents 2750.00
Dispenser, Fowlers Cherry Smash 1400.00
Dispenser, Green River, Pottery 135.00
Dispenser, Hires Root Beer, Spigot, 1920 .... 800.00
Dispenser, Howell's Orange Julep Syrup, Round 750.00
Dispenser, Ice Cream Cups, Nickel Plated, 1923, 7 1/2 X 6 In. 110.00
Dispenser, Jersey–Creme, Red & Gold Lettering, Pump, 1920 .... 1200.00
Dispenser, Kara–Van Iced Tea, Barrel Shape 35.00
Dispenser, Lemon Crush Syrup, 1910 .... 300.00
Dispenser, Needle & Shuttle, Boye 27.50
Dispenser, Orange Crush 290.00

Dispenser, Robinson Crusoe, Salted Peanuts, Counter 295.00
Dispenser, Sweet Chocolate, 1920, 17 X 2 In. 150.00
Dispenser, Wheat–Kist Nuts, Square 80.00
Display Basket, Kool, Embossed Penguin, Tin 25.00
Display Case, Esterbrook Drawlet Pen, Glass Lift Top, 1 Drawer 25.00
Display Case, Eversharp Pen, Etched Glass, 15 1/2 X 8 1/2 In. 100.00
Display, Adams California Fruit Gum, 1917, 6 X 4 X 6 In. 160.00
Display, Bar Holder, Swizzle Stick, Rheingold Beer, Chrome 20.00
Display, Hood's Sarsaparilla, Stand Up, Counter, 19 X 14 In. 280.00
Display, Ice Cream Cone, Dairy Queen, Papier–Mache, 25 In. 145.00
Display, Johnson & Johnson Medicated Plasters, Metal, Counter 125.00
Display, Johnson & Johnson, Corn Plasters, Bunion Pads, Tin 300.00
Display, Shelf, Furniture Polish, Wood, 20 X 15 X 8 1/2 In. 375.00
Display, SS United States World's Fastest Liner, 42 X 43 In. 175.00
Display, Sunbeam Toaster, Toast Moves Up & Down, 22 In. 375.00
Display, Twinkie Store, Electro–Mechanical, Clown, 19 X 12 In. 295.00
Door Plate, Junge's Bread, Porcelain, 1930s 30.00
Door Push, Camel Cigarettes, Dancing Pack, Girl's Legs, Tin 45.00
Door Push, Door, 7–Up 55.00
Door Push, Foss' Extracts, Porcelain 85.00
Door Push, Katz Brothers Burton Brewing, Reverse Glass, 10 In. 93.00
Door Push, Nochol Kola, Tin, 1930s 30.00
Earrings, Reddy Kilowatt 16.00
Emblem, John Deere, Plow & Deer In Circle, Iron, 17 X 14 In. 60.00
Eye Shade, Gambler's, Schells Deer Brand Beer, Green 12.00
　ADVERTISING, FAN, see Fan, Advertising
Figure, Anvil Overalls, Hard To Beat, High Point, N.C. 35.00
Figure, Blatz, Barrel Man, Pot Metal, 12 X 16 In. 25.00
Figure, Dog, Bucki Carbons Ribbons, Iron, 1 Ear Cocked Up, 2 In. 15.00
Figure, Dog, Nipper, Papier–Mache, 35 1/2 In. 800.00
Figure, Dog, RCA Victor, Papier–Mache, White, Black Paint, 11 In. 145.00
Figure, Dr.Kool, 4 In. 35.00
Figure, Eagle, On Globe, J.I.Case Threshing Machine, Iron, 4 Ft. 3800.00
Figure, Miss Curity, 21 In. 125.00
Figure, Old Crow Whiskey, Papier–Mache, 29 In. 395.00
Figure, Red Goose Shoes, Goose On Box Gave Free Eggs, Vinyl 150.00
Figure, Shoe, Lady's High Button, Tongue Out, Zinc, 9 1/2 In. 260.00
Figure, Teacher's Scotch, Cap & Gown 16.00
Figure, Tin Man, Made From Furnace Heating Parts, Life Size 1800.00
Flashlight, Schlitz, Amber Plastic, Bottle Shape, 1950, 10 In. 35.00
Fly Swatter, Socony, Lithographed Tin 30.00
Fly Swatter, Williams Ice Cream 17.00
Funnel, Lash's Bitters, Copper 75.00
Glass, Measuring, Speed Queen, Glass 3.50
Glass, Twin Kiss Root Beer, 3 In. 15.00
Goblet, Lion Brewery, Embossed 45.00
Grater, Fels Naptha, To Make Soap Chips, Tin, 9 In. 3.25
Gum Stand, Clark's Teaberry Gum, Glass, Pedestal 45.00
Hairnets, Elite, 1940s 2.50
Hairnets, Rexall Good Form, Blond 5.00
Hairnets, Vivian, 1930s 3.00
Hanger, Rummy Soda, Cardboard, 1930s, 4 X 4 1/2 In. 2.50
Hat, Crepe Paper, Brown's Ice Cream 15.00
Holder, Catalog, Sears & Roebuck 40.00
Holder, String, SSS For The Blood, Iron 85.00
Holder, Thread, Red Goose 850.00
Humidifier, For Cigar Showcase, Electric, Art Nouveau, 1880s 1450.00
Humidor, C.O.D.Moxie Cigar Co., Walnut, 14 In. 950.00
Humidor, Edgeworth, Tin 95.00
Humidor, Union Leader Smoking Tobacco 65.00
Ice Pick, Empire Lager, Black Horse Ale 27.00
Jar, Apothecary, Homer's Foot Powder, Etched Baseball Player 155.00
Jar, Chico's Peanuts, Glass, Lithographed Tin Lid, Base, 8 In. 275.00
Jar, Colgar's Toffy–Tulu, Clown Lid 125.00

Jar, Cordove Cigar, Glass	50.00
Jar, Display, Swift's Toilet Soap	335.00
Jar, F.R.Rice Mercantile, Amber, Pat.1894–1895	37.50
Jar, Horlick's Malted Milk, Tin Lid, Miniature	25.00
Jar, Kis–Me Gum, 8 In.	85.00
Jar, Malted Milk, Thompson's, Porcelain, Brass Lid	275.00
Jar, Noxzema Shaving Cream, Cobalt Blue, 8 In.	25.00
Jar, Nut House Peanuts, Embossed, 8 In.	275.00
Jar, Taylor, Taylored To Taste, Cover, Glass, Large	145.00
Kit, Pep Wood Plane, Kelloggs, Original Package	15.00
Knife & Bottle Opener, Pickwick Ale, 3 Oz.	23.00
Knife, Purina	16.00
Knife, Victor Adding Machine, Pocket	14.00
Knife, Walkover Shoes, Pocket	30.00
Knob, Beer Tap, Ansbach Light, Wooden, 11 In.	8.00
Knob, Beer Tap, Culmbacher Dark, Wooden, Brown	6.00
Knob, Beer Tap, Hamm's, Ceramic, With Bear, 4 1/2 In.	15.00
Label, 1st Cabinet, Washington, Hamilton, Cigar, 1900, 6 X 8 In.	9.50
Label, Auditorium Brand Coffee	5.00
Label, Dubuque, Export Beer, Pre–Prohibition	33.00
Label, Grape, Nude Black Child, Grape Box, 1930s, 4 X 13 In.	1.50
Label, Heinz, Pure Food Products, Barrel End, 1940s, 8 In.	10.00
Label, JECF Harper's Druggists, Horse & Cattle Powder	1.50
Label, Lago Lager, Lagomarcino Grupe Co., Black, Gold, Red, White	31.00
Label, Longwood Plantation, Mammy, Hotcakes, 7 X 8 In.	1.75
Lamp, Budweiser, Clydesdale Horses	575.00
Lamp, Charlie The Tuna, 11 In.	25.00
Lamp, Hanging, A & W Root Beer	25.00
Lantern, None Such Brand Products, Tin, Glass, 17 X 7 In.	850.00
Light Bulb, Edison Mazda, Red, 300 Watt, Carton, 1923, Large	20.00
ADVERTISING, LUNCH BOX, see LUNCH Box	
Match Dispenser, National Mfg.Co., Cast Iron, Pat.1897	400.00
Match Holder, American Brewing Co., Stoneware, Blue, Gray, 3 In.	125.00
Match Holder, Tin, Green, Logo, 1940s	60.00
Match Safe, Checker's Cough Drops, Tin	25.00
Match Safe, Spring Wheat Flour	15.00
Milk Box, Return To Walker Gordon, Juliustown, N.J., Blue Paint	125.00
Milk Cap Extractor, Made Better Flavoring Extracts, Celluloid	20.00

Pocket mirrors range in size from 1 1/2 to 5 inches in diameter.
Most of these mirrors were given away as advertising promotions.

Mirror, 7–Up, 1940s Bubble Girl, 2 X 3 In.	1.50
Mirror, Adams Chicklets, Pocket	52.00
Mirror, Aetna Insurance, Fort Wayne, Indiana, Pocket	15.00
Mirror, American Line Steamship, Philadelphia, Pocket	45.00
Mirror, Anderson's Soups, Pocket	30.00
Mirror, Angelus Marshmallows, 2 Cupids, Pocket	45.00 To 75.00
Mirror, Beehive Overalls, Pocket	150.00
Mirror, Bell's Coffee, Pocket	28.00 To 45.00
Mirror, Benton Harbor, Michigan, Pocket	40.00
Mirror, Big Jo Flour, Pocket	20.00
Mirror, Boot & Shoe Worker's Union, Pocket	20.00
Mirror, Brotherhood Overalls, Bare–Chested Woman, Pocket	125.00
Mirror, Calendar, Gillette, Pocket	120.00
Mirror, Cawston Ostrich Farm, Pocket	25.00
Mirror, Central Bank Corp., Black, White, Paperweight, 4 In.	8.00
Mirror, Central Plumbing, Worcester, Pocket	12.00
Mirror, Ceresota Flour, Boy Cutting Bread, Pocket	32.00 To 70.00
Mirror, Ceresota Flour, White, Pocket	95.00
Mirror, Chas.G.Bosch Co. Plumbers, Pocket, Oval, 2 3/4 In.	50.00
Mirror, Copperclad Stoves, Pocket	25.00
Mirror, Crane Whiskey, Pictures Crane, Pocket	25.00
Mirror, Dr.Hebras Viola Cream, Pocket	65.00
Mirror, Drink Chero–Cola, 2–Face Man, Smile & Don't, Pocket	30.00

Mirror, Duffy's Malt Whiskey, Chemist Picture, Pocket 55.00
Mirror, Garland Stoves, Celluloid, Pocket 19.00
Mirror, Good For 10 Cents, Pocket 150.00
Mirror, Good Friends Whiskey, Indian, Pilgrim, Pocket 185.00
Mirror, Great Majestic, Pocket 20.00
Mirror, Haires The Shoe Wizard, Pocket 20.00
Mirror, Hass Sheet Metal Works, Orange, Paperweight, 4 In. 8.00
Mirror, Hawarden, Iowa Monument, Pocket 145.00
Mirror, Hires Root Beer, Pocket 85.00
Mirror, Horlick's Malted Milk, Pocket ....65.00 To 110.00
Mirror, James Oliver Plows, Pocket 125.00
Mirror, Jesse French Pianos, Pocket 20.00
Mirror, Kernstown Whiskey, Sow, Piglets, Pocket 195.00
Mirror, Keystone State Normal School Team, 1914–15, Pocket 9.00
Mirror, Lava Soap, Pocket 50.00
Mirror, Lively Limes, A Cloverdale Soft Drink, 16 X12 In. 30.00
Mirror, Mascot Tobacco 45.00
Mirror, Mayme Gilmore, Sepia Photo, Early 1900s, Pocket 15.00
Mirror, Minneapolis Tractor, Pocket 65.00
Mirror, Morning Newspaper Bldg., Gloversville, N.Y., Pocket 21.00
Mirror, Morton's Salt, Umbrella Girl, Pocket 35.00
Mirror, Old Reliable Coffee, Pocket 37.50
Mirror, Order of Forestry, Pocket 35.00
Mirror, Osram Light Bulbs, Pocket 18.00
Mirror, Oxford Chocolates, Graduate Girl, Pocket 85.00
Mirror, Pan American Life Insurance, 1937, Pocket 15.00
Mirror, Panama Carbon Paper, Pocket 20.00
Mirror, Pingree Shoes, Picture of 1920s Girl, Pocket 15.00
Mirror, Pretty Lady, With Fancy Headdress, Pocket 10.00
Mirror, Queen Quality Shoes, Pocket 26.00
Mirror, Red Goose, Framed, Used To View Shoes Try–Ons 45.00
Mirror, Schaeffer Piano, Yellow, Pocket 48.00
Mirror, Seese Motor, Kingwood, W.Va., Pocket 20.00
Mirror, Shaeffer Piano, Upright Picture, Oval, Pocket 45.00
Mirror, Sharples Tubular Cream Separators, Oval, Pocket, 3 In. 60.00
Mirror, Shell Oil, Pictures Dog, Flushing Birds, 10 X 7 In. 35.00
Mirror, Stand, Dept. Store, 3–Way, Oak, Metal, Late 1800s, 7 Ft. 1100.00
Mirror, Star Soap, Pocket 18.00
Mirror, Studebaker Vehicle Works, South Bend, Ind., Pocket 25.00
Mirror, Superior Stock Food, Multicolor, 1900s, Pocket 10.00
Mirror, Swansdown, Pocket 47.50
Mirror, Swedish American Line, Pocket 27.00
Mirror, Tetlows Zephyr Powder, Philadelphia, Oval, Pocket 45.00
Mirror, Toggery Shop, Eagle River, Wis., Pocket 20.00
Mirror, Traveler's Insurance, Railroad, Locomotive, Pocket 38.50
Mirror, United Service Motors, Pictures Car, Pocket 20.00
Mirror, White Cat Union Suits, Pocket 45.00
Mirror, Woman, Flowing Hair, Holding Pink Roses, Pocket, 2 In. 25.00
Mirror, Woodmen of The World, Omaha, Pocket 45.00
Money Clip, Reid Separator, Celluloid On Metal, 1900s 10.00
Money, Paper, Poll Parrot, Premium 4.00
Mug, A & W Root Beer, Embossed, 3 1/4 In. ....3.00 To 10.00
Mug, Atlas Beer, Red Tropic Bar Colon–Panama, 4 1/2 In. 32.00
Mug, Baker's Chocolate, Jiminy Cricket 5.00
Mug, Booth Bros., Schmidts & Poth Beer 95.00
Mug, Bosco Bear, Ice Skating 15.00
Mug, Bosco, Brown & White 12.00
Mug, Cream of Wheat, Rastus Picture, Ceramic 25.00
Mug, Doe–Wah–Jack, Round Oak Stove, Indian, 1907 .... 85.00
Mug, Hire's Root Beer, Boy Print, Germany 98.00
Mug, Hire's Root Beer, Plastic 15.00
Mug, Hunter's Root Beer 45.00
Mug, Independent Brewing Ass'n, Chicago, Ill., Burg Brau, 6 In. 30.00
Mug, Kayo Hot Chocolate Knocks Me Out, Yellow, 1950s 25.00

Mug, Nestle 20.00
Mug, North Western Brewery, Chicago, Beige, Red Logo, 4 1/4 In. 136.00
Mug, Oliver Typewriter Co., Annual Conference, Menu, Dec.1905 .... 375.00
Mug, Richardson's Root Beer 19.50
Mug, Schuester Root Beer 40.00
Mug, Sterling Breweries, Anniversary, 1863-1963, White, 5 In. 47.00
Mug, TNT Root Beer, Glass 15.00
Mug, Twin Kiss Root Beer, 3 In. 15.00
Note Pad, Clabber Girl, 1900s 8.00
Note Pad, Rainer Beer, Girl On Horse, Celluloid 75.00
Notebook, Bromo Seltzer, Pharmacist's Giveaway 10.00
Oil Can, Texaco Home Lubricant, House & Star 10.00
Pail, Buffalo Peanut Butter 50.00
Pail, Coffee, Chief, 4 Oz. 55.00
Pail, Keystone Mincemeat, 1918, 9 X 13 X 13 In. 100.00
Pail, King-Kup Candies, Tin, Cartoon Litho, Frogs, Ducks 20.00
Pail, Lincoln Club Coffee 425.00
Pail, Nigger Hair Smoking Tobacco, Cover, 1890, 6 1/2 X 5 In. 325.00
Pail, Plow Boy Tobacco, Bail Handle, Tax Stamp 25.00
Pail, Pure Lard Kettle Rendered, Homer, N.Y., Gilt Pig, 7 In. 75.00
Pail, Shedd's Peanut Butter, 5 Lb. 23.00
Pail, Sultana Peanut Butter, Bail Handle, 4 X 4 In. 15.00
Pail, Teenie Weenie Peanut Butter, Monarch, 10 Oz. 75.00
Paper Clamp, Peacock Prophylactic, Tin Litho, 1950s, 2 1/2 In. 16.00
Paper Dispenser, Zig-Zag Cigarette, Metal 45.00
Paper Spindle, Walker's Austex Products, Celluloid 30.00
Peeler, Scraper, Potato Eye Remover, Morton Salt 5.00
Pencil Box, Red Goose, Tube, Lid 50.00
Pencil Sharpener, Baker's Chocolate, Figural, Iron, 2 .... 25.00 To 35.00
Pennant, Cloth, Ringling Bros.Barnum & Bailey, Circus Acts 35.00
Pin Holder, Gibbs Piano, Aluminum, Raised Floral Edge, 1900s 8.00
Pin, Borden's Elmer 15.00
Pin, Honey Bread, Multicolor, Yellow Ground, 1900s, 1 1/4 In. 5.00
Pin, Horlick's Malted Milk, Table, Fountain, 1900s, 7/8 In. 10.00
Pin, Johnson's Wax, Tan, Red, Black, 1930s, 5/8 In. 3.00
Pin, Kellogg's Toasted Corn Flakes, Girl, 1920s, 7/8 In. 20.00
Pin, Miller High Life Beer, Woman On Quarter Moon, 1 In. 19.00
Pin, Occident Flour, Early 1900s, 1 1/4 In. 8.00
Pin, Pickle, Heinz, Celluloid 8.00
Pin, Pretty Kitty Kelly, Columbia Broadcasting, 1 3/4 In. 12.00
Pin, Reddy Kilowatt 12.00
Pin, Sheboygan Maid Flour 5.00
Pin, Yellow Kid Bubble Gum, Early 1900s, 3/4 In. 20.00
Pitcher, Atlas Beer, Panama, Pottery, Bulbous, 2 Liter 125.00
Pitcher, Cream, Hotel Supply Co., Seagull Picture 15.00
Pitcher, Henderson's Wild Cherry Beverage 225.00
Pitcher, Horlick's 65.00
Pitcher, Lord Calvert 12.00
Pitcher, Milk, Wolf Grocery, Annapolis 25.00
Pitcher, Orange Crush 30.00
Pitcher, Pabst Blue Ribbon Beer 12.00
Plate, Ford, In Script, 9 In. 45.00
Plate, Miller Brewing Co., Commemorative, Dated 1980, 10 In. 71.00
Plate, Mobile Oil, 7 In. 25.00
Plate, Pabst Blue Ribbon Logo, McNichol China, 10 In. 22.00
Plate, Western Coke, Marguerite 325.00
Plate, Yellow Poppy, Malt Ranier, The Pure Malt Tonic, Gold Rim 27.00
Poker Chip, Stachelber & Co., Cigar Picture 10.00
Pot Holder, Hotpoint Stoves 10.00
Pot Scraper, Fairmount Creamery, Lithographed Tin 110.00
Pot Scraper, Henkels Flour, Lithographed Tin 88.00
Pot Scraper, Junket Powder, Lithographed Tin 154.00
Pot Scraper, Red Wing Milling Co., Lithographed Tin 282.50
Pot Scraper, Royal Graniteware, Lithographed Tin 247.50

Pot Scraper, Sharples Cream Separator, Lithographed Tin 121.00
Pot Scraper, Wards Extracts, Lithographed Tin 121.00
Pouch, Union Leader Tobacco, Uncle Sam, 4 1/2 In. 22.00
Puzzle, Flying Family On The Air, Radio, Cocomalt, Jigsaw, 1932 .... 40.00
Puzzle, New Idea Farm Equipment 25.00
Puzzle, Rin Tin Tin, Nabisco Shredded Wheat, Plastic Face 18.00
Puzzle, Tray, McDonald 12.00
Ring, Post Toasties Corn Flakes, Premium, 1949 .... 12.50
Ring, Sears Has Everything, Silvered Plastic, Flasher, 1960s 8.00
Rubber Boots, Candee, Salesman's Sample 65.00
Ruler, Edison Mazda Lamps, More Light For Less Money, 12 In. 8.00
Sack, Fair Flour, Cloth 15.00
Sack, Feed, MoorMan's Hog & Calf Feed 5.00
Sack, Franklin Sugar, 100 Lb. 8.00
Sack, Snow White Flour, 8 1/2 X 15 In. 1.50
ADVERTISING, SALT & PEPPER, see Salt & Pepper
Saucer, Baker's Instant Cocoa, Clock Face 6.00
ADVERTISING, SCALE, see Scale
Screen Door, Colonial Is Good Bread 250.00
Screwdriver, Velie Script, Dealer 25.00
Seed Packet, Elsie–Borden's Daisy, Unopened 30.00
Shoe, Heineken, Holland Beer, Scene, Wooden, Orange, 10 In. 35.00
Shoehorn, R.H.Macy, 34th Street, Tin 7.00
Shoehorn, Red Goose Shoes 10.00
Shoehorn, Red Wing Shoes, Plastic 7.00
Shopping List, Doe–Wah–Jack, Cardboard, Multicolor, 15 In. 30.00
Shot Glass, Gannymaded Pure Rye & Whiskey Dexterity Puzzle 28.00
Shot Glass, Green River Whiskey, Shot Mark, 4 In. 25.00
Sign, 20–Mule Team Borax, Woman, Product, Cardboard, 14 X 17 In. 550.00
Sign, Altes Lager Beer, Wooden Frame, Fiber Board, 9 X 15 In. 35.00
Sign, Ansco Film, Red, White & Blue Glass, 10 X 16 In. 45.00
Sign, Apothecary, Mortar & Pestle Form, Wooden, 22 1/2 In. 225.00
Sign, Arbuckle's Coffee, Embossed Tin, 5 1/2 X 20 In. 30.00
Sign, Ask For Wildroot, Red, White, Blue, 39 X 13 In. 45.00
Sign, Atlantic Gas, Porcelain, Red, White & Black, 10 X 12 In. 75.00
Sign, Ballantine Brew, Tin, Self–Framed, C.1909, 22 X 30 In. 700.00
Sign, Barnum's Animal Crackers, Trolley, 1924, 11 X 21 In. 475.00
Sign, Berghoff Brewing, Dog, Tin, 13 X 21 In. 250.00
Sign, Berkley Knit Ties, Man, Cardboard, Dated 1925, 8 X 10 In. 25.00
Sign, Blacksmith, Wooden, 28 In. 225.00
Sign, Blitz Weinhard Beer, Tin, Scalloped, Round, 11 1/2 In. 42.00
Sign, Briggs Seeds, Picture of Antique Auto, 1915, 24 X 18 In. 850.00
Sign, Brownie Soda, 5 Ft. 225.00
Sign, Browns Bread, Tin, 1920, 8 X 15 In. 150.00
Sign, Budweiser Beer, Embossed, Tin, 15 X 25 In. 16.00
Sign, Budweiser, Paper, Red, White Letters, 1920s, 11 X 21 In. 79.00
Sign, Bull Durham, A Royal Victory, Framed, 1909, 26 X 44 In. 825.00
Sign, Buster Brown Golden Sheaf Bakers, Frame, 22 X 30 In. 550.00
Sign, Butter–Nut Bread, Embossed Tin, 1930s, 35 X 12 In. 60.00
Sign, Call Again, Embossed Tin, 1930s, 35 X 11 In. 60.00
Sign, Canada Dry, Picture Logo, Porcelain, 4 X 20 In. 45.00
Sign, Canaries For Sale, Tin, Canary Yellow, 45 X 18 In. 200.00
Sign, Carnation Milk, Pictures Bottle, Porcelain, 14 X 15 In. 85.00
Sign, Champagne Velvet Beer, Tin, Self–Framed, 15 X 20 In. 150.00
Sign, Chas.E.Higgins German Laundry Soap, Cardboard, 5 In. 150.00
Sign, Chase & Sanborn, Reverse Painting, 1910, 18 X 24 In. 225.00
Sign, Chesterfield Cigarettes, Tin, Pack, 12 X 34 In. 35.00
Sign, Cinco Cigars, Reverse On Glass, Beveled, 14 X 30 In. 550.00
Sign, Cities Service, Clover, 2–Sided, Porcelain, 46 X 48 In. 60.00
Sign, City Mutual Fire of Lebanon, Penna., Tin.19 X 13 In. 50.00
Sign, Clabber Girl Baking Powder, Tin, 1940s, 11 X 30 In. 35.00
Sign, Clark's O.N.T.Spools, Children Whispering, 1900, 24 In. 190.00
Sign, Cleo Cola, Cleopatra, Embossed Tin, 10 X 30 In. 225.00
Sign, Cleveland's Superior Baking Powder, Cardboard, 25 In. 45.00

Sign,	Cliquot Club, Eskimos, Sled, Cardboard, 14 X 20 In.	25.00
Sign,	Continental Insurance, Soldier, Tin, Self–Framed, 31 In	1100.00
Sign,	Cook's Beer, Tin, 1940s, 24 X 16 In.	30.00
Sign,	Cook's Goldblume Beer, 2 Sides, Cardboard, 14 X 28 In.	45.00
Sign,	Copenhagen Snuff, Paper, C.1900, 15 X 21 In.	250.00
Sign,	Cork Whiskey, Bottle & Package, Tin, 1885, 14 X 22 In.	75.00
Sign,	Curyeas Maizena Glen Cove Starch, Litho, 13 X 16 In.	750.00
Sign,	Dairy Made Ice Cream, Baby, Ice Cream, 1915, 33 X 25 In.	450.00
Sign,	Dan Patch 1908, Framed, 21 X 28 In.	75.00
Sign,	DeLaval Cream Separators, Girl & Cow, Green, 31 X 20 In.	1180.00
Sign,	DeLaval Cream Separators, Girl & Cow, Red, 31 X 20 In.	1650.00
Sign,	Diamond Edge Tools, Embossed Tin, 1940s, 10 X 28 In.	35.00
Sign,	Dr.Baker, Specialist Rheumatism, Brass, 24 X 18 In.	95.00
Sign,	Dr.Daniels Cat & Dog Remedies, Cardboard, 10 X 18 In.	60.00
Sign,	Dr.Farley, Indian Medicine Man, Wood, 16 1/4 X 23 1/2 In.	2750.00
Sign,	Dr.Shoops, Embossed Tin, 1900, 9 X 6 In.	450.00
Sign,	Drink Jax Beer On Top, Horse & Rider, Tin, 40 X 16 In.	25.00
Sign,	Drink Mixer, Milky Way Rocket, Plastic, 1940, 10 X 4 In.	7.50
Sign,	Dublin Bay Smoking Tobacco, Cardboard, 11 X 14 In.	5.00
Sign,	Duxbak Hunting Clothes, Tin, Self–Framed, 1910, 19 In.	450.00
Sign,	Eastside Old Tap Lager, Celluloid, Red, Gold, 9 X 20 In.	25.00
Sign,	Edison Mazda Lamps, Parrish, Tin Litho, 2 Sides, 25 In.	4950.00
Sign,	El Wadora, Quality Cigar, 5 Cent, Tin, 1930s, 24 X 36 In.	60.00
Sign,	Elgin Watches, Farm Boy, Wooden, 1900, 22 X 15 In.	350.00
Sign,	Elgin, Boy, Tattered Clothes, Watch, 1920, 23 X 16 In.	50.00
Sign,	Elk's Head Beer, Oskosh, Porcelain, 14 1/2 X 21 In.	185.00
Sign,	Empire Soap, Inspirational Black, C.1915, 24 X 16 In.	950.00
Sign,	Erb Cigar, Metal, 2 Sides, Revolves Electrically, 24 In.	578.00
Sign,	Eye Exam, Sand Paint, Gold Letters, Brass Glasses, 34 In.	895.00
Sign,	Fairbanks Scales, Porcelain, Blue, White, 10 X 50 In.	135.00
Sign,	Family Paints, Sherwin Williams, Shield Shape, 28 In.	175.00
Sign,	Fehr's Beer, Man, Rocker, Woman, Bottle, 28 X 21 In.	100.00
Sign,	Five–O, Bottle Pictured, Tin, 1930s, 11 X 28 In.	35.00
Sign,	Fleckenstein Brewery, 3 Workers, Metal, 1910, 19 X 13 In.	550.00
Sign,	Fordson Tractor, Tin, 14 X 18 In.	55.00
Sign,	Gennett's Fountain Inn, Gold, Red, 48 1/2 X 57 In.	100.00
Sign,	George Lawrence Dog Chains, Leads, Tin Litho, 1915, 7 In.	120.00
Sign,	Ginger Mint Julep, Cherrywood Frame, 24 X 9 In.	50.00
Sign,	Globe, Show, Drug Store, Art Deco, Owens–Illinois, Pair	450.00
Sign,	Gold Label Beer, Porcelain Corner, 20 X 14 In.	300.00
Sign,	Gollam's Ice Cream, Enameled, 2 Sides, Litho, 1930, 27 In.	110.00
Sign,	Goodyear Tires, Porcelain, 24 X 66 In.	75.00
Sign,	Grape–Nuts, Girl With Large Dog, Tin, 30 X 20 In.	2200.00
Sign,	Grapette Soda, Embossed Tin, 1940s, 11 X 27 In.	30.00
Sign,	Green River, Black Man, Horse, 1899, 11 X 13 1/2 In.	55.00
Sign,	Hamilton Watch, Young Girl, Tin, 1904, 18 In.	200.00
Sign,	Hansel & Gretel Mild Blend Havana Cigar, Square, 17 In.	150.00
Sign,	Happy Days, I.W.Harper Whiskey, Milk Glass, 25 X 32 In.	1050.00
Sign,	Havana Favorite Cigar, Cardboard, 8 X 10 In.	6.00
Sign,	Hires, Josh Slinger, 1914, 6 X 11 In.	160.00
Sign,	Holihan's, Holly 7, Tin Over Cardboard, 7 X 10 In.	11.00
Sign,	Hudepohl Beer, Deer, Barrel, Reverse On Glass, 22 X 16 In.	875.00
Sign,	Hunt Club Shoes, Tin, 14 X 19 In.	47.50
Sign,	Idaho Brewing Co., Boise City, Idaho, Tin, 18 X 24 In.	7500.00
Sign,	Imported Pilsner, Girl, Curved Corners, Metal, 17 X 21 In.	264.00
Sign,	Indian Motorcycle, Black, White, Paper, 1940, 38 X 50 In.	550.00
Sign,	Int'l.Stock Food Co., Directum, C.1902, 24 X 31 In.	375.00
Sign,	Ivory Soap Girl, Proctor & Gamble, Framed, 15 X 20 In.	350.00
Sign,	J.P.Coats Spool Cotton, Paper, 1895, 23 X 17 In.	160.00
Sign,	J.Read Inn, Figure With Glass, Painted, 49 1/2 X 35 In.	1100.00
Sign,	Jos.Doelger's Sons, Lager Beer, Tin, 1900s, 19 X 28 In.	660.00
Sign,	Kist, Everybody Loves To Get, Tin, 1950s, 26 X 20 In.	40.00
Sign,	Kodak Developing & Printing, Porcelain, 20 X 24 In.	175.00
Sign,	Krueger, Beer & Ale, Electric, 13 X 19 In.	55.00

Sign, La Flor De Carvalho, Tin, Oak Frame, 15 X 21 In. 255.00
Sign, La Raphaella Liqueur, Lithograph, 1907, 48 X 36 In. 300.00
Sign, Land–O–Lakes Seed Dealer, Tin, 24 X 36 In. 16.00
Sign, Locksmith, Cut–Out Key, Openwork Bracket, Iron, 39 In. 1500.00
Sign, Lowells Orange Julep, Lithograph, 1920, 9 X 28 In. 90.00
Sign, Ma's Cola, Bottle In Front of Cap, Tin, 1940s, 11 X 28 In. 30.00
Sign, Maestro, Man Smoking Cigar, Die–Cut, 14 X 18 In. 25.00
Sign, Marathon Gasoline, Steel, 1930s, 48 X 18 In. 65.00
Sign, Mayos Cut Plug, Rooster, Porcelain, 13 X 6 1/2 In. 325.00
Sign, Miller Beer, Lobster, Self–Framed, Tin, 1910, 20 X 15 In. 450.00
Sign, Milliner's, Iron Top Hat, Removable Glove, 43 1/2 In. 1025.00
Sign, Milwaukee Beer, Gentleman, Bakelite, Round, 13 In. 190.00
Sign, Mini–Lax, Embossed Tin, 1930s, 20 X 16 In. 40.00
Sign, Mobil Gas, Winged Horse, Porcelain, 6 Ft. 300.00
Sign, Mortar & Pestle, Armstrong Drug Co., Sheet Iron, 46 In. 325.00
Sign, Moxie Eclipse, Hall of Fame, Embossed, 1930, 54 X 19 In. 50.00
Sign, Never Split Seats, Toilet, Tin, Self–Framed, 13 X 9 In. 325.00
Sign, Nichol Kola, Embossed Metal, 1930s, 18 1/2 X 11 In. 40.00
Sign, North Tavern, N.Sutton, N.H., Wooden, C.1815, 55 1/2 In. 2200.00
Sign, Nova Scotia Fire Insurance, Porcelain, 12 X 19 In. 65.00
Sign, Odo–Ro–No, Bottle Shape, Cardboard, Art Deco, 30 In. 45.00
Sign, Oilsum, America's Finest Oil, Porcelain, 19 1/2 X 27 In. 175.00
Sign, Old Gold Cigarettes, Wm.Kimball, Framed, 14 X 29 In. 200.00
Sign, Oliver Plows & Implements, Plow Picture, Tin, 10 X 28 In. 65.00
Sign, Orange Crust, Tin, 36 X 8 In. 50.00
Sign, Palm Cigars, Embossed Tin, 1930s, 6 X 20 In. 20.00
Sign, Pangburn's Chocolates, Counter, 7 X 9 In. 25.00
Sign, Parliament Cigarettes, Tin, 12 X 24 In. 24.00
Sign, Patrick Henry Beer, Silhouette, Tin, 36 X 19 In. 25.00
Sign, Paul Webb Mountain Boys, Imperial Pottery, 9 In. 265.00
Sign, Penn Cigars, 9 1/2 X 6 1/2 In. 50.00
Sign, Peter Pan Ice Cream, Embossed Tin, 1930s, 16 X 20 In. 65.00
Sign, Pevely Baby's First Best Milk, Baby, Bottle, 29 X 20 In. 170.00
Sign, Phillip Morris, Color, Cardboard, 1930s, 23 X 19 In. 40.00
Sign, Physician, Gold Letters, Sand Paint, 18 1/2 X 31 1/2 In. 225.00
Sign, Pinch Hit Tobacco, Players, Tin, 13 1/4 X 9 1/4 In. 150.00
Sign, Poll–Parrot Shoes, Cardboard, Framed, 6 X 12 In. 65.00
Sign, Ponds–Ginger Brandy, Tin, 1915, 6 X 9 In. 50.00
Sign, Power Lube Motor Oil, Porcelain, 2 Sides, 22 X 28 In. 450.00
Sign, Purity Ice Cream, Porcelain, 2 Sides, 20 X 28 In. 55.00
Sign, Rainbo Is Good Bread, Tin, 2 3/4 X 17 1/2 In. 10.00
Sign, Rainbow Beverages, Embossed Tin, 1930s, 11 X 28 In. 35.00
Sign, Red Dot Cigar, Cigar Shape, Cardboard, 36 1/2 In. 46.00
Sign, Red Jacket Tobacco, Baseball, Cardboard, 22 X 28 In. 125.00
Sign, Red Man Tobacco, Pictures Indian, Tin, 14 X 4 1/2 In. 28.00
Sign, Red Raven, Bird, Hugged By Girl, Metal, 1900, Round, 24 In. 1500.00
Sign, Red Rose Coffee, Color, Tin, 19 X 27 In. 48.00
Sign, Remer's Tea Store, Baby, Pillow, Lithograph, 32 X 13 In. 65.00
Sign, Richmond Cigarettes, 17th Century Man, Tin, 1900, 28 In. 875.00
Sign, Royal Crown Cola, Embossed Tin, 1940s, 21 X 4 In. 30.00
Sign, Salada Tea, Purple, Yellow & Black, Porcelain, 15 X 3 In. 95.00
Sign, Satom Slom Powder, Lithograph, 1903, 42 X 26 In. 85.00
Sign, Schaefer Beer, Painting On Glass, 1930, 13 X 21 In. 25.00
Sign, Scissors, Wooden Carved & Painted, 19th Century, 72 In. 6250.00
Sign, Sherwin Williams, 2 Sides, Porcelain, 9 X 21 In. 90.00
Sign, Shoe Rebuilding, Painted Wood, Green Border, 73 X 11 In. 150.00
Sign, Shoe Shine, Sidewalk, 24 In. 110.00
Sign, Simonds Saw Blade Co., Man, Axe, Metal, 1910, 20 X 14 In. 350.00
Sign, Skeleton Key Form, Brown Painted Wood, 76 In. 350.00
Sign, Snow King Baking Powder, St.Nick, Cardboard, 24 X 36 In. 350.00
Sign, Squire's Pork Products, Lithographed Tin, Framed, 24 In. 2100.00
Sign, Star Soap, Paper, C.1900, 21 X 13 In. 550.00
Sign, Statue of Liberty, Schlitz Brewing Co., Tin, 40 X 30 In. 145.00
Sign, Steam Fire Proof Safes, Lithographed Tin, 10 X 14 In. 250.00

Sign, Stegmaier, Gold Medal, Bottle, Tin, Cardboard, 8 X 13 In. 29.00
Sign, Storz Beer, 70 Years of Quality, Round, 9 In. 38.00
Sign, Stroh's Is Spoken Here, Chicago, Mirror, 14 X 22 In. 51.00
Sign, Trade, Half Opened Jack Knife, Silver Gilt Ends, 32 In. 850.00
Sign, Trade, Violin, Brass, Iron & Tin, Life–Size 1500.00
Sign, True Fruit, J.Hungerford–Smith, Oil On Tin, 37 X 25 In. 425.00
Sign, Twin City Fire Insurance, Reverse On Glass, 19 X 11 In. 65.00
Sign, Valley Brew, Red Letters, Tin Over Cardboard, 9 X 13 In. 40.00
Sign, Viceroy Cigarettes, Tin, 17 X 26 In. 50.00
Sign, We Give & Redeem American Stamps, Tin, 10 X 30 In. 35.00
Sign, Welch's Grape Juice, Bottle Shape, 20th Century, 30 In. 885.00
Sign, Will's Gold Flake Cigarettes, Celluloid, 15 X 20 In. 175.00
Sign, Willard Treatment, Stomach Distress, Tin, 18 X 6 1/2 In. 40.00
Sign, Winchester Cigarettes, Porcelain, 18 X 30 In. 60.00
Sign, Wright's Dentomyrh Toothpaste, Framed, 19 X 13 In. 80.00
Sign, Wrigley's Gum, Cardboard, 1930s, 11 X 21 In. 50.00
Sign, Wrigley's Gum, Man, Pack Gum, 11 X 21 In. 180.00
Sign, Wrigley's Soap, Victorian, Lithographed Tin, 14 X 19 In. 225.00
Soap, Bendix Washing Machine, Figural, Salesman's, 1940s, Box 35.00
Soap, Ivory, Alfred Hitchcock Presents 9.00
Soap, Octagon 5.00
Soap, Sinclair Heating Oils, Oil Truck, Figural, Perfume 8.00
Spoon, Calumet, Indian Handle 28.00
Spoon, Coffee Measuring, A & P, Metal 8.00
Spoon, Dairimaid Milk, Curled Handle, Chrome–Silver 10.00
Spoon, Monarch, Silver Plate 25.00
Spoon, Nestle Quik, Stainless Steel 5.00
Spoon, Rolex, Figural, Silver Plated, 4 In. 15.00
Spoon, Spaghetti Ohs 12.50
Spoon, Toledo Pie Co., Real Good Pies, Metal, 11 In. 2.25
Spoon, Tony The Tiger 12.50
Spoon, Weatherbird Shoe 4.50
Stand, Smoking, Moxie, Figural, Man, Green Cap, In Tails, 35 In. 375.00
Stickpin, Anchor Buggy 12.50
Stickpin, DuPont Powders, Dog On Point, 1 Leg Up 60.00
Stickpin, Nipper, Celluloid 85.00
Stickpin, Reddy Kilowatt, Original Folder, 1955 .... 30.00
Stickpin, Remington, 30 Caliber Shell Shape 40.00
Stickpin, Richmond Bicycle, Celluloid, Late 1890s 18.00
Stickpin, Round Oak Stove Co. 30.00
Straw Box, Jersey Cream 850.00
String Holder, 7–Up, Tin 300.00
String Holder, Freeman's Face Powder, Mortar & Pestle Shape 100.00
String Holder, Red Goose Shoes, Cast Iron 1200.00
String Holder, Red Goose Shoes, Tin Tilting Goose 1700.00
String Holder, Yum Yum Bread, Metal 85.00
Stud, Lapel, Swell Newport Bicycles, Celluloid, 1896 .... 15.00
Teapot, Banquet Tea, A Wonderful Flavor, Embossed Letters, 1920 .... 50.00
Teapot, Lipton, Cream, Signed 45.00
Teapot, Salada Tea 10.00
Teapot, Van Dyke Coffee & Tea Co., Stoneware, Miniature 75.00
ADVERTISING, THERMOMETER, see Thermometer
Thermos, Monarch Coffee, Good Pilots Deserve Good Coffee, 1920 .... 160.00
Tie Tac, Goodyear Blimp, Dirigible, Silver Plated 10.00

 The English language is sometimes confusing. Tin cans or canisters were first used commercially in the United States in 1819 and were called "tins." Today the word "tin" is used by most collectors to describe many types of containers, including food tins, biscuit boxes, roly poly tobacco containers, gunpowder cans, talcum powder sprinkle–top cans, cigarette flat–fifty tins, and more. Beer cans are listed in their own section. Things made of undecorated tin are listed under Tinware.

Tin, Abbey Tobacco, Pocket 375.00

Tin, Advance Agent Cigars, Lindbergh, 8 X 6 X 4 In. 150.00
Tin, Angelus Marshmallow, 5 Lbs. 20.00
Tin, Antonella Tobacco, Paper Label, Pocket 400.00
Tin, Anza Coffee, Screw Lid, 1 Lb. 22.00
Tin, Armour Lard, 4 Lb. 10.00
Tin, B.F.Gravely & Sons Tobacco, Pocket 1400.00
Tin, Bagley's Sweet Tips Tobacco, Pocket 45.00
Tin, Baker's Cocoa, Label, Sample 45.00
Tin, Barrington Hall Coffee, Red, Green, White, Key Type, 1 Lb. 12.00
Tin, Barsco Waterproof Dressing, Bliss & Richardson, 3 In. 4.00
Tin, Bayle Peanut Butter, Boy and Girl Scouts, 1 Lb. 20.00
Tin, Beebrand Whole Red Pepper, 1 Oz. 5.00
Tin, Belmont Tobacco, Vertical, Pocket .... 225.00 To 245.00
Tin, Big Ben Tobacco, Horse, Pocket 15.00
Tin, Blanke's Majov Coffee, Blue, Gold, Cream, 8 X 5 In. 165.00
Tin, Blue Boar Tobacco, Round, Pocket 35.00
Tin, Blue Heaven Smoking Mixture, Small 5.00
Tin, Bobwhite Tobacco, 3 X 2 X 1 In. 250.00
Tin, Bokar Coffee, 1 Lb. 15.00
Tin, Bond Street Pipe Tobacco, Pocket 18.50
Tin, Bowl of Roses Tobacco, Pocket, 3 1/2 X 3 X 1 In. 225.00
Tin, Briggs Pipe Mixture, Brown, Pocket 8.00
Tin, Briggs Tobacco, Brown, Red, White, 4 X 3 In. 10.00
Tin, Buckingham Tobacco, Trail Package 25.00
Tin, Buffalo Brand Peanuts, Standing Buffalo, 10 Lb. ....80.00 To 175.00
Tin, Bugler Tobacco, Canister 18.00
Tin, Bull Dog, Dog, Frame, Pocket 195.00
Tin, Bull's Eye Revolver Gun Powder 32.00
Tin, Bunte Marshmallow, Picture of Boy & Can 125.00
Tin, Burley Boy Tobacco, Pocket .... 400.00 To 450.00
Tin, Butternut Coffee, Graphics, Key Type, 1 Lb. 10.00
Tin, Cadillac Tobacco, 2 X 8 In. 750.00
Tin, Calabash Pipe Tobacco, Brown, Yellow, Floral, 4 X 2 X 3 In. 40.00
Tin, California Perfume Co., Sample 40.00
Tin, Calumet Baking Powder, 1 Lb. 4.50
Tin, Calumet Baking Powder, Embossed, 6 Oz. 14.00
Tin, Calumet Baking Powder, Indian, Red, 6 X 2 In. 55.00
Tin, Camel Tube Patch, 1946, 4 X 2 In. 18.50
Tin, Campbell's Brand Coffee, Bloomington, Ill., 10 Lb. 55.00
Tin, Campbell's Shag Tobacco, Pocket 225.00
Tin, Candy, Gloria Swanson 20.00
Tin, Canova Coffee, 3 Lb. 65.00
Tin, Captain Jacks Oysters, Blue, White, 1 Gal., 7 In. 8.00
Tin, Cardinal Sample Tobacco, Pocket 375.00
Tin, Cardinal Tobacco, Pocket 1200.00
Tin, Carter's Midnight Typewriter Ribbon, Smith Corona 5.00
Tin, Cashmere Bouquet, Pink, Colgate–Palmolive, 4 Oz. 17.00
Tin, Castle Blend Tea, Lithographed Tin, Horseshoe Shape, 7 In. 50.00
Tin, Caswell Coffee, 3 Lb. 26.00
Tin, Central Union Cut Plug, Red, 6 X 5 X 3 In. 35.00
Tin, Champ Pomade, Boxer In Ring, Oval, 4 In. 40.00
Tin, Charles Denby Cigars, Blue, White, Red, Black, 5 X 5 In. 10.00
Tin, Charm of The West Tobacco, Embossed Silver, Flat, Pocket 195.00
Tin, Checkers Tobacco, Red & Black Squares, Stamp, Canister 595.00
Tin, Chocolate Cream Brand Coffee, 1 Lb. 15.00
Tin, Christie Biscuits, Truck, 5 1/2 X 10 In. 1250.00
Tin, City Club Tobacco, Pocket, Short 375.00
Tin, Clabber Girl Baking Powder, 10 Oz. 6.00
Tin, Climax Cut Plug Tobacco, 7 Oz. 30.00
Tin, Club Lido Tobacco, Pocket 385.00
Tin, Coach & Four Tobacco, Pocket 225.00
Tin, Colgate Toothpowder, 1906 .... 45.00
Tin, Comfort Powder, 10 Oz. 7.00
Tin, Continental Cubes Tobacco, Pocket .... 200.00 To 395.00

Tin, Continental Cubes, Concave, Tin, Picture of Washington 225.00
Tin, Cook Coffee, Canister, 5 Lb. 22.00
Tin, Crosby Square Pipe Mixture, Wheeling, W.Va., 5 In. 10.00
Tin, Cross Swords Tobacco, Square Corner, Pocket 50.00
Tin, Davis Baking Powder, 8 Oz. 5.00
Tin, Deerwood Coffee, Deer, Mountains, 1922, 5 3/4 X 4 In. 63.00
Tin, DeVoe's Makings Tobacco, Pocket 400.00
Tin, DeWitt's Golden Liniment, 3 3/4 In. 8.00
Tin, Dial Smoking Tobacco, Red, White, Black, Yellow, 4 X 7 In. 10.00
Tin, Diana Brand Confections, Green, Red, Black, 9 1/2 In. 15.00
Tin, Dill's Best Cut Plug, 2 3/4 X 3 3/4 X 3/4 In. 20.00
Tin, Dill's Best, Girl In Oval, Pocket 10.00
Tin, Dixie Kid Tobacco, Black Child, 6 X 5 X 5 In. 275.00
Tin, Dixie Mix, Dromedary Outline, 6 1/4 X 3 1/2 In. 4.00
Tin, Dixie Queen Cut Plug, Woman, 6 X 5 X 4 In. 130.00
Tin, Djer Kiss Talcum Powder, Snowflake Graphics, 5 1/2 In. 15.00
Tin, Dr.Lyons Tooth Powder, 2 Oz. 8.00
Tin, Droste Cocoa, 5 Lb. 40.00
Tin, DuPont Superfine Gunpowder 65.00
Tin, Eagle Brand Coffee, Eagle Litho, Tin, 1 Lb. .... 30.00 To 75.00
Tin, Eatonic For Your Stomach's Sake, Cardboard, 2 In. 3.50
Tin, Edgeworth Tobacco, Upright, Pocket 6.00
Tin, Edgeworth, Plug Slice, 3 1/4 X 4 1/4 In. 15.00
Tin, Edgeworth, Sample 45.00
Tin, Epicure Tobacco, Pocket .... 50.00 To 85.00
Tin, Evening In Paris Talcum Powder 10.00
Tin, ExLax, Sample 4.00
Tin, Express Tobacco, 2 X 8 In. 800.00
Tin, Fairway Brand Golden Corn, Paper Label, 1 Lb.4 Oz. 9.00
Tin, Fast Mail Tobacco, Flat, Pocket 375.00
Tin, Fast Union Leader, Pocket 39.00
Tin, Flor De Murat Cigar, Revenue Stamp, 3 1/2 X 5 In. 15.00
Tin, Forest & Stream Pipe Tobacco, Red, White, Duck, 4 X 4 In. 25.00
Tin, Forest & Stream Tobacco, 2 Fishermen 250.00
Tin, Forest & Stream Tobacco, Ducks, Pocket .... 25.00 To 45.00
Tin, Four Roses Tobacco, Flip Top, Red, Silver, Green, 4 X 3 In. 125.00
Tin, Franko–American Coffee, Pry Lid, 6 X 3 X 4 In., 1 Lb. 17.00
Tin, Frazier Axle Grease 8.00
Tin, Frontenac Peanut Butter, 12 Oz. 65.00
Tin, Ft.Bedford Instant Coffee, 6 Oz. 7.00
Tin, Full Dress Tobacco, Round Bottom, Pocket 65.00
Tin, Gail & Ax Tobacco, Canister 275.00
Tin, Gem Ever Ready Blades, 1919, 3 1/4 X 11 In. 750.00
Tin, George Washington's Instant Coffee, 2 Oz. 10.00
Tin, Glendora Coffee, Pry Lid, 3 Lb. 95.00
Tin, Gold Dust Scouring Cleanser, Half Contents, 14 Oz. 19.00
Tin, Gold Dust Tobacco, Pocket 200.00
Tin, Gold Medal Steel Cut Brand Coffee, Blue, Gold, White, 1 Lb. 10.00
Tin, Gold Shore Tobacco, Vertical, Pocket 350.00
Tin, Golden Sceptre Tobacco, Pocket 425.00
Tin, Golden Sun Cream Tartar, 1912, 2 Oz. 5.00
Tin, Golden Vine Brand Salted Peanuts, Brundage Bros., 10 Lb. 60.00
Tin, Golden West Coffee, Cowgirl, 3 Lb. 75.00
Tin, Granger Tobacco, Pocket 775.00
Tin, Gun Powder, Bull's–Eye Revolver Smokeless, 1 Lb. 50.00
Tin, Hand Made Tobacco, Pocket .... 135.00 To 175.00
Tin, Hash Brown Blend Tobacco, Flat 75.00
Tin, Havana Ribbon Brand Cigar, Gold, Blue, Red, White, 5 X 3 In. 10.00
Tin, Hi–Plane Tobacco, 2 Engines, Pocket 55.00
Tin, Hi–Plane Tobacco, 4 Motors, Pocket 200.00
Tin, High–Grade Tobacco, Green, Vertical, Pocket 995.00
Tin, Hillcrest Brand Curry Powder, 2 Oz. 5.00
Tin, Hindoo Tobacco, Pocket .... 375.00 To 675.00
Tin, Hinz's Eagle Brand Coffee, Paper Label, 1 Lb. 35.00

Tin, Home Brand Cloves Spice, Yellow, Gold, Black, 2 Oz. 5.00
Tin, Honey Moon Tobacco, Man On The Moon .... 60.00 To 85.00
Tin, Hoosier Boy Coffee, Paper Label 150.00
Tin, Hostess Holiday Fruit Cake, Hinged Cover, 3 X 6 In. 10.00
Tin, Hudson Bay Tea, Red Ground, 3 X 3 X 5 1/2 In. 95.00
Tin, Huntley & Palmer, Books, With Bookends, 4 X 9 In. 175.00
Tin, Huntley & Palmer, Egyptian Vase, 1924 .... 35.00
Tin, Huntley & Palmer, Nankin, Ginger Jar, 1910, 7 X 5 In. 67.00
Tin, Huntley & Palmer, Reptile 75.00
Tin, Huntley & Palmer, Slant Top Desk, Wood Grained, 7 In. 65.00
Tin, IGA Cocoa, Cardboard, Metal Top & Bottom, 2 Lb. 13.00
Tin, Index Cocoa, Girl Picture, Montgomery Ward, 5 Lb. 110.00
Tin, Iodex Ointment, 1 3/4 In. 4.50
Tin, Jack Sprat Coffee, Label, 2 Lb. 45.00
Tin, Jack Sprat Evaporated Milk, Paper Label, 1 Lb. 12.00
Tin, Japanese, Potpourri, Somers, 4 1/2 In. 40.00
Tin, Johnson & Johnson Mustard Plasters, 4 X 5 X 1/4 In. 45.00
Tin, Kentucky Club Rough Cut Pipe Tobacco, Canister, 5 1/4 In. 10.00
Tin, Kentucky Club Rough Cut Tobacco, Horse, Rider, 1 Lb. 10.00
Tin, Key West Perfectos, Canister 20.00
Tin, King Edward Tobacco, Pocket 300.00
Tin, King George's Navy Chewing Tobacco, 2 Lb., 4 3/4 In. 20.00
Tin, King George's Navy Tobacco, Navy, Red, Hinged, 3 X 5 In. 20.00
Tin, Kleeko Coffee, 1 Lb. 35.00
Tin, Knock–Em–Dead, Bed Bug Killer 75.00
Tin, Koenigs Coffee, Sailboat 230.00
Tin, Kohr's Lard, Red, 4 Lb. 40.00
Tin, LandFords Ground Nutmeg, 1 1/2 Oz. 6.50
Tin, Levi Nickerson's, Elastic Oil Dressing, 3 X 5 In. 5.00
Tin, Log Cabin Syrup, Cartoon All Sides 120.00
Tin, Log Cabin Syrup, Mother Flipping Pancakes 120.00
Tin, Loose–Willes, Robin Hood & His Men, Octagon, 9 In. 65.00
Tin, Lord Cecil Brand Coffee, Horse, Carriage, 3 Lb. 35.00
Tin, Lucky Strike, Sample 45.00
Tin, Lustre Creme Hair Dressing, 1 3/4 Oz. 5.00
Tin, Luzianne Brand Coffee, Pry Off, Black Mammy, Coffee Pot 20.00
Tin, Luzianne Coffee & Chicory, Dated 1928, 3 Lb. 95.00
Tin, Maltby's Coconut, Red, Gold, Black, Ginna & Hines Mfg. 90.00
Tin, Mammy's Favorite Brand Coffee, 1915, 4 Lb. 170.00
Tin, Man–Zan, For Rectal Discomforts, Sample 8.00
Tin, Manhattan Cocktail Tobacco, Pocket 250.00
Tin, Mapacuba Cigars, 5 In. 75.00
Tin, Martinson's Coffee, 1 Lb. 20.00
Tin, Maryland Club Tobacco, Flip Lid, Pocket 800.00
Tin, Master Mason Tobacco, Pocket 1800.00
Tin, Matchless Coffee, Screw Lid, 1 Lb. 65.00
Tin, Matoaka Tobacco, Pocket 1100.00
Tin, May Day Coffee, 1 Lb. 20.00
Tin, Mayo Cut Plug, Handle, Blue 35.00
Tin, McCormack Tea, 5 In. 7.00
Tin, Mellow Smoke, Pocket 35.00
Tin, Mennen Borated Talcum Toilet Powder, Shaker Top, 4 In. 7.00
Tin, Model Tobacco, Silver, 15 Cents, Pocket 12.00
Tin, Mohawk Chief Tobacco, 6 X 6 X 4 In. 600.00
Tin, Monarch Cocoa, C.1923, 1 Lb. 25.00
Tin, Monarch Tea, Lion Over Tea Plantation, 4 X 2 X 2 In. 45.00
Tin, Moses Cough Drops, 5 Lb. 350.00
Tin, Nic–Nac Tobacco, Yellow, 14 X 8 In. 800.00
Tin, Nigger Hair Tobacco, Pocket .... 100.00 To 400.00
Tin, Nursery Talcum, Family, 1 Lb. 15.00
Tin, O.P.S.Brand Coffee, Blue, Gold, White, 3 Lb. 25.00
Tin, Ointment of Seven Oils, Internal & External, Round, 2 In. 4.00
Tin, Old Colony Mixture, Gold, Pocket, 1910 .... 10.00
Tin, Old Colony Tobacco, Silver, Pocket 70.00

Tin, Old Master Coffee, 1930, 6 X 4 X 4 In. 170.00
Tin, Old Squire Tobacco, Pocket 125.00
Tin, Our Mother's Cocoa, Metal Pry Off Lid, Cardboard, 2 Lb. 7.00
Tin, Oven Kist Biscuits, Truck, Canadian, 4 X 7 1/2 In. 350.00
Tin, Ox Heart Peanut Butter, 5 Lb. 60.00
Tin, Pall Mall Cigarettes, Christmas, 7 X 8 In. 12.50
Tin, Palmers Jack Frost Marshmallow, 10 X 6 In. 55.00
Tin, Par Talc, Golfer 75.00
Tin, Pat Hand Tobacco, 5 Cent, Pocket .... 50.00 To 60.00
Tin, Patterson's Seal Cut Plug, 3 1/2 X 3 1/2 X 5 1/2 In. 25.00
Tin, Peacock Rubber Prophylactics, Litho Peacock, 1950s 15.00
Tin, Pearson's Red Top Snuff 22.00
Tin, Penick Syrup, Young Boy On Front, Paper Label, 10 Lb. 35.00
Tin, Phillips 66 Philube, 1 Lb. 10.00
Tin, Picobac Tobacco, Hand, Gold Leaves, Pocket, 4 In. .... 20.00 To 40.00
Tin, Pinkussohn's Tobacco, Pocket .... 25.00 To 40.00
Tin, Pipe Major Tobacco, Pocket 175.00
Tin, Piper Heidsieck Tobacco, 8 X 3 X 3 In. 35.00
Tin, Pitcher, Sears Roebuck, Cross Country Motor Oil, Figural 75.00
Tin, Player's Tobacco, Sailor, 1916 .... 14.00
Tin, Plow Boy Tobacco, Label, Round 42.00
Tin, Polar Bear Celery Seed, Blue, White, Red, Yellow, 1 Oz. 5.00
Tin, Polar Bear Prophylactic, Polar Bear Picture 15.00
Tin, Poppers Ace Cigars, Photo of Bi–Plane, 1910, 5 X 3 In. 160.00
Tin, Portage Brand Cigar, Red, White, Black, 5 X 9 In. 8.00
Tin, Possum Cigars, Am Good & Sweet, Red 70.00
Tin, Postmaster Cigars, 2 For 5 Cents, Orange, Round 35.00
Tin, Postmaster Tobacco, St.Bernard, 7 X 5 In. 48.00
Tin, Premier Coffee, 1 Lb. 3.00
Tin, Prexy Tobacco, Yellow Striped Robe, Pocket 750.00
Tin, Prince Albert, Now King, Pocket 250.00
Tin, Prince Albert, Pocket 10.00
Tin, Puritan Tobacco, Dark Gray Ad Letters, Pocket 165.00
Tin, Pusches Hand Made Brand Cigar, Gold, Black, Red, 6 X 4 In. 12.00
Tin, QBoid Tobacco, Oval, Pocket 50.00
Tin, Queentex Condoms, Lipstick–Shaped 10.00
Tin, Rat Stop, Poison, 2 Oz. 7.00
Tin, Red Belt Tobacco, Pocket 30.00
Tin, Red Owl Stores Savory Spice, Red, White, Blue, 1 1/2 Oz. 5.00
Tin, Reeds Butterscotch Wafers, 20 Lb. 40.00
Tin, Reeses Corn Remover, 12 Pads 6.00
Tin, Repeater Tobacco, 4 X 6 In. 45.00
Tin, Rex Tobacco, Pocket 80.00
Tin, Rexall Baby Talcum, Baby On Front, 3 1/2 Oz. 30.00
Tin, Rhody Tobacco, Canister 260.00
Tin, Richardson's U–All–No After Dinner Mints, 1907, 2 X 1 In. 5.00
Tin, Rip Long Cut Tobacco, Box, 6 X 3 X 2 In. 350.00
Tin, Roly Poly, Brownie 550.00
Tin, Roly Poly, Dutchman, Mayo 375.00
Tin, Roly Poly, Mammy, Mayo, 7 In. .... 225.00 To 325.00
Tin, Roly Poly, Santa, 1980s, 5 In. 35.00
Tin, Roly Poly, Satisfied Customer, Dixie Queen .... 450.00 To 495.00
Tin, Roly Poly, Storekeeper, U.S.Marine Cut Tobacco .... 275.00 To 350.00
Tin, Roosevelt Tobacco, 1930s, 5 X 3 1/2 In. 30.00
Tin, Rose Leaf Tobacco, Compass, Pictures Frog, Pocket 50.00
Tin, Round Trip Smoking Tobacco, Lunch Box Type, 6 X 4 In. 60.00
Tin, Royal Baking Powder, Dated 1938, 12 Oz. 15.00
Tin, Royal Crown Men's Pomade, Sample 6.50
Tin, Royal Shield Tea, Multo–Color, Embossed, 9 X 9 X 5 In. 48.00
Tin, Sailor Girl Oysters 45.00
Tin, Salicon For Headache, Color Litho, Sample, 1 X 1/1/4 In. 5.00
Tin, Saratoga Chips Sliced Plug, U.S.Tobacco Co., 3 1/4 In. 10.00
Tin, Savory Coffee, Contents, Key Type, 1 Lb. 12.00
Tin, Schepps Cake, Paintings Top & Sides, Large 67.50

Tin, Seneca Spice Tobacco, Pocket 11.00
Tin, Sheik Prophylactics, White Sheik Silhouette 25.00
Tin, Singer Household Oil 10.00
Tin, Sir Walter Raleigh, Orange, Black, White, Pocket .... 10.00 To 12.00
Tin, Snap Shots Tobacco, 4 X 2 In. 750.00
Tin, Standard Oil of Indiana Oil, Brass Label, 5 Gal. 85.00
Tin, Stanwix Tobacco, Pocket 1350.00
Tin, Star Maid Peanuts, Picture of Girl, 10 Lb. 85.00
Tin, Sterling Brand Thyme, Blue Label, 1 1/2 Oz. 4.00
Tin, Sun Cured Tobacco, Pocket 850.00
Tin, Sweet Clover Tobacco, Flat, Pocket 375.00
Tin, Sweet Cuba Tobacco, Pie Shape 30.00
Tin, Sweet Cuba Tobacco, Round, 11 In. 75.00
Tin, Sweet Tip Top Tobacco, 1926, 6 X 5 In. 8.00
Tin, Sweet Violet Tobacco, Pocket .... 475.00 To 550.00
Tin, Tao Tea Balls, Cover, Round, 3 3/4 X 1 1/2 In. 2.50
Tin, Taxi Tobacco, Pocket .... 1800.00 To 2000.00
Tin, Texaco Gun Oil, Canister 45.00
Tin, Texaco Lighter Fluid, 4 Oz. 7.00
Tin, Texaco Oil, Rectangular, 2 Qt. 85.00
Tin, Thorough Bred Udder Balm, Directions, Square, 3 In. 17.50
Tin, Three Feathers Tobacco, Pocket 275.00
Tin, Tiger Tobacco, Red, 12 X 8 X 6 In. 130.00
Tin, Totem Tobacco, Pocket 1500.00
Tin, Toyland Peanut Butter, 2 Lb. 195.00
Tin, Trojan Blasting Caps 50.00
Tin, Trojan Prophylactics 25.00
Tin, Trout–Line Tobacco, Pocket, 3 X 2 In. 700.00
Tin, Trout–Line Tobacco, Pocket, 3 X 3 In. 225.00
Tin, Turkey Coffee, Whole Bean Lid, American Can Co., C.1910 .... 550.00
Tin, Tuxedo Tobacco, 50th Anniversary, Canister, 1906, 1 Lb. 20.00
Tin, Tuxedo Tobacco, Canister, 1906, 1 Lb. 20.00
Tin, Tuxedo Tobacco, Man Smoking, Pocket 20.00
Tin, Twilight Brand Coffee, Pull Lid, Yellow, Blue, Silver, L Lb. 20.00
Tin, Twin Oaks Tobacco, Flat Lid, Pocket 75.00
Tin, Twin Oaks Tobacco, Flip Top, Pocket 85.00
Tin, U.S.Marine Tobacco, Pocket 150.00
Tin, U.S.Marine Tobacco, Unopened, Pocket 325.00
Tin, Union Leader Tobacco, Uncle Sam, Canister 40.00
Tin, Unity Tobacco, Pocket 1275.00
Tin, Upland Queen Brand Cinnamon, Gold, Blue, White, Black, 8 Oz. ... 5.00
Tin, Vanity Dusting Powder, Peacock, 5 In.Diam. 15.00
Tin, Velvet Tobacco, Pocket 8.00
Tin, Vick's, Sample 10.00
Tin, Virginity Tobacco 275.00
Tin, Wagon Wheel Tobacco, Pocket .... 400.00 To 600.00
Tin, Waldin Brand Coffee, Yellow, Black, White, Sears, Roebuck 65.00
Tin, Wampum Coffee, Bare Breasted Indian Maiden 250.00
Tin, Wedding Breakfast Coffee, 1 Lb. 34.00
Tin, Weiserts 54 Tobacco, Pocket 700.00
Tin, Weldon Slice Smoking Tobacco, Yellow, Brown, Green, 5 In. 8.00
Tin, Wentworth Oyster, 1/2 Gal. 20.00
Tin, Wessanen's Cocoa, 1/4 Lb. 20.00
Tin, Whip Tobacco, Pocket .... 275.00 To 350.00
Tin, White House Brand Coffee, Key Type, Blue, White, Gold, 1 Lb. ... 12.00
Tin, Whitman's Caddy Peanut Brittle, 1920s Golfer With Caddy 125.00
Tin, Williams Aftershaving Talc, 3 Oz. 8.00
Tin, Willoughby Tayler Tobacco, 6 X 6 X 4 In. 20.00
Tin, Wishbone Coffee, 5 Lb. 85.00
Tin, Wishbone Coffee, Pail, 4 Lb. 40.00
Tin, Yacht Club Tobacco, 4 X 2 In. .... 300.00 To 350.00
Tin, Yacht Club Tobacco, 4 X 3 X 2 In. 70.00
Tin, Yankee Boy Tobacco, Blond Boy, Pocket 775.00
Tin, Yankee Boy Tobacco, Brunette Boy, Pocket 400.00

Tin, Zig–Zag Candy, Sample 35.00

> A tip tray is a decorated metal tray less than 5 inches in diameter.
> It was placed on the table or counter to hold either the bill or the
> coins that were left as a tip. A change receiver could be made of
> glass, plastic, or metal. It was kept on the counter near the cash
> register and held the money passed back and forth by the cashier.

ADVERTISING, TIP TRAY, see also Advertising, Change Receiver

Tip Tray, American Line 95.00
Tip Tray, Ballentine Beer, Woodgrain, 3 Rings, 4 In. 50.00
Tip Tray, Bartholomay Brewery 150.00
Tip Tray, Bartholomay's Brewery 60.00
Tip Tray, Buffalo Brewing 175.00
Tip Tray, Camel Cigarettes 20.00
Tip Tray, Carnation Dairy 70.00
Tip Tray, Clover Brand Shoes, Kittens, 2 1/2 In. 40.00
Tip Tray, Columbus 125.00
Tip Tray, Cottolene Lard, Blacks Picking Cotton 150.00
Tip Tray, Cottolene, Best For Frying, 1910 ....78.00 To 100.00
Tip Tray, Cudahys 95.00
Tip Tray, DeLaval 85.00
Tip Tray, Dorns Carnation Chewing Gum, Taste The Smell, 1910 .... 80.00
Tip Tray, Dowagaic Grain Drills 28.00
Tip Tray, Elverso, Man, In Chair, Cigar, 4 1/2 X 6 1/2 In. 49.00
Tip Tray, Fairy Soap, Have You A Fairy In Your Home 57.00
Tip Tray, Garcia Grande, Multicolored Joker, 4 X 6 In. 33.00
Tip Tray, Grin Belt 35.00
Tip Tray, Hommel's Champagne 60.00
Tip Tray, Hyroler Whiskey 20.00
Tip Tray, Hyroler Whiskey, Green, White, Black, Man In Tuxedo 38.00
Tip Tray, Imperial Dry Ginger Ale, Pictures Bottle 40.00
Tip Tray, International Harvester, Horse 35.00
Tip Tray, Jack Daniels Whiskey 20.00
Tip Tray, James Quirk Milling Co., Minneapolis 45.00
Tip Tray, Jap Rose Soap, Graphics 275.00
Tip Tray, Lemon–Kola 90.00
Tip Tray, Los Angeles Brewery, 4 In. 125.00
Tip Tray, Luden's Cough Drops, 5 Cent Box Center, 1920 .... 80.00
Tip Tray, Marilyn Monroe, Nude, 1953, 4 In.Diam. 25.00
Tip Tray, Miller Beer, Mallards 10.00
Tip Tray, Miller High Life Beer, Black Border, Gold Script 15.00
Tip Tray, Monticello Whiskey, It's All Whiskey, 1910, 4 X 6 In. 50.00
Tip Tray, Old Reliable 125.00
Tip Tray, Portland Exposiition, 1905 .... 60.00
Tip Tray, Red Cross Stoves 12.00
Tip Tray, Red Raven, Ask The Man, Girl & Red Raven, 1900 .... 25.00
Tip Tray, Resinol Soap & Ointment, Woman With Roses, 1910 .... 35.00
Tip Tray, Rienzi 175.00
Tip Tray, Roosevelt Bears, Tin, 1906 .... 110.00
Tip Tray, Ruhstaller, Lady With Dove 125.00
Tip Tray, Sears Roebuck 50.00
Tip Tray, Shriner Grain Belt Beer 35.00
Tip Tray, Stegmaier, 4 3/8 In. ....35.00 To 55.00
Tip Tray, Stollwerck Chocolate & Cocoa 15.00
Tip Tray, Sullivan's Cigar, Brown, Black, Gold, 6 X 4 In. 48.00
Tip Tray, Tivoli Brewing Co., Pre–Prohibition Bottle, 4 In. 25.00
Tip Tray, Torrey's Mt.Vernon Rye 60.00
Tip Tray, Universal Stoves 90.00
Tip Tray, Waterman Pens, Brass 195.00
Tip Tray, Welsbach Mantels, Eagle Picture, 4 In.Diam. 40.00
Tip Tray, White Rock 75.00
Tip Tray, William Tell Flour, Flower of Family Portrait, 1907 .... 35.00
Tobacco Cutter, Brighton, Little Imp 65.00
Tobacco Cutter, Reynolds Brown's Mule Tobacco 46.00

Tobacco Cutter, Star	65.00
Token, Sanitary Dairy, Barnesville, Ohio, Aluminum	2.50
Token, Union Coffee Co., N.Y., Gutta Percha, Jefferson Bust	21.00
Top Hat, Moet & Chandon, Bakelite	15.00
Towel, Beach, Hamm's Beer	6.00
Toy, Car, Pan American Airlines, Friction, Tin, Box, 1960s, 10 In.	25.00
Toy, Crinkle The Cat, Kellogg, Cloth, 1935	80.00
Toy, Dandy The Duck, Kellogg, Cloth, 1935	80.00
Toy, Dinkey The Dog, Kellogg, Cloth, 1935	80.00
Toy, Frisbee, Kodak	10.00
Toy, Milk Truck, Meeker Dairys, Gong Bell	200.00
Toy, Periscope, Morton Salt	20.00
Toy, Playset, Ronald McDonald, Complete	25.00
Toy, Pop, Kelloggs, Rubber, 7 1/2 In. ....*Illus*	25.00
Toy, Rocket, Milky Way, Plastic Premium, 1940, 10 X 4 In.	7.50
Toy, Soldier, International Harvester Cub Cadet, Iron, 7 In.	13.00
Toy, Top, Jenkins One Price Pianos, Cast Iron	52.00
Toy, Top, Kleenmaide Bread, Plastic	16.00
Toy, Top, Poll Parrot Shoes	32.00
Toy, Wagon, J.P.Coats, Wooden Wheels	825.00
Tray, A New Diehl, Diehl Brewing Co., Topless Girl, 1933, 12 In.	46.00
Tray, Akron Brewing Co., Lady, Tiger, C.1910, 13 In.	80.00
Tray, Anheuser–Busch, Lady, Letter, Eagle, 13 X 16 In.	400.00
Tray, Baker's Breakfast Cocoa, Baker's Lady, Home, 1915, 6 In.	180.00
Tray, Baker's Chocolate, Green & Red Design, Oval, 13 X 17 In.	200.00
Tray, Ballantine Beer, Silver Finish, Floral, Oval, 20 In.	18.00
Tray, Baltimore Brewing Co., 1930s, 13 In.	175.00
Tray, Bartel's Brewery, Wilkes Barre, Penna., 13 In.	165.00
Tray, Beer Union, Dutch Girl, Beer, Boy, 1914, 13 X 10 In.	180.00
Tray, Bevo Beverage, Wood Grain Border, Team of Horses, C.1900	125.00
Tray, Budweiser, Levee Scene, 12 In.	145.00
Tray, Budweiser, Oval, Girl With Parasol, 12 In.	10.00
Tray, Budweiser, Waiter, With Tray, Red Rim, Black Ground, 11 In.	30.00
Tray, Champagne Velvet, Cherubs	295.00
Tray, Christian Feighn–Span Breweries, 1916	45.00
Tray, Cincinnati Creme, Waiter	135.00
Tray, Columbia Ice Cream, Loyal Friends, Horse, Dog, C.1913	150.00
Tray, Congress Beer, Haberle Brew, Label, 12 In.Diam.	45.00
Tray, Crescent Brewing Co., Nampa, Idaho, Pretty Girl	110.00
Tray, DeCourseys Ice Cream, Red, White, 13 1/4 X 10 1/2 In.	15.00
Tray, DeLaval Cream Separator	130.00
Tray, Drink Old Timbrook, Woman	50.00
Tray, Elgear Fortier Soda, 1910	75.00
Tray, Enterprise Brewing, Lady With Flowers	300.00
Tray, Fairy Soap, Little Girl Sitting On Soap, 14 In.	40.00
Tray, Falstaff Beer, 1971	35.00
Tray, Feigenspan Beer, Woman	20.00
Tray, Ferris Brick Co., 1903	25.00
Tray, Fink Brewing Company, Right To The Point, C.1914, 16 In.	160.00
Tray, Florida Brewing Co., Dogs Smoking, Drinking, 1910	150.00
Tray, Goebel Beer, Picture of Dutch Girl	125.00
Tray, Goetz Beer	25.00
Tray, Green River Whiskey, Picture Black Man & Horse, 12 In.	225.00
Tray, HA Youn & Co., Lake City, Minn.	95.00
Tray, Harvard Brewing Co., Bathing Beauty, Glass, Beer, 12 In.	95.00
Tray, Hires, Woman	95.00
Tray, Home of Falstaff, Fireplace Drinking Scene, 24 In.	125.00
Tray, Ice Cream, Picture of 3 Girls	325.00
Tray, J.H.Cutter Whiskey, Sunrise, Sailing Vessel, 1915, 16 In.	325.00
Tray, Jersey Creme, Woman	195.00
Tray, Jeweler & Optical Baby	22.00
Tray, John H.Leemhuis, Fine Boots & Shoes, Blue Earth, Minn.	125.00
Tray, Kentucky Taylor	20.00
Tray, Le Bon Coffee, Sheep Fold, 1904, 12 X 17 In.	75.00

Tray, Liberty Brewing Co., Auburn, N.Y., Shonk, 12 In.	560.00
Tray, Lionel Trains, 1950	100.00
Tray, Little Cuba Cigars, Metal, 1930s	30.00
Tray, Louisville Refining Co.	35.00
Tray, Marilyn Monroe, 1953, 4 In.	25.00
Tray, Martha Washington Wine	95.00
Tray, Miller High Life, Girl On Moon, 13 In.Diam.	50.00
Tray, Mirinda Orange Soda	25.00
Tray, Moehn Brewery Co., Round, 1909, 13 In.	600.00
Tray, Moxie, 9 1/4 X 5 In.	40.00
Tray, Old Pepper Whiskey, Oval	450.00
Tray, Oldenberg, Picture of Brewery, 10 X 13 In.	4.00
Tray, Orange Julep	115.00
Tray, Pacific Bee, 1912	175.00
Tray, Peil's Beer, Pictures Elves	68.00
Tray, Rainier Beer, Victorian Girl, On Bearskin Rug, 1900	275.00
Tray, RCA, Nipper, His Master's Voice, Metal, 11 1/2 X 14 In.	5.00
Tray, Red Raven, Papa Has A Headache	535.00
Tray, Robin Brand Carbonated Ice Cream, Children, Round	295.00
Tray, Robin Brand Ice Cream, Woman, Telephone	175.00
Tray, Rolling Rock, Blue, White, Horse Head, 13 In.	8.00
Tray, Rupert Beer, Comic Butcher Shop, 13 In.Diam.	75.00
Tray, Salt Lake City Brewing Co.	27.50
Tray, Schlitz Beer, Schlitzerland, 1957	35.00
Tray, Schlitz Beer, World Globe, 1930s	20.00
Tray, Schmidt's Valley Forge Beer, 1930	20.00
Tray, Semon's Ice Cream, 2 Children Eating, 1930, 13 1/2 In.	200.00
Tray, Sen–Sen, Aluminum	22.00
Tray, South Side Clothing Co., Girl, Flowing Hair, 5 In.	68.00
Tray, Storz Brewing Co., Omaha, Nebr., Glass, Bottle & Can	75.00
Tray, Terre Haute Brewing, Angles, Oval	295.00
ADVERTISING, TRAY, TIP, see Advertising, Tip Tray	
Tray, Union Beer	148.50
Tray, Weiland Beer, San Francisco, Pre–Prohibition, Pretty Lady	150.00
Tray, Yellowstone Whiskey, Bottle On Falls, Rectangular	125.00
Tumbler, Allen's Red Tame	15.00
Tumbler, Bevo The Beverage, Barrel, 3 1/2 In.	35.00
Tumbler, Bluebonnet, White, Geese, Hops, Estra Pale Beer, 4 In.	44.00
Tumbler, Bosco, Mickey Mouse,, 1939	35.00
Tumbler, Coors, Barrel, Nevada Centennial 1864–1964, 3 In.	18.00
Tumbler, Elsie The Cow	10.00
Tumbler, Erie Brewery Co.	15.00
Tumbler, Gold Bond Beer, Cleveland, Ohio, Shell, 4 In.	26.00
Tumbler, Hirim Walker, Enameled Glass	3.00
Tumbler, Howard Johnson	15.00
Tumbler, Juice, Norton Orange Maid, Glass Straws, Box, 6 Piece	15.00
Tumbler, Los Angeles Brewing, Santa Barbara Mission, 2 3/4 In.	40.00
Tumbler, Michelob, A Short Beer, Shell Red Ribbon, Black, 3 In.	13.00
Tumbler, Michelob, All Red Logo, 5 1/2 In.	106.00
Tumbler, Michelob, Black A, Pre–Prohibition, Stemmed, 6 In.	51.00
Tumbler, Mitchell's, All Red Triangle Design, 6 1/4 In.	112.00
Tumbler, Mitchell's, Red Diamond Shape Logo, Barrel, 3 In.	86.00
Tumbler, Old Crow Whiskey, Footed, 6 Piece	30.00
Tumbler, Premium Quality Falstaff, Red, 5 1/4 In.	10.00
Tumbler, R.C.Cola, Gold Rim, 1950s, Box, 6 Piece	35.00
Tumbler, Winnie The Pooh & Friends, Sears, 5 In.	6.00
Vase, National Sewing Machine Factory, Side Handles, 2 X 3 In.	5.00
Warmer, Peanut, Lights Up, Lift Lid, Bell Rings, 1920s	500.00
Whistle, Weatherbird Shoes	15.00

Agata glass was made by Joseph Locke of the New England Glass Company of Cambridge, Massachusetts, after 1885. A metallic stain was applied to New England Peachblow and the mottled design characteristic of agata appeared.

AGATA, Celery, Square, Crimped Edge, 6 3/4 In. 895.00
  Finger Bowl, Ruffled Top 650.00
  Toothpick, Pinched Scalloped Rim 795.00
  Tumbler, 3 3/4 In. 550.00
  Tumbler, Lemonade, Gold Tracery, 5 1/8 In. 1250.00

Akro agate glass was made in Clarksburg, West Virginia, from 1932 to 1951. Before that time, the firm made children's glass marbles. Most of the glass is marked with a crow flying through the letter A.

AKRO AGATE, Ashtray, Dark Jade 5.00
  Ashtray, Green & White 4.00
  Ashtray, Green Marble 5.00
  Ashtray, Hotel Edison, 4 In. 26.00
  Ashtray, Turquoise 5.00
  Bowl, Pumpkin, 6 In. 20.00
  Box, Cigarette, Mexicali 27.50
  Cup, Chiquita, Purple 16.00
  Dish Set, Child's, Playtime, Box 42.50
  Dish, Scotty Dog Cover, Chartreuse 90.00
  Dish, Southern Belle Cover 50.00
  Flowerpot, Blue, 3 1/2 In. 7.00
  Inkwell, Pug Dog, Removable Head Over 165.00
  Jar, Mexicali, Orange In White 32.00
  Lamp, Electric, 2–Light, Red & White 55.00
  Lamp, Marble Base, Cream & Orange, 11 1/2 In. 190.00
  Match Holder & Ashtray, Cornucopia 25.00
  Match Holder, Transparent Teal Blue 40.00
  Pitcher, Water, Octagonal, Blue 11.00
  Planter, Green, White, 5 1/2 In. 8.00
  Plate, Concentric Ring, Green, Blue 4.50
  Powder Box, Colonial Lady, Blue Top, White Bottom 50.00
  Powder Box, Colonial Lady, Pink 14.00
  Powder Jar, Apple, Orange, White Lid, Marbelized 95.00
  Powder Jar, Colonial Lady, Pink 25.00
  Powder Jar, Mexicali, Blue & White, Cover 20.00
  Saucer, Chiquita, Yellow 6.00
  Shaving Mug, Cover, Black & White 20.00
  Smoke Set, Red & White, Box, 5 Piece 48.00
  Sugar, Chiquita, Blue 6.50
  Sugar, Stippled Band, Amber 15.00
  Tea Set, Child's, Concentric Ring, Green Marbelized, 19 Piece 120.00
  Teapot, Swirl Autumn Colors 18.00
  Teapot, Transparent Green, Cover 35.00
  Tumbler, Yellow, Octagonal 13.00
  Vase, 7 Darts, 8 3/4 In. 60.00
  Water Set, Child's, Transoptic Stippled Band, Green, 7 Piece 55.00
  Water Set, Transparent Green, Disc, Interior Panel, Small, 7 Pc. 65.00

Alabaster is a very soft form of gypsum, a stone that resembles marble. It was often carved into vases or statues in Victorian times. There are alabaster carvings being made even today. Because the alabaster is very porous, it will dissolve if kept in water, so do not use alabaster vases for flowers.

ALABASTER, Compote, Brown, Scalloped, 7 3/4 X 4 1/2 In. 18.00
  Dish, Oatmeal, White, Agate–Like, Oval, 7 3/4 X 4 1/2 In. 28.00
  Figurine, Cherubs, Doing Alphabet, 17 In., Pair ....*Illus* 1870.00
  Figurine, Girl In Classical Dress, Signed Marron, 13 1/2 In. 100.00
  Group, Young Girl On Rocky Outcropping, 2 Sheep, 26 1/2 In. 750.00
  Plate, LaScalla Opera, Box, Certificates, 1976–82, 7 Piece 155.00
  Torchere, Stylized Relief Leaves & Veins, Conical, C.1930, 19 In. 6050.00
  Urn, Griffins, Scrolls, Animal Handles, Ovoid, Plinth, 4 Ft., Pair 1210.00

Alexandrite is a name with many meanings. It is a form of the mineral chrysoberyl that changes from green to red under artificial light. A man–made version of this mineral is sold in Mexico today. It changes from deep purple to aquamarine blue under artificial light. The Alexandrite listed here is glass made in the late nineteenth and twentieth centuries. Thomas Webb & Sons sold their transparent glass shaded from yellow to rose to blue under the name Alexandrite. Stevens and Williams had a cased Alexandrite of yellow, rose, and blue. A. Douglas Nash Corporation made an amethyst–colored Alexandrite. Several American glass companies of the 1920s made a glass that changed color under electric lights and these were called Alexandrite too.

ALEXANDRITE, Bowl, Irregularly Ruffled Edge, 3 X 5 In.	830.00
Goblet, Textured Leaves On Stem, Wafer Base, 8 1/2 In.	1750.00
Pitcher, Flower–Shaped Top, Amber, Rose & Lavender, 5 1/2 In.	1700.00
Vase, Jack–In–The–Pulpit, Honeycomb Pattern, 4 In.	925.00

Alhambra is a pattern of tableware made in Vienna, Austria, in the twentieth century. The geometric designs are in applied gold, red, and dark green. Full sets of dishes can be found in this pattern.

ALHAMBRA, Compote, Low–Footed, Austria, 8 1/2 In.	85.00
Cup & Saucer, Austria, Demitasse	45.00

Aluminum was more expensive than gold or silver until the 1850s. Chemists learned how to refine bauxite to get aluminum. Jewelry and other small objects were made of the valuable metal until 1914 when an inexpensive smelting process was invented. The aluminum collected today dates from the 1930s through 1950s. Hand–hammered pieces are the most popular.

ALUMINUM, Ashtray, 6 Incised Flowers, Buenilum, 6 1/2 In.	3.00
Ashtray, Siesta Scene, Everlast, 5 1/4 In.	2.50
Basket, Acorn Design, Scalloped, Continental 536, 11 3/4 X 6 In.	12.00
Basket, Cake, Chrysanthemum, Rolled Up, Continental 510, 10 In.	8.00
Bowl, Bamboo, Everlast, 10 In.	6.00
Bowl, Dogwood, Everlast, 11 In.	6.50
Bowl, Floral, Hand Forged, 11 In.	6.50
Bowl, Flower, Leaf, Buenilum	5.00
Bread Tray, Chrysanthemum, Continental 566, 12 In.	6.50
Bread Tray, Chrysanthemum, Handle, Continental 755, 13 X 7 In.	6.50
Bread Tray, Pineapple, Kensington	22.00
Bread Tray, Tulip, Rodney Kent 406	7.00

Alabaster, Figurine, Cherubs,
Doing Alphabet, 17 In., Pair

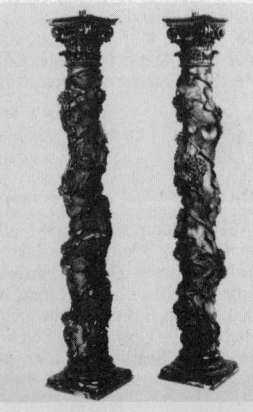

Architectural, Columns, Carved,
Gilded, Twisted, Grapes, 78 In.

Candlesticks, Acanthus Leaf Base, Continental 511, 6 In., Pair 8.50
Candy Dish, Blossom, Bows, Pedestal, Cover, Rodney Kent 457, 6 In. 6.50
Candy Dish, Rosette Center, 3 Sections, Continental 756, 7 In. 7.00
Canister Set, Red Apples, 5 Piece 55.00
Casserole Holder, Warmer Stand, Flower Bud Design, Handles 15.00
Cheese & Cracker Set, Tulip Center, Cover, Rodney Kent 460, 12 In. 14.00
Coaster, Flying Ducks, Reeds, Water, Set of 10 .... 9.00
Coaster, Roses, Everlast, Set of 4 .... 3.50
Coaster, Tulip, Rodney Kent 446, Set of 6 .... 5.00
Ice Bucket, Handle, Cromwell, 5 In. 9.00
Lazy Susan, Fruit & Flowers, Cromwell, 16 In. 25.00
Lazy Susan, Poppy, Wheat, Daffodil, Hand Wrought, 14 1/2 In. 10.00
Lazy Susan, Tulip, Rodney Kent 413, 18 In. 14.00
Platter, Cromwell, Handles, 16 In. 30.00
Relish, Palm Frond, Haeger, Bruce Cox, 25 In. 30.00
Server, 2 Tiers, Acorns, Continental 525, 17 1/2 In. 12.00
Server, 2 Tiers, Bamboo, Everlast 10.00
Server, Hors D'Oeuvres, Hubcap, 13 1/2 In., 2 Piece 115.00
Shaker, Cocktail, Buenilum, Art Deco Top 15.00
Silent Butler, Pinecones, Needles, Everlast 8.00
Silent Butler, Tulip, Rodney Kent 439 .... 8.50
Tray, Blossoms, Ivy, Keystone Paisley 423, 18 In. 8.50
Tray, Floral, Leaf, Fluted, Crimped, Farber-Schlevin, 15 In. 8.50
Tray, Grape Cluster, Loop Handle, Buenilum, 17 1/2 In. 10.00
Tray, Hammered, Double Looped Open Handles, Cromwell 8.00
Tray, Plain, Leaf & Bud Handles, Continental 22, 15 1/2 In. 12.00
Tray, Vegetables, Keystone Paisley 310, 13 X 10 In. 7.00
Tumbler, Green 1.00
Warmer, Wooden, 3 Covered Pots, Holder, 15 X 10 1/2 In. 325.00
Water Set, Art Deco Colors, 7 Piece 20.00

AMBER, see Jewelry

Amber glass is the name of any glassware with the proper yellow-brown shading. It was a popular color just after the Civil War and many pressed glass pieces were made of amber glass. Depression glass of the 1930s–1950s was also made in shades of amber glass. All types are being reproduced.

AMBER GLASS, Bouquet Holder, Glass Slipper, 1876 .... 35.00
Box, Pansies, Cover, Melon-Sectioned Shape, 6 1/2 In. 210.00
Compote, Daisy & Button, Octagonal, Scalloped, C.1920, 8 1/2 In. 150.00
Cuspidor, Applied White Rim, 6 In. 40.00
Jug, Applied Lip & Handle, 5 1/4 In. 525.00
Pitcher, Blue Grapes & Leaves, Blue Handle, 8 1/4 In. 195.00
Pitcher, Chalet, Crystal Rim & Feet, Marked, 8 1/2 In. 95.00
Pitcher, Diamond-Quilted, Figure of Man With Bird, 11 1/8 In. 125.00
Pitcher, Inverted Thumbprint, Clear Rope Handle, 6 1/4 In. 150.00
Pitcher, Water, Enameled Flowers, Gold Trim, 10 1/2 In. 175.00
Smoke Bell, Daisy & Button, Smoke 70.00
Syrup, Hercules Pillar 110.00
Water Set, Hobnail, Amber, 7 Piece 595.00
Water Set, Willow Oak, 9 Piece 250.00

AMBERETTE, see Pressed Glass, Klondike

Amberina is a two-toned glassware made from 1883 to about 1900. It was patented by Joseph Locke of the New England Glass Company. The glass shades from red to amber.

AMBERINA, see also Baccarat; Bluerina; Plated Amberina
AMBERINA, Bowl, Enameled Pastel Floral, Gold Allover Vines, Ruffled, 9 In. 299.00
Bowl, Fluted, Gold Flowers, Berries & Branches, 8 1/8 In. 365.00
Bowl, Melon Sectioned, Enameled Flowers, Leaves, 9 1/2 In. 295.00
Bowl, Ruffled Top, Libbey, Marked, 5 In. 145.00
Bowl, Swirled, Gold Flowers & Leaves, Footed, 4 1/2 X 4 3/4 In. 265.00
Bowl, Thumbprint Pattern, Tricorner, 2 1/4 X 4 1/2 In. 275.00
Candy, Cover, Stem Handle, 7 In. 195.00

Castor, Pickle, Inverted Thumbprint, Enameled Florals, Sterling 595.00
Celery Dish, Scrolled, Scalloped, Frosted, 10 In. 325.00
Celery Vase, Venetian Diamond, Squared Scalloped Top, 6 1/4 In. 345.00
Compote, Honeycomb, 5 3/4 In. 85.00
Cruet, Drape Pattern, Original Stopper 395.00
Cruet, Enameled Flowers, Ball Stopper, Amber Handle, 9 In. 265.00
Cruet, Fuchsia 250.00
Cuspidor, Woman's, Optic Ribbing, 2 1/2 X 5 1/4 In. 280.00
Decanter, Cranberry, Amber Applied Handle, Flowers, 9 In. 265.00
Decanter, Pedestal Foot, Amber Stopper, Enameled Flowers, 14 In. 235.00
Decanter, Wine, Pedestal Foot 235.00
Dish, Daisy & Button, Square, 5 1/2 In. 115.00
Dish, Swirl To Cranberry, Cover, Amber Handles, 4 In. 365.00
Finger Bowl, Fluted, 2 3/4 X 5 1/2 In. 225.00
Lamp, Hall, Hanging, Hobnail, Brass Trim, 10 X 9 In. 345.00
Mug, Applied Amber Handle, Plated 2100.00
Pitcher, Inverted Thumbprint, Squared Dimpled Shape, 5 7/8 In. 165.00
Pitcher, Milk, Diamond–Quilted, 6 1/2 In. 140.00
Pitcher, Optic Diamond–Quilted, 4 1/4 In. 235.00
Pitcher, Swirl, Reeded Amber Handle, 19th Century, 8 1/2 In. 350.00
Pitcher, Water, Drape Pattern, Square Mouth, 7 1/8 In. 295.00
Pitcher, Water, Inverted Thumbprint, Amber Handle, 7 1/2 In. 175.00
Punch Cup, Diamond–Quilted, Amber Reeded Handle, New England 75.00
Punch Cup, Optic Rib & Honeycomb 55.00
Spooner, Diamond–Quilted, Square Scalloped Top, 4 1/2 In. 235.00
Sugar, Cover, Daisy & Button, 5 1/2 In. 535.00
Toothpick, Diamond–Quilted, Fuchsia 225.00
Toothpick, Venetian Diamond, 3–Cornered 210.00
Tumbler, Baby Thumbprint 30.00
Tumbler, Diamond–Quilted, 3 3/4 In. 195.00
Tumbler, Inverted Thumbprint .... 45.00 To 65.00
Tumbler, Thumbprint 72.00
Tumbler, Wheeling, Plated, 4 In. 450.00
Vase, Amber Ruffled Rim, Swirl Pattern, 10 1/2 In. 165.00
Vase, Applied Leaves, Crystal Ruffled Top, Loop Feet, 6 1/2 In. 395.00
Vase, Calla Lily Shape, Amber Spiral Trim, 13 3/4 In. 195.00
Vase, Crystal Ruffled Top, Crystal Leaves, Crackled, 6 1/8 In. 395.00
Vase, Jack–In–The–Pulpit Top, Amber Edging, 11 5/8 In. 175.00
Vase, Jack–In–The–Pulpit, Swirl Pattern In Body, 12 In. 440.00
Vase, Paneled Lily, 7 In. 150.00
Vase, Square Mouth, Gold Enameled Floral, Rigaree Neck, 3 3/4 In. 175.00
Vase, Swirl, Enameled Flowers, Green Leaves, 5 1/8 In. 335.00
Vase, Swirled Cylinder, Amber Rope, 6–Footed, 10 In. 145.00
Vase, White Enameled Flowers, Green Leaves, Cylindrical, 10 In. 335.00
Wine, Inverted Thumbprint 140.00

 The American Encaustic Tiling Company was founded in Zanesville, Ohio, in 1875. The company planned to make a variety of tiles to compete with the English tiles that were selling in the United States for use in fireplaces and other architectural needs. The first glazed tiles were made in 1880, embossed tiles were added in 1881, faience tiles in the 1920s. The firm closed in 1935 and reopened in 1937 as the Shawnee Pottery.

AMERICAN ENCAUSTIC TILING CO., Bookends, Cupid, Rabbit, Beige Glaze, 1926   125.00
Fireplace Set, Complete, Flowered, Geometric 275.00
Tile, Black Marbelized 20.00
Tile, Cherub, Warming Hands By Fire, 6 In. 65.00
Tile, Chicken In Relief 50.00
Tile, Figure of A Woman 75.00
Tile, Floral 25.00
Tile, Torches 65.00

Amethyst glass is any of the many glasswares made in the dark purple color of the gemstone called amethyst. Included in this section are many pieces made in the nineteenth and twentieth centuries. Very dark pieces are called black amethyst and are listed under that heading.

AMETHYST GLASS, Bottle, Barber's, Gold & White Design, Pewter Top 70.00
Bowl, 4 Sections, Attached Chrome Base, Signed, 1920s 22.00
Creamer, Sawtooth & Waffle Variant, Applied Handle, 4 In. 100.00
Goblet, Applied Foot & Stem, 6 In., Pair 90.00
Powder Jar, Diagonal Bands Molded Roses, Rose Finial Cover 22.00
Rose Bowl, Clear Applied Branch & Leaf, 8–Crimp Top 135.00
Sugar, Applied Foot, Domed Lid, Galleried Rim, 7 In. 650.00
Vase, Coralene Flowers, Amber Feet, Fluted Top, 6 X 5 In. 325.00
Vase, Ormolu Trim, Bacchus Head Handles, 12 1/2 In., Pair 750.00
Water Set, Daisies, Blue & Coral Flowers, Gold Trim, 7 Piece 295.00
    AMPHORA, see Teplitz
    ANDIRON AND RELATED FIREPLACE ITEMS, see Fireplace

Stuffed animals or fish, rugs made of animal skins, and other similar collectibles are listed in this section. Collectors should be aware of the endangered species laws that make it illegal to buy and sell some of these items. Any eagle feathers, many types of cats, such as leopard, and many forms of tortoiseshell can be confiscated if discovered by the government.

ANIMAL TROPHY, Alligator, 3 Ft. 125.00
Bearskin Rug, With Head 375.00
Bearskin, Brown, Full Head, Open Mouth 300.00
Buck Deer, 8–Point, Mounted 50.00
Buffalo Skull, 1870s 95.00
Grizzly Bear, Walking, Full Mount 4000.00
Insect Display, Collector's Photograph, 1891, Framed, 50 In. 700.00
Moose Head, Stuffed 425.00
Owl, Stuffed, On Tree Branch, 16 In. 150.00
Parrot, Victorian, Large 90.00
Walleye Pike, Mounted, 23 In. 30.00
Wild Black Boar's Head, 4 Large Tusks 125.00

Animation cels are painted drawings on celluloid that are needed to make an animated cartoon. Hundreds of cels are made, then photographed in sequence to make a cartoon showing moving figures. Early examples made by the Walt Disney Studios are popular with collectors today.

ANIMATION ART, Cel, Adventures of Ichabod & Mr.Toad, 1969, 8 1/2 X 9 In. 550.00
Cel, Alice In Wonderland, 1951, 10 1/4 X 12 In. 715.00
Cel, Alice In Wonderland, 9 Bizarre Creatures, 1951 .... 2475.00
Cel, Alice In Wonderland, Dodo Bird, Tears, 1951, 10 X 12 In. 715.00
Cel, Alice In Wonderland, White Rabbit, Dodo Bird, 1951 .... 990.00
Cel, Aristocats, Kitten Beloiz 175.00
Cel, Bambi, With Stag In Forest, 1942, 8 1/2 X 7 In. 880.00
Cel, Beatles, Profile Head of John Singing, Help 605.00
Cel, Beatles, Yellow Submarine, Ringo Starr, Mr.Mayor, 1968 .... 880.00
Cel, Betty Boop, Full–Figured Profile 165.00
Cel, Black Cauldron, Horned King 145.00
Cel, Bugs Bunny, Bugs In Top Hat & Cane, Hand Inked, Framed 175.00
Cel, Bugs Bunny, Chased By Giant Dragon, Frame 325.00
Cel, Cinderella, Lucifer, 1950, 7 1/2 X 11 3/4 In. 935.00
Cel, Cinderella, Stepmother, Holding Staff 2200.00
Cel, Cinderella, With King, 1950, 5 1/2 X 8 1/2 In 1200.00
Cel, Daffy Duck, Blowing Blue Tuba, Framed 195.00
Cel, Day The Earth Made Playoffs, Baseball, Framed, 11 In. 85.00
Cel, Donald Duck, Orphans Benefit 750.00
Cel, Dumbo, Pink Elephant Dream, 1941, 8 X 10 In. 3025.00
Cel, Eeyore, Background Paintings 190.00

Cel, Fantasia, Baby Pegasus Seated, 1940, 8 X 11 In. 550.00
Cel, Fantasia, Sorcerer's Apprentice, 1940, 9 X 11 In. 2475.00
Cel, Ferdinand The Bull, Smiling Matador, 1938, 9 X 11 In. 2500.00
Cel, Fred Flintstone & Barney, With Gypsy Fortune Teller 175.00
Cel, George Jetson In Futuristic Computer Room 115.00
Cel, Jiminy Cricket, Swinging Umbrella 300.00
Cel, Jiminy Cricket, Umbrella, I'm No Fool, TV Series, 4 In. 325.00
Cel, Jungle Book, King Louie & Baloo, 1967, 11 1/2 X 15 In. 990.00
Cel, Jungle Book, King Louie, 1967, 12 1/2 X 15 1/4 In. 385.00
Cel, Krazy Kat, Girlfriend On Camel, Hand Painted, Framed 245.00
Cel, Lady & The Tramp, Lady Looking At Fish Bowl, 1955 .... 4950.00
Cel, Lady and The Tramp, Peg The Pekinese, 1955, 13 X 15 In. 2475.00
Cel, Little Hiawatha, 1937, 9 1/2 X 10 In. 440.00
Cel, Little John, Framed & Matted 365.00
Cel, Lucy, Peanuts, Girl Talk, 6 Girls Eating Lunch 250.00
Cel, Mickey Mouse, Simple Things, Framed, 1953, 15 X 16 In. 985.00
Cel, Mickey Mouse, Two–Gun Mickey, 1934 .... 185.00
Cel, Mickey, Donald, Pluto, 1978 .... 125.00
Cel, Pepe Lepew, Crown Running & Holding Noses 275.00
Cel, Peter & The Wolf, Ivan The Cat, 1946, 9 1/2 X 7 1/2 In. 275.00
Cel, Peter and The Wolf, Ivan The Cat, 1946, 9 X 7 In. 275.00
Cel, Peter Pan, Tinkerbell, 1953, 8 1/2 X 10 3/4 In. 2200.00
Cel, Pink Panther, Pink Outline, With Flyswatter 80.00
Cel, Pinocchio & Dutch Marionette, Disney Seal 1600.00
Cel, Pinocchio, Holding Apple, Disney Studios, 6 X 6 In. 475.00
Cel, Pinocchio, Jiminy Cricket, Top Hat, 1939, 9 X 8 In. 880.00
Cel, Pogo, Signed Walt Kell, Hand Painted Ground 750.00
Cel, Robin Hood, Little John & Bear, Framed 325.00
Cel, Sleeping Beauty, Briar Rose, Broom, 1959, 9 X 7 In. 660.00
Cel, Sleeping Beauty, Malificent & Raven Diablo, Framed 3000.00
Cel, Snow White & 7 Dwarfs, Bashful Playing Accordion, 1937 .... 1540.00
Cel, Steamboat Willie, 1928, 9 X 11 In. 770.00
Cel, Sword In The Stone, Sir Ector, 1963, 7 1/2 X 10 1/2 In. 330.00
Cel, Sylvester The Cat, Carrying Book, Graduation Cap 115.00
Cel, Three Little Pigs, With Shotgun, 1932, 9 X 11 In. 2200.00
Cel, Uncle Scrooge, Handing Money To Nephew 195.00
Cel, Winnie The Pooh & Tigger Too, 1974, 12 X 15 In. 1650.00
Cel, Winnie The Pooh & Tigger Too, Tigger 185.00
Cel, Winnie The Pooh, Pooh Bear, Honey Pot, 1968, 10 X 14 In. 495.00
Cel, Winnie The Pooh, Santa Claus Holding Winnie 165.00
Cel, Yogi Bear, On Park Bench, Lying Down 95.00
Cel, Yosemite Sam, With 6 Guns, Double Image, Framed 175.00
APPLE PEELER, see Kitchen, Peeler, Apple

 This section includes a variety of collectibles, usually very large, that have been removed from buildings. Hardware, backbars, doors, paneling, and even old bathtubs are now wanted by collectors. Pieces of the Victorian, Art Nouveau, and Art Deco styles are in greatest demand.

ARCHITECTURAL, Backbar, Golden Oak, C.1900, 8 Ft.11 1/2 In. X 14 Ft. 2200.00
Backbar, Oak, Mirror Back, Top Drawers, 12 X 9 Ft. 3400.00
Barn Ventilator, Round Hex Sign, Weathered 3800.00
Bathroom Tissue Holder, Porcelain, White .... 6.00 To 12.00
Bathtub, Child's, Metal 85.00
Bathtub, Copper, Oak Rim, Steel Clad Bath Co., Label, 1891 .... 1595.00
Bathtub, Tin, 1900, Round 210.00
Bathtub, Tin, Wooden Base, Oval 60.00
Columns, Carved, Gilded, Twisted, Grapes, 78 In. ....*Illus* 2860.00
Corbel, Bullfinch, From Boston State House, 4 Piece 650.00
Door Hinge, Brass, Says Texas Capitol, Walnut Base, Pair 4950.00
Door, Jail, Framing, Lock, Hinges, Food Access Window, Steel 150.00
Door, Oak, Beveled Glass, Pair 525.00
Doorway, Exterior, Federal, Pine, Carved, Painted, 1800, 120 In. 1650.00
Doorway, Stained Glass, Grain Painted, Pine, Arched Pediment 3200.00

Downspout, Copper, C.1880, 16 X 10 In., Pair 195.00
Dumbwaiter, Mahogany, Piecrust, 3–Footed, 36 X 26 In. 180.00
Eagle, On Base, Lead, 19th Century, 20 In., Pair 4125.00
Fence, Spearheads, Iron, 4 X 80 Ft. 400.00
Finial, Opening Bud, Sheet Copper, 15 1/2 In. 95.00
Fountain, Cupid & Dolphin, Bronze 2100.00
Gazebo, Arch Form, Painted White Wrought Iron, 120 X 120 In. 4300.00
Hinge, Moravian, Stag Horn, Pintles, 1760, 12 X 5 In., Pair 1800.00
Hinge, Y, Wrought Iron, 18 In., Pair 60.00
Lamppost, Lotus & Acanthus Top, Fluted, Bronze, 58 In., Pair 1100.00
Lamppost, Tin, Gas, Dated 1800s 18.00
Letter Slot, Scrolls, Florals, Yale & Towne, 8 3/4 In., Pair 840.00
Mantel, Carved Maple, Beveled Mirror 2300.00
Mantel, Lion Heads Over Frieze, Oak, 8 Ft.6 In. X 7 Ft.4 In. 1600.00
Mantel, Recessed Panels & Moldings, Pine, 53 1/2 In. 400.00
Mantel, Tiger Oak, Beveled Mirror, Carved & Side Poles 800.00
Molding, Chinese, Teak, Gold Leaf, 11 X 32 In., 3 Piece 350.00
Ornament, Cherub Head, Wings, Oak, Red Paint, 13 In. 395.00
Panel, Virgin Mary With Jesus, Heraldic Crest, 6 1/4 In., Pr. 185.00
Post Office, Complete, 1910 .... 1750.00
Pull Bell & Door Knocker, Ornate Cast Iron 65.00
Sign, Arms of Austria & France, Pine Frame, 54 X 20 In. 330.00
Soda Fountain, Marble Top & Front 1500.00
Staircase, Shaker, Original Mustard Paint 1200.00
Statue, Putti, 4 Seasons, Garden, Cement, 1930, 25 In., 4 Piece 650.00
Street Sign, Grant Pl.& Jackson Ave., White On Blue, C.1920 .... 195.00
Streetlight, Electric, Helious Arc Lamp Co., 1896 .... 155.00
Window, Stained, Countryside Cottage Scene, 1900s, 12 X 5 Ft. 4500.00

Arequipa Pottery was produced from 1911 to 1918 by the patients of the Arequipa Sanitorium in Marin County Hills, California.

AREQUIPA, Bowl, Striated Brown Clay, 4 In. 295.00
Vase, Matte Green, Marked, 5 In. 400.00
Vase, Mottled Wine Color, 4 X 6 In. 195.00
ARGY–ROUSSEAU, see G. Argy–Rousseau

Arita is a port in Japan. Porcelain was made there from about 1616. Many types of decorations were used, including the popular Imari designs, which are listed under Imari in this book.

ARITA, Charger, Hunting Scene, Samurai Pursuing Tiger, Signed, 16 1/2 In. 350.00

Art Deco, or Art Moderne, a style started at the Paris Exposition of 1925, is characterized by linear, geometric designs. All types of furniture and decorative arts, jewelry, book bindings, and even games were designed in this style.

ART DECO, Bowl, Fruit, Swan, Blue, Outstretched Wings, 9 X 9 In. 75.00
Candlestick, 2–Light, Frosted Horseshoe Shape, 20 Prisms 135.00
Figurine, Dancer, Outstretched Arms, Multicolor, German 165.00
Figurine, Oriental, Hedi Schoop, California Pottery, Pair 75.00
Figurine, Woman, Bronze & Ivory, Signed Omerth, C.1925, 9 In. 950.00
Finger Bowl, Undertray, Sapphire Blue, Rayed Design, Lutz–Type 25.00
Frame, Picture, Green Mirror, 11 X 13 In. 70.00
Ice Chopper, Glass 10.00
Jar, Honey, Bee Shape, Silver, Red Glass, Large 125.00
Man's Head, Top Hat, Bow Tie, Primitive, Tin, Square Base 1200.00
Night–Light, Nude, Sitting, Ceramic, Early 1920s 45.00
Pitcher, Red Geometric, Yellow Top, Czech–Style, Japan, 4 3/4 In. 6.00
Salt & Pepper, Bakelite, Yellow, 3 1/2 In. 10.00
String Holder, Dog, With Fly 48.50
Sugar & Creamer, Cover, Chrome–Plated Hammered Copper 25.00
Trinket Box, Sandoz, 7 1/2 In. 375.00

Art glass means any of the many forms of glassware made during the late nineteenth century or early twentieth century. These wares were expensive and production was limited. Art glass is not the typical commercial glass that was made in large quantities, and most of the art glass was produced by hand methods.

ART GLASS, see also separate headings such as Burmese; Cameo Glass; Tiffany; etc.

ART GLASS, Basket, Blue, Amber Edge Ruffles, Crisscross Handle, 8 1/4 In.	165.00
Basket, Clear Vaseline Band, White Rim, Thorn Handle, 7 1/2 In.	350.00
Basket, Pink & White Candy Stripe, Thorn Handle, 7 In.	295.00
Basket, Pink Overlay, Clear Applied Flowers, White Inside, 9 In.	365.00
Basket, White, Rose Lining, Square Foldover, Clear Handle, 6 In.	145.00
Basket, Yellow, Green, Mother-of-Pearl, Victorian	220.00
Biscuit Jar, Blue-Green To Yellow, Gold Bamboo Design, 9 In.	900.00
Bowl & Undertray, Palm Tree, Opalescent, Lalique-Style, Barolac	165.00
Bowl, Amber, Blue Rigaree & Feet, Stevens & Williams Type, 6 In.	65.00
Bowl, Custard, Cranberry Interior, Enameled Flowers, U.S., 9 In.	50.00
Bride's Basket, Cranberry Coin Spot, Pleated, Marked, 10 In.	225.00
Candlestick, Banquet, Emerald Cut, 16 In.	185.00
Candlestick, Lustre Blue, Opalescent Veined, 10 3/8 In.	60.00
Cheese Cover, Inverted Thumbprint, Cut Glass Knob, 6 1/4 In.	150.00
Cup & Saucer, Celeste Blue, Crystal Handle, Demitasse	32.00
Dish, Opalescent, Overshot, Berries, Triangular, Austria, 10 In.	200.00
Epergne, Jade Green & White, 19th Century, France, 11 In.	200.00
Jar, Dresser, Opaque White, Mayflowers, Celluloid Top, 5 5/8 In.	50.00
Mug, Lemonade, Baluster Shape, Optic Vertical Ribs, 6 Piece	150.00
Pitcher, Guttate Pattern, Pink, Handle, 9 1/2 In.	245.00
Ring Tree, Red Flowers, Leaves & Stems, St.Louis, 3 1/4 In.	145.00
Salt, Yellow, Victorian, Sterling Silver Top, England	78.00
Spittoon, Woman's, Red, Blue & Yellow Design, Eisch, 4 1/2 In.	125.00
Syrup, Pink & Blue Wildflowers, Opaque White, 5 In.	150.00
Tray, Raised Sculptured Fruit & Leaves, Oval, Michel, 18 X 8 In.	350.00
Tumbler, Green Opaque, New England Glass	400.00
Tumbler, White Birds & Florals, Rose Ground, England	135.00
Tumbler, Yellow, Diamond-Quilted, Mother-of-Pearl, Floral Design	140.00
Vase, Amethyst, Square Top, Enameled Daisies & Lilies, 11 In.	110.00
Vase, Blue, Enameled Floral Design, 5 1/2 In.	83.00
Vase, Bud, Stick Type, Black Luster Base, 8 In., Pair	40.00
Vase, Crackle Finish, Ruffled, Cranberry, Austria, 12 In.	175.00
Vase, Cupid Chasing Butterfly, Black Ground, George Jones, 6 In.	475.00
Vase, Hyacinth, Gold Luster, Swirl, Foliate Design, Austria, 5 In.	240.00
Vase, Lava, Bulbous Bottom, Long Neck, 10 In.	1100.00
Vase, Mottled Tortoiseshell Design, Egg Shape, Clear Feet, 5 In.	25.00
Vase, Overall Cane Flowers, Paperweight Base, 11 1/4 In.	250.00
Vase, Pulled Feather, Orient & Flume, 8 In.	90.00
Vase, Purple, Threading, Beading, 3 1/4 In.	115.00
Vase, Tulip Shape, Lutz-Type, 7 In.	578.00
Wine, Cranberry To Crystal, Notched Stem, St.Louis, 7 1/2 In.	120.00

Art Nouveau is a style of design that was at its most popular from 1895 to 1905. Famous designers, including Rene Lalique and Emile Galle, produced furniture, glass, silver, metalwork, and buildings in the new style. Ladies with long flowing hair and elongated bodies were among the more easily recognized design elements. Copies of this style are being made today. Many modern pieces of jewelry can be found.

ART NOUVEAU, see also Furniture; various glass categories; etc.

ART NOUVEAU, Tray, Card, Metal, Beautiful Lady, Marked	55.00
Tray, Card, Repousse, Engraved, Meriden Silver Plate, 6 1/2 In.	78.00
Vase, Cornucopia, Mother-of-Pearl, Glass,, Fluted, 9 5/8 In.	295.00

The first American art pottery was made in Cincinnati, Ohio, during the 1870s. The pieces were hand thrown and hand decorated. The art pottery tradition continued until the 1920s when studio potters began making the more artistic wares.

ART POTTERY, see also under factory name

ART POTTERY, Ashtray, Gustav Stickley, 6 In.	185.00
Bowl, Black & Gold Stylized Bird, Waylande Gregory, 4 In.	185.00
Bowl, Cover, Black Gold Wash, Waylande Gregory, 3 1/4 In.	325.00
Bowl, Mottled High Glaze, Signed Clayton, 1904, 6 In.	135.00
Bowl, Red, White & Gold, Waylande Gregory, 3 1/2 In.	45.00
Figurine, Bird In Flight, Waylande Gregory	1075.00
Figurine, Doves, Gold Trim, Ivory, Waylande Gregory, Pair	550.00
Figurine, Quail, Feeding, Black & White, Waylande Gregory, Pair	550.00
Figurine, Rooster, Sgraffito Texture, Waylande Gregory	1075.00
Group, Madonna & Child, G.Kemper, Germany, C.1900, 21 1/2 In.	200.00
Group, Schoolgirls, Flowered Base, Marked CV & LL, 12 X 25 In.	350.00
Jar, White Pansies, E.Diers	650.00
Jardiniere, Mottled Green Glaze, Square, 13 In.	550.00
Jug, Ceramic Stopper, Multicolored Flowers, Anton Lang, 6 In.	95.00
Jug, Seaweed On Rose Ground, Beech & Hancock, 9 1/8 In.	100.00
Plate, Swirled Turquoise Sections, Albright, 10 In.	395.00
Plate, White & Black Scenic, Signed Lessell, 8 In.	595.00
Thimble Mug, Brown High Glaze, Marked, Dated 2/06, 2 X 2 In.	195.00
Thimble Mug, Dark Green, Marked, 1 X 1 In.	95.00
Umbrella Stand, Matte Green, Domed Triangular Cutout, 26 In.	325.00
Vase, Egyptian Scene, Camels, Oasis, Drilled, Lessell, 12 1/2 In.	795.00
Vase, Flambe Design, Bats, Bernard Moore, 9 1/2 In.	395.00
Vase, Gold Lines, Swastika Keramos, 8 In.	175.00
Vase, Salmon Flowers, Blue Ground, T.J.Wheatley, 1879, 29 In.	1950.00
Vase, Translucent Green, Mottled, Wannopee, 13 1/2 In.	350.00

ARTHUR OSBORNE, see Ivorex

AURENE   Aurene glass was made by Frederick Carder of New York about 1904. It is an iridescent gold or blue glass, usually marked "Aurene" or "Steuben."

AURENE, Bowl, With Frog, 12 In.	1300.00
Candlestick, Twist, Pair	2000.00
Cuspidor, Woman's, Gold	435.00
Perfume Bottle, Blue, Silver Iridescent, 6 In.	500.00
Perfume Bottle, Etched, Label, Fleur-De-Lis Seal, 7 In.	200.00
Perfume Bottle, Gold Luster, No Stopper, Signed 1414, 5 3/4 In.	50.00
Perfume Bottle, Long Dipper, Blue, 7 1/2 In.	575.00
Vase, Blue, Ribbed, Script Signed, 6 In.	500.00
Vase, Flared, Gold Interior, Calcite Exterior, 6 In.	180.00
Vase, Handles, Blue, 14 1/2 In.	2300.00
Vase, Ruffled, Iridescent Rim, 5 1/2 In.	300.00

AUSTRIA, see Royal Dux; Kauffmann; Porcelain

Auto parts and accessories are collectors' items today. Gas pump globes and license plates are part of this specialty. Prices are determined by age, rarity, and condition.

AUTO, Cap, Studebaker, 2 In.	30.00
Case, 21 Viles of Oil Products, Salesman's Sample, 1890	185.00
Catalog, General Motors, Unfolded Poster, 1941, 6 X 9 1/4 In.	33.00
Catalog, Hudson Super Six, Black & White Models, 16 Pages, 1919	22.00
Catalog, Model T Ford Parts, 61 Pages, 1914	35.00
Clicker, Mustang, Tin, 1967	10.00
Clock, Dashboard, 1932 Ford, Luminous Dial, Westclox, 2 1/2 In.	20.00
Clock, Dashboard, Cadillac Jaeger, 1930-31	125.00
Clock, Elgin, Long Set Stem	45.00
Clock, Phinney-Walker, 8-Day	40.00
Clock, Waltham, 1911	85.00
Coil Tester, Model T	400.00

Credit Card, Amoco, 1981 .... 9.00
Credit Card, Arco, 1975 .... 12.00
Credit Card, Arco, 1977 .... 4.00
Credit Card, Arco, Lifetime 20.00
Credit Card, Chevron, 1967 .... 15.00
Credit Card, Gulf, 1950 .... 50.00
Credit Card, Gulf, 1974 .... 12.00
Credit Card, Humble, 1962 .... 18.00
Credit Card, Mobil, 1960 .... 20.00
Credit Card, Shell Oil, 1940s 50.00
Credit Card, Sinclair, 1941 .... 105.00
Credit Card, Sinclair, 1948 .... 75.00
Credit Card, Sinclair, 1970 .... 12.00
Credit Card, Standard Oil, 1971 .... 24.00
Credit Card, Standard Oil, 1973 .... 12.00
Credit Card, Sunoco, 1975 .... 5.00
Credit Card, Texaco, 1961 .... 18.00
Credit Card, Texaco, 1962 .... 12.00
Extinguisher, Pyrene, Brass 15.00
Fan, Chevrolet, 1932 .... 6.00
Fog Lights, Brackets, 1947 Chrysler 65.00
Gas Gauge, Ford, Wooden, 5 In. 3.95
Gas Pump Globe, American, Megal 275.00
Gas Pump Globe, Atlantic 225.00
Gas Pump Globe, Dino 175.00
Gas Pump Globe, Erie, Porcelain Clock Face 700.00
Gas Pump Globe, Essolene, Metal 210.00
Gas Pump Globe, Farm Bureau Service, Special, 1930–40 .... 85.00
Gas Pump Globe, Kendall 50.00
Gas Pump Globe, Sinclair H–C Gasoline 145.00
Gas Pump Globe, Sky Chief Texaco 135.00
Gas Pump Globe, Standard Oil, Flame Shape, Signed 200.00
Gas Pump Globe, Tydol Gas, Metal Frame, 1930s 275.00
Gas Pump Globe, Visible Gasoline, Etched, 1 Piece 495.00
Gas Pump Globe, Wadham, Glass 200.00
Goggles, Touring Car 32.50
Grill Ornament, Ford, 1940s 10.00
AUTO, HOOD ORNAMENT, see also Lalique
Hood Ornament, Crawford, Porcelain 250.00
Hood Ornament, DeSoto, 1928 .... 200.00
Hood Ornament, Eagle, Franklin, Brass, 1911 .... 85.00
Hood Ornament, Eskimo Sled Dog In Harness, Art Deco, Metal 35.00
Hood Ornament, Horse Sulky & Driver, Chrome, 4 X 7 In. 30.00
Hood Ornament, Indian Head, Pontiac ....45.00 To 58.00
Hood Ornament, Lion, Franklin 200.00
Hood Ornament, Mack Truck Bulldog, Chrome 48.00
Hood Ornament, Plymouth, Swan, Outspread Wings, Chrome 75.00
Hood Ornament, Policeman, Tin, 1915, 8 In. 150.00
Hood Ornament, Pontiac, 1929 .... 150.00
Hood Ornament, Winged Lady, 1931 Plymouth 100.00
Hood Ornament, Woman, Flowing Hair 68.00
Horn Cap, Chevrolet 10.00
Horn, Claxon, Push–Down Friction Operated 75.00
Horn, Copper, 10 1/2 In. 13.00
Hubcap, Lafayette 5.00
Hubcap, Whippet, Pair 7.50
Knob, Gearshift, Cobalt Blue Swirl 15.00
Knob, Gearshift, Orange & White Swirl 20.00
Knob, Gearshift, Orange, With White 32.00
Lamp, Kerosene, Model T 65.00
Lens Set, Coastal Gasoline, Seagulls 250.00
License Plate, California, 1934 .... 10.00
License Plate, California, 1935, Pair 35.00
License Plate, Harold's Club Or Bust, Reno, Nevado, 1940, 14 X 7 In. ... 45.00

Auto, License Plate, Ohio, 1973

License Plate, Illinois, 1937	15.00
License Plate, Illinois, Soybean, 1944	15.00
License Plate, Michigan, 1934, Pair	21.00
License Plate, Missouri, 1931, Carton	32.50
License Plate, New Hampshire, 1918, Porcelain	75.00
License Plate, Ohio, 1930	4.00
License Plate, Ohio, 1973 ....*Illus*	1.00
License Plate, Pennsylvania, 1915, Pair	30.00
Manual, Chevrolet Truck Shop, 1948–51	35.00
Manual, Owner's, Buick, 1941	14.50
Manual, Owner's, Edsel, 1959	35.00
Manual, Repair, Chevrolet, 1929	22.00
Mirror, Rearview, Edsel	50.00
Motometer, Hupmobile	45.00
Motometer, Overland	28.00
Pump, Tire, Enginair Spark Plug, Wooden Box	30.00
Radiator Cap, Ford, Model T	15.00
Speed Armature, Chevrolet, 1950	40.00
Spray Can, Green Striped Logo	30.00
Sprayer, Window, Metal, Finger Plunger, Pocket Clip, 6 1/2 In.	12.00
Sticker, Milwaukee Automobile Show, Color, 1920	7.50
Tire Gauge, Buick, Dial–Type	100.00
Tire Gauge, Leather Case, U.S., 1911	35.00
Tire Gauge, Pierce Arrow–Schrader	90.00
Traffic Light, Cast Iron, Wired, Floor Stand	185.00
Vase, Marigold, Carnival Glass	42.50

Autumn Leaf pattern china was made for the Jewel Tea Company beginning in 1933. Hall China Company of East Liverpool, Ohio, Crooksville China Company of Crooksville, Ohio, Harker Potteries of Chester, West Virginia, and Paden City Pottery, Paden City, West Virginia, made dishes with this design. Autumn Leaf has remained popular and was made by Hall China Company until 1978. Some other pieces in the Autumn Leaf pattern are still being made.

AUTUMN LEAF, Bean Pot, 2 Handles, Jewel Tea	95.00
Berry Bowl, 5 In.	5.50
Berry Bowl, Ruffled	4.00
Bowl Set, Nested	55.00
Bowl, 6 In.	20.00
Bowl, Cover, Oval, Jewel Tea	55.00
Bowl, Vegetable, Cover, Oval, Jewel Tea, 10 In.	35.00
Bread Plate	2.25
Butter, Cover, 1 Lb.	155.00
Butter, Jewel Tea, Hall	75.00
Cake Carrier, Tin, Jewel Tea	37.50
Cake Plate, Footed, Jewel Tea	100.00
Casserole, 1 Qt.	60.00

Casserole, Cover, 2 Handles, 9 3/4 In.	25.50
Clock, Electric, Jewel Tea	320.00
Coaster Set, Jewel Tea, 8 Piece	45.00
Coffeepot, Drip, Jewel Tea, 8 Cup	32.00 To 50.00
Coffeepot, Short Spout	110.00
Cookie Jar, Jewel Tea	55.00
Cup & Saucer, Jewel Tea	2.50
Drip Jar, Jewel Tea	12.00
French Baker, 3 Sections, Jewel Tea	28.00
Gravy Boat	15.00
Jug, Ball	22.00
Jug, Ice Lip	24.00
Mixing Bowl, Jewel Tea, 9 In.	25.00
Mustard, Underplate	35.00
Pitcher, Ball Jug, Large	30.00
Pitcher, Jewel Tea, 5 3/4 In.	15.00
Plate, 6 In.	3.00
Plate, 7 In.	2.50 To 6.50
Plate, 10 In.	14.00
Plate, Hall, 7 In.	5.00
Plate, Hall, 9 In.	5.00
Platter, 13 1/2 In.	15.00
Platter, Hall, 9 In.	10.00
Salt & Pepper, Hall	18.00
Salt & Pepper, Range	12.00
Soup, Dish, Hall	12.00
Stack Set, Jewel Tea, 3 Piece	30.00
Sugar & Creamer, Cover	35.00
Tablecloth, Plastic, 54 X 72 In.	90.00
Tea Set, Aladdin, Jewel Tea, 3 Piece	48.00
Teapot, Aladdin, Gold Trim	22.00
Thermos	275.00
Tidbit, 3 Tiers	35.00 To 45.00
Tin, Fruit Cake	8.00 To 12.50
Trivet, Round	12.00
Tumbler, Frosted, 14 Oz.	12.00 To 15.00
Tumbler, Frosted, Flat, 5 1/2 In.	11.00
Tumbler, Juice, Frosted, Hall, 3 3/4 In.	25.00
Vase, Bud	200.00
Warmer, Round, Jewel Tea	95.00

AVON, see Bottle, Avon

Baccarat glass was made in France by La Compagnie des Cristalleries de Baccarat, located 150 miles from Paris. The factory was started in 1765. The firm went bankrupt and began operating again about 1822. Cane and millefiori paperweights were made during the 1860 to 1880 period. The firm is still working near Paris making paperweights and glasswares.

BACCARAT, Bobeche, Rose Teinte, Diamond Point Swirl, Marked, 3 1/4 In.	40.00
Bonbon, Oval, Folded Lip, Applied Ribbon	75.00
Bowl, Amberina Swirl, 2 X 5 1/2 In.	60.00
Bowl, Rose Teinte Swirl, 5 In.	60.00
Candlestick, Ball, Rose Teinte, Signed, 1 1/4 X 1 3/4 In., Pair	95.00
Cookie Jar, Cut	125.00
Decanter, Applied Fleur-De-Lis Medallions, 11 In.	55.00
Decanter, Cranberry Shaded To Yellow, 9 In.	75.00
Decanter, Crystal, Pair	350.00
Figurine, Frog, Sitting, Crystal	90.00
Figurine, Leaping Dolphin	85.00
Figurine, Porcupine, Crystal, Signed	185.00
Figurine, Wild Boar, Crystal, Signed	155.00
Inkwell, Swirls, Silver Plated Lid, Flowers, Square, 2 3/4 In.	65.00
Lamp, Fairy, Saucer Base, Rose Teinte, Sunburst, Marked, 4 In.	235.00
Lamp, Frosty Orange, 18 In.	265.00

Lantern, Pink Glass, Birds, Branches, Geometric Pattern, 36 In.	1100.00
Paperweight, Flat Bouquet of White Pompon, Red Clematis, Pansies	6900.00
Paperweight, Garland, Tomato–Red Ground	1000.00
Paperweight, Pansy, 1 Stem, Gold To Velvety Purple, 2 In.	500.00
Paperweight, Pompon, Garland	1050.00
Paperweight, Sulfide, Abraham Lincoln	50.00 To 60.00
Paperweight, Sulfide, Admiral DeGrasse	70.00
Paperweight, Sulfide, Alexander The Great	40.00
Paperweight, Sulfide, Charlemagne	50.00
Paperweight, Sulfide, Dwight D.Eisenhower	275.00
Paperweight, Sulfide, George Washington	50.00
Paperweight, Sulfide, Harry Truman, Gold Base	65.00 To 85.00
Paperweight, Sulfide, John F.Kennedy, Green Base	110.00
Paperweight, Sulfide, Julius Caesar	40.00
Paperweight, Sulfide, Napoleon	40.00
Paperweight, Sulfide, Peter The Great	40.00
Paperweight, Sulfide, Pope John XXIII	30.00
Paperweight, Sulfide, Queen Elizabeth I	40.00
Paperweight, Sulfide, Sir Winston Churchill	575.00
Paperweight, Sulfide, Thomas Paine	50.00
Paperweight, Sulfide, Woodrow Wilson	250.00
Paperweight, Tethered Horse, Faceted	375.00
Paperweight, Water Bearers, Cobalt Blue, 1956	125.00
Perfume Bottle, Amethyst Lilies, Gold	350.00
Perfume Bottle, Houbigant, Panel Cut, Gold Trim	125.00
Perfume Bottle, Intaglio Cut Flowers, Paneled, Black	275.00
Perfume Bottle, Pagonara, Gardenia Royal, Signed	110.00
Perfume Bottle, Possession	150.00
Perfume Bottle, Possession, By Cordey	45.00
Perfume Bottle, Rose Teinte Swirl, 4 1/4 In.	65.00
Perfume Bottle, Rose Teinte Swirl, 6 3/4 In.	65.00
Perfume Bottle, Rose Teinte Swirl, 7 1/2 In.	70.00
Perfume Bottle, Shape of Woman's Hand, 1920s	200.00
Perfume Bottle, Vega	165.00
Perfume Bottle, Vogue Souvenir, Signed	125.00
Pitcher, Harcourt, Large	145.00
Pitcher, Water, With Bowl, Scalloped, 2 Piece	1575.00
Plate, Dessert, Crystal, Center Mark, 10 Piece	302.00
Plate, Dessert, Hand Blown, 10 Piece	275.00
Powder Jar, Rose Teinte, Cover, 4 1/4 X 3 1/2 In.	95.00
Ring Tree, Rubina	120.00
Sauce, Rose Teinte Swirl, Footed, 3 In.	50.00
Shot Glass, Concentric Millefiori Base	130.00
Tray, Green Cut To Clear, Signed, 14 X 10 In.	975.00
Tumbler, Rose Teinte Swirl, 4 1/2 In.	55.00
Vase, Birds, Scenic, Opalescent, Signed, 10 In.	350.00
Vase, Jack–In–The–Pulpit, Amethyst, 12 In.	50.00
Water Set, Rose Teinte, Embossed Diamond Swirls, Tray, 8 Piece	595.00

Badges have been used since before the Civil War. Collectors search for examples of all types, including law enforcement and company identification badges. Well–known prison or law enforcement badges are most desirable. Most are made of nickel or brass. Many recent reproductions have been made.

BADGE, Chauffeur, Illinois, 1940s	10.00
Chauffeur, Missouri, 1919	28.00
Chauffeur, Oregon, 1927	13.00
Florida Correctional Officer, State Seal	25.00
Hartford Police, Silver, Eagle, Stars, State Seal, T–Bar Pin, 1860–70	330.00
Heinz Manufacturing Co., Safety Committee, Philadelphia	20.00
Indianapolis Transit Co.	15.00
Interurban Freight Stage, La., 1923	15.00
Meridian Police, 9 In.	20.00
Police, New York, Copper, C.1860, 3 In.	30.00

Police, Portland, Star In Circle 85.00
Postal Telegraph Co., Employee's Number, Telegraph Machine Center 89.00
San Quentin, Guard, Death Row, Brass 6.00
U.S.Deputy Marshall, Oklahoma Territory, Pre–1907 .... 95.00
Unveiling Soldiers & Sailors Monument, Shield Shape, 1892 .... 15.00
W.M.A.Transit Co. 10.00
Women's Relief Corps., 1883 .... 15.00
Wyatt Earp, On Card 10.00

   BAG, BEADED, see Purse

Metal banks have been made since 1868. There are still banks,
mechanical banks, and registering banks (those which show the total
money deposited on the face of the bank). Many old banks have
been reproduced since the 1950s in iron or plastic.

BANK, Abe Lincoln, Glass 15.00
Andy Gump, Polychrome Paint, Cast Iron, 4 3/8 In. 600.00
Andy Panda, Suitcase, Tin 35.00
Apple & Bug, Cast Iron, Painted 850.00
Apple, Cast Iron 550.00
Army Safe, Cast Iron, Metal Sides, Red & Silver, 4 X 2 1/2 X 2 3/4 In. 63.00
Army Tank, Cast Iron, 1918, 2 1/2 In. 40.00
Astro Boy, Plastic, Japan 115.00
Atlas Batteries, Tin 15.00
Bam Bam, 1971, 13 In. 25.00
Barney Rubble, 1971, 13 In. 25.00
Barrel, Kopp's Mustard, Glass 6.00
Barrel, National Fidelity Life Ins., Wooden 25.00
Barrel, Papier–Mache, 1890s 50.00
Baseball Set, Snoopy, Red Cap, Papier–Mache, 8 In. 15.00
Baseball, On 3 Bats, American League, Chrome 495.00
Battleship Oregon, Cast Iron .... 250.00 To 275.00
Bear & Pig, Cast Iron, 5 1/2 In. 825.00
Bear, Sitting, Cast Iron 120.00
Bear, Standing, Cast Iron 75.00
Beehive, 3 Buzzing Bees, Cast Iron 75.00
Beer Can, American Can Co., 75th Anniversary 3.00
Ben Franklin, Cast Iron 30.00
Billiken, On Throne, Cast Iron .... 110.00 To 145.00
Billiken, Silver Paint, Cast Iron, 4 3/8 In. 32.00
Birdcage, Cast Iron .... 50.00 To 60.00
Black Girl, 2 Faces 100.00
Black Man, Bare Toes, Cast Iron, 5 In. ....*Illus*   85.00
Black Man, Cast Iron 265.00
Black Woman, 2 Faces, Cast Iron 235.00
Block, ABC, Silver Plate 17.00
Bokar Coffee 6.50
Book, Central Valley Bank, Key 25.00
Book, Green, Embossed Rock of Gibralta 15.00
Book, Sun Life Insurance 17.50
Book, Thrift Pays Dividend, Key 50.00
Bosco, Lithographed Tin 40.00
Boy Scout, Cast Iron .... 68.00 To 160.00
Bucket, Brass Banded, Wooden 375.00
Budget, Louis Marx & Co., Key 25.00
Buffalo, Cast Iron 110.00
Building, 4 Towers, Iron 32.00
Building, Bank, Cast Iron, 1870s 40.00
Building, Bank, Domes, Cast Iron 42.50
Building, Capitol, Marx Budget, Tin, Red, White & Blue, 5 In. 20.00
Building, Church, Cast Iron, Large 295.00
Building, Empire State, Cast Iron 25.00
Building, Independence Hall, Glass, 7 1/4 In. 70.00
Building, Independence Hall, Tower, Moore 400.00
Building, Japanning With Gold Trim, 5 1/4 In. 100.00

Building, State Bank, Moore No.1079, Solid Front 275.00
Building, Towers, Cast Iron, Silver, Gold, 4 In. 20.00
Bulldog, Cast Iron, Small 45.00
Bulldog, Georgia, Composition 14.00
Bulldog, Standing, Brown & White, Cast Iron 135.00
Cabin & Trees, Painted Scene, Redware, 4 1/4 In. 85.00
Calumet Baking Powder, Tin, 4 In. 75.00
Camel, Cast Iron 85.00
Camel, Gold, Saddle, A.C. Williams, C.1920, 7 1/4 In. 170.00
Candy Jar, Railroad Tank Car Shape, Pressed Glass, 5 1/4 In. 35.00
Captain Kidd, Cast Iron .... 250.00 To 400.00
Captain Kirk, Hard Rubber, 1975, 11 In. 15.00
Car, Maroon, Cast Iron 750.00
Car, Yellow Cab, Cast Iron 595.00
Casey Jones, Locomotive, Bronzed 15.00
Cat, Black, Flowers & Ribbons, Redware 15.00
Cat, With Ball, Cast Iron, 5 1/2 In. 110.00
Cat, With Bow, Cast Iron, 4 1/4 In. 45.00
Centennial Independence Hall, Iron, Marked, 1876, 7 X 10 X 3 In. 295.00
Chest of Drawers, Bakelite 45.00
Chevrolet, 1954 .... 75.00
Chinaman's Head, Pottery 150.00
Church, Tin 25.00
Cigarette, Chrome 14.00
Clock, My Own Bank, 1940s 15.00
Clown, Cast Iron 125.00
Clown, Silver Plate 45.00
Clown, Tin, Chein 45.00
Covered Wagon, Banthrico, Metal 15.00
Cow, Cast Iron, 3 1/4 X 5 1/4 In. 60.00
Cow, Cast Iron, Gilt Paint, 5 1/2 In. 220.00
Cow, Hornless, Cast Iron 45.00
Cow, Sirloin Steak House 20.00
Cylinder, Blue & White Sponge Spatter Design, Stoneware, 5 1/4 In. 545.00
Dalmatian, Cast Iron, 15 In. 59.00
Deer, Cast Iron 75.00
Dime Register, Chein, Tin 10.00
Dime Register, Junior 150.00
Dime Register, National Canners Association 20.00
Dime Register, Nickeled Cast Iron 175.00
Dime Register, Sen-Sen, Tin, 1912 .... 125.00
Dime Register, Uncle Sam, 3 Coin 22.00
Dime, Feed The Kitty, Metal 25.00
Dino, 1971, 13 In. 25.00
Dinosaur, Sinclair Oil Co., 1950s, 9 In. 11.00
Do You Know Me, Gold, Red & Green Trim, Cast Iron, 6 1/2 In. 250.00
Dog House, Snoopy, Papier-Mache, 6 In. 7.00
Dog, Fido, Cast Iron .... 65.00 To 100.00
Dog, Newfoundland, With Pack, Cast Iron 75.00
Dog, On Barrel, Cast Iron 85.00
Dog, On Tub, Cast Iron 125.00
Dog, Retriever, Aluminum, 7 1/2 In. 25.00
Dog, Retriever, With Pack, Cast Iron, 3 3/4 In. 75.00
Dog, Scotty, Black, Cast Iron 110.00
Dog, St. Bernard, With Barrel, Porcelain 35.00
Dog, With Pack, Cast Iron, 5 1/2 X 8 In. 95.00
Dog, With Pack, I Hear A Call, Cast Iron, Dated July 20, 1900 .... 95.00
Donkey, Cast Iron .... 50.00 To 110.00
Duck, On Top Hat, Save For A Rainy Day, Cast Iron, 5 1/2 In. 130.00
Duck, On Tub, Cast Iron 195.00
Duck, Second National Bank, Tin 135.00
Duck, With Umbrella, Cast Iron 50.00
Dutch Boy, Cast Iron .... 75.00 To 175.00
Dutch Girl, Cast Iron 90.00

Eagle, On Globe, Cast Iron	295.00
Elephant, Circus, Cast Iron	175.00
Elephant, Listerine Razor Blades	15.00
Elephant, Lucky Jumbo, Glass, Label	35.00
Elephant, On Tub, Cast Iron	85.00 To 125.00
Elephant, Red, White Metal, 5 In.	20.00
Elephant, Seated, Pot Metal, 1936, 5 1/4 In.	65.00
Elmer Fudd, Metal, Box	150.00
Elsie The Cow, Metal	48.00
Elsie The Cow, Plastic	65.00
Elves, Lithographed Tin, Vending, 1923, 8 In.	385.00
Feed The Kitty, Cast Iron, Coins Go Into Mouth	65.00
Foxy Grandpa, Cast Iron	110.00
Fred Flintstone, 1971, 13 In.	25.00
Frog, Cast Iron, Large	115.00
Gas Pump, H.C.Sinclair, Tin	20.00
Gazebo, Glass, 4 In.	30.00
General Pershing	120.00
Girl & Sheep, Cast Iron, 4 3/8 In.	310.00
Glass Block, Esso	20.00
Globe, Advertising Airlines, Tin	15.00
Globe, Pedestal, Cast Iron	225.00
Good Luck, Billiken	75.00
Goose, Cast Iron	225.00
Goose, On Pedestal	170.00
Graf Zeppelin, Cast Iron	195.00
Happy Hooligan, Bennington	350.00
Head, Scotsman With Cigar, Majolica, 3 1/2 In.	35.00
Horse, Feet On Tub, Cast Iron	225.00
Horse, Gold & White Paint, Cast Iron, 4 In.	100.00
Horse, Horseshoe With Good Luck, Painted, Cast Iron, 4 X 5 In.	90.00
House, Cast Iron	40.00
House, Haunted, Cast Iron	95.00
Humpty Dumpty, Tin, Chein	145.00
Indian, Hand To Head, Tomahawk, Full Figure, Cast Iron	175.00
Knob Finial, 2–Tone Orange Glaze, Stoneware, 3 7/8 X 4 In.	55.00
Krazy Kat, Graduation, 7 X 3 1/2 In.	20.00
Leprechaun, Lefton	35.00
Liberty Bell, Carnival Glass, 3 5/8 In.	8.50
Liberty Bell, Cast Iron, 1926, 4 In.	40.00
Liberty Bell, Opaque White, Metal Bottom, Robinson & Loble, 4 3/8 In.	10.00
Liberty Bell, White Metal, Dark Finish, Wood Base, 7 In. *Illus*	125.00

Bank, Liberty Bell,
White Metal, Dark
Finish, Wood Base,
7 In.

Bank, Mechanical,
Artillery, Polychrome
Paint, Cast Iron,
6 In.

Bank, Mechanical, William Tell, Cast Iron, 10 1/2 In.

Lifesavers Candy	45.00
Lincoln's High Hat, Cast Iron	80.00
Lion, Cast Iron, 3 1/2 In.	45.00
Lion, Cast Iron, 5 1/2 In.	55.00
Lion, Circus, Sitting Up On Haunches, On Tub, Iron, Gold, 4 1/4 In.	50.00
Lion, Circus, Sitting Upright On Tub, Cast Iron ....95.00 To 120.00
Lion, Ears Up, Cast Iron	48.00
Lion, Full Mane, Cast Iron, Some Paint, 4 X 5 In.	100.00
Lion, Standing, Cast Iron, Gilt Paint, 5 3/4 In.	50.00
Log Cabin, Greenish–White Glaze, Pottery, 5 1/4 In.	445.00
Log Cabin, Maple Sugar, Chalkware	75.00
Lord of The Rings, Vinyl, Gandolf, Box, 18 In.	60.00
Lucky Joe, Nash's Prepared Mustard, Glass, Red Lips, 5 In.	22.00
Mailbox, Allis Chalmers ....22.00 To 26.50
Mailbox, Dark Green, Cast Iron, 9 In.	20.00
Mailbox, Hanging, Blue & Gold, Cast Iron	48.00
Mailbox, John Deer, Cast Iron, Box	18.00
Mailbox, Sidewalk, Green, Decal Lettering, Tin, Cash Door, 9 X 4 In.	30.00
Main Street, Gold, Cast Iron, 6 5/8 In.	350.00
Main Street, Trolley, Cast Iron	425.00
Mammy, Cast Iron ....65.00 To 95.00
Mammy, Ceramic, 6 1/2 In.	28.00
Mammy, With Spoon, Cast Iron	115.00
Man, Cap, With Cigar, Pottery	40.00
Mandarin, Cast Iron, 2 Figures Carrying Person	3400.00
Marathon Motor Oil	12.50
Mary & Lamb, Cast Iron	250.00

 Mechanical banks were first made about 1870. Any bank with moving parts is considered mechanical. The metal banks made before World War I are the most desirable. Copies and new designs of mechanical banks have been made in metal or plastic since the 1920s.

Mechanical, African Native, Tin Lithographed, Germany, 5 1/2 In.	3575.00
Mechanical, Always Did 'Spise A Mule	575.00
Mechanical, Andy Gump	850.00
Mechanical, Apple	1200.00
Mechanical, Artillery, Polychrome Paint, Cast Iron, 6 In. ....*Illus*	1100.00
Mechanical, Artillery, Type 1, Bronze, 8 In.	770.00
Mechanical, Artillery, Type 1, Cast Iron, 7 3/4 In.	495.00
Mechanical, Atlas	2800.00
Mechanical, Bad Accident, Mule Pulls Man In Cart	1200.00
Mechanical, Bamboula, Cast Iron, C.1890, 7 In.	330.00
Mechanical, Bank of Education, Cast Iron, 4 In.	3025.00
Mechanical, Barking Dog On Base, Wood & Tin, 9 1/2 In.	2750.00
Mechanical, Baseball Player, Cast Iron	1775.00
Mechanical, Baseball, Dark Town Battery, Painted, 10 X 7 In.	1430.00
Mechanical, Bear & Tree Stump, Cast Iron, Judd Mfg.Co., C.1875, 5 In.	825.00
Mechanical, Bear, Dancing, Man With Organ Grinder Next To Building	300.00
Mechanical, Bill E.Grin, J.W.Schmitt, Cast Iron, 1915, 4 1/2 In.	1100.00
Mechanical, Bird, On Church Roof	650.00
Mechanical, Boy On Trapeze ....800.00 To 2100.00
Mechanical, Boy, Robbing Nest, Cast Iron	5700.00
Mechanical, British Clown, Tin Lithographed, Germany, C.1920, 5 1/2 In.	3300.00
Mechanical, Bucking Mule, H.L.Judd Co., 1884, 4 3/4 In.	1320.00
Mechanical, Bull Tosses Boy In Well, Brass, No.67, 6 3/4 In.	3025.00
Mechanical, Bulldog Savings Bank, Cast Iron, 1878, 8 1/2 In.	4400.00
Mechanical, Bulldog, Cast Iron ....695.00 To 1100.00
Mechanical, Bureau, Bird's-Eye Maple, Advertising, C.1875, 9 In.	880.00
Mechanical, Bureau, Wood, Serrell Patent, 1869, 5 3/4 In.	1550.00
Mechanical, Butting Buffalo, Butts Black Man On Tree Trunk	2000.00
Mechanical, Butting Goat, Tree Stump, Cast Iron, 1887, Judd Co., 5 In.	1100.00
Mechanical, Cabin, Cast Iron, J.& E.Stevens Co., 1885, 4 3/4 In.	770.00
Mechanical, Calamity, Polychrome Paint, Cast Iron, 7 1/2 In.	5300.00

Mechanical, Calumet, Tin, Edward E.Barnes, 1924, 5 In. 660.00
Mechanical, Cash Register, Crescent, J.& E.Stevens Co., 1890, 6 In. 660.00
Mechanical, Chief Big Moon, Cast Iron, J.& E.Stevens Co., 1899, 10 In. 1980.00
Mechanical, Chief Big Moon, Polychrome Paint, Cast Iron, 10 In. 1400.00
Mechanical, Circus, Cast Iron, Shepard Hardware Co., 1888, 7 In. 4125.00
Mechanical, Clown, Harlequin, Cast Iron 7000.00
Mechanical, Clown, On Globe, Cast Iron, 9 In. ....990.00 To 2075.00
Mechanical, Clown, Tin 75.00
Mechanical, Confectionery, Cast Iron 3500.00
Mechanical, Cow, Kicking, Dark Polychrome Paint, Cast Iron, 9 5/8 In. 165.00
Mechanical, Cowboy, Lithographed Tin, Germany, 1920, 6 In. 2750.00
Mechanical, Creedmore .... 340.00 To 700.00
Mechanical, Dapper Dan, Lithographed Tin, Clockwork, Marx, 1910, 10 In. 605.00
Mechanical, Darkie In Cabin, Cast Iron .... 395.00 To 450.00
Mechanical, Darktown Battery, Cast Iron, 10 In. .... 1320.00 To 2750.00
Mechanical, Dentist, Cast Iron, J.& E.Stevens, 1890, 9 1/2 In. 3025.00
Mechanical, Dog On Turntable, Cast Iron, 5 In. .... 330.00 To 500.00
Mechanical, Donkey & Silo, Sheet Metal, 8 1/2 In. 1540.00
Mechanical, Double Window, Tin, 6 1/2 In. 495.00
Mechanical, Eagle & Eaglets, Cast Iron, 6 In. .... 700.00 To 750.00
Mechanical, Eagle, With Eaglets In Nest 750.00
Mechanical, Elephant, Swings Trunk, Small .... 150.00 To 165.00
Mechanical, Elephant, Tin 75.00
Mechanical, Elephant, With 3 Clowns, Cast Iron .... 1000.00 To 1350.00
Mechanical, Elephant, With Howdah, Tusk, Cast Iron, Hubley, 7 1/2 In. 770.00
Mechanical, Elves, Tin Lithographed, Huntley & Palmer, 1923, 8 3/4 In. 385.00
Mechanical, Football Player, Cast Iron, 8 In. 110.00
Mechanical, Football Player, J.Harper, England, C.1895 .... 4000.00
Mechanical, Frog, Cast Iron, 1882 .... 605.00
Mechanical, Frog, On Rock 250.00
Mechanical, Frog, On Round Base 400.00
Mechanical, Give Me A Penny 200.00
Mechanical, Hall's Excelsior, Monkey, Cashier, 1869 .... 120.00
Mechanical, Harold Lloyd, Lithographed Tin, Germany, 1920, 6 In. 4800.00
Mechanical, Hen & Chick, J.& E.Stevens, Cast Iron, C.1901, 9 3/4 In. 2200.00
Mechanical, Hindu, Cast Iron, Patent 1–24–1882 .... 550.00
Mechanical, Horse Race 3850.00
Mechanical, Horse, On Tub 150.00
Mechanical, Humpty Dumpty ....875.00 To 1000.00
Mechanical, Humpty Dumpty, Plastic .... 45.00 To 65.00
Mechanical, Indian & Bear, Cast Iron ....500.00 To 1200.00
Mechanical, Jolly Nigger, Polychrome Paint, Cast Iron, 6 1/2 In. 325.00
Mechanical, Jonah & Whale, Cast Iron, 1890 .... 1200.00
Mechanical, Kick Inn, Wooden, Label 390.00
Mechanical, Lion & Monkeys, Cast Iron .... 1200.00 To 1700.00
Mechanical, Maggie & Jiggs 1900.00
Mechanical, Magician, J.& E.Stevens Co., C.1901 .... 2600.00 To 2950.00
Mechanical, Mammy & Child, Cast Iron 2500.00

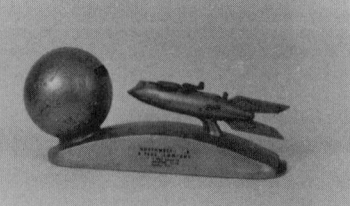

Bank, Mechanical, Rocket Ship, Strato Bank, 7 In.

Mechanical, Monkey & Coconut 1800.00
Mechanical, Monkey, Tips Hat When Coin Dropped, Tin, Chein 125.00
Mechanical, Nigger Most Polite, Put In A Coin, Lithographed Tin 2500.00
Mechanical, Organ Grinder, Cast Iron 650.00
Mechanical, Organ, Boy & Girl 1200.00
Mechanical, Organ, Cat & Dog, Polychrome Paint, Cast Iron, 7 1/4 In. 550.00
Mechanical, Owl, Turns Head .... 300.00 To 595.00
Mechanical, Paddy & Pig 1400.00
Mechanical, Pelican, With Rabbit, Cast Iron 4000.00
Mechanical, Pig, In High Chair, Cast Iron, C.1890, 5 1/4 In. 495.00
Mechanical, Preacher, Black, Pulpit, Clockwork, Wooden Base 2250.00
Mechanical, Professor Pug Frog, Cast Iron 6700.00
Mechanical, Punch & Judy, Cast Iron, 1884 .... 1200.00
Mechanical, Rabbit, Standing, Holding Nut 650.00
Mechanical, Rocket Ship 35.00
Mechanical, Rocket Ship, Strato Bank, 7 In. ....*Illus*   45.00
Mechanical, Rooster, Crowing, Lighographed Tin, Germany, 1937, 7 In. 1320.00
Mechanical, Santa Claus, Next To Chimney .... 1000.00 To 1800.00
Mechanical, Speaking Dog, Cast Iron .... 600.00 To 795.00
Mechanical, Speaking Dog, Shepard Hardware 250.00
Mechanical, Springing Cat, Cast Iron 6000.00
Mechanical, Stump Speaker, Shepard, 1886 .... 1550.00 To 2200.00
Mechanical, Tammany Boss Tweed, Fat Man, Sitting, 1870s 220.00
Mechanical, Tammany, Cast Iron, 6 In. .... 140.00 To 385.00
Mechanical, Teddy & Bear 900.00
Mechanical, Ticket Collector, Circus, Iron, H.L.Judd Co., 1879, 5 In. 1100.00
Mechanical, Trick Dog .... 425.00 To 950.00
Mechanical, Trick Dog, 6-Part Base 1125.00
Mechanical, Trick Pony, C.1900 .... 890.00
Mechanical, Uncle Sam, Shepard Hardware, C.1886 .... 1500.00 To 1800.00
Mechanical, William Tell, Cast Iron, 10 1/2 In. ....*Illus* 825.00
Mechanical, Wireless, Tin 250.00
Mechanical, World's Fair, Gold Paint, Cast Iron, 8 1/4 In. 900.00
Mechanical, Zoo, Building With Animals In Windows 650.00
Minuteman, C.1940 .... 145.00
Monkey, Bennington 45.00
Monkey, Dressed Like Napoleon, Porcelain 175.00
Mutt & Jeff, Cast Iron, 5 1/4 In. 220.00
Ocean Spray Cranberry Sauce Can 29.00
Pass The Hat, Cast Iron 75.00
Peter Pan Bread, Tin 25.00
Pig, Anchor Hocking, 6 In. 12.50
Pig, Arizona Bank & Trust Co., Plastic, Blue Eyes, 4 1/4 X 8 In. 35.00
Pig, Bisque, Felt Hat 30.00
Pig, Brown Spots, Green On Base, White Clay, Yellow Glaze, 5 1/2 In. 85.00
Pig, Clear Glaze, Brown Dots, White Clay, 6 In. 45.00
Pig, First Dakota National Bank, 3 3/4 X 4 1/2 In. 25.00
Pig, Holes For Eyes, Pottery, Austria 35.00
Pig, Marbelized Glaze, Pottery, 5 In. 25.00
Pig, Pink, Allover Flowers, Kay Finch, 6 X 8 In. 40.00
Pig, Seated, Gold, Red Trim, Cast Iron, 3 In. 45.00
Pig, Seated, Gold, Red Trim, Cast Iron, 4 5/8 In. 65.00
Pig, Sitting, Black, Cast Iron 35.00
Pig, Wedding of Prince Charles & Diana 20.00
Pig, White, Brown Spots, Stoneware 40.00
Piggy, Mama, Bisque 20.00
Pirate, On Treasure Chest, Cast Iron 30.00
Pirate, White Metal, Polychrome Paint, 5 3/4 In. 35.00
Policeman, Black Man's Face, Bronze Color 135.00
Policeman, Cast Iron 275.00
Porky Pig, Dressed As Cowboy Sheriff, China 125.00
Potbelly Stove, Cast Iron 25.00
Prussian Helmet, Coat of Arms, Silver Plate, 5 In. 150.00
Rabbit, Begging, Cast Iron 135.00

Bank, Black Man, Bare Toes,
Cast Iron, 5 In.

Bank, Register, Uncle Sam, Steel,
Durable Toy & Novelty, 6 In.

Radio, Cast Iron 105.00
Radio, Emerson, Box, 1940s 50.00
Radio, Glass .... 20.00 To 52.50
Raggedy Ann, Nodder 35.00
Ranger, In Uniform, Cast Iron, 7 In. 50.00
Red Goose, Cast Iron 275.00
Refrigerator, Cast Iron 75.00
Refrigerator, Electrolux, Metal 50.00
Refrigerator, Frigidaire, Pot Metal, 4 X 2 In. 35.00
Refrigerator, G.E., Cast Iron 75.00
Refrigerator, Norge, White Metal 16.00
Register, Cast Iron 18.00
Register, Happy Days, Chein 20.00
Register, Penny, Cast Iron 375.00
Register, Uncle Sam, Steel, Durable Toy & Novelty, 6 In. .... *Illus* 45.00
Reindeer, Antlers, Black, Germany, 7 X 4 In. 175.00
Revolutionary, Spirit of 1776, 3 Figures, Cast Iron 75.00
Rival Dog Food, Can Shape .... 6.00 To 12.00
Rocky & Bullwinkle, Ceramic 75.00
Rooster, Cast Iron 135.00
Rooster, Chalkware, 13 In. 20.00
Rooster, Gold, Red Trim, Cast Iron, 5 1/2 In. 975.00
Rumpelstiltskin, Cast Iron 300.00
Safe, Cast Iron, 4 In. 40.00
Safe, Coin, Brass Plaque, Fidelity Investment, 4 X 2 In. 22.00
Safe, Columbus, Cast Iron, Combination, 5 1/4 In. 85.00
Safe, Lacy Design, Iron, Combination, 3 X 2 1/2 In. 45.00
Safe, National, Combination Lock 125.00
Safe, Security, Black, Gold, Lion's Head, Combination, 1887, 8 In. 100.00
Safe, Security, Combination Lock, Nickel Plated, 5 1/2 In. 35.00
Safety Deposit, Cast Iron 65.00
Sailor, Cast Iron 195.00
San Diego Chargers, Helmet Shape, Ceramic 5.00
Santa Claus, Asleep In Chair, Pot Metal 30.00
Santa Claus, Baltimore Savings & Loan, White Metal 75.00
Santa Claus, Papier–Mache, 7 1/2 In. 22.00
Schmoo, Li'l Abner, 8 In. 60.00
Seal, On Rock, Cast Iron 300.00
Sharecropper, Cast Iron 80.00
Sherwin Williams, Paint Can Shape 10.00
Ship, Arcade, Cast Iron, 7 1/2 In. 250.00
Ship, Side Wheeler, Gold, Red Trim, Cast Iron, 7 3/4 In. 325.00

Sitting Bear, Glass, Snow Crest Beverage, 7 In. 18.00
Skeleton, Hand From Coffin For Coin, Tin, Windup, Japan, 6 1/2 In. 33.00
Skier, Alpine, Big Nose, Papier–Mache, 7 In. 10.00
Snoopy, Ceramic 25.00
Snoopy, Lying On Top of Yellow Banana, Ceramic, 7 In. 15.00
Snoopy, On Doghouse, United Features, 1970 .... 10.00
Snoopy, Sitting On Top of Strawberry, 5 In. 10.00
Snoopy, With Woodstock, Jogger, Blue, 6 In. 5.00
Soldier, Cast Iron, 6 In. 90.00
Soldier, Fires Coin Into Tree, Southern Comfort, Metal 60.00
Soldier, In Blue, Cast Iron, 5 3/4 In. 30.00
Sow & Piglets, Pottery, Black, Brown, Matt Glaze, 5 1/4 In. 125.00
Statue of Liberty, Cast Iron 65.00
Sun–Maid Raisins, Box 35.00
Tank, Cast Iron, 1918 .... 145.00
Telephone, Black Porcelain, Wall 30.00
Telephone, Pay, Bakelite, 5 Cent, 10 Cent, 25 Cent 35.00
Telephone, Swank Shoe Polish 35.00
Thermo Anti–Freeze, Tin, Unused 15.00
Thrifty Chick, Box, 8 3/4 In. 23.00
Tootsie Roll, Hasbro 40.00
Tower Motor Oil, Tin 35.00
Treasure Chest, Gold, Cast Iron, 2 3/4 In. 35.00
Truck, Sealtest Dairy Products 35.00
Trunk, Cast Iron 165.00
Turkey, Black, Cast Iron, 3 1/2 In. 50.00
TV, Emerson, Plastic 10.00
Two Kids, Cast Iron, 4 1/2 In. 650.00
Uncle Don Savings 22.00
Uncle Remus, Cast Iron 300.00
Uncle Sam Hat, Slot Inside Brim, Milk Glass 45.00
Uncle Sam, Stoneware 95.00
Uncle Sam, With Arab 175.00
Uncle Wiggily, Tin 125.00
Windmill, Rotating Blades, Continental Silver, 5 1/2 In. 45.00
Wolf Head 17.00
World Globe, Tin, Chein 17.00

There is much confusion about the terms Banko, Korean ware, and Sumida. We are using the terms in the way most often used by antiques dealers and collectors. Korean ware is now called "Sumida" and is listed in this book under that heading. Banko is a group of rustic Japanese wares made in the nineteenth and twentieth centuries. Some pieces are made of mosaics of colored clay, some are fanciful teapots. Redware and other materials were also used.

BANKO, Tea Set, Flying Cranes, Yellow Enamel, 5 Piece 140.00
Teapot, 5 Faces 200.00
Teapot, Brown, Enameled Birds, Signed, 6 In. 60.00
Vase, Carved Pagoda & Trees, 7 1/4 In. 85.00
Vase, Terra–Cotta Carved Teahouse Scene, Dark Brown Glaze, 4 1/2 In. 45.00

Barbershop collectibles range from the popular red and white striped pole that used to be found in front of every shop to the small scissors and tools of the trade. Barber chairs are wanted, especially the older models with elaborate iron trim.

BARBER, Cabinet, Oak, Glass Door 150.00
Cabinet, Sterilizer, Marble 325.00
Cabinet, Wall, Beveled Mirror, Towel Bar, Sectioned Interior, Oak 180.00
Chair, Child's, Elephant, Wooden 5500.00
Chair, Child's, Fire Engine, With Ladders, Restored 1800.00
Chair, Child's, Koken, Horsehead At Front 1950.00
Chair, Hercules, Carved Oak, Brass Base 1400.00
Chair, Koch's, Porcelain On Cast Iron 250.00
Chair, Koken, Cast Iron Legs, Hoof Feet 750.00

Chair, Koken, Wooden, Restored 750.00
Chair, T.A.Koch, Chicago, Oak 900.00
Clippers, Oster, Chrome 7.50
Clippers, Winchester, Box 40.00
Curling Iron, Insulated Handles, 10 1/2 In. 6.00
Hair Cutter, Ucan, Nickel Plate, 2 In. 10.00
Hat Rack, Koken, White Porcelain Feet 450.00
Mug Cupboard, Occupational 600.00
Pole, 7 1/2 Ft. 1500.00
Pole, Ball Finial, Spherical Knot In Middle, American, 6 Ft.6 In. 600.00
Pole, Chrome 225.00
Pole, Joe's, Red, White & Blue Stripes, Wooden, 65 In. 165.00
Pole, Koken, Sidewalk–Type, 8 Ft. 2750.00
Pole, Leaded Glass, Floor Model, Restored 5500.00
Pole, Lighted Top, Spinner, Electric, Cast Iron, 1920 .... 625.00
Pole, Marvey, Electric 100.00
Pole, Paidar, Model 374 .... 500.00
Pole, Red, White, Black, Blue, Silver, Cast Iron & Sheet Metal, 90 In. ... 175.00
Pole, Red, White, Wooden, Wall Mount, Silver Ball Top & Bottom, 36 In. ... 450.00
Scissors, Pebbled Handle, Sheffield, England 6.50
Sterilizer, Copper, Small Round Mug Rack On Top 175.00

Barometers are used to forecast the weather. Antique barometers with elaborate wooden cases and brass trim are the most desirable. Mercury column barometers are popular with collectors. It is difficult to find someone to repair a broken example, so be sure your barometer is in working condition.

BAROMETER, Aneroid, Etched Steel Face, Thermometer, Tiffany, 6 5/8 In. 300.00
Banjo, George III, With Thermometer & Level, Mahogany, 37 1/2 In. 325.00
D.E.Lent, Rochester, N.Y., Mahogany 1210.00
Federal, Marine Stick, Brass, Mahogany, Mercury, Wall, 35 In. 4500.00
Louis XIV, Portrait Medallion, Brass Trim, Marquetry, 46 In. 7975.00
Louis XV, Thermometer, Father Time On Top, Brass Trim, 4 Ft.6 In. 4500.00
Oak, From Island Queen, Louisville Packet Boat 495.00
Queen Anne, Chinese Figures, Birds, Black Lacquer, 39 In. 4500.00
Silver, Enameled Red, Over Guilloche Ground, Russia, 6 3/4 In. 3300.00
Stick, Boston, 1850 .... 1250.00
Stick, Mahogany, Dolphin Gimbal, Reynolds & Son, 38 1/2 In. 4200.00
Stick, Mahogany, Molded Top, Exposed Tube, D.E.Lent, 36 1/2 In. 1100.00
Stick, Thermometer, W.Jewitt & Co., Liverpool, 36 In. 1300.00
Wheel, Mercury, Wood Inlaid Case, England, 1840–60 .... 795.00
Wheel, Rosewood & Mother–of–Pearl, Egilbert, Belfast, 42 In. 850.00

Basalt is a special type of ceramic invented by Josiah Wedgwood in the eighteenth century. It is a fine–grained, unglazed stoneware.

BASALT, Creamer, Embossed Floral Design, 4 5/8 In. 15.00
Pot, Embossed Floral Bands, Ribbed, Black, 9 In. 45.00
BASEBALL CARDS, see Card, Baseball

Baskets of all types are popular with collectors. Indian, Japanese, African, Shaker, and many other kinds of baskets can be found. Of course, baskets are still being made; so the collector must learn to tell the age and style of the basket to determine the value.

BASKET, African, Stitching In Purple & Tan, 2 3/8 X 2 1/4 In. 40.00
Baby, Wicker, 37 In. 50.00
Beaded, Tasseled, Chinese, Large 45.00
Birchbark & Porcupine Quill, Wisconsin, C.1910, 2 1/2 X 5 /4 In. 65.00
Bushel, Oak Splint 60.00
Bushel, Woven Splint, Bentwood Handles, 12 In. 85.00
Bushel, Woven Splint, Bentwood Rim Handles, 12 1/2 In. 150.00
Buttocks, Bentwood Handle, Zigzags Red & Green, 7 3/4 In. 165.00
Buttocks, Pennsylvania, 19 X 20 In. 285.00
Buttocks, Woven Splint, 3 1/4 X 4 1/2 In. 140.00
Buttocks, Woven Splint, 3 Horizontal Bands, Bentwood Handle, 5 In. ... 190.00

Buttocks, Woven Splint, 6 1/2 X 10 X 13 In. 90.00
Buttocks, Woven Splint, 8 X 13 X 19 In. 100.00
Buttocks, Woven Splint, Bentwood Handle, 10 X 5 1/2 In. 25.00
Buttocks, Woven Splint, Bentwood Handle, 5 In. 135.00
Buttocks, Woven Splint, Bentwood Handles, 6 1/4 In. 300.00
Buttocks, Woven Splint, Varnish Finish, 3 1/4 X 7 In. 25.00
Cheese, Woven Splint, 24 1/2 In. 195.00
Egg, Woven Splint, Radiating Ribs, Bentwood Handle, 15 X 8 1/2 In. 85.00
Franco–American Co., Dated 1897, Small 75.00
Gathering, Center Handle, Green, 9 X 24 In. 50.00
Horse Feeding, Woven Splint, Bentwood Handles, Round, 16 In. 55.00
Laundry, Woven Splint, Open Rim Handles, Oval, 27 1/2 X 11 1/2 In. 45.00
Laundry, Woven Splint, Wooden Bottom, Brown Patina, Oval, 19 X 22 In. 40.00
Lightship, Swing Handle, Captain Thomas James, Large 5000.00
Melon, Eye of God, 14 In. 135.00
Nantucket, Black, Tightly Woven, 4 X 6 In. 350.00
Nantucket, Concentric Rings On Bottom, Swing Handle, 5 X 8 1/2 In. 750.00
Nantucket, Turned Base, Shaped Swing Handle, 8 1/2 X 11 In. 650.00
Nantucket, Woven Splint & Cane, Bentwood Rim & Handles, 6 1/2 In. 500.00
Oriental, Double Lids, Hinge In Center At Handle, 3 1/4 In. 45.00
Picnic, 2 Swing Handles, Hinged Cover, Natural, 20 1/4 X 12 In. 23.00
Pie, Woven Splint, Cover, Curlicue Designs, 5 1/4 X 12 In. 45.00
Rye Straw, Beehive Shape, 13 1/2 X 10 3/4 In. 155.00
Rye Straw, Bowl Shape, Bentwood Ring Base, Woven Handle, 18 X 9 In. 400.00
Rye Straw, Rim Handles, Cloth Lining, 10 1/2 In.Diam. 30.00
Splint, Bentwood Handle, 4 X 7 X 8 In. 55.00
Splint, Carved Bentwood Rim Handles, 4 1/2 X 13 X 14 1/2 In. 45.00
Splint, Natural, 6 1/2 X 12 In. 125.00
Splint, Oak, Handle, Round, 9 X 16 In. 70.00
Splint, Potato Stamp Design, Double Handles, 6 1/2 X 13 In. 75.00
Splint, Square Bottom, C.1860, 9 1/2 X 14 In. 130.00
Storage, Rye Straw, Lid, 18 In. 140.00
Wall, New England, 17 In. 450.00
Wicker, With Alcohol Burner 45.00
Wool, Woven Brown Ash Splint, Double Handles, Round, 24 X 32 In. 850.00
Woven Splint, 2 Tiers, 3 Curved Wooden Legs, Curlicue Design, 25 In. 30.00
Woven Splint, Bentwood Handle, 12 X 19 X 22 In. 70.00
Woven Splint, Bentwood Handle, Round, 4 3/4 X 7 1/2 In. 150.00
Woven Splint, Bentwood Handle, Spring Clip, Hinged Lid, 4 In. 110.00
Woven Splint, Bentwood Handles, Blue, Purple, 5 In. 115.00
Woven Splint, Bentwood Handles, Dark Brown Patina, Round, 6 In. 225.00
Woven Splint, Bentwood Handles, Square Base, Brown Patina, 6 In. 90.00
Woven Splint, Bentwood Swivel Handle, Round, 14 X 8 1/4 In. 725.00
Woven Splint, Bentwood Swivel Handle, Round, 8 X 14 In. 345.00
Woven Splint, Brown, Natural, Potato Print Design, 7 In. 70.00
Woven Splint, Flower Design Around Rim & Base, Miniature 55.00
Woven Splint, Handle, 5 1/4 X 8 1/2 In. 40.00
Woven Splint, Melon Rib, 4 1/2 In. 215.00
Woven Splint, Melon Rib, Bentwood Handle, 7 In. 195.00
Woven Splint, Melon Rib, Oval, Swivel Handle, White, 8 In. 110.00
Woven Splint, Radiating Ribs, Bentwood Handle, 7 1/2 X 14 X 15 In. 45.00
Woven Splint, Rectangular, Bentwood Handle, 10 In. 75.00
Woven Splint, Round, Bentwood Handles, 5 3/4 In. 125.00
Woven Splint, Round, Dark Stained Finish, 10 1/2 In. 65.00
Woven Splint, Round, Swivel Handle, 9 In. 250.00
Woven Splint, Round, Swivel Handle, Wooden Bottom, 8 In. 95.00
Woven Splint, White Paint, Bentwood Handle, 9 X 10 In. 55.00
Woven, Brown & Gold Lacquered Design, Oriental, 18 In. 45.00

BATCHELDER Ernest Batchelder made ceramic and copper items in Los Angeles,
LOS ANGELES California. He died in 1957.

BATCHELDER, Tile, Grape Design, 7 X 12 In. 95.00
  Vase, Drip Glaze, Blue, White, 8 In. 190.00

Batman and Robin are characters from a comic strip by Bob Kane that started in 1939. In 1966, the characters became part of a popular television series. There have been radio and movie serials that featured the pair.

BATMAN, Animation Cel	65.00
Bank	35.00
Batcar, With Batman, Corgi, 1966, 5 In.	55.00
Batcoin, Metal, Metallic Blue, 1966	5.00
Bicycle Ornament, 1966	25.00
Button, I'm A Batman Crimefighter, 1966, 1 1/4 In.	8.00
Button, Society Deputy Crime Fighter, I Hate The Riddler, 3 In.	8.00
Clock, Talking Alarm, 1977	125.00
Comic Book, American Golden Age Batman, No.5	200.00
Comic Book, Matching Wits With Penguin, April–May 1952, No.70	81.00
Comic Book, No.1, Spring, 1940	771.00
Comic Book, No.26, December–January 1944–45	179.00
Comic Book, No.58	100.00
Costume	20.00
Flasher Display Disc, 1966, Set of 6	9.50
Game, Board, 1966	20.00 To 25.00
Lunch Box, Thermos	22.00
Mug, 1950	25.00
Night–Light, Robin, 8 In.	15.00
Spoon & Fork	15.00
Strip, Comic Art, Bob Kane, 1966	250.00

Battersea enamels are enamels painted on copper and made in the Battersea district of London from about 1750 to 1756. Many similar enamels are mistakenly called "Battersea."

BATTERSEA, Box, Industry Best Recompence	247.50
Box, Shape of Bird	770.00

J.A. Bauer moved his Kentucky pottery to Los Angeles, California, in 1909. The company made art pottery after 1912 and dinnerwares after 1929. The factory went out of business around 1958.

BAUER, Ashtray Set, Cobalt Blue, Yellow, Red & Green, Copper Holder, 4 Piece	75.00
Ashtray, Gray, Gunmetal Interior, 5 X 5 X 2 1/2 In.	80.00
Ashtray, Sombrero, Cobalt Blue	35.00
Ashtray, Sombrero, Yellow	30.00
Bowl, Ring, Yellow, 5 In.	9.00
Carafe, Green, Cover	16.00
Carafe, Orange Ring, Wooden Handle	20.00
Carafe, Turquoise	114.00
Carafe, Water, Cover, Wooden Handles, Green	16.00
Carafe, Wooden Handle, Yellow	35.00
Casserole, Speckled, Cover, Metal Tray	18.00
Casserole, Yellow Ring, Cover, 9 1/2 In.	50.00
Coffee Server, Monterey, Orange, Wooden Handle, 8 Cup	50.00
Coffee Server, Ring, Cobalt Blue, Copper Handle	45.00
Coffeepot, Monterey, Wooden Handle, 8 Cup	50.00
Cup & Saucer, Black Ring	50.00
Cup, Ring, Burgundy	15.00
Figurine, Swan, Blue, 6 In.	18.00
Goblet, Ring, Yellow, Footed	35.00
Jug, Water, Ring, Cobalt Blue	50.00
Mixing Bowl, Yellow, 11 In.	23.00
Pitcher, Copper Cover & Handle, Yellow	45.00
Pitcher, Ring, Green, 9 1/2 In.	7.00
Pitcher, Ring, Orange, 9 1/2 In.	10.00
Pitcher, Yellow, 5 1/2 In.	14.00
Planter, White Swan	45.00
Plate, Black Ring, 9 In.	24.00
Plate, Ring, 9 1/2 In.	10.00

Relish, Blue Ridge, Verna Shell	25.00
Rose Bowl, Yellow	14.00
Sugar & Creamer, Open, Black	11.00
Sugar & Creamer, Tray, Monterey, Orange, 3 Piece	69.00
Sugar, Cover, Black Ring	47.50
Teapot, Monterey, Red	38.00
Teapot, Yellow Ring	25.00
Tumbler, Black, 6 Oz.	35.00
Tumbler, Cobalt Blue, 6 Oz.	30.00
Tumbler, Ring, Black, 6 Oz.	25.00
Tumbler, Ring, Wooden Handle, 3 1/2 In.	16.00
Tumbler, Wooden Handle, Orange, 3 1/2 In.	15.00
Vase, Hi–Fire Cobalt Blue, 6 In.	17.50
Vase, Pillow, Turquoise, 2 Handles, 6 1/2 X 10 In.	45.00

Porcelains of all types were made in the region known as Bavaria. In the nineteenth century, the mark often included the word "Bavaria." After 1871, the words "Bavaria, Germany" were used. Listed here are pieces that include the name Bavaria in some form, but major porcelain makers such as Rosenthal are listed in their own categories.

BAVARIA, Basket, Roses, Entwined Branches, Gold, Pearl Luster, 5 X 3 In.	75.00
Berry Set, Roses, P.K.Silesia, 7 Piece	35.00
Bowl, Blue, Pink, Orange Luster, Flowered Sides, Scalloped, 9 In.	22.00
Bowl, Hand Painted Grapes, Gold Trim, Footed, 10 In.	65.00
Cake Plate, Green, Gold, Salmon, Floral, Gold Trim, 10 1/2 In.	15.00
Candy, Rose Buds, Ivys, Festoons, 4 In.	9.00
Coffee Set, Pot, Cover, Sugar & Creamer, White, Gray Design	30.00
Dish, Boat Shape, Open Handles, Roses, Yellow, Black Panels, 8 In.	12.00
Dish, Floral Centers, Square, 5 In.	8.00
Plate, Roses, Gray–Green, 8 In.	15.00
Plate, Service, Floral, Gold Edge, 12 Piece	495.00
Platter, Floral Band, Fruit Basket Border, 14 In.	16.00
Platter, Gold, Salmon, Floral Medallion, Handle, 11 In.	18.00
Sugar & Creamer, Hand Painted Water Lily Pattern, Aqua	85.00
Vase, Gold Flowers, Ivy Overall, Round, 4 1/2 In.	10.00

The Beatles became a famous music group in the 1960s. They first appeared on American network television in 1964. The group disbanded in 1971. Collectors search for any items picturing the four members of the group or any recordings. Because these items are so new, the condition is very important and top prices are paid only for items in mint condition.

BEATLES, Ashtray, Ringo, China, Blue, Black & White, Gold Rim, 5 In.	175.00
Autograph & Sketch, John Lennon, On Notepad, 6 X 8 1/4 In.	790.00
Bank, Dime Register	15.00
Book, Coloring, Beatles On Broadway, 1964	8.00
Book, Coloring, My Name Is John, Art My Hobby, Saalfield	150.00
Book, Punch–Out, Whitman, Unpunched, Mobile, 1964, 10 X 14 In.	600.00
Book, Yellow Submarine, Paperback	10.00
Calendar, 1964, Black & White Photos, Spiral, 9 X 11 In.	195.00
Card Set, 180 Piece	85.00
Change Purse, Pictures On Side, 1964, 4 X 5 In.	7.50
Doll, Sgt.Pepper, Porcelain, Star Shine Inc., 18 In., 4 Piece	450.00
Drawing, Ink, 4 Beatles, She Loves You, Ya Ya, 10 X 16 In.	496.00
Figure, Beatle, With Red Guitar, Gray Jacket, Plastic, 3 In.	12.00
Game, Flip Your Wig, 1964 ....85.00 To	160.00
Immigration Form, Canada, John Lennon, Signed, 1969	250.00
Knife, Pocket, Beatles Picture, 6 In.	5.75
Letter, Fan Club, Signed John, Ringo, George, Paul	2200.00
Lunch Box, Thermos, Blue	160.00
Mirror, Black Apple Outline, Apple Records, 14 X 11 In.	950.00
Mug, Blue Montage, Broadhurst Bros. Burslem, 4 1/2 In.	225.00
Nodder, Car Mascot, Set	650.00

Nodder, Ringo, 7 In.	50.00
Pencil Case, Pictures, Red, White & Blue, Signed & Dated 1964	11.75
Photograph, John Lennon & Yoko Ono, Drawn Face, Framed, 8 X 10 In.	500.00
Photograph, Publicity, BBC Postmark On Envelope, Sept.21, 1963	125.00
Photograph, With 4 Signatures, Framed	750.00
Pillow	150.00
Pin, Flasher, I Love Ringo, 4 Beatles	3.00
Pin, John Lennon, Blue Ground, 1964, 3/4 In.	15.00
Pin, Yellow Submarine, 1968, England	15.00
Plate, 4 Pictures & Names, Bone China, Gold Trim, Raised Outer Rim	225.00
Plate, John Lennon World Tribute, Black & White, Parkhurst	29.00
Pop–Out Art, Yellow Submarine, Paper, 1968	50.00
Postcard, War Is Over, John Lennon, Christmas, 1970, 6 X 8 In.	5.00
Poster, All Things Must Pass, George Harrison, 1970, 12 In.	35.00
Poster, Beatles At Hollywood Bowl, 1964, 36 X 36 In.	275.00
Poster, Hard Day's Night, 30 X 40 In.	20.00
Poster, Promotion, Mechanical, Love Songs, 31 X 26 In.	1650.00
Puzzle, Jigsaw, Cavern Club Scene, 11 X 8 In.	285.00
Puzzle, Jigsaw, Yellow Submarine, 650 Piece	42.00
Record Album, Hard Day's Night, United Artists	36.00
Record Album, Let It Be, Mobile Fidelity, Sealed, 12 In.	16.00
Record, Season's Greetings, Trifold, U.S.Fan Club, 1964, 7 In.	175.00
Record, Sergeant Pepper's Lonely Hearts Club Band	15.00
Record, Take It Away, Paul McCartney, Columbia, 7 In.	10.00
Scarf, Pictures & Signatures, 1964, 22 X 22 In.	11.50
Sheet Music, Hey Jude	10.00
Sheet Music, I Want To Hold Your Hand	8.00 To 10.00
Sheet Music, She Loves You	8.00
Sheet Music, We Can Work It Out	10.00
Shirt, John Lennon, Beige Cotton, Indian Label	495.00
Sketch, John Lennon, Autographed	790.00
Stickpin, Yellow Submarine, 8 Figures	15.00
Suit, Wool, John Lennon's, Black, C.1963, 2 Piece	5225.00
Suit, Wool, John Lennon's, Gray, C.1964, Millings, London, 2 Piece	3300.00
Ticket, Merseyside Civil Service Club, 1971, Signed, 4 X 5 In.	1650.00
Tie Tac, Ringo	15.00
Tin, Talcum Powder	425.00
Toy, Yellow Submarine, Corgi	100.00
Tray, Serving, Metal, Color, 13 X 13 In.	25.00
Wallet, 1960s	50.00

Beehive, Plate, Lohengrin, Royal Vienna, 10 In., Pair

"Beehive, Austria," or "Beehive, Vienna," are terms used in English–speaking countries to refer to the many types of decorated porcelain bearing a mark that looks like a beehive. The mark is actually a shield, viewed upside down. It was first used in 1744 by the Royal Porcelain Manufactory of Vienna. The firm made porcelains, called "Royal Vienna" by collectors, until it closed in 1864. Many other German, Austrian, and Japanese factories have reproduced Royal Vienna wares, complete with the original shield or "beehive" mark. This listing includes the expensive, original Royal Vienna porcelains and many other types of beehive porcelain. The Royal Vienna pieces include that name in the description.

BEEHIVE, Bowl, Cloisonne–Type, Flowers, Birds, Red, Square, Royal Vienna, 9 In.	125.00
Cracker Jar, Pearlized Porcelain, Lilies	225.00
Dish, Orchid, 3 5/8 X 7/8 In.	6.00
Hair Receiver, Cover, Diamond, Floral, Crown Mark, Royal Vienna	80.00
Plate, Cupid & Psyche, Cobalt & Gold Border, Signed C.Herr	225.00
Plate, Ein Geheimnis Scene, Gilt Frame, Royal Vienna, 9 1/2 In.	733.00
Plate, Lohengrin, Royal Vienna, 10 In., Pair *Illus*	660.00
Plate, Woman In Green Velvet, Forster, Royal Vienna, 9 1/2 In.	650.00
Platter, Cartouche, Openwork Handles, Kaufmann, Royal Vienna, 17 In.	253.00
Powder Box, Figural & Floral, Royal Vienna, C.1890	200.00
Urn, Figures, Leaf Handles, Finial, Royal Vienna, C.1880, 24 1/2 In.	3300.00
Urn, Hand Painted Portrait, Raised Gold, Royal Vienna, 8 In.	225.00
Urn, Mythological Scene, Gold, Kauffmann, Royal Vienna, 9 1/2 In.	110.00
Vase, Hand Painted Girl, Bird, Gold Rim, Royal Vienna, 6 1/4 In.	150.00
BEER BOTTLE, see bottle, beer	

Beer was sold in kegs or returnable bottles until 1934. The first patent for a can was issued to the American Can Company in September of that year; and Gotfried Kruger Brewing Company, Newark, New Jersey, was the first to use the can. The cone-top can was first made in 1935, the aluminum pop-top in 1962. Collectors should look for cans in good condition, with no dents or rust. Serious collectors prefer cans that have been opened from the bottom.

BEER CAN, ABC Ale	.75
Acme, 12 Oz.	14.00
Alligator Light, Aluminum, Florida Brewery	.75
Ballantine Bi–Cent, Falstaff, Aluminum, 12 Oz.	1.10
Beck's Beer, Aluminum, Germany	1.00
Becker's	65.00
Beverwyck, Cone Top	24.00
Big Kirin	10.00
Black Label, Heileman, Aluminum, White, Black & Red	.80
Blatz, Heileman, White, Gold & Maroon	.70
Bounty Hunter, River City, 1983	1.50
Braumeister, Flat Top	14.00
Brown Derby, Contents, 12 Oz.	24.00
Buffalo Brew, North Dakota	1.50
Burgermeister, Music Box	10.00
Busch, Olympics, White, Blue & Gold	.80
Calgary Amber Lager, 9 Oz.	2.00
Carlsberg, Green Can, Toronto, Canada	1.00
Carta Blanca, Aluminum, Mexico	1.00
Christian Moerlein	.75
Cloud Nine Malt Liquor	3.00
Colt 45 Malt Lager, 12 Oz.	15.00
Coors Extra Gold Draft, Gold, Black & White	.85
Dixie Light, World Expo, Aluminum	1.00
Eagle, Stevens Point, White, Gold & Blue	.75
Falls City, Aluminum, 16 Oz.	.75
Falstaff, Cone Top	45.00
Falstaff, Pearl, Aluminum, White, Brown, Gold, 16 Oz.	1.50

Genesee Cream Ale, Aluminum, 16 Oz.	.75
Grain Belt, Cone Top	22.50
Harley–Davidson, Huber, Aluminum, Orange, Black, White, 12 Oz.	2.50
Iron City, 1975 Steelers, Stainless Steel	2.00
Iron City, Pirates	.75
Kessler, Cone Top, Helena, Montana	62.00
Keyes Premium Lite, Aluminum	.75
Maine Jaycees, Sponsored By Ballantine, 1960–61	25.00
Michelob, Aluminum, Factory, Gold, Red, Black, 12 Oz.	4.00
Mickey Gilley's, Inside Texas, Aluminum	1.00
Midnight Dragon, Multicolor, 16 Oz.	1.50
Molson Light, Double Neck, Aluminum, Canada	1.00
Oertel's 92, Cone Top	45.00
Olympia Light, White, Gold & Blue, Aluminum	.50
Oranjeboom, Holland	1.00
Rathskeller, Aluminum, Silver, Red, Black, 12 Oz.	.75
Rheingold Extra Dry, 16 Oz.	.75
Rocky Mountain, Cone Top	15.00
Rolling Rock, Aluminum, 16 Oz.	.75
Royal Bohemian, Cone Top	30.00
Schaefer, Tapered Neck, Aluminum, 12 Oz.	.50
Schell, Andy's Crossroads, Straight, 12 Oz.	1.10
Schell, Bob's BCCA, Straight, White, Red, Beige, 12 Oz.	2.50
Stag, Heileman, Gold, White & Red, 16 Oz.	.90
Stroh's, Aluminum, 10 Oz.	.50
Suntory, Barrel Shape, Japan, 10.1 Oz.	1.00
Wisconsin Dells, Stevens Point, Aluminum, Yellow, White, 12 Oz.	.95
World's Fair, 1984, San Antonio, Aluminum, Blue, White, Gold, 12 Oz.	.90

Bells have been made of porcelain, china, or metal through the centuries. All types are collected. Favorites include glass bells, figural bells, school bells, and cowbells. Be careful not to buy a bell made from an old glass goblet.

BELL, Brass, Raised Figures, Yoke, Cincinnati, 1847, Large	1050.00
Dinner, Cast Iron, 45 Lbs., 14 1/2 In.	195.00
Dinner, Sterling Silver, Art Nouveau Foliate Handle, 5 1/2 X 2 In.	45.00
Dutch Girl, Brass	42.00
Hotel, Brass, Large	60.00
Lion, Bell On Back, Hotel, Brass	75.00
Old Lady With Hat, Brass, 5 1/2 In.	110.00
School, Steel Spring Between Bell & Wooden Handle, 9 1/2 In.	75.00
Shop, Brass, Coiled Wire Spring	75.00
Sleigh, 4 Graduated On Iron Strap	75.00
Sleigh, Brass, 12 Graduated On Leather Strap	125.00
Sleigh, Brass, Horse's Belly, Leather Strap, Buckle, 51 Bells	160.00
Smoke King Oscar, 3 1/4 In.	22.00
Tap, 3 Footed, 3 1/2 In.	18.00
Temple, Birds In Relief, Bronze, Tibetan, 9 1/4 In.	95.00
Victorian Lady, Brass, 4 In.	48.00

Belle Ware glass was made in 1903 by Carl V. Helmschmied. In 1904 he started a corporation known as the Helmschmied Manufacturing Company. His factory closed in 1908 and he worked on his own until his death in 1934.

BELLE WARE, Bowl, Large	265.00
Pin Tray	135.00
Syrup, Apple Blossom Design, Hinged Lid, Egg Shape	110.00
Vase, Stylized Orchid Blossom, 6 In.	385.00

Belleek china is made in Ireland, other European countries, and the United States. The glaze is creamy yellow and appears wet. The first Belleek was made in 1857. All pieces listed here are Irish Belleek. The mark changed through the years. The first mark, black, dates from 1863 to 1890. The second mark, black, dates from 1891 to

1926 and includes the words "Co. Fermanagh, Ireland." The third mark, black, dates from 1926 to 1946 and has the words "Deanta in Eirinn." The fourth mark, same as the third mark but green, dates from 1946 to 1955. The fifth mark, green, dates from 1955 to 1965 and has an R in a circle added in the upper right. The sixth mark, green, dates after 1965 and the words "Co. Fermanagh" have been omitted. The seventh mark, gold, was used after 1980 and omits the words "Deanta in Eirinn."

BELLEEK, see also Ceramic Art Co.; Haviland; Lenox; Ott & Brewer; Willets

BELLEEK, **Basket,** 4 Strands, Pearl Finish, Oval, Fermanagh, 12 1/2 In.	2090.00
Basket, Cover, 4 Strands, Painted, Fermanagh, 12 1/2 In.	2750.00
Basket, Cover, Applied Florals, Oval, Fermanagh, 9 In.	1540.00
Basket, Cover, Painted, Fermanagh, 10 3/4 In.	2475.00
Basket, Cover, Pearl Finish, Fermanagh, Round, 11 In.	1650.00
Basket, Lily, Painted, 1st Mark, 8 1/2 In.	1100.00
Basket, Pearl Finish, Heart Shape, Fermanagh, 4 1/2 In.	275.00
Basket, Pinched Envelope, Flowers, 2nd Black Mark, 6 In.	475.00
Basket, Rathmore, Oval, Fermanagh, 12 In.	1760.00
Basket, Strands, Oval, Fermanagh, 12 1/2 In.	1045.00
Basket, Straw, Cob Luster, 2nd Mark, 4 1/2 In.	415.00
Basket, Sydenham, Twig, 3 Strands, 10 1/2 In.	1540.00
Basket, Twig, Pearl Finish, Marked, 8 1/2 In.	2475.00
Bowl, Echinus, Cover, Footed, 6th Mark, 8 In.	385.00
Bowl, Lotus, 1st Green Mark, 3 1/2 In.	10.00
Bowl, Shell, Footed, Green Mark, 5 In.	45.00
Bracket, Wall, Grapevine, 2nd Mark, 13 1/2 In.	550.00
Bread Plate, Limpet, 4 Handles, 1st Black Mark	147.00
Brooch, Pink, Blue & White Flowers	225.00
Bust, Charles Dickens, Bisque & Pearl, 1st Mark, 18 In.	5500.00
Bust, Clytie, Porcelain & Bisque, 1st Black Mark, 11 3/4 In.	1995.00
Bust, John Wesley, 1st Black Mark, 8 1/4 In.	1950.00
Bust, Lord James Butler, Bisque & Pearl, 1st Mark, 11 1/2 In.	1430.00
Bust, Queen of The Hops, Bisque Finish, 1st Mark, 11 1/2 In.	3850.00
Butter, Cottage Cover, 1st Green Mark, 6 1/2 X 5 In.	140.00
Butter, Cottage Cover, Twig Handle, Yellow Roof, 1st Green Mark	160.00
Cache Pot, Quilted Diamond, 1st Green Mark	75.00
Cake Plate, 4 Strands, Pearl Finish, Hexagonal, 9 3/4 In.	385.00
Candleholder, 3 Branches, Tree, Seat For Boy, Cream, 14 X 7 In.	3200.00
Candlestick, Shepherd Sleeping With Dog, Gilt, 1st Mark, 7 In.	100.00
Coffeepot, Shamrock & Shell	80.00
Cracker Jar, Shell, Green Mark	85.00
Creamer, Girl, Figural	55.00
Creamer, Lily, 1st Green Mark	32.00
Creamer, Nautilus, 1st Black Mark	200.00
Creamer, Scale, Pink Rim & Handle, 2nd Black Mark, 3 1/4 In.	82.00
Creamer, Shell, Fluted, 1st Black Mark	115.00
Cup & Saucer, Boullion, Shamrock, 4 Sets	120.00
Cup & Saucer, Eggshell, Ridged Pattern, 2nd Black Mark	340.00
Cup & Saucer, Grass, 1st Black Mark	425.00
Cup & Saucer, Harp & Shamrock, 2nd Black Mark	80.00
Cup & Saucer, Hexagon, Green Trim, 2nd Black Mark	81.00
Cup & Saucer, Hexagonal, White, 2nd Black Mark	125.00
Cup & Saucer, Ivy, Cob Luster Finish, 3rd Black Mark	145.00
Cup & Saucer, Mask, 3rd Black Mark, Demitasse	130.00
Cup & Saucer, Neptune, Green Tint, 2nd Black Mark	135.00
Cup & Saucer, Shamrock, 3rd Black Mark, Demitasse	67.00
Cup & Saucer, Shamrock, Black Mark	22.00
Cup & Saucer, Shamrock, Twig Handle, 3rd Black Mark	80.00
Cup & Saucer, Shell	70.00
Cup & Saucer, Tridacna, 3rd Black Mark	40.00
Cup & Saucer, Tridacna, Pink Tint, 1st Black Mark	125.00
Cup & Saucer, Twig Handle, 3rd Black Mark	80.00

Dejeuner Set, Cob Luster, 2nd Mark, 12 Piece 1200.00
Dejeuner Set, Harp, Shamrock, Tea Ware, 2nd Black Mark, 8 Piece 1320.00
Dish, Heart Shape Shell, 4th Green Mark, 6 In. 47.00
Dish, Leaf, Green Tint, 2nd Black Mark 45.00
Dish, Muffin, Cover, Artichoke, 9 1/4 In. 525.00
Egg Stand, Hand & Ring Finial, 1st Black Mark 325.00
Ewer, Aberdeen, 2nd Green Mark 250.00
Ewer, Mask Below Handle, Green Trim, 2nd Black Mark, 8 1/2 In. 795.00
Ewer, Roman Transfer Pattern, Earthenware, 1st Mark, 8 1/2 In. 990.00
Figurine, Affection, Pearl Finish, 2nd Mark, 15 In. 880.00
Figurine, Belgian, Woman, Gold Mark 225.00
Figurine, Boy & Basket, 3rd Green Mark 295.00
Figurine, Erin With Celtic Cross, 1st Mark, 17 1/2 In. 5500.00
Figurine, Girl & Basket, 3rd Green Mark 295.00
Figurine, Greyhound, 3rd Black Mark 615.00
Figurine, Leprechaun, 3rd Green Mark 75.00
Figurine, Meditation, No.2, Green Mark 495.00
Figurine, Round Tower, 3rd Green Mark 375.00
Figurine, Seahorse & Shell, Painted & Gilt, 1st Period, 4 In. 715.00
Figurine, Spaniel On Pillow, 3rd Green Mark 95.00
Figurine, Tobacco Brewer With Two Barrels, 2nd Mark, 8 1/4 In. 3025.00
Figurine, Virgin Mary, 3rd Green Mark 350.00
Flowerpot, Naiads, Painted & Gilt Finish, 2nd Mark, 10 1/2 In. 1540.00
Flowerpot, Oak, Pearlescent, Roses & Chrysanthemum, 1st Mark, 13 In. 2090.00
Flowerpot, Shell, Pearl Luster, 2nd Black Mark, 9 In. 1760.00
Frame, Mirror, Lily of The Valley, 1st Mark, 16 1/2 X 13 1/2 In. 2200.00
Honey Pot, Grass, 1st Black Mark 350.00
Ice Pail, Prince of Wales, Gilt Finish, 1st Mark, 18 1/2 In. 5500.00
Jam Jar, Ribbon, Pearlescent, 1st Mark, 5 1/4 In. 248.00
Jam Jar, Shamrock, Barrel Shape, 3rd Black Mark 85.00
Jug, Lily, Stoneware, 1st Black Mark, 6 1/2 In. 180.00
Jug, Milk, Limpet, 2nd Green Mark 85.00
Mug, Thor, Twigs & Thorns, Pink Handle, 2nd Black Mark 140.00
Mug, Transfer Pattern, 1st Black Mark 275.00
Mustache Cup, Shamrock 225.00
Mustache Cup, Tridacna, Painted Finish, 1st Black Mark, 2 1/2 In. 220.00
Pitcher, Indian, Full Headdress 475.00
Pitcher, Lemonade, Red Roses, Green Ground, Signed, 5 1/2 In. 135.00
Planter, Shell Form 140.00
Plaque, Child Looking In Mirror, Lithophane, 5 1/2 X 5 1/2 In. 440.00
Plate, Artichoke, Gilt Finish, 1st Mark, 8 1/4 In., 2 Piece 220.00
Plate, Basket Weave & Shamrock, 3rd Black Mark 90.00
Plate, Greek, 1st Black Mark, 9 1/4 In. 250.00
Plate, Limpet, 3rd Black Mark, 8 1/2 In. 50.00
Plate, Shamrock, Rim Gilt Finish, 8 1/2 In. 165.00
Plate, Shell, 1st Black Mark, 8 1/2 In. 80.00
Plate, Tridacna, 1st Black Mark, 6 3/4 In., 4 Piece 195.00
Plate, Tridacna, 2nd Black Mark, 6 In. 40.00
Salt Dip, Ruffled, Floral Design, Morris & Willmore 35.00
Saucer, Shamrock, 1st Black Mark 20.00
Sugar & Creamer, Canterbury, 1st Black Mark 120.00
Sugar & Creamer, Harp, Shamrock, 3rd Black Mark 125.00
Sugar & Creamer, Lily, 4th Black Mark 55.00
Sugar & Creamer, Lotus, 3rd Black Mark 83.00
Sugar & Creamer, Neptune, 3rd Black Mark 60.00
Sugar & Creamer, Shamrock, 2nd Black Mark 150.00
Sugar & Creamer, Shamrock, 3rd Black Mark ....75.00 To 100.00
Sugar & Creamer, Tridacna, Boat Shape, 3rd Black Mark 100.00
Sugar, Scroll, Green Tint, Gold Trim, 2nd Black Mark 75.00
Sugar, Scroll, Tinted & Gilt Finish, 2nd Black Mark, 2 1/2 In. 120.00
Sugar, Shell, Blue Mark, Large 175.00
Sugar, Shell, Coral & White, 1st Black Mark, 6 1/2 In. 575.00
Teakettle, Grass, Painted, 1st Mark, 6 1/2 In. 495.00
Teapot, Brown & Gilded, 1st Black Mark, 6 1/2 In. 900.00

Belleek, Urn, Nymph
Playing Violin,
Hand Painted, Signed, 18 In.

Bisque, Figure,
Sailor's Valentine,
Paper Flowers, 7 In.

Teapot, Harp, 3rd Black Mark	325.00
Teapot, Harp, Shamrock, 3rd Black Mark	325.00
Teapot, Neptune, 2nd Black Mark	250.00
Teapot, Neptune, Blue Trim, Shell Feet, 2nd Black Mark	250.00
Teapot, Neptune, Green Trim, 2nd Black Mark	300.00
Teapot, Neptune, Shell Feet & Finial, 2nd Black Mark	300.00
Teapot, Neptune, Tinted Finish, 2nd Black Mark, 5 In.	248.00
Teapot, Shamrock, Harp Design, 1986	110.00
Teapot, Shell	100.00
Teapot, Sugar & Creamer, Shamrock, 3rd Black Mark	275.00
Teapot, Tinted Finish, 2nd Black Mark, 5 In.	275.00
Teapot, Tridacna, Tinted, 1st Mark, 3 3/4 In.	385.00
Tray, Chinese Tea Ware, 1st Mark, 15 In.	880.00
Tray, Floral Design, Hexagonal, 2nd Mark, 16 1/2 In.	1430.00
Tray, Tinted Finish, Hexagonal, 2nd Mark, 16 3/4 In.	605.00
Trivet, Blue, Round, 1st Black Mark	50.00
Tub, Irish Shamrock, 2 Handle, 2nd Green Mark	40.00
Urn, Nymph Playing Violin, Hand Painted, Signed, 18 In. ....*Illus*	880.00
Vase, Aberdeen, 3rd Green Mark, 6 In.	165.00
Vase, Aberdeen, 3rd Green Mark, 7 In.	195.00
Vase, Bud, Hand Painted Roses	100.00
Vase, Cover, 2nd Mark, 9 1/2 In.	825.00
Vase, Double Fish, Luster Finish, 1st Mark, 12 In.	605.00
Vase, Figural, Owl, Marked, 8 In.	37.00
Vase, Flared Top, Spider Mums, Burgundy Red, 1889, 10 1/4 In.	235.00
Vase, Frog, Black Eyes, Parian Body, 2nd Black Mark, 4 3/4 In.	850.00
Vase, Fruit Design, 7 In.	75.00
Vase, Hand Painted Roses, Beige Ground, 15 In.	365.00
Vase, Leaning Boy, Pearl & Bisque, 1st Mark, 7 In.	660.00
Vase, Princess, Applied Flowers, 2nd Black Mark, 9 In.	795.00
Vase, Shamrock & Harp, 2nd Black Mark, 9 In.	300.00
Vase, Trellis, Roses, 2nd Black Mark, 4 In.	115.00
Vase, Triple Fish, Painted & Gilt Finish, 2nd Mark, 5 3/4 In.	3575.00
Vase, Trumpet, Gilded Horse, 1st Black Mark, 5 In.	550.00

Bennington ware was the product of two factories working in Bennington, Vermont. Both firms were out of business by 1896. The wares include brown and yellow mottled pottery, Parian, scroddled ware, stoneware, graniteware, yellowware, and Staffordshirelike vases.

BENNINGTON, Bottle, Book Form, Flint Enamel, Marked Kossuth, 1849, 6 In.	300.00
Bottle, Book, Buntline's Companion, Flint, Enameled, 7 5/8 In.	325.00

Bottle, Book, Flint, Enameled, 1849 Mark, 6 In.	925.00
Bottle, Coachman, 1849, 10 3/8 In.	200.00 To 750.00
Bottle, Toby, Brown & Yellow Mustache, 1849 Mark, 10 3/4 In.	900.00
Bottle, Toby, Gray, Light Brown Sponged, 1849 Mark, 10 1/8 In.	600.00
Bowl, Mixing, 12 In.	72.00
Coffeepot, Flint Enamel Glaze, Mark of 1849, 12 1/2 In.	375.00
Creamer, Flowers & Leaves, Dark Brown, Large	60.00
Crock, Butter, Peacock On Fence	65.00
Crock, Floral Spray, Lug Handles, Marked, 10 1/2 In.	425.00
Crock, Spread Wing Eagle, On Stump, 3 Gal.	6000.00
Cuspidor, Flint Enamel, 1840, 8 1/2 In.	65.00
Cuspidor, Geometric Blown–Out Mold, Flint, 5 X 5 In.	75.00
Cuspidor, Grape Leaf Clusters, C.1850	95.00
Cuspidor, Shell Pattern, Side Vent, 8 1/2 In.	90.00 To 110.00
Cuspidor, Spatterware, 11 In.	125.00
Humidor, Marked 1849, 7 1/4 In.	25.00
Inkwell, Phrenology Head	175.00
Inkwell, Sleeping Child Holding Hat, Brown Glaze	150.00
Jug, Bird, Flower Branch, Marked J.Norton & Co., 4 Gal.	700.00
Jug, Bluebird On Branch, J.& E.Norton, 1 Gal.	495.00
Knob, For Drawer, Mottled, 1 7/8 In.	.50
Marble, Mottled Brown, 5 In.	35.00
Mug, Nude Handle, 1933, 6 1/2 In.	45.00
Paperweight, Dog On Pillow, 1849, 2 3/4 X 4 1/4 In.	250.00
Piggy Bank, Yellow & Brown, 3 3/4 In.	55.00
Pitcher, Anchor & Chain Design, 10 In.	95.00
Pitcher, Grape Design, Star On Bottom	75.00
Pitcher, Milk, Leaves & Grapes	125.00
Pitcher, Rockingham Glaze, Mark of 1849, 12 1/4 In.	150.00
Pitcher, Toby, 11 In.	350.00
Pitcher, Toby, Gentleman, Grapevine Handle, Marked, 10 3/4 In.	300.00
Pitcher, Tulip Design, Small	65.00
String Holder, Dog	165.00
Teapot, China Men, Large	100.00
Vase, Corn, 8 1/2 In.	30.00
Vase, Parian Eagle, Gilt Enameling, 7 3/8 In.	45.00

Berlin, a German porcelain factory, was started in 1751 by Wilhelm Kaspar Wegely. In 1763, the factory was taken over by Frederick the Great and became the Royal Berlin Porcelain Manufactory. It is still in operation today. Pieces have been marked in a variety of ways.

BERLIN, Figurine, Man Holding Flute, 9 In.	350.00
Figurine, Sandpiper, Walking Among Tall Grass, 8 1/4 In.	290.00
Mug, Gold Wash Interior, 1817, Small	145.00
Plate, Raised Fruit, Floral Decoration, 10 In.	150.00

Bernard Moore was an art potter working in England from about 1905 to 1915. He used his name as his mark.

John Beswick started making earthenware in Staffordshire, England, in 1936. The company is now part of Royal Doulton Tableware, Ltd. Figurines of animals, especially dogs and horses, Beatrix Potter animals, and other wares are still being made.

BESWICK, Character Mug, Captain Cuttle	38.00
Figurine, Alice In Wonderland, King of Hearts	45.00
Figurine, Alice In Wonderland, Queen of Hearts	45.00
Figurine, Appaloosa	125.00
Figurine, Bay Colt	30.00
Figurine, Bay Stallion	40.00
Figurine, Birds, Double, No.926	35.00
Figurine, Cat, Seated, Blue Eyes, Pink Nose, White, 11 In.	55.00
Figurine, Hawk, Marked, Original Gold Sticker, 7 In.	38.00
Figurine, Hawk, No.2316, 7 In.	35.00

Figurine, Kenga, Ceramic, 3 In.	12.00
Figurine, Owl, From Pooh, Ceramic, 3 In.	12.00
Figurine, Palomino	40.00
Figurine, Rabbit, From Pooh, Ceramic, 3 In.	12.00
Figurine, Sheep Dog, 10 In.	100.00
Group, Bunratty Castle, Limited Edition	30.00
Mug, Nursery Rhyme	15.00
Toby Jug, Behind Every Great Man, Worthingtons Ale, 9 In.	65.00
Vase, Blown–Out Palm Trees, Cobalt Blue, Gold, 6 1/2 In.	28.00

Betty Boop, the cartoon figure, first appeared on the screen in 1931. Her face was modeled after the famous singer Helen Kane and her body after Mae West. In 1935 a comic strip was started. Although the Betty Boop cartoons were ended by 1938, there has been a revival of interest in the Betty Boop image in the 1980s and new pieces are being made.

BETTY BOOP, Ashtray, Betty Boop & Bimbo, Marked Fleisher Studios	80.00
Button, Betty Boop For President, Litho, 1980, 1 1/2 In.	3.00
Coverlet, Green, Orange, Fleischer Studios, 1930s, 12 X 15 In.	85.00
Doll, Bisque, 5 In.	55.00
Doll, Celluloid, Movable Arms, 8 In.	95.00
Figure, Celluloid, Nude, Movable Arms, Occupied Japan, 3 In.	11.00
Figure, Stand–Up, Wooden, 16 In.	15.00
Figurine, Chalkware	2.00
Light Bulb, Christmas Tree	40.00
Ornament, Christmas Tree, Jointed, Wood	150.00
Purse, Celluloid	25.00
Quilt, Doll's, Fleischer Studios	160.00

The bicycle was invented in 1839. The first manufactured bicycle was made in 1861. Special ladies' bicycles were made after 1874. The modern safety bicycle was not produced until 1885. Collectors search for all types of bicycles and tricycles.

BICYCLE, Basket, Splint	60.00
Book, Gendron Wheel Co., Toledo, Ohio, 28 Pages, 1896, 6 X 7 In.	67.50
Built For 2, Remington Arms, Chain Drive	400.00
Columbia, Boy's, 1955	1700.00
Columbia, Large Wheel, Small Wheel, C.1880	3500.00
Columbia, Model 65	600.00
Hopalong Cassidy, Chrome Studs, Saddle Bags, Leather Fringe, 2 Guns	3000.00
Horn, Yoder, 1950s	7.00
J.C.Higgins, Boy's, Chrome Exhaust, 1948	2700.00
Peerless Roadster, Wooden Rims, Rubber Tires, Black, Red Trim	1400.00
Tricycle, 2 Large Rear Wheels, Upholstered Seat, 61 In.	605.00
Tricycle, Mercury	55.00
Tricycle, Wooden, C.1860	2400.00

Bing and Grondahl is a famous Danish factory making fine porcelains from 1853 to the present. Underglaze blue decoration was started in 1886. The annual Christmas plate series was introduced in 1895. Dinnerwares, stoneware, and figurines are still being made today. The firm has used the initials B & G and a stylized castle as part of the mark since 1898.

B&G
JØBENHAVN
MADE IN
DENMARK

BING & GRONDAHL, Cup & Saucer, Plate, Composer	35.00
Figurine, Ballerina, No.2325	178.00
Figurine, Boy Holding Book, Wearing Cape, No.1720	160.00
Figurine, Boy Kissing Girl, No.2162	210.00
Figurine, Boy Stirring Pot, Cat At Side, No.2305	175.00
Figurine, Bulldog, No.1676	45.00
Figurine, Buttoning My Shoe, No.2317	175.00
Figurine, Clown, No.2511	50.00
Figurine, Come To Mom, No.2324	140.00
Figurine, Dancing School, No.1845	295.00
Figurine, First Book, No.2247	135.00

Figurine, Friends, No.2249 .... 140.00
Figurine, Gentleman, No.2312 .... 240.00
Figurine, Girl Holding Butterfly, Pink, No.2185 .... 150.00
Figurine, Gold Crested Kinglet, No.2458 .... 45.00
Figurine, Good Morning, No.1624 .... 95.00
Figurine, Hans Christian Andersen With Girl 350.00
Figurine, Ida, No.2298 .... 178.00
Figurine, Kaj, No.1617 .... 160.00
Figurine, Little Match Girl, No.1655 .... 178.00
Figurine, Love Refused, No.1614 .... 225.00
Figurine, Marianne, No.2373 .... 190.00
Figurine, Mary, No.1721 .... 150.00
Figurine, Merry Sailor, No.1661, 8 1/2 In. 160.00
Figurine, Nude Woman Suckling Baby, Signed, 12 In. 195.00
Figurine, Peacock 1600.00
Figurine, Pierrot, No.2353 .... 245.00
Figurine, Polar Bear, 12 In. 168.00
Figurine, Prejudiced, No.2175 .... 240.00
Figurine, Two Friends, No.1790 .... 185.00
Figurine, Who Is Calling?, No.2251 .... 140.00
Figurine, Young Sailor, Holding Rope, No.2321 .... 160.00
Figurine, Youthful Boldness, No.2162 .... 255.00
Pendant, Dog, 1979 .... 10.00
Plate, Cat Portrait 26.00
Plate, Christmas, 1915 .... 95.00
Plate, Christmas, 1964 .... 50.00
Plate, Christmas, 1971 .... 12.00 To 14.00
Plate, Christmas, 1981 .... 35.00
Plate, Intruder, Kurtard, Box 9.00
Plate, Mother's Day, 1970, Birds 22.00
Plate, Mother's Day, 1972, Horses 24.00
Plate, Mother's Day, 1974, Bears 20.00
Plate, Mother's Day, 1975, Deer 18.00
Plate, Mother's Day, 1977 .... 15.00
Plate, S.S.Rotterdam, Holland Amer.Cruise, Blue, 1980, 8 In. 13.00
Plate, Statue of Liberty 75.00
Tureen, Cover, Seagull 200.00
Vase, Dandelions, 10 In. 50.00
Vase, Relief Flowers, Hand Painted, Signed, 8 1/2 In. 65.00
Vase, Sea Gulls, Gold Tipped Wings, 8 In. 95.00
Vase, Windmill, 10 In. 55.00

All types of old binoculars are wanted by collectors. Those made in the eighteenth and nineteenth centuries are favored by serious collectors. The small, attractive binoculars called opera glasses are listed in their own section.

BINOCULARS, Bardou & Son, Paris 65.00
Bushnell, Deluxe 95.00
Egyptian Figures, Occupied Japan 40.00
Stanhope, Miniature With Picture 39.00
Tom Corbett, Metal 45.00

Old birdcages are collected for use as homes for pet birds and as decorative objects of folk art. Elaborate wooden cages of the past centuries can still be found. The brass or wicker cages of the 1930s are popular with bird owners.

BIRDCAGE, Brass, Frame Building Shape 85.00
Carrier, Homing Pigeon 195.00
Domed, Tin, Pierced Galleried Tray, U.S., 18 X 14 In. 300.00
Fretwork, Ornate 650.00
Hendryx, Brass 68.00
Peaked Dome, Sliding Under Tray, Wire & Mahogany, 27 1/2 In. 3025.00
Porcelain Feeder, Etched Glass Guards, Brass, 11 3/4 X 9 1/4 In. 125.00
Victorian, Cut Fretwork, Bird Claw Hook, Stand 650.00

Wood & Wirework, 19th Century	575.00
Wooden Frame, Wire Bars	45.00

Bisque is an unglazed baked porcelain. Finished bisque has a slightly sandy texture with a dull finish. Some of it may be decorated with various colors. Bisque gained favor during the late Victorian era when thousands of bisque figurines were made. It is still being made.

BISQUE, see also named porcelain factories

BISQUE, Bowl, Waves & Frolicking Cherubs, Boat Shape, Germany, 11 1/4 In.	30.00
Box, Comb Shape, Roses, Gold, Comb Cover	15.00
Bust, Boy & Girl, Blond Hair, Floral Shirts, Germany, 10 In., Pair	275.00
Candleholder, Figural, King & Queen, Braided Hair Forms Handle, Pair	75.00
Figure, Sailor's Valentine, Paper Flowers, 7 In. *Illus*	125.00
Figure, Swinger, Baby, In Pink Blanket, Used Under Hanging Lamp	135.00
Figurine, Baby, Hands In Green Ink Pot, 3 5/8 X 2 X 3 In.	95.00
Figurine, Bow, Carrying Basket, Short Pants, Beret, Germany, 14 In.	225.00
Figurine, Dog Holding Basket of Puppies, Brown & White, 5 1/2 In.	95.00
Figurine, Happy Hooligan, 8 1/2 In.	40.00
Figurine, Romeo & Juliet, Floral Trousers, Floral Dress, 19 In., Pair	450.00
Figurine, Young Woman & Man Under Umbrella, Wire Handle, 6 In.	175.00
Frame, Picture, Shaded Blue, Gold, Germany, 4 In.	20.00
Holy Water Font, Angel, Blue, White	25.00
Night–Light, Glass Eyes, Blue Neck Bow, 4 1/4 In.	195.00
Plaque, Maiden Seated On Vines, C.1850, 10 3/4 X 8 3/8 In.	550.00

Black amethyst glass appears black until it is held to the light, then a dark purple can be seen. It has been made in many factories from 1860 to the present.

BLACK AMETHYST, Ashtray, Cloverleaf, 5 3/4 In.	60.00
Ashtray, Daisy & Button, 2 1/4 X 3 3/4 In.	4.50
Berry Set, Daisy & Lattice, 7 Piece	47.50
Bowl, 3 Horizontal Stippled Bands, Handles, 5 In.	10.00
Bowl, Console, Double Handles, 8 1/2 In.	20.00
Bowl, Flared, 10 In.	25.00
Box, Enameled Lady, Mary Gregory Style, Hinged, 4 X 5 In.	245.00
Box, Jewelry, Silver Plated Fittings, Velvet Lined	500.00
Box, Patch, Hinged Cover, Enameled Flower, Leaves, 2 In.	75.00
Console Set, Fluted Bowl, 3 Piece	70.00
Creamer	10.00
Decanter, 2 Sides Pinched, C.1900, 9 1/2 In.	90.00
Dish, Hen On Nest Cover, White Head	35.00
Planter Box, Nude Dancers On Sides, L.E.Smith	45.00
Pomade Jar, Bear, 3 3/4 In.	275.00
Rose Bowl, Greek Key, Silver Enameled	22.50
Salt & Pepper, Art Deco	20.00
Vase, Art Deco Design, 12 In.	40.00
Vase, Silver Roses, Butterflies, Urn Shape, 11 3/4 In.	35.00

Black memorabilia has become an important area of collecting since the 1970s. Any piece that pictures a black person is included in this category and objects range from sheet music to salt and pepper shakers. The best material dates from past centuries, but many recent items are of interest even if not yet expensive.

BLACK, Ad, Cream of Wheat, Best Dish In Cookbook, 1907, 16 X 20 In.	30.00
Ad, Cream of Wheat, Black Boy Jumping Fence, 1916, 18 X 15 In.	22.50
Ad, Cream of Wheat, Black Grandpa, Newspaper, 1916, 9 X 13 In.	30.00
Ashtray, Boy With Donkey	12.00
Ashtray, Coon Chicken Inn, Glass, Picture of Black	45.00
Aunt Jemima, Spice Set	95.00
Bag, Clothespin, Mammy	35.00
Bag, Fertilizer, Old Black Joe With Banjo Picture, 20 X 36 In.	36.00
Bank, Mammy, Cast Iron	45.00
Bank, Mammy, With Note & Pencil Holder	95.00

Bank, Nodder, Bisque	20.00
Bell, Table, Mammy, 4 In.	50.00
Billhook, Johnson's Hat Co., Shows Black Man	9.00
Book, Little Black Sambo Magic Drawing, Dated '28, Unused	50.00
Book, Little Black Sambo, Golden, Large, 1978	18.50
Book, Little Black Sambo, Saalfield, 1942	55.00
Book, Little Black Sambo, Soft Cover	15.00
Book, Little Black Sambo, Whitman, 1961	24.50
Book, Little Brown Baby	45.00
Book, Little Pickaninnies, 1929	15.00
Book, Ten Little Niggers, McLoughlin, 1880	178.00 To 185.00
Book, Tip Top Entertainment Minstrel Album, 1936, 66 Pages	25.00
Book, Uncle Tom's Children, 1943, Richard Wright	40.00
Bottle Stopper, Head of Black Man	22.00
Box, Cotton, With Black Child, Souvenir	35.00
Box, Gold Dust Twins, Washing Powder, Cardboard	20.00
Box, Recipe, Mammy	100.00
Box, Shoeshine, Mason Advertising	65.00
Broadside, 50 Dollars Reward, Negro Woman Sarah, 1854, 14 X 12 In.	495.00
Broadside, Carncross Minstrels, Blue Ink, 1882, 11 X 31 In.	125.00
Button, Aunt Jemima Breakfast Club, Eat A Better Breakfast	15.00
Cigarette Holder & Tray, Figural	35.00
Cookie Jar, Aunt Jemima, F & F Molding	195.00
Cookie Jar, Aunt Jemima, McCoy	125.00
Cookie Jar, Black Face, White Baker Hat, Ceramic	60.00
Cookie Jar, Chef, National Silver	150.00
Cookie Jar, Mammy, Green Dress, McCoy	75.00
Cookie Jar, Mammy, Lid In Tummy	75.00
Cookie Jar, Mammy, National Silver	115.00 To 150.00
Cover, Toaster, Mammy	35.00
Creamer, Toby, Grotesque Black, Germany	85.00
Decanter, Black Americana, 6 Flowerpot Shot Glasses, 11 1/2 In.	50.00
Dish Towel, Mammy, Cotton Linen, Blue, White	28.00
Doll, Aunt Jemima, 1949, Rubber	25.00
Doll, Aunt Jemima, Cloth, 10 In.	37.50
Doll, Aunt Jemima, Quaker Oats, Cloth, Uncut	85.00
Doll, Baby, Boy, Vinyl Head & Limbs, Cloth Body, Sleep Eyes, 22 In.	25.00
Doll, Baby, Bye–Lo Type, Bisque, Glass Eyes, Christening, 11 In.	25.00
Doll, Baby, Bye–Lo, Vinyl, Christening Clothes, Horsman, 1972, 15 In.	27.50
Doll, Baby, Magic Skin, Hard Plastic Head, Sleep Eyes, 1940s, 16 In.	45.00
Doll, Betsy Wetsy, Box, 1983	65.00
Doll, Bisque, Jointed, Pigtails, Ribbons, 4 In.	38.00
Doll, Child, Composition, Cloth Body, Mohair Wig, 1930s, 20 In.	67.50
Doll, Child, Vinyl, Sleep Eyes, Braids, Dressed, 29 In.	35.00
Doll, Cloth, Black Boy, Composition Head, 10 In.	65.00
Doll, Cloth, Black Girl, Looks Like Little Lulu, 15 In.	35.00
Doll, Cloth, Lamb's Wool Pigtails, Button Eyes, Red Dress, 25 In.	695.00
Doll, Cloth, Tufted Hair, 20 In.	30.00
Doll, Darkey Doll, Cloth, Cocheco Mfg.Co., Uncut, 1893	195.00
Doll, Kidskin Fleece Wig, Ball–Jointed, Composition, French	525.00
Doll, Lady, Primitive, Cloth, Separate Fingers, Human Hair, 24 In.	350.00
Doll, Mammy, Cloth, Primitive, 1930s, 6 In.	55.00
Doll, Michael Jackson, Assorted Clothes, 11 1/2 In.	6.00
Doll, Paper Eyes, Fabric Mouth, Polka Dot Dress & Scarf, 11 1/2 In.	42.00
Doll, Papier–Mache Head, Brown Eyes, Cloth Body, Girdle, Shoes, 14 In.	325.00
Doll, Toaster, Mammy, Stuffed, Red Print, Bandana, Hoop Earrings, 18 In.	20.00
Doll, Uncle Mose, Rubber, 1949	25.00
Doll, Wooden Head, Painted Face, 1937 Newspaper Under Skirt, 9 In.	125.00
Doll, Yellow, White, Dress, Bandana, Apron, Embroidered Face, 16 In.	85.00
Doorstop, Aunt Jemima, Blue Dress, 12 In.	350.00
Egg Timer, Chef	25.00
Fan, Coon Chicken Inn	20.00
Figurine, Boy, Goose, Early Bird Catches The Worm, Chalkware	8.00
Figurine, Boy, In Swing, Plaid Pants, Bisque, 6 1/2 X 3 3/4 In.	135.00

Figurine, Boy, Top Hat, Sitting On Pottie, Nightgown, Bisque, 4 1/2 In. 65.00
Figurine, Man, Sitting On Cotton Bale, Banjo, Bisque, 6 1/4 In. 95.00
Fishing Lure, Black Man, Box 110.00
Flour Sack, Aunt Jemima, Quaker Oats Co., 25 Lb. 25.00
Game, Blackface Skill, Litho, Germany 55.00
Game, Ring Toss, Black Man Figural Holder, Painted Wood 26.00
Hot Plate, Full Figure, Mammy 8.00
Jar, Head, Black Boy, Straw Hat Lid, Pottery, Buff Clay, 5 In. 85.00
Lamp, Mammy Head, Ceramic Pinup, Wall 180.00
Mannequin, Girl, 39 In. 125.00
Match Holder, 3 Blacks, Hanging Ma's Bloomers, Porcelain 25.00
Match Holder, Black, With Watermelon, Flemish Art, 1910 .... 95.00
Match Holder, Children, Melon, Bale of Cotton, Metal 65.00
Memo Pad, Black Chef 39.00
Mixing Bowl, Black Mammy, Red Dots On Dress, Metlox 98.00
Mold, Pancake Griddle, Aunt Jemima 35.00
Nodder, Boy On Cotton Bale, With Watermelon 50.00
Note Pad Holder, Black Girl 16.00
Oilcloth, Aunt Jemima, 4-Piece Family, Plastic 110.00
Ornament, Christmas Tree, Mammy, Spoon, Glass, Painted, 1930–40, 3 In. 95.00
Pad, Mammy, Plastic 22.00
Pail, Sambo's Axle Grease, Black Boy, Handle, Tin, 10 Lb. 48.00
Peg Board, Mammy, We Needs Grocery List 80.00
Perfume Bottle, Black Boy, Germany, 3 In. 25.00
Picture, Haverly's Genuine Colored Minstrels, Color, Framed 418.00
Pie Bird, Chef, Yellow 60.00
Pin, Aunt Jemima Breakfast Club, 3 1/2 In. 2.00
Pin, Aunt Jemima, Pencil Clip, Celluloid, Over Tin, 1 In. 1.50
Pin, Trixy Molasses, Picaninny, 2 1/4 In. 25.00
Pincushion, Mammy 21.00
Pitcher, Baby, Black Boy On Toy Horse, Bear, White Girl, Wagon, 4 In. 65.00
Plaque, Black Sambo, Chalkware 15.00
Plate, Coon Chicken Inn, 6 1/2 In. 65.00
Postcard, Dixie Land, De Ole Cabin Home, P.Tuck 4.00
Postcard, Le Negre Joyeaux Dansant Le Cakewalk, French 18.00
Postcard, Picking Cotton Near New Orleans, Black Men, Children, 1912 .... 4.00
Poster, Baseball Championship, Satchel Paige, Jul.4, 1935, 32 X 17 In. 2400.00
Poster, I Am A Man, Memphis Striker's Protest, 1968, 22 X 28 In. 15.00
Poster, J.W.Baird's Mammoth Minstrels, Sepia Tone, 21 X 14 In. 90.00
Poster, True Blue, Lady, With Baby, Husband Picture, 1919, 16 X 20 In. 60.00
Poster, Uncle Tom's Cabin, New Orleans, Middaugh, 1900s, 28 X 21 In. 80.00
Powder Box, Butler Head, Ceramic 125.00
Print, Cream of Wheat, Block Story, Otto Schneider, 14 X 11 In. 15.00
Print, Cream of Wheat, Girl & Box, Framed, 12 X 13 In. 150.00
Puzzle Box, Woosy Jig, Dancing Blacks 18.00
Puzzle, Clippo Show, 2 Black Dolls, 7 X 8 In. 27.00
Puzzle, Little Black Sambo & Tiger, Color, 8 X 10 In. 18.00
Rack, Pot Holder, Mammy, Wooden, Red, 8 In. 16.00
Range Set, Aqua, 4 Piece 120.00
Recipe Box, Aunt Jemima 85.00
Script, Amos 'N Andy, Radio, Amos' Wedding, 1935 .... 20.00
Sheet Music, Aunt Jemima, Song Tells About Her Pancakes, 25 In. 25.00
Sheet Music, Mammy's Chocolate Soldier 15.00
Sheet Music, Old Black Joe 14.00
Sheet Music, Pickaninny's Paradise 15.00
Sheet Music, Rag Baby Rag, Black Rag Doll Picture, 1909 .... 10.00
Sign, Cortez Cigars Co., 5 Black Babies Picture, 5 X 9 In. 200.00
Sign, Original Fook's Blackberry Punch, Boy, Cardboard, 5 X 14 In. 40.00
Sprinkler, Sambo, Metal 195.00
Stereo Card, Black Child, Straw Hat, Watermelon, Cotton Picking, 3 Pc. 27.00
Storybook, Little Brown Baby 45.00
String Holder, Butler 125.00
String Holder, Mammy, Japan 85.00
String Holder, Young Mammy, Holding Flowers 68.50

Syrup, Aunt Jemima 36.00
Tablecloth, Blacks, Watermelons, Banjo, 52 X 50 In. 95.00
Tablecloth, Pickaninny 85.00
Tablecloth, Watermelons, Banjos, 52 X 50 In 95.00
Teapot, Mammy Face 95.00
Thermometer, Black Boy Standing Behind It, Wood 8.00
Thermometer, Brown Boy, Pressed Wood, 1949 .... 25.00
Tin, Murray's Superior Hair Dressing, Picture of Black People 7.00
Tin, Southern Biscuit, 1926 .... 29.00
Toaster Cover, Doll, Mammy, Cloth 22.00
Toaster Cover, Mammy, 1920s 65.00
Toothpick, Coon Chicken Inn 150.00
Towel, Kitchen, Blacks, 27 X 15 In. 35.00
Toy, Acrobat, Wooden, Original Package 35.00
Toy, Alabama Coon Jigger, Dances At End of Hand–Held Stick, Wooden 75.00
Toy, Black Family, Cast Iron, Hubley 350.00
Toy, Black Woman, Strikes Bell, Turns In Circles, D.K.Hatfield, 1875 .... 2250.00
Toy, Bojangles Dances Again, Tin Litho, Wooden Man, Clown Toy Co., Box 295.00
Toy, Drum, With Black Children, Tin, Ohio Art 45.00
Toy, Face, Black Boy's, Pull String & Eyes Move, Tin, Germany 75.00
Toy, Hey Hey The Chicken Snatcher, Marx, Tin, 1926, 9 In. 65.00
Toy, Jack–In–The–Box, Uncle Tom, Wood, 19th Century, Square, 4 In. 550.00
Toy, Man's Head, Pull String, Bug Eyes Spin, Tin, 2 1/2 In. 28.00
Toy, Minstrel Man, Wood, Jointed, Put On Phonograph Record, 5 1/2 In. 60.00

Blown glass was formed by forcing air through a rod into molten glass. Early glass and some forms of art glass were hand blown. Other types of glass were molded or pressed.

BLOWN GLASS, Apple, Clear, Yellow Tints, Paperweight, 5 1/2 In. 75.00
Bell Cover, Grass Green, South Jersey, 1850–80 .... 625.00
Bottle, Figural, Hound, Silver Plated Head, Austria, 10 In. 180.00
Bottle, Polychrome Enameling, 1/2 Post, 20th Century, 7 1/2 In. 15.00
Bowl & Underplate, White, Pink Latticinio, Flecks, 7 In., Pair 190.00
Bowl, Aqua, Applied Flared Foot, 8 1/4 In. 50.00
Bowl, Enameled Flowers & Birds, Green, 20th Century, 7 X 6 In. 10.00
Bowl, Flared Rim, Amethyst, 7 In. 75.00
Canister, Aqua, Open Flared Mouth, 9 In. 45.00
Canister, Corseted Cylinder Shape, Cover, 15 1/2 In. 35.00
Carafe, Water, Enameled Design, Cobalt Blue, 10 1/2 In. 33.00
Creamer, Violet Cobalt Blue, Applied Handle, 4 1/4 In. 50.00
Creamer, White Looping, Applied Handle, 3 In. 75.00
Decanter, McK–GIII–5, 3 Applied Rings, Stopper, 7 In. 175.00
Decanter, Paperweight Rooster Side, South Jersey, Amber, 11 In. 80.00
Floater, Rope 20.00
Fly Catcher, Footed, Bulbous, Applied Feet, Stopper, 9 In. 145.00
Mug, Child's, Ruby, For A Good Boy, Gilt Leaves & Bow, 2 3/4 In. 45.00
Mug, Enameled Bird, Applied Handle, 3 5/8 In. 35.00
Pitcher, Applied Handle, Horizontal Bands, Cobalt Blue, 6 In. 100.00
Pitcher, Bulbous Base, Pattern of Swirl Ribs, 10 In. 140.00
Pitcher, Cobalt Blue, Applied Handle, Swirled Ribs, 5 7/8 In. 125.00
Pitcher, Cut Panels & Strawberry Diamonds, Handle, 8 1/4 In. 150.00
Pitcher, Geometric, Ribbed Barrel, McK–GI–29, Mt.Vernon, N.Y. 1210.00
Pitcher, Handle, 3 1/8 In. 85.00
Pitcher, Violet Cobalt Blue, Applied Handle, Berry, 5 1/2 In. 100.00
Pitcher, Water, Reeded Handle, Amber 115.00
Rolling Pin, Aqua, 6 In. 85.00
Salt, Master, Medium Blue, Design, 4 X 2 1/2 In. 132.00
Shade, Hurricane, Floral Design, 21 In., Pair 900.00
Sugar & Creamer, Open, Cobalt Blue, Applied Handle, 4 3/8 In. 250.00
Sugar, Open, Violet Cobalt Blue, Diamond, Applied Foot, 3 In. 425.00
Sugar, Open, White Looping, Applied Blue Rim, 3 3/4 In. 175.00
Sugar, Witch Ball Cover, Opalescent Loops, Pittsburgh, 9 In. 500.00
Tumbler, Canary, Footed, Flared, 4 1/4 In. 35.00
Tumbler, Swirled Ribs, Opalescent, 3 1/8 In. 25.00

Vase, Aqua, Applied Bulbous Base, 11 1/2 In. 55.00
Vase, Floral, Applied Spiral Snake Neck, Green, 12 In. 25.00
Vase, Floral, Black Enameled Silhouette Dancing Couple, 7 In. 65.00
Vase, Jar Shape, 15 1/4 In. 25.00
Vase, Moorish Hand Painted Design, Bohemian Style, 2 Handles 75.00
Wine, Emerald Green, Wafer Stem, 4 3/8 In., 5 Piece 100.00

    BLUE AMBERINA, see Bluerina
    BLUE GLASS, see Cobalt Blue
    BLUE ONION, see Onion

Blue Willow pattern has been made in England since 1780. The pattern has been copied by factories in many countries, including Germany, Japan, and the United States. It is still being made. Willow was named for a pattern that pictures a bridge, birds, willow trees, and a Chinese landscape.

BLUE WILLOW, Berry Bowl, Royal Pottery, 4 3/4 In. 8.00
Bowl, Cover, Figures On Bridge, Birds In Flight, 7 In. 760.00
Bowl, Homer Laughlin, 6 In. 3.50
Bowl, Japan, 5 In. 3.50
Bowl, Japan, 6 In. 4.00
Bowl, Royal China, 9 1/8 In. 16.00
Bowl, Soup, Fluted, Scroll Design Rim, 8 In. 8.00
Bowl, Vegetable, Cover, Grimwades, C.1906 .... 95.00
Bowl, Vegetable, Occupied Japan, 10 1/4 In. 12.00
Bowl, Vegetable, Rectangular, Allerton, 9 X 11 In. 60.00
Bowl, Vegetable, Royal China 20.00
Bread Plate, Japan 2.50
Butter, Strainer & Cover, Ridgway 130.00
Cake Plate, Tab Handles, Royal China, 10 In. 15.00
Canister, Sugar, Cover, Japan, 7 X 18 In. 25.00
Castor, Pepper, Soft Paste, English, 1800s 178.00
Cup & Saucer, Allerton 18.00
Cup & Saucer, Child's .... 12.00 To 20.00
Cup & Saucer, Coalport 25.00
Cup & Saucer, Japan 7.00
Cup & Saucer, Occupied Japan 6.00
Cup, Crown Kanedai 6.00
Cup, Meakin 15.00
Demitasse Set, Tall Pot 95.00
Dinner Service, Child's, England, 21 Piece 450.00
Eggcup, Double, Japan 18.00
Eggcup, Japan 13.00
Gravy, Oval, 3 X 5 1/2 In. 20.00
Grill Plate, Child's 35.00
Grill Plate, Grimwades, Blue 30.00
Grill Plate, Japan 10.00
Grill Plate, Maastricht, 11 In. 10.00
Hot Plate, Enameled Design, Asbestos, 7 In. 6.50
Ladle, Gravy 60.00
Ladle, Soup 265.00
Lamp, Oil, Domed Shade 45.00
Lavebo, English 46.00
Mug 11.00
Mustard, Cover, Patterned Ladle 40.00
Napkin Holder, Tile, Japan, Square 15.00
Plate, Allerton, 5 3/4 In. 5.00
Plate, Burslem, 7 1/2 In. 8.00
Plate, Chen–Si, 9 1/2 In. 75.00
Plate, Homer Laughlin, 7 1/4 In. 3.50
Plate, Maastricht, 9 1/8 In. 15.00
Plate, Metal, 10 1/8 In. 9.50
Plate, Occupied Japan, 9 In. .... 7.00 To 12.00
Plate, Royal, 12 In. 12.00
Plate, Royal, 9 In. 7.50

Plate, Stanley Hotel Ware, 11 In. 8.00
Plate, Swinnertons, 9 3/4 In. .... 15.00 To 20.00
Plate, WA Adderly & Co., 10 1/4 In. .... 10.00 To 25.00
Plate, Wood & Son, 10 In. 18.00
Platter, 17 1/4 In. 95.00
Platter, Child's 30.00
Platter, Japan, Oval, 12 In. 25.00
Platter, Mayer, Stoke, Staffordshire, 18 1/4 In. 75.00
Platter, Oval, Occupied Japan, 13 In. 12.00
Platter, Topaz, 1929, England, 14 In. 115.00
Salt & Papper, 3 1/4 In. 30.00
Salt & Pepper, Brown Plastic Bottom, 4 In. 9.00
Salt & Pepper, House of Blue Willow, 3 1/4 In. 20.00
Salt & Pepper, Royal 9.00
Saltshaker, 3 3/8 In. 12.00
Saucer, Child's, Occupied Japan 12.00
Saucer, Homer Laughlin .... .50
Saucer, Occupied Japan 2.50
Saucer, Royal 1.00
Shaker, Flared Bottom, Square, Japan, 3 1/4 In. 13.00
Snack Plate, Off–Center Ring, Japan, 7 1/4 In. 5.00
Sugar & Creamer, Straight Side, Cover, Japan 20.00
Sugar, Cover, Child's, 2 1/2 In. 15.00
Sugar, Cover, Handles, Meakin 35.00
Sugar, Tab Handle, Open 5.00
Tablecloth, 52 X 64 In. 75.00
Teapot, Pink, Royal 22.00
Teapot, Sadler, 2 Cup 40.00
Tureen, Sauce, Underplate, Cover, English, C.1860, 5 1/2 X 7 In. 195.00

> Bluerina is a type of art glass which shades from light blue to ruby.
> It is often called blue amberina.

BLUERINA, Vase, 8 In. 300.00

> The Boch Freres factory was founded in 1841 in La Louviere in
> eastern Belgium. The wares resemble the work of Villeroy & Boch.
> The factory is still in business.

BOCH FRERES, Vase, Frieze of Deer, Marked, 1925, 15 In. 2400.00
Vase, Grazing Deer, Crackled Ground, 14 In. 1375.00

> Osso China Company was reorganized as Edward Marshall Boehm,
> Inc., in 1953. The company is still working in England and New
> Jersey. In the early days of the factory, dishes were made, but the
> elaborate and lifelike bird figurines are the best known ware.
> Edward Marshall Boehm, the founder, died in 1961; but the firm
> has continued to design and produce porcelain. Today, the firm
> makes both limited and unlimited editions of figurines and plates.

BOEHM, Figurine, Black Capped Chickadee, On Holly Branch, 9 In. 450.00
Figurine, Canada Geese, With Gosling, White Bisque, Porcelain, Pair 585.00
Figurine, Cardinal, Female, No.415, Grape Vines, Grapes 600.00
Figurine, Cedar Waxwing, Signed, Pair 3000.00
Figurine, Deer Mouse 75.00
Figurine, Fledgling, Cedar Waxwing, No.432 .... 115.00 To 150.00
Figurine, Fledgling, Eastern Bluebird, No.442 .... 135.00 To 150.00
Figurine, Fledgling, Kingfisher, No.449 .... 150.00
Figurine, Fledgling, Western Bluebirds, No.494 .... 195.00 To 395.00
Figurine, Indigo Bunting 375.00
Figurine, Kestral, Pair 1800.00
Figurine, Lesser Prairie Chickens, Pair 1250.00
Figurine, Madonna, White Glaze, 10 In. 450.00
Figurine, Nuthatch 550.00
Figurine, Rabbit, Sitting, White, Signed, 2 1/2 X 3 In. 350.00
Figurine, Yellow Rose, On Bark, No.200 .... 120.00
Letter Opener, Porcelain Eagle, Bicentennial, 1876 .... 95.00

Plate, Baby Bald Eagle, Young America 1776, 13 In. 400.00

Bohemian glass is an ornate overlay or flashed glass made during the Victorian era. It has been reproduced in Bohemia, which is now a part of Czechoslovakia. Glass made from 1875 to 1900 is preferred by collectors.

BOHEMIAN GLASS, Bell, Atlantic City, 1903, 6 1/2 In. 35.00
Bottle, Dresser, Florals, Child's Portrait, Cranberry, 10 In. 250.00
Bottle, Dresser, White On Cranberry, Floral, Stopper, 10 In. 250.00
Bowl, Engraved Foliage Design, Castle, Deer, 6 X 4 In. 35.00
Candlestick, Ruby, Deer, Etched, 8 3/4 In. 60.00
Compote, White To Green, Multicolored Floral Design, 9 In. 125.00
Cruet, Deer & Castle 85.00
Decanter, Cranberry Etch To Clear, Clear Bottom, 12 In., Pr. 155.00
Decanter, Cranberry Overlay, 14 In. 85.00
Decanter, Engraved, Cut Panels, Stopper, 10 1/2 In., Pair 140.00
Decanter, Fluted Neck, Ruby Cut To Clear, 15 1/2 In. 125.00
Fruit Compote, White Cut To Green, Floral Design, 9 In. 125.00
Garniture Set, Portraits, Green Ground, 14 1/2 In., 3 Piece 2640.00
Goblet, Ruby, Scrolls, 5 3/4 In. 50.00
Jar, Dresser, White On Cranberry, Floral Reserve 200.00
Lamp, Oil, Engraved Amber, Marble Base, C.1845 .... 155.00
Mug, Beer, Cranberry Etched To Clear, 5 1/2 In., Pair 35.00
Pitcher, Lemonade, Deer & Castle 125.00
Pokal, Stags, In Forest, Etched, 15 In., Pair 260.00
Punch Set, Vintage Pattern, 13 Piece 475.00
Rose Bowl, Deer & Castle, Etched 150.00
Spooner, Frosted Amber, Amethyst 25.00
Syrup, Deer & Castle 100.00
Tumble-Up Set, Amber, Green & White Engraved Stags, 7 Piece 60.00
Tumbler, Flashed Amethyst, Ship Design 75.00
Vase, Amber, Green, Blue, Red, White, Swirl, 7 1/2 In. 75.00
Vase, Cased With White, Enameled Flowers, 8 1/4 In. 160.00
Vase, Cobalt Blue Overlay, Cut, Scalloped, 8 1/4 In. 105.00
Vase, Deer & Castle, Cut To Clear Teardrops, 11 1/4 In. 95.00
Vase, Emerald Green, White & Gold Enameling, 9 In., Pair 425.00
Vase, Engraved Grapes & Leaves, Crisscrosses, 6 In. 90.00
Vase, Green, White Cased & Cut, Enameled Flowers, 8 1/4 In. 148.00

Bone dishes were considered a necessary part of a table setting for the Victorian table. The crescent-shaped dish was kept at the edge of the dinner plate so the bones removed from the fish could be stored away from the uneaten food. Some bone dishes were made in more fanciful shapes and many resemble fish.

BONE DISH, Blue Transfer Picture, Landscape, Crescent Shape, Staffordshire 25.00
Clarice Cliff, Tonquin, Green 15.00
Fish-Shape, Pink, Blue 55.00

Bookends have probably been used since books became inexpensive. Early libraries kept books in cupboards, not on open shelves. By the 1870s bookends appear, especially homemade fretcarved wooden examples. Most bookends listed in this book date from the twentieth century.

BOOKENDS, Art Deco, Black Man In Loin Cloth With Panther, Cast Brass 75.00
Boy & Girl, Zigler, Signed, 1921 .... 250.00
Colonial Lady, Cast Iron 25.00
Discus Thrower, Bronze Finish, 7 In. 40.00
Dutch Boy & Girl, Rocky Terrain, Bronze, 4 1/4 In. 175.00
Eagle, Cast Iron 65.00
Elephants, Bronze Finish 55.00
End of The Trail, Bronze Finish .... 25.00 To 38.00
End of Trail, Iron, 4 1/2 In. 25.00
Female Figure, Bronze, Lorenzl, 11 1/2 In. 3500.00
German Shepherd, Head, Figural .... 25.00 To 40.00

Goddess Kwan Yin, Seated, Brass Frame, 4 1/2 X 3 In. 75.00
Golfer, Knickers, Caddy, Metal 65.00
Golfer, Swinging Clubs, Bronze Finish, 9 1/2 In. 250.00
Hartford Fire Insurance Co., Brass, 1910–35 .... 35.00
Horse, Brown & White, Styron No.352 .... 15.00
Indian Bust, Cast Iron 45.00
Liberty Bell, Bronze Finish 22.50
Lily Pad & Frog, Metal 35.00
Lincoln, Full Figural Bust, Bronze Finish, 5 1/2in. 45.00
Lion, Art Deco, Cast Iron 17.00
Longfellow, Bust, Platform, Metal 39.50
Monk, Reading, Bronze Finish, TVA, 1922 .... 20.00
Nude Boys, Reading, Bronze Finish 27.00
Nudes & Gazelles, Brass 85.00
Old Ironsides, Cast Iron 40.00
Old Man & Dog, Ellis 185.00
Old Man & Woman, Hand Carved Wood, 6 In. 20.00
Oriental Kneeling Man, Woman Face To Face, Fan, Bronze 50.00
Owl, Cast Iron 18.00
Pharaoh, Egyptian Style, Copper, Plaster Filled, Signed, 7 In. 85.00
Pouter Pigeon, Clear Glass 75.00
Pyramids & Sphinx, Bronze 185.00
Race Horses, Jennings Bros. 55.00
Roaring Lion, Bronze Colored Metal 30.00
Scotty On Stepped Deco Back, Bronze Finish 75.00
Seahorses, E.T.Hurley, Bronze 700.00
Ship Captain At Wheel, Glogett Studios, Bronze Finish 25.00
Ship's Wheel, Wood & Brass 14.00
Ships, Cast Iron 20.00
Sleeping Lions, Antonio Canova, Bronze Finish 40.00
Stag, Hartford Fire Insurance, Bronze, 1935 .... 135.00
Steam Engine, Brass, Marble Base 45.00
Teddy Roosevelt, Bronze Finish 21.00
Thinker, Bronzed Spelter 48.00
Tree Form, Dutch Boy & Girl, Full Figural, Vienna Bronze 175.00
Washington On Horseback, Bronze, Signed Paul Herzel 55.00

Bookmarks were originally made of parchment, cloth, or leather. Soon woven silk ribbon, thin cardboard, celluloid, wood, silver, tortoiseshell, and metals were used. Examples made before 1850 are scarce, but there are many to be found dating before 1920.

BOOKMARK, Beaver, Red Painted Mouth, Alaskan Ivory 40.00
Butterfly, Multicolored, Die Cut Celluloid, Early 1900s 15.00
Cunningham Pianos, Multicolored, Die Cut Celluloid, 1900s 10.00
Eisenhower Bust, American Silk Label, Red, Green, 2 X 7 In. 32.50
Empire State Building, Woven 20.00
Heintz's Shoes, 4 Vintage Children, 1910 .... 15.00
Indian Girl, Figural, Leather 10.00
Indian, Leather 10.00
Ludwig Piano 4.00
Owl, Full Figure, Sterling Silver, 3 In. 45.00
Price Baking Powder, 1903 Calendar On Back 13.00
Statue of Liberty, Woven Silk, American & French Flags, 9 In. 75.00
Victorian Child, Hop Ointment, 1887 .... 4.00
     BOSTON & SANDWICH CO., see Sandwich Glass; Lutz

As soon as the commercial bottle was invented, the opener to be used with the new types of closures became a necessity. Many types of bottle openers can be found, most dating from the twentieth century. Collectors prize advertising and comic openers.

BOTTLE OPENER, 4–Eyed Man, Cast Iron .... 35.00 To 60.00
4–Eyed Woman, Cast Iron .... 55.00 To 60.00
Acorn, Georg Jensen 95.00
Alligator, Iron, 6 3/8 In. .... 18.00 To 35.00

Alligator, Polychrome Paint, 6 1/4 In.	75.00
Auto Jack	10.00
Bar Bum	25.00
Bear Head	45.00
Bird, Chrome	12.00
Black Face, Cast Iron, Large Smile, White Teeth, Red Bow Tie	75.00
Blue Ribbon	5.00
Blumer's	12.00
Boy & Alligator, Arms Down, Cast Iron	155.00
Camel	225.00
Canada Dry, Wall	4.00 To 7.00
Canada Goose, Cast Iron	60.00
Canadian Cream Ale, Wooden	9.00
Canvas Back Duck	65.00 To 110.00
Chipmunk	7.00
Clown Head	45.00
Coat, Black	10.00
Corkscrew, Wing Type, Brass, Italy	8.50
Cowboy Cactus	35.00
Cowboy With Guitar	345.00
Cowboy, Sign Post	75.00
Dog, Brass	5.00
Dog, Cocker	20.00
Dog, Dachshund, Collar, Brass	25.00
Dog, Pointer, Cast Iron, 4 1/2 In.	25.00 To 45.00
Dog, Spaniel, Cast Iron	37.00
Dolphin	15.00
Donkey, Brass	15.00
Donkey, Cast Iron	20.00 To 46.00
Donkey, Flat, Brass	12.00
Dr.Brown's Celery Tonic	8.00
Dr.Pepper	12.00
Drunk On Ashtray	22.50
Duck, Canvas Back	75.00
Elephant	25.00
Elephant, Iron	22.00
Elephant, Seated, Flat, Cast Iron	135.00
False Teeth	100.00
Falstaff, Choicest Product of Brewers Art, Metal, Hand	6.00
Fish, Aluminum	25.00
Fish, Stainless Steel & Wood, 9 1/2 In.	10.00
Fisherman	20.00
Flamingo	55.00 To 85.00
Foundryman	100.00
Goat, 4 3/8 In.	30.00
Goat, Seated, Cast Iron	40.00
Goat, White & Green Paint, 4 3/8 In.	45.00
Goose, Black, White & Green Paint, Cast Iron, 3 5/8 In.	75.00
Hand	25.00
Handy Hans	250.00
Indian Bust, Headdress	22.00
Indian With Papoose	16.00
Indian, Iroquois	15.00
Jayhawk	25.00
Lion Head, Health's Sake Drink Pep To Lac, 3 In.	20.00
Lobster, Cast Iron, Red Paint, 3 1/2 In.	55.00 To 65.00
Mademoiselle	25.00
Mallard Duck	10.00 To 65.00
Man, Clinging To Lamppost, Iron, Original Paint	45.00
Man, Helmet, Long Pants, Wide Belt, Jacket, Brass	23.00
Miss 4–Eyes	30.00
Monkey, Aluminum	1.00
Monkey, Cast Iron	95.00 To 225.00
Northern Mattress Co., Spoon	5.00

Bottle Opener, Prostitute, On Lamppost,
Cast Iron, 4 1/2 In.

Bottle, Figural, Dog, All's Well,
Pottery, Japan, 4 In.

Orange Crush	20.00
Palm Tree	105.00
Palm Tree, Drunk	30.00
Parrot, Cast Iron	28.00 To 42.00
Parrot, Large Beak, 5 3/8 In.	25.00
Parrot, Metal, Corkscrew	15.00
Pelican, Black & Red Paint, Cast Iron	25.00 To 65.00
Pig, Aluminum	22.00
Pretzel	8.00 To 25.00
Prostitute, On Lamppost, Cast Iron, 4 1/2 In. ....*Illus*	25.00
Sailor, Cast Iron	55.00
Sea Gull, Cast Iron	35.00 To 45.00
Southern Select	20.00
Squirrel, Cast Iron, 3 1/2 In.	75.00
Straw Hat, Sign Post	30.00
Swordfish	85.00
Timberjack	25.00
Turtle, Corkscrew Tail	20.00
Uncle Sam	45.00
Wolf, Brass	25.00

Bottle collecting has become a major American hobby. There are several general categories of bottles, such as historic flasks, bitters, household, and figural. For modern bottle prices and more old bottle prices, see the book "The Kovels' Bottles Price List" by Ralph and Terry Kovel.

BOTTLE, Amber Bleach, 4 Gal.	8.00
Apothecary, Design, 14 X 23 In.Diam.	75.00
Apothecary, Green, Glass Top, Automatic Bottle Machine, 1 Qt.	45.00
Apothecary, Label Fused To Glass, Acid Nitric, 6 1/2 In.	15.00
Apothecary, Marked Walsh, England, Sapphire Blue, 10 1/4 In.	130.00

Avon started in 1886 as the California Perfume Company. It was not until 1929 that the name Avon was used. In 1939, it became Avon Products, Inc. Each year Avon sells figural bottles filled with cosmetic products. Ceramic, plastic, and glass bottles are made in limited editions.

Avon, Bust, Teddy Roosevelt	15.00
Avon, Tiffany Lamp Perfume, 1973	13.00
Bar, Pillar Mold, Black Amber, Bulbous Lip, Applied Ring, 11 1/2 In.	1550.00
Barber, Emerald Green, Enameled Design, Open Pontil	48.00
Barber, Enameled Stag, Amethyst	110.00

Barber, Milk Glass, Painted 125.00
Barber, Wapler, Cobalt Blue 85.00

Beam bottles are made to hold Kentucky Straight Bourbon, made by the James B. Beam Distilling Company. The Beam series of ceramic bottles began in 1953.

Beam, Circus Wagon 30.00
Beam, Donkey & Elephant, 1968, Pair 40.00
Beam, Hatfield 30.00
Beam, McCoy 30.00
Beer, Acme, 1950s, 1 Qt. 10.00
Beer, Buffalo Brewing Co., Buffalo Jumping Through Horseshoe, Amber 20.00
Beer, Gambrinius Bottling Co., Monogram, 1 Qt. 15.00
Beer, Gettelman's, Embossed, 12 In. 14.00
Beer, Honolulu Brewing Co., Aqua, 1 Qt. 25.00
Beer, John Rapp & Son, San Francisco, Split 15.00
Beer, Lucky Sunny, Green, Pictures Smiling Boy 25.00
Beer, San Antonio Triple XXX Brewing Assn., Crown Top, Aqua, 7 In. 25.00
Beer, Standard Bottling Co., In Circle, 1 Pt. 15.00
Beer, United States Brewing Co., Chicago, Red Amber, 1 Qt. 16.00
Beer, Willington Type, Olive Amber 65.00
Beer, Wilson's, Embossed, 12 In. 10.00
Bitters, Atwoods, Sample 12.00
Bitters, Beggs Dandelion, Chicago 100.00
Bitters, Burdock Blood 15.00
Bitters, Carmeliter Stomach, New York 75.00
Bitters, Dewitts Stomach, Amber 45.00
Bitters, Doyles Hop 20.00
Bitters, Dr.Hoofland's German Bitters 45.00
Bitters, Dr.Hostetter's Stomach 15.00
Bitters, Dr.Thomas Mayapple, Tax Stamp Dated June 21, 1881, Amber 50.00
Bitters, Dr.Von Hopf's Curaco, Chamberlain, Amber, Square, 9 In. 25.00
Bitters, Dr.Walker's Vinegar Bitters, Green 8.00
Bitters, Drake's Plantation, 6–Log, Reddish–Puce 150.00
Bitters, Electric, Large 20.00
Bitters, Kaiser Wilhelm Bitters 35.00
Bitters, Kimball's Jaundice, Light Olive Amber 395.00
Bitters, McKeever's Army, Connonballs Stacked On Drum, Amber 1775.00
Bitters, Peychaud's Cordial 20.00
Bitters, Pineapple Form, Bluish–Green 2200.00
Bitters, Royal Italian, Amethyst 495.00
Bitters, Vermo Stomach, Partial Label, Contents 35.00
Bitters, Wait's Kidney & Liver Bitters, Calif., Dark Amber, Bimal 45.00
Bourbon, Golden Wedding, 4 In. 18.00
Burgie Man, Smiling, Decanter, 2 Sides, 1971, 9 In. 32.00
Chestnut, 16 Swirled Ribs, Blown, 6 In., 1 Pt. 135.00
BOTTLE, COCA–COLA, see Coca–Cola, Bottle
Cosmetic, Dr.D.Jaynes Hair Tonic, Philadelphia, OP 39.00
Cosmetic, Hind's Fragrance Cream, 6 1/2 Oz. 7.00
Cosmetic, Woodbury Cold Cream, 3.6 Oz. 8.00
Cosmetic, Woodbury Hand Cream, 5.9 Oz. 6.00
Cream, Zinc Top, Bulbous, 4 In. 20.00
Creamer, 3–Mold, Hollow Handle, Clear, 1820, 3 3/4 In. 300.00
Figural, Book, Cobalt Blue, History of Bourbon, 5 X 7 X 2 3/4 In. 225.00
Figural, Book, History of Holland, Blue Glaze, 5 1/2 In. 350.00
Figural, Book, Marked Coming Thro The Rye, Blue Glaze, 5 In. 165.00
Figural, Clock, Happy Time, Embossed Face On Reverse, Screw Lid 6.00
Figural, Clock, Railway Chronometer, 5 1/4 In. 95.00
Figural, Dog, All's Well, Pottery, Japan, 4 In. ....*Illus* 35.00
Figural, House, Embossed Windows, Doors, 2–Tone Glaze, 6 1/4 In. 85.00
Figural, Lion, Standing, Gilt, Cork Rear, 9 X 5 In. 24.00
Figural, Nude, Frosted, Bands Above Head, 1880's Type, 13 1/2 In. 59.00
Figural, Pig, Dark Brown Glaze, Embossed Train, 6 5/8 In. 200.00
Figural, Pretzel, Ceramic, Large 75.00

Figural, Sad Hound Dog, Sitting, Amethyst 23.00
Figural, Shoe, Scroddleware, Yellow, White, Brown, Clear Glaze, 5 In. 250.00
Figural, Stork, Top Hat Stopper, Specs, Umbrella Under Arm, 16 In. 825.00
Figural, Violin, Amethyst, 9 1/2 In. 25.00
Flask, Cannon, A Little More Grape Capt.Bragg, Deep Amber 525.00
Flask, Corn For The World, Baltimore Glass Works, Green, 1 Qt. 900.00
Flask, Daisy & Button, Pewter Top 45.00
Flask, Diamond Pattern, Chestnut Shape, Amethyst 575.00
Flask, Double Eagle, Aqua, 1/2 Pint, 6 In. 70.00
Flask, Dr.Von Hopf's Curaco, Amber, 8 In. 29.00
Flask, Eagle, Frigate Reverse, Aqua, C.1840, 1 Pt. 135.00
Flask, Eagle–Eagle Snake, Pittsburg 3250.00
Flask, Figural, Whisk Broom, Stand–Up, Bisque, Germany 60.00
Flask, G.A.R.Design, Glass 495.00
Flask, John Q.Adams, Eagle, Portrait 9300.00
Flask, McK G II–972, Eagle & Cornucopia, Olive Amber, 1 Pt., 7 In. 95.00
Flask, McK G III–061, Eagle, Willington Glass Co., Medium Green 302.50
Flask, McK G VIII–4, Calabash, Hunter & Fisherman, Puce 225.00
Flask, McK G VIII–8, Keene, Sunburst, P.& W., Open Pontil, Olive Amber 290.00
Flask, McK G XIII, Flora Temple, Dark Aqua 445.00
Flask, Our Candidates, McKinley & Teddy Roosevelt, 1900, 5 In. 420.00
Flask, Pig, Anna Pottery, Map Type 1750.00
Flask, Pike's Peak, Aqua 65.00
Flask, Pocket, 26 Ribs, Open Pontil, Sapphire, 5 3/4 In. 335.00
Flask, Railroad & Eagle, Marked Railroad Lowell 130.00
Flask, Sprunce, Stanley & Co., San Francisco 250.00
Flask, Stoddard Type, Yellow Citron, Crude, 1/2 Pt. 18.00
Flask, Summer Tree, Cobalt Blue 5300.00
Flask, Wm.Harrison Cabin, Aqua 5500.00
Food, Cathedral Pepper Sauce, Aqua, Bimal, 8 In. 20.00
Food, Hershey Chocolate Corp., Lebanon, Pa., Emblem, 1 Pt. 27.50
Food, Lang's Pickles, 1 Gal. 10.00
Food, Sandwich Mustard, Open Pontil 100.00
Foot, E.R.Durkee & Co., Peppersauce, Blue Green, Horizontal Ribs 29.00
Fruit Jar, A.G.Smalley & Co., Boston & New York, 1/2 Pt. 10.00
Fruit Jar, Acme LG Co., 1893, 1/2 Gal. 215.00
Fruit Jar, Amber, Cohansey Cover, P.Lorrilard On Bottom 25.00
Fruit Jar, Aqua, Double Collar, 1 1/4 In.Pontil, Cork, 3/4 Qt. 600.00
Fruit Jar, Atlas E–Z Seal, Amber, Glass Lid, 1 Qt. 35.00
Fruit Jar, Atlas E–Z Seal, Apple Green, Qt. 15.00
Fruit Jar, Atlas E–Z Seal, Aqua, 58 Oz. 45.00
Fruit Jar, Atlas E–Z Seal, Aqua, Glass Lid, 1 Pt. 23.00
Fruit Jar, Atlas, Clear, Glass Lid, 1 Qt. 11.00
Fruit Jar, Ball Ideal, Blue, 1/2 Pt. 28.00
Fruit Jar, Ball Mason, Olive Green, Pint 15.00
Fruit Jar, Ball Perfect Mason, Amber, 1/2 Gal. 35.00
Fruit Jar, Ball Perfect Mason, Blue, Zinc Lid, 1 Qt. 14.00
Fruit Jar, Ball Perfect Mason, Deep Olive Green, 1 Pt. 50.00
Fruit Jar, Ball Perfect Mason, Emerald Green, 1/2 Gal. 45.00
Fruit Jar, Burlington, 1 Qt. 45.00
Fruit Jar, C.F.Spencer's Patent, Rochester, N.Y., Aqua, Qt. 95.00
Fruit Jar, Canadian Queen, Amber, 1 Qt. 300.00
Fruit Jar, Canton Domestic, Pt. 150.00
Fruit Jar, Canton, Cobalt Blue, 1870–90, 1/2 Gal. 2000.00
Fruit Jar, Carter's Butter & Fruit Preserving, Glass Lid, Bail, 1897 .... 115.00
Fruit Jar, Clark's Peerless, Cornflower Blue, Pt. 25.00
Fruit Jar, Cross Crown, 1 Qt. 45.00
Fruit Jar, Crown, Olive Green, 1 Qt. 45.00
Fruit Jar, Dillon Glass Co. 25.00
Fruit Jar, Egco Imperial, Mono, Aqua, Midget 40.00
Fruit Jar, Electric, World Globe, Aqua, Qt. 80.00
Fruit Jar, Fearman's Mincemeat, Amber, 1 Qt. 55.00
Fruit Jar, Forest City, Amber, 1 Qt. 75.00
Fruit Jar, Franklin Dexter, Aqua, 1/2 Gal. 35.00

Fruit Jar, Freeblown, Milk Glass 742.00
Fruit Jar, Globe, Amber, Lid & Bail 45.00
Fruit Jar, Globe, Tin, Wire & Iron Closure, Amber, 1 Pt. 45.00
Fruit Jar, Globe, Tin, Wire & Iron Closure, Amber, 8 7/8 In. 25.00
Fruit Jar, Improved Jam, 1/2 Gal. 115.00
Fruit Jar, J.E.Taylor, Aqua 18.00
Fruit Jar, J.M.Clark & Co., Green, Round Shoulder, 1/2 Gal. 70.00
Fruit Jar, Lightning, Amber, Glass Lid, 1/2 Gal. 55.00
Fruit Jar, Lightning, Aqua, 1/2 Gal. 40.00
Fruit Jar, Lightning, Aqua, Glass Lid, 1 Qt. 28.00
Fruit Jar, Mason, 1858 Trademark, Aqua, 1/2 Gal. 90.00
Fruit Jar, Mason, 3 Gal. 300.00
Fruit Jar, Mason, Pat.Nov.30th, 1858, 1 Pt. 6.00
Fruit Jar, Mason, Pat.Nov.30th, 1858, Deep Aqua 20.00
Fruit Jar, Mason, Pat.Nov.30th, 1858, Reverse Cross, Amber, 1/2 Gal. 75.00
Fruit Jar, Millville Atmospheric, Aqua, Qt. 30.00
Fruit Jar, Rau's Improved Groove Ring, Crystal 45.00
Fruit Jar, Safety Seal, Clear 2.50
Fruit Jar, Schram Automatic Sealer, Flag, Pt. 10.00
Fruit Jar, Swayzee's Improved Mason, Dark Olive, 1/2 Gal. 40.00
Fruit Jar, Trademark Lightning, Amber, 1 Qt. 30.00
Fruit Jar, Trademark Lightning, Amber, 1/2 Gal. 32.00
Fruit Jar, Wan–Eta Cocoa, Aqua 12.00
Fruit Jar, Whitney Mason, Pat'd 1858, Aqua, Pt. 12.00
Ginger Ale, Felix The Cat 55.00
Henry Ward Beecher, Clear, 6 1/2 In. 30.00
Horseradish, As You Like It, Brown & White Stoneware, 1/2 Pt. 35.00
Ink, Benjamin Franklin Head, Figural, Aqua 125.00
Ink, Block House Fort Pitt, Figural 100.00
Ink, Bricket J.Taylor 150.00
Ink, Carter's, American Blue, 2 1/2 Oz. 5.50
Ink, Carter's, Cobalt Blue, Cathedral, 9 1/2 In. 115.00
Ink, Carter's, House Shape 200.00
Ink, Carter's, Hunting Red, 2 1/2 Oz. 6.00
Ink, Carter's, Ma & Pa Ink, Germany, Pair 130.00
Ink, Carter's, Midnight Blue–Black, Owl Picture 7.00
Ink, Caws, Black Crow, Cork Top 10.00
Ink, Crolius, Pottery, Gray & Blue Glazed, 3 1/4 In. 1000.00
Ink, E.Water's Ink, Troy, N.Y., Amber, 6 1/2 In. 450.00
Ink, Farley's Ink, Pontil 200.00
Ink, Figural, Bell, Cobalt Blue 35.00
Ink, Higgins Drawing, Blue, 8 Oz. 8.50
Ink, Igloo Shape, Cobalt Blue 250.00
Ink, Laughlin & Bushfield, Wheeling, Va., Aqua, 8 Sides 80.00
Ink, Levinson's Ink, Amber, 2 1/2 In. 150.00
Ink, Pennsylvania Dutch, Brass Top 100.00
Ink, Quink, Cobalt Blue, Diamond Shape, Box 10.00
Ink, R.F., Amethyst, Rolled Mouth, 1840–60, 2 3/8 In. 200.00
Ink, S.Fine, Black Ink, Green, 3 In. 192.50
Ink, S.I.Comp, House Shape 150.00
Ink, Sanford, Square 5.00
Ink, South Jersey, Lily Paperweight Base & Stopper, 8 3/4 In. 225.00
Ink, Stoneware, Marked England, 1 Pt. 6.00
Ink, Wood's Black Ink, Amber, Cone, Embossed Shield 100.00
Jam Jar, Emerald Green, Blown Glass, New York, 1820–59 .... 125.00
Juice, Home Dairy, Eureka, Calif., Black, 1/2 Pt. 4.50
Medical, DeWitt's Golden Liniment, 1 7/8 In. 6.00
Medical, DeWitt's Laxative, 6 Oz. 7.00
Medicine, Atlas Medicine Co., Henderson, N.C., Amber, Logo 8.00
Medicine, Black Cohash Tincture, Amber, Crown Lip, Label, 4 3/4 In. 5.00
Medicine, Chemist's, Cobalt Label Under Glass 330.00
Medicine, Collin's Cough Elixir, 8 Panels, Bimal, 6 1/4 In. 15.00
Medicine, Crosby's Balsamic Cough Elixir, Bimal, 4 1/2 In. 6.00
Medicine, DeCosta's Radical Cure 33.00

Medicine, Dr.D.Jayne's Alterative, OP, Large Oval, 7 In. 29.00
Medicine, Dr.Groga's Blood & Liver Syrup 35.00
Medicine, Dr.Haynes Arabian Balsam, Embossed, Label, The Doc, 4 In. 8.00
Medicine, Dr.Hess, Louse Killer, Liquid, 5 Oz. 4.00
Medicine, Dr.King's New Life Pills, Clear 350.00
Medicine, Dr.Lazarus's Essence of Chiretta, Cobalt Blue 30.00
Medicine, Dr.Legears, Antihistamine Tabs For Dogs, 10 Tablets 5.00
Medicine, Dr.Pierce's Favorite Prescription, Bimal, 8 1/4 In. 12.00
Medicine, Dr.Weiss Blackberry Ginger & Wild Cherry Tonic, 1900 .... 130.00
Medicine, Dr.Wistar's Balsam of Wild Cherry, 8 Panels, Bimal, 5 In. 23.00
Medicine, Forestine Kidney Cure, Amber, 9 1/4 In. 75.00
Medicine, Kerolysin–Upjohn Co., Milk Glass, Paper Label, 2 1/2 In. 4.00
Medicine, Kodal Dyspepsia Cure, Aqua, 9 In. 10.00
Medicine, Larkin Anodine Liniment, Cork Top 8.00
Medicine, Mel–Pinus Cough Syrup, Litho Label, Cork, C.1890, 8 In. 10.00
Medicine, Old Indian Liver & Kidney Tonic, Cherokee Medicine Co. 50.00
Medicine, Peacock Chemical Co., Clear, 1890, Paper Label, 6 In. 8.00
Medicine, River Swamp Chill & Fever Cure, Embossed Alligator 175.00
Medicine, South American Stomach & Liver Cure, Clear, 9 1/2 In. 70.00
Medicine, Tonsiline Throat Cure, Embossed Giraffe, Box 15.00
Medicine, Warner's Safe Compound, 5 In. 340.00
Medicine, Warner's Safe Kidney & Liver Cure, Amber, Rochester, N.Y. 30.00
Medicine, Warner's Safe Kidney & Liver Cure, Embossed, Amber 225.00
Medicine, Warner's Tippecanoe, Light Amber 70.00
Milk, Alpha Dairy, Baby & Chef's Hat, Square, Pryo 10.00
Milk, Arden Milk Western Dairy Products Inc., Embossed, 1/2 Pt. 6.00
Milk, Ayrhill Farms, Adams, Mass., 1 Qt. 7.00
Milk, Billing's Dairy, Green, 1/2 Oz. 12.50
Milk, Borden's Capital Dairy Co., Boy, Brown Pyro, 1/2 Pt. 12.00
Milk, Borden, Ruby Red 850.00
Milk, Bowman, Red Letters, 20 In. 325.00
Milk, Brighton Place, Green 200.00
Milk, Bryant & Chapman, Red, 3/4 Oz. 12.50
Milk, Butler Dairy, Willmantic, Conn., 1 Qt. 12.00
Milk, College Dairy, Phone 2545, Modesto, Calif., Brown Pyro, 1/2 Pt. 35.00
Milk, Dairy Gold, Pyro, Round, Yellow Pyro, Black, 1/2 Pt. 17.00
Milk, Drink Hoffman's Milk, Cream Top, Emblem, 1/2 Pt. 13.00
Milk, Fairview Farms You Can Whip Our Cream, Amber, Square, 1 Qt. 9.00
Milk, Farmers Dairy Inc., Martinsburg, W.Va., Cream Top, 1 Pt. 15.00
Milk, Gold Medal Creamery, Long Beach, Slug Plate, Cream Top, 1 Qt. 12.50
Milk, Golden State Brand Dairy Products, Emblem, Red Pyro, 1/2 Pt. 14.00
Milk, Hagan Buttermilk, 15 Cent Deposit Back, Red Pyro, 1/2 Gal. 25.00
Milk, Jersey Milk Cream & Butter Co., Embossed, Amethyst, 1 Pt. 10.00
Milk, Kern County Hospital, Embossed, Round, 1/2 Pt. 25.00
Milk, Linger Light Dairy, 1 Gal. 45.00
Milk, Lone Oak Farm, Emblem, Square, 3/4 Oz. 25.00
Milk, Miller Dairy, Orange, Green Bottle Washer, Squat, 1 Qt. 10.50
Milk, National Dairy Sealtest Products Corp., Red, 1/2 Oz. 12.50
Milk, Northern Dairy Grade A Dairy Products, Orange, Square, 1 Gal. 25.00
Milk, Palmer's Dairy, Emerald Green, 2 1/2 Oz. 12.00
Milk, Round Top Farms, Cream Top, 1/2 Pt. 28.00
Milk, Springdale Fars, Millington, N.J., Cream Top, 1 Qt. 18.00
Milk, Sun Valley Dairy Multi–Vitamin, Green, Yellow Pyro, 1/2 Gal. 20.00
Milk, Titusville Dairy Co., Titusville, Pa., Red, Black, 1 Pt. 40.00
Milk, Union Dairy Co., Pint 7.00
Milk, V.M.I.Co., Amber, Embossed, 1 Qt. 65.00
Milk, Valley Gold, Orange Baby, Blue, Plastic Handle, Square, 1 Gal. 10.00
Milk, Victoria Guernsey, San Bernardino, Calif., Orange, Squat, 1 Qt. 12.00
Mineral Water, Avon Springs 850.00
Mineral Water, Ballston Spa, Emerald Green, 1 Pt. 64.00
Mineral Water, Clarke & Co., Green 75.00
Mineral Water, Guilford Mineral Spring Water, Guilford, Vt., 1 Qt. 29.00
Mineral Water, White Rock, Amber, Contents, 1922, 10 In. 10.00
Nurser, Acme, Star Emblem, 6 In. 22.50

Nurser, Cat & Kittens, Emblem, 8 Oz. 20.00
Nurser, Embossed Bulldog 15.00
Nurser, Evenflo, With Nipple, 1950 .... 5.00
Nurser, Hygia, Ball 4.00
Nurser, Little Jack Horner In The Corner, Batavia Dairy Co., 4 Oz. 15.00
Nurser, Pale Green, 16 Ribs & Diamonds, Blown Glass, 6 5/8 In. 125.00
Nurser, Sonny Boy, Emblem, 8 Oz. 18.00
Nurser, Temp–Guard, Eisele & Co., Red Pyro, Thermometer Inset, 8 Oz. 25.00
Oil, Sperm Sewing Machine, Embossed 12.00
Orange Crush, Patent July 20, 1920 .... 25.00
BOTTLE, PERFUME, see Perfume Bottle
Pickle, Arched Shoulders, Square, Aqua, 1/2 Gal. 40.00
Pickle, Cathedral, 1870 .... 45.00
Poison, Cobalt Blue, Vertical Ribbed, 32 Oz., 9 3/4 In. 25.00
Poison, Not To Be Taken, Cobalt Blue, Octagonal, 5 1/2 In. 15.00
Poison, Save The Calves Abortion Remedy, Cork Top, Cow, 1917 .... 25.00
Seltzer, Quality Beverages, Manitowoc, Wisc., Large Red Logo, 11 In. 25.00
Snuff, Bird & Flower Design, Green Quartz, Jar Shape, 3 1/2 In. 230.00
Snuff, Bird & Flower, Jar Form, Rock Crystal, 3 1/2 In. 100.00
Snuff, Blue & White Porcelain, Jade Top 75.00
Snuff, Buddha Seated On Cloud, Agate, 2 In. 450.00
Snuff, Buddha's Hand Form, Imperial Yellow Glass, 2 1/2 In. 1200.00
Snuff, Carved Ivory, Elephant Heads On Sides, Trunk Forms Holder 475.00
Snuff, Carved Ivory, Screw Top, Spoon, Teak Stand, C.1910 .... 50.00
Snuff, Carving of Squirrels In Grape Arbor, Blue Agate, 2 1/4 In. 440.00
Snuff, Double Neck, Relief Carving On Front, 2 3/8 In. 450.00
Snuff, Emperor & Empress, Ivory, Pair 125.00
Snuff, Fishermen On Riverband, 2–Color Carnelian Agate, 2 1/8 In. 220.00
Snuff, Flowering Branch, Mask Ring Handles, Cameo Agate, 2 1/4 In. 303.00
Snuff, Free–Form Design, Flattened Ovoid, Shadow Agate, 2 1/8 In. 330.00
Snuff, Fruit & Vine, Relief Flowers, Butterflies, Jadite, 3 1/2 In. 1650.00
Snuff, Fruit Form, Relief Leaves & Vines, Red & Green Jadite, 2 In. 248.00
Snuff, Ivory, Japanese Polychrome, Passion Flower & Vine, 3 1/8 In. 605.00
Snuff, Ivory, Sage, Jar On Back, Stroking Beard, 4 1/4 In. 275.00
Snuff, Jar Shape, 8 Ivory Carved Figures, Landscape, 4 1/2 In. 385.00
Snuff, Leaping Carp Form, Mandarin Duck Stopper, Jadite, 3 In. 413.00
Snuff, Leaping Carp Form, Pagoda Stopper, Smoky Crystal, 3 5/8 In. 120.00
Snuff, Painted Interior of 2 Groups of Kittens 410.00
Snuff, Painted Interior of Pandas & Bamboo, Chinese 170.00
Snuff, Pebble Form, Inclusions of Quail & Millet, Jade, 2 3/4 In. 385.00
Snuff, Pilgrim Flask Form, Bamboo, Turquoise Stopper, 2 1/4 In. 660.00
Snuff, Relief Carp, Amber–Green Ground, Ovoid, Coral Stopper, 2 In. 685.00
Snuff, Reverse Painted Scene of Family, Flowers, Jade Stopper, 3 In. 185.00
Snuff, Sage & Monkey, Bats & Tree, Carved Rock Crystal, 2 3/4 In. 495.00
Snuff, Spade Shape, Green Glass Stopper, Aventure, 2 1/8 In. 110.00
Snuff, Temple Jar Form, Lion's Head Handle, Cloisonne, Blue, 3 In. 285.00
Snuff, Turquoise, Cabochons, Lapis Lazuli, 4 In. 165.00
Snuff, Vase Form, Red & White Swirl Pattern, White Cased, 2 1/8 In. 155.00
Snuff, Young Child Beside Jar, Aquamarine, 2 In. 688.00
Snuff, Young Man On Horseback, Removable Head Stopper, Ivory, 3 In. 413.00
Soda, Aloha Soda Works, Kaulela, 6 1/2 Oz. 9.00
Soda, Canadian Club, On Key Chain, 2 1/2 In. 6.00
Soda, Clipper Root Beer, Clark's Beverages, Amber, White, 10 Oz. 7.00
Soda, Cliquot Club, Embossed, Paper Label 8.00
Soda, Dr.Townsend's Sarsaparilla, Albany, N.Y., Olive Amber, Pontil 135.00
Soda, Felix The Cat Ginger Ale 60.00
Soda, Highland Spring Bottling Co., Inc., Frostie Picture, 12 Oz. 2.00
Soda, Hutch Sodas, J.M.Rice, Norwalk, Ohio, Light Green, Slug Plate 14.00
Soda, J.C.Schoch's, Philadelphia, Teal Blue, Graphite Pontil 95.00
Soda, Kohl & Beans, Graphite Pontil, Medium Green 85.00
Soda, Moxie, Needham Heights, Mass., Red, White, 7 Oz. 3.00
Soda, Orange Crush, 1920 .... 25.00
Soda, RC Royal Crown Cola, 10 Oz. 6.00
Soda, RC Royal Crown Cola, 6th Annual Raft Race, 1975, 16 Oz. 12.00

Soda, Robinson Wilson & Legallee, Boston, Blue Green, Iron Pontil 69.00
Soda, Royal Soda Works, Light Green, Crown Cap 12.00
Soda, Smiley, 18 In. 150.00
Spring Water, Masena, Embossed Dove Monogram, Blue, 1 Qt. 95.00
Stoddard, Olive–Green, Blown Glass, 1842–73, 1 Gal. 350.00
Syrup, Allen's Red Tame Cherry, 5 Cent Glass Label 1500.00
Syrup, Little Brown Jug, Crock, Dated 1921, 1 Pt. 7.00
Tonic, Dr.Weiss Blackberry Ginger & Wild Cherry, 1900, 12 1/4 In. 130.00
Veterinary, Dr.Hess Fly Spray, 8 Oz. 5.00
Veterinary, Dr.Hess Louse Killer, 5 Oz. 4.00
Veterinary, Dr.Legear's Household Insect Spray, 1 Qt. 5.00
Veterinary, Dr.Legear's Poultry Inhalant, 4 Oz. 3.25
Veterinary, Pratts In–Tes–Trol, 1 Pt. 5.00
Vinegar, White House, Jug, Pouring Lip, White House Embossed, Cork 10.00
Wheaton, Dwight Eisenhower, 1969, Box 20.00
Wheaton, Franklin Roosevelt, 1st Edition, Box 35.00
Wheaton, Jean Harlow 7.50
Wheaton, John F.Kennedy, 1st Edition, Box 75.00
Wheaton, Nixon–Agnew, Purple 7.50
Wheaton, Teddy Roosevelt, 1970, Box 15.00
Wheaton, Thomas Jefferson, 1970, Box 10.00
Wheaton, Woodrow Wilson, 1967, Box 20.00
Whiskey, Back Bar, Black Cat, White & Black Enamel Lettering 1870.00
Whiskey, Davy Crockett Pure Old Bourbon 45.00
Whiskey, Decanter, Ezra Brooks, Locomotive, Red & Black, 12 In. 30.00
Whiskey, Duffy Malt, Honey Amber, Pat.Aug.24, 1886, Bubbles 8.50
Whiskey, Duffy, Malt, Clear To Frosted, 1860–90, 9 5/8 In. 125.00
Whiskey, Hayner Distillery Co., 1 Qt. 15.00
Whiskey, Hermitage Rye, V.Van Bergen & Co., Amber 50.00
Whiskey, J.Q.C.Wisharts Pine Tree Tar Cordial, Green, 1859, 1/2 Pt. 79.00
Whiskey, Liquor Galliano, Figural, Box, Miniature 10.00
Whiskey, Mount Vernon Pure Rye Whiskey, Amber, Emblem, Miniature 22.00
Whiskey, Paul Jones, Dark Amber, Wicker, Blob Seal, 1 Qt. 22.00
Whiskey, Schade & Buysings Schapps, Olive Green, 9 In. 25.00
Whiskey, Three Feathers, Sealed, Wis.Tax Stamp, Miniature 19.00
Whiskey, Udolpho Wolfe's Aromatic Schnapps, Olive, Iron Pontil 47.00
Wild Turkey No. 1 .... 215.00

Boxes of all kinds are collected. They were made of thin strips of inlaid wood, metal, tortoiseshell, embroidery, or other material.

BOX, see also Advertising, Box; Ivory, Box; Porcelain, Box; Shaker, Box; Tinware, Box; and various Porcelain categories.
BOX, 4–Masted Schooner, Recessed Mahogany Carved, Chain Ends, 5 X 12 In. 145.00
Alms, Relief Carved Stars, Fans, Flowers, Brass Stud Trim, 10 3/4 In. 85.00
Band, Bentwood, Floral & Classical Buildings Wallpaper Covered, 19 In. 135.00
Band, Wallpaper Covered, Floral, Gray Ground, Bent Poplar, 11 1/4 In. 135.00
BOX, BATTERSEA, see Battersea, Box
Bentwood, Overlap Joint, Iron Tacks, Green Paint, Oval, 9 1/4 In. 575.00
Bentwood, Wooden Spring Clip Lid, 5–Finger, Geometric, Oval, 9 In. 65.00
Bible, Cotter–Pin Hinges, 2 Covered Tills, Blue Paint, 14 X 19 In. 375.00
Bible, Flat Cover, Incised Line Design, England, Oak, 9 1/4 X 15 1/4 In. 115.00
Bible, Slant Lid, Inlaid T.E.1755, Oak, 13 1/2 X 24 1/2 X 15 1/2 In. 200.00
Blanket, Yellow Ochre Ground, Bootjack Ends, 10 X 14 In. 1800.00
Bride's, Painted Husband & Wife On Cover, Florals On Sides, 8 X 19 In. 742.50
Candle, Fruitwood, Hanging, Dovetailed, Sliding Lid, 19 1/2 In. 600.00
Candle, Hanging, Ebony Line Inlay, Scalloped Crest, English, 12 1/4 In. 225.00
Candle, Hanging, Hinged Lid, Cylindrical, Tin, 17 1/2 In. 85.00
Candle, Hanging, Pine, Square Cut Nails, Blue, 6 X 13 X 13 In. 285.00
Candle, Hanging, Reddish Brown Finish, Peaked Backboard 40.00
Candle, Hanging, Splashes of White Paint, Pine, 13 1/2 In. 135.00
Candle, Notched, Beveled Top, Old Paint, C.1830, 7 X 9 X 16 In. 150.00
Candle, Open, Blue Paint, 11 1/2 In. 300.00
Candle, Pine & Poplar, Red Traces, Slide Lid, Rounded Corners, 9 In. 55.00
Candle, Slide Lid, 3 Finger Holds, Jacob Weber, 1840s, 4 1/8 In. 770.00

Candle, Thumb Niche In Sliding Top, Painted, Norwegian, 12 1/4 In. 85.00
Candy, Hooded Lady On Top, Art Deco, Metal, Pink Glass Insert 22.50
Collection, Church, Pencil Post Handle, Walnut, Dark Finish, 24 3/4 In. 75.00
Colored Leaves & Quarter Rounds, Brass Escutcheon, 11 X 7 1/4 In. 1000.00
Comb, Wooden, Castle Shape, Painted 50.00
Copper Tacks, Bentwood, Round, Miniature 250.00
Crayon, American Crayon Co., Slide Lid, Wooden 115.00
Deed, Domed Lid, Tin 44.00
Deed, Leather Covered, Red 20.00
Design On Dome Top, 2 Black Pinwheels, 4 Compass Stars, 28 3/4 In. 200.00
Document, Classical Figure Inset Discs, English 160.00
Document, Cowhide, Bail Handle, Leather Hinges, Brass Tacks, 1790, 12 In. 125.00
Document, Inlaid With Ivory, Ebonized Wood, 9 X 11 1/2 In. 187.00
Document, Iron, Brass, Bound Walnut, Geometric Patterns, 8 1/2 In. 275.00
Dome Top, Alligatored, Wallpaper Lined, Brass Handle, 11 3/4 In. 85.00
Dome Top, Black Paint, Yellow Striping, Wrought Iron Lock, 29 1/4 In. 205.00
Dome Top, Burl Veneer, Contrasting Edging, 9 1/2 In. 225.00
Dome Top, Designs, Pine & Poplar, 14 In. 195.00
Dome Top, Herringbone Straw Inlay, Tin Hinges & Hasp, 11 1/2 In. 80.00
Dome Top, Polychrome Floral Design, German Inscription, 13 In. 100.00
Dome Top, Rainbow Painted, Pine, C.1840, 17 1/2 X 11 In. 3150.00
Dome Top, Red & Black Graining, Striping, Pine, 27 In. 175.00
Dome Top, Wooden, Paint Design 137.00
Dough, Breadboard Top, Old Red Base, Poplar, 27 1/2 X 51 1/2 In. 700.00
Dough, Commercial, C.1896 .... 115.00
Dough, Dovetailed Pine Boards, Rattail Hinges, 19th Century, 20 In. 650.00
Dough, English Country, Oak, Early 19th Century 300.00
Dough, Mennonite, 1850-60, Small 65.00
Egg, Dark Green Paint, Cover, Square 55.00
Embroidered, Velvet, Blue, Red, Grey, Green, Floral Print Design, 3 In. 325.00
Farebox, Trolley Conductor's, Johnson, 6 Sections 25.00
Figured Grain, Beveled, Fiddle Back Mahogany, Cover, 14 In. 185.00
Figures & Houses, Carved, Brass Fittings, Camphorwood, Chinese, 10 In. 125.00
Geometric Design, Wallpaper Covered, Bentwood, 10 1/2 In. 125.00
Glove, Woman's, Carved Wood, Lined, 4 X 18 1/2 In. 65.00
Gray, Yellow, Green & Salmon Paint, 25 In. 330.00
Hanging, Dovetailed Case, 2 Sections, Hinged Slant Lid, 14 X 12 1/4 In. 275.00
Hat, Dobbs Fifth Avenue, Cardboard 12.00
Hat, Flowered Wallpaper, 1900s, 3 7/8 X 9 1/4 In. 175.00
Hat, Flowered Wallpaper, 1900s, 5 1/8 X 6 In. 75.00
Hourglass Shape, Hinged Lid, Plywood Sides & Bottom, 25 In. 75.00
Inlaid Mother-of-Pearl Lid, Tortoiseshell, Lined, C.1810, 11 3/8 In. 850.00
Jacobean Style, Raised Case, Fruitwood, 56 In. 200.00
Jewelry, Barrel-Cart Shape, Porcelain Horse, Brass, Glass Dome, 7 In. 400.00
Jewelry, Black Glass Inserts, Ormolu, Hinged, Marked Moreau, 4 X 3 In. 245.00
Jewelry, Casket, Burl & Brass Inlay, English Walnut, C.1850 .... 245.00
Jewelry, Gold & Silver Lacquer Floral, Meiji Period 575.00
Jewelry, Japanese Lacquer & Mother-of-Pearl, Village Scene, 13 1/2 In. 225.00
Jewelry, Matte Tan Exterior, Glossy Rose Inside, 3 1/2 X 6 1/2 X 4 In. 300.00
Jewelry, Red Lacquer, Regency, Gilt St.George & Dragon, 6 X 12 X 9 In. 3575.00
Knife, Domed Cover, Fruit Finial, Duncan Phyfe, 26 In., Pair 2090.00
Knife, George III, Lid, Interior Star, Mahogany, 14 In., Pair 3740.00
Knife, George III, Rosewood, Mahogany, Serpentine Front, C.1800, 14 In. 350.00
Knife, Glass, Dur-X, Pat.112059 .... 10.00
Knife, Heart-Shaped Handle, Dovetailed, Walnut 165.00
Knife, Hepplewhite, Inlaid Mahogany, Pair 2250.00
Knife, Maple, Turned Wooden Handle, Old Finish, 10 1/4 X 13 1/4 In. 135.00
Knife, Scalloped Edges, Zoar, Ohio, Walnut, 14 1/4 X 10 In. 250.00
Knife, Scrolled Edges, Divider, Handle, Mahogany, 9 1/4 X 15 In. 135.00
Knife, Serpentine & Blocked, American, Mahogany, C.1800 .... 357.00
Knife, Silver, George II, 13 In. 825.00
Knife, Walnut, 4 Compartments 275.00
Landscape Scene On Lid & Front, Pine, 20th Century, 19 In. 375.00
Leather Bound, Brass Tacks, Brass Bale Handle, 11 1/4 In. 35.00

Leather, Embossed Floral & Line, Mother-of-Pearl Cover, 1910, 8 3/4 In. 175.00
Letter, Dome Top, Carved Ebony, 6 1/2 X 5 X 10 In. 65.00
Lime Green Glass, Sanded Gold Scrolls, Pink Flowers, 3 3/4 X 5 1/2 In. 165.00
Mouse On Cover, Gilt Trim, Gold Tassel, Keg Shape, Oriental, 8 In. 270.00
Notions, Burnt Wood, Colors, Dated 1913 .... 25.00
Painted & Incised Pinwheels On Cover, 6 1/2 X 2 3/4 In. 300.00
Painted Flowers On Cover, Swags Around Side, Bentwood, 6 3/4 In. 80.00
Pantry, Bentwood, 3-Finger Construction, Green Paint, Round, 10 1/2 In. 300.00
Pantry, Copper Nails, Natural Finish, 7 1/2 X 3 1/2 In. 60.00
Pantry, Cover, Wire Bail & Wood Handle, 9 1/2 In. 165.00
Pantry, Donut, Theorem Design, Yellow, 19th Century, Penna., Small 650.00
Pantry, Original Green Paint, Fingered, Oval 75.00
Pantry, Pegs Hold Top & Bottom Boards, Cover, Natural, 7 X 4 1/2 In. 28.00
Pantry, Straight Lap Cover, Marked J.Loring, Blue-Green, 6 1/2 In. 110.00
Pantry, Wooden, Cover, 8 3/4 X 3 1/2 In. 22.00
Pantry, Wooden, Iron Reinforcements At Tips of Fingers 250.00
Pencil & Quill, Slide Cover, T Head Nails, 2 X 2 1/2 X 7 In. 150.00
Pencil, Bullet, 31 Piece 25.00
Pencil, Jackie Coogan 38.00
Pencil, Mother Goose, Wooden 15.00
Pencil, Winchester, Green 46.00
Pine, Brown Flame Graining, 13 1/2 In. 75.00
Pine, Dome Top Dovetailed, Wrought Iron Lock, 18 3/4 In. 125.00
Pine, Original Red Flame Graining, Inlaid Ivory Escutcheon, 11 In. 100.00
Pine, Painted, Tulips, Leaves, 4 Bun Feet, 5 1/2 X 12 X 7 In. 6500.00
Pipe, Carved Vine, Floral & Tulip Design, Softwood 700.00
Pipe, Cutout Crest, Dark Varnish, 18 1/2 In. 30.00
Poplar, Red & Black Graining, Brushed Designs, Keyhole Cover, 30 In. 775.00
Post Office, Joey Stivic, Box 50.00
Powder, Half Doll Top, Green Hoop Skirt, Hat, Arms Extended, 7 1/2 In. 87.00
Red, Black Graining, Black Borders, Yellow Foliage Design, 9 3/4 In. 325.00
Red, Ship American Privateer 1812 On Lid, 11 1/2 X 8 5/8 X 5 1/8 In. 2200.00
Salt Box, Double, Treenware, Sliding Lids, 18 In. 70.00
Salt, Ceramic, Wooden Lift Lid, German 75.00
Salt, Hanging, Maple, Dovetailed, 8 X 7 1/2 X 8 1/2 In. 175.00
Shaving, Wooden, Mirror In Lid, 3 5/8 In. 30.00
Shoe, High-Button 115.00
Silver Plate, Cedar Lined, Chase, 8 In. 40.00
Silver, Chinese Jade Insert, 20th Century, 800 Silver, 3 3/4 X 7 In. 225.00
Sliding Lid, Dovetailed, Cherry, 7 1/2 In. 145.00
Sliding Lid, Dovetailed, Poplar, 15 In. 75.00
Sliding Lid, Red Stain, Poplar, 8 In. 10.00
Spice, 6 Round Containers, Wood, Sliding Door, Penna. 135.00
Stamp, Dragons, Enameled Ground, Brass, Chinese, C.1920 .... 37.50
Storage, Primitive, Wooden, Slant Top 50.00
Strong Box, Black Paint, Gold Trim, Brass Escutcheon, Steel, 9 3/4 In. 35.00
Strong Box, Padlock, M.W.& Co., Steel, Brass Key Slot 25.00
           BOX, TEA CADDY, see Tea Caddy
Tin, Copper, Enameled Boat Scene, 1780 .... 2235.00
Tinder, Exterior Candle Socket, Damper, Strike & Flint, 18th Century 425.00
Tobacco Storage, Oak, Dovetailed, Lined, Hinged Cover, 11 X 8 X 8 In. 26.50
Tooled, Mahogany, Maple & Butternut, Brassbound Corners 625.00
Trinket, Red, Blue Stamps, Birds, Stars & Hex Signs, 5 1/2 X 8 1/2 In. 1500.00
Wall, Country, Apple Green Paint, 3 Graduated Pockets, 17 In. 395.00
Wall, Green Putty Paint, 16 In. 1210.00
Wall, Paneled Door, Painted Green, Scandinavian, 19 1/2 X 20 In. 400.00
Wall, Red & White Painted, Carved Pine, Dated 1821, 16 X 7 In. 2310.00
Wooden, Hinged Lid, Bone Carving Applied Over Surface, Hunting Scene 1210.00
Writing, Exotic Wood Inlaid Cover, Lock, 14 3/4in. 370.00
Writing, Fitted Interior, Brass Bound Rosewood, 13 3/4 In. 105.00
Writing, Fitted Interior, Cherry, 20 In. 225.00
Writing, Officer's, Mahogany, Fitted, 18 X 13 X 22 In. 1550.00
Wrought Iron & Strap Hinges, Painted, Pine, 8 1/2 X 20 1/2 In. 65.00

The Boy Scout movement in the United States started in 1910. The first Jamboree was held in 1937. Collectors search for any material related to scouting, including patches, manuals, and uniforms. Girl Scouts are listed under their own heading.

BOY SCOUT, Ax, Leather Cover	18.00
Badge, Merit, Eagle, Bronze	70.00
Bank, Leader Shape, Staff In Hand, Cast Iron, 5 3/4 In.	74.00
Belt Slide, National Jamboree, Silvered Metal, Design, 1957	3.00
Binoculars, Tan Leather, 1920s	85.00
Book, Afloat In France, Carter, 1917	8.00
Book, Boy Scouts of The Air, Stuart, 1912	9.00
Book, Handbook For Leaders, 1950	9.00
Book, Test, Saalfield, 1916	25.00
Book, The Boy Scout, Davis, 1914	19.00
Book, Under The Stars & Stripes, Saalfield, 1918	25.00
Booklet, Bird Study Merit Badge, Illustrations, 1925	16.00
Bugle, Rexcraft	38.00
Button, Committee, Boy Scouts of America, 1940s, 2 In.	20.00
Button, I'll Be Invested Scout Circus, Colors, 1930s, 1 1/4 In.	22.00
Button, Scout Logo, Navy Blue, Gold Litho, 1930s, 5/8 In.	6.00
Button, Walter W.Head Acorn Award, Gold, 1930s, 1 In.	12.00
Camera, Box, 1955	35.00
Canteen, Canvas Carrier	14.00
Card, Membership, 1920	5.00
Compass, 1940s	25.00
Diary, 255 Pages, 1931	15.00
Drums, 1908	20.00
Figurine, Copper, Wood Base, 1950s, 5 In.	25.00
First Aid Kit, Contents & Booklet, 1933	20.00
Flashlight, Emblem On End	20.00
Handbook, Canvas Lined Cover, Signed Leyendecker, 1917, 498 Pages	35.00
Handbook, For Scoutmaster, 1923	25.00
Handbook, Official Firemaking Equipment For Boy Scouts, Box	55.00
Handbook, Rockwell Cover, 1945	7.00
Hat, Campaign, Stetson, Size 7 1/4	30.00
Hat, Master's, Box	95.00
Holder, Neckerchief, Bronze, Eagle, Domed, 1 1/2 X 1 1/4 In.	8.00
Indian Beadcraft Kit	30.00
Knife, Kutmaster	12.00
Knife, Official, Imperial	12.00
Knife, Stainless Steel, 2 Blades, Engraved, 1950s, Zippo	8.00
Map, 1960 Golden Jamboree, Colorado	8.00
Match Safe, Pocket, Round	30.00
Medal, Eisenhower Paper Campaign, 1945	50.00
Mess Kit, Carrier	10.00
Mug, San Diego Council, 1981, Ceramic	5.00
Patch, BSA Eagle Scout, Silver Mylar Rolled Edge, Eagle, 1980s	5.00
Patch, District Commissioner, White Outline, Yellow Eagle, 1950	21.00
Patch, Eagle Scout, Emblem, White Edge, Red Twill, 1970s	12.00
Patch, Hawkeye Area Council, 25th Anniversary, Blue, Design	15.00
Patch, National BSA Jamboree Trading Post, Yellow Edge, 1985	5.00
Pin, Collar, Asst.District Executive, Gold Wreath, 7/8 In.	35.00
Pin, Hat, BSA Jr.Asst.Scoutmaster, 3 Green Bars, Package, 1940s	45.00
Pin, Lapel, BSA, 30 Year Veteran, Blue Enameled, 1/2 In.	10.00
Plate, National Jamboree, 1973	12.00
Pocket Flap, Black Eagle Lodge, Black Rolled Edge	5.00
Pocket Flap, O.A.Lodge 123, Emblem, White Twill, Red Cut Edge	10.00
Postcard, Firemaker Girl, Boy Scout & Campfire, Unused, 1912	12.50
Shirt, Lone Scout, Tan, Removable Buttons, Logo, 1930	35.00
Song Book, 1956	7.00
Statues, Bronze Finish, Marble Base,, 4 In.	8.00
Tin, First Aid	12.00
Watch Fob, Scout Holding U.S.Flag, Brass, Colors Worn, 1920	30.00

Whistle, On Chain 12.00

Bradley & Hubbard Manufacturing Company made lamps and other metalwork in Meriden, Connecticut, from the 1840s. Their lamps are especially prized by collectors.

BRADLEY & HUBBARD, Candelabra, Triple, Matching Candlesticks, 7 1/2 In. 150.00
Candlestick, Flower Shape, Signed 60.00
Candlestick, Square Base, 12 In., Pair 85.00
Card Holder, Egyptian Design 20.00
Desk Set, Brass, 4 Piece 100.00
Desk Set, Textured Black, Brass Corners, 5 Piece 175.00
Inkwell, Double, Deer Head, Antlers Hold Pens 125.00
Lamp, Cone Shape, Bulbous Squat Body, Panel Shade 650.00
Lamp, Factory Security, Glass Insert, Brass 110.00
Lamp, Kerosene, Pull-Down, Store, Brass Fount, Tin Shade 110.00

Brass, Candleholder, Roman Foot, 6 In.

Bronze, Figurine, Cranes,
Beaks Open, Japanese, 62 In., Pair

Bronze, Crystal Ball, Stand, Frothy Wave Form, 8 3/4 In.

Lamp, Oil, Leaded Stained Glass Shade, Signed 340.00
Lamp, Prairie School, C.1900 .... 650.00
Lamp, Reverse Painted Classical Ruins, 15 In. 350.00
Letter Opener, Bronze 20.00
Match Holder, Figural, Fly, Iron 50.00
Mirror, Bacchus' Head, Beveled, Bronze, 9 1/2 X 14 In. 125.00
Plaque, Art Nouveau, Bust of Woman, Blue Gown, Signed 395.00
Trivet, Woman's Head, Cast Brass 60.00

Brass has been used for decorative pieces and useful tablewares since ancient times. It is an alloy of copper, zinc, and other metals.

BRASS, see also Bell; Tool; Trivet; etc.
BRASS, Ashtray, Oak Leaf 25.00
Barrel, Stenciled High Grade Sweepstakes Ensilage Corn, 8 X 11 In. 75.00
Bed Warmer, Brass, Floral Engraved Lid, Turned Wooden Handle, 42 In. 325.00
Bed Warmer, Copper, Turned Wooden Handle, Salesman's Sample, 9 In. 125.00
Bed Warmer, Turned Wooden Handle, Salesman's Sample, 9 In. 200.00
Bed Warmer, Wooden Handle, Miniature, 9 In. 105.00
Bowl, Engraved Dragons, Marked China, 10 In. 5.00
Bowl, Pouring Spout, Iron Handles, Hammered, 14 1/2 In. 40.00
Box, Miniature On Ivory, Signed, 4 3/4 X 5 In. 245.00
Box, Tobacco, Civil War, 1863, Hinged, 3 X 2 X 1 In. 125.00
Box, Tobacco, Tooling, Oval, 3 In. 45.00
Brazier, Turkish, Hand Tooled, Round, 10 In. 75.00
Bucket, 10 In. 30.00
Bucket, Waterbury, Forged Bail, Spun, 1873 .... 90.00
Candleholder, Roman Foot, 6 In. ....*Illus* 125.00
BRASS, CANDLESTICK, see Candlestick
Cigarette Lighter, Table, Engraved Leaves, India, 4 1/2 In. 7.00
Cigarette Set, Floral Design, Chinese, C.1930, 3 Piece 45.00
Compass, Surveying, W.F.Young, Philadelphia, Late 18th Century 750.00
Cuspidor, Bulldog Cut Plug, Raised Bulldog, 11 In. 125.00
Desk Set, Silvered, G.W.Junker & Co., 1860, 9 Piece 7800.00
Door Knocker, Kissing Couple Against Roses, 5 1/2 In. 80.00
Door Knocker, Urn Shape 20.00
Door Knocker, Victorian Woman's Head, 4 1/2 In. 28.00
Eagle, Spread Wings, Paris, 1900 .... 1200.00
Figure, Drunk In Tails, Clutching Signpost, Coat of Arms, 4 1/2 In. 18.00
Figurine, Rhino, Studded Carnelians, Turquoise Eyes, Filigree, 4 In. 28.00
Figurine, Squirrel, Solid, English, 1 1/2 X 2 In. 22.00
Girandole Set, Indians, Black Marble Base, 17 1/2 & 19 In., 3 Piece 500.00
Glove Hook, Figural, Bird, Brass 45.00
Jar, Fruit Finial, Glass Insert, 2 1/2 X 2 1/8 In. 75.00
Kettle, Butter, Large 425.00
Ladle, Polished, 20 In. 55.00
Ladle, Richard Lee, Mass., 1788–1820, 11 1/2 In. 900.00
Memo Clip, Lion & Unicorn, Merry Phipson & Parker, Oct.3, 1843, 7 In. 65.00
Mortar & Pestle, 3 X 3 In. 20.00
Mortar & Pestle, Diagonal Zigzag, Square Handle, 3 X 4 In. 70.00
Nutcracker, Lion, 4 3/4 In. 32.00
Pail, Ansonia Brass Co., Wrought Iron Bale Handle, Spun, 10 1/2 In. 45.00
Pail, Iron Bail Handle, Hayden's Patent, 8 1/2 X 13 In. 35.00
Pail, Stationary Wrought Iron Bail Handle, 6 X 15 In. 45.00
Paper Clip, Spencerian, 4 In. 15.00
Pen Rest, Figural, Turbaned Man Rides Backwards On Donkey, 3 X 4 In. 30.00
Pitcher, Art Deco, Hagenauer–Werkstatte, 15 In. 85.00
Scissors, Art Nouveau, With Letter Opener, Velvet Lined Sheath 75.00
Seal, Wax, Bee 4.00
Seal, Wax, Leaf 3.50
Shoehorn, Curved & Sculptural, Seamed, 18th Century, 9 1/2 In. 260.00
Skimmer, Punch, English, C.1770 .... 495.00
Soap Dish, Victorian Bathtub, 4 Carved Legs, 5 1/2 X 2 3/4 In. 15.00
Spurs, Nickel Trim, Floral Tooling, 6 In. 45.00
Stand, Umbrella, Dish Bottom, Vertical Rods, Rail, 19 In. 65.00

Teakettle, Amber Glass Handle, Gooseneck Spout, English, 8 In. 65.00
Teakettle, Gooseneck, Heater Stand, Insulated Handle 495.00
Teapot, Pewter Lines, Amber Handle, Footed, Gooseneck Spout, 9 In. 200.00
Telescope, Leather, 3–Draw, France 65.00
Tobacco Cutter, Steel Blade, 6 1/2 In. 20.00
Toothpick, Engraved Flowering Tree Design, China, 2 X 2 In. 10.00
Trivet, Red Riding Hood & Wolf, 10 1/2 In. 45.00
Umbrella Stand, Scenes On Each Side, Hammered, Liner, 26 In. 185.00
Urn, Cover, Applied Vining Flower Design, 10 In. 90.00
Warmer, Carriage, Charcoal 75.00
Warming Pan, Etched Cover, Band of Stars, Peacock On Branch, 42 In. 250.00
Warming Pan, Fitted Cover, Stylized Floral Design, Pan, 10 1/2 In. 200.00
Wreath, Figural, Jungle Animal, Contemporary, 16 1/2 In., Pair 250.00
BREAD PLATE, see various Pressed Glass patterns

Brides' baskets of glass were usually one–of–a–kind novelties made in American and European glass factories. They were especially popular about 1880 when the decorated basket was often given as a wedding gift. Cut glass baskets were popular after 1890. All brides' baskets lost favor about 1905.

BRIDE'S BASKET, Art Glass, Meriden Holder, Sapphire Blue, Courting Scene 285.00
Cranberry, White 350.00
Filigree Floral Design, Victorian Silver Plated Holder 48.00
Optic Petal Design, Reed & Barton Frame, Blue, 13 1/2 In. 225.00
Pink With Enameling, Lady, Silver Plated Holder 650.00
Red & Gold Design, Gold Edge, 4 X 10 In. 875.00
Rubina Verde, Silver Plated Holder, 12 In. 600.00
Satin Glass, Floral, Gold Overlay, Silver Frame, 11 1/2 In. 525.00
Tapestry Herringbone, Mother–of–Pearl, C.1892 .... 1250.00
White Exterior, Blue Interior, Adelphi Holder, 11 3/4 In. 600.00
White Exterior, Cranberry Interior, Silver Plated Holder 185.00
BRIDE'S BOWL, Butterscotch Art Glass, Silver Plated Holder 325.00
Cameo, Deep Blue, White Floral, Amber Edge, Webb 1250.00
Cranberry Glass, Enameled Flowers, Silver Plated Stand, 1880s 375.00
Diamond Quilted, Hunter Scene On Silver Plated Frame, 12 In. 375.00
Fluted & Crimped Edge, Enameling, Silver Plated Holder 585.00
Gold Leaves, White Flowers, Silver Plated Holder, 11 1/2 In. 595.00
Pink To White, Ruffled Rim, Silver Plated Holder 250.00
Ruffled, Flowers, Pink To Blue, Silver Plated Stand, 8 3/4 In. 195.00

Bristol glass was made in Bristol, England, after the 1700s. The Bristol glass most often seen today is a Victorian, lightweight opaque glass that is often blue. Some of the glass was decorated with enamels.

BRISTOL, Biscuit Jar, Enameled Flowers, Silver Plated Fittings 145.00
Box, Hinged Cover, Egg Shape, Flowers, Leaves, Gold Trim, 6 1/2 In. 225.00
Box, Jewelry, Multicolor Florals, Omolu Rings, 5 In. 375.00
Box, Ring, Lift–Off Lid, Gold Flowers & Leaves, Turquoise, 1 3/4 In. 45.00
Decanter, Rose To Deep Rose, Flowers, Marbelized Stopper, 11 In. 95.00
Ewer, Floral & Bird Design, Light Green, 8 1/4 In., Pair 150.00
Ewer, White Satin, Gold Floral, 11 In. 50.00
Lamp, Kerosene, Ball Shape, Brass Hardware, Miniature 75.00
Lustres, Prisms, Gold Trim & Designs, 12 1/4 In., Pair 550.00
Perfume Bottle, Gold Trim Ball Stopper, Pink Roses, 5 3/8 In. 75.00
Perfume Bottle, Green, Gold, Green & White Design, Glass Stopper 50.00
Pitcher, Gold Band, Enameled Flowers & Leaves, 2 1/4 In. 60.00
Rose Bowl, 4–Crimp, Gold Scallops & Flowers, 4 In. 95.00
Rose Bowl, 4–Crimp, Rope Garlands, White Enamel Trim, 4 In. 75.00
Rose Bowl, 6–Crimp, Ball Feet, Gold Bands, Turquoise, 5 In. 135.00
Rose Bowl, 6–Crimp, Gold Florals & Leaves, 3 Ball Feet, 4 1/2 In. 118.00
Salt, Orange Flowers, Silver Plated Frame, Claw Feet, Tan, 2 1/4 In. 135.00
Saltstorks, Branches, Green, Bucket Shape, 1 3/4 X 2 3/8 In. 75.00
Sugar & Creamer, Floral Design, Opaque White, Cover 40.00
Toilet Set, Cockatoo On Perch, Enameled, Tufts Silver, 3 Piece 375.00

Tumbler, Gold Beaded Swags, Hand Painted Flowers, Star Bottom 12.00
Vase, Allover Flowers & Leaf Design, Goat Head Handles, 8 1/2 In. 60.00
Vase, American Cattle, Signed, 17 In., Pair 235.00
Vase, Aqua & Gold Flowers, Flared, Enamel On Custard, 7 1/4 In. 60.00
Vase, Bachelor's Buttons, Brown Foliage, Gold Outlining, 8 1/2 In. 48.00
Vase, Blue & White, Gold Trim, 6 In. 35.00
Vase, Bud, Hand Painted, 5 In. 37.50
Vase, Coach & Horses Medallion, Scrolls, Foliage, Gold Trim, 14 In. 145.00
Vase, Dutch Windmill Scene, White Ground, 7 In. 30.00
Vase, Enameled Floral, Pink Cased, 14 In., Pair 45.00
Vase, Gold, Blue & White, 13 In., Pair 110.00
Vase, Pink, Urn Shape, Gold Design, 9 1/2 In. 18.50
Vase, Pink, White Floral, 12 In. 90.00
Vase, Scenic, Cottage Scene, 11 In. 135.00
Vase, Stylized Flower & Leaf, Goat's Head Handles, 8 1/2 In. 60.00
Vase, Turquoise, Calla Lily, Gold Design, Flowers, 5 1/2 In. 45.00
  BRITANNIA, see Pewter

Bronze is an alloy of copper, tin, and other metals. It is used to make figurines, lamps, and other decorative objects.

BRONZE, Ashtray, Alabaster Figure of Dog Attached, Austrian, 2 3/4 In. 88.00
Ashtray, Frank Lloyd Wright, Copper–Plated, Triangles, 3 5/8 In. 2200.00
Ashtray, Oakleaf, Oval, Noroia, Israel, 5 X 3 In. 5.00
Bookends, Figural, Tree Form, Dutch Boy & Girl, Vienna, 4 3/4 In. 175.00
Bookends, The Thinker 15.00
Bust, Austrian, Goethe & Schiller, Pedestal, 4 In., Pair 115.00
Bust, Boy In Top Hat, 14 In. 175.00
Bust, Gentleman, Fur Trimmed Hat, Marble Base, Russia, 1870, 12 In. 1300.00
Bust, Georges Coudray, Young Woman, Bow In Hair, 20 1/2 In. 950.00
Bust, Heber, Woman & Child, 1911, 7 1/2 In. 770.00
Bust, Laporte, Young Woman, Armless, Looking Left, Marble Base, 10 In. 250.00
Bust, Leonard, Cupid, Quiver About Shoulder, 20 1/2 In. 880.00
Bust, Man With Mustache, Harriet Randolph Hyatt, 1891 .... 1650.00
Bust, Man, Exhausted Expression, Italian, 19th Century, 19 In. 1400.00
Bust, Man, Schematically Rendered Features, 12 In. 150.00
Bust, Man, Shoulder Length, Square Base, Brown Patina, 10 In. 150.00
Bust, Mayer, Woman, Le Matin, Arms Behind Neck, C.1900, 22 1/4 In. 1320.00
Bust, Villanis, Woman, Tanagra, Upswept Hair, C.1900, 24 1/4 In. 990.00
Bust, Woman, Bianca, Egyptian Style Headdress, Marble Base, 17 In. 650.00
China, Empress, Ceremonial Robe & Headdress, 19th Century, 10 In. 395.00
Cranes, Beaks Open, Japanese, Pair, 62 In. ....*Illus* 1320.00
Crystal Ball, Stand, Frothy Wave Form, 8 3/4 In. ....*Illus* 3025.00
Cuspidor, Marked Burley & Co., Small 35.00
Dinner Gong, L.& J.G.Stickley, Arched Frame, Shelf, 1907, 17 In. 8500.00
Figure, Classical Female, Draped Robes, Elbow On Rock, 12 3/4 In. 825.00
Figurine, Athena, Green Marble Base, 8 3/8 In. 195.00
Figurine, Austria, Buffalo, On Marble Ashtray, 2 3/4 X 11 In. 275.00
Figurine, Barbedienne, Duke Lorenzo Medici, In Battle Armor, 38 In. 3250.00
Figurine, Bayre, Lion, Full Mane, 6 X 11 In. 395.00
Figurine, Bayre, Lion, Signed, 15 In. 75.00
Figurine, Bergmann, Tiger, Polychrome Paint, Signed, 4 X 8 In. 1400.00
Figurine, Bologna, Mercury, 20th Century, 30 In. 225.00
Figurine, Bonheur, Bull, On Grassy Ground, C.1886, 20 In. 4400.00
Figurine, Borghese Gladiator, Marble Base, 19 1/4 In. 880.00
Figurine, Bracque, Nude Woman & Faun, C.1925, 19 3/4 In. 3300.00
Figurine, Buddha Head, Siamese, 19th Century, 5 In. 60.00
Figurine, Buddha, On Lotus Throne, Black Patina, 6 1/4 In. 115.00
Figurine, Bull, Sloping Quartz Support, 19th Century, 13 In. 8250.00
Figurine, Callery, Maquette For Free–Form, Marble Base, 8 1/2 In. 605.00
Figurine, Chalon, Woman, Riding Horse, Marble Base, Pedestal, 39 In. 3350.00
Figurine, Chinese, Buddha, Seated, Lotus Plinth, 12 1/2 In. 400.00
Figurine, Chinese, Guan Yin, Seated, Lotus Crown, 7 1/2 In. 500.00
Figurine, Chiparus, Javelin Thrower, C.1925, 34 In. 2475.00
Figurine, Clemente Sampinato, Horse, Bucking, Rider, Signed, 1972 .... 1650.00

Figurine, Colinet, Nude, Arms Outstretched, Marble Base, 12 1/2 In. 550.00
Figurine, Cranes, Beaks Open, Japanese, 62 In., Pair ....*Illus* 1320.00
Figurine, Cumberworth, Bearded Man, Woman, 38 1/2 In., Pair 7700.00
Figurine, Cyrus Dallin, Appeal To The Great Spirit, 1920s 1975.00
Figurine, Dallin, Indian Chief, On Horse, Dated 1890, 12 In. 2500.00
Figurine, Dancing Woman, Gilt, Flowing Gown, Flower In Hair, 18 In. 4250.00
Figurine, De Bologne, Mercury, On Demon Mask, C.1900, 33 In. 885.00
Figurine, De Luco, Charioteer, Holding 2 Rearing Horses, 23 X 27 In. 6000.00
Figurine, Delagrange, Woman, Dancing, Flowing Cape, 16 3/4 In. 8250.00
Figurine, Diana With Stag, Ormolu Base, French, 16 3/4 In. 3575.00
Figurine, Dilabrierre, The Hunt, 19th Century 3500.00
Figurine, Dubois, Lute Player, Singing, C.1865, 24 1/4 In. 1200.00
Figurine, Elephant, Cold-Painted, Indian, Mahout, 9 1/4 In. 2100.00
Figurine, Elephant, Indian, Mahout, 9 X 10 In. ....*Illus* 2100.00
Figurine, Ewe, Reclining, Oval Base, 4 1/2 In. 950.00
Figurine, Falconet, Bather, Standing Woman Nude, 19 In. 600.00
Figurine, Fournier, Shakespeare, Standing, Open Book, 20 1/2 In. 605.00
Figurine, France, Girl, With Bow, Artist Signed, 26 In. 800.00
Figurine, Germain, Man Playing Lyre, In Loin Cloth, 25 In. 4840.00
Figurine, Giovanni, Playing, Singing, Leaning Against Rail, 19 In. 1300.00
Figurine, Godard, Female, Early 20th Century, 17 1/2 In. 1980.00
Figurine, Harpokrates, Seated, Naked, Skull Cap, 7 1/4 In. 500.00
Figurine, Horse, Stallion, Japanese, 72 In. ....*Illus* 4840.00
Figurine, Hu, Chinese, 10 1/4 In. 230.00
Figurine, Ibis, Egyptian, Faience, Standing, Curving Beak, 3 3/4 In. 500.00
Figurine, Japanese, Rabbit, Sitting, Humorous, Crossed Legs, 21 In. 660.00
Figurine, Johann Gutenberg, Standing, Holding Bible Page, 16 In. 400.00
Figurine, Julien Causse, Woman, On Rocky Terrain, C.1900, 14 1/2 In. 400.00
Figurine, Karl, Amazon Riding Horse, 12 3/4 In. 1760.00
Figurine, Lavergne, Courtier, Tricorn, Lace At Neck, C.1880, 13 In. 345.00
Figurine, Le Faguays, Signalman, Archer, Silvered & Ivory, 16 In. 4950.00
Figurine, Lion, 1 Paw Resting On Bronze Sphere, 19 1/2 In. 2200.00

Bronze, Figurine, Elephant, Indian, Mahout, 9 X 10 In.

Figurine, Lobster, C.1900, Japan, 8 7/8 In. 110.00
Figurine, Lorenzl, Kneeling Woman, With Alabaster Bowl, 8 1/2 In. 500.00
Figurine, Madrassi, Wounded Soldier, On Ground, 20 1/4 In. 1650.00
Figurine, Man, Standing, Archer Wearing Loincloth, Brown, 17 In. 600.00
Figurine, Masse, Gentlemen, Dueling, C.1910, 13 In., Pair 1500.00
Figurine, Masson, Setter, Seated On Ground, Late 19th Century, 12 In. 1980.00
Figurine, Maubach, La Source, Maiden Pouring Water, 13 1/2 In. 675.00
Figurine, Mene, Irish Setter, Long-Eared, Standing, 12 3/8 In. 990.00
Figurine, Mene, Setter, Uneven Terrain, Fallen Oak Bough, 13 1/2 In. 1430.00
Figurine, Moigniez, Falcon In Flight, Marble Base, 24 In. 1100.00
Figurine, Moreau, Le Retour Des Hirondelles, 1891, 27 In. 2500.00
Figurine, Moreau, Peasant Girl, Red Marble Base, 36 In. 3500.00
Figurine, Moreau, Young Woman, Seated On Rocky Ledge, 28 1/4 In. 1750.00
Figurine, Morisc, Napoleon On Horseback, Marble Base, 13 3/4 In. 1200.00
Figurine, Muller, 2 Farmers, Weary Woman, Man With Scythe, 15 In., Pr. 3410.00
Figurine, Napoleon, Horseback, Marble Base, 13 3/4 In. ....*Illus* 1320.00
Figurine, Nude, With Waterjug, Art Nouveau, 9 In. 175.00
Figurine, Paul Jouve, Buffalo Locked In Combat, C.1905, 22 In. 4125.00
Figurine, Paul Jouve, Lion Devouring Boar, C.1925, 37 3/4 In. 9460.00
Figurine, Pinto, Mother & Child, Veined Marble Base, 25 1/2 In. 660.00
Figurine, Pradier, Hunter, Quiver & Bow, Holding Prey, 20 1/4 In. 2750.00
Figurine, Remington, Rattlesnake, 22 1/2 In. 950.00
Figurine, Rigaud, Female Figure, Silvered & Ivory, 22 1/4 In. 4950.00
Figurine, Riviere, Masked Venetian Harlequin, C.1925, 26 In. 9350.00
Figurine, Rousseau, Seminude Woman, Holding Instrument, 37 In. 3200.00
Figurine, Sailor, Standing Barefoot, Holding A Rope, C.1900 .... 475.00
Figurine, Sauvage, Venus De Milo, Green Patina, 34 1/2 In. 850.00
Figurine, Saya Greene, Isadora Duncan Dancing, 1915, 19 In. 950.00
Figurine, Scotty Dog, Mackarness, Male, Show Stance, 7 3/4 In. 175.00
Figurine, Seifest, Satyr Stealing Goslings, Chased By Goose, 15 In. 450.00
Figurine, Sheep Dog, Austrian, 2 1/2 X 3 In. 250.00
Figurine, Tivier, Peasant Woman Holding Sickle, Head Scarf, 13 Ub. 335.00
Figurine, Whippet, Full-Bodied, 20 1/2 X 27 In., Pair 1000.00
Figurine, Willis, Horse, Jockey 2975.00
Figurine, Woman, Standing, Classical Greek Dress, Water Jar, 42 In. 1500.00
Figurine, Young Boy, With Firecrackers, C.1900, 29 1/2 In. 1435.00
Figurine, Zach, Ballerina, Veined Pink Marble Base, 19 1/2 In. 1650.00
Figurine, Zach, Fashionable Woman With Umbrella, 25 1/4 In. 7700.00
Figurine, Zach, Female Jockey, 16 3/4 In. 2420.00
Figurine, Zach, Girl With Cigarette, Marble Base, 27 3/4 In. 8250.00
Figurine, Zach, Girl, Seated, Broken Eggshell, Marble Base, 7 1/2 In. 4200.00
Figurine, Zach, Standing Equestrienne, Cold Painted, 17 1/2 In. 3100.00
Figurine, Zach, Working Man, Green Marble Base, 12 3/4 In. 885.00
Fremiet, Stallion, Standing, Front Foot Up, Marble Base, 15 1/4 In. 700.00
Gong, Stand, Barrel Form, Dragon Finial, Marble Base, Chinese, 15 In. 5000.00
Group, Allegorical, Labor, Blacksmith, Woman Crowning Him, 29 In. 2200.00
Group, Bacchanalian, Female Satyr, Attended By Infant Satyrs, 14 In. 1430.00
Group, Bitter, 2 Doe Drinking From Satyr's Shell, Marble, 9 X 35 In. 1875.00
Group, Buhot, 3 Cavorting Putti, Oval Base, 15 5/8 In. 1875.00
Group, Chiparus, 3 Female Nudes, Dancer, Flutist, 1925, 19 5/8 In. 5500.00
Group, Fratin, Lion & Boar, Lion Carrying Dead Prey, 21 In. 1210.00
Group, Fremiet, Equestrian, Jockey On Horseback, 20 3/4 In. 4500.00
Group, Godet, Equestrian Group, Cape, Sword At Side, 21 3/4 In. 3850.00
Group, Gratchev, Troika, Lady, Gentleman, Wrapped In Furs, 19 1/2 In. 6600.00
Group, Hager, Two Elephants, Man On Head of Leader, 39 3/4 In. 4200.00
Group, Japanese, Kylin On Rockery, 9 In. 350.00
Group, Lambert-Rucki, Ke Bauser, Embracing Couple, 18 1/2 In. 6600.00
Group, Leonard, 2 Birds Scavenging, Late 19th Century, 20 In. 1200.00
Group, Levy, Woman, On Marble Pillar, Snarling Panthers Below, 21 In. 2475.00
Group, Louis Marie, 2 Lovers, Woman Swooning, Man On Raft, 21 1/2 In. 1775.00
Group, Man Battling A Satyr, 17 In. 1300.00
Group, Mene, Horse & Jockey, Vainqueur Du Derby, C.1863, 17 1/2 In. 5500.00
Group, Mercury With Caduceus, Ceres With Wheat, 33 & 33 1/8 In., Pr. 1750.00
Group, Puech, Winged Sea Siren, Young Man On Shoulder, 35 1/2 In. 3300.00

Bronze, Figurine, Horse, Stallion,   Bronze, Figurine, Napoleon, Horseback,
Japanese, 72 In.   Marble Base, 13 3/4 In.

Group, Vincent–Becquerel, 2 Leaping Deer, Signed, C.1925, 28 3/4 In. 2300.00
Group, Zach, 3 Dancing Ladies, Pink Marble Base, 11 3/4 X 15 In. 2100.00
Group, Zach, Dancing Couple, Woman On Man's Shoulder, 17 In. 2000.00
Group, Zach, Girl, On Rearing Horse, Green Marble Base, 15 1/4 In. 2650.00
Incense Burner, Silver Crest, Marked 2233-2 .... 45.00
Incense Burner, Silver Shakudo Bird, Tree, Dragon Cover, 7 3/4 In. 1100.00
Jardiniere, Parcel Gilt, Waisted Ovoid, Pod Form Handles, 20 In., Pr. 4500.00
Jardiniere, Tubular Handles, Knob Feet, Landscape, Chinese, 10 In. 300.00
Lamp, Flower Stalk, Steuben Shade, G.Gurschner, C.1900, 25 3/4 In. 4675.00
Lamp, Nude, Egyptian Headdress, Bronze Clad, Loetz Shade, 19 In. 400.00
Lamp, Table, Columns Held By 3 Winged Guardians, Marble Base, 24 In. 300.00
Lantern, Temple, Crane, Man, Gilt, Late 19th Century, Japanese, 25 In. 995.00
Letter Opener, Ball & Claw Handle 110.00
Mirror, Dressing, Circular, Women Support, Marble Base, 8 1/2 In., Pr. 2750.00
Mirror, Ivory Lady Portrait, Mother–of–Pearl Mount, Signed, 11 In. 2000.00
Mold, Clown, For Making Rubber Toys, 11 In. 225.00
Mold, Santa Claus, For Making Rubber Toys, 12 In. 275.00
Nude, Foundry Stamp, Signed, 1902, 19 In. 495.00
Pitcher, Nude Maiden Handle, Molded Fish Design, Ledru, 15 1/2 In. 1600.00
Planter, Ornate Dragon Design, Liner, 5 X 5 3/4 In., Pair 1000.00
Plaque, 3 Women, Symbols of Long Life & Wealth, 11 3/4 In., Pair 175.00
Plaque, Farmyard Scene, Child, Goose, Dog, Bird, Oval, 10 3/4 In. 90.00
Plaque, Fraser, Teddy Roosevelt, With Quote, Label, 10 X 12 3/4 In. 175.00
Sarcophagus, Female Nude Inside, Franz Bergman 2100.00
Shoe, Baby's 12.00
Trophy, Golf, Nouveau Sterling Overlay, Golfer, 12 In. 160.00
Urn, Bacchante's Face, Red Enameled Ground, Art Nouveau, 8 In. 550.00
Urn, Dragons At Bottom, Bird Handles, Flowers At Side, 28 In. 925.00
Urn, Fruit, Basket, Baluster Body, Cupid, Dolphin, Handles, 17 In., Pair 2500.00
Vase, Bamboo Section Form, Crane Design, Cylindrical, 8 In., Pair 75.00
Vase, Beaker, Oriental Archaic Style, 10 1/2 In. 140.00
Vase, Child's Form Applied At Middle, Flared, L.Fuller, 5 3/4 In. 1450.00
Vase, Figure of Dragonfly Lady, Louchet Seal, 10 1/2 In. 1750.00
Vase, Gilded Cherub Faces In Swirling Sea, Louchet, 1896, 6 In. 315.00
Vase, Gilt Bird, Chrysanthemums, Shakudo Cover, Miyao, 7 3/4 In. 1980.00
Vase, Inlaid Hawk, Songbirds & Swimming Carp, Japanese, 4 1/2 In. 750.00
Vase, Mermaid & Waves, Handle, 4 3/4 X 6 In. 99.00
Vase, Silver Overlay of Thistles & Leaves, Marked, 12 In. 275.00

Brownies were first drawn in 1883 by Palmer Cox. They are characterized by large round eyes, downturned mouths, and skinny legs. Toys, books, dinnerware, and other objects were made with the Brownies as part of the design.

BROWNIES, Book, Bomba The Merry Old King, Palmer Cox	20.00
Book, Cock Robin, Palmer Cox, Illustrated	35.00
Book, Monkey Jack, Palmer Cox, 1902	20.00
Book, Palmer Cox Primer, Busy Brownies, Soft Cover, 1898	15.00
Book, Queer People, Palmer Cox, 1894	35.00
Bottle, Soda, Embossed, 1926	25.00
Box, Oatmeal	35.00
Calendar, Ramon's, 1940	14.00
Creamer, Pipe Smokers, Motto, Palmer Cox, 2 1/2 In.	58.00
Cup & Saucer, 3 Brownies, Multicolored, Palmer Cox	35.00
Cup & Saucer, Golfing, Palmer Cox	85.00
Cup, Palmer Cox	25.00
Match Holder, Bisque	45.00
Paper Holder, Brass, Large	30.00
Paperweight, Brownies Scene On Bottom, Glass, Palmer Cox	135.00
Paperweight, Scrolling, Chinaman, Irishman, 2 Others, Palmer Cox	195.00
Plate, Engaged In Wicked Activities, Palmer Cox	95.00
Tray, Pin, Brownie Crawling On Edge, Palmer Cox, Pairpoint	130.00
Trivet, Tea, 6 Brownies, Palmer Cox, 6 1/4 In.	85.00

George Brush started working in 1901 in Zanesville, Ohio. He started his own pottery in 1907, but it burned to the ground and he joined McCoy in 1909. After a series of name changes, the company became The Brush Pottery in 1925. Collectors favor the figural cookie jars made by this company.

BRUSH, Bowl, Onyxware, 5 In.	30.00
Console, Built-In Candleholder Ends, Ivory, 14 In.	7.00
Cookie Jar, Brown Cow, Kitten On Back	45.00 To 85.00
Cookie Jar, Cinderella's Pumpkin	55.00 To 72.00
Cookie Jar, Covered Wagon, Dog On Top	158.00
Cookie Jar, Donkey With Cart, Gray Ears Down	75.00
Cookie Jar, Elephant With Ice Cream Cone	50.00
Cookie Jar, Granny	75.00
Cookie Jar, Humpty Dumpty	45.00
Cookie Jar, Little Boy Blue	75.00
Cookie Jar, Little Red Riding Hood	110.00
Cookie Jar, Old Woman's Shoe	75.00
Cookie Jar, Panda Bear	50.00 To 75.00
Cookie Jar, Raggedy Ann	50.00 To 75.00
Cookie Jar, Squirrel On Log	23.00 To 50.00
Cookie Jar, White Hen On Nest	35.00
Planter, Green, Flared, Scalloped, 4 Footed, 11 1/4 X 5 1/4 In.	5.00
Vase, Mottled Rust & Gray, Akimbo Handles, 8 1/4 X 5 1/2 In.	14.00
Vase, Vestal Nude, Green, 10 In.	65.00
Wall Pocket, Owl	90.00

BRUSH MCCOY, see McCoy

Buck Rogers was the first American science fiction comic strip. It started in 1929 and continued until 1965. Buck has also appeared in comic books, movies, and, in the 1980s, in a television series. Any memorabilia connected with the character Buck Rogers is collectible.

BUCK ROGERS, Atomic Disintegrator	70.00 To 140.00
Atomic Pistol, Box	425.00
Badge, Litho Multicolored Portrait, White Ground, 1930s	90.00
Badge, Solar Scout Member	38.00
Book, Buck Rogers & The Doom Comet, Big Little Book, Whitman	18.00
Book, Buck Rogers & The Overturned World, Whitman, 1941	22.00
Book, Collected Works, 1969	25.00
Book, Dangerous Mission, Pop-Up, Blue Ribbon Press, 1934	239.00

Book, Paint, 1935, Whitman 40.00
Book, Strange Adventures In Spider Ship, Pop–Up 195.00
Booklet, Premium From Kelloggs, 32 Pages 40.00
Booklet, Solar Scouts, Premium 110.00
Chemical Laboratory Kit, 1930s 886.00
Destroyer, Tootsietoy, Box 150.00
Dixie Cup, Photo Picture, 1930s 50.00
Doll Set, 3 3/4 In., 6 Piece 12.00
Doll, Space Clothes, Mego, 12 In. 12.00
Doll, Space Suit, 12 In. 12.00
Figure Set, Buck, Wilma, Dr.Huter, Ardala, 2 Robots, Britain, 1935 .... 3850.00
Figurines, Lead, 1935, Wilma, Tiger Man, Asterite, Killer Kane 60.00
Flying Saucer 60.00
Game, Board, Gigantica, Cosmic Wars & Secrets of Atlantis, 1934 .... 395.00
Game, Ring of Saturn, Instructions 575.00
Gun, Atomic 140.00
Gun, Sonic Ray, Plastic, Code Book & Box 55.00
Kit, Space Ranger, 1950s 35.00
Kite, 1950s 65.00
Map, Solar 450.00
Paint Book, 1938 .... 85.00
Pin, Club Member, Red, White & Blue, 1 In. 38.00
Pin, Solar Scout 50.00
Pistol, Disintegrating 160.00
Pistol, Rocket, Daisy, 1934, 9 1/2 In. 90.00
Sonic Ray Gun, Box 75.00
Space Kit, Sylvania, 1952 .... 135.00
Stamp Set, Rubber, 1930s, 23 Piece 125.00
Strato Kite, Envelope, 1946 .... 35.00
Super Dread Not, Balsa Wood 20.00
Toy, Battle Cruiser, Buck Rogers, Tootsietoy 135.00
Toy, Flash Blast Attack Ship, Tootsietoy, Die Cast 65.00
Toy, Rocket Ship, Marx, Box 575.00
Toy, Venus Duo Destroyer, Tootsietoy 100.00
Watch, Pocket .... 195.00 To 225.00

 Buffalo pottery was made in Buffalo, New York, after 1902. The company was established by the Larkin Company, famous manufacturers of soap. The wares are marked with a picture of a buffalo and the date of manufacture. Deldare ware is the most famous pottery made at the factory. It is khaki–colored transfer-decorated ware.

BUFFALO POTTERY DELDARE, Candlestick, 1909, 9 1/2 In., Pair 800.00
Chamberstick, Handle, Signed, Dated 1909 .... 595.00
Chop Plate, Evening At Lion Inn, 14 In. 525.00
Chop Plate, Fallowfield Hunt, The Start, 14 In. 495.00
Creamer, Breaking Cover, 1908 .... 135.00
Cup & Saucer, Ye Olden Days .... 175.00 To 180.00
Cup Plate, Ye Olden Days, 4 1/4 In. 290.00
Fruit Bowl, Ye Village Tavern, 1908 .... 360.00 To 450.00
Humidor, Dr.Syntax Returned Home .... 650.00 To 750.00
Humidor, Ye Lion Inn 750.00
Mug, At The Three Pigeons, , 1909, 4 1/2 In. 270.00
Mug, Fallowfield Hunt, 4 1/2 In. 225.00
Mug, Ye Lion Inn, 1909, 4 1/2 In. 270.00
Pitcher, Demand Annual Rent 495.00
Pitcher, Fallowfield Hunt, 1908, 6 In. 400.00
Plaque, Fallowfield Hunt, 1908, 12 In. 400.00
Plaque, Lost Sheep In Winter, 13 1/2 In. 1500.00
Plaque, Three Pigeons, 12 In. .... 400.00 To 475.00
Plaque, Ye Lion Inn, 1908, 12 In. 400.00
Plate, Art Nouveau, 8 1/4 In. 350.00
Plate, Fallowfield Hunt To The Death, 8 1/2 In. 125.00
Plate, Fallowfield Hunt, 9 1/4 In. 145.00

Plate, Ye Olden Times, 9 1/4 In. .... 165.00 To 175.00
Plate, Ye Town Crier, 8 1/4 In. 140.00
Plate, Ye Village Gossips, 1909, 10 In. 130.00
Plate, Ye Village Street, 7 1/4 In. .... 140.00 To 225.00
Saucer, Ye Olden Days, 1908 .... 50.00
Sugar & Creamer, Village Life Ye Olden Days 325.00
Tankard, Great Controversy, 12 1/2 In. 695.00
Teapot, Dr.Syntax 400.00
Tray, Dancing Minuet, 1909, 12 X 9 In. .... 398.00 To 500.00
BUFFALO POTTERY, Bowl, Roses, Poppies, Gold Trim, 10 1/2 In. 75.00
Fish Set, Different Fish, Sea Ground, Signed 240.00
Game Set, Deer, 6 Piece 100.00
Pitcher, Cinderella .... 350.00 To 365.00
Pitcher, Deer Hunter 295.00
Pitcher, George Washington 300.00
Pitcher, Robin Hood, Dated 1909, 8 1/2 In. 185.00
Plate, American Scenery, Niagara Falls, 10 In. 100.00
Plate, Tercentenary, Souvenir, 1908, 7 1/2 In. 35.00
Teapot, Argyle, Blue, 1914 .... 175.00
Washstand Set, Pitcher, Bowl, Soap Dish, Mustache Cup 175.00

Burmese glass was developed by Frederick Shirley at the Mt. Washington Glass Works in New Bedford, Massachusetts, in 1885. It is a two-toned glass, shading from peach to yellow. Some have a pattern mold design. A few Burmese pieces were decorated with pictures or applied glass flowers of colored Burmese glass.

BURMESE, see also Gunderson
BURMESE, Bell, Clear Handle, 9 3/4 In. 575.00
Bowl, Crimped Rim, 2 1/4 X 3 3/4 In. 245.00
Bowl, Crimped Rim, 2 1/4 X 3 3/4in. 275.00
Creamer, Strawberry In Pontil, Mt.Washington 300.00
Finger Bowl, Folded Rim, Mt.Washington, 2 3/4 X 6 In. 285.00
Lamp, Fairy, Clarke Pyramid Base, 4 In. 275.00
Lamp, Fairy, Double Branch, Brass Branches, Cut Pedestal, 16 1/2 In. 595.00
Lamp, Fairy, Flower Bowl Base, Clarke Insert, 5 1/2 In. 295.00
Mustard Pot, Silver Hinged Cover 98.00
Perfume Bottle, Silver Closure 675.00
Pitcher, Peachblow, Blown Wooden Mold, Shiny, Miniature 150.00
Rose Bowl, 2 1/4 In. 225.00
Rose Bowl, Glossy, 4 X 5 1/2 In. 325.00
Rose Bowl, Mt.Washington, 2 1/2 In. 200.00
Sugar & Creamer, Fishscale, White Lining, Creamer 3 1/2 In. 685.00
Sugar & Creamer, Yellow Handles, 2 3/4 In. 785.00
Toothpick, Hexagonal Rim, Florals, Berries & Oak Leaves 350.00
Toothpick, Pink Blush On Upper Portion 335.00
Tumbler, Diamond–Quilted, 2 3/4 In. 375.00
Vase, 8 Yellow Ribs, Pink Between, 4 1/4 In. 470.00
Vase, Applied Pink Flowers, Matte, 8 X 5 In. 450.00
Vase, Blue & Yellow Flowers, Signed, 3 1/2 In. 250.00
Vase, Bud, Floral Design, 8 1/4 In. 510.00
Vase, Bud, Floral Design, Silver Plated Frame, 8 1/4 In. 510.00
Vase, Floral Sprays, 2 1/4 In. 225.00
Vase, Leaves & Berries, Dimpled On 4 Sides, 6 In. 380.00
Vase, Lily, Tricorner Top, Candy Coloring, 9 3/4 In., Pair 975.00
Vase, Pink Leaves & Flowers, Textured Stems, 8 In. 500.00
Vase, Swirled, 12 7/8 In. 200.00
BURMESE, WEBB, see Webb Burmese
Whiskey Glass, Diamond–Quilted, Mt.Washington 80.00

Buster Brown, the comic strip, first appeared in color in 1902. Buster and his dog Tige remained a popular comic and soon became even more famous as the emblem for a shoe company, a textile firm, and others. The strip was discontinued in 1920, but some of the advertising is still in use.

BUSTER BROWN, Bank, Buster Brown & Tige, Cast Iron .... 125.00 To 150.00
Bank, Buster Brown & Tige, Mechanical 150.00
Bank, Good Luck, Cast Iron, Arcade .... 155.00 To 225.00
Book of Travels, 1912 .... 45.00
Booklet, Buster's Experiences, Pond's Extract, 1904, 12 Pages 30.00
Button, Buster Brown Bread, Multicolor, Gold, 1900s, 1 1/4 In. 8.00
Cake Plate, Adult 65.00
Camping Set 85.00
Card, Bread, Advertising, Buster & Tige 10.00
Clicker, Buster Brown Shoes, 1930s 20.00
Cup & Saucer, Child's, Buster Brown, Tige, Singing Tea Kettle 50.00
Dictionary, Dated 1927 .... 20.00
Dish, Child's, Feeding, Tige In Bowl, Ceramic 35.00
Doll, Hosiery 95.00
Easter Egg, Tin Litho 85.00
Figurine, Tiger At Feet, Composition, 28 In. 140.00
Froggy The Gremlin 28.00
Hatchet 75.00
Hose Support, Multicolor, Early 1900s, 5/8 In. 12.00
Knife & Fork, Child's, With Tige 45.00
Letterhead 10.00
Mannikin, Boy & Matching Girl, 32 In. 275.00
Mirror, Hand 12.50
Mug, Pouring Tea For Tige 45.00
Napkin Ring, With Tige, Celluloid 30.00
Pencil Case, Pencil Shape 65.00
Periscope .... 14.00 To 25.00
Pitcher, Green & White, 3 1/2 In. 45.00
Plate, Tige Doing Tricks, 4 3/4 In. 15.00
Playing Cards, Box, 1913 .... 30.00
Ruler, 12 In. 12.00
Shoe Tree, Pink, Original Bag 70.00
Sign, Buster Brown Bread, Tige & Bundle of Wheat, 22 X 30 In. 350.00
Socks, Original Label, 1 Pair 22.50
Teapot, Creamer, China, 6 In. 50.00
Waffle Iron, Back Side Has Picture of Buster & Tige 75.00
Whistle, Airplane, Tin, Germany 30.00
Whistle, Buster Brown Shoes, Tin 20.00
Yo–Yo 3.00
    BUTTER MOLD, see Kitchen, Mold, Butter
    BUTTERMILK GLASS, see Custard Glass

Buttons have been known throughout the centuries, and there are millions of styles. Gold, silver, or precious stones were used for the best buttons, but most were made of natural materials like bone or shell, or from inexpensive metals. Only a few types are listed for comparison.

BUTTON, Black Glass & Silver, Glass Stones, Silver Color Swirl, 7 Piece 5.00
Fire Dept.Uniform, City of Fall River, 7/8 In. 15.00
Knotted Band Top, Brass, 1 In., 8 Piece 6.00
Mold, Brass 385.00
Paperweight, Designed From Full–Size Paperweight 3.00
Police, Chicago, Brass, 11 Piece 150.00
Railroad Uniform, Train Picture 10.00
U.S.Uniform, Spanish American War, WW I, WW II, Group of 9 .... 5.00

Buttonhooks have been a popular collectible in England for many years but only recently have gained the attention of American collectors. The buttonhooks were made to help fasten the many buttons of the old–fashioned high–button shoes and other items of apparel.

BUTTONHOOK, Floral Design, Sterling Silver 20.00
Folding, Muse, Atlanta, Pat.April 4, 1902 .... 15.00
Repousse, Sterling Silver, 7 1/2 In. 27.00

The Bybee Pottery was started in 1845 and is still working. The Lexington, Kentucky, firm makes pottery that is sold at the factory. Pieces are marked with the name or with the name enclosed by the outline of the state of Kentucky.

BYBEE, Candlestick, Mottled Green, Spiral Stick, 6 X 3 In., Pair 45.00
Vase, Dusty Rose, Pinched Lip, 4 X 3 1/4 In. 25.00

Calendars made to hang on the wall or to be displayed on a desk top have been popular since the last quarter of the nineteenth century. Many were printed with advertising as part of the artwork and were given away as premiums. Calendars with gun or gunpowder or Coca–Cola advertising are most prized.

CALENDAR PAPER, 1838, Atlantic Oil, Hunters In Canoe, Sunset 40.00
1863–64, Francis & Loutrel Stationers & Printers, 1 Sheet 9.50
1886, Burlington Northern Railroad, 12 X 23 In. 12.00
1887, Hood's Sarsaparilla 35.00
1888, Mrs.Winslow's Soothing Syrup, Desk, Victorian Baby 9.00
1889, Prang, All Holidays Pictured 50.00
1890, Walter A.Wood Mowing & Reaping Machine Co., Postcard 25.00
1893, Cinderella, Maud Humphrey 70.00
1894, Drummond Chewing Tobacco, Bawdy Woman, 20 X 24 In. 65.00
1894, Hood's Sarsaparilla, Sweet Sixteen, Cardboard 10.00
1895, Cherub, Ida Waugh, Tissue Paper Between Pages 65.00
1895, Hanford's Celery Cure, Syracuse, New York 50.00
1895, Hood's Sarsaparilla, Heart Shape 50.00
1896, Waverley Cigar, Young Woman Portrait, 15 X 19 3/4 In. 65.00
1899, Hood's Sarsaparilla, 6 X 10 In. 12.50
1900, L.Neutzenhelzer 11.00
1900, Scott's Emulsion, Lithograph of Children 10.00
1900, U.S.Rubber, Victorian Children 32.00
1901, Grand Union Tea Co., Children & Women 45.00
1901, Grand Union Tea, Progress of The Century 95.00
1902, Bell–Cap–Sic Plaster 30.00
1902, Quaker Oats, Queens of Homes & Nations 40.00
1903, Hood's Sarsaparilla, Four Friends 40.00
1904, Embossed Babies, Crying, Smiling 40.00
1905, Grand Union Tea 45.00
1905, Westlecher Herald, Lithograph of Children 40.00
1906, A & P, Child 30.00
1907, John Dousman Milling, Cowgirl, Carboard, 10 X 20 In. 50.00
1908, Bell–Cap Plasters, Children, With Dog, Colorful 38.00
1909, Antikamnia Pills, Photograph of Pretty Woman 10.00
1911, Aug.Baetzhold & Sons, Man & Woman, Framed, 19 X 26 In. 286.00
1911, Pretty Lady Photo, Holding Camera, 3 X 5 In. 25.00
1912, Bristol, Fishing, No Pad 465.00
1912, Colgate Co., Pocket, Each Page Different Product 55.00
1912, New York Telephone Co. 15.00
1914, Ashland Brewery 65.00
1914, Suel Printing Co., Embossed Flowers, 14 X 19 In. 111.00
1915, Bathing Beauty 20.00
1916, J.J.Thompson, Framed, Under Glass, 21 1/2 X 14 1/2 In. 30.00
1916, Shapleigh Hardware 48.00
1920, Chevrolet 200.00
1920, Chevrolet Motor Cars, 30 X 16 In. 35.00
1920, Compliments of Joseph Horejski, Smoked Meats 48.00
1921, Diamond Shoe 10.00
1922, Peters Ammunition, 14 X 26 In. 10.00
1922, Peters Cartridge Co., Lest We Forget 385.00
1922, Remington Arms, 14 X 26 In. 10.00
1923, Waterman's Fountain Pen, 3 1/2 X 6 In. 3.25
1923, Winchester, Philip Goodwin 300.00
1924, Parrish, Pocket 25.00
1924, Remington, Old Mike Painting Decoys, Framed 950.00

1925, Bank of Belfast	72.50
1925, Dodge Bros.	35.00
1926, Atkins Silver Steel Saws	23.00
1926, Calendar of Friendship, Parrish, 53 Pages	20.00
1926, Peters Cartridge Co., Quail In Tall Grass	250.00
1926, Prudential Insurance Co.	17.00
1926, Ziegler Confectioners, 20 X 15 In.	12.00 To 15.00
1927, Armstrong, Pompeian Beauty	30.00
1927, Keller & Son, Cypress, Ill., 20 3/4 X 10 In.	125.00
1927, People's Drugstore, Waycross, Ga., Black Children	55.00
1927, Seymour Hardware, Carboard, Full Pad, 10 X 16 1/2 In.	8.00
1927, Winchester	185.00 To 250.00
1928, Buster Brown, Girl & Doll	45.00
1930, Azda, Ectasy, Parrish	235.00
1930, Dr.Daniel's Veterinary	14.00
1931, Sinclair Gasoline, Cardboard, 10 X 16 In.	8.00
1932, Northwestern Lithographing Co., 23 3/4 X 35 In.	45.00
1933, Winchester, Maas & Steffens	185.00
1934, Seiberling Tires, Art Deco, 10 1/4 X 16 1/4 In.	8.00
1934, Wrigley's Gum, Myrt & Marge	15.00
1935, Nu–Grape, Full Pad	65.00
1936, Deep Rock Oil, Flapper Girl, 6 X 12 In.	22.00
1936, Lum & Abner, With Party Book	15.00
1936, Mobilgas, Magnolia Trail South, 12 X 11 In.	32.00
1937, American Book Co., Lessons Reprint, McGuffey Reader	20.00
1937, Bridgeport Brewing Co., Full Pad, 9 X 14 1/2 In.	30.00
1937, Chicago Heights Pattern, 18 X 27 In.	45.00
1937, International Harvester	15.00
1937, Nyal Drug, Custer, So.Dakota	8.00
1938, Christmas, Hintermeister Artwork, Hunters In Canoe	35.00
1938, DeLaval	10.00
1938, International Harvester	20.00
1938, Mother & Child Picture	11.00
1938, Oxford Hardware	7.00
1940, Beerston, New York	10.00
1940, Vargas, For Esquire Magazine, 12 Girls, 10 X 14 In.	100.00
1941, Bear Scientific Garage, Ferocious Bear, Unused	65.00
1941, Ft.Dodge Laboratories, Etched Scottish Terrier	6.50
1941, Ghost Town	4.50
1941, Hudson Bay	115.00
1942, Brick Farm Implement, Cardboard, 10 X 16 In.	8.00
1942, Clico Club Ginger Ale, 12 X 24 In.	25.00
1942, Templed Hills, Parrish	95.00
1942, Vargas, 12 Pages, 8 X 14 In.	111.00
1943, Hercules Powder Co.	85.00
1943, Parrish, Box	250.00
1944, Vargas, 12 Pages, 8 1/2 X 12 In.	36.00 To 50.00
1945, Parrish, Box	300.00
1945, Rockwell, The American Way	55.00
1945, Sinclair H.C.Gasoline	15.00
1946, Gloria, E.Moran, 1946, 10 X 17 In.	20.00
1946, Hercules, N.C.Wyeth	75.00
1946, Royal Crown Cola	50.00
1946, Truman & Previous Presidents, 10 X 17 In.	8.50
1946, Vargas, Large	30.00
1947, Audubon, 12 Pages of Birds, 12 X 9 In.	35.00
1947, Hunting Scene	25.00
1948, Dr Pepper	50.00
1948, Jewel Tea	15.00
1948, Union Pacific R.R.	28.95
1948, Veedol Flying A Gasoline Motor Oil, 10 X 18 In.	12.00
1949, RC Cola, Wandra Hendrix Picture	45.00
1949, Squirt, Lady, Black Lace Dress, 20 X 14 In.	37.00
1949, Union Pacific	22.00

1951, Producer's Dairy Co., Babies	10.00
1953, Oliver Tractor	20.00
1954, Nu–Grape	31.00
1955, Marilyn Monroe, Nude, 10 X 17 In.	22.00 To 45.00
1957, ABC Cleaner, Moline, Ill., Nude Picture	10.00
1958, Foreman's Cleaners & Laundry, G–String Girl, 16 In.	15.00
1958, Hamm's Beer, Seminude	12.50
1958, Playboy, Wall, No Jacket	15.00
1963, Boy Scout, Rockwell	30.00
1963, Traveler's Insurance, Currier & Ives Print	25.00
1964, Sinclair, Dinosaur, World's Fair	20.00
1968, Base, Pad, Crown Gasoline, Orange Lettering, 19 X 8 In.	45.00
1968, Robert F.Kennedy Memorial	10.00
1969, Union Pacific Centennial	20.00
1970, Union Pacific Railroad	11.00
1972, Schlitz, 6 Circus Ads, Iowa Distributor, 16 In.	15.00
1972, Vargas Girls	30.00
1982, Marble Arms Corp.	25.00

 Calendar plates were very popular in the United States from 1906 to 1929. Since then, plates have been made every year. A calendar and the name of a store, a picture of flowers, a girl, or a scene were featured on the plate.

CALENDAR PLATE, 1907, Florals, Advertising	38.00
1909, Four Corners, Iowa	35.00
1909, Months Border, Center Roses, Advertising Shelorta, Pa.	45.00
1909, Mountain Scene	20.00
1910, 18th–Century Couple	20.00
1910, Cherries, Rose Border, Carnation McNicol, 8 1/2 In.	29.00
1910, Cherub Center, Nippon	10.00
1910, Chicago, Roses	12.00
1910, Cupid Ringing In The New Year, Advertising	30.00
1910, Elgin, Illinois	25.00
1910, Lewellen, Nebraska, Advertising	21.00
1910, Poole Hardware Co., Duke, Oklahoma, 6 In.	35.00
1910, Star Union Brewing, Peru, Ill., Tin	75.00
1910, T.B.Woolard Grocery Store, Peoria, Ill.	16.00
1911, Dutch Winter Scene, Advertising, Trenton, N.J.	60.00
1911, Girl, On Jumping Horse	26.00
1911, Victorian Girl In Horseshoe Center, Republic, Mich.	22.00
1911–12, Compliments John Caldwell, Poppies, 8 1/2 In.	20.00
1912, Glider Plane	25.00
1912, Hot Air Balloon	75.00
1912, Sunbonnet	50.00
1912, Utica, Nebraska	18.00
1913, Smith & Brown, Quebec, Canada	25.00
1915, Panama Canal Map	12.00
1917, Peru, Ill., Advertising On Back	30.00
1918, Poppies	25.00
1919, Walnut Grove, Minn.	42.00
1920, Victory	28.00
1921, Tabor & Pukwana, So.Dakota	60.00
1921, Western Ammunition	85.00
1922, Dog Hunting Scene, 9 In.	35.00
1924, Hunting Scene	55.00 To 65.00
1928, Deer In Field, Williamsville, Illinois, 8 3/4 In.	50.00
1930, Dutch Boy & Dog, Sounemin, Illinois, 9 In.	60.00
1955, Good Luck, Fiesta	35.00
1961, Pink	10.50
1974, Staffordshire	10.00

Camark Pottery started in 1924 in Camden, Arkansas. Jack Carnes founded the firm and made many types of glazes and wares. The company was bought by Mary Daniel, who still owns the firm. Production was halted in 1983.

CAMARK, Ashtray, Blue, 1 1/2 In.	4.00
Ashtray, Maroon, Melon Rib, 3 1/4 In.	2.00
Basket, Black, 4 1/2 X 5 3/4 In.	6.00
Basket, Cabbage Leaf, Olive, Double, Center Handle, 4 1/2 X 5 1/2 In.	6.50
Bowl, Flower, Yellow, Melon Shape, Low, 6 In.	6.00
Bowl, Green, Leaf Shape, 12 X 9 1/2 In.	8.00
Bowl, Green, Melon Rib, Scalloped, 9 1/2 X 4 In.	14.00
Candlestick, Dolphin, Pair	25.00
Console Set, Double Bird, Frog, Yellow Matte, 4 Piece	45.00
Cornucopia, Cream, Horizontal Rib, 8 X 9 In.	8.00
Ewer, Blue, Small	10.00
Flower Frog, 2 Ducks, Green, 24 Holes, 9 X 6 In.	11.00
Pitcher, Black, Bead & Scroll, 3 1/4 In.	4.00
Pitcher, Maroon, Aladdin Lamp Style, Art Deco, 8 X 5 1/2 In.	10.00
Planter, Figural, Elephant, Black, Trunk Up, 6 1/4 X 5 1/2 In.	10.00
Strawberry Pot, Yellow, Hanging, 8 Cup, 4 3/4 X 5 1/2 In.	6.00
Vase, Brown, 7 In.	18.00
Vase, Gold Iridescent, 1926, 7 In.	145.00
Vase, White, Fluted, 10 X 12 In.	8.00
Vase, Yellow, Leaf Shape, Footed, Flared, Split Top, 5 In.	5.00
Wall Pocket, Blue, Label	25.00
Wall Pocket, Scoop, Green, Striker	32.50

Cambridge art pottery was made in Cambridge, Ohio, from about 1895 until World War I. The factory made brown glazed decorated wares with a variety of marks including an acorn, the name "Cambridge," the name "Oakwood," or the name "Terrhea."

CAMBRIDGE POTTERY, Teapot, Terra–Cotta, White Interior	25.00 To 45.00
Vase, Bud, Oakwood, Streaked Brown, Flowers, 7 1/4 In.	65.00
Vase, High Glaze, Yellow Streaks, Oakwood, 6 1/2 In.	58.00
Vase, Oakwood, Glossy Green, Gold Streaks	55.00

Cambridge Glass Company was founded in 1901 in Cambridge, Ohio. The company closed in 1954, reopened briefly, and closed again in 1958. The firm made all types of glass. Their early wares included heavy pressed glass with the mark "Near Cut." Later wares included Crown Tuscan, etched stemware, clear and colored glass. The firm used a C in a triangle mark after 1920.

CAMBRIDGE, see also Depression Glass

CAMBRIDGE, Aero Optic, Goblet	13.00
Alpine Caprice, Jug, Doulton, 6 In.Tumbler, 9 Piece	250.00
Apple Blossom, Bowl, Yellow, 10 In.	45.00
Apple Blossom, Box, Cigarette, Open, Brass Stand, Yellow	35.00
Apple Blossom, Candlestick, 3–Light, Yellow, Pair	85.00
Apple Blossom, Compote, Pink, 7 In.	85.00
Apple Blossom, Cordial, Yellow	75.00
Apple Blossom, Cup	5.00 To 10.00
Apple Blossom, Fruit Bowl, Amber, Liner	12.90
Apple Blossom, Goblet, Iced Tea, Crystal, 12 Oz.	18.00
Apple Blossom, Goblet, Water, Yellow	25.00
Apple Blossom, Jug, 80 Oz.	135.00
Apple Blossom, Sherbet, Yellow	18.00
Avocado, Candlestick, 3 1/2 In., Pair	110.00
Ball Shape Line, Decanter, Amethyst, Stopper, 32 Oz.	30.00
Ball Shape Line, Goblet, Heatherbloom Bowl, Crystal Stem	30.00
Ball Shape Line, Jug, Emerald Green, 80 Oz.	65.00
Bashful Charlotte, Flower Frog, Crystal, 11 In.	100.00
Bashful Charlotte, Flower Frog, Green, Frosted, 13 1/2 In.	175.00
Bashful Charlotte, Flower Holder, Crystal, 8 In.	35.00

Blossom Time, Mayonnaise, Footed 22.00
Buffalo Hunt, Console, Mystic Blue 250.00
Buzz Saw, Tumbler 12.50
Calla Lily, Candlestick, Crystal 8.00
Calla Lily, Candlestick, Yellow, Pair 38.00
Candlewick, Candlestick, Pair 18.00
Candlewick, Sugar 5.00
Candlewick, Tray, Center Handle 28.00
Caprice Alpine, Bowl, 4–Footed, 12 1/2 In. 68.00
Caprice Alpine, Candy Box, Cover, 3–Footed, 6 In. 45.00
Caprice, Ashtray, Blue, Triangular 10.00
Caprice, Ashtray, Shell Shape, Blue, Pink, Amber, 4 Piece 45.00
Caprice, Bonbon, Blue, Square Handle, 4 X 4 1/2 In. 16.00
Caprice, Bowl, Crystal, 10 1/2 In. 25.00
Caprice, Bowl, Footed, Alpine, Crystal, 13 1/4 In. 45.00
Caprice, Box, Cigarette, Blue 37.00
Caprice, Cabaret Plate, 4–Footed, 14 In. 55.00
Caprice, Candlestick, 3–Light, Blue, Pair 70.00
Caprice, Cocktail, Blue 20.00
Caprice, Creamer, Blue, Medium 13.00
Caprice, Cup & Saucer, Amber 35.00
Caprice, Cup & Saucer, Blue 30.00
Caprice, Cup & Saucer, Crystal 12.50
Caprice, Cup, Demitasse, Green 12.00
Caprice, Jelly, 2 Handles, Square, 4 In. 12.00
Caprice, Mayonnaise Liner, Blue, 6 1/2 In. 15.00
Caprice, Plate, Amber, 8 1/2 In. 18.00
Caprice, Plate, Blue, 8 1/2 In. 27.00
Caprice, Plate, Cabaret, Blue, 14 In. 65.00
Caprice, Plate, Crystal, 5 1/2 In. 3.50
Caprice, Plate, Lemon, Handle, 6 1/2 In. 7.00
Caprice, Relish, 5 Sections, 12 In. 45.00
Caprice, Saltshaker, Egg Shape 15.00
Caprice, Sherbet, Blue 27.50
Caprice, Sugar & Creamer, Footed, Blue, Pair 40.00
Caprice, Tumbler, Iced Tea, 12 Oz. 16.50
Caprice, Tumbler, Iced Tea, Footed, Thin 40.00
Caprice, Tumbler, Juice, Blue, 5 Oz. 30.00
Caprice, Vase, Crystal, 4 1/2 In. 35.00
Caprice, Vase, Green, 4 In. 40.00
Carmen, Ashtray, Card 60.00
Carmen, Brandy Snifter, 20 Oz. 50.00
Carmen, Cocktail, 3 1/2 In. 18.00
Carmen, Compote, Nude, 7 In. 160.00
Carmen, Decanter, Cordial, Red, Stopper, 30 Oz. 100.00
Carmen, Ivy Bowl, Red 55.00
Cascade, Candlestick, Emerald Green, Pair 45.00
Cascade, Cheese & Cracker, Green 56.00
Cascade, Plate, Luncheon, Green 10.00
Cattails & Heron, Cocktail Shaker, Cobalt Blue, Sterling, 10 In. 50.00
Chantilly, Bottle, French Dressing, Sterling Top 100.00
Chantilly, Candy Dish, 3 Sections, Amethyst 95.00
Chantilly, Candy Dish, Cover, 3 Sections, Sterling Holder 55.00
Chantilly, Cocktail Shaker .... 75.00 To 85.00
Chantilly, Cornucopia, Sterling Silver Base, 12 In. 145.00
Chantilly, Decanter, Sterling Base 110.00
Chantilly, Pitcher, Milk, Sterling Base, 6 In. 165.00
Chantilly, Plate, 10 1/2 In. 40.00
Chantilly, Sherbet, 4 1/4 In. 10.00
Chantilly, Tumbler, Iced Tea, Footed 16.00
Chantilly, Tumbler, Water, Crystal 13.95
Chantilly, Vase, Farber Ware, 10 In. 50.00
Chantilly, Wine, 2 1/2 Oz. 10.00
Cherry, Bowl, Handle, Blue, 9 In. 15.00

Cherry, Plate, Child's, Blue 7.50
Cherry, Tumbler, Blue, Footed, 4 3/8 In. 15.00
Claret, Nudes, Dark Green 120.00
Cleo, Candlestick, Amber, Pair 45.00
Cleo, Cup & Saucer, Blue 25.00
Cleo, Ice Bucket 50.00
Cleo, Plate, Blue, 8 In. 7.00
Cleo, Relish, Topaz, 2 Sections 18.00
Cleo, Tumbler, Water, Blue, Footed, 5 In. 45.00
Colonial, Creamer, Child's 4.00
Colonial, Sugar & Spooner, Cover, Child's .... 43.00 To 48.00
Columbia, Plate, 11 In. 6.00
Coronation, Bowl, Ruby, 8 In. 10.00
Coronation, Sherbet, Pink 3.25
Crown Tuscan, Candleholder, Swan, Pair 150.00
Crown Tuscan, Compote, Nude, 7 In. 140.00
Crown Tuscan, Dish, 4–Footed, Oval, Crystal, 8 In. 50.00
Crown Tuscan, Napkin Ring, Seashell, 7 1/2 X 9 In. 150.00
Crown Tuscan, Plate, Shell, 5 In. 23.00
Crown Tuscan, Swan, 8 1/2 In. 145.00
Crown Tuscan, Vase, Diane, Gold Etched, Large 65.00
Crown Tuscan, Vase, Keyhole, 12 In. .... 45.00 To 75.00
Cubist, Bowl, Pink, 6 1/2 In. 6.50
Cubist, Creamer, Green 6.50
Cubist, Saltshaker, Green 13.00
Cubist, Sherbet, Green 5.50
Decagon, Bowl, Amber, Handle, 6 In. 18.00
Decagon, Cup & Saucer, Blue 12.50
Decagon, Ice Bucket, Pink 40.00
Decagon, Ice Pail, Handle, Blue 55.00
Decagon, Plate, Amber, 6 In. 3.00
Decagon, Sandwich Tray, Center Handle, Pink 38.00
Decagon, Sugar & Creamer, Blue 23.00
Decagon, Sugar & Creamer, Tray, Green 35.00
Decagon, Sugar, Blue .... 7.00 To 8.00
Decagon, Sugar, Creamer & Tray, Green 35.00
Decagon, Sugar, Pink 6.00
Diane, Bowl, 4–Footed, Green, Large 40.00
Diane, Bowl, Flared, 4–Toed, 12 In. 35.00
Diane, Candy Dish 65.00
Diane, Goblet, 9 Oz. 22.00
Diane, Ice Bucket, Chrome Handles 55.00
Diane, Plate, 8 In. 14.00
Diane, Relish, 3 Sections, 8 In. 22.00
Diane, Relish, 5 Sections, 10 In. 75.00
Diane, Sherbet, Stem 11.00
Diane, Sherbet, Yellow 35.00
Diane, Vase, 6 In. 48.00
Doric Column, Candlestick, Jade Green, Pair 220.00
Draped Lady, Flower Frog, Amber, 8 1/2 In. 190.00
Draped Lady, Flower Frog, Blue, 8 1/2 In. .... 300.00 To 310.00
Draped Lady, Flower Frog, Green, 8 1/2 In. 139.00
Draped Lady, Flower Frog, Green, 9 In. .... 105.00 To 135.00
Draped Lady, Flower Frog, Peachblow, 8 1/2 In. 65.00
Draped Lady, Flower Frog, Pink, 8 1/2 In. 147.00
Eagle, Wing Spread, 6 In., Pair 145.00
Elaine, Bowl, 10 In. 27.00
Elaine, Bowl, Flat, 11 In. 45.00
Elaine, Jug, Ball, Tumblers, 80 Oz., 4 Piece 185.00
Elaine, Oyster Cocktail, 4 1/2 In. 15.00
Elaine, Plate, Gadroon, 8 In. 12.00
Elaine, Sugar & Creamer 25.00
Elaine, Tumbler, Crystal, Footed, 5 Oz. 10.00
Everglades, Compote, Topaz, C.1930 .... 75.00

Everglades, Plate, 16 In. 45.00
Everglades, Sugar & Creamer, Amber 45.00
Everglades, Vase, Square Top, 8 In. 25.00
Feather, Punch Cup 15.00
Fernland, Table Set, Child's, Green, 4 Piece 80.00
Figurine, Buddha, Green, 6 1/2 In. 150.00
Figurine, Swan, Pink, Small 20.00
Gadroon, Relish, 3 Sections, Green 10.00
Gadroon, Relish, Divided 10.00
Gadroon, Sugar & Creamer, Individual 14.00
Georgian, Tumbler, Green, 2 1/2 In. 8.00
Gloria, Candlestick, 3–Light, Pair 65.00
Gloria, Cocktail Shaker, Amber 225.00
Gloria, Cocktail, Green, Footed, 3 In. 20.00
Heatherbloom, Bottle, Oil, Green, Stopper, 7 3/4 In. 75.00
Heatherbloom, Jug, Ball, 80 Oz. 195.00
Heirloom, Compote, Pink, 9 In. 30.00
Helios, Candlestick, 7 In., Pair 90.00
Heliotrope, Candlestick, 7 1/2 In. 65.00
Heliotrope, Candlestick, 9 3/4 In., Pair 100.00
Heron, Flower Frog, 12 In. 149.00
Heron, Flower Frog, Crystal, 9 In. 60.00
Inverted Strawberry, Sugar, Open 15.00
Inverted Thistle, Water Set, Green, Gold Trim, 6 Piece 185.00
June, Tumbler, Ice Blue 32.40
Keyhole, Candlestick, Double, Crystal, 5 In. 15.00
Keyhole, Ivy Bowl, Ruby 60.00
Keyhole, Vase, Crystal, 10 In. 20.00
Kid, Flower Frog, Mocha 213.00
Kid, Flower Frog, Peach 249.00
Late Thistle, Pitcher, Water, Near Cut, Ruby Flashed, 8 1/4 In. 265.00
Laurel Wreath, Bowl, 8 In. 9.00
Laurel Wreath, Plate, 8 In. 6.00
Mandolin Lady, Flower Frog, Green, Bent Back, 9 In. 425.00
Mandolin Player, Flower Frog, Green 90.00
Manor Cut, Cordial 15.00
Martha, Bonbon, Handle, 7 In. 12.00
Martha, Candlestick, 4 In. 12.50
Martha, Oyster Plate 10.00
Meadow Rose, Goblet, Water, 10 Oz. 18.00
Minerva, Bonbon, Gold Encrusted, 7 In. 22.00
Minerva, Goblet, Water, Crystal 14.50
Moonlight, Bowl, Blue, 5 In. 20.00
Moonlight, Plate, Blue, 10 1/4 In. 47.50
Mt.Vernon, Celery, Oval, Crystal 15.00
Mt.Vernon, Decanter, Amber, 40 Oz. 60.00
Mt.Vernon, Mug, Carmen 38.00
Mug, Iridescent, Cobalt Blue Handles, 5 In., 6 Piece 155.00
Nude Stem, Champagne, Carmen 105.00
Nude Stem, Claret 105.00
Nude Stem, Cocktail, Carmen 75.00
Nude Stem, Cocktail, Ebony Stem 65.00
Nude Stem, Wine, Black Nude, Crystal Top & Base 75.00
Oval Star, Butter, Cover, Child's 32.00
Paneled Daisy, Celery 27.50
Patrician, Cookie Jar, Crystal 100.00
Pomona, Tray, Sandwich 85.00
Portia, Condiment Set, 5 Piece 50.00
Portia, Cordial, 1 Oz. 50.00
Portia, Goblet, 10 Oz. 15.00
Portia, Relish, 3 Sections, 12 In. 20.00
Primrose, Candlestick 85.00
Primrose, Candlestick, Tall 330.00
Rosalie, Cocktail, Black Stem 25.00

Rosalie, Goblet, Green Stem, 8 1/4 In. 12.00
Rosalie, Ice Tub 37.50
Rosalie, Seafood, Liner, Green 15.00
Rose Lady, Flower Frog, Crystal, 8 1/2 In. 200.00
Rose Lady, Flower Frog, Green, High Base, 9 5/8 In. 180.00
Rose Point, Basket, 2 Handles 38.00
Rose Point, Bonbon, Footed, 2 Handles 30.00
Rose Point, Bowl, Handles, Footed, 6 In. 40.00
Rose Point, Bowl, Mayonnaise, Ladle, Footed 45.00
Rose Point, Butter Tub, Cover 125.00
Rose Point, Butter, Cover, 1/4 Lb. 225.00
Rose Point, Candleholder, Keyhole, 6 In. 38.00
Rose Point, Candy Container, Cover, 3 Sections 85.00
Rose Point, Candy Dish, 3 Sections, 6 1/2 In. 55.00
Rose Point, Cocktail Shaker, Sterling Silver Base & Top 135.00
Rose Point, Compote, Cheese, Gold Trim 40.00
Rose Point, Cruet, Vinegar 150.00
Rose Point, Goblet, Carmen 45.00
Rose Point, Goblet, Water, 10 Oz. 22.00
Rose Point, Ice Bucket, Hammered Chrome Handle, Tongs 145.00
Rose Point, Juice, Footed 35.00
Rose Point, Lamp, Hurricane, Prisms, 18 In. 100.00
Rose Point, Mayonnaise Set, 3 Piece .... 60.00 To 65.00
Rose Point, Mustard 100.00
Rose Point, Nappy, 2 Handles, 8 1/2 In. 49.50
Rose Point, Plate, 4-Footed, 12 1/2 In. 75.00
Rose Point, Relish, 3 Sections, Handle, 15 In. 250.00
Rose Point, Relish, 5 Sections, 12 In. 48.00
Rose Point, Relish, Handle, 3 Sections, 6 1/2 In. 40.00
Rose Point, Sherbet, Low 22.00
Rose Point, Sherbet, Tall 30.00
Rose Point, Sugar & Creamer, Individual 45.00
Rose Point, Sugar & Creamer, Piecrust Edge 22.50
Rose Point, Tumbler, Iced Tea, Footed 27.00
Rose Point, Vase, 11 3/4 In. 149.75
Royal Lace, Butter, Cover, Cobalt Blue 395.00
Rubina, Vase, Sweet Pea, 7 In. 135.00
Seashell, Sugar & Creamer, Crystal 18.00
Shell, Sugar & Creamer 18.00
Snowflake, Cake Plate, Pink, 13 In. .... 40.00 To 65.00
Starlight, Cocktail, Original Label 9.00
Swan, Amber, 12 In. 45.00
Swan, Black, 3 1/2 In. 50.00
Swan, Black, 8 In. 250.00
Swan, Carmen, 6 1/2 In. 265.00
Swan, Crystal, 6 1/2 In. 28.00
Swan, Crystal, 8 In. 75.00
Swan, Dark Emerald, 8 1/2 In. 165.00
Swan, Ebony, 8 1/2 In. 98.00
Swan, Green, 3 In. 36.00
Swan, Milk Glass, 4 1/2 In. 135.00
Swan, Milk Glass, 8 1/2 In. 250.00
Swan, Peach, 3 In. 37.00
Swan, Pink, 6 1/2 X 8 In. 100.00
Sweetheart, Creamer 25.00
Sweetheart, Sugar, Near Cut 35.00
Tally Ho, Compote, Cheese, Red 26.00
Tally Ho, Cup & Saucer, Red 25.00
Tally Ho, Decanter, Amber 50.00
Tally Ho, Plate, Carmen, 2 Handles, 11 1/2 In. 30.00
Tally Ho, Sandwich Plate, 2 Handles, Amber, 11 1/2 In. 15.00
Tally Ho, Sugar & Creamer 12.00
Tally Ho, Tumbler, Blue, 10 Oz. 40.00
Tumbler, Amethyst, 2 Oz. 5.00

Twisted Optic, Pitcher Set, Royal Blue, 6 Piece 250.00
Vesper, Sherbet, Blue, Low 18.00
Wedding Ring, Plate, 8 In. 5.00
Wedding Ring, Sherbet, 4 1/2 In. 6.00
Wildflower, Bonbon, 7 In. 22.00
Wildflower, Bonbon, Footed, Gold Trim 25.00
Wildflower, Candy Dish, Cover, 4 Footed, Gold Trim 68.00
Wildflower, Compote, 7 In. 35.00
Wildflower, Cruet 69.00
Wildflower, Decanter, Gold Trim, 28 Oz. 180.00
Wildflower, Plate, Blue, Footed, Square, 6 In. 15.00
Wildflower, Plate, Crystal, 8 In. 19.00
Wildflower, Relish, 2 Sections, Gold Encrusted, 6 In. 20.00
Wildflower, Relish, 3 Sections, 6 1/2 In. 16.00
Wildflower, Relish, 5 Sections, Crystal, 12 1/2 X 10 1/2 In. 40.00
Wildflower, Torte Plate, 14 In. 35.00
Willow, Cheese & Cracker Set, Pink Etch On Pink, Oval, 12 In. 95.00

Cameo glass was made in much the same manner as a cameo in jewelry. Parts of the top layer of glass were cut away to reveal a different colored glass beneath. The most famous cameo glass was made during the nineteenth century.

CAMEO GLASS, see also under factory names

CAMEO GLASS, Bowl, Carved Flowers, Branches, Spray On Back, English, 4 In. 2250.00
Bowl, White, Pink Ground, Flowers, Leaves, Butterfly, 4 X 3 In. 1800.00
Cordial, Green On White, Cranberry On White, Vesier, 5 In., Pair 350.00
Dish, Brown Leaves, Burgun & Schverer, C.1900, 3 7/8 In. 2200.00
Lamp, Mushroom, Butterflies, French, 14 In. 900.00
Perfume Bottle, Cut Floral & Vine, Black Matte, Vandermark 125.00
Perfume Bottle, Pink Flowers On Clear, Sterling Top, English 1000.00
Plaque, Landscape, Pine Trees, Lake, Jacques Gruber, 7 X 16 In. 2500.00
Powder Box, St.Louis 225.00
Rose Bowl, Flowers, Leaves, 3-Color, English, 2 1/2 In. 950.00
Shade, Bullet Shape, Flowers, Gold Cut To White, Pebbly, 6 In. 225.00
Shade, Gaslight, Maidenhair Fern, Powder Blue, English, Pair 1500.00
Shade, Hanging, Red Leaves, Frosted Ground, French 450.00
Tumbler, Allover Cut Leaf, Vine & Flower, St.Louis, 3 1/2 In. 335.00
Tumbler, Burnt Orange, White Enamel Flowers, 3 3/4 In. 90.00
Tumbler, Florentine, Amber, White Enamel Flowers 55.00
Vase, Cranberry Red & Opaque White, English, 10 1/2 In. 1975.00
Vase, Flowers, Citron On Opaque White, English, 4 1/2 In. 750.00
Vase, Flowers, Citron, Opaque Top & Bottom, English, 4 7/8 In. 650.00
Vase, Flowers, Leaves, Stick Shape, Bun Base, De Vianne, 13 In. 625.00
Vase, Flowers, Purple Iridescent, Twisted Form, French, 8 In. 510.00
Vase, Frosted Cranberry, White Bands, Bottle Shape, 10 1/2 In. 1995.00
Vase, Frosted Etched Ground, Topaz, Honesdale, 16 In. 495.00
Vase, Lace, Shaded Pink, White Enameled, 10 1/2 In. 395.00
Vase, Lavender Lily-of-The-Valley, Frosted White, Arsall, 6 In. 475.00
Vase, Opaque Irises, Leaves, Frosted Blue, English, 12 In. 2250.00
Vase, Opaque White, Turquoise, Blue Ground, English, 3 3/8 In. 675.00
Vase, Raspberries & Foliage, Green, Lavender, Pink Ground, 4 In. 1400.00
Vase, Raspberries & Foliage, Pink, Arsall, 14 In. 1400.00
Vase, Sailing Ship, Lighthouse, Yellow, Michel, 10 1/4 In. 1215.00
Vase, Shamrocks, Acanthus Leaves, Chartreuse, English, 3 1/8 In. 675.00
Vase, Stick, Chartreuse Satin, White Floral, 4 1/8 In. 750.00
Vase, Sunset Scene, Trees & Mountains, Signed Barz, 10 1/4 In. 325.00
Vase, Turquoise Satin, Floral, White Lining, English, 2 1/4 In. 650.00
Vase, White Carved Flowers, Frosted Citron, English, 2 3/4 In. 550.00
Vase, White Irises, Frosted Blue, English, 12 In. 2250.00

CAMPAIGN, see Political

The Campbell Kids were first used as part of an advertisement for the Campbell Soup Company in 1906. The kids were created by Grace Drayton, a popular illustrator of the day. The kids were used

in magazine and newspaper ads until about 1951. They were presented again in 1966; and in 1983, they were redesigned with a slimmer, more contemporary appearance.

CAMPBELL KIDS, Bank, Mechanical	185.00
Book, Menu	25.00
Bowl, ABC	16.00
Cookbook, Help For The Hostess, 64 Pages	35.00
Cup, Yellow Handle & Hair, Plastic, Trademark	8.50
Doll, Bicentennial, 10 In., Pair	75.00
Doll, Composition, Effanbee, 12 In., Pair	250.00
Doll, Ideal Toy Co.	16.00
Plate, Buffalo	92.00
Postcard, C.1929	11.00
Puzzle, Grocery Shopping	20.00
Salt & Pepper	12.00 To 35.00
Spoon	12.50 To 15.00

Camphor glass is a cloudy white glass that has been blown or pressed. It was made by many factories in the Midwest during the mid–nineteenth century.

CAMPHOR GLASS, Biscuit Jar, Hand Painted Florals	75.00
Paperweight, Reclining Lion Shape, Gillinder, 5 5/8 In.	80.00
Powder Jar, Lovebirds On Cover	15.00
Vase, Chrysanthemum, Pierced Brass Foot, 7 1/2 In.	35.00

CANARY GLASS, see Vaseline Glass

A candlestick is designed to hold one candle; a candelabrum has more than one arm and holds many candles. The eccentricity of the English language makes the plural of candelabrum into candelabra.

CANDELABRUM, 2–Light, Bras De Lumiere, Regency, Ormolu, C.1720, 10 In., Pair	2300.00
2–Light, Cut Glass, Star, Prisms, Irish, 24 In.	2800.00
2–Light, Louis XVI, Beaded Pan, 18th Century, 14 In., Pair	5170.00
3–Light, Cut Glass, Chains of Faceted Glass, Prisms, 27 In.	9900.00
3–Light, Louis XV, Gilt, Bronze, Putto Holds Branch, 34 In., Pair	2750.00
3–Light, Napoleon III, Bronze, Female Support, 22 In., Pair	3300.00
3–Light, Shellwork Arms, Sheffield, C.1830, 21 5/8 In., Pair	1045.00
3–Light, Sterling Silver, Convertible, Gorham, 14 In., Pair	195.00
4 Looped Arms, Pendant Chains, Bronze & Slate, 25 1/2 In.	250.00
4–Light, Winged Female On Sphere, Bronze, Marble, 21 In., Pair	3300.00
5–Light, Griffins, Paw Feet, Bronze, 22 In., Pair	225.00
5–Light, Porcelain, Gold Design, German, Pair	450.00
5–Light, Sheffield, Removable Branches, C.1820	300.00
5–Light, Silver Plate, Circular Base, 19 In., Pair	1800.00
6–Light, Louis XVI, Bronze, Pedestal, Marble Plinth, 22 In., Pair	2200.00
7–Light, Napoleon III, Central Spire, Gilt Bronze, 28 In.	200.00
George III Style, Jasperware & Gilt Metal, 32 1/4 In.	1760.00
Neoclassical Style, Champleve, Gilt & Metal, 21 In., Pair	300.00

Candlesticks were made of brass, pewter, Sandwich glass, sterling silver, plated silver, and all types of pottery and porcelain. The earliest candlesticks, dating from the sixteenth century, held the candle on a pricket (sharp pointed spike). These lost favor because in times of strife the large church candlesticks with prickets became formidable weapons, so the socket was mandated. Candlesticks changed in style through the centuries and designs range from classic to rococo to Art Nouveau to Art Deco.

CANDLESTICK, 1–Light, Twisted Shaft, Sheffield, 4 1/2 In.	66.00
Adjustable Bobeche, Dish, Handle, India, 1877, 5 1/2 In., Pair	150.00
Altar, Foliate Bands, Bronze & Alabaster, 23 1/2 In., Pair	350.00
Banquet, Emerald Cut, 16 In.	185.00
Beta Model, Jarvie, Pair	6000.00
Brass Insert, Turned Walnut, 12 3/4 In., Pair	60.00
Brass, Cobras, Snakes Trail Forms, 7 X 8 In., Pair	60.00

Brass, Dolphin, 10 1/2 In., Pair 265.00
Brass, Faux Bobeche, Chicago, C.1910, 11 1/2 In., Pair 600.00
Brass, Hogscraper, Wedding Band, E.Clark, 8 1/2 In. 350.00
Brass, Multi–Knopped Column, Circular Drip Pan, 4, 30 In. 150.00
Brass, Push–Up, 11 3/4 In., Pair 80.00
Brass, Push–Up, 7 1/8 In., Pair 90.00
Brass, Push–Up, 8 1/2 In., Pair 50.00
Brass, Push–Up, Marked, The Queen of Diamonds, 11 1/4 In., Pair 210.00
Brass, Push–Up, Queen Anne, Scalloped Feet, Pair 800.00
Brass, Push–Up, Victorian, 8 7/8 In., Pair .... 60.00 To 80.00
Brass, Queen Anne, Petal Base 395.00
Brass, Twist Stem, Saucer Base, 6 1/2 In., Pair 50.00
Brass, Victorian, Push–Up, Polished, 8 7/8 In., Pair 150.00
Brass, Wide Base, Soldered Stem, 9 1/4 In., Pair 1050.00
Brass, Winged Serpent, Pair 40.00
Bronze, Art Nouveau Shape, Robert Jarvie, C.1903, 14 In., Pair 3400.00
Bronze, Cylindrical Socket, Flared, Drip Plate, 1910, 9 In., Pair 425.00
Bronze, Floriform, Disc Base, Bulbous Socket, Jarvie, 13 3/4 In. 1000.00
Bronze, Leaf & Floral Tri–Foot, Louis Philippe, 12 1/8 In., Pr. 400.00
Bronze, Louis Philippe, Gilt, Bobeche, Winged Putto, 13 In. 500.00
Bronze, Voluted & Stem, Cabochon & Butterfly On Stem, Pair 6600.00
Chamber, Ormolu, Malachite, Square Base, Vine, 3 1/2 In., Pair 1760.00
Chandelier & Sconce Set, Cut Glass, Metal, Lobmeyer, 24 In. 185.00
Coiled Cobra, Brass, 8 1/2 In., Pair 48.00
Cut Glass, Metal & Jasperware, English, 9 3/8 In., Pair 440.00
Flared Candle Cup, Shaped Stem, 18th Century, 7 In., Pair 2400.00
Gilt–Bronze & Cut Glass, Faceted Panels, C.1800, 13 In., Pair 4400.00
Grape Stalk Shape, Paw Feet, Gilt & Bronze, 10 1/2 In., Pair 1320.00
Hexagonal, Cut Design On Edge, Crystal, Pair 120.00
Hog Scraper, Push–Up, Tin Plate, 6 3/4 In. 125.00
Louis XVI, 4–Light, Ormolu, Acanthus Leaves Foot, 16 In., Pair 6050.00
Paktong, Square Candlecup, Fluted Standard, English, 10 In., Pr. 885.00
Peacock Stem, Red & Black Enameling, Brass, Indian, 12 1/2 In. 50.00
Picket, Embossed Copper, Silver Plate, 21 In., Pair 100.00
Pricket Form, Brass, 18th Century, English, Pair 450.00
Pricket, Embossed Copper & Brass, 28 In., Pair 550.00
Push–Up, Hog Scraper, Plated Tin, 5 1/2 In. 105.00
Push–Up, Iron, 5 1/4 In. 65.00
Push–Up, Victorian, Brass, 8 1/4 In., Pair 60.00
Push–Up, Wedding Stick, Iron & Brass, C.1830, 7 1/4 In., Pair 650.00
Queen Anne, Brass, Octagonal Base, 7 In. 200.00
Regency, Female Sphinx On Marble Platform, 10 /4 In., Pair 3850.00
Rust & Brown Enameled Iron, Saucer, Short Chamber 49.00
Sconce, 5 Cups, Hanging, Iron, Strawberries, Painted, 34 In. 105.00
Shaped Standard, Domed Base, Bell Metal, 5 3/4 In., Pair 3300.00
Telescoping, Sheffield, 8 1/2 In., Pair 125.00
Tinder Box, With Flint, Damper, Tin, 4 1/4 In. 65.00
Traveling, Brass, Saucer, Unscrews, 1860, 2 1/2 X 3 1/2 In. 49.00
Wooden Turned, Dark Finish, 24 In., Pair 135.00
Wrought Iron Twisted Stem, Tripod, Strap Feet, 17 1/2 In., Pair 85.00
    CANDLEWICK, see Imperial; Pressed Glass

Candy containers have been popular since the late Victorian era.
Collectors have long favored the glass containers; but now all types,
including tin and papier-mache, are collected. Probably the earliest
glass container sold commercially was the Liberty Bell made in 1876
for sale at the Centennial Exposition. Thousands of designs were
made until the cost became too high in the 1960s. By the late 1970s,
reproductions were being made and sold without the candy.

CANDY CONTAINER, Airplane, Spirit of Goodwill, Glass 130.00
  Amos 'N' Andy, Glass 450.00
  Amster Danner, Clear Glass 95.00
  Army Bomber 45.00
  Auto, Screw Cap 15.00

Auto, Streamlined, Amber	22.00
Automobile, Airflow, V.G.Co., Jeanette, Pa.	525.00
Automobile, Sedan, Glass, Clear, 12 Vents, 4 In.	65.00
Automobile, Victory Glass	20.00
Automobile, Yellow Paint, Tin Closure, Agadjanian, 6 Vents	70.00
Automobile, Coupe, Glass, Clear, Long Nose, Marked Avor, 3 In.	60.00
Baby Jumbo Pencil, Glass, Clear, Wooden Closure, 6 In.	50.00
Ball, Angel, Santa, Cabin, Composition, 4 1/2 In.	85.00
Basket, Grape, Milk Glass	50.00
Belsnickle, Red Coat, Feather Tree, Papier–Mache, 8 In.	375.00
Belsnickle, Red, Germany, 12 In.	450.00
Belsnickle, White Coat, Grey, Brown, Papier–Mache, 11 In.	550.00
Boat, Battleship, On Waves, 5 1/4 In.	85.00
Boat, Battleship, Victory Glass	22.00
Boat, Cruiser	35.00
Boot, Christmas, Glass, Paper Label	22.00
Boot, Glass, 3 In.	12.00
Boot, Glass, 6 In.	16.25
Boot, Papier–Mache, Red, Silver Holly On Side, 7 1/4 In.	20.00
Boot, Santa Boot, Plastic	10.00
Boot, Santa Claus Boot, Red, Snow, Papier–Mache, 8 In.	29.00
Candelabra, Glass, E & A	45.00
Candlestick, Colonial, Pair	25.00
Cannon, 4–Wheel Mount	475.00
Cat, Black, For Luck, 4 1/2 In.	70.00
Chicken On Egg, Germany	37.50
Chicken On Nest, Glass, Clear, 5 In.	12.00 To 32.00
Christmas Angel, Holds Feather Tree, Papier–Mache	125.00
Clock, Mantel	125.00
Clown, Nodder, Papier–Mache, Germany	125.00
Coach, Pulled By Rabbit, Cardboard, Whitman's	45.00
Dirigible, Los Angeles, 5 3/4 In.	200.00
Dog, Bulldog, 3 In.	10.00
Dog, Bulldog, Sitting, T.H.Stough	45.00
Dog, Cobalt Blue Glass	30.00
Dog, Hound Pup, Hat, Screw Lid, Geneva, Ohio	18.00
Dog, Hound, Frosted	14.00
Dog, Scotty, 5 1/4 In.	10.00 To 18.00
Dog, Scotty, Tin Closure, Crosetti Co.	3.50
Dog, Sitting, Glass, Metal Cap	10.00
Dog, With Basket In Mouth, Christmas, Papier–Mache, Germany	200.00
Duck, On Nest, Red Tin Bottom, Glass, 3 3/8 X 3 1/2 In.	42.50
Duck, Swimming	95.00
Duckling, Ugly, Closure	135.00
Easter Egg, Papier–Mache, Germany	27.00
Egg, Hand Painted Mother, Children, Christmas Tree, Wooden	75.00
Egg, Victorian Children, Wicker Basket, Tin, 2 X 2 1/2 In.	28.00
Father Christmas, French, 24 In.	875.00
Father Christmas, White, Gold Boots, French, 8 In.	375.00
Fire Engine, Clear Glass, 5 1/2 In.	45.00
Fire Engine, Ladders, Truck, Tin Wheel, 2 1/8 X 4 3/4 In.	70.00
Fish, Glass Eyes	250.00
Girl's Head, Bisque, Dove On Shoulder	350.00
Girl, Celluloid Face, Tree, Pressed Cotton, 4 X 3 In.	125.00
Girl, In Winter Garb, Bisque, 4 1/2 In.	60.00
Globe, World, On Nickel Plated Stand, Sticker	500.00
Goose With Chick	135.00
Gun, Fancy Grip, Soft Circles, 5 1/4 In.	30.00
Hat, Napoleon Style, Glass, With Candy	125.00
Hat, Uncle Sam, Milk Glass, Painted Stars & Stripes	85.00
Head, Bisque, Flocked Doves On Shoulder & Hem, 10 In.	350.00
Hen On Nest, Glass	17.00 To 30.00
Horn, Contents	15.00
Horse & Cart, 2 Wheels, 4 1/2 In.	10.00

Horse & Cart, 2 Wheels, 9 In.	14.00
Independence Hall, 5 1/2 X 4 1/2 In.	75.00
Iron, Clear Glass, 4 1/2 In.	15.00
Jeep, Cardboard Closure	14.00
Kettle, Boston Baked Beans, Simulated Leather Handle	165.00
Kewpie	160.00
Lantern, Aqua Globe	26.00
Lantern, Brass Frame, Pat.Apr.25, 1882	22.50
Lantern, Clear Glass, Ribbed Design, Metal Top, 4 1/2 In.	18.00
Lantern, Halloween, Germany	18.00
Lantern, Train	35.00
Lynn Doll Nurser, No Closure	20.00
Man's Head On Top Hat, Crepe Paper Hair, Germany	27.50
Monkey, Seated	40.00
Nude Baby	50.00
Orange Crate, Wooden, With Candy	10.00
Owl	60.00
Pencil, Glass, Original Candy	48.00
Policeman, Papier–Mache, 14 In.	150.00
Pumpkin	65.00
Puss 'N' Boots	75.00
Rabbit & Chick, In Baby Carriage, Closure, 1 3/4 X 4 In.	225.00
Rabbit & Hen, Next To Nest	80.00
Rabbit, Coming Out of Egg, With Umbrella, Papier–Mache	115.00
Rabbit, Eating Carrot, Glass, Clear, 4 1/2 In.	40.00
Rabbit, Fur, Glass Eyes, Concealed Candy Cache	270.00
Rabbit, Laid Back Ears, Glass, Clear, 2 In.	55.00
Rabbit, Nodder	25.00
Rabbit, Papier–Mache, Germany, 7 In. .... 15.00 To	20.00
Rabbit, Playing Golf, Papier–Mache, Germany	225.00
Rabbit, Plush, 11 In.	150.00
Rabbit, Pulling Cart, Wooden, Cardboard, Germany, 8 In.	120.00
Rabbit, Removable Head, 5 1/2 In.	43.50
Reindeer, Germany .... 65.00 To	395.00
Rocking Horse With Clown, Blue Glass	225.00
Rooster Pulling Cart, Porcelain	25.00
Safety First	335.00
Santa Claus, Bisque Head, Holding Bag, 1900's, 8 In.	450.00
Santa Claus, Body Opens In Center, Papier–Mache	39.50
Santa Claus, Chenille Covered, Cardbord Face	35.00
Santa Claus, Clay Face, Felt Clothes, Japan, 5 In.	150.00
Santa Claus, Composition Face & Hands, Riding Sleigh	450.00
Santa Claus, Germany, 1930s, 11 In.	135.00
Santa Claus, Molded Beard & Hair, Red Cap, 5 1/2 In.	125.00
Santa Claus, Next To Square Chimney, 3 5/8 In.	95.00
Santa Claus, On Chimney, Cotton Ball Body, 8 In.	35.00
Santa Claus, Papier–Mache, White, Red Highlights, 8 In.	45.00
Santa Claus, Plastic Head, 6 In.	35.00
Santa Claus, Riding Sleigh With Yule Logs	450.00
Santa Claus, Short Coat, Germany, 20 In.	1400.00
Santa Claus, White With Red, 1930s, 10 In.	48.00
Santa Claus, Wooden Head, White Cotton, Schoenhut, 15 In.	1250.00
Skookum, Glass	100.00
Snowman, Papier–Mache, Germany	85.00
Snowman, Red Top Hat, Holding Twig, 8 1/2 In.	80.00
Snowman, Wax, With Candy	25.00
Soda Fountain, Plastic, With Candy	40.00
Spark Plug .... 78.00 To	95.00
Speedboat, Glass	15.00
Stagecoach Wagon, Clear Glass, Metal Closure, 3 In.	50.00
Stork, Cotton	22.00
Stork, Glass Eyes, 30 In. .... 125.00 To	225.00
Stork, Papier–Mache, Germany	95.00
Suitcase, With Roosevelt Teddy Bears On Front, Milk Glass	135.00

Swan Boat	400.00
Teddy Bear, Milk Glass	85.00
Telephone, Glass, With Receiver	52.00
Telephone, Upright	32.00
Train	25.00
Train, Engine, Whistle, Contents	40.00
Train, Locomotive–888, Clear Glass, 4 1/5 In.	11.00
Train, Pink	15.00
Truck, Panel, Glass	12.00
Trunk, Milk Glass	110.00
Turkey, Papier–Mache, Germany	25.00 To 45.00
Willys Jeep	22.00 To 25.00

 Canes and walking sticks were used by every well–dressed man in the nineteenth century, but by World War I the style had changed. Today canes are used by few but the infirm. Collectors prize old canes made with special features such as hidden swords, whiskey flasks, or risque pictures seen through peepholes. Examples with solid gold heads or made from exotic materials such as walrus vertebrae are among the higher priced canes.

CANE, Blown Glass, Knob Baton Top, Clear, Maroon & Vaseline Swirled, 39 In.	135.00
Cap Bomb, Iron Ball Bomb Working End, Wooden Ball Knot Other End	55.00
Carved & Painted Eagle With Snake, 35 In.	5.00
Carved Bamboo, Carving of Warriors & Cattle, Japanese	110.00
Carved Ivory Handle, Bust of Pharaoh, Ebony, 35 1/2 In.	66.00
Carved Ivory Head of Negro	242.00
Carved Serpents, Liberty Cap, Red, Black, Brown & Natural, 36 In.	45.00
Carved Snake & Undraped Lady	907.00
Cranberry Glass, 15 3/4 In.	150.00
Gold Head, Inscribed Grace Chandler, Brunswick, Maine	1017.00
Handle, Floral, Unger	135.00
Handle, Gold, Amethyst Border, Presentation, Dated 1869, 4 In.	3300.00
Handle, Smoking Woman, Unger	135.00
Optic Rib, Thin Ruby Swirls Inside Full Length, Crook Handle, 47 In.	225.00
Riding Crop, William IV, Silver Seated Fox Handle, London, 1836, 31 In.	3850.00
Tri–Head, Bulldog, Cat & Owl	5.00
Vertabrae & Horn, Serpent's Head, 35 In.	395.00
Walking Stick, Bone Cutout On Handle, India	150.00
Walking Stick, Carved Hand Grasping Shaft That Forms Handle, 36 In.	35.00
Walking Stick, English, 37 In.	20.00
Walking Stick, Gold Mounted Knop, Engraved Foliage, Wood Shaft, 33 In.	825.00
Walking Stick, Ivory Uncle Sam's Head, Star Tortoiseshell Inlaid	1150.00
Walking Stick, Opera, Fist Shape Handle, Snuffbox In Handle, 43 In.	880.00
Walking Stick, Primitive Lion, Natural, 38 In.	35.00
Walking Stick, Sapling Growth, Vining Branch, Brown Paint, 32 In.	10.00
Walking Stick, Silver Fox Head Mount, 35 In.	1050.00
Walking Stick, Snake Coiled Around Shaft, 34 In.	150.00
Walking Stick, Snake Shape, Red–Brown, North Western R.R., 38 In.	20.00
Walking Stick, Stag Horn Handle, Silver Trim, 35 In.	40.00
Walking Stick, Sterling Silver Head of Punch, 37 1/2 In.	1200.00 To 1210.00
Walking Stick, Twisted, Aqua With Amber Center, Glass, 38 In.	45.00

Canton china is blue–and–white ware made near Canton, China, from about 1785 to 1895. It is hand decorated with Chinese scenes.

CANTON, Bowl, Reticulated Sides, Oval, 8 3/4 X 9 3/4 In.	275.00
Bowl, Scalloped Rim, Quatre–Foil Shape, 9 1/2 X 9 1/2 In.	250.00
Bowl, Vegetable, Fruit Finial On Cover, Rectangular, 10 In.	55.00
Bowl, Vegetable, Rain Cloud Border, 6 Lobes, Scenes, 9 3/4 In.	1000.00
Bowl, Vegetable, Rain Cloud Border, Floral Outside, 8 X 9 1/2 In.	325.00
Bowl, Vegetable, Rain Cloud Border, Oriental Scenes, 9 3/4 In.	1000.00
Chop Plate, Blue & White, Landscape Scene, 14 In. ....*Illus*	330.00
Chop Plate, Rain Cloud Border, Slanted Rim, 11 3/4 In.	800.00
Dish, Leaf, Rain Cloud Border, Canton Scenes, 8 X 6 In., Pair	400.00
Dish, Octagonal, Pierced Tray Insert, 19th Century, 11 X 9 In.	425.00

Dish, Serving, Oblong, 12 In. 275.00
Dish, Serving, Oval, 9 1/4 In. 200.00
Dish, Serving, Oval, 10 3/8 In. 325.00
Dish, Shrimp, Scene With Bridge, Rain Cloud Border, 10 1/2 X 10 In. 600.00
Fruit Basket, Undertray, Handleless, Center Scene, 9 1/4 X 11 In. 700.00
Fruit Basket, With Underliner, Bridge Scene Inside, 4 X 9 1/2 In. 900.00
Fruit Bowl, Scalloped Rain Cloud Border, Scene, 9 3/4 X 12 3/4 In. 1200.00
Jug, Cider, Domed Cover, Strap Handle, Scene, 19th Century, 8 In. 750.00
Jug, Cider, Foo Dog Lid, Intertwined Handles, 9 1/4 In. 1350.00
Pitcher, Figural, Fish, Tail Forms Handle, Cobalt Blue, 9 In. 155.00
Pitcher, Water, Scene With Bridge, 19th Century, 8 In. 700.00
Plate, 8 5/8 In. 600.00
Plate, Hot Water, 9 1/2 In. .... 150.00 To 245.00
Platter, Cut–Corner, 8–Sided, 14 3/8 X 11 1/2 In. 200.00
Platter, Orange Peel Glaze, 14 1/4 In. 350.00
Platter, Orange Peel Glaze, 16 In. 475.00
Platter, Oval, 11 In. 220.00
Platter, Rain Cloud Edge, Bridge Scene, Cut Corner, 15 X 18 1/2 In. 275.00
Punch Bowl, Rain Cloud Border, Bridge Scene, Marked, 16 1/4 In. 1600.00
Salad Bowl, Rain Cloud Border, Scenes Inside & Out, 10 In. 900.00
Sauceboat, Undertray & Spoon, Scalloped Sides, Scenes, 8 In. 400.00
Tea Caddy, Seascape, Rain Cloud Border, 6–Sided, Hexagonal, 6 3/4 In. 1000.00
Teapot, Ball Finial, Urn Shape, Scrolled Spout, 19th Century, 8 In. 700.00
Teapot, Domed Cover, Bud Finial, Canton Bridge, 5 3/4 In. 1550.00
Teapot, Domed Top, 9 In. 300.00
Tray, Reticulated Rim, Orange Peel Glaze, 10 1/4 In. 375.00
Tureen, Cover, Cut–Corner Body, Boar's Head Handles, 9 X 12 In. 450.00
Tureen, Cover, Rectangular Cut Corner, Boar's Head Handles, 10 In. 450.00
Tureen, Sauce, Undertray, Domed Cover, Leaf Finial, Scene, 4 1/2 In. 550.00
Tureen, Soup, Cover, Leaf Finial, Canton Scene, 8 1/2 X 11 3/4 In. 950.00
Tureen, Soup, Flower Finial, Scene, Sprig Handles, 11 X 13 1/2 In. 1900.00

Capo–di–Monte porcelain was first made in Naples, Italy, from 1743 to 1759. The factory moved near Madrid, Spain, reopened in 1771, and worked to 1834. Since that time the Doccia factory of Italy acquired the molds and is using the N and crown mark. Societe Richard Ceramica is a modern–day firm often referred to as Ginori or Capo–di–Monte. This company uses the crown and N mark.

CAPO–DI–MONTE, Bowl, Cherubs, Center Scene, Pierced For Hanging, 12 In. 85.00
Bowl, Seminude Cherubs, Scene Center, Pierced, Hanging, 12 In. 85.00
Cup & Saucer, Cherubs & Birds, Gold Trim 25.00
Dish, Relief Figures, Scalloped, 6 X 4 In. 25.00

Canton, Chop Plate, Blue & White,
Landscape Scene, 14 In.

Chinese Export, Aquarium, Famille Rose,
Peaches, Bats, 21 In.

Figurine Set, Goddess, 7 1/2 To 8 1/2 In., 12 Piece	330.00
Figurine, African Crowned Crane, 1 Foot, Water, Armani, 14 In.	150.00
Figurine, African Crowned Crane, Water Plants, Signed, 14 In.	150.00
Figurine, Angel, Playful Pose, 6 In., Pair	75.00
Figurine, Beggar, 4 3/4 In.	121.00
Figurine, Beggar, Umbrella Under Arm, Mending Coat, 12 In.	150.00
Figurine, Boy & Girl, On Teeter–Totter, Signed, 8 X 11 In.	125.00
Figurine, Chestnut Vendor, Old Woman, Copper Stove, 10 In.	250.00
Figurine, Classical Roman, 10 In., Pair	50.00
Figurine, French Soldier, 7 In., Pair	200.00
Figurine, Man In Wheelbarrow, Pushed By Man, 10 X 12 In.	350.00
Figurine, Pearl Fisherman, Bag In Hand, Signed, 9 1/2 In.	175.00
Figurine, Photographer, Girl, Seated On Brick Wall, 9 1/2 In.	150.00
Figurine, Sheep Herder & Woman, 12 In.	700.00
Group, Man With Cigar, Offering Bone To Dog, Marked, 9 In.	125.00
Lamp, Dolphins At Base, Metal, C.1920, 20 In.	75.00
Lamp, Embossed Dionysian, Fitted, 26 In.	60.00
Lamp, Table, Silk Shade, Pair	395.00
Lamp, Tiered, Foliage, Cherubs, Brass Dolphin Base, 1920s	115.00
Mug, Figural Handle	5.00
Neptune Group, 8 Sea Horses, 7 3/4 42 In., 12 Piece	688.00
Plaque, Battle Scenes, 5 3/8 X 9 5/8 In., Pair	209.00
Plate, Christmas, 1947	48.00
Platter, Draped Ladies, Marked, 19 In.	85.00
Urn, Cover, Cherubs, Grapes, Bacchus Head Handles, 15 In., Pr.	425.00

Captain Marvel was introduced in February 1940 in Whiz comic books. An orphan named Billy Batson met the wizard Shazam and whenever he said the magic word he was transformed into a superhero. A movie serial was released in 1940. The comic was discontinued in 1954. A second Captain Marvel appeared in 1966, a third in 1967. Only the original was transformed by shouting "Shazam."

CAPTAIN MARVEL, Button, Membership, Tin Litho, 1943	25.00
Dime Bank, 1948	150.00
Game, Puzzle, Captain Marvel's Picture, 1944	18.00
Game, Shazam	75.00
Magic Flute, On Original Card, 4 1/2 X 7 1/4 In.	40.00
Paper Doll, Book, Uncut	38.00
Tie Clip, Brass, Dimensional Portrait, 1940s	20.00
Toy, Clock, With Mary Marvel, Fuzzy Bear, Envelope, 1944	15.00
Toy, Race Car, Windup	165.00

Captain Midnight began as a radio show in September 1940. The first comic book appeared in July 1941. Captain Midnight was really the aviator Captain Albright, who was to defeat the Nazis. A movie serial was made in 1942 and a comic strip was published for a short time. The comic book Captain Midnight ended his career in 1948. The radio premiums are the prized collector memorabilia today.

CAPTAIN MIDNIGHT, Book, Big Little Book, and The Secret Squadron	20.00
Book, Joyce of The Secret Squadron, Hardcover	7.00
Booklet, Trick & Riddle, Skelly Oil	15.00
Code–O–Graph	75.00
Coin, 1940	15.00
Coin, Medal of Membership, Picture of Midnight	6.50
Decoder, 1941	38.00
Decoder, 1946	75.00
Decoder, 1947	35.00
Decoder, 1949	50.00
Display, Skelly Oil, Die Cut Cardboard, 1939, 6 Ft.11 In.	828.00
Flight Wings, Mysto–Magic Weather, Brass, Skelly Oil, 1939	20.00
Magic Book, 1939	15.00
Medal of Membership, 1940	14.00
Mug, Ovaltine, 15th Anniversary	35.00

Mug, Shake–Up	50.00
Pamphlet, Captain Midnight Membership, Ovaltine, 1941	115.00
Patch, 15th Anniversary, In Sealed Wrapper, 1957	40.00
Poster, Die Cut Cardboard, Skelly Oil Sponsor, 1939	828.00
Sign, Radio Display, 1930s, 3 X 7 Ft.	825.00
Spinner Disc, Patsy, Ramsy, Metal, Skelly Oil, 1940	14.00
Toy, Decoder	20.00
Trick Book	8.00
Whistle, Code–O–Graph, Red & Blue Plastic, 1947	38.00

CARAMEL SLAG, see Chocolate Glass

The cards listed here include advertising cards, greeting cards, baseball cards, playing cards, valentines, and others. Color pictures were rare in the nineteenth century, so companies gave away colorful cards with pictures of children, flowers, products, or related scenes that promoted the company name. These were often collected and stored in albums. Greeting cards are also a nineteenth–century idea that has remained popular. Baseball cards also date from the nineteenth century when they were used by tobacco companies as giveaways. The gum cards were started in 1933, but it was not until after World War II that the bubble gum cards favored today were produced. Today over 1,000 cards are issued each year by the gum companies.

CARD, see also Postcard

CARD, Advertising, A & P, Die–Cut, Grandmother In Boat, Late 1800s, Large	20.00
Advertising, Arbuckle's Coffee	6.00
Advertising, Arm & Hammer, Duck Series No.4, 30 Piece	25.00
Advertising, Austen's Forest Flower Cologne, Girl, Picking Flowers	7.00
Advertising, Best Tonic, Phillip Best Brewing Co., 1880s, 19 X 25 In.	20.00
Advertising, Boraxine, Cat, 1882	10.00
Advertising, Brooke Bond Tea, Famous People, 1969, Set of 50	17.50
Advertising, C.Foster Clothiers, Repeal of Silver Purchase Law, 1894	7.50
Advertising, Dr.Morse's Indian Root Pills, Girl With Puppies	6.00
Advertising, Edward Sharp & Sons, Magic Trick, 1970, Set of 25	10.00
Advertising, Everett Piano, People, Window, Piano Player	25.00
Advertising, Great Republic, Clipper Ship, 8 X 5 3/4 In.	4180.00
Advertising, Ivorine, Wonderful Cleanser, Lady, Donaldson Bros., Litho	4.00
Advertising, J & P Coats Thread, 1880, 2 1/2 X 4 In.	17.50
Advertising, Larkin, Pictures of Presidents, 23 Piece	100.00
Advertising, McKelvey Department Store, Black Buggy Driver	12.50
Advertising, Mechanical, Royal Baking Powder	35.00
Advertising, Orphan Boy	3.00
Advertising, Quakeress Cigar	4.00
Advertising, Sensation Cut Plug	7.50
Advertising, Turkish Trophies Cigars	10.00
Advertising, Union Pacific Tea Company, We Had A High Old Time	4.00
Advertising, Wm.Kimball & Co., Cigarettes, 1880s, 4 X 6 1/2 In.	12.50
Advertising, Woman Suffrage, Hold To Light	22.00
Advertising, Zu Zu Ginger Snaps, Trolley, Framed	400.00
Baseball, Chili Davis, Topps, 1982	1.25
Baseball, Complete Set 589, Topps, 1961	380.00
Baseball, Cy Young, Polar Bear Tobacco Co.	115.00
Baseball, George Herman, Babe Ruth, Big League Chewing Gum, No.80	440.00
Baseball, Hank Aaron, Topps, 1956	85.00
Baseball, Hank Aaron, Topps, 1966	30.00
Baseball, Jesse Barfield, Rookie, Topps, 1982	4.00
Baseball, Mickey Mantle, Bowman, 1954	155.00
Baseball, Mickey Mantle, Topps, 1961	35.00
Baseball, Pee Wee Reese, Topps, 1958	16.00
Baseball, Pete Rose, Topps, 1965	125.00
Baseball, Reggie Jackson, Topps, 1969	90.00
Baseball, Roger Maris, Topps, 1968	7.00
Baseball, Sandy Koufax, Topps, 1955	165.00
Baseball, Satchell Paige, Topps, 1953	110.00

Baseball, Willie Mays, Jello, 1963 .... 10.00
Christmas, Winchester, Canada, 1950 .... 6.00
Cigarette, Mitchell, Wonderful Century, 1937, Set of 50 .... 60.00
Cigarette, Ogden's Gold, Lord Baden Powell 5.00
Cigarette, Ogden's Gold, Sarah Bernhardt 5.00
Cigarette, Ogden's Gold, Winston Spencer Churchill 3.50
Cigarette, Players, Firefighting Appliances, 1930, Set of 50 .... 150.00
Cigarette, Players, Flag K7 Military, Color, 1928, Set of 50 .... 37.50
Football, Set, Topps, 1958, 132 Piece 170.00
Lobby, Babe Ruth Story, 1948 .... 45.00
Lobby, Big Store, 3 Marx Brothers, 1941 .... 120.00
Lobby, Gone With The Wind, 1947 .... 200.00
Lobby, House of Wax, 1955 .... 42.00
Lobby, Klondike Annie, 1936, Mae West 247.50
Lobby, Mister Roberts, 1955 .... 17.50
Lobby, My Little Chickadee, Mae West, W.C.Fields, 1940 .... 275.00
Lobby, Red River, John Wayne 35.00
Lobby, Seven Year Itch, Mariyln Monroe, Tom Ewell 55.00
Lobby, Spellbound, Hitchcock, Ingrid Bergman, Gregory Peck 80.00
Lobby, Suspicion, Cary Grant, Joan Fontaine, 1941 .... 65.00
Lobby, That Hagen Girl, Ronald Reagan & Shirley Temple 85.00
Lobby, The Fight Never Ends, Joe Louis 50.00
Lobby, Three Stooges 68.00
Playing, Alaska Steamship 25.00
Playing, Army & Navy Game, Anma Card Co., 1941 .... 67.00
Playing, Autumn Scene, Rockwell 17.50
Playing, B.P.Grimaud Paris, Dated April 1890, 53 Cards 125.00
Playing, Bluebird Bus System, 1947 .... 22.00
Playing, Columbian Souvenir, Clark, 1893 .... 57.00
Playing, Edison–Mazda, Reveries, Parrish, Complete 225.00
Playing, Frisco Railway, Red 15.00
Playing, Great Lakes, Souvenir, 1909 .... 40.00
Playing, Harlequin Transformation, Tiffany, 1879 .... 608.00
Playing, Jack Daniel's, Gentlemen's, 1972, Double Deck 38.00
Playing, Marilyn Monroe, 1956 .... 10.00
Playing, Marilyn Monroe, Nude, Brown & Big, 1950 .... 48.00
Playing, Niagara Falls Souvenir, Oval Photos, Niagara PCC, 1901 ...... 38.00
Playing, Old Crow, Box 25.00
Playing, Pan–American Expo, Oval Scenes, 1901 .... 76.00
Playing, Panama Souvenir, Inaugural Edition, 1910, Box 86.00
Playing, Peanuts, Hallmark, 1960 .... 27.00
Playing, Pep Boys, Caricature, Manny, Moe & Jack, Arrco, 1930, Box 114.00
Playing, Pompeian Massage Cream, 1915 .... 85.00
Playing, Reveries, Parrish 95.00
Playing, Ringling Bros. & Barnum & Bailey Circus, Miniature 12.00
Playing, Santa Fe Trains, Congress 16.00
Playing, Schiaparelli, Double Deck, Unopened, Box 18.00
Playing, Southern Pacific Lines, Barkalow, 1935, Sealed In Box 57.00
Playing, Southern Pacific Lines, Oval Photos, 1920, Part Box 86.00
Playing, Trophy Whist No.39, USPCC, 1895, Box 67.00
Playing, Union Made Cigars, Advertising Back, PCC, 1890 .... 29.00
Playing, Washington, D.C., Each Card Has Scene, 1925 .... 40.00
Playing, White Pass & Yukon Route, Black, White Photos, 1900 .... 86.00
Valentine, A Present From Barbados, Sailor's, Wooden Hinged Case 1350.00
Valentine, Black Cat, Die Cut, Legs, Tail & Head Move, 5 1/2 In. 8.50
Valentine, Boy, Dressed As Pilot, Movable 12.00
Valentine, Boy, Jester's Clothes, Poem, Marcus Ward, 1878, 4 X 5 In. 14.00
Valentine, Calling Card, Flowers, Gedenke Mein, Howland, 2 X 3 5/16 In. .. 10.00
Valentine, Drawing, Red, Black Ink, He's Given, Heart, Framed, 7 X 9 In. 300.00
Valentine, Embossed Roses & Heart, Hand Written Verse, 3 X 3 7/8 In. 20.00
Valentine, Folder, Silver & White Lace, Bluebird, Meek, 4 X 5 5/8 In. 35.00
Valentine, Human Hair Circlettes, Hearts, Ribbons, 19th Century, 4 Pc. 500.00
Valentine, Lilies & Leaves, Signed Meek, Dated 1855, 4 3/4 X 7 In. 30.00
Valentine, Medallion, Embossed, Hand Written Verse, Meek, 1860, 6 In. 52.00

Valentine, Movable Face, Tuck	10.00
Valentine, Popeye, 1943	5.00
Valentine, Punch & Judy, Mechanical	10.00
Valentine, Radio & Children, Germany	45.00
Valentine, Roses & Ferns Wreath, Printed, Howland, 2 5/8 X 3 3/4 In.	8.00
Valentine, Sachet, Gold & White Cameo Lace Allover, Doves, 3 X 4 In.	20.00
Valentine, Sachet, Lovers, Cameo Lace, Signed Mansell, 2 3/4 X 4 In.	35.00
Valentine, Sachet, Padded, Lace Border, Verse, 3 1/4 X 4 3/4 In.	30.00
Valentine, Sleepy Playing Accordion, 1938	25.00
Valentine, Snow White, Mechanical, 1938	32.00
Valentine, White Cameo Lace, Horizontal, Howland, 4 7/8 X 3/3/8 In.	18.00
Valentine, White Lace, Girl, Puzzle, Signed Whitney, 3 X 4 1/2 In.	13.00
Velentine, Boy, Mechanical, Stand Up, 1910, 7 In.	5.75

CARDER, see Aurene; Steuben

Carlsbad, Germany, is a mark found on china made by several factories in Germany. Most of the pieces available today were made after 1891.

CARLSBAD, Biscuit Jar, Hand Painted Red Iris	95.00
Box, Angels, Gold On Green	175.00
Creamer	95.00
Plate, Portrait, Victorian Lady, Signed Marie Lecxinska, 8 In.	30.00
Plate, Salad, Pink & Blue Flowers Band, Gold Trim, Set of 6	24.00
Platter, Fish, Oval, 9 X 20 1/2 In.	66.00
Tureen, Pink & Blue Flowers Band, Gold Trim, Round	25.00
Vase, Gourd Shape, Stick Neck, Floral Design, Marked, 12 1/2 In.	225.00
Vase, Portrait of Monk Reading Newspaper, Handles, 8 1/2 In.	65.00

Carlton ware was made at the Carlton Works of Stoke-on-Trent, England, about 1890. The firm traded as Wiltshaw & Robinson until 1957. It was renamed Carlton Ware Ltd. in 1958.

CARLTON WARE, Ashtray, Man Smoking, Funny Verse	30.00
Biscuit Jar, Multicolored Florals, Silver Plated Fittings	110.00
Bowl, Royal Rouge, 1920s, 4 1/2 In.	85.00
Box & Ashtray Set, Pagoda, Enameled, Cobalt Blue, Gold, 3 Piece	85.00
Candlestick, Cream Luster, Tied Bow, 4 In., Pair	35.00
Dish, Rouge Royale, Art Deco Gold Trim, Oval, 10 1/2 In.	115.00
Fruit Bowl, Applied Yellow & Brown Bananas, 9 In.	36.00
Jam Jar, Art Deco, Orange	65.00
Pitcher, Buttercup Flowers, Lime Green, 5 In.	35.00
Rose Bowl, 4 In.	75.00
Salad Set, Flowers Inside & Out of Bowl, 9 3/4 In., 3 Piece	385.00
Sardine Holder, Silver Plate	60.00
Sugar & Creamer	23.00
Sugar Shaker, Figural, Sheaves of Wheat, Marked, 5 In.	40.00
Vase, Rouge Royale, Pink Luster Inside, Gold Handle, 7 In.	175.00

Carnival, or taffeta, glass was an inexpensive, pressed, iridescent glass made from about 1907 to about 1925. Over 1,000 different patterns are known. Carnival glass is currently being reproduced.

CARNIVAL GLASS, see also Northwood

CARNIVAL GLASS, Acanthus, Bowl, Amethyst, 7 1/2 In.	80.00
ACORN BURRS & BARK, see Acorn Burrs	
Acorn Burrs, Punch Set, Marigold, 7 Piece	675.00
Acorn Burrs, Sauce, Purple	40.00
Acorn Burrs, Spooner, Amethyst	125.00 To 150.00
Acorn Burrs, Table Set, Purple, 4 Piece	595.00
Acorn Burrs, Tumbler, Purple	60.00 To 65.00
Acorn Burrs, Water Set, Amethyst, 5 Piece	700.00
Acorn Burrs, Water Set, Marigold, 5 Piece	650.00
Acorn, Bowl, Marigold, 7 1/4 In.	58.50
Acorn, Bowl, Marigold, 7 5/8 In.	25.00
Advertising, Bowl, Gevuriz Brothers, Amethyst	200.00
Advertising, Bowl, Isaac Benesch & Sons, Amethyst	245.00

AMARYLLIS, see Tiger Lily
AMERICAN BEAUTY ROSES, see Wreath of Roses
APPLE & PEAR, see Two Fruits
APPLE BLOSSOM BORDER, see Blossoms & Band

Apple Blossom Twigs, Plate, Flat, Peach	375.00
Apple Blossoms, Bowl, Marigold, 7 In.	45.00
Apple Tree, Pitcher, Water, Marigold	185.00
Apple Tree, Tumbler, Marigold	25.00 To 45.00
Apple Tree, Water Set, White, 4 Piece	750.00
April Showers, Vase, Green, 12 In.	42.00

ARGONAUT SHELL, see Nautilus
AUTUMN, see Wild Berry

Autumn Acorns, Bowl, Amethyst, 8 3/4 In.	45.00
Autumn Acorns, Bowl, Red, 7 In.	200.00

BANDED MEDALLION & TEARDROP, see Beaded Bull's Eye

Basket, Bushel, Aqua	425.00
Basket, Bushel, Blue	135.00
Basket, Bushel, Round, Ice Green	235.00

BATTENBURG LACE NO.1, see Hearts & Flowers
BATTENBURG LACE NO.2, see Captive Rose
BATTENBURG LACE NO.3, see Fanciful

Beaded Cable, Candy Dish, Marigold	35.00
Beaded Cable, Rose Bowl, Aqua	325.00 To 350.00
Beaded Cable, Rose Bowl, Green	70.00 To 75.00
Beaded Cable, Rose Bowl, White	485.00

BEADED MEDALLION & TEARDROP, see Beaded Bull's Eye

Beaded Shell, Mug, Purple	95.00
Beaded Shell, Tumbler, Amethyst	65.00
Beaded Shell, Tumbler, Purple	30.00
Beads, Bowl, Green, 7 1/2 In.	70.00
Birds & Cherries, Bonbon, 2 Handles, Blue	135.00
Birds & Cherries, Bowl, Blue, 9 In.	475.00

BIRDS ON BOUGH, see Birds & Cherries
BLACKBERRY A., see Blackberry
BLACKBERRY B., see Blackberry Spray

Blackberry Spray, Hat, Aqua	75.00
Blackberry Spray, Hat, Marigold	40.00
Blackberry Wreath, Bowl, Amethyst, 6 In.	68.00
Blackberry Wreath, Bowl, Blue, Ruffled, 10 In.	550.00
Blackberry, Basket, Marigold, Open Edge	32.50
Blackberry, Bowl, White, 7 In.	50.00
Brocaded Palms, Dish, 2 Handles, Ice Green, 7 In.	75.00
Broken Arches, Punch Set, Purple, 8 Piece	925.00
Butterfly & Berry, Berry Bowl, Master, Marigold	50.00
Butterfly & Berry, Berry Set, Blue, 5 Piece	255.00
Butterfly & Berry, Bowl, Footed, Marigold, 4 1/2 In.	30.00
Butterfly & Berry, Bowl, Footed, Marigold, 8 1/2 In.	50.00
Butterfly & Berry, Bowl, Marigold, 8 1/2 In.	65.00
Butterfly & Berry, Tumbler, Blue	35.00 To 47.00
Butterfly & Berry, Vase, Marigold, 6 In.	35.00
Butterfly & Berry, Water Set, Blue, 7 Piece	510.00
Butterfly & Berry, Water Set, Marigold, 11 Piece	450.00
Butterfly & Fern, Tumbler, Amethyst	40.00
Butterfly & Fern, Tumbler, Green	50.00
Butterfly & Fern, Water Set, Green, 7 Piece	850.00

To clean carnival glass, use a mixture of 1/2 cup ammonia and 1/8 cup white vinegar.

Butterfly & Fern, Water Set, Marigold, 7 Piece 695.00
    BUTTERFLY & GRAPE, see Butterfly & Berry
    BUTTERFLY & PLUME, see Butterfly & Fern
    BUTTERFLY & STIPPLED RAYS, see Butterfly
Butterfly, Bonbon, Purple 45.00
Buzz Saw, Cruet, Green 175.00
Buzz Saw, Cruet, Green, Miniature 525.00
Cable, Hatpin Holder, Ice Blue 1300.00
    CACTUS LEAF RAYS, see Leaf Rays
Captive Rose, Plate, Amethyst, 9 In. 185.00
    CATTAILS & FISH, see Fisherman's Mug
    CATTAILS & WATER LILY, see Water Lily & Cattails
Chatelaine, Tumbler, Purple 400.00
Cherry & Cable, Creamer, Marigold 175.00
Cherry & Cable, Sugar, Cover, Marigold 150.00
Cherry Chain, Plate, Marigold, 6 1/4 In. 45.00
    CHERRY WREATHED, see Wreathed Cherry
Cherry, Compote, Marigold, 3 Footed 60.00
Cherry, Creamer, Marigold 65.00
    CHRISTMAS CACTUS, see Thistle
    CHRISTMAS PLATE, see Poinsettia
    CHRISTMAS ROSE & POPPY, see Six–Petals
    CHRYSANTHEMUM WREATH, see Ten Mums
Chrysanthemum, Bowl, Marigold 50.00
Circled Scroll, Whimsey, Purple, 7 In. 90.00
Coin Dot, Bowl, Amethyst, 7 In. 45.00
Coin Dot, Bowl, Ruffled, Amethyst, 9 1/2 In. 68.00
Corinth, Bowl, Aqua, 7 In. 85.00
Corn Vase, Vase, White 395.00
Cosmos & Cane, Butter, Cover, Amber 235.00
Cosmos & Cane, Table Set, Amber, 4 Piece .... 575.00 To 595.00
Cosmos & Cane, Tumbler, Amber 125.00
Cosmos, Bowl, Green, 6 In. 60.00
Courthouse, Bowl, Ruffled, Amethyst 425.00
Crackle, Water Set, Dome Foot, Marigold, 7 Piece 175.00
Cut Arcs, Dish, Ruffled, Marigold, 8 1/2 In. 35.00
Dahlia, Berry Set, White, 5 Piece 595.00
Dahlia, Creamer, White 145.00
    DAISY & LATTICE BAND, see Lattice & Daisy
Daisy & Plume, Rose Bowl, Marigold 90.00
Daisy & Plume, Rose Bowl, Purple 95.00
Dandelion, Mug, Blue 395.00
Dandelion, Tumbler Set, Marigold, 6 Piece 200.00
Diamond & Rib, Vase, Marigold, 10 In. 25.00
Diamond & Sunburst, Wine, Marigold 25.00
Diamond Lace, Bowl, Amethyst, 5 In. 15.00
Diamond Lace, Bowl, Marigold, 9 In. 32.00
Diamond Lace, Bowl, Ruffled, Purple, 9 In. 45.00
Diamond Lace, Water Set, Amethyst, 7 Piece 400.00
    DIAMOND POINT & DAISY, see Cosmos & Cane
Diamond Point, Vase, Purple, 9 In. 57.50
Diamond Ring, Bowl, Marigold, 9 In. 40.00

Candlesticks will melt or even explode if candles burn too low. Support the arm of a candelabrum when putting in the candles.

To remove easily wax that has dripped on a candlestick, put the candlestick in the freezer for about an hour. The wax will flake off.

Diamond Ring, Bowl, Purple, 9 In. 57.50
   DOGWOOD & MARSH LILY, see Two Flowers
Dogwood Spray, Bowl, Amethyst, Domed Base 65.00
Dogwood Spray, Compote, Purple 40.00
Double Star, Tumbler, Green 60.00
Double–Stem Rose, Bowl, Purple, 8 1/4 In. 70.00
Dragon & Lotus, Bowl, Footed, Amethyst, 9 In. 125.00
Dragon & Lotus, Bowl, Footed, Blue, 9 In. 45.00
Dragon & Lotus, Bowl, Marigold, 9 In. 20.00
   DRAPE & TIE, see Rosalind
Dutch Twins, Ashtray 25.00
   EGYPTIAN BAND, see Round–Up
   EMALINE, see Zippered Loop Lamp
Embroidered Mums, Bowl, Blue, 9 In. 350.00
   FAN & ARCH, see Persian Garden
Fan–Tail, Bowl, Marigold, 3–Footed, 9 In. 50.00
Fanciful, Bowl, White, 8 1/2 In. 135.00
Fanciful, Plate, Marigold, 9 In. 70.00
Fanciful, Plate, Purple, 9 In. 225.00
Fashion, Pitcher, Purple 600.00
Fashion, Punch Cup, Marigold 15.00
Fashion, Punch Set, Marigold, 12 Piece 250.00
Fashion, Tumbler, Marigold 18.00
Fashion, Water Set, Marigold, 7 Piece 230.00
   FEATHER & HOBSTAR, see Inverted Feather
   FENTON'S ARABIC, see Illusion
   FENTON'S BUTTERFLY, see Butterfly
   FIELD ROSE, see Rambler Rose
Fine Cut & Roses, Candy Dish, Footed, Green 65.00
Fine Cut & Roses, Candy Dish, Footed, Purple 45.00
Fine Cut & Roses, Rose Bowl, Purple 85.00
Fine Rib, Bowl, Green, 10 1/2 In. 60.00
Fine Rib, Vase, Blue, 9 In. 42.00
   FINECUT & STAR, see Star & File
   FISH & FLOWERS, see Trout & Fly
Fisherman's Mug, Mug, Purple 75.00
   FISHERMAN'S NET, see Treebark
Fishscale & Beads, Plate, Ruffled, White, 7 In. 60.00
   FLORAL & DIAMOND POINT, see Fine Cut & Roses
Floral & Grape, Water Set, Marigold, 4 Piece 175.00
Floral & Grape, Water Set, White, 5 Piece .... 650.00 To 695.00
   FLORAL & GRAPEVINE, see Floral & Grape
   FLORAL & WHEAT SPRAY, see Floral & Wheat
   FLUFFY BIRD, see Peacock
Flute, Bowl, Purple, 3 1/2 In. 68.00
Flute, Butter, Cover, Green ....95.00 To 105.00
Flute, Compote, Marigold, 6 In. 400.00
Flute, Toothpick, Amethyst 36.50
Flute, Toothpick, Marigold 65.00
Flute, Vase, Amethyst, 9 In. 82.00
Folding Fan, Compote, Peach, 7 3/4 In. 95.00
Four Flowers, Bowl, Purple, 9 1/4 In. 135.00
Frosted Block, Plate, Clambroth, 9 In. 35.00
Fruit Salad, Punch Set, Marigold, 7 Piece .... 350.00 To 500.00
Fruits & Flowers, Bonbon, Aqua 475.00
Fruits & Flowers, Bonbon, Handle, Blue, Basketweave 125.00

To remove a dried cork that has fallen inside a bottle: pour some household ammonia in the bottle and let it set for a few days. Most of the cork should dissolve and can easily be removed.

Fruits & Flowers, Bonbon, Pedestal, Handles, Blue ....90.00 To 110.00
Fruits & Flowers, Bowl, Amethyst, 9 1/2 In. 55.00
Garden Path Variant, Chop Plate, Peach, 11 In. 325.00
Garland, Rose Bowl, Blue 65.00
Golden Grapes, Bowl, Marigold, 7 In. 35.00
Golden Harvest, Decanter, Stopper, Marigold 125.00
Golden Harvest, Wine, Marigold 20.00
Golden Wedding, Bottle, Whiskey, Marigold, 1 Pt. 25.00
Good Luck, Bowl, Fluted, Cobalt Blue, 8 3/4 In. 225.00
Good Luck, Bowl, Fluted, Marigold, 8 3/4 In. .... 145.00 To 150.00
Good Luck, Bowl, Ruffled, Green, 8 3/4 In. .... 225.00 To 245.00
Graceful, Vase, Green, 5 1/2 In. 65.00
Grape & Cable, Banana Boat, Green 75.00
Grape & Cable, Banana Boat, Purple .... 175.00 To 235.00
Grape & Cable, Banana Bowl, Marigold 135.00
Grape & Cable, Bowl, Amethyst, 8 3/4 In. 98.50
Grape & Cable, Bowl, Red, 6 In. 60.00
Grape & Cable, Bowl, Scalloped, Green, 6 1/2 In. 25.00
Grape & Cable, Butter, Cover, Green 250.00
Grape & Cable, Butter, Cover, Marigold .... 110.00 To 175.00
Grape & Cable, Cookie Jar, Purple 300.00
Grape & Cable, Cup & Saucer, Amethyst 350.00
Grape & Cable, Hatpin Holder, Marigold 135.00
Grape & Cable, Perfume Bottle, Stopper, Amethyst 165.00
Grape & Cable, Pin Tray, Amethyst 175.00
Grape & Cable, Plate, Footed, Marigold, 9 In. 70.00
Grape & Cable, Plate, Green, 9 In. 110.00
Grape & Cable, Plate, Hand Grip, Purple, 6 1/2 In. 70.00
Grape & Cable, Powder Jar, Purple 115.00
Grape & Cable, Punch Bowl, Green, 2 Piece 475.00
Grape & Cable, Punch Set, Marigold, 7 Piece 320.00
Grape & Cable, Shot Glass, Purple, 6 Piece 875.00
Grape & Cable, Spooner, Green 90.00
Grape & Cable, Spooner, Marigold 75.00
Grape & Cable, Tumbler, Purple .... 27.50 To 50.00
Grape & Cable, Water Set, Green, 7 Piece 240.00
Grape & Cable, Water Set, Purple, 7 Piece 375.00
Grape & Cable, Whiskey, Amethyst .... 135.00 To 155.00
Grape & Gothic Arches, Sugar, Creamer & Spooner, Blue 245.00
Grape & Gothic Arches, Tumbler, Marigold 25.00
Grape Arbor, Tumbler, White 85.00
Grape Arbor, Water Set, Marigold, 5 Piece 195.00
    GRAPE DELIGHT, see Vintage
    GRAPEVINE DIAMONDS, see Grapevine Lattice
Grapevine Lattice, Tumbler, Purple .... 35.00 To 50.00
Harvest Poppy, Compote, Purple 475.00
    HARVEST TIME, see Golden Harvest
Heart & Vine, Bowl, Green, 8 1/2 In. 95.00
Heart Band, Mug, Marigold 85.00
Hearts & Flowers, Bowl, Blue 450.00
Hearts & Flowers, Bowl, White 215.00
Hearts & Flowers, Compote, Aqua ....695.00 To 1175.00
Hearts & Flowers, Compote, White .... 150.00 To 165.00
Heavy Grape, Berry Bowl, Master, Purple .... 50.00 To 80.00
Heavy Grape, Chop Plate, Marigold 120.00
    HERON & RUSHES, see Stork & Rushes
Herringbone & Iris, Bowl, Fluted, Marigold, 12 In. 12.00
    HOBNAIL, see also Hobnail category
Hobnail, Cuspidor, Amethyst 250.00
    HOBSTAR & TORCH, see Double Star
Hobstar, Cookie Jar, Marigold 150.00
Hobstar, Punch Set, Marigold, 14 Piece 300.00

HOLLY SPRAY, see Holly Sprig
Holly Sprig, Bowl, Ruffled, Paneled, Amethyst, 8 1/4 In. 55.00
Holly Whirl, Bonbon, Marigold 45.00
Holly Whirl, Bowl, Green, 9 1/2 In. 75.00
Holly, Bowl, Blue, 8 In. 30.00
Holly, Bowl, Green, 9 In. 45.00
Holly, Bowl, Ice Cream, Amethyst, 8 1/4 In. 75.00
Holly, Chop Plate, Blue, 10 In. 160.00
Holly, Plate, Marigold, 9 3/4 In. 95.00
HONEYCOMB COLLAR, see Fishscale & Beads
HORSE MEDALLIONS, see Horses' Heads
Horses' Heads, Bowl, Fluted, Cobalt Blue, 7 1/8 In. 118.00
Horses' Heads, Bowl, Green, 7 1/2 In. 135.00
Horses' Heads, Bowl, Marigold, 8 In. 65.00
Horses' Heads, Bowl, Nut, Footed, Marigold 70.00
Illusion, Bonbon, Wavy Edge, Handle, Purple 50.00
Imperial Grape, Berry Set, Purple, 7 Piece 225.00
Imperial Grape, Bottle, Water, Purple 125.00
Imperial Grape, Bottle, Water, Smoky 475.00
Imperial Grape, Bowl, Marigold, 5 In. 18.00
Imperial Grape, Decanter, Purple 155.00
Imperial Grape, Goblet, Water, Marigold 105.00
Imperial Grape, Plate, Marigold, 6 1/2 In. 42.00
Imperial Grape, Punch Bowl, Green, 2 Piece 475.00
Imperial Grape, Punch Set, Purple, 6 Piece 800.00
Imperial Grape, Water Bottle, Purple .... 140.00 To 160.00
Imperial Grape, Water Set, Marigold, 7 Piece .... 200.00 To 220.00
Imperial Grape, Wine, Marigold .... 20.00 To 30.00
Imperial Pansy, Relish, Green 32.00
Inverted Coin Dot, Pitcher, Water, Marigold 125.00
Inverted Feather, Cracker Jar, Green 175.00
Inverted Strawberry, Powder Jar, Cover, Green .... 135.00 To 195.00
Iris Herringbone, Butter, Cover 45.00
Iris Herringbone, Dish, 4 1/2 In. 5.00
Iris Herringbone, Pitcher, Water, Marigold 37.50
IRISH LACE, see Louisa
Jack-In-The-Pulpit, Vase, Marigold, 8 In. 35.00
Kittens, Banana Boat, Marigold 115.00
Kittens, Cup & Saucer, Marigold 250.00
Kittens, Cup, Marigold, Child's 110.00
LABELLE ELAINE, see Primrose
LABELLE POPPY, see Poppy Show
LABELLE ROSE, see Rose Show
LATE IRIS, see Iris Herringbone
Lattice & Daisy, Tumbler, Marigold .... 20.00 To 38.00
Lattice & Poinsettia, Bowl, Footed, Blue, 8 1/2 In. 290.00
Leaf & Beads, Bowl, Marigold, Footed 50.00
Leaf & Beads, Candy Dish, Footed, Marigold 65.00
Leaf & Beads, Rose Bowl, Aqua 270.00
Leaf & Little Flowers, Compote, Amethyst 400.00
Leaf Chain, Bowl, Green, 6 In. 275.00
Leaf Chain, Plate, Marigold, 7 1/2 In. 50.00
Leaf Column, Vase, Purple, 6 In. 80.00
LEAF MEDALLION, see Leaf Chain
LEAF PINWHEEL & STAR FLOWER, see Whirling Leaves

Put about 15 inches of plastic "popcorn" in the bottom of your grandfather clock case. If the weights fall, as sometimes happens, this will
prevent damage to the bottom boards.

Leaf Rays, Nappy, Handle, Marigold 30.00
Leaf Tiers, Bowl, Marigold, 5 In. 17.50
Lion, Bowl, Ruffled, Marigold, 7 In. 165.00
Little Flowers, Bowl, Blue, 9 In. 95.00
Little Stars, Bowl, Ruffled, Purple, 7 1/2 In. 65.00
Loganberry, Vase, Amber 375.00
    LOOP & COLUMN, see Pulled Loop
    LOOPED PETALS, see Scales
Lotus & Grape, Bonbon, Handles, Marigold 47.50
Lotus & Grape, Candy Dish, Footed, Marigold 33.00
Louisa, Bowl, 3–Footed, Amethyst, 8 1/2 In. 37.50
Louisa, Plate, Footed, Amber 150.00
Lustre Rose, Bowl, Footed, Marigold, 8 1/2 In. 35.00
Lustre Rose, Butter, Cover, Marigold ....45.00 To 100.00
Lustre Rose, Sugar & Creamer, Marigold 40.00
Lustre Rose, Water Set, Marigold, 7 Piece 250.00
    MAGNOLIA & POINSETTIA, see Water Lily
    MAINE COAST, see Seacoast
Many Fruits, Bowl, Purple, 10 1/2 In. 95.00
Many Stars, Bowl, Ruffled, Marigold, 9 In. 345.00
Maple Leaf, Spooner, Marigold 50.00
Maple Leaf, Tumbler, Amethyst 35.00
Maple Leaf, Water Set, Marigold, 7 Piece 125.00
    MARYLAND, see Rustic
    MELINDA, see Wishbone
    MELON & FAN, see Diamond & Rib
Morning Glory, Vase, Funeral, Amethyst, 17 In. 230.00
Morning Glory, Vase, Purple, 8 In. 30.00
    MULTI FRUIT & FLOWERS, see Many Fruits
    MUMS & GREEK KEY, see Embroidered Mums
Nautilus, Sugar, Peach 250.00
Nautilus, Whimsey, Peach 350.00
Nippon, Bowl, Ruffled, Ice Blue 225.00
Nippon, Bowl, Ruffled, Ice Green 385.00
Nuart Shade, Shade, Greek Key Rim, Marigold, 4 1/2 In. 20.00
    OAK LEAF & ACORN, see Acorn
Octagon, Bowl, Marigold, 8 1/2 In. 40.00
Octagon, Sugar, Cover, Marigold 25.00
Open Rose, Bowl, Marigold, 8 In. 22.00
    ORANGE TREE & CABLE, see Orange Tree Orchard
    ORANGE TREE & SCROLL, see Orange Tree Variant
Orange Tree, Bowl, Ice Cream, Green, 8 In. 215.00
Orange Tree, Bowl, Ice Cream, Green, 9 In. 195.00
Orange Tree, Bowl, Marigold, 8 1/2 In. 30.00
Orange Tree, Bowl, White, 8 In. 75.00
Orange Tree, Breakfast Set, Blue, 3 Piece 125.00
Orange Tree, Butter, Cover, Marigold 135.00
Orange Tree, Goblet, Marigold 20.00
Orange Tree, Hatpin Holder, Blue ....180.00 To 245.00
Orange Tree, Mug, Blue ....45.00 To 60.00
Orange Tree, Mug, Red 150.00
Orange Tree, Orange Bowl, Footed, Blue 225.00
Orange Tree, Powder Jar, Cover, Blue ....75.00 To 95.00
Orange Tree, Punch Set, Marigold, 6 Piece 365.00
Orange Tree, Table Set, Cobalt Blue, 4 Piece 495.00
Orange Tree, Tumbler, Blue 45.00
Orange Tree, Water Set, Blue, 8 Piece 495.00
Oriental Poppy, Pitcher, Marigold 295.00

Plastic should be cleaned gently. Wipe with a damp cloth, then dry.
Do not use an abrasive cleaner. Soapy water can be used.

Oriental Poppy, Water Set, White, 7 Piece 2500.00
Palm Beach, Creamer, Marigold 65.00
Pansy, Dish, Pickle, Amber 165.00
Pansy, Nappy, Green 28.00
Pansy, Nappy, Purple 28.00
Panther, Berry Bowl, Marigold 25.00
Panther, Bowl, Footed, Marigold, 9 1/4 In. 135.00
Panther, Sauce, Footed, Green 110.00
  PARROT TULIP SWIRL, see Acanthus
Peach, Berry Set, White, 5 Piece .... 375.00 To 395.00
Peach, Tumbler, Blue 45.00
Peacock & Dahlia, Bowl, Marigold, 7 In. 48.00
Peacock & Grape, Bowl, Amethyst, 9 In. 47.00
Peacock & Grape, Plate, Marigold, 9 1/4 In. 185.00
Peacock & Urn, Bowl, Amethyst, 10 1/2 In. 265.00
Peacock & Urn, Bowl, Blue, 8 1/2 In. 110.00
Peacock & Urn, Bowl, Blue, 9 In. 125.00
Peacock & Urn, Bowl, Ice Cream, Blue, 11 In. .... 675.00 To 795.00
Peacock & Urn, Bowl, Ice Cream, White, 11 In. 350.00
Peacock & Urn, Bowl, Marigold, 9 In. 55.00
Peacock & Urn, Bowl, Marigold, 10 In. 195.00
Peacock & Urn, Bowl, Ruffled, Blue, 8 1/2 In. .... 110.00 To 120.00
Peacock & Urn, Bowl, White, 10 In. 275.00
Peacock & Urn, Compote, Footed, Marigold 30.00
Peacock & Urn, Plate, Fluted, 9 In. 120.00
Peacock At The Fountain, Berry Bowl, Marigold 90.00
Peacock At The Fountain, Compote, Blue 575.00
Peacock At The Fountain, Compote, Purple 800.00
Peacock At The Fountain, Punch Cup, Marigold 20.00
Peacock At The Fountain, Punch Set, Marigold, 6 Piece 500.00
Peacock At The Fountain, Spooner, Marigold .... 55.00 To 75.00
Peacock At The Fountain, Water Set, Marigold, 7 Piece 575.00
  PEACOCK EYE & GRAPE, see Vineyard
  PEACOCK ON FENCE, see Peacock
Peacock, Bowl, Marigold, 9 In. 185.00
Peacock, Plate, Blue, 9 In. 725.00
Persian Garden, Bowl, Ice Cream, Master, Purple 550.00
Persian Garden, Bowl, Ice Cream, White, 6 In. 75.00
Persian Garden, Plate, Marigold, 6 1/2 In. 135.00
Persian Garden, Plate, White, 6 3/4 In. 235.00
Persian Medallion, Bonbon, 2 Sides Up, Handles, Blue 45.00
Persian Medallion, Compote, Cobalt Blue, 6 3/4 In. 75.00
Persian Medallion, Plate, Marigold, 6 In. 23.00
Persian Medallion, Plate, Marigold, 7 1/2 In. 60.00
Petals & Fan, Bowl, Amethyst, 5 3/8 In. 40.00
Petals & Fan, Bowl, Fluted, Amethyst, 11 In. 375.00
  PINE CONE WREATH, see Pine Cone
Pine Cone, Plate, Marigold, 6 3/4 In. 35.00
Pineapple, Bowl, Marigold, 5 In. 25.00
  POINSETTIA & LATTICE, see Poinsettia
Poinsettia, Pitcher, Milk, Marigold 65.00
  POLKA DOT, see Inverted Coin Dot
Polo, Ashtray, Marigold 25.00
  PONY ROSETTE, see Pony
Pony, Bowl, Marigold, 8 1/2 In. 65.00
Poppy Show, Bowl, Green 750.00
Poppy Show, Plate, White 1350.00
Pretty Panels, Tumbler, Marigold 45.00
Primrose, Bowl, Green, 9 1/2 In. 75.00
  PRINCESS LACE, see Octagon

Pulled Loop, Vase, Green, 9 In. 40.00
Pulled Loop, Vase, Purple, 10 In. 35.00
Raindrops, Bowl, Ruffled, Footed, Amethyst, 9 In. 85.00
Rambler Rose, Tumbler, Marigold .... 35.00 To 45.00
Rambler Rose, Water Set, Purple, 7 Piece 995.00
Raspberry, Pitcher, Milk, White 650.00
Raspberry, Sauce, Purple 90.00
Raspberry, Tumbler, Green 38.00
Raspberry, Water Set, Green, 7 Piece .... 695.00 To 895.00
Raspberry, Water Set, Marigold, 7 Piece 300.00
Rays & Ribbons, Bowl, Green, 9 In. 60.00
Rays & Ribbons, Bowl, Marigold 45.00
Ripple, Vase, Amber, 15 1/2 In. 75.00
Ripple, Vase, Amethyst, 8 3/4 In. 28.00
Rococo, Vase, Marigold, 4 In. 110.00
Rosalind, Bowl, Marigold, 10 In. 105.00
    ROSE & RUFFLES, see Open Rose
Rose Show, Bowl, Amethyst, 8 3/4 In. 265.00
Rose Show, Bowl, White, 8 3/4 In. 325.00
Rose Show, Plate, Blue, 9 In. 750.00
    ROSES & LOOPS, see Double–Stem Rose
Round–Up, Bowl, Ice Cream, White 175.00
Round–Up, Plate, Blue 275.00
Rustic, Vase, Blue, 12 In. 32.00
    SAILBOAT & WINDMILL, see Sailboats
Sailboats, Bowl, Ruffled, Marigold 6 In. 40.00
Scales, Bowl, Amethyst, 5 In. 35.00
Scales, Bowl, Purple, 7 In. 57.50
Seacoast, Pin Tray, Green 250.00
Seaweed, Bowl, Ruffled, Amethyst, 10 In. 350.00
Singing Birds, Berry Set, Green, 7 Piece .... 435.00 To 450.00
Singing Birds, Mug, Blue .... 110.00 To 195.00
Singing Birds, Mug, Green 250.00
Singing Birds, Mug, Purple .... 65.00 To 75.00
Singing Birds, Water Set, Purple, 7 Piece 550.00
Single Flower, Bowl, Peach, 9 In. 55.00
Six–Petals, Bowl, Peach, 7 1/2 In. 80.00
Ski Star, Bowl, 8 Flutes, Purple, 11 In. 475.00
Ski Star, Plate, Grip Handles, Dome Footed, Peach 125.00
Smooth Rays, Bowl, Green, 8 1/2 In. 58.00
Smooth Rays, Bowl, Marigold, 8 In. 30.00
Soda Gold, Cuspidor, Marigold 45.00
Soda Gold, Water Set, Marigold, 7 Piece 235.00
    SPIDER WEB, see Soda Gold
Split Diamond, Creamer, Marigold, Miniature 35.00
Split Diamond, Sugar, Marigold 30.00
Stag & Holly, Bowl, 3 Footed, Marigold, 10 1/8 In. 95.00
Stag & Holly, Bowl, Footed, Amber, 10 In. .... 500.00 To 725.00
Stag & Holly, Bowl, Footed, Aqua, 10 1/2 In. 450.00
Stag & Holly, Bowl, Footed, Marigold, 11 In. ....85.00 To 110.00
Stag & Holly, Bowl, Green, 10 3/4 In. 195.00
Stag & Holly, Bowl, Spatula Footed, Marigold, 9 In. 80.00
Star & File, Rose Bowl, Marigold 60.00
Star Medallion, Bowl, Marigold, 6 In. 20.00

A drawer that is stuck can be helped by heat. Remove any nearby drawers, then aim a blow dryer set on medium at the wood. Once the drawer is opened, rub the runners with soap or a candle.

Star Medallion, Pitcher, Milk, Marigold 50.00
Star of David & Bows, Bowl, Footed, Amethyst, 7 In. 75.00
    STAR OF DAVID MEDALLION, see Star of David & Bows
    STIPPLED CLEMATIS, see Little Stars
    STIPPLED DIAMOND & FLOWER, see Little Flowers
    STIPPLED LEAF, see Leaf Tiers
    STIPPLED LEAF & BEADS, see leaf & Beads
Stippled Petals, Banana Boat, Marigold 50.00
    STIPPLED POSY & PODS, see Four Flowers
Stippled Rays, Bowl, Amethyst, 8 In. 42.00
Stippled Rays, Plate, Marigold, 6 3/4 In. 25.00
Stippled Rays, Sugar & Creamer, Stemmed, Marigold 65.00
    STIPPLED RIBBONS & RAYS, see Rays & Ribbons
Stork & Rushes, Bowl, Marigold, 9 1/2 In. 90.00
Stork & Rushes, Mug, Amethyst 275.00
Stork & Rushes, Mug, Blue 795.00
Stork & Rushes, Tumbler, Amethyst 40.00
    STRAWBERRY, see Wild Strawberry
Strutting Peacock, Sugar & Creamer, Purple 80.00
    SUNFLOWER, see Dandelion
    SUNFLOWER & WHEAT, see Fieldflower
Swirled Hobnail, Cuspidor, Marigold 500.00
Swirled Hobnail, Rose Bowl, Purple 250.00
Swirled Hobnail, Rose Bowl, Scalloped Rim, Marigold 225.00
Target, Vase, White, 12 In. 125.00
    TEARDROPS, see Raindrops
Ten Mums, Water Set, Blue, 7 Piece 1450.00
Thistle, Banana Boat, Blue 325.00
Three Fruits, Bowl, Amethyst, 9 1/2 In. 98.50
Three Fruits, Bowl, Ruffled, Basket Weave Base, Green, 9 In. 60.00
Three Fruits, Plate, 12 Sides, Purple, 9 1/4 In. 150.00
Three Fruits, Plate, Marigold, 9 In. .... 55.00 To 95.00
Thumbprint, Vase, Marigold, 15 In. 45.00
Tiger Lily, Tumbler, Marigold 27.50
Tiger Lily, Water Set, Green, 5 Piece 275.00
Tiger Lily, Water Set, Marigold, 5 Piece 300.00
Tree Trunk, Vase, Green, 9 In. 235.00
Treebark, Plate, Marigold, 8 In. 10.00
Treebark, Tumbler, Marigold 12.00
Treebark, Vase, Marigold, 7 1/2 In. 15.00
Treebark, Water Set, Marigold, 6 Piece 100.00
Triands, Celery Vase, Marigold 50.00
Trout & Fly, Bowl, Green, 8 3/4 In. 495.00
Trout & Fly, Bowl, Marigold, 8 3/4 In. 375.00
Twins, Bowl, Green, 5 In. 32.50
Two Flowers, Bowl, Footed, 11 In. 130.00
Two Flowers, Bowl, Spatula Feet, Green, 8 In. 85.00
Venetian, Rose Bowl, Green 1200.00
Victorian, Bowl, Fluted, Purple, 11 In. 235.00
Vineyard, Pitcher, Water, Peach 75.00
Vintage, Bowl, Blue, 10 In. 95.00
Vintage, Bowl, Piecrust Rim, Green, 8 1/2 In. 40.00
Vintage, Epergne, Purple, 5 In. 95.00
Vintage, Fernery, Marigold 45.00
Vintage, Ice Cream Set, Blue, 5 Piece 450.00
Vintage, Rose Bowl, Purple 50.00
Waffle Block, Bowl, Square, Marigold, 8 In. 35.00
Water Lily & Cattails, Bonbon, Marigold, 2 Handles 50.00
Water Lily & Cattails, Tumbler, Marigold .... 50.00 To 65.00

Water Lily, Bowl, Footed, Green, 10 In.	135.00
Water Lily, Bowl, Footed, Marigold, 5 In.	30.00
Whirling Leaves, Bowl, Green, 9 In.	125.00
Wide Panel, Epergne, 4–Lily, Green ....600.00 To	1275.00
Wild Berry, Powder Jar, Marigold	165.00
Wild Flower, Compote, Amethyst	600.00
Wild Strawberry, Bowl, Basketweave Exterior, Green, 9 In.	65.00
Wild Strawberry, Bowl, Candy Ribbon Rim, Amethyst, 10 In.	350.00
Wild Strawberry, Bowl, Stippled, Purple	165.00
Windflower, Bowl, Marigold, 9 In.	65.00
WINDMILL MEDALLION, see Windmill	
Windmill, Bowl, Green, 8 In.	40.00
Windmill, Pitcher, Milk, Purple	350.00
Windmill, Pitcher, Water, Marigold	70.00
Windmill, Water Set, Marigold, 7 Piece	85.00
Wishbone, Bowl, Amethyst, 10 In.	85.00
Wishbone, Bowl, Marigold, 8 In.	65.00
Wishbone, Epergne, 1–Lily, Purple	495.00
Wishbone, Plate, Footed, Purple, 8 1/4 In.	245.00
WISTERIA & LATTICE, see Wisteria	
Wisteria, Tumbler, Ice Blue	375.00
Wreath of Roses, Rose Bowl, Marigold, 3 1/2 In.	35.00
Wreathed Cherry, Berry Set, Purple, 7 Piece	275.00
Zig Zag, Bowl, Green, 9 In.	100.00
Zippered Loop Lamp, Lamp, Finger, Marigold	800.00
Zippered Loop Lamp, Lamp, Oil, Smoke, 8 In.	450.00

The first carousel or merry–go–round figures carved in the United States were made in 1867 by Gustav Dentzel. Collectors discovered the charm of the hand–carved figures in the 1970s and they were soon classed as folk art. Most desirable are the figures other than horses, such as pigs, camels, lions, or dogs. A jumper is a figure that was made to move up and down on a pole, a stander was placed in a stationary position.

CAROUSEL, Calliope, Tangley, 43 Notes	6500.00
Figure, Camel, PTC, C.1905, Park Paint	4700.00
Figure, Deer, Wooden, 6–Point Antlers, Park Paint, 61 X 59 In.	8500.00
Figure, Elephant, Charles Dare, Glass Eyes, 1885–95, 26 X 34 In.	3300.00
Figure, Elephant, Englarged Ears, Saddle Blanket, Painted, 70 In.	2750.00
Figure, Horse, Eagle Head Between Ears, Yellow, Black, 46 In.	3000.00
Figure, Horse, Herschel–Spillman, C.1904	2900.00
Figure, Horse, Inside Stander, PTC	2485.00
Figure, Horse, Jumper, Armitage–Herschell, C.1890	1850.00
Figure, Horse, Jumper, Herschell–Spillman, C.1915	3500.00
Figure, Horse, Jumper, Spillman, Wooden, Hair Tails, 1922	3000.00
Figure, Horse, Stander, Inside Row, Head Tucked	6350.00
Figure, Lady, Calliope, Standing At Attention, Painted	6000.00
Figure, Lion, Spiral Base Handle, Wooden Base, C.1900	2400.00
Figure, Rooster, Running, Child's Size	2500.00
Figure, Zebra, Wood Carved	950.00
Rocket, Car	195.00

The word "carriage" has several meanings, so this section lists baby carriages, buggies for adults, horse–drawn sleighs, and even strollers. Doll–sized carriages are listed under "toy."

CARRIAGE, Baby Buggy, Chippewa, C.1920	350.00
Baby Buggy, Eastlake–Style	880.00
Baby Buggy, Wicker, Original Wooden Wheels & Handles, 1889	850.00
Baby Buggy, Wicker, Wire Wheels	310.00
Baby Buggy, Wicker, Wooden Spokes, 1886	175.00
Baby Buggy, Wire Wheels, Plush Upholstery, Wicker	1150.00
Baby Buggy, Woven Wicker, Seagrass, Manufacturer's Label, 1910	325.00

Baby Stroller, Wicker, Green Frame, Heywood–Wakefield, 38 X 43 In.	425.00
Baby Walker, Encircling Bentwood Ring, Wooden, 16 In.	65.00
Baby Walker, Victorian, Walnut	110.00
Buckboard, Pony, Wooden Spoke Wheels, Green & Yellow, 22 X 55 In.	275.00
Sleigh, Hand Painted, Stenciled, Keene, N.Y.	1650.00
Sleigh, Push, Child's, Metal Tipped Runners, Wood, Fabric Lined	220.00
Sleigh, Upholstered, Push	1295.00
Surrey, 2 Seats, Red Fringe, J.P.Moore & Sons	3500.00
Surrey, Child's, 2 Large Wheels, Leather, Original Condition	450.00
Wagon, Goat, Green, Dreadnaught, 2 Large Back Wheels	2400.00
Wagon, Goat, Late 1800s, 36 In.	495.00
Wagon, Goat, Studebaker, Original Paint & Tongue	2000.00

An eye on the cash was a necessity in stores of the nineteenth century, too. The cash register was invented in 1884. John and James Ritty invented a large clocklike model that kept a record of the dollars and cents exchanged in the store. John Patterson improved the cash register with a paper roll to record the money. By the early 1900s, elaborate brass registers were made. At about the time of World War I, the fancy case was exchanged for the more modern types.

CASH REGISTER, Hallwood Leader, Columbus, Ohio	475.00
Michigan, Model 342, Nickel Plate, Amount Purchased	400.00
Monitor, Barber Shop, Pin Striping	850.00
National, 9 Drawers, 1 Door, On Bombe Oak Base	1100.00
National, Model 12 No. 1, Brass, C.1900	800.00
National, Model 38, Drawer, Brass, 1896	750.00
National, Model 46, Brass	1600.00
National, Model 47, Brass	600.00
National, Model 250, Polished	795.00
National, Model 311, Copper Over Brass	950.00
National, Model 313, Candy Store	795.00
National, Model 313, Polished .... 595.00 To	795.00
National, Model 317, Polished Bronze .... 695.00 To	750.00
National, Model 342, Nickel Over Brass, Amount Purchased	500.00
National, Model 432–3–C, 1904	1000.00
National, Model 452 E–L, Manual & Electric	1100.00
National, Model 532, Floor Model	450.00
Woodie, Model 442, Brass, 1911 .... 750.00 To	850.00

Castor sets holding just salt and pepper castors were used in the seventeenth century. The sugar castor, mustard pot, spice dredger, bottles for vinegar and oil, and other spice holders became popular by the eighteenth century. These sets were usually made of sterling silver. The American Victorian castor set, the type most collected today, was made of silver plated Britannia metal. Colored glass bottles were introduced after the Civil War. The sets were out of fashion by World War I. Be careful when buying sets with colored bottles; many are reproductions.

CASTOR SET, see also various Porcelain and Glass categories

CASTOR SET, 4–Bottle, Child's, Diamond Pattern, Holder	135.00
5–Bottle, Gothic, Pressed Glass, Pewter Stand	95.00
5–Bottle, Pressed Glass, Bellflower, Pewter Stand	325.00
6–Bottle, Metal Frame, With Bell	135.00
6–Bottle, Rogers	60.00

The pickle castor was a glass jar about six inches in height, held in a special metal holder. It became a popular dinner table accessory about 1890. The jar had a top that was usually silver or silver plate. The frame, also of a silver metal, had a handle that arched above the jar and a hook that held a pair of tongs. By 1900, the pickle castor was out of fashion. Many examples found today have reproduced glass jars in old holders.

CASTOR, PICKLE, see also various Glass categories

CASTOR, Pickle, Amber, Thumbprint, Silver Plated, Ornate Cover, Tongs, 10 In.	175.00
Pickle, Beaded Edge, Blue, 4 1/4 In.	87.00
Pickle, Blue Glass Insert, Tongs	190.00
Pickle, Chrysanthemum Base, Reverse Swirl Insert, Cranberry	395.00
Pickle, Cosmos, Milk Glass, Frame, Lid, Tongs	350.00
Pickle, Cranberry & Vaseline Spatter, Leaf Mold Insert	395.00
Pickle, Cranberry Glass Insert, Silver Plated Frame, Tongs	350.00
Pickle, Daisy & Button, Lime, Tongs, Rogers	255.00
Pickle, Flattened Diamond Point Sides, Webster & Co., 11 1/2 In.	115.00
Pickle, Frosted Crisscross Diamond, Clear, Tongs	150.00
Pickle, Frosted, Clear Glass, Handle Raises Lid, Reed & Barton	275.00
Pickle, Hobnail, Embossed Trim At Base of Frame, Brass Bail, Simpson	425.00
Pickle, Inverted Thumbprint, Enameled Flowers, Leaves, Plated Holder	425.00
Pickle, Inverted Thumbrprint Insert, Ruby, Silver Top	125.00
Pickle, Jacob's Ladder Crystal Insert, Stand	130.00
Pickle, Openwork Arched Top, Zipper Panels, Strawberry Finial, Fork	100.00
Pickle, Optic Jar, Enameled Flowers, Coffee Color, Aurora	295.00
Pickle, Panel & Button Insert, Cut Floral At Base, Meriden	175.00
Pickle, Silver Frame, Turn Handle & Lid Raises, Reed & Barton	225.00
Pickle, Spatter Leaf Mold Insert, Ruffled Frame, Silver, Cranberry	395.00
Pickle, Thumbprint, Enameled Floral, Square Base, Cranberry, Rogers	395.00
Pickle, Thumbprint, Ribbed Base, Bail, Cranberry, Webster	250.00
Pickle, White Interior, Pairpoint Holder, Peach Finial, Signed	550.00
Pickle, Zipper Insert, Twist Fork, Silver Plate	125.00

CATALOG, see Paper, Catalog
CAUGHLEY, see Salopian

Celadon is a Chinese porcelain having a velvet–textured green–gray glaze. Japanese, Korean, and other factories also made a celadon–colored glaze.

CELADON, Bowl, Applied Copper Rim, Korean, 10 X 17 1/2 In.	1595.00
Cruet, 18th Century	525.00
Jar, Cover, Raised Floral, Green Foliage, Gold Trim, 6 In.	85.00
Jardiniere, Louis XVI Style, Ram's Head Handles, C.1885, 9 In.	3300.00
Plate, Enameled Birds & Flowers, 10 In., 8 Piece	280.00
Teapot, Cat Shape, 6 In.	125.00
Tile, Hand Painted Scene, Chinese, 1730–50, 16 X 11 1/2 In.	625.00
Vase, Blue & White, Birds & Flowers, 23 1/2 In.	95.00
Vase, Teardrop Body, Floral Design, Green Glaze Ground, 11 1/2 In.	450.00

Celluloid is a trademark for a plastic developed in 1868 by John W. Hyatt. Celluloid Manufacturing Company, the Celluloid Novelty Company, Celluloid Fancy Goods Company, and American Xylonite Company all used Celluloid to make jewelry, games, sewing equipment, false teeth, and piano keys. Eventually, the Hyatt Company became the American Celluloid and Chemical Manufacturing Company—the Celanese Corporation. The name "Celluloid" was often used to identify any similar plastic. Celluloid toys are listed under toys.

CELLULOID, Box, Collar, Horses On Cover	45.00
Box, Collar, Small Design	15.00
Box, Glove, Woman's	45.00
Box, Shaving, Traveling, Mirror, Brass Slant Front, 5 X 7 1/2 In.	95.00
Cigarette Case, Woman's Hand Clasp	10.00
Comb, Lady's, Bakelite, Handmade, France	8.50
Dresser Set, Case, 14 Piece	200.00
Dresser Set, Hand Painted Blue Flowers, Beveled Mirror, 3 Piece	45.00
Dresser Set, Tray, Black Art Nouveau Handle, Leather Case, 8 Pc.	95.00
Frame, Easel Back, 4 1/2 X 5 3/4 In.	12.00
Mirror, Hand, Pelo's Juvenile Band, Iron River, Mich., 3 1/2 In.	20.00
Pin, Flag, Lapel, Old Glory, World War I, 1 In.	2.00
Rattle, Blue Boy Playing Mandolin, Ball Hanging From Ring	28.00
Rattle, Stocking Filled With Presents, From Santa, 4 In.	85.00
Salt & Pepper, Penguins, Willie & Millie	15.00

The Ceramic Art Company of Trenton, New Jersey, was established in 1889 by J. Coxon and W. Lenox and was an early producer of American Belleek porcelain. Pieces made by this company are listed here. Do not confuse this ware with the pottery made by the Ceramic Arts Studio of Madison, Wisconsin, from 1941 to 1957.

CERAMIC ART CO., Pitcher, Berries, Leaves, Maroon Border, Palette, 12 In.	195.00
Salt, Pink & Red Roses, Pink, Gold Trim, 3 Legged, Palette	22.00
Vase, Flowers, Leaves, Hexagonal, Green Palette, 1919, 8 In.	85.00
Vase, Pinecones, Birds, 12 In.	325.00

Chalkware is really plaster of Paris decorated with watercolors. One type was molded from Staffordshire and other porcelain models and painted and sold as inexpensive decorations in the nineteenth century. Figures of plaster, made from about 1910 to 1940 for use as prizes at carnivals, are also known as chalkware.

CHALKWARE, Bank, Dog, Carnival, Large	55.00
Bank, Santa Claus, In Chair	30.00
Bookends, Ship	14.00
Bust, American Indian, Hole In Head, Reliable On Headband, 6 In.	75.00
Bust, Hiawatha, C.1900, 18 In.	100.00
Bust, Joe E. Louis, Artist, 1935	175.00

CHALKWARE, FIGURINE, see also Kewpie

Figurine, Cat, Seated, Curled Tail, Painted, Penn., 15 1/2 In.	8800.00
Figurine, Cat, Seated, Smoked Grain Design, Mid-1800s, 11 In.	2420.00
Figurine, Dog, Seated, Polychrome Paint, 6 1/4 In.	85.00
Figurine, Dog, Seated, Red, Yellow & Black Paint, 7 5/8 In.	10.00
Figurine, Doulton-Type Lady, 1800s, 5 In.	12.00
Figurine, Doulton-Type Lady, 1800s, 7 In.	18.00
Figurine, Drum Majorette, 14 1/2 In.	15.00
Figurine, Horse, Open Mouth, Oriental, Green, 21 In.	395.00
Figurine, Man On Keg With Accordion, Hampden Ale, 15 In.	65.00
Figurine, Rabbit, Crouching, Painted, Penna., Mid-1800s, 5 1/2 In.	715.00
Figurine, Rooster, 7 In.	15.00
Figurine, Stag, Recumbent, Grained Design, Mid-1800s, 5 1/2 In.	440.00
Garniture, Pomegranate, Leaves, Square Base, 19th Century, 11 In.	495.00
Group, 3 Monkeys, Hear, See & Speak No Evil, 2 In.	5.00
Group, Rooster, Hen & Chick	22.50
Watchstand, Dog, On Fluted Column, Painted, 19th Century, 11 In.	935.00
Whistle, Bird, Folded Feathers, Yellow, 2 1/2 X 4 In.	1100.00

Charlie Chaplin, the famous comic and actor, lived from 1889 to 1977. He made his first movie in 1913. He did the movie "The Tramp" in 1915. The character of the Tramp has remained famous and is in use today in a series of television commercials for computers. Dolls, candy containers, and all sorts of memorabilia picture Charlie Chaplin. Pieces are being made even today.

CHARLIE CHAPLIN, Ashtray, Figural, Smoking Cigar, Lego	20.00
Book, Charlie Chaplin's Funny Stunts, 12 Pg., 12 X 16 In.	130.00
Book, In The Army, 1917	12.00
Booklet, Great Dictator, Movie, Color Lithograph	80.00
Button, City Lights, 1931, 3/4 In.	20.00
Button, Modern Times, Orange & Blue, 1936, 3/4 In.	30.00
Candy Container, Standing Next To Barrel	195.00
Cartoon Strip, Full Color, 1915	30.00
Doll, Walks With Cane, Composition Head	750.00
Figurine, Metal, Hand Painted, 1900s, 3 In.	25.00
Lobby Card Set, For Movie Sunnyside	760.00
Newspaper Strip, Full Color, Dated 1915, Matted	30.00
Pencil Box, Tin, Henry Cline	50.00
Poster, The Cure, Export & Import Film, C.1923, 41 X 81 In.	2500.00
Poster, The Floor Walker, CC Pictures, C.1920, 41 X 81 In.	4800.00
Poster, The Rink, Export & Import Film, C.1924, 27 X 41 In.	1600.00
Program, Charlie Chaplin In The Circus, 1927	85.00

Toy, Walking, Windup 125.00

Charlie McCarthy was the ventriloquist's dummy used by Edgar Bergen from the 1930s. He was famous for his work in radio, movies, and television. The act was retired in the 1970s.

CHARLIE MCCARTHY, Book, Paint, C.1938 .... 20.00
  Card, Get–Well, Talking, Original Package 40.00
  Doll, Composition, 12 In. 125.00
  Doll, Composition, Open–Close Mouth, Sheriff Badge, 16 In. 95.00
  Doll, Effanbee, 1937, 17 In. 260.00
  Game, Flying Hats 30.00
  Game, Question & Answer, 1938 .... 35.00
  Puppet, Cardboard, 21 In. 40.00
  Record, Lessons In Ventriloquism, E.Bergen, 33 1/3 RPM 25.00
  Spoon ....9.00 To 15.00
  Toy, Charlie McCarthy's Radio Party, 1938, Spinner 6.00
  Toy, Mortimer Snerd Drives Krazy Car, 1930s 650.00

Chelsea grape pattern was made before 1840. A small bunch of grapes in a raised design, colored with purple or blue luster, is on the border of the white plate. Most of the pieces are unmarked. The pattern is sometimes called "Aynsley" or "Grandmother." Chelsea sprig is similar but has a sprig of flowers instead of the bunch of grapes. Chelsea thistle has a raised thistle pattern.

CHELSEA GRAPE, Cake Set, 25 Piece 125.00
  Coffeepot 150.00
  Plate, 7 In. 15.00
  Sugar, Cover 50.00
    CHELSEA KERAMIC ART WORKS, see Dedham
CHELSEA SPRIG, Bowl, 6 In. 15.00
  Cup & Saucer 25.00
  Dish, 7 1/2 In. 55.00
  Plate, 8 In. 25.00
CHELSEA THISTLE, Cup & Saucer 125.00
  Sugar Bowl 75.00
  Teapot 125.00

Chelsea porcelain was made in the Chelsea area of London from about 1745 to 1784. Ceramic designs were borrowed from the Meissen models of the day. Pieces were made of soft paste. The gold anchor was used as the mark but it has been copied by many other factories. Recent copies of Chelsea have been made from the original molds.

CHELSEA, Bowl, Lotus Mold, Insect & Floral Bouquet Inside, Marked, 7 5/8 In. 990.00
  Cup & Saucer, Arched Panels, Dot Diaper Border, Cinquefoil Saucer 2475.00
  Cup & Saucer, Cinquefoil Saucer, Mazarine Blue, 1760, 2 3/8 In. 6050.00
  Dish, Cabbage Leaf, Center Floral Sprig, C.1759, 9 1/2 In. 1650.00
  Dish, Peony, Irregular Petals, Feathered In Red, C.1756, 9 In. 7150.00
  Dish, Salmon & Gold Phoenix In Flight, C.1753, 7 3/4 In. 880.00
  Dish, Seed–Molded Center, Petals, Stem Handle, C.1755, 8 3/4 In. 6600.00
  Figurine, Beggar Lady With Child, Marked, 6 In. 295.00
  Patch Box, Cover, Woman's Face, Diamond Eyes, C.1755, 1 1/16 In. 1100.00
  Plate, Cluster of Peas, Plums & Cherries, Butterflies, C.1760, 8 In. 825.00
  Plate, Floral Bouquet & Sprigs, C.1756, 8 3/8 In. 330.00
  Plate, Green Twig, Sprays of Leaves, Rosebuds, C.1770, 7 3/4 In. 1760.00
  Plate, Striated Tulip, Red Center, Scalloped, C.1758, 9 In. 7700.00

Chinese export porcelain comprises all the many kinds of porcelain made in China for export to America and Europe in the eighteenth and nineteenth centuries.

    CHINESE EXPORT, see also Canton; Celadon; Nanking; Rose Medallion
CHINESE EXPORT, Aquarium, Famille Rose, Peaches, Bats, 21 In. ....*Illus*   412.50
  Bowl, Dutch Ship Vryburg, Square, 10 In. 80.00
  Bowl, Painted Flowers, Famille Rose Colors, 11 1/2 In. 750.00

Box, Cover, Fitzhugh, Chrysanthemums, Medallion, 7 1/4 In.	400.00
Box, Eagle, Cover, 8 In.	50.00
Charger, Famille Jaune, Bat & Peach Design, 21 In.	468.00
Dish, Enameled Figures, Trees, 5 Sides, Porcelain, 1870, 8 In.	80.00
Figurine, Oriental Man, Smoking Pipe, Pantaloons, 6 In.	38.00
Flask, Medallions, Birds, Floral, Footed, Hexagonal, 5 1/2 In.	56.00
Ginger Jar, Children, Rosewood Cover, Stand, 10 X 8 In., Pair	850.00
Jug, Cream, Flower & Leaf, Bird's Beak Spout, C.1780, 5 In.	210.00
Mug, Mandarin, C.1810	445.00
Pitcher, Bird & Butterfly, 19th Century, 10 In.	600.00
Pitcher, Cover, Button & Leaf Finial, Strap Handles, 10 In.	750.00
Plate, Bird, Butterfly Border, Garden Center, 7 3/4 In., Pair	425.00
Platter, Central Medallion, 4 Fan Floral Reserves, 19 In.	400.00
Platter, Notched Rim, Bamboo & Foliate Rim, 16 1/2 X 13 In.	650.00
Punch Bowl, Mandarin, C.1830	880.00
Rice Bowl, Stand, Blue & White, C.1870	78.00
Soup, Dish, Figural & Symbolic Design, Enamel, 10 In., Pair	550.00
Tea Bowl & Saucer, Mandarin, C.1825	88.00
Teapot, Polychrome Arms & Crest, Sir Robert Eden, C.1785	3520.00
Teapot, Rooster, Early 19th Century, 3 In.	345.00
Temple Jar, Peony, Blue & White, Kang Hsi Mark, 13 1/2 In.	138.00
Tureen, Cover, Landscape Design, Mask–Head Handles	1550.00
Vase, Famille Rose, Bronze Ormolu, C.1760	1800.00
Vase, Rose Mandarin, Double Gourd Shape, 24 In.	2200.00
Vase, Speckled Navy & Cream, Ring Handles, 9 X 6 In.	75.00

Chocolate glass, sometimes mistakenly called caramel slag, was made by the Indiana Tumbler and Goblet Company of Greentown, Indiana, from 1900 to 1903. Fenton Art Glass Co. also made chocolate glass from about 1907 to 1915.

CHOCOLATE GLASS, Berry Bowl, Cactus, 7 1/4 In.	115.00
Bowl, Beaded Triangle, 4 1/4 In.	200.00
Bowl, Cactus, 8 1/4 In.	50.00 To 125.00
Butter, Cover, Holly Panel	45.00
Compote, Cactus, 5 1/4 In.	80.00
Compote, Chrysanthemum Leaf, 4 1/2 In.	300.00
Compote, Jelly, Geneva	110.00
Compote, Jelly, Melrose, 6 In.	110.00
Cracker Jar, Cactus	145.00
Creamer, Cactus, 5 1/4 X 3 3/4 In.	85.00
Creamer, Geneva	135.00
Creamer, Leaf Bracket	75.00 To 95.00
Cruet, Cactus	155.00 To 175.00
Cruet, Leaf Bracket	175.00
Cruet, Wild Rose With Bowknot	335.00 To 365.00
Dish, Cat On Hamper Cover	335.00
Dish, Dolphin, Cover, Beaded, Sawtooth Edge	675.00
Dish, Hen On Nest Cover	375.00 To 415.00
Lamp, Wild Rose With Festoon, 9 1/2 In.	675.00
Mug, Cactus	85.00
Mug, Indoor Drinking Scene, 5 In.	135.00
Mug, Serenade	150.00
Mug, Shuttle	65.00
Mug, Stein, Outdoor Drinking Scene, Spout	125.00
Nappy, Cactus	145.00
Nappy, Leaf Bracket, Heart Shape	30.00
Nappy, Masonic	140.00
Nappy, Shuttle	185.00
Salt & Pepper, Cactus	85.00
Saltshaker, Leaf Bracket	100.00
Sauce, Cactus, Set of 4	125.00
Sauce, Leaf Bracket	20.00
Sauce, Wild Rose With Bowknot	70.00
Sugar & Creamer, Cactus	35.00

Table Set, Leaf Bracket, 4 Piece 400.00
Toothpick, Cactus .... 45.00 To 65.00
Toothpick, Leaf Bracket 195.00
Toothpick, Sheaf of Wheat 750.00
Tumbler, Cactus .... 55.00 To 75.00
Tumbler, Cattail & Waterlily 42.50
Tumbler, Fleur–De–Lis 100.00
Tumbler, Sawtooth 75.00
Tumbler, Uneeda Milk Biscuit .... 120.00 To 135.00

The first decorated Christmas tree in America is claimed by many states, including Pennsylvania (1747), Massachusetts (1832), Illinois (1833), Ohio (1838), and Iowa (1845). The first glass ornaments were imported from Germany about 1860. Dresden ornaments were made about 100 years ago of paper and tinsel. Manufacturers in the United States were making ornaments in the early 1870s. Electric lights were first used on a Christmas tree in 1882. Character light bulbs became popular in the 1920s, bubble lights in the 1940s, twinkle bulbs in the 1950s, plastic bulbs by 1955. In this book a Christmas light is a holder for a candle used on the tree. Other forms of lighting include light bulbs.

CHRISTMAS TREE, Cellophane Needles, Chalk Base, Bubble Lights, 29 In. 50.00
Cellophane, White, 28 In. 75.00
Feather, 2 Sections, 66 In. 500.00
Feather, 34 In. 215.00
Feather, 36 In. 375.00
Feather, 40 In. 325.00
Feather, 48 In. 375.00
Feather, Berries, 13 In. 115.00
Feather, Blue–Green, Candleholders On Tips, 58 In. 565.00
Feather, Candleholders, Berries, Germany, 23 In. 195.00
Feather, Frosted Tips, Berries, White Base, 55 In. 525.00
Feather, Germany, 2 Sections, 7 1/2 Ft. 800.00
Feather, Glass Icicles, Beads & Ornaments, 60 In. 400.00
Feather, Green With Red Berries, 46 In. 350.00
Feather, On Musical Tin Base, 24 In. 300.00
Feather, Poinsettia Decals, Green, White Base, 31 In. 230.00
Feather, Red Berries, Wooden Base, Germany, 16 1/2 In. 105.00
Feather, Red Berry Ends, Painted Wood Base, Germany, 42 In. 200.00
Feather, Round Base, White, 14 In. 145.00
Feather, West Germany, 1950s, 27 In. 175.00
Fence, 5 Sides, Goose Feathers, Germany 310.00
Fence, Red & Green, Center Gate, Square, 4 X 19 In. 92.00
Fence, Red, Green, Folding, Double Gate, Wooden, 26 X 36 In. 78.00
Fence, Wooden, 2 Gates 80.00
Garland, Red Tissue Tinsel, National Tinsel, 32 Ft. 13.00
Light Bulb, Ball With Star 10.00
Light Bulb, Basket of Flowers 22.50
Light Bulb, Bear, Eyes To Side, Pink, 2 3/4 In. 80.00
Light Bulb, Bulldog, Sitting, Black Collar, 2 In. 25.00
Light Bulb, Clown, Mazda, 2 1/2 In. 180.00
Light Bulb, Cottage 10.00
Light Bulb, Elephant, Raised Trunk 18.00
Light Bulb, Father Christmas, 8 In. 125.00
Light Bulb, Fearless Fossdick 20.00
Light Bulb, Humpty Dumpty, Brick Wall, Glo–Ray, 3 In. 265.00
Light Bulb, Indian Head, Brown Skin, Headdress, 2 1/2 In. 350.00
Light Bulb, Log Cabin, 2 In. 24.00
Light Bulb, Owl 27.50
Light Bulb, Pine Cones, Plastic, String, 12 In. 14.00
Light Bulb, Pinocchio 10.00
Light Bulb, Popeye 125.00
Light Bulb, Reliance, 6 Original Bulbs, Box 100.00
Light Bulb, Santa Claus, Box, Japan, 8 In. 135.00

Light Bulb, Santa Claus, Double Face .... 10.00 To 25.00
Light Bulb, Santa Claus, Frosted, 10 In. 65.00
Light Bulb, Santa, Milk Glass, Full Figure 30.00
Light Bulb, Silly Symphony, Box 160.00
Light Bulb, Snowball, General Electric, 5 Bulbs 15.00
Light Bulb, Star of Bethlehem, Treetop, Box 10.00
Light Bulb, Sylvania Fluorescent, Box, 7 Bulbs 70.00
Light Bulb, Teddy Bear 15.00
Light, Diamond Point Pattern, Green Glass, 3 1/2 In. 38.00
Light, Eye Pattern, Tin Cover, Sapphire Opalescent 115.00
Light, Pinecone, Clip–On, Glass, 4 In. 35.00
Ornament, Airship 95.00
Ornament, Angel, Gossamer Wings 8.00
Ornament, Angel, Red Head, Gold Harp 7.00
Ornament, Angel, Spun Glass Wings 30.00
Ornament, Angel, Standing, Tinsel Hanger 65.00
Ornament, Angel, Treetop, Box 15.00
Ornament, Angel, Treetop, Holds Banner, Dresden, 6 1/2 In. 185.00
Ornament, Apple, Sparkly Yellow, Pressed Cotton, 2 1/2 In. 28.00
Ornament, Baby In Stocking 6.00
Ornament, Baby Jesus, On Straw Nest, Wax, 3 In. 52.00
Ornament, Baby With Pacifier, Blown Glass 140.00
Ornament, Ball, Campbell's Soup, 1982 .... 3.00
Ornament, Basket of Fruit, Blown Glass 30.00
Ornament, Bear, Annealed Legs, Glass 295.00
Ornament, Bell, 3 Santa Claus Faces 15.00
Ornament, Bird, Clip–On, Glass, Silver, Green Wings, 1930 .... 8.00
Ornament, Bird, Red, Blown Glass 25.00
Ornament, Birdcage, Sequined Base Over Cardbaord, 3 In. 60.00
Ornament, Blue Pulled Swirls, Iridescent, C.1905, 2 In. 68.00
Ornament, Boxer 58.00
Ornament, Bulldog, On Red Pillow, 2 1/4 In. 80.00
Ornament, Camel, Dresden 50.00
Ornament, Candy Bag, Little Girl Celluloid Face, Mesh 75.00
Ornament, Carrot, Orange Paint Over Silver, Glass, 3 3/4 In. 35.00
Ornament, Cat In Shoe, Silver, Pre–1914, 3 1/4 In. 250.00
Ornament, Chandelier, Embossed Silver, Dresden, 5 3/4 In. 32.50
Ornament, Charles Lindbergh 28.00
Ornament, Church, Papier–Mache 7.50
Ornament, Clown's Head, Glass, Molded Teeth, C.1910, 3 In. 95.00
Ornament, Clown, Red & Yellow Suit, Blown Glass, 3 1/4 In. 30.00
Ornament, Coffeepot, Coralene Flowers, 3 In. 13.00
Ornament, Corn, Glass, Pink, Green, Gold Leaves, 1900–20, 3 In. 22.00
Ornament, Cow, Papier–Mache, Brown & White, 5 X 2 In. 45.00
Ornament, Crib, Baby, Beaded, Tinsel Wrapper, Sebnitz, 2 In. 140.00
Ornament, Cuckoo Clock, Bird, Pinecone Weights, 3 1/4 In. 35.00
Ornament, Cupid, Tinsel Wrapper 80.00
Ornament, Devil's Head, 2 Faces, Blown Glass, 6 In. 300.00
Ornament, Dog In Pink Bag, Blown Glass 130.00
Ornament, Dog On Ball, Polychrome, 3 1/2 In. 75.00
Ornament, Dog, Dresden 50.00
Ornament, Dog, Golden Dog, 2 Faces, Blown Glass 150.00
Ornament, Dog, Multicolored, Glass, 3 In. 15.00
Ornament, Elephant, Dresden 50.00
Ornament, Elephant, Glass Eyes, Pressed Cotton, 3 X 6 In. 195.00
Ornament, Elephant, Gold, Pink Blanket, White, 1910, 3 1/4 In. 115.00
Ornament, Elk, Dresden 50.00
Ornament, Father Christmas, Embossed Leaves Over Head 180.00
Ornament, Father Christmas, Full Figure, Celluloid, 5 In. 52.00
Ornament, Fish, Embossed, Gold, Dresden, Flat, 5 In. ....*Illus* 45.00
Ornament, Flying Dove, White, Dresden, 1 1/2 X 3 In. 125.00
Ornament, Football, Glass 95.00
Ornament, Girl's Head, Glass, Painted, Silver Cap, 1910, 2 In. 195.00
Ornament, Girl, In Basket, Gold Hat, Painted, 1920, 2 In. 35.00

Ornament, Girl, In Robe, Flowers In Hair, Blown Glass, 4 In. 100.00
Ornament, Grapes, Child's Face & Arms, Blown Glass 230.00
Ornament, Horn, Glass, Pearly Pink, Pink Flowers, 1920, 5 In. 15.00
Ornament, Horn, Patriotic, Red, Silver & Blue, C.1915, 3 In. 10.00
Ornament, Horse, Brown Fabric, Glass Eyes, 4 3/4 In. 30.00
Ornament, Horsehead In Horseshoe, 2 1/4 In. 65.00
Ornament, Ice Skate, Silver, Hanger, Dresden, 2 1/2 In. 195.00
Ornament, Icicle, Clear Plastic 7.00
Ornament, Icicle, Tin, Twisted, Diamond Ray Jeweled, 2 Boxes 32.00
Ornament, Keystone Cop, Red–Gold Hair & Mustache, 3 1/2 In. 225.00
Ornament, Lamp, On Rocker, Germany, 5 X 6 In. 350.00
Ornament, Lion's Head, Silvered, Blown Glass, 3 1/4 In. 120.00
Ornament, Madonna, Baby, Blue Robe, Glass, Painted, 1950, 5 In. 20.00
Ornament, Mickey Mouse, Glitter On Body, Papier–Mache 55.00
Ornament, Miss Muffet, Glass, Painted, Hat, 1910, 2 1/2 In. 35.00
Ornament, Moon Mullins 65.00
Ornament, Mrs.Claus, Polychrome, 4 1/2 In. 95.00
Ornament, Mushroom, 3 In. 30.00
Ornament, Mushroom, Clip–On 10.00
Ornament, Orphan Annie 50.00
Ornament, Parrot, Full–Bodied, Glass Eyes, Dresden, 6 In. 400.00
Ornament, Peach, Frosted Pink, Gold Fabric, 1910, 2 1/4 In. 22.00
Ornament, Peacock, 1930s 20.00
Ornament, Pickle, Silvered Green Over Paint, 3 3/4 In. 65.00
Ornament, Pinecone 7.00
Ornament, Pocket Watch, White, Red Rim & Numerals, 1 3/4 In. 30.00
Ornament, Rabbit, With Carrot, Cotton 16.00
Ornament, Red Ball Wrapped In Gold & Silver Wire 5.00
Ornament, Red Devil's Head, Clip–On, Blown Glass 300.00
Ornament, Reindeer, Celluloid 3.00
Ornament, Reindeer, Glass Eyes, Dresden, 8 X 9 In. ...._Illus_ 170.00
Ornament, Reindeer, Red Glass Eyes, Celluloid, 5 1/4 In. 5.00
Ornament, Sailboat, Victorian Children, Dresden, 3 3/4 In. 55.00
Ornament, Santa Claus, Head, Pearly Silver, 1910, 3 In. 95.00
Ornament, Santa Claus, Blown Glass, 3 1/2 In. 28.00
Ornament, Santa Claus, Crepe Paper Clothes ...._Illus_ 140.00
Ornament, Santa Claus, Die Cut 15.00
Ornament, Santa Claus, Holding Tree, 3 1/2 In. 18.00
Ornament, Santa Claus, Jack–In–The–Box, 3 In. 25.00
Ornament, Santa Claus, On Skis, Celluloid, 4 In. 35.00
Ornament, Santa Claus, Paper Face, Cotton, 4 3/4 In. 210.00
Ornament, Santa Claus, Pipe Cleaner Body, 6 Reindeer, 6 In. 88.00

Christmas Tree, Ornament,   Christmas Tree, Ornament, Fish,   Christmas Tree, Ornament,
Santa Claus, Crepe Paper   Embossed, Gold, Dresden,   Reindeer, Glass Eyes,
Clothes   Flat, 5 In.   Dresden, 8 X 9 In.

Ornament, Santa Claus, Red, Pearl, Gold Tree, 4 In. 30.00
Ornament, Sheep With Dog, Wooden, Germany, Set of 7 .... 58.00
Ornament, Sheep, Wood & Papier-Mache 23.00
Ornament, Sheep, Wooly, Germany, 2 1/2 In. 35.00
Ornament, Skis, Pair 35.00
Ornament, Sled, White, Germany, 6 1/2 In. 55.00
Ornament, Snow Angel, Gold, Red Coat, Flat, Dresden, 6 3/4 In. 125.00
Ornament, Snowman, Wax 6.00
Ornament, Spinning Wheel, Beaded, Tinsel, Sebnitz 65.00
Ornament, Stork, Clip-On 45.00
Ornament, Street Light, Tinsel Wick, Clip-On, 4 1/2 In. 25.00
Ornament, Swan, On Tinsel Nest 28.00
Ornament, Teapot, Blown Glass, Green 30.00
Ornament, Teapot, Silver 20.00
Ornament, Teddy Bear, Jointed, Wool Over Wood, Glass Eyes 32.00
Ornament, Teddy Bear, On Swing, Wood & Wire, White 190.00
Ornament, Tomato, Red, C.1920, 2 In. 30.00
Ornament, Windmill, Dresden Blades, White, 2 1/2 In. 18.00
Ornament, Wine Bottle, Cotton Batting, Pink, 4 In. 10.00
Ornament, Woodpecker, On Stump, Spun Glass Tail, 2 In. 165.00
Ornament, Zeppelin, American Flag, White Glass, 1915, 4 In. 285.00
Stand, 2 Embossed Santa Claus Faces, Cast Iron, 11 In. 125.00
Stand, Bells, Trees, Open Work Design, Cast Iron, 9 X 9 In. 50.00
Stand, Embossed Poinsettias, Eight Sockets, 13 1/4 In. 25.00
Stand, Farm Scenes, Gathering Wood, Sleds, Snow, Metal 49.00
Stand, Igloo Shape, Made From W.W.I Helmet, Iron 40.00
Stand, Santas & Poinsettias, Tin 40.00

Almost anything connected with Christmas is collected. Ornaments, feather trees, tree stands, santa claus figures, special dishes, even games and wrapping paper. A Belsnickle is a nineteenth-century figure of Father Christmas.

CHRISTMAS, Belsnickle, Blue & Charcoal, 4 1/4 In. 135.00
Belsnickle, Blue, 8 In. 550.00
Belsnickle, Orange, 3 In. 150.00
Belsnickle, Papier-Mache, Chenille Trim, 11 In. 550.00
Belsnickle, Red & Turquoise, 4 1/4 In. 125.00
Belsnickle, Yellow Coat, Red & Blue Cheille Trim, 12 1/2 In. 1300.00
Belsnickle, Yellow Gold Coat, 12 In. ....*Illus* 1300.00
Blotter, Merry Christmas, Celluloid 15.00
Book, A Visit From Santa Claus, Linen, McLaughlin 55.00
Book, Santa Claus In Storyland, Pop-Up Box, 1950 .... 45.00
Box, Cookie, Santa Claus, 1940s 25.00
Bracelet, 6 Charms, Santa In Chimney, 14K Gold, 1950s 275.00
Candle, Santa Claus, Wax, 10 In. 12.00
Candlestand, Amber Glass, Diamond Point, Wire Holder, 3 3/4 In. 38.00
Candy Box, Santa Claus, Nodder, Papier-Mache, 15 In. 25.00
Candy Box, Santa Claus, Zeppelin, American Flag, Early Airplanes 95.00
Centerpiece, Crystal Pine Tree, Plastic Ornaments, Box, 1940s 14.00
Charm, Santa Claus, Celluloid, Red, White, Yellow Sack, 3/4 In. 12.00
Church, White, Cardboard, Cellophane Window, 2 X 3 X 7 In. 38.00
Costume, Santa Claus, Ben Cooper, Box, 1950s 40.00
Dinner Set, Child's, Little Duchess, China, Pinecone Pattern, Box 75.00
Father Christmas, Papier-Mache, Germany, 1910, 4 In. 95.00
Handkerchief, Santa Claus, Cotton, Oriental Print Works, Nast 500.00
Lamp, Santa, Pressed Glass, Original Socket & Cord, 7 3/4 In. 45.00
Manger, Heavy Cardboard, 1940s 20.00
Mask, Santa Claus, Painted Face, 28 In. 285.00
Mold, Food, Rudolph Reindeer, 4 In. 10.00
Nativity Scene, Papier-Mache, German, Stick Leg Animals, 13 Piece 135.00
Nativity Scene, Plastic, West Germany, Box 8.00
Pen Wipe, Bisque Doll Head, Felt, Victorian, Dated Christmas 1890 .... 95.00
Pillow, Made Up of 24 Christmas Hangings, Nast 300.00
Pin, Santa Claus, Chimney Scene, 1900s, 1 1/4 In. 40.00

Christmas, Belsnickle,
Yellow Gold Coat, 12 In.

Christmas, Toy, Santa Claus,
Rubber, Rempal, 10 In.

Pin, Santa Claus, Dark Blue Ground, 1911–20, 1 1/4 In.	35.00
Pin, Santa Claus, Multicolor Litho, 1950s, 1 1/4 In.	20.00
Pinata, Santa Claus, Red Cape, Boots, Cotton Beard, 24 In.	60.00
Planter, Santa Claus In Sleigh, Brad Keeler	40.00
CHRISTMAS, PLATE, see Collector Plate	
Print, Cracker Scrap, St.Nicholas, Reverse Painted, 24 X 32 In.	250.00
Print, Santa Claus, Delivering Toys, 8 X 10 In.	15.00
Reindeer, Green Pottery	2.50
Santa Claus, Bag of Toys, Cutout Windows, 15 X 12 In.	15.00
Santa Claus, Celluloid Face, Papier–Mache	50.00
Santa Claus, Composition Face, Plush, Occupied Japan, 4 1/2 In.	25.00
Santa Claus, In Sleigh, 1 Large Reindeer, Cotton	190.00
Santa Claus, Mask Face, Eyes Light Up, 1940s	100.00
Santa Claus, Mechanical, Papier–Mache, 36 In.	160.00
Santa Claus, Molded Painted Face, Cloth, 29 In.	225.00
Santa Claus, Papier–Mache Face, Cotton Body, 2 1/2 In.	15.00
Santa Claus, Papier–Mache Face, Red Wool Costume, 6 3/4 In.	135.00
Santa Claus, Papier–Mache, Crepe Suit, Cotton Beard, 26 In.	70.00
Santa Claus, Pennsylvania Dutch, Blue, 4 1/2 In.	265.00
Santa Claus, Pennsylvania Dutch, Yellow, 10 In.	275.00
Santa Claus, Plastic, 1950s	5.00
Santa Claus, Standing, Long Coat, Lantern, 4 In.	55.00
Santa, Stuffed Body, Papier–Mache Boots, Red Costume, 32 In.	75.00
Spoon, Enameled Christmas Design Handles, Gold Wash, Meka, 6 Pc.	95.00
Stocking, Mesh, With Toys, Thanhauser, Phila., 1940s, Unused, 21 In.	25.00
Toy, North Pole Village, Flat Metal, 1930, Germany, 1 To 3 In.	395.00
Toy, Santa Claus, Rubber, Rempal, 10 In. ....*Illus*	25.00
Village, 13 Wooden Buildings, Furnished, Electrified, Sleighs	2400.00
Wreath, Holly, Red Berries, Electric Socket, Iron, 12 X 8 3/8 In.	250.00
Wreath, Window, Chenille Wrap, Electric	25.00

Art Deco chrome items became popular in the 1930s. Collectors are most interested in high–style pieces made by the Connecticut firms of Chase Brass and Copper Company and Manning Bowman.

CHROME, Ashtray, Mack Truck Bulldog	40.00
Ashtray, Spinning Bucket, 2 Figural Cigarette Grips, Hamilton, 5 In.	11.00
Candlestick, 3 Arms, Amber & Clear Glass, Chrome Base	50.00
Cigarette Case, Map of Scotland, Tallent–England	27.00
Cocktail Mixer, Black Bands On Cover & Bottom, Chase, 11 1/2 In.	22.00
Cocktail Set, Handle Shaker, 6 Flared Goblets, 7 In.	35.00
Cocktail Set, Shaker, 4 Cups, 4 Muddlers, Chase	90.00
Cocktail Shaker, Art Deco, Black, With Filter, Chase	30.00
Cocktail Shaker, Art Deco, Ice Drainer, Chase	75.00
Cocktail Shaker, Art Deco, Manning Bowman	30.00
Cocktail Shaker, Penguin	325.00
Compote, Nude Stem, Scalloped, Fancy Grape, Leaf, 7 3/4 In.	27.00
Cordial Set, Caddy, Green Plastic Handle, 6 Striped Tumblers	20.00
Cordial Set, Horizontal Rib Glass, 6 Jiggers	25.00
Crumb Set, Farber Bros., Krome Kraft	12.00
Crumber, Chase Brass	35.00
Decanter Set, Music Box Plays How Dry I Am, 5 Piece	30.00
Decanter, Sherry, Amber Glass, Disc Stopper, Farber, 14 3/4 In.	25.00
Figurine, Lady's Head, Stylized, Hagenauer, 14 3/4 & 14 In., Pair	2750.00
Flask, Hip, Leather Cover, 10 Oz.	15.00
Ice Bucket, Art Deco, Cover, Maroon Bakelite Handles	15.00
Ice Bucket, Walking Penguins Around, Art Deco, Cover, Wooden Handles	20.00
Lighter, Table, Airplane	35.00
Napkin Holder, Cocktail, Catalin Handle, Chase	25.00
Pitcher, 4 Goblets, Chase	225.00
Salad Servers, Bakelite Handle	45.00
Stand, Smoker's, Lazy Boy, Art Deco, Chase	250.00
Tray, Basket, Handle, Farber, 7 X 5 In.	7.00

Cigar Store Figure, Indian Princess,
Fisher Cigars, 78 In.

Clarice Cliff pieces marked in black are worth two to three times as much as pieces marked in any other color.

A damaged porcelain clock face is difficult to repair. The damage will lower the price of a clock by 20 to 30 percent.

If you buy an Art Deco bronze and ivory figure, be very careful to examine the ivory. Even slight cracks or other damage lower the value.

Outdoor bronze garden figures should be waxed at least twice a year for protection.

Tray, Folding, Chase Brass 18.00
Tray, Leaf & Scroll, Pierced Double Rim, Kromkraft–Farber, 13 In. 12.00
Tray, Manning Bowman, 3 1/2 X 7 1/2 In. 2.50
Vase, Bud, Cylinder, Chase, 3 1/2 In. 16.00

Carved wooden or cast iron figures were used as advertisements in front of the Victorian cigar store. The carved figures are now collected as folk art. They range in size from counter type, about three feet, to over eight feet high.

CIGAR STORE FIGURE, Indian Princess, Fisher Cigars, 78 In. ....*Illus* 4290.00
Indian, Signed F.F.Artell, C.1910, 7 Ft. 2900.00
Turk, Wooden, Original Paint, 70 In. 8000.00

Cinnabar is a vermilion or red lacquer. Some pieces are made with hundreds of thicknesses of the lacquer that is later carved.

CINNABAR, Box, Cover, 3 1/2 X 5 In. 95.00
Box, Fruit Shape, Floral Designs, 5 In. 95.00
Cabinet, 4 Doors, Ritual Vessels & Flowers, China, 36 X 24 In. 650.00

Civil War mementos are important collectors' items. Most of the pieces are military items used from 1861 to 1865.

CIVIL WAR, Bed, Collapsible, Field Officer's 395.00
Belt & Buckle, Confederate 2100.00
Belt, Sword, Uion, Leather 20.00
Book, Four Years In The Saddle, Colonel Harry Gilmor, 1866 .... 175.00
Booklet, Vicksburg For The Tourist, Pres.Hayes Center, Fremont 10.00
Broadside, Let Us Protect Washington, 12 X 18 1/2 In. 418.00
Canteen, Bull's–Eye 95.00
Canteen, Charcoal Filter, Brass Label Dated July 1, 1861 .... 150.00
Canteen, Leather Strap 60.00
Cap, Beekman Street Hospital, Surgeon, Union 550.00
Carpetbag, Owned By Abraham Lincoln, Given To Soldier 4180.00
Coffeepot, Field 120.00
Cup, Collapsible, Pewter, Brown Japanned Tin Case 65.00
Epaulets, Tin Box 190.00
Helmet, U.S.Army, Spike, 1861, 11 In. 225.00
Holster, Cylinder Pouch & Capper, Kriegsmarine 600.00
Knife, Utility, 2–Piece Wood Scale Grip, 7 In.Blade, Brass Rivets 85.00
Mold, Pistol Ball, 45 Caliber, Scissors Form, Dark Patina, 5 In. 45.00
Print, Camp Bates, 3rd N.Y.Vol.Cavalry, 1860s, 24 X 17 3/4 In. 110.00
Shaving Mug, Tin, Handle & Side Pocket 75.00
Spurs, Officer's, Brass 125.00
Stirrups, Marked U.S., Iron, Pair 50.00
Sword, Officer's 135.00
Telescope, Pocket 30.00
Tobacco Box, Brass, R.Mainwaring From Brother Joseph, 1863 .... 125.00
Uniform, Union, Complete 495.00
Wreath, Reunion, Human Hair, Framed, 12 X 10 1/2 In. 135.00
     CKAW, see Dedham

Clambroth glass, popular in the Victorian era, is a grayish color and is semiopaque like clambroth.

CLAMBROTH, Bottle, Barber, Floral Design 38.00
Bowl, Scalloped, 3 X 12 In. 45.00
Box, Opaline, Egg Shape, Gilt Brass Fittings, With Nest, 4 In. 175.00
Compote, Opaline, Ornate Gilt Base, Lion Finial, 4 X 6 1/4 In. 225.00
Eggcup, Cover, Diamond Point 950.00
Eggcup, Diamond Point, Blue 650.00
Jigger, Paneled, Streak of Ash, 2 1/2 In. 75.00
Scoop, Pickle 25.00
Souvenir, Canoe, Pawnee, Oklahoma, Flowers, Gold Trim 17.50
Spill, Horn of Plenty, Flint 650.00
Vase, Enameled Daisies, Bristol, 10 1/2 In. 25.00

Clarice Cliff NEWPORT POTTERY ENGLAND   Clarice Cliff was a designer who began working at several English factories in the 1920s. She died in 1972.

CLARICE CLIFF, Bone Dish, Tonquin	35.00
Bowl, Balloon Trees, House, Handle, 5 In.	125.00
Bowl, Bizarre, Marked, 6 In.	60.00
Bowl, Cover, D Shape, 8 In.	100.00
Bowl, Plum, 6 In.	10.00
Bowl, Vegetable, Tonquin, Pink	20.00
Coffee Set, Bonjour Pot, Conical Handled Cups, 9 Piece	1800.00
Creamer, Balloon Tree, House, D Shape	150.00
Creamer, Crocus, Large	80.00
Creamer, Sailboats	85.00
Cup & Saucer, Tea Plate, Bizarre, Marked	110.00
Dish, Temple Scene, Bizarre, Oblong, 6 3/4 In.	105.00
Gravy Boat, Underplate, Tonquin	20.00
Honey Pot, Beehive, Autumn Crocus, Bizarre	295.00
Jam Jar, Celtic Harvest, Fruit Handles, Marked, 5 In.	95.00
Jug, Gay Day, 6 In.	575.00
Pitcher, Celtic Harvest, Sheaves of Wheat, Marked, 11 In.	195.00
Pitcher, Fantasque, House & Tree Landscape, 4 1/4 In.	195.00
Plate, Autumn Crocus, 6 1/2 In.	75.00
Plate, Cotswold, 11 In.	55.00
Plate, Spring Crocus, 6 1/2 In.	65.00
Plate, Tonquin, Brown Transfer, 9 1/2 In.	10.00
Soup, Dish, Sunshine, 9 In.	35.00
Sugar Shaker, Bizarre, Flowers, Marked, 5 3/4 In.	125.00
Sugar Shaker, Crocus, Cone Shape, Marked, 5 3/4 In.	135.00
Sugar, Fantasque	70.00
Tumbler, Bizarre, Art Deco, 4 1/4 In.	110.00
Vase, Bizarre, Floral Design, Marked, 5 3/8 In.	165.00
Vase, My Garden, Raised Flowers At Base, Marked, 7 In.	100.00
Vase, Raised Florals, Blue & Cream Ground, Marked, 8 1/2 In.	165.00
Vase, Raised Parakeets, Marked, 12 1/2 In.	175.00
Vase, Tonquin, Flared, 5 1/2 In.	25.00
Vase, Trumpet, Blown–Out Parakeets, Yellow, Green	325.00
Vase, Trumpet, Brown, Orange, Tan & Cream Bands, 8 1/4 In.	525.00

Clewell ware was made in limited quantities by Charles Walter Clewell of Canton, Ohio, from 1902 to 1955. Pottery was covered with a thin coating of bronze, then treated to make the bronze turn different colors. Pieces covered with copper, brass, or silver were also made. Mr. Clewell's secret formula for blue patina bronze was burned when he died in 1965.

CLEWELL, Compote, Signed, 5 In.	80.00
Jar, Seed Form, 5 1/2 In.	175.00
Mug, Medallions On Sides	95.00
Mug, Rivets & Monogram	125.00
Vase, Bulbous, Signed, 4 In.	210.00
Vase, Copper, 6 In.	350.00
Vase, Geometric Designs, Copper Overlay, 9 In.	250.00

Clews pottery was made by George Clews & Co. of Brownhill Pottery, Tunstall, England, from 1806 to 1861.

CLEWS, see also Flow Blue

CLEWS, Plate, Don Quixote & Shepherdess, Dark Blue, 10 In.	250.00
Plate, Dr.Syntax, 10 In.	150.00
Plate, Landing of Lafayette, Blue, 10 In.	195.00
Plate, Peace & Plenty, Blue, 10 In.	250.00

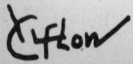   Clifton Pottery was founded by William Long in Clifton, New Jersey, in 1905. He worked there until 1908 making a line called "Crystal Patina." Clifton Pottery made art pottery. Another firm, Chesapeake Pottery, sold majolica marked "Clifton ware."

CLIFTON, Bowl, Robin's–Egg Blue, 1905 .... 90.00
Humidor, Unglazed Terra–Cotta, Indian Geometric Rim & Lid 110.00
Teapot, Green Crystalline, Cover, 5 3/4 In. 70.00
Teapot, Indian Ware, Mottle Yellow Luster, Gold Trim, 7 1/2 In. 57.00
Vase, Crystal Patina, 1905, 8 1/4 In. 90.00
Vase, Indian Ware, Red, Black & White Geometric Design 165.00

Clocks of all types have always been popular with collectors. The eighteenth–century tall case, or grandfather's clock, was designed to house a works with a long pendulum. In 1816, Eli Terry patented a new, smaller works for a clock; and the case became smaller. The clock could be kept on a shelf instead of on the floor. By 1840, coiled springs were used and even smaller clocks were made. Battery–powered electric clocks were made in the 1870s.

CLOCK, Advertising, 7–Up, Plastic 25.00
Advertising, 7–Up, Square Metal Frame 65.00
Advertising, Accutron, Light–Up, 1950s 25.00
Advertising, Ballantine Beer, Moving 3–Ring Pendulum, Electric 33.50
Advertising, Blatz Man, Mechanical 45.00
Advertising, Borden, Electric 45.00
Advertising, Calumet Baking Powder, Regulator .... 365.00 To 850.00
Advertising, Calvert Reserve, Electric 25.00
Advertising, Canada Dry, Plastic Face, Metal Frame, 16 X 16 In. 40.00
Advertising, Dr Pepper, Cap Shape 22.00
Advertising, Dr Pepper, Diamond Shape, 1950s 35.00
Advertising, Duquesne Beer, Lighted, Reverse Painted 350.00
Advertising, Elsie The Cow, Bordens Ice Cream 85.00
Advertising, Ever–Ready Safety Razor, Face In Center Shaving 825.00
Advertising, Fan Tan Gum, Alarm 110.00
Advertising, Gem Razor, Man On Dial, Pendulum 1495.00
Advertising, General Electric, Refrigerator, With Monitor Top 150.00
Advertising, Geraldine Cigars, Baird Clock Co. 330.00
Advertising, Grapette, 1950s 30.00
Advertising, Keebler Bulldog 75.00
Advertising, Kendall Motor Oil 150.00
Advertising, Kodak Film, Pictures Are Priceless, 15 1/2 In. 35.00
Advertising, Lucky Strike, School 575.00
Advertising, Molliscorium, Baird 650.00
Advertising, National Beer of Texas, State Shape, Plaque, 10 X 12 In. 45.00
Advertising, Nu–Grape Soda, Light–Up 47.50
Advertising, Oldsmobile Service, Neon, 1930s 300.00
Advertising, Pan American Exposition, Frying Pan, 1901 .... 145.00
Advertising, Pumpkin Pie Shape 850.00
Advertising, R.C.Cola, Wood Frame, Metal Face 250.00
Advertising, Remington, It's Time To Buy Cutlery, Tin, 1930 .... 2200.00
Advertising, Seagram's, Digital, Number 7 Shape 95.00
Advertising, Silverwood's Ice Cream, Glass Face, Bubble Cover 100.00
Advertising, Squirt, Electric, Square Glass Face, 1950s 70.00
Advertising, Star Brand Shoes 50.00
Advertising, Starkist Foods, Alarm, 1969 .... 20.00
Advertising, Uneeda Boy, Regulator, Wisconsin Clock Co., 32 X 15 In. 500.00
Advertising, Western Union, Battery Operated 75.00
Advertising, Whistle Orange Soda, Metal 45.00
Advertising, William's Garage, Electric, Aztec, 1935 .... 1200.00
Alarm, Animated, Woody Woodpecker, Columbia, 1950 .... 145.00
Alarm, Barbie, Talking 20.00
Alarm, Double Bell, Parker, Nickel 250.00
Alarm, Gilbert, War, Box 60.00
Alarm, John Wayne 75.00
Ansonia, Box Regulator, Oak 395.00
Ansonia, Double Statue, Fisherman & Hunter 1100.00
Ansonia, Fire Screen Form, Painted & Metal, C.1880, 20 1/4 In. 550.00
Ansonia, Florentine, Velvet 275.00
Ansonia, Long Drop, Time & Strike, Oak 350.00

Clock, French, Mantel,
Bronze, C.1900, 18 In.

Clock, French, Mantel, Bronze, Cupid,
Psyche, Empire Design, 25 In.

Clock, French, Mantel, Woman, Basket, Fruit,
Deer, Bronze & Alabaster

Clock, Seth Thomas, Mantel, Ship's Bell,
Bronze Wave Base, 23 In.

Clock, McCabe, Regency, Brass,
Ebonized, Striking, 26 1/2 In.

Never wind an old clock counterclockwise. Clocks that are wound
from the back should be wound
counterclockwise because that is
clockwise from the front of the
clock.

Ansonia, Louis XIV Style, Cast Iron, Porcelain Dial .... 250.00 To 285.00
Ansonia, Mantel, Brass Lion Handles, Cast Iron 100.00
Ansonia, Mantel, Cherub Base, Violinist On Top, Gilded, 30 In. 375.00
Ansonia, Porcelain Dial, Visible Escapement, Brass & Glass 240.00
Ansonia, Porcelain Dial, Yellow, Flowers, Royal Bonn 285.00
Ansonia, Racket Alarm, Strikes Hour & Half Hour 100.00
Ansonia, Regulator, Brass Cased Crystal, Beveled Glass Panels, 11 In. 250.00
Ansonia, Royal Bonn Case, 1895, 8 In. 275.00
Ansonia, School, Long Drop, Time & Strike, England 250.00
Ansonia, Statue, Florida 1800.00
Ansonia, Statue, Shakespeare 495.00
Ansonia, Tambour, Octagonal, Miniature 65.00
Ansonia, Versailles, Painted Cupids, Cast Metal 375.00
Ansonia, Wall, Roman Numerals, Arts & Craft 700.00
Atkins, Short Drop Regulator, Ripple–Front Rosewood, Wagon Spring 2650.00
Banjo, Brass Framed Dial, Reverse Painted Panel, New England, C.1830 .... 600.00
Banjo, Federal, Mahogany, Eglomise, 1825, Mt.Vernon Scene, 29 In. 2095.00
Banjo, New Haven, Reverse Painting of Mt.Vernon, Miniature 135.00
Banjo, War of 1812 Depicted On Glass, C.1815 .... 6500.00
Boulle, Louis XV, Wistariahurst 6050.00
Bracket, Brass Face, Walnut Case, Carl Stritzcku, 19th Century 700.00
Bracket, Gilt Design, Green Japanned, Danl.De St.Leu, C.1720, 20 In. 8250.00
Bracket, King George II, 1730–50, English 5000.00
Bracket, Louis XV, Brass, Tortoiseshell Boulle, C.1730, 4 Ft.4 In. 3850.00
Bracket, Regency Style, Gilt Bronze, Boulle Marquetry, 5 Ft.6 In. 2970.00
Carriage, Champleve Enameling, Chinese Style, Brass, 6 In. 825.00
Carriage, Minute Repeating, Quadrangular Case, C.1900 .... 1650.00
Cartel, Louis XVI, Floral Wreath, Porcelain Dial, Bagues & Fils 600.00
Chelsea, Engine Room, Phenolic Case, Black Dial 90.00
Clown, German Weight Driven, Moving Eyes 45.00
Cowboy, Waving Hat, Rearing Bronco, Copper, Electric, 18 X 18 In. 95.00
Cuckoo, Black Forest, Carved Leaf & Bird Design, Half & Hour Song 95.00
Cuckoo, Black Forest, Quail On Quarter Hour, Cuckoo On Hour, 1914 .... 500.00
Cuckoo, Carved Stag On Top, Deer & Game Scene, Germany 300.00
Cuckoo, Wooden, Glass Eyes, Germany, 9 X 7 In. 20.00
Dresden Style, Scrolled Brass Front, 10 1/2 In. 385.00
French, Arched Pediment, Onyx Pilasters, 8–Day, Strike, 16 1/2 In. 400.00
French, Hanging, Porcelain, Round, 9 In. 110.00
French, Mantel, Bronze, 2 Cherub Heads, C.1900, 20 In. 750.00
French, Mantel, Bronze, C.1900, 18 In. ....*Illus* 440.00
French, Mantel, Bronze, Cupid, Psyche, Empire Design, 25 In. ....*Illus* 2200.00
French, Mantel, Drum Shape, Columns, Sunburst Pendulum, 17 1/4 In. 330.00
French, Mantel, Gilt Bronze, Alabaster, Woman, Basket of Fruit, 18 In. 650.00
French, Mantel, Gilt Bronze, Man Reads Oedipus, C.1900, 18 In. 400.00
French, Mantel, Lady & Suitor At Top, Porcelain, 18 7/8 In. 440.00
French, Mantel, Marble Columns Over Dial, Gilt Bronze, 13 1/2 In. 500.00
French, Mantel, Porcelain, Onyx & Ormolu Trim, 2 Urns, 16 In., 3 Piece 350.00
French, Mantel, Urn Form, Alabaster, Enamel Dial, Brass Mounts, 17 In. 286.00
French, Mantel, Woman, Basket, Fruit, Deer, Bronze & Alabaster ....*Illus* 650.00
French, Openwork & Carved Stem Design, Brass Pendulum, C.1900, 22 In. 1210.00
French, Picture Frame, Enameled Dial, Inlaid Case, Square, 21 In. 235.00
German, Cuckoo, Quail & Cuckoo, 3 Weights, Dated 1914, 21 X 13 In. 500.00
Gilbert, Alarm, Oak, Dated 1904 .... 95.00
Gilbert, Banjo, 23 In. 85.00
Gilbert, Banjo, Lyre, With Barometer & Thermometer 145.00
Gilbert, Mantel, Black Wood, Cast Foot & Pillars 100.00
Gilbert, Parlor, Occidental, Mirror Sides, Walnut 600.00
Gilbert, Regulator, Jeweler's, No.16, Walnut, Floor Model 5800.00
Gilbert, Regulator, No.14 .... 1050.00
Gilbert, Regulator, No.16, Jewelers, Floor Model, Walnut 5800.00
Gilbert, School, Admiral, Calendar, Oak 250.00
Glo–Dial, Neon 250.00
Granger & Quelaines, Monk's, Enameled Face, 2 Iron Weights, 53 In. 800.00
Gustav Stickley, Mantel, Oak, Door, Leaded Window, 14 X 8 1/2 In. 3000.00

Hall, Herschede, 5 Crown Tubes, Mahogany, 7 1/2 In. 9500.00
Henry Voisin, Mantel, Louis XVI, Marble, Ormolu, 18th Century, 17 In. 6325.00
Hickory Dickory Dock, Philadelphia Label 1000.00
Howard, Banjo, No.5, Rosewood Grained Case 2500.00
I.B.M., Master, Wall, Weight 400.00
Ingersoll, Shelf, Double Dial Calendar 700.00
Ingraham, Alarm, Bugs Bunny 225.00
Ingraham, Banjo, Treasure Island 395.00
Ingraham, Bugs Bunny, Alarm 127.50
Ingraham, Calendar, Dewdrop, Grain Painted Rosewood 325.00
Ingraham, Grecian, 8–Day, Time & Strike, Label 240.00
Ingraham, Mantel, 8–Day, Walnut 175.00
Ingraham, Regulator, Bonnet, Pendulum, Alligatored, 38 X 16 In. 325.00
Ingraham, Regulator, Calendar & Time, Oak Case 375.00
Ingraham, Regulator, Wall, Brass Pendulum, Key, Oak, 38 1/2 In. 325.00
Ingraham, Wall, Ionic, Figure 8 .... 375.00
International, Time Recorder, Oak Case, Glass Side Doors, 35 1/2 In. 225.00
Japanese, Bronze, Sky & Water Dragon, French Movement, 1905 .... 2200.00
John Holm, Wall, Gilt Cartel Type, Stockholm, 26 In. 365.00
Joshua Farrer, Tall Case, Mahogany, 18–Day, 1800, English 3400.00
Kieninger, 2 Weights, 29 1/2 In. 145.00
Kit–Kat, Animated, Black, Rhinestone Collar .... 35.00 To 45.00
Kitchen, Red Wing, Aunt Jemima, Ceramic 100.00
Kroeber, Shelf, 30–Hour, Brass Movement 145.00
LeCoultre, Atmos, 15 Jewels, 9 1/8 X 8 1/4 In. 285.00
LeCoultre, Chamfered Case, Gilt Metal & Glass, 9 1/2 In. 192.00
Liberty & Co., Mantel, Pewter, Copper, Enameled, C.1900 .... 2850.00
Lighthouse, Napoleon III, Brass, Champleve, Nautical Design, 20 In. 4500.00
Louis XVI Style, Marble, 3 Graces, Rotary Dial, Gilt Bronze, 35 In. 7425.00
Louis XVI, Cartel, Ormolu, Bearded Mask Bottom, 18th Century, 29 In. 2975.00
Louis XVI, Garniture, Gilt Bronze, Mask Ring Handles, C.1870, 3 Piece 995.00
Lux, Black Sambo, Moving Eyes & Tie 425.00
Lux, Red Petunia, Pendulum, Box 250.00
Lux, Schmoo, Pink 135.00
Lyre, Wall, Mahogany, Partial London, England Label, Replaced Finial 3000.00
Malachite, Dial Between 2 Gilt Metal Columns, 8 1/2 In. 1100.00
Mantel, Art Deco, Silvered Bronze, Dragonflies, Round Top, 1925, 12 In. 900.00
Mantel, Bronze, Musical Cherubs, Enameled Dial, Figures, 25 In. 2000.00
Mantel, Egyptian Revival, Bronze, Bailey, Banks & Biddle, 16 In. 1320.00
Mantel, Empire, Ormolu, Hippolytus, Chariot, 19th Century, 19 1/4 In. 6600.00
Mantel, Female With Arms On Top, Bronze & Onyx, C.1890, 18 1/2 In. 1400.00
Mantel, Fisherman, Gilded Cast Metal, Brass Works, Enamel Dial, 14 In. 60.00
Mantel, Florals On Black Ground, Cast Iron, Owen & Clark, 20 1/2 In. 95.00
Mantel, Louis Philippe, Figural, Gothic Rose Window, Maiden, 27 In. 1650.00
Mantel, Louis Philippe, Gilt & Bronze, Seated Child, Swags, 16 In. 2200.00
Mantel, Louis Philippe, Ormolu, Fisherman, Seated, 16 1/2 In. 2200.00
Mantel, Louis XVI, Ormolu & Marble, Balthazar, C.1780, 15 3/4 In. 4400.00
Mantel, Napoleon III, Figural, Reclining Female Figure, C.1870, 15 In. 1550.00
Mantel, Napoleon III, Frieze Over Dial, Time & Strike, Brass, 23 In. 1700.00
Mantel, Napoleon III, Slate, Time & Strike, C.1870, 14 3/4 In. 300.00
Mantel, Silver, Victorian, Cartouche Shape, 1899, 7 1/2 In. 2750.00
Mantel, Skeleton–Type, Fusee Movement, Glass Dome, 17 1/2 In. 550.00
Mauser Mill Co., Brass Plate, Cathedral, Electric, 4 1/2 X 6 In. 58.00
McCabe, Regency, Brass, Ebonized, Striking, 26 1/2 In. ....*Illus* 2200.00
Middletown, Figural, Cherub, Rabbit, Standing On Leaf, Silver Plate 225.00
New Haven, Banjo, Whitney 165.00
New Haven, Cathedral, 30–Hour, Brass Movement, Alarm 135.00
New Haven, Cherubs, Rhinestone Around Face, Bronze On Copper, 10 In. 145.00
New Haven, Flower Girl, Seated Woman, Birds, Scrollwork Base, 12 In. 455.00
New Haven, Open Escapement, Lions' Heads At Side, Cast Iron 175.00
New Haven, School, English–Type, Inlay, C.1900 .... 175.00
New Haven, Walnut, Tambour, Striking, 1915 .... 65.00
Nottingham, Tall Case, Oak, Mahogany, Hunting Scene, Cornice, 86 In. 1400.00
Pedestal, Rouge Marble, Green Onyx Hood, Enamel Dial, 4 Ft.2 In. 7150.00

Pillar & Scroll, American, Mahogany, Floral Spandrels, 1830, 29 In.	1200.00
Pillar, Japanese, Reverse Painted Escapements, Brass Weight Works	850.00
Postal Telegraph, Synchronous	120.00
Regency Style, Boulle Marquetry, Gilt Bronze, Pedestal, 1870, 7 Ft.	4125.00
Regulator, Brass Weight–Driven 8–Day Movement, L.A.Hunt, 1865, 66 In.	375.00
Regulator, Master, Stromberg, Oak, 1915, 5 Ft.	550.00
Scott, Tall Case, Mahogany, 8–Day, Strike, Arched Dial, C.1840, 7 Ft.	1400.00
Sessions, Banjo, Small	100.00
Sessions, Cherub On Top, 11 In.	125.00
Sessions, Held By Art Deco Nude, Metal, 1930s	165.00
Sessions, Mantel, Lions' Heads	75.00
Sessions, Regulator, 2 Weights, Oak	750.00
Sessions, Walnut Ship, Chrome Sails, Box	125.00
Seth Thomas, Alamantine, 1880	300.00
Seth Thomas, Alarm, Weight Driven, Reverse Painted Stork	200.00
Seth Thomas, Art Deco, Skyscraper Style, Key Wind	150.00
Seth Thomas, Banjo, Pomfret, Jeweled Movement, Burled Walnut	150.00
Seth Thomas, Banjo, Time & Strike, Pendulum	375.00
Seth Thomas, Banjo, Treasure Island, Time & Strike	395.00
Seth Thomas, Bracket, 1/4 Hour Westminster Chimes, Mahogany	200.00
Seth Thomas, Cincinnati, Reverse Glass of Sleeping Fisherman	335.00
Seth Thomas, Commemorative, Great White Fleet, Paper Label	235.00
Seth Thomas, Firehouse, 30–Day, Rings Bell	950.00
Seth Thomas, Half–Column, 30–Hour	475.00
Seth Thomas, Kitchen, Alarm, 30–Hour, C.1840	260.00
Seth Thomas, Kitchen, Oak, 8–Day, Time & Strike	200.00
Seth Thomas, Locomotive, Key Wind, Brass	295.00
Seth Thomas, Mantel, Oak, Arts & Crafts	1320.00
Seth Thomas, Mantel, Ship's Bell, Bronze Wave Base, 23 In. ....*Illus*	990.00
Seth Thomas, Mantel, Time & Strike, 4 Pillars, 2 Bronze Lions, C.1870	185.00
Seth Thomas, Metals Series, Brass Trim, No.6	125.00
Seth Thomas, School, Octagon Drop, Oak	250.00
Seth Thomas, Shelf, Concord, Cities Series, Walnut	225.00
Seth Thomas, Sonora Adamantine, 4 Bells	335.00
Seth Thomas, Tall Case, Wooden Works, 93 1/2 In.	1900.00
Seth Thomas, Watchman's, Oak, Nickel Trim, 1898, 5 Ft.	1000.00
Shelf, Empire, Reverse Painted Glass, Garner Curtis, Mahogany, 29 In.	700.00
Ship's Bell, 8–Day, Brass, Beveled Glass, German Movement	225.00
Silas Hoadley, Tall Case, Cherry, 8–Day Wooden Movement, Painted Face	2700.00
Silver, Viennese, Female Figures, Birds, Lapis Lazuli, 1885, 6 1/2 In.	3300.00
Spanish American War & McKinley, Commemorataive, Pressed Wood	330.00
Standard, Master, Electric, Wall, 5 Ft.	450.00
Street, Bartlesville, Okla., 2 Sides, Dial 30 In., 15 Ft.	4000.00
Swedish, Wood, 1–Day, Blue Ground, Red & Cream Floral, Hour Hand, 1840	4500.00
Swiss, Table, Gilt Metal & Glass, Circular Face, 9 1/2 In.	195.00
Tall Case, 8–Day Brass Weights, Fretwork Above Door, C.1815, 86 In.	5100.00
Tall Case, 9 Chimes, German Works, Mahogany, C.1905	3600.00
Tall Case, A.Hurt, George II, Oak, 1 Weight, 77 1/2 In. ....*Illus*	800.00
Tall Case, Brass & Silver Dial, Mahogany, C.1890, 94 In.	1265.00
Tall Case, Brass Finials, Glazed Door, 8–Day, Key Wind, Ithaca, 85 In.	450.00
Tall Case, Brass Rosettes, Reverse Glass Panels, English, 93 In.	5700.00
Tall Case, Chinoiserie, Dark Green Ground, Pendulum, Europe, 104 In.	1650.00
Tall Case, Chippendale, Pennsylvania, Walnut, C.1785, 7 Ft.7 In.	4950.00
Tall Case, Chippendale, Walnut, David Rittenhouse Dial, C.1770	9000.00
Tall Case, Cincinnati, 5 Tubes, C.1900	1300.00
Tall Case, Colonial Mfg.Co., Westminster Chimes, Mahogany, 92 In.	1225.00
Tall Case, Dutch Rococo, Arched Bonnet, Burr Walnut, 7 Ft.10 In.	9350.00
Tall Case, Federal, Mahogany, Arched Hood, Painted Dial, 93 In.	4000.00
Tall Case, Federal, Will Claggett, Inlaid Cherry, C.1805, 91 1/2 In.	4675.00
Tall Case, Fretwork, Wooden Dial, 30–Hour, New England, C.1830, 85 In.	1300.00
Tall Case, Garrett, Philadelphia, 1790–1802, 96 In.	7500.00
Tall Case, George III, Mahogany, Bristol, Arched Door, C.1770, 103 In.	4250.00
Tall Case, George III, Mahogany, Painted Dial, Roman Numerals, 99 In.	4500.00
Tall Case, George III, Oak & Mahogany, Signed Dial, Spandrels, 80 In.	1600.00

Clock, Tall Case, A.Hurt,
George II, Oak, 1 Weight, 77 1/2 In.

Clock, Tall Case, Oak, Mahogany,
Turned Columns, English, 86 In.

Tall Case, George III, Painted Face, Inlaid Mahogany, 7 Ft.8 In. 605.00
Tall Case, H.Hahn, Moon Phases, Date, Walnut, C.1810, 7 Ft.9 1/2 In. 7975.00
Tall Case, Hepplewhite, Cherry, Line Inlay, Moon Dial 5000.00
Tall Case, Italian Renaissance, Carved Spandrels, 3 Chimes 8000.00
Tall Case, John Baker, Oak, Bonnet, Seven Oaks, Key, English, 83 In. 1300.00
Tall Case, John Mill, Montrose, Quarter Columns, Mahogany, 85 1/2 In. 2800.00
Tall Case, Luman Watson, Cherry, Pine 2778.00
Tall Case, Mahogany, Ebonized, Anchor Escapement, C.1820, 91 In. 3600.00
Tall Case, Mahogany, Oak, 8–Day, Musical, Pagoda, London, 1780, 91 In. 5500.00
Tall Case, Oak, Mahogany, Turned Columns, English, 86 In. ....*Illus* 1540.00
Tall Case, Pennyslvania, Painted, John Shaffer, 1870 .... 3850.00
Tall Case, Peter Tawney, Chinoiserie, Black Japanned, 7 Ft.8 In. 3850.00
Tall Case, Pine, Bonnet, Brass Works, Calendar, Pendulum, 88 In. 1100.00
Tall Case, Quarter Hour Strike, 8 Bells, Mahogany, English, C.1810 .... 9500.00
Tall Case, Reed, Watson, Pine Case 3800.00
Tall Case, Silas Hoadley, Painted Dial, Painted Design, Pine, 62 In. 4400.00
Tall Case, Smith Patterson Co., Brass & Steel Face, Moon Dial, 92 In. 1100.00
Tall Case, Solomon Curtis, Philadelphia 3900.00
Tall Case, Tho.Butterfield, Burled Walnut Veneer, Pendulum, 87 In. 4300.00
Tall Case, Thomas Cherington, George III, Mahogany, Musical 5500.00
Telechron, Radio Shape, Bakelite 90.00
Terry, Piller & Scroll, Mahogany, Reverse Painted, Pendulum, 32 In. 650.00
    CLOCK, TIFFANY, see Tiffany, Clock
Victorian, Garniture, Black & Rouge Marble, Architectural Form, 3 Pc. 1540.00
Viennese Enamel, Hinged Lid, Classical Scenes, 8 In. 1500.00
Wag–On–The–Wall, Brass Works, Wooden Plates, Wooden Case, 13 In. 225.00
Wag–On–The–Wall, Moon Phase Dial, Scenic Panel, Connecticut, 17 In. 1900.00
Waltham, Aircraft, Sweep Second Hand, Date, 24–Hour Black Dial 75.00
Waltham, Banjo, Weight Driven 1275.00
Waltham, Tall Case, Westminster, 5 Tubes, Quartered Oak, 7 Ft.10 In. 6800.00
Waterbury, Carriage, Brass, 4 1/2 In. 125.00
Waterbury, Ironstone, Brass, Flowers, Blue & Gilt Trim, 13 In. 175.00

Waterbury, Mantel, 8–Day, Weights & Pendulum 75.00
Waterbury, Regulator No.8, Jeweler's, Pinwheel, Deadbeat, 96 In. 6000.00
Waterbury, Tall Case, Westminster Chime, Carved Mahogany 2200.00
Waterbury, Wall, Porcelain Dial, Chimes 385.00
Watson, Tall Case, Hepplewhite, Oval Medallion On Door 2750.00
Welch, Calendar, Damorosch 500.00
Welch, Double Dial Calendar, Arditi Model, Gale's Pat.Movement 650.00
Welch, Regulator, Wall, Store 395.00
Welch, School, 8–Day, Mahogany 295.00
Welch, Shelf, Rosewood Patti No.2, 8–Day & Time, Pat.1878, 10 X 8 In. 2500.00
Westclox, Alarm, Baby Ben 45.00
Westclox, Alarm, Moonbeam, Celluoid 25.00
Willard, Banjo, Urn At Top, Reverse Painted Mount Vernon, 29 3/4 In. 2090.00
Williams & Hughes, Moon Phase Dial, 8–Day Time & Strike, Weight 1325.00

Cloisonne enamel was developed during the tenth century. A glass enamel was applied between small ribbonlike pieces of metal on a metal base. Most cloisonne is Chinese or Japanese. Pieces marked "China" are twentieth–century examples.

CLOISONNE, Box, Cover, Allover Silver Wire & Pink Enamel Design, 1898, 6 In. 3135.00
Box, Cover, Blue Floral, Footed, 3 1/2 X 4 In. 85.00
Box, Hinged Cover, Allover Flowers, Hanging Grapes, 3 3/4 In. 85.00
Box, Hinged Cover, Blue & Gold, 5 In. 35.00
Box, Hinged Cover, Brass Frame Forms Feet, Scrolls, 4 1/2 X 3 In. 165.00
Charger, Bird, Flowers, Turquoise, Scalloped Border, Japan, 12 In. 375.00
Charger, Dragon Center, Faces Around Inner Band, 17 1/2 In. 475.00
Charger, Fish, Butterfly & Flower Center, 12 1/2 In. 475.00
Dish, Sweetmeat, 3 Sections, Blue Floral, 8 1/2 In. 125.00
Figurine, Rooster Standing On Rookery, China, 38 In. 300.00
Figurine, Tan War Horse, Chinese, 12 In. 50.00
Jar, Cover, Gold Spike Finial, Flowers, 8 In., Pair 375.00
Jar, Cover, Pink Cherry Blossom, Black, 1880, 3 3/4 In. 9350.00
Jug, 3 Panels, Dragon, Bird, Flowers & Butterlfies, 5 In. 240.00
Mirror, Swivel Base & Mirror, Bird & Flowers, 18 In. 375.00
Plate, 7 Birds In Flight, 10 1/2 In. 125.00
Plate, Flying Bird, Water Lily Blossom, Frogs, 10 3/4 In. 325.00
Salt Dip, 1 Black, 1 Red, Footed, Pair 18.00
Snuff Bottle, Flower & Butterfly Panels, Blue, Pear Shape, 3 In. 80.00
Tea Jar, Dragon & Pearl With Cloud Scrolls 65.00
Teapot, Butterflies, Goldstone, 4 1/2 In. 225.00
Vase, Alternating Shield Panels of Dragon, Phoenix Bird, 12 In. 385.00
Vase, Brown Sparrows, Japan, Late 19th Century, 18 In. ....*Illus* 3000.00
Vase, Colored Bird Sitting In Foliage, Blue Ground, 2 3/8 In. 275.00
Vase, Double Cloisons, Red Ground, Teak Base, 8 3/4 In., Pair 450.00
Vase, Double Gourd, Cloud, Scroll Panels, 9 1/2 In. 350.00
Vase, Flowers, Enamel, Globular Form, Wide Neck, Japan, 18 In. 3000.00
Vase, Flowers, Yellow Ground, Baluster Form, 19th Century, 37 In. 275.00
Vase, Iris, Wisteria, Blue, Japan, 6 In. 70.00
Vase, Lotus Blossoms, Cylindrical, 4 1/2 In. 65.00
Vase, Overall Polychrome Chrysanthemums, Turquoise, 13 In. 175.00
Vase, Pink Flowers, Black, 8 In. 90.00
Vase, Prunus, Dogwood, Green, 5 In. 95.00
Vase, Purple Floral, Butterflies, Foil Ground, 7 In. 255.00
Vase, Stylized Corners, Pigeons & Rose Bushes, Japan, 13 In. 400.00
Vase, Urns With Flowers, Black Ground, Bulbous, 7 In. 70.00
Vase, Wisterias & Foliage, Japan, 6 1/2 In., Pair 390.00

Antique and collectible clothes of all types are listed in this section. Dresses, hats, shoes, underwear and more are found here. Other textiles are to be found in the Textile, World War I, World War II, Quilt, and Coverlet sections.

CLOTHING, Apron, Blue & White Checks, Long 20.00
Apron, Blue & White Homespun 48.00
Baseball Uniform, Carlisle, Penna., 1930s 125.00

Bathing Suit, Woman's, Body Suit, Overdress, Dotted, 20th Century 25.00
Bathing Tunic, Sateen, 1915 .... 25.00
Bed Jacket, Floral Print, Pink Rayon, Lace Trim, 1940s 10.00
Bed Jacket, Scalloped Collar, Pockets, Ribbon Trim, Ecru 7.00
Bib, Baby's, Sheer, Tiny Embroidery Work 10.00
Blouse, Beading, Red Silk 25.00
Blouse, High Neck, White Lacy Yoke, 1905 .... 10.00
Blouse, Long Sleeves, Crocheted, Roses, Orange, Drawstring Neck 12.00
Bonnet, Amish, Black 35.00
Bonnet, Baby's, Fishnet Openwork, Double Scalloped Rim 4.00
Bonnet, Black Lace, Silk Ribbons, Ostrich Boa, 1890s 50.00
Bonnet, Black Velvet, Sequins, Silk Band, Lace, Feathers, 1900s 40.00
Bonnet, Hand–Woven Fabric, Hand Gathered & Stitched, 19th Century 65.00
Bonnet, Silk, Crochet Lace, Handmade, 1900 .... 35.00
Bow Tie, Clip–On, White On White, Silk 4.50
Camisole, Peach Rayon Knit, Thin Straps, Drawstring Top 2.50
Cap, Lace, Floral & Leaf Lace Edge, Dutch 30.00
Cape, Beaded, Circular Pattern, Black, 1875 .... 65.00
Cape, Black Organza, White Leaves, Pearls, 20 In. 14.00
Cape, Black Wool, Black Beaded Circle Pattern, 1875 .... 175.00 To 225.00
Cape, Crocheted, Purple Zigzag Bottom, Button Front 14.00
Cape, Fuchsia, Silk, Velvet, Fox Collar, Long, 1920s 60.00
Cape, Off–White Wool, Lined, Floor Length, 1950s 95.00
Cape, Taffeta, C.1890 .... 20.00
Chinese Costume, Jacket, Skirt, Pants, Silk Brocade, 1860s 750.00
Coat, Alaskan Seal, Black, Mink Trim, 1940s 100.00
Coat, Child's, Silk Brocade, Embroidered, Chinese, 1850s 250.00
Coat, Cotton, Silk, Black, Embroidered, Button, 1850s 125.00
Coat, Man's, Cashmere, Full Length 200.00
Coat, Man's, Pendleton Wool, Brown 75.00
Coat, Opera, Red Silk Velvet, Ermine Collar, Full Length 95.00
Coat, Raccoon, Man Or Woman, Medium 135.00

Coalport, Plate, Peeled Half Lemon,
Dated 1808, 9 1/2 In.

Collar, Honiton Lace, Large	135.00
Crinoline, 3 Tiers, Embroidered Flowers, Barbizon, Size 14	13.00
Dress, Baby's, Embroidered, Lace, Ruffles, Tiny Buttons Down Front	25.00
Dress, Baby's, Puffed Sleeves, Embroidered, Pale Yellow	10.00
Dress, Battenberg Lace Skirt With Train, Blouse & Silk Sash	500.00
Dress, Beige Chiffon, Drop Waist, Lace Trim, 1930s	70.00
Dress, Black & White Striped Silk, C.1900, Size 12	38.00
Dress, Black Crepe, Red Velvet Trim, Short, 1930–40	15.00
Dress, Black Lace, Size 14, 1920s	75.00
Dress, Black Satin, Bustle, Lace Trim, 2 Piece	85.00
Dress, Black Silk, C.1890, 2 Piece	60.00
Dress, Black Taffeta, Pink Flowers, Long	80.00
Dress, Black, Net Overskirt, Ruffled Waist, Scalloped Neck, 1920s	12.50
Dress, Black, Silk & Lace, Beaded Collar, 1920s	250.00
Dress, Blue & White Calico	98.00
Dress, Chemise, Sequins, Art Deco	85.00
Dress, Child's, Handkerchief Linen, Tatted	38.00
Dress, Christening, French Seams, Lace Edging, C.1900	24.00
Dress, Christening, Lace Trim, White Lawn, C.1880	65.00
Dress, Eyelet Full Skirt, Long Sleeves, Medium Size	45.00
Dress, Flapper, Black, Crystal Beads	90.00
Dress, Flapper, Brown, Copper & Lavender Beads	90.00
Dress, Flapper, Embroidered Panels	135.00
Dress, Flapper, Red, 1920s	15.00
Dress, Flapper, Royal Blue, With Feather Headband, Size 16	45.00
Dress, Girl's, Brown Dots, Cotton, Mother-of-Pearl Buttons, 1900	25.00
Dress, Gold Lame, Silk & Velvet Floral Applied Design	55.00
Dress, Graduation, Rows of Lace, Full Skirt, Large Collar	55.00
Dress, Knitted Boucle, Vertical Stripes, Drop Waist, Miss Joan	16.00
Dress, Metallic Thread, Rayon, Tiers of Stripes, Long, 1940s	12.00
Dress, Prom, Strapless, Tier Skirt, Blue, 1950s	25.00
Dress, Red Silk, Crystal Beaded Bodice, Full Skirt, 1950	35.00
Dress, Sienna Velveteen, Gold Stenciled, Venetian Beads, Fortuny	4500.00
Dress, Strapless, Bolero, 1950s	38.00
Dress, Taffeta, Bronze, Metallic Lace, Rhinestones, 1920s	65.00
Dress, Victorian, Mourning, Black Silk	70.00
Dress, Victorian, Ribbed, Wide Eyelet Collar & Hem, Long Sleeves	50.00
Dress, Wedding, 2 Petticoats, Skirt & Blouse, 1890, 4 Piece	850.00
Dress, Wedding, Early 1900s, 2 Piece	98.00
Dress, Wedding, Satin & Lace, Train With Inserts of Lace, 1940s	75.00
Dress, Wedding, White Lawn, Embroidered & Tucked, C.1900	175.00
Dress, Wedding, White Lawn, Embroidered Yoke, Ruffles, Size 10	135.00
Gloves, Crocheted, Victorian	8.00
Gloves, White Kid, Long, Unused	30.00
Gloves, Woman's, Hand Tatted	20.00
Hat, Baby's, Crocheted, Cloth Lined, Hand Stenciled	5.00
Hat, Beaver, Signed, Lancaster, Pa., Original Wallpaper Box, C.1830	250.00
Hat, Child's, Peach & Green Silk Organdy	25.00
Hat, Fur, Leopard Skin, Pillbox Style	35.00
Hat, Straw, Black, Broad Rim, Ostrich Plumes, 1930s	20.00
Hat, Union Parade, Black, Gold Letters, Sunburst Design, No.1, 1789	3750.00
Hat, Widow's, Veiling, World War I	35.00
Hose, Seamed, Wilborn, Wrapper	2.00
Jacket, Band, University of Illinois, Wool, Insignia, 1939	30.00
Jacket, Bolero, Black Sequins, 1950s	75.00
Jacket, Long Black Monkey Fur, Hip Length, Medium	325.00
Jacket, Smoking, Black Velvet, 1903	75.00
Jacket, Woman's, Velvet, French, 1920, Size 12	40.00
Kabuki Robe, Gold Thread, Black, Silk, Japan, 19th Century	1000.00
Leggings, Child's, Black, Knit	8.00
Mantilla, Black Floral Lace, Triangular, 48 X 48 X 89 In.	28.00
Muff, Teddy Bear, Steiff, White	695.00
Nightgown, Child's, White, Lace Panel, Tucked	10.00
Nightgown, Edwardian, White, 1905	55.00

Nightgown, Pink Rayon, Lace Straps & Neck, Embroidered Flowers 12.00
Nightgown, Silk, Hawaiian, Openwork, Embroidered, Unworn, Size 32 .... 100.00
Nightshirt, Child's, Crochet Trim, Ecru Linen, 1912 .... 20.00
Opera Coat, Woman's, Gold Sequins, 1920s 500.00
Pajamas, Embroidered Silk, Black, 1930s, Small 30.00
Pajamas, Negligee, Satin, Aqua, Pink, Japan, 1940s, Size 12 .... 50.00
Pants, Child's, Bib, Little Boy Blue, Nursery Rhymes, Size 3 .... 12.00
Petticoat, Double Ruffle, Victorian 35.00
Petticoat, Tucked & Tatted Lace Inserts, C.1900, Size 10 .... 50.00
Petticoat, Victorian, With Tucks 10.00
Poncho, Crocheted, Red & Navy Stripes, Fringe, 21 In. 8.00
Robe, Dragon, Cloud, Chrysanthemum Design, Chinese, Floor Length 1200.00
Robe, Smoking, Man's, Maroon Satin 60.00
Romper Suit, Boy's, Blue Collar & Cuffs, Embroidered Collar, 1 Pc. 12.00
Scarf, Battenberg Lace, Grapes, Leaves, 9 In. 60.00
Scarf, Black Lace, Floral, Scalloped, 60 X 80 In. 25.00
Scarf, Man's, Rayon Damask, Setters, Rabbits, Reeds, Fringe, 46 In. 9.00
Shawl, Embroidered Boteh, Trefoil Border, 5 Ft.9 In. X 5 Ft.6 In. 350.00
Shawl, Multicolored Floral Design, Platinum Ground, 68 X 70 In. 135.00
Shawl, Paisley, Ivory Center, Red Border, 63 X 126 In. 120.00
Shawl, Paisley, Kashmir, 59 X 128 In. 75.00
Shoes, Baby's, Leather, Pair 17.50
Shoes, Child's, Stride Rite, White 30.00
Shoes, Girl's, Berk's Vigortone, Black 25.00
Shoes, Girl's, Lady Frances, Black T–Strap 25.00
Shoes, Girl's, Peterman, Black, Strap, Buckle 25.00
Shoes, High Button, Western Shoe Co., Toledo, Unused 100.00
Shoes, Man's, Black, High Top, Lace & Hook, Franklin Shoe Co. 60.00
Shoes, Mans, Ball Brand Rubber Boots 9.00
Shoes, Nurse's, Clara Barton, Box, 6 1/2–D 17.00
Shoes, Woman's, Black, High Button, Lace 20.00
Shoes, Woman's, Brown Leather, High Top 8.00
Shoes, Woman's, Brown Suede Lace, High Top, Lace 45.00
Skirt, Black Silk, Ruffled, Full 40.00
Skirt, Dirndl, Floral Print On Navy, Floor Length 6.00
Skirt, Grass, Hawaii 10.00
Skirt, Ruffles & Tucks, Lace On Upper Section, Size 10 .... 35.00
Slip, Princess, Ruffled Bottom, Embroidered Inserts, Size 8 .... 85.00
Socks, Men's, Silver Point Hose 8.00
Spats, Bond Street, Gray 22.00
Stockings, Child's, Yorktown Hosiery, Black 7.00
Stockings, Woman's, Anna, Brown Cotton 6.00
Stockings, Woman's, B.V. May, Silver Gray Cotton Top & Sole 8.00
Stockings, Woman's, Black Silk & Cotton 7.00
Stockings, Woman's, Seam Up Back, Rayon & Cotton Sole 8.00
Stockings, Woman's, Silk, Paramount, Brown Silk & Cotton 7.00
Stockings, Woman's, Yorktown Mills, Cotton 6.00
Stole, Gray Squirrel 20.00
Straw Hat, Farmer's, Salesman's Sample, Tagged 25.00
Suit, Man's, Blue Pinstripe, Wool, Size 32 .... 45.00
Suit, Walking, Woman's, C.1890, 2 Piece 100.00
Sunbonnet, Baby's, Tucked White Organza, Applied Lace, Visor 9.00
Sweater, Cashmere, Mink Collar, 1950s 25.00
Sweater, Ivory Wool, Beaded, Fully Lined, Pearls, Size 42 .... 40.00
Uniform, London Bobby's, 9 Piece 495.00

 Cluthra glass is a two–layered glass with small air pockets that form white spots. The Steuben Glass Works of Corning, New York, made it after 1903. Kimball Glass Company of Vineland, New Jersey, made Cluthra from about 1925. Victor Durand signed some pieces with his name.

CLUTHRA, see also Steuben
CLUTHRA, Vase, 6 In. 900.00
   Vase, Burgundy Rim, Dark Rose Base, Steuben, 10 1/2 In. ....*Illus* 1045.00

Vase, White, Kimball, 1968, 6 1/4 In. 175.00

> Coalbrookdale was made by the Coalport porcelain factory of England during the Victorian period. Pieces are decorated with floral encrustations.

COALBROOKDALE, Vase, Flowers, Leaves, Urn Shape, Lid, 10 In. 300.00

> Coalport ware has been made by the Coalport Porcelain Works of England from 1795 to the present time. Early pieces were unmarked. About 1810–1825 the pieces were marked with the name "Coalport" in various forms. Later pieces also had the name "John Rose" in the mark. The crown mark has been used with variations since 1881.

COALPORT, Bastille Burner, Cottage 75.00
Bowl, Trinket, Floral Cover, June Time, White 15.00
Chocolate Pot, White, Birds, Flowers, 6 In. 65.00
Coffee Set, Tray, Pink, Gilt, Demitasse, Late 19th Century, 8 In. 176.00
Decanter, Navy Floral, White Ground, 12 In. 45.00
Figurine, Annette, 1920 Mark, 6 In. 50.00
Figurine, Stella, 8 1/4 In. 75.00
Plate, Cherub & Flowers, Encrusted Gold Garlands, Signed, 9 In. 395.00
Plate, Floral Bouquets, Gilt Scroll Rim, C.1825, 10 3/8 In., 12 Pc. 1100.00
Plate, Peeled Half Lemon, Dated 1808, 9 1/2 In. ....*Illus* 3575.00
Platter, Tobacco Leaf, Nicotiana Blossom, 1805–10, 10 3/4 In., Pr. 2475.00
Vase, Pilgrim Flask Shape, Gold Carp, Sea Grasses, Pink, 7 In., Pair 715.00
Vase, Shell, Ivory, 4 In. 75.00

> Cobalt blue glass was made using oxide of cobalt. The characteristic bright dark blue identifies it for the collector. Most cobalt glass found today was made after the Civil War.

COBALT BLUE, Bottle, Apothecary, 1879 .... 100.00
Bottle, Barber's, Pewter Top 40.00
Decanter, Wine, Floral Silver Deposit, Bulbous, 13 3/4 In. 130.00
Dish, Camel Cover, Westmoreland, 6 1/4 In. 79.50
Eggcup, Octagonal, Scalloped Rim, 4 Raised Ribs, Flint 195.00
Epergne, Enameled Daisies, Yellow Centers, Leaves, 15 In., 2 Pc. 325.00
Figurine, Bird & Nest, Small 85.00
Figurine, Shoe 55.00
Patch Box, Enameled Dots, White & Green Leaves, 1 1/4 X 4 In. 100.00
Salt & Pepper, Christmas, Art Glass 225.00
Salt, Silver–Plated Holder, Hanging Spoon, 2 1/4 X 3 3/8 In. 100.00
Spooner 49.00
Sugar & Creamer 50.00
Tumbler, Inverted Thumbprint, 3 7/8 X 2 7/8 In. 40.00
Vase, Bud 55.00

> Coca–Cola was first served in 1886 in Atlanta, Georgia. It was advertised through signs, newspaper ads, coupons, bottles, trays, calendars, and even lamps and clocks. Collectors want anything with the word "Coca–Cola," including a few rare products like gum wrappers and cigar bands. The famous trademark was patented in 1893, the "Coke" mark in 1945. Many modern items and reproductions are being made.

COCA–COLA, Ad, Magazine, Coca–Cola Chewing Gum 20.00
Airplane, Turner Toy Co., 1920s, 27 In. 950.00
Ashtray, Metal, Red, 1961 .... 2.25
Automaton, Bathing Girl, C.1930 .... 935.00
Badge, Duster Girl, Convention, Celluloid, Pin–Back, 1910 .... 3400.00
Blotter, Blond, Brunette & Redhead Ladies, 1944 .... 7.00
Book Cover, Football, 1957 .... 10.00
Book, 1932 Los Angeles Olympics, Spiral Bound, 61 Page 10.00
Bookmark, 1903 .... 310.00
Bookmark, Heart Shape, Celluloid, 1898, 2 X 2 1/4 In. 425.00
Bookmark, Heart Shape, Celluloid, 2 Sides, 1900, 2 X 2 1/4 In. 1250.00

Bookmark, Hilda Clark, Heart Shape, Celluloid, 1900, 2 X 2 1/4 In. 375.00
Bookmark, Lillian Nordica, 1905, 2 X 6 In. 575.00
Bookmark, Owl, 1906, 1 X 3 1/2 In. 700.00
Bottle Carrier, Cardboard, 1937 .... 30.00
Bottle Opener, Bottle Cap Shape, Silver Finish, 3 In. 22.00
Bottle Opener, Drink Coca–Cola In Bottles, Metal, Hand 6.00
Bottle Opener, Lady Form, Grand Island, Nebr., Key Chain, 3 In. 58.00
Bottle, 59th Anniversary, Gold, Pacific Coast Bottling Co. 60.00
Bottle, Amber ....7.25 To 25.00
Bottle, Hutchinson, Property of Coca–Cola Bottling Co., Script 700.00
Bottle, Rochester, New York 170.00
Bottle, Seltzer, Blue 175.00
Bottle, Super Max, Max Headroom, 16 Oz., 4 Oz. Free .... .75
Box, Wooden, 1930s 65.00
Brochure, Toonerville Trolley, 1930 .... 75.00
Calendar, 1905, Lillian Nordica 2000.00
Calendar, 1910, Framed 4070.00
Calendar, 1917, Constance, 8 X 19 1/2 In. 860.00
Calendar, 1918, Ladies With Parasol, Framed 600.00
Calendar, 1919, Girl With Bottle, No Pad 500.00
Calendar, 1930, Bathing Beauty, Hayden, Framed 500.00
Calendar, 1931, Barefoot Boy, Fishing, Dog, Rockwell, Framed 725.00
Calendar, 1937, Boy Fishing, Wyeth, Framed 600.00
Calendar, 1945, Boy Scout, Rockwell 500.00
Calendar, 1946, Boy Scout, Rockwell 475.00
Calendar, 1951, 6 Pages, Pretty Ladies 25.00
Calendar, 1955, 6 Pages, Canadian 40.00
Cap, Vendor's, Drink Coca–Cola In Bottles 9.00
Card Set, Nature Study, Box, 1928, 96 Cards 25.00
Card, Playing, 52 Different Women, Box 29.00
Card, Playing, Bobbed–Haired Girls, 1928 .... 350.00
Card, Playing, Colored Back, 1943, Box 67.00
Card, Playing, Constance, With Straight–Sided Bottle, 1915 .... 1000.00
Card, Playing, Drink Coca–Cola In Bottles, Red, 1938 .... 65.00
Card, Playing, Girl, With Coke, Double Deck, 1939 .... 525.00
Cartoon, Coke Gunnery Crew, Shoot Pepsi Skywriting Plane, 1940s 58.00
Chair, Beanbag 100.00
Change Purse, Coca–Cola Bottling Co., Leather, Wrapper, 1907 .... 240.00
Christmas Wreath, Drink Coca–Cola, Die Cut, 1917 .... 600.00
Clicker, Plastic, Metal, 1960s 1.00
Clock, Coke, Electric, 1942 .... 275.00
Clock, Gilbert, Regulator, 1920s 2600.00
Clock, Ingraham, Regulator, Store, 1905 .... 1250.00
Clock, Rotating Sign 510.00
Coaster Set, Santa Claus, 6 Piece 7.00
Coaster, Coke, With Santa Claus, Pair 9.00
Coin–Operated Machine, No.56 .... 400.00
Compact, With Gold Bottle, 1960 .... 10.00
Cooler, Carrying Case, Catalogue, 1939, Salesman's Sample 3310.00
Cooler, Red, Drink Coca–Cola In Bottles, 1930s 65.00
Cooler, Wooden, Tin Lining, Lift–Up Top, Legs, 1900s, 3 Ft.4 In. 900.00
Coupon, Coke, Rockwell, 1928 .... 5.00
Cutout, Coca–Cola Girls, 5 Branches of Service From 1944 .... 1200.00
Cutout, Delicious, Man, Large Leaves Ground, Cardboard, 1927 .... 190.00
Decanter, Mack Truck, Pacesetter, Porcelain 225.00
Dispenser, Syrup, Ceramic, Wheeling Pottery Co., 1896 .... 1500.00
Display, 1940, 1896 Dispenser 650.00
Display, Sundblom Santas, 1950s 500.00
Display, Window, Coca–Cola Circus, 1932 .... 2200.00
Display, Window, Uncle Remus, Cardboard, 1931 .... 4100.00
Door Pull, Porcelain, 1940s, 30 X 4 In. 125.00
Door Push, Green, White, Red, Enamel, 8 X 4 In., Pair 375.00
Electric Light, Coke Bottle Shape, Glass, Tin Cap 3640.00
Flyswatter, 1940s 10.00

Game, Test Your Skills, Have A Coke 350.00
Globe, Milk Glass, Drink Coca–Cola, Metal Piece Top 1050.00
Gun, Paper Snap, Christmas Design 5.00
Ice Pick & Bottle Opener, 1930s 15.00
Ice Pick, Dutch Coca–Cola 7.00
Jar, Pepsin Gum, Rooster On Top, 1908 .... 850.00
Key Chain, Golden Anniversary 2.00
Key Ring, Hook–On, Screwdriver, Cigar Cutter, Pulaski, Tenn., 1910 .... 240.00
Knife, Bone Handle, 1 Blade & Opener, A.Kastor & Bros., 1915 .... 200.00
Knife, Bottle Shape, Brass, 2 1/4 In. 15.00
Knife, Pen, Cola Clan Convention, 1976 .... 5.00
Knife, Pocket, Winchester, Bottle Shape 25.00
Label, Diamond Shape, For Straight–Sided Bottle 12.00
Lampshade, Leaded Glass, Marked On Band, 1920s 3700.00
License Plate, Enjoy Coca–Cola, Aluminum, 6 X 11 7/8 In. 3.00
Lighter, Miniature Bottle Shape, 1950 .... 12.00
Menu Board, Good With Food, Plastic, Metal Frame, 18 X 30 In. 25.00
Menu, Girl, Drinking Coke, Menu On Back, 1902 .... 500.00
Mirror, Elaine, 1916, Pocket 285.00
Mirror, Norman Rockwell, 2 X 3 In. 2.00
Music Box, Cooler, Girl On Top 800.00
Napkin, Rice Paper, 1911 .... 110.00
Needle Case, Coke, 1925 .... 40.00
Night–Light, Printed Courtesy of Your Dealer, 1945 .... 8.50
Note Pad, Celluloid, 1902 .... 450.00
Patch, Uniform, 1984 Olympics 5.00
Pencil Holder, Ceramic Dispenser, 75th Anniversary, 7 In. 60.00
Pencil Sharpener, Bottle Shape 25.00
Pencil, Lead, Red, Gold, White, 7 In. 5.00
Pencil, Mechanical, Red, Silver Bottle Pocket Clip, Box 10.00
Picnic Carrier, Things Go Better With Coke, 1960s 110.00
Pin, Olympic, Calgary, White, Dominion–Made, 1988 .... 4.00
Postcard, Girl & Horse, Color, Germany, 1950 .... 5.75
Poster, Baseball, Willie Mays, 22 X 17 In. 10.00
Poster, Commemorative, 1776–1976 .... 10.00
Rack, Display, Metal, 8 Cartons, 6 For 25 Cents, 1930s 1400.00
Rack, Stair–Step, 6–Pack Carton, Drink Coca–Cola, 35 X 16 In. 575.00
Radio, Bakelite 625.00
Radio, Can Shape 12.00
Radio, In Case, Top Handle, Refreshes You, 1950s, 8 X 10 1/2 In. 1400.00
Radio, Transistor, 6 Oz.Coke Bottle Shape, 8 In. 25.00
Ruler, Compliments, Your Coca–Cola Bottling Co., Wooden, 12 In. 1.75
Sewing Kit, 1950s 1.75
Sign, Arrow, Take Home A Carton, Tin Die Cut, 2 Sides, 18 X 11 In. 100.00
Sign, Bottle In Center, Flat, Round, Dated 1936, 4 Ft. 450.00
Sign, Bottle, Reproduction, Leaded Glass, 4 Ft. 1025.00
Sign, Circus, Clown & Ice Skater, Framed, 1950, 16 X 27 In. 350.00
Sign, Coca–Cola, Cigars, Neon, 12 X 23 In. 2400.00
Sign, Coke, Cardboard, 2 Sides, 1956, 36 X 20 In. 20.00
Sign, Coke, Triangular, Hanging, 1936 .... 375.00
Sign, Drink Coca–Cola, Girl With Bottles, 1929, 3 1/2 X 14 In. 800.00
Sign, Drink Coca–Cola, Multicolored, Tin, 1970s, 24 X 18 In. 47.00
Sign, Drink Coca–Cola, Tin, Self–Framed, 1955, 18 X 54 In. 95.00
Sign, Drink Coca–Cola, Tin, Wooden Frame, 1942, 24 X 69 In. 450.00
Sign, Fishtail, Bottle, Green Frame, 31 X 11 In. 55.00
Sign, Hilda Clark, Paper, 1901, 15 X 20 In. 3800.00
Sign, Ice Cold Coca–Cola Sold Here, Dated 1931, 15 X 30 In. 150.00
Sign, Ice Cold, Sold Here, 1916 Bottle, Tin, 19 X 27 In. 285.00
Sign, Lillian Russell, Cardboard, 5 X 3 In. 200.00
Sign, Pause That Refreshes, 2 Sides, Masonite, 1935, 21 X 13 In. 750.00
Sign, Picnic Scene, Cardboard, Framed, 1923, 14 X 24 In. 2000.00
Sign, Porcelain, 1939, 26 X 12 In. 400.00
Sign, Reverse On Glass, Oval, 1932 .... 2500.00
Sign, Round, Flat, Bottle In Center, 1936, 4 Ft. 450.00

Sign, Take Home A Carton, 6 Pack, 25 Cents, Round, 1930s 135.00
Sign, Trolley, Delicious, Refreshing, Fountains In Bottles, 5 Cent 750.00
Stamp Holder, Celluloid, Compliments of Coca–Cola Co., 1901 .... 450.00
Sterilizer, Ray Glass, Drink Coca–Cola, Ultraviolet, 1924 .... 1100.00
Tap Knob, Plastic 5.00
Teaching Kit, Transportation Series, Original Mailer, 1943 .... 350.00
Thermometer, 2 Bottles, C.1941, 17 X 6 In. 300.00
Thermometer, Embossed Gold Bottle, Dated 1937 .... 75.00
Thermometer, Gold Bottle, 1938 .... 140.00
Thermometer, Sign of Good Taste, Tin, 30 X 8 In. 85.00
Thermometer, Wooden, 1905 .... 275.00
Ticket, Rubber Bowl, Spotlight Salute, Harry James, 1944, 7 In. 8.50
Tip Tray, 1899, Hilda Clark, 5 1/2 In. 2600.00
Tip Tray, 1912, Hamilton King, 6 X 4 1/4 In. 150.00
Tip Tray, 1914, Betty ....65.00 To 135.00
Tip Tray, 1917, Elaine ....125.00 To 160.00
Toy, Ball On String, Toss Into Cup On Stick, 6 In. 3.75
Toy, Coke Dispenser, Chilton, Box 45.00
Toy, Truck, Delivery, Metal, Yellow, Black, Red, 1970, 4 In. 15.00
Toy, Truck, Metalcraft No.215, Box, 1930s 200.00
Toy, Truck, Original Bottles, Metalcraft, 1930s, 11 In. 300.00
Toy, Truck, Rubber Wheels, Headlights, Metalcraft, 1930s 900.00
Toy, Truck, Smitty's Toys, Wooden Coca–Cola Blocks, 1940s 850.00
Toy, Truck, Wooden, Delicious & Refreshing, 1940s 700.00
Tray, 1904, Lillian Nordica, With Bottle 1300.00
Tray, 1906, Relieves Fatigue, Oval 2550.00
Tray, 1912, Hamilton King Girl, Rectangular 195.00
Tray, 1914, Betty, Oval ....195.00 To 250.00
Tray, 1917, Elaine, Rectangular 385.00
Tray, 1921, Summer Girl 550.00
Tray, 1922, Autumn Girl 190.00
Tray, 1923, Flapper Girl 100.00
Tray, 1925, Girl At Party 160.00
Tray, 1927, Girl With Bobbed Hair 500.00
Tray, 1931, Farm Boy With Dog, Rockwell ....200.00 To 360.00
Tray, 1932, Yellow Bathing Suit Girl, Rectangular 175.00
Tray, 1935, Madge Evans 110.00
Tray, 1936, Hostess ....75.00 To 120.00
Tray, 1937, Running Girl ....85.00 To 100.00
Tray, 1938, Girl In The Afternoon ....60.00 To 125.00
Tray, 1940, Sailor Girl 75.00
Tray, 1941, Girl Ice Skater ....55.00 To 60.00
Tray, 1942, 2 Girls At Car ....60.00 To 100.00
Tray, 1943, Girl With Wind In Her Hair 20.00
Tray, 1961, Pansy Garden 15.00
Tray, 1961, Thanksgiving 25.00
Tumbler, 1920s 12.50
Vending Machine, Model UMC 39 .... 375.00
Wallet, Leather, 1930s 45.00
Watch Fob, Bulldogs, Petretti, 1920 .... 225.00
Watch Fob, Girl, With Straight–Sided Bottle, Celluloid, 1910 .... 725.00
Watch Fob, Swastika, 1920s 75.00
Watch, Drink Coke, Pocket 85.00
Wrapper, Spearmint Gum, 1910 .... 300.00

 Coffee grinders of home size were first made about 1894. They lost favor by the 1930s. Large floor–standing or counter model coffee grinders were used in the nineteenth–century country store. The renewed interest in fresh–ground coffee has produced many modern electric and hand grinders, and reproductions of the old styles are being made.

COFFEE GRINDER, Arcade, Glass Top 65.00
    Arcade, Wall 80.00
    Crescent, Brass Hopper, Red Paint, Floor Model 525.00

Dovetailed Wooden Box, 1 Drawer, Hand Crank, Iron Handle 55.00
Enterprise, Double Wheel, 14 In. 225.00
Enterprise, Floor Model 900.00
Enterprise, No.3, Double Wheel, Counter 595.00
Enterprise, Red Stenciling, Eagle Finial 1000.00
Enterprise, Wall, Painted Tin Cup, Iron 195.00
Goodridge, Barrett & Co., Wall, Gold Hopper, 1900 .... 80.00
Griswold, Cast Iron 325.00
J.Wright, Store, Cast Iron, Double Wheel 75.00
Keen Kutter, Simmons Hardware, Lap, Metal 30.00
LaHaska, Lap, Brass Cup, Forged Iron Handle, Hole 220.00
Lap, Pine Base, Drawer, Cast Iron Handle 50.00
Mahogany, Drawer, Screw-Off Top, Iron Handle, 10 In. 175.00
National Coffee Mill, Paper Label 95.00
Open Iron Cup & Crank Handle On Top, Drawer, Wooden 75.00
Parker, Wall, Tin 45.00
Persepolis, Counter Top 450.00
Rittenhouse, Nailed Drawer, Pewter Hopper, Iron Crank, 9 In. 215.00
Tin Top With Hopper, Iron Crank, Wooden Drawer, 8 In. 105.00
Universal, Metal 22.50
Wooden Iron Lid & Handle, Wooden Loop Knob 50.00

Coin spot is a glass pattern that was named by the collectors. It features coinlike spots as part of the glass. Colored, clear, and opalescent glass was made with the spots. Many companies used the design in the 1870–90 period. It is so popular that reproductions are still being made.

COIN SPOT, Bride's Basket, Pleated & Ruffled, Silver Holder, 10 1/4 In. 225.00
Bride's Bowl, Frosted Blue Edging, Ormolu Base, 8 1/2 X 9 In. 695.00
Bride's Bowl, Frosted Blue Rim, Ormolu Base, 8 1/2 X 14 In. 650.00
Cruet, Polished Pontil, Cranberry 200.00
Ewer, Opalescent 27.00
Lamp, Kerosene, Finger, Clear Opalescent 350.00
Muffineer, Cranberry 125.00
Pitcher, Cranberry ....75.00 To 120.00
Pitcher, Milk, Blue, Opalescent, 5 1/2 In. 45.00
Pitcher, Water, Pale Blue, Clear Handle, Crimped Rim 150.00
Spooner, Blue, Opalescent 50.00
Syrup, Ring Neck, Northwood 210.00
Vase, Mother-of-Pearl, White Lining, Blue, 7 3/4 In. 195.00
Vase, Ruffled Rim, Cranberry, 7 1/4 In. 85.00
Vase, Ruffled, Mother-of-Pearl, Flowers, Gold Leaves, 8 1/2 In. 495.00
Vase, Ruffled, Satin Glass, Pink & Lavender Flowers, 11 In., Pair 1850.00
Water Set, Green, 7 Piece 200.00

The vending machine is an ancient invention dating back to 200 B.C. when holy water was dispensed in a coin-operated vase. Smokers in seventeenth-century England could buy tobacco from a coin-operated box. It was not until after the Civil War that the technology made modern coin-operated games and vending machines plentiful. Slot machines, arcade games, and dispensers are all collected.

COIN-OPERATED MACHINE, Autostereoscope, Mills, Table Model, Stand 650.00
Bowling, Ten Pins, Rock-Ola 850.00
Candy Bar, Brownie, Floor Model, Wooden 475.00
Candy, Life Savers, 10 Cent, 1950s 85.00
Cigar, 3 Slots, Different Types, 31 1/4 In. 1450.00
Cigar, Bennett, 5 Cent, Oak & Glass, Holds 4 Boxes 2000.00
Cigar, Doremus, Cast Iron 2250.00
Cigar, Mack, 5 Cent, 1940s 350.00
Cigarette, Cigarola 3300.00
Coin Changer, Brandt, Dragons 125.00
Fortune-Teller, Dice, 1 Cent 250.00
Fortune-Teller, Grandma Prophecies 2700.00

Fortune–Teller, Madam X	60.00
Glamour Rating, Wooden, Table Model, 1 Cent	235.00
Grip Tester, Arcade	1500.00
Gum, Adams, 1 Cent, Octagonal	200.00
Gum, Atlas Master	140.00
Gum, Blinkey Eye Soda Mint Gum, Cast Iron, Wood	5720.00
Gum, Columbia, 16 X 8 In.	160.00
Gum, Homerun Ball	250.00
Gum, Pulver Too Choos, Porcelain, Tin, Foxy Grandpa	900.00
Gum, Pulver Yellow Kid, 1 Cent, Clockwork	750.00
Gum, Pulver, Dola–Pepsin	850.00
Gum, Pulver, Red	550.00
Gum, Stick, Wall, 5 Cent, 1940s	125.00
Gum, Yuchu Sweet Breath	225.00
Gum, Zeno Chewing, Key Wound, Clockwork Mechanism	425.00
Gumball, Abbey	40.00
Gumball, Adams, C.1910	875.00
Gumball, Advance, 1 Cent, 1923	175.00
Gumball, Advance, Glass Football Globe	150.00
Gumball, Atlas, 1 & 5 Cent, 1950	95.00
Gumball, B & O, Hit The Target, Rocket Ship	85.00
Gumball, Coast Vending, Baseball Flip, 1950s	125.00
Gumball, Columbus, Model 14X	375.00
Gumball, Hit The Target, Gambling, 1 Cent, 1950s	85.00
Gumball, Homerun	325.00
Gumball, Log Cabin	285.00 To 375.00
Gumball, Masters, 1 Cent, 1923	130.00
Gumball, Rex, Silent Salesman	1000.00
Gumball, Victor, Baby Grand, 1 Cent, Oak	100.00
Gumball, Victor, Key, 1 Cent, 1950	35.00
Gumball, Victor, Topper, 1950	50.00
High Top No.777, Mills, 10 Cents, Rebuilt	850.00
Horse Race, Bally, Spark Plug Pay–Out	1600.00
Kicker & Catcher, Game	300.00
Lighter Fluid, Firefly–Fluidor	125.00
Love Analyst, Mutoscope	650.00
Love Letter, Disposition Register, Personality	750.00
Love Tester, Exhibit, Thermometer	650.00
Love Tester, Row of Light Bulbs On One Side	750.00
Match Dispenser, Griswold	110.00
Mutoscope, Empire State Building, Walnut Cabinet	2500.00
Nut, Challenger, 3 Columns	300.00
Nut, Jennings–In–The–Bag	375.00
Nut, Stollwerck, Porcelain	650.00
Nut, U–Chew, 1 Cent	55.00
Owl, Upright, Ornate, Mills, Restored	6500.00
Peanut, Abbey	75.00
Peanut, Advance, Big Mouth, Model 11	175.00
Peanut, Bartholomew	225.00
Peanut, Brice Williams	275.00
Peanut, Brodie, Master 1 Cent, Long Beach, 1923	150.00
Peanut, Columbus, Model A	275.00
Peanut, Columbus, Model M, 1930s	150.00
Peanut, Northwestern, Model 60	35.00
Peanut, Perk–Up, 5 Cent	75.00
Peanut, Selmor, Cast Iron, 1 Cent	200.00
Peanut, Silver King, 5 Cent	100.00
Peanut, Victor, Baby Grand, Oak & Metal, 1 Cent	135.00
Pencil, National, Cast Iron	750.00
Perfume, Bull Shape, Iron, Give Horn Tug & Spritz	900.00
Perfume, Bull's Head, Cast Iron, Glass, Instructions	3520.00
Perfume, Coty	195.00
Perfume, Steer Head, Iron, 1 Cent, 1900	900.00
Perfume, Whiffs of Fragrance, 4 Bottles	6070.00

Pinball, Arcade, Shooter, 3 Animal Targets, 25 In.	150.00
Pinball, Bally, Coney Island Bingo, 1951	260.00
Pinball, Bally, Eight–Ball	325.00
Pinball, Bally, Elton John, Captain Fantastic	850.00
Pinball, Gottlieb, Bank A Ball, 1960s	350.00
Pinball, Pacific Amusement Mfg.Co., 1933	750.00
Pinball, Williams Mfg.Co., Cyclone, 1947	325.00
Popcorn, Popperette, 10 Cent	1275.00
Prophylactic Condom, All Original	65.00
Shock, Advance, Marquee, 1 Cent	295.00
Shooting Gallery, Farm Yard, Floor Model	1275.00
Skilltest, 1 Cent, Oak	400.00
Slot, Arcade, Roulette Wheel	1000.00
Slot, Bally, Hold & Draw	350.00
Slot, Bally, Poker Spinner	2000.00
Slot, Bally, Progressive, 1973	1300.00
Slot, Bally, Skill–Roll Nickel	200.00
Slot, Bally, Sparkplug	2250.00
Slot, Buckley Bonanza, 5 Cent, 1940s	800.00
Slot, Buckley, Long–Shot Horse Race	595.00
Slot, Caille, Jumbo Success	1600.00
Slot, D.N.Schall Improved Chicago, Counter Top	5000.00
Slot, Jennings, Challenger, 5 & 25 Cent	3200.00
Slot, Jennings, Duchess, 3 Reels, 5 Cent	1400.00
Slot, Jennings, Dutch Boy	1300.00
Slot, Jennings, Operator's Bell, 1920s	1700.00
Slot, Jennings, Tic–Tac–Toe, Sun Chief, 25 Cent	1800.00
Slot, Jennings, Victory Chief, 5 Cent	900.00
Slot, Mills, Black Beauty, 5 Cent, Table	950.00
Slot, Mills, Black Cherry	1400.00
Slot, Mills, Bursting Cherry, 5 Cent, 1939	950.00
Slot, Mills, Castlefront, 5 Cent	1700.00
Slot, Mills, Dewey, 5 Cent	8900.00
Slot, Mills, Diamond, 5 Cent, 1939	950.00
Slot, Mills, Four Bells, 4 Player, 5 Cent	5000.00
Slot, Mills, Futurity, Gold Aware, 25 Cent	2600.00
Slot, Mills, Golden Falls, 25 Cent	1800.00
Slot, Mills, Hi–Top, 25 Cent	1100.00
Slot, Mills, Judge, 5 Cent	6900.00
Slot, Mills, Owl Jr., Counter Top	6000.00
Slot, Mills, Perfection, Upright, Jackpot Watch	2100.00
Slot, Mills, Poinsettia	700.00
Slot, Mills, Q.T.Bell, 10 Cent, 1935	1600.00
Slot, Mills, War Chief, 25 Cent	1400.00
Slot, Mills, War Chief, 5 Cent	1500.00
Slot, Pace Bantam, 10 Cent	1150.00
Slot, Pace, Deluxe, Chrome, 5 Cent	1500.00
Slot, Pace, Mayfair Superstar Aristocrat, 25 Cent	1000.00
Slot, Pace, Races, Black & Gold	7500.00
Slot, Pace, Silver Dollar	1500.00
Slot, Rock–Ola, Model 1428	2600.00
Slot, Watling, 5 Cent Treasury, 3 Reels, 1936, 24 In.	2970.00
Slot, Watling, Rol–A–Top, 5 Cent	2300.00
Stamp, Cast Iron, 10 Cent	95.00
Stamp, Porcelain, C.1946	300.00
Stamp, Uncle Sam, 6 Cent	50.00
Stereopticon, 1 Cent, 500 Colored Cards, Pat.1913	495.00
Strength Tester, Gottleib, Counter Top	100.00
Talking Grandma, 1906	7500.00
Trade Stimulator, Arcade, Poison This Rat, 1942	475.00
Trade Stimulator, Buckley, Bang Tail	395.00
Trade Stimulator, Caille, Puritan Bell, Cast Iron	750.00
Trade Stimulator, Churchill Downs, Penny Drop	500.00
Trade Stimulator, Groetchen, Penny Smoke	325.00

Trade Stimulator, Gum, Kelly, Oak Case 1800.00
Trade Stimulator, Imps, 1940 .... 295.00
Trade Stimulator, Jackpot Sue, Punchboard 135.00
Trade Stimulator, Jennings, Hit The Target, Indian 550.00
Trade Stimulator, Kelley, Gum, Oak Case 1800.00
Trade Stimulator, Mills, Little Perfection 475.00
Trade Stimulator, Mills, Puritan Bell, Restored 600.00
Trade Stimulator, Mills, Success, Floor Model 1750.00
Trade Stimulator, Mills, Target Practice, Penny Flip 375.00
Trade Stimulator, Pol–O–Reel 345.00
Trade Stimulator, Rock–Ola, Hold & Draw 375.00
Trade Stimulator, Shipman, Spin–It 75.00
Viewer, Girlie, Exhibit Supply, 3–D, 1940s 200.00

Collector plates are modern plates produced in limited editions. Some will be found listed under the factory name, such as Bing & Grondahl, Royal Copenhagen, Royal Doulton, and Wedgwood. Pictures and more price information can be found in "Kovels' Price Guide for Collector Plates, Figurines, Paperweights and Other Limited Editions."

COLLECTOR PLATE, Crown Parian, Captain Freddie, Red Skelton, 1981 .... 60.00
Fairmont, DeGrazia Holiday Series, Bell of Hope, 1977 .... 119.00
Fairmont, DeGrazia Holiday Series, Little Prayer, 1981 .... 70.00
Fairmont, John Wayne, 1980 .... 40.00
Fairmont, W.C.Fields, Red Skelton, 1981 .... 75.00
Gorham, Rockwell Christmas Series, Tiny Tim, 1974 .... 24.00
Knowles, Biblical Mothers Series, Bathsheba, Solomon, 1983 .... 109.00
Knowles, Gone With The Wind, Mammy Lacing Scarlett, 1982 .... 50.00
Knowles, Gone With The Wind, Rhett & Bonnie, 1985 .... 39.00
Knowles, Wizard of Oz, Wonderful Wizard, 1979 .... 55.00
Leyendecker, With Bell, Santa Loves You, 1977 .... 43.00
Pickard, Robin Hood, 1985 .... 60.00
Rockwell Museum, Tribute To J.F.K., 1983 .... 50.00
Rockwell Society, Christmas Series, Christmas Dream, 1978 .... 25.00
Rockwell Society, Heritage Series, Cobbler, 1978 .... 120.00
Rockwell Society, Heritage Series, Music Maker, 1981 .... 22.50
Royal Orleans, Marilyn, Seven Year Itch, 1983 .... 25.00
Schmid, Mother's Day, Minnie Mouse & Friends, Box, 1976 .... 20.00
Vague Shadows, Perillo, Apache Boy, 1981 .... 130.00

Comic art, or cartoon art, is a relatively new field of collecting. Original comic strips, magazine covers, and even printed strips are collected. The first daily comic strip was printed in 1907. The paintings on celluloid used for movie cartoons are listed in this book under Animation Art.

COMIC ART, Book Cover, Felix The Cat, O.Messmer, Ink 167.00
Book, Best From Boy's Life, No.1, Classic, Oct.1957 .... 8.50
Bungle Family, 45 Panels, Tuthill 850.00
Page, Turrible Tales of Kaptain Kiddo, Black Man, G.Drayton, 1911 .... 30.00
Strip, Alley Oop, Ink, V.T.Hamlin, July 31, 1966, 16 X 24 In. 101.00
Strip, Felix The Cat, Ink, O.Messmer, Sept.15, 1935, 16 X 20 In. 731.00
Strip, Fritzi Ritz, Ink, Ernie Bushmiller, 15 X 22 1/2 In. 44.00
Strip, Nancy, Ink, Ernie Bushmiller, Oct.18, 1944, 5 X 19 In. 77.00

Commemorative items have been made to honor members of royalty and those of great national fame. World's fairs and important historical events are also remembered with commemorative pieces.

COMMEMORATIVE, see also Coronation; World's Fair

COMMEMORATIVE, Brooch, Queen Wilhemina, Circled Seed Pearls, Box, 1903 .... 350.00
Compact, King George Coronation, Marcasites & Chrome 48.00
Cup & Saucer, Queen Mother's Birthday, A.W.Hockridge 100.00
Fan, Philadelphia Exposition, 1876, Fabric, Bone Stick, 10 In. 150.00
Lamp, Admiral Dewey's, Fluid, Ship, Artillery Shell, 13 In. 350.00
Loving Cup, Andrew & Sarah Wedding, Rampant Lion Handles 75.00

Loving Cup, Charles & Diana Wedding, Rampant Lion Handles 85.00
Mug, Child's, Our Country Martyrs, Lincoln, Garfield, Crystal 25.00
Mug, Cleveland–Thurman, Crystal 110.00
Mug, Investiture of Prince Charles, Guyatt, 1969 .... 85.00
Mug, King George V, Sepia Portrait 45.00
Pitcher, George & Elizabeth Coronation, 1937 .... 30.00
Plate, Birth of Princess Margaret, Parakeets & Roses, 1903 .... 85.00
Plate, King George V, Silver Jubilee, Glass, Scalloped, 10 In. 65.00
Plate, King George VI, Queen Elizabeth, Visit To Canada, 1939 .... 25.00
Plate, Queen Elizabeth II, Silver Jubilee, 9 In. 35.00
Plate, Victoria & Albert, Full Figures, Luster Edge, 9 In. 78.00
Tumbler, Queen Victoria, Silver Jubilee 185.00

A woman did not powder her face in public until after World War I. By 1920 the beauty parlor, permanent waves, and cosmetics had become acceptable. A few companies sold cake face powder in a box with a mirror and a pad or puff. Soon the compact was being designed by jewelers and made of gold, silver, and precious materials. Cosmetic companies began to sell powder in attractive compacts of less valuable metal or plastic. Collectors today search for Art Deco designs, commemorative compacts from world's fairs or political events, and unusual examples. Many were made with companion lipsticks and other fittings.

COMPACT, Art Deco, Enameled Sterling Silver, Birmingham, 1937 .... 70.00
Art Deco, Richard Hudnut, Sterling Silver, 2 1/2 In. 95.00
Arthur Murray, First Prize, Deep Gourge Front, Silver 18.00
Blue Enamel & Sterling Silver, Portrait 60.00
Coty, Art Deco, Gold & Black, 3 1/4 In. 30.00
Dorset, Fifth Avenue, Embossed Rose 20.00
Dorset, Woman's Profile, 1940s, 3 In. 35.00
DuBarry, Copper, Round Design, Powderette 6.00
Elgin, Red Enameled Flowers, Gold, Box 20.00
Enamel Lid, Scene of Fireworks, Coty, Silver 50.00
Figural, Sparrow, Lipstick In Head, Pill Box In Tail, Dali Design 290.00
Gold, Finger Holder, Chain, Tiffany, 1920s 325.00
Gold, Raymond Yard, Diamond Clasp 1400.00
Gold, Sapphire & Diamond, Cobochon Thumbpiece, Rectangular 1100.00
Limoges, Victorian Enameled Scene, Gold, Signed 40.00
Lipstick With Mirror, Comb In Case, Gray, Rhinestones 20.00
Loose Powder, Elgin–American, Silver, 4 In. 50.00
Mexican Silver, Aztec Figure Engraved On Lid, 2 1/2 In. 20.00
Morhill, Mother–of–Pearl, Abalone, Pagoda On Black 12.00
Silver Inlay, Pink Flamingos, 1940s 35.00
Sterling Silver, Floral Design, 4 In. 85.00
Sterling Silver, Lavender Top, Enameled, 2 1/2 In. 75.00
Sterling Silver, Sunburst Design, 19 Natural Sapphires 135.00
Tortoiseshell, Celluloid, Large 28.00
Turtle Shell Pattern Top, Round, Silver, 4 In. 45.00
Volupte, Gold Plated, Raised Oak Leaves & Circles 12.00

The term "contemporary glass" refers to art glass made since 1950. Some contemporary glass factories, such as Orrefors or Baccarat, are listed under their own categories.

CONTEMPORARY GLASS, Bowl, Blue, Red Flower Center, Labino, 5 X 2 In. 450.00
Fountain Piece, Pink, Gold, Labino, 1979, 6 In. 1800.00
Jar, Dresser, Blue & White Flowers, Opaque, Monroe, 3 In. 80.00
Vase, Crystal, Paperweight Base, Erickson, 9 1/2 In. 22.00
Vase, Handkerchief, Red & White, Venini, 9 1/4 In. 950.00
Vase, Harlequin, Multicolored, Labino, 1975, 6 1/2 In. 1600.00
Vase, Iridescent, White Flower, Vandermark, 1981, 10 In. 175.00
Vase, Turquoise, Mottled Design, Brian Maytum, 7 1/2 In. 40.00
Vase, Venini, Red, White, 9 1/4 In. ....*Illus* 1045.00
Vase, White Flowers, Aqua Ground, Vandermark, 6 In. 125.00

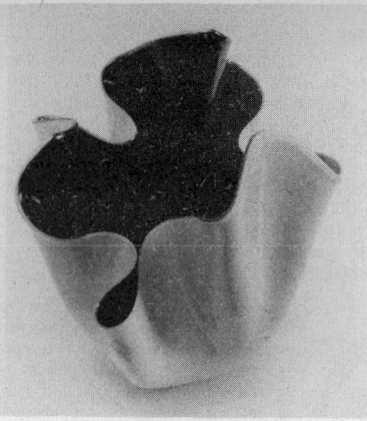

Cluthra, Vase, Burgundy Rim,
Dark Rose Base, Steuben, 10 1/2 In.

Contemporary Glass, Vase, Venini,
Red, White, 9 1/4 In.

 Cookbooks are collected for various reasons. Some are wanted for the recipes, some for investment, and some as examples of advertising. Cookbooks and recipe pamphlets are included in this section.

COOKBOOK, 20 Lessons In Domestic Science, 1916	15.00
250 Cake Recipes, 1949	5.00
365 Ways To Cook Hamburger, Betty Crocker, 1960	12.00
500 Tasty Sandwiches, 1941	5.00
American Family Receipt Book, 1907	30.00
American Woman's, Hard Cover, 1939	9.00
Aunt Ellen For Griswold, Booklet, 1938	6.00
Aunt Jenny's Spry Shortening, 1940s	7.00
Baker's Best Chocolate, 1932	18.00
Baker's Chocolate, 1945	5.00
Borden's, World's Fair, 1939	20.00
Brer Rabbit's Molasses Recipes, 1936	8.00
Business of Home Making, Western Stoneware Co., Illustrated	30.00
Calumet Baking Powder, 1918	15.00
Calumet Baking Powder, 1931	7.00
Campfire Marshmallows, 1920s	5.00
Carnation Milk, Mary Blake, 1928	7.00
Clabber Girl, 1934	8.00
Cooking The Modern Way, 1948	3.00
Cooking Way Down South In Dixie, 1949	3.00
Cream of Wheat, 1900s	9.00
Crisco, The Whys of Cooking, 1921	5.00
Dainty Dishes For Slender Incomes, 1900	25.00
Delineator Recipes, 1930	4.50
Dromedary, 1919	5.00
Edgewater Beach Hotel, Salad Book	30.00
Elsie The Cow, 1952	17.50
Family Circle, Cake & Cookie, 1953	10.00
Family Food Supply, Metropolitan Life Ins.Co., 1900s	8.00
Fannie Farmer Catering For Special Occasions, 1911	45.00
Farmer's Guide, April 16, 1929	1.50
Fleischmann's Yeast, Excellent Recipes For Baking, 1910	10.00
Fleischmann, 65 Delicious Dishes, 1919	11.00
Fleischmann, Choice Recipes, 1902, 50 Pages	13.50
Gold Medal Flour, 1909	15.00
Gold Medal Flour, 1916, 72 Pages	22.00
Good Luck Margarine, 1932	5.00

Griswold, 1919	5.00
Heinz, 1939	5.00
Hershey Chocolate, 1930	7.50
Hood's Sarsaparilla, 1888	12.50
Hotel St.Francis, 1919	30.00
Imperial, 1890	35.00
Jell–O, 1915	10.00
Jell–O, Booklet, 1926	4.00
Jell–O, Jack Benny	10.00
Jell–O, Parrish, 1924	40.00
Jewett Chafing Dish, Buffalo, N.Y., Recipes & Pictures, 1902	18.00
Kalamazoo Heating Co., Golden Jubilee, 1951, 48 Pages	8.00
Karo, 1920s	8.00
King Midas Mill Baking, Booklet	3.00
Knox Gelatin, 1936	8.00
Macon Cookbook, 1909	17.00
Methacol, Mammy On Cover, 1921	14.00
Monkeys, Rock Star, Singers & Swingers In The Kitchen, 1967	30.00
Nebraska Ladies' Club	7.50
New Royal, 1920	8.00
Ontario Ladies Cookbook, Gravenhurst, C.1900, 82 Pages	3.25
Pigby's, Reliable Candy Teacher, 1923	18.00
Pillsbury Bake–Off, No. 1	10.00
Price Baking Powder, 1921	5.00
Royal Baking Powder, 1920	7.00
Royal Desserts, 1932	5.00
Rumford Baking Powder, Common Sense Cookbook, 1900s	10.00
Rumford, 1934	12.00
Rumford, Complete Cookbook, Lilly Hoxworth Wallace, 1908	15.00
Runkle's Cocoa Delights, 1920s	8.00
Salad Dressing, Yacht Club, Manual of Salads, 1919	8.00
Snowflake Marshmallow Creme, 1916	8.00
Snowflake Wesson Oil, Booklet, 1929	4.00
Staley's Salad Oil & Syrups, Approved Recipes, 1900s	7.00
Storz, 1952, 300 Pages	15.00
Swan's Down, 1925	8.00
Swift's Jewel Shortening, 1935	8.00
Walter Baker Chocolate & Cocoa, With Figural Spoon	100.00
Watkins, Almanac Home Doctor & Cookbook, 1913	15.00
Watkins, Green, Copyright 1930	5.00

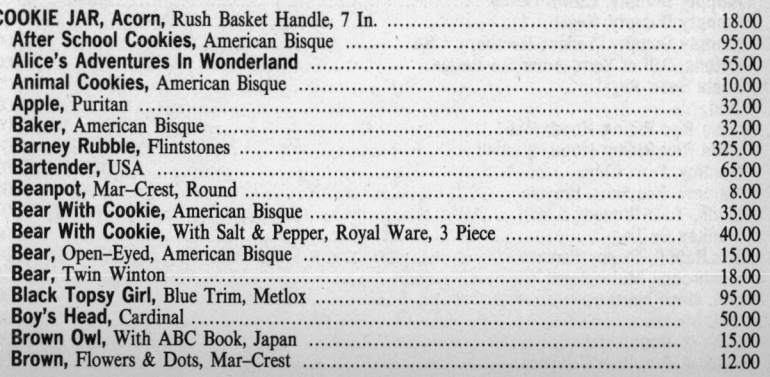

Cookie jars with brightly painted designs or amusing figural shapes became popular in the mid–1930s. Many companies made them and collectors search for cookie jars either by design or by maker's name. Listed here are examples by the less common makers. Major factories are listed under their own names in other sections of the book.

COOKIE JAR, Acorn, Rush Basket Handle, 7 In.	18.00
After School Cookies, American Bisque	95.00
Alice's Adventures In Wonderland	55.00
Animal Cookies, American Bisque	10.00
Apple, Puritan	32.00
Baker, American Bisque	32.00
Barney Rubble, Flintstones	325.00
Bartender, USA	65.00
Beanpot, Mar–Crest, Round	8.00
Bear With Cookie, American Bisque	35.00
Bear With Cookie, With Salt & Pepper, Royal Ware, 3 Piece	40.00
Bear, Open–Eyed, American Bisque	15.00
Bear, Twin Winton	18.00
Black Topsy Girl, Blue Trim, Metlox	95.00
Boy's Head, Cardinal	50.00
Brown Owl, With ABC Book, Japan	15.00
Brown, Flowers & Dots, Mar–Crest	12.00

C3pO, Star Wars	85.00
California Pelican	35.00
Cat On Beehive, American Bisque	22.50
Cat On Roof	22.50
Chef, American Bisque	30.00
Chef, Pearl China	225.00
Children Going To School, Tin, Copper, Black	20.00
Churn, American Bisque	10.00
Clock, American Bisque	17.00
Clock, Gold Design, American Bisque	35.00
Clown Head	30.00
Coffeepot, American Bisque	95.00
Cookie Monster	30.00
Cookie Train, American Bisque	32.00
Cookie Tree, Keebler	13.00
Cookie Truck, American Bisque	26.00
Cookstove, Regal China	12.00
Cylinder, Nursery Rhyme, Flamingo Decal, Blue, White, 9 In.	12.00
Dad's Oatmeal, Label	175.00
Derby Dan, Pfaltzgraff	55.00
Dog In Doghouse	22.50
Donald Duck, American Bisque	225.00
Donald Duck, Marked WD Products, Japan	95.00
Dumbo, Turnabout, Walt Disney Productions	45.00
Dutch Boy, Blue Tie, Stripes, Great Northern	45.00
Dutch Girl, Delft Blue, Occupied Japan	22.00
Dutch Girl, Great Northern	85.00
Dutch Girl, Pottery Guild	45.00 To 50.00
Dutch Girl, Twin Winton	24.00
Ear of Corn, Stanfordware	45.00 To 85.00
Elephant, American Bisque	45.00
Elsie The Cow, In Barrel, Pottery Guild	118.00
Elsie The Cow, Westfall	45.00
Elves & Schoolhouse	24.00
Ernie	85.00
Farmer Pig, American Bisque	50.00
Fred Flintstone	75.00
Gingerbread Man & Baker, Hexagonal, Says Cookies	15.00
Goldilocks, Royal Ware	90.00
Grandma, Hand Painted, Multicolored, Brayton Laguna, 13 In.	135.00
Granny, American Bisque	35.00
Grape Cluster, Metlox	20.00
Happy Birthday, Yellow	22.00
Hen With Chicks, Morton	60.00
Horse, Sitting, American Bisque	55.00
Hubert Lion, Regal	150.00
Humpty Dumpty, Crown Devon	45.00
Humpty Dumpty, Regal	150.00
Humpty Dumpty, Yellow, Ransburg, USA	12.00
Kittens, Ball of Yarn, American Bisque	12.00
Koala Bear, Regal	150.00
Lion, Metlox	35.00
Little Red Riding Hood, Hull	65.00
Little Red Riding Hood, Westfall	40.00
Mammy, Pearl China	200.00 To 350.00
Mammy, Red Skirt, Brayton	400.00
Monk, Twin Winton	16.00 To 25.00
Monkey On Log	28.00
Mrs.Rabbit, Floppy Ears	40.00
Mushroom, Multicolored	24.00
Owl, Great Northern	30.00
Owl, Metlox	25.00
Peek-A-Boo, Regal	425.00
Peek-A-Boo, Van Tellingen	250.00

Pelican, California	35.00
Pillsbury Doughboy, American Bisque	35.00
Pirate, Twin Winton	25.00
Poodle Behind Counter, Twin Winton	20.00
Poodle, American Bisque	35.00
Quaker Oats, Regal	85.00
Rabbit In Hat, American Bisque	25.00 To 40.00
Rabbit, Bow, White On White, Brick Bottom	16.00
Radio, Old Style, Maroon	20.00
Raggedy Andy, Poppytrail By Metlox	35.00
Ring For Cookies, American Bisque	95.00
Rooster, American Bisque	30.00
Rooster, Glamour Boy, Artcraft, Calif.	38.00
Rooster, Poppytrail By Metlox	35.00
Roses, Blue & Cream	65.00
Sailor Elephant, Twin Winton	24.00
Sailor Mouse, Twin Winton	25.00
Santa Claus, American Bisque	60.00
Santa On Rooftop	18.00
Sheriff, Robbinson Ransbottom	30.00
Shoe, Doranne of Calif.	25.00
Snoopy, On Red Roof, United Features Syndicate, 1970, 11 In.	38.00
Southern Belle, Pan American Art	36.00
Space Ship, American Bisque	50.00 To 55.00
Standing Pig, Blue Overalls	38.00
Sugar Dairy, Twin Winton	21.00
Teddy Bear, On Lid, Mottled Purple, Winfield	50.00
Thou Shalt Not Steal	20.00
Train, Sierra Vista	25.00
Train, Twin Winton	30.00
W.C. Fields	75.00
White Chick, American Bisque	18.00
White Kitten, Poppytrail By Metlox	25.00
Wooden Soldier, American Bisque	20.00
Yarn Doll, American Bisque	25.00
Yellow Chick, American Bisque	18.00
Yogi Bear, Dated 1961	150.00

COORS U.S.A.   Coors ware was made by a pottery in Golden, Colorado, owned by the Coors Beverage Company. It was produced from the turn of the century until the pottery was destroyed by fire in the 1930s. The name "Coors" is marked on the back.

COORS, Ashtray, Rosebud, Brown	4.50
Batter Bowl, Rosebud, Red	30.00
Bowl, Rosebud, 6 In.	15.00
Cake Plate, Rosebud, Maroon, 11 In.	10.00
Cake Set, Rosebud, 7 Piece	15.00
Casserole, Cover, Green, 3 1/2 Pt.	35.00
Cookie Jar, Rosebud, Utility, Green	20.00
Custard Cup, Green	9.00
Dish, Laboratory, Crucible	4.00
Jar, Utility, Blue, 2 1/2 Pt.	20.00
Mixing Bowl, Handle, Orange	24.00
Planter, Orange Matte, 3–Footed, 8 3/4 In.	25.00
Plate, Rose, 6 In.	9.00
Salt & Pepper, Range, Blue	15.00
Salt & Pepper, Rosebud, Tapered, Ivory	20.00
Teapot, Rose, Large	48.00
Urn, Mottled Green, High Glaze, 7 In.	45.00
Urn, White, Blue Interior, 7 1/2 In.	20.00
Urn, Yellow & White, 7 In.	35.00
Vase, Bulbous Bottom, Flared Rim, Matte Green, 8 1/4 In.	22.00
Vase, Coral & Green, Matte Finish, 5 In.	25.00
Vase, Green, White Interior, 8 1/2 In.	20.00

Vase, Orange, White Interior, 6 In.	30.00
Vase, Ribbed, Handles, Turquoise, 5 In.	10.00
Vase, Rope Handles, Large	25.00

Josiah Spode established a pottery at Stoke–on–Trent, England, in 1770. In 1833, the firm was purchased by William Copeland and Thomas Garrett and the firm mark was changed. In 1847, Copeland became the sole owner and the mark changed again. W. T. Copeland & Sons continued until a 1976 merger when it became Royal Worcester Spode. Pieces are listed in this book under the name that appears in the mark. Copeland Spode, Copeland, and Royal Worcester have separate listings.

COPELAND SPODE, 5 Piece Table Set, Moss Rose, Setting For 12	350.00
Cup & Saucer, Gainsborough	11.00
Cup & Saucer, Tower	12.00
Figurine, Bird, Rock Thrush, On Branch, 6 In.	38.00
Mug, King George V, Sepia Printed Design	125.00
Pitcher, Cameos, Hunters, Horses, Fallen Moose, C.1900, 4 In.	50.00
Pitcher, Pewter Top, Classical Woman Figures, 5 1/2 In.	125.00
Plate, Ermine, 9 1/4 In.	9.00
Plate, Rosebud Chintz, Square, 9 In.	15.00
Plate, Scenes of Ruins, Blue Transfer, 10 1/2 In.	25.00
Plate, Wicker Lane, 6 1/2 In.	5.00
Teapot, Hunt Scene, 6 1/2 In.	85.00 To 115.00
Tobacco Jar, Raised Design, Brown & Tan	60.00
COPELAND, Bust, Angel, Sleeping, Wings Tucked Under Chin, C.1860, 9 In.	175.00
Bust, Wellington, Black Basalt	1250.00
Coffee Set, Tray, C.1880, 9 Piece	1900.00
Coffeepot, Hunting Scene, Blue Ground, C.1890	165.00
Gravy, Underplate, Blue Willow, Light Blue Mandarin Border, 2 Pc.	45.00
Plate, Bird Nest, Flowers, Grasses, Black & White, 7 1/4 In.	15.00
Plate, Blue Willow, Light Blue Mandarin Border, 10 In.	10.00
Platter, Blue Willow, Light Blue Mandarin Border, 15 In.	45.00
Soup, Dish, Blue Willow, Light Blue Mandarin Border, 10 In.	10.00

COPPER LUSTER, see Luster, Copper

Utilitarian items, such as teakettles and cooking pans, have been handcrafted from copper in America since the days of the early colonists. Copper became a popular metal with the Arts and Crafts makers of the early 1900s and decorative pieces such as bookends and desk sets were made. Other pieces of copper may be found in the Bradley & Hubbard, Roycroft, and Kitchen categories.

COPPER, Ashtray, Sombrero, 5 1/2 In.	6.50
Atomizer, Rosewater, Pink Enameled, Vase Shape, Spout, Handle, 5 In.	330.00
Basin, Brass Rim, Cast Brass Handle, Italy, 16 In.	45.00
Berry Pail, Brass Bail, C.1860, 4 X 5 1/2 In.	40.00
Boiler, Cover, Red Wooden Handles	75.00
Bookends, Indian Chief, Full Headdress	40.00
Bowl, Fruit, Pedestal, Reticulated, Manning Bowman, 4 X 7 In.	25.00
Bowl, Hammered, Cupped, Scalloped, Gregorian Copper, 8 1/2 In.	17.00
Bowl, Silver Rim, Bulbous, Wide Mouth, Arthur Stone, 4 1/4 In.	325.00
Box, Hammered, Loop Finial, G.Stickley, 1905, 4 1/2 X 7 1/8 In.	375.00
Can, Watering, Brass Basket Handle, Spout, 7 In.	22.00
Candlestick, Abalone Inlay, Charles Burdick, C.1909, 11 3/4 In., Pair	4000.00
Candy Pan, Dovetailed, Rounded Bottom, Iron Rim Handles	95.00
Centerpiece, Hammered, Scroll Strapwork, Domed Circular Foot, 9 In.	50.00
Chamberstick, Hammered, Strap Handle, Dish Base, G.Stickley, 9 In.	400.00
Coffeepot, Brass Handle & Finial, Art Deco, 11 1/2 In.	250.00
Coffeepot, Majestic	25.00
Dinner Pail, Interior Compartments, Wire Bail & Wooden Handle, Lisk	40.00
Finial, Flag Pole, Full–Bodied Eagle, Outstretched Wings, 6 In.	200.00
Flask, Brass Eagle, Clasped Handles, U.S.In Shield	50.00
Food Warmer, Attached China Insert	135.00
Humidor, Old Mission, 6 1/2 In.	250.00

Humidor, Tookay Shop Mark, Karl Kipp, 1911–15	1100.00
Ink Filler, School Desk, American	65.00
Jar, Hammered, Enameled Floral Cover, Dirk Van Erp, 4 X 4 In.	100.00
Jar, Hammered, Enameled Ship Cover, G.Twitchell, 2 X 6 1/2 In.Diam.	600.00
Kettle, Apple Butter, Tripod Base	135.00
Kettle, Candy, Wrought Iron Rim Handles, 9 X 21 In.	85.00
Kettle, Rounded Bottom, Iron Side Handles, 12 X 23 1/2 In.	95.00
Kettle, Wrought Iron Handles, Dovetailed, 11 X 21 1/2 In.	80.00
Lightning Rod, Glass Sphere, Roof Mounting Plate, 5 In.	30.00
Mask, Dance, Jaguar Form, Turtle Appendages, Mexico, 14 In.	225.00
COPPER, MOLD, see Kitchen, Mold	
Pen Holder, Statue of Liberty	16.00
Planter, Hanging, Cauldron-Shape Bowl, Copper Chain, 4 In.	6.50
Plaque, Hammered, Dark Patina, Robert Jarvie, 20 In.Diam.	6050.00
Pot, Jelly Boiler, Iron Handles, 17 In.	110.00
Samovar, Tray & Waste Bowl, Copper, Small	45.00
Sconce, Karl Kipp	300.00
Tankard, Iron Handles, Gustav Stickley, C.1905, 8 1/4 In.	720.00
Teakettle, Bail Handle, Curved Spout, Portugal	12.00
Teakettle, Brass Handle, Hannam & Gillett, 13 1/4 In.	150.00
Teakettle, Brass Lid Finial, Stamped Heiss, Phila., 6 3/8 In.	450.00
Teakettle, Brass Trim, Gooseneck Spout, Oval	145.00
Teakettle, Gooseneck Spout, Fancy Handle, 18th Century, 2 Cup	395.00
Teakettle, Gooseneck Spout, Swivel Handle, 6 1/4 In.	25.00
Teakettle, Gooseneck Spout, Swivel Handle, 8 In.	90.00
Teakettle, Swivel Handle, Polished, 8 In.	65.00
Teakettle, Wrought Iron Side Handle, Gooseneck Spout With Flap	65.00
Teapot, Stand, Wooden Handle, Warmer, Gorham Co., Anchor	120.00
Tinder Box, Candle Socket, 5 In.	50.00
Tray, Gustav Stickley, Handles, Logo, C.1907, 23 1/4 In.	785.00
Tray, Hammered, Pierced Handles, Alternating Leaf, G.Stickley, 20 In.	650.00
Tray, Hammered, Pierced, Riveted Strap Border, Square, Van Erp, 9 In.	950.00
Vase, Hammered Zigzag, Gold Enameled, Oviform, Linossier, 4 In.	880.00
Vase, Trumpet Form, Logo, Gustav Stickley, C.1907, 10 5/8 In.	1020.00

Coralene glass was made by firing many small colored beads on the outside of glassware. It was made in many patterns in the United States and Europe in the 1880s. Reproductions are made today.

CORALENE, Bowl, Fruit, Fruits, Flowers, Orange, Silver Plated Holder, Meriden	350.00
CORALENE, JAPANESE, see Japanese Coralene	
Plate, Pink Poppies On Bisque, Green, 7 3/4 In.	90.00
Vase, Cobalt & Gold Border, Yellow & Orange Beading, 8 1/2 In.	325.00
Vase, Cylinder, 2 Small Handles, Nasturtiums, Leaves, 8 1/4 In.	405.00
Vase, Pink & Lavender Irises, Green Ground, 9 In.	455.00
Vase, Ruffled Top, Yellow Bird On Branch, Blue, C.1900, 5 1/2 In.	210.00
Vase, Wheat Pattern, Mother-of-Pearl, White Lining, 5 3/8 In.	495.00

Boleslaw Cybis was one of the founders of the Cordey China Company in 1942 in Trenton, New Jersey. The firm produced gift shop items. In 1969 it was acquired by the Lightron Corp. and operated as the Schiller Cordey Co., manufacturers of lamps. About 1950 Boleslaw Cybis began making Cybis porcelains, which are listed in their own section in this book.

CORDEY, Box, Female Oriental Dancer, Flowing Robe, Cover, 3 X 4 X 2 In.	45.00
Box, Leaves On Cover, Pink Roses, Gold Trim, 5 X 5 In.	45.00
Bust, Gentleman, No.3001	45.00
Bust, Girl, No.5011	55.00
Bust, Napoleon, No.5038, Green Jacket	90.00
Figurine, Bird, No.2037, Wings Fold In, Claws Hold Stump, 8 1/2 In.	115.00
Figurine, Boy & Basket, No.304	90.00
Figurine, Boy & Hat, No.303	95.00
Figurine, Chinese Mandarin, No.5071, Full Figure Woman, 12 In.	75.00
Figurine, Colonial Man & Woman, No.5041 & 5089, 11 In.	135.00
Figurine, Lamb, No.6025	85.00

Figurine, Woman & Basket, No.302	85.00
Figurine, Woman & Basket, No.304	85.00
Figurine, Woman & Fan, No.300, 16 In.	85.00
Figurine, Woman Wearing Pink Hat, Man Wearing Tricorner, Pair	110.00
Figurine, Woman, No.306, 16 In.	115.00
Figurine, Woman, No.5084	100.00
Figurine, Woman, Peach Skirt, Fuchsia Bodice, Pink, Green Fan, 16 In.	120.00
Figurine, Woman, Ringlets, Roses, Leaves, Bustle, 10 3/4 In.	80.00

There has been a need for a corkscrew since the first bottle was sealed with a cork, probably in the seventeenth century. Today collectors search for the early, unusual patented examples or the figural corkscrews of recent years.

CORKSCREW, 2–Sided Man, Jigger, Bottle Opener & Spoon, Silver Plate, 1932	110.00
Alpeter, With Bottle Opener, Box, 1901	18.00
Attached Ivory Brush, Brass & Steel, English	250.00
Benjamin Franklin, Brass	22.50
Butterfly, Murphy	75.00
Carved Ivory Tusk Handle, Sterling Cap	185.00
Charter Whiskey, Wooden	12.00
Crucifix, Ivory, With Sheath, Sterling Silver	375.00
Folding, Blue Steel, 4 X 2 1/2 In.	18.00
Hollweg Handy	85.00
Koppitz–Melchers Brewing Co., Purse Select Reverse Side	16.00
Listerine, Tin Litho	10.00
Magnolia Brewery, Houston Ice & Brewing	11.00
Naughty Boy, Brass	10.00
Nude Mermaid, Celluloid, Geschutz Mark	250.00
Sperry, Single Lever	1500.00
W.C.Fields	27.00
Wooden Grip, Hand Forged Iron Shank, 4 1/2 In.	12.00

Coronation cups have been made since the 1800s. Pottery or glass with a picture of the monarch and date have been souvenirs for many coronations. The pieces that mention King Edward VIII, the king who was never crowned, are not rare; and collectors should be sure to check values before buying.

CORONATION, see also Commemorative

CORONATION, Beaker, George V	45.00
Box, Elizabeth & Philip, 1955, Tin, 11 1/4 X 7 3/4 X 2 In.	10.00
Card, In Album, George VI, Queen Elizabeth, 50 Players, 1937	50.00
Cup & Saucer, Edward VII & Alexandria	45.00
Decanter, George V, Queen Mary, Coat of Arms, Crown Stopper, 1911	150.00
Mirror, George V, Pocket	25.00
Mug, Edward VIII, Myott, Dame Laura Knight	35.00
Mug, Queen Elizabeth, June 2, 1953	240.00
Paper Dolls, Coloring Book, Queen of England, Uncut	55.00
Paperweight, Queen Elizabeth & Prince Philip	250.00
Pitcher, George V, 6 1/2 In.	65.00
Plate, George VI, Wedgwood	40.00
Plate, King George VI, Scalloped Edge, Glass, 10 In.	55.00
Tumbler, King George VI, Sepia Portrait	55.00
Watch Fob, Queen Victoria	55.00

Cosmos is a pressed milk glass pattern with colored flowers made from 1894 to 1915 by the Consolidated Lamp and Glass Company. Tablewares and lamps were made. A few pieces were also made of clear glass with painted decorations.

COSMOS, Butter, Cover	115.00
Butter, Cover, Pink Band	195.00 To 200.00
Butter, Pink Band, Cover	200.00 To 235.00
Creamer, Pink Band	165.00
Lamp, Shade, 14 In.	250.00 To 350.00
Salt & Pepper, Pink Band	135.00

Spooner, Pink 75.00
Spoonholder, Raspberry, Opaque White, 4 1/4 In. 600.00
Sugar, Cover, Pink Band .... 125.00 To 135.00
Tumbler, Opaque White 80.00

Linen or wool coverlets were made during the nineteenth century. Most of the coverlets date from 1800 to 1850. Four types were made: the double woven, jacquard, summer and winter, and overshot. Later coverlets were made of a variety of materials. Quilts are listed in this book in their own section.

COVERLET, Double Weave, Geometric Design, Pine Tree Border, 71 X 82 In. 250.00
Double Weave, Geometric, Tricolor, 73 X 86 In. 350.00
Double Weave, Irish Chain Design, 2 Piece, Blue, White, 74 X 86 In. 350.00
Double Weave, Snowflake & Pine Tree, 78 X 90 In. ....*Illus* 105.00
Jacquard, American Flag, Liberty Head Medallion, 1852, 83 X 55 In. 800.00
Jacquard, Centennial, Memorial Hall, 1776–1786, 76 X 82 In. 225.00
Jacquard, Columbia Pattern, Eagle Carrying Hail Columbia Banner 300.00
Jacquard, Dancing Cherubs, Tassels, 106 X 125 1/2 In. 1500.00
Jacquard, Double Weave, Blue, White, Floral Medallion, 82 X 82 In. 175.00
Jacquard, Double Weave, Floral Medallion Center, 78 X 82 In. 95.00
Jacquard, Floral Border, 1850, 78 X 88 In. ....*Illus* 900.00
Jacquard, Floral Design, Birds, Red, White, 78 X 88 In. 275.00
Jacquard, Floral Medallion, 83 X 83 In. 225.00
Jacquard, Floral Medallion, Miby H.Stager, 80 X 80 In. 550.00
Jacquard, Floral, Blue, White, 80 X 92 In. ....*Illus* 350.00
Jacquard, Head of George Washington, Boats, Horses, 82 X 76 In. 695.00
Jacquard, Single Weave, Floral Design, Red, Blue, Green, 80 X 90 In. 400.00
Jacquard, Star Flowers, Dated 1857, Red, Blue, 82 X 92 In., 1 Piece 450.00
Jacquard, Star Medallion Center, Blue, Green, Red, 76 X 82 In. 125.00
Jacquard, Vining Rose, Bird Border, Henry Miller, 1847, 74 X 86 In. 275.00
Jacquard, Washington On Horse Back Corners, 75 X 88 In. 750.00
Linsey–Woolsey, Circle, Flower & Leaf Design, 74 X 63 In. 900.00
Linsey–Woolsey, Quilted Panels, Geometric & Floral, 71 X 76 In. 600.00
Overshot, Blue & White Optical Pattern, 77 X 96 In. 125.00
Overshot, Blue & White Optical Pattern, 80 X 104 In. 150.00
Overshot, Blue & White, Signed C S, Fringed, 8 X 72 In. 175.00
Overshot, Blue, Red, Natural White, 2 Piece, Woven, 72 X 84 In. 180.00
Overshot, Eagle & Star, Date Woven Into Border, 1838, 76 X 84 In. 125.00
Overshot, Floral Medallion, Geometric Field, 3–Color, 88 X 83 In. 300.00
Overshot, Flower Type Pattern, Wide Borders, 74 X 82 In., 2 Piece 325.00
Overshot, Navy Blue, Natural White, 64 X 96 In., 2 Piece 345.00
Overshot, Optical Pattern, Blue, Green, Red, 72 X 86 In., 2 Piece 300.00

Coverlet, Double Weave,
Snowflake & Pine Tree,
78 X 90 In.

Coverlet, Jacquard,
Floral, Blue, White,
80 X 92 In.

Coverlet, Jacquard,
Floral Border, 1850,
78 X 88 In.

Overshot, Optical Pattern, Navy Blue, 60 X 88 In. 500.00

 Guy Cowan made pottery in Rocky River, Ohio, a suburb of Cleveland, from 1913 to 1931. The Cowan Pottery made art pottery and wares for florists. A stylized mark with the word "Cowan" was used on most pieces. A commercial, mass–produced line was marked "Lakeware." Collectors today search for the Art Deco pieces by Guy Cowan, Viktor Schreckengost, Waylande Gregory, or Thelma Frazier Winter.

COWAN, Bookend, Elephant Pull, Single 110.00
Bowl, Console, Seahorse, Iridescent Blue 32.00
Bowl, Cream, Apple Green Interior, Scallopped, Footed, 9 1/2 X 4 In. 22.00
Bowl, Luster, 12 In. 45.00
Candelabra, 3–Light Scroll, 4 1/2 X 7 In., Pair 60.00
Candleholder, Cliffwood, Rose To Purple, 1923, Pre–Morton, 6 In. 60.00
Candleholder, Leaping Gazelle, Glossy Caramel, 5 3/4 In. 70.00
Candleholder, Triple, Ivory, 8 In., Pair 48.00
Candlestick, Angels, Brown 165.00
Candlestick, Art Deco, Orange Luster, 1 1/2 X 5 In., Pair 10.00
Candlestick, Blue Luster, 2 1/4 In., Pair 20.00
Candlestick, Figural, Seahorse, Ivory, Glossy, 4 1/4 In. 10.00
Candlestick, Ivory, 4 In., Pair 17.00
Candlestick, Seahorse, Green, 4 1/2 In., Pair 23.00
Figurine, Egret, Ivory, 11 1/2 In. 125.00
Flower Frog, Art Deco Nude, White, 6 1/2 In. 35.00
Flower Frog, Leaf Form, Green Glaze, Signed 35.00
Flower Frog, Nude Veiled Woman, Art Deco 60.00
Flower Frog, Nude Woman, 6 In. 125.00
Flower Holder, Mushroom, Cream Color 50.00
Ginger Jar, Cover, Purple Luster, 5 1/2 In. 48.00
Lamp, Relief Stork, Brown Highlights, 10 In. 295.00
Lamp, Squirrel, Pheasant & Heron In Relief, Off–White 60.00
Planter, Strawberry, Underplate, Red–Orange Glaze, Marked, 6 In. 50.00
Sugar, Creamer & Tray, Geometric Shapes 25.00
Vase, Apple Green, Trumpet Flared, Ribbed, Footed, Flower Frog, 7 In. 49.00
Vase, Aqua, 9 1/2 In. 15.00
Vase, Blue Luster, 7 In. 35.00
Vase, Blue Luster, Octagonal, 6 3/4 In. 45.00
Vase, Bud, Seahorse, Ivory, 8 1/4 In. 43.00
Vase, Lavender, High Gloss, Signed, 3 X 3 1/2 In. 22.00
Vase, Oriental Glaze, Beehive Shape, 8 X 8 In. 225.00
Vase, Seahorse, Green, 7 In. 33.00
Wall Pocket, Purple Luster, Signed, 8 1/2 In. 45.00

 Cracker Jack, the molasses–flavored popcorn mixture, was first made in 1896 in Chicago, Illinois. A prize was added to each box in 1912. Collectors search for the old boxes and toys and advertising materials. Many of the toys are unmarked.

CRACKER JACK, Badge, Police Star 10.00
Bookmark, Scotty Dog 15.00
Coin, Pair 6.00
Delivery Truck 35.00
Doll, Advertising 28.00
Mirror, Red, White, Blue, More Your Eat, More You Want, Pocket 60.00
Mustache, Paper, Unpunched 25.00
Riddle Cards, 20 Cards, 1 Missing 35.00
Sailor .... 20.00 To 35.00
Skeezix 35.00
Top, Always On Top, Litho Tin, 1930s 25.00
Top, Cracker Jack–Angelus, Tin Litho, 1930s 25.00
Top, Sheet Metal, Wooden Center, Red, White & Blue 10.00
Wheelbarrow, Tin Litho 30.00
Whistle, Blue & White 6.00
Whistle, Tin, Single Barrel, Embossed, 2 1/8 In. 12.00

Crackle glass was originally made by the Venetians, but most of the ware found today dates from the 1800s. The glass was heated, cooled, and refired so that many small lines appeared inside the glass. It was made in many factories in the United States and Europe.

CRACKLE GLASS, Bowl, Overshot Casing, Embossed Ivy Branches, 8 In.	85.00
Creamer, Enameled Fish & Plants, Mt.Washington, 4 1/2 In.	125.00
Cruet, Amber	35.00
Cruet, Teal, West Virginia	25.00
Cruet, Vinegar, Stopper	175.00
Pitcher, Clear Handle, Green, 5 In.	17.50
Pitcher, Green Handle	20.00
Pitcher, Light Blue, Amber Applied Handle	135.00
Water Set, Marigold, 9 Piece	195.00

Cranberry glass is an almost transparent yellow–red glass. It resembles the color of cranberry juice. The glass has been made in Europe and America since the Civil War. It is still being made and reproductions can fool the unwary.

CRANBERRY GLASS, see also Northwood; Rubena Verde; etc.

CRANBERRY GLASS, Basket, Clear Thorn Handle & Ruffle, , 9 1/2 X 4 1/2 In.	195.00
Bell, Wedding, Opaque White Base Rim, 14 3/4 In.	198.00
Biscuit Jar, Ribbed, Ruffled Trim, Vaseline Collar, 8 In.	540.00
Bottle, Barber, Melon Ribbed, Applicator Top, 7 1/4 In.	85.00
Bottle, Wine, Gold & Silver Leaves, 10 1/2 In.	165.00
Bowl, Hobnail, Fluted Top, 5 X 6 In.	65.00
Bowl, Opalescent Threaded, Footed, Clear Rigaree, 3 1/2 In.	135.00
Box, Enameled Fowers On Hinged Cover, 2 7/8 X 3 3/4 In.	195.00
Box, Hinged Lid, Enameled Work, 1 1/4 X 2 In.	75.00
Box, Hinged Lid, Orchid & Hearts, Enameling, Beading, 4 In.	160.00
Box, Patch, Metal Filigree Around Hinged Lid, 2 1/4 In.	135.00
Castor, Pickle, Inverted Thumbprint, Rockford Frame	285.00
Compote, Scalloped Edge, Gold Trim, 9 X 9 1/4 In.	275.00
Cordial Set, Tray, Enameled Flowers, C.1950, 8 Piece	145.00
Cracker Jar, White Lace Design	345.00
Cruet, Clear Hobnail Stopper, Clear Handle	55.00
Cruet, Griffin Bust On Handle, Pewter Mounts, 9 1/8 In.	245.00
Cruet, Melon Shape, Over Clear, Faceted Stopper	98.00
Cruet, White Enameled Flowers & Leaves, 7 1/2 In.	165.00
Decanter, Flattened, Clear Rope Handle, Stopper, 9 5/8 In.	135.00
Decanter, Openwork Vintage Design, 12 1/2 In. ....*Illus*	5280.00
Decanter, Pewter Lid, Bubble Stopper, French, 15 1/2 In.	395.00
Dish, Cheese, Cover, Thumbprint	195.00
Dish, Sweetmeat, Ruffled, Silver Plated Holder, 5 3/4 In.	95.00
Dresser Set, Gold Flowers & Leaves, 5 Piece	725.00
Epergne, 4 Long Stem Lilies, Clear Rigaree, 10 In.	575.00
Epergne, 5 Ruffled Trumpets, Clear Applied Design, 23 In.	425.00
Finger Bowl, Enameled Flowers	50.00
Finger Bowl, Underplate, Crimped, Optic Diamond, 6 1/2 In.	135.00
Globe, Hobnail, 5 1/2 X 9 In.	100.00
Gold Flowers & Leaves, Outlined In White, 10 3/4 In., Pr.	225.00
Jug, Claret, Hinged Cover, Pewter Encased, 9 1/2 In.	245.00
Lamp, Drape Pattern, Amber Scallops, 6 1/2 In.	300.00
Lamp, Finger, Optic Pattern, Clear Handle, 5 1/2 In.	135.00
Lamp, Hall, Victorian, Tapered Ribbed, Brass Mount, 13 In.	70.00
Lamp, Hanging, Ovoid Swirled Globe, Brass Mounts, 10 In.	130.00
Light Fixture, Hanging, Coin Spot, Brass, Electrified	900.00
Liqueur Set, Enameled Flowers, Leaves, Swallows, 8 Piece	375.00
Loving Cup, Silver Overlay, 3 Handles, 3 1/2 In.	495.00
Mayonnaise, Underplate, Threaded	68.00
Perfume Bottle, Laydown, Spangle, Silver Hinged Top	325.00
Perfume Bottle, Spiral Trim, Bubble Stopper, 6 7/8 In.	110.00
Pitcher, Bulbous, Clear Handle, 5 In.	150.00

Cranberry Glass, Decanter,
Openwork Vintage Design,
12 1/2 In.

Feel the edges of the design of the glass. Cut glass has sharp edges; pressed-glass designs were molded into the glass.

Never put anything hot in a cut glass bowl. It was not made to withstand heat and will crack.

Pitcher, Enameled Flowers, Gold Rim, 12 1/4 In.	195.00
Pitcher, Gold Scroll, Leaves, Enameled Outline, 4 In.	70.00
Pitcher, Hobnail, Fluted Top, Clear Handle, 8 In.	195.00
Pitcher, Ice Bladder, Clear Rope Handle, 11 1/4 In.	375.00
Pitcher, Inverted Coin Spot, 8 In.	265.00
Pitcher, Inverted Thumbprint, Clear Reeded Handle, 6 In.	60.00
Pitcher, Inverted Thumbprint, Clear Ribbed Handle, 9 In.	225.00
Pitcher, Lattice & Dot Enameled Design, 3 5/8 In.	95.00
Pitcher, Thumbprint, Ruffled Top, Clear Handle, 8 1/2 In.	95.00
Pitcher, Water, Applied Green Handle	120.00
Pitcher, Water, Clear Rope Handle, Bulbous, 7 3/8 X 5 In.	245.00
Pitcher, Water, Paneled Sprig	195.00
Pitcher, Water, Squared Mouth, Ribbed Handle, 9 In.	200.00
Pitcher, Water, Tankard Shape, Clear Handle, 9 1/8 In.	165.00
Pokal, Venetian, Gilt Highlights, Cover, 11 3/4 In.	99.00
Punch Bowl, Lid, Enemeled Flowers, Gilded Design, 17 In.	1360.00
Punch Set, Compote, Enameled Florals, 9 Piece	850.00
Relish, Vaseline Edge, Silver Plated Holder	120.00
Rose Bowl, Painted Floral Desigh, 6 In.	35.00
Salt & Pepper, Opalescent, Original Cover	165.00
Salt & Pepper, Optic, Bulbous, Pewter Tops, 3 1/2 In.	135.00
Salt, 3 Clear Scroll Feet, Master, 1 3/4 X 3 In.	45.00
Salt, Coal Hod Shape, Silver Plated Holder, 3 In.	75.00
Saltshaker, Inverted Thumbprint, Silver Plated, 2 1/2 In.	50.00
Sugar Shaker, Paneled Sides, Screw-On Top	65.00
Sugar Shaker, Paneled Sprig	175.00
Syrup, Inverted Rib, Clear Handle, 5 3/4 In.	350.00
Toothpick, Ribbed Lattice	75.00
Toothpick, Swirled Windows	85.00
Tray, Dresser, White & Gold Enameled, 10 1/4 X 7 1/2 In.	95.00
Tumbler, Paneled Sprig	45.00
Tumbler, Thumbprint, 3 3/4 In.	85.00
Vase, Cased White, Enameled Flowers, 7 In.	195.00
Vase, Clear Applied Ruffle & 3 Feet, 4 3/4 X 2 3/4 In.	75.00
Vase, Clear Rosette Patterned Foot, 5 7/8 In.	88.00
Vase, Coin Dot, 8 In.	65.00
Vase, Crystal Leaves & Flower, Wishbone Feet, 9 1/4 In.	125.00
Vase, Crystal Leaves Top, Rigaree Below, 9 3/8 In.	145.00
Vase, Cylinder, Gold Flowers, Leaves, Dot Trim, 7 1/4 In.	65.00
Vase, Diamond-Quilted, Ruffled Top, 4 1/2 X 3 1/2 In.	95.00
Vase, Enameled Daisies & Leaves, 9 3/8 In., Pair	225.00
Vase, Enameled Flowers & Leaves, 2 3/4 X 1 1/2 In.	55.00

Vase, Enameled Flowers, Yellow Buds & Branches, 6 3/4 In.	75.00
Vase, Enameled Scrolls, Front & Back Florals, 3 1/4 In.	40.00
Vase, Fan Top, Clear Wishbone Feet, Enameled Floral, 11 In.	195.00
Vase, Flattened Oval, Rigaree, Hodgitt's Patent, 6 3/4 In.	145.00
Vase, Gold Scrolls & Leaves, Blue Flowers, 10 1/2 In.	225.00
Vase, Hobnail, Opalescent Border, Legged, Hobbs, Brockunier	595.00
Vase, Interior Ribs, Enameled Florals, Foliage, 8 1/2 In.	125.00
Vase, Lacy Foliage, Gold Balls, Clear Pedestal, 5 1/4 In.	100.00
Vase, Ruffled Top, Gold Rose Garlands, 5 X 4 1/2 In.	150.00
Vase, Sanded Gold Leaves & Trim, 11 1/4 In.	245.00
Vase, Scalloped, White Enameled Stag Scene, 10 1/4 In.	135.00
Vase, Trumpet, Crystal Spiral Trim, 8 3/8 In.	85.00
Vase, Urn Shape, Crystal Applied Handles, 7 3/8 In., Pair	145.00
Vase, White Vine, Leaves, Grapes, Ormolu Foot, 10 1/2 In.	265.00
Water Set, Enameled Lattice Design, Clear Handle, 7 Piece	525.00
Wine, Swirl Pattern, Clear Stem, 6 Piece	200.00

Creamware, or queensware, was developed by Josiah Wedgwood about 1765. It is a cream-colored earthenware that has been copied by many factories.

CREAMWARE, see also Wedgwood

CREAMWARE, Basket, Chestnut	1250.00
Candle Shield, Floral Decal	120.00
Food Warmer, Bust of Jefferson, Eagle & Shield, 6 In.	3550.00
Mold, English Crown, Mid-19th Century, 3 3/4 X 5 3/4 X 4 1/4 In.	60.00
Mold, Grape, Buff Color, 3 3/4 X 8 X 7 In.	70.00
Mold, Pudding, Bunch of Grapes & Leaf, Oval, 3 X 5 X 7 In.	110.00
Mug, Knights of Pythias	175.00
Pitcher, Humanoid Looking Into Bottom Handle, 8 1/2 In.	467.50
Pitcher, Lafayette, Washington, Inscriptions, C.1825, 4 3/4 In.	825.00
Tureen, Grape Form, Vine Forms Handle, Leaf Form Base, Ladle	715.00
Umbrella Stand, Floral Decal	150.00

Crown Derby is the nickname given to the works of the Royal Crown Derby factory, which began working in England in 1859. An earlier and more famous English Derby factory existed from 1750 to 1848. The two factories were not related. Most of the porcelain found today with the Derby mark is the work of the later Derby factory.

CROWN DERBY, see also Derby; Royal Crown Derby

CROWN DERBY, Tureen, Underplate, Posie, Oval	495.00
Vase, Ivory, Flowers, Jeweling, Small Neck, Globular, C.1878	350.00
Vase, Peonies, Gold, Japanese Style, Bulbous, 12 In.	2300.00
Vase, Potpourri, Fruit, Insect, Urn Form, Pinecone Cover, 5 In.	358.00

Crown Ducal is the name used on some pieces of porcelain made by A. G. Richardson and Co., Ltd., England. The name has been used since 1916.

CROWN DUCAL, Figurine, Rabbit, 6 In.	40.00
Ice Bucket, Cover, Scenes of Oriental Lanters, Wicker Handle	45.00

Crown Milano glass was made by Frederick Shirley about 1890. It had a plain biscuit color with a satin finish. It was decorated with flowers and often had large gold scrolls.

CROWN MILANO, Biscuit Barrel, Floral Engraved Lid, Gold Encrusted Flowers	900.00
Biscuit Jar, 16 Panels, Harbor Scene, Marked, 5 1/2 X 9 In.	735.00
Biscuit Jar, Ribbed, Floral, Silver Plated Handle & Lid, 8 In.	475.00
Biscuit Jar, Stylized Florals, Enamel Dots, Marked	485.00
Bowl, Flowers Outlined In Gold, Signed, 7 X 9 1/2 In.	950.00
Bowl, Opaque White, Melon Ribbed, 6 3/4 In.	110.00
Creamer, Melon Ribbed, Silver Plated Rim & Handle, 3 1/8 In.	100.00
Creamer, Silver Plated Mount, Roses, Mt.Washington, 3 3/4 In.	200.00
Cup, Floral Sprays, Gold Scrolls, Demitasse, 2 X 3 In.	285.00
Dish, Sweetmeat, Cover, Melon Ribbed, Pink Top & Bottom, 4 In.	825.00

Jar, Silver Plate Cover & Handle, Pansies, Mt.Wshington, 4 In.	300.00
Jardiniere, Gold & Floral Design, Signed, 5 1/2 X 8 1/4 In.	250.00
Perfume Bottle, Enamelled Florals, Gold Outlining, 4 1/2 In.	325.00
Sugar & Creamer, Violets, Gold Trim, Lusterless White	910.00
Tray, Ruffled Edge, Raised Gold Scrolls, Marked, 9 1/2 In.	325.00
Vase, Colonial Children, Opaque Satin, Gold, Signed, 13 3/4 In.	1100.00
Vase, Entwined Arms, Gold Ribbon, Framed By Wreath, Signed	480.00
Vase, Floral Paisley, Snipped Top, Gold Edge, 13 1/2 In.	800.00
Vase, Flying Bats, Gold Crescent Moon	2350.00
Vase, Multicolored Enamel Dot Design, 12 1/2 In.	930.00
Vase, Pansies, Gold Trim, 3 Leaf Handles, 8 In.	1870.00
Vase, Roses, Thorn Branches, 2 Applied Handles, 10 1/2 In.	585.00
Vase, Squares of Enamel of Geometric Design, Handles	535.00
CROWN TUSCAN, see Cambridge	

Cruets of glass or porcelain were made to hold vinegar, oil, and other condiments. They were especially popular during Victorian times but have been made in a variety of styles since the eighteenth century.

CRUET, see also Castor Set

CRUET, Amber, Enameled, Scenic Medallion, Niagara Falls	69.00
Fluted Scrolls, Blue Opalescent, Stopper	135.00
Forget-Me-Not, Challinor	58.00
Hobnail, Amber, Push-Up Bottom	52.50
Liqueur, Cranberry Glass, Pewter, Cherub, Flat Bulbous, French, 9 In.	225.00
Satin Bubble Lattice, Blue Opalescent, Stopper	145.00
Scroll With Acanthus, Blue Opalescent, Stopper	145.00
Shoshone, Red Flashed, Stopper	145.00

There are many marks that include the words "CT Germany." The first mark with those words was used by a company in Altwasser, Germany, in 1845. The initials stand for C. Thielsch, a partner in the firm. The Hutschenreuther firm took over the company in 1918 and continued to use the "CT."

C. T.

CT GERMANY, Bowl, Flowers, Blue & Gold Border, 10 In.	75.00
Cracker Jar, Melon Rib, Brown Floral, Leaf Design, Twig Handle	80.00
Ramekin, Pin Roses, Scalloped, Altwasser	10.00

Cup plates are small glass or china plates that held the cup while a gentleman of the mid-nineteenth century drank his coffee or tea from the saucer. The most famous cup plates were made of glass at the Boston and Sandwich factory located in Sandwich, Massachusetts. There have been many new glass cup plates made in recent years for sale to gift shops or the limited edition collectors. These are similar to the old plates but can be identified.

CUP PLATE, Diamond Point Edge, 8-Point Star Center	20.00
Eagle	62.00
Garfield, Crystal	125.00
Landing of Lafayette, Dark Blue, Clews	500.00
Major Ringgold	245.00

Currier & Ives made the famous American lithographs marked with their name from 1857 to 1907. The mark used on the print included the street address in New York City, and it is possible to date the year of the original issue from this information. Earlier prints were made by N. Currier and used that name from 1835 to 1847. Many reprints of the Currier or Currier & Ives prints have been made. Many collectors also buy the insurance calendars that were based on the old prints. The words large, small, or medium folio refer to size.

CURRIER & IVES, Abraham Lincoln The Nations Martyr	75.00
American Field Sports, On A Point, 1857, Large Folio	275.00
Autumn Fruits, 1861, Medium Folio	220.00
Battle of New Orleans, Framed, 1842	150.00
Beauties of Billards, 1869, 16 1/8 X 24 3/4 In.	900.00

Begging A Bite, 15 1/2 X 11 1/2 In. 95.00
Bowling Club Bowled Out, Darktown, 1888, Small Folio, Pair 385.00
Celebrated Trotting Mare Lucy Passing Stand, 9 X 14 In. 575.00
Christ Walking On The Sun, 8 X 12 In. 40.00
Col. Michael Corcoran, Batttle of Bullrun, 8 X 12 In. 35.00
Coming Up Smiling, Signed, 9 1/4 X 13 In. 240.00
Conklin's Bay Gelding Rarus, 16 3/4 X 26 In. ....*Illus* 1400.00
Crack Trotter, Coming Around, 1880, Red Flag Oil 220.00
Darktown Fire Brigade, A Prize Squirt, Framed, No.1386 .... 175.00
Death of Washington, Frame, 13 X 17 1/2 In. 45.00
Farmer's Home, Autumn, Framed, Large Folio 1650.00
General George Washington, 14 X 10 In. 55.00
Golden Fruits of California, 1869, Large Folio 1045.00
Great Fire At Boston, Nov.9th & 10th 1872, 8 X 12 5/8 In. 125.00
Hudson, From West Point, 1862, Medium Folio 990.00
Indian Pass, Rocky Mountains, Medium Folio 550.00
Landing of The Pilgrims, Framed, 13 X 17 In. 85.00
Lawn Party, Music & Bully Time, Darktown, 1888, Small, Pair 418.00
Life In The Woods, Starting Out, 1860, Framed, Large Folio 3850.00
Life of A Fireman, The Ruins, Walnut Frame, 16 X 25 In. 1700.00
Little May Blossom, 14 X 16 In. 95.00
Love Is The Lightest, Framed, 1847, 11 X 8 In. 200.00
Midnight Race On The Mississippi, Large Folio 4620.00
Morning In The Woods, 1865, Large Folio 660.00
Morning Prayer, 18 X 20 In. 65.00
Napoleon, Hero of 100 Battles, Framed, 14 X 17 In. 85.00
Niagara Falls, From Goat Island, Medium Folio 275.00
Niagara Falls, Matted, Framed, 11 5/8 X 14 5/8 In. 55.00
Noah's Ark, 12 X 14 In. 235.00
Norman, Burning of The Clipper Ship, Framed, Small Folio 660.00
Norman, Loss of Steamship Swallow, 1845, Small Folio 352.00
Oaken Bucket, Woodworth Verse, 1864, 15 15/16 X 23 3/8 In. 1000.00
Old Manse, Framed, 12 1/2 X 8 1/2 In. 375.00
Old Oaken Bucket, 10 X 12 In. 55.00
Old Oaken Bucket, Small Folio 130.00
On De Half Shell, Black, 1885, 18 X 13 In. 1475.00
Presidents of The United States, 10 X 14 In. 40.00
Summer Time, Hand Colored, Frame, 13 1/2 X 17 1/2 In. 95.00
Tree of Temperance & Intemperance, Frame, 1872, Set 200.00
Where Do You Buy Our Cigars, Man, Owl, Trade Card, 1880 .... 50.00

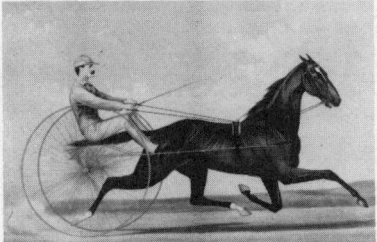

Currier & Ives, Conklin's Bay Gelding Rarus,
16 3/4 X 26 In.

Custard glass and milk glass can now be repaired by black light-proof methods. Be very careful when buying antiques.

A signature adds 25 percent to the value of the glass.

Don't cook acid foods in copper pots unless they have tin linings. The combination of acid and copper creates a poison.

Custard glass is an opaque glass sometimes called "buttermilk glass." It was first made in the United States after 1886 at the La Belle Glass Works, Bridgeport, Ohio. It is being reproduced.

CUSTARD GLASS, see also Maize

CUSTARD GLASS, Alba, Sugar Shaker	125.00
Argonaut Shell, Butter, Cover, Northwood, Gold Trim	260.00
Argonaut Shell, Creamer & Sugar	49.00
Argonaut Shell, Spooner, Gold Trim	100.00
Argonaut Shell, Table Set, Gold Trim, 4 Piece	650.00
Argus Swirl, Berry Bowl, White Swirls, Pink Opaque, C.1896	85.00
Beaded Cable, Rose Bowl, Northwood	145.00
Beaded Circle, Berry Bowl, Master	80.00
Beaded Circle, Creamer, Gold Trim	125.00
Beaded Circle, Spooner, Gold Trim	115.00
Beaded Circle, Sugar, Cover, Gold Trim	165.00
Beaded Swag, Goblet, Dow City, Iowa, Roses	60.00
Bees On Basket, Toothpick, Handle	75.00
Canadian, Lamp, Flat Finger, Green	295.00
Chrysanthemum Sprig, Celery Vase, Blue	1250.00
Chrysanthemum Sprig, Berry Bowl, Blue, Gold Trim, Small	145.00
Chrysanthemum Sprig, Berry Set, Gold Trim, 7 Piece	565.00 To 595.00
Chrysanthemum Sprig, Butter, Cover, Blue	950.00
Chrysanthemum Sprig, Celery Vase, Blue, Gold Trim	1050.00
Chrysanthemum Sprig, Condiment Tray, Gold Trim	650.00
Chrysanthemum Sprig, Cruet	175.00
Chrysanthemum Sprig, Cruet, Blue, Gold, Original Stopper	600.00
Chrysanthemum Sprig, Cruet, Gold Trim	450.00
Chrysanthemum Sprig, Jelly, Footed	40.00
Chrysanthemum Sprig, Pitcher, 4 1/2 In.	50.00
Chrysanthemum Sprig, Salt & Pepper	198.00 To 200.00
Chrysanthemum Sprig, Spooner, Blue	225.00
Chrysanthemum Sprig, Toothpick, Gold Trim	310.00
Chrysanthemum Sprig, Tray, Condiment	425.00
Chrysanthemum Sprig, Tumbler, Blue	95.00
Chrysanthemum Sprig, Water Set, Silver Trim, 7 Piece	700.00
Dancing Ladies, Lamp, Hanging, Northwood, Nutmeg Finish	695.00
Dandelion, Mug, Nutmeg	195.00
Delaware, Banana Bowl, Metal Holder	225.00
Delaware, Creamer, Blue Design, Individual	50.00
Delaware, Tumbler	45.00
Fan, Creamer, Gold Trim	90.00
Fan, Pitcher, Water	255.00
Geneva, Banana Boat	100.00
Geneva, Berry Bowl, Northwood, Green, Small	15.00
Geneva, Butter, Cover, Green, Gold Trim	95.00
Geneva, Table Set, Green, 3 Piece	35.00
Geneva, Toothpick, Green & Red Design	135.00
Georgia Gem, Berry Bowl, Master, Green	40.00
Georgia Gem, Berry Set, Cornflower Pattern, 7 Piece	295.00
Georgia Gem, Butter, Cover, Gold Trim	165.00
Georgia Gem, Hair Receiver, Williams, Iowa, Red Roses	55.00
Georgia Gem, Sauce, Floral Design	30.00
Georgia Gem, Spooner, Cane Insert	65.00
Georgia Gem, Spooner, Floral Design, Green	38.00
Georgia Gem, Toothpick, Gold Trim	55.00
Georgia Gem, Toothpick, Lewiston, Maine, Yellow	30.00
Gothic Arches, Goblet	29.00
Gothic Arches, Water Set, Green, Gold Trim, 7 Piece	225.00
Grape & Cable, Banana Boat, Nutmeg Stain	225.00
Grape & Cable, Bowl, Ruffled Edge, 7 1/2 In.	45.00
Grape & Cable, Cracker Jar, Northwood, Nutmeg Stained	725.00
Grape & Cable, Sugar, Open, Nutmeg Stain, 3 X 4 In.	35.00
Grape & Gothic Arches, Goblet, Nutmeg Stain, 6 Piece	275.00

Grape & Gothic Arches, Tumbler, Gold Tirm	60.00
Grape & Thumbprint, Water Set, Nutmeg Stain, Northwood, 7 Pc.	1250.00
Grape, Punch Cup, Nutmeg Stain, Northwood	75.00
Grape, Sauce, Footed, Northwood	45.00
Harvard, Toothpick, Gold Band	55.00
Heart & Thumbprint, Lamp, Oil, Floral Design, 9 1/2 In.	250.00
Heart & Thumbprint, Sugar, Green, Individual	95.00
Intaglio, Berry Bowl, Green & Gold Design	50.00
Intaglio, Berry Set, Footed & Stemmed, 9 In., 6 Piece	250.00
Intaglio, Butter, Cover, Gold Design, Northwood	175.00
Intaglio, Pitcher, Water, Green & Gold Design	350.00
Intaglio, Salt & Pepper, Green & Gold Design	175.00
Intaglio, Salt & Pepper, Northwood	135.00 To 150.00
Intaglio, Table Set, 4 Piece	495.00
Intaglio, Tumbler, Green & Gold Design	70.00
Inverted Fan & Feather, Berry Bowl, Green, Gold Trim, Small	20.00
Inverted Fan & Feather, Compote, Jelly	450.00
Inverted Fan & Feather, Creamer, Gold Trim	135.00
Inverted Fan & Feather, Spooner, Pink, Gold Trim	115.00
Inverted Fan & Feather, Toothpick	475.00
Inverted Feather, Butter, Cover, Northwood	300.00
Iris, Cruet	285.00
IVORINA VERDE, see Winged Scroll	
Jackson, Creamer	20.00
Jackson, Saltshaker	35.00
Jackson, Water Set, 5 Piece	335.00
Jefferson Optic, Toothpick, Souvenir	50.00
Leaf & Berry, Sugar & Creamer, Child's, Red Trim	42.50
Leaf Chain, Creamer, Northwood, Cobalt Blue, Gold Trim	75.00
Leaf Chain, Tumbler, Northwood, Green, Gold Trim	35.00
Leaf Medallion, Creamer, Cobalt Blue, Gold Trim	95.00
Leaf Umbrella, Sugar Shaker, Yellow Cased	165.00
Louis XV, Berry Bowl, Marigold	150.00
Louis XV, Creamer, Northwood, Green, Gold Trim	38.00
Louis XV, Pitcher, Water	200.00
Louis XV, Spooner	65.00
Louis XV, Sugar, Cover, Gold Trim	100.00
Louis XV, Table Set, 4 Piece	325.00 To 675.00
MAIZE, see Maize category	
Maple Leaf, Butter, Cover	150.00 To 225.00
Maple Leaf, Jelly, Footed, Low	45.00
Maple Leaf, Spooner	75.00
Maple Leaf, Sugar, Cover	75.00
Memphis, Tumbler, Northwood, Green, Gold Trim	15.00
Peacock At The Fountain, Ice Cream Dish, Master, Nutmeg	295.00
Peacock At The Urn, Dish, Ice Cream, Nutmeg Stain, Master	295.00
Pods & Posie, Butter, Cover, Gold Trim	125.00
Punty Band, Spittoon, Woman's, Heisey	75.00
Punty Band, Toothpick, Rose Design	65.00
Quihote, Toothpick, Horse Island, Maine, Yellow	28.00
Ribbed Drape, Cruet	250.00
Ribbed Drape, Table Set, Butter, Sugar, Creamer, Spooner	575.00
Ribbed Thumbprint, Toothpick, Souvenir, Benedict, N.D.	55.00
Ring Band, Berry Set, Heisey, 6 Piece	225.00
Ring Band, Butter, Cover, Hand Painted	125.00
Ring Band, Spooner, Hand Painted	65.00
Ring Band, Sugar & Creamer, Cover	250.00
Ring Band, Sugar, Cover, Hand Painted	95.00 To 125.00
Sengbusch, Inkwell	55.00
Star & Punty, Mug, Ottawa, Illinois, 3 1/4 In.	28.00
Vermont, Toothpick, Blue Design	80.00
Victoria, Spooner	55.00
Water Lily, Cracker Jar	185.00

Cut Glass, Bowl, Arabian Pattern, 8–Sided,
Signed, 9 1/2 In.

Cut Glass, Punch Bowl, Fan, Hobstar,
Waffled Design, 14 In.

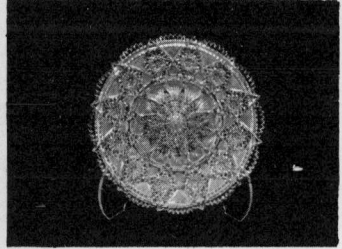

Cut Glass, Tray, Rex,
Signed Tuthill, 12 1/2 In.

Wild Bouquet, Cruet	300.00
Wild Bouquet, Custard	750.00
Wild Bouquet, Sugar, Cover, Design, Gold Trim, Knob Finial	205.00
Winged Scroll, Berry Set, 7 Piece	200.00
Winged Scroll, Butter, Cover, Gold Trim	150.00
Winged Scroll, Celery	295.00
Winged Scroll, Creamer	85.00 To 95.00
Winged Scroll, Spooner, Gold Trim	55.00 To 65.00
Winged Scroll, Toothpick, Gold Trim	295.00
Winged Scroll, Water Set	375.00

Cut glass has been made since ancient times, but the large majority of the pieces now for sale date from the brilliant period of glass design, 1880 to 1905. These pieces have elaborate geometric designs with a deep miter cut. Modern cut glass with a similar appearance is being made in England and Ireland. Chips and scratches are often difficult to notice but lower the value dramatically.

CUT GLASS, see also listings under factory name

CUT GLASS, Banana Boat, Fans, Hobstars, Needlepoint, Scalloped Rim, 10 In.	375.00
Banana Boat, Harvard Pattern, Cosmos	185.00
Banana Bowl, Hobstars, Russian, 2 Tone Effect, 13 In.	850.00
Basket, Brilliant Cut, 19 1/2 X 13 1/2 In.	3000.00
Basket, Star & Feather, Geometric Cutting, 18 In.	1375.00
Basket, Stars, Miters & Fans On Handle, Star Base, 10 X 9 1/2 In.	275.00
Berry Bowl, Maple City Pattern, Notched Prism Flares, 9 In.	300.00
Bonbon, Hobstar Bottom	285.00
Boot, Riding, Flutes, Swags, Crosscut, Dorflinger, 10 1/2 In.	795.00
Bottle, 12 Point Star, Needlepoint, Diamonds, Fans, Stopper, 6 In.	115.00
Bottle, Pattern Cut Collar, Signed Hoare, 12 3/4 In.	425.00
Bottle, Sachet, Zipper & Feather, Hobstar Cover, 3 7/8 In.	90.00
Bottle, Water, Russian Cut, Flared Rim, Convex Diamonds At Neck	395.00
Bottle, Water, Strawberry Diamond, 32 Point Star Bottom, 8 In.	135.00
Bottle, Water, Strawberry Diamond, Fan, Notched Panel, 7 3/4 In.	95.00

Bowl, Alhambra Pattern, 9 In. 1250.00
Bowl, Allover Buttons & Flowers, Oval, 4 X 8 In. 125.00
Bowl, Arabian Pattern, 8–Sided, Signed, 9 1/2 In. ....*Illus* 1375.00
Bowl, Bellevue Pattern, Taylor Bros., 6 1/4 X 3 In. 450.00
Bowl, Brilliant & Rock Crystal, Hawkes, 10 In. 2200.00
Bowl, Creswick, Rolled Side, Hoare, 7 In. 200.00
Bowl, Grapefruit, Underplate, Kalana Lily, Dorflinger 100.00
Bowl, Harvard & Floral Panels, Scalloped Rim, Oval, 11 1/4 In. 118.00
Bowl, Hobstar, Crosshatch & Fern Pattern, American, 12 In. 950.00
Bowl, Hobstar, Notches, Fan, 4 X 8 In. 375.00
Bowl, Hobstars & Stars, Scalloped Serrated Rim, Star Base, 8 In. 110.00
Bowl, Hobstars, Split Vesicas, Needlepoint, Scalloped Rim, 8 In. 135.00
Bowl, Hobstars, Variant Cane, Fans, Split Vesicas, 8 In. 150.00
Bowl, Laurel Leaf, Leaf Base, Fluted Rim, 2 3/4 X 6 In. 37.00
Bowl, Myrtle Pattern, 3 1/2 X 9 1/2 In. 475.00
Bowl, Overall Rayed Stars, Hobstar Base, Pedestal, 4 X 9 1/4 In. 500.00
Bowl, Peg, Laurel Pattern, 1907, Laurel Cut Glass Co., 2 Piece 1575.00
Bowl, Scalloped Rim, Hawkes, 3 3/8 X 7 1/8 In. 165.00
Bowl, Six 40 Point Hobstars, Jeweled Centers, 3 1/2 X 8 1/4 In. 1550.00
Bowl, Strawberry Diamonds, Buzz Saws, Hobstar Bottom, 8 In. 185.00
Box, Jewel, Hobstars, Vesicas, Prims, Fans, Hinged, 6 In. 525.00
Bread Tray, Diamond Points, Hobstar, Buttons & Caning, 12 In. 225.00
Butter, Cover, Child's, Hobstars, Fans & Cross Hatching 135.00
Butter, Cover, Hobstars, Diamond Points, 3 Sizes of Caning 325.00
Butter, Cover, Orland Pattern, Bergen, 5 X 7 1/4 In. 465.00
Butter, Cover, Russian Pattern, 5 1/2 X 7 1/2 In. 850.00
Candelabra, 3–Light, Brazilian Pattern, Hawkes, Pair 6100.00
Candlestick, Classical Floral & Draped, Hawkes, 12 In., Pair 300.00
Candlestick, Comet Pattern, 10 In., Pair 700.00
Candlestick, Fancy Prism Pattern, Teardrop, 18 In. 3000.00
Candlestick, Hobstars Alternating Cane, Teardrop Stem, 8 In., Pr. 600.00
Candlestick, Teardrop, Prism Pattern, Hobstar Base, 18 In., Pair 3000.00
Candy Dish, 4 Hobstars, Needlepoint, Fans, Scalloped Rim, 6 In. 75.00
Canoe, Hobstars, Fan & Diamond, 9 In. 160.00
Carafe, Hobstar Within Hobstar, Fans, Notched Panel Neck, 7 In. 115.00
Carafe, Strawberry & Fan, Notched Panel Neck, 8 In. 125.00
Carafe, Water, Hobstars, Notched Panel Neck, 7 1/4 In. 135.00
Carafe, Water, Sharp Cutting, Hobstar Bottom 200.00
Carafe, Water, Sultana Pattern, Signed Libbey, 8 X 6 In. 135.00
Casserole, Palm Pattern, Hobstar Cover, Taylor Bros., 9 In. 1450.00
Celery, Hobstar Foot, Pedestal, 7 1/2 In. 1850.00
Celery, Hobstar, Mini–Caning, Strawberry Diamond, 10 1/2 In. 145.00
Celery, Hobstars, Fans, Diamond, Notched, Scalloped Rim, 11 In. 145.00
Celery, Intaglio Flowers, Butterflies, Notched Rim, 11 X 5 In. 65.00
Celery, Pinwheels, Hobstars, Signed Clarke, 4 1/2 X 11 7/8 In. 130.00
Celery, Polished Leaf Sprays, Cut Flowers, Butterflies, 5 In. 70.00
Chamberstick, Brilliant Cut, Signed J.Hoare, 3 X 6 1/2 In. 1500.00
Champagne Cooler, Signed J.Hoare, 9 1/4 X 14 In. 6750.00
Cheese Dish, Arcadia Pattern, 6 X 9 In. 950.00
Cheese Dish, Hobstars, Diamonds, Fans, Cover 350.00
Cheese Dish, Underplate, Hobstar, Brilliant, Cover, 10 X 8 In. 650.00
Cigar Jar, Zipper, 5 1/2 X 14 In. 100.00
Claret Jug, American Brilliant Period, Notched Prism, C.1895 .... 300.00
Clock, Harvard Pattern, 5 1/2 X 4 In. 600.00
Clock, Waterbury, Harvard Pattern, 5 1/2 In. 165.00
Cologne, Rayed Base, Dorflinger, 6 1/2 In. 250.00
Cologne, Russian & Swirl Pattern, Signed Hawkes, 5 In., Pair 875.00
Compote, Angora Pattern, Quaker City 450.00
Compote, Arcadia Pattern, Scalloped Hobstar Foot, 9 X 5 3/4 In. 525.00
Compote, Arcadia, Cover, J.D.Bergen Cut Glass Co. 1650.00
Compote, Boat Shape, Cut Stem, Fan & Shell Rim, Irish, 13 1/2 In. 825.00
Compote, Brilliant, Notched, Paneled, Compartments, Sterling, 1905 ..... 500.00
Compote, Cut Daises, Leaves, 8 In. 75.00
Compote, Elmira Pattern, White Luster, 5 3/4 X 5 In. 325.00

Compote, Hobstars & Fan, Pedestal, 8 X 7 In.	165.00
Compote, Hobstars, Notched Stem, Roll Top	225.00
Compote, Intaglio Cut, Teardrop Stem, 8 In.	115.00
Compote, Wreath & Thistle, Teardrop Stem, 8 In.	145.00
Cruet, Diamonds & Fans	85.00
Cruet, Hobstars, Button & Cane, Star Base, 5 3/4 In.	65.00
Cruet, Hobstars, Fans, Cross Hatching, Zipper Neck, Signed Fry	150.00
Cruet, Hobstars, Fans, Notched Prism, Teardrop Stopper	127.50
Cruet, Oil, Stopper, Signed Hawkes, 7 1/2 In.	85.00
Cuspidor, Lady's, Bishop's Hat, Dorflinger, 8 1/4 X 2 5/8 In.	325.00
Decanter, 8 Hobstars, Needlepoint, Fans, Cut Neck, 10 1/2 In.	235.00
Decanter, Buzz Saw, Needlepoint, 16 Point Star Base, 11 In.	160.00
Decanter, Chamfered Corners, Square, Stopper, 9 1/2 In., Pair	150.00
Decanter, Cordial, Creswick Pattern, Matching Stopper, Egginton	2600.00
Decanter, Hobstars, Diamond & Fan, Notched Panel Neck, 10 1/2 In.	260.00
Decanter, Intaglio Engraved Flowers & Leaves, 15 In.	125.00
Decanter, Lismore, Waterford	165.00
Decanter, Pinwheels, Diaper Cuttings, Ruby To Clear, 9 1/2 In.	195.00
Decanter, Raised Block, Star Base, Dorflinger, 12 In.	425.00
Decanter, Stars and Lobes, Baluster–Shaped Body, 20th C., 27 In.	935.00
Decanter, Sterling Silver Eagle Spout, Hawkes, 14 In.	3400.00
Dish, Heart Shape, Hand Painted White Flowers, Luce, 5 1/2 In.	15.00
Dish, Hobstar, Fan, Triangular Vesicas, 6 1/2 In.	85.00
Dish, Strawberry Diamond, Fan, 24 Point Star, 6 In.	75.00
Dresser Box, Hobstars, Fan Cutting	1100.00
Fernery, Allover Hobstars & Fans, Silver Rim, Monroe Co., 8 In.	450.00
Fernery, Hobstar In Pinwheel, Feathering, 3 Footed, 7 1/4 In.	125.00
Fernery, Pinwheels, Spraying Fans, Chromed Liner, 7 3/8 In.	135.00
Finger Bowl, Lotus, 2 3/4 X 4 3/4 In.	85.00
Finger Bowl, Russian, Double Miter Circular Band Base	125.00
Finger Bowl, Russian, Star Bottom	65.00
Flower Basket, Cut On Heavy & Clear Blank, 15 In.	1090.00
Fruit Bowl, Drape, Straus, 8 1/2 X 10 In., 2 Piece	1400.00
Fruit Bowl, Tomatoes, Leaves, Cucumbers, Cabbage, 9 In.	450.00
Goblet, Supreme, Persian Cut, Blaze Base, Blacks, Hoare, 10 Piece	8000.00
Hat, Napoleon, Hobstar & Diamond Point, Fan, 11 1/2 In.	350.00
Humidor, Strawberries, Hobs, Stars, Fan, 9 In.	350.00
Ice Bucket, Allover Diamond Miters, Star Base, Silver Fittings	225.00
Ice Bucket, Chain of Hobstars, 24 Point Hobstar Base, 6 1/2 In.	1000.00
Ice Bucket, Zipper, Cut Sterling Silver Rim	200.00
Jam Jar, Fan Cut, Rayed Base, Silver Plated Spoon	40.00
Jar, Cherry Blossom, Cover, Baluster, 17 1/4 In.	633.00
Jar, Cherry, Lorraine, Dorflinger, 6 1/2 In.	385.00
Jar, Hobstars, Rays, Crosscut, Cover, 7 X 4 1/2 In.	165.00
Jar, Pickle, Hobstar & Diamond Panels, Silver Plated Frame	65.00
Jar, Star Cut Inset Lid, Stars & Miters, 4 1/2 X 6 1/2 In.	135.00
Jardiniere, Diamond Panels, Gilt Bronze Band, Paw Feet, 7 In., Pr.	1320.00
Jug, Claret, Star & Thumbprint, Star Cut Base, 19th Century, Pair	225.00
Jug, Whiskey, Panel, Chartreuse Cut To Clear	600.00
Knife Rest, Dumbbell, Cut Ends, 4 1/2 In.	27.00
Knife Rest, Prism Cut, Star At End, Dumbbell Shape, 5 1/2 In.	40.00
Ladle, Punch Bowl, Montrose, Cranberry To Clear, Dorflinger	2500.00
Lamp, Boudoir, Hobstars, Fans, Pinwheels, Prisms, 13 In.	850.00
Lamp, Hobstars, Diamond Point, Step Cut Neck, 12 In.	450.00
Loving Cup, 2 Handles, Signed Sinclaire, 9 1/4 X 8 1/2 In.	1475.00
Loving Cup, Notched Prism, Sterling Silver Collar, 7 In.	750.00
Muffineer, Pinwheel, Beading, Flares At Base, 6 In.	155.00
Nappy, Notched Rim, Intaglio Floral, Leaf Spray, Ring Handle	55.00
Parfait, Kalanna Lily, Dorflinger, 6 In.	75.00
Pitcher, 24–Point Hobstar Base, Triple Notched Handle, 7 1/2 In.	750.00
Pitcher, Amethyst To Clear, Engraved, Dorflinger	6500.00
Pitcher, Amethyst To Clear, Sterling Collar, Roses, Swirls, Leaves	6500.00
Pitcher, Bands of Hobstars, Fans With Notched Prisms, 8 1/2 In.	275.00
Pitcher, Champagne, Hobstar, Paperweight Base, Buds, Leaves, 15 In.	600.00

Pitcher, Crosshatch & Swag Cut, Thumbprint Faceted Neck	85.00
Pitcher, Diamond & Horizontal Miters, Corset Shape, Stuart, 6 In.	98.00
Pitcher, Eleanor, J.Hoare, 12 In.	2200.00
Pitcher, Fans, Swag & Diamond Miters, Piecrust Rim, 7 1/4 In.	110.00
Pitcher, Fans, Swags, Diamonds, Piecrust Rim, 7 1/4 In.	110.00
Pitcher, Green Cut To Clear, Gold Washed Collar ....*Illus*	1800.00
Pitcher, Green To Clear, Gold Collar, Hobstars, Cross	2600.00
Pitcher, Green To Clear, Silver Gold Washed Collar, Dorflinger	2600.00
Pitcher, Rayed Base, Signed Fry, 9 X 5 In.	675.00
Pitcher, Sawtooth Triangles, Fans, Zigzag Miters, 8 In.	150.00
Pitcher, Tankard, Green To Clear, Hobstars, Bull's-Eye, Prism	1800.00
Pitcher, Water, Butterfly & Daisy, 11 1/2 In. .... 195.00 To	225.00
Pitcher, Water, Feather & Diamond Point, 7 In.	175.00
Pitcher, Water, Russian, 3 In.Sterling Top, 1890	225.00
Pitcher, Water, Wreath & Thistle, 10 In.	158.00
Pitcher, Zipper Cut, Sterling Silver Top, 10 1/2 In.	195.00
Plate, Butterfly, Square, 7 In.	200.00
Powder Box, Diamond & Fan Cutting, Sterling Cover, 5 X 3 In.	24.00
Powder Box, Fans, Diamond Point, Crosshatch, Green To Clear, 5 In.	135.00
Powder Box, Hinged Cover, Murillo, Star Base, 5 In.	345.00
Powder Jar, Diamond Miters, Star Bottom, Star Cut Lid, 3 3/4 In.	75.00
Powder Jar, Swirled Comet, Cover, Signed Bergen	425.00
Punch Bowl, Apple Green Cut To Clear, Dorflinger, 2 Part	6100.00
Punch Bowl, Apple Green To Clear, Dorflinger, 2 Sections	6100.00
Punch Bowl, Compote Base, Newport, Signed Hoare, 12 1/2 In.	1500.00
Punch Bowl, Fan, Hobstar, Waffled Design, 14 In. ....*Illus*	1210.00
Punch Bowl, On Stand, Fan, Hobstar, Waffled, 14 In.	1100.00
Punch Bowl, Stand, Cane, Hobstar, Fan & Medallion, 18 1/2 In.	2000.00
Punch Bowl, Strawberry, Diamond & Fan, Half-Round Form, 15 In.	550.00
Relish, 3-Lobed, J.Hoare, 6 In.	28.00
Relish, Brighton, Hoare, 7 In.	85.00
Rose Bowl, Allover Russian, 9 X 8 1/2 In.	700.00
Rose Bowl, Fan, Hobstar & Diamond Point, 4 In.	125.00
Rose Bowl, Florence Hobstar, Meriden Silver Holder	245.00
Rose Bowl, Turquoise Cut To Clear, Flared, Hawkes	5600.00
Rose Bowl, Turquoise To Clear, Chrysanthemum Pattern	5600.00
Salad Set, Russian, Starred Buttons, 12 1/2 In.Plate, 10 In.Bowl	2000.00
Salt, Pineapple & Fan, Serrated Rim, 1 1/2 X 2 In.	40.00
Sherbet, Fan, Scalloped Foot, 8 Piece	160.00
Sherbet, Underplate, Thumbspring & Diamond, Green Cut To Clear	48.00
Sugar & Creamer, 8-Pointed Hobstars, Fans, Triple Notched Handle	380.00
Sugar & Creamer, Bee & Flower	95.00
Sugar & Creamer, Diamond Point, Notched Prism Rays, Pedestal	275.00
Sugar & Creamer, Drape, Straus	275.00
Sugar & Creamer, Geometric & Floral	85.00
Sugar & Creamer, Notched Prism-Cut Handles, 4 1/2 In.	325.00
Sugar & Creamer, Pineapple	75.00
Sugar & Creamer, Rose	75.00
Sugar & Creamer, Royal, Hunt	250.00
Sugar Shaker, Diamond & Star, Silver Plated Finial, 5 5/8 In.	68.00
Sugar Shaker, Diamond Cuts, Amber, 5 1/2 In.	95.00
Sugar Shaker, Hobstars, Notched Prism, Sterling, Pear Shape, 5 In.	175.00
Sugar Tray, Cosmos, 9 In.	60.00
Syrup, Hinged Lid, Allover Hobstars, Rows of Buttons, Rayed Base	195.00
Syrup, Vertical Notched Prism	110.00
Tankard, Hobstar & Cane, Cut Handle, 14 1/2 In.	550.00
Teapot, Brilliant, Hobstar, Strawberry Diamond, Intaglio Base, Fry	1450.00
Tobacco Jar, Emerald Green To Clear, Marlboro Pattern, 9 1/2 In.	4700.00
Toothpick, Diamond & Hobstar, Bulbous Bottom, 2 1/2 In., Pair	40.00
Toothpick, Paneled Crosshatch & Zipper	25.00
Tray, Bonbon, Russian, Pattern In Foot, 3 X 8 In.	395.00
Tray, Castle Scene, Kohinoor Gallery, Engraved, Hawkes, 10 In.	1700.00
Tray, Cheese & Cracker, Brilliant Cutting, 10 In.	375.00
Tray, Cross Pattern, Rosettes, New York, C.1900, 14 1/4 In.	440.00

Tray, Dresser, Brilliant Allover, 15 1/2 X 7 In. 245.00
Tray, Edge of Hobstars, Diamond Point & Fan, Oval, 16 X 10 In. 575.00
Tray, Encore, 13 X 5 1/2 In. 200.00
Tray, Fans, Hobstars, 14 X 9 In. 350.00
Tray, Festoon Variation, Hawkes, Round, 13 In. 3000.00
Tray, Ice Cream, Brilliant Period, Sawtooth Edge, Hobstars, 17 In. 400.00
Tray, Leaf Sprays, Pinwheels, Daisies, Star Centers, 12 1/2 In. 175.00
Tray, Rex, Signed Tuthill, 12 1/2 In. ....*Illus* 7300.00
Tray, Royal, Thick Blank, Hunt, Round, 12 In. 800.00
Tray, Serving, Expanding Star, 12 In. 975.00
Tumbler, Brilliant Period, Hobstar Base, Egginton, 4 Piece 125.00
Tumbler, Drape, Hobstar Base, Signed Straus, 4 Piece 325.00
Tumbler, Iced Tea, Leaves, Rye, Berries, Copper Wheel Engraved 50.00
Tumbler, Lamberton Coat of Arms 90.00
Tumbler, Pineapple & Hobstar, 3 1/2 In., 4 Piece 160.00
Tumbler, Pinwheels, Miters, Star Bottom, 9 Oz., 6 Piece 175.00
Urn, Louis XVI, Diamond Border, Bronze Handles, 14 1/2 In., Pair 2750.00
Vase, Allover Cut Leaves, Floral Etch, 12 In. 45.00
Vase, Allover Grapes & Leaves, Notched Rim, 5 3/8 In. 185.00
Vase, Auto, Cut Florals & Foliage, Silver Rim, 8 In. 32.00
Vase, Brilliant Cut, Hobstar, American, 7 In. 100.00
Vase, Brilliant, Ruffled, Hobstars, Fans, Notched, Bulbous, 7 In. 400.00
Vase, Butterfly, Flowers & Leaves, Rayed Base, 11 1/2 In. 110.00
Vase, Cobalt Blue To Clear, Geometric, Stars, 6–Petal, 10 In., Pair 400.00
Vase, Cranberry To Clear, Roses, Scalloped Notched Rim, 12 In. 395.00
Vase, Cupid Faces, Hobstars, Sterling Silver, Muser, 8 1/2 In., Pr. 1150.00
Vase, Diamond Cut, Cranberry, Pedestal Foot, 7 1/4 In. 175.00
Vase, Geometric & 6 Panel Cutting, Cobalt Overlay, 10 3/4 In. 450.00
Vase, Green To Clear, Urn Shape, Gilt Trim, 5 1/4 In. 75.00
Vase, Hobstar, Cane, Hobnail, 2 Handles, 18 In. ....*Illus* 3600.00
Vase, Hobstar, English Diamond, Brilliant, 7 X 9 In. 425.00
Vase, Hobstars Panel, Cane, Rayed Star, Notched Handles, 9 In. 1500.00
Vase, Hobstars, Fans, Diamond Point, Bowling Pin Shape, 12 In. 425.00
Vase, Kalana Pansy, Flared Top & Bottom, Dorflinger, 12 In. 140.00
Vase, Kalana Wild Rose, Amethyst Flowers, Dorflinger, 10 In. 185.00
Vase, Lotus, Green, On Standard, 16 In. 3200.00
Vase, Montrose, Bowling Pin Shape, Dorflinger, 10 In. 2550.00
Vase, New York, Trumpet, Ruffled Free–Form Rim, Hoare, 14 In. 280.00
Vase, Pinwheel, Bulbous, 8 1/2 X 7 In. 350.00
Vase, Sweet Pea, Crosshatch & Hobstars 135.00
Vase, Trumpet Shape, Hobstars In Diamond Field At Top, 9 3/4 In. 100.00
Vase, Urn Shape, 4 Hobstars, Comet Swirls, Base, Egginton, 14 In. 2000.00

Cut Glass, Pitchers, Green Cut To Clear

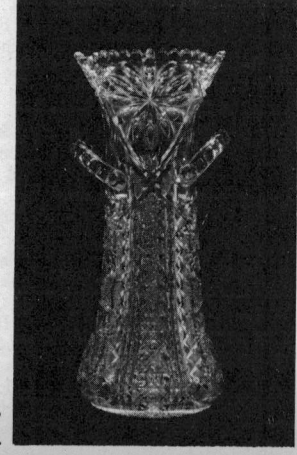

Cut Glass, Vase, Hobstar,
Cane, Hobnail, 2 Handles, 18 In.

Vase, Violet, Ashland, Overback, 3 1/2 X 3 In. 175.00
Water Set, Hobstar, Pitcher & 6 Glasses 250.00
Water Set, Hobstars, Pinwheel, Double Notched Handle, 7 Piece 270.00
Wine Set, Grape, Amber To Clear, 9 Piece .... 225.00 To 245.00
Wine, Amethyst To Clear, Hobstar & Fern, Teardrop Stem 475.00
Wine, Cranberry To Clear, Double Teardrop, Bell Shape, 8 1/2 In. 375.00
Wine, Cranberry To Clear, Strawberry Diamonds, Fans, 8 Piece 1760.00
Wine, Crosscut Diamond & Fan, Cranberry 150.00
Wine, Rhine, Russian Cut, Green To Clear, Teardrop Stem 390.00
Wine, Russian, Hollow Stem 95.00
Wine, Strawberry & Diamond, Cranberry To Clear 150.00

> Cut velvet is a special type of art glass, made with two layers of blown glass, which shows a raised pattern. It usually had an acid finish or velvetlike texture. It was made by many glass factories during the late Victorian years.

CUT VELVET, Rose Bowl, Diamond Quilted, 3 In.Diam. 175.00
Vase, Diamond Quilted, Blue, 7 In. 150.00
Vase, Vertical Ribs, Shades of Pink, Bottle Shape, 8 3/4 In. 145.00

CYBIS

> Boleslaw Cybis came to the United States from Poland in 1939. He started making porcelains in Long Island, New York, in 1940. He moved to Trenton, New Jersey, in 1942 as one of the founders of Cordey China Co. and started his own Cybis Porcelains about 1950. The firm is still working. (See also Cordey.)

CYBIS, Bust, Baby Boy, Signed 450.00
Bust, Madonna, 4 In. 125.00
Figurine, Baby Owl, 4 1/4 In. 60.00
Figurine, Beatrice 350.00
Figurine, Bunny, Bisque, White 75.00
Figurine, Calla Lily 1800.00
Figurine, Duckling 75.00
Figurine, Foal 125.00
Figurine, Little Princess 350.00
Figurine, Little Red Riding Hood .... 195.00 To 295.00
Figurine, Madonna, Crown of Roses, 14 In. 175.00
Figurine, Melissa, Girl In Cape Holding Rabbit, 10 In. 400.00
Figurine, Pandora 135.00
Figurine, Portia, No.126, Cape, Violet Dress, Gold Design, 13 1/2 In. 1495.00
Figurine, Queen Esther, Marked, 1976, 13 1/2 In. 1250.00
Figurine, Raccoon .... 185.00 To 195.00
Figurine, Snail 185.00
Figurine, Turtle, Frog Perched On Back, 3 X 4 1/2 In. 150.00
Figurine, Wood Wren With Dogwood 260.00
Figurine, Young Boy Sitting On Back of Grasshopper 315.00

> There are some collectibles that are identified by the name of the country, not a factory mark. Anything marked "Czechoslovakia" is popular today. The name, first used as a mark after the country was formed in 1918, appears on glass and porcelain and other decorative items. The name is still used in some trademarks.

CZECHOSLOVAKIA, Basket, Marbelized, Maroon, Black Interior, Pottery, 1930s 20.00
Box, Red Glass, Cut Floral Design, Cover, Signed, 4 In. 68.00
Console Set, Art Deco, Orange & Black Trim, Pottery 125.00
Creamer, Parrot, Yellow, Orange & Green, 4 1/2 In. 22.00
Decanter Set, Green Glass, Gold Trim, 6 Shot Glasses 85.00
Decanter, Opalescent, Crackle, Ruby Handle, Cone Shape, Glass 175.00
Dish, Red, Black Enameled Design, Cover 85.00
Ewer, Mottled Glaze, Brown Streaks, Pottery, 16 In. 95.00
Figurine, Art Deco Lady, White Gown, Pottery, Erphila, 10 In. 75.00
Figurine, Cockatoo, Orange, Yellow, Porcelain, 17 In. 1365.00
Figurine, Elephant, Trunk Down, Gray, Pottery, 4 1/2 In. 40.00
Figurine, Horsehead, Stylized, White Luster, 5 In. 22.00
Figurine, Man, Leaning On Post, Cigarette, Pottery, 5 3/4 In. 375.00

Daum Nancy, Vase, Bud, Hammered
Fire Polished, Olive, Amber, 7 In.

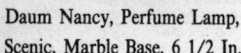

Daum Nancy, Perfume Lamp,
Scenic, Marble Base, 6 1/2 In.

D'Argental, Vase, Cameo,
Woodpecker, Trumpet Vines, Orange, 20 In.

Figurine, Parrot, On Tree Stump, 3 Sections, Pottery, 5 In.	18.00
Perfume Bottle, Art Deco, Blue, Crystal, 6 1/4 In.	185.00
Perfume Bottle, Blue, Brass & Jewels, 4 1/4 In.	125.00
Perfume Bottle, Cut Hobstars, Noted Wheels, 7 1/2 In.	65.00
Perfume Bottle, Molded Daffodils Stopper, Crystal, 7 In.	95.00
Pitcher, Rooster, Erphila, Yellow, Red, Pottery, 9 1/2 In.	37.50
Pitcher, Streaked Green, Blue Threads, Topaz, Glass, 10 In.	115.00
Salt & Pepper, Chicken, Marked	8.00
Tea Set, Lemon Yellow, Cameo Portraits, 6 Setting, 23 Piece	150.00
Tray, Tidbit, White, Rooster, Toothpick Holes, 11 In.	30.00
Vase, Canary Yellow, Black Handles, Glass, 13 In.	75.00
Vase, Emerald Green, Raised Floral, Glass, Square, 11 In.	220.00
Vase, Fan, Blue Applied Threading, Amber Ground, 9 1/2 In.	85.00
Vase, Genie Face, Speckled Orange Luster, 2 Handles, 10 In.	35.00
Vase, Green, Brown, Honeycomb Design, Ditmer Urbach, 8 In.	35.00
Vase, Panel of Embossed Flowers, Crackle Glass, 7 1/2 In.	22.00
Vase, Pitcher, Luster Shell, 5 In.	25.00
Vase, Spatter Cobalt Blue, 4 1/2 In.	40.00
Vase, Tangerine Blue, Ruffled, Glass, 8 In.	95.00
Vase, Wild Horses Relief, Frosted Glass, 7 In.	65.00
Vase, Yellow, Blue & Black Drippings, Erphila, 3 X 5 In.	26.00

D'Argental is a mark used by the St. Louis, France, glassworks. The
firm made multilayered, acid–cut cameo glass in the late nineteenth
and twentieth centuries. D'Argental is the French name for the city
of Munzthal, home of the glassworks. Later they made enameled
etched glass. Compagnie des Cristalleries de St. Louis is still
working.

D'ARGENTAL, Lamp, Cameo, Wildflowers, Gilt Bronze Mounts, C.1920, 16 2/4 In.	9350.00
Vase, Cameo, Cottage In Trees, Castle On Hilltop, 7 In.	700.00
Vase, Cameo, Flowers & Leaves, Frosted Ground, Amethyst, 6 In.	425.00
Vase, Cameo, Harbor Scene, Sailboats, City In Distance, 12 In.	1650.00

Vase, Cameo, Landscape, Gold Ground With Trees, Lake, 9 5/8 In.	895.00
Vase, Cameo, Leaves & Flowers, Brown Neck & Base, 4 In.	575.00
Vase, Cameo, Red Poppies, Amber Ground, Signed, 5 7/8 In.	400.00
Vase, Cameo, Rocky Shore, Lighthouse, 5 In.	675.00
Vase, Cameo, Scene of Chateau, Trees On Hill, 12 1/8 In.	895.00
Vase, Cameo, Woodpecker, Trumpet Vines, Orange, 20 In. ....*Illus*	9350.00
Vase, Carved Flowers, Leaves, Beige, Brown, 4 In.	495.00

DAUM
NANCY
†

Jean Daum started a glassworks in Nancy, France, in 1875. The
company, now called "Cristalleries de Nancy," is still working. The
"Daum Nancy" mark has been used in many variations. The name
of the city and the artist are usually both included.

DAUM NANCY, Beaker, Green, Floral Gilt Design, Footed, 4 1/2 In.	72.00
Bowl, Butterflies, Translucent Green, Yellow, Blue, 3 3/4 In.	2400.00
Bowl, Flattened Lip, Violets, Leaves, Signed, C.1910, 8 In.	6050.00
Bowl, Free–Form, Squared, Lead Crystal, 10 In.	210.00
Bowl, Red & Burgundy Overlay, Daisies, Signed, C.1910, 4 In.	5500.00
Bowl, Shasta Daisies, Leaves, Signed, C.1910, 6 1/4 In.	2475.00
Box, Amethyst, Gold Tracing	875.00
Box, Wildflowers On Lid, Gilt, Enameled, Signed, 1910, 5 1/8 In.	3575.00
Lamp, Boudoir, Grape Cluster Design	6500.00
Lamp, Domical Shade, 3–Sided Base, Signed, C.1925, 18 1/8 In.	4950.00
Lamp, Landscape, Blue, Green, Violet, Flowers, 7 In.	1800.00
Lamp, Marble Base, Forest Lake Scene, Green, Brown, 7 In.	2100.00
Lamp, Perfume, Marble Base, Frosted Lake Scene, 6 In.	2300.00
Lamp, Sailing Boats Scene, Art Deco Bronze Figural Base	2900.00
Mustard, Pink Flowers, Yellow Ground, Signed	525.00
Perfume Bottle, Green, Gold Cameo Flowers, Signed, 3 In.	1250.00
Perfume Lamp, Scenic, Marble Base, 6 1/2 In. ....*Illus*	2100.00
Pitcher, Claret, Grapes, Vines, Signed, 13 In.	895.00
Pitcher, Clover Flowers, Leaves, Enamel & Gold, 3 1/2 In.	500.00
Pitcher, Vine, Leaves, Berries, Mottled Green & Purple, 2 1/2 In.	1430.00
Ring Dish, Double Cut Daisies, Foliage, Amethyst Spike	400.00
Ring Tree, Amethyst Floral Over Blue	370.00
Sconce, Stylized Flowers Vasiform, Gold Shades, 20 3/4 In., Pair	9900.00
Tankard, Ornate Silver Plated Handle, White Frosted Ground	2800.00
Tumbler, Purple Violets, Green Leaves, 4 3/4 In.	1250.00
Vase, 5 Ships On Lake, Dark Trees, Mottled, Signed, 8 1/2 In.	2650.00
Vase, Acid Etched Circles, Signed, C.1925, 9 In.	3300.00
Vase, Amber, Sailing Vessel, Signed, 4 In.	935.00
Vase, Berry–Laden Leafy Branches, Signed, C.1910, 17 In.	3575.00
Vase, Blossoms, Yellow, Enameled, Conical, Footed, 13 3/8 In.	6600.00
Vase, Bud, Hammered Fire Polished, Olive, Amber, 7 In. ....*Illus*	2420.00
Vase, Bud, Lead Crystal, 7 In.	95.00
Vase, Cameo, Forest, Setting Sun Ground, Signed, 14 In.	3400.00
Vase, Cameo, Mottled Gray, Yellow Glass, Violet, Handles, 16 In.	4400.00
Vase, Cameo, Streaked, Green, Maroon, Thistles, Gold, 7 In.	2250.00
Vase, Carved Leaves & Flowers, Textured Ground, 5 1/2 In.	595.00
Vase, Cross of Lorraine, Cameo, Green, Gold, Bulbous, 4 In.	750.00
Vase, Cut Iris Blossoms, Leaves,, Signed, C.1910, 22 In.	6050.00
Vase, Diamond Cross Section, Amethyst, Gold Flowers, 7 In.	1295.00
Vase, Dimpled Sides, Stalks of Freesia, Signed, C.1915, 5 1/2 In.	2420.00
Vase, Falling Leaves, Yellow Overlay, Signed, C.1910, 15 7/8 In.	2750.00
Vase, Flowering Tree Branches, Red & Yellow, Flared, 13 1/8 In.	3850.00
Vase, Fruiting Peach Branches, Signed, C.1910, 23 3/4 In.	4950.00
Vase, Fuchsia & Leaf Design, Square, 4 In.	525.00
Vase, Grape Clusters, Leafy Vines, Signed, C.1915, 13 3/4 In.	3850.00
Vase, Green Lakeland Scene, Mottled Salmon & Amber, 22 In.	5280.00
Vase, Hammered & Fire Polished, Amber, White Ground, 6 3/4 In.	2200.00
Vase, Hammered & Frosted Surface, Amber, 6 3/4 In.	2100.00
Vase, Hemispherical, Green Ground, Signed, 1920, 8 In.	1980.00
Vase, Islets, Mountains, Lake, Signed, C.1910, 6 In.	4400.00
Vase, Junks Sailing In Bay, Ovoid, Signed, C.1910, 16 1/2 In.	2200.00

Vase, Lake Scene, Pines, Frosted Body, 6 1/2 In.	425.00
Vase, Lakeside Scene, Signed, C.1910, 17 5/8 In.	7425.00
Vase, Landscape, Chinese Red Overlay, Signed, C.1910, 23 1/4 In.	4950.00
Vase, Leafy Vines, Clusters of Berries, Signed, C.1910, 9 7/8 In.	3850.00
Vase, Leaves, Stems, Mottled Green, Brown, Square, 4 3/4 In.	1760.00
Vase, Mottled Orange, Amber, Blown Into Metal Frame, 9 In.	1200.00
Vase, Orange Fruit, Green Leaves, Matte, 19 In.	1950.00
Vase, Peach, Thistle Flowers, Gold, Silver, 6 In.	650.00
Vase, Pendent Grape Clusters, Leaves, Signed, C.1910, 24 1/8 In.	6100.00
Vase, Pinched In & Out, Red Ground, Gray Mottling, Signed, 14 In.	450.00
Vase, Rambling Rose Branches, Signed, C.1915, 15 3/8 In.	4400.00
Vase, River Landscape, Signed, C.1910, 14 3/4 In.	6325.00
Vase, River Landscape, Trees, Signed, C.1910, 12 1/2 In.	2860.00
Vase, River, Cypress Trees, Holls, Signed, C.1915, 15 1/2 In.	3025.00
Vase, Scrolling Foliage, Blue Ground, Signed, C.1910, 17 3/4 In.	7975.00
Vase, Simulated Rainfall, Leaves, Signed, C.1910, 15 7/8 In.	2750.00
Vase, Streaked, Wildflowers, Leaves, Signed, C.1910, 11 1/4 In.	2200.00
Vase, Striated & Mottled, Parrot Tulips, Signed, C.1910, 19 In.	6050.00
Vase, Swans In Pond, Grasses, Trees, Signed, C.1910, 4 3/8 In.	4675.00
Vase, Thistles & Leaves, Purple Ground, Gold Outlining, 12 In.	600.00
Vase, Tree Landscape, River, Yellow Ground, Signed, 12 3/8 In.	650.00
Vase, Tulips, Leaves, Silver Deposit, Signed, C.1915, 10 1/8 In.	3630.00
Vase, Tulle Netting, Lotus Blossoms, Gold Outlining, 11 3/4 In.	600.00
Vase, Water, Village, Trees, Sailboat, Signed, 5 1/2 X 5 In.	475.00
Vase, Wheel–Carved, Cameo, Upright Leaves, Gold, Red, 12 In.	3025.00

Davenport pottery and porcelain were made at the Davenport factory in Longport, Staffordshire, England, from 1793 to 1887. Earthenwares, creamwares, porcelains, ironstone, and other ceramics were made. Most of the pieces are marked with a form of the word "Davenport."

DAVENPORT
LONGPORT
STAFFORDSHIRE

DAVENPORT, Creamer, Tavern Scene, Trees In Relief, 4 1/2 In.	150.00
Plate, Amoy, Flow Blue, 9 In.	75.00
Plate, Strawerry, Rimless Base, 6 1/2 In.	115.00
Plate, Village Scene, Purple Transfer, C.1840, 9 In.	40.00
Platter, Cyprus, Flow Blue, Ironstone, 1848, Octagonal, Large	325.00
Sugar, Cyprus, Flow Blue, Ironstone, 1848	75.00

Davy Crockett, the American frontiersman, was born in 1786 and died in 1836. He became popular again in 1954 with the introduction of a television series about his life. Coonskin caps and buckskins became popular and hundreds of different Davy Crockett items were made.

DAVY CROCKETT, Album, Record	20.00
Belt, With Davy Crockett Buckle, Engraved Leather	20.00
Book Bag, 1950s	15.00
Book, Golden, King of The Wild Frontier	4.00
Card, Lobby, Indian Scout, 1949	20.00
Chest, Toy, Wooden, Large	75.00
Clock, Wall, Weight Driven, Box	275.00
Collar, Leather, Studded	15.00
Cookie Jar, American Bisque	65.00 To 78.00
Cookie Jar, McCoy	200.00
Cookie Jar, Standing, American Bisque	225.00
Cup	8.00
Doll, Effanbee, Box, 14 In.	35.00
Doll, Ventriloquist	45.00
Jacket & Pants, Leather, Fringed	95.00
Key Chain, Paper Illustration, Clear Styrene Plastic, 1950s	20.00
Knife, Fess Parker	30.00
Lamp, Chalkware	150.00
Mug, Brown	7.00
Mug, Red, White	12.00
Neckerchief, Pink, Leather Studded Collar	15.00 To 25.00

Necktie	20.00
Pen, Ballpoint, 1 Ft.	9.50
Pencil Case, Contents Complete	75.00
Pin, Red, Yellow, Black, Orange, 1 3/8 In.	2.50
Pin, Yellow & Red Litho, Mid–1950s	18.00
Poster, King of The Wild Frontier, 1955	50.00
Puzzle, Complete, 1950s	20.00
Puzzle, Inlaid	18.00
Record, Adventures of Davy Crockett, 33 1/3 RPM, 1950s	20.00
Ring, Copper Plastic, Coonskin Cap Picture, Mid–1950s	7.00
Sheet Music, Ballad of Davy Crockett, Name On Cover	15.00
Tomahawk	11.00
Tumbler, 4 1/4 In. ....5.00 To	10.00

William de Morgan made art pottery in England from the 1860s to 1907. He is best known for his luster–glazed Moorish–inspired pieces. The pottery used a variety of marks.

DE MORGAN, Tile, Geometric Pattern, Green, Black, 8 In.	250.00
Vase, Griffin, Iridescent, 10 In.	2500.00

de Vez

De Vez is a name found on special pieces of French cameo glass made by the Cristallerie de Pantin about 1890. Monsieur de Varreaux was the art director of the glassworks and he signed pieces "de Vez."

DE VEZ, Box, Cameo, Oriental Scenic Design, Cover, 5 1/4 In.	975.00
Box, Cover, Cobalt Blue Butterflies, Signed, 2 1/2 X 3 1/2 In.	475.00
Night–Light, Cameo Glass, Skyline City Scene, Signed, 6 3/4 In.	895.00
Squirrel, Sitting On Oak Tree, Red, Gold, Yellow, 23 In.	4250.00
Vase, Brown Scenic, Blue & Brown, 8 In.	650.00
Vase, Burgundy To Amber, Trees, Winding River, Signed, 8 In.	1100.00
Vase, Cameo, Fishing Scene, Frosted Gold Ground, 4 1/4 X 4 In.	595.00
Vase, Cameo, River & Tree Scene, C.1900	1000.00
Vase, Castle Scene On High Hill, Lake & Trees, Signed, 9 In.	1250.00
Vase, Floral Tree Farming Scene, Village On Island, Signed, 6 In.	795.00
Vase, Flowers, Green, Allover Stippling, Cameo, 2 1/4 X 4 In.	275.00
Vase, Lakeside Scene, Cameo, Dark Brown, Rust, Amber, Signed, 4 In. ...	450.00
Vase, Landscape Along River, Mountains, Signed, 5 1/4 In.	495.00
Vase, Landscape Scene, River, Branches Frame Top, Signed, 9 1/2 In.	575.00
Vase, Man In Boat Fishing, House On Island, Marked, 4 1/4 In.	595.00
Vase, Meteor Rock, Village, Frosted Ground, Signed, 8 1/2 In.	895.00
Vase, Sailboats, Cameo, 3 Cuttings, Signed, 9 5/8 X 3 1/4 In.	750.00
Vase, Sailboats, Clouds, Gold Ground, Signed, 6 3/4 In.	550.00
Vase, Sailboats, Clouds, Shore Background, Signed, 8 5/8 In.	750.00
Vase, Sailboats, Mountains In Background, Signed, 8 1/8 In.	695.00
Vase, Scenic, Island, Village, Boat & Mountain Range, 6 In.	900.00
Vase, Tree In Foreground, Islands, Foliage, Signed, 9 1/8 In.	650.00

Decoys are carved or turned wooden copies of birds or fish. The decoy was placed in the water or propped on the shore to lure flying birds to the pond for hunters. Some decoys are handmade, some are commercial products. Today there is a group of artists making modern decoys for display, not for use in a pond.

DECOY, Black Duck, Charles Thomas, Carver, J.Lincoln, Painter, 18 In., Pair	600.00
Black Duck, Cork Body, Lou Rathmel	3250.00
Black Duck, Cork, Scaled Paint Head, 8 1/2 X 21 1/2 In.	75.00
Black Duck, Glass Eyes, Lead Weight, Charles Thomas, 8 X 18 In., Pair	550.00
Black Duck, Hollow, Exaggerated Neck Carving, Nathan Cobb, Jr.	8800.00
Black Duck, Sleeping, Cork	125.00
Black Male Premier Grand Duck, Mason	630.00
Black–Breasted Plover, Russ Burr	2200.00
Blue Goose, Swimming, Ben Schmidt, Immature, 1920s	6900.00
Blue–Winged Teal, Ken Anger	8000.00
Bluebill Drake, Doc McClewen, Hollow, Laminated Body, 13 3/4 In.	45.00
Bluebill Drake, Glass Eyes, Shot Scars, Greenlake, Wisconsin, 13 In.	65.00

Bluebill Drake, Hollow Body, 15 1/2 In. 200.00
Bluebill Drake, Hollow Body, Rasped Head,, Glass Eyes, 13 1/4 In. 55.00
Bluebill Drake, Old Repaint, Glass Eyes, 13 3/4 In. 75.00
Bluebill Drake, One-Armed Kellie, Glass Eyes, 10 In. 355.00
Bluebill Drake, Primitive, Pratt, Worn Paint, Glass Eyes, 13 1/2 In. 55.00
Bluebill Drake, Recessed Eyes, Exaggerated Tail, C.1920, 12 3/4 In. 375.00
Bluebill Drake, Schmidt, Glass Eyes, 14 1/4 In. 275.00
Bluebill Drake, Turned Head, Glass Eyes, 16 In. 160.00
Bluebill Drake, Turned High Head, Glass Eyes, 14 In. 85.00
Bluebill Drake, Verne Cheesman 4675.00
Bluebill Hen, Cork Body, Shang Wheeler 775.00
Bluebill Hen, One-Armed Kellie, Glass Eyes, 10 1/4 In. 325.00
Bluebill Hen, Verne Cheesman 5775.00
Brant Goose, Hollow-Carved, Nathan Cobb, C.1860 .... 5500.00
Canada Goose, Hollow, George Peterson, C.1880 .... 5500.00
Canada Goose, Ira Hudson 2200.00
Canada Goose, Sentinel Hollow-Carved, C.1920, By Scott Osbourne 3300.00
Canada Goose, Slat Constructed Body, Galvanized Sheet Metal, 31 In. 95.00
Canada Goose, Standing, Wooden Body, Cast Iron Head, C.1910 .... 6050.00
Canada Goose, Watch Gander, Setting Goose, C.1930, 16 1/2, 13 1/2 In. 1800.00
Canada Goose, White, Curly Maple, Tapered Legs, 29 In. 550.00
Canvasback Drake, Brass Tack Eyes, Primitive, Original Paint, 15 In. 125.00
Canvasback Drake, Hollow Body, Glass Eyes, 15 1/4 In. 105.00
Canvasback Drake, Paint Yellowed Over Varnish, Glass Eyes, 12 In. 100.00
Canvasback Drake, Primitive, Wisconsin, Repaint, Glass Eyes, 16 In. 45.00
Canvasback Drake, R.Madison Mitchell, Chesapeake Bay, 15 1/2 In. 275.00
Canvasback Goose, Glass Eyes, Original Paint 275.00
Crow, Folding, Tin, Screws Into Fence Post 100.00
Crow, Full-Bodied, Composition, Glass Eyes, Life Size 65.00
Crow, Glass Eyes, Papier-Mache 23.00
Crow, Wooden, Original Paint 175.00
Dowitcher, Bowman 7500.00
Duck, Carry Light, Milwaukee, Wis., Papier-Mache, Wooden Bottoms 40.00
Duck, Gundlefinger, Chrome Finish 95.00
Duck, Old Squaw, 1870, Stamped JHZ 3000.00
Duck, Pine, White, Gray, Black, 27 In. 412.00
Eider Hen, Gus Wilson, Bill Tucked To Breast 2475.00
Fish, Bufflehead, Spearing 2750.00
Fish, Metal Fins, Wooden, Black Paint, Silver Polka Dots, 6 In. 65.00
Fish, Pickerel, 6 Metal Fins, Brown Wood, Inchworm Line Tie 160.00
Fish, Trout, 3 Dimensional, Wooden, Signed Moeller 1739, 16 X 22 In. 400.00
Goldeneye Drake, Joseph Lincoln 4000.00
Goldeneye Hen, Mason 7700.00
Goose, Virginia, Doug Jester 1350.00
Green-Winged Teal, Charles McCoy, Pair 3300.00
Grouse, General Fibre Co., 1940s 55.00
Heron, Root Head, 19th Century 1300.00
Herring Gull, Juvenile, G.E.Wallace 3250.00
Labrador Duck, Zabriskie 1500.00
Loon, Horseshoe Weight, Signed Ted Anderson 140.00
Mallard Drake, Bobbing Head, Glass Eyes, 17 In. 65.00
Mallard Drake, Fred Mott, Pekin, Ill., Hollow Body, 16 3/8 In. 85.00
Mallard Drake, Hollow Body, Glass Eyes, Marked Evans Decoy, 16 In. 85.00
Mallard Drake, Peru, Ill. 180.00
Mallard Hen & Drake, Mason, Original Paint, Pair 800.00
Mallard Hen, Glass Eyes, White Paint On Tail, 18 1/4 In. 200.00
Mallard Hen, Ignatious Valentine Stachowik, Illinois, 16 1/4 In. 250.00
Mallard Hen, Light Hollow Construction, Tack Eyes, C.1930, 17 In. 145.00
Mallard Hen, Mason, Hollow Body, Glass Eyes, 17 1/2 In. 325.00
Merganser Drake, Swimming, Carved Wings, Gus Wilson 6050.00
Merganser Hen, Shourds, Original Paint 3000.00
Merganser, Woodring Family, Pair 1600.00
Northern Pike, Broad Fins, Double Tail, Minnesota, Red & Yellow 90.00
Owl, Papier-Mache, Large Glass Eyes, 16 1/2 In. 60.00

Pintail Drake, Ken Anger 5500.00
Pintail Drake, Zabriskie 700.00
Plover, Black Bellied, Russ Burr 2300.00
Premier Redhead Hen, Mason 290.00
Redhead Drake, John Blair, Removable Head, With Brass Collar, 1900s 450.00
Redhead Hen, Crowell, Oversized, Miniature 1320.00
Redhead Hen, Mason, Oversized 310.00
Redhead Hen, Sleeping, Hollow Carved, Albert Laing 3000.00
Redhead Hen, Sleeping, Hollow, Albert Laing Type, 19th Century 3000.00
Ruddy Duck, Alvirah Wright, 1865–1951 .... 9900.00
Shorebird, Folding, Tin, Straters, 1874, 11 In., Pair 150.00
Shorebird, Tack Eyes, Randall, 11 1/2 In. 145.00
Shorebird, Tin, Driftwood Mounted, Pair 1150.00
Sickle–Billed Curlew, On Stand, Lloyd Johnson, C.1940 .... 375.00
Snipe, Folding, Tin 45.00
Snow Goose, Ardell Watefalck, N.C. 120.00
Sucker, Wisconsin, Wood Surface, 5 Metal Fins 875.00
Teal, Hollow Carved, Initials J.W.C., Lindsay, Ont., 1920s 400.00
Whittled Surface, Brown Paint, 16 In. 40.00
Wigeon, Crowell 7700.00
Yellowlegs, Painted Wing Detail, Wood Stand 495.00
Yellowlegs, Painted Wing, Eye, Mounted On Driftwood 490.00
Yellowlegs, Painted Wing, Wooden Stand, Late 19th Century 495.00
Yellowlegs, Tack Eyes, Shaped Tail, Pegged Bill, 5 1/2 X 11 In., Pair 400.00

Chelsea Keramic Art Works was established in 1872 in Chelsea, Massachusetts, by members of the Robertson family. The factory closed in 1889 and was reorganized as the Chelsea Pottery U.S. in 1891. It became the Dedham Pottery of Dedham, Massachusetts, in 1895. The factory closed in 1943. It was famous for its crackleware dishes, which picture blue outlines of animals, flowers, and other natural motifs.

DEDHAM, Ashtray, Dutch Boy, 4 7/8 In. 2000.00
Ashtray, Elephant, Stamped, 1929–43, 4 In. 375.00
Bacon Rasher, Butterfly, 20th Century, 12 In. 350.00
Bouillon Cup, Rabbit, 2 Handles, 3 In. 374.00
Bowl, Azalea, Shallow, Stamped, 9 1/2 In. 250.00
Bowl, Center, 3–Petal Floral, Cut Corner, Stamped, 3 1/2 X 9 In. 1000.00
Bowl, Rabbit Border, Blue Mark, 4 1/2 In. 275.00
Bowl, Rabbit Border, Blue Mark, 5 3/8 In. 400.00
Bowl, Rabbit Border, Date 1931, Square, 8 1/4 In. 700.00
Bowl, Rabbit Border, Marked, 12 1/2 In. 750.00
Bowl, Rabbit Silhouette, Stamped, 2 5/8 In. 650.00
Bowl, Rabbit, 3 1/2 X 8 1/4 In. 495.00
Bowl, Rabbit, Shallow, Stamped, C.1896, 12 In. 300.00
Bowl, Rabbit, Signed, 1 3/4 X 3 1/4 In. 225.00
Bowl, Turkey Border, Rabbit Mark, 5 1/2 In. 350.00
Candlestick, Lily, Low, Pair 375.00
Charger, 1 Eared Rabbit Border, Marked, 12 In. 900.00
Chop Plate, Crab, Impressed Rabbit, 12 In. 1100.00
Chop Plate, Rabbit, 12 In. 595.00
Creamer, Night & Morning, 4 7/8 In. 475.00
Cup & Saucer, Crab, 1931, Stamped, 2 5/8 X 6 1/8 In. 700.00
Cup & Saucer, Elephant 325.00
Cup & Saucer, Iris 190.00
Cup & Saucer, Magnolia 195.00
Cup & Saucer, Rabbit, Stamped, 2 3/4 In. .... 190.00 To 200.00
Cup & Saucer, Rabbit, Stamped, 20th Century, 3 X 6 1/2 In. 150.00
Cup & Saucer, Swan, Stamped, 4 In. 200.00
Cup Plate, Alternating Tulips & Daisies, Chelsea Keramic Art Works 900.00
Cup Plate, Pineapple, Chelsea Keramic Art Works, 4 1/2 In. 550.00
Cup, AAPA Convention, 1983, 4 In. 9.00
Cup, Coffee, Rabbits, Signed 195.00
Cup, Rabbit Border, 2 Handles, Blue Mark, 3 1/2 In. 400.00

Dish, Rabbit, Lotus Edge, Stamped, 9 1/8 In.	750.00
Dish, Rabbit, Oval, Double Stamp, C.1929, 14 In.	425.00
Dish, Serving, Cover, Blue Rabbit Border, Marked, 11 In.	450.00
Dish, Serving, Rabbit, Button Finial Domed Cover, Flared, 7 1/2 In.	475.00
Flower Arranger, Rabbit Form, 6 1/8 In.	850.00
Humidor, Brass Screw–Top Handle, White Elephants, Cover, 8 1/2 In.	2975.00
Jar, Cover, Scotty Dog, Button Finial, Stamped, 6 In.	1200.00
Knife Rest, Rabbit, 21 1/2 In.	425.00
Mug, Rabbit, Handles, Stamped, 2 3/4 In.	400.00
Paperweight, Rabbit Form, Marked, 3 1/2 In.	250.00
Pitcher, Night & Morning, Early 20th Century, 5 In.	475.00
Pitcher, Rabbit, Angled Handle, Bulbous, Stamped, 5 1/2 In.	325.00
Pitcher, Rabbit, Pear Shape, Angled Handle, Stamped, 7 In.	500.00
Plate, Azalea, 8 1/2 In.	195.00
Plate, Azalea, Stamped, C.1920, 8 1/4 In.	150.00
Plate, Bird In Potted Orange Tree Border, Rabbit Mark, 10 1/4 In.	800.00
Plate, Butterfly, Experimental, Stamped, 6 In.	700.00
Plate, Chestnut, Stamped, 8 1/2 In.	110.00
Plate, Clover, Raised Design Border, C.P.U.S., 1881–95, 8 3/4 In.	325.00
Plate, Crab, Stamped, 8 1/2 In.	600.00
Plate, Crab, Waves Border, 8 5/8 In.	750.00
Plate, Dolphin, Stamped, C.1896, 8 1/2 In.	500.00
Plate, Dolphin, Upside–Down, 1893, Stamped C.P.U.S., 10 In.	750.00
Plate, Duck, Stamped, 8 1/2 In., 4 Piece	600.00
Plate, Duck, Stamped, C.1930, 8 1/4 In.	225.00
Plate, French Mushroom, Stamped, 6 In.	450.00
Plate, Grape, Stamped, C.1929, 8 1/2 In.	150.00
Plate, Horsechestnut	195.00
Plate, Iris, Stamped, C.1896, 10 In.	200.00
Plate, Lobster, Impressed Rabbit, 8 1/2 In.	450.00
Plate, Lobster, Stamped, 6 In.	750.00
Plate, Lobster, Stamped, 8 1/2 In.	600.00
Plate, Magnolia, Stamped, 1896, 8 1/2 In. 140.00 To	200.00
Plate, Magnolia, Stamped, 1929, 6 In.	100.00
Plate, Pineapple Border, Cloverleaf, 10 1/8 In.	800.00
Plate, Polar Bear Border, O Mark, 10 In.	1100.00
Plate, Polar Bear, C.1929, Stamped, 7 In.	475.00
Plate, Polar Bear, Stamped, 9 3/4 In.	500.00
Plate, Pond Lily Border, Cloverleaf, 10 1/4 In.	2500.00
Plate, Poppy, Artist, 1896–1932, 8 1/4 In.	550.00
Plate, Rabbit, 6 In.	95.00
Plate, Rabbit, 8 1/2 In.	165.00
Plate, Rabbit, 9 3/4 In.	145.00
Plate, Rabbit, Stamped, 10 In.	375.00
Plate, Scotty Dog, Stamped, 1932, 8 1/2 In.	1700.00
Plate, Snow Tree Border, O Mark, 8 5/8 In.	400.00
Plate, Snowtree, Stamped, Early 20th Century, 8 1/2 In.	125.00
Plate, Snowtree, Stamped, Early 20th Century, 10 In.	275.00
Plate, Standing Bird, Stamped, 8 1/2 In.	1700.00
Plate, Strawberry, Marked, 6 In. 1300.00 To	1600.00
Plate, Tapestry Lion, Stamped, 20th Century, 8 1/2 In.	1700.00
Plate, Tercentenary, Fish Border, Molded Rim, Marked, 8 7/8 In.	2300.00
Plate, Turkey Border, Turns To Left, Impressed, 8 5/8 In.	1600.00
Plate, Turkey, Early 20th Century, Stamped, 8 1/2 In.	250.00
Plate, Turtle Border, Double, Blue Ground, Marked, 6 In.	850.00
Plate, Upside–Down Dolphin Border, Cloverleaf Mark, 10 1/8 In.	1500.00
Plate, White Poppy, Blue, Rabbit Mark, 8 3/4 In.	400.00
Plate, Woodcock, Flying, Stamped, 8 1/2 In.	650.00
Salt & Pepper, Rabbit Border, Marked D.P., 3 3/4 In.	450.00
Sugar & Creamer, Berry	400.00
Tea Tile, Rabbit, Round, Stamped Twice, 6 In.	250.00
Teapot, Rabbit Border, Rabbit Mark, 7 7/8 In.	700.00
Teapot, Rabbit, Button Finial Domed Cover, 20th Century, 7 In.	450.00
Tray, Rabbit Border, Stamped, 14 1/8 In.	700.00

Tray, Rabbit Pattern, Bubble Bursts, 1905, Stamped, 13 In.	550.00
Vase, Experimental, Mottled Green Glaze, Cylindrical, HR, CKAW, 11 In.	475.00
Vase, Experimental, Red & Brown Drip Glaze, Short Neck, CKAW, 9 In.	2000.00
Vase, Pink Glaze, Green Blush, Marked, Late 19th Century, CKAW, 13 In.	6750.00
Vase, Volcanic, Gray, Blue & Brown Glaze, Wide Mouth, HR, CKAW, 10 In.	1000.00
Vase, Wide Mouth, Iridescent Red Glaze, Label, 6 1/2 In.	2500.00

John and Elizabeth Degenhart started the Crystal Art Glass of Cambridge, Ohio, in 1947. Quality paperweights and other glass objects were made. John died in 1964 and his wife took over management and production ideas. Over 145 colors of glass were made. In 1978, after the death of Mrs. Degenhart, the molds were sold. The D in a heart trademark was removed, so collectors can easily recognize the true Degenhart piece.

DEGENHART, Plate, Face, Amberina	35.00

Degue

Degue is a signature found acid-etched on pieces of French glass made in the early 1900s. Cameo, mold blown, and smooth glass with contrasting colored rims are the types most often found.

DEGUE, Vase, Green Flowers, Frosted Ground, 3 1/2 In.	450.00
Vase, Scene In Navy Cut To Pink, House On Island, Signed, 5 1/2 In.	475.00

Delatte Nancy

Delatte glass is a French cameo glass made by Andre Delatte. It was first made in Nancy, France, in 1921. Lighting fixtures and opaque glassware in imitation of Bohemian opaline were made. There were many French cameo glass makers, so be sure to look in other appropriate sections.

DELATTE, Box, Cover, Florals, Pink Ground, Signed, 6 In.	590.00
Box, Dresser, Red, Green, Frosted	525.00
Vase, Bird On Branch, Fruit On Reverse, Signed, 6 1/2 In.	750.00
Vase, Landscape Along River, Salmon Pink, Signed, 7 1/2 In.	595.00
Vase, Magenta Florals & Leaves, Signed, 4 1/4 In.	375.00
Vase, Water, Trees On Island, Pedestal Foot, Signed, 9 3/4 In.	950.00
DELAWARE, see Custard Glass; Pressed Glass	
DELDARE, see Buffalo Pottery Deldare	

Delft

Delft is a tin-glazed pottery that has been made since the seventeenth century. It is decorated with blue on white or with colored decorations. Most of the pieces sold today were made after 1891, and the name "Holland" appears with the Delft factory marks.

DELFT, Coffee Grinder, Hanging, Scene, Blue & White	78.00
Creamer, Cow	10.00
Garniture Set, 3 Jars, 2 Vases, 19th Century, Blue & White, 5 Piece	1540.00
Jar, Exotic Birds, Flowering Plants, Mounted As Lamp, 11 In.	1750.00
Pitcher, Oriental Scenes, 9 In.	75.00
Planter, Violin, Blue Floral & Leaf Design, English, 5 1/2 X 15 In.	95.00
Plaque, Portrait of Woman, Hanging Hole, 16 1/2 In.	395.00
Plaque, Winter Canal Scene, Signed Bonneville, 15 In.	105.00
Plate, Bird On Flowering Branch, English, 9 In.	190.00
Plate, Blue & White Landscape, English, 8 3/4 In.	170.00
Plate, Floral, Blue & White, Yellow Rim, Signed B.P.J., 9 In.	175.00
Plate, Old Man, Pipe, Harbor Scene, Boch Freres Louiviere, 9 1/2 In.	35.00
Plate, Oriental Design, Bianco Sopra Bianco Edge, 8 7/8 In.	225.00
Plate, Oriental Design, English, 9 In.	150.00
Plate, Polychrome Floral Design, 9 3/8 In.	275.00
Plate, Polychrome Squirrel, English, 9 In.	175.00
Plate, Scene of Archer Shooting, Octagonal, English, 8 1/2 In.	375.00
Platter, Blue Design, Marked, 17th Century, 20 In.	275.00
Reamer, Germany, 2 Piece	45.00
Salt & Pepper	5.00
Smoking Pot, House Shape, With Chimney, 4 In., Pair	30.00
Stein, Lithophane, Blue & White, 1/2 Liter	200.00
Tile, Blue & White, Frame, 6 X 6 In.	20.00
Tile, Canal Scene, Registered Number, 9 In.	75.00

Tile, Donkey Inside 3–Band Circle, Medallion Each Corner, 6 In. 50.00
Tile, Man, Fish Tail, Blue & White, Framed, 9 3/4 In. 20.00
Tile, The Mayflower, Blue, Brown, 6 In. 15.00
Vase, Cover, Floral Design, English, 10 1/2 In. 77.00
Vase, Dutch Woman Carrying Basket, Dragon Handles, 6 In. 240.00
Vase, Floral, Blue & White, Signed B.P., 8 In. 275.00
Vase, Peacock, Thooft & Labouchere, 9 In. 265.00
Vase, Windmill Medallion, Bulbous Bottom, 8 In., Pair 120.00
Vessel, Canteen Shape, Floral, Blue, White, Black, Grove & Loops, 7 In. 250.00

Dental cabinets, chairs, equipment, and other related items are listed here. Other objects may be found listed under Medical.

DENTAL, Cabinet, 3 Tiers, Mirrors, Glass Trays, Walnut, 41 X 5 Ft.3 In. 2500.00
Cabinet, Allison, 21 Drawers & Compartments, Blond & Dark Wood, 1930 .... 400.00
Cabinet, Etched Glass, 16 Drawers, Lower Cupboards, Mahogany, C.1920 .... 1100.00
Cabinet, Golden Oak, Original Glass Knobs, Marble Trim 1500.00
Cabinet, Leaded Glass Doors, Bird's–Eye Maple Drawers, Marble Base 1500.00
Cabinet, Quartersawn Oak 3200.00
Chair, S.S.White, 1902 .... 1500.00
Mirror, Ivory Handle 175.00
Pin, Dental Hygiene, Graphic Design, 1920s, 5/8 In. 5.00
Pin, Odontological Society, Black, Orange, 1930s, 7/8 In. 5.00
Pliers, 1890 .... 22.00

DENVER
CT&
PTCo

William Long of Steubenville, Ohio, founded the Lonhuda Pottery Company in 1892. In 1900 he moved to Denver, Colorado, and organized the Denver China and Pottery Company. This pottery worked until 1905 when Long moved to New Jersey and founded the Clifton Pottery. Long also worked for Weller Pottery, Roseville Pottery, and American Encaustic Tiling Company.

DENVER, Bowl, Gnarled Trees, Blue Ground, White, Signed, 6 In. 475.00
Frog, Green Glaze, Marked, Terra Cotta Co., 3 X 3 In. 65.00
Vase, White Tree, Blue Ground, Marked, 7 In. 475.00

Depression glass was an inexpensive glass manufactured in large quantities during the 1920s and early 1930s. It was made in many colors and patterns by dozens of factories in the United States. The name "Depression glass" is a modern one. For more descriptions, history, pictures, and prices of Depression glass, see the book "Kovels' Depression Glass & American Dinnerware Price List."

DEPRESSION GLASS, Adam, Ashtray, Green 16.00
Adam, Bowl, Cover, Pink, 9 In. .... 30.00 To 58.00
Adam, Bowl, Green, 10 In. 15.00
Adam, Bowl, Pink, 5 3/4 In. 25.00
Adam, Butter, Cover, Green .... 245.00 To 255.00
Adam, Butter, Cover, Pink .... 60.00 To 70.00
Adam, Cake Plate, Green 14.00
Adam, Candlestick, Green, Pair 75.00
Adam, Candy Jar, Cover, Pink 39.00
Adam, Cup & Saucer, Green 20.00
Adam, Grill Plate, Green .... 8.00 To 10.00
Adam, Plate, Green, 7 3/4 In. 8.00
Adam, Plate, Pink, 9 In. 12.50
Adam, Relish, Green 9.00
Adam, Salt & Pepper, Pink 30.00
Adam, Saltshaker, Pink 15.00
Adam, Tumbler, Iced Tea, Green, 5 1/2 In. .... 27.00 To 30.00
Adam, Tumbler, Pink, 4 1/2 In. 18.50
Adam, Vase, Green, 7 1/2 In. 75.00
Akro Agate, Bowl, Cereal, Child's, Red 25.00
Akro Agate, Plate, Child's, White, 3 3/8 In. 3.50
   AMERICAN BEAUTY, see English Hobnail
American Pioneer, Plate, Green, 8 In. 5.00

American Pioneer, Sherbet, Pink, 4 3/4 In. 19.00
American Pioneer, Sugar, Green, 2 3/4 In. 14.50
American Sweetheart, Bowl, Monax, 6 In. 10.00
American Sweetheart, Bowl, Pink, 9 In. 23.00
American Sweetheart, Cup & Saucer, Monax .... 8.00 To 8.50
American Sweetheart, Pitcher, Pink, 7 1/2 In. 385.00
American Sweetheart, Plate, Monax, 8 In. 6.00
American Sweetheart, Plate, Monax, 9 In. .... 5.00 To 6.50
American Sweetheart, Plate, Pink, 8 In. .... 5.00 To 6.00
American Sweetheart, Platter, Pink 19.00
American Sweetheart, Salver, Pink, 12 In. 13.00
American Sweetheart, Soup, Dish, Pink 26.00
American Sweetheart, Sugar & Creamer, Monax 10.00
American Sweetheart, Sugar, Monax .... 5.00 To 7.00
American, Mug, 4 1/2 In. 33.00
Anniversary, Bowl, Crystal, 9 In. 4.00
Anniversary, Butter, Cover, Crystal 22.00
Anniversary, Cake Plate, Crystal 4.00
Anniversary, Compote, 3-Footed, Crystal 3.00
Anniversary, Cup & Saucer, Crystal 2.00
Anniversary, Soup, Dish, Iridescent 2.50
Anniversary, Sugar, Cover, Crystal 6.00
Anniversary, Wine, Pink 12.00
    APPLE BLOSSOM, see Dogwood
Aunt Polly, Butter, Cover, Blue .... 125.00 To 150.00
Aunt Polly, Plate, Blue, 6 In. 5.00
Aunt Polly, Salt & Pepper, Blue 160.00
Aunt Polly, Sherbet, Iridescent .... 5.00 To 6.00
Aunt Polly, Tumbler, Blue 12.50
Aunt Polly, Vase, Green, 6 1/2 In. 20.00
    AURORA, see Petalware
Aurora, Bowl, Cobalt Blue, 5 3/8 In. 5.00
Aurora, Tumbler, Cobalt Blue 12.50
Avocado, Bowl, Pink, 5 1/4 In. 18.00
Avocado, Plate, Pink, 6 3/4 In. 9.00
Avocado, Sherbet, Pink 50.00
    B PATTERN, see Dogwood
    BALLERINA, see Cameo
Bamboo Optic, Cup & Saucer, Green 6.00
Bamboo Optic, Cup, Pink 4.00
Bamboo Optic, Plate, Green, 12 3/4 In. 11.00
Bamboo Optic, Plate, Pink, 8 In. 4.25
    BANDED CHERRY, see Cherry Blossom
    BANDED FINE RIB, see Coronation
    BANDED PETALWARE, see Petalware
    BANDED RAINBOW, see Ring
    BANDED RIBBON, see New Century
    BANDED RINGS, see Ring
Baroque, Bowl, 2 Sections, Blue, 6 1/2 In. 16.00
    BASKET, see No. 615
Beaded Block, Bowl, 2 Handles, Amber, 4 1/2 In. 32.00
Beaded Block, Bowl, 2 Handles, Ice Blue, 4 1/2 In. 32.00
Beaded Block, Pitcher, Crystal 35.00
Beaded Block, Plate, Square, Green, 7 3/4 In. 6.00
    BERWICK, see Boopie
    BEVERAGE WITH SAILBOAT, see White Ship
    BIG RIB, see Manhattan
    BLOCK, see Block Optic
Block Optic, Compote, Pink 32.00
Block Optic, Creamer, Cone Shape, Green 10.00
Block Optic, Cup & Saucer, Green .... 8.50 To 9.00
Block Optic, Cup, Green .... 3.00 To 3.50

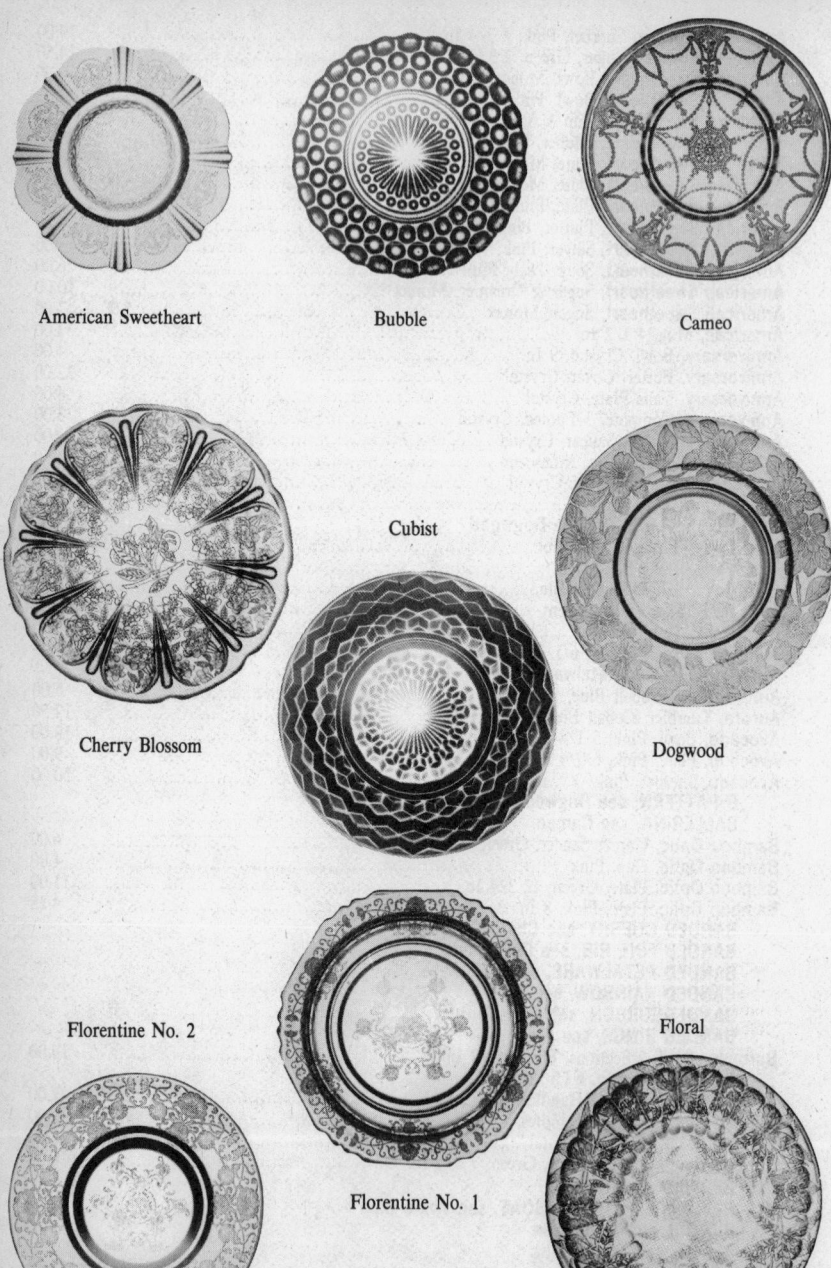

American Sweetheart

Bubble

Cameo

Cubist

Cherry Blossom

Dogwood

Florentine No. 2

Florentine No. 1

Floral

Block Optic, Cup, Yellow 6.00
Block Optic, Ice Bucket, Metal Handle, Crystal 16.00
Block Optic, Plate, Green, 10 1/4 In. 12.00
Block Optic, Plate, Green, 9 In. ....9.00 To 12.00
Block Optic, Sandwich Server, Center Handle, Pink 30.00
Block Optic, Sherbet, Green, 3 1/4 In. 3.00
Block Optic, Sherbet, Pink, 3 1/4 In. 2.00
Boopie, Goblet, Crystal, 4 1/2 In. 1.25
Boopie, Goblet, Footed, Crystal, 5 1/2 In. 1.25
Boopie, Sherbet, Crystal 1.25
Boopie, Sherbet, Red 5.00
    BOUQUET & LATTICE, see Normandie
    BRIDAL BOUQUET, see No. 615
Bubble, Bowl, Blue, 4 1/2 In. ....4.00 To 6.00
Bubble, Bowl, Blue, 5 1/4 In. ....5.00 To 7.00
Bubble, Bowl, Blue, 8 3/8 In. 17.00
Bubble, Bowl, Crystal, 5 1/4 In. ....2.25 To 5.00
Bubble, Bowl, Crystal, 8 3/8 In. 4.50
Bubble, Creamer, Blue ....15.00 To 30.00
Bubble, Creamer, Green 5.00
Bubble, Cup & Saucer, Blue 4.00
Bubble, Cup & Saucer, Red 8.50
Bubble, Cup, Blue 3.00
Bubble, Cup, Green 2.00
Bubble, Plate, Blue, 6 3/4 In. ....1.00 To 2.50
Bubble, Plate, Blue, 9 3/8 In. 4.50
Bubble, Platter, Oval, Blue, 12 In. 7.00
Bubble, Soup, Dish, Blue ....5.00 To 8.50
Bubble, Sugar & Creamer, Green 12.00
Bubble, Tumbler, Crystal, 6 Oz. 6.00
Bubble, Tumbler, Red, 16 Oz. 12.00
    BULLSEYE, see Bubble
Burple, Bowl, Crystal, 4 1/2 In. 1.50
Burple, Bowl, Crystal, 8 1/2 In. 2.00
Burple, Bowl, Green, 4 1/2 In. 3.50
    BUTTERFLIES & ROSES, see Flower Garden with Butterflies
    BUTTONS & BOWS, see Holiday
By Cracky, Pitcher, Crystal 12.00
By Cracky, Plate, Amber, Octagonal, 8 In. 2.00
By Cracky, Plate, Green, 6 In. 1.25
By Cracky, Sherbet, Crimped, Green 3.00
By Cracky, Sherbet, Round, Canary 3.00
    CABBAGE ROSE, see Sharon
    CABBAGE ROSE WITH SINGLE ARCH, see Rosemary
Cameo, Bowl, 3–Footed, Green, 11 In. 35.00
Cameo, Butter, Cover, Green 140.00
Cameo, Cake Plate, 3–Footed, Green, 10 In. 15.00
Cameo, Candy Jar, Cover, Green, 4 In. ....32.00 To 45.00
Cameo, Cookie Jar, Cover, Green ....27.50 To 40.00
Cameo, Decanter, Stopper, Green 100.00
Cameo, Dish, Mayonnaise, Green 19.00
Cameo, Goblet, Water, Green, 6 In. 38.00
Cameo, Grill Plate, Green ....5.00 To 7.00
Cameo, Grill Plate, Yellow ....3.50 To 6.50
Cameo, Jam Jar, Cover, Green 90.00
Cameo, Pitcher, Green, 8 1/2 In. ....18.00 To 26.00
Cameo, Plate, Closed Handles, Green, 10 1/2 In. ....3.50 To 12.00
Cameo, Plate, Green, 6 In. ....1.25 To 3.00
Cameo, Plate, Green, 8 In. ....5.00 To 6.50
Cameo, Plate, Green, 9 1/2 In. 9.50
Cameo, Plate, Yellow, 9 1/2 In. 7.00
Cameo, Salt & Pepper, Green 50.00
Cameo, Sherbet, Green, 4 7/8 In. 20.00
Cameo, Sugar & Creamer, Green, 3 1/4 In. 22.50

Cameo, Sugar & Creamer, Yellow, 3 1/4 In. 22.00
Cameo, Sugar, Green, 3 1/4 In. 11.00
Cameo, Tumbler, Footed, Green, 5 In. .... 10.00 To 12.00
Candlewick, Berry Bowl, 2 Handles, Crystal, 8 1/2 In. 12.50
Candlewick, Bowl, Flared, Crystal, 10 In. 20.00
Candlewick, Plate, Crystal, 6 In. 4.50
Candlewick, Plate, Crystal, 9 In. 12.00
Candlewick, Sugar & Creamer, Footed, Crystal 50.00
Cape Cod, Plate, Crystal, 10 In. .... 25.00 To 30.00
Cape Cod, Relish, 2 Sections, Handle, Crystal, 8 1/2 In. 20.00
    CAPRICE, see Cambridge
    CHAIN DAISY, see Adam
Cherry Blossom, Bowl, 2 Handles, Green, 9 In. 30.00
Cherry Blossom, Bowl, 2 Handles, Pink, 9 In. 18.00
Cherry Blossom, Bowl, Green, 4 3/4 In. 12.00
Cherry Blossom, Bowl, Green, 5 3/4 In. 20.00
Cherry Blossom, Bowl, Green, 8 1/2 In. .... 14.00 To 16.00
Cherry Blossom, Bowl, Pink, 5 3/4 In. .... 17.00 To 22.00
Cherry Blossom, Butter, Cover, Green .... 52.50 To 70.00
Cherry Blossom, Butter, Cover, Pink 55.00
Cherry Blossom, Creamer, Delphite .... 14.50 To 15.00
Cherry Blossom, Creamer, Pink 10.00
Cherry Blossom, Cup & Saucer, Green 28.00
Cherry Blossom, Cup & Saucer, Pink .... 12.50 To 16.00
Cherry Blossom, Dinner Set, Child's, Delphite, 4 Piece 190.00
Cherry Blossom, Grill Plate, Pink, 9 In. 15.00
Cherry Blossom, Mug, Green, 7 Oz. 115.00
Cherry Blossom, Pitcher, Crystal, 6 3/4 In. 32.00
Cherry Blossom, Pitcher, Footed, Green, 8 In. 42.00
Cherry Blossom, Pitcher, Green, 36 Oz. 32.00
Cherry Blossom, Pitcher, Pink, 6 3/4 In. 25.00
Cherry Blossom, Plate, Green, 9 In. 12.00
Cherry Blossom, Plate, Pink, 7 In. 13.00
Cherry Blossom, Plate, Pink, 9 In. .... 12.00 To 13.00
Cherry Blossom, Platter, Crystal, 13 In. 22.00
Cherry Blossom, Platter, Pink, 11 In. 16.00
Cherry Blossom, Saucer, Pink .... 2.00 To 6.00
Cherry Blossom, Sherbet, Green 12.50
Cherry Blossom, Sherbet, Pink .... 7.00 To 8.00
Cherry Blossom, Soup, Dish, Pink 35.00
Cherry Blossom, Sugar & Creamer, Child's, Delphite 60.00
Cherry Blossom, Sugar & Creamer, Pink 20.00
Cherry Blossom, Sugar, Cover, Green .... 11.00 To 20.00
Cherry Blossom, Sugar, Pink, Cover 20.00
Cherry Blossom, Tray, Sandwich, Green, 10 1/2 In. 8.50
Cherry Blossom, Tumbler, Footed, Green, 3 3/4 In. 12.00
Cherry Blossom, Tumbler, Footed, Pink, 3 3/4 In. 8.00
Cherry Blossom, Tumbler, Footed, Pink, 4 1/2 In. 20.00
Cherry Blossom, Tumbler, Pink, 4 1/4 In. 12.00
Cherry Blossom, Water Set, Delphite, 6 Piece 115.00
    CHERRY, see Cherry Blossom
    CHERRY–BERRY, see also Strawberry
Cherry–Berry, Bowl, Green, 7 1/2 In. 30.00
Cherry–Berry, Sugar, Pink, 2 7/8 In. 17.00
Chico, Tumbler, Ruby, 2 3/4 In. 5.50
Chico, Tumbler, Topaz, 4 3/8 In. 6.50
Chinex Classic, Cup & Saucer, White 4.75
Chinex Classic, Cup, Floral, White 4.50
Chinex Classic, Plate, White, 11 1/2 In. 6.00
    CHRISTMAS CANDY RIBBON, see Christmas Candy
Christmas Candy, Creamer, Teal Blue 11.00
Christmas Candy, Plate, Crystal, 11 1/4 In. 6.00
Christmas Candy, Soup, Dish, Teal Blue 30.00

Circle, Creamer, Green 3.00
Circle, Cup & Saucer, Green 3.50
Circle, Sherbet, Green Foot, 4 3/4 In. 4.50
Circle, Sherbet, Green, Gold Rim, 3 1/8 In. .... 3.00 To 3.25
Circle, Sherbet, Pink, 3 1/8 In. 2.25
Circle, Sugar, Green .... 3.00 To 7.00
Circle, Wine, Green Foot, 4 1/2 In. 6.50
    CIRCULAR RIBS, see Circle
    CLASSIC, see Chinex Classic
    CLEO, see Cambridge
Cloverleaf, Bowl, Green, 5 In. 22.00
Cloverleaf, Bowl, Pink, 4 In. 10.00
Cloverleaf, Candy Dish, Cover, Green 40.00
Cloverleaf, Creamer, Topaz 12.00
Cloverleaf, Cup & Saucer, Black 14.00
Cloverleaf, Cup & Saucer, Green 8.50
Cloverleaf, Cup & Saucer, Pink 7.00
Cloverleaf, Plate, Black, 6 In. 20.00
Cloverleaf, Plate, Pink, 8 In. 5.00
Cloverleaf, Salt & Pepper, Topaz 85.00
Cloverleaf, Saucer, Green 1.25
Cloverleaf, Sherbet, Topaz 8.00
Cloverleaf, Sugar & Creamer, Black 25.00
Cloverleaf, Sugar, Green 5.50
Cloverleaf, Tumbler, Footed, Green, 10 Oz., 5 3/4 In. 16.00
Cloverleaf, Tumbler, Green, 9 Oz. 28.00
Colonial Block, Bowl, Crystal, 4 In. 2.50
Colonial Block, Bowl, Green, 7 In. 10.00
Colonial Block, Creamer, Green .... 5.00 To 6.50
Colonial, Creamer, Green 14.00
Colonial, Goblet, Claret, Green, 5 1/4 In. 20.00
Colonial, Goblet, Cordial, Green 25.00
Colonial, Goblet, Water, Green 22.00
Colonial, Grill Plate, Green 20.00
Colonial, Pitcher, Crystal, 7 In. .... 15.00 To 16.00
Colonial, Pitcher, Ice Lip, Green, 7 3/4 In. 50.00
Colonial, Plate, Crystal, 8 1/2 In. 3.50
Colonial, Platter, Green 16.00
Colonial, Tumbler, Iced Tea, Green, 12 Oz. 65.00
Columbia, Bowl, Crystal, 5 In. 6.00
Columbia, Bowl, Ruffled, Crystal, 10 1/2 In. 14.00
Columbia, Butter, Cover, Crystal 12.00

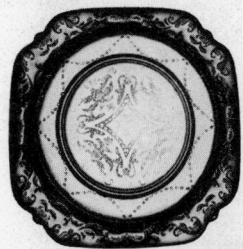

Madrid

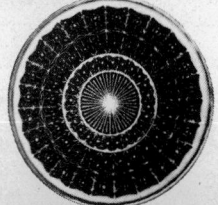

Holiday

Glassware, old or new, requires careful handling. Stand each piece upright, not touching another. Never nest pieces. Wash in moderately hot water and mild detergent. Avoid wiping gold- or platinum-banded pieces while glasses are hot. Never use scouring pads or silver polish on glass. For an automatic dishwasher, be sure the water temperature is under 180°F.

Columbia, Chop Plate, Crystal, 11 In. ....6.00 To 10.00
Columbia, Plate, Crystal, 9 1/2 In. 4.00
Coronation, Bowl, Ruby Red, 4 1/4 In. .... 4.50 To 5.00
Coronation, Bowl, Ruby Red, 8 In. 10.00
Coronation, Cup, Pink 3.25
Coronation, Plate, Pink, 6 In. .... 2.00 To 3.00
Cracked Ice, Sherbet, Pink 7.00
    CREMAX, see Chinex Classic
    CRISS CROSS, see X Design
    CUBE, see Cubist
Cubist, Bowl, Green, 4 1/2 In. 5.00
Cubist, Bowl, Pink, 4 1/2 In. 4.00
Cubist, Candy Jar, Cover, Green 22.00
Cubist, Candy Jar, Cover, Pink 20.00
Cubist, Creamer, Pink 3.50
Cubist, Pitcher, Green 140.00
Cubist, Plate, Green, 6 In. 2.00
Cubist, Plate, Green, 8 In. 4.50
Cubist, Plate, Pink, 6 In. 1.50
Cubist, Plate, Pink, 8 In. 22.00
Cubist, Sherbet, Footed, Green .... 4.50 To 6.00
Cubist, Sugar, Green, 3 In. 6.00
Cubist, Sugar, Pink, 3 In. 4.50
Cubist, Tumbler, Amber, 4 In. 10.00
    DAISY, see No. 620
    DAISY PETALS, see Petalware
    DANCING GIRL, see Cameo
Della Robbia, Bowl, Amber, 4 3/4 In. 12.00
Della Robbia, Bowl, Green, 4 3/4 In. 12.00
Della Robbia, Plate, Amber, 9 In. 17.00
Dewdrop, Lazy Susan, 5 Sections, 13 1/2 In. 8.00
Dewdrop, Water Set, Crystal, 7 Piece 25.00
    DIAMOND, see Windsor
    DIAMOND PATTERN, see Miss America
    DIAMOND POINT, see Petalware
Diamond Quilted, Bowl, Green, 5 1/2 In. 3.00
Diamond Quilted, Bowl, Pink, 7 In. 4.00
Diamond Quilted, Creamer, Green 5.50
Diamond Quilted, Plate, Pink, 8 In. 3.75
Diamond Quilted, Saltshaker, Green 8.00
Diamond Quilted, Sugar, Green 5.00
Diamond Quilted, Table Set, Child's, 3 Piece 32.00
Diana, Bowl, 5 In. 2.25
Diana, Bowl, Amber, 5 In. 3.50
Diana, Bowl, Amber, 11 In. .... 6.00 To 7.00
Diana, Bowl, Scalloped, Crystal, 12 In. 4.00
Diana, Creamer, Crystal 1.25
Diana, Cup & Saucer, Pink 20.00
Diana, Plate, Crystal, 11 3/4 In. 4.25
Diana, Platter, Oval, Amber, 12 In. 15.00
Diana, Soup, Cream, Crystal 5.00
Diana, Sugar & Creamer, Crystal 4.50
Dixie, Tumbler, Pink, 5 1/4 In. 4.50
Dogwood, Bowl, Pink, 5 1/2 In. 14.25
Dogwood, Bowl, Pink, 8 1/2 In. 35.00
Dogwood, Cup & Saucer, Green 24.00
Dogwood, Cup & Saucer, Pink 13.00
Dogwood, Grill Plate, Pink ....5.00 To 10.00
Dogwood, Pitcher, Pink, 8 In. .... 115.00 To 135.00
Dogwood, Plate, Pink, 6 In. .... 3.00 To 4.00
Dogwood, Plate, Pink, 9 1/4 In. .... 15.00 To 17.50
Dogwood, Saucer, Pink .... 2.00 To 2.50
Dogwood, Sherbet, Pink 20.00

DORIC & PANSY, see also Pretty Polly Party Dishes

Doric & Pansy, Bowl, Handle, Ultramarine, 9 In.	30.00
Doric & Pansy, Cup & Saucer, Ultramarine	18.00
Doric & Pansy, Saucer, Ultramarine	3.00
Doric & Pansy, Tray, Handle, Crystal, 10 In.	9.00
Doric & Pansy, Tray, Handle, Ultramarine, 10 In.	17.00

DORIC WITH PANSY, see Doric & Pansy

Doric, Bowl, Green, 5 1/2 In.	25.00
Doric, Butter, Cover, Green	65.00
Doric, Butter, Cover, Pink	55.00
Doric, Candy Dish, 3 Sections, Green	6.00
Doric, Candy Dish, 3 Sections, Pink	4.50
Doric, Candy Dish, Cover, Pink	25.00
Doric, Creamer, Green	4.50
Doric, Plate, Green, 7 In.	8.50 To 12.50
Doric, Plate, Green, 9 In.	7.00 To 8.00
Doric, Salt & Pepper, Pink	18.00 To 30.00
Doric, Sherbet, Footed, Green	6.00
Doric, Sugar, Pink	5.00
Doric, Tumbler, Green, 4 1/2 In.	35.00 To 45.00

DOUBLE SHIELD, see Mt. Pleasant
DOUBLE SWIRL, see Swirl
DRAPE & TASSEL, see Princess
DUTCH, see Windmill
DUTCH ROSE, see Rosemary
EARLY AMERICAN, see Princess Feather
EARLY AMERICAN HOBNAIL, see Hobnail
EARLY AMERICAN ROCK CRYSTAL, see Rock Crystal
ENGLISH HOBNAIL, see also Miss America

English Hobnail, Ashtray, Hat, Crystal, 4 In.	4.00
English Hobnail, Bowl, Crystal, 6 In.	4.00
English Hobnail, Candy Dish, Amber, 1/2 Lb.	35.00
English Hobnail, Decanter, Crystal, 20 Oz.	25.00
English Hobnail, Salt & Pepper, Square Base, Crystal	33.00
English Hobnail, Sherbet, Footed, Crystal	8.00
English Hobnail, Sugar & Creamer, Footed, Crystal	20.00
English Hobnail, Tumbler, Crystal, 3 3/4 In.	4.50
Fairfax, Bowl, Oval, Amber, 10 1/2 In.	14.00

FAN & FEATHER, see Adam
FINE RIB, see Homespun

Fire–King, Bowl, Blue, 5 3/8 In.	10.00
Fire–King, Hot Plate, Blue	5.50
Fire–King, Measuring Cup, Blue, 8 Oz.	10.00
Fire–King, Mixing Bowl, Blue, 8 3/8 In.	10.00
Fire–King, Pie Plate, Blue, 8 3/8 In.	7.00

FLAT DIAMOND, see Diamond Quilted

Floragold, Bowl, Shell Pink, 4 1/2 In.	3.00
Floragold, Butter, Cover, Oblong, Iridescent	11.00
Floragold, Butter, Cover, Round, Iridescent	32.00
Floragold, Coaster/Ashtray, Crystal	2.50
Floragold, Coaster/Ashtray, Iridescent	3.00
Floragold, Creamer, Iridescent	4.00
Floragold, Pitcher, Iridescent	22.50 To 28.00
Floragold, Plate, Iridescent, 5 3/4 In.	4.50
Floragold, Salt & Pepper, Iridescent	29.00 To 35.00
Floragold, Salt & Pepper, Shell Pink	30.00
Floragold, Sugar, Cover, Iridescent	10.00
Floragold, Tray, Indented, Iridescent, 13 1/2 In.	22.50
Floragold, Tumbler, Iridescent, 10 Oz.	9.00
Floral & Diamond Band, Butter, Cover, Green	55.00 To 95.00
Floral & Diamond Band, Butter, Cover, Pink	85.00

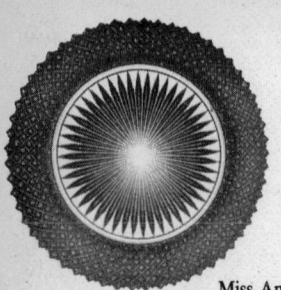

Mayfair Open Rose

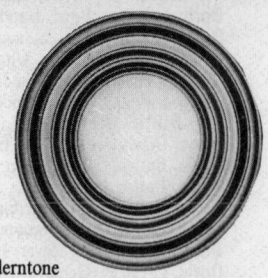

Miss America

Moderntone

FLORAL RIM, see Vitrock

Floral, Bowl, Cover, Green, 8 In.	32.00
Floral, Bowl, Pink, 4 In.	12.00
Floral, Bowl, Vegetable, Oval, Green	11.50
Floral, Butter, Cover, Pink	70.00
Floral, Butter, Green	35.00
Floral, Candy Jar, Cover, Green	27.00
Floral, Coaster, Pink	7.00
Floral, Cup, Green	8.00 To 9.00
Floral, Ice Tub, Pink	500.00
Floral, Pitcher, Green, 10 1/4 In.	170.00
Floral, Pitcher, Green, 5 1/2 In.	400.00
Floral, Pitcher, Green, 8 In.	20.00 To 30.00
Floral, Pitcher, Pink, 10 1/4 In.	145.00
Floral, Pitcher, Pink, 8 In.	17.00
Floral, Plate, Green, 6 In.	3.00
Floral, Platter, Green, 10 3/4 In.	12.00
Floral, Platter, Pink, 10 3/4 In.	10.50
Floral, Refrigerator Dish, Cover, Green	50.00
Floral, Relish, 2 Sections, Green	10.00
Floral, Relish, 2 Sections, Pink	12.00
Floral, Salt & Pepper, Footed, Green	36.00 To 39.00
Floral, Salt & Pepper, Pink, 4 In.	35.00
Floral, Tumbler, Footed, Green, 4 3/4 In.	12.00
Floral, Tumbler, Footed, Pink, 4 3/4 In.	12.00
Floral, Tumbler, Footed, Pink, 5 1/4 In.	30.00
Florentine No.1, Ashtray, Green, 5 1/2 In.	16.50
Florentine No.1, Berry Bowl, Yellow, 5 In.	9.00
Florentine No.1, Bowl, Pink, 5 In.	6.50
Florentine No.1, Butter, Cover, Crystal	165.00
Florentine No.1, Butter, Cover, Pink	115.00 To 175.00
Florentine No.1, Butter, Cover, Yellow	135.00
Florentine No.1, Creamer, Crystal	7.50
Florentine No.1, Cup & Saucer, Crystal	7.00
Florentine No.1, Grill Plate, Crystal	7.00
Florentine No.1, Pitcher, Green, 6 1/2 In.	25.00
Florentine No.1, Plate, Yellow, 10 In.	11.00
Florentine No.1, Salt & Pepper, Pink	45.00
Florentine No.1, Saucer, Yellow	3.00
Florentine No.1, Sherbet, Green	5.75
Florentine No.1, Sugar & Creamer, Green	15.00
Florentine No.2, Bowl, Green, 8 In.	11.00
Florentine No.2, Butter, Cover, Amber	90.00
Florentine No.2, Butter, Cover, Green	85.00
Florentine No.2, Candlestick, Green, Pair	35.00
Florentine No.2, Candy Dish, Cover, Crystal	65.00
Florentine No.2, Compote, Ruffled, Cobalt Blue, 3 1/2 In.	30.00
Florentine No.2, Creamer, Green	4.75

Florentine No.2, Cup, Green 4.50
Florentine No.2, Custard Cup, Green 45.00
Florentine No.2, Gravy Boat, Amber 32.50
Florentine No.2, Plate, Amber, 10 In. 11.00
Florentine No.2, Plate, Green, 8 1/2 In. 3.00
Florentine No.2, Relish, 3 Sections, Amber 12.00
Florentine No.2, Sherbet, Amber 6.00
Florentine No.2, Sherbet, Footed, Green 6.00
Florentine No.2, Soup, Cream, Green ....7.00 To 10.00
Florentine No.2, Sugar, Cover, Amber 23.00
Florentine No.2, Sugar, Green 4.50
Florentine No.2, Tumbler, Amber, 4 In. 22.50
Florentine No.2, Tumbler, Green, 4 In. .... 7.00 To 9.00
    FLOWER, see Princess Feather
    FLOWER & LEAF BAND, see Indiana Custard
    FLOWER BASKET, see No. 615
Flower Garden With Butterflies, Compote, Crystal 85.00
Flower Garden With Butterflies, Plate, Blue, 10 In. 65.00
Flower Garden With Butterflies, Plate, Crystal, 8 In. 22.00
Flower Garden With Butterflies, Sandwich Server, Crystal 75.00
    FLOWER RIM, see Vitrock
Forest Green, Bowl, Green, 10 In. 45.00
Forest Green, Bowl, Square, 4 1/4 In. 3.25
Forest Green, Cup & Saucer, Square, Green 4.00
Forest Green, Pitcher, Green, 22 Oz. 13.00
Forest Green, Pitcher, Green, 3 Qt. 22.00
Forest Green, Plate, Square, Green, 6 3/4 In. 3.00
Forest Green, Punch Set, Green, 10 Piece 55.00
Forest Green, Vase, Bud, Crimped, Green, 6 3/8 In. 2.50
Forest Green, Vase, Corset Shape, Green, 5 7/8 In. 2.25
Forest Green, Vase, Green, 6 3/8 In. 2.00
Forest Green, Water Set, Green, 9 Piece 28.00
Fortune, Bowl, Pink, 4 1/2 In. 2.25
Fortune, Candy Dish, Cover, Pink 15.00
    FOSTORIA, see American
    FROSTED BLOCK, see Beaded Block
Fruits, Cup, Green 4.50
Fruits, Saucer, Green 3.00
Fruits, Sherbet, Pink 5.50
Georgian, Bowl, Green, 4 1/2 In. 5.00
Georgian, Butter, Cover, Green .... 55.00 To 70.00
Georgian, Creamer, Green, 4 In. 9.00
Georgian, Cup, Green 5.00
Georgian, Plate, Green, 6 In. 1.75
Georgian, Sugar & Creamer, Cover, Green, 3 In. 38.50
Georgian, Sugar, Green, 3 In. 8.00
Georgian, Sugar, Green, 4 In. 9.00
    GLADIOLI, see Royal Lace
Gothic Arches, Plate, Amber, 10 1/2 In. 12.00
Gothic Arches, Plate, Green, 8 In. 7.00
    HAIRPIN, see Newport
    HANGING BASKET, see No. 615
Harp, Cake Plate, Crystal .... 12.00 To 13.00
Harp, Cake Stand, Blue 15.00
Harp, Coaster, Crystal .... 1.00 To 3.00
Harp, Plate, Gold Trim, Crystal, 7 In. 4.00
Harp, Tray, Pink 20.00
Heritage, Bowl, Crystal, 8 1/2 In. 12.50
Heritage, Cup & Saucer, Crystal 5.00
Heritage, Plate, Crystal, 12 In. 7.00
    HEX OPTIC, see Hexagon Optic
Hexagon Optic, Plate, Green, 6 In. 1.25
Hexagon Optic, Tumbler, Green, 3 3/4 In. 2.25

HINGE, see Patrician
Hobnail, Cup & Saucer, Crystal 3.00
Hobnail, Cup, Pink 3.50
Hobnail, Pitcher, Crystal, 18 Oz. 16.00
Holiday, Bowl, Pink, 5 1/8 In. 7.50
Holiday, Candlestick, Pink 20.00
Holiday, Cup & Saucer, Pink 7.00
Holiday, Plate, Pink, 9 1/2 In. 10.00
Holiday, Sherbet, Pink 4.00
Homespun, Bowl, Pink, 4 1/2 In. 4.50
Homespun, Butter, Cover, Pink .... 40.00 To 45.00
Homespun, Dinner Set, Child's, Pink, 14 Piece 220.00
Homespun, Platter, Pink, 13 In. 14.00
Homespun, Sherbet, Pink 4.00
Homespun, Tumbler, Footed, Pink, 6 1/4 In. 8.50
Homespun, Tumbler, Pink, 4 In. 6.00
Homespun, Tumbler, Pink, 5 1/4 In. 18.00
Homestead, Cup, Pink 3.00
HONEYCOMB, see Hexagon Optic
HORIZONTAL FINE RIB, see Manhattan
HORIZONTAL RIBBED, see Manhattan
HORIZONTAL ROUNDED BIG RIB, see Manhattan
HORIZONTAL SHARP BIG RIB, see Manhattan
HORSESHOE, see No. 612
Imperial Plain Octagon, Bowl, Amber, 9 1/4 In. 11.00
Imperial Plain Octagon, Bowl, Green, 8 3/4 In. 10.00
Imperial Plain Octagon, Plate, Green, 8 In. 3.00
Imperial Plain Octagon, Tray, Handle, Green, 10 1/2 In. 4.50
Indiana Custard Bowl, 7 1/2 In. 9.00
Indiana Custard, Butter, Cover, Ivory .... 53.00 To 55.00
IRIS & HERRINGBONE, see Iris
Iris, Bowl, Ruffled, Crystal, 11 In. 8.00
Iris, Bowl, Salad, 9 1/2 In. 6.50
Iris, Butter, Cover, Crystal 25.00
Iris, Butter, Cover, Iridescent .... 20.00 To 33.00
Iris, Candy Jar, Cover, Crystal .... 72.00 To 80.00
Iris, Creamer, Crystal .... 5.00 To 7.00
Iris, Cup & Saucer, Crystal 40.00
Iris, Cup, Iridescent .... 7.00 To 11.00
Iris, Goblet, Crystal, 8 Oz., 5 3/4 In. 13.00
Iris, Goblet, Wine, Crystal 10.00
Iris, Pitcher, Footed, Crystal, 9 1/2 In. 20.00
Iris, Pitcher, Footed, Iridescent, 9 1/2 In. 22.50
Iris, Plate, Iridescent, 9 In. 15.00
Iris, Saucer, Crystal 3.50
Iris, Soup Dish, Crystal 80.00
Iris, Sugar, Cover, Crystal 10.00
Iris, Tumbler, Footed, Crystal, 6 In. .... 10.00 To 11.00
Iris, Tumbler, Footed, Crystal, 7 In. 12.00
Iris, Vase, Iridescent, 9 In. 24.00
IVEX, see Chinex Classic
JADITE, see also Jane–Ray
Jadite, Bowl, Jadite, 4 1/4 In. 3.00
JANE–RAY, see also Jadite
Jane–Ray, Bowl, Jadite, 5 In. .... 2.00 To 3.00
Jane–Ray, Cup & Saucer 1.50
Jane–Ray, Cup & Saucer, Jadite .... 1.50 To 3.50
Jane–Ray, Mug, Coffee, Jadite 4.50
Jane–Ray, Plate, 9 In. .... 2.00 To 3.00
Jane–Ray, Plate, Jadite, 5 1/2 In. 1.00
Jubilee, Creamer, Yellow 14.50
Jubilee, Cup & Saucer, Yellow 11.00
Jubilee, Goblet, Yellow, 10 Oz., 6 In. 22.00

Jubilee, Plate, Yellow, 7 In. 6.50
Jubilee, Plate, Yellow, 8 3/4 In. 8.50
Jubilee, Sugar & Creamer, Yellow .... 25.00 To 35.00
    KNIFE & FORK, see Colonial
    LACE EDGE, see also Coronation
Lace Edge, Bowl, 3–Footed, Pink, 10 1/2 In. 135.00
Lace Edge, Bowl, Pink, 6 3/8 In. 12.00
Lace Edge, Bowl, Pink, 9 1/2 In. 11.00
Lace Edge, Butter, Cover, Pink .... 45.00 To 75.00
Lace Edge, Candy Jar, Cover, Pink .... 32.00 To 43.00
Lace Edge, Compote, Pink, 7 In. 14.00
Lace Edge, Cookie Jar, Cover, Pink 35.00
Lace Edge, Grill Plate, Pink ....9.00 To 12.50
Lace Edge, Plate, Pink, 7 1/4 In. 15.00
Lace Edge, Plate, Pink, 8 3/4 In. .... 10.50 To 12.50
Lace Edge, Plate, Pink, 10 1/2 In. .... 14.00 To 17.00
Lace Edge, Platter, Pink 15.00
Lace Edge, Relish, 3 Sections, Pink, 10 1/2 In. 20.00
Lace Edge, Sherbet, Pink 75.00
Lace Edge, Tumbler, Footed, Pink, 5 In. 40.00
    LACY DAISY, see No. 618
Lariatte, Relish, 2 Sections, Crystal 13.50
Laurel, Bowl, Ivory, 11 In. 22.00
Laurel, Cheese Dish, Cover, Green 38.00
Laurel, Cheese Dish, Cover, Ivory 10.00
Laurel, Creamer, Ivory, Tall ....9.50 To 10.00
Laurel, Plate, Ivory, 6 In. ....2.00 To 2.25
Laurel, Plate, Ivory, 9 1/8 In. 5.00
Laurel, Sherbet, Jade 6.50
Laurel, Sugar, Jade, Tall 6.00
    LILY MEDALLION, see American Sweetheart
    LINCOLN DRAPE, see Princess
Lincoln Inn, Sugar & Creamer, Red 30.00
    LITTLE HOSTESS, see Moderntone Little Hostess
    LOOP, see Lace Edge
    LORAIN, see No. 615
    LOUISA, see Floragold
    LOVEBIRDS, see Georgian
    LYDIA RAY, see New Century
Madrid, Bowl, Amber, 5 In. ....3.50 To 5.00
Madrid, Bowl, Amber, 9 1/2 In. 14.00
Madrid, Bowl, Green, 8 In. 15.00
Madrid, Bowl, Vegetable, Oval, Blue, 10 In. 15.00
Madrid, Butter, Cover, Amber .... 52.00 To 90.00
Madrid, Butter, Cover, Green 68.00
Madrid, Cake Plate, Round, Amber, 11 1/4 In. 14.00
Madrid, Cake Plate, Round, Pink, 11 1/4 In. 12.00
Madrid, Candlestick, Amber, Pair 20.00
Madrid, Cookie Jar, Cover, Amber 35.00
Madrid, Creamer, Green 6.50
Madrid, Cup & Saucer, Blue 12.00
Madrid, Cup, Amber ....3.00 To 4.00
Madrid, Cup, Blue 11.00
Madrid, Grill Plate, Green 13.50
Madrid, Jello Mold, Amber, 4 Piece 8.00
Madrid, Pitcher, Square, Amber, 60 Oz., 8 In. 30.00
Madrid, Pitcher, Square, Blue, 60 Oz., 8 In. ....80.00 To 130.00
Madrid, Plate, Amber, 71/2 In. 5.00
Madrid, Platter, Blue, 11 1/2 In. 17.50
Madrid, Platter, Green, 11 1/2 In. 10.00
Madrid, Salt & Pepper, Flat, Amber .... 30.00 To 32.00
Madrid, Salt & Pepper, Flat, Green 54.00

Madrid, Saucer, Amber 2.50
Madrid, Sherbet, Amber .... 3.00 To 3.50
Madrid, Sherbet, Blue 9.50
Madrid, Sherbet, Green 6.00
Madrid, Soup, Cream, Amber 7.00
Madrid, Sugar & Creamer, Cover, Amber 30.00
Madrid, Sugar, Blue 10.00
Madrid, Tumbler, Amber, 3 7/8 In. 10.00
Madrid, Tumbler, Amber, 4 1/4 In. 8.50
Madrid, Tumbler, Amber, 5 1/2 In. 17.00
Madrid, Tumbler, Blue, 5 1/2 In. 25.00
MAGNOLIA, see Dogwood
Manhattan, Ashtray, Round, Crystal 8.00
Manhattan, Bowl, Crystal, 9 In. 11.00
Manhattan, Bowl, Handles, Crystal, 4 1/2 In. 5.00
Manhattan, Bowl, Handles, Crystal, 5 3/8 In. 5.50
Manhattan, Candlestick, Crystal 6.00
Manhattan, Candy Dish, 3–Footed, Pink 7.50
Manhattan, Compote, Pink 15.00
Manhattan, Creamer 5.00
Manhattan, Plate, Crystal, 6 In. 3.00
Manhattan, Plate, Crystal, 10 1/4 In. .... 8.00 To 10.00
MANY WINDOWS, see Roulette
MAYFAIR, see Mayfair Open Rose
Mayfair Open Rose, Bowl, Blue, 5 1/2 In. 35.00
Mayfair Open Rose, Bowl, Pink, 10 In. 14.00
Mayfair Open Rose, Butter, Cover, Pink 35.00
Mayfair Open Rose, Candy Dish, Cover, Pink 30.00
Mayfair Open Rose, Cookie Jar, Cover, Blue 185.00
Mayfair Open Rose, Cookie Jar, Cover, Pink 32.00
Mayfair Open Rose, Cup & Saucer, Blue 55.00
Mayfair Open Rose, Cup & Saucer, Cup Ring, Pink 34.00
Mayfair Open Rose, Cup, Pink 12.00
Mayfair Open Rose, Decanter, Stopper, Pink .... 80.00 To 105.00
Mayfair Open Rose, Fruit Bowl, Pink, 12 In. 30.00
Mayfair Open Rose, Goblet, Pink, 2 1/2 Oz., 4 In. 65.00
Mayfair Open Rose, Grill Plate, Blue, 9 1/2 In. 25.00
Mayfair Open Rose, Pitcher, Pink, 6 In. 33.00
Mayfair Open Rose, Platter, Open Handles, Blue, 12 In. 35.00
Mayfair Open Rose, Salt & Pepper, Flat, Blue 110.00
Mayfair Open Rose, Salt & Pepper, Pink .... 38.00 To 42.00
Mayfair Open Rose, Sandwich Server, Green .... 18.00 To 24.00
Mayfair Open Rose, Saucer, Cup Ring, Pink 18.00
Mayfair Open Rose, Soup, Cream, Pink 34.00
Mayfair Open Rose, Sugar, Blue 47.00
Mayfair Open Rose, Tumbler, Footed, Pink, 3 1/4 In. 42.50
Mayfair Open Rose, Tumbler, Footed, Pink, 5 1/4 In. 25.00
Mayfair Open Rose, Tumbler, Pink, 4 1/2 In. 22.00
MEADOW FLOWER, see No. 618
MEANDERING VINE, see Madrid
MISS AMERICA, see also English Hobnail
Miss America, Bowl, Oval, Crystal, 10 In. 6.00
Miss America, Bowl, Pink, 6 1/4 In. .... 9.00 To 13.00
Miss America, Cake Plate, Crystal 16.50
Miss America, Candy Jar, Cover, Pink .... 90.00 To 95.00
Miss America, Compote, Pink 12.00
Miss America, Creamer, Pink 12.00
Miss America, Cup & Saucer, Crystal 10.00
Miss America, Goblet, Crystal, 4 3/4 In. 15.00
Miss America, Goblet, Pink, 4 3/4 In. 48.00
Miss America, Grill Plate, Crystal 4.50
Miss America, Grill Plate, Pink 13.50
Miss America, Plate, Crystal, 8 1/2 In. 3.00

No. 612

Mt. Pleasant

Don't use ammonia on glasses with gold or silver decorations.

If two tumblers get stuck when stacked, try putting cold water into the inside glass, then put both into hot water up to the lower rim.

Miss America, Plate, Crystal, 10 1/4 In.	6.50
Miss America, Plate, Pink, 10 1/4 In.	15.00
Miss America, Platter, Oval, Pink	16.00 To 20.00
Miss America, Salt & Pepper, Crystal	20.00
Miss America, Sugar, Crystal	3.50
Miss America, Tumbler, Crystal, 5 3/4 In.	20.00
MODERNE ART, see Tea Room	
Moderntone Little Hostess, Teapot, Turquoise	20.00
Moderntone, Bowl, Platonite, 5 In.	2.25
Moderntone, Bowl, Platonite, 8 3/4 In.	5.00
Moderntone, Butter, Cover, Cobalt Blue	65.00
Moderntone, Creamer, Cobalt Blue	7.00
Moderntone, Cup & Saucer, Cobalt Blue	8.00
Moderntone, Custard Cup, Cobalt Blue	10.50
Moderntone, Plate, Cobalt Blue, 5 7/8 In.	3.00
Moderntone, Plate, Cobalt Blue, 8 7/8 In.	8.50 To 9.50
Moderntone, Plate, Platonite, 8 7/8 In.	4.00
Moderntone, Platter, Yellow, 12 In.	11.00
Moderntone, Salt & Pepper, Cobalt Blue	32.50
Moderntone, Salt & Pepper, Platonite	8.00
Moderntone, Sherbet, Cobalt Blue	8.00
Moderntone, Sherbet, Platonite	2.25
Moderntone, Sugar, Crystal	6.00
Moderntone, Sugar, Pink	4.50
Moderntone, Tumbler, Green, 5 Oz.	12.50
Moderntone, Tumbler, Platonite, 9 Oz.	3.50
MOLLY, see Imperial Plain Octagon	
Moondrops, Butter, Cover, Cobalt Blue	330.00
Moondrops, Candlestick, Wings, Cobalt Blue, Pair	80.00
Moondrops, Cup & Saucer, Ruby	9.50 To 12.50
Moondrops, Decanter, Rocket Top, Crystal	55.00
Moondrops, Plate, Ruby, 8 1/2 In.	11.00
Moondrops, Plate, Ruby, 9 1/2 In.	8.50
Moondrops, Sugar & Creamer, Ruby, 2 3/4 In.	20.00
Moondrops, Whiskey Set, Ruby, 7 Piece	95.00
Moonstone, Candleholder, Crystal, Pair	14.00
Moonstone, Candy Jar, Cover, Crystal	17.00
Moonstone, Plate, Crystal, 6 1/4 In.	2.50
Moonstone, Plate, Ruffled, Crystal, 10 In.	14.00
Moonstone, Powder Box, Cover, Crystal	11.00 To 15.00
Mt.Pleasant, Bowl, Mayonnaise, 3 Footed, Black, 5 1/2 In.	16.00
Mt.Pleasant, Bowl, Square, 2 Handles, Cobalt Blue, 8 In.	20.00

Mt.Pleasant, Creamer, Black 11.50
Mt.Pleasant, Plate, Cobalt Blue, 7 In. 6.00
Mt.Pleasant, Sugar & Creamer, Cobalt Blue, Platinum Trim 24.00
Mt.Pleasant, Sugar & Creamer, Tray, Black 95.00
New Century, Bowl, Green, 8 In. 12.00
New Century, Goblet, Wine, Green, 12 Piece 125.00
New Century, Pitcher, Cobalt Blue, 9 1/2 In. 48.00
New Century, Salt & Pepper, Green 25.00
New Century, Sherbet, Green 6.00
New Century, Tumbler, Amethyst, 5 Oz., 3 1/2 In. 6.50
Newport, Creamer, Amethyst 10.00
Newport, Plate, Amethyst, 8 1/2 In. 7.50
Newport, Plate, Cobalt Blue, 8 1/2 In. 3.75
Newport, Soup, Cream, Amethyst 10.00
Newport, Sugar & Creamer, Cobalt Blue 20.00
Newport, Sugar, Cover, Cobalt Blue 8.00
Newport, Tumbler, Cobalt Blue, 4 1/2 In. 25.00
    NO. 601, see Avocado
No.610, Bowl, Green, 8 1/2 In. 15.00
No.610, Relish, 4 Sections, Pink 45.00
No.612, Creamer, Green 10.00
No.612, Cup, Green 6.50
No.612, Tumbler, Yellow 12.00
No.615, Relish, 4 Sections, Yellow 18.00
No.615, Sugar, Green 10.00
No.615, Tumbler, Crystal, 4 3/4 In. 15.00
No.616, Cup, Crystal 5.00
No.616, Plate, Green, 11 In. 17.00
No.616, Plate, Platinum Trim, 8 In. 4.00
No.618, Bowl, Crystal, 6 In. 19.00
No.618, Cup & Saucer, Amber 8.00
No.618, Cup & Saucer, Crystal ....8.00 To 10.50
No.618, Cup, Crystal 5.00
No.618, Plate, Crystal, 6 In. 2.50
No.618, Relish, Crystal .... 10.00 To 15.00
No.618, Sherbet, Crystal .... 12.00 To 14.50
No.618, Soup, Cream, Crystal 16.00
No.618, Sugar & Creamer, Amber 15.00
No.618, Sugar & Creamer, Crystal ....7.00 To 10.00
No.618, Sugar, Crystal 5.00
No.618, Tumbler, Crystal, 4 1/4 In. 15.00
No.620, Bowl, Amber, 4 1/2 In. 6.00
No.620, Bowl, Amber, 9 3/8 In. 20.00
No.620, Bowl, Vegetable, Oval, Amber, 10 In. 12.00
No.620, Grill Plate, Amber 12.00
No.620, Grill Plate, Crystal, 10 1/4 In. 7.50
No.620, Plate, Amber, 7 3/8 In. 5.00
No.620, Plate, Amber, 9 3/8 In. 5.00
No.620, Platter, Amber 9.00
No.620, Saucer, Amber 1.00
No.620, Sherbet, Amber 5.50
No.620, Soup, Cream, Amber 6.00
No.620, Sugar & Creamer, Amber 12.00
    NO. 622, see Pretzel
    NO. 624, see Christmas Candy
Normandie, Bowl, Amber, 5 In. 2.25
Normandie, Bowl, Oval, Amber, 10 In. 11.00
Normandie, Cup & Saucer, Pink ....5.00 To 8.50
Normandie, Plate, Pink, 8 In. ....5.00 To 5.50
Normandie, Plate, Pink, 11 In. 40.00
Normandie, Saucer, Pink 1.25
Normandie, Sherbet, Amber 5.00
Normandie, Sherbet, Pink ....3.00 To 6.25
Normandie, Sugar, Cover, Amber 70.00

OATMEAL LACE SCROLL, see Princess Feather
Old Cafe, Bowl, Closed Handles, Pink, 9 In. 7.00
Old Cafe, Bowl, Crystal, 3 3/4 In. 6.50
Old Cafe, Candy Dish, Crystal 4.00
Old Cafe, Pitcher, Pink, 80 Oz. .... 65.00 To 75.00
Old Cafe, Plate, Pink, 10 In. .... 15.50 To 17.00
Old English, Eggcup, Crystal 4.50
OLD FLORENTINE, see Florentine No. 1
OPALESCENT HOBNAIL, see Moonstone
OPEN LACE, see Lace Edge
OPEN ROSE, see Mayfair Open Rose
OPEN SCALLOP, see Lace Edge
OPTIC DESIGN, see Raindrops
Orange Blossom, Bowl, White, 5 1/2 In. 1.75
OREGON GRAPE, see Woolworth
ORIENTAL POPPY, see Florentine No. 2
OXFORD, see Chinex Classic
Oyster & Pearl, Bowl, Crystal, 10 1/2 In. .... 15.00 To 16.00
Oyster & Pearl, Bowl, Heart Shape, White, Pink 5.00
Oyster & Pearl, Bowl, Pink, 10 1/2 In. 7.50
Oyster & Pearl, Bowl, Red, 10 1/2 In. .... 30.00 To 32.00
Oyster & Pearl, Candleholder, Fired-On Green, Pair 12.00
Oyster & Pearl, Candleholder, Pink, Pair 12.00
Oyster & Pearl, Candleholder, Red, Pair 30.00
Oyster & Pearl, Plate, Crystal, 13 1/2 In. .... 9.00 To 9.50
Oyster & Pearl, Plate, Red, 13 1/2 In. .... 26.00 To 30.00
Oyster & Pearl, Relish, Pink, 10 1/4 In. .... 5.00 To 8.00
PANELED ASTER, see Madrid
PANELED CHERRY BLOSSOM, see Cherry Blossom
PANSY & DORIC, see Doric & Pansy
PARROT, see Sylvan
Patrician, Bowl, Amber, 5 In. 4.50
Patrician, Bowl, Amber, 8 1/2 In. 30.00
Patrician, Bowl, Green, 5 In. 6.00
Patrician, Butter, Cover, Amber .... 55.00 To 58.00
Patrician, Butter, Cover, Green .... 70.00 To 75.00
Patrician, Cookie Jar, Cover, Amber .... 52.00 To 80.00
Patrician, Cookie Jar, Cover, Crystal 58.00
Patrician, Cookie Jar, Cover, Green 275.00
Patrician, Cup & Saucer, Green 11.00
Patrician, Cup, Pink 8.00
Patrician, Grill Plate, Amber 9.00
Patrician, Grill Plate, Yellow, 11 In. 9.00
Patrician, Pitcher, Amber, 8 In. 80.00
Patrician, Plate, Amber, 7 1/2 In. 7.00
Patrician, Plate, Amber, 9 In. .... 5.50 To 7.50
Patrician, Plate, Green, 6 In. 4.00
Patrician, Plate, Green, 7 1/2 In. 8.50
Patrician, Sherbet, Amber 6.00
Patrician, Soup, Cream, Amber .... 8.00 To 11.00
Patrician, Soup, Cream, Pink 15.00
Patrician, Sugar & Creamer, Amber .... 9.00 To 12.00
Patrician, Tumbler, Amber, 4 1/2 In. .... 17.50 To 20.00
Patrician, Tumbler, Footed, Green, 5 1/4 In. 36.00
Pear Optic, Cup & Saucer, Green 3.50
Pear Optic, Cup, Green 3.00
PEBBLE OPTIC, see Raindrops
PETAL, see Petalware
PETAL SWIRL, see Swirl
Petalware, Bowl, Crystal, 5 3/4 In. 2.75

Petalware, Bowl, Monax, 5 3/4 In. 4.50
Petalware, Bowl, Monax, 9 In. 12.00
Petalware, Creamer, Monax 4.50
Petalware, Cup & Saucer, Cremax 5.00
Petalware, Cup & Saucer, Monax 5.00
Petalware, Plate, Cremax, 6 In. 1.50
Petalware, Plate, Monax, 6 In. .... 1.50 To 2.00
Petalware, Plate, Monax, 9 In. 4.00
Petalware, Plate, Pink, 8 In. 1.00
Petalware, Sugar, Cremax 4.00
Petalware, Sugar, Monax 4.00
    PIE CRUST, see Cremax
    PINEAPPLE & FLORAL, see No. 618
    PINWHEEL, see Sierra
Pioneer, Bowl, 11 In. 9.00
    POINSETTIA, see Floral
    POPPY NO. 1, see Florentine No. 1
    POPPY NO. 2, see Florentine No. 2
    PRETTY POLLY PARTY DISHES, see also Doric & Pansy
Pretty Polly Party Dishes, Cup & Saucer, Pink 28.00
Pretty Polly Party Dishes, Cup & Saucer, Ultramarine 22.50
Pretty Polly Party Dishes, Sugar, Pink 30.00
Pretzel, Celery, Crystal 1.50
Pretzel, Creamer, Crystal 4.50
Pretzel, Cup & Saucer, Crystal 3.00
    PRIMUS, see Madrid
Princess Feather, Plate, Crystal, 8 In. 6.00
Princess, Bowl, Hat Shape, Green, 9 1/2 In. 25.00
Princess, Bowl, Vegetable, Oval, Green .... 14.00 To 16.50
Princess, Butter, Cover, Green .... 60.00 To 70.00
Princess, Butter, Cover, Pink 65.00
Princess, Candy Dish, Cover, Green 40.00
Princess, Cookie Jar, Cover, Green 35.00
Princess, Creamer, Topaz 10.00
Princess, Cup & Saucer, Green 12.00
Princess, Cup & Saucer, Topaz .... 7.50 To 10.00
Princess, Pitcher, Green, 6 In. .... 28.50 To 34.00
Princess, Pitcher, Green, 8 In. 28.50
Princess, Pitcher, Pink, 8 In. 35.00
Princess, Plate, Topaz, 5 1/2 In. 2.50
Princess, Plate, Topaz, 9 In. .... 8.00 To 10.00
Princess, Sherbet, Green .... 10.00 To 17.50
Princess, Sugar, Topaz 9.25
Princess, Tumbler, Footed, Topaz, 5 1/4 In. 14.00
    PRISMATIC LINE, see Queen Mary
    PROVINCIAL, see Bubble
    PYRAMID, see No. 610
Queen Mary, Bowl, Crystal, 8 3/4 In. 5.50

Royal Lace

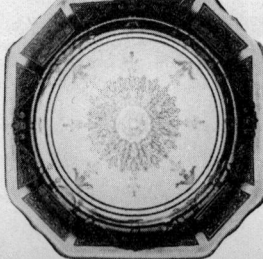

Princess

Normandie

Queen Mary, Bowl, Pink, 4 In. 3.00
Queen Mary, Butter, Cover, Crystal .... 15.00 To 19.00
Queen Mary, Candleholder, Double, Crystal, Pair 12.00
Queen Mary, Candy Dish, Cover, Pink 25.00
Queen Mary, Creamer, Pink .... 3.50 To 4.00
Queen Mary, Cup & Saucer, Crystal 6.50
Queen Mary, Plate, Crystal, 9 3/4 In. 8.75
Queen Mary, Plate, Pink, 9 3/4 In. 20.00
Queen Mary, Plate, Pink, 12 In. 10.00
Queen Mary, Sherbet, Footed, Pink .... 3.00 To 4.50
Queen Mary, Sugar, Pink 4.50
Queen Mary, Tumbler, Pink, 4 In. .... 4.00 To 5.50
Radiance, Butter, Cover, Ice Blue 98.00
Radiance, Sugar & Creamer, Ice Blue 20.00
Raindrops, Cup & Saucer, Crystal 5.00
Raindrops, Cup & Saucer, Green 5.00
Raindrops, Sherbet, Green .... 4.00 To 4.50
Raindrops, Whiskey, Crystal 4.00
    RASPBERRY BAND, see Laurel
    REX, see No. 610
    RIBBED, see Manhattan
    RIBBON CANDY, see Pretzel
Ribbon, Bowl, Green, 4 In. 4.00
Ribbon, Bowl, Green, 8 In. .... 10.00 To 18.00
Ribbon, Candy Dish, Cover, Green .... 25.00 To 28.00
Ribbon, Plate, Green, 6 1/4 In. .... 1.25 To 2.00
Ribbon, Salt & Pepper, Green .... 17.50 To 18.00
Ribbon, Tumbler, Green, 6 In. 17.00
Ring, Creamer, Crystal 3.00
Ring, Cup & Saucer, Crystal, Silver Trim 5.50
Ring, Cup, Green 3.50
Ring, Pitcher, Crystal, 8 In. 10.00
Ring, Pitcher, Pink, 80 Oz., 8 1/2 In. 12.00
Ring, Plate, Green, 6 1/4 In. 1.50
Ring, Plate, Green, Off–Center Ring, 6 1/2 In. 4.50
Ring, Tumbler, Footed, Crystal, 6 1/2 In. 5.00
Ring, Tumbler, Green, 5 1/8 In. 4.50
Rock Crystal, Bonbon, Crystal, 7 1/2 In. .... 9.00 To 12.00
Rock Crystal, Cake Plate, Footed, Green 40.00
Rock Crystal, Cup & Saucer, Crystal .... 11.00 To 13.00
Rock Crystal, Goblet, Footed, Crystal, 7 1/2 In. 12.00
Rock Crystal, Sugar, Amber 30.00
Rock Crystal, Tumbler, Crystal, 5 Oz. 9.00
Rock Crystal, Tumbler, Crystal, 9 Oz. 12.00
Rose Cameo, Tumbler, Footed, Green, 5 In. 10.00
    ROSE LACE, see Royal Lace
Rosemary, Bowl, Amber, 5 In. .... 4.00 To 4.50
Rosemary, Bowl, Oval, Amber, 10 In. .... 8.50 To 10.00
Rosemary, Creamer, Amber .... 6.00 To 6.50
Rosemary, Cup, Amber 4.00
Rosemary, Plate, Amber, 6 3/4 In. 3.75
Rosemary, Plate, Amber, 9 1/2 In. .... 4.00 To 5.00
Rosemary, Platter, Oval, Amber 10.00
Rosemary, Sugar, Amber .... 6.00 To 6.50
Rosemary, Sugar, Pink 9.00
Rosemary, Tumbler, Amber, 4 1/4 In. 18.00
Roulette, Bowl, Green, 9 In. 8.00
Roulette, Cup & Saucer, Green .... 4.00 To 6.50
Roulette, Plate, Green, 8 1/2 In. .... 3.00 To 4.25
Roulette, Tumbler, Footed, Green, 5 1/2 In. 15.00
Roulette, Tumbler, Pink, 5 1/8 In. 7.50

Roulette, Whiskey, Pink 5.00
Round Robin, Cup, Green 3.00
Roxana, Bowl, Yellow, 4 1/2 In. 4.00
Royal Lace, Bowl, Oval, Cobalt Blue, 11 In. 35.00
Royal Lace, Bowl, Oval, Green, 11 In. 11.00
Royal Lace, Bowl, Rolled Edge, Pink, 10 In. 27.50
Royal Lace, Bowl, Round, Pink, 10 In. .... 12.50 To 15.00
Royal Lace, Butter, Cover, Crystal 65.00
Royal Lace, Butter, Cover, Green .... 280.00 To 300.00
Royal Lace, Candlestick, Rolled Edge, Pink, Pair 40.00
Royal Lace, Cookie Jar, Cover, Cobalt Blue 250.00
Royal Lace, Cookie Jar, Cover, Crystal 20.00
Royal Lace, Cookie Jar, Cover, Green .... 50.00 To 60.00
Royal Lace, Cup & Saucer, Pink .... 12.50 To 14.00
Royal Lace, Green, 9 7/8 In. 18.00
Royal Lace, Pitcher, Cobalt Blue, 48 Oz. .... 70.00 To 75.00
Royal Lace, Pitcher, Cobalt Blue, 8 1/2 In. .... 145.00 To 160.00
Royal Lace, Pitcher, Crystal, 8 1/2 In. 30.00
Royal Lace, Plate, Pink, 6 In. 3.00
Royal Lace, Plate, Pink, 8 1/2 In. 4.00
Royal Lace, Plate, Pink, 9 7/8 In. .... 9.00 To 10.00
Royal Lace, Platter, Green .... 22.00 To 22.50
Royal Lace, Saucer, Crystal 2.50
Royal Lace, Sherbet, Metal Holder, Cobalt Blue 17.00
Royal Lace, Toddy Set, Amethyst 105.00
Royal Lace, Tumbler, Green, 4 1/8 In. 20.00
Royal Lace, Tumbler, Pink, 4 1/8 In. 11.00
Royal Ruby, Bowl, Red, 11 1/2 In. 15.00
Royal Ruby, Creamer, Flat, Red 4.50
Royal Ruby, Cup & Saucer, Red 4.00
Royal Ruby, Cup, Round, Red 2.25
Royal Ruby, Cup, Square, Red 2.25
Royal Ruby, Plate, Red, 7 In. 3.00
Royal Ruby, Punch Cup, Red .... 1.50 To 2.00
Royal Ruby, Soup, Dish, Red 7.00
Royal Ruby, Sugar, Flat, Red 4.50
Royal Ruby, Tumbler, Footed, Red, 2 1/2 Oz. 6.00
Royal Ruby, Tumbler, Red, 13 Oz. .... 3.00 To 5.00
Royal Ruby, Vase, Red, 6 1/2 In. .... 4.00 To 4.50
    RUSSIAN, see Holiday
S Pattern, Cake Plate, Amber, 13 In. 45.00
S Pattern, Cup & Saucer, Crystal 4.00
S Pattern, Cup, Thick, Crystal 2.00
S Pattern, Plate, Amber Band, 6 In. 2.00
S Pattern, Plate, Crystal, 8 In. 1.50
S Pattern, Sugar, Amber Band, Thin 5.00
S Pattern, Sugar, Footed, Thin, Crystal 3.25
S Pattern, Tumbler, Crystal, 4 In. 3.00
    SAIL BOAT, see White Ship
    SAILING SHIP, see White Ship
Sandwich Anchor Hocking, Bowl, Crystal, 4 7/8 In. 5.00
Sandwich Anchor Hocking, Bowl, Crystal, 8 In. 5.50
Sandwich Anchor Hocking, Butter, Cover, Crystal 28.00
Sandwich Anchor Hocking, Cup & Saucer, Crystal 3.00
Sandwich Anchor Hocking, Punch Cup, Opaque White 1.00
Sandwich Anchor Hocking, Punch Set, Crystal, 13 Piece 27.00
Sandwich Anchor Hocking, Sugar, Crystal 3.00
Sandwich Indiana, Ashtray, Club Shape, Crystal 2.00
Sandwich Indiana, Bowl, Crystal, 4 1/4 In. 3.00
Sandwich Indiana, Cup & Saucer, Crystal 3.50
Sandwich Indiana, Plate, Crystal, 10 1/2 In. 6.50
    SAWTOOTH, see English Hobnail
    SAXON, see Coronation
    SCROLL & STAR, see Princess Feather

Swirl

Sharon

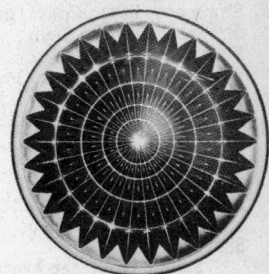

Windsor

SHAMROCK, see Cloverleaf
Sharon, Bowl, Amber, 5 In. 5.00
Sharon, Bowl, Amber, 8 1/2 In. .... 2.50 To 4.50
Sharon, Bowl, Pink, 5 In. 6.00
Sharon, Bowl, Pink, 8 1/2 In. 12.00
Sharon, Butter, Cover, Amber 35.00
Sharon, Butter, Cover, Pink 40.00
Sharon, Cake Plate, Pink, 11 1/2 In. 20.00
Sharon, Candy Jar, Cover, Amber 35.00
Sharon, Candy Jar, Cover, Green 120.00
Sharon, Candy Jar, Cover, Pink 35.00
Sharon, Creamer, Pink 10.00
Sharon, Cup & Saucer, Amber .... 10.00 To 10.50
Sharon, Cup & Saucer, Pink 13.50
Sharon, Cup, Pink .... 7.00 To 9.00
Sharon, Jam Dish, Pink 135.00
Sharon, Pitcher, Ice Lip, Pink .... 85.00 To 100.00
Sharon, Plate, Amber, 9 1/2 In. 6.50
Sharon, Plate, Pink, 9 1/2 In. .... 9.00 To 10.00
Sharon, Salt & Pepper, Pink 30.00
Sharon, Saltshaker, Amber 15.00
Sharon, Sherbet, Pink .... 8.00 To 9.00
Sharon, Sugar & Creamer, Amber 10.00
Sharon, Tumbler, Footed, Amber, 6 1/2 In. 40.00
Sharon, Tumbler, Footed, Pink, 6 1/2 In. .... 25.00 To 28.00
Sharon, Water Set, Pink, 7 Piece 185.00
SHEFFIELD, see Chinex Classic
SHELL, see Petalware
Sierra, Bowl, Green, 5 1/2 In. 8.00
Sierra, Pitcher, Pink, 6 1/2 In. 40.00
Sierra, Plate, Green, 6 1/2 In. 60.00
Sierra, Salt & Pepper, Pink 25.00

Sierra, Tumbler, Green, Footed, 4 1/2 In. 55.00
    SMOCKING, see Windsor
    SNOWFLAKE, see Doric
Spiral Flutes, Sugar, Amber 8.00
    SPIRAL OPTIC, see Spiral
Spiral, Butter Tub, Green 8.00
Spiral, Plate, Green, 8 1/2 In. .... 2.00 To 2.50
Spiral, Sherbet, Amber 2.50
Spiral, Sherbet, Pink 2.75
    SPOKE, see Patrician
Starlight, Sherbet, Crystal 6.50
    STIPPLED ROSE BAND, see S Pattern
    STRAWBERRY, see also Cherry–Berry
Strawberry, Bowl, Green, 4 In. 10.00
Strawberry, Butter, Cover, Green .... 100.00 To 135.00
Strawberry, Butter, Cover, Pink 111.00
Strawberry, Pitcher, Green 110.00
Strawberry, Sherbet, Green .... 6.00 To 6.75
Strawberry, Sugar, Cover, Green, Large 38.00
Sunburst, Cup, Crystal 3.00
Sunflower, Ashtray, Green 6.00
Sunflower, Ashtray, Pink 4.50
Sunflower, Cake Plate, Green .... 8.00 To 15.00
Sunflower, Cake Plate, Pink .... 8.50 To 9.00
Sunflower, Creamer, Pink 5.00
Sunflower, Plate, Pink, 9 In. 8.00
Sunflower, Sugar, Pink 11.00
    SWEET PEAR, see Avocado
Swirl, Bread Plate, Ultramarine 3.00
Swirl, Butter, Cover, Pink 125.00
Swirl, Candy Dish, 3–Footed, Pink .... 3.50 To 4.00
Swirl, Cup & Saucer, Pink 2.50
Swirl, Cup & Saucer, Ultramarine 10.25
Swirl, Cup, Utramarine 7.00
Swirl, Plate, Ultramarine, 6 1/2 In. 3.50
Swirl, Sandwich Server, Ultramarine 11.00
Swirl, Sugar & Creamer, Ultramarine 19.00
Swirl, Vase, Ultramarine, 8 1/2 In. 14.00
    SWIRLED BIG RIB, see Spiral
    SWIRLED SHARP RIB, see Diana
Sylvan, Bowl, Amber, 5 In. 7.00
Sylvan, Butter, Cover, Green .... 200.00 To 300.00
Sylvan, Cup, Green .... 16.00 To 20.00
Sylvan, Grill Plate, Round, Green 20.00
Sylvan, Plate, Green, 9 In. 10.00
Sylvan, Sherbet, Footed, Amber .... 6.00 To 9.00
Sylvan, Soup, Amber, 7 In. 25.00
    TASSELL, see Princess
Tea Room, Banana Boat, Footed, Green 60.00
Tea Room, Bowl, Oval, Pink, 9 1/2 In. 39.00
Tea Room, Candleholder, Green, Pair 26.00
Tea Room, Creamer, Green 8.00
Tea Room, Sugar, Footed, Green 13.00
Tea Room, Vase, Ruffled, Green, 9 In. 60.00
Thistle, Bowl, Pink, 5 1/2 In. 13.00
Thistle, Cup & Saucer, Pink 18.00
Thistle, Plate, Pink, 8 In. .... 6.00 To 8.00
    THREADING, see Old English
    THREE PARROT, see Sylvan
    THUMBPRINT, see Pear Optic

Tulip, Celery, 9 1/2 In. 6.00
Twisted Optic, Candy Jar, Green 25.00
Twisted Optic, Plate, Yellow, 8 In. 7.00
    VERNON, see No. 616
Versailles, Goblet, Cocktail, Blue 47.00
Versailles, Plate, Blue, 9 1/2 In. 30.00
    VERTICAL RIBBED, see Queen Mary
Victory, Bowl, Pink, 6 1/2 In. 7.50
Victory, Cup & Saucer, Amber 6.00
Victory, Cup & Saucer, Green 6.00
Vitrock, Creamer, White 3.00
Vitrock, Cup, White 2.00
    VIVID BANDS, see Petalware
    WAFFLE, see Waterford
Waterford, Butter, Cover, Crystal .... 12.00 To 20.00
Waterford, Butter, Cover, Pink 85.00
Waterford, Cake Plate, Crystal, 10 1/4 In. 3.50
Waterford, Creamer, Crystal 2.50
Waterford, Cup, Crystal .... 2.50 To 4.00
Waterford, Cup, Green 2.50
Waterford, Pitcher, Crystal, 80 Oz. 21.00
Waterford, Pitcher, Pink, 80 Oz. 70.00
Waterford, Plate, Crystal, 7 1/8 In. 2.50
Waterford, Relish, 5 Sections, Crystal 12.00
Waterford, Salt & Pepper, Crystal .... 5.00 To 5.50
Waterford, Sandwich Plate, Crystal, 13 3/4 In. 5.00
Waterford, Sherbet, Crystal .... 1.25 To 2.00
Waterford, Sugar & Creamer, Cover, Crystal 6.50
    WEDDING BAND, see Moderntone
    WESTMORELAND SANDWICH, see Princess Feather
    WHITE SAIL, see White Ship
White Ship, Pitcher Set, Blue, 7 Piece 70.00
White Ship, Roly Poly, Blue 7.00
White Ship, Water Set, 6 Piece 40.00
    WILD ROSE, see Dogwood
    WILDFLOWER, see No. 618
    WILDROSE WITH APPLE BLOSSOM, see Flower Garden with Butterflies
Windmill, Ice Bucket, Blue 20.00
Windmill, Ice Bucket, Holder, 7 Tumblers, Blue 105.00
    WINDSOR DIAMOND, see Windsor
Windsor, Butter, Cover, Crystal 18.00
Windsor, Butter, Cover, Pink .... 17.50 To 28.50
Windsor, Candlestick, Crystal, Pair 10.00
Windsor, Chop Plate, Green 19.00
Windsor, Chop Plate, Pink 20.00
Windsor, Cup & Saucer, Pink 8.00
Windsor, Cup, Pink 4.00
Windsor, Plate, Green, 9 In. 7.00
Windsor, Plate, Pink, 9 In. .... 9.00 To 9.50
Windsor, Platter, Green, 11 1/2 In. 11.00
Windsor, Salt & Pepper, Green 32.00
Windsor, Saucer, Pink .... 1.25 To 2.25
Windsor, Sherbet, Green 4.50
Windsor, Sugar, Cover, Pink 12.00
Windsor, Tray, Crystal, 4 X 4 In. 2.00
Windsor, Tumbler, Footed, Crystal, 7 1/4 In. 6.00
Windsor, Tumbler, Pink, 4 In. .... 7.50 To 10.00
    WINGED MEDALLION, see Madrid
Woolworth, Creamer, Pink 6.00
Woolworth, Pitcher, Ruffled Edge, Green, 8 1/2 In. 7.50

Woolworth, Plate, Green, 8 1/2 In.	7.00
Woolworth, Plate, Pink, 8 1/2 In.	7.00
Woolworth, Plate, Scalloped, Green, 8 1/2 In.	9.00
Woolworth, Relish, Divided, Chrome Holder, Green	8.00
Woolworth, Sugar, Green	9.00
X Design, Bowl, 7 5/8 In.	3.00
X Design, Bowl, Crystal, 8 3/4 In.	4.00
X Design, Bowl, Crystal, 10 1/2 In.	8.00
X Design, Dish, Refrigerator, Cover, Green, 4 X 8 In.	15.00

Derby porcelain was made in Derby, England, from 1756 to the present. The factory changed names and marks several times. Chelsea Derby (1770–1784), Crown Derby (1784–1811), and the modern Royal Crown Derby are some of the most famous periods of the factory.

DERBY, see also Chelsea; Crown Derby; Royal Crown Derby

DERBY, Bough Pot, Flowers, Vertical Panels of Gold, Marked, C.1835, 8 In.	1100.00
Candlestick, Punch As Nightwatchman, Holding Lantern, 9 1/2 In.	1350.00
Dish, On Shore of Posilipo Center, Lozenge Shape, C.1805, 12 In.	1100.00
Figurine, Boy, Holding Spaniel With 1 Hand, Other Raised, Marked	65.00
Figurine, Gardener, Holding Flask, Before Tree, C.1775, 11 1/4 In.	660.00
Figurine, Sheep, Ram & Ewe, Standing Before Cage, C.1780, 3 5/8 In.	495.00
Plate, Basket Mold, Fruit Sprigs, 4 Insects, C.1760, 10 1/16 In.	1980.00
Plate, Center Cluster of Flowers & Sprigs, C.1825, 10 In., Pair	2150.00
Platter, Botanical, Oval, C.1795, 10 1/2 In.	2640.00
Platter, Iron Red & Green Dots, Salmon Ground, C.1820, 20 In.	1430.00
Vase, Welsh Coast Scene, Bloor, 1820–40	850.00

The DeVilbiss Company has made atomizers of all types since 1888 but no longer makes the perfume bottle tops so popular with collectors. These were made from 1920 to 1968. The glass bottle may be by any of many manufacturers even if the atomizer says DeVilbiss.

DEVILBISS, Atomizer, Gold Crackle	37.00
Atomizer, Penguin	75.00
Atomizer, Squat, White, Gold Design, Tan Netting, Marked, 4 In.	59.00
Bottle, Throat Sprayer, Cobalt Blue	28.00
Lamp, Perfume, Lighthouse Shape, Trees, Moon, Brass Frame, 8 In.	145.00
Perfume Bottle, Atomizer, Gold Crackle, 4 3/4 In.	35.00
Perfume Bottle, Atomizer, Gold, Cranberry, Etched	35.00
Perfume Bottle, Atomizer, Opalescent Feathers, Gold Cap, Label	38.00
Perfume Bottle, Atomizer, Raspberry Pink	35.00
Perfume Bottle, Atomizer, Swirled White Opalescent, Feathers	20.00
Perfume Bottle, Blown, Gold Design	55.00
Perfume Bottle, Etched Vintage	60.00
Perfume Bottle, Intaglio Cut Floral, 1908	45.00
Perfume Bottle, Penguin, Atomizer, Lenox	195.00
Perfume Bottle, Pink, Silver Overlay, 1935 Junior Hop	45.00
Perfume Bottle, White Feather, Opaline	35.00

The comic strip "Dick Tracy" started in 1931. He was the hero of movies from 1937 to 1947, starred in a radio series in the 1940s and a television series in the 1950s. Memorabilia from all these activities is collected.

DICK TRACY, Badge, Detective Club, Brass	5.75 To 15.00
Badge, Detective, Hidden Coin Area	30.00
Badge, Inspector General, Promotional Paper	375.00
Badge, Junior G–Man, Brass, Gold & Black Accents, 1930s	10.00
Badge, Secret Service Patrol, Black, White, Gold Litho, 1938	15.00
Book, Better Little Book, Special F.B.I.Operative, Whitman, 1943	29.00
Book, Big Little Book, and The Bicycle Gang	20.00
Book, Capture of Boris Arson, Pop–Up, 1935, 20 Page	144.00
Book, Coloring, 1946	20.00
Book, Meets The Night Crawler, 1945	15.00

Button, Pink Back 17.00
Button, Secret Service Patrol Member, 1938 .... 18.00
Camera .... 20.00 To 42.00
Car, Squad, Tin, 7 In. 55.00
Card, Candy, Dick Tracy Carmels, 1930s Series Scene, 4 Piece 21.00
Doll, Bonnie Braids 250.00
Doll, Honeymoon, 1950s 150.00
Flashlight, Pocket, Secret Service, Tubular Plastic, 1939 .... 75.00
Game, Dick Tracy Detective, Board, 14 X 20 In. 48.00
Game, Playing Cards, 1934 .... 35.00
Game, Selchow & Righter, 1961 .... 25.00
Game, Super Detective Mystery, Cards, Magnifying Glass, Box, 1941 .... 35.00
Handcuffs 40.00
Lunch Box .... 25.00 To 35.00
Puppet 40.00
Ring, Adjustable, Silvered Metal, Quaker Oats, 1939 .... 175.00
Salt & Pepper, Dick & Junior, Chalkware 40.00
Suspenders, Box 50.00
Target, Tin, 1941, 9 1/2 X 9 1/2 In. 40.00
Wallet, Badge, Card, Kit 30.00
Wallet, Medal Badge & ID Card, 1950s 18.00
Wings, Air Detective, Brass, Airplane Center, 1938 .... 12.00
Wrist Radio, Battery Operated, 2-Way Talk & Signal, Remco, Box 30.00
     DICKENS WARE, see Royal Doulton; Weller

The Dionne quintuplets were born in Canada on May 28, 1934. The publicity about their birth and their special status as wards of the Canadian government made them famous throughout the world. Visitors could watch the girls play, reporters interviewed the girls and the staff, and thousands of special dolls and souvenirs were made picturing the quints at different ages. Emilie died in 1954, Marie in 1970. Yvonne, Annette, and Cecile still live in Canada.

DIONNE QUINTUPLETS, Book, Soon We'll Be Three, Whitman, 1936 .... 25.00
Book, Souvenir Views Quintland, Northern Ontario, 1938 .... 15.00
Book, Story of Dionne Quintuplets, Whitman No.937, 1935 .... 22.50
Book, We're 2 Years Old, 1936 .... 15.00
Calendar, 1936 .... 22.00
Calendar, 1937 .... 40.00
Calendar, 1946 .... 15.00
Calendar, 1949 .... 15.00
Calendar, 1950, Sweet Sixteen, Yellowed 18.00
Calendar, 1953, Girls At Piano, Full Pad 15.00
Doll Set, Composition 285.00
Doll, Bisque, Japan, 5 Piece 45.00
Doll, Toddler, Open Mouth, Wig, Original Clothes, 16 In. 295.00
Handkerchief 28.00
Paper Doll, Palm Olive Mailer, Cut, 1937 .... 45.00
Poster, 5 of A Kind, Movie, 1938, Cutdown To 12 X 16 In. 40.00

Walt Disney and his company introduced many comic characters to the world. Collectors search for examples of the work of the Disney Studios and the many commercial products modeled after his characters. These collectibles are called "Disneyana."

DISNEYANA, Album, Snow White & 7 Dwarfs, 1938 .... 35.00
Bank, Dime Register, Mickey Mouse, Lithographed, 1939 .... 75.00
Bank, Mickey Mouse Club, Smoky Glass 30.00
Bank, Mickey Mouse's Head, Painted Face, 1968 .... 14.50
Bank, Mickey Mouse, Movable Head & Arm, Plastic, Hong Kong, 6 In. 10.00
Bank, Mickey Mouse, Silver Plate, England 25.00
Bank, Mickey Mouse, Standing, Iron, 9 1/2 In. 50.00
Bank, Mickey Mouse, Suitcase, Tin 145.00
Bank, Pinocchio's Head, 1970s 15.00
Blocks, Mickey Mouse, 6 Different Pictures, Suitcase, 12 Blocks 29.00
Boat, Pull Toy, Donald Duck Tricky Rider, Red, White, Plastic 20.00

Book, America On Parade, Souvenir	12.00
Book, Big Little Book, Donald Duck Lays Down The Law, 1948	33.00
Book, Big Little Book, Mickey Mouse & Night Prowlers	10.00
Book, Big Little Book, Mickey Mouse & Pluto The Racer, 1936	30.00
Book, Big Little Book, Mickey Mouse & The Magic Lamp, 1942	44.00
Book, Big Little Book, Mickey Mouse and The Bat Bandit, 1935	30.00
Book, Big Little Book, Mickey Mouse In Blaggard Castle, 1934	98.00
Book, Big Little Book, Mickey Mouse Sails For Treasure Island	18.00
Book, Big Little Book, Mickey Mouse The Detective, 1934	35.00
Book, Big Little Book, Mickey Mouse, Silly Symphonies Stories	62.00
Book, Brer Rabbit, Tales By Uncle Remus	28.00
Book, Coloring, Pinocchio, 1939	19.00
Book, Coloring, Visit To Walt Disney, 1971	15.00
Book, Donald Duck & His Nephews, Cloth Bound, 1939–40	20.00
Book, Donald Duck & The Witch, Golden	5.00
Book, Dumbo of The Circus, Garden City	18.00
Book, Giant Funbook, Mickey Mouse, Whitman, 448 Pages, 1980, Unused	12.00
Book, Mickey Mouse & The Mouseketeers, Ghost Town Adventure	3.00
Book, Mickey Mouse Sees The USA, 1944	60.00
Book, Mickey Mouse The Kitten–Sitter, Little Golden Book	3.00
Book, Mickey Mouse, 1931	60.00
Book, Penny Series, Goofy & Wilbur, 1938–39	10.00
Book, Pinocchio, Cloth Bound, 1939–40	20.00
Book, Pop–Up, Goofy & Chimp, 1979	7.50
Book, Pop–Up, Mickey Mouse, 1933	195.00
Book, Pop–Up, Minnie Mouse, 1933	175.00
Book, Snow White & 7 Dwarfs, Linen–Like	27.00
Book, Song, Snow White & 7 Dwarfs, 1938	25.00
Booklet, Cartoon, Wheaties, 1951	25.00
Bottle Cap, Mickey Mouse, Tin Litho, 1930s	8.00
Bowl, ABC, Donald Duck, Beetleware, Walt Disney	15.00
Bowl, Cereal, Mickey Mouse, 1930s	75.00
Bracelet, Charm, Pluto, Nephew of Donald Duck, Sterling Silver	95.00
Bread Wrapper, Donald Duck, Debos, Red, Brown, Blue, 17 X 16 In.	15.00
Bubble Buster, Mickey Mouse	35.00
Bubble Pipe, Donald Duck, Plastic, Lido, Package, 1950s	5.00
Bucket, Sand, Shovel, 3 Little Pigs	75.00
Cake Mold, Dumbo	20.00
Camera, Bugs Bunny	15.00
Camera, Donald Duck, Box	45.00 To 60.00
Camera, Instant, Bugs Bunny, 1975	11.00
Candle Holder, Birthday Cake, Plastic, Best, 1950s, 5 Piece	5.00
Candy Container, Donald Duck, Hollow Bisque, Marked, 6 In.	30.00
Card, Bubble Gum, Mickey Mouse, No.8, 1930s	12.00
Card, Christmas, Mickey, Minnie, Pluto, Little Pigs, 1933, 7 X 9 In.	266.00
Card, Feeling Better, 3 Cheers, Hall Bros., Unused, Envelope	15.00
Card, Game, Donald Duck, Whitman	18.00
Card, Game, Mickey Mouse, Russell	9.00
Card, Game, Snow White, Russell	7.00
DISNEYANA, CEL, see Animation Art	
Charm, Minnie Mouse, Figural, Painted Metal, 1930s	25.00
Charm, Pluto, Plastic, Gray, 1 In.	4.00
Clicker, Jiminy Cricket, United Way Premium, 1950s, 1 3/4 In.	12.00
Clock Radio, Electronic, Mickey Mouse	50.00
Clock, Alarm, Big Bad Wolf, Ingersoll, 1930s	600.00
Clock, Alarm, Cinderella, Bradley, 2 Bells, 1970s, Small	35.00
Clock, Alarm, Mickey Mouse, Bradley, Locomotive Shape	18.00
Clock, Alarm, Walking Pie–Eye Mickey, Arm Movement, Bradley, 1970s	65.00
Clock, Bambi, Bayard, Box	200.00
Clock, Pinocchio, Bayard, Box	350.00
Clock, Snow White, Bayard, Box	400.00
Club House, Mickey Mouse, Cardboard, 1950s, 50 In.	125.00
Coat Rack, Snow White & 7 Dwarfs, Wooden, 3 Pegs, 12 1/2 X 7 In.	68.00
Comic Book, Donald Duck Fun Book	101.00

Comic Book, Donald Duck, In Golden Christmas Tree, Carl Barks 100.00
Comic Book, Dumbo, 4 Colors 1.00
Cookie Cutter, Minnie Mouse, Tin 12.00
Cookie Jar, Donald Duck On Train, 10 In. 25.00
Cookie Jar, Donald Duck, Jose Carioca, Turnabout, Painted 95.00
Cookie Jar, Dumbo 55.00
Cookie Jar, Mickey & Minnie Turnabout, Leeds 90.00
Cookie Jar, Mickey Mouse, On Drum 78.00
Costume, Mickey Mouse, Mask, Blouse, Bloomers, 1934 .... 375.00
Crayons, Donald Duck, Mickey Mouse, Metal Box, Transgram Co. 35.00
Creamer, Dumbo 22.00
Dental Certificate, Disney Characters, Framed 30.00
Doll, Donald Duck, Sieberling, 6 In. 145.00
Doll, Dopey, Cloth, Dean, 11 In. 65.00
Doll, Dopey, Composition, Clothes, Knickerbocker, 1940s, 12 In. 100.00
Doll, Goofy, Plastic, Hinged Ears, Red Turtleneck, Blue Jeans, 7 In 17.00
Doll, Grumpy, Cloth, Plastic Hands, Purple Hat, Pink Pants, 7 In. 9.00
Doll, Happy, Red Hat, Yellow Jacket, Blue Pants, Japan, 8 In. 8.00
Doll, Mickey & Minnie Mouse, Cloth, 18 In., Pair 1500.00
Doll, Mickey Mouse, Stuffed, California, 16 In. 22.00
Doll, Minnie Mouse, Wooden, 5 In. 190.00
Doll, Pinocchio, Blue Shorts, Pink Cap, Jointed, Poland, 8 In. 30.00
Doll, Pinocchio, Composition, Knickerbocker, 1940s, 14 In. 340.00
Doll, Pinocchio, Composition, Walt Disney Prod., 9 In. 125.00
Doll, Pinocchio, Knickerbocker, 14 In. 175.00
Doll, Snow White, Suitcase, Madame Alexander, 1952, 18 In. 550.00
Door Plate, Disneyland 18.00
Doorstop, 7 Dwarfs, Cast Iron, 9 1/2 In. 600.00
Drum, Snow White 45.00
Figurine, Baby Flower, American Pottery 60.00
Figurine, Bambi, American Pottery 60.00
Figurine, Bashful & Happy Playing Instruments, 2 In. 40.00
Figurine, Cinderella, Ceramic Arts Studio 70.00
Figurine, Daisy Duck, 5 In. 20.00
Figurine, Dalmation, Ceramic, 6 Different Puppies, 5 In. 60.00
Figurine, Donald Duck, 1940, Rubber, 6 In. 4.50
Figurine, Donald Duck, Bill Open, Hands On Hip, Bisque, 3 In. 68.00
Figurine, Donald Duck, Bisque, Porcelain, Bird Watching, WDP, 4 In. 12.00
Figurine, Donald Duck, Blue Sailor Hat, Jacket, Pink Bowtie, 6 In. 25.00
Figurine, Donald Duck, Marx, Green, Plastic, 6 In. 6.00
Figurine, Donald Duck, Sailor Suit, Green Scooter, Bisque, 3 In. 55.00
Figurine, Donald Duck, Sieberling, Cracking Paint, 1930s, Large 90.00
Figurine, Dopey, Bisque, Japan, 2 In. 20.00
Figurine, Dumbo, Yellow Hat, Rubber Head, Plastic Body, 7 1/2 In. 14.00
Figurine, Elmer The Elephant, Sieberling, 1930s 70.00
Figurine, Ferdinand The Bull, Sieberling 35.00
Figurine, Figaro, Multi Products 85.00
Figurine, Goofy, Bisque, Right Hand Back, Left To Side, 1 3/4 In. 45.00
Figurine, Goofy, Green Plastic, Louis Marx, 1971, 6 1/4 In. 5.00
Figurine, Grumpy, Bisque, 2 In. 15.00
Figurine, Mickey Mouse, Green, Plastic, Marx, 1971, 5 3/4 In. 5.00
Figurine, Mickey Mouse, Standing, Ceramic, Japan, 1970s, 3 In. 8.00
Figurine, Minnie Mouse With Umbrella, Bisque, 4 3/4 In. 95.00
Figurine, Minnie Mouse, Mandolin, Bisque, Japan, 1930s, 3 1/2 In. 68.00
Figurine, Pinocchio, Green, National Pottery, 3 In. 40.00
Figurine, Pinocchio, Wood Jointed, Composition Head, 8 In. 22.00
Figurine, Pluto, Bisque, Sitting, 2 1/4 In. 35.00
Figurine, Pluto, Ceramic, 6 In. 30.00
Figurine, Rabbit, From Bambi, Goebel, 1930s, 2 1/2 In. 28.00
Figurine, Sleepy, Bisque, Japan, 3 In. 20.00
Figurine, Sneezy, Bisque, 2 In. 20.00
Figurine, Snow White & 7 Dwarfs, Bisque, Japan, 5 In. 170.00
Figurine, Snow White & 7 Dwarfs, Ceramic, Japan, 3 1/2 To 4 In. 150.00
Figurine, Snow White & 7 Dwarfs, Hard Rubber, 2 1/2 In. 20.00

Date Mickey Mouse from his appearance. He has changed in the 60 years since his introduction in "Steamboat Willie." Originally he didn't have pupils in his eyes. His legs were like pipe cleaners, now they have shape. He had a neck and white inside his ears in his middle years, but none when young or old. His nose has gotten shorter and more tilted.

Disneyana, Holder, Toothbrush,
3 Little Pigs, 4 In.

Figurine, Snow White, Bisque, 5 In.	30.00
Figurine, Snow White, Carnival Chalkware	35.00
Figurine, Thumper, American Pottery, 3 In.	60.00
Figurine, Tinkerbell, Ceramic, Japan, 4 In.	12.00
Freez–Ur–Pop, Mickey Mouse Club, Plastic, 1950s, Package, 5 Piece	5.00
Game, 101 Dalmatians, Walt Disney	15.00
Game, Card, Old Maid, Mickey Mouse, Instructions, Box	50.00
Game, Card, Snow White, 1946	10.00
Game, Disneyland Monorail, 1960	25.00
Game, Mickey Mouse, Board, Parker Bros., Based On Club Song, 1976	20.00
Game, Mickey Mouse, Library of Games, Queen Holden, 1940s	110.00
Game, Mickey Mouse, Pin Tail	75.00
Game, Mickey Mouse, Scatterball	250.00
Game, Pinocchio The Merry Puppet Game, Milton Bradley	60.00
Game, Pinocchio, Parker Brothers	10.00
Game, Puzzle, Robin Hood, Drum, Mickey Mouse	55.00
Game, Uncle Remus, Pinball, Walt Disney, 1950s	100.00
Game, Who's Afraid of The Big Bad Wolf, 1933	125.00
Guide, Disneyland, 1961, 28 Pages, 8 X 11 1/2 In.	45.00
Guitar, Mickey Mouse, Plastic, 21 In.	20.00
Gum Ball Machine, Clear Face, Yellow Bottom, Plastic, 1968	24.00
Gum Ball Machine, Mickey Mouse, Hasbro, 1968, 9 In.	15.00
Handkerchief Holder, Dopey, Handkerchief, Clear Plastic Box	25.00
Handkerchief, Mickey Mouse, 1930s	8.00
Handkerchief, Snow White, Walt Disney Ent., 1930s, 8 1/2 In.	35.00
Harmonica, Mickey Mouse Club, Sealed In Original Package	10.00
Hat, Mouseketeer, Black	9.00
Holder, Toothbrush, 3 Little Pigs, 4 In. ....*Illus*	55.00
Jardiniere, Tinker Bell, Ivory, Reserves, 1940, Vernon Kilns, 12 In	110.00
Jukebox, Characters, Light–Up Jr.Jukebox, 1955	385.00
Key Chain, Mickey Mouse, Gold Colored Metal, Hawaiian Clothes	10.00
Lamp, Rubber Mickey Mouse, Plastic Base, Paper Shade, 16 In.	28.00
Lithograph, Sailing The Spanishy Main, Uncle Scrooge, Donald	1949.00
Lobby Card, Aristocats	55.00
Lobby Card, Pinocchio, Rerelease	50.00
Lunch Box, Rescuers, Thermos, Tin Litho, Aladdin	10.00
Lunch Box, School Bus, Walt Disney	6.00
Lunch Box, Snow White	22.00
Magazine, Life, Bounces & Bonanzas For W.Disney, April, 1961	8.00
Magazine, Mickey Mouse, April 1937	52.00
Magazine, Mickey Mouse, Dec.1933, Vol.1, No.2	80.00
Magazine, Walt Disney, Feb.1958, Annette On Cover	34.00
Map, Donald Duck's Race To Treasure Island, Standard Oil, 1939	60.00
Mask & Vest, Mickey Mouse Club	10.00
Mask, Ferdinand The Bull, Canvas, Oil Painted	40.00
Mask, Pinocchio, Gillette Blue Blades, 1939	15.00
Mask, Pinocchio, Paper, Elastic, Gillette, 1940s	14.00
Money Set, Mickey Mouse, 5 Coins, Credit Card, Wallet, Clip	9.00

Mug, Donald Duck, Glass, 1970s, 5 1/2 In. 5.00
Mug, Mickey, Donald On Train, Plastic 5.00
Nodder, 3 Little Pigs 25.00
Nodder, Mickey Mouse, Celluloid 45.00
Pail, Mickey & Minnie Mouse, Walt Disney Enterprises 150.00
Pail, Mickey, Minnie, Pluto, Donald, Tin, Ohio Art, 1930s, 8 In. 95.00
Pail, Snow White, Ohio Art 7.00
Paper Doll, Annette, Mouseketeer, 1956, Whitman, Unused 18.00
Paper Doll, Mickey Mouse & Minnie Mouse, Stepping Out, Uncut 7.50
Paper Doll, Minnie Mouse, 1930, 4 Outfits 28.00
Paper Doll, Mouseketeers, Karen, Cubby, Cheryl, Bobby, 1963 .... 20.00
Paperweight, Jiminy Cricket, 1958 .... 25.00
Paperweight, Mickey Mouse, Cast Lead, 1930s 385.00
Patch, Minnie Mouse, Profile, Disneyland, Plastic Package 19.00
Pen, Mickey Mouse, Happy Birthday, 1928–78 .... 1.25
Pencil Pouch, Mickey & Minnie Mouse, Colgate, 1987, 9 1/2 X 6 In. 3.00
Pencil Pouch, Mickey & Minnie, Promotional, Colgate, 9 X 6 In. 3.50
Pencil Sharpener, Donald Duck, Celluloid 28.00
Pencil Sharpener, Donald Duck, Orange, Bakelite, 1 In.Diam. 22.00
Pencil Sharpener, Donald Duck, Red, 1940s, Round, 1 3/8 In. 20.00
Pin, 10th Anniversary of Walt Disney World, 3 In. 5.00
Pin, Mickey Mouse Club, 1930s, 3/4 In. 35.00
Pin, Mickey Mouse, Cap & Gown, Disneyland Grad Nite, '82, 3 In. 5.00
Pin, Mickey Mouse, Head, Walt Disney Productions, 1960s, 1 1/2 In. 8.00
Pin, Mickey Mouse, Official Store, 1937 .... 45.00
Pin, Mickey Mouse, Prize Photographer, Tin 75.00
Pin, Mickey Mouse, Waving, 1 1/4 In. 22.00
Pin, Minnie Mouse, Profile, Disneyland, Pink & White, 3 In. 5.00
Pin, Snow White Jingle Club, Kamen, 1938, 1 1/4 In. 28.00
Pin, Sport Goofy, Yellow Letters, Orange, 3 In. 3.00
Planter, Bambi & Thumper, Leeds 20.00
Planter, Cinderella, Evans Shaw 95.00
Planter, Donald Duck 12.50
Planter, Snow White, Leeds China 28.00
Planter, Thumper 25.00
Planter, Wall, Bambi 30.00
Plate, Disneyland, Castle, 1950s, 4 In. 15.00
Plate, Donald Duck, 50th Birthday 20.00
Plate, Goofy, Golden Jubilee, Schmid 12.00
Plate, Mickey's 50th Birthday, Schmid, Box, 1978, Large 125.00
Postcard, 3 Little Pigs, Sleeping Beauty Castle Behind 2.00
Postcard, Donald Duck, Scrooge, Nephews, Litho, Carl Barks, 1983 .... 7.75
Postcard, Mickey Mouse, England, Pencil Writing On Back, 1930s 22.00
Postcard, Mickey Mouse, Goofy, Discovery Island, Pirates 5.50
Postcard, Mickey Mouse, Pluto, Hunt A Bear 14.00
Postcard, Snow White & 7 Dwarfs, Forest Friends 15.00
Poster, 101 Dalmations, 1961, 14 X 36 In. 72.00
Poster, A Goofy Lunch Pulls Your Punch, 1943, 12 1/2 X 19 In. 20.00
Poster, Bambi, 1942, 11 X 14 In. 162.00
Poster, Donald Duck, Breakfast Like Bird, Work Like Horse, 1943 .... 20.00
Poster, Donald Duck, Crazy With The Heat, 1947 .... 200.00
Poster, Donald Duck, Cured Duck, 1945, Daisy, Broom 147.00
Poster, Donald Duck, Flying Jalopy 266.00
Poster, Goofy, How To Sleep, 1953 .... 106.00
Poster, How To Dance, Goofy In Tuxedo, Walt Disney Prod., 1953 .... 425.00
Poster, Littlest Outlaw, 1953 .... 20.00
Poster, Ludwig Von Drake, Symposium of Songs, Orange, 27 X 41 In. 45.00
Poster, Now You See Him Now You Don't 10.00
Poster, Pinocchio, All Characters, 22 X 26 In. 15.00
Poster, Pinocchio, Stromboli, 1945 .... 55.00
Poster, Scorcerer's Apprentice, Fantasia, Night On Bald Mountain 25.00
Poster, Snow White & 7 Dwarfs, 1937, 22 X 28 In. 847.00
Poster, Sword In The Stone, Original Release 12.00
Poster, The Three Caballeros, 1944, 22 X 28 In. 126.00

Poster, Touchdown Mickey, 1930 .... 3500.00
Poster, Waterbirds, True Life Adventure, Full Color 45.00
Program, Fantasia, Walt Disney, 1940 .... 35.00
Program, Souvenir, Song of The South, 1946, 20 Pages, 10 X 12 In. 110.00
Puppet, Hand, Mickey & Minnie Mouse 22.00
Puppet, Hand, Pinocchio, Plastic Head, Cloth Body 10.00
Puppet, Hand, Zorro 35.00
Puzzle, Donald Duck & Daisy, Eating Hot Dog, Box, 5 1/8 X 7 In. 7.00
Puzzle, Jigsaw, Mickey Mouse, Marx, Box 325.00
Puzzle, Mickey Mouse, 12 Sections, Make Story, 1950s 55.00
Puzzle, Pinocchio, Jaymar, Box 15.00
Radio, Mickey Mouse, General Electric 60.00
Radio, Mickey Mouse, Plastic 85.00
Record, Cinderella, Story Book Set, RCA Victor, 78 RPM 27.00
Record, Dumbo, Narrated By Shirley Temple, 78 RCA Record Set 30.00
Record, Little Toot, Capitol Record, 78 RPM 12.00
Record, Pinocchio, Give A Little Whistle, Golden, 45 RPM, 1950s 10.00
Record, Pinocchio, Original Sound Track, RCA Victor, 78 RPM 50.00
Record, Pinocchio, RCA Victor, 78 RPM, 1940s 50.00
Record, Snow White & Seven Dwarfs, Album, Words, Music, 1938 .... 20.00
Record, Zip–A–Dee–Doo–Dah, Art Carney Narrates, 78 RPM, 1950s 10.00
Ring, Mickey Mouse, Figure Mounted On Plastic, Expandable, 1930s 10.00
Ring, Mickey Mouse, Sterling Silver, 1930s 50.00
Roller, Peek–In, Mickey Mouse, Inflatable, 5 Balls, Bell, 15 In. 15.00
Rug, Hooked, Donald Duck, Carrying 2 Buckets On Shoulders 18.00
Rug, Mickey & Minnie Mouse, Playing Tennis 36.50
Rug, Snow White & 7 Dwarfs, 27 X22 In. 60.00
Salt & Pepper, Donald Duck, Walt Disney Productions 30.00
Salt & Pepper, Dumbo, Large 28.00
Sand Set, Snow White, Tinkertoy, Disney Enterprises, Box, 1938 .... 375.00
School Bag, Donald Duck 85.00
Shaggy Dog, Kal Kan Sponsored Contest, Box, 1967 .... 150.00
Sheet Music, Cinderella, Bibbidi–Bobbidi-Boo, Disney 10.00
Sheet Music, Supercalifragilisticexpialidocious, Mary Poppins 12.00
Sheet Music, Whistle While You Work, Snow White .... 10.00 To 12.00
Sheet Music, Who's Afraid of The Big Bad Wolf 20.00
Sheet Music, You Belong To My Heart, 3 Caballeros 10.00
Slide Set, 3 Little Pigs, Booklet, Box, 1930s, 6 Piece 65.00
Slide Set, Snow White & 7 Dwarfs, Booklet, Box, 1938, 6 Piece 75.00
Slide Set, Snow White, Color, 3 Dimensional, Radex, Box 35.00
Soldier, Mickey Mouse, Box, Set of 8 .... 200.00
Spoon, Mickey Mouse, Silver Plate, Branford 10.00
Spoon, Mickey Mouse, Silver Plate, Mickey On Handle, 5 In. 30.00
Spoon, Mickey Mouse, Wm. Rogers, 1930 .... 15.00
Stamp, Rubber, Daisy Duck, Red Plastic, 1 1/8 X 1 1/2 In. 3.00
Stationary, Peter Pan, 1952, 8 1/2 X 11 In. 17.00
Stool, Mickey Mouse Club House, 1940's 40.00
Storyboard, Bambi, Charcoal, Crayon, 1942, 6 X 8 In. 581.00
Storyboard, Sneezy, 1937, 4 1/2 X 4 In. 181.00
Straws, Donald Duck, Box, 1940s 10.00
Target Board, Mickey Mouse, Walt E.Disney 48.00
Tea Set, Alice In Wonderland, 1949, Box 40.00
Tea Set, Donald Duck Picnic, Tin, Ohio Art, 1930s, 9 Piece 60.00
Tea Set, Mary Poppins, Tin 18.00
Tea Set, Mickey & Minnie Mouse, Pluto, Box, 1950s, Disneyland 65.00
Tea Set, Mickey Mouse, Tin, Ohio Art, 9 Piece 80.00
Thermos, Mickey Mouse 18.00
Top, Musical, Snow White & 7 Dwarfs, Chein, 6 1/2 In. 24.00
Toy, Acrobats, Mickey Mouse, Stombecker 60.00
Toy, Car, Crazy, Mickey Mouse, Marx 250.00
Toy, Car, Matchbook, Goofy's Beetle, Flying Ears 12.00
Toy, Car, Mickey Mouse Dipsy, Marx 285.00
Toy, Cart, Shopping, Minnie Mouse, Battery Operated 125.00
Toy, Donald Duck, Acrobat, Linemar, Windup 70.00

Toy, Donald Duck, Celluloid, 1930, 6 In. 160.00
Toy, Donald Duck, Crazy Car 350.00
Toy, Donald Duck, Hangs From Red Ring, Jumps, 1940, 5 In. 15.00
Toy, Donald Duck, Long Bill, Walks, Celluloid, 1930s 1750.00
Toy, Donald Duck, Pluto In Rubber Car, 6 1/2 In. 65.00
Toy, Donald Duck, Push, Wooden, Donald Holding Suitcase, 4 In. 15.00
Toy, Donald Duck, Walks, Pushing Barrow, 1940, 3 X 3 1/2 In. 9.00
Toy, Donald Duck, Windup, Composition, 11 In. 560.00
Toy, Donald Duck, Windup, Lithographed Tin, Chein 48.00
Toy, Dopey, Yellow Coat, Purple Hat, Squeeze, Rubber, 7 1/2 In. 16.00
Toy, Drum, Mickey Mouse Club 28.00
Toy, Figaro, Windup, Marx 65.00
Toy, Goofy, Windup, Tail Spins, Head & Feet Move, Linemar 325.00
Toy, Handcar, Mickey & Minnie Mouse 525.00
Toy, Handcar, Mickey Mouse, Windup, Papier–Mache, Tin, Lionel, 9 In. .. 445.00
Toy, Kanga & Roo, Squeeze Figure, Roo In Pouch, 7 3/4 In. 12.00
Toy, Medical Kit, Mickey Mouse, Hasbro 18.00
Toy, Mickey Mouse, Cloth Shoes, Knickerbocker, 20 In. 275.00
Toy, Mickey Mouse, Fire Engine, Rubber 30.00
Toy, Mickey Mouse, Knickerbocker, 22 In. 495.00
Toy, Mickey Mouse, On Horse, Key Wind, Celluloid & Wood, 1930s 3250.00
Toy, Mickey Mouse, Peek–In Roller, Inflatable, Plastic, 1977, 15 In 15.00
Toy, Mickey Mouse, Soaky Toys, For Bathtub, Colgate–Palmolive 8.00
Toy, Mickey Mouse, Somersaults, Litho On Wood, Squeeze Handles 37.00
Toy, Mickey Mouse, Steiff, 1930s 275.00
Toy, Mickey Mouse, Sun Rubber, 8 In. 15.00
Toy, Mickey Mouse, Talks, Plastic, Large Head, Hasbro, 1970s, 7 In. 35.00
Toy, Mickey Mouse, Talks, Plastic, Large Head, Mattel, 1982, 7 In. 28.00
Toy, Mickey Mouse, Tencennial Streetcar, Plaque, Pride Lines, 1981 ..... 350.00
Toy, Mickey Mouse, Tractor, Sun Rubber 35.00
Toy, Mickey Mouse, Xylophone Player 85.00
Toy, Minnie Mouse, Pushes Carriage, Yellow, Red, Plastic, 6 In. 35.00
Toy, Movie Projector, Mickey Mouse Club, Mattel, Plastic 22.00
Toy, Piano, Mickey Mouse, Wooden, Mickey & Minnie Dance, 10 In. 1050.00
Toy, Pluto, Walks, Box, 1950s 450.00
Toy, Projector, Mickey Mouse Club, Mattel, Plastic 22.00
Toy, Roll–A–Tune, Musical, Jolly Blinker Co., 9 In. 30.00
Toy, Sand Filter, Mickey & Minnie Mouse, Pluto, Clarabelle 225.00
Toy, Sweeper, Litho of Mickey & Minnie Mouse, Ohio Art, Tin 150.00
Toy, Sweeper, Mickey & Minnie, 1936, Ohio Art Co. 100.00
Toy, Telephone, Mickey Mouse 145.00
Toy, Train, Disneyland, Windup, Tin, Marx, 13 In. 25.00
Toy, Wagon, Tiny–Tot, Marked WDP 39.00
Transfer, Mickey Mouse, Iron–On 4.00
Tray, Snow White & Doc, Rabbits & Deer Border, Tin 45.00
Tumbler Set, Snow White, 8 Piece 100.00
Tumbler, America On Parade, Mickey Holding Flag, Coca–Cola, 6 In. 8.00
Tumbler, Cinderella, 1950s, 5 1/4 In. 8.00
Tumbler, Disney On Parade 10.50
Tumbler, Donald Duck & Goofy, Blue, Banner Top, 4 3/4 In. 25.00
Tumbler, Dopey, Walt Disney 8.00
Tumbler, Grumpy, Blue, Libbey Premium, 4 3/8 In. 16.00
Tumbler, Mickey & Minnie Mouse, Happy Birthday, Pepsi–Cola, 6 In. .. 9.50
Tumbler, Mickey Mouse Club, Goofy Fishing, Rowboat, 32 Oz. 5.00
Tumbler, Mickey Mouse, Pie–Eyed 20.00
Tumbler, Mickey's Christmas Carol, Goofy As Marley, 6 In. 7.00
Tumbler, Pinocchio, Red, Libbey Premium, 4 3/4 In. 18.00
Tumbler, Sleeping Beauty, Samson 12.00
Tumbler, Star/Ship Royal, Premier Cruise, Walt Disney World, 8 In 6.00
Tumbler, Water, Snow White & 7 Dwarfs, Doc, 5 In. 5.00
Tumbler, Water, Snow White & 7 Dwarfs, Happy, 5 In. 5.00
Tumbler, Water, Snow White & 7 Dwarfs, Sneezy, 5 In. 5.00
Tumbler, Water, Snow White & 7 Dwarfs, Snow White, 5 In. 5.00
Umbrella, Mary Poppins, Yellow 5.00

Umbrella, Mickey Mouse 20.00
Valentine, Mechanical, Sleepy Playing Accordian 15.00
Vase, Snow White, Picking Flowers, Cream, Tan, Multicolor, 6 In. 12.00
Walker, Jiminy Cricket, Plastic 12.00
Waste Can, Mickey Mouse, 50th Anniversary 10.00
Watch Fob, Mickey Mouse, Black Enamel 55.00
Watch, Pocket, 3 Little Pigs, Red Dial 450.00
Watch, Pocket, Mickey Mouse, 1976 .... 125.00
Watch, Pocket, Mickey Mouse, With Fob 395.00
Watch, Pocket, Mickey Mouse, Yellowed, Watch Fob, 1933 .... 600.00
Watering Can, 3 Little Pigs 20.00
Watering Can, Mickey Mouse, Tin, 1930s 50.00
Wristwatch, Alice In Wonderland, U.S.Time 20.00
Wristwatch, Bubble, Mickey Mouse, Box 175.00
Wristwatch, Cinderella, U.S.Time 20.00
Wristwatch, Donald Duck, Expandable Metal Strap 60.00
Wristwatch, Mickey Mouse, 1935 .... 350.00
Wristwatch, Mickey Mouse, Animated Hands, Bradley 45.00
Wristwatch, Mickey Mouse, Bradley, Red Strap, Swiss, 1970s 20.00
Wristwatch, Mickey Mouse, Electric, Timex, New Band, 1968 .... 200.00
Wristwatch, Minnie Mouse, Animated Hands, Bradley 40.00
Wristwatch, Minnie Mouse, Golf, 17 Jewel, Elgin 200.00
Wristwatch, Minnie Mouse, Swiss 15.00
Wristwatch, Snow White 25.00
   DOCTOR, see Medical; Dental

Doll entries are listed by marks printed or incised on the doll, if possible. If there are no marks, the doll is listed by the name of the subject or country.

DOLL, A.B.G., Girl, Bisque Head, Sleep Eyes, Jointed, Antique Dress, 35 In. 950.00
A.B.G.1123 1/2, Bisque, Cloth & Leather Body, Sailor Dress, 28 In. 1095.00
A.M. 1, Character Child, Closed Mouth, Original Costume, 13 In. 2350.00
A.M. 15, Bisque, Fur Eyebrows, 36 In. 850.00
A.M. 240, Kewpie, Googly, 10 In. 2800.00
A.M. 323, Googly, 5–Piece Composition Body, Molded Shoes, 7 1/2 In. 450.00
A.M. 323, Googly, All Original, 8 In. 695.00
A.M. 323, Googly, Closed Mouth, 7 In. 650.00
A.M. 325, Googly Boy, Bisque, Original Clothes, 12 In. 1450.00
A.M. 327, Character, 25 In. 500.00
A.M. 341, Baby, Sleep Eyes, 8 In. 110.00
A.M. 341, Dream Baby, 16 In. 500.00
A.M. 351, Sleep Eyes, Open Mouth, Lower Teeth, Baby Body, 18 In. 300.00
A.M. 351–3K, Black Baby, Bisque, Jointed Body, Yellow Pants, 13 1/2 In. 650.00
A.M. 352, Character Baby, Hard Stuffed Cloth Toddler Body, Dressed 410.00
A.M. 353, Oriental, Baby Body, Straight Wrists, Marked, 13 In. 785.00
A.M. 390, Ball–Jointed Composition Body, 24 In. 450.00
A.M. 390, Bisque Head, Open Mouth, Jointed, Composition, 27 In. 385.00
A.M. 390, Bisque, Sleep Eyes, Original Clothes, 11 In. 80.00
A.M. 390, Composition, Wooden Body, 18 In. 300.00
A.M. 590, Bisque Tongue, Paperweight Eyes, Ball–Jointed, 18 In. 1350.00
A.M. 985, Bent Limb Body, Christening Gown, Bonnet, 23 In. .... 550.00 To 800.00
A.M. 985, Bent Limp Body, Long Christening Gown, Slip, Bonnet, 23 In. 550.00
A.M. 985, Character Baby, 16 In. 695.00
A.M. 985, Character Baby, 19 In. 375.00
A.M. 985, Child, Sleep Eyes, Baby Body, White Christening Dress, 9 In. 250.00
A.M. 990, Character Baby, Bisque Head, Open Mouth, Fixed Eyes, 20 In. 440.00
A.M. 995, Character Baby, Brown, 5 Piece Body, Gown, Bonnet, 18 1/2 In. 425.00
A.M. 996, Toddler, Open & Close Eyes, Jointed, Dressed, 21 In. 550.00
A.M., Alma, Kid Body, Sleep Eyes, 17 In. 225.00
A.M., Baby Gloria, Bisque, 13 In. 195.00
A.M., Child, Bisque Head, Jointed, Alice In Wonderland Dress, 24 In. 275.00
A.M., Florodora, Lace Dress, Hat, Shoes, 14 In. 275.00
A.M., Florodora, Sleep Eyes, Human Hair Curls, 20 In. 295.00
A.M., Googly, Sleep Blue Eyes, Toddler Body, 7 In. 600.00

A.M., Just Me, Bisque, 7 In. 1250.00
A.M., Mabel, 19 In. 200.00
Action Jackson, Mego, Box 22.00
Active Sindy, Brown, Ballerina, Blue Eys, Pedigree From England 55.00
Advertising, Baby Ruth Candy 18.00
Advertising, Betsy & Billy Permanent Dolls, Cloth, Uncut, 1913 .... 150.00
Advertising, Big Boy Set, Dolly, Big Boy & Nuggett, 3 Piece 9.00
Advertising, Buddy Lee, Phillips 66, Plastic, Overalls, Plaid Shirt 135.00
Advertising, Buddy Lee, Standard Oil, No Cap 70.00
Advertising, Burger King, Cloth .... 5.00 To 9.50
Advertising, C-H Sugar, Hawaiian Girls, Cloth, 14 In. 3.00
Advertising, Ceresota Flour Boy, Cloth, Uncut, 1920s 200.00
Advertising, Chiquita Banana, Cloth 15.00
Advertising, Chiquita Banana, Kelloggs, Cloth, Uncut, 1944 .... 30.00
Advertising, Chore Girl, Cloth 8.00
Advertising, Cover Girl, Darci 10.00
Advertising, Cresta & Heckler's Unbleached Flour, Mail Bag 30.00
Advertising, Domino Sugar 20.00
Advertising, Dutch Boy Paint 250.00
Advertising, Dy-O-La Dye Girl, Cloth, Uncut, 1920s 125.00
Advertising, Eskimo Pie .... 8.00 To 20.00
Advertising, Frosty Root Beer 15.00
Advertising, Gerber, Baby, 1966 .... 35.00
Advertising, Gerber, Baby, 1970 .... 60.00
Advertising, Green Giant, Vinyl 10.00
Advertising, I.G.A.Tablerite Kid 5.00
Advertising, Jack Frost Sugar, Cloth 25.00
Advertising, Kellogg, Clown, In Barrel 5.00
Advertising, Kellogg, Crackle, Rubber 17.00
Advertising, Kellogg, Freckles, Cloth, Uncut, 1935 .... 75.00
Advertising, Kellogg, Snap, Crackle, Pop, Cloth, 1954 .... 50.00
Advertising, Kelly Girl, Cloth, Knickerbocker, 1978, 12 1/2 In. 6.00
Advertising, Little Debbie 20.00
Advertising, Little Miss Revlon, Brunette, All Original 35.00
Advertising, Maxwell House Coffee, Cloth, In Package 25.00
Advertising, McDonald, Professor Gadget 12.00
Advertising, Miss Revlon, 12 In. 36.00
Advertising, Miss Revlon, 22 In. 60.00
Advertising, Miss Revlon, In Suitcase, Commercial Wardrobe, Large 125.00
Advertising, Miss Sunbeam, Cut Mohair Wig, Hard Plastic 40.00
Advertising, Nabisco Cookies, Box 15.00
Advertising, Petite Princess, Wood, Display For Furniture, Large 70.00
Advertising, Pillsbury Doughboy & Girl, Dated 1971-72, 2 Piece 22.00
Advertising, Pillsbury Pop 'N' Fresh, 1972, 13 In. 7.00
Advertising, Ronald McDonald 5.00
Advertising, Roseland, Male & Female Dancer, Signed, 11 In., Pair 25.00
Advertising, Sailor, Holland America Cruises 15.00
Advertising, Uneeda Nabisco Boy, Painted Hair, Composition 275.00
Advertising, United Airlines, Hawaiian 385.00
Alabama, Indestructible Doll, Marked, 24 In. 2300.00
    DOLL, ALEXANDER, see Doll, Madame Alexander
Alice, Kid Body, Blue Sleep Eyes, Pink Velvet Dress, Bonnet, 13 In. 300.00
Amberg, Edwina, Molded Hair, Ball-Jointed Waist, Dressed, 14 In. 275.00
Amberg, Newborn Baby, 1914, 14 In. 450.00
American Character, Sweet Sue Bride, Vinyl Skull Cap, Original, 24 In. 125.00
American Schoolboy, Blond Molded Hair, Brown Eyes, 14 In. 245.00
American Schoolboy, Kid Body, Bisque Head, Stationary Eyes, 15 In. 350.00
Amish, Cloth, Handmade, Faceless, Apron, 1930s 77.00
Archie, & His Gang, Set, Vinyl, In Comic Attire, Stands, 18 In., 5 Piece 125.00
    DOLL, ARMAND MARSEILLE, see Doll, A. M.
Automaton, Black Lady Seated On Taboret Playing Harp 1600.00
Babe Ruth, Original Striped Suit, Cap, 30 In. 385.00
Baby Boo, Baby Peek 'N' Play 20.00
Baby First Steps, Skates, All Original, 17 In. 50.00

Baby Jane, Original Dress, 1935, 16 In.	850.00
Baby Sally, Open Red Pajama Flap, Hungerford	40.00
Baby Snooks, Original Clothes, Paper Tag, 1938	200.00
Baby Yokum, Vinyl, Box, 16 In.	95.00
Babyland, Girl, Cloth, Sailor Outfit, 13 In.	275.00
Bahr & Proschild, 585, Baby, 26 In.	550.00

DOLL, BARBIE, see Doll, Mattel, Barbie

Bebe, Cork Pate, Composition Jointed Body, Label, C.1890, 24 In.	3575.00
Bebe, Googly, Impish Smile, Jointed Body, Sailor Outfit, 9 In.	2200.00
Bebe, No.9, Walker, 24 In.	950.00
Bebe, Smiling Portrait, Swivel Head, Kid Body, Walking Costume, 21 In.	6050.00
Beck & Gottschalck, Toddler, Bisque, Character, Flirty Eyes, 29 In.	1100.00
Belton, Brown Glass Eyes, 13 In.	1350.00
Belton, Glass Eyes, Painted Stockings, 6 In.	125.00
Belton, Trousseau, Open–Close Mouth, 2 Outfits, Box, 12 In.	2850.00

DOLL, BERGMANN, see also Doll, S & H; Doll, Simon & Halbig

Bergmann, German Girl, 31 In.	900.00
Berjusa, Baby, Human Hair, Sucks Thumb, 24 In.	70.00
Betina & Bernard, Steiff, Pair	600.00
Betsy Wetsy, Hair, American Character, 10 In.	•20.00
Blondie & Dagwood Bumstead, Stand, 19 In., Pair	45.00
Borgfeldt, Alma, 1901, 21 In.	350.00
Borgfeldt, Baby, Composition Body, 26 In.	450.00
Borgfeldt, Rosebud, Leather Body, 20 In.	225.00
Bride Set, 4 Bridesmaids, 2 In Blue & 2 In Pink, C.1915, 5 Piece	1800.00
Bruckner, Cloth, Dated 1901, 12 In.	125.00
Bruno Schmidt 2048, Tommy Tucker, 28 In.	1200.00
Bubbles, Toddler, Slant Hip, 16 In.	175.00
Buddy Lee, Cowboy, Overalls, Vinyl	135.00
Bye–Lo, All Bisque, Jointed, Original Clothes, 4 In.	300.00
Bye–Lo, Baby, Bisque Head, Painted Hair, C.1925, 6 In.	200.00
Bye–Lo, Baby, Composition Hands, Christening Gown, 11 1/2 In.	425.00
Bye–Lo, Baby, Sleep Eyes, Plastic Hands, 12 In.	275.00 To 300.00
Bye–Lo, Bisque Head, Marked Head & Body, Putnam, 10 In.	375.00
Bye–Lo, Bisque, Painted Eyes, Old Clothes, Marked, 6 1/2 In.	475.00
Bye–Lo, Boy, Bisque, Bent Limb, Painted Eyes, 7 In.	150.00
Bye–Lo, Closed Mouth, Body Signed, Large	1000.00
Bye–Lo, Rubber, Incised, 1922, 14 1/2 In.	350.00
Cabbage Patch, Lydia Judith	38.00
Cameo, Joy, Composition, 15 In.	195.00
Cameo, Margie, 10 In.	165.00
Cameo, Scootles, Boy & Girl, 12 In., Pair	57.50
Cameo, Scootles, Boy & Girl, 16 In., Pair	67.50
Cameo, Scootles, Original Clothes, C.1925, 16 In.	400.00
Capezio, Toe Dancer, En Pointe, Sleep Eyes, Plastic, Silver Tutu, 18 In.	95.00
Cat In The Hat, Box	35.00
Cat, Composition Face, Clothed Teddy Body, Herman Teddy, 10 In.	95.00
Celluloid, Girl, Composition, Original Dress, France, 8 1/2 In.	20.00
Celluloid, Girl, Jointed, Original Clothes, 7 In.	18.00
Celluloid, Long Braids, German Costume, Germany, 13 In.	75.00
Century, Baby, Bisque Head, Composition Hands, Cloth Body, 10 In.	114.50
Chad Valley, Bambina, Glass Eyes, 18 In.	725.00
Chad Valley, Black, Calico Dress, Painted Blue Shoes, Socks, 9 In.	375.00
Chad Valley, Bonzo, Blue, Yellow & Red Suit, 9 In.	350.00
Chad Valley, Boy, Curly Mohair Wig, Socks, Shoes, Clothes, Label, 9 In.	250.00
Charlie Brown, Hungerford, 10 In.	20.00
Child, Bisque Head, Wooden, Ball–Jointed, Eyelet Dress, Germany, 25 In.	345.00
China Head, Blond, Redressed Petticoats & Bloomers, 23 In.	285.00
China Head, Flat Top, Old Baby Clothes, Cloth Body, 30 In.	400.00
China Head, Pink Luster, Braided Bun, Cloth Body, Molded Bosom, 14 In.	1600.00
China Head, Sawdust Stuffed Body, 1890s, 10 In.	135.00
China Head, Wavy Black Hair, Excelsior Cloth Body, 1880s, 21 In.	150.00
Cloth, Printed, Undies, High Top Shoes & Socks, 1920s, 25 In.	200.00
Cloth, Tabby Kittens, Uncut, Arnold Print Works, 1894	50.00

Cochran, Indian, Composition, Human Hair, 20 In. ....*Illus*	3250.00
Coleco, Bald Boy, 2 Dimples, Blue Eyes, Corduroy Teddy Suit	55.00
Coleco, Bride & Groom, Japanese, Pair	195.00
Coleco, Preemie Girl, Rosebud Gown, Bonnet, 1 Dimple, Green Eyes	35.00
Columbian, Cloth, Oil Painted, Emma Adams, C.1890 ....*Illus*	9500.00
Cosmopolitan, Ginger, White Ruffled Dress, Pink Picture Hat, Box	125.00
Daniel & Cie, Paris Bebe, Standing, Jacket, 26 In.	4000.00
Degas Girl, Original Clothes	125.00
Dennis The Menace, 9 In.	12.50
DEP 7, Girl, Jointed, Composition, Squeaker, Old Clothes, 18 In.	1050.00
DEP 154, Rivet–Jointed Kid Body, Cork Stuffed, Label, 17 1/2 In.	450.00
DEP, Tete Jumeau Bebe, Long Curls, Closed Mouth, 26 In.	1600.00
Dolly Dingle, Baby, White Eyelet	50.00
Dolly Dingle, Composition, Signed G.G.Drayton, 13 1/2 In.	275.00
Dolly Parton, Goldberger, 1970s	32.00
Dream Baby, Blue Sleep Eyes, Celluloid Hands, Cloth Body, 13 1/2 In.	250.00
Dream Baby, Blue Sleep Eyes, Tagged Dress, 9 In.	150.00
Dressel, Child, Bisque Head, Sleep Eyes, Ball–Jointed, 24 In.	335.00
E.D., Bisque Head, Open Mouth, Jointed, Silk Dress, Bonnet, 11 1/2 In.	550.00
E.J., Bisque, Applied Tears, Paperweight Eyes, Dressed, 18 In.	6500.00
Ed Norton, Honeymooners Series	65.00
Eden Bebe, Bisque Head, Closed Mouth, Paperweight Eyes, Paris, 12 In.	1600.00
Eden Bebe, Bisque, Paperweight Eyes, Long Curls, Dressed, 26 In.	1850.00
Eden Bebe, Bisque, Upper Teeth, Jointed Body, Pleated Skirt, 22 1/2 In.	1595.00
Eegee, My Fair Lady, Platinum Blond, Black & Silver Costume, 20 In.	65.00
Eegee, Susan Stroller, Hard Plastic Body & Limbs, Cries, 23 In.	50.00
Effanbee, Anne Shirley, Short Blond Wig, 15 In.	100.00
Effanbee, Babe Ruth	89.00
Effanbee, Baby Button Nose, Black, 1986, 14 In.	30.00
Effanbee, Baby Dainty, 15 In.	75.00
Effanbee, Baby Tinyette, Cowgirl Outfit, Tagged	225.00
Effanbee, Babyette, Composition, 16 In.	90.00
Effanbee, Brunette, I Am Buttercup, Box	50.00
Effanbee, Bubbles, Baby Clothes, 1924, 22 In.	175.00
Effanbee, Butter Ball, Dated 1969, Box	60.00
Effanbee, Candy Kid, Composition, 1940s, 12 1/2 In.	165.00
Effanbee, Candy Kid, Composition, Dressed, C.1945, 12 1/2 In.	165.00
Effanbee, Coco, Bisque Arms, Legs, Real Hair, 15 1/2 In.	95.00
Effanbee, Cuddles, 23 In.	90.00
Effanbee, Dwight D.Eisenhower	75.00
Effanbee, Evangeline, Hand Painted, 16 In.	95.00
Effanbee, George Washington	22.00
Effanbee, Girl, Anchors Aweigh	45.00
Effanbee, Groucho Marx .... 45.00 To	75.00
Effanbee, Harry S. Truman	75.00
Effanbee, Honey Walker, 25 In.	110.00
Effanbee, John Wayne, Cavalry Outfit, Box	75.00
Effanbee, Judy Garland	95.00
Effanbee, Liberace	250.00
Effanbee, Louis Armstrong	175.00
Effanbee, Lovum, 20 In.	75.00
Effanbee, Mae West .... 75.00 To	90.00
Effanbee, Marilyn Monroe	80.00
Effanbee, Mary Jane, 27 In.	85.00
Effanbee, Mary Lee, 1924, 27 In.	175.00
Effanbee, Mary Lee, Composition, Box, 16 In.	200.00
Effanbee, Mary Poppins, Box, 14 In. .... 30.00 To	50.00
Effanbee, Miss Italy, 11 In.	45.00
Effanbee, Most Happy Family, Mom, Fluffie & Mickie, Blue Coats, 1957	225.00
Effanbee, Orange Blossom, Oriental Girl	42.00
Effanbee, Patsy Joan, Composition, Original Dress, 16 In.	375.00
Effanbee, Patsy, 1926, 14 In.	65.00
Effanbee, Patsy, 1927 Style Pinafore Sundress, Teddy Bear, 14 In.	47.50
Effanbee, Patsy, Sleep Eyes, Dressed	150.00

Effanbee, Patsykin, Magic Skin Body, 9 In. 125.00
Effanbee, Pocahontas, Box, 14 In. 30.00
Effanbee, Puppet, MacAwful The Scot 60.00
Effanbee, Robin Hood, Box, 14 In. 30.00
Effanbee, Skippy, Original Clothes 250.00
Effanbee, Skippy, World War II, Doughboy Uniform 325.00
Effanbee, Snow White, Box, 14 In. 35.00
Effanbee, Susan B.Anthony 150.00
Effanbee, Suzanne, 14 In. .... 195.00 To 275.00
Effanbee, Suzie Sunshine, 18 In. 55.00
Effanbee, Sweetie Pie, Composition, Lamb's Wool Wig, 24 In. 175.00
Effanbee, Sweetie Pie, Flirty Eyes, Caracul Wig, 22 In. 95.00
Effanbee, Toddler, 30 In. 265.00
Effanbee, Twinkie, Flirty Eyes, Jointed Knees & Elbows, 20 In. 45.00
Effanbee, W.C.Fields .... 160.00 To 175.00

Doll, Cochran, Indian,
Composition, Human Hair, 20 In.

Doll, Simon & Halbig 1469, Bisque,
Flapper, Socket Head, 14 In.

Doll, K & K, Character Child, Sleep
Eyes, Open Mouth, 18 In.

Doll, Franz Schmidt, Laughing,
Sleep Eyes, Open Mouth, 16 In.

Effanbee, Wee Patsy, Composition, 6 In. .... 115.00 To 325.00
Effanbee, Wicked Witch, Box, 14 In. 30.00
Emma Clear, Black Hair, Dressed, Marked, Dated, 21 In. 350.00
Emma Clear, Parian, Pierced Ears, Elaborate Outfit 185.00
Eskimo, Leather, Fur, 8 In. 40.00
Eubank, Mark Twain 65.00
F.B.J. 230, Bisque, Upper Teeth, Jointed Body, Silk Dress, 25 1/2 In. 1250.00
F.B.J. 236, Character, Bisque, Sleep Eyes, Jointed, Dress, 20 In. 1550.00
F.B.J. 236, Character, Toddler Body, Bisque, Print Dress, 26 In. 1950.00
F.B.J. 236, Chunky Toddler Body, Cotton Print Dress, 26 In. 1895.00
F.B.J. 236, Toddler, Bisque Head, Open–Close Mouth, Knit Dress, 17 In. 1195.00
F.B.J. 301, Bisque, Sleep Eyes, Ball–Jointed, Dress, Hat, 29 In. 995.00
F.B.J. 301, Bisque, Sleep Eyes, Satin Dress, Bonnet, 34 In. 1895.00
F.B.J. 301, Bisque, Sleep Eyes, Teeth, Velvet Dress, 33 In. 1375.00
F.B.J. 301, Bisque, Upper Teeth, Ball–Jointed, Satin Dress, 34 In. 1950.00
F.G., Ballerina, Automaton, 16 1/2 In. 3150.00
F.G., Bisque Head, Long Curls, Ball–Jointed Body, Taffeta Dress, 23 In. 2800.00
F.G., Bisque, Set Eyes, Swivel Head, Silk Dress, Underclothes, 11 In. 975.00
F.G., Blue Paperweight Eyes, Chunky Body, Straight Wrists, 10 In. 3850.00
F.G., Brown Curls, Ball–Jointed Body, Silk Taffeta Dress, 23 1/2 In. 2800.00
F.G., Fashion, Bisque Swivel Head, Leather Body, Silk Dress, 11 In. 950.00
F.G., French Fashion, Swivel Head, Closed Mouth, Leather Body, 17 In. 1495.00
F.G., Mechanical, Plays Music Box As Strumming Guitar, Dressed, 16 In. 3250.00
Fashion, Bisque, Swivel Head, Kid Torso, Costume, 10 1/2 In. 1195.00
Foxy Grandpa, Cloth, Cartoon Character, 1905, 16 In. 100.00
Franz Schmidt, Laughing, Sleep Eyes, Open Mouth, 16 In. ....*Illus* 4000.00
French, Bisque, Swivel Head, Blue Glass Stationary Eyes, 18 In. 3500.00
French, Fashion, Bisque, Kid Leather Body, Striped Dress, 9 /12 In. 695.00
French, Fashion, Bisque, Swivel Head, Kid Body, Jointed Limbs, 20 In. 3850.00
French, Fashion, Trade Lady, Swivel Head, Bisque Shoulders, 24 In. 1400.00
French, Lady, Papier–Mache, Breather, Cloth Body, Silk Dress 1200.00
French, Leather Body, Fur Wig, Smiler, 12 In. 1250.00
French, Open Mouth, Composition, Plaid Dress, Hat, 1907, 30 In. 2395.00
French, Pushcart Woman, Vending Fruit & Vegetables 850.00
French, Smoker Automaton, Toreador Outfit, 18 1/2 In. 2000.00
Frozen Charlie, Tinted Face & Neck, Blond Hair, 15 1/2 In. 685.00
Frozen Charlotte, 5 1/2 In. 95.00
Frozen Charlotte, Bisque, Golden Curly Hair, Blue Eyes, 3 In. 125.00
Frozen Charlotte, Molded Black Hair, Arms Extended, 3 1/2 In. 65.00
Furga, Bicycle Girl, Elaborate Hairstyle, Italy, 17 In. 195.00
G.I.Joe, Army, First Talker, Molded Hair, Comic Book 75.00
G.I.Joe, German Uniform 125.00
G.I.Joe, Life Jacket, Navy Attack 20.00
G.I.Joe, Painted Hair, Nude 60.00
G.I.Joe, State Trooper, Cello Bag 80.00
G.K.10.22, Fashion, Kid Body, Turned Dome Head, Cobalt Eyes, 14 In. 600.00
Gaultier, Fashion, Bisque, Kid Body, Underclothes, Silk Skirt, 11 In. 1100.00
Gaultier, Fashion, Bisque, Swivel Head, Original Clothes, 11 In. 1100.00
Gebruder Heubach 165, Ball–Jointed Body, Flirty–Eyed, 29 In. 750.00
Gebruder Heubach 8192, Character Girl, Jointed, Blue Lashes, 21 In. 375.00
Gebruder Heubach, Laughing Child, Dimples, Cloth Body, 9 In. 350.00
Gebruder Heubach, Lennie, Dressed, 14 In. 425.00
German, Amelia Earhart, Bisque, 3 1/8 In. 85.00
Gilbert, James Bond, Package, 1965, Set of 7, All Different 18.00
Girl, Bisque Head, Crepe Paper Clothes, 6 In. 45.00
Goebel, Bisque, Ball–Jointed Body, 22 In. 210.00
Goebel, Character Girl, Molded Flowers In Hair 375.00
Goebel, Girl, All Original, Box, 18 In. 495.00
Goebel, Hansel & Gretel, Vinyl, Pair 150.00
Gotz, Girl, Long Brown Hair, Ribbon Wreath, Country Dress, Shoes, 20 In. 55.00
Gotz, Toddler, Long Brown Pigtails, Brown Eyes, Pouty, 20 In. 95.00
Greek, Woman, Cotton Costume, 8 In. 12.00
Handwerck 99, Blue Eyes, Blue Dress, 20 In. 375.00
Handwerck 109, Blue Eyes, Clothes & Shoes, 18 In. 375.00

When storing dolls (old or new), be sure to remove any sticky tape that might have been used to hold bows, etc., in place. The glue from the tape will eventually discolor the fabric. If dolls are to be stored a long time, put tissue between the clothing and the doll to keep bright colors from "bleeding" onto the doll; remove metal, which might rust; and save the box and all tags.

Doll, Columbian, Cloth, Oil
Painted, Emma Adams, C.1890

Handwerck 109, Blue Sleep Eyes, Pierced Ears, Original Wig, 19 In.	495.00
Handwerck 283/35, Child, 38 In.	1400.00
Handwerck, Bisque Head, Open Mouth, Ball–Jointed, Dressed, 19 In.	575.00
Handwerck, Bisque Head, Open Mouth, Eyes, Leather Body, 15 In.	295.00
Handwerck, Bisque, Ball–Jointed Body, Red Velvet Dress, Bonnet, 24 In.	365.00
Handwerck, Brown Sleep Eyes, Ball–Jointed, 24 In.	450.00
Happy, Baby Toddler, 27 In.	275.00 To 325.00
Harold Lloyd, Cloth	75.00
✓**Heidi Ott,** Alex, Boy, Brown Human Hair, Blue Eyes, Signed, 12 In.	150.00
Heidi Ott, Lucie With Baby, Pair	195.00
Heidi Ott, Mein Liebling	365.00
Heidi Ott, Quinta, 18 In.	495.00
Heller, Annette, With Teddy	400.00
Hendren, Baby, Composition, 25 In.	250.00
Hertel & Schwab 152, Baby, 12 In.	550.00
Hertel & Schwab 152, Character Boy, 13 1/2 In.	275.00
Hertel & Schwab 152, Mohair Wig, Gray Sleep Eyes, 4 Teeth, 18 In.	475.00
Heubach 320, Breather Baby, 12 In.	250.00
Heubach 342, Painted Bisque, Character Face, 16 In.	300.00
Heubach 7628, Open–Close Mouth, Composition Body, Ball–Jointed	875.00
Heubach 8306, Character Boy, Open–Close Mouth, Eyes To Side, Dressed	625.00
Heubach Koppelsdorf 251, Boy, Tyrolean, Costume, 9 In.	150.00
Heubach Koppelsdorf 300, Bisque, Sleep Eyes, Knit Dress, 10 In.	275.00
Heubach Koppelsdorf 339, Bisque, Christening Gown, 15 In.	550.00
Heubach Koppelsdorf 342, Character, 28 In.	550.00
Heubach Koppelsdorf, Bisque, Ball–Jointed, Pink Dress, 18 In.	275.00
Heubach Koppelsdorf, Girl, Flapper, Molded Shoes, 11 1/2 In.	265.00
Heubach, Boy, Black Suit, 13 In.	375.00
Heubach, Boy, Crooked Smile, 10 1/2 In.	325.00
Heubach, Boy, Laughing, Marked 6, 18 In.	600.00
Heubach, Boy, Smiling, Molded Hair, Intaglio Eyes, Composition, 19 In.	950.00
Heubach, Coquette, Marked, 11 In.	550.00
Heubach, Dolly Dimple, Sleep Eyes, Blond Hair, 23 In.	1750.00
Heubach, Girl, Bisque, Blond Wig, Blue Eyes, 9 1/2 In.	185.00
Heubach, Girl, Blue Glass Eyes, Kid Body, Jointed, Marked, 19 In.	595.00
Honey West, TV Private Eye, Anne Francis, 1965	60.00
Horsman, Bye–Lo Baby, Black, 1979, 14 In.	22.00
Horsman, Dolly Dimples, Grace Drayton, Composition	275.00
Horsman, Ella Cinders, Composition, Dressed, 18 In.	375.00
Horsman, Girl, Hard Plastic, Ice Skating Outfit, 18 In.	60.00
Horsman, Girl, Sleep Eyes, Brown Braids, Composition Body, 12 In.	130.00
Horsman, Hand Knit Dress & Bonnet, 13 In.	50.00

Horsman, He Bee, She Bee, Sailor Outfits, 11 In., Pair	80.00
Horsman, Mary Poppins, 1964, 12 In.	45.00 To 60.00
Horsman, Ronald Reagan	55.00 To 60.00
Ideal, Baby Coos, Open Yawning Mouth, Painted Eyes, 1962	95.00
Ideal, Betsy McCall, 1952, 14 In.	85.00
Ideal, Betsy McCall, Beauty Box, 12 In.	45.00
Ideal, Betsy McCall, Riding Clothes, 8 In.	75.00
Ideal, Betsy McCall, Walking Jamie	235.00
Ideal, Betsy McCall, Wendykin, Marked, 8 In.	65.00
Ideal, Bonnie Braids, 14 In.	80.00
Ideal, Bonnie Walker, 16 In.	85.00
Ideal, Crissy, Brown Ponytail, Dressed	85.00
Ideal, Crissy, Grow Hair, Dressed, 20 In.	425.00
Ideal, Deanna Durbin, Dressed, Button, 24 In.	425.00
Ideal, Deanna Durbin, Flirty, Original Pin, 25 In.	850.00
Ideal, Deanna Durbin, Original Dress & Wig, 18 In.	250.00
Ideal, Fanny Brice, Baby Snooks, 12 In,	210.00
Ideal, Goody-Two-Shoes, Feathered Eyelashes, Dressed, 1965, 18 In.	57.50
Ideal, Kerry, Grow Hair	10.00
Ideal, Kissy, Name Ribbon On Dress, Red Shoes, 1962, 22 In.	75.00
Ideal, Kissy, Original Clothes, Box, 16 In.	45.00
Ideal, Kissy, Original Clothes, Box, 22 In.	65.00
Ideal, Linus, Cloth, 8 In.	5.00
Ideal, Little Miss Marker, Box	10.00
Ideal, Magic Skin Latex Baby, Hard Plastic, 1949, 18 In.	125.00
Ideal, Mama, Composition Head & Limbs, Molded Hair, 1920s, 28 In.	67.50
Ideal, Patti Playpal, Black, Original Clothes, Re-Issue, 36 In.	85.00
Ideal, Patti Playpal, Brown Hair, Rosy Color, 32 In.	150.00
Ideal, Patti Playpal, Brunette, Redressed, 1960	140.00
Ideal, Rub-A-Dub, 17 In.	20.00
Ideal, Snoozy, Stuffed Latex Cloth Body, 20 In.	55.00
Ideal, Tammy & Family, With Dad, Clothes, In Case, Box	135.00
Ideal, Tara, Grow Hair, Box	125.00
Ideal, Thumbelina, Mama Voice, White Dress, 18 In.	35.00
Ideal, Tiny Tears, 12 In.	38.00
Ideal, Tippy Tumbles, Works, 1976, 16 In.	20.00
Ideal, Toni, Bleached Hair & Lashes, 1949, 14 In.	25.00
Ideal, Toni, Brunette, No Solutions, Box, 16 In.	245.00
Ideal, Toni, Wardrobe, 18 In.	90.00
Ideal, Tressy, Grow Hair, Box	85.00
Ignatz Mouse, Wooden, Jointed, 9 In.	250.00
DOLL, INDIAN, see Indian, Doll	
DOLL, J.D.K., see also Doll, Kestner	
J.D.K.211, Toddler, Bisque Head, Brown Sleep Eyes, Open Mouth, 2 Teeth	425.00
J.D.K.214, Blond Long Curls, Bisque, Sleep Eyes, Old Dress, 28 In.	750.00
J.D.K.243, New Outfit, 16 In.	5000.00
J.D.K.260, Character Child, Brown Eyes, Jointed, Swivel Head, 28 In.	900.00
Jackie Coogan, All Original, 14 In.	225.00
Jackie Robinson, Composition, Dodger's Uniform	425.00
Jane Withers, 20 In.	950.00
Japanese, Bisque Head, Hands & Feet, Sleep Eyes, Red Silk Kimono	95.00
Jerri, Annette	500.00
Jerri, Christmas Carol	350.00
Jerri, Laura Ingalls	325.00
Jerri, Tammy	325.00
Jerry Mahoney, Composition	25.00
Joey Stivic, Archie Bunker's Grandson, 1976	25.00
John Bull, Palmer Cox, Cloth, Uncut	45.00
John Travolta, Dressed, 12 In.	16.00
John-John, Celluloid, Japan, 24 1/2 In.	200.00
Julia, No.1128, Talking, Box	100.00
Jumeau 1907, Bisque, Open Mouth, Row of Teeth, Composition Body, 16 In.	1150.00
Jumeau 1907, Bisque, Upper Teeth, Jointed Wrists, Dressed, 32 In.	2600.00
Jumeau, Automaton, On Fainting Couch, 24 In.	3400.00

Jumeau, Bisque Head, Ball–Jointed Body, Underclothes, Dress, 16 In. 2250.00
Jumeau, Bisque Head, Ball–Jointed Composition Body, Dressed, 31 In. 2450.00
Jumeau, Bisque Head, 19 In. 3300.00
Jumeau, Bisque, Jointed Body, Underclothes, Satin Dress, 11 In. 2495.00
Jumeau, Bisque, Paperweight Eyes, Ball–Jointed, Dressed, 19 In. 5000.00
Jumeau, Bisque, Paperweight Eyes, Satin Dress, Lace, Bonnet, 18 1/2 In. 1195.00
Jumeau, Bisque, Set Eyes, Jointed Wrists, Silk Dress, Lace Trim, 26 In. 3200.00
Jumeau, Bisque, Sleep Eyes, Taffeta Dress, Lace Overskirt, 24 In. 1250.00
Jumeau, Bisque, Upper Teeth, Blond Long Curls, Satin Dress, 34 In. 2800.00
Jumeau, Bisque, Upper Teeth, Jointed Wrists, Satin Dress, 18 1/2 In. 1950.00
Jumeau, Bisque, Upper Teeth, Jointed Wrists, Taffeta Dress, 29 In. 2250.00
Jumeau, French, Automaton, Musical, Closed Mouth, Maroon Box, 16 In. 3000.00
Jumeau, Open Mouth, Blue Eyes, Jointed, Composition, Silk Dress, 24 In. 1395.00
Jumeau, Paperweight Eyes, Human Hair Wig, Thanos, 27 In. 550.00
Jumeau, Portrait Fashion, Original Clothes, 25 In. 3500.00
Jumeau, Portrait, French Body, Jointed, Closed Mouth, Maroon Hat, 17 In. 5000.00
Jumeau, Sleep Eyes, Upper Teeth, Jointed Body, 26 1/2 In. 1195.00
Jumeau, Upper Teeth, Curls, Ball–Jointed Body, Dress, Straw Hat, 15 In. 675.00
K & K, Character Child, Sleep Eyes, Open Mouth, 18 In. ....*Illus* 248.00
K * R 80, Child, 33 In. 1100.00
K * R 100, Kaiser Baby, Bent Limb, 10 In. 325.00
K * R 101, Marie, 17 In. 2700.00
K * R 114X, Character Boy, Flocked Hair, Composition, Jointed, 15 In. 3000.00
K * R 117, Character Child, Flirty Blue Eyes, Silk, Lace Dress, 21 In. 1595.00
K * R 117N, Flirty Eyes, Long Wig, 25 In. 1950.00
K * R 117N, Sleep Eyes, Wood & Composition, Ball–Jointed, 35 1/2 .... 2090.00
K * R 121, Baby, Brown Sleep Eyes, Not Crying, White Dress, 25 In. 1150.00
K * R 126, Baby, Tremble Tongue, 23 In. 850.00
K * R 126, Character Baby, Blue Sleep Eyes, Brown Hair, Clothes, 16 In. 500.00
K * R 126, Jill, Baby, Tremble Tongue, Sleep Eyes, 20 In. 575.00
K * R 126, Sleep Eyes, Bent Limb, 21 In. 625.00
K * R 126, Toddler Body, Black, 16 1/2 In. 850.00
K * R 127, Baby, Bent Limb Body, Solid Dome, Painted Hair, 14 In. 1100.00
K * R 131, Googly, Box, 12 In. 4800.00
K * R 728, Boy, Tyrolean, Costume, Celluloid 300.00
K * R 728, Character Baby, Celluloid, 19 In. 390.00
K * R, Boy, Bisque Head, Painted Hair & Eyes, Pants, Shirt, 17 1/2 In. 975.00
K * R, Boy, Bisque, Jointed Body, Leather Leggings, Hat, 18 1/2 In. 650.00
K * R, Character Baby, Dimpled, Jointed Body, Dressed, 22 In. 675.00
K * R, Santa Girl, Ball–Jointed, Big Tummy, Sleep Eyes, 10 In. 650.00
Kate Greenaway Style, Parian Head, Roses, Blue Ribbons, 13 In. 775.00
Kathe Kruse, Bastel, Redhead, Freckles, 10 In. 140.00

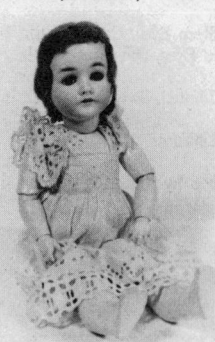

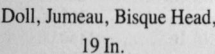

Save your doll's packaging, tags, and inserts. These can triple the price when the doll is sold.

Doll, Jumeau, Bisque Head,
19 In.

Doll, Queen Louise, Bisque,
Sleep Eyes, Jointed Body,
19 In.

Kathe Kruse, Bess, Black Girl, 10 In. 165.00
Kenner, Alien, Ugly, 1979 .... 185.00
Kenner, Bionic Woman, 1977 .... 16.00
Kenner, Shaun Cassidy, 1978 .... 18.00

DOLL, KESTNER, see also Doll, J.D.K.

Kestner 4, Bisque Head, Sleep Eyes, Wood & Composition Body, 9 In. 660.00
Kestner 20, Baby, Bisque, Fat Cheeks, Sleep Eyes, Curly Wig, 28 In. 1300.00
Kestner 142, Character Baby, Bisque, 13 In. 195.00
Kestner 143, Ball–Jointed Body, Sleep Eyes, Plaster Pate, 19 In. 750.00
Kestner 143, Brown Sleep Eyes, Red Dress, Lace Trim, 19 In. 745.00
Kestner 143, Character Child, Brown Sleep Eyes, Jointed, Dress, 15 In. 650.00
Kestner 143, Character Toddler, Jointed, Sleep Brown Eyes, 16 1/2 In. 775.00
Kestner 148, Brown Sleep Eyes, Blond Hair, Kid Body, Chemise, 14 In. 250.00
Kestner 150/9, Sleep Eyes, Open Mouth, Teeth, 8 In. 375.00
Kestner 154, Kid Body, 27 In. 545.00
Kestner 154, Sleep Eyes, Fur Eyebrows, Open Mouth 350.00
Kestner 168, Girl, Original Clothes, 22 In. 395.00
Kestner 171, French Type Body, Ball–Jointed, 25 In. 525.00
Kestner 191C, Lady Body, 19 In. 850.00
Kestner 192, Sleep Eyes, Open Mouth, Blond Wig, 7 In. 375.00
Kestner 196, Fur Brows, 17 In. 350.00
Kestner 214, Character, Pouty Lip, Bobbed Wig, Navy Dress, 20 In. 595.00
Kestner 243, Oriental Child, Painted Hair, 13 In. 4400.00
Kestner 323, Googly, Blue Eyes, Pigtails, 11 In. 975.00
Kestner, Character, Bisque, Open Mouth, Human Hair, C.1915, 22 In. 750.00
Kestner, Florodora, Black Hair, Dressed, 22 In. 275.00
Kestner, Gibson Girl, Original Dress, 21 In. 2300.00
Kestner, Leather Body, Open–Close Mouth, Plaster Pate, 18 In. 595.00
Kestner, Pouty, All Bisque, Bare Feet, Sleep Eyes, 10 In. 1850.00
Kestner, Pouty, Character Boy, 13 1/2 In. 500.00
Kestner, Turned Head, Blond Mohair Wig, Dressed, 21 In. 750.00

DOLL, KEWPIE, see Kewpie, Doll

Kewpie, Boy & Girl, Black, School Outfits, Cameo, Pair 50.00
Kewpie, Bride & Groom, Cameo, 16 In., Pair 67.50
Kewpie, Doctor & Nurse, Cameo, 12 In., Pair 45.00
Kley & Hahn 525, Character Toddler, Sleep Eyes, 14 1/2 In. 1750.00
Kley & Hahn 546, Blue Glass Eyes, 20 In. 3700.00
Kley & Hahn, Baby, Christening Outfit 400.00
Knickerbocker, Barney Rubble, 14 In. 10.00
Knickerbocker, Bozo, Tagged, 4 Ft. 195.00
Knickerbocker, Fred Flintstone, 14 In. 10.00
Knickerbocker, Raggedy Andy, Bend–Em 10.00
Knickerbocker, Sandy, 22 In. 25.00
Konig & Wernicke 1070, Character Baby, 25 In. 700.00
Konig & Wernicke 1070, Character Baby, Jointed Wrists, 19 In. 550.00
Krueger, Rattle Head, Celluloid Head, Oilcloth Body 65.00
LaMotte, Bonnet Head, Dressed, 16 In. 225.00
Lanternier & Cie, La Georgienne, French Walker Body, 21 In. 550.00
Lanternier, Toto, Character, Bisque, Stationary Eyes, 21 In. 695.00
Lenci, Aureilia, Holding Felt Goose, 12 In. 125.00
Lenci, Boy, Tyrolean Costume, 16 In. 550.00
Lenci, Clown, Felt, Jointed Arms & Legs, Hand Painted Features, 15 In. 375.00
Lenci, Curly Blond Hair, Striped Green Dress, 12 In. 220.00
Lenci, Felt Swivel Head, Blue Side–Glancing Eyes, C.1930, 17 In. 1500.00
Lenci, Girl, Tags, Box, 13 In. 1850.00
Lenci, Glenda, 17 In. 350.00
Lenci, Golfer, 22 In. 250.00
Lenci, Little Hatmaker, Certificate, Box, 1984, 20 In. 345.00
Lenci, Lucia, Tags, 14 In. 950.00
Lenci, Marta, 17 In. 350.00
Lenci, Mascot, Felt Hair, All Original, Tagged, 9 In. 200.00
Lenci, Nanni, Trenchcoat, 22 In. 250.00
Limbach, Toddler, 5 In. 150.00
Linda Williams, All Original, 1959, 14 In. 35.00

Linus, Hungerford, 10 In.	20.00
Lissy 1225, Meg, Pink Cotton Dress, White Apron, Box	200.00
Lissy, Bisque, Pin–Jointed Kid Body, Original Dress & Hat, 21 In.	365.00
Little Love, Composition Head, Limbs, 1940s, 18 In.	65.00
Little Max, From Joe Palooka, Original Clothes, 1950s, 19 In.	35.00
Madame Alexander, Agatha, Box .... 280.00 To 350.00
Madame Alexander, Alice In Wonderland, 1966, 14 In.	75.00
Madame Alexander, Alice In Wonderland, Hard Plastic, 1951, 14 In.	275.00
Madame Alexander, Angelica Van Buren	66.00
Madame Alexander, Baby Victoria, 20 In.	40.00
Madame Alexander, Baby, Spice	100.00
Madame Alexander, Baby, Sugar	100.00
Madame Alexander, Ballerina, Blue, 8 In.	150.00
Madame Alexander, Beth, 1966, 8 In.	85.00
Madame Alexander, Black Baby, Gingham Dress, Rubberized, 1965, 14 In.	55.00
Madame Alexander, Brenda Starr, Hard Plastic, Extra Clothes, 12 In.	185.00
Madame Alexander, Bride, Box, 1966, 14 In.	200.00
Madame Alexander, Bride, Hard Plastic, Ivory Gown, 1950, 18 In.	55.00
Madame Alexander, Brigitta, 1965, 14 In.	65.00
Madame Alexander, Carmen Miranda, Composition, Tagged Dress, 14 In.	300.00
Madame Alexander, Caroline, Corduroy Outfit, Shoes, Tag	190.00
Madame Alexander, Cinderella, 12 In.	105.00
Madame Alexander, Cissette, Godey, Red Hair, Yellow Dress, Box, 1969	495.00
Madame Alexander, Cissette, Street Clothes, 1958, 9 In. .... 105.00 To 175.00
Madame Alexander, Cissy, Fashion Parade, Gown, Fur Cape, 1956, 13 In.	625.00
Madame Alexander, Cissy, Hard Plastic, High Heels, Dress, 1955, 20 In.	200.00
Madame Alexander, Cissy, Tulle & Purple Velvet Gown, Jewels, 21 In.	500.00
Madame Alexander, Cornelia, 1973	350.00
Madame Alexander, Cousin Mary, Blond, Blue Organdy Dress, Box, 1963	800.00
Madame Alexander, Cowboy & Cowgirl, Box, 1967, Pair	1450.00
Madame Alexander, Cry Baby, Dressed, Dated 1965	50.00
Madame Alexander, Deanna Durbin, 21 In.	275.00
Madame Alexander, Dilly Dally Sally, Composition, 1937, 7 In.	180.00
Madame Alexander, Elise, Bride, Box	125.00
Madame Alexander, Elise, Bridesmaid, Blond, Blue Eyes, Pink, Box	70.00
Madame Alexander, Elise, Bridesmaid, Red Hair, Pink Clothes, Box	125.00
Madame Alexander, Elizabeth Monroe .... 44.00 To 55.00
Madame Alexander, Flora McFlimsey, Freckle–Faced, Composition, 24 In.	500.00
Madame Alexander, Gene Tierney, Composition, 1945, 14 In.	525.00
Madame Alexander, Goldilocks, Box, 1978	85.00
Madame Alexander, Grandma Jane, Box .... 260.00 To 300.00
Madame Alexander, Hansel & Gretel, Pair	85.00
Madame Alexander, Hedy LaMarr, 1949, 17 In.	600.00
Madame Alexander, Hiawatha	710.00
Madame Alexander, Jane Withers, Tagged Dress & Straw Hat, 1937, 13 In.	495.00
Madame Alexander, Jeannie, Walker, Composition, 14 In.	170.00
Madame Alexander, Jo, Hard Plastic, Jumper, Apron, 11 3/4 In.	125.00
Madame Alexander, Josephine, 12 In.	60.00
Madame Alexander, Julia Tyler	55.00
Madame Alexander, Kate Greenaway, Tagged, 13 In.	425.00
Madame Alexander, Kathy, Cry Baby, Vinyl, Bonnet & Bloomers, 15 In.	90.00
Madame Alexander, Kelly, Plastic, Blue Eyes, Closed Mouth, 1958, 21 In.	550.00
Madame Alexander, Lady Hamilton, 12 In.	72.00
Madame Alexander, Laurie, Vinyl, 1969 In.	65.00
Madame Alexander, Leslie, Black, Box, 17 In.	300.00
Madame Alexander, Little Edwardian, Brunette, Box.8 In.	1150.00
Madame Alexander, Little Genius, 2 Tagged Outfits, 8 In.	130.00
Madame Alexander, Little Genius, Turquoise Polka Dot Dress	135.00
Madame Alexander, Little Lord Fauntleroy, 12 In. .... 80.00 To 110.00
Madame Alexander, Littlest Kitten, Blond, Organdy Dress, 8 In.	265.00
Madame Alexander, Lord Nelson, 12 In.	58.00
Madame Alexander, Louisa Adams	44.00
Madame Alexander, Madalaine DuBain, Composition, Red Satin Outfit	375.00
Madame Alexander, Madame Pompadour, 1970, 21 In.	850.00

Madame Alexander, Madelaine, Flowered Southern Bell Dress, 18 In. 275.00
Madame Alexander, Maggie Mixup, Guardian Angel, Dress, No Halo, 8 In. 325.00
Madame Alexander, Margaret O'Brien, Composition, Straw Hat, 1946 .... 495.00
Madame Alexander, Margot, 1951 .... 165.00
Madame Alexander, Marie Antoinette .... 185.00 To 225.00
Madame Alexander, Marlo Thomas, Plastic, 1967, 17 In. 560.00
Madame Alexander, Marme, 1966, 8 In. 85.00
Madame Alexander, Martha Randolph 33.00
Madame Alexander, Mary, Mary, Box, 8 In. 135.00
Madame Alexander, McGuffey Ana, 8 In. 375.00
Madame Alexander, McGuffey Ana, 15 In. 250.00
Madame Alexander, McGuffey Ana, Composition, 16 In. 250.00
Madame Alexander, McGuffey Ana, Composition, Original Clothes, 13 In. 90.00
Madame Alexander, McGuffey Ana, Pigtails, Pinafore, 1937, 20 In. 350.00
Madame Alexander, McGuffey Ana, Tagged, Dress, Hair Bow, 18 In. 255.00
Madame Alexander, Monet, 21 In. .... 195.00 To 320.00
Madame Alexander, Nurse & Baby, Blue & White Striped Outfit, 8 In. 550.00
Madame Alexander, Penny, Painted Eyes & Face, 34 In. 375.00
Madame Alexander, Peter Pan, 1969 .... 350.00
Madame Alexander, President's Wives, 2nd Set, Box .... 595.00 To 600.00
Madame Alexander, President's Wives, 3rd Set, Box .... 595.00 To 635.00
Madame Alexander, Prince Charles, Navy Suit & Hat, 1957, 8 In. 250.00
Madame Alexander, Princess Elizabeth, 27 In. 475.00
Madame Alexander, Princess Elizabeth, Long Gown, Shoes, Tagged, 16 In. 230.00
Madame Alexander, Puddin', Box, 1966, 20 In. 85.00
Madame Alexander, Quizkin, Floral Romper, Sunbonnet, Blue Shoes, 1953 .... 385.00
Madame Alexander, Rosebud, 18 In. 150.00
Madame Alexander, Rosebud, 23 In. 150.00
Madame Alexander, Scarlett & Rhett, 12 In., Pair 150.00
Madame Alexander, Scarlett O'Hara, Bent Knee, 1971, 8 In. 375.00
Madame Alexander, Scarlett O'Hara, Flowered Gown & Hat, 1971, 8 In. 450.00
Madame Alexander, Scarlett O'Hara, Green Velvet, 21 In. 195.00
Madame Alexander, Scarlett O'Hara, Taffeta Dress, Box, 1977, 21 In. 395.00
Madame Alexander, Shari Lewis, 1959, 21 In. 350.00
Madame Alexander, Sweet Sue Walker, Original Clothes, 1950s, 14 In. 58.00
Madame Alexander, Uncle Wiggily, Cloth, No Clothes, 18 In. 245.00
Madame Alexander, Victoria, Box, 1975, 16 In. 80.00
Madame Alexander, Victoria, Christening Gown, 14 In. 60.00
Madame Alexander, Walker, Straight Leg, 1955, 7 1/2 In. 95.00
Madame Alexander, Wendy Ann, Bride, Tagged, 18 In. 275.00
Madame Alexander, Wendy Ann, Composition, Swivel Waist, 14 In. 175.00
Madame Alexander, Wendy Likes A Rainy Day, Raincoat, Boots, 9155, 8 In. 350.00
Madame Alexander, Winnie Walker, Pink Formal Gown, Tag, 18 In. 285.00
Madame Alexander, Zorina, Ballerina, 1937, 17 In. 875.00
Madame Hendren, Composition, 26 In. 140.00
Mail Baby, Fabric, 5 In. 110.00
Marilyn Monroe, Dress, 11 In. 40.00
Marilyn Monroe, Offical 20th-Century Fox, Box, 11 In. 47.00
Marilyn Monroe, Porcelain, White Sequin Dress, World, 1983 .... 300.00
Marionette, Goofy, Pelham, Box 125.00
Marionette, Hillbilly, Hazell's No.806 .... 150.00
Marionette, Horse, Wooden, Painted Designs 175.00
Marionette, Jiminy Cricket 35.00
Marionette, Oliver Hardy, Chalkware, Larry Harmon Features, 12 In. 85.00
Marionette, Peter Pan & Wendy, Composition, Pair 225.00
Marionette, Pinocchio, Jointed Legs, 10 1/2 In. 60.00
Marotte, China Head, On Stick, 3-Point Hat With Bells, Red & Yellow 75.00
Martha Chase, Baby, Jointed Elbows & Knees, C.1889, 27 In. 1550.00
Martha Chase, Hospital Boy, Nightgown, Paste-Painted, 1918, 24 In. 875.00
Mary Hartline, 8 In. 60.00
Mary Poppins, 15 In. 65.00
Mary Vasquez, Spain, Little Boy, Felt, Glass Eyes, 10 In. 75.00
Mattel, Baby Brother Tenderlove, Sexed, 1975, 13 In. 19.00
Mattel, Barbie, Astronaut, Box 20.00

Mattel, Barbie, Astronaut, Silver Asbestos Jumpsuit, Boots	125.00
Mattel, Barbie, Benefit Performance, Porcelain	175.00
Mattel, Barbie, Blond Twist, Rose & White Suit	125.00
Mattel, Barbie, Brunette, 1960	65.00
Mattel, Barbie, Bubble Cut, Blonde, 1962	45.00
Mattel, Barbie, Fashion Queen .... 25.00 To 65.00
Mattel, Barbie, Happy Birthday	14.00
Mattel, Barbie, Live Action, No.115, 1971	60.00
Mattel, Barbie, Mardi Gras	25.00
Mattel, Barbie, Miss America .... 15.00 To 45.00
Mattel, Barbie, No.3, Blonde	250.00
Mattel, Barbie, Nurse's Uniform	175.00
Mattel, Barbie, Platinum Swirl Ponytail, 1964	225.00
Mattel, Barbie, Queen, Box, 1963	200.00
Mattel, Barbie, Saturday Date	85.00
Mattel, Barbie, Singing In The Shower	80.00
Mattel, Barbie, Ski Queen	80.00
Mattel, Barbie, Sleep–Eye, 1964	550.00
Mattel, Barbie, Standard, 1971	135.00
Mattel, Barbie, Star Dream	25.00
Mattel, Barbie, Sweet Dreams	75.00
Mattel, Barbie, Talking, Blond, Pink Bathing Suit, Net Top, 1969	30.00
Mattel, Barbie, Twist & Turn, 1967	20.00
Mattel, Barbie, Twist & Turn, Blond, Rooted Eyelashes, Suit, 1966	40.00
Mattel, Barbie, Twist & Turn, Dressed, 1966	65.00
Mattel, Barbie, White Astronaut, Box	18.00
Mattel, Charmin' Chatty, Red Hair, Sailor Suit, Saddle Shoes, 25 In.	67.50
Mattel, Charmin' Chatty, With Record	40.00
Mattel, Chatty Baby, Blonde, Dressed, 1960s, 18 In.	47.50
Mattel, Chatty Cathy, Original Dress	40.00
Mattel, Cheryl Ladd, 1978	15.00
Mattel, Donnie Osmond, 1976	20.00
Mattel, Francie, 1966	45.00
Mattel, Ken, Graduation	40.00
Mattel, Ken, No.1111, Talking, Box	75.00
Mattel, Ken, Rally Days	40.00
Mattel, Ken, Red Trunks, Striped Jacket, Painted Hair, 1962	55.00
Mattel, Ken, Sailor, Box	350.00
Mattel, Ken, Sun Valley, 1974	40.00
Mattel, Ken, Touchdown Outfit, Red	28.00
Mattel, Ken, Western, 1981	20.00
Mattel, Marie Osmond, 1976	20.00
Mattel, Skipper, Box	50.00
Mattel, Small Talk, Wrist Tag, 11 In.	12.00
Mattel, Stacy, Talking, Blue & Silver Suit	200.00
Mattel, Tutti, Walking My Dolly, Box	150.00
Mattel, Woody Woodpecker, Talks	30.00
Mego, Cher, Stylable Hair, Poseable, 1976, 12 In.	35.00
Mego, Farrah Fawcett–Majors, 1977	24.00
Mego, John Boy & Mary Ellen Walton, 8 In., Pair	10.00
Mego, Kirk & Spock, Star Trek, 1979, 12 1/2 In., Pair	47.00
Mego, Spiderman, Box, 12 In.	100.00
Mego, Toni Tennille, 12 1/2 In.	5.00
Mein Liebling, My Little Lover, Glass Eyes, Vinyl, Germany, 24 In.	115.00
Michael Jackson, Show Accessories, 11 In.	20.00
Monkee, Mickey	20.00
Morimura, Character Boy, 18 In.	275.00
Muhammad Ali, Boxing Room, Champ & His Opponent	55.00
Nancy Ann Storybook, Bisque, Original Clothes & Box	35.00
Nancy Ann Storybook, Saturday's Child, Nylon Dress, Broom, Box	100.00
Nancy Ann Storybook, Sunday's Child, White Taffeta Dress, Blond Hair	80.00
Nancy Ann Storybook, Sweet Alice, Brunette, Red Bodice, Striped Skirt	65.00
Nancy Ann Storybook, Sweet October Maiden Rather Shy, Brunette, Tag	85.00
Nancy Ann Storybook, Western Miss, Blonde, Green Checked Dress, Hat	85.00

Norah Wellings, Black, Glass Eyes, Original Clothes, 15 In. 250.00
Norah Wellings, Character, All Original, 17 In. 150.00
Norah Wellings, Old Lady, 24 In. 500.00
Norah Wellings, Sailor, With Lifesaver, 8 In. 55.00
Nuthead Family, Black, 9 Piece 350.00
Nuthead, White, Pair 25.00
Old Woman, Wooden Chair, Rag, Wax Head & Hands, Cloth Costume, 16 In. 95.00
Painted Character Face, Straw–Filled Body, Composition, 17 In. 50.00
    DOLL, PAPER, see Paper Doll
Papier–Mache Head, Old Clothes, 1880, 34 In. 450.00
Papier–Mache, Boy & Girl, Oriental, Bisque, 1920, Pair 110.00
Papier–Mache, Braided Bun, Cluster Side Curls, Old Clothing, 14 In. 800.00
Papier–Mache, Molded Hair, Wooden Limbs, Kid Body, 11 In. 500.00
Parian, Boy, Bisque Feet & Hands, 8 In. 175.00
Parian, Boy, Original Clothes, 4 1/2 In. 75.00
Parian, Junior Bridesmaid, 7 1/4 In. 175.00
Peanuts & Lucy, Molded Plastic, 9 In., Pair 24.00
Peasant Girl, Bisque Head, Painted, All Original, 11 In. 125.00
Peggy Nisbet, Prince Charles & Lady Diana, Wedding Attire, Pair 100.00
Peter Pan & Tinkerbell, Bisque, 1940s, Pair 75.00
Pierrot, Head 65.00
    DOLL, PINCUSHION, see Pincushion Doll
Poor Pitiful Pearl, 16 In. 45.00
Poor Pitiful Pearl, Vinyl, 1950s, 12 In. 60.00
Puppet, Black Boy, White Boy, Levers Activate Mouth, Wooden, 32 In., Pr. 3400.00
Puppet, Donald Duck, Pelham, Handmade, Box 60.00
Puppet, Lion, Steiff 45.00
Puppet, Monkey, Steiff 35.00
Puppet, Punch & Judy, Papier–Mache, Litho Paper, Wooden Stage, 7 Piece 850.00
Queen Louise, Bisque, Sleep Eyes, Jointed Body, 19 In. ....*Illus* 330.00
Queen Louise, Regal Clothes, Crown, 17 In. 335.00
R & B, Bisque, Long Curls, Ball–Jointed, Maroon Satin Dress, 28 1/2 In. 3500.00
Rag, Babyland, Hand Painted, American, C.1900 .... 1850.00
Rag, Black, Painted Face, Calico Dress, Sandals, 24 In. 475.00
Rag, Black, Red Jacket & Shoes, Black Pants, Mid–19th Century, 9 In. 150.00
Rag, Painted Face, Sailor Clothes 145.00
Raggedy Andy, George, 50 In. 500.00
Raggedy Ann, Oilcloth Face, 1920s 95.00
Ralph Cramden, Honeymooners Series 65.00
Red Riding Hood, Composition, Sears Roebuck 50.00
Reggie, Jointed, Orange T–Shirt, Marx, 1975, 9 In. 12.00
Revalo, Ball–Jointed Body, 15 In. 285.00
Revalo, Coquette, Molded Hair With Bowl, Composition Body 695.00
Robin Woods, Alice In Trunk 200.00
Robin Woods, Beatrice 96.00
    DOLL, S & H, see also Doll, Bergmann; Doll, Simon & Halbig
S & H 1250, Kid Body, Real Lashes, 18 In. 500.00
S & H 1428, Bisque Head, Character Baby, Blond, Jointed, 14 In. 1250.00
S & H 1906, Sleep Eyes, Ball–Jointed, Human Hair Wig, Tyrolean Dress 495.00
S & H, Bisque Head, Sleep Eyes, Brown Hair, Jointed, Composition, 24 In. 165.00
S & H, Sleep Eyes, Open Mouth, Old Clothes, 18 In. 450.00
S.F.B.J. 60, 5 Piece Body, 15 In. 275.00
S.F.B.J. 235, Jewel Eyes, Laughing Mouth, Molded Hair, 17 In. 1600.00
S.F.B.J. 236, Toddler, Light Brown Hair, Stemped, 20 1/2 In. 1850.00
S.F.B.J. 247, Twerp, Long Hair, Dressed, 24 In. 3500.00
S.F.B.J. 251, Character Toddler, 16 In. 1150.00
S.F.B.J., Bisque Head, Upper Teeth, Sleep Eyes, Dressed, 29 In. 1450.00
S.F.B.J., Mulatto Boy, Jewel Eyes, Painted Hair, Dressed, 18 In. 1850.00
S.F.B.J., Nurse, World War I, 7 In. 175.00
S.F.B.J., Walker, Bisque, Upper Teeth, Pink Dress, Bonnet, 23 In. 995.00
Samurai, Full Armor Suit, Seated, Glass Fronted Case, 11 3/4 In. 200.00
Samurai, Seated, Meiji Period, C.1880 .... 650.00
Scandia House, Troll, Cloth Body, Plastic Arms, Head, White Hair, 11 In. 10.00
Schmidt 1272, Character Baby, 19 In. 375.00

Schmitt & Fils, Girl, Wearing Factory Frock, 20 In.	6900.00
Schmitt, Bisque, Long Blond Curls, Straw Hat, Dress, 19 1/2 In.	9200.00
Schoenau & Hoffmeister, Bisque, Ball-Jointed, Drop-Waist Dress, 24 In.	355.00
Schoenau & Hoffmeister, Sleep Eyes, Ball-Jointed, Dressed, 28 In.	475.00
Schoenhut, Boy, Stand, 19 In.	725.00
Schoenhut, Clown, Wooden, Original Clothes, 8 In.	98.00
Schoenhut, Girl, Carved Pageboy-Type Curls, Intaglio Eyes	6000.00
Schoenhut, Pouty Baby, Original Paint, Undressed, 13 1/2 In.	325.00
Schoenhut, Pouty Boy, Blonde Wig, 11 In.	590.00
Schoenhut, Pouty, 16 In.	325.00
Scootles, 1973, 14 In.	150.00
Scootles, Girl, Cheerleader, 16 In.	40.00
Shader, Elena, China, Box	2000.00
Shader, Francoise, Box	1200.00
DOLL, SHIRLEY TEMPLE, see Shirley Temple	
Simmone, Fashion, Kid Over Wood Body, Bisque Arms & Lower Legs, 18 In.	7500.00
DOLL, SIMON & HALBIG, see also Doll, Bergmann; Doll, S & H	
Simon & Halbig 46, Boy & Girl, Sailor Outfit, Original & Wig, 17 In.	1450.00
Simon & Halbig 151, Character, Side-Glancing Painted Eyes, 17 In.	6500.00
Simon & Halbig 921, Bisque, Black Hair, Sleep Eyes, Bent Limb, 4 In.	440.00
Simon & Halbig 939, Original Wig & Clothes, 9 In.	1550.00
Simon & Halbig 949, Ball-Jointed Body, Dressed, 15 In.	1200.00
Simon & Halbig 949, Pouty Face, Closed Mouth, 23 In.	2300.00
Simon & Halbig 1039, Roullet & Decamp Movement, Silk Dress, 18 In.	950.00
Simon & Halbig 1078, Bisque Head, Sleep Eyes, Jointed, 30 In.	880.00
Simon & Halbig 1079, Lace Party Dress, 37 In.	1700.00
Simon & Halbig 1079, Pale Complexion, Antique Dress, 40 In.	1995.00
Simon & Halbig 1079, Sleep Eyes, Open Mouth, Jointed, Velvet, 15 In.	350.00
Simon & Halbig 1159, Lady, Molded Bust, Straight Wrists, 22 In.	1300.00
Simon & Halbig 1248, Santa Claus, Mohair Wig, Sleep Eyes, 32 In.	1850.00
Simon & Halbig 1469, Bisque, Flapper, Socket Head, 14 In. ....*Illus*	6750.00
Simon & Halbig, Bisque, Open Mouth, Jointed, Antique Dress, 41 In.	2700.00
Simon & Halbig, Bisque, Pierced Ears, Sleep Eyes, Dressed, 18 In.	575.00
Simon & Halbig, Bisque, Upper Teeth, Ball-Jointed Body, Dressed, 32 In.	895.00
Simon & Halbig, Composition Body, Hair, Feathered Eyebrows, 24 In.	500.00
Simon & Halbig, Eyes Move Side To Side When String Is Pulled, 17 In.	685.00
Simon & Halbig, Girl, String Makes Eyes Move, 16 In.	600.00
Simon & Halbig, Indian, Bisque Head, Composition, All Original, 7 In.	155.00
Skookum, Indian Brave, 19 In.	35.00
Skookum, Papoose, Indian, Worn Face, Sparse Hair, 3 1/2 In.	7.50
Snoopy, Flying Ace, Brown Helmet, Goggles, Scarf, 7 In.	5.00
Star Wars, Life-Size, Stand Ups	350.00
Steiff, Clownie, Felt, Pressed Rubber Head, Glass Eyes, Tag & Button	135.00
Steiff, Golliwog, 11 In.	5000.00
Steiff, Leprechaun, Glass Eyes, Felt	35.00
Steiner, 2 Rows of Teeth, Cryer, Paperweight Eyes, 18 In.	2950.00
Steiner, Bebe, Kicking, Crying, Bisque, 2 Rows of Teeth, Dressed, 17 In.	2250.00
Steiner, Bisque Head, Mamma, Voice Box, 1880s	2640.00
Steiner, Bisque, Jointed Body, Lever For Eye Mechanism, C.1890, 25 In.	4675.00
Steiner, Brown Paperweight Eyes, 24 In.	5400.00
Steiner, Composition Body, Open-Close Mouth, Paperweight Eyes, 18 In.	3500.00
Steiner, Crepe De Chine Chemise & Bloomers, 8 In.	3500.00
Steiner, Fashion, Pierced Ears, Open-Close Mouth, 18 In.	3500.00
Steiner, Sleep Eyes, Bisque, Clothes, Original Wig, 9 In.	130.00
Stoneware, Head, Molded Features, Tan Glazed Hair, Primitive, 4 In.	400.00
Terri Lee, Auburn Hair, Green Party Dress, Felt Hat, 16 In.	150.00
Terri Lee, Black Long Hair, Aqua Pajamas, 16 In.	125.00
Terri Lee, Bride, Box	400.00
Terri Lee, Brown Hair, Red Plaid Dress, 16 In.	125.00
Terri Lee, Brunette, Hairnet, Taffeta, Sequin Net Overskirt, 16 In.	175.00
Tete Jumeau, Bisque Head, Closed Mouth, Brown Eyes, Jointed, 19 In.	3300.00
Tete Jumeau, Bisque, Ivory Lace Dress, Bonnet, Pink Stockings, 17 In.	2500.00
Tete Jumeau, Brown Human Hair Wig, Sleep Eyes With Lashes, 26 1/2 In.	1175.00
Tete Jumeau, Brown Paperweight Eyes, 17 In.	4400.00

Tete Jumeau, Closed Mouth, Paperweight Eyes, Replaced Hair, 15 In. 2495.00
Tin Head, Baby Smile, Old Outfit 75.00
Tin Head, Cloth Body, Stuffing, Painted, Germany, 13 In. 40.00
Topsy Turvy, Red Riding Hood, Grandma & Wolf, 12 1/2 In. 38.00
Topsy, 3 Pigtails, Composition, 10 In. 65.00
Topsy, Black, 3 Tufts of Hair, Painted-On Clothes, 3 In. 20.00
Troll, Dam Things Establishment, 1964, 12 In. 65.00
Twins, Boy & Girl, Painted Booties, Original Dresses, 4 In., Pair 109.00
Uncle Sam, Bisque, Composition Body, Glass Eyes, Germany, 12 In. 1650.00
Unis 251, Character, Toddler Body, Striped Cotton Dress, Socks, 19 In. 1550.00
Unis 301, Bisque, Upper Teeth, Shirt, Red Pants, Jacket, 13 1/2 In. 350.00
Unis, Black, 12 In. 400.00
Valentine, Toddler, 18 In. 20.00
Vichy, Bisque, On Scooter, 12 In. 3750.00
Vinta, Baby, Composition, Labeled Gown, Tin Eyes, 24 In. 180.00
Vogue, Baby Dear, Black, Vinyl, Cloth, 18 In. 40.00
Vogue, Baby Dear, Dark Hair, Brown Eyes, 1965, 25 In. 30.00
Vogue, Crib Crowd Baby, Painted Blue Eyes, Worn Wig, 1948-50 .... 395.00
Vogue, Fairy Godmother, 1951 .... 250.00
Vogue, Ginny Baby, 15 In. 30.00
Vogue, Ginny Groom, Painted Eyes 225.00
Vogue, Ginny Nun, Box, 1956 .... 175.00 To 295.00
Vogue, Ginny, Porcelain, Jointed, Knees Bend, Pink Taffeta Gown, 1984 .... 30.00
Vogue, Ginny, Sailor Outfit, 1977 .... 25.00
Vogue, Jan, Blonde, Pearl Earrings, Label, 10 In. 60.00
Vogue, Jill, Angel-Cut Red Hair, Strapless Dress, Box 165.00
Vogue, Jill, Felt Circle Skirt 60.00
Vogue, Too Dear, 18 In. 125.00
Wagner & Zetske Nu 200/6, Character, Socket Head, Sleep Eyes, 21 In. 455.00
Wellings, Royal Mountie, Tag, 14 In. 69.00
Wizard of Oz, Throne Chair, Crystal Ball, 8 In. 17.00
Wooden Peg, Hand Painted Face, 12 In. 195.00
Wooden, Jointed Arms & Legs, Wool Costume, Germany, C.1830, 15 In. 1000.00
Wooden, Penny, 1900s, 12 In. 35.00
World, Amy Carter, In Wicker Basket, Box 60.00
World, Witch, Flashing Eyes, 1972, 6 1/2 In. 25.00
Xavier Roberts, Fudge Boy & Girl, Bronze Edition, Pair 500.00
DONALD DUCK, see Disneyana

Iron doorstops have been made in all types of designs. The vast
majority of the doorstops sold today are cast iron and were made
from about 1890 to 1930. Most of them are shaped like people,
animals, flowers, or ships.

DOORSTOP, 2 Eagles, Cast Iron 560.00
2 Men In Livery, Iron, Painted, 12 In. 900.00
3 Walking Geese, Cast Iron, 8 In. 125.00
Aunt Jemima, 3-Dimensional, Iron 175.00
Aunt Jemima, Blue Dress, Cast Iron, 12 3/4 In. 350.00
Basket of Flowers, White Paint, Cast Iron 37.00
Bellhop, Black, Cast Iron 1150.00
Blacksmith, Full Figure, Nickel Over Cast Iron, 6 1/2 In. 45.00
Buffalo, Full Figure, Iron, No.10 .... 85.00
Bundle of Wheat, Iron 75.00
Cat, Fireside, Gold Bell, Bowl, White Paint, Cast Iron 145.00
Cat, Fireside, Hubley, Signed 210.00
Cat, Full-Bodied, Cast Iron, Black, Polychrome Features, 10 In. 95.00
Cinderella Carriage, Cast Iron 275.00
Cockatoo, Red, Yellow & Green, Cast Iron, 14 In. 175.00
Colonial Woman, Purse In Hand 50.00
Conestoga Wagon & Oxen, White Paint, Cast Iron, 10 1/4 In. 105.00
Cottage, Hubley 50.00
Covered Wagon, W.H.Howell Co., Red, Cast Iron, 6 3/4 In. 60.00
Dog, Boston Bull, Full Figure, Cast Iron, 10 1/2 In. .... 55.00 To 70.00
Dog, Bulldog, Sitting, Cast Iron, Original Paint 100.00

Dog, Cocker Spaniel, Cast Iron 275.00
Dog, English Bulldog, White, Black Spots, Iron, 5 3/4 X 8 3/4 In. 175.00
Dog, English Setter, Cast Iron, Original Paint 105.00
Dog, Full-Bodied, Black, White, Hubley, Cast Iron, 10 In. 175.00
Dog, Full-Bodied, Cast Iron, Black, White, Polychrome, 8 In. 25.00
Dog, German Shepherd, Cast Iron, Original Paint .... 40.00 To 90.00
Dog, German Shepherd, Full Figure .... 135.00 To 175.00
Dog, German Shepherd, Leather Collar, Cast Iron 150.00
Dog, Irish Setter, Cast Iron, Original Paint 55.00
Dog, Police, Full Figure, 9 3/4 In. 65.00
Dog, Retriever, Full Figure, Black, White Paint, 14 3/4 In. 65.00
Dog, Scotty, Cast Iron, Original Paint 45.00
Dog, Scotty, Pair, Cast Iron, Word Listen On Base, 8 X 5 In. 55.00
Dog, Scotty, Sitting, Cast Iron 85.00
Dog, Setter, Brass, 7 1/2 X 6 In. 45.00
Dog, St.Bernard, Metallic Brown & Black Paint, Iron, 9 1/4 In. 135.00
Dog, Wirehair Terrier, Cast Iron, 5 1/2 X 5 1/2 In. 75.00
Dog, With Bone, Full Figure, Hubley, Cast Iron, 4 1/8 In. 105.00
Dog, Wolfhound, Full Figure, Cast Iron, 15 1/2 In. 135.00
Dragon, Black, Cast Iron 55.00
Drum Major, Red Jacket, Cast Iron 325.00
Elephant, Full Figure, Solid, Cast Iron, Black, 5 3/4 In. 25.00
Elephant, Metallic White Paint, Cast Iron, 8 1/4 In. 145.00
Fat Man, Full Figure, Polychrome Paint, Cast Iron, 5 1/2 In. 105.00
Fawn, Taylor-Cook, Cast Iron 275.00
Flower Basket, Iron, 9 1/2 In. 69.00
Frog, Green & Yellow Paint, Cast Iron, 7 1/4 In. 135.00
Frog, Standing On Lily Pad 170.00
Gentleman, Full Figure, Polychrome Paint, 16 In. 350.00
George Washington, Cast Iron, C.1929 .... 650.00
Girl, Art Deco, Cast Iron 195.00
Girl, Feather In Bonnet, Cast Iron, Original Paint 125.00
Gnome, Cast Iron .... 300.00 To 375.00
Golfer, Club Up, Cast Iron 375.00
Horse, Full Figure, Chestnut Paint, Cast Iron, 11 In. 110.00
Horse, Full Figure, Palimino, Iron, 8 2/3 In. 55.00
House, With Woman, Cast Iron 185.00
Indian, With Bow, Red Paint, Iron, 12 1/2 In. 225.00
Lighthouse, Cottage, Cast Iron .... 140.00 To 190.00
Lion, Rearing, Painted, Cast Iron, 14 1/2 In. 85.00
Lobster, Black, Upright, Cast Iron, 1900s, 12 In. 130.00
London Royal Mail Coach, Brass Finish 75.00
Mammy, Black, Cast Iron 395.00
Mammy, Hubley, Cast Iron, 8 1/2 In. 265.00
Minuet Girl, Cast Iron 135.00
Napoleon, Riding Horse, Brass, Step-Down Base, 6 X 6 1/2 In. 85.00
Naughty Nellie, Iron 525.00
Parrot, Iron, 6 In. 85.00
Parrot, Iron, 8 In. 75.00
Parrot, Polychrome Paint, Cast Iron, 6 1/2 In. 30.00
Peacock, Bronze 95.00
Peacock, Full Plumage, Iron, 6 1/2 X 6 1/2 In. 125.00
Petunias & Asters 85.00
Pheasant, Hubley 100.00
Punch, Cast Iron 180.00
Puppy, On Pillow, Cast Iron 325.00
Rabbit, Grandpa, Cast Iron 165.00
Racehorse, Virginia Metalcrafters, Cast Iron, 1949 .... 125.00
Rooster, Hubley, Cast Iron 385.00
Santa Claus, Holding Tree, Drum & Horn, White Metal, 1915, 5 In. 200.00
Santa Claus, Sack of Toys Over Shoulder, White Metal, 1915 .... 190.00
Schooner, Brass, 9 In. 85.00
Scotsman, With Spear, Gold & Black Paint, Cast Iron, 15 In. 85.00
Ship, Cast Iron, Polychrome Paint, 12 1/2 In. 10.00

Ship, Sailing, Cast Iron, 11 In. .... 32.00 To 68.00
Spanish Galleon, Cast Iron, 10 X 11 In. 45.00
Urn With Flowers, Cast Iron, 6 1/2 In. 40.00
Vase of Roses, Hubley, 10 1/8 X 8 In. 150.00
Wagon Train, Cast Iron 125.00
Warrior, Bradley & Hubbard, Cast Iron 590.00
Woman, Hoop Skirt, Cast Iron 110.00
Woman, Pink Bonnet, Holding Bouquet, Cast Iron, 7 1/2 In. 65.00

Doulton pottery and porcelain were made by Doulton and Co. of Burslem, England, after 1882. The name "Royal Doulton" appeared on their wares after 1902. Other pottery by Doulton is listed under Royal Doulton.

DOULTON, Ashtray, Figural, Bird, Green Leaves Around Dish, Marked, 4 1/2 In. 275.00
Biscuit Jar, 4 Views of Switzerland, Gold Trim, Marked, 8 1/2 In. 155.00
Biscuit Jar, Blue Border Top & Bottom, Silver Fittings, 6 3/4 In. 175.00
Biscuit Jar, Dutch Man & Woman, Silver Plated Fittings, 6 1/4 In. 225.00
Biscuit Jar, Floral, Leaves, Gold Trim, Marked, 6 1/2 In. 165.00
Biscuit Jar, Silicon Glaze, Ferns & Plants, Lambeth, 7 1/4 In. 275.00
Bottle, Grazing Sheep, Hinged Metal Top, Marked, 5 1/4 In. 85.00
Flask, Embossed Tobacco Leaves, Man Smoking Pipe, Lambeth, 8 In. 115.00
Flask, Whiskey, Kingsware, Bonnie Prince Charlie 295.00
Flask, Whiskey, Kingsware, Falstaff 350.00
Flask, Whiskey, Kingsware, Jovial Monk 325.00
Flask, Whiskey, Kingsware, Mr. Micawber 275.00
Group, 3 Mice In Carriage, Pulled By Mouse, Lambeth 1475.00
Group, Mice Playing Banjo, Accordian, Tambourine, Lambeth, 3 3/4 In. 500.00
Group, Playgoers, Mice, Punch & Judy Show, Lambeth, 1886, 5 In. 2588.50
Jug, Brown & Yellow Transfer, Geo.Marland, C.1890, 6 7/8 In. 95.00
Jug, Dewar's Whiskey, Kingsware, Uncle Sam 200.00
Jug, Simulated Leather, Silver Band, Stoneware, Marked, 6 1/8 In. 110.00
Pitcher, Festoon Pattern, Blue & White, Gold Trim, Burslem, 7 In. 85.00
Plate, Coronation, Queen Mary, Burslem, 1902 .... 60.00
Plate, Exotic Flowers, Gold Outlined, Burslem, 9 In., 4 Piece 320.00
Platter, Blue Garland Edge, White, Burslem, 20 X 15 In. 125.00
Saltshaker, Raised Dog Design, Brown Pottery 22.00
Shaving Mug, Kingsware, Sterling Rim 545.00
Spittoon, Browns, Gold, Burslem 225.00
Toby Jug, Huntsman, Kingsware, Set of 4 .... 1500.00
Vase, Brown, Aqua, Bulbous, Handle, Lambeth, 1882, 3 1/4 In. 75.00
Vase, Comical Hunt Scene, Marked, 4 3/8 X 4 1/2 In. 85.00
Vase, Cows In Pastoral Scene, Gold Trim Top, Marked, 4 5/8 In. 100.00
Vase, Floral, Cream & Gilt Ground, Burslem, 8 1/2 In. 110.00
Vase, Flow Blue Scenic, Cottage Amid Trees, Marked, 9 1/2 In. 110.00
Vase, Gold Enameled Panel, Hand Painted Flowers, 11 In. 125.00
Vase, Incised Natural Foliage, Ocher & Brown, C.1891, 24 1/2 In. 400.00
Vase, Iris, Gold Design On Band Under Rim, 15 3/4 In. 370.00
Vase, Multicolored Flowers, Gold Outlining, Burslem, 5 1/2 In. 100.00
Vase, Sheep, Cows & Donkeys Grazing, Hanna Barlow, 1876, 6 1/2 In. 375.00
Vase, Stoneware, Gold Enameled Panel, Cobalt Blue, 11 In. 95.00
    DR. SYNTAX, see Adams; Staffordshire

Moriage is a type of decoration on Japanese pottery. Raised white designs are applied to the ware. Dragonware is a form of moriage pottery. White dragons are the major raised decorations. The background colors are gray and white, orange and lavender, or orange and brown. It is a twentieth-century ware.

DRAGONWARE, Cup & Saucer, Orange Luster Inside, Brown Rim, Japan 10.00
Demitasse Set, Gray, Pink, Gold, Yellow, Handle, 6 Cups & Saucers 135.00
Dish, Divided, Holes For Cane Handle, 4 Sections, 9 In. 26.00
Plate, Brown Rim, Gray Bird, Raised Dragon, Beige, 7 In. 13.00
Saucer, Brown Rim 2.50
Sugar & Creamer, Niagara Falls, Gray-Green Luster, Gold Handles 25.00
Tea Service, Brown Trim, Pastel Ground 65.00

Tea Set, Moriaga, 3 Piece	65.00
Teapot, Miniature	12.00
Tray, Condiment Set, Cruets, Salt & Pepper, Mustard, Cover, 10 In.	75.00
Vase, 5 1/2 In.	22.00
Vase, Brown, Orange, White Dragon, Turquoise, Flared, 8 In., Pair	175.00
Vase, Orange Luster, Pink, Handle, 9 In.	90.00

Dresden china is any china made in the town of Dresden, Germany. The most famous factory in Dresden is the Meissen factory. Figurines of eighteenth–century ladies and gentlemen, animal groups, or cherubs and other mythological subjects were popular. One special type of figurine was made with skirts of porcelain–dipped lace. Do not make the mistake of thinking that all pieces marked "Dresden" are from the Meissen factory. The Meissen pieces usually have crossed swords marks and are listed under Meissen.

DRESDEN, Biscuit Jar, Pale Violets, Crown Germany Mark, 7 1/2 In.	135.00
Bowl, Boat Shape, Painted Floral Interior, Wreath Handles, 17 In.	325.00
Bowl, Clementine, Long–Haired Maiden, Luster Inside, 7 1/2 In.	320.00
Bowl, Flowers, Shell Shape, 9 In.	450.00
Cake Plate, Reticulated Border, Marked, 10 In.	90.00
Cake Plate, Reticulated Bowl, Floral, 5 1/2 X 7 1/2 In.	125.00
Clock, Scrolled Brass Front, Porcelain, 10 1/2 In.	385.00
Ewer Vase, Women & Cupid, Flattened Oval, Gold Trim, Marked, 12 In.	795.00
Figurine, Ballerina, Pink & White Dress, Blue Shoes, Arms Out, 6 In.	170.00
Figurine, Ballerina, Red Shoes, Flower In Hair, 7 In.	225.00
Figurine, Deer, Glass Eyes, 8 In., Pair	350.00
Figurine, Frog Band, Instruments, 4 3/4 In., 7 Piece	775.00
Figurine, Lady Marquise De Vereuil, No.1667, With Fan, 1875, 8 In.	350.00
Figurine, Lady With Greyhound, Seated, Vase of Flowers, 8 In.	325.00
Figurine, Parrot On Stump, 8 In.	165.00
Figurine, Persian Cat, Sitting, Marked, 8 1/2 In.	275.00
Figurine, Woman, Holding Mask, 8 3/8 In.	121.00
Fruit Bowl, Open Lattice Work, Flower Design, Gold Trim, 8 1/2 In.	350.00
Fruit Bowl, Openwork Pointed Rim, Oval, Inside Florals, 4 X 9 In.	175.00
Group, French Parlor Scene, Lace Skirts, 19 In.	660.00
Group, Mother Reading To Her 2 Children, Lace, 8 X 8 In.	650.00
Group, Woman, In Sedan Chair, Suitors Around Her, 9 1/2 In.	495.00
Lamp, Banquet, Cherubs In Floral Reserves of Gold, 21 1/2 In.	425.00
Lamp, Rustic Scene, Children, 15 In.	185.00
Luncheon Set, Gilt Foliate Scrolls, Swags, Blue, Porcelain, 24 Piece	375.00
Plaque, Partially Draped Lady, Waving Sash, Baroque Frame, 6 In.	450.00
Plate, Dessert, Floral, Gilt Borders, 8 1/2 In., 12 Piece	209.00
Plate, Victorian Men & Women, Gold, 11 In., 10 Piece	225.00
Shelf, Corner, Mirrored, Porcelain	50.00
Sugar & Creamer, Tray, Courting & Fishing, Gilt Interior, 3 Piece	465.00
Tea Set, Corinthian Greek Design, Scrolls, Porcelain, 4 Piece	275.00
Urn, Cover, Boat Shape, Floral Baskets, Gold Trim, 1870, 10 X 7 In.	750.00
Urn, Putti, Applied Floral, Cover, 10 3/4 In.	193.00
Vase, Cobalt Blue, Center Medallion Courting Scene, Gold, 8 In.	325.00

Duncan & Miller is a term used by collectors when referring to glass made by the George A. Duncan and Sons Company or the Duncan and Miller Glass Company. These companies worked from 1893 to 1955, when the use of the name "Duncan" was discontinued and the firm became part of the United States Glass Company. Early patterns may be listed under Pressed Glass.

DUNCAN & MILLER, Amberette, Bowl, 1880, 8 In.	75.00
American Way, Candleholder, Blue Opalescent, Pair	55.00
American Way, Candleholder, Ruby, Pair	55.00
Block, Candy Dish, Cover, Square	40.00
Button & Arches, Water Set, Ruby, C.1897, 7 Piece	250.00
Canterbury, Basket, Handle, Oval, Opalescent Blue, 10 In.	135.00
Canterbury, Bowl, 10 1/2 In.	25.00
Canterbury, Bowl, Divided, Handles, Blue, 8 In.	18.00

Canterbury, Bowl, Ruby, 8 In.	45.00
Canterbury, Box, Cigarette, Blue, 3 1/2 In.	45.00
Canterbury, Candy Dish, Chartreuse	22.00
Canterbury, Cigar Jar, Cover	55.00
Canterbury, Cocktail, 4 1/4 In.	3.00
Canterbury, Compote, Blue, 7 In.	30.00
Canterbury, Compote, Silver Overlay	22.50
Canterbury, Condiment Set, Tray, 6 Piece	65.00
Canterbury, Cordial	36.00
Canterbury, Cup	10.50
Canterbury, Decanter, Crystal	95.00
Canterbury, Dish, Mayonnaise, Divided, Underliner	25.00
Canterbury, Goblet, 9 Oz.	6.00
Canterbury, Ice Bucket, Blue	85.00
Canterbury, Nappy, 2 Handles, Pink Opalescent	23.00
Canterbury, Pitcher, Martini	55.00
Canterbury, Plate, Chartreuse, 7 1/2 In.	10.00
Canterbury, Plate, Yellow, 7 3/4 In.	7.00
Canterbury, Salt & Pepper	15.00
Canterbury, Shot Glass	14.00
Canterbury, Sugar & Creamer, Blue	65.00
Canterbury, Sugar & Creamer, Miniature	18.00
Canterbury, Tumbler, Footed, 3 3/4 In.	15.00
Canterbury, Tumbler, Footed, 4 1/4 In.	13.00
Canterbury, Vase, Crimped, Opalescent Blue, 10 In.	18.00
Canterbury, Vase, Ruffled, Blue, 4 3/4 In.	30.00
Canterbury, Vase, Violet, Blue, Crimped, 2 3/4 In.	16.00
Canterbury, Wine, Yellow, 5 In.	10.00
Caribbean, Ashtray, Footed, 4 1/2 In.	15.00
Caribbean, Bowl, Fruit, Blue, Footed, Handle, Oval, 9 In.	55.00
Caribbean, Box, Cigarette, Cover, Round	30.00
Caribbean, Candlestick, Prisms, Pair	75.00
Caribbean, Cocktail Shaker, Blue	250.00
Caribbean, Cocktail, Hourglass, Blue	25.00
Caribbean, Creamer, Blue	30.00
Caribbean, Cruet, Blue	65.00
Caribbean, Goblet, Water, Blue	45.00
Caribbean, Mustard, Cover	47.00
Caribbean, Nappy, Handle, Blue, 10 In.	95.00
Caribbean, Pitcher, Green, 3 Qt.	16.00
Caribbean, Plate, Blue, 7 1/2 In.	28.00
Caribbean, Punch Bowl	75.00
Caribbean, Punch Ladle	12.00
Caribbean, Punch Set, Red Handles, 15 Piece	205.00
Caribbean, Relish, 5 Sections, Round, 10 In.	55.00
Caribbean, Salt & Pepper, Blue, 3 In.	95.00
Caribbean, Syrup, 9 Oz., 4 1/4 In.	43.00
Caribbean, Syrup, Cover, Blue, 8 In.	250.00
Caribbean, Wine, Egg, 2 1/2 In.	17.00
Cathay, Champagne, Ruby Base	6.00
Cathay, Cocktail, Ruby Base	6.00
Cathay, Goblet, Water, Ruby Base, 10 Oz.	8.00
Chanticleer, Vase, Blue, 4 In.	60.00
Chanticleer, Vase, Ruffled, Blue Opalescent, 3 In.	35.00
Diamond Ridge, Cracker Jar, Cover	155.00
Diamond Ridge, Creamer, Individual, Oval	22.00
Dogwood, Vase, Half Round, Milk Glass	35.00
Duck, Ashtray, 4 In.	12.00
Duck, Ashtray, 8 In.	12.00
Duck, Box, Cigarette, 5 In.	10.00
First Love, Bowl, 3 Sections, Sterling Base, 8 In.	35.00
First Love, Candlestick, Double, 8 1/2 In.	150.00
First Love, Candy Dish, Cover, 3 Sections	70.00
First Love, Champagne	25.00

First Love, Goblet, 10 Oz.	25.00
First Love, Ice Bucket, Handle	75.00
First Love, Martini Set, Pitcher & 4 Cocktails	250.00
First Love, Nappy, Handle, Round, 6 In.	25.00
First Love, Plate, 2 Handles, 11 In.	35.00
First Love, Relish, 3 Sections, 7 In.	24.00
First Love, Relish, 3 Sections, Handles, 9 In.	30.00
First Love, Sugar, 3 In.	20.00
First Love, Torte Plate, 15 In.	65.00
First Love, Urn, 2 Handles, 7 In.	65.00
First Love, Vase, Cornucopia, 3 Feathers, 8 In.	75.00
First Love, Vase, Crimped, 5 In.	25.00
First Love, Wine	25.00
Georgian, Salt & Pepper, Ruby	18.00
Grecian, Vase, Ruby, 6 3/4 In.	55.00
Hat, Blue Opalescent, 4 In.	48.00
Hobnail, Basket, Pink Opalescent, 10 In.	95.00
Hobnail, Bowl, Console, Pink Opalescent, Oval, 12 In.	32.00
Hobnail, Candlestick, Pink Opalescent, 4 In., Pair	20.00
Hobnail, Candy, Blue Opalescent, Cover, 9 1/2 In.	85.00
Hobnail, Celery, 2 Handles, Oval, 12 In.	25.00
Hobnail, Cocktail, Pink Opalescent	13.00
Hobnail, Cologne Bottle, Stopper, 8 Oz.	28.00
Hobnail, Cup & Saucer	6.00
Hobnail, Goblet, Pink Opalescent, 9 Oz.	15.00
Hobnail, Hat, 10 In.	65.00
Hobnail, Ivy Ball, Blue Opalescent	50.00
Hobnail, Plate, Pink Opalescent, 8 1/2 In.	18.00
Hobnail, Plate, Torte, Pink Opalescent, 13 In.	30.00
Hobnail, Punch Ladle, Blue Opalescent	65.00
Hobnail, Saucer, Champagne, Pink Opalescent	13.00
Hobnail, Sherbet, Pink Opalescent, Footed	13.00
Hobnail, Tray, Pink Opalescent, Footed, 6 In.	14.00
Hobnail, Tumbler, Iced Tea, Pink Opalescent	15.00
Hobnail, Tumbler, Juice, Pink Opalescent	13.00
Hobnail, Vase, Oval, 4 1/2 In.	19.00
Hobnail, Water Set, Pink Opalescent, 8 Tumblers	395.00
Lily of The Valley, Champagne	28.00
Lily of The Valley, Goblet	30.00
Lily of The Valley, Mayonnaise, 3 Piece	65.00
Lily of The Valley, Plate, Canterbury, 9 In.	25.00
Lily of The Valley, Wine	30.00
Mardi Gras, Lamp Shade, Frosted Lower Part, 4 1/2 In.	26.00
Mardi Gras, Pitcher, Water, 9 1/2 In.	65.00
Mardi Gras, Sherbet	18.00
Mardi Gras, Wine	27.00
Murano, Bowl, Flower, Milk Glass, 10 X 6 In.	50.00
Nautical, Bookends, Rope & Anchor	325.00
Nautical, Ice Bucket, Blue	150.00
Nautical, Relish, 7 Sections, Blue, 11 In.	150.00
Pall Mall, Duck, Solid, 4 In.	40.00
Pall Mall, Swan, Biscayne Green, 7 In.	45.00
Pall Mall, Swan, Crystal Head & Neck, 10 In.	50.00
Pall Mall, Swan, Ruby, 10 1/2 In.	45.00
Pall Mall, Swan, Silver Deposit, 7 In.	28.00
Pall Mall, Swan, Solid, 5 In.	20.00
Pall Mall, Swan, Sterling Floral Design, 7 In.	28.00
Pall Mall, Swan, Wheat Cutting, 10 In.	27.00
Pall Mall, Swan, Yellow, 8 In.	40.00
Puritan, Bowl, 4 3/4 In.	5.00
Puritan, Cup & Saucer, Pink, Demitasse, Footed	22.00
Puritan, Platter, Oval, 12 In.	20.00
Radiance, Pitcher, Blue, 1/2 Gal.	95.00
Radiance, Pitcher, Sapphire Blue, 1/2 Gal.	95.00 To 125.00

Radiance, Punch Cup, Colored Handles 4.00
Ridge, Cracker Jar 75.00
Sandwich, Ashtray, Square, 2 3/4 In. 7.00
Sandwich, Bonbon, Heart, Handle 14.00
Sandwich, Box, Cigarette, Cover 19.00
Sandwich, Cake Stand 70.00
Sandwich, Candlestick, 4 In., Pair 37.50
Sandwich, Coaster ....8.00 To 10.00
Sandwich, Compote, Footed 20.00
Sandwich, Creamer, 5 Oz. 12.00
Sandwich, Cruet 22.50
Sandwich, Cup & Saucer ....9.50 To 12.00
Sandwich, Goblet, 5 3/4 In. 10.00
Sandwich, Nappy, Handle, 5 1/2 In. 12.00
Sandwich, Plate, 6 In. 8.00
Sandwich, Plate, 16 In. 35.00
Sandwich, Plate, Deviled Eggs, Green, 12 In. 50.00
Sandwich, Plate, Green, 8 In. 8.00
Sandwich, Plate, Sandwich, 14 In. 60.00
Sandwich, Relish, 2 Sections, 7 In. 15.00
Sandwich, Relish, 3 Sections, 10 In. 40.00
Sandwich, Sherbet, 5 Oz. 8.00
Sandwich, Sugar & Creamer, Tray 24.00
Sandwich, Sugar & Creamer, Yellow 25.00
Sandwich, Tumbler, Footed, 5 1/2 In. 12.00
Sandwich, Tumbler, Iced Tea, Footed, 5 1/2 In. ....8.00 To 10.00
Sandwich, Tumbler, Juice, Flat 6.00
Sandwich, Tumbler, Juice, Footed, 3 3/4 In. 6.00
Sandwich, Wine ....9.00 To 18.00
Sanibel, Bowl, Pink, 14 In. 35.00
Shell & Tassel, Compote, Pedestal, 6 In. 33.00
Spiral Flutes, Bowl, Green, Flanged, 8 1/2 In. 17.50
Spiral Flutes, Bowl, Green, Flat Rim, 7 5/8 In. 12.00
Spiral Flutes, Compote, Green, 4 1/2 In. 12.00
Spiral Flutes, Cup & Saucer, Green 14.00
Spiral Flutes, Cup & Saucer, Pink 6.00
Spiral Flutes, Finger Bowl, Amber, 4 3/8 In. 6.00
Spiral Flutes, Goblet, Water, Green, 7 Oz. 7.00
Spiral Flutes, Nut Dish, Footed, Green 12.50
Spiral Flutes, Plate, Green, 6 3/4 In. 6.00
Spiral Flutes, Plate, Green, 10 3/4 In. 18.00
Spiral Flutes, Seafood Cup, Green 15.00
Spiral Flutes, Sherbet, 3 1/2 In. 4.00
Spiral Flutes, Soup, Dish, Flanged, Green, 6 3/4 In. 4.00
Spiral Flutes, Sugar & Creamer, Amber 7.00
Spiral Flutes, Tumbler, Footed, Green, 2 1/2 Oz. 5.00
Spiral Flutes, Vase, Green, 8 3/4 In. 30.00
Swan, Chartreuse, 7 In. ....22.00 To 28.00
Swan, Clear Neck, Red 25.00
Swan, Crystal Neck, Ruby, 10 1/2 X 14 In. 125.00
Swan, Crystal, 10 In. 45.00
Swan, Red Neck, Milk Glass 200.00
Swan, Red, Clear Neck, 7 In. 28.00
Swan, Ruby Floral Design, 8 In. 55.00
Swan, Ruby, 6 In. 30.00
Swan, Ruby, 8 In. 40.00
Swan, Spread Wings, Blue Opalescent, 11 In. 210.00
Sylvan, Swan, Opalescent Blue, 7 In. 55.00
Sylvan, Swan, Opalescent Pink, 7 In. 65.00
Sylvan, Vase, 6 In. 55.00
Teardrop, Ashtray, 3 1/4 In. 20.00
Teardrop, Ashtray, Individual, 3 In. 5.00
Teardrop, Bowl, 5 In. 6.00
Teardrop, Bowl, 6 In. 8.00

Teardrop, Bowl, Fruit, 5 In.	5.50
Teardrop, Bowl, Salad, Low	30.00
Teardrop, Cake Plate, Handles, 13 1/2 In.	35.00
Teardrop, Candelabra, 2–Light, Bobeches, V Prisms, 9 In., Pr.	90.00
Teardrop, Candy Dish, Heart, 7 1/2 In.	15.00
Teardrop, Champagne	12.00
Teardrop, Claret	20.00
Teardrop, Cocktail	15.00 To 18.00
Teardrop, Creamer, 16 Oz., 5 1/4 In.	20.00
Teardrop, Cruet, 4 3/4 In.	15.00
Teardrop, Cruet, On Tray, 3 Piece	30.00
Teardrop, Cruet, Stopper, 3 Oz.	16.00 To 20.00
Teardrop, Cup & Saucer	5.00 To 7.50
Teardrop, Dish, Mayonnaise, Liner	15.00
Teardrop, Finger Bowl, Underplate, 5 1/4 In.	8.50
Teardrop, Goblet, 6 In.	8.00
Teardrop, Ice Bucket	30.00
Teardrop, Nut Dish, Divided, Handle	7.50
Teardrop, Plate, 8 1/2 In.	5.50 To 7.50
Teardrop, Relish, 2 Sections, Heart Shape	12.50 To 18.00
Teardrop, Relish, 5 Sections, 12 In.	13.00
Teardrop, Sherbet, Footed, 5 Oz.	8.00
Teardrop, Sugar & Creamer, Teardrop Handles	18.00
Teardrop, Tumbler, Footed, 6 In.	15.00
Teardrop, Whiskey, Footed, 3 In.	12.00
Teardrop, Wine	15.00 To 20.00

Durand glass was made by Victor Durand from 1879 to 1935 at several factories. Most of the iridescent Durand glass was made by Victor Durand, Jr., from 1912 to 1924, at the Durand Art Glass Works in Vineland, New Jersey.

DURAND, Bowl, Pulled Feather, Royal Blue & White, 8 In.	325.00
Bowl, Spanish Yellow, Paneled, Footed, Green Rim, 5 X 2 3/4 In.	40.00
Compote, Green, White, Iridescent, Signed, 5 1/4 In.	325.00
Garniture Set, Pulled Feather Design, Emerald & Green, Bowl, 14 In.	800.00
Lamp, Gold Glass, Applied Threading, 22 In.	575.00
Lamp, King Tut, Table	295.00
Plate, Feather Pattern, Ruby, Opalescent, Clear, Bubbles, 8 In.	150.00
Rose Bowl, Blue Iridescent, Random Streaks, 4 In.	375.00
Tazza, Pale Amethyst, Handle, Signed & No.744, 5 3/4 X 6 5/8 In.	225.00
Urn, King Tut Design, Feathers & Plums, Gold Aurene, Signed, 10 In.	475.00
Vase, Amethyst Ribbed, 6 In.	300.00
Vase, Blue, Hearts, Vines, Signed, 10 In.	950.00
Vase, Butterfly, Threaded Glass, Blue, Signed, 6 1/4 X 5 1/4 In.	695.00
Vase, Feather Design, Cranberry, Artist Note Inside, 1925, 10 In.	850.00
Vase, Gold Design, Signed, 6 3/4 In.	425.00
Vase, Gold Threaded, Marked, 8 In.	275.00
Vase, Jack–In–The–Pulpit, Pansy Face, Gold, Signed, 10 1/2 In.	1425.00
Vase, King Tut Design, Gold Lined, Signed, 7 1/2 In.	550.00
Vase, Leaf & Vine Design, C.1924, 11 In.	2200.00
Vase, Peacock Blue, Glass Threaded, Signed, Numbered, 8 In.	950.00
Vase, Red, Signed, 10 In.	950.00
Vase, Shoestring Pattern, Silver Feather Pulls, Signed, 6 In.	900.00
Vase, Swirled Shades of Blue, Blue Interior, 6 7/8 In.	425.00
Vase, Teardrop, Iridescent Blue, 5 1/8 In.	200.00
Vase, Trumpet, Gold Iridescent, Circular Base, Signed, 15 In.	875.00

Elfinware was made from about 1918 to 1940. It is a Dresden–like porcelain that was sold in dime stores and gift shops. Many pieces were decorated with raised flowers. The small pieces are marked with the name "Elfinware" or with a crown and M mark. The words "Germany" or "Made in Germany" also appear on some pieces.

ELFINWARE, Basket	22.00
Box Set, Largest 4 3/4 In., 5 Piece	110.00

Box, Germany, Flowers On Cover, 2 1/2 X 1 1/2 X 1 3/4 In.	35.00
Figurine, Sheep Pulling Card, Flowers, Pink Bows, Signed	25.00
Perfume Bottle, Green Luster, Pink Roses, Greenery, 8 1/2 In.	55.00
Powder Box, Pink Roses, Greenery, Green Luster, 4 1/2 In.	25.00
Salt, Basket Form	18.00
Shoe	20.00
Slat Basket	25.00

Elvis Presley, the famous singer, lived from 1935 to 1977. He became famous by 1956. Elvis appeared on television, starred in twenty-seven movies, and performed in Las Vegas. Memorabilia from any of the Presley shows, his records, and even memorials made after his death are collected.

ELVIS PRESLEY, Badge, English Fan Club, Star Shape, Brass, 2 1/2 In.	7.50
Book, Elvis Greatest Song Hits, 120 Pages, 8 1/2 X 11 In.	8.75
Book, Pop–Up, Musical, Hardbound, Full Color, 8 X 11 In.	10.00
Book, Valentine Pop Special No.6, Foldout Poster	45.00
Bracelet, 1950s	12.00
Bracelet, Cuff, American Indian Style, Turquoise & Coral	3200.00
Calendar, Memorial, Elvis Photos, 1979, 8 1/2 X 11 In.	7.00
Calendar, Pocket, RCA, Elvis & Santa, 1978	2.50
Card, 1976 Calendar, Picture, Wallet Size	5.00
Card, Movie, Window, Viva Las Vegas	47.00
Case, Overnight, Blue, Mirror, 1956 Guitar Pose, 12 X 8 In.	850.00
Cassette, Greatest Moments In Music, RCA	7.00
Decanter, Musical, Yours Elvis, 1955	65.00
Dog Tags, 1950s	12.00
Doll, Vinyl, Box, 21 In.	80.00
Doll, White, Flame Suit, World Doll, 20 In.	70.00
Doll, World Doll, 21 In.	95.00
Figurine, Royal Orleans	106.00
Guitar, Original Case, Presley Enterprises Copyright, 1956	1556.00
Guitar, White, Brown, Photo On Neck, Selcol, 1950s, 33 In.	425.00
Jewelry Box, Brass Turtle, Blue Stones, 6 X 3 1/2 In.	700.00
Key Chain, Guitar Shape, Color Photo	5.50
Knife, Elvis Photo, Color, 2 Blades, Pocket	4.00
Knife, Guitar Shape, Pearl Insert With Picture	9.75
Magazine, Elvis The King, Memorial Issue, 1977, 66 Pages	1.50
Magazine, Motion Picture, Sorrow He Hides From Fans, 1974	8.00
Magazine, Photoplay Tribute, 128 Pages, 1977	15.00
Mirror, Love Me Tender, Color, Signed & Dated 1956	2.00
Mirror, With Guitar In Performance, 1956, 2 X 3 In.	2.00
Necklace, American Indian Style, Thunderbird Pendant, 28 In.	1650.00
Paper Doll Book, With Priscilla, Uncut	40.00
Photograph, Elvis & Priscilla Presley Wedding, 8 X 10 In.	650.00
Plate, Memorial, 1977	35.00
Postcard, 12 Different Cards, Concert, Buffalo, N.Y., 1957	10.00
Poster, Charro, 1969, 41 X 27 In.	20.00
Record, Album, Confidentially, 29 Photos	30.00
Record, Album, Remember The King	25.00
Record, Burning Love, Pickwick, 1972	5.00
Record, Canadian Tribute, Gold Vinyl Import, LP	40.00
Record, Girls, Girls, Girls, RCA, LP	5.00
Record, I Forgot To Remember To Forget, 45 RPM	25.00
Record, Love Me Tender, RCA, 45 RPM	10.00
Record, Loving You, RCA, LP	15.00
Record, Our Memories of Elvis, RCA	5.00
Ring, American Indian Style, Tiger's–Eye, Silver Cording	880.00
Robe, Karate GI, Gold–Plated Bezels, Studs, Jewels, Size 4	4675.00
Scarf, Blue Acetate, Facsimile Signature, 34 X 34 In.	330.00
Scarf, Pictures of Elvis, Square, 22 In.	8.50 To 10.00
Sheet Music, G.I.Blues	8.00
Sheet Music, Heartbreak Hotel, Photo Cover, 1956	20.00
Sheet Music, Loving You	8.00

Enamel, Infuser, Gold Washed Silver,

Green, Red, White

To test ivory to see if it is real, heat
the tip of a needle or pin until it is
red hot. Put the point on the ivory
in an inconspicuous spot. If it
goes in more than a tiny pinprick,
it is not ivory.

Always keep a rug on a pad. It will
wear out sooner on a bare floor.

Shirt, Silk	1760.00
Song Sheet, Framed & Glazed, Autographed The King	780.00
Tape Measure, Heart Shape, Words of Love Me Tender, Box	5.75
Teddy Bear, Elvis Bearsley, N.American	250.00
Tray, Full Color Bust of Elvis, Round, 12 In.	14.75
Underwear, Fan's, Handwritten Messages, Size 14	440.00
Watch, Pocket, Character, Bradley, Windup, Package	35.00
Wristwatch, In Concert, Box	45.00

In the eighteenth and nineteenth centuries, workmen from Russia, France, England, and other countries made small boxes and table pieces of enamel on metal. One form of English enamel is called "Battersea" and is listed under that name.

ENAMEL, Box, Emerald Green Glass, White Flowers, Hinged Cover, 3 X 5 In.	135.00
Cigar Case, Silver–Gilt, Dragons, White Beads, Saltykov, 1896, 5 In.	1980.00
Coffeepot, Blue & White, Pewter Lid & Handle	95.00
Easter Egg, Silver–Gilt, Floral, Border, Ovchinnikov, 1900, 2 1/2 In.	6600.00
Ewer, Wine, Geometric, Blue Ground, Persia, 8 In.	825.00
Figurine, Dog, Seated, Flint, 10 3/4 In.	650.00
Infuser, Gold Washed Silver, Green, Red, White ....*Illus*	55.00
Jardiniere, Gilt–Bronze, Corner Angular Handles, Champleve, 10 In.	1980.00
Jug, Cream, Silver, Floral, Deep & Sky Blue, Russia, C.1910, 3 5/8 In.	2530.00
Kovsh, Flower Panels, Cream, Blue, Beaded Border, Saltykov, 1900, 9 In.	4510.00
Kovsh, Flowering Foliage, Silver–Gilt, Ovchinnikov, 1910, 12 1/4 In.	8250.00
Pitcher, Paneled, Mask Spout, Flint, 10 3/4 In.	200.00
Plaque, Maidens, Garden, Cupids, Wooden Frame, Viennese, 15 1/8 In.	3740.00
Salt & Pepper, Owl, Gilded Silver, 1 Purple, 1 Blue, Norway, 2 In., Pr.	75.00
Screen, 3–Fold, Courting Scenes, Brass Frame, French, 5 X 5 In.	165.00
Sugar & Creamer, Stylized Design, Swing Handle, Silver–Gilt, Russia	2750.00
Syrup, Castle Scenes Front & Back, Metal Trim, Classic Head Finial	245.00
Teapot, Dogwood Blossom, Iron, Pewter, Copper Handle, Oval, 8 X 10 In.	295.00
Toothpick Case, Gold, 3 Doves, Stylized Foliage, French, 1800, 3 In.	4675.00
Toothpick Case, Silver–Gilt, Blue, Diamonds, Pearl, Britzin, 3 5/8 In.	4950.00
Vase, Mythological Scenes, Lobed Body, Domed Foot, Viennese, 6 In.	1540.00

ES Germany porcelain was made at the factory of Erdmann Schlegelmilch from 1861 to 1925 in Suhl, Germany. The porcelain was sold decorated or undecorated. Other pieces were made at the factory in Saxony, Prussia, and are marked "ES Prussia." Reinhold Schlegelmilch, a brother, made the famous wares marked "RS Germany."

ES GERMANY, Bowl, 3 Girls, Prov.Saxe, 9 3/4 In.	100.00
Candy Dish, Portrait of Napoleon, Gold Trim, 8 In.	125.00
Dish, Tidbit, Center Handle, Berries, 6 1/2 In.	15.00
Plate, Women, Cherubs, 8 In., Pair	65.00
Salt & Pepper, Yellow Rose, Marked	175.00
Sugar & Creamer, Cover, Gold Floral Band, Textured Body	50.00
Teapot, Sponged Gold, Green Laurel Wreath With Portraits	80.00

Tray, Dresser, Red Roses 45.00

All types of Eskimo artifacts are collected. Carvings of whale or walrus teeth are listed under Scrimshaw. Baskets are in the Basket category. All other types of Eskimo art are listed here.

ESKIMO, Basket, Cover, Globular, Dyed Fishskin Embroidery, 7 1/2 X 7 In. 300.00
  Cribbage Board, Walrus Tusk Ivory, Wood Inlay, 15 In. 200.00
  Doll, Carved Wood, Woman, Baby In Backpack, Greenland, 15 1/2 In. 800.00
  Doll, Oil Skin Head, Cropped Hair, Leather Clothes, Handmade, 15 In. 65.00
  Figurine, Hunter, Black Stone, Incised, 4 In. 85.00
  Group, Carved Ivory, 4 Figures, 2 Fossilized Harpoon Heads 220.00
  Knife, Carved Bird Head Finial On Hilt, Hide Sheath, 8 1/2 In. 400.00
  Model, Kayak, Carved Wooden Man, Sealskin Parka, Seal Float, 25 In. 225.00
  Model, Kayak, Doll, Standing, Harpoons, Oars, Labrador, 1920s, 31 In. 650.00
  Muc-Lucs, Liner, Reindeer Fur, Khaki Cloth, Seal Fur Interior, 16 In. 95.00
  Muc-Lucs, Seal Fur, Wolverine Trim, Red Felt Binding, 9 1/2 In. 25.00
  Pants, Leather, Baby Reindeer Fur, Red Velvet & Felt Trim, 32 In. 20.00
  Scrimshaw, Man & Woman, Fish, Rabbit, Carved Antler, 15 1/2 In. 100.00
  Snow Goggles, Wooden, Visor-Like Rim, Pierced Viewing Field, 6 In. 400.00

ETLING FRANCE Etling glass is very similar in design to Lalique and Phoenix glass. It was made in France for Etling, a retail shop. It dates from the 1920s and 1930s.

ETLING, Bowl, 3 Flowers, Centers Form Feet, Opalescent, 8 1/2 In. 275.00
  Bowl, Fern Fronds, Stippled Ground, White Opalescent, 13 3/4 In. 95.00

ФАБЕРЖЕ Faberge was a firm of jewelers and goldsmiths founded in St.
КФ Petersburg, Russia, in 1842, by Gustav Faberge. Peter Carl Faberge, his son, was jeweler to the Russian Imperial Court from about 1870 to 1914.

FABERGE, Brooch, Scroll, Moonstone Cabochons, 4 Garnet Pendulums, 1 1/2 In. 1320.00
  Buckle, Silver, Gold, Translucent Rose Pink Enamel, 1900, 2 7/8 In. 3300.00
  Cigarette Case, Gold, Sunray, Monogram, Sapphire Thumb, 3 1/2 In. 4125.00
  Compote, Silver, Stylized Enameled Foliage, 1910, 2 1/4 In. 3300.00
  Cup, Vodka, Silver, Enameled Red Band, Guilloche, Marked, 1 7/8 In. 3850.00
  Icon, Mother Of God Iverskaya, Silver Frame, 1900, 2 1/2 In. 5225.00
  Jug, Cream, Silver-Gilt, Scroll Handle, Cylinder Shape, 2 7/8 In. 2200.00
  Napkin Ring, Silver, Plain, Gold Monogram, 1896, Oval, 2 1/4 In. 1430.00
  Saltcellar, Silver, Stylized Enameled Foliage, Bulbous, 1910, 2 In. 2860.00
  Stickpin, Gold, Sapphire, 3 Diamonds, 1900, 2 3/4 In. 9900.00
  Tray, Silver, Fluted Border, Cutout Handles, Monogram, Oval, 18 In. 8800.00

Definitions of the words differentiating the types of pottery and porcelain are difficult because there is so much overlapping of meaning. Faience is tin-glazed earthenware, especially the wares made in France, Germany, and Scandinavia. It is also correct to say that faience is the same as majolica or Delft, although usually the term refers only to the tin-glazed pottery of the three regions mentioned.

FAIENCE, Candlestick, Green, 1925, 7 In. 78.00
  Cistern, Cover, On Stand, Lamp Mounted, Dolphin Spout, 19 In., Pair 1540.00
  Inkwell, Roses & Foliage, 9 In. 100.00
  Plate, Ballooning Scenes, Tin Glaze, St.Clement, 9 5/8 In., 10 Piece 300.00
  Urn, St.George & Dragon, Lion Handles, 20th Century, 16 In. 85.00
  Vase, Enameled Flowers, Fish, Angels, Mounted As Lamp, 37 In. 250.00
  Vase, Green, 10 In. 350.00
  Vase, Sailboats, Fishermen, Urn Shape, Elaborate Handle, 9 1/4 In. 1650.00

Fairings are small souvenir china boxes and figurines that were sold at country fairs during the nineteenth century. Most were made in Germany. Reproductions of fairings are being made, especially of the famous "twelve months of marriage" series.

FAIRING, Box, Alone At Last, 2 Domestic Scenes, C.1880, 3 1/2 X 4 In. 75.00
  Figurine, Tug of War, Baby, Doll, Dog, 2 3/4 X 5 1/4 In. 175.00

Fairing, Figurine, Welsh Tea Party,
  Germany, 4 In.

> Don't lock furniture with an antique lock. If it sticks, it is almost impossible to open the door or drawer without damaging the wood.

Figurine, Welsh Tea Party, Germany, 4 In. ....*Illus*   35.00
FAMILLE ROSE, see Chinese Export

 Fans have been used for cooling since the days of the ancients. By the eighteenth century, the fan was an accessory for the lady of fashion, and very elaborate and expensive fans were made. Sticks were made of ivory or wood, set with jewels or carved. The fans were made of painted silk or paper. Inexpensive paper fans printed with advertising were giveaways in the late nineteenth and early twentieth centuries and are listed in this book under Advertising, Fan. Electric fans were introduced in 1882.

FAN, Advertising, 1900 New Home Sewing Machine Calendar, Mother, Dog 45.00
Advertising, Agate Ironware Co., Paper, 1884 ....   690.00
Advertising, Coon Chicken Inn 20.00
Advertising, Droos Horn Funeral Home, Sheboygan, Wis., Paper, Wood 35.00
Advertising, Franklin Ice Cream, Die Cut Sundae 18.00
Advertising, Gold Dust Twins, St.Louis World's Fair, 1904 ....   100.00
Advertising, Jack Daniels, Songs On Back 4.00
Advertising, Moores & Ross Ice Cream, Die Cut 40.00
Advertising, Moxie, Eileen Percy, Actress, 1923 ....   37.50
Advertising, Moxie, Rocking Horse, 1920s 18.00
Advertising, Nature's Remedy & Tums, Boy With Lollipop, Cardboard 24.00
Advertising, New York Telephone, Baseball Shape & Markings 25.00
Advertising, Putnam Dye 5.50
Advertising, Spillville S & S Memorial, Wooden 30.00
Advertising, Winchester Store 21.00
Advertising, Zig-Zag, Honeycomb Inside 40.00
Black Lace, Black Box 125.00
Electric, Ceiling, 2-Speed, Hunter 120.00
Electric, Ceiling, G.E., 4 Blades, 1920 ....   75.00
Electric, Master, Cast Iron Bottom, 4 Blades, Fabric Cord, Green Paint 45.00
Electric, Super Blue Line, Brass Blades, 8 In. 26.00
Feather, Celluloid Handle 36.50
Folding, Paddles Are Wood, End Plates Japanned Tin, 1867 ....   12.00
Hand Painted Floral On Silk, Ivory Sticks, Japan, 12 1/2 In. 125.00
Hand Painted Flowers On Satin, Ivory Sticks, Hunt Allen, C.1890, 24 In. 125.00
Hand Painted Pagoda, Tree House, Fuji, Black Silk, Bamboo Slats, 14 In. 25.00
Hot Air, Jost, 21 In. 2500.00
Ivory, Flowers, Cranes, Lotus, Insects, Gold Lacquer, Abalone, Japanese 2860.00
Ivory, Silk, Thousand Face, Lacquered Box, Japan, 19th Century, 14 In. 700.00
Lace, Painted Figures, S.Mocholi, Tortoise Sticks, C.1900, 11 5/8 In. 100.00
Lafayette Portrait, Oval Portrait, Tassels, Wood, Paper, 9 1/2 In. 275.00
Ostrich Feather, Black Carved Sticks, 11 X 23 In. 95.00
Ostrich Feather, Celluloid Handle, Cawston Ostrich Farm, Box 50.00
Ostrich Feather, Tortoise Handle, Hand Painted Flowers, Blue 380.00
Paper, Bamboo, Florals, Occupied Japan 10.00
Philadelphia Expo, 3 Buildings, Fabric, Black Print, 1876, 10 1/2 In. 150.00
Silk & Mother-of-Pearl, French 125.00

Solid Ivory, French, Hand Painted	500.00
White Net, Yellow & Orange Flowers, Bone Sticks, 13 X 30 In.	75.00

> Federzeichnung is the very strange German name for a pattern of mother-of-pearl satin glass. The pattern had irregularly shaped sections of brown glass covered with a pattern of gold squiggle lines. It was first made in the late nineteenth century.

FEDERZEICHNUNG, Vase, Brown, White Lining, 10 In.	1750.00
Vase, Maze of Air Traps, Brown, Gold Enamel, 7 In.	1215.00

> Fenton Art Glass Company, founded in Martins Ferry, Ohio, by Frank L. Fenton, is now located in Williamstown, West Virginia. It is noted for early carnival glass produced between 1907 and 1920. Many other types of glass were also made.

FENTON, Apple Blossom, Vase, 4 1/2 In.	55.00
Apple Blossom, Vase, 8 In.	85.00
Aqua Crest, Bowl, 7 In.	27.50
Aqua Crest, Compote, Footed, 6 In.	10.00
Aqua Crest, Plate, Pink, 12 In.	25.00
Aqua Crest, Vase, Crimped, 3-Lobed, 4 1/4 In.	18.00
Art, Bowl, Red Flakes, Turned In Rim, C.1924, 9 In.	125.00
Blackberry, Compote, Amethyst, Miniature	85.00
Burmese, Bowl, Blue To Pink, Ruffled, 8 1/2 In.	35.00
Burmese, Rose Bowl, Tree Scene, Hand Painted, 4 In.	25.00
Burmese, Vase, Tulip, 7 In.	32.00
Coin Dot, Chandelier, Cranberry, Sticker	400.00
Coin Dot, Vase, Clear Dots On White Ground, Crimped, 8 In.	32.00
Coin Dot, Vase, Tritop, Green, 6 1/2 In.	95.00
Coin, Compote, Jelly, Green	15.00
Daisy & Fern, Cruet, Stopper	120.00
Diamond Lace, Vase, Fan, Blue Opalescent, Piecrust, Footed, 6 In.	31.00
Diamond Optic, Basket, Hat Shape, Ruby Overlay, 6 1/4 In.	49.00
Diamond Optic, Candy Dish, Dolphin Green, Footed, 4 In.	55.00
Dolphin, Bowl, Green Swirl, 8 1/2 In.	55.00
Dolphin, Bowl, Pink, 8 1/2 In.	47.00
Dot Optic, Hat, 4 X 5 1/2 In.	55.00
Dot Optic, Pitcher, Blue Opalescent, 9 In.	120.00
Dot Optic, Salt & Pepper, Paper Label	30.00
Dot Optic, Sugar Shaker, Cranberry	40.00
Emerald Crest, Cake Server, Pedestal	68.00
Emerald Crest, Plate, 8 In.	25.00
Figurine, Dog, Scottie, Blue, Milk Glass	40.00
Floral & Grape, Tumbler, Blue	32.00
Fluted, Shade, Green, 4 In.Base, 8 In.	30.00
Georgian, Cup & Saucer, Ruby	17.00
Georgian, Sugar & Creamer, Ruby	35.00
Georgian, Wine, Ruby, 4 1/2 Oz.	18.00
Gold Crest, Compote, 8 In.	17.00
Gold Crest, Vase, Triangular, Label, 8 In.	25.00
Hobnail, Basket, Blue Opalescent, Footed, 10 In.	50.00
Hobnail, Basket, Yellow, 4 In.	65.00
Hobnail, Bowl, Pastel Rose, Footed, 7 1/2 In.	18.00
Hobnail, Bowl, Ruffled, Cranberry, 6 In.	22.00
Hobnail, Candleholder, Topaz, C.1942, Pair	62.00
Hobnail, Compote, Green, Footed, Cover, 8 1/2 In.	45.00
Hobnail, Condiment Set, Milk Glass, 7 Piece	65.00
Hobnail, Cracker Jar, Topaz Opalescent	210.00
Hobnail, Cruet, Cranberry, 5 In.	35.00
Hobnail, Epergne, 3-Light, Aqua	95.00
Hobnail, Jam Jar, Spoon	37.00
Hobnail, Pitcher, Ice Lip, Round, 9 In.	25.00
Hobnail, Rose Bowl, Ball Shape, Amber, Beige Ruffled, 4 1/2 In.	40.00
Hobnail, Sugar & Creamer, Topaz, 3 1/2 In.	22.00
Hobnail, Vase, Blue Opalescent, 1942, 5 1/2 In.	51.00

Hobnail, Vase, Cranberry, Double Crimped, 4 1/2 In. 25.00
Hobnail, Vase, Jack-In-The-Pulpit, Cranberry, 5 In. 68.00
Hobnail, Vase, Trumpet, White, 3 3/4 X 3 3/4 In. 9.00
Hobnail, Water Set, Cranberry, 11 Piece 600.00
Holly, Bowl, Green, 9 In. 425.00
Lincoln Inn, Bowl, Cereal, Pink 45.00
Lincoln Inn, Cigarette Set, Blue, 3 Piece 25.00
Lincoln Inn, Cocktail, Stemmed, Amberina 20.00
Lincoln Inn, Compote, Green .... 20.00 To 65.00
Lincoln Inn, Cup & Saucer, Cobalt Blue 35.00
Lincoln Inn, Goblet, Footed, Red 22.00
Lincoln Inn, Goblet, Stemmed, Aqua 22.50
Lincoln Inn, Goblet, Stemmed, Cobalt Blue 22.00
Lincoln Inn, Goblet, Stemmed, Green 15.00
Lincoln Inn, Goblet, Water, Dark Green 20.00
Lincoln Inn, Nappy, Pink, Handle 35.00
Lincoln Inn, Plate, Pink, 8 In. 15.00
Lincoln Inn, Salt & Pepper, Black 250.00
Lincoln Inn, Salt & Pepper, Pink 125.00
Lincoln Inn, Sherbet, Stemmed, Aqua 17.50
Lincoln Inn, Sherbet, Stemmed, Crystal 11.00
Lincoln Inn, Vase, Jade, 10 In. 175.00
Mandarin, Bowl, Red, Black Stand, 8 In. 145.00
Ming, Plate, Pink, 3-Footed, 8 In. 18.00
Orange Tree, Punch Bowl, Marigold, 10 X 10 In., 2 Piece 175.00
Orange Tree, Punch Cup, Marigold 20.00
Peach Crest, Pitcher, 6 1/4 In. 25.00
Peach Crest, Vase, 5 1/2 In. 22.00
Peach Crest, Vase, 6 1/2 In. 36.00
Persian Medallion, Rose Bowl 55.00
Plymouth, Goblet, Water, Red 17.50
Plymouth, Sherbet, Red 12.50
Plymouth, Shot Glass, Ruby 14.00
Plymouth, Tumbler, Flat, Red, 5 In. 15.00
Plymouth, Tumbler, Juice, Ruby 12.00
Poinsettia, Pitcher, Milk 85.00
Priscilla, Compote, Cover, Blue, 7 1/2 In. 28.00
Priscilla, Goblet 28.50
Ring, Lemonade Set, Black Handles, 9 Piece 195.00
Rosaline, Basket, Diamond Optic, Footed, Threaded, 8 In. 44.00
Rose Crest, Bonbon, Triangular, 5 1/2 In. 15.00
Rose Crest, Vase, 6 In. 25.00
Rustic, Vase, Funeral, Carnival Glass, 21 In. 500.00
September Morn, Bowl, Flower Frog, White, Petal Form 135.00
September Morn, Flower Frog, Chinese Yellow 395.00
Silver Crest, Ashtray, 7 In. 42.00
Silver Crest, Basket, Clear Ruffled Rim, Handle, 6 1/2 X 8 In. 24.00
Silver Crest, Basket, Crimped, 8 In. 20.00
Silver Crest, Bowl, Crimped, 10 In. 17.50
Silver Crest, Bowl, Hand Painted Roses, Aqua Stars, Gold Trim, 7 In. 15.00
Silver Crest, Bowl, Triangular, 8 In. 9.00
Silver Crest, Cake Stand, Crimped, 5 X 13 In. 32.00
Silver Crest, Candleholder, Crimped Rim, Ball Shape 12.00
Silver Crest, Candy, Cover, Footed 35.00
Silver Crest, Compote, Ruffled, 3 3/8 X 8 In. 18.00
Silver Crest, Vase, Spanish Lace, 8 In. 28.00
Silvertone, Candlestick, Cornucopia, Pink 17.00
Wreath of Roses, Rose Bowl 45.00

fiesta

Fiesta, the colorful dinnerware, was introduced in 1936 by the
Homer Laughlin China Co., redesigned in 1969, and withdrawn in
1973. The simple design was characterized by a band of concentric
circles, beginning at the rim. Cups had full-circle handles until
1969, when partial-circle handles were made. Harlequin and Riviera

were related wares. For more information and prices of American dinnerware, see the book "Kovels' Depression Glass & American Dinnerware Price List."

FIESTA, Ashtray, Cobalt Blue	20.00
Ashtray, Forest Green	25.00
Ashtray, Gray	65.00
Ashtray, Old Ivory	25.00 To 30.00
Ashtray, Yellow	20.00 To 25.00
Bowl Set, Nested, Red, Yellow, Ivory, Green, Cobalt Blue, 7 Piece	350.00
Bowl, Betty Crocker, General Mills, Turquoise, 8 1/2 X 3 In.	22.00
Bowl, Cereal, Green	10.00
Bowl, Cereal, Old Ivory	10.00
Bowl, Dessert, Gray, 6 In.	25.00
Bowl, Fruit, Light Green, 5 1/2 In.	10.00
Bowl, Fruit, Medium Green, 4 3/4 In.	125.00
Bowl, Fruit, Red, 4 3/4 In.	15.00
Bowl, Mixing, No.2, Cobalt Blue, 6 In.	24.00 To 34.00
Bowl, Mixing, No.3, Old Ivory, 7 In.	27.00
Bowl, Mixing, No.3, Turquoise, 7 In.	9.00
Bowl, Mixing, No.4, Mauve Blue, Kitchen Kraft, 8 In.	75.00
Bowl, Mixing, No.4, Old Ivory, 8 In.	30.00 To 33.00
Bowl, Mixing, No.5, Red, 9 In.	50.00
Bowl, Mixing, No.6, Chartreuse, Kitchen Kraft, 10 In.	125.00
Bowl, Mixing, No.6, Yellow, Kitchen Kraft, 10 In.	50.00
Bowl, Salad, Green	15.00
Bowl, Salad, Individual, Turquoise	32.00
Bowl, Salad, Yellow, Footed	125.00
Bowl, Serving, Cobalt Blue, 14 In.	100.00
Bowl, Serving, Green	12.50
Bread Plate, Old Ivory	5.00
Bread Plate, Yellow	5.00
Cake Plate, Green, Kitchen Kraft	20.00 To 30.00
Cake Plate, Yellow, Flat	220.00
Calendar Plate, 1955, Old Ivory, 9 In.	35.00
Candleholder, Bulb, Yellow, Pair	37.00
Carafe, Light Green	80.00
Carafe, Yellow	55.00 To 75.00
Casserole, Cover, Red, Kitchen Kraft	65.00
Casserole, French, Yellow	110.00
Casserole, Old Ivory, Cover	55.00
Casserole, Yellow	40.00 To 50.00
Chop Plate, Chartruese, 13 In.	28.00
Chop Plate, Cobalt Blue, 13 In.	16.00
Chop Plate, Forest Green, 13 In.	28.00
Chop Plate, Light Green, 15 In.	17.00 To 18.00
Chop Plate, Red, 15 In.	30.00
Chop Plate, Turquoise, 13 In.	12.00 To 19.50
Chop Plate, Yellow, 15 In.	13.00 To 17.00
Cocktail Set, Metal Based Tumbler, Cobalt Blue, 6 Piece	75.00
Coffee Server, Cobalt Blue	75.00
Coffeepot, Chartreuse	110.00
Coffeepot, Cobalt Blue, After Dinner	130.00
Coffeepot, Light Green	70.00
Coffeepot, Old Ivory	75.00
Coffeepot, Red, After Dinner	140.00
Compote, Sweets, Green	25.00
Compote, Sweets, Turquoise	22.00
Creamer, Light Green	8.00
Creamer, Old Ivory	10.00 To 12.00
Creamer, Red	15.00 To 20.00
Creamer, Rose	13.00 To 18.00
Creamer, Turquoise	8.00 To 12.00
Cup & Saucer, Cobalt Blue	17.50 To 25.00

Cup & Saucer, Dark Green	25.00
Cup & Saucer, Gray	19.50 To 20.00
Cup & Saucer, Medium Green	35.00
Cup & Saucer, Red	25.00 To 55.00
Cup & Saucer, Turquoise	14.00 To 15.00
Cup & Saucer, Yellow, After Dinner	20.00
Cup, Cobalt Blue	8.00
Cup, Turquoise	12.00 To 55.00
Egg Cooker, Hankscraft, Red, Glass Insert, 4 Piece	49.00
Eggcup, Chartreuse	38.00 To 55.00
Eggcup, Cobalt Blue	25.00 To 28.00
Gravy Boat, Cobalt Blue	25.00
Gravy Boat, Light Green	25.00
Gravy Boat, Old Ivory	16.00
Gravy Boat, Red, Liner	85.00
Gravy Boat, Turquoise	6.50 To 16.00
Grill Plate, Cobalt Blue	15.00
Grill Plate, Green	12.00
Jar, Cover, Green, Kitchen Kraft, Large	155.00
Jar, Nesting, Green, Yellow & Red Lid, Kitchen Kraft	95.00
Jug, Turquoise, 2 Pt.	45.00
Jug, Yellow	38.00
Mug, Dark Green	43.00 To 50.00
Mug, Gray	43.00 To 55.00
Mug, Rose	35.00
Mug, Yellow	29.00
Mustard, Cobalt Blue	90.00
Nappy, Chartreuse, 8 1/2 In.	20.00 To 23.00
Nappy, Medium Green, 8 1/2 In.	55.00
Nappy, Metal Holder, Rose	50.00
Pie Plate, Yellow, Kitchen Kraft, 10 In.	20.00
Pitcher, Disc, Light Green	35.00
Pitcher, Disc, Old Ivory	35.00
Pitcher, Disc, Red	65.00 To 85.00
Pitcher, Disc, Rose	85.00 To 110.00
Pitcher, Disc, Yellow	25.00 To 32.50
Pitcher, Ice Lip, Cobalt Blue	75.00
Pitcher, Jug, Green	15.00
Pitcher, Martha Washington	24.75
Pitcher, Red, 30 Oz.	150.00
Plate, Chartreuse, 6 In.	3.50
Plate, Chartreuse, 7 In.	5.00
Plate, Chartreuse, 10 In.	12.00
Plate, Cobalt Blue, 9 In.	8.00 To 10.00
Plate, Cobalt Blue, 10 In.	10.00 To 24.00
Plate, Gray, 9 In.	8.00 To 27.00
Plate, Green, 10 In.	12.00
Plate, Medium Green, 6 In.	4.00 To 7.00
Plate, Old Ivory, 10 In.	10.00
Plate, Red, 6 In.	3.50
Plate, Red, 9 In.	9.00 To 11.00
Plate, Rose, 10 In.	12.00
Plate, Turquoise, 6 1/2 In.	4.00
Plate, Turquoise, 12 In.	15.00
Plate, Yellow, 6 1/2 In.	3.00
Plate, Yellow, 7 In.	3.00 To 7.00
Plate, Yellow, 9 In.	6.00 To 7.00
Plate, Yellow, 10 In.	6.00 To 10.00
Platter, Forest Green, 12 In.	15.00
Platter, Gray	25.00
Platter, Green, Holder, Kitchen Kraft	65.00
Platter, Turquoise, 7 1/2 In.	6.00
Relish, Aqua Base, Red Center, 4 Multicolored Sections	140.00
Relish, Old Ivory, 2 Cobalt Blue Inserts	85.00

Salt & Pepper, Forest Green	18.00
Salt & Pepper, Red	16.00
Salt & Pepper, Red, Kitchen Kraft	60.00
Saltshaker, Forest Green	8.00
Saltshaker, Light Green	4.50
Saucer, Chartreuse	3.50
Saucer, Cobalt Blue	1.50
Saucer, Gray	4.00
Saucer, Rose	2.50
Saucer, Turquoise	.50 To 2.50
Server, Kitchen Kraft, Mexicana	25.00
Sit 'N Sip Cup	13.50
Soup, Cream, Cobalt Blue	22.00 To 26.00
Soup, Cream, Rose	33.00
Soup, Cream, Yellow	16.00 To 20.00
Soup, Dish, Flat, Cobalt Blue	18.00
Soup, Dish, Turquoise	18.00
Soup, Dish, Yellow	18.00
Soup, Onion, Cover, Cobalt Blue	200.00
Spoon, Red	40.00
Spoon, Yellow, Kitchen Kraft	36.00 To 65.00
Sugar & Creamer, Cobalt Blue	25.00
Sugar, Cover, Chartreuse	30.00
Sugar, Cover, Forest Green	25.00
Sugar, Cover, Gray	35.00
Sugar, Cover, Light Green	15.00
Sugar, Cover, Red	25.00
Sugar, Cover, Turquoise	19.50
Sugar, Yellow	4.50
Syrup, Cobalt Blue, Label	135.00
Teapot, Chartreuse	125.00
Teapot, Green	35.00 To 75.00
Teapot, Red, Large	105.00
Teapot, Rose	100.00
Tray, Relish, Old Ivory, Cobalt Blue	85.00
Tray, Utility, Light Green	14.00
Tray, Utility, Old Ivory	9.50
Tumbler, Gray, 5 Oz.	20.00
Tumbler, Water, Light Green	22.50
Tumbler, Water, Old Ivory	25.00
Vase, Bud, Cobalt Blue	29.00 To 40.00
Vase, Bud, Turquoise	30.00
Vase, Yellow, 10 In.	85.00
Vase, Yellow, 12 In.	295.00

 Findlay, or onyx, glass was made using three layers of glass. It was manufactured by the Dalzell Gilmore Leighton Company about 1889 in Findlay, Ohio. The platinum, ruby, or black pattern was molded into the glass. The glass came in several colors, but was usually white or ruby.

FINDLAY ONYX, Celery	300.00 To 325.00
Creamer	165.00
Pitcher, Cream, Opalescent Applied Handle, 4 1/2 In.	575.00
Saltshaker	335.00
Spooner	300.00
Sugar Shaker	275.00
Sugar, Open, White On Raspberry, 3 3/4 X 4 1/4 In.	570.00
Tumbler	240.00
Water Set, 7 Piece	1195.00

 It is said that every little boy wanted to be a fireman or a train engineer 75 years ago and the collectors today reflect this interest. All types of firefighting equipment are wanted, from fire marks to uniforms to toy fire trucks.

Some Shaker chairs have a number impressed on the top of the front leg or back post. This indicates where the chair belonged. Each room had a number.

Firefighting, Bucket,
Leather, Black

Firefighting, Helmet,
Leather, Shield On
Front, NFD, Black

FIREFIGHTING, Alarm Box, Cast Iron, Red, 6 Ft.	700.00
Alarm Box, Gamewell Fire Telegraph, Flame Finial, 6 1/2 Ft.	1200.00
Alarm Box, Gamewell, Red, Cast Iron	45.00 To 60.00
Alarm Box, Victor	2000.00
Ax, Fireman's	35.00
Badge, Chief, Stromburg Fire Dept., Nickel Plated, 2 3/4 In.	17.50
Badge, Presentation, New York, Gold	480.00
Badge, Presentation, Ohio, Gold	500.00
Bell, Brass Gong	200.00
Bell, Muffin	325.00
Belt, Independence 39, Red & White On Black Leather, 41 In.	50.00
Bucket, Dated 1834, Pair	725.00
Bucket, Leather, Black ....*Illus*	360.00
Bucket, Leather, Hand Painted Scene, Green, 12 In.	900.00
Bucket, Leather, Old Black Paint, White Painted Label, 11 In.	225.00
Bucket, Leather, Red Paint, Gold Trim, 11 On Face, 11 1/2 In.	475.00
Bucket, Leather, Tomlinson, Yellow Paint, C.1830	350.00
Bucket, Polychrome Eagle & Banners, New England, July 1806	650.00
Button, New York State Fire Dept., Middleville, 1897, 1 1/4 In	5.00
Button, Pumper, Horses, White Ground, Back Pin, 1896, 1 1/2 In.	8.00
Button, York Fire Dept., Celluloid, Brass Pin, 1900s, 1 1/2 In.	8.00
Cap, Fireman's, Leather, White, Says Foreman 1, 9 1/2 In.	175.00
Cart, Hose & Brass Nozzle, Studebaker Factory, South Bend	500.00
Extinguisher, Comet	35.00
Extinguisher, Exscelsior Fire Appliance Co., 22 In.	35.00
Extinguisher, Fyr Fyter, Child, Logo, C.1924	18.00
Extinguisher, Presto	12.00
Extinguisher, Pyrene, With 3 Qts.Liquid	15.00
Extinguisher, Safety First Co., 12 In.	25.00
Extinguisher, Si–Reen, Dist.P.F.O'Brien & Son	8.00
Extinguisher, Texaco, Brass	75.00
Grenade, Harden, Ribbed, Blue Glass	45.00
Grenade, Harden, Sapphire Blue	65.00
Grenade, Harden, Turquoise, Small	65.00
Grenade, Red Comet, Firemaster, Box, 6 Piece	140.00
Grenade, Red Comet, Hanger, Box	35.00
Grenade, Red Comet, Metal Bracket	30.00
Hat, Fireman's, Parade, Lafayette Medallion, 1840, 6 3/4 In.	5500.00
Hat, Fireman's, Parade, Penna., Western Hose Co., 1836, 7 In.	7155.00
Hat, Fireman's, Parade, Thomas Jefferson Medallion, 1850, 6 In.	7425.00
Hat, Fireman's, Parade, Western Hose Co., Felt	7150.00
Hat, Fireman's, Wool, Philadelphia Co., 19th Century	4400.00
Hat, Top, Parade, Felt, Neversink Fire Company, 1850, 6 1/2 In.	6050.00
Hat, White Paint, Gilt Trim, 1860, 15 In.	65.00
Hatchet, Handmade, 19th Century	42.00
Helmet, Chief's, Hi–Eagle, Aluminum, Shield, Brass Trumpets	225.00
Helmet, Fire Chief, Texaco	25.00
Helmet, Leather, Black, Shelton & Cheever, Boston, Tiger No.1	375.00

Helmet, Leather, Cairns & Bro., Lehigh High Eagle, Shield	750.00
Helmet, Leather, Shield On Front, NFD, Black ....*Illus*	350.00
Helmet, Leather, White, Eagle, White Shield, Lowell VFA, Mass.	225.00
Helmet, New Bedford, Mass.	1900.00
Helmet, Parade, Eagle, Columbia Hose No.1, Whitestone, NY	150.00
Invitation, Dance, Torrent Engine Co., No.3, 1856, 6 X 8 In.	55.00
Lamp, Engine, Frederick Macy No.6, Brass, White Mfg., 15 In.	1000.00
Lamp, Fire Dept.Identification, Tin, 8 Panes, 4 Sides, 29 In.	300.00
Lamp, Oil, Fire Dept.King	135.00
Lamp, Side, Engine, Engraved Volunteer	750.00
Lantern, Dietz, Friendship Company	450.00
Lantern, Hand, Dietz King, On Oil Pot	75.00
Lantern, Red, Brass, Globe, 5 3/8 In.	65.00
Lantern, Wristlet, Candle, Toleware, 4 Glass Panels, 4 X 8 In.	100.00
Lithograph, Steam Engine No.12, 12 X 17 In.	800.00
Mark, Hydrant & Hose, Letters F.A., C.1830, 7 1/2 X 11 1/2 In.	550.00
Model, Ladder Wagon, Chief C.Leonard, Newburgh, N.Y., 1874	5750.00
Nozzle, Brass & Copper, 30 In.	85.00
Nozzle, Hose, Brass, Double Handle, Akron Brass Mfg., 16 In.	135.00
Oil Can, American LaFrance	450.00
Photograph, Fireman In Uniform, C.1915	9.00
Pitcher, Water, Presentation, Dated 1892	500.00
Plate, Calendar, Fire Dept.Gettysburg, 1915–75	12.00
Print, Pacific Engine 8, San Francisco, 18 X 23 In.	475.00
Sign, Village Volunteer Fire Brigade, Silver, Black, 84 In.	600.00
Telegraph Alarm, Gamewell, Spiral Column Base, 6 Ft.6 In.	1200.00
Trumpet, Fire, Toleware, Red, Black, Tassel Rings, 23 X 6 In.	1200.00
Trumpet, Presentation, Coin Silver, July 4, 1856, 16 1/4 In.	1300.00
Trumpet, Presentation, Nickel Plated, 1890, Octagonal, 19 In.	900.00
Trumpet, Speaking, Brass, Engraved W.Stachlen, 1858, 19 In.	1200.00
Trumpet, Toleware, Initials A.W.B., 2 Tassel Rings, 23 X 6 In.	1200.00
Uniform, Peace Dale, R.I., Hat, Badge	525.00

The fireplace was used to cook and to heat the American home in past centuries. Many types of tools and equipment were used. Andirons held the logs in place, firebacks reflected the heat into the room, and tongs were used to move either fuel or food. Many types of spits and roasting jacks were made and are listed under Kitchen.

FIREPLACE, Andirons, Bell Metal, Ball Top, Incised Pot On Fireplace Crane	100.00
Andirons, Bell Metal, Lemon Finial, 18th Century, 17 In.	935.00
Andirons, Bell Metal, Lemon Top, Tools & Jamb Hooks, Boston	3850.00
Andirons, Brass & Wrought Iron, American Federal, 19th Century	550.00
Andirons, Brass & Wrought Iron, Ball Top, Arches, 28 1/2 In.	200.00
Andirons, Brass Ball, 13 In.	75.00
Andirons, Brass Finials, Knife Blade, Wrought Iron, Pair	45.00
Andirons, Brass, Acorn Finials, Log Stops, Victorian, 33 X 26 In.	800.00
Andirons, Brass, Art Deco, Figural, Swan, 14 1/2 In.	495.00
Andirons, Brass, Ball Top, 21 1/2 In.	275.00
Andirons, Brass, Ball Top, Turned Shafts, American, C.1830	550.00
Andirons, Brass, Beehive Design, Log Stops, C.1800, 20 In.	2000.00
Andirons, Brass, Belted & Ball Finials, C.1800, 14 3/4 In.	300.00
Andirons, Brass, Belted Ball Finials, Arched Legs, Molineux	350.00
Andirons, Brass, Boston Tyle, Ball Tops, Arched Legs, C.1800	375.00
Andirons, Brass, Button Knob Finials, Ringed Shafts, 1835	350.00
Andirons, Brass, Early 19th Century	650.00
Andirons, Brass, Federal, Acorn Top, American, C.1800, 21 1/4 In.	1430.00
Andirons, Brass, Federal, Spired Baluster Finials, 26 In.	450.00
Andirons, Brass, Figural, Portrait Head, Gothic, 25 X 27 In.	800.00
Andirons, Brass, Hessian Soldiers, Revolutionary Style	145.00
Andirons, Brass, Lemon Top, Log Stops, Boston, C.1800, 17 1/2 In.	850.00
Andirons, Brass, Neo–Classical Design, 20th Century, 29 In.	115.00
Andirons, Brass, Nob Finials, Oval Knob, Arched Legs, C.1835	300.00
Andirons, Brass, Prairie School Style, Block Top, 17 X 25 In.	350.00
Andirons, Brass, R.Whittingham, 1800s, 22 In.	1500.00

Andirons, Brass, Signed J.Davis 5600.00
Andirons, Brass, Spurred Curved Legs, Ball Log Stops, 15 1/2 In. 275.00
Andirons, Brass, Steeple–Top, Pair of Matching Tools, B.Edmonds 3600.00
Andirons, Brass, U–Shaped Top & Base, D.Deskey, 13 X 20 In. 275.00
Andirons, Brass, Urn Top, Penny Feet, Philadelphia 1760.00
Andirons, Bronze, Fluted Column, Scrolled Feet, 32 In. 500.00
Andirons, Iron, Animal Heads, Green Eyes, Red Eyes 1650.00
Andirons, Iron, Baseball, Batter & Pitcher, R.B.S.'09, 20 In. 2400.00
Andirons, Iron, Black Man Dressed In Tails & Vest 345.00
Andirons, Iron, Circular Finial, Brass Trim, Hand Made, 24 In. 125.00
Andirons, Iron, Comic Black Men, Black Paint, 16 1/2 In. 400.00
Andirons, Iron, Dwarf's Caricature Shape 450.00
Andirons, Iron, Leaf Terminals, Scotland, C.1900 .... 1760.00
Andirons, Iron, Lion's Heads, Copper Ball Finial, 18 1/2 In. 95.00
Andirons, Iron, Owls, Glass Eyes, Dated 1887, 16 In. 450.00
Andirons, Iron, Sphinx Heads, Animal Feet 28.00
Bellows, Bellow's Whiskey, Wooden, 16 In. 35.00
Bellows, Crank & Wheel Operated, 10 X 28 In. 295.00
Bellows, Crescent Moon, Geometric Inlays, Walnut, 19th Century 1320.00
Bellows, Primitive, Oak, Tooled Brass Design, Copper Tack, 24 In. 25.00
Bellows, Turtle Back, Floral Design, Brass Nozzle, Leather, 19 In. 350.00
Bird Spit, Crown Shape 385.00
Bird Spit, Tin, Draining Corners 90.00
Broom, Hearth, Birch Splint, C.1860, 10 1/2 In. 30.00
Bucket, Chestnut, Staved, Large 45.00
Chenet, Louis XV, Gilt Bronze, Satyr, 19th Century, 13 In., Pair 1045.00
Chenet, Louis XV, Male & Female Oriental Figure, 18 In., Pair 6000.00
Chenet, Louis XV, Ormolu, Mid–19th Century, 18 In. ....*Illus* 6000.00
Chenet, Louis XV, Putto, Seated, Foliate Base, 14 1/2 In., Pair 3850.00
Chestnut Roaster, Reticulated, Brass, English, 23 In. 150.00
Chimney Pot, Clay, 35 1/2 In. 45.00
Coal Bucket, Brass 82.50
Coal Rack, Forged Iron 35.75
Door, For Oven, Strap Latch, Movable Draft, Lincoln Foundry 350.00
Fan, Brass, Embossed Griffon Base, 25 X 38 In. 75.00
Fan, Fire Screen, White, Silk Fringed, Ivory Handles, 22 X 12 In. 280.00
Fender, 2 Horizontal Bars, Urn Finials, Brass, 48 In. 145.00
Fender, Brass & Iron, Double Rail, 32 In. 90.00
Fender, Brass & Wire, Ball Finials, 19th Century, 45 1/4 In. 950.00
Fender, Brass, 2 Rails, Columnar Posts, Ball Finials, 54 In. 290.00
Fender, Brass, Baroque Style, Urn–Form Ends, 17 X 44 In. 350.00
Fender, Brass, Leather, English, 19th Century 550.00

Fireplace, Chenet, Louis XV, Ormolu,
Mid–19th Century, 18 In.

Try to rearrange your furniture once a year to avoid noticeable sun fading.

Very dirty lacquer can be cleaned with a paste of flour and olive oil.

Remove the musty smell from a bureau drawer by sprinkling fresh ground coffee inside. Leave it for 24 hours.

Fender, Brass, Pierced Design, Claw Corners, 14 X 44 In.	155.00
Fender, Brass, Tubular Finial Rails, Late 19th Century, 42 In.	150.00
Fender, Wire & Brass, Half Oval Shape, C.1900, 12 X 50 In.	200.00
Fender–Roaster, Adjustable, Hand Wrought Iron	140.00
Fire Screen, Iron, 28 Mesh Squares, Loop Handles, 27 X 45 In.	650.00
Fire Screen, Louis XV, Tilt, Signed L.Dromard, Paris	750.00
Fire Screen, Needlepoint, Ribbon, French Gilded, 19th Century	350.00
Fire Screen, Victorian, Rosewood, Glass Bead, Angel, Cherub, 63 In.	250.00
Fire Tongs, Brass, Iron, 19th Century, 34 In.	95.00
Fireback, Crossed Bow, Quiver, Birds, Cast Iron, 19 X 23 1/2 In.	50.00
Fireback, Serpents Over Scroll Border, Cast Iron, 27 In.	225.00
Fireboard, Cats, With Wicker Cat House, Veneered, Victorian	1750.00
Fireboard, Striping, Double Rose Sprig, Shenandoah Valley, 29 In.	375.00
Grate, Fleur–De–Lis Design On Crest, Black, Cast Iron, 21 1/2 In.	50.00
Grate, Minerva Head, Cast Nickel Steel, 18 1/2 X 20 1/2 In.	285.00
Grate, Pierced Brass Fender, Etched Foliage, C.1800, 31 In.	1870.00
Gypsy Pot, 3–Legged, Long Hangers, Iron	55.00
Holder, Tool & Candleholder, Cherubs, Bronze & Brass, 5 Ft.	2700.00
Hood, 3–Sided, Trapezoidal Front, Shell Reserve, Oak, 87 In.	225.00
Kettle Stand, Iron, Cabriole Legs, Pierced Sheet Metal, 10 In.	250.00
Mantel, Curved China Cabinet Top, Quartersawn Oak	1200.00
Mantel, Eastlake, Ebonized & Parcel Gilt, C.1870, 50 X 64 In.	550.00
Mantel, Italian Renaissance, Carved Acanthus, Walnut, 60 X 65 In.	1900.00
Meat Hook, Triple–Forged Iron	37.50
Peel, Hearth & Oven, Long Handle, Cast Iron	75.00
Roaster, Apple, Double Shelf, Tin, 11 1/2 X 12 In.	155.00
Roasting Stick, 2 Hooks At End, Rotating Bar, Iron, 24 In.	185.00
Screen, Adjustable Silk–Lined, Trestle Ends, 38 X 20 In.	155.00
Screen, Carved Foliage, Embroidered Inset, Giltwood, 43 1/2 In.	2750.00
Screen, Gothic, Needlepoint Cottage Scene Under Glass	1450.00
Screen, Peacock Shape, Summer, Polychromed, 36 In.To Top Feathers	675.00
Screen, White Metal	60.00
Shelf, Kettle, Steel, Cabriole Legs, Pierced Top, 13 X 13 In.	65.00
Shovel, Tongs, Brass Grips, Eagle Etched, Steel, English, 34 In.	2420.00
Spider, Iron, Half Ball Shape, Footed, 18th Century, 5 1/2 In.	350.00
Spit, Clockwork, Key, Iron, Tin Sides, Brass Handle, 40 X 14 In.	375.00
Tilter, Kettle, Hand Forged Iron, 18th Century	295.00
Trammel, Chain, Wrought Hooks, 4 1/2 Ft.	22.00
Trammel, Iron, Original Tilter & Iron Teapot, 1805	1150.00
Trammel, Wrought Iron, Adjusts From 20 In.	65.00
Trivet, Horse In Center, 3–Footed, Brass, 6 In.	65.00
Trivet, Revolving, 3–Legged, Hand Forged Iron, 1800s, 27 X 9 In.	147.00

MF Porcelain was made in Herend, Hungary, by Moritz Fischer. The factory was founded in 1839 and continued working into the twentieth century. The wares are sometimes referred to as "Herend" porcelain.

FISCHER, Basket, Reticulated Sides, Flowers & Leaves, C.1840, 11 3/4 In.	650.00
Dinner Set, Scalloped Rims, Rose Bud Center, Marked, 55 Piece	1500.00
Ewer, Multicolored Floral Design, Gold Trim, 15 3/4 In.	350.00
Figurine, Girl & Goose, Enameled, Marked, 7 1/8 In.	95.00
Figurine, Madonna & Child, 14 In.	350.00
Figurine, Parrot, No.5000	165.00
Figurine, Peasant Child, Holding Piglets, 7 In.	225.00
Sugar, Polychrome Butterflies, Rose Finial, Marked, 3 7/8 In.	55.00
Teapot, Rothchild Bird, Bird Finial, Gold Trim	795.00
Vase, Stylized Flowers, Gold At Neck & Base, 10 1/2 In., Pair	310.00

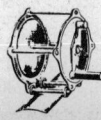 Fishing reels of brass or nickel were made in the United States by 1810. Bamboo fly rods were sold by 1860, often marked with the maker's name. Metal lures, then wooden and metal lures were made in the nineteenth century. Plastic lures were made by the 1930s. All fishing material is collected today and even equipment of the past thirty years is of interest if in good condition with original box.

FISHING, Basket, Trout, Birch Bark, Paul Reschng, Narrow Lake, June 1927 .... 798.00
  Bucket, Minnow, Copper 105.00
  Cabinet, Lures, Weber, Fish Logo 250.00
  Creel, Basket, Splint 37.50
  Creel, Wooden 45.00
  Fly Rod, F.E.Thomas 126.50
  Fly Rod, Gillum Deluxe, 7 Ft. 900.00
  Fly Rod, Kendryx Reed, 9 Ft. 200.00
  Fly Rod, Leonard, 6 1/2 Ft. 650.00
  Fly Rod, Montague 82.50
  Fly Rod, Payne, 8 1/2 Ft. 1300.00
  Fly Rod, Split Bamboo, Round Case 60.00
  Fly Rod, Winchester, Metal 55.00
  Fly Rod, Winchester, No.6055 .... 135.00
  Knife, Ka–Far, Trout 110.00
  Lure, Baby Crab, Heddon–Dowagiac, Box, 1909 .... 15.00
  Lure, Brown Frog, Louis Rhead 700.00
  Lure, Bud Stewart, Strawberry Color 775.00
  Lure, Carter Bestever, 3 In. 35.00
  Lure, Expert Innow, Keeling, 3 In. 50.00
  Lure, Frog Legs, Mechanical, Hard Plastic, Box 30.00
  Lure, Frog, Mechanical, Halik, Rubber 35.00
  Lure, Heddon Vamp 15.00
  Lure, Injured Minnow, Best–O–Luck, 4 In. 40.00
  Lure, LeBoeuf Creeper, LeBoeuf Mfg.Co., Wesleyville, Penna., Box 35.00
  Lure, Lucky 13, Heddon–Dowagiac, Box 25.00
  Lure, Mouse, Wooden, 5 In. 20.00
  Lure, Oreno Wobbling, Bass 25.00
  Lure, Pikaroon, Moonlight Bait, 5 1/2 In. 40.00
  Lure, Pikie Minnow, Creek Chub, Jointed, 5 In. 25.00
  Lure, Revolution, Mickey Mouse Prop, Shakespeare, Aluminum, 4 In. 50.00
  Lure, Sambo In Barrel, Barrel Pushes Up, Box, 4 1/2 In. 45.00
  Lure, South Bend Minnow, Oreno, 4 In. 25.00
  Lure, Swimming Mouse, Shakespeare, 3 1/2 In. 35.00
  Lure, Vamp Spook, Heddon, 4 1/4 In. 18.00
  Lure, Winchester, No.9204, Red 250.00
  Lure, Winchester, No.9206 .... 275.00
  Minnow Trap, Blown Glass 275.00
  Plug, Heddon 2120xrs 25.00
  Plug, Paw Paw 2204 .... 25.00
  Plug, Wooden Body, Comstock Flying Helgramite 9075.00
  Reel, A.W.Gamage, Brass, Walnut, 19th Century, 5 1/2 In. 195.00
  Reel, Bass, Vomhofe, German Silver, Dated July 14, 1896 .... 400.00
  Reel, Goodwin Granger Champion, C.1934, 8 1/2 In. 300.00
  Reel, Kovalosky, No.12/0, Leather Case 2200.00
  Reel, Meek, No.30 .... 75.00
  Reel, Meisellbach 35.00
  Reel, Pflueger, No.1944 .... 30.00
  Reel, Saltwater, Vomhofe, Large 350.00
  Reel, Shakespeare 1958 Triumph 16.00
  Reel, Shakespeare President, Level Wind, Round Side Plates 35.00
  Reel, Shakespeare, 1920 .... 25.00
  Reel, Takapart, Left Hand, 1909 .... 30.00
  Reel, Winchester, No.4250, Take Down, Satin Finish 130.00
  Reel, Wooden, Large 75.00
  Rod & Reel, Winchester, No.4350 Reel, No.5510 Rod 150.00
  Rod, Casting, Montague, Split Bamboo 25.00
  Rod, Winchester, No.5650, Steel, Canvas Bag 60.00
  Spinner, J.T.Buhl, Whitehall, N.Y. 30.00
  Tackle Box, Leather, Brass Fittings, 1800s 325.00
  Tackle Box, Winchester 45.00
  Tackle Box, Winchester Casting Reel, Lures, 2 1/2 X 5 X 19 In. 240.00
  Torch, Triple Light, Tin, Back Reflector 35.00
  Trap, Minnow, C.F.G.Orvis, Glass 65.00

Trap, Minnow, Checotah, Glass	35.00
Trap, Minnow, McSwain, Jonesboro, Ark., Glass	45.00
Wrench, Linesman, 14 In.	60.00

FLAG, see Textile, Flag

 Flash Gordon appeared in the Sunday comics in 1934. The daily strip started in 1940. The hero was also in comic books from 1930 to 1970, in books from 1936, in movies from 1938, on the radio in the 1930s and 1940s, and on television from 1953 to 1954. All sorts of memorabilia are collected, but the ray guns and rocket ships are the most popular.

FLASH GORDON, Badge, Flash Gordon Club, Fleshtone Litho, 1930s, 1 In.	125.00
Book, Better Little Book, Flash Gordon In Jungles of Mongo	40.00
Book, Big Little Book, Power of Men of Mongo	35.00
Book, Flash Gordon & Tournaments of Mongo, Whitman, 1935	48.00
Book, Paint, 1936, Whitman	30.00
Click Gun, Tin Litho, Marx, Box, 1935	150.00
Display Card, 2 Rockets, Holding Belt, Pioneer, 14 X 16 In.	48.00
Doll Set, 4 Piece	65.00
Figure, Syroco, 1944	195.00
Kite	22.00
Lid, Dixie Cup, Buster Crabbe, Universal Chapter, 2 3/4 In.	25.00
Pin, Flash Gordon Club, Black, Red, White, 1 1/8 In.	60.00
Pistol, Arresting Ray, Litho Tin	250.00
Ray Gun	35.00
Rocket Ship .... 295.00 To	325.00
Space Compass	30.00
Water Pistol, Yellow Plastic, Whistle Base, Marx, 1950, 4 In.	75.00

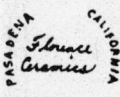 Florence Ceramics were made in Pasadena, California, from World War II to 1977. Florence Ward created many colorful figurines, boxes, candleholders, and other items for the giftshop trade. Each piece was marked with an ink stamp that included the name Florence Ceramics Co. The company was sold in 1964 and although the name remained the same the products were very different. Mugs, cups, and trays were made.

FLORENCE CERAMICS, Figurine, Abigail, White, Gold, 9 In.	90.00
Figurine, Bird, White, 14 1/2 In.	18.00
Figurine, Choir Boy, 6 In.	12.00
Figurine, Dalla, Gray	45.00
Figurine, David & Betsy, White & Gold, 7 1/2 In., Pair	65.00
Figurine, Delia, 8 In.	55.00
Figurine, Elaine .... 30.00 To	45.00
Figurine, Ellen	44.00
Figurine, Emily, 8 In.	40.00
Figurine, Irene, White, 6 In. .... 30.00 To	45.00
Figurine, Jim, Rose Colored Outfit, Green & Gold Trim	68.00
Figurine, Kay, 6 In.	24.00
Figurine, Lillian	110.00
Figurine, Louis XVI & Marie Antoinette, Pair	350.00
Figurine, Louise, 7 1/4 In.	65.00
Figurine, Madeline, Pink Dress, Blue Scarf	95.00
Figurine, Matilda, 9 In. .... 75.00 To	85.00
Figurine, Melanie, 7 In. ....*Illus*	75.00
Figurine, Mermaid Rosie	90.00
Figurine, Oriental Boy & Girl, Pair ....55.00 To	110.00
Figurine, Priscilla, Pink Dress, 8 In.	65.00
Figurine, Rebecca	75.00
Figurine, Rhett, 9 In.	145.00
Figurine, Roberta, 8 3/4 In.	95.00
Figurine, Sarah	115.00
Figurine, Scarlett, 9 In. ....75.00 To	125.00
Figurine, Story Hour, 3 Seated Figures	350.00
Figurine, Sue Ellen, Blue, Signed, 8 1/2 In.	75.00

Figurine, Sue, 6 In.	50.00 To 65.00
Figurine, Vase, Swedish Lady, Green, 9 In.	75.00
Figurine, Victor	80.00
Figurine, Victoria	300.00
Figurine, Vivian, Green Dress, 8 In.	110.00
Flower Holder, Chinese Couple, 8 In., Pair	110.00
Planter, Blond Girl	14.00
Planter, Boy	18.00
Planter, Chinese Girl, White, Green Trim, Label	25.00
Planter, Man & Woman, Pair	35.00
Planter, May	30.00
Plaque, Matilda, Gray & Maroon	70.00
Plaque, Scarlett, Gray Dress, 9 In.	90.00
Plaque, Sue, White Dress, 5 1/2 In.	55.00
Plaque, Vivian, Rose Dress	70.00
Vase, Girl Sitting With Bird	24.00
Vase, Girl With Parasol, Blue & White	28.00

 Flow blue, or flo blue, was made in England about 1830 to 1900. The plates were printed with designs using a cobalt blue coloring. The color flowed from the design to the white plate so that the finished plate has a smeared blue design. The plates were usually made of ironstone china.

FLOW BLUE, Berry Bowl, Raleigh, Burgess & Leigh	20.00
Bone Dish, Amoy, 8 In.	75.00
Bone Dish, Marguerite, Grindley	35.00
Bowl, Abbey, Geo.Jones, Round, 8 In.	85.00
Bowl, Alhambra, 10 1/2 In.	44.00
Bowl, Cover, Amoy, 10 1/4 In.	395.00
Bowl, Cover, Bamboo, Oval, Cover, C.1845	295.00
Bowl, Cover, Cashmere, Cover, 9 3/4 In.	725.00
Bowl, Cover, Fairy Villas, Adams, C.1891, 12 1/2 In.	195.00
Bowl, Cover, Holland, Johnson, 10 1/2 In.	175.00
Bowl, Cover, Kenworth, 10 1/2 In.	225.00
Bowl, Cover, Marguerite, Grindley, 10 1/2 In.	195.00
Bowl, Cover, Normandy, Oval, 10 In.	225.00
Bowl, Cover, Oxford, 6–Sided, Ford & Sons, 10 1/2 In.	295.00
Bowl, Del Monte, Cover, Vegetable	95.00
Bowl, Duchess, Tulip, Grindley	40.00
Bowl, Florida, Grindley, 7 In.	55.00
Bowl, Hat, La Belle	65.00
Bowl, Holland, Johnson, 9 1/4 In.	75.00

Florence Ceramics, Figurine,
Melanie, 7 In.

Folk Art, Whirligig, Washer Woman,
Mass., 1910, 27 In.

Bowl, Honey, Cyprus 65.00
Bowl, Keswick, Wood & Sons, 9 1/2 X 12 In. 40.00
Bowl, La Belle, 1 Handle 165.00
Bowl, La Belle, Oval, 9 1/2 In. 65.00
Bowl, La Belle, Scalloped, Oval, 9 1/2 In. 65.00
Bowl, Leicester, Gold Trim, 12 1/2 X 8 In. 130.00
Bowl, Manhattan, Flanged, 9 In. 48.00
Bowl, Manila, Oval, Till & Sons, 10 In. 75.00
Bowl, Oregon, Mayer, 10 3/4 In. 150.00
Bowl, Oriental, Cover, Footed, Oval, 11 1/4 X 8 3/4 In. 295.00
Bowl, Paris, 7 In. 35.00
Bowl, Pekin, Staffordshire, 9 1/2 In. 70.00
Bowl, Scinde, Alcock, 10 3/4 In. 250.00
Bowl, Touraine, Stanley, 10 1/2 In. 90.00
Bowl, Waldorf, 9 In. 65.00
Bowl, Waste, Watteau, 7 In. 70.00
Bowl, Watteau, Scalloped Edge, 4 3/4 In. 42.50
Butter Chip, Argyle 20.00
Butter Chip, Clarissa, Johnson Bros. 17.50
Butter Chip, Hofburg .... 22.00 To 80.00
Butter Chip, La Belle 20.00
Butter Chip, Linda, 4 Piece 75.00
Butter Chip, Marguerite, Grindley .... 20.00 To 25.00
Butter Chip, Nonpareil 30.00
Butter Chip, Richmond 24.00
Butter, Cover, Manhattan, Grindley 250.00
Butter, Cover, Touraine, Stanley 275.00
Butter, Florida, Grindley 295.00
Cake Plate, Delft, Ridgway 40.00
Casserole, Claremont, Johnson Bros. 135.00
Chamber Pot, Geneva, Doulton 175.00
Charger, Oriental, Ridgway, 12 1/2in. 125.00
Charger, Pekin, Jones, 11 1/2 In. 110.00
Coffeepot, Abbey, Jones 255.00
Creamer, Abbey, Jones 60.00
Creamer, Amoy 225.00
Creamer, Chapoo 235.00
Creamer, Chusan, Clementson 175.00
Creamer, Marguerite, Grindley 125.00
Creamer, Touraine, Stanley 140.00
Creamer, Tulip 75.00
Cup & Saucer, 3 Handles, Pelew, Chalinnor 75.00
Cup & Saucer, Cashmere 115.00
Cup & Saucer, Chapoo, Wedgwood 150.00
Cup & Saucer, Clayton, Demitasse 65.00
Cup & Saucer, Fairy Villas 50.00
Cup & Saucer, Glenwood, Johnson 65.00
Cup & Saucer, Idris, Grindley 50.00
Cup & Saucer, Manhattan 55.00
Cup & Saucer, Marguerite, Grindley 65.00
Cup & Saucer, Marquis, Grindley 65.00
Cup & Saucer, Pelew, Handleless, Chalinor 95.00
Cup & Saucer, Raleigh, Burgess & Leigh 35.00
Cup & Saucer, Temple, Handleless, Podmore & Walker 125.00
Cup & Saucer, Vine, Wedgwood 44.00
Cup Plate, Amoy .... 65.00 To 95.00
Cup Plate, Amoy, Davenport, 4 1/8 In. 35.00
Cup Plate, Excelsior, Fell 65.00
Cup, Astoria, Johnson 25.00
Dinner Set, Lugano, Ridgway, Service For 6, 49 Piece 2200.00
Dinner Set, Oregon, Johnson Bros., 80 Piece 2900.00
Dish, Pickle, Scinde 125.00
Gravy Boat, Georgia, Johnson 65.00
Gravy Boat, Marguerite, Grindley 75.00

Gravy Boat, Melbourne, Grindley	65.00
Gravy Boat, Poppy, Douglas	75.00
Gravy Boat, Raleigh, Burgess & Leigh	60.00
Gravy Boat, Rose, Underplate	120.00
Gravy Boat, Scinde, Alcock	195.00
Jam Jar, Abbey, G.Jones	75.00
Jardiniere, Babes In Woods, Woman & Girl, Marked, 8 3/4 X 10 In.	395.00
Luncheon Set, La Francais, Service For 4, 41 Piece	495.00
Mug, Watteau, Doulton	125.00
Pitcher & Bowl, Lobelia	450.00
Pitcher, La Belle, Bulbous, 6 1/2 In.	140.00
Pitcher, Milk, Cashmere, Morley, 7 5/8 In.	625.00
Pitcher, Milk, Water Lily, Adams, 8 1/2 In.	95.00
Pitcher, Milk, Watteau, Doulton, 7 In.	195.00
Pitcher, Norbury, C.1910, 6 In.	55.00
Pitcher, Pansy, Warwick, Bulbous, 6 In.	125.00
Pitcher, Pelew, 11 3/4 In.	550.00
Pitcher, Water, Scinde, Walker, 12 1/2 In.	850.00
Plate, Alaska, Grindley, 6 3/4 In.	25.00
Plate, Amoy, 10 1/2 In.	95.00
Plate, Arabesque, 10 1/2 In.	95.00
Plate, Argyle, 10 In.	50.00
Plate, Ashburton, Grindley, 1891, 8 In.	35.00
Plate, Asiatic Pheasants, 8 3/4 In.	25.00
Plate, Beaufort, 8 1/2 In.	42.00
Plate, Candia, 7 In.	30.00
Plate, Canton, 6 In.	32.50
Plate, Cashmere, Ridgway, 9 In.	95.00
Plate, Chen–Si, 7 1/2in.	65.00
Plate, Chinese, Allerton, 9 In.	23.50
Plate, Chusan, 10 In.	55.00
Plate, Dorothy, 8 In.	18.00
Plate, Duchess, 10 In.	35.00
Plate, Excelsior, 9 In.	45.00
Plate, Fairy Villas, Adams, 10 In.	30.00
Plate, Florida, Grindley, 6 In.	20.00
Plate, Florida, Grindley, 9 In.	45.00
Plate, Geneva, Doulton, 6 1/2 In.	25.00
Plate, Gironde, 10 In.	55.00
Plate, Glenwood, Johnson, 8 In.	65.00
Plate, Glenwood, Johnson, 10 In.	55.00
Plate, Harvest, 10 In.	50.00
Plate, Hong Kong, 8 1/4 In.	70.00
Plate, Hong Kong, 10 1/2 In.	90.00
Plate, Kyber, Adams, 8 In.	40.00
Plate, LaHore, Phillips, 10 1/2 In.	90.00
Plate, Lancaster, 7 1/2 In.	30.00
Plate, Lois, New Wharf, 9 3/4 In.	35.00
Plate, Lorne, 6 In.	22.00
Plate, Lorne, 7 In.	32.00
Plate, Lorne, 10 In. .... 45.00 To	65.00
Plate, Manilla, 9 In.	90.00
Plate, Manilla, 10 In. .... 70.00 To	75.00
Plate, Marguerite, Grindley, 10 In.	65.00
Plate, Nonpareil, 9 In.	45.00
Plate, Normandy, 10 In.	65.00
Plate, Oregon, Mayer, 9 1/2 In.	75.00
Plate, Oriental, New Wharf Pottery, 7 In.	18.00
Plate, Oriental, Ridgway, 9 In.	42.00
Plate, Paris, 9 In.	50.00
Plate, Pelew, Challinor, 9 1/2 In.	55.00
Plate, Pelew, Challinor, 10 3/4 In.	85.00
Plate, Raleigh, Burgess & Leigh, 9 In.	35.00
Plate, Scinde, Alcock, 10 1/2 In.	55.00

Plate, Shanghai, 7 In. .... 38.00 To 40.00
Plate, Shanghai, 9 1/2 In. .... 50.00 To 75.00
Plate, Shanghai, Grindley, 10 In. 28.00
Plate, Shapoo, Boote, 7 1/2 In. 60.00
Plate, Shell, 6 1/2 In. 50.00
Plate, Shell, Challinor, 9 1/2 In. 85.00
Plate, Shell, Challinor, 11 In. 95.00
Plate, Temple, Podmore & Walker, 7 3/4 In. 50.00
Plate, Temple, Podmore & Walker, 9 In. 70.00
Plate, Togo, 8 3/4 In. 18.00
Plate, Tokio, Polychromed, Mayers, 8 In. 30.00
Plate, Tonquin, 9 1/2 In. 80.00
Plate, Touraine, Alcock, 8 In. 50.00
Plate, Touraine, Stanley, 8 3/4 In. 48.00
Plate, Vermont, 7 In. 22.00
Plate, Vermont, Burgess & Leigh, 10 1/2 In. 65.00
Plate, Vine, Wedgwood, 9 In. 40.00
Plate, Virginia, 10 In. 35.00
Plate, Waldorf, Bird Center, Copeland, 10 In. 95.00
Plate, Wampoa, Mellow & Venables, 7 1/4 In. 55.00
Plate, Watteau, 10 1/2 In. 55.00
Plate, Watteau, Doulton, 8 1/2 In. .... 38.00 To 45.00
Plate, Watteau, Doulton, 9 1/2 In. 50.00
Plate, Watteau, Vermont, 10 In. 48.00
Plate, Whampoa, M & V, 7 1/2 In. 55.00
Plate, Whampoa, M & V, 10 1/2 In. 90.00
Platter, Albany, Grindley, 14 In. 130.00
Platter, Argyle, 17 In. 155.00
Platter, Argyle, Grindley, 13 In. 70.00
Platter, Argyle, Grindley, 17 In. 210.00
Platter, Astoria, 12 In. 65.00
Platter, Carlton, Alcock, 13 1/2 In. 200.00
Platter, Cashmere, 13 X 10 In. 275.00
Platter, Chapoo, Wedgwood, 15 3/4 In. 375.00
Platter, Chinese, Wedgwood, 14 X 17 In. 325.00
Platter, Coburg, Edwards, 17 7/8 In. 345.00
Platter, Florida, Grindley, 14 In. .... 125.00 To 145.00
Platter, Hartington, Grindley, 16 X 11 1/2 In. 65.00
Platter, Holland, Johnson, 12 In. .... 85.00 To 110.00
Platter, Keele, 9 In. 70.00
Platter, Kenworth, Johnson, 12 X 16 In. 197.50
Platter, LaHore, Phillips, 16 X 12 In. 300.00
Platter, Lakewood, Royal Wood, 12 In. 75.00
Platter, Lakewood, Royal Wood, 14 In. 95.00
Platter, Lotus, Grindley, 16 X 12 In. 125.00
Platter, Madras, Oriental, 18 X 15 In. 325.00
Platter, Marechal Niel, Grindley, 12 In. 65.00
Platter, Marguerite, Grindley, 11 In. 85.00
Platter, Marie, 17 1/2 In. 160.00
Platter, Meissen, 12 X 16 In. 95.00
Platter, Melbourne, Grindley, 14 In. 110.00
Platter, Mulberry, Washington Vase, 16 X 12 In. 148.00
Platter, Nonpareil, Burgess Leigh, 18 In. 295.00
Platter, Normandy, 8 In. 85.00
Platter, Normandy, 14 In. 100.00
Platter, Oriental, Kaolin Ware, 10 X 13 1/2 In. 150.00
Platter, Oxford, Ford & Sons, 11 1/2 X 8 1/2 In. 125.00
Platter, Oxford, Ford & Sons, 14 X 11 In. 195.00
Platter, Peach Royal, 12 In. 65.00
Platter, Peach Royal, 16 X 13 In. 125.00
Platter, Peking, 17 In. 67.50
Platter, Raleigh, Burgess & Leigh, 14 In. 125.00
Platter, Regent, 15 In. 135.00
Platter, Rhone, T.Goodfellow, Octagonal 175.00

Platter, Richmond, Doulton, 13 1/2 X 17 In. 185.00
Platter, Richmond, Meakin, 16 In. 85.00
Platter, Royal, 9 1/2 X 12 In. 98.00
Platter, Scinde, Alcock, 13 3/4 In. 220.00
Platter, Scinde, Alcock, 16 In. 465.00
Platter, Scinde, Alcock, 18 X 15 In. 325.00
Platter, Tivoli, 10 In. 55.00
Platter, Tonquin, Adams, 14 X 10 In. 235.00
Platter, Touraine, 10 1/2 X 7 In. 60.00
Platter, Touraine, Stanley, 12 1/2 In. 125.00
Platter, Turkey, Wedgwood, 13 X 17 In. 195.00
Platter, Verona, Wedgwood & Son, C.1870, 9 1/2 X 11 In. 125.00
Platter, Virginia, Embossed Handles, Maddox, 18 X 15 In. 325.00
Platter, Waldorf, 10 1/2 X 8 In. 75.00
Platter, Watteau, Doulton, 10 1/4 X 8 1/4 In. 95.00
Potty, Vernon, Royal Doulton 125.00
Sauce, Chapoo 32.00
Sauce, Gainsborough 30.00
Sauce, Normandy, 5 1/4 In. 30.00
Sauce, Waldorf 20.00
Saucer, Nonpareil 15.00
Saucer, Princeton 15.00
Soup, Dish, Argyle, Grindley 50.00
Soup, Dish, Astoria, Johnson, 10 In. 45.00
Soup, Dish, Clifton, Grindley, 5 Piece .... 150.00 To 175.00
Soup, Dish, Gironde, Flanged, 9 In. 55.00
Soup, Dish, Lotus, 4 In. 100.00
Soup, Dish, Marechal Niel, 8 In. 40.00
Soup, Dish, Princeton, Flanged, 9 In. 32.00
Soup, Dish, Sabraon, Flanged, 9 In. 95.00
Soup, Dish, Shanghai, 7 3/4 In. 28.00
Soup, Dish, Tokio 150.00
Soup, Dish, Waldorf, New Wharf Pottery 55.00
Sugar, Columbia, Clementson 250.00
Sugar, Cover, Circassia 150.00
Sugar, Cover, Hofburg 85.00
Sugar, Cover, Lobelia 125.00
Sugar, Cover, Marguerite, Grindley 125.00
Sugar, Cover, Scinde, Alcock 345.00
Sugar, Idris 125.00
Sugar, LaHore, Phillips 150.00
Sugar, Marguerite, Grindley 125.00
Sugar, Shanghai, Grindley 125.00
Syrup, Claremont, Pewter Top, Burgess & Leigh, 6 1/2 In. 95.00
Syrup, Warwick, Pansy, Metal Cover 145.00
Tea Set, Child's, Wagon Wheel, 13 Piece 675.00
Tea Tray, Watteau, Doulton, 16 X 14 In. 350.00
Teapot, Abbey, G.Jones 325.00
Teapot, Athens, Meigh 350.00
Teapot, Chapoo .... 350.00 To 525.00
Teapot, Chusan, Clementson 275.00
Teapot, Lobelia 150.00
Teapot, Manhattan 285.00
Teapot, Manilla 395.00
Teapot, Sabraon 300.00
Toothbursh Holder, Togo 45.00
Tureen, Cover, Vermont, Burgess & Leigh 130.00
Tureen, Soup, Cover, Paisley, Mercer 275.00
Tureen, Soup, Le Pavot, Grindley, 12 In. 265.00
Tureen, Soup, Vermont, With 8 Soup Dishes 435.00
Tureen, Tonquin, Stanley, 1845 .... 450.00
Wash Basin, Chapoo 475.00
Wash Basin, Chatsworth, Grindley 250.00
Wash Set, Princess, Woods & Sons, 7 Piece 1250.00

Waste Bowl, Singan, Goodfellow 215.00
FLYING PHOENIX, see Phoenix Bird

Folk art is listed in many sections of the book under the actual name of the object. See categories such as Box; Cigar Store Figure; Weather Vane; Wooden; etc.

FOLK ART, Bird, Long Beak, Carved Wood, Orange Paint, Spots, 4 1/2 In. 75.00
Birdhouse, Canvas, Japanese Lantern Shape, Painted, Hanging 45.00
Box, Man In Interior, Swivel Lid, Primitive, Wooden, 4 In. 60.00
Branch, 2 Carved Faces On Urn Base, Green With Polychrome, 9 In. 20.00
Bust, Man With Beard, 5 In. 95.00
Cage, Squirrel, Grand Hotel, House Shape 3200.00
Cupboard, Relief Carving, 1 Drawer, Fall Front Door, Miniature 25.00
Desk Set, Pond With Alligator, Fish, Turtle, Ducks, Ceramic, 12 In. 385.00
Dollhouse, 4 Rooms, Grain Painted Woodwork, Carved People, 30 Pc. 2200.00
Dummy Board, Boy, Red Jacket, Plumed Hat, Painted Oak, 37 In. 1750.00
Figure, Athlete Struggling With A Serpent, 19 In. 155.00
Figure, Bear, Sitting, Holding Brass Ashtray, Wooden, 8 1/2 In. 145.00
Figure, Coiled Snake, Wooden, 11 1/4 In. 75.00
Figure, Dog, Sandstone, W.H.Vickers, Jan.20th, 1889, 3 X 2 In. 65.00
Figure, Drunk, Keystone Cop, Lamp Post 100.00
Figure, Eagle, Wood, Brown, Gray, White & Yellow Highlights, 24 In. 75.00
Figure, Horse, 2–Tone Varnish Finish, Wooden, 10 In. 65.00
Figure, Horse, Carved, Horsehair, 6 X 6 In. 45.00
Figure, Lion, Polychrome Paint, 5 1/2 In. 45.00
Figure, Mermaid Embraces A Diver, Wooden, 12 In. 275.00
Figure, Penguin, Black, White, Yellow Eyes, 20th Century, 10 1/2 In. 85.00
Figure, Turkey, Spring Legs, Carved Wood, 5 7/8 In. 65.00
Finial, Hitching Post, Stylized Horsehead, Copper Eyes, 14 1/2 In. 700.00
Head, Man's, Movable Eyes & Mouth, Pennsylvania Carnival, 1926 .... 2250.00
Horse, Pine, Cream Paint, Black Trim, Saddle, 14 1/2 In. 105.00
Mask, Mexican Dance, Polychome Paint, Carved Wood, 19 In. 35.00
Mask, Mexican Dance, Polychrome Paint, Man, Crown Headdress, 14 In. 20.00
Model, Coach, Goose Heads Under Front, Wooden, 15 In. 55.00
Model, House, Tissue Paper Windows, Brown Paint, Wooden, 15 In. 55.00
Plaque, Chip Carved, American Flags, Pinwheels, Painted, 31 In. 30.00
Rug, Felt, Wool, Animal, Figural Design, C.1910, 4 Ft. 10 In. 3250.00
Shelf, Corner, Folding, Walnut, Carved Foliage, 16 1/2 In. 50.00
Sign, Clothespin, Wood, Giant 650.00
Silhouette, Crown, Tack Eyes, Wooden, Iron Mounting Bracket, 17 In. 35.00
Tiger, Carved & Painted, Elijah Pierce, 5 In. 425.00
Toy, Parrot, Balancing, Tack Eyes, Hook, Balancing On Rod, 24 In. 135.00
Toy, Pecking Chickens 45.00
Toy, Pull, 6 Hungry Chicks, Hand Carved, John Sanford, 1948, 15 In. 225.00
Toy, Rooster & Hen, Coop, Wood Carved, Mechanical, 1900, 6 X 4 In. 160.00
Whimsey, Spoon, Chain & Man's Head, 24 In. 75.00
Whirligig, 2 Dancing Men, Windup, On Stands 380.00
Whirligig, Bear & Logger, Axes On Log 40.00
Whirligig, Cow, At Trough, Man On Stool, Sheet Metal, 23 In. 750.00
Whirligig, Dancing Man & Indian, Articulated Legs 30.00
Whirligig, French Soldier, Arms Hold Metal Blades, 8 In. 550.00
Whirligig, Girl Churning Butter 100.00
Whirligig, Horse & Sulky 3400.00
Whirligig, Indian In Canoe, Polychrome Paint, 12 1/2 In. 95.00
Whirligig, Indians In Canoe, 2–Dimensional 550.00
Whirligig, Keystone Kop 3800.00
Whirligig, Lighthouse, Wooden, Metal, No Directional, Green, White 325.00
Whirligig, Man At Sawhorse, Sawing Log, Wood & Metal, 14 X 14 In. 300.00
Whirligig, Red Fan, 2 Figures, Cutout Star, Painted Metal, Wood 250.00
Whirligig, Uncle Sam, Chopping Or Sawing Wood, 19 In. 45.00
Whirligig, Washer Woman, Mass., 1910, 27 In. ....*Illus* 350.00
Whirligig, Windmill, House & Woman, Polychrome Paint, 59 X 24 In. 75.00
Whirligig, World War I Doughboy, C.1918, 24 In. 2000.00
Wreath, Human Hair 175.00

Cold feet have been a problem for generations. Our ancestors had many ingenious ways to warm feet with portable foot warmers. Some warmers held charcoal, others held hot water. Pottery, tin, and soapstone were the favored materials to conduct the heat. The warmer was kept under the feet, then the legs and feet were tucked into a blanket, providing welcome warmth in a cold carriage or church.

FOOT WARMER, Congregational Church of Gospel Hill, Cincinnati, Ember Pan 130.00
Henderson .... 52.50 To 85.00
Lantern & Heater Combination, Triple Thread, Iron, Pat.1853 .... 160.00
Pierced Tin, Cherry Case, Punched Design, 6 X 9 In. 135.00
Punched Tin, Hardwood Frame, 9 In. 155.00
Punched Tin, Wooden Frame, Black Paint, 8 3/4 In. 105.00
Tin, Pierced, Wooden Frame, Wire Handle, Door 165.00
Victorian, Wooden, Sliding Heart–Shaped Vents, Tin Pan, Carpet 40.00
Wood & Tin, 1800–20 .... 225.00

Fostoria glass was made in Fostoria, Ohio, from 1887 to 1891. The factory was moved to Moundsville, West Virginia, and most of the glass seen in shops today is a twentieth–century product. The company was sold in 1983; new items will be easily identifiable, according to the new owners, Lancaster Colony Corporation.

FOSTORIA, see also Milk Glass
FOSTORIA, Acanthus, Grill Plate, 7 1/2 In. 3.00
Alexis, Vase, Sweet Pea 15.00
American Lady, Champagne, Burgandy 20.00
American Lady, Cordial, Crystal, 1 Oz. 25.00
American Lady, Goblet, 10 Oz. 12.00
American Lady, Goblet, Claret, Cobalt Blue, 4 5/8 In. 42.00
American Lady, Tumbler, Footed, Amethyst, 5 1/4 In. 18.00
American, Appetizer Set, Amethyst, 7 Piece 205.00
American, Ashtray, Oval, 3 7/8 In. 8.00
American, Basket, Black, 11 In. 38.00
American, Bonbon, 3–Footed, 7 In. 14.00
American, Bowl, 16 In. 125.00
American, Bowl, 3–Footed, 8 In. 30.00
American, Bowl, Flared, 5 In. 8.00
American, Bowl, Flared, 10 In. 30.00
American, Bowl, Mayonnaise, 4 5/8 In. 16.00
American, Bowl, Vegetable, Oval 25.00
American, Box, Cigarette 45.00
American, Butter, Cover, Round 73.50
American, Cake Stand, Footed, Square, 10 In. .... 55.00 To 75.00
American, Cake Stand, Round 70.00
American, Candlestick, 3 In. 10.00
American, Candlestick, 6 In. 50.00
American, Candy Dish, Cover, 3 Sections 75.00
American, Carafe, Water, Ice Tube, Chrome Handle 45.00
American, Celery, Oblong, 10 1/4 In. 14.00
American, Chamberstick, With Fingerhold, 2 In. 20.00
American, Coaster 6.00
American, Cocktail, Plain Bowl 45.00
American, Cookie Jar, Cover .... 300.00 To 320.00
American, Cordial, Footed, 2 7/8 In. 5.50
American, Creamer & Sugar 15.00
American, Cruet, Stopper, 6 1/4 In. 25.00
American, Cup & Saucer .... 8.00 To 9.00
American, Decanter, 10 In. 55.00
American, Decanter, Sterling Silver Stopper 125.00
American, Fruit Bowl, Footed, 16 In. 140.00
American, Fruit Stand, Footed 130.00
American, Goblet, 3 1/2 In. 10.00
American, Goblet, 9 Oz., 5 1/2 In. 7.50

American, Ice Tub, 6 1/2 In. 40.00
American, Jelly, Cover 30.00
American, Jug, 1/2 Gal. 55.00
American, Napkin Ring, Set of 4 .... 25.00
American, Nappy, Cover, 5 In. 25.00
American, Nappy, Square 12.00
American, Pitcher, Straight Side, Ice Lip, 1/2 Gal. 65.00
American, Plate, 6 In. 6.50
American, Plate, 8 1/2 In. 14.00
American, Plate, Torte, 19 In. 95.00
American, Platter, Round, 12 In. 140.00
American, Punch Bowl, Tom & Jerry 119.00
American, Punch Cup, Flared, Amethyst 10.00
American, Punch Cup, Footed 7.00
American, Punch Set, Bowl, 14 In., 14 Piece 295.00
American, Relish, 3 Sections, Amethyst, 11 1/2 In. 35.00
American, Relish, Oblong, 8 In. 13.00
American, Relish, Oblong, 9 X 6 In. 50.00
American, Salt & Pepper, 3 1/2 In. .... 10.00 To 12.00
American, Salt, Individual 6.00
American, Sandwich Plate, 11 1/2 In. 20.00
American, Saucer 2.00
American, Sherbet, Flared, Hex Stem, 4 1/4 In. 10.00
American, Soup, Cream, 7 1/2 In. 12.00
American, Straw Holder 235.00
American, Sugar & Creamer, Individual 15.00
American, Sugar Shaker, Chrome Top 50.00
American, Syrup 35.00
American, Tidbit Tray, 3–Footed, 7 In. 18.00
American, Tray, Luncheon, 12 In. 29.00
American, Tumbler, Blue, Footed, 6 In. 22.00
American, Tumbler, Footed, 4 1/4 In. 7.00
American, Tumbler, Iced Tea, Flat 11.00
American, Tumbler, Iced Tea, Footed, 12 Oz. 14.00
American, Tumbler, Water, Pink 20.00
American, Urn, Square, 7 1/2 In. 33.00
American, Vase, Bud, 8 1/2 In. 12.00
American, Vase, Cupped, 10 In. 175.00
American, Vase, Straight, 12 In. 95.00
American, Vase, Sweet Pea 90.00
Arcady, Champagne 12.00
Arcady, Cup & Saucer 18.50
Arcady, Sherbet 12.50
Arcady, Tumbler, Iced Tea 14.75
Avon, Plate, Miss America Type Edge, 1978, 8 In. 10.00
Baroque, Bowl, Footed, Topaz, 7 In. 24.75
Baroque, Bowl, Yellow, Flared, 12 In. 27.00
Baroque, Candlestick, Topaz, 5 In., Pair 35.00
Baroque, Candy Dish, Cover, 3 Sections, Topaz 55.00
Baroque, Console Set, 3 Piece 90.00
Baroque, Cup & Saucer, Topaz 15.00
Baroque, Ice Bucket, Topaz .... 40.50 To 50.00
Baroque, Mayonnaise Bowl, Flared, Topaz 18.00
Baroque, Relish, 4 Sections 25.00
Baroque, Sherbet 8.00
Baroque, Sugar & Creamer, Topaz, Miniature 24.75
Baroque, Tumbler, Footed, 5 1/2 In. 12.50
Baroque, Vase, Topaz, 8 In. 30.00
Beacon, Goblet 9.00
Bell, Christmas, 1978 .... 17.00
Beverly, Cocktail, Amber, 3 Oz. 18.00
Beverly, Creamer, Footed, Amber 20.00
Beverly, Cup & Saucer, Amber .... 10.00 To 16.00
Beverly, Plate, Amber, 7 1/2 In. 6.00

Beverly, Plate, Amber, 8 1/2 In. 7.00
Beverly, Soup, Cream, Amber 8.00
Beverly, Sugar, Green 15.00
Beverly, Tumbler, Footed, Amber, 12 Oz. 13.00
Bookends, Elephant, 7 1/4 X 6 1/2 In. 75.00
Bookends, Horse, Rearing, 6 X 7 1/2 In. 55.00
Bookends, Owl, 7 1/2 In. 300.00
Bookends, Seahorse 95.00
Brazilian, Cracker Jar, Custard, C.1898 .... 60.00
Buttercup, Champagne 12.00
Buttercup, Console 32.00
Buttercup, Jug, Footed, 53 Oz. 195.00
Buttercup, Plate, Torte, 13 3/4 In. 22.00
Camellia, Bowl, Lily Pond, 11 1/4 In. 35.00
Camellia, Plate, 6 In. 5.75
Camellia, Sugar & Creamer, Tray 29.75
Century, Bonbon, 3–Footed 15.00
Century, Bowl, Flared, Etched, 11 In. 30.00
Century, Bowl, Oval, 9 1/2 In. 30.00
Century, Compote, 4 3/8 In. 17.00
Century, Cruet 37.50
Century, Dish, Pickle, 8 1/2 In. 15.00
Century, Jug, Ice Lip, 3 Pt. .... 80.00 To 95.00
Century, Pitcher, 16 Oz. .... 30.00 To 40.00
Century, Plate, Crystal, 7 1/2 In. 5.00
Century, Relish, 3 Sections, Crystal, 11 In. 25.00
Century, Sugar & Creamer, Footed .... 15.00 To 18.00
Chintz, Champagne, 6 Oz. 9.95
Chintz, Cruet, Stopper 50.00
Chintz, Cup & Saucer 18.00
Chintz, Decanter, Oil, Stopper 55.00
Chintz, Goblet, Water 18.00
Chintz, Marmalade, Cover 50.00
Chintz, Plate, 2 Handles, 10 In. 29.50
Chintz, Plate, Torte, 14 In. 30.00
Chintz, Relish, 2 Sections 19.50
Chintz, Salt & Pepper 60.00
Chintz, Sugar & Creamer, Footed 18.00
Chintz, Tray, Sandwich 38.00
Chintz, Tumbler, Footed, 6 In. 10.50
Chintz, Wine 22.00
Christina, Champagne 10.00
Christina, Goblet, 10 Oz. 12.00
Coin Dot, Urn, Cover, Amber, 13 In. 77.00
Coin, Ashtray, Amber, 5 In. 9.00
Coin, Bowl, Oval, Blue, 9 In. 45.00
Coin, Bride's Bowl 30.00
Coin, Candleholder, Amber, Frosted, Low, Pair 33.00
Coin, Candlestick, Amber, 4 1/2 In., Pair 40.00
Coin, Candlestick, Amber, 8 In. 27.00
Coin, Candlestick, Ruby, 8 In., Pair 125.00
Coin, Candy Dish, Amber, Cover, 4 In. 37.00
Coin, Compote, Amber 60.00
Coin, Compote, Ruby, 7 X 8 In. 48.00
Coin, Creamer, Ruby 25.00
Coin, Cruet, Olive Green 55.00
Coin, Lamp, Finger, Amber, Opalescent Shade 98.00
Coin, Nappy, Amber, Handle, Frosted, 5 3/8 In. 15.00
Coin, Pitcher, Crystal, 1 Qt. 36.00
Coin, Sugar & Creamer, Cover, Amber 37.50
Coin, Toothpick, Amber 20.00
Coin, Vase, Bud, 8 In. 18.00
Coin, Vase, Triangular Top, Green Opalescent, 6 1/2 In. 95.00
Coin, Wedding Bowl, Cover, Amber 50.00

Colonial Dame, Cordial, Green 14.00
Colonial Dame, Goblet, Water, Green 8.00
Colonial, Cordial, 1 Oz. 11.00
Colony, Bonbon, 3–Footed 15.00
Colony, Bowl, Cupped, 3–Footed, 6 In. 18.00
Colony, Bowl, Topaz, 9 1/2 In. 85.00
Colony, Butter, Cover .... 65.00 To 75.00
Colony, Candlestick, 8 1/2 In. 45.00
Colony, Cheese & Cracker Set .... 35.00 To 40.00
Colony, Compote, 3 In. 8.00
Colony, Creamer, Individual 8.00
Colony, Cup & Saucer 8.00
Colony, Goblet, 9 Oz., 5 1/8 In. .... 6.00 To 10.00
Colony, Mayonnaise Set, 3 Piece 32.50
Colony, Plate, 7 In. 10.00
Colony, Salt & Pepper, Tray 18.00
Colony, Server, Center Handle 29.50
Colony, Sugar & Creamer .... 10.00 To 12.00
Colony, Tidbit, 3–Footed, 7 1/2 In. 14.00
Colony, Tumbler, Juice, 4 1/2 In. 12.00
Colony, Vase, Cupped, 7 In. 26.00
Colony, Vase, Flared, 7 1/2 In. 32.00
Coronet, Cruet, Stopper 22.00
Coronet, Vase, Handles, 6 1/2 In. 38.00
Corsage, Bowl, Flared, 12 In. 27.50
Dolly Madison, Champagne 22.00
Dolly Madison, Goblet, Water 25.00
Dolly Madison, Sherbet 20.00
Dolly Madison, Tumbler, Iced Tea 25.00
Engagement, Sherbet 13.00
Engagement, Tumbler, Juice 15.00
Fairfax, Bowl, Amber, 12 1/4 In. 25.00
Fairfax, Bowl, Centerpiece, With Flower Frog, Amber, 15 In. 50.00
Fairfax, Butter, Cover .... 60.00 To 70.00
Fairfax, Candy Dish, Cover, 3–Footed 40.00
Fairfax, Celery, Amber 15.00
Fairfax, Champagne, Orchid, 6 In. 26.00
Fairfax, Compote, Green, 7 In. 20.00
Fairfax, Cup & Saucer, Flat, Amber 7.00
Fairfax, Cup & Saucer, Orchid 15.00
Fairfax, Cup & Saucer, Pink, Demitasse .... 15.00 To 19.00
Fairfax, Cup, Topaz 4.00
Fairfax, Goblet, Topaz Bowl 6.00
Fairfax, Goblet, Water, Orchid 25.00
Fairfax, Gravy, Liner, Orchid 95.00
Fairfax, Pitcher, Azure 135.00
Fairfax, Pitcher, Pink, Footed 160.00
Fairfax, Plate, Amber, 6 In. 2.50
Fairfax, Plate, Amber, 8 3/4 In. 6.00
Fairfax, Plate, Azure, 7 In. 7.50
Fairfax, Plate, Topaz, 9 1/2 In. .... 4.50 To 8.50
Fairfax, Relish, 2 Sections, Amber, 8 1/2 In. .... 8.50 To 15.00
Fairfax, Relish, Orchid, 8 1/2 In. 15.00
Fairfax, Shaker, Topaz 12.50
Fairfax, Sugar, Cover, Amber, Large 12.00
Fairfax, Sugar, Footed, Amber 7.00
Fairfax, Table Set, Blue, 4 Piece 210.00
Fairfax, Tray, Service, Insert, Pink 95.00
Fairfax, Whiskey, Footed, Orchid 30.00
Fairfax, Wine, Orchid 30.00
Fascination, Tumbler, Ice Tea 10.00
Fascination, Tumbler, Juice 10.00
Fascination, Wine 10.00
Figurine, Cat, Amber, Seated, Head Turned, 3 3/4 In. 25.00

Figurine, Chanticleer, Ebony Glass, 10 3/4 In. 110.00
Figurine, Deer, Standing, Blue, 2 1/8 X 4 3/8 In. 35.00
Figurine, Fish, Shrimper 20.00
Figurine, Gosling, Looking Down 18.00
Figurine, Mallard, Wings Up 68.00
Figurine, Mermaid 65.00
Figurine, Polar Bear, Frosted 50.00
Figurine, Seal, Frosted 50.00
Gadroon, Juice, Footed 4.50
Grape, Candy Dish, 3 Sections, Cover 88.00
Hartford, Toothpick 80.00
Heather, Bonbon, Tricornered, 7 1/8 In. 15.00
Heather, Candy Dish 40.00
Heather, Cup & Saucer 15.00
Heather, Dish, Pickle, 8 3/4 In. 18.00
Heather, Nappy, Tricornered, 3 Footed, 7 In. 22.50
Heather, Sherbet, 4 3/4 In. 20.00
Heather, Sugar 14.00
Heirloom, Bowl, Opalescent Blue, Oblong, 13 In. 65.00
Heirloom, Candleholder, Opalescent Blue, 9 1/2 In. 25.00
Heirloom, Candlestick, Opalescent Pink, Flora 37.00
Hermitage, Decanter, Stopper, Amber 25.00
Hermitage, Decanter, Topaz 75.00
Hermitage, Ice Bucket, Tab Handle 35.00
Hermitage, Mustard, Topaz, 2 Piece 45.00
Hermitage, Pitcher, Amber, 6 1/2 In. 75.00
Hermitage, Pitcher, Footed, Topaz, 3 Pt. 70.00
Hermitage, Relish, 2 Sections, 6 In. 12.00
Hermitage, Sugar & Creamer, Topaz, Footed 15.00
Hermitage, Tumbler, Footed, Green, 2 3/4 In. 10.00
Hermitage, Tumbler, Footed, Topaz, 9 Oz. 8.00
Hermitage, Tumbler, Orchid, 9 Oz. 8.00
Hermitage, Vase, Footed, 6 In. .... 12.00 To 14.00
Hermitage, Water Set, Blue, 6 Piece 150.00
Holly, Champagne 15.00
Holly, Goblet, Cocktail 18.00
Holly, Goblet, Water 12.00
Holly, Relish, 3 Sections, 12 In. 32.00
Holly, Server, Sandwich, Center Handle 25.00
Holly, Sherbet 14.00
Holly, Sugar & Creamer 36.00
Holly, Tumbler, Iced Tea, Footed 18.00
Holly, Tumbler, Juice, Footed 15.00
Jamestown, Goblet, Water, Blue 15.00
Jamestown, Sherbet, Amber 10.00
Jamestown, Sherbet, Ruby 12.00
Jamestown, Sugar 10.00
Jamestown, Tumbler, Iced Tea, Amber 5.00
Jamestown, Tumbler, Iced Tea, Blue 15.00
Jamestown, Tumbler, Juice, Footed, Amber 10.00
Jamestown, Wine, Amber 12.00
Jenny Lind, Flask, Cologne, Stopper 95.00
June, Berry Bowl, Blue, 5 In. 30.00
June, Bowl, Footed, Topaz, 6 In. 16.00
June, Cake Plate, Handles, Topaz 45.00
June, Candy Dish, Topaz, Cover 85.00
June, Celery, Topaz, 11 1/4 In. 30.00
June, Claret, Topaz, 6 Oz. 35.00
June, Cup & Saucer, Blue 32.00
June, Finger Bowl, Liner, Topaz 45.00
June, Goblet, Water, Topaz 25.00
June, Ice Bucket, Topaz .... 60.00 To 65.00
June, Pitcher, Water, Topaz 325.00
June, Plate, Topaz, 10 1/4 In. 35.00

June, Relish, 3 Sections, 10 In.	28.00
June, Relish, Pink, 8 1/2 In.	15.00
June, Sherbet, Low	12.00
June, Sugar & Creamer	35.00
June, Tumbler, Juice, Footed, Blue, 3 3/4 In.	25.00
June, Tumbler, Water, Footed, Blue	27.00
June, Vase, Topaz, 8 In.	145.00
Kimberly, Sherbet	4.00
Kimberly, Wine	5.00
Lafayette, Bowl, Amber, Oval, 6 In.	12.00
Lafayette, Cup & Saucer, Green	15.00
Lafayette, Salad Bowl	65.00
Laurel, Champagne	8.00
Laurel, Cordial, Amethyst	13.00
Lido, Champagne	5.00
Lido, Goblet	12.00
Lido, Mayonnaise Set, 3 Piece	20.00
Lido, Sherbet	9.00
Lucerne, Toothpick	25.00
Manor, Plate, 7 In.	7.00
Mardi Gras, Vase, Signed, Dated, 7 1/4 In.	88.00
Mayfair, Sandwich Plate, Center Handle, Topaz, 11 In.	25.00
Mayfair, Sherbet, Amber	9.00
Mayflower, Bowl, Flared, Crystal, 12 In.	14.50
Mayflower, Plate, 9 1/2 In.	22.50
Meadow Rose, Bowl, 12 In.	30.00
Meadow Rose, Ice Bucket, Bail, Tongs	70.00
Meadow Rose, Salt & Pepper	65.00
Meadow Rose, Sandwich, Center Handle	40.00
Meadow Rose, Tumbler, Iced Tea, Footed	22.00
Midnight Rose, Champagne, Crystal	18.50
Midnight Rose, Cup & Saucer	12.00
Midnight Rose, Mayonnaise, Underplate, 2 Part	28.00
Midnight Rose, Sherbet	18.00
Midnight Rose, Tumbler, Footed, 5 3/4 In.	24.00
Mother of Pearl, Goblet, 9 Oz., 7 In.	6.00
Mother of Pearl, Sherbet, 4 1/2 In.	5.00
Mystic, Plate, Green, 7 1/2 In.	4.50
Navarre, Bowl, 11 1/2 In.	50.00
Navarre, Candlestick, Pair	32.50
Navarre, Compote, 5 1/2 In.	30.00
Navarre, Console Set, Footed	75.00
Navarre, Cup & Saucer	15.00
Navarre, Goblet, 5 1/2 In.	15.00
Navarre, Mayonnaise, Divided	40.00
Navarre, Pitcher, Footed	250.00
Navarre, Plate, 7 1/2 In.	11.00
Navarre, Platter, 14 In.	25.00
Navarre, Wine	23.00
Oak Leaf, Vase, Blue, 6 In.	90.00
Oak Leaf, Vase, Green, 6 In.	75.00
Paradise, Bowl, Orchid, 12 In.	35.00
Pioneer, Cup & Saucer, Green	4.00
Pioneer, Plate, Bread, Green	2.00
Plymouth, Sherbet, Royal Blue, 4 1/2 In.	25.00
Priscilla, Compote, Cover, Green, Gold Trim	115.00
Priscilla, Cup, Gold Trim	8.00
Priscilla, Salt & Pepper, Sterling Silver Tops	25.00
Priscilla, Tumbler	15.00
Raleigh, Cruet, Green Stopper	30.00
Raleigh, Salt & Pepper	18.00
Rambler, Candleholder, 3–Light	25.00
Rambler, Cup & Saucer	15.00
Randolph, Candleholder, Lace Edged Base, 6 In.	15.00

Red Coin, Sugar & Creamer 12.00
Reflection, Champagne 10.00
Reflection, Goblet, Footed 25.00
Rhapsody, Sherbet, Turquoise 7.00
Rhapsody, Tumbler, Iced Tea, Footed 5.50
Romance, Champagne 19.00
Romance, Cocktail, 3 1/2 Oz. .... 14.50 To 20.00
Romance, Cordial, 3/4 Oz. 38.00
Romance, Goblet, 7 3/8 In. 22.00
Romance, Relish, 3 Sections 32.00
Romance, Sherbet, Low 12.00
Romance, Tumbler, Footed, 6 In. 20.00
Rose, Mayonnaise, 3 Piece 35.00
Rose, Relish, 3 Sections, 12 In. 38.00
Royal, Cup & Saucer, Green 15.00
Royal, Grapefruit, Green, Footed 12.00
Royal, Plate, Green, 8 1/2 In. 4.00
Royal, Platter, Green, 13 In. 12.00
Seville, Sugar, Cover, Green 45.00
Shirley, Bowl, Flared, 11 In. 15.95
Shirley, Cake Plate, Handle, 10 In. 25.00
Shirley, Cheese & Cracker Set 40.00
Shirley, Cup & Saucer 18.00
Shirley, Ice Bucket 60.00
Shirley, Plate, 7 1/2 In. 8.00
Shirley, Relish, 3 Sections, 10 In. 28.00
Shirley, Sugar & Creamer 20.00
Shirley, Tumbler, Footed, 9 Oz. 14.00
Silver Mist, Sherbet, Tall 6.00
Sunray, Decanter 90.00
Sunray, Egg Plate, Oval 50.00
Swirl, Tumbler, Amber 18.00
Sylvan, Cracker Jar 110.00
Sylvan, Cruet 60.00
Thelma, Cake Plate, Handle, Green 25.00
Trojan, Bowl, Footed, Topaz Stem, 12 In. 30.00
Trojan, Cocktail, Topaz 25.00
Trojan, Cruet, Topaz 250.00
Trojan, Plate, Topaz, 7 1/2 In. 6.00
Trojan, Relish, Topaz, Oval, 2 Sections 18.00
Trojan, Sherbet, Topaz Stem 40.00
Trojan, Wine, Topaz, 10 Oz., 6 1/4 In. 24.00
Tuxedo, Toothpick 130.00
Valencia, Candy Dish, Triangular, Handles 12.00
Vernon, Bowl, Flower Frog, Amber Center, 13 In. 40.00
Vernon, Candlestick, Amber, Pair 38.00
Vernon, Candy Dish, Cover, Green 30.00
Vernon, Compote, Amber 25.00
Versailles, Bowl, Handle, Green, 6 In. 22.00
Versailles, Bowl, Scroll Handles, Topaz, 10 In. 45.00
Versailles, Candleholder, 5 1/2 In. 40.00
Versailles, Candy Container, Topaz, Cover 55.00
Versailles, Cordial, Topaz, 4 In. .... 48.00 To 55.00
Versailles, Cruet, Topaz 325.00
Versailles, Cup & Saucer, Topaz 18.00
Versailles, Goblet, Water, Topaz 27.00
Versailles, Pitcher, Blue .... 440.00 To 450.00
Versailles, Plate, 6 In. 4.00
Versailles, Plate, Topaz, 6 In. .... 2.50 To 5.00
Versailles, Platter, Topaz, 8-Sided, 13 3/4 In. 35.00
Versailles, Server, Center Handle, Blue 52.00
Versailles, Sherbet, Pink, Tall 19.00
Versailles, Sherbet, Topaz Stem, Low 20.00
Versailles, Sugar & Creamer, Pink 45.00

Versailles, Sugar, Topaz, Individual 15.00
Versailles, Tumbler, Topaz & Pink, Footed, 5 1/4 In. 25.00
Versailles, Wine, Topaz 40.00
Vesper, Celery, Green, 11 In. 17.00
Vesper, Cocktail, Amber, 3 Oz. 18.00
Vesper, Cup & Saucer, Green, Footed 16.00
Vesper, Goblet, Water, Amber .... 18.00 To 25.00
Vesper, Plate, Amber, 6 In. 6.00
Vesper, Plate, Amber, 7 1/2 In. 6.00
Vesper, Server, Center Handle, Amber 30.00
Vesper, Sugar & Creamer, Amber, Footed 45.00
Vesper, Tumbler & Coaster Set, Green, Footed, 12 Piece 120.00
Victoria, Bowl, Frosted, 9 In. 30.00
Victoria, Nappy, 5 In. 12.00
Victoria, Vase, Frosted & Clear, 6 In. 85.00
Vintage, Sherbet, 5 Oz. 4.00
Virginia, Goblet, Water 12.00
Virginia, Lamp, Candle 85.00
Wakefield, Champagne 12.00
Wedding Ring, Sherbet 13.00
Willowmere, Cruet 65.00
Willowmere, Goblet, 7 In. 17.00
Willowmere, Plate, 8 In. 15.00
Willowmere, Wine, 6 In. 16.00
Windsor, Berry Bowl, Pink 4.00
Windsor, Bowl, Pink, Boat Shape 15.00
Windsor, Plate, Pink, Handle, 10 1/4 In. 10.00
Windsor, Sherbet, Pink 5.00
Woodland, Claret 3.00

FOVAL, see Fry Foval
FRAME, PICTURE see Furniture, Frame

Francisware is a named glassware made by Hobbs, Brockunier and Company of Wheeling, West Virginia, in the 1880s. It is a clear or frosted hobnail or swirl pattern glass with amber-stained rim. Some pieces were made by a pressed glass method, others were mold blown.

FRANCISWARE, Carafe, Wooden Handle, Turquoise 22.00
Cruet, Swirl, Frosted 375.00
Syrup, Hobnail, Frosted, Amber Stain 135.00
Table Set, Swirl, Amber, Frosted, Cover, Hobb, 4 Piece 225.00

Frankart, Inc., New York, New York, mass-produced nude "dancing-lady" lamps, ashtrays, and other decorative Art Deco items in the 1920s and 1930s. They were made of white lead composition and spray-painted. "Frankart Inc." and the patent number and year were stamped on the base.

FRANKART, Ashtray, Fighting Rams 38.00
Bookends, Dog 85.00
Bookends, Horsehead 90.00
Bookends, Sailor Boy & Dog 65.00
Bookends, Wild Horsehead 75.00
Bookends, Woman's Head 150.00
Lamp, 2 Nudes Kneeling Toward Vaseline Globe .... 325.00 To 450.00
Lamp, Art Deco, Nude On Knees, Head & Arms Back, Paperweight Globe 475.00
Lamp, Girl Holds Bucket On Shoulder, 1922, 14 In. 425.00
Lamp, Head of Shriner, Scimitar & Sword, Atlantic City, N.J., 1927 .... 195.00
Lamp, Horse, Art Deco 75.00
Lamp, Kneeling Nudes, Embracing, Crackle Glass Globe, 9 In. 425.00
Lamp, Nude, Parchment Shade, 14 In. 585.00

Frankoma Pottery was originally known as The Frank Potteries when John F. Frank opened shop in 1933. The factory is now working in Sapulpa, Oklahoma. Early wares were made from a light

cream–colored clay, but in 1956 the company switched to a red burning clay. The firm makes dinnerwares, utilitarian and decorative kitchen wares, figurines, flowerpots, and limited edition and commemorative pieces.

FRANKOMA, Ashtray, Covered Wagon, Tan	4.00
Bean Pot, Green Bronze, Handle, Cover, 6 1/2 X 8 1/2 In.	11.00
Bookends, Bucking Bronco, Stepped Base	35.00
Bookends, Indian Chief, Brown	35.00
Bookends, Indian Chief, Green	75.00
Bookends, Mountain Girl, Green	175.00
Bookends, Nude, Seated, Hair Over Face, Black	125.00
Bookends, Nude, Seated, Hair Over Face, Green	135.00
Boot, Cowboy, Ivory, 4 1/2 In.	8.00
Candlestick, Christ The Light of The World, Oral Roberts, Pair	25.00
Candy Dish, Brown, Beige Leaf	3.00
Canteen, Turquoise, Indian Design, Rawhide Strap	29.00
Casserole, Wagon Wheel, Tan	15.00
Cider Set, 1933 Mark, 5 Piece	750.00
Creamer, Wagon Wheel, Brown	3.00
Cup & Saucer, Mayan Aztec, Woodland Moss	5.00
Cup & Saucer, Prairie, Green	4.00
Cup, Wagon Wheel	4.00
Dish, 4–Leaf Clover, Turqoise, 6 In.	12.00
Dish, Wagon Wheel, 13 1/4 X 7 In.	9.00
Ewer, Handle, Green, 8 In.	8.00
Figurine, Bowl Maker, Red, No.123	85.00
Figurine, Elephant, Walking, Prairie Green	50.00
Figurine, Fan Dancer, Brown, Green	110.00
Figurine, Gardener Girl	48.50
Figurine, Martha The Money Maker	20.00
Figurine, Swan, Prairie Green, 1942–57, Miniature	15.00
Flower Frog, Hobby Horse, Blue, No.182	75.00
Fondue Set, Green, 3 Piece	30.00
Jardiniere, Tulip, 5 In.	25.00
Jug, 1934 Mark, 3 Cup	75.00
Jug, Cork, Green, 6 1/2 In.	9.00
Mask, Indian Chief, Turquoise, 3 In.	7.00
Mug, Ada, Green	15.00
Mug, Donkey, 1975, Autumn Yellow	5.00 To 9.00
Mug, Donkey, 1976, Red	19.00
Mug, Elephant, 1969, Flame	30.00 To 35.00
Mug, Elephant, 1970, Blue	20.00
Mug, Elephant, 1971, Black	50.00
Mug, Elephant, Nixon–Agnew, 1969, Flame	85.00
Mug, Hank Aaron	20.00
Mug, Indian Chief	45.00
Mug, Plainsman, Green, 16 Oz., 5 3/8 In.	3.50
Mug, Uncle Sam, Red	11.00
Pie Bird, Green, Brown, Blue & White	10.00
Pitcher, Batter, Red Bud	26.00
Pitcher, Green, Marked, 9 1/2 In.	40.00
Pitcher, Red, 5 In.	10.00
Planter, Boat Shape, White, 12 1/2 X 5 In.	9.00
Planter, Dutch Shoe, 9 In.	7.00
Plate, Bicentennial, Patriots–Leaders, 1973	29.50
Plate, Bicentennial, Symbols of Freedom, 1976	25.50
Plate, Christmas, 1968	15.00 To 20.50
Plate, Christmas, 1969	7.00
Plate, Christmas, 1971	23.50
Plate, Easter, 1972	12.00 To 13.00
Plate, Parrot, Green, 7 1/2 In.	14.00
Plate, Prairie, Green, 9 In.	3.50
Plate, World's Fair, New York, 1939, Potter At His Wheel, Turquoise	35.00

Salt & Pepper, Aztec, Curved 8.00
Salt & Pepper, Wagon Wheel 8.00
Sugar, Cover, Barrel 6.00
Tea Set, Plainsman, Gold Bronze, 6–Cup Teapot, 3 Piece 35.00
Teapot, Green, Cover, 2 Cup 8.00
Teapot, Wagon Wheel, Small 15.00
Tray, Prairie, Green, 9 In. 3.50
Trivet, Cherokee Alphabet 11.00
Trivet, Kansas Centennial 17.50
Trivet, Will Rogers 18.00
Vase, Aqua, 12 1/2 In. 60.00
Vase, Cactus, No.5 .... 35.00
Vase, Goose, Green, 9 In. 19.50
Vase, Green, Cylinder, 10 X 4 In. 10.00
Vase, Moss, Octagonal, 6 In. 9.50
Vase, Ram's Head, 6 In. 21.50
Wall Pocket, Acorn, Black, No.190 .... 15.00
Wall Pocket, Acorn, Green, Brown 35.00
Wall Pocket, Brown, 1st Mark In Sapulpa, 2 1/2 In. 50.00
Wall Pocket, Phoebe 50.00

The Fraternal section lists objects that are related to the many different fraternal organizations in the United States. The Elks, Masons, Odd Fellows, and others are included. Furniture is listed in the Furniture section.

FRATERNAL, see also Shaving Mug

FRATERNAL, B.P.O.E., Ashtray, Bronze 30.00
B.P.O.E., Bottle, Jim Beam, Centennial 7.00
B.P.O.E., Shaving Mug 50.00
Eastern Star, Badge, Worthy Matron 35.00
Eastern Star, Pin, Gold & Pearl 30.00
Eastern Star, Ring, 14K White Gold, Mine Cut Diamond, Filigree 225.00
Elks, Plate, Grand Lodge Reunion, Metal, 1907 .... 45.00
F.O.E., Cufflinks, Enameled 3.00
Knights of Columbus, Watch Fob, Enameled 21.50
Knights of Pythias, Watch Fob 8.50
Knights of Pythias, Watch Fob, 14th Degree, Silver, Brass 47.50
Knights Templar, Clock, New Haven, Ogee Case 350.00
Knights Templar, Hat, Ostrich Plumage 60.00
Knights Templar, Watch Chain, Helmet, Enameled Fob 57.50
Loyal Order of Moose, Book, General Laws, 112 Pages, 1915 .... 15.00
Masonic, Apron, Silk, Ruffled, J.T.Porter, Middletown, Conn., 1818 .... 275.00
Masonic, Ashtray, Brass, 1934 .... 25.00
Masonic, Badge, Past Master's, Grand Lodge, Burlington, Iowa, 1912 .... 42.50
Masonic, Fire Mark, Cast Iron 200.00
Masonic, Goblet, St.Paul, 1908 .... 65.00 To 75.00
Masonic, Letter Opener & Cigarette Lighter, Combination, Germany 35.00
Masonic, Magic Lantern Slides 55.00
Masonic, Paperweight, 3 Engraved Symbols On Base, 2 1/2 In. 95.00
Masonic, Paperweight, Pittsburgh Syria Temple, 1924 .... 20.00
Masonic, Pitcher, Emblems, Concordia Lodge No.67, 1795–1913 .... 75.00
Masonic, Plate, Los Angeles, May 1906, 6 In. 45.00
Masonic, Ring, 32nd Degree, .75 Solitaire Diamond, C.1900 .... 500.00
Masonic, Ring, Zircon Stone, 14K Gold 145.00
Masonic, Spoon, Masonic Temple, Chicago, Indian Handle 45.00
Masonic, Sword 40.00
Masonic, Watch Fob, Carved Ivory 47.50
Masonic, Watch Fob, Eagle, Square & Compass, Sojourness National 42.50
Masonic, Watch Fob, Whitewell, Tenn., Shield 22.50
Odd Fellows, Banner, Painted Symbols, On Rod, 19 X 30 In. 65.00
Odd Fellows, Jewel, Badge, Coin Silver, 1860–65, 4 1/2 In. 195.00
Odd Fellows, Shaving Mug 50.00
Odd Fellows, Sign, Fruit–Filled Cornucopia, Painted, 13 In. 1760.00
Order of Foresters, Mirror, Pocket, 1915 .... 30.00

Shriner, Ashtray, Figural	30.00
Shriner, Cup, 1904	40.00
Shriner, Humidor, Glass	50.00
Shriner, Loving Cup, Niagara Falls, 3 Handles, 1905	50.00
Shriner, Watch Fob, Mother-of-Pearl	52.50

Fry glass was made by the H. C. Fry Glass Company of Rochester, Pennsylvania. The company, founded in 1901, first made cut glass and other types of fine glasswares. In 1922, they patented a heat-resistant glass called "Pearl Oven glass." For two years, 1926–27, the company made Fry Foval, an opal ware decorated with colored trim. Reproductions of this glass have been made. The company also made Depression glass.

FRY FOVAL, Berry Set, Creamer, Jade Green, Opalescent White, 1926	550.00
Cup & Saucer, Green	50.00
Goblet, Buttermilk, Green	65.00
Pitcher, Crackled, Green Handle, 6 1/4 X 6 In.	75.00
FRY, Baker, Square	25.00
Casserole, Cover, Metal Holder, 8 1/2 In.	32.50
Casserole, Cover, Oval	35.00
Casserole, Cover, Round	35.00
Lemonade Set, Blue Handles, 7 Piece	500.00
Pie Plate, Metal Holder, 9 In.	22.00
Platter, Oval, 13 In.	20.00

Fulper is the mark used by the American Pottery Company of Flemington, New Jersey. The art pottery was made from 1910 to 1929. The firm had been making bottles, jugs, and housewares from 1805. Doll heads were made about 1928. The firm became Stangl Pottery in 1929. Fulper art pottery is admired for its attractive glazes and simple shapes.

FULPER, Bell, Hollyhock, Blue	60.00
Bookends, Peacock, Blue Flambe .... 195.00 To 275.00	
Bowl, Blue & Yellow, Drip Glaze, 10 In.	80.00
Bowl, Blue Flambe, Yellow Ground, Art Deco Feet, 10 X 4 1/2 In.	150.00
Bowl, Console, Black Streaks, Black, 12 In.	195.00
Bowl, Green, Black Streaks, 5 In.	40.00
Bowl, Handles, Copper Overlay, 3 In.	395.00
Bowl, Lily, Brown Mirror, 7 In.	80.00
Bowl, Purple Over Rose, Purple Speckles, 8 3/4 X 4 3/8 In.	80.00
Box, Figural, Spanish Girl .... 120.00 To 135.00	
Candleholder, Lily Pad, Light & Dark Brown, Pair	80.00
Ewer, Pink & Blue Matte, Miniature	55.00
Figurine, Owl, Blue & Green, 5 In.	45.00
Jardiniere, Handles, Brown, 4 In.	95.00
Jug, Built-In Music Box, How Dry I Am, 3 Sides, Green Glaze, 10 In.	85.00
Jug, Copperdust Music	250.00
Lamp Base, Black Flambe, 16 In.	325.00
Lamp, Green To Rose, Factory, Brass Plated Fittings, 25 1/2 In.	120.00
Lamp, Perfume, Frosted & Painted Flowers, Electrified	65.00
Lamp, Perfume, Woman In Pink	110.00
Lamp, Pinch Bottle, Leopard Skin, Crystalline Green Glaze, 7 In.	295.00
Pitcher, Green Crystalline, 4 In.	50.00
Vase, 5 Graduating Concentric Rings, Blue, 3 3/4 In.	60.00
Vase, Black On Green Flambe, 4 3/4 In.	65.00
Vase, Chinese Form, Rose & Green Flambe, 10 1/2 In.	195.00
Vase, Column, Scattered Crystals, 8 1/2 In.	250.00
Vase, Copper Dust On Green, Paper Label, Marked, 9 1/2 In.	450.00
Vase, Copper Dust, Mocha, Dark Brown, Handles, 6 In.	70.00
Vase, Cornucopia, Blue Drip Over Speckled Brown, 8 In.	70.00
Vase, Flambe, Rose To Green, Scattered Crystals, 8 In.	145.00
Vase, Flambe, Traces of Crystalline, Rose & Green, 8 In.	125.00
Vase, Green & Rose, Handles, 8 In.	55.00
Vase, Green Over Matte Rose, Bulbous Pitcher Shape, 4 1/2 X 3 In.	38.00

Furniture, Armchair, Chinese,   Furniture, Armchair, Rococo,
Carved Rosewood Dragon   Gentleman's, Walnut, Victorian

Vase, High Gloss Blue, Mirror Glaze At Top, 5 1/2 In.	95.00
Vase, Iridescent Green, Black Glaze, 2 Handles, 9 In.	50.00
Vase, Lava Glaze, 6 In.	105.00
Vase, Olive Over Crystalline Copper, Handles, Bulbous, 7 1/2 X 6 In.	74.00
Vase, Purple Matte, High Glaze Drip, 9 In.	150.00
Wall Pocket, Greek Key	95.00

All types of furniture are listed in this section. Examples dating from the seventeenth century to the 1950s are included. Prices for furniture vary in different parts of the country. Oak furniture is most expensive in the West; large pieces over eight feet high are sold for the most money in the South, where high ceilings are found in the old homes. Condition is very important when determining prices. These are NOT average prices but rather reports of unique sales. If the description includes the word "style," the piece resembles the old furniture style but was made at a later time. It is not a period piece.

FURNITURE, Armchair, see also Furniture, Chair

FURNITURE, Armchair, Banister Back, Crest Over 4 Spindles	5500.00
Armchair, Caned Back & Seat, Leather Cushion, Walnut	400.00
Armchair, Child's, Adirondack, Graduated, 3 Piece	175.00
Armchair, Child's, Slat Back, Shaped Finials, Maple, 26 In.	300.00
Armchair, Child's, Twig	400.00
Armchair, Child's, Windsor, Sack Back, Painted Black Over Red	1430.00
Armchair, Child's, Yew Wood, England	250.00
Armchair, Chinese, Carved Rosewood Dragon ....*Illus*	1155.00
Armchair, Congressional, Oak, Carved Shield Crest, Upholstered	2300.00
Armchair, Federal, Carved Teakwood, Chinese Export	1200.00
Armchair, Federal, Mahogany, Serpentine Crest, Slip Seat, Pair	5500.00
Armchair, George II Style, Pierced Shell, Upholstered Back, 1900	650.00
Armchair, George III, Walnut Stain, Upholstered Back & Arms, Pr.	1000.00
Armchair, George III, Yewwood, Urn Splat, Saddle Seat, Pad Feet	1800.00
Armchair, Gothic Revival, Imitation Grained Rosewood, Upholstery	130.00
Armchair, Haywood–Wakefield, Wicker	900.00
Armchair, Hepplewhite, Walnut, Pierced Splats, Slip Seats, Pair	360.00
Armchair, Hermes, Leather Upholstered, Metal Frame, C.1940	3025.00
Armchair, Karpen Co., Cutout Sides	1200.00
Armchair, L.& J.G.Stickley, Fixed Back, Upholstered, 1912	4750.00
Armchair, Ladder Back, 4 Slat Back, Rush Seat, Sausage Turnings	350.00
Armchair, Ladder Back, 4 Slats, Acorn Finials, Birch, 46 1/2 In.	400.00
Armchair, Ladder Back, Dark Brown Finish, Rush Seat, English	500.00
Armchair, Leather Button Upholstered, Mahogany, C.1825	5500.00

Armchair, Library, George III, Serpentine Crest Rail, Mahogany 450.00
Armchair, Louis XIV, Gilded, Aubusson Cover, Pair 2800.00
Armchair, Louis XVI, Molded Back, Needlepoint Cover, Walnut 275.00
Armchair, Mahogany, Gargoyle Carved, American, C.1900 .... 170.00
Armchair, Marquetry, Dutch Neoclassical, 33 In. 200.00
Armchair, Morris, Angle Bend Arms, Gustav Stickley, Upholstered 5225.00
Armchair, Morris, L & J.G.Stickley, Straight Arm, Model 498 .... 6325.00
Armchair, Pierced & Carved Frame, Ebonized Burmese, C.1900 .... 600.00
Armchair, Regency, Upholstered Seat, Salesman's Sample 675.00
Armchair, Rococo, Gentleman's, Walnut, Victorian ....*Illus* 110.00
Armchair, Shepherd's Crook, Cabriole Legs, Brocade Upholstery 300.00
Armchair, Sleepy Hollow, Back Crest, Horsehair Upholstery, 1880 .... 300.00
Armchair, Thonet, 15 Spindles Top To Floor, Wooden Seat, 1911 .... 4180.00
Armchair, Victorian, Henry Clay Pattern, Laminated Rosewood 4500.00
Armchair, Windsor, Bow Back, Black Paint Over Blue Green 2050.00
Armchair, Windsor, Bow Back, H Stretcher, Olive Green Paint 450.00
Armoire, Baroque Style, Double Doors, Carved Masks, Oak, 98 In. 1800.00
Armoire, French Provincial, Beveled Mirrored Door, Walnut, 98 In. 650.00
Armoire, Single Door, New Orleans, Prudent Mallard, Rosewood 5500.00
Armoire, Sliding Shelves, Drawer, English, Mahogany, C.1905, 86 In. 600.00
Armoire, Victorian, Carved, 10 X 10 Ft. 5400.00
Bar, Art Nouveau, Leaded Glass Panels, England, 94 X 73 In. 800.00
Bed Steps, Ebony Inlay On Risers, Top Compartment Door, Mahogany 675.00
Bed Steps, Mahogany, English, 19th Century 3950.00
Bed Steps, Sheraton, Leather & Gilt Tooling, Mahogany, 28 3/4 In. 925.00
Bed, Baby's, Pencil Post Legs, Walnut, 27 1/2 X 46 In. 50.00
Bed, Bird's-Eye Maple, Paneled Headboard, Tapered Posts 1595.00
Bed, Brass, Eastlake Style, Victorian, 61 X 55 In. 650.00
Bed, Cannonball, Maple 425.00
Bed, Cannonball, Rope, Brown Repaint, 39 X 54 X 76 In. 500.00
Bed, Canopy, Fluted Posts, Damask Hangings, Silk Canopy, Mahogany 4000.00
Bed, Child's, Empire, Curly Maple 1200.00
Bed, Child's, Sheraton, Maple, Turned Posts, Spindles, 48 In. 1750.00
Bed, Continental Neoclassical, Walnut, 7 Ft.X 3 In.X 40 In. 5500.00
Bed, Day, L.& J.G.Stickley, 4 Slats, Rail Stretcher, 30 X 80 In. 1800.00
Bed, Federal, Curly Maple, Acorn Turnings, 3/4 Size 575.00
Bed, Federal, Low Post, Red Over Red Grain Paint, 1800-30 .... 4600.00
Bed, Finger Carved Serpentine Molding, Green Paint, Single 50.00
Bed, Folding Field, Shoe Feet, Removable Headboard, 51 X 74 In. 1000.00
Bed, Four-Poster, Cherry, Single, Pair 630.00
Bed, Four-Poster, Pine, Turned Posts, American, Single 200.00
Bed, Four-Poster, Regency, Walnut, Reeded, Rope Twist, 84 In. 950.00
Bed, Four-Poster, Rope, Cherry, 1850 .... 425.00
Bed, French Empire, Burl Veneer, Ormolu Trim, 58 X 75 X 59 In. 110.00
Bed, G.Stickley, 4 Slats Ends, Oak, C.1907, Single, Pair 3600.00
Bed, Half-Tester, Victorian, Cherry, C.1870, 8 Ft.9 In. 2500.00
Bed, Half-Tester, Victorian, New Orleans 7325.00
Bed, High Back, Oak, 3/4 Size 25.00
Bed, Hired Man's, 1/4 Size Rope, Pine, Red Paint, Early 1800s 50.00
Bed, Hired Man's, Oak & Maple 150.00
Bed, Hired Man's, Red Wash, Built For 2 .... 900.00
Bed, Iron, Brass Finial, Single 90.00
Bed, Iron, White, Brass Finials, Single 25.00
Bed, L.& J.G.Stickley, Double 3800.00
Bed, Louis XVI, Painted Portrait Reserves & Foliage, Single 500.00
Bed, Mitchell & Rammelsburg, Cincinnati, Ohio 4125.00
Bed, Neoclasical, Walnut, Continental, 7 Ft.X 40 In. 3500.00
Bed, Reddish Brown Paint, Hard & Soft Wood, 51 X 52 1/2 X 70 In. 450.00
Bed, Reeded Front Posts, Tapered Rear Posts, Maple, C.1840, 64 In. 1100.00
Bed, Rope, Tulipwood, 1790s 575.00
Bed, Rope, Turned & Scrolled, Pine, Maple, C.1860 .... 650.00
Bed, Rope, Turned Posts, Original Red Paint, 29 In. 350.00
Bed, Rope, Walnut, C.1850 .... 325.00
Bed, Sheraton, Pine Headboard, Maple & Tiger Maple, C.1820 .... 1250.00

Bed, Sleigh, American Classical, Carved Mahogany, C.1830, Single 1100.00
Bed, Sleigh, Federal, Carved, Mahogany, Early 19th Century 2000.00
Bed, Sleigh, Sheraton 2500.00
Bed, Sleigh, Walnut, 1840 .... 285.00
Bed, Spindle, Walnut, Germany, Full Size 800.00
Bed, Tall Post, Rope, Cherry, Paneled Pine & Poplar, 56 X 72 In. 275.00
Bed, Tester, Burled Posts & Headboard, C.1810 .... 1950.00
Bed, Tester, Canopy, Federal, New England, Maple, C.1820, 82 In. 4950.00
Bed, Tester, George II, Fluted Posts, Mahogany, C.1750, 4 Ft. 4125.00
Bed, Tester, George III, Pine & Walnut, 4 Ft. 935.00
Bed, Trundle, Ball Finials, Walnut, 45 X 60 In. 240.00
Bed, Trundle, Rope, Cannonball Finials, 39 X 60 In. 200.00
Bed, Victorian, Carved Walnut Head & Foot, Removable Post, Full 800.00
Bed, Washed Gold Medallion, Brass, Full Size 3500.00
Bed, Yellow Bird'-Eye Grain Painted, Paneled, Ball Finial, C.1850 .... 1995.00
Bedroom Set, American Furniture Co., Indiana, Mahogany, 3 Piece 350.00
Bedroom Set, Art Deco, Classic Waterfall Front, Vanity, 4 Piece 1395.00
Bedroom Set, Burled Walnut, 4 Piece 500.00
Bedroom Set, Eastlake, Burled Walnut, Marble, 3 Piece 2500.00
Bedroom Set, French Style, Walnut Veneer, Bow Chest, 8 Piece 500.00
Bedroom Set, Marble Tops, Renaissance, Walnut, 3 Piece 3000.00
Bedroom Set, Renaissance Revival, Carved, Oak, 3 Piece .... 5000.00 To 6875.00
Bedroom Set, Renaissance Revival, Walnut, C.1880, 4 Piece 7425.00
Bedroom Set, Victorian Renaissance, Walnut, Marble Tops, 3 Piece 3000.00
Bedroom Set, Victorian, High Back Bed, Marble Dresser, Washstand 2700.00
Bench, Bootjack Ends, Green Repaint, Pine, 18 X 70 1/2 In. 65.00
Bench, Bucket, Blue Paint, Oak, 31 In. 60.00
Bench, Bucket, Pine, 2 Shelves, Original Green Paint, 41 In. 4250.00
Bench, Bucket, Red, White Paint, Bootjack Feet, Primitive, 23 In. 425.00
Bench, Cabinet Maker's, 2 Vises, Swing-Out Shelf, 28 X 77 In. 250.00
Bench, Cast Iron, Gilt, Red Plush Upholstery, 46 In. 95.00
Bench, Church, Wedding Scene Back, Gray Alligatored Paint, 1850 .... 1300.00
Bench, Deacon's, Folds Down To Become Bed, Pine 850.00
Bench, Deacon's, Repainted Green, Taylor Thompson 1000.00
Bench, Deacon's, Windsor, Original Paint, C.1840 .... 1850.00
Bench, Fireside, Mahogany 105.00
Bench, Garden, Cast Iron, Branches & Foliage, Gray Repaint, 49 In. 1100.00
Bench, Hall, Oak, Gustav Stickley, No.224 .... 6700.00
Bench, Iron, Lion's Heads, Upholstered Seat 130.00
Bench, Iron, Wooden Slats, Green, 40 X 65 In. 595.00
Bench, Kidney Shape, Cast Iron Base, Upholstered, 45 In. 65.00
Bench, Louis XV, Upholstered Seat, Cream Painted, 4 Ft. 4675.00
Bench, Mahogany, Carved Crest, English Inscription, 48 In. 625.00
Bench, Mammy's, Arrow Back, 19th Century, 73 In. ....*Illus* 715.00
Bench, Mennonite, Spool Turned, Arms, Red Paint 2400.00
Bench, Mission, Mahogany, Cushion Seat, Pierced Slats 475.00
Bench, Pine, Mortised & Pinned Legs, Dark Brown, 8 X 48 X 14 In. 325.00
Bench, Pine, Square Nail Construction, 20 In. 150.00

Furniture, Bench, Mammy's, Arrow Back, 19th Century, 73 In.

Furniture, Bookcase,
Carved Rosewood, Maple
Interior, 9 Ft.2 In.

Furniture, Bookcase,
Federal, Mahogany,
Glazed Doors, 89 In.

Bench, Railroad, 2–Sided, Oak	875.00
Bench, Rococo Revival, American, Walnut, C.1860, 36 In., Pair	850.00
Bench, Roycroft, Ali Baba, Carved Baba On Seat, Half Log Seat	8250.00
Bench, Shaker, Pine, Bootjack Ends, Hancock, C.1840, 18 X 39 In.	4000.00
Bench, Shaker, Yellow Pine, Watervliet, 1850, 16 X 34 In.	350.00
Bench, Steel, Eiffel Tower Open Construction, French, Pair	1200.00
Bench, Upholstered Seat, Scrolled Armrests, Mahogany, 8 Ft.	9000.00
Bench, Vanity, Wicker, White Paint, 1890	375.00
Bench, Wainscot, Plank Seat, Scrolled Arms, Oak, 55 3/4 In.	500.00
Bench, Walnut, Cutout Ends, Arts & Crafts, 16 3/4 X 36 In.	250.00
Bench, Water, Pine, Primitive, Brown Finish, 23 In.	175.00
Bench, Window, William IV, Scrolled Ends, Rosewood, C.1860, 5 Ft.	4950.00
Bench, Windsor, Curved Oak Crest Rail, 80 In.	2750.00
Bergere, Directoire, Green Paint, Gilt, Upholstered Back, 32 In.	1200.00
Bergere, George III, Ebonized, Arched Back, Serpentine Seat	800.00
Bergere, Gilt Wood, Carved Fern Fronds Arms, Crest, Majorelle	3500.00
Bin, Pine, Green Repaint, Primitive, Dovetaile, Iron Hinges, 28 In.	100.00
Bookcase, 3 Door, Limbert	1650.00
Bookcase, 5 Shelves, Lower Cupboard, Burl Walnut, 7 Ft.5 In.	2475.00
Bookcase, 8 Slat Gallery, Gustav Stickley, 1 Door, 60 X 28 In.	4250.00
Bookcase, Carved Doors, Barley Twist Half Posts, Oak, English	650.00
Bookcase, Carved Rosewood, Maple Interior, 9 Ft.2 In. ....*Illus*	6500.00
Bookcase, Corner, Mahogany, 3 Sections	200.00
Bookcase, F.W.Hutchings, Maple, Glass Doors, 19th Century, 9 Ft.	6500.00
Bookcase, Federal, Mahogany, Glazed Doors, 89 In. ....*Illus*	4125.00
Bookcase, Glazed Double Doors, Old Red Paint, 7 Ft.7 In.	3800.00
Bookcase, Glazed Sliding Doors, Lion's Head Capitals, Oak, 61 In.	800.00
Bookcase, Gothic Revival, 4 Grilled Doors, Oak, C.1900, 83 In.	1000.00
Bookcase, Gustav Stickley, Gallery, 16 Panes, 2 Doors, 56 X 36 In.	2750.00
Bookcase, L.&J.G., Gallery, 16 Pane Door, 1907, 55 In.	3250.00
Bookcase, Lawyer's, Quarter Sawn Oak, Bow Front, 5 Stacks, Macey	1095.00
Bookcase, Leaded Glass Windows, Stickley	8800.00
Bookcase, Onondaga, 3 Doors, Gallery, Keyed Tenons, 56 X 70 In.	4250.00
Bookcase, Onondaga, Gallery, 2 Doors, 12 Panes Each, 57 In.	4750.00
Bookcase, Revolves, French, Rosewood, Nudes Hold Marble, 19 In.	1800.00
Bookcase, Rococo Revival, Fold–Down Drawer, Walnut, C.1860, 86 In.	700.00
Bookcase, Roycroft Molded Cornice, 1 Door, 1904, 60 1/2 In.	5000.00
Bookcase, Side–By–Side, Mahogany, Glass Doors, Drop Front Desk	280.00
Bookcase, Victorian, Walnut, Double Doors, Lower Drawer, 46 In.	665.00
Bookcase, Walnut, Round Mirror, 2 Doors, 2 Drawers, Candle Shelves	350.00
Bookrack, G.Stickley, Ladderback Form, C.1913, 7 X 12 In.	1100.00
Box, Blanket, Walnut, Lift Top, Dovetailed, Carved Moldings, 24 In.	400.00
Box, Campaign, Military Officer's, Teak, 14 X 9 X 19 In.	1345.00
Breakfast Set, Wrought Iron, Upholstered, 20th Century, 5 Piece	450.00
Breakfront Bookcase, George III, 4 Glazed Doors, 84 X 94 In.	2900.00
Breakfront, Chinese Style, Drexel, Glass Shelves, Painted, 3 Piece	1395.00
Breakfront, Hepplewhite, Banded Drawers, Mahogany, 80 1/2 In.	775.00
Breakfront, Louis XVI, Mirrored, Marble Top, 19th Century, 70 In.	1100.00

Buffet, Oak, Claw Feet, Glass Center Door, Mirror, C.1915 .... 195.00
Bureau Bookcase, Glazed Doors, Ebonized Satinwood, 7 Ft.4 In. 4400.00
Bureau Bookcase, Gothic Arch Doors, 3 Drawers, Mahogany, C.1850 .... 1900.00
Bureau Bookcase, Queen Anne, Candle Slides, Walnut, 6 Ft.6 In. 6000.00
Bureau, Cockbeaded Case, 4 Drawers, Birch, C.1800, 34 1/2 X 37 In. 1500.00
Bureau, Federal, 4 Graduated Drawers, Wavy Birch, 39 In. 1200.00
Bureau, Federal, Bowfront, Cherry, Mass., 1790, 35 In. ....*Illus* 5300.00
Bureau, Federal, Tiger Maple, Cherry, C.1800, 38 In. ....*Illus* 1400.00
Bureau, Graduated Drawers, Quarter Columns, Mahogany, 44 1/2 In. 165.00
Bureau, Oak, Gustav Stickley, Mirror, 2 Top Drawers, 66 X 48 In. 4000.00
Bureau, Shaker, Pine, Red Stain, New Lebanon, 1830, 6 1/2 X 14 In. 500.00
Bureau, Slant Front, Leather Surface, Drawers, Walnut, 36 In. 2000.00
Cabinet, Bedside, Tray Top, Cupboard Doors, Mahogany, C.1790 .... 1700.00
Cabinet, Card File, Brass Pulls, 15 Drawers, 38 X 33 In. 295.00
Cabinet, Card File, Oak, 8 X 20 X 20 In. 65.00
Cabinet, China, Corner, Oak, 5 Shelves, Glass Door 1250.00
Cabinet, Corner, Arched, 1 Center Drawer, Burl Walnut, 7 Ft.7 In. 9000.00
Cabinet, Corner, Candle Shelf, Painted, 9 3/4 In. 250.00
Cabinet, Corner, George III, Inlaid Walnut, 6 Ft.1 In., Pair 4950.00
Cabinet, Corner, Pine, Gudgeon Hinges, 18th Century, 89 In. 7500.00
Cabinet, Cupboard, Pennsylvania, Poplar & Pine, C.1860, 83 In. 3250.00
Cabinet, Curved Glass, Custom Made For Miniatures, 73 X 35 In. 450.00
Cabinet, Eastlake, 3 Glazed Doors, Oak, C.1890, 107 1/2 In. 1200.00
Cabinet, Female Figures Flank 2 Drawers, Walnut, 36 1/2 In. 825.00
Cabinet, Hoosier, Oak, Maple, Painted, Original Hardware, Label 700.00
Cabinet, Hoosier, Reverse Roll Porcelain Top 450.00
Cabinet, Hoosier, Zinc Top, 1908 .... 675.00
Cabinet, Italian Renaissance, Carved Frieze, 3 Doors, Oak, 95 In. 2500.00
Cabinet, Japanese, 6 Inside Drawers, Keyaki Wood, 16 X 17 1/2 In. 550.00
Cabinet, Japanese, Hardwood, 2 Doors, Block Legs, 40 In. 2250.00
Cabinet, Kitchen, Oak, Painted, Flour Bin, Frosted Glass Doors 220.00
Cabinet, Liquor, Inlaid, Marble Top, Mounted Ormolu, French, 62 In. 400.00
Cabinet, Louis XV Style, Marquetry, Marble Top, 30 In., Pair 300.00
Cabinet, Louis XV, Serpentine Front, Painted Scenes, 55 1/2 In. 935.00
Cabinet, Louis XVI, Marquetry, Floral Design, 57 In. ....*Illus* 1650.00
Cabinet, Magazine, Gustav Stickley 1650.00
Cabinet, Music, Mahogany, Mirror Back 125.00
Cabinet, Music, Oak, 6 Open Shelves, 1902, 30 In. ....*Illus* 1870.00
Cabinet, Music, Roycroft, Side Designs, Logo, Oak, C.1910, 42 In. 7200.00
Cabinet, Neoclassical, Mahogany, Austria, 1830, 72 In. ....*Illus* 2900.00
Cabinet, On Stand, Chinoiserie Design, Black Lacquer, 55 1/2 In. 1200.00
Cabinet, On Stand, Glazed Doors, 5 Shelves, Pine, 94 1/2 In. 335.00
Cabinet, On Stand, Italian Renaissance, Walnut, 49 In. ....*Illus* 600.00
Cabinet, Paktong Lock, Japan, 19th Century, 40 In. ....*Illus* 2250.00
Cabinet, Renaissance Revival, Ebonized, Porcelain Plaques, 1870 .... 2800.00
Cabinet, Renaissance Revival, Partial Gilt, Walnut, C.1865, 52 In. 1900.00
Cabinet, Serpentine Front, Drawer, Painted Floral, French, 22 In. 100.00
Cabinet, Spanish Baroque, Fruitwood, 2 Doors, 65 X 41 In. 1100.00

Furniture, Bureau, Federal, Bowfront,
Cherry, Mass., 1790, 35 In.

Furniture, Bureau, Federal, Tiger
Maple, Cherry, C.1800, 38 In.

Furniture, Cabinet, Louis XVI, Marquetry,
Floral Design, 57 In.

Furniture, Cabinet, Music, Oak,
6 Open Shelves, 1902, 30 In.

Furniture, Cabinet, Neoclassical,
Mahogany, Austria, 1830, 72 In.

Furniture, Cabinet, Paktong Lock,
Japan, 19th Century, 40 In.

Furniture, Cabinet, On Stand,
Italian Renaissance, Walnut, 49 In.

Cabinet, Spice, Hanging, 6 Drawers, Knobs, Walnut, 14 3/4 In. 125.00
Cabinet, Spice, Light Maple, Brass Knob Pulls, 7 Drawers 74.50
Cabinet, Stand, Maghogany, Mullioned Door, Drawer, C.1900, 58 In. 320.00
Cabinet, Table, German Baroque, Walnut, Scrolled Crest, 37 In. 850.00
Cabinet, Thomas Godey, Bronze Plaque of Mother & Child 4620.00
Cabinet, Venetian Style, Shaped Doors, Watteau Scenes, 45 In. 500.00
Cabinet, Wood & Brass Inlay On Doors, A.Fabre, C.1930, 33 1/2 In. 2300.00
Candlestand, Adjustable, Rotating Plate, Wooden, 34 1/2 In. 425.00
Candlestand, Candle, Walnut, Pedestal, 3 Legs, Varnished, 30 In. 37.50
Candlestand, Cherry Column, Legs of Curly Maple, 25 In. 95.00
Candlestand, Cherry, Handmade, 25 1/2 In. 325.00
Candlestand, Cherry, Tripod, Octagonal Top, Molding, 26 1/4 In. 350.00
Candlestand, Chippendale, Maple, Octagon, C.1780, 28 X 17 X 17 In. 850.00
Candlestand, Curly Walnut Post, Walnut, 24 1/2 In. 55.00
Candlestand, Down–Curving Legs, Red Painted Maple & Pine, 25 In. 600.00
Candlestand, Federal, Curly Maple, New England, 26 In. 1430.00
Candlestand, Federal, Tiger Maple, C.1810, 26 1/2 In. 475.00
Candlestand, Federal, Tilt Top, Oval, Pedestal, Mahogany, 29 In. 2970.00
Candlestand, George III, Cabriole Legs, Maple, 24 In. 192.00
Candlestand, George III, Tilt Top, Fruitwood, 28 In. 770.00
Candlestand, Hepplewhite, Cherry, Maple, Walnut, Country, 29 In. 325.00
Candlestand, Hepplewhite, Cherry, Oval 1 Board Top, 26 1/2 In. 500.00
Candlestand, Hepplewhite, Oval Top, Mahogany, 28 1/2 In. 85.00
Candlestand, Hepplewhite, Tilt Top, Birdcage, Curly Maple 1650.00
Candlestand, Hepplewhite, Tilt Top, Curly Maple, 28 1/2 In. 700.00
Candlestand, Italian Baroque, Walnut, Tripartite Legs, 40 In. 700.00
Candlestand, Line & Diamond Inlay, Cherry, C.1810, 29 1/2 In. 2750.00
Candlestand, Octagonal Maple Top, Cherry Pedestal, 30 In. 600.00
Candlestand, Pine, Cut Corner, Roanoke Valley, Nutting 325.00
Candlestand, Serpentine Sides, Inlaid Birch, C.1790, 27 1/2 In. 900.00
Candlestand, Shaker, Cherry, Round Top, New Lebanon, Refinished 2600.00
Candlestand, Threaded Arm, Curly Maple Base, 13 1/2 In. 65.00
Candlestand, Tilt Top, Iron Latch, Chestnut, 28 In. 300.00
Candlestand, Tilt Top, Octagonal, New England, Mahogany, C.1790 .... 2400.00
Candlestand, Tilt Top, Rosewood Banding, Mahogany, 21 3/4 In. 500.00
Candlestand, Tilt Top, Snake Feet, Mahogany, 28 In. 80.00
Candlestand, Tripod Base, Spring Clip For Rush, Iron, 33 In. 225.00
Candlestand, Tripod, Penny Feet, Iron, Pin & Chain, 22 1/4 In. 400.00
Candlestand, Vase, Ring Pedestal, Red–Brown Paint, Cherry, C.1780 .... 900.00
Canterbury, Divided Top, Center Handle, Drawer, Mahogany 2550.00
Canterbury, Lyre Form, Drawer, Floral Marquetry, 23 In. 200.00
Canterbury, Regency, 3 Drawers, Grained Rosewood, 1820, 3 Ft.2 In. 6650.00
Canterbury, Victorian, Walnut, 4 Arched Banister Sections, 1860 .... 1000.00
Carrier, Wine, Carrying Handle, 6 Sections, Mahogany, 20 In. 2475.00
Cellarette, George III, Hinged Lid, Divided, Mahogany, C.1800 .... 1320.00
Cellarette, On Stand, Brass–Bound Mahogany, C.1800, 26 In. 6050.00
Chair Set, 2 Slat Ladder Back, Splint Seat, Red & White Paint, 4 .... 60.00
Chair Set, 3 Ladder Back, Gustav Stickley, Leather Seat, 4 .... 2250.00
Chair Set, 3 Slat, Rush Seat, L.& J.G.Stickley, Decal, C.1910, 4 .... 1800.00
Chair Set, 4 Horizontal Slats, Gustav Stickley, C.1904, 4 .... 2500.00
Chair Set, 6 Half Spindle, Pillow Back, Painted, Stenciled, 1840, 6 .... 2450.00
Chair Set, Arm & Lady's, Carved Crest Rail, Walnut, C.1870, 4 .... 2475.00
Chair Set, Austrian, Rosewood, Plush Velvet Seats, Refinished, 6 .... 510.00
Chair Set, Ball & Claw Feet, Mahogany, C.1900, 12 .... 3300.00
Chair Set, Balloon Back, Cherry Colored Finish, 6 .... 350.00
Chair Set, Balloon Back, Rosewood Grain Paint, Stencil, 6 .... 1650.00
Chair Set, Bamboo Turned, Ebonized, E.W.Vaill, Worcester, Mass., 5 .... 935.00
Chair Set, Barley Twist, Green Velour Seats, 4 .... 150.00
Chair Set, Black & Green Striping, Floral & Lyre, 4 .... 900.00
Chair Set, Black, Yellow Striping, Cane Seat, 3 .... 270.00
Chair Set, Chippendale, Mahogany, 2 Armchairs, White Finish, 8 .... 1560.00
Chair Set, Chippendale, Mahogany, Green Slip Seat, 2 Armchairs, 6 .... 570.00
Chair Set, Curved Stiles, Shaped Splat Crests, Cane Seat, 6 .... 685.00
Chair Set, Dining, Chippendale Style, 6 Side, 2 Arm, Silk Seats, 8 .... 600.00

Chair Set, Dining, George III, Pierced Splat, Mahogany, 6 .... 2000.00
Chair Set, Dining, George III, Turned Slats, Rush Seat, 7 .... 425.00
Chair Set, Dining, L.& J.G.Stickley, Upholstered Seat, 6 .... 1600.00
Chair Set, Dining, Queen Anne, Hickory Chair Co., Mahogany, 12 .... 2508.00
Chair Set, Dining, Slat Back, Gustav Stickley, 4 .... 3000.00
Chair Set, Dining, Victorian, Carved, Oak, 8 .... 1875.00
Chair Set, Dining, William IV, Mahogany, 1 Armchair, 1830, 9 .... 4950.00
Chair Set, Dining, William IV, Rosewood, C.1830, 6 .... 715.00
Chair Set, Empire, Black Paint, Gold Stenciled Design, Caned, 4 .... 180.00
Chair Set, Empire, Cane Seat, Mahogany, 4 .... 200.00
Chair Set, Empire, Cane Seat, Vase Splats, 6 .... 120.00
Chair Set, G.Stickley, Decal, Leather Seat, Oak, 37 1/2 In., 8 .... 7250.00
Chair Set, George I, Walnut, Upholstered, Trapezoidal Seat, 4 .... 1600.00
Chair Set, George II, Mahogany, Cabriole Leg, 2 Armchairs, 1820, 6 .... 3150.00
Chair Set, George III, Painted Scenes, Crest Rails, Upholstered, 4 .... 8250.00
Chair Set, George III, Pierced Baluster Splat, Mahogany, 6 .... 5500.00
Chair Set, Gondola Form Back, French, Walnut & Burl, C.1925, 4 .... 2850.00
Chair Set, Hitchcock, Polychrome Design, Rush Seat, 4 .... 450.00
Chair Set, Ladder Back, Oak, L.& J.G.Stickley, 4 .... 357.00
Chair Set, Larkin, Pressed Crest & Bottom Rail, Spindle Back, 4 .... 500.00
Chair Set, Louis Philippe, Inlaid Brass & Pewter, Ebony, 1840, 4 .... 2475.00
Chair Set, New York, Painted Grapes Tablet, Painted, 1820–30, 9 .... 2800.00
Chair Set, Plank Seat, Green Paint, Stencil Design, 6 .... 725.00
Chair Set, Plank Seats, Turned Spindles, Tan Paint, 6 .... 330.00
Chair Set, Pressed Back, 6 Spindle, Cane Seat, 6 .... 325.00
Chair Set, Queen Anne, Mahogany, Flame Stitched Slip Seats, 8 .... 3800.00
Chair Set, Regency, Arched Curved Crest, Pad Seat, Mahogany, 4 .... 550.00
Chair Set, Renaissance Revival, Oak Frames, Marquetry Panels, 10 .... 1980.00
Chair Set, Shaker, Maple, Red Varnish, 1820, North Family, 4 .... 5000.00
Chair Set, Shaker, Tilting, 4 .... 900.00
Chair Set, Sheraton, Alligatored Red Paint, 2 Arm, 6 Side, 8 .... 525.00
Chair Set, Sheraton, Black Paint, Yellow Striping, Eagle Slats, 6 .... 1050.00
Chair Set, Spindle Back, Oak Carved, 8 .... 1325.00
Chair Set, Step–Down, Plank Seat, Bamboo Turned Legs, Painted, 9 .... 3100.00
Chair Set, T–Back, Oak, Leather Sets, 6 .... 180.00
Chair Set, Victorian, Saber Legs, Rose Carved Crests, Walnut, 6 .... 450.00
Chair Set, Walnut, Straight, Cane Seat, Hooked Seat Covers, 6 .... 350.00
Chair Set, Windsor, Arrowback, American, C.1810, 6 .... 5600.00
Chair Set, Windsor, Bow Back, 7 Spindles, Painted, C.1810, 6 .... 7975.00
Chair Set, Windsor, Fruit & Flower Painted Rests, Plank Seat, 6 .... 3000.00
Chair Set, Windsor, George IV, Yewwood, Bow Back, 4 .... 1200.00
Chair Set, Windsor, Hoop Back, Taylor, Philadelphia, Arms, 1798, 4 .... 4500.00

Furniture, Chair, Savonarola
Style, Arms Ending in
Lion's Heads

Furniture, Chair, Bentwood,
Leather, Hoof Feet, Arms, 1888

Furniture, Chair, Horn,
Continental, 1890, Pair

Chair Set, Windsor, Rabbit, Painted Fruit & Foliage, Willard, 4 .... 1500.00
Chair Set, Windsor, Turned Spindles, Plank Seat, Painted, 4 .... 300.00
Chair Set, Windsor, Victorian, U–Shaped Back, Fruitwood, 4 .... 500.00
Chair Set, Windsor, Walnut, Ash & Maple, Saddle Seat, 36 In., 4 .... 2800.00
Chair Set, Yorkshire, Shaped Ladder Back, Rush Seat, Elm, 8 .... 3100.00
Chair Table, 3 Board Oval Top, Worn Feet, 47 1/4 X 46 3/4 In. 2000.00
Chair Table, Shaker, Pine, Birch, Canterbury, C.1840, 27 In.X 6 Ft. 4000.00
Chair, Adjustable Back, Arms, S.& J.G.Stickley 1600.00
Chair, American Gothic, Walnut, Pierced Crest, Rectangular Back 100.00
Chair, Arrow Back, Painted Design, Canary Yellow, Pair 1950.00
Chair, Balloon Back, Plank Seat, Brown & Yellow Paint, Pa., Pair 345.00
Chair, Banister Back, Black Repaint, Yellow Striping, Rush Seat 350.00
Chair, Banister Back, Maple, Bulbous Turned, Rush Seat, Pair 1700.00
Chair, Banister Back, Painted, Block & Vase, Posts, Rush Seat, Pair 2300.00
Chair, Banister Back, Rush Seat, New England, 18th Century 575.00
Chair, Barrel Back, Arms, Mahogany 110.00
Chair, Belter Style, Rosalie Pattern Upholstery, Pair 4400.00
Chair, Belter, Rose & Grape Carved Crests, Pair 4500.00
Chair, Bentwood, Leather, Hoof Feet, Arms, 1888 ....*Illus* 2750.00
Chair, Biedermeier, 3 Bar Splat, Fruitwood & Ebonized, 35 In. 550.00
Chair, Brace Back, 6 Spindles, Vase & Ring Stiles, C.1780 .... 1000.00
Chair, Broken Arched Crest Rail, Simulated Rosewood, American 110.00
Chair, C.Rohlfs, Pierced Backrest, Logo, Oak, 1900, 37 3/4 In. 5450.00
Chair, Cane Back & Seat, Spanish Foot, Mahogany 95.00
Chair, Carved & Upholstered Open Arms, Scrolling Acanthus Arms 750.00
Chair, Carved Acanthus Leaves, Pierced Splat, Mahogany, C.1750 .... 2750.00
Chair, Carved Crest Rail, Carved Trifid Front Feet, C.1740 .... 2200.00
Chair, Carved Foliage, Shields, Angels, Grotesque Face, Walnut 475.00
Chair, Carved Fruitwood Frame, Damask Upholstered, C.1840 .... 55.00
Chair, Carved Gothic Arches & Quatrefoil, Arms, C.1840 .... 1100.00
Chair, Child's, Cane Seat, Nursery Scene, 1920 .... 250.00
Chair, Child's, Corner, Acanthus Carving, English, 19th Century 1500.00
Chair, Child's, Cushion Seat & Back, Frank Lloyd Wright 8250.00
Chair, Child's, Ladder Back, Hickory 225.00
Chair, Child's, Morris Recliner, Mission Oak Style 125.00
Chair, Child's, Oak, Straight Back 37.50
Chair, Child's, Pennsylvania, Plank Seat, Painted, Gilt, C.1845 .... 440.00
Chair, Child's, Sheraton, Curly Maple, Yellow Painted Rush Seat 200.00
Chair, Child's, Spindle Back, Plank Seat, Stripped, Green Traces 35.00
Chair, Child's, Windsor, Comb Back, 7 Spindles, Red Paint 500.00
Chair, Child's, Windsor, New Hampshire, 18th Century 52.50
Chair, Child's, Woven Rush Seat, Arms, C.1840, 21 In. 145.00
Chair, Chippendale Style, Upholstered Seat, Pierced Splat, Walnut 200.00
Chair, Chippendale, Carved Apron, Foliage Brackets, Mahogany 300.00
Chair, Chippendale, Carved Mahogany, C.1780, 39 1/2 In. 3250.00
Chair, Chippendale, Center Shell, Pierced Splat, Mahogany, C.1780 .... 2970.00
Chair, Chippendale, Central Carved Fan Over Splat, Maple, C.1780 .... 450.00
Chair, Chippendale, Central Carved Fan, Slip Seat, C.1780 .... 450.00
Chair, Chippendale, Cherry, Original Leather Seat, New England 550.00
Chair, Chippendale, Cherry, Square Legs, Pierced Splat, Rush Seat 300.00
Chair, Chippendale, Floral & Leaf Design On Arms, Upholstered 275.00
Chair, Chippendale, Mahogany, Cross–Eyed Owl Splat, Salem 7150.00
Chair, Chippendale, Mahogany, Upholstered Seat, American, Pair 1925.00
Chair, Chippendale, Pierced Splat, Mahogany, C.1780, Pair 3950.00
Chair, Chippendale, Punch Carved Element, Maple, 1780, 38 In. 350.00
Chair, Chippendale, Raked & Molded Ears, Carved Mahogany, C.1775 .... 400.00
Chair, Chippendale, Scrolled Ears, Walnut, Pennsylvania, C.1750 .... 4125.00
Chair, Chippendale, Serpentine Crest, Solid Splat, Cutouts, Maple 225.00
Chair, Chippendale, Vase Splat, Pennyslvania, C.1780, Walnut 7425.00
Chair, Concave Crest, Stenciled & Painted, C.1820, 32 1/2 In. 200.00
Chair, Congressional, Carved Shield & Stars On Crest, Oak 2300.00
Chair, Continental, Fruitwood, Ivory Inlaid, Crest, 1790–1810, Pair 1485.00
Chair, Corner, Carved Putto & Lion Heads, Walnut, C.1890, Pair 400.00
Chair, Corner, Mahogany, Turned Legs, Curved Arms, Country 175.00

Chair, Corner, New England, Painted, Designs, Rush Seat, 1775 .... 4125.00
Chair, Corner, Sausage Turned Post, Scrolled Arm Rail, Rush Seat 1000.00
Chair, Corner, Scrolled Arms, Rush Seat, Maple & Chestnut, 30 In. 700.00
Chair, Corner, William & Mary, Crest Continuing To Scrolled Arms 950.00
Chair, Cube, Spindles, Brooks Mfg.Co. 1000.00
Chair, Cube, Spindles, Michigan Chair Co. 600.00
Chair, Curved Frame, Upholstered Back & Seat, Arms 100.00
Chair, Deer Horn 275.00
Chair, Desk, Gustav Stickley, Pierced Top Slat, Oak, C.1901 .... 1350.00
Chair, Desk, Wicker 175.00
Chair, Dressing, Birch, Rush Seat, Double Dowel, Mt.Lebanon, 1880 .... 1000.00
Chair, Dutch Rococo, Marquetry Inlaid Walnut, Pair 1210.00
Chair, Eastlake, Arms, Red & White, Pair 275.00
Chair, Empire, Mahogany, Lyre Back, Upholstered Seat, Paw Feet, Pr. 2750.00
Chair, Empire, Mahogany, Marquetry, Satin Inlaid, 1825 .... 250.00
Chair, English, Carved Knee Shells, Balloon Seat, Arms, Mahogany 600.00
Chair, Federal, Klismos, Carved Mahogany, Slip Seat, 1815–20, Pair 1320.00
Chair, Federal, Urn Form Splat, New York, C.1800, Mahogany 990.00
Chair, Folding, Labeled W.W.Vaill, Upholstered Seat 175.00
Chair, Folding, Rawhide Seat, Bronze Pegged Legs, C.1880 .... 325.00
Chair, Folding, Victorian, Original Upholstered Seat 125.00
Chair, Fountain Elms Pattern, Belter, Round Seat Apron 5500.00
Chair, Frank Lloyd Wright Design, Low Spindle Back, Oak, 1902 .... 8470.00
Chair, Freehand Design, Mustard Paint, Plank Seat, Pair 150.00
Chair, French Style, Carved Wooden Frame, Tufted Seat, Arms, Pair 170.00
Chair, G.Stickley, Rabbit Ear, Leather Seat, Oak, C.1901 .... 905.00
Chair, George I, Leather Upholstered, Arms, Walnut 5325.00
Chair, George III, Carved Arm Supports, Mahogany, C.1765 .... 5500.00
Chair, George III, Padded Back, Fret Carved Legs, C.1770 .... 8800.00
Chair, George III, Red Painted & Parcel Gilt, Bowed Seat, Pair 200.00
Chair, George III, Serpentine Crest, Pierced Splat, England, Oak 165.00
Chair, George III, Upholstered Back, Open Arms, Mahogany, Pair 2200.00
Chair, Glastonbury, Arms, 1680, Pair 1250.00
Chair, Gustav Stickley, 3–Slat Back, Leather Seat Cover 575.00
Chair, Gustav Stickley, Flat Arms, Square Cutouts, Willow, 1910 .... 3500.00
Chair, Hall, Mahogany, Floral Medallion Back, Germany 200.00
Chair, Hawaiian Planter's, Swivel Arms, Yew Wood, Mahogany, 1880 .... 425.00
Chair, High Back, Carved Mermaids, Velvet Upholstered, Walnut 250.00
Chair, Horn, Continental, 1890, Pair ....*Illus* 1650.00
Chair, Hunzinger, Tape Wrapped & Woven Steel Back & Seat, Walnut 200.00
Chair, Hunzinger, Walnut & Incised Leather, Rustic, C.1870 .... 300.00
Chair, Ice Cream Parlor, Oak 50.00
Chair, Inlaid Brass & Pewter, Ebony Veneer, C.1840, Pair 1450.00
Chair, Iron, Morning Glory Design, White, Green & Purple, Pair 440.00
Chair, Italian Rococo, Lacquered, Baluster Splat, 18th Century 500.00
Chair, Japanese, Tub, Dragon, Carved Hardwood, 19th Century, Pair 825.00
Chair, L.& J.G.Stickley, Arms, Oak, C.1912, 31 7/8 In. 3870.00
Chair, Ladder Back, 3 Slats, High Seat, Reddish Varnish 85.00
Chair, Ladder Back, 4 Arched Slats, Bulbous Arm Rests, Rush Seat 135.00
Chair, Ladder Back, Pencil Posts, 2 Slats, Splint Seat 25.00
Chair, Ladder Back, Sausage Turning, Scrolled Arms, 4 Slats 750.00
Chair, Ladder Back, Shaped Finials, Rush Seat, Maple, Pair 300.00
Chair, Ladder Back, Turned Posts, Arms, Rush Seat 175.00
Chair, Laminated Rosewood, Philadelphia, Upholstered Back & Seat 885.00
Chair, Landscape & Sidewheeler Scene On Crest, C.1840, Pair 1700.00
Chair, Library, George III, Padded Back & Arms, Mahogany, C.1775 .... 3300.00
Chair, Lolling, Contoured Arms, Mahogany, C.1790, 47 X 20 In. 4000.00
Chair, Lolling, Federal, Molded Arms, New England, C.1805 .... 3850.00
Chair, Lolling, Upholstered Back, Square Legs, Mahogany, 1780 .... 4500.00
Chair, Louis XV, Arched Needlepoint Back & Seat, Beechwood 425.00
Chair, Louis XV, Carved Arms, Apron, Beechwood, 19th Century, Pair 9350.00
Chair, Louis XV, Carved Crest Rail, Upholstered Back, Walnut 550.00
Chair, Louix XV, Upholstered Back, Shaped Seat, Arms, Walnut 2750.00
Chair, Lounge, Charles Eames, Contemporary, Leather Upholstered 495.00

Furniture, Rockers, Child's, Mt. Lebanon; Tilter, Mt. Lebanon, 1870–1880

Chair, Lounge, William IV, Carved Mahogany	1800.00
Chair, Lyre, Walnut, Gargoyles, Tufted Leather Seat, Refinished	250.00
Chair, Majorelle, Clematis Vines Back, Upholstered Seat, Pair	2640.00
Chair, Maple, Slat Back, Delaware River Valley, C.1770, 44 In.	700.00
Chair, Morris, Exposed Tenons, Medium Finish, L.& J.G.Stickley	600.00
Chair, Morris, Gustav Stickley, Bent Arm, 5 Slat Side, 1907	5500.00
Chair, Morris, Gustav Stickley, No.336	7150.00
Chair, Morris, Gustav Stickley, No.367	7700.00
Chair, Office, 11 Spindles, Flat Open Arms, G.Stickley	6750.00
Chair, Office, Oak, Swivel	195.00
Chair, Ogival Wings, Chippendale, Upholstered, Mahogany, C.1780	4125.00
Chair, Paddded Back, Open Arms, Gilt Design, C.1780, Pair	1980.00
Chair, Pierced Splat, Leather Arms, Wrought Iron & Brass, 47 In.	275.00
Chair, Portuguese, Carved & Pierced Rail, Scrolled Arms, Mahogany	375.00
Chair, Portuguese, Crowned Shell Flanked By Lions, Walnut, Pair	1760.00
Chair, Potty, Child's, Wicker	65.00
Chair, Potty, Child's, Windsor, Original Paint, Stenciled	325.00
Chair, Pressed Back, Art Nouveau Design	150.00
Chair, Pressed Oak, Black River, Spindles, Original Finish	160.00
Chair, Prince of Wales Rail, Arms, Black Paint, 1720, 46 3/4 In.	1350.00
Chair, Queen Anne Style, Painted Floral Design, Slip Seat, Pair	240.00
Chair, Queen Anne, Cherry, Vase Splat, Rush Seat, 19th Century	500.00
Chair, Queen Anne, John Elliott, Carved Walnut, C.1750	8525.00
Chair, Queen Anne, Maple, Pine, Turned Legs, Duck Feet, Rush Seat	1050.00
Chair, Queen Anne, Rush Seat, Pad Feet, New York, C.1740	2420.00
Chair, Queen Anne, Salmon Paint Under Black, Turned, C.1840	525.00
Chair, Queen Anne, Vase Form Splat, Arched Skirt, Maple, C.1755	3850.00
Chair, Queen Anne, Woodbury, Ct., Arms, C.1750	1760.00
Chair, Regency, Caned Back, Padded Caned Arms, 19th Century, Pair	9900.00
Chair, Regency, Caned Curule Form, H.Butts, Mahogany, C.1800, Pair	7700.00
FURNITURE, Chair, Rocker, see Furniture, Rocker	
Chair, Savonarola Style, Arms Ending In Lion's Heads ....*Illus*	900.00
Chair, Savonarola, Inlaid Brass, 1850	1850.00
Chair, Scalloped Crest Rail, Banister Back, Ash & Maple	250.00
Chair, Serpentine Crest Rail, Pierced Splats, Cherry, C.1790, Pair	450.00
Chair, Serpentine Rail, Square Stiles, Rush Seat, Maple, C.1780	275.00
Chair, Shaker, Birch, Cane Seat, Tilters, Enfield, 1840, 17 In.	5500.00
Chair, Shaker, Birch, Rush Seat, Enfield, 1840, 17 In.	1100.00
Chair, Shaker, Child's, Maple, Shawl Bar, Mt.Lebanon, Arms, 1870	1150.00
Chair, Shaker, Child's, Mt.Lebanon, Ash & Butternut, 1880, 28 In.	1000.00
Chair, Shaker, Maple, Cane Seat, Titers, Canterbury, C.1840, 41 In.	6000.00
Chair, Shaker, No.1, Mt.Lebanon, N.Y., Arms, Tape Seat	2050.00

Chair, Shaker, No.3, Armless	412.00
Chair, Shaker, No.3, Mt.Lebanon, Shaped Finials, C.1877, 33 5/8 In.	275.00
Chair, Shaker, No.5, Tape Back	742.00
Chair, Shaker, No.6, Mt.Lebanon	2200.00
Chair, Shaker, Queen Anne, Spoon Back, Rush Seat, Spanish Feet	450.00
Chair, Shaker, Revolving, Hickory, Pine, 8 Spindles, New Lebanon ....'......	5250.00
Chair, Shaker, Side, Cherry, Harvard, C.1830, 41 In.	3100.00
Chair, Shaker, Tilter, Barlow	5060.00
Chair, Shaker, Tilter, Mt.Lebanon, Tape Seat, C.1870, 36 1/2 In.	1100.00
Chair, Shaped Slats, Splint Seat, Curly Maple, C.1780	3300.00
Chair, Shaped Wings, Flaring Arms, Upholstered, Mahogany, 44 In.	1800.00
Chair, Shield Back, Inlaid Fan, Shaped Arms, Upholstered Seat	5000.00
Chair, Shield Back, Vertical Splats, Curved Arms, Painted, C.1780	3300.00
Chair, Slat Back, Leather Seat, Shop of The Crafters	40.00
Chair, Slipper, Gilt Design, Rosewood, Walnut & Holly	1500.00
Chair, Spindles, Adjustable Back, L.& J.G.Stickley, C.1905	2600.00
Chair, Spindles, Tall Back, G.Stickley, C.1907, 49 1/2 In.	8500.00
Chair, Swivel, Picket Fence Back, Red Paint, Wooden	25.00
Chair, Tapered Splat, Rush Seat, Painted Black, C.1740	3575.00
Chair, Tub, Leather Covered, Horseshoe Back, Carved Oak, C.1835	6050.00
Chair, Twig, Painted White, Pair	700.00
Chair, Upholstered Back, Padded Arms, Mahogany, C.1770	7150.00
Chair, Victorian, Caned Seat, Black Walnut	115.00
Chair, Victorian, Grape Back, Walnut, Original Black Upholstery	181.50
Chair, Wallace Nutting, No.361	250.00
Chair, Wicker, Upholstered Back & Seat	52.50
Chair, William IV, Leather Button Upholstery, Mahogany, C.1830	7700.00
Chair, Windsor, 7 Spindles, Bamboo Turnings, Saddle Seat	300.00
Chair, Windsor, 7 Spindles, Bamboo, Plank Seat, 17 In.	155.00
Chair, Windsor, 7 Spindles, Bow Back, Bamboo Turnings, Shaped Seat	200.00
Chair, Windsor, 7 Spindles, Bow Back, Turned Legs	200.00
Chair, Windsor, 7 Spindles, Continous Arm, Ash, Pine, Maple, C.1780	1600.00
Chair, Windsor, 8 Spindles, Arms, English, Center Carved Splat	925.00
Chair, Windsor, 9 Spindles, Bow Back, Signed John Letchworth	1100.00
Chair, Windsor, Arched Bow, Shaped Seat, Black Over Black, Pair	6800.00
Chair, Windsor, Bamboo, Brown, 17 1/2 In.	85.00
Chair, Windsor, Birdcage, 7 Spindles, Painted Gold, C.1810, 32 In.	200.00
Chair, Windsor, Birdcage, Medallion Between Spindles, Arms, C.1810	1000.00
Chair, Windsor, Black Over Green, Marked Adams, 1790s	2450.00
Chair, Windsor, Black, Painted Shell Designs On Flat Spindles	500.00
Chair, Windsor, Bow Back, 7 Spindles, Rhode Island, C.1780	1600.00
Chair, Windsor, Bow Back, Continous Arms, Pair	1200.00
Chair, Windsor, Bow Back, Knuckle Arms, Green	375.00
Chair, Windsor, Bow Back, Plank Seat, 7 Spindle Back	175.00
Chair, Windsor, Bow Back, Potty Seat, Black	125.00
Chair, Windsor, Bow Back, Spindles, Painted Brown, C.1800	450.00
Chair, Windsor, Brace Back, Brown Finish, Split Seat	250.00
Chair, Windsor, Brace Back, Continuous Arm, Ash, Maple, W.MacBride	1100.00
Chair, Windsor, Child's, Thumb Back, Yellow, Red & Black, 1800	795.00
Chair, Windsor, Comb Back, Fanback, 7 Spindles, Arms, Ash, Chestnut	1400.00
Chair, Windsor, Comb Back, Nutting	160.00
Chair, Windsor, Continous Arm, Ash, Pine & Maple, C.1780	1600.00
Chair, Windsor, Continous Arms, Branded I.C.Kitchel, C.1780	550.00
Chair, Windsor, Ended Out Feet, Arms, English	700.00
Chair, Windsor, Fanback, 6 Spindles, Maple, C.1780	600.00
Chair, Windsor, Fanback, 7 Spindles, Black, Connecticut, C.1780	700.00
Chair, Windsor, Fanback, 7 Spindles, Saddle Seat, Green, 36 In.	1900.00
Chair, Windsor, Fanback, 8 Spindles, Vase Stiles, Ash, Maple, C.1700	500.00
Chair, Windsor, Fanback, Ash & Maple, Pennsylvania, 1780, 38 In.	650.00
Chair, Windsor, Fanback, Carved Ears, 1770–90, 36 In.	1600.00
Chair, Windsor, Fanback, Conn.River Valley, 18th Century, Pair	5000.00
Chair, Windsor, Fanback, Eared Arms, Splayed Base, Black, Penna.	3100.00
Chair, Windsor, Fanback, England, Ash & Maple, C.1780	600.00
Chair, Windsor, Fanback, Maple, New England, 1780, 4 Pc. ....*Illus*	600.00

Chair, Windsor, Hoop Back, 7 Spindles, Painted Black, New England 1540.00
Chair, Windsor, Pierced Splat, English Elmwood, C.1780, Pair 2200.00
Chair, Windsor, Rod Back, 7 Incised Back Posts, C.1815, Pair 1000.00
Chair, Windsor, Rod Back, Gragg, Boston, Ash & Maple, Pair 500.00
Chair, Windsor, Rod Back, H Stretcher, Pair 1250.00
Chair, Windsor, Sack Back, 6 Spindles, Ash & Chestnut, C.1800 .... 2300.00
Chair, Windsor, Sack Back, 7 Spindles, Shaped Arms, Painted, C.1800 .... 600.00
Chair, Windsor, Sack Back, Ash, Chestnut, Painted, New Eng., 1800 .... 2300.00
Chair, Windsor, Sack Back, Rhode Island, C.1790, Pair 1350.00
Chair, Windsor, Sack Back, Scrolled Hand Holds, Painted, C.1800 .... 1320.00
Chair, Windsor, Spindle Back, Bow Back, Bulbous Turnings 500.00
Chair, Windsor, Spindle Back, Saddle Seat 950.00
Chair, Windsor, Spindle Back, Splayed Base, H Stretcher 225.00
Chair, Windsor, Straight Arms, Elmwood, C.1780, Pair 3025.00
Chair, Windsor, Yewwood, Elm, England, C.1800 .... 3500.00
Chair, Wing, Carved Mahogany, Hoof Front Feet 450.00
Chair, Wing, George I, Padded Back & Arms, Walnut, C.1720 .... 4950.00
Chair, Wing, George III, Barrel Back, Loose Cushion Seat, C.1780 .... 2420.00
Chair, Wing, George III, Loose Seat, C.1780, Mahogany 1540.00
Chair, Wing, Outscrolled Padded Arms, Cushioned Seat, Mahogany 1750.00
Chair, Wing, Queen Anne, Upholstered Back, Walnut, Pair 2000.00
Chair, Wing, Serpentine Crest Rail, Padded Back, Arms, 50 In. 600.00
Chair, Wing, Upholstered Back, Serpentine Rail, Brass Feet, Arms 2090.00
Chair, Wing, Woven Flame Stitch Upholstered, Arms 300.00
Chair, Wingback, Child's, Crewel–Like Upholstery 100.00
Chair, Wingback, Duck Feet, Silk Damask Upholstered, Arms 1700.00
Chair, Wingback, Floral Damask Upholstered, Arms, Mahogany 400.00
Chair, Writing Arm, Drawer Under Seat & Arm, 5–Spindle, 1826 .... 1000.00
Chair, Yellow, Cornucopia & Stars Back, C.1825, Pair 4400.00
Chair, Youth, Black & Yellow Striping, Floral On Crest, 33 In. 150.00
Chaise, Louis XV, Beechwood, Upholstered Back, 34 1/2 In., Pair 800.00
Chaise, Louis XV, Caned Back & Seat, Loose Cushion, Painted Green 175.00
Chest, 2 Drawers, Green Mottled Marble Top, 29 X 29 X 16 In. 4125.00
Chest, 3 Drawers, Corner Posts, Walnut & Poplar, 37 X 41 In. 225.00
Chest, 3 Drawers, Faux Bamboo, Mirror, C.1900, 50 In. 60.00
Chest, 3 Drawers, Slide, Bronze Pulls, Mahogany, C.1780, 38 In. 9900.00
Chest, 3 Drawers, Walnut, Scrolls, Molded Feet, Italian, 35 1/2 In. 2600.00
Chest, 3 Small Drawers, 4 Drawers, Stenciled Ends, Penna., 1886 .... 4100.00
Chest, 4 Drawers, Bird'–Eye Maple Drawer Fronts 1000.00
Chest, 4 Drawers, Inlaid Marquetry Facade, 48 1/2 X 43 In. 175.00
Chest, 4 Drawers, Oval Brasses, Pine, 31 1/4 In. 1900.00
Chest, 4 Drawers, Walnut & Mahogany Banding, English, 34 In. 4000.00
Chest, 4 Graduated Drawers, Overhanging Top, Maple, C.1780, 39 In. 2750.00
Chest, 4 Molded Drawers, New England, Maple, 33 3/4 In. 3500.00
Chest, 4 Tiger Maple Fronted Drawers, Cherry, Dated 1822 .... 2800.00
Chest, 5 Drawers, Curly Maple Facings, Walnut, 41 3/4 X 44 In. 1000.00
Chest, 5 Drawers, Edge Beading, Brasses, Mahogany, 41 1/4 In. 750.00

Furniture, Chair, Windsor, Fanback, Maple, New England, 1780, 4 Pc.

Furniture, Chest, Bowfront, Federal,
Inlaid Mahogany, 37 In.

Furniture, Chest–On–Chest,
George III, Mahogany,
1780, 75 X 44 In.

Furniture, Commode, Louis XV, Ormolu,
Marquetry, 3 Drawers, 43 In.

Furniture, Cupboard, Oak,
French, 72 X 44 In.

Chest, 5 Graduated Drawers, New Hampshire, Maple, C.1780, 42 In.	3500.00
Chest, 6 Small Drawers, Red Painted & Carved Pine, 15 In.	2750.00
Chest, Beveled Mirror, Hat Box, Oak	700.00
Chest, Blanket, 1 Drawer, Green Paint, 29 1/2 In.	550.00
Chest, Blanket, 1 Drawer, New England	1050.00
Chest, Blanket, 2 Drawers & Till, Painted Poplar, 26 1/2 X 37 In.	275.00
Chest, Blanket, 2 Drawers, New England, Late 18th Century, Pine	2900.00
Chest, Blanket, 2 Drawers, Painted Tiger Maple, 36 3/4 In.	400.00
Chest, Blanket, 3 Drawers, Lift Top Over False Drawers, Pine	2000.00
Chest, Blanket, 3–Board Top, Pine & Poplar, 25 1/2 X 50 1/4 In.	250.00
Chest, Blanket, Baffle With Till & Shelf, Pine, 57 1/2 In.	45.00
Chest, Blanket, Bear Trap Lock, Initials M.A.D., Pine, 52 In.	300.00
Chest, Blanket, Brown Graining, Till With Lid, Poplar, 31 X 46 In.	95.00
Chest, Blanket, Chippendale, 3 Dovetailed Drawers, 28 In.	625.00
Chest, Blanket, Chippendale, Dovetailed Case, Ogee Feet, 30 In.	900.00

Chest, Blanket, Chippendale, Pine, Till, 3 Drawers, 1800s, 19 In. 4180.00
Chest, Blanket, Chippendale, Walnut, Till, 2 Drawers, Penna., 28 In. 2860.00
Chest, Blanket, Dovetailed Case, 6–Board, Pine, 17 X 38 1/2 In. 125.00
Chest, Blanket, Dovetailed Case, Biscuit Corners, 38 In. 1700.00
Chest, Blanket, Dovetailed Case, Till, Poplar, 22 X 38 1/4 In. 175.00
Chest, Blanket, Dovetailed Case, Turned Ball Feet, 21 3/4 In. 500.00
Chest, Blanket, Dovetailed Drawer, Till, Strap Hinges, Lock, Pine 250.00
Chest, Blanket, Grain Painted, C.1790, 39 1/2 X 46 In. 4600.00
Chest, Blanket, Hinged Top, England, Maple, Pine, 1800, 49 1/2 In. 3100.00
Chest, Blanket, Iron Strap Hinges, Orange Paint, Pine, 34 1/4 In. 125.00
Chest, Blanket, Lift Lid, Drawer, Mauve, 18th Century, 26 X 36 In. 1400.00
Chest, Blanket, New York State, Blue, C.1840 .... 3900.00
Chest, Blanket, Painted Design, Jacob Werrey, Signed 4500.00
Chest, Blanket, Painted, Stenciled, Initials E.S., Dated 1871 .... 500.00
Chest, Blanket, Pennsylvania, Design, Poplar, 27 X 49 1/2 In. 3700.00
Chest, Blanket, Pennsylvania, Painted, Design, 1804, 50 In. 3300.00
Chest, Blanket, Pine, 6 Board, Blue Over Putty Paint, 41 X 22 In. 675.00
Chest, Blanket, Poplar, Brown Vinegar Grained, Lift Lid, 13 In. 2000.00
Chest, Blanket, Red Flame Graining, Case & Till, Poplar, 44 In. 250.00
Chest, Blanket, Red Flame Graining, Iron Handles, 49 1/2 In. 550.00
Chest, Blanket, Shaker, 1 Drawer, Poplar, New Lebanon, 35 In. 3000.00
Chest, Blanket, Shaker, 2 Drawers, Poplar, Blue Paint, Watervliet 5500.00
Chest, Blanket, Shaker, Drawer, Pine, Bootjack Ends, 1840, 35 In. 2500.00
Chest, Blanket, Shaker, Pine, Red, Enfield, C.1850, 22 X 41 In. 850.00
Chest, Blanket, Soap Hollow, 1874 On Front, 16 1/2 X 20 X 8 In. 8100.00
Chest, Blanket, Soap Hollow, 2 Drawers, Dated 1850, Initials J C 4000.00
Chest, Blanket, Yellow Graining, Brown Trim, 22 1/4 In. 150.00
Chest, Blanket, Yellow Graining, Pine, Miniature 1075.00
Chest, Block Front, 4 Drawers, Mahogany, Boston, C.1775, 32 In. 9900.00
Chest, Bombe, Marquetry, 9 Drawers, Marble Top, Bronze Trim 950.00
Chest, Bowfront, Federal, Inlaid Mahogany, 37 In. ....*Illus* 2750.00
Chest, Bowfront, Federal, Line & Fan Inlay, Walnut, C.1815, 38 In. 1450.00
Chest, Bowfront, Mahogany, 4 Drawers, Reeded Post, 39 X 41 In. 500.00
Chest, Bowfront, Mahogany, 4 Graduated Drawers, 37 1/2 In. 770.00
Chest, Bridal, Oak, Roycroft, Keyed Tenons, 1912, 26 X 36 In. 6750.00
Chest, Carved Facade, Iron Hinges, English, Oak, 1667, 56 In. 600.00
Chest, Cedar, Chippendale, Mahogany, Carved Fan, Ball & Claw Legs 600.00
Chest, Cherry, 4 Dovetailed Drawers, Reeded Feet, 37 1/2 In. 1150.00
Chest, Cherry, 4 Graduated Drawers, Connecticut, 1780–1800, 35 In. 9350.00
Chest, Cherry, Birds's–Eye Maple, Paw Feet, 6 Drawers, 47 In. 450.00
Chest, Cherry, Curly Maple, 4 Dovetailed Drawers, Pine Top, 47 In. 625.00
Chest, Child's, Brown Paint, Yellow Striping, 5 Drawers, 13 In. 130.00
Chest, Child's, Shaker, Poplar, Red Stain, Watervliet, 1850, 15 In. 900.00
Chest, Chippendale, 4 Cockbeaded Drawers, Maple, 36 In. 2800.00
Chest, Chippendale, 4 Dovetailed Drawers, Bracket Feet, 36 In. 1300.00
Chest, Chippendale, 4 Drawers, Cherry, Bracket Feet, 37 In. 1100.00
Chest, Chippendale, 4 Drawers, Queen Anne Feet, Mahogany 305.00
Chest, Chippendale, 4 Drawers, Walnut, C.1780, 36 X 33 In. 3410.00
Chest, Chippendale, 4 Graduated Drawers, Mahogany, 1780, 32 In. 6500.00
Chest, Chippendale, 4 Overlapping Drawers, Cherry Facade, 36 In. 85.00
Chest, Chippendale, 5 Drawers, Maple, 42 X 19 X 19 In. 3500.00
Chest, Chippendale, 5 Overlapping Drawers, Cherry, 36 X 47 In. 4750.00
Chest, Chippendale, 5 Quarter Sawed Drawers, Oak, Mahogany, Eng. 1250.00
Chest, Chippendale, 6 Graduated Drawers, Cherry, C.1780, 44 In. 4950.00
Chest, Converted To Butler's Desk, Fold–Down, Oak, 38 X 42 In. 550.00
Chest, Dome Top, Oak, Reddish Finish, Dovetailed Case, 26 3/4 In. 70.00
Chest, Dome Top, Tooled Iron Strapping, Pine, 49 In. 200.00
Chest, Dressing, 4 Drawers, Slide In Top Drawer, Mahogany, 31 In. 2475.00
Chest, Empire, 2 Small Top Drawers Over 3 Large Drawers, Walnut 600.00
Chest, Empire, 4 Drawers, Cherry, 42 1/4 X 46 In. 280.00
Chest, Empire, 4 Drawers, Cherry, Curly Maple Banded Drawer, 1830 .... 1050.00
Chest, Empire, 5 Drawers, Rope Twist Pilasters, Cherry, 44 In. 450.00
Chest, Federal, 4 Drawers, Birch, Mahogany, Splashboard, 46 In. 2090.00
Chest, Federal, 4 Drawers, Cherry, Conn., 1800–15, 34 X 42 In. 1650.00

Chest, Federal, 4 Graduated Drawers, Inlaid Mahogany, 37 X 42 In. 3080.00
Chest, Federal, 6 Drawers, Rope Turned Pilasters, Cherry, 95 In. 950.00
Chest, Federal, Bowfront, Cherry, Bird's-Eye Maple, C.1820, 42 In. 3950.00
Chest, Federal, Cherrywood, 8 Drawers, Cornice, 1800s, 64 In. 4180.00
Chest, French Style, 7 Drawers, Marble Top, Walnut, 52 In. 250.00
Chest, George II, 11 Drawers, Burl Walnut, C.1730, 76 In. 9250.00
Chest, George III, 2 Short, 3 Long Drawers, Mahogany, 40 3/4 In. 2000.00
Chest, George III, Mahogany, Crossbanded, Serpentine, 31 X 41 In. 8000.00
Chest, Georgian, 4 Drawers, Mahogany, Inlaid, English, 1830, 32 In. 2500.00
Chest, Hepplewhite, 4 Drawers, Cherry, French Splayed Feet, Apron 2600.00
Chest, Hepplewhite, 4 Drawers, Swirl Front, Mahogany, C.1800 .... 2950.00
Chest, Hepplewhite, 5 Drawers, Banded Inlay, Cherry, 42 1/2 In. 850.00
Chest, Hepplewhite, Mahogany Veneer, Scalloped Apron, 40 1/2 In. 950.00
Chest, Iron Bands, Hinges & Handles, Dated 1854 .... 1400.00
Chest, Lid, Till, Brown Graining, Iron Handles, 34 In. 110.00
Chest, Lift Top, Orange & Brown Design, C.1835, 43 1/2 In. 1400.00
Chest, Lift Top, Roller Graining, 6 Board, Poplar, 42 3/4 In. 700.00
Chest, Lift Top, Till, 6 Board, Tiger Maple, 22 1/2 X 47 In. 4200.00
Chest, Lingerie, Attached Beveled Mirror, Oak 795.00
Chest, Lingerie, Louis XVI, 7 Drawers, Marble Top, Marquetry 700.00
Chest, Louis XV, Bombe, Gilt Bronze, Marble Top 4400.00
Chest, Mule, 1 Drawer, Gray Paint, Miniature 525.00
Chest, Mule, 2 Drawers, Lift Lid, Pine, 40 1/2 X 40 3/4 In. 550.00
Chest, Mule, George III, 2 Drawers, Hinged Cover, Oak, 1760, 43 In. 250.00
Chest, Mule, George III, Hinged Top, Oak, C.1800 .... 850.00
Chest, Mule, Hinged Top Over Paneled Case, C.1750, 48 In. 375.00
Chest, Mule, Pine, Brown Over Yellow Grain Painted, C.1840 .... 1050.00
Chest, Mule, Walnut, Breadboard Lid, Dovetailed Drawer, 47 In. 950.00
Chest, Pine, Oak, Board, Mass., Compass Design, Initials, 1650-1710 .... 1760.00
Chest, Pine, Original Dark Blue Paint, Floral Design, 50 In. 250.00
Chest, Queen Anne, 5 Graduated Drawers, Pine, Red Paint, 40 In. 6000.00
Chest, Red Over Black, Label Maria Kruger, 46 3/4 In. 300.00
Chest, Regency, 3 Drawers, Ebony Inlaid Mahogany, C.1815, 38 In. 4950.00
Chest, Scandinavian, Incised Floral, Painted Flowers, Pine, 36 In. 325.00
Chest, Serpentine Front, Mahogany, Rhode Island, 1780, 32 1/2 In. 4625.00
Chest, Serpentine, 4 Drawers, Floral Design, Ormolu, French, 48 In. 450.00
Chest, Shaker, 3 Drawers, Painted, Sabbathday Lake 3850.00
Chest, Shaker, 3 Drawers, Pine, Grained, Sabbathday, 31 X 36 In. 3500.00
Chest, Shaker, 3 Drawers, Pine, Watervliet, 1850, 33 X 34 In. 800.00
Chest, Sheraton, 4 Drawers, Cherry, Poplar, Cockbeaded, Escutcheons 1095.00
Chest, Sheraton, Cherry, String Inlay, Signed Wm.McCormack, 1820s 1950.00
Chest, Sidelock, 6 Drawers, Inlaid Walnut, Galleried Top 1980.00
Chest, Slide & 4 Graduated Drawers, Mahogany, C.1780, 31 1/2 In. 5500.00
Chest, Spanish, Vine Carved Panels, Chestnut, 17th Century, 28 In. 250.00
Chest, Spice, Raised Panel Door, 12 Drawers, Walnut, 25 1/4 In. 800.00
Chest, Storage, Shaker, Yellow Stain, Hancock, Mass., C.1840 .... 3000.00
Chest, Sugar, Hinged Overhanging Top, Walnut Veneer, 30 3/4 In. 800.00
Chest, Sugar, Walnut Dovetailed Case, String Inlay 2000.00
Chest, Tall, 5 Drawers, Maple, Bracket Foot Base 2000.00
Chest, Tall, 6 Drawers, Bow Sided, Harvey Ellis For Stickley 9500.00
Chest, Tall, 6 Drawers, Door, Spindled Rail, Walnut, 64 X 40 In. 1200.00
Chest, Victorian, 5 Drawers, Carved Crest, Luce Furniture Co., Oak 600.00
Chest, William & Mary, 2 Short, 2 Long Drawers, Oak, C.1700, 28 In. 2750.00
Chest, Wine, Carved, Italian, 18th Century 1750.00
Chest, Yellow Paint, Floral Stencil, Portland, Dated 1821, 15 In. 5500.00
Chest-On-Chest, 8 Drawers, Mahogany, Charleston, S.C., 6 Ft.6 In. 8250.00
Chest-On-Chest, 8 Drawers, Original Brasses, Mahogany, 70 1/2 In. 4400.00
Chest-On-Chest, Beaded Molding, Tiger & Bird's-Eye Maple, 62 In. 3595.00
Chest-On-Chest, Chippendale, Cherry, C.1800, 38 1/4 In. 1100.00
Chest-On-Chest, George III, Mahogany, 1780, 75 X 44 In. ....*Illus* 2800.00
Chest-On-Frame, 2 Drawers, Hinged Top, Black Japanned, 46 In. 1540.00
China Cabinet, Curved Glass, Golden Oak, Small 325.00
China Cabinet, G.Stickley, 1 Glass Pane Door 4500.00
China Cabinet, H.Harris, Ribbon Inlay, Mahogany, 78 1/2 In. 1045.00

China Cabinet, L.& J.G.Stickley, 2 Doors, Oak, C.1912, 5 Ft.10 In. 3575.00
China Cabinet, Oak, 2 Glass Doors, 32 In.Wide 100.00
China Closet, 16 Panes, Gustav Stickley, Signed 4000.00
China Closet, L.& J.G.Stickley, 1 Door, Red Decal, Oak, 54 3/8 In. 4230.00
Coffer, Arched Top, Grain Painted, Scandinavian, Pine, 35 1/2 In. 375.00
Coffer, Carved Oak, Figures, Rosettes, 64 In. ....*Illus* 770.00
Coffer, Jacobean, Carved Paneled Case, Oak, 17th Century, 35 In. 300.00
Commode, 2 Drawers, Shaped Apron, Walnut & Parquetry, 16 In. 385.00
Commode, 3 Drawers, 1 Door, Maple 55.00
Commode, 3 Drawers, Kingwood & Bronze Mounted Parquetry, 36 In. 1300.00
Commode, Bed, Mahogany, White Marble Top, Victorian 340.00
Commode, Bombe, Marble Top, Fruitwood Marquetry, Gilt Bronze 2200.00
Commode, Charles X, Marble Top, Walnut, Bracket Feet, 23 In. 3575.00
Commode, Charles X, Walnut, 3 Drawers, Ormolu, Marble Top, 51 In. 3575.00
Commode, Eastlake, Walnut, Marble Top, 1870 .... 525.00
Commode, Ebonized Wood & Mother-of-Pearl Inlay, J.Leleu, 6 Ft. 7150.00
Commode, Empire, 4 Drawers, Mahogany, Black Marble Top, 37 In. 825.00
Commode, Griffin & Rococo Design, Inlaid Walnut, 52 1/2 In. 2400.00
Commode, Italian Renaissance, 3 Drawers, Walnut, 13 In. 900.00
Commode, Italian Rococo, Walnut, Cabriole Legs, 34 In. 5100.00
Commode, Louis XV, Marble Top, Canted Drawers, Tulipwood, 35 In. 2800.00
Commode, Louis XV, Marble Top, Tulipwood, C.1890, 4 Ft.10 In. 2090.00
Commode, Louis XV, Ormolu Mounted, Marquetry, Marble Top, 46 In. 800.00
Commode, Louis XV, Ormolu, Marquetry, 3 Drawers, 43 In. ....*Illus* 1430.00
Commode, Louis XV-XVI, Violet, Beige Marble Top, C.1900, 34 In. 1900.00
Commode, Louis XVI, Marble Top, Fruitwood, 4 Ft. 3000.00
Commode, Mahogany, Serpentine, Molded Marble Top, American, 36 In. 250.00
Commode, Rococo, 2 Drawers, Walnut, Serpentine, Italy, 34 X 50 In. 5100.00
Commode, Serpentine Top, 4 Long Drawers, Dutch, Mahogany, 32 In. 1200.00
Commode, Shaped Rectangular Top, 2 Drawers, Inlaid Walnut, 36 In. 2090.00
Commode, Walnut Parquetry, 3 Drawers, Italy, 1780 .... 5800.00
Commode, Walnut, 2 Small Over 2 Large Drawers 300.00
Console, Continental, Walnut, Triple Arch Design, Columns, 66 In. 2200.00
Console, Florentine, Carved & Gilded Marble Top, Mirror, 2 Piece 4400.00
Console, Jacobean, Gilded Acanthus Apron, Green Marble, 50 In. 825.00
Console, Louis XVI, Gray Paint, Gilt, Mirror, 2 Piece 4750.00
Console, Louis XVI, White, Black D-Shape Marble Top, 26 In., Pair 900.00
Console, Marble Top, 3 Drawers, Curved Side Doors, 35 3/4 In. 1300.00
Cooler, Wine, Regency, Parcel Gilt & Ebony Inlay, Mahogany, 26 In. 4950.00
Couch, Country, Olive Yellow Upholstery, Round Legs, 77 In. 1600.00
Couch, Fainting, Folds Out To Bed, Eastlake, 1875 .... 475.00
Couch, Hepplewhite, Mahogany, Olive Linsey Woolsey, 78 1/2 In. 2750.00

Furniture, Coffer, Carved Oak, Figures, Rosettes, 64 In.

Cradle, Child's, Renaissance Revival, Carved Walnut 8500.00
Cradle, Country, Dowel Spindles, Original Paint 275.00
Cradle, Double Hood, Pennsylvania, For Twins 895.00
Cradle, High Head & Footboard, Pressed Design, Porcelain Castors 250.00
Cradle, Oak, Rockers, White Porcelain Knobs On Rim, 41 1/2 In. 105.00
Cradle, Pine, Dovetailed, American, 36 In. 135.00
Cradle, Rocking, Sausage Turned Spindles, Walnut 260.00
Cradle, Scalloped Sides, Cherry, 39 In. 125.00
Cradle, Self–Rocking, Victorian, Missouri, Patent 1862 .... 1375.00
Cradle, Stylized Foliage, Iron Fold–Up Hood, Bentwood, 26 1/2 In. 45.00
Cradle, Wicker, Heywood–Wakefield 675.00
Cradle, Windsor, Reddish–Brown Paint, C.1830 .... 2500.00
Credenza, Frieze Drawer Over Cupboard Doors, Walnut, 39 1/2 In. 7500.00
Credenza, Italian Baroque, Walnut, Crossbanded Top, 36 In. 8200.00
Credenza, Italian Baroque, Walnut, Serpentine, Crossbanded, 52 In. 8200.00
Credenza, Recessed Shelf, Mirrored Back, Rosewood, 53 In. 2100.00
Crib, Lower Enclosed Base For Heated Brick, Pine, 30 In. 250.00
Cupboard & Side Cupboard, Shaker, Butternut, Enfield, 8 Ft.6 In. 6000.00
Cupboard, 1 Door, Drawer, Shelves, Painted, Scandinavia, 29 1/2 In. 1400.00
Cupboard, 1 Panel Hinged Door, Red & Grained Pine, 26 3/4 In. 600.00
Cupboard, 2 Glass & 2 Wooden Doors, Shelf, Wisc.German, 1840s 1395.00
Cupboard, 2 Piece, Pine, Poplar, 12 Panes Glass, Red Paint, 89 In. 1250.00
Cupboard, 4 Doors, Red Wash, Traces of Graining, 2 Piece 3200.00
Cupboard, Bedside, 1 Flap, Divided Interior, Mahogany, 28 1/2 In. 2100.00
Cupboard, Bedside, Tambour Slide, Hand Holds, Mahogany, 31 1/4 In. 2850.00
Cupboard, Brown Over Yellow Graining, 12 Pane, C.1840, 2 Piece 2300.00
Cupboard, Built–In–Wall, Yellow Grained, Door, Pine, 78 In. 80.00
Cupboard, Cape Breton, 3 Open Shelves, 4 Doors, 1 Piece 7500.00
Cupboard, Carved Frieze, Drawers, Bird's–Eye Maple, 82 3/4 In. 1200.00
Cupboard, Child's, Primitive, Butternut, White Paint Trace, 24 In. 105.00
Cupboard, Chimney, Blue, 2 Doors 650.00
Cupboard, Chimney, New Hampshire, 1875, 5 1/2 Ft. 695.00
Cupboard, Chimney, Pine, Raised Panel, 2 In.Sides, New Eng., 1830 .... 675.00
Cupboard, Clothes, Pine, 1 Door, Red 500.00
Cupboard, Corner, 2 Drawers, 8 Panes On Door, Cherry, 83 1/2 In. 1700.00
Cupboard, Corner, 2 Drawers, Walnut, Paneled Doors, 81 1/4 In. 1100.00
Cupboard, Corner, 3 Drawers, Softwood, Spoon Holders, 2 Piece 2000.00
Cupboard, Corner, 4 Doors, Paneled, Cream Over Blue Paint 2700.00
Cupboard, Corner, 12 Pane Door, Pie Shelf, 2 Drawers, Walnut 5610.00
Cupboard, Corner, 12 Pane Glass Doors, Virginia, Walnut, 1820 .... 2000.00
Cupboard, Corner, 12 Panes In Top Door, 2 Blind Doors, Cherry 4500.00
Cupboard, Corner, Blind Bottom Doors, Glass On Top, Walnut, 1840 .... 4000.00
Cupboard, Corner, Cherry, W.Penna, C.1810, 7 Ft.8 In., 1 Piece 6500.00
Cupboard, Corner, Cherry, Walnut, 4 Doors, 2 Drawers 1700.00
Cupboard, Corner, Chippendale, Cherry, Hanging, Penna., 1790, 45 In. 6500.00
Cupboard, Corner, Chippendale, Inlaid Walnut, C.1780, 7 Ft.6 In. 5775.00
Cupboard, Corner, Graining, Paneled Doors, Poplar, 82 3/4 In. 1350.00
Cupboard, Corner, Hanging, Double Doors, Pine, 44 X 31 1/2 In. 275.00
Cupboard, Corner, Paladin Glass Doors, Bonnet Top, 42 In. 575.00
Cupboard, Corner, Paneled Doors, Cornice, Cherry, 76 1/2 In. 650.00
Cupboard, Corner, Pie Shelf, Single Board Door, Poplar, 72 In. 300.00
Cupboard, Corner, Poplar, 2 Glass Paned Doors, 2 Doors, 86 In. 875.00
Cupboard, Corner, Walnut, Blind Door, Framed Molding, S.Va., C.1830 .... 3500.00
Cupboard, Court, Carved Pilasters, Acanthus Scrolls, 44 In. 750.00
Cupboard, Dutch, Blind Door, Green Paint, 2 Piece 5000.00
Cupboard, Figural Cornice, Pierced Cabinets, Teakwood, 83 In. 385.00
Cupboard, Hoosier Top, Oak, 4 Glazed Doors, 48 In. 330.00
Cupboard, Hoosier, Oak, White Shelf, Gray Graniteware Edge 525.00
Cupboard, Jacobean Style, Carved Lion Masks, 2 Doors, Oak, 71 In. 700.00
Cupboard, Jam, Batten Door, Original Blue Paint 450.00
Cupboard, Jelly, 1 Board Doors, Old Red Paint, Poplar, 33 X 36 In. 400.00
Cupboard, Jelly, Brown Graining Over Paint, Board Doors, 55 In. 275.00
Cupboard, Jelly, Brown Graining, Batten Doors, 75 1/2 In. 375.00
Cupboard, Jelly, Butternut, 1 Door, 54 X 41 In. 300.00

Cupboard, Jelly, Cast Iron Thumb Catch, Pine, 34 1/2 In. 450.00
Cupboard, Jelly, Pennsylvania, Brown–Red Graining, 2 Doors 2100.00
Cupboard, Jelly, Pine, Brown Patina, Double Doors, 55 3/4 In. 550.00
Cupboard, Jelly, Pine, Green Repaint, Cutout Feet, 2 Doors, 58 In. 1200.00
Cupboard, Jelly, Red Paint, 1 Door, Gallery, Small 1900.00
Cupboard, Jelly, Single Board Doors, Green Paint, Poplar, 36 In. 200.00
Cupboard, Jelly, Yellow Paint, Board & Batten Door, Poplar, 62 In. 400.00
Cupboard, Kitchen, 3 Frosted Glass Doors, Porcelain Work Top 640.00
Cupboard, Kitchen, 4 Doors, 2 Drawers, Spoon Carved Oak 475.00
Cupboard, Kitchen, Punched Tin Doors, Sides, 2 Lower Doors, 1 Pc. 215.00
Cupboard, Oak, French, 72 X 44 In. ....*Illus* 1540.00
Cupboard, Open Top, Molded Cornice, English, Oak, 74 1/2 In., 2 Pc. 1900.00
Cupboard, Paneled Doors, 3 Drawers, Pine & Poplar, 90 In. 1000.00
Cupboard, Paneled Doors, Drawers, Pie Shelf, Poplar, 85 1/4 In. 1500.00
Cupboard, Pewter, 3 Shelves, 4 Bottom Doors, New England, C.1800 .... 4250.00
Cupboard, Pewter, Cape Breton, Double Step Back, Open Top 1600.00
Cupboard, Pewter, Open Faced, New England, Pine, C.1780, 65 5/8 In. 2800.00
Cupboard, Pewter, Red Paint, Black Stained Top, Poplar, 59 1/4 In. 1000.00
Cupboard, Pine, Mirror In Top Door, White Paint, 31 X 15 X 7 In. 29.00
Cupboard, Pine, Poplar, 4 Paneled Doors, 45 X 88 In., 2 Piece 1425.00
Cupboard, Pine, Raised Panels, 4 Doors, Virginia, C.1840 .... 1850.00
Cupboard, Poplar, Walnut, 1 Paneled Door, Base Drawer, 1847, 58 In. 2600.00
Cupboard, Queen Anne, 2 Tombstone Paneled Doors, Yellow Paint 425.00
Cupboard, Shaker, Hanging, Pine, Stained, North Family, 1850, 27 In. 6000.00
Cupboard, Shaker, Pine, 4 Door, Hancock, 1860, 5 1/2 X 3 1/2 Ft. 1000.00
Cupboard, Shaker, Pine, Red Stain, Tyringham, C.1840, 43 1/2 In. 1750.00
Cupboard, Single Paneled Door, Painted Pine, 36 X 19 1/2 In. 375.00
Cupboard, Step Back, Blue Paint, C.1830, 79 X 48 In. 2800.00
Cupboard, Step Back, Chamfered Drawers, Front Molding, C.1800 .... 4600.00
Cupboard, Step Back, Kitchen, 4 Doors, 5 Small Center Drawers 600.00
Cupboard, Step Back, Oak, 92 In. 725.00
Cupboard, Step Back, Pine, 2 Paned Glass Doors, 2 Drawers, 85 In. 2700.00
Cupboard, Step Back, Pine, Butterprint Design, Refinished, 2 Piece 1200.00
Cupboard, Step Back, Walnut, 2 Glass Doors, 2 Blind Doors, 92 In. 1075.00
Cupboard, Step Back, Walnut, Poplar, Refinished, 2 Piece 2000.00
Cupboard, Storage, Japanese, Cedar & Pine, C.1860 .... 850.00
Cupboard, Walnut & Poplar, Double Raised Paneled Doors, 1830 .... 3200.00
Cupboard, Walnut, American, Gallery Top, 2 Drawers, 45 X 40 In. 375.00
Cupboard, Walnut, Paneled Doors, 2 Drawers, 79 3/4 In. 1000.00
Cupboard, Walnut, Raised Paneled Doors, Pennsylvania, 1 Piece 3650.00
Cupboard, Water, Green Over Red, Missouri, Mid–19th Century 725.00
Cupboard, Yellow, Grain Painted, 2 Glass Pane Doors, 19th Century 1650.00
Cupboard, Zoar Type, Blue Paint Traces, 4 Drawers, 1 Side Door 1150.00
Daybed, Federal, Cherry, Sleigh Type 470.00
Daybed, Iron, Converts To Full Bed 4.00
Desk Bookcase, Fold–Out Writing Surface, Mahogany, 70 1/2 In. 4000.00
Desk Table, Boudoir, Mahogany, Rope Turned Legs, 2 Drawers 1050.00
Desk, Artist's, Adjustable Swivel Seat, Slant Top, Maple, 42 In. 275.00
Desk, Arts & Crafts Style, Kimbel, Slant Lid 3355.00
Desk, Black Glass Top, French, Rosewood, C.1930, 6 Ft.1/2 In. 1760.00
Desk, Bookeeper's, Walnut, 2 Drawers, Turned Legs 180.00
Desk, Bookkeeper's, Lift Lid, 1 Drawer, Cherry, 52 X 25 1/4 In. 600.00
Desk, Butler's, Biedermeier, Fruitwood, 4 Drawers, 36 X 50 In. 1700.00
Desk, Butler's, Empire, Cherry, Mahogany Facade, 49 X X 47 In. 375.00
Desk, Butler's, Empire, Curly Maple, Drop Lid, 2 Bottom Drawers 700.00
Desk, Butler's, Georgian, 3 Graduated Drawers, Mid–19th Century 1500.00
Desk, Campaign, Folding, C.1860 .... 770.00
Desk, Campaign–Dressing Table, Mahogany, Kneehole, England, C.1780 .... 2950.00
Desk, Chalet, Gustav Stickley, Gallery, Keyed Tenon Sides, 46 In. 1600.00
Desk, Chippendale, 9 Drawers, Leather Top, Mahogany, 59 In. 1900.00
Desk, Chippendale, Ball & Claw Feet, Bill of Sale, 1927, English 1100.00
Desk, Chippendale, Oxbow Form, Mahogany, Original Brasses, 41 In. 5850.00
Desk, Chippendale, Slant Front, Walnut, Maple, Bracket Feet, 40 In. 6600.00
Desk, Colonial Revival, Slant Front, Walnut, 1860–75 .... 875.00

Furniture, Desk, Roll Top, Mahogany,
3/4 Galleried Top, 1845

Furniture, Desk, Slant Front, Chippendale,
Cherry, 36 In.

Desk, Covered In Python Skin, Carl Sringer 2400.00
Desk, Cylinder Roll, Renaissance Revival, Walnut & Burl 2850.00
Desk, Cylinder, Eastlake, Walnut, C.1882 .... 2300.00
Desk, Dark Cherry, 17 Drawers, Tall 825.00
Desk, Dark Patina, Primitive, Table Top, 15 1/2 In. 55.00
Desk, Double Sided, Brass Mounts, Mahogany Veneer, 48 X 36 In. 385.00
Desk, Drafting, Oak, 4 Drawers 150.00
Desk, Gentleman's, Slant Lid, Chippendale, Mahogany, N.Y., 48 In. 1250.00
Desk, George II, Fitted Interior, 4 Drawers, Walnut, C.1740, 40 In. 4300.00
Desk, George II, Walnut, Slant Front, 6 Drawers, C.1750, 40 In. 1800.00
Desk, Georgian, Slant Lid, Mahogany, 5 Banded Drawers, 28 In. 2900.00
Desk, Glass Doors, Trestle Base, Carved Mahogany, 2 Piece 412.00
Desk, Gustav Stickley, Fall Front, Oak, C.1910, 45 X 36 In. 2475.00
Desk, Gustav Stickley, Leather Top, Brass Tacks, Kneehole, 47 In. 1000.00
Desk, Gustav Stickley, Letter Rack, Decal, Oak, C.1901, 34 N. 4595.00
Desk, Hepplewhite, Slant Front, Walnut Inlay, French Feet, 35 In. 4000.00
Desk, Inlay On Drawers, Dovetailed Case, Dated 1800, 30 In. 4200.00
Desk, Lady's, Mahogany, Curved Lid, Compartmented Interior, 34 In. 2800.00
Desk, Lady's, Slant Front, Roycroft, Drawer, Club Feet, 44 X 39 In. 1800.00
Desk, Lap, Campaign Style, English, Mahogany, C.1830 .... 310.00
Desk, Lap, Fitted, Brass Corners, Walnut Burl, 6 X 13 X 9 In. 95.00
Desk, Lap, Mother-of-Pearl Inlay, Key, Fitted, Mahogany, 1800s 70.00
Desk, Lap, Papier-Mache & Mother-of-Pearl Flowers, C.1850 .... 225.00
Desk, Lap, Papier-Mache & Mother-of-Pearl, Mid-19th Century 195.00
Desk, Larkin, Mission Style, Oak, Green Leaded Glass Doors 275.00
Desk, Library, Eastlake, Leather Top, Apron, Scalloped Corners 500.00
Desk, Library, Hartman, Fumed Oak, C.1900 .... 350.00
Desk, Library, Mahogany, Shaped Gallery, Inlaid, England, 1875 .... 2250.00
Desk, Louis XV, Inlaid Cylinder, Gilt Bronze Mounted 6000.00
Desk, Louis XV, Walnut, Open Compartment, Cabriole Legs, 43 In. 1600.00
Desk, Mahogany, Secretary, Secret Sections, Schuylerville, 1867 .... 715.00
Desk, Northwind, Mahogany, C.1890 .... 1430.00
Desk, Paolo Barracchi, Yew & Palisander, 6 Ft.6 In. 1650.00
Desk, Partners', Gilt Leather Surface, 2 Pedestals, 4 Ft.9 In. 7150.00
Desk, Partners', Hepplewhite, Inlaid Mahogany, 30 1/2 X 48 In. 275.00
Desk, Partners', Mahogany, Cabriole Legs, Spanish Foot, 1920 .... 550.00
Desk, Partners', Oak, 42 X 54 In. 100.00
Desk, Partners', Sheraton Style, 1920 .... 1200.00
Desk, Pedestal, Georgian, Mahogany, Leather Top, English, 51 In. 6500.00
Desk, Plantation, Curly Maple, C.1850 .... 1600.00
Desk, Plantation, Oak, Pegged, Turned Legs, Late 19th Century 1500.00
Desk, Post Office, 104 Holes, C.1900 .... 1000.00
Desk, Postal Gallery, Gustav Stickley 1400.00
Desk, Queen Anne, Maple, Chestnut, Stepped Interior, R.I., 1760 .... 9200.00
Desk, Roll Top, C Roll, Oak, With Oak Chair 350.00
Desk, Roll Top, Eastlake 450.00
Desk, Roll Top, Mahogany, 3/4 Galleried Top, 1845 ....*Illus* 550.00
Desk, Roll Top, Oak, Swivel Chair 159.50

Desk, Roll Top, Pigeonholes, Oak, 54 In. 950.00
Desk, Roll Top, S Roll, Bird's–Eye Maple Interior, Oak, 60 In. 4500.00
Desk, Roll Top, S Roll, Cherry, Double Pedestal, 50 In. 850.00
Desk, Roll Top, S Roll, Oak, 8 Drawers 1400.00
Desk, Roll Top, S Roll, Quarter Sawn Oak, Tiger Stripe, 48 In. 1850.00
Desk, Roll Top, Secretary, Oak, Carved Door 1550.00
Desk, Schoolmaster's, Chestnut, Lift Front, 1 Drawer 110.00
Desk, Schoolmaster's, Hepplewhite, New England 995.00
Desk, Schoolmaster's, Slant Top Lid, Gray On Red, Pine, 44 3/4 In. 250.00
Desk, Sewing, Shaker, Child's, Walnut, Poplar, 1850, 31 X 23 In. 2200.00
Desk, Sewing, Shaker, Pine, 3 Side Drawers, C.1830, 32 1/2 In. 3250.00
Desk, Shaker, Trustee's, Poplar, Birch, 2 Drawer, 1840, 46 X 37 In. 2000.00
Desk, Sheraton, Yellow Birch, Drop Leaf, Top Door, 1810 .... 5700.00
Desk, Slant Front, 4 Drawers, Fitted Interior, Cherry, 43 In. 1900.00
Desk, Slant Front, 7 Interior Drawers, Hardwood, 42 1/4 In. 2200.00
Desk, Slant Front, Black Japanned, Fitted Interior, 39 X 22 In. 825.00
Desk, Slant Front, Chippendale, Birch, Massachusetts 6275.00
Desk, Slant Front, Chippendale, Cherry, 36 In. ....*Illus* 3520.00
Desk, Slant Front, Chippendale, Curly Maple, Bracket Feet, 41 In. 3500.00
Desk, Slant Front, Chippendale, Stained Maple, 40 X 24 In. 3025.00
Desk, Slant Front, Fall Front, Mahogany Interior, Cherry, C.1780 .... 3500.00
Desk, Slant Front, George II, Mahogany, 6 Drawers, C.1750, 40 In. 1700.00
Desk, Slant Front, Hepplewhite, Curly Maple, Penna., 1790–1810 .... 7400.00
Desk, Slant Front, Mahogany, Chippendale, 18th Century, 39 3/4 In. 4950.00
Desk, Slant Front, Maple & Tiger Maple, C.1790 .... 7500.00
Desk, Slant Front, Maple, Walnut Faced, Fitted, 6 Drawers, 47 In. 1000.00
Desk, Slant Front, Ship Chandler's, Pine 600.00
Desk, Slant Front, Tiger Maple, Bracket Feet, 1780, 41 X 36 In. 4500.00
Desk, Slant Front, Valanced Compartments, Mahogany, C.1790 .... 2800.00
Desk, Slant Front, Walnut, Ohio, 1820 .... 3800.00
Desk, Slant Front, Walnut, Tiger Maple, Lancaster Co., Dated 1810 .... 2800.00
Desk, Slant Front, Wavy Birch & Tiger Maple, 41 X 36 In. 2000.00
Desk, Slant Front, William & Mary, Pine, Maple, Red, 1710–25, 34 In. 6000.00
Desk, Spool, Oak, Back Shelves, Inkwell, Pencil Stand, 1900s, 30 In. 395.00
Desk, Usonian, Frank Lloyd Wright, With Chair 6600.00
Desk, Walnut, L Shape, Pullout, Compartment, Moore 6160.00
Desk, Wicker, Full Skirt, Gallery 625.00
Desk, Wicker, Kneehole, Glass Top, 5 Ft. 395.00
Desk, Wooton Rotary, Walnut, 60 X 33 X 31 In. .... 1700.00 To 3900.00
Desk–On–Frame, Lift Slant Lid, Fitted, Cherry, C.1810, 47 In. 600.00
Dining Set, Heritage Herendon Furn.Co., Leather Seat, 1956, 7 Pc. 6600.00
Dining Set, Jacobean, Oak, Turned Legs, 2 Armchairs, 9 Piece 650.00
Dining Set, L.& J.G.Stickley, Round Table, 6 Chairs 650.00
Dining Set, Lion's Heads, Claw Feet, Round Table, Oak, 11 Piece 6500.00
Dining Set, Mission, Quarter Sawn Oak, 6 Chairs, 102 X 54 In. 1500.00
Dresser, 2 Drawers, Oak, Carving Over Swing Mirror, Hatbox 525.00
Dresser, 3 Drawers, Eastlake, Marble Top, Burled 240.00
Dresser, 3 Drawers, Victorian, Spoon Carving, Square Mirror 125.00
Dresser, 4 Drawers, Gustav Stickley, Harvey Ellis Design 3750.00
Dresser, Arched Cornice, Mirror, Marble Top, Walnut, C.1870, 95 In. 450.00
Dresser, Bamboo Mirror, Cherry, Mahogany, 3 Drawers 600.00
Dresser, Carved Walnut, Marble Top, Mirror, Crest ....*Illus* 8800.00
Dresser, Cottage, Renaissance Revival, Pine, Yellow Paint, 1860–70 .... 595.00
Dresser, L.& J.G.Stickley, 2 Top & 2 Bottom Drawers, Mirror 2420.00
Dresser, Princess, 5 Drawers, Oak, Serpentine, Wishbone Mirror 160.00
Dresser, Princess, Mahogany, Drop Front, Tall Mirror 275.00
Dresser, Victorian, White Marble Top, Carved Pulls 875.00
Dry Sink, 2 Doors, West Virginia, Original Green Paint 850.00
Dry Sink, Child's, Gray Paint, Over Mustard, Zinc Liner 860.00
Dry Sink, Child's, Pine, 16 X 18 In. 250.00
Dry Sink, Child's, Scraped To Original Paint, 23 X 32 In. 610.00
Dry Sink, Double Door, High Back, Oak 450.00
Dry Sink, Hutch, Poplar, Walnut, Copper, Scalloped Doors, N.C., 1850 .... 2750.00
Dry Sink, Pine, Basswood Panels, Red Paint, C.1870, 33 X 49 In. 3200.00

Dry Sink, Pine, Gallery, 3 Drawers, Cutout Feet, Moravian 2400.00
Dry Sink, Pine, Mortised & Pinned, Turned Feet, 2 Drawers, Penna. 795.00
Dry Sink, Poplar, 43 X 43 1/2 In. 385.00
Dry Sink, Poplar, Red, Cutout Feet, 2 Doors, '48, 48 X 36 In. 2100.00
Dry Sink, Recessed Top, 1 Drawer, Cupboard, Grained & Painted 650.00
Dry Sink, Small Drawer, Paneled Doors, Pine & Poplar, 48 1/2 In. 600.00
Dumbwaiter, George III, Tripod Base, Mahogany, 29 X 23 1/2 In. 175.00
Etagere, Belter, Rosewood 4000.00
Etagere, Cabinet Base, Marble, 9 Mirrors, Rosewood, 8 Ft.8 In. 6500.00
Etagere, George III, Brass Supports, Mahogany, 34 In. 990.00
Etagere, Roux, New York 9350.00
Etagere, Sheraton, Turned Columns, English, Mahogany 750.00
Etagere, Walnut, Turned Columns, 64 1/2 In., Pair 700.00
Fauteuil, Beechwood, Italian Neoclassical, Oval Back, Bowed Seat 550.00
Fauteuil, Louis XV, Shield Back, Cabriole Legs, Gilded, Upholstery 1000.00
Fauteuil, Louis XVI, Beechwood, Upholstered, Bowed Seat, 36 In. 500.00
Fauteuil, Louis XVI, Upholstered Back, Bowed Seat, 35 1/2 In. 450.00
File, Letter, 3 Stacking Sections, 36 Drawers, Brass Pulls, 56 In. 375.00
Flower Cart, Wicker 375.00
Footstool, Bamboo, English 50.00
Footstool, Cast Iron, Red Velvet Cover 65.00
Footstool, Extended Corner Posts, Upholstered, Roycroft, 1912 .... 325.00
Footstool, Federal, Slip Seat, Carved Mahogany, C.1810 .... 4675.00
Footstool, Gustav Stickley, Leather, Dark Finish, 1902–04, 17 In. 300.00
Footstool, Gustav Stickley, Painted, Original Tacks & Leather 950.00
Footstool, Gustav Stickley, Rush Seat, C.1907, 17 1/2 In. 650.00
Footstool, Horseshoe Shape, Words Put Your Feet Here On Top 80.00
Footstool, L.& J.G.Stickley, Leather Cover, Oak, C.1910, 16 In. 720.00
Footstool, L.& J.G.Stickley, Upholstered, Arched Seat Rail, 1912 .... 400.00
Footstool, Painted Brown, Stenciled Vine, Flowerhead, 5 X 13 In. 225.00
Footstool, Poplar, Worn Dark Finish, Scalloped, 8 X 14 3/4 In. 110.00
Footstool, Scalloped, Walnut, 7 1/4 X 8 3/4 X 16 In. 75.00
Footstool, Shaker, Maple, Rush Seat, 9 1/2 X 13 In. 500.00
Footstool, Shaker, Tripod, Yellow Stain, Leather Seat 5500.00
Footstool, Shell Carving On Knees, Slipper Feet, Upholstered 175.00
Footstool, Steer Horn 12.00
Footstool, Victorian, S.Allman, Upholstered 300.00
Footstool, Walnut, Needlepoint Floral Design, Turquoise, 1920 .... 350.00
Footstool, William IV, Box, Mahogany, C.1830 .... 305.00
Footstool, Windsor, Bamboo Legs, Black Repaint, Oilcloth, 10 In. 175.00
Footstool, Windsor, Oval Top, Splayed Turned Legs, 7 X 12 In. 45.00
Footstool, Windsor, Red Paint Over Black, Upholstered Oval Top 30.00

Furniture, Dresser, Carved
Walnut, Marble Top,
Mirror, Crest

Furniture, Highboy, Oak,
2 Short, 3 Long Drawers
On Top, 63 In.

Furniture, Lowboy,
Queen Anne, Burled Walnut,
28 In.

Frame, ABC's, Numbers, Vases, Flowers, Dated 1888, 16 X 20 1/2 In. 295.00
Frame, Picture, Victorian, Carved Walnut, Leaf, 39 X 33 In., Pair 400.00
Frame, Shadow Box, Ebony & Gilded Trim, Walnut, 32 X 37 In. 200.00
Garden Seat, Scrolled Crest, Vine & Flower, Iron, 32 In. 200.00
Garden Set, Fern Pattern, Iron, Settee & 2 Chairs 3300.00
Hall Stand, Beveled Mirror, 9 Pegs, Umbrella Holder, Bamboo, 38 In 700.00
Hall Stand, Beveled Mirror, Original Hooks, Brass Trim, Oak 795.00
Hall Stand, Beveled Mirrors, Side Umbrella Holders, Mahogany 2250.00
Hall Stand, Birds, Floral, Bamboo, Japanned, Mirror, English, 76 In. 500.00
Hall Stand, Glove Box, Beveled Mirror, Oak 300.00
Hall Stand, Gothic, Oak 2420.00
Hall Stand, High Back, Carved, Oak 700.00
Hall Stand, Mirror, Bronze Foliate Coat Hooks, Oak, 91 X 53 In. 2300.00
Hall Stand, Mirror, Umbrella Supports, Walnut, C.1870, 94 In. 600.00
Hall Stand, Oak, Fancy Hooks, Beveled Mirror, Narrow 500.00
Hall Stand, Umbrella Holder, Mirror, Walnut, 7 Ft.6 In. 850.00
Hall Stand, Victorian, Lift Top, Oak, Mirror 385.00
Hall Stand, Walnut, Brass Hardware, Mirror, Arms 800.00
Hall Tree, Mahogany, Fluted, Acanthus Shaft, Hairy Paw Feet, 75 In 225.00
Hamper, Hinged Lid, Wooden Spring Catch, Wicker, 31 X 24 X 21 In. 25.00
Hat Rack, Wall, Bentwood 45.00
Headboard, Jacobean, Recessed Panels, Geometric Inlay, Oak, 60 In. 1450.00
High Chair, Bentwood, Caned Seat & Back, Tray 175.00
High Chair, Bentwood, Kohn Wein 165.00
High Chair, Bentwood, Oak, 1890 .... 195.00
High Chair, Captain's Chair Back, 29 In. 85.00
High Chair, G.Stickley, 8 Spindles, Hinged Tray, Decal, Oak, C.1904 .... 935.00
High Chair, Pressed Back, Spindle Arms & Back, Wooden Tray 80.00
High Chair, Shaker Style, 2 Slats, C.1880, 35 1/2 In. 400.00
High Chair, Spindle Back, Bent Arms, Footrest, No Tray 95.00
High Chair, Top Folds Down, Becomes Walker, Hardwood, English 225.00
Highboy, 4 Graduated Drawers, Drop Pendants, Walnut, C.1760 .... 6000.00
Highboy, 5 Drawers, Trumpet Legs, Maple & Pine, 59 3/4 In. 1900.00
Highboy, Chippendale, 8 Drawers, Walnut, Pennsylvania, 5 Ft.8 In. 7425.00
Highboy, Chippendale, Figured Curly Maple, Miniature 8800.00
Highboy, Compass Star Inlay, Scalloped Skirt 5250.00
Highboy, Maple, 5 Graduated Top Drawers, 3 Bottom Drawers, C.1800 .... 6800.00
Highboy, Oak, 2 Short, 3 Long Drawers On Top, 63 In. ....*Illus* 2200.00
Highboy, Queen Anne, 4 Graduated Drawers, Tiger Maple, C.1770 .... 7000.00
Highboy, Queen Anne, Mahogany Veneer & Mahogany, 78 1/2 In. 1200.00
Highboy, Queen Anne, Walnut, New England, C.1740 .... 6500.00
Highboy, Short Fan–Carved Drawer, Lower Drawers, Cherry, 67 In. 4250.00
Highboy, Short, Long Drawers, Painted Tiger Maple, C.1730, 62 In. 3300.00
Highboy, Walnut, 10 Dovetailed Drawers, Bonnet Top, 39 X 15 In. 4900.00
Highboy, William & Mary, 5 Drawers, Maple, C.1730, 39 X 39 In. 1200.00
Highboy, William & Mary, Trumpet Legs, Bun Feet, Pine, 5 Ft.7 In. 2300.00
Huntboard, Poplar, 2 Drawers, 43 X 58 In. 3500.00
Huntboard, Walnut Top, Pine Sides, Cherry Legs, S.C., C.1880 .... 4500.00
Huntboard, Walnut, Pine, 3 Drawers, C.1820 .... 4800.00
Hutch, Wall, 5 Tier, White Paint, Blue Trim, 22 X 16 1/2 In. 125.00
Hutch, Wall, Side Drop Leaves, 1 Drawer, Oak, 1920s, 57 X 30 In. 250.00
Ice Cream Set, Marble Top Table, 3 Piece 80.00
Ice Cream Set, Twisted Wire Legs, Oak Top Table, 5 Piece 225.00
Icebox, Chestnut, American, 47 In. 220.00
Icebox, Oak, 2 Doors, Refinished 625.00
Icebox, Oak, Hudson, Lift Top, Front Door 360.00
Icebox, Oak, Lift Top, 1 Drawer 205.00
Icebox, Oak, Snow White, Lift Top, 1 Door, Small 360.00
Kas, Walnut, Center Door Pull, Interior Wooden Hooks, Zoar, 6 Ft. 3800.00
Lectern, Trefoil, Bird's–Eye Maple Column, Cherry, 35 1/4 In. 1000.00
Library Steps, Armchair, Caned Seat, 6 Steps, Mahogany, C.1820 .... 6050.00
Library Steps, Chair, Metamorphic, Regency, Mahogany, C.1820 .... 2750.00
Library Steps, Federal, Topform Feet, Maple & Pine, 21 In. 1325.00
Linen Press, Chippendale, Connecticut Valley 5500.00

Linen Press, George III, Mahogany, Mahogany Veneer, C.1840 .... 2200.00
Linen Press, Inlaid Doors, Inner Slides, Mahogany, C.1800, 80 In. 5500.00
Linen Press, Lower 4 Drawers, Cupboard Top, Original Brasses 4250.00
Linen Press, Oval Inlaid Doors, 4 Drawers, Mahogany, 6 Ft.4 In. 4400.00
Love Seat, 3 Flower Carved Crests, Walnut 475.00
Love Seat, Empire, Feather Carving, Shiny Mauve Upholstery 2400.00
Love Seat, Louis XV, Down Filled Seat, C.1890 .... 1350.00
Love Seat, Rosalie Pattern, Upholstered, Belter Style 4400.00
Love Seat, Victorian, Shaped Back, Walnut, 5 1/2 Ft. 523.00
Love Seat, Wicker, White Paint, Pink & Green Cushion, 70 In. 715.00
Lowboy, Chippendale, Mahogany, 3 Drawers, English, 16 X 32 In. 1200.00
Lowboy, Queen Anne, 1 Long, 3 Short Drawers, Mahogany, 29 In. 495.00
Lowboy, Queen Anne, Burled Walnut, 28 In. ....*Illus* 2750.00
Lowboy, Queen Anne, Fan Carved Center Drawer, Cherry, 31 1/2 In. 600.00
Lowboy, Queen Anne, Inlaid Top, 3 Drawers, Walnut, C.1785, 28 In. 2500.00
Lowboy, William & Mary, Walnut Burl Veneer On Pine, 32 In. 1400.00
Magazine Stand, Limbert, 3 Shelves 1045.00
Magazine Stand, Limbert, Cutout 650.00
Meridienne, Rosewood, J.H.Belter, Upholstered 5600.00
Mirror, 1/2 Column Frame, Reverse Painted Glass, 31 X 15 1/4 In. 150.00
Mirror, Adjustable, Cast Iron Floral Frame, 16 3/4 In. 65.00
Mirror, American Chippendale, Old Red Paint, 18 X 9 In. 2100.00
Mirror, Baroque, Gilt Wood, Beaded Molding, Scrolls, 54 In., Pair 7000.00
Mirror, Beaded & Leaftip Edge, Top Medallion, Gilt, 30 X 14 In. 495.00
Mirror, Beaded Frame, Urn Pedestal, Gilt Wood, 4 Ft.2 In., Pair 44500.00
Mirror, Beveled Glass, Quatrefoil Frame, 18 1/2 X 20 In., Pair 230.00
Mirror, Brass Rosettes, Reverse Glass Painting of Girl, 35 In. 105.00
Mirror, Carved & Gilded Phoenix, Mahogany, 37 1/4 X 18 1/4 In. 1200.00
Mirror, Carved Crests, Black & Gold, 9 1/2 X 17 In. 95.00
Mirror, Carved Pilasters, Brass Rosettes, Mahogany, 28 1/4 In. 150.00
Mirror, Carved Prince of Wales Feathers, 26 1/4 X 14 In. 225.00
Mirror, Center Beveled Panel, Engraved Frame, 37 1/2 X 39 In. 625.00
Mirror, Cheval, Beveled, Mahogany Lyre Frame, Oval, 68 In. 300.00
Mirror, Cheval, Mahogany, Swivels In Wishbone Clawfoot Stand 1500.00
Mirror, Chippendale Style, Gilded Phoenix, 20th Century, 36 In. 100.00
Mirror, Chippendale, Benjamin Randolf, Mahogany, 5 Ft.3 In. 6875.00
Mirror, Chippendale, Gesso Eagle, Mahogany, 26 X 14 3/4 In. 175.00
Mirror, Chippendale, Gilded Liner, Mahogany, Pine, 22 1/4 X 42 In. 600.00
Mirror, Chippendale, Gilded Liner, Side Draperies, 43 1/4 In. 500.00
Mirror, Chippendale, Gold Leaf, Carved Ho–Ho Birds, 76 In. 825.00
Mirror, Chippendale, Inlaid Mahogany, C.1780, 38 X 19 1/2 In. 3190.00
Mirror, Chippendale, Mahogany Frame, Gilt Florals, 4 Ft.X 25 In. 3850.00
Mirror, Chippendale, Mahogany On Pine, 14 1/2 X 24 1/2 In. 150.00
Mirror, Chippendale, Mahogany, Inlaid Border, 28 1/2 In. 200.00
Mirror, Chippendale, Mahogany, Scroll, Molded Frame, 12 X 20 In. 375.00
Mirror, Chippendale, Scroll, Beveled, Mahogany Veneer, 38 1/2 In. 215.00
Mirror, Chippendale, Scroll, Molded Frame, 11 3/4 X 10 3/4 In. 150.00
Mirror, Chippendale, Walnut & Parcel Gilt, 43 X 25 In. 2475.00
Mirror, Classical, Giltwood Eagle, Mahogany, 32 1/2 X 19 In. 247.00
Mirror, Convex, Gilded, Doe Finial Top, Candle Arms 200.00
Mirror, Convex, Molded Frame, Gilding, 17 1/2 In. 95.00
Mirror, Cornucopia Panel, Ball Drop Cornice, 26 1/2 X 36 In. 250.00
Mirror, Cornucopias, Gilded Cast Plaster Frame, Oval, 27 1/2 In. 50.00
Mirror, Courting, Reverse Painted Hunting Scene, Mahogany, 19 In. 700.00
Mirror, Dresser, Walnut, Folding, Drawer, 14 X 12 In. ....*Illus* 500.00
Mirror, Dressing, Chippendale, 3 Drawers, Mahogany, 24 X 18 In. 132.00
Mirror, Dressing, Line Inlaid Frame, 3 Drawers, Mahogany, C.1800 .... 1100.00
Mirror, Dressing, Slant Front, 3 Drawers, Mahogany, 29 In. 1430.00
Mirror, Eglomise Panel, 2 Part, 30 X 17 In. 275.00
Mirror, Empire, Columns, Corner Blocks, Sponging, 24 1/2 X 12 In. 55.00
Mirror, Empire, Mahogany Veneer, Black, Stencil, 15 X 30 In., 2 Pc. 180.00
Mirror, Federal, Architectural, Mahogany, 2 Part Frame, 27 In. 3200.00
Mirror, Federal, Inlaid Shell At Top, Inlaid Mahogany, 33 In. 825.00
Mirror, Federal, Urn Crest With Flowers & Garlands, Oval, 56 In. 900.00

Furniture, Mirror, Dresser, Walnut, Folding, Drawer, 14 X 12 In.

Furniture, Mirror, Shaving, Large Shell, Trailing Vine, 16 In.

Mirror, Filled Cornucopias, Eagle Finial, Oval, 26 1/2 In.	135.00
Mirror, Floral Frieze On Cornice, Marble Brackets, 96 In.	650.00
Mirror, George I, Gilt Wood, Leaf Carved Frame, C.1720, 26 1/2 In.	2100.00
Mirror, George II, Carved Border, Walnut, 33 1/2 X 18 1/4 In.	2750.00
Mirror, George III, Acanthus Carved Column Form Frame, 43 In.	660.00
Mirror, George III, Acanthus Frame, Gilt Wood, 71 X 43 In.	350.00
Mirror, George III, Beaded Frame, Gilt Wood, C.1790, 35 X 23 In.	935.00
Mirror, George III, Icicles, Scrolls & Leaf Frame, 6 Ft. X 4 Ft.	9350.00
Mirror, George III, Mahogany, Scroll Cut & Molded Frame, 24 In.	225.00
Mirror, George III, Oval Plate, Foliate & Scroll Frame, 46 In.	6325.00
Mirror, Gilded Florentine Frame, 27 1/2 X 35 In.	325.00
Mirror, Gilded Walnut, Arched Crest, Side Draperies, Italy, 59 In.	450.00
Mirror, Gilt Wood, Oval Molded Frame, C.1830, 21 In., Pair	1700.00
Mirror, Gold Stenciling, Girl, Reverse On Glass, 26 3/4 X 13 In.	475.00
Mirror, Hepplewhite, Inlaid & Gilded, Mahogany, 20 X 36 1/4 In.	850.00
Mirror, Hepplewhite, Inlaid Mahogany, Gilt, N.Y., 1790, 59 X 22 In.	3850.00
Mirror, Italian Neoclassical, Gilt Wood, Urn Finial, 31 In.	500.00
Mirror, Italian Rococo, Beveled, Leaf Frame, 25 X 17 In.	1200.00
Mirror, Italian Rococo, Gilt Wood, Cartouche Shape, 21 In., Pair	375.00
Mirror, Italian Rococo, Gilt Wood, Etched Glass, Crest, 31 In., Pr.	3900.00
Mirror, Louis XV, Gilt Wood, Beveled Plate, 37 In.	700.00
Mirror, Mahogany Frame, Reverse Painted House, 24 X 13 3/4 In.	75.00
Mirror, Mantel, 3 Plates, Leaf & Scroll Frame, Gilt, 4 Ft.4 In.	192.00
Mirror, Mantel, Black Frame, C.1830, 32 1/2 X 57 1/2 In.	4200.00
Mirror, Mantel, C Scroll & Shell, Spiral Columns, 75 In.	1500.00
Mirror, Mantel, Empire, Black Banister Frame, 1830, 32 X 57 In.	4200.00
Mirror, Mantel, Mahogany & Parcel Gilt, 31 X 47 In.	825.00
Mirror, Mantel, Rococo, Gilt Wood, Leaf, Scroll Frame, 52 In.	500.00
Mirror, Molded Frame With Leaves, Top Urn, C.1770, 5 Ft.4 In.	9350.00
Mirror, Molded Frame, Eagle, Gold & Bronze Paint, 22 X 27 In.	400.00
Mirror, Napoleon III, Florals, Gilt Champleve & Bronze, 17 In.	475.00
Mirror, Napoleon III, Foliage & Beading Border, Oval, 4 Ft.10 In.	2090.00
Mirror, Ornate Gold Frame, 51 1/4 X 39 1/4 In.	295.00
Mirror, Oval Plate, Carved Berried Foliage Frame, 34 X 29 In.	550.00
Mirror, Painting On Glass, Building, Gilded Frame, 17 X 29 In.	125.00
Mirror, Phoenix Bird, Mahogany & Gilt Wood, 43 1/2 X 23 In., Pair	8525.00
Mirror, Pier, Gilt Gesso Frame, Marble Ledge Base, 9 Ft., Pair	1650.00
Mirror, Pier, Gold Leaf Frame, Gesso Ornaments, 71 X 35 In.	850.00
Mirror, Plateau, Beveled Glass, Flower Border, 10 X 13 In.	105.00
Mirror, Plateau, Beveled Rim, Cast Metal Frame, 11 1/4 In.	25.00
Mirror, Plateau, Double Bevel Edge, Silver Plate	105.00
Mirror, Plateau, Forbes, Silver Plated Mounting, Round, 22 In.	245.00

Mirror, Plateau, Notched Ball & Claw Feet, Silver Plate Frame 95.00
Mirror, Plateau, Notched Beveled Mirror, Victorian, 16 In. 85.00
Mirror, Plateau, Ornate Handle, Bronze, 14 X 17 In. 195.00
Mirror, Plateau, Scalloped, Removable Claw Feet, 18 X 36 In. 375.00
Mirror, Prince of Wales Feathers, Mahogany, 25 1/2 X 12 3/4 In. 325.00
Mirror, Queen Anne, Beveled, Walnut Frame, 33 1/2 X 18 1/4 In. 950.00
Mirror, Queen Anne, Mahogany Frame, 2–Part Glass, 33 1/4 X 18 In. 750.00
Mirror, Queen Anne, Shaped Crest, Original Glass, 17 1/2 X 9 In. 475.00
Mirror, Queen Anne, Walnut On Pine, Scrolled Crest, 11 X 21 In. 1700.00
Mirror, Red Sponging On Yellow Ground, 25 1/2 X 13 In. 125.00
Mirror, Regency, Gilt Wood, Reverse Painted Panel, C.1820, 36 In. 1300.00
Mirror, Relief Carved Crest, Beveled Glass, 23 3/4 X 45 In. 305.00
Mirror, Reverse On Glass Harbor Scene, Gilded, 32 X 19 1/4 In. 700.00
Mirror, River Landscape Panel, Gilt Wood & Eglomise, 42 In. 2475.00
Mirror, Scroll, Ebony Line Inlay On Frame, 24 1/2 X 14 In. 200.00
Mirror, Scrolled Crest & Drop, Walnut, England, 31 X 16 1/8 In. 300.00
Mirror, Shaving, 3 Sections, Beveled Glass, Brass Hinges, Oak 110.00
Mirror, Shaving, Base Cutout Compartment, Butternut, 22 1/4 In. 25.00
Mirror, Shaving, Bowfront, Dovetailed Case, 2 Drawers, 21 In. 400.00
Mirror, Shaving, Hanging, Butternut, 15 1/4 X 9 3/4 In. 75.00
Mirror, Shaving, Hepplewhite, 2 Drawers, Bowfront, 19 1/4 In. 150.00
Mirror, Shaving, Hepplewhite, Inlaid Mahogany, Oval, 20 X 24 In. 85.00
Mirror, Shaving, Large Shell, Trailing Vine, 16 In. ....*Illus* 413.00
Mirror, Shaving, On Stand, Mahogany, Ebony Inlay, 21 X 22 In. 400.00
Mirror, Shaving, Queen Anne, Gilt Liner, 3 Drawers, England, 24 In. 650.00
Mirror, Shaving, Victorian, Walnut, Curved Marble Shelf 275.00
Mirror, Sheraton, Gilded Tabernacle, Half Columns, 28 X 15 In. 185.00
Mirror, Spanish, Gilt Wood, Acanthus Carved Frame, 34 In. 750.00
Mirror, Spherules Over Panel, Gilt Wood, C.1810, 46 X 30 1/2 In. 2860.00
Mirror, Sunflower Top, Carved Swag, Parcel Gilt, 13 1/2 X 31 In. 880.00
Mirror, Swan's Neck Pediment, Mahogany & Parcel Gilt, 4 Ft.3 In. 2310.00
Mirror, Tabernacle, 20 X 10 In. 225.00
Mirror, Tabernacle, C.1830, 42 3/4 X 26 In. 425.00
Mirror, Tortoiseshell, Silk Stumpwork, C.1690, 21 X 17 In. 4675.00
Mirror, Urn & Swag Draped Design, Gilt, 43 In. 85.00
Mirror, Urns of Flowers, Fruit, Cherubs, Gold Leaf, 5 Ft.6 In. 4000.00
Mirror, Vase Finial, Gilded Molding, Mahogany, 49 X 21 In. 6250.00
Mirror, Venetian, Rococo, Gilt Wood, Mid–18th Century, 31 X 21 In. 1100.00
Mirror, William & Mary, Cushion Molded, C.1690, 30 1/2 X 27 In. 2310.00
Mirror, Wrought Steel & Parcel Gilt, C.1870, 49 1/2 X 33 In. 400.00
Parlor Set, Baroque, Masks, Dragons Lions On Crest Rails, 3 Piece 850.00
Parlor Set, Carved Walnut, Green Damask Covers, 3 Piece 6000.00
Parlor Set, Chinese Export, Rosewood, Carved Dragons, 5 Piece 5000.00
Parlor Set, Empire, Mahogany, Tufted Upholstery, 1860s, 3 Piece 800.00
Parlor Set, Heywood Bros., Settee, Armchair & Rocker, C.1900 .... 6500.00
Parlor Set, Victorian, McCracken, Carved, 6 Piece 3850.00
Parlor Set, Victorian, Prudent Mallard, Rosewood, 7 Piece 6050.00
Parlor Set, Wicker, Heywood Wakefield, Caned Seats, C.1900, 4 Pc. 6500.00
Pedestal, Biedermeier Style, Ebonized Trim, Walnut, 38 In. 450.00
Pedestal, Continental, Carved Cherubs, Tripod Base, 54 In., Pair 2200.00
Pedestal, Neoclassical, Ebony, Ivory Inlaid Mahogany, 48 3/4 In. 2530.00
Pedestal, Rotating Top, Marquetry Panel 1 Side, C.1850, 40 In. 1500.00
Pedstal, Carved, Green, 44 In. 325.00
Pew, Church, Pine, 36 X 48 In. 95.00
Pie Safe, 12 Tiers, 1 Drawer, Punched Tin 800.00
Pie Safe, 12 Tins, 2 Doors, 1 Bottom Drawer, Blue Paint 1800.00
Pie Safe, Cherry, Urn & Grape Design, 1830–50, 51 X 52 In. 6200.00
Pie Safe, Graduated Eagle Tins On Sides, Painted 2250.00
Pie Safe, Hanging, Punched Tin Panels, Pine & Poplar, 19 In. 1250.00
Pie Safe, Hanging, Punched Zinc Panels All 4 Sides, Pine, 29 In. 75.00
Pie Safe, Heart & Tulip Tins, Bottom Drawer 795.00
Pie Safe, Oak, 2 Tin Upper Doors, 2 Blind Doors, 2 Drawers 360.00
Pie Safe, Poplar, 1 Door, High Feet, 1850 .... 595.00
Pie Safe, Poplar, Tin, Geometric, 4 Shelves, 1850, 5 Ft.X 34 In. 595.00

Pie Safe, Red Wash & Pinwheel Tin Inserts, Mid–19th Century 695.00
Pie Safe, Tins Painted Green, Shenandoah Valley, C.1840 .... 1400.00
Pie Safe, Tulip & Heart Tins, Red, Cutout Bottom, Wisc. 595.00
Pie Safe, Walnut, Mercer County, Ky., 19th Century 1900.00
Pie Safe, Walnut, Stepback Top, Shelf, Original Tins, C.1880 .... 995.00
Rack, Blanket, Turned Supports & Finials, Mahogany, 75 X 28 In. 440.00
Rack, Pipe, Pine, Dark Brown, Molded Cornices, 17 In. 3300.00
Rack, Plant, 3 Shelves, Open, Pine, Hanging, Brown, 35 X 37 In. 475.00
Rack, Plant, Hanging, Scalloped Sides, Spindle Rails, Oak, 42 In. 600.00
Recamier, Twig, 1922 .... 2450.00
Rocker, Adirondack Twig, Blue–Green .... 150.00 To 220.00
Rocker, Amish Style, Hickory, Bentwood Arms 260.00
Rocker, Amish, Stamped East Goshen, Michigan 475.00
Rocker, Arms, Brown Graining, Floral Design, Replaced Rush Seat 275.00
Rocker, Arrow Back, Red & Black Graining 200.00
Rocker, Bentwood, Looped Back, Arms, Rockers, J.& J.Kohn, C.1900 .... 6600.00
Rocker, Boston, Pale Yellow Paint, Blue, Gold & Black Stenciled 275.00
Rocker, Cane Back, Red & Black Graining 50.00
Rocker, Child's, Adirondack, 31 In. 50.00
Rocker, Child's, Bentwood, Red 45.00
Rocker, Child's, Ladder Back, 3 Slats, Cushion Seat, 25 1/2 In. 60.00
Rocker, Child's, Ladder Back, 3 Slats, Turned Finials 55.00
Rocker, Child's, Ladder Back, Arms, Red Paint, 26 In. 65.00
Rocker, Child's, Ladder Back, Green, Woven Cane Seat, Arms 75.00
Rocker, Child's, Pressed Back 130.00
Rocker, Child's, Rung Back, Square Cloth Tape Seat 25.00
Rocker, Child's, Shaker, Mt.Lebanon, Taped Seat, 28 1/2 In. 1500.00
Rocker, Child's, Shaker, No.0, Arms, Mt.Lebanon, 1880–1920, 23 In. 1500.00
Rocker, Child's, Shaker, No.0, Original Tape, Decal .... 1100.00 To 3300.00
Rocker, Child's, Shaker, No.0, Slat Back, Mt.Lebanon, Roll Bar, Arms 800.00
Rocker, Child's, Shaker, No.0, Splint Seat 2000.00
Rocker, Child's, Shaker, Taped Back, Mt.Lebanon, 23 In. 1500.00
Rocker, Child's, Stenciled Wood, Carpet Seat, Folding, 1870 .... 225.00
Rocker, Child's, Twig 75.00
Rocker, Child's, Victorian, Caned 100.00
Rocker, Crest Rail of Carved Serpents, Oak 300.00
Rocker, Graduated Slats, Shaped Handholds, Tiger Maple, 40 In. 500.00
Rocker, Gustav Stickley, 4 Slats, Leather Seat, Red Decal, 1902 .... 475.00
Rocker, Gustav Stickley, 5 Vertical Slats, Oak, C.1902 .... 495.00
Rocker, Gustav Stickley, Flat Arms, Leather Seat, Tacks, 1907 .... 250.00
Rocker, High Back, Brown Graining On Yellow 85.00
Rocker, High Balloon Back, Plank Seat, Red Repaint 45.00
Rocker, Hitchcock, Stenciled Name On Back of Seat, Arrow Splats 650.00
Rocker, Hunzinger Bros., Wire Cloth Webbing, Walnut, Signed 550.00
Rocker, L.& J.G.Stickley, Tall Back, Arched Apron, Arms 1100.00
Rocker, Ladder Back, 3 Slats, Splint Seat 55.00
Rocker, Ladder Back, 4 Slats, Rush Seat, Arms 70.00
Rocker, Ladder Back, Arms, Rush Seat, 4–Slat Back, 1850s 190.00
Rocker, Ladder Back, Arms, Woven Splint Seat 100.00
Rocker, Lincoln, Arms, Red & Black Grained, Yellow Striping 75.00
Rocker, Mahogany, Lion's Head, Carved Back & Arms 175.00
Rocker, Mission, Oak, Shop of The Crafters, Cinncinnati 250.00
Rocker, Oak, Caned Seat, Spindle Back & Arms 90.00
Rocker, Oak, Splint Seat, Legs Bolted To Rockers 125.00
Rocker, Oak, Stenciled, C.1900 .... 80.00
Rocker, Paper Rush Seat, Canadian 75.00
Rocker, Plank Seat, Painted, Stenciled, New England, C.1830 .... 715.00
Rocker, Platform, Arched Back, Downswept Arms, Wicker, 47 In., Pair 1400.00
Rocker, Platform, Eastlake Style, Cherry 90.00
Rocker, Potty Chair, Solid Back, Serpentine Edge, Grain Painted 475.00
Rocker, Pressed Back, Oak, Pressed Board Seat 90.00
Rocker, Pressed Back, Oak, Pressed Leather Seat 49.00
Rocker, Pressed Back, Oak, Stenciled, C.1900 .... 80.00
Rocker, Pressed Back, Spindle Back & Arms, Oak 215.00

Rocker, Pressed Back, Spindle Back & Arms, Round Leather Seat 90.00
Rocker, Red & Black Graining, White Striping, Gilt Stencil 90.00
Rocker, Red Flame Graining, Yellow & White Striping 120.00
Rocker, Roycroft, Mahogany, Leather Seat, Signed 300.00
Rocker, Sewing, Ladder Back, No.4, Varnish Finish, Rush Seat 125.00
Rocker, Sewing, Lyre Back, Claw Carvings 27.50
Rocker, Sewing, Pressed Back, Cane Seat & Back 115.00
Rocker, Sewing, Spindle Back 75.00
Rocker, Shaker, Armless, Maple, Shawl Bar, Striped Tape, Mt.Lebanon 1150.00
Rocker, Shaker, Armless, Maple, Stained, Mt.Lebanon, 1880, 15 In. 475.00
Rocker, Shaker, Child's, Maple, Walnut, Mt.Lebanon, 23 In. 2000.00
Rocker, Shaker, Elder's, Maple, Cherry, Birch, New Lebannon, 1850 .... 1800.00
Rocker, Shaker, Maple, Black Walnut, Mt.Lebanon, 39 In. 1300.00
Rocker, Shaker, Maple, Ebony, Taped Seat, Back, 1880, 39 In. 750.00
Rocker, Shaker, Maple, Green, Splint Seat, Sabbathday Lake, 1820 .... 700.00
Rocker, Shaker, Maple, Rush Seat, Watervliet, 1820, 17 X 39 In. 900.00
Rocker, Shaker, No.1, Mt.Lebanon, Tape Seat 1395.00
Rocker, Shaker, No.2, Mt.Lebanon, Shawl Bar 795.00
Rocker, Shaker, No.3, Mt.Lebanon, Tape Seat 795.00
Rocker, Shaker, No.4, Decal 522.50
Rocker, Shaker, No.7, Maple, Ebony, Green Tape, 1870, 14 1/4 In. 1250.00
Rocker, Spindle Back, Stenciled 100.00
Rocker, Spinning Wheel, Original Ocher Paint 550.00
Rocker, Thonet, Ebonized Bentwood, C.1880, 36 1/2 In. 300.00
Rocker, Twig, Green Over Blue, C.1860 .... 325.00
Rocker, Wicker, Bar Harbor Style 110.00
Rocker, Wicker, Platform, White 295.00
Rocker, Wicker, Victorian, Curlicues, Lattice Panels 625.00
Rocker, Wicker, Victorian, Ornate Back & Platform 850.00
Rocker, Wicker, White Paint, Arms, Cream, Navy, Rust, Green Coverlet 110.00
Rocker, Windsor, 7 Tapered Spindles, Plank Seat, New England, 1815 .... 3200.00
Rocker, Windsor, Bow Back, 7 Tapered Spindles, Painted, C.1790 .... 300.00
Rocker, Windsor, Comb Back, 6 Spindles, Arms, Pine & Ash, C.1820 .... 325.00
Rocker, Yellow Striping, Stenciled Design, Arms 100.00
Screen, 3–Panel, Blue & Peach Peacock Design Wallpaper, 72 In. 425.00
Screen, 3–Panel, Blue & Silver Fabric, Crane Hunt, Japan, 67 In. 715.00
Screen, 3–Panel, Embroidered Sections, G.Stickley, 65 1/4 In. 9500.00
Screen, 3–Panel, Jacobean Style, Carved Oak, Each Panel 78 In. 325.00
Screen, 3–Panel, Silver Gilt Frame, White, Glass Panels, 71 In. 275.00
Screen, 3–Panel, Teakwood, Indian, C.1860, 6 Ft. X 6 Ft.3 In. 600.00
Screen, 4–Panel, Coromandel, Lacquer, Immortals, Brown, 34 X 44 In. 2200.00
Screen, 4–Panel, Embossed Leather, Center Flowers, 82 1/4 In. 2750.00
Screen, 4–Panel, Fowl, Gold Stenciled Foliage, 65 1/2 X 87 In. 500.00
Screen, 4–Panel, Lacquered, Birds, Red, China, C.1900, 72 X 18 In. 475.00
Screen, 4–Panel, Tooled Leather, Science, Industry, Arts, Commerce 3400.00
Screen, 8–Panel, U Shaped Plywood Panels, Folding, Eames, 67 In. 1650.00
Screen, Birds, Ivory Heads, Mother–of–Pearl Flowers, 2 Ft.5 In. 1300.00
Screen, Inlaid Ivory Design of Pagodas, Rosewood, 32 In. 350.00
Screen, Pole, William IV, Carved Mahogany, C.1835 .... 400.00
Screen, Renaissance, Tapestry Panels, Carved, Walnut, C.1890 .... 880.00
Secretaire, Biedermeier, Fall Front, Walnut, Ormolu Mounted, 5 Ft. 7700.00
Secretaire, Fall Front, Fitted Interior, Rosewood, C.1820, 63 In. 9350.00
Secretary Bookcase, Arched Glazed Doors, Walnut, C.1865, 86 In. 600.00
Secretary Bookcase, Black Oak Veneer, Glass Side Door, Mirror 245.00
Secretary Bookcase, Federal, Mahogany, Curly Maple, 1825, 92 In. 7500.00
Secretary Bookcase, George III, Inlaid Mahogany, Sycamore, 8 Ft. 4100.00
Secretary Bookcase, George III, Mahogany, 4 Drawer, 86 In. 3000.00
Secretary Bookcase, George III, Mahogany, Mullioned Doors, 90 In. 2800.00
Secretary Bookcase, Mullioned Doors, Mahogany, C.1815, 76 1/2 In. 4125.00
Secretary Bookcase, Pressed Carved, Paw Feet, Mirror, 5 Shelves 650.00
Secretary Bookcase, Victorian, Walnut, Cylinder Top, Glass Door 800.00
Secretary Chest, Drop Front Drawer Over Drawers, Walnut, 45 In. 2250.00
Secretary Desk, Painted, Swedish, C.1820 .... 4950.00
Secretary Desk, Slant Front, Pine, C.1800, 84 1/2 In. 4750.00

Secretary, Biedermeier, Fall Front, Bird's–Eye Maple Veneer	8800.00
Secretary, Black Walnut, Tiger Maple Interior, New England, 1865	1900.00
Secretary, Chippendale, Cherry, Bonnet Top, Mass., 1770–80, 7 Ft.	4750.00
Secretary, Empire, Fall Front, Glass Doors, C.1850	1600.00
Secretary, Empire, Flame Grain Veneer, Ionic, 37 X 23 X 80 In.	2300.00
Secretary, Fall Front, Marquetry, Walnut.C.1700, 5 Ft.2 In.	7150.00
Secretary, Fall Front, Oak, Oval Mirror, 3 Drawers	350.00
Secretary, Governor Winthrop, Drop Front, Claw Feet, Mahogany	650.00
Secretary, Painted Drawers, Bird's–Eye Maple, C.1830, 67 In.	850.00
Secretary, Plantation Style, Walnut, Spool Legs, 1 Drawer, 79 In.	800.00
Secretary, Slant Front, Lift Lid, Red Paint, Poplar, 66 1/2 In.	1000.00
Secretary, Tiger Maple Veneer, Cherry & Mahogany, C.1800, 53 In.	4800.00
Server, Concave Top, Frieze Drawer, Tambour Doors, Mahogany	1540.00
Server, Federal, Maple, Arched Splashboard, 3 Drawers, 47 In.	6600.00
Server, L.& J.Stickley, Backsplash, 1 Long, 2 Short Drawers, Oak	1200.00
Server, Limbert, 1 Drawer, Backsplash, 2 Shelves, 1905, 41 X 42 In.	1600.00
Server, Pine, Oak, Breadboard Ends, 3 Drawers, 36 X 45 In.	850.00
Settee, Brass Inlaid Crest, Carved Arms, Mahogany, C.1830, 72 In.	2600.00
Settee, Chairback, Queen Anne, Walnut, 45 X 62 In. ....*Illus*	3000.00
Settee, Chippendale, Arched Back, Upholstered, 19th Century	950.00
Settee, DeWolfe, Grape Design, Off–White Ground, Cast Iron, 44 In.	440.00
Settee, English Classical Revival, C.1850	1800.00
Settee, Federal, Carved Tassle Swags, Brass Paw Feet, 6 Ft.7 In.	3500.00
Settee, Federal, Reeded Arms, Loose Cushion Seat, Mahogany, C.1825	1980.00
Settee, George III, 5 Shield Back, Painted Bouquets, 6 Ft.6 In.	3300.00
Settee, George III, Oak, Upholstered Seat, Pad Feet, 39 In.	475.00
Settee, George III, Shaped Crest, Upholstered Seat, Mahogany	1000.00
Settee, German Neoclassical, Walnut, Upholstered Back, 35 In.	600.00
Settee, Green Covering, Pennsylvania, 6 Ft.	2700.00
Settee, Louis XV, Carved Arched Back, 19th Century, Pair	1000.00
Settee, Louis XVI, Padded Back & Open Arms, Bleached Beechwood	495.00
Settee, Mission, Gustav Stickley, Leather Covered Cushion, Oak	3850.00
Settee, Mission, Oak, Leather Upholstery	60.00
Settee, Mission, Stickley Brothers, Oak, Slat Back, 76 In.	3500.00
Settee, Nutting, Walnut, C.1820	700.00
Settee, Queen Anne, Walnut, Triple Chairback, Crest Rail, 45 In.	3000.00
Settee, Regency, Chairback, Rosewood, Brass Marquetry, 1820, 63 In.	4250.00
Settee, Regency, Upholstered Back, Rosewood & Brass, 91 In.	450.00
Settee, Rococo, John Henry Belter, Carved Roses, Rosewood, C.1855	6050.00
Settee, Rococo, Upholstered Back, Sides & Seat, 58 In.	500.00
Settee, Serpentine Upholstered Back, Scrolled Arms, 7 Ft.11 In.	2090.00
Settee, Sheraton, Mahogany, Inlaid, Reeded Legs, 60 In.	3000.00
Settee, Sheraton, Pa.Style, Maple, Pine, Buttermilk Paint, 71 In.	1650.00
Settee, Shield Back, Burled Trim On Crests, Walnut, Small	400.00
Settee, Upholstered Back & Seat, Carved Mahogany, C.1815, 84 In.	8800.00
Settee, Upholstered Back, Seat, Curved Arms, Cherry, 1825, 73 In.	2000.00
Settee, Victorian, Rosewood, Blue Velvet, 1870	850.00
Settee, Victorian, Shield Back, Rose Carving On Skirt, Walnut	925.00

Furniture, Sideboard, Hepplewhite, Mahogany,
Bowfront, 35 1/2 In.

Furniture, Settee, Chairback, Queen Anne, Walnut, 45 X 62 In.

Settee, William & Mary, Outscrolled Padded Arms, Walnut 2310.00
Settee, Windsor, 22 Spindles, Incised Seat, 6 Legs, Painted, C.1810 .... 2750.00
Settee, Windsor, 24 Tapered Spindles, Plank Seat, C.1825, 84 In. 3575.00
Settee, Windsor, 47 Tapered Spindles, Green Paint, 1800, 7 Ft. 7700.00
Settle, Charles II, Acanthus Leaves On Rail, Open Seat, C.1680 .... 265.00
Settle, Child's, Shaped & Tenoned Wings, Painted, 22 X 25 In. 1500.00
Settle, Gustav Stickley, Cushion Seat, Oak, C.1910, 77 3/4 In. 8975.00
Settle, Gustav Stickley, Even Arm, Slatted .... 5250.00 To 8500.00
Settle, Hall, Gustav Stickley, Lift Seat .... 5000.00 To 6750.00
Settle, Hall, L.& J.G.Stickley, Lift Seat, 9 Slats, 42 X 37 In. 4500.00
Settle, L.& J.G.Stickley, Horizontal Back Rails 3500.00
Settle, L.& J.G.Stickley, No.225, Slatted Back 700.00
Settle, Michigan Chair Co., Spindle, Even Arm, Plank Seat, 83 In. 1000.00
Settle, Onondaga, Even Arm, Tall Tapering Posts, 1905, 39 X 76 In. 4750.00
Settle, Plank Seat, Spindle Back, Curved Arms, 96 In. 375.00
Settle, Plank Seat, Yellow Brown Steel Comb Repaint, 73 In. 325.00
Shelf, Corner, Hanging, 4 Curved Shelves, Mahogany, 35 X 23 In. 600.00
Shelf, Federal, 5 Graduated Shelves, Birch, 49 1/2 X 33 1/2 In. 700.00
Shelf, Hanging, 2 Dovetailed Drawers, Yellow Graining, 36 1/2 In. 400.00
Shelf, Hanging, 3 Shelves, 1 Drawer, Dark Finish, 35 In. 675.00
Shelf, Hanging, 4 Shelves, Scalloped Ends, Pine, 36 1/2 X 24 In. 175.00
Shelf, Hanging, Cutout, Polychromed Floral, Persian, Folds, 19 In. 45.00
Shelf, Hanging, Pine, Varied Arrangements, Towel Bar, 57 1/2 In. 425.00
Shelf, Hanging, Poplar, Pit Sawn Backboards, 34 1/4 In. 300.00
Shelf, Hanging, Scalloped, Lower Compartment, Poplar, 22 1/2 In. 165.00
Shelf, Hanging, Walnut, Jigsaw Work, 12 1/4 X 21 1/4 In. 65.00
Shelf, Hanging, Wicker, Heywood–Wakefield 550.00
Shelf, Hanging, Wooden Carved Scrolled Bracket, 24 1/2 In. 95.00
Shelf, Screw Construction, Zoar, Ohio, 22 In. 200.00
Sideboard, 3/4 Galley, Drawer, Doors, Mahogany, 66 1/2 In. 1500.00
Sideboard, Brushed Steel, Marble Top, J.Leleu, C.1930, 5 Ft.10 In. 7150.00
Sideboard, Cherry, Curly Maple, Bird's–Eye Maple Columns, C.1830 .... 895.00
Sideboard, Empire, 3 Drawers, Flame Grained, Mahogany, 44 3/8 In. 500.00
Sideboard, Empire, Curly Maple, Paneled Doors, 49 In. 750.00
Sideboard, Federal, Convex Doors, Inlaid Mahogany, C.1805, 72 In. 7150.00
Sideboard, Federal, Line Inlaid Edge, Mahogany, C.1815, 67 In. 9900.00
Sideboard, Federal, Mahogany, Bowed, Cockbeaded, 1800–15, 74 In. 1550.00
Sideboard, Federal, Serpentine Front, Mahogany, C.1800, 69 In. 6325.00
Sideboard, Federal, Tambour, Drawers, Mahogany, C.1805, 67 1/2 In. 5775.00
Sideboard, George III, 1 Long Drawer, Side Drawers, Mahogany 2860.00
Sideboard, Gruber, Oak, Ormolu, 3 Glass Top Doors, 106 In. 9900.00
Sideboard, Gustav Stickley, 4 Middle Drawers, 2 Side Doors 2750.00
Sideboard, Gustav Stickley, 8 Legs, Plate Rail, 50 X 68 In. 9250.00
Sideboard, Gustav Stickley, Side Cupboards, 4 Center Drawers 2750.00
Sideboard, Hepplewhite, Mahogany, Bowfront, 35 1/2 In. ....*Illus* 6160.00
Sideboard, L.& J.G.Stickley, 4 Central Drawers, Oak.C.1912, 6 Ft. 1430.00
Sideboard, L.& J.G.Stickley, Plate Rail, 3 Drawers, 44 X 60 In. 3000.00
Sideboard, Limbert, Shallow Mirror, 3 Small Drawers, 47 X 60 In. 2100.00
Sideboard, Mahogany, 3 Drawers, 4 Cabinets, C.1815, 6 Ft.1/2 In. 3025.00
Sideboard, Mahogany, Central Drawer, Side Drawers, 6 Ft.3 In. 9350.00
Sideboard, Mahogany, Interior Plate Racks, Inlaid, 9 Ft.11 In. 7150.00
Sideboard, Mahogany, Long Drawer, Cabinet Doors, Inlaid, 72 In. 2500.00
Sideboard, Mahogany, Ovolo Corners, Center Drawer, 2 Doors, 1790 .... 7500.00
Sideboard, Mahogany, Serpentine Front, Line Inlaid, 7 Ft.8 In. 3520.00
Sideboard, Mahogany, Tambours Above Drawers, 86 In. 2800.00
Sideboard, Oak, Carved Arch On Columns, Marble Top, 82 In. 1900.00
Sideboard, Oak, Carved Facade, 3 Drawers, 2 Doors, 65 1/2 In. 395.00
Sideboard, Peter Hunt, Drawer Over Door, Painted, C.1940, 45 In. 850.00
Sideboard, Sheraton, Bowfront, Banded Top, Mahogany, C.1800 .... 3400.00
Sideboard, Sheraton, Mahogany, 2 Cockbeaded Drawers, 1815, 38 In. 2700.00
Sideboard, Walnut, Mirror, Hand Carved Posts, Medallions On Doors 2500.00
Sofa, Belter, Rosalie Pattern, Velvet Upholstered 5900.00
Sofa, Camelback, Chinese Fretwork Legs, Silk Upholstered, 86 In. 1200.00
Sofa, Chippendale, Camelback, Mahogany, C.1780, 81 In. 3575.00

Furniture, Sofa, Classical, Mahogany Veneered

Furniture, Sofa, Federal, Green Moire Upholstery, Paw Feet, 76 In.

Sofa, Classical, Mahogany Veneered ....*Illus* 4800.00
Sofa, Crest Continuing To Shaped Arms, Mahogany, C.1790, 78 In. 2500.00
Sofa, Empire Swan, Carved Mahogany, Bird's–Eye Maple Insets 5225.00
Sofa, Empire, Claw Foot, Fan Armrest, Down Cushion, C.1840 .... 3000.00
Sofa, Empire, Walnut, Rosewood Veneer, Reupholstered, C.1840 .... 1400.00
Sofa, Federal, Acanthus Carved Crest, Green Moire, 76 In. 1500.00
Sofa, Federal, Flat Upholstered Back, Arms, C.1820, 70 3/4 In. 1000.00
Sofa, Federal, Green Moire Upholstery, Paw Feet, 76 In. ....*Illus* 1650.00
Sofa, Flower & Leaf Carving, Velour Cover, Mahogany Frame 3000.00
Sofa, Frank Lloyd Wright Design, C.1937, 7 Ft.6 In. 1650.00
Sofa, George II, Mahogany, Camelback, 4 Cabriole Legs, 76 In. 850.00
Sofa, Haines–Connelly School, Carved Mahogany, C.1805, 81 In. 8250.00
Sofa, Horsehair, Black, Carved, Victorian 2200.00
Sofa, Louis XV, Floral & Foliate Crest, Carved, Upholstery, 80 In. 1200.00
Sofa, Regency, Gold & Green Paint, Striped Upholstered, 85 In. 4600.00
Sofa, Rosewood Laminated, Henry Clay Pattern, Upholstery, C.1850 .... 5775.00
Sofa, Rosewood, Roses Carved Across Back, Gold Velvet, Victorian 5500.00
Sofa, Scroll Arms, Saber Legs, Carved Mahogany, C.1820 .... 1750.00
Sofa, Upholstered Back & Scroll Arms, C.1900, 63 In. 600.00
Sofa, Walnut, 4 Crest Back, Serpentine Seat, Portuguese, 100 In. 600.00
Sofa, William Hancock, Drawers In Arms, Boston, 1826, 89 1/2 In. 4800.00
Stand, 1 Drawer, 1 Board Top, Cherry, 28 In. 275.00
Stand, 1 Drawer, Dovetailed Cherry, 21 X 21 1/4 In. 250.00
Stand, 1 Drawer, Dovetailed, Pine Top, Hard & Soft Wood, 29 In. 300.00
Stand, 1 Drawer, Shaker, Pine, Birch, Red Finish, 27 X 19 X 16 In. 650.00
Stand, 3 Drawers, Rounded Corners Top, Painted & Stenciled 975.00
Stand, Basin, Corner, Federal, Curly Maple, C.1820, 40 1/2 In. 2000.00
Stand, Book, Little Journeys, Roycroft, Shelves, Oak, C.1915, 26 In. 720.00
Stand, Book, Neoclassical, Rosewood, 3 Tiers, English, 1850, 38 In. 5250.00
Stand, Cherry, Dovetailed Walnut Drawer, Turned Legs, 28 1/2 In. 275.00
Stand, Cherry, Maple Legs, 1 Dovetailed Drawer, 28 1/2 In. 275.00
Stand, Chinese, Cinnabar, Scene On Top, 10 3/4 X 15 3/4 In. 205.00
Stand, Corner, Cutout & Inlaid Design 300.00
Stand, Corner, Scalloped Shelves & Supports, 8 Shelves 570.00
Stand, Curly Maple Drawer Front, Walnut, 29 In. 195.00
Stand, Drop Leaf, 1 Drawer, Lothrop Brand 880.00
Stand, Eastlake, Brown Marble Top, Porcelain Castors 220.00
Stand, Empire, Drop Leaf, Spool Legs 140.00
Stand, Empire, Mahogany, Ormolu Trim, Marble Top, 15 X 29 In. 225.00
Stand, Federal, Birch, Drawer, New England, C.1810, 28 1/2 In. 700.00
Stand, Federal, Cherry, Bird's–Eye Maple, 1 Drawer, Eared, 27 In. 2100.00
Stand, Federal, Inlaid, Drawer, Cherry, N.Hampshire, 28 1/2 In. 2400.00
Stand, Federal, Leaves, Drawer, Mahogany, 29 1/2 In. 1100.00
Stand, Federal, Tilt Top, Mahogany, Square, Pedestal, Mass., 27 In. 2420.00
Stand, Fern, White Wicker ....50.00 To 100.00
Stand, Gothic, Oak, Knight Finials, 1850, 89 X 50 In., Pair 1700.00
Stand, Gustav Stickley, Round Overhanging Top, 25 X 20 In. 800.00
Stand, Gustav Stickley, Splashback, Red Decal, Oak, 28 7/8 In. 1810.00

Stand, Hepplewhie, Ovolo Corners, Walnut, 26 In. 375.00
Stand, Hepplewhite, 1 Drawer, Curly Top, Cherry Base, 28 In. 300.00
Stand, Hepplewhite, 2 Board Top, 1 Dovetailed Drawer, 28 In. 925.00
Stand, Hepplewhite, Cherry Base, Poplar Top, 28 1/2 In. 155.00
Stand, Hepplewhite, Maple, 1 Dovetailed Drawer, Curly Top, 28 In. 150.00
Stand, Hepplewhite, Pine, Tapered Legs, 28 1/4 In. 225.00
Stand, Hepplewhite, Walnut, 1 Dovetailed Drawer, 29 In. 200.00
Stand, Hexagonal Top, Porcelain Plaque, Bronze, Tulipwood, C.1870 .... 880.00
Stand, Louis XV, Marquetry, Marble, Ormolu, 2 Drawers, 26 In., Pair 590.00
Stand, Magician's, Pine, Green, Black, Orange, 14 X 14 In. 250.00
Stand, Magician's, Pine, Painted, Scrolled Iron Base, 40 In. 250.00
Stand, Marble Top, Daisy Carved Drawer Pull, Rosewood 825.00
Stand, Marquetry Inlaid, 2 Lower Shelves, 2 Drawers 800.00
Stand, Muffin, Mahogany, 3 Tiers, Inlaid Floral Design, 36 In. 200.00
Stand, Music, Gustav Stickley, Open Shelf, 1904, 42 In. 3600.00
Stand, Music, Lyre Form, Cast Iron, 16 1/2 In. 55.00
Stand, Pine Apron & Top, Triangular Base, Ash Legs, 28 1/2 In. 200.00
Stand, Plant, 5 Arms, Plus Lower Middle Shelf, Iron 1250.00
Stand, Plant, Adirondack, Black, Silver Design, 36 In. 50.00
Stand, Plant, Amish, Pine, Dark Paint, Scrubbed Top, 1865–70 .... 310.00
Stand, Plant, Biedermeier, Fruitwood 1800.00
Stand, Plant, Faceted Standard, Gilt, Rosewood, C.1825, 41 In. 4675.00
Stand, Plant, Renaissance Revival, Giltwood, 1880 ....*Illus* 675.00
Stand, Plant, Iron Base, Gilded Acanthus Leaves 975.00
Stand, Plant, Iron, Wire, Tier, Revolving, 19th Century 2200.00
Stand, Plant, Stick & Ball, C.1800, 20 In. 675.00
Stand, Plant, Wire, 2 Shelves, Pointed Crown 135.00
Stand, Portfolio, Renaissance, Carved Walnut, American, C.1865 .... 935.00
Stand, Portfolio, William IV, Carved Rosewood, C.1830 .... 3300.00
Stand, Rattan, Blue Design 27.50
Stand, Sewing, Cherry, Tiger Maple Drawer 350.00
Stand, Sewing, New York State, Tiger Maple 2500.00
Stand, Shaker, 1 Drawer, Chestnut, Pine, Canterbury, 1850, 25 In. 2000.00
Stand, Shaving, Adjustable Support, Walnut, C.1835, 63 1/2 In. 300.00
Stand, Shaving, Marble Top, Platform Base, Mahogany, C.1830 .... 715.00
Stand, Shaving, Mirror, Candlestick, Iron, Wood, Gilt Traces, 1800 .... 565.00
Stand, Shaving, Mirror, Neoclassical, Shell Inlaid, Vines, 25 In. 375.00
Stand, Sheraton, 1 Drawer, Curly Maple, Cherry Legs 175.00
Stand, Sheraton, 2 Drawers, Cherry, Drop Leaves 300.00
Stand, Smoking, Art Deco, Dragon's Head & Green Onyx Trim 165.00
Stand, Smoking, Brass, Steuben Ashtray, O.Bach, 40 In. ....*Illus* 600.00
Stand, Teakwood, Marble Top, Chinese, 20 1/4 In., Pair 275.00

Furniture, Stand, Work,
Classical Revival, Cherry
Inlaid, 1830

Furniture, Stand, Smoking,
Brass, Steuben Ashtray,
O.Bach, 40 In.

Furniture, Stand, Plant,
Renaissance Revival,
Giltwood, 1880

Stand, Tiffany & Co., Papier–Mache, 4 Drawers, Jewel Box, Label 1325.00
Stand, Umbrella, Gustav Stickley, Metal Liner, C.1905, 33 In. 1810.00
Stand, Umbrella, Kutani, Orange, White, Figural, Landscape, 30 In. 850.00
Stand, Umbrella, Stickley, Model No.54, Shelf, Liner, 1907, 33 In. 440.00
Stand, Urn, George III, Japanned, Boats, 27 X 12 In. 450.00
Stand, Urn, Marble Top, Pierced Frieze, Chinese, Hardwood, 37 In. 300.00
Stand, Work, Classical Revival, Cherry Inlaid, 1830 ....*Illus* 475.00
Stand, Work, Shaker, Cherry, Pine, 1 Drawer, 1830, 21 X 16 X 14 In. 900.00
Stand, Writing, Empire, Fitted Desk In Drawer 165.00
Stool, 2 Hearts Carved On Seat, Red, New England, C.1880, Pine 2090.00
Stool, Desk, G.Stickley, Rush Seat, Decal, Oak, C.1908, 17 1/2 In. 905.00
Stool, Dressing, George III, Turkish Rug Cover, Mahogany, C, 1760 .... 8250.00
Stool, Frank Lloyd Wright, Oak, Cutout, 17 X 24 X 12 In. 2400.00
Stool, George II, Needlepoint Covered, Walnut, C.1760, 11 1/2 In. 5500.00
Stool, Joint, Oak, Carved Apron, 19th Century, 19 3/4 In. 200.00
Stool, Oriental, Carved Teak, 19 In., Pair 130.00
Stool, Piano, American Classical, Carved Mahogany, C.1830 .... 198.00
Stool, Piano, Cherry, Ball & Claw Feet 65.00
Stool, Piano, Claw & Glass Ball Feet ....85.00 To 125.00
Stool, Piano, Round Wooden Top, Adjusts, 4 Ball & Claw Feet 59.00
Stool, Piano, Round Wooden Top, Horsehair, Pedestal, 3 Wooden Feet 32.00
Stool, Piano, Spindle Back, Adjustable Height 100.00
Stool, Shaker, Birch, Adjustable Back, Brown Stain, Enfield, 38 In. 4400.00
Stool, Shaker, Weaver's, Cane Seat 550.00
Stool, Walnut, Needlepoint, C.1720, 17 1/2 X 21 In. 2300.00
Swing, Porch, Wicker, Dark Green 105.00
Swing, Wicker, Curved Back, Rolled Arms 395.00
Table, 2 Board Tilt Top, Pennsylvania, Walnut, C.1780, 27 3/4 In. 250.00
Table, 2 Drawers, Mahogany, Crossbanded Top, 28 In. 350.00
Table, 2 Drawers, Sepentine Top, Acanthus Knees, Mahogany, 29 In. 1300.00
Table, Altar, Carved Rosewood, Open Apron, 73 In. ....*Illus* 550.00
Table, American Renaissance, Walnut, White Marble Top, 1870 .... 1500.00
Table, Architect's, Hinged Lid, Brass Bound Mahogany, 29 1/2 In. 2475.00
Table, Art Moderne, Brass, 2 Tiers, Inset Onyx Top, Pair 1800.00
Table, Backgammon, Bird's–Eye Maple & Brass, 28 1/4 In. 1650.00
Table, Banquet, Ball & Claw Pedestal, 3 Leaves, Mahogany, 15 Ft. 5500.00
Table, Banquet, Empire, Mahogany, Pedestal, Swing Top, 25 X 53 In. 1000.00
Table, Banquet, Hepplewhite, Mahogany, Shaped Apron, 42 X 77 In. 500.00
Table, Banquet, Hepplewhite, Mahogany, String Inlay, D End, 108 In. 3900.00
Table, Beaded Edge Apron, Triangular Shape, Pine, 28 X 34 1/2 In. 150.00
Table, Billiard, Brunswick, Inlaid Design, Rack, Balls, 1917 .... 3400.00
Table, Billiard, Brunswick, Regina, Rosewood, 1917, 4 X 8 Ft. 3900.00
Table, Breakfast, Brass Inlaid, Rosewood, C.1830, 4 Ft.3 In. 4950.00
Table, Breakfast, English Regency, Mahogany, Reeded Legs, 1800–20 .... 2400.00
Table, Breakfast, George IV, Tilting, Mahogany, C.1825 .... 990.00
Table, Breakfast, Mahogany, Flared Legs, English, Oval, 38 X 47 In. 2500.00
Table, Breakfast, Satinwood Inlaid Mahogany, C.1845, 41 1/2 In. 3850.00
Table, Breakfast, Tilt Top, Mahogany, C.1830, 4 Ft.6 In. 6600.00
Table, Breakfast, Tilt Top, Tripod Base, Mahogany, 52 In. 450.00
Table, Cannon Form Base On 3 Balls, Painted Gilt & Black, 32 In. 900.00
Table, Card, Beaded Frieze On Ionic Lyre Base, Mahogany, 29 In. 1150.00
Table, Card, Chippendale, Mahogany, Card Drawer, C.1780, 28 1/2 In. 7700.00
Table, Card, Classical, Mahogany Veneered, New England, 1825, Pair 5000.00
Table, Card, Elliptical Hinged Top, New Hampshire, Birch, 1790 .... 1800.00
Table, Card, Empire, Flip Top, Hairy Claw Feet, 1810, 29 In. 1200.00
Table, Card, Empire, Mahogany, 1830, 29 1/2 In. ....*Illus* 400.00
Table, Card, Empire, Mahogany, Folding Top, Inlaid, Claw Feet, 1835 .... 1000.00
Table, Card, Federal, Curly Maple, Inlaid Mahogany, C.1810, 30 In. 3300.00
Table, Card, Federal, Double Top, Crotch Mahogany Veneer, C.1790 .... 4500.00
Table, Card, Federal, Flamed Birch, Inlaid Mahogany, C.1810, 30 In. 4400.00
Table, Card, Federal, Flamed Birch, Inlaid Mahogany, C.1815, 29 In. 1980.00
Table, Card, Federal, Inlaid & Veneered, Mahogany, England, C.1790 .... 1200.00
Table, Card, Federal, Inlaid Mahogany, Hinged Circular Top, 34 In. 6600.00
Table, Card, Federal, Mahogany, D Shape, Tapered Legs, 1800s, 29 In. 5500.00

Furniture, Table, Altar, Carved Rosewood,
Open Apron, 73 In.

Furniture, Table, Card, Empire, Mahogany,
1830, 29 1/2 In.

Furniture, Table, Center, Baroque,
Oak, C.1900, 55 X 37 In.

Furniture, Table, Dressing, Queen
Anne, Maple, New England, 33 In.

Furniture, Table, Center, Red Marble,
Indochina, 19th Century

Furniture, Table, Drop Leaf, Sheraton,
Walnut, 48 X 63 In.

Furniture, Table, Galle,
2 Tiers, 1900, 30 In.

Table, Card, Federal, String Inlaid Top, Mahogany, C.1800, 30 In. 3000.00
Table, Card, George I, Walnut, D–Shaped Top, 3 Drawers, 29 In. 850.00
Table, Card, George III, Frieze Drawer, Mahogany, 1780, 38 1/2 In. 350.00
Table, Card, Hepplewhite, Bird's–Eye Maple Apron, Mahogany 7500.00
Table, Card, Hepplewhite, Mahogany, Eagle, Flower Inlay, 35 In. 1200.00
Table, Card, Hepplewhite, Shell, Bellflower & Line Inlay, C.1780 .... 6000.00
Table, Card, L.Majorelle, Marquetry, C.1900, 28 1/4 In. 4950.00
Table, Card, New England, Inlaid & Veneered Mahogany, C.1810 .... 5000.00
Table, Card, Philadelphia, Carved Mahogany, C.1830, 36 1/2 In. 1320.00
Table, Card, Queen Anne, Swing Leg, 1 Drawer, 14 X 30 X 28 In. 1400.00
Table, Card, Regency, Baize Surface, Mahogany, 28 1/2 In. 200.00
Table, Card, Sheraton, Mahogany, Rope Turned Legs, Swing Leg, 1820 .... 1250.00
Table, Card, Spiral Carved Legs, Brass Inlaid, Mahogany, 30 In. 950.00
Table, Card, Square Leather Top, Mahogany, 27 1/4 X 29 In. 33.00
Table, Center, Baroque, Oak, C.1900, 55 X 37 In. ....*Illus* 3740.00
Table, Center, Carved Oak, Rope Twist Legs, 31 X 47 In. 250.00
Table, Center, Charles X, Mahogany, Parcel Gilt, Marble Top, 32 In. 8525.00
Table, Center, Chinese, Hardwood, Rose Marble Insert, 33 In. 1500.00
Table, Center, Classical, Mahogany, Gilt, Marble, Round, 31 X 38 In. 8250.00
Table, Center, Napoleon III, Bronze, Marble Top, 47 1/2 In.Diam. 9500.00
Table, Center, Red Marble, Indochina, 19th Century ....*Illus* 4000.00
Table, Charles X, Mahogany, Rosewood, Drawer, Launier Style, Pair 2400.00
Table, Cherry, Dovetailed Drawer, 1 Board Top, 29 In. 375.00
Table, Child's, Enameled Noah's Ark, Alphabet & Numbers 175.00
Table, Chinese, Ebonized, Circular Top, Rose Marble Insert, 31 In. 500.00
Table, Chinese, Polychrome Painted Red Lacquer, 16 X 37 1/2 In. 660.00
Table, Chinese, Red Lacquer, Circular, 19th Century, 18 1/2 In. 3300.00
Table, Chippendale, Applewood, Drop Leaves, 1 Drawer, X Stretcher 1760.00
Table, Claw Feet, Round, Oak, 54 In. 895.00
Table, Coffee, Brass Banded Top, E.Kohlmann, C.1930, 39 1/2 In. 1100.00
Table, Coffee, Mahogany, Ball & Claw Feet, Floral, Glass Insert 135.00
Table, Coffee, Oriental Coromandel Type 750.00
Table, Coffin Stand Base, Pencil Post Legs, 28 1/2 In. 125.00
Table, Console, 1 Drawer, Carved Mahogany Frame, 32 1/4 In. 400.00
Table, Console, Adam, Painted, Marble Top, Jasperware Plaque, Pair 5500.00
Table, Console, American Empire, Mahogany, Serpentine, 1840 .... 3500.00
Table, Console, Carved Frame, Marble Top, 33 1/4 X 47 In. 1850.00
Table, Console, Etched Glass Top, Iron, French, C.1925, 35 1/4 In. 2750.00
Table, Console, Mirrored, Gilt Stencil Over Black Paint 6050.00
Table, Console, P.De Poli, Mahogany, Enameled Copper Top, 37 In. 3080.00
Table, Console, Scrolled Frieze, Wrought Iron, 1935, 22 In. 150.00
Table, Corner, Bowed Triangular Top, Mahogany, 33 1/2 In. 825.00
Table, Crossbanded Top, 2 Drawers, Mahogany, C.1800, 30 1/4 In. 4400.00
Table, Crouching Blackamoor Support, Marble Top, Italian 9750.00
Table, Cupid, Arms Raised As Support For Glass Top, 30 In. 2250.00
Table, Dining, Double Pedestal Base, Serpentine Ends, Mahogany 225.00
Table, Dining, Drop Leaf, Federal, C.1800, 62 1/4 In. 1980.00
Table, Dining, Drop Leaf, Federal, Mahogany, 29 X 69 1/2 In. 2475.00
Table, Dining, Drop Leaf, Federal, Tiger Maple, C.1810, 39 1/2 In. 1100.00
Table, Dining, Drop Leaf, Mahogany, C.1850, 59 1/2 In. 400.00
Table, Dining, Drop Leaf, Queen Anne, Cherry, C.1765, 47 1/2 In. 3850.00
Table, Dining, Drop Leaf, Shaped Skirt, Maple, 1750–80, 43 1/2 In. 750.00
Table, Dining, Drop Leaf, Sheraton, 3 Legs, 48 X 63 In. 575.00
Table, Dining, Drop Leaf, Walnut, Eliptical, Turned Legs 3150.00
Table, Dining, Duncan Phyfe Style, 44 X 69 In. 1760.00
Table, Dining, Federal, Inlaid Mahogany, 3 Part, C.1795 .... 7700.00
Table, Dining, Federal, Mahogany Veneer, Cherry, C.1815, 2 Part 7700.00
Table, Dining, Gustav Stickley, 5 Legs, Signed, C.1904, 48 In. 2400.00
Table, Dining, Gustav Stickley, No.656, 4 Leaves 4300.00
Table, Dining, Mahogany, 2 Pedestal, Scimitar Legs, 44 X 66 In. 175.00
Table, Dining, Mahogany, 3 Pedestal, Scimitar Legs, 42 X 144 In. 600.00
Table, Dining, New England, Mahogany, Birch, 1825 .... 8500.00
Table, Dining, Oak, Claw Feet, Round, 54 In. 795.00
Table, Dining, Shaker, Trestle Base, 72 In. 4400.00

Table, Dining, Victorian, 3 Leaves, Carved, Oak, C.1880	2640.00
Table, Dragon Legs, Soapstone Top Insert, Teak Frame, 32 In.	550.00
Table, Drawer Each End, Elm Base, Oak Top, Seats 12, C.1800	4800.00
Table, Dresden Porcelain Top, C.1850, 33 X 27 In.	4200.00
Table, Dressing, 3 Drawers, Painted Designs, C.1830, 39 3/4 In.	300.00
Table, Dressing, 3 Drawers, Walnut & Burl Elm, 30 X 29 In.	990.00
Table, Dressing, 3 Long & 3 Small Drawers, Walnut, 27 1/2 In.	4950.00
Table, Dressing, Adirondack, Side Mirror	3400.00
Table, Dressing, Attached Mirror, Gustav Stickley	3800.00
Table, Dressing, Beau Brummel, Biedermeier	900.00
Table, Dressing, Carved Mahogany, Oval Mirror, 19th Century	2100.00
Table, Dressing, Chippendale, 3 Drawers, Beading, Oak, 30 1/4 In.	850.00
Table, Dressing, Chippendale, 3 Drawers, Mahogany, 29 X 31 1/4 In.	2100.00
Table, Dressing, Federal, 1 Drawer, Painted & Stenciled, C.1820	350.00
Table, Dressing, Federal, Blue Paint, Gold Design, C.1820, 30 In.	1900.00
Table, Dressing, George III, Satinwood, Interior Mirror, 35 In.	2100.00
Table, Dressing, Kneehole, English, Mahogany, 37 X 38 1/2 In.	385.00
Table, Dressing, Lady's, Swivel Mirror, Kneehole, 1910, 56 X 42 In.	800.00
Table, Dressing, Louis XV, Fruitwood, Rectangular Top, 28 In.	1200.00
Table, Dressing, Majorelle, Mahogany, Inlaid, 3 Mirrors, 67 In.	7700.00
Table, Dressing, Neoclassical, Continental, 4 Ft.10 In. ....*Illus*	4950.00
Table, Dressing, Pine, Grained & Stenciled, 3 Drawers, C.1820	995.00
Table, Dressing, Queen Anne, Fan Carving, Tiger Maple, 31 1/2 In.	1500.00
Table, Dressing, Queen Anne, Maple, New England, 33 In. ....*Illus*	1500.00
Table, Dressing, Red & Black Graining, 3 Drawers, Pine, 29 In.	550.00
Table, Dressing, Walnut, Marble, End Candlestands, 88 In.	800.00
Table, Dressing, Walnut, Shell, Plum Carving, Mirror, England	425.00
Table, Drop Leaf, 6 Legs, 2–Board Top, Curly Maple, 46 In.	1650.00
Table, Drop Leaf, Beaded Edge, Stained Fruitwood, 29 1/2 X 4 Ft.	330.00
Table, Drop Leaf, Cherry Top & Legs, Bird's–Eye Maple, C.1830	650.00
Table, Drop Leaf, Cherry, 6 Legs, Acanthus Carvings, 45 In.	350.00
Table, Drop Leaf, Chippendale, Mahogany, Swing Legs, 18 X 42 In.	275.00
Table, Drop Leaf, Chippendale, Walnut Top, 8 Legs, 27 3/8 In.	750.00
Table, Drop Leaf, D–Shaped Leaves, Mahogany, C.1760, 50 In.	425.00
Table, Drop Leaf, Dutch, Floral Marquetry, Mahogany, C.1840, 29 In.	2500.00
Table, Drop Leaf, Federal, Cherrywood, Icicle Feet, 39 In.	7150.00
Table, Drop Leaf, Federal, Mahogany, 29 X 18 X 47 In.	400.00
Table, Drop Leaf, Federal, Maple, C.1810, 28 1/2 In.	700.00
Table, Drop Leaf, George II, Mahogany, Tapered Legs, C.1740, 28 In.	850.00
Table, Drop Leaf, George II, Oval Top, Walnut, 28 1/2 X 41 In.	950.00
Table, Drop Leaf, George II, Rectangular Leaves, Oak, 1750, 48 In.	225.00
Table, Drop Leaf, George III, Elmwood, C.1770, 27 X 40 In.	125.00
Table, Drop Leaf, George III, Mahogany, 19th Century, 27 1/2 In.	200.00
Table, Drop Leaf, New England, Curly Maple, C.1815	1950.00
Table, Drop Leaf, Queen Anne, Mahogany, Duck Feet, 16 X 33 In.	1550.00
Table, Drop Leaf, Queen Anne, Tiger Maple, Pegged, 1720–50, 47 In.	2500.00
Table, Drop Leaf, Sheraton, Walnut, 48 X 63 In. ....*Illus*	633.00
Table, Drop Leaf, Squared Leaves, Tiger Maple, C.1800, 28 In.	4000.00
Table, Drop Leaf, Tiger Maple Top, Spiral Legs, Castors, 1800s	560.00
Table, Drum, Carved & Gilded, Mahogany, C.1825	4950.00
Table, Drum, Leather Top, 8 Drawers, English, C.1880, 46 In.	2900.00
Table, Duncan Phyfe Style, Kittinger, 38 In.	200.00
Table, Dupre–Lafon, 2 Tiers, Leather, Oak, Bronze, Pedestal, 17 In.	7700.00
Table, Dutch, Mahogany & Satinwood, 1 Drawer, C.1800, 30 1/2 In.	950.00
Table, Eastlake, Rectangular, Incised Lines, Walnut, 28 1/4 In.	110.00
Table, Empire, Mahogany, Ormolu, Figural Pediments, Marble, 23 In.	350.00
Table, Figural, Putto & Dolphin, 1937, 27 In., Pair ....*Illus*	3025.00
Table, Galle, 2 Tiers, 1900, 30 In. ....*Illus*	5500.00
Table, Galle, Nesting, Inlaid Pecking Birds, Fruitwood, C.1900, 4	4125.00
Table, Game, Bellflower Inlaid, C.1780	900.00
Table, Game, Cherry, Connecticut, Inlaid Apron, C.1815, 35 In.	4500.00
Table, Game, Drop Leaf, Mother–of–Pearl & Wood Inlay	695.00
Table, Game, Duncan Phyfe, Mahogany, Trick Leg, C.1805, 28 In.	5775.00
Table, Game, Dutch, Mahogany, Floral Inlay, Baize Surface, 28 In.	850.00

Table, Game, Ebonized & Parcel Gilt, C.1865, 30 X 27 1/2 In. 500.00
Table, Game, George I, Demilune, Wells, Walnut, C.1720, 28 1/2 In. 7150.00
Table, Game, George III, Mahogany, Backgammon Board In Drawer 3300.00
Table, Game, Germany, Elmwood, Inlaid Chessboard, 30 X 32 In. 600.00
Table, Game, Hepplewhite, Cherry, Backgammon Board Top, Drawer 275.00
Table, Game, Hepplewhite, Satinwood, Ebony, Swing Leg, England, 1770 .... 3950.00
Table, Game, Inlaid Marble Game Board, C.1870, 30 X 35 In. 6875.00
Table, Game, Las Vegas, Faro Board, Mahogany, Green Cloth Top 1700.00
Table, Game, Mahogany, Baize Lined Surface, Inlay, 28 X 36 In. 2750.00
Table, Game, Mahogany, Crossed Lyre Support, C.1820, 39 In., Pair 4125.00
Table, Game, Mahogany, Inlaid Mahogany, Baize Lined Surface 9350.00
Table, Game, Oak, Canvas Covered Surface, Shaped Frieze, 30 In. 660.00
Table, Game, Queen Anne, Duck Feet, Mahogany, 27 3/4 In. 3900.00
Table, Game, Queen Anne, Square Leather Covered Top, 28 3/4 In. 195.00
Table, Game, Queen Anne, Triple Top, Walnut, C.1710, 28 1/2 In. 6325.00
Table, Game, Regency, Penwork, Stylized Figures, C.1820, 27 In. 6600.00
Table, Game, Rosewood, Leather Lined Surface, Inlay, C.1820 .... 2750.00
Table, Game, Walnut, Crossbanded, 1 Drawer, Cabriole Legs, German 4250.00
Table, Gateleg, Bird's-Eye Maple Trim On Apron 700.00
Table, Gateleg, D-Shaped Leaves, Drawer, Oak, 42 14 In. 300.00
Table, Gateleg, Mortised Apron, Oak, 29 1/2 In. 225.00
Table, Gateleg, Oval Drop Leaf Top, Oak, 15 3/4 X 36 In. 400.00
Table, Gateleg, Oval Drop Leaf, Drawer, English, Opens To 60 In. 600.00
Table, Gateleg, Oval Twin Flap Top, Cherry, 31 X 42 In. 132.00
Table, Gateleg, Spanish Feet, 2 Drawers, Oak, C.1850, 40 1/2 In. 650.00
Table, Gateleg, Walnut, 1 Drawer, Turned Legs, 28 3/4 In. 1300.00
Table, Gateleg, William & Mary, Maple, 45 In.Extended ....*Illus* 1000.00
Table, George II, Marble Top, Walnut, Mid–18th Century, 32 In. 7700.00
Table, George III, Center Medallion On Drawers, Mahogany, 37 In. 2850.00
Table, George III, Mahogany, Serpentine, 3 Drawers, 58 In. 4500.00
Table, George III, Mahogany, Tripod, Octagonal Galleried Top, 1780 .... 2000.00
Table, Gilt Bronze Mounted, Tulipwood, Parquetry, C.1900, 44 In. 4950.00
Table, Gio Ponti, Marble Top, End Pedestals, 1950, 6 Ft.6 In. 3850.00
Table, Grapevine Frieze, Mahogany & Parcel Gilt, 40 1/2 In., Pair 6000.00
Table, Grueby Tile Top, C.1900, 21 X 15 1/4 In. 4000.00
Table, Gustav Stickley, Cut Corners, 1902, 29 X 24 In. 2000.00
Table, Gustav Stickley, Trestle Base, Lower Shelf, C.1903, 28 In. 2500.00
Table, Handkerchief, Triangular Top, Flaps, Mahogany, 28 In. 3575.00
Table, Handkerchief, Triangular, English 2500.00
Table, Harvest, Maple, Pine, C.1800, 29 X 72 X 31 In. 2800.00
Table, Hunt, 8 Legs, 2 Swing Legs, Irish, Mahogany, 17 Leaves 4300.00
Table, Hutch, 1 Drawer, Round Top, Pine, 29 1/2 X 38 In. 325.00
Table, Hutch, 2–Board Top, Canadian, Pine, 18th Century, 47 1/2 In. 2750.00
Table, Hutch, 2–Board Top, Maple & Birch, 1760s 1850.00
Table, Hutch, 2–Board Top, New England, Early 19th Century 2400.00
Table, Hutch, Drawer, Old Red Paint, Pine, 26 3/4 X 46 3/4 In. 1500.00
Table, Hutch, Lift Lid, Box Base, Painted Pine, C.1800, 30 X 48 In. 500.00
Table, Hutch, Massachusetts, Paint Decorated, C.1850 .... 2250.00
Table, Iberian, Baroque, Iron Mounted, Walnut, C.1680, 6 Ft.9 In. 8500.00
Table, Inlaid Marquetry, Walnut, Satinwood & Burl, 31 In. 1650.00
Table, Iron Pedestal, Brunswick, Balke, Collender Co., 46 In. 400.00
Table, Islamic, Center Fish, Birds, Men, Brass, Octagonal, 23 In. 605.00
Table, John B.Hill, Serpentine Top, Deerfield, 1816 .... 1980.00
Table, Kitchen, Porcelain Top, Blue Trim, 4 Matching Vinyl Chairs 95.00
Table, Lamp, Gustav Stickley, Oak, C.1909, 28 7/8 In. 1025.00
Table, Lamp, Hand Carved Mahogany, Dolphin Feet, Octagonal Top 850.00
Table, Lamp, Teakwood, Carved, Griffin Legs, Rose Marble, Round 325.00
Table, Library, Carved Garland, Scrolls, 2 Drawers, Oak, 66 In. 1400.00
Table, Library, Exposed Tenons, 1 Drawer, Arts & Crafts 350.00
Table, Library, Gustav Stickley, 2 Drawers, Shelf, 30 X 48 In. 800.00
Table, Library, Gustav Stickley, Leather Top, Clear Finish 2200.00
Table, Library, Roycroft, Drawers, Slats Side, Logo, Mahogany, 1910 .... 3150.00
Table, Library, Spanish, Walnut, 3 Drawers, Turned Legs, 32 In. 2000.00
Table, Library, Victorian, Carved, Walnut, C.1880 .... 1210.00

Furniture, Table,
Dressing,
Neoclassical,
Continental,
4 Ft.10 In.

Furniture, Table, Figural, Putto & Dolphin,
1937, 27 In., Pair

Table, Limbert, Cutout Sides, Oval, Lower Shelf 7500.00
Table, Limbert, Rectangular Cutout Legs, Octagonal 6000.00
Table, Limbert, Turtle Top, Blind Drawer, Cutouts, 1910, 48 In. 1700.00
Table, Louis XV Style, Serpentine Marble Top, Peg Feet, 29 In. 1200.00
Table, Louis XV, Brass Gallery, Inlaid Vases, Mahogany, 29 1/4 In. 1430.00
Table, Louis XV, Parquetry, Drawers, Gallery, Tulipwood, 28 1/2 In. 350.00
Table, Louis XV, Tulipwood Parquetry, Brass Edge, 26 X 19 In. 1540.00
Table, Mahogany, Round Cherry Inlaid Top, 20th Century, 33 In. 350.00
Table, Marble Top, Raised On Eagle, Wings Back, Pine, 35 1/2 In. 2200.00
Table, Marquetry, Geometric, Birds, Refinished, Pedestal, Square 225.00
Table, Napoleon III, Glass Center, Cast Iron, Round, 32 X 33 In. 7150.00
Table, Napoleon III, Pewter, Brass Inset, Tulipwood, C.1855, 30 In. 2200.00
Table, Nesting, Galle, Fishing Scenes, Signed, 26 & 27 In. 1545.00
Table, Oak, Leaves Roll Out In Accordion Fashion 375.00
Table, Oak, Scalloped Apron, Cabriole Legs, 1 Drawer, French, 1780 .... 2000.00
Table, Octagonal, Floral Carved Apron, Oak, C.1930, 28 1/2 In. 160.00
Table, Orchid, Perforated Removable Top, Handles, Mahogany, 31 In. 1925.00
Table, Papier-Mache, Victorian, Floral Center, Pedestal, English 695.00
Table, Pegged Construction, 2 Drawers, Walnut, 3 X 5 Ft. 2900.00
Table, Pembroke, 3 Drawers, 3 False Drawers, Mahogany, C.1800 .... 2310.00
Table, Pembroke, Cherry, 18th Century, 32 In. 475.00
Table, Pembroke, Chippendale, Drop Leaf Top, Country, 26 3/4 In. 300.00
Table, Pembroke, Corner Designs, Hardwood, 28 1/2 X 42 In. 500.00
Table, Pembroke, Curly Maple, Turned Legs, 29 1/2 In. 400.00
Table, Pembroke, English, Inlaid Urns On Posts, Mahogany, 29 In. 4750.00
Table, Pembroke, Federal, Hinged Leaves, Drawer, Mahogany, C.1815 .... 3500.00
Table, Pembroke, Federal, Inlaid Mahogany, C.1800, 28 3/4 In. 7700.00
Table, Pembroke, Federal, Mahogany, Rope Carved Legs, 28 3/4 In. 450.00
Table, Pembroke, George II, D-Shaped Flaps, Drawers, Mahogany 2300.00
Table, Pembroke, Hepplewhite, 3-Board Top, Cherry, 20 1/4 In. 250.00
Table, Pembroke, Hepplewhite, Square Legs, Scroll Edge Top, 33 In. 1075.00
Table, Pembroke, Mahogany, Satinwood Inlaid Drawers, Oval, C.1785 .... 2850.00
Table, Pembroke, Regency, Drawer, Mahogany, C.1810, 35 1/2 In. 450.00
Table, Pembroke, Sheraton, Curly Maple, 29 1/4 In. 1000.00
Table, Pembroke, Stringing, Drawer, Mahogany, C.1790, 28 3/4 In. 1000.00
Table, Petticoat, Empire, Mahogany, Marble Top 375.00
Table, Pier, Classical, Mahogany, Marble Top, 38 1/2 In. ....*Illus* 4510.00
Table, Pier, Classical, Mahogany, Marble, Acanthus, 38 X 43 In. 6050.00
Table, Pier, Mahogany, Marble Top, Metal Mounted, C.1820, 40 In. 6875.00
Table, Pier, Peter Hunt, Serpentine Shelf, Painted, C.1940, 33 In. 650.00
Table, Pine, 1 Drawer, Western Ontario, C.1860, 30 In. 1200.00
Table, Pine, With Lazy Susan, Round 1395.00
Table, Plank Top, Trestle Supports, Stuart, Pine, 102 In. 400.00
Table, Powder, Center Mirror, 3 Drawers, 18th Century, French 1100.00
Table, Pub, Pine, Flying Buttress Supports, England, 28 3/4 In. 200.00
Table, Queen Anne, Inset Glass Top, Walnut & Parquetry, 20 In. 440.00
Table, Queen Anne, Maple, Cabriole Legs, 1 Board Pine Top, 35 In. 5750.00
Table, Queen Anne, Swing Leg, Mahogany, 54 In. 650.00

Table, Ram's Head & Hoofs, Polished Steel, Glass Top, 48 In. 350.00
Table, Refectory, Carved Legs, Marquetry Apron, Oak, 31 1/2 In. 1075.00
Table, Refectory, Dutch Baroque, 6 Turned Legs, Oak, 61 In. 1700.00
Table, Refectory, Dutch Baroque, Oak, 19th Century, 61 In. 1700.00
Table, Refectory, Italian, Walnut, Inlaid Band, Scroll Legs, 78 In. 250.00
Table, Refectory, Renaissance, Oak, Rectangular Top, 106 1/2 In. 1500.00
Table, Refectory, Walnut, Acanthus Carved Legs, 108 In. 3600.00
Table, Regency, Edwards & Roberts, Rosewood, Gallery, Lyre, Drawer 750.00
Table, Renaissance Style, Carved Mermaids, Walnut, 28 1/2 In. 375.00
Table, Ring Turned Legs, Drawer, Maple, 18th Century, 45 In. 1000.00
Table, Rococo Revival, Marble Top, Rosewood, C.1850, 29 X 34 In. 1000.00
Table, Rosewood, Inset Marble Top, Lion Carved Legs, 32 In. 550.00
Table, Rosewood, White Marble Turtle Top 350.00
Table, Roycroft, 2 Open Shelves, Slat Sides, 30 X 26 In. 2000.00
Table, Sawbuck, Iron Rod Braces, Beaded Apron Edge, 47 1/2 In. 295.00
Table, Scrolling Vines On Drawer Front, Oak, C.1900, 37 X 55 In. 3400.00
Table, Serving, Open Shelves, Carved, Oak, C.1880 .... 490.00
Table, Serving, Queen Anne, Acanthus Knees, Mahogany, 30 In. 880.00
Table, Sewing, Classical, Mahogany, Maple Veneer, 2 Drawers, 1810 .... 6600.00
Table, Sewing, Drop Leaf, Bag Underneath 1100.00
Table, Sewing, Federal, Mahogany, 2 Drop Leaves, Bag Drawer, 29 In. 1870.00
Table, Sewing, Federal, Tambour, Inlaid Mahogany, Hinged, 29 In. 2860.00
Table, Sewing, George III, Mahogany, Floral Band, 1 Drawer, 28 In. 1800.00
Table, Sewing, Mahogany, 2 Drawers 2420.00
Table, Sewing, Oval, Glass Top, Walnut, 70 In. 750.00
Table, Sewing, Regency, 2 Drawers, Ivory Pulls, Rosewood, C.1880 .... 800.00
Table, Sewing, Work Drawer, Upholstered Bag, Lift Lid, 28 3/4 In. 750.00
Table, Shaker, Enfield, Pine & Poplar, 28 3/4 X 30 1/2 In. 425.00
Table, Shaker, Sewing, 1 Drawer, Pine, Canterbury, 1830, 17 X 21 In. 1700.00
Table, Shaker, Sorting, Poplar, Oak, Harvard, 1860, 28 X 17 In. 600.00
Table, Shaker, Tilt Top, Cherry, Birdcage, Spider Legs, 1850, 34 In. 800.00
Table, Shaker, Trestle, Cherry, Iron Brace, New Lebanon, 1835 .... 5500.00
Table, Sheraton, Cherry, Maple, Turned Legs, 36 In. 225.00
Table, Silk Inset Top, Porcelain Plaques, Mahogany, C.1870, 27 In. 1980.00
Table, Silver, George III, Carved Fretwork, Mahogany, 27 1/2 In. 4950.00
Table, Sofa, Mahogany, 2 Drawers, Acanthus Carved Base, 43 In. 800.00
Table, Sorting, Shaker, Oak, Tray Top, 1 Drawer, New Lebanon, 29 In. 2200.00
Table, Stuart, Plank Top, Shoe Feet, Pine & Oak, 29 X 102 In. 350.00
Table, Tapered Legs, Dark Varnish, Pine, 1/2 Round, 24 1/2 In. 260.00
Table, Tavern, 2 Drawers, Beaded Skirt, Painted Walnut, 29 1/4 In. 6000.00
Table, Tavern, Drawer, Beaded Edges, Ball Feet, Walnut, 28 X 30 In. 1500.00
Table, Tavern, English Country, Sycamore, Early 19th Century 300.00
Table, Tavern, Octagonal Top, Carved Pine, 26 X 30 In. 2200.00
Table, Tavern, Oval Top, Button Feet, Maple & Pine, C.1780, 28 In. 2750.00
Table, Tavern, Pine, Maple, New England, 18th Century, 36 X 26 In. 2600.00
Table, Tavern, Pine, New England, Breadboard Sides, 1 Drawer, 1820 .... 3500.00
Table, Tavern, Queen Anne, 3 Drawers, Walnut, C.1760, 29 X 57 In. 3025.00
Table, Tavern, Queen Anne, Maple, Pine, 1 Drawer, Breadboard Top 3750.00
Table, Tavern, Walnut, 1 Drawer Over Skirt, H Stretcher 1500.00
Table, Tavern, William & Mary, New England, Red Paint, 1710–40 .... 3575.00
Table, Tavern, Windsor, Worn Red Paint, 2 Board Pine Top, 29 In. 4700.00
Table, Tea, Birdcage Mechanism, Dish Top, Philadelphia, 34 In. 5500.00
Table, Tea, Birdcage, Connecticut, C.1760, 28 3/4 In. 6500.00
Table, Tea, Chippendale, American, Tiger Maple, C.1780. ^^ X 33 In. 1000.00
Table, Tea, Chippendale, New England, C.1790, Walnut, 1/4 In. 600.00
Table, Tea, George I, Frieze Drawer, Walnut, C.1725, 28 3/4 In. 3630.00
Table, Tea, Queen Anne, Tilt Top, Mahogany, C.1780 .... 2850.00
Table, Tea, Serpentine, New England, Mahogany, C.1780, 28 1/2 In. 4250.00
Table, Tea, Tilt Top, 2 Board Top, Cherry, 27 X 25 1/2 In. 250.00
Table, Tea, Tilt Top, Elongated Feet, Mahogany, 28 1/4 In. 1400.00
Table, Tea, Tilt Top, Mahogany, Massachusetts, C.1800, 29 1/2 In. 2200.00
Table, Tea, Tilt Top, Pennsylvania, Walnut, C.1760, 29 In. 3750.00
Table, Tea, Vase & Ring Pedestal, Mahogany, C.1780, 28 1/2 In. 4250.00
Table, Teapoy, Stepped Top, Mahogany, C.1830, 32 In. 600.00

Table, Textured Pewter Top, Wrought Iron Legs & Frame, 44 In.	2300.00
Table, Tilt Top, Acanthus Carved Legs, Mahogany, 28 1/2 In.	990.00
Table, Tilt Top, Acanthus Carved Stem, Mahogany, 26 In.	495.00
Table, Tilt Top, Birdcage Support, Walnut, Penna., 28 1/2 In.	1870.00
Table, Tilt Top, Chippendale, Mahogany, New England, C.1780, 30 In.	600.00
Table, Tilt Top, George II, Mahogany, Tripartite Legs, Pad Feet	750.00
Table, Tilt Top, George II, Walnut, Circular Top, Pad Feet, 36 In.	300.00
Table, Tilt Top, Lacquer & Papier–Mache, 24 In. ....*Illus*	302.50
Table, Tilt Top, Tripod, Parcel Gilt, Black Japanned, 29 1/2 In.	2310.00
Table, Tilt Top, Uncle Daniel, Winona, Ohio, Poplar, 1837, 27 In.	475.00
Table, Trestle, Stuart, Pine, Oak, Plank Top, 17th Century, 102 In.	350.00
Table, Tricolor Marquetry Top, Inlaid Pedestal, American, 29 In.	2300.00
Table, Veneered Drawer, Brass Mounted, Tulipwood, 28 X 13 1/2 In.	528.00
Table, Walnut, Fruit & Floral Carvings, European, 62 In.	1200.00
Table, Walnut, Parquet Dish Top, Foliate Tripod Bse, 24 In.	175.00
Table, Wash, Shaker, Pine, Blue Gray Paint, Sabbathday Lake, 32 In.	2900.00
Table, Wicker, Bar Harbor, Wooden Top, Painted, 72 X 30 X 23 In.	495.00
Table, Wicker, Mahogany Top, Early 20th Century, 54 In. ....*Illus*	750.00
Table, Wicker, Open Lower Shelf, Mahogany Top, 30 X 54 1/2 In.	750.00
Table, William & Mary, Inlaid, Floral Reserves, 22 X 76 In.	2500.00
Table, Work, 2 Drawers, 2 Board Top, Turned Legs, 27 X 29 In.	350.00
Table, Work, Breadboard Top, Red Paint, 29 X 44 In.	175.00
Table, Work, Carved Leafage At Corners, Mahogany Veneered, C.1830	900.00
Table, Work, Crotch Veneers, Oval Flanking Panel, Mahogany, C.1800	7000.00
Table, Work, Empire, 2 Drawers, Tiger Maple, C.1860, 27 3/4 In.	425.00
Table, Work, Federal, Rosewood Veneered Top, Mahogany, 30 1/2 In.	650.00
Table, Work, Hepplewhite, Polychrome Design, 1 Drawer, Satinwood	1900.00
Table, Work, Hepplewhite, Red Paint, Drawers, Poplar, 51 1/2 In.	385.00
Table, Work, Hepplewhite, Scrubbed Top, Drawer, Pine, 30 1/2 In.	400.00
Table, Work, Hepplewhite, Walnut Square Legs, Drawer, Leaf, 43 In.	135.00
Table, Work, Inlaid Edge, Bowed Frieze, Mahogany, 29 X 22 In.	1540.00
Table, Work, Maple Legs, Cherry Apron, Cherry Top, 33 X 41 3/4 In.	150.00

Furniture, Table, Tilt Top,
Lacquer & Papier–Mache, 24 In.

Furniture, Table, Gateleg, William
& Mary, Maple, 45 In.Extended

Furniture, Table, Writing,
Classical, Rosewood,
Stenciled, 1830

Furniture, Table, Wicker, Mahogany Top,
Early 20th Century, 54 In.

Furniture, Table, Pier, Classical,
Mahogany, Marble Top, 38 1/2 In.

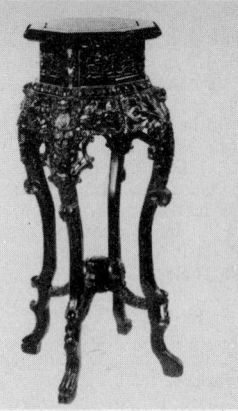

Furniture, Tabouret, Marble Insert, Lion
Legs, Rosewood, 32 In.

Furniture, Tabouret, Rosewood, Octagonal,
Chinese, 36 In.

Table, Work, Nailed Apron, 2 Drawers, Back Drop Leaf, 30 In. 200.00
Table, Work, Painted Gray, White Speckles, Pine, 75 3/4 In. 1100.00
Table, Work, Queen Anne, Walnut, 3 Overlapping Drawers, Pa., 58 In. 1800.00
Table, Work, Rosewood & Mother-of-Pearl, Chinese, C.1830, 19 In. 1000.00
Table, Work, Shaker, Birch, Breadboard Top, Canterbury, 1830, 45 In. 3500.00
Table, Work, Shaker, Birch, Cherry, Cream Paint, 1820, 26 X 42 In. 550.00
Table, Work, Shaker, Breadboard, White On Underside, Low 2000.00
Table, Work, Shaker, Pine, Birch, Scrubbed Top, Canterbury, 63 In. 1750.00
Table, Work, Shaker, Pine, Green, 1 Drawer, 25 X 23 In. 1000.00
Table, Work, Shaker, Pine, Oak, Drawer, Sabbathday Lake, 1860, 27 In. 300.00
Table, Work, Tilt-Up Top, Rope Carved Posts, Mahogany, 29 3/8 In. 500.00
Table, Work, Walnut, 2 Drawers, 3 Removable Board Top, 28 X 60 In. 1350.00
Table, Writing, Classical, Rosewood, Stenciled, 1830 ....*Illus* 1800.00
Table, Writing, Gothic Revival, Ebonized Oak, C.1880, 4 Ft.8 In. 7700.00
Table, Writing, Kneehole, Foliate Carved, Late 19th Century 4360.00
Table, Writing, Lady's, Fruitwood, Bronze Dore Trim, Marble, French 4500.00
Table, Writing, Regency, Ebony Inlaid Mahogany, C.1810, 29 1/2 In. 7700.00
Table, Writing, Stencil Design, Veneered Rosewood, C.1830, 30 In. 1800.00
Tabouret, Carved Rosewood, Inset Rouge Marble Top, China, 24 In. 250.00
Tabouret, Gustav Stickley, Cross Stretcher, 16 X 14 In.Diam. 375.00
Tabouret, L. & J.G.Stickley, Legs Through Top Stretcher, 20 In. 650.00
Tabouret, L.& J.G.Stickley, Octagonal Top, Oak, C.1912, 20 In. 1025.00
Tabouret, Limbert, Cutout 2250.00
Tabouret, Louis XV, Upholstered Seat, Walnut, 19 In. 475.00
Tabouret, Marble Insert, Lion Legs, Rosewood, 32 In. ....*Illus* 550.00
Tabouret, Rosewood, Octagonal, Chinese, 36 In. ....*Illus* 440.00
Tansu, Red Lacquer Frame, Wood Top, Silk Doors, 70 In. ....*Illus* 1265.00
Tea Cart, Victorian, Golden Oak 265.00
Tea Cart, Walnut, Imperial, Grand Rapids 200.00
Tea Cart, Wooden Wheels, Oak 80.00
Terrarium, English Gothic, Top Aquarium, Floor Stand, 1860 .... 3600.00
Tray, Butler's, Art Nouveau, Mahogany, Belgian, 1900 .... 8500.00
Tray, Butler's, Chippendale, Mahogany, English, 1780, 37 X 21 In. 2000.00
Tray, Butler's, Fold-Up Edges, Oak, Opens To 26 3/4 X 37 In. 325.00
Tray, Butler's, Folding Stand, Galleried, Mahogany, 27 3/4 In. 275.00
Tray, Butler's, Folding Stand, Mahogany, 18 1/2 X 26 1/4 In. 500.00
Tray, Butler's, Stand, Refinished Oak, 18 1/2 X 30 1/2 In. 140.00
Tray, Drawer, Handles, Bone Knobs, Mahogany, 11 1/2 X 12 1/2 In. 475.00
Tray, Galle, Castle Tower, Marquetry, Octagonal, 17 1/2 In. 1300.00
Tray, Galle, Marquetry, Irises, Handles, Fruitwood, Signed 1000.00
Tray, Inlaid Shell, Scalloped Rim, Mahogany, 15 1/2 X 23 In. 245.00

Tray, Tole, Floral, Mounted On Contemporary Base, French 1800.00
Vitrine, Bombe Form, Cherub & Floral Enamel Design, 32 1/2 In. 1265.00
Vitrine, Corner, Louis XV, Serpentine Top, Glazed Door, Mahogany 325.00
Vitrine, Glazed Door & Sides, Brass, Mirrored Back, 5 Ft., Pair 3575.00
Vitrine, Ivory, Ebony, Pewter, Mirrors, Portraits, Bugatti, 75 In. 7700.00
Vitrine, Louis XIV, 4 Shaped Glass Panels, Painted Design 770.00
Vitrine, Louis XV, Bronze Mounted, Kingwood, 6 Ft. 4000.00
Vitrine, Louis XV–XVI, Mahogany, Ormolu, Marble Top ....*Illus* 1500.00
Vitrine, Louis XVI, Curved Glass Sides, Mahogany, 29 1/4 In. 825.00
Vitrine, Marble Top, F.Linke, Paris, Mahogany, C.1900, 4 Ft.1 In. 3850.00
Vitrine, Napoleon III, Ebonized & Brass Mounted, C.1870, 31 In. 550.00
Wardrobe, American Classical, Carved Mahogany, C.1830, Triple 1145.00
Wardrobe, Biedermeier, Interior Shelves, 81 1/2 In. 475.00
Wardrobe, Ionic Columns, Stenciled, Mahogany, C.1825, 93 In. 7700.00
Wardrobe, Oak, Knockdown, Applied Carvings 600.00
Wardrobe, Pine, 2 Paneled Doors, 2 Drawers, Dated 1835, Va., 80 In. 4500.00
Wardrobe, Walnut, Knockdown, Ornate Top, Carved Keyhole, 92 In. 875.00
Washstand, Corner, Hepplewhite, Cherry, C.1800 ....*Illus* 330.00
Washstand, Dark Oak, Towel Bar 110.00
Washstand, Divided Wash Bowl, French, Metal, Manufacurer's Seal 750.00
Washstand, Drawer In Base, Gallery, Walnut, 37 1/2 In. 285.00
Washstand, Federal, Mahogany, 22 1/2 In. ....*Illus* 523.00
Washstand, Federal, Mahogany, Shaped Top, Turned Legs, 22 1/2 In. 475.00
Washstand, George III, Drawer In Lower Shelf, Mahogany, C.1770 .... 175.00
Washstand, Hepplewhite, Cherry, C.1800, 46 In. 300.00
Washstand, Hepplewhite, Pine, Worn White, Green Striped, Gallery 275.00
Washstand, Marble Top, Serpentine Front, Mahogany, C.1840 .... 1050.00
Washstand, Marble Top, Walnut 190.00
Washstand, Oak, Bow Front, Towel Bar 275.00
Washstand, Shaker, Pine, Bootjack Ends, Canterbury, 1830, 35 In. 3500.00
Washstand, Shaker, Walnut, Poplar, Green Over Varnish, New Lebanon 7000.00
Washstand, Splashboard, Drawer, Grain Painted, C.1830, 36 1/4 In. 275.00

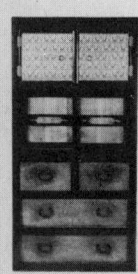

Furniture, Tansu,
Red Lacquer Frame,
Wood Top, Silk
Doors, 70 In.

Furniture, Vitrine,
Louis XV–XVI,
Mahogany, Ormolu,
Marble Top

Furniture, Washstand,
Corner, Hepplewhite,
Cherry, C.1800

Furniture, Washstand,
Federal, Mahogany,
22 1/2 In.

If you see any numbers or letters on the frame of a wooden piece, do
not remove or erase them. They may refer to a catalog; and, eventually,
you may be able to attribute the piece to the proper manufacturer.

Washstand, Venetian, Rococo, Lacquered, Cabriole Legs, 35 X 17 In. 5500.00
Washstand, Walnut, Backsplash, 2 Drawers & 2 Doors 185.00
Washstand, Walnut, Marble, Candle Shelves, John McKee, Kalamazoo 500.00
Wastebasket, Gustav Stickley, C.1905, 11 3/4 In. 2500.00
Wastebasket, Slat Sided, Gustav Stickley, 1906, 14 X 12 In. 1500.00
Wastepaper Basket, Stickley, Vertical Slats, Label, C.1910, 14 In. 1810.00
Whatnot, 3 Tiers, Casters, Mahogany, Victorian, 37 In. 5775.00
Whatnot, 3 Tiers, Victorian, Openwork, Carved Walnut, 41 In. 145.00
Whatnot, 5 Tiers, Walnut 220.00
Whatnot, Walnut, Original Mirrors, Original Silk Backing, Label 2860.00
Window Seat, Classical, Original Upholstery, C.1850 .... 1450.00
Window Seat, Neoclassical, Cushion, Green Paint, Italy, 6 Ft. 4400.00
Window Seat, Neoclassical, Gilt Wood, Upholstered, Cushion, 8 Ft. 3575.00
Window Seat, Overupholstered Seat, Mahogany, C.1800, 39 In. 2300.00
Window Seat, Serpentine Front, Mahogany, Mid–19th Century 385.00

G-ARGy-
ROUSSEAU   Gabriel Argy–Rousseau, born in 1885, was a French glass artist who
                produced a variety of objects in the Art Deco style. His mark, "G.
                Argy–Rousseau," was usually impressed.

G.ARGY–ROUSSEAU, Lamp, Boudoir, Floral Petal, Wrought Iron Base, 8 In. 8000.00
Pendant, Pate–De–Verre, Pinecone, Needles, C.1925, 2 1/4 In. 1430.00
Pendant, Red Berries, Silk Cord, Signed, C.1925, 2 3/4 In. 1100.00
Shade, Pate–De–Verre, Aztec Designs, Signed, 1925, 2 3/4 In. 2475.00
Vase, Fan Form Flowers, Ovoid, Signed, C.1925, 10 1/2 In. 7700.00

Emile Galle, the famous French designer, made ceramics after 1874.
The pieces were marked with the initials "E.G." impressed, "Em.
Galle Faiencerie de Nancy," or a version of his signature. Galle is
best known for his glass, listed in the next section.

GALLE POTTERY, Figurine, Owl, Raised Circular Base, Earth Tones, 12 3/4 In. 4400.00
Vase, Captain's, Decanter Shape, Chartreuse, Brown Buds, 6 In. 950.00
Watch Holder, Faience, 10 In. 355.00

Galle   Galle was a designer who made glass, pottery, furniture, and other
             Art Nouveau items. Emile Galle founded his factory in France in
             1874. After Galle's death in 1904, the firm continued to make glass
             and furniture until 1931. The name "Galle" was used as a mark, but
             it was often hidden in the design of the object. Galle Pottery is
             listed above and his furniture is listed in the Furniture section.

GALLE, Bowl, Exotic Flowers, Enameled, Dark Green, Signed, 4 1/2 In. 1300.00
Bowl, Leaves & Berries, Orange Ground, Cameo Signed, 2 1/2 In. 700.00
Bowl, Lobed, Enameled & Gilt Branches, Signed, C.1900, 11 1/4 In. 3850.00
Box, Butterflies On Domed Cover, Clematis, Signed, C.1900, 6 In. 2475.00
Box, Cameo, Cover, Poppy Blossoms, Gray Glass, 1900, 4 1/4 In. 900.00
Box, Frosted Ground, Pastel Colors, 3 X 5 1/2 In. 2250.00
Charger, Lotus Blossoms, Pads & Leafage, Signed, C.1900, 16 1/4 In. 7975.00
Charger, Overlaid Blue, Marguerites, Opaque Ground, Signed, 15 7/8 In. 6050.00
Compote, Forget–Me–Nots, Metal Gilt Base, Signed, 7 1/4 In. 850.00
Compote, Maple Leaves, Frosted Outside, Pink Pods Inside, 6 1/2 In. 850.00
Compote, Pink Enameled Flowers Inside, Carved Leaves Outside, 4 In. 850.00
Lamp, Blossom Sprays, Pelican On Bronze Base, Signed, 19 1/4 In. 8800.00
Lamp, Domed Green & White Branches Shade, Bronze Base, 18 1/2 In. 7700.00
Lamp, Meandering Clematis, Bronze Overlay, Signed, C.1900, 14 1/2 In. 9900.00
Night–Light, Cameo, Bronze Base, Jellyfish, Purple, Blue, Cream, 7 In. 800.00
Perfume Bottle, Cameo, Yellow Glass, Red Blossoms, C.1900, 10 In. 2475.00
Pitcher, Bleeding Hearts, Frosted Handle, Signed, 3 In. 750.00
Pitcher, Floral Design, Green, Mottled Red & Brown, 3 1/4 In. 1650.00
Powder Jar, Cameo, Art Glass, Red Carved Flowers, Signed 1500.00
Powder Jar, Green Ground, Red Carved Flowers, Signed, 6 In. 1650.00
Vase, 3 Color Cameo, Olive To Blue To Rose Floral, 10 In. ....*Illus* 1980.00
Vase, Algae & Starfish, Pinched, Scalloped, Chinese Style, 5 In. 7700.00
Vase, Allover Polished Orange Flowers, Lemon Ground, 7 1/2 In. 1350.00
Vase, Blue & Green Floral, Signed, 3 3/4 In. 695.00
Vase, Brown & Yellow Pansies Silhouette, Tricornered, 3 3/4 In. 625.00

Galle, Vase, 3 Color
Cameo, Olive To Blue
To Rose Floral, 10 In.

A video inventory is being offered in some cities. It is a color video-cassette recording done in your home with your voice describing the antiques. Keep it in a safe deposit box for a permanent record of your collection.

Vase, Brown & Yellow Peonies, Shaded Pink Ground, 5 In.	700.00
Vase, Bud, Berry & Leaf, Pale Green Ground, Cameo, Signed, 7 In.	1000.00
Vase, Bud, Leaves & Fruit, Golden Olive, Marked, 11 3/4 In.	750.00
Vase, Bud, Rose Fruit Branches, Pale Amber Ground, 8 In.	850.00
Vase, Butterflies Over Iris Blossoms, Signed, C.1900, 24 3/4 In.	7700.00
Vase, Cameo, 5 Petal Blossoms, Butter Yellow, Signed, 4 5/8 In.	3200.00
Vase, Cameo, Carved Purple Sweetpeas, Frosted Ground, 5 1/2 In.	695.00
Vase, Cameo, Enameled, Applied Design, Cylindrical Neck, 23 In.	6325.00
Vase, Cameo, Frosted Gray Glass, Violet, Blossoming Columbine, 15 In.	4620.00
Vase, Cameo, Landscape, Gray, Goldenrod, Yellow, Lake Scene, 24 3/4 In.	6600.00
Vase, Cameo, Peonies, Brown, Yellow, Pink Ground, 5 In.	700.00
Vase, Cameo, Yellow Glass, Teardrop Form, Tiger Lily Branches, 20 In.	6600.00
Vase, Carved Flowering Branches, Leaves, White Ground, 5 In.	850.00
Vase, Enameled Bumblebee, Dragonfly, Applied Handles, Oviform, 9 In.	3850.00
Vase, Ferns & Grass Leaves, Black Over Yellow, 10 1/2 In.	695.00
Vase, Ferns, Leaves, Buds, Etched, Frosted White, Conical, 13 3/4 In.	1980.00
Vase, Flask Form, Wild Poppy Blossoms, Signed, C.1900, 13 1/4 In.	7150.00
Vase, Floral & Leaf, Yellow Ground, Footed, Cameo, Signed, 5 In.	900.00
Vase, Floral Design, Brown & Lavender, Clear Ground, 4 In.	500.00
Vase, Green Leaves, Frosted Ground, Signed, 4 In.	325.00
Vase, Green, Red, Octopus, Coral, Verrerie Parlante, Signed, 6 In.	600.00
Vase, Hydrangea, Stems, Leaves, Etched, Frosted, Bulbous, 11 3/4 In.	2200.00
Vase, Iris Blossoms, Buds, Lavender & Amber, Signed, C.1900, 15 3/4 In.	6600.00
Vase, Jack–In–The–Pulpit Blossoms, Leaves, Signed, C.1900, 20 1/4 In.	7975.00
Vase, Landscape, Milky White Ground, Gray Blue, Signed, 6 1/4 In.	1250.00
Vase, Landscape, White Ground With Gray Blue, Signed, 6 1/4 In.	1250.00
Vase, Lavender Cut Flowers, Green Ground, Signed, 5 In.	1045.00
Vase, Leaves & Large Flowers, Lavender & Pink On Frost, 8 In.	2950.00
Vase, Oak Leaves & Acorns On Frosted Ground, 13 1/2 In.	1550.00
Vase, Oak Leaves, Acorns, Rust & Green, Salmon Ground, 13 1/2 In.	1550.00
Vase, Olive To Blue To Rose, Floral, Signed, 10 In.	3200.00
Vase, Overlaid Raspberry Over White, Morning Glories, Signed, 7 In.	4840.00
Vase, Plum Flowers & Leaves, Butterscotch Ground, Signed, 6 1/4 In.	875.00
Vase, Poppies, Leaves, Tangerine To Orange, Signed, 9 In.	3500.00
Vase, Shaded Green Pods From Branches, Leaves, Signed, 2 1/2 In.	650.00
Vase, Water Landscape, Blossoming Iris, Signed, C.1900, 9 3/8 In.	4125.00
Vase, Wisteria Flowers & Leaves, Ginger Jar Shape, Signed, 3 In.	735.00
Vase, Yellow, Red Overlaid, Plants, Berries, Signed, 5 1/4 In.	3080.00

Game plates are plates of any make decorated with pictures of birds, animals, or fish. The game plates usually came in sets consisting of twelve dishes and a serving platter. These sets were most popular during the 1880s.

GAME PLATE, Natural Habitat, Scalloped Rim, Each Different, Limoges, 6 Piece	450.00
Set, Each With Different Scene, Limoges, Platter, 12 Plates	1450.00
GAME SET, Each With Different Scene, Limoges, Platter, 12 Plates	1450.00

Children's games of all sorts are collected. Of special interest are any board games or card games. Other games may be found listed under Toy, Card, or the name of the character or celebrity featured in the game.

GAME, A Tumble Bum Dice Game, Remco, Box, 1950s	50.00
Addams Family, Milton Bradley, Spinner Board, 1973	30.00
Alice In Wonderland, McLoughlin Bros., 1905	110.00
Ally Slooper, Milton Bradley, Early 1900s, Box	75.00
Around The World With Nellie Bly, McLoughlin Bros., 1890	275.00
Auto Race, Gotham Pressed Steel Corp., C.1930, 10 X 22 In.	175.00
Autogiro Pocket Roulette, Box	30.00
Avilude, McLoughlin Bros.	32.00
Babe Ruth's Baseball Game, Board, Milton Bradley, C.1926	770.00
Bagatelle, Traveling, Mahogany Veneer, Ivory Pins, Cues, 36 X 18 In.	75.00
Ball Toss, Litho Paper Clowns, Cardboard & Wood, 13 3 4/ X 16 In.	45.00
Barney Google, Board	150.00
Base–Ball, McLoughlin Bros., Wooden Box, Metal Men, C.1886	2530.00
Baseball, Litho Metal, Wooden Players, Spinner, 14 X 9 In.	115.00
Baseball, Walter Johnson, Autographed, 1920s	175.00
Basketball, Baldwin, Tin	65.00
Batman, Board, 1965	15.00
Bernie Bierman's Big 10 Football, Jack Armstrong, Wheaties, 1936	90.00
Bingo Skill, Tin	15.00
Bingo, Marble, Wolverine, Box	55.00
Bionic Woman, 1976	12.00
Black Beauty, 1957	10.00
Black Sambo .... 50.00 To 55.00
Board, Alphabet, Foxy, Reversible	40.00
Board, Amish, Monogram MS, Baltic, Ohio	300.00
Board, Cribbage, Figures, Wild Animals, Ivory, China, 1900, 8 1/2 In.	80.00
Board, Cribbage, Rhinelander Beer	35.00
Board, Dart, Sambo, Tin, Wyandotte, Box	135.00
Board, Game of Aesop, H.M. Francis, C.1861, Framed, 28 1/2 X 23 In.	770.00
Board, Game of Asiatic Ostrich, William Darton, Framed, 1812	715.00
Board, Game of The Races, William Crosby, Framed, C.1844, 24 X 18 In.	1210.00
Board, Heedless Tommy, McLoughlin Bros., Framed, C.1875, 22 X 20 In.	275.00
Board, Mansion of Happiness, W. & W.B. Ives, C.1843, Frame, 18 X 14 In.	990.00
Board, National Snake Game, C.1855, Charles Magnus, Framed	1210.00
Board, Ouija, Parker Bros., Box	30.00
Board, Ouija, William Fuld	16.00
Board, Parcheesi, Book–Form Box, Painted, 18 In. ....*Illus*	750.00
Board, Parcheesi, Inlaid, Light & Dark Woods, 24 1/4 In.	75.00
Board, Parcheesi, Reverse Painted On Glass, Framed	200.00
Board, Parcheesi, Salmon Red, Green Mustard, Black, 19th Century	1500.00
Board, Running The Blockade, Civil War Scenes, C.Magnees, Framed, 1860s	2200.00
Board, Yellow Kid, Characters of Comic Strip, C.1890, 3 1/2 X 34 In.	467.50
Bobbsey Twins On Farm, Board, 1957	25.00

Game, Board, Parcheesi,
Book–Form Box, Painted,
18 In.

To remove the musty smell from a closed cupboard or box, try using rice. Parch several handfuls of uncooked rice in a shallow pan in the oven. Then put the pan and rice in the musty drawer. You may have to repeat the parching to keep the moisture and mildew from reappearing.

Boondoggle, Games of Comic Elections, Selchow & Righter 15.00
Bowling, Automatic Pin Setting, Box, 1920s 7.50
Bowling, Boxball, Wooden, Parker Bros. 35.00
Bowling, King Pin, Tin 125.00
Boys In Blue, McLoughlin Bros., Military Men Litho Cards, 1891 .... 175.00
Camelot, Board, Parker Brothers, 1930 .... 16.00
Candid Camera, Allen Funt, 1963 .... 15.00
Captain America, Milton Bradley, 1977 .... 10.00
Captain Gallant of The Foreign Legion 10.00
Captain Kidd, Board, Parker Brothers, C.1896, 16 1/2 X 14 1/2 In. 495.00
Card, 3 Little Pigs, Russell 7.00
Card, Dr.Busby, 1900 .... 15.00
Card, Dr.Quack, Russell 5.00
Card, Flinch, Kalamazoo, Mich., 1913 .... 45.00
Card, Foolish Questions, Rube Goldberg 35.00
Card, Fortune Telling, Dr.Jayne's Egyptian 15.00
Card, Going To The Market, 1915 .... 70.00
Card, Grandmama's Improved Geographical Game, 1880s 25.00
Card, Huckleberry Hound 5.00
Card, Law.Stevens, Wrapper, 1869 .... 133.00
Card, Little Hocus Pocus, Slide Top Wooden Box, C.1840, 9 X 5 In. 357.50
Card, Logomachy, McLoughlin Bros., 1899 .... 30.00
Card, Logomachy, Premium Edition, McLoughlin Bros., 1883 .... 125.00
Card, Madam Morrows Fortune Telling Cards, McLoughlin Bros., 1886 .... 65.00
Card, Rook, Parker Bros. .... 10.00 To 15.00
Card, Tom Barker Baseball, Players On Cards, 53 Piece, Case 825.00
Cat & Mice, McLoughlin Bros. 40.00
Cat & Mouse, Ages 4 To 10, Parker Bros. 18.00
Champion Spark Plug, Board, 1930s 40.00
Charlie Chan, 1937 .... 50.00
Charlie McCarthy, Game of Topper, Board, Whitman, 1938 .... 30.00
Checker Set, Standard Oil 30.00
Checkerboard, Backgammon Other Side, Inlaid Wood 40.00
Checkerboard, Gold & Silver Gilding, Pine, Square, 15 1/2 In. 255.00
Checkerboard, Hires Root Beer, 1892 .... 150.00
Checkerboard, Oilcloth, Black Ground, 25 1/2 X 26 In. 250.00
Checkerboard, Other Side Chinese Checker Star, Red Frame, 19 1/2 In. 155.00
Checkerboard, Painted, Side Faux Marble Pillars, 17 X 24 1/2 In. 1100.00
Checkerboard, Reverse Painted Glass, Black, Red, Green & Gold Leaf 55.00
Checkerboard, Standard Oil 25.00
Checkerboard, Traveling, Dated 1910 .... 50.00
Checkerboard, Well's Durham, Black Characters, Folding 275.00
Checkerboard, Whalebone & Ivory 7000.00
Checkerboard, Wooden, Portable 40.00
Checkers, Checkerboard, Folds In Wood Grocery Box, Advertising, 1880s 250.00
Checkers, Triple Play, Milton Bradley 12.00
Chess Set, Irory, Oriental Figures, Case Opens To Playing Board 375.00
Chess Set, Ivory, Hand Carved, Padded & Silk Lined Box, Board 1650.00
Chess Set, Ivory, Natural & Green Painted Pieces, Kings Are 4 1/4 In. 245.00
Chess Set, Ivory, Red & White, 19th Century 154.00
Chess Set, Old Crow Liquor, China Pieces, Leatherette Case, 32 Piece 3200.00
Chinese Checkers, Akro Agate, Box 20.00
Chinese Checkers, Board, Marbles, 1939 .... 15.00
Chiromagica, McLoughlin Bros, , C.1870, 11 1/2 In. 825.00
Chit Chat, Hugh Downs Game, Milton Bradley, 1963 .... 6.00
Chivalry, Parker Brothers, C.1880 ....*Illus*   468.00
Clipper Race, Board, Gabriel & Sons, Metal Ship Playing Pieces 10.00
Common Taters, Plastic, Hand Held, 1953 .... 6.00
Cootie, 1949 .... 20.00
Cracker Jack, Milton Bradley, 1976 .... 8.00
Cribbage Board, Ivory Figures & Wild Animals, C.1900, 8 1/2 In. 80.00
Croquet, Table, Litho On Wooden Box Cover, Milton Bradley 35.00
Crossword Lexicon, Parker Bros., 1937 .... 12.50 To 18.00
Daniel Boone, Board, Milton Bradley 35.00

Dating Game, Hasbro, 1967 .... 12.00
Dewey's Victory, Board, Parker Bros., C.1900 .... 467.50
Dominoes, Double Nine, Wooden, Halsam, Box 10.00
Dominoes, Lion Embossed, Wooden Box, 91 Piece 32.00
Dominoes, Marlboro Cigarettes 36.00
Dominoes, Victorian Children, Wooden Box 8.00
Donkey Party, 1930s 7.00
Easy Money, Board, Box, 1960 .... 16.00 To 20.00
Electric Jack Straws, Battery Operated, 1940s 25.00
Errand Boy, Board, McLoughlin Bros. 150.00
Fast Mail, Board, Milton Bradley, 20 X 10 In. 1100.00
Feeding Sambo, Pin Watermelon In Mouth, Lion Coffee, 1903, 12 X 20 In. 150.00
Fibber McGee and The Wistful Vista Mystery, 1940 .... 25.00
Finance, Parker Brothers, 1958 .... 9.00
Flintstones, Board, 1961 .... 20.00
Fortune Teller, Milton Bradley, 1905 .... 55.00
Fortunescope, The Prognosticator of Human Destiny, 1935 .... 14.00
Foto–Electric Football, 1941 .... 40.00
Fox & Hounds, Parker Bros., 1948 .... 20.00
Fun At The Zoo, Board, Parker Bros., C.1902 .... 248.00
Game of Bicycle Race, Board, McLoughlin Bros., C.1895 .... 550.00 To 935.00
Game of Bobb, Board, McLoughlin Bros., C.1898, 18 1/2 In. 425.00
Game of Chivalry, Board, Parker Bros., 1880, 15 3/4 In. 468.00
Game of Fish Pond, Board, Milton Bradley, C.1895 .... 75.00 To 165.00
Game of Golf, Board, McLoughlin Bros., C.1896, 13 1/2 X 15 1/2 In. 825.00
Game of Hide and Seek, Board, McLoughlin Bros., C.1895 .... 412.50
Game of Life's Mishaps, McLoughlin Bros., C.1891, 12 1/2 In. 605.00
Game of Mail, Express Or Accommodation, McLoughlin Bros., C.1895 .... 1000.00
Game of Playing Department Store, McLoughlin Bros., C.1898 .... 1320.00
Game of Politics, Davis & Company, C.1859, 24 In. 357.50
Game of Red Riding Hood, Board, Parker Bros., C.1895, 20 X 10 In. 440.00
Game of Stars & Stripes, Board, McLoughlin Bros., C.1900 .... 990.00
Game of The Man In The Moon, McLoughlin Bros., C.1901 ....*Illus* 5060.00
Game of The Visit of Santa Claus, Board, McLoughlin Bros., C.1899 .... 2090.00
Game of Tobogganing At Christmas, Board, McLoughlin Bros., 1899 .... 770.00
Game of Toll Gate, Board, McLoughlin Bros., C.1890, 15 X 13 In. 522.50
Game of Trip Around The World, Board, McLoughlin Bros., C.1897 .... 1300.00
Game of War At Sea, McLoughlin Bros., C.1898, 16 X 23 In. 715.00
Gee–Wiz Race, Tin Flywheel Horse Race, Wolverine, 1923 .... 50.00
Go Bang, Milton Bradley, 1890 .... 28.00
Golf, Get All Balls In Hole, Cardboard, Glass Top, Hand Held, 1930s 12.00
Gone With The Wind, Scarlett, One of Her Problems, 1940 .... 150.00
Hardy Boys, Treasure Game 17.00
Have Gun Will Travel, Board 15.00
Hearts, Wooden Dice, Cup, Directions, Parker Bros., 1914 .... 10.00
Higgly Piggly, Fame Game, Parker Bros., 1953 .... 25.00
High Bid, 1971 .... 8.00
Historical Perspectives, C.1830 .... 350.00
Historical Quiz, McLoughlin Bros. 48.00
Hold The Fort, Board, Civil War Cover, Parker Bros., 1890s 55.00
Home Baseball, McLoughlin Bros. 700.00
How To Succeed In Business Without Really Trying 15.00
Hunting, McLaughlin Bros., C.1904 ....*Illus* 900.00
Indian Backgammon, Russel Mfg., 1920 .... 15.00
Jolly Marble Game, Litho Paper On Wood, Late 19th Century 990.00
King of The Turf, Horse Race, 1940s 40.00
Knapp Electric Questioner, Buzzer, Knapp, 1929 .... 30.00
Knight's Journey, Parker Bros., 1929, 14 1/4 X 22 In. 467.50
Knight's Journey, Parker Brothers, C.1929 ....*Illus* 468.00
Kukla, Frank & Ollie, Parker Bros. 35.00
L'Attaque, World War II, England 25.00
Limited Mail & Express, Parker Bros., C.1894, 24 X 14 In. 715.00
Lindy Hop–Off, Board, Parker Bros., C.1927, 14 X 13 In. 412.50
Little Cowboy Game, Board, Parker Bros., C.1895, 20 1/2 X 10 1/2 In. 357.50

Game, Man In The Moon, McLaughlin Bros., C.1901

Game, Wonderful Game of Oz, Parker Brothers, C.1921

Little Lulu's Adventure, Milton Bradley, 1945	73.00
Lone Ranger, Board, 1966	12.00
Magic Pebble, Raggedy Ann, 1940	30.00
Magic Spelling With Bewitched Letters, McLoughlin Bros., 1900s	35.00
Mah Jong Set, Bamboo, Ivory	650.00
Majestic Game of Asiatic Ostrich, Board, William Darton, C.1812	1100.00
Man In The Moon, McLaughlin Bros., C.1901 .... *Illus*	5060.00
Mary Poppins, Board, Parker Bros., 1964	20.00
Merry Milkman, 1950s	17.00
Monopoly, C.B.Darrow, Pre–Parker, C.1934, 21 X 11 In.	2640.00
New Game of King's Quoits, Board, McLoughlin Bros., C.1893	247.50
North Pole Game, Board, Milton Bradley, C.1907	522.50
Peg'lty, Board, Parker Bros., 1925	22.00
Peg'lty, Board, Parker Bros., 1953	25.00
Peter Pan, Cardboard, Hunt–Wesson, 1969, 20 X 14 In.	6.50
Pick–Up Stix, Wooden, 1937	12.00
Pinball, Fish, Small	38.00
Pinball, Gotham Circus	54.00
Pinball, Poosh–M–Up's Rodeo, Bagatelle	35.00
Pirate & Traveler, Board, Milton Bradley, 1936	50.00
Pluto Big Bike Race, Whitman, Paper, 1974	7.00
Poker Chip, Ivory, Monogram MC, Black Line Around, 1870s, 1 3/4 In.	48.00
Poker Chips, Round Bakelite Caddy, Small	85.00
Poker Chips, Tiger Head, Clay, Red, White & Yellow, 1920s, 3 Piece	12.00
Price Is Right, 1960, Milton Bradley	10.00
Put–Take, Come To Buffalo, Celluloid, 1923	15.00
Puzzle, 3 Circus Scenes, Litho, Milton Bradley, Box	65.00
Puzzle, 6 Ivory Pieces, Makes Triangle, Chinese, 1830	57.50
Puzzle, Amos 'N Andy, O.K.Hotel, 1932	70.00
Puzzle, Animal Antics, McLoughlin Bros., Dated 1894, Box	295.00
Puzzle, Annie Oakley	15.00
Puzzle, Battle of Manila, McLoughlin Bros.	155.00

Puzzle, Birthday Party, Maud Humphrey, Signed & Dated '84 .... 65.00
Puzzle, Fishing Village, Campfire Marshmallows, No.3, Jigsaw 12.50
Puzzle, Flying Family, Jigsaw, Envelope, 1923 .... 30.00
Puzzle, Goldbergs, Pepsodent Radio Giveaway, 1932 .... 18.00
Puzzle, Hood's, Original Box, Picture Both Sides, Jigsaw 25.00
Puzzle, Hoppy The Marvel Bunny, Original Mailer, 1940s 7.00
Puzzle, Jack & Jill, Original Envelope 20.00
Puzzle, King Kong, RKO, 16 X 22 In. 45.00
Puzzle, Little Black Sambo, 2–In. Box 45.00
Puzzle, Locomotive Picture, McLoughlin Bros. 350.00
Puzzle, Munsters, 1965, 100 Piece, Box 40.00
Puzzle, Olympic Games, 1980 .... 10.00
Puzzle, On The Alert, Battleship, Planes, Tuco Brand, World War II 5.00
Puzzle, Our Gang, Drugstore Soda Fountain Scene, Dated 1932 .... 57.00
Puzzle, Pacific Coast Borax Co., 20 Mule Team In Death Valley, 1933 .... 25.00
Puzzle, Pan Am Giveaway, Colored, Original Envelope, 1933 .... 65.00
Puzzle, Parrish, Jigsaw, Box 175.00
Puzzle, Sculptured Wood, Straus, Jigsaw 125.00
Puzzle, Sliced Animals, Selchow & Righter Co., N.Y., 1920s 12.00
Puzzle, Sliced Nations, Selchow & Righter, 1881 .... 195.00
Puzzle, Sohio Standard Oil Company, Gene and Glenn, 1933 .... 20.00
Puzzle, Star Trek, Jigsaw, 1974, 10 X 14 In. 15.00
Puzzle, Steamer & Hose, Fire Engines, Horses, Milton Bradley, C.1900 .... 115.00
Puzzle, Uncle Sam, Horseshoe, 3 Rings, No.3, 1920 .... 17.50
Puzzle, Union News Co., Roly Poly 10.00
Puzzle, Vermont Maid Syrup, Original Envelope 27.00
Puzzle, Victorian Boy Sitting On Rocking Horse, McLoughlin Bros. 150.00
Puzzle, Wild West, McLoughlin Bros., 1890 .... 40.00
Puzzle, World War II, Tank Jeep Picture, Envelope, 8 X 11 In., 2 Piece 10.00
Puzzle, Zorro, Walt Disney Prod., Jigsaw, Box 10.00
Quiz Kids, Radio Question Bee, Whitman, 1941 .... 6.00
Realistic Baseball, Realistic Game & Toy Corp., Tin Litho, 1925 .... 110.00
Reward of Virtue, W. & S.B. Ives, Litho, Framed 1760.00
Rinaldo, Spinning Wheels, Paper Design, Stirn & Lyon, Wooden Box, 1880 .... 325.00
Risk, Wooden Pieces, Parker Bros., 1950 .... 10.00
Rival Policemen, Board, McLoughlin Bros., C.1896 .... 1760.00
Robot, Ted–No–Krazy, Box, 1930s 25.00
Roger Maris, Baseball, Metal, 1962 .... 65.00
Roulette Wheel, Mason & Co., C.1890 .... 2145.00
Salute, Military Theme, 1942, Selchow & Righter 35.00
Sergeant Preston, Board 20.00
Shoot The Chutes, Marble, Marx, Box 35.00
Shoot The Loop, Marble 25.00
Siege of Havana, Board, Parker Bros., C.1898 .... 522.50
Six Million Dollar Man, 1975 .... 12.00
Skip A Cross, Scrabble Game, 1950, Cadach–Ellis 10.00
Skippy, 1932, Milton Bradley 35.00
Sleeping Beauty, Board, Parker Bros., 1958 .... 25.00
Soupy Sales Go Go Go, Complete 25.00
Speed, Superman, Milton Bradley, C.1941 .... 100.00
Stagecoach, Board 12.00
Star Trek, 1979 .... 18.00
Steeple Chase, McLoughlin Bros. 130.00
Story of The Arctic Ship Resolute, 7 X 9 In. 3000.00
Stratomatic Basball, 1962 .... 14.00
Swayze, TV News Game, 1954, Milton Bradley 25.00
Swinging 'Round The Circle, McLoughlin Bros., 1887 .... 325.00
Table Tennis, Sheepskin Bats, Instructions, McLoughlin Bros., Box, 1902 .... 120.00
Tactics II, Avalon, Ill., 1960 .... 12.00
Target, Katzenjammer Kids, Box 15.00
Target, Pop The Bird, Cork Gun 26.00
Target, Red Ryder, Whitman, Box, 1939, 13 1/4 X 10 In. 75.00
Target, Ski Jump, Graphics On Box 185.00
Tell It To The Judge, Board, Eddie Cantor 32.50

Gaudy Dutch, Cup & Saucer, Rose   Gaudy Dutch, Basin, 12 In.

Gaudy Dutch,
Saucer, Floral

Tiny Wild Animals, 1895	25.00
Topsy Turvy, Board, McLoughlin Bros., C.1899	605.00
Touring, Parker Bros., 1926	25.00
Train For Boston, Board, Parker Bros., C.1900	990.00
Uncle Jim's Question Bee Game, NBC	25.00
Undersea World of Jacques Cousteau, Parker Bros.	17.00
Watergate Scandal, Instructions, 1973	10.00
Welfare, Banned By Government, Box	75.00
Wheel, C.1930	115.00
Whirlpool, Marble	25.00
Wide World Game, Board, Parker Bros., 1958	18.00
Winnie The Pooh, Parker Bros., 1959	35.00
Wonderful Game of Oz, Parker Brothers, C.1921 ....*Illus*	1045.00
Wyatt Earp, 1958	18.00
Zippy Zepps, Alderman Fairchild Co., C.1925, 18 X 9 In.	357.50

ГАРДНЕРЗ The Gardner porcelain works was founded in Verbiki, outside Moscow, by the English–born Francis Gardner in 1766. Gardner made porcelain tablewares, figurines, and faience.

GARDNER, Figurine, Man, Sitting, Holding Concertina, 6 3/4 X 4 3/4 In.	450.00
Group, 2 Children, Painting Easter Eggs, 5 3/4 In.	750.00
Group, Beggar, Holding Hat In Hand, 5 3/4 In.	830.00
Group, Man, Seated, Drinking From Kovsh, 6 1/8 In.	730.00
Tea Set, Flowers, Red Ground, 25 Piece	935.00

Gaudy Dutch pottery was made in England for America from about 1810 to 1820. It is a white earthenware with Imari–style decorations of red, blue, green, yellow, and black. Only sixteen patterns of Gaudy Dutch were made: Butterfly, Carnation, Dahlia, Double Rose, Dove, Grape, Leaf, Oyster, Primrose, Single Rose, Strawflower, Sunflower, Urn, War Bonnet, Zinnia, and No Name. Other similar wares are called "Gaudy Ironstone" and "Gaudy Welsh."

GAUDY DUTCH, Basin, 12 In. ....*Illus*	1815.00
Cup & Saucer, Rose ....*Illus*	182.00
Cup & Saucer, Single Rose	500.00
Plate, Single Rose, 10 In.	550.00
Plate, Toddy, War Bonnet, 5 1/4 In.	100.00
Plate, War Bonnet, 5 1/4 In.	450.00
Plate, War Bonnet, 7 In.	475.00
Saltshaker, Double, Slippers Shape	135.00
Saucer, Floral ....*Illus*	74.00
Tea Bowl & Saucer, War Bonnet	500.00
Teapot, Dahlia, Cover ....*Illus*	521.00
Teapot, War Bonnet	900.00
Urn, 7 1/2 In.	575.00

Some collectors have named the ironstone wares with the bright Gaudy Dutchlike patterns "Gaudy Ironstone." There may be other examples found in the listing for Ironstone or under the name of the ceramic factory.

GAUDY IRONSTONE, Bowl, Footed, Floral Design, Underglaze Blue, 5 1/4 In.	195.00
Bowl, Spatterware, Stick, Polychrome Floral Design, 3 In.	155.00
Pitcher & Bowl, Vulture's Head Handles, J.Heath, C.1830	695.00
Pitcher, Embossed Tulips, Underglaze Blue, 6 1/2 In.	75.00
Pitcher, Floral Design, Underglaze Blue, 8 1/4 In.	175.00
Pitcher, Morning Glory, 8 In.	185.00
Pitcher, Polychrome Design, Snake Handle, 8 3/8 In.	300.00
Plate, Floral Design, Underglaze Blue, Purple Luster, 9 In.	65.00
Platter, Morning Glory, Blue, Green, 13 3/4 In.	250.00
Soup, Dish, Flowers, Blues, Oranges, Masons, 10 In.	45.00
Vase, Poppies, Shoulder Handles, Urn, Royal Nishiki, 10 In.	180.00

Gaudy Welsh is an Imari–decorated earthenware with red, blue, green, and gold decorations. It was made after 1820.

GAUDY WELSH, Bottle, Cobalt Blue On White, Flowers, Mushroom Stopper, Pair	85.00
Cake Plate, Self–Handles, Tulip, 10 In. .... 85.00 To	90.00
Jug, Cream, Oyster Pattern, C.1820, 3 3/4 In.	90.00
Pitcher, Oyster Pattern, 5 X 5 In.	75.00
Teapot, Baluster Shape	145.00

In the late nineteenth century Geisha Girl porcelain was made in Japan for export. It was an inexpensive porcelain often sold in dime stores or used as free premiums. Pieces are sometimes marked with the name of a store. Japanese ladies in kimonos are pictured on the dishes. Borders of red, blue, green, gold, brown, or several of these colors were used. Modern reproductions are being made.

GEISHA GIRL, Berry Set, Red, Gold Trim, 6 Piece	90.00
Bowl, Cup & Saucer, Tea House, Red Trim	6.50
Bowl, Footed, 4 In.	5.00
Bowl, Garden, Red Trim, Marked, Fluted, 4 1/2 In.	8.00
Bowl, Multiple Patterns, Red, 8 In.	30.00
Bowl, Nut, Geisha In Garden, Red Trim, 3–Footed, 6 1/2 In.	15.00
Bowl, Rickshaw, Water, Boats, Flower, Red Rim, 6 In.	5.00
Chocolate Set, Geisha With Parasol, Red Trim, 7 Piece	125.00
Cocoa Pot, Parasol	28.00
Cup & Saucer, Orange Border	6.00
Hair Receiver, Green, Gold Piecrust Rim, Red Geishas, 4 1/4 In.	25.00
Mayonnaise Set, 2 Piece	25.00
Mug, Child's, Geisha In Sampan	25.00
Mug, Child's, Wait For Me	28.00
Nut Set, Floral Design On Outside, 7 Piece	35.00
Plate, Cobalt Blue Swirl Edge, Roses, 7 In.	12.50
Powder Jar, Cover, Red Border	12.00
Salt & Pepper, 2 Girls, Orange Top, Bulbous, 2 3/4 In.	18.00
Salt & Pepper, Garden Bench, Water Jar Shape	13.00
Sugar & Creamer, Geisha With Parasols, Red Trim, 3 1/2 In.	25.00
Teapot, Red	45.00

Gene Autry was born in 1907. He began his career as the "Singing Cowboy" in 1928. His first movie appearance was in 1934, his last in 1958.

GENE AUTRY, Badge, Club, Black & White Photo, Brown & Orange Rim	35.00
Book, Autry Golden Ladder Gang	6.00
Book, Gene Autry Songs & Scenes Songbook	55.00
Cap Gun, Kenton	48.00
Cap Gun, Repeater, Box	75.00
Comic Book, No.55	8.50
Guitar, Emenee, Box	200.00
Guitar, Melody Ranch, Wooden	195.00

Guitar, Round–Up, Wooden	195.00
Membership Card, Friendship Club, Magazine & Premium Photo	125.00
Nail Ring	40.00
Paper Doll, Uncut	35.00
Photograph, Red River Valley Movie, Signed	45.00
Program, Rodeo, Fort Madison, Iowa, 1948	20.00
Puzzle Tray	10.00
Record, Happy Trails	15.00
Record, Rodeo Album	30.00
Ring, Horseshoe Nail, On Card	65.00
Songbook, No.2, 1934	25.00
Thermos	45.00
Wristwatch, Gun Moves Up & Down, 1948	150.00

Black and blue decorated Gibson Girl plates were made in the early 1900s. Twenty–four different 10 1/2–inch plates were made by the Royal Doulton Pottery at Lambeth, England. These pictured scenes are from the book "A Widow and Her Friends" by Charles Dana Gibson. Another set of twelve 9–inch plates featuring pictures of the heads of Gibson Girls had all–blue decoration. Many other items also pictured the famous Gibson Girl.

GIBSON GIRL, Book, Charles Dana, 1907	75.00
Plate, Failing To Find Rest & Quiet In Country, 10 1/2 In.	95.00
Plate, Hostile Criticism, 10 1/2 In.	95.00
Plate, Rosenthal, 10 In.	38.00
Plate, She Becomes A Trained Nurse, 10 1/2 In.	70.00
Plate, She Contemplates The Cloister, 10 1/2 In.	85.00
Plate, She Decides To Die, 10 1/2 In.	75.00
Plate, She Finds Exercise Does Not Improve, 10 1/2 In.	70.00
Plate, She Goes Into Colors, 10 1/2 In.	98.00
Plate, She Goes To A Fancy Dress Ball As Juliet, 10 1/2 In.	90.00
Plate, She Longs For Seclusion, 10 1/2 In.	85.00
Plate, Winning New Friends, 10 1/2 In. .... 70.00 To 95.00

GILLINDER

Gillinder pressed glass was first made by William T. Gillinder of Philadelphia in 1863. The company had a working factory on the grounds at the Centennial and made small, marked pieces of glass for sale as souvenirs. They made a variety of decorative glass pieces and tablewares.

GILLINDER, Figurine, Ruth The Gleaner, Frosted	125.00
Figurine, Seated Buddha, Signed, Amber, 6 In. .... 150.00 To 165.00

The Girl Scout movement started in 1912, two years after the Boy Scouts. It began under Juliette Gordon Low of Savannah, Georgia. The first Girl Scout cookies were sold in 1928. Collectors search for anything pertaining to the Girl Scouts, including uniforms, publications, and old cookie boxes.

GIRL SCOUT, Badge, Hat, Tenderfoot, Eagle, Bronze, Trefoil, 1920s, 1 1/4 In.	32.00
Calendar, 1953	12.00
Doll, Effenbee, Dated 1965, Box, 8 1/2 In.	30.00
Handbook, 1947	10.00
Handbook, Official, 1st Edition, 1920	27.00
Hat, Box, 1960s	15.00

GLASS, CONTEMPORARY, see Contemporary Glass

Eyeglasses, or spectacles, were mentioned in a manuscript in 1289 and have been used ever since. The first glasses with rigid side pieces were made in London in 1727. Bifocals were invented by Benjamin Franklin in 1785. Lorgnettes were popular in late Victorian times.

GLASSES, Goggles, Aviator, Leather, With Snaps	7.00
Granny, 14K Gold Filled, Wire Frame, Case	10.00
Lorgnette, Folding, 14K Gold	150.00
Lorgnette, Gold & Mother–of–Pearl	22.50

Lorgnette, Gold Scrolled, Victorian	550.00
Lorgnette, Onyx & Diamond In Handle, 14K White Gold Mounting	250.00
Lorgnette, Sterling Silver, Filigree Handle	49.00
Lorgnette, Victorian, Chain, Filigree, Gold Filled, Leather Pouch	105.00
Opera, Brass, Sportiere–Paris	20.00
Opera, Metal, Leatherette, Occupied Japan	20.00
Opera, Mother–of–Pearl & Brass, French	65.00
Shooting, Winchester, Slip–On, Cloth Case	12.00
Steel, Case, Engraved Gold, Velvet Lined, Inscription, American, 1865	1100.00
Sun, Merit, Original Card, 1950s	25.00

Goebel   W. Goebel Porzellanfabrik of Oeslau, Germany, now Rodental, West Germany, has made many types of figurines and dishes. The firm is still working. The pieces marked "Goebel Hummel" are listed under Hummel in this book.

GOEBEL, Bottle, Comical Man With Cigar	195.00
Candleholder, Swan, Full Bee, Pair	35.00
Character Jug, Friar, Stylized Bee, 1 1/2 In.	30.00
Condiment Set, Monks, 4 Piece	40.00
Cookie Jar, Monk	165.00
Creamer, Cow	28.00
Dish, Cigarette, Cover, Dragon Finial, 1930s	135.00
Doorstop, Turtle, 9 X 14 In.	82.50
Egg Timer, Friar Tuck	30.00
Figurine, Bathing Beauty, Seated On Scalloped Shell, Marked, 3 In.	135.00
Figurine, Elmer & Tilly, Full Bee	98.00
Figurine, Piglet, No.320008–07, 4 In., Pair	50.00
Figurine, Sleeping Woman, Full Bee, 6 In.	100.00
Half Doll, Eyes Looking Down At Hand	375.00
Jug, Great Dane, Head, Brown & Black, Rust Collar, 1 3/4 In.	40.00
Plaque, Monks, Hanging	55.00
Plate, Manchurian Crane	90.00
Salt & Pepper, Cardinal Tuck	40.00
Salt & Pepper, Clown Shape, Red & Blue, 1930s	85.00
Salt & Pepper, Friar Tuck, Stylized Bee, 2 1/2 In.	30.00 To 45.00
Salt & Pepper, Turkey	17.50
Sugar & Creamer, Tray, Monks	45.00
Vase, Boy Seated, With Turtle, 3 Stump Openings, Full Bee, 4 3/4 In.	280.00

Goldscheider Wien   Porcelain has been made by three branches of the Goldscheider family. The family left Vienna in 1938 and started factories in England and in Trenton, New Jersey. The New Jersey factory started in 1940 as Goldscheider–U.S.A. In 1941 it became Goldscheider–Everlast Corporation. From 1947 to 1953 it was Goldcrest Ceramics Corporation. In 1950 the Vienna plant was returned to Mr. Goldscheider and the company continues in business. The Trenton, New Jersey, business is now Goldscheider of Vienna and imports all of the pieces.

GOLDSCHEIDER, Ashtray, Mauve	5.00
Dish, Half Figure of Girl On Lid, 6 1/2 X 8 In.	85.00
Figurine, April Showers, Pink, Umbrella, 6 1/2 In.	70.00
Figurine, Dog, Reclining, 11 In.	85.00
Figurine, Elephant, Gray, 7 In.	20.00
Figurine, Flying Duck, E.Straub, 13 In.	98.00
Figurine, Horse, Brown, 8 1/2 In.	75.00
Figurine, Lady With Muff, Blue & Tan Coat, Gown, 8 In.	85.00
Figurine, Lady, Art Deco, Artist Signed, 14 In.	175.00
Figurine, Lady, Holding Basket of Flowers, 7 1/2 In.	95.00
Figurine, Madonna & Child, 7 In.	75.00
Figurine, Madonna & Child, Label, 4 1/2 In.	30.00
Figurine, Madonna With Crown, 7 In.	65.00
Figurine, Madonna, Signed, 5 1/2 In.	35.00
Figurine, Rooster, 10 1/2 In.	65.00
Figurine, Sing Lo, Oriental, Bird, Pagods, Bird House, 7 1/4 In.	80.00

Figurine, Southern Belle, Holding Hat, 9 In. .... 100.00 To 105.00
Figurine, Swan, Bizarre, 11 X 10 In. 170.00
Lamp, Candle, Parrot In Stand, Porcelain, Pre–1930, 24 In. 2195.00
Music Box, Colonial Girl, 7 In. 85.00
Wall Mask, Curly–Haired Girl, Red Lips, Aqua Scarf, 11 1/4 In. 175.00
   GOLF, see Sports

Lawton Gonder opened Gonder Ceramic Arts, Inc., in 1941. He worked in the old Peters and Reed pottery in Zanesville, Ohio. Gonder pieces include lamp bases marked "Eglee" and many wares with Oriental–type glazes.

GONDER, Ewer, Mottled Beige Over Gray, Pink Interior, 5 1/2 X 7 1/2 In. 15.00
  Ewer, Turquoise, 5 In. 8.00
  Figurine, Collie, Gray, 9 In. 15.00
  Figurine, Coolie, Kneeling, Yellow, 6 In. 8.00
  Figurine, Oriental Water Carrier, Green, 14 1/2 In. 45.00
  Figurine, Panther, 19 In. 90.00
  Figurine, Swan, Gray & Pink, 5 1/2 In. 14.00
  Planter, Figural, Swan, Yellow, Pink Mottling, 5 In. 16.00
  Tumbler, Enamel Design, Purple 22.00
  Vase, Fan, Gray & Pink, 7 In. 14.00
  Vase, Flat, Swirls, Gray & Pink, 11 1/2 In. 20.00
  Vase, Leaf, 6 1/2 In. 15.00
  Vase, Turquoise & Yellow, 9 In., Pair 45.00

Goofus glass was made from about 1900 to 1920 by many American factories. It was originally painted gold, red, green, bronze, pink, purple, or other bright colors. Many pieces are found today with flaking paint and this lowers the value.

GOOFUS GLASS, Bowl, 8 Feathery Flared Florals, 9 In. 12.00
  Bowl, Carnations, Red & Gold, 9 In. 26.00
  Bowl, Red Carnations, 9 In. 35.00
  Plate, Florals, 10 In., Pair 25.00
  Plate, Gibson Girl, 8 In. 22.00
  Powder Jar 30.00
  Sugar, Grape Design, 1910 .... 50.00
  Vase, Grape, 13 In. 45.00
  Vase, Iris, Green, 12 1/2 In., Pair 40.00

Goss china has been made since 1858. English potter William Henry Goss first made it at the Falcon Pottery in Stoke–on–Trent. The factory name was changed to Goss China Company in 1934 when it was taken over by Cauldon Potteries. Production ceased in 1940. Goss china resembles Irish Belleek in both body and glaze. The company also made popular souvenir china, usually marked with local crests and names.

W.H.GOSS

GOSS, Ashtray, Pheasant, Hand Painted 22.50
  Candlestick, Owls, Leeds, 6 In. 75.00
  Creamer, Seal of Windsor Castle 17.00
  Night–Light, Shakespeare 70.00
  Sugar, Roses 10.00

Pottery has been made in Gouda, Holland, since the seventeenth century. Two firms, the Zenith pottery, established in the eighteenth century, and the Zuid–Hollandsche pottery, made the brightly colored wares marked "Gouda" from 1880 to about 1940. Many pieces featured Art Nouveau or Art Deco designs.

GOUDA, Ashtray, Glazed 15.00
  Biscuit Jar, Flowers & Leaves, Gold Outlining, Marked, 5 1/4 In. 45.00
  Bottle, Liqueur, Dutchman & Woman, Crown Mark, 10 In. 110.00
  Bowl, Florals, Ribbon Raised Handle, Marked, 7 1/4 In. 68.00
  Candlestick, Drip Pan, Multicolored Floral, Jade, Marked 120.00
  Candlestick, Green, Rust, Cobalt & Ocher, 3 3/4 In. 50.00
  Candlestick, Ring Handle, Saucer Top, Flared Base, 7 1/4 In. 75.00

Chamberstick, Drip Cup, Burgundy, Peach, Ring Handle, 7 1/4 In. 85.00
Compote, Olive & Orange Bands, Black, Regina, 1890, 4 1/2 X 8 3/4 In. 250.00
Dish, Flowers & Leaves, Anjer House, 6 In. 80.00
Dish, Satin Finish, Handled, 3 Sections, Art Deco, 4 In. 85.00
Figurine, Boy & Girl, Signed, Marken, 15 In., Pair 200.00
Figurine, Shoe, Turquoise, Blue, Orange & Yellow Design, 2 1/4 In. 65.00
Humidor, Tobacco, Flowers & Scrolls, Gold Trim, Marked, 5 1/4 In. 135.00
Humidor, Zenith 28.00
Lantern, Old Plazuid, Ring Handle, 9 1/2 In. 85.00
Lantern, Ring Handle, 9 1/2 In. 85.00
Mug, Stork, Cathedral Scene, 5 In. 40.00
Pitcher, Gray, Seafoam Green, Glossy Finish, 2 1/2 In. 10.00
Tumbler, Water, Flowers, Green Leaves, Black Ground, Art Deco, 3 In. 55.00
Vase, Art Nouveau Foliage, House Mark, 4 In. 55.00
Vase, Floral, Crackle Ground, Marked, 3 1/4 In.Pair 88.00
Wall Pocket, Art Nouveau Design, Black House Mark, 11 1/2 X 5 In. 110.00
Wall Pocket, Rust & Cream, Black Ground, 9 In. 120.00

 Graniteware is an enameled tinware that has been used in the
kitchen from the late nineteenth century to the present. Earlier
graniteware was green or turquoise blue, with white spatters. The
later ware was gray with white spatters. Reproductions are being
made in all colors.

GRANITEWARE, Ashtray, Sullivan's Cigars 20.00
Basin, Salesman's Sample, Blue & White 48.00
Bean Pot, Chocolate Brown, White 300.00
Bedpan, Cover, Gray 20.00
Berry Bucket, Child's, Cobalt Blue & White Swirl 38.00
Berry Bucket, Cover, Turquoise & White Swirl, 2 3/4 X 3 In. 180.00
Berry Bucket, Light Blue, White Spatter 35.00
Bucket, Dinner, Cobalt Blue, Pewter Finial 22.50
Bucket, Dinner, Thermos, Top Pie Tray, Gray 85.00
Bucket, Lunch, Coal Miner's, Mottled Brown & White 45.00
Butter, Cover, White 95.00
Cake Pan, 8 X 12 In. 11.00
Cake Pan, Angel Food, Cobalt Blue Swirl, White Interior 70.00
Cake Pan, Blue & White Swirl, 7 1/2 In. 47.00
Can, Cream, Gray, Bail Handle, 2 Qt. 45.00
Canister, Tea, Blue 35.00
Chamber Pot, Gray, Cover 50.00
Chamber Pot, Mottled Gray, 5 X 9 1/2 In. 45.00
Cheese Dish, Cover, Sky Blue 250.00
Churn, Butter, Blue & White Swirl 900.00
Coffee Boiler, Cobalt Blue Mottled 60.00
Coffee Boiler, Turquoise Blue Swirl 70.00
Coffeepot, Blue & White Swirl 65.00
Coffeepot, Blue & White Swirl, 10 In. 95.00
Coffeepot, Brown, White Spots, Hinged Cover, 10 X 7 In. 16.50
Coffeepot, Child's, Gray 240.00
Coffeepot, Cobalt Blue & White Swirl, 11 1/2 In. 95.00
Coffeepot, Gray, 1 1/2 Gal. 25.00
Coffeepot, Green & White Swirl, 1880s 200.00
Coffeepot, Lighthouse, 10 In. 32.50
Coffeepot, Mottled Gray, Knobbed Cover, 11 X 7 In. 18.00
Coffeepot, Teapot & Creamer, Blue Spatter, Pewter, 3 Piece 450.00
Colander, Blue & White Swirl 45.00
Colander, Dark Cobalt Blue, White Flecked, Wire Handle 24.00
Colander, Gray, 3 In. 14.00
Colander, Gray, Footed, Handles, 11 1/2 In. 30.00
Colander, Handles, Brown & White 36.50
Colander, Teardrop, Gray 75.00
Cook Set, Child's, Blue, 6 Piece 150.00
Cup & Saucer, Child's, Gray & White 52.00
Cup, Blue & White Swirl 30.00

Dipper, Blue, White Swirl 52.00
Dipper, Speckled Burgundy 20.00
Double Boiler, Blue Spatter 55.00
Double Boiler, Navy Blue & White Speckled 35.00
Dough Raiser, Gray, Matching Vented Lid 95.00
Dripolator, Cream & Green 30.00
Dutch Oven, Green, Original Label, 12 In. 45.00
Egg Poacher, Gray 185.00
Fish Mold, Blue, Small 210.00
Fish Poacher, Rack, White, Cobalt Blue Handle & Rim, 21 In. 35.00
Frying Pan, Gray, 8 1/2 X 15 1/2 In. 19.00
Funnel, Canning Jar, Gray 20.00
Grater, Nutmeg, Hinged Cover On Pocket Top, 5 1/4 In. 6.25
Jug, Batter, Gray, Cover, Tin Cap, Spout 150.00
Kettle, Coffee, Blue & White 45.00
Kettle, Gray, Bail Handle, 2 Gal. 12.00
Ladle, Cobalt Handle, Gray Bowl 21.00
Little Dolly's Cooking Set, Original Card, 12 Piece 265.00
Muffin Pan, Cobalt Blue & White Swirl, 8 In. 128.00
Mug, Barber, Navy Blue Trim, Patent 1905 .... 75.00
Pail, Mottled Gray, Bail, 5 X 3 3/4 In. 7.75
Pan, Blue & White, 10 In. 22.00
Pan, Sweet Bread Riser, Cover 80.00
Pie Pan, Speckled Blue, 10 In. 5.50
Pie Pan, White, Blue Rim, Heart Shaped Handles, 5 1/2 In. 34.00
Pie Plate, Brown & White Swirl 20.00
Pie Plate, Cobalt Blue Swirl, 9 In. 20.00
Pie Plate, Purple & White 30.00
Pitcher & Bowl, Green, White Swirl 595.00
Pitcher, Gray, 7 In. 45.00
Plate, Child's, Polly Flanders, Verse 25.00
Plate, Pink Roses, White 7.00
Pot, Blue, Bail, Large 15.00
Potty, Gray .... 13.00 To 30.00
Rack, Utensil, Turquoise 125.00
Roaster, Relief Marked Savory, Oval, Blue, 9 X 18 X 12 In. 25.00
Rolling Pin, Black & White 105.00
Saucer, Gray, 5 3/4 In. 4.00
Sieve, Gray, 10 In. 9.00
Skillet, Black & White, 5 1/2 In. 15.00
Skillet, Dark Blue Spatter, 6 In. 12.00
Skillet, Gray, 10 1/4 In. 30.00
Soap Dish, Cobalt Blue Swirl 40.00
Spatula, White 50.00
Spoon, Basting, White & Black, 15 In. 8.00
Spoon, Turquoise & White Spatter, 11 1/2 In. 6.00
Tea Steeper, Chrysolite 150.00
Teakettle, Chrysolite 350.00
Teakettle, Dome, Light Blue Mottled 70.00
Teakettle, Speckled Blue 28.00
Teapot, Cobalt Blue & White, Speckled, White Interior 47.00
Teapot, Gooseneck Spout, Gray, 9 In. 40.00
Teapot, Gooseneck Spout, Red Handle, Pyrex Knob 25.00
Teapot, Gooseneck, Blue & White Swirl, 2 Cup 300.00
Teapot, Mottled Gray, Gooseneck, Wooden Handle 32.00
Tub, Baby Bath, Oval, 25 In. 25.00
Tube Pan, Gray, 11 1/2 In. 25.00
Tumblers, Nesting, White, Germany, 4 Piece 55.00
Washboard, Soap Saver 11.00
Washboard, Turquoise Blue 125.00
Water Cooler, Cover, Spigot, Gray 165.00

Greentown glass was made by the Indiana Tumbler and Goblet Company of Greentown, Indiana, from 1894 to 1903. In 1899, the factory name was changed to National Glass Company. A variety of pressed, milk, and chocolate glass was made.

GREENTOWN, see also Chocolate Glass; Custard Glass; Holly Amber; Milk Glass; Pressed Glass

GREENTOWN, Bowl, Holly, 6 1/2 In.	85.00
Butter, Cover, Chrysanthemum, Gold Trim	175.00
Butter, Dewey	35.00
Butter, Leafy Chrysanthemum	145.00
Butter, Wild Rose With Bowknot, Frosted, Cover, Pastel Design	27.50
Cake Stand, Austrian Pattern	70.00
Condiment Set, Dewey, Amber, 4 Piece	210.00
Cracker Jar, Cactus	195.00
Creamer, Butterfly Handles, Frost Band	35.00
Creamer, Dewey, Green, 5 In.	65.00
Creamer, Frosted Flower Band	95.00
Creamer, Teardrop & Tassel, Opaque White	45.00
Cruet, Dewey, Amber	110.00 To 125.00
Cruet, Dewey, Green	775.00
Cup, Prize, Green	25.00
Dish, Chicken On Nest, Amber	145.00
Dish, Hen Cover, Amber	47.00
Dish, Rabbit Cover, Blue	175.00
Goblet, Beehive, Crystal	75.00
Goblet, Brazen Shield	45.00
Goblet, Octagonal, Teal Blue	150.00
Goblet, Open Rose, Buttermilk	25.00
Goblet, Overall Lattice	40.00
Goblet, Pleat Band	25.00
Goblet, Shuttle, 5 In.	40.00
Mug, Cover, Troubadour Scene, 6 1/2 In.	60.00
Mug, Serenade, Amber, 4 3/4 In.	75.00
Mug, Serenade, Blue	30.00
Mug, Troubador, Blue Milk Glass	16.00
Nappy, Austrian, Cover	45.00
Pitcher, Milk, Maple Leaf, Vaseline	85.00
Pitcher, Reticulated Cord, Amber, 9 In.	95.00
Pitcher, Water, Marilyn	300.00
Pitcher, Water, Racing Deer & Doe	150.00
Plate, Serenade, 8 1/4 In.	40.00
Relish, Teardrop & Tassle, Green, Oval	45.00
Salt & Pepper, Pleat Band	5.00
Saltshaker, Pleat Band	18.00
Sauce, Teardrop & Tassel	120.00
Sauce, Wild Rose & Bowknot	75.00
Spooner, Actress	75.00
Spooner, Butterfly Handles	35.00
Spooner, Daisy, Frosted	20.00
Spooner, Teardrop & Tassel, Opaque White	45.00
Stein, Drinking Scene, Nile Green	175.00
Stein, Serenade	35.00
Sugar & Creamer, Wild Rose With Bowknot	27.50
Sugar, Holly, Amber	55.00
Syrup, Crystal	95.00
Toothpick, Holly	110.00
Tumbler, Austrian	35.00
Tumbler, Cactus, 8 Piece	400.00
Tumbler, Dewey, Canary	70.00
Tumbler, Holly, Amber	180.00
Tumbler, Hummingbird, Amber	55.00
Tumbler, Teardrop & Tassel	20.00
Vase, Herringbone Buttress, Green, 6 In.	150.00

Water Set, Brazen Shield, Blue, 7 Piece	425.00
Water Set, Early Diamond, Gold Flashed, 7 Piece	250.00
Wine, Austrian, Canary	150.00
Wine, Cathedral, Blue	55.00
Wine, Diamond Prisms, 1880s	50.00
Wine, Finecut & Panel, Amber	30.00
Wine, Panel Jewel, Vaseline	55.00
Wine, Pleat Band	22.50
Wine, Shuttle	5.00

Grueby Faience Company of Boston, Massachusetts, was incorporated in 1897 by William H. Grueby. Garden statuary, art pottery, and architectural tiles were made until 1920. The company developed a matte green glaze that was so popular it was copied by many other factories making a less expensive type of pottery. This eventually led to the financial problems of the pottery.

GRUEBY, Bowl, Green Inside & Out, High Gloss, 8 In.	285.00
Paperweight, Scarab, Mottled Green Glaze, Paper Label, 4 In.	325.00
Tile, Griffin, Charcoal Gray, Green Glaze, 1908, 8 In.	275.00
Tile, Grove of Pines, Lake & Mountains, Marked, 8 X 8 In.	3140.00
Tile, Mermaid, Looking In Mirror, Orange Glaze, Blue Ground, 6 In.	200.00
Tile, Scene of Galleon In High Seas, Paper Label, 9 X 9 In.	2400.00
Vase, 2 Colors, Trefoil Rim, 8 1/2 In.	2640.00
Vase, 3 Tooled Petaled Flowers & Stems, Marked, C.1905, 13 3/4 In.	3900.00
Vase, Broad Vertical Leaves, Wide Mouth, 1905, S.W., 11 In.	2000.00
Vase, Brown–Green Glaze, Bulbous, Thumb Ribbed, 1905, 21 X 20 In.	4000.00
Vase, Bud & Blade Design, Yellow, Bulbous, Artist ER, 1907, 8 1/2 In.	800.00
Vase, Bulbous Bottom, Long Neck, Artist W.F., 8 In.	2200.00
Vase, Gourd, Rows of Alternating Leaves, 12 In.	6600.00
Vase, Green, Tooled Leaves, 13 1/2 In.	4290.00
Vase, Pumpkin Shape, Butterscotch Glaze, 6 1/2 In.	7150.00
Vase, Repeating Leaves, Tiffany Font, Cylindrical, 1905, 10 1/2 In.	4000.00
Vase, Repeating Vertical Lines, Swollen Cylindrical, 1770	1200.00
Vase, Tooled Sides, Leaves, Blue Drip Glaze, C.1905, 11 1/4 In.	4000.00
Vase, Upright Ribbed Leaves, Marked, C.1900, 12 3/8 In.	8800.00
Wall Pocket, Green, Molded Relief, Arts & Crafts Look	175.00

Included in this category are shotguns, pistols, and other antique firearms. Rifles are listed in their own section. Be very careful when buying or selling guns because there are special laws governing the sale and ownership. A collector's gun should be displayed in a safe manner, probably with the barrel filled or a part missing to be sure it cannot be accidentally fired.

GUN, Air Pistol, Winchester, Model 353	145.00
BB, Columbian, Cast Iron, 1908	175.00
BB, Daisy, Buck Jones, Compass In Stock, 1934	250.00
BB, Daisy, No. 99, Official, Educational	25.00
BB, Daisy, No. 299, 1960s	40.00
BB, Daisy, No.1894	30.00
BB, Markham King, 500 Shot, Dated 1910	75.00
BB, Red Ryder, 1940s	50.00
Colt, 45 Caliber, Model 1871	1100.00
Colt, Revolver, Navy, Model 1851, Accessories, 36 Cal., Mahogany Case	5000.00
Flintlock Box Lock, 45 Caliber, 3 In.Barrel, England, C.1770	245.00
Flintlock, Primitive Tin & Ivory Inlay, Middle East, 17 1/2 In.	55.00
Flintlock, Walnut Stock, Brass Fittings, 14 3/4 In.	350.00
Hanging Tag, Parker, No.194552, Dated 1921	37.50
Musket, Enfield, Britain, Civil War	80.00
Musket, Flintlock, Brown Bess, Walnut Stock, 52 In.	175.00
Musket, Flintlock, Walnut Full Stock, 55 1/2 In.	550.00
Pistol, 5 Shot, Ornate Barrel & Grip, World War I	65.00
Pistol, Air, Benjamin, Instructions, Parts List, Box, 1920s	65.00
Pistol, Air, Crossman 22, Model 116	55.00
Pistol, Allen & Wheelock, 32 Rimfire, Side Hammer, Brass Frame	350.00

Pistol, Boot, Primitive, Underslung Trigger	475.00
Pistol, Iver Johnson, 32 Caliber, Leather Case	70.00
Pistol, Lee, 32 Caliber, Double Action, Pearl Handle	27.50
Pistol, Marble's Game–Getter, 22 Caliber, 10–In.Barrel	510.00
Pistol, Octagon Double Barrel, Cap & Ball, Checkered Grips	95.00
Pistol, Pepperbox, Marked S. Sutherland, Richmond, Va.	600.00
Pistol, Percussion Box, Smooth Grip, England, C.1850	97.50
Pistol, Percussion, Octagonal Stepped To Round Barrel, 32 Caliber, 1840	115.00
Pistol, Pocket, Morgan & Clapp, 32 Caliber, Single Shot	165.00
Pistol, Walther, Automatic, 32 Caliber, Holster	325.00
Pistol, Winchester, Hi–Wall 38–55, Octagon Barrel, Lever Action	275.00
Remington, Model 721, 270 Caliber	240.00
Revolver, Colt 38, Pocket, 1/2–In. Octagonal Barrel, 5 Shot	450.00
Revolver, Confederate, Hardin & Sons	1650.00
Revolver, H & R, 22 Caliber, 12–In. Barrel	115.00
Revolver, Iver Johnson, 32 Caliber, Box	95.00
Revolver, Military, Belgium, C.1890	175.00
Revolver, Remington–Rider, Pocket, 31 Caliber, 3–In. Octagonal Barrel	285.00
Revolver, Smith & Wesson, 32 Caliber, C.1881	95.00
Shotgun, Crescent Fire Arms	145.00
Shotgun, Double Barrel, L.C.Smith Specialty, 12 Gauge	1250.00
Shotgun, Moore, Percussion, Powder Loaded, 1842	400.00
Shotgun, Remington, 38–40 Caliber, Pump, Walnut Stock & Forearm	190.00
Shotgun, Stevens Model .410, Single Shot, Hammer	90.00
Shotgun, Walther, 12 Gauge, Gold W On Trigger Guard	450.00
Shotgun, Winchester, Model 36, 9mm, Single Shot	60.00
Shotgun, Winchester, Model 37, Single Shot	75.00

Gunderson glass was made at the Gunderson–Pairpoint Glass Works of New Bedford, Massachusetts, from 1952 to 1957. Gunderson Peachblow is especially famous.

GUNDERSON, Bowl, Peachblow, Shaded Blue To Pink, 4 3/4 In.	80.00
Bride's Basket, Peachblow, Silver Holder	950.00
Butter, Cover, Peachblow, Applied Finial, Scalloped, 9 X 5 In.	395.00
Compote, Peachblow, 5 1/8 X 6 In.	220.00
Compote, Peachblow, Flared, Rim of Pink, C.1953, 5 1/8 In.	300.00
Vase, Peachblow, Classic, Serpentine Handles, Square Base, 8 In.	150.00
Vase, Peachblow, Crimped, 6 1/2 In.	160.00

Gutta–percha was one of the first plastic materials. It was made from a mixture of resins from Malaysian trees. It was molded and used for daguerreotype cases, toilet articles, and picture frames in the nineteenth century.

GUTTA–PERCHA, Case, Bobby Shafto, 1/6 Plate	75.00
Case, Children Playing With Toys, Double, 1/9 Plate	70.00
Case, Cluster of Cherries, Brown, 1/9 Plate	45.00
Case, Country Dance, Brown, 1/4 Plate	110.00
Case, Cupid & The Wounded Stag, 1/4 Plate	80.00
Case, Eagle At Bay, 1/6 Plate	95.00
Case, Gypsy Fortune Teller, 1/4 Plate	75.00
Case, Medallion of George Washington	120.00
Case, Ship's Stern, 1/9 Plate	65.00
Match Safe, Arm & Hammer	65.00
Snuffbox, 3 1/4 X 2 X 3/4 In.	15.00 To 16.00

Haeger Potteries, Inc., Dundee, Illinois, started making commercial art wares in 1914. Early pieces were marked with the name "Haeger" written over an "H." About 1938, the mark "Royal Haeger" was used. The firm is still making florist wares and lamp bases.

HAEGER, Ashtray, Gold Patina	10.00
Ashtray, Green, 1871–1971	30.00
Ashtray, Green, Rust, Hexagonal, 8 1/2 X 4 3/4 In.	5.00
Candlestick, 2–Light, Flowers On Leaf Shape, Black, 8 In., Pair	23.00
Centerpiece, Sculptured Leaves, Floral, Pink, Blue, Green, 24 In.	22.00

Cigarette Lighter, Aladdin Lamp	10.00
Console Set, Molded Grape Cluster, Pink Froth Over Plum, 3 Piece	50.00
Console Set, Ocean Waves, Pea Green, 7 1/2 & 6-In. Swans	18.00
Cornucopia, Gray, Footed Shell, Label, 5 X 8 In.	8.50
Figurine, Boxer Dog, Reclining, Label, 11 In.	42.00
Pitcher, Flowers, White, 12 In.	15.00
Planter, Blue Stork, Basket, 9 X 11 In.	15.00
Planter, Figural, Boy, Semidraped, Urn On Shoulder, Ivory, 12 In.	20.00
Planter, Madonna, Holds Child, Blue Stamp, 11 1/2 In.	25.00
Planter, Mermaid, Reclining, 22 In.	85.00
Platter, Leaf Shape, Green, Blue, Pierced, 13 3/4 X 10 3/4 In.	20.00
Vase, Art Deco, 9 1/2 In.	45.00
Vase, Blue Basket Weave, Triangular, 12 In.	25.00
Vase, Figural, Deer, Running, Ivory, Green Sticker, 9 1/8 In.	14.00
Vase, Figural, Swordfish, Mottled Pink, Blue, Green, 13 X 9 In.	30.00
Vase, Fish, Small & Large, Dark Green, Art Deco Scrolls, 11 In.	27.00
Vase, Leaf Shape, Gray Brown, Beaded Spirals, 9 1/2 In.	13.00
Violet Pot, Saucer, Violets, Paper Label	20.00
Window Box, Mottled Green, Paper Label, 13 X 6 X 4 1/2 In.	8.50

Hall China Company started in East Liverpool, Ohio, in 1903. The firm made all types of wares. Collectors search for the Hall teapots made from the 1920s to the 1950s. The dinnerwares of the same period, especially Autumn Leaf pattern, are also popular. The Hall China Company is still working. Autumn Leaf pattern dishes are listed in their own category in this book.

HALL, Ashtray, Advertising, Seaview Country Club	10.00
Ashtray, Attached Match Holder, Striker, Cobalt Blue	15.00
Ashtray, Cigar, Sea Spray, Round, 5 1/2 In.	12.00
Ashtray, DuPont Hotel	6.00
Ashtray, With Match Holder, Black	2.00
Baker, Pie, Cross & Flowers, Mother-of-Pearl	25.00
Bean Pot, Rose Parade	30.00 To 45.00
Bean Pot, Tab Handle, Chinese Red	40.00
Berry Bowl, Springtime, 5 1/2 In.	3.00
Bowl Set, Chinese Red, Banded, 3 Piece	30.00
Bowl, Advertising, Keen's English Chop House, 4 3/4 In.	16.50
Bowl, Batter, Banded, Cobalt Blue	30.00
Bowl, Crocus, 7 1/2 In.	22.50
Bowl, Morning Glory, Blue, No.2, Straight Side	8.00
Bowl, Poppy & Wheat, 5 1/2 In.	15.00
Bowl, Poppy, 9 In.	12.00 To 17.00
Bowl, Springtime, 5 1/2 In.	4.00
Bowl, Vegetable, Cameo Rose, Round, 9 In.	11.00
Cake Plate, Red Poppy	9.00 To 15.00
Cake Plate, Springtime	12.00
Cannister Set, Red Poppy, Metal, 4 Piece	40.00
Coffee Dispenser, Crocus	6.00
Coffee Set, Electric Perk, Sugar & Creamer, Wild Rose	60.00
Coffee Set, With Sugar & Creamer, Basket Weave	40.00
Coffeepot, Amory, Lettuce	10.00
Coffeepot, Beaver Falls, Maroon	10.00
Coffeepot, Big Boy, Maroon & Silver	35.00
Coffeepot, Bricks, Ivory, Floral	10.00
Coffeepot, Crocus, Step-Down	35.00
Coffeepot, Cube, Stock Brown, 1 Cup	20.00
Coffeepot, French Russet, Drip	34.00
Coffeepot, Heather Rose, Step-Down	35.00
Coffeepot, Ivory, Green, Silver	15.00
Coffeepot, Orange	40.00
Coffeepot, Poppy, Gold Key	35.00
Coffeepot, Red Poppy	25.00
Coffeepot, Red Poppy, Metal Insert	38.00
Coffeepot, Ritz, Canary	10.00

Coffeepot, Shaggy Tulip, 4–Part 60.00
Coffeepot, Sweep, Flowers 10.00
Coffeepot, Tulip, Drip 70.00
Coffeepot, Washington, Cream, Roses, Silver Spout, 18 Oz. 10.00
Coffeepot, Washington, Eggshell, White & Red Trim 26.00
Cookie Jar, Crocus 60.00
Cookie Jar, Poppy .... 30.00 To 40.00
Cookie Jar, Sundial, Blue Blossom 225.00
Creamer, Colonial 20.00
Creamer, Orange Poppy 18.00
Creamer, Rose White 12.00
Creamer, Taverne 9.00
Creamer, Zeisel, Tomorrow's Classic Bouquet 8.50
Cup & Saucer, Cameo Rose 5.50
Cup & Saucer, Serenade 5.50
Cup & Saucer, Springtime 7.00
Cup & Saucer, Wildflower 5.00
Cup, Heather Rose 4.50
Custard, Poppy 4.50
Custard, Rose, Yellow 4.00
Dish, Refrigerator, Taverne, Oblong 26.50
Dish, Refrigerator, Westinghouse, Orange 15.00
Drip Jar, Chinese Red, Cover 14.00
Drip Jar, Springtime 16.50
Drip–O–Lator, Blue & White, Silver Trim 20.00
Drip–O–Lator, Bullseye 15.00
Drip–O–Lator, Taverne 42.00
Gravy Boat, Crocus 25.00
Gravy Boat, Springtime 13.99
Gravy Boat, Wildfire 15.00
Jar, Refrigerator, Poppy, Loop Handle 17.00
Jug, Ball, Red, No.3 .... 12.00
Jug, Batter, Sundial, Blue 75.00
Jug, Brown, 2 Pt. 8.00
Jug, Radiance, 3 1/4 In. 19.00
Jug, Rose Parade, 5 In. .... 15.00 To 17.00
Leftover, Hotpoint, Yellow, 7 In. 7.00
Leftover, Poppy, Loop Handle 20.00
Leftover, Red Poppy, Loop Handle 20.00
Leftover, Taverne, Rectangular 25.00
Leftover, Westinghouse, Aristocrat, Ivory 20.00
Leftover, Westinghouse, Emperor, Red 14.00
Leftover, Westinghouse, Sunset, Aristocrat 18.00
Mixing Bowl Set, Crocus 35.00
Mixing Bowl, Indian, Banded, Red, 6 In. 9.00
Mixing Bowl, Rose Parade, 7 1/2 In. 25.00
Mixing Bowl, Rose White, 9 In. 14.00
Mixing Bowl, Sunshine 10.00
Mixing Bowl, Wildfire, 7 1/2 In. 8.00
Mug, Emerald Green 7.00
Mug, Irish Coffee, Brown 8.00
Pepper Shaker, Rose Parade 7.00
Pitcher, Chinese Red, 5 1/2 In. 16.00
Pitcher, Heather Rose, 6 In. 9.50
Pitcher, Milk, Orange 18.00
Pitcher, Poppy 18.50
Pitcher, Poppy & Wheat 35.00
Pitcher, Red Poppy 14.00
Pitcher, Schroon Manor, Schroon Lake, N.Y. 65.00
Pitcher, Water, Donut, Red 30.00
Pitcher, Water, Westinghouse, Hercules, Cobalt Blue 58.00
Pitcher, Wildflower, Sani–Grid 25.00
Plate, Cake, Springtime 9.00
Plate, Cameo Rose, 9 In. 5.00

Plate, Cameo Rose, 10 In.	4.00
Plate, Crocus, 6 1/4 In.	4.50
Plate, Poppy, 6 In.	3.50
Plate, Poppy, 10 In.	12.00
Plate, Red Poppy, 9 In.	6.00
Plate, Red Poppy, 10 In.	12.00
Plate, Richmond, 8 In.	3.50
Plate, Richmond, 9 1/4 In.	3.50
Plate, Springtime, 6 In.	2.00
Plate, Springtime, 9 1/4 In.	5.00 To 6.00
Plate, Tulip, 9 In.	3.00
Plate, Wildfire, 9 In.	7.00
Platter, Brown–Eyed Susan	18.00
Platter, Springtime, 13 1/2 In.	9.99
Punch Bowl Set, Old Crow Advertising, Box, 12 Piece	225.00
Range Set, Red Poppy, 3 Piece	35.00
Range Set, Royal Rose, 3 Piece	35.00
Relish, Century, Sun Glow	25.00
Roaster, Westinghouse, Blue	8.50
Rolling Pin, Taverne	65.00
Rolling Pin, Tulip	85.00
Salt & Pepper, Chinese Red	16.00
Salt & Pepper, Red Poppy, Teardrop	15.00
Salt & Pepper, Rose Parade	12.00 To 18.00
Salt & Pepper, Rose White	12.00
Salt & Pepper, Rose, Yellow	18.00
Salt & Pepper, Sani–Grid	15.00
Salt & Pepper, Wildfire, Egg Shape	20.00
Saltshaker, Red Poppy, Eggdrop Shape	5.00
Saltshaker, Taverne, Colonial	7.50
Shaker, Pepper, Rose White, Sani–Grid	5.50
Shaker, Pepper, Wildflower	8.00
Soup, Dish, Poppy	12.00
Sugar & Creamer, Bouquet, Blue	30.00
Sugar & Creamer, Parchment & Pine, Green	15.00
Sugar & Creamer, Poppy	12.00
Sugar & Creamer, Red Poppy	14.00
Sugar & Creamer, Taverne	27.00 To 30.00
Sugar, Light Green, Saf–Handle	6.00
Sugar, Rose Parade, Blue	9.00
Sugar, Saf–Handle, Cover, Yellow	7.00
Syrup, Chinese Red, Banded	30.00
Teapot, Airflow, Chinese Red	45.00
Teapot, Airflow, Cobalt Blue, Gold Trim	27.50 To 45.00
Teapot, Airflow, Navy Blue, Gold Trim	40.00
Teapot, Aladdin, Black, Infuser, Round	16.00
Teapot, Aladdin, Cadet, Infuser, Round	28.00
Teapot, Aladdin, Canary, Gold	18.00
Teapot, Aladdin, Light Blue	32.00
Teapot, Aladdin, Marine Blue, Infuser, Round, 6 Cup	35.00
Teapot, Aladdin, Marine, Gold	32.00
Teapot, Aladdin, New York, Black, 1 1/2 Cup	27.00
Teapot, Aladdin, Pink	20.00
Teapot, Aladdin, Sky Blue	40.00
Teapot, Aladdin, Turquoise Blue, Round Infuser, 6 Cup	35.00
Teapot, Albany, Ivory & Gold, 6 Cup	38.00
Teapot, Albany, Mahogany	20.00
Teapot, Albert, Celadon, 6 Cup	25.00
Teapot, Automobile, Black, Gold	375.00
Teapot, Automobile, Cobalt Blue	410.00 To 450.00
Teapot, Baltimore, Cadet Blue	25.00
Teapot, Baltimore, Delphinium Design, 6 Cup	27.00
Teapot, Basket, Turquoise, 6 Cup	85.00
Teapot, Bellevue, Black, 1 Cup	10.00

Teapot, Bellevue, Maroon	10.00
Teapot, Birdcage, Maroon & Gold	155.00
Teapot, Boston, Brown, 1 Cup	10.00
Teapot, Boston, Chinese Red, Metal Tip Spout, 2 Cup	15.00
Teapot, Boston, Cobalt Blue, 2 Cup	15.00
Teapot, Boston, Crocus	100.00
Teapot, Boston, Emerald Green & Gold, 8 Cup	28.00
Teapot, Boston, Gray, 2 Cup	20.00
Teapot, Boston, Maroon Design, 6 Cup	25.00
Teapot, Boston, Maroon, Gold	16.00
Teapot, Chinese Red, 4 Cup	22.00
Teapot, Cleveland, Emerald Green .... 28.00 To 65.00
Teapot, Cleveland, Maroon & Gold, 6 Cup	20.00
Teapot, Cleveland, Turquoise .... 25.00 To 28.00
Teapot, Cleveland, Turquoise & Gold, 6 Cup	37.00
Teapot, Cleveland, Yellow	35.00
Teapot, Cleveland, Yellow & Gold, 6 Cup	35.00
Teapot, Cloverleaf, Yellow, 6 Cup	18.00
Teapot, Colonial, Ivory, Floral Decal, 6 Cup	15.00
Teapot, Coverlet, Ivory, 6 Cup	18.00
Teapot, Cozy Cover, Chrome Cover, White	25.00
Teapot, Cozy Cover, Yellow, Gold Trim	20.00
Teapot, Crocus, New York	25.00
Teapot, Cube, Green, 2 Cup	22.50
Teapot, Cube, Stock Brown, 6 Cup	20.00
Teapot, Danielle, Green	20.00
Teapot, Disraeli .... 15.00 To 30.00
Teapot, Dresden, Streamline	50.00
Teapot, Dripless, Chartreuse	60.00
Teapot, French, Black, 6 Cup	10.00
Teapot, French, Blue, 6 Cup	10.00
Teapot, French, Ivory & Gold, 4 Cup	30.00
Teapot, French, Maroon, 2 Cup	25.00
Teapot, Globe, Dripless, Blue, Gold Trim	60.00
Teapot, Globe, Dripless, Jewel Tea	56.50
Teapot, Globe, Dripless, Yellow	70.00
Teapot, Globe, Emerald Green	35.00
Teapot, Hollywood, Black, Gold Trim, 6 Cup	40.00
Teapot, Hollywood, Chartreuse & Gold, 6 Cup	16.00
Teapot, Hollywood, Delphinium Blue, 4 Cup	25.00
Teapot, Hollywood, Ivory, 6 Cup	35.00
Teapot, Hollywood, Maroon, 6 Cup	25.00
Teapot, Hollywood, Monterey, 6 Cup	27.00
Teapot, Hollywood, Pink	13.00
Teapot, Hook Cover, Cobalt Blue, 6 Cup .... 35.00 To 40.00
Teapot, Hook Cover, Maroon, Gold	18.00
Teapot, Illinois, Maroon, 6 Cup	50.00
Teapot, Inverted Spout, Camelia	35.00
Teapot, Kansas, Emerald Green, Gold Trim	90.00
Teapot, Lipton, Black	14.00
Teapot, Lipton, Maroon, 6 Cup	14.00
Teapot, Lipton, Yellow .... 10.00 To 12.00
Teapot, Los Angeles, Cobalt Blue, 6 Cup	45.00
Teapot, Los Angeles, Ivory, 8 Cup	30.00
Teapot, Los Angeles, Maroon & Gold, 8 Cup	35.00
Teapot, McCormick, Black, 6 Cup	23.00
Teapot, McCormick, Maroon, Infuser	20.00
Teapot, McCormick, Pink, 6 Cup	23.00
Teapot, McCormick, Turquoise, Infuser	20.00
Teapot, Melody, Chinese Red	75.00
Teapot, Melody, Poppy	95.00
Teapot, Melody, Teal, Gold Trim	110.00
Teapot, Nautilus, Red	85.00
Teapot, New York, Black, 2 Cup	10.00

Teapot, New York, Brown	15.00
Teapot, New York, Crocus	40.00
Teapot, New York, Emerald Green Design, 6 Cup	20.00
Teapot, New York, Gold Design, On Green, 6 Cup	22.00
Teapot, New York, Green	18.00
Teapot, New York, Ivory, Gold	16.00
Teapot, New York, Turquoise & Gold, 6 Cup	20.00
Teapot, Newport, Jewel Tea, 1930s	125.00
Teapot, Parade, Cadet Blue, 6 Cup	25.00
Teapot, Parade, Canary, 6 Cup	18.00
Teapot, Parade, Maroon & Gold, 6 Cup	25.00
Teapot, Parade, Yellow	12.00 To 17.00
Teapot, Philadelphia, Black, 1 1/2 Cup	30.00
Teapot, Philadelphia, Cobalt Blue, Gold Trim, 4 Cup	30.00
Teapot, Philadelphia, Green, Gold	28.00
Teapot, Philadelphia, Pink Basket, 6 Cup	25.00
Teapot, Philadelphia, Tan, Wide Gold Bands	20.00
Teapot, Rhythm, Ivory	35.00
Teapot, Rose Parade	14.00 To 35.00
Teapot, Rose White, 3 Cup	22.00
Teapot, Saf–Handle, Canary, Gold	50.00
Teapot, Saf–Handle, Dark Green	10.00
Teapot, Saf–Handle, Maroon	20.00
Teapot, Sani–Grid, Cadet Blue, Pink & Blue Flowers, White Handle, 6 Cup	28.00
Teapot, Silver Basket, Canary	55.00
Teapot, Star, Cobalt Blue	30.00
Teapot, Star, Turquoise	20.00
Teapot, Streamline, Yellow, Gold	50.00
Teapot, Sundial, Teal, Gold Trim	55.00
Teapot, T–Ball, Maroon, Round	36.00
Teapot, T–Ball, Pink, Square	50.00
Teapot, T–Ball, Round, Silver Luster	35.00
Teapot, Tea For 2, Green	32.00
Teapot, Teataster, Cobalt Blue Design, 6 Cup	75.00
Teapot, Twinspout, Turquoise, 4 Cup	48.00
Teapot, Twinspout, Turquoise, 6 Cup	70.00
Teapot, Victoria, Celadon, 6 Cup	18.00 To 20.00
Teapot, Windshield, Cadet Blue	45.00
Teapot, Windshield, Ivory, Gold Dots, 6 Cup	32.00
Teapot, Windshield, Maroon	10.00 To 25.00
Tidbit, Sunshine	75.00
Tile, Tea, Silhouette	80.00
Tile, Tea, Taverne	60.00
Tumbler, Red Poppy, Red Band	15.00
Water Server, Hotpoint, Blue	28.00
Water Server, Westinghouse, Emperor, Delft Blue, Cover	50.00

Halloween is an ancient holiday that has been changed in the last 200 years. The jack–o'–lantern, witches on broomsticks, and orange decorations seem to be twentieth–century creations. Collectors started to become serious about collecting Halloween–related items in the late 1970s. The papier–mache decorations, now replaced by plastic, and old costumes are in demand.

HALLOWEEN, Apron & Cap, Crepe Paper	10.00
Black Cat, Arched Back, Papier–Mache	55.00
Candy Container, Witch	120.00
Clapper, Witch On Broom, 8 1/4 In.	42.00
Costume, Bewitched, Box	18.00
Costume, Blondie, Box	22.00
Costume, Cinderella, Box	40.00
Costume, Devil, Crepe Paper, Dennison	20.00
Costume, Flower, Crepe Paper, 1930s	18.00
Costume, Fred Flintstone	30.00
Costume, Meanie, Blue	70.00

Costume, Peter Rabbit	15.00
Costume, Santa Claus, Starched Cloth Mask	37.50
Costume, Witch, Crepe Paper, Dennison	25.00
Costume, Woody Woodpecker, Cotton Gauze Face Mask, Box	35.00
Costume, Zorro, Box	28.00
Figure, Dracula, Vinyl, Dressed In Tails, 12 1/2 In.	75.00
Game, Pumpkin Fortune	15.00
Jack-O'-Lantern, Black Cat On Fence, Papier-Mache .... 32.00 To 45.00
Jack-O'-Lantern, Laughing, Puffed, Orange, 5 In.	52.00
Jack-O'-Lantern, Papier-Mache, Tissue Paper Face, 7 1/2 In.	35.00
Jack-O'-Lantern, Papier-Mache, Wire Handle, Germany, 5 1/2 X 4 In	45.00
Jack-O'-Lantern, Pressed Paper, Germany	25.00
Jack-O'-Lantern, Tin, Bats On Back, Bail Handle, 1930, 5 X 6 In.	25.00
Lantern, Child's, Pumpkin Head, Glass, Battery Operated	65.00
Lantern, Child's, Skull Head, Glass, Battery Operated	45.00
Mask, John F.Kennedy, 1960	50.00
Mask, Pinocchio, 1939	15.00
Mask, Rabbit, Child's, Plastic	3.00
Mask, Skeleton, Hard Cloth	20.00
Mask, Witch, Paper, Tip-Top Bread Advertising On Back, 1948	24.00
Mask, Zorro, Black Sombrero	15.00
Noisemaker, Black Cat, On Domed Disc, Handle, Kircholf, 3 In.	15.00
Noisemaker, Composition Cat's Head, Twirl	85.00
Noisemaker, Lithographed, Tin, 1930s, Set of 6	28.00
Noisemaker, Pumpkin Head, Wood, Germany	85.00
Pumpkin, Paper, Foldout	8.00
Pumpkin, Plush	1250.00
Whistle, Cat, Papier-Mache	115.00
Witch, Pressed Paper, Germany	35.00

Hampshire pottery was made in Keene, New Hampshire, between 1871 and 1923. Hampshire developed a line of colored glazed wares as early as 1883, including a Royal Worcester-type pink, olive green, blue, and mahogany. Pieces are marked with the printed mark or the impressed name "Hampshire Pottery" or "J.S.T. & Co., Keene, N.H." Many pieces were marked with city names and sold as souvenirs.

HAMPSHIRE, Bowl, Blue Matte, 5 In.	50.00
Bowl, White Oakleaf, Green, 3 X 6 In.	65.00
Ewer, Dark Green Glaze, JST & Co., 7 In.	60.00
Ewer, Oyster Bay, L.I., Green & Brown, Signed, 5 1/2 In.	85.00
Lamp, Etched Glass Shade, Incised Floral Design, C.1910, 15 In.	300.00
Pitcher, Landing of The Pilgrims, 7 1/2 In. .... 75.00 To 95.00
Pitcher, Worcester Glaze, Transfer of Stone House, 7 1/2 In.	60.00
Shaving Mug, Scuttle, Molded Leafy Branches, Gold Trim, 4 In.	65.00
Urn, Art Nouveau Leaves, Handles, Pedestal, 8 X 6 In.	165.00
Vase, Bisque Body, High Glaze Black Rim, Dated 1914, 3 In.	195.00
Vase, Green Matte Glaze, Geometric, Art Pottery, 8 In.	154.00
Vase, Leaf Design, Green Matte Glaze, Handles, 5 1/2 In.	95.00
Vase, Puff, Blue Paint, 3 1/2 In.	65.00
Vase, Repeating Molded Tulip, Running Stem Design, 9 In.	350.00

Philip Handel worked in Meriden, Connecticut, from 1885 and in New York City from 1893 to 1933. His firm made art glass and other types of lamps. Handel shades were made not only of leaded glass in a style reminiscent of Tiffany but also of reverse painted glass. Handel also made vases and other glass objects.

HANDEL, Compote, Art Nouveau Design, Signed, 8 In.	235.00
Humidor, Cigar, Silver Plated Hinged Glass Lid, Bear Cubs Playing	615.00
Humidor, Hinged Cover, Owls, Tapered Form, 7 In.	600.00
Humidor, Hunting Dog, Signed	950.00
Humidor, Squirrels, Flattened Sphere, Pipe On Cover, 6 In. .... 500.00 To 750.00
Humidor, Stag, Cover With Pipe, 5 1/2 In.	525.00
Humidor, Yellow & Green On Frosted Ground	1150.00

Handel, Lamp, Desk, Roll Top, Leaded Glass, Green Slag, 18 In.

Jewelry Box, Footed, Signed 465.00
Lamp, 8 Panels, Peacock Feathers, Green, Yellow, Red, Marked, 22 In. 5850.00
Lamp, Art Nouveau, Mosaic Brown Shade, 7 In. 300.00
Lamp, Banker's, 2 Painted Peacocks 750.00
Lamp, Bird of Paradise, Signed, 18 In. 1200.00
Lamp, Boudoir, Cracked Ice Shade, Exotic Birds, Flowers, 7 In. 2400.00
Lamp, Bronze, Leaf & Bird Design, Forest Scene Shade, 24 In. 3520.00
Lamp, Copper Finish, Hand Painted Scene, 16 In. 425.00
Lamp, Cracked Ice Shade, Birds, Flowers Painted Inside, 8 In. 2640.00
Lamp, Desk, Adjustable Brass Base, Scenic Shade, Signed, 14 In. 1700.00
Lamp, Desk, Dragonflies Bell Shade, Bronze Candlestick Base, 12 In. 1600.00
Lamp, Desk, Roll Top, Leaded Glass, Green Slag, 18 In. ....*Illus* 1750.00
Lamp, Domed Shade, Pines, River, Reverse Painted, 18 In. ....*Illus* 4070.00
Lamp, Domed Shade, Roses, Bronzed Base, Signed, 7 In. 2100.00
Lamp, Enameled Band of Floral Designs On Shade, Signed, 18 In. 2300.00
Lamp, Exotic Birds & Flowers, Cracked Ice Shade, 7 In. 2400.00
Lamp, Floor, Bronze, Signed, 55 In., Pair 900.00
Lamp, Flower Border, Reverse Painting, Brass Base, 7 In. 1500.00
Lamp, Goose Girl, Geese Scene, Label, 14 1/2 In. 750.00
Lamp, Hanging, Reverse Painted Parrots, Brass Collar, Amber, 10 In. 1250.00
Lamp, Painted & Enameled Sunset Forest Scene, Signed, 18 In. 2400.00
Lamp, Painted Landscape Shade, Baluster Base, 14 In. 1300.00
Lamp, Painted Metal, Cracked Ice Shade, Inside Exotic Birds, 7 In. 2400.00
Lamp, Painted Shade, Suspended From Metal Frame, Signed, 57 In. 8250.00
Lamp, Painted Sunset Scene In Forest, Signed, 22 In. 2050.00
Lamp, Paneled, Palm Tree Filigree Over Slag Glass, Signed, 18 In. 2200.00
Lamp, Reverse & Obverse Painted Shade, Signed, 18 In. 1150.00
Lamp, Reverse Painted 6–Sided Shade, Wisteria, 7 1/2 In. 2000.00
Lamp, Reverse Painted Floral On Chipped Ice Shade, Signed, 14 In. 360.00
Lamp, Reverse Painted Japanese Design, Bronze Base, Signed, 7 In. 700.00
Lamp, Reverse Painted Palm Tree Scene, 6–Sided Shade, Signed 4250.00
Lamp, Reverse Painted Roses & Wildflower Shade, Signed, 15 In. 1450.00
Lamp, Reverse Painted Setting Sun With Autumn Foliage, 18 In. 5600.00
Lamp, Reverse Painted Shade, Blackberry Border, Signed, 23 In. 4000.00
Lamp, Reverse Painted Shade, Pines Along River, Signed, 18 In. 3700.00
Lamp, Reverse Painted Shade, Rose Border, Yellow Field, 22 In. 1600.00
Lamp, Reverse Painted Shade, Winter Forest Scene, Signed, 7 In. 1100.00
Lamp, Reverse Painted Snowfall At Dusk, Signed, 16 In. 1900.00
Lamp, Reverse Painted Wild Roses, Butterflies, Chipped Glass Base 2100.00
Lamp, Reverse Painted, Black–Eyed Susans, Yellow, Bronze, 18 In. 1900.00
Lamp, Reverse Painted, Palm Forest At Sunset, Fluted Base, 18 In. 9500.00
Lamp, Reverse Painted, Signed, 16 In. ....*Illus* 4400.00
Lamp, Scene of Windmill Against Red Sky, Signed, 18 In. 1700.00
Lamp, Scenic Shade, Brass, Signed, Numbered, 14 In. 1700.00
Lamp, Shepherd Scene Shade, 18 In. 9200.00
Lamp, Slag Glass, Octagonal Shade, Signed, 18 In. ....*Illus* 2420.00
Lamp, Squared Shade, Winter Forest Scene, Signed, 8 In. 1700.00
Lamp, Table, Leaded Glass, 25–In.Diam.Shade, Signed Base, 26 In. 2750.00

Lamp, Torch, Enameled Shade, Red & Green Flowers, Label	400.00
Lamp, Wisteria, 18–In.Diam.Shade, Signed, 28 In.	5500.00
Plate, Dogwood Branch, Teroma, 8 In.	210.00
Shade, Lamp, Arts & Crafts Style, Tooled Copper, Glass, 4 Panels	880.00
Shade, Painted Parchment, Harbor of Venice	800.00
Shade, Reverse Painted Tapestry, Flowers, Eagles, Signed, 18 In.	1800.00
Shade, Windwmill Scene, Blue–Gray Ground, Signed, 16 In.	7200.00
Tobacco Jar, Tavern Scene, Pipe Handle On Lid, 7 3/4 In.	145.00

HARDWARE, see Architectural

Harker Pottery Company of East Liverpool, Ohio, was founded by Benjamin Harker in 1840. The company made many types of pottery but by the Civil War was making quantities of yellowware from native clays. They also made Rockingham–type brown–glazed pottery and whiteware. The plant was moved to Chester, West Virginia, in 1931. Dinnerwares were made and sold nationally. In 1971 the company was sold to Jeanette Glass Company and all operations ceased in 1972.

HARKER, Ashtray, Chesterton, Gray, Round, 4 3/4 In.	5.00
Batter Set, Covers, Red Apple	50.00
Bean Pot, Calico Tulip, Individual	3.00
Bowl, Chowder, Cameo, Blue	4.50
Bowl, George & Martha Washington, 5 1/4 In.	2.00
Bowl, George & Martha Washington, 10 1/2 In.	4.00
Bowl, Modern Tulip, 6 In.	3.00
Bowl, Modern Tulip, 9 1/2 In.	7.00
Cake Plate, Cameo, Tab Handles, Blue	18.00
Cake Plate, Modern Age, 12 In.	10.00
Cake Plate, Tulip, 11 In.	10.00
Cake Server, Amethyst	12.00
Cake Server, Petit Point	12.50
Casserole, Cover, Cameo, Blue, 8 In.	32.00
Casserole, Cover, Petit Point, 8 In.	28.00
Cup & Saucer, Chesterton, Gray, White Trim	4.00
Cup & Saucer, George & Martha Washington	5.00
Cup & Saucer, Modern Tulip	3.50
Cup & Saucer, Silhouette	7.00
Eggcup, Double, Chesterton, Gray, White Trim	12.00
Gravy Boat, Chesterton, Gray, White Trim	10.00
Gravy Boat, Liner, Chesterton	10.00
Jug, Cover	26.00
Pie Baker, Petit Point, 10 In.	12.00

Handel, Lamp, Domed Shade, Pines, River, Reverse Painted, 18 In.

Handel, Lamp, Slag Glass, Octagonal Shade, Signed, 18 In.

Handel, Lamp, Reverse Painted, Signed, 16 In.

Pie Baker, Tulip 10.00
Pie Lifter, Petit Point 12.00
Pitcher, Dahlia, Cover, 4 1/2 In. 10.00
Pitcher, Water, Hand Painted Water Lilies, Gold Trim, C.1890, 9 In. 125.00
Plate, Cameo, Blue, 7 In. 3.00
Plate, Cameo, Brown, 7 1/8 In. 2.00
Plate, Chesterton, Gray, White Trim, 6 In. 1.75
Plate, Chesterton, Gray, White Trim, 9 1/2 In. 2.50
Plate, Chesterton, Gray, White Trim, Handles, 10 1/2 In. 7.50
Plate, George & Martha Washington, 6 1/4 In. 2.00
Plate, Modern Tulip, 6 1/2 In. 3.00
Plate, Modern Tulip, 9 In. 3.50
Plate, Modern Tulip, 11 3/4 In. 8.00
Plate, Modern Tulip, Square, 7 In. 3.00
Plate, Silhouette, 9 3/4 In. 7.00
Plate, Utility, Cameo Rose 10.00
Platter, Amy, 11 1/4 In. 12.00
Platter, Cameo, Blue 7.00
Platter, Modern Tulip, 14 In. 7.00
Rolling Pin, Amy 50.00
Rolling Pin, Cameo, Blue 75.00
Rolling Pin, Petit Point 45.00
Rolling Pin, Red Apple .... 45.00 To 65.00
Rolling Pin, Taverne 45.00
Salt & Pepper, Colonial Lady 18.00
Salt & Pepper, Range, Cameo, Blue 24.00
Snack Set, Chesterton, Cake Plate, Cup, 9 Piece 20.00
Snack Set, Chesterton, Teal, 8 1/4 In., 9 Piece 25.00
Spoon, Modern Tulip 16.00
Spoon, Petit Point 9.50
Spoon, Red Apple 12.00
Sugar & Creamer, Cover, Chesterton, Gray, White Trim 14.00
Sugar, Cameo, Blue, Cover 5.00
Sugar, Modern Tulip, Cover 6.00
Teapot, Cameo, Blue, 6 Cup 48.00
Water Server, Modern Tulip, Cover 18.00

Harlequin dinnerware was produced by the Homer Laughlin Company from 1938 to 1964, and sold without trademark by the F.W. Woolworth Co. It has a concentric ring design like Fiesta, but the rings are separated from the rim by a plain margin. Cup handles are triangular in shape.

HARLEQUIN, Ashtray, Basket, Turquoise 42.00
Ashtray, Saucer, Red 45.00
Ashtray, Saucer, Turquoise 35.00
Bowl, Cereal, Mauve, 5 In. 3.00
Bowl, Cereal, Yellow, 6 1/2 In. 4.00
Bowl, Rose, 5 1/4 In. 6.00
Bowl, Salad, Yellow 12.00
Butter, Cover, Green, 1/2 Lb. 55.00
Butter, Turquoise, 1/2 Lb. 45.00
Butter, Yellow 95.00
Candleholder, Yellow, Pair 165.00
Casserole, Mauve 40.00
Casserole, Red, Cover 45.00
Casserole, Rose, Cover 42.00
Casserole, Yellow .... 28.00 To 35.00
Cat, Mauve 45.00
Chop Plate, Rose, 13 In. .... 10.00 To 17.50
Creamer, Novelty, Red 15.00
Creamer, Turquoise 4.00
Creamer, Yellow .... 4.00 To 7.00
Creamer, Yellow, High Lip 38.00
Cup & Saucer, Green 6.00

Cup & Saucer, Mauve, After Dinner	30.00
Cup & Saucer, Rose	7.00
Cup & Saucer, Turquoise	6.00
Cup & Saucer, Yellow	6.50
Cup, Dark Green	5.00
Cup, Light Green	4.00
Cup, Maroon, After Dinner	30.00
Dinner Set, Service For 4, Box, 20 Piece	60.00
Eggcup, Mauve, Single	15.00
Eggcup, Red	18.00
Eggcup, Spruce, Double	18.00
Figurine, 2 Ducks, Maverick, Gold, White	23.00
Figurine, 2 Ducks, Maverick, White	8.00
Figurine, 2 Penguins, Maverick, White	8.00
Figurine, Donkey	25.00
Figurine, Lamb, Green	45.00
Figurine, Penguin, Blue	45.00
Figurine, Penguin, Green, 3 In.	60.00 To 65.00
Jug, Ball, Chartreuse	45.00
Jug, Ball, Light Green	28.00
Jug, Ball, Maroon	40.00
Jug, Ball, Rose	32.00 To 36.00
Jug, Tilt, Blue	14.00
Jug, Water, Maroon	35.00
Mixing Bowl, Forest Green, 6 In.	70.00
Pitcher, Milk, Yellow	25.00
Pitcher, Water, Green	30.00
Pitcher, Water, Maroon	45.00
Pitcher, Water, Turquoise	24.50
Pitcher, Water, Yellow	30.00
Plate, Chartreuse, 9 In.	8.00
Plate, Dark Green, 6 In.	3.00
Plate, Green, 9 In.	10.00
Plate, Red, 6 In.	2.50
Plate, Salad, Dark Green, Individual	15.00
Plate, Yellow, 10 In.	6.50 To 10.00
Platter, Chartreuse, 11 In.	7.00
Platter, Dark Green, 11 In.	8.00
Platter, Gray, 13 In.	13.00
Platter, Red, 11 In.	9.00
Platter, Turquoise	8.00
Platter, Yellow, Oval, 13 In.	9.00
Relish Insert, Yellow	15.00
Relish, Mauve	20.00
Salt & Pepper, Green	9.00
Saltshaker, Aqua	7.00
Sauce Boat, Turquoise	10.00
Shaker Holder, Donkey	14.00
Soup, Dish	10.00
Spoon Rest, Double, Yellow	150.00
Spoon Rest, Rhythm, Turquoise	130.00
Spooner, White	65.00
Sugar, Gray	13.00 To 15.50
Sugar, Yellow	6.00 To 10.00
Teapot, Blue	35.00
Teapot, Chartreuse	50.00
Teapot, Forest Green	65.00
Teapot, Rose	45.00
Teapot, Turquoise	29.00
Tumbler, Maroon	35.00
Tumbler, Turquoise	24.00
Tumbler, Yellow, Round	35.00

Haviland, Vase, Courting Scene, 1882–86, 20 1/4 In., Pair

Hatpins were fashionable from 1860 to 1920 when large, heavy hats required special long-shanked pins to hold them in place. Naturally, hatpin holders were made during the same years. The hatpin holder resembles a large saltshaker, but it often has no opening at the bottom as a shaker does. Hatpin holders were made of all types of ceramics and metal. Look for other prices under the names of specific manufacturers.

HATPIN HOLDER, Art Nouveau Lady, Sterling Silver, 6 1/2 In.	25.00
Cloissone, 12 In.	25.00
Hat, Pink, Purple Flowers, Obelisk Style, White, Nippon, 5 In.	20.00
Rhinestone, 8 1/2 In.	17.50
Rose Design, Porcelain, Gold, 2 1/4 In.	55.00
Royal Doulton, Dickensware, Sam Weller, 6 In.	110.00
RS Prussia Type, Trinket Tray Front, Floral, 4 1/2 In.	125.00
Ruffled Top, Small Rose, Gold Trim, Signed	80.00

Hatpins were popular from 1860 to 1920. The long pin, often over four inches, was used to hold the hat in place on the hair. The tops of the pins were made of all materials from solid gold and real gemstones to ceramics and glass. Be careful to buy original hatpins and not recent pieces made by altering old buttons.

HATPIN, Black Jetstone, Domed Top, Twisted Wire Forms Cage, 11 In.	10.00
Carnival Glass, Belle	175.00
Carnival Glass, Bumblebees	65.00
Carnival Glass, Cattails	65.00
Carnival Glass, Flying Bat	125.00
Carnival Glass, Four Hearts	85.00
Carnival Glass, Strawberry, Green	135.00
Carnival Glass, Top–O'–Morn	25.00
Eagle, Rhinestone	15.00
Egyptian Head Profile, Embossed Brass, 1 1/4 X 1 In.	18.00
Flowing Haired Woman, Art Nouveau	33.00
Fourleaf Clover, Sterling Silver, Round, 1 In.	20.00
Heart, Flowers & Scrolls, Embossed Brass, 1 7/8 X 2 In.	14.00
Large Amethyst Stone, Long	32.50
Openwork, Red Stones, Oval Moonstone Center, Brass, 10 In.	12.00
Oval Amethyst, Cameo Center	95.00
Poppy, Green, Cream, Austria	40.00
Pronged Rhinestones On Domed Top, Filigree Brass, 10 1/2 In.	14.00
Stove Advertising	65.00
Trumpet, Rhinestone	5.00
Victorian, Owl's Head	34.00
Woman's Face, Floral Mount, Art Nouveau, Gold	150.00

HAVILAND & CO. Haviland china has been made in Limoges, France, since 1842. The factory was started by the Haviland Brothers of New York City. Pieces are marked H & Co., Haviland & Co., or Theodore

Haviland. It is possible to match existing sets of dishes through dealers who specialize in Haviland china. Other factories worked in the town of Limoges making a similar chinaware. These porcelains are listed in this book under "Limoges."

HAVILAND, Cake Plate, Cherries & Green Leaves, 13 In.	67.00
Cake Plate, Louisiana, Florals, Multicolor, Gold Handles, 9 In.	28.00
Coffeepot, Pink Rosebuds, Theo.Haviland	38.00
Cup & Saucer, Apple Blossom	14.00
Plate, Dropped Rose, Scalloped Rim, 9 1/2 In.	75.00
Plate, Hand Painted Daisies, 8 1/2 In., Pair	48.00
Sugar & Creamer, Autumn Leaf	130.00
Teacup, 4 O'Clock	32.00
Tray, Perfume, Hand Painted Farm Scene, Scalloped, 8 1/2 X 7 In.	42.00
Vase, Courting Scene, 1882–86, 20 1/4 In., Pair ....*Illus*	3300.00

T. G. Hawkes & Company of Corning, New York, was founded in 1880. The firm cut glass blanks made at other glassworks until 1962. Many pieces are marked with the trademark, a trefoil ring enclosing a fleur-de-lis and two hawks. Cut glass by other manufacturers is listed under either the factory name or the general category "Cut Glass."

HAWKES, Basket, Basket Weave Cutting At Sides, Flared, 9 In.	275.00
Basket, Flared Bowl, Basket Weave Cut Around Side, 10 In.	235.00
Bottle, Vinegar, Etched Flowers, Vine, Stopper, Pat.June 10, 1918	85.00
Bowl, Brilliant & Rock Crystal, Hobstar Bottom, Signed, 10 In.	2200.00
Bowl, Queen's Pattern, Variant, Hobstars, Bull's-Eye Clusters, 9 In.	500.00
Bowl, Scalloped Rim, Sculptured Dahlias & Swirls, Marked, 9 1/4 In.	425.00
Candelabra, 3-Light, Brazilian Pattern, 17 X 12 1/2 In., Pair	6100.00
Candletick, Floral & Draped Design, 12 In., Pair	300.00
Celery, Intaglio Cut Fruit Baskets, Cornucopia, Florals	125.00
Cruet, Enameled, Etched	90.00
Cruet, Engraved Swag, Oil & Vinegar, 1915	27.00
Cruet, Etched Flowers, Vines, 1918	95.00
Cruet, Oil & Vinegar, Sterling Stoppers	75.00
Cruet, Vinegar	70.00
Fruit Bowl, Millicent Pattern, 9 In.	250.00
Nappy, Venetian, Black Cut, 3 Sides, 5 In.	295.00
Parfait, Louis XVI Style, Lapidary Cut, C.1910, 6 3/4 In., 6 Piece	1100.00
Pitcher, Boxer & Great Dane, Signed, C.1910, 9 In.	235.00
Plate, Centauri, 7 In.	110.00
Punch Bowl, Fan & Star, 12 1/2 X 10 1/2 In., 2 Piece	2350.00
Rose Bowl, Panels of Hobstars, Circles At Top & Bottom, 5 1/2 In.	250.00
Syrup, Brunswick, Sterling Silver Spout, Lid & Collar, Signed, 7 In.	265.00
Tray, Dresser, Sheraton, Oval, 10 X 7 In.	195.00
Vase, Bands of Hobstars, Ferns & Roses, 12 In.	225.00
Vase, Fleur-De-Lis, Chain of Leaves Circling Neck, Signed, 10 In.	75.00
Vase, Hobstar Chain, Diamond Field, Trumpet Foot, Serrated, 9 3/4 In.	95.00
Vase, Millicent Pattern, Glass Knob, Sterling Foot, 11 1/2 In.	250.00
Vase, Sheraton, Trumpet Shape, 10 In.	110.00
Vase, Trumpet, Rayed Star Foot, Nailhead & Panel Cut, 14 In.	150.00
Water Set, Flower Pattern, Signed, 6 Piece	285.00

Figural vases, generally showing a woman from the shoulders up, were used by florists primarily in the 1950s and 1960s. Head vases, made in a variety of sizes and often decorated with imitation jewelry and other life-like accessories, were manufactured in Japan and the U.S. Less elaborate examples were made as early as the 1930s. Religious themes, babies and animals are also common subjects.

HEAD VASE, Girl, Bubble Haircut, Green Dress, Pearls, Napcoware, 8 In.	25.00
Girl, Hat Tied With Pink Bow, VCAG Co., 6 In.	15.00
Girl, Umbrella, Pigtails, Semco, 5 In.	10.00
Lady, Planter, Pearls, 6 In. ....*Illus*	8.75
Woman, Brimmed Hat, White, Art Deco, USA, 9 X 8 In.	65.00

Spray the inside of a glass flower vase with a nonstick product made to keep food from sticking to cooking pots. This will keep the vase from staining if water is left in too long.

Head Vase, Lady, Planter,
    Pearls, 6 In.

Woman, Oriental Luster, Large	16.00
Woman, Oriental, Headband, Pearls, Inarco, 6 In.	17.50
Woman, Pearls, Inarco, Cleveland, 6 In.	8.75
Woman, Winking Eyelashes, Earrings, High Collar, Flat Hat, 6 In.	30.00

Heintz Art Metal shop made jewelry, copper, silver, and brass in Buffalo, New York, from 1906 to 1929. The most popular items with collectors today are the copper desk sets and vases made with applied silver designs.

HEINTZ ART, Humidor, Cigar, Golf Scene, Silver On Bronze, C.1920	165.00
Loving Cup, Silver Overlay, Essex Country Club, July 8–10, 1920	165.00
Loving Cup, Silver Overlay, Golf–Tabor Field Club, July 4, 1916	60.00
Loving Cup, Vermont State Golf Assoc., C.1913, 10 1/4 In.	120.00
Vase, Sterling On Bronze, 4 In.	30.00

Heisey glass was made from 1896 to 1957 in Newark, Ohio, by A. H. Heisey and Co., Inc. The Imperial Glass Company of Bellaire, Ohio, bought some of the molds and the rights to the trademark. Some Heisey patterns have been made by Imperial since 1960. After 1968, they stopped using the "H" trademark. Heisey used romantic names for colors such as "Sahara." Do not confuse color and pattern names.

HEISEY, see also Custard Glass; Ruby Glass

HEISEY, Albemarle, Compote, Sahara, 7 In.	65.00
Alexandrite, Sugar & Creamer, Dolphin Footed, 3 Handles	595.00
Apple, Jam Jar, Cover, Spoon, Cut, Crystal	135.00
Banty Rooster, Cocktail, Full Figure	75.00
Barbara Fritchie, Cocktail, Marked, 3 1/2 Oz.	15.00
Beaded Swag, Butter, Cover, Crystal, Gold Trim	65.00
Beaded Swag, Creamer	30.00
Beaded Swag, Goblet	60.00
Beaded Swag, Spooner	35.00
Beaded Swag, Sugar, Cover	45.00
Beaded Swag, Table Set, Gold Trim, 4 Piece	250.00
Beaded Swag, Tumbler, Gold	12.00
Beaded Swag, Wine, Red Flashed	40.00
Beehive, Plate, Limelight, 4 In.	49.50
Block & Dog, Salt, Open, Blue	50.00
Buzz Saw, Tumbler, Crystal	12.50
Cabachon, Compote, Jelly, 5 In.	17.50
Cambridge, Flower Holder, Seagull, 10 1/2 In.	95.00
Candlestick, 2–Light, C.1940, Pair	50.00
Candlewick, Ashtray, 6 In.	10.00
Candlewick, Bowl, 2 Part, 6 1/3 X 3 In.	10.00
Candlewick, Bowl, Belled, 10 1/2 In.	27.50
Candlewick, Bowl, Flared, 10 1/2 In.	25.00
Candlewick, Candy Dish, Cover, 2 Sections	45.00
Candlewick, Cheese Stand, 5 3/4 X 2 1/2 In.	16.00

Candlewick, Plate, 6 In. .... 6.00 To 7.00
Candlewick, Plate, 8 In. 8.00
Candlewick, Sugar & Creamer, Bead Handles, Floral, Leaf Cut, 6 Oz. 14.00
Candlewick, Tray, Handle, 10 In. 22.00
Cape Cod, Candy Dish, Cover, Footed 65.00
Cape Cod, Pitcher, Water, Footed 95.00
Cape Cod, Sugar & Creamer, Footed 13.50
Caprice, Cruet, Crystal 38.00
Caprice, Sugar & Creamer, Individual 12.00
Carcassone, Soda, Cobalt Blue Bowl, 12 Oz. 75.00
Cascade, Candlestick, 3–Light, Orchid, Pair 135.00
Cat In Hat, Salt, Open, Amber 15.00
Champ Terrier, Caramel Slag, 6 1/2 X 5 5/8 In. 125.00
Champagnes, Orchid Etch 18.00
Charter Oak, Champagne, Saucer, Marked, Flamingo 18.00
Charter Oak, Compote, Moongleam, 7 In. 75.00
Charter Oak, Goblet, Flamingo 19.00
Cheese & Cracker, Floral Design, Cover, Signed 160.00
Chintz, Goblet, 7 3/4 In. 12.50
Chintz, Tumbler, Footed, Crystal, 5 1/2 In. 9.95
Cockade, Bowl, Marked, 12 In. 40.00
Cocktail Shaker, Rooster Head 80.00
Coleport, Cigarette Set, Holder & 2 Ashtrays, Marked 42.50
Colonial Star, Plate, 6 1/2 In., 6 Piece 40.00
Colonial, Celery, Marked 30.00
Colonial, Champagne, Crystal 13.00
Colonial, Cocktail, Marked, Crystal, 3 Oz., 4 Piece 30.00
Colonial, Compote, Child's, Marked, 4 1/4 X 5 In. 14.00
Colonial, Compote, Marked, Crystal, 4 1/4 X 5 In. 14.00
Colonial, Creamer, Child's, Crystal 15.00
Colonial, Goblet, Water 10.00
Colonial, Jar, Fruit, Sanitary Crushed, Dated, 1 1/2 Qt. 115.00
Colonial, Nut Cup, Marked 6.00
Colonial, Pitcher 55.00
Colonial, Pitcher, Squat 85.00
Colonial, Pitcher, Water, Bulbous 65.00
Colonial, Plate, 4 1/2 In. 6.00
Colonial, Punch Cup, 4 Oz. 12.00
Colonial, Sugar & Creamer, Scalloped Tops 40.00
Continental, Compote, Footed, Marked, 7 In. 52.50
Continental, Wine 15.00
Country Club, Cocktail Shaker, Cover 25.00
Crystolite, Ashtray, Leaf, Individual 6.00
Crystolite, Bowl, Tricorner, Handle, 5 1/2 In. 18.00
Crystolite, Box, Cigarette, Signed 30.00
Crystolite, Box, Cover, 7 In. 50.00
Crystolite, Candelabrum, 2–Light, Bobeches, Prisms, Pair 60.00
Crystolite, Candelabrum, Bobeches, Prisms, 2–Light, Pair 60.00
Crystolite, Candelholder, 3–Light, Pair 45.00
Crystolite, Candy Dish, Handle, Cover, 5 1/2 In. 45.00
Crystolite, Champagne 12.00
Crystolite, Compote, Jelly 3.00
Crystolite, Cruet, Label, 3 Oz. 45.00
Crystolite, Goblet, 10 Oz. 12.00
Crystolite, Jam Jar, Cover 50.00
Crystolite, Lighter, Cigarette 9.50
Crystolite, Relish, 3 Sections .... 19.00 To 25.00
Crystolite, Sugar & Creamer 18.00
Diamond Optic, Plate, Pink, 7 In. 7.00
Diamond Optic, Plate, Pink, 8 1/2 In. 10.00
Diamond Optic, Platter, Sahara, 12 In. 18.00
Diamond Point, Ashtray, Individual 6.00
Diamond Point, Butter Chip 10.00
Diamond, Bowl, Cross–Hatch Bottom, Marked, 9 1/2 In. 125.00

Dolphin, Candlestick, Cobalt Blue, 9 In., Pair 2250.00
Domino, Sugar Cube Tray, Crystal 50.00
Duck, Salt, Open, Light Blue, Milk Glass 25.00
Duquesne, Goblet, Chintz Etch 22.00
Elaine, Relish, 2 Sections, Etched 8.50
Elfinware, Salt, Open, Handle, Signed 20.00
Empire, Candlestick, 3–Light, Center Insert, 9 In., Pair 650.00
Empress Etch, Tumbler, Iced Tea, Flamingo 32.50
Empress, Ashtray, Sahara 75.00
Empress, Basket, Allover Cut Wtih Butterflies, 15 In. 160.00
Empress, Bowl, Cover, Dolphin Finial, Marked, Marigold, 6 3/4 In. 55.00
Empress, Bowl, Dolphin Footed, Sahara, 11 In. 60.00
Empress, Bowl, Footed, Sahara, 8 1/2 In. 45.00
Empress, Candlestick, 6 In. 40.00
Empress, Compote, Oval, Crystal, 7 In. 35.00
Empress, Creamer, Sahara 25.00
Empress, Cruet, Moongleam Foot & Stopper 125.00
Empress, Cruet, Yellow 110.00
Empress, Cup & Saucer, Flamingo 30.00
Empress, Dish, Pink, 6 In. 25.00
Empress, Ice Bucket, Metal Handle, Yellow 95.00
Empress, Mayonnaise, Yellow, 3 Footed 35.00
Empress, Mustard, Sahara 65.00
Empress, Plate, Flamingo, 10 1/4 In. 85.00
Empress, Plate, Green, 8 In. 13.50
Empress, Plate, Green, Square, 6 In. 11.50
Empress, Plate, Sahara, 8 In. .... 15.00 To 18.00
Empress, Plate, Yellow, Square, 8 In. 14.25
Empress, Relish, 3 Sections, Marked, Marigold, 10 1/4 In. 38.00
Empress, Relish, Old Colony Etch, Marked, Round, 7 In. 29.50
Empress, Rose Bowl, Flamingo, 5 1/2 In. 55.00
Empress, Salt & Pepper, Sahara 70.00
Empress, Salt & Pepper, Silver Deposit, Crystal 40.00
Empress, Server, Center Handle 50.00
Empress, Sugar & Creamer, Sahara, Individual 70.00
Empress, Vase, Dolphin Feet, Silver Overlay, 9 In. 45.00
Fancy Loop, Pickle 30.00
Fancy Loop, Rose Bowl, Crystal, 6 In. 100.00
Fancy Loop, Sauce, Crystal, Gold Trim 12.00
Fancy Loop, Tankard, Martini 175.00
Fancy Loop, Toothpick 50.00
Fancy Loop, Tumbler, Green, Gold Trim 49.50
Fandango, Bowl, 6 In. 35.00
Fandango, Salt 20.00
Figurine, 2 Baby Rabbits, Head Down 95.00
Figurine, Clydesdale Horse, 7 In. .... 225.00 To 275.00
Figurine, Cygnet, Crystal, 2 In. 100.00
Figurine, Elephant 287.50
Figurine, Fighting Rooster, 8 In., Pair 300.00
Figurine, Giraffe, 1 Head Back, 1 Head Front, Pair 300.00
Figurine, Giraffe, Head Turned .... 150.00 To 175.00
Figurine, Goose, Half Wings 65.00
Figurine, Goose, Wings Down 300.00
Figurine, Goose, Wings Half Up 80.00
Figurine, Goose, Wings Up 70.00
Figurine, Horse, Clydesdale 400.00
Figurine, Horse, Plug 68.00
Figurine, Mallard, Wings Up 120.00
Figurine, Mallard, Wings Up, Marked 155.00
Figurine, Mother Rabbit 650.00
Figurine, Pelican, 10 In., Pair 200.00
Figurine, Pony, Rearing, Blue, Imperial 20.00
Figurine, Pouter Pigeon, Marked 375.00
Figurine, Scotty 135.00

Figurine, Sparrow, Crystal 75.00
Finecut & Block, Salt, Open, Amber 40.00
Fish, Bookends .... 125.00 To 160.00
Flamingo, Bowl, Oval–Handle, 6 1/2 In. 18.00
Flamingo, Dish, Nut, Individual, Marked 16.00
Flat Panel, Relish, 5 Sections, Wheelcut Flowers, Stemmed, 10 In. 35.00
Fox Chase, Plate, Etched Old Fashions, Deep 25.00
Frontenac, Goblet 12.00
Giraffe, 1 Head Back, 1 Head Front, Pair 300.00
Greek Key, Compote, Jelly, Marked 37.50
Greek Key, Cruet, 2 Oz. 80.00
Greek Key, Cruet, 6 Oz. 60.00
Greek Key, Pitcher, Milk, Marked, 5 In. 45.00
Greek Key, Punch Cup 15.00
Greek Key, Sherbet, 3 1/2 In. 12.00
Greek Key, Sherbet, Crystal, 3 1/2 In. 12.00
Greek Key, Straw Jar 150.00
Hawthrone, Sugar, Hotel 30.00
Horsehead, Bookends 100.00
Horsehead, Cigarette Box 70.00
Horseshoe, Candlestick, Pair 85.00
Ipswich, Bowl, Floral, Crystal, 11 In. 40.00
Ipswich, Candy Jar, Cover, Green 50.00
Ipswich, Centerpiece, 7 1/2 In. 90.00
Ipswich, Centerpiece, Prisms, Pair 125.00
Ipswich, Sherbet, Sahara 25.00
Kalonyal, Syrup 65.00
Kalonyal, Toothpick 120.00
Kimberly, Relish, Crystal 32.50
King Arthur, Goblet, Moongleam, Clear 25.00
King Arthur, Wine, Diamond, Pink, 2 1/2 Oz. 30.00
Kingfisher, Flower Block, Flamingo 300.00
Kingfisher, Flower Frog, Green 165.00
Kohinoor, Candelabra, 2–Light, Topaz, Pair 350.00
Kohinoor, Cocktail, Oyster 8.00
Kohinoor, Goblet, Footed, Low 19.00
Krystol, Bonbon, Divided, Crystal, 1907, 5 In. 20.00
Lariat, Basket, 10 In. 95.00
Lariat, Bonbon, Round, Crystal, 8 1/4 In. 25.00
Lariat, Bowl, 12 In. 25.00
Lariat, Bowl, Divided, Sticker, Marked 35.00
Lariat, Bowl, Underplate, Ladle, Divided, 7 1/4 In. 60.00
Lariat, Candlestick .... 8.00 To 10.00
Lariat, Candlestick, 3–Light, Pair .... 110.00 To 145.00
Lariat, Champagne 10.00
Lariat, Coaster .... 5.00 To 10.00
Lariat, Plate, Center Handle, 14 In. 39.00
Lariat, Plate, Cut, 13 In. 24.00
Lariat, Punch Set, 12 Cups, Glass Ladle, 21 In. 250.00
Lariat, Relish, 3 Sections 25.00
Lariat, Sugar & Creamer, Etched 24.00
Lariat, Sugar, Creamer & Tray, Crystal 40.00
Lariat, Tumbler, Juice, Moonglo 20.00
Leaf & Rib, Salt, Open, Amber 20.00
Locket On Chain, Spooner, Red Flashed, Gold 235.00
Lodestar, Sugar, Open 75.00
Lotus Wave, Bowl, Centerpiece, Cobalt Blue 125.00
Mercury, Candleholder, Pair 18.00
Mercury, Candlestick, Crystal, Pair 55.00
Minuet, Cup & Saucer, Empress Etch 35.00
Minuet, Tumbler, Iced Tea, Footed, 12 Oz. 34.00
Minuet, Wine 50.00
Moongleam, Compote, Marked, 5 In. 37.50
Moongleam, Decanter, 1 Pt. 130.00

Moongleam, Ice Bucket, Dolphin Footed, Empress Etch 125.00
Moongleam, Plate, 2 Handles, Octagonal, Floral Cutting, 12 In. 40.00
Moonglo, Cup, Yellow 13.00
Moonglo, Vase, 7 In. 40.00
Narrow Flute, Compote, Jelly, Handles, Marked, 5 1/2 In. 37.50
Narrow Flute, Dish, Nut, Marked & Dated 10.00
Narrow Flute, Jug, Bulbous, Crystal, 1 Qt. 40.00
Near Cut, Wine 8.00
New Era, Ashtray 8.00
Noonday Sun, Salt, Open 20.00
Octagon, Creamer, Flamingo 20.00
Octagon, Mayonnaise Set, Moongleam, 3 Piece 55.00
Octagon, Mayonnaise, Footed, Handle, Hawthorne, 5 1/2 In. 39.50
Octagon, Sugar & Creamer, Pink 25.00
Octagon, Tray, Handles, Cut, 10 In. 39.50
Old Colony, Cup & Saucer, Crystal 9.50
Old Colony, Plate, Crystal, Square, 8 In. 9.75
Old Colony, Saucer, Crystal 3.00
Old Colony, Vase, Empress, Sahara, 10 In. 90.00
Old Dominion, Goblet, Sahara 25.00
Old Dominion, Goblet, Sahara, 10 Oz. 30.00
Old Dominion, Goblet, Trojan Etch, 8 Oz. 22.00
Old Sandwich, Candlestick, Pair 130.00
Old Sandwich, Cocktail, Marked, Crystal, 4 Oz., 6 Piece 48.00
Old Sandwich, Cruet, Sahara 55.00
Old Sandwich, Salt & Pepper, Yellow 62.00
Old Sandwich, Shot Glass 14.00
Old Williamsburg, Candlestick, 1–Light, Crystal, 10 In. 160.00
Old Williamsburg, Celery Tray, Oval, Hotel, Marked, 9 In. 16.50
Olympiad, Sherbet 15.00
Orchard, Plate, Scalloped, 14 In. 40.00
Orchard, Sugar, Footed 20.00
Orchid Etch, Bottle, French Dressing 155.00
Orchid Etch, Cake Plate, Footed 225.00
Orchid Etch, Compote 35.00
Orchid Etch, Cordial 100.00
Orchid Etch, Cordial, 1 Oz. 110.00
Orchid Etch, Cup & Saucer .... 45.00 To 52.50
Orchid Etch, Goblet, Water 29.00
Orchid Etch, Measuring Cup 225.00
Orchid Etch, Plate, 10 1/2 In. 88.00
Orchid Etch, Relish, 3 Sections, 11 1/2 In. 75.00
Orchid Etch, Serving Plate, Center Handle 225.00
Orchid Etch, Sherbet 19.50
Orchid Etch, Sugar & Creamer 40.00
Orchid Etch, Wine 50.00
Orchid, Bowl, Footed, 6 In. 27.50
Orchid, Butter, Cover ....80.00 To 150.00
Orchid, Candlestick, Double, Pair 40.00
Orchid, Candy Dish, Chrome Cover 110.00
Orchid, Compote 43.00
Orchid, Cup & Saucer 53.00
Orchid, Goblet, Cocktail, 4 Oz. 38.00
Orchid, Goblet, Water 17.00
Orchid, Plate, 8 1/2 In. .... 18.00 To 20.00
Orchid, Plate, Rolled Edge, 14 In. 50.00
Orchid, Salt & Pepper, Footed 75.00
Orchid, Sugar & Creamer, Footed .... 48.00 To 65.00
Orchid, Torte Plate, 14 In. 45.00
Orchid, Tumbler, Juice, 5 Oz. 38.00
Orchid, Vase, Fan, Footed, 7 In. 65.00
Oxford, Sherbet 5.00
Panel Recess, Nappy, Oval, Marked, 10 In. 10.00
Paperweight, Rabbit 80.00

Paperweight, Tiger, Jade 35.00
Pearl & Oyster, Relish, Divided, Pink 7.00
Peerless, Berry Set, Marked, 7 Piece 95.00
Peerless, Sherbet, Flat Bottom, Marked 7.50
Peerless, Wine, 1 1/2 Oz. 11.00
Pied Piper, Bowl 90.00
Pineapple & Fan, Syrup, Green 385.00
Pineapple & Fan, Vase, Emerald Green, Gold Trim, 6 In. 52.50
Pineapple & Fan, Vase, Trumpet, Gold Trim, Crystal, 6 1/2 In. 18.00
Pinwheel & Fan, Hair Receiver 60.00
Pinwheel & Fan, Nappy, Marked 37.50
Pinwheel & Fan, Nappy, Marked, 8 In. 47.50
Plain Band, Creamer, Crystal 30.00
Plain Panel Recessed, Jug, Crystal, 1 Pt. 40.00
Plantation, Bowl, 12 In. 35.00
Plantation, Compote, 12 In. 48.00
Plantation, Cruet .... 80.00 To 125.00
Plantation, Mayonnaise Set, 3 Piece 75.00
Plantation, Relish, 3 Sections, Oval, 11 1/2 In. 30.00
Plantation, Syrup 60.00
Plate, Frog, Pink 110.00
Pleat & Panel, Champagne, Saucer, Flamingo 15.00
Pleat & Panel, Cruet, Flamingo 42.50
Pleat & Panel, Cruet, Flamingo, 3 Oz. 57.50
Pleat & Panel, Cruet, Moongleam, 3 Oz. 75.00
Pleat & Panel, Plate, Flamingo, 7 In. 9.00
Pleats, Basket 100.00
Polo, Soda Glass, Etch 75.00
Priscilla, Jug, Crystal, 3 Pt. 80.00
Provincial, Champagne, Heather 10.00
Provincial, Goblet, Heather 16.00
Punty Band, Cake Stand 65.00
Puritan, Ashtray, Paper Label, 4 1/2 In. 15.00
Puritan, Berry Set, Gold Rims, Marked, 7 Piece 90.00
Puritan, Jam Jar, Mushroom Cover 40.00
Puritan, Jug, Crystal, 1 Qt. 45.00
Puritan, Plate, Marked, 8 In. 12.50
Puritan, Punch Set, 13 Piece 195.00
Puritan, Punch Set, Crystal, 15 Piece 275.00
Queen Ann, Candelabra, 1–Light, Prisms, Pair 85.00
Queen Ann, Mustard, Cover, Paddle 35.00
Queen Ann, Sugar & Creamer, Flamingo, Individual 45.00
Radiance, Butter, Cover, Crystal 40.00
Recessed Panels, Candy, Gold Trim, Cover, 1/2 Lb., 9 In. 35.00
Regency, Candlestick, Crytal, Pair 45.00
Relish, 3 Sections, 10 In. 22.00
Revere, Candy Dish, Spire Top, 1 Lb. 78.00
Revere, Coaster, Marked, 4 In. 6.00
Ribbed Octagon, Sugar, Open, Moongleam 15.00
Ribbed Optic, Candlestick, Flamingo, Pair 30.00
Ridge & Star, Plate, Flamingo, 7 In. 5.00
Ridgeleigh, Bowl, Pillow, 10 In. 55.00
Ridgeleigh, Bowl, Vegetable, 8 In. .... 16.00 To 20.00
Ridgeleigh, Box, Cover, Round, 4 3/4 In. 45.00
Ridgeleigh, Candleblock, Round, 3 In. 18.00
Ridgeleigh, Candlestick, Square Base 30.00
Ridgeleigh, Coaster, Sahara, 3 1/2 In. 18.00
Ridgeleigh, Coaster, Zircon, 4 In. 39.50
Ridgeleigh, Fruit Bowl, 12 In. 25.00
Ridgeleigh, Jelly, 2 Part, 2 Handles, 6 In. 12.50
Ridgeleigh, Mustard, Cover, Spoon 48.00
Ridgeleigh, Plate, 8 In. 5.25
Ridgeleigh, Plate, Sandwich, 13 1/2 In. 22.00
Ridgeleigh, Punch Cup 15.00

Ridgeleigh, Relish, 3 Sections, Oblong, 10 1/2 In.	28.00
Ridgeleigh, Sauce, Marked, 5 1/2 In., 5 Piece	20.00
Ridgeleigh, Sugar & Creamer, Marked	32.00
Ridgeleigh, Vase, Marked, 6 In.	21.50
Ridgleigh, Bowl, Oval, Sahara, 11 In.	75.00
Ring Band, Butter, Cover, Gold Trim	225.00
Ring Band, Butter, Cover, Gold Trim, Custard Glass, 6 1/2 X 7 In.	150.00
Ring Band, Butter, Cover, Rose Design	200.00
Ring Band, Sugar, Cover, Custard Glass, Gold Trim, 6 3/4 In.	135.00
Ring Band, Toothpick, Enameled Roses	125.00
Ring Band, Toothpick, Geneva, N.Y.	45.00
Ring Band, Water Set, Custard Glass, 9 Piece	875.00
Rock Crystal, Sherbet, Red	26.00
Rococo, Compote	38.00
Rooster Head, Cocktail Shaker	65.00
Rooster Head, Wine, Tall	45.00
Rosalie, Champagne	12.00
Rosalie, Parfait, 6 In.	12.00
Rosalie, Sherbet, Stemmed	8.00
Rose Bowl, Saturn, Crystal, 6 In.	32.50
Rose Etch, Champagne	26.00
Rose Etch, Goblet	34.00
Rose Etch, Mayonnaise, Footed	38.00
Rose Etch, Saltshaker	30.00
Rose Etch, Vase, 7 In.	80.00
Rose Point, Vase, Keyhole, 10 In.	70.00
Rose, Butter, Cover	125.00
Rose, Champagne	32.00
Rose, Cocktail	28.00
Sahara, Bowl, Swan Handles	195.00
Sahara, Candleholder, 3-Light, Pair	120.00
Sahara, Relish, Divided	22.00
Satellite, Bowl, Marked, 13 In.	57.50
Saturn, Candle Block, 2-Light, Pair	125.00
Saturn, Mustard	23.00
Saturn, Vase, 5 In.	20.00
Sawtooth Band, Spooner, Crystal, Miniature	90.00
Seagull, Flower Frog, Crystal, 8 1/2 In.	42.50
Sheffield, Goblet	20.00
Sleigh, Salt, Open	30.00
Southwind, Sherbet	18.00
Spanish, Cocktail	38.00
Spanish, Sherbet	33.00
Stanhope, Cup & Creamer, Black Knobs	50.00
Stanhope, Cup & Saucer	16.50
Stanhope, Plate, 7 In.	10.00
Sunburst, Tumbler, Marked	32.50
Swan, Salt, Individual	6.00
Tally Ho, Ice Bucket	12.50
Teardrop, Pitcher, Ice Lip	65.00
Titania, Goblet, Sahara	27.00
Trident, Candleholder, 2-Light, Sahara, Pair	150.00
Tudor, Cruet, Marked, 6 Oz.	13.50
Tudor, Pitcher, Glass Cover, 1 Qt.	112.50
Twist, Bonbon, Moongleam	25.00
Twist, Bonbon, Sides Up, Handles, Green	30.00
Twist, Bowl, Floral, 9 In.	35.00
Twist, Bowl, Sahara, 12 In.	65.00
Twist, Celery Tray, Moongleam	15.00
Twist, Celery, Crystal, 13 In.	15.00
Twist, Cocktail, Oyster, Moongleam	35.00
Twist, Cruet, Green, 4 Oz.	75.00
Twist, Cruet, Pink, 2 1/2 Oz.	40.00
Twist, Cup & Saucer, Flamingo	25.00

Twist, Goblet, Flamingo, Etched, 9 Oz. 25.00
Twist, Ice Bucket, Moongleam 50.00
Twist, Mustard, Cover, Spoon, Moongleam 55.00
Twist, Nappy, Marigold, Marked, 8 In. 12.50
Twist, Platter, Green, 15 In. 65.00
Twist, Sugar & Creamer, Moongleam, Oval 40.00
Victorian, Tumbler, Barrel, Signed 150.00
Vintage, Tumbler, Intaglio Cut, Signed 90.00
Wabash, Champagne 9.00
Wabash, Goblet, Water 10.00
Wabash, Punch Cup 9.00
Wampum, Cigarette Set, Box & 4 Ashtrays 65.00
Warwick, Vase, 7 In., Pair 42.00
Warwick, Vase, Crystal, 9 In., Pair 75.00
Water Lily, Butter, Cover 50.00
Water Lily, Sugar 40.00
Waverly, Bowl, Rose Etch, 9 1/2 In. 50.00
Waverly, Candy Dish, Cover, Footed, Yellow 40.00
Waverly, Compote, Jelly, Narcissus Cut 35.00
Waverly, Plate, Crystal, 8 1/4 In. 9.00
Waverly, Plate, Orchid Etch, 10 1/2 In. 50.00
Waverly, Platter, Rose, 13 In. 45.00
Waverly, Relish, 3 Sections, Orchid Etch, 11 In. 75.00
Waverly, Sugar & Creamer, Narcissus Cut 42.50
Whirlpool, Candleholder, 3-Light, Pair 145.00
Whirlpool, Nut Dish, Individual .... 8.00 To 9.00
Whirlpool, Relish, 4 Sections, Limelight 165.00
Whirlpool, Sherbet 6.00
Whirlpool, Sugar & Creamer 22.00
Whirlpool, Tumbler, Ruby, Flat, Imperial 14.00
Wide Optic, Claret 14.50
Winchester, Decanter, Soda, 18 Oz. 155.00
Winged Scroll, Butter, Cover, Gold Trim 90.00
Wreath, Candy Dish, Brushed Gold Cover 48.00
Yeoman, Compote, Footed, Stem, Moongleam 39.50
Yeoman, Creamer, Hotel, Crystal 30.00
Yeoman, Creamer, Moongleam, Individual 35.00
Yeoman, Cruet, Pink 32.00
Yeoman, Mustard, Cover, Spoon, Flamingo, 3 Piece 115.00
Yeoman, Plate, Diamond Optic, Pink, 7 3/8 In. 8.00
Yeoman, Plate, Flamingo, 7 3/4 In. 12.00
Yeoman, Plate, Flamingo, 9 In. 11.00
Yeoman, Plate, Marigold, 8 In. 13.00
Yeoman, Plate, Sandwich, Handles, Enameled Design, 10 1/2 In. 42.00
Yeoman, Sugar Shaker, Pink 70.00
Zodiac, Ashtry, Ohio, 1953 .... 19.50
　HEREND, see Fischer

Gebruder Heubach, a firm working in Lichte, Germany, from 1820 to 1925, is best known for bisque dolls and doll heads, their principal products. They also manufactured bisque figurines, including piano babies, beginning in the 1880s, and glazed figurines in the 1900s. Dolls are not listed here, but are listed in the Doll section. Another factory, Ernst Heubach, working in Koppelsdorf, Germany, also made porcelains and dolls.

HEUBACH, Bowl, Molded Mermaids, Iridescent Purple 450.00
Box, Cover, Bell Shape, Figural Ribbon Finial, Signed 245.00
Figurine, Baby Stuart, No.7977, 10 In. 800.00
Figurine, Bear, Lounging On Steps, Formal Attire, Signed 225.00
Figurine, Begging Sheep Dog, Yellow Eyes, Coral Collar, Signed 200.00
Figurine, Black Boy, Polka Dot Romper, Sitting, 5 In. 775.00
Figurine, Dutch Child, Basket Attached To Back, 5 1/2 In., Pair 165.00
Figurine, Girl, Seated, Orange Hat, Pulling Off Socks, 5 In. 200.00
Figurine, Man, Ax In Hand, Woman Holding Baby, 12 1/2 In., Pair 720.00

Figurine, Pup, Floppy Ear, Signed, 3 1/2 In., Pair 85.00
Jug, Character, Man's Head, Marked, 4 1/2 In. 135.00
Match Holder, Striker, Porcelain 25.00
Planter, Boy, Waving, Colonial Dress, Boy Walking, 4 1/2 X 5 In., Pr. 125.00
Planter, Colonial Boy, Arms & Feet Away, 4 1/2 X 5 In. 80.00
Tramp Shoe, Mother Mouse At Top, Baby Coming Out At Base, 5 In. 165.00
Vase, Gypsy Woman With Tambourine In Forest, Signed, 9 In. 135.00

Higbee glass was made by the J. B. Higbee Company of Bridgeville, Pennsylvania, about 1900. Tablewares were made and it is possible to assemble a full set of dishes and goblets in some Higbee patterns. Most of the glass was clear, not colored.

HIGBEE, see also Pressed Glass
HIGBEE, Butter, Cover, Child's, Hawaiian Lei, Marked 32.50
Cake Stand, Paris Design 18.00
Creamer, Child's, Hawaiian Lei 27.50
Goblet, Paneled Thistle, Footed 25.00
Sugar & Creamer, Paneled Thistle 35.00
Sugar, Child's, Hawaiian Lei 30.00
Vase, Flared, Marked, 7 In. 30.00

HISTORIC BLUE, see Adams; Clews; Ridgway; Staffordshire

Hobnail glass is a pattern of glass with bumps in an allover pattern. Dozens of hobnail patterns and variants have been made and are made. Clear, colored, and opalescent hobnail have been made and are being reproduced. Other pieces of hobnail are also listed under Carnival Glass, Hobnail.

HOBNAIL, see also Fenton; Francisware
HOBNAIL, Bottle, Barber's, Amethyst, Original Stopper 100.00
Bottle, Barber's, Cranberry, Opalescent 30.00
Bowl, Burmese, Satin Glass, 10 1/4 In. 200.00
Candy Dish, Robin's-Egg Blue, Cover, 8 1/2 In. 50.00
Creamer, Square Mouth, Opalescent Amber, 8 In. 245.00
Goblet, Opalescent 25.00
Pitcher, Lemonade, Cranberry, Opalescent 300.00
Rose Bowl, & Pitcher, Amber, Handle, Gold Wash, 7 & 11 In., 3 Piece 250.00
Salt & Pepper, Powder Blue, Opalescent 35.00
Salt & Pepper, Red, Opalescent 35.00
Shade, Student, Deep Green, Ruffled Rim, Hobbs, 3 1/4 X 2 In. 95.00
Syrup, Cranberry, Opalescent 225.00
Toothpick, Blue 30.00
Vase, Cranberry, Opalescent, 5 In. 35.00
Vase, Cranberry, Round Top, Squat, 3 3/4 X 4 1/4 In. 80.00

Holly amber, or golden agate, glass was made by the Indiana Tumbler and Goblet Company of Greentown, Indiana, from January 1, 1903, to June 13, 1903. It is a pressed glass pattern featuring holly leaves in the amber-shaded glass. The glass was made with shadings that range from creamy opalescent to brown-amber.

HOLLY AMBER, Compote, Cover, 7 In. 500.00
Compote, Greentown 975.00
Cruet 375.00
Mug, Clear Amber Center, Amber White Handle, Indiana, 4 1/2 In. 535.00
Parfait 625.00
Sauce Dish, Greentown 225.00
Tray, Water 145.00
Tumbler, Holly Branch Panels, Clear Amber Rim 385.00
Tumbler, Panels of Holly Branch, Wreath In Base 385.00

Hopalong Cassidy was named William Lawrence Boyd when he was born in Cambridge, Ohio, in 1895. His first movie appearance was in 1919, but the first Hopalong Cassidy film was not until 1934. Sixty-six films were made. In 1948, William Boyd purchased the television rights to the movies, then later made fifty–two new programs. In the 1950s, Hopalong Cassidy was seen in comics, records, toys, and other products. Boyd died in 1972.

HOPALONG CASSIDY, Alarm Clock	75.00
Badge, 6 Point Star, 3–D Picture	13.50
Badge, Brown, Orange, Early 1950s	20.00
Badge, Sheriff, Copper	20.00
Bank, Savings, Green Plastic	30.00
Banner, Hands On Guns, Felt, 1950, 28 In.	12.50
Banner, On Horse, Felt, 1950, 28 In.	12.50
Belt	42.00
Binoculars, Black	40.00
Board, Target Practice, Tin	22.00
Book, Coloring, 1950, 10 X 14 In.	20.00
Book, Coloring, Acrobat Shoes	45.00
Book, Coloring, Hoppy Comes To Rimrock, 1950	15.00
Book, Pop–Up	38.00
Booklet, Recipe, Chicken of The Sea, 1951	25.00
Bottle, Beverage, Insulated	15.00
Bottle, Milk, Glass	35.00
Button, Pinback, Hoppy & Topper, Color, 1 3/4 In.	1.00
Button, Saving Rodeo, Tenderfoot Picture, Yellow, 1950	15.00
Button, Sheriff's Star, Brass, 6 Points, 2 In.	5.75 To 8.75
Camera, 1940s	50.00
Cap Gun, Broken Spring	25.00
Card, Topp's, Framed, 1955	20.00
Charm, Figural, Silver, Copyright William Boyd 1950	15.00
Chuck Wagon Set, Plate, Bowl, Cup, In Display Box	175.00
Clock, Alarm	350.00
Coin, Good Luck, Aluminum, Picture, Symbols, 1950s	8.00
Decal, 1951, 2 X 6 In.	2.00
Disk, Cardboard, From Milk Bottle, Early 1950s	4.00
Field Glasses	75.00
Figure, Hoppy & Topper, Hartland	85.00
Fork	8.00
Game Board, 1950	25.00
Gun & Holster	145.00 To 150.00
Gun, Zoomerang	60.00
Hat	30.00
Holster Set, 2 Guns, Black Leather Belt	30.00
Horseshoe, Good Luck Horseshoe, Bar 20 Ranch, 1950	4.50
Knife, Pocket	15.00
Lamp, Revolving Waterfall	175.00
Lamp, Wall, Aladdin, Holster Shape	325.00
Lunch Box, 1950	48.00
Lunch Box, Thermos	70.00
Milk Carton, Picture of Hoppy, 1970s	2.50
Money, Play	1.00
Mug, Blue Logo & Scene, Milk Glass	8.50
Neckerchief, Dated 1950	12.00
Neckerchief Slide	15.00
Night–Light, Gun	135.00
Night–Light, Hoppy	30.00
Outfit, Cowgirl, Colorful Picture On Box, Size 10	160.00
Pajamas & Robe, Black, Size 8	80.00
Pen, Ballpoint	75.00
Photograph, Hopalong, Horse, Autograph, Framed, 24 X 19 In.	95.00
Picture Frame, Cardboard	20.00
Picture, Gun & Theater	95.00
Pin	8.50 To 10.00
Plate, Blue	60.00
Postcard, Hoppy Savings Club	5.00
Poster, Matted, 1950s, 22 1/2 X 18 In.	45.00

Puzzle, TV	75.00
Radio, Black Metal	265.00
Record, Album, Hoppy & Singing Bandit	85.00
Record–Reader, 78 RPM, Booklet Combination	25.00
Ring, Metal Face	35.00
Roller Skates	45.00
Scarf, On Horse, 1950	18.00
Spurs	45.00
Thermos, Cover	26.00
Watch, Pocket	75.00
Woodburning Set, Box	185.00
Wristwatch .... 45.00 To 75.00	

Howdy Doody and Buffalo Bob were the main characters in a children's series televised from 1947 to 1960. Howdy was a redheaded puppet. The series became popular with college students in the late 1970s when Buffalo Bob began to lecture on campuses.

HOWDY DOODY, Bandana	5.50
Bank, Howdy Sitting On Pig, Ceramic, U.S.A.	95.00
Bank, Musical	29.50
Big Prize Doodle List, Color, 1954–55, 4 Pages	6.00
Book, Follow The Dots, Whitman No.1410, 1955	20.00
Card, Russell, Box, 1954	12.00
Clown, 30 In.	250.00
Cookbook, Welch Grape Juice Co., 1952	55.00
Cookie Jar, Howdy Doody	285.00
Cup, Ovaltine	30.00
Doll Set, 5 Piece	58.00
Doll, Box, 12 In. .... 13.50 To 15.00	
Doll, Clarabell The Clown	22.00
Doll, Cowboy Clothes, Package, 12 In.	8.00
Doll, Stuffed, Plastic Head, Red Cotton Body, Eegee Co., 19 In.	16.00
Ear Muffs, Figural	25.00
Game, Card	15.00
Game, Parker Bros., Box	75.00
Hat, Campaign, Paper	65.00
Marionette, Box .... 100.00 To 275.00	
Night–Light, Howdy Sitting, 1950s	125.00
Night–Light, Porcelain	34.50
Pencil Holder, Hat Is Open For Storage, Ceramic	17.50
Pin, Flipper, Howdy Doody Says, Paper, Wonder Bread, 1952–56	10.00
Puppet, Clarabell, Hand	40.00
Puppet, Flub–A–Dub, Hand	45.00
Puppet, Howdy Doody	75.00
Puppet, With NBC Mike	95.00
Puzzle, Poll Parrot	10.00
Record, Jacket, 1949, 2 Piece	30.00
Record, Laughing Circus, Pictures	18.00
Ring, Brass, Flashes Howdy To Logo, Poll Parrot, 1950s ...	48.00
Spoon, Iced Tea	20.00
Teaspoon	20.00
Toy, Pull, Box	85.00
Tumbler, Blue, Comicware	40.00
Tumbler, Welch	6.00
Ukelele, Emense Musical Toys, Case, 1950s	70.00
Wristwatch, Box	140.00
Wristwatch, Moving Eyes	250.00

Hull pottery was made in Crooksville, Ohio, from 1905. Addis E. Hull bought the Acme Pottery Company and started making ceramic wares. In 1917, A. E. Hull Pottery began making art pottery as well as the commercial wares. For a short time, 1921 to 1929, the firm also sold pottery imported from Europe. The dinnerwares of the 1940s, including the Little Red Riding Hood line, the high gloss artwares of the 1950s, and the matte wares of the 1940s, are all popular with collectors. The firm is still in business.

HULL, Ashtray, Capri, Swan, White	3.50
Bank, Little Red Riding Hood, Standing, 7 In.	175.00 To 200.00
Bank, Pig, Brown Glaze, USA	10.00
Bank, Piggy, 14 In.	48.00
Bank, Porky Pig	28.00
Basket, Blossom Flite, Square, 10 1/4 X 5 1/2 In.	16.00
Basket, Bow Knot, Blue Base To Pink Top, 6 1/2 In.	75.00
Basket, Dogwood, 7 1/2 In.	100.00
Basket, Dogwood, 10 1/2 In.	110.00
Basket, Girl, Blue Trim, 8 1/4 In.	16.00
Basket, Parchment & Pine, 16 1/2 In.	30.00
Basket, Rosella, 7 In.	75.00
Basket, Tokay, 10 1/2 In.	32.50
Basket, Tropicana	180.00
Basket, Water Lily, Pink, 10 1/2 In.	80.00
Basket, Wild Flower, Matte, Pink To Blue, 10 1/2 In.	120.00
Bowl, Blossom Flite, 16 1/2 In.	20.00
Bowl, Console, Bow Knot, Pink, 13 1/2 In.	80.00
Bowl, Console, Iris, 12 In.	100.00
Bowl, Console, Open Rose, 12 In.	125.00
Bowl, Console, Water Lily, Aqua, 13 1/2 In.	60.00
Bowl, Ebb Tide, 15 3/4 In.	30.00
Bowl, House In Garden, Brown, 5 1/4 In.	1.50
Bowl, Magnolia, Pink, 12 1/2 In.	47.00
Bowl, Parchment & Pine, 16 In.	15.00
Bowl, Sunglow, Pink, 5 1/2 In.	9.00
Bowl, Sunglow, Pink, 7 1/2 In.	16.00
Bowl, Woodland, 14 In.	40.00
Butter, Cover, Little Red Riding Hood	125.00
Candleholder, Butterfly, Pair	25.00
Candleholder, Parchment & Pine, Green, 5 In., Pair	28.50
Candleholder, Wild Flower, Russet & Yellow, Pair	45.00
Candlestick, Woodland, Chartreuse, Rose, 3 1/2 In., Pair	28.50
Canister, Cereal, Little Red Riding Hood	300.00
Canister, Coffee, Little Red Riding Hood	175.00 To 240.00
Canister, Salt, Little Red Riding Hood	325.00
Canister, Sugar, Little Red Riding Hood	225.00 To 250.00
Canister, Tea, Little Red Riding Hood	225.00
Centerpiece, Magnolia, Pink, Footed, 13 In.	38.00
Compote, Candy, Butterfly, Cream, Square, 4 3/4 X 5 1/4 In.	24.00
Console Set, Bow Knot, 3 Piece	180.00
Console Set, Bow Knot, Pink, Candleholder, 3 Piece	85.00
Console Set, Butterfly, 3 Piece	55.00
Console Set, Magnolia, 3 Piece	55.00
Console Set, Water Lily, 3 Piece	79.50
Console, Butterfly, 3–Footed	45.00
Console, Magnolia, Matte Yellow To Tan	50.00
Console, Woodland, Chartreuse, Pink, 14 In.	30.00
Cookie Jar, Baby Duck, Yellow	50.00
Cookie Jar, Boy, Barefoot	195.00
Cookie Jar, Little Red Riding Hood, Blue Apron Fringe	78.00
Cookie Jar, Little Red Riding Hood, Open Basket	90.00 To 95.00
Cookie Jar, Little Red Riding Hood, Poinsettias	150.00
Cookie Jar, Old McDonald Barn	75.00
Cornucopia, Blossom Flite, 10 1/2 In.	28.00
Cornucopia, Bow Knot, Blue, Double	90.00
Cornucopia, Bow Knot, Pink, 7 1/2 In.	40.00 To 50.00
Cornucopia, Butterfly, Glossy, 6 In.	15.00
Cornucopia, Calla Lily, 8 In.	28.00

Cornucopia, Dogwood, 3 3/4 In., Pair .... 44.00 To 49.00
Cornucopia, Ebb Tide, Mermaid 45.00
Cornucopia, Magnolia, Matte, Pink & Blue, Double, 12 In. 65.00
Cornucopia, Open Rose, Pink, Blue, 8 1/2 In. 35.00
Cornucopia, Parchment & Pine .... 15.00 To 22.00
Cornucopia, Water Lily, Peach, Rose, 6 1/2 In. 28.00
Cornucopia, Wild Flower, 8 1/2 In. 45.00
Cornucopia, Wild Flower, Pink, Blue, 7 1/2 In. 25.00
Cornucopia, Wild Flower, Yellow, Rose, 7 1/2 In. 38.00
Cornucopia, Woodland, Green, 11 In. 40.00
Cornucopia, Woodland, Pink, Green, 5 1/2 In. 20.00
Creamer, Little Red Riding Hood, Head Pour 65.00
Creamer, Little Red Riding Hood, Tab Handle 55.00
Cruet, House In Garden, Brown, 6 1/2 In. 5.00
Ewer, Calla Lily, 10 In. 100.00
Ewer, Continental, 12 1/2 In. 45.00
Ewer, Dogwood, 4 3/4 In. 35.00
Ewer, Dogwood, 8 1/2 In. .... 65.00 To 75.00
Ewer, Dogwood, 13 1/2 In. 175.00
Ewer, Ebb Tide, 14 In. 95.00
Ewer, Iris, 13 1/2 In. 235.00
Ewer, Magnolia, Pink, 7 In. 30.00
Ewer, Magnolia, Pink, 13 1/2 In. 85.00
Ewer, Magnolia, Rose, Green, 14 1/4 In. 120.00
Ewer, Magnolia, Yellow, Rose, 7 In. 30.00
Ewer, Magnolia, Yellow, Rose, 13 1/2 In. 125.00
Ewer, Mardi Gras, Cream, Rose 38.50
Ewer, Open Rose, 4 1/4 In. 30.00
Ewer, Open Rose, 8 1/2 In. 75.00
Ewer, Open Rose, White, 7 1/2 In. 46.00
Ewer, Parchment & Pine, 14 1/2 In. 45.00
Ewer, Rosella, 7 In. 35.00
Ewer, Serenade, Yellow, 6 1/2 In. 25.00
Ewer, Water Lily, Aqua, Gold Trim, 5 1/2 In. 45.00
Ewer, Wild Flower, Brown, 5 1/2 In. 42.00
Ewer, Wild Flower, Pink, 8 1/2 In. 55.00
Ewer, Wild Flower, Pink, 13 1/2 In. .... 100.00 To 110.00
Ewer, Wild Flower, Yellow, Pink Matte, 13 1/2 In. 125.00
Ewer, Woodland, 6 1/2 In. .... 20.00 To 30.00
Grease Jar, Sunglow, Pink 25.00
Hen On Nest, Bake & Serve, 8 In. 20.00
Hot Plate, Baby's, Little Red Riding Hood 95.00
Jar, Little Red Riding Hood, Bow Front, 9 In. 175.00
Jardiniere, Bow Knot, 5 3/4 In. 65.00
Jardiniere, Tulip, 7 In. 100.00
Jardiniere, Tulip, Beige, Blue, 5 In. 32.00
Jardiniere, Water Lily, 5 1/2 In. 30.00
Lamp, Little Red Riding Hood 700.00
Lamp, Woodland, Aladdin Shape 500.00
Lavabo, Butterfly, Cream, Blue, Hole, 2 Piece 60.00
Match Holder, Little Red Riding Hood .... 275.00 To 300.00
Mold, House In Garden, Gingerbread Man, Brown 12.00
Mug, Beer, House In Garden, Brown, 16 Oz. 4.00
Mustard, Cover, Little Red Riding Hood, Spoon .... 150.00 To 175.00
Pitcher, Butterfly 40.00
Pitcher, House In Garden, Brown, 9 1/2 In. 14.00
Pitcher, Little Red Riding Hood, 6 1/2 In. 120.00
Pitcher, Little Red Riding Hood, 8 In. .... 85.00 To 150.00
Pitcher, Rosella, Label 30.00
Pitcher, Serenade, Yellow, 9 In. 35.00
Pitcher, Sunglow, 5 1/2 In. 25.00
Planter, Dancing Girl .... 18.00 To 30.00
Planter, Kitten, Ivory, 7 X 7 3/4 In. 16.50
Planter, Little Red Riding Hood, Hanging 195.00

Planter, Madonna & Child 20.00
Planter, Parrot, Pink, Chartreuse, 9 1/2 X 6 In. 18.00
Planter, Pheasant, 6 X 8 In. 20.00
Planter, Poodle, Chartreuse, Dark Green, 8 In. 18.00
Planter, Rooster, Pink, Brown 14.00
Planter, Sunglow, Yellow, Hanging 35.00
Planter, Telephone 28.00
Planter, Twin Geese, Green, Rose, 7 1/4 In. 20.00
Plate, Magnolia, Green Leaves, 10 1/4 In. 4.50
Rose Bowl, Iris, Pink & Blue On Apricot, 4 In. 22.00
Salt & Pepper, House In Garden, Brown 3.50
Salt & Pepper, Little Red Riding Hood, Large .... 35.00 To 50.00
Salt & Pepper, Little Red Riding Hood, Small 25.00
Sugar & Creamer, Cover, Bow Knot 75.00
Sugar & Creamer, Little Red Riding Hood, Side Pour ...... 50.00 To 80.00
Sugar, Little Red Riding Hood .... 50.00 To 60.00
Sugar, Little Red Riding Hood, Open, 5 In. 35.00
Swan, Maroon 10.00
Swan, Pink 7.50
Tea Set, Blossom Flite, 3 Piece .... 75.00 To 85.00
Tea Set, Magnolia, 3 Piece .... 70.00 To 130.00
Tea Set, Parchment & Pine, 3 Piece 90.00
Tea Set, Serenade, Pink, 3 Piece 50.00
Tea Set, Water Lily, Beige, Brown, 3 Piece 105.00
Teapot, Bow Knot 50.00
Teapot, Butterfly 20.00
Teapot, Dogwood 60.00
Teapot, Little Red Riding Hood .... 95.00 To 160.00
Teapot, Magnolia, Pink 38.00
Teapot, Parchment & Pine 45.00
Teapot, Poppy 90.00
Teapot, Sugar, Salt & Pepper, Little Red Riding Hood 205.00
Teapot, Wild Flower 149.50
Teapot, Woodland .... 55.00 To 65.00
Vase, Blossom Flite, 2 Handles, 10 1/2 In. 35.00
Vase, Bow Knot, 5 3/4 In. .... 45.00 To 60.00
Vase, Bow Knot, 8 1/2 In. 55.00
Vase, Bow Knot, Blue, 6 1/2 In. 58.00
Vase, Bow Knot, Blue, 8 1/2 In. 65.00
Vase, Butterfly, 3–Footed, 10 In. 34.00
Vase, Butterfly, 9 In. 39.00
Vase, Calla Lily, 6 1/2 In. 40.00
Vase, Calla Lily, 7 1/2 In. 48.00
Vase, Calla Lily, Green To Rose, Side Handles, 8 7/8 In. 45.00
Vase, Capri, Green, Footed, 6 In. 8.00
Vase, Dogwood, Beige, 6 1/2 In. 45.00
Vase, Dogwood, Pink, 10 1/2 In. 85.00
Vase, Ebb Tide, 14 In. 37.00
Vase, Ebb Tide, Figural, Fish, 11 In. 30.00
Vase, Iris, 8 In. 48.00
Vase, Iris, 10 1/2 In. 85.00
Vase, Magnolia, 4 3/4 In. .... 18.00 To 22.00
Vase, Magnolia, Biege, Brown, Side Handles, 8 1/2 In. 32.00
Vase, Magnolia, Glossy Blue, 12 1/2 In. 75.00
Vase, Magnolia, Matte, 6 In. 19.00
Vase, Magnolia, Matte, 15 In. 175.00
Vase, Magnolia, Pink & Blue Matte, 12 1/2 In. 65.00
Vase, Magnolia, Pink, 6 1/2 In. 10.00
Vase, Magnolia, Yellow Matte, 6 1/2 In. 18.00
Vase, Magnolia, Yellow To Tan, 12 1/2 In. 58.00
Vase, Open Rose, 6 1/2 In. .... 25.00 To 55.00
Vase, Open Rose, Pink, 10 1/2 In. 175.00
Vase, Orchid, 9 In. 70.00
Vase, Orchid, Handles, 6 3/4 In. 14.00

Vase, Orchid, Rose, 6 In. 37.50
Vase, Poppy, 6 1/2 In. 45.00
Vase, Rosella, Base Handles, 8 1/2 In. 32.00
Vase, Rosella, Cream, 6 1/2 In. 24.00
Vase, Thistle, Pink, 6 1/2 In. .... 30.00 To 36.00
Vase, Tulip, 10 In. 100.00
Vase, Water Lily, 6 1/2 In. .... 14.00 To 23.00
Vase, Water Lily, Aqua, 9 1/2 In. 45.00
Vase, Water Lily, Pink, Turquoise, Side Handles, 6 1/2 In. 13.00
Vase, Water Lily, Yellow, Brown, 6 1/2 In. 24.00
Vase, Wild Flower, 12 1/2 In. 70.00
Vase, Wild Flower, Brown, 12 3/4 In. 70.00
Vase, Wild Flower, Cream To Pink, 7 1/2 In. 35.00
Vase, Wild Flower, Handles, 10 1/2 In. 55.00
Vase, Wild Flower, Mauve, Corn, 6 1/4 In. 55.00
Vase, Wild Flower, Pink, 10 1/2 In. 85.00
Vase, Wild Flower, Pink, Blue, 7 1/2 In. 28.00
Vase, Wild Flower, Pink, Pastel Green, Corn, 7 1/2 In. 40.00
Vase, Wild Flower, Yellow, Brown, 8 1/2 In. 36.00
Vase, Woodland, 6 1/2 In. 17.50
Vase, Woodland, Chartreuse, Pink, 8 1/2 In. 28.50
Vase, Woodland, Matte Finish, 12 1/2 In. 85.00
Vase, Woodland, Speckled Pink, Green, 11 In. 32.00
Wall Pocket, Goose, Flying, Pink & Gray 30.00
Wall Pocket, Little Red Riding Hood .... 150.00 To 285.00
Wall Pocket, Sunglow, Pink 20.00
Wall Pocket, Sunglow, Whiskbroom, Pink, 8 1/2 In. 25.00
Wall Pocket, Sunglow, Whiskbroom, Pink, Yellow Butterfly 20.00
Wall Pocket, Woodland, Glossy 30.00
Window Box, Woodland, 10 In. 24.00
Window Box, Woodland, Chartreuse, Pink, 9 In. 20.00

Hummel figurines, based on the drawings of Berta Hummel, are made by the W. Goebel Porzellanfabrik of Oeslau, Germany, now Rodenthal, West Germany. They were first made in 1934. The mark has changed through the years. The following are the approximate dates for each of the marks: "Crown" mark, 1935 to 1949; "U. S. Zone, Germany," 1946 to 1948; "West Germany," after 1949; "full bee," with variations, 1950 to 1959; "stylized bee," 1960 to 1972; "three line mark," 1968 to 1979; "vee over gee," 1972 to 1979; "new mark," 1979 to present.

HUMMEL, Ashtray, No.34, Singing Lesson, Stylized Bee 125.00
Bell, 1978 .... 56.00
Bell, 1980 .... 32.00
Bookends, No.61A & 61B, Playmates & Chick Girl, Full Bee 475.00
Candlestick, No. 117, Boy With Horse, Stylized Bee 60.00
Candy Box, Chick Girl, Full Bee 195.00
Figurine, No. 1, Puppy Love, Full Bee 175.00
Figurine, No. 1, Puppy Love, Stylized Bee 55.00
Figurine, No. 2/II, Little Fiddler, Stylized Bee 365.00
Figurine, No. 4, Little Fiddler, Stylized Bee 125.00
Figurine, No. 5, Strolling Along, Stylized Bee 120.00
Figurine, No. 6/0, Sensitive Hunter, Stylized Bee 145.00
Figurine, No. 6/I, Sensitive Hunter, Full Bee 420.00
Figurine, No. 9, Begging His Share, Full Bee 350.00
Figurine, No. 11/0, Merry Wanderer, Crown Mark 300.00
Figurine, No. 13, Meditation, Three Line Mark 70.00
Figurine, No. 13/0, Meditation, New Mark 118.00
Figurine, No. 15/0, Hear Ye, Hear Ye, Full Bee 150.00
Figurine, No. 16/I, Little Hiker, Stylized Bee 120.00
Figurine, No. 17, Congratulations, Stylized Bee 225.00
Figurine, No. 20, Prayer Before Battle, Full Bee 100.00
Figurine, No. 21, Heavenly Angel, Stylized Bee 110.00
Figurine, No. 21/0, Heavenly Angel, Full Bee 175.00

Figurine, No. 21/0, Heavenly Angel, Stylized Bee 80.00
Figurine, No. 27, Joyous News, Three Line Mark 30.00
Figurine, No. 28/II, Wayside Devotion, Vee Over Gee 212.00
Figurine, No. 30/0/A, Ba–Bee Ring, Full Bee 65.00
Figurine, No. 42/0, Good Shepherd, New Mark 98.00
Figurine, No. 43, March Winds, Crown Mark 225.00
Figurine, No. 47, Goose Girl, Full Bee 65.00
Figurine, No. 47/3/0, Goose Girl, Stylized Bee 120.00
Figurine, No. 49, To Market, Stylized Bee 90.00
Figurine, No. 50/2/0, Volunteers, New Mark 140.00
Figurine, No. 51/0, Village Boy, Stylized Bee 125.00
Figurine, No. 51/2/0, Village Boy, Three Line Mark 95.00
Figurine, No. 57/0, Chick Girl, Full Bee ....85.00 To 125.00
Figurine, No. 58/0, Playmates, Full Bee 175.00
Figurine, No. 66, Farm Boy, Crown Mark 195.00
Figurine, No. 66, Farm Boy, Stylized Bee 225.00
Figurine, No. 67, Doll Mother, New Mark 140.00
Figurine, No. 72, Spring Cheer, Vee Over Gee 115.00
Figurine, No. 78/III, Blessed Child, Full Bee 150.00
Figurine, No. 82/2/0, School Boy, Three Line Mark 75.00
Figurine, No. 83, Angel Serenade, Crown Mark 500.00
Figurine, No. 84/0, Worship, Crown Mark 300.00
Figurine, No. 87, For Father, Stylized Bee 200.00
Figurine, No. 97, Trumpet Boy, Stylized Bee 85.00
Figurine, No.109/0, Happy Traveller, Stylized Bee 200.00
Figurine, No.111, Wayside Harmony, Full Bee 150.00
Figurine, No.111/I, Wayside Harmony, Crown Mark 395.00
Figurine, No.112/3/0, Just Resting, Three Line Mark 89.00
Figurine, No.119, Postman, Stylized Bee 180.00
Figurine, No.124/0, Hello, Full Bee 180.00
Figurine, No.124/0, Hello, Stylized Bee 120.00
Figurine, No.129, Band Leader, Stylized Bee 132.00
Figurine, No.131, Street Singer, Stylized Bee 90.00
Figurine, No.132, Star Gazer, Full Bee 225.00
Figurine, No.132, Star Gazer, Stylized Bee 160.00
Figurine, No.135, Soloist, Stylized Bee 70.00
Figurine, No.136/I, Friends, Stylized Bee 150.00
Figurine, No.141/I, Apple Tree Girl, Crown Mark 375.00
Figurine, No.142/3/0, Apple Tree Boy, Full Bee .... 110.00 To 130.00
Figurine, No.142/3/0, Apple Tree Boy, Stylized Bee 65.00
Figurine, No.150/0, Happy Days, Vee Over Gee 115.00
Figurine, No.152A & 152B, Umbrella Boy & Girl, Stylized Bee 1550.00
Figurine, No.153/0, Auf Wiedersehen, With Hat, Full Bee 2200.00
Figurine, No.163, Whitsuntide, Full Bee 620.00
Figurine, No.172/O, Festival Harmony, Mandolin, Three Line Mark 175.00
Figurine, No.173/O, Festival Harmony, Flute, Three Line Mark 175.00
Figurine, No.177, School Girls, Full Bee 1350.00
Figurine, No.179, Coquettes, Three Line Mark 175.00
Figurine, No.184, Latest News, New Mark 160.00
Figurine, No.184, Latest News, Stylized Bee 260.00
Figurine, No.195/2/0, Barnyard Hero, Three Line Mark 125.00
Figurine, No.196, Telling Her Secret, Full Bee 640.00
Figurine, No.196/0, Telling Her Secret, Full Bee 215.00
Figurine, No.196/0, Telling Her Secret, Three Line Mark 130.00
Figurine, No.200/O, Little Goat Herder, Full Bee 175.00
Figurine, No.203/2/0, Signs of Spring, Full Bee 350.00
Figurine, No.218/0, Birthday Serenade, Vee Over Gee 120.00
Figurine, No.239/B, Girl With Doll, Vee Over Gee 26.00
Figurine, No.300, Bird Watcher, New Mark 135.00
Figurine, No.306, Little Bookkeeper, Three Line Mark .... 165.00 To 180.00
Figurine, No.311, Kiss Me, Three Line Mark 250.00
Figurine, No.317, Not For You, Three Line Mark 170.00
Figurine, No.348, Ring Around The Rosie, Stylized Bee 2500.00
Figurine, No.396, Ride Into Christmas, Three Line Mark 150.00

Holy Water Font, No. 29/0, Guardian Angel, Full Bee 1000.00
Lamp, No.234, Birthday Serenade, Three Line Mark 650.00
Plate, Anniversary, 1975 .... 120.00 To 155.00
Plate, Anniversary, 1985 .... 190.00
Plate, Annual, 1971 .... 465.00 To 500.00
Plate, Annual, 1973 .... 104.00
Plate, Annual, 1976 .... 70.00
Plate, Annual, 1980 .... 55.00
Plate, Christmas, 1971 .... 425.00

LORENZ
HUTSCHEN REUTER
Hutschenreuther Porcelain Company of Selb, Germany, was established in 1814 and is still working. The company makes fine quality porcelain dinnerwares and figurines. The mark has changed through the years, but the name and the lion insignia appear in most versions.
GERMANY

HUTSCHENREUTHER, Bowl, Gilded Floral, Nude Child, With Bouquet Cover, Marked 185.00
....
Cake Plate, Hand Painted Fruits, Gold Trim, 11 In. 75.00
Dresser Set, Floral, Geometric Borders, Crown Mark, 5 Piece 150.00
Figurine, 5 Dolphins Jumping, Bisque, 15 X 20 In. 400.00
Figurine, Bison, Small 75.00
Figurine, Buffalo, With Horns 80.00
Figurine, Cherub Feeding Fawn 285.00
Figurine, Dachshund 45.00
Figurine, Dancing Girls, 8 In. 100.00
Figurine, Figure Skater 165.00
Figurine, Finch On Branch 100.00
Figurine, Grosbeaks 175.00
Figurine, Kingfisher 110.00
Figurine, Madonna & Child, 6 In. 95.00
Figurine, Moose 375.00
Figurine, Nude Dancer, 1 Foot On of Top Gold Ball, 9 In. 225.00
Figurine, Parakeet, Pair 145.00
Figurine, Parrot, Perched On 4 In. Gold Ball, 9 In. 325.00
Figurine, Poodle, Sitting, 6 1/4 In. 120.00
Figurine, Rabbit, White, Long Ears 65.00
Figurine, Squirrel, With Acorn 85.00
Figurine, Thrush, Brown, Speckled Throat & Breast, 8 In. 125.00
Figurine, Woman Tennis Player, Signed G. Werner 395.00
Figurine, Young Ass 80.00
Group, Three Frolicking Nude Children, 4 1/2 X 9 In. 90.00
Group, Woman In Blouse & Skirt, Holding Child, 8 1/2 In. 275.00
Plate, Angels' Concert .... 83.00 To 112.50
Plate, Easter Bouquet 24.50
Plate, Legend of St. George 80.00
Plate, Parsifal 112.50
Plate, Portrait, Cobalt Blue & Gold, 10 In. 59.00
Plate, Roses of Redoute, 24K Gold Rim, Box, 6 1/4 In., 8 Pc. 260.00
Plate, Singing Angel No.1 .... 80.00
Plate, St.George 100.00
Plate, Tristan & Isolde 113.00
Tabby Cat, Sitting, Bisque, 6 3/4 In. 140.00

An icon is a special, revered picture of Jesus, Mary, or a saint. These are usually Russian or Byzantine. The small icons collected today are made of wood and tin or precious metals. Many modern copies have been made in the old style and are being sold to unsuspecting tourists in Russia and Europe.

ICON, Christ Pantocrator, Silvered Brass, Russian, 19th Century, 9 X 7 In. 200.00
Eastern Madonna With Attendants, Oil On Wood, 12 1/2 X 10 In. 150.00
Head of Christ, Silver & Enamel, Russian, 19th Century .... 425.00 To 685.00
Kazan Mother of God, Silver, Enamel, S.G., Moscow, 7 1/8 X 5 3/4 In. 2550.00
Madonna & Child, Silver Riza, Russian, 12 X 10 1/2 In. ....*Illus* 550.00
Mary With Dagger, Tin, Frame, 9 1/2 X 16 In. 195.00

Old iron heating grates have a new use. Put them on the outdoor mat to be used as mud scrapers.

Remove iron rust by soaking the piece in kerosene for 24 hours, or use any one of several commercial preparations made for its removal. Wash, dry, and coat the piece with a light oil to protect it.

Icon, Madonna & Child, Silver Riza,
Russian, 12 X 10 1/2 In.

Mother of God Tichvinskaya, Silver Gilt, S.G., Moscow, 10 5/8 X 9 In.	2100.00
Priest With Woman, 10 X 6 2/4 In.	95.00
Russian, Brass Riza, 19th Century	121.00
St. Andrew, Holding Fish & Scroll, Greek, 19th Century, 12 1/2 In.	325.00
St. John Chrysostom, 1/2 Length Figure, Gilt Bible, Greek, 3 In.	250.00
St. Michael, On Horseback, Tempera On Wood, Russian, 15 1/2 In.	475.00
St. Nicholas Flanked By Makarus & Female Saint, Greek, 12 X 10 In.	400.00
St. Nicholas, Standing With Christ & Virgin, Greek, 11 1/2 In.	250.00
Vigin & Child, Silver & Enamel Repousse, Russian, Late 19th Century	525.00
Virgin & Child On Upper Tier, Saints On Lower Tier, Greek, 11 1/2 In.	350.00
Virgin & Child, Remains of St. Spyridon, Inscription, Greek, 12 In.	400.00
Virgin & Child, Repousse Silver & Enamel, Russian, 19th Century	685.00
Virgin & Christ Child, Repousse & Enamel, Silver Base, Russian	495.00
Virgin & Christ, Child–King, God & Angels Look On, Green, 22 1/2 In.	1100.00
Virgin of Kazan, Sterling Silver Riza, Russian, 1892, 7 X 5 3/4 In.	275.00

Imari patterns are named for the Japanese ware decorated with orange and blue stylized flowers. The design on the Japanese ware became so characteristic that the name "Imari" has come to mean any pattern of this type. It was copied by the European factories of the eighteenth and early nineteenth centuries.

IMARI, Bottle, Snuff, Polychrome, 3 3/8 In.	20.00
Bowl, Bird, Landscape, Flowers, Blue Border, 9 1/2 In.	65.00
Bowl, Tree Pattern, Scalloped, Blue, 6 1/2 In.	125.00
Charger, 6 Medallions, Dragons & Florals, C.1760, 12 In.	365.00
Charger, Leaf Veining, 3 Bird Reserves, C.1760, 12 1/2 In.	525.00
Charger, Peonies, Brocade Pattern, Floral, 12 In.	350.00
Charger, Red & Gold, Dark Blue Scroll, Mid–19th Century, 18 1/4 In.	1100.00
Charger, Scalloped, 3 Gourd–Shaped Medallions, C.1790, 12 In.	415.00
Dish, Boat Shape, Raised Prow, Buildings, Flora & Fauna, 13 In.	375.00
Dish, Scalloped, Fluted, Floral Reserves, Vase of Flowers, 11 In.	310.00
Dish, Shell, Scalloped, Garden Scene, C.1800, 10 In.	225.00
Figurine, Cat, Seated, 11 In.	100.00
Jardiniere, Blue Flowers, Pale Blue, Gold Outline, 5 1/4 X 6 In.	18.00
Jardiniere, Diaper Pattern Borders, Dancing Figures, 10 1/4 In.	350.00
Plate, Bird, Flowers & Trees, 8 1/2 In.	75.00
Plate, Scalloped Basket of Flowers Center, Panels of Children, 8 In.	58.00
Plate, Scenes In Blue Rectangles, Brown Rim, Imperial Seal, 8 1/2 In.	60.00
Platter, Fish Form, Garden Scene, Signed, 16 X 11 In.	470.00
Platter, Garden Scene, Scalloped, Oval, C.1860	450.00
Punch Bowl, 5 Colors, 13 In.	1350.00
Punch Bowl, Scalloped Rim, Floral Decoration, Japan, 6 1/4 In.	900.00

Imari, Vase, Purple Foo Dog
Finial, Figures, Canopy,
Cover, 41 In.

To test the age of engraving on
glass, place a white handkerchief
on the inside. If the engraving is
old, the lines will usually show up
darker than the rest of the glass.
New engraving has a bright, pow-
derlike surface.

Tray, Alternating Blossom & Tree Panels, Garden, 10 1/4 In.	150.00
Umbrella Stand, Red & Blue, Porcelain, Late 19th Century	990.00
Umbrella Stand, Ukiyo-E Style Figural Design, 24 In.	275.00
Vase, Purple Foo Dog Finial, Figures, Canopy, Cover, 41 In. ....*Illus*	4000.00

Imperial Glass Corporation was founded in Bellaire, Ohio, in 1901.
It became a division of Lenox, Inc., in 1977 and was sold to Arthur
R. Lorch in 1981. It was sold again in 1982. It went bankrupt in
1982 and some of the molds and assets have been offered to other
companies. The Imperial glass preferred by the collector is stretch
glass, art glass, carnival glass, and the top-quality tablewares.

IMPERIAL, Azalea, Goblet, Paper Label	9.00
Bunny On Nest, Dish, Blue Satin Glass	25.00
Candlewick, Ashtray, 2 3/4 In.	4.00
Candlewick, Ashtray, 6 In.	5.00
Candlewick, Ashtray, Eagle, 6 1/2 In.	55.00
Candlewick, Bowl, 11 In.	43.00
Candlewick, Bowl, 2 Handles, 7 In.	14.00
Candlewick, Bowl, Blue, 5 In.	38.00
Candlewick, Bowl, Float, 13 In.	35.00
Candlewick, Bowl, Heart Shape, Crystal, 5 In.	10.00
Candlewick, Bowl, Sauce, 5 1/2 In.	10.00
Candlewick, Bowl, Vegetable, Divided, Handles, 8 1/2 In.	60.00
Candlewick, Butter, Cover, 1/4 Lb.	15.00 To 22.00
Candlewick, Cake Stand, 5 3/4 In.	45.00
Candlewick, Cake Stand, 11 In.	50.00
Candlewick, Cake Stand, Child's, Blue	25.00
Candlewick, Candlestick, Heart Finger	38.00
Candlewick, Celery, Oval, 11 In.	50.00
Candlewick, Compote, 2-Bead Stem, Crystal, 5 In.	14.00
Candlewick, Compote, 5 1/2 In.	11.00
Candlewick, Condiment Set, Glass Tray, Farberware Tray, 8 Piece	135.00
Candlewick, Cordial	65.00
Candlewick, Cruet	32.50 To 45.00
Candlewick, Cruet, Blown	28.00
Candlewick, Cup & Saucer	8.00 To 9.00
Candlewick, Decanter, Stopper, 11 1/2 In.	18.00
Candlewick, Egg Plate	80.00
Candlewick, Eggcup	32.00
Candlewick, Goblet, Footed	14.00
Candlewick, Gravy Boat	125.00
Candlewick, Ice Tub, 5 1/2 X 8 In.	85.00
Candlewick, Marmalade Set, 3 Piece	35.00
Candlewick, Mayonnaise, 3 Piece	20.00
Candlewick, Mustard, Cover	23.00 To 28.00
Candlewick, Perfume Bottle	35.00
Candlewick, Pitcher, 80 Oz.	98.00 To 185.00
Candlewick, Pitcher, Manhattan, 40 Oz.	205.00

Candlewick, Plate, 8 In. ....6.00 To 10.00
Candlewick, Plate, Center Handle, 11 3/4 In. 35.00
Candlewick, Plate, Off–Center Ring 9.00
Candlewick, Platter, Oval, 13 In. 70.00
Candlewick, Punch Set, Underplate, 13 Piece 295.00
Candlewick, Relish, 3 Sections, 10 1/2 In. .... 16.00 To 35.00
Candlewick, Relish, 4 Sections, 8 1/2 In. .... 12.00 To 15.00
Candlewick, Salt & Pepper, Tray 30.00
Candlewick, Sauce Boat, Liner .... 100.00 To 105.00
Candlewick, Soup, Cream, Liner 48.00
Candlewick, Spoon, Fork, Serving 20.00
Candlewick, Sugar & Creamer 24.00
Candlewick, Tray, Beaded Foot, Oval, 9 In. 11.00
Candlewick, Tray, Center Handle, 8 In. 20.00
Candlewick, Tray, Handles, 8 1/2 In. 17.00
Candlewick, Tray, Lemon 30.00
Candlewick, Vase, Crimped, 8 In. 25.00
Candlewick, Vase, Fan 18.00
Cape Cod, Bowl, 6 In. 6.50
Cape Cod, Bowl, Crimped, 9 1/2 In. 35.00
Cape Cod, Bowl, Deep, Oval, 11 1/2 In. 95.00
Cape Cod, Cake Stand, 10 1/2 In. 30.00
Cape Cod, Cake Stand, Allover Pattern, 11 In. .... 43.00 To 55.00
Cape Cod, Candlestick, 2 Arm 25.00
Cape Cod, Candy Dish, Reed Handle 65.00
Cape Cod, Celery, Oval, 10 1/2 In. 45.00
Cape Cod, Cocktail, 4 1/2 In. .... 6.00 To 8.00
Cape Cod, Compote, 10 X 5 1/2 In. 50.00
Cape Cod, Condiment Set, 5 Piece 47.00
Cape Cod, Creamer, Footed 5.00
Cape Cod, Cruet, Loop Handle 32.00
Cape Cod, Cruet, Olive Green 35.00
Cape Cod, Cruet, Silver Deposit 65.00
Cape Cod, Cup & Saucer 6.50
Cape Cod, Decanter, Square 45.00
Cape Cod, Mustard, Cover 16.00
Cape Cod, Mustard, Cover, Wooden Spoon 35.00
Cape Cod, Parfait 13.00
Cape Cod, Pitcher, Milk, 8 Oz. 17.00
Cape Cod, Pitcher, Milk, 16 Oz. 30.00
Cape Cod, Pitcher, Water, 60 Oz. 80.00
Cape Cod, Plate, 6 In. 2.00
Cape Cod, Plate, 8 In. 6.00
Cape Cod, Plate, 10 In. .... 25.00 To 33.00
Cape Cod, Plate, 16 In. 28.00
Cape Cod, Plate, 2 Handles, 11 In. .... 24.00 To 30.00
Cape Cod, Plate, Torte, 14 In. 24.00
Cape Cod, Punch Bowl Set, Blue, Ladle, 12 Cups 140.00
Cape Cod, Punch Set, 15 Piece 165.00
Cape Cod, Relish, 5 Sections, 11 In. 40.00
Cape Cod, Salt & Pepper, Flat .... 20.00 To 30.00
Cape Cod, Salt & Pepper, Footed ....8.00 To 10.00
Cape Cod, Salt & Pepper, Yellow 35.00
Cape Cod, Sherbet, 4 1/4 In. .... 3.00 To 5.50
Cape Cod, Soup, Coup, 1 Handle 19.00
Cape Cod, Sugar & Creamer, Tray 23.00
Cape Cod, Sundae, 6 Oz. 3.00
Cape Cod, Tumbler, Iced Tea, Footed, 12 Oz. 5.00
Cape Cod, Tumbler, Juice, Footed, 6 Oz. 5.00
Cape Cod, Tumbler, Old Fashioned 6.50
Cape Cod, Tumbler, Water, 10 Oz. 5.00
Cape Cod, Vase, 8 1/2 In. 35.00
Cape Cod, Wine, 3 Oz. .... 7.00 To 9.00
Catalina, Carafe Set, Orange, Wooden Handles, 5 Piece 75.00

Christmas, Plate, 1971	20.00
Diamond Block, Bowl, Blue, 6 1/2 In.	10.00
Diamond Block, Bowl, Green, Square, 5 3/4 In.	8.00
Diamond Block, Celery, Green, 8 1/4 In.	8.00
Diamond Block, Vase, 6 In.	6.00
Diamond Point, Bowl, Open Lace, 1950 Mark, 7 1/2 In.	8.00
Diamond Quilt, Candleholder, Twin, 4 1/4 In.	8.00
Duck On Nest, Dish, Caramel Slag, Glossy	35.00
Duck On Nest, Dish, Green Satin Glass	25.00
Empress, Bookends, Cathay Line	150.00
Figurine, Colt, Standing	50.00
Figurine, Donkey, Slag	60.00
Figurine, Minuet Girl, Ultramarine Blue, 4 1/2 In.	125.00
Flower Garden & Butterfly, Vase, Blue, 6 In.	90.00
Free Blown, Vase, Allover Leaf & Vine, Orange Interior, 9 1/2 In.	300.00
Freehand, Rose Bowl, Applied Threading, Gold	135.00
Hen On Nest, Dish, Beaded Brown, 4 1/2 In.	20.00
Monogah, Goblet, Springtime Etch	12.00
Mountain Boys, Planter, Paul Webb	95.00
Pansy, Bowl, Flat, Ruffled, 9 In.	80.00
Pillar Flutes, Cup, Blue	6.00
Pillar Flutes, Relish, Blue, Oval	12.00
Pillar Flutes, Vase, Bud, Blue	18.50
Provincial, Plate, 8 In.	12.00
Provincial, Sugar & Creamer, 6 In.	40.00
Red Slag, Basket, Handle, 4 1/2 X 5 1/2 X 5 In.	20.00
Red Slag, Bowl, Emblem, Roses, 9 In.	25.00
Red Slag, Toothpick	10.00
Star & File, Spooner, Child's	45.00
Swan On Nest, Dish, Ivory Satin Glass	25.00
Swan, Caramel Slag	30.00
Swan, Milk Glass	30.00
Tradition, Plate, Crystal, 8 In.	1.75
Twist, Cocktail	8.50
Twist, Parfait	14.00
Vine & Leaf, Vase, Tricorner Mouth, Iridescent, 11 3/4 In.	350.00
White Rabbit, Paperweight	45.00
Windmill, Water Set, White, Gold Trim, 7 Piece	75.00
Yeoman, Cup & Saucer, Moongleam	25.00
Zodiac, Compote, Yellow, 5 Sides	6.00

Indian Tree is a china pattern that was popular during the last half of the nineteenth century. It was copied from earlier Indian textile patterns that were very similar. The pattern includes the crooked branch of a tree and a partial landscape with exotic flowers and leaves. Green, blue, pink, and orange were the favored colors used in the design.

INDIAN TREE, Bowl, Johnson, 7 In.	6.50
Bowl, Vegetable, Cover, Johnson	35.00
Cup & Saucer, Johnson	7.00
Plate, Cauldon	8.00
Sugar & Creamer, Coalport, Pre–1920	65.00
Sugar & Creamer, Coalport, Pre–1921	75.00
Teapot, Sugar, Creamer & Nappy, Coalport	85.00
Teapot, Wood	25.00

Indian art from North America has attracted the collector for many years. Each tribe has its own distinctive designs and techniques. Baskets, jewelry, pottery, and leatherwork are of greatest collector interest. Eskimo art is listed in another section in this book.

INDIAN, Arm Band, Quill, Tin Cone Dangles On 1 Feather Remnant	110.00
Awl Case, Plains, Beaded Both Sides, Shell & Brass Closure, 11 In.	125.00
Ax, Sioux, Trade, With Beads	25.00
Baby Carrier, Apache, Beaded Hide, Bentwood Frame, Twig Bonnet	3300.00

Bag, Chippewa, Bandolier, Beaded, Floral 975.00
Bag, Chippewa, Fully Beaded 1 Side, 1880s, 10 X 11 In. 185.00
Bag, Crow, Beaded, White Heart, Green, Blue, Salmon, 31 In. 3000.00
Bag, Nez Perce, Corn Husk, Geometric Design, Orange, Black, 18 In, ... 325.00
Bag, Northern Plains, Beaded Sides, Flap, Quilled, Horsehair, 15 In. 900.00
Bag, Northern Plains, Beaded, Quilled 990.00
Bag, Plains, Horizontal Bead Bands, Yellow, White, Red, Purple, 17 In. 1450.00
Bag, Pueblo, Wild Floral, Beaded Geometric Design, C.1930 .... 90.00
Bag, Sioux, Doctor's, White, Caramel, Blue, Green, Sioux Script, 14 In. 1000.00
Bag, Sioux, Red, White, Dark Blue, Yellow, Fringe, C.1880, 6 In. 110.00
Basin, Agate, Pike County, Illinois, Tan, 4 1/8 In. 110.00
Basket, Aleut, Swing, Golden Rye Grass, Embroidered, Handle, 3 1/2 In. 425.00
Basket, Algonquin, Wool Wash, Potato Stencil, Painted, 13 X 18 In. 425.00
Basket, Apache, Burden, Mulberry, Cottonwood, Rawhide, Cloth, 1920 .... 1385.00
Basket, Apache, Burden, Tanned Leather, Tinklers, Wicker Design 115.00
Basket, Apache, Coiled, Devil's Claw, Gold Willow Ground, 19 1/2 In. 900.00
Basket, Chippewa, Melon, C.1930 .... 65.00
Basket, Deerfield, Wine, Green, Natural, 11 1/4 X 3 1/4 In. 105.00
Basket, Eastern Woodland, Splint, Colors & Natural, 18 X 20 In. 685.00
Basket, Fraser River, Cedar, Imbricated, 15 X 22 X 12 1/2 In. 125.00
Basket, Hopi, Coiled, Open Crosses, 4 1/2 X 7 1/2 In. 125.00
Basket, Hopi, Plaited Yucca Leaf, 3 1/2 X 12 In. 55.00
Basket, Hupa, Bowl Shape, Twined Geometric Design, 5 X 5 1/2 In. 60.00
Basket, Klamath, Child's Hat, 3 X 6 In. 125.00
Basket, Klamath, Wild Geese Flying Pattern, Pre-1910, 4 1/2 X 8 In. 145.00
Basket, Micmac, Cover, Round, 1930s, 8 1/2 In. 45.00
Basket, Navajo, Wedding, Abstract Design, Braided Rim, 12 In. 115.00
Basket, Nootka, Cover, Green, Red & Natural, 4 1/2 In. 90.00
Basket, Northwest Coast, Imbricated Design, 14 X 16 X 25 In. 180.00
Basket, Papago, Baking, Wire, 1 3/4 X 11 In. 65.00
Basket, Papago, Blue & Purple On Natural, Oval, 11 1/2 In. 48.00
Basket, Papago, Horse, Dogs, Snakes, Footed, 12 X 12 In. 300.00
Basket, Penobscot, Cover, Pre-1910, 5 In. 27.50
Basket, Penobscot, Cover, Sweetgrass, Miniature 36.00
Basket, Pomo, Coiled & Feathered 4675.00
Basket, Porcupine Quill Trim, 1908, 5 1/4 In. 65.00
Basket, Pueblo, Carrying Pouches, Each Pouch 10 X 10 In. 55.00
Basket, Seminole, Palmetto Fiber & Swamp Grass, Ceremonial, 4 In. 35.00
Basket, Southeastern, Storage, Twill Plaited, Cover, 15 1/2 In. 175.00
Basket, Washo, Pre-1910, 5 X 13 In. 145.00
Basket, Western Apache, Figural, Olla, Deer, Horses, Geometrics, 16 In. 3200.00
Basket, Western Reservation, Gathering, Yucca & Devil's Claw, 10 In. 148.00
Basket, Wine Brewing, Fret Design, 7 1/4 X 13 3/4 In. 500.00
Basket, Woodland, Woven Splint, Cover, 9 1/2 X 6 3/4 In. 65.00
Basket, Woodland, Woven Splint, Green Stripes, Bentwood Handle, 9 In. 55.00
Basket, Woodland, Woven Splint, Red & Green Bands, Cover, 16 In. 150.00
Basket, Woodland, Woven Splint, Red, Brown & Natural, 10 1/2 In. 85.00
Basket, Yokuts, Rattlesnake Design, Black Fern, 25 1/2 In. 6200.00
Beads, Hammered Brass, North Dakota, 1700s, 10 Piece 7.00
Beads, Trade, Venetian & Italian Glass, 31 In. 45.00
Belt Pouch, Ute, Beaded, Fringed, Tin Cone Suspensions 125.00
Belt, Mohawk, Wampum, Blue, White, Tube Beads, 6 Rows, 23 1/2 In. 200.00
Belt, Navaho, Coin Silver, 8 Oval Conchas 400.00
Belt, Navajo, Concha, Butterflies, Size 38 .... 145.00
Belt, Northern Plains, Beaded Panel, Leather, White Ground, 38 In. 100.00
Blanket, Navajo, Chief Pattern Revival, 3rd Phase, 1895 .... 4500.00
Blanket, Navajo, Chief's, Red, White, Blue, Brown, Full Size 2000.00
Blanket, Navajo, Hand Loomed, Geometric Ziggurat, C.1900, 94 X 66 In. 525.00
Blanket, Navajo, Saddle, Center Strips, Corner Tassels, 33 1/2 In. 60.00
Bolo Tie, Zuni, Floral Design, Turquoise, Stone, Silver 50.00
Bottle, Navajo, Tobacco, Silver, Turquoise, Stamped Design, Stopper 115.00
Bowl, Apache, Coiled Basketry, Devil's Claw, Willow, 5 X 12 1/2 In. 650.00
Bowl, Cahuilla, Basketry, 4 1/4 X 14 3/4 In. 200.00
Bowl, Coiled Basketry, Yucca, Martynia, Dogs Around Rim, 9 1/2 In. 225.00

Bowl, Eastern Woodlands, Figural, Human Figure On Hands, Knees, 8 In.	1500.00
Bowl, Hopi, Food, Feather Design, Footed, Pottery, 5 1/2 In.	50.00
Bowl, Hopi, Nampeyo Style, Geometric, Brown, Red, 8 1/4 In.	550.00
Bowl, Klikitat, Basketry, Zigzag, Gold Outlined, Open Work Top, 5 In.	150.00
Bowl, Papago, Basketry, Black Martynia, Yucca, 9 3/4 X 4 In.	65.00
Bowl, Pueblo, Blackware, Geometric Design, Signed Lucy, 3 1/4 X 5 In.	90.00
Bowl, Salish, Basketry, Storage, Leather Rim, Design, Brown, 9 X 16 In.	60.00
Bowl, Santa Clara, Blackware, Highly Polished, 6 In.	100.00
Bowl, Tlingit, Basketry, Rattle Top, Design, Brown, 3 1/2 X 3 3/4 In.	575.00
Bowl, Zia, Clouds, Figures, Leaves, Polychrome, 7 X 3 1/4 In.	120.00
Bowl, Zuni, Geometric, Deer Interior, Heart Line, 5 X 13 In.	1000.00
Box, Arapahoe, Peyote Ceremony, Whistle, Pipe, Drumstick, Staff	150.00
Box, Forest Indian, Cover, Beaded Birchbark, 5 1/2 X 7 In.	95.00
Box, Micmac, Birchbark, Embroidered, Cylindrical, Cover, 4 X 7 In.	800.00
Box, Navajo, Jewelry, Sterling, Stampwork, Footed, S.James, 5 In.	125.00
Box, Navajo, Pill, Silver, Turquoise In Lid, 1 X 1 1/8 In.	45.00
Bracelet, Navajo, Blue Turquoise, Red Coral, 2.2 X 1.5	110.00
Bracelet, Navajo, Old Concha, Turquoise, 2.7 X 2 In.	135.00
Bracelet, Navajo, Silver & Turquoise, 5 Stone Sets, 3/8 X 1/2 In.	75.00
Bracelet, Navajo, Silver, Linked Miniature, Conchas, 7 1/2 In.	15.00
Bracelet, Navajo, Sterling Silver, Turquoise, Dated 1911	456.50
Bracelet, Zuni, Mother–of–Pearl, White & Red Woodpecker	40.00
Bracelet, Zuni, Turquoise & Coral Chip Inlay, 1 In.	25.00
Breastplate, Sioux, Woman's Hair, Brass, Glass Trade Beads, 27 In.	500.00
Bridle, Ute, Horsehair, Forged Iron Bit, Heurmann's Pat., Tassels	375.00
Buckle, Navajo, Rosette Design, C.1900, 4 X 3 In.	110.00
Buckle, Turquoise & Coral Snake Design, Effie Costtelo	295.00
Buffalo Hide, Sioux, Box & Border Pattern, C.1830	1760.00
Canteen, Hopi, Stylized Bird Design, Pottery, 9 In.	150.00
Cap, Apache, Ceremonial, Beaded Hide, Fringed, Crosses	1760.00
Coat, Great Lakes, Fringed Hide, European Style, Embroidered	400.00
Cradle Board, Apache, Wood Frame & Slats, Cloth Shade, C.1930, 36 In.	190.00
Cradle Board, Nez Perce, Blue, White, Salmon, White Heart, 22 In.	650.00
Cradle Board, Sioux, C.1885	1000.00
Cradle Cover, Sioux, Beaded, Quillwork, Fringed, Trade Cloth, 13 In.	3000.00
Cradle Cover, Sioux, Quilled, 1870s	2000.00
Cradle, Nez Perce, Doll, Blue, White, Red, 19 In.	600.00
Cradle, Sioux, Beaded Hide Cover, Cowrie Shell Suspensions	1540.00
Cuff, 21 Turquoise Nuggets, Bennie T	1500.00
Dish, Northwest Coast, Paint Dish, Carved Frog, Stone, 6 3/4 In.	600.00
Doll, Kachina, Wooden, Polychrome, 9 In.	275.00
Doll, Micmac, East Coast, Blue & Yellow Silks, 18th Century, Pair	4950.00
Doll, Northern Plains, Beaded & Quilled, Sinew Sewn, C.1880	1760.00
Doll, Plains, Beaded Yoke, Cowrie Shell Design, Brass Buttons	1980.00
Doll, Plains, Rag, Painted & Fringed Outfit, 7 1/2 In.	95.00
Dress, Crow, Child's, Cowrie Shell Design, Black Velvet, C.1890	550.00
Dress, Crow, Trade Cloth, Cowrie Shells, 1890s	1500.00
Dress, Kwakiutl, Chief's Ceremonial	7700.00
Dress, Plains, Fringed, Deertail Type, Beaded Yoke, 19th Century	7920.00
Drum, Great Lakes, Sinew Sewn, Painted Thunderbird, 19th Century	1980.00
Garter, Great Lakes, Ribbonwork, Appliqued, Green Wool, Beaded, 36 In.	225.00
Gauntlet, Northern Plains, Geometric, Moosehide, White, Beads, 15 In.	300.00
Gloves, Sioux, Beaded, Fringed	715.00
Hat Band, Ute, Braided Horsehair, Engraved Silver Adornments	175.00
Hat, Northern California, Basketry, Geometric, Beige, Quills, 7 In.	150.00
Headdress, Plains, Leather, Dyed Feathers, Loom Beaded, 18 In.	50.00
Hide, Stretched, Indian Observes Indian Artist, 12 X 24 In.	200.00
Hide, Woodland, Plains, Beaded, Fringed, Wool & Cotton, 52 In.	900.00
Hoe, Notched, St.Clair, Miss.	325.00
Hood, Cree, Woman's, Beaded Blue Cloth, Floral & Foliate Patterns	4400.00
Horn, Moose Call, Birchbark, Square, Cone Shape, 1830, 23 In.	150.00
Jacket & Chaps, Orange & Green Beads, 1900, Wyoming, 2 Piece	900.00
Jacket, Great Lakes, Fringed Hide, Beaded, Machine Sewn	375.00
Jacket, Northern Plains, Child's, Fringed Hide	3025.00

Jacket, Plains, Horse & Indians Pictured, Beaded, Fringed	2600.00
Jacket, Plains, Yellow Ocher, Beaded, Fringed, European Style	4500.00
Jar, Acoma, Curvilinear Design, Step–Down Shoulder, 8 1/2 In.	475.00
Jar, Acoma, Pottery, Umber, Red, Curvilinear Design, Cream, 8 X 6 In.	125.00
Jar, Acoma, Water, Bird, Flower Design, Polychrome, 10 In.	1200.00
Jar, Apache, Coiled Basketry, Birds, Figure, 2 1/2 In. ....*Illus*	450.00
Jar, Apache, Coiled, Devil's Claw, Natural, Man, Birds, Horse, 2 1/2 In.	450.00
Jar, Hopi, Pottery, Polychrome Geometric Design, 4 1/2 X 5 In.	70.00
Jar, Pueblo, Blackware, Bear Paw Design, 6 1/4 X 5 1/2 In.	55.00
Jar, San Ildefonso, Blackware, Painted Swag Design, 5 In. ....*Illus*	425.00
Jar, San Juan Pueblo, Redware, Clouds, Signed Manulita, 7 1/2 In.	90.00
Jar, Zia, Birds In Red & Brown, Mid–20th Century, 9 1/4 In.	1200.00
Jar, Zia, Polychrome Pottery, Geometric, Parrot, 15 X 19 In.	6500.00
Jar, Zia, Red & White Design, Mid–20th Century, 11 In.	1250.00
Jug, Apache, Water, Bulbous, Red, 8 In.	295.00
Knife Sheath, Northern Plains, Beaded, Blue, Green, Yellow, 5 1/2 In.	90.00
Knife Sheath, Sioux, Beaded, Pumpkin, Fringe, 9 In.	400.00
Leggings, Plains, Beaded, Fringed, Sinew Sewn, 31 In.	100.00
Leggings, Sioux, Sinew Laced, C.1880	1500.00
Leggings, Sioux, Woman's, American Flag Design, White Ground	4125.00
Map, Choctaw, Nation Coal Leases, 1900	35.00
Mask, Hopi, Mud, Kachina, Leather, 12 X 12 In.	175.00
Mask, Kachina, Dance Bustle Ornament, Eagle Feathers, 1920, Pair	1200.00
Mat, Navajo, Germantown, Colored & Natural Yarn, Fringe, 14 1/2 In.	300.00
Maul, Plains, Stone, Rawhide Cover Head & Handle, 8 1/2 In.	185.00
Medicine Bundle, Navajo, Yei Rattle, Gourd, Sashes, Bull Roar, Bag	350.00
Micmac, Pouch, Beaded, Floral, Gold, Blue, Green, Salmon, 6 In.	140.00
Moccasins, Athabascan, Fringed, Beaded, Canada N.W.M.P., 16 X 11 In.	350.00
Moccasins, Blackfoot, Elk Hide, Made By Wild Coyote, 10 In.	65.00
Moccasins, Crown, Yellow, Green, White & Vermilion, C.1910	375.00
Moccasins, Huron, Smoke & Dyed Skin, Floral Silk Embroidery	350.00
Moccasins, Man's, High Ankle Back, Red, White & Blue Beads, 1900	275.00
Moccasins, Navajo, Child's, Leather, Beadwork On Vamp & Cuff	42.00
Moccasins, Northern Cheyenne, Beaded, Geometric, Tepee Doors, Adult	400.00
Moccasins, Northern Cheyenne, Child's, White, Caramel, Purple, 5 In.	140.00
Moccasins, Northern Plains, Child's, Blue, Geometric Design, 7 In.	130.00
Moccasins, Northern Plains, Painted, Beaded, Gold, Purple, 10 In.	250.00
Moccasins, Plains, Beaded, Quilled Hide, Hard Soles, 10 In.	150.00
Moccasins, Sioux, Red, Blue, White & Orange Beads, C.1890	350.00
Moccasins, Southern Plains, Green, Yellow, White Heart, Red, 9 In.	800.00
Moccasins, Stiff Leather, Beaded Diamond, 9 1/2 In.	145.00
Moccasins, Woodland, Beaded, Velvet	85.00

Indian, Jar, Apache,
Coiled Basketry,
Birds, Figure,
2 1/2 In.

Indian, Plate, San
Idlefonso, Blackware,
Feather Design,
6 1/4 In.

Indian, Jar, San
Ildefonso, Blackware,
Painted Swag
Design, 5 In.

Indian, Vase, Acoma, Pottery,
Cream Slip Over Geometric, 12 In.

Moccasins, Woodland, Lake, High Button, Beaded Cuffs, 11 X 10 In. 125.00
Mush Bowl, Modoc, Basketry, 8 X 4 In. 65.00
Necklace, Navajo, Pendant Set With Coral & Turquoise, 20 In. 40.00
Necklace, Navajo, Silver & Turquoise, Squash Blossom, 24 In. 350.00
Necklace, Navajo, Turquoise, Silver Squash Blossom, 15 In. 300.00
Necklace, Ojibway, Moose Teeth 125.00
Necklace, Pueblo, Turquoise, 17 In. 75.00
Necklace, Puma, Double Chain, Center Thunderbird, Silver 1200.00
Necklace, Puma, Thunderbirds Each Side, Double Beaded Chain, Silver 385.00
Necklace, Puma, Turquoise, Silver, 5 Birds, Double Beaded Chain 450.00
Necklace, Ring & Earrings, Zuni, Silver, Turquoise Squash Blossom 550.00
Necklace, Santo Domingo, Heishi & Turquoise, 30 In. 65.00
Necklace, Santo Domingo, Rolled Turquoise Heishi Jocla, 19 In. 45.00
Necklace, Santo Domingo, Shell Heishi, Turquoise Nuggets, 30 In. 45.00
Necklace, Sioux, Bear Claw 40.00
Necklace, Squash Blossom, 20 Turqoise Nuggets & Silver 450.00
Necklace, Zuni, Fetish, Turquoise, Shell, Jet, Coral, 2 Strands 210.00
Olla, Acoma, 12 1/2 In. 7260.00
Olla, Apache, Polychrome, C.1895, 7 1/2 In. 1800.00
Olla, Apache, Stepped Diamonds 1017.50
Olla, Paiute, 15 X 18 In. 225.00
Olla, Papago, Spiral Whirlwind Design, C.1900, 13 X 12 In. 425.00
Olla, Santo Domingo, Polychrome, 8-Arm Stars 6325.00
Olla, Zia, With Bird, Bell Signed, 7 X 10 1/2 In. 350.00
Panel, Huron, Floral Design On Moosehair & Porcupine Quills 1210.00
Pendant, Zuni, Abstract Bird, Coral, Jet, Turquoise, Pearl 140.00
Picture, Indian Chief, Braves, Canoe, Watercolor, Herget, 8 X 18 In. 175.00
Pin, Zuni, Turquoise, Stone, 1 In. 75.00
Pipe Bag, Buckskin Fringe, Beaded, C.1900, 10 X 8 In. 1050.00
Pipe Bag, Plains, Beaded, Fringed, Geometric, White Ground, 21 In. 250.00
Pipe Bag, Sioux, 2 Geometric Beaded Panels, Fringed, 30 In. 900.00
Pipe, Catlinite, Silver, Carved Wooden Stem, 30 In. 100.00
Pipe, Catlinite, Stem, 22 In. 600.00
Pipe, Cherokee, Head Effigy, North Carolina, 1700, 2 3/4 In. 175.00
Pipe, Cherokee, Human Effigy, 3 In. 175.00
Pipe, Effigy, Rat, Virginia 28.00
Pipe, Iroquois, Human Mask Face Bowl, C.1830 .... 425.00
Pipe, Southeastern Style, Stone, 8 1/2 X 3 In. 50.00
Pipe, Steatite, L Shape, West Virginia, 3 3/4 X 2 3/4 In. 180.00
Plaque, Hopi, Basketry, Kachina Figure, 12 1/2 In. 125.00
Plaque, Hopi, Coiled Basketry, 2nd Mesa, Star, Red, Green, 17 In. 60.00
Plate, San Idlefonso, Blackware, Feather Design, 6 1/4 In. ....*Illus* 425.00
Pot, Acoma, Head, Orange, Amber, Cream Slip, C.1920, 9 1/2 X 7 In. 290.00
Pot, Acoma, Orange, Amber, Cream, Signed, Duran, 8 1/2 X 5 In. 95.00
Pot, San Ildefonso, Black On Black, 6 1/2 X 4 3/4 In. 475.00
Pot, Stylized Eagle Design, Black Clay, Christiana Naraya, 7 In. 550.00
Pot, Zuni, Ceremonial, Rain Dance, C.1870 .... 4000.00
Pouch, Crow, Beaded, 4 Winds Pattern, Fringed, 9 X 7 In. 350.00
Pouch, Eastern Woodlands, Black Velvet, Beading Both Sides, 4 In. 60.00
Pouch, Northwest, Graphic Beaded, Red, White & Blue, C.1870 .... 2500.00
Pouch, Plains, Strike-A-Light, Beaded Front, Tin Cone Dangles, 6 In. 55.00
Pouch, Sioux, Beaded, Smoked Elk Hide, Yellow, White, Red, Blue, 9 In. 85.00
Pounder, Northwest Coast, Wolf's Head, Stone, 3 X 6 3/4 In. 1500.00
Print, Ojibwa, Rag Paper, Color, Documented, 1836, 20 X 27 In. 425.00
Purse, Micmac, Birchbark, Quill Design, Floral, 6 Sided 330.00
Purse, Woodland, Beaded, Small 75.00
Quirt, Crow, Carved, Painted Red Birch, Leather, Steel Beads Design 400.00
Quirt, Sioux, Beaded, Red Horsehair On End, 31 In. 45.00
Quiver, Sioux, Red Ocher, Leather, Elkhide Trim, Arrow, 1885, 30 In. 600.00
Rattle, Northwest Coast, Totemic Designs, Signed Lavalle, Abalone 650.00
Rattle, Northwest Coast, Wooden, Hooked Beak, Carved Teeth, Painted 1400.00
Ring, Snake, Turquoise, Effie Costtelo 85.00
Rug, Navaho, Red, Black, White Crosses, 60 X 84 In. 650.00
Rug, Navaho, Red, Brown, White, Gray, Diamond Design, 61 X 78 In. 525.00

Rug, Navaho, Throw, All Natural, 41 X 71 In. 400.00
Rug, Navaho, Throw, Brown, Beige, Gray, Squash Blossom, 62 X 41 In. 500.00
Rug, Navaho, Throw, Brown, White, Wool, 45 X 57 In. 325.00
Rug, Navaho, Throw, Geometric, Red, White, Black, Brown, 69 X 44 In. 600.00
Rug, Navaho, Whirling Log Design, Red, Gray, Brown, White, 66 X 97 In. 550.00
Rug, Navajo, 3 Yei Figures, Cornstalks, Rainbow God, 59 X 42 In. 375.00
Rug, Navajo, Concentric Diamonds, Gray–Brown Ground, 46 X 82 In. 225.00
Rug, Navajo, Figural, White, Beige, Black, Red, 42 X 51 In. 1300.00
Rug, Navajo, Ganado, Double Dye Red, Tan & Natural, 54 X 104 In. 400.00
Rug, Navajo, Ganado, Two-Dye Red, Brown, Black, Natural, 39 X 62 In. 600.00
Rug, Navajo, Homespun, Human Figure, White Ground, 40 X 66 In. 700.00
Rug, Navajo, Klagetch, Natural, Gray, Brown, Two-Dye Red, 44 X 72 In. 750.00
Rug, Navajo, Pictorial, Cornstalk, Birds, Anagram Sugar, 51 X 76 In. 1700.00
Rug, Navajo, Pictorial, Yei Figures, Birds, Cornstalks, 52 X 95 In. 1600.00
Rug, Navajo, Stripe Pattern, 56 X 74 In. 300.00
Rug, Navajo, Tapestry, Lula Cody, Cameron Trading Post, 23 X 35 In. 375.00
Rug, Navajo, Tapestry, Two Gray Hills, Spirit Line, 30 1/2 X 40 In. 450.00
Rug, Navajo, Teec Nos Pos, Yellow, Blue, Natural, C.1900, 44 X 58 In. 500.00
Rug, Navajo, Twill Weave, Aniline Stripe, Gray Design, 33 X 53 In. 175.00
Rug, Navajo, Two Gray Hills, 37 X 50 In. 75.00
Saddlebag, Apache, Cutwork Hide, Indigo, Cochineal Red, 1870 .... 3500.00
Saddlebag, Apache, Double, Red Wool Trade Cloth Panels, Hide 3410.00
Saddlebag, Hide Backing, Beaded, Horsehair Tassels, 1900, 18 In., Pair 2800.00
Seed Beater, Paiute, Black Stripe Design, Woven Handle, 11 X 9 In. 265.00
Serape, Saltillo, Serrated Diamond, Red, White Binding, 41 X 82 In. 1300.00
Shawl, Navajo, Woman's, Red & Black–Blue Wool 4125.00
Shirt, Sioux, Child's, Beaded Crosses Down Arms & Sides, C.1890 .... 3000.00
Skull Cracker, Plains, Blue & Yellow Beaded Design, Sinew, 36 In. 675.00
Snowshoes, Ojibwa, Child's 165.00
Spear, Dickson, Boone County, Missouri, Tan, Peach, 4 1/8 In. 165.00
Spear, Hardin, Gray, Sevier County, Ark., 3 1/4 In. 165.00
Spear, Hopewell, Pike County, Illinois, 3 3/4 In. 160.00
Spoon, Hopi, 5 3/4 In. 40.00
Spoon, Northwest Coast, Mountain Goat Horn, Incised Handle, 7 In. 175.00
Strip, Sioux, Faceted Metallic Beads On White, 3 X 31 In. 90.00
Tapestry, Navajo, Gray Hills, Nancy Gould, Spirit Line, 20 X 27 In. 250.00
Textile, Woven, Navajo, Yei Bichai Design, Dancers, 35 X 50 In. 375.00
Tomahawk, Eastern Woodlands, Forged Steel, Carved Handle, 18 In. 375.00
Totem Pole, Haida, Raven, Various Figures, 1900s, 26 3/4 In. 500.00
Tray, Apache, Rod Construction, Horses, Crosses, Sunburst, 18 In. 1100.00
Tray, Hopi, Coiled, Devil's Claw Checkerboard, 1950s, 6 X 12 In. 68.00
Tray, Jicarilla Apache, Basketry, Central Star Design, 17 1/4 In. 200.00
Tray, Papago, Coiled, Handles, Devil's Claw Checkerboard, 12 In. 68.00
Tray, Papago, Gambling, 15 In. 50.00
Tray, Papago, Leaf Flower Center, C.1940, 9 In. 45.00
Tray, Winnowing, Paiute, Triangular Shape, 23 X 16 In. 225.00
Tray, Yavapai, Basketry, Dogs & People Woven Into Design 4500.00
Trousers, Plains, Deerskin, Beaded, Machine Sewn, 40 In. Waist 190.00
Vase, Acoma, Pottery, Cream Slip Over Geometric, 12 In. ....*Illus* 1700.00
Vase, Southwest, Black, Signed Rose, 5 1/2 X 4 1/2 In. 395.00
Vessel, Hopi, Buff Smoked Ground, C.1900, 11 3/4 X 8 1/2 In. 200.00
Wall Hanging, Yei, Red, Orange, Coral, Gray, Natural, 24 X 39 In. 150.00
Wall Pocket, Woodland, Birchbark, Dyed Leather Decorated, 4 X 7 In. 35.00
War Club, Metal Blade, Scorched Handle, 7 In. Blade, 17 In. 75.00
War Club, With Knife, Carved Animal Head Wood, Metal Blade, Holder 500.00
Water Jar, Zia, C.1880 .... 3500.00

 An inkstand was made to be placed on a desk. It held some type of container for ink, and possibly a sander, a pen tray, a pen, a holder for pounce, and even a candle to melt the sealing wax. Inkstands date to the eighteenth century and have been made of silver, copper, ceramics, and glass.

INKSTAND, Floral, Geometric, Oriental Porcelain, Curl Handles, 4 Holes, 6 In. 85.00
   George II, Silver, Gadroon, 3 Bottles, Adridge & Stamper, 10 In. 2310.00

George III, Silver, Boat Shape, 2 Bottles, Elkington, 13 3/4 In. 1870.00

 Inkwells, of course, held ink. Ready–made ink was first made about 1836 and was sold in bottles. The desk inkwell had a narrow hole so the pen would not slip inside. Pottery, glass, pewter, silver, and other materials were used to make inkwells. Look in other sections for more listings of inkwells.

INKWELL, Aladdin's Lamp Shape, Flowers, Ribbons, Yellow, Porcelain, French 125.00
  Art Deco, Sterling Silver On Bronze 65.00
  Art Nouveau, Metal, Glass Insert, G.De Feure 340.00
  Barrel Shape, Enameled Bacchanalian Scenes, Viennese, 1885, 10 In. 1980.00
  Baseball, Metal 190.00
  Black Boy's Head, Hinged Cover, Metal, 8 In. 120.00
  Blockhouse, Cover, Pittsburgh, Penna., Painted Design, Crystal 60.00
  Blown Glass, Emerald Green, Open, 7 X 1 1/4 In. 55.00
  Blown Glass, Olive Green Swirl 990.00
  Bronze, Hinged Cover, Bail Handle, Gurschner, C.1900, 12 1/4 In. 1320.00
  Copper, Hammered, Gustav Stickley 750.00
  Cork & Acorn, Spout On Side, Cobalt Blue Glaze, English 65.00
  Cover, Moon & Forest Silhouette, Limoges, Yellow & Green, 2 1/2 In. 95.00
  Crystal, Silver Plated Tray, Embossed Cover 25.00
  Cut Glass, Paperweight, Hobstars, Sterling Silver, Gorham, 4 In. 450.00
  Double, Hand Painted Roses, Gold Trim, Ovington Bros., 8 In. 60.00
  Double, Lime Green Cut Glass, Stag's Head Center, 7 1/4 In. 235.00
  Double, Silver Plated Holder, Stag's Head Center, Green, 7 1/4 In. 235.00
  Double, Snail, Cast Iron, Crystal Bottles 150.00
  Evil Old Laughing Man, Metal, Glass Insert 65.00
  Fount–O–Ink, Bakelite, Metal, 5 1/2 X 3 1/2 In. 25.00
  Gilt Bronze, Floral Relief, Scroll, Leaf Design, Louis XV, 13 In. 400.00
  Gilt Bronze, Pen Tray, Monogram, Napoleon III, 9 3/4 In. 600.00
  Glass, Brass Trim 45.00
  Globe Insurance 35.00
  High Wheel Bicycle Shape, 2 Cut Glass Wells, Wooden, 6 1/2 In. 275.00
  Kettle Shape, Green Ribbed Opaline Glass, 19th Century 425.00
  Lap Desk, Milk Glass, Scroll Design, Fired–On Floral, Cover 75.00
  Melon Ribs, Jockey Hat Hinged Cover, Cranberry, White Overshot 225.00
  Metal Frame, 2 Revolving Glass Holders 85.00
  Peasant House, Removable Roof Is Lid, Pottery, Erphila, Brown 65.00
  Pewter, Marked W.Humiston, Troy, N.Y., 4 3/8 In. 200.00
  Pewter, Wide Flat Base, Pewter Insert, 6 7/8 In. 105.00
  Pyramid Shape, 6–Sided Panels, Cut Glass, Silver Plate, 3 3/4 In. 125.00
  Pyramid, Cut Glass, 6 Sides, Hinged Lid, 3 3/4 X 2 7/8 In. 115.00
  Russian Cut Glass, Sterling Silver, Gorham 950.00
  Saddled Camel, Metal, 6 In. 75.00
  Snail, In Stand 175.00
  Stag & Hounds, Brass, B & H Glass Inserts 70.00
  Stepped Bronze & Marble, Bottles Shaped Domes, Louisville, Ky. 1850.00
  Stoneware, Drum Shape, 3 Nib Holes, Gray Salt Glaze, 3 1/2 In. 175.00
  Traveling, Attached To Pen Holder, Brass, Early 19th Century 145.00
  Urn Shape, Grape Design, Marble Base, Bronze, 4 3/4 X 4 In. 150.00
  Viking Ships & Waves, Hinged Lid, Jennings Bros., Bronzed 75.00
  Wooden, Painted Design 65.00

 Insulators of glass or pottery have been made for use on telegraph or telephone poles since 1844. Thousands of different styles of insulators have been made. Most common are those of clear or aqua glass, most desirable are the threadless types made from 1850 to 1870.

INSULATOR, Beehive, Ram's Horn, Curlicue End Attachment 90.00
  Brookes, Embossed CPRR, Aqua 85.00
  Brookfield, Amber Streaks, Green 15.00
  California, Aqua 15.00
  Canadian Pacific, Purple 13.00
  Diamond, Olive Amber 5.00

Iron, Door Knocker, Pink & Blue   Iron, Figurine, Girl, With
Paint, 1930, 4 In.   Basket, 27 In.

Duquesne Glass Co., Light Blue	8.00
Foree Bain, Dated 1890	25.00
G.N.W., Light Green	20.00
Hard Rubber, Goodyear	25.00
Hemingray, Bigmouth, Clear	15.00
Hemingray, No.16	9.00
Hemingray, No.20	9.00
Lignum Vitae, Ram's Horn	50.00
McKee, Bluish Aqua	175.00
Mount Washington, Coblat Blue Insert	150.00
Mount Washington, Gray Insert	75.00
Porcelain, Cuban Pattern, Full Curl of Bighorn Ram	150.00
Pyrex Consolidated Design, 320, Carnival	25.00
W.Brookfield, Yellow Green	50.00
W.G.M.Co., Purple	15.00
Whitall Tatum, No.1, Purple	7.50

IRISH BELLEEK, see Belleek

Iron is a metal that has been used by man since prehistoric times. It is a popular metal for tools and decorative items like doorstops that need as much weight as possible. Items are listed here or under other appropriate headings such as Bookends, Doorstop, Kitchen, or Tool. The tool that is used for ironing clothes, an iron, is listed under Kitchen, Iron; or Kitchen, Sadiron.

IRON, Ashtray, Floor, Black, Nude Female Standing On Chrome Ball, 24 In.	440.00
Ashtray, Skillet, Wagner, 3 1/2 In.	15.00
Ashtray, Standing, Butler Shape, Holding Cigarette Box, Iron, 35 In.	325.00
Ax Holder, Conestoga Wagon, Fish Shape, Penna., 19th Century, 8 1/4 In.	3850.00
Basin, Bottom Marked Clark, 3 X 9 In.	15.00
Bean Roaster, Roy & Wilcox Co., Berling, Conn., Pat. April 17, 1849	245.00
Bill Spindle, Fancy Base	6.00
Boot Scraper, Dachshund, 10 1/2 In.	60.00
Boot Scraper, Dachshund, Painted Dark Green, 21 In.	260.00
Boot Scraper, Dolphin	325.00
Boot Scraper, Fighting Cock, Painted Wooden Block, 20 In.	475.00
Boot Scraper, Holcroft & Sons, Wolverhampton, 18 3/4 In.	45.00
Bootjack, Beetle, Yellow Stripe Down Back, 9 In.	25.00
Bootjack, Cricket, Tri State Foundry Co., Worn Black Paint, 10 1/2 In.	35.00
Bootjack, Naughty Nellie, Crudely Painted	110.00
Bowls, Nesting, Sheet Iron, Movable Wire Loop Handles, 5 Piece	260.00
Box, Hinged, Molded In Form of Pig, Interior Wells, 9 X 15 1/2 In.	3575.00
Buggy Step, Long Arm To Bottom of Wagon, 3 Arms	3.00
Burner, Incense, Snail	25.00
Candlestand, 2 Arms, Adjustable, Brass Finial, 3 Penny Feet, 54 In.	1500.00
Candlestand, Spring Slide, Single Socket Candleholder, 59 In., Pair	275.00
Candlestick, Hog Scraper, Wedding Band, 7 1/4 In.	250.00
Cauldron, Bail Handle, 27 In.	85.00
Curler, Wig, Scissors Shape, Ball Ends, 10 In.	75.00

Dispenser, Cigarette, Donkey, Crank Tail, Ejects Cigarette, 5 X 9 In.	85.00
Dispenser, Cigarette, Elephant	85.00
Door Knocker, Lion's Head, 3 Dimensional, 1800s, 3 1/2 X 7 1/2 In.	110.00
Door Knocker, Owl	95.00
Door Knocker, Pink & Blue Paint, 1930, 4 In. ....*Illus*	30.00
Doormat, Heart Shaped Links, 13 1/2 X 21 1/2 In.	155.00
Figurine, Cat, Victorian, Painted Mustard Color, 5 X 10 In.	250.00
Figurine, Deer, Sabatino Angelis, 1904, 7 1/4 X 6 In.	253.00
Figurine, Girl, With Basket, 27 In. ....*Illus*	275.00
Figurine, Guardian, Oriental, 15 In., Pair	150.00
Handcuffs & Chain, A.Hanna & Co., C.1860	40.00
Heater, Cover, Openwork, Rococo Design	275.00
Hitching Post, Horsehead, 10 1/2 In.	264.00
Hitching Post, Horsehead, Black Paint, 13 In.	100.00
Hitching Post, Horsehead, Ring In Nose, Round Post, 28 In.	500.00
Holder, Hose, Round, Ring In Top	20.00
Hook, Multiple Prong, 15 In.	65.00
Hook, Wall, Victorian, Embossed Florals & Leaves, 8 In.	15.00
Leg Irons & Chain, Southern, C.1850	25.00
Leg Irons & Handcuffs, Keys	170.00
Lock, Elbow, With Keeper, 4 1/2 In.	35.00
IRON, MATCH HOLDER, see Match Holder	
Nail Cup, Cobbler's, Star, 8 Divided Compartments	68.00
Ornament, Garden, Deer, Doe & Stag, Standing, H.Mansbach, Life Size, Pair	3750.00
Ornament, Garden, Fruit & Flower Form, 26 In., Pair	440.00
Ornament, Garden, Lion, 1 Awake, 1 Asleep, 45 In., Pair	7800.00
Peanut Roaster, Separate Bin To Catch Peanuts	425.00
Pipe Tongs, Spring Action, 16 3/8 In.	1250.00
Plaque, Fish Form, Green, Brown & Gold, 37 In., Pair	248.00
Rack, Utensil, Primitive, 5 Hooks, 9 X 14 In.	130.00
Rack, Utensil, Rooster Finial, Handmade, 18 1/2 In.	175.00
Shooting Gallery Figure, Bear, 10 In.	25.00
Shooting Gallery Figure, Bear, Yellow Paint, 5 1/4 In.	65.00
Shooting Gallery Figure, Donkey, Yellow Paint, 2 Parts, 22 1/2 In.	350.00
Shooting Gallery Figure, Doubles, Stars, Man In Moon, 9 1/2 In.	70.00
Shooting Gallery Figure, Duck, 1 White, 1 Yellow, Pair	90.00
Shooting Gallery Figure, Duck, Bracket, Black Paint, 5 3/4 In.	35.00
Shooting Gallery Figure, Elephant, Orange Paint, 9 In.	95.00
Shooting Gallery Figure, Indian In Canoe, White Paint, 9 In.	205.00
Shooting Gallery Figure, Quail, White Paint, 4 1/4 In.	50.00
Shooting Gallery Figure, Running Rabbit, Orange Paint, 11 In.	25.00
Shooting Gallery Figure, Shamrock, Orange & Yellow Paint, 4 1/2 In.	15.00
Shooting Gallery Figure, Squirrel, Orange Paint, 7 3/4 In.	25.00
Shooting Gallery Figure, Turkey, Orange Paint, 6 In.	20.00
Sign, Hooks Each End, Painting of Soldier, Dated 1810, 12 X 22 In.	175.00
Snow Bird, Eagles, Black & Silver Paint, Red Mouth, 6 5/8 In.	35.00
String Holder, Beehive, 5 1/2 X 6 In.	65.00
String Holder, Colonial Boy, Figural, Polychrome, 7 In.	400.00
Sugar Cutter, On Stand	295.00
Taper Jack, Tooled, 8 In.	1025.00
Teakettle, Wrought Handle, Marked No.7–9 Quarts, 14 In.	150.00
Tobacco Cutter, China Man	295.00
Tobacco Cutter, Counter Top, 3 Holes, El–Arabe Label, Nickel Plated	165.00
Tobacco Cutter, Enterprise	42.00
Tobacco Cutter, Figural, Gun	135.00
Tobacco Cutter, Horsehead, Black Beauty	325.00
Tobacco Cutter, Triumph	60.00
Trivet, Round, Stylized Tulip, 5 1/4 In.	50.00
Tsuba, Geometric Horseshoe, 2 1/2 In.	110.00
Tsuba, Gnarled Tree, Crane, Old Man, Openwork, Copper, Silver, Japan	155.00
Tsuba, Latticework Design, 2 3/4 In.	231.00
Tsuba, Stylized Flying Crane, 1 7/8 In.	110.00
Urn, Campana Form, Flared Rim, 19th Century, 26 1/2 In.	375.00
Urn, Campana Form, Handles, Root Form Base, C.1860, 41 1/4 In.	950.00

Urn, Grape Leaf Design, Handles, White & Green, 20 X 29 In.	300.00
Urn, Sectional, Painted White, 19th Century, 45 X 28 In.	385.00
Urn, Victorian, Scrolled Handles, Fluted Bowl, C.1870, 16 1/2 In., Pair	325.00
Windmill Weight, Bobtailed Horse	200.00
Windmill Weight, Buffalo, Fairbury, Nebraska	475.00
Windmill Weight, Bull, Fairbury, Nebraska	650.00
Windmill Weight, Chicken	1550.00
Windmill Weight, Elgin, Original Paint	725.00
Windmill Weight, Horse, Bobtail, Free Standing, 17 X 18 In.	350.00
Windmill Weight, Horse, Short Tail	160.00
Windmill Weight, Rooster On Ball	450.00
Windmill Weight, Rooster, 10 Ft.	525.00
Windmill Weight, Rooster, 18 X 15 1/2 In.	400.00
Windmill Weight, Rooster, Elgin Wind Power & Pump Co., 16 1/2 In.	600.00
Windmill Weight, Rooster, Flattened Body, Painted, 19th Century, 17 In.	1210.00
Windmill Weight, Rooster, Rainbow Tail	975.00
Windmill Weight, W	125.00

Ironstone china was first made in 1813. It gained its greatest
popularity during the mid–nineteenth century. The heavy, durable,
off–white pottery was made in white or was decorated with any of
hundreds of patterns. Much flow blue pottery was made of
ironstone. Some of the decorations were raised. Many pieces of
ironstone are unmarked but some English and American factories
included the word "Ironstone" in their marks.

**IRONSTONE, see also Chelsea Grape; Chelsea Sprig; Gaudy Ironstone;
Moss Rose; Staffordshire**

IRONSTONE, Bedpan, Urinal Spout, H.Laughlin, 1920	30.00
Bowl, Blue Flowers, Lavender, 4 In. ....*Illus*	20.00
Bowl, Underplate, Cover, Columbia Shape, Jos.Goodwin, C.1850	125.00
Bowl, Vegetable, Cover, Sydenham Shape, T & R Boote, Small	175.00
Cake Plate, Glamis Castle, Brown, Handles	22.50
Compote, Pedestal, Gothic Shape, J.Edwards, 1850s	50.00
Creamer, Grenade	60.00
Creamer, Laurel Wreath, Washington Transfer Medallion	245.00
Cup & Saucer, Green & Purple Transfer of Indian, Handleless	22.50
Cup & Saucer, Handleless, Elsmore & Forster	45.00
Cup & Saucer, Strawberry, Handleless	295.00
Cup & Saucer, Tree of Life, Wood & Sons, 1890	35.00
Cup & Saucer, Wheat & Clover, Handleless	150.00
Cup & Saucer, Wheat, J.& G.Meakin, Handleless, 1860s	30.00
Cup, Hot Toddy, Branch of Three Leaves	20.00
Cup, Wheat In The Meadow, Handleless	22.00
Dish, Serving, Cover, Embossed Leaves, Flowers, White, 11 1/2 In.	30.00
Dish, Spoon Bowl Shape, Fruit & Nut Handle, Meakin, 8 3/4 In.	15.00
Footbath, Seaweed Medallions, Pink, Malcolm & Mountford, 20 In.	800.00
Fruit Stand, Floral, Footed, C.1825, Pair	100.00
Gravy Boat, Blue Transfer, Eagle, 7 3/4 In.	65.00

Ironstone, Bowl, Blue Flowers,
Lavender, 4 In.

Small nicks and scratches in iron
can be covered with black crayon.
Wipe off the excess with paper.

To clean small pieces of iron, try
soaking them in white vinegar for
24 to 48 hours.

Jug, Otto Wagner & Bros., Liquor Dealer, Tiffin, Ohio, 1/2 Gal.	85.00
Ladle, Lavender Bird, Large	65.00
Mold, Food, Columns & Floral Design, White, 4 X 6 1/2 In.	45.00
Mold, Food, Double Ear of Corn, C.1870, 2 1/2 X 6 1/2 In.	45.00
Mold, Pudding, 2 Levels of Arches & Floral Design, Oval, 7 In.	45.00
Pitcher & Bowl, Black Transfer Oriental Design, Mason's, 13 In.	175.00
Pitcher, Brown Transfer, Florentine, Mayer, 9 1/2 In.	135.00
Pitcher, Dogs & Deer, Green Tree Handle	75.00
Pitcher, Grape Cluster, Vine Design, Brown, Star Mark, 9 In.	95.00
Pitcher, Imari Pattern, Mason, C.1813, 9 In.	795.00
Pitcher, Paneled, Blue Transfer, English, 10 In.	135.00
Pitcher, Snake Handle, Mason	195.00
Plate, Black Floral Transfer, Enameling, Marked, 10 1/8 In.	35.00
Plate, Blue Transfer, Eagle, Stick Spatter Rim, 8 3/4 In.	65.00
Plate, Floral Imari Design, Marked, 10 1/2 In., 6 Piece	465.00
Plate, Lisley & Powell, Copper Luster Trim, 7 1/2 In.	12.00
Plate, Oyster White. Copper Luster Trim, Scroll, Walley, 9 1/2 In.	25.00
Plate, Teaberry, Gold Luster, Impressed Mark, 9 3/4 In.	25.00
Plate, Trent Shape, John Alcock, 1881, 9 3/4 In.	18.00
Platter, Black Transfer of Birds & Flowers, 15 3/4 In.	75.00
Platter, Blue–Black Transfer Ornithology, Adams, 15 5/8 In.	35.00
Platter, Caledonian, Red & Green Transfer, Marked, 17 In.	45.00
Platter, Ceres Shape, Elsmore & Forster, 16 In.	55.00
Platter, Light Blue Floral Transfer, Indian, 17 In.	95.00
Punch Bowl, Berry Cluster, White	125.00
Punch Bowl, Scrolled Bubble, Parkhurst	195.00
Sauce, Cover, Ceres Shape, Elsmore & Forster, 1859	120.00
Shaving Mug, Ring Handle	15.00
Soap Dish, Cover, Rabbit & Sandpiper Transfer, Luster	88.00
Soap Dish, Rose, Meakin	40.00
Soup, Dish, Black & Orange Oriental Design, Mason's, 1849	85.00
Sugar, Cover, Ceres Shape, Elsmore & Forster	75.00
Syrup, Cock & Edge, Pewter Lid, Relief Grapes & Leaf, 5 1/2 In.	130.00
IRONSTONE, TEA LEAF, see Tea Leaf Ironstone	
Teapot, Ceres Shape, Copper Luster Trim	225.00
Teapot, Dr.Wall Type, Blue Stenciled Pheasant, Hinged Lid, 6 In.	400.00
Teapot, Embossed Ivy, William Adams, 10 In.	70.00
Teapot, Embossed Vintage, White, Lion & Unicorn Mark, 10 In.	60.00
Teapot, Trent Shape, Alcock	90.00
Teapot, Wedding Ring Design, Cover	45.00
Teapot, White, Ribbed, J.W.Pankhurst	330.00
Toilet Set, Stork In Rushes, Brown Transfer, 10 Piece	525.00
Tureen, Brown Classical Design, Primavesi, Cardiff, C.1850, Large	125.00
Tureen, Cover, Acorn Finial, J.Edwards, 1855, 11 1/2 X 6 3/4 In.	90.00
Tureen, Gothic, White, Cover, Ladle & Underplate, J.Edwards	385.00
Tureen, Malta Pattern, 13 In.	40.00
Tureen, Sauce, Cover, Ceres, Elsmore & Forster, Wedgwood	95.00
Tureen, Sauce, With Ladle, Embossed Design, Scrolled Leaf Handles	60.00
Tureen, Underplate, Blue & Gold Design, Ladle, Dimmock, 3 Piece	750.00
Waste Bowl, Ceres Shape, White	242.00
Water Cooler, Spigot Hole, 2 Handles, Replaced Cover, 30 Gal.	140.00
Wine Cooler, Gold Stylized Peony Blossom, Mermaid Handles, Pair	1760.00

Laszlo Ispanky began his American career as a designer for Cybis Porcelains. In 1966, he established his own studio in Pennington, New Jersey; since 1976, he has worked for Goebel of North America. He works in stone, wood, or metal, as well as porcelain. The first limited edition figurines were issued in 1966.

ISPANKY, Sign, Dealer's, Buffalo, Porcelain	75.00

"IVOREX"
OSBORNE.(COPYRIGHT.
MADE IN ENGLAND.

Arthur Osborne made Ivorex plaques in England in the beginning of the 1900s. The plaques, made of a material he called "sterine wax," pictured buildings or room interiors modeled in three dimensions.

Ivory, Figurine, Gautama
Buddha, Seated, Lotus
Pedestal, 9 In.

Ivory, Figurine, Shou
Lao, Chinese, 10 1/2 In.

Ivory, Figurine, Man, Protecting
Himself Against Weather, 13 In.

Ivory, Vase, Tusk, Cover, Carved
Birds, Demon, Monkey, Foliage

After Osborne's death his daughter Blanche ran the company. It
was closed in 1965, then purchased by W.H. Bossons Ltd. in 1971.
Production of the plaques started again in 1980.

IVOREX, Plaque, Lady Godiva, Stamped Osborne, 7 X 8 In. 28.00

The tusk of an elephant is ivory and to many that is the only true
ivory. To most collectors, the term "ivory" also includes such natural
materials as walrus, hippopotamus, or whale teeth or tusks, and
some of the vegetable materials that are of similar texture and
density. Other ivory items are listed under Scrimshaw or Netsuke.

IVORY, Boat, Rooster Figurehead, Household Gods, 15 1/4 X 12 In.	900.00
Brush Holder, Tusk, Figures, Animals In Garden, 4 3/4 In.	200.00
Bust, Lady, Silver Wrapped Hair & Drapery, Pedestal, 1900, 11 In.	2310.00
Carving, Wasps On Honeycomb, 3 Worms, Signed Senpo	440.00
Figurine, Apple, Carved Village Scene, Leaf & Stem, Chinese, 3 1/4 In.	150.00
Figurine, Bearded Man, Holding Fan, Japan, 8 1/2 In.	138.00
Figurine, Buddha, Wooden Stand, 5 3/4 In.	45.00
Figurine, Child With Scroll, Man Holding Banner, Signed, 9 1/8 In.	200.00
Figurine, Dove, Articulated Wings, Wood Base, 2 1/4 In.	440.00
Figurine, Fawn, 4 X 4 In.	132.00
Figurine, Flute Player, Buffalo, Stag, China, 5 1/2 In., Pair	325.00
Figurine, Gautama Buddha, Seated, Lotus Pedestal, 9 In. ....*Illus*	687.50
Figurine, Horse, Rearing, Jewels, Malachite Base, 20th Century, 7 In.	4400.00
Figurine, Man, Japanese, Standing, Basket of Fish, Foot On Log, 5 In.	150.00
Figurine, Man, Protecting Himself Against Weather, 13 In. ....*Illus*	1100.00
Figurine, Nude Woman, Long Hair, Wrists Crossed, C.1920, 11 7/8 In.	1650.00
Figurine, Old Oriental Women, 9 In., Pair	350.00
Figurine, Oriental Wise Man, Dragon Staff, 7 5/8 In.	145.00
Figurine, Rats Eating Coi, Japan, 6 In.	300.00
Figurine, Shou Lao, Chinese, 10 1/2 In. ....*Illus*	110.00
Figurine, Traveler On Rock, Staff, Child, 20th Century, 8 5/8 In.	150.00
Figurine, Two Street Urchins, Oval Base, 3 3/8 In.	25.00
Figurine, Woman, Flowing Robe, Long Hair, Black Pupils, 6 3/4 In.	160.00
Group, Lohan & Attendant, Standing On Oni, Japan, C.1900, 7 3/4 In.	154.00
Group, Sacred Virtue With Cherub, Mirror Back Plinth, French, 10 In.	1870.00
Group, Various Sized Rats, With Seal, Masayoshi, 3 1/2 In.	2600.00
Group, Woman, Holding Flower Ball, Child, Japan, 8 In.	176.00
Lorgnette, Carved Handle, French Fashion, 2 3/4 In.	150.00
Puzzle Ball, Concentric Circles, Figural Stand, 1900, 7 1/2 In.	225.00
Triptych, Napoleon Scene, Carved Walnut, C.1880, 12 In.	2200.00
Tusk, Box, Rhinoceros Forms Finial, 6 In.	250.00

Tusk, Chinese Carving, 18 Monks, Mountain Landscape, 16 In. 1320.00
Tusk, Figure Scenes, Buildings, Trees, Wood Base, Chinese, 8 In., Pair 550.00
Tusk, Figure, Quan Yin, Holding Basket of Lotus, Crown, Chinese, 39 In. 2310.00
Vase, Tusk, Cover, Carved Birds, Demon, Monkey, Foliage ....*Illus* 2300.00
Vase, Tusk, Monkey Design, Japanese, 8 In. 440.00

Jack Armstrong, the all–American boy, was the hero of a radio serial from 1933 to 1951. Premiums were offered to the listeners until the mid–1940s. Jack Armstrong's best–known endorsement is for Wheaties.

JACK ARMSTRONG, Book, Big Little Book, Mystery of Iron Key 12.00
Box, Magic Answer, Original Mailer, Extra Strips 65.00
Flashlight, Bullet Shape, Bisquick Ad For Compass, 4 In. 20.00
Flashlight, Signal 24.00
Game, Football, Wheaties Premium, 1936 .... 90.00
Pedometer .... 20.00 To 28.00
Ring, Egyptian Siren, Wheaties, 1938 .... 45.00

Jack–in–the–pulpit vases were named for their odd trumpetlike shape that resembles the wild plant called jack–in–the–pulpit. The design originated in the late Victorian years. Vases in the jack–in–the–pulpit shape were made of ceramic or glass.

JACK–IN–THE–PULPIT, Vase, Amberina, 7 1/2 In. 265.00
Vase, Clear Rigaree Trim, Cranberry, 7 In. 75.00
Vase, Cream Opalescent, Brown Leaf Overlay, 12 1/2 In. 160.00
Vase, Flower Petal Top, Green Interior, 6 5/8 In. 88.00
Vase, Fluted, Flared, Vaseline To Blue, 7 In. 85.00
Vase, Green Opalescent Stripes, Pink Flower, 9 In. 125.00
Vase, Leaf Chalice Pattern, Blue, 5 3/4 X 6 1/4 In. 45.00
Vase, Ruffled, Ribbed Body, Green Stem & Leaf, 8 1/4 In. 90.00
Vase, White Dot Enameled Flowers, 4 1/2 In. 75.00

Jackfield ware was originally a black glazed pottery made in Jackfield, England, from 1750 to 1775. A yellow glazed ware has also been called Jackfield ware. Most of the pieces referred to as "Jackfield" today are black–glazed, red–clay wares made at the Jackfield Pottery in Shropshire, England, in Victorian times.

JACKFIELD, Coffeepot, Victorian Girl Blowing Bubbles, Rolling Hoop, Gold 275.00
Teapot, Miniature 48.00

Two different minerals, nephrite and jadeite, are called jade. Nephrite is the mineral used for most early Oriental carvings. Jade is a very tough stone that is found in many colors from dark green to pale lavender. Jade carvings are still being made in the old styles, so collectors must be careful not to be fooled by recent pieces. Jade jewelry is found in this book under Jewelry.

JADE, Figurine, Court Lady, Floral Spray & Fan In Hands, Chinese, 8 In. 325.00
Figurine, Foo Dog, Collar Bells & Tassels, Black Eyes, 7 X 8 In., Pair 6875.00
Figurine, Lady, Standing, Flowing Robes, Phoenix On Rockwork, 6 1/2 In. 7000.00
Lamp, Urn Shape, Su Chow, 19th Century, 9 In., Pair 900.00
Screen, Hand Carved Nephrite, Chinese 385.00
Urn, Cover, Loose Rings On Dragon Handles, Dragon Finial, 12 In. 750.00
Vase, Archaic Style, Birds, 7 Loose Rings, Spinach Green, 11 In. 495.00
Vase, Farmer Mount, Foo Dog Finial, Crane & Foliage 4750.00

There are two types of jasperware. Some pieces have raised designs of white or a contrasting color made from colored clay. Other pieces are made by decorating the raised portions with a color.

JASPERWARE, see also various art potteries; Wedgwood
JASPERWARE, Box, Cupid Over Woman's Shoulder, Lavender, Green Border, 3 In. ... 125.00
Creamer, White, Queen Elizabeth I 25.00
Cup & Saucer, White Figures, Deep Blue, Saucer 5 1/4 In. 225.00
Hair Receiver, Adams, Dark Blue 75.00
Hair Receiver, Dark Blue, Horse & Hunt, Nickel Plated Top, Adams 75.00

Hair Receiver, Green, White, Heart Shaped, Bird, Floral 55.00
Match Holder, Cover, White Figures, Deep Blue, 3 3/4 In. 125.00
Plaque, Woman & Child, Celluloid Frame, Germany 16.50
Plaque, Woman, Butterfly Wings, Cupid, Green Border, 4 1/2 In. 125.00
Plate, Indian Smoking Peace Pipe, Green, 4 1/4 In. 25.00
Tile, Light Blue, Woman & Cherub, Japan, 3 7/8 X 3 1/16 In. 3.50

Jewelry, if made from gold and precious gems or plastic and colored glass, is still popular with collectors. Values are determined by the intrinsic value of the stones and metal and by the skill of the craftsmen and designers. Victorian and older jewelry have been popular since the 1950s. More recent interests are Art Deco and Edwardian styles, Mexican and Danish silver jewelry, and beads of all kinds. Copies of almost all styles are being made.

JEWELRY, Bar Pin, 4 Sapphires, Diamond, 14K Gold, Edwardian 1200.00
Bar Pin, Cameo, Enameled, 1930s 16.00
Bar Pin, Cat's Eye 55.00
Bar Pin, Victorian, Flower, Diamond, Onyx 412.00
Beads, Amber Glass, Art Deco, 35 In. 58.00
Beads, Ivory, Graduating Sizes, Ivory Clasp, American, 24 In. 40.00
Bracelet, 14K Gold, Rubies & Diamonds, Plaited Links, 1940 .... 4125.00
Bracelet, 3 Rows, Rhinestone, Weiss 40.00
Bracelet, 4 Pear-Shaped Jadeite Stones, 14K Yellow Gold, 1950s 165.00
Bracelet, 5 Carved Burmese Jadeite Cabochons, 14K Gold, C.1940 .... 4000.00
Bracelet, 7 Charms, Sewing Machine, Enamel Fish, Abacus, 14K Gold 275.00
Bracelet, 7 Oval Faceted Unfoiled Stones, Schiaparelli 75.00
Bracelet, Bangle, Celadon Jadeite, Chased Gilded Copper Mounts 1400.00
Bracelet, Bangle, Hinged, Pearls, Pierced Diamond, Victorian Style 660.00
Bracelet, Bangle, Lucien Iccard 18.00
Bracelet, Bangle, Sterling Silver, Georg Jensen, Curved Open Cuff 300.00
Bracelet, Bezel Set Cabochon Onyx Stone, Mexican Silver 45.00
Bracelet, Chanel Set Sapphire Links & Diamonds, 18K Gold 1300.00
Bracelet, Clear Round & Large Baguette Stones, Hobe, 3/4 In. 65.00
Bracelet, Coral Cameo Clasp, Chain Link, 14K Yellow Gold 200.00
Bracelet, Earrings, 18K Gold, Mother-of-Pearl, Diamond Plaques, 1920 .... 935.00
Bracelet, Faux Gemstones, Byzantine Type, Goldette Slide 50.00
Bracelet, Gold Links, Victorian 715.00
Bracelet, Hinged, 3 Red Stones, 2 Diamond Chips, 9K Gold, English 308.00
Bracelet, Interlocking Hearts, Sterling Silver, Signed Bent 95.00
Bracelet, Link, 14K Yellow Gold, 8 In. 425.00
Bracelet, Rhinestone Bows, Pearl Center, Hobe, 1 1/8 In.Wide 55.00
Bracelet, Rhinestone, Ice Blue, Schiaparelli 75.00
Bracelet, Rhinestone, Triple Row, Weiss 40.00
Bracelet, Scarab & Cultured Pearls, 14K Gold 175.00
Bracelet, Scottish Agate, Silver Mount, English, 1860, 7 1/2 In. 275.00
Bracelet, Scroll, 11 Circular Amethysts, Victorian 600.00
Bracelet, Silver & Onyx, Georg Jensen 80.00
Bracelet, Victorian Garter, Tricolor Clasp, Dated 1884 .... 150.00
Bracelet, White Onyx, Silver Bands, Bezel Set Stones, Mexican 45.00
Braclet, 14K Gold, Emerald, Diamond, Chevron Links, Schepps, 1945 .... 9900.00
Chain, 15K Yellow Gold, Interlocking, Belcher, 1860, 15 In. 850.00
Chain, Art Nouveau, Floral, Woman's Profile, Gold, 2-Strand, 30 In. 154.00
Chain, Art Nouveau, Silver, 2-Strand, Woman's Face Slide, 30 In. 187.00
Chain, Watch, 14K Gold, 41 In. .... 150.00 To 220.00
Chain, Watch, Large Links, Sterling Silver 375.00
Charm, Clarinet, 14K Gold 75.00
Chatelaine, Silver, Whistle, Dance Card Holder, Unger, 1911, 6 Piece 1500.00
Choker, Crystal, Drop, Haskell 85.00
Cigar Cutter, Birmingham, Gold, Knife Type, 1898, 1 1/2 In. 85.00
Cigar Cutter, El Roe-Tan Perfect Cigars 30.00
Cigar Cutter, Gold Filled, With Bottle Opener, Pocket 20.00
Clasp, Gold Filigree, Jade, Diamond, Edward Oakes, 1 In. 550.00
Clip, Draped Lady On Crescent Moon, Diamond In Hair, Pearls 175.00
Clip, Shield Shape, 54 Diamond Outlined, Platinum, 1930 .... 4950.00

Clip, T Shape, Gold, Sapphire, Diamond Border, Marcus & Co., 1940 .... 3850.00
Cuff Links, Mother–of–Pearl, Enameled, Seed Pearl Center, 1920s 275.00
Earrings, & 1 Pin, Chalcedony Gold, Victorian 1100.00
Earrings, 2 Beaded Balls, Chains, Tassels, 14K Gold, Victorian 350.00
Earrings, Art Deco, Step Cut Sapphire, Baguette Diamond 1760.00
Earrings, Clip, Green & White, Hobe 8.00
Earrings, Cloisonne Enamel Flowers, Cobalt Blue Ground, 14K Gold 120.00
Earrings, Dangle, Oval Cat's–Eye Stones, Screwbacks, 14K Gold 75.00
Earrings, Drop, Black Onyx Set With 95 Diamonds, 18K White Gold 3950.00
Earrings, Edwardian, Sapphire, Diamond, Chandelier Design, 1900 .... 9350.00
Earrings, Pave Diamonds, 14K Gold, Colored Cabochons, Clip–On 1200.00
Earrings, Rhinestone Crescent, Clip, Kenneth Lane, 2 In. 55.00
Earrings, Ruby, Diamond, Octagonal Cluster, Art Deco 1200.00
Fur Clip, Sterling Silver, Gilt, Napier 18.00
    JEWELRY, HATPIN, see Hatpin
    JEWELRY, INDIAN, see Indian
Lavalier, 1 Diamond, 2 Pearls 60.00
Lavalier, Chain, Pearl, 10K Yellow Gold 65.00
Locket, 18K Gold, Lock of Child's Hair, American, C.1810 .... 850.00
Locket, 8 Diamonds, 8 Sapphires, Heart Shape, 14K Gold Chain 200.00
Locket, Agate, Diamond Floret, Ruby, 14K Gold Swivel Bale, Victorian 1050.00
Locket, Heart Shape, 14K Yellow Gold, Monogram, Shreve 330.00
Muff Chain, Gold, 16 Sapphires Intervaled With Links, Victorian 1650.00
Necklace & Earrings, Black Oval Stones, Silver Beads, Schiaparelli 240.00
Necklace, 4 Strands of Garnet, Rose Quartz, 14K Gold Clasp, 18 In. 200.00
Necklace, Abalone, Diamond Shapes 125.00
Necklace, Amber Beads, Faceted, 18 In. 125.00
Necklace, Amber, Natural Shaped Gold & Brown, Transparent, 19 In. 65.00
Necklace, Art Nouveau, Gold, Lozenge Shape Synthetic Peridot 302.00
Necklace, Bakelite, Carved, Green & Cream, Art Deco, 16 In. 24.00
Necklace, Bakelite, Hanging Ink Bottle, Speller, Pen & Pencil, 1930s 45.00
Necklace, Center Oval Cabochon Citrine, Silver Griffins, Sterling 550.00
Necklace, Cherry Amber, Oval Beads, 16 In. 145.00
Necklace, Clear Stones, Chain, Eisenberg 75.00
Necklace, Crocheted, Venetian Bead Tassle, 1920s 28.00
Necklace, Crystal Beads, 4 Strands, Signed Laguna 55.00
Necklace, Enameled Eagle, Tourmaline, Silver Chain, 19th Century 525.00
Necklace, Freshwater Pearl Strands, Center Topaz, Rubies, 18K Gold 1300.00
Necklace, Fringe, Pink & Golden Topazes, 17 Drops, Victorian 700.00
Necklace, Goldstone Beads, Graduated, Gold Filled Clasp, 30 In. 60.00
Necklace, Green Agate, Sterling Silver, Georg Jensen, 1914, 14 In. 950.00
Necklace, Nouveau Face Pendant, Brass Chain, 1930s 45.00
Necklace, Opal & Diamond, 14K Gold, Serpents, C.1900 .... 880.00
Necklace, Pearls, Yellow Gold Floral & Diamond Shortener, 35 In. 440.00
Necklace, Pendant, Aquamarine, Diamond, Sapphire, Tiffany, 1940 .... 5500.00
Necklace, Pink & Lavender Crystal, 4 Strands, Haskell 75.00
Necklace, Star & Crescent Design, Diamond, Seed Pearl, Gold, 15 In. 330.00
Necklace, Tourmaline Chips, Foil Beads, Double Strand, 30 In. 40.00
Necklace, Victorian, 3 Emerald Pearls On Bars, Gold Scroll 275.00
Pendant, Agate Cameo, Etruscan Revival Frame, 15K Gold, Victorian 1150.00
Pendant, Baltic Amber, Carved Rose, Early 20th Century 375.00
Pendant, Black Bakelite Cameo, Yellow Bakelite Chain, Art Deco 38.00
Pendant, Bow, Diamond, European Style, 19th Century, Oval 3300.00
Pendant, Cameo, Encircled With Pearls, 10K Gold 90.00
Pendant, Cameo, Gold Chased Border, Georgian Chain, 1860s 1045.00
Pendant, Cameo, With Diamond, 14K Gold 140.00
Pendant, Gold, Carnelian Intaglio, Islamic, Mid–19th Century 198.00
Pendant, Heart Shaped Amethyst, Pearl, 1814 .... 660.00
Pendant, Lapis, 10 Rubies, 14K Gold 350.00
Pendant, Miniature Portrait, Young Man, American, C.1840, 1 1/4 In. 125.00
Pendant, Pin, Center Diamond, Surrounding Seed Pearls, 14K Gold 400.00
Pendant, Portrait, Gold Silver, Pearl Scroll, Late 19th Century 412.00
Pin & Earrings, Arrow Tip, Clear Rhinestones, Eisenberg 125.00
Pin & Earrings, Grape Cluster, Sterling Silver, G.Jensen, Wendel 225.00

Pin & Earrings, Onyx, Half Pearl Strap, Victorian 660.00
Pin & Earrings, Rhinestones, Around Faux Pearl, Art Deco, Valjean 16.00
Pin, 14K Gold, Black Opal Center, Diamonds, Enameled, 1900 .... 5500.00
Pin, Art Nouveau, Baroque Seed Pearls, Center Diamond, 14K Gold 275.00
Pin, Art Nouveau, Bird Within Green Enamel Leaves 150.00
Pin, Balloon, Rose Cut Rubies, Diamonds, 2 Figures, French 3465.00
Pin, Berries, Sterling Silver Leaves, Danecraft, 2 1/2 In. 45.00
Pin, Birds, In Flight, Sterling Silver, Rhinestone Bellies, Mazer 95.00
Pin, Bow Shape, Diamond, Sapphire, 2 Color 14K Gold, 1940 ....*Illus* 500.00
Pin, Bracelet & Earrings, Blue Shades, Prongs, Signed Weiss 55.00
Pin, Cameo, 5 Diamonds, Yellow Gold Filigree, 14K Gold, 2 1/2 In. 150.00
Pin, Cameo, Black & White, Pearls, Victorian 800.00
Pin, Cameo, Brown & White, Gold, Pearls & Locket Back, 1890s 1045.00
Pin, Christmas Tree, Clear Rhinestones, Gold Plate, Mylu, 2 1/2 In. 20.00
Pin, Cinnabar, Set In Silver, Marked China 45.00
Pin, Cross Shape, Pearl At Center, 14K Gold, 2 1 1/2 In. 110.00
Pin, Dogwood, Sterling Silver, Kalo, 1 3/4 In. 175.00
Pin, Dove, Gold, Turquoise Leaf Spray, French, 19th Century 350.00
Pin, Dragon, Foil, Cloisonne 60.00
Pin, Edwardian, Platinum, Step Cut Aquamarine, Diamond, 1900 .... 995.00
Pin, Enameled Religious Portrait, Seed Pearls, 19th Century 121.00
Pin, Fish, Sterling Silver, Abalone, Mexican 15.00
Pin, Gold Ribbon Scroll, Opal, Emerald, With Pendant, Victorian 275.00
Pin, Gold Scroll, Pearl Sprays, Pendant Drop Hook, 1870s 412.00
Pin, Gold, Black Tracery, Fringe Terminal, Victorian 250.00
Pin, Gold, Circular, Black Enameled, Half Pearl, Victorian 220.00
Pin, Illinois Bell Employee, 2 Diamonds, 1 Ruby, Bell Symbol 75.00
Pin, Insect, Rhinestone Trim, Spring Wings, Hattie Carnegie, 2 In. 60.00
Pin, Irish Wolfhound, Sterling Silver, Gilt, Monet, 1960s, 2 1/2 In. 60.00
Pin, Ivory, Faux Amber Center, Gold Metal, Yves St.Laurent, 2 In. 65.00
Pin, Key Shape, Silver, Semiprecious Stones, Foster, 3 1/2 In. 1100.00
Pin, Leaf, Faux Aquamarine Center, Haskell, 2 In. 45.00
Pin, Man's Portrait, 18th–Century Dress, 14K Yellow Gold Frame 250.00
Pin, Maple Leaves, Silver, Openwork, Silver Beads, Mary Gage, 2 In. 200.00
Pin, Onyx Coral, Pearl Blister Drop, Black Enameled, 1890s 385.00
Pin, Oval Cabochon Garnet, Gold, Box Chain Swag, Victorian 425.00
Pin, Peacock, Gold, Ruby, Pearl Breast & Neck, 1920 .... 950.00
Pin, Pear Shaped Pendant, Victorian, Gold, 2 In. 55.00
Pin, Peridot, 14K Yellow Gold, Gillot & Co., 1917, Fitted Box 1300.00
Pin, Pierced Foliate, Diamond, Emerald, 14K Gold, Edwardian 1900.00
Pin, Platinum, Diamond Filigree, Sapphire Arcs, 1920 .... 1210.00
Pin, Rhinestone Flower, Pink Aurora Borealis, Weiss, 2 1/2 In. 35.00
Pin, Rhinestones, Leaf Design, Ceil Chapman 25.00
Pin, Rock Crystal, Edwardian, Etched Maiden & Angels, 14K Gold 725.00
Pin, Saber Shape, Silver, Stones In Handle, Mary Gage, 5 1/4 In. 150.00
Pin, Sapphire & Diamond, Enameled, Oval, 2 In. 2530.00
Pin, Sapphire, Diamond, Silver & Gold Mount, Mid–19th Century 3575.00
Pin, Satsuma On Silver, Gold Enameled Dragons, 1 3/4 In. 150.00

Jewelry, Pin, Bow Shape,
Diamond, Sapphire, 2
Color 14K Gold, 1940

If you wear antique jewelry, check the claw settings to be sure the prongs are not worn or loose. It is cheaper to be careful than to replace lost stones.

Pin, Satsuma, Samurai Warriors, Marked, 1 1/4 In. 50.00
Pin, Seed Pearl, Onyx, Victorian 385.00
Pin, Shell Cameo, Classical Head, Silver, Signed, Dated 1935 .... 85.00
Pin, Shell Cameo, Sterling Silver Frame, Marcasites, 1 1/2 In. 165.00
Pin, Shell, Paste, Pinchback, C.1870 .... 75.00
Pin, Starburst, Amber, Green, Hobe, Dated 1965, Large 45.00
Pin, Sunburst, Seed Pearl, 14K Gold, Pendant Attachment, 1 1/2 In. 165.00
Pin, Tassel, Victorian, 18K Gold, Pearls, Black Enameled, 2 1/2 In. 475.00
Pin, Victorian, Branch With Leaves, Movable Rose, Diamonds, Pearl 1265.00
Ring, Aquamarine, Sapphires & Diamonds Surround, Gold, 1940 .... 2530.00
Ring, Art Deco, Square Center Emerald, 22 Diamonds, 14K Gold 1430.00
Ring, Art Nouveau, Sleeping Woman Shape, Gold 303.00
Ring, Carved Flower Amethyst, 18K Yellow Gold 200.00
Ring, Checkerboard Design, Rubies & Diamonds, 1890s 1760.00
Ring, Cocktail, 4K Rubies, 1K Diamond, Platinum, C.1940 .... 975.00
Ring, Diamond Cluster, Gold, Cabochon Opal, Garnet, Victorian 770.00
Ring, Diamond Cluster, Square, 14K White Gold, C.1900 .... 350.00
Ring, Diamond Cluster, Turquoise Cabochon, 1890s, Oval 770.00
Ring, Diamond, 2 Square Cut Synthetic Sapphires, Victorian 143.00
Ring, Diamond, Hexagonal Setting, Victorian 660.00
Ring, Edwardian, Burma Oval Ruby, Circle of Diamonds, 18K Gold 2200.00
Ring, Emerald & Diamond Rectangular Cluster, Edwardian, 1910 .... 8000.00
Ring, Gold, Star Sapphire, Rubies & Diamonds Surround, 1940 .... 1760.00
Ring, Man's, Alexandrite, 10K Gold, C.1960 .... 385.00
Ring, Man's, Maple Leaf, 14K Gold Coin 265.00
Ring, Masonic, Rectangular Black Onyx, 10k Gold, Size 8 .... 60.00
Ring, Onyx, Rose Diamond, Geometric Shape, Art Deco 325.00
Ring, Oval Emerald, Diamond, Platinum, Edwardian, Gorham 2700.00
Ring, Platinum, Ruby, Diamond Shoulders, Black Enameled, Art Deco 990.00
Ring, Silver & Onyx, Georg Jensen 80.00
Ring, Silver, French, Black Onyx, Rectangular, Signed Jean Despres 3575.00
Ring, Silver, French, Gold, Coral, Square, Signed Jean Despres 2750.00
Ring, Woman's, Diamond, 18K White Gold Floral Setting, 1910 .... 1760.00
Ring, Woman's, Garnet, Sterling Silver Band 85.00
Ring, Woman's, Platinum, Leaf Shape, Sapphires, Openwork, 1920 .... 3190.00
Ring, Woman's, Ruby, Art Deco, Square Platinum Mount, Diamonds 3575.00
Ring, Yellow Gold, Platinum, 12 Brilliant Diamond, Sapphires, 1940 .... 990.00
Slide Chain, Lady's Watch, Curb Links, Pearls, Turquoise, C.1896 .... 395.00
Stickpin, Cameo, 10K Gold, 3/4 In. 40.00
Stickpin, Floral, 4 Seed Pearls, Diamond, Gold 55.00
Stickpin, Garnet & Pearl, 10K Gold 32.00
Stickpin, Gold Color, Deer Leaping Over Plow 18.00
Stickpin, Sterling Silver, Sword Handle Head 10.00
Stickpin, Wishbone, Amethyst 55.00
JEWELRY, WATCH, see Watch

 John Rogers statues were made from 1859 to 1892. The originals were bronze, but the thousands of copies made by the Rogers factory were of painted plaster. Eighty different figures were made. Similar painted plaster figures were made by some other factories. Never repaint a Rogers figure because this lowers the value to collectors.

JOHN ROGERS, Group, Checker Players 1500.00
Group, Coming To Parson 300.00
Group, Fighting Bob 1500.00
Group, First Love, Draped Classical Figures, 19 1/4 In. 300.00
Group, Football 1980.00
Group, George Washington 1300.00
Group, Photographer 1000.00
Group, Shakespeare Scene 695.00
Group, Taking The Oath 350.00
Group, Uncle Ned's School 1500.00

Any memorabilia that refers to the Jews or the Jewish religion is collected. Interests range from newspaper clippings that mention eighteenth- and nineteenth-century Jewish Americans to religious objects, such as menorahs or spice boxes. Age, condition, and the intrinsic value of the material, as well as the historic and artistic importance, determine the value.

JUDAICA, Box, Hebrew Script, Israel On Lid, Hinged, 3 X 4 In.	30.00
Bust, Bronze, Black, Semitic Man, Pais, Yarmulka, Israel, 5 In.	18.00
Kiddush Cup, Applied Turquoise	35.00
Lamp, Hanging, Sabbath, Drip Pan, Brass, 18 In.	50.00
Menorah, 19th Century, Brass, 19 In.	200.00
Painting, Machitonim Tanz, Wedding Dance, Couple, 14 X 18 In.	65.00
Painting, Rabbi, Otto Eichinger, 1922, 10 X 8 In.	775.00
Plaque, Hebrew Engraving, Camel, Trees, Countryside, Brass, 11 In.	55.00
Spice Container, Flower Form, Sterling Silver, Teppich	145.00
Torah Finials, Crown, Silver Bells, Marked JZ, Silver, 15 3/4 In.	1500.00
Torah Shield, Inscribed Tablets, Lion On Columns, Austrian, Silver	275.00
Tray, Hebrew Inscription, Copper, 4 1/2 In.	8.00

Jugtown Pottery refers to pottery made in North Carolina as far back as the 1750s. In 1915, Juliana and Jacques Busbee set up a training and sales organization for what they named "Jugtown Pottery." In 1921, they built a shop at Jugtown, North Carolina, and hired Ben Owen as a potter in 1923. The Busbees moved the village store where the pottery was sold and promoted to New York City. Juliana Busbee sold the New York store in 1926 and moved into a log cabin near the Jugtown Pottery. The pottery closed in 1958. It reopened and is still working near Seagrove, North Carolina.

JUGTOWN, Bean Pot, Cover	38.00
Bowl, Lava Glaze, Piecrust Rim, 6 In.	125.00
Bowl, Rice, 6 In.	30.00
Chamberstick, Orange	35.00
Jar, Frogskin, Large	40.00
Jug, Frogskin Glaze, 9 In.	85.00
Jug, Frogskin Luster Glaze, Handle, 6 1/2 In.	75.00
Pitcher, Cobalt Blue Design, Salt Glaze	120.00
Pitcher, Speckled Brown, Incised Design, Bulbous, Circle, 8 1/2 In.	62.00
Pot, Orange Glaze, Embossed, 4 In.	30.00
Vase, Chinese Translation, 7 In.	250.00
Vase, Embossed Handles, Chinese Blue, 8 In.	210.00

Kate Greenaway, who was a famous illustrator of children's books, drew pictures of children in high-waisted Empire dresses. She lived from 1846 to 1901. Her designs appear on china, glass, and other pieces. Figural napkin rings depicting the Greenaway children are also to be found listed under Napkin Ring, Figural.

KATE GREENAWAY, Almanac, 1892	75.00
Book, Painting, The Little Folks, Hard Cover	50.00
Figurine, Boy, Shaker, Porcelain	45.00
Toothpick, Boy, Triangle Base, Silver Plate, Tufts	225.00
Toothpick, Girl, Green Basket At Side	80.00

"Kauffmann" refers to the type of work done by Angelica Kauffmann, a painter and decorative artist for Adam Brothers in England between 1766 and 1781. She designed small-scale pictorial subjects in the neoclassic manner. Most porcelains signed "Kauffmann" were made in the 1800s. She did not do the artwork on all pieces signed with her name.

KAUFFMANN, Butter Chip	18.00
Cup & Saucer	15.00
Ewer, Maiden & Cupid In Reserve, Gold Maroon, 6 In.	195.00
Humidor, Pewter Top, Signed, 6 1/2 In.	225.00

Plate, Queen Louise, Beehive Mark, 10 In. 110.00
Vase, Pastoral Scenes Both Sides, Meissen, 1730–63, 12 In. 275.00
Vase, Portrait, Flowers, Pearlized Ground, Signed, 10 1/2 In. 100.00
    KAYSERZINN, see Pewter

KELVA   Kelva glassware was made by the C. F. Monroe Company of Meriden, Connecticut, about 1904. It is a pale, pastel–painted glass decorated with flowers, designs, or scenes. Kelva resembles Nakara and Wave Crest, two other glasswares made by the same company.

KELVA, Box, Cover, Embossed Rococo, Large Pink Roses, 4 X 8 In. 1165.00
Box, Hinged Cover, Pink, White Flowers, Marked, 8 In. 650.00
Box, Jewelry, Mauve, Flowers 425.00
Box, Jewelry, Mottled Ground, Pink Apple Blossom, Signed, 6 In. 160.00
Box, Jewelry, Pink Flowers, Blue, 5 1/2 In. 475.00
Box, Pink Flowers, Blue–Gray Ground, Mirror In Lid, 4 1/2 In. 510.00
Box, Watch, Blue Floral, Beaded 270.00
Humidor, Cigar 550.00
Jar, Dresser, Pink Roses, Mottled Green, C.F.Monroe, 6 In. 600.00
Jar, Powder, Pink Ground, White Lily Design, 1870, 4 In. 660.00
Jewelry Box, Hinged Cover, Azaleas, Lined, Signed, 4 1/4 In. 335.00
Pin Tray, Ormolu Handles, Hexagonal 235.00
Powder Jar, White Lily Design, Satin Glass 600.00
Vase, Pink Flowrs, Green Ground, 13 1/2 In. 600.00

Kemple glass was made by John Kemple of East Palestine, Ohio, and Kenova, West Virginia, from 1945 to 1970. The glass was made from old molds. Many designs and colors were made. Kemple pieces are usually marked with a "K" ón the bottom. Many milk glass pieces were made with or without the mark.

KEMPLE, Pitcher, Water, Ivy & Snow, Milk Glass 65.00

The Kenton Hills Pottery made art wares, including vases and figurines that resembled Rookwood, probably because so many of the original artists and workmen had worked at the Rookwood plant.

KENTON HILLS, Lamp, Lotus Design, Peach Beige, Pear Shape, Hentschel, 12 In. 350.00

KEW-BLAS

Kew Blas is the name used by the Union Glass Company of Somerville, Massachusetts. The name refers to an iridescent golden glass made from the 1890s to 1924. The iridescent glass was reminiscent of the Tiffany glass of the period.

KEW BLAS, Compote, Iridescent Gold, Pink Highlights, 6 1/2 X 7 In. 495.00
Sherbet, Favrile Glass, 3 In. 66.00
Tumbler, Gold Luster, Pinched, Signed, 4 In. 235.00
Vase, Green, Gold Pulled Feather Design, Ivory Ground, 6 In. 550.00
Vase, Pulled Design On White Ground, Gold Interior, 5 1/2 In. 750.00
Vase, Zipper, Rose Bowl Shape, Green & Gold, Signed, 4 1/2 In. 575.00

Kewpies, designed by Rose O'Neill, were first pictured in the "Ladies' Home Journal." The pixielike figures were a success, and Kewpie dolls started appearing in 1911. Kewpie pictures and other items soon followed. Collectors search for all items that picture the little winged people.

KEWPIE, Bell, Figural, Kewpie Handle, Gold Paint 165.00
Brush & Comb, Joseph Kallus 38.00
Camera, No.3, Conley 25.00
Celluloid, Rose O'Neill, 1913 Label 40.00
Charm, Carved Bone 35.00
Clock, Tumbling Kewpies, Floral, German Works, Signed O'Neill 395.00
Creamer, Jasperware, Blue, Signed 165.00
Dish, Soup 145.00
Display, Cardboard, Kewpie, Says Drink Smile, 6 In. 3.50
Doll Set, Bisque, Lefton, 5 In., Set of 3 .... 14.00
Doll, Bisque Head, Composition Body, Rose O'Neill 4125.00

Doll, Bisque, Jointed, Heart On Chest, Signed, 5 In. 165.00
Doll, Bisque, Reclining, O'Neill, 3 1/2 In. 85.00
Doll, Bisque, Signed, Heart Stamp, Rose O'Neill, 5 1/2 In. 225.00
Doll, Black Girl & Boy, Matching School Clothes, 12 In., Pair 47.50
Doll, Black, Celluloid, Rose O'Neill, Signed, Dated 1913, 2 3/4 In. 110.00
Doll, Boy & Girl, Cheerleader Clothes, Jesco, 16 In., Pair 42.50
Doll, Bride & Groom, Bridal Clothes, Action, Blue Wing, 4 1/2 In., Pr. 500.00
Doll, Bride & Groom, Cameo, Jesco, 16 In., Pair 67.50
Doll, Brother, Black, School Clothes, Jesco, 12 In. 27.50
Doll, Cameo, Red Dress, Clothes, Box, 1960 .... 95.00
Doll, Chalkware, Signed, Painted, 4 In. 12.00
Doll, Chariot & Doves, 4 In. 2800.00
Doll, Composition, Jointed, Movable Arms & Legs, Crazed Face 50.00
Doll, Fireman Masquerade Costume, Jesco, 12 In. 27.50
Doll, Hugging, Bisque, Japan, 2 1/2 In. 65.00
Doll, Ice Skating, Olympic Winner, Cameo, Vinyl, JLK, 12 In. 50.00
Doll, Marked Kewpie Gal, Red & White Christmas Dress, 14 In. 85.00
Doll, Ragsy, 8 In. 29.00
Doll, Ring Bearer & Flower Girl, Cameo, Jesco, 12 In., Pair 57.50
Doll, School Outfit, Jesco, 16 In. 37.50
Doll, Seated, Thumb Sucker, Bisque, Stamped KW 288 .... 60.00
Doll, Sleeper, Clothes, Tag, Box, Cameo 85.00
Doll, Sunbonnet, Cameo, 11 1/2 In. 45.00
Doll, Thinker, Vinyl, Cameo, 6 In. 20.00
Doll, Traveler, With Doodle Dog 850.00
Doll, Way Down Home Country Clothes, Jesco, 8 In. 15.00
Figurine, At Tea Table, 4 1/4 In. 3300.00
Figurine, Celluloid, Rose O'Neill, 1913 Label 40.00
Figurine, Chalkware, 5 In. 15.00
Figurine, Doodle Dog, 3 In. 1200.00
Figurine, Farmer, With Rake, Box, 5 1/4 In. 950.00
Figurine, In Basket, 3 In. 950.00
Figurine, Sweeper, 4 1/4 In. 495.00
Figurine, With Drum, 3 1/2 In. 3200.00
Figurine, With Guitar, Bud Base, 5 1/4 In. 650.00
Figurine, With Ladybug & Basket, 4 1/4 In. 2500.00
Graduation Dress, Rose O'Neill, Pair 125.00
Match Holder 70.00
Matchbook, Advertising 20.00
Mold, Candy, Kewpies, Cast Iron, 6 X 10 In. 150.00
Paperweight, Metal 35.00
Perfume Bottle, Germany 35.00
Pitcher, 7 Kewpies, Blossoms Top, Blue Ground, O'Neill, 2 1/2 In. 200.00
Plaque, 3 Figures, Butterflies, Crescent Shape, Signed Rose O'Neill 265.00
Plate, Box, 1973, 8 In. 10.00
Plate, Bread 145.00
Poster, Unopened, Rose O'Neill, 1960 .... 25.00
Sheet Music, Kewpies & The Aeroplane 50.00
Stickpin, Gardener 100.00
Tea Set, Germany, 10 Piece 600.00
Vase, Bud, Doll Holding Teddy Bear, Bisque, 4 In. 400.00
Vase, Candlestick, Pewter Finish, 8 In. 250.00

       KIMBALL, see Cluthra
       KING'S ROSE, see Soft Paste

 All types of kitchen utensils, from eggbeaters to bowls, are collected today. Handmade wooden and metal items, like ladles and apple peelers, were made in the early nineteenth century. Mass–produced pieces, like iron apple peelers and graniteware, were made in the nineteenth century. Other kitchen wares are listed under manufacturers' names or under Iron; Advertising; Tool; or Wooden.

       KITCHEN, SALT & PEPPER, see Salt & Pepper
KITCHEN, Apple Corer, Bone, Mennonite, 1800–39 .... 45.00
     Apple Corer, Tapered Hollow Blade, T Bar Handle, 6 1/2 In. 13.00

Apple Dryer	75.00
Auger, Fruit, Sugar Devil, Wood Turned Bar Handle	150.00
Baker, Potato, Rumford, Tin, 1909	45.00
Baller, Melon, Green Wood Handle, Makes 1 1/4 In.Balls	2.50
Beater Jar, Brown Stripe, Wautoma, Wisconsin	45.00
Biscuit Pricker, Twisted Wire, 4 1/2 In.	65.00
Board, Bread, Pig Shape, Relief Carving 1 Side, 13 1/4 In.	300.00
Board, Bread, Pine, Paddle Shape, 8 X 17 In.	45.00
Board, Bread, Rectangular, Gooseneck, Munsing	22.00
Board, Bread, Round, Carved, Welcome, Wheat Design	75.00
Board, Bread, Wooden, Bread Carved On Rim, 11 In.	32.00
Board, Cookie, 4–Part Design, Cast Pewter, 3 3/8 X 4 In.	65.00
Board, Cookie, Goose, Sheep, Rooster, 3 1/2 X 1/2 In.	175.00
Board, Cookie, Pine, Almond Shaped Pewter Insert, F.B., 4 X 9 In.	575.00
Board, Cutting, Maple Speckle Burl, Shaped Handle, 1820, 8 X 13 In.	165.00
Board, Noodle, Pennsylvania, Handing Handle, Round, 16 In.	67.00
Board, Springerle, 6 Patterns, Cherry, 1800s, 3 1/2 X 6 1/2 In.	130.00
Boiler, Double, Blue & White, Enamel	15.00
Bowl, Dough, Wooden, C.1870, 18 In.	125.00
Bowl, Herb Masher, Treenware, Handle, C.1870, 4 X 2 In.	42.25
Bowl, Mustard Inside & Out, 18th Century, 17 5/8 X 7 1/2 In.	695.00
Bowl, Stove Top Candy Making, Copper	400.00
Bowl, Wooden, Almond Shape, Tab Handles, Brown, Varnished, 26 X 6 In.	250.00
Box, Dough, Cover, Breadboard Ends, Gray Paint, 23 3/4 In.	105.00
Box, Dough, Cover, Poplar, 33 In.	55.00
Box, Dough, Mortised & Pinned Apron, Poplar, 26 3/4 X 36 In.	250.00
Box, Dough, Traces of Green Paint, 42 In.	95.00
Box, Pantry, Butter Carrier, Wire Bail, Wooden Handle, 9 1/2 In.	165.00
Box, Pantry, Wooden, Red, 18 X 10 In.	175.00
Box, Salt, Slant Lid, Leather Hinges, Red Paint, C.1850, 7 X 12 In.	140.00
Box, Scouring, Hanging, Old Red, Poplar, 10 3/4 X 16 1/4 In.	155.00
Bread Mixer, Universal, Tin, Bucket Shape	35.00
Breadbox, Cattail, 2–Door, Tin	60.00
Broom Holder, Iron	80.00
Bucket, Lard, Wooden, Unusual Lid	20.00
Burner, Alcohol, Dated 1904	25.00
KITCHEN, BUTTER MOLD, see Kitchen, Mold, Butter	
Butter Paddle, Blade Drilled With Small Holes, 10 In.	65.00
Butter Paddle, Square Blade, Primitive Hex Signs On Handle, 11 In.	95.00
Butter Stamp, 5 Labels Louella, Marks Quantity, 2 1/2 X 23 In.	165.00
Butter Stamp, Acorn, 2 Large Leaves, Hand Carved, C.1880, 3 1/4 In.	95.00
Butter Stamp, Chip Carved Floral Design, 4 1/2 X 6 In. ....55.00 To	150.00
Butter Stamp, Cow, Boxwood Maple, Knob Handle, 1800, 1 5/8 In.	190.00
Butter Stamp, Cow, Geometric Border, Turned Handle, 4 In.	350.00
Butter Stamp, Cow, Knob Handle, 3 In.	190.00
Butter Stamp, Cow, Knob Handle, Birch, Hand Carved	395.00
Butter Stamp, Daisy & 2 Leaves, Plunger & Case, Early 1800s	95.00
Butter Stamp, Daisy & Acorn, 3 In.	95.00
Butter Stamp, Double Pattern, Tree & Leaves, Oval, 4 3/4 In.	395.00
Butter Stamp, Double Sheaf of Wheat, Hand Carved, 1800s, 2 X 3 In.	85.00
Butter Stamp, Double Strawberry, 2 X 2 In.	110.00
Butter Stamp, Eagle, Knob Handle, C.1820, 4 In.	395.00
Butter Stamp, Eagle, With Shield, Conger, N.Y., 3 1/8 X 3 3/8 In.	250.00
Butter Stamp, Lollipop, Cow, Primitive, Scrubbed Finish, 9 1/4 In.	450.00
Butter Stamp, Lollipop, Geometric Cross, 4 X 8 In.	170.00
Butter Stamp, Plain Imprint, Wooden, Plunger, 5 3/4 X 3 X 4 In.	14.50
Butter Stamp, Pressed Glass, Sheaf Design, 4 5/8 In.	85.00
Butter Stamp, Rayed Design, Round, Turned Handle, 7 In.	65.00
Butter Stamp, Rose, Cased, 2 X 1 1/2 In.	55.00
Butter Stamp, Semicircular, Stylized Floral Design, 3 1/2 X 7 In.	215.00
Butter Stamp, Sheaf of Wheat, Cherrywood, Early 1800s, 4 1/4 In.	95.00
Butter Stamp, Sheaf of Wheat, Round, 4 1/2 In.	130.00
Butter Stamp, Sheaf of Wheat, Turned Handle, Wooden, 4 1/4 In.	75.00
Butter Stamp, Strawberry, Brass Hanger, 4 1/8 In.	115.00

Butter Stamp, Stylized Pineapple, Turned Handle, 3 7/8 In. 65.00
Butter Stamp, Stylized Tulip, Wooden, 3 3/4 In. 95.00
Butter Stamp, Thistle & Leaves, Plunger, Wooden, 3 1/2 In. 55.00
Butter Stamp, Thistle, Hand Carved, Beveled Handle, 4 In. 295.00
Butter Stamp, Thistle, Turned Handle, 4 In. 75.00
Butter Stamp, Top of Crock, Cow In Bushes, 1 Piece Wood, Knob, 5 In. 30.00
Butter Stamp, Tulip, Ephrata Cloisters, C.1800, 4 1/4 In. 350.00
Butter Stamp, Wooden Knob Handle, Fleur-De-Lis, 4 In. 85.00
Cake Pan, Swans Down Cake Flour, Tin, Square, 8 X 2 In. 4.00
Can Opener & Corkscrew, King, Pat.1885 .... 4.50
Can Opener, Bull's Head, Iron, Iron Handle, English 22.00
Can Opener, Bull's Head, Wood Handle, English 26.00
Can Opener, Bull, Looped Tail Handle, Iron, 1850, 6 In. 28.00
Can Opener, Cow Handle, Cast Iron, 6 1/2 In. 10.00
Can Opener, Keen Kutter, 1893 .... 28.00
Can Opener, W.R.A.Company, Winchester Logo, Steel Blade 35.00
Canister, Marked Sugar, Blue Stenciled Design, Germany, 4 X 6 In. 35.00
Cap Lifter, Miracle Vacuum Jar 3.00
Cheese Ladder, Mortised & Pinned, Beveled, Handle Top, 44 In. 150.00
Cherry Pitter, Enterprise, Double .... 28.00 To 40.00
Cherry Pitter, Enterprise, No.1 .... 42.00
Cherry Pitter, Enterprise, No.18, Pat.1903 .... 32.00
Cherry Pitter, Goodell Co. 28.00
Cherry Pitter, Scott, Table Top, 4-Legged, Iron, 12 In. 77.00
Chopper, Double Blade, Green Handle 8.00
Chopper, Food, Double Blade, Wooden Handle 13.00
Chopper, Food, Maple Handle, Cast Iron Shank 22.00
Chopper, Food, S-Shaped Sides, Hand Forged Iron & Steel, 6 X 7 In. 150.00
Chopper, Food, Steel, W.Greaves & Sons, Wooden Handle 16.00
Chopper, Hand Forged Iron, Fastened To Thick Pine Board 48.00
Chopper, Incised Lines, Brass Ferrule, Steel Blade, Maple, 4 1/2 In. 40.00
Chopper, Nutmeat, Jar, Metal Top, 4 Chopper Measuring, Mechanical 6.00
Chopper, Onion, Federal, Red Handle, Label 15.00
Chopper, Parsley, Rotary Style, Tin Cup, Red Wood Handle, Parsilette 8.00
Chopper, Pumpkin, Hand Crank, Patent 1869 .... 350.00
Chopper, Single Blade, Natural Wood Handle, 6 In. 6.50
Chopper, Slaw, Red & Yellow Striping, Crank Handle, Tin & Cast Iron 140.00
Churn, Brass Bands, Porcelain Handles On Lid, Dasher, 23 In. 150.00
Churn, Chip Carved, Red Brown, Turned Legs & Spindles, 46 In. 225.00
Churn, Davis Swing, Mustard Paint, Vermont Machine Co. 350.00
Churn, Dazey No.10, 1 Qt. .... 750.00 To 1200.00
Churn, Dazey, 4 Qt. 40.00
Churn, Dazey, St.Louis, Clear, Embossed In Circle, 1 Qt. 585.00
Churn, Dog Powered Treadmill Type 400.00
Churn, Gem Dandy, Electric, Alabama Mfg.Co., Cow Jar, Metal, 16 In. 35.00
Churn, Glass, Red Metal Cover & Paddles, 1 Gal. 30.00
Churn, Glass, Wooden Paddle, 2 Qt. 20.00
Churn, Hanging, Wooden, 29 X 5 In. 85.00
Churn, Interlocking Laps, Old Red Paint, Standing, 19 In. 200.00
Churn, Lid, Stave Construction, Hand Crank, 14 In. 85.00
Churn, Metal Bands, Turned Wooden Lid, Dasher With Rod, Blue, 19 In. 275.00
Churn, Pine, Barrel 300.00
Churn, Presto, 1 Qt. 95.00
Churn, Presto, 2 Qt. 70.00
Churn, R.M.Fenner, Hand Crank 45.00
Churn, Stave Constructed, Red Paint, 19 1/2 In. 165.00
Churn, Swing, Davis, Black Stenciling, Dated 1879, 3 1/2 Ft. 425.00
Churn, Wapakoneta, Barrel, Decals 275.00
Churn, Wooden, Tiffin Union Churn No.2, Pat.1864, 20 X 14 X 33 In. 240.00
Cleaver, Meat, Hand Forged Iron, 13 In. 175.00
Cleaver, Meat, W.Brady, Wooden Handle, 18 In. 22.00
Clothes Sprinkler, Century, Aluminum 5.00
Clothes Washer, Portable, Porcelain, 1934, 5 Gal. 45.00
Clothespin, Diamond, Wooden, 30 Per Package 8.00

KITCHEN, COFFEE GRINDER, see Coffee Grinder

Coffee Maker, Silex, Glass, 1938, Box	20.00
Coffee Set, Bakelite Trim, Tray, Spoon, Manning Bowman, 1925, 5 Piece	85.00
Coffeepot, George Washington, Electric	22.00
Coffeepot, Porcelain, Blue & White, Blue Onion Type Design	100.00
Coffeepot, White Enameled, Scalloped Metal Trim Around Lid	125.00
Collander, Porcelain, White, Black Trim, Large	45.00
Corer & Peeler, Apple, Bonanza, Goodell, N.H., 16 X 18 In.	215.00
Corer & Scraper, Red Wood Handle, Wizard	3.00
Corer, Apple, Bulbous Handle, Metal Blade, Oak, C.1880	22.00
Corer, Apple, Green Wood Handle, A & P English Co.	4.00
Corn Sheller, Table Mount, Little Iowa, Cast Iron	20.00
Cover, Fly Screen, Dome Shape, Nest of 4	460.00
Cover, Food, Gray, Tin, Black Wood Knob, 1900, 10 In.	22.00
Cream Can, Sherman White Co., Greenville, Ohio, 5 Gal.	47.50
Cream Shipper, 4 Looped Legs, Crank Handle, Lid, Tin	85.00
Creamer, German Cooking Ware	29.00
Cup, Measuring, Kellogg, Glass, Green	18.00
Cup, Measuring, Rumford, Keen Kutter	11.00
Cup, Measuring, Spry	5.00
Cutter, Biscuit, Cottolene, Tin, Ring Handle	7.00
Cutter, Biscuit, Darr's Baking Powder	5.00
Cutter, Biscuit, Rumford Baking Powder	14.00
Cutter, Cabbage, 3 Blades, Indianapolis Sanitary Kraut Cutter, 1908	40.00
Cutter, Cabbage, 6 X 16 In.	9.00
Cutter, Cabbage, Box, Large	75.00
Cutter, Cabbage, Dovetailed Box, 3 Ft.	33.00
Cutter, Cabbage, Pine, 25 In.	22.00
Cutter, Cabbage, Pine, 8 1/2 X 20 In.	30.00
Cutter, Cabbage, Queen	17.50
Cutter, Cookie, Arrow, Tin, 4 In.	4.00
Cutter, Cookie, Bear, Tin	8.00
Cutter, Cookie, Bird, Aluminum, 4 3/4 In.	3.00
Cutter, Cookie, Camel, Aluminum, Strap Handle	4.00
Cutter, Cookie, Chicken, Lapped Edge, 2 3/4 X 3 In.	8.00
Cutter, Cookie, Christmas Tree, Strap Handle, 3 In.	2.50
Cutter, Cookie, Cow	14.00
Cutter, Cookie, Crescent, Tin	3.00
Cutter, Cookie, Dog, Flat Tin, Soldered Handle	12.00
Cutter, Cookie, Duck, Flat Tin, Soldered Handle	12.00
Cutter, Cookie, Fish, Strap Handle, Tin	18.00
Cutter, Cookie, Flower Form, 9 Petal, Tin, 3 3/8 In.	7.00
Cutter, Cookie, Gingerbread Boy, Aluminum, Handle, 6 In.	4.00
Cutter, Cookie, Hatchet, Strap Handle, 1830, 5 X 6 X 8 1/2 In.	85.00
Cutter, Cookie, Heart, Flat Tin, Soldered Handle	12.00
Cutter, Cookie, Horse, Tin, 4 1/2 In.	105.00
Cutter, Cookie, Indian, Tin, 8 In.	35.00
Cutter, Cookie, Lamb, Aluminum, 4 In.	3.50
Cutter, Cookie, Lion, Aluminum, Strap Handle, 3 In.	2.50
Cutter, Cookie, Multiple, Easter Designs, Oval, Tin, 7 5/8 X 11 In.	85.00
Cutter, Cookie, Pig, Strap Handle, Tin	18.00
Cutter, Cookie, Rabbit, Aluminum, 4 In.	3.00
Cutter, Cookie, Rabbit, Standing, Gray, Tin, 2 1/2 X 2 1/2 In.	10.00
Cutter, Cookie, Scalloped Mint Leaves, Strap Handle, Tin, 2 1/2 In.	130.00
Cutter, Cookie, Shamrock, Tin	15.00
Cutter, Cookie, Sheep, Tin	8.00
Cutter, Cookie, Standing Chick, Tin, 1930s, 2 1/4 X 2 3/4 In.	10.00
Cutter, Cookie, Star, Tin, 3 In.	4.00
Cutter, Cookie, Turkey, Aluminum, 4 In.	3.00
Cutter, Cookie, Violin, Tin, Flat Back, C.1830, 5 1/2 In.	55.00
Cutter, Cookie, Woman, Hands On Hips, Apron, 8 In.	500.00
Cutter, Doughnut, Flower Form, Gray, Tin, Scalloped	10.00
Cutter, French Fries, Ecko, 10 In.	12.00
Cutter, Noodle, Cast Iron, 10 In.	225.00

COLLECTIBLES UNDER $100

FISHER-PRICE TOYS

Many will remember "Buzzy Bee," "Snoopy Sniffer," "Teddy Bear Zilo," and "Corn Popper," the children's colorful and noisy wooden pull toys. Prices for the not-too-old toys by Fisher-Price are zooming, but some can still be found for under $100 if you go to

Teddy Bear Zilo, a 10½-inch high Fisher-Price wooden and paper toy sells for about $150. It was first made in the 1940s.

Gabby Goofies were introduced by Fisher-Price in 1956 and the design was updated in 1963. This is the later version.

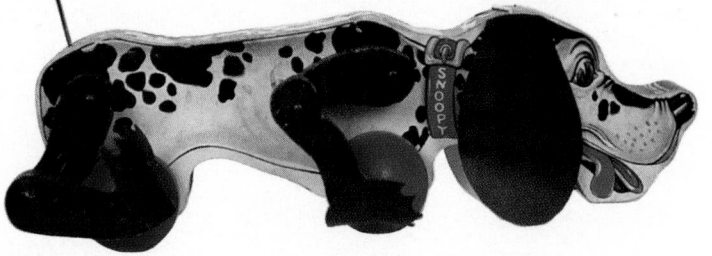

Snoopy Sniffer, a Fisher-Price toy made from 1938.

house sales and flea markets. Fisher-Price was founded in 1931 in East Aurora, New York. The toys were made from Ponderosa pine and decorated with permanently laminated paper lithographs. Collectors can date their toys from the appearance and the logo. The first few toys were marked "Fisher-Price Toy, Pat. Applied For." Later, each wooden toy was identified by a black and white square logo enclosing the name. The logo was changed in 1956 to the initails "FP" in a rectangle. There have been several other logo changes. Plastic was not used on any toys until 1949. The most familiar toys are pull toys that made music or noise. The company also made plain painted wooden toys, movable animals made of wooden beads on strings, and "pop-up kritters." Educational toys with many parts to be put together or counted, trucks, carpet sweepers, and Disney character toys were also produced. Value is determined by the condition and rarity. Teddy Zilo sells for $50; Mickey Mouse puddle jumper, $80; Merry Mousewife, $25; but some rare toys are already at $500. More information can be found in *Fisher-Price 1931-1963: A Historical, Rarity, Value Guide* by John J. Murray & Bruce R. Fox (Books Americana, Florence, AL, $16.95).

HEAD VASES

Collectors have not decided what to call this collectible. Some want to call them "lady head vases," some "pot heads," some "head vases," which is the name we use in this edition of the price book. In the late 1930s and 1940s, a few head-shaped vases were made to hold florists' arrangements. They were popular and large numbers of the head vases were made in the 1950s and 1960s. Today, there are still new examples to be found in gift shops and mail-order catalogs. The hair style of the lady's head often helps to date the vases. Collectors soon learn to differentiate the Betty Grable look of the forties from the Gidget look of the sixties. Vases and planters were made to resemble heads of men, women, teen-age girls, babies, famous people, Orientals, madonnas, clowns, and even animals. Special features that enhance the value are real-fake pearl jewelry, elaborate hat styles, Oriental heads, and examples by known makers. Look for Enesco, Lefton, Napco, and Inarco; they were all firms that imported head vases from Japan and Europe. Shawnee and Hull are American potteries that made head vases. Typical prices range from $8 to $35.

Head vases: girl with parasol, 7½ inches, $18; blonde girl with pearls, 7 inches, $22; girl with long eyelashes, 7 inches, $12.

ART POTTERY

Pottery pieces by Rookwood, Weller, Ohr, Paul Revere, Dedham, Newcomb and other American art potteries are now displayed in museums as part of the art of the country. Twenty-five years ago any piece from these potters sold for less than $100. Many books were written as art historians and antiques collectors began recognizing the value of American pottery. Museum exhibitions were held and

The Cowan Pottery made this vase with an inner flower holder and a removable, pierced top to help hold the flowers. It is 10 by 4½ inches. Price, $85.

This Florence Ceramics figurine is called "Melanie." She is worth $75.

There is an incised decorative band on this North Dakota School of Mines 6¼-inch vase. Value, $200.

American Encaustic Tiling Company, Art Deco-style figurine of a woman, 7 inches high, $85.

prices rose. The record price for an iris-glaze Rookwood vase in 1981 was $2,750. In 1988 a similar vase sold for $23,000. Top prices today are $17,600 for an Ohr vase and $32,000 for a Rookwood vase decorated with an Indian. There are still many top-quality pieces by small art potteries and studio potters that sell for less than $100. Look for pieces by American Encaustic, Arc-En-Ciel, Arthur Baggs, Cowan, Paul Cox, Denver, Dickota, Hampshire, Kenton Hills, Glen Lukens, Markham, Niloak, North Dakota School of Mines, Viktor Schreckengost, and Van Briggle. There were other potters who worked after 1950 and made pieces of interest. Look for Kay Finch (1935-1963), Sascha Brastoff (1953-present), Silver Springs (1930s-1965), Florence Ceramics (1930s-1964), Vernon Kilns (1916-1964), Hull (1905-1986), Shawnee (1937-1961), and Ceramic Arts Studio (1941-1955).

These vases may have been used as bookends. They were made by the North Dakota School of Mines. Value, $100.

CZECHOSLOVAKIAN ORANGE

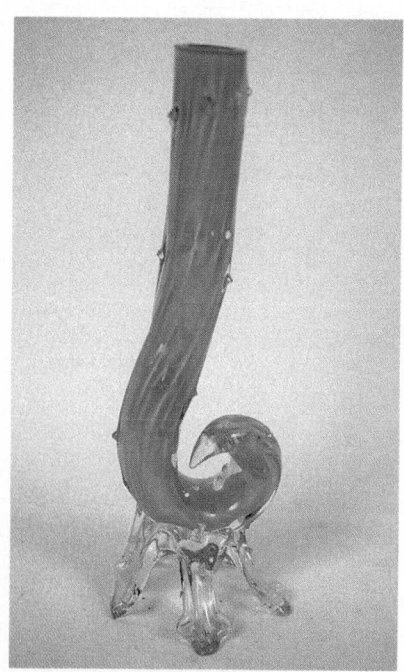

This 6½-inch Czechoslovakian orange glass vase is worth $50.

Colors used in decorating go in and out of fashion. Turquoise was a popular fifties color while violet was a favorite in 1910. Bright orange was in use during the 1920s and thirties, then lost favor for everything but Halloween decorations. It is coming back into style, so a collection of orange-colored Czechoslovakian glass or pottery should rise in price. Czechoslovakian firms made decorative pieces that were exported to other countries from 1918 to 1938. Pieces were inspired by Art Deco, traditional, and Egyptian designs. Flowers, dancing girls, and Greek figures were often depicted. Many pieces of mold-blown or pressed orange glass were made of bright orange and black or spatter glass. The colors are vivid, but the shapes are plain. Applied serpentine or floral ornaments were

A 5-inch Czechoslovakian pottery vase, $20, and a creamer from an
orange Art Deco set.

also used. Some pieces had metallic flakes in the glass. The orange
ceramics are either figurines with some orange decoration or tablewares with Art Deco designs of orange and sometimes black, bright
blue, and green. They are usually marked with the name Czechoslovakia. It is easy to find "Czech orange." The bright colors draw your
eye to a piece. The best pieces have strong Deco shapes or unusual
glass overlay and applied decorations. A 6½-inch orange glass vase
with an applied black snakelike decoration is about $50; an orange,
yellow, black, and blue spatter glass round covered bowl is $85. A
set of four cups and saucers, a teapot, creamer, and sugar in Deco
geometric designs of orange, black, and blue is $95. A 5-inch vase
with dot decoration is $20.

PRINTS

Currier & Ives prints were inexpensive, but popular, collectibles in the 1930s. Important collections were formed and many books listing the prints were written. The prints, made from 1857 to 1907, attained new status. Prints of popular subjects such as fires, trains, fighting animals, and quaint scenes of farm life are now selling for thousands of dollars. But collectors can still find prints of children, religious subjects, and still lifes for under $100. There have been many copies made of Currier & Ives prints and some have even been reproduced photographically. Be sure to examine prints carefully to determine if you are buying originals.

Another type of picture that will probably be going up in value in the next few years is the Nutting print. Wallace Nutting was a clergyman, photographer, furniture manufacturer, and author. He took photographs of landscapes, flowers, colonial interiors, architectural exteriors, and other attractive scenes between 1900 and

Wallace Nutting picture titled "The Way it Begins" sold recently for $715.

"Summer Wind" by Wallace Nutting is worth $110.

Summer Cloud

Wallace Nutting

1941. Millions of his photographs were printed and hand-colored. The matted and framed pictures were then sold. Over 10,000 different subjects were marketed. Serious collectors are beginning to amass large collections of "Nuttings." Some are just buying a few attractive pictures to hang on a wall. Interiors are usually worth more than exteriors. The unusual subjects such as foreign scenes, snow scenes, seascapes, and pictures with animals, men, or children are prized. All of the prints are signed and most often have a title. The record price for a Nutting in 1989 was $1,430 for a picture of fifteen cows by a stream. Prices for more common Nutting prints are: Honeymoon Windings, $35; Connecticut Blossom, $35; Brown Study, $72; Lady Reads Letter, $70.

ART DECO ALUMINUM

Aluminum was more expensive than gold when it was first used. Napoleon used aluminum, not solid gold plates, at important dinners. Charles Martin Hall, who discovered an inexpensive method of extracting aluminum from its ore in 1886, founded The Aluminum Company of America (Alcoa). Soon after, kitchen utensils, teapots,

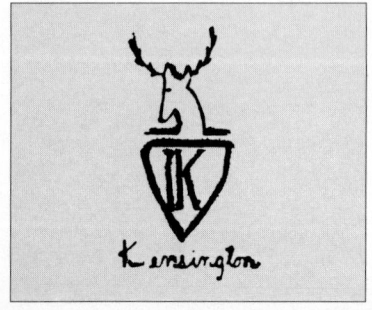

The Buenilum chrome casserole is 9 by 3½ inches, the Kensington aluminum plate is 12½ inches in diameter. Each would cost less than $100.

and pans were made. The best modern, decorative aluminum was made in the 1930s. Alcoa formed a subsidiary called Kensington, Inc. (1934-1952) that made a line of giftware. Important designers, such as Lurelle Guild, made everything from vases, bowls, ashtrays, and candlesticks to furniture. Other marks found on the high-style, polished aluminum are Argental, the trademark used by the Cellini Shop of Chicago, Illinois (1934-1965), and Buenilum, the mark of Buehner-Warner, Inc. (c. 1965). Those who do not like the severe Art Deco style might collect the handmade look of hammered aluminum. It was made by Rodney Kent, Wendell August Forge, and others.

VICTORIAN SILVER & SILVER PLATE

Victorian silver and silver plate of eclectic design have been almost ignored and have remained low priced for over fifty years. It is not unusual to find a silver basket with goat's legs for feet, a cupid on the handle, animal heads, flowers, and geometric patterns on the sides. Most collectors of the early 1980s searched for Art Nouveau or colonial pattern silver and ignored the ornate examples. In 1984 there was one serious collector who began buying American sterling and silver-plated examples with ornate naturalistic and figural designs. At that time the prices were low, but in 1989 when the collection was sold, the prices sky-rocketed. A silver bowl and spoon in the shape of ice, icicles, and polar bears sold for $44,000. It had only cost $3,600 in 1984. Small pieces of Victorian silver, especially serving pieces, are still a good buy. The best makers are Tiffany, Unger, Gorham, International Silver, and Meriden. Look for the unusual. Prices: silver-plated cheese scoop with Assyrian head, $58; silver-plated figural knife rest shaped like lions, $45; sterling silver Unger teaspoon with nude figural handle, $35.

This silver-plated basket is unmarked. It is typical Victorian style.

Wilcox Silverplate Company made this silver-plated fruit dish about 1890. There are grapes in the bottom, cherries on the rim. It is 9 inches long, value $175.

HOLIDAY
COLLECTIBLES

Christmas cards and ornaments were the first holiday-related items to interest collectors. Savvy collectors began buying ornaments for a few dollars each until 1977, when a book on the subject was published. Prices for rare ornaments are already high. A paper "Dresden" camel costs $400 and a blown glass potato $100. Now the search has begun for memorabilia from other holidays: Fourth of July fireworks and flag-decorated glass and china; Thanksgiving postcards, glass, and ceramic or paper turkeys; or Halloween pumpkins. Halloween is second only to Christmas as a collector's holiday. Look for the black, pressed cardboard cats and witches that were first made in the late 19th century. The Dennison Company started making crepe paper and pressed cardboard Halloween items in the early 1900s. Buy children's books, noisemakers, masks, dancing paper skeletons, papier-mâché "nodders," and candy containers imported from Germany. Embossed, die-cut cardboard wall decorations still cost less than $35. Patterns for costumes from Butterick, sold as early as the

The 6-inch valentine from the 1930s is worth $20, the 4-inch papier-mâché jack-o'-lantern with the original paper eyes sells for $45.

Now who do you sup-pose sent it?

1870s, and complete homemade or dimestore costumes (early 1900s) can still be found. The papier-mache pumpkins made for Halloween after the 1920s are selling from $35 to $125 each at many of the "country look" antiques shops. Plastic pumpkins were first introduced in the 1950s. Crepe paper black cats cost $15 and up. Halloween costumes list in this book for $15 to $40. Many holiday items can still be found at yard sales and in attics where prices range from free to a few dollars. Pieces marked "Germany" probably predate 1940. "U.S. Zone Germany" dates them from 1945 to 1949.

ENAMELS

Metal objects decorated with enamel have been made for centuries, but were unpopular in the early 20th century. About 1930, a few American artists began experimenting with enamel-decorated bowls, ashtrays, jewelry, plaques, and even huge wall panels. The designs reflected work of the Wiener Werkstätte in Vienna, the Art Deco motif of France, and later the abstract patterns favored by fifties' artists.

Mildred Watkins made this 7-inch enamel-on-copper dish called "Peace in a Dark World."

Metal foil was used with the enamel on this Mildred Watkins dish marked "Ladies of the Womens Art Club."

Antiques dealers and shops with middle-of-the market items sometimes have one or two enamels. They usually know the good from the bad and the important artist from the amateur. Enamels are priced by their decorative value. Look for enamels by Karl Drerup, Mildred Watkins, Claire Conover, Nekrassoff, Edward Winter, or Kenneth Bates. If there is an art institute in your area, ask about any of the exhibitions held in the fifties that included enamels. Groups of artists in Cleveland, Chicago, Boston, and New York made and exhibited many pieces; important artists were also found in California and Florida. Some of the best examples have foil under the enamel, strong geometric design, realistic figures, or cutout metal parts. Prices range from a few dollars for an ashtray at a house sale to $200 for a small bowl by Drerup to $1,250 for a larger plaque by Winter.

Mold, Barley Sugar, 3 Begging Dogs 50.00
Mold, Butter, Bird, Wooden, 5 X 3 In. 38.00
Mold, Butter, Cased Wood, Flower & Initials A.C., 11 1/4 In., 3 Pc. 110.00
Mold, Butter, Cow Imprint, Wooden, Plunger, 3 1/2 X 4 In. 27.00
Mold, Butter, Daisy, 2 Leaves, Geometric Border 95.00
Mold, Butter, Donkey, Standing, Plunger, Mid–1800s, 4 In. 395.00
Mold, Butter, Double Acorn 85.00
Mold, Butter, Double Wheat Sheaves, Chip Carved, 3 1/4 X 3 1/2 In. 85.00
Mold, Butter, Flower 20.00
Mold, Butter, Heart, Carved Case & Plunger 260.00
Mold, Butter, Heart, Case & Plunger, Early 1800s, 3 1/2 In. 260.00
Mold, Butter, Pineapple, Dated 1876 .... 40.00
Mold, Butter, Sheaf of Wheat, Oblong 85.00
Mold, Butter, Star & Rosette, Brass Hooks, Maple 50.00
Mold, Butter, Star, Wooden, 3 In. 24.00
Mold, Butter, Swan, Pine 135.00
Mold, Butter, Wheat, Round, 1 Lb. 55.00
Mold, Butter, Zero Creamery Butter, Round, 4 1/2 In. 65.00
Mold, Cake, Gingerbread Boy, Aluminum, 9 X 10 1/2 In. 15.00
Mold, Cake, Griswold, Tag 225.00
Mold, Cake, Lamb, Aluminum 20.00
Mold, Cake, Lamb, Cast Iron 55.00
Mold, Cake, Lamb, Griswold, No.866 .... 75.00
Mold, Cake, Lamb, Schaab Stove & Furnace Co. 125.00
Mold, Cake, Rabbit, Griswold, 12 In. 80.00
Mold, Cake, Santa Claus, Aluminum 25.00
   KITCHEN, MOLD, CANDLE, see Tinware, Mold, Candle
Mold, Candy, 7 Letter Ts, Oak, Each 12 In. 60.00
Mold, Candy, Acorn Shape, Oak, 12 In., 2 Piece 60.00
Mold, Candy, Acorns, Oak, 12 In., 2 Piece 60.00
Mold, Candy, Bunny, Resting, Glass, Marked British, 8 In. 35.00
Mold, Candy, Dutch Wooden Shoe, 2 Sections, 2 X 6 X 2 In. 65.00
Mold, Candy, Ship & Bird, 7 1/2 In., Pair 65.00
Mold, Cheese, Bentwood, Rope, Wood Tightening Belt, Round, 24 1/2 In. 45.00
Mold, Chocolate, 1 Rabbit Sitting, 8 X 5 In. 35.00
Mold, Chocolate, 2 Rabbits With Floppy Ears, Tin, 4 X 4 X 2 In. 85.00
Mold, Chocolate, 3 Rabbits Standing, Comic, 10 X 7 In. 35.00
Mold, Chocolate, 4 Rabbits Sitting, 10 X 5 In. 35.00
Mold, Chocolate, 6 Rabbits Standing, With Packs, 10 1/2 X 5 In. 35.00
Mold, Chocolate, Bird, Tin, 3 X 3 In. 60.00
Mold, Chocolate, Bunny, With Ball, Gray, Tin, 8 X 7 In. 50.00
Mold, Chocolate, Ear of Corn 45.00
Mold, Chocolate, Easter Egg, Racked Design, Gray, Tin, 4 X 5 X 3 In. 20.00
Mold, Chocolate, Rabbit, Tin, Iron Frame, 13 In. 65.00
Mold, Chocolate, Santa Claus 85.00
Mold, Chocolate, Santa's Boot, Dark Gray, 2 Sections, 3 X 2 3/4 In. 65.00
Mold, Chocolate, Sitting Hen, Randle & Smith, Birmingham, 5 In. 65.00
Mold, Chocolate, Sleigh Full of Toys, 10 Designs, Cast Iron 45.00
Mold, Chocolate, Snowman, Tin, 4 In. 15.00
Mold, Chocolate, Speckled Gray, Embossed, 2 X 3 In., 2 Piece 15.00
Mold, Cookie, Basket of Flowers, Cast Iron, 1800s, 3 1/2 X 5 1/2 In. 150.00
Mold, Cookie, Pineapple, Oval, Cast Iron, C.1800, 4 1/2 X 6 In. 190.00
Mold, Croquette, Tin 17.00
Mold, Fish, Danish, Copper, Large 68.00
Mold, Fish, Stands & Hangs, Tin, 11 In. 44.00
Mold, Food, Abstract Swirl Pattern, Tinned Inside, Copper, 4 X 7 In. 150.00
Mold, Food, Geometric Design, Copper 65.00
Mold, Food, Ironstone, Columns, Swirls, 6 In. 45.00
Mold, Food, Pineapple, Oval, Copper, 4 1/2 X 6 3/4 In. 75.00
Mold, Food, Pineapple, Tin 85.00
Mold, Food, Rabbit, Griswold .... 125.00 To 225.00
Mold, Food, Ring of Swirled Cones, Open Center, Tin, 8 3/4 In. 30.00
Mold, Food, Turk's Head, Griswold 75.00
   KITCHEN, MOLD, ICE CREAM, see Pewter, Mold, Ice Cream

Mold, Maple Sugar, 3 Hearts, Carved Design, 1800s, 7 X 22 1/2 In. 440.00
Mold, Maple Sugar, Duck, Wooden Block, Canada, 6 1/4 X 5 1/2 In. 8.50
Mold, Maple Sugar, Pine Wih Initials, C.1840, 9 In. 295.00
Mold, Maple Sugar, Turkey, Wooden Block, Canada, 5 3/4 X 5 1/4 In. 8.50
Mold, Maple Sugar, Wooden, 12 Sections, 37 X 2 1/2 X 3 1/2 In. 125.00
Mold, Melon, Tinned Copper, Large, 2 Piece 45.00
Mold, Patty, Griswold, Instructions, Box 34.00
Mold, Plum Pudding, Tin, England, 6 3/4 X 5 1/2 In. 15.00
Mold, Pudding, Center Prong, Tin, Early 1900s 35.00
Mold, Pudding, Fluted Slant Sided, Graniteware, 3 1/2 X 6 1/2 In. 65.00
Mold, Pudding, Pineapple, 5 X 5 X 6 1/2 In. 65.00
Mortar & Pestle, Rosebuds, White, Cranberry Border, AP, 3 3/4 In. 65.00
Mug, Blue & White, Enamel 3.50
Napkin Holder, Proud Rooster, Black, Iron 8.00
Opener, Jar, Jimmney 8.00
Opener, Wizard Jar Wrench, Metal 2.00
Paddle, Butter, Wooden Hook At End of Handle, Blade, 5 3/4 In. 21.00
Paddle, Maple Butter, Curl, Bird's–Eye Maple, 12 In. 175.00
Pail, Cedar, Blizzard, 1900s 65.00
Pan, Baking, Cobalt Blue Swirl, Long 95.00
Pan, Biscuit, Calumet Baking Powder Embossed, 11 X 7 1/2 In. 5.00
Pan, Braising, 2 Handles, Brass & Copper, 19th Century 132.00
Pan, Bread Rising, Rounded Lid, Large, Primitive 25.00
Pan, Bread, Deckers, Tin, Signed 8.00
Pan, Bread, Double, Tin 44.00
Pan, Bundt, Cast Iron, Fluted, 18th Century, 9 X 2 1/2 In. 95.00
Pan, Bundt, Tinware, 4 In. 10.00
Pan, Cake, Py–O–My Puddin' Cake On Bottom 10.00
Pan, Cake, Spring Form, Kreamer, Tin 10.00
Pan, Corn Fritter, Wheat Design, Iron 18.00
Pan, Cornstick, Griswold 24.00
Pan, Cornstick, Wagnerware 26.00
Pan, Griswold Crispy Corn Or Wheat Stick, 4 X 8 1/2 In. 75.00
Pan, Griswold, No.32, 7 Hole 25.00
Pan, Krusty Korn Kob, Wagnerware, Label 24.00
Pan, Muffin, 12 Hole, Open Frame, Cast Iron 60.00
Pan, Muffin, Fluted, Tin, 8 Cup 6.00
Pan, Muffin, Iron, G.F.Filley No.11 .... 50.00
Pan, Muffin, Wheat Design, Cast Iron, 7 Sections, 12 1/2 In. 75.00
Pan, Popover, Griswold, No.10, 1890s 25.00
Pan, Popover, Griswold, No.18 .... 75.00
Pan, Popover, Wagner, Iron 25.00
Pan, Roasting, Tinned, Dovetailed, Early 1800s, 3 1/2 X 8 X 13 In. 175.00
Pan, Sauce, Cast Iron Handle, Copper, 6 1/4 In. 20.00
Pan, Tube, 12 Sides, Tin 10.00
Pan, Twin Bread Loaf, Hinged Halves, Tin 44.00
Pan, Vienna Roll 42.00
Pancake Turner, Red Wood Handle 2.50
Pastry Roiler, Carved Bone, Brass Yoke, Cherry Handle, 6 1/2 In. 130.00
Pastry Wheel & Crimper, Iron Shaft, Hewn Wood Handle, Brass Disc 45.00
Peel, Cookie, Double Ram's Head Handle, 18th Century, 28 1/2 In. 260.00
Peel, Pie, Round Tapered Paddle, Hanging Hole, 28 In. 220.00
Peel, Replaced Handle, Salamander 40.00
Peeler, Apple, 2 Gears, Crank Handle, Pewter Fittings, C.1800 .... 350.00
Peeler, Apple, 2–Inch Blade, Hand Carved, 18th Century, 9 In. 150.00
Peeler, Apple, Goodell, Iron, Instructions, Box .... 25.00 To 42.00
Peeler, Apple, Mechanical, Cast Iron, Rolls In 1/2 Circle 85.00
Peeler, Apple, Reading Hardware Co. 45.00
Peeler, Apple, Rival, Commercial 295.00
Peeler, Apple, Sargeant & Foster, Mounted On Board, Iron 95.00
Peeler, Apple, Sinclair Scott, Heart–Shaped Gears 60.00
Peeler, Apple, Table Clamp, Cutter Arm, 14 In. 275.00
Peeler, Apple, White Mountain, Box, C.1950 .... 35.00
Peeler, Apple, Whitmore, 1866 .... 52.50

Peeler, Peach, Sinclair Scott, Iron 55.00
Percolator Pump, Pyrex, Range Top 5.00
Pie Bird, Benny The Baker 45.00
Pie Carrier, Wire 33.00
Pie Crimper, Wrought Iron, Twisted Handle, 7 1/4 In. 125.00
Pie Divider, Wire 40.00
Pie Lifter, Wire, C.1890 .... 33.00
Pie Lifter, Wire, Dated 1875 .... 30.00
Pie Lifter, Wooden Handle, 2 Tine 50.00
Pie Pan, Olympic Helms, Tin 10.00
Pie Plate, Brown Interior Glaze, Black Exterior, Clay, 10 1/2 In. 25.00
Pie Plate, Yellow, Advertising 35.00
Piebird, Yellow, Marked Josef 5.00
Poacher, Pottery, Red, Hankscraft 40.00
Popcorn Machine, Junior, Glass, Tin, 1940s, Box, 18 X 12 In. 170.00
Popcorn Popper, Aladdin 30.00
Popcorn Popper, Poppin Pete 35.00
Pot, 3 Short Legs, Cast Bronze, Ribbed Handle, 5 1/4 X 8 In. 145.00
Pot, Cast Iron, 3-Footed, 1860, Large 50.00
Pot, Fish Cooker, With Poaching Tray, Tin, C.1870, 7 X 9 X 15 In. 85.00
Pot, Wagnerware, Heart Shape, Cover, 2 1/2 Qt. 37.50
Potato Masher, Crisscross, Wooden Handle 4.00
Potato Masher, Metal, Red Wooden Handle 15.00
Potato Masher, Red Plastic Handle 2.00
Press, Cheese, Shoe Feet, Laced Pulleys, Wooden, 30 1/2 In. 85.00
Press, Fruit & Vegetable, Climax 15.00
Press, Lard, Walnut Wood, 18 In. 30.00
Rack, Dish Drying, 10 Spindles, 2 Oval Side Bars, 9 3/4 X 20 In. 8.50
Rack, Drying, Pine, Mortised & Pinned Construction, 22 X 23 In. 325.00
Rack, Hanging, Multiple Hooks, Iron, 1920s, 17 X 21 In. 105.00
Rack, Pie, Nickel Plated, Holds 8 Pies, C.1930 .... 65.00
Rack, Utensil, Scrolled Crest, 6 Hooks, Iron, 26 In. 225.00
Rack, Utensil, Wrought Iron, Scrolled, Twisted, 18 1/4 In. 200.00
Raisin Seeder, Everett, Wooden Handle, Wire Grid, C.1893 .... 55.00
Raisin Seeder, Mechanical, Cast Iron, 1891 .... 42.00
Reamer, Aid-O-Matic, Maroon 125.00
Reamer, Green 10.00
Reamer, Sunkist, Pink 50.00
Roaster, Coffee, Iron, Roys & Wilcox, Berlin, Conn.Pat.1859 .... 245.00
Roaster, Coffee, Roys & Wilcox & Co., Iron Frame, 3 Legs, Pat.1849 .... 245.00
Roaster, Coffee, Wooden Handle, Sheet Iron, C.1800, 50 In. 295.00
Roaster, Ring Base, Tripod Frame, Crank Handle, Iron, 15 1/2 In. 175.00
Roller, Strudel, Striped Tiger Maple, 16 In. 85.00
Rolling Pin, 1 Handle, Hang-Up Hook, Maple, 14 In. 20.00
Rolling Pin, 12 Designs In Squares, 15 In. 75.00
Rolling Pin, Advertising, Stoneware .... 225.00 To 238.00
Rolling Pin, Ball Ends, Ridge Lines, C.1870, 18 In. 35.00
Rolling Pin, Brown Lignum Vitae, Yellow Oak Handles, 20 In. 55.50
Rolling Pin, Cookie, Corrugated, Wooden, 11 In. 22.00
Rolling Pin, Curly Maple, 16 3/4 In. .... 38.00 To 45.00
Rolling Pin, Custard Glass, Tin Closure 125.00
Rolling Pin, Glass, Screw-On Metal Cap, 1910 .... 20.00
Rolling Pin, Glass, Wooden Handle, Dated Oct.21, 1879 .... 85.00
Rolling Pin, Hardwood, Bone Handles, 15 In. 165.00
Rolling Pin, Kelvinator, Milk Glass 68.00
Rolling Pin, Mahogany, Pewter Handles, 18 In. 400.00
Rolling Pin, Maple, 9 In. 8.00
Rolling Pin, Maple, Red Wood Handles, 17 1/2 In. 15.00
Rolling Pin, Maple, Turned Handles, 20 In. 15.00
Rolling Pin, Mortised & Pinned, Single Bar, 18th Century 350.00
Rolling Pin, Noodle, Wooden 35.00
Rolling Pin, Plainview, Nebraska, Stoneware 165.00
Rolling Pin, Pomeroy, Iowa, Need Good Flour To Knead Dough, Pottery ... 167.50
Rolling Pin, Red Design, Flowers, Ivy, Basket, China, 17 In. 52.00

Graniteware and other enameled kitchenwares should be cleaned with water and baking soda. If necessary, use chlorine bleach.

Kitchen, Scoops, Ice Cream

Rolling Pin, Springerle, 12 Designs	35.00
Rolling Pin, Stoneware, Flowers, Handle	165.00
Rolling Pin, Tiger Maple	18.00
Rolling Pin, Well, Minn., Amber Bands, Pottery	185.00
Rolling Pin, Wildflower, Advertising, Wisconsin, 1914	250.00
Rolling Pin, Wooden, Turned Handles, Maple, 14 In.	20.00
Rug Beater, Wire	9.00
Sadiron & Trivet, Child's, Marked Jewel	35.00
Sadiron, Asbestos, Detachable Handle, 1900, 5 In.	20.00
Sadiron, Brass, Gate Lifts, Vertical Handle, Opens For Heat Plug	58.00
Sadiron, Foliate Iron, Soapstone Rests Inside	126.50
Sadiron, Geneva Star	9.00
Sadiron, Trivet, Signed O.P.Frost, Handle, Christmas Tree Shape	180.00
Scale, Egg	12.00
Scoop, Airy Fairy	10.00
Scoop, Butter, Chip Carved Butter Print Handle, 10 1/2 In.	310.00
Scoop, Candy, Brass, Small	35.00
Scoop, Cheese, Oval Shallow Bowl, Stilton, Carved Wood, 11 1/2 In.	35.00
Scoop, Ice Cream Sandwich, Maryland Cream Pie Disher	275.00
Scoop, Ice Cream, Aluminum, 1940s	45.00
Scoop, Ice Cream, Banana, United Products ....*Illus*	605.00
Scoop, Ice Cream, Clewell, Tin, 1896	65.00
Scoop, Ice Cream, Clipper Fountain Supply ....*Illus*	330.00
Scoop, Ice Cream, Cone, White Metal, Advertising	37.50
Scoop, Ice Cream, Cutoff, No.20, Dover Mfg.Co.	605.00
Scoop, Ice Cream, Cylinder Type	185.00
Scoop, Ice Cream, Dover Double Scoop	120.00
Scoop, Ice Cream, Erie Specialty	60.00
Scoop, Ice Cream, Gear Mfg.Clipper Disher, 1905, Large	150.00
Scoop, Ice Cream, Gem City	10.00
Scoop, Ice Cream, Gilchrist, No.30, Brass, Nickel	38.00
Scoop, Ice Cream, Gilchrist, No.31	28.00 To 40.00
Scoop, Ice Cream, Gilchrist, No.33, Cone Shape ....*Illus*	248.00
Scoop, Ice Cream, Heart	2500.00
Scoop, Ice Cream, ICYPI, Square	193.00
Scoop, Ice Cream, Indestructo, No.3	85.00
Scoop, Ice Cream, Mechanical, Bakelite Handle, Bunny Products	12.50
Scoop, Ice Cream, Mosteller Rollover	500.00
Scoop, Ice Cream, Peerless, Bakelite Handle	20.00
Scoop, Ice Cream, Reliance, Sandwich Type	95.00
Scoop, Ice Cream, Reliance, Wafer Holder	250.00
Scoop, Ice Cream, Revolving, No.20	578.00
Scoop, Ice Cream, Triangular Cone Shape, Open Loop Handle, KW	29.00
Scoop, Scale, Dark Gray, Tin, 4 1/2 X 12 In.	20.00
Scoop, Sugar, Hand Carved, Wooden, Early 1800s, 7 1/2 In.	130.00
Scoop, Sugar, Red, White Handle, 1/4 Cup	4.00
Scoop, Sugar, Rolled Edges, Brass, C.1880	26.00
Scoop, Zeroll Ice Cream	16.00

Scraper, Butter, Maple, 1 Piece, 10 3/4 X 4 In. 6.00
Seal Breaker, For Bottle, Jenney, Cast Iron 10.00
Shredder, Salad, Bremwells, Finger Guard, Tin, 11 In. 7.00
Sieve, Dark Blue–Gray Paint, Woven Ash, C.1800, 20 1/2 In. 275.00
Sieve, Horsehair, Bentwood, 13 1/2 In. 45.00
Sifter, Bromwell, Green Wood Handle, 3–Cup 6.50
Sifter, Double Screen, Squeeze Handle, Tin 8.00
Sifter, Double, Red Wood Handle, Tin 18.00
Sifter, Flour, Blood's Patent, Wooden, Label, 1861 .... 195.00
Sifter, Flour, Bromwell, 5–Cup 6.00
Sifter, Flour, Calumet, 1–Cup 10.00
Sifter, Grain, 5 X 17 In. 75.00
Sifter, Wooden, Wire Mesh, 13 1/2 X 4 In. 19.50
Skillet, Arbuckle Appliance, Noblesville, Ind., Iron, 4 In. 15.00
Skillet, Griswold, No.0 .... 65.00
Skillet, Griswold, No.3 .... 10.00
Skillet, Griswold, No.8 .... 12.00
Skillet, Griswold, No.9 .... 12.00
Skillet, Hand Forged Iron, 12 In. 175.00
Skillet, Hand Forged Iron, Spider Leg 65.00
Skillet, Hanging, Pouring Spout, Hand Forged Iron, 12 In. 245.00
Skillet, Wagner Ware, 6 In. 21.00
Skillet, Wagner Ware, Iron, 4 3/8 In. 20.00
Skimmer, Marked F.B.S. Canton, O., Brass & Wrought Iron, 18 1/2 In. 35.00
Skimmer, Milk, Green Wood Handle, Aluminum, 4 In. 3.50
Skimmer, Pierced Holes, Tab Handle, Hanging Hole, Wooden, 6 1/2 In. 250.00
Skimmer, Pierced Oval Spoon–Shaped Bowl, Copper, 17 In. 130.00
Slicer, Bean, Tin & Cast Iron 25.00
Smoothing Board, Walnut, Red, Black, Horse Handle, Ano 1769, 27 In. 800.00
Soap Shaker, Tin, Square Type, Metal Handle 13.50
Sock Stretcher, Wooden 12.50
Spatula, Copper Blade, Wrought Iron Handle, 6 3/8 In. 65.00
Spatula, Fairmonte Better Butter, Metal Letters, 12 In. 2.25
Spatula, Hand Forged Iron, Open Ring Handle, American, 1820, 11 In. 65.00
Spatula, Iron Handle, Hook End, F.B.S., Canton, Ohio, 14 1/2 In. 150.00
Spice Box, 6 Small Round Cans Inside, Round 55.00
Spice Box, 7 Labeled Canisters, Round, Wooden 295.00
Spice Box, 8 Inner Stenciled Canisters, Round, Wooden, 1800s 225.00
Spice Box, Lapped Seams, Metal Lift Top, Tin, C.1820, 2 X 2 In. 20.00
Spice Cabinet, 8 Drawers, Hanging, Wooden 140.00
Spice Chest, House Front Shape, Chip Carved, Names In German 600.00
Spider, Wrought Iron, Handle, 7 1/4 In. 85.00
Spoon, Brass Bowl, Wrought Iron Handle, 9 1/2 In. 160.00
Spoon, Copper Bowl, Iron Handle, 10 1/4 In. 215.00
Spoon, Mixing, White, Hole For Hanging, Enamel, 10 In. 3.50
Spoon, Slotted, Natural Wood Handle, Steel, C.1920 .... 4.00
Spoon, Slotted, Rumford Baking Powder 12.00
Squeezer, Lemon, Clown Shape, Crown Mark 75.00
Squeezer, Lemon, Concealed Metal Hinges, Wooden Handle, 9 1/2 In. 25.00
Squeezer, Lemon, Hinged, Wooden, 2 Tapered Handles, Mid–1800s 40.00
Squeezer, Lemon, Mosteller, Cast Iron 250.00
Squeezer, Lemon, White Porcelain Strainer 37.50
Squeezer, Orange, Wooden, 20 In. 95.00
Steamer, Inserts, Spout Whistle, Tin, Copper Bottom, 5 3/4 In. 95.00
Steamer, Pretzel, Black Waiter, Ceramic 125.00
String Holder, Aunt Jemima 55.00
String Holder, Cat On Ball of Yarn, Ceramic 25.00
String Holder, Cat, Ceramic 10.00
String Holder, Chef's Head, Chalkware, 7 1/2 In. 85.00
String Holder, Chef, White 25.00
String Holder, Dome Shape, Cast Iron 28.50
String Holder, Dutch Boy, White Lead, Lithographed Tin 6160.00
String Holder, Dutch Girl, Chalkware 15.00
String Holder, Mammy, Full Figure, 8 1/2 In. 55.00

String Holder, Owl, Cast Iron	95.00
String Holder, Rolled Edges, Bell Shaped Clear Glass, Table Model	110.00
String Holder, Woman Knitting, Cat Playing With Yarn Ball, Tin	15.00
String Holder, Young Girl, Knitting Stocking, Full Figure	135.00
Tablespoon, Cow Horn, Arched Handle, 9 1/2 In.	30.00
Tea Infuser, Acorn, Aluminum	2.50
Tea Strainer, Metal, Wooden Handle, Drip Guard	6.00
Teakettle, Revere, Nickel Plated, Bakelite, Bird Whistle, 7 In.	25.00
Teakettle, Wagner Ware, Metal, Wooden Handle, Colonial, 5 Qt.	25.00
Teakettle, Wrought Iron Handle, Cast Iron, 9 3/4 In.	15.00
Teapot, Wagner, Cast Iron, 1 Gal.	60.00
Tenderizer, Meat, Metal Teeth, Wooden Handle, 3 1/2 X 4 In.	185.00
Thermometer, Candy, Taylor, Wooden Handle	10.00
Timer, Egg, Dutch Girl, Standing, Marked Germay	18.00
Toaster Grill, Flip-Fold, Cast Iron, C.1900, 18 X 14 In.	60.00
Toaster, Estate, 4-Slice	65.00
Toaster, Heart Handle, Iron	275.00
Toaster, Rotating, Hand Forged Iron, Handle & Ring, 18th Century	260.00
Toaster, Stove Top, Pierced Disc, Wire Ricks, 4 Slices, 8 3/4 In.	9.00
Toaster, Swing Handle, Iron	250.00
Toaster, Toast-A-Later, Bread Moves From One End To Other	85.00
Toaster, Universal, 1930s	17.00 To 30.00
Toaster, Wrought Iron, 16 In.	295.00
Tongs, Pickle, Country Store, 28 In.	95.00
Toothpicks, Part-T-Pac, Plastic	4.00
Tray, Knife, Black Walnut, 13 1/4 X 8 1/2 In.	37.00
Tray, Knife, Center Partition, Bar Carrying Handle, Slant Sides	110.00
Tray, Knife, Maple, Dovetailed Corners, Center Hand Hole, 12 X 7 In.	26.00
Vegetable Washer, Legs, Wire, 26 X 18 In.	105.00
Wafer Iron, Brass Pads, Hand Forged, 14 In.Handles	295.00
Waffle Iron, Child's, Wagner, Sidney, Ohio, Dated 1910	75.00
Waffle Iron, Cookstove, Super Maid, Cast Aluminum, 7 1/2 In.	60.00
Waffle Iron, Crescent, Wagner, Low Stand	20.00
Waffle Iron, Double Wafer, Cast Iron, Handle, 25 In.	85.00
Waffle Iron, Griswold No.8	20.00 To 35.00
Waffle Iron, Griswold, Heart & Star	100.00
Waffle Iron, Hearts, Cast Iron	60.00
Wash Fork, For Boiling Clothes, 1 Piece Oak, 2 Tines, 27 In.	7.50
Wash Stick, Heart Cutout & Carved Horse Handle, Natural, 26 In.	550.00
Washboard, All Tin, Curled Feet Base, C.1880, 24 X 12 In.	49.00
Washboard, Blue Agate, Soap Saver	75.00
Washboard, Blue Porcelain Scrub, Wooden	42.00
Washboard, Corrugated Rollers On Rocker Frame, Wooden, 13 X 24 In.	115.00
Washboard, Domestic Science, Label, Glass, 17 X 8 In.	15.00
Washboard, Graniteware, Cobalt Blue, Gray Mixture	40.00
Washboard, Hudson	14.00
Washboard, Lingerie, 7 In.	15.00
Washboard, National 801, Wood, Brass, Wood Soap Saver	12.00
Washboard, National No.862, Glass	8.00
Washboard, Rollers Along Lower Part, Wooden	27.50
Washboard, Soap Pocket, Wooden, Curved, 19th Century, 13 X 24 In.	110.00
Washboard, Standard Family Size No.2080, Columbus, Glass, Wood	12.00
Washboard, Wooden Scrub, Dubl Handy, 18 X 8 3/4 In.	34.00
Washing Agitator, 1874, 29 1/2 In.	71.50
Washing Machine, Copper Tub, Operated By Pushing & Pulling Lever	200.00
Washing Machine, Dexter, Wooden Tub, Complete	75.00
Washing Machine, Judd, Electrified, Copper Tub, Iron Gears, 1909	1250.00
Washing Machine, Laundry Queen, Copper Tub	195.00
Washing Machine, Maytag, Wringer Washer, Double Rinse Tubs	50.00
Washing Machine, Perfect, L.O.Lein, Albion, Wis., Wooden, Mar.29, 1889	385.00
Washing Machine, Rock-A-Bye, Wooden	375.00
Washtub, Wooden, Cover	295.00
Whisk, Coiled Wire, Wood Handle, Funnel Shape	5.00
Whisk, Wire, Spoon Shape, Red & Natural Wood Handle, C.1940	4.50

In the 1960s, the United States government passed a law that required knife manufacturers to mark their knives with the country of origin. This seemed to encourage the collectors, and knife collecting became an interest of a large group of people. All types of knives are collected, from top quality twentieth–century examples to old bone– or pearl–handled knives in excellent condition.

KNIFE, 2 Blades, Schmidt & Ziegler, Stag Handle	37.50
3 Blades, Corkscrew, Anheuser–Busch, Silver Plate	75.00
Bayonet, Plug, Civil War, 11 1/2 In.Wedge Leaf Shaped Blade, English	220.00
Bowie Type, Randall	280.00
Bowie, 2–Piece Staghorn Grip, Scabbard, Civil War, 5 1/4 In.Blade	115.00
Bowie, Rebel Guard, Blade, 17 In.	995.00
Buckskinner's, Elkhorn Handle	75.00
Butcher, Russell Green River Works, 15 In.	27.50
Butcher, Winchester, Wooden Handle, 12 1/2 In.	45.00
Cake, Red Wooden Handle	4.00
Case, Founder's, Walnut Case, Etched Blade, Stag Handle	90.00
Case, No.6165, Box	45.00
Case, XX, 9–Dot, 3 Blades, Bone Handle, 4 In.	28.00
Case, XX, Sheath	55.00
Colt, Black Leather Sheath, 10 In.	135.00
Dagger, Bone, Carved Court Scene, Japan, 14 In.Blade	145.00
Diamond Edge, 2 Blades, Yellow Pearl, Celluloid Handle, 2 3/4 In.	25.00
Dirk, Stocking, Chris Johnson, England, 4 In.False Edge Blade	85.00
Dog Head, Single Blade, Union Cutlery, Pocket	700.00
Figural, Bone Fish, Scheveninger, Detail of Fins, Single Blade, 4 In.	18.00
Folding, Swedish Flag, 4 Blades, Gold Tone, 3 1/2 X 1 In.	30.00
Hunting, Bone Handle, Blade Signed Geo.Wostenholm, 19th Century	880.00
Hunting, Deer Foot Carved Handle, 11 1/2 In.	95.00
Hunting, Red Goose Shoes	70.00
Leathermaker's, Brass Half Moon, Rosewood, C.S.Osborn & Co., 4 In.	35.00
Machete, Leather Sheath, Brazil	25.00
New York Knife Co., Walden, Walnut Handle, 5 1/2 In.	85.00
Pocket, Case, No.5265, 5 1/4 In.	250.00
Pocket, Marilyn Monroe, Nude, 1950's	3.00
Pocket, Miller Bros., Ivory	265.00
Pocket, Remington No.6723, 3 Blades	50.00
Pocket, Smith & Wesson, All Steel	17.50
Pocket, Volendam	35.00
Pocket, William Penn Cigars	35.00
Pocket, Winchester, No.3965	75.00
Queen, 3 Blades, Bone Handle, Marked No.9	28.00
Remington, 2 Marked Blades, Bone Handle, Curtiss Baby Ruth Candy	30.00
Remington, Missouri Pacific Quick Point	65.00
Remington, Model R1301, Reproduction, 1984	95.00
Remington, Pen, Pear Handle, 3 In.	35.00
Skinning, Case XX Kodiak, Bone Handle, Engraved, Sheath	65.00
Skinning, Kabar, Sheath, 5 In.	15.00
Skinning, Soligen, Leather Handle, 5 In.	8.00
Soligen, Bone Handle, Leather Sheath	11.00

KNOWLES, TAYLOR & KNOWLES, see KTK; Lotus Ware

KOCH The name "Koch" is signed on the front of a series of plates decorated with fruit, vegetables, animals, or birds. The dishes date from the 1910 to 1930 period and were probably decorated in Germany.

KOCH, Plate, Apples, 9 3/4 In.	65.00
Plate, Grape Clusters, Brown To Cream, Gold Rim, Signed, 7 1/2 In.	32.00
Plate, Grape Clusters, Dark Green To Brown, Signed, 8 1/2 In.	40.00
Plate, Hand Painted Grapes, Signed, 7 1/2 In.	25.00

KOREAN WARE, see Sumida

K P M

K.P.M

Most dealers and collectors use the term "KPM" to refer to Berlin porcelain, but the same initials were used alone and in combination with other symbols by several German porcelain makers. They include the Konigliche Porzellan Manufaktur of Berlin, initials used in mark, 1823–47; Meissen, 1723–24 only; Krister Porzellan Manufaktur in Waldenburg, after 1831; Kranichfelder Porzellan Manufaktur in Kranichfeld, after 1903; and the Kister Porzellan Manufaktur in Scheibe, after 1838.

KPM, Bowl, Wild Flowers, Twig Handle, Basket Shape, 14 In.	395.00
Box, Celadon, White Rim & Base, Dark Green Bee, Scepter, 3 X 2 3/4 In.	52.00
Box, Dark Green Insect Finial, 3 In.	50.00
Bust, Woman, Feathered Hat, Raised Gold, Beading On Gown	325.00
Charger, Hand Painted Scene, Wagner	5500.00
Coffeepot, Roses	325.00
Cup & Saucer, Floral Sprays Inside & Out, Gold Rim, Footed, Demitasse	12.50
Cup & Saucer, Gothic Gold Lines, Butterflies & Flowers	150.00
Cup & Saucer, Hunt Scene 1 Side, Country Manor Reverse, Oversized	633.00
Cup & Saucer, Medallion, Royal Blue, Gilt, Beading, Gold Wash Interior	150.00
Dish, 2 Sections, Center Handle, Marked, 19th Century, 12 1/4 In.	125.00
Dish, Gold Scrolls, Different Flower In Each of 3 Parts, 11 1/2 In.	145.00
Figurine, Carriage, 4 Horses, Woman Inside, Driver, Marked, 6 X 13 In.	175.00
Figurine, Carriage, 4 Horses, Woman, Man, Driver, Blue, White, Marked, 9 In.	175.00
Figurine, Tea Time, Seated Couple, Table, Blue Crown Mark, 7 X 11 In.	150.00
KPM, LITHOPHANE, see also Lithophane	
Plaque, 3 Children, Dancing In Field, 8 1/4 X 6 In.	2100.00
Plaque, Angel of Night, Carrying Child, Oval, Marked, 9 In.	1100.00
Plaque, Assumption of The Virgin, Onyx Frame, C.1900, 21 1/2 In.	2100.00
Plaque, Beautiful Woman With Scarf, Oval, 10 X 12 In.	3500.00
Plaque, Bust, Young Woman, Short Hair, Pendant, 7 1/2 X 5 3/4 In.	1300.00
Plaque, Cardinal Seated Beside Gentleman, Early Costumes, 12 X 15 In.	2600.00
Plaque, Chained Man, Lying On Bed, Bearded, Marked, 11 1/2 In.	2200.00
Plaque, Children Nestled At Base of Tree, Walking Woman, Marked, 11 In.	1875.00
Plaque, Flourishing Female, Framed, Signed Bock, 8 3/4 X 6 3/8 In.	3850.00
Plaque, Jesus As Child, Elders In Temple, Giltwood Frame, Stand	1750.00
Plaque, Lady, Red Hat, Looking Left, Oval, 6 3/4 In. ....*Illus*	1210.00
Plaque, Maiden, Gazing At Reflection In Hand Mirror, Marked, 13 1/4 In.	9075.00
Plaque, Mother & Children, Holding Infant, Marked, C.1900, 15 3/4 In.	6600.00
Plaque, Nude, Figure of Klutho, Spinning Thread of Life, 9 3/4 In.	8250.00
Plaque, Nymph & Pluto, Putto Stripping Clothing From Nude, 10 In.	3740.00
Plaque, Peasant Boy, Violin, Female Companion Sleeps, 15 X 12 1/4 In.	7700.00
Plaque, Peasant Girl, Spinning Flax, Boy, Playing Lute, 10 1/4 In.	3300.00
Plaque, Peninent Magdelene, Late 19th Century, 7 X 5 In.	1250.00
Plaque, Portrait of Gentleman, Signed Durschke, 10 In.	350.00
Plaque, Portrait of Ruth, Porcelain, 8 1/2 X 5 1/2 In. ....*Illus*	2400.00
Plaque, Psyche At Spring, Artist Signed & Numbered, C.1837, 6 X 8 In.	4000.00
Plaque, School Girl, Notebook, Basket, Porcelain, 9 1/4 In.	2600.00
Plaque, Woman In Field, 5 X 8 In.	2600.00
Plaque, Woman Preparing Meal, Other Winding Yarn, Porcelain, 12 In., Pr.	6500.00
Plaque, Young Girl, Classical Attire, Waterjug, Gold Frame, 9 X 11 In.	650.00
Plaque, Young Woman, Fur–Trimmed Garment, Marked, C.1900, 12 1/2 In.	8800.00
Plaque, Young Woman, Grecian Robe, Greek Temple, C.1900, 12 1/2 In.	4800.00
Plate, Floral Design, Gilt, Marked, 9 3/4 In., Pair	110.00
Plate, Medallion of Kneeling Nude, White, C.1878, 10 1/2 In.	65.00
Screen, Table, Child In Church, Lithophane & Bronze, Frame, 20 1/4 In.	500.00
Screen, Table, Lithophane, Bronze, 19th Century, 20 1/4 In. ....*Illus*	500.00
Vase, Roses, Blue Ground, Gold, Royal Porzellan, 9 In.	29.00

K.T.&K.
CHINA

KTK are the initials of the Knowles, Taylor & Knowles Company of East Liverpool, Ohio, founded by Isaac W. Knowles in 1853. The company made many types of utilitarian wares, hotel china, and dinnerwares. They made the fine bone china known as Lotus Ware from 1891 to 1896. The company merged with American Ceramic Corporation in 1928. It closed in 1934. Lotus Ware is listed in its own category in this book.

KTK, Bowl, Openwork At Ends, Flowers On Sides, White, 4 3/4 X 6 In.	650.00
Coffee Server, Leaf Fronds On Spout, Lace Base, Sponged Gold, 8 1/4 In.	50.00
Jug, Spring Lake Sour Mash, Klein Bros., Cincinnati, Ohio	125.00
Platter, Mexican Siesta, Ivory, Red Rim, 12 In.	6.50
Sugar, Cover, Applied Fishnet, Gold Bows	350.00
Teapot, Silver Finial	187.50

KKK   Any items relating to the Ku Klux Klan are now collected because of their historic importance. Literature, robes, and memorabilia are available. The Klan is still in existence, so new material is found.

KU KLUX KLAN, Bottle, Marked K.K.K., Green, Medium	20.00
Doll, Rag	14.00
Knife, Pocket, Special Edition	150.00
Paperweight, Crystal	95.00
Watch, G.F.Elgin, Size 16, Beaded Watch Fob	150.00

Kutani ware is a Japanese porcelain made after the mid–seventeenth century. Most of the pieces found today are nineteenth century. Collectors often use the term "kutani" to refer to just the later, colorful pieces decorated with red, gold, and black pictures of warriors, animals, and birds.

KUTANI, Bowl, Rice, Cover, Floral Design, Scholars, Mt.Fuji, 4 1/2 In.	65.00
Bowl, Ruffled, Flowers, Leaves, White & Red Ground, Gold, 5 1/4 In.	35.00
Chocolate Pot, Birds & Peonies, Garden Scene, 1860–90, 8 1/2 In.	125.00
Chocolate Pot, Reserve Panels of Peonies, People, 8 1/2 In.	125.00
Nut Set, Nishikide, Diaper Pattern, Gold Scene of Geisha, 7 Piece	75.00
Tea Set, Gold, 21 Piece	195.00
Teapot, Scholar & Pupils On White	35.00
Teapot, Tortoiseshell Designs, Cherry Blossoms, Gold Trim, 4 In.	55.00
Tray, Encrusted Gold Nishikid Diaper, Children, 12 X 6 1/4 In.	48.00
Umbrella Stand, Tree Trunk Shape, Painted Lily, Signed, 24 In.	700.00
Vase, 3 1/2 In.	110.00
Vase, Stick, Gourd, 9 In.	68.00

Lacquer is a type of varnish. Collectors are most interested in the Chinese and Japanese lacquer wares made from the Japanese varnish tree. Lacquer wares are made from wood coated with many coats of lacquer. Sometimes the piece is carved or decorated with ivory or metal inlay.

LACQUER, Box, Chrysanthemums, Japanese Style, Metal, Tiffany, 7/8 X 2 1/4 In.	1550.00
Box, Raised Gilt Floral & Birds, Oriental, Dark Brown, 14 1/2 In.	120.00
Box, Sewing, Chinese, Fitted Interior, Paw Feet, Hinged Top, 14 In.	400.00
Smoking Set, Tabako–Ban, Kiri Wood, Artist Signed, Japan	1750.00
Table, Red, Mythical Family, Foo Dogs, Carved, Chinese, 14 X 32 In.	65.00
Table, Tea, Chinese	385.00
Tray, Black, Oriental Household Scene, 15 3/4 X 20 1/4 In.	175.00

LADY HEAD VASES, see Head Vases

Lalique glass was made by Rene Lalique in Paris, France, between the 1890s and his death in 1945. The glass was molded, pressed, and engraved in Art Nouveau and Art Deco styles. Pieces were marked with the signature "R. Lalique." Lalique glass is still being made. Pieces made after 1945 bear the mark "Lalique."

LALIQUE, Ashtray, 8 Girls' Faces Around Edge, 4 1/2 In.	70.00
Ashtray, Caravelle	60.00
Ashtray, Caravelle, Frosted Boat, Signed	60.00
Ashtray, Cupid	135.00
Ashtray, Fish, Frosted & Clear, Signed, 6 In.	195.00
Beaker, 6 Panels of Standing Figures, Signed, 4 In., Pair	200.00
Bell, Bird Finial	125.00

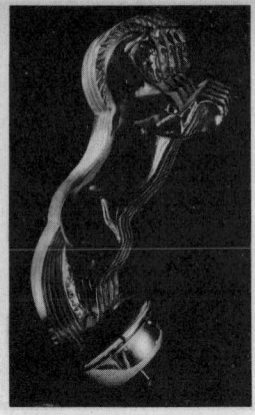

Lalique, Cross, Silver Plated,   Lalique, Hood Ornament, 5
Light, Engraved Signature, 16 In.   Rearing Horses, Profile, Chrome, 5 In.

Bowl, Fish Encircle Body, Signed, 9 In. 550.00
Bowl, Madagascar, Monkey Masks, Marked, C.1932, 11 3/4 In. 7975.00
Bowl, Mermaids, Opalescent, Signed, 8 In. 1325.00
Bowl, Mistletoe, Gray Wash, Marked, 4 X 9 1/4 In. 325.00
Bowl, Nemours, Blue Wash, 10 In. 1295.00
Bowl, Overlapping Ribbed Leaves, Canoe Shape, C.1925, 18 3/8 In. 1650.00
Bowl, Relief Nudes, Opalescent Blue, Signed, 8 In. 500.00
Bowl, Stylized Cherry Tree Center Medallion, Signed, 4 1/2 In. 75.00
Bowl, Swimming Fish & Bubbles, 8 In. 325.00
Bowl, Swimming Fish & Bubbles, 12 In. 450.00
Bowl, Swirl, 8 In. 275.00
Bowl, Swirling Rows of Graduating Bubbles Outside, Signed, 8 In. 450.00
Box, Clear & Amber Cover, Allover Blossoms, Signed, 4 In. 500.00
Box, Cover, Cyprins, Swimming Carp, Marked, C.1932, 10 In. 2475.00
Box, Dresser, Persian Cat On Cover, Signed, 4 In. 90.00
Chandelier, Coquilles, Glass Ceiling Mount, 4 Cords, Signed 1500.00
Charger, Opalescent Fish, Marked, 11 1/2 In. 495.00
Clock, Birds Mark Hours, Enameled Numerals, Signed, 8 1/4 In. 3650.00
Clock, Naiades, Blue Wash 2250.00
Clock, Parakeets, Branches, Circular Face, 4 1/2 In. 3300.00
Cordial, Amber Nude Panel, Signed, 5 Piece 575.00
Cross, Silver Plated, Light, Engraved Signature, 16 In. .... *Illus* 1430.00
Figurine, Buffalo, Frosted, Signed, 4 1/2 In. 190.00
Figurine, Elephant, Signed 425.00
Figurine, Lizard, Green, 6 1/2 In. 175.00
Figurine, Owl, Signed, 3 In. 85.00
Figurine, Rhinoceros, Black Base 795.00
Figurine, Suzanne, Lamp Mounted, Amber Glass, 14 1/2 In. 5000.00
Hood Ornament, 5 Rearing Horses, Profile, Chrome, 5 In. .... *Illus* 4400.00
Hood Ornament, Coq Nain, Marked 1600.00
Hood Ornament, Dragonfly, Frosted Glass, Inscribed, 6 1/4 In. 5000.00
Hood Ornament, Perche, Frosted, With Mount, Signed, 7 1/2 In. 2200.00
Hood Ornament, Tete D'Aigle, Eagle's Head, Frosted, 4 1/4 In. 3300.00
Ice Bucket, Bands of Leaves, Green Enameled Recesses, Signed 3870.00
Inkwell, Scarab Molded, Dark Amber, 1920, 3 1/2 In. 3000.00
Lamp, Thistle Pattern, Smoky 900.00
Liqueur, 6 Panels, Classical Ladies, Tapered Sides, 1920 .... 100.00
Paperweight, Black Demonic Mask, Clear Base, Signed 230.00
Paperweight, Football Shape, Clear & Frosted, 4 In. 125.00
Paperweight, Owl, Label, Marked, 1960s, 3 1/2 In. 95.00
Pendant, 2 Nudes, Holding Floral Urns, Frosted, Clear, Black Cord 1760.00
Pendant, Cherries, Red & Amber, Triangle Shape 975.00

Pendant, Floret, Tassel 495.00
Perfume Bottle, 4 Turtles At Sides, Heads Back, Signed, 4 1/2 In. 6000.00
Perfume Bottle, 5 Fleurs, Forvil, Sealed & Labeled, 5 1/2 In. 975.00
Perfume Bottle, Black, Classic Maidens, Ambre D'Orsay, 5 1/4 In. 1980.00
Perfume Bottle, Blue, Dans La Nuit 65.00
Perfume Bottle, Blue, Spherical, Glass Stopper, 6 5/8 In. 1650.00
Perfume Bottle, Bouquet De Faine 650.00
Perfume Bottle, Cactus, Marked 450.00
Perfume Bottle, Capricci, Ricci 195.00
Perfume Bottle, Coeur–Joie, Heart Shape, Nina Ricci, 6 In. 200.00
Perfume Bottle, Dahlia Mold, Frosted, Enameled, Nude Stopper, 9 In. 3080.00
Perfume Bottle, Draped Female Figures, Intaglio Mold, Signed, 6 In. 2100.00
Perfume Bottle, Fleurettes, Blue Stained, Large 475.00
Perfume Bottle, Flower Blossom, Brown & Black Patina, 3 In. 3950.00
Perfume Bottle, Flower Heads, Flask Form, Signed, 9 1/2 In. 6650.00
Perfume Bottle, Horizontal Bands, Enamel Bosses, Signed, 3 5/8 In. 2075.00
Perfume Bottle, Je Reviens, Turquoise, Signed, 4 1/2 In. 125.00
Perfume Bottle, L'Air Du Temps, Dove Stopper 25.00
Perfume Bottle, Lovebird Stopper 290.00
Perfume Bottle, Mimosa Trailing From Shoulder, Signed, 3 In. 240.00
Perfume Bottle, Mirrored Worth Store Display, Dark Blue, 4 In. 450.00
Perfume Bottle, Nude Maidens In Panels, Gilt Top, Amber, Marked 315.00
Perfume Bottle, Palerme 595.00
Perfume Bottle, Pearl Festoons, Signed, 6 5/8 In. 7200.00
Perfume Bottle, Perles 2500.00
Perfume Bottle, Ring Form, Inset With Lizards, Signed, 1 1/4 In. 1200.00
Perfume Bottle, Turtles, Amber, Signed, 5 1/2 In. 7250.00
Perfume Bottle, Tzigane, Corday, Signed 450.00
Plate, Annual, 1966, Dream Rose, 8 1/2 In. 165.00
Plate, Annual, 1968, Box 45.00
Plate, Annual, 1971 .... 75.00
Plate, Annual, 1976 .... 135.00
Plate, Black Leaf, 8 In. 105.00
Plate, Seashell, Opalescent, Marked, 9 In. 525.00
Plate, Seashell, Signed, 9 In. 845.00
Powder Box, 3 Nudes 325.00
Powder Box, Embossed Dancing Nudes, Garlands, Signed, 3 5/8 In. 245.00
Powder Box, Emiliane 265.00
Powder Box, Meridan 525.00
Powder Box, Roger, Black Enameling 2750.00
Scent Burner, Mermaids Around, Wave Form Cap, Opalescent, 7 In. 2100.00
Scent Burner, Sirens, Frosted & Gray Stain 2450.00
Seal, Fountain, Exposition Internationale, 1925, 3 1/4 In. 3550.00
Tray, Carnation Blossoms, Clear & Frosted, Signed, 15 1/2 X 10 In. 750.00
Tumbler, Jaffa Design, 16 Columns, Amber Body, Frosted, Signed, 1932 .... 215.00
Vase, 12 Sculptured Birds, 7 In. .... 250.00 To 255.00
Vase, 2 Applied Doves, Frosted Swirled Body, Footed, Signed, 5 In. 195.00
Vase, Alternating Panels of 6 Female Nudes, Signed, 9 1/2 In. 3650.00
Vase, Berries, Raised, Globe Shape, White Opalescent, Signed, 7 In. 650.00
Vase, Berry Finial, Sylvia, Berry Clusters, Signed, 8 3/4 In. 4850.00
Vase, Blown–Out Blossoms, Raised Branches, Signed, 6 1/4 In. 525.00
Vase, Blue Cornflowers, Clear Ground, 6 3/4 In. 1650.00
Vase, Cane & Berries, Blue Opalescent, 6 1/2 In. 450.00
Vase, Ceylon, Lovebirds, Signed, C.1932, 9 5/8 In. 3025.00
Vase, Charmilles, Marked, C.1932, 14 In. 7700.00
Vase, Cherries, Blue Opalescent, 8 X 8 In. 750.00
Vase, Dahlia Blossoms, Black Enameled Stamen, Signed, 5 In. 1450.00
Vase, Danaides, 6 Nudes Holding Urns, Signed, C.1932, 7 1/4 In. 2090.00
Vase, Fish, Protruding, Raised Bubbles, Signed, 5 In. 850.00
Vase, Formose, Pearly Opalescent, Marked, C.1932, 7 In. 2200.00
Vase, Formose, Tiers of Swimming Fish, Green, Marked, C.1932, 7 In. 6600.00
Vase, Gros Scarabees, Spherical, Marked, C.1932, 11 3/4 In. 9900.00
Vase, Languedoc, Frosted Sides, Marked, C.1932, 9 In. 4400.00
Vase, Lotus Blossoms, Stamen On Frosted Ground, Signed, 5 3/4 In. 525.00

Vase, Macaws On Berried Branches, Signed, 9 In. 1935.00
Vase, Male Nudes In Base, Holding Up Vessel, Signed, 5 1/4 In. 2660.00
Vase, Mythological Beasts, Tapered Neck, Frosted, Clear, 11 In. 1200.00
Vase, Overlapping Stylized Leaves, Amber Red, Signed, 5 In. 1815.00
Vase, Pan, Blowing Flute, Nudes, Notched, Cylinder, Signed, 3 1/2 In. 245.00
Vase, Parakeets, 9 1/2 In. 1900.00
Vase, Pattern of Wheat Stalks, Trefoil Top, Signed, 5 3/4 In. 795.00
Vase, Sparrows & Leaves, Clear & Frosted, 5 In. 395.00
Vase, Stylized Cocks Heralding Morning, Signed, 4 In. 3870.00
Vase, Stylized Frieze Egrets, Reeds, Molded, 9 7/8 In. 3850.00
Vase, Tourbillons, Thorny Branches, Amber, Signed, C.1932, 8 In. 8800.00
Vase, Vertical Bands of Lizards, Signed, 12 1/4 In. 1815.00
Vase, Wild Stallions Against Clouds, Signed, 11 1/4 In. 7200.00
Water Set, Fish Design, Blue, 5 Piece 1350.00
Wine, Stem of Dancing Nudes, Clear & Frosted, Signed, 6 In. 110.00

Interest is strong in lamps of every type, from the early oil-burning Betty and Phoebe lamps to the recent electric lamps with glass or beaded shades. Fuels used in lamps changed through the years; whale oil (1800–40), camphene (1828), Argand (1830), lard (1833–63), turpentine and alcohol (1840s), gas (1850–79), kerosene (1860), and electricity (1879) are the most common. Other lamps are listed by manufacturer or type of material.

LAMP, 3 Deer, Bronze Metal, Wooden Base, F.Lavelle, France, 12 X 14 X 20 In. 785.00
3–Light, Carved As Classical Urn, Bronze Mounted, Alabaster, 22 In. 250.00
Aladdin, B– 48, Green Bell Stem 145.00
Aladdin, B– 52, Washington Drape, Green 75.00
Aladdin, B– 54, Washington Drape, Green Beta Crystal 55.00
Aladdin, B– 62, Lincoln Drape, Ruby, With Burner, Short 250.00
Aladdin, B– 70, Solitaire, White Moonstone 1000.00
Aladdin, B– 75, Lincoln Drape, Ivory Alacite, With 401 Shade 220.00
Aladdin, B– 77, Lincoln Drape, Ruby, With Burner, Tall 125.00
Aladdin, B– 83, Beehive, Ruby 110.00
Aladdin, B– 88, Vertique, Yellow Moonstone .... 295.00 To 375.00
Aladdin, B–101, Corinthian, Amber 42.50
Aladdin, B–102, Corinthian, Green Crystal 45.00
Aladdin, B–104, Corinthian, Clear, Black Base 55.00
Aladdin, B–108, Cathedral, Painted Shade, Green Crystal Shade 100.00
Aladdin, B–110, Cathedral, White Moonstone 140.00
Aladdin, Boudoir, Rose Alacite 27.50
Aladdin, Electric, Glass Shade, Pink, White, Bird of Paradise, 8 In. 90.00
Aladdin, Electric, Urn Shape, 18 In. 38.00
Aladdin, Emeralite, Dual Shade 700.00
Aladdin, G– 24, Cupid, Green Base, Parchment Shade 75.00
Aladdin, G–144, Frosted White Moonstone 180.00
Aladdin, G–171, Mantle, Reverse Painted Moonstone With Bouquet 95.00
Aladdin, G–252, Anglia Finial 55.00
Aladdin, No. 6, Nickel, With 301 Shade 135.00
Aladdin, No. 104, Colonial 55.00
Aladdin, No. 325, Hand Painted Ball Shade 1050.00
Aladdin, No. 550, Swiss Scene Shade 400.00
Aladdin, No.1250, Green Variegated Vase 100.00
Aladdin, P–421U, Terra Cotta Base, Treebark Fabric Shade, 27 In. 75.00
Aladdin, P–467, Ceramic Base, Fruitwood Finish, Box 30.00
Argand, 2 Arms, Gilt Bronze, Prisms, 3 Caryatid, Electrified, 19 In., Pr. 2200.00
Argand, Gothic, Prism Hung, Electrified, Frosted & Cut Shade, C.1825 .... 1100.00
Argand, Ionic Column, Brass, Gilt Bronze Finish, 22 3/4 In. 750.00
Argand, Mica Shade, C.1830, 24 3/4 In. 695.00
Argand-Type Burner, Viscous Fuel, Lithophane Shade ....*Illus* 700.00
Astral, Brass Baluster Base, Cut Glass Shade, 1849, 23 In. 1100.00
Astral, Cast Brass Base, Fire Gilding, Cut Prisms, Frosted, 19 3/8 In. 350.00
Astral, Marble Base, Brass Column, Brass Font, Cut Prisms, 21 1/2 In. 275.00
Betty, Hanger, Wrought Iron, 4 In. 45.00
Betty, Pear Shaped Hinged Lid, Tin, 18th Century 220.00

Betty, Tin, Hanger, 6 1/4 In. 150.00
Betty, Tin, Wick Pick & Hook, American 350.00
Betty, Twisted Hanger, Wrought Iron, 4 In. 45.00
Betty, Wire Link Wick Pick, Iron Hook, C.1800 .... 295.00
Betty, Wrought Iron, Hanger, 4 3/4 In. 115.00
LAMP, BRADLEY & HUBBARD, see Bradley & Hubbard, Lamp
Candle, Folding, Tin, Mica Windows, Minors Pat., Jan.24, 1865, 5 1/4 In. 75.00
Candle, Hodge & Roberts, Green Glass, Gilt Bronze, English 2200.00
Candle, Hurricane, Tulip Shaped Shade, Scrolled Handles, 18 In., Pair 325.00
Candle, Scrolled Tubing, Jeweled Copper, 23 1/2 In. 185.00
Candle, Spring Loaded, Nickel–Plated Brass, Curved Glass Lens, 6 In. 45.00
Chandelier, 3–Light, Owl On Flowering Bush, English, 12 1/2 In. 440.00
Chandelier, 4–Light, Rococo Gilt Bronze, Figures On Support 7425.00
Chandelier, 5–Light, Art Deco, Polished & Lacquered Shades 495.00
Chandelier, 6–Light, Cut Glass Standard, Foliate Arms, 23 X 15 In. 825.00
Chandelier, 6–Light, Cut With Fans, Berry Finial, Prisms, 27 1/2 In. 3850.00
Chandelier, 6–Light, Louis XVI, Cut Glass, Cage Form, 2 Tiers, 39 In. 4950.00
Chandelier, 6–Light, Neoclassical, Cut Glass, Cobalt, Sweden, 28 In. 6050.00
Chandelier, 6–Light, Regency, Cut Glass, Faceted Glass Chain, 36 In. 2860.00
Chandelier, 7–Light, Rococo, Bronze, Nude Female, Electrified, 30 In. 2200.00
Chandelier, 8–Light, Electric Candles, Silk Shades, 17 X 23 In. 410.00
Chandelier, 8–Light, Masks Supporting Nozzles, Gilt Bronze, 19 In. 4125.00
Chandelier, 8–Light, Prisms & Stars, Wrought Iron & Cut Glass, 28 In. 1540.00
Chandelier, 9–Light, Wedgwood Plaques, Fruit Finial, Electric, 35 In. 2640.00
Chandelier, 10–Light, 3 Nude Men Center, Bronze, 1910, 25 1/2 In. 3850.00
Chandelier, 12–Light, 2 Tiers, Gilt Metal Frame, Prisms, Czech., 1950 .... 6500.00
Chandelier, 12–Light, Drip Cups, Brass, 19th Century, 25 1/2 In. 3520.00
Chandelier, 12–Light, Louis XV Style, Cut Glass & Ormolu, 44 In. 1800.00
Chandelier, Brass & Cut Glass, 1905, 7 1/2 X 4 1/2 In. 3500.00
Chanelier, Cast Brass Frame, Crystal, 20th Century, 35 In. 275.00
Coach, Beveled Glass, Tin With Brass Trim, Bracket Arms, 14 In., Pair 70.00
Coach, Brass, Beveled Glass, Polished & Electrified, 12 1/4 In., Pair 115.00
Coach, Candle Burning, Beveled Glass, Red Lens, 17 1/4 In., Pair 40.00
Coach, Hexagonal, Beveled Glass, Electrified, 38 In., Pair 340.00
Crusie, Double, Hanger, Wrought Iron, 4 1/2 In. 35.00
Crusie, Double, Stylized Bird Design, European, 8 1/2 In. 55.00
Crusie, Double, Wrought Iron, 6 3/4 In. 55.00
Electric, Airplane Shape, Cobalt Blue Glass, Airline Premium 750.00
Electric, Arab Selling Artifacts, Draped Booth, Namgreb, C.1900, 15 In. 1000.00
Electric, Architect's, Daylite Screen, Emeralite 365.00
Electric, Art Deco, 1 Cylindrical Light Between Marble Monoliths 120.00
Electric, Art Deco, Black, With Chrome Rings 65.00
Electric, Art Deco, Caramel, Original Paint 450.00
Electric, Art Deco, Fred Astaire, Ginger Rogers, Dancing The Carioca 85.00
Electric, Art Deco, Green Glass, Alligatored, Mica Shade, Floral, 23 In. 600.00
Electric, Art Deco, Statue of Liberty, Frosted 85.00
Electric, Art Deco, White Painted Metal, 5 Cylindrical Globes, 75 In. 100.00
Electric, Art Nouveau, Bronze, Leaded Floral Design, American, 23 In. 600.00
Electric, Banquet Style, Brass Plated Cast Metal, No Shade, 32 In. 35.00
Electric, Brass, Clear 2 Cylinder Pole, Glass Water Lily Shade, Floor 300.00
Electric, Bronze Figures of Dutch Man & Woman, Shades, 21 In., Pair 170.00
Electric, Bronze, Amorous Knight, Lover, Ivory, Green Onyx, 1920, 29 In. 2000.00
Electric, Bronze, Cracked Ice Shade, Reverse Painted Scene, 14 In. 300.00
Electric, Bronze, Girl, Porcelain Flowers, King Tut Shade, 15 In. 375.00
Electric, Bronze, Nude, Inside Columns, Minaret, Loetz Shade, 19 In. 400.00
Electric, Bronze, Silk Windmill Design Shade, Hanging Switch, Floor 170.00
Electric, Cameo, Purple, Green, Floral, Petal Design, 8 In. ....*Illus* 8080.00
Electric, Champleve & Bronze, 2–Light, Twist Mask, 22 In. 150.00
Electric, Chinese Bronze & Champleve Enamel, Floral Design, 58 In. 650.00
Electric, Classical Scribe, Wearing Toga, Crown, Bronze, 22 1/2 In. 550.00
Electric, Columnar Shaft, Silvered Bronze, Arched Legs, 4 Ft.2 In. 3575.00
Electric, Coraline Beaded & Beaded Fringed Shade, 21 In. 150.00
Electric, Desk, Arts & Crafts, Green Glass Shade, Cast Iron, 20 In. 350.00
Electric, Desk, Pittsburgh, Reverse Painted Glass, Oval Base, Floral 450.00

Electric, Desk, Verdelite, Double Knuckle, Cased Shade	385.00
Electric, Dietz, Post, Tubular Street Lamp, Wire Bail, 20 1/2 In.	200.00
Electric, Dietz, Tubular, Stenciled, Reflector, Square, 22 In.	160.00
Electric, Double Candelabras In Gilded Brass, Amethyst Beads, 14 In.	75.00
Electric, Econolite Corp., 2 Train Engines Picture, 9 1/2 X 6 In.	65.00
Electric, Elsie The Borden Cow, 10 In.	55.00
Electric, Emeralite, Brass Color, Stylized Leaf Design, 18 In.	205.00
Electric, Full Figural Nude Woman, Bronze, Lily Pad Base, 15 1/4 In.	1395.00
Electric, G.Stickley, Copper, Swollen Cylindrical, Round Foot, 21 In.	1500.00
Electric, Green Slag Glass Inset Shade, Wrought Iron, Floor	1300.00
Electric, Indian Sitting On Rock, Metal, Delaware Water Gap, Pa.	62.00
Electric, Jefferson, Reverse Painted Shade, Signed, 16 In.	1000.00
Electric, Jefferson, Reverse Painted, Country Road, Baluster, 18 In.	1400.00
Electric, Leaded Glass, Mushroom Shade, Bronze Tree Trunk, 14 In.	425.00
Electric, Limbert, Hammered Copper, Conical Mica Shade	4500.00
Electric, Mayflower Ship Shape, Cast Iron	40.00
Electric, Millefiori, 12 1/2 In.	135.00
Electric, Mission Style, Signed Burke, Paper Shade, 28.In.	150.00
Electric, Moe Bridges, Art Deco, Bronze Color, 26 In.	100.00
Electric, Newel Post, Bronze God, Holding Platen, Ruffled Shade, 27 In.	900.00
Electric, Open Weave Shade, Bulbous Bottom Base, Wicker, 24 In.	150.00
Electric, Oriental White Metal, Slag Glass, Statue of Liberty, 25 In.	400.00
Electric, Pairpoint, Reverse Painted Scenic Shade, Signed, 27 In.	3500.00
Electric, Phoenix, Rose Quartz, Lotus Branch, In Rushes, Chinese, 12 In.	5500.00
Electric, Pottery, Green, White Globe, Grasscloth Shade, 13 3/4 In.	76.00
Electric, Pottery, Mottled Turquoise Gray, Red Bubbles, 10 X 5 In.	80.00
Electric, Pottery, Oakleaf Cluster, Urn Shape, Plum, Footed, 10 In.	75.00
Electric, Reverse Painted Breaking Waves, Pittsburgh, 16 In.	1400.00
Electric, Reverse Painted Shade, Gold Finished Base, Desk	900.00
Electric, Seated Official, Gold Lacquer, 19th Century, Chinese, 16 In.	800.00
Electric, St.Clair, Glass, 4 Floral Sections, Brass Spacers, 1940s	1000.00
Electric, Stiffel, Floor, Brass	80.00
Electric, Tree Lamppost, Man, Woman, Seated, Occupied Japan, 10 3/4 In.	38.00
Electric, TV, Gold Ceramic Ballerina, Speckled Royal Blue	27.00
Electric, TV, Sailing Ship, Green	20.00
Electric, TV, Swan, Pink, Gold	18.00
Electric, Vase, Rose Quartz, Birds, Branches, Chinese, 7 1/2 In.	2250.00
Electric, Walnut, Large Fringed Shade	80.00
Electric, Wicker Shade, Brown Wicker	135.00
Electric, Wicker, 6 Ft.	650.00
Electric, Wooden Pyramid Base, Slag Glass, Arts & Crafts, 23 In.	1600.00
Electric, Wooden, Candle Shape, Trestle Base, Arts & Crafts, 17 In.	300.00
Fairy, Blue Satin Glass Shade, Seaweed Pattern, Pinched Top, 3 1/2 In.	120.00
Fairy, Burmese Base, Clarke Insert, Brass Frame, 7 X 7 In.	750.00
Fairy, Burmese, Clarke Base, 3 5/8 In.	150.00
Fairy, Citron Nailsea Shade, Clarke Cricklite Base, 4 3/4 In.	160.00
Fairy, Citron Yellow, White Loopings, Cricklite, England, 9 1/2 In.	225.00
Fairy, Clarke, Tin Handled Base, Odd Shaped Candle	220.00

Lamp, Reverse Swirl, Acorn Burner,
Blue Opalescent, 4 1/4 In.

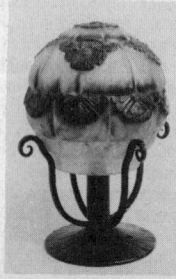

Lamp, Electric, Cameo, Purple,
Green, Floral, Petal Design, 8 In.

Lamp, Figural, Arab Antiquarian, Draped   Lamp, Gone With The Wind, Brass,

Carpet, Bronze, 15 1/2 In.   Glass, Maroon Shade, 1880, 29 In.

Fairy, Cleveland Pattern, Blue, White, Satin Stripe, 3 Parts, 6 1/4 In.	650.00
Fairy, Cut Standards With Darts, Star Base, Clarke Cricklite, 4 Piece	400.00
Fairy, Diamond Point, Amber Glass, Marked, 3 3/4 In.	62.00
Fairy, Embossed Satin Swirl, Marked Clarke Base, 5 In.	165.00
Fairy, Gray To White Overlay Satin, Marked Clarke, Ruffled, 6 1/4 In.	195.00
Fairy, Green Overlay, White Lined Dome Shade, Clarke Base, 4 X 4 In.	100.00
Fairy, Hanging, Jeweled Brass, 16 1/2 In.	150.00
Fairy, Mother–of–Pearl Quilt, Clarke Cricklite Base, 7 X 5 1/2 In.	675.00
Fairy, Nailsea Base, Clarke Pyramid Mark, 5 1/2 In.	485.00
Fairy, Owl Head, Clarke Base, Cranberry, 4 3/4 In.	195.00
Fairy, Peachblow Colored Shade, Clarke Base, Silver Plated Frame	330.00
Fairy, Puffy Shade, Reverse Painted, 8 In.	250.00
Fairy, Queen Victoria's Jubilee, Blue, 4 1/2 X 3 In.	185.00
Fairy, Verre Moire, Clarke Insert, Cranberry, 5 X 5 1/2 In.	425.00
Fairy, Verre Moire, Crimped Base, Clarke Insert, Green, 5 1/4 X 6 In.	425.00
Fairy, Verre Moire, Frosted Cranberry, White Looping Shade, 4 1/4 In.	165.00
Figural, Arab Antiquarian, Draped Carpet, Bronze, 15 1/2 In. ....*Illus*	1100.00
Finger, Aquarius Pattern, Pale Green Shade, Footed, 4 1/2 In.	60.00
Finger, Embossed Design, Crystal Handle, Cranberry, 5 1/4 In.	250.00
Finger, Emma, Opalescent Coin Spot	350.00
Finger, Flat, Torpedo .... 70.00 To 80.00	
Finger, Flat, Wheat In Shield	85.00
Finger, Flint, Double Wedding Ring	135.00
Finger, Inverted Thumbprint, Reeded Handle, Green, 6 1/4 In.	75.00
Finger, Oil Guard, Sept.10, 1870	75.00
Finger, Orange & Cobalt Blue Spatter Glass, Clear Handle	195.00
Finger, Pressed Glass, Quartered Block, 6 In.	110.00
Finger, Pressed Glass, Wheat In Shield, Flat	100.00
Finger, Purple Fishscale Pattern, Reflector	225.00
Finger, Sweetheart, Green Font, Clear Base	450.00
Fiscous Fuel, Argand–Type Burner, Lithophane Shade, 31 In. ....*Illus*	700.00
Fluid, Brass, Acorn Font, 8 In.	125.00
Fluid, Pewter, Cast Ear Handle, Handle, 7 1/2 In.	85.00
Fluid, Triple Cut Overlay, Blue To White To Clear, 12 1/4 In.	2300.00
Girandole, Etched Shade, Prisms On Arched Branches, Brass, 15 In., Pair	350.00
Glow Light, Ruby Glass Ribbed Globe & Font, Night–Light	195.00
Glow–Oil, Mushroom, Clear Bottom, Milk Top, 4 1/2 In.	60.00
Gone With The Wind, Blown–Out Lion Heads, Desert Scene, 23 1/2 In.	500.00
Gone With The Wind, Brass, Glass, Maroon Shade, 1880, 29 In. ....*Illus*	525.00
Gone With The Wind, Diamond–Quilted, Red Satin, 28 In.	425.00
Gone With The Wind, Holly Berry & Leaf, Chimney, White Satin, 23 In.	795.00
Gone With The Wind, Pillar, Red Satin, 25 In.	500.00

Gone With The Wind, Puffy Drape, Simulated Cord Quilted, 27 In. 650.00
Gone With The Wind, Red Floral, Green & White Ground, 24 In. 525.00
Gone With The Wind, Red Satin Glass, Gazebo Form 900.00
Gone With The Wind, Red Satin Glass, Teardrop Pattern 850.00
Gone With The Wind, Red Satin Regal Iris, Electrified, 27 In. 400.00
Gone With The Wind, Satin Finish Clear Glass, Roses, 24 In. 640.00
Gone With The Wind, Tulip, Red Satin, 22 In. 350.00
Hand, Figural, Shoe, Laces Tied In Bow, Crystal, 3 X 5 1/2 In. 350.00
     LAMP, HANDEL, see Handel, Lamp
Hanging, Brass Cottage Frame, Milk Glass Shade, Floral Design 100.00
Hanging, Hall, Blown Globe, Smoke Bell, Embossed Brass Trim, 20 In. 625.00
Hanging, Hall, Blown, Frosted Globe, Smoke Bell, Brass Trim, 27 In. 400.00
Hanging, Hall, Brass Frame, Cranberry, 4 1/2 X 12 In. 750.00
Hanging, Hall, Cylindrical, Amber Shade, Bull's-Eye Pattern, 27 In. 200.00
Hanging, Hall, Pink Opalescent Paneled Shade, Brass Frame 250.00
Hanging, Hall, Rubina With Optic Striping, Corset Waist 345.00
Hanging, Hall, Vaseline Glass, Hobnail Pattern, Chain, 15 In. 150.00
Hanging, Hand Painted & Transfer, Glass Shade, Brass, 13 1/2 In. 150.00
Hanging, Hobnail, Cranberry, Brass Frame, Prisms, Electrified, 19 In. 800.00
Hanging, Ornate Frame, Pink To Opalescent, 4 1/2 X 12 In. 750.00
Hanging, Victorian, Cranberry Hobnail, Prisms, Polished Frame 925.00
Jeweler's, Alcohol, Brass Blowing Tube, F.M.Roy & Co., 2 3/4 In. 39.00
Kerosene, Acorn Fittings, Tin, 7 1/2 In. 65.00
Kerosene, Amber Glass, Aquarius, Original Burner 115.00
Kerosene, Angle, Double, Embossed Brass, Milk Glass Shades, 27 In. 425.00
Kerosene, Artichoke Pattern, Milk Glass, Fired-On Paint, 7 1/2 In. 300.00
Kerosene, Banquet, Paneled Stem, Waffle Cut Foot, Font, Crystal, 23 In. 400.00
Kerosene, Banquet, Pink Stain Glass Font, Stem, Embossed Design, 26 In. 1465.00
Kerosene, Banquet, Reeded Colums, Corinthian Tops, Silver Plated, Pair 190.00
Kerosene, Banquet, Spiraled Column, Pink Globe, Wrought Iron, 33 In. 350.00
Kerosene, Banquet, Victorian, Rose To White Globe, Pierced Brass Base 150.00
Kerosene, Banquet, White Metal, Brass, Onyx Stem, Electrified, 21 In. 120.00
Kerosene, Beaded Drape, Red Satin Glass, Nutmeg Burner, 9 In. 300.00
Kerosene, Beaded Swirl Pattern, Cranberry, Nornet Burner, 8 In. 150.00
Kerosene, Blue Mother-of-Pearl, Raindrop Pattern, Nutmeg Burner, 8 In. 3000.00
Kerosene, Brass, Label, Burner, 8 3/4 In. 35.00
Kerosene, Brass, Single Spout Burner, Wick Advance Knob, 11 In. 65.00
Kerosene, Bronze, Squat Baluster Form, Dragons, Green Patina, 15 In. 450.00
Kerosene, Chocolate Glass, Wild Rose & Bowknot 695.00
Kerosene, Coleman, 4 Frosted Colored Panels 85.00
Kerosene, Coleman, Kerolite Mantle, Signed Chimney, Extra Wicks, Box 80.00
Kerosene, Coleman, Patent May 13, 1919 .... 185.00
Kerosene, Copper Finish, Rampant Lions, Cherub Handles, Globe, 24 In. 400.00
Kerosene, Cosmos, Milk Glass, Pink Bands, Colored Flowers, 7 1/2 In. 250.00
Kerosene, Daisy & Cube Pattern, Amber, 7 3/4 In. 325.00
Kerosene, Diamond & Fan, Amber 135.00
Kerosene, Diamond & Thumbprint Font, Clear, Pewter Collar, 6 1/4 In. 80.00
Kerosene, Dolphin, Pink 525.00
Kerosene, Embossed Design, Nutmeg Burner, Miniature 450.00
Kerosene, Embossed Flower, Scrolls, Burgundy Ground, Milk Glass, 8 In. 350.00
Kerosene, Embossed Owl, Milk Glass, Shades of Green & Brown, 8 In. 1300.00
Kerosene, Feather Duster, Amber 140.00
Kerosene, Feather Duster, Canary 150.00
Kerosene, Finger, Beaded Heart 130.00
Kerosene, Finger, Clear Heart 75.00
Kerosene, Finger, Custard Heart 250.00
Kerosene, Finger, Wreath & Daisy, Green 250.00
Kerosene, Greek Key, Brass Acorn Burner, P.& A. Mfg., 5 1/2 In. 40.00
Kerosene, Hand Painted Shade, Cosmos Burner, Green Opalescent, 20 In. 150.00
Kerosene, Hanging, Brass Fonts, Waffle Shades 135.00
Kerosene, Hanging, Bristol, Pink & Floral 250.00
Kerosene, Hanging, Ribbed Shade, Moves Up & Down On Weights, Brass 875.00
Kerosene, Little Buttercup, Green 110.00
Kerosene, Lomax, Handle, Footed, 1870 .... 40.00

Kerosene, Milk Glass, Rust Ground, Floral Design, 8 1/4 In. 400.00
Kerosene, Moon & Star, Amethyst Glass, Nutmeg Burner, 7 3/4 In. 65.00
Kerosene, Mountain Laurel, Oval Band Base, Chimney & Burner 75.00
Kerosene, Neverout, Safety 50.00
Kerosene, New York, Blue Font, Milk Glass Base 195.00
Kerosene, Opalescent Vaseline Stripe, Ringed Base 295.00
Kerosene, Peanut Pattern, Pressed Glass 65.00
Kerosene, Prince Edward, Green, 8 1/4 In. 135.00
Kerosene, Princess Feather 85.00
Kerosene, Raised Basket of Flowers, Glass Chimney & Shade, 5 In. 50.00
Kerosene, Reverse Swirl, Blue Opalescent, Acorn Burner, 4 1/4 In. 200.00
Kerosene, Ripley & Co., Pat.1868, Pressed Glass, Brass Collar, 4 In. 70.00
Kerosene, Riverside Panel, Green Font, Clear Stem 145.00
Kerosene, Snowflake, Blue 395.00
Kerosene, Snowflake, Cranberry 450.00
Kerosene, Snowflake, White 295.00
Kerosene, St.Louis, Amber Font 140.00
Kerosene, St.Louis, Amber Font, Clear Pedestal 140.00
Kerosene, Time & Light, Pride of America, Brass Collar, Clear 105.00
Kerosene, Zipper & Circle, Eagle Burner 47.00
Lacemaker's, All Glass, 10 In. 235.00
Lacemaker's, Cranberry Inverted Thumbprint Shade, Brass Base, 18 In. 450.00
Lacemaker's, Diamond–Quilted Shade, Brass Base, Cranberry, 16 1/2 In. 425.00
Lard, N.& H.C. Ufford, Iron Base, Brass Labels, Pat.1851, 13 In., Pr. 210.00
Lard, Saucer Base, Green Paint, Archer's Patent, C.1842, 7 In. 650.00
Lard, Saucer Base, Green Paint, Gilt Trim, Davis Patent, C.1856, 7 In. 150.00
Lard, Smith & Stonesifer, Front Leaves, C.1854, 8 In. 125.00
Lard, Smith & Stonesifer, Tin, Pat.6 In. 75.00
Library, Milk Glass Shade & Font, Flowers, Brass Frame, Prisms 300.00
Library, Milk Glass Shade, Butterfly & Floral, Brass Frame 215.00
Library, Milk Glass Shade, Floral Design, Pink Ground, Prisms 250.00
Miner's, American Safety Lamp & Miners Supply Co., Carbide, Brass, Tin 65.00
Miner's, Brass Collar & Lid, Spout, Patent 1908, 4 In. 45.00
Miner's, Brass, Copper, Hanger, 4 In. 250.00
Miner's, Copper, Wrought Iron Fittings, Copper Shovel, Hanger, 4 In. 300.00
Miner's, Justrite, Brass, Large 40.00
Miner's, Mine Safety Appliances Co., Brass Label, Tin, 11 1/2 In. 65.00
Miner's, Safety, Wolf, 3 Positions, Cap Igniter, Copper Shade, Key 145.00
Miner's, Vaolite, Copper Spout, Smokeless, Odorless, Tin, 3 1/2 In. 60.00
Napoleon III, Gilt Bronze Socle, Cut Glass, Electrifed, 1860, 14 In. 770.00
Oil, Beaded Loop, Pressed Glass, 11 In. 300.00
Oil, Bellflower, Pressed Glass, 7 In., Pair 350.00
Oil, Bellflower, Pressed Glass, Bracket 425.00
Oil, Black Amethyst Stem, Acanthus Leaves, American, 11 In. 135.00
Oil, Blown Glass, Aqua, Bell Font, Applied Handle, Pewter Snuffer, 4 In. 296.00
Oil, Boudoir, Hand Painted Glass Shade, Brass, Victorian, 17 1/2 In. 190.00
Oil, Bristol, Enameled Floral Design, Ball Base, Beige Ground, 6 In. 95.00
Oil, Bristol, Hanging, 34 Prisms, Climax Font, Brass, Painted Shade 250.00
Oil, Cameo Glass, Trumpet Top, Blue Over White, Marble Base, 23 In., Pr. 2200.00
Oil, Clear Daisy, Bull's–Eye Foot & Shoulders 60.00
Oil, Columbian Coin Pattern, Milk Glass, 10 5/8 In. 125.00
Oil, Cosmos, Yellow Band, Fishnet, Milk Glass, Miniature 60.00
Oil, Daisy, No.1, Milk Glass 195.00
Oil, Dog's Head Brand, Metal 26.00
Oil, Double Iron Bracket, Mercury Reflector, 1877–90 .... 175.00
Oil, Double Portrait Stem, Black Amethyst Base, Dated 1876 .... 125.00
Oil, Duplex, Pagoda Style, Cranberry Fluted Shade, 22 X 9 In. 350.00
Oil, Emblem Pattern, 6 3/4 In. 100.00
Oil, Erwin Fan, Green 135.00
Oil, Fern Pattern, Blue 65.00
Oil, Figural, Dolphin, Conch Shell Finial, Bronze, C.1850, 11 In., Pair 2860.00
Oil, Findlay, Cable Pattern, Clear, 3 5/8 In. 32.00
Oil, Fishscale, Pressed Glass, 10 In. 70.00
Oil, Florette, Pink Cased Font, Clear Base 415.00

Oil, Hawkeye Pattern, Milk Glass, Diamond Rib & Bead Stem, Blue 325.00
Oil, Jeweler's, Metal Base 65.00
Oil, Juno, Purple Slag 210.00
Oil, King Comet, Pressed Glass, 11 1/2 In. 110.00
Oil, Lincoln Drape, Cobalt Blue, Tall 800.00
Oil, Milk Glass, Acorn Burner, C.1912, Miniature 85.00
Oil, Milk Glass, Reclining Elephant 480.00
Oil, Mold Blown Ruby Glass Font, Flower & Foliage, Marble Base, C.1880 .... 225.00
Oil, Nellie Bly, Miniature 175.00
Oil, Poinsettia Pattern Leaded Glass Shade 200.00
Oil, Prince Edward, Pink Cased, Clear Base 645.00
Oil, Ripley Double Handle, 1868 .... 80.00
Oil, Sawtooth & Swag, Pressed Glass, 8 3/4 In. 75.00
Oil, Teardrop With Eyewinker, Plume Font 67.50
Oil, Twinkle, Blue Glass, Acorn Burner, 6 7/8 In. 225.00
Oil, Zipper Loop, Umbrella Shade, Ruby Stained, 10 1/2 In. 140.00
Organ, Brass, Cranberry Shade, Dated 1896 .... 125.00
LAMP, PAIRPOINT, see Pairpoint, Lamp
Pan, Brass, Twisted Wrought Iron Trunion Hanger, 16 1/2 In. 125.00
Pan, Wrought Iron, Sawtooth Trammel, Adjusts From 16 3/4 In. 225.00
Peg, Bearded Head Brass Holder, Embossed Shade, 16 In., Pair 1650.00
Peg, Canary Glass, Brass Collar, Brass Burners, 3 3/4 In., Pair 120.00
Peg, Cranberry Glass, Brass Collar, 6 1/4 In., Pair 240.00
Peg, Embossed Design, Brass Base, Ribbed Shade, Blue, 15 In., Pair 1475.00
Peg, Gold Flowers On Font & Shade, Etched Birds, Foliage 450.00
Peg, Petticoat, Pewter, Brass Fluid Burner, 4 1/4 In. 135.00
Peg, Yellow Overlay, Mushroom Shade, Brass Candlestick, 15 In. 525.00
Peg, Yellow-Green, White Enameled, Brass Collar, 6 3/8 In., Pair 310.00
Perfume, Art Deco, Woman's Head, White 95.00
Perfume, Bulldog, With Glass Eyes, 5 1/2 In. 145.00
Piano, Adjustable Mechanism, Brass Font, Wrought Iron Stem 160.00
Piano, Brass, Twisted Shaft, Foliate Design, Handel Shade ....*Illus* 495.00
Piano, Gold Bronze Stand, Etched Dragon Globe, Royal Bonn, 6 Ft. 4750.00
Reverse Painted Table, Wooded Area, Bronze Base, Classique, Table 1700.00
Reverse Swirl, Acorn Burner, Blue Opalescent, 4 1/4 In. ....*Illus* 200.00
Ripley, Marriage, Clambroth Connector, Opalescent White Base, 11 In. 1200.00
Rushlight, Spring Clip, Wrought Iron, 20 1/2 In. 200.00
Rushlight, Twisted Detail, Wrought Iron, 12 In. 150.00
Sconce, 2-Light, Brass, Double Stars, Cups, Burnished, 7 In., Pair 75.00
Sconce, 2-Light, Ormolu Frame, Crystal Spire, Russian, 21 In., Pair 5500.00
Sconce, 2-Light, Urn & Dolphin Crest Over Mirror, 22 1/2 In., Pair 200.00
Sconce, 3-Light, Louis XV, Bronze, Scrolled Back Plate, 28 In. 3850.00

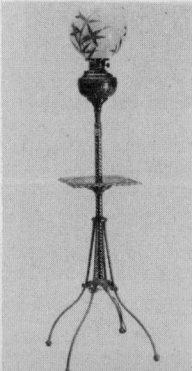 

Lamp, Piano, Brass Twisted Shaft,
Foliate Design, Handel Shade

Lamp, Argand-Type Burner,
Viscous Fuel, Lithophane Shade

Sconce, 5–Light, French Empire, Gilt Bronze, C.1815, Pair 2750.00
Sconce, Brass Wall Bracket, Clear Blown Shade, 9 1/2 In., Pair 410.00
Sconce, Brass Wall Bracket, Clear Blown Shade, 15 In., Pair 210.00
Sconce, Candle, Brass, Mirror Back, Urn & Minerva, 20 In., Pair 290.00
Sconce, Candle, Concave Reflector, Fluted Drip Cup, Tin, 9 3/4 In., Pr. 3000.00
Sconce, Candle, Porcelain, Brass Ormolu Frames, French, Pair 650.00
Sconce, Crimped Shell Top, Rolled Edge, Tin, C.1820, 13 In., Pair 40.00
Sconce, Glass, Scrolling Wrought Iron, E.Brandt, C.1925, 23 In., Pair 8800.00
Sconce, Louis XVI, Garlands & Ribbons On Backplate, Bronze, 27 In., Pr. 700.00
Sconce, Wall, Candle, Tin, Crimped Cup, 11 1/2 In. 140.00
Sinumbra, Etched Globe, Cornelius, Philadelphia, C.1845 .... 2100.00
Sparking, Blown Font, 3–Stepped Scalloped Base, Flint, 3 3/4 In. 295.00
Sparking, Blown Globular Font, 3–Stepped Base, 3 1/4 In. 750.00
Sparking, Brass Burner & Cap, Blown Glass Pedestal Base, 3 3/4 In. 85.00
Student, Brass, Dated 1863 .... 425.00
Student, Double Greenalite, Green Shades, Pot Metal Base, 18 In. 200.00
Student, Double, Acorn Shaped Fonts, Brass, Electrified 400.00
Student, Double, Green Ribbed Shade, Brass, 24 1/2 In. 135.00
Student, Double, Green Tam–O–Shanter Shade 550.00
Student, Double, White Milk Glass Shades, Brass, 10 1/2 In. 150.00
Student, Green Cased Shade, Brass, Electrified, 20 1/2 In. 195.00
Student, Lincoln, Brass, Horizontal Cylindrical Font, Pat.1879, 17 In. 395.00
Student, Manhattan Brass Co. 2500.00
Student, Manhattan, Nickel Plated Brass, Green Cased Shade, 20 1/2 In. 450.00
Student, Ribbed Green Cased Shade, Double Wick, Duplex, 19 3/4 In. 175.00
Student, White Milk Glass Shade, Brass, Olmsted Burner, 8 In. 1200.00
LAMP, TIFFANY, see Tiffany, Lamp
Torch, P.R.R., Dayton Malleable Iron Co., 9 In. 35.00
Torchere, 5–Light, Wrought Iron, 60 1/2 In., Pair 605.00
Torchere, Art Deco, Nude, Kneeling, Wrought Iron, Glass, 67 1/4 In. 2600.00
Torchere, Blackamoor, Drapery Covered Base, 46 1/2 In., Pair 3850.00
Torchere, Center Baluster, 3 Outer Supports, Black Japanned, 5 Ft., Pr. 4200.00
Traveler's, Swinging Font Cover, Oil Burner, L.H.Thurston, 9 In. 225.00
Vapo Cresolene, Cast Iron Frame, Gold Paint, 6 1/4 In. 25.00
Vouillotte, Empire, Gilt Bronze, Malachite Veneered, Pen Holder, 24 In. 2420.00
Whale Oil, Bigler, Canary Yellow, 10 1/2 In. 650.00
Whale Oil, Brass, Apron Font, 8 In. 95.00
Whale Oil, Bull's–Eye & Fleur–De–Lis, Sandwich, 10 In., Pair 375.00
Whale Oil, Clear Base, Double Burner, 6 1/8 In. 100.00
Whale Oil, Clear Blown Glass, Pewter Collar, 6 3/4 In. 80.00
Whale Oil, Clear Glass Octagon Font & Base, Pewter Collar, Miniature 125.00
Whale Oil, Cobalt Blue, Hexagonal Foot, Pewter Collar, 9 3/4 In. 145.00
Whale Oil, Conical Font, Faceted Side, C.1830, 11 1/2 In., Pair 500.00
Whale Oil, Heart With Diamond & Thumbprint, 10 In. 130.00
Whale Oil, Loop Pattern, Pressed Glass, Sapphire Blue, 9 1/4 In. 400.00
Whale Oil, Moon & Star, Marble Base, C.1845, Pair 302.50
Whale Oil, On Tin Pan, Closed Handle, Pewter, 2 1/2 X 5 In. 45.00
Whale Oil, Paneled, New England, 11 3/4 In., Pair 500.00
Whale Oil, Pear Shaped Font, Sandwich, Mass., C.1840, 11 1/2 In., Pair 375.00
Whale Oil, Peg, Brass Collar, Clear, 5 3/4 In. 135.00
Whale Oil, Peg, Petticoat, Alligatored Red Japanning, 4 In. 60.00
Whale Oil, Petticoat, Acorn Font, Tin, 5 1/4 In. 25.00
Whale Oil, Pewter, Acorn Font, R.Gleason, 8 3/8 In. 165.00
Whale Oil, Pewter, Bull's–Eye Lens, American, 9 1/4 In. 325.00
Whale Oil, Pewter, Roswell Gleason, 8 In. 325.00
Whale Oil, Pressed Glass, Blown Pear Shaped Font, 8 In. 125.00
Whale Oil, Pressed Stepped Base, Tin & Clear Glass, 7 In. 160.00
Whale Oil, Sawtooth, Flint, 1855–60, 10 3/4 In. 235.00
Whale Oil, Sparking, Ring Handle, Tweeney Lite, 3 In. 85.00
Whale Oil, Star & Punty Pattern, Bobeche, Brass Stem, C.1840, Pair 600.00
Whale Oil, Star Pattern, Sandwich, 10 1/2 In., Pair 400.00
Whale Oil, Sweetheart Pattern, Brass Collar, Double Burner, 8 3/4 In. 130.00
Whale Oil, Threaded Burner, 1 3/4 In. 350.00
Whale Oil, Tin, Clear Blown Globe, Ring Collar, N.E.Glass Co., 13 In. 175.00

Whale Oil, Tumbler, Tin & Glass, 1871 .... 395.00
Whale Oil, Twin Tube Burner, Ball Shaped Font, Brass, 8 In. 140.00
Whale Oil, Vine Pattern, Sandwich, 10 In. 175.00
Whale Oil, Waffle Pattern, Pressed Glass, 11 1/2 In. 175.00

A lantern is a special type of lighting device. It has a light source, usually a candle, totally hidden inside the walls of the lantern. Light is seen through holes or glass sections.

LANTERN, Barn, Glass Sides, Hinged Door, Wire Bail Handle, 12 In. 55.00
Barn, Hinged Door, Wire Hinges, Bale Handle, 10 3/4 In. 95.00
Barn, Tin, Spout Slides Down, Hanging Handle, 19 X 14 X 9 In. 97.50
Blown Glass, Blue–Green, Domed Cover, Hanging, Anglo–Indian, 13 In. 1540.00
Candle, Hurricane, Hanging, Glass Chimney, Tin, Pat.1894 .... 130.00
Candle, Square, Vented Top, Tin, 6 1/4 In., Pair 160.00
Carriage, Tin, Paw Feet, Black, Early 19th Century, 13 In. 75.00
Clear Blown Globe, N.E. Glass Co., Tin, 12 1/2 In. 65.00
Dietz, Beacon, No.60, 2 Ft. 415.00
Dietz, Buckeye Dash Lamp, Dated 1891 .... 35.00
Dietz, Comet, Small 15.00
Dietz, Globe, Purple 45.00
Dietz, Station, Hanging Hook, Clear Globe, Black & White, 22 In. 200.00
Hall, Brass Mounted, Colorless Glass, Inverted Bell Form, 15 In. 1320.00
Hanging, Heart Shape Cutouts, G. Stickley, C.1906, 13 X 6 In. 1600.00
Horn, English, 18th Century 595.00
Inverted Bell Form, Etched Drapery Swags, Crystal, 6 1/2 In. 1320.00
Kerosene, Hanging, French, Applied Oval Copper Label, 27 In., Pair 325.00
Kerosene, Hinged Door, Yellow Japanning, Tin, 16 Ih. 115.00
Kerosene, Talin Mfg.Co., Frosted Chimney, Brass & Copper, 15 In. 75.00
Kerosene, Triumph, No.2, Barn Style, Property of City of Rochester 25.00
Kerosene, Vent Top, Hinged Door, Painted Red, Tin, 22 In. 85.00
Police, Bulls's–Eye Lens, Blackout Shade, Tin, 6 3/8 In. 45.00
Rear Hinged Door, Punched Design, Semicircular, Tin, 12 In. 125.00
Reflector, Brass, Tin, Legged, Bail 85.00
Skater's, Berco Wonder Jr. 50.00
Skater's, Brass Frame, Teal Globe, 7 In. 170.00
Wall, Gustav Stickly, Opalescent Glass Globe, Pull Chain, Pair 5500.00

Le Verre Francais is one of the many types of cameo glass made in France. The glass was made by the C. Schneider factory in Epinay–sur–Seine from 1920 to 1933. It is a mottled glass, usually decorated with floral designs, and bears the incised signature "Le Verre Francais."

LE VERRE FRANCAIS, Bowl, Water Lily, Orange To Brown, Stippled Yellow, 4 In. 400.00
Lamp, Perfume, Cameo, 19 In. 325.00
Lamp, Red, White & Blue Mottled Shade, 17 1/2 In. 1200.00
Lamp, Reds & Purples, 21 In. 2650.00
Lamp, Stylized Flowers, Signed, 13 In. 2700.00
Vase, Art Deco Design, Oxidized Brass Finish, 20 In. 1300.00
Vase, Art Deco Floral, Stippled Yellow, Charder, 10 In. 1000.00
Vase, Geese In Flight, Rushes, Mottled Interior, 5 In. 700.00
Vase, Leaves, Pendant, Globular, Signed, C.1925, 12 1/2 In. 1980.00
Vase, Orange Floral, Stippled Peach, Charder, 12 1/2 In. 550.00
Vase, Pendant Honeysuckle, Blue, Amber, White, 20 In. 2420.00
Vase, Pink, Yellow & Green, Signed, 10 1/2 In. 350.00
Vase, Stylized Pendant Buds & Branches, Amber, 14 In. 770.00
Vase, Stylized Swans, Branches, White, Yellow, 21 3/4 In. 2090.00
Veilleuse, Inverted Gourd, Iron Blossoms, Charder, 7 In. 1320.00

Leather is tanned animal hide and it has been used to make decorative and useful objects for centuries. Leather objects must be carefully preserved with proper humidity and oiling or the leather will deteriorate and crack. This damage cannot be repaired.

LEATHER, Apron, Blacksmith's, Buckled Legs 65.00
Billy Club, Police, 1871, 14 In. 45.00

Box, Brass Fittings, Garden Scene, Figures, Pigskin, 9 3/8 X 13 In. 200.00
Box, Jewelry, Mounted In Ormolu & Enamel, A.Klein, 1896, 19 3/4 In. 1760.00
Bucket, Water, Victorian, Incised RCD, X–Form Handles, 28 In. 33.00
Canteen, American Revolution 500.00
Harness, Horse Show, Double Draft 750.00
Harness, Pony Show, Chrome Hames 700.00
Overcoat, Navy, Flying, Size 42 .... 200.00
Prayer Book, Edward VII, Victorian Embroidered, Red 25.00
Saddle Bag, With Letters of H. Olds & C.& W.Shaw, Flint, 1850–70 .... 220.00
Saddle, Camel, C.1890 .... 375.00
Saddle, English, Metal Plate Inscribed Barnsby & Son 350.00
Traveling Case, Zipper, Black, Fitted, Occupied Japan, 12 X 6 In. 75.00
Wallet, Ostrich Skin, 24K Gold Corners, Guarantee Tag, 1930s 45.00
Wallet, Red, Amity Handcrafted 4.00

LEEDS POTTERY, Leeds pottery was made at Leeds, Yorkshire, England, from 1774 to 1878. Most Leeds ware was not marked. Early Leeds pieces had distinctive twisted handles with a greenish glaze on part of the creamy ware. Later ware often had blue borders on the creamy pottery.

LEEDS, Chamber Pot, Blue & White 100.00
Creamer, Embossed Leaf Handle, 4 In. 100.00
Creamer, Gaudy Floral Decoration, 3 Colors, 5 1/2 In. 95.00
Mug, Gaudy Floral Decoration, 4 Colors, 4 5/8 In. 150.00
Mustard, Yellow Bands, Blue Tassle Design 155.00
Pitcher, Cream, King's Rose, Shell Pattern, Rust ....*Illus* 132.00
Plate, King's Rose, Large Rust Rose, 10 In. ....*Illus* 220.00
Plate, King's Rose, Rust, Yellow Buds, Green Leaves, 8 In. ....*Illus* 176.00
Plate, Toddy, Bell Flower 100.00
Sugar, Floral Design, 4 Colors, 5 5/8 In. 90.00
Teapot, 4 Colors, Gaudy Floral, 7 1/2 In. 45.00
Teapot, Peafowl 770.00
Tureen, Feather Edge, Blue 231.00
Tureen, Feather Edge, Green 286.00

The Geo. Zoltan Lefton Company has imported porcelains to be sold in America since 1940. The pieces are often marked with the Lefton name. The firm is still in business. The company mark has changed through the years and objects can be dated accurately by the shape of the mark.

MADE IN JAPAN

LEFTON, Ashtray, Figural, Swan 18.00
Bank, Grandpa In Rocker, 7 In. 14.00
Bust, U.S.Grant 30.00
Condiment Set, Stack, 3 Piece 10.00
Cookie Jar, Santa Claus, Seated In Rocker 85.00
Dresser Set, Rhinestones, Blue & White, 1956, 4 Piece 48.00
Figurine, Girl, 4 1/2 In. 10.00
Figurine, Victorian Lady 17.50

Leeds, Plates, Pitcher, King's Rose

Legras, Vase, Opaque Custard,   Limoges, Vase, Woman, Gazing Across
Green Foliate, 14 In.   Landscape, Enameled, 6 1/2 In.

Jug, Thomas Jefferson, Marked	37.00
Planter, Elephant	15.00
Plate, Cardinals	9.00
Ring Holder, Rhinestones, Hand Shape	10.00
Salt & Pepper, Santa Claus & Mrs.Claus, 1957	25.00
Tea Set, Fruit, Gold Trim, 24 Piece	225.00
Vase, Bisque Figure, 2 Hands, Raised Pink Roses, 7 In.	15.00

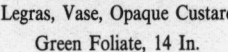

Legras was founded in 1864 by Auguste Legras at St. Denis, France. It is best known for cameo glass and enamel–decorated glass with Art Nouveau designs. Legras merged with Pantin in 1920 and became the Verreries et Cristalleries de St. Denis et de Pantin Reunies.

LEGRAS, Bowl, Art Deco Flowers Within Triangles, Yellow, 8 1/4 In.	200.00
Vase, Cameo, Art Glass, Pink Frosted Ground, Flared, Square, 5 In.	350.00
Vase, Cameo, Opaque Custard, Dark Red & Green Foliate, Signed, 14 In.	425.00
Vase, Cameo, Red Grapes & Vines, Frosted Ground, 13 1/2 In.	750.00
Vase, Cameo, Red Leaves, Bottle Shape, Textured Ground, 9 1/4 In.	200.00
Vase, Carved Maroon Leaves, Pink Ground, 9 In.	475.00
Vase, Enameled Leaves, 1 Layer Crystal Ground, 11 3/4 In.	510.00
Vase, Flattened Oval Top, Village Scene, Mountains, 4 1/2 In.	295.00
Vase, Floral Design, Enameled, Signed, 10 In.	150.00
Vase, Gold Luster, Enameled, 4 In.	80.00
Vase, Landscape, Shepherdess, Flock, Signed, 5 In.	770.00
Vase, Landscape, Trees, Stream, Green To Brown, Signed, 12 In.	635.00
Vase, Maroon Branches & Leaves, Frosted Ground, 9 In.	575.00
Vase, Opaque Custard, Green Foliate, 14 In. ....*Illus*	468.00
Vase, Red Leaves, Textured Ground, Bottle Form, 9 1/4 In.	200.00
Vase, Shepherd & Flock, On Hillside, Cameo, Square, 7 In., Pair	550.00
Vase, Shepherd & Flock, On Hillside, Cameo, Square, 8 1/2 In.	375.00
Vase, Thistle Design, Brown Shades, 8 In.	575.00

Walter Scott Lenox and Jonathan Cox founded the Ceramic Art Company in Trenton, New Jersey, in 1889. In 1906, Lenox left and started his own company. The company makes a porcelain that is similar to Irish Belleek. The marks used by the firm have changed through the years and collectors prefer the earlier examples.

LENOX, see also Ceramic Art Co.

LENOX, Bowl, Cheese & Cracker, Pleated Diamonds, Square, 1950s, 11 In., 2 Pc.	25.00
Box, Rose, Round, Large	85.00
Charger, Ming Pattern, Black Mark, 12 1/2 In.	75.00
Cigarette Set, Box & 2 Ashtrays, Pink, Green Mark	45.00
Cup & Saucer, Enamel Design, Palette Mark, 8 1/2 In.	45.00
Cup, Ming, Black Mark	15.00
Dish, Grape Leaf, 3–Lobed, Cream, Gold Edge, Gold Mark, 8 1/2 X 8 In.	25.00
Dish, Lotus Leaf, 10 1/2 In.	4.00
Figurine, First Waltz	125.00
Humidor, With Match Holder, Sailboats, Artist, Palette Mark, 1914	65.00
Jug, William Penn, Ivory, Green Mark, 7 In.	125.00
Lamp, Woman's Head, Ivory, Pink, Chrome Base, Signed	400.00
Pitcher, Girl's Mask At Spout, Textured Body, Pink, 7 1/2 In.	95.00
Pitcher, Lemons, Foliage & Blossoms, Green Trim, Marked, 10 3/4 In.	225.00
Pitcher, Pink, White Handle, 5 In.	48.00
Pitcher, Shell–Shaped Lip, Design At Top, White Handle, Gray, 5 In.	85.00
Plate, Chipmunks, 1976	60.00
Plate, Floral Center, Blue Border, Scalloped, Green Mark, 9 In.	25.00
Plate, Woodland Wildlife, Set of 10	450.00
Relish, 3 Sections, Hand Painted Wild Roses, Gold Handle, 9 3/4 In.	50.00
Salt & Pepper, Bird, White, Miniature	35.00
Salt & Pepper, Nipper	50.00
Saltshaker, Dog Nipper, His Master's Voice, RCA Victor	15.00
Setting For 12, Westchester Pattern, Gold Band, 104 Piece	2750.00
Sugar & Creamer, Cream, Handleless Sugar, Shell Spout, Oval, 3 1/2 In.	35.00
Sugar & Creamer, White Lining, Pink	35.00
Swan, Pale Peach, Gold, Green Wreath, 4 1/2 X 3 1/4 In.	30.00
Tankard, Lemonade, Lemons & Blossoms, Handle Extends To Base, 10 In.	185.00
Tankard, Lemonade, Plump Lemons, Green Handle, 10 3/4 In.	235.00
Tankard, Red Cherries & Raspberries, Hand Painted, 14 1/2 In.	195.00
Tea Set, George Washington Pattern, 3 Piece	105.00
Toby Jug, George Washington	350.00
Toby Jug, William Penn	125.00
Urn, Classic Chalice Shape, White, Green Mark, 5 1/2 In.	20.00
Vase, Cornucopia of Plenty, White, Green Mark, 8 In.	95.00
Vase, Flared Fluted Neck, Green Wreath Mark, 7 3/4 In.	60.00
Vase, Hand Painted Flowers, Leaves, Geometric, 1919, 8 In.	85.00
Vase, Ivory, Flared & Fluted Top, Bulbous, Blue Mark, 3 1/2 X 8 In.	28.50
Vase, Peach Tree, Ovoid, 6 1/2 X 10 In.	85.00
Vase, White Birds, Tree, Florals, Celadon Ground, 9 1/4 In.	155.00

Letter openers have been used since the eighteenth century. Ivory and silver were favored by the well–to–do. In the late nineteenth century, the letter opener was popular as an advertising giveaway and many were made of metal or celluloid. Brass openers with figural handles were also popular.

LETTER OPENER, 1934 Calendar, Metal, Advertising	9.00
Horsehead Handle, Silver Plate, Reed & Barton	75.00
Pan American Expo, Buffalo Figural Top, Brass, 1901	45.00
Red Cross Stoves, Milwaukee, Tin	7.00
Relief Flowers, Sterling Silver, Jacobi & Jenkins, 7 In.	125.00
Schlitz, Pearl Handle, 1 Blade, Logo Handle, Box, 9 In.	31.00
Seahorse Handle, Bronze, E.T.Hurley	325.00
Thompson's Malted Food Co., Celluloid	25.00
Washington Patent Lawyers, Brass	12.00

The Libbey Glass Company has made glass of many types since 1888. Libbey made cut glass and tablewares that are collected today. The stemwares of the 1930s and 1940s are once again in style. The Toledo, Ohio, firm was purchased by Owens–Illinois in 1935 and is still working under the name "Libbey" as a division of that company.

LIBBEY, see also Amberina; Cut Glass; Maize

LIBBEY, Berry Set, Paneled Holly, Opalescent Blue, Marked, 6 Piece	265.00
Bowl, Brazilian Rose Pattern, 6 X 5 In.	350.00
Bowl, Colonna Pattern, 9 In.	250.00
Bowl, Empress Pattern, 9 In.	300.00
Bowl, Hobstars, Fan Center, 8 X 9 In.	800.00
Bowl, Mayonnaise, Underplate, Hobstars & Flowers	125.00
Bowl, Raised Diamond, Radiant, Signed, 6 In.	125.00
Bowl, Rib Cut & Blocks, Wide Rim, 9 1/2 X 1 1/4 In.	45.00
Bowl, Senora Pattern, 9 In.	450.00
Bowl, Snowflake Pattern, Cut Glass, Signed, 9 In.	1000.00
Bread Tray, Feather, 12 X 7 1/2 In.	275.00
Candleholder, Cut Glass, Crosscut Hobnail, Signed, 3 1/2 X 2 In., Pr.	175.00
Candlestick, Figural, Camel, Pair	24.00
Candlestick, Teardrop Stem, Facet Cut, Rayed Base, Signed, 10 In.	425.00
Celery Dish, Hobstar, Fan & Diamond Point, Blown Out, 13 1/2 In.	225.00
Celery Vase, Regal Pattern, Signed, 12 1/4 X 5 1/4 In.	175.00
Chalice, Colonna Pattern, Cut Glass, Old Sword, Signed, 11 In.	850.00
Cordial, Cut Glass, Stratford, Teardrop Knobs On Hobstar Base, Pair	160.00
Cup & Saucer, Frosted Satin, Flower Petal, Columbia Exposition	85.00
Fernery, Intaglio Cut Fern & Feather, Peg Legs, Signed, 8 In.	365.00
Finger Bowl, Rock Crystal	75.00
Hat, Columbian Exposition, Signed & Dated	225.00
Lemonade Set, Imperial Pattern, Cut Glass, Ball Shape, 6 Tumblers	1750.00
Mayonnaise Set, Colonna Pattern	250.00
Nappy, Radiant Cut, Signed, 6 In.	105.00
Pitcher, Cane Pattern	725.00
Pitcher, Cream, Elsmere Pattern, Cut Glass, Wafer Foot, Old Sword	290.00
Pitcher, Elsmere Pattern, Wafer Foot, Notched Handle, Signed	200.00
Pitcher, Intaglio, Cut Glass, 6 Tumblers	1450.00
Pitcher, Sultana Pattern	450.00
Punch Bowl, Avon Pattern, 2 Piece	1095.00
Punch Bowl, Elite, Cut Glass, Large, 2 Piece	4100.00
Punch Cup, Baby Thumbprint Pattern, Amberina	75.00
Salad Set, Cherries Pattern, Cut Glass, Signed, 2 Piece	3200.00
Sherbet, Leaf & Floral, Faceted Stem, 4 X 3 1/2 In.	6.00
Sugar & Creamer, Heart Pattern	235.00
Sugar & Creamer, Lovebirds Pattern	575.00
Tazza, Wandering Foliate Design, 5 5/8 X 7 1/4 In., Pair	413.00
Toothpick, Little Lobe	100.00
Tray, Buzz Saws & Fan In Caning Allover, Signed, 8 X 11 In.	125.00
Tray, Neola, Cut Glass, Signed, 12 In.	2300.00
Tray, Orange Leaf, Intaglio, Round, 13 In.	450.00
Tray, Rajah Pattern, Thick Blank, Signed, 14 In.	2200.00
Tumbler, 2nd Little Pig, Fiddler, 1930s, 4 3/8 In.	15.00
Tumbler, Bashful, From Snow White & 7 Dwarfs, Red, 1938, 4 3/8 In.	18.00
Tumbler, Minnie Mouse, 1930s, 3 1/2 In.	25.00
Tumbler, Talisman, Footed, Ruby Threaded Design, 1932	40.00
Vase, Amberina, 7 7/8 In.	345.00
Vase, Blue Threading, Opalescent Body, Signed, 9 In.	245.00
Vase, Fine Ribbed, Cut Glass, 10 In.	145.00
Vase, Modern American, Spiral Rib, 9 1/2 In.	65.00
Vase, Pea, Intaglio Orchids & Leaves, Ruffled Top, 5 X 6 In.	175.00
Vase, Trumpet, Brilliant Cutting Overall, Signed, 12 In.	275.00
Vase, Trumpet, Harvard Pattern, Emerald Green Cut To Clear, 14 In.	1100.00
Vase, Wedgemere Pattern, Cut Glass, 18 In.	2400.00
Water Set, Bull's–Eye Band, Nailhead Banded Base, Signed, 5 Piece	250.00

Water Set, Poppy Pattern, Cut Glass, Signed, 9 Piece 4100.00
Whiskey, Amberina, Signed 65.00
Wine, Black Bear Silhouette, Signed 85.00
Wine, Harvard Pattern, 10 Piece 375.00

Cigarettes became popular in the late nineteenth century and with the cigarette came matches and cigarette lighters. All types of lighters are collected, from solid gold to the first of the recent disposable lighters. Most examples found were made after 1940.

LIGHTER, Cigar, Midland Jump, Oak, 1920s 225.00
Cigar, Monkey 20.00
Cigarette, 21 Club, Iron Jockey On Top 35.00
Cigarette, Airplane, Chrome 35.00
Cigarette, Aladdin Lamp, Chrome, Occupied Japan, 2 1/2 X 2 In. 9.50
Cigarette, Aladdin Lamp, Chrome, Occupied Japan, Table 25.00
Cigarette, Amico, Table, Brown China Donkey, Japan 15.00
Cigarette, Camel Cigarettes 5.00
Cigarette, Camera & Tripod 35.00
Cigarette, Camera, Luimise, Occupied Japan 18.00
Cigarette, Capitol, Patent 1912 .... 100.00
Cigarette, Carnation, 3 In. 12.00
Cigarette, Cartier, 18K Gold Plated, Box 225.00
Cigarette, Cartier, Florentined, 14K Gold 175.00
Cigarette, Case, Ronson, Sterling Silver, Gold Stripes, Pat.1934 .... 200.00
Cigarette, Chaselite, Pencil Shape, Chrome, Japan 30.00
Cigarette, Chess Knight, Table 15.00
Cigarette, Closed Book 15.00
Cigarette, Cradle Phone, Chrome, Occupied Japan 45.00
Cigarette, Dodge Truck, Oil Barrel Shape 25.00
Cigarette, Dunhill, Figural, Pistol, Wooden Handle 34.50
Cigarette, Dunhill, Revolver Shape 27.50
Cigarette, Dunhill, Sterling Silver 75.00
Cigarette, Elgin, Gold Plated, Pocket 27.50
Cigarette, Evans, Black & Gold Flowers, Butterfly, Table 30.00
Cigarette, Evans, Combined With Case, 1940s 30.00
Cigarette, Evans, Gold Plated, Flat 8.00
Cigarette, Evans, Musical, Anniversary Waltz, Chrome 65.00
Cigarette, Evans, Table, Plaid & Gold 12.50
Cigarette, Evans, Transfer of 1903 Auto, Bone China, 4 In. 25.00
Cigarette, Golf Ball, On Club Legs 35.00
Cigarette, Golf Club, 5 In. 45.00
Cigarette, Gun, Occupied Japan, Box 20.00
Cigarette, Hamm's, Bear On Log, Multicolored 33.00
Cigarette, Hamm's, Lake Scene, Multicolored 26.00
Cigarette, Harvey Avedon, Sterling Silver, 2 1/2 X 1 1/2 In. 27.50
Cigarette, Jack Daniels, Box 25.00
Cigarette, John Deere 8.00
Cigarette, Kreisler, Butane, Box 10.00
Cigarette, Lamp Shape, Art Deco, Table 25.00
Cigarette, Marathon, Tank Shape, 1930, Attleboro, Mass. 27.50
Cigarette, Massey Harris 10.00
Cigarette, Mastercraft, Tareyton, Pocket 8.50
Cigarette, Mountain Dew, Box 10.00
Cigarette, Paperweight, Mother-of-Pearl Dividers, Paris, Table 45.00
Cigarette, Pennsylvania Railroad 10.00
Cigarette, Perfect, Leica Camera, On Tripod, Occupied Japan 45.00
Cigarette, Quaker State Oil 8.00
Cigarette, R.J.Reynolds, Lucite, Large 35.00
Cigarette, Radio, Dials Move, Occupied Japan 45.00
Cigarette, Ronson, Man's, Brown & Chrome, With Case 20.00
Cigarette, Ronson, Pencil Shape, Chrome, Dark Blue 45.00
Cigarette, Ronson, Penlighter 9.00
Cigarette, Ronson, Woman's, Blue Enamel 31.75
Cigarette, Royal Crown Derby, Imari Pattern 55.00

Cigarette, Sam Kelso, Figural 16.00
Cigarette, Sarome Bluebird, Automobile, Box 90.00
Cigarette, Scotty Dog, Figural, 1940s 12.00
Cigarette, Sinclair Heating Oil, Enameled Flame Logo 30.00
Cigarette, Texaco Fire Chief, Enameled 10.00
Cigarette, Wedgwood, Blue & White Jasperware, Table 25.00
Cigarette, Woman's Head, Art Deco, Metal, Painted, Electric, 6 In. 100.00
Cigarette, Zippo, Bradford, Engraved, Silver, No.870 .... 28.00
Cigarette, Zippo, Raised Relief Tavern Scene, Danish 10.00
Cigarette, Zippo, Vintage, Brushed Brass 9.00
Tinder, Flintlock Pistol, Brass & Iron, Wooden Grip, England, C.1800 ...... 225.00
Tinder, Flintlock, Maple Pistol Stock, 7 1/2 In. 925.00

 Limoges porcelain has been made in Limoges, France, since the mid-nineteenth century. Fine porcelains were made by many factories including Haviland, Ahrenfeldt, Guerin, Pouyat, Elite, and others. Modern porcelains are being made at Limoges and the word "Limoges" as part of the mark is not an indication of age. Haviland is listed as a separate category in this book.

LIMOGES, Ashtray, Cobalt Blue, Gold Paisley Border, 4 1/2 In. 5.50
Bouillon Cup, Red Roses, Blue & Green Scrolls, Gold Rim & Handles 8.00
Bowl, Flowers, Ivory, Fluted, Scalloped, Scrolls, 8 5/8 X 1 3/4 In. 40.00
Bowl, Grapes Interior & Exterior, Rococo Gold Rim, 9 1/2 In. 185.00
Bowl, Hand Painted Grapes Inside & Out, Footed 75.00
Box, Pink Roses, Gold, Cover, 4 In. 20.00
Box, Puff, Courting Couple, Maroon, Gold, R.Pragout, 3 1/2 In. 20.00
Box, Reclining Cat, Enameled 80.00
Bread Plate, Hand Painted Narcissus 30.00
Butter Chip, Rose, Pink 35.00
Cachepot, Woman, Preparing Bath, Pseudo Ring Handles, 12 In. 295.00
Cake Plate, Hand Painted, Raised Edge, 11 1/2 In. 65.00
Candleholder, Floral Design, Hand Painted, Tall, Pair 50.00
Candlestick, Violets & Leaves, Gold Trim, 5 3/4 In. 100.00
Chocolate Pot, Melon Ribbed, Floral Design, Brown Handle, 9 In. 275.00
Chocolate Pot, Pink Roses 95.00
Compote, Enameled Cameo Center, Bronze Gilded, 4 X 8 In. 975.00
Cup & Saucer, Mustache, Robin's-Egg Blue, Gold Lace, O.Gutherz 40.00
Decanter, Liqueur, Fruit Design, Gold Trim, Pair 250.00
Dish, Pink Roses, Gold Trim, Crescent Shape, 8 1/2 In. 25.00
Figurine, Clown, Ruffled Collar, Broad Hat, Spectacles, 10 In. 145.00
Figurine, Parrot, Open Wings, On Stump, White, 18 In. 275.00
Humidor, Indians Smoking Peace Pipe, Gold, Orange, Signed, 6 1/2 In. ... 225.00
Humidor, Pinecones, Yellow, Coral & Brown, 6 1/2 In. 150.00
Humidor, Poppies, Deep Amber, Gold Cover, Artist Signed 75.00
Inkwell, Cover, Moon & Forest Silhouette, 1 1/2 X 2 1/2 In. 100.00
Jam Jar, Underplate, Hand Painted Currants 65.00
Jar, Cover, Purple Flowers, Gold Edging, 5 1/4 In. 97.50
Night-Light, Flowers, Cage Shape, Artist Signed, 1920, 6 1/2 In. 235.00
Pitcher, Cider, Fruit Trim, Gold Handle, Signed 165.00
Pitcher, Lemonade, Hand Painted Grapes, Gold Trimmed Top, 12 In. 165.00
Plaque, Game Birds, Gold Trim, 11 3/4 In. 245.00
Plaque, Hand Painted Fish, 12 In. 165.00
Plaque, Scenic, Lake Setting, Gold Border, 12 In. 150.00
Plaque, Woman & 5 Attendants, Framed, 12 X 17 In. 700.00
Plaque, Woman, Long Hair, Holding Roses, Artist Signed, 13 3/4 In. 265.00
Plaque, Yellowstone Park, Grand Waterfall, 10 X 13 In. 175.00
Plate, Basket of Fruit, Gold Rococo Border, R. Brisson, 16 In., Pair 650.00
Plate, Flight of The Unicorn, Tapestry, 8 Piece 425.00
Plate, Holly & Berries, Hand Painted, 9 1/2 In. 40.00
Plate, Pheasant & Quail, Gold Rococo Border, Barbois, 13 In., Pair 495.00
Plate, Pink Roses, Artist Signed, 8 1/2 In. 18.00
Plate, Portrait, Composer, Cobalt Blue Border, Gold, Fehl, 9 5/8 In. 175.00
Plate, Raspberries, Leaves, Scalloped, Signed, 1908, 9 In. 40.00

Loetz, Vase, Iridescent Blue Swirl   Loetz, Vase, Seashell Form, Footed,
Design, Ovoid Form, 7 1/2 In.   Green Gold Iridescent, 8 In.

Plate, Roses, Hand Painted, Gold Edge, 13 3/8 In.	195.00
Plate, Scene of Arab Riding Horse, Marked, 12 1/2 In.	250.00
Platter, Autumn, 16 In.	50.00
Platter, Underwater Scene, Oyster, Marked, 10 1/2 X 7 1/2 In.	65.00
Punch Bowl Set, Hand Painted, 14 In. Diam., 11 Piece	850.00
Punch Bowl, 3 French Military Panels, Green, Gilt, 17 1/2 X 8 In.	1210.00
Ramekin, Underplate, Stylized Leaf & Scroll Border, Black, Tan, Pink	15.00
Ring Tree, Floral, Hand Painted, 1890s	30.00
Rose Bowl, Poppies, Pastel Green, Gold Trim, 3–Footed, 5 1/4 In.	60.00
Sardine Set, Fish, Shells, Sea Design, Gold Trim, 3 Piece	235.00
Sugar & Creamer, Floral Border, Cream, Gold Handles	65.00
Sugar Shaker, Apples, Grapes, Leaves, Mottled Ground, 7 In.	55.00
Sugar Shaker, Pheasant In Grasses, Muted Gold, 6 In.	50.00
Tankard, Grapes, 14 In.	150.00
Tankard, Portrait of Monk, Glasses On Tip of Nose, 14 1/2 In.	395.00
Teapot, Yellow & White Plaid, Baskets of Flowers, Gold Handle	75.00
Tile, Mother In Blue Gown, Child With Blond Hair, 6 X 13 In.	595.00
Tobacco Jar, Gold Pipe On Lid	110.00
Tray, Boats On Sand, House, People, Scalloped, Gold Trim, 9 1/2 In.	53.00
Tray, Grape Design Allover, 16 X 12 In.	125.00
Trivet, Yellow Roses, Pastel, 3 Button Feet, E. Thau, 6 1/2 In.	55.00
Tureen, Soup, Cover, Gold Handles, Finial & Trim, Marked, 8 X 12 In.	165.00
Tureen, White, Leaf Border, Gold, Wm. Gubrin & Co., 8 1/2 X 14 In.	75.00
Vase, Acorns, Hand Painted, Gold Trim, Signed, 7 1/2 In.	110.00
Vase, Enamel On Copper, Turquoise, White, Black, Signed, 10 In.	1650.00
Vase, Flower Form, Gold Handle, Violet Design, Gold Trimmed, 3 In.	45.00
Vase, Pillow, Oriental Design, Reversed Dragon Handles, 8 1/2 In.	85.00
Vase, Trees, Hand Painted, 15 In.	225.00
Vase, Woman In Red, Stops To Smell Roses, Signed, 4 1/4 In.	275.00
Vase, Woman, Gazing Across Landscape, Enameled, 6 1/2 In. *Illus*	440.00

In 1927, Charles Lindbergh, the aviator, became the first man to make a nonstop solo flight across the Atlantic Ocean. He was a national hero. In 1932, his son was kidnapped and murdered, and Lindbergh was again the center of public interest. He died in 1974. All types of Lindbergh memorabilia are collected.

LINDBERGH, Book, Lone Scout of The Sky, 275 Pages	20.00
Book, National Geographic, Seeing America With Lindbergh, 1928	9.00
Book, Story of Lindbergh, Saleman's Sample, Order Blanks, 1927	50.00
Bookends, Figural	65.00
Bookends, Revolving Propellers	55.00
Box, Mirrored, Sepia Photograph of Lindy & Plane, 7 1/2 In.	75.00

Charm, Spirit of St. Louis, Capt. Lindbergh On Wing, Brass 25.00
Cigar Label, Spirit of St. Louis, Plane, 2 Points On Globe, 1927 .... 15.00
Night–Light & Fan, Plane, Spirit of St. Louis 775.00
Photograph, 25 Years Old, 6 X 8 In. 50.00
Photograph, Profile, May 1927 .... 35.00
Pin, Lucky Lindy, Lithographed, Photo, 1/2 In. 18.00
Pin, Welcome Lindy, Picture, 3/4 In. 15.00
Plate, Pan–Am Lindbergh–Sikorsky Flight, 1929 .... 25.00
Plate, Plane & Ocean, Face In Center, 8 In. 30.00
Postcard Set, Photography, 4 Piece 40.00
Stereo Card, Ambassador of Air, Spirit of St. Louis, Keystone 44.50
Tapestry, 19 X 56 In. 95.00
Watch, Pocket, With Fob 300.00

Lithophanes are porcelain pictures made by casting clay in layers of various thicknesses. When a piece is held to the light, a picture of light and shadow is seen through it. Most lithophanes date from the 1825–75 period. A few are still being made. Many lithophanes sold today were originally panels for lampshades.

LITHOPHANE, Lamp, Fairy, Peachblow, Signed Clarke, Crimped Edge Base 950.00
Lamp, Genre & Mont Blanc Scenes, Pair 935.00
Lamp, Green Glass Font, Marble Base, 23 1/2 In. 880.00
Lamp, Hunters, Mountains, Soldier, Spelter Base, 22 1/2 In. 950.00
Lamp, Moderator, 5–Panel Shade, French, 1830s, 23 In. 700.00
Lamp, White Cut To Green, Marble Base, Scenes 995.00
Lamp, Wrought Iron Base, 6 Sided Shade, 28 3/8 In. 985.00
Matchbox, Girl, Holding Basket, Collie In The Woods, Miniature 75.00
Miniature, Boy, Playing Soldier, Dog, Metal Frame, Velvet Ground 170.00
Panel, Niagara Falls, Trapezoid, 5 X 3 1/4 X 5 1/4 In. 150.00
Picture, Boy, Playing Violin, 2 Monkeys Dancing, Girl, 3 7/8 In. 95.00
Picture, Heidelberg Castle, 7 3/4 X 6 In. 185.00
Picture, Sailing Ship, Avramov, Spain, Marble Stand, 6 1/2 In. 95.00
Picture, Young Girl, In Bed, Marked PPM, 3 X 3 In. 85.00
Shade, Figures, Trapezoid, 1 Panel Missing 650.00
Stein, Jockey, Horsehead Thumblift 600.00
Tea Set, Japan, 8 Piece 175.00
Tea Warmer 195.00

Liverpool, England, was the site of several pottery and porcelain factories from 1716 to 1785. Some earthenware was made with transfer decorations. Sadler and Green made print–decorated wares from 1756. Many of the pieces were made for the American market and feature patriotic emblems, such as eagles, flags, and other special–interest motifs.

LIVERPOOL, Coffeepot, Eagle Transfer Under Spout 4250.00
Jug, Memorial To Washington, Plan of City of Washington, Large 2860.00
Jug, Polychrome Scenes Celebrating Agriculture 2750.00
Mug, Hero of The Lake, Black Transfer, 5 3/4 In. 2150.00
Mug, Washington, Black Transfer, 6 In. 1900.00
Pitcher, World In Planisphere, Map of World, 3–Masted Ship, 1799 .... 175.00

LLADRÓ

Juan, Jose, and Vicente Lladro opened a ceramics workshop in Almacera, Spain, in 1951. They soon began making figurines in a distinctive, elongated style. In 1958 the factory moved to Tabernes Blanques, Spain. The company makes stoneware and porcelain vases and figurines in limited and nonlimited editions.

LLADRO, Bell, Christmas, 1987 .... 22.00
Figurine, Afternoon Tea 110.00
Figurine, Anniversary Waltz 370.00
Figurine, At The Ball 308.00
Figurine, Clown With Concertina 335.00
Figurine, Clown With Puppy, 4 1/2 In. 88.00
Figurine, Court Jester 400.00
Figurine, Daydreamer 320.00

Figurine, Elephant, 10 In. 195.00
Figurine, Fantasy 150.00
Figurine, Feeding Time 260.00
Figurine, Girl On Carousel Horse 420.00
Figurine, Girl With Doll 220.00
Figurine, Girl, Seated, With Bird, Stump, Blues, Grays, 7 X 7 In. 125.00
Figurine, Happy Birthday ....78.00 To 100.00
Figurine, Intermezzo 250.00
Figurine, Isabel 175.00
Figurine, Little Gardener 390.00
Figurine, Love Letters 440.00
Figurine, Matrimony 290.00
Figurine, Midwife 135.00
Figurine, Music Time 500.00
Figurine, My Best Friend, 6 3/4 In. 119.50
Figurine, Nativity, Stable, 5 Pieces, Box, Unused 200.00
Figurine, Nude, 3/4 Figure, Dated 1958 .... 145.00
Figurine, Oriental Girl, No.4840 .... 285.00
Figurine, Peaceful Stroll 190.00
Figurine, Poetry of Love 500.00
Figurine, Polar Bear, Miniature, 3 1/2 In. 50.00
Figurine, Short-Eared Owl 150.00
Figurine, Singer, 8 In. 70.00
Figurine, Springtime 320.00
Figurine, St. Nicholas 320.00
Figurine, Summer Stock 500.00
Figurine, Violinist & Girl 490.00
Figurine, Wedding 125.00
Figurine, Will You Marry Me? 565.00
Figurine, Young Love 450.00
Plate, Christmas, 1972 .... 18.00
Plate, Mother's Day, 1972 .... 18.00

Locke Art is a trademark found on glass of the early twentieth century. Joseph Locke worked at many English and American firms. He designed and etched his own glass in Pittsburgh, Pennsylvania, starting in the 1880s. Some pieces were marked "Joe Locke," but most were marked with the words "Locke Art." The mark is hidden in the pattern on the glass.

LOCKE ART, Vase, Etched Poppies, Corset Shape, 7 In. 85.00
Vase, Serrated Edge, 7 In. 145.00

Johann Loetz bought a glassworks in Austria in 1840. He died in 1848 and his widow ran the company; in 1879, his grandson took over. Loetz glass was varied. Most collectors recognize the iridescent gold glass similar to Tiffany, but many other types were made. The firm closed during World War II.

LOETZ, Bowl, Alternating Turned-In Sides, White Floral, Purple, 3 X 11 In. 895.00
Bowl, Green Papillon, Silver Deposit, Signed, 2 1/2 In. 300.00
Bowl, Green, 5 X 10 In. 200.00
Bowl, Pink Design, 8 In. 275.00
Bowl, Rose, Deep Green, Lavender Design, 4 1/2 In. 150.00
Bowl, Ruffled Rim, 3 Applied Purple Handles, 6 1/2 In. 80.00
Bowl, Ruffled, 3 Silvery Applied Handles, Signed, 8 In. 100.00
Cookie Jar, Florette, Pink, Silver Plated Lid 265.00
Dish, Ribbed Shell Shape, Yellow Iridescent, Signed, 13 In. 450.00
Dish, Sweetmeat, Glass Threads, Silver Bail & Lid, 6 In. 275.00
Ewer, Applied Handles, Green Iridescent, 6 In. 450.00
Inkwell, Brass Hinged Lid, Lily Pad, Crystal Insert, 5 1/4 In. 250.00
Powder Box, Iridescent, Gold Enameled, Brass Mounts 100.00
Rose Bowl, Shaded Red Iridescent, 4 In. 50.00
Shade, Acorn Shape, White Applied Spiral, Green, 8 In. 275.00
Shade, Alligatored Red Over Yellow, Ruffled, 5 In., Pair 175.00
Shade, Flattened Acorn Form, Blue, Green, White Spiral, 8 In. 275.00

Shade, Irregular Amber Threading, Ovoid, 7 1/2 In. 150.00
Urn, Art Nouveau Thistles, Metal Frame, 6 X 11 In. 875.00
Vase, Amber Stringing, Striated Feathering, C.1900, 4 3/4 In. 2090.00
Vase, Applied Iridescent Grapes, Bottle Shape, 7 In. 90.00
Vase, Art Nouveau Free–Form, Swirled Ridges, Iridescent, 12 1/2 In. 410.00
Vase, Blown Twisted Shape, Gold Looping, 12 1/2 In. 750.00
Vase, Blue Snail Designs, 4 X 5 In. 550.00
Vase, Blue Swirled Design, Iridescent, Pinched Form, 8 In. 650.00
Vase, Blue Swirled Design, Pinched Ovoid Shape, 7 1/2 In. 650.00
Vase, Bottle Form, Applied Iridescent Grapes, 7 In. 90.00
Vase, Bottle Shape, Random Threading, Green, 9 3/4 In. 275.00
Vase, Dimpled Sides, Iridescent Blue–Green, 5 1/2 In. 450.00
Vase, Glass Strands Wind Up From Pontil To Neck, Oil Spots, 13 In. 325.00
Vase, Green Iridescent, Swirls, Bulls–Eye Design, Signed, 9 1/2 In. 195.00
Vase, Green, Blue Snake Entwined On Neck, Squat, 6 1/2 In. 350.00
Vase, Green, Drapery, Bottle Shape, Pinched Triangular, 10 In., Pair 450.00
Vase, Green, Opalescent Swirls, Ruffled, 8 In. 100.00
Vase, Green, Signed, 7 1/2 In. 135.00
Vase, Iridescent Blue Swirl Design, Ovoid Form, 7 1/2 In. ....*Illus* 715.00
Vase, Iridescent Dusty Rose Surface, Tapered, 10 In. 375.00
Vase, Iridescent, Pink Interior, Ruffled, 12 In. 200.00
Vase, Jack–In–The–Pulpit, Random Threading, Fluted Top, 6 3/4 In. 235.00
Vase, Lavender To Burgundy Ground, Gold To Green, Signed, 6 In. 440.00
Vase, Loopings On Opalescent Ground, 12 1/4 In. 225.00
Vase, Pinched Bottle Shape, Alligatored Surface, 9 In. 275.00
Vase, Pulled Feather, Green, 6 Silver Blue Feathers, 6 1/4 In. 4500.00
Vase, Pulled Feather, Orange & Silver Green, Iridescent, 6 In. 5500.00
Vase, Pulled Feather, Red, 10 In. 875.00
Vase, Purple Iridescent, 14 In. 650.00
Vase, Ruffled Rim, Blue, Pink Interior, 12 In. 200.00
Vase, Seashell Form, Footed, Green Gold Iridescent, 8 In. ....*Illus* 880.00
Vase, Swirl & Bull's–Eye Design, Green, 9 1/2 In. 195.00
Vase, Twisted, Treebark Design, Polished Pontil, 11 In. 275.00
Vase, Wave Pattern, Ruffled Rim, Bulbous Base, 12 3/4 In. 225.00
Vase, White Spider Web Ground, Bun Base, 14 1/2 In. 295.00

 The Lone Ranger is a fictional character introduced on the radio in 1932. Over three thousand shows were produced before the series ended in 1954. In 1938, the first Lone Ranger movie was made. Television shows were started in 1949 and are still seen on some stations. The Lone Ranger appears on many products and was even the name of a restaurant chain for several years.

LONE RANGER, Badge, Bond Bread 45.00
Badge, Deputy, Brass, Secret Compartment, Embossed Design, 1949 .... 70.00
Badge, Safety Club, Brass Star, Bond Bread, 1938 .... 20.00
Badge, Safety Scout Member, 1930s 22.00
Badge, Silver Cup, Premium, Ranger Riding Silver, 1 In. Diam. 12.50
Blotter, Bond Bread, C.1939 .... 16.00 To 20.00
Book, Big Little Book 15.00
Book, The Lone Ranger, Fran Striker, 1936, 218 Pages 8.50
Brush, Box 185.00
Buckle, Belt, Flasher, 1976 .... 25.00
Button, Plastic, Clothing, Gold, Black, Red, 1950s 12.00
Certificate, Pledge To Parents, 1938 .... 25.00
Clock, Alarm, Bradley, Box 35.00
Coloring Book, 1960 .... 5.00
Comic Book, Gold Key, No.14 .... 4.00
Comic Book, Legend of The Lone Ranger, Small 35.00
Comic Book, Lone Ranger Family Restaurant, 5 X 7 In. 5.00
Comic Book, March of Comics, No.174 .... 35.00
Comic Book, Story of Silver, Cheerios, 1954, 16 Pages 15.00
Comic Book, Whitman, No.18 .... 4.00
Costume, Child's, Box, 1940s 80.00
Costume, Halloween, 1980 .... 25.00

Coupon, Lone Ranger Cones, Dated 1940, 2 1/4 X 3 1/2 In.	1.00
Cowboy Outfit, Box	130.00
Cowboy Suit, Official, Yank Boy, 1947, 5 Piece	160.00
Dart Board, Tin, 1938, 16 X 28 In.	50.00
Display, Store, 12 Badges	165.00
Doll, Gabrielle, 8 1/2 In.	40.00
Doll, Lone Ranger & Silver, Box	65.00
Doll, Tonto, Composition, 1940s	250.00
Doll, Wood, Composition, 1930s, 16 In.	125.00
Figure, Chalkware	20.00
Figure, Hartland	5.00
Flashlight Pistol, Premium	65.00
Flashlight Ring, Instructions, Box	165.00
Flashlight, Signal & Siren, Silver Bullet Code, Box	70.00
Game, Box, 1938	50.00
Game, Fighting Mountain Lions	25.00
Game, Marble, Tin & Glass, 5 In.	30.00
Game, Target, Marx	40.00
Guitar, Jefferson	95.00
Guitar, Wooden	145.00
Gun & Hoister Set, 1950	85.00
Hat, Felt, 1940s	30.00
Holster Fob	15.00
Holster, Leather, 1940	30.00
Horseshoe, Rubber	15.00
Key Chain, Silver Bullet	20.00
Knife, Pocket, C.1940	35.00
Knife, Pocket, Metal, Plastic Sides, Picture, 1940s	20.00
Knife, Pocket, With Bullet	25.00
Lunch Box, Thermos	15.00
Model Kit, 3–D, Lone Ranger & Silver	28.50
Ornament, Christmas Tree	5.00
Paint Book, 1939	75.00
Paint Book, 1940	75.00
Paperweight, Snowball, Red Base, 1950s	28.00
Pedometer, Tin, 3 In.	22.00 To 40.00
Pen, Bullet Shape, Leather Belt Holder, Pictures Ranger, Tonto	50.00
Pencil Sharpener, Silver Bullet Form	35.00
Pencil, Silver Bullet, All Metal, T.L.R.Inc.	3.75
Photograph, Merita Bread Premium, Mailer, Letter	100.00
Photograph, Tonto, Merita Premium, Mailer, Letter	125.00
Pin, Star, Bond Bread Safety Club	28.00
Pistol, Smoke, Click, Plastic, Marx, 1950s	28.00
Pistol, Sparkler, Box	60.00
Play Set, Legend of Lone Ranger, 65 Piece	45.00
Poster, 50th Anniversary, Black, Gold	10.00
Prairie Wagon, Gabriel, Box	25.00
Radio, Desk Model, 1930s	545.00
Record, He Becomes The Lone Ranger, 45 RPM, Decca	5.00
Record, He Saves The Colonel's Son, 45 RPM, Decca	15.00
Ring, Atom Bomb, Adjustable, Brass, Bullet Shaped Tube, 1947	70.00
Ring, Flashlight, 1948	25.00 To 50.00
Ring, National Defenders	45.00
Ring, Secret Compartment	85.00
Ring, Six–Shooter, Adjustable, Brass, Spark Wheel, 1948	75.00
Ring, Weather	30.00
Scarf, Silver, Black Silk, 36 In.	22.00
Sign, Merita Bread, Embossed Tin, 24 X 36 In.	675.00
Sign, Merita Bread, Lone Ranger, Lithographed Tin, 22 X 34 In.	900.00
Signal Siren Flashlight, Original Box & Silver Bullet Code	70.00
Snow Globe, Roping Calf, Red Base, Decal	50.00
Target, Tin, 1938, 9 1/2 X 9 1/2 In.	40.00
Tie, With Slide	35.00
Toothbrush Holder	65.00

Watch, Moving Pictures 50.00

The Longwy Workshop of Longwy, France, first made ceramic wares in 1798. The workshop is still in business. Most of the ceramic pieces found today are glazed with many colors to resemble cloisonne or other enameled metal. The factory used a variety of marks.

LONGWY, Candelabrum, 3 Arms, Scrolling Brass, Pottery Standard, 11 In. 85.00
  Candlestick, Brass Standard, 8 Crystal Prisms, 9 3/4 In. .... 150.00 To 165.00
  Candlestick, Flowers On Base, Brass Standard, Prism, 3 1/4 In., Pair 160.00
  Plate, Bird, Flowers, Marked, 8 In. 125.00
  Tray, Bird Among Freesias, Foliage, 10 X 11 In. 200.00
  Vase, Bird, Palm Tree, Mountain, Blue Ground, 7 In. 295.00

Lotus Ware was made by the Knowles, Taylor & Knowles Company of East Liverpool, Ohio, from 1890 to 1900. Lotus Ware is a thin, Belleek–like porcelain. It was sometimes decorated outside the factory. Other types of ceramics that were made by the Knowles, Taylor & Knowles Company are listed under "KTK."

LOTUS WARE, Creamer, Fishnet & Floral 265.00
  Tea Set, Feather Design, 3 Piece 495.00
  Vase, Applied Reticulated Design 95.00

Low art tiles were made by the J. and J. G. Low Art Tile Works of Chelsea, Massachusetts, from 1877 to 1902. A variety of art and other tiles were made. Some of the tiles were made by a process called "natural," some were hand–modeled, and some made mechanically.

LOW, Tile, Florals, Amber 35.00

The Lowestoft factory in Suffolk, England, worked from 1757 to 1802. They made many commemorative gift pieces and small, dated, inscribed pieces of soft paste porcelain.

LOWESTOFT, see also Chinese Export
LOWESTOFT, Creamer, Spiral Flutes, Leaves At Base, C.1775, 3 3/4 In. 770.00
  Cup, Feeding, Spray of Flowers Transfer, Fruit, 1770–75, 3 1/4 In. 440.00
  Dish, Pickle, Leaf Shape, Stem Handle, Stylized Blossoms, 1768, Pr. 880.00
LOY–NEL–ART, see McCoy

Lunch pails and lunch boxes have been used to carry lunches to school or work since the nineteenth century. Today, most collectors want either early tobacco advertising boxes or children's lunch boxes made since the 1930s. The original Thermos bottle must be inside the box for the collector to consider it complete.

LUNCH BOX, Astronaut 30.00
  Bionic Woman 15.00
  Blondie, Thermos 30.00
  Blue Tiger 85.00
  Brown Beauty Tobacco, Tin, Pictures Aunt Jemima 150.00
  Captain America 15.00
  Central Union Tobacco, Moon 55.00
  Charlie's Angels, Thermos 5.00
  Daniel Boone, Fess Parker, American Tradition Co., Dated 1965 .... 18.00
  Dixie Kid, Black Boy 125.00
  Dixie Queen, Portrait 150.00
  Dukes of Hazzard, Thermos 18.00
  Fat Albert 10.00
  Flipper, Thermos 30.00
  Friends Smoking & Chewing Tobacco, Bail Handle, 1908 .... 35.00
  Gail & Ax Tobacco 35.00
  Gentle Ben .... 12.00 To 20.00
  Green Hornet, Thermos 35.00
  Grizzly Adams, Dome Top .... 10.00 To 15.00
  Gunsmoke, 1959 .... 50.00

Gunsmoke, Thermos, Aladdin, 1973 .... 65.00
Joe Palooka, Tin, 1948 .... 55.00 To 60.00
Just Suits Cut Plug, Red, Gold, Black, Side Opening, Tin, 7 3/4 In. 35.00
Lawman 50.00
Lost In Space 25.00
Mickey Mouse Club, Thermos 25.00
Monkees, Vinyl, Portrait, Thermos, 1967 .... 25.00
Monsters, Thermos 28.00
Nabisco 20.00
Patterson's Seal Cut Plug, Basket Weave 25.00
Peanuts 8.00
Pebbles & Bam Bam 35.00
Pedro Tobacco 120.00
Penny Post 225.00
Peter Rabbit, Candy, Tin 70.00
Planet of Apes 20.00
Porky Lunch Wagon, Dome Top, 1959 .... 55.00
Rainbow Tobacco 195.00
Red Indian Tobacco .... 175.00 To 200.00
Red Tiger Tobacco 60.00
Redicut Tobacco 145.00
School Bus, Disney 35.00
Sensible Tobacco, Tin 30.00
Snoopy, Peanuts, Thermos, 1965 .... 15.00
Space, 1999, Thermos, Barbara Bain, Martin Landau, Dated 1975 .... 18.00
Sports Figures, Ohio Art, Oval 18.00
Star Wars 10.00
Steve Canyon, Thermos .... 25.00 To 35.00
Sunset Trail 225.00
Super Heroes, Thermos 20.00
Tarzan 20.00
Tiger Tobacco, Red, Black, Tiger On Top, 9 X 6 X 6 In. .... 35.00 To 50.00
Tom Corbett, Thermos .... 75.00 To 95.00
U.S.Marine, Basket Weave 45.00
UFO, 1973 .... 22.00
Union Leader Cut Plug Tobacco 50.00
Union Leader, Red Eagle 20.00
Wagon Train, Thermos 20.00
Welcome Back Kotter, Thermos 6.00
Wild Bill Hickok, Thermos .... 25.00 To 35.00
Winner Tobacco, Trunk Style 65.00
LUNCH PAIL, Circus Performers, 4 X 6 In. 28.50
Pedro Tobacco 14.00
Red Tiger Tobacco 65.00
Star Trek, Thermos 10.00
Tiger Tobacco, Tiger Each End, Blue 160.00

Luneville, a French faience factory, was established in 1731 by Jacques Chambrette. It is best known for its fine biscuit figures and groups and for large faience dogs and lions. The early pieces were unmarked. The firm was acquired by Keller and Guerin and is still working.

LUNEVILLE, Cup & Saucer, Oversized 45.00
Plate, Floral, 9 In. 32.00
Platter, Rooster, Crazed, 15 In. 110.00
Vase, St.Clement, Applied Dragons & Birds, 1860s, 16 1/2 In., Pair 2600.00

Lusterware was meant to resemble copper, silver, or gold. It has been used since the sixteenth century. Most of the luster found today was made during the nineteenth century. The metallic glazes are applied on pottery. The finished color depends on the combination of the clay color and the glaze.

LUSTER, Blue, Plate, White Blossoms Allover, Leaf Mark, Japan, Set of 6 .... 12.00
Blue, Vase, Bronze Holder, Austrian, 9 In. 200.00

Canary, Figurine, Cat, Full–Bodied, 8 In. 525.00
Canary, Pitcher, Mask, 5 3/4 In. 425.00
Copper, Goblet, Sunderland Band, Pink Luster Over Cream, 4 .... 45.00 To 48.00
Copper, Pitcher, Basket of Flowers, Dolphin Handle, Mask Spout, 7 In. 85.00
Copper, Pitcher, Berry & Leaf, Bulbous, Harvest Ware, 4 1/4 X 4 In. 36.00
Copper, Pitcher, Berry & Leaf, Wade, 2 3/4 In. 22.00
Copper, Pitcher, Enameled Flowers, 4 1/2 In. 47.50
Copper, Pitcher, Lavender Band, Orange Flowers, 5 In. 75.00
Copper, Pitcher, Polychrome Floral, 8 3/8 In. 55.00
Copper, Sugar, Small 25.00
     LUSTER, COPPER, TEA LEAF, see Tea Leaf Ironstone
Copper, Teapot, Windmill Scene, Scroll, Hexagonal, Wood & Sons 36.00
     LUSTER, FAIRYLAND, see Wedgwood
Green, Sugar & Creamer, Ornate Holder, Japan 38.00
Pink, Cup & Saucer, Building With Clock 65.00
Pink, Cup & Saucer, Friendship, Applied Flowers, Gold & Pastels 58.00
Pink, Cup, Cloud, Sunderland, 3 In. 22.00
Pink, Mug, Primitive Design, Cream Ground 20.00
Pink, Pitcher, Waconda–Great Spirit Springs Souvenir, Germany, 4 In. 13.00
Pink, Plate, Cloud, Sunderland, 7 In. 25.00
Pink, Plate, Roses, White Seaweed, Open Handles, Germany, 9 In. 24.00
Pink, Spittoon, Fenton 45.00
Pink, Tumbler, Carnegie Library, Elroy, Wisc., Germany, 3 1/2 In. 10.00
Purple, Cup & Saucer, Embossed Baskets of Flowers 22.50
     LUSTER, SUNDERLAND, see Sunderland
Yellow, Bowl, 8 In. 850.00
Yellow, Mug, A Present For My Dear Girl, Eagle 715.00
Yellow, Pitcher, Peace & Plenty, 7 In. 1760.00
Yellow, Tea Set, 3 Piece 495.00

Lustre Art Glass Company was founded in Long Island, New York, in 1920 by Conrad Vahlsing and Paul Frank. The company made lampshades and globes that are almost indistinguishable from those made by Quezal. Most of the shades made by the company were unmarked.

LUSTRE ART, Shade, Bull's–Eye At Top, Leaf Swags, Raised Scrolls, 11 In. 250.00
Shade, Gold Aurene Interior, White Calcite Exterior, Signed 125.00
Shade, Gold Thread Over Green & Gold Leaves, 6 Piece 750.00
Shade, Threaded, Green & Gold, Opalescent, Signed 65.00

Lustres are mantel decorations, or pedestal vases, with many hanging glass prisms. The name really refers to the prisms, and it is proper to refer to a single glass prism as a lustre. Either spelling, luster or lustre, is correct.

LUSTRES, Cranberry Glass, Pair 375.00
Opalene, Blue, Gilt Tracery, Applied Jewels, 19 In., Pair 1000.00
Pink Cased, Enameled Florals, Gilt Trim, Bristol, 13 In., Pair 370.00

Petrus Regout established the De Sphinx pottery in Maastricht, Holland, in 1836. The firm was noted for its transfer–printed earthenware. Many factories in Maastricht are still making ceramics.

MAASTRICHT, Charger, Children Skating On Frozen Canal, Windmill, 15 1/2 In. 65.00
Plate, Oriental Pattern, Deep Blue, White, 9 In. 18.00
Tea Set, Child's, Petrus Regout & Co., 13 Piece 150.00
Tray, Polychrome, Delft, Round 38.00

Maize glass was made by W. L. Libbey & Son Company of Toledo, Ohio, after 1889. The glass resembled an ear of corn. The leaves were usually green, but some pieces were made with blue or red leaves. The kernels of "corn" were light yellow, white, or light green.

MAIZE, Butter, Cover, Green & Brown Leaves, Custard Glass 650.00
Butter, Cover, Green Leaves 650.00
Celery Vase, Blue Leaves, Marigold 165.00
Cruet, Libbey .... 175.00 To 195.00

Pitcher, Rows of Corn Kernels, Blue Husks, Clear Handle, 8 3/4 In.	585.00
Rose Bowl, Honey Amber, White Lining, 6 1/2 In.	25.00
Saltshaker, Blue Stalks	75.00
Saltshaker, Green Leaves, Custard Glass	135.00
Sugar Shaker, Pink, Cased, Pewter Top	100.00
Toothpick, Green & Gold Leaves, Flat Base	275.00
Tumbler, Yellow Leaves	135.00

 Majolica is a general term for any pottery glazed with an opaque tin enamel that conceals the color of the clay body. It has been made since the fourteenth century. Today's collector is most likely to find Victorian majolica. The heavy, colorful ware is rarely marked. Some famous makers include Wedgwood; Minton; Griffen, Smith and Hill (marked "Etruscan"); and Chesapeake Pottery (marked "Avalon" or "Clifton").

MAJOLICA, Ashtray, Figural, Swan	10.00
Basket, Birds & Strawberries On Top of Handles, Etruscan, 15 In.	1920.00
Basket, Ribbon Around Brown Handle, Blue Side Pouches, 11 In.	1050.00
Bowl, Cauliflower, Footed, Wedgwood, 10 1/2 In.	235.00
Bowl, Cupid Medallions, Gondola Shape, French, 20 In.	375.00
Bowl, Dogwood, Handle, Twisted Feet, 11 In.	425.00
Bowl, Grapes, Leaves, Scalloped, Grape Cluster Feet, Germany, 11 In.	35.00
Bowl, Green Leaf Corners, Sunflower Center, Double Handle, 11 In.	80.00
Bowl, Leaf Center, 9 1/2 In., 5 Piece	275.00
Bowl, Leaf, Open Handle, 9 In.	35.00
Bowl, Leaves, Acorns, Green, Cream, Signed, 12 In.	275.00
Bowl, Lobster, Claws At Ends, 12 X 6 1/2 In.	225.00
Bowl, Molded Green Leaves On Green Ground, Marked, 6 In.	30.00
Bowl, Napkin Shape, Morning Glory, 1880s	80.00
Bowl, Pond Lily, Holdcroft, Blue Interior, Twig Feet, 10 In.	350.00
Bowl, Raised Basket Design, Green To Brown, 2 3/4 X 3 1/4 In.	43.00
Bowl, Ram's Heads, Openwork, 8 1/2 X 15 In.	400.00
Bowl, Shell Shape, Green Rim, Flowers, 16 In.	100.00
Bowl, Shell, Coral Band, Turquoise, Marked GJ, 19 X 11 1/2 In.	950.00
Bowl, Shell, Lavender Interior, Brown Exterior, Footed, 8 1/2 In.	200.00
Bowl, Underplate, Blackberries, 5 1/4 In.	110.00
Box, Sardine, Blue, Yellow Trim, 8 1/2 In.	525.00
Box, Sardine, Pineapple, Attached Underplate, 9 In.	215.00
Box, Sardine, Wedgwood, 8 3/4 X 7 In.	365.00
Bread Tray, Bamboo & Fern, Wardles	85.00
Breadbox, Mottled Greens, Blues & Cream, 9 X 10 1/2 In.	400.00
Butter Chip, Dogwood, Cobalt Ground, Signed George Jones	40.00
Butter Chip, Etruscan	32.00
Butter Chip, Etruscan Shell & Seaweed	75.00
Butter Chip, Floral & Fern	18.00
Butter Chip, Geranium Leaf, Green, Brown	30.00
Butter Chip, Pansy, Signed Etruscan	30.00
Butter Chip, Sunflower, White, Tan & Brown Flower, Signed Wedgwood	35.00
Butter Keeper, Dogwood, Signed, 8 In.	550.00
Butter Keeper, Strawberries, Yellow Ground, Signed, 8 In.	195.00
Butter, Cover, Figural, Corn	48.00
Cake Plate, Green Outlined Berries, Green, 1884, 10 1/2 In.	65.00
Cake Plate, Running Deer & Dog, 11 In.	125.00
Cake Plate, White & Green, Blue Ground, Germany, 7 1/2 In.	56.00
Candlestick, Mustard Glaze, Figural Leaf Saucer, Handle, 5 In.	39.00
Carafe, Pineapple	210.00
Card Holder, Old Man & Woman, Arms Outstretched, Pair	125.00
Charger, Polychrome Fish, Lobsters, Frogs, 24 In.	715.00
Cheese Dome, Swan Finial, Etruscan Lily	1350.00
Cheese Keeper, Cover, Dogwood Pattern, Wicker Wrap, 5 1/2 In.	500.00
Cheese Keeper, Domed, Band of Raspberries, 8 1/2 X 11 In.	450.00
Cheese Keeper, Lid, Turquoise, Wedge Shape	250.00
Coffeepot, Bamboo, Etruscan, 7 In.	185.00
Compote, Cream, Green, Yellow, Blue Leaves, 5 1/2 In.	65.00

Compote, Daisy, Cobalt Ground, Pedestal, Signed, Etruscan, 9 In. 175.00
Compote, Dogwood, Cobalt Ground, Pedestal, George Jones Mark, 9 In. 300.00
Compote, Floral, Etruscan, 5 X 9 In. 200.00
Compote, Flowers, Green, Cobalt, Yellow Flowers, Green Leaves, 9 In. 85.00
Compote, Lily Pad, 3-Footed 165.00
Compote, Rose, Classical Series 65.00
Creamer, Basket Weave 55.00
Creamer, Brown Basket Weave Bottom, 3 1/2 In. 95.00
Creamer, Corn, Yellow & Green, 4 1/2 In. 25.00
Creamer, Green Ground, 2 Birds, Flowering Branch, Lavender, 6 In. 95.00
Creamer, Pineapple, Bulbous, 2 3/4 In. 75.00
Creamer, Rose Flower, Brown Fence Top & Handle, 4 1/2 In. 48.00
Creamer, Shell & Seaweed, Albino, Tan, Etruscan, 6 In. 115.00
Creamer, White Goat, 4 1/4 In. 140.00
Cup & Saucer, Bamboo, Etruscan 125.00
Cup & Saucer, Blackberry & Basket Weave, Tan Center, 7 In. 165.00
Cup & Saucer, Dragonfly & Fan 125.00
Cup & Saucer, Shell & Seaweed, Etruscan 280.00
Decanter, Duck 75.00
Decanter, Parrot 75.00
Dessert Set, Pink Rims, Open Handle On Master, 7 Piece 310.00
Dish, 2 Figural Koala Bears, Leaf Shape, 4 In. 175.00
Dish, Acorns, Open Handles, 12 1/2 In. 55.00
Dish, Asparagus, Footed, Blue Feet, 8 In. 260.00
Dish, Asparagus, Open Handle, Green, White, Lavender 500.00
Dish, Chip & Dip, Fan Shape, 17 In. 65.00
Dish, Fan, Various Colors, 6 1/2 In., 6 Piece 345.00
Dish, Fan, Yellow, Lavender, Brown & Blue, 6 1/2 In. 60.00
Dish, Floral, Basket Weave, Rope Border, Signed, 5 In. 80.00
Dish, Hen Cover, Green & Brown Bottom 175.00
Dish, Ice Cream, Double Pink Shell Handle, Water Lilies 375.00
Dish, Leaf, Acorn Design, Marked Gory, 12 In. 70.00
Dish, Leaf, Brown Open Handles, 12 In., 4 Piece 260.00
Dish, Leaf, Open Handle, Pink Flowers In Center, 11 1/2 In. 45.00
Dish, Low, Oval, Etruscan, 8 1/2 In. 285.00
Dish, Open, Green & Brown, 2 Handles, French, 16 In. 950.00
Dish, Sauce, Attached Asparagus Plate, Double Handle, 10 1/2 In. 150.00
Dish, Serving, Cover, Deer Heads In Relief, 14 In. 300.00
Dish, Serving, Strawberry, Marked, 10 1/2 In. 300.00
Dish, Strawberry, Minton, 8 In. 125.00
Figurine, American Salver Boy, Holding Tray, Straw Hat, 20 In. 1625.00
Figurine, Bird On Leafy Perch, Continental, 12 1/4 In. 225.00
Figurine, Rooster, Beside Hollow Tree Trunk, 24 In. 600.00
Garden Seat, Dark Blue, Green & Cream, 18 1/2 In. 180.00
Humidor, Cat, Gray, Lavender Lining, 9 In. 110.00
Humidor, Corn, Yellow & Green, 7 In. 65.00
Humidor, Dutch Children, Pipe On Cover, Fluted Chest Shape, 4 In. 55.00
Humidor, Lavender Band, Black Boy Faces, 10 In. 210.00
Humidor, Pouch Tied At Neck, Tasseled Cord On Lid, 5 1/2 In. 95.00
Inkwell, Attached Saucer, Painted Flowers & Butterfly, 6 1/2 In. 115.00
Jug, Here's To A Good Life, Silver Plated Collar, Wedgwood 575.00
Jug, Pewter Top, Cobalt Blue & Brown, 9 In. 120.00
Mallard Duck, Impressed W.S.&S., Bavarian, 1829–1860 .... 450.00
Match Holder, Striker, Green & Brown Tints, Signed, 5 In. 190.00
Mustache Cup, Bow Trim, English 195.00
Mustache Cup, Saucer, Rose & Rope, Lavender Inside, Yellow 225.00
Nut Dish, Standing Squirrel 175.00
Oyster Plate, 3 Lavender, 3 Yellow Indentations, 9 In. 125.00
Oyster Plate, 3 Turquoise, 3 Lavender Indentions, Brown, 10 In. 100.00
Oyster Plate, Minton, 10 In. 285.00
Oyster Plate, Shell & Seaweed, George Jones, 8 1/2 In. 210.00
Oyster Plate, White Shell, Turquoise Ground, 5 Indentations, 7 In. 200.00
Pitcher, Acorns & Leaves, 7 In. 95.00
Pitcher, Antelope Under Tree, 7 3/4 In. 115.00

Pitcher, Banana Tree, 7 In. 90.00
Pitcher, Bird & Fan, Wedgwood, 8 In. .... 485.00 To 500.00
Pitcher, Bird & Floral Branch, Lavender, Marked, 7 In. 75.00
Pitcher, Blackberries, Green Leaves, Brown Bands, 7 In. 75.00
Pitcher, Bow & Blackberry, Cream Base, Wine Leaves, Marked, 8 In. 185.00
Pitcher, Brewster, Shield With Crown & Key Mark, 9 1/2 In. 295.00
Pitcher, Butterfly Lip, Etruscan, 8 In. 175.00
Pitcher, Corn, Bulbous, Yellow & Green, 9 1/2 In. 110.00
Pitcher, Corn, Yellow & Green, 8 1/2 In. 75.00
Pitcher, Duck, 12 In. 95.00
Pitcher, Etruscan, Rustic, 8 1/4 In. 195.00
Pitcher, Fern & Bamboo, English, 4 1/2 In. 50.00
Pitcher, Fish, Blue & Cream, 12 In. 110.00
Pitcher, Fish, Dark Green Shaded To White, 11 In. 95.00
Pitcher, Fish, Floral, Aqua, Cream, Brown & Pink, 8 In. 165.00
Pitcher, Fish, Green Seaweed, Gold Fish, 9 In. 175.00
Pitcher, Fish, On Waves, Cobalt Blue, 8 1/4 In. 165.00
Pitcher, Fish, Seashells, Mottled Blue & Green, 24 1/2 In. 900.00
Pitcher, Flowers, Branch, Hawthorne, Mottled Ground, 9 In. 150.00
Pitcher, Goat, Dark Purple, Yellow & White, 9 3/4 In. 95.00
Pitcher, Grapes & Leaves, Cobalt Blue Panels, 8 In. 250.00
Pitcher, Hunt Scene, Hound Handle, Wedgwood, 6 In. 110.00
Pitcher, Hunting Scene, Emerald Green, Dog Handle, Wedgwood 225.00
Pitcher, Hunting Scene, Hound Handle, Wedgwood, 7 In. 160.00
Pitcher, Hunting Scene, Pig Spout, Tree Trunk Handle, 8 1/4 In. 160.00
Pitcher, Iris, Lavender, Yellow Band, Marked, 7 In. 90.00
Pitcher, Man's Torso, On Elephant Body, Brown Streaks, 9 X 5 In. 65.00
Pitcher, Mottled Cobalt, Green, Yellow & Brown, 7 In. 130.00
Pitcher, Owl & Fan, Triangular, 8 In. 160.00
Pitcher, Owl, Brown, Pink & Green, 10 In. 265.00
Pitcher, Owl, Green & Cream, 12 In. 125.00
Pitcher, Owl, Morley & Co., 8 1/4 In. 200.00
Pitcher, Pink Flowers, Turquoise Ground, Brown Handle, 6 1/2 In. 75.00
Pitcher, Pond Lily, 7 In. 160.00
Pitcher, Raised Flowers & Leaf, Floral Medallion, 12 1/2 In. 125.00
Pitcher, Ram, Lavender, Yellow Head, Handle, Marked, 7 In. 150.00
Pitcher, Shaded Green To Brown & Gold, Flowers, Scrolls, 6 1/2 In. 90.00
Pitcher, Shell & Seaweed, 4 In. 45.00
Pitcher, Stork In Rushes, 7 1/2 In. 125.00
Pitcher, Syrup, Sunflower, Pink Ground, Marked 1879, Signed, 8 In. 295.00
Pitcher, Turquoise, Brown Basket Weave, Lavender Inside, 6 1/2 In. 50.00
Pitcher, Victorian Flowers, 7 In. 105.00
Pitcher, Wild Rose, Basket Weave, Geometric Design, 7 In. 110.00
Pitcher, Wild Rose, Brown, 9 In. 165.00
Pitcher, Wild Rose, Butterfly Spout, Etruscan, 8 In. 130.00
Planter, Bird, Polychrome, Footed, Marked, 18 In. 600.00
Planter, Rooster, L.C.Belleuse, 21 In. 1200.00
Planter, Undertray, Brown Borders, 12 In. 700.00
Plaque, Mother, 2 Baby Alligators, Textured Green, 7 In. 295.00
Plaque, Royal Figure Seated On Horse, Impressed Elliot, 11 In. 350.00
Plate, Apple Blossom, 6 In. 38.00
Plate, Artichoke, White, Marked, 9 In. 27.50
Plate, Bamboo, Etruscan, 8 In. .... 85.00 To 110.00
Plate, Basket Weave, Blackberries, Blue, 8 1/4 In. 55.00
Plate, Begonia Leaf, Etruscan, 9 In. 35.00
Plate, Blackberries & Floral Design, Basket Weave, 8 In., Pair 110.00
Plate, Blackberry, Aqua, Gold, Avalon, 8 In. 58.00
Plate, Blackberry, Leaves, Cobalt Ground, 9 1/2 In. 90.00
Plate, Boy Carrying Cane, Walking Duck, Castle, Trees, 7 In. 25.00
Plate, Cauliflower, Etruscan, 8 In. 125.00
Plate, Cherub Riding Lion, Rose & Green, Etruscan, 9 In. 60.00
Plate, Deer & Dog, 8 In. 65.00
Plate, Dog & Doghouse, Mottled Back, 11 In. 75.00
Plate, Dogs In Center, Cream, Brown, Green, Yellow, 11 In. 125.00

Plate, Field Berries & Blossoms, Leaves, 8 1/2 In. 50.00
Plate, Floral, Bee & Butterfly, Basket Weave, Wedgwood, 9 In. 95.00
Plate, Fruit, Basket Weave, Green, Yellow & Pink, 9 In. 50.00
Plate, Grapevine, 8 In. 35.00
Plate, Green, Brown & Yellow Leaves, 8 1/2 In. 25.00
Plate, Leaf & Basket Weave, 8 In. 55.00
Plate, Leaf & Blackberry, 9 In. 85.00
Plate, Leaf, Rustic Brown, Marked, 8 1/2 In. 100.00
Plate, Leaves, Butterflies, Marked, 9 In. 32.00
Plate, Maple Leaf, Fern, Seaweed, Yellow Ground, Green, Brown, 8 In. 80.00
Plate, Mulberries, Leaves, Brown Basket Weave, 8 In. 39.00
Plate, Old Man Drinking Beer, Brown & Yellow, 10 1/2 In. 75.00
Plate, Overlapping Begonia Leaf, Etruscan, 9 In. 85.00
Plate, Recessed Center, Scrolled Flowers, Gnomes, 11 1/4 In. 115.00
Plate, Rose, Basket Weave Center, Etruscan, 7 In. 95.00
Plate, Shell & Seaweed, Pink, Green Seaweed, Marked, 9 In. 75.00
Plate, Shield & Knife, Cobalt With Green, Pink & Gray, 17 In. 60.00
Plate, Wedgwood, 8 3/4 In. 95.00
Plate, Wild Rose, Gray Ground, Basket Weave, Impressed, 9 In. 390.00
Platter, American Pub Scene, 11 1/2 In. 145.00
Platter, Asparagus, Aqua, Green, Lavender & White, 11 1/2 In. 175.00
Platter, Bamboo, Basket Weave, Impressed Back, 11 In. 175.00
Platter, Begonia Leaf, 11 X 9 In. 115.00
Platter, Bird, Floral, Blue, Pink, Brown, Gray, Yellow, 12 In. 200.00
Platter, Blackberry Leaf, Fox Peering On Edge, Green, Brown, 11 In. 750.00
Platter, Bread, Brown Center, Sheaves of Wheat, 13 In. 120.00
Platter, Figural, Fish, Lavender Mouth, 13 In. 155.00
Platter, Fish, Mottled Rim, Aqua Center, Red & Green Fish, 18 In. 400.00
Platter, Fruit, Green, Cream, Pink, Purple, Green, Marked, 12 In. 1300.00
Platter, Game, Green & Yellow Rim, 18 1/2 In. 300.00
Platter, Green, Black, Yellow, White, Lavender, 13 In. 225.00
Platter, Indians, 14 In. 225.00
Reamer, Daisies, Basket Weave 21.00
Relish, Begonia Leaf 55.00
Relish, Reticulated Center, Austria, 13 In. 55.00
Saucer, Pineapple 25.00
Shaving Jug, Cover, Soap, Wicker & Grape 125.00
Shell, Lavender Interior, 3 Twig Feet, George Jones, 7 In. 300.00
Shoe, Cobalt & Gray, 4 In. 60.00
Spittoon, Brown Bamboo Outside, Brown, Green & Yellow Inside 35.00
Spoon Rest, Begonia Leaf On Basket Weave 45.00
Spooner, Shell & Seaweed, Albino 75.00
Strawberry Basket, Tree Branch Handle, George Jones, 11 In. 650.00
Strawberry Bowl, Underplate, Green & Pink, E.Carleton, 9 In. 48.00
Sugar & Creamer, Crane & Fan, Pink Interior, 3 1/2 In. 85.00
Sugar, Cauliflower, Etruscan 175.00
Sugar, Cover, Basket Weave 65.00
Sugar, Cover, Pineapple, 4 1/2 In. ....75.00 To 125.00
Syrup, Blackberries, Bennett 145.00
Syrup, Corn, Pewter Lid, Green & Yellow, 6 In. 190.00
Syrup, Green Leaves, White Flowers, Blue, Pewter Lid 160.00
Syrup, Pineapple 225.00
Syrup, Pineapple, Green & Yellow, Pewter Lid, 5 3/4 In. 160.00
Syrup, Sunflower, Etruscan 275.00
Syrup, Sunflowers In Brown Vase, 5 In. 40.00
Syrup, Tin Cover, Green, Yellow, Brown, 5 1/2 In. 135.00
Tankard, Corn, Green & Yellow, 10 3/4 In. 55.00
Tea Set, Bird & Iris, Blue, Etruscan, 3 Piece 485.00
Tea Set, Child's, Cabbage Design, 12 Piece 120.00
Tea Set, Child's, Green Ground, Pink & Yellow, 21 Piece 700.00
Tea Set, Shell & Seaweed, 8 Piece 1600.00
Teapot, Bamboo, Etruscan 88.00
Teapot, Cabbage 38.00
Teapot, Cauliflower, Etruscan ....165.00 To 385.00

Teapot, Fish, Lion's Head, 3–Dimensional, Fish Finial 95.00
Teapot, Floral, Butterflies, Square 130.00
Teapot, Pineapple, Yellow & Green, 6 In. 150.00
Teapot, Shell & Seaweed, Albino, Etruscan 350.00
Toast Holder, Mottled Greens, Browns & Blues, 8 1/2 In. 290.00
Tobacco Jar, Figural, Turk 125.00
Toothpick, Figural, Boy With Basket 90.00
Tray, Begonia Leaf, Raspberry Colored Edge, 12 In. 80.00
Tray, Begonia, Green, Rose, Mottled Center, 12 X 9 In. 98.00
Tray, Bread, Lily–of–The–Valley, Turquoise, Handle, Marked, 14 In. 150.00
Tray, Geranium Blossoms & Leaves, Open Handles, 12 In. 85.00
Tureen, Cover, Wildlife Design, Minton, C.1863, 9 X 14 1/2 In. 1800.00
Tureen, Ducks On Cover, Wild Game, C.1863, 14 1/2 X 9 In. 1300.00
Tureen, Ducks, Chased By Foxes, Frog Finial 3600.00
Umbrella Stand, Ducks, Stylized Penguins, Blue Ground, 29 In. 468.00
Umbrella Stand, Elf Figure, Wicker Basket Type 2400.00
Umbrella Stand, Heron, On 1 Leg, Bullrushes, Holdcroft, 1875, 32 In. 1000.00
Urn, Cover, Onion Finial, Girl Tending Sheep, Painted Swags, 18 In. 450.00
Urn, Domed Cover, Painted Urns, Bouquets, V.Corrente, 28 In., Pair 650.00
Vase, Colonial Figures, Tree Trunk, 9 In., Pair 160.00
Vase, Figural, Woman With Fan, Standing At Tree Trunk, 12 In. 275.00
Vase, Hand, Cobalt & Brown, 5 In. 40.00
Vase, Iris Flowers, Germany, 10 1/2 In. 48.00
Vase, Panels of Iris, Pink & Lavender, 10 1/2 In. 150.00
Vase, Pink & Yellow Poppies, Cobalt Blue, 10 1/2 In. 125.00
Vase, Red Flower On Front, Brown Double Handles, 5 1/4 In. 40.00
Vase, Red, Beige & Gold Trim, 15 3/4 In. 95.00
Vase, Shell & Seaweed, Figural, 4 3/4 In. 110.00
Wall Pocket, Ducks & Flowers, 9 In. 60.00
Wall Pocket, Green, White Applied Flowers, 10 In. 80.00
Waste Bowl, Blackberry & Basket Weave, Signed, 5 In. 95.00

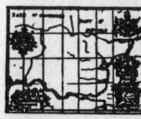 Maps of all types have been collected for centuries. The earliest known printed maps were made in 1478. The first printed street map showed London in 1559. The first road maps for use by drivers of automobiles were made in 1901. Collectors buy maps that were pages of old books, as well as the multifolded road maps popular in this century.

MAP, American Republic & Railways, Perry Spoulding, 1875 .... 195.00
Arkansas, Hand Colored, Paper, 14 X 17 In. 25.00
Atlas, Long's Classical, 1856 .... 75.00
Battlegrounds, Chickahominy, Siege of Richmond, 1862 .... 875.00
Boone County, Illinois, 1923 .... 75.00
Bridgeport, Conn., Folded, 1885, 40 X 40 In. 75.00
California, Hand Colored, Border, Colton, 1859, 1 Page 50.00
California, Richfield Travel Guide, 1950s 5.00
Canada & United States, Early Configurations, Framed 130.00
Confederate, Manassas & Vicinity, Civil War, 1861 .... 750.00
Crimean War, Europe & Railroads, Leather Portfolio 1250.00
Cultural & Historical, Hartford, Color Illustrations, 1933 .... 25.00
East Indies, Pinkerton, Hand Colored, 1809–15, 22 X 30 1/2 In. 75.00
Eastern Canada, 8 X 10 In., 2 Piece 15.00
Florida, Hand Colored, Colton, 1859, 1 Page 50.00
Florida, Thos.Copperthwait & Co., 1850 .... 55.00
France, Wall, 1915 .... 8.00
Ft.Snelling, Minnesota, Steel Engraved, C.1850, 8 7/8 X 11 1/4 In. 35.00
Globe, Copper Metal Stand, Library Size, C.1930, 46 X 24 In.Diam. 600.00
Globe, Footed Stand, 1930s 350.00
Globe, Newton's Celestial & Terrestrial, 1801 & 1845, 21 1/2 In., Pair 8500.00
Globe, On Iron Floor Stand, Early 20th Century, 44 1/2 In. 30.00
Globe, Rand McNally, Tin, Disney, 1940s 95.00
Globe, Table, Weber Costello, Bronze Finish Stand, 12 In.Globe, 21 In. 175.00
Globe, Texaco, 1 Piece 375.00
Hawaii, For Government Survey, F.L.Lowell, 1901, 38 1/8 X 34 In. 300.00

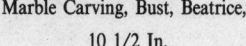

Marble Carving, Bust, Beatrice,
10 1/2 In.

Marble Carving, Pedestal, White,
C.1900, 32 X 15 In., Pair

Iowa, Hand Colored, Paper, 14 X 17 In.	25.00
Ireland, Hand Colored, Printed In France, 1750, 27 X 29 1/2 In.	275.00
Island of Maui, Lithograph, U.S.Geological Survey, 1883, 10 X 12 In.	100.00
Japan, Pinkerton, Hand Colored, 1809–15, 22 X 30 1/2 In.	75.00
Juneau County, Wisconsin, 1914	75.00
Louisiana, Color, 1895, Matted, 11 X 8 In.	16.50
Louisiana, Ink On Paper, Printed 1767, 6 1/4 X 8 In.	220.00
Lowell, Massachusetts, 1875, 27 X 22 In.	45.00
Manhattan, Battle of Harlem Hts., W.C.Rogers, 1868, 15 X 24 In.	50.00
Montana, Northern Pacific, Settlers, 4 Indian Reservations, 1882	50.00
Napoleon I's Campaign, 18th Century, 19 X 12 In.	44.00
New England, Automobile, 1911	4.50
New Mexico Territory, Rand–McNally, Color, 1912, 20 X 24 In.	30.00
New Mexico, Western Emigration, Rio Grande Settlements, 1882	50.00
New York & Brooklyn, Mitchell, 1872	35.00
New York City, 1776 Plan, Major Holland, Reprinted 1863, 15 X 17 In.	15.00
New York City, Street Guide, 192 Pages, 1945–46	3.50
New York Subways, 1940	4.00
North & South America, Calif.As Island, Mallet, French, 1681, 6 X 4 In.	685.00
North & South America, World, Sandwich Islands, German, 1812, 8 X 10 In.	225.00
Northeast & North Central U.S.Roads, Buick Motor Cars, 1930s, 12 In.	8.50
Ohio, Each County Separately Colored, Forts, Roads, 1831	45.00
Ohio, Johnson, Hand Colored, 1863, Framed	175.00
Old New York, The Bowery, Streets, 1862, 16 3/4 X 20 1/2 In.	35.00
Pacific Theater, World War II, Esso Gasoline	12.00
Railroad Route From Sacramento Valley To Columbia River, Civil War	250.00
Road Atlas, Wolverine, 1957	8.00
Road, Nebraska, Sinclair, 1931	7.00
Road, North & South Carolina, Esso, 1938	7.00
Road, Pennsylvania, Texaco, 1934	7.00
Road, San Francisco, Chevron Supreme, 1960s	5.00
Sauk County, Wisconsin, 1922	75.00

Southeastern Virginia, Manuscript, Fr.J.N.LeConte, C.1863 .... 275.00
U.S.& Territories, Gold, Silver, Railroad & Cities, Book Form, 1868 .... 100.00
U.S.Coastal Survey, San Francisco & Harbor, American, 1853, 28 X 31 In. 585.00
United States, Student's, Painted, C.1830, 16 X 21 In. 1430.00
Upper & Lower Canada, Colton, Hand Colored, 1855, 28 X 17 1/2 In. 20.00
Virginia, Color, 1895, Matted, 11 X 8 In. 16.50
Waltham, Mass., Beers, 1875 .... 48.00
Western Hemisphere, Engraved, In Latin, Bocklin, 1665, 7 X 8 1/2 In. 100.00
Weston, Missouri, Mayer, Steel Engraved, C.1850, 8 7/8 X 11 1/4 In. 35.00
Wind Directions, Jan Jansson, Framed, 17th Century, 25 X 29 In. 1500.00
World In 2 Hemispheres, DeLisle, Colored, Paris, 1720, 17 1/2 X 27 In. 2250.00
World, Roll–Down Type, Round Oak Case, 55 In. 150.00
World, Schoolroom, In Oak Case, 55 In. 250.00

Marble is used in many ways on antiques. Marble tops are popular for tables because they resist stains and damage. Listed here are marble carvings, large or small figurines, and groups of people or animals that have been a special art form since the time of the ancient Greeks. Reproductions, especially of large Victorian groups, are being made of a mixture using marble dust. These are very difficult to detect and collectors should be careful. Other carvings are listed under Alabaster.

MARBLE CARVING, Austrian Boy, Blowing Horn, Italian, 3 In. 3000.00
   Bust, Aphrodite, 19th Century, 24 In. 880.00
   Bust, Apollo, Long Curled Hair, 19th Century, 19 In. 2500.00
   Bust, Beatrice, 10 1/2 In. ....*Illus* 660.00
   Bust, Grecian, John Quincy Adams Ward, 1839–1910 .... 9500.00
   Bust, Marie Antoinette, 14 In. 155.00
   Bust, Seneca, Waisted Marble Socle, Continental, 23 In. 550.00
   Bust, Woman, Upswept Hair, Roses, Decollete, Evax, 1900, 32 In. 1350.00
   David, Standing, Italian, 44 3/4 In. 5225.00
   Female, Partially Nude, Flower Socle, Bastiani, 56 In. 7150.00
   Jardiniere, Putti, Grotesque Figures, Carrara, 32 In. 2750.00
   Obelisk, Black, Malachite Veneer, Stepped Base, 18 In., Pair 1540.00
   Pedestal, Reeded Support, Octagonal Base, Carrara, 44 In. 250.00
   Pedestal, White, C.1900, 32 X 15 In., Pair ....*Illus* 1650.00
   Table, Garden, 3 Caryatids Pedestal, Black Base, 1900, 25 In. 2250.00

The game of marbles has been popular since the days of the ancient Romans. American children were able to buy marbles by the mid–eighteenth century. Dutch glazed clay marbles were least expensive. Glazed pottery marbles, attributed to the Bennington potteries in Vermont, were of a better quality. Marbles made of pink marble were also available by the 1830s. Glass marbles seem to have been made later. By 1880, Samuel C. Dyke of South Akron, Ohio, was making clay marbles and The National Onyx Marble Company was making marbles of onyx. The Navarre Glass Marble Company of Navarre, Ohio, and M. B. Mishler of Ravenna, Ohio, made the glass marbles. Ohio remained the center of the marble industry and the Akron–made Akro Agate brand became nationally known. The most expensive marbles collected today are the sulfides. These are glass marbles with frosted white figures in the center.

MARBLE, Amber Glass Onion Swirl, 3/4 In. 85.00
   Bennington, Blue, 3 1/4 In. 8.00
   Bennington, Brown, 4 1/4 In. 10.00
   Blue & Red Banded Opaque, 3/4 In. 90.00
   Candy Swirl, 7/8 In. 50.00
   Clambroth, Blue Line, White, 1/2 In. 190.00
   Clambroth, Green Line, White, 1/2 In. 180.00
   Clambroth, White & Blue Lines, 9/16 In. 195.00
   Clambroth, White, Blue & Red Lines, 1 5/8 In. 150.00
   Latticinio Core Swirl, 1 3/4 In. 75.00
   Latticinio Swirl, 1 3/8 In. 75.00
   Latticinio, Orange, 7/8 In. 38.00

Lutz, Amber Glass, 7/8 In. 450.00
Lutz, Green Swirls, Coreless, 1 In. 150.00
Majolica, 1 1/2 In. 35.00
Mica, Emerald Green, 7/8 In. 35.00
Onionskin, Green, Lutz, 3/4 In. 295.00
Onionskin, Multicolor, 1 3/4 In. 160.00
Onionskin, Pink & Green, 1 1/2 In. 135.00
Onionskin, White & Blue, 7/8 In. 45.00
Opaque, Blue, 3/4 In. 50.00
Opaque, Pearl White, Solid, 3/4 In. 65.00
Opaque, White, 5/8 In. 30.00
Steelie, Hollow, 5/8 In. 15.00
Sulfide, Baseball Player, St.Clair, 2 In. 150.00
Sulfide, Bear, Sitting, 1 5/8 In. 80.00
Sulfide, Bear, Standing, 1 11/16 In. 240.00
Sulfide, Bear, Standing, 1 3/8 In. 180.00
Sulfide, Bear, Walking, 1 In. 110.00
Sulfide, Bird, On Post, 2 In. 225.00
Sulfide, Bird, With Long Feathers, 1 7/16 In. 150.00
Sulfide, Boy, On Stump, 1 5/8 In. 850.00
Sulfide, Boy, Sitting On Base, Ball Suit, Cap To Side, 2 In. 275.00
Sulfide, Boy, With Bat, White, Blue, Joe St.Clair, 1 3/4 In. 800.00
Sulfide, Boy, With Boat, 1 13/16 In. 1200.00
Sulfide, Camel, 1 5/8 In. 90.00
Sulfide, Child, Sitting, Hand On Chest, 1 1/4 In. 225.00
Sulfide, Cow, Reclining, 1 1/4 In. 75.00
Sulfide, Dog, Begging, 1 1/4 In. 75.00
Sulfide, Dog, Husky, 1 1/2 In. 150.00
Sulfide, Dog, Long–Haired, White, 1 1/4 In. 135.00
Sulfide, Dog, Lying Down, 1 7/8 In. 110.00
Sulfide, Dog, Sitting, 1 1/2in. 140.00
Sulfide, Dog, Sleeping, 2 In. 180.00
Sulfide, Eagle, On Post, 2 In. 285.00
Sulfide, Elephant, 1 3/8 In. 120.00
Sulfide, Elephant, 1 5/8 In. 275.00
Sulfide, Fish, 2 1/2 In. 450.00
Sulfide, Fox, 1 7/16 In. 130.00
Sulfide, Girl With Dress, 1 1/2 In. 1000.00
Sulfide, Goat, 1 3/4 In. 190.00
Sulfide, Goat, 2 1/32 In. 300.00
Sulfide, Hen, 1 1/4 In. 75.00
Sulfide, Horned Owl, Standing, 1 1/2 In. 100.00
Sulfide, Horse, Flowing Mane & Tail, Pink Arched Neck, 2 In. 2000.00
Sulfide, Horse, Grazing, 1 5/8 In. 180.00
Sulfide, Horse, Running, 1 1/2 In. 180.00
Sulfide, Lamb, 1 3/4 In. 220.00
Sulfide, Lamb, Grazing, 1 5/8 In. 140.00
Sulfide, Lion, 1 5/8 In. 200.00
Sulfide, Lion, 1 7/16 In. 75.00
Sulfide, Lion, 2 In. 125.00
Sulfide, Llama, 1 5/8 In. 140.00
Sulfide, Monkey, 1 1/8 In. 65.00
Sulfide, Pelican, 1 1/4 In. 275.00
Sulfide, Pig, 2 In. 100.00
Sulfide, Rabbit, 1 9/16 In. 180.00
Sulfide, Rabbit, Running, 1 15/16 In. 380.00
Sulfide, Rabbit, Seated, 2 1/4 In. 245.00
Sulfide, Rooster, 1 7/16 In. 140.00
Sulfide, Rooster, Yellow, 1 3/4 In. 175.00
Sulfide, Sheep, 1 1/4 In. 75.00
Sulfide, Squirrel, With Nut, 1 13/16 In. 220.00
Sulfide, Squirrel, With Nut, 2 In. 300.00
Swirl, Divided Core, Polished, 1 3/4 In. 65.00

The Marblehead Pottery was founded in 1905 by Dr. J. Hall as a rehabilitative program for the patients of a Marblehead, Massachusetts, sanitarium. Two years later it was separated from the sanitarium and it continued operations until 1936. Many of the pieces were decorated with marine motifs.

MARBLEHEAD, Basket, Hanging, Brown	175.00
Basket, Hanging, Green	85.00
Bowl, Blue, 9 X 2 In.	125.00
Bowl, Dark Blue, 6 In.	95.00
Candleholder, Matte Blue, Handles, Paper Label	68.00
Penholder, Fleishmann's Margarine, 1959	125.00
Pitcher, Schooner Medallion 1 Side, Galleon Other, 4 3/4 In.	650.00
Tile, 5 Color Flower Basket, Framed, 6 In.	475.00
Tile, Hand Painted Ship, 18 Sails, Framed, Marked, 6 In.	395.00
Vase, Black & Brown Squares, Green, Corset Shape, H.Tutt, 9 In.	5000.00
Vase, Blue & Brown Floral, Gray–Blue, Squat Bulbous, 3 1/4 In.	300.00
Vase, Blue Matte, 5 In.	110.00
Vase, Brown Lattice, Green, Straight Cylindrical, Label, 6 In.	2100.00
Vase, Dark Blue, 5 In.	58.00
Vase, Hanging Flowers, Blue, Gray Ground, 1910, 6 1/2 In.	1300.00

Mary Gregory glass is identified by a characteristic white figure painted on dark glass. It was made from 1870 to 1910. The name refers to any glass decorated with a white silhouette figure and not just to the Sandwich glass originally painted by Miss Mary Gregory. Many reproductions have been made and there are new pieces being sold in gift shops today.

MARY GREGORY, Bottle, Wine, Boy, Cranberry, Clear Bubble Stopper, 7 1/8 In.	195.00
Bottle, Wine, Girl, Bubble Stopper, Cranberry, 10 In.	195.00
Box, Boy Feeding Ducks, Royal Blue, White Trim, 3 1/2 In.	630.00
Box, Hinged Cover, Girl Feeding Bird, Blue, 5 5/8 X 6 In.	450.00
Box, Hinged Cover, Girl Holding Bird, Cobalt Blue, 5 1/2 In.	395.00
Box, Hinged Cover, Girl With Scarf, Amber, 4 X 3 5/8 In.	295.00
Box, Patch, Girl Picking Flowers On Cover, 2 1/8 In.	295.00
Box, Patch, Hinged Cover, Boy, Lime Green, 2 1/4 In.	165.00
Box, Patch, Hinged Cover, Girl, Lime Green, 2 3/8 In.	165.00
Box, Patch, Hinged Cover, White Figures, Cobalt Blue, 1 7/8 In.	175.00
Cookie Jar, Girl Sitting On Fence, Plated Fittings, Cranberry	450.00
Cruet, Boy In Garden, Green, Clear Stopper	175.00
Decanter, Wine, 3–Petal Top, Young Girl, Lime Green, 10 In.	145.00
Decanter, Young Boy In Riding Outfit, Amber, 13 1/2 In.	295.00
Decanter, Young Woman, Swan In Water, Cranberry, 9 1/2 In.	415.00
Dish, Cranberry, Footed, 4 1/4 In.	150.00
Dish, Trinket, Girl In Garden, Flowers, Atlantic City, 1898	135.00
Goblet, Boy Feeding Birds, Cranberry, 5 3/4 In.	110.00
Lamp, Fairy, Green On Crystal Base, 6 In.	495.00
Lamp, Kerosene, Girl, Dot Design Around Font, Cranberry	750.00
Match Holder, Boy, Barrel Shape, Cranberry, 2 1/4 In.	85.00
Mug, Boy & Girl, Facing, Olive Amber, 3 7/8 In.	118.00
Mug, Boy On 1, Girl On Other, Light Green, 3 3/8 In., Pair	115.00
Mug, Boy, Trees, Clear Handle, Cranberry, 3 3/4 In.	110.00
Mug, Girl, Boy, Facing, Barrel Shape, Amber, 4 1/4 In., Pair	145.00
Paperweight, Amber	90.00
Perfume Bottle, Girl Holding Branch, Silver Snowflakes, Blue	165.00
Pin Tray, Girl Holding Flower Amid Foliage, 4 1/2 X 2 In.	95.00
Pitcher, Boy, Riding Crop, Horn Around Chest, Cranberry, 7 In.	195.00
Pitcher, Boys Under Spout, Crystal Handle, Cranberry, 9 In.	415.00
Pitcher, Girl Chasing Butterfly, Crimped, Crystal, 9 1/2 In.	120.00
Pitcher, Girl Holding Balloon, Lime Green, 7 1/2 In.	195.00
Pitcher, Girl With Flower, Gold Trim, 9 In.	295.00
Pitcher, Girl, Gold Dress, Foliage, Sapphire Blue, 10 3/4 In.	275.00
Pitcher, Water, Girl Dancer, Urn Shape, Cobalt Blue, 7 In.	165.00
Plate, Girl In Swing, Black, 8 In.	38.00

Rose Bowl, Gold Trim On Collared Base, Cranberry, 2 X 2 In. 125.00
Shot Glass, Blue, 2 1/2 In. 85.00
Stein, Pewter Lid, Aqua Blue, 13 In. 295.00
Sugar Shaker, Cranberry 125.00
Tile, Blue, 5 In. 95.00
Toothpick, Girl Standing In Foliage, Sapphire Blue 195.00
Toothpick, Girl, Cranberry, 2 1/4 In. 85.00
Tray, Dresser, Cranberry, 6 X 9 In. 275.00
Tumble–Up, Victorian Lady, Emerald Green, 9 In. 125.00
Tumbler, Boy & Girl, Facing, Cranberry, 2 1/2 In., Pair 105.00
Tumbler, Boy & Girl, Facing, Gold Trim, Sapphire Blue 110.00
Tumbler, Boy, Cranberry, 3 In. 50.00
Tumbler, Green, Gilded Rim, 3 1/2 In. 100.00
Vase, Boy & Girl, Facing, Black Amethyst, 10 3/4 In., Pair 450.00
Vase, Boy & Girl, Facing, Cranberry, Cylinder, 6 1/4 In., Pair 225.00
Vase, Boy & Girl, Facing, Scalloped, Amber, 10 In., Pair 475.00
Vase, Boy Holding Butterfly Net, Shells, Green, 8 1/2 In. 125.00
Vase, Boy In Garden, Blue, 4 In. 85.00
Vase, Boy Running, Girl Facing, Lime Green, 6 In., Pair 225.00
Vase, Boy With Butterfly Net, Facing, Blue, 4 1/8 In., Pair 145.00
Vase, Boy, Sapphire Blue, 10 In. 85.00
Vase, Boy, Scalloped Top, Gold Trim, Pedestal, 11 1/4 In. 325.00
Vase, Boy, With Cane, Cranberry, 8 1/4 X 3 7/8 In. 195.00
Vase, Boy, With Hat & Oars, Cobalt Blue, 7 1/2 In. 95.00
Vase, Children Picking Apples, Cranberry, 17 In., Pair 1050.00
Vase, Cobalt, Brass Ormolu, 8 In., Pair 775.00
Vase, Girl & Flowers, Girl & Bird, Cranberry, 15 1/2 In., Pair 500.00
Vase, Girl, Carrying Umbrella, Scalloped Rim, Blue, 10 In. 90.00
Vase, Girl, Clear Pedestal Foot, Cranberry, 4 1/4 In. 105.00
Vase, Girl, Cranberry, 6 1/2 In. 98.00
Vase, Girl, On Tiptoes, Green, Cylinder, 6 X 1 3/4 In. 110.00
Vase, Girl, Sitting On Shore, Snail Handles, Green, 11 5/8 In. 265.00
Vase, Girl, With Butterfly Net, White Lining, Pink, 7 3/4 In. 145.00
Vase, Girl, With Hat, Umbrella & Basket, Black Amethyst, 17 In. 450.00
Vase, Girl, With Watering Can, Cranberry, 2 1/8 In. 95.00
Vase, Girls, Facing, Cobalt Blue, Pedestal, 7 1/2 In., Pair 225.00
Vase, Rooster, Amethyst, 7 In. 100.00

MASONIC, see Fraternal

Massier pottery is iridescent French art pottery made by Clement Massier in Golfe–Juan, France, in the late nineteenth and early twentieth centuries. It has an iridescent metallic luster glaze that resembles the Weller Sicard pottery glaze. Most pieces are marked "J. Massier."

MASSIER, Vase, Marsh Scene, Gold Ground, Greens, 8 In. 250.00

Large wooden matches were used in the nineteenth and twentieth centuries for a variety of purposes. The kitchen stove and the fireplace or furnace had to be lit regularly. One type of match holder was made to hang on the wall, another was designed to be kept on a tabletop. Of special interest today are match holders that have advertisements as part of the design.

MATCH HOLDER, American Steel Fence, Wall 75.00
Bacchus Head, Grapes & Leaves On Back Plate, Wall, Iron 85.00
Black Boy's Head, High Collar, Table Model, Milk Glass 25.00
Boot, Cast Iron 45.00
Carved Wood, Shell & Starflower, Black Paint, 2 X 4 1/2 In. 300.00
Cat In Well, Cast Iron 110.00
Ceresota, Prize Bread Flour Of World, Litho Tin, 4 1/4 In. 110.00
Checker's Cough Drops, Tin, Wall 25.00
Columbia Flour, Wall 825.00
Cowboy Boots, Bisque 20.00
Davenport Cigars, Celluloid On Tin, Wall, 1920s 15.00
DeLaval Cream Separator, Wall .... 115.00 To 247.00

Dockash Stove, Factory, Tin, Wall 33.00
Dog, Sitting Between 2 Wooden Pails, Metal, 6 X 4 In. 55.00
Doghouse, Amber Glass 50.00
Donkey, Basket Each Side For Matches, Striker, Wooden, 5 In. 36.00
Dreyer Bakery, St.Louis, Tin, Wall 35.00
Dutch Boy, Tin Litho, Wall, 6 X 3 In. 80.00
Elephant's Head, Glass 12.50
Elk Head, Cast Iron, Primitive, With Striker 60.00
Embossed Saucer, Sticker, Cast Iron, 3 1/2 In. 35.00
Fairy Soap, Metal, Wall 110.00
Fish, Amber Glass 12.00
Fletcher Triple Tested, Plastic 20.00
Game Bird, Rabbit, 2 Pockets, Cast Iron, Wall, 8 1/2 In. 130.00
Garland Stoves, Die Cut 175.00
Graniteware, 5 X 3 In. 7.00
Indian Head, Apple Green Glass 40.00
Indian Head, Light Blue 50.00
Judson Whiskey, Tin, Wall 55.00
Kool, Tin, Wall 15.00
Laxets, Tin, Wall 110.00
Leprechaun, Figural, Milk Glass 40.00
Lincoln, Ax, Tree & Goat, Marked Kindling Wood, Wall, 5 1/4 In. 75.00
Man, Figural, Ceramic 68.00
Michigan Stoves, Cast Iron, Wall 85.00
Milk Glass, Pillar & Panel 22.00
Miss Liberty's Head, Wall, 4 1/2 In. 80.00
Moonshine Still, Handmade Wood, Glass & Copper, 10 X 5 In. 22.00
Open Pocket Top, Closing Slant Top Lid, 2–Tier, Hanging 65.00
Pabst Chemical Co., Celluloid On Tin, Brown, Calendar, Wall 15.00
Rockford Watches, Tin 350.00
Rotating Barrel, Painted Green, Strike Surface, Wall 35.00
Self–Closing Lid, Cast Iron, Rectangular, Wall 40.00
Sharples Cream Separator, Litho Tin, Wall .... 135.00 To 200.00
Shoe, Blue Glass 30.00
Shoe, Brass 15.00
Silver, Repousse Cherubs, Foliate, W. Comyns & Sons, 2 1/2 In. 65.00
Spring Wheat Flour 15.00
Squirrel, Bisque, Double, Wall 30.00
Sterling Silver, Chased Foliage, Monogram, 2 3/4 In. 65.00
Tinware, Allumettes, Made In France, 4 3/4 X 2 1/2 In. 8.00
Traymore Tailors, Celluloid On Tin, Satisfaction, Wall, 1900s 20.00
Turtle, Cast Iron 45.00
Universal Stoves & Ranges, Best On Earth, Wall 52.00
Wall, Zephyr Flour 52.00

Early matches were made with phosphorus and could ignite unexpectedly. Match safes were designed to be carried in the pocket. The matches were safely stored in the tightly closed container. Examples were made in sterling silver, plated silver, or other metals. The English call these "vesta boxes."

MATCH SAFE, Alligator, Monon Route 275.00
American Shield Shape, Marked America, 1492–1892, 3 15/16 In. 140.00
Black Boy, Bisque 125.00
Black Cats, Antique Auto, Celluloid Top, 2 Bottom Strikers, 1911 .... 80.00
Bunch of Cigars, Silver Plate 85.00
Doctor's Bag, Sterling Silver 275.00
Dog With Whistle, Silver Plate 175.00
Figural, Pig, Opens At Head, Silver Plate, 1 1/2 In. 75.00
Figural, Punch, Opens At Base, Silver Plate, 2 3/8 In. 135.00
Frog, Encircling Brass Bucket, C.1870, 2 X 2 1/2 In. 150.00
Gladstone Face, Brass 75.00
Goldstone, Button On Side, Hinged Lid, Filigree Brass 75.00
Golfer, Sterling Silver 275.00
Horse, Enamel, Silver Plate 90.00

Hunter Baltimore Rye, Celluloid	65.00
Pyramidal, Counter, Ironstone, Strike Surface On Sides	25.00
Raised Head of Woman, Sterling Silver, Art Nouveau, 2 X 2 In.	75.00
Reads Upside Down & Reverse, Wedding Day, 6 Weeks After, Pocket	85.00
Repousse Floral, Sterling Silver, Marked	58.00
Table, Asphaltum Striker, Blue Tin, 2–Tier, 2 1/2 X 3 1/2 In.	85.00
Tadcaster–Heidelbrau, Celluloid, Multicolor, Early 1900s	30.00
Teddy Bear, Skating, Metal, 1905	65.00
Traveler's Insurance, Silver Plate	28.00
Walnut, Opens At Top, Striker Back, Silver Plate, 1 1/4 In.	75.00
Yellow Stencil Scrolls On Scalloped Back, Blue Japanned Tin	65.00

Matsu–no–ke was a type of applied decoration for glass patented by Frederick Carder in 1922. There is clear evidence that pieces were made before that date at the Steuben glassworks. Stevens & Williams of England also made an applied decoration by the same name.

MATSU–NO–KE, Basket, Teal, Thorny Handles, Crimped Trefoil Top	735.00
Bowl, Applied Flowers, Button Flowers, Pink Spatter, 5 X 6 In.	495.00
Bowl, Ruffled, Yellow Overlay, Flowers, Marked, 2 3/4 X 4 In.	425.00
Candleholder, 9 1/2 In.	295.00
Pitcher, Clear Thorn Feet, Thorny Handle, Crystal, 6 3/4 In.	550.00

Matt Morgan, an English artist, was making pottery in Cincinnati, Ohio, by 1883. His pieces were decorated to resemble Moorish wares. Incised designs and colors were applied to raised panels on the pottery. Shiny or matte glazes were used. The company lasted only a few years.

MATT MORGAN, Jug, Raised Sheaf of Wheat, Brown & Gold, 7 In.	475.00
Jug, Whiskey, Molded Cornstalks, Chain, Tag, C.1883, 7 In.	425.00
Vase, Spiders 1 Side, Branches Other, Red–Brown, M. Daly, 8 In.	375.00

McCoy pottery is made in Roseville, Ohio. The J. W. McCoy Pottery was founded in 1899. It became the Brush McCoy Pottery Company in 1911. The name changed to the Brush Pottery in 1925. The word "Brush" was usually included in the mark on their pieces. The Nelson McCoy Sanitary and Stoneware Company, a different firm, was founded in Roseville, Ohio, in 1910. The firm made art pottery after 1926. In 1933 it became the Nelson McCoy Pottery. Pieces marked "McCoy" were made by the Nelson McCoy Company.

MCCOY, Bank, Williamsburg Savings, Penholder, Gray, 7 1/4 In.	15.00
Basket, Green Leaves, Red Berries Body, Branch Handle, 9 In.	25.00
Basket, Hanging, Loy–Nel–Art, Brown, Green, 3–Toed	16.00
Bean Pot, Red	9.00
Bowl, Butterfly, Turquoise, 3 1/2 X 3 In.	4.00
Bowl, Dog Food, To Man's Best Friend–His Dog, Turquoise	15.00
Bowl, Tonecraft, Pedestal, Square	5.00
Candlestick, Black, Yellow Green, Cinnamon, 3 X 3 1/2 In., Pair	16.00
Coffeepot, Cowboy	45.00
Console Set, Matte Brown, Green, 3 Piece	26.00
Cookie Jar, Apple	35.00
Cookie Jar, Balloon	20.00
Cookie Jar, Bananas	60.00 To 85.00
Cookie Jar, Bank	95.00
Cookie Jar, Barn, Red	65.00
Cookie Jar, Barrel, Brown	9.00
Cookie Jar, Bean Pot, Brown	18.00
Cookie Jar, Bear, Brown, Red Bow	55.00
Cookie Jar, Bobby Baker	10.00 To 95.00
Cookie Jar, Caboose	25.00 To 55.00
Cookie Jar, Chef	45.00
Cookie Jar, Chipmunk	45.00 To 55.00
Cookie Jar, Circus Horse	65.00

Cookie Jar, Clown In Barrel, 10 In. 45.00
Cookie Jar, Clown, Bust .... 25.00 To 30.00
Cookie Jar, Clyde The Dog 25.00
Cookie Jar, Coffee Grinder .... 20.00 To 27.00
Cookie Jar, Coffee Mug .... 20.00 To 23.00
Cookie Jar, Colonial Fireplace .... 40.00 To 42.00
Cookie Jar, Cookie Boy, Blue 67.00
Cookie Jar, Cookie Cabin .... 28.00 To 35.00
Cookie Jar, Cookie Jug .... 12.00 To 15.00
Cookie Jar, Cookie Pot 20.00
Cookie Jar, Cookie Wagon 45.00
Cookie Jar, Cookstove, Black .... 20.00 To 25.00
Cookie Jar, Cookstove, White .... 20.00 To 25.00
Cookie Jar, Corn .... 75.00 To 85.00
Cookie Jar, Country Stove, Potbelly .... 10.00 To 20.00
Cookie Jar, Covered Wagon .... 25.00 To 45.00
Cookie Jar, Davy Crockett 135.00
Cookie Jar, Dutch Boy 46.00
Cookie Jar, Dutch Treat Barn .... 25.00 To 28.00
Cookie Jar, Elephant 45.00
Cookie Jar, Engine, Black .... 40.00 To 46.00
Cookie Jar, Fortune Cookies 18.00
Cookie Jar, Frontier Family .... 30.00 To 35.00
Cookie Jar, Fruit In Basket .... 27.00 To 65.00
Cookie Jar, Gingerbread Boy 22.00
Cookie Jar, Globe .... 45.00 To 100.00
Cookie Jar, Goodie Goose 25.00
Cookie Jar, Granny .... 36.00 To 40.00
Cookie Jar, Hamm's Bear 60.00
Cookie Jar, Have A Happy Day, Black Letters 20.00
Cookie Jar, House 65.00
Cookie Jar, Indian .... 110.00 To 225.00
Cookie Jar, Jug 13.00
Cookie Jar, Kangaroo, Blue .... 125.00 To 225.00
Cookie Jar, Keebler Elf 25.00
Cookie Jar, Kettle, Large 20.00
Cookie Jar, Kookie Kettle, Black .... 10.00 To 18.00
Cookie Jar, Lamb 45.00
Cookie Jar, Lemon 90.00
Cookie Jar, Lollipops .... 20.00 To 30.00
Cookie Jar, Mac Dog .... 36.00 To 55.00
Cookie Jar, Mammy .... 75.00 To 145.00
Cookie Jar, Mammy, With Cauliflower .... 425.00 To 495.00
Cookie Jar, Milk Can, White, Gold Angel Decal 16.00
Cookie Jar, Monkey, On Stump 22.00
Cookie Jar, Mr. & Mrs. Owl .... 35.00 To 70.00
Cookie Jar, Nabisco, Round 25.00
Cookie Jar, Pelican .... 40.00 To 45.00
Cookie Jar, Penguins, Kissing 16.00
Cookie Jar, Picnic Basket 35.00
Cookie Jar, Pig 25.00
Cookie Jar, Pineapple .... 25.00 To 35.00
Cookie Jar, Puppy, Holding Sign .... 38.00 To 65.00
Cookie Jar, Rabbit, White 14.00
Cookie Jar, Rocking Chair, Dalmatians .... 100.00 To 180.00
Cookie Jar, Rocking Horse 39.50
Cookie Jar, Sad Clown .... 29.00 To 35.00
Cookie Jar, Snow Bear 40.00
Cookie Jar, Spaceship, Friendship 7 .... 175.00
Cookie Jar, Squirrel On Log 10.00
Cookie Jar, Stagecoach 250.00
Cookie Jar, Strawberry .... 15.00 To 25.00
Cookie Jar, Teakettle .... 20.00 To 35.00
Cookie Jar, Teapot, White 10.00

Cookie Jar, Timmy Tortoise .... 17.00 To 18.00
Cookie Jar, Tugboat 20.00
Cookie Jar, W.C. Fields .... 75.00 To 95.00
Cookie Jar, Windmill 38.00
Cookie Jar, Wishing Well .... 18.00 To 20.00
Cookie Jar, Woodsy Owl .... 60.00 To 75.00
Cookie Jar, Wren House .... 45.00 To 82.00
Cornucopia, Brown, Green Base, Sanitary Stoneware, 6 1/4 In. 11.00
Creamer, Daisy 10.00
Decanter, Apollo Missile 100.00
Decanter, Pierce Arrow 40.00
Dish, Harmony, Green, White, Footed, 8 1/2 X 4 X 6 In. 6.50
Fern Box, Butterfly, Dull Brown, Green, 8 3/4 X 4 1/2 X 3 1/4 In. 8.50
Flowerpot, Basket Weave, Attached Saucer, Pink, 4 1/4 In. 4.00
Flowerpot, Greek Key, Attached Saucer, Green, 5 3/4 In. 5.00
Flowerpot, Leaves & Dots, Green, 3 3/4 X 2 3/4 In. 3.50
Jardiniere, Onyx Glaze, Browns, Tab Shoulder Handles, 8 1/2 In. 25.00
Jardiniere, Roses, Pink, 6 3/4 X 7 1/2 In. 12.00
Jardiniere, Tufted, Glossy Green, Relief With Leaves, 9 1/2 X 8 In. 30.00
Lamp, Cowboy Boots .... 20.00 To 25.00
Lamp, Gazelle In Relief, Art Deco 55.00
Mug, Barrel Shape, Glossy Green, 4 3/4 In. 5.00
Mug, Buccaneer, Brown 15.00
Mug, Green, Shield Mark 18.00
Mug, Pirate, Green 6.50
Mug, Smiley Face, White, Red Face 2.00
Pepper Shaker, Green 12.00
Pitcher, Bird, Cherries, Turquoise, 5 In. 10.00
Pitcher, Chick, Green 15.00
Pitcher, Nassau County Republican Committe, 6 3/4 In. 25.00
Pitcher, Water Lilies 25.00
Pitcher, Windmill, Blue Delft Type, White, Scrolled Handle, 6 X 5 In. 6.50
Planter, Banjo Player On Boat 45.00
Planter, Birds, White, Red Beaks, Green Head 6.50
Planter, Blossom Time, Ivory 8.50
Planter, Bowl, Glossy Green, End Handles, Oval, 10 1/4 In. 8.50
Planter, Bulb Bowl, Green, 8 X 2 3/4 In. 4.00
Planter, Carriage With Umbrella 45.00
Planter, Cart 15.00
Planter, Cowboy Boots 15.00
Planter, Double Leaves, White 3.00
Planter, Duck, Umbrella, High Gloss Yellow, Cream 12.00
Planter, Fish, Blue, Open Mouth, 3 1/4 In. 18.00
Planter, Frog .... 11.00 To 16.00
Planter, Gray, Pink Sculptured Bird, Square, 6 1/2 In. 25.00
Planter, Green Birds 6.00
Planter, Green Stump 4.00
Planter, Mammy 30.00
Planter, Oriental, Black, Hand Painted Chinese Design, 5 1/2 In. 6.00
Planter, Pelican, Cream 5.00
Planter, Pinecone Feet 10.00
Planter, Quail, Marked 25.00
Planter, Scotty Dog, White 17.00
Planter, Shell Dish, White, Footed, Loop Handle End, 8 X 4 X 6 In. 11.00
Planter, Spinning Wheel 15.00
Planter, Under The Spreading Chestnut Tree, White Horse 30.00
Planter, Wishing Well .... 12.00 To 15.00
Platter, Turkey, Brown, 11 X 16 In. .... 28.00 To 32.00
Salt & Pepper, Mango & Cucumber 25.00
Sugar & Creamer, Elsie & Elmer 39.00
Sugar, Pinecone 10.00
Tea Set, Daisy, 3 Piece 35.00
Tea Set, Grecian, 3 Piece 45.00
Tea Set, Ivy, 3 Piece 38.00

Tea Set, Pinecone, 3 Piece	35.00
Tea Set, Speckled Pink, 3 Piece	28.00
Teapot, Daisy	24.00
Teapot, Grecian	30.00
Teapot, Turtle	23.00
Tile, Mammy, Mosaic	395.00
Vase, Arcature, Bird, Gray, Maroon, Square, 6 1/2 In.	12.00
Vase, Blue, Bulbous, 8 In.	25.00
Vase, Double Tulip, Pink, Yellow, 8 In.	14.00
Vase, Flying Geese, 1935	20.00
Vase, Fruit Handles, Yellow, 6 1/2 In.	12.00
Vase, Green, Side Handles, Relief Design Base, Fluted, 8 1/4 In.	6.50
Vase, Lily, Cream, 8 1/2 In.	13.00
Vase, Loy–Nel–Art, 12 1/2 In.	190.00
Vase, Loy–Nel–Art, Berries, Green, Bulbous Base, 8 In.	10.00
Vase, Poppy, Pink, Green, 8 1/2 X 7 X 3 1/2 In.	14.00
Vase, Sailboat, Turquoise, Square Foot, Wave Relief, 9 1/4 In.	12.00
Vase, Wild Rose, Yellow Flower, Pink, Footed, 6 X 5 1/2 X 6 1/2 In.	6.00
Wall Pocket, Apple	20.00
Wall Pocket, Flowers	12.00
Wall Pocket, Owl	60.00
Wall Pocket, Pear	12.00
Water Sprinkler, Turtle, Green, 9 1/2 In.	20.00
Window Box, Icicles Over Turquoise, 10 1/4 X 5 X 3 In.	7.00

PRESCUT

The McKee name has been associated with various glass enterprises in the United States since 1836, including J. & F. McKee (1850), Bryce, McKee & Co. (1850 to 1854), McKee and Brothers (1865), and National Glass Co. (1899). In 1903, the McKee Glass Company was formed in Jeanette, Pennsylvania. It became McKee Division of the Thatcher Glass Co. in 1951 and was bought out by the Jeanette Corporation in 1961. Pressed glass, kitchenwares, and tablewares were produced.

MCKEE, see also Custard Glass

MCKEE, Baker, Custard, Oval, 7 In.	10.00
Bowl, Seville Yellow, 4 1/4 In.	6.00
Canister, Jadite, Cover, 48 Oz.	20.00
Clock, Mantel, Tambour, Green, 14 X 6 1/2 In.	375.00
Cordial, Majestic	16.50
Cordial, Rock Crystal, Footed	45.00
Creamer, Jade	9.00
Cruet, Prescut, Crystal	18.00
Cruet, Rock Crystal, Stopper	25.00
Cup, Tom & Jerry, White, Red Scroll	2.00
Eggcup, Custard, Footed	10.00
Eggcup, Green & White	9.00
Eggcup, Jade	8.00
Eggcup, Seville Yellow	10.00
Figure, Horse, Milk Glass	75.00
Flour Shaker, Red Sailboat, 1930s	8.00
Flour Shaker, Roman Arch, White	6.00
Goblet, Rock Crystal, Footed, Stem	8.00
Jar, Cover, Refrigerator, Jade, Round, 10 Oz.	18.00
Jar, Cover, Refrigerator, Jade, Round, 24 Oz.	18.00
Lamp, Art Deco, Dance De Lumiere, Frosted Nudes, Pink	250.00 To 400.00
Lamp, Bambi, Open Book	22.00
Lamp, No.2, Sapphire Blue	150.00
Laurel, Candleholder, Green, Pair	18.00
Measuring Cup, 2 Spout, Jade	100.00
Measuring Cup, Custard, 4 Cup	45.00
Measuring Cup, Jade, 4 Cup	25.00
Measuring Cup, Seville Yellow, 4 Cup	55.00
Mixing Bowl, Spout, 7 In.	10.00
Mug, Tom & Jerry, Glass	6.00

Pitcher, Aztec, 5 1/2 In. 15.00
Pitcher, Jade, 16 Oz. 17.00
Pitcher, Jade, 32 Oz. 35.00
Plate, Dinner, Rock Crystal, Scalloped 30.00
Plate, Doltec, 6 In. 2.50
Plate, Rock Crystal, 7 1/2 In. 5.00
Plate, Rock Crystal, Footed, 12 3/4 In. 18.00
Punch Set, Aztec, 26 Piece 165.00
Punch Set, Christmas Scene, Custard 48.00
Punch Set, Nortec, Pedestaled Stand, 9 Piece 95.00
Shaker, Custard, Square 15.00
Sherbet, Rock Crystal, Stemmed 6.00
Shot Glass, Bottoms Up, Custard Glass 125.00
Shot Glass, Rock Crystal, Red 10.00
Sugar Shaker, Seville Yellow, Square 15.00
Sugar, Cover, Pink 30.00
Sugar, White, Open 15.00
Tumble–Up, Butterscotch 50.00
Tumble–Up, With Coaster, Jadite 75.00
Tumbler, Custard, Flat, 4 In. 20.00
Urn, Horse 75.00
Vase, Nudes, Light Green, Triangular, 8 1/2 In. 85.00
Vase, Rock Crystal, 11 In. 35.00
Wine, Liberty, Ruby Stained, Niagara Falls, 1909 .... 44.50
Wine, Rock Crystal, 4 3/4 In. ....8.00 To 11.00

MECHANICAL BANK, see Bank, Mechanical

All types of equipment used by doctors or hospitals are included in
this section. Medical office furniture, operating tools, microscopes,
thermometers, and other paraphernalia used by doctors are included.
Medicine bottles are listed under Bottle. There are related
collectibles listed under Dental.

MEDICAL, Athletic Supporter, Boston 5.00
Bandage, Gauze, Bauer & Black 3.50
Belt, Electric, Dr. McLaughlin's 225.00
Bleeder, Brass, Blown Bleeder Cup, 2 Lancets & Knife Blade 60.00
Bleeding Vessel, Priest's, Kris To Maiden's Throat, Silver, C.1840 .... 295.00
Book, Dr. Gunn's Family Physician, Saalfield, 1000 Pages, 1901 .... 12.50
Bottle Sterilizer, Baby's 22.00
Bottle, Bromo Seltzer, Cobalt Blue, 6 In. 5.00
Bottle, Hospital, Pouring Spout, Label 27.00
Box, Pharmaceutical, 17 Brass Weights, Oak, 4 X 6 1/2 In. 40.00
Box, Surgeon's, Civil War, Campaign Style, Original Tools, C.1860 .... 1040.00
Broadside, Dr. Skinner's Magic Bitters, Portrait, 10 X 6 In. 45.00
Cabinet, Dr. Claris Veterinary, Oak, Glass Door, Carved Crest, 1900 ...... 160.00
Carrier, Human's Specimen, Says Vorsicht, Caution, Wooden, Cork Top 35.00
Chest, Apothecary, 20 Drawers, Brass Pulls, Poplar, 34 1/2 In. 600.00
Chest, Apothecary, 30 Drawers, Cherry & Poplar, 17 3/4 X 17 In. 400.00
Chest, Apothecary, 60 Drawers, Pressed Carving, Walnut 700.00
Chest, Druggist's, Brass Trim, Walnut 1050.00
Cupboard, Apothecary, 12 Drawers, Walnut & Poplar, 26 X 47 1/2 In. 350.00
Diploma, Louisville Medical Institute, Sheepskin, 1838, 22 X 29 In. 125.00
Ether Pump, Electric, Portable, Nickel Plated Brass, Wood, 1915 .... 250.00
Eyecup, Elder Flower Lotion, Cobalt Blue 25.00
Eyecup, Milk Glass 15.00
Eyecup, Orange Slag–Like Glass 15.00
Eyecup, Wyeth, Cobalt Blue 8.00
Feeder, Duck Shape 12.00
Fleam, 2 Blades, Folding, Brass Case, Sheffield 65.00
Fleam, 2 Steel Blades, Folding, Brass Case, Borwick 45.00
Fleam, Nickel Plate, 3 Blades 65.00
Foldout, Male & Female Anatomy, 1930s 15.00
Funnel, Apothecary, Clear Glass 85.00
Gynecological Instruments, Tiemann & Co., Leather Case 995.00

Hearing Aid, Rhein, London, Engraved Silver Plate, 1800s 250.00
Hearing Horn, Shephard & Dudley, Coiled 95.00
Holder, Thermometer, Vest Pocket, Abalone, Gold Filled 49.00
Hot Water Bottle, Cello–Brand, Copper, 1912 .... 27.00
Hot Water Bottle, Child's, Piggy 10.00
Hot Water Bottle, Metal 15.00
Hot Water Bottle, Teddy Bear In Cub Scout Uniform, Red Rubber 65.00
Hot Water Bottle, This Little Piggy Went To Market 45.00
Ice Bag, St. Regis, Wartime Materials Declaration, Box 23.50
Inhaler, Hygienic, Boots 120.00
Invalid Feeder, Child's, Red Cross 18.00
Jar, Nickel Plated, Hinged, Engraved Antiseptic, 8 In. 29.00
Kit, Surgical, Scalpels, Saws, Hemostat, Pocket, 5 Piece 45.00
Measure, Double, Pharmacist's, Hourglass Shape, Turned, Maple 53.00
Measure, This Cup Holds A Heaping Dessert Spoonful, Cobalt Blue 20.00
Medicine Chest, Doctor's, Victorian, Walnut, Mirrors, Brass, Gallery 395.00
Medicine Cup, Ceramic, Greensboro, N.C. Drugstore 15.00
Mold, Suppository, 12 Cavity, Nickel Plate 35.00
Mortar & Pestle, Cast Iron, 5 1/2 In. 35.00
Ophthalmoscope, May, 1930s 45.00
Pestle, Ceramic, Germany, Large 15.00
Pill Machine, 18 Roller Slots, Sliding Wood Handle 175.00
Print, Heart & Great Arteries, 4 Part, Matted, 1916, 8 3/4 X 5 In. 17.50
Ring Remover & Measuring Rod, Mortician's, Brass, Extends 22 In. 95.00
Saw, Bow, Surgeon's, Ebony Handle, 18th Century, 10 X 3 In. 195.00
Saw, Stainless Steel, Nickel Plated Handle, Feick, Star Brand 45.00
Scale, Apothecary, Troemer Co., 1920s 170.00
Scale, Druggist's, Brass Pans 75.00
Scalpel, Doctor's, Ivory, 1800s 30.00
Shock Pulsator, Medeotronics, No.50, Chiropractic, Electric 140.00
Sign, Apothecary, Mortar & Pestle Form, Painted Wood, 22 1/2 In. 225.00
Sign, Doctor Is Out, Adjustable Metal Hands, Cardboard, 5 X 7 In. 10.00
Spoon, Folding, Teaspoon One End, Tablespoon Other, Case, Sterling 95.00
Spoon, Medicine, Silver Plate, Cat, Kitten, Birds, R & B 45.00
Sterilizer, Alcohol, Case, 2 1/2 X 1 3/4 In 25.00
Syringe, Ear & Ulcer, Miller 2.25
Syringe, Veterinary, B.D.Champion 12.00
Teaspoon, Hooded, Marked A Tablespoon, Leather Case, Sterling 150.00
Thermometer, Gold Filled Trim, Abalone Case 75.00
Thermometer, Immisch, Gold 450.00
Tool, Apothecary, 6 In. Red Glass, Large Blob 1 End 15.00
Unit, 30 Steel Pins, Blisters, For Infection, Spring Loaded, 1870s 195.00
Vial, Bishop's Varalettes, Gout, Rheumatism, Gravel, Glass, 3 3/8 In. 5.00
Vibrator, Tired Feet, Machine 250.00
Wheelchair, Oak, Cane 95.00
MEDICINE, Spoon, Duffy's Malt Whiskey 38.00

Meerschaum pipes and other pieces of carved meerschaum, a soft mineral, date from the nineteenth century to the present.

MEERSCHAUM, Cheroot Holder, Carved Ivory Dog, Case 55.00
Cigar & Cigarette Holder, Swirling Bands, Beading, Flowers 48.00
Cigar Holder, Amber Stem, Clay Body, Case 42.00
Cigar Holder, Glass Bead Grape & Clusters, Carved Leaves 50.00
Pipe, Bacchus Head, Carved Wooden Case 245.00
Pipe, Carved Rosettes, Amber Stem, 4 1/4 In. 65.00
Pipe, Chieftan, Turban, Full Beard, Yellow Stem, 6 In. 28.00
Pipe, Female Hand Holds Bowl, English, Case, Amber Stem, 3 In. 85.00
Pipe, Gibson Girl, Amber Stem, Case, 4 1/2in. 70.00
Pipe, Hand Holding Bowl, Case 80.00
Pipe, Longhorn Mountain Goat, Case, 6 In. 48.00
Pipe, Man, Turban, Beard, Amber Stem 25.00
Pipe, Pasha's Head Form, Germany, C.1870 .... 45.00
Pipe, Sultan's Head, Amber Stem 70.00
Pipe, Turk's Head, Amber Stem, 5 1/2 In. 65.00

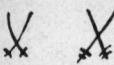

Meissen is a town in Germany where porcelain has been made since 1710. Any china made in the town can be called Meissen, although the famous Meissen factory made the finest porcelains of the area. The crossed swords mark of the great Meissen factory has been copied by many other firms in Germany and other parts of the world.

MEISSEN, Bone Dish, Wild Flower 65.00
  Bowl, 4 Cherubs, Reticulated, Blue Crossed Lines, 12 3/4 In. 300.00
  Bowl, 4 Floral Medallions, Floral Center, Gold Laced, 8 In. 65.00
  Bowl, Allover Raised Gold Relief, 10 1/2 In. 145.00
  Bowl, Pierced, Loop Handles, 8 Cherubs On Stem, Marked, 19 1/4 In. 4675.00
  Box, 3 Courting Couples, Country, Flowers On Cover, 19th Century 98.00
  Box, Applied Floral & Allover Leaf, Cover, C.1750, Round, 3 In. 375.00
  Box, Country Lovers, Fishscale Lattice, Gold Flowers, 1800s 95.00
  Box, Cover, Floral, Crossed Swords, Miniature 125.00
  Box, Patch, Woman's Face, Red Lips, Domino Mask, Cover, 1 7/16 In. 1320.00
  Box, Pill, Blue Enameled Flowers, Gold Highlights, Crossed Swords 120.00
  Candelabra, 3–Light, Flowers, Putti, Scrolled Base, 8 1/2 In., Pair 3190.00
  Candelabra, 4–Light, Man, Holding Child, Woman, Same, 17 1/4 In., Pair 1925.00
  Candelabra, 6–Light, Fluted Column, Bacchic Figures, 30 In. 700.00
  Candelabra, Girl & Boy Grape Pickers, C.1740, 19 In., Pair 2400.00
  Candy Dish, Wild Flower, Rococo Style, Divided 400.00
  Clock, Mantel, Figural, Putto, Lady, Standing, Poodle, 14 3/4 In. 3575.00
  Clock, Stand, 4 Children, Floral Garland, 20 In. ....*Illus* 3300.00
  Coffee Set, Pink Onion·Pattern, Crossed Swords, 21 Piece 975.00
  Coffeepot, 2 Arrows, Kalk 100.00
  Compote, Fruit, Coat of Arms, Pierced, Gold Interior, 10 X 7 X 8 In. 4500.00
  Compote, Relief Floral, Beaded Center, Floral Rim, Marked, 12 In. 350.00
  Cornucopia, Green Ivy Pattern, 4 1/2 In. 115.00
  Cup & Saucer, Floral, Gold, 1774–1814, Crossed Swords, Blue Star 250.00
  Cup & Saucer, Polychrome Roses, Marked 95.00
  Cup & Saucer, Swan Neck Handle, White, Gold Trim 30.00
  Dinner Set, Rose Pattern, Service For 12 .... 4000.00
  Dish, Sweetmeat, Blanc De Chine Type, Molded Flowers 35.00
  Dish, Sweetmeat, Flower Form, Stem Forms Handle, 7 1/2 In., Pair 825.00
  Figurine, Europa & The Bull, Marked, C.1848, 9 X 7 In. 450.00
  Figurine, Goat, Standing With Front Paws On Broken Bowl, 5 1/2 In. 275.00
  Figurine, Harlequins, Grotesquely Posed, 19th Century, 9 In. 1250.00
  Figurine, Oehme Panther, White, 1920 .... 325.00
  Figurine, Seated Girl, Holding Basket of Flowers 425.00
  Figurine, Stork, Crossed Swords, 8 1/2 In. ....*Illus* 605.00

Meissen, Clock, Stand, 4 Children, Floral Garland, 20 In.

Meissen, Figurine, Stork, Crossed Swords, 8 1/2 In.

Meissen, Vase, Pate–Sur–Pate, Gilt Borders, Handles, 12 1/2 In.

Meissen, Group, 2 Women, Children,   Meissen, Group, Woman, Boy, Eagle,
Net, Sea Life, 13 In.   Telescope, 11 In.

Figurine, Woman In Long Yellow Coat, 10 In.	300.00
Figurine, Woman Vendor, Holding Oyster Shell, Tray, 6 1/4 In.	495.00
Figurine, Young Dandy, Colorful Dress, Seated, Rockwork, Dog, 7 In.	600.00
Group, 2 Cherubs, Globe, Book, Telescope, Underglaze Mark, 6 In.	525.00
Group, 2 Women, Children, Net, Sea Life, 13 In. ....*Illus*	850.00
Group, Cherub Musical Quartet, 4 3/8 In.	198.00
Group, Hunt, Seated Figure of Diane, Dogs, Weapons, Marked, 15 In.	4950.00
Group, The Day's Catch, 18th Century, 12 3/4 In.	1430.00
Group, Winged Chariot, 4 Putti, Interlacing Circles, Marked, 13 In.	4950.00
Group, Woman, Boy, Eagle, Telescope, 11 In. ....*Illus*	1265.00
Inkwell, Cover, Orange Florals, Lavender Ground, Gold Trim, Marked	135.00
Jar, Cover, Grape Form, Stem Forms Handle, Marked, 6 In., Pair	1210.00
Lamp, Polychrome Genre Reserves, Round Font, Marked, 26 1/2 In.	200.00
Mug, Washington & Franklin Medallion, Porcelain	495.00
Pipe, Figural, Nubian Head, Bronze Cap, Porcelain, 3 In.	325.00
Plate, Allover Painted Flowers, Gilt Trim, Marked, 9 5/8 In., 12 Pc.	1980.00
Plate, Gold & White Design, Crossed Swords, C.1860, 9 In.	150.00
Plate, Hand Painted Floral Design, Marked, 10 1/2 In., 8 Piece	600.00
Plate, Leaf Shape, Cobalt Blue & Gold, Marked, 8 1/2 In.	125.00
Platter, Daisy & Button, Center Floral, Marked, 11 In.	190.00
Tazza, Red Flowers, Crossed Swords	375.00
Teapot, Marked, 1840	400.00
Teapot, Stenciled Military Battle Scenes, Marcolini Period	500.00
Tray, Sweetmeat, Reclining Figure, Crossed Swords	350.00
Tureen, Hand Painted Rose, Large	1800.00
Tureen, Sauce, Boy With Cornucopia Finial, Marked, 11 In.	165.00
Urn, Armorial Crest, Courting, Goddess Form, Double Handles, 28 In.	450.00
Vase, Cover, Encrusted Flowerheads, Vines, Marked, 15 In., Pair	1210.00
Vase, Flowers, Man & Woman In Garden, White Ground, 7 3/4 In.	95.00
Vase, Pate–Sur–Pate, Gilt Borders, Handles, 12 1/2 In. ....*Illus*	1400.00

Mercury, or silvered, glass was first made in the 1850s. It lost favor for a while but became popular again about 1910. It looks like a piece of silver.

MERCURY GLASS, Bowl, Beaded Handle, 5 In. 15.00
  Bowl, Ruffled, 3 In. 20.00
  Figurine, Heron, 10 In. 50.00
  Tieback, Pewter Post, Large, Pair 135.00
  Vase, Silver, Painted Flowers, 7 In. 25.00

Mettlach, Germany, is a city where the Villeroy and Boch factories worked. Steins from the firm are known as Mettlach steins. They date from about 1842. PUG means "painted under glaze." The steins can be dated from the marks on the bottom which include a date-number code. Other pieces may be listed in the Villeroy & Boch category.

METTLACH, Beaker, Stadt Tilsit, PUG 55.00
  Charger, No.212, Elf, 2 Bottles of Wine, Bird's Nest ....*Illus* 1650.00
  Mug, Bartholomay's Brewery 150.00
  Mug, No.1526, Keeper of Wine Cellar 40.00
  Pitcher, No.1028 .... 295.00
  Pitcher, No.2382, PUG 295.00
  Plaque, No.1048, Black & White King On Throne, Marked, 16 In. 650.00
  Plaque, No.1048, Opening Crypt of Charlemagne 550.00
  Plaque, No.2079, Regimental, Mounted Lancers, 15 1/2 In. 1500.00
  Plaque, No.2080, Regimental, Officer With Bugler 1500.00
  Plaque, No.2442, Trojan Warriors On Boat, Marked, 1899, 18 In. 1100.00
  Plaque, No.5080, Dutch Port Scene, C.1897, 17 1/2 In. 450.00
  Plaque, No.7074, Cupid & Woman Scene, Square, Marked, 1907, 8 In. ... 395.00
  Stein, No. 24, 1/2 Liter, Hunters 450.00
  Stein, No.1132, Alligator & Pyramid 395.00
  Stein, No.1164, 1/2 Liter, Musician & Girl 450.00
  Stein, No.1475, 1/2 Liter, Working Gnomes 500.00
  Stein, No.1530, 1/2 Liter, Man In Robe Smoking Pipe, 8 3/4 In. 365.00
  Stein, No.1536, Tapestry On Front of Man With Pipe, Pewter Lid 325.00
  Stein, No.1642, 1/2 Liter, Tapestry 395.00
  Stein, No.1655, 1/2 Liter, Young People Dancing 495.00
  Stein, No.1734, 1 1/4 Liter, Man & Woman Lovers, 12 1/2 In. 950.00
  Stein, No.1786, 1/2 Liter, St. Florian, Dragon Handle 690.00
  Stein, No.1976, 3/10 Liter, Verse 375.00
  Stein, No.2001, 1/2 Liter, Book, Scholar, Gold Trim, 5 3/4 In. 550.00
  Stein, No.2001A, 1/2 Liter, Book, Lawyer, Pewter Lid, 5 3/4 In. 550.00

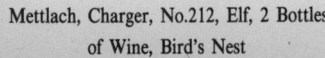

Mettlach, Charger, No.212, Elf, 2 Bottles
of Wine, Bird's Nest

Mustache Cup,
Blue & White, 3 In.

Stein, No.2002, 1/2 Liter, Munich .... 325.00 To 530.00
Stein, No.2015, 1/2 Liter, St.George & Dragon 500.00
Stein, No.2034, 1/2 Liter, Blue Etched Mosaic Design 395.00
Stein, No.2035, 1/2 Liter, Bacchus 425.00
Stein, No.2091, 1/2 Liter, St. Florian Pouring Water 690.00
Stein, No.2093, 1/2 Liter, Playing Card 645.00
Stein, No.2103, 1 1/2 Liter, Man On Barrel 1150.00
Stein, No.2180/955, 5 Liter, Drinking Scene 1300.00
Stein, No.2786, 1 Liter, St. Florian, Dragon Handle 875.00
Stein, No.2838, Etched, 6 1/2 In. 190.00
Stein, No.2872, 1/2 Liter, Cornell University 650.00
Stein, No.2893, 3 Liter, PUG 575.00
Stein, No.2967, 1/2 Liter, 2 Farmers With Pigs 275.00
Stein, No.3282, 1/2 Liter, Target Shooting 165.00
Tile, Duck, Villeroy & Boch 45.00
Tile, Wildlife Scene, Ducks, U & B, 6 X 6 In. 48.00
Tureen, No.3037, 6 Panels, Cover 500.00
Vase, No.1409, Beige Tapestry Ground, Dragon Handles, 11 1/4 In. 445.00
Vase, No.1591, Etched Design, 4 Scenes, Boy In Tree, 12 1/2 In. 465.00

Milk glass was named for its milky–white color. It was first made in England during the 1700s. The height of its popularity in the United States was from 1870 to 1880. It is now correct to refer to some colored glass as blue milk glass, black milk glass, etc. Reproductions of milk glass are being made and sold in many stores.

MILK GLASS, see also Cosmos; Vallerysthal
MILK GLASS, Baby's Bootie, Blue, Enameled Rim 50.00
Basket, Hobnail, 6 1/2 In. 7.50
Basket, Magnolia, Split Handle, Round, 4 3/4 In. 22.50
Basket, Paneled Grape, Flowers, Westmoreland, Oval .... 35.00 To 38.00
Bone Dish, Dewey, 6 3/4 In. 220.00
Bottle, Barber, Bay Rum 145.00
Bottle, Cologne, Ball Shape, Floral, Hollow Stopper, 9 In., Pair 65.00
Bottle, Cologne, Jenny Lind, Stopper 85.00
Bottle, Figural, Boy, In Long Cloak, Clear Stopper Head, 7 In. 47.50
Bottle, Joan of Arc, Head Stopper, French, 16 1/2 In. 285.00
Bowl, Acanthus, Blue 95.00
Bowl, Beaded Grape, Cover, Gold Trim, Westmoreland, Square 35.00
Bowl, Cover, Garlands, 3 Dolphin Feet, Shell Finial, 6 1/2 In. 38.00
Bowl, Daisy, Openwork Edge, Hand Painted 60.00
Bowl, Hobnail, Ruffled, White, 4 1/2 X 8 In. 16.00
Bowl, Raised Floral Center, Floral Edge, C.1880, 8 1/2 In. 250.00
Bowl, Serving, Paneled Grape, Westmoreland 45.00
Bowl, Thistle & Shamrock, Tree Bark Feet 15.00
Bowl, Thousand Eye, Blue, Pedestal, 8 In. 105.00
Box, Chocolate, Paneled Grape, Cover, Westmoreland, 4 X 6 In. 35.00
Box, Dresser, Blue, Jenny Lind Portrait, Cover, Late 1800s 85.00
Box, Dresser, Triple Scallop, Fruit, Leaves, Berries, 7 X 5 In. 65.00
Box, Fruit Design Cover, 7 X 5 In. 48.00
Box, Glove, Jenny Lind Cover 95.00
Box, Red & Gold Design On Cover, Clam Shape, McKee 45.00
Box, Seated Lion Cover 95.00
Bread Plate, Rock of Ages, 1875 .... 150.00
Butter, Cover, Child's, Flattened Diamond & Sunburst 25.00
Butter, Cover, Crossed Ferns 60.00
Butter, Cover, Diamond Point & Leaf 150.00
Butter, Cover, Lacy Dewdrop 45.00
Butter, Herringbone 22.00
Butter, Tree of Life Cover 125.00
Butter, Versailles, Painted Fired–On Floral Design, Cover 45.00
Cake Stand, Hant, 11–Point Star 125.00
Cake Stand, Paneled Grape, Skirt, Westmoreland 50.00
Candleholder, Clown 75.00
Candleholder, Dolphin, 4 1/2 In., Pair 15.00

Candleholder, Old Quilt, Pair 27.00
Candlestick, Child's, Swirl, Blue, 3 3/8 In. 35.00
Candy Dish, Cover, Della Robbia, White 22.00
Candy Dish, Cover, Square Pedestal, Blue 30.00
Candy Dish, Paneled Grape, Crimped, Westmoreland 23.00
Canister Set, Grape, Indiana Glass, 3 Piece 73.00
Celery, Flute, Blue, Crossblock Base 95.00
Charger, Gothic, 11 3/4 In. 39.50
Chop Plate, Open Rose, 10 In. 22.50
Cigar Holder, Indian, Satin Finish, 4 1/2 In. 150.00
Compote, Atlas, Chartreuse, 8 1/4 In. 100.00
Compote, Beaded Grape, Cover, Pedestal, Westmoreland 25.00
Compote, Cactus, Double Crimp, 6 In. 8.00
Compote, Crossed Fern, 7 In. 18.50
Compote, Della Robbia, 2 Piece 10.00
Compote, Flowers, Cover, Westmoreland, 12 1/2 In. 35.00
Compote, Lattice 40.00
Condiment Set, Hobnail, 7 Piece 65.00
Condiment Set, Tray, Cosmos, Miniature 90.00
Cookie Jar, Fruits, Westmoreland 65.00
Cookie Jar, Paneled Cherry Thumbprint 65.00
Creamer, Child's, Wild Rose 60.00
Creamer, Netted Oak 55.00
Creamer, Paneled Flower 35.00
Creamer, Paneled Wheat 45.00
Creamer, Swan 48.00
Cruet, Forget–Me–Not, Stopper 45.00
Cruet, Hobnail, Fenton, 5 In. 8.00
Cruet, Moonstone, Westmoreland 25.00
Cruet, Paneled Grape & Leaf, 6 1/2 In. 30.00
Cruet, Paneled Grape, Westmoreland 25.00
Cruet, Sawtooth, Westmoreland 25.00
Cuspidor, Gold Trim 45.00
Dish, Actress Cover, Oval, Old Gold Paint, 5 In. 25.00
Dish, Admiral Dewey On Battleship Cover 75.00
Dish, American Hen Cover, 6 1/4 In. 70.00
Dish, Battleship Cover, Gilt, 7 7/8 In. 50.00
Dish, Battleship Shape, Admiral Dewey Cover, 6 1/2 In. 70.00
Dish, Blue Dog White Head Cover 48.00
Dish, Cat Cover, Atterberry, Dated 1889 .... 175.00
Dish, Cat With Blue & White Head Cover, 5 1/2in. 50.00
Dish, Chick On Basket Cover, 2 Handles, White 38.00
Dish, Chicken On Nest Cover 20.00
Dish, Covered Wagon Shape, Cover, 6 In. 125.00
Dish, Crawfish Cover, On 2–Handled Base 135.00
Dish, Dog Cover, Blue, White Head, 5 1/2 In. 50.00
Dish, Drum With Cannon On Top 47.50
Dish, Emblem & Eagle Cover, 6 1/2 In. 50.00
Dish, Fox Cover, Lacy Base 65.00
Dish, Fox Cover, Ribbed Base, 1889 .... 150.00
Dish, Hand & Fan 75.00
Dish, Hen Cover, Blue, White Head, Basket Base, 5 1/2 In. 35.00
Dish, Hen Cover, Red Comb, 4 1/2 In. 20.00
Dish, Hen Cover, Stippled Nest, Beaded Rim, 5 1/2 X 7 In. 24.00
Dish, Hen Cover, White Head, Blue Body, Molded Eyes, 7 1/4 In. 90.00
Dish, Hen On Nest Cover, Westmoreland, 5 1/2 In. 18.00
Dish, Hen, On Lattice Nest, Westmoreland, 3 In. 15.00
Dish, Lamb On Split Rib Base 35.00
Dish, Paneled Grape & Leaf, Leaf, 4 Footed, Oval, 6 In. 15.00
Dish, Pintail Duck Cover, Basket Weave Base, Blue, 5 1/2 In. 95.00
Dish, Quail Cover 60.00
Dish, Rabbit Cover, Westmoreland 35.00
Dish, Reclining Lion Cover, Ribbed Base, Dated 145.00
Dish, Rooster Cover On Basket Weave, Colored Comb & Eyes 60.00

Dish, Rooster, Standing 28.00
Dish, Turtle Cover, On 2–Handled Base 135.00
Dish, Uncle Sam On Battleship Cover 55.00
Duck, Atterbury, Amethyst & White Head, L.G. Wright, 11 In. 35.00
Easter Egg, 6 In. 35.00
Easter Egg, Blown, Flat Bottom, Chick Design, 1900s 35.00
Easter Egg, Embossed Chick, 2 1/2 In. 25.00
Eggcup, Blackberry 50.00
Eggcup, Chick, Westmoreland 15.00
Eggcup, Dart & Oval 8.00
Epergne, 4–Light, Blue Trim, 17 In. 375.00
Epergne, Fenton, 2 Piece 45.00
Figurine, Owl, Red Jewel Eyes, 8 In. 42.50
Figurine, Rabbit, Atterbury, Dated, 9 In. 175.00
Figurine, Rooster, Footed, Westmoreland, 8 1/2 In. 35.00
Flowerpot, Grape, White 20.00
Frying Pan, Pan–American Souvenir, 6 7/8 In. 120.00
Globe, Lamp, Baby Face, 7 X 7 In. 25.00
Goblet, Blackberry 20.00
Goblet, Paneled Grape 12.00
Gravy Boat, Dolphin 67.00
Hat, Dobbs Advertising, Black 15.00
Inkwell, Pug Dog 165.00
Jar, 3 Bears Hunting, Dressed As Humans, Cover, 4 In. 110.00
Jar, Cover, Roosevelt Bears 85.00
Jar, E Pluribus Unum, Old Abe Cover 125.00
Lamp, Acanthus Leaves On Base, Ball Shade, 9 1/4 In. 225.00
Lamp, Beading Around Shields, Eagles With Arrows, 7 1/4 In. 195.00
Lamp, Block, 6 1/2 In. 110.00
Lamp, Coreopsis, Clear Chimney 125.00
Lamp, Japan, Miniature 12.50
Lamp, Log Cabin, Brass Collar, Kerosene Burner, 3 3/4 In. 300.00
Lamp, Moon & Stars Umbrella Shade, Blue, 7 1/2 In. 90.00
Lamp, Nellie Bly, Pink Blush, Rose Design, Miniature 150.00
Lamp, Pink Design, Shade, Miniature 350.00
Lavabo Set, Hobnail, 3 Piece 75.00
Lavabo, Thumbprint 65.00
Match Holder, Butterfly, Wall 21.00
Match Holder, Cornucopia 16.00
Match Holder, Diamond Point, Striker Around Rim, Hat Shape 24.00
Match Holder, Flag Shield Shape, Word America, Wall, 3 7/8 In. 175.00
Match Holder, Grape Panel, Footed 18.00
Match Holder, Hand Holding Fan, Pedestal 25.00
Match Holder, Paneled Rib 22.00
Mug, Child's, Beaded Handle, Painted, 3 In. 15.00
Mug, Pansy, Shell 22.00
Mug, Robin 30.00
Mug, Shaving, Garfield, 5 In. 125.00
Mug, Swan 195.00
Mustard, Cover, Fisherman & Sailing Ship, Gilt Trim 55.00
Mustard, Cover, Swirl 15.00
Nappy, Scroll & Eye 18.00
Paperweight, Washington Monument 135.00
Pen Tray, Gargoyle 25.00
Pitcher, Child's, Boudoir, Dutch 65.00
Pitcher, Child's, Owl, Glass Eyes 90.00
Pitcher, Garfield Drape 65.00
Pitcher, Jenny Lind 125.00
Pitcher, Medallion, Oval, Painted Flowers 85.00
Pitcher, Paneled Grape & Leaf, Marked, 8 1/4 In. 65.00
Pitcher, Water, Blackberry, Applied Handle, Dated Feb. 1870 .... 450.00
Pitcher, Water, Grape 12.00
Pitcher, Wild Rose, Ruffled, 9 3/4 In. 125.00
Planter, Paneled Grape, Westmoreland, 5 X 9 In. 28.00

Planter, Window, Paneled Grape, 8 X 3 In. 35.00
Plate, 3 Owls, Westmoreland 30.00
Plate, Angel Head, Blue, 9 In. 50.00
Plate, Apple Blossom, Lattice Edge, 10 1/2 In. 25.00
Plate, California Bear, 9 1/4 In. .... 110.00 To 135.00
Plate, Commemorating Columbus, 9 5/8 In. 40.00
Plate, Commemorating Life of Washington, 8 3/8 In. .... 15.00 To 20.00
Plate, Commemorating W.J. Bryan, 7 3/8 In. 20.00
Plate, Commemorating W.J. Bryan, Black, 9 1/4 In. .... 85.00 To 95.00
Plate, Commemorating Wm. McKinley, 7 1/2 In. 140.00
Plate, Commemorating Wm. McKinley, 9 1/8 In. 110.00
Plate, Dinner, Grape, Westmoreland 20.00
Plate, Dog & Cats, He's All Right 95.00
Plate, Eagle, Fleur-De-Lis, Flag, 7 1/4 In. 35.00
Plate, Federation Women's Clubs Bicentennial, Blue 18.00
Plate, Forget-Me-Not, Blue 30.00
Plate, Gilded Eagle, Patent Date, 7 1/4 In. 50.00
Plate, Home In The Wilderness, Imperial Mark, 10 1/2 In. 15.00
Plate, Indian Chief, 7 1/4 In. 30.00
Plate, Jefferson Davis 40.00
Plate, Niagara Falls, 7 3/8 In. 65.00
Plate, Rabbit In Center, White, 7 1/2 In. 32.00
Plate, Raised Sloop, Chain & Anchor Border, 7 3/8 In. 30.00
Plate, Ring & Petal, Square, 8 1/2 In. 18.00
Plate, Rock of Ages 135.00
Plate, Serenade, 6 1/2 In. 25.00
Plate, Spring Meets Winter 45.00
Plate, Washington Bicentennial, Black, 8 1/8 In. 30.00
Platter, Dewey, Patriotic Base 100.00
Platter, Dewey, Tile Base 35.00
Platter, Liberty Bell 210.00
Punch Cup, Fruits, Westmoreland 5.00
Punch Cup, Nursery Rhymes 15.00
Punch Cup, Wild Rose 16.00
Relish, Fish, 10 X 6 1/4 In. 19.00
Ring Tree, Enameled 38.00
Rolling Pin, Green Wooden Handles, Imperial 45.00
Rolling Pin, Kelvinator 68.00
Salt & Pepper, Allover Blown-Out Roses, 1 Rose, Other Yellow 45.00
Salt & Pepper, Apple Blossom, Northwood 60.00
Salt & Pepper, Basket Weave, Blue, No Tops 35.00
Salt & Pepper, Forget-Me-Not 40.00
Salt & Pepper, Grapes & Leaves, 4-Sided, 3 In. 18.00
Salt & Pepper, Hen & Rabbit 125.00
Salt & Pepper, Heron & Lighthouse, Cover 95.00
Salt & Pepper, Leaf Base 15.00
Salt, Blackberry, Round 32.00
Salt, Double, 1 1/2 X 2 1/2 In. 35.00
Salt, Master, Basket Weave, Atterbury 45.00
Saltshaker, Cotton Bale, Green 28.00
Saltshaker, Owl Head, Original Top 110.00
Sauce Boat, Underplate, Paneled Grape, Westmoreland 38.00
Sauce, Crossed Fern 12.00
Sherbet, American Hobnail 5.00
Spooner, Apple Blossom, Yellow Band 18.00
Spooner, Ceres .... 35.00 To 38.00
Spooner, Paneled Fern 35.00
Spooner, Paneled Grape 15.00
Spooner, Paneled Grape & Leaf, Footed, 6 In. 25.00
Spooner, Scalloped Rim, Painted Gold 35.00
Spooner, Wild Iris, Painted Gold 40.00
Spooner, Wild Rose .... 50.00 To 55.00
Sugar & Creamer, Beaded Grape, Westmoreland, Square 25.00
Sugar & Creamer, Cover, Marked Prescut 16.00

Sugar & Creamer, Della Robbia .... 22.00 To 24.00
Sugar & Creamer, Diamond Fan, Miniature 58.00
Sugar & Creamer, Grape .... 15.00 To 20.00
Sugar & Creamer, Paneled Grape, Westmoreland 50.00
Sugar Shaker, Apple Blossom 100.00
Sugar Shaker, Johnny Bull, Original Lid 95.00
Sugar Shaker, Leaning Pillars, Blue 30.00
Sugar Shaker, Netted Oak 65.00
Sugar, Child's, Lamb 175.00
Sugar, Cover, Apple Blossom, Design 150.00
Sugar, Cover, Beaded Swag, Flower Design, Gold Trim 65.00
Sugar, Cover, Panel Sprig, Design 65.00
Sugar, Cover, Princess Feather, Flint 125.00
Sugar, Cover, Tree of Life, Challinor 75.00
Sugar, Cover, Wild Iris, Painted Gold 55.00
Sugar, Open, Ceres 20.00
Swan, Open Back, Orange Bill, Large 45.00
Syrup, Daisy With Swirl, 7 1/2 In. 78.00
Syrup, Enamel Design 60.00
Syrup, Tree of Life 75.00
Table Set, Cactus, 3 Piece 75.00
Tankard, Water, Scroll 58.00
Tomahawk, Marbled, Blue, 7 1/4 In. 15.00
Toothpick, Basket 16.00
Toothpick, Button & Bulge 50.00
Toothpick, Horseshoe & Clover 30.00
Toothpick, Owl, Westmoreland .... 7.00 To 20.00
Toothpick, Parrot With Hat 65.00
Toothpick, Swan 22.50
Toothpick, Top Hat 9.00
Toothpick, Tramp's Shoe 28.00
Top Hat, Black, Hand Blown, 7 X 12 In. 150.00
Tray, Actress, 9 X 4 1/2 In. 22.00
Tray, Deviled Egg, Grape, Westmoreland .... 79.00 To 85.00
Tray, Dresser, Actress 45.00
Tray, Dresser, Versailles 27.50
Tumbler, Apple Blossom 25.00
Tumbler, Louisiana Purchase Exposition, 5 In. 5.00
Tumbler, Vermont 35.00
Urn, Cover, 10 In. 66.00
Vase, Blue, Fluted, 12 In., Pair 65.00
Vase, Crimped, 4 X 4 In. 6.50
Vase, Mephistopheles, Horns, Pointed Ears, 8 1/2 In. 55.00
Witch's Ball, Clear, White Loops, Opalescent Lace Stand, 6 In. 125.00

Millefiori means, literally, a thousand flowers. It is a type of glasswork popular in paperweights. Many small flowerlike pieces of glass are grouped together to form a design.

MILLEFIORI, Epergne, 3 Ruffled Trumpets & Bowl, 16 In. 225.00
Lamp, Canes 200.00
Sugar & Creamer, Cover, Blue 195.00
Toothpick 35.00
Vase, Multicolor Canes, Cobalt Blue, 6 1/4 In. 145.00
Vase, Ruffled, Pontil, 4 In. 85.00

Minton china has been made in the Staffordshire region of England from 1793 to the present. The firm became part of the Royal Doulton Tableware Group in 1968, but the wares continued to be marked "Minton." Many marks have been used. The one shown dates from about 1873 to 1891, when the word "England" was added.

MINTON, Bowl, Oriental Japan, Porringer Handle, 9 X 10 In. 75.00
Charger, Delft, 1871, 11 In. 55.00
Charger, Game Bird, Gold Scalloped Border, Coronet, 11 1/2 In. 165.00

Eggcup, Paisley Border, 1910	35.00
Ewer, Pate–Sur–Pate	200.00
Figurine, Cockatoo, Blue, Green, Ocher, Brown Streaked Glaze, 1910, Pr.	1200.00
Figurine, Pointer, White, 1876, 37 1/2 In.	7000.00
Figurine, Woman, Bisque, 14 In.	150.00
Jug, Applied Hops & Vine, Blue Ground, Marked, 6 1/4 In.	225.00
Oyster Plate, Majolica, Green, Brown Tints, 6 Wells	165.00
Plate, Oriental Japan, Cobalt Blue, Multicolored, White, 8 1/2 In.	35.00
Plate, Warwick Castle, 9 1/2 In.	45.00
Ramekin, Underplate, White, Gold Trim	20.00
Tile, Sprays of Pastel Flowers, White Ground, Footed, 6 X 6 In.	45.00
Urn, Cobalt Blue, Butterfly, Floral, Gilt, C.1870, 12 In.	578.00
MIRROR, see Furniture, Mirror	

Mochaware is an English–made product that was sold in America during the early 1800s. It is a heavy pottery with pale coffee-and-cream coloring. Designs of blue, brown, green, orange, black, or white were added to the pottery.

MOCHA, Bowl, Earthworm Design, Pale Blue Ground, Brown Stripes, 4 1/4 In.	425.00
Bowl, Flared Banded Rim, Earthworm Design, C.1830, 3 3/4 X 7 1/4 In.	200.00
Candlestick, C.1840, 8 1/4 In.	350.00
Creamer, Brown, Blue, 2 1/2 In.	150.00
Creamer, Floral Medallions	725.00
Creamer, Seaweed	650.00
Crock, Seaweed	100.00
Cup, Tan	80.00
Mug, Earthworm Desigh, Leaf Handles, Stripes, 4 7/8 In.	150.00
Mug, Seaweed, Blue, White Ground	200.00
Pitcher, 2 Bands White Earthworm Design, Blue, 6 X 16 In.	550.00
Pitcher, Earthworm, 6 In.	1300.00
Pitcher, Marbelized, 5 1/2 In.	1875.00
Pitcher, Milk, Moon Circles, Brown Band With Dot Swag, Ovoid, 7 In.	425.00
Pitcher, Milk, Tan Collar Band, Cat's Eyes Band, C.1825, 6 7/8 In.	475.00
Pitcher, Seaweed, Yellowware	275.00

Monmouth Pottery Company started working in Monmouth, Illinois, in 1892. The pottery made a variety of utilitarian wares. They became part of Western Stoneware Company in 1906. The maple leaf mark was used until 1930. If the word "Co." appears as part of the mark, the piece was made before 1906.

MONMOUTH, Ashtray, 3 Child's Footprints, 1 Week, 1 Year, 2 Years, Gray, 9 In.	10.00
Cookie Jar, Jug Shape, Stencils	125.00
Cookie Jar, Jug, With Cork	18.00
Dish, Cover, Sponge–Type Coloring	25.00
Mug, Band Center, Aqua, Squatty, Signed	2.00
Pitcher, Salt Glaze, Brown, 6 1/4 In.	22.00
Pitcher, Tan, Horizontal Ribs, 5 1/2 In.	7.00
Vase, Bulbous, Aqua, Label, 8 In.	48.00
Vase, Handles, Paper Label, Aqua, 8 In.	60.00
Vase, Lotus, Gray & Blue, Matte, 8 In.	19.00
Vase, Matte Green, 8 In.	8.50
MONT JOYE, see Mt. Joye	

William Moorcroft managed the art pottery department for James MacIntyre & Company of England from 1898 to 1913. In 1913, he started his own company, Moorcroft Pottery, in Burslem, England. He died in 1945, but the company continues. The earlier wares are similar to those made today, but color and marking will help indicate the age.

MOORCROFT, Bonbonniere, Tulips, Wild Flowers, Cream, 2 Handles, Cover, 8 In.	1850.00
Bowl, Large Leaves, Inside Blue & Green, Marked, 5 3/4 In.	145.00
Candlestick, Design, Cobalt Blue, 6 1/2 In.	45.00
Dish, Leaf Shape, Cobalt Blue, Footed, 4 1/2 In.	65.00
Dish, Potted, Cover, Round, 5 In.	135.00

Lamp, Anemone Design, Blue To Green Ground, C.1949, 9 3/4 In.	510.00
Lamp, Flambe Feather & Grapes, 11 In.	450.00
Planter, Cornflowers, MacIntyre Mark, 5 In.	2000.00
Tea Set, Anemone Design, Dark Blue Ground, C.1945, 3 Piece	600.00
Urn, Cornflowers, Pale Green, Silver Overlay, Handles, 6 In.	4000.00
Vase, Allover Floral Design, Cobalt Blue Ground, 3 1/2 In.	80.00
Vase, Cobalt Blue, 8 1/2 In.	135.00
Vase, Cobalt Ground, Colored Flowers, 4 1/4 In.	60.00
Vase, Florian Design of Tulips, MacIntyre, C.1903, 7 1/4 In.	1000.00
Vase, Florian Red Daisies, MacIntyre, C.1902, 5 1/2 In.	1200.00
Vase, Florian Ware, Iris Design, MacIntyre, 7 In.	880.00
Vase, Green & Gold Tulip Florian Design, C.1904, 7 1/8 In.	1005.00
Vase, Green & Peach Flowers, Bulbous, 7 In.	135.00
Vase, Hilly Landscape, Blue Ground, Hazeldine, Ovoid, 9 3/4 In.	600.00
Vase, Orchid Design, Mottled Green Ground, Marked, 7 1/4 In.	350.00
Vase, Orchids & Poppies, Signed, 6 In.	450.00
Vase, Pansies, Signed, 3 1/2 In.	275.00
Vase, Pomegranates & Grapes, Blue Ground, 1940s, 3 In.	125.00
Vase, Poppies, Green Ground, 7 In.	138.00
Vase, Red & Yellow Leaves, Purple & Red Grapes, Marked, 5 7/8 In.	325.00
Vase, Rust Pomegranates, Dark Blue, 3 1/2 In.	45.00

Some types of Japanese pottery and porcelain are decorated with a special type of raised decoration known as moriage. Sometimes pieces of clay were shaped by hand and applied to the item; sometimes the clay was squeezed from a tube in the way we apply cake frosting. One type of moriage is called dragonware and is listed under that name.

MORIAGE, Box, Scenic Lid, Club Shape, Enameled Design, Marked, 2 3/4 X 2 In.	38.00
Creamer, Allover Flowers, Green, Gold Trim	45.00
Ewer, Hand Painted Floral, White Lacy Slip, 8 1/2 In.	145.00
Ewer, Pink Orchids, Green Ground, 8 In.	150.00
Liqueur Dispenser, Green Keg, Elephant Stopper, 3 Barrel Tumblers	40.00
Pitcher, Blue & Brown Bird, Cream & Pink Ground, 6 In.	60.00
Pitcher, Net Over Hand Painted Flowers, 6 In.	75.00
Sugar Shaker, Barrel Shape, Roses, Enameled	75.00
Urn, Applied 3 In. Beaded Flowers, Gold Slipwork, Japan, 10 In.	185.00
Vase, Flowers, Serpentine Handles, 10 In.	155.00
Vase, Queen Anne's Lace & Pink Roses, 6 1/2 In., Pair	165.00
Vase, Violets, White Ground, 4 1/2 In.	35.00
Vase, White Lacy Slipwork, Floral Medallions, Lavender, 8 In.	175.00
Wine Cask, Dragon, Wooden Spout	45.00

The Mosaic Tile Company of Zanesville, Ohio, was started by Karl Langerbeck and Herman Mueller in 1894. Many types of plain and ornamental tiles were made until 1959. The company closed in 1967. The company also made some ashtrays, bookends, and related gift wares. Most pieces are marked with the entwined MTC monogram.

MOSAIC TILE CO., Figurine, Bear, Black, 10 1/4 X 5 3/4 In.	105.00
Figurine, German Shepherd, Lying Down, Tan, 10 1/2 X 6 In.	110.00
Tile, Bird, 6 In.	25.00
Tile, Dog, Lying, Off-White, 8 In.	120.00

Moser glass is made by Ludwig Moser und Sohne, a Bohemian glasshouse founded in 1857. Art Nouveau-type glassware and iridescent glassware were made. The most famous Moser glass is decorated with heavy enameling in gold and bright colors. The firm is still working in Czechoslovakia. Few pieces of Moser glass are marked.

MOSER, Basket, Applied Insects, Gold Metal Frame, 5 X 8 In.	1750.00
Bow, Hinged Cover, Floral Design, Gold Trim, Green, Signed	275.00
Candlestick, Cranberry Overlay, Bobeches, Gilded Scrolls, 14 In., Pair	1200.00
Console Set, Cranberry, 3 Piece	900.00
Decanter, Enameled Cameo Scenes, Signed	115.00

Ewer, Enameled Flowers, Multicolored Beads, Signed, 11 1/2 In.	710.00
Ewer, Leaf & Forget–Me–Nots, Enameled, Hollow Brown Stopper	590.00
Flask, Leaf Enameling, Brass Spigot, Fittings, Horn Shape, 7 1/2 In.	770.00
Jewelry Box, Enameled Flowers & Gilding, Ormolu Base & Trim	620.00
Lamp, Oil, Vintage, Panel Cut, Blue, Miniature	150.00
Liqueur Set, Barrel–Shaped Decanter, Fern Leaves, Gold Trim, 5 Piece	885.00
Perfume Bottle, Amethyst Prism Cut, Matching Stopper, 3 In.	225.00
Pitcher, Clear Shaded To Emerald, Zipper Pattern, 13 In.	195.00
Pitcher, Water, Allover Multicolored Leaves, Honey Amber, 7 In.	650.00
Pitcher, Water, Amber, Sapphire Blue Trim, Footed, 8 1/4 In.	275.00
Pitcher, Whimsey, Hand Enameled, Glass Rigaree, 10 In.	385.00
Powder Box, Gold Amazon Border On Cover & Bow, Signed	210.00
Relish, Amberina, Gold, Silver Enameling, 4–Footed	450.00
Tumbler, 3 Cut Panels, 3 Gold Encrusted Panels, Cabochon Jewel	345.00
Tumbler, Allover Gold & Enameled Flowers, Cranberry	85.00
Tumbler, Cranberry, Allover Gold Leaves & Flowers, 4 1/4 In.	75.00
Tumbler, Enameled Blue Floral	65.00
Tumbler, Melon Ribbed, Encrusted Gold Flowers, Various Colors, 12 Pc.	475.00
Vase, Amethyst, Enameled, C.1895, 16 In., Pair	1200.00
Vase, Cobalt Blue, Bulbous, Signed, 10 In.	115.00
Vase, Cranberry, Dimpled Sides, Enameled Oak Leaves & Wasp, 4 1/4 In.	450.00
Vase, Cranberry, Multicolor Enameled Oak Leaves, Gold Trim, 4 3/4 In.	225.00
Vase, Cut Floral, Green To Clear, 8 1/2 In.	325.00
Vase, Enameled Acorns & Oak Leaves, Gold Foliage, 5 In.	225.00
Vase, Enameled Flowers, Amethyst Jewels, 5 3/4 In.	225.00
Vase, Enameled Flowers, Paw Feet, Cranberry, Signed, 7 1/2 In.	375.00
Vase, Enameled Poppies, Gold Leaves On Branches, 10 1/2 In.	325.00
Vase, Floral, Cut Clear To Emerald, Tall Neck, Bulbous, 19 1/2 In.	700.00
Vase, Ground–Out Window Panels, Green To Clear, 6 X 5 In.	125.00
Vase, Heavy Gilding, 15 In.	620.00
Vase, Intaglio Cut, Paneled, Green To Clear, 9 In.	90.00
Vase, Multicolored Oak Leaves, Applied Acorns, Green, 3 1/2 In., Pr.	295.00
Vase, Poppies, Gold Leaves & Branches, Baluster Shape, 10 1/2 In.	325.00
Vase, Trumpet, Gold Design, Pink Flowers, Ruffled, Signed, 9 1/2 In.	150.00
Vase, Wishbone Feet, Multicolored Oak Leaves, Insect, 4 3/4 In.	700.00
Wine Taster, Paneled, Blue Shade To Clear, 2 1/2 In.	200.00

Moss rose china was made by many firms from 1808 to 1900. It has a typical moss rose pictured as the design. The plant is not as popular now as it was in Victorian gardens, so the fuzz–covered bud is unfamiliar to most collectors. The dishes were usually decorated with pink and green flowers.

MOSS ROSE, Creamer	12.00
Cup & Saucer, Scrolls, Gold Trim, Footed	8.00
Plate, Meakin, 8 In.	14.00
Plate, Pink Border, Ironstone, Powell & Bishop, 10 In.	18.00
Sugar, Cover, Moss Rose, Grindley, Ironstone	95.00
Tea Set, Child's, Teapot, 7 In. Platter, 11 Piece	65.00
MOTHER–OF–PEARL, Ewer, Diamond–Quilted, Thorny Handle, Pink, 12 3/4 In.	495.00

Mother–of–pearl glass, or pearl satin glass, was first made in the 1850s in England and in Massachusetts. It was a special type of mold–blown satin glass with air bubbles in the glass, giving it a pearlized color. It has been reproduced. Mother–of–pearl shell objects are listed under Pearl.

MOTHER–OF–PEARL, Biscuit Jar, Diamond–Quilted, Silver Plate Handle, 11 In.	735.00
Biscuit Jar, Painted Florals, Peachblow	225.00
Bowl, 8–Crimp Top, Air Trap Pattern, Green, 2 1/2 X 3 In.	200.00
Creamer, Blue Raindrop, Satin Glass, White Lining, 4 In.	225.00
Creamer, White Lining, Frosted Rim, Butterscotch, 4 1/2 In.	225.00
Cruet, Diamond–Quilted, Rose Colored Air Traps, 5 In.	685.00
Dish, Sweetmeat, Flower & Acorn, Red, Gold Design, 4 3/4 In.	755.00
Ewer, Rose Herringbone, 3–Petal Top, 6 3/4 In.	225.00
Globe, Ruffled Rim, Pink, White Interior, 7 1/2 X 9 1/2 In.	225.00

Lamp, Diamond–Quilted, Rainbow, 4 1/2 In. 525.00
Lamp, Peg, Ruffled Shade, Blue Swirl, 16 1/2 In. 760.00
Rose Bowl, 3–Crimp Top, Chocolate Brown, 3 In. 295.00
Rose Bowl, Blue Ribbon, White Lining, 9 Crimp, 2 1/2 In. 225.00
Rose Bowl, Diamond–Quilted, Blue, White Lining, 8 Crimp 245.00
Rose Bowl, Herringbone, Yellow, 4 In. 30.00
Rose Bowl, Peacock Eye, Red, White Lining, 3 In. 900.00
Rose Bowl, Rivulet Pattern, 8–Crimp Top, Green, 3 1/4 In. 275.00
Saltshaker, Raindrop, Blue 235.00
    MOTHER–OF–PEARL, SATIN GLASS, see also Satin Glass; Smith Brothers;
    etc.
Toothpick, Diamond–Quilted, Yellow, 2 1/2 In. 350.00
Tumbler, Rose To Pink, White Lining 110.00
Vase, Coralene, Snowflake, Gold Top Trim, 6 1/4 In. 425.00
Vase, Diamond–Quilted, Alternating Stripes, 6 1/8 In. 895.00
Vase, Diamond–Quilted, Blue, Ruffled, 4 1/8 In. 125.00
Vase, Diamond–Quilted, Vaseline Layer Over Top, 10 1/4 In. 495.00
Vase, Diamond–Quilted, White Lining, Pink, 10 1/8 In., Pair 550.00
Vase, Diamond–Quilted, Yellow, 6 In. 165.00
Vase, Dimpled Sides, Rose Red, 4 5/8 X 5 3/8 In. 225.00
Vase, Fan Shape Top, Yellow Herringbone, 7 1/2 In. 135.00
Vase, Fan Shape, Ruffled, Wafer Foot, Chartreuse, 3 1/2 In. 195.00
Vase, Flared Fluted Top, White Lining, Blue, 4 1/4 In. 210.00
Vase, Flowers, Leaves, Gold Enameling, Blue, 7 In., Pair 850.00
Vase, Fluted Top, White Lining, Blue Swirl, 6 1/4 In. 165.00
Vase, Herringbone, Blue, Ruffled, 7 1/4 In. 118.00
Vase, Peacock Eye, Ruffled, White Lining, 13 3/4 In. 325.00
Vase, Rainbow, 7 In. 1150.00
Vase, Raindrop, Blue, Satin Glass, White Lining, 8 1/4 In. 225.00
Vase, Ribbon, Chartreuse, Ball Shape, 4 1/4 In. 195.00
Vase, Ribbon, Gilded, 4 Medallions, White, 6 1/2 In. 1100.00
Vase, Ruffled Top, Rose Herringbone, 8 1/4 In. 175.00
Vase, Ruffled, Diamond–Quilted, Frosted Top, Yellow, 7 In. 495.00
Vase, Star–Shaped Top, 9 In., Pair 350.00
Vase, Thorny Handles & Feet, Blue, 9 3/4 In., Pair 795.00
Vase, Tiers of Air Traps, Cylindrical, 7 1/2 In. 685.00
MOUSTACHE CUP, see Mustache Cup

Mt. Joye is an enameled cameo glass made in the late nineteenth and the twentieth centuries by Saint–Hilaire Touvoir de Varraux and Co. of Pantin, France. This same company made De Vez glass. Pieces were usually decorated with enameling. Most pieces are not marked.

MT.JOYE, Rose Bowl, Enameled Violets, Frosted Clear Ground, 4 1/2 X 4 In. 400.00
Vase, Blue & Gold Leaves & Berries, Textured Ground, 19 1/2 In. 450.00
Vase, Enameled Vines & Fruit, Gold Trim, Signed, 8 1/2 In. 195.00
Vase, Pansies, Purple Frost, Cylindrical, 9 In. 450.00

The Mt. Washington Glass Works started in 1837 in South Boston, Massachusetts. In 1869 the company moved to New Bedford, Massachusetts. Many types of art glass were made there to the 1890s. These included Burmese, Crown Milano, Royal Flemish, and others.

MT.WASHINGTON, Biscuit Jar, Astrological Signs, Silver Rim & Bale 400.00
Biscuit Jar, Blown–Out Oak Leaf Base, Mums, Signed, 9 1/2 In. 550.00
Biscuit Jar, Crescents, White Beading, Off–White Body 325.00
Biscuit Jar, Melon Shape, Water Lilies In Gold & Green 550.00
Biscuit Jar, Pansy Design, Silver Plated Lid, Signed 225.00
Biscuit Jar, Ribbed, Silver Plated Fittings, Blue, 9 1/4 In. 1190.00
Bottle, Enameled Floral Sprays, Blue To Pink, 5 1/2 In. 1200.00
Bowl, Burmese, Applied Lemon Feathers, Footed, 9 X 7 In. 1250.00
Bowl, Hat Shape, 38 Ruffles 675.00
Bowl, Tulip Pattern & Shape, Cut Glass, 9 X 4 In. 550.00

Card Plate, Daisies & Clovers, Fluted, Self–Handle, 6 In.	110.00
Castor, Pickle, Pairpoint Frame, Tongs, Signed	495.00
Compote, Hobstar Scalloped Foot, 2 Handles, Pedestal	1300.00
Compote, Napoli, Blossoms On Underside, 10 X 6 1/4 In.	585.00
Condiment Set, Fluted, Spoon, Opaque White Satin, 3 Piece	225.00
Condiment Set, Foxglove, Silver Plated Stand, 3 Piece	495.00
Cookie Jar, Acorn & Leaves Design, Marked, 6 1/4 In.	595.00
Cracker Jar, Blown–Out Oak Leaf, Mums, Signed, 9 1/2 In.	750.00
Cracker Jar, Burmese, Oak Leaf & Acorn	750.00
Cruet, Burmese, Handle	700.00
Cruet, Melon Ribbed Body, Mushroom Stopper, 6 1/2 In.	935.00
Dish, Vertical Miter, Concave Sides, 6 In.	65.00
Figurine, Sleigh, Cased Glass	625.00
Hatpin Holder, Autumn Leaves, Mushroom Shape, 2 3/4 In.	165.00
Muffineer, Melon Shape, Foliage, Raised Blueberries, 4 In.	485.00
Perfume Bottle, Peachblow, Sprays of Flowers, 5 In.	600.00
Pitcher, Burmese, 8 1/2 In.	235.00
Pitcher, Burmese, Dickens Rhyme, Ivy Vines	2100.00
Pitcher, Burmese, Satin Finish, Squat, 2 Qt.	585.00
Plate, World's Fair, White Glass, Santa Maria, 1893, 6 1/4 In.	300.00
Rose Bowl, Pansies, Lusterless, White, 4 1/2 X 5 In.	75.00
Rosebowl, Crosscut Diamond, Wafer Foot, 6 In.	250.00
Salt & Pepper, Acorn Shape, Swirled, Pewter Top	130.00
Salt & Pepper, Burmese, Pillared, Double Screw Tops	260.00
Salt & Pepper, Egg Shape, Apple Blossom Design	90.00
Salt & Pepper, Egg Shape, Burmese, Original Top	110.00
Salt & Pepper, Egg, White To Pink Floral	95.00
Salt & Pepper, Enamel Design, Pewter Tops	60.00
Salt & Pepper, Lay Down, Pewter Lids	125.00
Salt & Pepper, Melon Shape, Enameled Flowers	95.00
Saltshaker, Chick In Egg, Rose Design, Silver Plated Head	310.00
Saltshaker, Chick In Egg, White Flowers, Pink	340.00
Saltshaker, Fig, Red Flashed	130.00
Saltshaker, Loop & Daisy	60.00
Saltshaker, Melon Rib	35.00
Saltshaker, Tomato	40.00
Saltshaker, Tomato, Satin Glass, Hand Painted, No Stopper	75.00
Shaker, Sugar, Frosted Glass, Pansies, Metal Top, Prongs, 4 In.	585.00
Sugar & Creamer, Burmese, Yellow Handles, 2 3/4 In.	785.00
Sugar Shaker, Acorn	95.00
Sugar Shaker, Berries & Leaves, Melon Ribbed, 3 3/4 In.	275.00
Sugar Shaker, Egg Shape, Bunches of Pink Flowers, 4 In.	195.00
Sugar Shaker, Green & Pink Leaves	120.00
Toothpick, Burmese, Urn Shape, Shasta Daisies	275.00
Toothpick, Tricornered, Diamond, White	295.00
Tray, Bristol Rose, 11 3/4 In.	1600.00
Tumbler, Peachblow	750.00
Vase, Burmese, Bowling Pin Shape, 12 1/2 In.	685.00
Vase, Burmese, Cupid Pedestal, Pairpoint Gilt Finish, 9 In.	485.00
Vase, Burmese, Pink To Yellow Matte, Tea Rose, C.1890, 8 In.	400.00
Vase, Burmese, Swallows, Shiny Finish, 4 1/2 In.	300.00
Vase, Gourd Shape, Burmese, 7 3/4 In.	395.00
Vase, Jack–In–The–Pulpit, Burmese, 6 7/8 In.	300.00
Vase, Lava Glass, Pink, Red, Blue, White, Green, Aqua, 1878, 9 In.	4730.00
Vase, Lily, Alabaster, 6 1/4 In.	12.00
Vase, Peachblow Pink To White, Enameled Florals, 10 In.	650.00
Vase, Peachblow, Daisies, Magenta Centers, 8 In.	2450.00
Vase, Trumpet, White Satin, Lavender Flowers, 13 1/2 In.	325.00
Vase, Tulip Shape, Peachblow, 7 1/2 In.	650.00
Wine, Fuchsia Amberina	175.00

Mud figures are small Chinese pottery figures made in the twentieth century. The figures usually represent workers, scholars, farmers, or merchants. Other pieces are trees, houses, and similar parts of the landscape. The figures have unglazed faces and hands but glazed clothing. They were originally made for fish tanks or planters. Mud figures were of little interest and brought low prices until the 1980s. When the prices rose, reproductions appeared.

MUD FIGURE, Chinese Man, 3 1/2 In.	20.00
Chinese Man, Book In Hand, Yellow Robe, 6 In.	45.00
Chinese Man, Seated, Small	75.00
Elder With Flute, Green Coat, 3 1/2 In.	15.00
Fisherman, 6 In.	36.00
Hut On Stilts, Village Scene	26.00
Man Standing On Carp's Head	75.00
Man With Bonsai, 3 In.	60.00
Man With Bonsai, Brass Planter, 3 1/2 In.	75.00
Man With Fan, 10 1/2 In.	100.00
Man, Bundle To Shoulder, 3 5/8 In.	26.00
Man, Goatee Tendrils, Bundle On Shoulder, 3 5/8 In.	30.00

Mulberry ware was made in the Staffordshire district of England from about 1850 to 1860. The dishes were decorated with a transfer design of a reddish brown, now called "mulberry." Many of the patterns are similar to those used for flow blue and other Staffordshire transfer wares.

MULBERRY, Bowl, Vegetable, Cover, Thomas Walker	75.00
Bowl, Vegetable, Tivoli, 10 In.	75.00 To 100.00
Compote, Jeddo, Pedestal, W.Adams & Sons	350.00
Creamer, Rhone Scenery	95.00
Pitcher, Moss Rose, 11 1/2 In.	350.00
Pitcher, Water, Washington Vase, Podmore & Walker, 8 In.	75.00
Plate, Beauties of China, M.V.Co., 9 In.	19.00
Plate, Bokhara, 10 In.	50.00
Plate, Castle Scenery, Furnival, 7 1/4 In.	22.00
Plate, Corean, 7 In.	40.00
Plate, Corean, 9 1/2 In.	50.00
Plate, Corean, 10 1/2 In.	55.00
Plate, Cyprus, Davenport, 7 In.	25.00
Plate, Jeddo, 10 1/4 In.	35.50
Plate, Marble Pattern, Octagonal, 7 In.	30.00
Plate, Rhone Scenery, T.J.& J.Mayer, 9 5/8 In.	35.00
Plate, Temple, 9 1/2 In.	50.00
Plate, Washington Vase, 9 In.	22.00
Plate, Washington Vase, 10 In.	45.00
Plate, Washington Vase, Podmore & Walker, 7 3/4 In.	25.00
Plate, Washington Vase, Podmore & Walker, 10 In.	26.00
Platter, Jeddo, 1850, 15 1/2 X 12 In.	115.00
Platter, Rhone Scenery, T.J.& J.Mayer, 13 1/2 X 10 1/2 In.	75.00
Platter, Washington Vase, 16 In.	150.00
Soup, Dish, Peru, Holdcroft, 10 3/4 In.	30.00
Teapot, Alcock	80.00
Teapot, Corean	195.00
Tureen, Vegetable, Cyprus	125.00

Muller Freres, French for Muller Brothers, made cameo and other glass from the early 1900s to the late 1930s. Their factory was first located in Luneville, then in nearby Croismaire, France. Pieces were usually marked with the company name.

MULLER FRERES, Bowl, Red Stylized Fish, Frosted Ground, Signed, 9 In.	650.00
Case, Bleeding Heart Vines, Signed, C.1910, 14 In.	4400.00
Lamp, Cameo Shade, Vine, Tendril, Orange, Amber ....*Illus*	1500.00
Lamp, Glass Shade & Base, Blue & Orange Mottling, 12 In.	795.00
Lamp, Helmet Form Shade, Cascading Blossoms, C.1925, 18 In.	2200.00

Lamp, Orange & Black Mottled, Luneville, 7 1/2 In.	350.00
Lamp, Red, Black, Purple, Red, Poppies, Frosted, 13 1/2 In.	600.00
Shade, Ball, Frosted Birds & Flowers, Luneville, 6 In.	195.00
Vase, 3 Cherubs, Landscape, Garland of Flowers, Signed, 5 In.	1550.00
Vase, Aubergine Grapes, Vines, Mottled Green, Cameo, 4 1/2 In.	250.00
Vase, Birds & Flowers, 12 In.	2600.00
Vase, Brown & Orange Tones, Signed, 8 In.	200.00
Vase, Brown, Tan, Yellow, Birds, Tree, Lake, 5 1/2 In.	2850.00
Vase, Cameo, Floral, Red, Green, Yellow, 10 1/2 In. ....*Illus*	4540.00
Vase, Cameo, Landscape Silhouette, Sunset, Signed, 2 3/4 In.	475.00
Vase, Continous Landscape Scene, 3–Color, Spherical, 4 In.	800.00
Vase, Enamel Design, Etching, C.1910, 13 3/4 In.	895.00
Vase, Floral Design, Green & Yellow, Signed, 10 1/2 In.	4100.00
Vase, Forest Landscape, Bridge, Signed, C.1920, 17 1/2 In.	6600.00
Vase, Frosted White, Mottled, Signed, 5 1/2 In.	245.00
Vase, Lakeside Scene, Signed, C.1920, 8 1/2 In.	2090.00
Vase, Landscape, River, Islets, Signed, C.1925, 19 3/4 In.	3575.00
Vase, Large Birds Sitting On Branch, Lake, 16 In.	2850.00
Vase, Millefiori Florettes, Blue, Red, Aqua, 8 1/2 In.	695.00
Vase, Orchid Type Flowers, Leaves, Frosted, Signed, 5 7/8 In.	895.00
Vase, Poppy Blossoms & Leaves, Signed, C.1920, 10 In.	5500.00
Vase, Scenic, Black To Gray, Man, Cattle, Signed, 4 1/2 In.	395.00
Vase, Shepherd & Flock, Green To Red, Signed, 4 1/2 In.	795.00
Vase, Shepherd & His Flock, Setting Sun, Signed, 4 1/2 In.	750.00
Vase, Shepherd, Sheep, Trees, Castle, 4 Colors, 12 In.	1275.00
Vase, Spider Chrysanthemums, Signed, C.1925, 18 In.	4125.00
Vase, Thorny Rose Branches, Blossoms, Signed, C.1925, 11 In.	2475.00

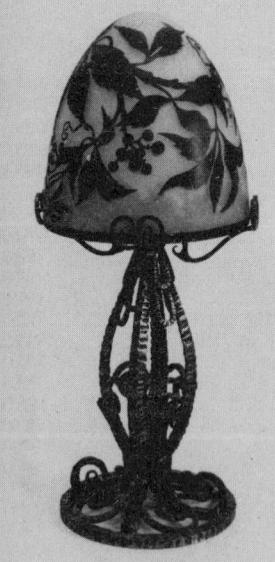

Muller Freres, Lamp, Cameo Shade,
Vine, Tendril, Orange, Amber

Muller Freres, Vase, Cameo, Floral, Red,
Green, Yellow, 10 1/2 In.

MUNCIE

The Muncie Clay Products Company was established by Charles Benham in Muncie, Indiana, in 1922. The company made pottery for the florist and gift shop trade. The company closed by 1939. Pieces are marked with the name "Muncie" or just with a system of numbers and letters like "1A."

MUNCIE, Pitcher, Matte Green Dripped Over Pink, 5 1/2 X 5 In.	13.00
Vase, Bud, Pink, Green, A.Johnson, 8 1/2 In.	12.00
Vase, Green, Rose, Handles, 9 X 5 1/4 In.	25.00
Vase, High Gloss Black, 7 In.	30.00
Vase, High Gloss Maroon, 8 In.	30.00
Vase, Pink, White Frosted, 4 In.	16.00
Vase, Top Hat, Green	18.00

Glass was made on Murano Island in Italy from 1291. The output dwindled in the late seventeenth century, but began to flourish again in the 1850s. Some of the old techniques of glassmaking were revived and firms today make traditional designs and original modern glass. Collectors have recently become interested in the Art Deco and fifties designs.

MURANO, Bowl, Swirl, Gold, 4 In.	15.00
Cordial Set, Tray, Enameled Flowers, Gold Trim, 1950s, 7 Piece	115.00
Figurine, Fisherman, Fishwife, Carrying Fish & Lobster, 12 In., Pair	275.00
Figurine, Rabbit, Gold Trim	45.00

Music boxes and musical instruments are listed in this section. Phonograph records, jukeboxes, phonographs, and sheet music are listed in other sections in this book.

MUSIC, Accordion, Empress, Bellows, Germany, 1890, Small	65.00
Accordion, Hohner, Case	125.00
Accordion, Lakeside, Case	135.00
Album, Picture, 4 In. Disc Movement	700.00
Ampico, Fisher, 9–Legged Art Case	5200.00
Autoharp, Favorite, Original Box	95.00
Autoharp, Oscar Schmidt, Amplifier, Wooden Case	95.00
Automaton, 2 Black Dancers, 1880–1900	715.00
Automaton, Ballet Dancer, Swings Leg, Upper Body, 1920, 17 1/2 In.	1100.00
Automaton, Mandolin Player, L.Lambert, C.1910, 21 In.	6600.00
Band Organ, Logan, Showcraft	1000.00
Band Organ, North Tonawanda, Brass Horn, Style 155	7000.00
Banjo, Ivory Keys, Inlaid Mother–of–Pearl Star, 20 Frets, 10 In. Head	60.00
Birdcage, Brass, Feathered Bird Moves To Music, French, 11 In.	412.00
Box, 5 Cylinders, Bells, Drum, Dancing Doll	5800.00
Box, 8 Tunes, Cylinder, Swiss, C.1920, 6 In.	650.00
Box, Ballerina, Art Deco, Tortoiseshell, Mirror, Cigarette Compartment	50.00
Box, Bremond, 6 Tunes, Inlaid Case	1495.00
Box, Child's, Boy Hugging Dog, Metal, Handle, Round, C.1900	125.00
Box, Criterion, Carved Oak, Floor Model, 15 Original Discs, 6 1/2 Ft.	8000.00
Box, Cylinder, Bells, 12 Tunes, Inlaid Table Model	3000.00
Box, Cylinder, Inlaid Rosewood, Bells & Drum, Swiss, 22 In.	500.00
Box, Kalliope, Upright, 12 Bells, 20 1/2 In. Disc	3850.00
Box, Mermod Freres, Ideal Concerta, 3 Cylinders, C.1886	4800.00
Box, Nativity Creche, Wooden, 15 Composition Figures	65.00
Box, Orcha Strone, Late 1800s	500.00
Box, Orguinette, Mechanical, Style 3, Double Reeds, Floor Model	2000.00
Box, Overture, 4 Overtures, Key Wind, Rosewood, 19 1/2 In.	4125.00
Box, Paillard, 12 Tunes, Zither Attachment, C.1880, 33 1/2 In.	2200.00
Box, Paillard, Cylinder, In Burl Walnut Side Table, Swiss	6325.00
Box, Piano, Hinged Top, Cigarettes & Matches Holder, Walnut, 3 1/2 In.	165.00
Box, Polyphon, Disc, Upright, 19 5/8 In.	4600.00
Box, Polyphon, Mahogany, C.1900, 6 1/2 In.	450.00
Box, Polyphon, Plays 24 Discs, 24 Extra Discs, Floor Model, 6 Ft.4 In.	8400.00
Box, Polyphon, Upright, 19 5/8 In. Disc	3850.00 To 4350.00
Box, Porky Pig, Mattel, 1964	15.00

Box, Regina, 2 Speeds, Double Comb, 20 Discs	3250.00
Box, Regina, Automatic Changer, Upright	9750.00
Box, Regina, Casket Model, Mahogany, 20 3/4 In.	6500.00
Box, Regina, Coin–Operated, 15 Discs, Cabinet	500.00
Box, Regina, Double Comb, Carved Case, Style 9, 12 Discs	4500.00
Box, Regina, Double Comb, Style 11, Oak	2450.00
Box, Regina, Hexaphone	3600.00
Box, Regina, Single Comb, Mahogany, 15 1/2 In.	2850.00
Box, Regina, Table Model	1375.00
Box, Reginaphone, Combination Box & Phonograph, Oak Horn	6000.00
Box, Rosewood, Tulipwood, Inlaid, Piccolo, Zither, 10 Tunes, 10 X 26 In.	1300.00
Box, Sewing, Rosewood, Piano Shape, Inlaid Ivory Keys, 11 1/2 In.	700.00
Box, Singing Bird, Silver, Enameled, Lady, Guilloche, Germany, 4 3/8 In.	4400.00
Box, Single Comb, Short Bedplate, Oak, 15 1/2 In.	3300.00
Box, Swiss, 8 Tunes, Also Gilbert & Sullivan, Cylinder, 1920, 6 In.	650.00
Box, Swiss, Bells, 12 Tunes, Inlaid Cabinet	3000.00
Box, Swiss, Jacot, 10 Tunes, Coin–Operated, Grain Painted Case, 20 In.	1300.00
Box, Symphonia, Upright, 25 In.Disc, 7 1/2 Ft.	8500.00
Box, Symphonion, 6 German Songs, 9–In. Disc, 12 X 11 In.	4950.00
Box, Symphonion, Disc, Style 106, Upright, 17 In.	8000.00
Box, Symphonion, Double Comb, 12 Discs, Oak Case, 18 X 9 In.	1495.00
Bugle, Infantry, World War I	175.00
Calliope, Cozatt, 44 Brass Pipes, Manual	5500.00
Calliope, Tangley, Model 43A	8000.00
Calliope, Tangley, Whistles	2500.00
Clarinet, McClellan Universal	150.00
Cornet, Cornopium, 12 In.	192.50
Cornet, Nova Concerto, Cup Mute, Brass, Case	40.00
Cornet, Rotary Valve, Brass Label M. Slater, N.Y., Civil War	190.00
Drum, American Flag, Insignia, Red Paint, Rope Laces, 16 1/4 In.	450.00
Drum, Slingerland, American Legion	50.00
Glockenspiel, Carrying Strap, Case	65.00
Graphophone, Treadle Shaver	3000.00
Guitar, Martin, Tenor, 4 Strings	600.00
Harmonica, American Glass, C.1830	5200.00
Harmonica, Bora Minevitch	20.00
Harmonica, Hohner, Grand Auditorium	175.00
Harmonica, Hohner, Marine, Box	15.00
Harmonica, Radio Band Jazz, 1920s, 11 In.	22.00
Harmonica, Rol–Monica Player, Bakelite, 1900s	165.00
Harmonica, Song Bird, Hotz, Germany, Box	10.00
Harmonica, Triple Concert, Brass, Wood, Germany	130.00
Harp, Seeburg, E Model, Gilded, Restrung	3350.00
Harp, Wurlitzer, Style A, Case	2500.00
Horn, To Call Field Hands In From Work, Toleware, 14 In.	12.00
Hurdy–Gurdy, Gypsy Figure, Barcelona, 1940	3800.00
Kazoo, Wurlitzer, 1923	35.00
Kinetoscope, Edison Exhibition	3000.00
Mandolin, Gibson, Style A	600.00
Mandolin, Inlaid Mother–of–Pearl, C.1840	195.00
Melodeon, G.A.Prince & Co., Hinged Top, Keyboard, Rosewood, 45 1/2 In.	450.00
Mouth Organ, Baseball Club Band, 2 Sound Horns, 1920s	18.00
Nickelodeon, 8 Instruments, Wonder Light	6495.00
Nickelodeon, Coinola, Cupid Cabinet	7500.00
Nickelodeon, Khul & Klat, 6 Rolls	850.00
Nickelodeon, Leaded Glass Front, 9 Instruments, Coin Slot, Rolls, Oak	7000.00
Nickelodeon, National, 8–Roll Changer, 150 Rolls	2650.00
Nickelodeon, Peerless, Style D, Art Glass Case, 3 Rolls	6500.00
Nickelodeon, Seeburg, Model L	5800.00
Nickelodeon, Seeburg, Style A, Lamps	7000.00
Nickelodeon, Western Electric, Mascot, Model C	7500.00
Orchestrion, Khul & Klat, Pneumatic Model, Rolls	2500.00
Organ, Aeolian Hammond, Player, Bench, 50 Rolls	3000.00
Organ, Aeolian, Model 1500	1500.00

Organ, Barrel, 36 Keys, Brass Reeds, Metal Flutes	3500.00
Organ, Beethoven, Reed, 88 Note	800.00
Organ, Bruder, 50 Keys, 158 Pipes	7000.00
Organ, Carousel, Gavioli, 100 Pipes, Music Book	7250.00
Organ, Estey, Ornate, Mirror, Rebuilt, 1870s	700.00
Organ, Estey, Reed, Full Peddle Board, 2 Keyboards, Electric	2700.00
Organ, Evans, Player, Pipe, Walnut, Mechanism Drawer, 1867, 19 X 6 Ft.	5000.00
Organ, G.Molinari, 23 Keys	3000.00
Organ, H.S.Taylor, 24 Keys	2750.00
Organ, Kimball, Electramatic Player	1050.00
Organ, Mason & Hamlin, Black Walnut	250.00
Organ, Monkey, Frati, 49 Note	6500.00
Organ, Monkey, Gavioli, Harmoniflute & Trombone	4500.00
Organ, Monkey, Molinari	3800.00
Organ, Packard, Candle Shelves, Beveled Mirror, Spoon Carving	750.00
Organ, Pipe, Aeolian Duo-Art, 15 Rank & Harp, 70 Rolls, 12 X 10 Ft.	6500.00
Organ, Pump, Chicago Cottage	525.00
Organ, Pump, Estey, Traveling, Folds Into Oak Trunk	575.00
Organ, Pump, Miller, Walnut, Restored, C.1890	325.00
Organ, Pump, Sterling, Walnut	150.00
Organ, Reed, Estey, 2 Keyboards, Electrified, Oak	2000.00
Organ, Reed, Story & Clark, Full Canopy Top	750.00
Organ, Roller, Wilcox & White	450.00
Organ, Seeburg, Horseshoe Console, Rolls	4500.00
Organ, Story & Clark, Pump, Church, Beveled Mirrors	550.00
Organ, Street, Wooden, 126 Pipes, 10 Tunes	7150.00
Organ, Wurlitzer, Bank, No.150, Rolls	425.00
Organ, Wurlitzer, Model D, Theater, Chinese Design, Percussion	4500.00
Organette, Wurlitzer, Style W, Rolls	630.00
Photograph, Yasha Heifetz, Autographed, Dated 1938	150.00
Piano & Phonograph, Seeburg Combination, Mahogany	7200.00
Piano Harp, MacKenzie, 1890	1200.00
Piano, Barrel, With Bell, Coin-Operated	4750.00
Piano, Bluthner, Grand, Rosewood, 6 Ft.6 In.	7500.00
Piano, Boardman & Gray, Grand, Rosewood, Early 1800s	400.00
Piano, C. Bechstein, Grand, Rosewood Hepplewhite, Bench, 1968, 72 In.	5500.00
Piano, Chicago Gerold, Ivory Keys, 1890s	1400.00
Piano, Chickering, Grand, Lyre, New Strings, 1882	3900.00
Piano, Chickering, Square Grand, Rosewood, C.1830	3200.00
Piano, Coinola, Stained Glass, Oak Case	5000.00
Piano, Columbia, Grand	2500.00
Piano, Decker Bros., Concert Grand, Rosewood, Restored, C.1875, 9 Ft.	9500.00
Piano, Doll & Son, Grand, Painted Oriental Figures, Ornate, C.1897	6000.00
Piano, Fischer, Ampico A, 9 Legs, Art Case	5200.00
Piano, Fischer, Upright Marque, Ampico	950.00
Piano, Jacob Zech, Grand, Rosewood, 1856	2500.00
Piano, Knabe, Ampico, Upright	1600.00
Piano, Knabe-Gayle, Rosewood, Duncan Phyfe Pedestal, 1840s	5000.00
Piano, Kranich & Bach, Baby Grand, Mahogany	750.00
Piano, Marshall Wendel, Ampico Grand, 50 Rolls	3500.00
Piano, Mason & Hamlin, Grand, Hepplewhite, Mahogany, 1917, 5 Ft.4 In.	5000.00
Piano, Mehlin, Upright Grand, Ivory Keys, 1902	1500.00
Piano, Nickelodeon, O-Type Rolls, Xylophone, Drums, Cymbal, Mandolin	7500.00
Piano, Peters Webb & Co., Grand, Rosewood, Octagon Legs, Square, 1866	2000.00
Piano, Player, Beckwith, 1920	4500.00
Piano, Player, Behr Brothers, Mahogany Case	600.00
Piano, Player, Bush & Gertz	650.00
Piano, Player, Cable, 1919	4500.00
Piano, Player, Cable, Nelson, Recordo, Upright	6500.00
Piano, Player, Chapell, Grand, 88 Note, Oak Art Case, 926, 7 Ft.	6500.00
Piano, Player, Chickering, Ampico, Grand, 1923	3500.00
Piano, Player, Coin-Operated, O-Roll, Restored	4000.00
Piano, Player, Dayton Auto Style, Tiger Oak, Refinished	4114.00
Piano, Player, Griggs, Oak Case, 850 Rolls	3500.00

Piano, Player, Grinnell Bros., Bench, Oak 1850.00
Piano, Player, Koehler & Campbell, 88 Keys, Cantonese Red 5500.00
Piano, Player, Strich Zeidler, Early 1900s 2950.00
Piano, Player, Welte 2500.00
Piano, Player, Welte Farrand, Upright 7000.00
Piano, Red Welte, Cabinet Style, Oak 4000.00
Piano, Reproducing, Chickering, Ampico Grand, Model A, 50 Rolls, 6 Ft. 6900.00
Piano, Reproducing, Chickering, Grand, Model A, 6 Ft.6 In. 7900.00
Piano, Reproducing, Mason & Hamlin, 200 Tapes, Walnut, 5 Ft.8 In. 7000.00
Piano, Reproducing, Stroud Aeolian, G.E.Motor, Walnut, 1926 .... 4600.00
Piano, Reproducing, Weber, Duo–Art, Player Grand, 1925, 5 Ft.9 In. 9500.00
Piano, Ryder & Talman, No.15 .... 8800.00
Piano, Seeburg, Upright Grand, Model XP, Coin–Operated 2500.00
Piano, Steinway, Duo–Art, Upright 9950.00
Piano, Story & Clark, Upright 2000.00
Piano, Stroud Duo–Art, Grand, Tubed Sides 3000.00
Piano, Stroud Duo–Art, Upright 800.00
Piano, Weber, Duo–Art, William & Mary, Art Case, Inlaid Panels 5500.00
Piano, Welte, Cabinet Style, Oak 2900.00
Piano, William Knabe, Grand, Ebonized, 60 In. 4500.00
Piano, Wm.Knabe, Baby Grand, Mahogany, Alligatored, Stool, 54 X 61 In. 1150.00
Pianola, Player, Steck, Baby Grand, Electrified, 100 Rolls, 1911 .... 6500.00
Pianotainer, Fox 5000.00
Pitch Pipe, Wm.Kratt, Ukulele, Box 8.00
Polyphone, Table Model, Six 16 1/2–In. Discs 2000.00
Stringed Instrument, Gourd With Carved Wood, Lacquered, Ivory Trim 127.50
Symphonium, Litho Scene Lid, 11 7/8 In. Metal Disc, 1900s 1500.00
Tambourine, Salvation Army 30.00
Trombone, King, Case 50.00
Trumpet, Barclay, Czechosolvakia, Case 195.00
Trumpet, Ludwig, Nickel, Wooden Case 195.00
Ukelin, C.1920 .... 85.00
Ukulele, 4 Strings 70.00
Vase, Hourglass Shape, Light Blue On Blue, 8 In. 35.00
Violin, Ruggeri, Francesco, Wooden Case, Bow Needs Hair, Needs Strings 100.00
Violin, Salvadore De Durro, Label, Case 200.00
Xylophone, J.C.Deagan Co., Chicago, Dated 1916 .... 650.00
Zither, Mahogany, Radio Mandolin Guitar Harp, Paper Label, 21 In. 22.50

The mustache cup was popular from 1850 to 1900 when the large, flowing mustache was in style. A ledge of china or silver held the hair out of the liquid in the cup. This kept the mustache tidy and also kept the mustache wax from melting. Left–handed mustache cups are rare but are being reproduced.

MUSTACHE CUP, Blue & White, 3 In. ....*Illus*   25.00
 Elegant Lady, Flower Transfer, Saucer, Large 20.00
 Fat Man's Face, I Am Not Greedy But I Like A Lot 80.00
 Indian Chief, American Flag, Footed, Eagle Mark, 4 In. 6.00
 Left–Handed, Multicolor Floral Spray, Scrolled Base, Handle 40.00
 Saucer, Beaded Rim, Eureka Silver Co., Dated 1901 .... 115.00
 Saucer, Bright Cut, Beading On Saucer Rim, Silver Plate, 1901 .... 125.00
 Scene, Race of The Century, 4 In. 38.00

MZ Austria
"MZ Austria" is the wording on a mark used by Moritz Zdekauer on porcelains made at his works from about 1900. The firm worked in the town of Alt–Rohlau, Austria. The pieces were decorated with lavish floral patterns and overglaze gold decoration. Full sets of dishes were made as well as vases, toilet sets, and other wares.

MZ AUSTRIA, Bowl, Art Nouveau Stylized Design, 10 In. 35.00
 Celery, 4 Portraits, 10 1/2 In. 100.00
 Plate, Flowers & Berries, 8 In. 17.50
 Plate, Pink & Green Roses, Vines, Round, 12 In. 34.00

Nailsea glass was made in the Bristol district in England from 1788 to 1873. It was made by many different factories, not just the Nailsea Glass House. Many pieces were made with loopings of either white or colored glass as decoration.

NAILSEA, Bell, Large	285.00
Bowl, White Loopings On Citron Ground, 4 1/4 In.	95.00
Cup, Cordial	32.50
Flask, Blue, Cranberry Looping, White Casing, 9 In.	185.00
Flask, Blue, White Looping, Interior Red Flashing From Pink, 7 In.	175.00
Flask, Clear, Cobalt Blue, 1 Pt.	150.00
Flask, Cobalt Blue, White Looping, 6 7/8 In.	170.00
Flask, Custard Blue, Pink Looping, Vertical Ribs, 6 3/4 In.	185.00
Flask, White Looping, Pigeon Blood To Cranberry, 7 3/4 In.	175.00
Flask, White Looping, White, Clear	80.00
Jar, Sweetmeat, Silver Plated Fittings, Spoon, Red Loopings, 4 In.	265.00
Lamp, Fairy, Clarke Base, Cranberry & White, 5 In.	190.00
Lamp, Fairy, Ruffled Base, Clarke Holder, Blue & White, 6 In.	485.00
Perfume Bottle, Silver Collar, Repousse Top, 1838, 5 1/2 In.	395.00
Pipe, Blown Glass, White Looping, 24 In.	200.00
Pipe, Cobalt Blue, Blown Glass, 18 In.	200.00
Pipe, Cranberry, Blue, White Looping, 17 In.	200.00
Pipe, Pale Yellow Opalescent, Applied Yellow Lip On Bowl, 16 In.	165.00
Spittoon, Art Glass	265.00

NAKARA

Nakara is a trade name for a white glassware made about 1900 by the C. F. Monroe Company of Meriden, Connecticut. It was decorated in pastel colors. The glass was very similar to another glass made by the company called "Wave Crest." The company closed in 1916. Boxes for use on a dressing table are the most commonly found Nakara pieces. The mark is not found on every piece.

NAKARA, Ashtray, Dotted Swags, Flowers, Ormolu Collar, 4 1/2 In.	295.00
Bowl, Crown Mold, Hand Painted Roses, 8 1/2 In.	850.00
Box, 2 Cupids, Green, 4 In.	275.00
Box, Bishop's Hat, Avocado Green, Pink Flowers, 9 1/2 In.	750.00
Box, Bishop's Hat, Florals, White Beading, Footed, Blue, 6 3/4 In.	850.00
Box, Cherubs On Cover, Green, Pink Tones, 4 In.	295.00
Box, Dotted Flowers On Cover, Allover Dotting, Hexagonal	275.00
Box, Dresser, Blue & Pink Floral, Rust Brown, C.F.Monroe, 4 3/4 In.	350.00
Box, Dresser, Children Playing Adults, C.F.Monroe, Square, 4 In.	350.00
Box, Hand Painted Florals, Brass Ormolu, Pink & Green, 4 1/2 In.	525.00
Box, Hinged Lid, Queen Louise, Blue, 4 1/2 In.	475.00
Box, Jewel, Cupids Carved On Lid, Lined, 2 1/4 X 3 3/4 In.	235.00
Box, Mirror In Hinged Cover, Blue Floral, Marked	365.00
Box, Petal Flowers, Pink Centers, Lined, 4 1/2 X 6 1/4 In.	950.00
Box, Powder, Portrait Cover, Marked	875.00
Box, Ring, Blue, Pink Flowers	395.00
Card Receiver, Hand Painted Flowers, Brass Rim, 4 1/2 In.	225.00
Cigarette Holder, Portrait, Pedestal On Ashtray, Metal Bottom	750.00
Dish, Trinket, Handle, 4 In.	175.00
Humidor, Cigar, Indian, Scene	850.00
Humidor, Indian, Full Feather Bonnet, Brass Lid, Marked, 7 3/4 In.	500.00
Tray, Ring, Pink Apple Blossom, White Dotting, Marked, 2 3/4 In.	175.00
Vase, Nosegay of Raised Dots, Gilt Metal Base, Marked, 14 In.	785.00
Vase, White Enameled Dots Outline Scrolls, Flowers, 8 3/4 In.	405.00

Nanking is a type of blue–and–white porcelain made in Canton, China, since the late eighteenth century. It is very similar to Canton, which is listed under its own name in this book. Both Nanking and Canton are part of a larger group now called "Chinese Export" porcelain. Nanking has a spear–and–post border and may have gold decoration.

NANKING, Bowl, Orange Peel Glaze, 1 5/8 X 10 In.	275.00

Platter, Warming, Fruit Finial On Cover, 7 1/2 X 18 X 13 In. 2000.00

 Napkin rings were in fashion from 1869 to about 1900. They were made of silver, porcelain, wood, and other materials. They are still being made today. The most popular rings with collectors are the figural napkin rings of silver plate. Small, realistic figures were made to hold the ring. Good and poor reproductions of the more expensive rings are now being made and collectors must be very careful, especially when buying any of the Kate Greenaway rings.

NAPKIN RING, Cut Glass, Hobstars, Strawberry Diamond, Fans 80.00
Figural, 2 Turtles Under Ring, Meriden 125.00
Figural, Art Deco Man, From Waist Up, Top Hat, Cape, Noritake 15.00
Figural, Baby By Ring, Derby 125.00
Figural, Baker, Tufts 135.00
Figural, Barrel, Branches, Leaves, Silver Plate 45.00
Figural, Barrel, Cupid Each End, Meriden 225.00
Figural, Baseball Player, Bat & Ball, Silver Plate, Rogers 230.00
Figural, Bear, Meriden 125.00
Figural, Bird On Top of Ring, Barking Dog, Reed & Barton 125.00
Figural, Boy On Turtle With Umbrella, Pairpoint 165.00
Figural, Boy Removing Socks, Derby 185.00
Figural, Boy Wearing Coat, Carrying Books 320.00
Figural, Boy's Head, Ceramic 18.00
Figural, Boy, Drum 230.00
Figural, Cherub On Ring Leashed To Swan, Silver Plated 225.00
Figural, Cherub With Spear, Riding Dolphin, Meriden 245.00
Figural, Child Riding Turtle, Silver Plate 125.00
Figural, Dog Pulling Sled, Silver, Meriden 125.00
Figural, Dolphins, Holding Ring With Tail 135.00
Figural, Draped Girl, Seated, Leaning On Ring 275.00
Figural, Eagle, Holding Ring 80.00
Figural, Eagles Each Side, Meriden 85.00
Figural, Elk, Antlers, Pulling Ring On Wheels, Silver Plate 250.00
Figural, Fans Support Ring, Meriden 95.00
Figural, Girls, Climbing Ladder 400.00
Figural, Half Boy, Half Fish, Rogers & Smith 235.00
Figural, Horse, Pulling Ring, Wheels Revolve 295.00
Figural, Kewpie, Silver Plate 125.00
Figural, Kitten Pulling Cart, Wheels Revolve, Sterling 275.00
Figural, Lion Stands With Paws On Ring, 3 In. 250.00
Figural, Lion, Ring Back 120.00
Figural, On Sheet of Music, Violin Against Ring, Silver Plate 300.00
Figural, Oriental Man, Sterling Silver 225.00
Figural, Parrot On Perch, Tufts 125.00
Figural, Peacock Roosting On Top, Meriden 175.00
Figural, Prancing Horse Pulling Cart, Silver Plate 295.00
Figural, Sailors, Rogers 225.00
Figural, Seated Cupid, Pairpoint 120.00
Figural, Squirrel & Bird, Seated Beside Ring 260.00
Figural, Squirrel, Silver 95.00
Figural, Teddy Bear, Sitting, Ceramic 22.00
Figural, Triangle With Wishbone Each Side, Meriden 90.00
Figural, Viking Standing Beside Ring, Meriden 125.00
Figural, Winged Cherub With Horn, Ring On Base, Silver Plate 150.00
Figural, Winged Cupid, On Head of Dolphin, Silver Plate 180.00
Goodwill Soap, For Family Use, Litho Paper, 2 In. 10.00
Silver, Cartouche, NM Script, N & H, England, 1893, 1 3/4 In., Pr. 90.00

NASH   Nash glass was made in Corona, New York, after 1919 by Arthur Nash and his sons. He worked at the Webb factory in England and for the Tiffany Glassworks in the United States.

NASH, Goblet, Chintz, 8 In. 50.00
Mustard, Lantern Shape 38.00
Parfait, Phantom Luster, Impressed Design, 6 1/2 In. 125.00

Plate, Chintz, 6 1/4 In. 18.00
Vase, Chintz, Allover Alternating Green & Blue Stripes, Signed, 11 In. 325.00
Vase, Chintz, Blue & Green Stripes, Flare–Out Top, 10 In. 300.00

Nautical antiques are listed in this section. Any of the many objects that were made or used by the seafaring trade, including ship parts, models, and tools, are included. Other pieces may be found listed under Scrimshaw.

NAUTICAL, Ashtray, Battleship, USS Guam, Silver Plate, Engraved, Switzerland 30.00
Ashtray, Pacific Far East Lines 65.00
Basket, Sewing, Nantucket, Cover, Handle 1100.00
Bill of Lading, Philadelphia & Southern Mail Steamship Co., 1870 .... 25.00
Booklet, Queen Mary, Souvenir, 1936 .... 11.00
Buoy, Marker, Wooden, Weathered White Paint, Stripes, 34 1/2 In. 25.00
Cabinet, HMS Canopus, 4 Drawers, Teak, 1897, 30 X 46 In. 1250.00
Card, Playing, Steamboat 999, USPCC, 1915, Steamboat Joker 38.00
Chandelier, 13 Lamps, 3 Levels, For Canal Boat, Tin, 25 In. 750.00
Chest, Sewing, Pine, Fall Front, 4 Drawers, Painted, 19th Century 3250.00
Chronometer, Hamilton, Key, Brass & Mahogany, 7 1/2 X 7 1/2 In. 1000.00
Chronometer, Parkinson & Frodsham, London, Rosewood Case, 1801 .... 1700.00
Clock, Light–Up, Evinrude 150.00
Compass, Mariner's, Green & Red 495.00
Compass, Ship's, Star, Brass, Dovetailed Wooden Box, Sliding Lid 50.00
Compass, U.S. Army, Brass, Dated 1918 .... 85.00
Compass, Wet Ship, Box 253.00
Cup & Saucer, Delta Steamship Co., Demitasse 65.00
Cup, Bouillon, American Mail Line 37.50
Desk, Table, Slant Lid, Wood, Scrimshaw, Abalone, 1850, 20 X 19 In. 3100.00
Diorama, American Whaler, Charles W. Morgan, Whale, 1860–70, 21 In. 7000.00
Diving Suit, Bronze Helmet, Gloves, Boston Marine Salv., 1880–95 .... 1500.00
Doorstop, HMS Hercules, Hercules Figure, 11 In. 245.00
Figurehead, Maiden Bust, Pensive, Painted Pine, C.1850, 11 In. 8800.00
Headlight, Oceanic II, Pair 400.00
Horn, Tugboat, Brass 300.00
Jar, Pickled Lime, S.S.Pierce, Label, Cork, 1 Gal. 45.00
Knife, Pocket, S.S.Washington 47.00
Lamp, Dietz, Red Lens, Wire Bail, Black Paint, 13 In. 65.00
Lamp, Hanging, Gimbal 950.00
Lamp, Spot, Brass, C.1910 .... 150.00
Lantern, Boat Signal 15.00
Lantern, Gillett & Forest, Electrified, Brass Trim, 25 In., Pair 300.00
Lantern, Hanging, Kerosene, Blown Globe, Brass, Copper, 15 1/2 In. 175.00
Lantern, Oil, Passageway, Davey & Co., London, 13 3/4 In., Pair 350.00
Menu, Imprinted On Place Mat, U.S.S.Wyoming, Thanksgiving 10.00
Mirror, Paperweight, Delta Line, Sailing Schedule, 3 1/2 In. Diam. 20.00
Model, 3–Master, 25 X 37 In. 350.00
Model, American Square Rigger, Cotton Sails, 30 X 40 In. 695.00
Model, Half–Hull, Hoope 3338 Tons, Painted, On Plaque 193.00
Model, Half–Hull, Virginia, Steam, Boxwood, Bath Iron Works, 1899 .... 2420.00
Model, Sailboat, 1 Cloth Masts, Painted, Varnished Deck, 29 In. 450.00
Model, Schooner, Blue Nose, Wooden Cradle, 35 X 38 In. 550.00
Model, Steamship, Wire & String Rigging, Canada, C.1930, 28 In. 650.00
Model, Stern–Wheeler, Letters U.S.A. 225.00
Model, U.S.Frigate, President, French Bone, 1799–1817, 24 In. 8000.00
Model, Victoria's Coronation, Hand Carved, Case, 23 X 34 In. 550.00
Model, Whale Boat, Fully Rigged, Glass Case, 32 In. 3700.00
Model, Whale Boat, Planked, Glass Case, Robert Boyle, 24 In. 3100.00
Pass, Vancouver Transportation Co., 1911 .... 20.00
Plate, Georgian Bay Steamboat, Boat Center, Great Lakes Scene 35.00
Postcard, Queen Mary, Churchman's Cigarettes, 1936, 50 Piece 125.00
Postcard, Red Star Line, Unused, Dated 1898 .... 35.00
Postcard, Ships of The World, Reddings Tea Co., 1964, 48 Piece 15.00
Quadrant, Amsterdam, 18th Century, Parts Missing 1750.00
Schedule, U.S.Lines Sailing, 1963 .... 5.00

Sextant, Brass, England	700.00
Sextant, Fitted Mahogany Case, Shepard, London, 10 X 11 1/2 In.	250.00
Sextant, Ivory, Ebony Trim, Box	660.00
Ship's Figurehead, Young Maiden, Wavy Hair, Yellow Ribbon, 11 In.	8800.00
Shot Glass, Matson Lines	6.00
Sign, Cunard Passener Fleet, 12 Ships, Names, 24 X 36 In.	115.00
Sign, Scandinavian–American Lines, Self–Framed Tin, 22 X 30 In.	195.00
Soup Cup, Logo Eastern Steamship Lines, Mayer China	117.50
Spoon, Battleship Indiana, Silver Plated, Demitasse	14.00
Spoon, Steamer Princess Victoria, Enameled, Canadian Prov. Shield	65.00
Swift, Double, On Whalebone Stand, 20 1/2 In.	2600.00
Tea Set, Cunard Lines, Gold, Myott, England, Art Deco, Square, 3 Pc.	50.00
Telescope, 3 Sections, Josiah Chadbourne, Maine, Brass, 40 In.	200.00
Telescope, Floor Tripod, T. Mason, Dublin	2100.00
Telescope, L. Casella, London, Tracking Rods, Wooden Case	3850.00
Tip Tray, Cleveland & Buffalo Line, Seeandbee, 1910, 5 X 6 1/2 In.	50.00
Toothpick, R.M.S.Saxonia, Sterling Silver & Gold	85.00
Valentine, Sailor's, Octagonal Frame, Modern Version, 9 In.	2500.00
Watch, Zenith, 8–Day, Mahogany & Brass, 4 3/4 X 4 3/4 In.	300.00
Wheel, Ship's, 1903, 36 In.	1900.00
Whistle, Boatswain's, Silver, Handwoven Cord	25.00
Whistle, Bosun's, Spherical Terminal, R.& W. Wilson, C.1840	1650.00
Whistle, Lunkenheimer, Brass, 30 X 10 In.	775.00
Whistle, Riverboat, Lunkenheimer, 3–Tiered Manifold, 3 Sizes	1350.00

Small ivory, wood, metal, or porcelain pieces were used as buttons on the end of the cord that held a Japanese money pouch. These were called "netsuke." The earliest date from the sixteenth century. Many are miniature, carved works of art.

NETSUKE, Ivory, 2 Fish, In Woven Reed Basket	110.00
Ivory, Animal, Recumbent, Scratching Nose, Shishi	1320.00
Ivory, Bamboo, Lotus & Peonies, Round	550.00
Ivory, Boar, Sleeping, Masatsugu	577.00
Ivory, Cat, Curled Around Basket, Rat, Signed Meigyokusai	440.00
Ivory, Deer, Lying On Ground, Looking Over Shoulder	275.00
Ivory, Dragon, Looking Straight Ahead, Signed Shosai	660.00
Ivory, Flower, 19th Century, Round	192.50
Ivory, Game Hen	60.00
Ivory, Kirin, Seated On Haunches, Head Turned	1320.00
Ivory, Man, Escaping From Breached Sake Jar, 19th Century	650.00
Ivory, Man, Hiding Baby Under Shell	120.00
Ivory, Man, Wide Brimmed Hat, Playing Horn	400.00
Ivory, Monkey, Playing Drums, Pop–Out Eyes, Signed, C.1860, 1 1/2 In.	60.00
Ivory, Mouse, 1 1/4 In.	65.00
Ivory, Nobleman, Sitting On Dragon, Signed, Round	275.00
Ivory, Octopus & Man, Holding Each Other, 19th Century, Kosai	770.00
Ivory, Puppies, Chewing Cord of Pull Toy, Signed Kangyoku	935.00
Ivory, Puppy, Lying On Fan, Inlaid Eyes	825.00
Ivory, Rabbit, Seated, Scratching Head, Signed Yasufusa	680.00
Ivory, Rat, Crawling, Tail Curled, Signed, Tomokazu	495.00
Ivory, Snake, Coiled, Signed Masayuki	357.00
Ivory, Snake, Coiled, Signed Meigyokusai	605.00
Ivory, Stylized Bird, Glass Eyes	275.00
Ivory, Theater Figure, Rotating Mask	150.00
Ivory, Thunder God, Mother–of–Pearl Hailstones, Sansui, Round	495.00
Ivory, Turtle, Lamb On Back, 1 3/4 In.	75.00
Ivory, Water Buffalo	110.00
Ivory, Zodiac, Animal Heads, Signed	220.00
Ivory, Zodiac, Signed Meigyokusai	715.00
Jade, Monk	250.00
Pottery, Face	195.00
Wood, Monk	20.00
Wood, Toad, Young On Back, Signed	275.00
Wood, Turtle, Legs & Tail Tucked In	330.00

New Hall Porcelain Manufactory was started at Newhall, Shelton, Staffordshire, England, in 1782. Simple decorated wares were made. Between 1810 and 1825, the factory made a glassy bone porcelain sometimes marked with the factory name. Do not confuse New Hall porcelain with the pieces made by the New Hall Pottery Company, Ltd., a twentieth–century firm.

NEW HALL, Box, Cigarette, Cover, Mr. Pecksniff, 4 1/2 X 4 In. 25.00

The New Martinsville Glass Manufacturing Company was established in 1901 in New Martinsville, West Virginia. It was bought and renamed the Viking Glass Company in 1944 and is still producing fine glasswares.

NEW MARTINSVILLE, Bonbon, Radiance, Amber, 6 In.	8.00
Bookends, Dove, Frosted, Solid, 6 In.	68.00
Bookends, Nautilus, Shell	30.00
Bookends, Sailing Ship .... 85.00 To 95.00	
Bowl, Florentine, Flared, 12 In.	15.00
Bride's Bowl, Caramel, Cinnamon & Orange, Crimped, 11 In.	115.00
Bride's Bowl, Green, Rose, Pleated Edge, 2 Rows Hobnails	95.00
Candlestick, Florentine, 5 In.	9.00
Candlestick, Moondrops, Ruffled, Amber, 3 In., Pair	20.00
Candlestick, Squirrel	22.00
Celery, Janice, 11 In.	12.50
Cologne, Amber, Fan Stopper, Lady, Cupid, Floral, 8 In.	35.00
Console Set, Sterling Silver Deposit	60.00
Console Set, Swan Bowl & Pair of Candlesticks, Amber	55.00
Decanter, Michael, Amber, Clear, V Beehive Stopper	15.00
Dish, Swan, Prelude, Crystal, 5 In.	25.00
Dish, Swan, Red, Oval, Cystal Neck & Head, 8 X 4 1/4 In.	26.00
Figurine, Bear, Baby	45.00
Figurine, Bear, Black, With Wheelbarrow, 2 Piece	195.00
Figurine, Bear, Mama .... 135.00 To 175.00	
Figurine, Chick, Baby	28.00
Figurine, Eagle	55.00
Figurine, Elephant, Pair	85.00
Figurine, Gazelle, Pair	165.00
Figurine, German Shepherd	39.00
Figurine, Horse, Rearing, Head Up, 6 1/2 X 8 1/4 In.	50.00
Figurine, Pelican, Lavender Tint, 8 In.	50.00
Figurine, Rooster, Light Purple	35.00
Figurine, Russian Wolfhound	78.00
Figurine, Seal, Crystal, 7 1/2 In.	37.00
Figurine, Seal, With Ball, Pair	110.00
Figurine, Squirrel .... 36.00 To 50.00	
Figurine, Swan, Crystal, 5 In.	10.00
Figurine, Tiger, Head Down, 8 1/2 X 5 1/4 In.	195.00
Figurine, Wolfhound, 9 1/4 X 7 In.	50.00
Mayonnaise Set, Florentine	4.00
Mustard, Janice, Blue, Cover	30.00
Pitcher, Oscar, Amber	15.00
Punch Cup, Radiance, Ice Blue	11.00
Relish, Prelude, 4 Sections	12.00
Relish, Radiance, 3 Sections, Amber, 8 In.	12.00
Saucer, Amber	1.00
Seal, With Candle, Small, Pair	120.00
Sugar & Creamer, Moondrops, Miniature	27.00
Sugar & Creamer, Tray, Radiance, Etched Crystal	30.00
Sugar, Amber	5.00
Sugar, Meadow Wreath	7.00
Toothpick, Carnation	37.00
Torte Plate, Prelude, 18 In.	35.00
Tumbler, Hairpin, Footed, Amethyst, 4 3/4 In.	14.00
Tumbler, Moondrops, Cobalt Blue, 9 Oz.	13.00

Newcomb, Jar, Lemons, Foliage Design,
Yellow, Blue, Green, 6 In.

Newcomb, Mug, Wobbly, Free–Form
Swirl Design, 4 3/4 In.

Newcomb, Tile, Joseph Meyer At Potter's
Wheel, Leona Nicholson

Newcomb, Vases, Trees, Spanish Moss,
1922, 12 In.

Tumbler, Moondrops, Handle, 2 Oz.	7.00
Vase, Peg, Janice, Violet	18.00
Whiskey Set, Radiance, Decanter & 6 Shot Glasses	130.00

Newcomb Pottery was founded by Ellsworth and William Woodward at Sophie Newcomb College, New Orleans, Louisiana, in 1896. The work continued through the 1940s. Pieces of this art pottery are marked with the printed letters "NC" and often have the incised initials of the artist as well. Most pieces have a matte glaze and incised decoration.

NEWCOMB, Candlestick, Black Gunmetal Glaze, C.1920, 10 1/4 In.	357.50
Cup, 3 Panels, College Seal, Medallion of Freesias, Phi Beta Seal	1320.00
Ink Pot, Incised, Marie LeBlanc, C.1930	60.00
Jar, Lemons, Foliage Design, Yellow, Blue, Green, 6 In. ....*Illus*	3190.00
Mug, Incised Pinecone, Marked B.M., 1908, 4 3/4 In.	175.00

Mug, Stylized Design, Gertrude R. Smith, C.1900 .... 1320.00
Mug, Stylized Design, High Glaze, Marie LeBlanc, 1902, 6 1/2 In. 1500.00
Mug, Wobbly, Free–Form Swirl Design, 4 3/4 In. ....*Illus* 5500.00
Pitcher, Geometric Design, Sadie Irvine, 1927, 8 1/4 In. 1100.00
Plate, Magnolia, Frances Lines Gensler, 1904, 9 1/4 In. 550.00
Plate, Portrait, High Glaze, Marie LeBlanc, 1898, 9 In. 1800.00
Tea Set, Alma Mason, Dated 1911, 7 Piece 5610.00
Teapot, Incised Floral Desigh, Ada Lonnegan, 1906 .... 2090.00
Tile, Joseph Meyer At Potter's Wheel, Leona Nicholson ....*Illus* 3960.00
Tile, Metallic Glaze, Round, May Dunn, 1984, 3 1/2 In. 140.00
Vase, Blue High Glaze, Signed, 3 1/4 In. 295.00
Vase, Blue, Mossy Trees, Moon, Signed A.F.Simpson, 5 In. 800.00
Vase, Cypress Trees, Spanish Moss & Moon, H.Bailey, 1933, 6 3/4 In. 1210.00
Vase, Cypress Trees, Spanish Moss, 1922, 12 In. ....*Illus* 2200.00
Vase, Elephant Ears, Freesia, Georgia B.Drennan, 1903, 6 1/4 In. 4840.00
Vase, Evening Sky, Oaks, Spanish Moss, Sadie Irvine, 1928, 5 1/4 In. 1485.00
Vase, Floral, 3 1/2 In. 595.00
Vase, Floral, Sadie Irvine, Label, 1927, 7 In. 990.00
Vase, Green Over Pale Green, Lavender, Rose, Bulbous, Dimples, 4 In. 200.00
Vase, Incised Design, Handles, Anna Frances Simpson, 1907, 4 In. 1300.00
Vase, Incised Oaks, Spanish Moss, A.F.Simpson, 1929, 8 1/2 In. 1760.00
Vase, Live Oaks, Spanish Moss, Moon, Aurelia Arbo, C.1935, 8 In. 1100.00
Vase, Marked 149 In Script, C.1920, 9 In. 575.00
Vase, Matte Brown, 3 In., Pair 185.00
Vase, Oak Tree, Spanish Moss, Moon, 1922, 12 3/4 In. ....*Illus* 4180.00
Vase, Oak Trees, Spanish Moss, Moon, Anna F.Simpson, 1930, 6 3/4 In. 550.00
Vase, Oak Trees, Spanish Moss, Moon, Sadie Irvine, 1923, 7 3/8 In. 1300.00
Vase, Oak Trees, Spanish Moss, Moon, Sadie Irvine, 1930, 5 1/2 In. 1200.00
Vase, Pink Flowers At Top, Blue Matte, Signed Irvine, 7 In. 850.00
Vase, Stylized Irises, Sadie Irvine, 1921, 6 In. 1045.00

ᴺᴵᴸᴼᴬᴷ   Niloak Pottery (Kaolin spelled backward) was made at the Hyten
              Brothers Pottery in Benton, Arkansas, between 1909 and 1946.
              Although the factory did make cast and molded wares, collectors
              are most interested in the marbelized art pottery line made of
              colored swirls of clay. It was called "Mission Ware."

NILOAK, Ashtray, Marbelized, 4 In. 75.00
Bowl, Mission Ware, Marbelized, 3 X 6 In. 45.00
Candleholder, Marbelized, Finger Hole, 5 In. 125.00
Candletick, Marbelized, 8 In., Pair 225.00
Elephant, Black 20.00
Ewer, Wing & Star, Pink, Green, Marked, 10 1/4 In. 18.00
Figurine, Elephant On Tub, Blue 18.00
Jar, Strawberry, Blue, 4 1/2 In. 12.00
Lamp, Marbelized, Bulbous, 7 In. 295.00
Pitcher, Green 18.00
Planter, Camel, 1930s, 3 X 6 In. 22.50
Planter, Deer, Figural, Blue 35.00
Planter, Dutch Shoe, Rose, Green Drip 15.00
Planter, Elephant On Drum, Light Blue 9.00
Planter, Shoe, Pink, Green, 5 In. 8.00
Planter, Window Box, Rose 20.00
Sugar & Creamer, Red Matte 24.00
Vase, Blue, Melon Rib, Wing Side Handles, Flared, Bulbous, 6 X 5 In. 10.00
Vase, Marbelized, Blue, Impressed Mark, 5 1/4 X 3 3/8 In. 60.00
Vase, Marbelized, Brown, Beige, Cream, 8 1/2 In. 75.00
Vase, Marbelized, Browns & Blues, Signed & Labeled, 5 1/2 In. 65.00
Vase, Marbelized, C.1912, 4 1/2 In. 45.00
Vase, Marbelized, Cylindrical, Signed, 10 In. 150.00
Vase, Marbelized, Dark Brown, Blues, Rust, Signed, 8 In. 95.00
Vase, Marbelized, Flared Lip, 4 1/2 In. 55.00
Vase, Marbelized, Flared Rim, Pinched Neck, 6 In. 32.00
Vase, Marbelized, Layers, Bulbous Bottom, 7 In. 45.00

Nippon–marked porcelain was made in Japan from 1891 to 1921. "Nippon" is the Japanese word for "Japan." A few firms continued to use the word "Nippon" on ceramics after 1921 as a part of the company name more than as an identification of the country of origin. More pieces marked Nippon will be found in the Dragonware, Moriage, and Noritake sections.

NIPPON, Ashtray, Desert Scene, 4 1/2 In.	45.00
Ashtray, Dog In Relief, Brown	12.00
Ashtray, Willow, Pagoda Design, Spittoon Style, Kyoto Hotel, Wreath	15.00
Asparagus Set, Blue Borders, Tray & 4 Plates, Green Mark, 12 X 7 In.	350.00
Bell, Roses, Gold Beading, Cobalt Blue	135.00
Berry Bowl, Pink Floral, Gold, Pierced, 3 Footed	25.00
Bowl, Allover Roses, Gold Border, 6 1/2 In.	45.00
Bowl, Beach Scene, House, Trees, Hand Painted, Signed, 7 1/2 In.	25.00
Bowl, Blown–Out Acorns & Leaves, 7 1/2 In.	95.00 To 115.00
Bowl, Child's, Blown–Out Boy	50.00
Bowl, Floral Center, Gold Border, 10 In.	75.00
Bowl, Flowers, Center Medallion, Open Handles, Green Wreath, 10 In.	88.00
Bowl, House, Lake Scene, Gold, Black, Bisque, Handle, 5 In.	15.00
Bowl, Moriage, Flowers, Rolled Edge	65.00
Bowl, Pink & Green Floral, Gold Beaded Trim, Maple Leaf, 6 1/2 In.	65.00
Bowl, Roses, Scrolled Border, Pink, Scalloped, Melon Ribbed, 10 In.	70.00
Bowl, Ruffled, Cutout Handles, Art Deco Floral Exterior, 7 1/4 In.	75.00
Bowl, Scene, Muted Colors, 3–Footed, Beaded Rim, Marked, 6 In.	22.00
Box, Trinket, Beaded Gold Roses, Pink Bands, Cylindrical, Wreath	50.00
Butter, Cover, Raised Gold, Flowers	55.00
Cake Set, Beach & Ocean Scene, Purple Plovers, 7 Piece	185.00
Cake Set, Green, Rust, Gold, Floral, 7 Piece	75.00
Candy Dish, Roses, Gold Trim, Ring Handle, 6 Lobed, 5 3/4 X 1 1/4 In.	38.00
Celery Set, Butterflies, Pierced Tray, 12 3/4 X 6 In., 7 Piece	58.00
Celery Set, Roses, Scrolls, Beading, Handles, 13–In. Bowl, 6 Salts	105.00
Cheese Dish, Sloping Cover, Cobalt Blue Flowers, Ivory, 8 In.	65.00
Chocolate Pot, Floral, Gold & Silver Deposit	95.00
Chocolate Pot, Gold Beading, Blue Maple Leaf Mark, 10 1/2 In.	180.00
Coffeepot, Allover Yellow Roses	65.00
Cup & Saucer, Azalea	15.00
Cup & Saucer, Chocolate, Alpine Scene, Raised Outlined, Gold Trim	12.00
Cup & Saucer, Flowers, Green Tones	10.00
Cup & Saucer, Pink Flowers, Gold Trim, Pale Lemon Base, Demitasse	12.00
Cup & Saucer, Pink Roses	20.00
Dish, Child's, Clown Suits, Blue Mark	75.00
Dish, Gold Scrolls, Beaded, Raised Outlined, Cream, 7 1/4 X 1 1/2 In.	48.00
Dish, Rose Center, Red, 7 In.	60.00
Doll, Watermelon Mouth, 5 In.	60.00
Dresser Set, Floral Medallion, Gold Filigree, Green, Cover, Square	95.00
Ewer, Horizontal Panels of Roses On Green, Beading, 8 1/2 In.	40.00
Fernery, Swan On Lake, Jewels, Gold Trim, 4 X 6 1/2 In.	145.00
Hair Receiver, Floral, Gold, 3 Long Legs, Rising Sun	30.00
Hair Receiver, Pink Roses, Leaf Swags, Gold Beading, Maple Leaf Mark	60.00
Hair Receiver, Purple Orchids, Pink Posies, Swags, Scrolls	65.00
Hatpin Holder, Border Pattern of Roses, Leaves, Beading, Marked	42.00
Humidor, Egyptian	185.00
Humidor, Enamel Beading, Turquoise Ground, Marked, 6 1/2 In.	65.00
Humidor, Indian In Canoe, Hexagonal	225.00 To 300.00
Humidor, Playing Cards, 7 1/2 In.	395.00
Humidor, Scenic, Signed, 5 1/4 In.	175.00
Humidor, Ships, 7 In.	350.00
Humidor, Yellow, Dark Green Trees, Round	225.00
Ice Cream Set, Raised Enameling, 5 Piece	495.00
Ladle, Mayonnaise, Floral Band, Ivory Handle, Gold Beading, Marked	113.00
Lemonade Set, Roses, Gold, 4 Mugs, 5 Piece	350.00
Mayonnaise Bowl, Bun Feet, Hand Painted Beaded Flowers	25.00
Mustard, Airplane, Marked	110.00

Mustard, Attached Plate, Spoon, Floral On White, Gold Trim 45.00
Pitcher, Gold & Enamel Flowers, Geometric, Oriental Mark, 7 3/4 In. 95.00
Pitcher, Gold Brocade, Rose Floral, 9 1/2 In. 125.00
Pitcher, Roses, Gold, Cover, Blue Mark, 4 In. 80.00
Plaque, Black Man, Playing Banjo, Flower Field, 7 1/2 In. 200.00
Plaque, Buffalo Scene, Marked 399.00
Plaque, Dutchman, Dogs, Boats, Maroon Diaper Border, 9 1/2 In. 225.00
Plaque, House, Autumnal Colors, 9 In. 115.00
Plaque, Moose, 7 3/4 In. 125.00
Plaque, Moriage Trees, 10 In. 115.00
Plaque, Sailboat, Sunset, Marked, 8 In. 95.00
Plaque, Scenic, Moriage Apple Tree, 9 In. 155.00
Plaque, Thatched Roof Cottage, Chickens, 7 3/4 In. 165.00
Plate, Azalea, 7 3/4 In. 10.00
Plate, Commemorative, Capitol At Washington, D.C., 7 3/4 In. 115.00
Plate, Floral, Gold Jewels, Scrolls, Center Medallion, 9 3/4 In. 65.00
Plate, Flying Geese, Jeweled, 10 In. 135.00
Plate, Gold Jewels, Scrolls, Floral Medallion, Marked, 9 3/4 In. 65.00
Plate, Sailboat, Trees, Pierced Handle, Green Mark, 5 In. 15.00
Plate, Trees, Meadow Scene, Hand Painted, Marked EE, 8 3/4 In. 22.00
Plate, Violets & Green Leaves, Gold Rim, Wreath Mark, 8 3/4 In. 25.00
Plate, Woodland, 7 1/2 In. 68.00
Powder Jar & Hair Receiver, Hunt Scene, Greek Key Design, Tan Green 87.50
Powder Jar, Flowers On Lid, Geometric Sides, Gold Trim, Marked 85.00
Powder Jar, Red & Yellow Roses, Cover, Footed 30.00
Punch Bowl, Roses, Gold Scrollwork Inside & Out, Aqua Jewels, 2 Pc. 395.00
Punch Set, Hand Painted Grapes, Gold Trim, 11 Cups 1050.00
Relish, Curled-In Edges, Red Flowers, Gold Trim, Boat Shape 28.00
Ring Tree, Gold Hand, Floral, Pink Luster Rim, Green Wreath 48.00
Salt & Pepper, Flying Geese, Turquoise 65.00
Saltshaker, Ginger Jar Shape, 2 Girls, River, 2 3/4 In. 5.00
Saltshaker, Ivory, White, Raised Gold, Bulbous, 3 Footed 12.00
Sherbet, Flowers, Ivory, Copper Holder, Manning Bowman 25.00
Stamp Box, Pink Trim, Gold Flower, Side Slot 40.00
Stein, Woodland, Moriage 150.00
Stickpin Holder, Cobalt Blue, Peach Flowers, Gold Beading 125.00
Stickpin Holder, Roses On Gold Ground, Hat Shape 135.00
Sugar & Creamer, Beading, Gold Trim, Orange Leaves, Green Mark 45.00
Sugar & Creamer, Cover, Polychrome Butterflies, Gold Trim 45.00
Sugar & Creamer, Geometric, Floral, Melon Ribbed, Oriental Mark 45.00
Sugar & Creamer, Pearlized, Beading, Green Wreath 195.00
Sugar Shaker, Roses, Gold Trim 35.00
Sugar, Cover, Butterflies 10.00
Syrup, Underplate, Sailboat On Front & Back 65.00
Table Set, Jeweled Floral Panels, Turquoise, Melon Ribbed, 4 Piece 150.00
Tea Set, Child's, Boy & Girl Silhouette, Pale Yellow, 13 Piece 285.00
Tea Set, Pastel Swan, Lake, Houses, Geometric Gold Border, 11 Piece 200.00
Tea Strainer & Bowl, Hand Painted Flowers, Gold Trim, Torii Mark 75.00
Tea Strainer, Flowers, Gold Trim, Green Mark 70.00
Tea Strainer, Pansies, Gold Beading, 2 Piece 60.00
Teapot & Creamer, Flowers, Gold Tracery, Gaudy Red 235.00
Teapot, Figural, Fat Samurai 135.00
Teapot, Gaudy Cobalt Blue, Red Roses, Gold 185.00
Tile, Scenic, Bluebirds, Trees, Green Wreath Mark 37.50
Tobacco Jar, Water & Swan Scene, Signed 95.00
Toothpick, Blue 35.00
Tray, Dresser, Bisque, Wavy Edge, Roses, Shaded Leaves, Marked 45.00
Tray, Lake, Trees, Building, 12 1/2 X 7 1/4 In. 125.00
Tray, Pin, Gold Handles, Gold Border, 14 Yellow Arches 30.00
Urn, Floral Medallions, Cobalt Blue & Gold, 8 In. 135.00
Urn, Oasis Scene, Melon Ribbed, Bisque Finish, Handles, 9 In. 495.00
Vase, Allover Gold, Turquoise Dots, Hand Painted Roses, 6 3/4 In. 150.00
Vase, Birds, Beaded Ring Handles, Scalloped, Green Mark, 8 1/2 In. 285.00
Vase, Desert Village & River, Female Figurehead On Boat, 8 In. 200.00

Vase, Dimpled, Thistle Pattern, 10 In. 295.00
Vase, Dutch Scene, Oriental Pattern, Green Wreath Mark, 18 In. 525.00
Vase, Floral, Green Mark, 6 In. 85.00
Vase, Gold Beading, Shoulder Handles, Green Wreath, 5 3/8 In. 75.00
Vase, House, Trees, Lake, Mountains, Shades of Brown, Gold, 7 In., Pr. 125.00
Vase, Hunt Scene, Blown–Out Stag & Hounds, 2 Handles, 6 1/2 In. 495.00
Vase, Hunt Scene, Blown–Out Stag & Hounds, 2 Handles, 9 In. 500.00
Vase, Jewels On Gilt Leaves, Trees, Gold Moriage, 8 In. 150.00
Vase, Moriage Applied Dragon, Gray Ground, Green Mark, 4 1/2 In. 88.00
Vase, Moriage, Green Mark, 5 1/4 In. 190.00
Vase, Nile River Scene, 10 1/4 In. 195.00
Vase, Orange Poppies, Blue Trim, Handles, Marked, 11 3/4 In. 225.00
Vase, Palm Trees, Water, 8 1/2 In. 125.00
Vase, Paneled, Indians, Gold Beads, Brown Ground, 9 1/4 In. 110.00
Vase, Raised Pink Magnolia, Moriage Beaded Top, 9 7/8 In. 125.00
Vase, Roses, Lake, Dragon Handles, Hand Painted, 8 In. 185.00
Vase, Ruins Scene, 9 3/4 In. 325.00
Vase, Sailing Ship, Jewels, 6–Sided, Handles, 11 In. 260.00
Vase, Scenic & Floral, Raised Gold Flowers, Wreath Mark, 10 1/2 In. 145.00
Vase, Scenic, 2 Handles, Gold Trim, Green Wreath Mark, 10 In. 195.00
Vase, Tree, Lake Sunset, Olive Handles, Jeweled, Square, 5 3/4 In., Pr. 140.00
Vase, Windmill Scene, Gold Beading, 10 In. 135.00
Vase, Wisteria Cascading, Moriage Streamers, Bisque, FML Mark 155.00

 Nodders, or nodding figures, or pagods, are porcelain figures with heads and hands that are attached to wires. Any slight movement causes the parts to move up and down. They were made in many countries during the eighteenth and nineteenth centuries. A few Art Deco designs are also known. Copies are being made.

NODDER, Ashtray, Fan, Legs Move, 6 In. ....*Illus* 25.00
Ashtray, Smoking Cigar, Man Wearing Derby 50.00
Boy Smoking, On Metal Ashtray, Austrian 47.00
Cat, Sitting, Has Bank & Thermometer On Front 15.00
Chinese Man, Bisque, Germany, 2 1/2 In. 60.00
Dog, Comical, 15 X 8 1/2 In. 125.00
Donkey, Celluloid, Occupied Japan, 6 1/2 X 5 1/2 In., 2 Piece 24.00
Dutch Girl, Papier–Mache, 1940, 5 1/2 In. 18.00
Dutch Girl, Schoenhut 275.00
Hound Dog, Sitting, West Germany 43.00
Hula Dancer, Plaster, Cotton Lei Around Neck, Uke, Thrifco, 6 1/2 In. 28.00
Irish Girl, Bisque, Germany, 3 In. 35.00
Kissing Indians, Brave & Princess, Seated On Bench, Plaster, Japan 35.00

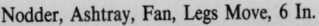

Nodder, Ashtray, Fan, Legs Move, 6 In.

Nodder, Oriental Lady, Bisque, 6 1/2 In.

Lord Plushbottom, Bisque, Germany	135.00
Man, Gilding On White, Blue, 7 In.	190.00
Max, Street Cleaner, Bisque, Sohess, Germany	65.00
Mr.Aily, Bisque, Germany	75.00
Mutt, Germany	85.00
Oakland A's	25.00
Oriental Lady, Bisque, 6 1/2 In. *Illus*	80.00
Skull, Occupied Japan, 3 In.	20.00
Skunk, Black & White Plaster, Red Base, Japan, 5 In.	15.00
Toothpick, Skull, Nodding Jaw, Bisque, 4 In.	275.00
Uncle Walt, Bisque, Germany	120.00
Uneeda Nabisco Boy, Painted Hair	250.00
Winnie Winkle, Bisque, Germany	125.00
Woman, Gilding On White, Blue, 7 In.	190.00

Noritake-marked porcelain was made in Japan after 1904 by Nippon Toki Kaisha. The best-known Noritake pieces are marked with the M in a wreath for the Morimura Brothers, a New York City distributing company. This mark was used until 1941. Another famous Noritake china was made for the Larkin Soap Company from 1916 through the 1930s. This dinnerware, decorated with azaleas, was sold or given away as a premium. There may be some helpful price information in the Nippon category since prices are comparable.

NORITAKE, Ashtray, Egyptian Woman, Art Deco, 5 In.	40.00
Ashtray, Figural, Clown Holding Knee, 5 In.	125.00
Ashtray, Figural, Dog	45.00
Ashtray, Horsehead, Scene, M In Wreath	85.00
Ashtray, Raccoon In Relief	225.00
Ashtray, Woman Golfer, 1920s	145.00
Basket, Florals, Red, Top Hat Shape, Ruffled, Handle, 6 X 4 1/2 In.	58.00
Basket, Pearl Luster Center, Black Border, Handle, Unicorns, 7 In.	38.00
Bonbon, Red Wreath Mark, 5 1/2 In.	6.00
Bouillon Cup, Underplate, Burgundy, Gold Trim	28.00
Bowl, Blown-Out Peanuts, Scalloped, Flowers, Brown Shaded, 7 In.	52.00
Bowl, Leaf Shape, Gold Etched, Magenta Mark, 9 In.	80.00
Bowl, Medallions, Peach Band, 2 Handles, 3 Ball Feet, Green Wreath	35.00
Bowl, Shell, Tree In Meadow, Footed	115.00
Bowl, Swan On Water, 8 In.	30.00
Bowl, Underplate, Water Lily Shape, Pink	45.00
Bowl, Vegetable, Azalea, 9 1/4 In.	50.00
Bowl, Vegetable, Azalea, Oval, 10 1/2 In.	35.00
Bowl, Vegetable, Tree In Meadow, Oval	22.00
Box, Trinket, Bird Finial, Blue Luster, Cover, 5 X 3 1/2 In.	38.00
Bread Plate, Azalea	5.00
Butter Tub, Insert, Azalea	35.00
Butter, Chelsea, 3 Piece	65.00
Butter, Cover, Green, Band of Daisies & Blue Flowers	30.00
Cake Plate, Azalea, Handles, Marked	28.00
Cake Plate, Celtic Pattern, Handles, 10 In.	12.00
Cake Plate, Tree In Meadow, Pierced Handles	16.00 To 20.00
Candlestick, Tobacco Leaf, 9 In.	30.00
Candlestick, Tree In Meadow, Red Wreath, 3 1/2 In., Pair	30.00
Candy Dish, Figural, Swan, Blue & Tan Luster, 5 1/2 X 2 1/2 In.	55.00
Casserole, Azalea, Cover	85.00
Casserole, Azalea, Gold Finial Cover	250.00
Celery & Salt Set, Marigold, Pearl Luster, Red Mark, 7 Piece	75.00
Celery, Tree In Meadow, 12 In.	25.00
Chamberstick, Blue Roses, Black Handles & Trim, 3 1/2 In., Pair	75.00
Cigarette Box, Cover, Figural, Bird, Butterfly, Floral, Red Mark	95.00
Compote, Painted Fruit Interior, Gold Trim, 2 Piece	125.00
Compote, Tree In Meadow	80.00
Condiment Set, Tray, Pelican	75.00

Condiment Set, Tree In Meadow, Loop Handle, Marked 22.00
Cookie Jar, Arab At Campfire, Metal Lid & Handle, 7 In. 175.00
Cracker Jar, Tree In Meadow, Gold Ball, 3–Footed, Green Wreath 125.00
Creamer & Sugar Shaker, Azalea 110.00
Creamer, Midori 10.00
Creamer, Tree In Sunset, Lakeside Scene, Green Wreath, 3 In. 10.00
Cruet, Azalea, Stopper 150.00
Cup & Saucer, Angel D'Amour 21.00
Cup & Saucer, Anniversary 44.00
Cup & Saucer, Autumn Day 15.50
Cup & Saucer, Azalea ....8.00 To 16.00
Cup & Saucer, Blossom Time 20.00
Cup & Saucer, Enchanteur 22.50
Cup & Saucer, Paisley 12.00
Cup & Saucer, Sheridan, Demitasse 35.00
Cup, Black Tango 13.00
Dinner Set, Laureate Pattern, 81 Piece 70.00
Egg Warmer, Handle, Blue Luster, Hand Painted Fruits, Gold Trim 68.00
Eggcup, Azalea ....45.00 To 50.00
Gravy Boat, Attached Underplate, Tree In Meadow 85.00
Gravy Boat, Azalea 35.00
Gravy Boat, Vineyard 15.00
Hair Receiver, Gold & White 75.00
Humidor, Azalea, Deco Shape, Square Top & Lid 115.00
Humidor, Blown–Out Camel & Rider, Large 595.00
Humidor, Blown–Out Dogs, Mottled Orange Ground, Marked 450.00
Humidor, Desert Scene, Exotic Figural Bird On Lid, 6 1/2 In. 225.00
Jam Jar, Underplate, Purple Flowers, Black & Gold Trim 35.00
Luncheon Plate, Azalea 10.00
Luncheon Set, Bold Flowers, Orange Borders, Red M, 20 Piece 55.00
Mayonnaise Set, Azalea, 3 Piece 35.00
Mayonnaise Set, Lakeside Scene, Artist Signed Bowl, 3 Piece 65.00
Mustard, Spoon, Red Mark 36.00
Napkin Ring, Gentleman, Art Deco 25.00
Plaque, Blown–Out Arabian Horses, 10 3/4 In. 750.00
Plate, 4 Action Kewpies, Gold Tirm, 10 In. 110.00
Plate, Anniversary, 9 3/4 In. 41.00
Plate, Apollo, 9 3/4 In. 4.00
Plate, Azalea, 6 1/2 In. 10.00
Plate, Azalea, 7 1/2 In. ....5.00 To 10.00
Plate, Azalea, 8 1/2 In. ....18.00 To 19.00
Plate, Bambury, 9 3/4 In. 21.50
Plate, Blossom Time, 7 1/2 In. 11.00
Plate, Blossom Time, 9 3/4 In. 20.00
Plate, Dresalda, 10 In. 22.00
Plate, Enchanteur, 9 3/4 In. 21.00
Plate, Fair Day, 9 3/4 In. 12.50
Plate, Heather, 7 1/2 In. 11.00
Plate, Hofgarten, 9 3/4 In. 16.00
Plate, Ice Flower, 9 3/4 In. 16.50
Plate, Imperial Garden 24.00
Plate, Roseland, 10 In. 10.00
Plate, Tree In Meadow, Red Wreath, 8 5/8 In. 9.00
Platter, Gold Beaded Floral Medallions, Border, Ivory Band, 16 In. 25.00
Platter, Petite Fleur, Blue Wreath, 10 1/4 X 14 In. 60.00
Powder Jar, Woman Smoking, Pink 245.00
Relish, Desert Scene, Blue 75.00
Salt & Pepper, Azalea, Individual 25.00
Salt & Pepper, Pink Flowers, Gold Tops 14.00
Salt, Open, Tilted Head of Swan 75.00
Salt, Swan, Luster, Spoon 15.00
Saltshaker, Azalea, Individual 10.00
Server, Candy, Florals, Orange Luster, Center Black Handle 25.00
Soup, Dish, Azalea 20.00

Sugar & Creamer, Azalea .... 20.00 To 40.00
Sugar & Creamer, Claire 30.00
Sugar & Creamer, Cover, House & Trees 20.00
Sugar & Creamer, Hand Painted, Gold Trim 25.00
Sugar & Creamer, Tree In Meadow, Gold, Red Wreath 25.00
Sugar Shaker & Creamer, Azalea 125.00
Sugar, Tree In Meadow 10.00
Tea Set, Child's, Azalea, Gold, Green Wreath Mark, 11 Piece 895.00
Tea Set, Peonies, Pearl Luster, Black Band, 9 Piece 45.00
Tea Set, Roses, M In Wreath, 11 Piece 58.00
Teapot, Azalea 85.00
Tile, Tea, Tree In Meadow, Round 20.00
Vase, Bluebirds, Cornucopia Shape, Raised Shell Base, 5 X 3 In. 35.00
Vase, Fan, Azalea 160.00
Vase, Floral Design, Phoenix Bird, Gold Handles, Marked, 11 1/2 In. 175.00
Wall Pocket, 3 Fledglings, Heads Out of Nest, Mother Watching 70.00
Wall Pocket, Applied Flowers, Blue, 8 In. 45.00
Wall Pocket, Bee & Butteryfly, Blue 35.00
Wall Pocket, Parrot, Art Deco, 8 In. 45.00

The Norse Pottery Company started in Edgerton, Wisconsin, in 1903. In 1904 the company moved to Rockford, Illinois. The company made a black pottery which resembled early bronze relics of the Scandinavian countries. The firm went out of business in 1913.

NORSE, Bowl, Sunburst Design On Sides, Otter Handles 110.00
Vase, 9 1/4 In. 95.00

The North Dakota School of Mines was established in 1892 at the University of North Dakota. A ceramic course was included and pieces were made from the clays found in the region. Students at the university made pieces from 1909 to 1949. Although very early pieces were marked "U.N.D.," most pieces were stamped with the university seal.

NORTH DAKOTA SCHOOL OF MINES, Bookends, Half Bowl Shape, Grunefelter, Pair   225.00

Bowl, Carved Flowers & Leaves, Signed, 7 In. 175.00
Bowl, Free–Form, Ruffled, Buff, Signed, 10 In. 50.00
Bowl, Light Green, Shaded, Marked, 4 X 2 In. 40.00
Bowl, Mottled Blue & Green, 6 1/2 In. 38.00
Bowl, Ox Cart, Signed, 3 1/2 In. 525.00
Bowl, Signed AMK, 4 In. 35.00
Coaster, Fawn Outlined In Buff, 3 1/2 In. 95.00
Jar, Cover, Indians On Horseback, 7 X 6 In. 395.00
Pitcher, Incised Floral, 8 In. 125.00
Plaque, Stockwell, 5 In. 150.00
Rose Bowl, Signed Bectel, Blue, 1946 .... 110.00
Vase, Blue Leaves At Top, Huckfield, 4 In. 425.00
Vase, Bud, Light Blue, 6 1/4 In. 95.00
Vase, Colored Bands, Mattson & Mix, 5 In. 225.00
Vase, Green To Purple, Huck, 1930, 5 1/2 In. 65.00
Vase, High Glaze Blue To Green, Signed, 3 In. 95.00
Vase, Maroon, Buff Lining, Signed, 8 X 5 In. 150.00
Vase, Prairie Dogs, Huckfield 495.00
Vase, Stylized Wheat Pattern, Signed, 6 In. 325.00
Vase, Yellow, Marked, 3 In. 60.00

The Harry Northwood Glass Company was founded by Harry Northwood, a glassmaker who worked for Hobbs, Brockunier and Company, La Belle Glass Company, and Buckeye Glass Company before founding his own firm. He opened one factory in Sinclaire, Pennsylvania, in 1896, and another in Wheeling, West Virginia, in

1902. Northwood closed when Mr. Northwood died in 1923. Many types of glass were made, including carnival, custard, goofus, and pressed. The underlined N mark was used on some pieces.

NORTHWOOD, Basket, Bushel, Northwood	225.00
Biscuit Jar, Leaf Umbrella, Cased Lemon	300.00
Bonbon, Persian Medallion, 5 X 7 In.	195.00
Bowl, Leaf & Beads, 10 In.	50.00
Compote, Hilltop Vines, White Opalescent	80.00
Compote, Jelly, Inverted Fan & Feather, Pink & Gold Design	280.00
Creamer, Acorn, Child's	85.00
Creamer, Argonaut Shell, Vaseline Opalescent	110.00
Creamer, Hobnail, Child's	60.00
Cruet, Apple Blossom, Milk Glass	145.00
Cup, Luster Flute, Ruby Stained Rim, Marked	20.00
Dish, Peacock Pattern, Blue, Carnival Glass	352.00
Nappy, Grape, Amethyst, Gold Overlay Handle, Marked, 6 1/2 In.	45.00
Pitcher, Water, Lilies-of-The-Valley, Blue, Ruffled, 12 3/4 In.	140.00
Pitcher, Water, Shell & Jewel, Crystal	35.00
Plate, Sunflower, Green, Gold Trim, Marked, 7 1/2 In.	18.00
Rose Bowl, Beaded Cable, Green	65.00
Rose Bowl, Leaf & Beads, Blue	125.00
Rose Bowl, White, Yellow & Puce Swirl, Blue Interior, 4 1/2 In.	250.00
Spooner, Cherry Thumbprint & Cable, Ruby & Gold	45.00
Spooner, Peach, Green, Gold Trim	75.00
Sugar Shaker, Royal Oak, Frosted Rubina, Cover	145.00
Tray, Argonaut Shell, Rolled Lip, Pedestal, Blue, 4 1/2 X 8 In.	30.00
Tray, Sandwich, Chinese Coral, 10 1/2 In.	45.00
Tumbler, Peach, Green, Gold Trim	30.00
Tumbler, Water, Cherry & Cable, Red Cherries, Gold Cable, Marked	30.00
Vase, Pull-Up Feather, Blue Lining, 5 1/2 In.	750.00
Vase, Pull-Up Feather, Gourd Shape, Yellow Ground, 9 3/4 In.	995.00
Vase, Tree Trunk, Amethyst, 10 In.	40.00

Nu-Art was a trademark registered by the Imperial Glass Company of Bellaire, Ohio, about 1920.

NU-ART, Ashtray, Elephant, Trunk Raised, Metal, Glass Insert, Signed	30.00
Bookends, Covered Wagon	15.00
Bookends, Girl, Doll, Spelter	30.00
Shade, Pillars, Crystal	40.00
Shade, Pillars, Electric, Clear	45.00
Shade, Pillars, Pastel & Clear	40.00
Shade, Pineapple, 6 Piece	350.00

Nutcrackers of many types have been used through the centuries. At first the nutcracker was a fancy hammer, but by the nineteenth century, many elaborate and ingenious types were made. Levers, screws, and hammer adaptations were the most popular. Because nutcrackers are still useful, they are still being made, some in the old styles.

NUTCRACKER, Alligator, Brass, 7 In.	16.00
Alligator, Green Paint, Cast Iron, 11 1/4 In.	95.00
Crocodile, Brass	20.00
Dog, Black & White Paint, Cast Iron, 10 3/4 In.	15.00
Dog, Marked Harper Supply Co., Cast Iron, 12 3/4 In.	65.00
Dog, St. Bernard, Bronze, 8 3/4 In.	58.00
Double, Enterprise	35.00
Eagle, Iron	185.00
Elephant, Twine Tail, Red Paint, Cast Iron, 5 X 9 3/4 In.	68.00
Knee, Iron, Lawrence	65.00
Man, Standing, Nightcap, Smoking Jacket, Full-Bodied, 7 1/2 In.	165.00
Man-In-The-Moon, Walnut, 4 1/2 In.	400.00
Maynut Cracker, Iron, Wharton, Tex., Dated 1914	35.00
Perfection, Clamp Type, Cast Iron	25.00

Polychrome Paint, Wooden, Germany, 11 1/2 In.	55.00
Punch & Judy, Brass, 1900	65.00
Rooster, Brass	28.00
Sailor & Girl, Kiss When Handles Are Squeezed, Brass, 6 In.	65.00
Santa Claus Head, Red Hat, Gold Trim, Carved, Wooden, 7 1/2 In.	250.00
Squirrel, Cast Iron, 5 In.	40.00 To 45.00
Squirrel, Cast Iron, Walnut Block, 1800s, 4 1/2 X 5 1/2 X 7 In.	95.00

The Nymphenburg porcelain factory was established at Neudeck-ob–der–Au, Germany, in 1753 and moved to Nymphenburg in 1761. The company is still in existence. Modern marks include a checkered shield topped by a crown, and a crowned "CT" with the year and a contemporary shield mark on reproductions of eighteenth–century porcelain.

NYMPHENBURG, Figurine, Doe	85.00
Figurine, Four Seasons, 4 White Figures	395.00

The words "Occupied Japan" were used on pottery, porcelain, toys, and other goods made during the American occupation of Japan after World War II, from 1945 to 1952. Collectors now search for these pieces. The items were made for export.

OCCUPIED JAPAN, Ashtray, Hand Painted Flowers, 3 X 2 1/2 In.	4.00
Ashtray, Jasperware, Classical Maidens, Doves, 2 3/4 In.	8.50
Ashtray, Pair of Baseball Mitts	8.00
Bookends, Girl Knitting, Boy With Umbrella	28.00
Cracker Jar, Wicker Bail Handle, Bird, Tree, 5 3/8 X 4 In.	45.00
Cup & Saucer, Blue Dragon, White Cottage Scene, Small	10.00
Cup & Saucer, Light Blue Flowers	24.00
Figurine, Bird, Crested, Blue & Red Overglaze, 3 1/4 In.	6.00
Figurine, Bride & Groom, Double, 1930s Clothes, 4 In.	20.00
Figurine, Cherub, Violin, Gold Trim, 4–Footed Pedestal, 8 In.	35.00
Figurine, Colonial Gentleman, 15 In.	85.00
Figurine, Girl, Hummel Type, Kerchief & Dress, 5 1/4 In.	20.00
Figurine, Gondolier With Gondola, Bisque, 8 X 10 In.	90.00
Figurine, Musician, Bee, String Base, Green Body, Shoes, 3 In.	11.00
Figurine, Newsboy, Bee, Green Body & Wings, Open Mouth, 4 In.	14.00
Figurine, Parrot, Branch, Flowers, Red, Green, Tan, 3 1/4 In.	11.00
Figurine, Shepherdess, Lamb On Shoulder, Paulux, 8 1/2 In.	30.00
Figurine, Siamese Cat, Red Pillow, Holds Gray Ball, 4 In.	16.00
Flower Pot, Attached Saucer, Floral, Gold Trim, 3 1/2 In.	6.00
Mug, Face, With Beard, 2 1/2 In.	10.00
Mug, Face, With Cigar, 2 1/2 In.	10.00
Planter, Colonial Musician, Man & Woman Front, 2 1/2 In.	5.00
Planter, Figural, Fawn, Tree, Foliage, 4 X 3 X 3 1/2 In.	4.50
Plaque, Colonial Woman, Man, Full Figural, 7 X 14 In., Pair	40.00
Plate, Grapes, Semiporcelain, 7 3/4 In.	10.00
Plate, Windmill, Tree, Sunset, Gold Rim, 5 1/8 In., 8 Piece	10.00
Salt & Pepper, Tomato, 3 In.	8.00
Salt & Pepper, Windmills, Delft	14.00
Sprinkling Can, Flowers, White, Elfin Ware Type, 6 1/2 In.	30.00
Tankard, Tavern Scene 1 Side, Malt Hops Other, 8 3/4 In.	18.00
Tea Set, Cobalt Blue, Marked, 11 Piece	30.00
Tea Set, Cottage, Figural, 7 Piece	65.00
Tray, Hand Painted Flowers, Wooden, 14 X 12 In.	35.00
Vase, Pink Lilies, Raised Gold, 7 1/2 In.	25.00
Wall Pocket, Blue Grapes, Leaves, Black, Sponged, 6 1/4 In.	14.00

George E. Ohr, a true eccentric, made pottery in Biloxi, Mississippi, between 1883 and 1918. The pottery was made of very thin clay that was twisted, folded, and dented into odd, graceful shapes. Some pieces were lifelike models of hats, animal heads, or even a potato. Some pieces were decorated with folded clay "snakes." Although reproductions would be almost impossible to make, there have been some reworked pieces appearing on the market. These have been reglazed, or snakes and other embellishments have been added.

OHR, Basket, Hanging, Gunmetal Over Brick Brown, Pimpled, 6 1/2 X 3 1/2 In.	360.00
Bird Feeder, Signed	650.00
Cup, Seaweed Green, Orange Speckles, Light Green, 2 Handles, Stamped	220.00
Jug, Unglazed, Signed, 5 In.	285.00
Pitcher, 2 Steamboats, Serpent Handle, 9 In.	1200.00
Pitcher, Chicken, 6 In.	350.00
Pitcher, Double Spout, Ring Handle, 11 In.	900.00
Pitcher, Grover Cleveland 1 Side, Wife Reverse, Navy, Handle, 8 In.	700.00
Pitcher, Steamboats, Serpent Handle, 9 In.	1200.00
Pitcher, Tree Trunk With Indian Head, Real Wood Branches, 11 In.	1100.00
Vase, Applied Crawling Serpent Top, 5 In.	6750.00
Vase, Dark Brown, Over To Cinnamon, Bowl, Impressed, 4 1/4 X 3 In.	220.00
Vase, Green Glaze & Clear On Ginger Clay, 3 In.	395.00
Vase, High Gloss, Pleated, Pinched–In Belly, 3 1/4 X 5 1/4 In.	225.00
Vase, Light Blue, Brown Shoulder & Rim, White Base, Classic, 4 1/4 In.	120.00
Vase, Mottled Black, Red, Gritty, 3 Horizontal Ribs, Stamped, 3 X 3 In.	220.00
Vase, Mottled Green, Over Speckled Tan, Brown, Corset Shape, 8 X 3 In.	300.00
Vase, Seaweed, Handles	220.00

OLD IVORY 84 Old Ivory china was made in Silesia, Germany, at the end of the nineteenth century. It is often marked with a crown and the word "Silesia." Some pieces are also marked with the words "Old Ivory." The pattern numbers appear on the base of each piece.

OLD IVORY, Berry Bowl, No.22, 10 In.	75.00
Berry Set, No.11, 5 Piece	135.00
Berry Set, No.16, 7 Piece	225.00
Berry Set, No.75, 5 Piece	135.00
Berry Set, No.84, 7 Piece	195.00
Bowl, No.11, 9 1/2 In.	32.50
Bowl, No.15, Silesia, 6 1/2 In.	25.00
Bowl, No.84, 10 In.	80.00
Bowl, Salad, Onondaga Pottery Co., 9 In.	8.00
Bowl, Vegetable, No.84, Silesia, 9 In.	75.00
Cake Plate, No. 6, Silesia	100.00
Cake Plate, No. 22	75.00
Cake Plate, No. 84, Pierced Handles .... 70.00 To	75.00
Cake Plate, No.121, Silesia	95.00
Cake Set, No.16, Pierced Handled Serving Plate, 7 Piece	250.00
Cake Set, No.84, 7 Piece	195.00
Celery, 12 3/4 X 5 1/2 In.	55.00
Celery, No.84, 11 1/4 X 5 1/2 In.	80.00
Chocolate Pot, No.11	250.00
Chocolate Pot, No.15, Silesia .... 250.00 To	275.00
Chocolate Pot, No.73, Silesia	285.00
Chocolate Set, No.11, 7 Piece	525.00
Chocolate Set, No.15, 9 Piece	795.00
Chop Plate, No.15, Silesia, 13 In.	125.00
Cracker Jar, No.15	350.00
Cracker Jar, No.16, Silesia	250.00
Creamer, No.16, Silesia	40.00
Cup & Saucer, No.15, Silesia	55.00
Cup & Saucer, No.84, Silesia	55.00
Cup, No.76, Silesia, 6 Piece	100.00
Dish, No.84, 11 1/4 X 5 1/2 In.	80.00
Dish, Pickle, No.84, 6 1/2 X 4 1/2 In.	38.00
Jardiniere, 7 X 10 In.	165.00
Mustard, No.16, Silesia	150.00
Nappy, No.16, Handle Inside Bowl	85.00
Oyster Bowl, No.16, Silesia	125.00
Plate, No. 11, Clairon, 7 3/4 In.	28.00

Don't wash ivory. The yellow color is preferred; white ivory has a much lower value.

Ivory will darken if kept in the dark. Keep a piano open so the keys will be in natural light. Keep figurines, chess sets, and other ivory in the open.

Onion, Plate, Blue & White

Plate, No. 73, 8 1/2 In., 6 Piece	200.00
Plate, No. 75, 6 In.	15.00 To 18.00
Plate, No. 84, 8 1/2 In.	38.00
Plate, No.121, Silesia, 7 In.	40.00
Plate, No.200, 6 In.	17.00 To 18.00
Plate, Thistle, 6 1/4 In.	14.00
Platter, No.15, Silesia, 11 1/2 In.	125.00
Relish, No.16, Silesia, 6 In.	95.00
Relish, No.33, 8 X 4 3/4 In.	75.00
Relish, No.84, 6 1/2 X 4 1/2 In.	38.00
Rose Bowl, Footed, Silesia	60.00
Salt & Pepper, Yellow Rose	75.00
Sugar & Creamer, No.84	150.00 To 300.00
Sugar, Cover, No.84, Silesia	45.00
Tea Set, No.205, Hand Painted Flowers, 4 Piece	150.00

OLD SLEEPY EYE, see Sleepy Eye

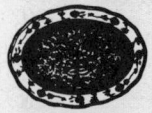

Onion pattern, originally named "bulb pattern," is a white ware decorated with cobalt blue or pink. Although it is commonly associated with Meissen, other companies made the pattern in the late nineteenth and the twentieth centuries. A rare type is called "red bud" because there are added red accents on the blue and white dishes.

ONION, Bowl, Dessert, Meissen, 4 Piece	40.00
Canister, Barrel Shape, Reiss, Pair	75.00
Canister, Word Rice, Germany	43.00
Canister, Words Granulated Sugar, Germany	43.00
Cruet, Vinegar, Stopper, Meissen, 1850, 5 1/2 In.	150.00
Cup & Saucer, Meissen	65.00
Cutting Board	63.00
Dish, Condiment, Underplate, Cover, Meissen, 8 X 4 In.	275.00
Figurine, Fairy Shoe, Meissen	175.00
Figurine, Shoe, Crossed Swords	175.00
Funnel, Blue & White, Meissen	75.00
Gravy Boat, Blue, White, Double Handle, Marked, 10 In.	204.00
Gravy, Attached Underplate, Meissen, 10 In.	165.00
Lazy Susan, 5 Curved Pieces, Wooden Turntable, Meissen, 17 In.	695.00
Plate, Blue & White ....*Illus*	50.00
Platter, Blue & White, Scalloped Edge, Oval, 26 In.	605.00
Platter, Bow Handles, 16 In.	450.00
Platter, Meissen, Anchor Mark, 10 1/2 In.	68.00
Platter, Meissen, Marked, 11 1/2 X 10 In.	150.00
Platter, Pewter Fitted Bottom, Oval, Meissen, 17 In.	295.00
Rolling Pin	75.00
Rolling Pin, Stoneware	250.00
Skimmer	90.00
Spoon Holder, Hanging	125.00
Tea Set, Doll's	95.00

Teapot, 7 In.	100.00
Tray, Bows On Ends, Meissen, C.1840, 15 X 11 In.	225.00

 Opalescent glass is translucent glass that has the tones of the opal gemstone. It originated in England in the 1870s and is often found in pressed glassware made in Victorian times. Opalescent glass was first made in America in 1897 at the Northwood glassworks in Indiana, Pennsylvania. Some dealers use the terms "opaline" and "opalescent" for any of these translucent wares.

OPALESCENT, see also Northwood; Pressed Glass; Spanish Lace

OPALESCENT, Banana Bowl, Alaska, Blue	175.00
Basket, Blue, Indented Hobs, Clear Thorn Handle, 1920, 7 X 6 In.	125.00
Basket, Clear Applied Leaves, Twisted Handle, Ruby, 7 1/4 In.	165.00
Basket, Diamond–Quilted, Applied Flowers, Vaseline, 7 In.	210.00
Basket, Ruffled, Twisted Thorny Pink Handle, Pink, 7 1/2 In.	195.00
Basket, Stripes, Shell Trim, Leaf Feet, Vaseline, 8 1/2 X 5 In.	225.00
Basket, Tree Bark, Handle, Blue, 5 In.	65.00
Berry Bowl, Alaska, Blue, Master	115.00
Berry Set, Circled Scroll, Blue, 5 Piece	275.00
Berry Set, Seaweed, Blue, 5 Piece	145.00
Berry Set, Wreath & Shell, Vaseline, 6 Piece	285.00
Berry Set, Wreath & Shell, White, 7 Piece	185.00
Bottle, Water, Reverse Swirl, Cranberry, 7 In.	150.00
Bowl, 3–Lobed Pinched Rim, Green, 2 3/8 X 6 In.	15.00
Bowl, Abalone, Handles, Green, 6 1/2 In.	30.00
Bowl, Art Nouveau Woman, Spelter Base, Vaseline, 12 1/4 In.	325.00
Bowl, Beaded Stars, 4–Sided, Green, 7 1/2 In.	38.00
Bowl, Daisy Wreath, Ruffled, Blue, 8 1/2 In.	240.00
Bowl, Grapevine Cluster, Blue, 4 X 5 1/2 In.	36.00
Bowl, Jeweled Heart, Ruffled, White, 5 3/4 In.	12.50
Bowl, Keyhole, White, 8 In.	30.00
Bowl, Keyhole, White, 9 In.	35.00
Bowl, Many Loops, 6 In.	18.00
Bowl, Overlapping Leaves, Footed, Green	22.00
Bowl, Pearl Flowers, Double Crimped, Blue, 9 In.	45.00
Bowl, Ruffles & Rings, Fluted, White, 8 1/2 In.	35.00
Bowl, Scroll With Acanthus, White, 5 1/2 In.	12.00
Bowl, Wheel & Block, Green, 10 In.	40.00
Bowl, Winter Cabbage, Green, 6 1/2 In.	35.00
Butter, Cover, Fluted Scrolls, Vaseline	65.00
Butter, Cover, Iris With Meander, White	110.00
Butter, Cover, Jackson, Blue	100.00
Butter, Cover, Regal, Crystal	125.00
Butter, Cover, Wreath & Shell, Blue	125.00
Butter, Cover, Wreath & Shell, White	110.00
Butter, Everglades, Cover, Blue	175.00
Celery Vase, Chrysanthemum Base, Cranberry	150.00
Celery Vase, Wreath & Shell, Blue	165.00
Celery, Regal, Blue	115.00
Celery, Spanish Lace, Blue, Ruffled, Bulbous	95.00
Compote, Button Panel, Fluted, White, 3 1/2 X 7 1/2 In.	40.00
Compote, Dolphin, Vaseline, 5 1/4 X 6 In.	45.00
Compote, Fluted, Vaseline, 1891, 8 1/4 X 10 In.	225.00
Compote, Jelly, Everglades, Blue, Gold Trim	85.00
Compote, Jelly, Intagalio, Vaseline	35.00
Compote, Jelly, Intaglio, Blue	30.00
Compote, Jelly, Iris With Meander, Blue	75.00
Compote, Jelly, Scroll With Acanthus, Blue	40.00
Compote, Popsicle Sticks, Green, 8 In.	43.00
Compote, Tokyo, Green	40.00
Condiment Set, Cosmos, 3 Piece	250.00
Creamer, Alaska	55.00
Creamer, Alaska, Yellow	70.00
Creamer, Beatty Honeycomb, Blue	50.00

Creamer, Beatty Rib, White 20.00
Creamer, Circled Scroll, Blue 95.00
Creamer, Double Greek Key, White, Northwood 80.00
Creamer, Everglades, Green 95.00
Creamer, Fluted Scrolls, Blue 55.00
Creamer, Intaglio, Blue .... 50.00 To 75.00
Creamer, Inverted Fan & Feather 35.00
Creamer, Jewel & Flower, White 45.00
Creamer, Ribbed Spiral, Blue 50.00
Creamer, Scalloped Skirt, Blue 40.00
Creamer, Wreath & Shell, Blue 85.00
Cruet, Alaska, Vaseline 245.00
Cruet, Argonaut Shell, Blue 295.00
Cruet, Cactus, Green 115.00
Cruet, Daisy & Fern 70.00
Cruet, Daisy & Fern On Swirl, Blue 95.00
Cruet, Double Circle, Blue 125.00
Cruet, Fancy Fans, Blue, Northwood 375.00
Cruet, Feather, Crystal 35.00
Cruet, Fluted Scrolls, Blue 150.00
Cruet, Fluted Scrolls, Canary 150.00
Cruet, Idyll, Blue 195.00
Cruet, Intaglio, White .... 55.00 To 60.00
Cruet, Jewel & Flower, Canary 395.00
Cruet, Paneled Sprig, Crystal 70.00
Cruet, Scroll With Acanthus, Blue 160.00
Cruet, Seaweed, Blue 135.00
Cruet, Stripe Pattern, Blue, 6 3/4 In. 125.00
Cruet, Swag With Brackets, Blue .... 275.00 To 360.00
Cruet, Wild Bouquet, Green 350.00
Cruet, Wild Bouquet, White 110.00
Cruet, Windows, Cranberry 375.00
Cruet, Windows, Swirl, Clear Stopper 65.00
Dish, Berry, Palm Beach, Vaseline, 4 In. 24.00
Dish, Sweetmeat, Silver Plated Holder, Pink, 5 1/2 In. 135.00
Dish, War of Roses, Boat Shape, 2 1/2 X 7 1/2 In. 60.00
Epergne, 3–Flower Shape, Green Base, Comes Apart, 19 1/2 In. 295.00
Epergne, 3–Light, Fluted Turned–Down Rims, Fluted Bowl, 24 In. 375.00
Epergne, 4–Lily, Vaseline Applied Trim, 20 In. .... 325.00 To 395.00
Epergne, 4–Trumpet, Cranberry, Canes, No Baskets 700.00
Lamp, Floral, Fluted Shade, Green, Brass Column, 21 1/2 In. 795.00
Lamp, Hobnail, Green, Fenton, Pair 65.00
Lamp, Oil, Coin Dot, Drilled For Electricity, 8 1/2 In. 195.00
Lamp, Oil, Vaseline Striped Font, Frosted Base & Stem 245.00
Lamp, Snowflake, Blue 250.00
Mug, Diamond Spearhead, Blue 68.00
Mug, Vintage Design, 2 1/2 In. 10.00
Pitcher, Daisy & Fern, Ball Shape, White 95.00
Pitcher, Drapery, Blue, Gold Trim 120.00
Pitcher, Jeweled Heart, Blue 225.00
Pitcher, Poinsettia, Blue 215.00
Pitcher, Swirl, Blue, Crimped Top 125.00
Pitcher, Water, Alaska, Blue .... 250.00 To 365.00
Pitcher, Water, Alaska, Enamel Design, Green 325.00
Pitcher, Water, Beatty Rib, Blue 120.00
Pitcher, Water, Buttons & Braids, Cranberry 295.00
Pitcher, Water, Buttons & Braids, Ruffled, Green 125.00
Pitcher, Water, Diamond Spearhead, Green 225.00
Pitcher, Water, Heavy Threading, Double Handle, Crystal, 9 In. 295.00
Pitcher, Water, Inverted Fan & Feather, Blue, 3 Tumblers 525.00
Pitcher, Water, Poinsettia, Blue 160.00
Pitcher, Water, Swirl, Ruffled Top, Blue, 8 3/4 In. 135.00
Rose Bowl, Fluted Scrolls, Blue 125.00
Rose Bowl, Honeycomb, Peach 175.00

Rose Bowl, Inverted Fan & Feather, Yellow 60.00
Rose Bowl, Wreath & Shell, Blue 50.00
Salt & Pepper, Lacy Medallion, Green, Gold Trim 60.00
Salt, Beatty Rib, White 24.00
Salt, Wreath & Shell, Blue 80.00
Saltshaker, Beatty Rib, Blue .... 20.00 To 55.00
Saltshaker, Daisy & Fern, Northwood, Cranberry 85.00
Sauce, Alaska, Blue 45.00
Shade, Cranberry, Swirled Windows, Hobbs, 5 X 2 In. 225.00
Shot Glass, Cranberry, Swirl 75.00
Spittoon, Woman's, Wreath & Shell, Vaseline 75.00
Spooner, Alaska, Vaseline 65.00
Spooner, Beaded Oval Medallion, Blue 35.00
Spooner, Child's, Twist, White 75.00
Spooner, Double Greek Key, White, Northwood 80.00
Spooner, Drapery, Blue 60.00
Spooner, Fluted Scrolls, Vaseline 40.00
Spooner, Hobnail Thumbprint Band, Blue 30.00
Spooner, Hobnail With Paneled Thumbprint, Vaseline 28.00
Spooner, Intaglio, Blue 60.00
Spooner, Palm Beach, Blue 95.00
Spooner, Reverse Swirl, Blue 65.00
Spooner, Scroll With Acanthus, Blue 60.00
Spooner, Thousand Eye 57.00
Spooner, Torpedo, Blue 65.00
Spooner, Water Lily With Cattails, Blue 70.00
Spooner, Wreath & Shell, Vaseline 95.00
Sugar & Creamer, Circled Scroll, Green 140.00
Sugar & Creamer, Cover, Peacock Pattern, Blue 125.00
Sugar & Creamer, Jewel & Flower, White 75.00
Sugar & Creamer, William & Mary, Vaseline 95.00
Sugar & Creamer, Wreathed Cherry, Vaseline 75.00
Sugar Shaker, Ribbed Opal Lattice, Cranberry .... 125.00 To 160.00
Sugar, Cover, Alaska, Blue 55.00
Sugar, Cover, Everglades, Blue 125.00
Sugar, Cover, Fluted Scrolls, Vaseline 85.00
Sugar, Cover, Jewel & Flower, White 60.00
Sugar, Cover, Seaweed, Cranberry 195.00
Sugar, Cover, Wreath & Shell, Vaseline 110.00
Sugar, Open, Drapery, Blue 35.00
Syrup Dispenser, Double Greek Key, Dated 1892 .... 600.00
Syrup, Coin Spot & Swirl, Blue 80.00
Syrup, Diamond Spearhead, Green 350.00
Syrup, Reverse Swirl, Blue 150.00
Syrup, Windows, Blue 175.00
Table Set, Alaska, Blue, 4 Piece 575.00
Table Set, Beatty Rib, Blue, 4 Piece 385.00
Table Set, Intaglio, Northwood, Green, Gold Trim, 4 Piece 550.00
Table Set, Twist, White, 4 Piece 600.00
Table Set, Wreath & Shell, Vaseline, 4 Piece 475.00
Tieback, Flower Form, Pewter Post, 4 1/2 In., Set of 11 .... 195.00
Toothpick, Beatty Rib, Blue 22.00
Toothpick, Diamond Spearhead, Green 28.00
Toothpick, Iris With Meander, Green .... 45.00 To 55.00
Toothpick, Paneled Sprig, White 60.00
Toothpick, Wild Bouquet, White .... 125.00 To 135.00
Toothpick, Wreath & Shell, Vaseline 225.00
Tumbler, Beatty Swirl, White 45.00
Tumbler, Block, Blue 25.00
Tumbler, Buttons & Braids, White 23.00
Tumbler, Daisy & Fern, Cranberry 35.00
Tumbler, Everglades 45.00
Tumbler, Herringbone, Cranberry 110.00
Tumbler, Iris, White 22.00

Tumbler, Jeweled Heart, Blue	50.00
Tumbler, Poinsettia, Cranberry	110.00
Tumbler, Reverse Swirl, Cranberry	35.00
Tumbler, Spanish Lace	15.00
Tumbler, Swag With Brackets, Blue	15.00
Tumbler, Wreath & Shell, Enameled Flowers, Blue	52.00
Vase, Iris With Meander, Green, 13 In.	25.00
Vase, Jack–In–The–Pulpit, 4 1/2 In.	65.00
Water Set, Daisy & Zipper, Blue, 5 Piece	280.00
Water Set, Iris With Meander, Vaseline, 6 Piece	475.00
Water Set, Jeweled Heart, Blue, 7 Piece	590.00
Water Set, Stripe, Light Green, 7 Piece	65.00
Water Set, Tray, Richelieu, Blue, 3 Piece	280.00
Wine, Lacy Medallion, Green, Gold Trim	30.00

Opaline, or opal glass, was made in white, green, and other colors. The glass had a matte surface and a lack of transparency. It was often gilded or painted. It was a popular mid–nineteenth–century European glassware.

OPALINE, Bouquet Holder, Blue, Henry N. Hooper & Co., Pair	302.00
Box, With 2 Perfume Bottles, Blue, Gilt Brass Fittings, 7 1/2 In.	575.00
Lamp, Black, 22 In., Pair	1250.00
Perfume Bottle, Blue, Panel Cut, Gilt Brass, Litho, 4 1/2 In., Pair	420.00
Perfume Bottle, Gold Overlay, Gold Flowers, Blue, 5 1/2 In.	95.00
Perfume Bottle, Green, Ornate Gilt Brass, Litho In Lid, 5 1/4 In.	275.00
Perfume Bottle, Green, Paris Scenes, Alabaster Base, France, 7 In.	300.00
Perfume Bottle, Pink, Enameled Stopper, 6 5/8 In.	105.00
Wine Cooler, Silver Frame, Liner, Blue	485.00

The stage is a long way from some of the seats at a play or an opera, so the patrons sometimes carried special opera glasses in the nineteenth and early twentieth centuries. Mother–of–pearl was a popular decoration.

OPERA GLASSES, French, Embossed Animals On Sides	225.00
Jessops, Leather Case	55.00
Mother–of–Pearl & Brass, Lemaire, France	75.00
Purple Mother–of–Pearl & Brass, Long Handle, London	75.00

Little Orphan Annie first appeared in the comics in 1924. The redheaded girl and her friends have been on the radio and are still on the comic pages. A Broadway musical show and a movie in the 1980s made Annie popular again and many toys, dishes, and other memorabilia are being made.

ORPHAN ANNIE, Bank, Ceramic	5.00
Book, Big Little Book, and The Gooneyville Mystery	20.00
Book, Coloring, 1930s	35.00
Bracelet	18.00
Card, Christmas, From Harold Gray, Annie & Santa, 1963	45.00
Cup, Saucer & Sugar, Lusterware	80.00
Doll, Annie & Sandy, Jointed, 7 & 4 In.	125.00
Doll, Dist. By Wellmade Toys, Box, 1973	12.00
Doll, Extra Outfit	25.00
Doll, Knickerbocker, 9 In.	7.00
Doll, Knickerbocker, 16 In.	14.00
Doll, Orphan Annie & Sandy, Jointed, Comic Litho, 7 & 4 In.	125.00
Doll, Rag, Knickerbocker, 1977, 16 In.	12.50
Figure, Annie, Sandy, Cardboard, Movable Arms, Legs, 7 & 4 In.	145.00
Figure, Stand–Up, Multicolored Tin Litho, Standing, 1930s	20.00
Figurine, Chalkware, Utah	20.00
Figurine, Daddy Warbucks, Chalkware, 1940s, 6 In.	24.00
Gameboard, Treasure Isle	45.00
Knitting Outfit, Box, 1930s	40.00
Lobby Card, 1938, 11 X 14 In.	20.00
Lunch Box, Aladdin, 1981	10.00 To 15.00

Mug, Ovaltine Premium 18.00
Mug, Ovaltine, Ceramic 50.00
Nodder, Daddy Warbucks, Bisque, Germany 135.00
Paper Doll, 1931 .... 40.00
Paper Doll, With Sandy, Gabriel 80.00
Pin, Decoder, Manual, 1935 .... 40.00
Pin, Decoder, Secret Compartment, Brass, Wheel, 1936 .... 25.00
Pin, Decoder, Telematic, Brass, Ovaltine, Wheel, 1938 .... 35.00
Pin, Secret Society, Bronze Colored Brass, 1934 .... 25.00
Puzzle, 1930s 30.00
Ring, Mystic Eye Detective, 1939 .... 13.00
Stove, Metal, 4 1/2 In. 35.00
Toothbrush Holder, Annie & Sandy .... 135.00 To 185.00
Toy, Limousine, Knickerbocker, Box 9.00
Toy, Sandy, Windup, Tin, No Suitcase, 5 In. 42.50
Wall Pocket ....75.00 To 125.00
Watch, Aztec Sun Dial, Radio Premium .... 35.00 To 85.00
Wristwatch .... 115.00 To 250.00

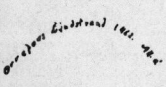

The Orrefors Glassworks, located in the Swedish province of Smaaland, was established in 1898. The company is still making glass for use on the table or as decorations. There is renewed interest in the glass made in the modern styles of the 1940s and 1950s. Most vases and decorative pieces are signed with the etched name.

ORREFORS, Bowl, Crystal, Signed, 2 X 11 In. 85.00
Figurine, Chef, Working Over Bowl, Crystal, 5 1/2 In. 135.00
Figurine, Man, Glass Blower, 4 1/2 In. 35.00
Perfume Bottle, Nude, Etched, 5 In. 95.00
Plate, Famous Places of Worship, Gold, Crystal 45.00
Plate, Notre Dame 35.00
Rose Bowl, Crystal 20.00
Sign, Dealer's, Solid Crystal, 3 X 4 In. 85.00
Vase, Abstract Face, Ariel, 6 7/8 In. ....*Illus* 4675.00
Vase, Blue Free–Form Pattern, Flared Neck, Bulbous, Graal, 7 In. 775.00
Vase, Brown Starfish, Kelp & Shells, Oviform, Small Opening, 7 In. 2650.00
Vase, Engraved Children, Oblong Shape, 6 X 4 3/4 In. 295.00
Vase, Engraved Sailboat, Birds On Reverse, Flattened Oval, 4 In. 105.00
Vase, Gondolier, Woman, Moonlit Landscape, Ariel, C.1945, 7 In. 1980.00
Vase, Paperweight, Underwater Scene, Marked, 4 1/4 In. 565.00
Vase, Starfish, Shells, Brown, Clear, Graal, 1948, Oviform, 7 In. 2400.00
Vase, Swimming Fish, Sea Grass, Signed, 5 3/4 In. 575.00

Orrefors, Vase, Abstract Face,
Ariel, 6 7/8 In.

When moving, remember there is no insurance coverage for breakage if the items are not packed by the shipper.

Be very careful if you try to oil the mechanism of a music box. Too much oil will cause damage.

Wine, Footed, 3 1/2 In. 10.00

Ott & Brewer Company operated the Etruria Pottery at Trenton, New Jersey, from 1863 to 1893. They started making belleek in 1882. The firm used a variety of marks that incorporated the initials O & B.

OTT & BREWER, Cup & Saucer, Tridacna, Gilt 125.00
  Pitcher, 6 1/2 In. 700.00
  Pitcher, Water, Acorn, Gold Trim, 9 In. 850.00

The four Overbeck sisters started a pottery in Cambridge City, Indiana, in 1911. They made all types of vases, each one-of-a-kind. Small, hand-modeled figurines are the most popular pieces with today's collectors. The factory continued until 1955 when the last of the four sisters died.

OVERBECK, Figurine, Lady, Blue Dress, Blond, Holding Flower Basket 180.00
  Figurine, Lady, Dark Hair, Blue Dress 150.00

Owens Pottery was made in Zanesville, Ohio, from 1891 to 1928. The first art pottery was made after 1896. Utopian Ware, Cyrano, Navarre, Feroza, and Henri Deux were made. Pieces were usually marked with a form of the name "Owens." About 1907, the firm began to make tile and discontinued the art pottery wares.

OWENS, Ewer, Pansies, 6 In. 170.00
  Ewer, Utopian, Pansies, Signed Steele, 6 In. 170.00
  Jardiniere, Lotus, Butterflies Rim, Shaded Tan, 10 1/2 X 7 1/2 In. 210.00
  Jardiniere, On Stand, 3 Griffins, Foliate, Chocolate Glaze, 45 In. 200.00
  Jug, Utopian, Rose Design, 10 1/4 In. 90.00
  Mug, Orange 35.00
  Tankard, Utopian, Floral, 12 In. 225.00
  Tile, Stylized Floral Medallion, Pale Green Ground, 9 In. 200.00
  Vase, Aqua Verdi, Bulbous Bottom, Pierced Neck, Handles, 6 3/4 In. 95.00
  Vase, Cattail, Feroz, Gunmetal Iridescent, 10 In. 325.00
  Vase, Utopian, Autumn Leaves, Dark Brown, Signed, 5 1/2 In. 150.00
  Vase, Utopian, Flowers, Signed, 11 In. 175.00
  Vase, Utopian, Twist Shape, Signed, 3 1/2 In. 105.00

Oyster plates were popular from the 1880s. Each course at dinner was served in a special dish. The oyster plate had indentations shaped like oysters. Usually six oysters were held on a plate. There is no greater value to a plate with more oysters although that myth continues to haunt antiques dealers. There are other plates for shellfish including cockle plates and whelk plates. The appropriately shaped indentations are part of the design of these dishes.

OYSTER PLATE, Brown Tracery Flowers, Gold Outlined, French & Co., Boston 25.00
  Garlands of Roses, 5 Shells, Gold Trim, Limoges, 8 3/4 In. 44.00
  Half Moon Shape, Copeland, 9 1/2 In. 110.00
  Majolica, Green, Cream, Yellow, Pink, Brown, 9 In. 155.00
  Shell Center, Floral Design, 5 Wells, Germany, 8 1/4 In. 58.00
  Turin, Seafood Design With Gold, 9 1/4 In. 65.00

Paden City Glass Manufacturing Company was established in 1916 at Paden City, West Virginia. It is best known for glasswares but also produced a pottery line. The firm closed in 1951.

PADEN CITY, Bookends, Eagles, Figural 220.00
  Bowl, Blue, Handles, 10 3/4 In. 18.50
  Bowl, Nora Bird, Pink, Footed, Oval, 9 In. 85.00
  Bowl, Orchid, Crystal, Footed, Square, 8 In. 35.00
  Bowl, Peacock & Wild Rose, Footed, 9 1/2 In. 110.00
  Bowl, Peacock, Pink, 10 1/2 In. 30.00
  Cake Plate, Peacock & Wild Rose, Pink, 10 In. 42.00
  Cake Stand, Pineapple Design 18.00
  Candlestick, Blue 35.00
  Candy Dish, Gazebo, Light Blue, Tall, Cover 75.00

Cheese & Cracker, Peacock & Rose 60.00
Compote, Crow's Foot, Red, 5 1/4 In. 25.00
Compote, Marie Cutting, Pink, 5 1/2 X 11 In. 48.00
Compote, Peacock & Rose, Pink, 6 1/2 In. 48.00
Cordial, Penny Line, Ruby 15.00
Cruet, Green, Stopper 35.00
Cup & Saucer, Penny Line, Ruby 10.50
Cup, Amethyst 5.00
Figurine, Chanticleer, 7 1/4 X 9 1/2 In. .... 55.00 To 85.00
Figurine, Cottontail Bunny, Blue 85.00
Figurine, Cottontail Bunny, Crystal 60.00
Figurine, Pheasant, 13 3/4 In. .... 85.00 To 95.00
Figurine, Pigeon, Pouter 50.00
Figurine, Pony, Tail Standing, 11 1/2 In. 95.00
Figurine, Squirrel On Log 40.00
Figurine, Swan, Dragon, 10 X 6 1/4 In. 200.00
Goblet, Amethyst, 8 Oz. 9.00
Goblet, Stemmed, Pink, 6 Piece 200.00
Gravy Boat, Underplate, Pink, Gold Trim 40.00
Mayonnaise, Liner, Nora Bird, Pink 60.00
Mayonnaise, Plate, Ardith, Yellow 35.00
Plate, Amethyst, 7 1/2 I. 5.00
Plate, Crow's Foot, Ruby, 9 In. 8.00
Plate, Patio, 11 In. 7.00
Plate, Sandwich, Peacock, Center Handle 50.00
Platter, Crow's Foot, Ruby, Oval 45.00
Reamer 42.50
Salt & Pepper, Cobalt Blue, 4 In. 30.00
Samovar, Painted Roses, Green 88.00
Sandwich Tray, Swan Handle 20.00
Server, Center Handle, Lucy, Cobalt Blue 35.00
Sherbet, Amethyst, 3 3/4 In. 7.00
Sherbet, Penny Line, Ruby 8.00
Soup, Cream, Crow's Foot, 8 1/2 In., 8 Piece 175.00
Sugar & Creamer, Catina, Amethyst, Footed 55.00
Sugar & Creamer, Peacock, Rose, Footed 95.00
Sugar, Nora Bird 35.00
Swan, Dragon, 10 X 6 1/4 In. 190.00
Tray, Peacock Reverse, Center Handle, Red, 10 In. 65.00
Tumbler, Iced Tea, Footed, Amethyst, 5 1/8 In. 10.00
Vase, California Popppy, Pink, 12 In. 125.00
Vase, Crow's Foot, Ruby, 11 In. 60.00
Vase, Flower Design, Crow's Foot, 10 In. 65.00
Vase, Milk Glass, Flower Design, Crow's Foot, 10 In. 66.00
Vase, Peacock & Wild Rose, Green, 10 In. 62.00
Wine, Penny Line, Ruby 9.00

The paintings listed in this book are not works by major artists but rather decorative paintings on ivory, board, or glass that would be of interest to the average collector. To learn the value of an oil painting by a listed artist you must contact an expert in that area.

PAINTING, On Board, Child, Red Dress, Primitive, 25 3/4 X 31 3/4 In. 500.00
On Board, Clark, California Coast, Framed, 1922, 7 X 9 In. 2750.00
On Board, Clydesdale Stallion, J.Kenyon, 19th Century, 25 X 18 In. 4000.00
On Board, Country Farm Scene, Norman Lloyd, Framed, 13 X 16 In. 135.00
On Board, East Coast Harbor, Sailors, Edgar Payne, 20 X 24 In. 550.00
On Board, Gentleman, High Collar, Frame, Oil, 1842, 20 3/4 X 17 In. 225.00
On Board, Hollyhocks, Oak Frame, 23 1/2 X 28 1/2 In. 40.00
On Board, Horse & Sleigh, Primitive, Charles Stockman, 21 X 27 In. 105.00
On Board, Indian Encampment, Hartwig, 16 1/2 X 21 3/4 In. 825.00
On Board, Jacobsen, Schooner Helen P., Oil, 1907, 16 X 24 In. 7500.00
On Board, Landscape With Skaters, Hessel, Gilt Frame, 17 X 19 In. 500.00
On Board, Rural Landscape, Cows, C.W.Middleton, 7 X 6 In. 247.00
On Board, Tree–Lined Country Home, Gussen Baum, 37 1/2 X 27 In. 20.00

On Board, Watermelon Slice, Fruit, Still Life, Frame, 6 In. 165.00
On Canvas, 3 Baby Chicks, Eating, Lobster, Oil, Frame, 13 X 17 In. 150.00
On Canvas, 5 Pups, Bowl of Milk, Primitive, Frame, 26 X 33 In. 375.00
On Canvas, Bonnie Lass, Scotsman, Girl, Dog, Oval, 14 X 17 In. 350.00
On Canvas, Classical Ruins of Aqueduct, Pastoral, 23 1/4 X 37 In. 350.00
On Canvas, Country Scene At Sunrise, Oil, 12 3/4 X 15 7/8 In. 85.00
On Canvas, Cows At The Pool, 2 Cows, Pond, Trees, Signed, 5 X 6 In. 950.00
On Canvas, F.D.R., Oil, Oval, 42 X 48 In. 450.00
On Canvas, Flowering Cactus, Komos, Frame, 16 1/4 X 28 1/4 In. 45.00
On Canvas, Flowers, Fruit & Fish, Oil, Frame, 30 1/2 X 37 1/2 In. 175.00
On Canvas, Gentleman & Lady, Primitive, Oil, 22 X 27 In., Pair 300.00
On Canvas, Hired Man's Dinner, Oil, 24 X 30 In. 1100.00
On Canvas, Interruption, Peasant Girl, Dressing Hair, 42 X 31 In. 850.00
On Canvas, Judith & Holofernes, Sack, Maidservant, 36 X 42 1/2 In. 250.00
On Canvas, Kitten In Shoe, Oil, Frame, 10 1/2 X 14 In. 125.00
On Canvas, Landscape, Moonlit Cottage By Sea, Oil, 12 X 20 In. 95.00
On Canvas, Loose Thread, Woman, Open Door, Blossom, 33 X 20 In. 2400.00
On Canvas, Man, Bearded, Helmet, Framed, 8 3/8 X 6 5/8 In. 175.00
On Canvas, Melancholy Reveries, Woman, Rose, Garden, 33 X 23 In. 500.00
On Canvas, Old Woman, Oil, Gilt Frame, 34 1/2 X 40 In. 325.00
On Canvas, Papal Benediction, Courtiers, Pope, Frame, 25 X 28 In. 850.00
On Canvas, Portrait, Young Woman, Empire Dress, 14 X 18 In. 350.00
On Canvas, Prince of Denmark, Gold Frame, 27 X 22 In. 475.00
On Canvas, Reclining Putto, Misty Landscape, 10 3/8 X 14 7/8 In. 275.00
On Canvas, Road Home, Woman, Windmill, Cottages, 17 X 23 In. 800.00
On Canvas, Royal Proclamation, King, Scroll, Guards, 24 X 28 In. 900.00
On Canvas, Train Station, Oil, 22 X 30 In. 550.00
On Canvas, Woman With Baby, Oil, Gilt Frame, 15 1/4 X 18 1/4 In. 550.00
On Canvas, Woman With Red Cape, Gilt Frame, 35 X 40 In. 550.00
On Canvas, Young Girl, Blond, Open Book, Oil, 13 1/4 X 15 1/2 In. 750.00
On Ivory, Amorous Victorian Couple, Signed, 2 1/2 X 3 1/4 In. 195.00
On Ivory, Blue Boy, Tile Frame, Brass Trim, 4 X 5 In. 185.00
On Ivory, Cleo DeMerode, Blond Hair, Gilt Frame, 3 1/2 In. 145.00
On Ivory, Lady, 18th–Century Clothes, Kraft, Easel Frame, 5 X 4 In. 1200.00
On Ivory, Lady, Feathered Hat, Gray Hair, Artist, 2 3/4 X 3 1/2 In. 165.00
On Ivory, Little Girl In Pink, Holding Rosebud, 2 3/4 X 2 1/4 In. 1100.00
On Ivory, Mary Pickford, Miniature 95.00
On Ivory, Panel, Gentleman, Period Dress, Landscape, 6 X 4 3/4 In. 175.00
On Ivory, Victorian Couple, 2 1/2 X 3 1/4 In. 125.00
On Ivory, Woman's Head, Inlaid Ivory Frame, 4 3/4 X 5 3/8 In. 85.00
On Ivory, Woman, Long Curls, Framed, 18th Century, Miniature 429.00
On Ivory, Woman, Tortoiseshell Frame, Signed Stieler, 3 3/4 In. 175.00
On Ivory, Young Woman In Empire Period Dress, 5 X 4 In. 100.00
On Masonite, County Fair, Oil, 24 X 36 In. 1300.00
On Panel, 3 Little Kittens, Framed, Signed, 3 X 4 In. 1100.00
On Panel, Boy & Sister, Basket of Produce, Leonide, 11 X 14 In. 1750.00
On Panel, Peter Reiner Van Stepraedt, Armor, Framed, 14 X 11 In. 1400.00
On Panel, Seascape, Sailing Vessels, Framed, Harris, 18 X 22 In. 450.00
On Panel, Woodland Nymph, Partially Draped Woman, 13 X 8 1/2 In. 900.00
On Paper, Cavalier, Cane, Watercolor, Signed, 13 1/2 X 8 1/2 In. 100.00
On Paper, Dogs, Plumed Hat, Table, Watercolor, 12 X 14 In. 165.00
On Paper, Hiker Beside Lake, W.Chase, Frame, 18 1/2 X 32 1/2 In. 35.00
On Paper, Peasant Mother, Child, E.Zampighi, Frame, 15 1/4 X 22 In. 1400.00
On Paper, Pennsylvania Barn In Winter, W. Howard, 21 X 16 3/4 In. 75.00
On Paper, Watercolor, Woman, Lacquered Frame, 4 1/2 X 5 1/2 In. 25.00
On Paper, Woman, Red & Yellow Frame, Watercolor, 8 X 9 In. 375.00
On Porcelain, Black–Haired Woman, With Tambourine, 7 X 9 In. 475.00
On Porcelain, Flowers, Butterfly, Castle, 19th Century, 6 X 5 In. 150.00
On Porcelain, Girl With Candle, Good Night, Germany, 5 X 3 In. 800.00
On Porcelain, Nude, Titled Solitude, Gilt Frame, Germany, 5 X 4 In. 2500.00
On Porcelain, Woman, Reading, Grotto, Bucker, Dresden, 11 X 14 In. 3520.00
On Serigraph, Abraham Lincoln, Leroy Nieman, 18 X 18 In. 385.00
On Silk, Court Ladies Scenes, Mountain Landscape, 34 X 9 In., Pair 250.00
On Tin, Young Lady In White Gown, 6 1/2 X 5 1/2 In. 425.00

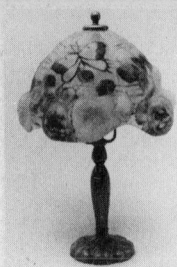

Don't hang an oil painting above a fireplace that is used frequently.

If possible, hang an oil painting on an inside wall away from direct sunlight. Leave a small gap behind the painting to allow air to circulate.

Pairpoint, Lamp, Puffy,
Boudoir, Gray, Butterflies,
    Red, 14 In.

On Velvet, Habana Cuba, Morro Castle, Framed	125.00
On Velvet, Theorum, Basket of Flowers	3520.00
On Wood, Saint With Angel, Arch Shape, 15 X 11 1/2 In.	160.00
On Wood, Windmills, Florentine Frame, 9 3/4 X 11 1/2 In.	275.00
Reverse On Glass, Crucifixion Scene, Framed, 11 1/2 X 13 In., Pair	70.00
Reverse On Glass, Garden Scene, Frame, C.1860, 16 5/8 X 23 In.	850.00
Reverse On Glass, Hongs of Canton In 1840s, 19th Century	7000.00
Reverse On Glass, Maidens, Child, Chinese Export, 16 1/2 X 23 In.	2750.00

The Pairpoint Manufacturing Company started in 1880 in New Bedford, Massachusetts. It soon joined with the glassworks nearby and made glass, silver plated pieces, and lamps. Reverse-painted glass shades and molded shades known as "puffies" were part of the production until the 1930s. The company reorganized and changed its name several times but is still working today. Items listed here are glass or glass and metal. Silver-plated pieces are listed under Silver Plate.

PAIRPOINT, Bowl, Pedestal, Etched Grape Design, 12 In.	395.00
Box, Cut Glass, Intaglio, Brilliant, Rayed Base, Hinged, Fitted	500.00
Box, Glove, Gold Iris Flowers & Leaves, 4 1/2 X 9 1/2 In.	750.00
Box, Gold Iris, White Ground, Opalescent Glass, 4 1/2 X 9 1/2 In.	675.00
Box, Scrolls & Vines of Wild Roses On Cover, 6 3/4 X 4 1/4 In.	660.00
Candle Lamp, Puffy, Cut & Frosted Amethyst, Floral Shade, Pair	380.00
Candleholder, Art Nouveau, 11 1/2 In., Pair	135.00
Candlestick, Art Nouveau Floral Engraving, 11 In., Pair	100.00
Candlestick, Cobalt Honeycomb Cut Glass, Prism, Plated, 14 In.	300.00
Castor, Pickle, Tongs, Threaded Insert	125.00
Cocktail Set, Rouge Flambe, Shaker & 6 Stemmed Tumblers	100.00
Cologne Bottle, Green, Clear Foot, Paperweight Stopper, 7 In.	200.00
Compote, Amber, Classical Engraved Design, Bubble In Stem, 12 In.	110.00
Compote, Classical Engraved, Amber, Bubble Ball Stem, 12 In.	110.00
Compote, Clear Pedestal Base, Cranberry, Pair	187.00
Compote, English Pattern, Star Ray Cut Base, 6 X 6 1/2 In, Pair	175.00
Compote, Engraved Design, Controlled Bubble Stem, 4 1/2 X 8 In.	70.00
Compote, Grape Pattern, Amethyst, 9 In.	85.00
Compote, Murillo Cut, 5 X 6 In.	55.00
Lamp, Desk, Cracked Shade, Signed, Small	325.00
Lamp, Floral, White Glass, Signed, No Shade, 12 In.	275.00
Lamp, Landscape Exeter Shade, Greek Revival Style, Signed	3150.00
Lamp, Oriental Pheasant, Shade On Bronzed Base, Signed, 9 In.	750.00
Lamp, Puffy, Boudoir, Gray, Butterflies, Red, 14 In. *Illus*	2750.00
Lamp, Puffy, Butterflies, Red & Yellow Flower Shade, Gray, 14 In.	2500.00
Lamp, Reverse Painted Floral Shade, Patinated Base, 17 In.	450.00
Lamp, Reverse Painted Garden Scene, Flowering Bushes, 16 In.	3150.00
Lamp, Reverse Painted Landscape, Signed, 18 In.	2100.00
Lamp, Reverse Painted Scenic Shade, 6-Sided, Signed, 27 In.	3500.00
Lamp, Reverse Painted Shade, Different Scene Each Side, Table	6750.00
Lamp, Reverse Painted Shade, Forest Scene, Metal Base, 18 In.	2500.00

Lamp, Reverse Painted Shade, Sailing Ships, Signed 1800.00
Lamp, Reverse Painted Shade, Scene On Base & Shade, Windmills 595.00
Lamp, Reverse Painted Shade, Winter Forest Scene, 18 In. 2150.00
Lamp, Reverse Painted, Golden Bird Border Shade, Urn Base, 20 In. 1900.00
Mirror, Plateau, Beaded Mirror, Reticulated Silver Frame, 10 In. 88.00
Paperweight, Controlled Bubbles, Engraved Egg, Colored Knob 50.00
Paperweight, Red Crimp Rose, Pedestal 210.00
Powder Box, Murillo Pattern, Butterfly & Flowers, 5 In. 245.00
Powder Box, Silsbee, 6 In. 325.00
Tray, Intaglio Peaches, Cherries & Leaves, Round, 13 In. 450.00
Tumbler, Cocktail, Rouge Flambe, Low, Pair 30.00
Urn, Cover, Wheel Engraved, Crystal & Amethyst 95.00
Urn, Flared Rim, Bubble Connector, Cobalt Blue, 13 In. 170.00
Vase, Cornucopia, Bubble Base, Ruby, 9 In., Pair 195.00
Vase, Flared, Footed, Crystal, 9 1/2 In. 70.00
Vase, Fruit Blossoms, Snowbirds, Silver White Ground, 12 In. 500.00
Vase, Horn of Plenty, Green Horn On Bubble Base, 8 1/2 In. 125.00
Vase, Ruby, 12 In. 80.00
Vase, Silsbee, 12 In. 350.00

PALMER COX, BROWNIES, see Brownies

The first paper dolls were probably the pantins, or jumping jacks, made in eighteenth–century Europe. By the 1880s, sheets of printed paper dolls and clothes were being made. The first paper doll books were made in the 1920s. Collectors prefer uncut sheets or books or boxed sets of paper dolls. Prices are about half as much if the pages have been cut.

PAPER DOLL, A Day With Debbie, Uncut 4.00
Baby Brother Tender Love, 1977, Uncut 7.00
Baby Sandy, With Booklet, Cut 35.00
Barbara Britton, Saalfield, 1954, Uncut 60.00
Barbie & Ken, Box 18.00
Barbie, Ken & Midge, Mattel, 32–Page Booklet, 1962 .... 10.00
Barbie, Uncut 6.00
Betsy McCall, Bag, Betsy McCall Goes To Wedding Article 25.00
Bette Davis, 13 Outfits 25.00
Betty Blue & Patty Pink, Merrill, 1949, Uncut 6.00
Betty Bonnet, Christmas, Framed, Uncut 35.00
Betty Grable, 14 Outfits, Cut 35.00
Birthday Party, Whitman, 1961, Uncut 27.00
Blondie Cutout Dolls, Whitman, 1945, Uncut 120.00
Blondie, 1944 .... 20.00
Blondie, Dagwood, Baby Dumpling, Cookie, 44 Outfits, 25 Hats 30.00
Blondie, Entire Bumstead Family, Whitman, 1949, 6 Pages, Uncut 75.00
Bonnie Braids, Uncut 60.00
Boy, Cotton Pants, Tuck, 7 1/4 In. 45.00
Bride & Groom, Merrill, 1949, Uncut 10.00
Courtly Beatrice, Tuck 90.00
Crissy, 1971, Cut 10.00
Deanna Durbin, 14 Outfits, Cut 45.00
Debby, Jaymar, 1950s, Uncut 22.00
Dinah Shore, 1954, Cut 33.00
Dolls of Christmas, Ernest Nister, London, Full Box 150.00
Dolly Dingle's Little Friend Peggs, Sheet, 1916 .... 12.00
Doris Day, Original Folder, 31 Outfits 48.00
Dorothy Lamour, 26 Outfits 25.00
Dr. Kildare & Nurse Susan 25.00
Dresses Worn By First Ladies, 1937, Uncut 60.00
Elvis Presley & Priscilla, Uncut, Outfits From His Movies 20.00
Esther Williams, Merrill, 1950, Uncut 45.00
Fairy Tale Figures, Hallmark, Album, 1948 .... 25.00
Fairy Tale Series, McLaughlin, Container 150.00
Fels Naptha, Cloth, 1933 .... 65.00
First Family, Uncut 15.00

Four Campus Queens, Uncut	6.00
Gene Autry, Whitman, 1951, Uncut	45.00
Girl Scouts, Uncut	20.00
Girl, Red Skirt, Tuck, 7 3/4 In.	45.00
Gone With The Wind, 108 Costume Pieces, Cut, Merrill, 1940	175.00
Gone With The Wind, Merrill, Punchout, 7 1/2 In. Rhett, 14 Piece	271.00
Gone With The Wind, Uncut, 5 Doll Book, Merrill	100.00
Gone With The Wind, Uncut, 18 Doll Book, Merrill	250.00
Grace Kelly, Whitman, 1955, Uncut	45.00
Greer Garson, 1944, Uncut	192.00
Hedy Lamar, 27 Outfits	45.00
Hedy Lamar, Merrill, Punchout	60.00
Here Comes The Bride, 1967, Uncut	6.00
Hood's Sarsaparilla, Clothes	50.00
Jane Russell, 1955	30.00
Jane Withers, Clothes, Doll, 1938, 13 1/2 In.	50.00
Janie, Playtime House, 1947, Uncut	20.00
Jeanette MacDonald, Merrill, Cut	60.00
Judy Garland, Whitman, 1940	41.00
Ladies of The White House, 1930	55.00
Lana Turner, Whitman, 1942	60.00
Lion Coffee, Shoemaker, Uncut	18.00
Little Lulu, Kleenex	18.00 To 20.00
Little Lulu, Oversized, 1960, 34 In., Uncut	90.00
Little Neighbor, 1940s	10.00
Lordly Lionel, Tuck	80.00
Lucille Ball, Uncut	42.00
Magic Mary Lou, Milton Bradley, 1955, Uncut	22.00
Malibu Skipper, Uncut	5.00
Mary Hartline, Kellogg's, Box, Uncut	60.00
Mary Martin, 1942, Uncut	73.00 To 85.00
Miss Molly Munsing, Munsingwear, Uncut Sheet	37.50
Munsters, 1966, Uncut	65.00
My Farm, Whitman, 1955, Uncut	15.00
My Little Margie, 1954, Uncut	75.00
National Velvet, 1962, Uncut	23.00
New Shirley Temple, 1942, Uncut	120.00
Nurse & Doctor, Saalfield, 1952, Uncut	16.00
Our Soldier Jim, 1943, Uncut	45.00
Pat Boone, Cut	15.00
Patsy Lou, McCall, 22 In.	35.00
Polly's Playmates, Spanish Dance, 1911, Uncut	25.00
Rita Hayworth, 26 Outfits	25.00
Rosemary Clooney, 1959, Uncut	35.00 To 65.00
Scrappy's Puppet Theater, 1936, Uncut	40.00
Sesame Street, 1976, Uncut	6.00
Shirley Temple, Sheet, 1976, Uncut	20.00
Snow White & Seven Dwarfs, Whitman	35.00
Sweet Alice, Original Envelope, Tuck, Complete, C.1890	119.00
Teddy Bear, Behr–Manning Sandpaper Co., Troy, N.Y., 1930s, Uncut	27.00
Teenager Tammie Lea, Box	8.00
Texas Rose, With Scissors, Uncut	15.00
That Girl, 1967, Uncut	40.00
Tillie The Toiler, Whitman, 10 Pages, 1942, Uncut	144.00
Trixie Belden, 1958, Uncut	35.00
Twiggy, 1967, Uncut	28.00
United We Stand, Children In Uniform	58.00
Wiggie The Mod Model, 1967, Uncut	6.00
World War II Doll, 62 Outfits	25.00

 Paper collectibles, including almanacs, catalogs, children's books, stock certificates, and other paper ephemera, are listed here. Paper calendars are listed separately under Calendar Paper.

PAPER, Almanac, Burcock Blood Bitters, Foster Milburn & Co., 1887–88	15.00

Almanac, Farmer's, New England Map, 1843, 48 Pages 10.00
Atlas, Cassell's, 35, 000 Index, 1930 .... 25.00
Atlas, Parke County, 1917 .... 52.50
Atlas, Rand McNally, State & Country, 1909 .... 30.00
B.W.Cigarette Papers, Blue Label 5.00
Backdrop, Punch & Judy, C.1910, 8 X 8 In. 1175.00
Bank Draft, Signed By 2 Mormon Apostles, Dated 1903 .... 175.00
Banner, I Am An American Day, Tuesday, Oct. 1940, 6 In. 4.00
Birth Record, Jeremiah Small, Falmouth, Mass., Oct., 1787, 15 X 12 In. 4400.00
Book, American Annual Golf Guide, Anderson, 1924 .... 50.00
Book, Big Little Book, Ella Cinders 20.00
Book, Big Little Book, Jungle Jim 26.00
Book, Big Little Book, Mickey Mouse Runs His Own Newspaper 39.50
Book, Big Little Book, Red Ryder and The Rimrock Killers 19.00
Book, Big Little Book, Tarzan In The Land of The Giant Apes 24.00
Book, Big Little Book, Terry & The Pirates and The Giant's Vengance 16.00
Book, Coloring, Carmen Miranda, Saalfield, 20 Pgs., Unused, 11 X 14 In. 271.00
Book, Coloring, Merry Christmas, Santa Claus, Unused, 1949 .... 8.00
Book, Coloring, Terry & The Pirates, 1946 .... 15.00
Book, Coupon, Irvington Ice & Coal, Indianapolis, 1920s, 48 Coupons 12.50
Book, Movie Flip, Funny Jungleland, Kellogg's, Dated 1909, 8 X 10 In. 18.00
Book, Navigation Dictionary, U.S.N., 1956 .... 5.00
Book, Nelson Eddy, Songs, Article, Photos, 1935, 8 1/2 X 11 1/2 In. 9.00
Book, Temperance Union, Blue By-Laws, Small 3.00
Bookplate, American Indian, With Pottery, Howard E.Wheelock, 3 X 4 In 2.00
Bookplate, Knights In Armour, Martha Riley Pratt, C.1920, 3 X 2 In. 2.00
Broadside, Nosh's Ark, Printer's Error, Should Be Noah's, 1870, 32 In. 3500.00
Broadside, White House Society, Brown Shoe Co., 1908, 19 X 29 In. 125.00
Calling Card, Cupid & Floral, Lizzie L. Kinney, 1880s, 3 X 2 In. 2.50
Calling Card, Floral Spray, Susie R. Lewis, 1880s, 3 X 2 In. 3.00
Cap, Milk Bottle, Roosevelt, Red, White & Blue 1.75
Catalog, A.H. Hoffman, Inc., Landisville, Pa., 1931, 12 X 6 In. 12.00
Catalog, American Radiator Co., N.Y., 1938, 85 Pages 12.00
Catalog, American Wholesale Corporation, 1920, 488 Pages, 10 X 13 In. 24.00
Catalog, Bakery, Confection & Ice Cream Supplies, 271 Pages, 1934 .... 45.00
Catalog, Baltimore Bargain House, Md., 1912, 18 Pages, 9 3/4 X 13 In. 16.00
Catalog, Barnes' Foot-Power Machinery, 45 Pages, 1872 .... 7.00
Catalog, Bathroom Furnishings, Standard, 55 Pages, 1929 .... 45.00
Catalog, Cavendish Brothers, West Huntington, Wallpaper Samples, 1925 .... 13.00
Catalog, Congoleum Pattern Book, 64 Pages, All Color, 1927 .... 20.00
Catalog, Craftsman Furnishings For The Home, Eastwood, N.Y., 1912 .... 375.00
Catalog, Delta Machinery, 52 Pages, 1941 .... 12.00
Catalog, Domestic Fashion Co., N.Y., Summer, 32 Pages, 1882 .... 24.00
Catalog, Eastman Kodak Co., Rochester, N.Y., 1925, 64 Pages 18.00
Catalog, Foster Stove Co., Ironton, Oh., 1928, 94 Pages, 7 X 10 In. 26.00
Catalog, Frank Marshall, Chicago., Ill., 1931, 20 Pages, 5 1/2 X 8 In. 36.00
Catalog, Funston Fur Co., Color Cover, 1930s 10.00
Catalog, Goodyear's Rubber Mfg. Co. & I.R. Glove Mfg.Co., 1900 .... 27.00
Catalog, H.E. Verran & Co., Inc., N.Y., 1917, 40 Pages, 9 1/2 X 7 In. 7.50
Catalog, H.M. Sheer Co., Quincy, Ill., 1905, 7 3/4 X 5 1/4 In. 15.00
Catalog, Higbee Co., Annual August Fur Sale, 1917,, 6 X 9 In. 19.00
Catalog, High Grade Metal & Tinware, 1903 .... 75.00
Catalog, International Typewriter Exchange, Chicago, 1927, 16 Pages 19.00
Catalog, Iver Johnson Fire Arms, Foldout Picture of Revolver 65.00
Catalog, John F. Woodruff Co., Conn., N.Y., Ye Style of 1903, 26 Pgs. 14.00
Catalog, L. Erikson Electric Co., Boston, Ma., No.91, 1925, 71 Pages 20.00
Catalog, L.& J.G. Stickley Furniture, 1910, 9 3/8 X 7 1/4 In. 100.00
Catalog, L.L. Bean, Freeport, Me., 1927, 24 Pages, 8 1/2 X 7 1/2 In. 17.00
Catalog, Leon Myers, Cigars & Tobacco Premiums, Est.1875 .... 15.00
Catalog, Lionel Train, 1937 .... 35.00
Catalog, Montgomery Ward Photography, 1943, 35 Pages 12.00
Catalog, Montgomery Ward, 1895, 624 Pages 17.00
Catalog, Montgomery Ward, 1935-36, 748 Pages 26.00
Catalog, Montgomery Ward, Christmas, 1942 .... 40.00

Catalog, Montgomery Ward, Fall & Winter, Mailing Wrapper, 1935–36	50.00
Catalog, Montgomery Ward, Spring & Summer, 1943	10.00
Catalog, Mutual Furniture Mfg. Co., Miamisburg, Ohio, 1930, 47 Pages	34.00
Catalog, National Bellas Hess, Fall–Winter, 1936, 158 Pages, 11 In.	14.00
Catalog, New Era Optical Co., Chicago, 1930, 11 1/2 X 9 3/4 In.	17.00
Catalog, Pneuvac Co., Worcester, Mass., C.1920, 17 Pages, 8 X 11 In.	23.00
Catalog, Progress Tailoring Co., Chicago, Spring & Summer, 1941	13.50
Catalog, R.H. White & Co., Boston, Fall & Winter, 1895–06, 112 Pages	34.00
Catalog, Rayburn Line, Lady's Corsets, Petticoats, Linens, 1900s	15.00
Catalog, S.S. Kresge, 5 Cent & 10 Cent Merchandise, 128 Pages, 1913	25.00
Catalog, Savage Fire Arms, 1946	20.00
Catalog, Sears, Roebuck, 1938–39	50.00
Catalog, Sears, Roebuck, Christmas, 1943	45.00
Catalog, Sears, Roebuck, Fall & Winter, 1934	11.00
Catalog, Sears, Roebuck, Sewing Machines, 1917, 24 Pages	11.00
Catalog, Sears, Roebuck, Spring & Summer, 1931	55.00
Catalog, Sears, Roebuck, Wallpaper, 1930	8.00
Catalog, Sears, Roebuck & Co., Chicago, 1928, 20 Pages, 6 X 9 In.	19.00
Catalog, Silver & Co., Brooklyn, N.Y., 40 Pages, 1905	26.00
Catalog, Spiegel, May, Stern Co., Christmas, Chicago, 1924, 58 Pages	18.00
Catalog, Stearns Conveyor Co., Cleveland, Ohio, 1926, 10 1/2 In.	5.00
Catalog, Underwood Typewriter Co., N.Y., 32 Pages, C.1906, 7 X 8 In.	13.00
Catalog, Victor Talking Machine Co., Camden, N.J., 1910, 24 Pages	24.00
Catalog, W.J. Holliday & Co., No.75, Illustrations, 1931, 582 Pages	16.00
Catalog, White Bicycles, Color Pictures, 1896	175.00
Catalog, Wilkinson Co., Chicago, 1893, 80 Pages, 10 3/4 X 7 3/4 In.	42.00
Catalog, Winchester, Spring Fishing, 1924	120.00
Credit Card, Phillips 66 Passport To Everywhere	5.00
Dispenser, Cigarette, Zig–Zag	24.00
Flier, Sherman Clothes Wringer, Woman, Flag Dress, Pre–1866, Envelope	37.50
Fraktur, Anna Abel, Birds On Vine, 1835, 11 X 8 1/2 In.	3575.00
Fraktur, Baptismal, Johann Frederick Lupold, 8 1/4 X 13 1/4 In.	2200.00
Fraktur, Birds On Leafy Vine, Spiky Flowers, Walnut Frame, 8 X 6 In.	3025.00
Fraktur, Birth & Baptismal, Nancy Klein, 1823, 10 1/4 X 7 1/2 In.	3025.00
Fraktur, Birth & Baptismal, Sarah Seifer, Angels, 9 X 6 1/2 In.	9350.00
Fraktur, Birth Letter, Parrots, Catharina Fing, 1811, 8 1/2 X 12 In.	4400.00
Fraktur, Birth, Berks Co., Penna., Birds, Angels, 15 1/4 X 18 2/3 In.	55.00
Fraktur, Birth, Geburts Und Taufschein, 1824, 14 1/2 X 17 1/2 In.	75.00
Fraktur, Birth, Grater Und Blumer, 1832, 15 1/2 X 18 3/4 In.	155.00
Fraktur, Dauphin County, Penna., Printer Ritter, 15 1/2 X 18 3/4 In.	135.00
Fraktur, David Bold Birth, 1806, Cutout Design, Penna., 13 X 17 In.	600.00
Fraktur, Frantz Matthaus Reichert, 1787, Tramp Art Frame	750.00
Fraktur, Haus Seegen AD 1785, Flowers, Crowns, Framed, 15 X 19 In.	400.00
Fraktur, Kate Butsbaugh, Jan. 2, 1865, Ink, 5 1/2 X 6 In.	105.00
Fraktur, Man, Top Hat, Swallowtail Coat, 1812, 7 1/2 X 12 In.	6875.00
Fraktur, Marriage Certificate, 1899, Pennsylvania, Frame, 16 X 20 In.	75.00
Fraktur, Samuel Angene, 1830, Fruit, Framed, 4 X 6 1/2 In.	1175.00
Fraktur, Sawtooth Central Circle, Martin Brechall, Dated 1807	1300.00
Fraktur, Vorschrift, Flowers, Red & Black Ink, 9 1/2 X 14 In.	85.00
Fraktur, Wedding, Angel Figures, Bird, Cupid, Pennsylvania, 1818	1500.00
Fratkur, Marriage Certificate, Wisconsin, 1887, 16 X 20 In.	75.00
Hunting License, New York State Residence, 1932	10.00
Land Sale, President Benjamin Harrison, 1891, 10 X 15 In.	150.00
Magazine, National Geographic, 1908	20.00
Magazine, National Geographic, Vol. 3, No. 1, 1891–92	180.00
Magazine, National Geographic, Vol. 4, No. 2, 1892–93	200.00
Menu, Cotton Club, 1936	110.00
Menu, Pioneer's Sons & Daughters, Chicago, Tremont House, 1989	10.00
Menu, Thanksgiving Day, U.S.Army Detachment Medical Corps, 1918	12.00
Newspaper, Brooklyn Daily Eagle, 4 Pages, 1853	4.00
Newspaper, Harper's Weekly, Gen. Sherman's Rear Guard, April 2, 1864	12.00
Newspaper, New York Herald, San Francisco Earthquake, April 22, 1906	18.00
Program, Annie Get Your Gun, Ethel Merman, 1947	12.50
Program, Clyde Beatty Circus, Magazine, Coca–Cola Ad Back Cover	10.00

Program, Folies Bergere, 1927 .... 17.00
Program, Graduation, Purdue University, Layafette, Ind., 1906 .... 20.00
Program, Ice Follies, Fitzwillis Cover, 1954, 9 1/2 X 12 In. 15.00
Program, Indiana St. Teachers Vs. Eastern Illinois Teachers, 1937 .... 8.50
Program, Romeo & Juliet, Norma Shearer & Leslie Howard, 1936, 14 Pgs. 65.00
Program, Sonja Henie, Hollywood Ice Revue, Plush Red Cover, 1947 .... 17.00
Program, Yehudi Menuhin, Civic Auditorium, San Jose, Cal., 1937 .... 50.00
Schedule, TWA Flight, Sepia, Map, July 1, 1933, 3 X 6 In. 25.00
Stock Certificate, Carrie S. Gold Mining Co., Cripple Creek, Colo. 20.00
Stock Certificate, Chatata Lead & Zinc Mining Co., Tennessee, 1903 .... 10.00
Stock Certificate, Grant Motor Car, 1919 .... 80.00
Stock Certificate, Home Insurance Co., 4 Women On Top of Globe 5.00
Stock Certificate, Little Mattie Mining, Milling & Power Co., 1903 .... 35.00
Stock Certificate, Okmulgee Oil Co., Muskogee, Indian Territory, 1896 .... 155.00
Stock Certificate, Pneumatic Scale Corporation, W.H. Doble, 1931 .... 35.00
Stock Certificate, Violet Milling & Mining Co., Washington, 1898 .... 20.00

Paperweights must have first appeared along with paper in ancient Egypt. Today's collectors search for every type from the very expensive French weights of the nineteenth century to the modern artist weights or advertising pieces. The glass tops of the paperweights sometimes have been nicked or scratched and this type of damage can be removed by polishing. Some serious collectors think this type of repair is an alteration and will not buy a repolished weight; others think it is an acceptable technique of restoration that does not change the value. Baccarat paperweights are listed separately under Baccarat.

PAPERWEIGHT, Advertising, Acme Lumber, San Francisco, Glass 20.00
Advertising, Aunt Jemima, Union Malleable Iron Co., 2 1/4 In. 38.00
Advertising, Boston's Cumner Jones & Co., 2 1/2 In. 353.00
Advertising, Brainard, Minnesota, Lake Scene, Glass, 3 In. 30.00
Advertising, Buffalo Speedometer Service Station, N.Y., Iron 45.00
Advertising, Crane Co., 75th Anniversary, Brass, 2 3/8 In. 30.00
Advertising, Dutch Boy Paint 25.00
Advertising, Georgia Department of Labor, Glass 14.00
Advertising, Goodyear Tires, Mirrored Bottom, 4 X 3 In. 12.50
Advertising, GW Munoz Garage, Glass 25.00
Advertising, James Hanley Brewing Co. 30.00
Advertising, Lehigh Sewer Pipe & Tile Co., Ft.Dodge, 4 In. 12.00
Advertising, Parker Bear, Best I Have Ever Had 195.00
Advertising, Prudential Insurance Co., 1875–1975, Brass 37.50
Advertising, Scottish Union Insurance Co., Brass, 3 7/8 In. 75.00
Baccarat, Concentric 130.00
Blue Overlay, Floral Cane Center, Thumbprint Cutting 100.00
Bust of George Washington, Frosted Intaglio, Clear, 2 3/4 In. 50.00
Bust of John J. Pershing, 1917, Reverse Gold Paint, 3 7/8 In. 160.00
Butterfly & Floral Canes, White Latticino Ground 300.00
Capitol, Clear, Rectangular, 4 1/4 In. 15.00
Cat & Tree Stump, Iron 25.00
Clichy Type, Clematis, Deep Blue Velvet, Bubbles, 2 1/4 In. 700.00
Columbus, Clear & Frosted, Flat, Circular, 3 1/4 In. .... 65.00 To 75.00
Dark Blue, Faceted Crystal, Large 90.00
Donkey, Democratic Symbol, Cast Iron 32.00
Eagle & N.R.A., Blue & Red Paint, Cast Iron, 3 5/8 In. 75.00
Flint Bottle Co., Allentown, Penna. 22.00
Floral, Multicolor, Joe St. Clair, Large 33.00
Frosted Ground, Acid Etched, 3 In. 100.00
Frosted, Washington, Clear, Flat, Circular, 3 1/8 In. 110.00
G.A.R. Encampment, 28th National, Pittsburgh, 1894, 3 In. 100.00
Glass, Don't Forget Your Father, 3 In. 55.00
Green Beehive, Signed Vandermark 65.00
Hamon, Pink Crocus, Pedestal 125.00
Kitten, Cast Iron, 3 In. 25.00
Kosta, Seaweed, Bubbles, Crystal, Beaded, Signed, 3 3/4 X 4 In. 72.00

Lincoln, Frosted Bust & Sides, Pressed Glass, 3 1/4 In.	10.00
Lookout Mountain, Tennessee, White	22.00
Lotton, Floral, Heart Shaped Green & Gold Leaves, Frosted, 1977	55.00
Masonic, Blue, Pink & White, Union Glass Co., 3 1/4 In.	10.00
McKinley, Pressed Glass, Frosted Head & Shoulders, 5 X 4 In.	25.00
Memorial Hall, Frosted, Oval, Black Glass, 6 In.	40.00
Millefiori, Canes In Concentric Rings, Murano, 2 1/4 In.	42.00
Millefiori, Teapot, Clear Frosted Spout & Handle	55.00
New Salem State Park, Illinois, Glass, 2 3/4 In.	30.00
Panama Pacific Exposition, Material From Canal, 3 1/2 In.	25.00
Red Floral, Signed Vandermark	65.00
Remember The Maine, White Ship, Multicolored Ground, 2 5/8 In.	100.00
Sandwich, Blue Poinsettia	400.00
Snow Dome, American Flag, Glass Globe, Plastic Base	20.00
Snow Dome, Baby Seal, Sitting On Rock, Black Bakelite Base	39.00
Snow Dome, Chief Sitting Bull, Black Ceramic Base	35.00
Snow Dome, Dog, Black Face, White Body, Brown Ceramic Base	30.00
Snow Dome, Empire State Building, Glass Globe, Plastic Base	20.00
Snow Dome, General Douglas MacArthur, Black Ceramic Base	45.00
Snow Dome, Girl, Blue & Red Snowsuit, Green Muffs, Ozarks Lake	45.00
Snow Dome, House, Red Roof, Pine Trees, Snow, Black Base	30.00
Snow Dome, Man & Monkey, Organ Grinder, Black Ceramic Base	30.00
Snow Dome, RCA Nipper Dog, Pink Water, Black Ceramic Base	65.00
Snow Dome, Snowman, Glass Globe, Plastic Base	10.00
Snow Dome, Snowman, Red Hat, Black Ceramic Base	30.00
Snow Dome, WAC Saluting, Pink Water, Black Ceramic Base	45.00
Snow Dome, Washington Monument, Glass Globe, Plastic Base	15.00
Snow Dome, White Bear, Glass Globe, Plastic Base	10.00
Snow Dome, World War II Airplane, Black Ceramic Base	45.00
Soldiers' Home, Marion, Ind.	16.00
Spread Eagle, Bronze, Camp Hancock	125.00
St. Clair, Apple, Carnival Glass, Cobalt Blue	70.00
St. Clair, Sulfide, Batter, Bat On Lap, Hat To Side, 2 In.	80.00
St. Louis, 6 Windows Revealing Millefiore Mushroom Center	275.00
St. Louis, Concentric Millefiori, Mushroom	2300.00
St. Louis, Doily Pattern Millefiori, Blue Flash Ground	190.00
St. Louis, Floral Bouquet, Thumbprint Cutting	400.00
St. Louis, Floral, Cane, Red, White & Blue Latticinio Ribbons	750.00
St. Louis, Newel Post, Brass Mounted, 1974	475.00
Standing Figure of Columbus, Holding Globe, Flat, 4 1/2 In.	210.00
Stankard, Raspberry Plant, Rectangular, 3 7/8 In.	2200.00
Stankard, Violet, 1978	750.00
Stankard, Yellow Meadow Wreath, Green	950.00
Temple Block, Salt Lake City, Reverse Painting Under Glass	18.00
Viking Ship, 8–Sided	175.00
Washington, Frosted Bust & Rim, Pressed Glass, 3 3/16 In.	70.00
White Eagle, In God We Trust On Banner, 3 1/2 In.	10.00
White House, Home Sweet Home, 3 1/2 In.	15.00
Women's Pavilion, Pressed Glass, Frosted Edge, Oval, 4 3/8 In.	60.00
World Columbian Exposition, Glass, 1893, 4 X 2 3/8 In.	45.00
Ysart, 4 Flower Bouquet, Surrounded By Gold Ribbon	450.00

Papier–mache is made from paper mixed with glue, chalk, and other ingredients, then molded and baked. It becomes very hard and can be painted. Boxes, trays, and furniture were made of papier–mache. Some of the nineteenth–century pieces were decorated with mother–of–pearl.

PAPIER–MACHE, see also Furniture

PAPIER–MACHE, Afghan Hound, Sitting, Life Size	375.00
Animal, Horse, Giraffe, Pig, Donkey, Painted, 3 To 5 In., 4 Piece	130.00
Bird, On Perch, Wood, White Polychrome, 4 5/8 In.	105.00
Boots, Santa	35.00
Carnival Mask, Horsehair Beard	275.00
Chickens, Rooster & Hen, Wooden Base, Gray & White, 3 1/4 In.	80.00

Coaster Set, Red, Flowers, Round Box, Occupied Japan, 8 Piece 28.00
Donkey, Gray Paper Felt Coat, Glass Eyes, 4 1/2 In. 65.00
Easter Egg, Large 33.00
Mask, Man's Face, With Beard, Larger Than Man's Head 350.00
Powder Box, Woman 35.00
Roly Poly, Clown, Germany, 10 In. 90.00
Rooster, Polychrome Trim, Orange Paint, Wooden Base, 4 3/4 In. 30.00
Soldier, French, Handlebar Mustache, Molded, 1890s, 19 In. 565.00
Tiger, Canton, Ohio, C.1930, Life Size, 36 X 72 In. 1400.00
Tray, Chippendale, Gold Leaf Design, Custom Stand, London, 1830 .... 3850.00
Tray, Gilt Flower Still Life, Black Lacquer, 28 1/2 X 22 In. 9350.00
Tray, House & Flowers, 14 X 12 In. 20.00
Tray, On Stand, Moths, Wisteria, Peach Blooms, Black Lacquer 2100.00
Tray, Pheasants, Florals, 19th Century, 22 1/2 X 28 3/4 In. 400.00
Tub, Silver Band, Iron Rim Handles, Amber Paint, 8 X 17 In. 20.00
Turkeys, Tom & Hen, Nodding Heads, Pewter Feet, 3 3/4 In., Pair 100.00
    PARASOL, see Umbrella

Parian is a fine–grained, hard–paste porcelain named for the marble it resembles. It was first made in England in 1846 and gained in favor in the United States about 1860. Figures, tea sets, vases, and other items were made of Parian at many English and American factories.

PARIAN, Box, Fairies, Pink & White, Art Nouveau 60.00
Bust, Dickens, 15 1/4 In. 140.00
Bust, George Washington, Painted Base, 10 1/2 In. 45.00
Candleholder, Three Graces At Base 37.50
Figurine, Bringing In The Wheat, Man & Woman, 11 In. 100.00
Figurine, Nude, Drapery On Legs, Standing Next To Urn, 9 1/2 In. 45.00
Figurine, Penelophon, The Beggar Maid, 2 Ft.6 In. 1800.00
Figurine, Swan Boat, Cherub Riders, Porcelain, Pair 50.00
Figurine, Young Girls, 1 Playing Harp, 1 Praying, 8 1/2 In., Pair 75.00
Jug, Embossed Classical Figures, White, 9 3/4 In. 155.00
Lamp, Horses, Dolphins, Cherubs, Cast Metal, Silk Shade, 39 1/2 In. 85.00
Match Holder, 2 Owls On Branch, 8 In. 85.00
Pitcher, Classical Women Representing Art, Science, 1862, 8 In. 110.00
Plaque, Scene From Dr. Faustus, 14 In., Pair 308.00
Vase, Landscape Scene, Leaf Form, 17 In., Pair 275.00
Vase, White Berries & Leaves, Blue, 6 In. 60.00

Vieux Paris, or Old Paris, is porcelain ware that is known to have been made in Paris in the eighteenth or early nineteenth century. These porcelains have no identifying mark but can be identified by the whiteness of the porcelain and the lines and decorations.

PARIS, Basket, Centerpiece, Reticulated, Anneau D'Or, C.1825 .... 220.00
Candleholder, Chinese Man & Woman, Standing, Pair 5500.00
Cup & Saucer, Paisley, C.1815 .... 200.00
Dessert Service, Floral Design, Blue, Gold Trim, 33 Piece 750.00
Figurine, Rooster, Yellow, Orange, Green, Blue, Label, 18 1/2 X 14 In. 290.00
Garniture Set, Louis XV, Blue Celeste, Clock & 2 Vases 2970.00
Inkstand, Eagle Form 165.00
Lamp Base, Flowers, White Ground, Baluster, 17 In. ....*Illus* 1600.00
Vase, Bucolic Scene, Amphora, C.1810 .... 220.00
Vase, Castle Scene, Cobalt Blue, 1825, 21 1/2 In., Pair ....*Illus* 4950.00
Vase, Everted Rim, Painted Courting Couple, Gilt Border, 22 In. 850.00
Vase, Fan, Floral, Vines, Gold, Cobalt Blue, 13 1/2 In. 325.00
Vase, Flared, Courting Couple, Gilt Accents, C.1850, 17 3/4 In., Pair 500.00
Vase, Flowers, Raised Scrolls, Gold, Mantel Type, Porcelian, 16 In. 145.00
Vase, French Court Scene, Rose Ground, Gold, White, Handles, 16 X 7 In. 245.00
Vase, Garniture, Neoclassical, C.1820, 15 1/2 In. 450.00
Vase, Reserves of Flowers, Scrolled Handles, 7 1/2 In., Pair 200.00
Vase, The Arts, Science & Literature, Mask Handles, C.1825, Pair 700.00

Pate–de–verre is an ancient technique in which glass is made by blending and refining powdered glass of different colors into molds. The process was revived by French glassmakers, especially Galle, around the end of the nineteenth century.

PATE–DE–VERRE, Figurine, Lady, Sitting, Green Bench, Grecian, 8 In. 3500.00

Pate–sur–pate means paste on paste. The design was made by painting layers of slip on the ceramic piece until a relief decoration was formed. The method was developed at the Sevres factory in France about 1850. It became even more famous at the English Minton factory about 1870. It has since been used by many potters to make both pottery and porcelain wares.

PATE–SUR–PATE, Card Tray, Chinese Pheasants, Gold Trim 120.00
Plate, Dinner, Set of 8 .... 1980.00
Tray, Cherub & Woman, White On Blue, Signed, 6 In. 45.00
Vase, Baluster Form, Everted Rim, Boy, White Body, 10 In., Pr. 200.00
Vase, Cupid Chasing Butterfly, Black Ground, 6 In. 535.00
Vase, Figure of Woman, Celadon Green Ground, 8 1/2 In. 350.00
Vase, Olive Green, Woman's Bust, 2 Handles, C.1880, 9 In. 275.00
Vase, Raised Flowers, Leaves, Roman Gold Handles, 10 3/8 In. 295.00
Vase, Shield Shape Body, Teal Blue Ground, Meissen, 12 In. 1400.00

Paul Revere pottery was made at several locations in and around Boston, Massachusetts, between 1906 and 1942. The pottery was operated as a settlement house program for teen–aged girls. Many pieces were signed "S.E.G." for Saturday Evening Girls. The artists concentrated on children's dishes and tiles. Decorations were outlined in black and filled with color.

PAUL REVERE POTTERY, Bowl, Blue, Shaded Pockmarks, Flared, Low, 5 In. 45.00
Bowl, Ducks, White On Green, Blue, SEG, 1910, 4 1/4 In. 250.00
Bowl, Midnight Ride, Inside Motto, 1941, 7 1/4 In. 1900.00

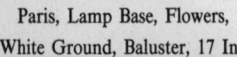
Paris, Lamp Base, Flowers, White Ground, Baluster, 17 In.

Paris, Vase, Castle Scene, Cobalt Blue, 1825, 21 1/2 In., Pair

Bowl, Mustard Glaze, Stamped 55.00
Bowl, White Geese, Blue & Green Ground, SEG, 11 1/2 In. 1200.00
Cup & Saucer, Black, White Cup Interior 95.00
Flower Frog, Robin's–Egg Blue, SEG 25.00
Plate, Running Rabbits, Blue Banded Ground, 6 1/4 In. 325.00
Plate, Undecorated 125.00
Tea Set, Teapot, Sugar, Creamer, Cup & Saucer, 35 Piece 750.00

Peachblow glass originated about 1883 at Hobbs, Brockunier and Company of Wheeling, West Virginia. It is a glass that shades from yellow to peach. It was lined with white glass. New England peachblow is a one–layer glass shading from red to white. Mt. Washington peachblow shades from pink to blue. Reproductions of all types of peachblow have been made. Some are poor and easy to identify as copies, others are very accurate reproductions and could fool the unwary.

PEACHBLOW, Biscuit Jar, Floral Design, Mother–of–Pearl, Silver Plated Mount 225.00
Butter, Cover, Inverted Thumbprint, Cut Clear Amber Knob, 7 In. 175.00
Creamer, New England, Vertical Shading of Pink & White 335.00
Creamer, Wheeling, Drape Pattern, Square Mouth, 4 1/2 In. 795.00
Cruet, Mahogany Spout, Cream Base, White Lining, Wheeling 1285.00
Cruet, Wheeling, White Lining, Trefoil Top, 6 1/2 In. 1285.00
Decanter, Handle & Stopper, New England Type, French, 11 In. 450.00
Finger Bowl, New England, 2 1/2 X 5 1/4 In. 335.00
    PEACHBLOW, GUNDERSON, see Gunderson
Lamp, Hobnail, Hanging 3250.00
Pear, Blown, Life Size, 4 7/8 In. 200.00
Perfume Bottle, New England, Pewter Fitting, 8 3/4 In. 350.00
Pitcher, Can Pattern, Green Cut To Clear, 8 1/2 In. 450.00
Pitcher, Enameled, Reeded Handle, Amber, 10 In. 650.00
Pitcher, Milk, New England, 9–Crimp Top, 1 Crimp Becomes Spout 1185.00
Pitcher, Overshot, Clear Applied Handle, 7 3/4 In. 200.00
Pitcher, Tankard, Diamond–Quilted, Mother–of–Pearl, 9 3/4 In. 175.00
Pitcher, Water, Amber Handle, White Lining, Wheeling, 8 1/2 In. 1550.00
Pitcher, Wheeling, Fuchsia To Amber, Applied Amber Handle, 4 In. 425.00
Punch Cup, New England, Reeded Opaque White Handle 225.00
Punch Cup, New England, Rose, White Handle & Interior, 2 3/4 In. 385.00
Punch Cup, New England, World's Fair, 1893 .... 395.00
Punch Cup, Wheeling, Satin Finish, Applied Amber Handle 225.00
Rose Bowl, New England, 7–Crimp Top, 2 1/2 X 3 In. 295.00
Rose Bowl, Open Bubbles, Sandwich, 3 7/8 In. 90.00
Rose Bowl, Satin Glass, Molded Shells, 4 In. 75.00
Toothpick, Lemon Yellow To Deep Raspberry, White Interior 145.00
Toothpick, Shiny Finish, Tricorner, 2 1/4 In. 400.00
Tumbler, Diamond–Quilted, Velvet Satin Glass 230.00
Tumbler, Peach To Creamy Yellow, Mt. Washington 170.00
Tumbler, Satin Finish, Wheeling, 3 5/8 In. 300.00
Vase, Diamond–Quilted, Mother–of–Pearl, Pinched Sides, 7 In., Pr. 225.00
Vase, Gunderson, Crimped Rim, 6 1/2 X 4 In. 160.00
Vase, Hobnail, Rose Bowl Shape, Double Crimp, 5 In. 25.00
Vase, New England, Opaque White Handles, Square Top, 4 In. 700.00
Vase, New England, Rose To White, Ribbed, 2 1/2 In. 335.00
Vase, Stick, Wheeling, 10 In. 1200.00
    PEACHBLOW, WEBB, see Webb Peachblow

Listed under Pearl are items made of the natural mother–of–pearl from shells. The glassware known as mother–of–pearl is listed by that name. Opera glasses made with natural pearl shell are listed under Opera Glasses. Natural pearl has been used to decorate furniture and small utilitarian objects for centuries.

PEARL, Gaming Counter, 1800s, Large 17.50
Knife, Dinner, Set of 4 .... 30.00
Manicure Set, Leather Case, 9 Tools 20.00

Peking glass is a Chinese cameo glass first made popular in the eighteenth century. The Chinese have continued to make this layered glass in the old manner, and many new pieces are now available that could confuse the average buyer.

PEKING GLASS, Bowl, Carved Flowers, Leaves, Butterfly, White Ground, 7 In.	260.00
Candlestick, Green Cased Center, Oakleaf Top, Dragon Foot	55.00
Candlestick, Metal Leaf Top, Dragon Toes Base, 1920s, 6 In.	85.00
Salt, Orange–Red Cut To White	165.00
Vase, Red On White, 12 3/8 In.	895.00

Peloton glass is a European glass with small threads of colored glass rolled onto the surface of clear or colored glass. It is sometimes called spaghetti, or shredded coconut, glass. Most pieces found today were made in the nineteenth century.

PELOTON, Dish, Sweetmeat, Multicolored, Rose Ground, Silver Lid, 5 1/2 In.	560.00
Pitcher, Overshot Surface, Crystal Body, 8 In.	305.00
Rose Bowl, 6–Crimp Top, Coconut Strings On Body, 2 1/2 In.	245.00
Rose Bowl, Yellow & White Coconut Strings, Shell Feet, 3 7/8 In.	275.00
Tumbler, Art Glass	210.00
Vase, 4–Point Top, 6 Petal Feet, Coconut Threading, 3 3/4 In.	245.00
Vase, Coconut Strings Over Outside, Pink Cased, 7 1/2 In.	225.00
Vase, Embossed Ribbing, Coconut Strings, Pink Lining, 5 7/8 In.	250.00
Vase, Outside Ribbing, Cloverleaf Top, Off–White, 3 1/2 In.	185.00
Vase, Ruffled Top, Yellow & White Coconut Strings, 5 3/8 In.	245.00
Vase, Stick, White Lining, Coconut Strings, Yellow, 6 3/4 In.	225.00
Vase, Tricornered Folded–Over Top, Coconut String, 4 1/4 In.	295.00
Vase, Tricornered Shape, Blue & White Coconut Strings, 5 In.	225.00
Vase, White Threading, Crystal, 3 1/8 In.	130.00

The first steel pen point was made in England in 1780 to replace the hand–cut quill as a writing instrument. It was 100 years before the commercial pen was a common item. The fountain pen was invented in the 1830s but was not made in quantity until the 1880s. All types of old pens are collected.

PEN & PENCIL, Conklin, Endura, Box	60.00
Eversharp, 14K Solid Gold, Case	425.00
Sheaffer, White Dot Triumph Valiant, Green, 1948	75.00
Waterman, 100 Year, Black, 1939	725.00
Waterman, Ideal, Box	50.00
PEN, Arnold, Green & Gray	4.00
Baseball Shape, Milwaukee Brewers, Ballpoint, 1970	12.00
Conklin, Black, 1926	40.00
Conklin, Endura, Lady's	10.00
Conklin, Fountain, Gold Overlay	100.00
Conklin, No.30, Cresent Fill	39.00
Conklin, No.40.Crescent Filler, 1918	165.00
Crocker, Ink–Tite, 1920	65.00
Diamond Metal Pen Co., Fountain	32.00
Eclipse, Canada	25.00
Eversharp, Fountain, Gold Nib, Desk	20.00
Eversharp, Ventura, Sterling Silver	75.00
Eyedrop Filler, Parker, Brown Rubber, C.1900	75.00
Goose Quill	24.50
Houston, Gold Filled Chain & Pin, 1920	75.00
Lettering, K & E, Box, 1926	20.00
Mont Blanc, No.22, Twist Filler, Black, 1979	70.00
Morrison, Gold Filled Filigree	45.00
Parker, 51, 1946	45.00
Parker, 51, Blue Diamond	25.00
Parker, Ballpoint, Sterling Silver	45.00 To 75.00
Parker, Challenger, Black	40.00
Parker, Deluxe Challenger, Black	55.00
Parker, Duofold, Big Red, 1924	395.00

Parker, Duofold, Big Red, 1928 .... 120.00
Parker, Duofold, Jr., Yellow 100.00
Parker, Duofold, Lucky Curve, Orange, Black, Fountain, Desk Set, 1911 ...... 75.00
Parker, Duofold, Red 65.00
Parker, Lady Duofold, Mandarin Yellow 95.00
Parker, Lady Duofold, Red, 1925 .... 55.00
Parker, Lucky Curve, Desk, Black, Yellow Taper, Onyx Base, 1927 .... 120.00
Parker, Lucky Curve, Mottled Red & Black, No.23, 1904 .... 235.00
Parker, Parkette, Silver–Red & Black, 1936 .... 35.00
Parker, Vacumatic, Black 65.00
Parker, Vacumatic, Gold Pearl 70.00
Parkerette 20.00
Sheaffer, Feather Touch, Black, Fountain, Box 35.00
Sheaffer, Featherweight, 14K Gold, Vacuum Fill 20.00
Sheaffer, Gold Filled Trim, Sovereign 875, 1937 .... 35.00
Sheaffer, K74SR, Deluxe, 1928 .... 50.00
Sheaffer, Lifetime, Emerald Pearl, Solid 14K Band & Clip, 1933 .... 495.00
Sheaffer, Lifetime, Green Mottled, Whitney Point 49.00
Sheaffer, Lifetime, Woman's, Green Jade, 1926 .... 45.00
Sheaffer, LT, Green & Gold Striped, 1940s 25.00
Sheaffer, Sentinel, Fountain, Box 35.00
Sheaffer, Tuck–A–Way, Gold Filled Trim, Black 25.00
Sheaffer, White Dot, Green, Chromium, Fountain, Box 35.00
Speed Ball, Oversize 29.00
Swan, Rosewood, 1915, Large 45.00
Swan, Self–Filling, Desk, Green Jade, 1926 .... 80.00
Townsend, Yellow, Large, Set, Box 25.00
Universal, Black 4.00
Wahl–Eversharp, Fountain, Pearl & Black, 14K Gold Tip 40.00
Wahl–Eversharp, Lady's, Ribbon Ring 18.00
Wahl–Eversharp, Skyline, Brown, Gold–Brown Cap, 1946 .... 50.00
Waltham, Fountain, Green Pearl, Arnold Green 20.00
Waterman, Fountain, Lever Fill, Red & Black Ripple, C.1925 .... 35.00
Waterman, Foutain, Ivy Vines, Sterling Circling Pen 125.00
Waterman, Ideal, No.52, 1920 .... 90.00
Waterman, No.20, Double Logo Barrel, Black 850.00
Waterman, No.56 .... 39.00
Waterman, No.58, Double Barrel 350.00
Waterman, Patrician, Moss Agate 400.00
Waterman, Sterling Silver Overlay 110.00
Waterman, Sterling Siver Filigree 325.00

The pencil was invented, so it is said, in 1565. The eraser was not
added to the pencil until 1858. The automatic pencil was invented in
1863. Collectors today want advertising pencils or automatic pencils
of unusual design. Boxes and sharpeners for pencils are also
collected.

PENCIL SHARPENER, Disc Type, Table Model, Pat.1907 .... 75.00
  Figural, Uncle Sam, Germany 28.00
  Gun In Holster, Germany 28.00
  Pat. Date 1904 .... 65.00
  Scotty 22.50
  World Globe, Germany 28.00
PENCIL, Carpenter's, Winchester 35.00
  Cross, Gold Filled, 1955 .... 32.00
  Derringer, Ivory & Metal, Mechanical, Miniature 100.00
  Esso Gas, Mechanical 13.00
  Eversharp, Mechanical, 14K Solid Gold, Dated 1919 .... 200.00
  Grand Prize Beer, Mechanical 9.00
  Holder, Porky Pig, By Stump, Pot Metal, Green Base 25.00
  Mickey Mouse 2.00
  Miracle Painting, Louis Marx 20.00
  Morrison, Navy Insignia, Mechanical 28.00
  Muriel Cigars, Mechanical, Wooden, 6 In. 20.00

Parker, Duofold, Black & Pearl, 5 In.	30.00
Parker, Duofold, Mandarin Yellow, 1928	70.00
R.M.S.Queen Elizabeth, Ship In Top, Mechanical	25.00
S.S.Ocean Monarch, Ship Floats In Oil, Mechanical	15.00
Sheaffer, Nickel Plate, 1919	30.00
Silver Plated, Lions International	12.00
Wahl–Eversharp, Art Deco, Pearl & Black, 1928	100.00
Wahl–Eversharp, Florals, Sterling Silver	30.00
Wahl–Eversharp, Silver Plate, 1925	42.00
Wahl–Eversharp, Woman's, Sterling Silver, 1921	18.50
Wahl–Eversharp, Yellow Gold Filled	18.00

Pennsbury Pottery   The Pennsbury Pottery worked in Morrisville, Pennsylvania, from 1950 to 1971. Full sets of dinnerware were made as well as many decorative items. Pieces are marked with the name of the factory.

PENNSBURY ASHTRAY, Such Schmootzers	20.00
PENNSBURY, Ashtray, Advertising, Doylestown National Bank & Trust Co., 1961	19.50
Bookends, Eagle	60.00
Bowl, Black Rooster, Heart Shape	25.00
Bowl, Cereal, Black Rooster	10.00
Bowl, Fruit, Black Rooster	8.00
Bread Plate, Black Rooster	5.00
Bread Tray, Wheat Pattern	25.00
Butter, Hex	30.00
Coffee Set, Floral Medallion Design, 5 1/2 Cup Pot, 3 Piece	50.00
Creamer, Daisy	18.00
Creamer, Rooster	12.00 To 18.00
Cruet, Amish Man, Figural Head Stopper	37.50
Cruet, Oil & Vinegar, Figural	75.00
Cup & Saucer, Black Rooster	15.00
Cup & Saucer, Red Rooster	18.00
Dish, Gray, 8 1/2 In.	24.00
Eggcup, Black Rooster	18.00
Figurine, Hen, Brown & White, Large	150.00
Figurine, Rooster, Cream, Brown, 11 In.	250.00
Figurine, Yellow Bird, Perched On Edge of Sign	175.00
Letter Holder, 2 Women Under Tree	37.00
Mug, Barbershop	25.00
Mug, Eagle	20.00
Pie Pan, Apple Tree	85.00
Pie Plate, Red Rooster, Deep, 9 In.	22.50
Pitcher, Black Rooster	30.00
Pitcher, Eagle, 6 In.	25.00
Pitcher, Rooster, 4 In.	11.00
Plaque, B & O R.R.1837	30.00
Plaque, B.& O.R.R., New Jersey	45.00
Plaque, Camden & Amboy R.R.	25.00
Plaque, Central R.R., New Jersey	45.00
Plaque, Hex, Round, 6 In.	18.00
Plaque, Washington Crossing Inn, 5 In.	16.00
Plate, Black Rooster, 10 In.	15.00
Plate, Christmas, Tree Top, 1966	15.00
Plate, Red Rooster, 11 X 14 In.	30.00
Plate, Red Rooster, 6 1/2 In.	12.00
Platter, Rooster, Oval, 11 In.	27.00
Salt & Pepper, Rooster	22.00
Snack Set, Rooster	45.00
Sugar & Creamer, Black Rooster	45.00
Teapot, Hex	50.00
Teapot, Rooster, Glaze Drip At Base of Handle	30.00
Tile, Dutch Couple, Falle Is Nix, Round, 4 In.	25.00
Tile, Round, 6 In.	25.00
Tray, Lovebirds, 5 X 7 In.	25.00
Wall Pocket, Floral	25.00

Wall Pocket, Green, Design, Square	43.00

Pepsi-Cola, the drink and the name, was invented in 1898 but was not trademarked until 1903. The logo was changed from an elaborate script to the modern block letters in the 1970 Pepsi label. All types of advertising memorabilia are collected and reproductions are being made.

PEPSI–COLA, Bottle Carrier, Wooden	40.00
Bottle, Amber Emblem, No Deposit, 1968, 16 Oz.	10.00
Bottle, Embossed, Contents, 8 Oz.	7.00
Bottle, Engraved Neck, 10 Oz.	8.00
Bottle, Paper Label, Amber, 1930s	45.00
Bottle, Red Dotted Neck, 10 Oz.	5.00
Bottle, Syrup, 1943	1.00
Bottle, Tin Cap, Contents, 3 In.	2.25
Bottle, World Series, Cincinnati Reds, Contents, 1975	30.00
Bottler, Amber, Paper Label, C.1930	43.00
Button, Pinback, Bigger Better, Old Logo, Yellow, Red, 2 In.	2.50
Calendar, 1909, Full Pad, Framed	2900.00
Calendar, 1944, 12 Pages, Color Picture, 15 X 20 In.	55.00
Carrier, Cardboard, 4 Embossed Bottles	35.00
Clock, 1970s	11.00
Clock, Advertising, Plastic	25.00
Clock, Lighted .... 80.00 To 95.00	
Clock, Plastic & Metal, Lights, Round, 16 In.	170.00
Cooler, Picnic, Raised Bottle Cap Logo	145.00
Curtain Pole	20.00
Dispenser, Napkin	450.00
Dispenser, Satisfying–Invigorating, Cures Indigestion, Rabbits	9350.00
Doorplate, Tin	40.00
Holder, Tin	12.00
Jug, Syrup, Embossed Glass, C.1910, 1 Gal.	275.00
Letterhead, 1940s	5.00
Lighter, Cigarette, Bottle Cap, 1960s	25.00
Money Clip, Bottle Cap, Bronze	25.00
Pencil Clip	1.75
Pencil, Bullet, Bigger Drink, Better, 5 Cents, Metal, Celluloid	2.50
Radio, Can Shape	12.00
Sign, 2 Dot, 12 Oz., 5 Cent, Cardboard, 8 X 12 In.	15.00
Sign, Bottle Cap, Yellow Ground, 1950s, 15 X 15 In.	90.00
Sign, Embossed Tin, 1940, 35 X 10 In.	195.00
Sign, Neon, Red & Blue	225.00
Sign, School Crossing, Figural, Safety Boy, Drive Slow Please	60.00
Slate Board	10.00
Thermometer, Have A Pepsi	65.00
Thermometer, Say Pepsi Please, 1960s, 8 X 8 In. .... 35.00 To 45.00	
Token, For Vending Machine, Brass, Spanish, 1950s	5.00
Tray, Coney Island Beach Scene, 12 In.Diam.	35.00
Tray, Oval, 1909	750.00
Tray, Singers, 1940s	25.00
Tray, Town, With Beach	20.00
Tray, Victorian Lady In Soda Fountain, 1890, 6 X 4 In.	110.00
Tumbler & Tray Set, Victorian Lady, 1974 Repro, 7 Piece	100.00
Tumbler, Goofy, Disneyana, Pepsi Series, 6 In.	5.00
Tumbler, Road Runner	5.00
Tumbler, Tweety, 6 1/4 In.	2.50

Cut glass, pressed glass, art glass, silver, metal, enamel, and even plastic or porcelain perfume bottles have been made. Although the small bottle to hold perfume was first made before the time of ancient Egypt, it is the nineteenth– and twentieth–century examples that interest today's collector. Examples with the atomizer top marked "DeVilbiss" are listed under that name. Glass or porcelain examples will be found under the appropriate name such as Lalique, Czechoslovakia, etc.

PERFUME BOTTLE, 3–Sided Pinched, Hammered Silver Overlay, 10 In.	675.00
Amber Glass, Flower Inside, Ornate, 11 In.	75.00
Amberina, Gilded Leaves & Butterflies, 11 In., Pair	650.00
Amberina, Swirled Stopper	90.00
Amethyst Luster, 4 1/4 In.	60.00
Apricot To Clear, Swirled Rib, Intaglio, Pair	3100.00
Arcadia, Cut Glass, Sterling Silver Top, Unger Bros., Pair	650.00
Art Deco Fans, Blue, Long Stopper, Occupied Japan, 3 1/2 In.	30.00
Baluster Carved, Amber, 2 1/2 In.	115.00
Blue, Flower Garden With Butterflies, No Stopper	75.00
Cabbage Rose With Butterfly Stopper, Frosted Amethyst	135.00
California Perfume Co., 4 Bottles, Black Box, Sample, 1931	325.00
Caron Nuit De Noel, Black Glass	55.00
Cathedral Type, Man, In Archway, Aqua, Open Pontil, 4 In.	59.00
Chatelaine, Art Nouveau, Yellow Metal, Ornate, C.1870	75.00
Ciro, Chevalier De La Nuit, Black Glass	295.00
Clare Fontaine, Lily-of-The-Valley, 1950	195.00
Colonial, Cut Glass, Dorflinger, 7 In.	140.00
Crown Top, Cockatoo	75.00
Cut Cranberry, Faceted Bubble Stopper, 5 1/2 In.	110.00
Cut Glass, Green To Clear, Dorflinger, 4 3/4 In.	350.00
Czechoslovakia, Nude, Blue Stopper, Crystal, 4 1/2 In.	135.00
Davis & Collamore, Green Glass, Gilt Vine Design, 5 In., Pr.	154.00
Diamonds, Fan, Hobstars, 3 X 3 1/2 In.	28.00
Doll, Holds Fan At Head, Top Half of Doll Is Stopper, Blue	75.00
Dorflinger, Bulbous, Faceted Stopper, Label, 6 In.	145.00
Enameled Blue, Stopper, Silver Plated Holder, J.Tufts	150.00
Enameled Floral, Silver, Slip–In Stopper, Russia, 1900, 3 In.	4400.00
Enameled Flowers, Leaves, Gold Trim, Blue, 4 3/4 In.	95.00
Engraved Irises, Crystal, 3 In.	95.00
Evening In Paris, Cobalt Blue	8.00
Fan Shape, Stopper, Clear	25.00
Fleur De Lis Design, White Enameled, Purple	125.00
Fleur De Rocaille	20.00
Gold, Jewels, Globe Shape, Hinged Cover, Kochli, 1890, 2 In.	4180.00
Green Glass, Silver Overlay	350.00
Green Opalescent, Atomizer, Fenton	40.00
Heart Shape, Cut Glass, Flowers Front & Back, 5 1/2 In.	70.00
Intaglio Cut, Floral, Flared Bottom, 6 1/4 In.	95.00
Intaglio Cutting of Flowers, Paperweight Base, 6 1/2 In.	30.00
Jeanne Lanvin, Black Glass, Round	195.00
Jersey Swirl, Aqua, Ribbed, Oval	120.00
Kaziun, Red Petals On Green Leaves, Center Stopper	1250.00
Lady, Porcelain, Figural, Germany	45.00
Laydown, Silver Crown–Shaped Hinged Cover, 4 In.	245.00
Malachite Glass, Lithyalin, Molded Roses, 5 1/2 In.	250.00
Mary Chess, Horse Shape	85.00
Metallic Gold Design, Flame Stopper, Clear Blown, Italy	55.00
Milk Glass, Cosmos, Stopper	165.00
Miracle, Lentheric, Large & Small, Pair	250.00
Perfume Doll, Yellow, Long Dabber, Yellow, Bavaria	85.00
Pressed Glass, Bellflower, Opaque Yellow Green, 7 In.	525.00
Pressed Glass, Fan Stopper, C.1935, 6 1/2 In., Pair	95.00
Pull–Up Design, Colored Striping, Sterling Cap, 2 1/2 In.	385.00
Sailor, Frosted Glass, Blue Tie, Black Hat & Shoes, 3 In.	25.00
Scarlett, Pinoud, Gone With The Wind	300.00
Scarlett, Yesteryear, Gone With The Wind, Dome, 1940	150.00
Silver, Gold Wash, Shell, Loops For Chain, Oval, 1 3/4 In.	36.00
Swan Handles, Duncan & Miller, 9 In.	135.00
Tomato Red Cut To Clear, New Atomizer Bulb	85.00

Woman Portrait, Floral Cameo, French, Pair 375.00
Zipper & Circular Cut, Brass Top, Raised Florals 65.00

ZPR
ZANE WARE
MADE IN USA

Peters & Reed Pottery Company of Zanesville, Ohio, was founded by John D. Peters and Adam Reed in 1897. Chromal, Landsun, Montene, Pereco, and Persian are some of the art lines that were made. The company became Zane Pottery in 1920, Gonder Pottery in 1941, and closed in 1957. Peters & Reed was unmarked.

PETERS & REED, Bowl, Berries, Stems, Leaves, Dark Blue, 8 1/2 X 3 1/4 In. 55.00
Bowl, Lotus & Pads In Relief, Matte Green, 9 1/2 In. 52.00
Jardiniere, Green Lion Heads, Beige, Fluted Base, 6 1/2 In. 65.00
Jardiniere, Moss Aztec, Grape Clusters, Ferrell, 7 1/2 In. 85.00
Jug, Sprigged Garlands, Brownware, Handle, 5 1/2 In. 55.00
Jug, Wine, Grapes & Leaves, 2–Tone Brown, 6 1/4 In. 68.00
Pitcher, Cavalier, 6 3/4 In. 80.00
Tankard, Brown Shaded To Green 20.00
Tankard, Sprigged–On Cavaliers, Brownware, Large 55.00
Vase, Applied Flower Swags, Brown, Handles, Squat Base, 5 In. 34.00
Vase, Brown Glaze, Wreath, 10 In. 40.00
Vase, Dark Blue, Cream Marble Glaze, 9 In. 58.00
Vase, Molded Flower Medallions, Brown, 6 Sides, 4 X 6 In. 50.00
Vase, Molded Hanging Leaves At Top, 15 In. 195.00
Vase, Moss Aztec, 10 In. 50.00
Vase, Moss Aztec, Iris, Corset Shape, 15 In. 80.00
Vase, Moss Aztec, Sculptured Ivy & Berries, 11 1/2 X 5 In. 45.00
Wall Pocket, Moss Aztec, 9 In. 150.00
PETRUS REGOUT, see Maastricht

PEWABIC

The Pewabic Pottery was founded by Mary Chase Perry Stratton in 1903 in Detroit, Michigan. The company made many types of art pottery including pieces with matte green glaze and an iridescent crystalline glaze. The company continued working until the death of Mary Stratton in 1961. It was reactivated by Michigan State University in 1968.

PEWABIC, Ashtray, Iridescent Green 80.00
Box, Handmade, Unglazed, Dated 1908, 3 In. 800.00
Candlestick, Orange Glaze, Glaze Bubble, 9 In. 65.00
Tile, College, Iridescent Plum, Marked 95.00
Tile, Oriental Dolphin, Burgundy & Turquoise, Square, 5 In. 120.00
Vase, Blue, 5 In. 500.00
Vase, Gray–Green Iridescent, Bulbous, Short Neck, Paper Label, 6 In. 250.00
Vase, Mottled Orange, Khaki Glaze Over Brown, 6 1/2 In. 265.00
Vase, Multicolor, 2 1/2 In. 275.00
Vase, Red & Green Iridescent, 2 1/2 In. 200.00

Pewter is a metal alloy of tin and lead. Some of the pewter made after 1840 has a slightly different composition and is called "Britannia metal." This later type of pewter was worked by machine; the earlier pieces were made by hand. In the 1920s pewter came back into fashion and pieces were often marked "Genuine Pewter." Nineteenth– and twentieth–century examples are listed here.

PEWTER, Basin, Eagle, Ashbil Griswold, Meriden, Conn., 7 3/4 In. 375.00
Basin, Incised Line, Thomas Boardman, No.37, Early 1800s, 8 In. 125.00
Beer Keg, European 240.00
Bowl, Rolled Rim, 3 Molded Feet, Conical, Liberty & Co., 1905, 4 In. 350.00
Buckle, Butterfly Shape, Art Nouveau 5.00
Candlestick, Ball Knopped, Trumpet Base, C.1660, 7 In. 3750.00
Candlestick, Bobeches, Flagg & Homan, C.1845, 10 In., Pair 250.00
Candlestick, Pushups, 9 In., Pair 250.00
Candlestick, Renaissance, 18 1/2 In., Pair 100.00
Cann, Lighthouse Form, Lyre Handle, English, 5 1/2 In. 1500.00
Caudle Cup, Strap Handle, WC Mark, C.1670, 2 1/2 In. 1050.00
Chamberstick, Van Hauten, 7 In. 48.00

Charger, Broad Rim, Leafage, Fleur-De-Lis, Rose Heads, 20 1/2 In. 950.00
Charger, Clement, English, 18 In. 375.00
Charger, Incised Rim Line, Deep Center, Marked London, 16 1/2 In. 225.00
Chocolate Urn, Flowers At Neck, Spigot, Red Paint & Gilt, 17 3/4 In. 1550.00
Coffee & Tea Set, Tudric, 5 Piece 950.00
Coffee Set, Kayserzinn, 4 Piece 495.00
Coffeepot, Copper Bottom, Engraved Flowers, Leaf Finial, 9 In. 150.00
Coffeepot, Domed Cover, Scrolled Handle, Rufus Dunham, C.1860, 12 In. 200.00
Coffeepot, J. Danforth, 10 1/4 In. 302.50
Decanter Set, Lilies, 19 In. Tray, WMF, C.1900, 8 Piece 1045.00
Ewer, Brushed, Royal Holland Pewter, 1950s 20.00
Ewer, Glass, Caryatid Handle, Classical Style, 14 In. 290.00
Flagon, Acorn Thumbpiece, 8 In. 45.00
Flagon, Domed Lid, I Stamped Inside Base, C.1700, 11 In. 4150.00
Flagon, Lewelny & Co., 12 In. 245.00
Inkwell, Ceramic Insert, Marked Alfred Browett, Birmingham, 8 In. 95.00
Inkwell, Dish, Porcelain Insert 85.00
Inkwell, Hinged Lid, Ceramic Insert, 7 In. 145.00
Knife Rest, Panther, Kayserzinn 65.00
Ladle, Spherical Bowl, Turned Handle, 15 In. 175.00
Lamp, Time Measuring, Clear Blown Ribbed Font, 14 1/2 In. 450.00
Liqueur Set, Orange, Mirrored Tray, French, 10 1/2 In., 7 Piece 550.00
Measure, Scottish Tappit Hen, C.1750 .... 995.00
Mold, Ice Cream, 2 Hearts, Word Love, 4 1/2 In. 10.00
Mold, Ice Cream, Airplane, 5 1/4 In. 55.00
Mold, Ice Cream, Baked Potato 25.00
Mold, Ice Cream, Banana, Large 27.00
Mold, Ice Cream, Banjo 50.00
Mold, Ice Cream, Battleship 65.00
Mold, Ice Cream, Bird's Nest, 7 Eggs 30.00
Mold, Ice Cream, Bunch of Grapes, 5 In. 21.50
Mold, Ice Cream, Cabbage With Bunny, 3 5/8 In. 22.50
Mold, Ice Cream, Candle In Candlestick 70.00
Mold, Ice Cream, Cherub Riding Easter Bunny, 4 In. 20.00
Mold, Ice Cream, Cob Brownie 60.00
Mold, Ice Cream, Cornucopia, 4 3/8 In. 15.00
Mold, Ice Cream, Cupid In Rose 33.00
Mold, Ice Cream, Dice 27.00
Mold, Ice Cream, Dove With Raised Wings, 4 1/2 In. 17.50
Mold, Ice Cream, Duck 30.00
Mold, Ice Cream, Dutch Shoe 27.00
Mold, Ice Cream, Floral 25.00
Mold, Ice Cream, Football Player, Early Uniform 75.00
Mold, Ice Cream, Football, 3 Sections, 3 1/4 In. 10.00
Mold, Ice Cream, Golfer In Knickers 75.00
Mold, Ice Cream, Hinged Log, 10 In. 40.00
Mold, Ice Cream, Maltese Cross, Roman Cross Center, 4 1/4 In. 10.00
Mold, Ice Cream, Man In Moon, E & Co, N.Y., 1888, 5 1/2 In. 70.00
Mold, Ice Cream, Open Book 27.00
Mold, Ice Cream, Rooster 40.00
Mold, Ice Cream, Steamship, 5 1/2 In., 2 Part 80.00
Mold, Ice Cream, Tulip, E & Co, N.Y., 4 1/8 In. 30.00
Mold, Ice Cream, Valentine Letter With Heart, 4 1/4 In. 15.00
Mold, Ice Cream, Washington Bust 55.00
Mold, Ice Cream, Washington Chopping Cherry Tree 55.00
Mold, Jello, Hollow Center, Aluminum Bottom, Westbend, 9 1/2 In. 6.50
Mug, Tavern, Thomas Abbott, C.1830, Qt., Pt., 1/2 Pt., 3 Piece 325.00
Napkin Ring, Relief Scene, Scrolled Border 14.00
Oil Can, Tin Bottom & Spout, 4 1/4 X 2 1/4 In. 12.00
Pitcher, Cover, G. Richardson, 7 1/2 In. 1237.00
Pitcher, Globular Baluster Body, Domed Lid, Handle, Spout, 7 1/2 In. 175.00
Pitcher, Handle, James Yates, C.1840, 1 Qt. 92.00
Pitcher, James Yates, 1 Pt. 50.00
Pitcher, R. Dunham, 6 3/4 In. 250.00

Plate, 10–Sided, Jonas Durand, C.1720, 9 1/4 In. 330.00
Plate, Austin, 8 3/4 In. 525.00
Plate, B & Co., English, 8 1/2 In. 85.00
Plate, Multiple Reeded, Richard Allen, 9 1/8 In. 410.00
Plate, Reeded, Baldwin of Wigan, Early 18th Century, 9 1/8 In. 400.00
Plate, S. Danforth, 8 In. 400.00
Plate, Scalloped, Block Zinn, 1840, 11 3/4 In. 155.00
Plate, T.C. & Thomas, 8 3/4 In. 55.00
Plate, Thomas Badger, Boston, Stamped, 8 1/2 In. 300.00
Plate, Townsend & Compton, 8 1/4 In. 35.00
Plate, Triple Reeded, Edward Leapidge, 9 In. 420.00
Plate, Wriggle Worked Tulip, Reeded Rim, C.1690, 8 1/4 In. 1600.00
Platter, Hot Water, Thomas Alderson, English, 15 1/2 X 22 In. 275.00
Porringer, I.C. Lewis, Meriden, Conn., Miniature 250.00
Porringer, R. Lee, 2 3/8 In. 600.00
Porringer, Tab Handle, Pennsylvania, 5 3/8 In. 475.00
Pot, Tall, J.B. Grave, 10 In. 175.00
Punch Bowl, Figure of Child On Cover, Ball & Claw Feet, Kayserzinn 575.00
Salt Box, Hanging, Scrolled Crest, Floral Engraving, 9 3/4 In. 85.00
Salt, Footed, William Will, 2 1/4 In. 425.00
Saucer, James I, C.1600, 5 1/4 In. 1200.00
Shaving Bowl & Pitcher, Figural Handle On Pitcher, 12 In. 120.00
Silent Butler, Wood Handle 8.00
Spoon, Badge of Greenwich Hospital, Dog–Nosed, C.1705, 8 In. 500.00
Spoon, Bird Claw On Back of Bowl, 6 3/8 In., 6 Piece 120.00
Spoon, Farmer George, George III, C.1770, 5 In. 450.00
Spoon, Feeding, A. Caron, 19th Century 275.00
Spoon, George III & Queen Caroline, C.1760, 8 In. 525.00
Spoon, Portrait of Queen Anne, Lace Back, C.1702, 7 In. 650.00
Spoon, Tryfid, Cast Heart, IN, London, C.1680, 7 In. 580.00
Spoon, Tryfid, Christopher Thorne, Dated Mark of 1675, 7 In. 525.00
Stein, Hinged Lid, Indian Head, Feather Headdress, 1904, 7 In. 165.00
Sugar & Creamer, Cover, 3 In. 30.00
Syrup, Button Finials, Scrolled Handle, Savage, MIDD, C.1835, 6 In. 200.00
Tankard, Ale, Lidless, 2–Banded, John Donne, London, C.1686, 1 Pt. 8000.00
Tankard, George III, Double Domed, C.1800, 7 3/4 In. 440.00
Teapot, Ear Handle, Vintage Finial, Smith & Morey, 8 1/2 In. 75.00
Teapot, Painted Panels, China, 8 In. 70.00
Teapot, Pear Shape, S Shaped Spout, C. Bradford, 1752–85 .... 2800.00
Teapot, Putnam, 7 3/4 In. 375.00
Teapot, Wood Finial, Joshua B. & Henry H. Graves, C.1850, 7 1/4 In. 200.00
Tobacco Jar, English, 5 In. 165.00
Vase, Art Deco, Gimbel Bros., Large 25.00
Vase, Cattails, Boy & Elfin Merman, Each Side, Baluster, WMF, 11 In. 1430.00
Vase, Kayserzinn, 4 3/4 In. 70.00

Phoenix Bird, or Flying Phoenix, is the name given to a blue–and–white kitchenware popular between 1900 and World War II. A variant is known as Flying Turkey. Most of this dinnerware was made in Japan for sale in the dime stores in America. It is still being made.

PHOENIX BIRD, Cake Tray 46.00
Celery, Hand Painted, Flying Turkey 75.00
Chamberstick 22.50
Chocolate Pot, Hand Painted, Flying Turkey, Cover 131.00
Creamer .... 10.00 To 14.50
Cup & Saucer 15.00
Cup & Saucer, Demitasse 19.00
Eggcup, Blue & White 20.00
Ginger Jar, 5 In. 55.00
Pitcher, Buttermilk 55.50
Plate, 6 In. 4.50
Plate, 7 In. ....7.00 To 15.00
Platter, 15 X 9 3/4 In. 58.50

Platter, Blue & White	75.00
Platter, Flying Turkey	60.00
Salt & Pepper .... 20.00 To	32.00
Saltshaker, Scalloped Base, 2 5/8 In.	10.00
Saltshaker, Shaped, 2 In.	10.00
Sugar	15.50
Sugar, Cover, 3 1/2 In. .... 20.00 To	23.50
Syrup	49.50
Tea Set, Floral Design, 13 Piece	50.00
Teapot .... 34.50 To	40.00
Tureen, Rice	83.50

Phoenix Glass Company was founded in 1880 in Pennsylvania. The firm made commercial products such as lampshades, bottles, and glassware. Collectors today are interested in the sculptured glassware made by the company from the 1930s until the mid–1950s. The company is still working.

PHOENIX, Bowl, Orchids, Rust Color, Footed, 11 In. .... 85.00 To	90.00
Bowl, Pinecone	31.00
Candlestick, Bird of Paradise, Green, 6 3/4 In., Pair	235.00
Centerpiece & 12 Plates, Nudes, 13 Piece	800.00
Lamp, Aqua Shell Pattern, Cream Ground, No Shade	165.00
Lamp, Foxglove, Marble Base, 14 1/2 In.	88.00
Lamp, Wild Roses, Turquoise, Creamy Ground, 14 In.	145.00
Snack Plate, Fruits, Pear Shape, 9 1/4 In., 6 Piece	10.00
Sugar & Creamer, Catalonian, Yellow	18.00
Urn, Nudes	320.00
Vase, Bronze Colored Grasshopper, Fan Shape, 8 1/4 In.	225.00
Vase, Bronze, Grasshopper, Custard Glass, Fan Shape, 8 In.	275.00
Vase, Catalonian, Flared, Aqua, 11 3/4 In.	52.00
Vase, Dancing Nudes, Pan Playing Pipes, 11 In.	325.00
Vase, Dogwood, Yellow, Green, Brown, White, 10 1/2 In. ....95.00 To	120.00
Vase, Flying Geese, Frosted, Pillow, 9 1/2 X 12 In.	145.00
Vase, Goldfish, Pink Purple, 9 In.	290.00
Vase, Lovebird, Blue Birds, Pillow Shape, White, 6 1/2 In.	79.00
Vase, Madonna, 10 In.	125.00
Vase, Pair of Lovebirds, Rectangular, Frosted, 6 1/2 In.	95.00
Vase, Peonies, 2 Pink Shades, Turquoise Leaves, 12 1/4 In.	150.00
Vase, Philodendron, White Leaves, Ivory Ground, 11 1/4 In.	85.00
Vase, Pink Birds, Blue Flowers, Ivory, 6 1/2 In.	50.00
Vase, Pink Flowers, Green Foliage, White Ground, Pillow, 7 1/2 In.	125.00
Vase, Rose Red Ground, Iridescent Flowers, Bulbous, 11 In.	175.00
Vase, Sculptured White Madonna, Blue Ground, Label, 10 1/4 In.	175.00
Vase, Sculputered Daisies, Gold On Clear, 7 In.	75.00
Vase, Thistle, Blue Ground, 17 In.	350.00
Vase, White Flowers, Lavender Ground, Pillow, 8 X 9 In.	89.00
Vase, Wild Rose, Blue Ground, 10 1/2 In.	145.00

The tin cases that held phonograph needles are collected today by music and phonograph enthusiasts and advertising addicts. The tins are very small, about 2 inches across, and often have attractive graphic designs lithographed on the tin.

PHONOGRAPH NEEDLE, Tin, Victor, Talking Machine, Pictures Nipper	8.00

The phonograph, invented by Thomas Edison in the 1880s, has been made by many firms. This section also includes other items associated with the phonograph. Records are listed in their own section.

PHONOGRAPH, Brunswick, 78 Victrola	275.00
Columbia, Cylinder, Model AA	300.00
Columbia, Eagle B, Decal	215.00
Edison, Amberola .... 225.00 To	275.00
Edison, Cylinder, Carrying Case	495.00
Edison, Diamond Disc	350.00

Edison, Fireside, Cygnet Horn	875.00
Edison, Gem, Keywind	375.00
Edison, Home, Cylinder, Morning Glory Horn	300.00
Edison, Home, Wood Cygnet	1500.00
Edison, Idealla	4200.00
Edison, Minuet, Cygnet Horn, 2 X 4 Ft.	575.00
Edison, Red Gem	750.00
Edison, Standard	380.00
Edison, Triumph, Flowered Horn	1250.00
Fern–O–Grand, Baby Grand Piano Shape, 2 X 3 X 3 Ft.	1500.00
Figure, Ragtime Rastus, Music, Hand Painted, Power, 5 1/2 In.	295.00
Figure, Siam Soo, Dancing, Music, Power Mechanism	475.00
Gramaphone, Edison	275.00
Graphonola, Deluxe	1500.00
Harmony, Cylinder, Oak, Red Horn	400.00
Harp Base Openworks Cylinder, Brass Horn	275.00
Jukebox, Amberola No.30	350.00
Jukebox, AMI Model JD1200, 45 RPM, 100 Selections	750.00
Jukebox, Engelhardt, Model A, With Xylophone	6500.00
Jukebox, Gem A	375.00
Jukebox, Knabe, Ampico, 5 Ft.8 In.	4000.00
Jukebox, Mills, Empress	2000.00
Jukebox, Mills, Ferris Wheel Type, 78 RPM	1800.00
Jukebox, Monarch	700.00
Jukebox, Pathe Gem	650.00
Jukebox, Rockola No.400	900.00
Jukebox, Rockola Princess	900.00
Jukebox, Seeburg E, With Xylophone	4000.00
Jukebox, Seeburg, Model 147, Reconditioned	2700.00
Jukebox, Seeburg, With Mandolin & Orchestrion Bells	7000.00
Jukebox, Wurlitzer, Model 10	2400.00
Jukebox, Wurlitzer, Model 24	1750.00
Jukebox, Wurlitzer, Model 105, Bubbler, 1946	5600.00
Jukebox, Wurlitzer, Model 600, 1936–38, 55 In.	2800.00
Jukebox, Wurlitzer, Model 750E	4200.00
Jukebox, Wurlitzer, Model 1015	8500.00
Jukebox, Wurlitzer, Model 1100	2500.00
Jukebox, Wurlitzer, No.1015, Crate	4295.00
Jukebox, Wurlitzer, Style A, Harp Case	2500.00
Kalamazoo Multiphone, 24 Cylinder	6500.00
Mastertone	170.00
Olympia, 10–In. Discs	240.00
RCA, Redhead, Bakelite, 45 RPM	30.00
Red Jem	750.00
Reginaphone, Metal Horn	4250.00
S. Hamilton Co., Table	125.00
Stradivara	95.00
Talkophone	350.00
Victor D, Wooden Horn	1500.00
Victor IV, Black Flower Horn	800.00
Victor VI, Papier–Mache Horn, Triple Gold Plated, 1910	1700.00
Victor, Model M	625.00 To 875.00
Victor, Model O	875.00
Victor, Model VV–100, Floor Model	325.00
Victor, No.5, Large Morning Glory Horn	500.00
Victor, RCA Decal, Large Horn, C.1920	1100.00 To 1700.00
Victor, Talking Machine, Walnut Cabinet	450.00
Victrola, Brunswick 78	275.00
Victrola, No.XVI, Upright, Electric, Oak	2750.00
Victrola, Victor Talking, Tiger Oak, File, 4 Records, 1905	300.00
Violano–Virtuoso, Mills, 9 Rolls, Mahogany	8500.00
Widdicomb, Windup, In Cabinet, Hinged Top, 4 1/2 Ft.	250.00

The first photograph was a view from a window in France taken in 1826. The commercially successful photograph started with the daguerreotype introduced in 1839. Today all sorts of photographs and photographic equipment are collected. Albums were popular in Victorian times. Cartes de visite, popular after 1854, were mounted on 2 1/2- by 4-inch cardboard. Cabinet cards were introduced in 1866. These were mounted on cards 4 1/4 x 6 1/2 inches. Stereo views are listed under Stereo Card.

PHOTOGRAPHY, Album, 1893 Columbian World's Fair, Administration Bldg.	55.00
Album, Musical, Victorian, Green Plush, Brass Trim	189.50
Albumen, Civil War Lady, W.L. Germon, Oval, 6 1/2 X 8 1/2 In.	25.00
Albumen, U.S.S.Maine Baseball Team, Mages, 1898	550.00
Ambrotype, Child In Military Uniform, Holding Musket	65.00
Ambrotype, Infantry Soldier, Hardee Hat, Musket, 1/9 Plate	100.00
Ambrotype, Kit Carson & Special Agent L.C. Baker, 1/2 Plate	3750.00
Ambrotype, Man & Woman, In Front of Falls, Cased, 1 Plate	385.00
Ambrotype, U.S.Marine, Uniform, Standing, 1/6 Plate	121.00
Cabinet Card, Actress, As Man, London, Late 1800s, 13 X 8 In.	25.00
Cabinet Card, Boy, In White Dress, Holding Wheelbarrel, Wright	11.25
Cabinet Card, Civil War Cabinet, Fisher, 1863, 3 1/2 X 6 In.	37.50
Cabinet Card, Girl With Doll	10.00
Cabinet Card, James Garfield	10.00
Cabinet Card, Lady In Oval, Asbury Park, N.J., 1889, 2 In.	7.50
Cabinet Card, Maple Run School, 1 Room, 1909, 8 X 10 In.	30.00
Cabinet Card, Midget, Age 25, 3 Ft. & 42 Lbs.	15.00
Cabinet Card, Pony Express Rider, Billie Johnson, July 22, 1886	330.00
Cabinet Card, President & Mrs. Hayes, 1878	35.00
Cabinet Card, Ruta & Evelyn Masson, 1882, T.H. Webster	11.25
Cabinet Card, Salvation Army Musicians, 3 Piece	32.00
Cabinet Card, Woman, With Pedestal Stereoscope & Views	30.00
Camera & Radio, Tom Thumb	345.00
Camera, AGFA, Pioneer, No.16	5.00
Camera, Angulon, Synchronized Shutter, 120 Mm	200.00
Camera, Ansco, C.1926	100.00
Camera, Ansco, Shur-Shot	12.50
Camera, Argus, C-3, Case	35.00
Camera, Argus, C-4, Candidate E	80.00
Camera, Blair, Plate Back, Kameret, 4 X 5 In.	375.00
Camera, Bolsey, Model B2, 35 Mm, Case & Flash	35.00
Camera, Burke & James, Inc., Graflex Strobe	85.00
Camera, Circuit, No.6	750.00
Camera, Conley Jr., Folding Plate, 4 X 8 In.	40.00
Camera, Conley, Red Bellows & Accessories, 1907	85.00
Camera, Coronet, Cameo, Box	65.00
Camera, Debrie, Movie & Still, 35 Mm, French, 1925	150.00
Camera, Eastman Kodak, Box, 50th Anniversary, 1938	450.00
Camera, Eastman, 2-C Autographic, Folding	20.00
Camera, Exakta, 35 Mm, Filters, L.28 X 50 Lens, Case	150.00
Camera, Expo	85.00
Camera, Goerz Angro, Case, Plate Holder	110.00
Camera, Goerz Dagor, Glass Negatives, Original Case	200.00
Camera, Goerz, Stereo-Binocular Detective, Case, 1899	2200.00
Camera, Hawkeye, No.2A, Model B, Box	25.00
Camera, Jiffy, Foldout, Art Deco	30.00
Camera, Keystone, Movie, 8 Mm, Case	20.00
Camera, Kodak, 1930, Instruction Manual, 50th Anniversary	45.00
Camera, Kodak, Bantam, Flash, 48 Mm, F 4.5 Anastar Lens	20.00
Camera, Kodak, Brownie, No.2	10.00
Camera, Kodak, Bull's-Eye, Model D, Wooden Interior, C.1898	45.00
Camera, Kodak, Compact Graflex, Handle, Bellows, 5 X 7 In.	150.00
Camera, Kodak, Jiffy	10.00
Camera, Kodak, Jr., Foldout, Box	40.00
Camera, Kodak, No.1-A, Folding, 1913	12.50

Camera, Kodak, No.3–A, Folding, Pocket, Model C	25.00
Camera, Kodak, Petite, Rose Color	50.00
Camera, Korona, IIE, Gundlach Optical Shutter, Cherry Body	65.00
Camera, Leica, Model 3A	300.00
Camera, Levy–Roth, Took Fifty 1/2–Frame Photographs, 1915	1400.00
Camera, Military, Used With Flash Powder, Olive Bellows	200.00
Camera, Minolta, No.16, Carrying Handle, Japan, Pocket Size	11.00
Camera, Minolta, XD11, D Winder, 50 Mm	185.00
Camera, Phoake, Box, Instruction Book	875.00
Camera, Polaroid Land, Speedline, Model 95B, Box	38.00
Camera, Praktica, B–100, 28 Mm	50.00
Camera, Retina III, Exenar, 50 Mm Lens, Case	125.00
Camera, Retina, IIIc, 35 Mm, Wide Angle & Portrait Lens	135.00
Camera, Revere 33, Stereo, Box & Carrying Case	135.00
Camera, Schacht, Macro Manual Universal, 50 Mm	75.00
Camera, Zeiss, Contaflex Super 50 Mm	100.00
Camera, Zeiss, Contax, 50 Mm, Sonnar, Meter, Leather Case	135.00
Camera, Zeiss, Unar, Premo Reflecting, Lens, 4 X 5 In.	1200.00
Carte De Visite, Abraham Lincoln, Seated At Table	105.00
Carte De Visite, Admiral Dot & Mother, Midget	27.50
Carte De Visite, Chinese Kindergarten, Los Angeles, Cal., 1897	15.00
Carte De Visite, Civil War Soldier, Full Uniform & Rifle	32.50
Carte De Visite, Deep Sea Diver, Full Gear, 1860s	40.00
Carte De Visite, Edgar Allen Poe	25.00
Carte De Visite, Edmund Ruffin, Seated, Rifle, Morris Island	198.00
Carte De Visite, Gentleman Opening Wine, Corkscrew, Glasses	30.00
Carte De Visite, Grant & Colfax	50.00
Carte De Visite, Henry Ward Beecher	12.00
Carte De Visite, J.W. Booth	55.00
Carte De Visite, Louisa May Alcott, Warren, Boston	40.00
Carte De Visite, Mrs. Lincoln	20.00
Carte De Visite, President Garfield	8.00
Carte De Visite, Sam Huston, Charles D. Fredricks Photo., N.Y.	385.00
Carte De Visite, View of Steamboat Quebec, People On Dock	40.00
Daguerreotype Case, Snowflake Medallion, Gutta–Percha, Man	16.00
Daguerreotype, Husband & Wife Portrait, 1/6 Plate, 2 Piece	37.50
Daguerreotype, Mother & Children, 1/4 Plate	45.00
Daguerreotype, Star Medallion, Woman, Leather, 3 X 4 In.	18.00
Daguerreotype, Woman Portrait, W.& E. Langeheim, 1/4 Plate	88.00
Daguerreotype, Young Couple Portrait, S. Root, 1/4 Plate	130.00
Daguerreotype, Young Man, 1800s, Case, 3 X 3 3/4 In.	35.00
Film Cutter, Eastman Kodak, Small	15.00
Lamp, Darkroom, Amber, Kodak, Oil	60.00
Lamp, Darkroom, Kodak, Kerosene	85.00
Light Meter, Argus, Germany	15.00
Magic Lantern, Bausch & Lomb, Model B, Slides, Songs, Case	235.00
Magic Lantern, Lilley Electric, Key, Instructions, Wooden Case	295.00
Movie Projector, Lindstrom, 7 Films, Chaplin, Popeye, Our Gang	155.00
Photograph, Anchorage, Alaska, 360 Bird's–Eye, 1920, 62 X 10 In.	150.00
Photograph, Carol Lombard, 1929, 8 X 10 In.	78.00
Photograph, Children, Pres. Taft Picture, Cal., 1909, 7 In.	15.00
Photograph, Dina Merill, Actress, Signed, 10 X 8 In.	45.00
Photograph, Dorothy Lamour, Standard Oil Premium, 8 X 10 In.	8.00
Photograph, Franklin D. Roosevelt, Governor, 1920–32, Set of 5	50.00
Photograph, Gary Cooper, The Texan, 1930, 8 X 10 In.	25.00
Photograph, Gen. Thomas, Civil War, Mounted, 8 1/2 X 6 1/2 In.	275.00
Photograph, Indian Mother, At Grave, Barry, 7 1/2 X 9 1/2 In.	375.00
Photograph, James Cagney, Standard Oil Premium, 8 X 10 In.	8.00
Photograph, Jimmy Allen, Skelly, 7 1/2 X 3 1/4 In.	47.00
Photograph, Norma Shearer, 1928, 11 X 14 In.	24.00
Photograph, Nude Woman, 6 Different, 1920s, 8 X 10 In., 6 Piece	32.00
Photograph, Richard E. Byrd, South Pole Expedition, 1933	50.00
Photograph, Rudolph Valentino, Autographed, 10 X 12 1/4 In.	35.00
Photograph, Tony Martin, Metal Frame, 8 X 10 In.	10.00

Photograph, World War I British Navy Balloon, Fleet 12.50
Photogravure, 2 Indian Dwellings, Edward S. Curtis, 5 X 7 In. 30.00
Photogravure, Jem Mace, Prize Ring Boxer, 1895, 14 X 10 1/2 In. 15.00
Photogravure, Mucha Lefevre, Utile Label, Curtis, 9 X 12 In. 165.00
Photogravure, Tablita Dancers & Singers, Curtis, 11 X 15 In. 225.00
Projector, Keystone, Junior, Box 125.00
Projector, Keystone, Moviegraph Model 575, Hand Crank 25.00
Projector, Movie, Lindstrom, Metal, 6 Films In Boxes 125.00
Timer, Developing, Kodak, Red 12.00
Tintype, 2 Baseball Players, Uniform, DeWitt, 1/6 Plate 110.00
Tintype, Armed Rebel, Bill Tucker, Savannah, Ga., 1/6 Plate 75.00
Tintype, Civil War Soldier, 1/4 Plate 65.00
Tintype, Cowboys Holding Whiskey Bottle, 2 1/2 X 3 1/2 In. 18.00
Tintype, Fireman, Holding Trumpet, 1/4 Plate 45.00
Tintype, Gambler, 1/4 Plate 25.00
Tintype, Girl, Urn, Bird, Fountain, Leather Case, 2 X 3 In. 15.00
Tintype, Indian & Agent, Southeastern, 1/6 Plate 88.00
Tintype, Little Girl Holding China Doll, 2 X 3 In. 10.00
Tintype, Naval Officer, 1/4 Plate 45.00
Tintype, Soldier, Bayonet, Plumed Hat, Uniform, 1/4 Plate 110.00
Tintype, Soldier, Firearm, Plumed Hat, Uniform, 1/4 Plate 85.00
Tintype, Stagecoach, 1/4 Plate 25.00
Tintype, Woman, Seated, 3/4 View, Civil War Era, 3 1/2 X 2 In. 12.50

About 1880, the well–decorated home had a shawl on the piano. Bisque piano babies were designed to help hold the shawl in place. They range in size from 6 to 18 inches. Most of the figures were made in Germany. Reproductions are being made. Other piano babies are listed under manufacturers' names.

PIANO BABY, Boy, On Stomach, Intaglio Eyes, Dimples, Marked, 11 In. 425.09
  Chubby Nude Toddler Boy, Seated, 7 In. 85.00
  Crawling On Stomach, Heubach, 7 In. 275.00
  Crawling, Blond Hair, White Nightie, Blue Bow, Heubach, 7 In. 225.00
  Crawling, Heubach 400.00
  Crawling, On Stomach, White Gown, Bisque 125.00
  Girl, Lying On Stomach, Legs Crossed, Yellow Floral Dress 195.00
  Girl, On Back, Playing With Toes, Intaglio Eyes, 8 In. 275.00
  Lying On Back, Playing With Toes, 12 In. 125.00
  Lying On Stomach, Bisque, 10 In. 175.00
  Lying On Stomach, Dog, Pacifier, 5 In. 38.00
  On Tummy, Looking Up, 6 In. 75.00
  Seated Chubby Girl, Green Dress, Gold Bead Trim, 6 1/4 In. 95.00
  Sitting and Reaching For Her Toes, Heubach, 6 /12 In. 285.00
  Sitting, Hand On Cheek, 6 In. 75.00
  Sitting, Leaning To Side, Yellow Dress, Holding Rattle, 8 In. 275.00
  Sitting, Pulling Off Pink Sock, Pink, White Bonnet, Signed, 9 In. 375.00
  White & Green Gown, Bonnet, Pink Trim, 4 1/2 In., Pair 195.00
  White Gown, Blue Trim, Dog Licking Face, Real Hair, 3 1/2 In. 165.00
  With Dog, Chewing Pacifier, 5 In. 65.00

Pickard China Company was started in 1898 by Wilder Pickard. Hand–painted designs were used on china purchased from other sources. In the 1930s, the company began to make its own china wares in Chicago, Illinois. The company now makes many types of porcelains including a successful line of limited edition collector plates.

PICKARD, Ashtray, Gold, Etched 45.00
  Bowl, Gooseberries, Foliage, Pierced Handle, Signed, 9 7/8 In. 125.00
  Bowl, Gooseberry, Signed, 5 X 2 1/4 In. 75.00
  Bowl, Lilies, Gold Trim, Signed Yeshik, 7 1/2 In. 165.00
  Creamer, Gold, No.698 .... 15.00
  Cup & Saucer, Artist Signed 90.00
  Cup & Saucer, Reflection of Silver, Gold & Floral 80.00

Hatpin Holder, Pink Roses, Shaded Ground, Signed, 5 In.	37.50
Pitcher, Cider, Leach, Water Lilies, Trees, Water, 1898–1904, 7 In.	350.00
Pitcher, Cider, Silver, Gold, Signed, 8 In.	295.00
Plate, Seashells At Water's Edge, Gold Rim, 8 1/2 In.	60.00
Relish, Floral Center, Gold Medallion, 11 X 6 3/4 In.	195.00
Soup, Dish, Rocail	27.50
Sugar & Creamer, Dutch Girl, Cover, Gold Maple Leaf .... 120.00 To	145.00
Sugar & Creamer, Poppy, Signed	295.00
Sugar & Creamer, Violets, Maple Leaf Mark	45.00
Sugar, Leaf & Scrolls	20.00
Tea Set, Gilt Design, 2 Waste Bowls, Oval 2–Handled Tray, 6 Piece	176.00
Tea Set, Oval Tray, 3 Piece	225.00
Toothpick, Blue, Gold Design	25.00
Vase, Floral, White Gold Band Base, Signed Challinor, 9 In.	395.00
Vase, Poppies, 8 In.	145.00
Vase, Red Poinsettias, Marked, 1905, 17 In.	640.00
Vase, Trees, Foliage, Water, Matte, 9 In.	445.00
Wine Set, Art Deco, Black Ground, Dripping Grapes, Hess, 10 Piece	625.00

PICTURE FRAME, see Furniture, Frame

Silhouettes and small decorative pictures are listed here. Some other types of pictures are listed under Print or Painting.

PICTURE, Cut Paper, 2 Eagles With Flags, Flower Urn Designs, 19th Century	1100.00
Embroidered Panel, Bird, Fish, Bats, Framed, Chinese, 9 X 10 1/2 In.	40.00
Feather, Carved Frame, Mexico, 6 X 9 In.	11.00
Hair Wreath, Victorian, Ribbon Tied Braid, Named, Frame, 13 X 17 In.	65.00
Needlepoint, Woman With A Lute, 28 X 36 In.	30.00
Needlework, Biblical Scene, Silk Panel, Gilt Frame, 16 X 19 In.	600.00
Needlework, God Bless Our Union, G. Washington, Framed, 8 X 10 In.	75.00
Needlework, Mary E. Strickler, Georgian House, 1820, 16 X 19 In.	900.00
Needlework, Silk, Moses Rescue, Bullrushes, Eglomise Glass, 23 In.	200.00
Needlework, Silk–On–Silk, The Little Slumberer, 1801	6050.00
Needlework, Urn, Memorial, Silk On Silk, Oval, 1797, 14 1/4 X 12 In.	550.00
Needlwork, Poem, Mary Louisa Deveau, 1839, 16 1/2 X 18 1/2 In.	675.00
Pen & Ink, Lion & Stag, Spencerian, M.W.Pierce, 21 X 26 1/2 In., Pr.	3200.00
Silhouette, Dancing Nudes, B. Major, 11 X 16 In.	35.00
Silhouette, Gentleman, Eglomise, Reverse Painted, Framed, 6 X 7 In.	235.00
Silhouette, Girls, Mother, Litho Ground, Edouart, 1843, 12 X 14 In.	4840.00
Silhouette, Lady, Bonnet, Ink, Gold Highlights, Framed, 4 X 4 5/8 In.	125.00
Silhouette, Levi Woodbury, Kellogg, Pine Frame, 13 1/2 X 17 1/2 In.	55.00
Silhouette, Man, Top Hat, Primitive, Black Paper, Framed, 4 X 6 In.	45.00
Silhouette, Old Woman In Bonnet, Frame, 4 1/2 X 5 1/4 In.	85.00
Silhouette, Pen & Ink, Woman, Lacy Collar, Black Frame, 4 X 5 In.	275.00
Silhouette, Young Man, Gilt, W. Seville, Frame, 4 3/8 X 5 1/4 In.	55.00
Silhouette, Young Woman, Gilt Frame, 4 X 4 3/8 In.	230.00
Silhouette, Young Woman, Hollow Cut, 4 3/4 X 5 3/4 In.	90.00
Silhouette, Young Woman, Mrs. Boyd, Oct. 1842, 3 7/8 X 4 7/8 In.	25.00
Theorem, Urn, With Flowers, Mid–19th Century, 15 X 18 3/4 In.	1980.00
Theorem, Velvet, Martha Morse, Keene, New Hampshire	5225.00
Tinsel, Bird Center, Blues & Reds, Floral Circle, Framed	895.00
Victorian Wreath, Chalkware Fruit, Parrot, Framed	525.00
Woodblock, Patterson, Windblown Trees, Framed, 7 1/8 X 10 1/4 In.	950.00

The Pigeon Forge Pottery was started in Pigeon Forge, Tennessee, in 1946. Red clay found near the pottery was used to make the pieces. Molded or thrown pottery with matte glaze and slip decoration was made. The pottery is still working.

PIGEON FORGE, Bowl, Gray, White Floral, Turquoise Interior, Squatty	8.00
Bowl, Yellow Glaze Inside, Garland of Dogwood, 5 1/2 In.	75.00
Candleholder, Brown, Handle, 3 In., Pair	5.00
Coaster, Yellow, Pair	18.00
Figurine, Owl, 4 In.	6.00
Mug, Hemlock Trees, Matte Green To Terra–Cotta, 4 1/4 In.	18.50
Sugar & Creamer, Individual	12.00

Sugar & Creamer, Terra–Cotta, Yellow Interior	8.00
Sugar, Creamer & Teapot, Dogwood Design, Yellow Interiors	35.00
Teapot, Hand Painted White Dogwood, Brown, 1 Cup	7.50
Vase, Brown Swirl Design, Tan, 6 3/4 X 5 In.	9.00
Vase, Dogwood, Squatty, Brown, 6 1/2 In.	8.00
Vase, Wedding, Brown, White Flower, 7 X 4 1/2 In.	8.00

The Pilkington Tile and Pottery Company was established in 1892 in England. The company made small pottery wares like buttons and hatpin heads but soon started decorating vases purchased from other potteries. By 1903, the company had discovered an opalescent glaze that became popular on the Lancastrian pottery line. The manufacture of pottery ended in 1937 but decorating continued until 1948.

PILKINGTON, Vase, Matte Intense Green, Squatty, 3 1/4 X 3 1/2 In.	48.00

The pincushion doll is not really a doll and often was not even a pincushion. The top half of the doll was made of porcelain. The edge of the half–doll was made with several small holes for thread, and the doll was stitched to a fabric body with a voluminous skirt. The finished figure was used to cover a hot pot of tea, a powder box, a pincushion, a whiskbroom, or a lamp. They were made in sizes from less than an inch to over 9 inches high. Most date from the early 1900s to the 1950s.

PINCUSHION DOLL, 1920s Woman, Porcelain, Arms Away From Body, Germany	250.00
Arms Extended, Gray Hairdo, Germany, 5 1/8 In.	125.00
Arms Extended, White Blouse, Apron, Hoop Skirt, 7 1/2 In.	125.00
Arms Out In Front, Lace Shawl, Mohair Wig, 3 1/2 In.	85.00
Blond Hair, Green Hat, Flowers In Hand Away, 3 3/4 In.	95.00
Bonnet Tied Under Chin, Arms Akimbo, Germany, 4 1/2 In.	75.00
Child, Brown Molded Hair, Parted In Middle, Arms Extended	60.00
Colonial Lady, Germany, 1 3/4 In.	30.00
Dancer, Lace Skirt	30.00
Dutch Girl	55.00
Fan In 1 Hand, Other On Hip, Art Deco Style Hat	36.00
Flapper, Arm Over Head, Black Hair, China, Box, 8 1/4 In.	195.00
Girl, Cloche Hat, Germany, 1 1/2 In.	25.00
Hand Away From Body, Other Holds Fan, Germany, 7 In.	50.00
Hands Away From Body, Gray Pompadour Hair, 4 1/2 In.	145.00
Hands Away, Wig, 7 1/2 In.	125.00
Harlequin, 3 In.	20.00
Holding Fan, Crocheted Skirt, Porcelain	24.00
Mary's Dress Shop, 5 In.	30.00
Mirror, Hand To Head, On Whisk Broom, 2 In.	30.00
Pierrette, Blue Skullcap, Hands Away, Signed Goebel	150.00
Victorian, Pink Satin Hat & Dress	30.00
Woman Holding Opera Glasses	135.00
Woman, Hair Wig, 1 Arm At Waist, Germany, 2 1/2 In.	45.00
PINK SLAG, see Slag, Pink	

Pipes have been popular since tobacco was introduced to Europe by Sir Walter Raleigh. Meerschaum pipes are listed under Meerschaum.

PIPE, Briar, Carved Bear	40.00
Briar, Carved Mutt & Jeff, Pair	65.00
Clambroth, Flowers & Merry Christmas On Bowl, Over Sized	20.00
Figural, Charlie Chaplin	75.00
Full–Bodied Alligator, Pottery	10.00
German Regiment, Briar & Bone, Dated 1903–05, 39 In.	225.00
German Shepherd, Red Cross Symbol On Collar, Dated 1918	55.00
Opium, 3 Tools Hanging From Short Chain, Metal, 1900s	65.00
Opium, Bamboo, Carved Fruit, Brass Bowl, Oriental, 21 1/2 In.	45.00
Pottery, Ancient Syria, 2nd Century B.C., 2 1/2 In.	35.00
Rest, Woman's Shoe Shape, Carved Detail, Granite, Pink, 6 In.	20.00

Shoe Kicking Ball, White Clay, 2 3/4 In.	6.50
Water, Enameled Brass, Chinese	50.00

Pirkenhammer is a porcelain manufactory started in 1802 by Friedrich Holke and J. G. Lilst. It was located in Bohemia, now Brezova, Czechoslovakia. The company made tablewares usually decorated with views and flowers. Lithophanes were also made. The mark of the crossed hammers is easy to remember as the Pirkenhammer symbol.

PIRKENHAMMER, Figurine, Girl Holding Basket, Flowers, 8 In.	250.00
Plate, Floral Design, 10 In.	65.00

Pisgah pottery pieces that are marked "Pisgah Forest Pottery" were made in North Carolina from 1926. The pottery was started by Walter R. Stephen in 1914, and after his death in 1941, the pottery continued in operation. The most famous types of Pisgah Forest ware are the cameo type with designs made of raised glaze and the turquoise crackle glaze wares.

PISGAH FOREST, Bowl, Harvest Scene, Chinese Blue, Signed	1050.00
Jug, High Glaze Turquoise, Dated 1935, 8 In.	110.00
Pitcher, Light Green, Stephen, 1949, 3 7/8 In.	38.00
Teapot, Small	55.00
Urn, Crackle Glaze, Chinese Blue, Pink Inside, 1939	65.00
Vase, Celadon, Handle, 6 3/4 X 4 3/4 In.	40.00
Vase, Dancing Couples, Blue, 10 In.	700.00
Vase, Gray High Glaze, Red Drip, 9 In.	295.00
Vase, Pink, 1938, 5 In.	45.00
Vase, Purple Crackle, Bulbous, 5 1/2 In.	68.00
Vase, Turquoise To Burgundy, Crackled, Corset, 5 1/2 X 4 In.	38.00
Vase, Turquoise, 4 3/4 In.	55.00
Vase, Urn Shape, Burgundy, 1954, 6 X 6 In.	40.00

Planters Nut and Chocolate Company was started in Wilkes–Barre, Pennsylvania, in 1906. The Mr. Peanut figure was adopted as a trademark in 1916. National advertising for Planters Peanuts started in 1918. The company was acquired by Standard Brands, Inc., in 1961. Some of the Mr. Peanut jars and other memorabilia have been reproduced and, of course, new items are being made.

PLANTERS PEANUTS, Alarm Clock	65.00
Ashtray, Figural, Ceramic	60.00
Bank, Plastic	6.00 To 13.00
Book, Painting, Famous Men, Envelope, 1935	25.00
Book, Story & Paint, America's Famous Men, 1939	15.00
Bookmark, Figural, Cardboard, C.1938	8.00
Bracelet, 6 Charms	18.00
Bracelet, Mr. Peanut, Brass, 1930s	28.00
Butter Maker, Mr. Peanut	15.00
Costume, Mr. Peanut Man, Large	950.00
Doll, Mr. Peanut, Cloth	10.00 To 16.00
Doll, Wood & Beads, 1930s, 8 1/2 In.	90.00
Glass, Cocktail, Red Bowl, Clear Figural Stem, Plastic	5.00
Jar, 1940 Leap Year, Lid	65.00
Jar, 8 Sides, No Cover	30.00
Jar, Embossed Peanuts At Corner, Peanut On Top	240.00
Jar, Embossed, Square	50.00
Jar, Fishbowl	75.00 To 100.00
Jar, Football Shape	200.00 To 285.00
Jar, Logo, 8 Sides, 5 Cents, 27 1/2 In.	48.00
Jar, Mr. Peanut, 4 Sides, Clear Glass, Domed Cover, 12 In.	65.00
Jar, Pennant, Partial Label	150.00
Jar, Planters Cocktail Peanuts, 8 Oz.	8.00
Jar, Streamline	45.00
Knife, Pocket	12.00
Lighter, Cigarette, Nut Shape	195.00

Mug, Red, Plastic, 4 In.	9.50
Night–Light, Figural	65.00
Nut Chopper	22.00
Nut Dish Set, New York World's Fair, 1940, 5 Piece	20.00
Nut Set, Mr. Peanut, Master & 7 Individual Bowls	28.00
Pencil, Mechanical, Figural Top	9.00
Pencil, Mechanical, Mr. Peanut	12.00
Pencil, Mechanical, Mr. Peanut, Original Wrapper	20.00
Pencil, Mr.Peanut	20.00
Pin, Tab, Yellow, Litho, 1930s, 5/8 In.	8.00
Pot, With Basket, Aluminum	65.00
Presidents of The U.S., 1932	22.00
Salt & Pepper, Green, Mr. Peanut, Plastic, 3 In.	9.00
Shaker, Beige, Black, Gloves, Spats, 4 In.	9.50
Shaker, Blue, Pair, 3 In.	8.00
Tin Container, Banner, 10 Lb.	40.00

> Plated amberina was patented June 15, 1886, by Edward D. Libbey
> and made by the New England Glass Works. It is similar in color
> to amberina, but is characterized by a cream colored or chartreuse
> lining (never white) and small ridges or ribs on the outside.

PLATED AMBERINA, Tumbler, 4 In.	2700.00
Vase, 8 In.	2000.00

> Plique–a–jour is an enameling process. The enamel is laid between
> thin raised metal lines and heated. The finished piece has
> transparent enamel held between the thin metal wires. It is different
> from cloisonne because it is transparent.

PLIQUE–A–JOUR, Bowl, Low	275.00

> All types of political memorabilia are collected, from buttons to
> banners. Items related to presidential candidates are the most
> popular, but collectors also search for material related to state and
> local offices. Many reproductions have been made.

POLITICAL, Ashtray, Thanks To Key Leader, Dick Nixon, Black Glass, 1960	8.00
Badge, Guest, Democratic National Convention, Chicago, 1944	20.00
Ballot, Democratic Party Ticket, Ward 18, Cook County, Ill., 1880	20.00
Bandana, Carter's Picture	144.00
Bandana, Grover Cleveland, A.E. Stevenson, 22 3/4 X 23 1/4 In.	195.00
Bandana, Roosevelt 1912 Flag, Red, White, Bust, 24 X 21 In.	20.00
Bank, Burro, New Deal On Side, Ceramic	35.00
Banner, Campaign, Teddy Roosevelt, Canvas, 44 X 51 In.	605.00
Banner, Fremont & Dayton, 2–Sided, 80 In.	1760.00
Banner, MacArthur Was Right, Silk, 3 X 20 In.	10.00
Beer Glass, Anti–Prohibition, 1932 Election	25.00
Blotter, Hugh Butler, Republican, U.S. Senator	7.50
Book, Coloring, JFK & Friends, Written As Primer, Unused	20.00
Bookmark, Harrison, Cello, Blue	65.00
Bottle Stopper, LBJ, Caricature, 5 1/2 In.	15.00
Box, Cigar, Warren G. Harding	35.00
Bracelet, Charm, Letters Spell Out Democratic, Brass, Copper, 1940	8.00
Bumper Sticker, Kenneth Fulbright, 1968	4.00
Button, Adlai, Estes, 1 3/8 In.	25.00
Button, Al Smith, A Winner For You, Photo, 3/4 In.	125.00
Button, Bryan & Stevenson, Bust, Red, White, Blue Ribbon, 1 1/4 In.	5.50
Button, Bryan, Clock Face, 1 1/4 In.	472.00
Button, Bryan, Shaking Hands With Labor, Cartoon	1534.00
Button, Coat, Garfield & Arthur, Brass, Raised Lettering, 3/4 In.	15.50
Button, Coolidge, Dawes, Jugate, Whitehead & Hoag, 1920s	23.50
Button, Davis, Bryan, Jugate, St. Joseph, Missouri	3860.00
Button, Dollars For Democrats, Stevenson, Kefauver, 1 1/4 In.	25.00
Button, Donkey, Al Smith, Enameled, Blue, Donkey Wearing Hat, 1 In.	10.50
Button, Douglas Johnson, Jugate, Hole Top	350.00
Button, Franklin D.Roosevelt, Inauguration, Jan.20, 1941, 7/8 In.	50.00

Button, Franklin Delano Roosevelt, Churchill, Jugate 395.00
Button, Goldwater For President, 1964, 7 In. 10.00
Button, Goldwater, Arrow, Black, Gold, 3/4 In. 2.00
Button, Help Hoover Help Business, 7/8 In. 88.00
Button, Hoover, Curtis, Jugate, Litho 175.00
Button, Hubert H. Humphrey, Jr. Memorial, 1978, 3 1/2 In. 6.00
Button, I Like Eisenhower, Litho, 1 1/4 In. 6.00
Button, Ike, In Morse Code, 1 In. 12.50
Button, Jimmy Carter For President In 1976, 1 1/2 In. 5.00
Button, John F. Kennedy, Picture, 3/4 In. 5.00
Button, John Glenn, First American In Orbit, Celluloid, 1 3/4 In. 9.00
Button, Ladies For Lyndon 1.25
Button, Landon & Knox, Sunflower Shape, Elephant Center, 3/4 In. 5.00
Button, Let's Back Ike, 2 1/2 In. 5.00
Button, McKinley, Hobart, Jugate, 1 1/4 In. 20.00
Button, Meet Mr. & Mrs. Nixon, Oval, 6 In. 47.50
Button, Mississippi Loves Carter, Yellow, Red, 3/4 In. 5.00
Button, Nixon, '72, 3/4 In. 2.50
Button, Parker, Davis, With Eagle, Gold Ground 110.00
Button, Pat For First Lady, Nixon, 1 In. 1.50
Button, Plate, Embossed Face of McKinley, Weller, 4 1/2 In. 50.00
Button, President Nixon, 1 In. 2.00
Button, President Polk, Peace & Friendship 50.00
Button, Reagan, of Course, Seattle, '84, Foxed, 1 In. 20.00
Button, Roosevelt & Wallace, 2 Round Photos, 1 In. 4.00
Button, Stevenson, Star Center With Date 1958, Celluloid 16.00
Button, Ted Kennedy In '72, 1 1/4 In. 3.00
Button, Truman, 3/4 In. 30.00
Button, Trust Humphrey, Black Letters, White Ground, 1 In. 2.00
Button, Uncommon Youth For Kennedy, 2 1/4 In. 200.00
Button, Vote Roosevelt, Labor's Choice 7.50
Button, Vote Stevenson 4.00
Button, William Taft, Black & White Photo, 7/8 In. 10.00
Button, Wilson, Multicolor, Blue & White Ground, 3/4 In. 12.00
Button, Win With Wilson, Center Picture 12.00
Calendar, Nixon To Kennedy Satirical Prints, 1972, 17 X 11 In. 10.00
Cane & Torch, Knob Unscrews Revealing Wick, Tin, 33 1/2 In. 110.00
Cane, With Horn, McKinley, Patriotism, Protection, Prosperity, Tin 225.00
Card, Campaign, President Jimmy Carter 5.00
Card, Greeting, Old Lady, Hat With Ronald Reagan Picture, 4 In. 2.50
Card, Mourning, J.F. Kennedy, E. Dickinson Poem, 1963, 7 X 5 In. 8.50
Card, Playing, Kennedy Kards, Humor House, 1963, Box 67.00
Card, Playing, The Alamo, LBJ Pack, E & S Co., 1965 .... 27.00
Card, Taft Or Bryan, Hostetter's Bitters, 1908 .... 11.00
Card, Trade, Ivory Polish, Mrs. Cleveland, 1880s, 2 1/2 In. 5.00
Carving Set, John F. Kennedy, Commemorative, Sheffield, 3 Piece 12.50
Charm, Picture, Flag On Reverse, Glass 25.00
Chess & Checkers Set, Political Campaign, 1968 .... 175.00
Cigar Label, In Honor of Pres. McKinley, 1901, 4 1/2 X 4 1/2 In. 10.00
Cigars, Landon 7.00
Clicker, Veterans For Nixon 3.50
Decal, John F. Kennedy For President, Shield Shape 12.00
Decal, Win With Ike, Picture 12.00
Dish, Zachary Taylor Cigar Band Trim, Clear, 5 1/2 In. 5.00
Elephant, Stuffed, Oilcloth, Painted Eyes, 2 Colors, 1940s 20.00
Fan, Dewey, Miles, Merritt Portraits In Pansies, Litho, 14 In. 200.00
Figurine, Cleveland & Harrison, Wrapped In Flag, Bisque, Scale 500.00
Figurine, Elephant, Life Begins In '40s, 1939 .... 200.00
Handkerchief, Herbert Hoover, Silk 95.00
Handle, Cane, McKinley 40.00
Hat Band, All The Way With L.B.J., Cardboard, Red, Blue, 1964 .... 4.00
Hat, Campaign, J.F. Kennedy 15.00
Hat, I Like Ike, Paper 12.00
Invitation, Roosevelt Memorial Service, Sepia Portrait, 1919 .... 27.00

Key Chain, Vote Eisenhower, 1950s	10.00
Lantern, Democratic County Officers, Cloth, Tin, 11 X 10 In.	187.00
Lantern, Parade, A. Lincoln, 1865, Paper, Tin Candle Socket, 13 In.	220.00
License Plate, President Carter's Official Inauguration, 1977	15.00
License Plate, Willkie	57.00
Light Bulb, Republican, Elephant Filaments	30.00
Magazine, Life, Kennedy Memorial Edition, 1963	8.00
Mirror, McKinley Memorial, Pocket	3.00
Mug, Cleveland, Thurman, Campaign of 1888	165.00
Mug, Elephant, Nixon & Agnew, Frankoma, 1969	60.00
Mug, McKinley One Side, Bryan Other, 2 Handles, 5 In.	125.00
Mug, New Deal	20.00
Mug, Nixon, Caricature, Signed & Dated, 1971, Rumph, 5 1/2 In.	85.00
Napkin, Richard Nixon, Caricature, Red, White & Blue	1.50
Necklace, Peanut, Jimmy Carter	6.00 To 12.00
Newspaper, Dewey Defeats Truman, Chicago Tribune	850.00
Paper Doll, Ronald Reagan, Centerfold Ramparts Magazine, 1965	50.00
Pen, Hubert Humphrey, Minority Whip, U.S. Senator	8.00
Pencil, Hoover For President, 1928	35.00
Pencil, Wendell Willkie, Mechanical	30.00
Pendant, Spiro Agnew, Chain, Box, 1968, 1 3/8 In.	7.00
Pendant, Votes For Women, Yellow, Black, 28 In.	150.00
Pipe, Z. Taylor Head, Old Rough & Ready, Red Clay, No Stem	50.00
Plate, J.F. Kennedy, In His Memory, Germany, 9 1/2 In.	12.00
Plate, James Garfield, Laurel Wreath Design, Clear, 10 In.	12.00
Plate, John F. Kennedy Center, Presidents All Around, 7 In.	15.00
Plate, Presidents, Up To Nixon	6.00
Plate, Taft, Eagle, Flags, Milk Glass, Embossed, 7 1/4 In.	75.00
Postcard, J.F. Kennedy, Sleeping, & Adlai Stevenson, Talking	5.00
Postcard, Lyndon B. Johnson, Coattail, With Nixon, Shaking Hands	12.00
Postcard, Miss Lillian Carter, Autograph	22.00
Postcard, President Theodore Roosevelt & Family	8.00
Postcard, Teddy Roosevelt & Family, Used, 1903	4.00
Postcard, Teddy Roosevelt, Billiken, South Africa, 1909, Unused	17.50
Postcard, Wm. Howard Taft, 1907	5.00
Poster, A Time For Greatness, Kennedy For President	22.00
Poster, Campaign, Humphrey, People's Democrat, 10 X 15 In.	9.00
Poster, Hoover, 16 X 22 In.	30.00
Poster, Lincoln & Johnson, C.1864, Litho, 30 X 24 In.	198.00
Poster, Vote Democratic, Progress With Roosevelt, 16 X 21 In.	50.00
Poster, Wendell Willkie, Wyoming Campaign, 1940, 11 X 14 In.	15.00
Poster, Wilson Needs Watson For US Senator, 1916, 19 X 9 In.	10.00
Program, Inauguration, Official Request Card, Ronald Reagan, 1981	12.00
Program, Richard Nixon, Inaugural, 1969	25.00
Puppet, Reagan, Boxing, Mechanical, Either Hand Can Punch, 11 In.	9.00
Puzzle, Jigsaw, Spiro Agnew, Dressed As Superman, 1970	18.00
Puzzle, Teddy & The Lions, New York, 1909, 5 X 6 In.	80.00
Record, Campaign, Adlai Stevenson, AFL–CIO, Cardboard, 1956, 7 In.	20.00
Ribbon, Eisenhower, Bust & Information, Red & Green, 7 X 2 In.	37.50
Ribbon, Republican, Precinct Committeeman	9.00
Ribbon, Willkie, Paper, Peoria, Ill.	85.00
Ring, Hoover, Silvered Brass	12.00
Ruler, Goldwater, A Leader Not A Ruler	8.00
Sheet Music, Harding's The Man For Me, 14 X 10 1/2 In.	35.00
Sheet of 25 Stamps, Nixon, Generation of Peace, 1972	10.00
Spoon, Grover Cleveland, White House Bowl, Sterling Silver	45.00
Spoon, McKinley, Sterling Silver	42.00
Sticker, Kennedy, Block Captain	12.00
Sticker, Landon, Knox, Yellow & Blue Sunflower, 1936, 2 X 9 In.	7.50
Stickpin, Franklin Delano Roosevelt, Photo, Plastic Frame	5.00
Stickpin, McKinley Homestead, Ribbon	40.00
Stud, GOP On Side of Elephant	4.50
Stud, McKinley, Lapel	12.00
T-Shirt, McGovern & Eagleton, Come Home America, 1972	17.50

Thimble, Coolidge, Dawes 12.50
Ticket, Lady Bird Johnson, Democratic Convention, Autographed 14.00
Tile, Bryan 30.00
Toby Jug, Herbert Hoover, Syracuse 65.00
Torch, Campaign, Embossed Eagle, Double Spout Burners, 23 In. 675.00
Tray, Keep Roosevelt, White House, Rectangular 35.00
Tray, McKinley, 12 X 17 In. 125.00
Tumbler, Taft For President, Sherman For Vice President 65.00
Watch Fob, For President, Al Smith, Metal, Celluloid Picture 55.00
Watch Fob, Next President William H. Taft, Old Strap Type 60.00
Watch Fob, Our Next Pres. William J. Bryan 60.00
Watch Fob, Sherman & Taft, 1908 .... 40.00
Watch Fob, Smith, Up From The Street 185.00
Watch Fob, Vote For Dr.A.A. Gossow, Coroner, St. Charles, Mo. 23.00
Watch Fob, Wilson, League of Nations 50.00
Watch, Dick Nixon, I'm Not A Crook, All American Time Co. 35.00
Watch, Ford In Auto, Caricature 35.00
Watch, Jimmy Carter, From Peanuts To President 35.00
Watch, Uncle Sam, Watergate 35.00
Wristwatch, Dickey Nixon, Dirty Times Co. 45.00

 Pomona glass is a clear glass with a soft amber border decorated with pale blue or rose-colored flowers and leaves. The colors are very, very pale. The background of the glass is covered with a network of fine lines. It was made from 1885 to 1888 by the New England Glass Company. First grind was made from April 1885 to June 1886. It was made by cutting a wax surface on the glass, then dipping it in acid. Second grind was a less expensive method of acid etching that was then developed.

POMONA, Bowl, Ruffled, 1st Grind, 5 In. 78.00
Bowl, Ruffled, Cornflowers, 2nd Grind, 3 X 5 1/2 In. 150.00
Celery Vase, Ruffled Rim, Cornflower Design, 1st Grind, 6 1/4 In. 350.00
Cruet, Pansy & Butterfly Design, 2nd Grind, 7 1/4 In. 465.00
Pitcher, Bird & Floral, Enamel 160.00
Pitcher, Cornflower, Amber Rim & Leaves, 1st Grind, 6 3/4 In. 365.00
Pitcher, Cornflower, Square Top, 1st Grind, 6 1/4 In. 395.00
Pitcher, Water, Inverted Thumbprint, Bluebird & Flowers, 6 3/4 In. 100.00
Punch Cup, Cornflower, 1st Grind 85.00
Punch Cup, Cornflower, 2nd Grind 90.00
Toothpick, Alternating Stripes of Amber, Frosted Tricornered Rim 225.00
Toothpick, Amber Ruffled Rim, 1st Grind 395.00
Toothpick, Tricornered, Diamond-Quilted, 2nd Grind 125.00
Tumbler, Cornflowers, 2nd Grind .... 55.00 To 95.00
Tumbler, Lemonade, Random Silvery Trails, 2nd Grind 185.00
Tumbler, Oakleaf Band, 2nd Grind 75.00
Tumbler, White Cornflowers, 2nd Grind, Green 100.00
Vase, Cornflower, 2nd Grind, 7 In. 175.00
Vase, Fan, Cornflower Design, Amber Ruffled Rim, 1st Grind, 3 X 6 In. 235.00
Vase, Fan, Scalloped Rim & Base, 1st Grind, 2 1/2 X 4 In. 350.00
Vase, Trifoil, Amber, 2nd Grind 115.00
Water Set, Butterfly & Pansy, 2nd Grind, Square Top Pitcher, 6 Piece 1415.00
PONTYPOOL, see Tole

 Popeye was introduced to the Thimble Theater comic strip in 1929. The character became a favorite of readers. In 1932, an animated cartoon featuring Popeye was made by Paramount Studios. The cartoon series continued and became even more popular when the old movies were used on television starting in the 1950s. The full-length movie with Robin Williams as Popeye was made in 1980.

POPEYE, Bank, Dime Register, 5 Dollars In Dimes, King Features, 1929, 5 In. 35.00
Book, Paint, 1930s, 10 X 12 In. 60.00
Bowling Set 35.00
Brush & Comb, Original Box, 1929 .... 55.00
Card Set, Popeye, 3rd Series, Color, Primrose Sweets, 1962, 50 Piece 12.50

Porcelain, Powder Box,
Raised Flowers, Ormolu,
Germany, 4 In.

Porcelain, Urn, Gold
Handles, Blue, Jacob Petit,
17 In., Pair

Porcelain, Bust, Man, Woman, Blue, White Costume Design, 16 In., Pr.

Card Set, Popeye, 4th Series, Color, Primrose Sweets, 1963, 50 Piece	10.00
Charm, Figural, Celluloid, Red Pants, Gray–Green Shirt, Japan, 1 In.	10.00
Charm, Figural, Painted Celluloid, 1930s	8.00
Comic Strip, Tru–Vue	10.00
Doll, Brutus, Popeye's Sparring Partner, Stand, 22 In.	25.00
Doll, Cloth, 1930s, 16 In.	140.00
Doll, Olive Oyl, Stand, 19 In.	22.50
Doll, Popeye, 18 In.	22.50
Doll, Swee'Pea, Stand, 17 In.	10.00
Doll, Swee'Pea, Uneeda, 1979, 8 In.	6.00
Doll, Wimpy, With Hamburger, Stand, 18 In.	22.50
Doll, Wooden, Jointed, 8 1/2 In.	250.00
Game, Ball Toss, Box	22.00
Game, Card, Leather Case, Dated 1934	30.00
Game, Pipe Toss, Box	35.00
Game, Popeye Treasure Map, 1958	22.00
Game, Skooz–It Pick A Picture, Olive Oyl, 1963	25.00
Gun Set, Halco, Late 50s	60.00
Hat, Earflaps, Unused, King Features, Late 1930s, Adult Size	48.00
Lantern, Linmar Marx, Box	595.00
Mask, Wrigley Premium, Mailing Envelope	65.00
Paint Box, Tin	20.00
Pen, Fountain	85.00
Pencil Sharpener, Bakelite	25.00
Pencil, Mechanical, Box, Large	50.00 To 75.00
Pez Holder	12.00
Pin, Figural, Metal, Enameled, 1930s, 1 1/2 In.	28.00
Soap, Figural, 1940s, 5 Piece	20.00
Toy, Kazoo & Charm, 2 Piece	25.00
Toy, Parrot In Cage, Windup	330.00
Toy, Pin The Pipe On Popeye, Box	32.00
Toy, Popeye & Olive Oyl Jiggers On Roof, Tin Litho, Marx, Box	4000.00
Toy, Popeye With Parrot Cage, Windup	225.00
Toy, Popeye, Blowing Bubbles, Linmar Marx, Battery Operated, Box	1795.00
Toy, Sitting On Can of Spinach, Battery Operated	1750.00
Toy, Walker, Chein	265.00
Tray, Tin, Oval, 1930s	30.00

 Major porcelain factories are listed in this book under the factory name. This section lists pieces that are by the less well–known factories.

PORCELAIN, Bottle, Figural, Lady, Bowl At Feet, Enameled, Jacob Petit, 13 In. 470.00

Bowl, Cover, Lovers In Woods, Bronze Handles, 8 1/2 In.	160.00
Bowl, Samurai Battle Scene, Allover Floral & Bird, 15 1/2 In.	375.00
Box, Cover, Nude Among Meshes, 6 1/2 In.	105.00
Brush Pot, Polychrome Floral Design, Birds, 11 1/4 In., Pair	60.00
Brush, Clothes, German Shepherd, Germany	30.00
Bust, Man, Woman, Blue, White Costume Design, 16 In., Pr. ....*Illus*	440.00
Candleholder, Child, Holding Flower Basket, Sitzendorf, 8 In.	110.00
Candlestick, 4 Putti, Sitzendorf	135.00
Casque, Chateau Des Etoiles, Roses, Cover, Signed Deco, 8 3/4 In.	400.00
Chocolate Pot, Lovers, Garden, White, Gold, NPS, Silesia, 1882, 9 In.	150.00
Chocolate Set, Oriental Pagoda, Cream Ground, Schoeleher, 29 Pc.	750.00
Compote, With Wax Fruit, Under Dome, C.1850, 21 In.	550.00
Condiment Set, Butterfly Form, Blue & White, China	150.00
Dish, Leaf Shape, Chintz Pattern, Frankenthal, 11 In., Pair	885.00
Dish, Pickle, Floral, White, Gold Highlights Edge, 11 X 4 In.	6.00
Ewer, Birds, Bonn	450.00
Figurine, Ballerina, Seated, Schaubachkunst, Germany, 10 In.	225.00
Figurine, Cornucopia Sleigh, White, Gold, Blue, Germany, 12 In.	236.00
Figurine, Dragon, On Blue Ocean Water, Red & Green, 18 In.	180.00
Figurine, Fortune Teller, Reading Girl's Palm, Hardy, 14 1/2 In.	550.00
Figurine, Girl & Lover On Bridge, Sitzendorf, 8 1/2 X 9 In.	760.00
Figurine, Lady, With Boots, Shaubachkunst, Germany	95.00
Figurine, Matador & Bull, Scheibe–Alsbach, 12 1/2 In.	350.00
Figurine, Monkey Band, 9 Piece, Sitzendorf, 6 In.	850.00
Figurine, Nude, 1 Sitting & 1 Lying, Rosenthal Style, 1950s, Pair	490.00
Figurine, Roman Slave Trader, Presenting Girl To Noble, 17 In.	1250.00
Figurine, Three Boys Holding Up Peach, Chinese, 9 X 10 1/2 In.	125.00
Figurine, Vulcan & Dionysus, Enameled, Marked, 6 3/8 In., Pair	290.00
Figurine, Whippet, Reclining, White, Blue Collar, 8 1/2 In.	45.00
Figurine, Woman On Sofa, Red Bodice, Ludwigsburg, C.1828, 6 In.	425.00
Foo Dog, Green, Yellow, Brown Base, 12 In.	38.00
Fruit Bowl, Grape Clusters, Austria, 1920	195.00
Ginger Jar, Floral Design, Crackle Glaze, Converted To Lamp, Pair	600.00
Group, 8 Figures & Piano, Lace, 16 X 28 X 14 1/2 In.	1760.00
Group, Isaac & Rebekah, Beside Prone Camel, W.Beattie, 20 1/2 In.	350.00
Group, Mother & Daughter, Drawing Water, Continental, 8 X 11 In.	175.00
Group, Youth & Maiden, Polychrome, Gilt, 5 3/4 In.	75.00
Jar, Cover, Flowers, Bats, Birds, Red Handles & Finial, 7 3/4 In.	65.00
Jar, Stylized Prunus, Blue & White, Chinese, 13 In., Pair	8800.00
Jar, Temple, Mythological Figures, Wood Cover, China, 1900, 14 In.	150.00
Jar, Wooden Lid, Polychrome Enameled Floral & Birds, 8 1/4 In.	75.00
Jug, Cabbage Leaf Mold, Caughley, C.1780, 8 3/4 In.	550.00
Jug, Cabbage Leaf Mold, Caughley, C.1780, 9 1/2 In.	495.00
Lamp, Figure of Woman In Evening Gown, Beaded, 13 In.	650.00
Pin Dish, Black, White, Pierrot	80.00
Pitcher, Chelsea Design, Black Transfer, Medallions, 8 1/4 In.	75.00
Planter, Putti, 3 Sections, Germany	200.00
Plaque, 2 Girls Kneeling In Prayer, Gilt Foliate Frame, 7 In.	375.00
Plaque, Daughter of Caliph After Sichel, Liebmann, 7 X 5 1/4 In.	633.00
Plaque, Greek Princess, Germany, Signed, 7 1/2 In.	425.00
Plate, Butterflies On Geometric Ground, 9 In., Pair	45.00
Plate, Polychrome Floral Design, 9 In., Pair	80.00
Plate, Portrait, Victorian Boy & Girl, Scalloped, England, Pair	58.00
Plate, Purple Plums, Blossoms, Gold Highlights, Germany, 12 In.	5.00
Plate, Transfer Portrait of Woman, Green & Gilt Edge, 10 In.	55.00
Powder Box, Raised Flowers, Ormolu, Germany, 4 In. ....*Illus*	175.00
Sprinkle Bottle, Chinese Man, Clemenson	20.00
Stand, Sweets, Man, Woman, Oval Lipped Bowl, 1890–1910, Germany, Pr.	525.00
Tea Set, Child's, Blue Flowers, Gilt Trim, 3 Piece	6.00
Tea Set, Child's, House That Jack Built, 11 Piece	85.00
Tea Set, Child's, White, Wooden Box, Label, French, 1900s, 15 Piece	175.00
Teabowl, Chinese Fishermen, Interior Design, Caughley, C.1785, Pr.	110.00
Teapot, Blue & White Faceted, China, 8 1/2 In.	70.00
Teapot, Courting Garden Scenes, Rosebud, Bail Handle, 9 In.	2250.00

Toothpick, Singing Frog, Germany	35.00
Tray, Dresser, Cherubs, Pink Border, Scalloped, 7 1/4 X 11 1/2 In.	35.00
Tureen, Squash Shape, Cover & Stand, J. Petit, C.1845, 9 1/2 In.	2475.00
Urn, Cherubs & Songbirds, Griffin Handles, Rorstrand, 28 In.	475.00
Urn, Cover, Portrait Scenes, Jacob Petit, Pair	1100.00
Urn, Gold Handles, Blue, Jacob Petit, 17 In., Pair............................*Illus*	1650.00
Vase, 5–Lobed Body, Flowers & Birds In White, Signed, 9 3/4 In.	800.00
Vase, Birds & Bouquets, Gilt Scrolls, J. Petit, 8 In., Pair	605.00
Vase, Birds In Flowering Trees, Blue & White, 22 3/4 In.	95.00
Vase, Blue & Celadon, Floral Design, Peacocks, 22 3/8 In.	75.00
Vase, Bud, Colonial Boy, Fountain & Tree, Figural, Germany, 7 In.	35.00
Vase, Bud, Thistles, Leaves, Paneled, Bulbous, Schellink, 2 2/3 In.	1045.00
Vase, Dragonflies, Rosenburg, Octagonal, 6 In.	850.00
Vase, Enameled Wise Men, Sorcerers, Tiger, Oriental, 18 1/2 In.	450.00
Vase, Famille Rose, Butterflies, Chinese, 12 1/2 X 16 In., Pair	360.00
Vase, Floral Design, Octagonal Body, Black, Floral Panels, C.1850	300.00
Vase, Floral With Peacock, Blue & White, Oriental, 22 3/4 In.	85.00
Vase, Hand Painted Flowers, Handles, Baluster Body, 17 In., Pair	1600.00
Vase, Outlined White Iris, Mottled Blue Ground, Danish, 5 In.	50.00
Vase, Rose Mandarin, Foo Dog Cover, 17 In., Pair	1540.00
Vase, Roses, Altwasser, Silesia, 12 In.	65.00
Vase, Several Women Painted, Eggshell, China, 6 1/2 In.	60.00
Vase, Temple, Ruffled, Colors Simulating Hiramakie, 38 In., Pair	1400.00
Vase, Urn Shape, Gold On Porcelain, Fraunfelter, No.93, 8 In.	200.00
Vase, Western Figures, Chinese, 11 In.	30.00
Wall Pocket, Flowers, Leaves, Blue Luster Ground, Japan	20.00
Wash Set, Fashoda, Floral, Dudson, Wilson & Tilley, 6 Piece	500.00

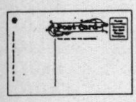

Postcards were first legally permitted in Austria on October 1, 1869. The United States passed postal regulations allowing the card in 1872. Most of the picture postcards collected today date after 1910. The amount of postage can help to date a card. The years the rates changed and the rates are: 1872 (1 cent), 1917 (2 cents), 1919 (1 cent), 1925 (2 cents), 1928 (1 cent), 1952 (2 cents), 1959 (3 cents), 1963 (4 cents), 1968 (5 cents), 1973 (8 cents), 1975 (7 cents), 1976 (9 cents), 1978 (10 cents), 1981 (12 cents), 1981 (13 cents), 1985 (14 cents), 1988 (15 cents).

POSTCARD, 2 Comic Characters, Holding Gun, Huge Rabbit, Leather, Unused, 1907	10.00
Adm. Peary, Glass Photo, Snow Baby's Father, G. Prince, 1910	97.00
Apollo, Photograph, Color, 11 Piece Set	8.50
Babe Ruth, 6 Piece	10.00
Bathing Girl, Embossed, 1911	8.00
Black Waiter, Stork, Pretty Girl, Cherries, Leather, 4 Piece Set	20.00
Bristol, Guide & Woman, Canoe, Fishing Scene, 1908	50.00
Broncho Billy, 1st Screen Cowboy, Films From 1908 To 1918	20.00
Buffalo Bill Cody, With Wild West Show In France, 1907	242.00
Cat, Squeaker Inside	10.00
Cats, Louis Wain, Tuck	35.00
Chicago, Milwaukee & St. Paul Railway, Yellowstone Park, 1910	5.75
Christmas Winter Scene, Hold To Light	25.00
Comic, Sgt. Dave Breger, 1935, 19 Piece	35.00
Coney Island, Color Litho, 18 Scenes, Foldout, 1950s	6.00
Dog, Boxer, Signed Rivst, Unused, 1920	5.00
Dogs, Alaska–Yukon Expo, 1909	5.00
DuPont, Powder Wagon	14.00
E. Broad Street, Columbus, Ohio, Homes & Autos, 1911	2.00
Enrico Caruso, Memorial, 1921	10.00
Flag Draped Outside Wall, Display, Photograph, 1910	5.00
Harvard, Army Football Game, Photograph, 1928	9.00
Hotel Vendome, San Jose, Calif., Color, C.1907	5.00
Hudson Motor Car, 1928	12.00
If My Wife Is A Suffragette I Should Worry, Used, 1913	12.50
Indianapolis Motor Speedway	3.00
Indians, Comanche Brave, P. Bosselman	7.00

Indira Gandhi, Photograph, Signed 40.00
Jamestown, Exposition, 1907, 11 Piece 50.00
Jane Withers, Star's Home Photo, Color, 1930s, Unused 5.00
Leather, C.1905 .... 3.75
Lemp Brewing Co., 1909 .... 10.00
Little Nemo, Chromo 65.00
Lombart Chocolate, Elephant In Jungle, Circus, C.1906, Unused 7.50
Madison Street At Clinton Street, 1906 .... 1.25
Maplewood Hotel, White Mountains, N.H., Menu, Folding, 1909 .... 4.00
Mickey Rooney, Star's Home Photo, Color, 1930s, Unused 5.00
Mississippi River, Cities, Towns, Steamers 25.00
Nelson Eddy Photograph, Opera, Signed 25.00
New Orleans Building & Battleship Illinois 6.00
Norvell–Shapleigh Hardware, Color 20.00
Oil Field Scene, Breckenridge, Tex. 3.00
Olympics, Melbourne, Australia, Poster Card, 1956 .... 10.00
Panama Canal, Foldout, 1913 Construction & History, Posted 1915 ..... 15.00
Pasadena, Tournament of Roses, 1950 .... 9.00
Phonograph Record, 33 1/3, 1950s 8.00
Photo, Businga's Prairie Lawn Farm, Hereford, Tx., 1909 .... 15.00
Photo, Phoenix, N.Y., Snowstorm, Trains On Tracks, Kellar, 1930s 5.00
Photo, Roundup In Panhandle, Hereford, Tx., Unused, 1909 .... 15.00
Riding Carousel, Riverview Park, 1915 .... 1.25
Ringling Bros. Circus, Sarasota, Fla., 1947 .... 15.00
Rookwood Pottery, Cincinnati, Sepia, 1911 .... 3.50
Roosevelt Bears 12.00
Russo–Japanese Peace Conference, Portsmouth, N.H., 1905 .... 12.00
San Francisco Street View, Before Earthquake, C.1904, Unused 6.00
Santa Claus In Auto 50.00
Santa Claus, Embossed, 6 Piece 50.00
Schoenhut Toys, All Different, 3 Piece 85.00
Steam Engine & Steel Separator, Racine, Wisconsin 10.00
Teddy Bear, Days of The Week, Dated 1907, 7 Piece Set 125.00
Thanksgiving, Embossed, Colorful, 3 Piece Set 15.00
U.S. Naval, Sea Bee 4.00
United For Victory, World War I 5.00
Votes For Women, Ballot Is Denied To Woman, 1910 .... 12.50
Votes For Women, Don't Let A Chance Slip, This Is Leap Year, 1908 .... 5.00
William S. Hart, England, 1920s 12.00
Yankee Doodle, Spirit of '76, Color, 1910, Unused 5.00

Posters have informed the public about news and entertainment events since ancient times. Nineteenth–century advertising or theatrical posters and twentieth–century movie and war posters are of special interest today. The price is determined by the artist, the condition, and the rarity. Other posters are listed under Advertising, World War I, and World War II.

POSTER, Abe Lincoln In Illinois, RKO, Raymond Massie, 1940 .... 150.00
Across Continent, Graphic Train, Color, Matted, Framed, 26 X 16 In. 220.00
Alaga Syrup, Picture of Willie Mays, 1960s, 22 X 15 In. 20.00
Alias A Gentleman, Wallace Beery, 1948, 41 X 27 In. 25.00
Anastasia, Ingrid Bergman, 1950s 30.00
Anheuser–Busch, Custer's Last Fight, 35 X 45 In. 160.00
Animal World, Special Effects By Ray Harryhausen, 1956, 41 X 27 In. 25.00
Army of 50 Clowns, Circus, 1960 .... 15.00
Austin Powder Co., Strauss, 1901 .... 395.00
Baldwin's Bilious & Liver Pills, 1905, 26 X 20 In. 40.00
Barnsdale's Moving Pictures, Russell Morgan Co., 1905, 28 X 42 In. 400.00
Bicycle, Cottereau & Cie, France, 58 X 34 In. 600.00
Buffalo Bill's Wild West, Congress Rough Riders, 1893, 26 X 22 In. 330.00
Buffalo Bill's Wild West, Matted, Framed, 14 X 19 In. 3520.00
Buffalo Bill, Folded, Rosa Bonheur, 1889, 56 X 32 In. 154.00
Buffalo Bill, Indian Maiden, W.J. Morgan, Framed, 1881, 28 X 15 In. 1540.00
Buffalo Brewing Co. 50.00

Camille, MGM, Greta Garbo, Robert Taylor, 1936	450.00
Cannatter Park, Amusement, Baltimore, C.1915, 24 X 36 In.	125.00
Circus, B.B. Street Parade, Strobridge Lithograph, 1909	418.00
Cleveland Cycles, Indian On Bicycle, Paris, 56 1/2 X 43 1/2 In.	250.00
Dan Patch, Hitched To Sulky, International Stock Food	350.00
Dawn Patrol, Errol Flynn, 1938, 22 X 28 In.	2750.00
Dr. Jekyll & Mr. Hyde, Spencer Tracy, 14 X 36 In.	400.00
Ecstacy, Parrish	95.00
Empire State Carousel, 1st Full–Sized Horse, 28 X 20 In.	10.00
Falcon's Adventure, Tom Conway, 1946, 41 X 27 In.	150.00
FBI Wanted, John Jenry Howland, 1939 Murder Suspect, 10 X 16 In.	9.00
Fillmore Rock, Chambers Bros., '67, 14 X 20 In.	20.00
Fleck's Lice Exterminator, Poultry & Livestock, 28 X 21 In.	140.00
Four Horsemen of Apocalypse, Metro Pictures, C.1921, 27 X 41 In.	325.00
Frank Sinatra, Reprise Records	5.00
Freedom From Fear, World War II, Rockwell, 20 X 28 In.	35.00
Great Lover, Paramount, Bob Hope, Rhonda Fleming, 1949	100.00
Henderson Motorcycle, 18 X 13 In.	70.00
Houdini, In Coffin, Otis Printing, 8 Pages, 1926, 76 X 96 In.	1818.00
I Walk Alone, Burt Lancaster, Lisabeth Scott, 1948, 81 X 81 In.	35.00
Imre Kiralfy's Grand Historical Spectacle America, 1893	605.00
Infallible Powder Co., Ducks, Marsh, Framed, 17 X 27 In.	950.00
Jungle Jim, Johnny Weissmuller, 1951, 14 X 17 In.	28.00
Karmi The Great, Levitation, Skeletons, Dated 1914, 41 X 28 In.	110.00
King of The Wild, Boris Karloff, 1931, 41 X 27 In.	350.00
King Solomon's Mines, Deborah Kerr, Stewart Granger, 1950, 3 Sheets	350.00
Lalla Rokh's Departure For Delhi, Strobridge Litho, 27 X 38 In.	165.00
Led Zepplin, Autographed By All Members	4125.00
Libeled Lady, Jean Harlow, William Powell, 1936, 27 X 41 In.	825.00
Lusitania, Damaged, Sinking, 1915	50.00
Magician Karmi, Multicolored, Blue Ground, 1914, 42 X 28 In.	125.00
Marilyn Monroe, 7 Year Itch, 1 Sheet	250.00
Marlin, Man With Dog, Stauss's MR–05, 1909	975.00
Monarch Fruits & Vegetables, 1920, 32 X 22 In.	50.00
Monarch Fruits & Vegetables, Shrink Wrapped, 1920, 32 X 22 In.	50.00
Packer's Tar Soap, Louis Rhead, Linen Mounted, 12 X 16 5/8 In.	110.00
Paul Cinquevalli, Boston Howard Athenaeum, Strobridge Litho, C.1900	1980.00
Pershing In France, Berlin Or Bust, World War I, Large Print	68.00
Pride & Prejudice, Greer Garson, Laurence Olivier, 1962, 41 In.	10.00
Prohibition, Liquor Business & Labor, Red, Black, 1900, 12 X 19 In.	20.00
Redfield Scopes, Moose, Large	10.00
Remington, Let Her Rain, Man, Duck Boat, Framed, 1925	285.00
Renault Racing On Back Roads, Dust Cloud, 1925, 63 X 46 In.	600.00
Ringling Bros. & Barnum & Bailey, Tiger & Lion, 34 X 21 In.	110.00
Rosemeade Paper Dealer, 11 X 9 In.	20.00
Royal Camel's Hair Skirt, 1870s, Framed, 14 X 20 In.	308.00
Save Freedom of Worship, Rockwell, 1943	35.00
Scout Buffalo Bill, On Horse, Full Color, Frame, 25 X 33 In.	4000.00
Spellbound, Ingrid Bergman, Mounted On Linen, 1948, 40 X 30 In.	400.00
Star Wars, Lucas Films, 60 X 38 In.	85.00
Tarzan & The Amazons, Johnny Weismuller, 1945	600.00
The Tigress, Jack Hold, Dorothy Revier, Otis Litho, 1926, 27 X 41 In.	250.00
Thin Man Goes Home, William Powell, 1944, 36 X 14 In.	350.00
This Island Earth, Classic Science Fiction	425.00
Uncle Sam, Pres. of Mexico Dancing, Laughing At Hitler, 14 X 20 In.	45.00
Use Fleck's Stock Food, Man Holding Large Box, 25 X 19 In.	50.00
W.C. Fields, The Bank Dick, Cartoon Type	665.00
Wallace & Co's Great World's Menagerie, Framed, 27 X 15 1/2 In.	880.00
Willie Shoemaker, Signed Andy Warhol	650.00
Winchester Ammunition, Bear, Out of Cabin, Framed, 1920s, 33 X 17 In.	850.00
Winchester Bullet, World War II	50.00
Wizard of Oz, 40 X 30 In.	225.00
Woman, Chased By Wolf, Art Nouveau, Monogram, Mounted, Trimmed, Square	28.00
World War II Veterans' Flight Training	10.00

A potlid is just that, a lid for a pot. Transfer–printed potlids had their heyday from the 1840s to the early 1900s. The English Staffordshire potteries made ceramic containers with decorative lids for bear's grease, shrimp or meat paste, cold cream, and toothpaste. Printed advertising and pictures of historical events, portraits of famous people, or scenic views were designed in black and white or color. Reproductions have been made. The most famous potlids were made by Pratt and are listed in that section.

POTLID, No By Heaven I Exclaimed	120.00
Washington Crossing Delaware, Taylor Perfumers, Philadelphia	65.00

Pottery and porcelain are different. Pottery is opaque; you can't see through it. Porcelain is translucent. If you hold a porcelain dish in front of a strong light you will see the light through the dish. Porcelain is colder to the touch. Pottery is softer and easier to break and will stain more easily because it is porous. Porcelain is thinner, lighter, and more durable. Majolica, faience, and stoneware are all pottery. Many types of pottery are listed in this book under the factory name.

POTTERY, Ashtray, Fred Flintstone, Wilma, Ceramic	15.00
Bird Whistle, Cream, Green, Splash, Shenandoah Pottery, 1860, 4 In.	260.00
Birdhouse, Log Cabin, Greenish White Glaze, 5 1/4 In.	600.00
Biscuit Jar, Multicolored Flowers, Silver Plate Fittings, G. Jones	95.00
Bowl, Cattail, 8 In.	8.00
Bowl, Incised Fern Design, Waylande Gregory, 4 In.	60.00
Bowl, Mottled, Cobalt Blue & Navy, Rolled In Top, Bretby, 8 X 4 In.	40.00
Bread Plate, Calico Fruit, 6 In.	8.00
Bread Plate, Cattail, 6 In.	7.00
Bust, Art Deco Lady, White Crackled Glaze, 9 In.	85.00
Canister Set, Dutch Design, 8 Piece	125.00
Canister, Rice, Blue Stenciled Design, 4 X 5 3/4 In.	40.00
Carpet Ball, Black, 3 1/2 In.	110.00
Casserole, Blue, Glidden, 5 1/2 X 8 In.	28.00
Casserole, Priscilla, Cover, Homer Laughlin	13.00
Cheese Dish, Cover, Brown & White Figures, English, 10 1/2 In.	225.00
Creche Set, High Gloss Tan, Fort Hays, 6 7/8 To 4 In., 3 Piece	145.00
Decanter, Oriental Sailors, Removable Hat, Robj, 11 1/4 In., Pair	3500.00
Dish, Cheese, Art Nouveau Floral Design, Gold Trim, Marked, 5 In.	110.00
Figurine, Antelope Head, Brown, Speckled Antlers, H. Pierce, 16 In.	55.00
Figurine, Cat, Sitting, White Clay, Brown Albany Slip Base, 5 In.	450.00
Figurine, Dog, Seated, Blue Sponged, White Clay, Ohio, 6 1/2 In.	800.00

Pottery, Figurine, Pig, Jay Finch, 6 In.

Pottery, Vase, Gazelles, Silver Overlaid, 1925, 14 1/2 In.

Figurine, Hen, Seated, Brown, Red Wattles, Kay Finch, 4 3/4 X 5 In.	30.00
Figurine, Horse, Art Deco, Cinnamon, Erect Tail, 3 X 3 In.	15.00
Figurine, Oriental Man & Woman, Hedi Schoop, 12 In., Pair	48.00
Figurine, Pig, Jay Finch, 6 In. ....*Illus*	85.00
Figurine, Pink Pig, Coming Out Cup, Germany	75.00
Figurine, Pink Pig, Playing Piano, Germany	95.00
Figurine, Shoe, Blue, Marked No.3	4.00
Figurine, Woman, Seated, Horses Standing, Straw Glaze, Chinese, 9 In.	2500.00
Head, Phrenological, Fowler's, Late 19th Century, 10 1/2 In.	600.00
Incense Burner, Daruma Form, Kyoto, Octagonal, 2 1/4 In.	200.00
Jar, Tobacco, Pig In Barrel Form, 6 1/4 In.	100.00
Jardinere, Matte Green, Pedestal, Arts & Crafts Shape	450.00
Jardiniere, Green–Brown, Checkerboard, Burley Winter, 10 X 11 In.	48.00
Jug, Ear Handles, Red–Gray, Brown Slip, Old Rye, 1901, 5 3/4 In.	5000.00
Jug, Foliate Design, Blue, Persian, 10 In.	50.00
Jug, Green Matte Glaze, Lanier Meaders, Grotesque, 9 In.	200.00
Lamp, Factory, Pink Roses, Gray & Tan, Cylinder, Limoges, 8 In.	250.00
Mug, Monk, Columbian Art Pottery, Trenton, N.J.	90.00
Pig, Painted With Large Roses, Wemyss	225.00
Pitcher & Bowl, Rose & Lily, Pioneer Pottery Co., C.1870	180.00
Pitcher, Black, Pink Roses, S. Ford Ltd., Burslem, England	75.00
Pitcher, Child's, Duck Shape, Spout In Bill, C.1890, 6 1/2 In.	50.00
Pitcher, Yellow & Gold Roses, White, East Liverpool Potteries	75.00
Planter, Black Panther, 1957, Lane	25.00
Planter, Figural, Turkey, Brown, Leg Raised, Kay Finch, 9 X 6 X 10 In	80.00
Plate, Calico Fruit, 7 In.	9.00
Platter, Cattail, Oval, 12 In.	15.00
Platter, Combware, Yellow & Brown, Late 18th Century, 14 In.	1985.00
Saucer, Empress, Sears, Roebuck	6.00
Saucer, Poppy, Sears, Roebuck	7.00
Shoe, High Button, White Clay, Brown Glazed, Ohio, 6 In., Pair	150.00
Spooner, Fish, Turquoise, Morton Pottery	6.50
Sugar Shaker, Woman, Boru	85.00
Swan, Crockery, 4 X 3 In.	37.50
Tea Set, Art Deco, Tan, Platinum Trim, Floral, Leigh Potters, 3 Piece	24.00
Tea Set, Black, Gold Brushed Design, 14 In. Tray, Brastoff, 4 Piece	125.00
Tea Set, Branch Handles, Applied Flowers, 12 Piece ....*Illus*	275.00
Teapot, Crocus, Enterprise	19.00
Teapot, Figural, Dachshund, Erphila, Germany, 8 In.	50.00
Vase, 2 Nudes, A.C.R. Eisenberger Co., 1928	1025.00
Vase, Albany Slip Interior, Double Stamped, 22 In.	1700.00
Vase, Dolphin With Cherub Rider, 13 In.	200.00
Vase, English Country Scene, Cream, Brown, Black, 1883, Bretby, 8 In.	75.00
Vase, Flowers, Streaked Brown Ground, Fluted, Rekston, 10 X 6 In.	290.00
Vase, Gazelles, Silver Overlaid, 1925, 14 1/2 In. ....*Illus*	7700.00
Vase, Green & Copper Patina, Ring Neck, Tapered, 11 In.	550.00
Vase, Hourglass, Rust, Gray & Lavender, Amaco, 6 In. ....*Illus*	24.00
Vase, Matte Green Glaze, Merrimac, Squat Bulbous, 1905, 4 1/2 In.	450.00
Vase, Molded Flowers & Stems, Matte Yellow Glaze, Shawsheen, 7 In.	1200.00
Vase, Mottled Emerald Over Black, Flask Shape, Blue Mountain, 4 In.	10.00
Vase, Mottled Orange–Green Glaze, Arts & Crafts, 10 1/4 In.	20.00
Vase, Pink Filigree, Cream, 3 Gold Feet, Bulbous, Collins, 6 1/2 In.	105.00
Vase, Yellow Floral, Brown Underglaze, Bottle Shape, Raku, 13 In.	132.00

Powder flasks and powder horns were made to hold the gunpowder used in antique firearms. The early examples were made of horn or wood; later ones were of copper or brass.

POWDER HORN, Copper, Hawksley, 1840–60	45.00
Map, New York, Brass Finial Horn, Wood Plug, 8 1/4 In.	1100.00
Never Stop When Fighting For The Right, R.C. Stahl 1847	450.00
Primitive, Wooden End Block, 8 In.	12.50
Rifleman's, Banded Copper Base & Spout, 1812 War, 11 1/4 In.	135.00
Silver Mount, Louisiana, Presented To Theodore Roosevelt	1320.00
Town Scene, Ship Portrait, Hunter, Crucifix, 16 1/2 In.	150.00

PRATT
FENTON

Pratt ware means two different things. It was an early Staffordshire pottery, cream–colored with colored decorations, made by Felix Pratt during the late eighteenth century. There was also Pratt ware made with transfer designs during the mid–nineteenth century in Fenton, England. Reproductions of the transfer–printed Pratt are being made.

PRATT, Jar, Pastel Floral, Cover, Hand Painted, 1 3/8 X 3 In.	75.00
Plate, Scene of Ruins, Sheep, Sleeping Girl, Marked, 8 5/8 In.	1700.00
Plate, Strathfieldsaye–Wellington, Blue Border	85.00
Potlid, A Pair, Old Man & Woman Playing Cards	95.00
Potlid, A Race, Horse Race At Fair	125.00
Potlid, City Scene	135.00
Potlid, Enthusiast, Old Man With Gout, Fishing In Tub	125.00
Potlid, Landing The Fare, Sailor Carrying Lady Through Surf	135.00
Potlid, Ning PO River	160.00
Potlid, Skewbald Horse, Ladies & Gentlemen With Horses	85.00
Potlid, Wimbledon, Queen Victoria At Rifle Association Meeting	135.00
Potlid, Wolf & Lamb, English Schoolboy Bully	85.00

Pressed glass was first made in the United States in the 1820s after the invention of glass pressing machines. Hundreds of patterns of pressed glass were made in complete table settings. Although the Boston and Sandwich Works was the most famous of the pressed glass factories, there were about sixteen other factories making pressed glass from 1830 to 1850, and still more from 1850 to 1900, when pressed glass reached its greatest popularity. It is now being widely reproduced. The pattern names used in this listing are based on the information in the book "Pressed Glass in America" by John and Elizabeth Welker. There may be pieces of pressed glass listed in this book in other sections. See Lamp, Ruby, Sandwich, and Souvenir.

100–LEAVED ROSE, see Hundred Leaved Rose
1000–EYE, see Thousand Eye
101, see One–Hundred–One
8–0–8, see Eight–0–Eight
ACANTHUS, see Ribbed Palm
ACORN MEDALLION, BEADED, see Beaded Acorn Medallion

PRESSED GLASS, Acorn, Butter	95.00
Acorn, Creamer, Child's	110.00
Acorn, Goblet	35.00
Acorn, Sugar, Child's	95.00
Actress, Bowl, 9 1/2 In.	58.00
Actress, Bread Plate, H.M.S. Pinafore	85.00
Actress, Butter	95.00
Actress, Cake Stand	130.00
Actress, Celery, Frosted	155.00
Actress, Cheese Dish, Cover	165.00
Actress, Compote, 6 X 7 In.	75.00
Actress, Compote, Frosted Dome Cover, 9 1/2 In.	75.00
Actress, Compote, Frosted, 7 In.	100.00
Actress, Creamer	60.00 To 75.00
Actress, Creamer, Frosted	75.00
Actress, Goblet	70.00 To 110.00
Actress, Jam Jar	85.00 To 95.00
Actress, Saltshaker, Annie	25.00 To 45.00
Actress, Sauce	25.00
Actress, Sauce, Footed, Frosted	85.00
Actress, Spooner	65.00
Actress, Sugar, Open	60.00
Actress, Tumbler, Blue	30.00
ADMIRAL DEWEY, see Spanish American	
Aida, Pitcher, Water	75.00
Alabama, Celery, Ruby & Amber Stained, Flat	125.00

Actress

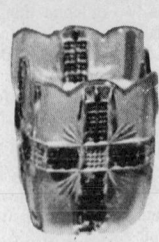

Amberette

Ashburton

Alabama, Saltshaker, Gold Trim	18.00
Alabama, Table Set, Ruby Stained, 5 Piece	425.00
Alabama, Tray, Water, 10 1/2 In.	28.00
Alaska, Banana Boat, Vaseline	175.00
Alaska, Berry Bowl, Green, Gold Trim, Silver Plated Stand	145.00
Alaska, Celery Tray, Green, Gold Trim	85.00
Alaska, Creamer, Blue	85.00
Alaska, Creamer, Vaseline	60.00
Alaska, Cruet, Green, Clear Stopper	275.00
Alaska, Spooner, Green, Gold Trim	65.00
Alaska, Sugar & Creamer, Scalloped Top, Vaseline	120.00
Alaska, Tumbler, Floral & Leaf Design, Vaseline	85.00
Albany, Butter, Cover	36.00
Albany, Celery Vase	28.50
Albany, Cruet	32.00
Albany, Pitcher, Water	30.00
Albany, Spooner, Green	45.00
Albany, Sugar, Cover	31.50
Alexis, Toothpick	18.00
Alligator Scales, Butter, Cover	40.00
Almond Thumbprint, Celery	25.00
Almond Thumbprint, Goblet	10.00 To 15.00
Almond Thumbprint, Wine	15.00
Amazon, Butter, Domed Cover, 5 1/4 In.	18.00
Amazon, Cake Stand	45.00
Amazon, Compote, Etched, 9 1/2 In.	55.00
Amberette, Berry Set, Amber, 5 Piece	135.00
Amberette, Butter, Cover, Amber, Frosted	215.00
Amberette, Salt & Pepper, Frosted & Amber	250.00
Amberette, Spooner, Amber, Frosted	300.00
Amberette, Sugar & Creamer, Amber, 5 In.	100.00
Amberette, Sugar, Frosted Panels, Amber Cross	225.00
Amberette, Toothpick	90.00
Amberette, Tumbler, Amber Cross, Frosted	145.00
American Flag, Platter, 38 Star, 8 X 11 In.	50.00
American Shield, Butter, Cover	50.00
American Shield, Table Set, 4 Piece	250.00
Anthemion, Pitcher, Water	45.00
Anthemion, Plate, 10 In.	55.00
Anthemion, Water Set, Green, 6 Piece	125.00
Anvil, Toothpick	35.00
Apollo, Berry Bowl, Emerald Green, Master	65.00
Apollo, Cake Stand, 10 In.	60.00
Apollo, Compote, Cover, 8 In.	65.00
Apollo, Compote, Open, 7 In.	30.00
Apollo, Lamp, 8 In.	65.00
Apollo, Lamp, Blue Base, Vaseline Font	245.00
Apollo, Sauce, Footed	15.00

Apollo, Sugar Shaker, Etched 30.00
Apollo, Tumbler, Frosted 30.00
Arched Ovals, Toothpick, Green, Gold Trim 40.00
Arched Ovals, Wine, Green 20.00
Argent, Wine 13.00
Argus, Eggcup 22.50
Argus, Goblet, Flint 33.00
    ARROWHEAD IN OVAL, see Style
Art, Banana Boat 55.00
Art, Butter, Cover 40.00
Art, Cake Stand 90.00
Art, Compote, Cover, 8 In. ....95.00 To 115.00
Art, Compote, Cover, High Standard, 6 In. 52.00
Art, Sugar, Cover 34.00
Ashburton, Celery Vase, Flint 60.00
Ashburton, Cordial 85.00
Ashburton, Cordial, Flint 47.50
Ashburton, Creamer, Handle, Thumbprint Under Spout, Flint 250.00
Ashburton, Cup, Applied Handle, Flint, 3 In., 4 Piece 220.00
Ashburton, Decanter, Pewter Stopper, Canary 1600.00
Ashburton, Eggcup ....16.50 To 30.00
Ashburton, Goblet, Flint 37.00
Ashburton, Sugar, Cover 145.00
Ashburton, Sugar, Flint, 7 1/4 In. 175.00
Ashburton, Tumbler, Flint, 3 1/2 In. 60.00
Ashburton, Wine, Straight Stem, Flint 36.00
Atlanta, Butter, Cover 48.00
Atlanta, Sugar & Creamer, Spooner, Cover, 3 Piece 125.00
Atlas, Creamer ....18.00 To 28.00
Atlas, Goblet, Etched Saratoga, 1892 .... 40.00
Atlas, Toothpick, Etched 32.50
Aurora, Bowl, 8 In. 23.00
Aurora, Celery 21.00
Aurora, Decanter, Original Stopper 41.00
Aurora, Wine ....15.00 To 20.00
Aurora, Wine Set, 3 Wines, Tray, Decanter 265.00
Austrian, Creamer, Child's 50.00
Austrian, Cruet 28.00
Austrian, Nappy 30.00
Austrian, Punch Cup 11.00
Austrian, Spooner, Round 25.00
Austrian, Vase, 8 1/4 In. 22.00
Aztec, Cruet 48.00
Aztec, Goblet 32.50
Aztec, Powder Jar 20.00
Baby Face, Celery 185.00
Baby Face, Sugar, Cover, Clear & Frosted 175.00
    BABY THUMBPRINT, see Dakota
Bag Ware, Creamer, Amber ....25.00 To 30.00
    BALDER, see Pennsylvania
    BALKY MULE, see Currier & Ives
Ball & Swirl, Butter, Cover 40.00
Ball & Swirl, Pitcher, Water 95.00
Ball & Swirl, Spooner 24.00
Baltimore Pear, Cake Stand 38.00
Baltimore Pear, Creamer ....25.00 To 28.50
Baltimore Pear, Sugar, Cover 41.50
Baltimore Pear, Table Set, 4 Piece 200.00
    BANDED BEADED GRAPE MEDALLION, see Beaded Grape Medallion,
    Banded
Banded Icicle, Goblet 20.00
    BANDED PORTLAND, when flashed with pink, is sometimes called
    "Maiden Blush."
Banded Portland, Cologne Bottle 51.00

Beaded Grape

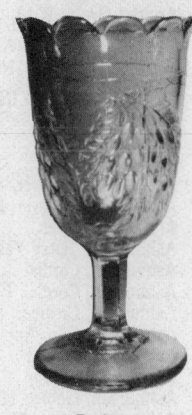

Bethlehem Star

Atlas

Barberry

Bellflower

Austrian

Banded Portland, Compote, Cover, 11 1/4 In. 65.00
Banded Portland, Cup 14.50
Banded Portland, Dish, Ruffled, 7 1/4 In. 24.00
Banded Portland, Pitcher, Water, Child's, Enameled, Green 20.00
Banded Portland, Vase, 6 In. 35.00
Banded Portland, Wine, Maiden Blush 65.00
     OTHER BANDED PATTERNS, see under name of basic pattern
Banner, Butter, Cover 85.00
     BAR & DIAMOND, see Kokomo
Barberry, Celery 32.00
Barberry, Compote, Cover, 8 In. 58.00
Barberry, Eggcup 20.00
Barberry, Goblet, Buttermilk 30.00
Barberry, Pitcher, Water 80.00
Barberry, Tumbler, Footed 25.00

BARLEY & OATS, see Wheat & Barley
BARLEY & WHEAT, see Wheat & Barley
Barley, Compote, Open, 9 In. 30.00
Barley, Goblet 17.00
Barley, Relish, 10 In. 10.00
Barred Forget–Me–Not, Cake Stand, 8 In. 32.50
Barred Forget–Me–Not, Cake Stand, 10 In. 41.50
Barred Forget–Me–Not, Plate, Closed Handle, 10 In. 15.00
BARRELED BLOCK, see Red Block
Bartlett Pear, Pitcher, Water 70.00
Basket Weave, Pitcher, Water, Amber 40.00
Basket Weave, Plate, Handles, 8 3/4 In. 7.00
Basket Weave, Tray, Water, Cabin Scene, Vaseline 65.00
Bead & Scroll, Berry Set, Gold Trim, 11 Piece 125.00
Bead & Scroll, Compote, Jelly 22.00
Bead & Scroll, Cruet 38.00
Beaded Acorn Medallion, Goblet 40.00
Beaded Acorn, Spooner 33.00
Beaded Arch, Mug, 2 In. 15.00
Beaded Block, Wine 12.00
BEADED BULL'S–EYE & DRAPE, see Alabama
Beaded Circle, Spooner, Green, Gold Trim 45.00
Beaded Coarse Bars, Cruet 25.00
BEADED DEWDROP, see Wisconsin
Beaded Fan, Butter 24.00
Beaded Grape Medallion, Banded, Sugar, Open 30.00
Beaded Grape Medallion, Goblet .... 25.00 To 27.00
Beaded Grape Medallion, Salt, 1 1/2 In. 35.00
Beaded Grape Medallion, Spooner 27.00
Beaded Grape, Compote, Green, Open, Square, 8 1/2 X 6 3/8 In. 56.00
Beaded Grape, Creamer 37.00
Beaded Grape, Cruet, Green ....95.00 To 110.00
Beaded Grape, Pitcher, Green, 6 In. 75.00
Beaded Grape, Relish, Green, 4 X 7 In. 20.00
Beaded Grape, Toothpick, Gold Trim 27.50
Beaded Loop, Bread Plate, 11 1/4 X 7 3/4 In. 27.00
Beaded Loop, Butter, Cover 40.00
Beaded Loop, Cake Stand 36.00
Beaded Loop, Carafe, Whiskey, Individual, 4 In. 31.00
Beaded Loop, Celery .... 27.50 To 28.00
Beaded Loop, Pitcher, Milk 35.00
Beaded Loop, Sugar, Cover, Ruby Stained 48.00

Bigler

Buckle

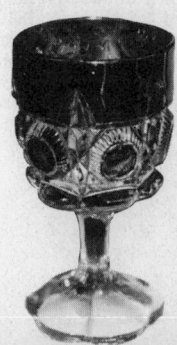

Bull's–Eye & Daisy

Beaded Medallion, Pitcher, Water, Child's 80.00
Beaded Mirror, Lamp, Square White Base, 8 3/4 In. 180.00
Beaded Oval & Scroll, Sauce, Flat, 4 1/2 In. 6.00
Beaded Panels, Wine, 1880s 14.50
Beaded Swirl & Disc, Butter 26.00
Beaded Swirl, Butter, Cover, Child's 45.00
Beaded Swirl, Cruet 58.00
Beaded Swirl, Punch Cup, Green, Gold Trim 9.00
Beaded Swirl, Table Set, Green, Gold Trim, 4 Piece 395.00
Beaded Tulip, Goblet 33.00
    BEARDED HEAD, see Viking
    BEARDED MAN, see Queen Anne
Beatty Rib, Toothpick 20.00
Beehive, Wine 24.00
Bellflower, Bowl, Low, Cover, 8 1/4 In. 225.00
Bellflower, Butter, Vine Cover, Flint 95.00
Bellflower, Compote, Open, Flint, 8 In. 80.00
Bellflower, Compote, Open, Single Vine, Flint, 7 3/4 In. 95.00
Bellflower, Decanter, 1 Qt., 12 1/2 In. 180.00
Bellflower, Double Vine, Goblet, Cut Pattern 225.00
Bellflower, Eggcup, Pale Amber 650.00
Bellflower, Goblet, Ruby Stained 65.00
Bellflower, Pitcher, Double Vine, 7 1/4 In. 385.00
Bellflower, Plate, 6 In. 135.00
Bellflower, Sauce, Apple Green 175.00
Bellflower, Spooner 37.50
Bellflower, Syrup, 10 Paneled Sides, Green Tint, 9 In. 700.00
Bellflower, Whiskey, Applied Handle 350.00
Belmont, Compote, Cover, Scalloped Rim 48.00
    BENT BUCKLE, see New Hampshire
Berry Cluster, Creamer 18.00
Bethlehem Star, Butter, Cover 60.00
Bethlehem Star, Cruet 27.00
Bethlehem Star, Pitcher, Water 42.00
Bethlehem Star, Tumbler .... 12.00 To 30.00
    BEVELED DIAMOND & STAR, see Albany
Beveled Star, Spooner, Green, Flint 30.00
Beveled Star, Table Set, Amber, 4 Piece 250.00
Bigler, Eggcup 35.00
Bigler, Plate, Amethyst, 6 In. 275.00
Bigler, Sauce, Canary, 4 1/4 In. 125.00
Birch Leaf, Bowl, Vaseline, Master 100.00
Birch Leaf, Goblet 15.00
Bird & Roses, Goblet, Etched 24.00
Bird & Strawberry, Bowl, 7 1/4 In. 85.00
Bird & Strawberry, Butter, Cover 90.00
Bird & Strawberry, Cake Stand 68.00
Bird & Strawberry, Compote, Cover, 4 1/2 In. 160.00

Bull's–Eye & Fan

Button Arches

Bull's–Eye with Diamond Point

Bird & Strawberry, Creamer .... 45.00 To 55.00
Bird & Strawberry, Punch Cup 10.00
Bird & Strawberry, Sugar, Cover 80.00
Bird & Strawberry, Tumbler 40.00
Bird & Strawberry, Wine 55.00
Bird In Eggshell, Toothpick 30.00
    BIRD IN RING, see Grace
Blackberry, Goblet, Opaque White 175.00
Blaine–Logan, Bread Plate, Frosted, 8 1/2 X 11 1/2 In. 250.00
Blaze & Mirror, Goblet 40.00
Bleeding Heart, Bowl, 8 In. 28.00
Bleeding Heart, Cake Stand, 9 1/2 In. 78.00
Bleeding Heart, Goblet 32.00
Bleeding Heart, Inkwell 65.00
Bleeding Heart, Mug 65.00
Bleeding Heart, Spooner 32.00
    BLOCK & CIRCLE, see Mellor
    BLOCK & FAN, see Romeo
    BLOCK & FINE CUT, see Fine Cut & Block
    BLOCK & STAR, see Valencia Waffle
Block With Fringe, Goblet 18.00
    BLOCK WITH STARS, see Hanover
Blocked Thumbprint, Tumbler, Flint 60.00
    BLOCKHOUSE, see Hanover
    BLUEBIRD, see Bird & Strawberry
Bohemian, Creamer, Cranberry, Gold Trim 65.00
Bohemian, Table Set, Green, Gold Trim, 4 Piece .... 335.00 To 450.00
Bohemian, Vase, Green, Gold Trim, Footed, 6 In. 75.00
Bordered Ellipse, Mug, Souvenir, Ruby Stained 35.00
Bordered Ellipse, Tumbler 25.00
Bowtie, Goblet 55.00
Bowtie, Pitcher, 6 1/2 In. 45.00
Bowtie, Pitcher, 8 In. 80.00
Bowtie, Pitcher, 9 In. 90.00
Bowtie, Relish, 5 X 8 In. 30.00
Box–In–Box, Butter, Cover, Ruby Stained 95.00
Box–In–Box, Relish, Ruby Stained .... 37.50 To 42.50
Box–In–Box, Toothpick, Ruby Stained 47.50
Branches, Pitcher, Water 50.00
Bridle Rosettes, Celery 20.00
Broken Column, Banana Boat 110.00
Broken Column, Bowl, 8 In. 37.50
Broken Column, Celery Vase 48.00
Broken Column, Compote, Cover, 5 In. 55.00
Broken Column, Cracker Jar .... 85.00 To 88.00
Broken Column, Cruet, Stopper 50.00
Broken Column, Cup, Cobalt Blue 52.50
Broken Column, Goblet 65.00
Broken Column, Pitcher, Water 95.00
Broken Column, Plate, 7 1/2 In. 65.00
Broken Column, Salt & Pepper 68.00
Broken Column, Sauce, 4 In. 17.00
Broken Column, Spooner .... 30.00 To 45.00
Broken Column, Sugar Shaker 110.00
Broken Column, Sugar, Cover, Red Notches 120.00
Broken Column, Tumbler 65.00
Brooklyn, Goblet, Flint 85.00
    BRYCE, see Ribbon Candy
    BUCKET, see Oaken Bucket
Buckle & Star, Compote, Cover, 7 1/2 In. 36.00
Buckle & Star, Compote, Open, 6 1/4 In. 17.00
Buckle & Star, Sugar 20.00
Buckle & Star, Wine 15.00
Buckle, Butter, Cover, Acorn Finial, Flint 45.00

Cabbage Rose

Cable

Cable with Ring

Cathedral

Celtic

Classic

Clear & Diamond Panels

Columbian Coin

Curtain

Buckle, Butter, Cover, Flint 125.00
Buckle, Goblet 15.00
Buckle, Goblet, Flint .... 41.00 To 50.00
Buckle, Spooner 20.00
Buckle, Sugar, Cover, Flint 35.00
Budded Ivy, Butter 26.00
Budded Ivy, Goblet 26.50
Budded Ivy, Spooner 19.00
Bull's-Eye & Daisy, Butter, Gold Trim 150.00
Bull's-Eye & Daisy, Creamer 75.00
Bull's-Eye & Daisy, Punch Cup 5.00
Bull's-Eye & Daisy, Water Set, Ruby Trim, 5 Piece 150.00
Bull's-Eye & Fan, Bowl, 5 In. 13.00
Bull's-Eye & Fan, Creamer, 5 1/2 In. 22.00
Bull's-Eye & Fan, Table Set, Gold Trim, 4 Piece 125.00
Bull's-Eye & Fan, Toothpick, Green 41.50
Bull's-Eye & Fan, Water Set, Cranberry Eyes, 7 Piece 160.00
Bull's-Eye & Fleur-De-Lis, Compote, 8 In. 25.00
Bull's-Eye & Fleur-De-Lis, Goblet 16.00
Bull's-Eye & Fleur-De-Lis, Goblet, Flint 80.00
Bull's-Eye & Rosette, Tumbler, Flint 27.00
Bull's-Eye Band, Goblet, Tulip Etch 110.00
Bull's-Eye Band, Tumbler 35.00
Bull's-Eye With Diamond Points, Cruet, Stopper, Square, Pair 80.00
Bull's-Eye With Diamond Points, Goblet 100.00
Bull's-Eye, Butter, Cover, Blue, Gold Trim .... 120.00 To 150.00
Bull's-Eye, Celery Vase, Flint, 9 1/4 In. 55.00
Bull's-Eye, Goblet, Flint 75.00
Bull's-Eye, Syrup, 6 3/4 In. .... 50.00 To 65.00
Bull's-Eye, Tumbler, Flint 75.00
Bullet, Table Set, 4 Piece 300.00
Bunker Hill, Bread Plate 45.00
       BUTTERFLY & FAN, see Grace
Butterfly Handles, Butter, Cover, Frosted Band 65.00
Butterfly Handles, Creamer 35.00
Butterfly Handles, Spooner .... 22.00 To 35.00
Butterfly, Nappy, Green 50.00
Butterfly, Pitcher, Water 125.00
Button Arches, Compote, Jelly, Ruby Stained 35.00
Button Arches, Creamer, Ruby Stained 45.00
Button Arches, Pitcher, Water, Frosted Band 75.00
Button Arches, Pitcher, Water, Tankard 32.00
Button Band, Pitcher, Water, Etched 55.00
Button Panel, Creamer, Gold Trim 50.00
Button Panel, Spooner, Gold Trim 55.00
Button Panel, Sugar, Cover, Gold Trim 80.00
Buttons & Bows, Spooner, Blue 40.00
Buttressed Sunburst, Goblet, 6 In. 10.00
Buzz & Saw, Creamer, Child's 20.00
Buzz Star, Butter, Cover 20.00
Buzz Star, Butter, Cover, Child's 14.00
Buzz Star, Sugar & Creamer, Child's, Cover 50.00
Cabbage Rose, Bowl, 7 1/2 In. 8.00
Cabbage Rose, Cake Stand, 11 In. .... 55.00 To 58.00
Cabbage Rose, Compote, Open, 7 In. 38.00
Cable With Ring, Creamer, Applied Handle, Flint 175.00
Cable With Ring, Sugar, Cover, Flint 65.00
Cable With Ring, Sugar, Open 40.00
Cable, Butter, Cover 90.00
Cable, Eggcup .... 25.00 To 48.00
Cable, Goblet 70.00
Cable, Spooner 35.00
Cable, Sugar, Cover 95.00
Cable, Syrup, C.1870 .... 135.00

Cadmus, Goblet 12.00
CALIFORNIA, see Beaded Grape
Canadian, Compote, Cover, 7 1/2 In. 125.00
Canadian, Compote, Cover, 8 In. 125.00
Canadian, Creamer 50.00
Canadian, Goblet 48.00
Canadian, Lamp, Heart, Green 175.00
Canadian, Pitcher, Water .... 75.00 To 95.00
Canadian, Wine .... 32.00 To 40.00

> The pressed glass pattern sometimes called Candlewick is listed in
> this section as Banded Raindrop. There is also a pattern called
> "Candlewick" which has been made by Imperial Glass Corporation
> since 1936. It is listed in this book under Imperial, Candlewick.

CANDY RIBBON, see Ribbon Candy
Cane & Rosette, Compote, Silver Plate Holder, 11 3/4 In. 75.00
Cane, Berry Set, Green, 6 Piece 75.00
Cane, Goblet, Vaseline 35.00
Cane, Pitcher, Water 42.50
Cane, Pitcher, Water, Blue 60.00
Cane, Spooner, Amber 42.00
Cane, Tray, Pin, Brush Shape 8.00
Cane, Tumbler, Amber 35.00
Cape Cod, Cake Stand, 10 1/2 In. 35.00
Cape Cod, Goblet, 10 Oz. 7.50
Cape Cod, Plate, Handle, 10 In. 45.00
Cape Cod, Wine 60.00
Capitol Building, Champagne 25.00
Captain Kidd, Mug, Child's 35.00
CARDINAL, see Cardinal Bird
Cardinal Bird, Creamer 35.00
Cardinal Bird, Goblet .... 35.00 To 45.00
Cardinal Bird, Sauce, 4 In. 10.00
CARMEN, see Paneled Diamond & Finecut
Carnation, Tumbler, Ruby Stained, Gold Trim 35.00
Carpenter's Hall, Bread Plate, 12 In. 70.00
Cathedral, Berry Bowl, Amber, 8 1/4 In. 48.00
Cathedral, Compote, Blue, 9 1/2 In. 65.00
Cathedral, Relish, Blue, Fish Shape 30.00
Cathedral, Sugar, Cover 35.00
Cathedral, Tumbler 20.00
Celtic Cross, Compote, Cover, 6 In. 85.00
Celtic Cross, Compote, Cover, Square, 11 1/2 In. 80.00
Celtic Cross, Spooner, Etched 40.00
Celtic, Cake Stand 22.00
CENTENNIAL, see also Liberty Bell; Washington Centennial
Centennial, Butter, Cover 75.00
Centennial, Goblet 20.00
Centennial, Table Set 395.00
CHAIN WITH DIAMONDS, see Washington Centennial
Chain With Star, Bread Plate, 11 In. 25.00
Champion, Celery Vase, Amber Stained 50.00
Chandelier, Butter, Cover 50.00
Chandelier, Cake Stand, 10 In. 65.00
Chandelier, Creamer 25.00
Chandelier, Goblet 65.00
Chandelier, Goblet, Etched 62.50
Chandelier, Spooner 35.00
Chandelier, Sugar Shaker 70.00
Chandelier, Tumbler .... 30.00 To 35.00
Charlie Chaplin, Toothpick 60.00
Checkered Diamonds, Goblet 15.00
Cherry & Cable, Butter, Cover 90.00

Cherry With Thumbprint, Sugar, Cover 60.00
Cherry, Spooner 18.00
CHURCH WINDOWS, see Tulip Petals
Circle & Swag, Bowl, 8 1/2 In. 20.00
Circle & Swag, Celery, 2 Handles 25.00
Classic Medallion, Creamer 25.00
Classic, Bowl, Warrior, 8 In. 145.00
Classic, Butter, Cover, Log Feet 225.00
Classic, Celery, Log Feet .... 100.00 To 200.00
Classic, Compote, Cover, Log Feet, 7 1/2 In. .... 200.00 To 250.00
Classic, Creamer, Log Feet 165.00
Classic, Creamer, Log Feet, Clear & Frosted 135.00
Classic, Dessert Set, Log Feet, 7 Piece 350.00
Classic, Pitcher, Water, Log Feet 300.00
Classic, Plate, John Alexander Logan, 11 3/8 In. 200.00
Classic, Plate, President Cleveland 160.00
Classic, Plate, Warrior .... 160.00 To 165.00
Classic, Spooner, Log Feet 120.00
Classic, Sugar, Cover 250.00
Classic, Table Set, Log Feet, 4 Piece 550.00
Clear & Diamond Panels, Spooner, Child's, Blue 40.00
Clear & Diamond Panels, Sugar, Child's, Cover, Blue 55.00
Cobb, Butter, Cover 37.00
Cobb, Cheese Dish, Cover 50.00
Cobb, Spooner 45.00
COIN SPOT, see Coin Spot Category
Colonial, Creamer, Flint 135.00
Colonial, Cruet 30.00
Colonial, Plate, Canary Yellow, 6 In. 250.00
Colorado, Butter, Cover, Green, Gold Trim 95.00
Colorado, Creamer, Coney Island, Green, 2 1/2 In. 18.00
Colorado, Creamer, Green, Child's 18.00
Colorado, Creamer, Green, Gold Trim .... 60.00 To 70.00
Colorado, Creamer, Green, Gold Trim, 3 1/2 In. 35.00
Colorado, Mug, Green, Gold Trim, 2 3/4 In. 15.00
Colorado, Nappy, Tricornered 32.00
Colorado, Saltshaker, Souvenir, Ruby Stained 75.00
Colorado, Sherbet, Green, Gold Trim .... 25.00 To 35.00
Colorado, Spooner, Blue, Gold Trim 75.00
Colorado, Spooner, Green, Gold Trim 55.00
Colorado, Table Set, Ruby Stained, 3 Piece 410.00
Colorado, Toothpick, Blue, Gold Trim 37.00
Colorado, Violet Bowl, Blue .... 35.00 To 50.00
Columbia, Table Set, Gold Trim, 5 Piece 150.00
Columbia, Table Set, Ruby & Gold Trim, 4 Piece 175.00
Columbian Coin, Compote, Frosted Coins 135.00
Columbian Coin, Goblet, Gold Trim 65.00
Columbian Coin, Mug, Gold Trim, 1 Pt. 100.00
Columbian Coin, Spooner, Gold Trim 42.00
Columbian Coin, Sugar & Creamer, Cover, Gilded 60.00
Columbian Coin, Toothpick 36.00
Comet, Goblet, Flint 95.00
COMPACT, see Snail
Constitution, Bread Plate 58.00
Constitution, Bread Plate, Liberty & Freedom 75.00
Cord & Tassle, Cake Stand, 9 In. 36.00
Cord & Tassle, Goblet 35.00
Cord Drapery, Butter, Cover 40.00
Cord Drapery, Cake Plate, Amber 155.00
Cord Drapery, Dish, Pickle, 7 3/8 In. 28.00
Cordova, Pitcher 30.00
Cordova, Syrup 85.00
Cornell, Butter, Cover, Green, Gold Trim 85.00
Cornucopia, Wine .... 12.00 To 15.00

COSMOS, see Cosmos Category

Cottage, Bowl, 9 1/4 X 6 3/4 In.	12.00
Cottage, Cake Stand, 9 In.	28.00
Cottage, Compote, 6 5/8 In.	10.00
Cottage, Creamer, Child's	28.00
Cottage, Cruet, Applied Leaves, Pink	68.00
Cottage, Goblet	18.00
Cottage, Plate, 10 In.	35.00
Croesus, Berry Bowl, Purple, Gold Trim, Master	155.00
Croesus, Berry Set, Amethyst, 5 Piece	295.00
Croesus, Bowl, Amethyst, Gold Trim, 6 1/4 In.	110.00
Croesus, Bowl, Footed, Amethyst, Gold Trim, 4 In.	28.00
Croesus, Butter, Cover, Green	165.00
Croesus, Butter, Cover, Green, Gold Trim	145.00 To 165.00
Croesus, Butter, Cover, Purple, Gold Trim	175.00 To 185.00
Croesus, Butter, Purple	275.00
Croesus, Celery Vase, Purple, Gold Trim	155.00
Croesus, Compote, Jelly, Green	195.00
Croesus, Cruet, Green, Gold Trim	175.00 To 225.00
Croesus, Fruit Bowl, Green, 7 In.	68.00
Croesus, Pitcher, Water, Green, Gold Trim	225.00
Croesus, Relish, Green	35.00
Croesus, Salt & Pepper, Green, Gold Trim	135.00
Croesus, Saltshaker, Amethyst, Gold Trim	110.00
Croesus, Saltshaker, Green, Gold Trim	30.00 To 65.00
Croesus, Sauce, Amethyst, Footed	54.00
Croesus, Sauce, Green, Gold Trim	25.00
Croesus, Spooner, Green, Gold Trim	75.00 To 85.00
Croesus, Sugar & Creamer, Purple, Gold Trim, Breakfast Size	195.00
Croesus, Sugar Shaker, Green, Gold Trim	135.00
Croesus, Sugar, Cover, Purple, Gold Trim	160.00 To 175.00
Croesus, Table Set, Green	395.00
Croesus, Table Set, Green, Gold Trim, 4 Piece	475.00 To 600.00
Croesus, Table Set, Purple, Gold Trim, 4 Piece	600.00 To 625.00
Croesus, Toothpick, Amethyst	90.00
Croesus, Tumbler, Green	30.00
Croesus, Tumbler, Purple	80.00
Croesus, Water Set, Green, Gold Trim, 7 Piece	520.00
Croesus, Water Set, Purple, Gold Trim, 5 Piece	475.00
Crossed Ovals, Spooner	19.00
Crossed Pressed Leaf, Goblet	28.00
Crowfoot, Butter, Cover	25.00

Dahlia

Deer & Dog

Be careful about putting antique
china or glass in the dishwasher.
Glass will sometimes crack from
the heat. Porcelains with gold
overglaze decoration often lose
the gold. Damaged or crazed
glass will sometimes pop off the
plates in large pieces.

Diagonal Band   Diamond Cut with Leaf   Diamond Point

Crowfoot, Cake Stand, 6 3/4 X 10 In. 35.00
Crowfoot, Cake Stand, 9 In. 48.00
Crowfoot, Goblet 20.00
Crowfoot, Sugar & Creamer 25.00
    CROWN JEWELS, see Chandelier; Queen's Necklace
Crystal Wedding, Cake Stand, 9 In. .... 55.00 To 75.00
Crystal Wedding, Champagne, Frosted 75.00
Crystal Wedding, Compote, Cover, 5 In. 65.00
Crystal Wedding, Compote, Cover, 7 In. .... 65.00 To 95.00
Crystal Wedding, Compote, Cover, C.1880, 7 X 9 In. 30.00
Crystal Wedding, Pitcher 70.00
Crystal Wedding, Sugar, Cover 55.00
    CUBE WITH FAN, see Pineapple & Fan
Cube, Butter, Cover 45.00
    CUPID & PSYCHE, see Psyche & Cupid
Cupid & Venus, Bread Plate .... 25.00 To 57.00
Cupid & Venus, Castor, Pickle 95.00
Cupid & Venus, Celery, 8 1/2 In. 48.00
Cupid & Venus, Cordial 85.00
Cupid & Venus, Goblet 79.00
Cupid & Venus, Jam Jar, Cover 45.00
Cupid & Venus, Pitcher, Milk .... 48.00 To 68.00
Cupid & Venus, Wine 85.00
Cupid's Hunt, Compote 45.00
Currant, Cake Stand, 11 In. 58.00
Currant, Celery 38.00
Currant, Creamer .... 35.00 To 45.00
Currier & Ives, Decanter Set, 6 Wines, 7 Piece 100.00
Currier & Ives, Goblet, Amber 55.00
Currier & Ives, Pitcher, Milk 40.00
Currier & Ives, Pitcher, Water 60.00
Currier & Ives, Sugar Shaker, Paneled Sides, Pierced Brass 85.00
Currier & Ives, Syrup, Blue 165.00
Currier & Ives, Wine .... 12.00 To 14.00
Curtain Tieback, Goblet .... 15.00 To 30.00
Curtain, Celery Vase .... 20.00 To 28.00
Curtain, Goblet 20.00
Cut Log, Cake Stand, 9 In. 63.00
Cut Log, Compote, Cover, 5 1/4 In. 85.00
Cut Log, Cruet .... 35.00 To 40.00
Cut Log, Dish, Handle, 5 In. 20.00
Cut Log, Mug, Large 18.50
Cut Log, Pitcher, Water 90.00
Cut Log, Vase, 16 In. 85.00
Cut Log, Wine 28.50
Dahlia With Petal, Bride's Basket, Green, 5 1/2 In. 85.00
Dahlia With Petal, Toothpick 55.00
Dahlia, Bread Plate 35.00

Dahlia, Cake Stand, 10 In.	35.00
Dahlia, Champagne, Amber	95.00
Dahlia, Goblet	35.00
Dahlia, Mug	35.00
Dahlia, Pitcher, 9 In.	19.00
Dahlia, Pitcher, Water, 8 1/2 In.	30.00
Dahlia, Pitcher, Water, Blue	145.00
Dahlia, Sauce, Blue, 4 In.	15.00
Dahlia, Spooner, Apple Green	60.00
Dahlia, Sugar	20.00
Dahlia, Sugar, Cover, Apple Green	120.00
Dahlia, Wine	30.00
DAISIES IN OVAL PANELS, see Bull's–Eye & Fan	
Daisy & Button With Crossbar, Bread Plate	49.00
Daisy & Button With Crossbar, Celery Vase, Amber	23.50
Daisy & Button With Crossbar, Cruet, Canary	125.00
Daisy & Button With Crossbar, Cruet, Stopper, Amber	75.00
Daisy & Button With Crossbar, Goblet	35.00
Daisy & Button With Crossbar, Pitcher, Water	75.00
Daisy & Button With Crossbar, Relish, Amber, 7 X 4 3/4 In.	15.00
DAISY & BUTTON WITH OVAL PANELS, see Hartley	
Daisy & Button With Rimmed Oval Panels, Relish, 6 3/4 In.	12.00
Daisy & Button With V–Ornament, Mug, Blue, 3 1/8 In.	23.00
Daisy & Button, Bowl, 10 In.	25.00
Daisy & Button, Butter, Cover, Etched	45.00
Daisy & Button, Butter, Cover, Triangular, Amber	60.00
Daisy & Button, Canoe, 8 In.	15.00
Daisy & Button, Dish, Yellow, Boat Shape, 10 In.	18.00
Daisy & Button, Match Holder, Hat Shape, Crimped Rim	30.00
Daisy & Button, Powder Jar, Cover, Amber .... 22.00 To 28.00
Daisy & Button, Relish, Square	5.00
Daisy & Button, Toothpick, Blue, Square	22.00
Daisy & Button, Tray, Water, Amber, 8 1/8 X 11 In.	31.00
Dakota, Bottle, Etched, 5 1/2 In.	45.00
Dakota, Cake Stand, Etched Fern & Berry	65.00
Dakota, Celery Vase, Etched	45.00
Dakota, Compote, Open, Etched Fern & Berry, 7 1/8 In.	60.00
Dakota, Creamer	45.00
Dakota, Creamer, Etched	65.00
Dakota, Goblet, Chautauqua, 1888	35.00
Dakota, Goblet, Etched Fern & Berry	35.00
Dakota, Pitcher, Water	65.00
Dakota, Salt & Pepper, Etched Leaf & Flower	95.00
Dakota, Saltshaker	35.00
Dakota, Sauce, Footed, Etched, 4 In.	24.50
Dakota, Spooner, Etched	35.00
Dakota, Table Set, Etched, 4 Piece	250.00
Dakota, Tankard, 12 In.	110.00
Dakota, Tumbler	18.00
Dakota, Waste Bowl, Etched Leaf & Flower	75.00
Dakota, Wine, Etched	39.00
Dart, Compote, Jelly	15.00
Darwin, Toothpick	35.00
Darwin, Toothpick, Amber	50.00
Deep Star, Goblet	20.00
Deer & Dog, Goblet	75.00
Deer & Dog, Jam Jar	100.00
Deer & Oak Tree, Pitcher, Water	100.00
Deer & Pine Tree, Bread Plate, Blue, 8 X 13 In.	80.00
Deer & Pine Tree, Compote, Cover	175.00
Deer & Pine Tree, Goblet	48.00
Deer & Pine Tree, Jam Jar, Cover	110.00
Deer & Pine Tree, Spooner	35.00
Delaware, Bowl, Green, Gold Trim, Octagonal, 9 In.	45.00

Delaware, Butter, Cover, Rose, Gold Trim 125.00
Delaware, Creamer, Green, Gold Trim 50.00
Delaware, Dessert Set, Rose Stained, 8 In., 6 Piece 260.00
Delaware, Sauce, Boat Shape, Cranberry, 2 X 6 In. 35.00
Delaware, Spooner, Green, Gold Trim 50.00
Delaware, Toothpick, Cranberry, Gold Trim 135.00
Delaware, Tumbler, Water, Cranberry, Gold Trim, 4 In. 40.00
Delaware, Vase, Amethyst Stained Flowers, 9 In. 58.00
Delaware, Vase, Rose & Gold Trim, 9 1/2 In. 100.00
Dewdrop & Raindrop, Cordial 10.00
Dewdrop & Raindrop, Pitcher, Water 50.00
Dewdrop & Raindrop, Wine 12.00
Dewdrop & Zig-Zag, Goblet, 4 Piece 7.50
Dewdrop Band, Goblet 11.00
Dewdrop In Point, Bread Plate 14.00
Dewdrop In Points, Cake Stand 28.00
Dewdrop With Sheaf of Wheat, Bread Plate 45.00
Dewdrop With Star, Butter 20.00
Dewdrop With Star, Pitcher, Water 125.00
Dewdrop, Creamer, Child's 30.00
Dewdrop, Goblet 20.00
Dewdrop, Goblet, Vaseline 30.00
    DEWEY, see also Spanish American
Dewey, Berry Bowl, Amber, Master 60.00
Dewey, Bowl, Footed, Amber, 8 In. 35.00
Dewey, Bust, Frosted, Marked Manila 1898, 5 1/8 In. 60.00
Dewey, Butter, Cover, Amber 35.00
Dewey, Butter, Cover, Green 95.00
Dewey, Pitcher, 9 In. 100.00
Dewey, Water Set, 7 Piece 225.00
Diagonal Band With Fan, Celery 23.00
Diagonal Band With Fan, Sauce, 6 Piece .... 75.00 To 80.00
Diagonal Band With Fan, Wine .... 15.00 To 22.50
Diagonal Band, Bread Plate, Amber 32.00
Diagonal Band, Goblet 28.00
Diagonal Band, Spooner .... 16.00 To 30.00
Diagonal Ribbon, Carafe & Tumbler 65.00
    DIAMOND CUT WITH FAN, see Holbrook
Diamond Cut With Leaf, Butter 20.00
Diamond Cut With Leaf, Goblet 21.00
    DIAMOND HORSESHOE, see Aurora
    DIAMOND MEDALLION, see Grand
Diamond Point Loop, Pitcher, Water, Amber 65.00
Diamond Point Loop, Plate, Amber, Square, 8 In. 24.00
Diamond Point Loop, Sugar, Cover, Amber 45.00
Diamond Point, Claret, Flint 125.00
Diamond Point, Goblet, Flint 60.00
Diamond Point, Pitcher, Water, Child's, Circles At Base 135.00

Diamond Thumbprint

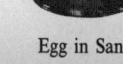

Egg in Sand

Excelsior

Diamond Point, Pitcher, Water, Flint 265.00
Diamond Point, Plate, Flint, 6 In. 25.00
Diamond Point, Salt, Acorn Finial On Cover, Flint, Master 195.00
Diamond Point, Spooner 17.00
Diamond Point, Sugar, Cover, Flint 70.00
Diamond Point, Toothpick 35.00
Diamond Point, Tumbler, 3 5/8 In. 28.00
Diamond Point, Wine, Vaseline 45.00
Diamond Quilted, Champagne 16.00
Diamond Quilted, Compote, Open, Vaseline, 7 1/2 In. 35.00
Diamond Quilted, Goblet, Amber 40.00
Diamond Quilted, Goblet, Blue 35.00
Diamond Quilted, Sauce, Amber, Footed, 5 1/2 In. 10.00
Diamond Quilted, Spooner, Vaseline 30.00
Diamond Quilted, Sugar, Cover, Vaseline 50.00
Diamond Quilted, Tumbler, Vaseline 22.00
Diamond Thumbprint, Champagne, Flint 450.00
Diamond Thumbprint, Compote, 7 1/2 In. 48.00
Diamond Thumbprint, Creamer, Scalloped Foot 385.00
Diamond With Double Fans, Punch Cup 6.00
Diamond, Butter, Cover, Blue 95.00
Diamonds & Clubs, Water Set, Green, Gold Trim, 5 Piece 175.00
Dice & Block, Cruet, Amber 85.00
Dickinson, Compote, 7 1/4 In. 22.50
Dickinson, Goblet, Flint 43.00
Dog With Hat, Toothpick 55.00
Dolly Madison, Spooner 35.00
Dolphin, Goblet 195.00
     DORIC, see Feather
Doric & Pansy, Child's Set, Pink, 14 Piece 225.00
Dots & Dashes, Goblet 18.00
Double Beetle Band, Mug, Child's, Blue .... 20.00 To 30.00
Double Beetle Band, Wine, Child's, Amber 32.00
Double Circle, Toothpick, Blue 75.00
     DOUBLE DAHLIA WITH LENS, see Dahlia with Petal
     DOUBLE DAISY, see Rosette Band
     DOUBLE LOOP, see Ribbon Candy
Double Spear, Spooner 20.00
     DOUBLE VINE, see Bellflower, Double Vine
     DOUBLE WEDDING RING, see Wedding Ring
Doyle No. 500, Butter, Cover, Child's, Amber 95.00
Doyle No.500, Table Set, Child's, Tray, Complete 350.00
Doyle's Comet, Sugar, Cover 35.00
Drapery, Spooner 27.00
Drum, Creamer, Child's 65.00
Drum, Sugar, Cover, Miniature 95.00
Drum, Table Set, Child's, 4 Piece .... 275.00 To 350.00
Duchess, Creamer, Green, Gold Trim .... 85.00 To 95.00
     E PLURIBUS UNUM, see Emblem
     EARL, see Spirea Band
Early Moon & Star, Sugar 24.00
Edgerton, Creamer .... 22.00 To 30.00
Egg In Sand, Sugar 8.00
Egyptian, Bread Plate, Cleopatra 48.00
Egyptian, Compote, Cover, Sphinx, 7 In. 225.00
Egyptian, Compote, Open, Sphinx, 8 In. 95.00
Egyptian, Creamer .... 40.00 To 48.00
Egyptian, Dish, Pickle, Oblong, 8 1/2 X 4 1/2 In. 20.00
Egyptian, Goblet .... 30.00 To 48.50
Egyptian, Spooner .... 28.00 To 55.00
Eight-O-Eight, Jar, Cover, 6 In. 35.00
Elephant Toes, Pitcher 45.00
     EMBLEM, see also American Shield; Bullet
Emblem, Dish, Pickle 55.00

Fine Cut & Block   Fine Rib with Cut Ovals   Flattened Diamond & Sunburst

Emerald Green Herringbone, Pitcher, Water	55.00
Emerald Green Herringbone, Syrup, Original Spring Lid	225.00
Emerald Green Herringbone, Tumbler, Green	21.00
Empress, Butter, Cover, Green	130.00
Empress, Pitcher, Water, Green	225.00
Empress, Salt & Pepper, Green, Gold Trim	150.00
Empress, Syrup, Hinged Lid, Green, Gold Trim	310.00
Empress, Table Set, Green, Gold Trim	395.00
Empress, Tumbler, Green, Gold Trim	45.00
ENGLISH HOBNAIL CROSS, see Amberette	
English Hobnail, Tray, Condiment, Child's, 4 3/8 X 3 1/4 In.	10.00
Esther, Berry Set, Green, Gold Trim, 6 Piece	225.00
Esther, Compote, Jelly, Green, Gold Trim	65.00
Esther, Cruet, Green, Gold Trim .... 165.00 To 235.00
Esther, Salt & Pepper, Green, Gold Trim .... 125.00 To 135.00
Esther, Spooner, Green, Gold Trim	65.00
Esther, Sugar, Cover, Green, Gold Trim ....75.00 To 115.00
Esther, Syrup, Green, Gold Trim	475.00
Esther, Toothpick, Green, Gold Trim	95.00
Esther, Tumbler, Green, Gold Trim	42.50
Esther, Water Set, Green, Gold Trim, 7 Piece	585.00
ETCHED DAKOTA, see Dakota	
Etta, Wine	10.00
Euclid, Butter, Cover, Child's	30.00
Euclid, Cake Stand, Footed, 12 In.	20.00
Eugenie, Celery, Flint	50.00
Eugenie, Compote, Cover, Oval, 9 X 6 1/2 In.	40.00
Eureka, Compote, 7 1/2 In.	28.50
Excelsior, Wine	25.00
Excelsior, Wine, Flint	42.50
Eyewinker, Butter, Cover .... 50.00 To 75.00
Eyewinker, Compote, Open, 8 1/2 X 9 1/2 In.	75.00
Eyewinker, Saltshaker	25.00
Faceted Flower, Pitcher, Water	35.00
Fan & Flute, Sugar, Red Flashed, Etched	30.00
Fan & Star, Spooner	22.00
FAN WITH DIAMOND, see Shell	
Fan, Bowl, Ice Cream, Cobalt Blue	195.00
Fancy Cut, Pitcher, Child's	31.00
Fancy Loop, Dish, 10 1/2 X 7 1/2 In.	19.00
Feather Duster, Cake Stand	22.00
Feather Duster, Compote, Jelly	6.00
Feather Duster, Tray, 10 3/8 X 7 3/4 In.	18.00
Feather, Bowl, 6 3/8 In.	6.00
Feather, Butter	45.00
Feather, Cake Stand, 8 1/2 In. .... 30.00 To 36.50
Feather, Cake Stand, 9 1/2 In.	40.00
Feather, Cake Stand, 11 In. .... 35.00 To 65.00

Feather, Cake Stand, Green, 9 In. 150.00
Feather, Compote, Jelly 18.00
Feather, Cruet 32.00
Feather, Dish, Pickle 15.00
Feather, Goblet 38.00
Feather, Goblet, Amber 130.00
Feather, Pitcher, Water .... 43.00 To 85.00
Feather, Plate, 10 In. .... 22.00 To 40.00
Feather, Salt & Pepper, Emerald Green 225.00
Feather, Sauce 10.00
Feather, Spooner .... 25.00 To 30.00
Feather, Sugar, Cover .... 28.00 To 55.00
Feather, Syrup, Spring Lid 135.00
Feather, Tumbler 45.00
Feather, Tumbler, Green .... 95.00 To 105.00
Feather, Wine 35.00
Fernland, Creamer, Child's 20.00
Fernland, Spooner, Child's 13.00
    FESTOON & GRAPE, see Grape & Festoon
Festoon, Cake Plate, 10 In. 40.00
Festoon, Plate, 7 1/2 In. 20.00
Festoon, Tray, Water 60.00
Festoon, Water Set, 8 Piece 225.00
Fickle Block, Tumbler 28.00
Fine Cut & Block, Cordial, Blue Blocks 65.00
Fine Cut & Block, Cordial, Yellow Blocks 55.00
Fine Cut & Block, Creamer, Pink 60.00
Fine Cut & Block, Cruet, Faceted Stopper, Blue, 5 1/2 In. 75.00
Fine Cut & Block, Wine 22.00
    FINE CUT & FEATHER, see Feather
Fine Cut & Panel, Goblet, Blue, 5 3/8 In. 48.00
Fine Cut & Panel, Wine, Amber 22.00
Fine Cut, Goblet, Buttermilk, Blue Blocks 35.00
Fine Cut, Pitcher, Water, 6 Panel, Amber Bars 135.00
Fine Rib With Cut Ovals, Wine, Flint 130.00
Fine Rib, Wine, Flint 43.50
Fish Atterbury, Pitcher, 1 Pt. 125.00
Fish Scale, Cake Stand, 8 1/4 In. 32.50
Fish Scale, Cake Stand, 9 In. 22.00
Fish Scale, Celery 26.00
Fish Scale, Compote, 8 1/2 In. 35.00
Fish Scale, Pitcher, Water 55.00

Frosted Circle

Frosted Eagle

Garfield Drape

Grape & Festoon

Grape & Festoon with Shield

Hamilton

Flamingo Habitat, Celery	45.00
Flamingo Habitat, Champagne, 5 1/2 In.	36.00
Flamingo Habitat, Creamer, Footed	40.00
Flamingo Habitat, Goblet	40.00
Flamingo Habitat, Wine	32.50
Flat Diamond & Panel, Claret, Flint	75.00
Flat Diamond & Panel, Plate, 10 3/4 In.	18.00
Flat Panel, Toothpick	35.00
Flatiron, Butter, Cover	36.00
Flattened Diamond & Sunburst, Butter, Child's	19.00
Flattened Diamond & Sunburst, Punch Bowl, Child's	25.00 To 27.00
Flattened Diamond & Sunburst, Punch Cup, Child's	7.00
Flattened Diamond & Sunburst, Sugar, Cover, Child's	18.00
Fleur-De-Lis & Drape, Butter, Cover	40.00
Fleur-De-Lis & Drape, Butter, Green, Footed	12.00
Fleur-De-Lis & Drape, Pitcher, Water	35.00
Fleur-De-Lis & Drape, Plate, Green, 8 1/4 In.	18.00
Fleur-De-Lis, Creamer	25.00
Fleur-De-Lis, Goblet	24.50
Flora, Creamer, Green, Gold Trim	45.00
Flora, Spooner, Green, Gold Trim	40.00
Flora, Sugar, Cover, Green, Gold Trim	60.00
FLORIDA, see Emerald Green Herringbone; Sunken Primrose	
FLORODORA, see Bohemian	
Flower & Pleat, Sugar Shaker	85.00
Flower & Pleat, Syrup, Embossed Flowers & Leaves	98.00
Flower & Pleat, Toothpick, Ruby Stained	110.00
Flower & Quill, Butter, Cover	40.00
Flower Band, Butter, Cover	15.00
Flower Band, Creamer, Clear & Frosted	70.00 To 75.00
Flower Band, Spooner	40.00
Flower Band, Sugar, Cover, Clear & Frosted	95.00
Flower Band, Sugar, Cover, Love Birds, Frosted	175.00
FLOWER FLANGE, see Dewey	
Flower Medallion, Bowl, 9 In.	30.00
FLOWER PANELED CANE, see Cane & Rosette	
Flower Pot, Bread Plate, In God We Trust	65.00
Flower Pot, Creamer	30.00
Flower Pot, Creamer, Vaseline	90.00
Flower Pot, Spooner, Amber	34.00
Flute & Cane, Pitcher, Milk	20.00
Flute, Goblet, Flint, 6 In., 6 Piece	90.00

Fluted Scrolls, Butter, Cover, Blue, 6 1/2 X 7 In. 145.00
Fluted Scrolls, Pitcher, Water, Blue 275.00
Fluted Scrolls, Sugar, Cover 65.00
Flying Birds, Goblet 75.00
      FLYING ROBIN, see Hummingbird
Flying Stork, Compote, Cover 110.00
Flying Stork, Spooner 55.00
Forget–Me–Not, Compote, Cover, 6 In. 40.00
Forget–Me–Not, Dish, Honey 5.00
Forget–Me–Not, Pitcher, Water 65.00
Forget–Me–Not, Relish, Boat Shape, 4 5/8 X 7 7/8 In. 13.00
Forget–Me–Not, Sugar Shaker, Green ....95.00 To 105.00
Four Petal, Sugar, Cover, Flint 135.00
Frost Crystal, Punch Set, Base, 12 Cups 90.00
      FROSTED PATTERNS, see also under name of main pattern
Frosted Circle, Butter 60.00
Frosted Circle, Cake Stand 55.00
Frosted Circle, Compote, Open, 5 1/4 In. 15.00
Frosted Circle, Spooner 21.00
Frosted Circle, Syrup, Spring Lid 95.00
      FROSTED CRANE, see Frosted Stork
Frosted Eagle, Celery, Rose Etched 75.00
Frosted Eagle, Creamer 50.00
Frosted Eagle, Sugar 38.00
      FROSTED FLOWER BAND, see Flower Band, Frosted
Frosted Fruits, Tumbler 65.00
Frosted Leaf, Eggcup, Flint 85.00
      FROSTED LION, see Lion, Frosted
      FROSTED RIBBON, see Ribbon, Frosted
      FROSTED ROMAN KEY, see Roman Key, Frosted
Frosted Stork, Bread Plate, Deer Medallion Border 80.00
Frosted Stork, Bread Plate, Handles, Oval, 11 5/8 X 8 In. 68.00
Frosted Stork, Sauce 25.00
      FROSTED WAFFLE, see Hidalgo
Fuchsia, Spooner 14.00
Fuchsia, Sugar, Open 12.00
Fulton, Tumbler 35.00
G.A.R., Bread Plate 145.00
Galloway, Butter, Cover 48.00
Galloway, Cake Stand 65.00
Galloway, Pitcher, Child's 17.00
Galloway, Relish 15.00
Galloway, Spooner, Maiden Blush 80.00
Galloway, Toothpick, Gold Trim 18.00
Galloway, Tumbler 15.00
Galloway, Wine, Gold Trim ....30.00 To 36.00
      GARDEN OF EDEN, see also Lotus & Serpent
Garden of Eden, Relish, Handle, 6 1/2 In. 6.00

Hildalgo

Holly

Horn of Plenty

Jeweled Heart   Jumbo   Leaf & Dart

Garden of Eden, With Serpent, Mug 34.00
Garfield Drape, Cake Stand 65.00
Garfield Drape, Compote, Cover, 8 In. 125.00
Garfield Drape, Creamer .... 37.50 To 38.50
Garfield Drape, Pitcher, Milk 95.00
Garfield Drape, Plate, We Mourn Our Nation's Loss 65.00
Garfield, Plate, 101 Border, 9 In. 20.00
Garfield, Tumbler 35.00
Gathered Knot, Toothpick, Sapphire Blue, C.1900 .... 125.00
Geneva, Compote, Jelly, Gold Trim 55.00
Geneva, Spooner, Gold Trim 55.00
George Peabody, Cup & Saucer 145.00
George Washington, Plate, 6 In. 75.00
Georgia, Sugar, Cover 37.00
Giant Bull's–Eye, Butter, Cover 30.00
Giant Bull's–Eye, Decanter, Wine 45.00
Giant Bull's–Eye, Relish, Oblong 15.00
Giant Sawtooth, Goblet 90.00
Giant Sawtooth, Goblet, Flint 100.00
Gibson Girl, Butter, Cover 55.00
Gibson Girl, Saltshaker, Frosted 110.00
Gibson Girl, Tumbler, Frosted .... 110.00 To 165.00
Girl With Goose, Compote 150.00
Gladstone, Bread Plate, For The Million, 5 In. 40.00
Goat's Head, Spooner, Frosted 47.50
     GOOD LUCK, see Horseshoe
Gooseberry, Spooner 25.00
Gothic Arch, Celery Vase, Flint 70.00
Gothic, Creamer, Footed, 5 3/4 In. 85.00
Gothic, Eggcup 40.00
Gothic, Sauce, Flat, 4 In. 10.00
Gothic, Sugar, Cover, Flint 70.00
Gothic, Wine, Flint 140.00
Grace, Creamer 38.00
Grace, Sauce, Flat 1.00
     GRAND ARMY OF THE REPUBLIC, see G.A.R.
Grand, Bread Plate 21.50
Grand, Butter 9.00
Grand, Cake Stand, 9 1/2 In. 35.00
Grand, Creamer 1.00
Grand, Goblet .... 20.00 To 21.50
Grant, U.S., Patriot & Soldier, Plate, Frosted Bust 75.00

GRAPE & CABLE, see Northwood's Grape

Grape & Festoon With Shield, Compote, Bird's Nest Finial	85.00
Grape & Festoon, Creamer	50.00
Grape & Festoon, Goblet	15.00
Grape & Festoon, Saucer, Set of 4	45.00
Grape Band, Pitcher, Water, Bulbous, Opaque, 8 In.	400.00
Grape Band, Sugar, Open	20.00
Grape Bunch, Eggcup	7.00
Grape With Thumbprint Band, Goblet	18.00
Grape With Thumbprint, Pitcher, Water, Cover	25.00

GRAPE, see Beaded Grape; Beaded Grape Medallion; Magnet & Grape; Paneled Grape; Paneled Grape Band

Grapevine With Ovals, Creamer, Child's	46.00
Grasshopper With Insect, Celery, Etched	47.00
Grasshopper With Insect, Goblet	35.00
Grasshopper With Insect, Sugar & Creamer	60.00
Gridley, Pitcher	125.00
Grooved Bigler, Waste Bowl, Flint, Purple, 4 1/2 In.	325.00
Guinevere, Pitcher, Water	24.00
Halley's Comet, Wine	27.00 To 30.00
Hamilton With Frosted Leaf, Compote, Scalloped Rim, 8 In.	135.00
Hamilton, Butter, Cover	65.00
Hamilton, Compote, Flint, 6 X 6 In.	75.00
Hamilton, Eggcup, Flint	45.00
Hand & Bar, Butter, Cover	80.00
Hand & Bar, Jam Jar	50.00
Hand, Celery Vase	38.00 To 41.50
Hand, Jam Jar	48.00
Hand, Wine	75.00
Hanover, Goblet	20.00
Hartford, Pepper Shaker	27.50
Hartley, Celery	21.00
Hartley, Pitcher, Milk	15.00 To 48.00
Harvard Yard, Butter, Cover	40.00
Hawaiian Lei, Bowl, 6 1/8 In.	14.00
Hawaiian Lei, Cake Stand, 9 1/2 In.	26.00
Hawaiian Lei, Sauce, Footed, 3 1/4 In.	7.00
Hawaiian Lei, Spooner, Child's	20.00
Heart Band, Creamer, Ruby Stained	24.00
Heart Plume, Nappy, Triangular, 5 3/4 In.	15.00
Heart Stem, Sugar & Creamer, Leaf Etched, 6 1/4 In.	55.00
Heart With Thumbprint, Bowl, 4 1/2 In.	30.00
Heart With Thumbprint, Bowl, 9 1/2 In.	41.50
Heart With Thumbprint, Bowl, Orange	125.00
Heart With Thumbprint, Card Tray	20.00
Heart With Thumbprint, Creamer, Individual	20.00
Heart With Thumbprint, Cruet, Stopper, Pair	115.00
Heart With Thumbprint, Goblet, Gold Trim	56.50
Heart With Thumbprint, Plate, 6 In.	22.00
Heart With Thumbprint, Punch Cup	15.00
Heart With Thumbprint, Relish, Heart Shape, Handle	24.00
Heart With Thumbprint, Saltshaker	48.00
Heart With Thumbprint, Sugar, Cover, Green, Gold Trim	25.00
Heart With Thumbprint, Sugar, Individual	19.00
Heart With Thumbprint, Tumbler	54.00
Heart With Thumbprint, Vase, 10 In.	48.00

HEARTS OF LOCH LAVEN, see Shuttle

Heavy Gothic, Bowl, 7 1/2 In.	18.00
Heavy Gothic, Bowl, Footed, 5 1/8 In.	12.00
Heavy Gothic, Wine	21.00
Henry Clay, Cup Plate, Bust of Clay In Center, 3 1/2 In.	15.00
Hercules Pillar, Goblet	45.00
Herringbone Buttress, Bowl, Green, 7 1/2 In.	125.00
Herringbone, Berry Bowl, Square, Green, Master	25.00

Herringbone, Berry Set, Scalloped, Square, Green, 7 Piece 75.00
Herringbone, Compote, Jelly, Green 45.00
Herringbone, Creamer, Green 40.00
Herringbone, Cruet, Green .... 110.00 To 125.00
Herringbone, Pitcher, Green 75.00
Herringbone, Tumbler, Green 21.00
Hexagon Block, Water Set, Ruby Stained, 7 Piece 165.00
Hickman, Bowl, 6 1/4 In. 8.00
Hickman, Cake Stand, 9 In. 32.00
Hickman, Compote, Jelly, 4 1/2 In. 30.00
Hickman, Condiment Set, Child's 50.00
Hickman, Creamer 25.00
Hickman, Goblet 35.00
Hickman, Ice Bucket 52.00
Hickman, Pitcher, Water 35.00
Hickman, Punch Cup, Footed 23.00
Hickman, Relish, Green 15.00
Hickman, Rose Bowl 28.00
Hickman, Sugar, Cover .... 33.50 To 35.00
Hickman, Toothpick 45.00
Hidalgo, Butter, Cover 25.00
Hidalgo, Creamer, Flowers 38.00
Hidalgo, Goblet, Frosted 18.00
Hidalgo, Tray, Water, Frosted 55.00
Hobbs' Hobnail, Lemonade Set, Amber Frosted, 4 Piece 425.00
Hobbs' Hobnail, Toothpick, Amber 20.00
Hobbs' Hobnail, Toothpick, Vaseline 22.00
    HOBNAIL, see Hobnail category
Hobnail With Thumbprint Base, Creamer, Child's, Amber 40.00
Hobnail With Thumbprint Base, Pitcher, 8 In. 30.00
Hobnail With Thumbprint Base, Sugar, Child's, Blue 55.00
Hobstar, Punch Cup 4.00
Holbrook, Punch Cup 5.00
Holly, Toothpick 110.00
Honeycomb With Diamonds, Eggcup 10.00
Honeycomb With Pillar, Goblet 17.50
Honeycomb, Butter, Cover, Cranberry 150.00
Honeycomb, Champagne, Flint 40.00
Honeycomb, Compote, Open, Flint, 7 1/4 X 10 In. 95.00
Honeycomb, Decanter, Stopper, Flint 45.00
Honeycomb, Goblet, Etched 42.00
Honeycomb, Spooner, 5 1/2 In. 15.00
Honeycomb, Toothpick, Flower Rim, Blue 33.50
Honeycomb, Tray, Water, Blue, 11 1/2 In. 40.00
Honeycomb, Tumbler, Bar, Flint 75.00
Honeycomb, Vase, Flint, 8 1/2 In. 40.00
Hooks & Eyes, Goblet 35.00
Hops Band, Bowl, Oval, 8 X 5 1/4 In. 8.00
Hops Band, Creamer 21.50
Hops Band, Goblet 19.00
Horizontal Threads, Butter, Cover, Child's 65.00
Horizontal Threads, Creamer, Child's 45.00
Horizontal Threads, Spooner, Child's 15.00
Horizontal Threads, Sugar, Cover, Child's 55.00
Horn of Plenty, Bowl, Green 25.00
Horn of Plenty, Eggcup, Flint .... 42.00 To 50.00
Horn of Plenty, Goblet, Flint .... 60.00 To 65.00
Horn of Plenty, Plate, Yellow, 6 1/4 In. 325.00
Horn of Plenty, Relish, Oval, Flint 85.00
Horn of Plenty, Salt, Flat, Flint 125.00
Horn of Plenty, Sauce, Flint, 4 7/16 In. 9.00
Horn of Plenty, Spooner, Yellow Stained Rim 145.00
Horn of Plenty, Sugar, Cover .... 75.00 To 110.00
Horn of Plenty, Sugar, Pagoda Cover 185.00

Liberty Bell

Lily-of-the-Valley

Lincoln Drape

Maine

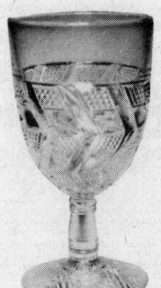

Mitered Diamond

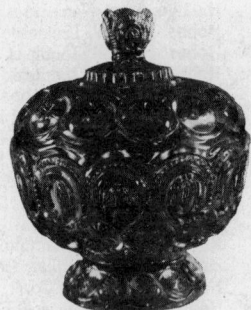

Moon & Star

New England Pineapple

Open Rose

Ostrich Looking at the Moon

Horse Mint, Butter, Cover 37.00
Horseshoe, Bowl, Cover, 8 In. 110.00
Horseshoe, Bread Plate 65.00
Horseshoe, Butter, Cover, Horseshoe Shape 175.00
Horseshoe, Cake Stand, 8 1/2 In. 55.00
Horseshoe, Celery 25.00
Horseshoe, Cheese Dish 86.00
Horseshoe, Compote, Cover, 7 1/2 X 12 In. 35.00
Horseshoe, Creamer .... 28.50 To 38.00
Horseshoe, Goblet .... 35.00 To 85.00
Horseshoe, Pitcher, 9 3/16 In. 64.00
Horseshoe, Pitcher, Milk 95.00
Horseshoe, Relish 22.50
Horseshoe, Sauce, 3 1/2 In. 7.50
Hotel Argus, Champagne, 5 In. 19.00
Huber, Champagne, Flint, 5 3/16 In. 30.00
Huber, Sugar, Cover, Flint 50.00
Huber, Whiskey, Flint, 3 In. 15.00
Huber, Wine, Flint 15.00
   HUCKLE, see Feather Duster
Hummingbird, Bowl, Amber, 6 In. 30.00
Hummingbird, Creamer 50.00
Hummingbird, Goblet 40.00
Hummingbird, Goblet, Amber 55.00
Hummingbird, Goblet, Blue 65.00
Hummingbird, Pitcher, Water, Blue 120.00
Hummingbird, Tumbler, Amber 55.00
Hundred–Leaved Rose, Sauce, Flat, 4 1/4 In. 5.00
Icicle With Star, Pitcher .... 25.00 To 30.00
Icicle, Goblet, Fluted 32.00
   IDA, see Sheraton
Illinois, Celery Tray 37.50
Illinois, Jam Jar, Cover 250.00
Illinois, Pitcher, Square 72.00
Illinois, Pitcher, Water, Metal Top, Green 175.00
Illinois, Pitcher, Water, Silver Plated Top, 9 3/4 In. 95.00
Illinois, Relish 15.00
Illinois, Sauce, Flat 12.00
Illinois, Straw Jar, Lid 65.00
Illinois, Sugar & Creamer 45.00
Illinois, Toothpick 25.00
Imperial Jewels, Bread Plate, Blue, 13 In. 75.00
Independence Hall, Bread Plate, 9 X 13 In. 45.00
   INDIANA SWIRL, see Feather
Intaglio Sunflower, Toothpick 28.00
Interlocked Hearts, Sugar & Creamer 25.00
Inverted Prism, Goblet, Etched 25.00
Inverted Strawberry, Berry Bowl, Child's 17.50

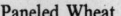

Paneled Wheat   Pleat & Panel   Pennsylvania

Inverted Strawberry, Punch Set, Child's, 6 Piece 135.00
Inverted Thistle, Sugar & Creamer, Ruby Flashed 60.00
Inverted Thistle, Water Set, Gold 185.00
Inverted Thumbprint, Goblet, Blue 30.00
Inverted Thumbprint, Pitcher, Water, Ruffled Top, Blue 55.00
Inverted Thumbprint, Syrup, Amber, Tapered 110.00
Inverted Thumbprint, Toothpick, Piecrust Rim, Amber 145.00
Iowa, Punch Cup ....9.00 To 18.50
Iowa, Salt & Pepper 35.00
Iowa, Toothpick 15.00
Iowa, Wine, Gold Trim ....28.00 To 35.00
Iris With Meander, Tumbler, Blue 30.00
Ivanhoe, Tumbler 27.50
Ivy In Snow, Cake Stand, 8 In. 40.00
Ivy In Snow, Goblet 16.00
Ivy In Snow, Tumbler 22.00
Ivy In Snow, Wine 22.00
Jacob's Coat, Butter, Cover 40.00
Jacob's Ladder, Bowl, 5 3/4 In. 10.00
Jacob's Ladder, Cake Plate, 11 In. 55.00
Jacob's Ladder, Celery Vase ....28.00 To 45.00
Jacob's Ladder, Compote, Cover, 9 1/2 In. 165.00
Jacob's Ladder, Creamer 30.00
Jacob's Ladder, Goblet 16.00
Jacob's Ladder, Honey, 3 3/4 In. 11.00
Jacob's Ladder, Pitcher, Water 155.00
Jacob's Ladder, Plate, 6 1/2 In. 30.00
Jacob's Ladder, Relish, Maltese Cross Handle ....20.00 To 22.00
Jacob's Ladder, Salt, Master ....19.00 To 35.00
Jacob's Ladder, Sauce, Round, 5 3/4 In. 8.00
Jacob's Ladder, Spooner 35.00
Jacob's Ladder, Sugar 22.00
Jacob's Ladder, Sugar & Creamer 55.00
Jacob's Ladder, Sugar, Cover 30.00
Jacob's Ladder, Syrup 85.00
Jacob's Ladder, Wine ....22.00 To 40.00
  JASPER, see Late Buckle
Jefferson Drape, Tumbler, Clear & Opalescent 30.00
Jefferson's Optic, Butter, Cover, Amethyst, Enameled Flowers 95.00
Jefferson's Optic, Creamer, Amethyst 55.00
Jefferson's Optic, Creamer, Amethyst, Enameled Flowers 65.00
Jefferson's Optic, Sugar, Cover, Green 30.00
Jewel & Dewdrop, Bowl, 8 In. 35.00
Jewel & Dewdrop, Bread Plate, Our Daily Bread, 10 1/2 In. 44.00
Jewel & Dewdrop, Bread Plate, Oval, 8 1/2 X 14 In. 36.00
Jewel & Dewdrop, Butter, Cover 75.00
Jewel & Dewdrop, Cake Stand, 8 In. 45.00
Jewel & Dewdrop, Compote, 7 1/4 In. 45.00
Jewel & Dewdrop, Goblet 65.00
Jewel & Dewdrop, Pitcher, Water ....42.00 To 55.00
  JEWEL & FESTOON, see Loop & Jewel
Jewel Band, Butter 9.00
Jewel Band, Creamer 20.00
Jewel Band, Pitcher, Water, Etched 58.00
Jewel, Wine, Amber 12.50
Jeweled Drapery, Goblet 14.00
Jeweled Heart, Cruet, Green 155.00
Jeweled Heart, Sugar Shaker, Beaded Lid, Blue 250.00
Jeweled Heart, Tumbler, Green 30.00
Jeweled Heart, Water Set, Gold Trim, 7 Piece 175.00
  JEWELED MOON & STAR, see Moon & Star Variant; Moon & Star
  JOB'S TEARS, see Art
  JUBILEE, see Hickman
Jumbo, Spoon Rack 700.00

Kalbach, Wine 14.00
Kaleidoscope, Celery, Etched 28.00
    KAMONI, see Pennsylvania
    KANSAS, see Jewel & Dewdrop
Kentucky, Punch Cup, Green 18.00
Kentucky, Salt, Master 10.00
Kentucky, Sauce, Green 16.00
Kentucky, Toothpick, Green 50.00
Kentucky, Tumbler, Green 28.00
Kentucky, Wine, Green .... 28.00 To 30.00
King's 500, Bowl, Rectangular, 5 1/2 X 8 1/2 In. 37.50
King's 500, Butter, Cover, Blue, Gold Trim 135.00
King's 500, Punch Cup, Cobalt Blue, Gold Eyes 18.00
King's 500, Sauce, Flat, Cobalt Blue, Gold Eyes, 4 1/4 In. 18.00
King's 500, Table Set, Cobalt Blue, 4 Piece 450.00
King's 500, Tumbler, Blue, Gold Trim 40.00
King's Block, Wine 13.00
King's Comet, Lamp, Stem, 7 1/2 In. 55.00
    KING'S CROWN, see also Ruby Thumbprint
King's Crown, Cheese Dish, Cover, Vintage Etch 650.00
King's Crown, Compote, Scalloped, Bell Shape 700.00
King's Crown, Cordial 12.00
King's Crown, Decanter, 14K Gold & White Design, 7 1/2 In. 135.00
King's Crown, Goblet, Souvenir, Green 20.00
King's Crown, Honey, Cover, Square 175.00
King's Crown, Lamp, 9 1/4 In. 195.00
King's Crown, Pitcher, Milk, Bulbous 75.00
King's Crown, Pitcher, Water, Etched 125.00
King's Crown, Spooner, Fern Etch 35.00
King's Crown, Table Set, Vintage Etch, 4 Piece 300.00
King's Crown, Water Set, Bulbous Pitcher, Vintage Etch, 7 Pc. 595.00
King's Crown, Wine 12.00
King, Pitcher, 8 1/2 In. 20.00
    KLONDIKE, see Amberette
Knights of Labor, Bread Plate, Oval 80.00
Knobby Bull's–Eye, Tumbler, Gold Trim 10.00
Kokomo, Goblet 28.00
Lacy Daisy, Berry, Small 6.00
Lacy Daisy, Butter, Cover 46.50
Lacy Daisy, Creamer 41.50
    LACY MEDALLION, see also Princess Feather
Lacy Medallion, Creamer, Green, Gold Trim, 3 5/8 In. 15.00
Lacy Medallion, Toothpick, Green 37.00
Lacy Medallion, Wine, Ruby Stained, Advertising 18.00
Ladder With Diamond, Saltshaker 8.00
Ladder With Diamond, Toothpick, Gold Trim 20.00
Ladders & Diamond With Star, Wine 20.00
Ladders, Card Tray, Folded Sides 15.00
Lamb, Sugar, Cover, Child's 75.00
Late Buckle, Wine, 4 1/4 In. 8.50
Late Paneled Grape, Sauce, Flat, 4 1/8 In. 10.00
    LATE THISTLE, see Inverted Thistle
    LATTICE & OVAL PANELS, see Flat Diamond & Panel
Lattice & Oval Panels, Tumbler, Flint 75.00
Lattice, Butter, Cover 18.00
Lattice, Cake Stand, 8 3/8 In. 36.00
Lattice, Goblet 25.00
Lattice, Relish, 5 1/4 X 9 1/4 In. 14.00
Leaf & Dart, Bowl, 6 X 9 In. 15.00
Leaf & Dart, Celery Vase .... 30.00 To 45.00
Leaf & Dart, Eggcup 12.00
Leaf & Dart, Honey, 3 1/2 In. 5.00
Leaf & Dart, Pitcher, Water 75.00
Leaf & Dart, Sugar, Cover .... 42.50 To 44.00

Leaf & Dart, Tumbler, 5 5/8 In. 25.00
Leaf & Flower, Celery Vase, Amber Stained 77.50
Leaf & Flower, Pitcher, Water, Amber Stained 95.00
Leaf & Flower, Syrup, Clear & Amber Stained 100.00
Leaf & Lattice, Bottle, Castor, Child's 5.00
Leaf & Star, Salt & Pepper, Ruby Stained 125.00
Leaf & Star, Spooner 20.00
Leaf Medallion, Saltshaker, Amethyst 92.50
Leaf Medallion, Spooner 75.00
Leaf Medallion, Sugar, Cover, Gold 55.00
Leaf Medallion, Table Set, Cobalt Blue, Gold Trim, 4 Piece 455.00
Leaf Umbrella, Saltshaker, Mauve 65.00
Leaf Umbrella, Sugar Shaker, Glossy Blue, Cased 165.00
Leaf Umbrella, Water Set, Yellow, Cased, 7 Piece 550.00
LEVERNE, see Star in Honeycomb
Liberty Bell, Bowl, Footed, 6 7/8 In. 40.00
Liberty Bell, Bread Plate, Signers .... 45.00 To 75.00
Liberty Bell, Butter, Cover ....80.00 To 140.00
Liberty Bell, Cake Plate 50.00
Liberty Bell, Creamer, Child's .... 100.00 To 120.00
Liberty Bell, Creamer, Reeded Handle ....65.00 To 100.00
Liberty Bell, Goblet .... 35.00 To 60.00
Liberty Bell, Plate, 10 3/4 In. .... 75.00 To 80.00
Liberty Bell, Platter, Oval, 8 1/2 In. 15.00
Liberty Bell, Relish 55.00
Liberty Bell, Salt, Oval, 2 1/4 In. 20.00
Liberty Bell, Sauce 20.00
Liberty Bell, Spooner .... 50.00 To 65.00
Liberty Bell, Spooner, Miniature 325.00
Liberty Bell, Sugar, Cover 95.00
Liberty Bell, Table Set, 4 Piece .... 350.00 To 395.00
Liberty Bell, Table Set, Child's 565.00
Lily-of-The-Valley, Celery 60.00
Lily-of-The-Valley, Compote, Cover 85.00
Lily-of-The-Valley, Compote, Cover, 8 In. 135.00
Lily-of-The-Valley, Creamer, Footed 78.00
Lily-of-The-Valley, Goblet, Buttermilk 30.00
Lily-of-The-Valley, Sugar, Open 45.00
Lincoln Drape With Tassel, Goblet 150.00
Lincoln Drape With Tassel, Goblet, Flint 125.00
Lincoln Drape, Compote, Open, Flint, 8 1/4 In. 110.00
Lincoln Drape, Eggcup 48.00
Lincoln Drape, Eggcup, Flint 65.00
Lincoln Drape, Spooner 45.00
Lincoln Drape, Syrup, Eagle Impressed On Tin Lid 195.00
LION'S LEG, see Alaska
Lion, Butter, Cover, Rampant Lion Finial 100.00
Lion, Celery 55.00
Lion, Celery, Frosted 55.00
Lion, Compote, Cover, Frosted 105.00
Lion, Compote, Cover, Rampant Lion Finial, Oval, 9 In. 88.00
Lion, Compote, Jelly, Square 50.00
Lion, Creamer, Child's 85.00
Lion, Cup & Saucer, Child's 50.00
Lion, Cup, Child's, Clear & Frosted 40.00
Lion, Dish, Cover, Double Lion Head Finial, Lion On Handles 125.00
Lion, Frosted, Berry Bowl, Collared Base, 8 In. 45.00
Lion, Frosted, Berry Bowl, Footed, Small 25.00
Lion, Frosted, Bread Plate, Lion Handles 85.00
Lion, Frosted, Butter, Cover, Child's 150.00
Lion, Frosted, Butter, Cover, Crouching Lion Finial, 5 7/8 In. 70.00
Lion, Frosted, Butter, Cover, Lion Head Finial, 5 7/8 In. 55.00
Lion, Frosted, Celery 55.00
Lion, Frosted, Celery, Footed 100.00

Lion, Frosted, Compote, 7 1/2 X 8 In. 72.00
Lion, Frosted, Compote, Cover, 10 1/2 In. 135.00
Lion, Frosted, Compote, Cover, Rampant Lion Finial 160.00
Lion, Frosted, Creamer 70.00
Lion, Frosted, Creamer, Footed 100.00
Lion, Frosted, Goblet 65.00
Lion, Frosted, Jam Jar ....85.00 To 135.00
Lion, Frosted, Pitcher, Water 375.00
Lion, Frosted, Relish 45.00
Lion, Frosted, Spooner .... 50.00 To 65.00
Lion, Frosted, Sugar, Cover, Rampant Lion Finial 150.00
Lion, Frosted, Sugar, Open, Collared Base, Etched 30.00
Lion, Frosted, Table Set, Sitting Lion Finial, 4 Piece 345.00
Lion, Goblet, Clear & Frosted 45.00
Lion, Pitcher, Child's, Frosted 65.00
Lion, Spooner, Square 52.00
Lion, Sugar, Child's, Cover 90.00
Lion, Sugar, Cover, Clear & Frosted 110.00
Lion, Sugar, Cover, Frosted, Rampant Lion Finial 65.00
Lion, Table Set, Child's, 4 Piece 450.00
Locket On Chain, Butter, Cover 68.00
Locket On Chain, Cake Stand 145.00
Locket On Chain, Syrup 235.00
Locket On Chain, Wine ....75.00 To 125.00
Log & Star, Cruet Set, Pedestal Base, Amber, 4 Piece 135.00
Log Cabin, Bowl, Cover, 7 3/4 In. 100.00
Log Cabin, Compote, Cover, Pedestal, 8 3/4 In. 200.00
Log Cabin, Mustard, Cover, Tecumseh Over Door 155.00
Log Cabin, Pitcher, Water 365.00
Log Cabin, Spooner, Sapphire Blue 395.00
Log Cabin, Sugar, Open 95.00
Loop & Block, Creamer, Ruby Stained 60.00
Loop & Block, Sugar, Cover, Ruby Stained 65.00
Loop & Dart With Round Ornaments, Creamer 14.00
Loop & Dart, Compote, Cover, 8 In. 45.00
Loop & Dart, Goblet 19.00
Loop & Fans, Bread Plate 22.50
Loop & Jewel, Creamer, 3 7/8 In. 24.00
Loop & Jewel, Dish, Square, 5 In. 8.00
Loop & Jewel, Relish, 8 1/4 X 4 1/4 In. 17.00
Loop With Dewdrop, Celery 23.00
Loop With Dewdrop, Creamer .... 22.00 To 30.00

Roman Rosette

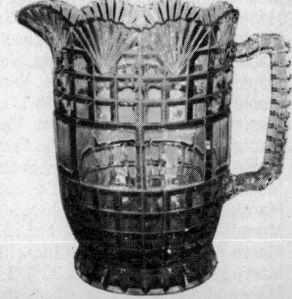

Ribbon Candy   Romeo

Rose in Snow   Selby   Sawtooth

LOOP WITH STIPPLED PANELS, see Texas
LOOP, see also Seneca Loop
Loop, Celery, 1850, 10 In. 75.00
Loop, Compote, Open, Cable Rim, 8 3/4 In. 20.00
Loop, Goblet 22.00
Loop, Goblet, Flint 21.00
Loop, Pitcher, Water, Flint 125.00
Loop, Spooner .... 16.00 To 18.00
Loop, Sugar, Open 50.00
LOOPS & DROPS, see New Jersey
Loops & Pyramids, Wine 16.50
Lotus & Serpent, Bread Plate 45.00
Lotus, Butter, Cover, Log Finial 90.00
Lotus, Ice Cream Tray, Garden of Eden 40.00
Louis XV, Water Set, Green, Gold Trim, 7 Piece 375.00
Louisiana, Bowl, Square, 6 1/2 In. 20.00
Lustre Flute, Sugar & Creamer, Green 55.00
Magna, Tumbler 6.00
Magna, Wine 18.00
Magnet & Grape With American Shield, Goblet 265.00
Magnet & Grape, Goblet, Buttermilk 45.00
Magnet & Grape, Goblet, Flint 250.00
Magnet & Grape, Wine, Frosted Leaves, 3 7/8 In. 150.00
MAIDEN BLUSH, see Banded Portland
Maine, Cake Stand, Green .... 38.50 To 58.00
Maine, Wine, Green .... 60.00 To 65.00
Majestic, Sauce, Flat, 4 In. 6.00
Majestic, Wine 15.00
Maltese Cross, Bread Plate, 10 In. 25.00
Manhattan, Bowl, Blue, Tricornered, Footed, 6 1/2 In. 15.00
Manhattan, Cake Stand, 10 In. 43.50
Manhattan, Goblet, Gold Rim 22.50
Maple Leaf, Bowl, Footed, Oval, Vaseline, 6 X 10 In. 40.00
Maple Leaf, Compote, Cover, Oval, Vaseline, 10 1/2 X 9 In. 150.00
Maple Leaf, Creamer, Log Feet, Vaseline 65.00
Maple Leaf, Pitcher, Log Feet, Vaseline, 8 In. 75.00
Maple Leaf, Plate, Vaseline, 10 1/2 In. 25.00
Maple Leaf, Spooner, Log Feet, Vaseline 65.00
Maple Leaf, Sugar, Cover, Log Feet, Vaseline 80.00
Maple Leaf, Table Set, Cover, Emerald Green, 4 Piece 225.00
Mardi Gras, Syrup 70.00
Marquisette, Goblet 22.00
Marquisette, Spooner .... 15.00 To 28.00
Marsh Fern, Cake Stand, 9 In. 42.50
Martyrs, Bread Plate, Oval, 12 1/2 In. 100.00
Maryland, Celery 25.00
Maryland, Pitcher, Milk 42.00
Maryland, Pitcher, Water 32.00

Maryland, Wine .... 30.00 To 35.00
Mascotte, Apothecary Jar, Dated 65.00
Mascotte, Butter, Cover 55.00
Mascotte, Celery Vase 40.00
Mascotte, Creamer 30.00
Mascotte, Spooner .... 26.00 To 28.00
Mascotte, Spooner, Etched 35.00
Mascotte, Sugar, Cover .... 48.00 To 56.00
Mascotte, Table Set, Etched, 4 Piece 165.00
Masonic, Dish, Pickle, Serpentine, Green 25.00
Massachusetts, Bottle, Bar 55.00
Massachusetts, Vase, Green, 6 1/2 In. 20.00
Master Argus, Tumbler, Footed, Flint 32.00
McKinley, Bread Plate, It Is God's Way .... 47.00 To 65.00
McKinley, Bread Plate, Protection, 9 1/4 In. .... 60.00 To 85.00
McKinley, Tumbler, Our Martyred President 9.00
Medallion Sunburst, Plate, 7 In. 15.00
Medallion Sunburst, Saucer, 4 1/2 In. 9.00
Medallion, Cake Stand 40.00
Medallion, Cake Stand, Amber 55.00
Medallion, Goblet 22.00
Medallion, Pitcher, Water 22.00
Medallion, Pitcher, Water, Amber 55.00
Medallion, Pitcher, Water, Blue .... 60.00 To 85.00
Medallion, Plate, Amber, 9 In. 35.00
Mellor, Goblet 25.00
Memphis, Table Set, Gold Trim, 4 Piece 175.00
Memphis, Table Set, Green, Gold Trim, 4 Piece 325.00
Memphis, Tumbler, Gold Trim 90.00
Memphis, Water Set, Green, Gold Trim, 7 Piece 225.00
Menagerie, Spooner, Fish, Child's, Amber 145.00
Menagerie, Spooner, Fish, Child's, Blue 75.00
Menagerie, Table Set, Child's, Blue, 4 Piece 4600.00
Michigan, Compote, Open, 10 In. 52.00
Michigan, Creamer, Green, Columbian Exposition, 1893 .... 30.00
Michigan, Creamer, Maiden Blush & Clear 80.00
Michigan, Goblet .... 20.00 To 35.00
Michigan, Pitcher, Water, Maiden Blush, Gold Trim 175.00
Michigan, Punch Cup, Green Stained, Forget–Me–Nots 35.00
Michigan, Spooner, Maiden Blush & Clear 70.00
Michigan, Sugar, Cover, Child's 65.00
Michigan, Sugar, Cover, Maiden Blush, Gold Trim 95.00
Michigan, Table Set, 4 Piece 145.00
Michigan, Vase, Bud 16.00
Michigan, Wine, Amber 45.00
Michigan, Wine, Blue 30.00
Mikado Fan, Creamer 42.00
Mikado Fan, Pitcher, Water 42.00
Mikado Fan, Spooner 24.00
Minerva, Bread Plate 48.00
Minerva, Cake Stand 75.00
Minerva, Goblet 75.00
Minerva, Plate, Handles, 10 In. 34.00
Minerva, Relish, Love's Request Is Pickles, Oval 30.00
Minerva, Sauce, Footed 15.00
Minerva, Spooner 32.00
Minerva, Table Set, 4 Piece .... 195.00 To 225.00
Minnesota, Butter, Cover 52.00
Minnesota, Nappy, Triangular, Handle 16.00
Minnesota, Relish, 7 1/4 X 5 In. 10.00
Minnesota, Toothpick, 3 Handles .... 19.00 To 20.00
Minnesota, Water Set, Gold Trim, 5 Piece 115.00
Minnesota, Wine 22.00
Mirror & Loop, Eggcup, Flint 30.00

Missouri, Cake Stand, 9 In. 35.00
Missouri, Pitcher, Milk 40.00
Missouri, Sugar, Cover 45.00
Missouri, Tumbler 28.00
Missouri, Tumbler, Green .... 22.00 To 25.00
Mitered Bars, Saltshaker 5.00
    MITERED DIAMOND POINTS, see Mitered Bars
Mitered Diamonds, Bowl, Amber, Square, 5 3/4 In. 7.00
Mitered Prisms, Cake Stand 28.00
Mitered Prisms, Cracker Jar, 10 In. 45.00
Moon & Star Variant, Spooner 30.00
Moon & Star Variant, Sugar, Cover 30.00
Moon & Star Variant, Tumbler, Gold Trim 16.00
Moon & Star, Berry Bowl, 8 1/4 In. 35.00
Moon & Star, Bowl, Cover, 6 In. 30.00
Moon & Star, Cake Stand 42.00
Moon & Star, Celery .... 25.00 To 27.00
Moon & Star, Compote, Cover 95.00
Moon & Star, Compote, Footed, 5 1/2 X 8 In. 30.00
Moon & Star, Creamer, 5 1/4 In. 375.00
Moon & Star, Cruet 75.00
Moon & Star, Goblet 12.00
Moon & Star, Pitcher, Water, Frosted Moons 175.00
Moon & Star, Sugar Shaker, Pewter Top, Amber Stained 60.00
Moon & Star, Sugar, Cover, Flint 175.00
Moon & Star, Syrup, 3–Mold 90.00
Moon & Star, Tumbler, Flint 60.00
    MOON & STORK, see Ostrich Looking At The Moon
Nail, Cake Stand, 7 1/2 X 10 1/2 In. 40.00
Nail, Celery Vase, Etched 25.00
Nail, Compote, Jelly 22.00
Nail, Goblet, Etched 45.00
Nail, Syrup .... 49.00 To 50.00
Nail, Wine 45.00
Nail, Wine, Etched 55.00
Nailhead, Butter, Cover 46.50
Nailhead, Cake Stand, 9 1/2 In. 25.00
Nailhead, Celery 23.00
Nailhead, Compote, Open, 8 In. 20.00
Nailhead, Creamer 25.00
Nailhead, Goblet .... 15.00 To 20.00
Nailhead, Relish, 5 1/4 X 8 3/4 In. 6.00

Shell & Tassel

Shell & Jewel

Shrine

Strawberry

Squirrel

Thistle

Nailhead, Sugar, Cover	27.00
Nailhead, Wine	18.50
Napoleon, Berry Bowl	25.00
Nellie Bly, Bread Plate, Oval, 11 3/4 In.	170.00
Nellie Bly, Lamp, Pink Design, Miniature	195.00
Nestor, Berry Bowl, Amethyst, Gold & Enamel Trim	25.00
Nestor, Butter, Cover, Flowers, Blue	105.00
Nestor, Butter, Cover, Green	105.00
Nestor, Creamer, Blue	65.00 To 70.00
Nestor, Creamer, Green	75.00
Nestor, Cruet, Amethyst	125.00
Nestor, Saltshaker, Blue	22.00
Nestor, Saltshaker, Blue, Gold & Enamel Trim	40.00
Nestor, Spooner, Blue	65.00 To 70.00
Nestor, Sugar, Cover, Green	95.00
Netted Oak, Sugar Shaker	45.00
Nevada, Sugar, Cover, Frosted Band of Flowers	65.00
New England Centennial, Goblet	80.00
New England Pineapple, Eggcup, Flint	50.00 To 65.00
New England Pineapple, Goblet, Flint	55.00 To 60.00
New England Pineapple, Spooner, Scalloped Rim	55.00
New Era, Butter, Cover	30.00
New Hampshire, Creamer, Individual	9.00
New Hampshire, Goblet, Gold Trim	20.00
New Hampshire, Mug	15.00
New Hampshire, Sugar, Open, Rose Stained, 2 3/4 X 3 In.	25.00
New Hampshire, Toothpick	25.00 To 30.00
New Hampshire, Tumbler	18.00
New Jersey, Bowl, Gold Trim, Oval, 8 1/2 In.	10.00
New Jersey, Butter, Cover	68.00
New Jersey, Celery Tray	25.00
New Jersey, Goblet, Gold Trim	36.50
New Jersey, Pitcher, Water, Gold Trim	40.00
New Jersey, Tumbler, Gold Trim	30.00
New Jersey, Vase, Green, 8 In.	25.00
New York Honeycomb, Celery Vase	45.00
New York Honeycomb, Goblet, Etched	25.00
Nicotiana, Goblet, Etched	12.00
Northwood's Grape, Orange Bowl, Green	75.00
Nursery Tales, Butter, Cover, Child's	55.00 To 75.00
Nursery Tales, Pitcher, Water, Child's	75.00
Nursery Tales, Punch Set, Child's, 7 Piece	185.00

Nursery Tales, Water Set, Child's, 7 Piece 195.00
Oak Leaf Band, Celery .... 35.00 To 36.00
Oak Leaf Band, Goblet 30.00
Oaken Bucket, Butter, Cover, Amber .... 65.00 To 75.00
Oaken Bucket, Creamer 28.00
Oaken Bucket, Pitcher, Water, Amber .... 45.00 To 65.00
Oaken Bucket, Pitcher, Water, Blue 110.00
Oaken Bucket, Spooner, Blue 50.00
Oaken Bucket, Sugar, Cover, Vaseline 58.00
Oaken Bucket, Table Set, Blue, 4 Piece 245.00
Odd Fellows, Goblet 40.00
Ohio, Creamer, Etched 25.00
Ohio, Goblet, Etched 45.00
    OLD ABE, see Frosted Eagle
One–Hundred–One, Celery 35.00
One–Hundred–One, Creamer .... 24.00 To 34.50
One–Hundred–One, Pitcher, Water 125.00
    ONE–O–ONE, see One–Hundred–One
    ONE–THOUSAND EYE, see Thousand Eye
Open Rose, Eggcup 25.00
Open Rose, Goblet 18.00
Open Rose, Spooner 30.00
Opposing Pyramids, Celery .... 15.00 To 18.00
Opposing Pyramids, Tankard 48.00
Opposing Pyramids, Wine 14.00
    OREGON, see also Beaded Loop; Skilton
Oregon, Butter, Cover 50.00
Oregon, Celery 25.00
Oregon, Compote, Jelly 22.00
Oregon, Goblet 22.00
Oregon, Relish, 7 1/2 X 3 3/4 In. 10.00
Oregon, Saltshaker 25.00
Oregon, Spooner 20.00
Oregon, Tumbler 45.00
    ORION, see Cathedral
Ostrich Looking At The Moon, Goblet 55.00
Oval & Fans, Salt & Pepper 30.00
    OVAL LOOP, see Question Mark
Oval Star, Butter, Cover, Child's 20.00
Oval Star, Pitcher 25.00
Oval Star, Spooner, Child's, 2 Handles, 2 1/4 In. 20.00
Oval Star, Table Set, Child's, 3 Piece 58.00
Overall Lattice, Wine, 6 Piece 50.00
Ovoid Panels, Goblet, Flint 30.00
    OWL, see Bull's–Eye with Diamond Points
    OWL IN FAN, see Parrot
Oxford, Berry Bowl, Fluted 25.00
Palm Beach, Compote, Apple Green 58.00
Palm Beach, Cruet 36.00
Palm Beach, Sugar, Cover 75.00
Palm Beach, Table Set, Red, Green & Gold On Clear, 4 Piece 375.00
Palm Leaf Fan, Cruet .... 25.00 To 30.00
Palm Stub, Goblet 25.00
Paneled 44, Bowl, Oval, 11 1/4 In. 30.00
Paneled 44, Candy, Cover, Platinum Trim 35.00
Paneled Acorn Band, Spooner .... 28.00 To 30.00
Paneled Cherry, Pitcher, Water, Red Cherries, Gold Branches 95.00
Paneled Daisy, Butter, Cover 40.00
Paneled Dewdrop, Celery Vase 38.00
Paneled Dewdrop, Sugar & Creamer, Cover 60.00
Paneled Diamond & Finecut, Sugar, Cover 30.00
Paneled Dogwood, Banana Boat, Green, Gold Trim .... 28.00 To 42.00
Paneled Dogwood, Bowl, Silver Plated Holder, Green, Gold Trim 95.00
Paneled Flowers, Goblet 14.00

Three Face   Thumbprint   Tree of Life

Paneled Forget–Me–Not, Cake Stand, 9 1/2 In.	30.00
Paneled Forget–Me–Not, Cake Stand, 11 1/2 In.	58.00
Paneled Forget–Me–Not, Compote, Cover, 7 In.	45.00
Paneled Forget–Me–Not, Compote, Cover, 11 In.	35.00
Paneled Forget–Me–Not, Goblet	35.00
Paneled Forget–Me–Not, Pitcher, Water	40.00
Paneled Graduated Thumbprints, Compote, Open, 5 In.	15.00
Paneled Grape Band, Eggcup, Flint	35.00
Paneled Grape, Creamer	25.00
Paneled Grape, Goblet	24.50
Paneled Grape, Parfait	35.00
Paneled Grape, Pitcher, Water	45.00
Paneled Grape, Sauce	15.00
Paneled Grape, Sugar	40.00
Paneled Grape, Vase	45.00
Paneled Grape, Water Set, Cover, 7 Piece	200.00
Paneled Grape, Wine, 4 In.	22.00
Paneled Heather, Compote, Open, 5 In.	15.00
Paneled Heather, Creamer	20.00
Paneled Heather, Table Set, Cover, 4 Piece	150.00
Paneled Herringbone, Goblet, Green	34.00
Paneled Iris, Wine	12.00 To 16.50
Paneled Palm, Creamer, Purple Stained, Gold Trim	40.00
Paneled Palm, Sugar, Cover, Cranberry Stained, Gold Trim	70.00
Paneled Sprig, Sugar Shaker	30.00
Paneled Star & Button, Creamer	32.00
Paneled Strawberry, Water Set, 6 Piece	195.00
Paneled Strawberry, Water Set, 8 Piece	175.00
Paneled Sunflower, Goblet	24.50
Paneled Thistle, Basket	35.00
Paneled Thistle, Butter	60.00
Paneled Thistle, Compote, Open, 7 1/4 In.	20.00
Paneled Thistle, Relish, 8 1/4 X 4 5/8 In.	8.00
Paneled Thistle, Sugar & Creamer, Higbee, Bee Mark	32.00
Paneled Wheat, Compote, Cover, 7 /2 In.	58.00
Parrot, Goblet	30.00 To 45.00
Parrot, Plate, Green, 9 In.	27.00
Pathfinder, Sugar, Cover	27.50
Pavonia, Cake Stand	45.00
Pavonia, Cake Stand, Etched	50.00
Pavonia, Creamer	37.00
Pavonia, Creamer, Etched	42.50
Pavonia, Goblet, Etched	32.00
Pavonia, Goblet, Etched, 6 Piece	185.00
Pavonia, Tankard, Etched	60.00
Pavonia, Tumbler, Ruby Stained	38.00
Pavonia, Wine	14.00
Pavonia, Wine, Ruby Stained	47.50

Peacock Feathers, Cruet 55.00
Peacock Feathers, Goblet 25.00
Peacock Feathers, Lamp, 9 In. 85.00
Peacock Feathers, Sugar, Cover 40.00
    PEACOCK'S EYE, see Peacock Feathers
    PEAR, see Bartlett Pear
Pennsylvania, Creamer, Child's 30.00
Pennsylvania, Creamer, Green, Gold Trim 28.00
Pennsylvania, Goblet 20.00
Pennsylvania, Goblet, Gold Trim 25.00
Pennsylvania, Pitcher, Milk, Gold Trim 55.00
Pennsylvania, Sauce 18.00
Pennsylvania, Shot Glass 12.00
Pennsylvania, Spooner .... 18.00 To 20.00
Pennsylvania, Sugar, Cover, Child's, Green 135.00
Pennsylvania, Table Set, Gold Trim, Child's 285.00
Pennsylvania, Wine .... 12.50 To 25.00
Pennsylvania, Wine, Green, Gold Trim 35.00
Pequot, Goblet 35.00
Persian, Relish, 5 X 9 1/4 In. 7.00
Petticoat, Creamer, Vaseline, Gold Trim 37.50
Petticoat, Cruet, Vaseline 275.00
Petticoat, Toothpick 65.00
Philadelphia Centennial, Goblet 30.00
Picket Fence, Table Set, 3 Piece 185.00
Picket, Bowl, Square, 4–Footed, 3 1/3 X 8 In. 8.00
Picket, Compote, 7 1/2 In. 30.00
    PILLAR & BULL'S–EYE, see Thistle
Pillar, Creamer, 8 Ribs, 6 In. 145.00
Pillar, Pitcher, Water, Flint, C.1845 .... 245.00
Pillow & Sunburst, Sugar & Creamer 7.00
Pillow & Sunburst, Toothpick, Gold Trim 25.00
Pillow Encircled, Cruet, Ruby Stained, Etched 95.00
Pillow Encircled, Tumbler 25.00
Pillow Encircled, Tumbler, Ruby Stained, Etched 32.50
    PINAFORE, see Actress
Pineapple & Fan, Creamer, Green, Gold 40.00
Pineapple & Fan, Spooner 25.00
Pineapple, Cake Stand 18.00
    PLAIN SMOCKING, see Smocking
Pleat & Panel, Cake Stand 75.00
Pleat & Panel, Compote, Open 35.00
Pleat & Panel, Creamer 30.00
Pleat & Panel, Goblet .... 25.00 To 35.00
Pleat & Panel, Jam Jar 54.00
Pleat & Panel, Plate, 7 In. 17.50
Pleat & Panel, Relish, Handle, 9 1/2 X 5 In. 24.00
Pleat & Panel, Sauce, Handle, 4 In. 14.00
Pleat & Panel, Tray, Handles, 9 1/2 X 5 In. 45.00
Pleat Band, Wine 18.00
Pleating, Table Set, Ruby Stained, 4 Piece 235.00
Plume & Block, Creamer, Ruby Stained 45.00
Plume, Berry Bowl, Flared 24.00
Plume, Butter, Cover, Etched 42.00
Plume, Cake Stand, 10 In. 38.00
Plume, Compote, Fluted, 7 In. 37.00
Plume, Compote, Open, 8 X 7 1/2 In. 35.00
Plume, Dish, Pickle 26.00
Pointed Jewel, Custard Cup 15.00
Pointed Jewel, Goblet 15.00
    POINTED THUMBPRINT, see Almond Thumbprint
Polar Bear, Goblet 110.00
Popcorn, Cake Stand, 9 In. 35.00
Popcorn, Cake Stand, 11 In. 68.00

PORTLAND WITH DIAMOND POINT BAND, see Banded Portland

Portland, Punch Bowl, Footed, 13 5/8 In. 150.00
Portland, Punch Cup 21.50
Portland, Wine 20.00
POTTED PLANT, see Flower Pot
Powder & Shot, Salt, Master 38.00
PRAYER RUG, see Horseshoe
Pressed Diamond, Butter, Cover, Blue .... 85.00 To 95.00
Pressed Diamond, Cake Stand, Blue, 11 In. 85.00
Pressed Diamond, Creamer, Blue .... 35.00 To 40.00
Pressed Diamond, Creamer, Canary 35.00
Pressed Diamond, Salt & Pepper 48.00
Pressed Diamond, Spooner, Scalloped, Amber 30.00
Pressed Diamond, Sugar, Cover, Blue .... 45.00 To 50.00
Pressed Diamond, Tumbler, Amber 22.00
Pressed Leaf, Goblet 21.50
Primrose, Pitcher, Milk 42.00
Primrose, Pitcher, Milk, Blue 65.00
Primrose, Plate, 4 1/2 In. 17.50
Primrose, Plate, Blue, 7 In. 28.50
Princess Feather, Celery 41.50
Princess Feather, Compote, Cover, 8 In. 95.00
Princess Feather, Spooner .... 20.00 To 32.50
Priscilla, Bowl, Findlay, 9 1/2 In. 38.00
Priscilla, Doughnut Stand 30.00
Priscilla, Relish, Divided, Findlay 20.00
Prism & Diamond, Spooner 20.00
Prism Band, Spooner 18.00
Prism With Diamond Points, Butter, Cover, Flint 45.00
Prism, Compote, Scalloped, 7 In. 25.00
Prism, Spooner, Flint 45.00
Prize, Compote, Jelly 28.00
Prize, Cordial, Green, Gold Trim 35.00
Prize, Creamer & Spooner, Ruby Stained 135.00
Prize, Toothpick 55.00
Prize, Wine, Green, Gold Trim .... 30.00 To 45.00
Psyche & Cupid, Creamer .... 42.00 To 60.00
Psyche & Cupid, Goblet 37.50
Psyche & Cupid, Pitcher, Water .... 45.00 To 57.50
Quaker Lady, Creamer 50.00
Quartered Block, Butter, Cover 27.00
Quatrefoil, Compote, Cover 45.00
Quatrefoil, Creamer 22.50
QUEEN, see also Daisy & Button, Paneled
Queen Anne, Compote, Cover, Low 85.00
Queen Anne, Puff Box, Amethyst, Cover, New Martinsville 18.50
Queen Anne, Spooner 32.00
Queen Anne, Syrup, 1880 .... 95.00

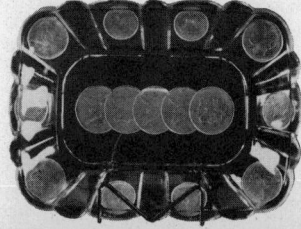

U.S. Coin

Waffle & Thumbprint

Washington Centennial

Queen's Necklace, Sugar Shaker 90.00
Queen's Necklace, Toothpick .... 45.00 To 60.00
Queen, Butter, Dome Cover, Sapphire Blue 60.00
Queen, Goblet, Amber 35.00
Question Mark, Tankard 78.00
Quixote, Cruet, Faceted Stopper 30.00
Quixote, Pitcher, Water 65.00
Quixote, Wine 14.50
Racing Deer, Water Set, Pedestal, 5 Piece 210.00
Railroad Train, Bread Plate 85.00
Ranson, Creamer 50.00
Ranson, Spooner 50.00
Ranson, Table Set, Vaseline, Gold Trim, 4 Piece .... 395.00 To 425.00
Ray, Creamer 25.00
Rayed Flower, Water Set, 7 Piece 75.00
Reardon, Cake Stand, Etched Flowers 25.00
Red Block, Goblet, Ruby Stained 25.00
Red Block, Tumbler 28.00
Red Block, Water Set, Ruby Stained, 7 Piece 295.00
Regal Block, Wine 18.50
    REGENT, see Leaf Medallion
Regina, Wine 16.50
Remember The Maine, Dish, Emerald, Cover, Battleship Shape 30.00
Reticulated Cord, Creamer .... 25.00 To 28.00
    REVERSE TORPEDO, see Bull's-Eye Band
Rex, Table Set, Child's, Teal Blue, 3 Piece 350.00
Rex, Water Set, Child's, 7 Piece 125.00
Rhode Island, Goblet 650.00
Rib & Bead, Toothpick, Ruby Stained 50.00
Ribbed Grape, Goblet, Flint 38.00
Ribbed Grape, Plate, Flint, 6 In. 35.00
Ribbed Ivy, Butter, Cover, Flint 95.00
Ribbed Ivy, Compote, Open, Flint, 8 1/2 In. 95.00
Ribbed Ivy, Goblet 35.00
    RIBBED OPAL, see Beatty Rib
Ribbed Palm, Celery Vase, Flint 75.00
Ribbed Palm, Creamer 155.00
Ribbed Palm, Eggcup 25.00
Ribbed Palm, Goblet, Flint 33.00
Ribbed Palm, Pitcher, Water, Flint 295.00
Ribbed Palm, Spooner 35.00
Ribbed Palm, Wine, Flint 50.00
Ribbon Candy, Cake Stand, 9 1/2 X 4 In. 38.00
Ribbon Candy, Creamer, Purple 18.50
Ribbon Candy, Doughnut Stand 28.00
Ribbon Candy, Pitcher, Milk 58.00
Ribbon Candy, Table Set, 4 Piece 145.00
Ribbon, Compote, Dolphin Stem, Clear & Frosted, 8 In. 225.00
Ribbon, Frosted With Double Bars, Goblet 25.00
Ribbon, Frosted, Butter, Cover 75.00
Ribbon, Frosted, Celery, Tapered 34.00
Ribbon, Frosted, Compote, Dolphin Pedestal 275.00
Ribbon, Frosted, Creamer 28.00
Ribbon, Frosted, Goblet 25.00
Ribbon, Frosted, Jam Jar 35.00
Ribbon, Frosted, Sauce 9.00
Ribbon, Goblet, Clear & Frosted 55.00
Ribbon, Jam Jar 50.00
Rising Sun, Wine, Gold Trim 7.50
Roanoke Star, Tumbler 12.00
Robin Hood, Sugar, Cover 30.00
    ROCHELLE, see Princess Feather
Rock of Ages, Bread Plate, Milk Glass Center, 1875 .... 150.00
Roman Key, Frosted, Eggcup, Flint 35.00

Roman Key, Frosted, Sugar, Cover, Flint 80.00
Roman Key, Goblet .... 35.00 To 40.00
Roman Rosette, Bread Plate, 11 X 8 In. 30.00
Roman Rosette, Bread Plate, 11 X 8 In. 35.00
Romeo, Sugar Shaker 65.00
Romeo, Tankard 38.00
Rooster, Creamer, Child's ....95.00 To 125.00
Rooster, Sugar, Cover, Dog Finial, Child's 145.00
Rope & Thumbprint, Sugar Shaker, Blue 75.00
ROPE BANDS, see Argent
Rose In Snow, Bottle, Stopper, 1/2 Pt. 135.00
Rose In Snow, Butter, Cover .... 40.00 To 48.00
Rose In Snow, Compote, Cover 55.00
Rose In Snow, Goblet, Amber 40.00
Rose In Snow, Plate, Handles, 9 1/2 In. 45.00
Rose Sprig, Celery 36.50
Rose Sprig, Goblet 25.00
Rose Sprig, Relish, Boat Shape, Blue 85.00
Rosette & Palms, Celery 25.00
Rosette & Palms, Compote, Open, 9 In. 15.00
Rosette & Palms, Goblet .... 22.00 To 23.00
Rosette Band, Compote, Jelly 28.00
ROSETTE MEDALLION, see Feather Duster
Rosette, Compote, Open, 4 1/2 In. 12.00
Rosette, Goblet .... 21.50 To 35.00
Royal Ivy, Creamer, Frosted 180.00
Royal Ivy, Pitcher, Water, Clear Handle, 8 5/8 In. 225.00
Royal Ivy, Pitcher, Water, Rainbow Cased 295.00
Royal Ivy, Rose Bowl, Clear To Cranberry .... 72.50 To 75.00
Royal Ivy, Spooner, Frosted 60.00
Royal Ivy, Sugar Shaker, Frosted 175.00
Royal Ivy, Sugar, Cover, Frosted 145.00
Royal Ivy, Table Set, Cranberry, Frosted, 4 Piece 695.00
Royal Ivy, Toothpick 125.00
Royal Ivy, Tumbler, Clear To Cranberry 75.00
Royal Lady, Butter, Cover 52.00
Royal Lady, Celery .... 38.00 To 42.00
Royal Lady, Spooner 40.00
Royal Oak, Butter, Cover, Acorn Finial 210.00
Royal Oak, Cruet, Frosted ....95.00 To 125.00
Royal Oak, Sugar Shaker, Frosted 75.00
Royal Oak, Toothpick, Cranberry 110.00
RUBY THUMBPRINT, see also King's Crown
Ruby Thumbprint, Sugar 15.00
Ruby Thumbprint, Wine, Souvenir LaPorte, Indiana, 4 1/2 In. 28.00
S–Repeat, Butter, Cover, Green, Gold Trim 125.00
S–Repeat, Decanter, Wine, Amethyst, Gold Trim 125.00
S–Repeat, Salt & Pepper, Blue 45.00
S–Repeat, Toothpick, Purple 65.00
S–Repeat, Tray, Condiment, Blue 55.00
S–Repeat, Tumbler, Blue, Gold Trim 30.00
S–Repeat, Tumbler, Purple, 4 Piece 200.00
Sawtooth & Star, Butter, Cover, Ruby Stained, Etched 110.00
Sawtooth & Star, Creamer, Ruby Stained, Etched 65.00
Sawtooth & Star, Cruet, Stopper, Ruby Stained 235.00
Sawtooth & Star, Spooner, Ruby Stained, Etched 50.00
Sawtooth & Star, Tumbler, Ruby Stained 37.50
SAWTOOTH BAND, see Amazon
Sawtooth, Celery 50.00
Sawtooth, Cordial, Ruby Stained .... 30.00 To 38.00
Sawtooth, Creamer, Scalloped Base, Flint 45.00
Sawtooth, Salt & Pepper, Amber 20.00
Sawtooth, Salt, Master 30.00
Sawtooth, Spill 46.50

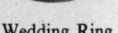

Wedding Ring   Westward Ho   Wheel & Comma   Wildflower

Sawtooth, Spooner	20.00
Sawtooth, Sugar, Cover, Flint	125.00
Sawtoothed Honeycomb, Creamer, Ruby Stained	55.00
Sawtoothed Honeycomb, Tumbler	40.00
SCALLOPED TAPE, see Jewel Band	
Scroll & Flower, Bread Plate	36.50
Scroll & Flower, Sugar, Cover	35.00
Scroll With Cane Band, Butter, Cover, Amber Stained	125.00
Scroll With Flowers, Bread Plate	35.00
Scroll With Flowers, Eggcup	15.00
Scroll With Flowers, Syrup, Dated	85.00
Scroll, Goblet	15.00
Scroll, Wine	15.00
Seashell, Spooner, Frosted Pedestal & Base	20.00
SEDAN, see Paneled Star & Button	
Seed Pod, Creamer, Blue, Gold Trim	45.00 To 70.00
Seed Pod, Sugar, Cover, Blue, Gold Trim	60.00
Seed Pod, Wine, 1870s	18.00
Selby, Goblet	8.00
Seneca Loop, Goblet, Flint	20.00
Sequoia, Bottle, Barber, 7 1/4 In.	22.50
Sequoia, Wine	16.00
Serenade, Mug, Light Blue, 4 3/4 In.	60.00
Serrated Prism, Syrup	35.00
Serrated Spearpoint, Wine	22.00
SHEAF OF WHEAT, see Wheat Sheaf	
Shell & Jewel, Berry Bowl, 4 1/2 In.	6.00
Shell & Jewel, Pitcher, Water	25.00 To 41.50
Shell & Jewel, Tumbler	20.00 To 22.50
Shell & Jewel, Water Set, Green, 7 Piece	245.00
Shell & Tassel, Bowl, 10 In.	22.00
Shell & Tassel, Bowl, Oval	45.00
Shell & Tassel, Compote, 8 X 8 In.	65.00
Shell & Tassel, Compote, Open, 9 1/2 In.	82.00
Shell & Tassel, Goblet	35.00
Shell, Butter, Cover	38.00
Sheraton, Bread Plate, Blue	55.00
Shields, Goblet	35.00
Shoe, Gillinder, Victorian, Frosted	20.00
Short Loop, Sugar, Cover, Etched With Stag	35.00
SHORT TEASEL, see Teasel	
SHOSHONE, see Victor	
Shrine, Pitcher, Water	30.00 To 40.00
Shuttle, Cake Stand	95.00
Shuttle, Celery Vase	60.00 To 65.00
Shuttle, Spooner	50.00
Shuttle, Sugar, Cover	70.00
Signers, Bread Plate, 9 1/2 X 13 In.	68.00

Single Rose, Tumbler, Green 32.00
Skilton, Goblet 32.00
Skilton, Tumbler, Ruby Stained 37.50
Slewed Horseshoe, Punch Set, 1909, 14 Piece 100.00
Smocking, Sugar, Cover, Flint 85.00
Snail, Butter, Cover 85.00
Snail, Compote, Open, 10 In. 145.00
Snail, Goblet, Etched 75.00
Snail, Jam Jar, Cover 125.00
Snail, Pitcher, Water, Etched, 11 3/4 In. 130.00
Snail, Rose Bowl, 5 In. 45.00
Snail, Salt & Pepper, Bulbous, Pewter Lids 110.00
Snail, Sugar, Cover 50.00
Snail, Syrup, Brass Lid 95.00
Snail, Tankard 75.00
Snake Drape, Goblet 22.00
Snakeskin With Dot, Creamer 20.00
Snowflake & Sunburst, Pitcher 27.50
Spanish American, Pitcher, Water, Cannon Balls .... 50.00 To 65.00
SPANISH COIN, see Columbian Coin
Spearheads, Celery .... 15.00 To 17.00
Spirea Band, Bowl, Blue, 7 5/8 In. 22.50
Spirea Band, Creamer, Dark Amber 36.50
Spirea Band, Goblet, Amber 18.00
Spirea Band, Goblet, Blue 35.00
Spirea Band, Wine, Amber 20.00
Spirea, Wine 18.50
Sprig, Compote, 6 1/2 In. 35.00
Sprig, Goblet 26.50
Square Fuchsia, Plate, Amber, Square, 10 In. 45.00
Square Panes, Butter, Cover, Etched 35.00
Square Panes, Cake Stand, 9 1/2 In. 48.00
Square Panes, Compote, Cover, Etched, 5 1/2 In. 75.00
Squirrel, Creamer 98.00
Squirrel, Pitcher, Water 110.00
STAR & PUNTY, see Moon & Star
Star In Bull's–Eye, Compote, Gold Trim, 6 1/4 In. 22.50
Star In Bull's–Eye, Punch Cup 10.00
Star In Bull's–Eye, Toothpick 22.00
Star In Honeycomb, Creamer, 6 In. 35.00
Star In Honeycomb, Wine 29.00
Star of David, Goblet 21.00
Star Rosetted, Plate, 1880 .... 60.00
Star Whorl, Wine, 1890s 8.50
Star, Punch Cup, Child's, Oval 7.50
Starred Block, Butter, Cover, Pedestal 90.00
Stars & Bars, Celery .... 23.00 To 27.00
Stars & Stripes, Tumbler, Blue 75.00
STATES, see The States
Statue of Liberty, Vase, Brown Stained 65.00
Stippled Chain, Goblet, Purple 22.00
Stippled Chain, Spooner 25.00
STIPPLED DAHLIA, see Dahlia
Stippled Grape & Festoon, Creamer 38.50
Stippled Grape & Festoon, Goblet .... 26.50 To 30.00
Stippled Ivy, Goblet 18.00
STIPPLED PANELED FLOWER, see Maine
Stippled Peppers, Goblet 8.00
STIPPLED SCROLL, see Scroll
Stippled Star, Spooner 25.00
STIPPLED VINE & BEADS, see Vine & Beads
STORK LOOKING AT THE MOON, see Ostrich Looking At The Moon
Strawberry & Currant, Goblet 25.00
Strawberry, Goblet, Jelly, 6 In. 17.50

Style, Butter, Cover 48.00
Style, Spooner, Child's 16.00
Sunbeam, Creamer, Child's 8.00
Sunbeam, Salt & Pepper, Green, Original Lid 40.00
Sunk Daisy, Compote, Stemmed, 8 In. 32.50
Sunk Daisy, Pitcher 40.00
Sunk Honeycomb, Cracker Jar, Cover 30.00
Sunk Honeycomb, Goblet, Ruby Stained, 6 Piece 150.00
Sunk Honeycomb, Mug, Souvenir, Ruby Stained 40.00
Sunken Primrose, Butter, Cover, Ruby Stained 150.00
    SUNRISE, see Rising Sun
Swag With Brackets, Butter, Cover, Amethyst 65.00
Swag Block, Eggcup 17.50
Swag With Brackets, Compote, Blue 35.00
Swag With Brackets, Salt & Pepper, Amethyst 25.00
Swag With Brackets, Tumbler, Green, Gold Trim 20.00
Swan, Creamer 45.00
Swan, Sugar, Open 40.00
Sweetheart, Table Set, Child's, 4 Piece 195.00
Swimming Swan, Goblet 80.00
Swinger, Toothpick, Ruby Stained, Gold Rim 35.00
Swirl, Berry Bowl, Amber, 9 1/2 In. 50.00
Swirl, Celery 30.00
Swirl, Creamer, Aqua 5.00
Swirl, Plate, Aqua, 9 In. 5.00
Tacoma, Pitcher, Water, Yellow 85.00
Tacoma, Spooner 20.00
Tacoma, Sugar, Cover 32.00
Tandem Bicycle, Celery .... 32.00 To 35.00
    TAPE MEASURE, see Shields
Tappan, Creamer, Child's, Amber 15.00
Tappan, Creamer, Child's, Amethyst 35.00
Tappan, Sugar, Cover, Child's, Amethyst 45.00
Tarentum's Atlanta, Spooner, Ruby Stained 40.00
Tarentum's Atlanta, Syrup, Pewter Top 55.00
Tarentum's Atlanta, Table Set, Ruby Stained 265.00
    TEARDROP, see Teardrop & Thumbprint
Teardrop & Tassel, Relish 15.00
Teardrop & Tassel, Tumbler, Cobalt Blue 45.00
Teardrop & Tassel, Tumbler, Green 250.00
Teardrop & Tassel, Wine 145.00
Teardrop & Thumbprint, Creamer 25.00
Teardrop & Thumbprint, Wine .... 11.00 To 16.00
Teasel, Celery 27.00
Tennessee, Cake Stand 48.00
Tennessee, Sugar, Cover 60.00
Tepee, Toothpick 21.00
Texas Star, Spooner 45.00
Texas Star, Wine 12.00
Texas, Bowl, 8 1/2 In. 26.00
Texas, Creamer, Gold Trim, Individual 18.00
Texas, Sugar & Creamer, Gold Trim, Individual 20.00
Texas, Toothpick .... 30.00 To 31.50
Texas, Vase, 9 In. 45.00
The States, Creamer, Individual 20.00
The States, Goblet 30.00
The States, Punch Cup 8.00
The States, Salt & Pepper, Glass Tops 30.00
The States, Wine 25.00
Theodore Roosevelt, Bread Plate, Oval, 10 3/8 In. .... 70.00 To 110.00
Thistle, Butter, Cover, Signed, Blue 45.00
Thistleblow, Wine 9.00
Thousand Eye, Bread Plate, Blue 48.00
Thousand Eye, Celery, Green 48.00

Thousand Eye, Compote, Open, Green, 8 1/2 In. 65.00
Thousand Eye, Cruet 30.00
Thousand Eye, Goblet .... 15.00 To 27.50
Thousand Eye, Mug, Child's 25.00
Thousand Eye, Plate, ABC, Blue, 6 In. 55.00
Thousand Eye, Plate, Folded Corners, Blue, 8 In. 25.00
Thousand Eye, Saltshaker, Amber 18.00
Thousand Eye, String Holder, Bell Shape 50.00
Thousand Eye, Tray, Water, Oval 30.00
Threaded, Celery 19.00
Three Face, Berry Bowl, Pedestal 35.00
Three Face, Butter, Cover 140.00
Three Face, Cake Stand, 9 3/8 In. 165.00
Three Face, Claret, Clear & Frosted 145.00
Three Face, Compote, 8 In. 195.00
Three Face, Compote, Cover, 4 1/2 X 6 In. 65.00
Three Face, Compote, Cover, Clear & Frosted, 4 In. 85.00
Three Face, Goblet .... 80.00 To 85.00
Three Face, Salt & Pepper 165.00
Three Face, Spooner 85.00
Three Face, Sugar, Cover 135.00
    THREE GRACES, see also Three Face
Three Graces, Bread Plate, 1875 .... 45.00
Three Panel, Mug, Amber .... 30.00 To 35.00
Three Panel, Pitcher, Milk 44.00
Three Panel, Table Set, Blue, 4 Piece .... 195.00 To 245.00
Three Presidents, Bread Plate 95.00
Three Presidents, Bread Plate, Frosted Center 55.00
    THREE SISTERS, see Three Face
Thumbprint & Hobnail, Salt, Master 225.00
Thumbprint & Twirl Stem, Wine 16.00
Thumbprint, Compote, Open, 7 1/2 In. 67.50
Thumbprint, Creamer, Ruby Stained, Etched 85.00
Thumbprint, Goblet 25.00
Thumbprint, Spooner, Ruby Stained, Etched 65.00
Thumbprint, Wine, Ruby Stained 35.00
Tic–Tac–Toe, Toothpick 13.00
Tile Band, Goblet 6.00
Tiny Fine Cut, Decanter, Ruby Stained, Gold Trim 75.00
Tiny Lion, Celery, Etched 45.00
Tiny Lion, Compote, Cover, Fluted, Clear & Frosted, 11 1/2 In. 175.00
Tiny Lion, Pitcher, Water 30.00
    TOBIN, see Leaf & Star
Togo, Goblet 20.00
Torpedo, Bowl, 8 7/8 In. 30.00
Torpedo, Cake Stand, 6 X 9 In. 85.00
Torpedo, Compote, Cover, 13 X 8 In. 130.00
Torpedo, Creamer 40.00
Torpedo, Goblet 50.00
Torpedo, Lamp, Allover Pattern, 9 In. 69.00
Torpedo, Pitcher, Water .... 65.00 To 88.00
Torpedo, Sugar, Cover 60.00
Torpedo, Tumbler 30.00
Torpedo, Wine 75.00
Tree of Life Portland, Compote, Open 75.00
Tree of Life Portland, Goblet, Flint 125.00
Tree of Life, Celery 42.50
Tree of Life, Compote, Black, Gold 385.00
Tree of Life, Compote, Hand, Frosted 80.00
Tree of Life, Goblet, 6 In. 20.00
Tree of Life, Saltshaker 42.00
Tree of Life, Sugar, Cover, 11 In. 25.00
Triangular Prism, Compote, Open, 7 1/4 In. 25.00
Triple Triangle, Butter, Cover 65.00

Triple Triangle, Butter, Cover, Ruby Stained 95.00
Triple Triangle, Goblet, Ruby Stained 34.50
Triple Triangle, Tumbler 18.00
Triple Triangle, Wine 35.00
Triple Triangle, Wine, Ruby Stained .... 28.00 To 38.00
Truncated Cube, Toothpick, Ruby Stained 35.00
Truncated Cube, Wine, Ruby Stained 35.00
Tulip & Honeycomb, Punch Set, Child's, 7 Piece .... 70.00 To 75.00
Tulip & Honeycomb, Sugar & Creamer, Child's 40.00
Tulip & Sawtooth, Decanter, Stopper 135.00
Tulip Band, Compote, 7 1/4 In. 20.00
Tulip Petals, Toothpick 25.00
Tulip With Honeycomb, Sugar & Creamer, Child's 38.00
Tulip With Sawtooth, Compote, Open 28.00
Tulip With Sawtooth, Spooner, Flint 26.00
Twin Snowshoes, Creamer 18.00
Twin Snowshoes, Creamer, Child's .... 25.00 To 40.00
Twin Snowshoes, Wine, Amethyst, Gold Trim 25.00
Twin Teardrops, Cruet 25.00
    TWINKLE STAR, see Utah
Twisted Hobnail, Toothpick 18.00
Two Band, Creamer 25.00
Two Band, Creamer, Child's 30.00
Two Band, Spooner, Child's 40.00
Two Panel, Compote, Cover, 6 1/2 In. 48.00
Two Panel, Creamer, Amber .... 38.00 To 60.00
Two Panel, Spooner, Amber 38.00
Two Panel, Wine, Blue 25.00
Two Panel, Wine, Green 50.00
U.S.Coin, Bread Plate, Frosted Dollar 400.00
U.S.Coin, Celery, Frosted Quarters 350.00
U.S.Coin, Compote, Flared, Frosted Quarters, Dimes, 8 3/8 In. 240.00
U.S.Coin, Relish, Frosted, 7 3/8 In. 250.00
U.S.Coin, Sauce, 4 In. 95.00
U.S.Coin, Sugar, Open, 8 1/4 In. 250.00
U.S.Coin, Toothpick, Dollar Obverse & Reverse 105.00
U.S.Coin, Toothpick, Frosted 225.00
U.S.Coin, Tumbler 50.00
Utah, Pitcher, Water .... 17.00 To 45.00
Utah, Wine .... 34.00 To 45.00
V–In–Heart, Creamer 9.00
Valencia Waffle, Compote, 6 1/4 In. 6.00
Valencia Waffle, Pitcher, Vaseline 57.00
Vermont, Pitcher, Water, Green, Gold Trim ....87.00 To 125.00
Vermont, Spooner 55.00
Vermont, Toothpick, Green 35.00
Vermont, Tumbler, Green, Gold Trim 24.50
Vermont, Water Set, Green, Gold Trim, 6 Piece 265.00
Victor, Cake Stand, Green 50.00
Victor, Cruet, Emerald Green 95.00
Victor, Sugar, Cover, Yellow Stained 40.00
Victor, Toothpick, Gold Trim 25.00
Victoria, Water Set, Green, Gold Trim, 7 Piece 275.00
Viking, Butter, Cover 45.00
Viking, Compote, Cover, 7 In. 90.00
Viking, Creamer 55.00
Viking, Jar, Apothecary, Original Stopper 110.00
Viking, Sauce, 4 In. 10.00
Viking, Sugar, Cover 65.00
Viking, Syrup, Clear & Frosted 155.00
Vine & Beads, Butter, Sugar, Creamer, Cover, Child's 120.00
    VIRGINIA, see also Galloway
Waffle & Thumbprint, Cake Stand, Flint, 12 In. 695.00
Waffle & Thumbprint, Celery Vase, Flint 135.00

Waffle & Thumbprint, Claret, Flint 110.00
Waffle & Thumbprint, Decanter, Bar Lip, Flint 85.00
Waffle & Thumbprint, Goblet, Baluster Knob Stem 52.00
Waffle & Thumbprint, Goblet, Bulb Stem 60.00
Waffle & Thumbprint, Wine, Flint 65.00
Waffle With Points, Compote, Cover 75.00
Waffle With Spearpoint, Goblet 10.00
Waffle, Champagne, Flint 145.00
Waffle, Eggcup 24.50
Waffle, Sugar, Cover, Flint 95.00
Waffle, Syrup 85.00
Washboard, Sugar, Cover 40.00
Washington Centennial, Bread Plate, Oval 115.00
Washington Centennial, Celery, Flint 50.00
Washington Centennial, Goblet 45.00
Washington Centennial, Tumbler 45.00
Washington, Wine, Flint 135.00
Wedding Bells, Pitcher, Water, Gold Trim 45.00
Wedding Ring, Goblet, Flint 53.00
Wee Branches, Creamer, Child's 80.00
Wellington, Water Set, Ruby Stained, 5 Piece .... 245.00 To 315.00
Westward Ho, Bread Plate 125.00
Westward Ho, Butter, Cover, Stemmed 70.00
Westward Ho, Compote, Cover, 11 In. .... 125.00 To 195.00
Westward Ho, Creamer .... 95.00 To 120.00
Westward Ho, Goblet, Water 80.00
Westward Ho, Jam Jar 15.00
Westward Ho, Pitcher, 9 1/2 In. 90.00
Westward Ho, Sauce, Footed 10.00
Westward Ho, Wine, Footed 200.00
Wheat & Barley, Cake Stand, 11 In. 40.00
Wheat & Barley, Compote, Jelly, Blue 30.00
Wheat & Barley, Creamer 55.00
Wheat & Barley, Goblet, Blue 20.00
Wheat & Barley, Pitcher, Milk 38.50
Wheat & Barley, Pitcher, Water, Amber 85.00
Wheat & Barley, Plate, 6 In. 35.00
Wheat & Barley, Salt & Pepper 42.00
Wheat & Barley, Spooner 25.00
Wheat & Barley, Tumbler 20.00
Wheat Sheaf, Bread Plate 35.00
Wheat Sheaf, Pitcher, Water 45.00
Wheel & Comma, Sauce 8.00
    WHIRLIGIG, see Buzz Star
Wild Bouquet, Spooner, Blue 60.00
Wild Rose With Bowknot, Butter, Child's, Cover, Green Satin 195.00
Wild Rose With Bowknot, Mustard, Pewter Lid & Spoon 38.00
Wild Rose With Bowknot, Water Set, Frosted, 6 Piece 125.00
Wildflower, Bowl, Apple Green, Square, 8 In. 30.00
Wildflower, Cake Stand, 9 1/2 In. 48.00
Wildflower, Candy Dish, Cut Floral Lid, Blue, 6 1/2 In. 35.00
Wildflower, Celery Vase, Blue 60.00
Wildflower, Celery, Amber 30.00
Wildflower, Goblet, Amber 35.00
Wildflower, Goblet, Apple Green 30.00
Wildflower, Pitcher, Water, Amber, Footed, 9 In. 55.00
Wildflower, Sauce, Pedestal 15.00
Wildflower, Spooner, Amber 32.00
Wildflower, Sugar, Open, Blue 30.00
Wildflower, Syrup, Pewter Top, Amber .... 145.00 To 150.00
Wildflower, Tumbler, Amber 30.00
Willow Oak, Bread Plate, 9 In. 20.00
Willow Oak, Compote, Amber 65.00
Willow Oak, Compote, Cover, Amber, 8 1/4 In. 65.00

Willow Oak, Creamer, Amber	38.00
Willow Oak, Goblet, 6 Piece	99.00
Willow Oak, Pitcher, Water	37.00
Willow Oak, Plate, 9 In.	20.00
Willow Oak, Plate, Tab Handle, 11 In.	27.00
Willow Oak, Salt & Pepper, Silver Lids	65.00
Willow Oak, Saltshaker, Pewter Lid, Amber	45.00
Willow Oak, Table Set, Amber, 4 Piece	395.00
Windflower, Compote, Open, 8 In.	15.00
Windflower, Goblet	43.00
Wisconsin, Cake Stand, 9 1/2 In.	45.00 To 55.00
Wisconsin, Castor, Pickle	135.00
Wisconsin, Pitcher, Water	45.00
Wisconsin, Punch Cup	18.00
Wisconsin, Spooner	35.00
Wisconsin, Syrup	78.00

WOODEN PAIL, see Oaken Bucket

Wreath & Shell, Berry Bowl Set, Vaseline, 6 Piece	245.00
Wreath & Shell, Creamer, Canary Yellow	95.00
Wreath & Shell, Spooner, Vaseline	87.50
Wyoming, Bowl, Footed, 7 In.	67.50
Wyoming, Butter, Cover	50.00 To 95.00
Wyoming, Cake Stand, 9 3/4 In.	52.00
Wyoming, Cake Stand, Clear, 4 X 9 3/4 In.	55.00
Wyoming, Compote, Open, 8 In.	52.50
Wyoming, Sugar, Cover	45.00
Wyoming, Syrup, Cover	95.00
X–Ray, Creamer, Green, Gold Trim, Individual	55.00
X–Ray, Sauce, Green, Gold Trim	22.50
X–Ray, Sugar, Cover, Green	45.00
X–Ray, Sugar, Cover, Green, Gold Trim, Individual	65.00
X–Ray, Table Set, Green, Gold Trim, 4 Piece	295.00
X–Ray, Toothpick, Green	55.00
X–Ray, Tumbler, Amethyst, Gold Trim	42.50 To 45.00

YALE, see Crowfoot

Zipper Slash, Creamer, Ruby Stained	45.00
Zipper Slash, Toothpick	20.00
Zipper Slash, Wine	24.00

Print, in this listing, means any of many printed images produced on paper by one of the more common methods, such as lithography. The prints listed here are of interest primarily to the antiques collector, not the fine arts collector. Many of these prints were originally part of books. Other prints will be found in the sections headed Currier & Ives, Advertising, and Poster.

PRINT, A. Bremet, President Jackson, Steamship, Framed, 17 X 20 In.	40.00
Albright, Fleeting Time Thou Hast Left Me Old, 13 3/4 X 9 1/2 In.	1875.00
Armstrong, Radiant Youth, 22 X 28 In.	125.00
Arnold, Snowfall, 1940, 9 3/4 X 13 1/2 In.	95.00

Audubon bird prints were originally issued as parts of books printed from 1826 to 1854. They were issued in two sizes, 26 1/2 in. by 39 1/2 in. and 11 in. by 7 in. The quadrupeds were issued in 28 in. by 22 in. size prints. Later editions of the Audubon books were done in many sizes and reprints of the books in the original size were also made. The bird pictures have been so popular they have been copied in myriad sizes by both old and new printing methods. This list includes originals and later copies because Audubon prints of all ages are sold in antiques shops.

Audubon, American Woodcock, 7 X 11 In.	275.00
Audubon, Barn Owl, 34 1/2 X 23 In.	880.00
Audubon, Black–Winged Hawk, 39 1/4 X 26 1/2 In.	440.00
Audubon, Bowen, 7 X 11 In.	125.00
Audubon, Canada Goose, Elephant Folio	6325.00

Audubon, Carolina Parrot, 12 X 20 In. 450.00
Audubon, Crested Grebe, 19 1/4 X 28 1/2 In. 440.00
Audubon, Evening Grosbeak, Male & Female, Framed, 26 1/2 X 39 1/2 In. 3025.00
Audubon, Golden Eagle, Elephant Folio, 38 X 26 In. 575.00
Audubon, Great Footed Hawk, 12 X 20 In. 475.00
Audubon, Green Heron, Elephant Folio 5445.00
Audubon, Marbled Godwit, 12 X 20 In. 350.00
Audubon, Marsh Hare, Stone Lithograph, American, 1848, 19 X 26 In. 1500.00
Audubon, Purple Sandpiper, 6 X 8 In. 22.50
Audubon, Soft-Haired Squirrel, 6 X 8 In. 22.50
Audubon, White-Crowned Pigeon, 26 1/2 X 39 1/2 In. 3500.00
Aylward, New York, Steamship, 27 X 37 In. 125.00
Bell, Mother & Child, Matted, 1905, 4 X 5 In. 12.50
Benton, Jesse James, Matted, Framed, 1936, 16 1/8 X 21 7/8 In. 5000.00
Benton, Shallow Creek, Signed, 1939, 14 1/4 X 9 1/2 In. 715.00
Brundage, Book, Good Samaritan, 4-Color, 1901, 8 X 10 In. 25.00
Cassells, Horses, London, 1870, 9 1/2 X 7 1/2 In. 67.50
Catesby, Carolina Parrot, 19th Century, Medium Folio 1100.00
Christy, Secrets of The Sea, Framed, 1904, 17 1/2 X 21 1/2 In. 100.00
Curtis, Arum Maculatum, London, 1780, 10 X 15 1/2 In. 685.00
Dessler, Woodcut, Chow At Table 13, 1937 .... 275.00
Edwards, Green Parrot, London, 1743, 9 1/4 X 7 1/4 In. 287.50
Fiene, Dyckman Street Church, 1926, 11 X 15 1/4 In. 210.00
Fisher, Bachelor Belles, 11 X 13 In. 125.00
Fisher, Her Infinite Variety, C.1909, 20 X 14 In. 40.00
Fisher, Lady, Sniffing Rose, 11 X 13 In. 10.00
Fisher, Oh Promise Me, Oval Tin Gilt Frame, 6 3/4 X 8 3/4 In. 45.00
Fox, 1st Raising of Stars & Stripes At Valley Forge, 13 X 17 In. 150.00
Fox, Blossom Time, 23 X 15 In. 45.00
Fox, Dawn, 11 X 17 In. 25.00
Fox, Daydreams, 16 X 12 In. 85.00
Fox, Dreamland, 14 X 22 In. 85.00
Fox, Flower Balcony, Framed, 17 X 29 In. 50.00
Fox, Fountain of Love, Framed, Signed, 10 X 16 In. 35.00
Fox, Girl of Golden West, 6 X 8 In. 45.00
Fox, Glorious Vista, 18 X 30 In. 90.00
Fox, High Up In The Mountains, 17 X 21 In. 55.00
Fox, Indian Summer, 20 1/2 X 32 1/2 In. 95.00
Fox, Lakeside, Mountains, Trees, 19 X 15 In. 34.00
Fox, Land of Dreams, 17 X 14 In. 58.00
Fox, Love's Paradise, 18 X 30 In. 110.00
Fox, Love's Paradise, Lady, Reclining, Bear Rug, Child, 11 X 19 In. 45.00
Fox, Magic Pool, 12 1/2 X 17 1/2 In. 75.00
Fox, Mt. Hood, Nature's Sublime Grandeur, 16 X 20 In. 125.00
Fox, Old Home, Framed, Signed, 16 X 20 In. 55.00
Fox, Stately Sentinels, Framed, 14 X 22 In. 42.00
Fox, Sunny South, Framed, 10 X 16 In. 38.00
Fox, Sunset Dreams, 18 X 30 In. .... 110.00 To 195.00
Fox, Thatched Roof House & Garden, No.12, Framed, 16 X 20 In. 57.50
Freeman, Deep In Hollywood, 1936, 9 1/2 X 12 1/8 In. 150.00
Frost, Fore, Golfing, American, 1896, 9 1/2 X 14 In. 287.50
Frost, Hunters In Camp, Preparing Meal, C.1900, 9 X 13 In. 27.50
Gag, Spinning Wheel, 1927, 7 7/8 X 10 In. 210.00
Gardiner, Candy Apples, Woodblock, 9 5/8 X 10 In. 375.00
George Hayward, Fulton Ferry Boat, 4 1/2 X 6 1/2 In. 75.00
Gillray, Caledonians In Moneyland, Cartoon, 1762, 9 1/2 X 13 In. 127.50
Golinkin, Through The Ceiling, 1928, 23 1/2 X 18 1/4 In. 450.00
Green, Off To Dreamland, Baby, 9 1/2 X 12 In. 12.00
Grezer, Morning of The Benevolent Sportsman, 19 X 24 In. 192.00
Gutmann, A Little Bit of Heaven, 14 X 19 In. 75.00
Gutmann, Be Sociable, Oval, Framed, 9 X 5 In. 30.00
Gutmann, Child, Blond, 10 X 14 In. 35.00
Gutmann, Excuse My Back, Cupid, Framed, 9 X 5 In. 45.00
Gutmann, Friendly Enemies, 11 X 14 In. 48.00

Do not mount old maps, prints, etc., on cardboard. The acid in the cardboard causes stains. Use an all-rag board and visit an art store.

Excessive humidity will cause mold. Keep the humidity level between 45 and 55 percent.

Print, Japanese, Kuniyoshi, Botaro
& Mother, Lotus Ground

Although paper is acid, ink fades, and insects and light cause damage, it is still possible to preserve paper antiques. Keep paper dry, cool, and sealed away from oxygen and ultraviolet light. Mylar plastic bags are the best for storage. Important papers should be deacidified by an expert. Dirt and other damage can be repaired.

Gutmann, On The Up & Up, Baby, Puppy, Crawling, 10 X 14 In.	20.00
Gutmann, To Love & To Cherish, 14 X 17 In.	110.00
Hencke, Dutch Woman, Children, Art Deco, Pastel, 20 X 22 1/4 In.	45.00
Hogarth, Time of The Day & Night, Cartoon, 1738, 20 X 24 In.	385.00
Homer, On The Bluff At Long Branch, Harpers Weekly, Aug.6, 1870	45.00
Homer, Post Office Brooklyn Fair, Sanitary Comm., 1864, 10 X 14 In.	30.00
Humphrey, 7 Little Girls In Meadow, Signed, Dated 1889	150.00
Humphrey, Playing Bride, Calendar Page, Equitable Assurance, 1904	75.00
Humphrey, Playing School, Calendar Page, Equitable Assurance, 1904	75.00
Icart, Apache Dancer, Pencil Signed, 22 X 15 1/2 In.	1100.00
Icart, Ballerina With Roses	800.00
Icart, Flower Vendor	1800.00
Icart, Japanese Goldfish	975.00
Icart, La Lettre, C.1928	145.00
Icart, Lady, Irish Wolfhounds, Drypoint Etch, 17 X 21 In.	1300.00
Icart, Le Bonnet Bleu	450.00
Icart, Les Hortensias, Drypoint Etch, Windmill Seal, 9 X 11 1/2 In.	900.00
Icart, Sleeping Beauty, 1927, 19 1/2 X 15 1/2 In.	1760.00
Icart, Symphony In Blue, Pencil Signed, 25 X 21 In.	1500.00
Icart, Young Woman With Bird, Signed, 1929, Oval Mat, 23 1/2 X 28 In.	650.00
Jacoulet, Calm On Truk Island, 1941	2750.00
Jacoulet, Daughters of The Wild, 1957	1980.00
Jacoulet, Joruri Singer, 1936, 14 1/4 X 9 1/2 In.	1870.00
Jacoulet, Midnight Prayer, Mongolian Lama, 1959	1100.00

 Japanese prints are listed as follows: Print, Japanese, name of artist, title or description, type, and size. Dealers use the following terms: Tate-e is a vertical composition. Yoko-e is a horizontal composition. The words Aiban (13 by 9 inches), Chuban (10 by 7 1/2 inches), Hosoban (12 by 6 inches), Oban (15 by 10 inches), and Koban (7 by 4 inches) denote size.

Japanese, Foujita, Woman, Green Dress, Hand To Face, 12 X 7 In.	325.00

Japanese, Hasui, Bridge Over Edo River, 1932, 15 X 10 In. 300.00
Japanese, Hiroshige, Night Rain At Niehaka, 1830, 9 X 14 1/4 In. 225.00
Japanese, Hiroshige, Snow Scene, Kameido Temple, 12 1/2 X 8 1/2 In. 600.00
Japanese, Koitsu, Mt. Fuji At Sunset, 1938, 10 X 15 In. 225.00
Japanese, Kunichika, Bijine, 1880, Matted, 9 1/2 X 14 In. 65.00
Japanese, Kunisada, Samurai In Interior, 13 X 8 1/2 In. 120.00
Japanese, Kuniyoshi, Botaro & Mother, Lotus Ground ....*Illus* 302.50
Japanese, Miyashita, Okutama Autumn, 20 X 27 In. 750.00
Japanese, Rotagowa Utamara, 3 Popular Beauties, 10 X 14 In. 1540.00
Japanese, Sadanobu, Samurai On White Horse, 17 X 11 In. 135.00
Japanese, Shiro, Misty Evening, 1935, 15 X 10 In. 425.00
Japanese, Shoson, Iris Flowers, 1926, 15 X 10 In. 425.00
Japanese, Sino-Jap. Battle Scene, Tokyo, 1890, 14 3/4 X 21 3/8 In. 285.00
Japanese, Tekiho, 2 Rabbits, 10 X 16 In. 135.00
Japanese, Yoshida, Half Moon Bridge, 1941, 7 X 10 In. 125.00
Japanese, Yoshida, Hirosaki Castle, 1935, 15 X 10 In. 300.00
Japanese, Yoshida, Kurobe River, 1926, 15 X 11 In. 300.00
Kellar, Little Girl, Dolly Wants To Go To Bed, 1900, 10 X 6 1/2 In. 25.00
Kellogg, Drunkard's Progress, 1st Glass To Grave, Framed, 13 X 16 In. 175.00
Kenyon, Bluebird Series, Signed, 1940s 95.00
Landseer, Stag At Bay, Handcolored, Matted, C.1880, 13 X 20 In. 85.00
Lynn Bogue, Hunt Duck, 1917 .... 30.00
Mannings, H.R.H. Prince of Wales, On Forest Witch, 16 X 21 In. 170.00
Markham, The Fit Yourself Shop, 1935, 12 3/4 X 9 3/4 In. 625.00
Maude Tousey Fangel, Darling Baby, Signed 25.00
Moran, Homeward Herd, Cattle, 1891, 7 X 13 In. 85.00
Morris, Snowy Owl, London, 1840, 8 1/2 X 5 1/2 In. 47.50
Moss, Children, With Fish, Framed 90.00
Mucha, Gismonda, Framed, 1894, 84 1/2 X 28 3/4 In. 3500.00
Nast, Another Such Victory, Political Cartoon, 1876, 9 X 13 5/8 In. 127.50

Wallace Nutting is known for his pictures, furniture, and books.
Nutting "prints" are actually hand-colored photographs issued from
1900 to 1941. There are over 10,000 different titles.

Nutting, Across The Charles, 11 X 14 In. 105.00
Nutting, Affectionately Yours, 13 X 16 In. .... 120.00 To 121.00
Nutting, Barre Brook, 14 X 17 In. 60.00
Nutting, Blossom Tree, Path, Matted, Framed, 3 X 3 3/4 In. 35.00
Nutting, Brown Study, 11 X 17 In. 72.00
Nutting, Canopied Mirror, 9 X 7 In. 210.00
Nutting, Cappuchini Pergola, 8 X 10 In. 180.00
Nutting, Connecticut Blossom, Carved Gilt Frame, 11 X 17 In. 48.00
Nutting, Critical Examination, 6 1/2 X 6 1/2 In. 55.00
Nutting, Dutch Sails, 4 1/4 X 9 In. 105.00
Nutting, Great Wayside Oak, 7 1/2 X 9 1/2 In. 165.00
Nutting, Hesitancy, 13 X 16 In. 429.00
Nutting, Hollyhock Cottage, 13 X 16 In. 210.00
Nutting, Honeymoon Windings, 13 X 11 In. 35.00
Nutting, Into The Birchwood, Framed, 17 X 21 In. 125.00
Nutting, Into The West, 8 X 15 In. 45.00
Nutting, Joy Path, Path In Floral Garden, Framed, 11 X 9 In. 48.00
Nutting, Lady Reads Letter, Framed, 10 X 8 In. 90.00
Nutting, Little River, 11 X 14 In. 120.00
Nutting, Maine Coast Sky, 14 X 17 In. 440.00
Nutting, Maple Sugar Closet, 14 X 17 In. 143.00
Nutting, Maple Sugar Cupboard, 14 X 17 In. 187.00
Nutting, May In The Berkshires, 7 X 9 In. 135.00
Nutting, Mother's Day Card, 5 X 6 In. 82.50
Nutting, Old Drawing Room, 13 In. 90.00
Nutting, Old Newbury Corner, 14 X 17 In. 155.00
Nutting, Pasture Dell, 13 X 16 In. ....*Illus* 1182.00
Nutting, Pergola Amalfi, Framed, 11 X 12 In. 100.00
Nutting, Pilgrim Daughter, 17 X 14 In. 120.00
Nutting, Pine Landing, Rowboat On Lake Shore, Framed, 10 1/2 X 13 In. 55.00

Print, Nutting, The Way It Begins, 13 X 16 In.

Nutting, Pride of The Lane, 16 X 14 In.		32.50
Nutting, Primrose Cottage, 16 X 12 In.		175.00
Nutting, River In Maine, 10 X 12 In.		55.00
Nutting, Springfield Blossoms, 13 X 16 In.		45.00
Nutting, Swan Cove, 20 X 28 In.	*Illus*	825.00
Nutting, Swimming Pool, 17 X 13 In.		70.00
Nutting, The Warner Doorway, Architectural, 14 X 17 In.		50.00
Nutting, The Way It Begins, 13 X 16 In.	*Illus*	660.00
Nutting, Turning of The Flapjack, 7 X 9 In.		190.00
Nutting, Vines & Thatch, 4 X 6 1/2 In.		105.00

Print, Nutting, Pasture Dell, 13 X 16 In.

Print, Nutting, Swan Cove, 20 X 28 In.

Nutting, Vista of Amalfi, 10 X 12 In. .... 209.00 To 210.00
Nutting, Warm Spring Day, 6 1/2 X 13 In. 240.00
Nutting, Warm Spring Day, Grazing Sheep, Frame, 16 1/2 X 19 1/2 In. 120.00
Nutting, Water Scene, A Little Killarney Castle & Cover, 11 1/2 In. 115.00
Nutting, Way Through The Orchard, 7 1/4 X 9 1/4 In. 50.00
Nutting, Wealth of May, 14 X 17 In. 210.00
Nutting, Woman By Fireplace, 8 3/4 X 12 3/4 In. 60.00
Nutting, Yellow Pansies, 10 X 10 1/2 In. 20.00
O'Brien, The Bookmaker & The Bettor, 1903 .... 200.00

Maxfield Frederick Parrish was an illustrator who lived from 1870 to 1966. He is best known as a designer of magazine covers, posters, calendars, and advertisements. All Parrish prints are wanted by collectors.

Parrish, Air Castles, Framed, 11 X 15 In. 135.00
Parrish, Arabian Nights, 12 Color Plates, 1909 .... 115.00
Parrish, Canyon, Framed, 12 X 15 In. 95.00
Parrish, Canyon, Framed, 16 1/2 X 19 1/2 In. 175.00
Parrish, Christmas Ever, 11 X 11 1/2 In. 65.00
Parrish, Cleopatra, 12 X 13 3/4 In. 18.00
Parrish, Cleopatra, Small 450.00
Parrish, Daybreak, 12 1/2 X 20 In. 220.00
Parrish, Daybreak, Black & Gold Frame, 21 X 33 In. 250.00
Parrish, Dinky Bird, Framed, 11 X 15 In. 135.00
Parrish, Dream Garden, 7 1/2 X 19 1/2 In. 125.00
Parrish, Evening, 11 1/2 X 14 1/2 In. 245.00
Parrish, Florentine Fete, Framed 135.00
Parrish, Garden of Allah, Framed, Label, 18 X 33 1/2 In. 235.00
Parrish, Golden Hours, Large 550.00
Parrish, Lute Players, 18 X 30 In. 110.00
Parrish, Polly Put The Kettle On, 8 X 11 In. 40.00
Parrish, Prince, Framed, 11 X 13 In. 60.00
Parrish, Quiet Solitude, 14 X 11 In. 20.00
Parrish, Reveries, 14 X 18 In. 235.00
Parrish, Reveries, 14 X 20 1/2 In. 350.00
Parrish, Rubaiyat, Die Cut Corners, Framed, 10 X 32 In. 295.00
Parrish, Spirit of Transportation, Large 795.00
Parrish, Summer's Eve, 14 X 11 1/4 In. 10.00
Parrish, Temple Hills, 10 1/2 X 8 In. 85.00
Parrish, Thy Rocks & Rills, 14 X 11 1/4 In. 10.00
Parrish, Thy Templed Hills, 8 X 10 In. 95.00
Parrish, Top Reveries, Large 550.00
Parrish, Waterfall, 15 X 20 In. 225.00
Parrish, White Birch, 8 3/4 X 11 In. 35.00
Petty, Girl, Telephone, Glass of Beer, Acme Beer, Plastic Coated Paper 85.00
Prang, Home of Abraham Lincoln, 14 X 16 In. 70.00
Remington, Indian Trapper 250.00
Remington, Night Herd, Harpers Weekly, Matted, 1886 .... 125.00
Rockwell, Doctor & Doll, Signed, Framed, 30 3/4 X 36 3/4 In. 9500.00
Rockwell, Hayseed Critic, Framed 1500.00
Rockwell, Jazz It Up 1200.00
Rockwell, Top Hat & Tails, Framed, 34 X 28 In. 710.00
Roland, Mushrooms, Paris, 1850, 8 X 10 In. 48.50
Rowlandson, Dr. Syntax At Liverpool, Cartoon, 1891, 5 X 7 In. 47.50
Rowlandson, Dr. Syntax Scene, Framed, 10 1/2 X 7 1/2 In. 60.00
Rowlandson, Syntax Preaching, Colored, Trimmed, Framed, 7 1/2 X 11 In. 65.00
Smith, First Love, Girl, Doll & Mother, 1905, 7 X 10 In. 25.00
Sturgess, Neck & Neck, English Hunt, London, 1880, 13 1/2 X 9 1/2 In. 87.50
Vargas, Bat Woman, Pinup 35.00
Willett, Seminude Lady, Pond, Swans, Trees, 1925, 17 X 30 In. 44.00
Woodcut, Coronation King Kaluakua, Honolulu, 1881, 14 X 10 In. 150.00
Woodcut, Hawaiian Feast, C.1900, 10 X 7 In. 45.00
Woodcut, Political Crisis, Sandwich Islands, 1874, 14 X 10 In. 45.00
Woodcut, Port of Honolulu, Sandwich Islands, 1849, 7 X 10 In. 85.00

Woodcut, Volcanic Eruption, Mauna Loa, 1872, 10 1/2 X 9 In. 287.50

How to carry a handkerchief and lipstick is a problem today for every woman, including the Queen of England. The purse has been recognizable since the eighteenth century. Leather and needlework purses were preferred. Beaded purses became popular in the nineteenth century, went out of style, but are again in use. Mesh purses date from the 1880s and are still being made.

PURSE, Alligator, Glass Eyes	60.00
Alligator, With Baby Alligator, Suede Lining	25.00
Beaded, Black Velvet	20.00
Beaded, Black, Bottom Fringe, Small	27.50
Beaded, Black, Drawstring Bag	40.00
Beaded, Carpetbag	35.00
Beaded, Colored Florals, Black Beads, Embossed Frame & Clasp	75.00
Beaded, Diamond, Floral Pattern, Black, Green, Gold, Germany, 10 In. ...	100.00
Beaded, Horizontal Stripes, Looped Fringe, Black & Green, Lined, 8 In. ..	33.00
Beaded, Pearl & White, Rhinestones	18.00
Beaded, Point De Beauvais Flowers, Enamel Clasp, 5 X 8 In.	30.00
Beaded, Purple Carnival, Crocheted, With Tassel	40.00
Beaded, Steel, Hung On Belt	35.00
Beaded, White Daisies, Brass Filigree Top	45.00
Chain Handle, Place For Coins, Rouge, Mirror, German Silver	30.00
Crocheted, Ribbon Handle, Small	6.00
Cut Steel, Oriental Prayer Rug Pattern, Ormolu Frame, 1925	500.00
Cut Steel, Self Pattern, 6 X 6 In.	85.00
Drawstring, Amethyst Beaded, Tassels	35.00
Flame Stitch, Silver Clasp, Rose, Gold & Green, Sarah E. Pope, 5 In.	850.00
Gold, Engraved Strapwork, Man, Pushing Lady On Swing, 1860, 3 3/4 In. ..	880.00
Leather, Sterling Silver Corners, Griffin Watch Corner	150.00
Leopard Skin, With Pillbox Hat	60.00
Mesh, 18k Gold, Cabochon Sapphire Clasp, Art Deco	990.00
Mesh, Birds, Chain Handle	45.00
Mesh, Evening, Mirror In Lid, Ruffled Bottom, Whiting & Davis	75.00
Mesh, Geometric Design, Signed, Mandalian, 4 1/4 X 7 1/4 In.	70.00
Mesh, Gun Metal, Floral Frame, Black, 6 X 4 1/4 In.	40.00
Mesh, Peacocks, Floral, Fringed	70.00
Mesh, Tan & White, Mandalian	65.00
Mesh, Turquoise & Pink, Mandalian, Scrolled Clasp, Chain Handle	60.00
Miser's, Crocheted Black, Cut Steel Beading	35.00
Mother–of–Pearl, 1893 Columbian Expo, Metal Corners, Bldg. Transfer ..	45.00
Needlepoint, Floral, 11 X 16 In.	25.00
Ostrich Feather, Corset, Red	45.00
Plastic, Clutch, Clear, Rhinestones	8.00
Plastic, Gold, Hinged Lid With Mirror, Wilardy, 5 X 10 3/8 In.	10.00
Silk, Schoolgirl's, Watercolor Paper Ends, 1812	1430.00
Silver, Engraved Design, English, Chester Hall, 1896, 4 X 3 In.	66.00
Snakeskin Design, Black & White Pouch	30.00
Sterling Silver, Attached Compact On Handle, Sapphire Clasp, Bliss	175.00
Sterling Silver, Russian, Klebnikov	550.00

Quezal　Quezal glass was made from 1901 to 1920 by Martin Bach, Sr., in Brooklyn, New York. Other glassware by other firms, such as Loetz, Steuben, and Tiffany, resembles this gold–colored iridescent glass. After Martin Bach's death in 1920, his son continued the manufacture of a similar glass under the name "Lustre Art Glass."

QUEZAL, Bowl, Flower, Feather Design, Opal Body, 4 In.	475.00
Ceiling Fixture, 2–Light, Enamel & Gold Iridescent, Signed	600.00
Ceiling Fixture, Center Globe, 3 Small Shades, Bronze, Signed	6000.00
Lamp, 3 Colors, 25 In.	6500.00
Salt, Gold Luster, Signed, 2 1/2 In.	100.00
Shade, Bell Shape, White Drag Loops, Gold Border, 6 3/4 In., Pair	350.00
Shade, Calcite Ribbed Exterior, Opal Interior, 6 In., Pair	475.00
Shade, Calcite, Gold Lined, Signed, 4 3/4 X 6 In.	135.00

Shade, Gold Aurene Inside & Out, 10 Spiral Ribs 135.00
Shade, Gold Iridescent Inside, Outside, Random Threading, 9 1/4 In. 650.00
Shade, Gold Lily, Ribbed, Signed, Pair 135.00
Shade, Green Feather, Gold Body, 5 In., Pair 650.00
Shade, Green Iridescent Leaves, Gold Threading, 5 Piece 950.00
Shade, Green Leaves, Gold Threading, White Pearlized, Set of 4 .... 400.00
Shade, Iridescent Gold Interior, Tulip Form, 4 X 5 In. 125.00
Shade, Iridescent Gold, Ribbed, Bell Shape, 5 1/2 In., Pair 120.00
Shade, King Tut, Gold, Signed, 3 1/4 In. .... 195.00 To 225.00
Shade, Leaf & Vine, Gold Lining, Baluster Shape, Signed, Pair 245.00
Shade, Pulled Feather Design, Green, Gold Interior, 5 1/2 In., Pair 320.00
Shade, Pulled Feather, Ribbed, Iridescent Gold, 15 1/2 In. 900.00
Shade, Pulled Feathers On Calcite, Gold Interior, Signed, 6 In., Pair 290.00
Shade, Ribbed Swirls, Iridescent Gold, Signed 100.00
Shade, Ruffled Stretch Edge, Gold, 3 1/2 X 6 In., 4 Piece 500.00
Shade, Snakeskin On Gold Upper Half, Green Snakeskin Border 185.00
Shade, Tulip, Gold Aurene, 5 In. 135.00
Tumbler, Dimpled At Base, Iridescent Gold, Signed, 4 1/2 In. 185.00
Vase, 3-Footed, Iridescent, Signed, 6 In. 625.00
Vase, Dark Blue Luster, Signed, 8 In. 350.00
Vase, Deep Ocher & Mustard, Silver Deposit, 1905-20, 5 3/4 In. 1540.00
Vase, Feathered Green, Gold, Opalescent, Bulbous, Signed, 7 In. 975.00
Vase, Jack-In-The-Pulpit, Gold Face, Pulled Feathers, Signed, 13 In. 3250.00
Vase, Peacock, Iridescent, Green Ground, Signed, 6 1/2 In. 550.00
Vase, Pulled Feathers Outlined In Gold, Signed, 11 1/2 In. 1150.00
Vase, Trumpet, Green Pulled Feather, Gold Overlay Design, 7 1/4 In. 1200.00

 Quilts have been made since the seventeenth century. Early textiles were very precious and every scrap was saved to be reused. A quilt is a combination of fabrics joined to a filler and a backing by small stitched designs known as quilting. An appliqued quilt has pieces stitched to the top of a large piece of background fabric. A patchwork, or pieced, quilt is made of many small pieces stitched together. Embroidery can be added to either type.

QUILT, Appliqued & Patchwork, Basket, Green & Red Calico, White, 76 X 89 In. 1300.00
Appliqued, 4 Oak Leaf Pinwheels, Scalloped Swag, 78 X 90 In. 750.00
Appliqued, Amish, Diamond In Square, 1930, Crib 850.00
Appliqued, Broderie Perse, Leafy Trees, Patchwork Border, 96 X 96 In. 5500.00
Appliqued, Cathedral Window, 104 X 108 .... 475.00
Appliqued, Cock's Comb, Swag & Flower Border, 88 X 90 In. 300.00
Appliqued, Double Wedding Ring, Cream, Lavender Border, 58 X 74 In. 100.00
Appliqued, Double Wedding Ring, Scalloped Edge, 72 X 90 In. 325.00
Appliqued, Floral Design, Red, Green Calico, Blue Chintz, 68 X 80 In. 70.00
Appliqued, Floral, Red, Pink, Green, White Ground, 1920s, Double Bed 850.00
Appliqued, Floral, Swag Border, Tulips, White Ground, 90 X 96 In. 1300.00
Appliqued, Lone Star, Blues & Grays, White Ground, 72 X 86 In. 525.00
Appliqued, Love Apple, Pumpkin Vine Border, C.1855, 84 X 88 In. 2475.00
Appliqued, Old Maid's Puzzle, Lavender, Pink, Dated 1940, 80 X 81 In. 70.00
Appliqued, Pinwheel & Star, Tulips, Scalloped Leaves, 88 X 90 In. 1430.00
Appliqued, Pinwheel, Green, White, Nursery Rhymes, 1927, Double Bed 325.00
Appliqued, Princess Feather, Swag & Tassel Border, 96 X 98 In. 1100.00
Appliqued, Red & Ecru Flowers, White Ground, 1900, 75 X 79 In. 350.00
Appliqued, Rose of Sharon, Radiating Oak Leaves, 84 X 83 In. 650.00
Appliqued, Stylized Flowers, Diamond Shaped Squares, 72 X 86 In. 325.00
Appliqued, Sun, Orange & Red, C.1870, 87 X 88 In. 695.00
Appliqued, Trip Around The World, Penna., 1900, Double Bed 295.00
Appliqued, Tulip Design, Lancaster County, C.1860, 80 X 80 In. 700.00
Patchwork, Album Block, Reds, Blues, Greens, 68 X 90 In. 100.00
Patchwork, Amish, Trip Around The World, Crib ...:....................................... 895.00
Patchwork, Baskets, Red & Blue, White Ground, C.1800, 82 X 82 In. 300.00
Patchwork, Blazing Star, 49 X 80 In. 100.00
Patchwork, Blue, Yellow & Red, Crib 105.00
Patchwork, Bold Stylized Design, Flowers, Blue, Red, Green, 84 X 88 In. 130.00
Patchwork, Bowtie, Multicolored, 69 X 80 In. 350.00

Patchwork, Broken Star, White & Solid Colors, 76 X 96 In.	275.00
Patchwork, Checkerboard, Alphabet, Green, White, 60 X 76 In.	150.00
Patchwork, Compass Stars, Calico, Pink On White, 72 X 82 In.	350.00
Patchwork, Compass Stars, White Ground, 76 X 88 In.	125.00
Patchwork, Complex T, T's At An Angle, Pennsylvania, 89 X 78 In.	450.00
Patchwork, Complex T, Wayne County, N.Y., 1860, 89 X 78 In.	450.00
Patchwork, Crazy, 11 Blocks, Fringed, 71 X 69 In.	350.00
Patchwork, Crazy, 19th Century, Crib	190.00
Patchwork, Crazy, Fringed, Dated 1884, 69 X 71 In.	600.00
Patchwork, Crazy, Satin & Black, 17 1/2 X 19 In.	350.00
Patchwork, Crazy, Silk, 92 X 78 In.	200.00
Patchwork, Cross & Crown, White Ground, C.1930, 78 X 92 In.	850.00
Patchwork, Dahlia, Stuffed Center Petals, 77 X 92 In.	165.00
Patchwork, Double Irish Chain, Brown & Blue On Cream, 84 X 102 In.	400.00
Patchwork, Double Wedding Ring, Blue Centers, 65 X 89 In.	395.00
Patchwork, Double Wedding Ring, Multicolored, 72 X 76 In.	250.00
Patchwork, Dresden Plate, 88 X 105 In.	425.00
Patchwork, Drunkard's Patch, 58 X 79 In.	165.00
Patchwork, Fan, Yellow, 55 X 68 In.	150.00
Patchwork, Farmer Boy & Girl, Pink & White, 58 X 74 In.	100.00
Patchwork, Flower & Garden, 102 X 88 In.	450.00
Patchwork, Friendship, Browns, Reds, 69 X 87 In.	167.00
Patchwork, Geometric Squares, Green Ground, 64 X 74 In.	150.00
Patchwork, Grandmother's Fan, 85 X 88 In.	350.00
Patchwork, Grandmother's Flower Garden, Multicolored, 72 X 84 In.	145.00
Patchwork, Grandmother's Flower Garden, Scalloped, 72 X 88 In.	235.00
Patchwork, Graphic, Blue & White, 3560 Pieces, 92 X 78 In.	225.00
Patchwork, Gray Plaid Hexagon, Knotted, 1930–40, 74 X 48 In.	45.00
Patchwork, Hexagonal Medallions, 70 X 90 In.	350.00
Patchwork, Irish Chain, 4 Part Medallions, 76 X 90 In.	300.00
Patchwork, Irish Chain, Blue & White, 67 X 78 In.	100.00
Patchwork, Irish Chain, Pink, White Calico, 66 X 72 In.	165.00
Patchwork, Irish Chain, Red & White, 68 X 79 In.	180.00
Patchwork, Kittens In Baskets, 56 X 88 In.	300.00
Patchwork, Log Cabin, Red Calico & White, Crib, 28 X 40 In.	295.00
Patchwork, Lone Star, 67 X 86 In.	90.00
Patchwork, Lone Star, Blue & White, 74 X 74 In.	475.00
Patchwork, Lone Star, White Ground, 72 X 82 In.	350.00
Patchwork, Monkey Wrench, Red, 65 X 72 In.	100.00
Patchwork, Monkey Wrench, Red, Blue, Calico, 1910, 78 X 80 In.	250.00
Patchwork, Nine Patch, Brown, Red, Printed Border, 74 X 88 In.	225.00
Patchwork, Nine Patch, Red & Blue, 72 X 74 In.	125.00
Patchwork, Nine Patch, Red, Yellow, Green & Blue Calico, 78 X 96 In.	495.00
Patchwork, Octagon Block, Multicolored, 64 X 74 In.	85.00
Patchwork, Picket Fence, 69 1/2 X 68 1/2 In.	237.50
Patchwork, Pineapple, Red & White, Crib, 31 1/2 X 37 In.	375.00
Patchwork, Pinwheel & Stars, 68 X 86 In.	110.00
Patchwork, Pinwheels, 775 Pieces, 70 X 80 In.	1200.00
Patchwork, Pinwheels, Album, Autographed Pieces, C.1851, 84 X 86 In.	375.00
Patchwork, Pinwheels, Pink Calico, White Ground, 70 X 72 In.	95.00
Patchwork, Poinsettias & Bows, All White, 90 X 108 In.	350.00
Patchwork, Postage Stamp, 1940s, 72 X 82 In.	150.00
Patchwork, Postage Stamp, Irish Linen, 1935–37, 106 X 89 In.	850.00
Patchwork, Postage Stamp, Red Border, Crib	195.00
Patchwork, Rob Peter & Pay Paul, Green & White, 1930s, 76 X 84 In.	300.00
Patchwork, Rocky Road To Kansas, Mauve, 72 X 80 In.	185.00
Patchwork, Rolling Star, Brown & Beige, 100 X 104 In.	275.00
Patchwork, Rose Dream, White & Pink, 74 X 77 In.	250.00
Patchwork, Rose of Sharon, 1920s, 74 X 72 In.	785.00
Patchwork, Schoolhouse, Multicolored Calico Houses, 78 X 72 In.	895.00
Patchwork, Seven Stars, Octagon Patches, 72 X 82 In.	210.00
Patchwork, Star, Chintz, 90 X 112 In.	150.00
Patchwork, Star, Gold, 68 X 82 In.	175.00
Patchwork, Star, Red, White & Blue, 1885, 68 X 72 In.	145.00

Patchwork, Star, Reds & Browns, 80 X 92 In.	65.00
Patchwork, Sunbonnet Sue, 68 X 92 In.	325.00
Patchwork, Sunburst & Flying Geese, 20th Century, 58 X 72 In.	400.00
Patchwork, Sunburst, Red & Yellow, C.1900, Square, 94 In.	375.00
Patchwork, Thousand Pyramids, Red & White, 64 X 76 In.	175.00
Patchwork, Tobacco Flannels, 75 X 80 In.	150.00
Patchwork, Triple Irish Chain, Signed & Dated 1876, 90 X 96 In.	1695.00
Patchwork, Wedding Ring, Colored Prints, 82 X 82 In.	345.00
Patchwork, Wedding Ring, Peach, 82 X 66 In.	175.00
Patchwork, Windmill, Golds & Pinks, 72 X 82 In.	165.00
Patchwork, Yellow & Green Calico, 80 X 80 In.	275.00

H.R.
Quimper

Tin–glazed, hand–painted pottery has been made in Quimper, France, since the late seventeenth century. The earliest firm, founded in 1685 by Jean Baptiste Bousquet, was known as HB Quimper. Another firm, founded in 1772 by Francois Eloury, was known as Porquier. The third firm, founded by Guillaume Dumaine in 1778, was known as HR or Henriot Quimper. All three firms made similar pottery decorated with designs of Breton peasants and sea and flower motifs. The Eloury (Porquier) and Dumaine (Henriot) firms merged in 1913. Bousquet (HB) merged with the others in 1968. The group was sold to a United States family in 1984. The American holding company is Quimper Faience Inc., located in Stonington, Connecticut. The French firm has been called Societe Nouvelle des Faienceries de Quimper HB Henriot since March 1984.

QUIMPER, Bookends, Seated Girl, Seated Boy, Signed, 7 1/2 In.	230.00
Bowl, Boy With Black Hat, Striped Pants, 3 X 6 1/2 In.	50.00
Box, Sardine, Woman With Sprays On Cover, 4 1/2 X 3 1/2 In.	235.00
Bust, French Peasant Woman, Chardson, 14 In.	895.00
Candlestick, Floral Sprays On Stem, Blue Candle Cup, 9 1/2 In.	115.00
Centerpiece, Floral Reserves, Signed, 16 X 8 In.	150.00
Chamberstick, Leaf–Shaped Handle	125.00
Chamberstick, Woman, Green Bodice, Apron, Handle, 3/4 X 6 In.	215.00
Charger, Shell & Seawood Edge, 2 Women & Sailor, 1920s, 15 1/2 In.	600.00
Charger, Woman In Rose–Colored Skirt, Scalloped, 15 1/2 In.	75.00
Compote, Peacock, Cobalt Blue, Off–White Ground, Marked, 9 X 4 In.	80.00
Cup & Saucer, Chocolate, Breton Border	50.00
Cup & Saucer, Woman In Orange Blouse, Man, Demitasse, Pair	160.00
Dish, Woman With Bouquet, Swan Finial, Cobalt Blue Design	165.00
Eggcup, Attached Plate, Boy & Girl	50.00
Eggcup, Rose Florals, Scalloped, Yellow Band, 2 1/2 In.	26.00
Figurine, Dancing Couple, 10 In.	250.00
Figurine, Girl, Hands Behind Back, Blue Skirt, Shawl, 9 3/4 In.	70.00
Figurine, Platter, Peasants, Yellow Ground, 14 1/2 In.	175.00
Figurine, Sailor Carrying Child & Bag, 4 3/8 In.	90.00
Group, Dancers, Man & 2 Women, Folk Dancing, 18 X 21 In.	450.00
Inkwell, Knobbed Lid, Woman With Flower, 3 1/4 X 5 1/2 In.	245.00
Jar, Ginger, Cover, Peacocks & Flowers, 16 1/2 In.	700.00
Jardiniere, Breton Couple, Bows On Handles, Signed, 13 In.	1800.00
Jardiniere, Swan Shape, Woman Seated On Rock, Signed, 8 X 11 In.	600.00
Keg, Wooden Stand, With 4 Small Cups, Henriot, 5 In.	175.00
Lamp, Bust of Woman, Wooden Base, 16 X 16 3/4 In.	80.00
Mirror, Garlands of Flowers, Woman & Man, 18 X 16 In.	1900.00
Oyster Plate, 7 Wells, 9 1/4 In.	98.00
Pitcher, Yellow, Henriot, Marked, 9 In.	200.00
Plaque, Peasant, Crescent, 9 In.	65.00
Plate, Baskets of Flowers, Rose Sponge Border, 6 3/4 In., Pair	70.00
Plate, Calendar, 1981	40.00
Plate, Fish Shape, Marked Henriot Quimper	175.00
Plate, Fish Shape, Peasant Reserve	175.00
Plate, Line Drawing of Young Women, Cream Ground, C.1950, 9 In.	20.00
Plate, Man In Pantaloons, Woman, Sprays of Flowers, 8 In., Pair	120.00
Plate, Peasant Man & Woman, 8 1/4 In., Pair	95.00
Plate, Yellow, Henriot, Mark, 11 In.	85.00

Platter, Fish, Yellow Ground, Hand Painted, 24 In.	175.00
Platter, French Peasant Man & Woman, Odetta Line	185.00
Platter, Sprays Circle Tray, Figures Inside, Signed, 9 X 15 3/8 In.	750.00
Platter, Yellow Border, Blue Stripes, Floral Logo Trim, 16 X 11 In.	225.00
Porringer, Underplate	32.00
Pot, Mustard Lines, Blue Spongeware Border, Handles, 2 X 1 In.	26.00
Relish Tray, Fisherman, Separate Butter Tub, Henriot, 15 In.	250.00
Salt Cellar, Double Baskets, Peasant Man	39.00
Salt Cellar, Peasant, Spatter Trim, 5 1/2 In.	48.00
Salt, Basket, Double Cup	40.00
Teapot, Musician Playing Pipe, Gold Bands On Hat, 8 1/4 In.	110.00
Teapot, Sprigs of Flowers, Lady, Gentleman, Scalloped, 7 1/2 In.	750.00
Tray, Man & Woman, Foliage, Scalloped, 17 X 14 In.	235.00
Tureen, Floral Sprays, Women On Cover, 6 1/2 X 9 In.	145.00
Tureen, Tray, Blue Sponge, 9 1/2 X 13 3/4 In.	450.00
Vase, Art Deco Women, Squat, 9 1/2 In.	145.00
Vase, Fan, Woman, Yellow Apron, Flowers, 4 3/4 X 7 3/4 In.	475.00
Vase, Floral Sprays, Man, Woman, 6 1/2 In., Pair	195.00
Vase, Head of Peasant Girl, Flower On Reverse, 10 In.	40.00
Vase, Man In Hat, Streamers, Cocoa Ground, 9 3/4 X 6 In.	160.00
Wine Taster, Spatter Handles, Inner Stripes, 3 1/8 In.	40.00

RADURA. Radford pottery was made by Alfred Radford in Broadway, Virginia, Tiffin and Zanesville, Ohio, and Clarksburg, West Virginia, from 1891 until 1912. Jasperware, Ruko, Thera, Radera, and Velvety Art Ware were made. The jasperware resembles the famous Wedgwood ware of the same name.

RADFORD, Vase, Lincoln & Eagle Cameos, 7 In.	395.00

The first radio broadcast receiving sets were sold in New York City in 1910. They were used to pick up the experimental broadcasts of the day. The first commercial radios were made by Westinghouse Company for listeners of the experimental shows on KDKA Pittsburgh in 1920. Collectors today are interested in all early radios, especially those made of Bakelite plastic or decorated with blue mirrors.

RADIO, AC Sparkplug	75.00
Arvin, Chrome	150.00 To 225.00
Arvin, White Metal Cabinet, Small	45.00
Arvin, Yellow & Turquoise Bakelite	600.00
Atwater Kent, Black & Silver Metal, Separate Speaker	650.00
Atwater Kent, Breadboard Type, Original Tubes & Speaker	750.00
Atwater Kent, Model 12, Breadboard Type, 1923	450.00
Atwater Kent, Model 30	100.00
B.F. Goodrich, Mantola, Wooden	25.00
Baseball Shape	475.00
Bendix, 2–Colored, Catalin	525.00
Bendix, Model 55LQU, Cream & Red	45.00
Bendix, Plastic, Chartreuse	75.00
Big Bird	22.00
Bosch, Wooden, Battery	45.00
Capehart, Phonograph, Changes & Plays 20 Record Stack, C.1937	500.00
Catalin, FADA 1000	650.00
Chief, Cannon Co., Earphones	12.00
Crosley Musical Chef, Built–In Kitchen Timer	35.00
Crosley Pup Regenerative Receiver	200.00
Crosley, Cathedral, Green Dial	175.00
Crosley, Model 124, Playtime Grandfather Clock, 1931	375.00
Crosley, Tombstone	65.00 To 85.00
Crosley, Tube Type, Portable, AC/DC, Wooden Case, 10 X 13 In.	40.00
Delco, Auto, Slide–Out, Transportable	35.00
Delco, Transportable, Car, Removable	45.00
DeWald, Marbelized, 1930s, Miniature	450.00
Emerson, Catalin, Brown & White Bakelite	175.00

Emerson, Model 520, Art Deco 275.00
Emerson, Trav–Ler, Brown Bakelite 10.00
Emerson, U.S.Signal Corp, Walkie–Talkie, 13 Tubes 50.00
Fada, Bullet, Yellow 625.00
Fada, Model 652, Red & Yellow 725.00
Fada, No.170T, Tombstone 100.00
Federal, Crystal Set 250.00
Firestone, Horizontal Wood Cabinet, 1940 .... 65.00
Garod, Art Deco, Brown Bakelite 18.00
General Electric, White Plastic, Late 1950s, Box 35.00
Getty Gas Pump, Box 30.00
Gilfillan, Art Deco, Ivory Bakelite 35.00
Granco, UHF Converter, Red, Yellow Dial 30.00
Grebe, Synchrophase Seven, Battery, 22 X 13 X 11 In. 100.00
Hospix, Television, Bedside, Early 1950s 55.00
Kellogg, Series 1000, Art Deco, Brown Bakelite, Chrome Dial 65.00
Knight's Helmet 35.00
Lear, Model 6615, Table, Wooden 50.00
Majestic, Chrome Front, Cathedral Type 225.00
Majestic, Model 90–B, Console 200.00
Mitchell, AM–FM 30.00
Mitchell, Rocketship, With Lamp, Bakelite, White Paint 85.00
Mork's Eggship, Box 18.00
Motorola, Bakelite, Red & Black 2800.00
Motorola, Catalin, Red & Black 2500.00
Motorola, Portable, 4 Tube, Metal, Model 5A7A 35.00
Peerless Reproducer, Model A–77707 .... 30.00
Peter Pan, Cathedral 300.00
Philco, Art Deco, With Phonograph, 1930s 22.00
Philco, Console, Oak Cabinet, 3 Band 10.00
Philco, Model 49–900, Bakelite 35.00
Philco, No.551, 1928 .... 160.00
Philco, Scantenna, AC/DC Battery, Pink, 1960s 25.00
Philco, Transitone 40.00
Philco, Twin Speaker, Bakelite 30.00
Philmore, Crystal Set, Box 22.50
Pioneer, Rocketship Shape, Crystal, Earphones, Brochure, 1940s 60.00
Raggedy Ann & Andy 20.00
RCA, No.4T, Cathedral 100.00
RCA, Radiola No.18, Speaker 240.00
RCA, Radiola No.20, 1925 .... 140.00
RCA, Shortwave 18.00
Sears & Roebuck, AM & FM, Wooden Case 25.00
Sentinel, No, 1U352–2, Red, Orange Knobs, 1950s 85.00
Shapleigh, Model 817, Battery, Cone Speaker 250.00
Silvertone, Gold Front, Brown 20.00
Silvertone, Sears, Oval, Deco 65.00
Skelco 20.00
Sonora, Model RCU208, Wooden, Table 25.00
Spark Plug, Novelty 75.00
Spiderman, Box 15.00
Spidola, 2 Colors, Russian 150.00
Stewart & Warner, Super Hetehodyne, Floor Model, Walnut Cabinet 250.00
Super Zenith, Transoceanic 78.00
Texaco Car Battery Shape, Battery, Original Box, 4 In. 10.00
Texaco Havoline Oil Can, Battery, 5 In. 10.00
Trutone, Table Model, Wooden Case, 12 X 20 In. 35.00
Westinghouse, Grandfather Clock, Art Deco .... 135.00 To 275.00
Westinghouse, Model H–600P4, Portable, Electric, Yellow, White 75.00
White, Air King Skyscraper 1650.00
Zenith Transoceanic, Model 8g995YT 78.00
Zenith, Art Deco, Lime Green 195.00
Zenith, Cloth Grill, Wood Cabinet Table, AM–FM 55.00
Zenith, Consol–Tone 15.00

Zenith, Holiday, Burgundy, Model 5g003Z	80.00
Zenith, Magic Eye, Floor Model, 1937	350.00
Zenith, Portable Shortwave	60.00
Zenith, Table, Battery Operated, 22 In.	75.00

Railroad enthusiasts collect any train memorabilia. Everything is wanted, from oilcans to whole train cars. The Chessie system has a store that sells many reproductions of their old dinnerware and uniforms.

RAILROAD, Air Horn, Locomotive	85.00
Ashtray, Chessie	40.00
Ashtray, Santa Fe, Super Chief, Glass	10.00
Badge, Cap, C.B.& Q.R.R.	40.00
Badge, Cap, I.C.R.R.	40.00
Badge, Cap, No.3, M.C.R.R., Baggage Master	45.00
Badge, Police, Illinois Central R.R., 5–Pointed Star, Nickel	60.00
Bell, 12–In. Apron, Brass, Cast Iron Yoke, 1880	750.00
Bell, 14–In. Apron, Cast Iron Yoke, 1890	1500.00
Bell, Crossing, 12 In.	150.00
Bell, Diesel, Brass	225.00 To 250.00
Bell, Locomotive, Brass	450.00
Bell, Train, Brass	250.00
Bond Certificate, New Orleans, Baton Rouge, Vicksburg Const., 1869	45.00
Book, C. & N.W. R.R., What I Saw At Chicago World's Fair	15.00
Booklet, Norfolk & Western, Souvenir Book of Virginia, 1960	15.00
Bottle, Milk, Missouri–Pacific, 1/2 Pt.	18.00 To 21.00
Bowl, Norfolk & Western, Dogwood, 4 1/2 In.	20.00
Bowl, Norfolk & Western, Dogwood, 6 1/2 In.	20.00
Bowl, Northern Pacific, Monad, 4 1/2 In.	45.00
Bowl, Santa Fe, California Poppy, 5 1/2 In.	27.00
Bowl, Yellow Bird, Norfolk & Western, White, Floral, Syracuse, 5 In.	85.00
Box, First Aid, Metal, C & O	20.00
Butter Chip, Atlantic Coast Line R.R., Carolina, 3 1/2 In.	15.00
Butter Chip, Baltimore & Ohio, Marked, 3 1/2 In.	42.00
Calendar, 1932, Santa Fe Railroad, Complete	45.00
Calendar, 1961, Santa Fe R.R., Indian Silversmith Picture	20.00
Calendar, Perpetual, Diesel, Missouri Pacific	125.00
Car, Post Office, Santa Fe, Fixtures, Rails, 1927	9950.00
Cup & Saucer, Baltimore & Ohio, Blue, 1927	95.00
Cup & Saucer, Union Pacific, Challenger	60.00
Cup & Saucer, Wabash	200.00
Cup, Norfolk & Western, Dogwood	30.00
Cup, Santa Fe, Violet & Daisy	35.00
Dish, Wabash, 4 1/2 In.	50.00
Finger Bowl, Northern Pacific, Silver	50.00
Fire Extinguisher, C.M.St.P. & R.Ry	48.00
Globe, CMSTP & O, 1895	325.00
Globe, Lantern, Red, Etched SALRY, 3 1/4 In.	10.00
Gravy Boat, Santa Fe, Egyptian Design, Fish Either Side	55.00
Hard Hat, C & O	20.00
Hat & Jacket, Pullman Conductor, 2 Piece	66.00
Ice Cream Shell, New York Central Lines, Limoges	20.00
Knife, C & O, Pocket	12.00
Lamp, Angle Lamp Co., 2 Hand Blown Shades, 1850s	675.00
Lamp, Caboose, N & W, Signed	90.00
Lamp, Switch, I.C.R.R., Red & Green Lens, Adlake, 16 In.	100.00
Lantern, Adams & Westlake Co., Kerosene	65.00
Lantern, Adlake No.300, Fount, With Burner	11.50
Lantern, Adlake, E.J. & E., Bell Bottom, Clear Globe	300.00
Lantern, Adlake, Red Glass, C & O	50.00
Lantern, B & O, 3 In. Clear Globe, 9 In.	85.00
Lantern, B.R. & P., Red Globe, Red Letters	235.00
Lantern, Boston & Maine, Red Globe	55.00
Lantern, Brakeman's, New York Central R.R.	55.00

Lantern, Brakeman's, Rock Island, Logo, Clear Globe, 3 1/2 In.	30.00
Lantern, C.M.St.P., Brass Top, Bell Bottom, Red Cast	195.00
Lantern, Caboose, Santa Fe, Pair	300.00
Lantern, Conductor's, Green Over Clear, 5 1/2 In.	550.00
Lantern, Conductor's, Onion Top Type	525.00
Lantern, Conductor's, Tall Globe, Bell Bottom, Nickel Over Brass	250.00
Lantern, Denver Trolley, Red Globe, Yellow	40.00
Lantern, Dietz 25, Mercury Reflector, Tin, 15 1/4 In.	35.00
Lantern, Dietz Acme Inspector Lamp, Erie, Tin, 14 1/4 In.	25.00
Lantern, Dietz, KCT Ry., Blue Globe, Marked, 5 1/2 In.	225.00
Lantern, Dietz, N.Y.N.H. R.R., Embossed Globe	60.00
Lantern, Missouri Pacific, Tall Globe	65.00
Lantern, N.Y.C. R.R., Dated 1911	52.00
Lantern, Santa Fe, Clear Globe, Marked Base	200.00
Lantern, Santa Fe, Clear Globe, Pat.1878, No Burner	185.00
Lantern, Square Tin Case, Smoke Shield, Handle, Hanging Socket	200.00
Lantern, Switch, Red & Blue Lenses	90.00
Lantern, Texas & Pacific Reliable	85.00
Lantern, Tin Bottom & Top, Brass Cap, Wire Bail & Cage, C.1860	100.00
Lantern, Twin Tube, Tin, Brass Cap, 11 1/2 In.	85.00
Lantern, Wabash R.R., Red Embossed Logo, Dated 1902	245.00
Ledger, Wheeling & Lake Erie R.R., Sept. To Dec. 1908	24.50
Lock, B & O R.R., Heart Shape, Bronze	40.00
Lock, B & O R.R., Signal, Yale Type, Key	20.00
Menu, Santa Fe Railroad, 1966	6.00
Mirror, New York Central System, Train, 2 X 3 In.	1.50
Mug, Denver & Rio Grande R.R., Graniteware, Cobalt Blue, White	130.00
Mustard, New York Central	27.50
Napkin, Burlington Route, Logo In Center Square	12.50
Napkin, California Zephyr, Center Logo	12.50
Napkin, Illinois Central R.R., Center Logo, 19 X 19 In.	12.50
Napkin, Illinois Central, Diamond Logo, White Linen, 19 X 19 In.	7.50
Napkin, Milwaukee Road Embossed, White Damask	12.00
Oil Can, Locomotive, Copper, 1860–80, Large	45.00
Ornament, Indian Chief, Silhouette, Headdress, Iron, 23 X 16 In.	1540.00
Pass, Annual, Missouri Pacific Railway Co., Dated 1887, 4 1/2 In.	10.00
Pin, Freedom Train, Common Heritage, 1940s, 1 1/4 In.	5.00
Pin, Great Northern Railway, Outing, Ribbons, 1915, 1 3/4 In.	12.00
Pitcher, Cereal Cream, Baltimore & Ohio	55.00
Plate, 1938, Centennial, Norfolk & Western	800.00
Plate, GM & O Logo, Rose Pattern, 6 1/2 In.	40.00
Plate, Missouri Pacific, State Flowers & Locomotive	250.00
Plate, Mo–Pac., Steam Train Center, State Flowers, 10 1/2 In.	195.00
Plate, Norfolk & Western, Centennial, 1938	800.00
Plate, Norfolk & Western, Dogwood, 10 1/4 In.	35.00
Plate, Pacific Lines, States Around Edge, 10 1/2 In.	75.00
Plate, Pennsylvania R.R., Broadway, 6 1/2 In.	30.00
Plate, Santa Fe, California Poppy, 7 1/2 In.	33.00
Plate, Santa Fe, California Poppy, 10 In.	33.00
Plate, Southern Pacific Lines, Wildflower, 9 1/2 In.	25.00
Plate, Southern Pacific, Prairie Mountain Wildflower, 10 1/4 In.	75.00
Plate, Union Pacific, Challenger, 6 1/2 In.	30.00
Plate, Union Pacific, Challenger, 9 1/2 In.	65.00
Plate, Union Pacific, Desert Flower, 6 1/2 In.	27.50
Plate, Wabash, 5 In.	60.00
Plate, Wabash, 10 In.	175.00
Platter, Boston & Albany, Berkshire, 6 1/2 X 10 1/2 In.	350.00
Platter, Missouri Pacific, Eagle, 10 1/2 In.	80.00
Platter, Santa Fe, Stamped Mimbreno, Syracuse China, 8 In.	95.00
Platter, Soo Line, 6 X 8 In.	200.00
Platter, Union Pacific, Portland Rose	175.00
Postcard, Arizona Depot, Black & White Photo, 8 X 10 In.	7.50
Postcard, Michigan Depot, Black & White Photo, 8 X 10 In.	7.50
Postcard, Texas Depot, Black & White Photo, 8 X 10 In.	7.50

Potty, Child's, Do Not Empty Out of Window, Central Pacific, Brass 120.00
Print Set, Southern Pacific Lines, Colored, 1943, 16 Piece 12.00
Print, Calendar, Chessie, 1940s, World War II Theme, 12 X 14 In. 27.50
Punch, Conductor's, S.D. Childs 10.00
Relish, Union Pacific, Historical Pattern 110.00
Rule Book, Illinois Central Trans. Dept., 1928, 125 Pages 10.00
Saucer, Chicago, Indianapolis & Louisville, 7 1/4 In. 100.00
Shovel, Rock Island Line .... 35.00 To 40.00
Sign, American Express Company Money Orders 320.00
Sign, Cattle Crossing, Full–Bodied Bull, Sheet Iron, 18 X 24 In. 150.00
Sign, Depot, Bay City Junction, Embossed Gold Letters, Iron, 1880 .... 850.00
Sign, One Mile To Station, Cast Iron 175.00
Soup Dish, Soo Line, Marked 100.00
Soup Dish, Southern Pacific Lines, Mountain Wildflower, 7 1/2 In. 25.00
Spittoon, NP R.R. Brass, Embossed Train 52.00
Spittoon, Pullman 60.00
Spittoon, Union Pacific R.R., Brass, 10 In. 150.00
Stepstool, Erie R.R., Passenger, Metal 150.00
Stock, Certificate, Chicago, Rock Island & Pacific Rwy.Co., 1903 .... 25.00
Swizzle Stick, Union Pacific R.R., Golden Spike Centennial 7.00
Tablecloth, Denver & Rio Grande R.R., Logo, 36 X 42 In. 15.00
Tablecloth, Illinois Central R.R., Center Logo, Gold, 50 X 60 In. 30.00
Tablecloth, Illinois Central, Center Diamond Logo, 36 X 42 In. 20.00
Tablecloth, Illinois Central, Diamond Logo, Linen, 36 X 36 In. 20.00
Tablecloth, Rio Grande, Stylized Lettering, White, 36 X 42 In. 15.00
Teapot, Canadian National 55.00
Time Check, Brass, Marked P & RRY Rutherford Car Shops, 1 3/8 In. 7.50
Timetable, Baltimore & Ohio, 4–28–1929 .... 12.00
Timetable, Employees, Illinois Central, Vicksburg Division, 1948 .... 6.00
Timetable, New Haven, 10–10–1926 .... 12.00
Timetable, Norfolk & Western, 1947 .... 14.00
Timetable, Old Colony, Providence Division, 4–7–1889 .... 10.00
Timetable, Pennsylvania, 9–28–1924 .... 12.00
Timetable, San Francisco, For Ferries, Cliff House, 1897, 4 X 2 In. 10.00
Towel, Property of Pullman Co. On Blue Stripe, White, 23 X 16 In. 6.00
Tray, Soo Line R.R., Routes Through N.D. & Montana, 1900s 265.00
Tumbler, Union Pacific 6.00
Uniform, Conductor's, Milwaukee R.R., Hat, 4 Piece 85.00
Uniform, Conductor's, NIRC, Hat, 3 Piece 60.00
Watch Fob, C & O 15.00
Watch Fob, Monis County Central R.R. 5.00
Watch, Father Time, Elgin, Gold Filled Case 95.00
Watch, New Haven, Car, For Mirror, Black Dial 67.50
Water Bag, Northern Pacific Railroad 20.00
Whistle, Dome Type, 3 Chime, Brass, 15 In. 375.00
Whistle, Steam, Brass, Polished, 8 In. 115.00
Wrench, Marked B & MRR, 15 In. 10.00
Wrench, Marked CM & STPRR, 12 In. 10.00
Wrench, Marked MOPACRY, 16 In. 10.00
Wrench, Monkey, B & R R.R., Marked Billings, 12 In. 12.00

The razor was used in ancient Egypt and subsequently wherever shaving was in fashion. The metal razor used in America until about 1870 was made in Sheffield, England. After 1870, machine–made hollow–ground razors were made in Germany or America. Plastic or bone handles were popular. The razor was often sold in a set of seven, one for each day of the week. The set was often kept by the barber who shaved the well–to–do man each day in the shop.

RAZOR, Blade Sharpener, Pull Cord 12.00
Blade, Marathon 2.00
Blade, Remington, Colorful Wrapper 6.00
Dehaven Diplomat, Safety, Box 18.00
Display Card, Blue Black, Gillette, 24 Blades 15.00
Display Card, Red, Gillette Razor, 10 Blades 10.00

Durham Duplex	6.00
Gillette, Brass, Original Box, 1940s	12.00
Gillette, Double Edge	6.00
Gillette, Man's, Plastic Case	12.00
Hone, Keen Kutter, No.15	15.00
Keen Kutter, Etched Blade, Ivory Handle	50.00
Keen Kutter, Junior, Box	16.00
Mauser Solingen, Celluloid Handle, Germany	25.00
Nude Picking Grapes, Oxford	32.00
Rolls, Sharpener, Instructions, Box	37.50
Safety, Winchester	35.00
Schick, 3–Speed Electric	17.50
Schick, Compact Electric, Leather Case	30.00
Straight, Art Nouveau Girl On Handle, Union Brand	45.00
Straight, Celluloid & Mother–of–Pearl, With Shaving Mug, Box	75.00
Straight, Indian Handle	40.00
Straight, Ivory Handle, Bamboo Design, England	37.50
Straight, Keen Kutter .... 25.00 To 30.00	
Straight, Salisbury Hardware, Plastic Handle, Germany	3.00
Straight, Tortoise Handle, Inlaid Silver Design, Sta–Sharp Logo	22.00
Straight, Tortoiseshell Case, Jefferson Steel	15.00
Straight, W.R. Case & Sons, Celluloid Handle	25.00
Strop, 4–Sided	9.00
Strop, Case Bros.	17.50
Strop, Keen Kutter	10.00

Reamers, or juice squeezers, have been known since 1767, although most of those collected today date from the twentieth century. Figural reamers are among the most prized.

REAMER, Amber, Federal Glass, Footed	30.00
Clown's Head, Orange Pitcher Bottom, Pottery, Japan, 5 1/2 In.	25.00
Clown's Head, Pitcher Bottom, Pottery, Mikoniware, Turtle Mark	25.00
Clown, 4 Colors, 2 Piece	45.00
Clown, Figural, Lime Top & Bottom, Japan, 5 In., 3 Piece	38.00
Clown, Japan	45.00
Cobalt Blue, Crisscross Pattern, Mold Mark	138.00
Delfite, Embossed, McKee, Small	285.00
Duck, Green Head, Orange Bill, Luster	43.00
Hazel Atlas, Pink	25.00
Jenny Ware, Ultramarine	65.00
Lemon, Mushroom Knob Handle, Wooden, C.1870	175.00
Orange, Figural, Ceramic	40.00
Pedestal, Pottery, Individual Juice Pitcher, Yellow, 2 Piece	120.00
Pottery, Yellow, Green, Japan	48.00
Skillet Shape, Seed Guard, Kwicky Juicer, Aluminum	5.00
Sunkist, Grapefruit, Pair	625.00
Sunkist, Jadite	35.00
Sunkist, Orange, Embossed Jadite	14.00
Sunkist, Pink	50.00
Sunkist, Ultramarine	950.00
Tufglas	45.00

The cylinder–shaped phonograph record for use with the early Edison phonograph was made about 1889. Disc records were first made by 1894; the double–sided disc by 1904. The high–fidelity records were first issued in 1944, the first vinyl disc in 1946, the first stereo record in 1958. The 78 RPM became the standard in 1926 but was discontinued in 1957. In 1932, the first 33 1/3 RPM was made but was not sold commercially until 1948. In 1949, the 45 RPM was introduced.

RECORD, Album, Bugs Bunny, Mel Blanc, Capitol, 78 RPM, 1947, 3 Records	28.00
Album, Glen Miller, RCA Victor, 14045 Extended Play, Limited Edition	110.00
Album, Judy Garland, 78 RPM, Decca, 1930s	30.00
Album, Waller On Ivories, Fats Waller, 78 RPM	18.00

Animals, Animalism	12.00
Annie Get Your Gun, Ethel Merman, Original Cast	7.00
Brooklyn Bridge, Buddah	6.00
Can–Can, F. Sinatra, S. MacLaine, Motion Picture Track, Capitol	6.00
Chipmunk Punk, The Chipmunks, Mercury, 1980	5.00
Electric Indian, Keem–O–Sabe	4.00
Feel Like Making Love, Roberta Flack, Atlantic	5.00
Hot Diggity Dog, Perry Como, 45 RPM	10.00
Hot Drums, Gene Krupa, Stack O Hits, 1981	5.00
John P. Sousa's Marches, LP	12.00
Judy Garland In Concert, San Francisco, Mark 56	7.00
Little Deuce Coupe, Beach Boys, Capitol	10.00
Mame, Angela Lansbury, Original Cast, Columbia	6.00
Move It Over, Hank Williams, MGM	15.00
My Fair Lady, Audrey Hepburn, Motion Picture Track, Columbia, 1964	4.00
Popular American Waltzes, Sammy Kaye, Columbia	4.00
Songs of The Fabulous '50s, Roger Williams	10.00
Thoroughly Modern Millie, Julie Andrews, Motion Picture Track, 1967	4.00
Voices From The Moon, Astronauts, Apollo 11, July, 1969, Philco–Ford	20.00
Wizard of Oz, Little Golden Record	15.00
Yellow Rose of Texas, Mitch Miller, Columbia	4.00

The Red Wing Pottery of Red Wing, Minnesota, was a firm started in 1878. The company first made utilitarian pottery. In the 1920s art pottery was made. Many dinner sets and vases were made before the company closed in 1967. Rumrill pottery was made for George Rumrill by the Red Wing Pottery and other firms. It was sold in the 1930s.

RED WING, Ashtray, Brown, Red	4.00
Ashtray, Deep Red Glaze	32.00
Ashtray, Embossed Indian Maid, Wing Shape	80.00
Bean Pot, Cover, Saffron	75.00
Beater Jar, Saffronware, Brown Stripe	60.00
Beater Jar, Titonka, Iowa	85.00
Bottle, Figural, Ear of Corn, Yellow, 10 In.	125.00
Bottle, Soda	8.50
Bowl, Brown–Blue Sponge	45.00
Bowl, Grapes, Leaves, Matte Green, Fluted, Flower Frog, 9 1/4 In.	24.00
Bowl, Lexington Rose, 5 In.	3.00
Bowl, Morning Glory, 5 1/4 In.	3.00
Bowl, Oak Leaves, Acorns, Matte Green, Dark Green Interior, 5 In.	8.50
Bowl, Random Harvest, 12 1/2 In.	22.50
Bowl, Spatter, Blue, Rust, Cream, 5 In.	125.00
Bowl, Spongeware, 6 In.	55.00
Bowl, Spongeware, Blue Stamp, 7 X 4 In.	17.50
Bowl, Tampico, 6 X 6 1/2 In.	12.50
Bowl, Vegetable, Bobwhite, 6 1/2 In.	6.00
Bowl, Vegetable, Divided, Bobwhite	35.00
Bread Tray, Bobwhite, 5 X 24 In.	60.00 To 75.00
Butter, Cover, Basket Weave, Blue	10.00
Butter, Cover, Bobwhite	55.00
Cake Plate, Tampico, 11 In.	25.00
Candleholder, Acorn & Leaf, Ivory & Tan	9.00
Candlestick, Stick–Type, Mottled Green & Tan, 6 In., Pair	10.00
Casserole, Cover, Saffron, Sponge	225.00
Celery, Random Harvest	8.00
Chop Plate, Ardennes, Dubonnet, Green Leaves Band, White Ground	12.00
Churn, Birch Leaves, Handles, 2 Gal.	135.00 To 220.00
Clock, Kitchen, Mammy, Electric	135.00
Clock, Tik–Tok Baker, Wall, Electric	40.00
Coffee Server, Cover, Pale Green, Waffle Weave, 12 3/4 In.	20.00
Coffee Server, Cover, Red	12.00
Console Set, Double Candleholders, Clear Centerpiece, 4 Piece	65.00
Console Set, Double Candlesticks, Ivory Matte	62.00

Console, Fawn Frog, Ivory & Tan, 10 X 15 In.Bowl, 10 1/2 In.Frog 28.00
Cookie Jar, Baker, Blue .... 30.00 To 45.00
Cookie Jar, Baker, Yellow 40.00
Cookie Jar, Bunch of Grapes, Yellow 18.00
Cookie Jar, Donkey Pulling Milk Truck 55.00
Cookie Jar, Dutch Girl, Blue 50.00
Cookie Jar, Dutch Girl, Brown 45.00
Cookie Jar, Dutch Girl, Yellow .... 35.00 To 55.00
Cookie Jar, Dutch People, Dancing 18.00
Cookie Jar, French Chef, Yellow, Marked 65.00
Cookie Jar, Katrina, Beige & Yellow 50.00
Cookie Jar, King of Tarts, Multicolor 175.00
Cookie Jar, Monk, Green 95.00
Cookie Jar, Monk, Yellow, Thou Shalt Not Steal .... 37.00 To 50.00
Cookie Jar, Pear, Green–Blue 25.00
Cornucopia, Antique White, 8 1/2 X 8 1/2 In. 12.00
Creamer, Bobwhite 20.00
Creamer, Driftwood 7.50
Creamer, Lexington Rose 7.50
Creamer, Morning Glory 5.00
Crock, Advertising, 20 Gal. 180.00
Crock, Butter, Cover, Blue Sponge 150.00
Crock, Butter, Floral, Blue & Gray 125.00
Crock, Butter, Gasser Co., 3 Lb. 65.00
Crock, Butter, Meadowbrook Butter, Blue Lettering 60.00
Crock, Butter, Sponge Band, Bail, No Lid 135.00
Crock, Elephant Ear, Blue, 2 Gal. 325.00
Crock, White, Large Wing, Gal. 345.00
Crock, White, Small Wing, Gal. 290.00
Crock, Wing, 1/2 Gal. 165.00
Cup & Saucer, Bobwhite .... 10.00 To 15.00
Cup & Saucer, Lexington Rose 6.00
Cup & Saucer, Pepe 4.00
Cup, Bobwhite 6.00
Cup, Morning Glory, Gray 4.00
Cup, Tampico 4.00
Feeder, Ko–Rec 85.00
Figurine, Cowgirl, Rust Color 65.00
Figurine, Deer, Blue 25.00
Figurine, Gopher On Football 100.00
Figurine, Pretty Red Wing 150.00
Figurine, Scotty Dog, Begging, Brown, 5 1/4 In. 35.00
Figurine, Tambourine Player, 10 1/4 In. 55.00
Flower Frog, Fish, White Angel 45.00
Gravy Boat, Attached Plate, Tampico 18.50
Gravy Boat, Bobwhite 28.00
Jar, Mason, 1 Gal. 315.00
Jar, Pantry, 10 Lb. 495.00
Jar, Preserve, North Star, 1/2 Gal. 165.00
Jar, Refrigerator, Stacking 95.00
Jug, Beehive, Large Wing, 5 Gal. .... 125.00 To 145.00
Jug, Birch Leaves Shoulder, 3 Gal. 75.00
Jug, Bird, 1/2 Gal. 185.00
Jug, Brown, 1 Gal. 65.00
Jug, North Star, Bail, 1/2 Gal. 650.00
Jug, Radams Microbe Killer, Raised Letters On Shoulder .... 250.00 To 375.00
Mug, Advertising, Gluek Brewing Co. 135.00
Mug, Brown, Blue Interior 10.00
Mug, Cherry Band, Commemorative 195.00
Mug, Chief Red Wing, Signed Christmas 1904 .... 2700.00
Mug, Transportation, Signed 75.00
Pail, Cover, Sponge Band No.3, Bail Handle, Signed 185.00
Pitcher, Advertising, Saffron 120.00
Pitcher, Advertising, Sundberg Bros., Sponge Band 175.00

Pitcher, Batter, Cover, Yellow 15.00
Pitcher, Bobwhite, 60 Oz. 25.00
Pitcher, Cover, Pipkin, Brown & White 165.00
Pitcher, Milk, Russian, Brown, 8 1/2 In. 40.00
Pitcher, Pine Ridge, Indian Design, Small 40.00
Pitcher, Ribbed, 8 In. 85.00
Pitcher, Water, Bobwhite 20.00
Planter, Coral & Green, 7 1/2 In. 10.00
Planter, Hanging, Incised Leaf Design 38.00
Planter, Hat Shape, Blue 6.00
Planter, Matte Green, Oblong 20.00
Planter, Piano 20.00
Planter, Speckled Gold, Vertical Flute, 12 X 4 1/4 In. 12.00
Planter, Speckled Pink, 12 1/2 X 6 1/2 In. 8.00
Planter, Turtle, White, Small 3.00
Plate, Antique Furniture With Rug, 10 3/4 In. 4.50
Plate, Bobwhite, 6 1/2 In. 3.00
Plate, Dinner, Bobwhite, 11 In. ....6.00 To 11.50
Plate, Dinner, Rose 6.50
Plate, Dinner, Zinnia 12.00
Plate, Hors D'Oeuvre, Bobwhite, Bird Shape 30.00
Plate, Lexington Rose, 7 In. 3.00
Plate, Lexington Rose, 10 In. ....4.00 To 9.00
Plate, Pepe, 7 1/2 In. 2.50
Platter, Bobwhite, 14 In. ....15.00 To 20.00
Platter, Capistrano, 15 In. 12.00
Platter, Driftwood, Anniversary Shape 12.00
Platter, Morning Glory, 13 In. 8.00
Platter, Tampico, Oval, 13 In. 18.50
Reamer & Juice Pitcher, Yellow, Pedestal, Individual 130.00
Relish, Bobwhite 25.00
Salt & Pepper, Bobwhite, Small 18.00
Salt, Beehive, Leaf, 5 Gal. 375.00
Salt, Beehive, Side Stamped RW, 5 Gal. 645.00
Saucer, Tampico 1.50
Spittoon, Brown 45.00
Spittoon, Salt Glaze 545.00
Sugar & Creamer, Bobwhite 35.00
Sugar & Creamer, Lexington Rose 7.00
Sugar, Cover, Bobwhite ....10.00 To 20.00
Sugar, Cover, Lexington Rose, Round 10.00
Sugar, Cover, Lexington Rose, Square 12.00
Sugar, Cover, Tampico 12.00
Sugar, Lexington Rose 7.50
Sugar, Morning Glory 4.00
Teapot, Bobwhite ....35.00 To 65.00
Teapot, Figural, Chicken, Yellow, 8 X 7 In. 22.00
Teapot, Lexington Rose 30.00
Trivet, Minnesota Centennial ....25.00 To 50.00
Urn, Grecian Design, 9 In. 45.00
Vase, Art Deco, Triangles, Ivory, Burnt Orange Interior, 6 1/2 In. 12.00
Vase, Bamboo Pattern, Green & Yellow, 12 1/2 In. 40.00
Vase, Basket Weave, Pink, 9 1/4 In. 18.00
Vase, Basket Weave, White, Green Interior 30.00
Vase, Burgundy Ribbed Roses, Ivory, 6 1/2 In. 21.00
Vase, Copper Oxide Green, Gourd Shape, Tall Narrow Neck, 12 In. 15.00
Vase, Egyptian, Green, White, 12 In. 45.00
Vase, Fan, Cornucopia Type, Ivory, Peach Interior, 7 3/4 In., Pair 25.00
Vase, Fan, Cream, Green Interior, 2 Leaves Shape, 7 1/2 In. 16.00
Vase, Figural, Elephant Head, Shoulder Handles, Green, 6 1/4 In. 32.00
Vase, Green, Pink Interior, Base Handles, 7 1/2 In. 14.00
Vase, Ivory & Green, 7 1/2 In. 18.00
Vase, Pitcher Shape, Raised Flower, Maroon, 7 In. 18.00
Vase, Red & White, 6 1/2 In. 30.00

Vase, Shell, Green, White Interior	12.50
Vase, Sitting Elephant, Teal, Matte Glaze, 5 In.	45.00
Vase, Storks, Green & Cream, Marked, 12 In.	75.00
Wall Pocket, Gardenia, Ivory	35.00
Wall Pocket, Mandolin, Ivory, 13 In.	20.00
Water Cooler, Cover, Spigot, Handles, 3 Gal. .... 285.00 To 325.00
Water, Cooler, Bobwhite	335.00
Wax Sealer, 1 Gal.	95.00
Wax Sealer, 1 Qt.	55.00

Redware is a hard, red stoneware that originated in the late 1600s and continues to be made. The term is also used to describe any common clay pottery that is reddish in color.

REDWARE, Bank, Engraved Words Liberty Bell, 1776	33.00
Bank, Ink Paper Label, N.L.Van Dyke, Black, 1842, 3 1/2 In.	85.00
Bank, Knob Finial, Gray Brown Glaze, Brown Streaks, 6 In.	175.00
Bank, Rooster, Yellow Slip Design, Primitive, 5 3/4 In.	300.00
Bottle, Pig Form, Dark Brown Glaze, 6 1/2 In.	170.00
Bottle, Pig Form, Green Glaze, Orange Spots, 8 1/4 In.	140.00
Bottle, Shoe Shape, Incised Laces, Clear Glaze, 7 1/2 In.	150.00
Bowl, Amber Glaze, Brown Splotches, 4 X 7 1/2 In.	235.00
Bowl, Brown Flecks, Irregular Band of Brown Sponging, 8 In.	220.00
Bowl, Brown Glaze, White Interior, 4 1/2 In.	100.00
Bowl, Clear Glaze, Brown Flecks, 8 5/8 In.	65.00
Bowl, Milk, Greenish Interior Glaze, 4 X 11 In.	40.00
Bowl, Milk, Orange Glaze, Red Slip Design, 8 1/2 In.	15.00
Bowl, Milk, Yellow Slip Swags, 2 1/2 X 10 In.	105.00
Bowl, Yellow Slip, Brown Glaze, Wavy Line, 9 1/4 X 3 1/8 In.	650.00
Charger, Cogwheel, Dark Green Drips, Clear Glaze, 10 X 16 In.	3525.00
Charger, Cogwheel, Yellow Slip, Clear Glaze, 13 1/2 In.	1065.00
Churn, Brown Finish, 1 Gal.	30.00
Churn, Butter, 4 Gal.	175.00
Collander, Mottled Glaze, Brown Sponging, 5 3/8 X 8 In.	325.00
Cookie Mold, Brown Bear, Sculpted Fur, Teeth, Claws, 1810, 3 X 5 In.	395.00
Crock, Brown Splotches, Clear Glaze, Applied Handles, 9 In.	175.00
Crock, Brownish Green Glaze, 1850, 1 Gal.	215.00
Cup Plate, Pine Tree, Yellow Slip, Bucks County	1325.00
Cup, Brown Spots, Ribbed Strap Handle, 3 1/4 In.	25.00
Cup, Brown Spotted Glaze, Handle, 2 1/4 X 4 In.	110.00
Desk Set, Bird Finial, Mounds of Rocks, Plants, 6 In.	90.00
Dish, Brown Dots & Splotches, 6 7/8 In.	70.00
Dish, Coggled, 3 Line Yellow Slip Design, 6 1/8 In.	220.00
Dish, Divided, Yellow Slip Design, 8 1/2 X 11 1/4 In.	35.00
Dish, Greenish Amber Glaze, Brown Splotches, 7 In.	100.00
Dish, Tulip Design In 4 Line Yellow Slip, 7 In.	725.00
Eggcup, Yellow Slip Design In Clock Pattern, 3 In.	18.50
Figurine, Cat, Gray Mottled Glaze, 10 1/4 In.	65.00
Flask, Brown Glaze, Incised Inscription, 4 1/8 In.	1750.00
Flask, Clear Glaze, Brown Splotches, Ovoid, 6 In.	250.00
Flask, Dark Brown Glaze, 5 In.	85.00
Flask, Dark Greenish Brown Glaze, 6 1/2 In.	75.00
Flask, Greenish Amber Glaze, Brown Flecks, 6 1/2 In. .... 65.00 To 75.00
Flask, Rust & Brown Glaze, 1810, 7 3/4 In.	250.00
Flask, Sgraffito Bird & Flowers, Foreign Inscription, 7 1/4 In.	100.00
Flowerpot, Attached Saucer, Crimped Rim, Amber Glaze, 6 5/8 In.	165.00
Hand Warmer, Molded Duck, Albany-Type Glaze, Loop Handle, 8 1/2 In.	130.00
Jar, Apple Butter, Interior Glaze, 7 1/2 In.	65.00
Jar, Apple Butter, Mottled Glaze, Ovoid, 7 1/2 In.	95.00
Jar, Brown Fleck Glaze, Tooled Handle, Ovoid, 5 3/8 In.	155.00
Jar, Brown Splotches, Dark Glaze, Ovoid, 4 5/8 In.	25.00
Jar, Brown Splotches, Handle, Amber	115.00
Jar, Brown Sponging, Clear Glaze, 8 1/4 In.	105.00
Jar, Cogwheel Design, Handles, New England, C.1830, 10 In.	2420.00
Jar, Cover, Brown Glaze, Yellow Slip Design, 6 1/4 In.	100.00

Jar, Dark Brown, Ovoid, Bulbous Lip, C.Link, 5 1/8 In. 85.00
Jar, Flange For Cover, Red Glaze, Green Rim, Ovoid, 11 In. 25.00
Jar, Fruit, Galena, 9 In. 125.00
Jar, Green Glaze, Orange Spots, 5 7/8 In. 90.00
Jar, Green Mottled Glaze, Label, Joseph Enterline, 1864, 9 3/4 In. 350.00
Jar, Incised Design, Penna., 1850–80 .... 450.00
Jar, Incised Lines, Sloping Shoulders, 6 3/8 In. 200.00
Jar, Minerva Head Handles, Acorn Finial, W.Scrafton, 9 3/4 In. 325.00
Jug, Brown Fleck Glaze, Strap Handle, 6 3/8 In. 85.00
Jug, Bulbous, Dark Brown Glaze, 4 In. 260.00
Jug, Coiled Snake Handle, Tan Glaze, 5 1/4 In. 115.00
Jug, Dark Brown Albany Glaze, Handle, 18th Century, 4 In. 260.00
Jug, Strap Handle, Shoulder Tooled Lines, Brown Flecks, 6 5/8 In. 425.00
Lamp, Grease, Brown Glaze, Saucer, Strap Handle, 4 1/2 In. 425.00
Lamp, Grease, Dark Brown Glaze, Coggled Rim, 5 1/4 In. 350.00
Loaf Dish, Yellow Squiggle Lines, Word Pork, C.1830, 11 3/4 X 9 In. 350.00
Loaf Pan, Coggled Rim, 4 Line Yellow Slip Design, 10 X 14 In. 375.00
Loaf Pan, Yellow Slip Design, 11 1/2 X 14 1/2 In. 35.00
Mold, Food, Turk's Head, Swirled Flutes, Black Sponging, 7 1/2 In. 25.00
Mug, Child's, Daisy, Yellow Stencil Design, 2 X 2 1/2 In. 49.00
Mug, Handle, Bloomfield, N.Y., 3 1/2 In. 350.00
Mug, Tooled Lines, Ribbed Strap Handle, 4 1/4 In. 55.00
Pedestal, Floral Bouquet Design, 36 In. 200.00
Pie Plate, Coggled Rim, Yellow Slip Design, I.S.Stahl, 1948, 8 In. 135.00
Pie Plate, Coggled Rim, Yellow Slip Inscription, 10 3/8 In. 300.00
Pie Plate, Coggled Rim, Yellow Slip Tulip Design, 9 1/4 In. 300.00
Pie Plate, Deep Dish, Stippled Rust Glaze, C.1820, 3 5/8 In. 110.00
Pie Plate, Sgraffito, 1930s 85.00
Pitcher, Incised Eagle & Shield, Glaze, Brown Flecks, 6 5/8 In. 750.00
Pitcher, Pinched Spout, Marked Jamestown Colony, 7 1/4 In. 15.00
Pitcher, Strap Handle, Greenish Glaze, Brown Flecks, 6 5/8 In. 435.00
Pitcher, Yellow Slip Design, 6 1/2 In. 25.00
Pot, Cover, Clear Glaze, Brown Splotches, 4 1/2 In. 100.00
Shaving Mug, Brown Amber Glaze, 4 1/4 X 5 In. 165.00
Shaving Mug, Plow Design, Brown Mottled Glaze, 3 3/4 In. 85.00
Sugar, Orange Glaze, Brown Splotches, 4 3/4 In. 155.00
Urn, Acanthus Leaves, Foliage Scrolls, 12 3/4 In. 200.00
Vase, Bud, Ovoid, 5 1/2 In. 93.50
Whistle, Bird, Finger Holes, 2 3/8 In. 165.00

REGOUT, see Maastricht

Richard "Richard" was the mark used on acid–etched cameo glass vases, bowls, night–lights, and lamps made in Lorraine, France, during the 1920s. The pieces were very similar to the other French cameo glasswares made by Daum, Galle, and others.

RICHARD, Goblet, Wine, Frosted Bowl, Rose Scene, Landscape, Signed, 7 3/4 In. 395.00
Vase, Holly Leaves & Berries, Mottled Interior, Marked, 9 1/2 In. 2900.00
Vase, House, Arched Bridge, River, Fin Feet, Signed, 8 In. 550.00
Vase, Landscape Along River, Frosted Ground, Signed, 3 3/8 In. 225.00
Vase, Landscape, Castle, Amber Ground, Lavender, Signed, 12 In. 990.00
Vase, Scarf–Dancing Lady, Frosted Ground, Signed, 10 In. 895.00
Vase, Ships Scene, Yellow & Brown, 4 1/2 In. 695.00

Ridgway pottery has been made in the Staffordshire district in England since 1808 by a series of companies with the name Ridgway. The transfer–design dinner sets are the most widely known product. They are still being made. Other pieces of Ridgway are listed under Flow Blue.

RIDGWAY, Bowl, Coaching Days, 3 Scenes, 9 In. 165.00
Bowl, Coaching Days, Meet At An Inn, 9 1/2 In. 75.00
Bowl, Shakespeare, 6 In. 25.00
Compote, 5 Whooping Cranes, Edwards & Son, 8 In. 65.00
Creamer, Coaching Days, Gold, Silver Luster Trim 55.00
Cup & Saucer, Boy Fishing On Lake 25.00

Cup & Saucer, Fishing Boats 25.00
Jug, Pickwick Scene, Black & Silver Luster Trim, 7 5/8 In. 70.00
Mug, Coaching Days, Changing Horses, Silver Handle & Rim, 4 In. 40.00
Mug, Coaching Days, Walking Up Hill, Silver Handle & Rim, 5 In. 45.00
Mug, New Haven & Eton, Copper Luster Handle & Rim, 4 In. 40.00
Mug, Niagara Falls 20.00
Mustard, Sailing Ship, 4 3/4 In. 55.00
Pitcher, Chester Pattern, Blue & White 45.00
Pitcher, Pickwick Scene, Black & Silver Luster Trim, 9 1/2 In. 100.00
Pitcher, Tam O'Shanter, Tan, 1835, 8 1/2 In. 165.00
Plate, Center Bouquet, Gilt Foliate Rim, C.1850, 10 In., 10 Piece 330.00
Platter, Warwick, Fruit & Wheat Underglaze, 12 In. 38.00
Tea Set, Child's, Chintz, Brown, 15 Piece 600.00
Tea Set, Child's, Stoke On Trent, C.1883, 24 Piece 250.00
Teapot, Coaching Days, 5 1/2 In. 165.00
Tile, Village In Foreground, Mt.Rainier, 6 1/4 In. 85.00
Wash Set, Poppy–Type Flower, Toothbrush Holder, 3 Piece 450.00

A rifle is a firearm that has a rifled bore and that is intended to be fired from the shoulder. Other firearms are listed under Gun.

RIFLE, Air Pellet, Custom Made Competition Grade 310.00
Air, Markham, 1888 .... 175.00
American Indian, 41 Caliber, Brass Tacks, Engraved H.E.Lemon, Pa. 900.00
Bayonette, Russian–Chinese 250.00
Browning, A–5 Belgium, 12 Gauge 300.00
Burnside 1860, Civil War, Lever Action 575.00
Colt, Lightning 175.00
Daisy, Air, Model 29, 350 Shot, Dated 1880–1915 .... 125.00
Edward Linder, Patent 1859 .... 1250.00
Flintlock, Asa Waters, Mass. 2800.00
Flintlock, Blunderbuss, U.S.Carved In Stock 950.00
Hamilton, 22 Caliber, C.1915 .... 110.00
Ithaca, Model 37, Featherlight 250.00
Japanese, 25 Caliber, Early World War II 130.00
Kentucky, Flintlock, Maple Full Stock, 61 1/2 In. 900.00
Kentucky, Percussion Lock, Maple Half Stock, 48 1/2 In. 800.00
Kentucky, Percussion Lock, Walnut Full Stock, 54 In. 575.00
Little Scout, 22 Caliber 85.00
M–I, 7 Ft. 415.00
Marlin, Lever Action, Model 1889, 32–20 Caliber, Octagon Barrel 275.00
Mauser, Bolt Action, 9mm., Marked A.G.Oberdorf 300.00
Musket, Colt No.3, Band, 1863 .... 1800.00
Muzzle Loader, Curly Maple, Full Stock, Engraved Eagle, Leaman 2300.00
Percussion, 2 Trigger 90.00
Remington, Model 30, Express Man, 1925 .... 270.00
Ruger, Model 10–22, Semi–Automatic, 22 Caliber 145.00
Sharp, Marked Bridgeport, Ct. 500.00
Spencer, Carbine 900.00
Springfield Armory, Model 1896 .... 310.00
Springfield, 1873 .... 395.00
Winchester, 1873, 32 Caliber 325.00
Winchester, Air, No.416, Boy's 95.00
Winchester, Carbine, 1892 .... 1000.00
Winchester, Model 1873, 32 WCF, With Octagonal Barrel 625.00
Winchester, Model 1895, 12, 13 Gauge, Unused 470.00
Winchester, Model 42, Vent Rib, Checkered Wood 750.00
Winchester, Model 94, 30/30 Carbine 135.00
Winchester, Model 94, 38–55, 1902 .... 400.00
Winchester, Pump, Model 1890, 22 Caliber, Round Barrel 275.00
Winchester, Saddle, 30–30 .... 200.00

Riviera dinnerware was made by the Homer Laughlin Co. of Newell, West Virginia, from 1938 to 1950. The pattern was similar in coloring and in mood to Fiesta and Harlequin. The Riviera plates and cup handles were square.

RIVIERA, Bowl, Cereal, Green, 6 In.	35.00
Butter, Yellow, 1/4 Lb.	85.00
Creamer, Red	7.00
Creamer, Yellow	4.00
Platter, Yellow, 11 1/2 In.	7.50
Syrup, Cover, Red	145.00
Teapot, Mauve Blue, Cover	45.00
Teapot, Yellow	35.00
Tumbler, Juice, Blue	35.00
Tumbler, Red, Handle	40.00 To 45.00
Tumbler, Yellow, Handle	38.00 To 42.50

Roblin Art Pottery was founded in 1898 by Alexander W. Robertson and Linna Irelan in San Francisco, California. The pottery closed in 1906. The firm made faience with green, tan, dull blue, or gray glazes. Decorations were usually animal shapes. Some red clay pieces were made.

ROBLIN, Vase, Brown Speckled Glaze, 3 In.	400.00

Rockingham, in the United States, is a brown glazed pottery with a tortoiseshell–like glaze. It was made from 1840 to 1900 by many American potteries. Mottled brown Rockingham wares were first made in England at the Rockingham factory. Other types of ceramics were also made by the English firm.

ROCKINGHAM, Bank, Shoe Shape, 5 1/2 In.	125.00
Bedpan, Dolphin Mouth, 16 1/2 In.	10.00
Bottle, Book Form, Gray Clay, Brown Sponging, 4 3/4 In.	150.00
Bottle, Clenched Fist, Spout, Upraised Thumb, 5 1/4 In.	225.00
Bottle, Fish, 10 3/4 In.	50.00
Bottle, Hound Head, Band of White Slip At Collar, 5 3/8 In.	205.00
Bottle, Shoe, Embossed Laces, 6 3/4 In.	200.00
Bottle, Shoe, Embossed Laces, Ann Reid, 1859, 6 In.	300.00
Bowl, 2 3/8 X 5 3/8 In.	10.00
Bowl, Embossed Tulip Design, 3 1/4 In.	55.00
Bowl, Milk, Canted Sides, 11 In.	65.00
Bowl, Mottled Brown & Yellow, National, 7 1/2 X 3 1/4 In.	40.00
Bowl, Oval, 3 5/8 X 13 In.	35.00
Bowl, Scalloped, 6 3/4 In.	75.00
Candlestick, 5 3/4 In.	25.00
Crock, Cover, 5 In.	50.00
Cup & Saucer, Rococo, C.1830	65.00
Cuspidor, Embossed Shell Design, 8 In.	25.00
Cuspidor, Scallop Design On Side, 3 1/2 X 6 1/2 In.	75.00
Dish, Oval, 8 X 10 3/4 In.	20.00
Dish, Shell Form, Rose Design, C.1835	55.00
Figurine, Cat, Seated, Freestanding Front Legs, 10 3/4 In.	175.00
Figurine, Dog, Seated, Freestanding Front Legs, 10 In.	55.00
Figurine, Poodle Holding A Basket, 5 In.	80.00
Flask, Book Shape, Flint, Life of Kossuth, 6 In.	375.00
Flask, Embossed Clasped Hands & Flowers, 7 7/8 In.	105.00
Flask, Embossed Horse Scenes, Dismounted Riders, 7 In.	325.00
Flask, Embossed Hunting Dogs, 7 In.	400.00
Flask, Embossed Leaves, Trees & Figures, 7 1/4 In.	95.00
Flask, Embossed Nymph With Vintage, 7 1/4 In.	130.00
Flask, Embossed Roses & Vintage, 7 1/4 In.	180.00
Flask, Embossed Roses, 6 In.	105.00
Flask, Morning Glories, 7 In.	125.00
Inkwell, Dog, English, 6 In. ....*Illus*	100.00
Inkwell, Paneled, Embossed Acanthus Leaves, 2 1/4 In.	135.00

Inkwell, Reclining Boy	135.00
Inkwell, Shoe Shape, Hole For Nib In Top, 5 1/2 In.	65.00
Loving Cup, 3 Handles, 5 3/8 In.	12.50
Mixing Bowl, 4 1/2 In.	35.00
Mixing Bowl, 6 1/4 In.	55.00
Mixing Bowl, 8 1/2 In.	85.00
Mixing Bowl, 9 5/8 In.	95.00
Mold, Cake, Turk's Head, 8 1/8 In.	45.00
Mug, Strap Handle, 3 1/8 In.	58.00
Pie Plate, Mottled Brown, Yellow, 9 1/4 In.	30.00
Pie Plate, Mottled Brown, Yellow, 10 1/2 In.	95.00
Pipe, Turkey Claw, Claw Clasps Bowl, C.1880	20.00
Pitcher, Acanthus Leaf & Grape, 9 3/4 In.	195.00
Pitcher, Acorn & Leaves, Small	37.00
Pitcher, Batter, Mottled Brown, Yellow, Handle, 7 In.	115.00
Pitcher, Daniel Boone, 9 In.	140.00
Pitcher, Embossed Game & Hound Handle, 8 In.	45.00
Pitcher, Figural, George Washington, 8 1/4 In.	225.00
Pitcher, Hunting Scene, 9 In.	140.00
Pitcher, Milk, Peacock	135.00
Pitcher, Tulip, 5 In.	95.00
Pitcher, Wellington Died Sep.14, 1832, Marked, 7 1/4 In.	75.00
Shaving Mug, Toby, 4 1/4 In.	300.00
Soap Dish, Drain Holes, Late 1800s	30.00
Teapot, Cherubs, Swags, Large	58.00
Teapot, Embossed Eagle & Shield, 8 1/2 In.	50.00
Teapot, Rebecca At The Well, 5 1/2 In.	50.00
Toby Jug, Snuff Taker, Glaze, 9 1/2 In.	265.00
Tumbler, 4 1/2 In.	55.00

ROGERS, see John Rogers

 Rookwood pottery was made in Cincinnati, Ohio, from 1880 to 1960. All of this art pottery is marked, most with the famous flame mark. The R is reversed and placed back to back with the letter P. Flames surround the letters. After 1900, a Roman numeral was added to the mark to indicate the year. The name and some of the molds were purchased in 1984; new items will be clearly marked.

ROOKWOOD, Ashtray, Figural, Dog	250.00
Ashtray, Figural, Elephant, White Matte, Dated 1933	195.00
Ashtray, Figural, Fish, Ivory	27.50
Ashtray, Figural, Owl, Blue, 1931	67.50
Bookends, Black Mirror Eagles	175.00
Bookends, Blue, Green, 1939, 6 1/2 X 6 In.	100.00
Bookends, Elephant, Celadon, Ovington Sticker, 1945	145.00
Bookends, Floral Basket	150.00 To 195.00
Bookends, Fruit, Green, 1937	125.00
Bookends, Panther, 1945	135.00 To 175.00
Bookends, Waterlily, Off–White, 1948	150.00

Rockingham, Inkwell, Dog, English, 6 In.

Future Royal Doulton collectors will be able to easily identify character jugs and figurines made before 1984. As of this year, the words "hand made" and "hand decorated" are added above the lion and crown mark, in the shape of an arch.

Rookwood, Ewer, Cream Star Flowers, Limoges Glaze Green, 10 In.

Rookwood, Mug, Diagonal Handle, Glazed Branch, 1890; Vase, Foliate, Almond Glaze, 1889; Jug, Spiders, Webs, Wave Ground, C.1883

Bookends, White Ship, Signed McDonald, 1925	210.00
Bookends, Woman, Reading, Yellow Matte Glaze, 7 In., Pair	250.00
Bowl, Flower Frog, Brown, Green, 3 Handles, 1922, 9 1/2 X 4 1/2 In.	65.00
Bowl, Yellow Flowers, Green Leaves, Handles, Signed, 1892, 8 1/2 In.	595.00
Bowl, Z Series, Turned–In Rim, 7 X 3 In.	55.00
Candleholder, Saucer Base, Finger Handle, Rose, 1924, Pair	85.00
Candlestick, Blue, 1924, 5 1/2 In., Pair	120.00
Candlestick, Dark Green Matte, 8 In.	95.00
Console Set, Elephant, Bowl Held Up By 3 Elephants, 1929, 3 Piece	395.00
Creamer, Green, 1945, 3 1/2 In.	15.00
Creamer, Rose, 1932, 3 1/2 In.	87.50
Cup & Saucer, Shipware, Blue	75.00
Ewer, Cluster of Leaves & Berries, Trefoil Top, 1900, 9 In.	350.00
Ewer, Cream Star Flowers, Limoges Glaze Green, 10 In. ....*Illus*	577.50
Figurine, Horsehead, Stylized, White, Signed McDonald, 1934, 6 In.	95.00
Figurine, Spanish Woman, 4 Colors, 11 In.	285.00
Flower Frog, Olive	18.00
Jug, Moss Green, Ferns, Wandering Jew Leaves, 4 1/2 X 2 5/8 In.	250.00
Jug, Pilgrim, Chickens, Handle, 1883, Signed Cranch, 7 1/2 In.	850.00
Jug, Spiders, Webs, Wave Ground, C.1883, 4 1/2 In. ....*Illus*	385.00
Lamp, Antelopes, Signed Barrett, 1946, 12 In.	675.00
Lamp, Kerosene, Chrysanthemums & Leaves, Brown Ground, 23 1/2 In.	750.00
Mug, Deer Portrait, E.T.H., 1904, 5 1/4 In.	550.00
Mug, Diagonal Handle, Glazed Branch, 1890, 5 3/4 In. ....*Illus*	578.00
Mug, Fall City Beer, Here's Good Luck To You, 1948, 5 In.	85.00
Mug, Vellum, Alpha Delta Phi, Moon & Star Design, 1905	150.00
Mustard, Cover, Yellow Flowers, Amelia Sprague, 1886, 4 In.	195.00
Mustard, Ginger Jar Shape, 6 In.	75.00
Paperweight, Donkey, Caramel, Signed Abel, 1935, 6 In.	110.00
Paperweight, Elephant, White, 1930, 4 1/4 In.	110.00
Paperweight, Lobster Shape	300.00
Paperweight, Nude	175.00
Pitcher, Clover, Grass, Green, Brown, Loop Handle, 1890, 12 1/2 In.	900.00
Pitcher, Cover, Ships, Blue, 5 1/2 In.	150.00
Planter, Ambrosia, Louise Abel, 1926	500.00
Plaque, Scenic, Signed, 8 X 5 In.	1600.00
Plate, Pink, 6 1/2 In.	25.00
Sugar & Creamer, Open, Aqua Matte Glaze, 1932	65.00
Tankard, Floral, LaMoro, 13 1/2 In.	375.00
Tea Set, Sailboats, White, Light Blue, 12 Sides, 1924, 16 Piece	450.00
Tea Set, Standard Glaze, Signed, 1888, 3 Piece	1250.00
Teapot, Sailing Ship	125.00

Tile, Ivy, Lavender Flowers, Ivory Ground	120.00
Toothpick, Embossed Acorns, Blue, Dated 1919	250.00
Tray, Pin, Nude Asleep On Side of Tray, 1947, 3 X 4 1/2 In.	105.00
Trivet, 7–Colored Parrot, 1919	195.00
Trivet, Parrot, Purple Shades, 1927	100.00
Urn, Impressed Circle of Beads, Matte Mint Green, 3 3/4 X 4 In.	110.00
Vase, 3 Birds In Flight, Standard Glaze, 1906, 9 In.	2000.00
Vase, 3 Cranes In Flight, Vellum, Lorinda Epply, 1909, 7 In.	400.00
Vase, Allover Green & Rust Leaves, 1945, 5 1/4 X 5 1/2 In.	325.00
Vase, Apple Blossom, Bisque Finish, Gold Trim, Matt Daly, 11 In.	800.00
Vase, Baluster Form, Incised Chrysanthemums, 1900, 8 3/4 In.	6050.00
Vase, Bishop, Standard Glaze, Floral, 8 In.	375.00
Vase, Black Scrolls & Leaves, Chartreuse, Footed, Flared, 6 1/4 In.	210.00
Vase, Blue Matte Glaze, Hexagonal, Lug Handles, 1921, 6 In.	120.00
Vase, Bluebirds, Field of Wildflowers, Vellum, 1930, 7 In.	1330.00
Vase, Branches With Blossoms, Iris Glaze, C.1900, 7 1/4 In.	350.00
Vase, Cherries, 3 Handles, E.T.Hurley, 4 1/4 In.	350.00
Vase, Chinese Style, Blue Matte Glaze, 1946, 10 In., Pair	110.00
Vase, Crocus, Blue & White, Marked, 1914, 9 3/8 In.	250.00
Vase, Dancing Women, Brown, Allover Stars, Handles, 1946, 9 In.	110.00
Vase, Deer, Off–White, Wax Matte, Art Deco, 4 1/2 In.	85.00
Vase, Dolphins, Yellow, 8 In.	55.00
Vase, Embossed Berries & Vines, Light Brown, Ball, 1946, 4 In.	50.00
Vase, Embossed Dancing Nudes, Cobalt Blue, 1936, 9 In.	95.00
Vase, Fish, Sea Green, Dated 1905, 6 In.	3000.00
Vase, Floral Band Top, Gray Base, Cylindrical, 1922, 8 1/2 In.	1000.00
Vase, Floral Band, Vellum, Dark Blue, 1917, 9 1/4 In.	325.00
Vase, Floral Vellum, 1911, 9 1/2 In.	350.00
Vase, Floral, Bands of Silver, Iris Glaze, Dated 1901, 5 In.	4000.00
Vase, Floral, Sallie Toohey, 1893, 9 In.	600.00
Vase, Flowers, Carrie Steinle, 1904, 4 X 4 In.	250.00
Vase, Foliate, Almond Glaze, ·1889, 12 1/2 In. ....*Illus*	550.00
Vase, Geometric Design In Relief, Green Matte, 5 1/2 In.	75.00
Vase, Gilt Incised Foliate, Off–White, L.F.Ashelby, 10 In.	425.00
Vase, Gold, Brown & Black Floral, Standard Glaze, 1906, 7 In.	395.00
Vase, Hand Painted Birds, Insects, Scene, Marked, C.1882, 21 In.	450.00
Vase, Incised Leaf Design, Turquoise Ground, 1931, 5 1/2 In.	125.00
Vase, Iris Design, Purplish Rust, Signed E.Barrett, 1944, 9 1/4 In.	375.00
Vase, Lake Scene, Vellum, Blue, Green, Signed L.E., 9 In.	900.00
Vase, Margaret Helen McDonald, 1919, 8 In.	295.00
Vase, Maroon, 4–Footed, Flared, Square, C.1950	55.00
Vase, Matte Purple Exterior, Black Interior, 7 1/2 In.	70.00
Vase, Mistletoe, 1915, 7 In.	125.00
Vase, Molded Flowers, Mottled Brown, Gray, 6 1/4 X 5 1/4 In.	60.00
Vase, Olive Floral, Signed O.G.Reed, 6 1/4 In.	200.00
Vase, Palm Leaves, Dark Green Glaze, H.Strafer, 1893, 4 1/4 X 8 In.	3500.00
Vase, Palm Trees On Lake, C.1916, 7 7/8 In.	800.00
Vase, Pastel Lines, 10 Sides, Delia Workum, 1928, 7 In.	350.00
Vase, Peacock Feather, Black Over Green Glaze, 1903, 7 1/2 In.	1570.00
Vase, Pink & Blue Gloss, 7 In.	45.00
Vase, Pink Flowers, Vellum, Cream, Gray Top, Urn Shape, 3 1/2 In.	300.00
Vase, Purple, Green, Blue Peacock Feathers, 1923, 10 In.	660.00
Vase, Raised Almond Foliate Design, C.1889, 12 1/2 In.	500.00
Vase, Religious Motif, Dated 1934, 5 1/2 In.	90.00
Vase, Sailboats In Harbor, Wide Mouth, 1908, 12 In.	1600.00
Vase, Scenic, Vellum, Small Glaze Drip, 8 In.	575.00
Vase, Scrolls, Leaves, Chartreuse, 6 1/4 In.	210.00
Vase, Sea Green, Sara E.Coyne, 1911, 8 1/2 In.	250.00
Vase, Speckle Dripping Over Gray, Blue & Green, 1932, 7 In., Pair	150.00
Vase, Standard Glaze, Epply, 6 In.	295.00
Vase, Stylized Dandelions, 4 1/2 In.	325.00
Vase, Swimming Fish, Shaded Blue, Vellum, Hurley, 1910, 7 In.	1000.00
Vase, Thorny Branched White Ground, Purple, 1927, 6 1/2 In.	700.00
Vase, Top Feather Swirl, Charles Stuart Todd, 1917, 7 In.	150.00

Vase, Trees Reflected In Lake, Vellum, E.Diers, 1920, 6 1/4 In. 500.00
Vase, Tulip, Blue Matte, 1916, 10 1/2 In. 125.00
Vase, Tulips, Wax Matte, 10 In. 125.00
Vase, Water Lilies & Pads, Yellow, 1950, 6 1/4 In. 78.00
Vase, White Buds, Green Leaves, Blue Ground, Z Mark, 5 In. 350.00
Vase, Woodland River Scene, Vellum, 1930, 9 In. 1090.00
Vase, Yellow Pond Lilies, Iris Glaze, Green Ground, 1908, 7 1/2 In. 910.00
    ROSALINE, see Steuben

 Rose bowls were popular during the 1880s. Rose petals were kept in the open bowl to add fragrance to a room, a popular idea in a time of limited personal hygiene. The glass bowls were made with crimped tops, which kept the petals inside. Many types of Victorian art glass were made into rose bowls.

ROSE BOWL, Cut Glass, 8 In. 140.00
  Diamond Quilted, Mother–of–Pearl, 9–Crimp Top, 4 In. 250.00
  Egg Shape, Fireglow Glass, 6–Crimp Top, 6 12 X 4 1/4 In. 165.00
  Enamel Design, Cut To Clear Overlay, Gold Trim, 3 In. 130.00
  Enameled Daisies, Satin Glass, Blue Overlay, 8–Crimp Top, 6 In. 165.00
  Mother–of–Pearl, Pink Herringbone, Deep Red To Pink, 3 1/2 In. 195.00
  Mother–of–Pearl, Satin, Diamond Quilted, Sky Blue, 5 1/2 In. 185.00
  Pansies, Leaves, Frosted Petal Feet, 4–Crimp Top, 5 3/4 In. 135.00
  Satin Glass, Blue, Blown, Crimped, Small 17.50
  Shaded White To Yellow, Crimped 50.00
  Shell & Seaweed, Yellow Overlay, 8–Crimp Top, 5 1/4 In. 125.00

    Rose Canton china is similar to Rose Medallion, except no people are pictured in the decoration. It was made during the nineteenth and twentieth centuries in greens, pinks, and other colors.

ROSE CANTON, Cup & Saucer, Butterfly & Cabbage 45.00
  Jar, Cover, Allover Design, Pair 785.00
  Teapot, 2 Cups In Wicker Basket, C.1890 .... 275.00

Rose Medallion, Punch Bowl,
Mandarin Figures, 6 X 14 1/2 In.

Royal Worcester, Vase, Japanese
Style, 1874, 8 1/2 In., Pair

Rose Medallion china was made in China during the nineteenth and twentieth centuries. It is a distinctive design picturing people, flowers, birds, and butterflies. Pieces are colored in greens, pinks, and other colors.

ROSE MEDALLION, Bowl, Gilt Bronze, Pierced Rim, Angular Handles, 12 In.	2750.00
Butter Chip, 10 Piece	360.00
Chop Plate, 4 Genre Panels, Florals, Butterflies, 13 3/4 In.	450.00
Creamer, People, Butterfly & Birds Panel, Gilt, 4 3/4 In.	200.00
Cup & Saucer, Birds, People	50.00
Cup & Saucer, Birds, People, Ruffled, Demitasse	30.00
Cup & Saucer, Genre Scenes, Wishbone Handle, 12 Sets	325.00
Fruit Basket, Undertray, Scenes On Rim, 9 1/2 X 11 In.	650.00
Plate, Birds, Figures, 6 In.	24.00
Plate, Birds, Figures, 7 1/2 In.	47.00
Plate, Birds, Figures, 9 1/2 In.	45.00
Plate, Genre Scenes, Floral & Bird Panels, 8 In., 12 Piece	350.00
Plate, Scenes, Bird & Butterfly Panels, 10 In., 12 Piece	700.00
Punch Bowl, C.1840, 12 In.	1200.00
Punch Bowl, Mandarin Figures, 6 X 14 1/2 In. ....*Illus*	1700.00
Rice Bowl, Seated Couples, 4 1/2 X 2 1/4 In.	10.00
Slop Jar	2475.00
Sugar & Creamer, People On Porch, Flowers, Cover, 5 1/2 In.	180.00
Tea & Coffee Set, Creamer, Sugar, Teapot & Coffeepot	1625.00
Tea Set, Bamboo Handles, Indoor Figures, Pear Shape, 3 Piece	170.00
Teapot, Basket, Cord–Wrapped Handles, C.1860	175.00
Teapot, Individual	135.00
Teapot, Melon Shape, Loop Handle	320.00
Teapot, People In Pavilion Panels, Gilt Floral Ground, 1890	450.00
Teapot, String–Wrapped Wire Handle, 6 In.	125.00
Urn, Gold Dragons, Foo Dog Handles, 37 X 17 In., Pair	1000.00
Vase, Figures & Scenes, 9 In.	245.00
Vase, Genre Scenes, Sprays, Butterflies, Flamed Base, 13 In.	425.00
Vase, Gold Handles, 6 Sides, 6 3/4 In.	120.00

ROSE O'NEILL, see Kewpie

Rose Tapestry porcelain was made by the Royal Bayreuth factory of Tettau, Germany, during the late nineteenth century. The surface of the porcelain was pressed against a coarse fabric while it was still damp, and the impressions remained on the finished porcelain. It looks and feels like a textured cloth. Very skillful reproductions are being made that even include a variation of the Royal Bayreuth mark, so be careful when buying.

ROSE TAPESTRY, Ashtray, Square, Blue Mark	165.00
Basket, 3–Color Roses, Blue Mark, 4 1/2 X 3 1/2 In.	225.00
Basket, Roses, White Ferns, Rope Handle, Gold Trim, 4 1/2 In.	335.00
Creamer, 3–Color Roses, Pinch Spout, Blue Mark	145.00
Creamer, Victorian Woman's Portrait, Blue Mark, 4 In.	250.00
Hair Receiver, 3–Footed, Royal Bayreuth	175.00
Hatpin Holder, Green Mark	335.00
Match Holder, Musicians Scene, Gold Trim, Wall	265.00
Nappy, Desert Scene, Blue Mark	110.00
Picture Frame, 5 1/2 X 4 1/4 In.	495.00
Pin Dish, 3–Color Roses, Red Rose Border, Cover	140.00
Plate, 3–Color, 6 In.	175.00
Relish, Small	225.00
Ring Box, Puffy Pillow Cover, Triangular, Marked, 3 In.	295.00
Ring Tree	175.00
Saltshaker	175.00
Shoe, Woman's High–Laced, Blue Mark	395.00
Toothpick, Old Man of The Mountain, Coal Scuttle Shape	295.00
Vase, Polar Bear, Handles, Blue Mark, 4 1/2 In.	250.00
Vase, White & Yellow Roses, Signed, 4 1/4 In.	190.00

Rosenthal porcelain was made at the factory established in Selb, Bavaria, in 1880. The factory is still making fine–quality tablewares and figurines. A series of Christmas plates was made from 1910. Other limited edition plates have been made since 1971.

ROSENTHAL, Ashtray, Fish Shape, Art Deco, Pair	35.00
Bowl, Red Berries, Gold Band, Pointed Handles, Oval, 9 X 4 1/2 In.	40.00
Bowl, Vegetable, Maria, Open, 10 In.	45.00
Cake Plate, Hand Painted Grapes, Open Handles, 12 In.	65.00
Cake Plate, Signed, 10 3/4 In.	45.00
Coffeepot, 10 In.	85.00
Creamer, Old Dutch	32.00
Cup & Saucer, Orchids Design, Signed R.Loewy	25.00
Cup, Demitasse, Portrait	22.00
Demitasse Set, White, Gold & Platinum Bands, 11 Piece	450.00
Eggcup, Moss Rose, Sterling Saucer Base	45.00
Figurine, Bird, Perched, Large	115.00
Figurine, Blackamoor, C.1930, 7 1/2 In., Pair	395.00
Figurine, Bullfinch, 3 1/2 In.	50.00
Figurine, Butterfly, Colored	95.00
Figurine, Dachshund Pup, 3 3/4 X 4 In.	90.00
Figurine, Dachshund, Signed F.Heindenreigh, 4 1/4 X 8 In.	280.00
Figurine, Deer Sitting, 4 X 3 1/2 In.	185.00
Figurine, Hen & Rooster	150.00
Figurine, Irish Setter, Sitting, 6 1/2 In.	270.00
Figurine, Mallard, U.S.Zone, 2 1/2 In.	45.00
Figurine, Naked Boy, Dancing With Goat, 6 1/2 In.	250.00
Figurine, Poodle, Sitting, Head Turned, Black	250.00
Figurine, Ram, Mottled Gray, 9 In.	195.00 To 230.00
Figurine, Stylized Maiden, Arm Around Afghan Hound, 9 In.	770.00
Hatpin Holder, Silver Deposit, Green	225.00
Paperweight, Satyr Listening To Singing Birds	275.00
Plate, Allover Roses, Blue & Gold Border, Signed, 10 1/4 In.	48.00
Plate, Christmas, 1951	450.00
Plate, Courtship, Pink Roses, Gold Scalloped, 10 In.	55.00
Plate, Queen's Rose, 10 1/4 In.	16.00
Plate, Rose Center, Gilt & Blue Borders, 11 In., 11 Piece	303.00
Platter, Maria, 15 In.	45.00
Sugar & Creamer, Blue Cherries, Pate–Sur–Pate	85.00
Tray, Dresser, Hand–Painted Poppies, Green, Gold Trim, Signed	35.00
Tray, Fluted, Victorian Woman, Clover Shape, Open Handles, 7 In.	50.00
Vase, Marsh Scene, Herons, Rust Ground, Ivory Design, 9 1/2 In.	250.00

The Roseville Pottery Company was organized in Roseville, Ohio, in 1890. Another plant was opened in Zanesville, Ohio, in 1898. Many types of pottery were made until 1954. Early wares include sgraffito, Olympic, and Rozane. Later lines were often made with molded decorations, especially flowers and fruit. Pieces are marked "Roseville."

ROSEVILLE, Ashtray, Bushberry	22.00
Ashtray, Hyde Park	18.00 To 22.00
Ashtray, Magnolia, 2 Handles	115.00 To 135.00
Ashtray, Pine Cone, Blue, 4 In.	85.00
Ashtray, Raymor, Gray, Pair	18.50
Ashtray, Snowberry, Blue	40.00
Ashtray, Zephyr Lily, Blue	45.00
Ashtray, Zephyr Lily, Brown	34.00
Bank, Monkey	125.00
Basket, Apple Blossom, Green, 12 In.	175.00
Basket, Bittersweet, Green, 10 In.	80.00
Basket, Bleeding Heart, Pink, 10 In.	100.00
Basket, Capri, 10 In.	50.00
Basket, Columbine, Blue, 12 In.	110.00 To 195.00
Basket, Columbine, Brown, 12 In.	95.00

Basket, Cover, Royal Capri, Allover Gold 300.00
Basket, Florane, Brown, 8 In. 68.00
Basket, Freesia, Brown 70.00
Basket, Gardenia, Tan, 10 In. 90.00
Basket, Hanging, Apple Blossom, Blue 90.00
Basket, Hanging, Apple Blossom, Green 95.00
Basket, Hanging, Bleeding Heart, Pink .... 125.00 To 130.00
Basket, Hanging, Bushberry, Brown 110.00
Basket, Hanging, Columbine, Blue 95.00
Basket, Hanging, Dahlrose 125.00
Basket, Hanging, Dogwood II 110.00
Basket, Hanging, Donatello, Chains 150.00
Basket, Hanging, Egypto, 11 In. 200.00
Basket, Hanging, Foxglove, Pink & White Blossoms, Blue 110.00
Basket, Hanging, Futura 245.00
Basket, Hanging, Imperial II 65.00
Basket, Hanging, Peony, Yellow 55.00
Basket, Hanging, Pine Cone, Chain 135.00
Basket, Hanging, Primrose, Pink, 6 In. 85.00
Basket, Hanging, Rozane, 1917, 6 X 10 In. 85.00
Basket, Hanging, Water Lily, Brown, 9 In. 70.00
Basket, Hanging, Zephyr Lily, Green, 7 1/2 In. 50.00
Basket, Magnolia, Blue, 8 In. 60.00
Basket, Magnolia, Blue, 10 In. 80.00
Basket, Magnolia, Blue, 12 In. 85.00
Basket, Magnolia, Brown, 10 In. 125.00
Basket, Ming Tree, 14 In. 145.00
Basket, Morning Glory, Green, 10 1/2 In. 595.00
Basket, Peony 75.00
Basket, Pine Cone, Brown, 10 In. 195.00
Basket, Pine Cone, Brown, Green, Attached Frog 165.00
Basket, Rozane, Green 145.00
Basket, Snowberry, Rust, 7 In. 45.00
Basket, Water Lily, Pink 75.00
Basket, Wincraft, Brown Berries, Brown, Glossy Yellow, 12 In. 60.00
Basket, Zephyr Lily, Brown, 8 In. 55.00
Bookends, Burmese, Figural, Black 150.00
Bookends, Burmese, Figural, White 150.00
Bookends, Clematis, Blue 65.00
Bookends, Foxglove 75.00
Bookends, Gardenia, Tan 80.00
Bookends, Iris 110.00
Bookends, Magnolia, Green .... 55.00 To 70.00
Bookends, Pine Cone, Brown 140.00
Bookends, Snowberry, Blue ....75.00 To 110.00
Bookends, Wincraft, Lime Green 50.00
Bookends, Zephyr Lily 75.00
Bowl, Apple Blossom, Green, 8 In. .... 40.00 To 50.00
Bowl, Apple Blossom, Pink, 10 In. 40.00
Bowl, Apple Blossom, Pink, 12 In. 40.00
Bowl, Baneda, Mauve, 11 In. 105.00
Bowl, Bittersweet, Green, 14 In. 75.00
Bowl, Blackberry, 9 1/2 In. 130.00
Bowl, Bushberry, 10 In. 40.00
Bowl, Cherry Blossom, Flowerpot Shape, Blue & Pink, 4 In. 95.00
Bowl, Clematis, Blue, 12 In. 70.00
Bowl, Clematis, Brown, 4 In. 38.00
Bowl, Columbine, 3 In. 30.00
Bowl, Columbine, Brown, 12 In. 50.00
Bowl, Corinthian, 6 In. 20.00
Bowl, Corinthian, 8 In. 48.00
Bowl, Dahlrose, 9 In. 28.00
Bowl, Dogwood II, 7 In. 40.00
Bowl, Earlam, 9 In. 85.00

Bowl, Earlam, Blue, 12 In. 85.00
Bowl, Ferella, Brown, 9 In. 200.00
Bowl, Florane, 1920s, 5 X 8 In. 48.00
Bowl, Florentine, 4 1/2 In. 25.00
Bowl, Florentine, 6 In. 35.00
Bowl, Florentine, Rim Handles, Brown, 7 In. 42.00
Bowl, Flower Frog, Donatello, 3 X 6 1/2 In. 50.00
Bowl, Flower Frog, Magnolia, Blue, 12 In. 145.00
Bowl, Foxglove, Blue, 5 In. 40.00
Bowl, Freesia, Blue, 14 In. 50.00
Bowl, Freesia, Brown, 12 In. 75.00
Bowl, Fuchsia, Blue, 4 In. 35.00
Bowl, Gardenia, Purple, Gray, 6 In. 50.00
Bowl, Geese, Landscape, Pedestal, Signed Frederick Rhead 825.00
Bowl, Imperial II, Yellow Splatter, Blue, 4 X 9 In. 110.00
Bowl, Ixia, Pink, 4 In. 35.00
Bowl, Ixia, Pink, 10 In. 58.00
Bowl, Laurel, Green, 6 1/2 X 2 1/2 In. 42.00
Bowl, Laurel, Yellow, 13 In. 80.00
Bowl, Magnolia, Green, 14 In. 40.00
Bowl, Magnolia, Handles, Green, 2 In. 45.00
Bowl, Medallion, Green, Gold Swags, 3 Pillar Legs, 3 X 4 In. 56.00
Bowl, Moderne, 8 In. 15.00
Bowl, Mostique, 8 In. .... 25.00 To 60.00
Bowl, Mostique, 10 In. 65.00
Bowl, Mostique, Gray, 8 X 3 In. 40.00
Bowl, Mostique, Handle, 9 In. 55.00
Bowl, Mostique, Ivory Matte, Label, 3 In. 25.00
Bowl, Peony, Pink, 4 In. 40.00
Bowl, Persian, 3 1/2 In. .... 65.00 To 75.00
Bowl, Pine Cone, Blue, 6 In. 95.00
Bowl, Pine Cone, Blue, Rectangular, 12 In. 125.00
Bowl, Pine Cone, Brown, 12 In. 85.00
Bowl, Pine Cone, Green, 3 In. 35.00
Bowl, Raymor, Lizard, Divided, 13 In. 32.00
Bowl, Rosecraft, Orange & Brown, 5 In. 45.00
Bowl, Rozane, Teal, 1940s, Dark Blue–Green, 11 In. 39.00
Bowl, Snowberry, Green, 7 X 2 In. 45.00
Bowl, Snowberry, Pink, 10 In. 45.00
Bowl, Sunflower, Mottled Green, Gold Sunflowers, 6 1/2 X 8 In. 150.00
Bowl, Thorn Apple, Pink, 6 In. .... 55.00 To 60.00
Bowl, Thorn Apple, Pink, 7 In. 28.00
Bowl, Thorn Apple, Turquoise, 9 In. 60.00
Bowl, Tuscany, Gray, 12 1/2 In. 65.00
Bowl, Wisteria, Blue, 9 In. 150.00
Bowl, Wisteria, Handles, Silver Label, 7 1/2 X 12 In. 125.00
Bowl, Zephyr Lily, Brown, Oval, 12 In. 35.00
Candleholder, Bushberry, 5 In., Pair 40.00
Candleholder, Carnelian I, Tan, 1 7/8 In., Pair 25.00
Candleholder, Clemana, Green, 4 1/2 In. 30.00
Candleholder, Clematis, Brown, 2 In., Pair 15.00
Candleholder, Columbine, Brown, 2 1/2 In., Pair 28.00
Candleholder, Ferella, Brown, 4 1/2 In. 140.00
Candleholder, Luffa, Green 70.00
Candleholder, Magnolia, Brown, 5 In., Pair 50.00
Candleholder, Peony, Gold, 4 3/4 In., Pair 35.00
Candleholder, Peony, Pink, 2 In., Pair 25.00
Candleholder, Primrose, 4 1/2 In., Pair 125.00
Candleholder, Snowberry, Pair 45.00
Candleholder, Teasel, Blue, Low 33.00
Candleholder, Tuscany, Gray, 3 1/2 In., Pair 48.00
Candleholder, Tuscany, Gray, 3 5/8 In. 25.00
Candleholder, Velmoss Scroll, 8 In., Pair 70.00
Candleholder, Water Lily, Brown, 2 In., Pair 50.00

Candleholder, White Rose, Low, Pair	30.00
Candleholder, Windsor, Red, Pair	165.00
Compote, Donatello, 4 In.	45.00 To 55.00
Compote, Florentine, Brown, 5 In.	40.00
Compote, Florentine, Footed, 10 In.	45.00
Compote, Mostique, Gray, 7 5/8 In.	65.00
Compote, Orion, Blue, 10 1/2 In.	48.00
Compote, Tuscany, 4 In.	30.00
Console Set, Columbine, Pink, 3 Piece	100.00
Console Set, Ferella, Built In Frog, 3 Piece	295.00
Console Set, Silhouette, Aqua, 3 Piece	55.00
Console Set, Snowberry, Green, 3 Piece	65.00
Console, Bittersweet, 14 3/4 In.	46.00
Console, Clematis, Brown, 14 In.	66.00
Console, Foxglove, Blue, 10 In.	70.00
Console, Gardenia, Gray, Boat Shape, 13 X 6 X 5 1/2 In.	55.00
Console, Mayfair, Brown, Footed, 12 In.	50.00
Console, Moss, Green, 13 In.	50.00
Console, Orian, Rose, Green, End Handles, 15 X 7 1/4 X 4 1/2 In.	68.00
Console, Snowberry, Rose, 11 X 2 3/4 In.	40.00
Console, Tuscany, Gray, Footed, 14 1/2 In.	65.00
Console, Wisteria, 12 3/4 X 6 3/4 X 3 In.	92.00
Console, Zephyr Lily, Green, 12 In.	45.00
Cookie Jar, Freesia, Blue	125.00
Cookie Jar, Water Lily, Brown	110.00 To 165.00
Cookie Jar, Zephyr Lily, Brown	125.00
Cornucopia, Apple Blossom, Blue, 6 In.	45.00
Cornucopia, Bleeding Heart, Green, 6 In.	20.00
Cornucopia, Bushberry, Double, Blue, 8 In.	45.00
Cornucopia, Magnolia, Green, 6 In.	20.00
Cornucopia, Mayfair, Brown, 3 In.	10.00
Cornucopia, Peony, Brown, Green, 6 1/4 In.	35.00
Cornucopia, Pine Cone, Brown, 6 In.	30.00 To 55.00
Cornucopia, Silhouette, Green, 1952	35.00
Cornucopia, Snowberry, Green, 8 In.	30.00
Creamer, Clematis, Green	18.00
Creamer, Magnolia, Blue	10.00
Creamer, Medallion	35.00
Cup & Saucer, Raymor, Light & Dark Green	18.00
Cup & Saucer, Raymor, Terra–Cotta	10.00
Cuspidor, Donatello, 3 Cherub Panels, Ivory Neck, 1915, 5 1/2 In.	179.00
Cuspidor, Mostique	137.50
Dish, Feeding, Dogs, Blue Luster Rim, Rolled Lip, 8 In.	40.00
Dish, Feeding, Old Woman & Children Rhyme	40.00
Dish, Feeding, Rabbits	40.00
Dish, Soup, Raymor, Medium Brown, Lug, Pair	12.00
Ewer, Bushberry, Brown, 15 In.	180.00
Ewer, Clematis, Blue	75.00
Ewer, Columbine, Blue, 7 In.	55.00
Ewer, Dawn, Green, 15 In.	250.00
Ewer, Foxglove, Blue, 10 In.	95.00
Ewer, Freesia, Tan, 6 In.	35.00
Ewer, Ming Tree, Turquoise, 10 In.	95.00
Ewer, Ming Tree, White, 10 In.	75.00
Ewer, Peony, Green, 6 In.	35.00
Ewer, Pine Cone, 12 In.	120.00
Ewer, Pine Cone, 18 In.	350.00
Ewer, Rozane, 9 1/2 In.	300.00
Ewer, Silhouette, Turquoise, 6 1/4 In.	40.00
Ewer, Snowberry, Blue, 15 In.	190.00
Ewer, Snowberry, Green, 6 In.	45.00
Ewer, Water Lily, Blue, 6 In.	35.00
Ewer, Water Lily, Pink, 15 In.	160.00
Ewer, Zephyr Lily, Blue, 10 In.	75.00

Ewer, Zephyr Lily, Brown, 15 In.	125.00
Flower Box, Sunflower, 11 In.	110.00
Flower Frog, Clematis, Green, 4 1/2 In.	24.00
Flower Frog, Florentine, Dark Brown, 3 1/2 In.	9.00
Flower Frog, Ixia, Green	30.00
Flowerpot, Freesia, Brown, 5 In.	36.00
Flowerpot, Pine Cone, Blue, 5 In.	38.00
Flowerpot, Rosecraft, Black, 8 In.	85.00
Flowerpot, Zephyr Lily, Green	45.00
Jardiniere, Baneda, Green, 6 In.	85.00
Jardiniere, Bittersweet, Gray, Pedestal, 8 In.	650.00
Jardiniere, Bushberry, Brown, 10 In.	250.00
Jardiniere, Cherry Blossom, Brown, 6 In.	145.00
Jardiniere, Clematis, Pedestal	345.00
Jardiniere, Corinthian, 9 X 13 In.	200.00
Jardiniere, Dahlrose, 4 1/2 X 6 3/4 In.	45.00
Jardiniere, Dahlrose, 6 X 8 In.	145.00
Jardiniere, Donatello, Ivory, 7 In.	100.00
Jardiniere, Florentine, Brown, 8 X 11 In.	140.00
Jardiniere, Fuchsia, Brown, 10 In.	365.00
Jardiniere, Futura, 6 In.	145.00
Jardiniere, Ivory II, 4 In.	45.00
Jardiniere, Jonquil, 4 In.	32.00 To 65.00
Jardiniere, Jonquil, 6 In.	110.00
Jardiniere, Luffa, 8 In.	200.00
Jardiniere, Magnolia, 3 In.	20.00
Jardiniere, Mostique, Green & Rose Design, 8 In.	75.00
Jardiniere, Normandy, 8 X 10 1/2 In.	250.00
Jardiniere, Normandy, 9 3/4 X 12 In.	290.00
Jardiniere, Persian, 8 X 10 In.	250.00
Jardiniere, Pine Cone, Blue, 8 In.	100.00
Jardiniere, Rozane, 1917, 10 X 13 In.	220.00
Jardiniere, Snowberry, Black	97.50
Jardiniere, Velmoss Scroll, 10 In.	170.00 To 250.00
Jug, Cherry Blossom, Brown, Label, 7 In.	120.00
Lamp, Ferella, Brown	550.00
Lamp, Florentine, 8 1/2 In.	100.00 To 125.00
Lamp, Florentine, Period Shade, 8 1/2 In.	125.00
Lamp, Ixia, Experimental, Flowers	390.00
Mug, Dutch, Creamware	55.00
Mug, Holland, Green	45.00
Mug, Magnolia, Blue, 3 In.	38.00
Mug, Raymor, Light Brown, Pair	40.00
Mug, Rozane, 1900	90.00 To 115.00
Mustard, Raymor, Brown	30.00
Owl, Thorn Apple, Blue, 6 In.	50.00
Pitcher, Aztec, 5 In.	175.00
Pitcher, Freesia, Brown, 10 In.	65.00
Pitcher, Pine Cone, Green, 9 In.	175.00
Pitcher, Pine Cone, Green, 10 In.	150.00
Planter, Bittersweet, Pointed Handles, Orange Pods, 8 X 9 1/2 In.	45.00
Planter, Chloron, 4 Cherub Heads, 3 X 6 In.	150.00
Planter, Donatello, 10 1/2 In.	40.00
Planter, Gardenia, Gray, 12 In.	50.00
Planter, Jonquil, 9 In.	75.00
Planter, Magnolia, 12 In.	45.00
Planter, Zephyr Lily, Brown, 8 In.	24.00
Plate, Juvenile, Rabbits	45.00 To 60.00
Plate, Juvenile, Tom, Tom The Piper's Son	75.00
Powder Jar, Donatello	240.00
Rose Bowl, Teasel, Blue, 4 In.	30.00
Strawberry Pot, Carnelian II, Aqua, 8 In.	60.00
Sugar & Creamer, Bittersweet, Gray	45.00

Sugar & Creamer, Snowberry, Pink 65.00
Tankard Set, Moose, 7 Piece 250.00
Tankard Set, Quaker, 5 Piece 950.00
Tankard, Rozane, 13 1/2 In. 695.00
Tea Set, Apple Blossom, Blue, 3 Piece 125.00
Tea Set, Apple Blossom, Green, 3 Piece 165.00
Tea Set, Magnolia, Blue, 3 Piece 95.00
Tea Set, Wincraft, 3 Piece 90.00
Tray, Dresser, Forget-Me-Not 85.00
Tray, Foxglove, Green, 15 X 7 1/2 In. 60.00
Tray, Zephyr Lily, Burnt Orange, Marked, 15 In. 65.00
Tumbler, Pine Cone, Brown 100.00
Umbrella Stand, Dogwood I, 20 1/4 In. 325.00
Umbrella Stand, Mostique, Gray, 20 1/4 In. 250.00
Umbrella Stand, Normandy, 20 In. 400.00
Urn, Blackberry, 6 In. 125.00
Urn, Cherry Blossom, Brown, 5 In. 105.00
Urn, Cherry Blossom, Brown, 8 In. 245.00
Urn, Moss, Blue, 8 In. 80.00
Urn, Pine Cone, Silver Base, 6 X 8 In. 35.00
Urn, Pine Cone, Single Handle, Green, 6 In. 70.00
Urn, Silhouette, Reclining Nude, Blue, Green, 8 1/2 In. 225.00
Urn, Velmoss II, Green, 5 In. 28.00
Vase, Apple Blossom, 9 In. 40.00
Vase, Baneda, Green, 7 In. 100.00
Vase, Baneda, Green, Label, 9 1/2 In. 165.00
Vase, Baneda, Handles, Blue, 6 In. 65.00
Vase, Bittersweet, Rust Berries, Pointed Handles, 4 In. 20.00
Vase, Bittersweet, Yellow, 8 In. 45.00
Vase, Blackberry, 4 In. 85.00
Vase, Blackberry, 6 In. .... 165.00 To 170.00
Vase, Bleeding Heart, Blue, 10 1/4 In. 85.00
Vase, Bleeding Heart, Green, 7 1/2 In. 48.00
Vase, Bud, Freesia, Brown, 7 In. 30.00
Vase, Bud, Magnolia, Blue, Waist Handles, 7 In. 42.00
Vase, Bud, Peony, Gold, Handle, 7 In. 25.00
Vase, Bud, Rosecraft, Yellow, 8 In. 47.00
Vase, Bushberry, Blue, 4 In. .... 20.00 To 25.00
Vase, Bushberry, Blue, 9 In. 40.00
Vase, Bushberry, Blue, 12 In. 135.00
Vase, Bushberry, Brown, 15 In. 165.00
Vase, Bushberry, Double, Green, 4 1/2 In. 35.00
Vase, Bushberry, Double, Rust, 4 1/2 In. 42.00
Vase, Bushberry, Green, Rectangular, 9 1/2 In. 50.00
Vase, Bushberry, Russet, 7 In. 45.00
Vase, Carnelian I, Green, Gold Trim, 9 1/4 In. 55.00
Vase, Carnelian I, Shoulder Handles, Blue, 18 In. 195.00
Vase, Carnelian II, Brown, 10 In. .... 45.00 To 55.00
Vase, Carnelian II, Pink & Purple, 10 In. 85.00
Vase, Cherry Blossom, Brown, 7 In. 135.00
Vase, Cherry Blossom, Pink & Blue, 5 In. 165.00
Vase, Cherry Blossom, Pink, 6 In. 175.00
Vase, Clematis, Blue, 7 In. 60.00
Vase, Clematis, Blue, 15 In. 165.00
Vase, Clematis, Brown, 6 In. 25.00
Vase, Clematis, Handles, Green, 4 In. 25.00
Vase, Clematis, Orange, 6 In. 30.00
Vase, Columbine, Brown, 14 In. .... 265.00 To 275.00
Vase, Columbine, Handles, Blue, 14 1/2 In. .... 150.00 To 175.00
Vase, Cosmos, Blue, 9 In. 50.00
Vase, Cosmos, Tan, 6 X 8 In. 90.00
Vase, Cremona, Pink, 10 In. 95.00
Vase, Dahlrose, Brown, 6 In. 39.00
Vase, Della Robbia, 8 1/2 In. 1150.00

Vase, Donatello, 7 In., Pair 95.00
Vase, Earlam, Green & Blue, 7 In. 125.00
Vase, Egypto, 12 1/2 In. 265.00
Vase, Falline, 6 In. 135.00
Vase, Florane, Bowl Shape, 7 1/2 X 5 In. 50.00
Vase, Florentine, 12 1/2 In. 95.00
Vase, Foxglove, Blue, 6 In. .... 35.00 To 40.00
Vase, Freesia, Blue, 19 In. 245.00
Vase, Fuchsia, Brown, 18 In. 375.00
Vase, Fuchsia, Green, 15 In. 295.00
Vase, Futura, Pink & Green, Glossy, 8 In. 225.00
Vase, Futura, Purple To Deep Pink, 8 1/4 In. 140.00
Vase, Gardenia, Brown, 14 In. 160.00
Vase, Imperial I, 9 In. 60.00
Vase, Iris, 4 In. 35.00
Vase, Iris, 8 In. 60.00
Vase, Ixia, 2 Handles, Blue–Green, 6 1/2 In. 30.00
Vase, Ixia, Yellow, 12 In. 125.00
Vase, Jonquil, 4 In. 40.00
Vase, Jonquil, Handles, 9 In. 110.00
Vase, La Rose, Footed, Rim Handles, 4 1/2 X 7 1/4 In. 45.00
Vase, Laurel, Green, 6 In. 65.00
Vase, Laurel, Yellow, 9 1/2 In. 125.00
Vase, Luffa, Green, 7 In. 62.00
Vase, Magnolia, Blue, Green, 13 In. 135.00
Vase, Magnolia, Brown, 7 1/4 In. 35.00
Vase, Magnolia, Brown, 9 In. 65.00
Vase, Magnolia, Green, 7 In. 45.00
Vase, Magnolia, Green, 8 In. .... 55.00 To 70.00
Vase, Magnolia, Green, 12 In. 65.00
Vase, Mock Orange, 10 In., Pair 110.00
Vase, Mongol, Bulbous, 10 1/2 In. 550.00
Vase, Monticello, 4 In. 65.00
Vase, Monticello, 5 In. 65.00
Vase, Morning Glory, 8 In. 150.00
Vase, Morning Glory, White, 15 In. 500.00
Vase, Mostique, Gray & Blue, 12 In. 125.00
Vase, Mostique, Gray, 6 In. 20.00
Vase, Orian, Blue Drip, Gold Label, 8 In. 50.00
Vase, Orian, Turquoise, 14 In. 175.00
Vase, Pauleo, Brown Underglaze, Swirl Overglaze, 13 In. 400.00
Vase, Pauleo, Mottled Green Over Brown, Green Wash, 12 3/4 In. 150.00
Vase, Pauleo, Plum, Bulbous, 8 1/2 In. 550.00
Vase, Peony, Gold & Green, 9 1/2 In. 48.00
Vase, Peony, Green, Shoulder Handles, 18 5/8 In. 220.00
Vase, Peony, Pink, 4 In. 20.00
Vase, Peony, Yellow, 9 In. 50.00
Vase, Pine Cone, Blue, 6 In. 45.00
Vase, Pine Cone, Brown, 6 In. 65.00
Vase, Primrose, Pink, 4 In. 45.00
Vase, Primrose, Pink, 7 In. 55.00
Vase, Primrose, Pink, 12 In. 210.00
Vase, Rosecraft Vintage, Bowl Shape, 4 X 6 In. 55.00
Vase, Rosecraft Vintage, Shoulder Handles, 6 X 3 3/4 In. 55.00
Vase, Rosecraft, 7 In. 65.00
Vase, Rosecraft, 12 1/2 In. 160.00
Vase, Rozane, Light Green, 8 In. 55.00
Vase, Russco, Blue, 7 In. 75.00
Vase, Russco, Brown, Bronze, Footed, 8 1/2 In. 98.00
Vase, Russco, Handles, Rust, Paper Label, 8 1/2 In. 55.00
Vase, Russco, Turquoise, 12 1/2 In. 90.00
Vase, Silhouette, Ivory, 6 In. 50.00
Vase, Silhouette, White, Green Floral Panel, 8 In. 24.00
Vase, Sunflower, 5 In. 65.00

Vase, Sunflower, 8 In. 195.00
Vase, Teasel, Blue, 15 In. 325.00
Vase, Thorn Apple, 10 1/2 In. 110.00
Vase, Topeo, Handles, Flat, 9 In. 165.00
Vase, Tourmaline, Blue, 6 In. .... 50.00 To 52.00
Vase, Tourmaline, Gold Highlights, 5 3/4 In. 37.00
Vase, Tuscany, Pink, Shoulder Handles, Bulbous, 10 In. 78.00
Vase, Volpato, Ivory, Fluted, 7 1/4 X 4 In., Pair 125.00
Vase, Water Lily, Brown, 4 In. .... 30.00 To 40.00
Vase, White Rose, Blue & Turquoise, Handles At Shoulders, 19 In. 275.00
Vase, White Rose, Blue, 6 1/4 In. 40.00
Vase, White Rose, Green & Brown, 8 In. 60.00
Vase, White Rose, Rose, Green, 6 In. 45.00
Vase, Wisteria, 2 Handles, Brown, Green & Lavender, 8 1/2 In. 135.00
Vase, Wisteria, Brown, 4 3/4 In. 80.00
Vase, Woodland, 4 Sides, 11 In. 385.00
Vase, Woodland, Seal, 7 In. 500.00
Vase, Zephyr Lily, 7 In. 37.00
Vase, Zephyr Lily, 12 In. 125.00
Vase, Zephyr Lily, 15 In. 135.00
Wall Pocket, Apple Blossom, Green .... 55.00 To 85.00
Wall Pocket, Carnelian I, Blue, 8 In. 65.00
Wall Pocket, Carnelian I, Green, 8 In. 75.00
Wall Pocket, Clematis, Brown, 8 In. 50.00
Wall Pocket, Corinthian, 9 In. 75.00
Wall Pocket, Cosmos, 6 1/2 In. 65.00
Wall Pocket, Cosmos, Double, Brown, 8 1/2 In. 115.00
Wall Pocket, Dahlrose, 9 In. 80.00
Wall Pocket, Donatello, 9 In. 95.00
Wall Pocket, Donatello, 10 In. .... 45.00 To 95.00
Wall Pocket, Donatello, 12 In. .... 95.00 To 125.00
Wall Pocket, Florane, 9 In. 75.00
Wall Pocket, Florentine, Brown, 5 In. 70.00
Wall Pocket, Freesia, Blue, 8 In. 35.00
Wall Pocket, Freesia, Brown, 8 In. 55.00
Wall Pocket, Freesia, Green, 8 In. 75.00
Wall Pocket, Futura, Panels, C.1928, 6 1/4 X 8 1/4 In. 125.00
Wall Pocket, Gardenia, Gray 115.00
Wall Pocket, Iris, Blue, 8 In. 195.00
Wall Pocket, La Rose, 7 1/2 In. 72.00
Wall Pocket, Lombardy, Glossy Turquoise Glaze 120.00
Wall Pocket, Magnolia, 6 1/2 In. 65.00
Wall Pocket, Mostique, Cone Shape, 9 1/2 In. 35.00
Wall Pocket, Orchid, Green, 9 In. 95.00
Wall Pocket, Pine Cone, Brown, 8 In. 135.00
Wall Pocket, Primrose, Brown, 8 In. 170.00
Wall Pocket, Rosecraft, Black, 10 In. .... 75.00 To 90.00
Wall Pocket, Silhouette, Magenta, 8 In. 75.00
Wall Pocket, Tuscany, Pink, 8 In. 65.00
Wall Pocket, White Rose, Green, 10 In. 75.00
Wall Pocket, Wincraft, Brown 70.00
Wall Pocket, Zephyr Lily, Brown .... 60.00 To 75.00
Window Box, Apple Blossom, 10 In. 37.00
Window Box, Ming Tree, 10 In. 70.00
Window Box, Wincraft, Chartreuse, 12 In., 2 Piece 42.00

Rowland & Marsellus Company is a mark which appears on historical Staffordshire dating from the late nineteenth and early twentieth centuries. Rowland & Marsellus is believed to be the mark used by the British Anchor Pottery Co. of Longton, England, for some pieces made for export to a New York firm. Many American views were made. Of special interest to collectors are the rolled edge, blue and white plates.

ROWLAND & MARSELLUS, Plate, Albany, Fort Frederick, Blue, White, Rolled Edge   45.00

Plate, Capitol, Washington, D.C., Blue 45.00
Plate, Faneuil Hall, Boston Harbor, Brown Transfer 35.00

Roy Rogers was born in 1911 in Cincinnati, Ohio. In the 1930s, he made a living as a singer; and in 1935, his group started work at a Los Angeles radio station. He appeared in his first movie in 1937. From 1952 to 1957, he made 101 television shows. Roy Rogers memorabilia is collected, including items from the Roy Rogers restaurants.

ROY ROGERS, Badge, Sheriff, Roy & Trigger, Deputy, Quaker Oats, 1940–50 .... 45.00
Bank, Boot, Metal, 5 1/2 In. 65.00
Belt, Leather, Tag 45.00
Blanket, Blue & White, Scenes, Signs, Reversible, 68 X 84 In. 65.00
Book, Big Little Book, Range Detective 10.00
Book, Ghost of Mystery Rancho, Inscription 65.00
Book, Little Golden Book, Roy Rogers & Cowboy Toby 10.00
Book, Pop–Up, 1934 .... 100.00
Book, Roy Rogers & Gopher Creek Gunman 20.00
Bow, Hardwood, Black Paint, Roy's Signature, No String, 48 In. 75.00
Button, 1950s 15.00
Button, Black & White Photo, 1940s 40.00
Camera ....8.00 To 10.00
Chaps, Plastic 30.00
Comic Book, No.10 .... 29.00
Comic Book, No.27 .... 18.00
Comic Book, No.36 .... 15.00
Comic Book, No.79 .... 9.00
Costume, Cowgirl, Dale Evans, Queen of The West, Box 160.00
Cowboy Boots 100.00
Cup, Plastic 16.00
Doll, Dale Evans & Roy Rogers, 1950s, Pair 125.00
Figurine, Dale Evans, Hartland 100.00
Figurine, Trigger, Whitman, 1950 .... 8.00
Flashlight, Signal Siren 12.00
Guitar, Copyright 1954, Case 65.00
Gun & Holster Set, Double 185.00
Gun, Cap, Trigger 25.00
Gun, Derringer, On Card 85.00
Gun, Tuck–A–Way, Store Card 25.00
Hat Band, White Fabric, Roy Rogers Symbols, Design, 1950, 20 In. 5.00
Hat Ring, Silver 35.00
Hat, With Hidden Cap Gun, Quick Shooter 225.00
Knife, Horseshoe, Pearl Insert 17.00
Lobby Card, Billy The Kid Returns, 1938, 11 X 14 In. 10.00
Lunch Box, Ranch, Thermos ....15.00 To 35.00
Lunch Box, Roy Rogers & Dale Evans 20.00
Neckerchief, Covered Wagons 12.00
Nodder 60.00
Pajamas 25.00
Photo, Premium, Original Envelope, Early 1940s 95.00
Photograph, Roy Rogers Riders, Comic Book Club Members, 1950s 40.00
Plate, Rodeo, Universal 25.00
Pop–Out Cards, Set of 21 .... 225.00
Poster, In Old Caliente, Republic, 1938, 41 X 81 In. 175.00
Poster, Movie, Twilight In Sierras, 1950, 27 X 41 In. 65.00
Puzzle, Whitman, 1952 .... 11.00
Record, Roy & Dale Evans, Original Picture Sleeve 20.00
Saddle 250.00
Sheet Music, Roy On Cover, 1952 .... 10.00
Slippers, Child's, Felt 45.00
Spurs 42.00
Sweatshirt 45.00
Thermos, Red Cap, Litho of Roy, Dale Evans, Trigger, Dog 6.00
Toy, Ranch, Marx 135.00

Toy, Zig Zag Stagecoach, Windup 145.00
Wristwatch, Ingraham 30.00
Yo–Yo 12.00

The Royal Bayreuth factory was founded in Tettau, Bavaria, in 1794. It has continued to modern times. The marks have changed through the years. A stylized crest, the name "Royal Bayreuth," and the word "Bavaria" appear in slightly different forms from 1870 to about 1919. Later dishes may include the words "U.S. Zone," the year of the issue, or the word "Germany" instead of "Bavaria."

ROYAL BAYREUTH, see also Rose Tapestry; Snow Babies; Sunbonnet Babies

ROYAL BAYREUTH, Ashtray, Devil 200.00
Ashtray, Elk 85.00
Bell, Dutch Girl & Boy, Marked, 3 1/4 In. 175.00
Bell, Goats Grazing, Wooden Clapper 125.00
Bell, Nursery Rhyme, Ring Around The Rosey, Children 295.00
Biscuit Jar, Grape Cluster, Pink Leaves, White Pearlized 250.00
Bonbon, Oak Leaf 65.00
Bowl, Boy In Barnyard Scene, Blue Mark, 11 In. 225.00
Bowl, Floral, Gold Trim, 10 1/2 In. 85.00
Bowl, Snow Girls, 6 In. 75.00
Box, Cover, Tomato, Blue Mark, 3 3/4 In. .... 40.00 To 50.00
Cake Plate, Hunter With Gun, Dog, Pierced Handle, 10 1/2 In. 250.00
Candleholder, Basset Hound, Black, Pair 325.00
Candleholder, Corinthian, Red & Black, Blue Mark 60.00
Candleholder, Elk Handle, Blue Mark 225.00
Candleholder, Riding Scene, Horse & Buggy, Shield Back 125.00
Candy Dish, Chickens Fighting, Chick At Top, Watching 275.00
Chocolate Pot, Yellow Poppy 525.00
Compote, Poppy, Green Leaf Stem, 5 3/4 X 3 1/2 In. 300.00
Creamer, 3–Colored Rose, Pinched Spout, 4 In. 150.00
Creamer, Alligator .... 165.00 To 195.00
Creamer, Art Nouveau Woman 450.00
Creamer, Bear 625.00
Creamer, Bell Ringer, Blue Mark .... 180.00 To 235.00
Creamer, Bird of Paradise 200.00
Creamer, Bull, Brown & White 160.00
Creamer, Butterfly, 3 3/4 In. 175.00
Creamer, Cat, Black .... 125.00 To 148.00
Creamer, Clown .... 150.00 To 185.00
Creamer, Corinthian, Black 48.00
Creamer, Corinthian, Yellow 85.00
Creamer, Cow, Black & Gray, Blue Mark, 3 1/2 In. 100.00
Creamer, Cow, Brown, Blue Mark, 4 In. 95.00
Creamer, Crow, Black 110.00
Creamer, Crow, Brown Eyes & Beak, Black, Blue Mark, 5 In. 125.00
Creamer, Desert Scene 44.00
Creamer, Devil & Card, Blue Mark, 4 In. 135.00
Creamer, Duck, Blue 135.00
Creamer, Eagle, Brown & Gray, Blue Mark, 4 In. 100.00
Creamer, Elk, Souvenir, Blue Mark 50.00
Creamer, Fish, Open Mouth, Marked 140.00
Creamer, French Poodle, Black, Marked 205.00
Creamer, Frog, Blue Mark 160.00
Creamer, Grape, Green 90.00
Creamer, Gray Cat Handle, Sapphire Blue, Marked 215.00
Creamer, Hound Dog, Sitting 65.00
Creamer, Hunt Scene, Green, Blue Mark, 3 1/4 In. 95.00
Creamer, Lamplighter, Green, Blue Mark .... 175.00 To 235.00
Creamer, Lemon .... 95.00 To 145.00
Creamer, Leopard, Blue Mark 750.00
Creamer, Lettuce Leaf, Lobster Handle, Marked .... 40.00 To 85.00
Creamer, Little Miss Muffet & Spider, Blue Mark, 4 1/2 In. 150.00

Creamer, Maple Leaf, Blue Mark 175.00
Creamer, Minstrels, Pinched Spout, Blue Mark, 4 In. 70.00
Creamer, Monkey, Brown 250.00
Creamer, Moose, Blue Mark 50.00
Creamer, Oak Leaf ....85.00 To 135.00
Creamer, Pansy, Purple, Blue Mark 125.00
Creamer, Parrot, Green, Blue Mark 210.00
Creamer, Perch, Blue Mark 150.00
Creamer, Poppy, Marked 90.00
Creamer, Robin, 2 1/2 In. 88.00
Creamer, Rooster 150.00
Creamer, Seal 295.00
Creamer, Shell, Lobster Handle 30.00
Creamer, St.Bernard 145.00
Creamer, Strawberry ....85.00 To 135.00
Creamer, Sunflower ....295.00 To 325.00
Creamer, Trout 150.00
Creamer, Turtle, Blue Mark 275.00
Creamer, Water Buffalo, Orange Lining, Blue Mark, 5 In. 110.00
Cup & Saucer, Oyster & Pearl, Demitasse 145.00
Cup & Saucer, Poppy, Blue Mark, Demitasse 125.00
Cup, Leaf & Tomato, Marked 85.00
Dish, Lobster, Cover, 4 1/2 X 4 3/4 In. 90.00
Dish, Shell, Mother-of-Pearl Luster, 2 1/8 In. 40.00
Dish, Tomato, Cover, On Lettuce Leaf, Marked, 3 3/4 In. 50.00
Dresser Set, Musicians, 6 Piece 620.00
Hair Receiver, Cows 145.00
Hatpin Holder, Farmer Holding Reins of Horses, Blue Mark 235.00
Hatpin Holder, Minstrel Figures, Underplate, Blue Mark 95.00
Hatpin Holder, Musicians, Signed 185.00
Hatpin Holder, Owl 350.00
Hatpin Holder, Penguin, Blue Mark 395.00
Hatpin Holder, Poppy, Red, Blue Mark 325.00
Humidor, Bell Ringer, Blue Mark 750.00
Humidor, Satyr With Nymphs, Blue Mark 185.00
Inkwell, Elk, Full Antlers, Marked 200.00
Match Holder, Burnt Match Tray Front & Back, Musicians 195.00
Match Holder, Clown, Hanging 275.00
Match Holder, Devil & Cards, Hanging 295.00
Match Holder, Elk, Blue Mark, Hanging 135.00
Match Holder, Enameled Stork, Yellow, 3 Handles, Blue Mark 195.00
Match Holder, Farmer & Horses, Hanging 95.00
Mug, Girl With Candle, Blue Mark, 7 In. 120.00
Mug, Little Jack Horner, Blue Mark 68.00
Mustard, Cover, Tomato, Green Mark 55.00
Mustard, Grape, Pearlized 100.00
Mustard, Grape, Yellow 85.00
Mustard, Tomato, Blue Mark 60.00
Nappy, Arab Scene, Tapestry, Blue Mark 120.00
Nut Dish, Oak Leaf, White, Blue Mark 60.00
Nut Dish, Poppy, Pink, Master 150.00
Pepper Shaker, Tomato 65.00
Pitcher & Bowl, Little Jack Horner, Blue Mark, Miniature 145.00
Pitcher, 2 Fishermen In Boat, 2 Handles, Blue Mark, 5 In. 110.00
Pitcher, 3 Fishermen In Boat, Blue Mark, 6 In. 135.00
Pitcher, Apple, Marked, 6 1/2 In. 260.00
Pitcher, Art Nouveau, Blue Mark, 6 1/2 In. 795.00
Pitcher, Butterfly, 4 1/2 In. 390.00
Pitcher, Chick, 4 1/2 In. 350.00
Pitcher, Clown, Red, Blue Mark, 4 1/2 In. .... 225.00 To 250.00
Pitcher, Clown, Yellow, 4 1/2 In. .... 295.00 To 395.00
Pitcher, Coachman, 6 1/2 In. 435.00
Pitcher, Conch Shell, Lobster Handle, Green, 8 1/2 In. 325.00
Pitcher, Coral Shell, 6 1/2 In. 235.00

Pitcher, Cow's Head, White & Black, 4 In.	60.00
Pitcher, Cows In Pasture, Allover Scene, Blue Mark, 9 In.	185.00
Pitcher, Desert Warrior, Jeweled, Blue Mark, 6 1/2 In.	140.00
Pitcher, Duck, 6 1/2 In.	495.00
Pitcher, Elk, Green Mark, 7 In.	275.00
Pitcher, Hunt Scene, Apple Green, 8 In.	100.00
Pitcher, Lobster, Marked, 4 1/2 In.	95.00
Pitcher, Musicians, 4 1/2 In.	140.00
Pitcher, Netherlands Scene, Blue Mark, 5 In.	85.00
Pitcher, Oak Leaf, Pearlized, Blue Mark, 4 1/2 In.	175.00
Pitcher, Oak, 6 1/2 In.	525.00
Pitcher, Orange, 6 1/2 In.	380.00
Pitcher, Owl, 4 1/2 In.	190.00
Pitcher, Robin, 6 1/2 In.	115.00
Pitcher, Scenic, 3 Bears, Gold Handle, Blue Mark, 4 1/4 In.	95.00
Pitcher, St.Bernard, 6 1/2 In.	450.00
Pitcher, Tomato, Green Ruffled Top & Handle, 4 In.	50.00
Plate, Donkey & Boy, Blue Mark, 6 In.	55.00
Plate, Grapes, Gold Leaves, Scalloped Edge, 7 1/4 In.	40.00
Plate, Jack & Jill, 6 In.	65.00
Plate, Jack & The Beanstalk, 7 In.	135.00
Plate, Lettuce, Yellow Flowers, Ring Handle, Blue Mark, 7 In.	40.00
Plate, Little Jack Horner, 6 In.	65.00
Plate, Little Jack Horner, Blue Mark, 7 3/4 In.	75.00
Plate, Peasant Musicians, 6 1/4 In.	60.00
Plate, Poppy, Blue Mark, 8 1/2 In.	35.00
Plate, Roses, Gold Tracery, Blue Mark, 9 In.	42.00
Powder Box, Sailboat, Men, Sea Gulls, 3 Gold Feet, 4 1/2 In.	85.00
Rose Bowl, Little Girl & Dog, Signed, 2 7/8 In.	65.00
Salt & Pepper, Jack & Jill On One, Little Boy Blue Other	195.00
Salt & Pepper, Lobster	25.00
Salt & Pepper, Shell	45.00
Salt & Pepper, Tomato, Leaf Base, 2 1/2 In.	40.00
Saltshaker, Dachshund	175.00
Saltshaker, Tomato, Leaf Base, 2 1/2 In.	20.00
Shaker, Chili Pepper, Red, Leaf Base, 4 In.	35.00
Stamp Box, Cover, Sitting Donkey Boy, Blue Mark	85.00
String Holder, Wall Bracket, Rooster	225.00
Sugar & Creamer, Apple, Yellow, Blue Mark	150.00
Sugar & Creamer, Grape, Blue & Green, Blue Mark	155.00
Sugar & Creamer, Grape, Mother–of–Pearl Luster	160.00
Sugar & Creamer, Tomato	115.00
Sugar, Cover, Cow Scene, Blue Mark	30.00
Sugar, Cover, Lobster	50.00
Sugar, Cover, Pansy	135.00
Sugar, Lemon	75.00
Sugar, Lobster	45.00
Tea Set, Nursery Rhyme, Child's	900.00
Tea Set, Tomato, Leaf Base, 5 Piece	185.00
Teapot, Pansy	265.00
Teapot, Sheep Scene, Red Ground	245.00
Toothpick, Grazing Goats, Blue Mark	135.00
Toothpick, Portrait of Woman, Coal Hod Shape, Handle	395.00
Tray, Dresser, Christmas Cactus, Blue Mark	450.00
Tureen, Cover, Figural, Rose, Underplate	250.00
Vase, Band of Roses, Butterflies, Blue Mark, 5 1/2 In.	45.00
Vase, Goose Girl, Natural Colors, Blue Mark, 4 X 2 1/2 In.	70.00
Vase, Hunting Scene, Lady On Horse, Blue Mark, 2 3/4 In.	48.00
Vase, Hunting Scene, Yellow, Blue Mark, 5 In.	95.00
Vase, Musicians, Gray Ground, Silver Top Band, 3 3/4 In.	45.00
Vase, Open Roses & Foliage On Green, Bulbous, 5 3/4 In.	60.00
Vase, Sheep, Pastoral, 5 1/4 In.	85.00
Vase, Yellow Roses, Green Ground, Gold Trim, 3 7/8 In.	55.00
Wall Pocket, Penny In Pocket Is A Merry Companion, Jester	165.00

Wall Pocket, White Satin Poppy, 9 X 5 1/2 In.	225.00
Watch Holder, Wall, Devil & Cards	250.00

Royal Bonn is the nineteenth– and twentieth–century trade name for the Bonn China Manufactory. It was established in 1755 in Bonn, Germany. A general line of porcelain was made. Many marks were used, most including the name "Bonn," the initials "FM," and a crown.

ROYAL BONN, Biscuit Jar, Flowers Outlined In Gold, Silver Plated Fittings	125.00
Biscuit Jar, Flowers, Leaves, Brass Fittings, Marked, 7 In.	100.00
Ewer, Encircling Gold Lizard Handle, Bird, Orchids, 12 1/2 In.	175.00
Ewer, Gold Twisted Lizard Handle, Bird, 12 1/2 In., Pair	350.00
Ewer, Parrot In Tree, 12 In.	100.00
Lamp, Piano, Kerosene, Gold Bronze Base, Frosted Shade, 6 Ft.	4500.00
Vase, Art Deco Design, Marked, 9 1/2 In.	95.00
Vase, Branch Handles, Hand Painted, Signed, 22 In.	400.00
Vase, Circle of Flowers, Gold, 9 1/2 In.	175.00
Vase, Flared, White Roses On Shaded Green Ground, 8 3/4 In.	95.00
Vase, Gold & Orange Floral, Brown & Yellow Ground, 8 X 5 In.	95.00
Vase, Green Floral, 12 1/2 In.	85.00
Vase, Iris, Bulbous, 6 In.	75.00
Vase, Lady In Garden, Ram's Head Handle, 8 In.	175.00
Vase, Lavender Hydrangeas, Green Ground, 12 In.	160.00
Vase, Painted Florals, Outlined In Gold, 14 In.	165.00
Vase, Portait of Woman, Brown & Gold Ground, Signed, 8 1/4 In.	550.00
Vase, Purple Florals, 8 In.	65.00
Vase, Rooster & Hen, Marked, 6 1/2 In.	125.00

Royal Copenhagen porcelain and pottery have been made in Denmark since 1772. The Christmas plate series started in 1908. The figurines with pale blue and gray glazes have remained popular in this century and are still being made. Many other old and new style porcelains are made today.

ROYAL COPENHAGEN, Basket, Fruit, Flora Danica, Marked, 10 1/4 In.	880.00
Candleholder, Brass Fittings, Blue & White	65.00
Chop Plate, Floral Design, Gilt, 13 In.	65.00
Coffee Server, Blue Fluted, Snail Handle, 9 3/4 In.	110.00
Decanter, Egeskov Castle, Blue, White, Stopper, 12 1/4 In.	53.00
Decanter, Rosenburg Castle, Blue, White, Stopper, 9 3/4 In.	48.50
Figurine, 2 Puppies Playing	80.00
Figurine, Ballet Girl, No.4975	575.00
Figurine, Boy & Girl With Book, No.4670	200.00
Figurine, Boy At Lunch, No.865	275.00
Figurine, Boy Cutting Stick, No.905	258.00
Figurine, Boy Standing At Shore, No.1186	200.00
Figurine, Boy With Boat, No.3272	50.00
Figurine, Boy With Drums	112.00
Figurine, Boy With Nude Girl, No.1760	850.00
Figurine, Boy With Teddy Bear, No.3468	268.00
Figurine, Child With Accordion, No.3667	172.00
Figurine, Collie, No.1701	195.00
Figurine, Drummer, No.3647	145.00
Figurine, Dutch Child, Enameled, Marked, 5 7/8 In.	65.00
Figurine, Elephant, No.1771, Gray, 6 In.	250.00
Figurine, Elephant, No.2998, Gray, 4 1/2in.	185.00
Figurine, Farmer, Large	225.00
Figurine, Faun With Lizard, No.433	285.00
Figurine, February, No.4524	265.00
Figurine, Girl On Stone, No.4027	195.00
Figurine, Girl With Cymbals, No.3677	108.00
Figurine, Little Mermaid, No.4431	815.00
Figurine, Lovebirds, No.402	125.00
Figurine, Mermaid, No.3321	90.00
Figurine, Nude, Lying On Side, No.4702	300.00

Figurine, Pan On Turtle	175.00
Figurine, Pan, On Top of Column, Holding Flute, 8 1/2 In.	375.00
Figurine, Pekinese, Sitting Up, Begging, 4 1/2 In.	110.00
Figurine, Poodle, No.4638	195.00
Figurine, Sandman, No.1129	700.00
Figurine, Shepherdess & Sheep, Marked, C.1930, 10 1/2 In.	250.00
Figurine, Soldier With Dog, No.1156	470.00
Figurine, Soldier With Princess, No.1180	615.00
Figurine, Soldier With Witch, No.1112	535.00
Figurine, Sparrows	95.00 To 100.00
Figurine, Squirrel, Sitting, Holding Nut, 2 1/2 In.	46.00
Figurine, Standing Nude, Holding Mirror, No.4639	400.00
Figurine, Turtle Doves, No.402, 5 1/2 In.	95.00
Figurine, Two Children, No.1761	570.00
Figurine, Young Mermaid, C.Thompson, 8 In.	110.00
Group, Penguins, Standing In Semicircle, 3 3/4 In.	190.00
Ice Dish, Domed Cover, Flora Danica, Marked, 12 In.	2530.00
Plaque, Allegorical Day & Night, White Parian, 11 In., Pr.	380.00
Plaque, Angel, Sleeping Babies, Owl, Pierced, Parian, 6 In.	30.00
Plate, Christmas, 1951	185.00 To 200.00
Plate, Christmas, 1962	170.00
Plate, Christmas, 1965	40.00
Plate, Christmas, 1971	35.00
Plate, Flora Danica, Marked, 7 1/2 In., 12 Piece	1320.00
Plate, Mother's Day, 1971	10.00
Plate, Shepherd, 1957	80.00
Platter, 1897 Mark, 12 In.	195.00
Platter, 1897 Mark, 17 1/2 In.	375.00
Platter, Cover, 1897 Mark, 14 In.	550.00
Relish, Leaf Shape	24.00
Vase, Blackberries & Blossoms, 7 In.	50.00
Vase, Blown–Out Figures, Celadon, Square, 8 3/4 In.	125.00
Vase, Cobalt Blue Flowers, White, Basket Weave Rim, 7 In.	48.00
Vase, Cover, Painted Landscape Scene, White, 16 1/2 In.	340.00

Royal Copley china was made by the Spaulding China Company of Sebring, Ohio, from 1939 to 1960. The figural planters and the small figurines, especially those with Art Deco designs, are of great collector interest.

ROYAL COPLEY, Figurine, Blackmoor, Pair	36.00
Figurine, Colonial Man, 8 In.	15.00
Figurine, Deer On Stump	18.00
Figurine, Dog With Mailbox	12.50
Figurine, Duck & Wheelbarrow	7.50 To 10.00
Figurine, Duck On Stump	12.00
Figurine, Kitten On Stump	12.50
Figurine, Oriental Boy, Red Jacket, Holds Urn, 8 In.	8.50
Figurine, Pheasant, 6 In.	5.00
Figurine, Pup In Basket	8.00 To 12.00
Figurine, Pup With Suitcase	15.00 To 20.00
Figurine, Teddy Bear, Mandolin	20.00
Figurine, Thrush, Brown, Green, Pink, Paper Label, 6 1/2 In.	7.00
Figurine, Woodpecker, 6 1/4 In.	8.00
Lamp, Black Boy, 12 In.	100.00
Pitcher, Juice, Yellow	24.00
Pitcher, Pear & Peaches In Relief, Pale Blue, 8 In.	16.00
Planter, 3 Bears, 6 1/4 In.	20.00
Planter, Bamboo, Oval, Pair	15.00
Planter, Bear On Stump	12.50
Planter, Big Blossom, Light Blue, Pink Flower	5.00
Planter, Chinese Boy	10.00
Planter, Doe & Fawn, 9 In.	18.00
Planter, Dog With Suitcase, Black & White	30.00
Planter, Fish, Yellow	5.00

Planter, Mill Plaque, 8 In.	25.00
Planter, Oriental Girl, Green Jacket, Basket, 7 1/2 In.	12.00
Planter, Peter Rabbit	16.50
Planter, Pirate, 8 In.	22.00
Planter, Rooster, Wheelbarrow	35.00
Planter, Star & Angel	12.00
Vase, Bud, Parrot, 5 In.	6.00
Vase, Daisies, Green, 8 In.	8.50
Vase, Mare & Foal, 8 1/2 In.	20.00
Wall Pocket, Apple, Pair	15.00
Wall Pocket, Bust, Oriental Girl, Arms Folded, 7 1/2 In.	15.00
Wall Pocket, Man, Woman, With Turbans, 8 In., Pair	34.00
Wall Pocket, Pirate, Pair	22.00

Royal Crown Derby Company, Ltd., was established in England in 1876. There is a complex family tree that includes the Derby, Crown Derby, Worcester, and Royal Crown Derby porcelains. The Royal Crown Derby mark includes the name and a crown. The words "Made in England" were used after 1921.

ROYAL CROWN DERBY, Creamer, Oriental Figures, Blue, White, Gold, 3 1/8 In.	25.00
Cup, Floral Sprays, Gold Trim, Fluted, Scalloped	10.00
Dish, Multicolored Flowers, White Ground, Gold, 5 In.	65.00
Ewer, Gold Design, Golden Yellow, 1896, 14 X 6 In.	425.00
Ewer, Gold Floral, Arabesque Design, C.1800, 7 1/2 In.	235.00
Pitcher, Multicolored Flowers, Gold Handle, 9 In.	395.00
Plate, Imari, 10 1/2 In., Set of 8	665.00
Plate, Mikado, Blue, White, 10 1/2 In.	35.00
Vase, Gold & Green Design, Pedestal, Bulbous, 11 1/2 In.	155.00
Vase, Gold Roses At Top, Gold Leaves, Marked, 3 1/4 In.	85.00
Vase, Sprays of Flowers, Green Body, 11 3/4 In.	145.00

"Royal Doulton" is the name used on Doulton and Company pottery made from 1902 to the present. Doulton and Company of England was founded in 1853. Pieces made before 1902 are listed in this book under Doulton. Royal Doulton collectors search for the out-of-production figurines, character jugs, and series wares.

ROYAL DOULTON, Animal, Alsatian, K 13	65.00
Animal, Boxer, HN 2643	75.00
Animal, Budgerigar, HN 199	135.00
Animal, Bulldog, HN 1047	85.00
Animal, Bulldog, K 1	75.00
Animal, Cat, Flambe, 12 In.	300.00
Animal, Chestnut Mare With Foal, HN 2522	950.00 To 1000.00
Animal, Cocker Spaniel & Pheasant, HN 1028	110.00
Animal, Cocker Spaniel, HN 1021	85.00
Animal, Collie, HN 1058	75.00
Animal, Dachshund, HN 1129	110.00
Animal, Doberman Pinscher, HN 2645	100.00
Animal, Elephant, HN 2640	825.00
Animal, Elephant, HN 2644	110.00
Animal, Fox, Flambe, 5 In.	40.00
Animal, Foxhound, Miniature, HN 7	35.00
Animal, French Poodle, HN 2631	100.00
Animal, Irish Setter, HN 1055	80.00
Animal, Irish Setter, HN 1056	115.00
Animal, Kitten, Laughing, Miniature, K 12	35.00
Animal, Monkeys, Embracing, Flambe, Pair	285.00
Animal, Pekinese, HN 1012	125.00
Animal, Pheasant, HN 2632	295.00
Animal, Pointer Dog, Grassy Base, HN 2624	250.00
Animal, Scottish Terrier, K 18	35.00
Animal, Terrier, K 8	80.00
Animal, Welsh Corgi, HN 2559	80.00
Animal, Welsh Corgi, K 16	80.00

Ash Pot, Farmer John 125.00
Ash Pot, Old Charley 115.00
Ash Pot, Paddy 115.00
Bank, Rabbit, With Drum 100.00
Biscuit Jar, Coaching Days 350.00
Bowl, English Scene, 7 3/4 In. 70.00
Bowl, Floral, 7 In. 70.00
Bowl, Fruit, Sir Roger De Coverly, Bowling, C.1937, 11 In. 70.00
Bowl, Hunt Scenes, Gold Trim, 14 1/2 In. 300.00
Bowl, Under The Greenwood Tree, Robin Hood Series, 8 In. 200.00
Candlestick, Bodian Castle, 6 1/2 In., Pair 75.00
Candlestick, Juliet, Shakespeare Series, 6 1/2 In. 85.00
Candlestick, Multicolored Flowers, White, 5 3/4 In., Pair 225.00
Chamber Pot, Gold Pin Striping, Marked, White, 9 1/2 In. 30.00

> Character jugs are the modeled head and shoulders of the subject.
> They are made in four sizes: large, 5 1/4 to 7 inches; small, 3 1/4
> to 4 inches; miniature, 2 1/4 to 2 1/2 inches; and tiny, 1 1/4
> inches. Toby jugs depict a seated, full figure.

Character Jug, 'Ard of 'Earing, D 6591, Small 445.00
Character Jug, 'Arriet, A Mark, Miniature 85.00
Character Jug, 'Arriet, Miniature .... 65.00 To 75.00
Character Jug, 'Arriet, Small 95.00
Character Jug, 'Arriet, Tiny 195.00
Character Jug, 'Arry, A Mark, Small 70.00
Character Jug, 'Arry, Large 175.00
Character Jug, 'Arry, Miniature .... 75.00 To 85.00
Character Jug, Anne Boleyn, Large 60.00
Character Jug, Anne of Cleves, Large .... 200.00 To 225.00
Character Jug, Anthony & Cleopatra, Large 170.00
Character Jug, Auld Mac, A Mark, Large 75.00
Character Jug, Auld Mac, Small 175.00
Character Jug, Auld Mac, Tiny 175.00
Character Jug, Beefeater, A Mark, Small 32.00
Character Jug, Buz Fuz, A Mark, Small ....80.00 To 110.00
Character Jug, Cap'n Cuttle, A Mark, Small 120.00
Character Jug, Captain Hook, Small 310.00
Character Jug, Cardinal, A Mark, Large 140.00
Character Jug, Cardinal, A Mark, Small 80.00
Character Jug, Cardinal, Tiny .... 160.00 To 195.00
Character Jug, Cavalier, A Mark, Small 60.00
Character Jug, Clown, Red Hair, Large 2350.00
Character Jug, Clown, White Hair, Large .... 895.00 To 925.00
Character Jug, Custer & Sitting Bull, Large .... 75.00 To 95.00
Character Jug, Davy Crockett, Santa Anna, LE, Large 85.00
Character Jug, Dick Turpin, A Mark, Miniature 45.00
Character Jug, Dick Turpin, Mask Down, Large 85.00
Character Jug, Dick Whittington, Large 365.00
Character Jug, Drake, A Mark, Large 145.00
Character Jug, Drake, A Mark, Small 85.00
Character Jug, Falconer, Large 95.00
Character Jug, Falstaff, Large 135.00
Character Jug, Farmer John, A Mark, Small 65.00
Character Jug, Fat Boy, Tiny 105.00
Character Jug, Field Marshall Smuts, Large 1395.00
Character Jug, Fortune Teller, Large 375.00
Character Jug, Fortune Teller, Small 265.00
Character Jug, Gardener, Large 145.00
Character Jug, Gardener, Miniature 50.00
Character Jug, Golfer, Large 250.00
Character Jug, Gondolier, Large 495.00
Character Jug, Granny, Large 225.00
Character Jug, Grant & Lee, Large .... 195.00 To 225.00
Character Jug, Groucho Marx, Large 80.00

Character Jug, Gulliver, Large	355.00
Character Jug, Henry Morgan, Large	85.00
Character Jug, Henry VIII, Small	35.00
Character Jug, Jarge, Large	295.00 To 305.00
Character Jug, Jarge, Small	185.00
Character Jug, Jester, A Mark, Small	75.00
Character Jug, Jimmy Durante, Large	70.00
Character Jug, John Barleycorn, A Mark, Small	38.00
Character Jug, John Peel, A Mark, Large	180.00
Character Jug, John Peel, A Mark, Miniature	75.00
Character Jug, John Peel, A Mark, Small	85.00
Character Jug, John Peel, Tiny	160.00 To 185.00
Character Jug, Johnny Appleseed, Large	255.00 To 295.00
Character Jug, Long John Silver, Large	95.00
Character Jug, Long John Silver, Small	35.00
Character Jug, Lord Nelson, Large	225.00
Character Jug, Louis Armstrong, Large	70.00
Character Jug, Mad Hatter, Miniature	50.00
Character Jug, Mae West, Large	80.00
Character Jug, Mephistopheles, Small	750.00
Character Jug, Merlin, Owl Handle, Large	67.50
Character Jug, Mikado, Large	425.00 To 450.00
Character Jug, Mr.Micawber, Miniature	50.00 To 65.00
Character Jug, Mr.Pickwick, Large	170.00 To 215.00
Character Jug, Neptune, 4 In.	40.00
Character Jug, Night Watchman, Miniature	45.00
Character Jug, North American Indian, Large	225.00 To 250.00
Character Jug, Old Charley, A Mark, Large	75.00
Character Jug, Old Charley, Large	85.00
Character Jug, Old Charley, Small	45.00
Character Jug, Old Charley, Tiny	85.00 To 105.00
Character Jug, Old King Cole, A Mark, Large	225.00
Character Jug, Old King Cole, A Mark, Small	110.00
Character Jug, Old King Cole, Small	90.00
Character Jug, Paddy, Small	65.00
Character Jug, Parson Brown, A Mark, Large	125.00
Character Jug, Pied Piper, Miniature	50.00
Character Jug, Punch & Judy Man, Large	525.00
Character Jug, Queen Victoria, Large	130.00 To 175.00
Character Jug, Rip Van Winkle, Large	65.00
Character Jug, Robin Hood, A Mark, Small	80.00
Character Jug, Robin Hood, Large	110.00 To 120.00
Character Jug, Robinson Crusoe, Miniature	35.00
Character Jug, Ronald Reagan, Large	275.00 To 450.00
Character Jug, Sam Weller, A Mark, Large	135.00
Character Jug, Sam Weller, A Mark, Miniature	75.00
Character Jug, Sam Weller, Tiny	100.00 To 105.00
Character Jug, Sancho Panza, Large	85.00
Character Jug, Sancho Panza, Small	60.00
Character Jug, Santa Claus, Large	235.00
Character Jug, Scaramouche, Small	365.00 To 425.00
Character Jug, Simon The Cellarer, A Mark, Large	145.00
Character Jug, Simple Simon, Large	425.00 To 450.00
Character Jug, Sleuth, Small	70.00
Character Jug, Smuggler, Large	85.00
Character Jug, St.George, Small	135.00 To 145.00
Character Jug, Toby Philpots, Miniature	50.00
Character Jug, Tony Weller, A Mark, Large	135.00
Character Jug, Tony Weller, A Mark, Miniature	50.00
Character Jug, Touchstone, A Mark, Large	185.00
Character Jug, Touchstone, Large	300.00
Character Jug, Town Crier, Large	175.00 To 195.00
Character Jug, Town Crier, Miniature	115.00
Character Jug, Ugly Duchess, Large	245.00 To 385.00

Character Jug, Ugly Duchess, Miniature 275.00
Character Jug, Ugly Duchess, Small 295.00
Character Jug, Uncle Tom Cobbleigh, Large 350.00
Character Jug, Viking, Large ....75.00 To 150.00
Character Jug, Viking, Small 80.00
Character Jug, W.C.Fields, Large 85.00
Charger, Lioness, 13 1/2 In. 60.00
Chop Plate, Tony Weller, Marked, 13 1/2 In. 185.00
Coffee Set, Geometric Design, Demitasse Spoons, 1932, 22 Pc. 1980.00
Creamer, Fish Head, Blue Mark, 4 1/2 In. 150.00
Decanter, Old Crow 55.00
Figurine, A La Mode, HN 2544 .... 170.00
Figurine, Adele, HN 2480 .... 99.50
Figurine, Adrienne, HN 2152 ....110.00 To 175.00
Figurine, Affection, HN 2236 .... 90.00
Figurine, Afternoon Tea, HN 1747 ....250.00 To 265.00
Figurine, Ajax, HN 2908 .... 350.00
Figurine, Amy, HN 2958 .... 75.00
Figurine, Angela, HN 1303 .... 1100.00
Figurine, Apple Maid, HN 2160 .... 300.00
Figurine, Autumn Breezes, HN 1934 ....135.00 To 225.00
Figurine, Autumn Breezes, HN 2147 .... 330.00
Figurine, Balinese Dancer, HN 2808 .... 690.00
Figurine, Ballerina, HN 2116 ....225.00 To 285.00
Figurine, Balloon Man, HN 1954 ....100.00 To 155.00
Figurine, Beat You To It, HN 2871 .... 260.00
Figurine, Bedtime Story, HN 2059 .... 200.00
Figurine, Belle O' The Ball, HN 1997 .... 245.00
Figurine, Benmore, HN 2909 .... 350.00
Figurine, Blacksmith of Williamsburg, HN 2240 ....140.00 To 160.00
Figurine, Bluebeard, HN 2105 ....175.00 To 250.00
Figurine, Boatman, HN 2417 .... 100.00
Figurine, Bonnie Lassie, HN 1626 .... 275.00
Figurine, Boy From Williamsburg, HN 2183 .... 150.00
Figurine, Breton Dancer, HN 2383 .... 675.00
Figurine, Bride, HN 2166 ....190.00 To 195.00
Figurine, Bridesmaid, HN 2148 .... 225.00
Figurine, Bridesmaid, HN 2196 .... 115.00
Figurine, Bridesmaid, M 30 .... 295.00
Figurine, Bunny, HN 2214 ....75.00 To 200.00
Figurine, Buttercup, HN 2309 ....145.00 To 195.00
Figurine, Buttercup, HN 2399 .... 114.00
Figurine, Camellia, HN 2222 .... 200.00
Figurine, Captain Cook, HN 2889 .... 265.00
Figurine, Carolyn, HN 2974 .... 160.00
Figurine, Carpet Seller, HN 1464 .... 185.00
Figurine, Cavalier, HN 2716 ....140.00 To 170.00
Figurine, Child From Williamsburg, HN 2154 .... 125.00
Figurine, Chinese Dancer, HN 2840 .... 685.00
Figurine, Chloe, HN 1765 .... 250.00
Figurine, Christmas Morn, HN 1992 .... 175.00
Figurine, Christmas Time, HN 2110 ....300.00 To 325.00
Figurine, Cissie, HN 1809 .... 65.00
Figurine, Clare, HN 2793 .... 170.00
Figurine, Clockmaker, HN 2279 .... 380.00
Figurine, Cobbler, HN 1706 .... 250.00
Figurine, Columbine, HN 1439 .... 575.00
Figurine, Cymbals, HN 2699 .... 700.00
Figurine, Cynthia, HN 2440 .... 99.00
Figurine, Daffy Down Dilly, HN 1712 .... 275.00
Figurine, Daisy, HN 1575 .... 425.00
Figurine, Dancing Years, HN 2235 .... 325.00
Figurine, Darling, HN 1319 .... 175.00
Figurine, David Copperfield, M 88 .... 55.00

Figurine, Daydreams, HN 1731 .... 115.00 To 195.00
Figurine, Detective, HN 2359 .... 145.00 To 170.00
Figurine, Diana, HN 1716 .... 300.00
Figurine, Dreamweaver, HN 2283 .... 225.00
Figurine, Drummer Boy, HN 2679 .... 325.00
Figurine, Duke of Edinburgh, HN 2386 .... 425.00
Figurine, Easter Day, HN 2039 .... 250.00
Figurine, Elegance, HN 2264 .... 115.00 To 195.00
Figurine, Enchantment, HN 2178 .... 120.00 To 195.00
Figurine, Ermine Coat, HN 1981 .... 200.00 To 350.00
Figurine, Esmeralda, HN 2168 .... 395.00
Figurine, Fair Lady, HN 2193 .... 120.00 To 195.00
Figurine, Farmer's Boy, HN 2520 .... 1450.00
Figurine, Fat Boy, M 44 .... 55.00
Figurine, First Dance, HN 2803 .... 170.00
Figurine, First Waltz, HN 2862 .... 190.00
Figurine, Fleur, HN 2368 .... 125.00
Figurine, Fleurette, HN 1587 .... 650.00
Figurine, Flower Seller's Children, HN 1342 .... 380.00
Figurine, Foaming Quart, HN 2162 .... 75.00 To 90.00
Figurine, Fortune Teller, HN 2159 .... 385.00
Figurine, Forty Winks, HN 1974 .... 165.00
Figurine, Four O'Clock, HN 1760 .... 850.00
Figurine, Gaffer, HN 2053 .... 325.00
Figurine, Gay Morning, HN 2135 .... 350.00
Figurine, Gentleman From Williamsburg, HN 2227 .... 145.00
Figurine, Giselle, Forest Glade, HN 2140 .... 295.00
Figurine, Good Catch, HN 2258 .... 110.00 To 120.00
Figurine, Good King Wenceslas, HN 2118 .... 260.00
Figurine, Grandma, HN 2052 .... 296.00
Figurine, Greta, HN 1485 .... 185.00 To 190.00
Figurine, Gypsy Dance, HN 2230 .... 175.00
Figurine, Harlequin, HN 2737 .... 475.00
Figurine, Helen of Troy, HN 2387 .... 775.00
Figurine, Her Ladyship, HN 1977 .... 250.00
Figurine, Hilary, HN 2335 .... 135.00
Figurine, Home Again, HN 2167 .... 60.00
Figurine, Honey, HN 1909 .... 275.00
Figurine, Honey, HN 1910 .... 375.00
Figurine, Honey, HN 1963 .... 465.00
Figurine, Hornpipe, HN 2161 .... 595.00
Figurine, Hostess From Williamsburg, HN 2209 .... 135.00 To 215.00
Figurine, In The Stocks, HN 2163 .... 525.00
Figurine, Jack Point, HN 2080 .... 1095.00
Figurine, Jack, HN 2060 .... 95.00
Figurine, Janet, HN 1537 .... 95.00 To 150.00
Figurine, Janet, HN 1916 .... 195.00
Figurine, Janine, HN 2461 .... 148.00
Figurine, Jean, HN 2032 .... 360.00
Figurine, Jester, HN 2016 .... 100.00 To 200.00
Figurine, Jill, HN 2061 .... 95.00 To 175.00
Figurine, Joan, HN 2023 .... 325.00
Figurine, Jolly Sailor, HN 2172 .... 525.00
Figurine, Jovial Monk, HN 2144 .... 125.00 To 170.00
Figurine, King Charles, HN 2084 .... 795.00
Figurine, Kirsty, HN 2381 .... 150.00
Figurine, Kurdish Dancer, HN 2867 .... 590.00
Figurine, Lady Betty, HN 1967 .... 245.00
Figurine, Lady Charmian, HN 1949 .... 165.00 To 275.00
Figurine, Lady Fayre, HN 1557 .... 430.00
Figurine, Lady Pamela, HN 2718 .... 145.00
Figurine, Lalla Rookh, HN 2910 .... 350.00
Figurine, Lambing Time, HN 1890 .... 130.00
Figurine, Last Waltz, HN 2315 .... 200.00

Figurine, Leisure Hour, HN 2055	300.00
Figurine, Lilac Time, HN 2137	325.00
Figurine, Lisa, HN 2310	145.00
Figurine, Little Bridesmaid, HN 1433	110.00 To 145.00
Figurine, Little Child Rare & Sweet, HN 1542	475.00
Figurine, Little Miss Muffet, HN 2727	135.00
Figurine, Little Nell, M 51	55.00
Figurine, Lobster Man, HN 2317	95.00
Figurine, Lori, HN 2801	70.00
Figurine, Lucy Lockett, HN 524	950.00
Figurine, Lynne, HN 2329	125.00 To 185.00
Figurine, Maisie, HN 1619	375.00
Figurine, Margaret of Anjou, HN 2012	495.00
Figurine, Margaret, HN 1989	350.00
Figurine, Marguerite, HN 1928	285.00 To 325.00
Figurine, Mary Had A Little Lamb, HN 2048	97.00
Figurine, Mask Seller, HN 2103	150.00
Figurine, Masque, HN 2554	160.00
Figurine, Matilda, HN 2011	550.00
Figurine, Maureen, HN 1770	225.00 To 250.00
Figurine, Mayor, HN 2280	395.00
Figurine, Maytime, HN 2113	235.00 To 375.00
Figurine, Melanie, HN 2271	100.00 To 175.00
Figurine, Melissa, HN 2467	142.00
Figurine, Memories, HN 2030	250.00 To 325.00
Figurine, Mendicant, HN 1365	250.00
Figurine, Mexican Dancer, HN 2866	590.00
Figurine, Miss Demure, HN 1402	145.00 To 195.00
Figurine, Moor, HN 2082	795.00
Figurine, Mrs.Bardell, M 86	45.00 To 55.00
Figurine, New Companions, HN 2770	145.00
Figurine, Newsboy, HN 2244	425.00
Figurine, Nicola, HN 2839	230.00
Figurine, Ninette, HN 2379	115.00 To 225.00
Figurine, Noelle, HN 2179	350.00
Figurine, North American Indian Dancer, HN 2809	680.00
Figurine, Old Balloon Seller, HN 1315	100.00 To 105.00
Figurine, Old King Cole, HN 2217	495.00
Figurine, Old Meg, HN 2494	130.00 To 225.00
Figurine, Old Mother Hubbard, HN 2314	240.00
Figurine, Olga, HN 2463	175.00
Figurine, Oliver Twist, M 89	55.00
Figurine, Orange Lady, HN 1759	165.00 To 215.00
Figurine, Paisley Shawl, HN 1392	250.00
Figurine, Paisley Shawl, HN 1987	200.00
Figurine, Pantalettes, HN 1362	395.00
Figurine, Parisian, HN 2445	155.00
Figurine, Past Glory, HN 2484	155.00 To 170.00
Figurine, Patchwork Quilt, HN 1984	295.00
Figurine, Pearly Boy, HN 1482, Pearly Girl, HN 1483, Pair	545.00
Figurine, Penelope, HN 1901	245.00
Figurine, Pensive Moments, HN 2704	185.00
Figurine, Perfect Pair, HN 581	850.00 To 900.00
Figurine, Pied Piper, HN 2102	160.00 To 250.00
Figurine, Pirate King, HN 2901	425.00
Figurine, Polish Dancer, HN 2836	685.00
Figurine, Polly Peachum, HN 698	275.00 To 295.00
Figurine, Potter, HN 1493	165.00 To 275.00
Figurine, Pretty Polly, HN 2768	90.00
Figurine, Prince of Wales, HN 2883	375.00
Figurine, Princess of Wales, HN 2885	425.00
Figurine, Professor, HN 2281	150.00
Figurine, Proposal, Woman, HN 715	850.00
Figurine, Prue, HN 1996	235.00

Figurine, Queen Elizabeth II, HN 2878	375.00 To 450.00
Figurine, Rachel, HN 2919	145.00
Figurine, Rag Doll, HN 2142	65.00
Figurine, Rendezvous, HN 2212	375.00
Figurine, Reverie, HN 2306	225.00
Figurine, River Boy, HN 2128	225.00
Figurine, Romany Sue, HN 1758	695.00
Figurine, Roseanna, HN 1926	320.00
Figurine, Rosemary, HN 2091	395.00
Figurine, Rowena, HN 2077	525.00
Figurine, Rumplestiltskin, HN 3025	90.00
Figurine, Sabbath Morn, HN 1982	245.00
Figurine, Sailor's Holiday, HN 2442	170.00
Figurine, Sairey Gamp, HN 1896	295.00
Figurine, Sam Weller, M 48	55.00
Figurine, Shepherd, HN 1975	140.00 To 225.00
Figurine, Shore Leave, HN 2254	150.00 To 175.00
Figurine, Silks & Ribbons, HN 2017	100.00 To 105.00
Figurine, Simone, HN 2378	115.00 To 225.00
Figurine, Sir Ralph, HN 2370	595.00
Figurine, Sir Richard, HN 2371	580.00
Figurine, Sir Thomas, HN 2372	585.00
Figurine, Sir Walter Raleigh, HN 1751	925.00
Figurine, Skater, HN 2117	325.00
Figurine, Sleepy Darling, HN 2953	175.00 To 200.00
Figurine, Soiree, HN 2312	145.00
Figurine, Solitude, HN 2810	175.00
Figurine, Southern Belle, HN 2229	140.00 To 225.00
Figurine, Spook, HN 50	2500.00
Figurine, Spring Flowers, HN 1807	225.00 To 245.00
Figurine, Spring, HN 2085	325.00 To 395.00
Figurine, Springtime, HN 3033	225.00
Figurine, St.George & Dragon, HN 2856	3250.00
Figurine, St.George, HN 2051	300.00
Figurine, Stiggins, M 50	55.00
Figurine, Suitor, HN 2132	275.00
Figurine, Sunday Best, HN 2206	185.00
Figurine, Sunday Best, HN 2698	100.00
Figurine, Sunday Morning, HN 2184	250.00
Figurine, Susan, HN 2056	280.00 To 450.00
Figurine, Sweet & Twenty, HN 1298	325.00
Figurine, Sweet & Twenty, HN 1549	200.00
Figurine, Sweet Anne, HN 1496	155.00 To 250.00
Figurine, Sweet Maid, HN 1505	850.00
Figurine, Tailor, HN 2174	650.00
Figurine, Taking Things Easy, HN 2677	200.00
Figurine, Tall Story, HN 2248	150.00
Figurine, This Little Pig, HN 1793	75.00
Figurine, Tiny Tim, M 56	55.00
Figurine, To Bed, HN 1805	145.00 To 150.00
Figurine, Tony Weller, M 47	55.00
Figurine, Top O' The Hill, HN 1849	140.00 To 225.00
Figurine, Twilight, HN 2256	250.00
Figurine, Tz'U–Hsi Empress Dowager, HN 2391	650.00
Figurine, Uriah Heep, M 45	55.00
Figurine, Veronica, HN 1517	275.00
Figurine, Victorian Lady, M 1	295.00
Figurine, Wardrobe Mistress, HN 2145	475.00
Figurine, West Indian Dancer, HN 2384	690.00
Figurine, Willy–Won't He, HN 2150	395.00
Figurine, Wizard, HN 2877	140.00 To 170.00
Figurine, Young Miss Nightingale, HN 2010	575.00
Goblet, Christmas, 3 French Hens, 1982	23.00
Group, Failure of Pears Soap, Scrubbing Black Child	802.00

Hatpin Holder, Sam Weller, 6 In.	110.00
Jardiniere, Cobalt, White Farm Country Scene, Stamped, 10 In.	150.00
Jardiniere, Welsh Ladies, Walking To Church, 7 1/8 In.	325.00
Jug, Kingsware, Drink Wisely	185.00
Jug, Old London, Series	250.00
Jug, Portia, Marked, 6 3/8 In.	110.00
Jug, Sea Shanty, Sailors, Ship, Verses, Marked, 6 3/4 In.	150.00
Lighter, Falstaff	110.00
Lighter, Long John Silver	110.00
Match Holder, Striker, Ashtray, Club, Heart, Spade, Diamond	80.00
Match Holder, Striker, Pedestal, Dewar's	125.00
Mug, Bunnykins, 1954	45.00
Pitcher, 2 Men At Table, 6 1/2 In.	125.00
Pitcher, Babes At Beach, 4 In.	58.00
Pitcher, Battle of Hastings, 4 3/4 In.	88.00
Pitcher, Bodian Castle, C.1930, 7 In.	50.00
Pitcher, Falstaff, Flared Spout, C.1909, 6 3/4 In.	85.00
Pitcher, Goldsmith, 9 In.	115.00
Pitcher, Izaak Walton, Saying At Base, Marked, 12 1/2 In.	225.00
Pitcher, Motto, Glasgow, Tan, Brown, Lambeth, C.1880, 7 1/4 In.	175.00
Pitcher, Oliver Goldsmith House, Pre–1930, 6 1/2 In.	98.00
Pitcher, Sailing Scene, Hand Painted, 7 X 5 In.	145.00
Pitcher, Sir Toby Belch, Maxim, C.1910, 8 In.	75.00
Plate, Admiral	45.00
Plate, Babes In Woods, Forest, Girls Looking At Light, 10 In.	430.00
Plate, Babes In Woods, Mother & Daughter, 8 3/4 In.	230.00
Plate, Balmoral Castle, 11 1/2 In.	50.00
Plate, Benevolent Sportsman, Dated 1934, 10 1/2 In.	70.00
Plate, Blue & White Castle Scene, 9 1/2 In.	40.00
Plate, Bunnykins, Mailbox Scene, Barbara Vernon	30.00
Plate, Burslem, Floral, Gold Tracery, Lacy Border, 9 In.	60.00
Plate, Christmas, 1979	25.00
Plate, Cypress, 10 1/2 In.	65.00
Plate, English Country Scene, 10 1/2 In.	38.00
Plate, Falstaff, 10 In.	70.00
Plate, Gamebird, 1904, 10 In.	125.00
Plate, Gondolier, 10 In.	45.00
Plate, Huntsman, 11 1/2 In.	50.00
Plate, Imperial Palace, 11 1/2 In.	50.00
Plate, Jackdaw of Rheims, 9 1/2 In.	35.00
Plate, Jester, 10 In.	48.00
Plate, King Arthur's Knights, 10 In.	35.00
Plate, Man On Horse, Green Field, Vine & Grape Border, 9 In.	35.00
Plate, Shakespeare, 10 In.	70.00
Plate, Shylock, 10 In.	70.00
Plate, Soldiers of Revolution, Georgia	950.00
Plate, Soldiers of Revolution, South Carolina	950.00
Plate, Valentine, 1976	20.00
Sugar Shaker, Thatched Roof Cottage, Church, 7 1/4 In.	135.00
Sugar, Cover, Sairey Gamp, Miniature	875.00
Sugar, Open, Coaching Day, Stagecoach & Passengers	75.00
Tea Set, Bayeux Tapestry, 3 Piece	175.00
Teapot, Dutch Harbor, Windmill Design, Signed Noke	210.00
Tile, Tea, King Arthur's Knights	80.00
Toby Jug, Best Is Not Too Good, Large	300.00
Toby Jug, Sam Weller, Seated, A Mark	135.00
Toby Jug, Winston Churchill, Seated, Small	45.00
Tray, Gaffers, Man In Smock, Top Hat, Cane, 6 1/4 In.	55.00
Tray, Zunday Zmocks, Marked, 1 1/2 X 6 1/2 X 9 3/8 In.	95.00
Trivet, Monk Portrait & Ladies, Blue, Buff Ground, 6 1/2 In.	45.00
Vase, Babes In Woods, Blindman's Bluff, Gold Trim, 4 3/8 In.	245.00
Vase, Cardinal Wolsey, Dressed In Red, Marked, 8 1/2 In.	165.00
Vase, Coaching Days, 8 In.	235.00
Vase, Coaching Days, Stagecoach, Horses, Passengers, 4 1/8 In.	118.00

Vase, Cobalt, Flowers, Tan Tapestry Body, Impressed, 10 In.	200.00
Vase, Dickens Ware, Barnaby Rudge, Square, 4 3/4 In.	70.00
Vase, Dickens Ware, Sam Weller, Square, 3 3/4 In.	65.00
Vase, Dunolly Castle, Artist J.Hughes, 4 1/2 In.	165.00
Vase, Fish & Seaweed, Luster, 8 In., Pair	150.00
Vase, Lambeth, Art Deco Fruit Design, 7 1/2 In.	110.00
Vase, Robin Hood Series, Guy of Gisborne, Marked, 5 1/2 In.	95.00
Vase, Romeo & Juliet, Facing Pair, 11 7/8 In.	425.00
Vase, Welsh Ladies, Women & Children On Path To House, 7 In.	165.00

The Duxer Porzellanmanufaktur was founded in Dux, Bohemia, in 1860 by E. Eichler. By the turn of the century, the firm specialized in porcelain statuary and busts of Art Nouveau-style maidens, large porcelain figures, and ornate vases with three-dimensional figures climbing on the sides. The firm is still in business.

ROYAL DUX, Bust, Lady, With Lyre, Gown Over Head, Pink Triangle Mark, 9 In.	395.00
Centerpiece, Maiden, Cherubs, Holding Up Shell Bowl, 15 X 20 In.	950.00
Figurine, Art Deco Lady, Pink Triangle, No.3262, 13 In.	525.00
Figurine, Bear With Guitar, 4 In.	55.00
Figurine, Bird, No.2819, Marked	125.00
Figurine, Bohemia Shepherdess, Sheepskin Robe, Turban, 14 3/4 In.	575.00
Figurine, Camel Driver, 17 X 14 In.	1800.00
Figurine, Children With Cow, Marked, 12 X 13 In.	695.00
Figurine, Cockatoo, Marked, 16 1/2 In., Pair	500.00
Figurine, Dancing Couple, Floral Design On Dress, Marked, 9 In.	150.00
Figurine, Dancing Couple, Gold Trim Plinth, Marked, 9 In.	85.00
Figurine, Elephant, 9 In.	45.00 To 90.00
Figurine, Girl, Seated, Bird On Shoulder, 4 1/2 In.	75.00
Figurine, Harvester & Wife, Blue & Gold, Marked, 21 In., Pair	750.00
Figurine, Hunting Dog With Birds, Marked, 17 1/2 In.	195.00
Figurine, Monkey With Horn, 4 1/2 In.	55.00
Figurine, Nude Woman, Standing, 12 In.	185.00
Figurine, Nude, Seated, Butterfly On Knee, Marked, 8 In.	225.00
Figurine, Owl, White, Pink Triangle Mark, 10 In.	75.00
Figurine, Peasant Boy & Girl, Sheaving Wheat, 1910, 19 1/2 In.	750.00
Figurine, Resting Deer, Marked, 9 X 6 In.	125.00
Figurine, Shepherd & Shepherdess, 14 In., Pair	850.00
Figurine, Spanish Dancer, Fan In One Hand, Smiling, 9 In.	295.00
Figurine, Stalking Tiger, Marked	145.00
Figurine, Water Carrier, Man, 20 In.	1100.00
Figurine, Water Carrier, Woman, 20 In.	1100.00
Figurine, Woman, Art Deco, Blue Dress, Flesh Tones, Marked, 10 In.	295.00
Figurine, Woman, Long Head Scarf, Jug In Hand, 11 1/4 In.	400.00
Figurine, Woman, Smiling, Hand On Hip, Mantilla & Fans, 9 In.	350.00
Figurine, Woman, With Basket, Holding Child, Marked, 8 1/2 In.	395.00
Group, Camels, Marked, 18 In.	450.00
Vase, Floral & Leaf Design, Circular Mark, 13 In.	95.00
Vase, Geisha Girl, Incised White, 12 In.	395.00

Royal Flemish glass was made during the late 1880s in New Bedford, Massachusetts, by the Mt. Washington Glass Works. It is a colored satin glass decorated with dark colors and raised gold designs. The glass was patented in 1894. It was supposed to resemble stained glass windows.

ROYAL FLEMISH, Biscuit Jar, Melon, Silver Plated Handle & Lid, 6 1/2 In.	750.00
Castor, Pickle, Pairpoint Frame	595.00
Vase, 5 Roman Medallions, Gold Borders, C.1890	1985.00

ROYAL HAEGER, see Haeger
ROYAL IVY, see Pressed Glass, Royal Ivy
ROYAL OAK, see Pressed Glass, Royal Oak
ROYAL RUDOLSTADT, see Rudolstadt
ROYAL VIENNA, see Beehive

Worcester porcelains were made in Worcester, England, from about 1751. The firm went through many different periods and name changes. It became the Worcester Royal Porcelain Company, Ltd., in 1862. Today collectors call the porcelains made after 1862 "Royal Worcester." In 1976, the firm merged with W. T. Copeland to become Royal Worcester Spode. Some early products of the factory are listed under Worcester.

ROYAL WORCESTER, Biscuit Jar, Flowers, Leaves, Silver–Plated Fittings, 6 In.	285.00
Candleholder, Brass, 12 In.	175.00
Candleholder, Gold Mouse, Marked, 1892, 2 1/2 In.	395.00
Candlesnuffer, Hat With Pink Plume	60.00
Candlesnuffer, Monk	95.00
Candlestick, Flower Saucer, Gold Wash Trim	45.00
Cup & Sauce, Doreen	25.00
Cup & Saucer, Panels of Flowers, Gold Trim, Marked	120.00
Dish, 3 Cupids, Heart Shape, C.1895, 6 In.	155.00
Ewer, Flowers, Gold Outlined, Salamander Handle, 9 In.	435.00
Ewer, Flowers, Salamander Handle, 1880, 11 1/2 In.	495.00
Ewer, Gilded Serpent Handle, Owl In Tree, 1894, 7 In.	325.00
Ewer, Ivoryware, Crane, Flower, Gold Flecked, 1884, 10 In.	220.00
Ewer, Rust & Yellow Flowers, Gold Outlined, 6 5/8 In.	225.00
Figurine, 2 Ducks, White & Gold, Signed Kenneth Potts	35.00
Figurine, Amaryllis	300.00
Figurine, Anne Boleyn, Holding Fan, Fan Collar, 8 1/2 In.	350.00
Figurine, Babes In The Woods	225.00
Figurine, Boy With Basket, Gold Trim, 1893, 8 1/2 In.	525.00
Figurine, Burmah, Signed, 5 In.	150.00
Figurine, Dreaming, No.2875, Phoebe Stabler, 1931	450.00
Figurine, Dutch Girl	125.00
Figurine, First Dance, No.3629	200.00
Figurine, Fortune Teller	285.00
Figurine, Goat Woman	300.00
Figurine, Goosie Goosie Gander	200.00
Figurine, Grandmother's Dress, Green	135.00
Figurine, Irishman, Marked, 1891, 6 7/8 In.	395.00
Figurine, January Boy	95.00
Figurine, John Bull, Marked, 1891, 6 7/8 In.	395.00
Figurine, Mother McCree	285.00
Figurine, My Favorite	250.00
Figurine, Parakeet On Stump, 6 In.	78.00
Figurine, Sabbath Child	125.00
Figurine, Scotsman, Marked, 1891, 6 1/4 In.	395.00
Figurine, Sisters	295.00
Figurine, Two Babies	185.00
Figurine, Woman, Holding Bird, 1896, 9 1/2 In., Pair	850.00
Figurine, Yankee, Beige & Brown, 7 In.	350.00
Flower Holder, Double, Apricot, Aqua, Gold, C.1898, 10 In.	275.00
Flower Holder, Roses, Brass Mesh Cover, C.1910, 5 1/8 In.	325.00
Jam Jar, Figural, Strawberry, Silver Lid, Spoon, 1898, 4 In.	88.00
Jug, Flowers, Gilded, Multicolored, C.1862, 6 In.	250.00
Jug, Owl On Branch, Gold Serpent Handle, C.1885, 11 1/4 In.	925.00
Jug, Wine, Colored Flowers, Gold Trim, 9 3/4 In.	325.00
Jug, Wine, Gold Over Handle, 1884, 10 In.	325.00
Mush Set, 1862 Mark, 3 Piece	65.00
Nautilus Shell, Supported By Coral Branches, 6 3/4 In.	375.00
Oyster Plate, Scalloped, Gold Trim, 4 Piece	85.00
Patch Box, Floral	98.00
Pie Bird, Black, Box	35.00
Pitcher, Floral Outlined In Gold, Mask Spout, 4 In.	70.00
Pitcher, Floral Spray On Beige, Gilt Handle, 8 1/4 In.	300.00
Pitcher, Floral Sprays, Beige Ground, 7 In.	300.00
Pitcher, Floral, Gold Outlined, Marked, 1903, 6 In.	125.00
Pitcher, Florals In Gold, Cream Ground, 1895, 3 3/4 In.	65.00

Pitcher, Gold & Cream, Flat Back, 8 In.	135.00
Pitcher, Horn, C.1906, 9 1/2 In.	175.00
Pitcher, Leaf, Cream Color, Green Mark, 4 1/4 In.	45.00
Pitcher, Thread–Wrapped Gold Handle, Florals, 10 In.	275.00
Plaque, Edward VIII, Embossed, 5 In.	65.00
Plate, 3 Cupids In Field, Heart Shape, C.1895, 6 In.	155.00
Plate, Fruit, Signed R.Sebright, 8 1/2 In.	325.00
Plate, Game Bird, Red Edge, Gold Design, 9 1/8 In.	85.00
Plate, Jeweled, Hand Painted, 1888, 9 In.	70.00
Rose Bowl, Locke	30.00
Thimble, Bluebird Design	50.00
Vase, Allover Gold Rayed, Serrated Wheels, 1887, 9 In.	178.00
Vase, Bamboo Trees, Flying Crane, Marked, 8 3/4 In.	495.00
Vase, Birds On Moonlit Night, 2 Handles, Gold, 12 In.	325.00
Vase, Blue Flowers, Gold Trim, 1898, 6 7/8 In.	225.00
Vase, Costumed Child Each Side, Encircled By Ivy, 6 In.	160.00
Vase, Cover, Egg Shape, Hoofed Feet, C.1910, 6 In.	560.00
Vase, Flowers, 2 Pierced Handles, C.1890, 6 1/2 In.	225.00
Vase, Flowers, Foliage, Gold Trim, C.1898, 7 In., Pair	435.00
Vase, Japanese Style, 1874, 8 1/2 In., Pair ....*Illus*	825.00
Vase, Raised Leaves, Flowers, Handles At Top, Marked, 14 In.	875.00
Vase, Roses & Lilies, Gold Trim, Marked, 7 In.	125.00

Roycroft products were made by the Roycrofter community of East Aurora, New York, in the late nineteenth and early twentieth centuries. The community was founded by Elbert Hubbard, famous philosopher, writer, and artist. The workshops owned by the community made furniture, metalware, leatherwork, embroidery, and jewelry. A printshop produced many signs, books, and the magazines that promoted the sayings of Elbert Hubbard. Furniture by the Roycroft community is listed in the furniture section.

ROYCROFT, Blotter Corner, Hammered Design, 4 Piece	110.00
Book, Story of Passion, Irving Bacheller	150.00
Bookends, Copper, Leather Owl Inserts	75.00
Bookends, Fleur–De–Lis Design, Hammered Copper	25.00
Bookends, Poppies, Arched, Hammered Brass On Copper, 8 In.	75.00
Bowl, Hammered, Silver Patina, 6 X 2 1/4 In.	40.00
Box, Hinged Lid, Mahogany, Brass Strapwork, 1910, 9 1/2 X 23 In.	825.00
Candleholder, Hammered Brass, U–Shaped Stem, 2 Bobeche, 6 In., Pair	300.00
Candlestick, Flared Rim, Bobeche, Stamped, 10 In., Pair	475.00
Candlestick, Wide Foot, Upturn At Rim, 6 3/8 In., Pair	1145.00
Catalog, Roycroft Shop, Christmas Greeting Enclosed, 1910	150.00
Crumb Set, 2 Piece	65.00
Desk Set, Hammered Copper, 3 Piece	150.00
Goblet Set, Tray, Hammered Silver Wash, 7 Piece	225.00
Hat, Doughboy, Copper, 5 X 2 In.	110.00
Lamp, Hammered Copper & Mica, C.1908, 14 In.	1100.00
Lamp, Mushroom Shade	2000.00
Mirror, Hanging	990.00
Pin Tray, Hammered, Marked	25.00
Vase, American Beauty, Large	750.00
Vase, Brass Wash, Acid Cut Band, Signed, 5 In.	175.00
Vase, Copper, 10 In.	200.00
Vase, Silver Squares At Rim, 4 Buttress Handles, C.1910, 7 3/4 In.	2300.00
Vase, Stylized Bands of Applied Silver, Logo, C.1915, 6 1/4 In.	1850.00
Vase, Stylized Floral Design, Hammered Copper	275.00
Vase, Vertical Lines of Bellflowers, Signed, 10 In.	700.00
ROZANE, see Roseville	

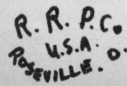

RRP is the mark used by the firm of Robinson–Ransbottom. It is not a mark of the more famous Roseville Pottery. The Ransbottom brothers started a pottery in 1900 in Ironspot, Ohio. In 1920, they merged with the Robinson Clay Product Company of Akron, Ohio, to become Robinson–Ransbottom. The factory is still working.

RRP, Cookie Jar, Chef With Eggs 25.00
 Cookie Jar, Dutch Boy, Gold Trim 75.00
 Cookie Jar, Old King Cole 150.00
 Cookie Jar, Wise Bird 30.00
 Jardiniere, Majolica, Brown, Green Base, Spike & Disc Design, 7 X 8 In. 28.00
 Pitcher, Batter, 5 Kitchen Tools, Yellow, 6 3/4 In. 18.00
 Planter, Figural, Bug, Turtle Head, Yellow, Green, 7 X 3 1/2 X 2 1/4 In. 7.00
 Planter, Figure–8 Shape, Brown, Swirled Scales, 8 1/2 X 4 1/2 In. 7.50
 Vase, Acanthus Leaf, White, 10 In. 14.00

The RS Germany mark was used on porcelain made at the factory of Reinhold Schlegelmilch from about 1910 to 1956 in Tillowitz, Germany. It was sold decorated and undecorated. The Schlegelmilch family made porcelains marked in many ways. Each type is listed separately. See also ES Germany, RS Poland, RS Prussia, RS Suhl, and RS Tillowitz.

RS GERMANY, Ashtray, Nightwatch Scene, Brown Ground 250.00
 Basket, Lily–of–The–Valley Design, Gold Rim, 6 3/4 X 5 1/2 In. 155.00
 Berry Set, White Flowers & Leaves, Shadows, 7 Piece 125.00
 Bowl, 3 Stylized Blue Orchids, Gold Trim, 10 In. 75.00
 Bowl, Cottage Scene, Steeple Mark, 10 1/2 In. 550.00
 Bowl, Multipetal Florals, Green Leaves, Gold Trim, Marked, 13 In. 68.00
 Bowl, Pastel Roses, Handles, Square, Blue Mark, 5 3/4 In. 35.00
 Bowl, Scene of Woman With Cows, Cottage, Handles, 10 In. 255.00
 Cake Set, Tulip Design, 7 Piece 135.00
 Celery, Art Deco, Artist Signed, 1930 .... 45.00
 Chocolate Set, Floral, Buds, Fronds, Aqua To Green, 7 Piece 225.00
 Condiment Set, Mustard, Salt, Underplate, Azalea, Blue Mark, 3 Pc. 125.00
 Cracker Jar, White Rose Design, Classic Shape, 4 1/2 In. 145.00
 Creamer, Lily–of–The–Valley Design, White, 3 1/2 In. 30.00
 Creamer, Orchid Florals, Gold Scalloped Rim, 3 1/2 In. 65.00
 Cup & Saucer, Lily, Demitasse 18.00
 Dish, Mayonnaise, Underplate, Ladle, Poppies, Blue Mark 68.00
 Hatpin Holder, Dogwood Flower 70.00
 Hatpin Holder, Green & White Daffodils 55.00
 Mustache Cup, Floral 45.00
 Mustard, Attached Underplate, Boating Scene 44.00
 Pitcher, Milk, Bronze & Pink Roses, Signed, 8 1/2 In. 80.00
 Plate, Blown–Out Irises, Marked, 10 1/2 In. 240.00
 Plate, Blue Flowers, Gold Veins To Petals, Gold Trim, 9 In. 80.00
 Plate, Orange Blossoms, Muted Green & Rose Ground, 8 1/2 In. 25.00
 Relish, Flowers, Green Trim 50.00
 Relish, Pink & White Roses, Marked, 6 X 10 In. 55.00
 Relish, White Poppy, Gold Trim, Green Ground, 9 1/4 In. 22.00
 Server, 2 Tiers, White Lilies, Beige Ground, Gold Trim 65.00
 Sugar & Creamer, Cottage Scene 160.00
 Sugar & Creamer, Forget–Me–Nots, Puffy Medallions, Footed 45.00
 Sugar & Creamer, Surreal Dogwood 85.00
 Tankard, Blown–Out Rose Buds, Marked, 14 1/2 In. 395.00
 Vase, Nightwatch Scene, Gold & Red Trim, Double Handles, 6 In. 395.00

The RS Poland (German) mark was used by the Reinhold Schlegelmilch factory at Tillowitz from about 1945 to 1956. This is one of many of the RS marks used. See also ES Germany, RS Germany, RS Prussia, RS Silesia, RS Suhl, and RS Tillowitz.

RS POLAND, Bowl, Portrait, Scalloped Base, 9 1/4 In. 325.00
 Cup & Saucer, Pink Roses, Gold Trim, Footed, Demitasse 125.00
 Planter, Band of Pink Flowers, Pedestal, 6 3/4 X 6 1/2 In. 230.00
 Plate, Dogwood & Pine, 8 In. 85.00
 Urn, Cover, Pink & White Roses, Brown Ground, Marked, 11 1/2 In. 800.00
 Vase, Floral, Gold & Brown Ground, Marked, 8 3/4 In. 135.00
 Vase, Roses, Garlands, Gold Band At Top, Marked, 8 3/4 In. 145.00
 Vase, Single Rose On Brown Ground, 4 1/4 In. 105.00

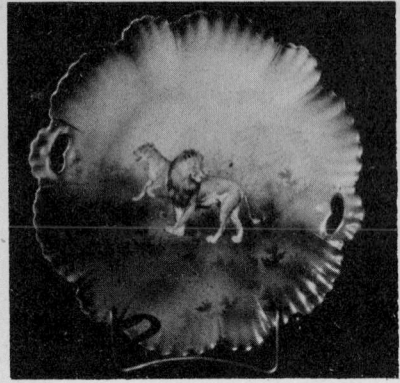

RS Prussia, Cake Plate, Lion, Open Handle,   RS Prussia, Urn,
10 1/2 In.   Hummingbird

"RS Prussia" is a mark that appears on porcelain made at the factory of Reinhold Schlegelmilch from the late 1870s to 1914 in Tillowitz, Germany, or on items made at the Erdmann Schlegelmilch factory in Suhl, Germany, from about 1910 to 1956. It was sold decorated or undecorated. The factories were owned by brothers. See also ES Germany, RS Germany, RS Poland, RS Silesia, RS Suhl, and RS Tillowitz.

RS PRUSSIA, Berry Bowl, Embossed Poppy Or Carnation Mold, 6 1/2 In.	168.00
Berry Set, Magnolias, Pastel Ground, Pebbled Gold Bands, 7 Piece	180.00
Berry Set, Rose & Daisy, 5 Piece	225.00
Berry Set, Snowball Mold, 5 Piece	295.00
Biscuit Jar, Bluebirds, Red Mark, 7 In.	450.00
Biscuit Jar, Cherub, Red Mark	325.00
Bowl, 5 Portrait Medallions, Gold Border, Red Mark, 9 1/4 In.	795.00
Bowl, 8 Blown–Out Sections, Grape & Leaf Edge, Red Mark, 10 In.	475.00
Bowl, Blown–Out Carnation Mold, Roses, Yellow Ground, 9 1/2 In.	215.00
Bowl, Blown–Out Iris Mold, Pink Roses, Red Mark, 10 1/2 In.	85.00
Bowl, Blown–Out Iris, 10 1/2 In.	250.00
Bowl, Cabbage, Red Mark, Miniature	150.00
Bowl, Carnation Mold, Floral, Red Mark, 10 1/4 In.	265.00
Bowl, Carnation Mold, Roses, Footed, Red Mark, 6 In.	150.00
Bowl, Cobalt Blue, 10 1/2 In.	650.00
Bowl, Dogwood & Pine, Lettuce Mold, Red Mark, 7 In.	200.00
Bowl, Duo Portrait, 11 In.	4000.00
Bowl, Fleur–De–Lis, Wishbone Shape, Red Mark, 10 1/2 In.	165.00
Bowl, Floral Center, Hexagonal, Marked, 10 1/2 In.	125.00
Bowl, Fruit Design, Gold, Low, 8 1/2 In.	140.00
Bowl, Hidden Image Portrait, 10 In.	325.00
Bowl, Masted Ships, Jeweled, 11 In.	2500.00
Bowl, Pompon & Roses, 10 3/4 In.	96.00
Bowl, Portrait, 3 Medallions, Floral Center, 10 1/2 In.	550.00
Bowl, Red Roses, Gold Band Border, St.Killian Mark, 10 X 3 In.	120.00
Bowl, Satin Finish Roses, Shadow Leaves, Red Mark, 13 In.	160.00
Bowl, White Flowers, Red Mark, 11 In.	115.00
Bun Tray, Four Seasons, Red Mark	8000.00
Cake Plate, Blown–Out Lily Mold, Yellow Roses, Red Mark, 11 In.	110.00
Cake Plate, Green, Pink, Yellow Roses, Pierced Handles	100.00
Cake Plate, Icicle Mold, Basket of Flowers, Marked, 10 In.	195.00
Cake Plate, Iris Mold, Poppies In Center, Marked, 10 3/4 In.	250.00
Cake Plate, Keyhole Pattern, Melon Boy, Jewels, Red Mark	175.00
Cake Plate, Lion, Open Handle, 10 1/2 In. ....*Illus*	5400.00

Cake Plate, Pheasant, Pine Trees, 11 In. 375.00
Cake Plate, Spring Season, Keyhole, Green, Pink & Gold, Red Mark 795.00
Cake Plate, Swallows, Chickens & Ducks, Open Handles, 10 In. 1000.00
Celery, Cloverleaf Mold 250.00
Celery, Diane The Huntress & Flora, Poppies & Daisies 895.00
Celery, Dogwood Blossoms, Red Mark, 12 1/2 In. 100.00
Celery, Iris Mold, Roses In Center, Marked, 6 1/4 X 10 In. 225.00
Celery, Pink Roses, 4 Embossed Iris, Open Handle, Yellow, 12 In. 245.00
Celery, Roses, Red Mark, 6 X 12 In. 300.00
Celery, Swan Scene, Scalloped, Red Mark, 12 1/2 In. 395.00
Chocolate Pot, Calla Lily Design, Satin Finish, Red Mark 295.00
Chocolate Pot, Cobalt Blue Carnation Mold, Red Mark 1200.00
Chocolate Pot, Floral, Cobalt & Gold Trim, Pink Florals 750.00
Chocolate Set, Pink Roses, Green & Yellow, Red Mark, 9 Piece 650.00
Chocolate Set, Swan, Red Mark, 7 Piece 2500.00
Coffee Set, Shaded Green, White Ground, Scalloped Rim, 8 Piece 650.00
Cracker Barrel, Laurel Chain, Red Mark, 7 In. 365.00
Cracker Jar, Blown-Out Flower Rim, Pagoda Finial On Lid 235.00
Cracker Jar, Crimson Roses Over Yellow & Green, Red Mark 230.00
Creamer, Castle Scene, Red Mark 525.00
Cruet, Pair of Birds, 6 In. 185.00
Cup & Saucer, Carnation Mold, Cobalt Blue, Demitasse 295.00
Cup & Saucer, Castle Scene, Browns, Set of 4 .... 800.00
Cup & Saucer, Chocolate, Pheasant 75.00
Cup & Saucer, Diagonal Swirls, Roses, Holly, Gold Trim 115.00
Cup & Saucer, Dogwood & Pine, Red Mold 115.00
Cup & Saucer, Floral, Footed, Demitasse 110.00
Cup & Saucer, Pink Roses, Shaded Green, Red Mark 65.00
Demitasse Set, Floral Design, Satin Finish, 9 Piece 1000.00
Dish, Iris Mold, 3-Footed 175.00
Ewer, Floral, Gold Floral Handle, Marked, 4-Footed, 10 1/2 In. 325.00
Ferner, Peach & White Roses, Green Ground, Signed, 7 1/2 In. 225.00
Flowers, Red Mark 175.00
Gravy Boat, Underplate, Rose Clusters, Gold Trim, Red Mark 105.00
Hair Receiver, Jeweled, Tiffany Coloring, Satin, 5 In. 295.00
Hair Receiver, Pink Rose, Yellow & Green 125.00
Hatpin Holder, Holly & Leaves 275.00
Hatpin Holder, Water Lilies On Water 175.00
Jam Jar, Flower Shape 195.00
Lemonade Set, Colonial Couple, Green, Silver Deposit, 9 Piece 750.00
Mustache Cup, Roses, Blue Swirls, Gold Trim 40.00
Mustache Cup, Shell, Floral 145.00
Mustache Cup, Underplate, Pearlized Luster, Poppies, 4-Footed 295.00
Mustard, Basket, Red Mark 120.00
Mustard, Cover, Spoon, Lilies, Red Mark 190.00
Mustard, Ladle, Satin Finish, Red Mark 125.00
Mustard, Lily Mold 48.00
Mustard, Satin Finish, Roses & Daisies 125.00
Nappy, Raised Flowers, Center Floral, Red Mark 75.00
Nut Set, Roses, Leaves, Gold Tracery, Red Mark, 7 Piece 300.00
Pitcher, Cider, Pink Roses, Gold Enameling, Red Mark, 6 1/2 In. 495.00
Pitcher, Fall Season, 9 1/2 In. 2250.00
Pitcher, Pink Roses, Green Ground, Gold Trim, Footed, 6 In. 225.00
Plaque, Mill Scene, Green Ground, 11 1/4 In. 710.00
Plate, Apple Girl, Red Mark, 9 In. 875.00
Plate, Castle Scene, Iris Mold, 9 1/2 In. 600.00
Plate, Castle, Fleur-De-Lis Mold, Browns, 8 1/2 In., Pair 650.00
Plate, Melon Boy, Jeweled, Red Mark, 6 In. 350.00
Plate, Open Roses, Red Mark, 8 1/2 In. 45.00
Plate, Peach & Pink Center Rose, Raised Gold Border, 7 3/4 In. 135.00
Powder Jar, Stippled Floral, Red Mark 100.00
Relish, Dogwood & Pine, Red Mark 65.00
Relish, Hidden Images, 12 In. 150.00
Relish, Pink Roses, Yellow Ground, Red Mark, 10 In. 115.00

Relish, Ruffled, Open Ends	85.00
Relish, Surreal Dogwood, Oval, 9 In.	150.00
Salt & Pepper, Mill Scene, Red Mark	295.00
Salt & Pepper, Single Lily, White, Red Mark	175.00
Saltshaker, Pink & Peach Roses, Blown–Out Shoulder & Bottom	35.00
Shaving Mug, Hidden Image, Lip	250.00
Shaving Mug, Scuttle, Flowers, Shell Molding	125.00
Spooner, Floral, Handles, Red Mark	150.00
Sugar & Creamer, Castle Scene, Pedestal, Red Mark	550.00
Sugar & Creamer, Cover, Blown–Out Flowers, 4 3/4 In.	145.00
Sugar & Creamer, Cover, Jeweled Floral, Gold Trim, Jewels, 5 In.	165.00
Sugar & Creamer, Floral Design, Gold Trim, Red Mark	200.00
Sugar & Creamer, Lily–of–The–Valley, Melon Ribbed, Pedestal	395.00
Sugar & Creamer, Pink Asters, Green Tint, Red Mark	95.00
Sugar & Creamer, Red & Yellow Roses, Mold 505, Signed	135.00
Sugar & Creamer, Roses, Stippled Mold, Blue, Red Mark	85.00
Sugar & Creamer, Stippled Pink & Yellow Roses, Red Mark	90.00
Sugar & Creamer, Water Lily, Icicle Mold, Red Mark	260.00
Sugar Shaker, Colonial Figure	225.00
Sugar Shaker, Roses, Scalloped Base, Red Mark, 4 3/4 In.	235.00
Sugar, Cover, Lavender Flowers, Green Tones, Red Mark	75.00
Talcum Shaker, Scalloped Base, Roses, Gold Trim, Red Mark	95.00
Talcum Shaker, Shaded Tea Roses, Scalloped Rim & Base, Red Mark	155.00
Tankard, Pink & Red Roses, Red Mark, 13 1/2 In.	765.00
Tankard, Yellow & Pink Roses, Cream & Pink Ground	295.00
Teapot, Blown–Out Carnations, Gold Spout & Handles	295.00
Teapot, Leaf Base	175.00
Toothpick, Basket of Roses, Red Mark	130.00
Toothpick, Green Iridescent, Shadow Florals, Red Mark	85.00
Tray, Dresser, Blown–Out Irises, Open Handles, 1 1/4 X 11 In.	165.00
Tray, Dresser, Carnation Mold, 11 X 7 1/2 In.	245.00
Tray, Dresser, Pink & Green Carnations, Red Mark, 11 X 7 In.	245.00
Tray, Dresser, Swallow, Medallion Mold	450.00
Tumbler, Large Rose, Off–White, Gold Bands, Red Mark	55.00
Urn, Hummingbird ....*Illus*	2100.00
Vase, Floral Design, Open Gold Handles, Green Rim, 10 In.	125.00
Vase, Lavender Violets, Red Mark, 6 3/4 In.	175.00
Vase, Pink Roses, Gold Leaves, Blown–Out Iris Mold, 7 1/2 In.	325.00
Vase, Roses, Daisies, Snowballs In Dish, Marked, 9 1/2 In.	345.00
Vase, Roses, Double Handle, Red Mark, 9 1/4 In.	135.00
Vase, Yellow Floral, Ormolu Handles, Cranberry, 10 1/2 In.	395.00

The RS Silesia mark appears on porcelain made at the Reinhold Schlegelmilch factory in Tillowitz, Germany, from about 1920 to the mid–1930s. The Schlegelmilch family made porcelains marked in many ways. Each type is listed separately. See also ES Germany, RS Germany, RS Poland, RS Prussia, RS Suhl, and RS Tillowitz.

RS SILESIA, Plate, Flowers, Gold Border, 10 In.	25.00
Vase, Violets, 7 In.	60.00

RS Suhl was a mark used by the Erdmann Schlegelmilch factory in Suhl, Germany, from c.1900 to the mid–1920s. The factory worked from 1861 to 1925. The Schlegelmilch family made porcelains in many places. See also ES Germany, RS Germany, RS Poland, RS Prussia, RS Silesia, and RS Tillowitz.

RS SUHL, Vase, Women Winding Flax, Feeding Chickens, Handles, 6 1/2 In.	475.00
Vase, Yellow Roses On Green, Raised Handles, 14 In.	325.00

The RS Tillowitz mark was used by the Reinhold Schlegelmilch factory at Tillowitz, near Silesia, from about 1920 to the mid–1930s. Table services and ornamental pieces were made. See also ES Germany, RS Germany, RS Poland, RS Prussia, RS Silesia, and RS Suhl.

RS TILLOWITZ, Cake Plate, Fuchsias, Silesia, 10 In.	48.00

Jam Jar, Underplate, Floral 50.00

 Rubena Verde is a Victorian glassware that was shaded from red to green. It was first made by Hobbs, Brockunier and Company of Wheeling, West Virginia, about 1890.

RUBENA VERDE, Bride's Bowl, Ruffled, Cased 125.00
  Epergne, Opalescent Rim, 16 In. 285.00
  Punch Cup, Paneled, Applied Handle, Opalescent Lining 30.00
  Rose Bowl 95.00
  Sugar Shaker, Enameled Florals 295.00
  Tumbler, Inverted Thumbprint, 3 7/8 In. 200.00
  Vase, Fluted Top, Paneled Optic Effect, 10 3/4 In. 175.00
  Vase, Pedestal Bowl, Drape Pattern, 9 1/4 In. 180.00
  Vase, White Flowers, Navy Scrolls, Gold Jewels, 9 1/2 In., Pair 250.00

Rubena is a glassware that shades from red to clear. It was first made by George Duncan and Sons of Pittsburgh, Pennsylvania, about 1885. This coloring was used on many types of glassware. The pressed glass patterns of Royal Ivy and Royal Oak are listed under Pressed Glass.

RUBENA, Biscuit Jar, Flowers, Gold & White Stems, Metal Top, 8 1/4 In. 235.00
  Carafe, Water, Threaded, Northwood 135.00
  Castor, Pickle, Inverted Thumbprint, Leaf On Lid, Dogs On Base 490.00
  Decanter, Thumbprint, Cranberry To Clear, Faceted Crystal Stopper 225.00
  Dish, Sweetmeat, Clear Shell Trim, Silver Plated Holder, 6 In. 115.00
  Pitcher, Scallop–Within–Scallop, 10 In. 295.00
  Pitcher, Water, Bulbous, Inverted Thumbprint, Rope Handle, 8 In. 265.00
  Rose Bowl, Allover Gold Lacy Floral, Cranberry To Clear, 4 3/4 In. 120.00
  Sugar Shaker, Bubble, Opalescent 250.00
  Sugar Shaker, Medallion Sprig 235.00
  Toothpick, Optic 40.00
  Vase, Enameled Mums, Scalloped & Speckled Gold Rim, 13 In., Pair 550.00
  Vase, Gold & White Enameled Flowers, 12 In. 125.00
  Vase, Jack–In–The–Pulpit, 12 In. 375.00
  Water Set, Embossed Floral Design, Gold Outlined, 13 1/2 In., 6 Pc. 885.00

Ruby glass is the dark red color of the precious gemstone known as a ruby. It was a popular Victorian color that never went completely out of style. The glass was shaped by many different processes to make many different types of ruby glass. There was a revival of interest in the 1940s when modern shaped ruby table glassware became fashionable. Sometimes the red color is added to clear glass by a process called flashing or staining. Flashed glass is clear glass dipped in a colored glass, then pressed or cut. Stained glass has color painted on a clear glass. Then it is refired so the stain fuses with the glass. Pieces of glass colored in this way are indicated by the word "stained" in the description.

RUBY GLASS, see also Cranberry Glass; Pressed Glass; Souvenir
RUBY GLASS, Biscuit Jar, Vertical Banding 150.00
  Box, Enameled Floral Bouquet On Hinged Cover, 4 1/2 In. 215.00
  Carafe, Mirror & Fan, Flashed 65.00
  Celery, Bead & Drapery 295.00
  Centerpiece, Scalloped Dish, Baluster Vase, Flashed, 23 In. 1760.00
  Claret, Georgian, 4 1/2 Oz. 18.00
  Compote, Sawtooth, Westmoreland, 10 In. 32.00
  Creamer, Flashed, Plattsmouth Carnival, 1905 .... 38.00
  Cup, Laverne, Minn., Stained 25.00
  Flask, Nickel Silver Cap, Base Becomes Cup, 5 3/4 In. 205.00
  Mug, Heart Band, Niagara Falls 20.00
  Pitcher, 12 Ribs, Applied Handle, Pittsburg, 1815–40, 4 In. 395.00
  Pitcher, J.H. Morgan, Civil War Officer, 1906, Stained, 4 In. 45.00
  Pitcher, Water, Torquay 250.00
  Plate, Salad, 6 Piece 20.00
  Sugar & Creamer, Georgian 35.00

Sugar & Creamer, Popeye	30.00
Sugar Shaker, Bulging Loops	250.00
Tumbler, Thumbprint, Ruby Stained, Etched	45.00
Vase, Stick, Gold & White Enameled Design, Austrian, 9 In.	200.00
Water Set, Button Arches, 7 Piece	250.00

Rudolstadt was a faience factory in the Thuringia region of Germany from 1720 to about 1791. In 1854, Ernst Bohne began working in the area. From about 1887 to 1918, the New York and Rudolstadt Pottery made decorated porcelain marked with the RW and crown familiar to collectors. This porcelain was imported by Lewis Straus and Sons of New York, which later became Nathan Straus and Sons. The word "Royal" was included in their import mark. Collectors often call it "Royal Rudolstadt." Late nineteenth– and early twentieth–century pieces are most commonly found today.

RUDOLSTADT, see also Kewpie

RUDOLSTADT, Bust, Queen Louise, C.1880, 8 1/2 In.	140.00
Coaster Set, Kewpie, 10 In. Tray, 6 Coasters	425.00
Cracker Jar, Floral, Signed Kahy	85.00
Creamer, 3 Action Kewpies, 3 3/4 In.	215.00
Creamer, Gilt Floral Design, C.1900, 5 3/4 In.	55.00
Figurine, Girl, Carries Tray, Decanter, Bisque, Schneider, 9 In.	45.00
Figurine, Woman, Gentleman, 13 In., Pair	325.00
Pin Dish, Iris	25.00
Plate, Roses, Gold, 6 In., 6 Piece	28.00
Tea Set, Floral, Matte Glaze, Marked, 3 Piece	143.00
Teapot, Enameled Flowers, Green Leaves, Rose Finial, 6 1/2 In.	165.00
Vase, Floral Design, Gold Handles, 15 In., Pair	175.00
Vase, Pansy Design, Cream, Green, Handles, 10 In.	100.00
Vase, Purple Flowers On Cream Ground, Pierced Neck, 13 3/4 In.	195.00

Rugs have been used in the American home since the seventeenth century. The Oriental rug of that time was often used on a table, not on the floor. Rag rugs, hooked rugs, and braided rugs were made by housewives from scraps of material.

RUG, Afshar, Linked Stepped Diamonds, C.1875, 7 Ft.8 In. X 5 Ft.2 In.	5225.00
Afshar, Vases of Flowers, Corner Spandrels, 3 Ft.9 In. X 3 Ft.7 In.	3500.00
American Indian, Thunderbird Center, Turquoise, 7 Ft.X4 Ft.4 In.	300.00
American, Yarn Sewn, Figure of Dog, Blossoming Rose, 24 1/2 X 37 In.	5775.00
Anatolian, Hourglass Medallion, Leaf Border, 4 Ft.6 In. X 2 Ft.10 In.	200.00
Anatolian, Medallion On Red, 4 X 6 Ft.	200.00
Aubusson, Central Floral Bouquet, C.1900, 6 Ft.7 In. X 2 Ft.11 In.	2300.00
Aubusson, Clown & Bear Corner, C.1930, 10 Ft.5 In. X 5 Ft.8 In.	2975.00
Aubusson, Wool & Metallic Thread, C.1900, 8 Ft.8 In. X 4 Ft.6 In.	6050.00
Aushak, Medallion, 17th Century, 18 Ft. X 9 Ft.7 In.	9900.00
Avar, Many–Necked House Design, 3 Ft.2 In. X 5 Ft.6 In.	1300.00
Baktiari, Angular Vine Medallion, 14 Ft. X 11 Ft.3 In.	3575.00
Baktiari, C.1920, 12 Ft.8 In. X 7 Ft.	9900.00
Baluch, Prayer, Graphic Mix of Designs, 3 Ft.9 In. X 4 Ft.5 In.	4750.00
Baluch, Prayer, Lustrous Wool, White Highlights, 3 Ft.9 In.X 4 Ft.5 In.	5225.00
Baluch, Repeating Stars Inset In Squares, 2 Ft.11 In. X 5 Ft.5 In.	150.00
Bergama, Archaic Border, Center Medallion, 6 Ft.8 In. X 4 Ft.6 In.	7800.00
Bidjar, Center Medallion, 7 Ft.6 In. X 10 Ft.9 In.	2750.00
Bidjar, Herati Designs, Turtle Border, 3 Ft.10 In.X 7 Ft.	1400.00
Braided, Horse Design, Striped Ground, 26 X 65 In.	185.00
Carpet, Kashan, Blue, Ivory, Red, Floral, Green, Coral, 13 Ft.6 In.	6750.00
Caucasian, Dated 1302, 8 Ft.11 In. X 5 Ft.2 In.	8800.00
Caucasian, Geometric, 3 Ft. X 4 Ft.6 In.	175.00
Caucasian, Gold Field, Allover Afghan Design, 5 Ft.10 In. X 3 Ft.3 In.	550.00
Caucasian, Medallions, 19th Century, 7 Ft.7 In. X 4 Ft.5 In.	800.00
Caucasian, Rows of Hexagonal Medallions, 7 Ft.2 In. X 4 Ft.3 In.	1200.00
Chinese, Bamboo Design, Camel Ground, 1900s, 7 Ft.10 In.X 10 Ft.6 In.	495.00
Chinese, Butterflies & Flowers Design, 9 X 12 Ft.	250.00
Chinese, Circular Medallion, Blue Foo Dogs, Brown Ground, Floral Sprays	325.00

Chinese, Figural Design, Blue & Ivory Ground, 9 X 12 Ft.		2950.00
Chinese, Lobed Center Medallion, Vines, 15 Ft.7 In.X 10 Ft.2 In.		4100.00
Chinese, Pictorial Scene of Pavilion, 5 Ft.3 In. X 2 Ft.6 In.		350.00
Chinese, Rice Pattern, Vine Border, 2 Ft.10 In.X 4 Ft.9 In.	*Illus*	1980.00
Chinese, Stylized Lotus Blossom Medallions, 11 Ft.7 In. X 8 Ft.8 In.		850.00
Crosshatch, Turquoise Field, Wool, France, C.1925, 20 Ft.11 In.		6160.00
Ersari, Rows of Guls, C.1900, 8 Ft.1 In. X 6 Ft.10 In.		2300.00
Ersari, Rust Field, Rows of 5 Guls, Sawtooth Leaf Border, 8 X 11 Ft.		1700.00
Esparta, Floral Vinery Lattice, 14 Ft.9 In. X 6 Ft.		1100.00
European, Needlepoint, Dated May 26, 1903, 6 Ft.3 In. X 4 Ft.6 In.		2300.00
Fereghan, Blue Allover Herati Pattern, 6 Ft.8 In. X 4 Ft.		1200.00
Hamadan, 3 Linked Diamond Medallions, Blue Ground, 5 Ft.X 6 Ft.4 In.		600.00
Hamadan, Abrashed Field, Allover Harati Design, 4 Ft. X 5 Ft.11 In.		300.00
Hamadan, Abrashed Field, Hooked Arrows, 4 Ft.8 In. X 2 Ft.6 In.		300.00
Hamadan, Allover Floral Lattice, Vines, 6 Ft.5 In. X 3 Ft.4 In.		350.00
Hamadan, Blue Ground, Palmette Lattice, Ivory Border, 6 Ft.7 In.X 4 Ft.		150.00
Hamadan, Blue, Rosettes, Red, Coral, Blue, Tan, Ivory, 6 Ft. 9 In.		350.00
Hamadan, Center Medallion, Detached Sprays, C.1830, 6 Ft.6 In. X 5 Ft.		725.00
Hamadan, Central & Corner Medallions, 5 Ft.1 In. X 7 Ft.5 In.		715.00
Hamadan, Diamond Medallions, Camel Field, 11 Ft.6 In. X 3 Ft.3 In.		325.00
Hamadan, Floral Sprays, 3 Borders, 2 Ft.8 In. X 3 Ft.10 In.		100.00
Hamadan, Lattice Overall, 9 Ft.6 In. X 2 Ft.9 In.		550.00
Hamadan, Mina Khani Design, Red, Gold, Olive, 6 Ft.6 In.X 4 Ft.6 In.		850.00
Hamadan, Stylized Floral Figure, 20th Century, 6 Ft.4 In.X 4 Ft.6 In.		650.00
Hemp, Floor Mat, Flat Weave, Nile Pattern, 3 Ft.1 In.X 3 Ft.2 In., Pair		800.00
Hemp, Floral Medallion, Lattice Work, Neutral Ground, India, 12 X 9 Ft.		475.00
Hemp, Nile Pattern, Mustard, Brown, Neutral, India, 14 Ft.X 2 Ft.6 In.		550.00
Herat, Trellis of Palmettes, 15 Ft.2 In. X 6 Ft.5 In.		7150.00
Heriz, 8–Lobed Flower Medallion, 9 Ft.4 In.X 6 Ft.7 In.		1400.00
Heriz, Allover Stylized Blossoms, 9 Ft.10 In. X 6 Ft.		2300.00
Heriz, Angular Lobed Medallion, Pendants, 15 Ft.2 In.X 11 Ft.2 In.		4500.00
Heriz, Blue Corner Spandrels, 9 Ft.5 In. X 11 Ft.2 In.		4180.00

Rug, Hooked, Snowflake Design,
2 Ft.8 In.X 5 Ft.2 In.

Rug, Chinese, Rice Pattern, Vine Border,
2 Ft.10 In.X 4 Ft.9 In.

Rug, Tabriz, 72 Flower & Tree Designs, 12 Ft.2 In.X 14 Ft.2 In.

Heriz, Blue Medallion Insert, Rosette, 14 Ft.10 In.X 11 Ft.2 In.	1300.00
Heriz, Diamond Medallions, Rose Polygon, Blue Border, 3 Ft.X 3 Ft.3 In.	250.00
Heriz, Lobed & Pendented Medallion, 11 Ft.8 In. X 8 Ft.11 In.	2200.00
Heriz, Scalloped Blue, Rose Medallion, Floral, 11 Ft.6 In.X 8 Ft.6 In.	350.00
Heriz, Square Medallion, Diamond Insets, 10 Ft.10 In. X 7 Ft.8 In.	2400.00
Heriz, Vine–Filled Medallion, C.1900, 5 Ft.7 In. X 4 Ft.10 In.	4125.00
Hooked, 3–Masted Ship, Full Sail, Pennants, American, 32 X 60 In.	475.00
Hooked, 6 Rows of Squares, Radiating Stripes, 5 Ft.10 In. X 5 Ft.2 In.	1400.00
Hooked, Allover Rosettes & Leaves, Geometric Field, 6 Ft.8 In. X 6 Ft.	600.00
Hooked, Appliqued Felt Flowers, Wool Twill, 27 1/2 X 41 In.	100.00
Hooked, Arctic Scene, Grenfell, Early 20th Century, 46 X 34 In.	2900.00
Hooked, Beaver, Maple Leaves In Corners, 19 X 32 In.	295.00
Hooked, Black Horse, Prancing, Eliza Lynes, 1909, 40 X 30 In.	3400.00
Hooked, Center Vase, Bouquet of Roses, American, C.1860, 31 1/2 X 53 In.	700.00
Hooked, Depicting 3 Trains, 4 Ft.2 In. X 3 Ft.2 In. ....*Illus*	660.00
Hooked, Depicting 3 Trains, 4 Ft.2 In.X 3 Ft.2in. ....*Illus*	660.00
Hooked, Eagle On Spiral Field, 3 Ft. 1 In. X 10 Ft.2 In.	445.00
Hooked, Eagle, Spiral Field, 3 Ft.1 In.X 10 Ft.2 In. ....*Illus*	440.00
Hooked, Farmer, With Sheaves of Corn, Sitting Dog, C.1920, 26 X 42 In.	395.00
Hooked, Floral Design, Garlands, Beige Field, 4 Ft. 6 In. X 6 Ft. 6 In.	180.00
Hooked, Florals, Diamonds, 24 X 38 In.	25.00
Hooked, Flowering Tree, Birds On Branch, 3 Ft.3 In. X 5 Ft.	200.00
Hooked, Flowering Tree, Peacock, 3 Ft. X 4 Ft.5 In.	250.00
Hooked, Flowers, Birds, Animals, Border of Ships, Anchors, 57 X 45 In.	675.00
Hooked, Girl Chasing Duck, 27 X 50 In.	450.00
Hooked, Girl, Water Can, Flowers, Browns, Blues, White, Red, 27 X 39 In.	245.00
Hooked, Horse–Drawn Carriage, 5 Ft.6 In.X 3 Ft.1 In. ....*Illus*	358.00
Hooked, Hunting Dog, Chickens, Fence, House, Trees, 22 X 39 In.	495.00
Hooked, Man–In–The–Moon & Sun–With–Face Corners, 1923, 36 X 37 1/2 In.	1200.00
Hooked, Oriental Design, 4 X 6 Ft.	90.00
Hooked, Prancing Horse, Before Brick Wall, 41 1/2 X 51 In.	3025.00
Hooked, Rag, 2 Dogs, Black Ground, 29 X 40 In.	225.00
Hooked, Railroad, 30 X 34 In.	300.00
Hooked, Red Heart Sprouting Stemmed Tulips, Vines, Penna., 32 X 50 In.	650.00
Hooked, Runner, Flower & Leaf Design, Border, 18 Ft.	1250.00
Hooked, Sambo & Tigers, 3 Ft.2 In.X 2 Ft.5 In. ....*Illus*	385.00
Hooked, Ship Under Full Sail, American Flag, Rough Sea, 31 X 40 In.	850.00
Hooked, Snowflake Design, 2 Ft.8 In.X 5 Ft.2 In. ....*Illus*	138.00
Hooked, Star Flowers, Sheared Yarn, 30 X 46 In.	100.00
Hooked, Sunburst Pattern, 43 X 66 In.	22.50
Hooked, Thunderbird Design, 4 Ft. 3 In.	1200.00
Hooked, Tree of Life, Green Border, 74 X 30 In.	350.00
Hooked, Variegated Shades of Beige, Flower Border, 9 Ft. X 7 Ft.6 In.	2800.00
Hooked, Victorian House, Porches, Red & Green, Canadian, 26 X 40 In.	145.00
Hooked, Victorian Lady & Gentleman Silhouette, 24 X 36 In.	175.00
Hooked, Winter Scene, Jeanne Brodener, 10 X 12 In.	145.00
Indo–Chinese, Medallion, Mythological Mask, Wool, C.1900, 18 X 18 Ft.	8250.00
Indo–Persian, Palmettes, Rosettes & Cloud Bands, 11 Ft.8 In. X 9 Ft.	650.00
Kapoutrang, Red Field, Detached Floral Sprays, 12 Ft. X 8 Ft.9 In.	1800.00
Karabagh, 3 Blue Medallions, Crab Design, 4 Ft.4 In. X 6 Ft.8 In.	450.00
Karabagh, Hexagonal Medallions, Blue–Black Field, 5 Ft. X 2 Ft.8 In.	325.00
Karadja, Medallions Inset With Florals, 8 Ft.7 In. X 2 Ft.10 In.	600.00
Karadja, Medallions, Small Stylized Flowers, 6 Ft.2 In. X 4 Ft.10 In.	900.00
Kashan, Branches, Floral Sprays, Silk, C.1900, 5 Ft.3 In. X 1 Ft.8 In.	4950.00
Kashan, Diamond Medallion, Blue Field, 7 Ft.2 In. X 4 Ft.5 In.	2400.00
Kashan, Diamond Medallion, Navy Field, 6 Ft.8 In. X 4 Ft.6 In.	1100.00
Kashan, Elongated Medallion, Rust Field, 13 Ft.6 In. X 8 Ft.8 In.	6750.00
Kashan, Pictorial, 4 Ft.3 In. X 6 Ft.9 In.	1800.00
Kashan, Prayer, Vase of Flowers, Blue Field, 2 Ft.5 In. X 1 Ft.11 In.	350.00
Kashan, Red Floral Medallion, Blue Field, 7 Ft. X 4 Ft.4 In.	1100.00
Kazak, 3 Diamond Medallions, C.1900, 7 Ft.2 In. X 4 Ft.10 In.	2530.00
Kazak, 4 Lesghi Star Medallions, Leaf Edge, 7 Ft.8 In. X 4 Ft.2 In.	800.00
Kazak, 5 Ft.2 In. X 6 Ft.5 In.	3600.00
Kazak, Cane Design Field, 6 Ft. X 4 Ft.4 In.	1760.00

Kazak, Caucasus, Royal Blue, Medallions, Animals, Flowers, 1900, 10 Ft.	750.00
Kazak, Center Medallion, Checkerboard Corners, 5 Ft.6 In. X 3 Ft.3 In.	375.00
Kazak, Cloudband, C.1900, 6 Ft.10 In. X 4 Ft.4 In.	2420.00
Kazak, Column of Stylized Flowering Plants, 8 Ft.2 In. X 3 Ft.7 In.	500.00
Kazak, Diamond Medallions, Stylized Human Figures, 7 Ft. X 3 Ft.11 In.	850.00
Kazak, Empty Red Field, Multiple Edge Borders, 4 Ft.10 In.X 3 Ft.9 In.	1650.00
Kazak, Geometric Design In Squares, 4 Ft.5 In. X 7 Ft.6 In.	275.00
Kazak, Octagonal Center, 7 X 6 Ft.	3000.00
Kazak, Pinwheel Medallions, C.1900, 8 Ft.9 In. X 5 Ft.11 In.	6600.00
Kazak, Royal Blue Medallions, C.1900, 6 Ft.7 In. X 5 Ft.2 In.	2970.00
Khotan, Aubergine Field, C.1850, 11 Ft.7 In. X 6 Ft.	2530.00
Kirman, 8–Pointed Medallion, Ivory Field, 8 Ft. X 4 Ft.10 In.	2700.00
Kirman, Central & Corner Medallions, 3 Ft.11 In. X 7 Ft.	468.00
Kirman, Central Rosette, Floral Medallion, 6 Ft.4 In. X 4 Ft.2 In.	750.00
Kirman, Floral Bouquets, Royal & Sky Blue, Tan, Pink, 10 Ft.6 In.X 8 Ft.	600.00
Kirman, Flowering Vine Medallion, C.1900, 7 Ft.2 In. X 4 Ft.7 In.	1980.00
Kirman, Foliate Medallion, Red Field, 8 X 10 Ft.	2700.00
Kirman, Lobed Medallion On Gold Field, 9 Ft.9 In. X 6 Ft.4 In.	5500.00
Kirman, Medallion Design, Ivory Field, 2 Ft.3 In. X 11 Ft.9 In.	550.00
Kirman, Sprays of Summer Flowers, 20th Century, 12 Ft.8 In. X 9 Ft.	2400.00
Kirman, Tile Design, Trees, Branches, C.1880, 20 Ft.4 In. X 13 Ft.7 In.	8800.00
Konagend, Honeycomb Design, Flowerheads, Dated 1881, 5 Ft. X 4 Ft.4 In.	1800.00
Konya, Graphic Pattern, Octagons, 4 Ft.7 In. X 7 Ft.10 In.	4500.00
Konya, Medallions On Gold Field, 10 Ft.9 In. X 3 Ft.5 In.	2300.00
Kuba, Alternating Rosettes & Carnations, 4 Ft.X 3 Ft.8 In.	1500.00
Kuba, Angular Blue Medallions, Rust Field, 4 Ft.10 In. X 3 Ft.8 In.	400.00
Kuba, Coral Flowerheads, 4 Ft.6 In. X 3 Ft.1 In.	1000.00
Kuba, Keyhole Medallion Center, C.1880, 6 Ft.2 In. X 3 Ft.6 In.	4675.00
Kuba, Rows of Colored Carnations, 4 Ft.5 In. X 3 Ft.2 In.	475.00
Kuba, Tile Pattern, Dated 1845, 7 Ft.5 In. X 3 Ft.9 In.	7500.00
Kurdish, 2 Diamond Pole Medallions, Animals, 9 Ft.4 In. X 4 Ft.3 In.	550.00
Kurdish, 2 Large Medallions, Blue Field, 9 Ft.6 In. X 4 Ft.8 In.	600.00
Kurdish, Allover Boteh Design, 4 Ft.6 In. X 10 Ft.4 In.	275.00
Kurdish, Allover Floral Design, 4 Ft.9 In. X 7 Ft.2 In.	1870.00
Kurdish, Checkerboard Diamond Pattern, 4 Ft.8 In. X 5 Ft.5 In.	700.00
Kurdish, Diagonal Stripes, Star Border, 9 Ft.8 In. X 3 Ft.7 In.	500.00
Kurdish, Midnight Blue Ground, Floral Guards, 9 Ft.6 In.X 2 Ft.7 In.	200.00
Kurdish, Repeating Palmettes, Geometric Florals, 3 Ft.6 In. X 15 Ft.	550.00
Kurdish, Staggered, Open Botehs, Striped Border, 7 Ft. X 3 Ft.6 In.	350.00
Kurdish, Stepped Diamond Medallion, 6 Ft.4 In. X 3 Ft.10 In.	275.00
Lillihan, Red Rosettes, Vine Meander Border, 11 Ft.9 In.X 9 Ft.	500.00
Luri, Field Divided By Ivory Latch–Hooks, 7 Ft. X 3 Ft.9 In.	2000.00
Mahal, Design of Rust, Royal Blue, Ivory, Rosettes, 12 Ft.X 8 Ft.8 In.	200.00
Mahal, Rosettes, Detached Floral Sprays, 12 Ft.6 In. X 10 Ft.	700.00
Mashad, Medallion, Palmette Corner Spandrels, 6 Ft.8 In. X4 Ft.8 In.	1900.00
Mat, Stenciled Rush, Flat Weave, Floral, Neutral Ground, 1915, 6 X 9 Ft.	450.00
Moghan, Diamond Medallions, Arrowhead Border, 7 Ft.4 In. X 3 Ft.6 In.	150.00
Mudjur, Red Field, Spandrels & Arrow Design, 5 Ft.5 In. X 4 Ft.	850.00
Needlepoint, Roses In Vertical Stripes, Portuguese, 5 Ft.2 In. X 8 Ft.	935.00
Persian, Hexagonal Medallion, Blossom Border, 10 Ft.6 In. X 7 Ft.	850.00
Persian, Rust Medallion, Ivory Field, 10 Ft. X 6 Ft.8 In.	650.00
Persian, Sarouk Pattern, 6 X 16 Ft.	370.00
Persian, Vase Pattern, 17th Century, 9 Ft.4 In.X 5 Ft.9 In.	3950.00
Persian, Vase Pattern, Late 17th Century, 5 Ft.8 In. X 4 Ft.3 In.	7775.00
Persian, Yellow Field, Flower Vases, Birds, 22 X 14 In.	4675.00
Portuguese, Stylized Floral Design, Wool, 13 Ft.4 In.X 14 Ft.6 In.	885.00
Rag, Stripes of Reds, Browns, Yellows & Blues, 78 X 105 In.	350.00
Rag, Stripes, Pennsylvania, 76 X 93 In.	275.00
Sarkisla, Hooked Diamonds, Late 19th Century, 4 X 6 Ft.	1200.00
Sarouk Fereghan, Floral Medallions, C.1900, 6 Ft.8 In. X 4 Ft.2 In.	4400.00
Sarouk, Allover Detached Floral Sprays, Red Field, 9 Ft. X 12 Ft.2 In.	1600.00
Sarouk, Central Medallion, Floral Borders, 3 Ft.2 In. X 11 Ft.	885.00
Sarouk, Flowers, Blue, Green, Tan–Gold, 2 Ft.7 In.X 1 Ft.10 In.	200.00
Sarouk, Hexagonal Medallion, Rosette Border, 4 Ft.10 In.X 3 Ft.5 In.	325.00

Rug, Hooked, Horse-Drawn Carriage,
5 Ft. 6 In. X 3 Ft. 1 In.

Rug, Hooked, Eagle, Spiral Field,
3 Ft.1 In. X 10 Ft.2 In.

Rug, Hooked, Depicting 3 Trains,
4 Ft.2 In. X 3 Ft.2 In.

Rug, Hooked, Sambo & Tigers, 3 Ft.2 In. X 2 Ft.5 In.

Sarouk, Palmettes, Vines, Boteh, 20th Century, 11 Ft. X 8 Ft.10 In.	1700.00
Sarouk, Teal, Coral Pink Medallion, Floral Field, 6 Ft.X 8 Ft.X 8 In.	2000.00
Savonnerie, Scattered Blossoms & Stars, C.1900, 10 Ft.8 In. X 10 Ft.	8250.00
Scandinavia, Wool Pile, Oriental Style, 3 Ft.4 In. X 4 Ft.11 In.	200.00
Senna, Linked Boteh, Florals, C.1900, 6 Ft.5 In. X 4 Ft.4 In.	4400.00
Senna, Stepped Medallion, C.1900, 6 Ft.8 In. X 4 Ft.	7150.00
Serab, Hexagonal Medallions, Flowers, 14 Ft.6 In. X 2 Ft.6 In.	1000.00
Seychour, Royal Blue, Stylized Vinery, 5 Ft.5 In. X 3 Ft.5 In.	2860.00
Shirvan Kilim, Horizontal Bands, 9 Ft.3 In. X 5 Ft.7 In.	2200.00
Shirvan, Medallions On Blue Field, 5 Ft.4 In. X 3 Ft.4 In.	1400.00
Shirvan, Red, Medallion, Blue Ground, C.1920, 4 Ft. X 5 Ft.	750.00
Spanish, Leaf–Formed Cartouches, Floral Border, 19 Ft.4 In. X 12 Ft.	2550.00
Spanish, Palmettes, Clusters of Gold, 13 Ft.8 In. X 8 Ft.	1500.00
Suzani, Spiraling Carnations, Silk On Linen, 7 Ft.5 In. X 4 Ft.9 In.	2200.00
Tabriz, 7 Borders, Central Design, 8 Ft.2 In. X 10 Ft.8 In.	5500.00

Tabriz, 72 Flower & Tree Designs, 12 Ft.2 In.X 14 Ft.2 In. ....*Illus*   7150.00
Tabriz, 72 Vignettes of Flowers, Trees, 12 Ft.2 In. X 14 Ft.2 In. 6500.00
Tabriz, Design, Ivory Ground, 8 Ft.8 In.X 12 Ft. 3600.00
Tabriz, Fish In Pond, 4 Ft.6 In. X 6 Ft. 1870.00
Tabriz, Foliate Design, Ivory Ground, 7 X 10 Ft. 450.00
Tabriz, Pattern On Ivory, 6 Ft.6 In. X 9 Ft.9 In. 1975.00
Tabriz, Tree With Birds, 4 Ft.6 In. X 7 Ft.3 In. 1850.00
Talish, 8–Pointed Stars On Gold Field, 7 Ft.3 In. X 3 Ft.5 In. 6700.00
Tekke, Brick Red Field, 5 Rows of Guls, 7 Ft.11 In. X 6 Ft.6 In. 2530.00
Turkoman, 60 Octagonal Medallions, 9 Ft.11 In. X 6 Ft.8 In. 550.00
Ushak, 4 Rows of Linked Medallions, Red Field, 1 Ft.X 13 Ft.6 In. 550.00
Wilton, Square & Linear Design, English, Wool, 8 Ft.6 1/2 In. 1980.00
Wool, 1 Side Stars, 4 Knights, Blue, Brown, Rust, 7 Ft.X 7 Ft.6 In. 400.00
Wool, Blue Willow, Semicircle, 70 X 24 In. 95.00
Wool, Pile, Beige Scrolls, Navy Flowers, Niedecken, 1923, 11 Ft.X 12 Ft. 2500.00
Yazd, Central Medallion, Indigo Field, 8 Ft.4 In. X 12 Ft. 2200.00

Rumrill Pottery was designed by George Rumrill of Little Rock, Arkansas. From 1930 to 1933, it was produced by the Red Wing Pottery of Red Wing, Minnesota. In 1938, production was transferred to the Shawnee Pottery in Zanesville, Ohio. Production ceased in the 1940s.

RUMRILL, Console Vase, Candleholders, Mottled Green 20.00
Jug, Ball, Cork Stopper 28.00
Jug, Shaded Orchid & Green, Melon Shape 40.00
Planter, Light Blue, White Interior, 2 Candleholders, 12 X 3 In. 50.00
Salt & Pepper, Brown & Green, Handle, 2 1/2 In. 3.50
Sign, Dealer, Matte Blue 95.00
Vase, Elephant–Head Handles, Burnt Orange, Ball Shape, 6 1/2 In. 24.00
Vase, Green & Copper Ladder Handles, 6 In. 18.00
Vase, Handles, Green, Ivory Inside, 7 1/2 In. 45.00
Vase, Molded Leaves, Green, Brown Splotches, Urn Shape, 6 In., Pair 30.00
Vase, Off–White, 7 1/2 In. 12.00
Vase, White, Turquoise Interior, Emblem Handles & Rings, 7 In. 18.00

Ruskin is a British art pottery of the twentieth century. The Ruskin Pottery was started by William Howson Taylor; his name was used as the mark until about 1899. The factory, at West Smethwick, Birmingham, England, stopped making new pieces in 1933 but continued to glaze and sell the remaining wares until 1935. The art pottery is noted for the exceptional glazes.

RUSKIN, Bowl, Turquoise Luster, 9 In. 320.00
Candlestick, Pink Luster, 7 In., Pair 250.00

Russel Wright designed dinnerwares in modern shapes for four companies. Iroquois China Company, Harker China Company, Steubenville Pottery, and Justin Therod and Sons made dishes marked "Russel Wright." The Steubenville wares, first made in 1938, are the most common today. This section lists the dinnerwares and other pieces by Wright. He was a designer of domestic and industrial wares, including furniture, aluminum, radios, interiors, and glassware.

RUSSEL WRIGHT, Aluminum, Server, 2 Tiers, Bamboo Handles 39.00
Ashtray, American Modern, Chartreuse 2.00
Ashtray, Bauer 185.00
Ashtray, Pinch, Sterling, Suede Gray 60.00
Bowl, American Modern, 10 In. 8.25
Bowl, American Modern, Chutney, Large 15.00
Bowl, American Modern, Mottled Mustard, 9 3/4 X 7 In. 14.00
Bowl, American Modern, Olive, 11 In. 14.00
Bowl, American Modern, Spruce Green, 10 X 7 X 2 1/2 In. 10.00
Bowl, Cereal, Iroquois 4.25
Bowl, Cereal, Iroquois, Apricot 3.50
Bowl, Cereal, Iroquois, Speckled Brown 5.00

Bowl, Divided, Cover, Iroquois, Blue, 10 In. 23.50
Bowl, Fruit, Iroquois, Avocado 3.00
Bowl, Fruit, Iroquois, Oyster 3.00
Bowl, Salad, American Modern, Cedar Green 30.00
Bowl, Salad, American Modern, Chutney 27.00
Bowl, Vegetable, Cover, Divided, Iroquois, Chartreuse 30.00
Bowl, Vegetable, Divided, Iroquois, Oyster 18.00
Bowl, Vegetable, Divided, Iroquois, Parsley Green 18.00
Bowl, Vegetable, Iroquois, Apricot 5.00
Bowl, Vegetable, Iroquois, Lettuce Green, 8 In. 15.00
Bread Plate, American Modern, Cantelope 3.00
Bread Plate, American Modern, Coral 2.50
Bread Plate, American Modern, Seafoam 2.50
Bread Plate, Iroquois, Avocado 2.50
Bread Plate, Iroquois, Parsley Green 2.50
Bread Plate, Iroquois, White 2.50
Butter, American Modern, Black Chutney 50.00
Butter, American Modern, Gray 25.00
Butter, Cover, Iroquois, Pink .... 45.00 To 50.00
Butter, Cover, Iroquois, White 50.00
Butter, Iroquois, Apricot, 1/2 Lb. 60.00
Butter, Iroquois, Avocado, 1/2 Lb. 50.00
Butter, Iroquois, Pink, 1/2 Lb. 60.00
Casserole, American Modern, Cedar Green, Stick Handle 40.00
Casserole, Cover, American Modern, Coral 25.00
Casserole, Cover, Iroquois, Brown 24.00
Casserole, Cover, Iroquois, Nutmeg, 2 Qt. 21.00
Casserole, Iroquois, Yellow, 2 Qt. 17.00
Celery Vase, American Modern, 13 In. 15.00
Celery, American Modern, Chartreuse .... 12.00 To 15.00
Coffeepot, American Modern, Chartreuse, After Dinner 23.00
Coffeepot, American Modern, Coral, After Dinner 35.00
Cordial, American Modern, Seafoam 25.00
Cordial, American Modern, Smoke 25.00
Creamer, American Modern, Chartreuse .... 7.00 To 8.50
Creamer, Stacking, Iroquois, Apricot 7.00
Creamer, Stacking, Iroquois, White 7.00
Cup & Saucer, American Modern, Rose 20.00
Cup & Saucer, American Modern, Rose, Demitasse 25.00
Cup & Saucer, Iroquois, Blue 5.00
Cup, American Modern, Chartreuse, Demitasse 7.50
Cup, Child's, American Modern, Gray 3.50
Cup, Iroquois, Avocado 4.00
Cup, Iroquois, Blue 8.00
Cup, Iroquois, Charcoal 4.00
Cup, Iroquois, Light Blue .... 4.75 To 6.00
Cup, Iroquois, Pink 4.00
Decanter, Wine, Iroquois, Lemon 65.00
Mug, Iroquois, Chartreuse, Old Style 40.00
Mug, Iroquois, Pine 35.00
Pitcher, Cover, American Modern, Coral 125.00
Pitcher, Iroquois, Brown, 5 3/4 In. .... 16.00 To 17.00
Pitcher, Water, American Modern, Coral 45.00
Pitcher, Water, American Modern, Seafoam Green 34.50
Plate, American Modern, Cedar Green, 7 In. 5.00
Plate, American Modern, Chartreuse, 10 In. 6.00
Plate, American Modern, Gray, 10 In. 6.00
Plate, American Modern, Olive, 10 In. 6.00
Plate, American Modern, Pink, 6 In. 2.50
Plate, American Modern, Rose, 10 In. 6.00
Plate, American Modern, Seafoam, 10 In. 6.00
Plate, Cattail, Square, 10 In. 12.00
Plate, Iroquois, Avocado, 10 In. 6.00
Plate, Iroquois, Lettuce Green, 9 In. 5.00

Plate, Iroquois, Pink, 10 In. .... 4.50 To 6.00
Plate, Iroquois, White, 10 In. 6.00
Plate, Iroquois, Yellow, 10 In. 6.00
Plate, Steubenville, Black Chutney, 10 In. 7.00
Platter, American Modern, Chartreuse, 12 In. 13.00
Platter, American Modern, Gray, 12 In. 13.00
Platter, Iroquois, Avocado, Oval, 12 In. 13.00
Platter, Iroquois, Ice Blue, Oval, 12 1/2 In. 20.00
Platter, Iroquois, Lettuce Green, Oval, 12 In. 13.00
Platter, Iroquois, Oyster Gray, Oval, 14 1/2 In. 25.00
Platter, Straw Yellow, 10 1/2 In. 12.00
Relish, American Modern, Divided 45.00
Salt & Pepper, American Modern, Coral 8.00
Salt & Pepper, American Modern, Gray 10.00
Salt & Pepper, Stacking, Iroquois, Avocado 10.00
Saltshaker, American Modern, Chutney 5.50
Saucer, American Modern, Glacier Blue 3.00
Saucer, American Modern, Seafoam 2.50
Saucer, American Modern, White 3.00
Saucer, Iroquois, Apricot 2.50
Saucer, Iroquois, Parsley Green 2.50
Skillet, Cover, Iroquois, Nutmeg 65.00
Stack Set, American Modern, Gray, Large 25.00
Sugar & Creamer, Stacking, Iroquois, Blue 14.00
Sugar, American Modern, Chutney 4.00
Sugar, Stacking, Iroquois, Forest Green 8.00
Teapot, American Modern, Cedar Green 40.00
Teapot, American Modern, Gray 15.00
Tray, American Modern, Chartreuse 55.00
Tumbler, Stemmed, American Modern, Chartreuse 12.00
Vase, Bauer, Ovoid, 9 In. 175.00
Vase, Pillow, Green, Large 350.00

SABINO FRANCE   Sabino glass was made in the 1920s and 1930s in Paris, France.
Founded by Marius-Ernest Sabino, the firm was noted for Art Deco
Sabino   lamps, vases, figurines, and animals in clear, colored, and opalescent
France   glass. Production stopped during World War II but resumed in the
1960s with the manufacture of nude figurines and small opalescent
glass animals. The new pieces are a slightly different color and can
be recognized.

SABINO, Blotter, French & American Flags In Relief, Rocker, Opalescent 165.00
Figurine, Nudes In Art Deco Jungle, Marked, 7 X 6 In. 545.00
Figurine, Rooster, Signed, White Opalescent, 3 1/2 In. 27.00
Knife Rest, Ducks 32.00
Knife Rest, Poodle 32.00
Lamp, Beehive, Citrine 175.00
Perfume Bottle, Dancers 95.00
Vase, Raised Parrots, Vine, Blue Opalescent, Script Signed, 8 In. 300.00

Salopian ware was made by the Caughley factory of England during
the eighteenth century. The early pieces were blue and white with
some colored decorations. Another ware called "Salopian" today is a
tableware decorated with color transfers. This ware was made during
the late nineteenth century.

SALOPIAN, Sugar, Deer, Cover 375.00

Matched sets of salt and pepper shakers were first used in the
nineteenth century. Collectors are primarily interested in figural
examples made after World War I. Huggies are pairs of shakers
which appear to embrace each other. Many salt and pepper shakers
are listed in other categories and can be located through the index
at the back of this book.

SALT & PEPPER, 7-In.Clown & 5-In.Dog, White, Brayton Laguna 95.00
Alligators, Black, Marked Japan 5.00

Amish Couple, Iron	8.00
Amish Man, Horse & Carriage, Iron	15.00
Aunt Jemima, Uncle Mose, 3 1/2 In.	15.00 To 25.00
Babies, Huggies, Van Tellingen	22.00
Barney Google & Snuffy Smith, Chalkware, Painted	25.00
Bear, Brown, Van Tellingen	25.00
Bear, Huggies, Japan	8.00
Bears, Black & Brown, Rosemeade	30.00
Bears, Huggies, Brown, Van Tellingen	17.00
Bears, Huggies, Pink	15.00
Black Boy & Dog, Van Tellingen	25.00
Black Cats, Sitting Cross–Legged, Large, Rosemeade	36.00
Boy & Girl, Cleminson	22.00
Boy, With Puppy, White & Brown, Van Tellingen	19.00
Bride & Groom, Cork Stopper, Japan, 4 In.	8.00
Bride & Groom, Humorous, Gray Hair, Gold Trim, 5 In.	10.00
Budweiser, Plastic Cap, Label	2.00
Bunnies, Huggies, Green	15.00
Bunnies, Huggies, Pink, Van Tellingen	16.00 To 18.00
Bunnies, Huggies, Yellow, Van Tellingen	10.00
Campbell's Soup	10.00
Cats, Boxing	5.00
Chefs In Tuxedos, Plastic, Magic Chef	10.00
Chefs, I'm Salt & I'm Pepper, 1 Piece	12.00
Children Holding Watermelons, Pair	28.00
Cow & Calf, Ceramic Art Studio	25.00
Dog & Doghouse	20.00
Ducks, Huggies, Van Tellingen	12.00
Ducks, Huggies, White	22.50
Dutch Boy & Girl, Huggies, Van Tellingen	15.00
Dutch Boy & Girl, Van Tellingen	15.00
Dutch Cookies, Gold	6.00
Ears of Corn, Rosemeade	22.00
Elephant	25.00
Elephant, Yellow, Chalkware	6.00
Elf & Toadstool	10.00
English Bobbies, Large, Twin Winton	11.00
Eskimo Children, Standing, 3 1/2 In.	8.00
Fat Men Doing Push–Ups, 5 In.	10.00
Fox & Goose	30.00
Gas Pump Shapes, Phillips 66	12.00
GE Refrigerator, Glass	18.00
His Master's Voice, Lenox	110.00
Humpty–Dumpty, Sitting	8.00
Indian & Squaw, With Papoose, M.P.I., 1949	7.00
Indian Playing Drums, 4 1/2 In.	10.00
Lambs, Huggies, White, Van Tellingen	7.00
Liberty Bell, Chalkware	8.00
Lovebugs, Wine, Van Tellingen	16.00
Mama & Baby Bear, Brown, Ceramic Art Studio	22.00
Mama & Baby Bear, White	24.00
Mammy & Chef, Fort Dodge, 3 In.	25.00
Mammy & Chef, Red Clothes, White Apron, 8 In.	50.00
Mammy, F & F Mold, Langniappe of New Orleans	35.00
Man & Woman, Occupied Japan	23.00
Model A Ford, Plastic	12.00
Model A Ford, With People, Plastic	12.00
Monkey & Barrel	9.00
Monkeys, Ceramic Arts	26.00
Moose, With Movable Eyes	9.00
Mouse & Cheese	25.00
Mr. & Mrs. Snowman	12.00
Mules In Dress Pants	6.00
Natives, Pearl Earrings, Wood, 2 1/2 In.	6.50

Niagara Falls, Maid of The Mist, 3 Piece	8.00
Nodder, Bull, Bullfighter, Mexican Souvenir, 4 In.	55.00
Nodder, Skeleton	65.00
Owl, Glass Eyes	75.00
Peach Mermaid, With Sailor, Huggies, Van Tellingen	32.00
Penguins	25.00
Penguins, Ceramic Arts Studio, Madison, Wisc.	22.00
Pheasants, Metal	10.00
Pheasants, Rosemeade	25.00
Phillips 66, Orange	8.00
Pigs, Van Tellingen	75.00
Pony, 1 With Rider, White, Brayton Laguna, 1939	95.00
Pop–Up Toaster, Metal, Bakelite	15.00
Puppies, Huggies, Yellow	20.00
Rabbits, Huggies, Blue, Long Ears	10.00
Rooster & Hen Tops, Sugar & Creamer Bottom, 6 In.	15.00
Root Beer, Souvenir, Rochester, Minn., 6 In.	30.00
Rose, Blue Ridge	38.50
Royal Canadian Mounted Police, Niagara Falls, Can.	7.00
Sailor & Girl, Van Tellingen	25.00
Scotty Dogs, Chalkware	6.00
Shoeshine Box, Metal	10.00
Skunks	5.00
Squirt, 5 1/2 In.	13.00
Trout, Bright Colors, 5 In.	8.00
Tuna, Yellow–Blue	10.00
Turkey, Brown, Red Head, Kay Finch, 3 1/4 In.	9.00
Washington D.C., On Bell, Holds 2 Glass Containers	9.00
Watering Can, Brown, Spongeware Type, 1940s	6.00
Westinghouse Washer & Dryer, Plastic, 3 X 5 In.	15.00

Salt glaze has a grayish–white, pitted, orange–peel–textured surface. It is a method of decoration that has been used since the eighteenth century. Salt-glazed pieces are still being made.

SALT GLAZE, Chamber Pot, Beaded Rose Cluster & Spearpoints, Black, White	175.00
Crock, Albany Slip, Lug Handles, 19th Century, 12 1/2 In.	425.00
Crock, Bee–Sting, Ears, 10 Gal.	170.00
Crock, Blue Geometric, Ears, H.Brunson, 4 Gal.	210.00
Crock, Blue, E.B.Taylor, Richmond, Va., Blue	115.00
Crock, Design On Entire Front, Cobalt Blue, 4 Gal.	295.00
Crock, Reverse Pine Tree, Gray & Cobalt Blue, C.1880, 2 Gal.	95.00
Jar, Storage, 2 Handles, 19th Century, 12 Gal.	250.00
Jug, 2 Incised Masted Ships, Cobalt Blue, P.Cross, C.1810, 15 In.	3850.00
Jug, Apostle, Hinged Pewter Top, Marked, Tan, 9 3/4 In.	265.00
Jug, Brushed Cobalt, Squiggle, Orange Peel, Turkey Eye Drips	250.00
Jug, Cobalt Blue Swirled Leaves, Shield With Saying, 10 In., Pr.	150.00
Jug, Universe, 4 Medallions, People, Animals, Maps, 9 5/8 In.	295.00
Pitcher, Blue Flowers, 9 In.	135.00

Salt & Pepper, Souvenir From Mexico

Soap Dish, Cat's Head, Black, White 150.00
Wall Pocket, Figural, Bacchus Head, Grapes & Leaves 475.00

ABCDE Samplers were made in America from the early 1700s. The best examples were made from 1790 to 1840. Long, narrow samplers are usually older than square ones. Early samplers just had stitching or alphabets. The later examples had numerals, borders, and pictorial decorations. Those with mottoes are mid–Victorian.

SAMPLER, Alphabet, House, Stylized Birds, Plants, Homespun, 18 X 17 3/4 In. 475.00
Alphabet, Numbers, Vines, Flowers, 13 1/2 X 13 1/2 In. 285.00
Alphabet, Red, Green, Matted, Framed, 1871, 9 X 11 1/2 In. 185.00
Alphabets, Numbers, Rachel Hartley, Framed, 1787, 18 X 22 1/2 In. 500.00
Alphabets, Springdale, Iowa, Dated 1860, 10 1/2 X 10 In. 225.00
Cross–Stitch, Girl Scene, Punched Paper, Floral, Framed, 21 X 22 In. 45.00
Deity & Humanity of Christ, Mary Ann Redar, 1787, 15 X 18 In. 550.00
Family Record, Phebe Entrikin, Dec., 1805, 30 1/4 X 33 1/2 In. 200.00
Family Register, Hannah Green, Leyden, Mass., 1828, Square, 18 In. 3080.00
Floral Border, Ann Turner, 8 Years, 17 1/2 X 20 1/4 In. 200.00
Floral Border, Colored Crosses, M.B., 19 3/4 X 20 In. 710.00
Floral, Sarah Coleman, 1814, 13 X 14 1/2 In. 2200.00
Lady In Bonnet, Flowers, Spun Linen, Signed, Dated 1941, 10 X 13 In. 175.00
Needlepoint, 4 Styles of The Alphabet, C.1890, 22 X 9 In. 80.00
Needlepoint, Dog, Birds, Flowers, Mesh Foundation, 16 X 17 In. 225.00
Needlepoint, Mary Turner, December 1857, 28 1/4 X 28 1/2 In. 550.00
Needlepoint, Memorial, Ann Eliza Maude, May 18, 1884, Framed, 28 In. 275.00
Pastoral Scene, Sarah Younge, September, 1797, 13 1/2 X 15 3/4 In. 2600.00
Petit Point, Girl At Cottage Door, 9 X 10 In. 60.00
Petit Point, Girl At Cottage Door, Framed, 8 X 9 In. 59.00
Red Silk Edges, Maria, 1838, 9 1/2 X 19 3/4 In. 425.00
Stylized Design of People, Ships, Birds, Dated 1842, 16 X 20 In. 250.00
Verse, Anne Chase, 13 Years, Newport, 1721, 12 1/4 X 8 1/2 In. 7150.00
Verse, Bible, Floral With Anchor, 1807, 19 3/4 X 19 1/2 In. 575.00
Verse, Do No Sinful Action, Mary Welch, 1878, 15 X 15 1/2 In. 245.00
Verse, Eliza Mehia, 1833, Floral, Brick House, 22 X 26 In. 2500.00
Verse, Florence Aspinwall, Framed, Dated 1889, 12 X 16 In. 295.00
Verse, Linen Ground, 1795, 11 3/4 X 11 1/2 In. 1450.00
Verse, Solomon's Temple, Ann Stranilands, 1836, 21 X 16 3/4 In. 895.00
Verse, Sprigs, Celia Humphrey, Age 12 Years, 1834, 16 X 15 1/2 In. 700.00
Vine Border, Ann Tindau, May 10, 1799, Age 11 Years, 13 3/4 X 19 In. 1000.00

Samson and Company, a French firm specializing in the reproduction of collectible wares of many countries and periods, was founded in Paris in the early nineteenth century. Chelsea, Meissen, Famille Verte, and Chinese Export porcelain are some of the wares that have been reproduced by the company. The firm uses a variety of marks on the reproductions. It is still in operation.

SAMSON, Salt, Master, Woman On Dolphin Shape, Marble, 19th Century, 7 In. 550.00

Sandwich glass is any one of the myriad types of glass made by the Boston and Sandwich Glass Works in Sandwich, Massachusetts, between 1825 and 1888. It is often very difficult to be sure whether a piece was really made at the Sandwich factory because so many types were made there and similar pieces were made at other glass factories.

SANDWICH GLASS, see also Pressed Glass, etc.
SANDWICH GLASS, Bowl, Lacy, 6 1/4 In. 200.00
Candlestick, Amethyst, Pair 1270.00
Compote, Loop, White Clambroth, 1850–70, 7 X 9 In. 1650.00
Compote, Panel Flowers Form Bowl, Pedestal, 1810, 11 In. 330.00
Creamer, Holly With Cord & Tassel 115.00
Creamer, Star & Buckle 450.00
Lamp, Transfer On Cobalt Blue Base, Miniature 395.00
Peg Lamp, Thumbprint & Fan, Camphene, Ball Shape, 5 1/2 In. 260.00
Perfume Bottle, 6 Convex Circles, 6 Ovals, Green, 5 In. 395.00

Perfume Bottle, Hexagonal, Blue	395.00
Salt, Christmas, Cobalt Blue, Signed, Dated 1877	110.00
Salt, Lafayette, Lacy Boat	130.00
Salt, Ram's Horn, Dull Amber	350.00
Salt, Shell, Pedestal Base	950.00
Spillholder, Star, Electric Blue, Pair	1760.00
Spillholder, Waffle & Thumbprint, Amethyst, Pair	1925.00
String Holder, Ruby On Clear, Bull's-Eye Pattern	195.00
Tumbler, Ten Panels, Sapphire Blue	135.00

Sarreguemines

Utzschneider and Company, a porcelain factory, made ceramics in Sarreguemines, Lorraine, France, from 1770. Transfer-printed wares and majolica were made in the nineteenth century. The nineteenth-century pieces, most often found today, usually had colorful transfer-printed decorations showing peasants in local costumes.

SARREGUEMINES, Plate, Song, Cadet Rousselle, 7 1/2 In.	28.00
Plate, Song, Marlborough, 7 1/2 In.	28.00
Plate, Strawberries, Floral Trim, Aqua Ground, 8 1/2 In.	68.00
Urn, Blue, Gold, Cover, 4 Ft.	1700.00

Satin glass is a late nineteenth-century art glass. It has a dull finish that is caused by a hydrofluoric acid vapor treatment. Satin glass was made in many colors and sometimes had applied decorations. Satin glass is also listed by factory name or in the mother-of-pearl category in this book.

SATIN GLASS, Basket, Raindrop, Mother-of-Pearl, Blue, Brier Handle, 9 1/2 In.	250.00
Bowl, Fluted, Red Cherries, Green Leaves, Teal Blue, 7 1/2 In.	450.00
Box, Embossed Design, Enameled Pink Rose, Blue, 5 3/4 In.	240.00
Bride's Bowl, Enameled Flowers, Ruffled, 9 1/4 In.	225.00
Bride's Bowl, Rose To Pink, Enameled Flowers, 5 1/4 X 11 In.	275.00
Butter, Cover, Thistle, Pink	50.00
Candlestick, Green, 3 Molds, 8 1/4 In., Pair	26.00
Candlestick, Yellow, Brown Roses Bottom, 8 3/4 In., Pair	150.00
Celery, Enameled Flowers, Butterflies, Silver-Plated Stand	450.00
Ewer, Daisies, Forget-Me-Nots, Frosted Handle, 8 1/2 In.	145.00
Ewer, Rainbow, Stripes, Swirl Over White Interior, 8 1/2 In.	575.00
Jar, Dresser, Gold Flowers, Yellow, Cover, 3 1/2 In.	100.00
Jar, Powder, Heart Shape, Pink Peony Design, C.1900, 3 In.	105.00
Lamp, Fairy, Diamond-Quilted, Raspberry, 2 Piece	375.00
Perfume Bottle, Green Fern, Bamboo Leaves, Sterling Silver Top	350.00
Rose Bowl, 4-Crimp Top, Rose, Pink Overlay, Pansies, 5 1/2 In.	135.00
Rose Bowl, 8-Crimp Top, Blue Overlay, Frosted Feet, 6 In.	135.00
Rose Bowl, 8-Crimp Top, Yellow Overlay, Foliage, 4 1/2 In.	125.00
Rose Bowl, Charteuse, Mother-of-Pearl, 12-Crimp, Lining, 3 In.	265.00
Rose Bowl, Cut Velvet, 6-Crimp Top, White Lining, 3 1/2 In.	225.00
Rose Bowl, Cut Velvet, Diamond-Quilted, 4-Crimp Top, 3 1/2 In.	195.00
Rose Bowl, Painted Leaves & Flowers, Green, 4 In.	50.00
Rose Bowl, Shell, Pink, 3 1/2 In.	75.00
Saltshaker, Diamond-Quilted, Mother-of-Pearl, Blue, Pink, Pair	140.00
Sugar Shaker, Moon & Star, Pewter Top	60.00
Tumbler, Oyster White, Flowers & Insect Design	20.00
Vase, Apricot Top Fading To White Bottom, Ruffled, 6 5/8 In.	110.00
Vase, Apricot, Gold Drape In Mother-of-Pearl, 7 1/2 In.	300.00
Vase, Blue Overlay, Ruffled Top Ewer, White Lining, 9 In., Pair	175.00
Vase, Cased Jack-In-The-Pulpit, Dimpled Base, Cranberry, 7 In.	260.00
Vase, Diamond-Quilted, Blue, Bottle Shape, Pontil, 10 1/4 In.	120.00
Vase, Diamond-Quilted, Pink, Cut Velvet, 7 1/8 In.	150.00
Vase, Ewer, Blue Overlay, Frosted Edging, Applied Handle, 9 In.	89.00
Vase, Fleurette, Pink Overlay, White Lining, Germany, 5 1/2 In.	195.00
Vase, Floral, Lime Green, English, 6 1/4 In., Pair	100.00
Vase, Flowers, Leaves, Outlined In Gold, 5 1/2 In.	125.00
Vase, Striped, Cut Velvet, White Lining, Square, 7 3/4 In.	145.00
Vase, Thumbprint Design, Blue, White Lining, 7 In., Pair	60.00
Vase, Thumbprint, Blue, White Lining, 7 In., Pair	60.00

SATIN GLASS, WEBB, see Webb

 Satsuma is a Japanese pottery with a distinctive creamy beige crackled glaze. Most of the pieces were decorated with blue, red, green, orange, or gold. Almost all the Satsuma found today was made after 1860. During World War I, Americans could not buy undecorated European porcelains. Women who liked to make hand-painted porcelains at home began to decorate plain Satsuma. These pieces are known today as "American Satsuma."

SATSUMA, Bowl, Millefleur, 3 3/4 In.	125.00
Bowl, Mountain Scene, Stream, Trees, 5 Sides, C.1925, 6 In.	295.00
Bowl, Scholars, Red & Gold, 11 In.	195.00
Brooch, Samurai Warriors, Marked, 1 1/4 In.	50.00
Cookie Jar, White & Gold Flowers, Orange Ground, 7 1/2 In.	125.00
Cup & Saucer, Bamboo With Birds, Gold Trim, Signed	55.00
Cup & Saucer, Blue, Warriors, Demitasse, Artist Hozan	210.00
Cup & Saucer, Scenic Medallions, Gold Jewels, Demitasse	35.00
Figurine, Manjushii Sitting On Lion, C.1860, 17 1/2 X 19 In.	2750.00
Figurine, Samurai Warrior, Applied Beading, Pair	42.00
Hatpin Holder, Allover Floral, Cream Ground, C.1900	40.00
Jar, Multicolored Flowers, Crackle, Lion Dog Handles, Cover, 13 In.	125.00
Jar, Pierced Cover, Lords & Attendants, Enameled, C.1885, 7 In.	125.00
Lamp, Figural, Elephant With Geisha Girl, 9 1/2 In.	65.00
Plaque, Lake, Waterflowl, Peonies, Gold Outlined, 1895, 9 3/4 In.	225.00
Plate, Bamboo With Birds, Gold Trim, Signed, 6 3/4 In.	38.00
Plate, Ladies & Lords, Gold Trim, 10 In.	25.00
Plate, Warrior, 12 In.	962.00
Powder Box, Woman In Garden, Gold Trim, Signed, 3 1/2 In.	225.00
Tea Set, Village Scene, Lake, Pastel, Cream Ground, 1920, 3 Piece	275.00
Teapot, Thousand Robed Figures, Melon-Ribbed Body, 8 In.	95.00
Teapot, Wrapped Swing Handle, Miniature	325.00
Vase, 2 Chinamen, Flowers, 9 In.	55.00
Vase, 2 Men, Floral On Back, Beaded, Neck Handles, Taisha, 11 1/2 In.	100.00
Vase, 2 Panels of Geisha, Cobalt Blue Ground, C.1910, 3 1/2 In.	90.00
Vase, 4 Sides, Scenes, Blue-Green, 7 1/2 In.	425.00
Vase, Allover Fishnet With Butterflies, Bow At Top Rim, 4 3/4 In.	135.00
Vase, Baluster Shape, Arhats & Kwannon, 1920, 9 1/2 In.	260.00
Vase, Building Landscape, Azaleas, Outlining, Crackle, Taisho, 6 In.	68.00
Vase, Cover, Foo Dog Finial, Handles & Feet, 13 1/2 In.	125.00
Vase, Double Gourd, Panels of Geisha, C.1880, 3 1/2 In.	125.00
Vase, Double, Serpent Handle, Flowers, Butterflies, 11 1/2 In.	450.00
Vase, Enamel & Gold Deities, Signed, C.1930, 12 1/4 In., Pair	275.00
Vase, Figures of Woman, Man & 3 Children, Signed, C.1925, 12 1/2 In.	125.00
Vase, Floral Reserves, Chrysanthemum Body, Mounted As Lamp, 18 In.	250.00
Vase, Floral, Bird, Rust Shade To Ocher, Beaded, 13 In.	105.00
Vase, Florals, Cream Ground, Elephant Handles, C.1895	75.00
Vase, Flowers, Foliage, Butterflies, Period Clothes, 12 In.	200.00
Vase, Flowers, Red Ground, Kiri Handles, 13 In.	80.00
Vase, Flowers, Scene, Floral Border, Shoulder Handles, 12 1/2 In.	95.00
Vase, Haloed Man & Woman, Gold Trim, Foo Dog Handles, 10 1/2 In.	75.00
Vase, Hummingbirds, Butterfly, Flowers, Brick To Yellow, 12 1/4 In.	95.00
Vase, Jeweled Floral, Brown Bands, Elephant Handles, 12 In., Pair	150.00
Vase, Lilies, Outlined, Twisted Shoulder Handles, Awata, 14 In.	170.00
Vase, Men, Courtesans & Children, Elephant Handles, C.1905, 6 In.	395.00
Vase, Ovoid Body, Children Playing Games, 19th Century, 3 5/8 In.	300.00
Vase, Painted Earthenware Body, Warrior, C.1900, 18 1/2 In., Pair	1980.00
Vase, Purple & White Wisteria, Cream Ground, 8 1/2 In.	145.00
Vase, Raised Peony Design, Rust Ground, C.1930, 21 1/4 In., Pair	200.00
Vase, Samurai & Immortals, Hododa, 5 In.	100.00
Vase, Samurai Warriors, Gold Battle Armor, Crackle Glaze, 7 In.	195.00
Vase, Scenes of Warriors, Children, Hexagonal, 7 1/2 In.	775.00
Vase, Scenic, Raised Beaded Flowers, Gold Handles, 12 In.	40.00

Special scales have been made to weigh everything from babies to gold. Collectors search for all types. Most popular are small gold–dust scales and special grocery scales.

SCALE, Acme, Egg, Pat.June 24, 1924, 19 To 30 Oz.	19.00
Angldile, Elkhart, Ind., 1900s	350.00
Apothecary, 2 Pans, Inlaid Case, Weights	50.00
Balance, Hanging, Wrought Steel, Hooks Each End, 19 1/2 In.	65.00
Balance, Improved Circular Spring, Front Dial, Brass, 10 In.	39.00
Balance, Tin & Iron, 20 1/2 In.	187.00
Balance, Twisted Stem, Cast Base, Wrought Iron, 16 1/2 In.	60.00
Butter, Hanging, Wooden, Carved Notched Bar, C.1820	350.00
Champion, Meat, Wall Mount	25.00
Chatillon, Hanging, Brass	15.00
Chatillon, No.50, Brass	30.00
Chatillon, Tubular Brass Spring, Up To 30 Lbs.	55.00
Columbia, Kitchen, Brass Case	55.00
Computing Scale Co., Small	90.00
Correct Weight, Platform, Penny, Iron, 6 Ft.	600.00
Detectogram, Candy, Cap, 3 Lbs.	45.00
Egg Grading, Graduated Brass Arm, Rectangular Board Mounted, Label	130.00
Egg, Walnut Case, Slides In & Out, Large	195.00
Enterprise, No. L–5, Candy, Nickel–Plated Brass Cradle Pan	62.00
Eureka, Balance, Iron Frame, Glass Face, Brass Pan, 18 X 15 In.	260.00
Forschners, Brass	39.00
Grocery, Hanging, Tin, Weighs To 30 Lbs.	45.00
Hamet Riglander & Co., Gold Miner's, Portable, C.1850	45.00
Hanson, Postal, No.1509, 1949	25.00
Herbet & Sons, London, Lion	1250.00
Jennings, 1 Cent, Porcelain Round Top	650.00
Jiffy–Way, Egg	15.00
Lobster, Brass, 5 3/4 In.	15.00
Lollipop, Penny, Red Porcelain Finish	575.00
Moderne Peerless, Art Deco Enameling, 1 Cent	165.00
National, Candy, Decal, Restored	350.00
National, Counter Top, 1910, Small	350.00
Ohaus, Dial–O–Gram Balance, Weighs Grams Only, Carrying Case	60.00
Parker Bros., Pocket, 2 1/2 In.	75.00
Peerless, Penny, Tiled Platform, Mirrored Front	320.00
Pelouze, Confectionary, Copyright 1899	38.00
Pelouze, Family Scale, 24 Lb.	45.00
Pillsbury, Advertising, Hanging, 8 In.	45.00
Sears Roebuck, Egg	20.00
Silver, Digital	260.00
Spices, Cross Bar, Round Pans, Clothes Pin Center Balance	550.00
Standard Computing, Butcher's, Enamel	75.00
Stimpson, Grocery, Computer, Brass, Pat.1907, Large	425.00
Toledo, Counter Top, Copper Tray, 10 Lb.	200.00
Troener, Jeweler's, With Weights & Accessories	750.00
Watling Jr., Tom Thumb, 1 Cent, 5 Cent, 10 Cent	425.00
Watling, Fortune, 1 Cent	195.00 To 250.00
Winchester, Brass Bucket	250.00
Wrigley of Chicago, Counter, Brass Pan & Face Dial, 1800s	125.00

Schafer & Vater, makers of small ceramic items, are best known for their amusing figurals. The factory was located in Volkstedt–Rudolstadt, Germany, from 1890 to 1962. Some pieces are marked with the crown and R mark, but many are unmarked.

SCHAFER & VATER, Bottle, Figural, Fox Trot	120.00
Bottle, Figural, Smiling Pear	125.00
Bowl, Egyptian Face, 3 1/2 In.	75.00
Box, Figural Girl Cover, Bonnet, Black Skirt, 3 X 5 1/2 In.	90.00
Box, Victorian Lady & Man On Cover, Marked, 3 1/2 In.	58.00
Boy & Dog In Wheelbarrow, Tray Behind, 3 X 4 In.	100.00

Creamer, Dutch Girl With Basket On Back, 3 3/4 In.	60.00
Creamer, Girl With Jug, Black Pocketbook, 5 In.	70.00
Creamer, Mother Goose Wearing Hat, 4 In.	160.00
Figurine, Scotsman In Kilt, Mind Your Business, 5 1/4 In.	130.00
Hatpin Holder, Egyptian, Pink	150.00
Hatpin Holder, Sphinx Design, Cream Tower, 5 1/8 In.	110.00
Jug, Black Woman, Bizarre, 4 In.	135.00
Lamp, Boudoir, Jasperware, Art Nouveau	100.00
Match Holder, Laughing Man, Open Mouth, Multicolored	90.00
Match Holder, Man, Mustache, Tongue Out, Multicolored	75.00
Pin Tray, Boy, Girl, Dog, Multicolored, Cassandra, 3 3/4 In.	110.00
Pin Tray, Skeleton & Coffin, Brockton Fair, 1912, 4 X 5 In.	150.00
Pitcher, Chinaman, Monkey On Back, Open Mouth, 5 1/2 In.	110.00
Pitcher, Clown With Mandolin, Open Mouth, White Ruff, 5 In.	105.00
Pitcher, Comical Elf	80.00
Pitcher, Dutch Maid, Blue & White	70.00 To 100.00
Pitcher, Figural, Comical Pierrot	95.00
Pitcher, Goat In Overcoat, Blue, 5 In.	100.00
Pitcher, Maid, With Jug & Keys, Multicolored, 3 1/2 In.	95.00
Pitcher, Mother Goose, Bonnet, Shawl, Blue, 5 1/2 In.	85.00
Pitcher, Oriental Kneeling, Screaming Baby In Lap, 5 In.	125.00
Planter, Figural, Girl, With Rooster, Chick	115.00
Rose Bowl, Cupid & Women, Blue & White	75.00
Salt & Pepper, Apple & Pear, Smiling	85.00
Shaving Mug, Blown–Out Elks, Oak Trees	100.00
Teapot, Apple, Smiling, 1 Cup	125.00
Toothpick, Smiling Pig, Insect	65.00
Vase, Figural, Boy Faces Wall, I'm So Discouraged, 4 In.	125.00

Schneider

Schneider Glassworks was founded in 1903 at Epinay–sur–Seine, France, by Charles and Ernest Schneider. Art glass was made between 1903 and 1930. The company still produces clear crystal glass.

SCHNEIDER, Bowl, Thorn–Covered Seed Pods, Mottled Interior, 5 1/2 X 11 In.	860.00
Compote, Peach Bowl, Blue Edge, Amethyst Base, 7 1/2 X 6 1/4 In.	380.00
Vase, 7 Cranes In Flight, Hills, Marsh, 19 In.	3900.00
Vase, Blue Dripping From Top, Red, Signed, 15 In., Pair	1200.00
Vase, Daisy Blossoms, Burgundy Centers, Signed, C.1925, 12 3/8 In.	2550.00
Vase, Wheel–Carved Flowerheads, Signed, C.1925, 8 1/2 In.	1550.00

Scrimshaw is bone or ivory or whale's teeth carved by sailors and others for entertainment during the sailing–ship days. Some scrimshaw was carved as early as 1800. There are modern scrimshanders making pieces today on bone, ivory, or plastic.

SCRIMSHAW, see also Ivory, Nautical

SCRIMSHAW, Bodkin, Heart & Scroll Pierced, Whalebone, 19th Century, 8 In.	220.00
Cane, Whalebone, Stylized Horsehead Handle, Mahogany Shaft	1400.00
Dipper, Whalebone, Apple Wood Handle	195.00
Ditty Box, Whalebone, Manuel Rogers, Lid, 10 1/4 In.	3300.00
Jagging Wheel, 2 Hearts, Star, Ebony Spacers, C.1875, 6 1/4 In.	1760.00
Jagging Wheel, Elongated Elliptical Loop Handle, C.1875, 9 In.	770.00
Jagging Wheel, Hearts, Circles, Oblong, Fluted Wheel, C.1875, 5 In.	1100.00
Jagging Wheel, Pierced Handle, Whalebone, C.1875, 5 1/8 In.	1100.00
Jagging Wheel, Relief Carved Star, Whalebone, C.1875, 6 1/4 In.	1760.00
Jewelry Set, Silver Filigree, Chinese, 5 Piece	145.00
Letter Opener & Page Cutter, Walrus Tusk, Hunt Scene, 16 1/2 In.	1350.00
Needle, Knitting, Whalebone, Clenched Fists, Pair	1500.00
Pie Trimmer, Nude Woman, Legs Straddling Wheel, Ivory, 6 5/8 In.	3250.00
Seam Rubber, Whalebone, Sleeve & Hand Handle, 1840, 4 1/4 In.	1320.00
Swift, 19th Century, 19 1/4 In.	2600.00
Swift, Mid–19th Century, 21 In.	2750.00
Tooth, Sperm Whale, Whaling Ship, Mottoes, Hayes, 1857, 7 1/2 In.	1870.00
Tooth, Whale, Boat & Lighthouse, Signed, 4 In.	175.00
Tooth, Whale, San Francisco View, Whaling Scene Other Side, 6 In.	3500.00

Tooth, Whale, Seminude Tahitian Girl, Warrior Other Side, 8 In. 4250.00
Tooth, Whale, Whaling Scene, South Seas Warrior Other Side, 7 In. 2000.00
Tooth, Whale, Whaling Ship, Verse Other Side, 7 1/8 In. 2750.00
Walking Stick, Fisted Handle 4800.00
Walrus Tusk, Whaling Ship, Birds, Men In Boats, 1842, 23 1/2 In. 1000.00
Whalebone, Thick Loop Handle, Initials S.S., 1875, 5 1/2 In. 1210.00

Prescott W. Baston made the first Sebastian miniatures in 1938 in Marblehead, Massachusetts. More than 400 different designs have been made and the collectors search for the out-of-production models. The mark may say "Copr. P. W. Baston U.S.A.," or "P. W. Baston, U.S.A.," or "Prescott W. Baston." Sometimes a paper label was used.

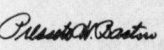

SEBASTIAN MINIATURES, Doctor .... 55.00 To 65.00
    Donald McKay, Signed 35.00
    George Washington, With Cannon, C.1947 .... 50.00
    House of Seven Gables 125.00
    Huckleberry Finn, Label 60.00
    In The Candy Store 55.00
    John Alden 70.00
    John F.Kennedy, In Rocking Chair 28.00
    Johnny Appleseed, Signed 22.50
    Lobsterman, Blue Label 30.00
    Madonna of The Goldfinch, Signed 27.00
    Mark Twain Home In Hannibal, Missouri 75.00
    Mr.Beacon Hill 55.00
    Mr.Obocell, Green Label, 1950 .... 225.00
    Old Lady Testing Soup On Cookstove, C.1947 .... 50.00
    Oliver Twist & Beadle, Green Label, 1949 .... 55.00
    Pilgrims 75.00
    Priscilla, Spinning Wheel 200.00
    Robert E.Lee 75.00
    Sailor, Signed 28.00
    Sairey Gamp, Marblehead Label 60.00
    Shaker Man & Woman, Arlington, 1941, Pair 225.00
    Three Men In A Tub, Signed 35.00
    SEG, see Paul Revere Pottery

Sevres porcelain has been made in Sevres, France, since 1769. Many copies of the famous ware have been made. The name originally referred to the works of the Royal Porcelain factory. The name now includes any of the wares made in the town of Sevres, France. The entwined lines with a center letter used as the mark is one of the most forged marks in antiques. Be very careful to identify Sevres by quality, not just by mark.

SEVRES, Box, Hinged Cover, Courting Scene On Front, Blue & Gold, Signed 485.00
    Box, Napoleon III, Bronze, Roses, Reclining Female Cover, 7 1/4 In. 2750.00
    Box, Trinket, Gold Cover, Woman's Portrait, Gold Bands At Top, 4 In. 395.00
    Cachet Pot, Pansies & Roses Front, Rose Sprig Back, 7 X 6 3/4 In. 375.00
    Casket, Porcelain Figural Scenes, Hinged Top, Bronze, 1900, 10 In. 2475.00
    Cruet, Gold Scrolls, Floral, Clear Handle, C.1890, Label, 8 1/2 In. 435.00
    Dish, Footed Ormolu Holder, Center Flowers, 6 1/2 In. 90.00
    Figurine, Owl, Perching On Half-Round Base, Paper Label, 5 In. 95.00
    Figurine, Woman, Holding Bowl At Shoulder, Marked, 1925, 16 7/8 In. 1870.00
    Lamp, Cherubs, Ceramic Flowers, Bronze Plateau Base, C.1880 .... 775.00
    Plate, Bronze Beaded Rim, Floral Reserves, Signed, 1846, 13 1/2 In. 425.00
    Plate, Duchess De Bourgoyne, 1846, 9 In. 225.00
    Plate, Francois II, Portrait, 7 3/4 In. 65.00
    Plate, Louis-Philippe Monogram, Late 19th Century, 10 1/4 In., 6 Pc. 825.00
    Plate, Madame Lavalliere, Gold Scalloped Rim, Crown Mark, 9 1/2 In. 95.00
    Plate, Madamoiselle De Barry, Navy Border, Gold, 9 1/2 In. 135.00
    Sugar & Creamer, Tray, Pink Roses, White, Silver Bands Marked, 3 Pc. 95.00
    Tea Service, Cobalt Blue, Battle Scenes, Gilt Edges, Marked, 34 Piece 8800.00
    Urn, Colonial Woman, Water, Scroll Handles, Marked, 10 In. 155.00

Urn, Cover, Bronze Mounted, Figures, Landscape, C.1900, 19 1/4 In., Pr.	1210.00
Urn, Cover, Cupid In Bronze Mount & Finial, Signed, 11 In.	1250.00
Urn, Domed Cover, Shield–Shaped Reserves, 12 1/4 In., Pair	1000.00
Urn, Floral Garlands, Ormolu Mounts, 19 In., Pair	275.00
Vase, Cover, Landscape & Figures Panels, Bronze Mounted, 17 In., Pair	1870.00

Sewer tile figures were made by workers at the sewer tile and pipe factories in the Ohio area during the late nineteenth and early twentieth centuries. Figurines, small vases, and cemetery vases were favored. Often the finished vase was a piece of the original pipe with added decorations and markings. All types of sewer tile work are now considered folk art by collectors.

SEWER TILE, Cowboy Boot, Tooled Designs, 3 1/4 In.	10.00
Dog, Blue & Brown Spots, 6 1/2 In.	125.00
Dog, Seated, Free–Standing Front Legs, 10 1/4 In.	125.00
Dog, Seated, Initialed E.J.E., 10 3/4 In.	325.00
Dog, Seated, Mottled Brown Glaze, 8 In.	65.00
Dog, Seated, Paint Traces, 8 In.	90.00
Dog, Seated, Right & Left Facing, 5 3/4 In., Pair	200.00
Dog, Spaniel, Seated, 8 In.	70.00
Dog, Spaniel, Seated, Bank Shape, 10 In.	90.00
Frog, Tooled Feet, Grinning, 8 1/4 In.	250.00
Lamp Base, Folk Art Tree, Grapes, Squirrels, 10 1/2 In.	175.00
Lamp, Tree Trunk Shape, 7 3/4 In.	25.00
Lion, Oval Base, 15 In.	150.00
Lion, Yellow Glaze, 8 3/4 In.	200.00
Planter, Tree Stump, 10 1/2 In.	65.00
Raccoon, Unglazed, 15 In.	125.00
Vase, Figural, Fish, Hand Stippling, 10 7/8 In.	250.00

All types of sewing equipment are collected, from sewing birds that held the cloth to old wooden spools.

SEWING, Basket, Woven Wicker, Floral Enameling, Black, 9 In.	25.00
Basket, Woven, Footed, Cover, Large	22.00
Bird, 2 Pincushions, Dated 1853	300.00
Bird, 2 Pincushions, Nickel Plated Brass, 4 3/4 In.	105.00
Bird, Brass, Blue Velvet, 5 In.	175.00
Bird, Nickel Plated Brass, 5 In.	85.00
Bird, Table Clamp, Black & Bronze Paint, 5 In.	95.00
Bird, With Dog	325.00
Box, Regency, Rosewood, Musical, Piano Shape, 11 1/2 In. ....*Illus*	700.00
Box, Winged Feet, Garden Scenes, Fitted Interior, Chinese Lacquer	475.00
Cabinet, Lift Top, Coats, 4 Drawers	450.00
Caddy, Cherry, Curly Maple Drawer, Pincushion Top, Red Paint, 11 In.	205.00
Caddy, Thread, Wire Spindles, Pincushion, Walnut, 1887, 8 1/2 X 9 In.	65.00
Case, Boye Rotary Needle Case, Top Door, Metal, Round, 17 In.	60.00
Clamp, Dolphin	395.00
Clamp, With Thread Reel, Steel	295.00
Darner, Striped Tiger Maple, Turned Handle, 6 1/2 In.	95.00
Darner, Toadstool Shape, Wooden Handle, Steel Spring Around Top	4.50
Egg, Wooden, Open To Brass Thimble, 1930	30.00
Goose, Tailor's, Twisted Handle, Holly Mfg.	30.00
Guide, Coats & Clark Thread	2.00
Hem Gauge, Griffin, Sterling Silver	150.00
Hem Gauge, Sterling Silver	60.00
Kit, Calvert Whiskey, Pocket	5.00
Machine, Beckwith, Patent 1872	275.00
Machine, Minnesota, Treadle	65.00
Machine, New Home, Pressed Design, Brass Pulls	45.00
Machine, New Home, Treadle	75.00
Machine, Signature Jr., Electric, Plastic Case, Foot Pedal, Green	48.00
Machine, Singer, Child's, Box, 1940s	65.00
Machine, Singer, Clamp, Needle & Thread, 6 X 6 1/2 In.	95.00
Machine, Singer, Portable, Walnut Case	88.00

Machine, Treadle, Pedestal, Drop-Leaf, Unusual Style 1675.00
Machine, Union Special, Double Locked Stick, Model 42576 .... 185.00
Machine, Wheeler & Mason, Oak, Electrified 110.00
Machine, Wheeler-Wilson, C.1870 .... 75.00
Machine, White, Tiger Striped Oak 80.00
Needle Book, Pictures Dirigible China Clipper 15.00
Needle Book, Sunbonnet Girl 14.00
Needle Case, Carved Vegetable Ivory, 2 In. 44.00
Needle Case, Engraved Floral, Sterling Silver, French, 2 1/4 In. 65.00
 SEWING, PINCUSHION DOLL, see Pincushion Doll
Pincushion, Beaded Bird, Implements On Bird, Red, 7 X 9 In. 130.00
Pincushion, Black Child Seated On Polka Dot Cover, Bisque, 2 In. 40.00
Pincushion, Carved, High-Top Shoe, Glass Buttons 125.00
Pincushion, Cat With Ball, Japan 18.00
Pincushion, Crocheted Heart, Green Crocheted Lace Ruffle, 8 X 7 In. 8.00
Pincushion, Gray Full-Bodied Mouse, Green Velvet, 4 X 4 In. 130.00
Pincushion, Gray Mouse Sitting On Velvet Ball, 1800s, 4 X 4 In. 120.00
Pincushion, Hat, Crocheted, Brim, White, Lavender Ribbons, 5 1/2 In. 3.50
Pincushion, Heart Shape, Entwined Ribbon, Hanger, 5 1/2 X 6 1/2 In. 20.00
Pincushion, Mama Mouse Pushing Carriage 15.00
Pincushion, Rabbit, Tape Measure Tongue, Corduroy 35.00
Pincushion, Table Clamp, Wooden, Red Velvet, Brown, M.D., 7 1/2 In. 175.00
Pinking Machine, Heavy Duty, Cast Iron 38.00
Punch, Embroidery, Ivory 17.00
Quilt Frame, On Stand, Roll Type 22.50
Ribbon Threader, 14K Gold, Set of 3 .... 95.00
Scissors, Buttonhole, Henry Sears & Son, Pat.1865 .... 37.00
Scissors, Buttonhole, Mushroom End, Tooled Shaft, Step-Down Blade 130.00
Scissors, Buttonhole, Tin 10.00
Scissors, Buttonhole, Wolcott, Teardrop Hole, 9 In. 25.00
Scissors, Embroidery, 14 K Gold 125.00
Scissors, Stork 12.00
Shuttle, Lydia Pinkham, Celluloid 25.00
Shuttle, Tatting, Sterling Silver 40.00
Spool Cabinet, 4 Drawers, Embossed Spool With Wings, Cherry 800.00
Spool Cabinet, Gallery Top, Stenciling, Belding Bros. 925.00
Spool Dispenser, Spool of Thread Shape, J & P Coates 700.00
Spool Rack, Red, Wooden Pegged Construction, Holds 16 Spools, 12 In. 135.00
Swift, Iron Table Clamp, 22 In. 35.00
Tape Measure, 2 Dogs Sitting On Pillow, Celluloid 53.00
Tape Measure, Acorn, Sterling Silver 65.00
Tape Measure, American Dry Goods, Co., Omaha 45.00
Tape Measure, Beetle, Tin 5.00
Tape Measure, Elephant, Celluloid, 4 1/2 In. 20.00
Tape Measure, Fab, Celluloid 25.00
Tape Measure, Frigidare, Celluloid 30.00
Tape Measure, Hardware Co., Celluloid, Mirror 1 Side, 1900s 15.00
Tape Measure, Harris Drug Store, Texas 25.00
Tape Measure, Illinois Surgical, Celluloid 25.00
Tape Measure, Levine Bros., Cincinnati, Ohio 12.00
Tape Measure, Lewis Lye, Celluloid 25.00
Tape Measure, Little Girl Holding Rose, Advertising Diamond Rings 65.00
Tape Measure, Lufkin National Bank, Spring Type, Round 7.50
Tape Measure, Lux Clock, Tan, Black & Blue 45.00
Tape Measure, Lydia Pinkham Medicines .... 16.00 To 32.00
Tape Measure, Mead Johnson & Co., Celluloid 12.00
Tape Measure, Owl 25.00
Tape Measure, Paint Co., Paint Can Picture, Celluloid, 1900s 10.00
Tape Measure, Pennsylvania Salt Mfg. 22.50
Tape Measure, Poodle, Silver Plate 110.00
Tape Measure, Radial Tire 8.00
Tape Measure, RCA, Silver Plated Case 15.00
Tape Measure, Russell Grader Mfg.Co., Celluloid 32.50
Tape Measure, St.Louis Exposition, 2 Views, 1904 .... 35.00

Tape Measure, Swinging Mirror, On Stand	85.00
Tape Measure, Turtle, Sterling Silver	95.00
Tape Measure, Washington D.C.Scenes, Celluloid	15.00
Thimble, Greek Key Band, Sterling Silver, Size 9	30.00
Thread Holder, Tat–It, J & R Coats, Plastic	1.50
Tracing Wheel, Black Wooden Handle	5.00

Shaker–produced items are characterized by simplicity, functionalism, and orderliness. There were many Shaker communities in America from the eighteenth century to the present day. The religious order made furniture, small wooden pieces, and packaged medicines, herbs, and jellies to sell to "outsiders." Other useful objects were made for use by members of the community. Shaker furniture is listed in this book under Furniture.

SHAKER, Apple Peeler, Cherry, Pegged, Double Wooden Wheel, 1840, 26 In.	450.00
Basket, Ash & Hickory, Rectangular Form, Hoop Handle, 1850, 15 In.	600.00
Basket, Ash, Rectangular Hoop Handle, Signed The Old House, 10 In.	325.00
Basket, Black Ash, Double Handle, 11 X 14 In.	300.00
Basket, Cheese, Black Ash & Maple, New Lebanon, 20 In.	1000.00
Basket, Cheese, Black Ash, Alfred, C.1840, 6 3/4 X 21 In.	800.00
Basket, Cutlery, Ash, Carved Medial Handle, 5 1/2 X 17 X 8 In.	1100.00
Basket, Gathering, Ash, Brown Patina, Swing Handle, 14 X 18 In.	1200.00
Basket, Gathering, Maple, Ash, New Lebanon, C.1830, Square, 12 In.	1900.00
Basket, Lid, Splint, Cheese Weave, Center Handle, 2 1/2 X 3 1/4 In.	260.00
Basket, Maple & Ash, Carved Handles, 14 X 9 In.	750.00
Basket, Maple & Ash, Flared Top, Enfield, C.1850, 17 In.	1400.00
Basket, Maple, 2 Handles, Enfield, 1850, 6 3/4 X 7 1/2 In.	550.00
Basket, Maple, Splint, Hoop Handle, 1850, 10 X 9 In.	600.00
Basket, Pie, Ash, Green Stain, Double Swing Handle, 6 In.	1000.00
Basket, Sewing, Maple, Side Handles, Corner Pocket, 7 1/2 In.	450.00
Basket, Sewing, Poplarware, Pink Satin Lining, 2 Compartments	300.00
Basket, Swing Handle, Black Ash, New Lebanon, 17 In.	1950.00
Basket, Woven Split Poplar, Bentwood Handle, 4 X 5 7/8 X 2 1/4 In.	175.00
Basket, Woven Split Poplar, Cover Inscribed Lucy Bandby, 4 X 7 In.	185.00
Bonnet, Canterbury, N.H.	2500.00
Bonnet, Woven, Poplarware, Brown Linen	200.00
Boot Jack	225.00
Bottle, Horseradish, Clear, Label	175.00
Bowl, Chopping, Maple, Yellow Stain, Signed First Order, Groveland	700.00
Box, Bureau, Butternut, Bird's Eye, Enfield, 1850, 8 X 4 In.	450.00
Box, Bureau, Cherry, 2 Compartment, Hancock, C.1840, 3 X 35 In.	800.00
Box, Cheese, Hickory & Pine, Green, Copper Nails, Hancock, 6 X 16 In.	850.00
Box, Chip, Pine, Hickory Handle, Brown, Watervliet, 1830, 20 In.	4500.00
Box, Chip, Pine, Hickory Handle, Mustard & Black, Red, 24 X 15 In.	1800.00
Box, Copper Tacks, 3–Finger Construction, Oval, 12 In.	300.00
Box, Cover, Copper Tacks, Dovetailed, 9 1/2 In.	125.00
Box, Desk, Chestnut, Cherry, Pine, Quill Pen, Ink Bottle, 1850, 16 In.	700.00
Box, Document, Pine, Blue, Brass Handle, Sabbathday Lake, C.1850, 6 In.	550.00
Box, Maple & Pine, Salmon Paint, Round, 1840, 6 X 11 In.	450.00
Box, Maple, Pine, Red, 3–Finger, Sabbathday Lake, 1830, 2 X 5 In.	1750.00
Box, Pine, Ash, Putty Brown, C.1840, 3 X 7 In.	1550.00
Box, Pine, Maple, Yellow, Sister's Workshop, 1820, 4 X 9 In.	4800.00
Box, Red Stained, Pinned Handle, 12 In.	295.00
Box, Seed, Pine, Fresh Garden Seeds Raised Label, 5 X 14 X 7 In.	700.00
Box, Seed, Pine, Mustard Paint, Shaker Vegetable Seed, 5 X 22 In.	1100.00
Box, Seed, Pine, Red Paint, Mt.Lebanon, 3 1/2 X 23 1/2 In.	1300.00
Box, Sewing, 3–Finger, Carrier, Fitted, Swing Handle, 3 X 8 1/4 In.	300.00
Box, Sewing, Bentwood, Swivel Handle, Copper Tack Construction, 6 In.	135.00
Box, Sewing, Drawer, Ivory Eyelets For Thread, Silk Pincushion	165.00
Box, Sewing, Swivel Handle, Cloth Lining, Pincushion, 7 3/4 In.	425.00
Box, Spit, Maple, Pine, Chrome Yellow, 2–Finger, Canterbury, 2 X 11 In.	900.00
Box, Storage, Bentwood, 3–Finger, 1–Finger Cover, Bird, 9 1/2 In.	500.00
Box, Storage, Mahogany, Key, 1840, 7 X 18 In.	1600.00
Box, Storage, Poplar, Brown Paint, Key, Watervliet, 1840, 7 X 15 In.	900.00

Bucket, Cover, Pine, Blue, Mt.Lebanon, C.1850, 15 X 9 In. 800.00
Bucket, Cover, Pine, Natural, Diamond Bail Plate, Enfield, 9 In. 1450.00
Bucket, Cover, Pine, Original Red Paint, Diamond Bail Plate, 9 In. 1000.00
Bucket, Lunch, Pine, Ash, Swing Handle, Canterbury, C.1830, 8 1/2 In. 400.00
Bucket, Pine, Apple Red, Diamond Bail Plate, Enfield, 1840, 7 1/2 In. 450.00
Butter Churn, Pine, Blue Finish, Dairy House, Mt.Lebanon, 1840, 22 In. 550.00
Cape, Dark Blue Wool, Gray Satin Trim, Mother–of–Pearl Buttons 250.00
Cape, Sister's, Beige Wool, Mother–of–Pearl Buttons, 32 In. 225.00
Carrier, Pine, Dovetailed, Box Shape, 12 X 8 In. 590.00
Carrier, Pine, Maple, Yellow Paint Traces, 3–Finger, Harvard, 10 In. 750.00
Carrier, Pine, Maple, Yellow, Oval, Canterbury, 1830, 7 X 10 In. 900.00
Carrier, Red Paint Traces, C.1840, Oval, 14 X 10 In. 750.00
Carrier, Seed, Square, Pine, Red Stain, 1830, 9 X 10 In. 1000.00
Case, Needle, Woven Poplarware 40.00
Chest, Spice, 13 Drawer, Walnut, Watervliet, C.1850, 17 X 17 In. 800.00
Chest, Spice, Pine, 3 Drawers Over 2, Arched Base, 7 X 10 X 5 In. 650.00
Churn, Butter, Red Box, 4 Stick Legs, Windows In Lid, Crank Handle 395.00
Cloak Hanger 45.00
Cloak, Blue Wool, Purple Satin, Enfield Label, 4 Ft. 8 In. 300.00
Cloak, Sister's, Wool, Royal Purple, Satin Brocade, 48 In. 1750.00
Cutter, Herb, Pine, Iron Chopper, Watervliet, C.1850, 8 In. 250.00
Dipper, Ash, Original Cream Yellow, Curved Handle, 6 1/2 In. 550.00
Doll, Porcelain Head, Kid Body, Wool Cloak, 15 In. 600.00
Dust Pan, 10 1/2 In. 4180.00
Dust Pan, Ladle, Tin, Flared, Sabbathday Lake 200.00
Dust Pan, Long Handle 880.00
Dust Pan, Tin, Red Paint, Tall Handle 520.00
Duster, Maple Handle, Red Feathers, Sabbathday Lake, 1850, 8 In. 350.00
Flax Wheel, Oak & Maple, Natural Finish, 34 X 35 In. 600.00
Flax Wheel, Oak & Maple, Signed SRAL, Complete With Distaff 300.00
       SHAKER, FURNITURE, see Furniture
Holder, Mirror, Cherry, Maple, Brass Bead Hangers, Varnish, 16 X 9 In. 400.00
Lamp Filler, Oil, Tin, 6 In. 350.00
Milk Tub, Pine, Blue Exterior, Cream Interior, Enfield, 1840, 5 In. 450.00
Mirror, Hand, Birch, Diamond Shape, Copper Nails, Enfield, 1850, 5 In. 175.00
Mortar & Pestle, Maple, Walnut Pestle, 1830, Harvard, Ma., 4 X 3 In. 550.00
Neckerchief, Silk, Hand Woven, Initialed RB 46, 1846, Square, 35 In. 450.00
Pail, Mustard Yellow Paint, Blue Bands 1500.00
Peggin, Pine Staves, Brown Stain, Hickory Handle, 1830, 8 In. 400.00
Pincushion, Sabbathday Lake, Round, 3 In. 73.50
Pincushion, Thread Holder, On Stand, Signed 115.00
Pitcher, Union Porcelain Works, Small 165.00
Press, Straw, Cherry, Mortised, Pegged, Knob, 1830, 18 X 13 In. 800.00
Rack, Drying, Chestnut, Arched Foot, New Lebanon, 1840, 38 X 24 In. 400.00
Rack, Drying, Pine, Red Paint, Watervliet, 1850, 4 Ft. 6 3/4 In. 1000.00
Rake, 10 Teeth, 3 Arched Concentric Half Circle Braces 125.00
Rug, Scatter, Silk, Diamond Pattern, Black, Red, Blue, 1840, 20 In. 250.00
Sampler, Blue Wool, Beige Ground, 3 Alphabets, Enfield, 1819 .... 3750.00
Scoop, Flour, Copper Fasteners, Turned Handle, 7 X 14 In. 130.00
Scoop, Flour, Finger Grip Turned Handle, 11 In. 150.00
Screen, Infirmary, Pine, 3 Panels, 3 Pegs, New Lebanon, 1850, 6 Ft. 900.00
Seed Planter, 12 Beveled Pegs, Tapered, Mortised Into Board, 67 In. 130.00
Sewing Carrier, Lid, Crystalized Surface 875.00
Sewing Carrier, Pine, Natural, Canted Sides, Fitted, Dated 1798, 9 In. 1600.00
Shawl, Gray & Cream, Wool, Striped Border, Sabbathday Lake, 5 Ft. 300.00
Sheet Music, The Little Shaking Quakers, Frank L, Bristow 500.00
Shovel, Birch, Carved 1 Piece, Enfield, C.1850, 36 In. 900.00
Shovel, Grain, Carved From 1 Piece of Wood 150.00
Shovel, Grain, Wooden, 1 Piece 200.00
Spice Box, Cover, Copper Tacks, Harvard Society, 4 3/4 X 6 1/4 In. 200.00
Spoolholder, Cherry, Red Velvet Pincushion, Thimble Holder, Scissors 500.00
Stove, Cast Iron, Canted Sides, New Lebanon, 1840, 19 X 29 In. 600.00
Stove, Iron, Curved Ash Catcher, Square Tapered Legs, 15 X 32 In. 1200.00
Strainer, Cheese, Milk Bleached, Round, 9 In. 190.00

Swift, Maple & Poplar 150.00
Tool, Butter Curler & Butter Baller, Pair 175.00
Trade Card, Shaker Family Pills 25.00
Tub, Cream, Pine, Blue Paint, White Interior, 1840, 5 X 10 In. 850.00
Wheel, Wool, Hardwoods, Natural Finish, 1820, Stamped Canterbury, N.H. 750.00
Winder, Yarn, Maple, Natural Finish, Clock Reel, 1839, 37 In. 550.00

Shaving mugs were popular from 1860 to 1900. Many types were made, including occupational mugs featuring pictures of men's jobs. There were scuttle mugs, silver plated mugs, glass–lined mugs, and others.

SHAVING MUG, Bird & Wheat, Barber Pole Handle 45.00
Brush Rest, Milk Glass Insert, Gold Trim, Silver Plate, 4 In. 65.00
Double Cup, Wild Root, Buffalo China 75.00
English Fox Hunt Scene, Marked Germany 85.00
Floral, Think of Me, Marked 15 .... 3.00
Golden Knights, Advertising, Crystal 60.00
Lotus Flowers & Bud, Outlined In Gold, Leaves, Nippon 125.00
Masonic Degree, C.T.Altwasser 65.00
Milk Glass, With Brush 18.00
Mr.& Mrs.Garfield, Milk Glass 110.00
Occupational, 2 Flags & Bugle, 10th Dragoons, Drum On Reverse 295.00
Occupational, A.J.Bradsher, M.D., Name In Gold 75.00
Occupational, Artist, With Palette, Germany 160.00
Occupational, Barber 90.00
Occupational, Blacksmith At Anvil 225.00
Occupational, Bricklaying 150.00
Occupational, Butcher, Sheep's Head 110.00
Occupational, Carpenter's Tools & Name 165.00
Occupational, Doctor 45.00
Occupational, Doctor With Carriage 165.00
Occupational, Duck Hunter, Boat, Dog 185.00
Occupational, Editor 695.00
Occupational, Farmer Plowing With Horses, Name In Gold 285.00
Occupational, Fireman 155.00
Occupational, Fireman, Horse–Drawn Engine 475.00
Occupational, Florist, With Container of Flowers 90.00
Occupational, Herbs Drying On Rough Cut Log, Name 225.00
Occupational, Horse Rancher 185.00
Occupational, Horseshoe With Flowers, Name 115.00
Occupational, House Painter 475.00
Occupational, Milkman, Milk Wagon Drawn By Horse, Name In Gold 525.00
Occupational, Minister, Holding Bible 180.00
Occupational, Musician 250.00
Occupational, Railroad Conductor 350.00
Occupational, Sailboat, Gold Trim, Limoges 135.00
Occupational, Sailor, With Girl 400.00
Occupational, Slot Machine, Upright 2850.00
Occupational, Steam Engine Operator 250.00
Occupational, Steam Engine Train, Geo.Blakley 350.00
Occupational, Steam Engine, Name 145.00
Occupational, Telegraph Operator, With Gold Key 160.00
Occupational, Textile Machinist, Lace Machine 385.00
Occupational, Tinsmith 200.00
Occupational, Trainer of Show Dogs, Dog Holding Trade Sign 495.00
Occupational, Trolley Driver, Horse–Drawn 650.00
Occupational, Undertaker 275.00
Occupational, Watchmaker, With Watch, Multicolored 260.00
Odd Fellows, Name 65.00
Patriotic, Eagle Design 100.00
Pink Luster, Lily-of-The–Valley, Octagonal, Twig Handle 30.00
Porcelain Liner, Marked Wallace Bros.Silver 15.00
Sailboat, Gold Trim, Limoges 135.00
Scuttle, Roses, Blue & White 35.00

Shawnee
USA

The Shawnee Pottery was started in Zanesville, Ohio, in 1935. The company made vases, novelty ware, flowerpots, figurines, dinnerwares, and cookie jars. Shawnee produced pottery for George Rumrill during the late 1930s. The company stopped working in 1961.

SHAWNEE, Bank, Bulldog	45.00
Bank, Figural, Farmer Pig	40.00
Bookends, Flying Geese	24.00
Bowl, Corn King, Box, 3 Piece	55.00
Bowl, Corn King, No.6, 6 In.	20.00
Box, Cigar, & Ashtrays, Indian Design	35.00
Bridge Set, Ashtray, 4 Piece	18.00
Butter, Corn King	25.00
Butter, Cover, Corn Queen	25.00
Casserole, Corn King, 1 1/2 Qt.	45.00
Casserole, Corn King, Cover, Large	65.00
Casserole, Corn King, Individual	30.00
Casserole, Corn King, No.74	30.00
Casserole, Fruit	18.00
Cereal, Corn King	25.00 To 26.50
Coaster & Ashtray Bridge Set, 4 Piece	18.00
Cookie Jar, Clown, Gold Trim	70.00
Cookie Jar, Clown, Seal, Balancing Ball Cover	145.00
Cookie Jar, Cookie House	360.00
Cookie Jar, Corn King	60.00 To 95.00
Cookie Jar, Drummer Boy	90.00
Cookie Jar, Dutch Boy, Gold Trim	120.00
Cookie Jar, Dutch Boy, Plain	30.00
Cookie Jar, Dutch Boy, Yellow Pants	28.00
Cookie Jar, Dutch Girl, Gold Trim	73.00 To 120.00
Cookie Jar, Dutch Girl, Yellow Skirt	50.00
Cookie Jar, Elephant, Pink With White Collar	30.00 To 65.00
Cookie Jar, Hexagon With Baker, Gingerbread Boy	25.00
Cookie Jar, Jug, Gold Trim	80.00
Cookie Jar, Lucky Elephant	50.00 To 90.00
Cookie Jar, Lucky Elephant, Decal, Gold Trim	150.00
Cookie Jar, Mugsy, Gold Trim	120.00
Cookie Jar, Octagon, Gold Trim	20.00 To 25.00
Cookie Jar, Owl	40.00 To 80.00
Cookie Jar, Owl, Gold Trim	90.00 To 150.00
Cookie Jar, Pig, Clovers	40.00
Cookie Jar, Pink Elephant	35.00 To 50.00
Cookie Jar, Puss 'N Boots	44.00 To 75.00
Cookie Jar, Puss 'N Boots, Gold Trim	60.00 To 175.00
Cookie Jar, Smiley Pig	50.00 To 55.00
Cookie Jar, Smiley Pig, Gold Trim	70.00
Cookie Jar, Smiley Pig, Red Scarf	22.00
Cookie Jar, Smiley Pig, Red Scarf, Tulips	45.00
Cookie Jar, Treasure Craft Ice Wagon	12.00
Cookie Jar, Winking Owl	85.00
Cookie Jar, Winnie Pig, Bank Head	85.00 To 125.00
Cookie Jar, Winnie Pig, Blue Collar	155.00
Cookie Jar, Winnie Pig, Gold Trim	70.00
Cookie Jar, Winnie Pig, Green Collar	50.00 To 55.00
Cookie Jar, Winnie Pig, Peach Collar	85.00
Creamer, Corn King, 5 In.	12.00 To 15.00
Creamer, Corn Queen	6.00
Creamer, Elephant	9.00 To 18.00
Creamer, Elephant, Decal, Gold	60.00
Creamer, Pig, Gold Leaf	45.00
Creamer, Puss 'N Boots, Gold, Decal	35.00
Creamer, Smiley Pig	20.00
Creamer, Smiley Pig, Gold Trim	47.00

Darner, Woman	18.00
Figurine, Dog, Pekingese	20.00
Figurine, Duck, Blue	12.00
Figurine, Gazelle	35.00
Figurine, Oriental, With Parasol	5.00
Figurine, Poodle, Miniature	10.00
Figurine, Puppy	20.00
Figurine, Rabbit	20.00
Figurine, Squirrel	12.00
Figurine, Teddy Bear	20.00
Figurine, Tumbling Bear	20.00
Jug, Corn King	22.00
Mixing Bowl, Corn King, 5 In.	20.00
Mixing Bowl, Corn King, 6 1/2 In.	20.00
Mixing Bowl, Corn King, 8 In.	30.00
Mug, Corn King	25.00
Pitcher, Bopeep, 7 In.	25.00
Pitcher, Chanticleer	24.00 To 40.00
Pitcher, Chanticleer Rooster, Flower Decals, Gold Trim, 10 In.	130.00
Pitcher, Corn King, No.70	10.00
Pitcher, Little Boy Blue, 7 In.	25.00 To 40.00
Pitcher, Rooster	25.00 To 30.00
Pitcher, Smiley Pig	40.00
Pitcher, Smiley Pig, Peach, Blue & Gold Flowers	125.00
Planter, Boy, At Fence	4.00
Planter, Boy, With Chicken	10.00
Planter, Boy, With Dog	2.00
Planter, Boy, With Wheelbarrow	10.00
Planter, Bridge	6.00
Planter, Buddha	12.00
Planter, Bull, With Leaf	35.00
Planter, Butterfly	3.00
Planter, Canopy Bed	28.00
Planter, Cat, Playing Saxophone	18.00
Planter, Cherub, Gold Trim	10.00
Planter, Chick, With Cart	10.00
Planter, Circus Cage	16.00
Planter, Deer	9.00
Planter, Doe & Fawn, Yellow Deer On Green	10.00
Planter, Doe Sitting In Front of Log	28.00
Planter, Donkey, With Basket, Head Down	12.00
Planter, Donkey, With Basket, Head Up	12.00
Planter, Donkey, With Cart, Large	12.00
Planter, Donkey, With Cart, Small	3.00
Planter, Dutch Boy & Girl	7.00
Planter, Dutch Children At Well	10.00
Planter, Elephant & Leaf	35.00
Planter, Elephant, Small	4.00
Planter, Elf Shoe	6.00
Planter, Four Birds, On Perch	30.00
Planter, Girl & Basket	8.00
Planter, Girl At Fence	10.00
Planter, Globe	16.00
Planter, Highchair	30.00
Planter, Lamb In Boat, Marked	12.50
Planter, Oriental Man With Basket	10.00
Planter, Piano	14.00
Planter, Polynesian Girl	10.00
Planter, Pony	16.00
Planter, Pump	8.00
Planter, Rickshaw Boy, Gold Trim	8.00
Planter, Squirrel, Gold Trim	9.00 To 10.00
Planter, Swan, Yellow	15.00
Planter, Train Set, Caboose, Boxcar, Coal Car, Locomotive	85.00

Planter, Wishing Well 18.00
Plate, Corn King, 10 In. .... 18.00 To 25.00
Refrigerator Dish, Crisscross, Green, 8 X 8 In. 25.00
Relish, Corn King .... 15.00 To 20.00
Relish, Corn Queen 16.00
Salt & Pepper, Baker 15.00
Salt & Pepper, Bopeep, Gold, 3 Holes 16.00
Salt & Pepper, Cat, Gold Trim 20.00
Salt & Pepper, Chefs 12.00
Salt & Pepper, Corn King, 5 1/2 In. .... 12.50 To 15.00
Salt & Pepper, Corn, 3 1/4 In. 10.00
Salt & Pepper, Daisy, Small 12.00
Salt & Pepper, Duck 18.00
Salt & Pepper, Dutch Boy 14.00
Salt & Pepper, Dutch Girl 14.00
Salt & Pepper, Farmer Pig, With Shovel 7.00
Salt & Pepper, Flowerpot, 3 1/2 In. .... 8.00 To 12.00
Salt & Pepper, Fruit 9.00
Salt & Pepper, Milk Can .... 6.00 To 10.00
Salt & Pepper, Mugsey, 5 In. .... 16.00 To 32.00
Salt & Pepper, Owl, Blue Eyes 12.00
Salt & Pepper, Owl, Green Eyes 4.00
Salt & Pepper, Puss 'N Boots .... 6.00 To 15.00
Salt & Pepper, Sailor Boy 6.00
Salt & Pepper, Smiley Pig, Large 20.00
Salt & Pepper, Swiss Kids 20.00
Salt & Pepper, Watering Can 8.00
Salt & Pepper, Wheelbarrow 8.00
Salt & Pepper, Winnie Pig, Large 20.00
Sugar & Creamer, Corn King, Gold Trim 35.00
Sugar, Corn King, Cover 15.00
Sugar, Corn Queen, Cover 12.00
Table Set, Corn King, 4 Piece 115.00
Teapot, Corn King .... 25.00 To 40.00
Teapot, Corn King, Individual 38.00
Teapot, Daisy 25.00
Teapot, Elephant, Yellow 60.00
Teapot, Flower 20.00
Teapot, Granny Ann .... 40.00 To 45.00
Teapot, Granny Ann, Gold Decals, Purple Apron 60.00
Teapot, Red Flower 20.00
Teapot, Tom, Tom, The Piper's Son .... 25.00 To 55.00
Utility Jar, Corn King 25.00
Vase, Bowknot 12.00
Vase, Doe In Shadowbox 14.00
Vase, Doves 16.00
Vase, Gazelle, With Baby 50.00
Vase, Swan 10.00
Wall Pocket, Birdhouse .... 12.00 To 15.00
Wall Pocket, Bopeep 10.00
Wall Pocket, Bow 6.00
Wall Pocket, Girl, With Rag Doll .... 14.00 To 22.50
Wall Pocket, Little Jack Horner 14.00
Wall Pocket, Mantel Clock 14.00
Wall Pocket, Telephone 14.00
Water Jug, Smiley Pig, 2 Qt. 36.00

The Shearwater pottery is a family business started by Mr. and Mrs. G. W. Anderson, Sr., and their three sons. The local Ocean Springs, Mississippi, clays were used to make the wares in the 1930s. The company is still in business.

SHEARWATER, Rum Keg, Pirate 65.00
Vase, Aquatic Scene, Blue Glaze, Signed, C.1930, 11 In. 2100.00
Vase, Incised Stylized Fish, Signed, C.1930, 9 In. 885.00

Vase, Pillow, Molded Leaf Form, Copper Green To Pink, 6 X 6 In. 95.00

Sheet music from the past centuries is now collected. The favorites are examples with covers featuring artistic or historic pictures. Early sheet music covers were lithographed but by the 1900s photographic reproductions were used. The early music was larger than more recent sheets and you must watch out for examples that were trimmed to fit in a twentieth–century piano bench.

SHEET MUSIC, Alcoholic Blues, Owl On Moon, 1916 Prohibition	10.00
Alice In Wonderland	15.00
Aloha Soldier Boy, 1918	16.50
Amelia Earhart's Last Flight, 1939	20.00
Anniversary Song, Jolson	6.00
As Time Goes By, Bogart, Berman, Henreid, Casablanca, 7 Pages	45.00
Aunt Jemima, Pancake Lyrics	25.00
Babe Ruth, 1928	35.00
Babe Ruth, With Advertising Pin, 1928	50.00
Barney Google, Barney & Spark Plug Picture, 1923	25.00
Big Stick, Musical For TR's Foreign Policy, 1907	12.50
Blue of The Night, Crosby	4.00
Close To You, Frank Sinatra	3.00
Did I Remember, Harlow	10.00
Dodge Brothers March	12.00
Don't Cry Swanee, Al Jolson	3.00
Fire Drill March	10.00
Footlight Parade	10.00
For Me & My Gal, Judy Garland	10.00
For You A Rose, 1917	11.00
Frankie & Johnny, Mae West	15.00
Freedom Train, Irving Berlin, 1947	10.00
From Here To Eternity	5.00
Fuehrer's Face, 1942	25.00
Gang's All Here	5.00
Gen.Jo' Wheeler's March, Dedicated To Pres.W.McKinley, 1899	15.00
Girl of Mine, Armstrong Cover	17.00
Gone With The Wind, 1937	50.00
Good Night Sweetheart	3.00
I'll Walk Alone, Dinah Shore, 1944	10.00
I'm Just A Vagabond Lover, Rudy Vallee, 1929	6.00
I'm Nobody's Baby, Mickey Rooney & Judy Garland	10.00
If I Had A Talking Picture of You, Janet Gaynor, 1929	10.00
In Our Little Wooden Shoes, Shirley Temple	10.00
Just As The Sun Went Down, Civil War	20.00
K–K–K–Katy, World War I, 7 X 10 1/2 In.	7.50
Making Eyes, Pretty Woman, 1905	18.00
Mystic Shrine March, Sousa Cover	12.00
Old Spinning Wheel, Baby Rose Marie, 1933	10.00
On The Atchison, Topeka & The Santa Fe, Judy Garland, 1945	15.00
On The Fall River Line	10.00
On The Good Ship Lollipop, Shirley Temple .... 12.00 To	25.00
Over The Rainbow, Wizard of Oz	15.00
Over Yonder Where Lilies Grow, 1918	20.00
Paperdoll, Frank Sinatra	6.00
Pennies From Heaven	4.00
Please Mister President, Rudy Vallee, Capitol, 1933	10.00
Poor Little Fool, Ricky Nelson	10.00
Pray For The Lights To Go Out, Preacher	15.00
Rag Baby Rag, 1909	15.00
Rum & Coca–Cola, Andrew Sisters	15.00
Sack Waltz, Teddy Bears	20.00
Saturday Night, Frank Sinatra	3.00
Sipping Cider, Fatty Arbuckle	10.00
Snow White, 1937	25.00
St.Louis Woman, Mae West	15.00

Sunbonnet Sue, Pretty Sue Cover, 1908	20.00
Sweet Little Buttercup, Woman, Flowers, 1917	20.00
Tennessee, Pretty Woman Cover, 1917	18.00
They're On Their Way To Mexico, Liberty Sending Troops, 1914	15.00
Three Little Words, 1930	15.00
Three Little Words, Amos & Andy, 1930	15.00 To 30.00
Trolley Song, Judy Garland	12.00
True Love, Frank Sinatra	6.00
We're All Americans All True Blue, Kate Smith, 1940	10.00
Who's Afraid of The Big Bad Wolf, Mickey Mouse, Irving Berlin	15.00

SHEFFIELD, see Silver–English; Silver Plate

The name Shelley first appeared on English ceramics about 1912. The Foley China Works started in England in 1860. Joseph Ball Shelley joined the company in 1862 and became a partner in 1872. Percy Shelley joined the firm in 1881. The company went through a series of name changes and in 1910 the then Foley China Company became Shelley China. In 1929 it became Shelley Potteries. The company was acquired in 1966 by Allied English Potteries, then merged with the Doulton group in 1971. The name Shelley was put into use again in 1980.

SHELLEY, Bowl, Underplate, Floral, Side Handles, Cover, Artist, 1929, 3 Piece	75.00
Cake Plate, Rosebud	48.00
Cup & Saucer, Briar Rose	30.00
Cup & Saucer, Dainty Blue	35.00
Cup & Saucer, Rock Garden	25.00
Saltshaker	25.00
Sugar & Creamer, Daffodil Time	35.00
Vase, Art Deco, Multicolor Drip Glaze, 5 In.	50.00
Whimsey, Piano, Goss–Type	35.00
Whimsey, Purse	30.00

Shirley Temple, the famous movie star, was born in 1928. She made her first movie in 1932. Thousands of items picturing Shirley have been and still are being made. Shirley Temple dolls were first made in 1934 by Ideal Toy Company. Millions of Shirley Temple cobalt blue glass dishes were made by Hazel Atlas Glass Company and U.S. Glass Company from 1934 to 1942. They were given away as premiums for Wheaties and Bisquick. A bowl, mug, and pitcher were made as a breakfast set. Some pieces were decorated with the picture of a very young Shirley, others used a picture of Shirley in her 1936 "Captain January" costume. Although collectors refer to a cobalt creamer it is actually the 4 1/2 inch high milk pitcher from the breakfast set. Many of these items are being reproduced today.

SHIRLEY TEMPLE, Book, 5 Stories, 1958	20.00
Book, Shirley Temple's Fairyland, TV, Random House, 1958	12.00
Button, Photo, Mid–1930s, 1 1/4 In.	15.00
Charm, Shirley & Her Dog Corky, Gold, Cloisonne	6.50
Doll, 1972, 14 In.	75.00
Doll, 1973, 16 In.	125.00
Doll, Button, S & H, Box, 20 In.	650.00
Doll, C.1958, 12 In.	150.00
Doll, Composition, 13 In.	450.00
Doll, Composition, Arranbee, 19 In.	295.00
Doll, Composition, Clear Eyes, Fur Coat & Hat, 15 In.	495.00
Doll, Composition, Ideal Novelty & Toy Co., 18 In.	110.00
Doll, Composition, Ideal, 18 In.	250.00
Doll, Composition, Japan, 8 In.	150.00
Doll, Composition, New Wig, Redressed, 25 In.	495.00
Doll, Composition, Sailor Suit, Ideal Novelty & Toy, 20 In.	137.50
Doll, Flirty Eyes, 1930s, 27 In.	600.00
Doll, Ideal, 1950s, 12 In.	110.00
Doll, Ideal, 1957, 12 In.	65.00
Doll, Little Colonel Clothes, Composition, 22 In.	650.00

Doll, Little Ranger, Composition, 11 In.	675.00
Doll, Nude, With Doll Pin, Ideal, 17 In.	27.00
Doll, Porcelain, 16 In.	130.00
Doll, Tagged Dress, Shoes, 1957, 15 In.	90.00
Doll, Vinyl, New Red & White Dress, Ideal, 15 In.	150.00
Doll, Vinyl, Plastic, Party Dress, 19 In.	71.50
Doll, Yellow Dress, Ideal Pin, 1957, 17 In.	185.00
Figurine, Captain January	49.00
Figurine, Heidi	49.00
Figurine, Pink Flocked Dress, 6 1/2 In.	80.00
Figurine, Salt Glaze, 4 1/2 In.	40.00
Game, Little Colonel, Selchow & Righter, 1935	70.00
Mirror, 20th Century Fox, America's Sweetheart, Pocket, 1936	24.75
Mirror, Christmas Greetings, 3 In.	4.25
Mirror, Movie Advertising	25.00
Mug, Cobalt Blue, 5 Oz.	21.00 To 35.00
Outfit, Texas Ranger, For 27-In. Doll	100.00
Paper Doll, 4 Outfits, In Suitcase, 1957, 12 In.	65.00
Paper Doll, Life–Like Hair, 10 Dresses, 75 Accessories, Box	36.00
Paper Doll, Now I Am 8, Saalfield, 1937	20.00
Pen & Pencil Set	160.00
Photograph, National Milk Week, Bottle In Hand, 1937	40.00
Pitcher, Cobalt Blue, 9 Oz.	22.00 To 37.00
Plate, Baby Take A Bow, 1st Edition, Box	45.00
Postcard, 1949	12.00
Poster, Adventures In Baltimore, R.Young, 1949, 81 X 41 In.	18.00
Poster, Christmas, Lobby	350.00
Poster, Our Little Girl, Joel McCrea, Fox, 1935, 36 In.	1350.00
Poster, Rebecca of Sunnybrook Farm, Fox, 1938	975.00
Poster, Wee Willie Winkie, Fox, 1937	1900.00
Record Set, Dumbo, Shirley Narrates, RCA, 78 RPM, 1940s	32.00
Sheet Music, Animal Crackers In My Soup	16.00
Sheet Music, Oh My Goodness	10.00
Sheet Music, On The Good Ship Lollipop	10.00
Sheet Music, Poor Little Rich Girl	14.00
Sheet Music, When I'm With You	8.00
Sign, Drink Milk Daily, 1938, 3 X 10 In.	10.00
Ticket, Theater, Little Miss Marker, 10 Cent	10.00

SHRINER, see Masonic

Silver deposit glass was made during the late nineteenth and early twentieth centuries. Solid sterling silver was applied to the glass by a chemical method so that a cutout design of silver metal appeared against a clear or colored glass. It is sometimes called silver overlay.

SILVER DEPOSIT, Console Set, Black Amethyst, Label, Ovington's NY	120.00
Rose Bowl, Greek Key, Black Amethyst	22.50
Trivet, 3/8 In. Glass, Round, 8 In.Diam.	25.00
Vase, Art Deco, Germany, 4 In.	125.00

Listed in this section are many of the current and out–of–production silver and silver plated flatware patterns made in the past eighty years. Other silver is listed under Silver–American, Silver–English, etc. Most silver flatware sets that are missing a few pieces can be completed through the help of one of the many silver matching services listed in "The Kovels' Collectors' Source Book."

SILVER FLATWARE SILVER PLATE, Alhambra, Iced Tea Teaspoon, Rogers	8.00
Alhambra, Teaspoon, Rogers	7.00
Ambassador, Butter Knife, Master	5.00
Ambassador, Sugar Spoon	7.00
Arbutus, Butter Pick, Gorham	45.00
Astoria, Strawberry Fork, Wallace, Set of 6	38.00
Belmont, Soup Ladle, Rogers, 11 1/2 In.	35.00
Berkshire, Gravy Ladle	18.00
Berkshire, Pie Server	35.00

Berkshire, Soup Ladle 55.00
Berwick, Bouillon Spoon 12.00
Bird of Paradise, Butter Server, Individual 5.00
Bird of Paradise, Community, Service For 12 .... 275.00
Bird of Paradise, Salad Fork 6.00
Brilliant, Nut Pick, 4 Piece 8.00
Carnation, Cream Ladle 30.00
Carnation, Dinner Knife 24.00
Charter Oak, Cocktail Fork 20.00
Classic, Olive Spear, Community, 8 1/4 In. 6.00
Columbia, Soup Ladle 95.00
Daffodil, Iced Tea Spoon 10.00
Danish Princess, Butter Server, Individual 4.00
Exeter, Knife, Community 2.00
Exquisite, Service For 8, Rogers, 35 Piece 115.00
Fair Oak, Punch Ladle 70.00
First Love, Pastry Fork, Engraved Bowl 10.00
Flirtation, Spoon & Fork, Baby's, Oneida 12.00
Grape, Service For 8, Rogers, C.1934, 44 Piece 185.00
Grenoble, Tablespoon, Rogers 6.00
Heritage, Ice Cream Fork 8.00
Jasmine, Service For 6, Community, 42 Piece 85.00
King Edward, Butter Server, Individual 4.00
Lafayette, Vegetable Fork 15.00
Lakewood, Pastry Fork 5.00
Lavigne, Cocktail Fork 18.00
Lavigne, Fruit Spoon 21.00
Leonora, Pickle Fork, Twist Handle, Rogers 15.00
Lilyta, Butter Knife, Master 5.00
Magic Rose, Service For 8, Community, 40 Pc. 120.00
Mayfair, Butter Knife, Wm. Rogers 3.00
Meadowbrook, Soup Spoon, Oval 7.00
Modern Baroque, Knife 6.00
Mystic, Dinner Fork, Rogers 3.50
Mystic, Dinner Fork, Rogers, 6 Piece 18.00
Old Colony, Olive Spoon 25.00
Old Colony, Pickle Fork 12.00
Old Colony, Soup Spoon, Oval, Rogers 6.50
Orange Blossom, Dinner Knife 35.00
Orange Blossom, Grapefruit Spoon, Rogers 3.00
Orange Blossom, Ice Cream Fork, Gorham, 9 Pc. 225.00
Orange Blossom, Orange Spoon, Set of 6 .... 25.00
Oriental, Youth Set 22.50
Oxford, Ladle, Shell Bowl, Wm. Rogers 15.00
Regent, Cocktail Fork, Gorham 5.00
Rose & Leaf, Iced Tea Spoon 7.00
Sheraton, Salad Fork 1.50
Sheraton, Teaspoon 1.50
Troy, Soup Ladle 45.00
Victorian Classic, Knife, Community, 9 In. 6.00
Vintage, Berry Serving Spoon, Moselle 48.00
Vintage, Butter Server, Flat, Rogers 6.00
Vintage, Cocktail Fork, Rogers 16.00
Vintage, Cold Meat Fork, Moselle 55.00
Vintage, Cold Meat Fork, Rogers 22.00
Vintage, Dinner Fork, Rogers 8.00
Vintage, Gravy Ladle, Rogers 25.00
Vintage, Punch Ladle 495.00
Vintage, Soup Ladle 120.00
Vintage, Sugar Tongs, Gorham 50.00
SILVER FLATWARE STERLING, Adam, Pie Server, Whiting 195.00
Aegean Weave, Spoon, Slotted, Wallace 38.00
Alencon Lace, Butter Knife, Master, Gorham 20.00
Amarylis, Luncheon Knife, Lunt 20.00

American Classic, Cold Meat Fork, Easterling	35.00
Arabesque, Jam Spoon, Whiting, 7 1/4 In.	30.00
Athenian, Horseradish Spoon, Reed & Barton	45.00
Avalon, Pastry Server, Pierced, International	125.00
Awakening, Gravy Ladle, Towle	30.00
Bacchus, Punch Ladle, Gorham	850.00
Baltimore Rose, Sauce Ladle, Schofield	85.00
Baltimore Rose, Serving Spoon, Schofield	85.00
Baronial, Salad Serving Spoon, Gorham	120.00
Baronial, Soup Ladle, Gorham	300.00
Bouquet, Bouillon Ladle, Gold Wash, Durgin	155.00
Bouquet, Seafood Fork, Durgin	25.00
Bridal Rose, Baby Spoon, Curved Handle, Alvin	45.00
Bridal Rose, Berry Fork & Spoon, Alvin	325.00
Bridal Rose, Berry Spoon, Gold Wash, Alvin	195.00
Bridal Rose, Cold Meat Fork, Alvin	150.00
Bridal Rose, Cream Soup Spoon, Alvin	40.00
Bridal Rose, Jelly Spoon, Alvin	55.00
Bridal Rose, Salad Serving Ladle, Alvin	150.00
Bridal Rose, Sardine Fork, Alvin	125.00
Buttercup, Bonbon Spoon, Gorham	30.00
Buttercup, Dinner Knife, Gorham	22.00
Buttercup, Fish Fork, Gorham	135.00
Buttercup, Gravy Ladle, Gorham	75.00
Buttercup, Ice Tongs, Gorham	275.00
Buttercup, Jam Spoon, Gorham	70.00
Buttercup, Orange Spoon, Gorham	25.00
Buttercup, Oyster Ladle, Gorham	295.00
Buttercup, Punch Ladle, Gorham	595.00
Buttercup, Tomato Server, Gorham	85.00
Cabot, Berry Spoon, Wallace	40.00
Cambridge, Bouillon Spoon, Gorham	13.00
Cambridge, Fork, Gorham	24.00
Cambridge, Ice Cream Spoon, Durgin	250.00
Cambridge, Lettuce Fork, Gorham, 9 3/8 In.	55.00
Cambridge, Mustard Ladle, Gorham	95.00
Candlelight, Fork, Towle, 7 1/4 In.	15.00
Candlelight, Gravy Ladle, Towle, 6 3/4 In.	45.00
Canterbury, Salad Serving Set, Towle, 2 Piece	150.00
Century, Stuffing Spoon, Dominick & Haff	150.00
Chamford, Beef Fork, Reed & Barton	25.00
Chantilly, Berry Fork, Gorham	20.00
Chantilly, Berry Spoon, Gilt Bowl, Gorham	115.00
Chantilly, Fried Oyster Server, Gorham	295.00
Chantilly, Stuffing Spoon, Gorham	375.00
Chantilly, Sugar Shell, Gorham, 6 In.	25.00
Chantilly, Tablespoon, Gorham, 8 3/8 In.	45.00
Chapel Bells, Cream Soup Spoon, Alvin	15.00
Charles II, Pastry Fork, Dominick & Haff	27.00
Chateau, Cold Meat Fork, Lunt	30.00
Classic Rose, Gravy Ladle, Reed & Barton	36.00
Classic Rose, Teaspoon, Kirk	12.00
Cluny, Sugar Tongs, Gorham	125.00
Colfax, Gravy Ladle, Durgin	36.00
Contour, Cold Meat Fork, Towle	35.00
Craftsman, Iced Tea Spoon, Towle	21.00
Cromwell, Cheese Scoop, Durgin, Small	70.00
Cromwell, Cucumber Fork, Durgin	75.00
Cromwell, Lettuce Spoon, Durgin	95.00
Cromwell, Oyster Ladle, Durgin	295.00
Cromwell, Strawberry Fork, Durgin	25.00
Cromwell, Tea Infusing Spoon, Durgin	195.00
Cupid, Serving Spoon, Dominick & Haff	37.00
D'Orleans, Teaspoon, Towle	12.00

Dawn Star, Service For 8, Wallace, 32 Piece 585.00
Decor, Grapefruit Spoon, Gorham 22.00
Decor, Gravy Ladle, Gorham 65.00
Della Robbia, Dinner Knife, Alvin 22.00
Diamond, Service For 8, Reed & Barton 752.00
Domestic, Sardine Fork, Gorham 30.00
Dorothy Vernon, Fish Fork, Whiting, 10 Piece 325.00
Dover, Strawberry Fork, Gold Wash, Towle, 6 Piece 145.00
Dresden, Demitasse Spoon, Whiting, 6 Piece 125.00
Dresden, Sauce Ladle, Gorham, 5 7/8 In. 35.00
Edgewood, Jelly Cake Server, International 125.00
Eloquence, Service For 12, Lunt, 84 Piece 2800.00
Empress, Soup Ladle, Durgin 395.00
Essex, Luncheon Knife, Durgin 18.00
Etruscan, Sardine Fork, Gorham 60.00
Etruscan, Service For 8, Gorham, 32 Piece 700.00
Fairfax, Asparagus Tongs, Durgin 395.00
Fairfax, Bottle Opener, Durgin 38.00
Fairfax, Food Pusher, Durgin 40.00
Fairfax, Gravy Ladle, Durgin, 6 In. 50.00
Fairfax, Service For 8, Case, Durgin, 66 Piece 995.00
Fairfax, Teaspoon, Gorham 7.00
First Frost, Service For 12, Oneida, 48 Piece 930.00
Florence, Sugar Shell, International 35.00
Florentine, Grapefruit Spoon, Gorham, 6 Piece 175.00
Florentine, Gumbo Soup Spoon, Gorham 45.00
Florentine, Mustard Ladle, Wendt 75.00
Francis I, Carving Set, Reed & Barton 95.00
Francis I, Ice Tongs, Reed & Barton 350.00
Francis I, Oyster Ladle, Reed & Barton 380.00
Francis I, Sugar Spoon, Reed & Barton 17.00
French Provincial, Gravy Ladle, Towle, 6 7/8 In. 45.00
French Scroll, Service For 12, Alvin, 60 Piece 995.00
Frontenac, Asparagus Fork, International 395.00
Frontenac, Cake Server, Pierced, International 295.00
Frontenac, Cold Meat Fork, International 110.00
Frontenac, Lettuce Fork, International 195.00
Frontenac, Mustard Ladle, International 150.00
Frontenac, Parfait Spoon, International 85.00
Frontenac, Pie Server, International 95.00
Frontenac, Preserve Spoon, International 75.00
Frontenac, Sugar Sifter, International 150.00
Frontenac, Sugar Tongs, International .... 55.00 To 75.00
Georgian Colonial, Jelly Server, Wallace 20.00
Georgian Maid, Soup Spoon, International 18.00
Georgian, Fruit Spoon, Towle 45.00
Georgian, Sardine Tongs, Towle 275.00
Grand Colonial, Luncheon Knife, Wallace 20.00
Grande Baroque, Dressing Spoon, Wallace 95.00
Grande Baroque, Sauce Ladle, Wallace 45.00
Grande Renaissance, Sugar Shell, Reed & Barton 24.00
Grecian, Sugar Sifter, Whiting 125.00
Hamilton, Luncheon Knife, Alvin 13.00
Hamilton, Teaspoon, Alvin 10.00
Hampshire, Cold Meat Fork, Durgin 34.00
Heiress, Berry Spoon, Durgin 30.00
Heiress, Cold Meat Fork, Heirloom 30.00
Heiress, Gravy Ladle, Durgin 30.00
Heiress, Service For 12, Oneida, 48 Piece 888.00
Honeysuckle, Teaspoon, Whiting 11.00
Hyperion, Dessert Spoon, Whiting 45.00
Hyperion, Orange Spoon, Whiting 28.00
Hyperion, Sardine Fork, Whiting 95.00
Imperial Chrysanthemum, Cream Ladle, Gorham 53.00

Imperial Chrysanthemum, Food Pusher, Gorham	55.00
Imperial Chrysanthemum, Sugar Tongs, Gorham	55.00
Imperial Queen, Sardine Fork, Whiting	55.00
Intaglio, Berry Spoon, Reed & Barton	275.00
Irian, Fork, Wallace, 7 In.	35.00
Japanese, Ice Cream Spoon, Gorham	75.00
Juliana, Service For 12, Watson, 60 Piece	1050.00
Juliana, Service For 12, Watson, 72 Piece	1200.00
Kimberly, Cold Meat Fork, Lunt	35.00
King Albert, Ice Tongs, Whiting	295.00
King Albert, Sugar Spoon, Whiting	20.00
King Edward, Cold Meat Fork, Whiting	80.00
King Edward, Gravy Ladle, Whiting	110.00
King Edward, Salad Serving Fork, Gorham	65.00
King George, Dessert Spoon, Gorham	18.00
King's Shell, Meat Fork, J.Conning, C.1850	522.50
La Parisienne, Fish Slicer, Reed & Barton	350.00
Labors of Cupid, Salad Set, Dominick & Haff	850.00
Lady Constance, Grapefruit Spoon, Towle	14.00
Lady Constance, Vegetable Spoon, Towle	85.00
Lady Diane, Service For 12, Towle, 48 Piece	875.00
Lady Hilton, Service For 12, Westmoreland	1100.00
Lafayette, Cucumber Server, Towle	30.00
Lancaster Rose, Chip Beef Fork, Gorham	30.00
Lancaster Rose, Soup Ladle, Gorham, 12 In.	245.00
Lancaster, Asparagus Fork, Gorham	235.00
Lancaster, Carving Set, Gorham, 2 Piece	80.00
Lancaster, Ice Cream Spoon, Gorham, 6 Piece	200.00
Lancaster, Lettuce Fork, Gorham	65.00
Lancaster, Mustard Ladle, Gorham	75.00
Lancaster, Salad Serving Set, Gorham	165.00
Lancaster, Soup Ladle, Gorham	270.00
Lancaster, Sugar Tongs, Gorham	30.00
Lancaster, Tablespoon, Gorham	32.00
Lancaster, Teaspoon, Gorham	8.00
Lansdowne, Citrus Spoon, Gorham	15.00
Lansdowne, Demitasse Spoon, Gorham	13.00
Lansdowne, Ice Cream Fork, Gorham	14.00
Lansdowne, Salad Serving Set, Gorham, 2 Piece	185.00
Les Cinq Fleurs, Jam Spoon, Reed & Barton	75.00
Les Cinq Fleurs, Sauce Ladle, Reed & Barton	195.00
Lily of The Valley, Cream Soup Spoon, Whiting	53.00
Lily of The Valley, Sugar Tongs, Whiting	145.00
Lily, Berry Spoon, Whiting, 9 In.	235.00
Lily, Poultry Shears, Whiting	90.00
Louis XIV, Olive Fork, Towle	30.00
Louis XIV, Olive Spoon, Towle	30.00
Louis XV, Butter Chip, Whiting	35.00
Louis XV, Cheese Knife, Whiting	125.00
Louis XV, Cucumber Server, Whiting	55.00
Louis XV, Ice Tongs, Whiting	295.00
Louis XV, Olive Spoon, Whiting	35.00
Louis XV, Sardine Fork, Whiting	75.00
Louis XV, Sugar Sifter, Whiting	55.00
Louis XV, Tea Strainer, 2 Handles, Whiting	75.00
Louis XVI, Service For 18, Whiting, 331 Piece	8000.00
Luxembourg, Cold Meat Fork, Gorham, 8 In.	55.00
Lyric, Cold Meat Fork, Gorham	40.00
Madame Jumel, Cream Ladle, Whiting	40.00
Madame Jumel, Gravy Ladle, Whiting	75.00
Madrigal, Cocktail Fork, Lunt	10.00
Majestic, Lemon Fork, Alvin	20.00
Majestic, Teaspoon, Alvin	17.00
Mandarin, Ice Cream Fork, Whiting	23.00

Marlborough, Jelly Server, Watson 22.00
Marlborough, Steak Knife, Lunt 25.00
Mayflower, Carving Set, Jenkins & Jenkins 125.00
Mazarin, Ice Cream Knife, Dominick & Haff 250.00
Mazarin, Strawberry Fork, Dominick & Haff 30.00
Mazarin, Teaspoon, Dominick & Haff 11.00
Mazarin, Tomato Server, Dominick & Haff 90.00
Medallion, Fish Slice, Gorham 275.00
Medici, Dessert Spoon, Gorham 30.00
Medici, Tablespoon, Gorham 40.00
Milburn Rose, Service For 8, Westmoreland, 40 Pc. 795.00
Modern Class, Cocktail Fork, Whiting 14.00
Monticello, Beef Fork, Lunt 75.00
Monticello, Fish Slicer, Lunt 25.00
Monticello, Olive Spoon, Lunt, Long 75.00
Monticello, Sauce Ladle, Whiting 26.00
Moonglow, Berry Spoon, International 40.00
Mount Vernon, Chocolate Spoon, Lunt 45.00
Mount Vernon, Olive Spoon, Lunt 45.00
Mount Vernon, Sardine Fork, Lunt 75.00
Mount Vernon, Tomato Server, Rogers, 7 3/4 In. 90.00
Mythologique, Fork, Gorham 55.00
Mythologique, Pea Server, Gorham 395.00
Mythologique, Serving Spoon, Gorham 75.00
Mythologique, Soup Spoon, Oval, Gorham 40.00
Mythologique, Teaspoon, Gorham 27.00
New Castle, Pea Server, Gorham 90.00
New Standish, Mustard Spoon, Durgin 32.00
New Standish, Olive Spoon, Durgin 32.00
New Standish, Serving Spoon, Durgin, 8 3/4 In. 50.00
Norfolk, Olive Spoon, Gorham, 8 3/8 In. 30.00
Normandie, Teaspoon, Wallace 18.50
Nuremberg, Cold Meat Fork, Alvin 95.00
Oak, Sauce Ladle, Smith 33.00
Old Colonial, Berry Spoon, Towle 225.00
Old Colonial, Bonbon Spoon, Towle 95.00
Old Colonial, Ice Cream Fork, Towle, 6 Piece 180.00
Old Colonial, Lettuce Fork, Towle, 9 1/2 In. 95.00
Old Colonial, Pickle Fork, Towle 60.00
Old Colonial, Sauce Ladle, Towle 45.00
Old Colonial, Strawberry Fork, Towle, 6 Piece 165.00
Old Colony, Grapefruit Spoon, Gorham, 5 3/4 In. 12.00
Old English, Tomato Server, Towle 45.00
Old French, Dinner Knife, Gorham 20.00
Old Medici, Cake Knife, Gorham 275.00
Old Newbury, Soup Spoon, Oval, Towle 14.00
Old Newbury, Teaspoon, Towle 6.00
Orient, Serving Fork, 4 Prongs, Alvin, 9 1/4 In. 65.00
Oval Twist, Berry Spoon, Whiting 125.00
Oval Twist, Preserve Spoon, Whiting 75.00
Paris, Dessert Spoon, Gorham 37.00
Paris, Fork, Gorham, 6 3/4 In. 28.00
Paris, Salad Fork, Gorham 40.00
Paul Revere, Baked Potato Fork, Towle 95.00
Paul Revere, Bouillon Ladle, Towle 195.00
Paul Revere, Punch Ladle, Towle 295.00
Pembroke, Teaspoon, Gorham 9.00
Plymouth, Olive Spoon, Gorham 75.00
Plymouth, Salt Spoon, Watson, Master 20.00
Plymouth, Sardine Fork, Gorham 60.00
Plymouth, Teaspoon, Gorham 10.00
Pompadour, Asparagus Fork, Whiting 275.00
Pompadour, Cheese Scoop, Whiting 90.00
Pompadour, Cream Soup Spoon, Whiting 25.00

Pompadour, Ice Cream Fork, Whiting 35.00
Pompadour, Youth Set, Whiting, 3 Piece 135.00
Prelude, Cream Soup Spoon, International 11.00
Prelude, Luncheon Fork, International 17.00
Prelude, Service For 8, International, 48 Piece 1050.00
Priscilla, Cake & Waffle Server, Wallace 70.00
Puritan, Cold Meat Fork, Stieff 40.00
Queen Elizabeth, Food Pusher, Towle 58.00
Radiant, Asparagus Server, 7 Tine, Whiting 275.00
Raphael, Berry Spoon, Alvin 450.00
Regent, Fork, Alvin, 6 7/8 In. 14.00
Renaissance, Sauce Ladle, Dominick & Haff 40.00
Repousse, Asparagus Serving Fork, Kirk 525.00
Repousse, Cheese Spreader, Stieff 28.00
Repousse, Cream Ladle, Kirk 40.00
Repousse, Demitasse Spoon, Kirk 12.00
Repousse, Gravy Ladle, Kirk 65.00
Repousse, Ice Tongs, Kirk 125.00
Repousse, Oyster Fork, Kirk, 6 Piece 195.00
Repousse, Salad Fork, Kirk 25.00
Repousse, Tablespoon, Kirk 50.00
Revere, Jelly Cake Server, International 295.00
Rhapsody, Cheese Server, International 20.00
Rhapsody, Cocktail Fork, International 18.00
Rhapsody, Slotted Spoon, International 40.00
Rococo, Dessert Spoon, Dominick & Haff 30.00
Rococo, Orange Spoon, Dominick & Haff 22.00
Rococo, Oyster Server, Dominick & Haff 150.00
Rococo, Teaspoon, Dominick & Haff 22.00
Romance of The Sea, Knife, Wallace, 9 3/4 In. 30.00
Romance of The Sea, Teaspoon, Wallace 17.00
Romance of The Stars, Spoon, Slotted, Fine Arts 30.00
Rose, Asparagus Fork, Stieff 575.00
Rose, Cake Server, Stieff 25.00
Rose, Cream Soup Spoon, Stieff 18.00
Rose, Sugar Shell, Stieff 13.00
Royal Danish, Gravy Ladle, International 65.00
Silver Plumes, Gravy Ladle, Towle 40.00
Snowflake, Service For 8, International, 52 Piece 665.00
Sonja, Service For 8, International, 32 Piece 560.00
Spanish Lace, Service For 12, Wallace, 60 Piece 1176.00
Spring Glory, Gravy Ladle, International 44.00
St.Cloud, Coffee Spoon, Gorham 18.00
St.Cloud, Dinner Fork, Gorham 27.00
St.Cloud, Serving Spoon, Gorham 37.00
St.Cloud, Teaspoon, Gorham 18.00
Stradivari, Service For 12, Wallace 2200.00
Strasbourg, Mustard Ladle, Gorham 95.00
Tapestry, Salad Fork, Reed & Barton 22.00
Tara, Service For 12, Reed & Barton, 60 Piece 1275.00
Trianon, Chocolate Spoon, Dominick & Haff, 6 Pc. 175.00
Trianon, Cream Ladle, Dominick & Haff 85.00
Trojan, Fish Serving Set, Reed & Barton 295.00
Tuileries, Soup Ladle, Gorham 175.00
Versailles, Fork, Gorham, 6 3/4 In. 29.00
Versailles, Ladle, Gorham, C.1900 .... 225.00
Versailles, Stuffing Spoon, Gorham 700.00
Vintage, Punch Ladle, Double Lip Bowl, Wallace 200.00
Violet, Cheese Scoop, Whiting 225.00
Violet, Food Pusher, Whiting 75.00
Violet, Horseradish Spoon, Wallace 55.00
Violet, Ice Cream Fork, Whiting 35.00
Virginia Carvel, Bonbon Spoon, Towle 20.00
Virginia Carvel, Cold Meat Fork, Towle, 9 1/2 In. 40.00

Silver Plate, Bowl, Nut, Squirrel,
Meriden Britannia, 1875

Clean silver with any acceptable commercial polish. Don't use household scouring powder on silver, no matter how stubborn the spot may be. Use a tarnish-retarding silver polish to keep your silver clean. It will not harm old solid or plated wares. Do not use "instant" silver polishes.

Virginia Carvel, Cucumber Server, Towle	30.00
Virginia Carvel, Gravy Ladle, Towle	36.00
Wild Rose, Iced Tea Spoon, Reed & Barton, 12 Pc.	300.00
Wildflower, Fork, Royal Crest	24.00
Wildflower, Teaspoon, Royal Crest	16.00
William & Mary, Fork, Lunt, 7 In.	19.00
Willow, Sauce Ladle, Gorham	28.00
Wood Lily, Pie Knife, Flat, Smith	175.00

Ⓔ Ⓟ Ⓝ Ⓢ   Silver plate is not solid silver. It is a ware made of a metal, such as nickel or copper, that is covered with a thin coating of silver. The letters "EPNS" are often found on American and English silver plated wares. Sheffield silver is a type of silver plate.

SILVER PLATE, Basket, Repousse, E.G.Webster & Son, N.Y.	65.00
Basket, Rope Bail Handle, Punch Work, Simpson, Hall & Miller	550.00
Basket, Wilcox Quadruple, Bird, Animals, Handle, 1890	65.00
Bowl, Nut, Squirrel, Meriden Britannia, 1875 ....*Illus*	1090.00
Box, Collar Button, Footed, 2 1/2 In.	20.00
Box, Hairpin, Hinged Lid, 4 Ball Feet, Floral Scrolls, Webster	24.00
Box, Scalloped Lid, Repousse Children, Metz, C.1790, 2 1/4 In.	38.00
Butter, Engraved Dome Cover, Insert, Rogers & Smith	60.00
Butter, Figural, Lady, Cherub On Handles, Pedestal, Victorian	800.00
Butter, Swivel Lid, Glass Insert, 4 5/8 X 5 In.	40.00
Caddy, Mustard, Victorian, Glass, Metal Filigree Holder, Spoon	45.00
Cake Basket, Forbes Silver Co.	35.00
Candelabra, 3–Light, Matthew Boulton, C.1825, 24 3/4 In., Pair	3025.00
Candelabrum, 4–Light, Sheffield, C.1815, 29 3/4 In., Pair	3575.00
Candlestick, Columnar, Acorns, Oak Leaves, 12 1/2 In., Pair	470.00
Candlestick, Columnar, George III Style, Husk Swag, 9 In., Pr.	440.00
Candlestick, Georgian, Corinthian Columns, Square, 14 In., Pair	100.00
Candlestick, Stepped, Electrified, English, 1900, 32 In., Pair	1320.00
Card Receiver, Tray, Girl With Bonnet, Dog, Wilcox, 8 In.	215.00
Carving Set, Stag Horn Handles, Steel Blades, 16 3/4 In.	35.00
Castor, Pickle, Tongs, Crystal Insert	110.00
Castor, Pickle, Tongs, Daisy & Button Jar	255.00
Cheese Scoop, Assyrian Head, 8 3/4 In.	58.00
Coaster, Wine, George III Style, Engraved Swags, 5 In., Pair	247.00
Coffee Urn, Acorn Shape, Looped Handles, Sheffield, 18 In.	500.00
Coffeepot, Leaf & Floral Designs, Swivel Stand, C.1890	275.00
Cover, Meat, Inlaid Coat of Arms, Sheffield, 11 1/2 X 19 In.	230.00
Creamer, Figural, Cow, Cover, Collis & Co., C.1850, 6 7/8 In.	825.00
Demitasse Pot, Hinged Lid, Braid Design, Sheffield, 7 1/4 In.	45.00

Dish, Entree, Cover, 1810, Engraved Crest, Sheffield, 11 In. 250.00
Dish, Ice Cream Sundae, Reed & Barton, 4 1/2 In., 6 Piece 90.00
Egg Caddy, Center–Handled Tray Holds 4 Spoons, Rogers 50.00
English, Server, Hot Water Reservoir, Sheffield, C.1800 .... 3850.00
Goblet, Wine, Gold Wash Inside, Engraved Grapes, Leaves, 8 Pc. 40.00
Hair Receiver, Repousse, Wilcox 25.00
Holder, Figural, Cherub, Holds Sapphire Bud Vase, Middletown 150.00
Hot Water Urn, Pagodas, Trees, Sheffield, C.1810, 16 3/8 In. 715.00
Humidor, Boy, Lying On Back, Top Hat For Matches, Meriden 250.00
Mirror & Brush Set, Art Nouveau Floral, Derby, Dated 1900 .... 48.00
Mirror, Hand, Art Nouveau, Children's Faces, Wings In Relief 90.00
Mirror, Hand, Art Nouveau, Ornate Flowers, 11 X 5 In. 75.00
  SILVER PLATE, NAPKIN RING, see Napkin Ring
Nut Basket, Figural, Simpson, Hall & Miller, 4 X 6 1/2 In. 60.00
Pitcher, Vintage Designs, Marked Hand Chased, 10 3/4 In. 95.00
Platter, Meat, George III, Engraved Crest, 22 1/4 In. 467.00
Platter, Well & Tree, Gadrooned Rim, Gorham, 16 X 23 1/2 In. 145.00
Platter, Well & Tree, Reed & Barton, 22 1/2 In. 137.00
Punch Bowl & Ladle, Band of Arabesques, Lion Masks, English 700.00
Salt, Lion's Head, Footed 23.00
Server, Cover, 2 Sections, Paw Feet, 19 In. 110.00
Spoon, Folding, Bone Handles, 6 3/4 In. 5.00
  SILVER PLATE, SPOON, SOUVENIR, see Souvenir, Spoon, Silver Plate
Spooner, Bird Finial, Rogers, 1901, 9 In. 28.00
Stand, Perfume, Applied Leaves, Holds Bristol Bottle, Meriden 225.00
Sugar & Creamer, Hotel McAlpin 20.00
Sugar & Creamer, Tuft 35.00
Sugar Bowl Spoon Holder, Bird, Squirrels In Handles, 12 Hooks 65.00
Syrup, Figural, Child Blowing Horn On Hinged Lid 45.00
Tankard, Ornate, Porcelain Lined, Woodman Cook Co., 13 X 7 In. 195.00
Tazza, Cut Glass, Swan, Reeded Pedestal, 11 X 8 3/4 In., Pair 2000.00
Tea & Coffee Set, 22–In.Tray, Paneled Design, Orivit, 6 Piece 2200.00
Tea Set, Rogers, Smith & Co., C.1875, 7 Piece ....*Illus* 605.00
Toast Rack, English, Christopher Dresser, 1878 .... 7900.00
Toothpick, Village Pump, Simulated Wood Trough, 1880, 5 In. 155.00
Tray, Bread, Ornate Openwork Rim, Hartford 55.00
Tray, Gadrooned Rim, Gallery, Wooden Bottom, Sheffield, 20 In. 85.00
Tray, Galleried, Engraved Design, Elkington, Oval, 24 X 17 In. 275.00
Tray, Stylized Floral Engraving, Key Fret, Oval, 30 In. 20.00
Tray, Tea, Curling Handles, Acanthus, Horse, Motto, 25 In. 715.00
Tureen, Neo–Classical Design, Floral Swags, 8 1/4 In. 55.00
Vase, Rose, Trumpet Form, American, C.1910 .... 160.00

Silver Plate, Tea Set, Rogers, Smith & Co., C.1875, 7 Piece

Waiter, Engraved Crest, 2 Handles, 27 In.	138.00
Waiter, Key Fret, Stylized Floral, American Aesthetic, 30 In.	20.00
Wine Coaster, Vintage Design, English, 4 Piece	220.00
Wine Cooler, English, 7 1/2 In., Pair	430.00
Wine Cooler, Lion Mask & Ring Handles, C.1800, 7 1/2 In., Pair	1980.00
Wine Cooler, Tree Form Handles, English, 10 In., Pair	935.00

SILVER, SHEFFIELD, see Silver Plate; Silver–English

The silver listed in this book is subdivided by country. Silver–American is the first listing, followed by Silver–Austrian, Silver–Canadian, Silver–Chinese, Silver–Danish, etc. There are also other pieces of silver and silver plate listed under special categories, such as Napkin Ring or Tiffany, and under Silver Flatware.

SILVER–AMERICAN, see also Tiffany Silver; Silver–Sterling

SILVER–AMERICAN, Basket, Footed, Cobalt Liner, Watson, 3 X 5 In.	75.00
Basket, Fruit, Meadows & Co., C.1835	1100.00
Basket, Pierced Loop Design, Whiting, C.1915, 21 1/4 In.	2090.00
Beaker, J.Watts, Philadelphia, C.1835	595.00
Beaker, Monogram JMH, Cylindrical, Garner, 3 1/2 In., Pair	1320.00
Bell, Lobed Body, Cherub Heads, Gorham, C.1890, 4 3/8 In.	660.00
Bowl, 3 Ball Feet, Applied Band, Grimm, 6 In.	425.00
Bowl, 5 Vertical Bands, Fruits, Leaves, Tiffany & Co., 9 In.	1325.00
Bowl, Cyma Border, Footed, Gorham, 10 In.	130.00
Bowl, Dessert, Bird's Wing, Spencer Orgell, 22 In.	2650.00
Bowl, Double Flutes, Ball–Footed, Cellini Craft, 10 In.	2350.00
Bowl, Flared, Hammered, Seth Ek, 1907, 3 1/2 In.	140.00
Bowl, Flared, Repousse Panels, Footed, Glendenning, 6 In.	3100.00
Bowl, Fluted, 6 Sections, Self–Footed, Grimm, 10 In.	895.00
Bowl, Fluted, Hammered, Chicago Silver Co., 9 In.	1350.00
Bowl, Fruit, Footed, Repousse, C.1853 ....*Illus*	4400.00
Bowl, Fruit, Scroll & Floral Border, Gorham, 9 3/4 In.	200.00
Bowl, Fruit, Shell Border, Monogram, Gorham, 1870, 10 In.	495.00
Bowl, Punch, Circular Foot, 1907, Tiffany & Co., 13 In.	3525.00
Bowl, Ripple Design, William Waldo Dodge Jr., 11 In.	1375.00
Bowl, Self–Formed Foot, Pronounced Hammering, Grimm, 6 In.	225.00
Bowl, Serpentine, Flowers & Leaves, 4–Footed, Gorham, 11 In.	4950.00
Bowl, Server, Arrowhead, Hammered, Gaylord, 6 In.	65.00
Bowl, Stand, Crest, Engraved, Crichton & Co., 12 In.	1875.00
Bowl, Trophy, 1921, 2 Handles, Crichton & Co., 9 In.	1200.00
Box, Cigar, Scrolled, 1890, Bailey, Banks & Biddle, 9 In.	2875.00
Box, Cigarette & Lighter, 1940, Cartier, 7 In.	3100.00
Box, Enamel Design, Holmes & Edward, C.1898, 1 X 1 3/4 In.	110.00
Bread Tray, Everted Rim, Dominick & Haff, 1901, 16 1/2 In.	600.00
Bread Tray, Self–Footed, Applied Rim, Grimm, 12 In.	425.00
Butter Pick, Orient, Alvin	42.00
Butter, Cover, Waved Rims, Gorham, 1887, 5 1/2 In., Pair	2200.00
Cake Basket, Grapes & Vines, Bail Handle, Marquand, 11 In.	4950.00
Cake Server, S.Coctrell, Mississippi, C.1860	280.00
Candelabra, 3–Light, Reed & Barton, Pair	220.00
Candle Stand, Triangular, 1947, Tiffany & Co., 9 In.	550.00
Candlestick, Fan Shape, William Durgin, 10 In., Pair	1950.00
Candlestick, Hurricane Insert, Towle, Pair	135.00
Candlestick, King's Pattern, Reed & Barton, 12 1/4 In., Pr.	550.00
Candlestick, Reed & Barton, C.1900, 10 1/4 In., Pair	750.00
Candy Dish, Leaf Form, Stem Handle, Allan Adler	575.00
Casket, Jewel, Figural Cherub, Seated, Mechanical, Rogers	450.00
Casket, Jewel, Hinged, Lined, 1940, Cartier, 14 In.	3410.00
Centerpiece, Palm Tree, Webb & Co., 1880, 19 In. ....*Illus*	4950.00
Centerpiece, Pierced, Border, Footed, Gorham, C.1870, 13 In.	400.00
Centerpiece, Repousse, Chased Flowers, S.Kirk, 11 X 18 In.	3100.00
Chalice, Crosses, Red, Blue, Green, Black, 1930, 7 In.	1100.00
Cheese Scoop, Chantilly Pattern, Durgin	165.00
Coaster, Sunburst Cut Glass Insert, Frank N.Whiting, 8 Pc.	65.00
Coffee & Tea Set, Foliate & Scroll, Gorham, C.1890, 7 Pc.	2750.00

Silver–American, Bowl, Fruit, Footed, Repousse, C.1853

Silver–American, Coffee Set, Lobed, Floral, 10–In.Pot, 3 Piece

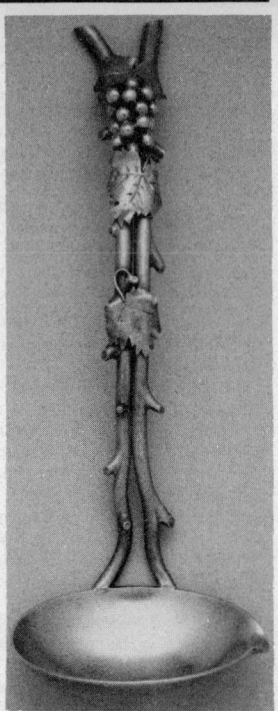

Silver–American, Ladle, Punch, Gilt, C.1855

Silver–American, Mirror, Dressing Table, Dominick & Haff, 17 In.

Silver–American, Centerpiece, Palm Tree, Webb & Co., 1880, 19 In.

Silver–American, Creamer, H.Potter, C.1900, 6 In.

Coffee & Tea Set, Globular, Samuel Kirk, 1824–29, 4 Piece	4950.00
Coffee & Tea Set, Lancaster Rose, Poole, C.1940, 6 Piece	3000.00
Coffee & Tea Set, Swags, Black, Starr & Frost, 1910, 6 Pc.	8250.00
Coffee & Tea Set, Tray, Gorham, C.1910, 8 Piece	6600.00
Coffee & Tea Set, Tray, Theodore Starr, 1900–24, 7 Piece	6000.00
Coffee Service, Pointed Antique, Reed & Barton, 5 Piece	6000.00
Coffee Set, Lobed, Floral, 10–In.Pot, 3 Piece ....*Illus*	2310.00
Coffeepot & Teapot, Bright Cut, J.Sayre, C.1805, 9 7/8 In.	1550.00
Coffeepot, Baluster, Acanthus Handle, Wriggins, 11 1/2 In.	665.00
Coffeepot, Lily–of–The–Valley, Domed, R.Williams, 11 In.	1765.00
Compote, Champagne Glass Form, 1910, Shreve & Co., 12 In.	1100.00
Compote, Pierced, Monogram, Dominick & Haff, 9 X 4 In.	700.00
Creamer, Diamond Design, W.Thomson, C.1809, 6 3/8 In.	475.00
Creamer, Double Handle, 3–Footed, Jacob G.Lansing, C.1750	6050.00
Creamer, H.Potter, C.1900, 6 In. ....*Illus*	400.00
Creamer, Shell Feet, Theodore B.Starr, C.1900, 3 1/2 In.	145.00
Crumber, Oval Thread, A.Coles, C.1850, 13 1/4 In.	295.00
Cup, Chased Foliage, Adolph Himmel, New Orleans, 4 Oz.	690.00
Cup, Foliate, Engraved, 3 Handles, Reed & Barton, 8 In.	500.00
Decanter, Scrolled Over Glass, Faceted Stopper, 1900	700.00
Dish, Kensington Style, Arthur Stone, 6 In.	465.00
Dish, Leaf & Bead Design, Handles, Cellini Craft, 7 X 9 In.	650.00
Dish, Leaf Form, Stem Handle, Alfredo Sciarotta, 12 In.	495.00
Dish, Sideboard, Digby, Scott & Benjamin Smith, 1805	9350.00
Dresser Set, Repousse, Powder Jar, Dominick & Haff, 3 Pc.	325.00
Dressing Table Set, Traveling, 1915, Tiffany & Co.	2545.00
Egg Coddler, Stand, Ball, Tomkins & Black, C.1850, 15 In.	2400.00
Ewer, Presentation, Bigelow, Kennard & Co., C.1851, Large	1500.00
Fish Server, Tuscan Pattern, Ball, Thompson, Black, 1833	275.00
Fish Slice & Fork, Dolphins, Engraved Blade, A.Cole	595.00
Fish Slice, Scroll, Floral Handle, Marked Shiebler, 12 In.	195.00
Flagon, Baluster, Scroll Handle, Cooper, 1840–51, 12 7/8 In.	1100.00
Flagon, Pear Shape, Francis W.Cooper, C.1850, 13 In.	550.00
Flask, Basket Weave, Glass, Hinged Cap, Gorham, 6 1/2 In.	385.00
Flask, Racehorse & Jockey, ADB Monogram, Gorham, 1885, 8 In.	2450.00
Food Pusher, Scrolling Leaf Design, Webster	50.00
Fork & Knife, Baby, Bunny Rabbits, Lewis Wise, 4 In.	225.00
Fork, Dinner, Hayden & Brother Co., C.1840, 6 Piece	245.00
Fork, Dinner, Onslow Design, Porter Blanchard, 8 In.	95.00
Fork, Meat, 2 Lions Across Neck, Porter Blanchard, 9 In.	135.00
Fork, Seafood, Lily–of–The–Valley, Whiting, C.1900, 12 Pc.	175.00
Fork, Serving, Notched Neck, Porter Blanchard, 10 In.	350.00
Frame, Nouveau, Mother–of–Pearl, Easel, Marcus, 5 X 8 In.	4180.00
Fruit Knife, Reeded Handle, Gorham, Case, C.1900, 12 Piece	140.00
Goblet, Prelude Pattern, International, 12 Piece	1100.00
Goblet, Wine, Hand Hammered, Whiting, 1923, 5 In., 12 Piece	575.00
Hook, Chatelaine, Heart Shape, Chain, 1795–1800, 2 1/2 In.	345.00
Jam Jar, Cover, Bombe Shape, Colin V.G.Forbes, C.1820, 7 In.	1750.00
Jug, Milk, Hyde & Goodrich, C.1850	750.00
Julep Cup, Hudson & Dolfinger, Beading, C.1854, 3 3/4 In.	650.00
Julep Cup, Hyde & Goodrich, Marked New Orleans, C.1850	475.00
Julep Cup, Jones, Shreve, Brown & Co., C.1854, 2 7/8 In.	450.00
Kettle, On Lampstand, Swing Handle, Obadiah Rich, C.1840	1650.00
Ladle, Condiment, A.Sanborn, Lowell	30.00
Ladle, Condiment, J.J.Rider, Salem	30.00
Ladle, Condiment, Palme & Bachelder	30.00
Ladle, Fiddle & Thread Pattern, H.P.Buckley, New Orleans	660.00
Ladle, Fiddle, Coin Silver, Conning, 1840–65, 14 In.	950.00
Ladle, Fiddleback, Wm.Kendrick, Louisville, Ky.	495.00
Ladle, Gold–Washed Bowl, N.G.Wood & Son, 7 1/4 In., Pair	155.00
Ladle, Gravy, Fiddle, Coin Silver, O & AK Childs, 1857–61	375.00
Ladle, Mustard, A.F.Burband, C.1840	30.00
Ladle, Mustard, B.Pitman, C.1840	30.00
Ladle, Mustard, Coffin Fiddle, J.Boutier, C.1810	78.00

Ladle, Mustard, Gurney Bros., C.1840	30.00
Ladle, Mustard, H.G.Stone, C.1840	35.00
Ladle, Mustard, J.Blackman & Co., Conn., C.1835	32.00
Ladle, Mustard, S.Brown, C.1830	30.00
Ladle, Mustard, Wreath of Flowers, J.Fries, C.1825	75.00
Ladle, Punch, Fontainebleau, Inscribed, Gorham, 1880	225.00
Ladle, Punch, Gilt, C.1855 ....*Illus*	2200.00
Ladle, Punch, J.Musgrave, Philadelphia, C.1790, 16 In.	675.00
Ladle, Punch, Medallion, Twist Handle, Bailey & Co., 1870	450.00
Ladle, Punch, R.E.Smith, C.1830	412.50
Ladle, Sauce, Prince Albert, Bennett & Caldwall, C.1850	75.00
Ladle, Soup, C.H.Zimmermann, C.1854	250.00
Ladle, Soup, Coin, Medallion, Schulz & Fischer, 1868, 13 In.	465.00
Ladle, Soup, J.McMullin, C.1850	750.00
Ladle, Soup, Oval End, Shreve, Crump & Low, 12 1/2 In.	250.00
Letter Opener, Relief of Flowers, Jacobi & Jenkins, 7 In.	125.00
Loving Cup, 3 Handles, Art Nouveau, Gorham, 12 In.	2200.00
Match Box Cover, On Ashtray, Repousse, Kirk, 3 Piece	75.00
Mirror, Dressing Table, Dominick & Haff, 17 In. ....*Illus*	1320.00
Mirror, Heart Shape, Cherubs, Dominick & Haff, 17 1/2 In.	1650.00
Mug, Chased Hoops, Scroll Handle, Joseph Lownes, C.1810	3025.00
Pitcher, Allover Floral, Handle & Cover, Sam L.Kirk, 17 In.	2700.00
Pitcher, Engraved Floral Belt, Dominick & Haff, 9 In.	650.00
Pitcher, Faceted Vase Shape, Square Handle, Gorham, 9 In.	450.00
Pitcher, Grapevine Design, Marked, 1899, 8 7/8 In.	6875.00
Pitcher, Leaf & Bead Ornaments, 1920, Randahl Shop, 9 In.	975.00
Pitcher, Leaf Bead Handle, Cellini Craft, 8 In.	2400.00
Pitcher, Pedestal Base, Thomas Shields, C.1770, 5 In.	1650.00
Pitcher, Vase Shape, Domed Cover, Churchill, 1815, 11 In.	1540.00
Pitcher, Water, Baluster Body, S-Form Handle, 7 In.	750.00
Pitcher, Water, C-Scroll Handle, Floral, Dominick & Haff	650.00
Pitcher, Water, Flared Shape, Loop Handle, Chicago, 9 In.	4100.00
Pitcher, Water, Hexagonally Paneled	4100.00
Pitcher, Water, Lord Saybrook Pattern, Meriden Co., 8 In.	600.00
Pitcher, Wedgwood Pattern, International, 4 1/2 Pts.	225.00
Platter, Oval, Engraved Border, Beaded Rim, 19 In.	275.00
Porringer, Blossom & Leaf Design, Chicago Silver Co.	475.00
Porringer, Bowed Sides, William Simpkins, C.1730, 5 In.	1450.00
Porringer, Lion Crest, John Edwards, C.1724	2700.00
Porringer, Pierced Handle, John Burt, C.1720, 5 1/8 In.	1450.00
Porringer, Pierced Keyhole Handle, RH Engraved, 8 X 5 In.	1200.00
Porringer, Pierced, Heart Design, Franklin Porter, 7 In.	595.00
Powder Jar, Silk & Feather Puff, Gorham, C.1900	200.00
Punch Bowl, Ladle, Fluted Sides, Grimm, 11 In.	2900.00
Punch Bowl, Repousse & Chased Flowers, Kirk, C.1900, 9 In.	2475.00
Punch Bowl, Ring Handle, Shields, 1930, Meriden, 18 In.	3850.00
Salad Set, Empire, Theodore Starr, C.1894	110.00
Salt, Open, Grapes & Leaves, P.Krider, Pair	425.00
Salver, Floral, Shell Feet, Bailey & Co., C.1848, 6 5/8 In.	495.00
Sauce Boat, Handle Edge, Openwork, Allan Adler, 3 X 7 In.	975.00
Scoop, Cheese, Chantilly Pattern, Durgin	165.00
Server, Jelly, Leaf Shape, Gaylord, 6 1/2 In.	65.00
Serving Set, Chop, Swedish Modern, Allan Adler, 2 Pc.	495.00
Serving Set, Salad, Diamond Etched, Porter Blanchard, 9 In.	695.00
Shoehorn, Flowers, Pierced Hole At End, 6 In.	125.00
Spoon, Berry, Beggs & Smith, C.1840	120.00
Spoon, Bright Cut, E.Burr, C.1800, 9 1/2 In.	58.00
Spoon, Bright Cut, N.Geffroy, Newport, R.I., 1800, 9 3/8 In.	145.00
Spoon, Citrus, Clark & Biddle, C.1870, 12 Piece	795.00
Spoon, Coffin End, Dyer & Eddy, C.1805, 10 In.	45.00
Spoon, Dessert, Fiddle Tip, Bailey & Parker, 7 1/4 In., Pr.	50.00
Spoon, Dessert, Fiddle Tip, C.A.W.Crisby, 7 1/4 In.	22.00
Spoon, Dessert, Fiddle, J.E.Munger, C.1839, 7 5/8 In.	45.00

Spoon, Dessert, P.Dickenson, 7 1/4 In. 22.00
Spoon, Dessert, Pinched Fiddle, P.Carleton, 7 7/8 In. 25.00
Spoon, Dessert, R.Putney, C.1812, 7 1/2 In. 55.00
Spoon, Dressing, Fiddle Thread, JBA, Gregg Hayden, 1846–52 .... 475.00
Spoon, Fiddle, Finless, C.Brewer, C.1824, 9 3/8 In. 40.00
Spoon, Fiddle, Finned, J.H.Chedell, C.1827, 9 1/2 In. 24.00
Spoon, Fiddle, Shell Back, W. Walker, C.1810, 9 1/2 In. 65.00
Spoon, Martini, Hammered, Applied Monogram, Kalo, 13 3/4 In. 150.00
Spoon, Oval End, S.Williamson, C.1795, 9 1/2 In. 85.00
Spoon, Pitcher, Pointed End, Porter Blanchard, 12 In. 135.00
Spoon, Salt, J.Musgrave, C.1790, Pair 160.00
Spoon, Salt, Master, Art Nouveau Flower, Arrow Mark 45.00
Spoon, Salt, Olive, H.Harker, C.1850, Pair 45.00
Spoon, Salt, Shell Bowl, Bright Cut, Standish Barry, 1795 .... 75.00
Spoon, Salt, Shell Bowl, Fiddle Tip, Hotchkiss, Schroeder 30.00
Spoon, Serving, Pierced, Porter Blanchard, 10 In. 350.00
Spoon, Soup, Bigelow Bros. & Kinnard, Boston, C.1845 .... 18.00
Spoon, Soup, Fiddleback, O.D.Seymour, Hartford, C.1850 .... 25.00
Spoon, Soup, Henry Gooding, Boston, 1830 .... 15.00
Spoon, Soup, Monogrammed, John Lynch, C.1830, 12 Piece 600.00
Spoon, Soup, Onslow, Engraved, Porter Blanchard, 6 In. 85.00
Spoon, Star, Monogram H, Coin Silver, D.B.Hempsted 20.00
Spoon, Stuffing, Fiddle Thread, Gale, Wood & Hughes, C.1850 .... 100.00
Spoon, Stuffing, Sunset Pattern, Allan Adler, 14 1/2 In. 350.00
Spoon, Tea Caddy, Shovel Bowl, Scalloped, Coin Silver, 4 In. 75.00
Spoon, U.S.Capitol Building, Coin Silver, Leonard & Wilson 225.00
Sugar & Creamer, Acanthus Design, John B.Jones, Boston 700.00
Sugar & Creamer, Applied Strap Rim, Shreve, 3 In. 475.00
Sugar & Creamer, Beaded Rims, Wreath Design, Gorham 165.00
Sugar & Creamer, Melon, Gadroon, Ball Feet, C.L. Boehme 2150.00
Sugar & Creamer, Pardon Miller, C.1822, 6 3/8 In. 800.00
Sugar & Creamer, Rose Point, Wallace 175.00
Sugar Basket, Medallion, Bail Handle, Krider, C.1860, 7 In. 528.00
Sugar Shell, B.S. Farringon, Rhode Island, C.1850 .... 30.00
Sugar Shell, Bright Cut Handle, Lena, A.F. Adams, 6 In. 32.00
Sugar Shell, Coe & Upton, H.I. Sawyer, N.Y., C.1850 .... 30.00
Sugar Shell, Fiddle Tip Handle, N. Harding & Co. 28.00
Sugar Shell, Hotchkiss & Schreuder, Syracuse, C.1850 .... 30.00
Sugar Shell, O.D. Seymour, Hartford, Conn., C.1850 .... 30.00
Sugar Shell, Scalloped Bowl, Marked F & H, 7 In. 30.00
Sugar Shell, Scalloped Bowl, Snell & Scott, 1840, 6 3/4 In. 38.00
Sugar Shell, Shovel Shape, Norton & Seymour, 6 1/2 In. 30.00
Sugar Shell, Swift & Truman, C.1840 .... 30.00
Sugar Shell, Willard & Hawley, Syracuse, C.1845 .... 30.00
Sugar Shell, Wood & Hughes, N.Y., Humboldt Pattern, C.1860 .... 35.00
Sugar Sifter Ladle, Threaded, Sterling Silver Mfg.Co. 20.00
Sugar Sifter Spoon, R. Blackington, 4 5/8 In. 20.00
Sugar Tongs, Basket of Flowers, Benedict & Scudder, C.1825 .... 175.00
Sugar Tongs, Bright Cut, B. Wenman, New York City, C.1805 .... 150.00
Sugar Tongs, Bright Cut, S.Alexander, Philadelphia, C.1790 .... 125.00
Sugar Tongs, Fiddle, H. Lewis, Philadelphia, C.1820 .... 75.00
Sugar Tongs, H. Porter & Co., New York City, C.1830 .... 175.00
Sugar Tongs, I. Kenkins, Albany, N.Y., C.1813 .... 125.00
Sugar Tongs, M. Pettit, New York City, C.1810 .... 75.00
Sugar Tongs, Mood & Ewan, C.1825 .... 125.00
Sugar Tongs, Sheaf of Wheat, B. Benjamin, N.Y., C.1825 .... 175.00
Sugar Tongs, Sheaf of Wheat, C. Brewer & Co., C.1825 .... 125.00
Sugar Tongs, Stylized Tulip Bowl, Hammered, P. Blanchard 50.00
Sugar, Cover, Chased Fruit, C.Terfloth & Kichler, 7 1/2 In. 2300.00
Sugar, Cover, Repousse, S–Scroll Handles, A.E. Warner, 5 In. 475.00
Sugar, Cover, Urn Shape, Gallery Edge, Pineapple, Marked INR 5500.00
Sugar, Flower Finial, A.E. Warner, Jr., C.1865, 5 1/2 In. 475.00
Sugar, Rococo Repousse, Gorham, Dated 1903 .... 180.00
Tablespoon, Basket of Flowers, J.O.Beebe, C.1833, 8 7/8 In. 55.00

Tablespoon, Basket of Flowers, L. Brock, 1830, 8 3/4 In. 40.00
Tablespoon, Bird Back, G. Walker, Philadelphia, C.1790 .... 195.00
Tablespoon, Bird Back, S. Richards, Philadelphia, C.1790 .... 165.00
Tablespoon, Bird Back, S. Williamson, C.1790 .... 195.00
Tablespoon, Coffin End, J.Ridgway, C.1800, 9 1/4 In. 60.00
Tablespoon, Coffin End, Ward & Bartholomew, 1804, 8 3/4 In. 60.00
Tablespoon, Daniel Russell, C.1742, 8 1/4 In. 795.00
Tablespoon, Eagle, Wm. Rogers, 8 3/4 In., Pair 60.00
Tablespoon, Fiddle Thread, J. Stockman, C.1828, 8 1/2 In. 60.00
Tablespoon, Fiddle Tip, E.E. Bailey, 8 3/4 In. 30.00
Tablespoon, Fiddle, Robert Wilson, C.1803, 8 7/8 In. 55.00
Tablespoon, H & B, Shell Back, Fiddle Shell, 8 1/2 In. 40.00
Tablespoon, H. Nichols, Flared Handle, C.1839, 8 5/8 In. 38.00
Tablespoon, Mobile, Coin Silver, Fiddle, Conning, 8 1/2 In. 75.00
Tablespoon, Oval End, John Proctor Trott, C.1795, 8 3/8 In. 110.00
Tablespoon, Oval End, Thomas Underhill, 8 In. 300.00
Tablespoon, Peter Vergereau, Double Drop, C.1721, 8 1/8 In. 300.00
Tablespoon, Radian, Whiting, C.1896, 4 Piece 135.00
Tablespoon, Rattail, John Edwards, C.1700, 7 1/8 In. 575.00
Tablespoon, Reverse Tip, G.G.Clark, 8 1/4 In., Pair 75.00
Tablespoon, Slashed Drop, Samuel Parmelee, C.1760, 8 In. 475.00
Tankard, Hinged Lid, Silver Mounts, Gorham, 7 3/4 In. 1485.00
Tazza, Ribbed Border, Engraved, Crichton & Co., 7 In., Pair 440.00
Tea & Coffee Set, Ovoid Forms, Gorham, 5 Piece 500.00
Tea Set, Floral Borders, Bennett & Caldwell, C.1844, 3 Pc. 1200.00
Tea Set, Repousse Grapes, Leaves, Shreve & Co., 10 In. 440.00
Tea Set, Squared Handles, Maynard & Potter, 1920s, 6 Piece 2100.00
Tea Set, Stylized Flowers, Ivory Finial, Hartwell, 3 Piece 4950.00
Tea Set, Urn Finials, William Gale & Son., C.1850, 4 Piece 1550.00
Tea Set, Vase Shape, Ball, Tompkins & Black, C.1845, 4 Piece 1650.00
Tea Strainer & Stand, Grimm, 1 X 7 In. 225.00
Tea Urn, Domed Cover, Pineapple, 2 Rings, Gebelein, 16 In. 5300.00
Teapot, Baluster Finial, Whiting, Dated 1877, 5 3/4 In. 550.00
Teapot, Domed Lid, Ribbon Finials, Boston, C.1861, 8 In. 300.00
Teapot, Lobed Urn Form, J. Sayre, C.1810, 10 3/4 In. 1325.00
Teaspoon, Anthony Rasch, Monogrammed, C.1821, 12 Piece 2860.00
Teaspoon, Basket of Flowers, B.C. Frobisher, Pair 75.00
Teaspoon, Basket of Flowers, H. Gooding, C.1830, 5 1/8 In. 30.00
Teaspoon, Bird Back, Moore & Ferguson, C.1800, 6 Piece 495.00
Teaspoon, Coffin End, J. Clark, C.1807, 5 3/8 In. 35.00
Teaspoon, Coffin End, J. McFarlane, C.1800 .... 45.00
Teaspoon, Coffin End, Mv. Homes, Jr., C.1800, 5 5/8 In. 35.00
Teaspoon, Eagle Back, J. Kucher, Philadelphia, C.1790 .... 95.00
Teaspoon, Fiddle Tip, A.W. Stearns, 6 Piece 95.00
Teaspoon, Fiddle Tip, T.M. Lamb, 9 Piece 135.00
Teaspoon, Fiddle, J.B. McFadden, C.1840, 5 7/8 In. 28.00
Teaspoon, Fiddle, J.H. Chedell, C.1827, 5 1/2 In. 14.00
Teaspoon, Fiddle, M. Merriman, C.1820, 6 1/8 In. 15.00
Teaspoon, Figural, Nude Handle, Unger Bros. 35.00
Teaspoon, J.S. Porter, Utica, 1805 .... 14.00
Teaspoon, James Hansell, Philadelphia, 1816–50, 6 Piece 225.00
Teaspoon, Lily–of–The–Valley, Whiting, C.1900, 12 Piece 110.00
Teaspoon, Narcissus, Unger 25.00
Teaspoon, Nautilus Design, A.C. Benedict, C.1840, 6 In. 14.00
Teaspoon, Oval End, J. Bedford, C.1800, 5 5/8 In. 40.00
Teaspoon, Oval Tip, C.F. Stone, 6 Piece 110.00
Teaspoon, P.O. Daniel, Boston, C.1830 .... 13.50
Teaspoon, Pointed End, B. Cleveland, C.1790, 5 1/2 In. 55.00
Teaspoon, R.H. Bailey, Flared Handle, C.1839, 5 7/8 In. 25.00
Teaspoon, Sheaf of Wheat, Griffen & Hoyt, 1819, 6 1/8 In. 40.00
Teaspoon, Shell, Scallop Back, Edward Lang, C.1768, 5 In. 185.00
Teaspoon, Urn Back, W. Mannerback, Penna., C.1825 .... 35.00
Teaspoon, Wolcott & Gelston, Boston, 1824 .... 13.50
Tongs, Basket of Flowers, Stebbins & Howe, 6 1/4 In. 135.00

Tongs, Bright Cut Design, A. Miller, 6 1/4 In. 130.00
Tongs, Sandwich, Swedish Modern Pattern, Allan Adler, 8 In. 295.00
Tongs, Spoon Ends, B.C. Frobisher, 6 In. 65.00
Tongs, Sugar Cube, V–Shape Teeth, C.B. Dyer, 5 In. 110.00
Tray, Calling Card, Chippendale, Wallace, 1910 .... 115.00
Tray, Cinderella, Gorham, Round, 14 In. 225.00
Tray, Cocktail, Ripple, William Waldo Dodge Jr., 9 In. 995.00
Tray, Floral, Scroll, Streve, Crump & Low, C.1880, 14 1/2 In. 850.00
Tray, Gorham, Round, Pierced Scroll Border, Monogram, 1899 .... 400.00
Tray, S–Scroll, Shell Border, Monogram, Towle, 11 1/2 In. 247.00
Tray, Scrolling Foliage, Wallace Silversmiths, 20 In. 385.00
Tray, Serpentine, Scalloped, H Center, Gorham, 16 1/2 In. 1210.00
Tureen, Sauce, Stags Head Handles, Cover, W.K. Vanderslice 2420.00
Vase, Celtic Style Design, Medallions, Towle, 1900, 10 In. 550.00
Vase, James Caldwell, Philadelphia, 16 In. 1500.00
Vase, Pierced Flared Rim, Flowers, Lebolt, 1905, 25 In. 6100.00
Vase, Trumpet, Flared, Kalo Shops, 14 In. 750.00
Warmer, Brandy, Side Handle, Dark Brown, Allan Adler, 5 In. 750.00
Yo–Yo, Gorham 125.00
SILVER–AUSTRIAN, Cruet Set, 8 Blue Flash Glass Bottles, 1859, 10 3/4 In. 2425.00
Vase, Urn Form, With Sardonyx, 8 1/4 In. 440.00
SILVER–CHINESE, Bowl, Prunus Trees, Crescent Moons, 19th Century, 9 In. 995.00
Saltshaker, Figural, Bird, Resting, Feathers, 1 1/4 In. 75.00
Tea Strainer, Carved Jade Handle, 6 1/2 In. 275.00
SILVER–CONTINENTAL, Box, Cigarette, Enameled, Gilded Leaves, Cabochons, 5 In. ... 665.00
Candlestick, Chamber, Rock Crystal, Handle, 5 3/4 In. 1875.00
Candlestick, Renaissance, Horseheads, 9 In., Pair 1875.00
Figurine, Knight, Ivory Face, Floral, 16 In. ....*Illus* 4400.00
Fish, Opens, Glass Eyes, 8 In. ....*Illus* 200.00
Goblet Set, Twig Rims, Repousse Grape & Vine, 6 In., 12 .... 2900.00
Mug, 1809 .... 650.00
Napkin Ring, Female Medallion, C.1865 .... 110.00
Salt, Master, Dolphin, PB & C Punch, 2 3/4 In., Pair 110.00
SILVER–DANISH, Bowl, 4 Grape Handles, Hammered Foot, Georg Jensen, 14 In. 8250.00
Bowl, Openwork Leaves Base, Georg Jensen, Post–1945, 12 In. 7775.00
Candy Dish, Blossom, Georg Jensen, 1925–32 .... 850.00
Compote, Flared, Berries, 1930, Georg Jensen, No.252, 9 In. 3300.00
Compote, Openwork Stem, Georg Jensen, 11 1/8 In. 7750.00
Compote, Stem of Foliage & Beads, G.Jensen, 1930, 11 3/8 In. 6875.00
Fruit Bowl, 4 Handles, Grape Design, Georg Jensen, 11 In. 5250.00
Grape Shears 60.00
Hors D'Ouevre Fork, Off–Set Middle Tine, Georg Jensen 35.00
Knife, Butter, Cactus, Georg Jensen 40.00
Lemon Fork, Acorn Pattern, Georg Jensen 45.00
Pitcher, Water, Georg Jensen, Ebony Handle, C.1934, 9 In. 4950.00
Platter, Beaded Rim, Octagonal, Georg Jensen, 12 In. 412.00
Salt Dip, Acorn, Georg Jensen .... 195.00 To 225.00
Server, Handle Band Meets Blade, Georg Jensen, 2 1/2 In. 40.00
Serving Fork, Acorn Pattern, Georg Jensen 300.00
Serving Spoon, Georg Jensen, Pair 550.00
Tea Strainer, Acorn, Georg Jensen .... 195.00 To 225.00
Vase, Fluted, Cylindrical, 1920, Kay Fisker, 8 1/4 In. 1760.00
SILVER–DUTCH, Ashtray, Pierced Rim, Birds, Scene Inside, 1929, 6 3/8 In. 58.00
Ashtray, Pierced Rim, Drinking Scene of Men, C.1929, 6 3/8 In. 60.00
Berry Spoon, Scalloped Bowl 40.00
Bonbon Spoon, Scalloped Bowl, Ship Scene, 1886 .... 55.00
Candle Case, Traveling, Cigar Shape, Floral Repousse 175.00
Candlestick, Repousse Scenes & Figures, 1920, 11 1/2 In., Pair 145.00
Decanter, Square Crystal Bottle, Cherub Finial, C.1890, 8 In. 300.00
Model, 3–Masted Ship Under Sail, Figures, 8 1/2 In. 300.00
Parlor Set, Doll's, Settee, Armchair, Side Chair, Table 145.00
Punch Strainer, Pierced, 2 Handles, 18th Century, 5 In. 950.00
Serving Spoon, Banjo Player Figural Handle 60.00
Snuffbox, Raised Figural Design, 19th Century, 3 In. 175.00

Sponge Box, Stylized Star & Scrolls, 1875, 1 5/8 In. 75.00
Spoon, Lion Holding Shield Finial, C.1900, 6 9/16 In. 30.00
Windmill, 4 Troy Oz. 165.00

English silver is marked with a series of four or five small hallmarks. The standing lion mark is the most commonly seen sterling quality mark. The other marks indicate the city of origin, the maker, and the year of manufacture. These dates can be verified in many good books on silver.

SILVER–ENGLISH, Basket, George III, Rococo Shell & Flower ...._Illus_ 2530.00
Basket, Liquor, Rope Handle, Footed, Sheffield, 8 In. 330.00
Beaker, Engraved Border, Marked WB, 1784, 3 1/2 In. 475.00
Bell, Table, Victorian Period, Silver & Ivory, 1864, 6 In. 1550.00
Bowl, Inscription, For Clare Booth Luce, 1945, 3 1/4 In. 175.00
Bowl, Pierced, Scrolled, Sheffield, 1897–98, 9 In. 275.00
Bowl, Vegetable, Cover, Gadrooned, Rectangular, 1888, 11 In. 300.00
Box, Cut Glass, Scroll Engraved, Monogram, 1846–47, 2 X 3 In. 75.00
Box, Pill, Agate Cover, Marked, Oval, 1 1/4 X 2 In. 55.00
Box, Woman, Child & 3 Sheep Scene Lid, 1932–33, 3 1/4 In. 75.00
Cake Basket, George II, Leaves Border, Pierced, Storr, 12 In. 6100.00
Cake Basket, George III, Diaperwork, 1799, 14 In. 2200.00
Candelabra, 3–Light, Walker, Hall & Sons, 1926, 22 In., Pair 3025.00
Candelabrum, 5–Light, Dogs Flushing Partridge, C.1845 .... 7150.00
Candlestick, Drapery & Rams Shades, 21 In., 4 Pc. ...._Illus_ 2090.00
Candlestick, George II, Contemporary Arms, Cafe, 10 In., Pair 3100.00
Candlestick, Georgian, John Parsons & Co., C.1788, Pair 625.00
Cann, George II, Foliate Design, 4 3/4 In. ...._Illus_ 990.00
Cann, George II, Repousse & Rococo, R. Beale, 4 3/4 In. 900.00
Card Holder, Playing, Word Bridge, Lion Head Ends 185.00
Case, Card, Hinged Lid, Carvings, Scroll, Flowers, 3 X 2 In. 145.00
Castor, George II, Baluster, Pierced Cover, S.Wood, 5 5/8 In. 1100.00
Centerpiece, Gold Aurene, Sheffield, C.1925, 4 1/2 In. 650.00

Silver–Continental, Fish, Opens, Glass Eyes, 8 In.

Silver–Continental, Figurine,
Knight, Ivory Face, Floral, 16 In.

Felt gives off hydrogen sulphide, which tarnishes silver. Do not use felt liners in drawers or felt bags to store silver.

Silver–English, Candlestick, Drapery & Rams Shades, 21 In., 4 Pc.

Silver–English, Cann, George II, Foliate Design, 4 3/4 In.

Silver–English, Wedding Cup, C.1820, 7 In.

Centerpiece, Seated Putti, Pedestal, S. Smith, 1881, 11 In.	4400.00
Chamberstick, With Snuffer, 5 3/4 In., Pair	190.00
Coaster, Goblet, George III, Acanthus Leaf, Wm. Ely, 6 Pc.	1100.00
Coaster, Wine, Sheffield, 1780, 4 3/4 In.	1450.00
Coffeepot, George I, Rococo Cartouche, T. Tearle, 8 1/4 In.	8250.00
Coffeepot, George II, Armorial, Cylindrical, I.Cookson, 9 In.	3080.00
Creamer, Chased Design, Hester Bateman, 1778, 4 1/4 In.	300.00
Creamer, George II, Baluster, S. Laundy, 3 1/8 In.	665.00
Cruet Set, Pierced, Drapery Swags, T. Daniel, 6 In., Pair	2100.00
Cruet Stand, George III, Cobalt Cruets, 1797, 11 Oz.	2200.00
Cup, Child's, Edwardian Period, 1901, Goldsmith, Silversmith	1000.00
Cup, Child's, George III Period, Smith, Hayter, 1795	625.00
Cup, George III, Bell Shape, Gilt Inside, Fernell, 7 In., Pr.	1325.00
Cup, Tumbler, George II, Henry Brind, C.1750, 4 In., Pair	5850.00
Dessert Set, Vermeil, Ivory Panels, Crichton Bros., 36 Pc.	1700.00
Dish, Reeded Rim, L.A. Crichton & Co., C.1927, 11 In., Pair	2100.00
Dish, Vegetable, Gadrooned Border, Cover, JHS, 11 In.	300.00
Dish, Vegetable, Hinged Lid, Hot Water Reservoir, 12 3/4 In.	45.00
Epergne, Frame, 4 Arms, No Inserts, Sheffield	400.00
Fish Slice, George III, Dublin, George Nangle, 1805, 11 In.	550.00
Flagon, Inscription, Paw & Ball Feet, Elkington, 9 3/4 In.	1765.00
Frame, Art Nouveau, Figural Design, 9 1/2 X 7 In.	175.00
Frame, Picture, Blue & Green Enameled, Repousse, 7 3/4 In.	2645.00
Goblet, Engraved Crest, Sheffield, Dated 1810, 5 1/2 In.	385.00
Goblet, George III, 1817, 6 1/4 In.	1975.00
Grater, Nutmeg, Bright Cut, Egg Shape, 1800, 1 1/2 In.	325.00
Grater, Nutmeg, Victorian Period, 1851, 1 7/8 In.	600.00
Inkstand, 3 Bottle, 4 Paw Feet, W. Plummer, 1762, 10 In.	1760.00
Inkstand, George III, John Eames, 1806, 10 In.	1850.00
Inkstand, George III, William Elliot, 1818, 11 In.	9995.00
Inkwell, Boat Shape, 2 Wells, Bradbury, 1897, 10 3/4 In.	445.00
Jardiniere, Pierced Body, Foliate Feet, T.W. Dobson	5500.00
Jug, Cream, George III, Dublin, James Scott, 1795, 5 1/4 In.	1250.00
Jug, Hot Water, George III, Crest, Wakelin & Taylor, 11 In.	1100.00
Ladle, George IV, Robert Garrard, 1829, 2 1/2 In.	1850.00
Letter Opener, George V, Enamel, Ivory, 1931, 9 1/2 In.	950.00
Mirror, Maiden In Garlands Frame, Art Nouveau, 33 1/2 In.	9350.00
Pail, Cream, George III, Peter & Ann Bateman, 1798, 5 1/2 In.	3850.00
Pap Boat, Geroge III, Peter & Ann Bateman, 1794, 5 In.	525.00
Pepper Shaker, Baluster Form, Engraved Crest, 5 1/4 In., Pr.	275.00
Plate, Entree, Sheffield, 1810, 15 1/4 In., Pair	1500.00
Plate, George II, Gadroon, Crest, Wickes, 9 3/4 In., 6 Piece	6600.00

Silver-English, Basket, George III,
Rococo Shell & Flower

Silver-English, Tray, George IV,
Floral, Shell Design, 32 In.

Silver-English, Salt, Open, Blue Liner,
C.1790, 2 1/2 In., Pair

Platter, Turkey Dome, Gadroon, Border, Sheffield, 24 In.	2400.00
Porringer, Hammered, Loop Handle, C.R. Ashbee, 1902, 4 In.	1800.00
Punch Bowl, Lion Head & Ring Handles, Sheffield, 18 In.	325.00
Punch Bowl, Shell & Swag, Pedestal, Lobed Swirl, 1895, 10 In.	5250.00
Rattle, George IV, Unite & Hillard, 1829, 5 In.	975.00
Rose Bowl, Georgian, Scrolled Double Handles, 1935, 2 In.	125.00
Salad Servers, Shreve Brown & Co., Engraved Tines, 1857	425.00
Salt, Fluted Design, Footed, With Spoon, Box, 1889, 2 Sets	375.00
Salt, George IV, Gadrooned Rim, William Eley II, 4 Piece	1300.00
Salt, Open, Blue Liner, C.1790, 2 1/2 In., Pair ....*Illus*	600.00
Salver, Footed, 1827, 45 Oz.	2750.00
Salver, George II, Center Crest, Isaac Cookson, 10 3/4 In.	1100.00
Salver, Shell & Scroll Rim, Armorials, Wm. Bennett, 25 In.	5500.00
Samovar, Cannonball, Engraved Shield, 17 In.	495.00
Samovar, Cannonball, Georgian, Sheffield, C.1803	450.00
Sauce Ladle, George III, G. Smith, 1798, 7 In., Pair	485.00
Sauce Tureen, Shell & Scroll Legs, Paul Storr, 1817	4500.00
Scoop, Engraved Arms On Handle, S. Hennell, 1837	110.00
Spoon, Marrow, George III, James Hobbs, C.1820	245.00
Spoon, Serving, Bright Cut Design, G. Giles, 1790, Pair	132.00
Spoon, Serving, Bright Cut Design, H. Bateman, 1789, Pair	350.00
Spoon, Serving, George III, H.Bateman, Dated 1789, 3 Piece	335.00
Spoon, Stuffing, Engraved Crest, Stamped Mayer, 1852	165.00
Spoon, Stuffing, George III, Eley & Fearn, 1806, 11 3/4 In.	950.00
Spoon, Stuffing, George III, Eley, Fern & Chawner, 1789	160.00
Spoon, Stuffing, George IV, William Eley, 1829	185.00
Spoon, Stuffing, Georgian, Thomas Jenkins, 1804	120.00
Spoon, Stuffing, S. Godbehere & E. Wigan, 1787	100.00
Spoon, Tea Caddy, George III, 1804, 3 In.	200.00
Sugar Tongs, P Over PM, Scissors Type, A. Barrier, 1775	285.00
Tablespoon, Chased Bowl, 1812, Pair	242.00
Tablespoon, George III, 1797, Pair	180.00

Tankard, George III, Curved Handle, David Windsor, 6 In. 1000.00
Tankard, George III, Sebastian & James Crespell, 1768, 6 In. 5500.00
Tart Slice, George III, John Troby, 1796, 12 In. 850.00
Tea & Coffee Set, William IV & Victorian, 1830–89, 4 Piece 2200.00
Tea Set, George III, Hand Made, Ebony Handles, Finial, 6 Pc. 900.00
Tea Set, Georgian, A M & Co., 1921, Miniature, 5 Piece 300.00
Tea Set, Queen Anne, Tea Kettle, Crichton Bros., 1916, 5 Pc. 2300.00
Teapot, George III, Hester Bateman, 1790, 6 1/4 In. 7950.00
Teapot, Georgian, Square Bombe, R.S. Hennel, 1810, 6 In. 850.00
Teapot, Rib & Leaf Design, Paul Storr, 1811, 6 1/2 X 10 In. 1430.00
Teapot, William Elliot, Ivory Heat Stops, 1814, 4 1/2 In. 500.00
Toast Caddy, 6–Slice, Sheffield, 1907 .... 115.00
Toast Caddy, Cathedral Shape, Sheffield, 1907 .... 130.00
Toast Rack, George III, Solomon Houghman, 1801, 7 1/2 In. 2100.00
Toddy Ladle, George III, Wooden Handle, 1770, 11 In. 1500.00
Travel Set, Manicure, Ivory Shoehorn, London, 1864, 40 Pc. 2500.00
Tray, Gadrooned Border, Acanthus Handles, J.S.Hunt, 30 In. 2500.00
Tray, Gadrooned Border, Footed, Oval, 12 1/2 In. 605.00
Tray, George IV, Floral, Shell Design, 32 In. ....*Illus* 3520.00
Tray, Hot Water, Turkey Domed, Double Handle, Garrard, 14 In. 1600.00
Tray, Serving, Rope Twist Border, Sheffield, 31 In. 1100.00
Tray, Tea, Tiered Border, Inscription, 1910, 23 X 15 1/2 In. 1550.00
Tumbler, Swirled Rib, Gold Washed Interior, J.S.B., 4 Piece 300.00
Vinaigrette, Watch Shape, Joseph Willmore, 1823, 1 3/8 In. 545.00
Waiter, Gadroon, Shells, Ebenezer Coker, 1766, 8 In., Pair 1325.00
Waiter, George III, H In Center Reeded, Scofield, 8 In.Diam. 995.00
Wedding Cup, C.1820, 7 In. ....*Illus* 275.00
Wine Cooler, Liner, Sheffield, Crewick, C.1813, Pair 3500.00
Wine Funnel, George III, William Eley, 1809, 5 1/2 In. 1200.00
SILVER–FRENCH, Box, Cover, Coral Mounts, Cartier, C.1935, 7 In. 6600.00
Box, Jade, 2 Compartment, Boin–Taburet, 1920, 8 1/2 In. 7700.00
Clock, Desk, Enamel Dial, Rose Diamonds On Hands, Cartier 3200.00
Desk Sealer, Hollow Repousse Handle, C.1850 .... 30.00
Dish, Shell Shape, Lion Rampant, Scroll, P.A.T., 9 5/8 In., Pr. 2100.00
Pitcher, Pod Shape, Rosewood Base, C Handle, 1930, 10 In. 8800.00
Salt Spoon, Gold Overlay, Shell–Shaped Bowl, Twist Handle 55.00
Saucepan, Straight Sides & Spout, Rosewood Handle, 12 In. 300.00
Snuffbox, Hinged Lid, Colonial Man, Maidens, Square, 2 In. 180.00
Strainer, Pierced Bowl, 8 In. ....*Illus* 60.50
Sugar Basket, Cobalt Blue Interior, C.1830 .... 590.00
Tea & Coffee Set, Pear Shape, Acanthus, H. & Cie., 1900, 4 Pc. 2750.00
Tray, Beaded Rim, Floral Garlands, Armorial, 1860, 36 1/4 In. 7150.00
Tray, Judgement of Paris, French & English Marks, 20 1/2 In. 1800.00
Tureen, Cover, Rosewood Handles, J. Puiforcat, C.1930, 10 In. 8800.00
Wine Taster, Coiled Serpent Handle, Fournier, 1760, 3 In. 1450.00
Wine Taster, Flute Chased, Dots, Charvet, 1763, 3 1/2 In. 1760.00
SILVER–GERMAN, Beaker, Granulated Band, Cylindrical, Hoffler, 1680, 3 5/8 In. 1450.00
Berry Bowl, Undertray, Foliate Scrolls, Birds, Scroll Feet 475.00
Box, Dresser, Hinged, Floral, Musical Designs, 1860, 3 In. 165.00
Box, Gadroon, Cover, Gilt Interior, Widemann, 1700, 3 1/2 In. 1650.00
Candlestick, C.1760, 8 In., Pair ....*Illus* 4840.00
Candlestick, Swirled Lobed Base, J.J.Bauer, C.1760, 8 In., Pr. 4400.00
Cart, Pulled By Winged Cherubs, Crystal Dish, 6 X 3 In., Pair 700.00
Cup, Double, Gourd Shape, John George Smith, 1899, 17 In. 1980.00
Fruit Set, Leaf & Scroll, 1900, 16 Piece 195.00
Plaque, St. George Slaying Dragon, 40 1/2 X 29 1/2 In. 4675.00
Salt, Swan Shape, 3 X 2 1/4 X 1 1/2 In. 75.00
Teapot, Key Border, Straight Sided, J.A.Kordell, 1800, 5 In. 1875.00
Tureen, Scroll Buttresses, Cover, Wilkens, 1920, 8 In. 2975.00
Vinaigrette, Gold Interior, Swan In Oval Mark, 17th Century 325.00
Vinaigrette, Inner Hinged Lid, Gold Wash, Marked, 1 1/2 In. 295.00
Vinaigrette, Swan In Circle, Hinged Lid, 1 1/2 X 1 1/8 In. 325.00
SILVER–HOLLAND, Spoon, Demitasse, Figural Flower Handle, Set of 8 .... 32.00
SILVER–IRISH, Cup, George II, 2 Handles, Bell Shape, T. Sutton, 7 1/2 In. 2100.00

Jug, Floral, Lion's Head Under Spout, Domed Cover, 1815, 9 In. 1200.00
Salver, Queen Anne, Capstan Foot, J.Walker, 1706–08, 13 1/2 In. 4950.00
Sauce Boat, George III, Lion Mask, Paw Feet, Walker, 7 1/4 In. 2475.00
Spoon, Stuffing, George IV, Smith & Gamble, 1825 .... 155.00
Teaspoon, William Cummins, 1825, 10 Piece 125.00
SILVER–ITALIAN, Candelabra, 5–Light, Rococo, Gianmaria, 10 7/8 In., Pair 3850.00
Candlestick, Acanthus Leaf Base, 9 3/4 In., Pair 1200.00
Pitcher, Ice Compartment, Strap Handle, 9 In. 1100.00
SILVER–JAPANESE, Hairpin, Geisha, 1 Prong, Bat & Designs, 3 1/4 In. 35.00
Teapot, Wooden Handle, Urn Shape, Marked Toshikazu, 9 In. 650.00
Tray, Cut Corners, Convex Rim, Dragons, Handles, 26 In. 4000.00
Tray, Dragon Handles, Monogram, 26 In. ....*Illus* 4000.00
Vase, Cloissone, Urn Shape, Turtle In Triangle, 8 In., Pair 3600.00
SILVER–MEXICAN, Bowl, Art Deco, 3 Handles, Wm. Spratling, 6 1/2 In. 595.00
Bowl, Kidney Shape, 3–Footed, 8 3/4 X 6 In. 225.00
Box, Egg Shape, Lift–Off Top, 2 3/8 In. 75.00
Butter, Ball Finial, Domed Cover, Round, 7 1/8 In. 275.00
Candlestick, 3–Light, Pedestal Base, 10 In., Pair 900.00
Plate, Gadroon Border, 8 5/8 In., 6 Piece 950.00
Plate, Juarez, 6 In. 60.00
Platter, Raised Ovals, Leaf & Scroll Rim, 16 X 9 1/2 In. 650.00
Platter, Shaped Rim, Rey Midas, 15 3/4 In. 200.00
Salt & Pepper, Bird Shape, Taxco, 3 1/2 In. 125.00
Sauce Ladle, Pointed Tip, Rest On Back, Leaf Bowl, 7 In. 55.00
Tea Set, Campana Shape, Green Onyx, Jean Puiforcat, 3 Pc. 5225.00
Tray, Undulating Rim, Floral Design, 15 3/4 In. 325.00
Tureen, Circular, Cover, Jean Puiforcat, 1945, 12 In. 6325.00
Vase, Scalloped Rim, Marked, Miniature, Pair 45.00
SILVER–NORWEGIAN, Salt, Viking Ship Shape, Blue Liner, Spoon, 3 1/4 In. 48.00
Strainer, Cup, Gold Washed, 4 1/2 In. ....*Illus* 230.00
Stuffing Spoon, L. Drammen, 1855, 17 In. 250.00
Sugar Shaker, Diamonds, Block Base, Enamel, 4 Sides, 5 In. 175.00
SILVER–PORTUGUESE, Candlestick, Pear Stem, Lara Oporto, 1815, 8 1/2 In., Pair ... 990.00
Tea & Coffee Set, Tray, Baroque Shells, J.P.C., 5 Piece 7150.00

ІБ 88
ᚼ·Я
Russian silver is marked with the cyrillic, or Russian, alphabet. The numbers 84, 88, or 91 indicate the silver content. Russian silver may be higher or lower than sterling standard. Other marks indicate maker, assayer, or city of manufacture. Many pieces of silver made in Russia are decorated with enamel.

SILVER–RUSSIAN, Badge, Officer's, Rifle Brigade 375.00
Bank, Hinged Cover, Scene of Peasants, 1879, 4 3/4 In. 1900.00
Cake Basket, Grapevine Border, Swing Handle, Seipel, 14 In. 2420.00
Candlestick, Fruiting Grapevines, Bell Base, 12 In., Pair 475.00
Centerpiece, Cut Glass, Shellwork, Floral, Kurlyukov, 11 In. 2640.00
Cigarette Case, City Scene, Niello, C.1900 .... 365.00
Cigarette Case, Imperial Opera House, N.S.Sapozhnik, C.1889 .... 412.50
Crucifix, Chain, Blue Enameled, Khlebnikov, Dated 1889 .... 750.00

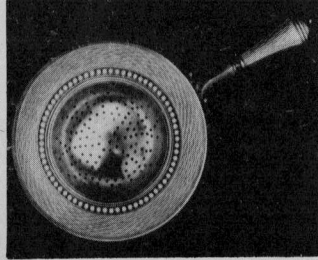

Silver–Norwegian, Strainer, Cup,
Gold Washed, 4 1/2 In.

The English use this old system for cleaning silver: Put the silver in a bowl, cover it with sour milk, and let it stand overnight. Rinse it in cold water the next morning, and dry it with a soft cloth.

Silver–German, Candlestick,
C.1760, 8 In., Pair

Silver–Japanese, Tray, Dragon Handles,
Monogram, 26 In.

Cup, Pedestal, Cover, Silver Gilt, Dubrovin, 6 In.	500.00
Cup, Vodka, Pre–Revolution Period, 2 In.	125.00
Hot Water Pot, Acanthus Leaf Finial, Efimov, 1806, 6 1/4 In.	1210.00
Kovsh, Silver Gilt & Plique–A–Jour Enamel	8800.00
Salt, Embossed, 3 Legs, Clear Liner	85.00
Tablespoon, Ovchinnikob	125.00
Tea Set, 6–In. Teapot, Baluster Body, 1896, 3 Piece	1000.00
Teapot, Teak Handle, Rose Band, Tuchaski, 1855, 5 1/2 In.	750.00
SILVER–SCOTCH, Buckle, Edinburgh, 1 1/4 X 1 5/8 In., Pair	25.00
Salt & Pepper, Kitchen, William IV, McKay, 1837, 2 In.	880.00
Spoon, Stuffing, Cunningham & Simpson, C.1810	132.00
Toddy Ladle, Whalebone Twisted Handle, Bowl Dated 1709	295.00

Sterling silver is made with 925 parts silver out of 1,000 parts of metal. The word "sterling" is a quality guarantee used in the United States after about 1860. The word was used much earlier in England and Ireland. Pieces listed here are not identified by country. Other pieces of sterling quality silver are listed under Silver–American, Silver–English, etc.

SILVER–STERLING, Basket, Scrolled Handle, Gadrooned Border, Kent, 9 1/2 In.	225.00
Bib Clip, Box	65.00
Bonbon Spoon, Heart Shaped, Chrysanthemum Pattern	175.00
Bowl, Hammered, Scalloped, Raised Ribs, KLF & Son, 9 1/2 In.	450.00
Bowl, Presentation, Leafy Scrolls, Medallion, 10 In.Diam.	125.00
Box, Heart Shape, Repousse Cows, Dutch Sheepherder, 3 In.	250.00
Box, Pill, Hinged, Engraved Scroll On Lid, 2 In.	45.00
Butter, Cover, Stylized Blossom Finial, Redlich, 4 3/4 In.	400.00
Candleholder, S–Curve Design, Pair	60.00
Candlestick, Hammered, Bobeche, Flared Rim, 10 1/4 In., Pair	200.00
Caviar Spreader, Mother–of–Pearl Blade	35.00
Chatelaine, Dance Set, Whalebone Pages, 3 Piece	225.00
Cigarette Set, Pedestal Bases, Ashtray & Holder	45.00
Corncob Holder, Corn Shaped Handle, 2 3/4 In., Pair	24.00
Dish, Chrysanthemum & Poppies, 15 In. *Illus*	358.00
Dish, Embossed Florals & Scrolls, Whiting, 8 1/4 In.	70.00
Dish, Flower Garden Border, 14 1/2 In. *Illus*	440.00
Dish, Poppies, 13 In. *Illus*	468.00
Dresser Set, Floral Design, Mirror, Brush, Buttonhook	170.00
Dresser Set, Madame DeMaitenon, Monogram, C.1930, 9 Piece	375.00
Frame, Ball Feet, Easel Back, Oval, 8 1/4 X 11 3/4 In.	165.00
Frame, Easel Back, Inscription On Top, 8 1/4 X 10 5/8 In.	135.00
Grape Shears, Stuart Devlin	375.00

Hair Crimper, Repousse Scrolled Handle, 6 In. 30.00
Hairbrush, Woman's, Art Nouveau Roses 50.00
Hatpin, Bear By Tree 125.00
Horn, Victorian, Ornate Handle, Floral 45.00
Kettle, On Stand, 11 1/2 In. 275.00
Knife Set, Fruit, Reeded Handle, Case, C.1900, Set of 12 .... 140.00
Match Safe, Engraved Both Sides, Harry From Lady Mullen 50.00
Medal, Nurses', Victoria Infirmatory, New Castle, 1 3/4 In. 20.00
Picnic Kit, Folding Knife, Fork, Spoon, Corkscrew, 4 5/8 In. 135.00
Pie Server, Coin, Marked Drew & Adele, 8 1/4 In. 75.00
Pitcher, Water, High Relief, Floral Design, 9 In. ....*Illus* 1265.00
Platter, Applied Leaf & Scroll, Large Ovals, 15 3/4 In. 650.00
Pusher, Stork Delivering Baby Handle 52.00
Rattle, Bone Ring 65.00
Rattle, Mother–of–Pearl Handle, With Bells & Whistle 165.00
Salad Set, Porringer, Spoon & Fork, Pierced Handles, Kalo 325.00
Salt & Pepper, 4 1/4 In., 4 Piece 450.00
Salt & Pepper, Concave Corners, Mause, 5 1/4 In. 58.00
Salt, Double, Cherubs, Handle, Marked, 4 In. 165.00
Shears, Poultry, Winchester Pattern 70.00
Sherbet, Etched Glass Insert, Velvet Box, Set of 8 .... 395.00
Shoehorn, Pierced Hole At End, Gorham, Flowers, 6 In. 125.00
Spoon, Child's, Who Killed Cock Robin 30.00
  **SILVER–STERLING, SPOON, SOUVENIR, see Souvenir, Spoon, Sterling
  Silver**
Spout Strainers, Boat Form, Lion Head, Pair ....*Illus* 176.00

Silver–Sterling, Dishes

Silver–Sterling, Pitcher, Water, High Relief, Floral Design, 9 In.

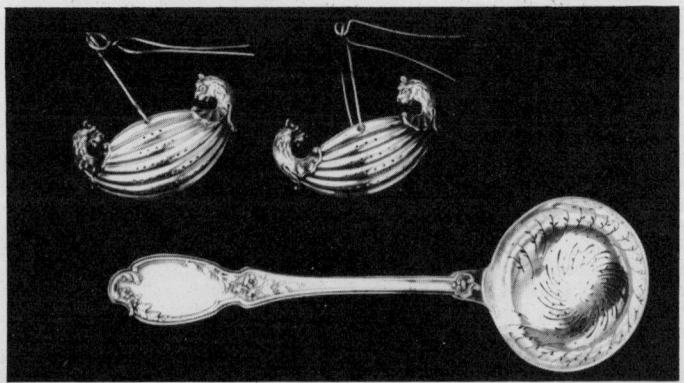

Silver–Sterling, Spout Strainers, Boat Form, Lion Head, Pair
Silver–French, Strainer, Pierced Bowl, 8 In.

Silver–Sterling, Tea Set, Shreve, Stanwood & Co., 1869, 3 Piece

Tea & Coffee Set, Footed, Ovoid Form, Gorham, 5 Piece 500.00
Tea & Coffee Set, Victorian, Vase Shape, J.E.B., 1889, 4 Pc. 1980.00
Tea Set, 10 Piece, Miniature 198.00
Tea Set, Castles, Ridges, Hunter, A.G.Schultz, C.1910, 5 Pc. 2100.00
Tea Set, Reeded Edges, Ivy Borders, 7 In.Teapot, 3 Piece 500.00
Tea Set, Shreve, Stanwood & Co., 1869, 3 Piece ....*Illus* 500.00
Tea Strainer, Ivory Handle, Marked 256w 65.00
Teapot, Engraved Designs, Ivory Finial, 20 Oz. 250.00
Teapot, George III, Floral Chasing, Hinged Cover, 4 In. 425.00
Tongs, Leaf Ends 100.00
Tray, Iris Design, Fluted Handles, Lebkuecher, 10 1/2 In. 550.00
Tray, Pierced Handle, Rolled Rim, McAuliff & Hadlem, 10 In. 250.00
Whistle, With Loop, Repousse, 1 1/2 In. 50.00
SILVER–VIENNESE, Clock, Desk, On Tails of Dolphins, Enameled, 1880, 7 In. 3300.00
Cup, Cover, Busts, Fruits, Enamel, Lapis–Lazuli, 1880, 11 In. 6050.00
Ewer, Stand, Mythological Enameled, Caryatid Handle, 9 In. 2850.00
Nef, Enamel, Silver–Gilt, Mythological Scenes, 8 3/4 In. 3300.00
Salt, Shell Form, Rock Crystal Dolphin, 1880, 6 In. 2200.00

 Sinclaire cut glass was made by H.P. Sinclaire and Company of Corning, New York, between 1905 and 1929. He cut glass made at other factories until 1920. Pieces were made of crystal as well as amber, blue, green, or ruby glass. Only a small percentage of Sinclaire glass is marked with the S in a wreath.

SINCLAIRE, Bookends, Flowers, Ovals, Sterling Silver Border, 8 In. 1025.00
Bowl, 8 Flower Medallions, Silver Thread, Signed 850.00
Bowl, Fish Pattern, Swirling Water, Intaglio, Signed, 9 1/2 In. 600.00
Candlestick, Cobalt Blue, White Rim, 9 1/2 In., Pair 160.00
Candlestick, Gooseberry, Large Teardrop, Intaglio, 14 In., Pair 700.00
Candlestick, Vintage Grapes Pattern, Green, 10 3/4 In., Pair 345.00
Celery, Geometric Cut, Hobstars 225.00
Epergne, Wreath & Flower Pattern, Signed, 2 Part 550.00
Finger Bowl, Floral, Foliage, Crystal, Underplate, Marked 58.00
Finger Bowl, Underplate, Overall Intaglio Cut Floral, Swags 70.00
Mug, Chocolate, Underplate, Sunflower Pattern, Signed 400.00
Perfume Bottle, Hobstars, Prism, Straw, Teardrop Stopper, Pair 700.00
Tray, Intaglio, 5 In. 75.00
Tray, Lace Hobnail Pattern, Engraved Border, Signed, 12 In. 2200.00
Vase, Floral Swags, Geometric Engraving, 9 1/2 In. 145.00
Vase, Silver Thread Pattern, 10 In. 1075.00
Vase, Urn Shape, Pattern Cut Base, Signed, 17 In. 350.00
Water Set, Brilliant & Intaglio Pattern, Signed, 9 Piece 550.00

 Slag glass resembles a marble cake. It can be streaked with different colors. There were many types made from about 1880. Pink slag was an American Victorian product of unknown origin. Purple and

blue slag were made in American and English factories. Red slag is a very late–Victorian and twentieth–century glass. Other colors are known but are of less importance to the collector.

SLAG, Blue, Dish, Horse On Nest Cover, 5 In.	25.00
Blue, Toothpick, Inverted Strawberry, Cambridge	8.00
Canary, Hen, Boyd, 5 1/2 In.	18.00
SLAG, CARAMEL, see Chocolate Glass	
Green, Cruet, Imperial, Octagon	55.00
Green, Dish, Squirrel Cover, Greentown	285.00
Pink, Bowl, Inverted Fan & Feather, 5 1/2 X 9 In.	750.00
Pink, Punch Cup, Inverted Fan & Feather	195.00 To 250.00
Pink, Sauce Dish, 4 Ball Feet, 2 1/2 X 4 1/2 In.	230.00
Pink, Sauce, Inverted Fan & Feather	200.00
Pink, Spooner	195.00
Pink, Tumbler, Inverted Fan & Feather	395.00
Purple, Boot, With Spur	45.00
Purple, Bowl, Cover, Cherries & Leaf, 3 Sections, 7 1/2 In.	75.00
Purple, Bowl, Fluted Shell, Pedestal, 8 1/2 In.	63.00
Purple, Box, Dog, Imperial	65.00
Purple, Box, Lion, Cover, Imperial	75.00
Purple, Butter, Cover, Block & Star, Paneled	60.00
Purple, Candy Dish, Ocean Shell, Northwood, 1901	38.00
Purple, Celery, Jewel Pattern, 8 1/4 In.	75.00
Purple, Compote, Cover	100.00
Purple, Creamer, Raised Cherries	95.00
Purple, Creamer, Wreathed Cherry	85.00
Purple, Cruet, Imperial	35.00 To 55.00
Purple, Dish, Hen On Nest Cover	30.00
Purple, Jar, Owl, Cover, Satin, Imperial	65.00
Purple, Mug, Robin	20.00
Purple, Plate, Heart Shape, Ribbons, Open Hearts Border	22.50
Purple, Platter, Oval, 13 1/2 In.	85.00
Purple, Rooster, Lavender Top, Westmoreland	165.00
Purple, Rose Bowl, Beaded Cable, Footed	27.00
Purple, Spooner, Oval Medallion	85.00
Purple, Spooner, Oval Panel	50.00
Purple, Toothpick	45.00
Purple, Tumbler, A Present From The Bristol Exposition 1893	45.00
Red, Basket, Milk Glass Handle, Imperial, Tall	70.00
Red, Bowl, Grape & Cable, 9 1/2 In.	65.00
Red, Candleholder, Imperial, Pair	25.00
Red, Dish, Cat On Nest, Westmoreland	47.00
Red, Dish, Horse On Nest, 5 In.	30.00
Red, Dish, Rooster On Nest Cover, 5 In.	30.00
Red, Goblet, Eagle	15.00
Red, Vase, Dancing Girls, Imperial Glass, 8 1/2 In.	25.00

Sleepy Eye collectors look for anything bearing the image of the 19th–century Indian chief with the drooping eyelid. The Sleepy Eye Milling Co., Sleepy Eye, Minnesota, used his portrait in advertising from 1883 to 1921. It offered many premiums, including stoneware and pottery steins, crocks, bowls, mugs, and pitchers, all decorated with the famous profile of the Indian. The pottery was popular and was made by Western Stoneware and other potteries long after the flour mill went out of business in 1921. Reproductions of the pitchers are being made today. The original pitchers came in only five sizes: 4 in., 5 1/4 in., 6 1/2 in., 8 in., and 9 in. The Sleepy Eye image was also used by companies unrelated to the flour mill.

SLEEPY EYE, Butter Box	75.00
Calendar, 1904	400.00
Cookbook, Paper Cover	65.00
Creamer, Numbered 42 S, 3 1/2 In.	150.00
Crock, Salt	410.00

Fan, Sleepy Eye Flour, Indian Head Shape, Cardboard, 1900 .... 145.00
Flour Sack, 11 X 12 In. 68.50
Mug, Blue & White, 4 1/2 In. 120.00
Mug, Brown & Green, Cream Ground, Brush 400.00
Mug, Brown, Western Pottery, 1952 .... 50.00
Mug, Minnesota 1150.00
Pitcher, No.2, Brown & White 675.00
Pitcher, No.3, Blue & White, 7 In. 250.00
Pitcher, No.4, Blue & Gray 200.00
Pitcher, No.4, Blue On Cream, 8 In. 275.00
Pitcher, No.5, Blue & Gray 200.00
Pitcher, No.5, Blue & White 190.00
Pitcher, No.5, Blue Gray, 9 1/4 In. 600.00
Pitcher, Sesquicentennial, 1981 .... 100.00
Postcard 65.00
Salt .... 300.00 To 395.00
Sign, Sleepy Eye Flour, Tin 960.00
Sign, Sleepy Eye Milling Co., Indian Chief, Round 700.00
Stein, Brown & White, 7 3/4 In. .... 750.00 To 900.00
Stein, Brown & Yellow, 7 3/4 In. 500.00
Trade Card, Set of 10 .... 700.00
Vase, Blue, Gray, Cylinder, 9 In. 165.00
Vase, Cattail, Blue, 9 In. .... 250.00 To 285.00
Vase, Cattail, No.2, Blue & White 150.00
Vase, Flemish, Indian & Cattails, 8 1/2 In. 295.00
SLOT MACHINE, see Coin–Operated Machine

Smith Bros. Co. Smith Brothers glass was made after 1878. Alfred and Harry Smith had worked for the Mt. Washington Glass Company in New Bedford, Massachusetts, for seven years before going into their own shop. They made many pieces with enamel decoration.

SMITH BROTHERS, Biscuit Jar, Floral Design 70.00
Box, Cover, White Cartouches, Yellow, Pink Roses, Green Stems 345.00
Dish, Sweetmeat, Flowers On Base & Cover, Marked, 5 1/4 In. 635.00
Figurine, Swan, Black Amethyst, 9 In. 60.00
Jar, Dresser, Melon–Ribbed, Pansies, Cover, Signed, 5 1/2 In. 300.00
Jar, Dresser, Melon–Ribbed, Words Hail Happy Morn, 3 1/4 In. 125.00
Mustard, Columned Ribs, Flowers On Blue Dots At Rim, 3 In. 155.00
Plate, Santa Maria, 7 3/4 In. 200.00
Powder Box, Melon–Ribbed, Glass Lid, Iris Blossoms, 4 In. 335.00
Rose Bowl, Pansies, Cream Ground, Marked, 4 1/4 In. 305.00
Salt, Melon–Ribbed Mold, Beaded Edge 90.00
Sugar & Creamer, Twisted Metal Handle, Rim & Cover 45.00
Tobacco Jar, Hand Painted Flowers, Silver Lid 225.00
Tray, Pink Ground, White Daisies, Marked, 8 X 4 In. 385.00
Vase, Enameled Storks, Marsh, Pink Ring, Silver Plated, 8 In. 125.00
Vase, Scenic, 6 In. 65.00
Vase, Wisteria Design, 9 1/2 In. 950.00

Snow Babies, made from bisque and spattered with glitter sand, were first manufactured in 1864 by Hertwig and Company of Thuringia. Other German and Japanese companies copied the Hertwig designs. Originally, Snow Babies were made of candy and used as Christmas decorations. There are also Snow Babies tablewares made by Royal Bayreuth. Copies of the small Snow Babies figurines are being made today and can easily confuse the collector.

SNOW BABIES, Box, Cover, Blue Mark 125.00
Box, Piano Shape, Royal Bayreuth 80.00
Cup & Saucer, Billowy Girl, Blue Mark 120.00
Mug, Blue Mark, 3 1/2 In. 75.00
On Sled, Pink Pants, 2 1/2 In. 99.00
Santa Climbs Down Chimney, 3 In. 44.00
Seated On Polar Bear, 2 1/4 In. 55.00

Slide Down Ramp, 2 Babies, 2 1/4 In. 22.00
Standing, With Pair of Skis 38.50
Tea Set, Sledding, Kettle–Style Handle, Royal Bayreuth, 6 Pc. 325.00
Vase, Miniature 25.00
   SNUFF BOTTLE, see Bottle, Snuff

Taking snuff was popular long before cigarettes became available. The snuff was kept in a small box. The gentleman or lady would take a small pinch of the ground tobacco or snuff in the fingers, then sniff it and sneeze. Snuffboxes were made of many materials, including gold, silver, enameled metal, and wood. Most snuffboxes date from the late eighteenth or early nineteenth centuries.

SNUFFBOX, Bird's Bill 1200.00
   Brass, Hinged Lid, Paddle Riverboat, Heart Shape, 3 1/2 In. 395.00
   Burled Wood, Turquoise Lined, Hinged, 1840, 2 1/2 In. 95.00
   Carved Horn, Hinged, Pair of Shoes Shape, Covered 80.00
   Enameled, American Trade Open & Free, Balston, 1807, 1 1/2 X 1 In. 495.00
   Enameled, Silver, Putto & Young Woman, French, Marked, 3 3/8 In. 450.00
   Enameled, Washington Portrait, Balston, 1800–10, 2 X 1 1/2 In. 1980.00
   Gold Wash, Gentleman, 17th Century Clothes, 18th Century, 2 In. 650.00
   Gold, Enameled White Flowers, Black Ground, Swiss, 1830, 3 1/8 In. 4125.00
   Gutta Percha, 3 14 X 2 X 3/4 In. 17.50
   Papier–Mache, Dr.Syntax, Shooting Pony 130.00
   Papier–Mache, Hand Colored Engraving of Youth, 2 5/8 In. 40.00
   Silver Gilt, George III, Napoleon Hinged Cover, Robinson, 3 In. 1650.00
   Silver Plated, Diamond Pattern Top, Parker 90.00
   Silver, Cowrie–Shell, George II Coin Hinged Lid, Roosevelt, 4 In. 825.00
   Silver, Engine–Turned Design, Cartouche, Continental, 3 1/4 In. 100.00
   Silver, Gold Washed, Engine Overall Design, J.Willmore, 1825, 3 In. 395.00
   Silver, Gold Washed, JB, Reeded Lid & Base, Vienna, 1880, 3 3/8 In. 200.00
   Silver, Hinged Cover, Dead Woman Lying In Coffin 175.00
   Silver, Hinged Lid, Colonial Man Greeting 2 Women, French, 2 In. 175.00
   Silver, Pillow Shaped Raying Shell, CW In Shield, French, 2 In. 150.00
   Silver, Reeded Ground, Cartouche, French, 1850, Rectangular, 3 In. 125.00

Soapstone is a mineral that was used for foot warmers or griddles because of its heat–retaining properties. Soapstone was carved into figurines and bowls in many countries in the nineteenth and twentieth centuries. Most of the soapstone seen today is from China or Japan. It is still being carved in the old styles.

SOAPSTONE, Bookends, Jardiniere, Trailing Plants, Flower, Green, 5 X 4 In. 40.00

If your papier-mâché doll heads or furniture are cracking, try arresting the cracks with a thin coat of white household glue.

If there is goldwash in a bright-cut silver design, the wash is a later addition. Victorian pieces were made with bright cutting against the gold to show the design in two colors.

Soapstone, Figurine, Goddess, Pouring Wine, Acolyte, 14 3/4 In.

Box, Heart Shape, Mother–of–Pearl Flowers, 2 1/2 X 2 1/2 In. 12.00
Figurine, Egyptian Style, Incised Calligraphy, 9 1/2 In. 50.00
Figurine, Goddess, Pouring Wine, Acolyte, 14 3/4 In. ....*Illus* 1320.00
Figurine, Lion, Reclining On Rocky Ledge, L.Riche, 15 1/2 In. 1430.00
Figurine, Ram, C.1900, 2 1/2 X 3 In. 65.00
Group, Monkey, 2 Babies, Bird, Brown, 5 X 6 In. 48.00
Inkwell, Beveled Sides, 1 1/2 X 1 3/4 In. 50.00
Plaque, On Stand, Tan, Bird, Tree, Rocks, Twigs, Oval, 9 1/2 In. 75.00
Signature Stamp, Old Man's Head Shape, Black, Base, 4 1/2 In. 78.00
Toothpick, Monkey 28.00
Vase, Lotus, 5 In. 20.00
Vase, Phoenix Bird & Flowers, China, 9 In. 65.00
Vase, Vine With Flowers & Leaves, 9 In. 48.00

> Soft paste is a name for a type of pottery. Although it looks very
> much like porcelain, it is a chemically different material. Most of
> the soft–paste wares were made in the early nineteenth century.
> Other pieces may be listed under Gaudy Dutch or Leeds.

SOFT PASTE, Chamber Pot, Floral Decoration, Blue, White, Leaf Handle, 3 In. 315.00
Creamer, Floral Decoration, Blue, Green, 4 In. 115.00
Cup & Saucer, Floral Design, Handleless, Red, Magenta, Yellow 35.00
Cup & Saucer, Handleless, Red Tulips On Black Stem, C.1800 .... 70.00
Cup & Saucer, Handleless, Roses & Swags 40.00
Cup, Stirrup, Enameled Wording, Success To Maesmaur Fox, 6 In. 500.00
Jug, Pink Luster, Commemorative, 1826 .... 595.00
Pitcher, Blue Checked Pattern, English, C.1820 .... 350.00
Pitcher, Polychrome Enameling, Embossed Design, 5 1/2 In., Pair 95.00
Plate, King's Rose, 7 1/2 In. 115.00
Platter, Blue Feather Edge, 16 3/8 In. 175.00
Punch Bowl, Gothic Pattern, English, 15 In. 900.00
Tea Set, Mother & Child, Classical Attire, 8 Piece 350.00
Teapot, Floral Decoration, 4 Colors, Acorn Final, 6 1/2 In. 75.00
Tureen, Blue Feather Edge, Foliage Scroll Handles, 5 1/2 In. 285.00

> What could be more fun than to bring home a souvenir of a trip?
> Our ancestors enjoyed the same thing and souvenirs were made for
> almost every location. Most of the souvenir pottery and porcelain
> pieces of the nineteenth century were made in England or Germany,
> even if the picture showed a North American scene. In the
> twentieth century, the souvenir china business seems to have gone to
> the manufacturers in Japan, Taiwan, Hong Kong, England, and
> America. Another popular souvenir item is the souvenir spoon,
> made of sterling or silver plate. These are usually made in the
> country pictured on the spoon.

SOUVENIR, see also Coronation; World's Fair
SOUVENIR, Album, Winter Olympics, Nazi Germany, 1936 .... 95.00
Ashtray, Century of Progress Expo, Art Deco, Sky Ride, 1933, 5 In. 30.00
Ashtray, Rudolph Valentino, Tin Lithograph 50.00
Bag, Shoulder, Olympics, Munich, Germany, Woven, 1972 .... 20.00
Bathtub, Pottery, Hot Springs National Park, Miniature 5.00
Bell, Atlantic City, Ruby Cut To Clear, 1903 .... 45.00
Booklet, Pan-Am, Singer Sewing Machine Co., 12 Pages, 1901 .... 35.00
Bowl, Apollo Ll, Ruffled, Gold, Scenes, 7 In. 8.00
Bowl, Prospect Point, Niagara Falls, Reticulated, Bavaria, 5 In. 8.50
Bucket, New Orleans Expo, Wooden, 1885, Miniature 25.00
Button, Astronaut Glenn, 1962, 1 3/4 In. 8.00
Button, Women's Relief Corps, Ribbon, Pendant, C.1890 .... 17.00
Capitol Building, Baton Rouge, Bronze, 7 In. 20.00
Creamer, Boston Christian Science Church 12.00
Cup & Saucer, Houses of Parliament, Victoria BC, Royal Winton 9.00
Dish, Court House, Burlington, Kansas, 6 In. 20.00
Hat, Welsh, Stovepipe, Souvenir of Wales, Porcelain, Name On Brim 22.00
Hatchet, Hazleton, Penna., White Milk Glass, 6 In. 25.00
Mug, Lake Preston, South Dakota 30.00

Pennant, Hollywood, Multicolored, Black Ground, 1940s, 25 In. 8.00
Pickle Fork, Sterling Silver, Golden Gate Bridge, Kirk, 1939 .... 20.00
Pitcher, 1000 Islands, Green Luster, Jonroth, England, 3 1/4 In. 8.00
Plate, Bundles For Britain, Steubenville, Backstamp 18.00
Plate, Niagara Falls, Gold Scalloped, Flowers, Germany, 7 1/2 In. 16.00
Plate, Niagara Falls, Lace Edge 10.00
Plate, Rainbow Falls, Watkins Glen, N.Y., Gold Trim, Adams, 10 In. 11.00
Plate, Yosemite, California Scenes On Border, 1940s 15.00
Shovel, Gold Scoop, Clear Handle, Kearney, Nebraska, Glass 20.00
Spoon, Silver Plate, Connecticut, 1915 .... 20.00
Spoon, Silver Plate, Florida 20.00
Spoon, Silver Plate, GAR, U.S. Veteran 10.00
Spoon, Silver Plate, Ireland 7.00
Spoon, Silver Plate, New Hampshire 20.00
Spoon, Silver Plate, North Carolina 5.00
Spoon, Silver Plate, Ohio 20.00
Spoon, Silver Plate, Puerto Rico 10.00
Spoon, Sterling Silver, 1891 Niagara, Indian, Demitasse 50.00
Spoon, Sterling Silver, Actor's Fund Fair, Gorham, May, 1982 .... 150.00
Spoon, Sterling Silver, Alaska, 5 Scenes, 5 1/4 In. 35.00
Spoon, Sterling Silver, Alaska, Gold Dredge, 5 In. 20.00
Spoon, Sterling Silver, Alaska, Ketchikan, 3 1/2 In. 15.00
Spoon, Sterling Silver, Alaska, Skyline 54.00
Spoon, Sterling Silver, Atlantic City 12.00
Spoon, Sterling Silver, Bangor, Maine, 4 In. 24.00
Spoon, Sterling Silver, Bermuda, 4 In. 15.00
Spoon, Sterling Silver, Brooklyn, 1896, 5 In. 22.00
Spoon, Sterling Silver, Bunker Hill, 3 1/4 In. 15.00
Spoon, Sterling Silver, Cedar Rapids High School 20.00
Spoon, Sterling Silver, Chattanooga, Tenn., Ornate Handle 25.00
Spoon, Sterling Silver, City Hall, Woodstock, Illinois 15.00
Spoon, Sterling Silver, City Hall, Worcester, Massachusetts 22.50
Spoon, Sterling Silver, Colorado, Figural Handle 58.00
Spoon, Sterling Silver, Coney Island, 4 1/4 In. 18.00
Spoon, Sterling Silver, Court House, Bemidji, Minn. 32.50
Spoon, Sterling Silver, Court House, Coles County, Illinois 15.00
Spoon, Sterling Silver, Court House, LaSalle County, Illinois 15.00
Spoon, Sterling Silver, Cripple Creek, Colorado 40.00
Spoon, Sterling Silver, Dallas, Kneeling Indian On Globe 85.00
Spoon, Sterling Silver, Denver, Colorado, Prospector On Handle 28.00
Spoon, Sterling Silver, Disneyland Castle, 4 1/4 In. 25.00
Spoon, Sterling Silver, Elburn Windmill, Illinois 15.00
Spoon, Sterling Silver, Elks, Figural 60.00
Spoon, Sterling Silver, Genter City, Minn. 22.50
Spoon, Sterling Silver, George Washington 12.00
Spoon, Sterling Silver, Hawaiian, Dime Bowl, Dated 1883, 3 In. 125.00
Spoon, Sterling Silver, Hendersonville, N.C. 17.50
Spoon, Sterling Silver, Higbee School, Memphis, Tenn. 35.00
Spoon, Sterling Silver, High School, Carrollton, Illinois 15.00
Spoon, Sterling Silver, High School, Louisiana, Missouri 22.50
Spoon, Sterling Silver, Hot Springs, Ark., Indian Design, Demitasse 45.00
Spoon, Sterling Silver, Houston, Texas, Demitasse 35.00
Spoon, Sterling Silver, I.O.O.F. Building, Akron, Ohio 25.00
Spoon, Sterling Silver, Indian Enameled Scene Bowl, Demitasse 25.00
Spoon, Sterling Silver, Indian Maiden Handle, Monogram, Watson Co. 60.00
Spoon, Sterling Silver, Iowa, 1905 .... 24.00
Spoon, Sterling Silver, LaCrosse, Ear of Corn Handle 28.00
Spoon, Sterling Silver, Landing of Pilgrims 12.00
Spoon, Sterling Silver, Library, University of Illinois, Urbana 15.00
Spoon, Sterling Silver, Mammoth Cave, Ky., Entrance 22.50
Spoon, Sterling Silver, Minnehaha Falls, Minn., Corn Stalk Handle 95.00
Spoon, Sterling Silver, Miss Canada, Sharpley, 1893 .... 36.00
Spoon, Sterling Silver, Mt. Hood, Washed Gold Bowl 30.00
Spoon, Sterling Silver, N.Y. Skyline Handle, Brooklyn Bridge, 1913 .... 42.00

Spoon, Sterling Silver, New Cliff House, San Francisco, Bowl Scene 15.00
Spoon, Sterling Silver, New Greenwood Hotel, Riverside, Cal., 5 In. 18.00
Spoon, Sterling Silver, New Orleans, Dated 1895, 5 1/4 In. 25.00
Spoon, Sterling Silver, Niagara Falls, Indian Handle, W.H. Glenny 40.00
Spoon, Sterling Silver, Ohio State Prison 25.00
Spoon, Sterling Silver, Pike's Peak, Full Headdress Indian 85.00
Spoon, Sterling Silver, Port Comfort, Texas, 3 3/4 In. 15.00
Spoon, Sterling Silver, Portland, Oregon, 3 3/4 In. 15.00
Spoon, Sterling Silver, Public School, Maroe, Illinois 15.00
Spoon, Sterling Silver, Queen City, Cincinnati, Ohio 25.00
Spoon, Sterling Silver, Sloss Furnaces, Birmingham, Alabama 25.00
Spoon, Sterling Silver, Soldier & Sailor Monument, Cleveland, Oh. 25.00
Spoon, Sterling Silver, Spring Lake, New Jersey, Beach Scene, Ship 27.50
Spoon, Sterling Silver, St. Joseph Hospital, Elgin, Illinois 15.00
Spoon, Sterling Silver, State Capitol, Helena, Mont., Demitasse 40.00
Spoon, Sterling Silver, Stork, Figural, 1910 .... 35.00
Spoon, Sterling Silver, Sturbridge, Mass., 4 1/4 In. 20.00
Spoon, Sterling Silver, Sulphur Springs, N.Y., Bow, Arrow, Tomahawk 85.00
Spoon, Sterling Silver, Tacoma, England, Demitasse 16.00
Spoon, Sterling Silver, Tampa, Florida, Alligator Handle 20.00
Spoon, Sterling Silver, Tijuana, Mexico, Bullfight 22.50
Spoon, Sterling Silver, Union Stock Yard, Chicago 14.00
Spoon, Sterling Silver, Washington, D.C. .... 12.00 To 27.50
Spoon, Sterling Silver, William Penn, Figural 60.00
Tape Measure, Pan–Am, Celluloid, Other Side Longhorn Steer, 1901 .... 18.00
Toilet, Porcelain, Coney Island, Gentlemen Only, Germany, Miniature 15.00
Tumbler, Kentucky Derby, 1954 .... 60.00
Tumbler, Kentucky Derby, 1961 .... 35.00
Tumbler, Kentucky Derby, Aluminum, 1957 .... 150.00
Tumbler, Liberace, With Piano, Etched, 7 Piece 90.00
Tumbler, Water, Union Station, St. Louis, Mo., Porcelain, Carlsbad 36.00
Whistle, Police, Compliments of N.Y. Evening Telegram, 1910 .... 15.00

Spangle glass is multicolored glass made from odds and ends of colored glass rods. It includes metallic flakes of mica covered with gold, silver, nickel, or copper. Spangle glass is usually cased with a thin layer of clear glass over the multicolored layer.

SPANGLE GLASS, see also Vasa Murrhina
SPANGLE GLASS, Basket, Cased White Interior, Amber & Gold 135.00
Basket, Clear Looped Handle, Yellow 145.00
Basket, Pink Ruffled Rim, Mica In White Body, 10 In. 225.00
Basket, Tortoiseshell Color, 6 In. 125.00
Bowl, Gold Mica, Tan, Clear Handles 100.00
Cracker Jar, Bird, Floral, Yellow, Silver Plated Lid & Handle 125.00
Cruet, Touch of Blue At Base, Silver Mica Flakes 435.00
Ewer, Multicolored Mica Flecks, White Cased, 6 1/4 In. 70.00
Pitcher, Ruffled Top, Melon Shaped Bottom, Mica Flakes, 9 In. 185.00
Pitcher, Water, Cranberry, Clear Handle 165.00
Vase, Opaque Fronds, Mica Flakes, 11 X 25 In. 210.00
Vase, Ruby, Mica Flecks, Ground Pontil 85.00

Spanish lace is a type of Victorian glass that has a white lace design. Blue, yellow, cranberry, or clear glass was made with this distinctive white pattern. It was made in England and the United States after 1885. Copies are being made.

SPANISH LACE, Bride's Basket, Silver Frame, Cranberry 200.00
Cake Stand, Blue, 5 X 13 In. 68.00
Cruet, Blue 90.00
Cruet, Yellow 125.00
Jam Jar, Cover, Cranberry 450.00
Pitcher, Ruffled Top, Cranberry, 10 In. 195.00
Pitcher, Water, White 140.00
Sugar Shaker, Yellow 135.00
Sugar, Cover, White 40.00

Syrup, Spring Lid, Yellow 325.00
Vase, Opalescent Yellow, 8 In. 4.00
Vase, Yellow, 6 1/2 In. 65.00
Water Set, Green, 7 Piece 525.00

Spatter glass is a multicolored glass made from many small pieces of different colored glass. It is sometimes called "End–Of–Day" glass. It is still being made.

SPATTER GLASS, Basket, 6–Point Top, White Lining, Thorn Handle, 6 3/4 In. 125.00
Basket, Clear Thorn Handle & Feet, Overlay, 8 1/2 X 6 In. 175.00
Basket, Flowers, Gold Outlined, Exposition Paris, 1889, 9 In. 295.00
Celery, Ribbed Pillar, Blue 135.00
Cup & Saucer, Stick, Green Flower Design, Red Band 55.00
Pitcher, Clear Cirles Surrounded By Spatter, 2 Qt. 350.00
Sugar & Creamer, Cased White, Clear Feet & Handle, 4 1/4 In. 135.00
Sugar Shaker, Iridescent Colors, Silver Plated Top, Cover 140.00
Vase, Aventurine, Melon Sections Top, Green, 7 1/8 In. 110.00
Vase, Jack–In–The–Pulpit, Yellow, 5 In. 88.00
Vase, Yellow, Orange, Bulbous, Green Shades Center, 8 1/2 In. 120.00
Water Set, Embossed Swirl, White Lining, Clear Handle, 5 Pc. 325.00

The creamware or soft–paste dinnerware decorated with spatter designs in color is called, of course, spatterware. The earliest pieces were made in the late eighteenth century, but most of the spatterware found today was made from about 1800 to 1850 or is a late nineteenth– and twentieth–century form of kitchen crockery that has added spatter designs. The early spatterware was made in the Staffordshire district of England for sale in America. The kitchen type is an American product.

SPATTERWARE, Bowl, Blue & White, Blue Bands, 8 X 3 1/2 In. 85.00
Bowl, Flowers, Blue Stick Floral, Belgium, 4 3/4 X 2 In. 38.00
Bowl, Gaudy Floral Design, 11 1/4 In. 35.00
Creamer, Peacock Design, Blue, English 275.00
Cup & Saucer, Handleless, Thistle 350.00
Cup & Saucer, Peafowl 295.00
Cup & Saucer, Rainbow, Cluster of Buds, Red, Yellow, Green 600.00
Cup Plate, Blue, 4 1/4 In. 45.00
Cup, Child's, Primitive Peafowl In Blue, Yellow, Green & Black 45.00
Cup, Peafowl, Blue Ground, Handleless 85.00
Mixing Bowl, Blue & White, 11 In. 105.00
Mixing Bowl, Yellowware, Blue & Brown, 11 1/4 X 5 3/4 In. 70.00
Mug, Blue & White, 19th Century, 5 In. 115.00
Pitcher, Blue & White, 9 In. 125.00
Pitcher, Blue, 17 In. 160.00
Pitcher, Milk, Peafowl, Red, Rope Twist Handle, 5 7/8 In. 145.00
Plate, Acorns, Oak Leaves, Blue Ground, Greens, Black, 9 1/2 In. 400.00
Plate, Peafowl Center, Red, 9 In. 195.00
Plate, Red & Green Thistle, Blue Ground, 9 3/8 In. 375.00
Saucer, Blue, Red & Blue Stripes, Brown Stick Design, 4 3/4 In. 55.00
Sugar, Blue & Green, 4 4/5 In. 85.00
Sugar, Ruffled, Yellow Lining, Yellow, White, Maroon, 5 1/2 In. 65.00

Spelter is a synonym for a zinc alloy. Figurines, candlesticks, and other pieces were made of spelter and given a bronze or painted finish. The metal has been used since about the 1860s to make statues, tablewares, and lamps that resemble bronze. Spelter is soft and breaks easily. To test for spelter, scratch the base of the piece. Bronze is solid; spelter will show a silvery scratch.

SPELTER, Figurine, Lady, Holding 3 Bowls, Art Nouveau 325.00
Figurine, Man On Rearing Horse 35.00
Lamp, 3 Nudes At Base, Bronzed, 21 In., Pair 130.00
Lamp, Figural, 4–Light, Young Woman In Gown, Holding Fan, 38 1/2 In. 550.00

The old spinning wheel in the corner has been the symbol of earlier times for the past 100 years. Although spinning wheels date back to medieval times, the ones found today are rarely more than 200 years old. Because the style of the spinning wheel changed very little, it is often impossible to place an exact date on a wheel.

SPINNING WHEEL, Distaff With Flax, Dark Finish, 49 1/2 In.	275.00
Flax Holder, Wooden, Miniature	95.00
Flax Pole, Original Paint, Bobbin Pole Has Water Cup, 2 Pc.	395.00
Flax, Salmon, Mustard, Turquoise, Green & Royal Blue Paint	3500.00
Flax, Signed & Dated 1848	330.00
Maple, Grain Painted, Ivory, Pewter Castle Design, 1830–50	3800.00
Red, White & Blue Stripes, Cutout Design, Upright, 38 In.	325.00
White Paint, 27 1/2 In.	134.00
Worn Green Paint, Turned, Chip Carved, 42 In.	145.00

Spode pottery, porcelain, and bone china were made by the Stoke-on-Trent factory of England founded by Josiah Spode about 1770. The firm became Copeland and Garrett from 1833 to 1847, then W.T. Copeland or W.T. Copeland and Sons until 1976. It then became Royal Worcester Spode Ltd. The word "Spode" appears on many pieces made by the factories. Most collectors include all the wares under the more familiar name of Spode. Porcelains are listed in this book by the name that appears on the piece.

SPODE, see also Copeland; Copeland Spode

SPODE, Casserole, Cover, Buttercup, Oval	100.00
Cup & Saucer, Buttercup	20.00
Dish, Sweetmeat, Floral, Orange Clobbering, Blue, White, 1810, 8 X 4 In.	825.00
Jam Jar, Butterfly	10.00
Mug, Christmas Tree	3.00
Plate, Buttercup, 5 1/2 In.	5.00
Plate, Dessert, Irene Pattern, 8 In.	30.00
Plate, Fox & Lion, Green, 10 In.	75.00
Plate, Peplow, 10 In.	7.50
Platter, Blue Willow, 18 3/4 In.	210.00
Platter, Peplow, 11 In.	15.00
Saucer, Neoclassical, White & Gold, C.1820, Pair	55.00
Tray, Buttercup, 6 1/2 X 11 In.	35.00

Spongeware is very similar to spatterware in appearance. The designs were applied to the ceramics by daubing the color on with a sponge or cloth. Many collectors do not differentiate between spongeware and spatterware and use the names interchangeably. Modern pottery is being made to resemble the old spongeware, but careful examination will show it is new.

SPONGEWARE, Bean Pot, Blue	125.00
Bean Pot, Cover, Monmouth, Illinois	95.00
Bowl Set, 5 To 11 In., 7 Piece	650.00
Bowl, Blue & White, 10 In.	100.00
Bowl, Blue & White, Monmouth Pottery, 7 In.	85.00
Bowl, Blue, 8 X 10 In.	137.50
Bowl, Blue, Yellow, 8 X 2 1/2 In.	85.00
Bowl, Brown & Cream, Flat, 5 In.	12.00
Bowl, Brown, Yellow, 5 X 2 In.	20.00
Bowl, Cream & Brown, 9 1/2 In.	30.00
Bowl, Paneled, 7 In.	50.00
Bowl, Signed George R. Alblaster, Clairon Co.	200.00
Bowl, Yellow, Blue, 8 In.	45.00
Casserole, Green & Brown, Cream Ground, Cover	65.00
Chamber Pot, Cover	195.00
Coffeepot, Blue & White, Gooseneck Spout, Ohio, 10 In.	725.00
Crock, Beater, Blue Stripe	18.00
Crock, Butter, Blue & White	225.00
Cup, Child's, Children & Dog Scene, 3 In.	24.00

Custard, Brown On Yellow	18.00
Custard, Brown, 5 1/2 In.	22.00
Inkwell, Blue & White	275.00
Jug, Water	395.00
Mixing Bowl, Green & Brown, Cream Ground	65.00
Pie Plate, Brown	100.00
Pitcher, 8 1/2 X 5 In.	375.00
Pitcher, Batter, Blue & White	65.00
Pitcher, Blue & White, 8 In.	75.00
Pitcher, Blue, 6 1/2 In.	295.00
Pitcher, Brown On Cream, Squared Handle, 7 In.	55.00
Pitcher, Brown, Green, Cream, 4 3/4 In.	55.00
Pitcher, Grapes & Shield, Green, 3 Mugs, Large	125.00
Pitcher, Hot Water, Blue	300.00
Pitcher, Milk, Tankard Style, Blue & White, 2 1/2 Qt.	395.00
Pitcher, Ribbed Sides, Brown & Green On Yellow, 5 1/2 In.	85.00
Pitcher, Water, Blue, Stopper	175.00
Platter, Blue, 12 In.	250.00
Salt & Pepper, Green, White	58.00
Slop Jar, Cover, Blue & White	265.00
Soap Dish, Blue	235.00

Sporting goods, equipment, brochures, and related items are listed here. Other sections of interest are Bicycle, Fishing, Gun, Rifle, Sword, Toy, and Weapons.

SPORTS, Almanac, Mutual Baseball, 1954	8.00
Ball, Target, Blue, Windowpane Pattern	65.00
Baseball Bat, Louisville Slugger, Steve Garvey Autograph	15.00
Baseball Bat, Louisville Slugger, Wooden, Salesman Sample, 8 In.	15.00
Baseball Bat, Mages, Georgia Sport Store, Wooden, 15 In.	25.00
Baseball Glove, Mickey Mantle, The Comet	20.00
Baseball, Babe Ruth Autograph & 15 Others	1760.00
Baseball, Bob Feller Autograph	25.00
Baseball, Bobby Doerr Autograph	25.00
Baseball, Frank Robinson Autograph	25.00
Baseball, Mickey Mantle Autograph	45.00
Bat, Louisville Slugger, Dizzy Dean Trademark, Joe Medwick, 22 In.	60.00
Bat, Tiger Striped Ash, 1918, 32 1/2 In.	150.00
Billiard Table, E.J.Riley, Green Felt Lined, Fluted Legs, Walnut	3575.00
Blanket, Baseball, Gowdy, 1914	30.00
Blanket, Baseball, W. Johnson, 1914	95.00
Book, A New Way To Play Better Golf, Rex Lardner, 1932	10.00
Book, How To Play Golf, Sam Snead, 1946	10.00
Book, St. Louis Cardinals Yearbook, 1963	7.50
Bottle, Golfer, One Up & Two To Go, Black Glass, 3 Sides, 9 In.	325.00
Boxing Gloves, Everlast	45.00
Camp Stove, Screw On Brass Lids, G.W.S.& S.	20.00
Card, Football, Frank Gifford, Philadelphia Gum Co., 1964	10.00
Card, Football, Jack Kemp, Topps, 1964	9.00
Card, Football, Jackie Jensen, Leaf Gum, 1948	20.00
Card, Football, Jim Brown, Fleer Gum Co., 1961	12.00
Card, Football, Roger Staubach, Topps, 1973	3.50
Card, Football, Sammy Baugh, Bowman Gum Co., 1948	22.00
Crawler, Crazy, Heddon, Box	35.00
Creel, Splint, Brown Patina, C.1800	220.00
Creel, Trout, Carrying Strap, 12 In.	50.00
Crow Call, Faulks, Wooden, Box	5.00
Crow Call, Hertus	10.00
Display Case, Counter Top, 3 Drawers, Weber Tackle Co., Oak	350.00
Duck Call, Perdew	2475.00
Football Guide, Spalding, 1930	35.00
Golf Ball, Winchester	135.00
Golf Club, Brassie, Driver & Spoon, Bert Dargie, Mid–1920s, 3 Piece	425.00
Golf Club, Wooden Shaft, 6 Piece	30.00

Goose Call, Walnut, Green Head 15.00
Harmless Archery Set, Complete, Box 35.00
Hockey Head, Colgate, Bobby Orr, 1972, 10 Different Scenes 15.00
Ice Skates, Brass Acorn At End of Curved Tip, Wooden, C.1820, 12 In. 250.00
Ice Skates, Dutch Queen, Wooden 65.00
Ice Skates, Steel Frame, Wood Pad To Curve, Brass Acorn Finial 220.00
Ice Skates, Winchester, Clamp–On .... 17.50 To 24.00
License, Hunting, Tin, Pennsylvania, 1939 .... 23.00
Moose Call, Birchboard, 21 In. 125.00
Mug, Milwaukee Braves, World's Baseball Champions, 1957 .... 25.00
Plate, Arnold Palmer, Signed 98.00
Plate, Baseball, Caught On The Fly, American Sports, ABC, 7 1/4 In. 275.00
Pocket Billiard, Table, Regina, Rack & 12 Cues, 1917 .... 6000.00
Pool Table, Brunswick & Balke, Rosewood, Mahogany, 4 X 8 Ft. 7500.00
Pool Table, Brunswick, Oak, 1890s, 4 1/2 X 9 Ft. 3500.00
Pool Table, Leather Pockets, Slate Top, 1901, 9 Ft. 700.00
Postcard Set, Photograph, Babe Ruth, Goudey, 1930s, 21 Piece 42.00
Postcard, Yankee Stadium 9.00
Poster, Football Player, Muslin, Welcome Visitors, 1930, 35 X 23 In. 28.50
Poster, Ted Williams, Coca–Cola, 22 X 14 In. 100.00
Program, Official Football, 1946 .... 18.00
Putter, Walter Hagen, Silver–Wrapped Handle 352.00
Ring, Boxing Bell, With Gavel, Walnut Base, 1905 .... 285.00
Ring, New York Mets World Championship, 1969 .... 990.00
Roller Skates, Brownie, Box 20.00
Roller Skates, Child's, Painted, Brass Acorns, Tipped Off, 1820 .... 250.00
Scent Bottle, Funsten Animal Bait, Embossed Neck, Paper Label, 1904 ...... 32.00
Score Card, Baseball, St. Louis & Pittsburgh, 1935 .... 20.00
Score Counter, Baseball, Glove, Multicolored Celluloid, 1911–20 .... 30.00
Scorecard, Los Angeles Dodgers, Reds, Centennial Issue, 1869–1969 .... 10.00
Shorebird Whistle, Tin 48.00
Tennis Racket & Display Stand, Winchester 285.00
Vest, Catcher's, Baseball, Leather 10.00
Watch, Pocket, New York Yankee World Champions, Wittnauer, 1952 .... 1540.00
Yearbook, Baseball, Boston Red Sox, 1977 .... 6.00
Yearbook, Baseball, Boston Red Sox, 1981 .... 5.00
Yearbook, Baseball, Minnesota Twins, Media Guide, 1986 .... 4.00
Yearbook, Football, Miami Dolphins, Rookie Marino's Year, 1984 .... 6.00
Yearbook, Philadelphia Athletics, 1953 .... 18.00
Yearbook, Washington Senators, 1953 .... 18.00

Pottery and porcelain have been made in the Staffordshire district in
England since the 1700s. Hundreds of kilns are still working in the
area. Thousands of types of pottery and porcelain have been made
in the many factories that worked and still work in the area. Some
of the most famous factories have been listed separately, such as
Adams, Davenport, Ridgway, Rowland & Marsellus, Royal Doulton,
Royal Worcester, Spode, Wedgwood, and others. Some Staffordshire
pieces are listed under sections like Fairing, Flow Blue, Shaving
Mug, etc.

STAFFORDSHIRE, see also Flow Blue; Mulberry
STAFFORDSHIRE, Bank, Cottage 165.00
Bowl, Strawberries, Woman, 10 In. 72.00
Bowl, Upper Ferry Bridge Over River Schuylkill, 12 3/4 In. 325.00
Bowl, Vegetable, Red Transfer Palestine, Adams, 12 1/4 In. 45.00
Bust, George Washington, 8 1/4 In. 687.00
Bust, George Washington, Blue Coat, Yellow Vest, 7 3/4 In. 285.00
Cake Plate, Oriental Scene, G.W. Turner & Sons, 1840, 10 In. 60.00
Chamber Pot, Cover, Florentine, Blue Scene 118.00
Chamber Pot, English Cathedral, Blue, 9 1/2 X 15 1/2 In. 350.00
Cheese Dish, Bovine Head Cover, C.1840 .... 500.00
Creamer, Cow, Standing, 1830, 4 3/4 In. 350.00
Cup & Saucer, Handleless, Floral, Gaudy .... 30.00 To 40.00
Cup & Saucer, Handleless, Medium Blue Transfer of Camels 25.00

Cup & Saucer, Handleless, Pet, Pink 50.00
Cup & Saucer, Light Blue Transfer, Garden Scenery, 6 Piece 40.00
Cup & Saucer, Mount Vernon, Dark Blue 325.00
Cup Plate, Blue Transfers, 6 Piece 35.00
Cup Plate, English Country House, Dark Blue, 3 7/8 In. 75.00
Cup Plate, Winter Season, Man & Dog, Brown Transfer, 4 In. 82.00
Cup, Stirrup, Dog Head, Polychrome Enamel, 5 In. 475.00
Cup, Stirrup, Fox Head, Polychrome Enamel, 3 1/2 In. 250.00
Dish, Pudding, Pains Hill, Surrey, R. Hall, C.1825, 11 1/2 In. 350.00
Figurine, 2 Men, Dog, Robin Hood, 15 In. ....*Illus* 247.50
Figurine, Birds On Twig 40.00
Figurine, Boy On Horseback, 9 1/2 In. 250.00
Figurine, Cherub, Nude, Tree, C.1800, 6 1/2 In., Pair ....*Illus* 300.00
Figurine, Cobbler & His Wife, C.1860, 12 1/2 In., Pair 950.00
Figurine, Cricket Player, 10 In. ....*Illus* 240.00
Figurine, Dog, Red & White, Polychrome Trim, 5 1/2 In., Pair 80.00
Figurine, Dog, Red Spots, Polychrome Features, 3 1/2 In. 85.00
Figurine, Dog, Rust & White, Gilt Trim, Glass Eyes, 13 1/4 In. 155.00
Figurine, Dog, Tray, 13 1/2 In. ....*Illus* 451.00
Figurine, Dog, White, Gilt, Polychrome Features, 8 3/4 In., Pr. 250.00
Figurine, Farrier, 16 In. ....*Illus* 275.00
Figurine, Girl, On Horse, 6 X 9 In. 375.00
Figurine, Lamb, Sanded Coat, Black Spots, Stripe, 2 5/8 In. 85.00
Figurine, Man & Woman, Holding Spaniels, 9 In., Pair 900.00
Figurine, Man, Plumed Hat, Cloak, Knee Boots, Dog, 17 In. 350.00
Figurine, Officer, 18 In. ....*Illus* 192.50
Figurine, Poodle, 5 In. 275.00
Figurine, Poodle, White, C.1840, 2 In. 100.00
Figurine, Queen Victoria, 11 In. ....*Illus* 302.50
Figurine, Queen Victoria, Sampson–Smith, C.1840, 17 In. 495.00
Figurine, Riding Goats, 5 3/4 In. 90.00
Figurine, Sankey, Man In Black Waistcoat, 17 In. 400.00
Figurine, Scotsman, 6 1/2 In. 325.00
Figurine, Spaniel, Gray, 5 1/4 In. 150.00
Figurine, Spaniel, Pearlware, Green Mound Base, 5 In., Pair 1100.00
Figurine, Spaniels, Red & Orange, 6 1/4 In. 275.00
Figurine, The Brownings, Reclining, C.1860, 8 X 9 In., Pair 450.00
Figurine, Whippet, 4 In., Pair 350.00
Figurine, Whippet, 5 In., Pair 275.00
Figurine, Whippet, With Hare, 10 In. 395.00
Figurine, Whippets, Reclining, 3 1/4 In. 225.00
Figurine, Woman, Basket, Dog, 5 1/2 In. 100.00

Staffordshire, Figurine, 2 Men,
Dog, Robin Hood, 15 In.

Staffordshire, Figurine, Cricket Player, 10 In.;
Queen Victoria, 11 In.

Staffordshire, Figurine, Cherub, Nude, Tree,
C.1800, 6 1/2 In., Pair

Staffordshire, Pitcher & Bowl, Blue
Willow, 10 1/2 In.Bowl

Figurine, Woman, Seated, With Cat, 3 1/2 In.		125.00
Figurine, Zebra, 9 In.	Illus	248.00
Garniture Set, Dragon Handles, 1830, 10 3/8, 9 5/8, 9 1/2 In.		775.00
Group, Boxing Match, Herman, Sayers, 9 1/4 In.	Illus	357.50
Group, Man & Woman With Rabbit & Hutch, 7 In.	55.00 To	150.00
Group, Queen Victoria On Horseback, 8 1/2in.		275.00
Group, Scotsman & Woman With Large Clock, 14 In.		225.00
Incense Burner, Cottage, Polychromed, 4 3/8 In.		15.00
Jug, Cover, Standing Figure, Tricornered Hat		140.00
Jug, Figural, Owl, Yellow Eyes & Beak, 6 In.		95.00
Jug, Seated Man With Pitcher		90.00
Mug, Child's, Industry Is Fortune's Handmaid, Boat On Ocean		135.00
Mug, Come Away Pompey, Going To Market On Reverse, 3 In.		85.00
Mug, Frog, Pink Luster Straps, Masonic Wording, C.1850		250.00
Mug, God Speed The Plough, Black Transfer, Handles, 3 7/8 In.		95.00
Mug, Grandmamma's Tales, Rock–A–Bye Baby Reverse, 2 1/2 In.		85.00
Patch Box, Reclining Spaniel Shape		935.00
Pitcher & Bowl, Blue Willow, 10 1/2 In.Bowl	Illus	193.00
Pitcher, Apprentices Drinking, Playing Cards, 7 In.		78.00
Pitcher, Black Transfer, Oriental Scene, Black Ground, 8 In.		75.00
Pitcher, Eagle, Shield & Star Design, White		225.00
Pitcher, Esplanade, Castle Garden, New York, Dark Blue, 9 In.		300.00
Pitcher, Lafayette At Franklin Tomb, Dark Blue, 6 In.		425.00
Pitcher, Pink Sunderland Luster, C.1810, 6 In.		250.00
Plate, Adelaide's Bower, Black, 8 1/2 In.		35.00
Plate, Arms of New York, T.Dark Blue, Mayer, 10 In.		425.00
Plate, Asiatic Pheasants, Black, 10 1/4 In.		45.00
Plate, Bank of United States, Philadelphia, 10 1/4 In.		275.00
Plate, Bathalha, Portugal, Medium Dark Blue, 9 3/4 In.		85.00
Plate, Building & Sheep Center, States Border, 8 3/4 In.		225.00
Plate, Cambrian, Black, 10 1/2 In.		50.00
Plate, Canova, Light Blue, 10 1/2 In.		55.00
Plate, Capitol Washington, Misspelled, Dark Blue, 10 1/8 In.		400.00
Plate, Castles, White Gadroon Border, Dark Blue, 9 In.		95.00
Plate, Christ Church Oxford, Medium Blue, 10 In.		22.50
Plate, City Hotel, New York, Medium Blue, 8 3/4 In.		200.00
Plate, Columbia College, New York, Dark Blue, 7 1/2 In.		3000.00
Plate, Commodore McDonnough's Victory, Woods, Blue, 10 In.		395.00
Plate, Compton Verney, Medium Blue, Warwickshire, 8 5/8 In.		25.00
Plate, Corinth, Light Blue, 8 In.		40.00
Plate, Dam & Water Works, Philadelphia, Light Blue, 10 In.		300.00
Plate, Dark Blue Transfer of Rabbit Hunter, 9 1/8 In.		75.00
Plate, Doctor Syntax Mistakes, Dark Blue, Clews, 9 7/8 In.		150.00
Plate, Doctor Syntax Taking Possession, Dark Blue, 10 In.		125.00
Plate, Fairmount Near Philadelphia, Stubbs, 10 1/4 In.		165.00
Plate, Falls of Killarney, Dark Blue, 5 1/2 In.		45.00
Plate, Gaudy Floral, Red Transfer, Ashworth, 10 3/8 In.		35.00
Plate, Highlands, Hudson River, Dark Blue, Enoch Wood, 5 In.		875.00

Plate, Italian Building, Purple, 9 In.	40.00
Plate, Lambton Hall, Durham, Medium Blue, 10 In.	30.00
Plate, Landing of Lafayette, Dark Blue, Clews, 6 3/4 In.	195.00
Plate, Marine Hospital, Louisville, Dark Blue, Wood, 9 1/8 In.	300.00
Plate, Nahant Hotel Near Boston, Medium Blue, 9 In.	200.00
Plate, Nonpareil, Brown, 10 In.	40.00
Plate, Ontario Lake Scenery, Heath, Blue, 10 1/2 In.	50.00
Plate, Ontario, Light Blue, 7 1/2 In.	40.00
Plate, Palestine, Green Border, Red Center, 10 1/2 In.	70.00
Plate, Palestine, Light Blue Transfer, Adams, 9 1/2 In.	30.00
Plate, Parisian Chateau, Brown, 9 In.	40.00
Plate, Pine Orchard House, Catskill Mountains, 10 1/4 In.	350.00
Plate, Quadrupeds, I. Hall, Dark Blue, 9 3/4 In.	180.00
Plate, Transylvania University, Lexington, Wood, 9 1/4 In.	250.00
Plate, Winter View, Pittsfield, Mass., Dark Blue, Clews, 10 In.	125.00
Platter, Alms House, Bushes, Ridgway, 12 3/4 X 16 1/2 In.	600.00
Platter, Christianburg Danish Settlement, Africa, 18 1/2 In.	400.00
Platter, Columbus, Ohio, Dark Blue, 14 1/2 In.	1750.00
Platter, Embossed Scroll, Scalloped, 16 3/4 In.	10.00
Platter, Floral Design, Blue, Red, Yellow, Gaudy, 18 In.	425.00
Platter, Letter of Introduction, Wilkie, 12 In.	250.00
Platter, New York From Heights Near Brooklyn, 16 1/2 In.	1400.00
Platter, Parisian, 13 1/4 In.	55.00
Platter, Park Scene, Brown Transfer, 18 In.	70.00
Platter, Purple Floral Transfer, 16 3/4 In.	95.00
Platter, Red Transfer Caledonia, Adams, 19 1/2 In.	180.00
Platter, Still Life With Bird Scene, Blue Transfer, 19 In.	255.00
Platter, Tree & Well, Landing of Gen. Lafayette, 18 1/2 In.	1250.00
Platter, Undertray, Mountain Scene, C.1830, 11 X 17 1/2 In.	375.00
Platter, Winter View of Pittsfield, Clews, 16 3/4 In.	1250.00
Powder Box, Hoop–Skirted Woman, 2 Piece	80.00
Punch Bowl, Hunt Scene Medallions, Pink Luster, 11 1/2 In.	450.00
Salt & Pepper, Forget–Me–Not	20.00
Soup, Dish, Boston Hospital, Dark Blue, 8 3/4 In.	300.00
Soup, Dish, Dark Blue Transfer, Impressed Adams, 10 1/8 In.	100.00
Sugar & Creamer, Cottage	38.00
Sugar, Oriental Scenery, Dark Blue, Cover, 6 7/8 In.	175.00
Tea Set, Canadian Historical, Blue, 3 Piece	795.00
Tea Set, Child's, Little Nell, Blue & White, 21 Piece	275.00
Tea Set, Strawberry Pattern, Pearlware, C.1820, 3 Piece	300.00
Teapot, Cottage & Castle, Octagonal, Flower Finial, 6 In.	95.00
Teapot, Floral, With Ruins, Dark Blue, Wood, 6 7/8 In.	100.00

Staffordshire, Figurine, Dog, Tray, 13 1/2 In.
Staffordshire, Figurine, Zebra, 9 In.

Teapot, Forget–Me–Not, Myott	45.00
Teapot, Pagoda, Floral, Dark Blue, 6 3/4 In.	250.00
Teapot, Parisian, G. Philips	95.00
Teapot, Whooping Cranes, Foliage, Brown & White, Dated 1877	95.00

STAFFORDSHIRE, TOBY JUG, see Toby Jug

Tureen, Blue & White, Underplate, Ladle	80.00
Tureen, Sauce, Stand, Cover, Dated 1825, 3 Piece	600.00
Tureen, Sauce, Underplate, Bramber Church, Sussex, Blue, 8 In.	275.00
Tureen, Soup, Ladle & Underplate, Solar Rays, Black Transfer	150.00
Tureen, Underplate, Pass In Catskill Mountains, Navy, 8 In.	1250.00
Vase, Washington, Light Blue, 10 In.	65.00
Whistle, Figural, Child Riding Bicycle	195.00

The Fulper Pottery had a long history that entwined with the Stangl Pottery in 1910 when Johann Martin Stangl started work. He bought into the firm in 1913, became president in 1926, and in 1929 changed the company name to Stangl Pottery. The pottery made dinnerwares and a line of limited–edition bird figurines. The company went out of business in 1972.

STANGL, Ashtray, Flying Geese, 10 In.	27.50
Ashtray, Pansies, 4 In.	3.00
Ashtray, Pointer Dog Center, Round, 8 In.	20.00
Ashtray, Woodcock, Large	17.00
Basket, White, Rope Twisted Handle	25.00
Berry Bowl, Thistle	3.50
Bird, Bird of Paradise, No.3408	70.00 To 85.00
Bird, Blue–Headed Vireo, No.3448	35.00 To 50.00
Bird, Bluebird, No.3276	75.00
Bird, Bluebirds, No.3276D	120.00 To 140.00
Bird, Broadbill Hummingbird, No.3629	90.00
Bird, Broadtail Hummingbird, No.3626	95.00
Bird, Canary, No.3747, Head Turned Left, Blue Flower	125.00
Bird, Cardinal, No.3444	55.00 To 65.00
Bird, Cerulean Warbler, No.3456	40.00 To 45.00
Bird, Chestnut–Backed Chickadee, No.3811	65.00 To 75.00
Bird, Chickadees, Group, No.3581	140.00 To 160.00
Bird, Cock Pheasant, No.3492	170.00
Bird, Cockatoo, No.3405, 6 In.	40.00
Bird, Cockatoo, No.3584, 12 In.	110.00 To 200.00
Bird, Duck Feeding, No.3250C	45.00
Bird, Evening Grosbeak, No.3813	95.00

Staffordshire, Figurine,
Farrier, 16 In.

Staffordshire, Figurine,
Officer, 18 In.

Staffordshire, Group, Boxing
Match, Herman, Sayers, 9 1/4 In.

Bird, Golden–Crowned Kinglet, No.3848 .... 35.00
Bird, Goldfinches, Group, No.3635 .... 150.00 To 225.00
Bird, Gray Cardinal, No.3596 .... 50.00 To 65.00
Bird, Hen Pheasant, No.3491 .... 170.00
Bird, Hummingbirds, No.3599D .... 255.00 To 260.00
Bird, Indigo Bunting, No.3589 .... 70.00
Bird, Kentucky Warbler, No.3598 .... 40.00
Bird, Key West Quail Dove, No.3454 .... 225.00 To 250.00
Bird, Kingfisher, No.3406 .... 35.00
Bird, Kingfishers, No.3406D 95.00
Bird, Lovebird, No.3400 .... 48.00 To 50.00
Bird, Lovebirds, No.3404D .... 55.00 To 100.00
Bird, Oriole, No.3402 .... 35.00
Bird, Oriole, No.3402S 42.00
Bird, Orioles, No.3402D .... 85.00 To 95.00
Bird, Painted Bunting, No.3452 .... 100.00
Bird, Parakeets, No.3582D .... 105.00 To 150.00
Bird, Parrot, No.3449 .... 85.00 To 145.00
Bird, Parula Warbler, No.3583 .... 40.00
Bird, Red–Breasted Nuthatch, No.3851 .... 50.00
Bird, Red–Headed Woodpecker, No.3752D 285.00
Bird, Red–Headed Woodpeckers, No.3752 .... 300.00
Bird, Redstarts, No.3490D .... 165.00 To 170.00
Bird, Rivoli Hummingbird, No.3627 .... 105.00
Bird, Rooster, No.3445 .... 95.00
Bird, Rufous Hummingbird, No.3585 .... 35.00 To 45.00
Bird, Western Tanager, No.3749 .... 165.00 To 225.00
Bird, Wilson Warbler, No.3597 .... 48.00
Bird, Wren, No.3401 .... 40.00 To 45.00
Bird, Wrens, No.3401D .... 75.00 To 85.00
Bird, Yellow Warbler, No.3447 .... 50.00 To 80.00
Bowl, Country Garden, 8 In. 9.00
Bowl, Golden Harvest, 12 1/2 In. 13.00
Bowl, Green, Scalloped, Oval, 9 1/2 X 4 1/2 In. 11.00
Bowl, Terra Rose Green, Leaf Handle, 6 X 2 1/4 In. 4.50
Bowl, Thistle, 12 In. 25.00
Bowl, Wild Rose, Divided, 10 1/2 X 7 In. 11.00
Cake Plate, Fruit & Flowers, Pedestal 15.00
Cake Stand, Terra Rose Green, 8 1/4 X 4 In. 16.00
Candle Warmer, Terra Rose, Green 10.00
Carafe, Yellow, Blue, Ribbed, Wooden Handle, 7 3/4 X 5 1/2 In. 15.00
Celery, Tulip, 9 1/2 In. 6.00
Chop Plate, Kumquat, 12 1/2 In. 12.00
Coffee Warmer, Golden Harvest 13.00
Coffeepot, Town & Country, Green & White Spatter 55.00
Cornucopia, Terra Rose, 6 1/2 In. 18.00
Cornucopia, Terra Rose, Blue, Leaf Shape, 7 1/2 In. 14.00
Creamer, Country Garden 4.00
Creamer, Prelude 3.00
Cup & Saucer, Colonial, Blue 4.50
Cup & Saucer, Country Garden, Tulip, Blue Flower 5.00
Cup & Saucer, Fruit 5.00
Cup & Saucer, Golden Harvest 6.00
Cup, Amber Glo 3.00
Cup, Prelude 5.00
Cup, Town & Country, Black 9.50
Dish, Serving, Bella Rosa, 2 Sections 14.00
Dish, Terra Rose, Basket Handle, Green, Pear Sections, 7 X 8 In. 10.00
Dish, Terra Rose, Green, Cover, 5 1/2 X 3 In. 9.00
Figurine, Buffalo, 3 1/2 X 2 1/2 In. 100.00
Figurine, Dog, Seated, Brown & Black, 5 In. 250.00
Gravy Boat, Underplate, Fruit & Flowers 4.00
Juvenile Set, Little Bo Peep, 3 Piece 45.00
Mold, Gelatin, Town & Country 55.00

Napkin Ring, Town & Country, Black 6.00
Nut Dish, Poppy, 4 In. 2.50
Pitcher, Black, Gold, 12 In. 12.00
Pitcher, Brushed Turquoise, 6 1/2 In. 12.50
Pitcher, Country Garden, Small 8.00
Pitcher, Fruit, 1/2 Gal. 45.00
Pitcher, Water, Bittersweet Pattern 20.00
Planter, Terra Rose, Blue, 5 1/2 X 3 In. 5.50
Plate, Apple Delight, 8 In. 3.50
Plate, Blueberry, 8 In. 7.00
Plate, Country Garden, Tiger Lily, 8 1/4 In. 3.50
Plate, Dahlia, 10 In. 4.50
Plate, Garland, 6 In. 1.50
Plate, Golden Harvest, 6 In. 1.50
Plate, Golden Harvest, 8 In. 4.00
Plate, Golden Harvest, 10 In. .... 4.25 To 5.50
Plate, Orchard Song, 6 In. 2.00
Plate, Prelude, 6 In. 2.00
Plate, Prelude, 8 In. 3.00
Plate, Prelude, 10 In. 4.00
Plate, Rings of Gold, Teal & Blue, 14 In. 22.00
Plate, Sailboat, Hand Painted, NMS, 10 In. 25.00
Plate, Star Flower, 6 In. 2.00
Plate, Thistle, 8 In. 3.50
Plate, Thistle, 10 In. 4.50
Plate, Thistle, 12 1/2 In. 11.00
Plate, Tidbit, Fruit & Flowers, 2–Tier 10.00
Plate, Town & Country, Black, 8 In. 9.50
Plate, Town & Country, Black, 12 1/4 In. 20.00
Plate, Town & Country, Server, Center Handle, Black 10.00
Plate, Town & Country, Yellow, 10 In. 15.00
Plate, Tulip, 12 In. 12.00
Plate, White Face, 8 In. 3.00
Salt & Pepper, Golden Harvest 8.50
Salt & Pepper, Magnolia 12.00
Salt & Pepper, Thistle 10.00
Saucer, Town & Country, Black 3.00
Server, Bella Rose, Center Handle 10.00
Server, Dahlia, Center Handle 10.00
Server, Sgraffito, Center Handle 10.00
Server, Thistle, Center Handle 12.00
Snack Set, Orchard Song, Off–Center Ring & Cup, 8 In. Plate 6.00
Sugar & Creamer, Country Garden, Cover 7.50
Sugar & Creamer, Thistle 12.00
Sugar & Creamer, Tray, Amber Glow, 3 Piece 25.00
Sugar, Cover, Orchard Song 4.00
Sugar, Creamer & Tray, Mottled Gold 60.00
Syrup, Colonial, Blue .... 8.00 To 10.00
Teapot, Bella Rosa 25.00
Vase, Figural, Lady's Head, Blue Hairnet & Neckline, Cream, 6 1/2 In. 45.00
Vase, Pale Blue To Yellow, Side Handles, Reeded, Scalloped, 7 In. 11.00
Vase, Terra Rose, 7 In., Pair 30.00
Vase, Yellow Rose, 4 X 4 In. 9.00
Water Set, Blue, 1 Qt. Pitcher, 4 3 1/2 In. Tumblers, 1902 .... 35.00

We named Star Holly in an article in the 1950s. It was thought to
be an early nineteenth–century art glass, but it is really a type of
milk glass made by the Imperial Glass Company of Bellaire, Ohio,
in 1957. The pieces were made to look like Wedgwood jasperware.
White holly leaves appear against colored borders of blue, green, or
rust. It is marked on the bottom of every piece. Some identical
molded glass was made without the added color. Unfortunately,
misinformation is difficult to correct, and even some museums have
mislabeled the Star Holly as earlier than 1957.

STAR HOLLY, Goblet 75.00

Steins have been used by beer and ale drinkers for over 500 years. They have been made of ivory, porcelain, stoneware, faience, silver, pewter, wood, or glass in sizes up to nine gallons. Although some were made by Meissen, Capo–di–Monte, and other famous factories, most were made in Germany. The words "Geschutz" or "Musterschutz" on a stein are the German words for patented or registered design, not company names. Steins are still being made in the old styles.

STEIN, Bottle, Coach Scene, Enameled, Blown Glass, 9 In. 130.00
  Capo–Di–Monte, War Scene, Helmet Finial, 1 Liter 95.00
  Cavalier, Maiden, Gambrenus Finial, Merkelbach & Wick, 2 Liter 235.00
  Chess Game, 3–D Hunter Lid, Pottery, 1 Liter 85.00
  Clown, Character ....*Illus* 2760.00
  Drinking Scene, 3–D Barmaid Lid, Pottery, 1/2 Liter 125.00
  Dutch Boy Stein Bank, Porcelain, 1/2 Liter 275.00
  Floral, Camel, Verse, Enameled, Blown Glass, 1/2 Liter 145.00
  Floral, Split Hoof Feet, Pewter, 2 Liter 230.00
  Fluted Body, Helmet On Lid, Pressed Glass, 4/10 Liter 175.00
  Frederick III, Character ....*Illus* 2300.00
  Frog Shape, Porcelain, Pewter Pierced Thumb Lift, W.Germany, 7 In. 80.00
  Hunter With Pipe, Porcelain, Pewter Thumb Lift, Germany, 8 1/2 In. 150.00
  Knights With Castle Body, Pottery, 5 Liter 275.00
  Man Fishing, Saying In Square, Blue Gray, Tree Bark Handle, Stoneware 350.00
  Masonic Crest Engraved, Blown Glass, Clear, Pewter Base, 8 3/4 In. 450.00
      STEIN, METTLACH, see Mettlach, Stein
  Munchener Frauenkirche, Character, Porcelain ....*Illus* 1380.00
  Munich Child Scene, Art Nouveau Body, Stoneware, 1 Liter 110.00
  Munich Child, Pottery, 1 Liter 325.00
  Musterschutz, Figural, Pig Smoking Pipe, 1/2 Liter 525.00
  Nobleman, Hunting Scene, Carved Ivory, Metal Hinged Cover, 10 In. 2640.00
  Nurenberg Tower, Stoneware, 1/2 Liter 235.00
  Olympia Beer, 10 In. 16.00
  Raised Figures, Lovers & Cupid, Gerz, 4 Liter, 21 In. 235.00
  Ram Barrel, Monkey Handle, Pottery, 1/2 Liter 120.00
  Round Horse, Character, 1895 ....*Illus* 1380.00
  Royal Canadian Air Force, Jet Plane Finial, Lithophane 95.00
  Ruby Body, Clear Handle, Pewter Overlay, Munich Child, 1/2 Liter 240.00
  Sailors, Embossed, Eagle Thumb Lift, S.M.S. Pfeil, 1 Liter, 1909–12 .... 1200.00
  Shooting Prize, Target Lid, Stoneware, 1/2 Liter 135.00
  Sitting Monkey, Figural, Top Hat, German Verse, Pottery 245.00
  Skull 1 Side, Devil Other, Bisque, 1/2 Liter, 4 X 5 1/2 In. 400.00
  St. Augustine, Alligator Handle, Pottery, 1/2 Liter 175.00
  Sterling Ale, Stoneware, Pewter Cover, 6 Liter, 16 In. 475.00
  Wolf Shape, Porcelain, Pewter Thumb Lift, Germany, 10 In. 120.00

Stereo cards that were made for stereopticon viewers became popular after 1840. Two almost identical pictures were mounted on a stiff cardboard backing so that, when viewed through a stereoscope, a three–dimensional picture could be seen. Value is determined by maker and by the subject. These cards were made in quantity through the 1930s.

STEREO CARD, 2 Dead Confederate Artillery Soldiers, Petersburg 76.00
  Broadway, R.C. Roche, Ealry Glass, C.1859 .... 120.00
  Bryan & Wife, 1900 .... 6.00 To 9.00
  Buffalo Indian Chief, Buffalo & People On City Street 45.00
  Colonel Duryea & Staff, Civil War, 1860s 12.50
  Colorado Central R.R.Extension, Construction Scene, Gardner 90.00
  Dead Soldiers, At Gettysburg, 1863, 2 Piece 60.00
  Evacuation of Confederate Forces, Fort Sumter, G.N. Barnard 22.50
  Funeral Scene, Herman Buchholz 4.00
  Gettysburg Battlefield, Slain Soldiers, 1863 .... 8.00
  Gettysburg Hero John Burns Recovering From Wounds, 1860s 12.50

Grand Canyon, Arizona, Underwood, Box, 18 Piece	50.00
Group Series, What Is Home Without A Mother–In–Law	4.00
Indian Massacre, Dining Outdoors On Prairie, Zimmermann, 1862	65.00
Interior Faneuil Hall, Boston	4.00
Interior Ft. Sumter, 1860s	8.00
Keystone Views, Historic Sites, 2 1/2 X 5 In., 50 Piece	125.00
Lincoln's Funeral, Anthony, 1865	30.00
McKinley Memorial, Keystone, 1899	8.00
Pedestrian Bridge, California Mountain Scenery	4.00
President Grant, Cottage By Sea, 1872 Copyright, G.W. Pach	28.00
Providence Railroad Station, Boston, Mass., John P. Soule	4.00
R.R. Depot, Los Angeles, Calif., Continent Stereoscopic Co.	50.50
Ruins In Richmond, G.O. Brown, 1865, 2 Piece	52.50
San Francisco Earthquake & Fire, 9 Piece	155.00
Sears Roebuck & Co., Views of Departments, Box, 50 Piece	48.00
Slave Pen, Alexandria, Virginia, Civil War, 1860s	12.50
Thomas Edison, In Laboratory, Closeup Pose	95.00
Vice Admiral David Farragut, U.S.N., Gallery View	50.00
View On Wharf, City Point, Va., After Explosion, Gardner	43.00
Wedding, H.C. White Co., Box.1902, 10 Piece	32.50
Winter At Horseshoe Bend On Penn.R.R., R.A. Bonine	4.00
Wm.H. Harrison & M. VanBuren Portrait, 4 X 7 In.	55.00
Wrecked Battleship Maine, Keystone, 1898	7.00

The stereoscope, or stereopticon, was used for viewing stereo cards. The hand viewer was invented by Oliver Wendell Holmes, although more complicated table models were used before his was produced in 1859.

STEREOSCOPE, Graphoscope, Wood, 11 X 7 X 6 In.	225.00
Stereopticon, Double, Walnut Case, Pat.1859, Alexander Reckerg	600.00
Viewer, Brewster, Burled Wood	150.00
Viewer, Keystone, Velvet Rim	30.00
Viewer, Velvet Rim, Aluminum Hood, Wooden	30.00

STERLING SILVER, see Silver–Sterling

Steuben glass was made at the Steuben Glass Works of Corning, New York. The factory, founded by Frederick Carder and T. C. Hawkes, Sr., was purchased by the Corning Glass Company. They continued to make glass called "Steuben." Many types of art glass were made at Steuben. The firm is still making exceptional quality glass but it is clear, modern–style glass.

STEUBEN, see also Aurene

STEUBEN, Ashtray, Rosaline & Alabaster	85.00
Basket, Crystal, 7 1/2 X 8 In.	170.00
Beaker, Agnus Dei, Crystal, Pedestal, 7 In.	300.00
Bowl, 3 Applied Designs At Base, Colorless, Signed, 8 In.	160.00
Bowl, Aurene & Calcite, 10 In.	245.00 To 275.00
Bowl, Boat Shape, Bubbles, Amber, 9 1/2 In.	110.00
Bowl, Calcite, Gold Aurene Interior, Rolled Lip, 10 In.	275.00
Bowl, Centerpiece, Gold Calcite, 10 1/4 In.	75.00
Bowl, Cluthra, White, Signed, 5 1/2 In.	250.00
Bowl, Fleur–De–Lis, Clear, 13 1/2 In.	225.00
Bowl, Gold, White Base, 12 In.	295.00
Bowl, Green Jade, Signed, 8 In.	95.00
Bowl, Green Swirl, 6–Sided, Amber Foot, 9 3/4 In.	425.00
Bowl, Petal Rim, Crystal, 13 In.	100.00
Bowl, Swirl, Porpoise Cover, Engraved President 1964, 12 In.	325.00
Bowl, Tied Bow Mold, Oval, Signed, 11 In.	495.00
Bowl, Trillium, 10 1/2 In.	200.00
Bowl, Turned–In Rim, Jade Green, 11 In.	125.00
Bowl, Verre De Soie, 9 In.	135.00
Bowl, White, Cluthra, 5 1/2 In.	250.00
Box, Verre De Soie, Cover, Fruit Design	175.00
Bunch of Grapes, Crystal, Signed, 7 1/2 In.	550.00

Candleholder, Green, Cerise Blue Handle, 5 In., Pair	395.00
Candlestick, Amber Twisted Around Clear Stem, 10 In., Pair	425.00
Candlestick, Canary, Domed Foot, Signed, 12 In., Pair	385.00
Candlestick, Crystal, 8 In., Pair	265.00
Candlestick, Green Body, Sapphire Blue Ring Handles, 3 3/4 In., Pr.	295.00
Candlestick, Oriental Poppy, 6 In., Pair	1500.00
Centerpiece, Gold Aurene, Signed, 11 3/4 X 4 1/2 In.	650.00
Centerpiece, White Calcite Pedestal, Ivrene, 8 In.	300.00
Champagne, Alabaster Twisted Stem, Jade, Signed, 5 1/2 In.	110.00
Compote, Centerpiece, Cylinder Base, Applied Design, 11 In.	250.00
Compote, Fruit, Calcite, Gold Fruit, 8 In.	290.00
Compote, Hollow Blue Mica Stem, Swirled Amber Base, Signed, 8 In.	495.00
Compote, Oriental Poppy, Cranberry Swirl, Green Tinted Base, 14 In.	1300.00
Cordial, Van Dyke, Rosa Swirled Stem, 5 3/4 In.	125.00
Cup & Saucer, Blue Aurene, Demitasse	775.00
Cuspidor, Woman's, Gold Aurene	395.00
Dish, Olive, Side Lip, Crystal, 7 In.	110.00
Epergne, Pink, Clear Thorn, Trumpet Form, 10 In.	139.00
Figurine, Bunch of Grapes, Crystal, 6 In.	250.00
Figurine, Dolphin, Curling Tail, Signed, 11 In.	1980.00
Figurine, Duck, Crystal, 5 1/2 In.	275.00
Figurine, Horse, 9 In., Pair	1350.00
Figurine, Penguin, Crystal, 4 In.	150.00
Figurine, Swan, 4 In.	175.00
Finger Bowl, Ruby, Gold, Abstract Threading, Signed, Pair	50.00
Fruit Bowl, Crystal, 8 Leaf Petals Around Base, 12 In.	400.00
Goblet, Engraved Floral Swags, Jade, Signed, 8 1/2 In.	225.00
Goblet, Gold Ruby, Clear Base, 6 1/4 In.	80.00
Goblet, Swirled Stem, Cranberry, 8 In.	150.00
Hand Cooler, Napping Cat, Signed, Encased, 3 In.	150.00
Lamp, Black Cut Over Cameo, Draped Classical Women, Slag Shade	1175.00
Lamp, Dragon On Field of Clouds, Bronze Mounts, Blue, Signed, 15 In.	2800.00
Lamp, Gold Pulled Feather, Brass Base, Opalescent Body, 16 In.	1150.00
Lamp, Mei Ping Form, Dragons, Clouds, 15 In.	2800.00 To 3050.00
Lamp, Yellow Quartz, Acid Cut Back, 9 1/2 In.	750.00
Ornament, Fruit Form, Pineapple, Bunch Grapes, Apple, Pear, Signed	412.00
Ornament, Galapagos Island, Etched, Mountain Form, Signed, 12 In.	4125.00
Ornament, Mouse On Swiss Cheese, 18K Gold, Signed, 5 In.	2420.00
Ornament, Table, Baffin Island, Glacier Form, Etched Eskimo, 8 In.	4950.00
Ornament, Table, Crete, Etched Mythical Figures, Signed, 10 In.	5500.00
Ornament, Table, Crusoe's Island, Mountain, Etched Robinson, 10 In.	4125.00
Ornament, Table, Easter Island, Engraved Island, Signed, 8 In.	4950.00
Ornament, Table, Excalibur, Silver, Gold, Signed, 8 In.	1870.00
Ornament, Table, Hawaii, Cloud, Engraved 3 Natives, Signed, 13 In.	4650.00
Ornament, Table, Oceanus Atlanticus Bermudas, Signed, 15 In.	4950.00
Ornament, Table, Partridge In Pear Tree, Signed, 6 1/4 In.	1760.00
Ornament, Table, Tahiti, Island, Etched Natives, Signed, 11 In.	3575.00
Paperweight, Crown, Crystal, 4 In.	175.00
Paperweight, Heart Shape, Fitted Leather Box	688.00
Paperweight, Teardrop & Spiral Weight Threads	130.00
Parfait, Rosaline, Alabaster	150.00
Perfume Bottle, Crackle Glass, Green Faceted Stopper, 5 In.	225.00
Perfume Bottle, Gourd Shape, Faceted Sided, Latticework, C.1925	5775.00
Perfume Bottle, Melon Ribbed, Gold, Signed, Numbered, 5 1/2 In.	550.00
Plate, Alabaster, Jade Green Rim, 8 5/8 In.	50.00
Plate, Amethyst, 8 1/2 In., Pair	209.00
Plate, Engraved Rose, 8 In.	250.00
Plate, Gold Aurene, 5 7/8 In.	70.00
Plate, Gold Aurene, 8 1/2 In.	75.00
Plate, Jade Green, 8 1/2 In.	35.00
Plate, Swirled Pattern, Gold Ruby, 8 1/2 In.	90.00
Platter, Matching Footed Bowl In Center, Gold Aurene, 14 In.	495.00
Punch Cup, Green, Applied Threads At Top, Handle, Signed, 2 3/4 In.	95.00
Saucer, Jade Green, 6 In.	50.00

Shade, Gold Aurene, Bell Shape, 5 In.	50.00
Shade, Gold Leaf & Vine, Calcite	115.00
Shade, Moss Agate, Marble Base, Between Bronze Nudes, 6 In.	1950.00
Shade, Pulled Gold Aurene Feathers, Green Outline, Calcite, 5 In.	135.00
Shade, Red Aurene Design, Closed Top, Opening For Wire, 4 1/2 In.	1150.00
Shade, Yellow Feather, Gold Lined, 5 1/2 In.	115.00
Sherbet & Underplate, Aurene & Calcite	135.00
Sherbet, Aurene On Calcite	85.00
Sherbet, Underplate, Gold Aurene	335.00
Sugar, Cover, Apple Finial	220.00
Sugar, Cover, Bubbly, Green Reeded Top, Pedestal, Signed, 3 3/4 In.	85.00
Tumbler, Iced Tea, Jade Green, Translucent White Handle, 6 In.	125.00
Urn, Green Jade, Alabaster Handles, 10 In., Pair	1500.00
Vase, 3 Calla Lilies Form, Ivrene, 13 In., Pair	1100.00
Vase, 3–Prong Tree Trunk, Topaz, 6 In.	125.00 To 250.00
Vase, Amphora Form, Alabaster Handles, Jade, 10 In.	550.00
Vase, Applied Shapes On Side Turned Half Around, Signed, 6 1/2 In.	145.00
Vase, Aurene, Swirl Gold & Green Peacock Feathers, Baluster, 8 In.	3300.00
Vase, Blue Aurene, Vertical Ribs, Pinched Belly, Signed, 6 In.	585.00
Vase, Bristol Yellow, Black Random Threads, Signed, 12 X 12 In.	850.00
Vase, Brown Geese In Flight, Yellow, Jade, Art Glass, 10 In.	2500.00
Vase, Bubbly Glass, Dark Amber, Signed, 7 In.	135.00
Vase, Bud, Rosaline, Alabaster Foot, Signed, 8 1/4 In.	110.00
Vase, Bud, Teardrop Base, Motto, 7 In.	130.00
Vase, Butterfly, Blue Aurene, Signed, 5 1/8 In.	565.00
Vase, Cluthra, Burgundy Rim, Shaded To Dark Dusty Rose, 10 In.	950.00
Vase, Cluthra, Green, Signed, 10 1/2 In.	1050.00
Vase, Cluthra, Jade Green, 11 X 10 In.	1100.00
Vase, Cluthra, White, 10 In.	675.00
Vase, Cone Shape, Clear Foot, Electric Blue, 12 In.	180.00
Vase, Conical, Fluted Quatrefoil Base, Signed, 14 In.	300.00
Vase, Cornucopia, Crystal, 8 In.	225.00
Vase, Cut Floral Design, Rose On Alabaster, Flared, 12 In.	950.00
Vase, Dark Blue, Jade Ribbed, 5 1/2 In.	2000.00
Vase, Diagonal Ribbing, Green Jade, Square Top, 5 1/2 In.	150.00
Vase, Diamond, Green Stem & Foot, Signed, 11 In.	250.00
Vase, Diamond, Mica Flecks, Silvrina Air Trap, Blue, 10 In.	750.00
Vase, Electric Blue, Clear Foot, Straight Optic, Cone Shape, 12 In.	180.00
Vase, Etched Art Deco Design, Black Foot, 6 1/2 In.	100.00
Vase, Fan, Amethyst, Signed, 8 1/2 In.	130.00
Vase, Fan, Clear Top, Blue Ball & Foot, 6 1/2 In.	125.00
Vase, Fan, Etched Ship, 8 3/4 In.	275.00
Vase, Fan, Grotesque, 11 In.	500.00 To 1200.00
Vase, Fan, Jade & Alabaster, Signed, 8 In.	400.00
Vase, Fan, Oriental Poppy, Cranberry, Opalescent White Stripe, 8 In.	1700.00
Vase, Fan, Ribbed Crystal, Pink Threading, 8 1/2 In.	115.00
Vase, Fan, White Iridescent, Wave Textured, Pedestal, 8 In.	600.00
Vase, Floral, Rosaline Cut To Alabaster, 7 In.	1695.00
Vase, Gold Aurene Ribbed, Signed, 5 In.	350.00
Vase, Gold Aurene, Crimped Rim, Signed, 4 1/4 In.	275.00
Vase, Gold Aurene, Dimpled Sides, 3 Handles, 9 In.	950.00
Vase, Gold Mica Flakes, Air Traps, 10 In.	850.00
Vase, Grotesque, Apple Green To Crystal, 11 1/2 In.	550.00
Vase, Grotesque, Flemish Blue To Clear, 9 1/2 In.	375.00
Vase, Ivory, Oriental Shape, Wide Mouth, 10 1/4 In., Pair	700.00
Vase, Ivory, Ribbed, Bulbous Body, Flared Neck, Signed, 5 In.	135.00
Vase, Ivrene, Handle, 13 In.	575.00
Vase, Jack–In–The–Pulpit, Aurene, Paper Label, 6 1/4 In.	1100.00
Vase, Jack–In–The–Pulpit, Ivrene, 6 In.	595.00
Vase, Jade, Alabaster Handles, Amphora Form, 10 In.	550.00
Vase, Marian Blue, Topaz Threaded Rim, 6 In.	85.00
Vase, Matzu Pattern, Jade Over Alabaster, 8 In.	995.00
Vase, Oriental Poppy, Lamp Mounted, 11 In.	700.00
Vase, Paperweight, Lily, 8 1/2 In.	250.00

Vase, Prunt On Each Side, Flared, Crystal, Signed, 4 3/4 In.	125.00
Vase, Ribbed, Blue Aurene, Signed, 6 In.	500.00
Vase, Ribbed, Gold Aurene, Signed, 5 In.	350.00
Vase, Rosaline, Alabaster Base, Signed, 7 In.	275.00
Vase, Rose Over Alabaster, 12 In.	1375.00
Vase, Rose, Flared, Footed, Alabaster Cut, Floral Design, 12 In.	950.00
Vase, Stick, Gold Aurene, Round Base, Signed, 8 1/4 In.	325.00
Vase, Stick, Gold Aurene, Signed, 6 In.	175.00
Vase, Trumpet, Calcite, Aurene Interior, Ruffled Rim, 6 In.	305.00
Vase, Verre De Soie, 12 In.	165.00
Vase, White Flowers, Green Leaves, Vines On Gold Aurene, 4 1/2 In.	2600.00
Vase, White To Pink, 3 Prong, Signed, 10 In.	1450.00
Vase, Wide Mouth, Oriental Shape, 10 1/4 In., Pair	700.00
Wine, Jade Bowl, Alabaster Stem, Signed, 6 Piece	395.00

Stevengraphs are woven pictures made like fancy ribbons. They were manufactured by Thomas Stevens of Coventry, England, and became popular in 1862. Most are marked "Woven in silk by Thomas Stevens" or were mounted on a cardboard that tells the story of the Stevengraph. Other similar ribbon pictures have been made in England and Germany.

STEVENGRAPH, At Old Jerome, New York Raceway	275.00
Bookmark, A Birthday Gift	50.00
Bookmark, Happy May Thy Birthday Be	45.00
Bookmark, Home Sweet Home, No Tassel	40.00
Bookmark, Norwich, Conn., 250th Anniversary	50.00
Bookmark, Sir Garibaldi	90.00
Bookmark, To My Father	40.00
Declaration of Independence, Frame, 7 1/4 In.	160.00
For Life Or Death, Heroism On Land, Matted & Framed	225.00
Heroism On Land, Fire Engine	285.00 To 300.00

Stevens & Williams of Stourbridge, England, made many types of glass, including layered, etched, cameo, and art glass, between the 1830s and 1930s. Some pieces are signed "S & W." Many pieces are decorated with flowers, leaves, and other designs based on nature.

STEVENS & WILLIAMS, Bowl, Crimped Amber Rim, Floral Design, 6 X 7 1/2 In.	325.00
Bowl, Pansy, Cranberry, Applied Clear Rigaree & Handles	225.00
Bowl, Ruffled Top, Pale Orange, 2 1/2 X 3 3/4 In.	145.00
Bride's Basket, Herringbone Mother–of–Pearl, 1892	1250.00
Bride's Bowl, Bird On Each Side, Silver Holder	750.00
Bride's Bowl, Silver Plated Holder, Square	475.00
Bride's Bowl, Triangular Shape, Holder	295.00
Dish, Sweetmeat, Bamboo Design, Metal Fittings, 5 In.	865.00
Dish, Sweetmeat, Raised Gold, Metal Fittings, 3 In.	865.00
Ewer, Amber Handle Forms Branch, Cherries, 5 1/4 In.	110.00
Ewer, Amber Rim, Handle & Branch, Opaque, 6 1/4 In.	95.00
Jam Jar, Rose Bowl Shape, Silver Plated Holder, 6 In.	110.00
Jar, Sweetmeat, Applied Leaves, Silver Plated Fittings	195.00
Liqueur Set, Tray, Flowers, Leaves, Clear Stopper, 7 Pc.	750.00
Muffineer, Cranberry	325.00
Muffineer, Quilted Phlox, Pink	165.00
Perfume Bottle, Green & Crystal Swirl Striped, 9 In.	165.00
Perfume Bottle, Swirl Design, Gold Trim, 13 In.	325.00
Pitcher, Candy Cane Striped, Bulbous	135.00
Rose Bowl, Arboresque, Opaque White, Crimped, 3 1/2 In.	125.00
Rose Bowl, Box Pleated Top, Beaded, Cranberry, 3 1/2 In.	175.00
Rose Bowl, Box Pleated Top, Gold Prunus, 5 In.	475.00
Rose Bowl, Cranberry, 4 1/4 In.	225.00
Rose Bowl, Crystal Acanthus Leaves Form Feet, 6 In.	175.00
Rose Bowl, Crystal Leaves Loop To Form Feet, 7 In.	155.00
Rose Bowl, Egg Shape, Pleated Top, Gold Prunus, 5 In.	475.00
Rose Bowl, Green–Amber, 2 3/4 In.	165.00
Rose Bowl, Thumbprint Pattern, Blue, 2 3/4 In.	175.00

Rose Bowl, Yellow–Amber, 2 3/4 In. 165.00
Sherbet, Matching Plate, Cherries & Pears, Royal Blue 325.00
Tankard, Snakes, Topaz, Blue Icicles Rim, 10 X 7 In. 185.00
Toothpick, Crimped Top, Clear Pedestal, 4 In. 75.00
Tumbler, Applied Amber Pear & Apple, 3 3/4 In. 225.00
Tumbler, Diamond–Quilted, Striped, Marked, 3 5/8 In. 225.00
Vase, 3 Applied Leaves, Amber Top, Cream, 7 1/4 In., Pr. 325.00
Vase, Amber Branch & Leaves, 1 White Blossom, 4 1/2 In. 80.00
Vase, Applied Amber Leaves, Branches, 13 1/2 In. 275.00
Vase, Applied Plums, Green & Amber Leaves, 7 1/4 In. 300.00
Vase, Applied Purple Fruit, Iridescent, 8 1/2 In. 90.00
Vase, Applied Rose Leaves, Pink Lining, 7 1/4 In., Pair 325.00
Vase, Art Glass, Floral Carving, Cameo, Red, 10 In. 3600.00
Vase, Blossoming Vines, Peonies, Silver Deposit, 12 In. 2475.00
Vase, Bud, Cranberry Swirl, Silver Mica 80.00
Vase, Cameo, 3 Geese Panels, Palm Trees, 3 1/2 In. 275.00
Vase, Clear & Rose Branch, Amber Acorn, 4 1/2 In. 75.00
Vase, Colored Swirls, Enamel Florals, Pear Shape, 13 In. 280.00
Vase, Crimped Top, Cranberry, 4 In. 175.00
Vase, Egg Shape, Pulled Feather, Crystal Feet, 7 3/4 In. 875.00
Vase, Flowers, White Lining, Pink Overlay, 6 3/8 In. 165.00
Vase, Irregular Threading, Marked, Crystal, 8 1/4 In. 325.00
Vase, Jack–In–The–Pulpit, Applied Flowers, 8 1/2 In. 135.00
Vase, Jack–In–The–Pulpit, Rainbow Frosted Shade, 12 In. 500.00
Vase, Mother–of–Pearl, Purple Swirl, Marked, 7 In. 895.00
Vase, Raised Flowers, Branches, Opaque White, 5 1/4 In. 60.00
Vase, Ruffled Leaf, Blue Interior, 3–Petal Top, 6 In. 135.00
Vase, Ruffled Leaf, Green & Amber Sides, 6 1/2 In. 145.00
Vase, Ruffled, Cream Outside, Pink Inside Top, 6 1/2 In. 145.00
Vase, Stick, Intaglio Cut, Emerald Green, 17 1/4 In. 550.00
Vase, Vaseline Branches & Leaves, Cherries, 9 1/2 In. 165.00
Vase, Vaseline Opalescent, Trumpet Shape, Holder, 7 In. 135.00

Henry William Stiegel, a colorful immigrant to the colonies, started his first factory in Pennsylvania in 1763. He remained in business until 1774. Glassware was made in a style popular in Europe at that time and was similar to the glass of many other makers. It was made of clear or colored glass and was decorated with enamel colors, mold blown designs, or etching. It is almost impossible to be sure a piece was made by Stiegel, so the knowing collector now refers to this glass as Stiegel type.

STIEGEL TYPE, Bottle, Nailsea Type, Blue, Octagonal, Pewter Top, 1/2 Pt. 650.00
Flask, Enameled 85.00
Tumbler, Hunter's, Flip, Flint, 4 In. 225.00

Stoneware is a coarse, glazed, and fired potter's ceramic that is used to make crocks, jugs, bowls, etc. It is often decorated with cobalt blue decorations. Stoneware is still being made.

STONEWARE, Basket, Braided Coil Handle, Scalloped Shell Rim, Oval, 8 1/2 In. 300.00
Batter Jar, Tin Lid, 2 Birds, Pennsylvania 950.00
Batter Jar, Wm.Rooke, Easton, Wire Bail Handle, Tin Cover, 12 In. 160.00
Batter Pail, Cowden & Wilcox, Floral, Bail Handle, Handles, 1 Gal. 1540.00
Batter Pail, Profile of Man, Top Hat, 1 Gal. 1870.00
Bean Pot, Chain Link 45.00
Beater Jar, Blue Stripe Around Body 42.00
Beater Jar, Hansell, Iowa, Blue Stripe, Advertising 65.00
Bottle, 3 Pinched Sides, Cobalt Blue On Indents, 10 1/2 In. 135.00
Bottle, J. Rosche, Blue At Neck, 10 1/4 In. 15.00
Bottle, Pig, Dark Brown Albany Slip, 6 7/8 In. 275.00
Bottle, Walte's Distillery Pure Canada Malt Whiskey, 1 Qt. 67.50
Bowl, Apricots & Honeycomb, Blue & White, 9 In. 75.00
Bowl, Chain Pattern, Blue, 9 In. 50.00
Bowl, Greek Key, 8 In. 65.00
Bowl, Milk, Label, Lyons, Cobalt Blue 2 & Foliage, 12 3/4 In. 475.00

Bowl, Wedding Ring, Blue & White, 10 In.	125.00
Bowl, Wedding Ring, Blue, 7 In.	85.00
Bowl, Wildflower, 8 In.	40.00 To 60.00
Butter, Apricot	295.00
Butter, Basketweave, Blue & White	275.00
Butter, Cover, Apple Blossom	245.00
Butter, Cover, Apricot & Honeycomb	210.00
Butter, Cover, Apricot, Blue & White	175.00
Butter, Cover, Eagle, Bail	585.00
Butter, Cover, Edelweiss	65.00
Butter, Draped Window	325.00
Butter, Robinson Clay	275.00
Canister, Cover, Oatmeal, Blue & White	275.00
Canister, Cover, Raisins, Blue & White	235.00
Canister, Cover, Rice, Snowflake	125.00
Canteen, Grand Army of The Republic, Dated 1900	450.00
Chamber Pot, Blue & White, Bluebird Decal	95.00
Chicken On Nest, Salt, Yellow, Brown, 3 In.	195.00
Chicken Waterer, Blue Hens & Chicks	130.00
Chicken Waterer, Rooster & Chicken Design	95.00
Chicken Waterer, Thos. Haig, Phila., 7 1/4 In.	465.00
Chicken Waterer, Western	30.00
Chicken Waterer, White	80.00
Churn, A.O. Whittemore, Havana, N.Y., Fruit Compote Design, 5 Gal.	412.50
Churn, Bee–Sting Design, 4 Gal.	40.00
Churn, Bee–Sting Design, 5 Gal.	75.00
Churn, Buckeye Pottery, McComb, Ill., White Bristol Glaze, 2 Gal.	55.00
Churn, Burger Brothers, 6 Gal.	325.00
Churn, Bust of Man In Tuxedo, Cobalt Blue, 2 Handles	7500.00
Churn, C.W. Braun	800.00
Churn, Cobalt Blue Floral, Applied Handles, 17 In.	450.00
Churn, Evan R. Jones, Man In Tuxedo, 6 Gal.	7500.00
Churn, Flowers, Hart	800.00
Churn, Galena, Ill., 4 Gal.	665.00
Churn, Impressed 2 In Circle, Incised Lines, Blue Design, 14 In.	175.00
Churn, Incised Line On Rim, No.2, Leaf Scrolls, 1840, 13 3/4 In.	225.00
Churn, Lid, Hamilton & Jones, Penna., Stenciled Label, 18 3/4 In.	325.00
Churn, N. Norton, Ear Handles, Cobalt Blue Brush Marks, C.1830	200.00
Churn, Peoria Pottery, Earred, Foliage, 5 Gal.	195.00
Churn, Prancing Lion, J. Burger, 5 Gal.	7250.00
Churn, S. Weiss, General Merchandise, Lamar, Ind., Brown, Small	525.00
Churn, W.E. Welding, Brantford, Ont., C.1880, 3 1/2 In.	4750.00
Churn, Western Stoneware, Blue Leaf, Squiggle Design, 2 Gal.	135.00
Churn, White Hall, Lid, Dasher, Triangular Mark, 4 Gal.	250.00
Coffeepot, Swirl, Blue & White	525.00
Coffeepot, Top Half White, Bottom Half Blue, Blue Band	275.00
Colander, Brown Glaze, Cylindrical, Handle, 6 1/2 X 13 In.	65.00
Cookie Jar, Flying Birds	390.00
Cooler, Blue Stenciled Design & Ice Water, White Glaze, 14 In.	25.00
Cooler, Blue, White Sponge Spatter, Albany Slip Interior, 14 In.	25.00
Cooler, Cobalt Blue Incised Lines, Keg Shape, 12 In.	110.00
Cooler, Cover, Monmouth–Western, Cold Drink In Leaf, 6 Gal.	275.00
Cooler, Crest Scenes With Deer, Brass Spigot, 13 1/4 In.	200.00
Cooler, Cupid, Cover, 6 Gal.	595.00
Cooler, Eagle, Grayish White, Stenciled Blue Label, 27 In.	190.00
Cooler, Embossed Woman At Well, Light Blue, Metal Spigot, 17 In.	185.00
Cooler, Keg Shape, Embossed Bands, Cobalt Blue Trim, 10 1/2 In.	65.00
Cooler, Nickel Plated Spigots, Cherry Cheer 5 Cents, 11 3/4 In.	255.00
Cooler, Tan, Buff Base, Bail Handle, Pewter Bung, 13 X 7 In.	85.00
Cream Pot, Cover, Ear Handles, E.L. Farrar, No.2, C.1852	85.00
Crock, 3 Large Squiggles, Blue, Salt Glaze	62.00
Crock, Apple Butter, Schuler Restaurant, Cover	45.00
Crock, Applied Handles, Stenciled Design, No.2, 9 1/4 In.	65.00
Crock, B.T. Stofer & Co., Lowell, Ill., Salt Glazed, 10 Gal.	2600.00

Stoneware, Crock, Cover, Cobalt,
Floral Design, 12 In.

Don't put cracked pottery or porcelain in the dishwasher. It will often break even more.

For emergency repairs to chipped pottery, try coloring the spot with a wax crayon or oil paint. It will look a little better.

Crock, Basket of Flowers, J.A. & C.W. Underwood, 6 Gal.	1210.00
Crock, Bird Design, Cowden & Wilcox	1650.00
Crock, Bird On Stump, Ellenville, C.1850	575.00
Crock, Bird, Ft.Edward, Cobalt Blue, 3 Gal.	310.00
Crock, Bird, Whites, Utica, N.Y., 1 Gal.	687.00
Crock, Blue Songbird Design, 2 Gal.	495.00
Crock, Bright Cobalt Blue Floral, Handles, 6 Gal.	500.00
Crock, Brushed Daubs, No.3, 11 1/4 In.	90.00
Crock, Burger & Lang, Floral Design, 2 Handles, 6 Gal.	1100.00
Crock, Butter, Cobalt Blue Stenciled Label, 9 In.	375.00
Crock, Butter, Cover, Design Around, 1 Gal.	495.00
Crock, Butter, Cover, Stylized Floral Design, 8 1/2 X 14 In.	900.00
Crock, Butter, Lambrecht, 4 5/8 In.	30.00
Crock, Cake, Blue Band, Wooden Lid	200.00
Crock, Canning, Ponaghho, W. Virginia, Gray, 2 Qt.	90.00
Crock, Clark & Bros., Cannelton, Ind., Ear Handles, 5 Gal.	85.00
Crock, Cobalt Blue Foliage Design, Applied Handles, Ovoid, 14 In.	1550.00
Crock, Cobalt Blue Label Macomb Pottery Co., 10 In.	45.00
Crock, Cobalt Blue Maple Leaf One Side, Flowers Other, 4 Gal.	57.00
Crock, Cobalt Blue Maple Leaf, Western, 3 Gal.	45.00
Crock, Cobalt Blue Rooster, 6 In Circle, 13 1/2 In.	130.00
Crock, Cobalt Blue Slip, Bird, 7 3/4 In.	250.00
Crock, Cover, Cobalt, Floral Design, 12 In. ....Illus	1210.00
Crock, Cover, J.R. Bell, Stylized Tulips, Handles	1200.00
Crock, D. Kellogg, Whately, Rolled Rim, Lug Handles, 11 1/2 In.	300.00
Crock, E. Charlestown, Straight Sides, C.1810, 1 Gal.	100.00
Crock, Eagle, Eagle Pottery Co., McComb, Ill., Salt Glaze, 6 Gal.	120.00
Crock, Empire City Pottery, Blue Tulip, 1 1/2 Gal.	200.00
Crock, F.H. Cowden, Harrisburg, Stenciled, 10 In.	70.00
Crock, Flowers, Cobalt Blue Quill Work, 11 In.	150.00
Crock, Fort Edward, Pecking Chicken, 2 Handles, 4 Gal.	1150.00
Crock, Fort Edward, Standing Deer, Handles, 4 Gal.	4400.00
Crock, Gray, Blue Leaf, Straight Sides, 2 Gal.	150.00
Crock, Hamilton & Jones, Greensboro, Pa., Tan Glaze, 10 1/2 In.	125.00
Crock, Harrington & Burger, Lug Handles, Eaglet, 14 3/4 In.	5500.00
Crock, Heinz Apple Butter Label, 7 X 4 In.	190.00
Crock, Impressed Label, Tailed Birds, Cobalt Blue Slip, 9 1/4 In.	350.00
Crock, Indian Head, Cobalt Blue, 4 Gal.	57.00
Crock, J.A. & C. W. Underwood, Basket of Flowers, 6 Gal.	1210.00
Crock, J.R. Bell, Floral, Cobalt, 1874, 12 In.	1100.00
Crock, James Hamilton, Greensboro, Pa., 1 Gal.	85.00
Crock, John Remmey, Cobalt Blue Design, Lug Handles, 11 1/4 In.	950.00

Crock, Macomb Stoneware Co., 5 Gal.	4.00
Crock, Monmouth Pottery Co., Monmouth, Ill., Salt Glazed, 5 Gal.	65.00
Crock, N. Clark & Co., Cobalt Blue Flower & 3, Handles, 13 In.	375.00
Crock, N. White & Co., Bird Perched On Compote, C.1865, 5 Gal.	1800.00
Crock, Norton & Fenton, Ovoid, 4 Gal.	470.00
Crock, Profile of Man In Top Hat, 1 Gal.	1870.00
Crock, Salt, Blue & White	100.00
Crock, Salt, Blue & White, Hanging, Butterfly	110.00
Crock, Scalloped Design, Applied Handles, Blue Slip, 9 In.	55.00
Crock, Stenciled Eagle With Banner, E. Pluribus Unum, 14 In.	125.00
Crock, Stylized Flower, Cobalt Blue Quillwork, 12 In.	400.00
Crock, Thomas Brothers, Huntington, Pa., Fern Leaf, 2 Gal.	435.00
Crock, Tin Cover, Wire Bail Handle, Copenhagen's Snuff, 9 1/4 In.	50.00
Crock, W.H. Farrar & Co., Cobalt Blue Bird & Flower, 10 In.	600.00
Crock, Wedding Ring, 8 In.	40.00
Crock, White Hall Sewer Pipe & Stoneware Co., 12 Gal.	60.00
Cup, Bowtie, Flower Transfer, Blue & White	45.00
Cup, Mustache, Brown Albany Slip, Snake Handle, 4 1/2 In.	90.00
Cuspidor, Blue Stripes, White Glaze, Brown Interior, 3 1/4 In.	95.00
Cuspidor, Grape Clusters, Green Glazed, 8 In.	25.00
Cuspidor, R.D.P. Phila., Cobalt Blue Foliage, 4 X 7 1/4 In.	215.00
Custard, Brown On Yellow	18.00
Figurine, Cat, White & Brown Spotted Glaze, 3 1/8 In.	350.00
Figurine, Dog, Seated, Gray Salt Glaze, 7 1/2 In.	800.00
Flask, Cobalt Blue Design, Flattened Ovoid Shape, 9 In.	1000.00
Flask, Mottled Glaze, Bubble Blue At Lip, 7 1/2 In.	105.00
Flask, S. Harrison Lincoln, Impressed Designs, 6 1/2 In.	115.00
Flask, Stylized Leaf Or Flower, Cobalt Blue, 5 7/8 In.	325.00
Flowerpot, Cobalt Blue Leaf & Dot, 10 3/4 X 13 In.	75.00
Flowerpot, Flared Sides, Cobalt Blue Rim Design, 6 1/4 In.	65.00
Flowerpot, Floral Design, Cobalt Blue, Impressed Label, 12 In.	275.00
Humidor, Cobalt Blue, Court Jester, Smoking Pipe	38.00
Inkwell, 2 Quill Holders, 2 X 4 In.	130.00
Jar, Abraham Rhodenbaugh, Blue Design, 11 1/4 In.	150.00
Jar, Applied Handles, Cobalt Blue, Impressed Label, 13 In.	225.00
Jar, Applied Handles, Cobalt Blue, Ovoid, 9 3/4 In.	35.00
Jar, Applied Handles, Weeping Willow, Cobalt Blue, 14 In.	450.00
Jar, Applied Rim Handle, Impressed 3, Gray Salt Glaze, 10 1/2 In.	60.00
Jar, C.E.Pharis & Co., No.2, Label, Ovoid, Handles, 11 In.	190.00
Jar, Canning, 3 Blue Stripes, 8 1/2 In.	85.00
Jar, Canning, Blue Design At Shoulder, 8 1/4 In.	100.00
Jar, Canning, Blue Song Bird On Branch, Blue & Gray, 2 Gal.	495.00
Jar, Canning, Blue Stenciled Star, 9 In.	85.00
Jar, Canning, Brushed Cobalt Blue Stripes, 10 1/2 In.	115.00
Jar, Canning, Cobalt Blue Design, Applied Handles, 6 1/2 In.	475.00
Jar, Canning, Cobalt Blue Design, Ovoid, 10 In.	105.00
Jar, Canning, Cobalt Blue Floral, Ovoid, 8 1/4 In.	175.00
Jar, Canning, Cobalt Blue Stripes & Foliage, 7 7/8 In.	135.00
Jar, Canning, Greensboro, Pa., Cobalt Stenciled Label, 7 3/4 In.	65.00
Jar, Canning, Hamilton & Jones, Stenciled Blue Floral, 6 1/4 In.	75.00
Jar, Canning, J.F. Enrix, Penna,, Stenciled Label, 6 1/4 In.	65.00
Jar, Canning, Jas. Hamilton & Co., Cobalt Blue Label, 9 1/2 In.	125.00
Jar, Canning, Jas. Hamilton & Co., Greensboro, Pa., 8 In.	105.00
Jar, Canning, Loammi Kendall, No.3, Pear Shape, C.1850	125.00
Jar, Canning, Republican State Convention, Cleveland, 1877, 1 Qt.	585.00
Jar, Canning, Stenciled Cobalt Blue Design, 9 1/2 In.	600.00
Jar, Canning, Tooled Lines, Straight & Wavy Lines, 7 1/2 In.	135.00
Jar, Canning, Weir, 1 Qt.	47.50
Jar, Canning, Williams & Reppert, Blue Stenciled, 9 3/4 In.	95.00
Jar, Cobalt Blue Designs, Handle, 8 In.	125.00
Jar, Cobalt Blue Floral, No.6, 16 1/2 In.	75.00
Jar, Cobalt Blue Floral, Ovoid, 12 3/4 In.	225.00
Jar, Cobalt Blue Lines & Commas, Ovoid, 6 1/4 In.	150.00
Jar, Cobalt Blue Straight & Wavy Lines, Ovoid, 6 3/8 In.	140.00

Jar, Cobalt Blue Tulips, Primitive, 10 1/4 In. 55.00
Jar, Cobalt Blue, Brownish Purple, Applied Open Handles, 6 In. 105.00
Jar, Cobalt Blue, Floral Design, Applied Handles, 14 In. 300.00
Jar, Cobalt Blue, Houses, Dog, Church, Handles, 20 In. 3600.00
Jar, Cobalt Blue, Stenciled & Freehand, 22 1/4 In. 1250.00
Jar, Cobalt Blue, Wide Strap Ear Handles, Floral, 14 In. 425.00
Jar, E. Fowler, Beaner, Pa., Stylized Cobalt Blue Floral, 12 In. 350.00
Jar, Eagle, McCarthey, Maysville, Ky., Handles, 3 Gal. 1150.00
Jar, Floral, Cobalt Blue, 6 1/2 In. 145.00
Jar, Floral, Cobalt Blue, Primitive, 8 5/8 In. 100.00
Jar, Floral, Cobalt Blue, Primitive, 9 1/4 In. 125.00
Jar, Flower, Cobalt Blue, Applied Handles, 9 In. 325.00
Jar, Hamilton & Jones, Stenciled & Freehand Label, 13 In. 150.00
Jar, Handles, Cobalt Blue Bird, Initials, Dated 1830, 9 1/4 In. 1650.00
Jar, Handles, Cobalt Blue, Quill Work, Impressed Label, 11 In. 1100.00
Jar, Incised Design, Woman's Bust In Medallion, C.1880, Large 375.00
Jar, J. & E. Norton, Bennington, Vt., Eagle On Stump, 3 Gal. 6600.00
Jar, J. & E. Norton, Spread-Wing Eagle On Stump, 3 Gal. 6600.00
Jar, J. Iambright, Newport, Ohio, Blue Slip Label, Ovoid, 18 In. 135.00
Jar, L.W.July 1, 1830 Written At Bottom, Incised Bird 1650.00
Jar, Lyons, Blue Design, 2 Gal. 900.00
Jar, Lyons, Impressed Label, 3 Leaf Clover, 9 In. 135.00
Jar, Mallory & Atkinson, Clarington, Ohio, 3 In. 375.00
Jar, Neff Bros., Cobalt Blue Stenciled Label, Ovoid, 20 1/4 In. 35.00
Jar, New York Stoneware Co., Blue Foliage, 10 1/2 In. 150.00
Jar, Palestine Pottery Co., Stenciled Label, 11 1/2 In. 225.00
Jar, Peoria Pottery, Brown Glaze, 4 Gal. 95.00
Jar, Protruding Lips, Brush Strokes, Ovoid, 10 In. 55.00
Jar, Ripley Potters, Tooled Design, Braided Handles, 11 In. 1350.00
Jar, Snuff, Blue Band, Cork Stopper 50.00
Jar, Stewart & Logan, Parnassus, Stenciled Label, Ovoid, 8 1/4 In. 525.00
Jar, Straight & Wavy Lines, Ovoid, 6 1/2 In. 170.00
Jar, Williams & Reppert, Greensboro, Pa., 12, Cobalt Blue, 22 In. 400.00
Jug, A. Hertz, Gloversville, Cobalt Blue Quill Work, 10 3/4 In. 60.00
Jug, A.O. Whittemore, Havanah, N.Y., Beehive Shape, Blue Flowers 120.00
Jug, Adam Caire, Po'Keepsie, N.Y., Floral, 14 In. 200.00
Jug, Albany Slip, Double Ear Handles, 15 1/2 In. 35.00
Jug, Bartmannkruge, Mask & Flower, Ovoid, 17 In. 700.00
Jug, Bartmannkruge, Mask & Flower, Salt Glaze, Ovoid, 8 3/4 In. 350.00
Jug, Blue Flower, Handle, 1 Gal. 190.00
Jug, Boston, L. Norton, No.2, 2-Tone Brown, Marked, C.1800 .... 175.00
Jug, Boston, Ocher Glaze At Top Half, C.1795, 1 Gal. 150.00
Jug, Burger Bro's & Co., Rochester, N.Y., 1867-71, 2 Gal. 325.00
Jug, Charlestown, 2-Tone Tan Glaze, Ovoid, 15 In. 500.00
Jug, Charlestown, Impressed Hearts Below Mark, Ovoid, C.1810 .... 225.00
Jug, Cobalt Blue Foliage, Ovoid, 9 1/2 In. 95.00
Jug, Cobalt Blue Foliage, Ovoid, 12 1/2 In. 200.00
Jug, Cobalt Blue, 3-Masted Ship, Gray Salt Glaze, 13 1/4 In. 1300.00
Jug, Cobalt Blue, Bird, Branch, Impressed Label, 11 In. 625.00
Jug, Cobalt Blue, Flower Design, Handle Has Blue Dots, 9 3/4 In. 725.00
Jug, Cobalt Blue, Flower, Gray Salt Glaze, Brown, 13 In. 200.00
Jug, Cook Grocery Co., White, Shoulder, 1 Gal. 47.50
Jug, Cowden & Wilcox, Bird Design, 4 Gal. 2000.00
Jug, Cowden & Wilcox, Harrisburg, Pa., No.2, Floral, 12 3/4 In. 275.00
Jug, Double Ear Handles, Impressed Eagle, Floral Design, 21 In. 400.00
Jug, E.L. Farrar, Grayish Glaze, Strap Handles, C.1880 .... 85.00
Jug, Edgefield Pottery, Storage, Loops, 2 Gal. 1900.00
Jug, Erie Distilling Co., Buffalo, N.Y., Freehand Design, 2 Gal. 100.00
Jug, Evan Jones, Pittston, Penna., 3 Gal. 450.00
Jug, F.H.Smith, Label, Olive Brown Albany Slip, Ovoid, 11 1/4 In. 65.00
Jug, F.Hawkins, Harvest, Foliage Design, 5 1/2 In. 500.00
Jug, Floral Design, Cobalt Blue, Impressed Label, 16 3/4 In. 225.00
Jug, G.I. Lazier, C.1870, 3 Gal. 2000.00
Jug, Grotesque, Facial Picture, White Eyes & Teeth, Ohio, 7 In. 375.00

Jug, H.A. Cook, Evansville, Ind., Beehive, 1 Gal. 125.00
Jug, Harvest, Wire Bail, Impressed Label, 9 3/4 In. 200.00
Jug, Haxstun, Ottman & Co., Bird, 1 Gal. 325.00
Jug, Henry Smith Wines & Liquors, Dunkirk, N.Y., 1 Gal. 110.00
Jug, Incised Bird, Branch, Berries, Impressed Label, 13 In. 875.00
Jug, J. & E. Norton, Pheasant, Cobalt Blue, Salt Glazed, 17 In. 2700.00
Jug, J.A. & C.W. Underwood, Peacock Sitting In Tree, 3 Gal. 1900.00
Jug, Jas. Hamilton Co., Greensboro, Penna., Ovoid, 2 Gal. 125.00
Jug, Julius Norton, No.2, Ovoid, C.1840 .... 175.00
Jug, Kintoe Scotch Whiskey, New York, 1 Qt. 35.00
Jug, Klinok Wickenberg & Co. Grocers, Blue Flower, 13 3/4 In. 350.00
Jug, L. Norton, Bennington, Cobalt Blue Single Flower, 18 In. 350.00
Jug, Leaf Design, Handle, 1 Gal. 190.00
Jug, Lithia Spring Water, Londonberry, N.H., 3 Gal. 385.00
Jug, Medford, Grayish Glaze, Ovoid, C.1840, 2 Gal. 100.00
Jug, Molasses, A. Standish, No.1, Blackish Glaze, C.1855 .... 100.00
Jug, Monmouth, Beehive, 6 Gal. 250.00
Jug, N.Clark and Co., Mount Morris, N.Y., Stamped, Ovoid, 2 Gal. 3000.00
Jug, Nichols & Boynton, Burlington, Vt., Blue Design, 1856, 2 Gal. 200.00
Jug, Ottman Brothers, Dyer, Albany, N.Y., Blue Slip, 1 Gal. 155.00
Jug, Ovoid, Blue At Shoulder & Handle, 11 1/2 In. 40.00
Jug, P.H.Smith, Impressed Label, 12 In. 85.00
Jug, Pine Tree Shaped Zigzag, Cobalt Blue Quillwork, 12 In. 175.00
Jug, Ribbed Strap Handle, Ovoid, 7 1/2 In. 75.00
Jug, S. & E. Norton, Cobalt Pheasant Perched On Stump, 17 In. 2700.00
Jug, Salt Glaze, Incised Ship, Strap Handle, Signed, 1810, 15 In. 3850.00
Jug, Schiltz Hotel, Albany, N.Y. 85.00
Jug, Spring Water, Pueblo, Colorado 45.00
Jug, Stetzenmeyer, Rochester, Flower 1550.00
Jug, Straight Sides, Small Bird Perched On Branch, 1 Gal. 250.00
Jug, T. Crafts & Co., No.3, Brown Glaze, Strap Handles, C.1845 .... 100.00
Jug, Viall Ruckel & Co., Ear Handles, Cobalt Blue Quill, 19 In. 2000.00
Jug, Ward Brothers, Drugstore Advertising, 1/2 Gal. 65.00
Jug, Williams & Reppert, Stenciled & Freehand Label, 13 3/4 In. 200.00
Meat Tenderizer, Brown Albany Slip, Turned Handle, 9 In. 85.00
Meat Tenderizer, Marked, Pat.Dec.25, 1877, Wooden Handle, 10 In. 60.00
Meat Tenderizer, Oak Handle, Pat.December 25, 1887 .... 176.00
Meat Tenderizer, Wildflower, Blue & White 265.00
Mold, Floral Design, Fluted, Beige, 5 X 5 1/2 In. 29.25
Mortar & Pestle, Large 50.00
Mortar & Pestle, Small 32.50
Mug, A.T. Kerr & Co., Incised Label, 4 1/4 In. 55.00
Mug, Auld Lang Syne, Bearded Man Handle, Blue, White 60.00
Mug, Embossed Bands In Cobalt Blue, 6 3/4 In. .... 55.00 To 75.00
Mug, Grain Belt Beer, Minneapolis, Monmouth 85.00
Mug, Pale Ale, Smith, N.Y. 375.00
Mug, Pewter Lid, Cobalt Blue Design, 4 1/4 In. 135.00
Mug, Whites, Utica, Blue & White, Handle, 4 1/2 In. 55.00
Paperweight, Open Book, Gray Salt Glaze, 4 X 5 In. 275.00
Pie Plate, Cobalt Design, 9 1/2 In. 1100.00
Pitcher & Bowl Set, Rose & Fish Scale, Blue & White, 5 Piece 600.00
Pitcher & Bowl, Bowtie, Blue & White .... 350.00 To 450.00
Pitcher, A. Conrad, Cobalt Blue Label, Tooled Ridges, 13 1/2 In. 1050.00
Pitcher, Basketweave & Morning Glories, 10 1/2 In. 175.00
Pitcher, Blue & White, Scene On Front, 10 In. 130.00
Pitcher, Buttermilk, Eskimo, 7 In. 32.00
Pitcher, Castle Scene, Blue, 1 Qt. 140.00
Pitcher, Cattail, Blue & White, 7 In. 150.00
Pitcher, Cobalt Blue Floral Design, 9 In. 150.00
Pitcher, Cobalt Blue Stenciled Design, 10 1/2 In. 475.00
Pitcher, Cow, Blue & White, 10 In. .... 135.00 To 145.00
Pitcher, Cow, Green & Cream, 10 In. 125.00
Pitcher, Dark Brown Albany Slip, 7 1/4 In. 20.00
Pitcher, Dutch Children & Dog, Blue & White, Cobalt Slip, 9 In. 125.00

Pitcher, Dutch Children, Kissing, Blue & White, 10 In. 95.00
Pitcher, Flemish Figures, Tavern, Blue & White, 9 1/2 In. 290.00
Pitcher, Flowers, Cobalt Blue Slip, 7 3/8 In. 275.00
Pitcher, Flowers, Cobalt Blue, Impressed Mark, 13 In. 500.00
Pitcher, Flowers, Cobalt Blue, Impressed Mark, 8 3/4 In. 425.00
Pitcher, Grapes & Rick-Rack, Blue & White, 10 In. 125.00
Pitcher, Grapes In Medallion, Beaded Band, Green, 9 In. 49.00
Pitcher, Grapes On Lattice, Green, 9 In. 40.00
Pitcher, Green Spongeware, 6 In. 75.00
Pitcher, Incised Floral & Figure On Keg, 9 3/4 In. 450.00
Pitcher, Indian Boy & Girl, Blue & White, 10 In. 165.00
Pitcher, Indian Girl & Boy, Brown, 10 In. 65.00
Pitcher, Leaf & Scroll, Blue & White, 6 In. 45.00
Pitcher, Lincoln Cabin, White, 8 In. 185.00
Pitcher, Matilda Dundora From Harry, Presentation, 7 3/8 In. 260.00
Pitcher, Milk, 2 Blue Bands, Brown Glaze Inside, 1/2 Gal. 85.00
Pitcher, Milk, Brown & Cream, 8 1/2 In. 14.00
Pitcher, Poinsettia, Blue & White, 10 In. 185.00
Pitcher, Rose On Trellis, Light Green, 9 In. 85.00
Pitcher, Stag & Pine Trees, 10 In. 335.00
Pitcher, Stylized Floral In Cobalt Blue, 8 3/4 In. 260.00
Pitcher, Tavern Scene, Flemish Figures, 9 In. 240.00
Pitcher, Tooled Lines, Cobalt Blue Foliage Design, 11 In. 475.00
Pitcher, Tulip, Rust & Cream, 10 In. 65.00
Pitcher, Western, Maple Leaf On Bottom, 1 Pt. 35.00
Pitcher, Windmill, Blue & White, 8 In. ....90.00 To 135.00
Planter, Gray, New York State, Attached Plate, 5 X 6 In. 50.00
Punch Set, Castle Scenes, Germany, 9 Piece 250.00
Rolling Pin, Blue Handles 18.00
Rolling Pin, O.O. Hartley, Home of Quality Groceries, Phone 53 .... 365.00
Rolling Pin, Wildflower, Blue & White, 7 In. ....200.00 To 245.00
Salt Box, Hanging, Wooden Cover, Blue Design 60.00
Salt Box, Lid, Blue Bands, Raised Letters Salt 115.00
Salt Crock, Wildflower & Fern 98.00
Salt, Hanging, Swastika 170.00
Salt, Hanging, Wooden Lid, Apple Blossom, Blue & Gray 130.00
Salt, Hanging, Wooden Lid, Daisy & Snowflake 135.00
Salt, Lid, Apricot, Blue & White 125.00
Smoking Set, G. Oliver Moody, Robinson Clay Products, 1910, 8 In. 200.00
Soap Dish, Blue, Rose 125.00
Soap Dish, Cover, Basket Weave With Flower 275.00
Soap Dish, Fish Scale, Rose 95.00
Spittoon, Cowden & Wilcox, Leaf Design 412.50
Spittoon, Embossed, Earthworm Sponging, Blue & White 85.00
Spittoon, Leaf & Diamond, Sponged, Half Moon Pattern, Blue, White 95.00
Sugar & Creamer, Button Knob On Cover, Flower & Leaf, C.1750 .... 215.00
Tea Dispenser, Brown, 1940s 125.00
Tea Set, Child's, Gray, Green, Pink, Peach Pastels, USA, 15 Piece 40.00
Teapot, Swirl, Blue & White 575.00
Totem Pole, Carved Indian Faces Base, Maple Leaf, Canada, 16 In. 65.00
Washboard, Albany Slip, Wooden Frame, 24 1/2 X 13 3/4 In. 45.00
Water Cooler, Cupid, Cover, 6 Gal. 675.00
Water Fountain, Cobalt Blue Design, Impressed 1 1/2, 11 1/2 In. 300.00
Wax Sealer, Lid, 1 Qt. 45.00
Whimsey, Stump, Vine & Bird Finial, Tan Salt Glaze, 5 3/4 In. 275.00

Most items found in an old store are listed under advertising in this book. Store fixtures, cases, cutters, and other items that have no advertising as part of the decoration are listed here.

STORE, Backbar, Drugstore, Stained Glass Doors, Mirror, 1930s, 14 X 8 Ft. 3500.00
 Bell, Spring Action, Brass 45.00
 Bin, Grain, Green Paint, 1900s, 39 X 33 1/2 In. 575.00
 Cabinet, 15 Drawers, Counter Top, Paneled Back, 8 Ft. 200.00
 Cabinet, Display, Gum, Wooden, Glass, Open Back, 15 X 18 X 9 In. 125.00

Cabinet, Hardware, Bolt, Original Condition 550.00
Ceiling Sheet, Metal, Pressed, 2 X 8 Ft. 1.75
Collar Case, Illinois Showcases Co., 48 X 6 X 7 In. 225.00
Counter, Bulk Nail, Oak, 9 Ft. 800.00
Counter, Feed & Seed, Oak, 3 Large Pullout Bins 800.00
Counter, Store Wrap, Oak, Raised Panel, 72 X 30 X 32 In. 225.00
Cupboard, Whiskey, Step–Back, Painted 680.00
Display Case, Curved Glass 240.00
Display Case, Oak, 4 Shelves, From Dime Store, 1920s, 5 Ft.X 28 In. 600.00
Display Case, Oak, Sliding Doors, Glass, Adjustable Shelves, 8 X 3 Ft. 550.00
Display Rack, Griswald, Metal 45.00
Holder, Buggy Whip, Iron, Wooden Ball On Top 160.00
Machine, Coin Counting & Table, Bank, Table Top Model 275.00
Mannequin, Toddler, Composition, 1940s 125.00
Model, Horse, Wooden, Dappled, Tack Shop, Kentucky, C.1880, Full Size 5500.00
Paper Holder, Store Counter, Wooden, Iron, 24 In. 16.50
Peanut Roaster, Stand, Eagle On Inside Lid, Steam Whistle, Copper 1500.00
Peanut Warmer, Defiance, Glass, A.Dutch, 1897–1902, 18 X 24 In. 975.00
Pie Case, Stainless Steel, Plate Glass, Back Opens, 1940s 160.00
Popcorn Popper, Floor Model, Burch, 1930s 2900.00
Popcorn Popper, Holcolm & Hoke, Butterkist, Floor Model, Mahogany 2650.00
Rack, For Pocket Watches, Nickel Plated, Brass Acorn Trim 175.00
Seed Counter, 21 Rear Drawers, Oak, Glass Front, 10 Ft. 1050.00
Service Bell, Counter, Zindia 8.00
Showcase, Candy Store, Brass Corners, 27 X 60 In. 695.00
Showcase, Curved Glass, Nickel Plating, Mirror Back 240.00
Soda Dispenser, Silver Plated, Engraved, Bigelow, 26 In., Pair 2500.00
Soda Fountain, 5 Porcelain Syrup Dispensers, Marble Handles 400.00
Straw Holder, Lay Down Type, Heisey 750.00
Straw Holder, Soda Fountain, Clear Glass, 1930s 77.00
Straw Holder, Soda Fountain, Green Depression Glass, 1930s 126.50
Straw Holder, Sweetheart 1540.00
Table, Butcher's Block, Primitive, Square, 2 Ft. 85.00
Table, Butcher's Block, Wooden, 3 Turned Legs, 32 X 25 1/2 In. 185.00

Stoves have been used in America for heating since the eighteenth century and for cooking since the nineteenth century. Most types of wood, coal, gas, kerosene, and even some electric stoves are collected.

STOVE, Buck, Original Utensils, Stove Pipe, 18 In. 800.00
Camp, Display Box, 1920s 25.00
Camp, Wrought Iron, Turned Wooden Handle, Black Paint, 9 X 16 In. 375.00
Child's, Enameled, Uses Pea–Sized Coal 2250.00
Coal, Perfect Favorite, Cast Iron & Nickel 110.00
Cook, Alcazar 50.00
Cook, Copper Clad 60.00
Cook, Home Comfort, Wood Burning, White Porcelain, Dated 1864 .... 975.00
Cook, Majestic, Wood & Coal, Warming Oven, Ash 1 .... 450.00
Cook, Majestic, Wood, Green Porcelain, Water Reservoir, 52 X 24 In. 160.00
Cook, Woodburning, Cast Iron, 6 Burners, Copper Hot Water Reservoir 1500.00
Crescent, Cast Iron, Utensils 70.00
Holman's Divlermoon, No.12, Cast Iron, 61 In. 5000.00
Mighty Oak, Small 31.00
Parlor, American Gothic, Signed J.B. Sexton & Co., Baltimore, C.1861 .... 440.00
Parlor, Comfort, Gray Graniteware, 62 X 34 In. 650.00
Parlor, Estate Oak, Salesman's Sample 3430.00
Parlor, Gas, Glendwood Perfect Favorite, Isinglass Sides, Front, 1890 .... 2500.00
Parlor, Topic No.6, Side Door, Revolving Grate, Cast Iron 550.00
Patent Model, Magazine Cooking & Heating Stove, Papers, 1877 .... 225.00
Pot Belly, Cast Iron, C.1870 .... 300.00
Quick Meal, 58 X 29 In. 135.00
Wood, Ceramic, European, 4 Ft. 3500.00
  STRAWBERRY, see Soft Paste

Stretch glass is named for the strange stretch marks in the glass. It was made by many glass companies in the United States from about 1900 to the 1920s. It is iridescent. Most American stretch glass is molded; most European pieces are blown and may have a pontil mark.

STRETCH GLASS, Basket, Gray, 10 1/2 In.	90.00
Bowl, Amber, 3 1/2 X 12 In.	28.00
Bowl, Blue, 10 1/2 In.	38.00
Bowl, Blue, 3 X 10 In.	26.00
Bowl, Blue, 9 3/4 In.	24.00
Bowl, Cupped–In, 10 1/2 In.	28.00
Bowl, Flared, 12 In.	28.00
Candlestick, Colonial, White, 10 1/2 In., Pair	175.00
Candlestick, Pair, 1 1/2 X 3 7/8 In.	22.00
Card Tray, Blue	23.00
Compote, Bark Pattern Stem, Vaseline, Northwood, 5 1/2 In.	135.00
Compote, Painted Flowers On Rim, Flared, 9 1/2 In.	65.00
Dish, Log Foot, Collar Bottom, 11 In.	24.00
Lemon Dish, Hand Painted Flowers, Center Handle, Vaseline	23.00
Tumbler, Diamond, Blue	18.00

Sumida, or Sumida Gawa, is a Japanese pottery. The pieces collected by that name today were made about 1895 to 1970. There has been much confusion about the name of this ware, and it is often called "Korean Pottery" or "Poo ware." Most pieces have a very heavy orange–red, blue, or green glaze, with raised three–dimensional figures as decorations.

SUMIDA, Bowl, 4 Figures, 8 1/2 In.	325.00
Humidor, Raised Oriental Figures, Oval Seal On Base, 6 3/8 In.	275.00
Mug, Applied Figure Making Offering To Bird, 5 In.	50.00
Mug, Children, Signed, 5 In.	135.00
Mug, Oriental Man On Side, Glossy Top, Marked, 4 5/8 In.	95.00
Tankard, Children, Signed, 12 1/2 In.	575.00
Teapot, 2 Characters, Ryosai Cartouche	425.00
Vase, 4 Oriental Children, Red Ground, 9 1/2 In.	175.00
Vase, Oriental Man, Glossy Glazed Top, Red Base, 6 3/4 In.	125.00
Vase, Raised Figure of Oriental Man, Marked, 6 5/8 In.	125.00

Sunbonnet Babies were first introduced in 1902 in the "Sunbonnet Babies Primer." The stories were by Eulalie Osgood Grover, illustrated by Bertha Corbett. The children's faces were completely hidden by the sunbonnets. The children had been pictured in black and white before this time, but the color pictures in the book were immediately successful. The Royal Bayreuth China Company made a full line of children's dishes decorated with the Sunbonnet Babies. Some Sunbonnet Babies plates have been reproduced but are clearly marked.

SUNBONNET BABIES, Bell, Cleaning, Wooden Clapper	595.00
Book, ABC, 1929	25.00 To 35.00
Candleholder, Cleaning, Handle, Tall	395.00
Candleholder, Washing, Handle, Flat, Short	295.00
Candlestick, Fishing, Sewing, Royal Bayreuth, Pair	475.00
Chamberstick, Cleaning, Blue Mark	295.00 To 495.00
Compote, Fishing, Royal Bayreuth Blue Mark, 6 X 4 1/2 In.	495.00
Creamer, Cup & Saucer, Cleaning	120.00
Creamer, Ironing, Double Spouted, Handle, 2 1/2 In.	395.00
Cup, Oversize	68.00
Flowerpot, Sweeping, Bulbous Base, Royal Bayreuth	295.00
Flowerpot, Washing & Ironing, Insert, 4 In.	495.00
Match Holder, Hanging, Sewing, Handles	495.00
Nappy, Washing & Ironing, Rolled In Rim, Handle, 5 In.	295.00
Pitcher, Cleaning, Twisted Handle, 3 1/4 In.	150.00
Pitcher, Milk, Fishing, Blue Mark	295.00

Pitcher, Sugar & Creamer, Plate, Royal Bayreuth, 4 Piece 400.00
Plate, 1912 .... 55.00
Plate, 1974, 7 Piece 175.00
Plate, Fishing, Royal Bayreuth, Marked, 6 In. 150.00
Postcard, 12 Months of Year, Unused 125.00
Rose Bowl, Cleaning, Royal Bayreuth 295.00
Toothpick, Sweeping, Handle, Coal Hod Shape, Blue Mark 450.00
Vase, Cleaning, Cylinder, Royal Bayreuth, Marked, 4 In. 395.00

Sunderland luster is a name given to a special type of pink luster made by Leeds, Newcastle, and other English firms during the nineteenth century. The luster glaze is metallic and glossy and appears to have bubbles in it.

SUNDERLAND, Creamer, Black Transfer, Ladies All I Pray Make Free, 2 3/4 In. 95.00
Creamer, Poem, Sailor's Tear, Ship On Reverse, 1800s, 5 In. 250.00
Jug, Mariner's Arms, Compass, Sailor's Farewell, Peace & Plenty 1195.00
Pitcher, Luster, Georgian Handle, Pink, C.1810, 6 In. 250.00
Plaque, Black Transfer, Praise Ye The Lord, 6 3/4 X 7 3/4 In. 175.00
Plaque, Black Transfer, Prepare To Meet Thy God, 7 X 8 In. 175.00
Plaque, Black Transfer, Thou God Seest Me, 6 5/8 In. 130.00
Plaque, Thou God Seest Me, Marked Dixon, 8 1/2 X 7 1/2 In. 150.00

Superman was created by two seventeen–year–olds in 1938. The first issue of "Action" comics had the strip. Superman remains popular and became the hero of a radio show in 1940, cartoons in the 1940s, a television series, and several major movies.

SUPERMAN, Bank, Dime Register 110.00
Book, Pop–Up, Random House, 1979 .... 5.00
Button, Brookdale Ford, Tin Tab, Yellow Ground, 1972, 1 3/4 In. 3.00
Button, Read Superman, Action Comics Magazine, 1940, 3/4 In. 85.00
Card Set, Primrose Confectionary, Color, 1967, 50 Piece 37.50
Card, Valentine, 1940s 20.00
Catalog, Gilbert Hall of Science, 1948 .... 75.00
Comic Book, No.42 .... 44.00
Comic Book, No.47 .... 22.00
Comic Book, No.73 .... 14.50
Cookie Jar, Brown Phone Booth, California Original 158.00
Doll, Mego, 12 In. 25.00
Game, Quoits, Official Club Card, Box 45.00
Goggles, Swim, Box 35.00
Hairbrush, Avon 22.00
Horseshoes, Box 80.00
Kite, Box, 1975 .... 18.00
Kryptonite Rocks, Box, 1975 .... 18.00
Lobby Card, Superman & Mole Men, George Reeves, 1951 .... 125.00
LP Record, Patch, Secret Decoder, Club Card & Button, Box, 1966 .... 35.00
Lunch Box, 1967 .... 50.00
Mug, 50th Anniversary 5.50
Muscle Building Set, Box 75.00
Pin, Lapel, 1940s, Cloisonne, Figure of Superman Hands On Hips 15.00
Pin, Promo For Movie, Color, 3 In. 2.00
Puzzle Set, Box, 1940s, 7 X 10 In., 3 Piece 58.00
Record Player, 1978 .... 100.00 To 175.00
Ring, Flasher 8.00
Ring, Movie, 1976 .... 10.00
Wristwatch, Lois Lane, Logo, 50th Anniversary, Superman Watches 25.00
Wristwatch, Superman, Logo, 50th Anniversary, Superman Watches 25.00

In 1933, the Kraft Food Company began to market cheese spreads in decorated, reusable glass tumblers. These were called "Swankyswigs." They were discontinued from 1941 to 1946, then made again from 1947 to 1958. Then plain glasses were used for most of the cheese, although a few special decorated Swankyswigs have been made since that time. A complete list of prices can be found in "The Kovels' Illustrated Price Guide to Depression Glass and American Dinnerware."

SWANKYSWIG, Antique, Black	2.00
Antique, Brown	1.75
Antique, Orange	1.75
Antique, Red	1.75
Bachelor Button	1.50
Band, No.2, Red, Black, 3 3/8 In.	1.50
Betsy, Blue	1.50
Betsy, Brown	1.50
Bird & Elephant	1.50
Bustling Betsy, Blue	2.00
Carnival, Orange	3.50
Carnival, Yellow, 3 1/2 In.	5.00
Cat & Rabbit	1.50
Checkerboard, Green, 3 1/2 In.	20.00
Circle & Dot, Black, 3 1/2 In.	4.00
Circle & Dot, Dark Blue	4.00
Circle & Dot, Green	3.00
Cornflower, Dark, 3 1/2 In.	1.50
Cornflower, Light, 3 1/2 In.	1.50
Cornflower, No.1, Blue, 3 1/2 In.	2.00
Cornflower, No.2, Dark Blue	1.50
Cornflower, No.2, Red	1.75
Cornflower, No.2, Yellow	1.75
Daisy, Red, White, Green, 3 3/4 In.	1.50
Duck & Horse	1.50
Forget–Me–Not, Dark Blue, 3 1/2 In.	1.50
Forget–Me–Not, Light Blue	1.75
Forget–Me–Not, Red	1.75
Jonquil, Yellow	2.00
Kiddie Kup, Green	2.00
Kiddie, Brown	1.50
Kiddie, Green	1.50
Sailboat, No.1, Blue, 4 1/2 In.	12.00
Squirrel & Deer	1.50
Star, Black, 3 1/2 In.	3.00
Star, Green, 3 1/2 In.	3.00
Tulip, No.1, Dark Blue	2.00
Tulip, No.1, Green	3.00
Tulip, No.1, Red	2.50
Tulip, No.3, Dark Blue	1.50 To 2.00

 All types of swords are of interest to collectors. The military dress sword with elaborate handle is probably the most wanted. Be sure to display swords in a safe way, out of reach of children.

SWORD, 5th U.S. Colored Cavalry, Solid Silver Grips, 1860s	6500.00
Bayonet, French, 1883	30.00
Bayonet, With Sheath, Revolutionary War	550.00
Brass Handguard, Curved Blade, World War II, Germany	65.00
Broad, Hanger, Brass Hilt, Stirrup Guard, 23 3/4-In. Blade, 1790–1800	147.50
Emerson & Silver, Trenton, N.J., Brass Hilt, 43 In.	190.00
Field General's, Presentation, Isham Hayne, Belt, 1850s	800.00
Katana, Officer's, Japanese, World War II	215.00
Militia, Fluted Handle, Knight Head, 1840s	95.00
Saber, Cavalry Officer's, Leather Grip, Osbornes, British, 1812 War	195.00
Saber, Crown GR Mark, Plain Stirrup Form Hilt, 27-1/2 In. Blade, U.S.	285.00
Saber, U.S. Officer's, Eagle Head, Curved Blade, Walnut Grip, 1812 War	275.00

SYRACUSE China 1871

Syracuse is a trademark used by the Onondaga Pottery of Syracuse, New York. The company was established in 1871. It is still working. The name became the Syracuse China Company in 1966. It is known for fine dinnerware and restaurant china.

SYRACUSE, Ashtray, Terrier, Signed C. Gora, 4 In.	10.00
Breakfast Set, White, Cranberry & Gold Border, 5 Piece	20.00
Compote, Underplate, 5 Ladies Medallions, Floral Bands, 7 & 9 In.	25.00
Cup & Saucer, Pale Roses, Leaves, Scrolled, Sprayed Gold	18.50
Dinner Set, Oriental Pattern, Service For 10, 65 Piece	295.00
Soup, Dish, Coventry	5.00
Sugar & Creamer, Woodbine, Open	18.00
TANKARD, see Stein	
TAPESTRY, PORCELAIN, see Rose Tapestry	

A tea caddy is a small box made to hold tea leaves. In the eighteenth century, tea was very expensive and it was stored under lock and key. The first tea caddies were made with locks. By the nineteenth century, tea was more plentiful and the tea caddy was larger. Often there were two sections, one for green tea, one for black tea.

TEA CADDY, Brass Hinge & Hook, Pear Shape, Wooden, Foil Lined, 6 /4 In.	1400.00
Charles X, Mother–of–Pearl, Carved Mythological Scene, 4 X 7 In.	3025.00
Chippendale Style, Mahogany, English, 9 In.	110.00
Copper, Design, Oval Cover	42.50
Decoupage, Brass Mounts, England, 9 In.	170.00
Dome Top, Burl Veneer, 3 Interior Lidded Compartments, 12 In.	200.00
Domed Lid, Rope Border, Mahogany & Satinwood, C.1800, 10 1/2 In.	2475.00
Federal, Inlaid Mahogany, Hinged Lid, 1790–1810, 5 X 9 X 4 In.	770.00
George II, Silver, Bright Cut Borders & Swags, Vincent, 5 1/2 In.	1750.00
George III, Brass Lifting Handles, Silvered Interior, Mahogany	650.00
George III, Fruitwood, Apple Shape, 4 1/2 In. ....*Illus*	1050.00
George III, Inlaid Mahogany, Coffered Cover, 5 X 10 X 5 5/8 In.	550.00
George III, Silver, Tassie–Style Plaques, 1783, Gilbert, 5 1/4 In.	2100.00
Gilt Enameling, Cranberry Glass, 5 X 4 1/4 In.	175.00
Gold Figures On Black Lacquered Box, 2 Pewter Compartments	175.00
Pear Shape, 1 Piece of Wood, 19th Century	1400.00
Porcelain, Blue & White, China, 8 1/2 In.	45.00
Repousse of People, Scenes, Scrolls, 6 Sides, Derby	68.00
Silver Plated, Embossed Children & Cherub Designs, 4 In.	65.00
Silver, Chased Flowers, Stippled, Vase Shape, Domed Cover, 5 In.	600.00
Stenciled Eagle, Flag, Cameo of Man, Tin, C.1880	20.00

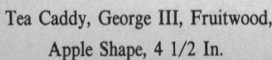
Tea Caddy, George III, Fruitwood, Apple Shape, 4 1/2 In.

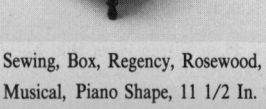
Sewing, Box, Regency, Rosewood, Musical, Piano Shape, 11 1/2 In.

Television, Philco, Predicta, 1959, 48 1/2 X 19 In.

Sterling Silver, Georgian, Mappin & Webb, Miniature, 1 In. 90.00
Tortoiseshell Veneer, Ivory Stringing, 2 Sections, 5 1/2 In. 750.00

There was a superstition that it was lucky if a whole tea leaf unfolded at the bottom of your cup. This idea was translated into the pattern of dishes known as "tea leaf." By 1850, at least twelve English factories were making this pattern; and by the 1870s, it was a popular pattern in many countries. The tea leaf was always a luster glaze on early wares, although now some pieces are made with a brown tea leaf.

TEA LEAF IRONSTONE, Bowl, Vegetable, Cover, Handles, Meakin, 11 1/2 In. 140.00
Butter, Cover, Bamboo, Meakin 125.00
Cracker Jar, Mellor–Taylor Co. 85.00
Creamer, Chelsea 195.00
Creamer, Dolphin Handle, Edwards 195.00
Cup & Saucer, Handleless, Fan 90.00
Cup & Saucer, Handleless, Lily-of-The-Valley, Shaw 75.00
Cup & Saucer, Handleless, Luster 18.00
Cup & Saucer, Luster, Elsmore & Forster 30.00
Cup & Saucer, Meakin, Bamboo 50.00
Cup Plate, Meakin 45.00
Pitcher, Burgess, 12 1/2 In. .... 165.00 To 175.00
Pitcher, Wash, Blown–Out Flowers, Burgess, 11 1/2 In. 245.00
Pitcher, Water, Edwards 80.00
Plate, 8 In. 14.00
Plate, Luncheon, Meakin 18.00
Plate, Luster, 7 1/2 In. 12.00
Plate, Morning Glory, 10 In. 25.00
Platter, Meakin, 10 X 14 In. 25.00
Relish, Oval 8.00
Soap Dish 20.00
Sugar & Creamer, Cover, Marked, 4 In. 150.00
Sugar, Fishhook & Bamboo, Shaw 125.00
Sugar, Shaw 85.00
Teapot, Bamboo, Meakin 135.00
Teapot, Morning Glory, E.& F. 265.00
Toothbrush Holder, Meakin 135.00
Toothbrush Holder, Wedgwood 35.00
Tureen, Sauce, Cable, Shaw 225.00

Teco is the mark used on the art pottery line made by the American Terra Cotta and Ceramic Company of Terra Cotta and Chicago, Illinois. The company was an offshoot of the firm founded by William D. Gates in 1881. The Teco line was first made in 1885 but was not sold commercially until 1902. It continued in production until 1922. Over 500 designs were made in a variety of colors, shapes, and glazes. The company closed in 1930.

TECO, Bookends, 5–Color Glaze, 5 X 7 In. 585.00
Bowl, Bulb, Stylized Leaf Design, Matte Green, 2 X 9 In. 200.00
Candleholder 650.00
Tile, Tea 160.00
Tray, Chicago Cubs Logo, Black, 3–Color 300.00
Vase, 4 Pinched Sides, Square Top, Round Bottom, Stamped, 4 1/2 In. 350.00
Vase, Art Deco, Aventurine Glaze, Gold To Black, Bulbous, Large 2200.00
Vase, Bulbous Bottom, Long Cylindrical Neck, 5 In. 850.00
Vase, Bulbous Bottom, Narrow Neck, 9 1/2 In. 550.00
Vase, Concentric Rings Below Lip, Paneled Body, C.1903, 12 1/4 In. 9900.00
Vase, Dakota, Signed, 6 X 9 In. 575.00
Vase, Green Matte, 5 In. .... 75.00 To 175.00
Vase, Green, 8 X 5 In. 375.00
Vase, Green, Bulbous, 7 1/2 In. 375.00
Vase, Green, Matte, 4 Handles 1100.00
Vase, Green, Matte, 4 Open Handles, Baluster, 1908, 6 1/2 In. 850.00
Vase, Melon Shape Base, Sprouting Blossom Form Neck, 10 In. 2185.00

Vase, Wall, 7 In. 550.00

The first teddy bear was a cuddly toy said to be inspired by a hunting trip made by Teddy Roosevelt in 1902. Morris and Rose Michtom started selling their stuffed bears as "Teddy bears" and the name stayed. The Michtoms founded the Ideal Novelty and Toy Company. The German version of the teddy bear was made about the same time by the Steiff Company. There are many types of teddy bears and all are collected. The old ones are being reproduced.

TEDDY BEAR, Amber Plush, Straw Filling, Snout Nose, Hump Back, 1915, 19 In. 300.00
  Black Willie, Straw Stuffed, Long Snout, Germany, 1950s, 16 In. 400.00
  Bordi, Pine Cone Forest, Gray, Growler, 1985, 18 In. 295.00
  Brown Wooly Coat, Articulated Limbs & Head, Glass Eyes, 18 In. 45.00
  Christopher, Gold Mohair, Jointed, 20 In. 195.00
  Dark Red Hair Cloth, Button Eyes, Embroidered Features, 20 In. 95.00
  Gold Hair Cloth, Articulated Limbs, Glass Eyes, 18 In. 105.00
  Gold Mohair, Growler, Jointed, Australian, 1940s, 13 In. 140.00
  Hermann Teddy, Brown Mohair, Musical, Teddy Bears Picnic, 14 In. 95.00
  Hump, Growler, Fully Jointed, Silk Blush, Germany, 1940s 245.00
  Hump, Mohair, Straw, Button Eyes, Red Suit, 1920, 17 In. 275.00
  Jointed Arms & Legs, Straw Stuffed, Glass Eyes, Brown, Germany 210.00
  Knickerbocker, C.1950, 27 In. 50.00
  Long Red & White Mohair, Straw Stuffed, Jointed, Germany 125.00
  Margaret Strong, Gold, Signed, 60 Cm. 395.00
  Mechanical, Arms Move, Brushes Boot, Head Side To Side, Keywind 125.00
  Merrythought, White Mohair, Growler, Brown Eyes, 1930s 150.00
  Minnie, Gray Mohair, Jointed, Squeaker, 9 In. 122.50
  Mohair, Jointed, 12 In. 925.00
  Muff, 1940s 40.00
  Muff, Gold Mohair, Glass Eyes, U.S., 1910 .... 550.00
  Music Box, Long White Mohair, Squeeze, 12 1/2 In. 950.00
  Nesbitt, Cowboy, Rusty, 17 In. 65.00
  Orange Plush, Musical, 16 In. 2100.00
  Plush, Wide–Apart Ears, Glass Eyes, Long Snout, 30 In. 550.00
  Schuco, 2–Faced, C.1940, Tiny 750.00
  Schuco, Beige Mohair, 18 In. 585.00
  Schuco, Gold Mohair, Growler, 1930s, 21 In. 688.00
  Schuco, Gold Mohair, Jointed, 1960s, 2 1/2 In. 138.00
  Schuco, Gold, 2 1/2 In. 138.00
  Schuco, Jointed 110.00
  Schuco, Tumbling, Keywind, Mohair Head, Red, Gold Suit, 4 In. 350.00
  Steiff, Baby, Printed Button, 14 In. 1100.00
  Steiff, Camp Fire, 1983, Signed 225.00
  Steiff, Dickey Bear 110.00
  Steiff, Doll, Bisque Head, Brown Sleep Eyes, 12 In. 600.00
  Steiff, Giengen Bear, Gold 90.00
  Steiff, Golden Brown Mohair, 18 In. 1700.00
  Steiff, Hump, 9 In. 175.00
  Steiff, Jointed, Gold Mohair, 7 In. 223.00
  Steiff, Light Brown, Stitched Nose, Silver Button, 1950s, 11 In. 335.00
  Steiff, Richard, Gray, 12 In. 150.00
  Steiff, Roly Poly 75.00
  Steiff, Tan Mohair, Silver Button, Tags, 9 In. 62.50
  Swivel Neck, Straw Filled, Jointed Hump Back, C.1915, 20 In. 325.00
  White Wool, Jointed, Eyebrows, English, 1950s, 23 In. 71.50

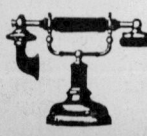

The first telephone may have been made in Havana, Cuba, in 1849, but it was not patented. The first publicly demonstrated phone was used in Frankfurt, Germany, in 1860. The phone made by Alexander Graham Bell was shown at the Centennial Exhibition in Philadelphia in 1876, but it was not until 1877 that the first private phones were installed. Collectors today want all types of old phones, phone parts, and advertising.

TELEPHONE, Book, How To Build Rural Telephone Lines, Early 1900s 15.00
  Book, Western Electric Magneto Telephones & Supplies, 1910 .... 50.00
  Button, To Hell With Bell Tel, Written On Bell, 1960s, 7/8 In. 5.00
  Candlestick, AT&T, Made Into Lamp, 1915 .... 140.00
  Candlestick, Battery Operated 105.00
  Candlestick, Oak Ringer Box, 1920 .... 95.00
  Candlestick, Stromberg–Carlson, Oil Can, Renickeled 350.00
  Candlestick, Western Electric, 1915 .... 75.00
  Candlestick, Western Electric, Brass, New Wiring, 1904 Pat. 100.00
  Chicago Oil Can 150.00
  Copper, Roycroft 1700.00
  Dispatcher's, Railroad, With Headset, Candlestick Type 100.00
  Kellogg, Candlestick, 1901 .... 165.00
  Kellogg, Candlestick, 1907 .... 85.00
  Kellogg, Wall, Metal 50.00
  Kellogg, Wall, Wooden, No Ringer Box, Small 60.00
  Montgomery Ward, Wall, Oak 190.00
  Phone Booth, Mahogany, Fan, Light, Working 320.00
  Phone Booth, Oak, Glass, Pull Chain Light Fixture, Coin Phone 2500.00
  Railroad Dispatcher's, Candlestick 75.00
  Railroad, Portable, 4–Sectioned Connecting Pole, Case 70.00
  Sign, Public Telephone Bell System, Porcelain, 2 Sides, 18 In. 95.00
  Sign, Telephone Cable Underground, Porcelain, 3 1/2 X 7 In. 20.00
  Simplex International, Cincinnati, Oak, Wall Mount, Intercom 225.00
  Stromberg–Carlson, Wall, Wooden, Rewired To Touchtone 185.00
  Telephone Bell Box, Dovetailed Oak 25.00
  U.S.Army, Camp, 1917 .... 125.00
  Wall, Cranker, Oak, Dial, 12 In. 69.00
  Wall, Oak 285.00
  Western Electric, Wall, Oak 175.00
  Windup Cat, Bell 125.00

Although the first television transmission took place in England in 1925, collectors find few sets which pre-date 1946. The first sets had only five channels, but by 1949 the additional VHF channels were included. The first color television set became available in 1951.

TELEVISION, Philco, Predicta, 1959, 48 1/2 X 19 In. ....*Illus* 605.00
  Stromberg–Carlson, Oak, Art Deco, 1940s, 9–In. Picture 250.00
  Zenith, Table, 1950s, 16 In. Picture 110.00

Teplitz refers to art pottery manufactured by a number of companies in the Teplitz–Turn area of Bohemia during the late nineteenth and early twentieth centuries. The Amphora Porcelain Works and the Alexandra Works were two of these companies.

TEPLITZ, Basket, Arabian Horseman, Enameled 95.00
  Basket, Multicolored Roses, Green Leaves, Amphora, 5 X 9 In. 145.00
  Bust, Classical Lady, Upswept Hair, Restored, 19 In. 500.00
  Bust, Young Woman, Curled Hair, Floral Socle, C.1900, 26 In. 3600.00
  Ewer, Figural Frog, Lily Pad Design, Amphora, 7 X 7 In. 700.00
  Ewer, Flowers On Cream Ground, Gold Trim, Frond–Type Handle 125.00
  Ewer, Pink Flowers & Leaves, Twisted Gold Handle, 6 X 5 In. 65.00
  Ewer, Variegated Poppies, Handle, Marked, 9 In. 80.00
  Figurine, Girl Pulling Rooster's Tail, 5 1/2 In. 55.00
  Figurine, Grecian Maiden With Basket of Flowers, Amphora, 12 In. 600.00
  Figurine, Young Woman, Above Shell, Assorted Symbols, 21 In. 1700.00
  Group, Woman Standing, Shell, Assorted Symbols, 21 In. ....*Illus* 1870.00
  Humidor, Painting of Boxer Dog, 8 In. 395.00
  Lamp, Gilded Seashells, Rococo Base, Florals, Amphora, 21 In. 800.00
  Pitcher, Indian Design, Blue, Stillmacher 95.00
  Pitcher, Warrior & Horse 75.00
  Planter, Fruits, Florals, Mushroom Shape, Amphora, Handles, 9 X 9 In. 195.00
  Vase, Applied Dog & Frog At Base, Bronze Finish, Amphora, 11 In. 750.00
  Vase, Applied Flower, Man's Face, Cream Ground, 11 In. 225.00

Teplitz, Group, Woman Standing, Shell,
Assorted Symbols, 21 In.

Thermometer, Silhouette, Mayfield Coal & Supply, 5 1/2 In.

Vase, Art Deco Design, Large Bird, 14 X 35 In.	285.00
Vase, Art Nouveau, Woman's Head,, Forest Scene Back, Amphora, 7 In.	550.00
Vase, Basket Weave, Applied Blackberries, Amphora, 1920s, 16 1/2 In.	395.00
Vase, Bird, Flowers, Leaves, Iridescent Ground, 4 Handles, 9 In.	135.00
Vase, Black Birds In Flight, Forest Ground, Amphora, 9 1/4 In.	250.00
Vase, Bottle Shape, Double Gourd Form, Scrolled, Amphora, 7 3/4 In.	143.00
Vase, Colored Flowers Around Center, Shadow Flowers, Amphora, 9 In.	175.00
Vase, Embossed Flowers, Leaves, Gold Trim, Marked, 10 5/8 In.	175.00
Vase, Flowers Outlined In Gold, Gold Trimmed Handles, 15 In.	265.00
Vase, Flowers, Gold Tracery, Gargoyle Draped Around Neck, 17 In.	675.00
Vase, Incised Bird & Flowers, Art Deco, Amphora, 9 In.	125.00
Vase, Ivory Bisque, Blue Florals, Raised Gold Paste, 6 3/4 In.	65.00
Vase, Jeweled Shell Design, Rose, Green & Blue, Amphora, 10 In.	85.00
Vase, King & Queen, Enameled, Church On Reverse, Amphora, 16 1/2 In.	295.00
Vase, Owls, Jeweled Rim, Open Handles, Amphora, 10 In.	155.00
Vase, Parrots, Tab Handles, Blue Dot Border, Marked, 6 1/2 In.	175.00
Vase, Portrait, Scenic Background, Amphora, 7 In.	595.00
Vase, Twisted Shape, Daisies, White, Aqua, Coral, Cobalt, Gold, 9 In.	185.00
Wall Pocket, Figural, Parrots	45.00

Terra–cotta is a special type of pottery. It ranges from pale orange
to dark reddish–brown in color. The color comes from the clay,
which is fired but not always glazed in the finished piece.

TERRA–COTTA, Bowl, Dandelion, Green Rim, Hammered, 8 1/4 X 2 3/4 In.	18.50
Bust, Chinaman, Long Queue, B. Carpeaux, Paris, 15 In.	1550.00
Bust, Woman's Head, Orange–Yellow Hair	95.00
Bust, Young Girl, Borghese Label, 16 In.	95.00
Bust, Young Girl, Nude, Hair Held By Scarf, Houdin, 19 1/4 In.	1100.00
Candelabra, Louis XVI, Putti Supports, Electrified, 11 In.	475.00
Pitcher, Picasso, Brown Facial Features	1250.00
Pot, Wide Neck, Flaring Rim, Arched Handle, Slip Design, 6 In.	200.00
Vase, Sculpted Allegorical Scenes, C.H. Rimmer, 1898, 12 In.	300.00

Textile includes many types of printed textiles, table and household linens, and clothing. Some other textiles will be found under Clothing, Coverlet, Rug, Quilt, etc.

TEXTILE, Antimacassar, Crocheted, Rose Center, Ivory, Arms, 6 X 16 In., Pair	4.00
Antimacassar, Crocheted, Turquoise, Saying, Back, 10 1/2 X 15 In.	8.00
Antimacassar, Ecru Linen, Cutwork, Embroidered, Back & Arms, 3 Piece	10.00
Antimacassar, White Linen, Blue Crocheted, Back, 11 X 10 In., Pair	5.00
Apron, Wrap-Around, Made From Occidental Flour Sacks	15.00
Bedspread, Battenburg & Net, Matching Shams, Double	150.00
Bedspread, Crewel, Allover Blossoms, Vines, Fringed, 104 X 95 In.	1200.00
Bedspread, Crocheted, 18 Squares of Animals, Children, 82 X 56 In.	175.00
Bedspread, Crocheted, Irish Type, 65 X 100 In.	59.00
Bedspread, Crocheted, Popcorn, White, 88 X 92 In.	95.00
Bedspread, Crocheted, White Muslin, Embroidered Floral, 80 X 80 In.	45.00
Bedspread, Net, Appliqued, Cutout For Posts, With Sham, Full Size	50.00
Bedspread, Peacock Design, Chenille, 92 X 93 In.	65.00
Bedspread, Peacock Design, Lace, 88 X 109 In.	125.00
Bedspread, Seersucker, White, Pink Stripes, Embroidered, 70 X 85 In.	12.00
Bedspread, White Linen, White Embroidered Flowers, Full Size	225.00
Blanket Cover, Reversible Cotton Damask Seersucker, 60 X 80 In.	10.00
Blanket, Wool Homespun, Natural, Blue Plaid, 74 X 82 In., 2 Piece	120.00
Blanket, Wool, Baby, Red, Navy, Nursery Rhymes, Fringed, 40 X 48 In.	30.00
Carriage Cover, Baby, White Percale, Lace, Tucked, 1910, 31 X 40 In.	22.00
Case, Handkerchief, Embroidered, Red Inside, Ribbons	35.00
Curtain, Ecru Lace, Open Filet, 3 Rows Holes Top, 34 X 76 In., Pair	15.00
Curtain, Ecru Sheer, Crocheted Lace Band Edge, 24 X 62 In., Pair	20.00
Curtain, Lace Panel, Floral, Machine, White, 28 X 50 In.	3.00
Doily, Battenburg Lace, Square, 16 In.	17.50
Doily, Crocheted, Pineapple, Ecru, 9 1/2 X 15 In.	4.00
Doily, Crocheted, Pineapples, Cream, 12 & 16 In., 2 Piece	7.00
Doily, Ecru & White Linen, Embroidered Floral, Square, 19 In.	6.00
Doily, Venetian Lace, Pair	25.00
Doily, White Linen, Embroidered Flowers, Rings, 18 In.	5.00
Flag, American, 38 Stars, Not Staggered, Colorado, 1876, 6 X 6 Ft.	200.00
Flag, American, 39 Stars, Silk, Framed, 30 1/2 X 41 1/4 In.	200.00
Flag, American, 46 Stars, 5 X 8 Feet	85.00
Flag, American, 46 Stars, Wool	9.00
Flag, American, 48 Stars, Felt, 8 X 16 Ft.	12.00
Handkerchief, Cotton, Children, Goat Cart, Red, Black, 11 X 11 In.	50.00
Hankerchief, Printed Indian Heads, Blue Border, 18 X 18 1/2 In.	85.00
Lap Robe, 1 Side Brown, Other Black, Velvet, 62 X 45 In.	45.00
Mattress Cover, Blue & White Homespun, Button Closure, 48 X 76 In.	115.00
Mattress Cover, Blue & White Homespun, Machine Sewn, 66 X 86 In.	200.00
Mattress Cover, Purple & White Cotton, Button Closure, 50 X 70 In.	105.00
Napkin, Cocktail, Cross-Stitch Flower Sprays, Square, 10 In., 4 Pc.	3.50
Panel, Felt, Colored Paper Detail, Woman With Goat, 13 X 14 3/4 In.	350.00
Panel, Needlepoint, Floral & Ivy Wreath, Frame, 22 1/2 X 22 1/2 In.	45.00
Piano Scarf, Birds & Flowers, Green Silk	38.00
Piano Scarf, Geometric, Reversible Cotton, Fringed, 78 X 59 In.	43.00
Piano Scarf, Jacquard, Floral, Reversible, Fringed, Square, 35 In.	22.00
Picture, Needlework, Basket of Flowers On Pink Mat, 11 X 12 In.	200.00
Picture, Needlework, Hector & Andromache, Catherine Jones, 1810	650.00
Picture, Needlework, Mythological Figures, D.Cone, 1805, 17 X 22 In.	8000.00
Pillow Sham, Flower Sprays, Red Embroidered Sayings, 28 In., Pair	75.00
Pillow Sham, Morning Glory Circle, Red Embroidery, 29 X 31 In.	34.00
Pillow, Embroidered Pinecone, Linen, Gustav Stickley, 1912, 19 In.	250.00
Pillow, Linen, Embroidered Stylized Leaf, Green, 1910, 21 X 15 In.	550.00
Pillowcase, Baby's, Blue, Scalloped, White Embroidered Flowers	9.00
Pillowcase, Baby's, Embroidered Child, Wheelbarrow of Flowers	18.00
Pillowcase, Percale, 3/4 In. Crocheted Circle Border, 30 In., Pair	18.00
Pillowcase, Tatting, Sugar Bag	10.00
Pillowcase, White, Embroidered, Ruffled, European, 1930s, 30 In.	60.00
Runner, Cluny Lace, Ecru, Stylized Flowers, Scalloped, 13 X 46 In.	12.00

Runner, Cutwork, Embroidered, Butterfly & Bow, 17 X 34 In. 35.00
Runner, Lacy Border, Battenburg Lace, Oval, 16 1/2 X 34 In. 82.00
Runner, Sideboard, Geometric Designs, Velvet, Black, 40 X 13 In. 20.00
Sheet, Muslin, Drawn Thread Lace Band, Cutwork, Floral, 108 X 84 In. 65.00
Spread, Wool Brocade, Blue & Green, Fringed, Italy, 78 X 108 In. 95.00
Table Cover, Brown Linen, Embroidered, 20th Century, 26 In. 375.00
Table Cover, Lace, Washington & Columbus, Columbian Expo, 6 X 8 Ft. 450.00
Table Cover, Linen, Stylized Leaf Embroidered, 1912, 31 In. Diam. 250.00
Table Piece, Crocheted, Staff of Life, 8 X 16 In. 18.00
Tablecloth, Banquet, Linen, 8 Napkins, 86 X 72 In. 45.00
Tablecloth, Battenburg Lace, Round, 64 In. 295.00
Tablecloth, Battenburg, Banquet, 90 X 68 In. 150.00
Tablecloth, Blacks Playing Banjo, Eating Watermelon, 53 X 64 In. 55.00
Tablecloth, Block Printed Floral, Indian, 72 X 112 In. 35.00
Tablecloth, Cluny Lace, 84 X 118 In. 145.00
Tablecloth, Crocheted Cotton Lace, 150 X 68 In. 95.00
Tablecloth, Crocheted, 58 X 82 In. 50.00
Tablecloth, Crocheted, Florals, 42 X 51 In. 60.00
Tablecloth, Crocheted, Medallions, Square, 78 In. 45.00
Tablecloth, Ecru Cotton Damask, 6 Napkins, 54 X 74 In. 52.00
Tablecloth, Embroidered Linen, Floral, 12 Napkins, 134 X 67 In. 350.00
Tablecloth, Handmade Lace, China, 72 X 90 In. 55.00
Tablecloth, Linen, Crocheted, Embroidered, 54 X 68 In. 200.00
Tablecloth, Linen, Drawn Work, 72 X 92 In. 250.00
Tablecloth, Linen, Handwork Insert & 9–In. Border, 100 X 144 In. 775.00
Tablecloth, Luncheon, Red & White Linen, Fringed 17.50
Tablecloth, Net Fillet, 62 X 85 In. 85.00
Tablecloth, Quaker Lace, Cupid Design, Unused, 1940s 55.00
Tablecloth, Rose Design Center, Double Woven, White, 82 X 86 In. 68.00
Tablecloth, Rose Design, 6 Napkins, Irish Linen, 55 X 70 In. 55.00
Tablecloth, Roses, Irish Damask, 8 Napkins, 1940, 70 X 84 In. 85.00
Tablecloth, Shamrock Pattern, Irish Linen, 1935, 84 X 144 In. 160.00
Tablecloth, Venetian Lace, 66 X 82 In. 325.00
Tablecloth, Wide Stripes, Handwoven Linen, American, 104 X 60 In. 150.00
Tapestry, 18th–Century Garden Scene, Plush, 78 X 48 In. 26.50
Tapestry, 18th–Century Ladies & Musicians Scene, 25 X 76 In. 58.00
Tapestry, 4 Kittens, 19 X 38 In. 25.00
Tapestry, Blindman's Bluff, Famco, 76 X 48 In. 850.00
Tapestry, Early 20th Century Paris Scene, 34 X 26 In. 35.00
Tapestry, Exotic Bird, Flowering Garden, 57 X 46 In. 1210.00
Tapestry, Foliage, Vintage & Flowers, Gold Ground, 84 X 92 In. 725.00
Tapestry, Forest Scene, Small Cottage, Hand Woven, 64 X 83 In. 400.00
Tapestry, Mother Bear, With Cubs, 38 X 20 In. 25.00
Tapestry, Party In Venice, Belgium, 19 X 36 In. 47.50
Tapestry, Victorian Figures, Garden Scene, Belgium, 20 X 52 In. 65.00
Tapestry, Water, Ducks, Fox, 48 X 74 In. 55.00
Vanity Set, Scarf & Pillow, Pink Organdy, Stamped Lady, Uncut, 1926 .... 45.00
Wall Hanging, Blue Velvet, Hand Painted Floral Spray, 24 X 17 In. 20.00

The thermometer was invented in 1731. It measures temperature of either water or air. All kinds of thermometers are collected, but those with advertising messages are the most popular.

THERMOMETER, 7–Up, Porcelain, 15 X 6 In. 35.00
7–Up, Silver, Yellow & Red, Canada, 6 X 30 In. 35.00
Biltrite Heels & Shoes, Embossed Heel & Sole 85.00
Blackstone Cigars, Blue Porcelain, 36 X 12 In. 150.00
Braun's Town Talk Bread, Tin 60.00
Camel Cigarettes, Tin 23.00
Candy, Red Handle, Nickel Silver 10.00
Carved Holder With Frog, Foxglove, Butterflies, 12 1/4 In. 35.00
Century of Progress, Shape of Key, Wall, 1925, 8 1/2 In. 22.00
Chew Wow Tobacco, Relax & Enjoy It, Metal, 39 In. 125.00
Eliott's, Abiline, Texas 15.00
Ex–Lax, Porcelain, 36 In. 60.00

Gold Medal Motor Oil, Kunz Oil Co., Minneapolis	200.00
Goodyear, 14 In. Diam.	40.00
Grapette, The Juicy Soda	65.00
Hills Bros. Coffee, Porcelain, Pat. March 16, 1919, 8 X 21 In.	75.00
Home Stove Co., Indianapolis, Ind.	12.00
Kayo Chocolate, Tin	100.00
Lenox Chocolates, Black, White, Gold, 9 In.	20.50
Mail Pouch Tobacco, Porcelain, 8 X 48 In.	250.00
Maple Sugar, Copper	40.00
Maple Syrup, Brass	65.00
Marvel's Cigarette, Painted, Tin, 11 1/2 In.	20.00
Medley Bros. Whiskey, Dated 1947	40.00
Moxie, Frank Archer Pointing, 1930, 25 X 10 In.	675.00
Nature's Remedy, Porcelain, 5 X 27 In.	150.00
Nesbitt's Orange	40.00
Orange Crush, Light Blue Ground, 16 X 6 In.	24.00
Orange Crush, Round, Large	20.00
Oshkosh B'Gosh	59.00
Pinaud's Hair Tonic	4070.00
Poll Parrot Shoes For Boys & Girls, Celluloid Parrot Below	150.00
Prestone, Red, White & Blue, Porcelain, 10 In.	70.00
RC Cola, 13 X 6 In.	20.00
Rislone Oil, Cab Picture, 10 X 24 In.	55.00
Rueter & Co. Highland Spring Brewery, Brass, Pat.1885, 9 In.	175.00
Salem Cigarettes, Pack Picture, Triangular, 6 X 8 In.	10.00
Sign, Velvet Tobacco, Porcelain, 39 X 12 In.	225.00
Silhouette, Mayfield Coal & Supply, 5 1/2 In. ....*Illus*	10.00
Sprague Meter Co., Gas Meter Picture, Wooden, 1930s	25.00
Squirt, Metal, 14 In.	20.00
St. Lawrence Flour, Canadian, Porcelain, 30 X 8 In.	80.00
Sweet & Pure Flour, Porcelain, Graphic, 27 X 7 In.	325.00
Wheatley Cereal, Wooden, 1920s	40.00
Williams Barbers Soap, White & Gold Metal, 1891, 24 In.	150.00
Woodward, Wooden	15.00

Tiffany glass was made by Louis Comfort Tiffany, the American glass designer who worked from about 1879 to 1933. His work included iridescent glass, Art Nouveau styles of design, and original contemporary styles. He was also noted for his stained glass windows, his unusual lamps, bronze work, pottery, and silver. Other types of Tiffany are listed under Tiffany Pottery, Tiffany Silver, or at the end of this section under Tiffany. The famous Tiffany lamps are under Tiffany, Lamp. Reproductions of some types of Tiffany are being made.

Louis C. Tiffany

Louis C Tiffany Furnaces Inc Favrile

TIFFANY GLASS, Basket, Cut Prism, Cane & Thumbprint, Stepcut Foot, 14 In.	825.00
Bonbon, Green Edge, Ribbed, Signed, 2 1/2 X 5 3/4 In.	475.00
Bowl, 4–Point Star Pattern, Lavender Interior, Marked, 8 In.	760.00
Bowl, Blue Iridescent, Signed, 6 In.	650.00
Bowl, Blue Iridescent, Signed, 7 3/4 In.	475.00
Bowl, Favrile, Blue, Signed, 11 3/4 In.	425.00
Bowl, Favrile, Gold, Wide Rim, Signed, 11 1/2 In.	475.00
Bowl, Favrile, Iridescent Blue, Opalescent, Signed, 10 1/4 In.	350.00
Bowl, Gold, Blue & Red Highlights, 2 X 7 In.	550.00
Bowl, Herringbone & Snowflake, Green, Signed, 8 1/4 In.	575.00
Bowl, Nut, Gold Iridescent, Signed, 2 1/4 X 5 In.	250.00
Bowl, Scalloped Edge, Stand–Out Ribs, Signed, 8 1/2 In.	700.00
Bowl, Vine & Tendril Design, Matching Frog, 5 X 12 In.	850.00
Butter Chip, Scalloped, Gold, Paper Label, 4 In.	175.00
Candlestick, Paneled, Iridescent Blue, 4 In., Pair	500.00
Candlestick, Twisted Stem, Yellow, Signed, 1920, 12 In., Pair	2750.00
Candy Dish, Gold Iridescent, Signed, 1 1/4 X 5 In.	175.00
Cologne Bottle, Feather Pattern, Mustard, Stopper, 5 3/4 In.	650.00
Compote, Favrile, Gold Iridescent, Short Pedestal, 3 In.	395.00
Compote, Gold Dore Base, Blue, Signed, 9 In.	750.00

Compote, Herringbone, Blue & Pastel, Signed, 5 1/4 In. 525.00
Compote, Light Green, Signed, 6 In. 700.00
Compote, Pink Top, Laurel Leaves Under Bowl, Stem, 5 3/4 In. 650.00
Compote, Quilted, Gold, Blue & Green, Signed, 6 X 6 In. 500.00
Dish, Favrile, Blue Iridescent, Scalloped, Center Well, Round 350.00
Dish, Favrile, Ivory Iridescent Center, Blue Edge, 7 In. 350.00
Dish, Gold Iridescent, Wavy Rim & Ribs, Signed, 6 3/4 In. 350.00
Fernery, Grapevine, Green Patina, Signed, 10 1/2 In. 650.00
Floriform, Favrile, Green Feather Design, Ruffled, 5 In. 650.00
Flower Bowl, Favrile, Gold Iridescent, Loops, 11 1/2 X 2 In. 1350.00
Flower Bowl, Flower Frog, Favrile, Blue, Signed, 10 1/2 In. 600.00
Paperweight, National Air Force Salute, Emblem, Etched 50.00
Parfait, Pastel Turquoise, Signed 325.00
Perfume Bottle, Gold Iridescent, Double Gourd, Stopper, 6 In. 495.00
Perfume Bottle, Iridescent Blue, Double Gourd, Stopper, 5 In. 633.00
Plate, Pastel Turquoise, Signed, 11 In. 325.00
Salt, Ruffled Edge, Red–Gold Color, Signed, 1 1/4 In. 200.00
Scarab, Red Iridescent, 3/4 In. 85.00
Shade, Feather, Scalloped, Gold Iridescent, 2 7/8 In., Pair 195.00
Shade, Lily, Gold Iridescent, Signed 200.00
Sherbet, Gold Iridescent, Signed, 3 In. 200.00
Tile, Iridescent Blue, Brass Mounted, Signed, 6 In. 125.00
Toothpick, Square Dimpled Gold Aurene, Blue, 2 In. 250.00
Vase, 3–Sided, Amber Swirls, Blue, Signed, 1899, 4 3/8 In. 3300.00
Vase, Agate–Type, 5 1/2 In. 1850.00
Vase, Amphora, Pinched Handles, Signed, 3 1/2 In. 275.00
Vase, Blue Aurene, Bottle Shape, Flattened Globular, 10 In. 1200.00
Vase, Blue Iridescent, 4 In. 675.00
Vase, Blue Scalloped, Signed, Numbered, 11 In. 1450.00
Vase, Bud, Geometric Design, Dark Blue Luster, Signed 650.00
Vase, Bud, Gold Iridescent, Signed, 5 In. 425.00
Vase, Bulging Waist, Green & Black Design, C.1901, 7 3/4 In. 2475.00
Vase, C–Scroll Handles, Ovoid, Amber Base, C.1909, 3 3/8 In. 880.00
Vase, Chain Link Design, Amber Iridescent, Egg Shape, 12 In. 4000.00
Vase, Chocolate Brown, Zigzag Designs, C.1904, 4 In. 3300.00
Vase, Cypriote, Paper Label, C.1915, 6 1/2 In. 2310.00
Vase, Cypriote, Pyriform, Wavy Lines At Sides, 1892, 5 3/8 In. 1760.00
Vase, Cypriote, Rounded Base, Slender Body, Signed, 5 1/4 In. 950.00
Vase, Favrile, Amber & Green Separated By Gold Design, 8 In. 1895.00
Vase, Favrile, Blue Iridescent, Diagonal Loop Design, 6 In. 2500.00
Vase, Favrile, Blue, Pedestal Base, Raised Ribs, 8 3/4 In. 1500.00
Vase, Favrile, Gold Iridescent, Green Leaf, Vine, 9 X 4 In. 1600.00
Vase, Favrile, Green Feather Pulls, Gold Iridescent, 10 In. 3850.00
Vase, Favrile, Peacock Blue, Tapered To Flared Top, 4 In. 1500.00
Vase, Favrile, Yellow Swirls Over Gold, Signed, 8 1/2 In. 875.00
Vase, Flori–Form, Green, Amber, Signed, Numbered, 10 In. 3500.00
Vase, Floriform, Green Pulled Feather, White, Signed, 13 In. 2350.00
Vase, Floriform, Onion–Form Cup, Signed, C.1904, 12 5/8 In. 3520.00
Vase, Floriform, Pulled Green Feathers, White, Signed, 13 In. 2150.00
Vase, Free–Form, Folds In Body, Blue, Signed, 4 1/2 In. 1400.00
Vase, Gold Iridescent, Bronze Tripod Holder, 9 1/2 In., 2 Pc. 450.00
Vase, Green & Opalescent Mottled, Signed, Label, 8 3/4 In. 100.00
Vase, Intaglio Carved Flowers, Green, 2 Handles 5400.00
Vase, Intaglio, Gold Iridescent, 3 Curved Arms, 7 1/2 In. 2500.00
Vase, Jack–In–The–Pulpit, Amber, Pink, Marked, 1905, 16 In. 9900.00
Vase, Millefiori, Flattened Ovoid Shape, 6 In. 1950.00
Vase, Millefiori, Florettes & Leaves, Vines, Signed, 4 1/2 In. 1950.00
Vase, Millefiori, Florettes, Leaves, Red, Gold, 4 X 4 In. 1950.00
Vase, Millefiori, Trailing Vines, Favrile, Signed, 4 1/2 In. 1500.00
Vase, Oyster White Outside, Pink Inside, 4 5/8 In. 475.00
Vase, Paneled, Gold Iridescent, Signed, C.1900, 4 In. 220.00
Vase, Paneled, Veined, Gold Luster, Signed, 4 In. 475.00
Vase, Paperweight, 5–Petaled Blossoms, C.1917, 6 In. 5500.00
Vase, Paperweight, Amber, Heart–Shaped Leaves, 1918, 4 1/2 In. 9900.00

Vase, Pulled Feather At Base, Emerald Green, Signed, 8 In. 1200.00
Vase, Pulled Feather, Floriform, Amber Foot, Opalescent Body 950.00
Vase, Shaded Opalescent Ground, Blue, Green, Stick Neck, 7 In. 1950.00
Vase, Striated Amber Feathering, Signed, C.1907, 6 1/8 In. 2200.00
Vase, Striated Feathering, Signed, C.1905, 11 1/2 In. 3575.00
Vase, Swirl, Favrile, Paperweight, Green, Amber, Lavender, 7 In. 5500.00
Vase, Trumpet, Green & Gold, Signed, 13 In. 2900.00
Vase, Trumpet, Spear–Type Green Leaves Sides, Signed, 8 In. 250.00
Vase, Urn Shape, Handles, Stand–Up Collar, Signed, 5 In. 1250.00
Wine, Clear Stem & Foot, Green Inside & Out, 4 3/4 In. 275.00
Wine, Faceted Cut Stem, Gold Iridescent, Signed, 5 In. 225.00
TIFFANY POTTERY, Plaque, Dragonfly, Silver Medal, 13 In. 1300.00
Vase, Bouquet of Queen Anne's Lace Mold, Signed, 8 1/4 In. 1935.00
Vase, Flowers, Pedestal Shape, Brown Glaze, LCT, 4 1/2 In. 225.00
Vase, Green & Brown Glaze, 5 1/4 In. 625.00
Vase, Lady Slippers, Mottled Green, Cylindrical, 12 1/4 In. 3750.00
Vase, Leaves Raised In Relief, Turned–In Top, Label, 11 In. 1500.00
Vase, Overlapping Leaves From Top To Body, 3 1/2 In. 750.00
Vase, Tulips In Relief, Stems Trailing To Base, 7 In. 1200.00
TIFFANY SILVER, Asparagus Tongs, Olympian 750.00
Berry Spoon, Conch, Ailanthus 495.00
Berry Spoon, Faneuil 140.00
Berry Spoon, Oval Thread, Gold Washed Shovel 365.00
Bonbon Spoon, Blackberry 165.00
Bouillon Spoon, Richelieu 25.00
Bowl, 1/2–Inch Openwork Near Top, Signed, 9 In. 425.00
Bowl, 5–Petal, Signed, 5 1/4 In. 95.00
Bowl, Bamboo Form, Openwork Sides, 10 In. 1210.00
Bowl, Concave Sides, Ring Foot, 9 In., Diam. 500.00
Bowl, Oblong, Octagonal Beaded, Pierced Rim, 12 In. 450.00
Bowl, Presentation, Wing–Form Buttress, Art Deco, 6 1/2 In. 800.00
Bowl, Vermeil, Hammered, Arts & Crafts, 1900, 3 X 9 In. 2750.00
Butter Plate, Engraved Design, 3 In. 45.00
Butter Spreader, Holly & Mistletoe 75.00
Butter, Domed Cover, 4 Raised Feet, Hammered, 5 3/4 In. 8250.00
Cake Knife, Japanese Style, 1880, 12 In. 715.00
Cake Plate, Molded Rim, Baluster Stem, C.1910, 3 1/8 X 9 In. 375.00
Candlestick, Bamboo Form, 7 In., Set of 4 .... 1650.00
Carving Set, Olympian, 2 Piece 325.00
Chalice, Strap Work, Embossed Design, Handles, 6 1/2 In. 1700.00
Cigarette Case, Basket Weave Design 150.00
Claret Ladle, Chrysanthemum 395.00
Compote, Grape Leaves, Vines, Gilded Pedestal, Marked, 10 In. 1400.00
Compote, Interlaced Laurel Vines, Marked, 9 In., Pair 800.00
Dessert Spoon, Audubon 80.00
Dessert Stand, Flower Heads, Ferns, C.1880, 7 1/2 In., Pair 2750.00
Dish, 5–Petal Leaf, Ball Feet, 3 1/4 In. 75.00
Dish, Asparagus, Liner, Flowers, Angels, 1902, 12 In. 4400.00
Dish, Asparagus, Liner, Scroll Rim, C.1891, 13 3/4 In. 1870.00
Dish, Lily Pad, Hammered, C.1879 .... 247.50
Dish, Mint, Seashell On Ball Feet, 5 1/4 In. 65.00
Dish, Shell–Form, Scalloped, 6 In., Pair 660.00
Dressing Set, Chased Flowers, Putti, Monogram, 1890s, 8 Pc. 1100.00
Dressing Table Set, Foliage, 1907, 17 Piece 2310.00
Fish Knife, Saratoga 85.00
Fish Serving Set, Wave Edge 595.00
Food Pusher, Cordis 60.00
Glove Stretcher, C.1875 .... 135.00
Ice Cream Server, Richelieu, Gold Washed Bowl 425.00
Ice Cream Spoon, Olympian 95.00
Ice Tongs, Faneuil 235.00
Ice Tongs, Wave Edge 375.00
Iced Tea Spoon, Beekman, 8 Piece 680.00
Ladle, Soup, Broom Corn, 11 In. 525.00

Lighter, Table, Paneled, Evans, C.1945 .... 35.00
Luncheon Fork, Shell & Thread 48.00
Meat Platter, Gadrooned Border, C.1907, 20 1/2 In. 1760.00
Mug, Child's, Parade, Engraved Constance, 1897, 3 1/2 In. 880.00
Mug, Naval Pennants, Inscription, C.1884, 5 1/4 In. 1430.00
Olive Spoon, Broom Corn 95.00
Olive Spoon, Chrysanthemum .... 150.00 To 195.00
Oyster Ladle, Beekman 395.00
Pen, Ballpoint, 4 1/2 In. .... 85.00 To 95.00
Pitcher, Cocktail, Rooster Stirrer, 8 In. 300.00
Pitcher, Hammered Surface, Strap Handle, C.1880, 7 1/2 In. 2200.00
Pitcher, Water, Reeded, Pedestal, 4 Pt., 9 In. 700.00
Pudding Spoon, Chrysanthemum 525.00
Salad Fork, Hampton 72.00
Salt & Pepper, Figural, Begging Rat, 1906-7, 2 3/8 In. 900.00
Salver, George II Style, 20th Century, 12 1/4 In., Pair 1870.00
Sandwich Tongs, English King 550.00
Sardine Fork, Holly 195.00
Sauce Ladle, Faneuil 75.00
Silent Butler, Saratoga 425.00
Soup Ladle, Chrysanthemum Pattern, C.1880, 10 3/4 In. 880.00
Soup Spoon, San Lorenzo, 6 Piece 350.00
Soup Spoon, Winthrop 50.00
Sugar & Creamer, Japanese Style, Stamped, 5 3/8 & 5 1/2 In. 1000.00
Sugar Sifter, Vine & Gourds 275.00
Sugar Spoon, Faneuil 50.00
Sugar Tongs, Chrysanthemum 325.00
Sugar Tongs, San Dustan 95.00
Sugar, Persian Style, Agee Cartouches, 1875, 5 1/2 In. 880.00
Tablespoon, Persian 125.00
Tazza, Pedestal Base, Reeded Border, 3 1/8 In. 750.00
Tea Set, Basket Weave Spout, Ball Finials, C.1880, 3 Piece 1100.00
Tea Set, Globular, C Scroll Handles, Marked, C.1891, 3 Piece 1980.00
Tea Set, Rectangular, Cut Corners, Early 1900s, 4 Piece 1800.00
Teaspoon, English King 55.00
Teaspoon, Morning Glory 95.00
Teaspoon, Palm 18.00
Tomato Server, Beekman 275.00
Tomato Server, Flemish Pattern 195.00
Tomato Server, Renaissance 375.00
Tongs, Chicken Claw, English King 575.00
Tray, Chrysanthemum, C.1891, 11 In. 1320.00
Tray, Shell, Round, 13 1/2 In. 1200.00
Tray, Tea, Floral Border, Pierced Handles, 1902-07, 18 In. 1320.00
Vase, Anemones & Foliage Body, 1891-1902, 15 3/8 In., Pr. 6325.00
Vase, Base Rim of Leaf Tips, Monogram, C.1920, 15 1/4 In. 2310.00
Vase, Trumpet, Stylized Buds & Leaves, C.1908, 20 In. 1650.00
Youth Set, Beekman, 3 Piece 130.00
TIFFANY STERLING, Compote, Scalloped, Scroll Design, 9 In., Diam. 600.00
Fork, Olive, Chrysanthemum Pattern 165.00
Pitcher, Cut Glass, Cylindrical Body, 10 1/2 In. 400.00

    Tiffany objects made from a mixture of materials, such as bronze
    and glass boxes, are listed here. Tiffany lamps are included in this
    section.

TIFFANY, Ashtray, Geometric Border, Bronze, Signed, 2 X 7 In. 165.00
Ashtray, Raised Ribs In Body, Bronze, Oval, Signed, 1/2 X 4 In. 110.00
Ashtray, Zodiac, Bronze, Gold Dore, Curved Line Design, 4 X 3 In. 135.00
Basket, Green Top Edge, Optic Pattern, Bronze Holder, 6 In. 750.00
Blotter Ends, American Indian, Dore, 19 In., Pair 350.00
Blotter, Chinese, Rocking, Bronze 85.00
Blotter, Ninth Century, Bronze, Jewels, Knob Handle, 5 3/4 In. 275.00
Bonbon, Ninth Century, Bronze, Gold Dore, 1 1/2 X 4 In. 150.00
Bookends, Venetian, Bronze, 14K Gold Plate, Row of Minks, 6 X 5 In. 550.00

Bookends, Woman Buddha, Line Pattern Border, Bronze, Signed, 6 In.	350.00
Bookends, Zodiac, Bronze	300.00
Bowl, Applied Ship Design, Bell Shape, Dore Bronze, Signed, 8 In.	210.00
Bowl, Flower, Favrile, Vine, Tendril Design, Gold Iridescent, 12 In.	850.00
Bowl, Flower, Vine Tendril Design, Gold, Frog, 5 X 12 In. ....*Illus*	935.00
Bowl, Turtle, Hammered Metal, Folded Over Rim, Tiffany, 4 X 8 In.	6050.00
Box, Cover, Grasshoppers, Enameled Copper, Marked, 5 1/4 In.	4675.00
Box, Dolphins In Relief At Base, Bronze, Signed, 5 X 3 1/4 In.	325.00
Box, Grapevine, Bronze Over Green Slag Glass, 3 X 4 1/2 In.	350.00
Box, Grapevine, Bronze, 2 X 4 X 6 1/2 In.	475.00
Box, Jewelry, Pine Needle, Bronze & Glass, Signed, Square, 7 In.	950.00
Box, Pine Needle, Bronze, 1 1/2 X 3 X 4 1/4 In.	175.00
Box, Pine Needle, Green Slag Glass & Bronze, 2 1/2 X 6 1/2 In.	275.00
Box, Stamp, Grapevine, 3 Sections, Bronze & Glass, Signed, 4 In.	350.00
Box, Stamp, Ninth Century, Bronze, Jewels, Domed Top, 4 X 2 In.	395.00
Box, Zodiac Symbols Allover, Hinged Lid, Signed, 4 1/2 X 3 1/2 In.	450.00
Calendar Holder, Grapevine, Bronze	625.00
Calendar Holder, Grapevine, Bronze & Green Glass	475.00
Candelabra, 8–Light, Bronze, Claws, Bobeches, Snuffer, 15 1/4 In.	4950.00
Candleholder, Damascene, Silver Lines, Blue, 10 In.	850.00
Candlestick, 2–Light, Gilt Bronze, Central Stem Bud, 9 In., Pair	2090.00
Candlestick, Bronze Body, Enameled Bobeches, Signed, 10 1/4 In., Pr.	1100.00
Candlestick, Classical Design, Gilt Bronze, 9 3/4 In., Pair	750.00
Candlestick, Cobra, Bronze, Signed	350.00
Candlestick, Emerald Green Stem, Bronze Base, 9 In., Pair	1200.00
Candlestick, Magnolia, Green Reticulated, Bronze, 17 In.	2000.00
Candlestick, Stick Body, Tripod Base & 4 Feet, Green Glass, 12 In.	1200.00
Castor Set, Cut & Etched Bottles, Silver, Signed	225.00
Clock, American Eagle, Bronze & Green Onyx, Stem Wind	2500.00
Clock, Mantel, Favrile Glass & Bronze, Signed, 1902–20, 9 1/8 In.	4125.00
Clock, Ninth Century, Bronze, Multicolored Enameled, 5 1/2 In.	975.00
Clock, Scotch Plaid, Enameled Dial, Time & Strike, 9 1/2 In.	200.00
Clock, Shelf, Beehive, Copper, Roman Numerals, Brass Base, 11 X 7 In.	1100.00
Compote, Abalone, Gold Dore, 8 In.	325.00
Compote, Blue Opalescent, Gold Dore Base, Signed, 10 X 9 In.	750.00
Compote, Gold Dore, Bronze, Footed, Knob Shaped Pedestal, 4 In.	225.00
Cross, Bishop's, 18K Gold, 5 Amethyst Cabochon Carved Symbols	1760.00
Desk Set, Indian Pattern, 1906, 6 Piece	850.00
Desk Set, Spider Web, Gold Dore, 5 Piece	1650.00
Figurine, Kangaroo, Bronze, 3 X 2 In.	235.00
Frame, Abalone Discs In Pattern, Signed, Bronze, 6 X 6 1/2 In.	550.00
Frame, Adam, Bronze, Gold Dore, Ribbon, Wreath, Sunburst, 7 X 6 In.	475.00
Frame, Bronze, Glass, Pine Needle, 9 1/2 X 8 In.	950.00
Frame, Bronze, Spider Web, Glass, Signed, 7 X 6 1/2 In.	165.00
Frame, Grapevine, Green Slag Glass, Bronze, 14 1/2 X 12 1/2 In.	2800.00
Frame, Grapevine, Signed, 8 X 9 1/2 In.	775.00
Frame, Louis XVI, Easel, Gold Dore, Floral Wreath Top, 6 X 5 1/2 In.	475.00
Frame, Pine Needle, Gold Dore Over Amber Slag Glass, 8 1/2 X 6 In.	2200.00

Tiffany, Bowl, Flower, Vine Tendril Design,
Gold, Frog, 5 X 12 In.

Frame, Venetian, Bronze, 11 3/4 X 9 In. 2200.00
Frame, Zodiac, Bronze, Gold Dore, Signed, 7 X 8 In. 750.00
Globe, Line & Swirl Design, Bronze Holder, White Shade, 13 In. 2600.00
Holder, Note Pad, Ninth Century, Bronze, Jewels, 7 1/2 X 4 1/2 In. 300.00
Holder, Note Pad, Venetian, Signed, 7 1/2 X 4 1/2 In. 250.00
Humidor, Pine Needle, Bronze & Glass, 2 1/2 In. 750.00
Inkwell, Art Nouveau, Bronze, Gold Dore, Raised Swirls, 8 X 6 In. 1200.00
Inkwell, Bookmark Pattern, Gold Dore, Octagonal, 4 3/4 In. 450.00
Inkwell, Bronze, Flowing Curved Tray, Art Nouveau, 6 In. 1200.00
Inkwell, Chinese, Line Design, Octagonal, Bronze, Signed, 4 In. 550.00
Inkwell, Cut Glass, Silver Mounted, C.1880, Massive 750.00
Inkwell, Grapevine, Bronze Hinged Lid, Amber Slag Glass, 3 X 7 In. 750.00
Inkwell, Nautical, Hinged Cover, Sea Designs, Dolphin Feet, Signed 700.00
Inkwell, Pine Needle, Glass & Bronze, 3 X 3 In. .... 375.00 To 525.00
Lamp, 10 Panels Fabrique Amber Glass, Bronze, Gold Dore, 16 In. 3500.00
Lamp, 3–Light, Flowers Frame Vase, Steuben Shades, 13 1/2 In. 8500.00
Lamp, 3–Light, Lily, Favrile, Gilt Bronze, 16 1/2 In. 4400.00
Lamp, 3–Light, Lily, No.319, Quezal Shades, Signed 1800.00
Lamp, Acorn Leaded Glass Hemispherical Shade, Bronze, 22 3/4 In. 6050.00
Lamp, Acorn, Bamboo Base, Gold, Signed Base & Shade, Repaired 4250.00
Lamp, Bridge, Gold Dore, Bell Shade, Feather, Adjusts 48 To 60 In. 1800.00
Lamp, Bronze & Enamel, Bell–Shaped Shade, Signed, 15 1/2 In. 2500.00
Lamp, Bronze, Pale Amber Panels Shade, Lenen Fold, 14 In. 4500.00
Lamp, Candlestick, 2–Arm, Chinese Gold Shade, 18 3/4 X 10 In. 2500.00
Lamp, Candlestick, Allover Green & Leaf Design, Signed, 15 In. 3500.00
Lamp, Candlestick, Composition Base, Bronze, Gold, Signed, 14 1/2 In. ... 1150.00
Lamp, Candlestick, Double–Arm, Chinese Gold Shades, 18 3/4 In. 2500.00
Lamp, Candlestick, Favrile, Twisted Body, Bronze, Signed, 17 In. 1500.00
Lamp, Candlestick, Gold Dore Bronze, Tulip–Shaped Shade, 14 1/4 In. ... 1800.00
Lamp, Candlestick, Pine Needle Shade, Bronze Base & Tassels, 23 In. 1800.00
Lamp, Columned Bronze Base, Green Damascene Shade, Signed, 18 In. ... 5500.00
Lamp, Desk, Arms Hold Shade, Bronze, Gold & Blue, 13 1/2 In. 1800.00
Lamp, Desk, Bronze Base, Inlaid With Mother–of–Pearl 300.00
Lamp, Desk, Bronze Counter Balance, Gold Patina 1100.00
Lamp, Desk, Bronze, Gold Dore, Arms Form Harp Around Shade, 19 In. ... 2200.00
Lamp, Desk, Chinese, Bronze & Amber Slag Glass, Signed, 16 1/4 In. 3000.00
Lamp, Desk, Counter–Balance, Favrile, Bronze, Yellow Shade, 7 In. 6050.00
Lamp, Desk, Counter–Balance, Gold Favrile Shade, Gilt Bronze, 7 In. 2500.00
Lamp, Desk, Damascene Shade, Gold Patina, 13 1/4 In. 3200.00
Lamp, Desk, Double Column Base, Green Bell Damascene Shade, 18 In. 5500.00
Lamp, Desk, Gold Favrile, Trailing Vine Design, Cloth Shade, 23 In. 1400.00
Lamp, Desk, Green Bell Form, Signed, 18 1/2 In. 3600.00
Lamp, Desk, Harp, Bronze, Foliate Design, 18 In. 900.00
Lamp, Desk, Harp, Damascene Shade, Signed, 13 In. 3200.00
Lamp, Desk, Zodiac, Bronze Shade, Adjustable Front & Back, 10 In. 950.00
Lamp, Double–Arm, Bronze Base, Flower Form Shades, Signed, 13 In. 3800.00
Lamp, Feather Design Shade In Pink, White & Gold, Gilt Bronze 4400.00
Lamp, Gilt Bronze, Mother–of–Pearl Shade, Relief Border 935.00
Lamp, Green & Gold Feather–Pull, White, Matching Base, 16 In. 5500.00
Lamp, Green & White Geometric Leaded Glass Shade, Bronze, 21 In. 8800.00
Lamp, Green Bell Shape Shade, Double Column Brass Base 6100.00
Lamp, Hanging, Grecian Style, Bronze, Green, 12 In. 485.00
Lamp, Library, Stylized Petals & Vines, Bronze, Stamped, 22 1/2 In. 6050.00
Lamp, Lily, Quezal Pulled Feather Shade, 3–Light, Signed 1800.00
Lamp, Linen Fold, Amber Glass Paneled Shade, Signed, 14 In. 4500.00
Lamp, Palm & Pomegranate 7250.00
Lamp, Panel, Turtle Back Glass, Tripod Base, Bronze 3950.00
Lamp, Piano, 3–Light, Lily Favrile Glass Shades, 8 1/4 In. 3300.00
Lamp, Piano, Lily, 3–Light, Gilt–Bronze, Stamped, 8 1/4 In. 3300.00
Lamp, Pompeian Bronze Base, Silver Iridescent Shade, 54 In. 6050.00
Lamp, Student, Bronze, Art Glass Shade 3600.00
Lamp, Table, Acorn, Leaded Glass Shade, Brass Base, 18 X 10 In. 2800.00
Lamp, Table, Bell Form Shade, Gold Pulled Feather, Signed 3600.00
Lamp, Table, Blown Glass Shade, Yellow–Green, Bronze, 21 In. 3500.00

Tiffany, Lamp, Table, Inlaid   Tiffany, Smoking Stand, Gilt, 1870-75, 9 1/4 In.
Mother-of-Pearl Shade, Gilt Bronze

Lamp, Table, Inlaid Mother-of-Pearl Shade, Gilt Bronze ....*Illus*	850.00
Lamp, Table, Mosaic Dragonfly Base	2300.00
Lamp, Table, Pineapple Design, Bronze, Stamped, 23 1/2 In.	5500.00
Lamp, Table, Red Leaded, Green Turtleback, Adjustable Base, 21 In.	8000.00
Lamp, Table, Vines & Petals, 4 Petal Feet, Bronze, 18 1/2 In.	3850.00
Lamp, Table, Vines, Stylized Buds, Petal Feet, Bronze, 18 1/2 In.	3300.00
Lamp, Turtleback, Bronze & Glass, Electrified, 16 In.	9500.00
Lamp, White & Yellow Geometric Leaded Glass Shade, Bronze, 18 In.	4950.00
Letter Opener, Chinese, Bronze	145.00
Letter Opener, Grapevine, Amber Glass In Handled & Beaded Edge	250.00
Letter Opener, Grapevine, Glass In Handle, Beaded, Signed, 9 In.	250.00
Letter Rack, Bronze, 2 Sections, Indian Scroll Design, 5 In.	400.00
Letter Rack, Louis XVI, Bronze, Gold Dore, 2 Compartments, 9 In.	500.00
Letter Rack, Ninth Century, Bronze, Jewels, 6 X 2 1/2 In.	550.00
Letter Rack, Ninth Century, Bronze, Jewels, Gold-Plated, 6 In.	450.00
Letter Rack, Pine Needle, Bronze, Amber Slag Glass, 10 X 6 1/2 In.	650.00
Letter Scale, Pine Needle, Bronze, Amber Slag Glass, 3 X 2 3/4 In.	550.00
Magnifying Glass, Grapevine, Green Slag Glass Handle, 8 1/2 In.	600.00
Magnifying Glass, Zodiac, Gold Dore, 4-In. Diam. Mirror, 8 3/4 In.	395.00
Match & Cigarette Holder, Pine Needle, Bronze	325.00
Memo Pad, Calendar, Zodiac, Bronze, 1926	375.00
Night-Light, Blue Enamel Design, 5 Ball Feet, Bronze & Glass, 7 In.	650.00
Night-Light, Putti, Marble, Gold Favrile Shade, 8 1/2 In.	500.00
Night-Light, Scarab	2500.00
Paper Clip, Grapevine, Bronze, Amber Glass, Gold Dore, 2 1/2 X 4 In.	225.00
Paper Clip, Zodiac, Bronze, Gold Dore, Signed	200.00
Paperweight, Bulldog, Sitting, Bronze, Signed, 1 1/2 X 2 1/4 In.	475.00
Paperweight, Grapevine, Green Slag Glass, Bronze Handle, 3 3/4 In.	325.00
Paperweight, Lioness, Recumbent Position, Bronze, 1 1/2 X 5 In.	550.00
Paperweight, Pine Needle, Bronze, Amber Slag Glass, 3 3/4 In. Diam.	325.00
Pen Tray, Louis XVI, Bronze, Oval Shape, 8 3/4 X 3 1/4 In.	250.00
Pen Tray, Zodiac, Bronze .... 110.00 To 125.00	
Penholder, Grapevine, Green Slag Glass, 3 Bronze Arms, 4 X 5 In.	400.00
Perfume Bottle, Green Leaves, Vines, Gold Ground, Signed, 4 1/2 In.	1250.00
Planter, Geometric, Bronze, Gold Dore, Liner, 8 1/2 X 2 1/2 In.	400.00
Rattle & Teether, Sterling & Mother-of-Pearl, Fitted Case, C.1920	140.00
Sconce, Candle, Wall, Shields, Mottled Glass, 9 In.	950.00
Sconce, Turtleback, Glass & Bronze, Pair	4500.00
Sconce, Twisted & Scroll Bronze Rope Trim, Leaded Green Glass	1400.00
Shade, Lamp, Leaded Glass, Filigree Bronze, Pendant Spheres, 19 In.	3300.00
Smoking Stand, Lighter, Gilt, 1870-75, 9 1/4 In. ....*Illus*	4620.00
Table, Glass & Bronze, Bamboo Type Legs, 1899, 17 7/8 X 30 1/8 In.	3850.00

Tray, Art Nouveau Circle Design, Bronze, Enameled, 10 In. 325.00
Tray, Card, Enameled Body, Free–Form Pattern, Bronze, Signed 250.00
Tray, Geometric Rim, Bronze, Enameled, 5 Ball Feet, 8 1/4 In. 325.00
Tray, Pen, Grapevine, Divided Into 3 Sections, Signed, 9 1/2 In. 250.00
Tray, Venetian, 2 Sections, Signed, 3 1/2 X 10 In. 175.00
Vase, Bud, Wall Hung, Faceted Base, Bronze & Glass, Signed, 9 1/2 In. 700.00
Vase, Flare–Out Ruffled Top, Bronze Holder, Signed, 5 3/4 In. 400.00
Vase, Fluted, Brass & Lapis Enamel Base, Marked, 17 In. 1250.00
Vase, Molded Hollyhocks In Bloom, Signed, Bronze, 16 3/4 In. 3390.00

The Tiffin Glass Company of Tiffin, Ohio, was a subsidiary of the United States Glass Co. of Pittsburgh, Pennsylvania, in 1892. The U.S. Glass Co. went bankrupt in 1963, and the Tiffin plant employees purchased the building and the inventory. They continued running it from 1963 to 1966, when it was sold to Continental Can Company. In 1969, it was sold to Interpace; and in 1980, it was closed. The black satin glass, made from 1923 to 1926, and the stemware of the last twenty years are the best–known products.

TIFFIN, Ashtray, Twilight, Cloverleaf Shape, 3 In. 20.00
Basket, Flower, Embassy, Ruby & Crystal, 9 In. 85.00
Candle Frog, No.72 .... 45.00
Candlestick, 2–Light, Bobeche, Prism, Pair 55.00
Candlestick, 3–Light, Round Ribbed Base, 4 1/2 In., Pair 28.00
Candlestick, Flanders, Blown Glass, Pink, Pair 75.00
Candy Dish, Cover, King's Thumbprint, Plum 25.00
Celery, June Night, 10 1/2 In. 30.00
Champagne, Cerise, Crystal 18.00
Champagne, Classic Dancer 18.00
Champagne, Flanders, Topaz 20.00
Champagne, Thistle 5.00
Cocktail, Byzantine 13.00
Cocktail, June Night, 4 Oz. 20.00
Cocktail, Persian Pheasant, 3 1/2 Oz. 10.00
Compote, Twist Stem, Yellow, 6 3/4 X 7 1/2 In. 40.00
Console Set, Drop, Hollow Stem, Amethyst, 3 Piece 88.00
Console Set, Teardrop Hollow Stem 4 3/4–In. Candlesticks, 3 Piece 88.00
Cordial, Cherokee Rose, 5 1/4 In. .... 28.00 To 45.00
Cordial, June Night 25.00
Creamer, Cerise, Footed, Crystal 25.00
Creamer, LeFleur, Yellow 22.50
Cup & Saucer, Flanders, Crystal 35.00
Decanter, Flanders, Clear Faceted Stopper, Pink 150.00
Decanter, Flanders, Pink 250.00
Figurine, Swan, Citron, 10 1/2 In. 85.00
Finger Bowl, Spiral Optic, Green, Crystal 7.50
Goblet, Cherokee Rose .... 14.00 To 22.00
Goblet, Classic Dancer, Footed 22.00
Goblet, Persian Pheasant, 10 Oz. 12.00
Goblet, Water, Cerise, Crystal 22.50
Goblet, Water, Cherokee Rose, Stemmed, 9 Oz. .... 18.50 To 24.00
Goblet, Water, June Night 16.00
Lamp, Bowl of Flowers On Black Base 225.00
Lamp, Green Parrot, Boudoir 275.00
Lamp, Parrot, Blue 195.00
Lamp, Red Lovebirds & Flower Basket, Boudoir 250.00
Lamp, Santa Claus In Chimney, Boudoir, Pair 950.00
Oyster Cocktail, Spiral Optic, Green, Crystal, Footed 7.50
Parfait, Classic Dancer 25.00
Pitcher, Byzantine, Yellow, 64 Oz. 325.00
Pitcher, Cover, Flying Nun, Green 475.00
Plate, Byzantine, Crystal, 10 1/2 In. 35.00
Plate, Empire Twilight, 8 In. 17.50
Plate, Flanders, Crystal, 8 In. .... 10.50 To 12.00
Plate, Flanders, Crystal, 10 1/2 In. 35.00

Plate, Flanders, Pink, 8 In. 17.50
Plate, Flanders, Scalloped, Crystal, 8 In. 12.00
Plate, Flanders, Yellow, 8 In. 18.50
Plate, Flanders, Yellow, 10 In. 35.00
Relish, Fuchsia, 3 Sections, 12 In. 40.00
Relish, June Night, 3 Sections, 6 1/2 In. 20.00
Rose Bowl, Black Poppy 35.00
Rose Bowl, Black Poppy, Amethyst, 7 1/2 In. 55.00
Salt & Pepper, Cerise, Crystal 75.00
Sherbet, Cherokee Rose, Footed 13.50
Sherbet, June Night, Low 12.00
Sugar & Creamer, Flanders, Crystal 95.00
Sugar, Flying Nun, Green 65.00
Sugar, Fuchsia 22.00
Tumbler, Iced Tea, Cherokee Rose 18.00
Tumbler, Iced Tea, Flanders, Topaz, Footed, 5 1/2 In. 25.00
Tumbler, June Night, Footed, 9 Oz. ....8.00 To 17.00
Vase, Blue, Crystal Ball Stem, 9 1/2 In. 25.00
Vase, Bud, Cherokee Rose, 11 In. 17.00
Vase, Cerise, Crystal, 10 1/2 In. 25.00
Vase, Crystal, Sand Carved, 12 1/2 In. 77.00
Vase, Flowers & Leaves, Black, Gold Deposit, 8 In. 65.00
Vase, Magnolia, Sand Carved, 12 3/4 In. 45.00
Vase, Parrot, Black Satin Glass, Silver Deposit, 6 3/4 In. 105.00
Vase, Teardrop, Swedish Modern, Light Amber, 8 3/4 In. 32.50
Wine, Cherokee Rose, 6 In. 16.00

Tiles have been used in most countries of the world as a sturdy building material for floors, roofs, fireplace surrounds, and surface toppings. Many of the American tiles are listed in this book under the factory name.

TILE, 3 Poppy Pods On 1 Edge, Dark Green Glaze, Marked, 6 X 6 In. 125.00
5–Color Tree Scene, White Border, Frame, 6 In. 195.00
Calendar, 1915, Jones, McDuffie & Stratton, Boston Custom House 48.00
Calendar, 1916, M.I.T., Wedgwood 50.00
Calendar, 1922, St. Paul's Church, Boston 45.00
Dark Green Tree, Leaves, Blue Ground, Marked VBP Co., 6 X 6 In. 125.00
Embossed Floral, Cream & Brown, Columbia Encaustic Tile, 4 1/4 In. 24.00
Figural, Black, White, Robertson 85.00
Figural, Multicolored, Mercer 42.00
Floral, Trent Green, Arts & Crafts 20.00
Flower Medallion, Green Leaf, Mottled Brown, Signed Trent 7.50
Hummingbirds, Flowers, Wire Holder, Wheeling, Square, 6 In., Pair 15.00
Ivory & Rust Sailing Ship, California, Faience, Square, 5 5/8 In. 400.00
Nouveau Leaves, 2–Color Gray–Green, Marked, 8 X 3 In. 95.00
Occupational Scenes, Spanish, 3 X 3 In., 7 Piece 28.00
Olive, Symmetrical Medallion, Glossy, Signed Trent 5.00
Parrot, Hand Painted, Marked, Signed C.J. Jones, 6 In. 135.00
Roof, Mythical Bird, Perched, Convex Base, Green Glaze, Ming, 11 1/2 In. 50.00
Sailing Ship, 6 Colors, California, Faience 320.00
Scene of Owl, Moon, Stars, Framed, 4 In. 195.00
Sheep, Village Scene, J. & JG., Signed A.O., 17 1/2 X 9 1/2 In. 1000.00
Yellow Bud, Green Leaves, Black Ground, Framed, 5 X 5 In. 125.00

Tin has been used to make household containers in America since the seventeenth century. The first tin utensils were brought from Europe; but by 1798, tin plate was imported and local tinsmiths made the wares. Painted tin is called "tole" and is listed separately. Some tin kitchen items may be found listed under Kitchen. The lithographed tin containers used to hold food and tobacco are listed under Advertising, Tin.

TINWARE, Box, Cutlery, Handle, 2 Lidded Sections 40.00
Cage, Squirrel, Exercise Wheel, 32 In. 100.00
Can, Brass Stopper, Initial K Front, C.1870, 7 1/4 X 3 1/2 In. 22.75

Candle Snuffer, Cone Shape, Twisted Wire Handle, 1860, 4 1/2 In. 44.00
Candleholder, Tinder Box, Flint Interior, 4 1/4 X 3 1/2 In. 325.00
Candleholder, Traveling, Pocket, 2 1/2 In. 220.00
Candlestick, Crimped Short Saucer Base, C.1830, 4 In. 55.00
Candlestick, Saucer Base, Iron Socket, C.1860 .... 55.00
Coffeepot, Inverted Cone Form, Pierced Design, Penna., 12 In. 2750.00
Comb Box, Mirror Back, Hanging 35.00
Container, Bread & Cake, Japanned Roll Back Lid, Kreamer, 13 In. 95.00
Dryer, Mitten, Pierced, Upright Hollow Holders, 13 X 23 In. 130.00
Dutch Oven, 28 1/4 In. 110.00
High Hat, Red, Black Wide Belt Around, 8 In. 1400.00
Horn, 50 1/2 In. 40.00
Lantern, Candle, Whirling Swastika Pattern, Gilt Paint, 17 In. 220.00
Measure, Flanged Lip, Rolled Seams, C.1860, 1/2 Pt. 30.00
Mold, Candle, 12 Tube, A.D. Richmond, New Bedford, 14 1/2 In. 650.00
Mold, Candle, 12 Tube, Resoldered Handles, 10 3/4 In. 75.00
Mold, Candle, 18 Tube, 10 1/2 In. 95.00
Mold, Candle, 24 Tubes, Pine, Floor Standing, 7 X 20 X 18 In. 1200.00
Mold, Candle, 48 Tube, Ring Handle, 10 1/2 In. 495.00
Planter, Painted Green, Iron Frame, 9 X 18 In. 85.00
Pocket, Letters Say Comb & Brush, 8 X 5 In. 9.50
Sconce, Candle, Crimped Crest, 10 1/4 In., Pair 270.00
Sconce, Candle, Crimping On Crest, 5 3/4 In. 300.00
Teapot, Anniversary, Sheet Tin, Man & Woman Figure Lid, 1856, 9 In. 8250.00
Watch Holder, Lift Lid, 3 1/2 X 1 3/4 In. 7.50

TOBACCO CUTTER, see Advertising

Because tobacco needs special conditions of humidity and air, it has been stored in special containers since the eighteenth century. The tobacco jar is often made in fanciful shapes.

TOBACCO JAR, 6 Carved Faces, Face On Lid, Wooden, English, C.1810 .... 2000.00
Carved Faces, Lead Liner, Carved Mahogany, C.1857 .... 700.00

The toby jug is a very special form of pitcher. It is shaped like the full figure of a man or woman. A pitcher that shows just the top half of a person is not correctly called a toby. More examples of toby jugs can be found under Royal Doulton and other factory names.

TOBY JUG, Beefeater, 7 1/2 In. 50.00
Chelsea Pensioner, Shorter & Sons, 1920–30, 6 1/2 In. 50.00
Gentleman, Seated, Tricorner Hat Spout, H & K Tunstall, 5 1/2 In. 30.00
Gray–Haired Gentleman, Lancaster's Ltd., England, 2 1/2 In. 30.00
Head, John Bull, Green Rope Handle, Japan, 4 In. 12.00
Man, Seated, Green Coat, Mug & Pipe, Wood & Sons, 7 1/4 In. 75.00
Old King Cole, 6 In. 55.00
Pearlware, Seated, Jug of Ale, Staffordshire, C.1780, 11 1/2 In. 440.00
Polychrome Enameling, Staffordshire, Marked, 8 1/2 In. 55.00
Punch, Striped Outfit, Staffordshire, C.1890, 10 1/4 In. 265.00

Tole is painted tin. It is sometimes called "japanned ware," "pontypool," or "toleware." Most nineteenth-century tole is painted with an orange–red or black background and multicolored decorations. Many recent versions of toleware are made and sold.

TOLE, see also Tinware

TOLE, Ballot Box, Cylindrical, Gilt Stenciled, Virginia, C.1850 .... 415.00
Box, Deed, Blue Japanning, Yellow Striping, Stenciled Lid, 3 1/4 In. 55.00
Box, Document, Black Ground, Yellow, Red, Black Swags, 13 In. 440.00
Box, Domed Lid, Swag, Brown & Black, 19th Century, 13 1/2 In. 440.00
Bread Tray, Black Paint, Striping & Stenciling, Pair 80.00
Bread Tray, Brown Ground, Fruit & Leaf Design, Oblong, 12 In. 715.00
Bread Tray, Fruit & Leaf, Brown, Pierced Handles, 19th Century, 12 In. 715.00
Canister, Black Ground, Floral, Cylindrical Form, Hinged, 6 1/2 In. 1200.00
Canister, Tea, Chinese Figures Amid Scrolls, Black Lacquer, 16 In. 1750.00
Chamberstick, Floral, Dish Base, Loop Handle, Brown–Black, 19th Century 2750.00

Chandelier, White Paint, Gold Trim, Electrified 375.00
Chocolate Pot, Fruit, Brown–Black, 19th Century, American, 9 In. 3850.00
Coal Hod, Cast Iron Feet & Handles, English, 21 1/2 In. 12.50
Coffeepot, Brass Finial, Polychrome Fruit & Floral, Penna., 11 1/4 In. 3300.00
Coffeepot, Straight Side Spout, Polychrome Fruit & Leaves, 8 1/2 In. 1550.00
Coffeepot, Stylized Leaf Design, Red, 19th Century, Penna., 9 1/2 In. 1650.00
Deed Box, Domed Hinged Lid, Polychrome Cherries & Leaves, 9 1/4 In. 450.00
Deed Box, Fruit & Leaf, Brown–Black, Domed Lid, Brass Handle, 7 X 9 In. 385.00
Food Warmer, Green Paint, Gold Stenciled Design, 8 1/2 In. 35.00
Mug, Floral, Black, Strap Handle, 19th Century, American, 5 3/4 In. 715.00
Planter, Green Paint, Gold Design, Cast Brass Paw Feet, 14 In. 265.00
Plaque, Figures of Woman, Oval, English, 8 1/2 X 6 1/4 In., Pair 210.00
Scale, Store, Cast Iron, Removable Pan, 4 Size Weights 75.00
Spice Box, 7 Interior Canisters, Brown Japanning, Gold Striping, 8 In. 45.00
Spice Caddy, Center Handle, Lift Lids, Floral Design, 6 X 9 In. 150.00
Spice Set, Hinged Cover Box, Handle, Stenciled, 9 1/2 In., 6 Piece 52.00
Sugar, Cover, Floral Design In Red, Blue & Yellow, 3 1/4 In. 885.00
Tea Caddy, Pennsylvania Dutch, Bird & Floral, Signed, 4 In. 32.00
Tea Caddy, Reverse Painted Glass Sides, Brass Cap 345.00
Tray, English Garden Scene, Stenciled, Hand Painted, Mid–19th Century 3500.00
Tray, Fruit & Leaf Design, Brown Ground, 12 In. 885.00
Tray, On Stand, Birds of Paradise, Gilt, Black Lacquer, 18 X 31 In. 1750.00
Tray, On Stand, Landscape, Red Lacquer, Pierced Handles, 18 X 28 In. 1450.00
Tray, Schoolyard, Children, Stencil & Freehand, 21 5/8 X 30 1/4 In. 1300.00
Tray, Stenciled Flowers & Peacock, Black, 17 1/2 X 24 In. 65.00
Tray, Stenciled Train, Passengers, Landscape, 15 3/4 X 20 In. 100.00
Tray, Town Scene, R. Porter Style, Pierced Gallery, C.1830, 22 X 17 In. 1900.00
Urn, Domed Lid, Gilt & Painted, Parrot Head Handles, 11 1/2 In., Pair 3000.00

Tom Mix was born in 1880 and died in 1940. He was the hero of over 100 silent movies from 1910 to 1929, and 25 sound films from 1929 to 1935. There was a Ralston Tom Mix radio show from 1933 to 1950, but the original Tom Mix was not in the show. Tom Mix comics were published from 1942 to 1953.

TOM MIX, Badge, Decoder 30.00
Badge, Portrait 30.00
Badge, Wanger, Diecut Brass, Red, Blue & Gold Foil Insert, 1938 .... 75.00
Bandana 50.00
Belt, Buckle, Championship 45.00
Belt, Glow In The Dark, Secret Compartment Buckle .... 120.00 To 135.00
Book, Draw & Paint, 1935, Whitman, 96 Pages 45.00
Boots, Leather, Box .... 125.00 To 325.00
Bracelet, Identification, Silvered Metal, Letter B, Ralston, 1947 .... 30.00
Button, Ralston Straight Shooters, Litho, 1946 .... 10.00
Catalog, Straight Shooter Premiums, 1935 .... 10.00
Compass Magnifier, Glow In The Dark, Ivory Plastic, Ralston, 1946 .... 20.00
Compass, Arrowhead 35.00
Compass, Straight Shooters, Brass, Magnifying Glass, 1940, Ralston 55.00
Decoder, Six Gun, Brass, Dial Pistol, Ralston Purina, 1941 .... 60.00
Emblem, Cloth 28.00
Game, Puzzle, Jigsaw, Rexall Drugs, Tom On Horse, 1930s 35.00
Gun, Wooden, Breaks Down ....85.00 To 125.00
Knife, Pocket, Metal, Marbled Yellow Plastic, Inscription, 1939 .... 15.00
Label, Cigar, 1920s, 11 X 8 In. 34.00
Manual, Straight Shooter, Life of Tom Mix, 16 Page, 1934 .... 66.00
Mask, Die Cut, Ralston Purina Premium, 1934, 12 X 14 In. 216.00
Periscope 25.00
Pin, Yankee Boy Play Clothes 65.00
Poster, Safety, Black, Green, Listen To Tom Mix, Photo, 17 X 21 In. 25.00
Puzzle, Jigsaw, Rexall, Original Mailer 25.00
Puzzle, Premium, 1930 .... 85.00
Ribbon, Service, Glow In The Dark, Instructions, Envelope 125.00
Ring, Look–Around, Adjustable, Brass, Ralston Purina, 1946 .... 35.00
Ring, Magnet .... 40.00 To 50.00

Ring, Mystery Look-In, Adjustable, Brass, Tom & Tony Photo, 1938 .... 125.00
Ring, Slide Whistle, Adjustable, Brass, Ralston Purina, 1949 .... 35.00
Rocket Parachute, Straight Shooters, Box 125.00
Rocking Horse, Wooden, 1930s .... 285.00 To 325.00
Six Gun, 1933 .... 85.00
Spinner, Good Luck 20.00
Spurs, Glow In The Dark 45.00
Telephone Set 40.00
Telescope, Black Enameled Metal, Decal, Ralston Purina, 1938 .... 25.00
Watch Fob, Brass, Clear Plastic Dome With Gold Ore, 1940 .... 35.00

Tools of all sorts are listed here, but most are related to industry. Other tools will be found listed under Iron; Kitchen; Tinware; and Wooden.

TOOL, Adze, B. Perard, 6 In. 95.00
Adze, Cooper's, English Style, Marked No.2, New Handle, 9 In. 35.00
Adze, English Style, 4 In. 28.00
Alidade, Surveyor's, Brass, K & E 55.00
Anvil, Jeweler's, O.W.B., Steel, 3 X 1 3/4 In. 22.00
Anvil, Shoemaker's, Iron, 9 X 3 X 10 In. 15.00
Auger, Adjustable, Woods Patent, Hollow, Cuts 1/4 In.To 1 1/4 In. 35.00
Auger, Cast Iron, Wooden Handle, Marked May 23, 1878, 15 In. 65.00
Auger, Hand Forged, Wooden Handle, Initials, Norway, Dated 1829 .... 130.00
Auger, Ratcheting, 1 Side Unscrews To Form L Handle, 15 In. 45.00
Auger, Ratcheting, Shipwright's, Adjustable Jaws, 15 In. 65.00
Auger, Steel Bit, Wooden T-Shaped Handle, 18 X 14 In. 5.00
Awl, Collar, Wooden Handle, Ferrules, Shoulders, 12 In., Pair 25.00
Ax Blade, Goosewing, Forged Iron & Steel, 18th Century 295.00
Ax, Aluminum, Modern Woodsmen of America, Original Handle 10.00
Ax, Broad, Beatty, 11-In. Blade, Handle, 25 In. 85.00
Ax, Broad, Douglas Mfg.Co. 40.00
Ax, Broad, Maker Marked In Circle, Hickory Handle, 12 In. 300.00
Ax, Felling, Tin 12-In. Head, 10 In. Bit, Black Painted Handle, 38 In. 195.00
Ax, Goosewing, Punch Design, 11 1/2 In. 200.00
Ax, Keen Kutter .... 30.00 To 40.00
Ax, Marble, No.5, Safety 85.00
Ax, Redman Lodge, T.O.T.E., 1908, Pot Metal 5.00
Bee Smoker, 1907 .... 35.00
Bee Smoker, Bellows, Root Co. 12.00
Bench, Harness Stitching, Nailed Drawer, Gallery With Tool Holder 385.00
Bill Hook, Suffolk Style, Original Handle, W. Gilpin, 16 In. 40.00
Bit Extender, Keen Kutter 22.00
Blow Torch, Brass, Standard Hardware, Mt. Joy, Penna. 8.00
Blow Torch, Otto Bernz, Brass, Patent 1902 .... 25.00
Blower, Champion, Model 50, Variable Speed, For Blacksmith Forge 125.00
Blower, Hand, Champion, Model 1455, For Blacksmith Forge 25.00
Boring Brace, Labeled R. Marple Inventor, Sheffield, 14 1/2 In. 135.00
Box, Carpenter's, Green Paint, 1 Tray, Iron Handles 70.00
Box, Painting On Inside Lid, H.R.N., Pine, Early 20th Century, 20 In. 90.00
Brace With Screwdriver Bit, Iron, Brass Trim At Handle, 12 1/2 In. 10.00
Brace, Can Take Several Different Sized Bits, Removable Wooden Pads 325.00
Brace, Carpenter's, Curly Maple 80.00
Brace, Chairmaker's, Beech, Owner's Name, Varnished, 12 3/4 In. 145.00
Brace, Sheffield, Plated, Ebony Head, Rotating Handle 995.00
Brace, Ultimatum, Framed, William Marples, Beech, Ivory Ring 495.00
Brace, Winchester No.3523 .... 65.00
Brace, Winchester No.3543 .... 45.00
Branding Iron, WMR, Cast Iron, Oak Handle, 17 In. 35.00
Bucket, Maple Sap, Red, Metal Staves 40.00
Bucksaw, Bentwood Frame, 30 In. 30.00
Buggy Jack, Iron, 4 Piece 16.00
Buggy Jack, Wooden, Tag 25.00
Buggy Steps, Cast Iron, 7 3/4 In., Pair 5.00
Bung Auger, Center Bit Syle, Handle Ring, 2 In. 13.00

Caliper, Double, Hand Forged 45.00
Caliper, Double, Hanging Hole, 17 1/2 In. 75.00
Caliper, Inside–Outside Leg, Dancing Master, 3 1/2 In. 30.00
Caliper, Jeweler's, Brass & Copper Rivet, Inlaid Circles, 3 1/2 In. 85.00
Caliper, Lufkin, 3881, Fully Bound, 3 Ft. 30.00
Caliper, Lufkin, Fully Bound, 1 Ft. 25.00
Caliper, Stamped W.T.I., 1863, 18 In. 85.00
Caliper, Vernier, Darling Brown & Sharp, Large 100.00
Caulking Mallet, With 11 Caulking Irons, Cahill Forge & Foundry Co. 160.00
Chain, Surveyor's, Brass Handles, 100 Ft. 125.00
Chamfer Knife, J. & I.J.White, 6 1/2 In. 36.00
Check Writer, Beebe Indelible, Cast Iron, Brass, 1897 .... 175.00
Cheese Thief, Cast Iron Handle, 6–In. Blade 25.00
Chest, Stanley, 7 Original Tools, Oak, 10 3/4 X 25 In. 100.00
Chisel & Gouge, Wood Carving, Brass Ferrules, Addis, 9 Piece 70.00
Chisel Set, Millers Falls, Bottom of Box, 5 Piece 65.00
Chisel, Hexagonal Cold Haft, 8 In. 8.00
Chisel, Lathe, James Swan, Set of 8 .... 50.00
Chisel, Lock Mortise, Beech Handle, W. Preston, London, 26 X 1 In. 55.00
Chisel, Mortising, W. Beatty & Son, 20 In. 15.00
Chisel, Turned Handle, Blade Marked Fulton, 28 1/2 In. 50.00
Clamp, Broom Maker's, Eccentric Lever Handle, 2 Ft. 45.00
Clamp, Instrument Maker's, Dowl Shape, J. Stamm, Mount Joy, Lan., Wooden 100.00
Clamp, Woodworker's, Parallel-Jaw, Wooden Threads, 10 In. 25.00
Cobbler's Bench, 1 Underslung Drawer, Pine, 14 X 38 In. 65.00
Cobbler's Bench, Blue Paint, Pennsylvania, 19th Century 1275.00
Cobbler's Bench, Leather Covered Seat, Drawer of Tools, Pine 75.00
Cobbler's Bench, Leather Seat, Drawer, Pine & Poplar, 28 X 60 In. 175.00
Cobbler's Bench, Whittled Legs, Dividers, 18 1/2 X 19 X 27 In. 95.00
Compass, Iron, Wing Nut, 10 To 12 In. 18.00
Corn Drier, 10 Place 8.00
Corn Planter, 1894 .... 30.00
Cow Poke, Bentwood Arch, 16–In. Cross Piece At Bottom, 25 In. 13.50
Cranberry Picker, Carved Handle, Wooden Teeth, 6 X 9 In. 240.00
Curry Comb, Forged Iron, Claw Handle, Wooden Handle 15.00
Cutter, Whey, 5 Steel Arms, Brass Ferrule, 21 In. 35.00
Damper, Griswold 4.00
Dividers, Angle, Stanley, No.30 .... 40.00
Dividers, Wing, Metal, 24 In. 30.00
Drawknife, Coach Maker's, Wooden Handle, Brass Ferrule, 7 In., Pair 60.00
Drawknife, Greenlee Reliance, Folding Handles 15.00
Drawknife, Smith's, Made From Old File, Ash Handles, 13 In. 18.00
Drill Kit, Jeweler's, Baleen Bow, Without String, 11 Bit Stocks 395.00
Drill, Breast, Stanley, No.741, Level Vial 20.00
Drill, Hand, Cast Iron, Brass Handle, 1 Bit, 11 In. 95.00
Eye Hook, With Spike, Wrought Iron, 4 1/4 In. 65.00
Fence Cutter, Stanley, Wooden Box, 55 In. 290.00
Flashlight, Eveready, Beveled Glass 75.00
Flashlight, Miner's, Winchester 17.00
Float, Planemaker's, Hardwood Handle, Brass Ferrule, 13 In. 95.00
Flue Hammer, Scotch Pattern, 2 1/2–In. Driving Face 20.00
Funnel, Wooden, With Tin Drain Pipe, Primitive 75.00
Gambrell, To Spread Hog Carcasses, Carved Wood, 37 X 6 In. 5.00
Gauge, Butt, Stanley No.93, Thumb Screw Has S. & W. Hart Logo 65.00
Gauge, Mortise, Brass Fittings, Rosewood, 8 In. 20.00
Gauge, Stanley No.77, Rosewood, Brass 15.00
Goffering Iron, Kendrick No.13 .... 95.00
Grain Cradle 30.00
Grain Measure, Mustard Paint, 1800s 30.00
Grain Tester, Also Called Thief, Brass, 3 Ft. 90.00
Gristmill, Enterprise, No.50, Single Wheel 60.00
Hacksaw, 2–Man, Atkin & Sons, Moses Haden Blade, Dated 1901 .... 75.00
Hacksaw, Iron Frame, Wooden Handle, Brass Ferrule, 14 In. 65.00
Hammer, Bricklayer's, Square–Headed 17.00

Hammer, Cooper's Nantucket, New Handle, 4 1/2 In. 15.00
Hammer, Cooper's, Bung, Hickory, 21–In. Handle 65.00
Hammer, Double Claw, Handle 150.00
Hammer, Driving, Cooper's, Nantucket, 4 3/4–In. Head 15.00
Hammer, Mason's, Keen Kutter .... 40.00 To 45.00
Hammer, Nail Holding, Cheney, Unused, Box 295.00
Hammer, Packing Case, Oak Handle, French, 18th Century 295.00
Hammer, Slate, Marked Auld & Conger, Cleveland, O., 11 1/2 In. 30.00
Hammer, Tack, Thomas A. Conklins, Pat. Dec.10, 1867 .... 75.00
Hammerhead, Veneering, C. Hammond, Philadelphia, 2 3/4 X 4 1/2 In. 40.00
Handcuffs, C.1850, Pair 40.00
Hatchet, Camper's, Collins, Leather Sheath, 3 1/4 In.Bit 45.00
Hatchet, Keen Kutter, No.2 1/2, Marble 450.00
Hatchet, Lattino, Numbered Handle 65.00
Hatchet, Marble No.2 1/2, With Nail Puller 425.00
Hatchet, Marble, Black Molded Handle With Hound Chasing Rabbit 195.00
Hatchet, Marble, No.2 1/2, With Nail Puller 425.00
Hatchet, Shingling, Keen Kutter 15.00
Hawsing Iron, Shipwright's, Hand Forged, 26 In. .... 59.00 To 85.00
Haystack Measurer, 1 Pint, Dovetailed Construction, 6 In. 25.00
Heading Knife, Flat Back, William Greaves & Sons, 11 In. 18.00
Hedge Trimmer, Hand Crank, Commercial, 1914 .... 550.00
Herb Grinder, Cast Iron, Boat Shape, Wheels 935.00
Hook, Hog, Hand Forged Iron, Wooden T Handle, 9 X 15 In. 5.75
Inclinometer, L.L. Davis, No.5, Mahogany, 3 1/2 X 30 In. 195.00
Inshave, Cooper's, Long Handled 45.00
Jack, Buggy, Wood Frame, Iron Steps, Eccentric Lever Action, 24 In. 20.00
Jack, Conestoga Wagon, Dated 1809 .... 195.00
Jack, Conestoga Wagon, Painted Orange & Black, Signed P.N., Dated 1863 .... 95.00
Jigsaw, W.F. & J. Barnes, Rockford, Ill., Stand, 1876 .... 800.00
Jointer, Steers, Double Plane, Patent 1885 .... 195.00
Key Cutter, Russwin, Hand Cranked 65.00
Knife, Curved Blade, Wooden Handles, Brass Ferrules, Marked, 14 1/2 In. 15.00
Knife, Leather, P. Hyde, Rosewood, Brass Handle 14.00
Knife, Race, Cabinet Maker's, Steel With Walnut Handle, Weise 65.00
Lathe, Jeweler's, Brass, Rosewood Case, Mudler, 1853 .... 195.00
Level & Grade Finder, Combined, Edward Helb, Railroad, Pa., Wooden Box 350.00
Level, A. Mathieson & Son, Scotland, Rosewood & Brass, 10 In. 85.00
Level, Disston, 25 In. 45.00
Level, John Rabone & Sons, England, Sliding Bubble Protector, Rosewood 80.00
Level, Sight, Brass, Rosewood, 8 1/2 In. 45.00
Level, Stanley, No. 40, Pocket, Pat. June 23, '96, Japanned, 3 1/4 In. 12.00
Level, Stanley, No.102, 1896 .... 19.50
Level, Torpedo Style, Rosewood & Brass 21.00
Level, Wrought Iron Handle, Adjustable Ends, Wooden, 62 In. 35.00
Lid Lifter, Stove, Nickel Plated, Coil Handle 3.00
Lock Mortise Chisel, Swan Neck Style 25.00
Loom, Rug Weaving, C.1885 .... 150.00
Mallet, Carpenter's, Stamped S. Ley, Burl, 14 In. 20.00
Mallet, Mechanic's, Malleable Iron Socket, Hickory Face & Handle 20.00
Marking Gauges, Adjustable, Mahogny & Brass, W. Tarring 45.00
Marking Gauges, Adjustable, Wood & Brass, Lambert 55.00
Meat Cleaver, Winchester, No.7642 .... 30.00
Micrometer, Starrett Co., 1906 .... 9.00
Microscope, Bausch & Lomb, 2 Turrets 147.50
Microscope, Bausch & Lomb, Brass .... 167.50 To 195.00
Microscope, Bausch & Lomb, Wooden Case, 1915, Large 325.00
Microscope, Brass, Case, Germany, 1920s, Small 75.00
Microscope, Brass, Walnut Case, American 90.00
Microscope, Drum, Brass Sliding Tube 50.00
Microscope, Spender, Brass & Iron, Wooden Case 110.00
Microscope, Weitz & Weztlar, Box 192.00
Miter Jack, For Working 45 Degree Angles 95.00
Miter Plane, Cabinet Maker, Stanley, No.9 .... 1100.00

Mortise Gauge, Thumb Screw, Ebony & Brass 45.00
Nail Puller, Keen Kutter 35.00
Nailing Machine, Shingle, P.J. Linde, Pat.Jan.26, 1899 .... 25.00
Niddy–Noddy, Mortised, Wooden Pins, Carved Maple 40.00
Oil Stone, Honing Block, Spear Shape, Pine Frame, C.1810, 13 In. 65.00
Paddle, Wool Carding, 1800s 25.00
Padlock, Logo Shape, Keen Kutter 80.00
Padlock, Winchester, 6 Levers 75.00
Pipe Wrench, 10 In. 20.00
Pipe Wrench, Keen Kutter, 36 In. 75.00
Plane Table & Tripod, Surveyor's, Dietzen 60.00
Plane, A. Kelly & Co., 22 In. 25.00
Plane, A. Kelly & Co., 26 In. 25.00
Plane, Bailey, No.5 .... 17.50
Plane, Bell, Wood Wedge Type, 8 In. 10.00
Plane, Block, Cabinetmaker's, Q Iron, Stanley, No.9 .... 1395.00
Plane, Block, Ohio, No.19314 .... 200.00
Plane, Block, Stanley, No.62, Angle Block 400.00
Plane, Block, Stanley, No.9314, Wood Knob 200.00
Plane, Carpenter's, Wooden, 22 In. 40.00
Plane, Circular, Evan's, No Brass Nameplate 160.00
Plane, Circular, Stanley–Victor, No.20, Japanned 80.00
Plane, Coach Maker's, Set of 5 .... 325.00
Plane, Compass, Wood Wedge Type, 8 In. 18.00
Plane, Core Box, Stanley No.57, Rosewood Handle, Extension, Tumbuckle 250.00
Plane, Dado, A. Howland & Co., Brass Depth Stop, 1869–74, 9 7/16 In. 35.00
Plane, Fales, Depth Stop, 4 Sets of Blades & Bottoms 300.00
Plane, Greenfield, No.70, Tool Pump, 1 1/2 Size, 14 In., Fence 150.00
Plane, Grooving, Jo Fuller, Providence, R.I., 10 In. 140.00
Plane, Guntz, No.18, 14 In. 14.00
Plane, Heintzleman, No.5 .... 18.00
Plane, Jack, Chaplin, No.1207, Metal 50.00
Plane, Jack, Diamond Edge, No.5C 45.00
Plane, Jack, Ducharme, Feltcher & Co., Wood, Wedge Handle, Button, C.1855 .... 22.00
Plane, Jack, Keen Kutter, Metal 20.00
Plane, Keen Kutter, No.10 .... 10.00
Plane, Miter, Rosewood & Brass, 10 In. 395.00
Plane, Molding, Cabinet Maker's, Signed 17.50
Plane, Mother, For Sash Template, Beech, 9 1/2 In. 295.00
Plane, Norris Panel, No.14/1/2, Iron 450.00
Plane, Nosing, Ohio Tool Co., C.1851, 9 1/2 In. 35.00
Plane, Ocontz Sandusky Blade, Wood, 3 1/2 X 3 1/2 X 16 In. 70.00
Plane, Ohio Tool, No. 72, Hollow, Round, Wooden 12.50
Plane, Ohio Tool, No.114, Panel Raising, 3 Size 175.00
Plane, Plow, Boxwood, A. Howland & Co., No.96 .... 395.00
Plane, Plow, Greenfield Tool, No.529 .... 75.00
Plane, Plow, S.E. Barton, No.35, 1 Blade, Handle, Plated 80.00
Plane, Plow, Sandusky Tool Co., No.137, Ebony, Ivory Tips 5700.00
Plane, Plow, Wedge Arm, Horton & Crane 245.00
Plane, Rabbet, Beech, F., Nicholson Wrentham, 9 7/8 In. 1495.00
Plane, Rabbet, Side, Sims, London, Beech, Pair 58.00
Plane, Rabbet, Stanley, No.10 1/2, Carriage Maker 45.00
Plane, Sandusky Tool Co., No.137 .... 900.00
Plane, Sash Fillister, Beech, Brass Tips, A. Mathieson & Son, Scotland 68.00
Plane, Scraper, Stanley, No.112 .... 65.00
Plane, Siegley, No.6, Japanned 40.00
Plane, Smoothing, Chaplin's Improved Patent No.1205, Rubber Handle 100.00
Plane, Smoothing, Metallic Plane Co., 2 3/4 In.Blade, 9 3/4 In. 125.00
Plane, Smoothing, Stanley, No.54 .... 125.00
Plane, Stanley, Liberty Bell On Blade 70.00
Plane, Stanley, No. 1, Rosewood 370.00
Plane, Stanley, No. 2 .... 140.00
Plane, Stanley, No. 5 .... 25.00
Plane, Stanley, No. 10 1/4, Steel Wheel, Hardwood Handle, Knob, 1940s 500.00

Plane, Stanley, No. 18–16 Block 45.00
Plane, Stanley, No. 37 .... 150.00
Plane, Stanley, No. 40 .... 20.00
Plane, Stanley, No. 45, 22 Blades, For Montgomery Ward 185.00
Plane, Stanley, No. 45, With Attachments 100.00
Plane, Stanley, No. 55, Blades 350.00
Plane, Stanley, No. 79, Side Rabbet, Japanned 65.00
Plane, Stanley, No. 90, Dated March 1900 .... 75.00
Plane, Stanley, No.144, Corner Rounding, 1/4 In. 210.00
Plane, Steers, No.406, Metallic 60.00
Plane, Sun, Maple Carved, Steel Plate, Signed French & Co., Cooper 80.00
Plane, Threaded Adjustable Fences, Sandusky Tool Co., 12 In., Pair 110.00
Plane, Toothing, D.R. Barton 30.00
Plane, Tower & Lysons, Metallic, O.R. Chaplins Pat., 24 In. 75.00
Plane, Winchester, 5 Cent, Red Logo On Cap, Pre–1926 .... 100.00
Plane, Winchester, No.8045 .... 45.00
Pliers, Leather Punch, With Cutter, Pat. July 16, 1872 .... 14.00
Plow Plane, Sandusky, No.119, Brass Adjusting Screws, Mahogany 145.00
Plow Plane, Stanley, No.45, 22 Boxed Blades 225.00
Plow Plane, Stanley, No.55, 38 Boxed Blades 175.00
Plumb Bob, Brass, 2 1/2 In. 15.00
Plumb Bob, Brass, 5 In. 75.00
Plumb Bob, Brass, Steel, 2 In. 65.00
Plumb Bob, With Pulley, Brass 65.00
Priming, Winchester 42.00
Pulley, Wooden, 3 Metal Wheels 22.00
Pump, Wooden, Stenciled J.P. Bodine, Flemington, N.J. 245.00
Punch, Shingle, 32 In. 35.00
Rack, Candle Dipping, Rack & Ladder, Rods & Grid, C.1770 .... 325.00
Reamer, Wheelwright's, Hooked, Handle 65.00
Repair Kit, Shoe, For Home, Economical Cobbler, Wooden Box, Lasts 20.00
Rope Machine, Iron Gears, Twine Holder, Patent Nov. 12, 1901 .... 75.00
Rope Maker, 3 Hook, Bendyke Mfg.Co., Pat.Nov.12, 1901 .... 135.00
Rope Twisting, Hand Crank, Wood & Cast Iron, 7 X 7 In. 45.00
Router, D, Kidney Shape, Mahogany, Wing Nut, 6 1/2 X 4 In. 55.00
Router, Keen Kutter, No.71 .... 80.00
Router, Stanley, No.71 .... 35.00
Rule, Architect's, SR& L, No.86 1/2, Ivory, Leather Case 400.00
Rule, Lufkin, Boxwood, Level & Angle Scale 145.00
Rule, Stanley, No.40, Ivory 85.00
Rule, Stanley, No.85, Ivory 150.00
Rule, Steel Hooked, L.S.S.Co., Athol, Mass., 4 Scales, 12 X 1 In. 15.00
Rule, Tape, Nickel Plated, Lufkin Mezurall, No.926, 1/2 X 6 Ft. 15.00
Ruler, Upson Nut Co., No.68, 4 Fold, Brass Hinged, 24 In. 17.00
Ruler, With Slide, Pelouze Mfg., Pat.Oct.2, '94, 4 In. 25.00
Ruler, Wooden, 1881, 15 In. 10.00
Sander, Wood, Fuller 15.00
Sash Template, 2 Saddle Type, 1 Side Template, Beech, 6 To 8 In. 10.00
Saw, 2–Man, Flexible Fast–Cut Blade, 43 In. 60.00
Saw, Aluminum Blade, Hardwood Handle, Superior, No.88A, 54 In. 595.00
Saw, Bow, Beech, 9 X 13 In. 65.00
Saw, Bow, Winding Stick, Cord, Hardwood Frame, 23 1/2 In. 35.00
Saw, Ice Pond, E.C. Atkins, Indianapolis, Ind., No.4, 4 1/2 Ft. Blade 65.00
Saw, Ice, Hand, Malleable Iron Handle, Henry Disston & Sons, 30 In. 35.00
Saw, In Mortised & Chamfered Chestnut Frame, 25 X 34 In. 45.00
Saw, Keyhole, Keen Kutter 15.00
Saw, Miter Box, Atkins, 5 X 26 In. 17.00
Saw, Pad, Brass Ferrule, Rosewood Handle 22.00
Saw, Piercing, Jeweler's, Maple Handle, Germany 25.00
Saw, Scroll, W.F. Barnes, Rockford, Ill., Pedal Power, Pat. Feb.1876 ...... 900.00
Scoop, Cranberry, Wooden, Dark Finish, 11 1/2 X 16 In. 285.00
Scorifier, Wiegand & Snowden, Smelting Gold & Silver, Fitted Case 245.00
Scorper, Cooper's, C. Drew & Co. 20.00
Scraper, Cabinet, Patent Dates 6/2/14 & 6/23/14, Box 65.00

Scraper, Winchester, No.3075	60.00
Screwdriver Set, Winchester, 2 In.To 10 In., 4 Piece	16.00
Screwdriver, Smith, Steel Ferrule, Beech, 16 In.	15.00
Scribe, Carpenter's, Wooden Sliding Block, Thumbscrew	4.50
Scribe, Timber, Folding, Rosewood Handle, Hammer Brand	35.00
Scribing Plate, Double Ended, J. Porritt, Brass, 6 X 6 In.	25.00
Sharpening Stone, Maas & Steffens, Case	15.00
Shaving Horse, Cooper's, For Shaping Barrel Staves	110.00
Shears, Sheep, Keen Kutter	12.00
Shoe Last, Cast Iron, 7 In.	15.00
Shoe Shine Box, Oak	70.00
Shovel, Cleaning Grease Lamps, Wrought Iron, 7 In.	210.00
Shovel, Grain, D Handle, Hand Carved, C.1810	195.00
Shovel, Grain, Maple, 1 Piece of Wood, Early 19th Century, 36 In.	325.00
Shucking Peg, Metal, Leather Strap	15.00
Skin Tape, Ass, Lufkin, No.713, Enameled Brass Case, 50 Ft.	17.00
Slide Rule, Keuffel & Ester, Leather Case, 1924	28.00
Smoothing Board, Carved Horse Handle, 32 In.	75.00
Smoothing Board, Chip Carved Design, Wooden, 15 1/2 In.	150.00
Snow Knocker, Smith, 4 1/2-In. Shaped Head, 7 1/2 In.	30.00
Spinning Jenny, Female Figure Working At Spinning Wheel, Mechanized	440.00
Spoke Shave, C.T. Co., Circular	38.00
Spoke Shave, Rosewood, F. Brittain, Sheffield, 10 1/2 X 2 1/2 In.	25.00
Spoke Shave, Stanley, No.67, 2 Soles, Rabbeting Fence	73.00
Square, Bevel, Brass Wing Nut, Walnut Handle, 8 3/4 In.	9.50
Square, Brass & Steel, 5 1/4 To 3 In.	20.00
Square, Keen Kutter, Steel, 12 X 8 In.	25.00
Staking Set, Jeweler's, K & D Special, No.4040, Mahogany Case	60.00
Staking, Tri-Duty, Moseley 120 Punches, 25 Stumps, Wooden Case	100.00
Steam Gauge, Pressure Check, Crosby, 1895	135.00
Swift, Shaker, Maple, Collapsible, 21 In.	150.00
Swift, Wooden, With Table Clamp, Small	45.00
Swift, Yarn Winder, Umbrella, Table Clamp, Shelf, Wooden Screw & Nut	95.00
Tape Loom Board, Pine, Rosehead Nails, 18th Century, 9 X 41 In.	350.00
Tape Loom, Pine, Adjustment Gear, Table Model, American, 8 X 16 In.	350.00
Telegraph Key, Vibroplex, No.4, Carrying Case, Key	105.00
Thread Winder, Mother-of-Pearl	16.00
Threshing Counter, Wooden, Drilled Hole Rows, 4 X 8 In.	45.00
Threshing Fork, 2-Tine, 6-Ft. Handle	37.50
Timber Scribe, Hook & Spike, Walnut Handle, New York, 6 In.	65.00
Tin Snips, Brass	35.50
Tongs, Coal, Cast Iron, Small	20.00
Tongs, Ember, Scissor Type, Accordion Toggle, Hand Made, 8 In.	175.00
Tool Set, Shipwright's, Rosewood, Owner's Mark, 4 Piece	545.00
Tool, Traveler, Measure Circumference of Wheel, Iron	100.00
Torch, Factory, Cast Iron, Double Spout, Screw On Lid, 7 1/2 In.	60.00
Torch, Oil Derrick, Cast Iron, Oil Well Supply Co., Pittsburgh, 8 In.	55.00
Trammel, Lighting, Wrought Iron, Elongated S Shape, 5 3/4 In.	85.00
Transit, Bostrom Rady, Perfect Optics, Wood Case	165.00
Transit, Surveyor's, S. Browning & Son, Boston, Mass., Brass, Box	325.00
Transit, W. & L.E. Gurley Co., C.1860	525.00
Traveling Wheels, Wheelwright's, Wooden Handle, Wrought Iron, 13 In.	25.00
Tray, Berry Carrying, Wooden, Green Paint, Arched Handle, 12 X 17 In.	175.00
Tray, Berry Picker's, Holds 4 1-Qt. Baskets, Bentwood Handle, 13 In.	41.00
Tray, Nail, Wooden, Center Divider, 5 Sections, Leather Strap, 23 In.	22.00
Try & Miter Square, Combination, Square Mfg.Co., 10 X 8 In.	65.00
Try & Miter Square, Steel, Ballard Drop Forge Co., 10 X 7 In.	65.00
Turf Cutter, Hand Forged	50.00
Verometer, Eyeglass Tester, Electric, Bausch & Lomb	175.00
Vise Bench, Broom Maker's	65.00
Vise, Leather Maker's, Sit On Base To Secure Vice, 22 In.	25.00
Well Pulley, Wooden, Rope	15.00
Wheel, Bookbinder's, Brass Edge, Handle, 1/4 In.Wide	45.00
Wheelbarrow, Wooden, Red Paint, Stenciled, Cast Iron Front Wheel	160.00

Wing Nuts, Wrought Iron, Ram's Horn Design, 2 In., 6 Piece	60.00
Wrench, Crescent, Westcott, No.76, Keystone Mfg. Co., 6 In.	12.00
Wrench, Frank Mossberg Co., No.74, 4 1/2 In.	15.00
Wrench, John Deere	30.00
Wrench, Maytag	7.50
Wrench, Monkey, Trimo No.6, Trimont Mfg.Co., Drop Forged	18.00
Wrench, Monkey, Winchester, 9 Lb., 21 In.	115.00
Wrench, Rope Bed, Wooden, 17 In.	32.00
Wrench, Winchester S, No.1528	32.00
Wrench, Windmill, International Harvester	15.00 To 30.00
Yarn Winder, Chip Carved Detail, Click Mechanism, 35 In.	75.00
Yarn Winder, Click Counter, Weasel	100.00
Yarn Winder, Squirrel Cage	265.00
Yoke, Goose, Bows, Hickory, Chestnut, Hand Hewn, 1830, 5 1/2 X 12 In.	130.00

Toothpick holders are sometimes called "toothpicks" by collectors. The variously shaped containers made to hold the small wooden toothpicks are of glass, china, or metal. Most of the toothpick holders are Victorian.

TOOTHPICK, see also other categories such as Bisque; Silver Plate; Slag; etc.

TOOTHPICK, Amethyst, Toltec, Footed	7.00
Barrel, With Snake, Milk Glass	30.00
Boot, Pattern, Milk Glass, 3 In.	15.00
Chick & Half Eggshell, Words Just Out, 4 1/4 In.	70.00
Chick & Wishbone, Silver Plate	65.00
Clown, Royal Bayreuth, Blue Mark	495.00
Coal Hod Shape, Amber	20.00
Coin, Green, Pedestal	27.50
Francisware, Amber	45.00
Frog Pulling Shell, Crystal	85.00
Geisha Girl, 3 Girls, Blue Top, Ribbed, 2 1/4 In.	18.00
Hat, English Hobnail, Crystal	9.50
Lake Geneva, Wisc.	40.00
Owl, Feathers Outlined With Brown, Bisque	50.00
Owl, Japan	18.00
Porcelain, Yellow Rose, Gold Rim Handles, Flared Base, 2 In.	10.00
Porcupine, Meriden	40.00 To 42.00
Rabbit In Tree	25.00
Rose Whimsey, Applied Shell Feet	195.00
Ruby Flash, State Fair, 1913	18.00
Shriners Sheaf of Wheat, Cranberry, Gold, 1908	495.00
Statue of Liberty, Amber	45.00
Statue of Liberty, Light Blue Glass	50.00
Top Hat, Blown Glass, Rolled Curved Edge, American	57.00
Tramp Shoe, Right Foot, Painted, Milk Glass	23.00

TORQUAY

Torquay is the name given to ceramics by several potteries working near Torquay, England, from 1870 until 1962. Until about 1900, the potteries used local red clay to make classical style art pottery vases and figurines. Then they turned to making souvenir wares. Items were dipped in colored slip and decorated with painted slip and sgraffito designs. They often had mottos or proverbs, and scenes of cottages, ships, birds, or flowers. The "Scandy" design was a symmetrical arrangement of brush strokes and spots done in colored slips. Potteries included Watcombe Pottery (1870–1962); Torquay Terra–Cotta Company (1875–1905); Aller Vale (1881–1924); Torquay Pottery (1908–1940); and Longpark (1883–1957).

TORQUAY, Bottle, Devon Violets	30.00
Bowl, Ruffled, Indian Village, Michigan, Motto Ware	30.00
Celery, Blue Design	195.00
Cheese Keeper, House Pattern	38.50
Creamer, Cottage, Motto Ware, 3 1/2 In.	32.00
Dish, Sweetmeat, Blue Design	195.00

Jam Jar, House Pattern	26.50
Jug, Puzzle, Aller Vale	50.00
Loving Cup, Cockerel, 3 Handles, Motto Ware	30.00
Match Holder, Sailing Ships, Striker, Aller Vale	60.00
Mug, Waste Not	25.00
Pitcher, Pheasant, Blue Ground, 5 In.	40.00
Pitcher, There's No Fun Like Work, 4 1/2 In.	35.00
Pot, Open, Cottage Scene, 1 1/2 X 1 3/4 In.	35.00
Spooner, Bkye Design	95.00
Sugar & Creamer, Cottage, Motto Ware	40.00
Sugar, Blue Design	105.00
Syrup, Cobalt Blue, Enameled Design, Squatty	165.00
Teapot, Motto Ware, 6 In.	55.00
Tile, Pray Place Your Lamp Upon This Tile, Motto Ware, 7 X 4 In.	115.00
Vase, Shamrocks, Verse, Flared, Handles, Motto Ware, 4 1/2 X 4 In.	45.00
Vase, Tulip, Longpark, 5 1/2 In.	48.00

> Tortoiseshell glass was made during the 1800s and after by the Sandwich Glass Works of Massachusetts and some firms in Germany. Tortoiseshell glass is, of course, named for its resemblance to real shell from a tortoise. It has been reproduced.

TORTOISESHELL GLASS, Ewer, Amber Handle, 9 1/2 In.	85.00
Pitcher, Amber Handle, 7 X 5 1/2 In.	95.00
Pitcher, Center Joined With Bronze Discs, 9 In.	175.00

> The shell of the tortoise has been used as inlay and to make small decorative objects since the seventeenth century. Some species of tortoise are now on the endangered species list, and objects made from these shells cannot be sold legally.

TORTOISESHELL, Box, Ivory Inlay, Rectangular, 8 3/4 In.	2400.00
Box, Singing Bird, Inlaid Silver, Chevob, Geneva, 3 7/8 In.	3025.00
Box, Writing, Inlaid Hinged Lid, Fitted, 14 1/4 X 11 In.	1875.00
Comb, Art Nouveau, Sterling Silver Vermeil	55.00
Tea Caddy, Ivory Inlay, Hinged Lid, 2 Sections, 4 1/2 In.	2640.00
Tea Caddy, Ivory Stringing, Fitted Interior, 12 In.	1985.00

> Toys are designed to entice children; and today, they have attracted new interest among adults who are still children at heart. All types of toys are collected. Tin toys, iron toys, battery operated toys, and many others are collected by specialists. Dolls, Games, Teddy Bears, and Bicycles are listed under their own categories. Other toys may be found under company or celebrity names.

TOY, Acrobat, Magnetic, Tin, 4 Items On Original Card, 1940s	20.00
Adding Machine, Wolverine ....8.00 To 15.00	
Admiral Peary, N. Pole Explorer Set, Metal, Germany, 1920s, 1/2 To 2 In.	395.00
African Man With Ostrich, Lehmann	210.00
Aircraft Carrier Set, American Eagle, 3 Fighter Planes, Pistol, Box	265.00
Airplane, Army Scout, Steelcraft, Wingspan 22 In.	125.00
Airplane, Army, Camouflaged, Windup, Guns, Marx	235.00
Airplane, B–17 Bomber, Wooden, 1943	95.00
Airplane, Biplane, Friction Drive, Tin, 1921	1015.00
Airplane, Bristol Bulldog, Battery Operated, Box	325.00
Airplane, Camouflage, Windup, Tin, Marx, 5 In.	140.00
Airplane, Comet Jetliner, Passenger, Tin Litho, Friction, Japan, 16 In. ...	495.00
Airplane, Dagwood, Tin, Windup, Box	550.00
Airplane, Fighter Jet, Friction, Japan, Box	85.00
Airplane, Fold Up Wings, Landing Gear, Metal, Hubley, 10 In.	20.00
Airplane, Giant Flyer, Spirit of St.Louis Style, Tip Top Toys, 1920s	525.00
Airplane, Helicopter, Battery Operated, Tin & Plastic, Japan, Box, 13 In.	60.00
Airplane, Helicopter, Traffic Control, Battery, Tin Litho, Late 1950s	145.00
Airplane, Kilgore, 5 3/4 In.	150.00
Airplane, Mail Plane, Pilot, Windup, Strauss, 1920s, 13 In.	425.00
Airplane, Model, World War II, 1940	8.00
Airplane, Mono Coupe, Arcade, Cast Iron	50.00

Airplane, Navy, Metal, Folding Wings, Retractable Wheels, Hubley, 9 In. 295.00
Airplane, Navy, Metal, Rubber Wheels, Blue, Red Nose, Hubley, 11 1/4 In. 165.00
Airplane, Roll Over, Marx ....115.00 To 135.00
Airplane, Sea, Hot Job, Windup, Ohio Art, Box 120.00
Airplane, Skybird Flyer, 2 Planes Fly Around Tower, Box 250.00
Airplane, Spirit of St. Louis, Linemar 100.00
Airplane, Spit Fire, British, Metal, Camouflaged, Dinky 95.00
Airplane, Swissair Airliner, Radiant 5600, Schuco 285.00
Airplane, Testor Gas, Spirit of '76 .... 40.00
Airplane, Tin, With Pilot, English, Tin, 11 In. 90.00
Airplane, Twin Engine, Windup, Tin 25.00
Airplane, U.S. Air Force Bomber, Tin Litho, 4 Props, Japan, 14 1/2 In. 1295.00
Airplane, U.S. Navy Jet, Black Knight, Friction, Tin, Japan, 9 1/2 In. 495.00
Airplane, U.S. Navy, Prop, Tin Litho, Friction, Japan, 7 In. 125.00
Airplane, Wen–Mac Yellow Jacket, Plastic 12.00
Airplane, World War II Navy Fighter, Hubley 15.00
Airport, Tin Litho, Marx 40.00
Alabama Coon Jigger, Windup, Tin, Strauss, 10 In. ....425.00 To 500.00
Alligator, Rider, Walker, Windup, 15 In. 175.00
Alligator, Steiff, 28 In. 95.00
Andy Gump, Tootsietoy 302.50
Ark, Paul's Soap Wagon, Litho On Wheels, Germany 120.00
Army Trench Set, Built–Rite, Box, 6 Soldiers 58.00
Astro Spaceman, Red, Silver, Battery Operated, Japan 1675.00
Astrophones, Box, 1950 .... 30.00
Atlantic City Rollo Chair, Tin, Windup, Marx, C.1910 .... 950.00
Baby Bottle, Anesco Toy 7.50
Baby Chick In Egg, Tin, Key Wind 25.00
Baby Tortoise, Windup, Occupied Japan, Box 45.00
Ball & Jacks, Original Container 10.00
Barn, With 5 Animals, Litho Wood, Converse 250.00
Barney Google, Rides Sparkplug, 1920s 1950.00
Basket, Nursery Rhyme, Metal, Chein 22.00
Battle Cruiser, Buck Rogers, Tootsietoy, Box, 1937 .... 200.00
Battleship, Tin Litho, Friction, Marx, 14 1/2 In. 125.00
    TOY, BEAR, see also Teddy Bear
Bear, Dancing, Windup, Straw Stuffed, Felt Clothing, Germany, 17 In. 3500.00
Bear, Drummer, Windup, Box 45.00
Bear, Musical, Crank, Mattel 32.00
Bear, Playing Drum, Guntherman 550.00
Bear, Smoking, Walks & Puffs, Battery Operated 48.00
Bear, Tumbling, Fur, Roullet Et Decamps 1500.00
Bear, Wool Nap, On Cast Iron Wheels, Button In Ear, Steiff, 10 X 11 In. 800.00
Bed, Doll's, 4–Poster, White, Gold Knobs, Wooden 20.00
Bed, Doll's, Brass, Head & Foot Spindles, 11–In. Side Rails, 15 X 16 In. 155.00
Bed, Doll's, Canopy, Headboard, Mattress, Dust Ruffle, 1900 .... 80.00
Bed, Doll's, Canopy, Padded Board Mattress, 27 X 27 X 16 In. 325.00
Bed, Doll's, Cast Iron, Green, Ornate 700.00
Bed, Doll's, Twisted Wire, Scrolled Side, Head, Foot, 5 X 7 X 10 In. 98.00
Bell, Heart Spoke Wheels, Red & Silver, Cast Iron, 3 1/2 In. 100.00
Bell, Male & Female Figure, Pull, American, Cast Iron & Tin, 7 1/4 In. 1210.00
    TOY, BICYCLE, see Bicycle
Big Tim Marionette Theater Stage, 2 Marionettes, Dated 1929 .... 100.00
Binoculars, Space Patrol 395.00
Bison, American, Steiff, Button In Ear, 6 X 10 In. 110.00
Blackboard, Easel Style 155.00
Blimp, U.S. Navy, Model Kit, Ideal, Box 20.00
Blocks, ABC, Nesting, Paper Litho, Wood, Dated 1881, Stack To 42 In. 950.00
Blocks, Alphabet, Hills, Cover Has Children, Parlor Scene 135.00
Blocks, Blondie & Dagwood, Interchangeable, Box, 1951 .... 35.00
Blocks, Brownie Portrait Cubes, Palmer Cox, Wooden, 1892, 5 X 13 In. 200.00
Blocks, Building, Hills, Father Christmas On Cover 235.00
Blocks, Building, Plastic, Lego Plastics, Inc., No.73, Instructions 25.00

Blocks, Litho, Interchangeable To Form 6 Different Animals 550.00
Blocks, Paper Litho of Fairy Tales, Puzzle 35.00
Blocks, Puzzle, Wooden, Makes 6 Puzzles, Children, Dolls, Dogs 110.00
Blocks, Stacking, Victorian Children & Animals, Germany, 6 Piece 275.00
Blocks, Wooden, Seneca Spelling, 16 Piece 40.00
Boat, America Ocean Liner, Tin, Key Wind, U.S. Zone Germany, 14 In. 395.00
Boat, Battleship, Tin Litho, Black, Gray, White, W. Germany, 14 In. 895.00
Boat, Cabin Cruiser, Windup, Tin, 1940s 30.00
Boat, Cabin Cruiser, Wooden, 28 In. 55.00
Boat, Fire, Tom Thumb Toys, 15 In. 125.00
Boat, Gunboat, Iron Wheels, Center Flywheel, Tin, 5 X 15 In. 275.00
Boat, Luxury Liner, Wolverine, Box 80.00
Boat, Nautilus Submarine, Tin Litho, Hand Crank, 1959–63, Japan, 17 In. 695.00
Boat, Navy Cruiser, Docking Slip, Tellicum Toys, Wooden, Painted, 17 In. 150.00
Boat, Ocean Liner, Marklin 4950.00
Boat, Ocean Liner, Passenger, White, Blue, Lifeboats, Fleischmann, 20 In. 750.00
Boat, Paddlewheel, Tin Litho, Windup, England, 1940s, 10 In. 145.00
Boat, Pull, With Blocks, Litho, Marked Philadelphia, 32 In. 175.00
Boat, S.S. America, Pull Toy, Tin Litho, Wyandotte, 9 In. 75.00
Boat, Side–Wheeler, Windup, Tin, 8 1/2 In. 795.00
Boat, Sloop Margaret, Gaff Rig, 19th Century, 71 X 60 In. 2900.00
Boat, Submarine, Green, Black, Red, Gold, Marklin, Restored, 14 1/2 In. 1795.00
Boat, Swamp, Tin, Windup, Pontoons, Man On Top, Bing 695.00
Boat, Tin, Green, Red, White, Japan, 16 1/2 In. 245.00
Boat, Torpedo, Black, Gray, 1930, Bing, 11 In. 1125.00
Boat, U.S. Cargo, Radio Control, Handmade, Wooden, 1940–50, 4 1/2 X 1 Ft. 695.00
Boat, U.S. Navy Submarine, Tin, Crank Power, Blue, Red, Gray, Japan, 10 In. 595.00
Boat, U.S. Submarine, Tin, Gray, White, Japan, 11 In. 595.00
Bobsled, Red, Yellow Striping, Small 80.00
Bombo The Monk, Windup 120.00
Bottle Sterilizer, Doll's, Bottles & Brush, Graniteware, Green 125.00
Brave Eagle, Beats Drum, War Whoops, Battery Operated, T–N Co. 120.00
Bread Box, Tin, Ivory, Gold Lettering 22.00
Buckeye Ditcher, Kenton, Cast Iron, 9 In. 525.00
Bull, Fighting, Remote Control, Box 35.00
Bulldozer, Battery–Operated, Linemar, 8 In. 70.00
Bulldozer, With Man, Windup, Marx 65.00
Bulldozer, Worn Paint, Tonka, 1950s 30.00
Bus, 7 Windows, Blue, Kenton, Cast Iron, 5 1/2 In. 200.00
Bus, ACF, Hubley, Cast Iron, 11 1/2 In. 250.00
Bus, Arcade, Cast Iron, 4 1/2 In. 65.00
Bus, Buddy L, 1938 .... 220.00
Bus, Cast Iron, Red, Tires, 10 Split Windows On Each Side, 5 X 1 3/4 In. 85.00
Bus, Double–Decker, Clockwork, Tin, French, Passengers, Driver, 9 1/4 In. 2200.00
Bus, Double–Decker, Exide, Dinky Toys, England 40.00
Bus, Double–Decker, Litho Tin, Driver, Ticket Taker, Carr & Co., 10 In. 1450.00
Bus, Double–Decker, Tin, Ober 395.00
Bus, Fageol Safety Coach, Hubley, Cast Iron, 12 In. 625.00
Bus, Fiat, Rio, Italy 40.00
Bus, Greyhound Lines, Lithographed Passengers, Marusan, 12 1/2 In. 475.00
Bus, Greyhound, Metal, Tootsie Toy 20.00
Bus, Greyhound, Sightseeing, Friction, 10 In. .... 65.00 To 75.00
Bus, Greyhound, Vista Cruiser, 66, Matchbox, Lesney 130.00
Bus, Greyhound, White Rubber Tires, 1930s, Tootsietoy, 6 In. 60.00
Bus, Jackie Gleason, Mechanical, 1950s 554.00
Bus, Overland, Tootsietoy 110.00
Bus, Remote Control, Gold, Radicon, Modern Toys, C.1952, 13 In. 225.00
Bus, School, Hubley 20.00
Bus, Trailways, Friction 45.00
Bus, Windup, Robot Bus Stamped On Side 85.00
Busy Bridge, Windup, Marx 375.00
Butter & Egg Man, Mechanical, Marx, Box 1750.00
Butterfly, Push Toy, Tin, Cast Iron Wheels, On Stick 145.00
Cable Car, San Francisco, Windup, Box 40.00

Cackling Hen, Pull Toy, Fisher-Price, Wooden, Wyandotte 92.50
Camel, Walking, Windup, Tin, C.1900 .... 150.00
Camera, Bugs Bunny 15.00
Cannon, Army, Green & Red Paint, Cast Iron, 25 In. 85.00
Cannon, Iron, Pine Frame, Sliding Carriage, Mid-1800s, 3 X 3 X 9 In. 130.00
Cannon, Kilgore, Slide Cracker, Steel Ball 85.00
Cannon, Wood Carriage, Cast Iron Spoked Wheels, Brass, 10 In. 40.00
Cannon, World War II, Litho Design, Windup, Tin, Marx 67.50
Cap Gun, Big Bill, Cast Iron, 1920s 22.00
Cap Gun, Bigger Bang, Cast Iron 37.00
Cap Gun, Border Patrol, Automatic, Kilgore 15.00
Cap Gun, Border Patrol, Iron, Kilgore, 1935, 5 In. 15.00
Cap Gun, Buc-A-Roo, Kilgore, Box, 7 1/2 In. 52.00
Cap Gun, Buffalo Bill, Cast Iron, Box, 1930s 60.00
Cap Gun, Buffalo Bill, Long Barrel, Cast Iron 125.00
Cap Gun, Buffalo Bill, Stevens, Chrome, White Handle 33.00
Cap Gun, Cast Iron, Miniature, 1890s 110.00
Cap Gun, Cast Nickel Steel, 1898, 5 In. 100.00
Cap Gun, Colt 45, Plastic, Hubley, 1958, 13 1/2 In. 50.00
Cap Gun, Comet, Single Shot 28.00
Cap Gun, Cowboy Jr., Die Cast, Hubley 45.00
Cap Gun, Cowboy King, Stevens, 9 In. 42.00
Cap Gun, Daisy, Cast Iron 30.00
Cap Gun, Daisy, Holsters, Box, Pair 27.50
Cap Gun, Derringer Style, Ejectable Cap Firing 15.00
Cap Gun, Echo, 4 1/2 In. 24.00
Cap Gun, Fanner 50, Metal, Silver, Stag Grips, 1961 .... 40.00
Cap Gun, Flintlock Jr., Hubley, 7 1/2 In. 28.00
Cap Gun, Gunsmoke 15.00
Cap Gun, Holster, Western Boy, Iron, Silver, Blue, White, 1940 .... 30.00
Cap Gun, Hubley, Sticker 30.00
Cap Gun, Invincible, Kilgore 48.00
Cap Gun, Jr. Police Chief, Silver Finish, Kenton, 1938, 4 In. 15.00
Cap Gun, King, Cast Iron 35.00
Cap Gun, Lawmaker, Kenton, Cast Iron, Box, 1939 .... 65.00
Cap Gun, Lawman, Cast Iron, Box 75.00
Cap Gun, Long Tom, Kilgore, Box, 10 In. 110.00
Cap Gun, Nichols Mustang 500 .... 200.00
Cap Gun, Oh Boy, Crank 55.00
Cap Gun, Peace Maker, Cast Iron 29.50
Cap Gun, Pinto, 3 1/2 In. 9.00
Cap Gun, Pluck, Cast Iron, 3 1/2 In. 50.00
Cap Gun, Presto, Iron, Silver, Red, Kilgore, 1940, 6 In. 15.00
Cap Gun, Punch & Judy, Animated 950.00
Cap Gun, Rick-O-Shay Jr., Cast Iron 25.00
Cap Gun, Rodeo, Hubley, 7 1/2 In. ....9.00 To 19.00
Cap Gun, Sambo, Cast Iron, 4 1/2 In. 155.00
Cap Gun, Scout, Iron, Stevens, 1940, 6 In. 15.00
Cap Gun, Sea Serpent, Figural, Animated 295.00
Cap Gun, Secret Service, Shoulder Holster, Kilgore, 6 1/2 In. 2.00
Cap Gun, Smoking Rex, Hubley, 7 1/2 In. 23.00
Cap Gun, Stallion 41-40, Silver, White, Stag Grip, Nichols, 10 In. 35.00
Cap Gun, Stallion 45, Metal, White Plastic, Nichols, 11 1/2 In. 40.00
Cap Gun, Starter, Iron, Silver Finish, 22 Cal., Kenton, 1925, 6 In. 15.00
Cap Gun, Super Defense, Tin & Iron 25.00
Cap Gun, Sure-Shot, Hubley, 7 1/2 In. 21.00
Cap Gun, Texan 38, Cartridges, Hubley 150.00
Cap Gun, Texan, Hubley 20.00
Cap Gun, Tim Holt, Cast Iron 7.00
Cap Gun, Trooper, Cast Iron 10.00
Cap Gun, Trooper, Hubley, 6 1/2 In. .... 14.00 To 15.00
Cap Gun, Wyatt Earp, 2 Guns, Holsters, Marked Coyote, Hubley, Box, 8 In. 65.00
Car, 2 Figures, Windup, Tin, Lehmann, 5 In. 95.00
Car, 5 Different Styles To Build, Schoenhut, Wooden, 1920s Style, Box 275.00

Car, Ambulance, Red Cross, With Siren, 1955 .... 99.00
Car, Ambulance, U.S. Army, Tin Litho, Lupor 25.00
Car, Autobus, No.590, Windup, Tin, Red & White, C.1910 .... 2100.00
Car, Beetle Bug 100.00
Car, Bentley S2 Coupe, Gold, Dinky Toys, England 25.00
Car, Bumper, Carnival, Windup 45.00
Car, Cadillac, Black & White, 1940s, Lustrous Paint 275.00
Car, Captain Marvel 85.00
Car, Carbine, STP, Turbine, Buddy L 25.00
Car, Chauffeur, Headlights Work, Karl Bubb, 1930s, 10 In. 850.00
Car, Chevrolet Caprice Pace Car, Corgi 22.00
Car, Chevrolet Pick–Up, Cameo Carrier, Tootsietoy, 1955 .... 10.00
Car, Chevy Camero Carrier, Tootsietoy, 1950s, 4 In. 18.00
Car, Chitty, Chitty, Bang, Bang, Aurora, Box 75.00
Car, Convertible, Wyandotte, Metal 90.00
Car, Copmobile, With Microphone, Dick Tracy, Battery, Ideal, 1963 ...... 75.00
Car, Corgi, James Bond, Box 40.00
Car, Corvette, Black & White, 8 In. 80.00
Car, Coupe, Battery Lights, Windup, Marx, 8 In. 125.00
Car, Coupe, Fire Chief, Siren, Girard 180.00
Car, Coupe, Sun Rubber 20.00
Car, Crazy, Dippy Dora, Marx 125.00
Car, Crazy, Peter Rabbit Drives, Metal, Plastic, Marx, Box 650.00
Car, DeSoto, White, 2 Door Sport, Promotional, 1960 .... 135.00
Car, Donald Duck, Sun Rubber 42.00
Car, Duesenberg J, 1931, France 20.00
Car, Fiat, 1929, 525–N, Papal, France 20.00
Car, Fire Chief's, 1959 Olds, Tin, Friction, 10 In. 42.00
Car, Fire Chief's, Battery Operated Siren, Marx 260.00
Car, Fire Chief, Siren Coupe, Battery Operated, Key Wind, Girard 250.00
Car, Flivver, Center Door, Certificate, Buddy L, Box 590.00
Car, Ford Coupe, Schuco, Tin, Plays Music, 6 X 4 In. 50.00
Car, Ford Roadster, Steel Plate, Maroon & Black, Red Trim, 20 In. 1320.00
Car, Ford Sedan, Arcade, Cast Iron, 6 1/ 2in. 275.00
Car, G–Man, With Sparking Gun 50.00
Car, GI Joe, Atomic 235.00
Car, Graffiti Jalopy, Tin, Friction, Linemar, Celluloid Driver, 1930s 235.00
Car, Humphreymobile, Red Smokestack, Box 650.00
Car, Jalopy, Tin, Black Touring Sedan, Marx, 7 In. .... 165.00 To 250.00
Car, Jumping, Marx, Windup 100.00
Car, Lark Studebaker, Convertible, Black, Promotional, 1962 .... 65.00
Car, Leaping Lena, Stauss 150.00
Car, Limousine, Pressed Steel, 1920s, 13 In. 150.00
Car, Lincoln Zephyr, 1937, Hubley, 7 1/4 In. 225.00
Car, Long Hood, Metal Masters, 1940s 40.00
Car, Loop The Loop, Wolverine, Box 175.00
Car, Messerschmitt, Bandai, Red, 7 1/2 In. 575.00
Car, Milton Berle, Marx, Box 230.00
Car, Mirakocar 1001, Schuco, No Key 88.00
Car, Monza Funny Car, Peanut L, AMT, Smile Grill, Box 25.00
Car, Old Jalopy, Marx, Tin, Windup, C.1940 .... 150.00
Car, Packard, 1930, Original Paint, 28 In. 7500.00
Car, Packard, Straight 8, Cast Iron, Hubley 8500.00
Car, Passenger, C.P.R.R., Red Paint, Cast Iron, 8 In. 55.00
Car, Pierce Arrow, AC Williams, 5 In. 150.00
Car, Police, Bandai, Friction 30.00
Car, Porsche 356A Coupe, Dinky Toys, England 80.00
Car, Racer, Rubber Ties, 3–D Tin Driver, Friction, Japan, 4 In. 27.00
Car, Racing, Berlin/Paris, Clockwork, Drives Rear Axle, C.1905, 6 In. ... 1760.00
Car, Racing, Blue, Bing, 5 3/4 In. 285.00
Car, Racing, Boat Tail, Bear Cat, Tin Plate, Wheels, Windup, 6 In. 40.00
Car, Racing, Electricar, Yellow, 11 1/2 In. 110.00
Car, Racing, Gas Powered, Roy Cox Thimble Drome, Metal, 9 In. 125.00
Car, Racing, Golden Arrow, Kingsbury, 20 In. 210.00

Car, Racing, Green, Strauss	300.00
Car, Racing, Metal Wheels, Ace	35.00
Car, Racing, Metal, Windup, Driver, Marx, 13 In.	65.00
Car, Racing, Mr. Rat Fink In Lotus Ford, Slot Car, Ed Roth, Revell, 1960s	175.00
Car, Racing, Remco Shark	150.00
Car, Racing, Roadster, Black, Red Wheels, Cast Iron, 1907, 8 In.	260.00
Car, Racing, Rusher Mach I Mustang, Metal, Battery Operated	27.00
Car, Racing, Tin Litho, Pull Rod Action, Elenee, 10 In.	160.00
Car, Racing, Windup, 35 Cent Price Tag, Marx	30.00
Car, Racing, Windup, Metal, No Driver, Marx, 5 In.	13.00
Car, Racing, Windup, Plastic, Blue, Yellow, Marx, 8 In.	29.00
Car, Racing, Windup, Tin, Marx, 5 In.	35.00
Car, Racing, Y–53 Jet, Friction, 12 In.	165.00
Car, Rambler, Yellow Taxi Company Logo, Promotional, 1962	125.00
Car, Roadster, Kilgore, 3 1/2 In.	70.00
Car, Roadster, Metal, Mechanical, Windup, Yellow Convertible, 1950, 11 In.	95.00
Car, Sedan, Pressed Steel, Wyandotte, 1920s, 6 1/2 In.	185.00
Car, Space Patrol, Battery Operated, 1950s	500.00
Car, Space Rocket Patrol, Tin, Friction	50.00
Car, Speedway Coupe, Marx, No–Light Version	325.00
Car, Speedway Coupe, Windup, Tin, Marx	300.00
Car, Sports, Kiddie–Toy, Metal, Rubber Tires, Hubley, Box, 7 1/8 In.	55.00
Car, Station Wagon, Woody Cadillac, Wyandotte, 21 In.	165.00
Car, Studebaker Golden Hawk, Dinky Toys, England	30.00
Car, Touring, Clockwork, Rubber Tires, Hafner, Steel, C.1904, 10 In.	775.00
Car, Touring, Friction, Iron Wheels, Tin, 10 3/4 In.	50.00
Car, Touring, People At Windows, Chauffeur, Penny Toy, Germany	135.00
Car, Town Estate, Tin	85.00
Car, Tut–Tut, Key Wind, Tin Plate, Lithographed, 7 In.	850.00
Car, Whoopee, Cowboy, 1930s	265.00
Car, With Driver, Mettoy, 1930s, 13 In.	650.00
Car, Yesteryear, 1912 Simplex, Matchbox, Green, Box, 1968	32.00
Carpenter's Set, Metal, Wood Box, Poland, 12 Piece	16.00
Carriage, Doll's, 3–Wheel, Wicker, Umbrella	700.00
Carriage, Doll's, Brown Wicker, French Lace, 4 Wheels, 33 X 37 In.	135.00
Carriage, Doll's, Cartoy, Wire Wheels, Black Cloth, 30 In.	150.00
Carriage, Doll's, Gray Wicker, Metal Under, 3 Wheels, 33 X 40 In.	119.00
Carriage, Doll's, Heywood–Wakefield, Natural Wicker	170.50
Carriage, Doll's, Leatherette & Tin, Miniature	2000.00
Carriage, Doll's, Leatherette, Large	95.00
Carriage, Doll's, Metal, 8 X 9 In.	140.00
Carriage, Doll's, Oilcloth Canopy, Upholstery, Carpet, Stenciled, C.1875	465.00
Carriage, Doll's, Plastic Over Wicker, Chrome Trim, Kinderwagen–Haus	300.00
Carriage, Doll's, Push, Horse & Cart, 3 Wheels	475.00
Carriage, Doll's, Tin, White, Hood Recovered, 5 X 5 In.	175.00
Carriage, Doll's, Victorian Wicker, Braided Edges, Wood Handle, 27 In.	375.00
Carriage, Doll's, Victorian, With Parasol, Dated 1895, Dollhouse Size	185.00
Carriage, Doll's, Wicker, Brown, French Lace, Wooden Balls, 33 X 15 In.	345.00
Carriage, Doll's, Wicker, Burgundy Fabric, Metal Undercarriage, 33 In.	120.00
Carriage, Doll's, Wicker, Gray, Burgundy Fabric, 33 X 13 X 40 In.	300.00
Carriage, Doll's, Wicker, Painted	120.00
Carriage, Doll's, Wicker, White, 3 Wheels, 37 X 13 In.	390.00
Carriage, Doll's, Wicker, Wire Spoke Wheels	130.00
Cash Register, Junior Merchant, Tin	50.00
Cash Register, Little Folk's, Tin	55.00
Cash Register, Tom Thumb	15.00
Cash Register, Wolverine, Tin	6.00
Cat, Black, Straw Stuffed, 1920s, Steiff, 16 In.	250.00
Cat, Snuffy, Sitting, Steiff, 8 In.	35.00
Cedar Chest, Doll's, C.1920, 7 X 9 X 18 In.	50.00
Cement Mixer, Buddy L	525.00 To 750.00
Cement Mixer, Jaeger, Cast Iron, Kenton, 7 In.	365.00
Chair, Doll's, Bliss	400.00
Chair, Doll's, Red, Yellow & Green Stripes, 19th Century, 21 In.	495.00

Chalk, Playtime, White 5.50
Chalk, Small Fry, Pressman Toy Co. 6.00
Chap The Obedient Dog, Battery Operated, Box, 12 In. 90.00
Charley Weaver, Bartender, Battery Operated 31.00
Chicken In Cage, Papier-Mache Rooster, Tail Pops Out When Door Opens 55.00
Chimpanzee, Steiff, White, 8 In. 90.00
Chinaman, Pulling Cart, Walking, Tin, Original Paint, 1910 .... 125.00
Chow-Chow Dog, White, Stuffed, Steiff, 8 In. 25.00
Circus Bandwagon, Hubley Toys, Lancaster, Pa. 2200.00
Circus Set, Animals, Balls, Stands, J.Wanamaker Price, 1920s, 4 To 9 In. 435.00
Circus Wagon, Musical, With Elephant, Steiff 275.00
Circus Wagon, Royal, Driver, Hubley, Cast Iron 245.00
Circus, Flying, Hubley, Metal American Eagle, Cobra, Box 175.00
Clicker, Frog, Tin 4.00
Clock, Teaching, Fisher-Price 15.00
Clown & Donkey, Windup, Lehmann, 1911 .... 265.00
Clown On Unicycle, Windup 130.00
Clown, Happy-Sad, Battery Operated 85.00
Clown, On Balky Mule, Tin, Windup, Box 135.00
Clown, On Scooter, Windup, Germany 225.00
Clown, Playing Xylophone, Wolverine, Tin, Windup 635.00
Clown, Roller Skating, Windup, Tin, Japan, 6 In. 65.00
Clown, Sign, Eat At Joe's, Windup, Tin, Tips Hat 85.00
Clown, Skating, Windup 145.00
Clown, Squeaky, Fisher-Price, 1958 .... 60.00
Clown, Unicyclist, Rides Tightrope, W. Germany 35.00
Clown, Windup, With Spinner, Chein 85.00
Clown, With Cart, Windup, Tin, Lehmann, 7 1/2 In. 75.00
Coal Elevator, Lionel 135.00
Code Lites, Twin, Navy Blinker, Gray Plastic, Compass, Hasbro 28.00
Coffee Grinder, Little Tot, Label 67.50
Coffee Set, Tin, Children & Kitten Design, Tray, Ohio Art, 7 Piece 32.00
Coin Changer, Metal, Box 15.00
Command Center, G.I. Joe 25.00
Construction Set, American Model Builder, Manual, Box, 1913 .... 48.00 To 70.00
Construction Set, Blondie Comic, Dog & Doghouse, Instruction, 1930, Box 120.00
Cosmetic Kit, Deb-U-Teen, Hasbro, 1950s 18.00
Courtland Ice Cream Man, Schuco 85.00
Covered Wagon, 2 Horse, Gibbs 395.00
Cow, On Wheels, Hide Covered, 21 In. 950.00
Cow, Pull Toy, Leather Covered, Bellows In Head Makes Sound 525.00
Cow, Pull Toy, Papier-Mache, Leather Horns, Red Board, Germany, 6 X 7 In. 225.00
Cowgirl Outfit, Annie Oakley, Box 45.00
Cradle, Doll's, Hooded, Red Paint, Late 19th Century 225.00
Cradle, Doll's, Pine, Red Paint, Pinstriped, Floral, 7 X 7 1/2 X 16 In. 175.00
Crane, Traveling Aerial, Tonka 225.00
Crayon & Stencil Set, Wyatt Earp 35.00
Crayon, Chalk, Colonial Artists, Wooden Box 15.00
Crayons, Crayowax Drawing, 8 Piece 5.00
Crayons, Small Fry, Pressman Toy Co. 6.00
Crayons, Tom Sawyer, 1932 .... 30.00
Crayons, Winky Dink, Box, 1950s 8.00
Creeper, Windup, Celluloid Face, Arms & Legs, Japanese Beer Can Body 45.00
Creeple Peeple, A Thing Maker, Iridescent Creatures, Mattel, 1960s 25.00
Cupboard, Doll's, 18 X 15 In. 87.50
Cupboard, Doll's, Open Top Shelves, Early 20th Century 295.00
Cyclist, Wonder, Marx, Tin, Windup 300.00
Dancing Man On Board, Painted 165.00
Dart Board, Tarzan In The Jungle, 1935, 8 X 18 In. 40.00
Derrick, Cast Iron, Arcade, 10 In. 275.00
Desk, Doll's, Rolltop, Oak, Chair, 1900s 350.00
Distance Finder, Sgt. Preston 35.00
Docking Rocket, Automatic Docking Action, Battery Operated, Japan, Box 295.00
Dog, Bulldog, On Wheels, Cloth Covered, Papier-Mache & Wood, 1900s 255.00

Dog, Bulldog, Walking, Clockwork, Leather Covered, Decamps, C.1890, 11 In.	440.00
Dog, Cocker Spaniel, Steiff, 4 In.	40.00
Dog, Cocker Spaniel, Straw Stuffed, Steiff, 10 In.	70.00
Dog, Dachshund, Steiff, 7 In.	45.00
Dog, Dalmation, Collar, Red Heart ID Tag, Steiff, 15 In.	175.00
Dog, Dancing, Lindstrom	45.00
Dog, German Shepherd, Fur, Stuffed, Vinyl Head, My Toy, 1965, 36 In.	45.00
Dog, Puppy, Red Collar, Terrier Style, Steiff, 6 In.	47.50
Dog, Puppy, Rope Skipping, Windup, Tin, Box, 5 In.	80.00
Dog, Rempel, Rubber, 5 In. ....*Illus*	6.00
Dog, Terrier, Steiff, 6 1/2 In.	47.50
Dog, Walking, Windup, Tin, Germany, 8 In.	80.00
TOY, DOLL, see Doll	
Doll Carrier, Barbie, Vinyl, Red, 1960s	8.00
Dollhouse, 2 Stories, Glazed Windows, Hinged Face, 4 Rooms, 31 X 31 In.	330.00
Dollhouse, 2 Stories, Tin, Windows, Keystone, 1940s	50.00
Dollhouse, 3 Stories, Metal, Litho, Marx, Furnished, 16 X 30 In., Box	100.00
Dollhouse, 3 Stories, Townhouse, American, Dec.1862, Lizzie C. Ball	6050.00
Dollhouse, 4 Fireplaces, Glass Windows, Shingled Roof, 4 Rooms, 27 In.	595.00
Dollhouse, Clapboard, Hardwood Floor, Copper Roof, Large	70.00
Dollhouse, Colonial, 3 Stories, White Paint, 2 Chimneys, Large	240.00
Dollhouse, Colonial, 6 Furnished Rooms, Hardwood Floors, Electrified	495.00
Dollhouse, Folding Litho On Cardboard, Box, 1894	285.00
Dollhouse, Furniture & Piano, Renwal, 8 Piece	35.00
Dollhouse, Furniture, Bathroom Fixtures, Arcade, 3 Piece	85.00
Dollhouse, Furniture, Breakfront, Renwal	15.00
Dollhouse, Furniture, Candelabra, Petite Princess	20.00
Dollhouse, Furniture, Chair, Dining Room, Wooden, 4 Piece	35.00
Dollhouse, Furniture, Dining Room Set, Renwal, C.1950	22.50
Dollhouse, Furniture, Dining Room, Tootsietoy, 7 Piece	65.00
Dollhouse, Furniture, Dining Table, 3 Chairs, Strombecker, Walnut	35.00
Dollhouse, Furniture, Doll, Cupboard, Oak	125.00
Dollhouse, Furniture, Kitchen, Cast Iron, Arcade, Complete, 5 Piece	1075.00
Dollhouse, Furniture, Kitchen, Cook 'N Serve Set, 3 Figures, C.1950	35.00
Dollhouse, Furniture, Living Room Set, Davenport Chair, Tables, Red	32.00
Dollhouse, Furniture, Living Room, Daisy, Tootsietoy, 1927, Box, 7 Piece	110.00
Dollhouse, Furniture, Metal, Tootsietoy, 11 Piece	85.00
Dollhouse, Furniture, Parlor Set, Heart Design, Lead, 3 Piece	65.00
Dollhouse, Furniture, Refrigerator, Stove & Sink, Wolverine	55.00
Dollhouse, Furniture, Sofa & Wing Chair, Wynietoy	75.00
Dollhouse, Townhouse, Electric Lights, Contents, Germany, 1910, 28 In.	795.00
Dolly Dressmaker, Battery Operated, Box	200.00

Toy, Dog, Rempel, Rubber, 5 In.

Toy, Drummer, Windup, Black
Felt Coat, Red Nose, 6 In.

Donkey With Bee, Windup, Chein	35.00
Donkey, Leather Ears, Jointed, Wooden, Schoenhut, 9 In.	85.00
Donkey, Pop–Up, Fisher–Price	10.00
Donkey, Schoenhut	115.00
Donkey, Windup, Schuco	185.00
Dresser, Doll's, Mirror, 3 Drawers, Wooden, 12 X 9 X 4 In.	45.00
Dresser, Doll's, Victorian, Swing Mirror, Painted Flowers	48.00
Dresser, Doll's, Walnut, Dated 1881	450.00
Dresser, Doll's, Wooden, Small Mirror	50.00
Drum, Gulliver's Travels, Chein, C.1939	38.00
Drummer Boy, Battery Operated, Linemar	250.00
Drummer, Windup, Black Felt Coat, Red Nose, 6 In. ....*Illus*	55.00
Dry Sink, Stepback, Red Paint, 2 X 15 X 9 In.	450.00
Duckling, Nodding Head, Papier–Mache, Plush Flannel Covering, 4 1/4 In.	35.00
Dutch Village Set, Wooden, 19th Century	1600.00
Eggbeater, Tin, Green Wooden Handle	3.50
Elephant, Dumbo The Acrobatic Elephant, Marx	368.50
Elephant, Mohair, Red Blanket, Button, Steiff, 4 In.	97.00
Elephant, Schoenhut	145.00
Elephant, Steiff, U.S. Zone, 4 In.	92.50
Elephant, With Calliope, Steiff, Box	550.00
Elevator, Coal, Remote Control, Lionel, Box	135.00
Erector Set, Builds Ferris Wheel, Directions, Metal Case, Gilbert	165.00
Erector Set, Electric Motor, Red Metal Case, A.C. Gilbert, No.6 1/2	75.00
Erector Set, Engineer's Series, Motor, Instructions, Metal Case	120.00
Erector Set, Ferris Wheel, Revolving Swing, Ladd, 1930s, 17 In.	350.00
Erector Set, Master Builder, Litho Cover	25.00
Erector Set, Rocket Launcher, Motor, 1938 Instructions	45.00
Erector, Set No. 2 1/2, Gilbert, 1930s	39.00
Farm Set, Wooden, Litho Animals, Figures, Machinery, 1920s	175.00
Farm Tractor Set, Wooden, Milk Cans, Hay Wagon, Peter Mar, 1940s, 3 Piece	375.00
Felix The Cat, Mohair, Ear Button, Chad Valley, 14 In.	195.00
Felix, Schoenhut, 4 In.	95.00
Felix, Soaky Toys, Colgate–Palmolive, For Bathtub	12.00
Ferdinand The Bull, Composition, Jointed Leg, 10 X 9 1/2 In.	100.00
Ferdinand The Bull, Windup, Marx, 1938	135.00
Ferris Wheel, 4 Figures, Flags, Tin, Carette, Manual, Early 1900s, 15 In.	2200.00
Ferris Wheel, Manually Operated, 6 Gondolas, Flags, Figures, Tin, 17 In.	2750.00
Ferris Wheel, Motorized, Germany	465.00
Ferris Wheel, Orange & Red, 17 In.	175.00
Finger Painting Set, Tom Sawyer	15.00
Fire Engine, 1 Man Front & Back, Cast Iron, Williams	275.00
Fire Engine, Aerial Ladder, Structo, Red, Chrome Trim, 34 In.	175.00
Fire Engine, Auburn, Rubber, Red, 7 1/2 In.	15.00
Fire Engine, Composition Figures, Rubber Tires, French, C.1910	6000.00
Fire Engine, Hook & Ladder, Horse Drawn, 3 Horses, Iron, Harris, 19 In.	120.00
Fire Engine, Ladders, Tootsietoy	90.00
Fire Engine, Red, Battery Operated, Banda, 8 In.	16.00
Fire Engine, Tin, Marx, 1920s, 9 1/2 In.	45.00
Fire Engine, Weight Driven, Wood, Tin & Steel	375.00
Fire Pumper, 2 Horses, Driver, Cast Iron, Ives	2500.00
Fire Pumper, 3 Galloping Horses, Wilkins Toys, 1895	3500.00
Fire Pumper, 3 Horses, Red & Black, Gold Trim, Cast Iron, 13 1/2 In.	200.00
Fire Pumper, Clockwork, Driver & Fireman, Gunthermann, C.1900, 8 In.	1870.00
Fire Pumper, Kenton, 8 In.	165.00
Fire Pumper, Keystone, Cast Iron	900.00
Fire Pumper, Red, Nickel Wheels, Cast Iron, 6 3/4 In.	150.00
Fire Truck, Aerial Ladder, Marx .... 115.00 To	135.00
Fire Truck, Aerial, Buddy L	750.00
Fire Truck, Extension Ladder, Nylint, 30 In.	225.00
Fire Truck, Hook & Ladder, 2 Horses, Cast Iron, 20 3/4 In.	230.00
Fire Truck, Hook & Ladder, Horse Drawn, 2 Drivers, 3 Ladders, Cast Iron	345.00
Fire Truck, Hubley, 1920s, 9 In.	210.00
Fire Truck, Hubley, Cast Iron, 13 1/4 In.	425.00

Toy, Horse, Gliding, Hide Cover, Horsehair Mane, Tail, 34 X 47 In.

Toy, Sled, Red Paint, Stenciled,
Late 19th Century, 41 X 11 In.

Fire Truck, Keystone Water Tower With Pump, Sheet Metal, Red, 31 In.	900.00
Fire Truck, Kingsbury, 24 In.	265.00
Fire Truck, Pumper, Ladder Truck, Directions, Keystone, Box	165.00
Fire Truck, Pumper, Ladder Truck, Rescue Squad, Tonka	495.00
Fire Truck, Removable Ladders, Al's Cycle Shop, Canada, 20 In.	75.00
Fire Truck, Windup, Tin, Kingsbury, 1910	650.00
Fire Wagon, Horse Drawn, Windup, Tin–Plated	6000.00
Fire Wagon, Horse, Cast Iron, 1910, 15 In.	185.00
Fireman, Climbing A Ladder, Windup, Tin	60.00
Fireman, Climbing Ladder, Windup, Tin, Signed Louis Marx	150.00
Fli–Back Paddle & Ball, Wooden	5.00
Flintstone, Incline Walker	20.00
Flipo, See Me Jump, Windup, Tin, Marx, 3 1/2 In.	85.00
Flossie Fish, Steiff, 5 In.	40.00
Fly Chaser, 2 Keys, Windup, Green, Cast Iron Base, 1894, 40 In.	200.00
Fort Apache Play Set, Carry–All, Metal, Marx, 19 X 12 X 4 In.	75.00
Fort Apache, Marx, Box	65.00
Fox, Swivel Head, Movable Legs, Steiff, 11 In.	500.00
Frankenstein Monster, Battery Operated, Growls, Waves, Pants Fall Down	180.00
French Farm Set, Papier–Mache Animals, Scenic Interior Box, 1900, Box	349.00
Frog, Windup, Tin	125.00
G.I.Joe, Backpack, Mountain Troops	20.00
G.I.Joe, Drag Bike, Box	35.00
G.I.Joe, Grenade Launcher	25.00
G.I.Joe, Jeep, Windup, Unique	145.00
G.I.Joe, M–1 Rifle	10.00
G.I.Joe, Rescue Raft, Box	35.00
TOY, GAME, see Game	
Garage, Blue Limousine, Red Touring Car, Bing, 6 1/2 In.	700.00
Garage, Double Door, Arcade, 1930s	165.00
Garage, Wooden, Sturdibilt	95.00
George The Drummer Boy, Tin, Windup, Marx, 9 In.	70.00 To 115.00

Gertie The Galloping Goose, Windup 210.00
Gino, Blows Bubbles, Battery Operated, Roscoe 85.00
Giraffe, Button In Ear, Steiff, 4 Ft. 410.00
Giraffe, Circus Car, Steiff 275.00
Girl On Swing, Gibbs .... 185.00 To 197.00
Glockenspiel, Schoenhut, Box 150.00
Go'n Back Mule, Key Wind, Fisher-Price, 1931 .... 550.00
Goat With Bell, Pull, White Paint, Red & Black Trim, Tin, 5 1/4 In. 275.00
Goat, Glass Eyes, Schoenhut .... 295.00 To 350.00
Gold Ore Detector, Sgt. Preston 95.00
Goose, Golden, Windup, Dated 1924, Marx 129.00
Goose, Pecking, Windup, Tin, Marx, 8 3/4 In. 75.00
Goose, Schoenhut, Full Size 385.00
Gorilla, Remote Control 95.00
Graf Zeppelin, Tipp, Large 5000.00
Grasshopper, Cast Iron, Hubley 700.00
Grocery Store, Toy Town, Miniature 1980.00
Guitar, Doctor Doolittle, 1950s 25.00
Guitar, Mattel 20.00
Gun & Holster, Bonanza, Double Set 165.00
Gun & Holster, Wyatt Earp, Esquire, Box 250.00
Gun, BB, Daisy Pump, 1940s 25.00
Gun, Blazer Ray, Transistorized, Box, 1966 .... 125.00
Gun, Bulldog, Cast Iron, Dated 1923 .... 45.00
Gun, Bullet Loading Fanner 50, Mattel, Box 150.00
Gun, Canteen, Leather Holster Set, Ramar of The Jungle, Daisy, Box 185.00
Gun, Colt, Cast Iron, 1880 .... 45.00
Gun, Commando Tommy, W.W.II, Cardboard, Pop With Snap of Wrist, 10 In. 6.50
Gun, Daisy Liquid, 1915 .... 20.00
Gun, Derringer, Hubley, 7 In. 35.00
Gun, Flashlight, Official Space Patrol, Plastic, Box 175.00
Gun, Flintlock, Hubley, Celluloid Case 26.00
Gun, G–Men, Big Shot, Repeater, Chein 38.50
Gun, Machine, Tom Corbett, Marx 30.00
Gun, Space, Electronic, Remco, Box, 1950s 35.00
Gun, Sure Shot, Hubley, Matching Set 25.00
Ham 'N Sam, Linemar, 1950s 850.00
Handcar, 2 Men, Tin, Windup, Japan 165.00
Handcar, Peter Rabbit Chick Mobile, Lionel, 1936 .... 925.00
Handcar, Railroad, 2 Figures, Windup, Tin, 5 1/2 In. 95.00
Haunted House, Marx 650.00
Hedge Hog, Original Clothes, Steiff, 7 In. 35.00
Helmet, Jet, Steve Canyon, Box, 1959 .... 35.00
Hippo, Schoenhut 400.00
Hobbyhorse, Health Rider, Wooden 27.50
Hobbyhorse, Hide Cover, Cast Iron Wheels, 1900s 500.00
Hobbyhorse, On Wooden Base, Metal Wheels, Hide Covered 995.00
Hobbyhorse, Polychrome Paint, Wood, Labeled Hobby Toddler, 33 In. 65.00
Hobbyhorse, Spring Action, Painted, Early 1900s 250.00
Hockey Player, Windup, Steiff, Tags 195.00
Hoe, Metal, Wooden 7.00
Hoop, Reg.Size 28.00
Horse & Buggy, Pull, Red & White Paint, Black Trim, 7 5/8 In. 300.00
Horse & Cart, Chester Gump, Cast Iron, Arcade 550.00
Horse & Jockey, Push, Wooden Rod, Cast Iron 250.00
Horse & Wagon, Borden's Milk 145.00
Horse & Wagon, Hooded, Driver, Tin, Plastic Wheels, U.S.A., 10 1/2 In. 125.00
Horse & Wagon, Ladders, 2 Drivers, 3 Horses, Cast Iron 725.00
Horse With Bell, Pull, Yellow Paint, Red & Black Trim, Tin, 5 1/2 In. 250.00
Horse, Brown Saddle, Glass Eyes, Schoenhut 155.00
Horse, Covered Wagon, Canvas, Gibbs, 19 In. 395.00
Horse, Gliding, Hide Cover, Horsehair Mane, Tail, 34 X 47 In. ....*Illus* 1400.00
Horse, On Wheels, Papier–Mache, Victorian, 7 In. 125.00
Horse, Pull Toy, Black Plush, Rabbit Fur Mane, Tack Eyes, 15 In. 675.00

Horse, Pull Toy, Black, Horsehair Mane & Tail, 19th Century, 20 In. 370.00
Horse, Pull Toy, Papier–Mache 170.00
Horse, Riding, Wheels, All Original, 24 X 36 In. 1125.00
Horse, Rocking, American, 33 In. 535.00
Horse, Rocking, Arabian, Large 700.00
Horse, Rocking, Carved Wood, White, Black Hooves, Red Trim 650.00
Horse, Rocking, Carved Wood, Wicker Seat, Painted, 19th Century, 36 In. 225.00
Horse, Rocking, Glass Eyes, Leather Ears, Brass Fittings, C.1870 .... 1100.00
Horse, Rocking, Original Gray Finish, 1900 .... 145.00
Horse, Rocking, Polychrome Paint, Tin, 7 In. 320.00
Horse, Rocking, Pull Toy, Felt, Horsehair Mane & Tail, 1900s, 30 X 41 In. 1700.00
Horse, Rocking, Removable Tin Rider, Tin Legs, 6 1/2 In. 375.00
Horse, Rocking, Toys & Fancy Goods Co., C.1850 .... 4500.00
Horse, Rocking, Wooden Silhouettes, Wicker Seat, White, Red Trim, 37 In. 70.00
Horse, Velveteen, 10 In. 250.00
Horse, With Sulky & Rider, Cast Iron, 6 In. 90.00
Horse, Wooden Wheels, Felt, Steiff, Printed Button, 15 In. 750.00
Hot–Air Balloon, Tin Plate, Windup 3400.00
House, Tin Litho, Yellow, Lighthouse On Side 1155.00
Hungry Cub, Windup, Pours Milk, Drinks, Black Plush, Rubber, Japan, 6 In. 55.00
Ice Cream Cycle, Windup 300.00
Ice Cream Man, Windup, Occupied Japan, Box 80.00
Indian Joe, Beating Drums, Battery Operated 100.00
Indian, Nutty Man, Battery Operated, Marx, Box 80.00
Iron, Dover Dolly 23.00
Iron, Little Lady, Electric, Kokomo, Box 29.00
Ironing Board & Iron, Bo Peep, Wolverine 15.00
Ironing Board, Red & White Metal 15.00
Ironing Board, Tin, Red 20.00
Ironing Board, Wolverine 15.00
J. Fred Muggs, Pull Toy, Hill Co. 38.00
Jane West, Horse, Marx 30.00
Jazzbo Jim 450.00
Jeep, Desert Patrol, Masudaya, Box, 12 1/2 In. 195.00
Jeep, Jumping, Marx 125.00
Jeep, Willys, Metal, Army Green, 10 In. 35.00
Jet Liner, Comet, Friction, Box 250.00
Jiminy Cricket, Linemar, Box 225.00
Jockey, On Horse, Bell Ringer, Wheeled Platform, Nickel Plated 450.00
Jockey, On Horse, On Wheels, Bell Ringer, Cast Iron 250.00
Jocko The Monkey, Windup, Linemar, Box 50.00
Jojo, Bozo The Clown, Tin, Japan 10.00
Jug Saw Jr., Electric, Burgess Vibrocrafters, Safe–Fun Constructive 38.00
Jump Rope, Redwood Handles, 1950s 15.00
Jumpin' Jeep, Marx, Tin, Windup .... 125.00 To 165.00
Kangaroo, Steiff, Tagged, 5 In. 80.00
Kiddie Flippers, Swim King 15.00
Kiddy Car, Wire Wheels, The Irish Mail, Hill Standard & Co., 40 In. 160.00
King Pin Jr. Bowling Alley 38.00
King Zor Dragon, Battery Operated 40.00
Kit, Airplane, Taylorcraft, Guillows 15.00
Kit, Animated Sailor, Rube Goldberg's 35.00
Kit, Brother Rat Fink, On Bike, Ed Roth, Revelle, Dated 1964, Unassembled 33.00
Kit, World War II Battleship, Paper, To Assemble, Package, 10 X 7 In. 12.50
Kitchen Set, Refrigerator, Stove, Sink, Wolverine 20.00
Komikal Kop, Cop Sitting In Car, Back Trunk, Marx 300.00
Lady, With Parasol, Friction, Germany, Early 1900s, 6 1/2 In. 1320.00
Ladybug, Ride–On, Steiff 125.00
Lamb, Riding, On Wheels, All Rubber 150.00
Lamb, Sleeping, 1949, Steiff 55.00
Lamby, White Wool, Bell & Ribbon, Steiff, 1950s, 9 In. 135.00
Lantern, Battery Operated, Ohio Art, Box 12.00
Lawn Mower, Tin Litho, Marked Rotor Mower, Chein, 10 X 10 In. 20.00
Leopard, Lying Down, Stitched Nose, Glass Eyes, Steiff, 8 In. 30.00

Leopard, Schoenhut, Full Size .... 275.00 To 315.00
Li'l Abner Dogpatch Band, Windup, Tin, Box, 1945 .... 500.00 To 550.00
Liddle Kiddles Klub House, With Furniture 25.00
Lila Auto Sisters, Lehmann, Tin, Windup, C.1908. .... 2100.00
Limousine, Bing, Tin, 6 1/4 In. 295.00
Limousine, Chauffeur & Passengers Litho, J. Chein, Windup, 6 In. 210.00
Limousine, Fischer, Tin, 5 1/4 In. 495.00
Lincoln Logs, J.L. Wright, Dated 1923, Single Set, Box 49.00
Lincoln Logs, Settler's Cabin, Box 28.00
Linda Kangaroo & Baby, Button, Tag, Steiff, 11 In. 120.00
Lion, Bubble Blowing, Battery Operated, Box 85.00
Lion, Tag & Button, Steiff, Large 285.00
Little King, Pull String, Wood, 1939, 3 1/2 In. 145.00
Llama, Moves Head & Chews, Llama Fur, Mechanical, 24 In. 285.00
Log Cabin, Joel Ellis, Wooden Box, 1860s, Large 225.00
Log Camp Building Set, Roy Toys, Set No.5, Box 40.00
Lone Ranger, Hi-Ho Silver, Tin, Windup, Marx, Box, 1938 .... 350.00
Loom, Davis, 1953, Box, Unused 25.00
Loom-Weave, 1936 .... 25.00
Ludwig Von Drake, On Go-Cart, Windup, Tin, Linemar 185.00
Machine Gun On Tripod, Smiths Automatic, Metal, 12 In. 80.00
Machine Gun, G-Man, Windup, Metal, Marx, 25 In. 20.00
Magic Trick, Kennard's Escape 3.00
Man From U.N.C.L.E. Playset, Plastic, MGM Inc., Rifle, 1966, 5 1/2 In. 85.00
Mandrake The Magician Magic Kit, Transogram, Box, 1949, 15 X 11 In. 18.00
Marbles, Clay, Bag 20.00
Mary & Her Lamb, Windup, Celluloid Figures, Metal Base 190.00
Mask, Nixon, 1960s 45.00
Meat Market, Hometown, Marx 65.00
Men Playing Pool, Windup, Tin 180.00
Merry Mousewife, Fisher-Price, 1962 .... 25.00
Merry-Go-Round, Lever Operated, Tin, C.1930 .... 175.00
Microscope Kit, Gilbert 25.00
Microscope, Porter Chemical Co., Manual & Instructions, 1954 .... 20.00
Midget Racers, Hubley, Box, 3 Piece 500.00
Military Academy Toy Set, Tin Building, Soldiers & Horses, Box, L. Marx 55.00
Milk Pail, Farm Scene, Marx, Tin 20.00
Minstrel Team, Hott & Tott, Unique Art, Box 490.00
Monkey, Bubble Blowing, Battery Operated, Box .... 45.00 To 100.00
Monkey, Drinking, Jocko, Battery Operated, Tin 50.00
Monkey, Felt Hands & Feet, Schuco, 3 In. .... 95.00 To 100.00
Monkey, On Wheels, Clown Hat, Jointed Head, Ribbon & Bell, Steiff 300.00
Monkey, Rag, Felt Face, Glass Eyes, Cloth & Felt Costume, 15 In. 12.50
Monkey, Schuco, 3 1/2 In. 125.00
Monkey, Windup, Checkered Body, Japanese 45.00
Monkey, Yes/No, Schuco, 13 In. 187.50
Monster Kit, Frankenstein, Rapco, 1974, Box, 12 X 9 1/2 X 3 In. 65.00
Moon Crawler, Battery Operated 28.00
Motor Car Constructor Set, Meccano, Box 1050.00
Motorboat, Tin, Lindstrom 60.00
Motorboat, Wood, Open Cockpit, Battery Operated, Japan, 12 X 4 In. 45.00
Motorcycle, Army, Windup, Marx, 8 In. 95.00
Motorcycle, Cop, Barclay Champion, 5 In. 150.00
Motorcycle, Curvo 1000, U.S. Zone, Key Wind 185.00
Motorcycle, Distler, Tin, Windup, Green & Brown, C.1910, 7 In. 1750.00
Motorcycle, Double Rider, Kilgore, 4 1/4 In. 150.00
Motorcycle, Harley Davidson, Cast Iron 75.00
Motorcycle, Indian, 4 Cylinder, Cast Iron, Hubley, 9 3/4 In. 675.00
Motorcycle, Mechanical, Police, Marx, 1930s, 8 In. 425.00
Motorcycle, Mystic, Windup, Tin, Marx, Box 75.00
Motorcycle, Police Siren, Tin, Windup, Box, 1930s, 8 1/2 In. 250.00
Motorcycle, Police, Cast Iron, 4 In. 75.00
Motorcycle, Technofix, 7 In. 125.00
Motorcycle, Tin, Windup, Blue & Brown, Gunthermann, C.1910 .... 1950.00

Motorcycle, With Policeman, Barclay 18.50
Motorcyle, With Rider, Champion, Cast Iron 95.00
Motorcyle With Policeman, Champion 150.00
Mouse Band, Merry Makers, Marx 500.00
Mouse, Tumbling, Windup, Japan 40.00
Mr. Robot, Key Wind, Battery Operated, Yonezawa 1200.00
Mr. Strongpup Weightlifter, Battery Operated 80.00
Mule, Balky, Tin, Litho, Windup, Lehmann, 7 1/2 In. .... 255.00 To 290.00
Mule, Balky, Windup, Marx .... 75.00 To 100.00
Naughty Boy, Tin, Lehmann 895.00
Naval War, Composition, Schoenhut, Dated 1916, Box 139.00
Noah's Ark, 16 Figures, Wooden, Handmade 175.00
Noah's Ark, 50 Animals, Dove Painted On Roof, Germany 2100.00
Noah's Ark, Lift Top, Carved & Painted Animals, 20th Century, 24 In. ... 275.00
Noah's Ark, Twin, Wooden, Paper Litho, Bliss-Type, Germany 175.00
Noah's Ark, Wooden, 14 Wooden Animals, Peter Mar, 1940 .... 195.00
Ocelot, Steiff 165.00
Oven, Suzy Home-Maker, Electric, Box 18.00
Owl, Wooden, Wings Flap, Black, Brown, Yellow, 5 1/2 X 11 In. 395.00
Pail, Sand, Tin, Children, Dog, Ohio Art, 3 In. 19.00
Paint Box, The Little Artist, Christmas 1899 .... 40.00
Paint Set, Blondie, Tin Container, King Features, 1946, 5 X 4 X 5 In. ... 10.00
Palm Puzzle, Kitty & Mouse, Paper, Glass, Eyeballs Roll, Germany, 1950s 8.00
Panda, Schuco, 3 1/2 In. 200.00
Panda, Standing, Steiff, 3 In. 145.00
Panda, Straw Filled, Jointed, 1920s, 28 In. 160.00
Pedal Car, 1931 Lincoln 9000.00
Pedal Car, 2 Passenger, Twin Sidelights, Horn, 80 In. 3850.00
Pedal Car, Cannonball Express, No.9 Trailing Cart, 1930s 200.00
Pedal Car, Casey Jones 425.00
Pedal Car, Covered Wagon 350.00
Pedal Car, Dr Pepper, 1950s 695.00
Pedal Car, Fire Chief's, Wooden, 1940s, 30 In. 95.00
Pedal Car, Fire Engine 105.00
Pedal Car, Hupmobile, Restored, 1920s 1995.00
Pedal Car, Landspeeder, Star Wars 95.00
Pedal Car, License Lifts To Say Stop, Lubricating Outfit In Trunk 3100.00
Pedal Car, Mobo Bronco 270.00
Pedal Car, Peerless Speedster 800.00
Pedal Car, Radio Cruiser 1900.00
Pedal Car, Red Convertible, Chrome Trim, Mercedes Hood Ornament, 43 In. ... 950.00
Pedal Car, Roadster, Black & Yellow Trim, Green, 34 In. 600.00
Pedal Car, Steelcraft, C.1920 .... 800.00
Pedal Car, Thunderbird, 1961 .... 100.00
Pedal Car, Tractor, Attachable 2-Wheel Cart, Sears 95.00
Pedal Car, Tractor, John Deere, Cast Iron 300.00
Pedometer, Sgt. Preston 25.00
Phone, Candlestick, Metal, Wooden, With Bell, 8 In. 30.00
Phonograph, Ragtime Rastus, With Boxing Blacks, C.1915 .... 275.00
Phonograph, RCA Nipper, Plastic, Box, 1950s 14.50
Phonograph, Siam Soo, 1909 .... 525.00
Piano, 8 Keys, Japan 40.00
Piano, Baby Grand, 18 Keys, Fold Down Top, Schoenhut 275.00
Piano, Baby Grand, Floor Model, 18 Keys, Rosewood, Schoenhut 295.00
Piano, Foot Pedals, Schoenhut 35.00
Piano, Jaymar 25.00
Piano, Painted Angels, Schoenhut, 6 1/4 In. 85.00
Piano, Upright, 14 Keys, Schoenhut, 20 X 20 X 10 In. 50.00
Piano, Upright, Crandall's Florence of Montrost, French, 1900, 20 In. ... 325.00
Piano, Walnut, Cupid Ends, Petite Muses Panel, Steel, Schoenhut 165.00
Pig & Rider, Lehmann 800.00
Pig, Pinky, Pull Toy, Fisher-Price 25.00
Piggy Cook, Flips Egg Over In Flying Pan, Battery Operated, Box 145.00
Pinocchio Acrobat, Tin, Windup, C.1939 .... 225.00

Pip–Squeak, Bird In Cage, Litho Paper Roof	75.00
Pip–Squeak, Goose, Flannel Coat, Glass Eyes, Papier–Mache Head, 6 In.	135.00
Pip–Squeak, Man, Papier–Mache Head, Wool & Felt Costume, Germany, 6 In.	30.00
Pip–Squeak, Nesting Duck On Wheels, Beak Opens, Papier–Mache, 6 In.	95.00
Pistol, Atomic, Space Patrol, Box	375.00
Pistol, Flashlight Atomic, Rex Mars, Marx, Box	155.00
Pistol, Me & My Buddy, Tin, Wyandotte	49.00
Pistol, Water, Figural, Airplane, Marx, Box, 1940	150.00
Play Barn, 3 Story, Loft, Horse & Cart, Stables For Kastor & Puck	100.00
Play Doh Fun Factory, 1960	12.00
Playhouse, With Puppets, Pillsbury	85.00
Pluto Drum Major, Linemar, Battery Operated	380.00
Pluto, Pulling Wagon, Tin, Linemar, 9 In.	135.00
Pluto, Tin, Windup, Linemar, 5 In.	240.00
Pluto, Watch Me Roll Over, Windup, Tin, Marx, 8 1/2 In.	85.00
Polar Bear, Fishing, Battery Operated, Box	140.00
Police Car, Tin Litho, Friction, Gun Hood, 1950s, W.Germany, 13 In.	65.00
Police, Motorcycle, Sidecar, Removable Rider, Hubley, 4 In.	75.00
Pony, Standing, Windup, Schuco	225.00
Poodle, Lying Down, Steiff, 1950s, 14 In.	85.00
Poodle, Schoenhut	275.00 To 450.00
Pool Player, Penny Toy	110.00
Pool Players, Ranger Steel, Windup	185.00
Pool Table, 2 Players, Tin	165.00
Powerful Katrinka	7000.00
Professor Pug Frog's Great Bicycle Feat	4500.00
Projector, Movie, Hand Crank	65.00
Projector, Movie, Keystone Junior, Box	125.00
Puddle Jumper, Mickey Mouse, Fisher–Price	80.00 To 145.00
Puppet, Barney Google, Soft Vinyl Head, Cloth Body, Gund, King Features	40.00
Puppet, Mr. Ed	12.00
Puppet, Pelham, Box	95.00
Puppet–Maker, Wilson, 1937	65.00
Push, Musical, Wire Wheels, Litho of Clowns, Animals, 42 1/2 In.	40.00
Quacking Duck, Windup, Box	35.00
Quilt, Doll's, Patchwork, Tumbling Baby Blocks, Velvet, 16 X 19 In.	65.00
Rabbit, Drinking Soda, Windup	15.00
Rabbit, On Wheels, Script Button, Tag, Steiff, 8 In.	95.00
Rabbit, Pulling Cart, Chein	50.00
Rabbit, Shaking Celluloid Maracas, Windup	35.00
Rabbit, Straw Filled, Cloth Clothes, 23 In.	45.00
Rabbit, Walking, With Drum, Battery Operated, Box	48.00
Rabbit, Windup, Chein	25.00
Radio, Rex, Battery Operated, Box, 1917	325.00
Ragtime Band, Box	20.00
Railroad Station, , Mansard Roofs, Tin, Bing, 1900, 23 In.	1210.00
Railroad Station, Loading, Hinged Doors, Tin, Marklin, 1902, 14 1/2 In.	4950.00
Railroad Station, Schoenhut, Large	250.00
Railroad Station, Talking, 1950s	125.00
Railroad Station, Talking, Marx, Box	150.00
Railroad Station, Waiting Platforms, Tin, Germany, C.1890, 25 1/2 In.	3850.00
Railroad Station, With Telegraph & Ticket Window, Schoenhut	495.00
Range Rider, Box	295.00
Rapid Transit, Friction, Blue Paint, White & Red Trim, 20 3/4 In.	250.00
Record Player, Bee–Gee, Battery Operated	7.00
Red Robin Farm, Converse, 1910	319.00
Refrigerator, Coldspot Jr., Coors Open, Wooden, 17 In.	20.00
Refrigerator, Electric, Wolverine	24.00
Refrigerator, Frigidaire	35.00
Refrigerator, Petite Princess, Box	75.00
Rider On Cycle, Uniform, Bride, Windup, Lehmann	1400.00
Riding Hoppy Pony, Marx, 1960s	100.00
Ring, Character, Flicker, 3 Stooges	20.00
Ring, Detector, Terry & Pirates, Gold	65.00

Ring, Flasher, Monkees 30.00
Ring, Romper Room, Aluminum, Adjustable, Jack–In–The–Box Clown, 1960s 8.00
Road Roller, With Figure, Cast Iron, Huber 500.00
Roaring Gorilla, Battery Operated 60.00
Robby The Robot, Battery Operated, Black, Red, Nomura, 14 In. 2495.00
Robot Commando, Ideal 90.00
Robot R–35, Square Battery Box, 1950s 600.00
Robot, Astronaut 210.00
Robot, Attacking Martian, Windup, Box 75.00
Robot, Battery Operated, Remote Control, Eyes Light Up, Masudaya 1200.00
Robot, Fighting, Rock–Em, Sock–Em, Marx, Box 85.00
Robot, Lost In Space, Box 75.00
Robot, Mr. Mercury 500.00
Robot, Planet Robot 350.00
Robot, Space Explorer, Battery Operated, Rotating Antenna, Japan, Box 295.00
Rocket Fighter, Marx 295.00
Rocket, Interplanetary, Box, 14 In. 40.00
Roller Coaster, Chein, 1950s 285.00
Roller Coaster, Ride On, Wooden Cart, 30 Ft. Track, Original Paint 675.00
Roller Skates, Doll's, Box 10.00
Rolling Pin, Wooden, Small 15.00
Roly Poly, Musical, Colored Suit, Blue Hat, Schoenhut, 8 In. 185.00
Roly Poly, Santa Claus, Polychrome, Papier–Mache, 6 In. 300.00
Rudolph The Reindeer, Standing, Plush, Montgomery Ward, 1939, 15 In. 44.00
Safe, Wooden Interior, Drawer, Cast Iron, Decals, Gold Trim, 8 3/4 In. 55.00
Sand Loader, Green, Barber 95.00
Sand Mill, Tin Litho, Chein, 11 1/2 In. 95.00
Santa Claus & Sleigh, Celluloid, Windup, Occupied Japan 22.50
Santa Claus, Flips Book Pages, Windup 68.00
Santa Claus, Holding Package, Walks When Pushed, 2–Sided, 12 X 6 In. 85.00
Santa Claus, On Skooter, Battery Operated, Box 100.00
Santa Claus, Standing, Ringing Bell, Battery Operated 50.00
Santa Claus, Walking, With Drum, Battery Operated 75.00
Santos Navigable Balloon, Instructions, Labeled Box 1100.00
Scale, Candy, Cast Iron 55.00
Scooter, Brake, Metal, Radio 25.00
Seal, Monkey On Back, Windup, Chein 45.00
Seesaw, Pull Toy 200.00
Service Station Center, Tin Litho 125.00
Service Station, Roadside, Marx, 1930s 385.00
Settee, Doll's, Wicker 38.00
Sewing Machine, American Girl 20.00
Sewing Machine, Blue Floral Country Design, Lindstrom, 1809 .... 47.00
Sewing Machine, Chain Driven, West Germany 55.00
Sewing Machine, Electric, Lindstrom 70.00
Sewing Machine, Junior Miss 14.00
Sewing Machine, Little Modiste, W. Germany .... 30.00 To 35.00
Sewing Machine, Maroon, Casige, Germany 65.00
Sewing Machine, Sew–Ette 20.00
Sewing Machine, Singer, Box .... 65.00 To 82.50
Sewing Machine, Singer, Model 20–10, Case 70.00
Sewing Machine, Stitch Mistress .... 20.00 To 40.00
Sewing Machine, Straco, Box 18.00
Sewing Set, Cardboard Dolls, Dresses, Scissors, Transogram, Box, 1936 .... 55.00
Shooting Gallery, Carnival, Ohio Art, Tin, 16 X 11 In. 50.00
Shooting Gallery, Daisy Cork Gun, Wyandotte 75.00
Shooting Gallery, Rubber Ball, Schoenhut 850.00
Shooting Gallery, Windup, Tin, Wyandotte, 14 1/2 X 10 1/2 In. 55.00
Sifter, Flour, Tin, 3 1/2 In. 4.00
Skybird Flyer, Zeppelin & Plane Fly Around Tower, Tin, Windup, 1930s 285.00
Sled, Called Go Devil, Iron Runners, 1800s 135.00
Sled, Clyde & Roy Thoms, Red Ground, Penna., Late 19th Century, 30 In. 325.00
Sled, Gold Stencils, Blue & Yellow, Figure of Boy, 41 In. 475.00
Sled, Gray, Large Letters Sibyl Across, Wooden, Iron, M.W. Styke, 5 Ft. 890.00

Sled, Green Paint, Gold Inscribed Racer, American, C.1870, 10 1/2 In. 600.00
Sled, Handholds, Landscape Scene of Lake, Hills, Painted, C.1880, 42 In. 225.00
Sled, Painted Scene Center, Red, White Striping, Feathering, Wood, Iron 595.00
Sled, Red Deck, Pinstriping Around Word Fairy, Metal Runners, 33 In. 550.00
Sled, Red Paint, Stenciled, Late 19th Century, 41 X 11 In. ....*Illus* 475.00
Sled, Santa Claus Embossed On Top, Reindeer Each Side, Wooden, 42 In. 185.00
Sled, Scroll & Floral Bouquet, Pinstriped, Green, Bentwood Runners 1800.00
Sled, Skater Picture, South Paris, Maine 291.50
Sled, Wooden, Iron Runners, 34 In. 75.00
Sleigh, Cast Iron Swan Head Finials, Wooden, Striping, 33 1/2 In. 325.00
Sleigh, Child's, Push, Red, Yellow Striping, Wooden Runners, 52 In. 250.00
Smokey Bear, Battery Operated, Box 90.00
Smokey The Bear, Dakin 18.00
Smokey The Bear, Soaky Toys, Colgate-Palmolive, For Bathtub 10.00
Smoking Grandpa, Rocking Chair, Battery Operated, Metal, San Co., 6 In. 25.00
Soldier Set, Tin, Marx, 31 Piece 95.00
Soldier, Artillery, Britain, 6 Horses, 3 Riders 160.00
Soldier, Band of Royal Berkshire Regiment 2970.00
Soldier, Crawling, Tin & Clockwork, Marx 75.00
Soldier, Crawling, Windup, Ohio Art, Box 115.00
Soldier, Dragoon Guards, Mounted At Gallop, Box, 5 Piece 1300.00
Soldier, Egyptian Cavalry, Mounted, Officer Holding Sword, Box, 5 Piece 200.00
Soldier, English Archers, Livery of Black Prince, Courtney, 2 Piece 400.00
Soldier, Figures of Napoleon & His Marshalls, 8 Piece 650.00
Soldier, Gestapo, German, Elastolin 45.00
Soldier, Life Guards, Mounted, At Gallop, Box, C.1935, 5 Piece 475.00
Soldier, Marine Band, Britain, 10 Piece 130.00
Soldier, Mounted, Britain, 39 Piece 450.00
Soldier, Queen's Own Cameron Highlanders, Marching, C.1945, Box, 8 Piece 250.00
Soldier, Queen's Own Hussars, Mounted, Review Order, Box, 5 Piece 130.00
Soldier, Royal Sussex Regiment, Marching, Review Order, 7 Piece 300.00
Soldier, Royal Welch Fusiliers, Marching, Goat Mascot, C.1935, 8 Piece 300.00
Space Tank, Windup, Japan, Box 85.00
Sparkler, Starlight, Ronson 18.00
Speedboat, Sea Dart, Friction 45.00
Speedboat, Windup, Lindstrom, Small 130.00
Spiderman, On Spidercycle 20.00
Star Wars Play Set, Box 22.00
Steam Engine, Flywheel On Side, Alcohol Or Canned Heat, Weeden, No.20 .... 65.00
Steam Engine, Fowler, Maroon & Yellow Wheels, Corgi, Box 60.00
Steam Roller, Alcohol Fired, Reversible Steam Engine, Germany 250.00
Steam Roller, Steel, Keystone, 1920s, Large 225.00
Steam Shovel, Earth Moving, Metal, Sturditoy Contracting Co., 20 In. 20.00
Steam Shovel, Hubley, 4 3/4 In. 40.00
Steam Shovel, Lumar Contractor 120.00
Steam Shovel, Mounted On 10-Wheel Mack Truck, Cast Iron, 10 In. 345.00
Steam Shovel, Structo 25.00
Steam Shovel, Tonka Toys 20.00
Steam Shovel, Wyandotte 68.00
Sterilizer, 4 Bottle, Brush, Funnel, Measuring Cup, Blue Graniteware 28.50
Stove, Black, Tin Plate, Nickel Trim, 6 Burners, Oven, 12 X 15 In. 115.00
Stove, Cast Iron, Kenton 35.00
Stove, Coal, Tin Plate, Litho, Embossed Doors, Pots & Pans, 1900s, 5 In. 145.00
Stove, Crescent, Cast Iron, 11 In. 90.00
Stove, Dollhouse, Crescent, Cast Iron, 8 1/2 In. 45.00
Stove, Eagle, Cast Iron, Accessories 65.00
Stove, Eagle, White Paint 45.00
Stove, Empire, Electric, Box, 15 In. 66.00
Stove, Empire, Electric, White Metal & Tin 15.00
Stove, Graniteware, Green 25.00
Stove, Jewel Range Jr., Cast Iron, Detroit, Flute, Damper, Ash Pan 495.00
Stove, Little Chef, Metal, 1950s, Box 25.00
Stove, Little Chief, Electric 49.00
Stove, Little Miss Housekeeper 22.50

Stove, Petite Princess, Box 70.00
Stove, Queen, Black Paint, Cast Iron, 6 1/2 In. 40.00
Stove, Raggedy Ann 15.00
Stove, Suzy Homemaker, Electric, Box 15.00
Stove, Tin, Sparking, Keywind, Ohio Art, Box 22.00
Stove, Western Electric Jr. Range, Black Tin, Nickel Trim & Top, 15 In. 95.00
Stove, Wolverine, Electric, 12 In. 24.00
Streetcar, Sandy Andy, Wolverine, Box, 1920s, 13 In. 400.00
Streetcar, Union Depot, City Hall Park, Red, Silver Trim, Tin, 16 In. 100.00
Stroller, Doll's, Wicker, Brown, 24 X 36 X 11 In. 300.00
Stroller, Doll's, Wood Wheels, Metal 225.00
Submarine, Pressed Metal, Windup, Wolverine 55.00
Submarine, Tin, Windup, Wolverine, 13 In. .... 44.00 To 65.00
Sulky–Trike, Trotting Horse & Seat, Rempel Mfg., 49 X 23 X 25 In. 475.00
Sweeper, Susy Goose, Kiddie Brush & Toy Co. 22.00
Swing, Doll's, Betsy Wetsy, Windup 145.00
Swing, Doll's, Collapsible, Oak Splint Design, 1890s 165.00
Swing, Doll's, Double Seating, Red & Green, 15 1/2 In. 55.00
Sylvester The Penguin, Soaky Toys, Colgate–Palmolive, For Bathtub 2.00
Table, Alphabet, Enamel Top 125.00
Table, Enamel Top, Blue & White 95.00
Tambourine, Ohio Art, 1970s 12.00
Tank, Anti–Aircraft, Battery Operated, Tin Litho, Pop–Up Driver, China 165.00
Tank, Camouflaged, Pop–Up Soldier, Marx, C.1930s 120.00
Tank, Gama, Germany, 6 1/4 In. 325.00
Tank, Roll Over, Popeye, Linemar 395.00
Tank, Sonny–Andy, Wolverine 180.00
Tank, U.S. Army, Battery Operated, Pop–Up Driver, Metal, 1940–50 .... 145.00
Tank, Windup, Gama, Germany, 5 1/4 In. 225.00
Tank, World War I, Pop–Up Gunner, Marx 200.00
Target, Gang Buster, 4 Bad Guys, Tin Litho, Marx, 1940, 16 X 24 In. 50.00
Target, Shooting Gallery, Flying Bird, Cast Iron 55.00
Taxi, Austin, Dinky 35.00
Taxi, Clockwork, Pressed Steel, Converse, Stenciled Design, 10 1/2 In. 770.00
Taxi, Folding Luggage Rack, Yellow, Cast Iron, Hubley, 7 3/4 In. 450.00
Taxi, Luggage Rack, Yellow, Hubley, 8 In. 450.00
Taxi, Trickey, Windup, Red & Yellow, Marx 65.00
Taxi, Yellow Cab, Dent, 7 3/4 In. 330.00
Taxi, Yellow, Cast Iron, Hubley, 8 In. 675.00
Taxi, Yellow, Chein, 7 1/4 In. 200.00
Tea Set, Barbie Anniversary 55.00
Tea Set, Blue Chrysanthemum, Pink Luster Edge, Little Hostess, 23 Piece 95.00
Tea Set, Doll's, Floral, China, English, 6 Cups & Saucers 44.00
Tea Set, Fern Bisel Peat, Tin Litho, Ohio Art, Box, 15 Piece 145.00
Tea Set, Green & Gold Wheat Sheafs, White Ground, Japan, Box, 23 Piece 65.00
Tea Set, Little Hostess, Box, 1920s, 23 Piece 95.00
    TOY, TEDDY BEAR, see Teddy Bear
Telephone, Tin, Black, Cradle Type 12.00
Telephone, Wall, Gong Bell Toy Co., Wooden Handle, Cowboy Design 42.00
The Thing, Addams Family, Battery Operated 20.00
Theater, Jackie Gleason Story Stage, T.V.Stage, Curtains, Scripts, 1955 .... 150.00
Theater, Movieland, Drive–In, Remco, 1959 .... 40.00
Theater, Paperdoll, Wizard of Oz, 18 Characters, 6 Sheets, 8 X 11 In. 11.00
Thunder Gun, Smokey Joe, Shoots Table Tennis Balls, Newell 30.00
Tidy Tim, With Tools, Windup, Tin, Marx, 7 1/2 In. 375.00
Tiger Race, Tonka, Sunlight Mfg. 125.00
Tin Soldiers Set, Gun, Shoots Rubber Tipped Dart, Marx, C.1945 .... 110.00
Tinkertoys, Wooden, In Tubes, 1950 .... 20.00
Tommy Gun, Untouchables, Box 55.00
Tonto, With Saddle, No Accessories, Hartland 65.00
Tool Box, Buddy L, Wooden, Red, Decal, Black Top, 23 In. 145.00
Tool Chest, Busy Boy 19.00
Tool Chest, Dovetailed Wood, No.120 .... 45.00

Tool Chest, Inside Litho, Boys' Building 60.00
Tool Chest, Small Fry, Deluxe 16.00
Toonerville Trolley, Slush, Cast Iron 350.00
Top, Apple, Chien 32.00
Top, Humming, Children In Planes, Ohio Art, 12 In. 22.50
Top, Spinning, Road Race Inside, Box, Large 48.00
Tower, Hoisting, Original Chutes 925.00
Tower, Switch Signal, Lionel, No.437 .... 260.00
Toy Town Grocery Store, Diorama of Store Props, Parker Bros. 1980.00
Tractor Trailer, Lowboy, With Steam Shovel, Tonka, C.1955 .... 125.00
Tractor Trailer, Structo 300.00
Tractor, Allis Chalmers, Ertl WD45, Box 20.00
Tractor, Arcade, Cast Iron .... 60.00 To 70.00
Tractor, Carrying Bin, Arcade, Cast Iron 125.00
Tractor, Caterpillar, U.S. Army, 4 Actions 65.00
Tractor, Caterpiller, Dozer, Cast Iron, Arcade, 8 1/2 In. 200.00
Tractor, Dump, Friction, Tin Litho, Man On Seat, Box 80.00
Tractor, Farm, Arcade, Cast Iron 125.00
Tractor, Farmall No.560 .... 130.00
Tractor, Field Marshall, Dinky Toys, England 100.00
Tractor, Fordson, Driver, Cast Iron .... 65.00 To 95.00
Tractor, International No.1586, Cab, Box 12.50
Tractor, John Deere, Model M, Box 12.00
Tractor, Key Wind, Marx, 7 In. 55.00
Tractor, Massey Harris Ferguson, Dinky Toys, England 30.00
Tractor, Minneapolis–Moline, Rubber Tires, Metal, 1940s, 5 In. 35.00
Tractor, Robot Driven, Marvelous Mike, Box 275.00
Tractor, Spring Seat, Rubber Tires, Hubley 20.00
Tractor, Steam Type, With Hay Wagon, Structo, 1920s 635.00
Tractor, Steam, Mamod, 10 In. 40.00
Tractor, With Hay Wagon, Windup, Cast Iron, Structo 675.00
Train Set, American Flyer, Wide Gauge, Original Box, C.1925 .... 650.00
Train Set, Clockwork, Locomotive, Tender, Passenger Car, Marklin, 1905 .... 2400.00
Train Set, Ranger Fast Freight, Mechanical 85.00
Train Set, Tin, Windup, Commodore 95.00
Train, Baggage Car, Lionel, No.332, Olive Green 210.00
Train, Boxcar, Rubber Stamped, Lionel, No.114 .... 90.00
Train, Caboose, Lionel, No.517 .... 180.00
Train, Caboose, P.R.R., Red Paint, Cast Iron, 4 7/8 In. 35.00
Train, Casey Jr., Windup, Green Plastic Engine, Marx, 1950s 55.00
Train, Climber Engine & Tender, Dayton Hill 175.00
Train, Diesel, Pull Train, Metal, Loud Bell, Wolverine, 17 In. 32.00
Train, Engine & Car, KCS Model R.R., Marx, 1950s 35.00
Train, Engine & Tender, Windup, Tin, 13 In. 200.00
Train, Engine, Commodore Vanderbilt, Marx 150.00
Train, Engine, Lionel, No.2055 .... 185.00
Train, Engine, Lionel, No.8, Standard Gauge 160.00
Train, Engine, Riding, Keystone 100.00
Train, Engine, Tender & Dining Car, Windup, Great Britain, 12 In. 45.00
Train, Gondola, Lionel, No.12, Gray 110.00
Train, Honeymoon Express, Linemar, Box 120.00
Train, Honeymoon Express, Streamline, Marx, Box 100.00
Train, Lionel Train Set, No.264, Instructions, 5 Piece, Box 700.00
Train, Locomotive, 3 Cars, Transformer, Tracks, Lionel, 1940 .... 225.00
Train, Mechanical, New Silver Mountain, 1969, 15 In. 25.00
Train, Painted Tin, Bergmann, 4 Piece 2000.00
Train, Santa Fe, 3 Tin Litho Passenger Cars, Marx 130.00
Train, Tin Litho, Wooden Wheels, Wolverine, 15 In. 35.00
Train, Union Pacific, 3 Cars, Red, White & Blue, Marx 60.00
Trencher, Buddy L, Box 3700.00
Tricky Dick, String Balance, Cardboard & Wood, Noreck, Original Card 68.00
Tricycle, 1920 .... 175.00
Tricycle, 1930s, 2 Piece 195.00
Tricycle, Iron Fittings, Gold Striping, Wooden, 44 1/2 In. 400.00

Tricycle, Metal, Kilgore, 3 In.	50.00
Trolley Car, Friction, 23 In.	225.00
Trolley, Broadway, Tin Litho, J. Chein, 1930s, 8 In.	175.00
Truck, Aerial Sand Loader, Tonka	95.00
Truck, Albion Concrete Mixer, Dinky Toys, England	70.00
Truck, Allied Van Lines, Tonka	95.00
Truck, Army, Metal Masters, 1940	20.00
Truck, Army, Steelcraft	245.00
Truck, Auto Transport, Marx, 23 In.	18.50
Truck, Bedford Articulated Lorry, Dinky Toys, England	130.00
Truck, Beer, Wooden Kegs, Barclay	75.00
Truck, Bell Telephone, Hubley, Cast Iron, 5 1/4 In.	400.00
Truck, Borden's Milk Cream Tanker, Metal, Yellow, 1970, 6 In.	16.00
Truck, Car Hauler, Rubber Tires, 2 Metal Cars, Barclay	27.00
Truck, Cement Mixer, Hubley Kiddie	20.00
Truck, Chain Drive, Tootsietoy	45.00
Truck, Coal, Tin Litho, 1920s	230.00
Truck, Coca–Cola, Yellow, Bottle, Smith Miller	525.00
Truck, Delivery, Model T, Buddy L, Box	925.00
Truck, Delivery, No.210, Fliver, Black, Silver, Red, Buddy L, 12 In.	550.00
Truck, Delivery, Steel, Wyandotte, Box, 9 1/2 In.	135.00
Truck, Dippy Dumper, Windup, Tin, Celluloid Popeye	450.00
Truck, Dump, Battery Operated Headlights, Red, Black, Wyandotte, 10 In.	55.00
Truck, Dump, Blue, Marx, 1950s	40.00
Truck, Dump, Buddy L, Steel Plate, Rear Rubber Tires, 1933, 23 In.	275.00
Truck, Dump, Dinky, Box, 1948	50.00
Truck, Dump, Driver, Penny Toy, Germany	135.00
Truck, Dump, Friction, Box	95.00
Truck, Dump, Irco, 5 1/2 In.	12.00
Truck, Dump, Mack, Red, Arcade, 12 In.	450.00
Truck, Dump, Original Paint, Wyandotte, 12 In.	55.00
Truck, Dump, Red Body, Arcade	650.00
Truck, Farm, Ertl, 15 In.	55.00
Truck, Farm, Lazy Day Farms, Metal, Marx, 1950s	20.00
Truck, Farm, Tonka, Set	195.00
Truck, Fast Freight, Buddy L, 1940s, 20 In.	105.00
Truck, Ford, Buddy L, C.1920, 12 In.	395.00
Truck, Ford, Stake Bed, Cast Iron, 4 In.	135.00
Truck, Heinz, Metal Craft	525.00
Truck, Hercules, Original Orange & Black Paint, Chein	300.00
Truck, J & B Express, Cast Iron, Kenton, 15 1/2 In.	2500.00
Truck, Johnston Road Sweeper, Dinky Toy, England	70.00
Truck, Lift, Dinky Toy	25.00
Truck, Livestock Lines, Marcrest, 17 In.	38.00
Truck, Livestock, Marx	50.00
Truck, Load of Wooden Building Blocks, Pull Toy, Wooden, 1930s, 15 In.	45.00
Truck, Mack, Tootsietoy, 3 In.	25.00
Truck, Mail, Structo, 16 In.	385.00
Truck, Mobil Gas Tank, Flying Red Horse, Tin, Toymaster	25.00
Truck, Mobil Gas, Friction, Japanese	45.00
Truck, Moving Van, Wooden, Buddy L, 27 In.	325.00
Truck, NBC TV, Box, 10 In.	425.00
Truck, Overland Freight, Structo, Box	125.00
Truck, Parcel Post, Strauss, 1920s	850.00
Truck, Railway Express, Hubley, 4 In.	95.00
Truck, Railway Express, Wrigley Advertising, Tootsietoy	125.00
Truck, Rapid–Delivery, Tin, Chein	225.00
Truck, REA Express, Wood, Buddy L, 16 In.	150.00
Truck, Rescue Vehicle, Tonka, Box, 19 In.	65.00
Truck, Riding, Buddy L, 1934	375.00
Truck, Semi, Mack, Wyandotte	40.00
Truck, Snap–On Tools, Red, White, Black, Ralstoy Co., 4 In.	25.00
Truck, Sprite Boy, Yellow, Decals, Marx, 20 In.	250.00
Truck, Stake, Delivery, Marx, Box	435.00

Truck, Stake, Friction, Linemar, Box	95.00
Truck, Stake, Tootsietoy	45.00
Truck, Stanton, With Winch	34.00
Truck, Structo Farms, Cast Iron	65.00
Truck, Swinging Tailgate, Steering Action, Keystone, 1920s	425.00
Truck, Tank, Buddy L	500.00
Truck, Telephone Service Van, Dinky Toy, England	80.00
Truck, Telephone, Auburn, Rubber, Yellow, 7 In.	15.00
Truck, Texaco Oil Tanker, Metal, 1970, 6 In.	19.00
Truck, Texaco Tanker, Buddy L, Box, 25 In.	125.00
Truck, Tonka, 16 In.	60.00
Truck, Tow, Buddy L	65.00
Truck, Tow, Cast Iron, Keystone	550.00
Truck, Tow, Nickel Grill, Cast Iron, Hubley, 9 In.	250.00
Truck, Tow, Plymouth, Cast Iron, 4 1/2 In.	150.00
Truck, Windup, 5 Advertising Trailers, Litho Tin, 1934	575.00
Truck, Wrecker, Arcade, Cast Iron	135.00
Truck, Wrecker, Cast Iron, Hubley, 3 3/4 In.	55.00
Truck, Wrecker, Wooden, Buddy L, 1940s	120.00
Truck, Wrecker, Wyandotte	65.00
Truck, Wrigley's Chewing Gum, Metal, Green, Black, 1970, 4 In.	10.00
Truck, Yellow Cab Baggage, Cast Iron	9900.00
Trunk, Doll's, Tole Painting	65.00
Trunk, Steamer, Doll's, Blue, Metal, Cass Toys, Large	60.00
Tugboat & Barge, Tom Thumb Toys, 15 In.	135.00
Turkey, Windup, Painted Tin, Germany, 4 3/4 In.	440.00
Tut–Tut, Tin, Windup, Lehmann, C.1910	1550.00
Typewriter, Berwin	25.00 To 55.00
Typewriter, Dial, Marx	35.00 To 40.00
Typewriter, Girl Friday, Battery Operated, Japan, 1950s	65.00
Typewriter, Junior Dial, Marx	20.00
Typewriter, Marx	7.00 To 15.00
Typewriter, Simplex, Box, 10 In.	24.00
Typewriter, Tin, Portable, Unique Art	22.50
Typewriter, Tom Thumb	22.00
Typewriter, Tom Thumb Jr., Box	20.00
Typewriter, Wood Base, Tinplate, Lithography Wood Top	95.00
Uncle Sam On Bicycle, String Balance, Tin Lithograph, Gibbs	475.00
Unicyclist, Hobo, Rides On String	265.00
Van, Child's Riding, Canteen Vending Service, Steel, 22 X 15 In.	50.00
Van, Special Delivery, Tootsietoy	65.00
Vehicle, Space Patrol, Tin Litho, Box	400.00
Village Set, Wooden, Keystone, Box	68.00
Village, McLaughlin Bros., Box, 1897	75.00
Waffle Iron, Stover Toy Co., Box, 1930s	165.00
Waffle Iron, Wooden Handles, Wagner, Dated 1910	75.00 To 100.00
Wagon, Blaxer, Blue	150.00
Wagon, Borden's Delivery, Pull, Horse Moves Up & Down, 1910, 14 X 30 In.	375.00
Wagon, Buckled Down Canvas Top & Driver, Penny Toy, Germany	135.00
Wagon, Cannon Ball, Original Paint	110.00
Wagon, Coaster, Wood, Original Paint, Iron Wheels, Ball Bearings	286.00
Wagon, Express, Metal Wheels, Original Paint, Small	62.50
Wagon, Green Paint, Red Iron Spoke Wheels, 1900s	800.00
Wagon, Ladder & Horse, Cast Iron, Nickel Finish, 7 1/2 In.	85.00
Wagon, Milk, Horse Drawn, Pennwood Toys, Box, 15 In.	125.00
Wagon, Milk, Toyland, Marx	225.00
Wagon, Oriole Flyer, Small	150.00
Wagon, Overland Circus, 2 Horses & Riders, Driver, Polar Bear, C.1920	770.00
Wagon, Red Frame, Roll–Up Canvas Top	1050.00
Wagon, Red Racer, Small	150.00
Wagon, Roller Coaster, Red Paint, Green Stenciled, Wooden Wheels, 34 In.	725.00
Wagon, Sand & Gravel, 2 Horses, Cast Iron	350.00
Wagon, Sand & Gravel, Drawn By White & Black Horses, Cast Iron	395.00
Wagon, Spokes, Wooden	475.00

Wagon, Tin Sides, Wooden Bed, Iron Wheels	185.00
Wagon, Wooden, Red & Green Paint, Low Front Wheels, High Back Wheels	315.00
Walker, Boy, Celluloid Head, Lead Feet, Dressed, Windup, Germany	145.00
Walkie Talkie, Metal, Tudor Metal Products	20.00
Walking Turk, Clockwork, Enoch Rich Morrison, American, Box, C.1862	1350.00
Washboard, Midget Washer, Glass	12.00
Washboard, Wood & Glass	28.00
Washing Machine, L. Marx, 5 In.	32.50
Washing Machine, Little Miss Whirlaway	37.50
Washing Machine, Ringer, Glass Tub	40.00
Washing Machine, Sunny Suzy, 1930s	60.00 To 80.00
Washing Machine, Tin, Green & Yellow, Wringer	40.00
Washtub & Washboard, 4 & 6 In., 2 Piece	20.00
Washtub, Wringer, Wooden, American Wringer Co., Round	185.00
Water Tower, Horse Drawn, Cast Iron	3500.00
Weasel Landing Craft, No.29C, Balsa, Roberts, Box	50.00
Wheelbarrow, Child's, Green Paint, Yellow Striping, Red Flower, 28 In.	175.00
Wheelbarrow, John Deere, All Wood	265.00
Wheelbarrow, Young's Toys, Charleston, W.Va.	65.00
Whip, Windup, Playland, Box, Large	395.00
Whistle, Bird, White Clay, Clear, Running Brown, 3 1/2 In.	50.00
Whistle, Dragnet	5.00
Whistle, Mystic Sun God	25.00
Xylophone Player, Windup, Occupied Japan, Box	55.00
Zebra, Straw Stuffed, Steiff, 12 1/2 In.	120.00
Zeppelin, Metalcraft, 27 1/2 In.	250.00
Zeppelin, Tin, Germany	1128.00 To 1500.00

Tramp art is a form of folk art made since the Civil War. It is usually made from chip–carved cigar boxes. Examples range from small boxes and picture frames to full–sized pieces of furniture.

TRAMP ART, Boat, Framed Behind Glass	195.00
Box, Comb, Double, Porcelain Buttons	150.00
Box, Comb, Folding, Wooden	45.00
Box, Sawtooth Cut, Velvet Lining, 5 1/2 X 11 1/4 X 8 In.	125.00
Chest, Jewelry, Graduated Chip Carved, Mirror, Hinged Cover	32.00
Church, 6 Drawers, Made From Cigar Boxes	825.00
Frame, Bowties, Leaves, Angle Cut, 14 X12 In.	125.00
Frame, Gilt, 12 1/2 X 10 1/2 In.	48.00 To 65.00
Frame, Shell Art Base, Dated 1907, 14 X 12 1/2 In.	195.00
Frame, With Sail	345.00
Lamp, Made of Marbles & Popsicle Sticks	50.00
Mirror, 12 X 19 In.	37.00
Processional Piece, Feed My Lambs, Square, Pole	850.00
Spice Box	395.00

Animal traps may be handmade. One of the most unusual is the mousetrap made so that when the mouse entered the trap, it was hit on the head with a mallet. Other traps were commercially manufactured and often are marked with the name of the manufacturer. Many traps were designed to be as humane as possible, and they would trap the live animal so it could be released in the woods.

TRAP, Bear & Fox	25.00
Bear, Hand Forged	300.00
Bear, Hudson Bay Kodiak	600.00
Bear, Large	160.00
Bear, Signed S. Newhouse, Oneida Community, N.Y., Iron, 32 In.	305.00
Bee, Wooden, Slide Cover, Glass Bottom, 4 1/2 X 3 1/2 X 4 In.	6.00
Fish, Basketry, Philippines, 16 In.	15.00
Fly, Blown Glass, C.1840, 6 1/2 X 5 In.	85.00
Fly, Sur Ketchum, 1930s	12.00
Grizzly Bear, Stamped 1886, Large	350.00
Mouse, Catch Alive, Box, Blue Tin Grid & Door	130.00

Mouse, Peerless	65.00
Mouse, Quadruple, 4 Sliding Gates, Handmade	95.00
Mouse, Sure Catch	10.00
Mouse, Wood & Wire, Catches 4	35.00
Rat, Old Style, Large	38.00
Triumph, Model 34x, Tooth	75.00
Wolf, Oneida Newhouse, No.4 1/2, Jaw Spread, 24 In.	95.00

TREEN, see Wooden

Trivets are now used to hold hot dishes. Most trivets of the late nineteenth and early twentieth centuries were made to hold hot irons. Iron or brass reproductions are being made of many of the old styles.

TRIVET, 2–Ply Twisted Ware, 19th Century, 6 In.	100.00
3 Curled Legs, Revolving, Hand Forged Iron, 8 1/2 In.	200.00
Bars Ray Out From Center, Iron, Canada	5.50
Campbell Soup, Bamboo, Cast Iron	10.00
Child's, Arrow Shape Prongs, Iron, 6 X 1 In.	40.00
Cross With Crown, Colebrookdale Iron Co., Pottstown, Penna.	20.00
Cutout Hearts, Cast Brass, 8 1/2 In.	55.00
Double Heart, Turned Feet, Cast Iron, 4 X 6 X 1 In.	95.00
E Center, Enterprise Mfg.Co., U.S.A., Cast Iron	24.00
Enterprize, Cast Iron	15.00
F Center, Fanner Mfg. Co., Cleveland, Ohio, Cast Iron	28.00
Favorite Stoves & Ranges, Cast Iron	20.00
Fireplace, Iron, Sliding	80.00
Folding Roasting Fork Rest, Pierced & Tooled Iron, 21 1/2 In.	75.00
Fox & Tree, Cast Brass, 8 1/8 In.	165.00
George Washington, Handle, Footed, Cast Iron	25.00
God Bless Our Home, Around Horseshoe, Dated 1892	56.00
Greyhound, Cast Brass, 9 1/4 In.	85.00
Hang–Up Rat Tail, 5 Rod, Revolving, Iron, 12 In.	200.00
Heart Shape, Ram's Horns, Wrought Iron, Scrolled Feet, 6 In.	325.00
Heart Shape, Wrought Iron, Turned Handle, Brass Ferrule, 12 3/4 In.	200.00
Howell, Cast Iron	15.00
I Want U, Strause Gas Iron Co., Penna.	19.00 To 22.00
Iridescent Inlaid Border, Burdick Studio, 1908, 5 5/8 In.	325.00
J.R. Clark Co., Minneapolis, Open Lettering	30.00
Kettle Stand, Wrought Iron Legs, Pierced Brass Top, Handle, 12 In.	135.00
Lattice Design, Cast Brass, 7 1/2 In.	30.00
Lyre Shape Center, Lacy Openwork Around Rim, Iron	8.00
Lyre Shape, Brass Top, Iron Legs, Wooden Handle, 12 1/2 In.	105.00
Monarch Coffee	8.00
Oak Leaf, End of Leaf Folds Over, 3–Legged, Early 1800s, 8 1/2 In.	85.00
Revolving Pinwheel, Cast Iron, 9 1/2 In., 2 Piece	135.00
Sadiron, Rosenbaum Mfg.Co., RCO In Center, 10 1/2 In.	75.00
Sadiron, Star & Fan, Cleveland Foundry	14.00
Scalloped Gallery, Wooden Handle, Cast Bronze, 11 In.	25.00
Scrolled, Wrought Iron, 8 1/2 In.	135.00
Spider Web Shape, Wire, Hexagonal, 6 Footed, 7 1/2 In.	35.00
Twisted Triangle, Long Handle, Wrought Iron, 10 In.	45.00
Waffle, Square, O.M. Co., Cast Iron, Square, 4 3/4 In.	5.00
Warming, Buck Stove, Fits On Stove	25.00

Trunks of many types were made. The nineteenth–century sea chest was often handmade of unpainted wood. Brass–fitted camphorwood chests were brought back from the Orient. Leather–covered trunks were popular from the late eighteenth to mid nineteenth centuries. By 1895, trunks were covered with canvas or decorated sheet metal. Embossed metal coverings were used from 1870 to 1910. By 1925, trunks were covered with vulcanized fiber or undecorated metal.

TRUNK, Brown & Yellow Striped, Wood & Metal Banding, Louis Vuitton, C.1900	350.00
Brown Graining, Bowed Sides, Iron Lock & Hasp, 27 1/2 In.	175.00

Child's, Dome Top, Pine, Restored, 18 X 11 In. 225.00
Dome Top, Allover Sponge Design, Yellow Ocher Base, Wood, 18 In. 425.00
Dome Top, Dovetailed, Wooden, Old Green Paint, 17 X 8 1/2 X 7 In. 85.00
Dome Top, Painted Vines & Leaves, Wire Bail Handles, 12 X 23 In. 4950.00
Flat Top, Oak Staves, Brass Corners, Lock & Key, 12 X 20 In. 185.00
Fur Trimmed, Metal–Bound 70.00
Leather Trim, Brass Tacks, Brass Bail Handle, Iron Lock, 8 In. 110.00
Leather, Glove & Hat Boxes, Dated 1876 .... 190.00
Red Florals, Black Ground, Painted Leather, Chinese, C.1800, 36 In. 375.00
Stagecoach, Owner's Name & Address, Brass Lock, Late 1800s 275.00
Steamer, Louis Vuitton 275.00
Turtle Top, Decorative Tin Inserts, Oak Slats, Black Trim 65.00

The Tuthill Cut Glass Company of Middletown, New York, worked from 1902 to 1923. Of special interest are the finely cut pieces of stemware and tableware.

TUTHILL, Banana Boat, Intaglio Pear, Brilliant Period, Signed 300.00
Basket, 1000 Eye Pattern, Flashed Hobstar Base, Twist Handle 875.00
Bowl, Blazed Cross Hobstars, Wheat Border, Signed 750.00
Bowl, Intaglio Rim & Base, Rolled Rim, 12 In. 350.00
Bowl, Intaglio Rose Design, Signed, 9 1/2 In. 250.00
Bowl, Phlox, 3 1/2 X 8 In. .... 250.00 To 300.00
Bowl, Rex Variation, 8 1/2 In. 750.00
Bowl, Whipped Cream, Lotus Pattern 275.00
Box, Wheel Pattern, Hinged Cover, Signed, 7 1/2 X 4 In. 2300.00
Candlestick, Fluted Teardrop Stem, Cut Knob, 8 1/2 In. 195.00
Candlestick, Vintage Pattern, Signed, 10 In. 375.00
Compote, Cosmos 200.00
Compote, Geometric & Intaglio, 7 1/2 In. 310.00
Compote, Jelly, Cosmos Pattern, Signed 225.00
Dish, Cut Glass, Signed, 4 X 9 In. 110.00
Dish, Fan Shaped Shell, Signed, 10 1/2 In. 5100.00
Dish, Vintage, Oval, Signed, 7 1/4 X 9 3/4 In. 595.00
Nappy, 3 Sections, Handles, Hobstar & Fans 295.00
Perfume Bottle, Cut Apricot To Clear, Pair 3100.00
Plate, Rosemere, Intaglio, Brilliant, Signed, 8 In. 400.00
Plate, Rosemere, Signed, 10 In. 650.00
Sugar & Creamer, Phlox, Signed 220.00
Sugar & Creamer, Primrose In A Swirl Comb, Signed 335.00
Tray, 4 Fruits, Scalloped Border, Signed, Round, 12 In. 1600.00
Tray, Rex, Deep, Signed, 12 1/2 In. 7300.00
Tray, Vintage, Handles, Signed, 13 1/2 X 8 1/2 In. 2100.00
Vase, Blackberry, Signed, 10 In. 335.00
Vase, Sweet Pea, Woodlily, Signed, 4 X 5 1/2 In. 325.00
Vase, Wild Rose, Signed, 10 3/4 In. 850.00
Water Set, Geometric, Signed, 7 Piece 885.00
Water Set, Primrose, Brilliant & Intaglio, Signed, 7 Piece 1300.00

The first successful typewriter was made by Sholes and Glidden in 1874. Collectors divide typewriters into two main classifications: the index machine, which has a pointer and a dial for letter selection, and the keyboard machine, most commonly seen today.

TYPEWRITER, Blickensderfer, No.5, Dated 1892 .... 60.00
Blickensderfer, No.7, Oak Case 60.00
Corona, Folding 30.00
Corona, July 10, 1917, Small 42.00
Demountable, Patent 1924 .... 40.00
Royal, Gold Trim 150.00
Royal, Unique Keyboard, Original Case, 1917 .... 45.00
Simplex, Model D, Index Type, Box 45.00
Tin, Carter's Typewriter Oil, 3 Oz. 6.00
Tin, M & M Miracle Typewriter Ribbon, Remington Portable 4.50
Tin, Paragon Typewriter Ribbon 5.00
Underwood, Standard, Dated 1912 .... 25.00

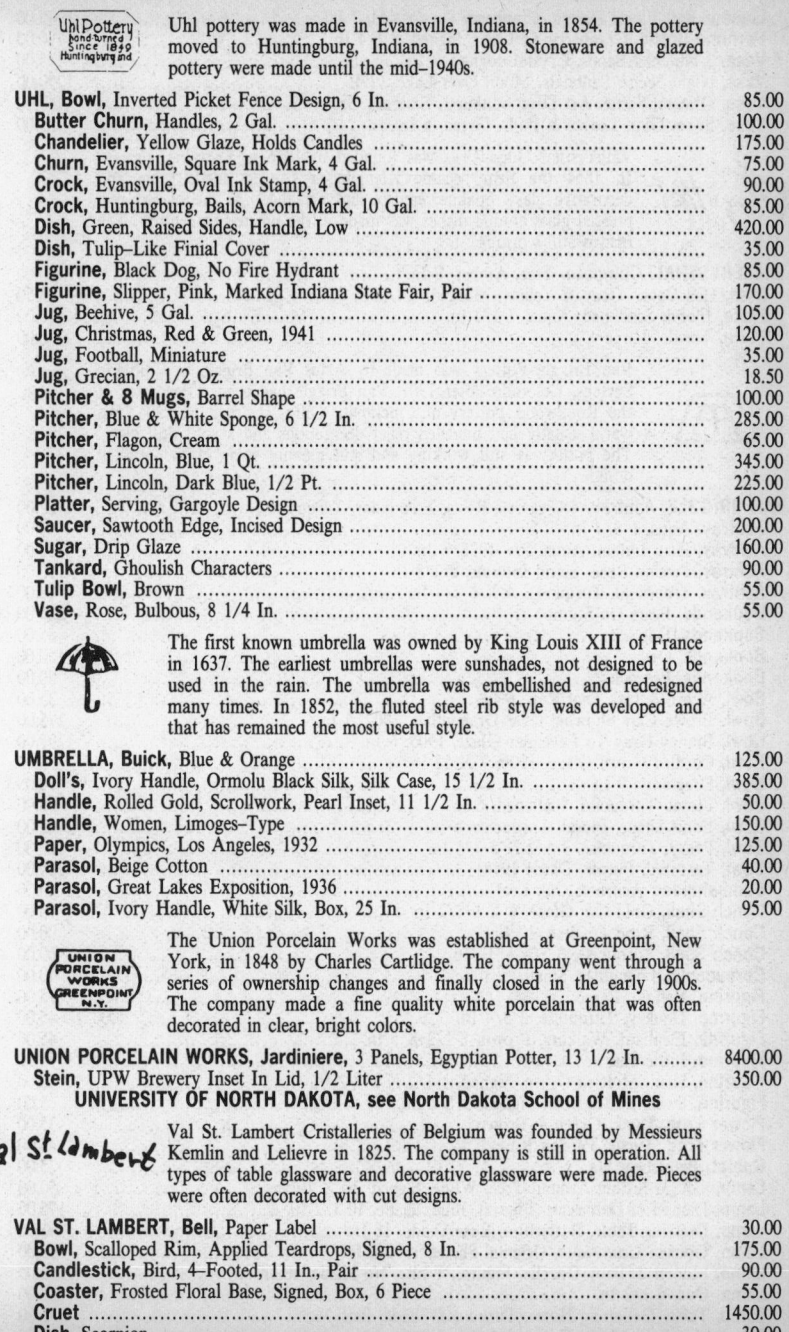

Uhl pottery was made in Evansville, Indiana, in 1854. The pottery moved to Huntingburg, Indiana, in 1908. Stoneware and glazed pottery were made until the mid–1940s.

UHL, Bowl, Inverted Picket Fence Design, 6 In.	85.00
Butter Churn, Handles, 2 Gal.	100.00
Chandelier, Yellow Glaze, Holds Candles	175.00
Churn, Evansville, Square Ink Mark, 4 Gal.	75.00
Crock, Evansville, Oval Ink Stamp, 4 Gal.	90.00
Crock, Huntingburg, Bails, Acorn Mark, 10 Gal.	85.00
Dish, Green, Raised Sides, Handle, Low	420.00
Dish, Tulip–Like Finial Cover	35.00
Figurine, Black Dog, No Fire Hydrant	85.00
Figurine, Slipper, Pink, Marked Indiana State Fair, Pair	170.00
Jug, Beehive, 5 Gal.	105.00
Jug, Christmas, Red & Green, 1941	120.00
Jug, Football, Miniature	35.00
Jug, Grecian, 2 1/2 Oz.	18.50
Pitcher & 8 Mugs, Barrel Shape	100.00
Pitcher, Blue & White Sponge, 6 1/2 In.	285.00
Pitcher, Flagon, Cream	65.00
Pitcher, Lincoln, Blue, 1 Qt.	345.00
Pitcher, Lincoln, Dark Blue, 1/2 Pt.	225.00
Platter, Serving, Gargoyle Design	100.00
Saucer, Sawtooth Edge, Incised Design	200.00
Sugar, Drip Glaze	160.00
Tankard, Ghoulish Characters	90.00
Tulip Bowl, Brown	55.00
Vase, Rose, Bulbous, 8 1/4 In.	55.00

The first known umbrella was owned by King Louis XIII of France in 1637. The earliest umbrellas were sunshades, not designed to be used in the rain. The umbrella was embellished and redesigned many times. In 1852, the fluted steel rib style was developed and that has remained the most useful style.

UMBRELLA, Buick, Blue & Orange	125.00
Doll's, Ivory Handle, Ormolu Black Silk, Silk Case, 15 1/2 In.	385.00
Handle, Rolled Gold, Scrollwork, Pearl Inset, 11 1/2 In.	50.00
Handle, Women, Limoges–Type	150.00
Paper, Olympics, Los Angeles, 1932	125.00
Parasol, Beige Cotton	40.00
Parasol, Great Lakes Exposition, 1936	20.00
Parasol, Ivory Handle, White Silk, Box, 25 In.	95.00

The Union Porcelain Works was established at Greenpoint, New York, in 1848 by Charles Cartlidge. The company went through a series of ownership changes and finally closed in the early 1900s. The company made a fine quality white porcelain that was often decorated in clear, bright colors.

UNION PORCELAIN WORKS, Jardiniere, 3 Panels, Egyptian Potter, 13 1/2 In.	8400.00
Stein, UPW Brewery Inset In Lid, 1/2 Liter	350.00

UNIVERSITY OF NORTH DAKOTA, see North Dakota School of Mines

Val St. Lambert Cristalleries of Belgium was founded by Messieurs Kemlin and Lelievre in 1825. The company is still in operation. All types of table glassware and decorative glassware were made. Pieces were often decorated with cut designs.

VAL ST. LAMBERT, Bell, Paper Label	30.00
Bowl, Scalloped Rim, Applied Teardrops, Signed, 8 In.	175.00
Candlestick, Bird, 4–Footed, 11 In., Pair	90.00
Coaster, Frosted Floral Base, Signed, Box, 6 Piece	55.00
Cruet	1450.00
Dish, Scorpion	30.00
Goblet, Cranberry Overlay	200.00

Liqueur Set, Floral Design, Cranberry On Crystal, 7 Piece	1795.00
Perfume Bottle, Cranberry To Clear, Signed, 5 1/4 In.	190.00
Vase, 3 Notched Bands, Crystal, Signed, 7 In.	115.00
Vase, Night Scene, Sailboats, Moon Over Lake, 11 In.	1250.00
Vase, Oriental Scene, Art Deco Sunburst, Emerald Green	280.00
Vase, Sweet Gum Leaves & Balls, Green, 6 In.	325.00

Vallerysthal Glassworks was founded in 1836 in Lorraine, France. In 1854 the firm became Klenglin et Cie. It made table and decorative glass, opaline, cameo, and art glass. A line of covered, pressed glass animal dishes was made in the nineteenth century. The firm is still working.

VALLERYSTHAL, Compote, Tree, Amber, 9 In.	160.00
Dish, Hen Cover, Gray & Yellow, Marked, 4 1/4 In.	42.50
Plate, Floral, Scalloped, Aqua, 7 1/2 In.	10.00
Plate, Thistle, Large	95.00

Van Briggle Pottery was made by Artus Van Briggle in Colorado Springs, Colorado, after 1901. Van Briggle had been a decorator at the Rookwood Pottery of Cincinnati, Ohio. He died in 1904. His wares usually had modeled relief decorations and a soft, dull glaze. The pottery is still working and still making some of the original designs.

VAN BRIGGLE, Ashtray, 4 Cigarette Rests, Triangular, Turquoise	22.00
Ashtray, Aqua, 6 3/4 In.	17.00
Ashtray, Hopi Indian, Aqua, Pre–1922, 6 In.	65.00
Ashtray, Persian Rose, Spiral Interior, 5 3/8 In.	12.00
Ashtray, Trapezoid, Turquoise, 4 X 6 3/4 In.	18.00
Bookends, Bears On Stump	225.00
Bookends, Dog	85.00
Bookends, Owl ....75.00 To 150.00
Bookends, Peacocks	50.00
Bowl, Acorn & Oak Leaf Rim, 6 In.	35.00
Bowl, Brown Clay Showing Over Dragonflies, 1907, 5 In.	275.00
Bowl, Bumpy Gray To Lavender Glaze, 1905, 6 In.	295.00
Bowl, Curdled Green Glaze, 1906, 7 X 12 In.	675.00
Bowl, Dragonfly, 9 In.	70.00
Bowl, Floral, Turquoise, Scalloped, 6 In.	26.00
Bowl, Lotus Shape, Floral, Turquoise, 6 In.	22.00
Bowl, Pansy, Turquoise, 3 1/2 X 3 3/4 In.	23.00
Bowl, Textured, Purple, Dated 1918	325.00
Candleholder, Acorn & Oak Leaf	20.00
Conch Shell, Gold Ore Glaze, 4 X 9 1/2 In.	75.00
Conch Shell, Rose To Blue, 17 In.	90.00
Conch Shell, Turquoise, 5 3/4 X 17 In.	60.00
Cornucopia, Triangular, Small	40.00
Figurine, Buffalo, Large	75.00
Figurine, Donkey, Turquoise, 3 3/4 In. ....28.00 To 45.00
Figurine, Elephant, Walking, Brown, 8 1/2 X 5 In.	45.00
Figurine, Little Star	75.00
Figurine, Snail, Mottled Green, Signed, 4 1/2 X 2 1/2 In.	40.00
Figurine, Swan, Matte Rose, Signed, 3 1/2 In.	65.00
Flower Frog, Duck, Green & Brown	35.00
Flower Frog, Turtle, Persian Rose	45.00
Goblet, Bethlehem Star	25.00
Lamp, Cougar Sitting Around Tree, White, Signed, 10 X 10 In.	50.00
Lamp, Damsel of Damascus, Figural, Blue, Shade, 10 1/2 In.	175.00
Lamp, Dressing Table, Butterflies, Rose Shade, 16 In.	95.00
Lamp, Grecian Urn, Aqua, Original Shade, 11 1/2 In.	55.00
Lamp, Mother & Baby Gazelle, Figural, White, No Shade, 10 In.	225.00
Lamp, Owl, 6 1/2 In.	185.00
Lamp, Table, Galloping Horse, Turquoise, Shade, Pair	195.00
Paperweight, Elephant, Green, 2 1/4 In.	35.00
Paperweight, Rabbit	45.00

Pitcher, Gold Ore Glaze, Marked, 1956, 4 In. 95.00
Plate, Green, Colorado Springs, 6 1/2 In. 75.00
Plate, Tawny Yellow, 1912, 4 In. 175.00
Rose Bowl, Spade Leaves Around Top, Turquoise, Marked, 5 In. 58.00
Soap Dish, Shell Girl, Aqua, Colorado Springs, Pre–1922 .... 75.00
Sugar & Creamer, Child's, Persian Rose, 2 X 2 In. 30.00
Teapot, Bamboo Reeded Handle, Turquoise, Purple Glaze 175.00
Urn, Turquoise, 3 1/2 In. 22.00
Vase, 3 Indians, Aqua, Pre–1922, 11 In. 175.00
Vase, Art Nouveau, Persian Rose, 1920s, 7 1/2 In. 95.00
Vase, Bird of Paradise, White, 8 3/4 In. 18.50
Vase, Blue Over Green Glaze, Marked, 1922–26, 7 1/2 In. 75.00
Vase, Brown Glaze, 10 In. 130.00
Vase, Brown, Signed L.F., 4 In. 50.00
Vase, Burgundy, Blue & Gray, 4 In. 35.00
Vase, Chocolate Brown & Green, 8 In. 55.00
Vase, Concave Neck, Classic Shape, 3 3/4 In. 30.00
Vase, Copper Clad, 1907, 3 1/2 In. 775.00
Vase, Cowboy Boot, 6 In. 35.00
Vase, Crocus, 5 In. 35.00
Vase, Dragonfly, Handles, Signed, 8 In. 150.00
Vase, Dragonfly, Rose & Blue, 8 In. 23.00
Vase, Indian, 3 Faces, Maroon, 10 In. 150.00
Vase, Leaf Mold, Blue & Green, 5 1/2 In. 27.50
Vase, Leaf Mold, Blue & Turquoise, 5 1/2 In. 27.50
Vase, Maroon Matte, Dated 1914, 8 In., Pair 225.00
Vase, Maroon, 1904, 6 In. 375.00
Vase, Matte Purple Glaze, 1907, 6 X 6 In. 375.00
Vase, Matte Purple, 1907, 4 1/2 In. 475.00
Vase, Molded Moths, Turquoise, 4 In. 45.00
Vase, Mt. Craig, Brown, 1920s, 4 X 5 In. 50.00
Vase, Persian Rose, Crocus, Bubble Glaze, 8 In. 35.00
Vase, Persian Rose, Flowers In Relief, 4 1/2 In. 48.00
Vase, Raspberry Color, 2 Handles, 1905, 10 In. 495.00
Vase, Rose & Blue Matte, 3 3/4 In. 22.00
Vase, Sunflower, Maroon & Blue, 1920s, 9 X 9 In. 345.00
Vase, Thick Turquoise Glaze, 1912, 8 In. 325.00
Vase, Triple Horn of Plenty, Center Candleholder, 4 1/4 In. 65.00
Vase, Tulip, Gold Ore Glaze, 4 In. 65.00
Vase, Turquoise, Heart Shape, Leaves, 1916, 4 X 4 In. 105.00
Vase, Turquoise, Stylized Peacock Feathers, 1920s, 7 1/2 In. 85.00
Vase, Upright Blossoms & Leaves, Marked, Dated 1920, 13 1/4 In. 825.00

Vasa Murrhina is the name of a glassware made by the Vasa
Murrhina Art Glass Company of Sandwich, Massachusetts, about
1884. The glassware was transparent and was embedded with small
pieces of colored glass and metallic flakes. Some of the pieces were
cased. The same type of glass was made in England. Collectors often
confuse Vasa Murrhina glass with aventurine, spatter, or spangle
glass. There is much confusion about what actually was made by the
Vasa Murrhina factory.

VASA MURRHINA, see also Spangle Glass
VASA MURRHINA, Basket, Art Glass, Green, Ribbon Candy, Brier Handle, 7 In. 100.00
Basket, Blue, Applied Thorny Handle, White Lining, 7 1/2 In. 175.00
Basket, Ruffled, Mica Flakes, Clear Handle, 4 X 6 In. 118.00
Bowl, Gold Flecks, Scalloped, Crimped, Low, 9 1/4 In. 135.00
Epergne, Blue, Ormolu, Clear Ruffled, Mica Flaking, 12 3/4 In. 295.00
Ewer, Ruffled Top, Thorny Handle, Mica Flakes, 7 1/2 In., Pair 225.00
Jug, Cream, Pigeon's Blood, Green, Yellow, Clear Handle, 6 In. 140.00
Pitcher, Melon–Ribbed, Raspberry To White, Mica, 8 1/2 In. 170.00
Rose Bowl, 8–Crimp Top, Mica Flaking, White Inside, 3 3/4 In. 125.00
Rose Bowl, Blue Overlay, White Lining, Wishbone Feet, 4 In. 85.00
Rose Bowl, Rose, 8–Crimp Top, Mica Flaking, 5 X 5 1/2 In. 145.00

Saltshaker, Leaf Mold, Cranberry 95.00
Sugar & Creamer, Cover, Gold Flakes, Melon Sectioned 225.00
Tumbler, Leaf Mold, Cranberry 65.00
Vase, Blue Mist, 14 In. 100.00
Vase, Blue Overlay, White Lining, Thorn Handle, Mica, 8 In. 125.00
Vase, Clear Thorny Handles, White Inside, 7 1/4 In. 110.00
Vase, Melon–Ribbed Body, Mica Flecking, Ruffled, 9 1/2 In. 75.00
Vase, Pink, Mica Flakes, White Lining, 9 3/8 In. 145.00
Vase, Rose, Silver Mica Flakes In Coral Pattern, 8 1/4 In. 125.00
Vase, Stick Neck, Hand Painted Flowers, Maroon, Cream, 7 In. 95.00
Vase, White Casing, Gold Metallic Flakes, 9 In. 70.00

Vaseline glass is a greenish–yellow glassware resembling petroleum jelly. Some vaseline glass is still being made in old and new styles. Pressed glass of the 1870s. was often made of vaseline–colored glass. Some pieces of vaseline glass may also be listed under Pressed Glass in this book.

VASELINE GLASS, Bowl, Basket Weave, Opal Lattice, Square, 4 1/2 In. 32.00
Bowl, Footed, 6 In. 50.00
Butter, Cover, Cherry 50.00
Butter, Cover, Daisy & Button, Knob Finial, 6 1/2 In. 125.00
Cake Set, Acid Etched Border, 13 Piece 200.00
Celery, Daisy & Button With Crossbars 36.00
Cruet, Alaska 195.00
Cruet, Jewel & Flower 375.00
Cruet, Tray, 6 1/2 In. ....Illus 65.00
Decanter, Ribs Swirled In Neck, Pillar Mold, 11 1/4 In. 270.00
Doorknob 65.00
Epergne, 3–Lily, Fluted Bowl, Applied Rigaree, 24 X 12 In. 395.00
Epergne, 4–Lily, Threaded 395.00
Figurine, Liberty, 8 1/2 In. 80.00
Goblet, Rose In Snow 65.00
Goblet, Sunken Buttons 37.50
Goblet, Thousand Eye 35.00
Hat, Hobnail, Opalescent Rim, 4 X 2 1/2 In. 35.00
Lemonade Set, Floral Cutting, 7 Piece 215.00
Mug, Child's, Heron & Peacock 45.00
Mustard, Cover, Petticoat 110.00
Perfume Bottle, Matching Stopper, 7 In. 250.00
Pitcher, Applied Handle, 9 1/2 In. ....85.00 To 120.00
Pitcher, Thumbprint Pattern, 7 In. 20.00
Rose Bowl, Honeycomb 65.00
Salt, Santa & Sleigh 95.00
Table Set, Alaska, Enamel Design, 4 Piece 535.00
Toothpick, Dog With Hat 55.00
Toothpick, Petticoat In Turned–Over Hat Mold 110.00
Tray, Condiment, Handles 22.00
Wine, Fine Cut & Panel 30.00

Vaseline Glass, Cruet, Tray, 6 1/2 In.

The pattern numbers on Van Briggle pottery can help date a piece. Numbers below 899 were used before 1912. AA alone was used before 1920; AA-USA was used from 1922 to 1929.

Venetian glass has been made near Venice, Italy, from the thirteenth to the twentieth century. Thin, colored glass with applied decoration is favored, although many other types have been made.

VENETIAN GLASS, Ashtray, 3–Lobed Shape, Silver Deposit, Murano, 5 X 7 In. 15.00
  Bowl, Concave Sides Form Square Top, Goldstone 48.00
  Candy Jar, Ruby, Applied Flowers, 24K Gold, Footed, Large 95.00
  Dish, Alternating Gold & Red Ray Design, 7 In. 35.00
  Figurine, Bird, Latticinio, Gold Flecked Bill, 3 1/2 In. 48.00
  Figurine, Fish, Gold Flecked Fins, Ruby, 9 3/4 In. 68.00
  Figurine, Rooster, Standing, Gold Dusted, Amber, 9 3/4 In. 95.00
  Group, 10 Birds In Tree, 20 In. 150.00
  Vase, Inverted Ribbing At Neck, Scalloped, Red, 12 In. 115.00
  Wine, Latticinio Striped, Cranberry, Clear, Opal & Goldstone 75.00
  Wine, Threaded, Sea Serpent Stem, 6 In., 4 Piece 110.00

Verlys glass was made in France after 1931. It was made in the United States from 1935 to 1951. The glass is either blown or molded. The American glass is signed with a diamond–point–scratched name, but the French pieces are marked with a molded signature. The designs resemble those used by Lalique.

VERLYS, Ashtray, Frosted Doves, Floral Border, Signed, 4 1/2 X 3 1/2 In. 35.00
  Ashtray, Swallows 25.00
  Bowl, Chrysanthemum, 10 X 6 In. 95.00
  Bowl, Ducks & Fish In Relief, Clear & Frosted, 13 1/2 In. .... 135.00 To 145.00
  Bowl, Pinecone, 1 3/4 X 6 In. 35.00
  Bowl, Pinecone, Frosted, Signed, 6 In. .... 35.00 To 60.00
  Bowl, Poppies, Label, 13 In. .... 75.00 To 90.00
  Bowl, Sculptured Bluebirds & Dragonflies, Frosted, 12 In. 110.00
  Bowl, Tassel, Frosted, Signed, 11 1/2 In. 110.00
  Bowl, Thistle, 3–Footed, 8 1/2 In. 140.00
  Bowl, Thistle, 8 1/2 In. 68.00
  Bowl, Water Lily, 13 3/4 In. 175.00
  Box, Cigarette, Sea Gulls 100.00
  Candy Dish, Cover, Dragonfly, 7 In. 280.00
  Charger, Wild Duck, Blue, 13 1/2 In. .... 235.00 To 245.00
  Dish, Roses, Frosted, 5 1/4 In. 65.00
  Figurine, Oriental Woman, 9 1/2 In. 375.00
  Figurine, Pigeon, Frosted, 4 1/4 In. 315.00
  Tray, Orchid, 14 In. 65.00
  Vase, 4 Seasons, Art Deco Woman In Relief, Signed, 8 1/4 In., Pair 310.00
  Vase, Autumn & Spring, Crystal Etched, 8 1/4 In. 275.00
  Vase, Frosted Cherries, 7 In. 95.00
  Vase, Gems, Opalescent & Clear, Signed, 6 1/2 In. 82.00
  Vase, Icicle, Crystal Etched, Signed, 8 In. 125.00
  Vase, Winter & Summer, Carl Schmidt, Signed & Dated 145.00

Vernon Potteries, Ltd., started in Vernon, California, in 1931. It became Vernon Kilns by 1948. The company made dinnerware and figurines until it closed in 1958. Collectors search for the brightly colored dinnerware and the pieces designed by Rockwell Kent, Walt Disney, and Don Blanding.

VERNON KILNS, Ashtray, Red, Alexandria, Va. 9.00
  Ashtray, Texas 12.00
  Berry Bowl, Bouquet, 6 In. 5.00
  Bowl, Homespun, 8 1/2 In. 4.00
  Bowl, Organdie, 9 In. 8.00
  Bowl, Sprite, Walt Disney, Pink, 1940 .... 125.00
  Butter, Cover, Organdie 15.00
  Carafe, Cover, Tam O'Shanter 25.00
  Chop Plate, Brown–Eyed Susan, 12 1/2 In. 15.00
  Chop Plate, Lei Lani, 13 In. 40.00
  Chop Plate, Organdie .... 10.00 To 12.50
  Coffeepot, California, Maroon 28.00

Coffeepot, Hawaiian Flowers, Blue	85.00
Creamer, Moby Dick, Blue	48.00
Creamer, Organdie	4.00
Cup & Saucer, Colossal, Gray	40.00
Cup & Saucer, Coral Reef	18.00
Cup & Saucer, Organdie	5.00
Cup & Saucer, Tam O'Shanter, Colossal	70.00
Cup, Coral Reef	12.00
Figurine, Evelyn Venable	225.00
Figurine, Satyr, Fantasia	250.00
Pitcher, Art Deco, Gray Gloss, Ice Lip, Vernonware, 11 1/2 In.	17.00
Pitcher, Raffia, 8 1/2 In.	20.00
Pitcher, Water, Organdie	15.00
Plate, Alamo, Under 6 Flags	18.00
Plate, Bouquet, 12 1/4 In.	15.00
Plate, Chatelaine, Topaz, 15 In.	25.00
Plate, Chopin, 8 1/2 In.	20.00
Plate, Commemorative, Will Rogers	20.00
Plate, Coral Reef, 9 1/2 In.	9.00
Plate, Cotton Patch, Black Figures, Old South	28.00
Plate, Cypress Swamp, 8 In.	7.00
Plate, Cypress Swamp, Black Figures, Old South	28.00
Plate, Eisenhower, 10 In.	10.00
Plate, El Jebel, Temple of Mountains, Denver, Colo., Colored	25.00
Plate, French Repro La Muette De Portici, 8 1/4 In.	18.00
Plate, Hawaiian Flowers, Maroon, 10 1/2 In.	30.00
Plate, Honolulu	10.00
Plate, House On River, Old South	15.00
Plate, Illinois	10.00
Plate, Lei Lani, 10 1/2 In.	25.00
Plate, Mendelssohn, Brown, 8 1/2 In.	10.00
Plate, Mission Dolores, San Francisco De Asis, 8 1/2 In.	20.00
Plate, Mission San Carlos Borromeo, 8 1/2 In.	20.00
Plate, New Orleans Sports Picture, Blue, White, 10 3/8 In.	7.00
Plate, Organdie, 6 In.	1.50
Plate, Organdie, 9 3/4 In.	4.00
Plate, Pennsylvania, Brown Map	30.00
Plate, Salamania, 9 1/2 In.	45.00
Plate, Santa Claus, 10 In.	20.00
Plate, Southern Mansion, Black Figures, Old South	28.00
Plate, St.Louis, Van Gelder, 1948	22.00
Plate, Tobacco Field, Black Figures, Old South	28.00
Plate, Utah, 1943	20.00
Platter, Organdie, 10 X 6 1/2 In.	5.00
Salad Bowl, Organdie, 10 1/2 In.	22.00
Salt & Pepper, Fantasia Mushrooms, Disney	75.00 To 100.00
Salt & Pepper, Hop Low, Fantasia	100.00 To 150.00
Salt & Pepper, Mushroom Shape, Fantasia, Marked Disney	60.00
Salt & Pepper, Mushrooms	100.00
Salt & Pepper, Organdie	8.00
Salt & Pepper, Turquoise	12.00
Sandwich Plate, Rose, 12 1/2 In.	7.50
Saucer, Hawaiian Flowers, Blue	9.00
Sugar & Creamer, Fantasia	275.00
Sugar & Creamer, Hawaiian Flowers	55.00
Sugar, Cover, Organdie	6.00
Teapot, Hawaiian Flowers, Blue	75.00
Teapot, Organdie	22.00
Tidbit, Gingham, 2 Tiers	14.00
Tumbler, Gingham, 5 1/2 In.	10.00
Tumbler, Organdie, 5 1/2 In.	15.00
Tumbler, Streamline	15.00
Vase, Fish Bowl Shape, Medium Blue, 6 X 8 In.	135.00

Verre de soie glass was first made by Frederick Carder at the Steuben Glass Works from about 1905 to 1930. It is an iridescent glass of soft white or very, very pale green. The name means glass of silk, and it does resemble silk. Other factories have made verre de soie, and some of the English examples were made of different colors. Verre de soie is an art glass and is not related to the iridescent, pressed, white Carnival glass mistakenly called by its name.

VERRE DE SOIE, see also Steuben
VERRE DE SOIE, Bowl, Signed, Steuben, 3 X 8 In.	85.00
Box, Cover, Fruit Finial, Steuben	175.00
Console Set, Flared Rim, 16–In.Bowl, 3 Piece	675.00
Perfume Bottle, Blue Feather, Lundberg, 1986, 3 In.	95.00
Pitcher, Water, Applied Design, Venetian Period	450.00
Vase, Abstract, Ruby Threading, Wide Rim, Steuben, 3 1/8 In.	50.00
Vase, Corset Shape, Flared, 6 1/4 X 3 3/4 In.	140.00
Vase, Quilted Cranberry, Threaded, Signed Steuben	165.00
Vase, Stump, Steuben	500.00

Vienna Art plates are round metal serving trays produced at the turn of the century. The designs, copied from Royal Vienna porcelain plates, usually featured a portrait of a woman encircled by a wide, ornate border. Many were used as advertising or promotional items and were produced in Coshocton, Ohio, by J.F. Meeks Tuscarora Advertising Co. and H.D. Beach's Standard Advertising Co.

VIENNA ART, Plate, Anger Baking Co., Child, 1905	45.00
Plate, Compliments of Fair Store, Rockport, Ind.	45.00
Plate, Frank Jones BRG Co., Portsmouth, N.H., 10 1/4 In.	25.00
Plate, Jill	145.00
Plate, Nude	475.00
Plate, Portrait, Floral Border, Tin, 10 In.	30.00 To 40.00
VIENNA, see Beehive	

The Villeroy & Boch Pottery of Mettlach was founded in 1841. The firm made many types of pottery, including the famous Mettlach steins. It is confusing for the collector because although Villeroy and Boch made most of its pieces in the city of Mettlach, Germany, they also had factories in other locations. There is a dating code impressed on the bottom of most pieces that makes it possible to determine the age of the piece.

VILLEROY & BOCH, see also Mettlach
VILLEROY & BOCH, Bowl, Blue & White Pattern, Square, 3 X 10 In.	125.00
Coffee Set, Farm Scenes, Cream Ground, Crazed, 3 Piece	285.00
Mixing Bowl Set, Nested, 3 Piece	56.00
Pitcher, Milk, Isabelle, Blue	22.00
Plaque, Scenic, 12 In.	65.00
Plate, Little Rascal Series, Heinrich	25.00
Plate, Snow Maiden, Heinrich	140.00
Plate, Tsar Bear, No.2	60.00
Plate, Vietnam	17.00
Plate, Windmill Scene, 11 In., Pair	200.00
Plate, Windmill Scene, Blue & White, 18 In.	225.00
Trivet, Scene	75.00
Tureen, Soup, Underplate, Dresden Pattern	275.00
Vase, Classical Women, Vines, Leaves, 1842 Shield Mark	80.00

VOLKMAR
Corona N.y

Volkmar pottery was made by Charles Volkmar of New York from 1879 to about 1911. He was associated with several firms, including the Volkmar Ceramic Company, Volkmar and Cory, and Charles Volkmar and Son. Volkmar had been a painter, and his designs often look like oil paintings drawn on pottery.

VOLKMAR, Vase, Mottled Yellow Glaze, Brown Streaking, 4 In.	275.00

Volkstadt was a soft–paste porcelain manufactory started in 1760 by Georg Heinrich Macheleid at Volkstadt, Thuringia. Volkstadt–Rudolstadt was a porcelain factory started at Volkstadt–Rudolstadt by Beyer and Bock in 1890. Most pieces seen in shops today are from the later factory.

VOLKSTADT, Figurine, Lovers At Swan Pond, Watching Swans, 9 X 8 1/2 In. 575.00
  Figurine, Woman With Mandolin, Man In Red Coat ....975.00 To 1050.00
  Group, Ostriches, Blue, Gray & Pink, Karla Ens, 7 1/2 In. 125.00
    WALLACE NUTTING photographs are listed under Print, Nutting. His reproduction furniture is listed under Furniture.

Frederich Walrath was a potter who worked in New York City, Rochester, New York, and at the Newcomb Pottery in New Orleans, Louisiana. He died in 1920. Pieces listed here are from his Rochester period.

WALRATH, Pitcher, 3–Color, Stylized Flower, Signed, 1911, 10 1/2 In. 350.00
  WALT DISNEY, see Disneyana
  WALTER, see A. Walter

Warwick china was made in Wheeling, West Virginia, in a pottery working from 1887 to 1951. Many pieces were made with hand painted or decal decorations. The most familiar Warwick has a shaded brown background. The name "Warwick" is part of the mark and sometimes the word "IOGA" is also included.

WARWICK, Bowl, Green Floral, Scroll, Molded Floral Blank, 5 1/2 X 2 In. 6.50
  Bowl, Orange Poppies On Brown, Open Handles, 10 3/4 In. 57.00
  Child's Set, Boy Hunting Scene, 3 Piece 55.00
  Dish, Shriner's Emblem, Oblong, 9 1/2 In. 9.50
  Jardiniere, Flow Blue Type Scenes, 4 3/4 X 5 In. 50.00
  Mug, F.O.E., Eagle, Brown, Ring Handle, 4 Piece 165.00
  Mug, Green Floral, Scroll, Floral Molded Blank, Handle, 3 1/4 In. 15.00
  Mug, Indian, Full Headdress 85.00
  Mug, Monk 145.00
  Pitcher, 4 Mugs, Cheerful Monks, Red Caps, 7 1/4 In. 265.00
  Pitcher, Lemonade, Portrait, Brown Glaze, IOGA 165.00
  Pitcher, Pink Floral, Leaves, Ferns, White, Scrolled Blank, 6 In. 22.00
  Pitcher, Poppies, Brown To Beige, Scrolled Handle, IOGA, 9 1/2 In. 95.00
  Plate, Indian Portrait, Yellow To Brown Ground, 10 In. 65.00
  Plate, Monk, IOGA, 9 1/2 In. 75.00
  Soup, Cream, Underplate, White, Gold Trim 10.00
  Vase, Crabapples, Golden Yellow, Brown, Aladdin's Lamp Shape, 5 In. 110.00
  Vase, Dark & Light Roses, Leaves, Green Ground, IOGA, 7 1/4 In. 65.00
  Vase, Hibiscus, Double Twig Handles, 10 1/2 In. 145.00
  Vase, Pink Flowers, White, 4 1/2 In. 40.00
  Vase, Portrait, Gypsy Girl, Twig Handles, 10 1/2 In. ....95.00 To 135.00
  Vase, Portrait, Lady With Red Roses, 12 In. 170.00
  Vase, Portrait, Woman & Child, Twig Handles, Gold Trim, 14 In. 145.00
  Vase, Pretty Girl, Red & Brown, 11 1/2 In. 250.00
  Vase, Senator, IOGA, 10 In. 200.00
  Vase, Trumpet Shape, Woman's Portrait, Ruffled Rim, 13 In. 165.00
  Vase, Twig Handle, Brown, Orange, Bouquet Shape, 12 In. 135.00
  Wash Set, Green, Pink, Gold, 5 Piece 365.00

Watch fobs were worn on watch chains. They were popular during Victorian times and after. Many styles, especially advertising designs, are still made today.

WATCH FOB, A.C.4000 Avery Tractor 40.00
  Adams Road Machinery, Grader 45.00
  Adams Road Machinery, Little Rock 12.00
  Alaska–Yukon–Pacific Exposition, 1909 .... 58.50
  Allis–Chalmers 23.00
  Alpha Portland Cement 35.00
  American Hoist Co., Bronze, Crane, Truck, 1 1/2 In. 25.00

American Legion, 1939	27.00
American Legion, 41st Convention, Cut–Out of Minnesota, 1959	35.00
American Racing Pigeon Union, Milwaukee, 1928	35.00
Appleman Gumbo Bit	65.00
Apsley Rubber Co.	22.00
Armour, Cow Head	20.00
Army Shoe, Gold Celluloid, On Black Cardboard, 1920	12.00
Arrowhead, With Saddle, Souvenir Texas	18.50
Aultman & Taylor, Chicken	75.00
Baltimore, Maryland Yacht Club, Brass, 1927	30.00
Black Diamond Plow Bolts	12.00
Blue Brute Cement Mixers	37.50
Buesher Tru–Tone, Musical Instruments	13.50
Bulldog, With Cigar Cutter, Bronze	95.00
Case Centennial Tractor Plow	38.00
Caterpillar Bulldozer	10.00
Chi–Nomel Paint, Chinese Boy	25.00 To 40.00
Clark's Rye Whiskey	37.00
Colt Firearms	67.50
Columbian Exposition, 1893	18.00
Columbian Exposition, Chicago, Gold Filled, 1893	30.00
Culver Summer Naval School, Raised Anchor In Center, Copper	40.00
Davenport High School	42.00
Dean & Berry, Paints & Varnishes	35.00
DeLaval Separator	55.00
Dr Pepper, Billiken	65.00
E–Z–Ola Polish, Chicago	19.00
El Paso Saddlery, Saddle Shape, 1889	125.00
Elcar	35.00
Elk's Tooth	35.00
Elk's Tooth, 14K Gold	45.00
Elks, Stamp Holder, Sterling Silver, 1910	75.00
Euclid Co., Bronze Finish, Bulldozer, 1 1/2 In.	25.00
Euclid Earth Moving Equipment, Silver, Truck, Garden, 1 1/2 In.	25.00
F.C.Ayers Mercantile Co., Denver, Colo., Ears of Corn	40.00
Fairbanks–Morse	40.00
Gardner Denver, Jackhammer	20.00
General Motors Diesel	25.00
Gipp's Beer, Peoria, Ill.	10.00
Grays Tonic, Horsehead In G	40.00
Gyro–Flo, Ingersoll–Rand, White Metal	45.00
Hair, 5 Strands, Chain, George Washington	67.50
Hercules Buggy, Presented To Guy Cooper, Evansville, Ind.	275.00
Hoards's Dairyman, W.D.Howard, White Metal	35.00
Hunter–Trader–Trapper	225.00
Inter–Southern Life Insurance, Brass, Building	22.00
International Harvester, Two Worlds	70.00
Jackhammer, Denver, Colorado	42.50
Kenney Machinery Co., Tiger Face	30.00
Kin Booster, Trumpet	30.00
LaPlant Choate, Earth Mover	45.00
LaSalle University	8.50
Leisy Brewing, Porcelain & Brass	100.00
Lima Earth Moving Equipment	24.00
Link–Belt Shovel Crane, Leather Strap	28.00
Lion's Head, Ruby Eyes, Cigar Cutter, Yellow Gold	65.00
Lorain Tractor, Double Side	60.00
Mack Trucks, Raised Bulldog With Collar, Brass	55.00
Marlin, 1911	48.00
Massey–Harris Tractors	75.00
Mexican Border Service, Bronze, 1916	30.00
Michigan Excavator Crane, Bronze Finish, Tractor, Shovel, 2 In.	25.00
Motorola, 25th Anniversary, Silver Plate, 1928–53	35.00
National Cash Register	125.00

National Sportsman	35.00
New York To Paris, With Compass	65.00
Old Reliable Coffee, Man Smoking Pipe	35.00
Oliver Chilled Plow	32.50
Orville Wright, Kitty Hawk, Early Biplane	125.00
Panama Pacific Exposition, Celluloid, 1915	17.00
Parker, Davis, 1904	20.00
Paul Revere Insurance	10.00
Paydozer–Payloader, Rectangular, Brass & Enamel	60.00
Peru Beer Co.	70.00
Peter's Weatherbird Shoes	45.00
Phoenix Brewery, Buffalo, N.Y., Eagle	115.00
Polarine Oil, Polar Bear, White Metal	65.00
Poll Parrot Shoes, Color	35.00
Railroad Conductor's, Gold	65.00
Red Diamond Overalls	22.00
Red Diamond Overalls, Celluloid On Fiber	65.00
Red Owl Coal, 50th Year	40.00
Red Owl Coal, Enameled, Oval	85.00
Remington, 1816–1916	50.00
Roszell's Ice Cream, Celluloid On Fiber	70.00
Rumely, Metal, C.1900	200.00
Sanico Stove, Brass	65.00
Shoe Bench Ade Smith Birscoe Shoe Co., Steadfast, Silver	62.00
Stamford, Texas, State of Texas Shape, 1933	110.00
Star Brand Shoes	22.00
Stickney & Poor Spice Co.	37.00
Stutzman Stone Co., Red, White, Yellow Enamel, 1 3/4 In.	10.00
Tractomotive, Cut–Out, Nickel Over Brass	65.00
U.S. Mexican Border Service, 1916	45.00
Utica, New York Trust Deposit Band	22.00
Wallis Tractor	60.00
Walter Wood Harvesting Machines, St.Louis Fair On Reverse, 1904	45.00
Warner House, No.11, Jonesboro, Arkansas, Brass	16.00
Washburn–Crosby Co., Foods, Celluloid In Shield	60.00
Washington, D.C., Pictures of Buildings On Links, 11 In.	87.50
Wolf Milling & Flour Machinery	28.00
Yellowstone Park, Deer	20.00

The pocket watch was important in Victorian times because it was not until World War I that the wristwatch was used. All types of watches are collected: silver, gold, or plated. Watches are listed by company name or by style.

WATCH, Alice In Wonderland, Wristwatch, U.S.Time	20.00
American Watch Co., Pocket, Railroad, Key Wind, Coin Silver, No.79295	375.00
Appleton Tracy, Pocket, Hunting Case	250.00
Arrow Watch Co., Pocket, 17 Jewel	100.00
Benrus, Wristwatch, Alarm	125.00
Boliva, Wristwatch, Woman's, 14K White Gold, No.218	1500.00
Bucherer, Pocket, 17 Jewel	60.00
Buhre, Pocket, Gold, Open Face, Imperial Presentation, 1900, 1 7/8 In.	1450.00
Bulova, Wristwatch, 14k Gold Filled, Rectangular, C.1920s	250.00
Bulova, Wristwatch, Accutron, Deep Sea, Stainless Steel	125.00
Bulova, Wristwatch, Man's, Self–Winding, Gold Filled, Leather Band	125.00
Bulova, Wristwatch, Woman's, 14K White Gold, 16 Jewel, Fancy Dial, 1920	85.00
Bulova, Wristwatch, Woman's, Diamonds, 21 Jewel	150.00
Burlington, Pocket, 17 Jewel, 16 Size, Gold Filled Case	185.00
Capt & Geneva, Pocket, Open Face, Blue Guilloche, 18 Jewel, Chain, 1912	1200.00
Cartier, Wristwatch, 17 Jewel, Swiss Movement, Lizard Strap	175.00
Chronograph, Open Face, Silver Key Wind, English, 1880s	125.00
Cinderella, Wristwatch, U.S.Time	20.00
Cinor, Lapel, Woman's, Silver	95.00
Corum, Wristwatch, 14K Gold, Swiss Jeweled Movement, Black Band	325.00
E.Howard, Hunting Case, White Dial, Roman Chapters, 14K Gold	550.00

Elgin, H.H.Taylor, Pocket, Gold–Filled Case 70.00
Elgin, Pendant, Nurse's, Sterling Silver Case 165.00
Elgin, Pocket, 7 Jewel, Nickel & Silver Swing–Out Case 45.00
Elgin, Pocket, 15 Jewel, Engraved Coin Hunter's Case 110.00
Elgin, Pocket, 17 Jewel, Engraved Case, Floral Design ....90.00 To 100.00
Elgin, Pocket, 17 Jewel, Fob, 14K Gold, C.1890 .... 550.00
Elgin, Pocket, 17 Jewel, Overland, Nickel Swing–Out Case 45.00
Elgin, Pocket, Father Time, Railroad, 21 Jewel, Gold Filled Case 95.00
Elgin, Pocket, H.H.Taylor, 15 Jewel, Engraved Case 100.00
Elgin, Pocket, Hunting Case, Gold–Filled, C.1850 .... 495.00
Elgin, Pocket, Masonic Symbols On Dial, 17 Jewel, 1913 .... 465.00
Elgin, Pocket, No. 6 Size, 14K Box Hinge Hunting Case 750.00
Elgin, Pocket, No. 8 Size, 14K Gold Hand Engraved Hunter Case 350.00
Elgin, Pocket, No.16 Size, Scenic Hunting Case, 15 Jewel, Colored Dial 250.00
Elgin, Woman's, Wristwatch, 14K Rose Gold, Leather Strap, Round 75.00
Elgin, Wristwatch, Man's, Rectangular, 14K Gold, 1940s 225.00
Elgin, Wristwatch, Man's, Rectangular, Leather Band, 14K Gold 150.00
Elgin, Wristwatch, Man's, Square, Gold Filled 35.00
Ellory, Pocket, Open Face 150.00
Eterna, Wristwatch, 17 Jewel, 14K Yellow Gold 155.00
Girard Perregaux, Wristwatch, Woman's, Rectangular, 14K Yellow Gold 300.00
Graf Zeppelin, Pocket, Box 250.00
Gruen, Wristwatch, Curvex, Yellow Gold Filled, Box 145.00
Gruen, Wristwatch, Man's, Curvex, 10K Gold 150.00
Hamilton, Pocket, 17 Jewel, Lever Set 65.00
Hamilton, Pocket, 21 Jewel, 2–Tone Movement, Gold–Filled Hunter Case 175.00
Hamilton, Pocket, Masonic, Symbols For Numerals, 17 Jewel, 1935 .... 425.00
Hamilton, Pocket, Military, Aviator's, World War II, 22 Jewel 250.00
Hamilton, Pocket, Railroad, 21 Jewel, White Gold Case, 1915 .... 195.00
Hamilton, Pocket, Railroad, No.922 .... 100.00
Hamilton, Pocket, Railway Special, Model 922B 185.00
Hamilton, Wristwatch, 14K White Gold, Square, C.1930 .... 185.00
Hamilton, Wristwatch, 14K Yellow Gold, Square, C.1940 .... 195.00
Hamilton, Wristwatch, 17 Jewel, Platinum, Diamond, 14K Gold Mesh Band 500.00
Hamilton, Wristwatch, Diamond Dial, Platinum, 1935 .... 1195.00
Hamilton, Wristwatch, Model 982, 19 Jewel, Inlaid Medallions 300.00
Hamilton, Wristwatch, Woman's, Diamond Dial, Platinum, 1935 .... 1195.00
Hampden, Pocket, 7 Jewel, Alaska Metal, Swing–Out Case 45.00
Hampden, Pocket, Woman's, Diamond, Engraved Gold Filled Case, 1907 .... 135.00
Hampden, Wristwatch, Woman's, 15 Jewel, Yellow Gold 90.00
Henry Beguelin, Pocket, 18K Gold, Hunter, Roman Numerals, Rope Chain 275.00
Howard, Pocket, 14K Gold, Box, 1920s 210.00
Howard, Pocket, 19 Jewel, White Gold Filled Case 295.00
Howard, Pocket, 21 Jewel, 14K Gold Chain, Knife, $1.00 Gold Coin 1000.00
Howard, Pocket, Open Face, Presentation, 14K Gold, 21 Jewel, 1925 .... 625.00
Howard, Pocket, Series, V, Hunting Case, L Size, 14K Gold 825.00
Howard, Wristwatch, 17 Jewel, Open Face, 8–Sided Case, 14K Gold 350.00
Illinois, Pocket, 15 Jewel, Swing–Out From Back, Coin Case 85.00
Illinois, Pocket, 17 Jewel, Gold–Filled Case 90.00
Illinois, Pocket, Bunn Special, 21 Jewel, Engraved Hunter's Case 275.00
Illinois, Pocket, Bunn Special, 23 Jewel, Open Face 595.00
Illinois, Pocket, Key Wind, Hunting Case 395.00
Illinois, Pocket, King Special, 17 Jewel, Engraved, Open Face Case 275.00
Illinois, Pocket, Lever–Set, 17 Jewel, Etched Train On Back 125.00
Illinois, Pocket, Plymouth, 17 Jewel, Size 18, Hunting Case 225.00
Illinois, Pocket, Sangamo Special, 23 Jewel, Bridge Movement 350.00
Illinois, Pocket, Time King, Open Face, 19 Jewel, 10K Gold 80.00
Ingersoll, Pocket, Bicycle 400.00
Ingersoll, Pocket, Midget, Silver Case, 1 1/2 In. 25.00
Ingersoll, Wristwatch, Mickey Mouse, Red Band, 1950s 50.00
John Wayne, Wristwatch 55.00
Jules Jurgensen, Pocket, 14K Gold, C.1940 .... 210.00
Jules Jurgenson, Wristwatch, 14K Gold 250.00
Lady Bulova, Wristwatch, 2 Diamonds, 21 Jewel, Art Deco Band 150.00

Lange, Pocket, No.4791, Key Wind, Roman Numerals, C.1865, Dresden	2300.00
Lapel, Figural, Alarm Clock, Dangles From Bow Pin, Rhinestones	75.00
LeCoultre, Wristwatch, Alarm, Yellow Gold Filled	120.00
Leonidas, In Lady's Ring, Art Nouveau, 14K White Gold, 15 Jewel, 1 In.	198.00
Longines, Pocket, Hunting Case, Silver, Scenic	105.00
Longines, Wristwatch, 14K Gold, Swiss Jeweled Movement, Strap	175.00
Longines, Wristwatch, Woman's, 14K White Gold	200.00
Lord Elgin, Wristwatch, Man's, 14K Yellow Gold Filled, 21 Jewels	65.00
M.I.Tobias, Pocket, Open Face, Roman Numerals, 18K Gold, Chain, Key	200.00
Majestime, Wristwatch, Spiro Agnew, Box	100.00
Movado, Wristwatch, Man's, 17 Jewel, 18K Yellow Gold	450.00
Movado, Wristwatch, Woman's, 17 Jewel, 14K Yellow Gold, Round	250.00
Mr.Spock, Wristwatch, 20th Anniversary, Digital, Box	30.00
New Haven, Pocket, Bulldog, Box	35.00
Omega, Pocket, Blue Dial, Yellow Gold Filled, Thin	1250.00
Omega, Wristwatch, Man's, Square Case, 17 Jewel, Gold	225.00
Omega, Wristwatch, Swiss Movement, Diamond Set Bezel, 14K Gold	300.00
Omega, Wristwatch, Woman's, 17 Jewel, 18 Diamonds	500.00
Oudin, Pocket, Gold, Hunter, Russian Imperial Eagle Cover, 1900, Chain	2850.00
Pocket, Railroad, Jeweled Gilt Movement, Second Dial, Chain, Silver	1000.00
Pocket, Woman's, Enamel, Silver Cherubs Kissing	300.00
R2D2-C3PO, Wristwatch, Bradley, Box	35.00
Repeater, Pocket, Quarter Hour, Open Face, Arabic Numbers, 18K Gold	1100.00
Reymond, Pocket, 21 Jewel, North Shore, Swiss	100.00
Rockford, Pocket, 15 Jewel, Key Wind, 1880	125.00
Rockford, Pocket, 7 Jewel, Coin Hunter's Case	130.00
Rolex, Pendant, Woman's, Ball-Type, 17 Jewel, Sterling Silver, Box	175.00
Rolex, Wristwatch, Man's, Oyster Speed King, Leather Band, Stainless	400.00
Rolex, Wristwatch, Oyster, Perpetual Date, Cotton Bowl Classic, 1968	900.00
Rolex, Wristwatch, Oyster, Perpetual, White Face, Jubilee Band	650.00
Rolex, Wristwatch, Prima Movement, Diamonds Surrounded By Sapphires	1900.00
Rolex, Wristwatch, Stainless Automatic, Matching Band, Box	380.00
Rolex, Wristwatch, Woman's, Calendar, Stainless Steel	475.00
Ronald McDonald, Wristwatch	25.00
Seth Thomas, Pocket, 15 Jewel, Silveroid, Engraved Steam Locomotive	45.00
Shreeve & Co., Wristwatch, Woman's, 15 Jewel, 14K Gold, 1930s	85.00
South Bend, Pocket, Open Face, 19 Jewel, 14K Yellow Gold Filled	85.00
Spiro Agnew, Wristwatch	50.00
Swiss, Belt Buckle, Sterling Silver Cover, Square Dial, Second Hand	400.00
Swiss, Pocket, 17 Jewel, Hunting Case, Destino	95.00
Tissot, Pocket, Sweep Second Hand, Yellow Gold Filled, Thin	150.00
Tissot, Wristwatch, Shriner's, Automatic	175.00
Tobias, Pocket, Key Wind, 9K Gold Dial, Engraved Scene On Case, 1850	375.00
Tobias, Pocket, Scenic, 9K Gold, Key Wind, Liverpool, 1850	400.00
Tom Corbett, Wristwatch, Space Ship Card	150.00
Waltham, Pocket, 11 Jewel, Coin Swing-Out Case, Screw Down Crown	75.00
Waltham, Pocket, 14K Gold, Hunter, Roman Numerals, Swiss Jewels	225.00
Waltham, Pocket, 21 Jewel, Gold-Filled Case	335.00
Waltham, Pocket, Coin Silver, 1890s	95.00
Waltham, Pocket, Hunting Case, Coin Silver, 1898	75.00
Waltham, Pocket, Open Face, 14K Yellow Gold Filled, 1889	90.00
Waltham, Pocket, Opera, Skeletonized, 14K Gold	350.00
Waltham, Pocket, P.S.Bartlett, 15 Jewel, Coin Hunter's Case	120.00
Waltham, Pocket, Railroad, 15 Jewel, Moose Head Fob	85.00
Waltham, Pocket, Railroad, Crescent Street, 21 Jewel, Train On Back	175.00
Waltham, Pocket, Size 18, Nickel Case, C.1920	45.00
Waltham, Pocket, Sterling Hunter's Case, Nickel Movement	105.00
Waltham, Pocket, Swing-Out Case, 15 Jewel, Rose Gold Sawmill, Trees	165.00
Waltham, Pocket, With Fob Chain, 10K Gold, C.1875	220.00
Waltham, Wristwatch, Woman's, 4 Small Diamonds, 14K White Gold	40.00
Warick, Wristwatch, Lady's, 14K Gold, 15 Jewels, Monogram	30.00
Westclox, Pocket, Scotty	25.00
Wittenaur, Wristwatch, Chronograph	75.00
Woman's, Wristwatch, Diamond, 14K Gold Wide Bangle Bracelet, 1930	990.00

Woman's, Wristwatch, Onyx, Diamond, Art Deco, Tonneau, Platinum, 1920s 400.00

Waterford–type glass resembles the famous glass made from 1783 to 1851 in the Waterford Glass Works in Ireland. It is a clear glass that was often decorated by cutting. Modern glass is being made again in Waterford, Ireland, and is marketed under the name "Waterford."

WATERFORD, Decanter, Modern Ship, Diamond Cutting 140.00
  Epergne, Crystal, 18 In. 500.00
  Mustard, Cover, 4 1/2 In. 45.00

The Watt family bought the Globe pottery of Crooksville, Ohio, in 1922. They made pottery mixing bowls and dishes of the type made by Globe. In 1935 they changed the production and made the pieces with the freehand decorations that are popular with collectors today. Apple, Starflower, Rooster, Red & Blue Tulip, and Autumn Foliage are the best–known patterns. The plant closed in 1965.

WATT, Bean Pot, Apple, No.76 .... 60.00 To 75.00
  Bean Pot, Flowerbud 55.00
  Bowl, Apple, 4 In. ....*Illus* 25.00
  Bowl, Apple, 7 In. 25.00
  Bowl, Apple, Deep, Cover, No.601 .... 50.00
  Bowl, Apple, No. 6 .... 25.00
  Bowl, Apple, No. 8 .... 33.00
  Bowl, Apple, No. 60 .... 28.00
  Bowl, Apple, No.104 .... 30.00
  Bowl, Cereal, Starflower 16.50
  Bowl, Flower & Cherries, No.52, 6 In. 18.00
  Bowl, Flower & Cherry, 6 In. 14.00
  Bowl, Red Flower, Black Stripe Inside, 11 In. 30.00
  Bowl, Red Flower, Red & Green Stripe Inside, 5 1/2 In. 12.00
  Bowl, Ribbed Apple 28.00
  Bowl, Rooster 48.00
  Bowl, Rooster, Domed Lid, 9 In. 55.00
  Bowl, Rose Parade, 7 1/2 In. 15.00
  Bowl, Says Chips 22.00
  Bowl, Spaghetti, Autumn 50.00
  Bowl, Spaghetti, Flower & Leaf Design 65.00
  Bowl, Spaghetti, Red Flower, Green & Red Center Rings, 13 In. 65.00
  Bowl, Spaghetti, Red Flowers 40.00
  Bowl, Starflower 28.00
  Bowl, Tulip 11.00

Watt, Bowl, Apple, 4 In.

Webb, Vases, Cameo, Blue, Opalescent White, 11 3/4 In; Cameo, Pinwheel, Handles, Woodall, 5 1/2 In.; Cameo, Floral Branch, Red, Baluster, 9 1/4 In.; Knob, Cameo, Black, 2 1/4 In.

Canister, Cover, Flower Buds, No, 80, Large 100.00
Casserole, Cover, Apple, No. 66, 7 In. 125.00
Casserole, Cover, Pennsylvania Dutch Tulip 16.00
Casserole, Eagle 150.00
Casserole, French Handle, No.18 .... 20.00
Cookie Jar, Apple, No.503 .... 179.00
Cookie Jar, Poinsettia 50.00
Creamer, Apple 32.00
Creamer, Rooster 75.00
Creamer, Tulip 75.00
Honey 28.00
Mixing Bowl, Apple, Advertising, 7 In. 25.00
Mug, Apple, No.121 .... 125.00
Nesting Bowls, Flowerbud Pattern, No.5, 6 & 7 .... 45.00
Nesting Bowls, No.4, 5, 6 & 7 .... 75.00
Pepper Shaker, Advertising 25.00
Pepper Shaker, Wheat 15.00
Pie Plate, Apple .... 50.00 To 80.00
Pie Plate, Apple Blossom, Advertising 65.00
Pie Plate, Apple, Advertising .... 70.00 To 85.00
Pie Plate, Apple, No.33 .... 65.00
Pitcher, Apple, 5 In. 18.00
Pitcher, Apple, No.15 .... 25.00 To 35.00
Pitcher, Apple, No.16 .... 36.00 To 45.00
Pitcher, Apple, Reinkes Dairy, Thorp, Wisconsin 45.00
Pitcher, Apple, Square 135.00
Pitcher, Bleeding Heart, No.15 .... 38.00 To 45.00
Pitcher, Brown Leaf 32.00
Pitcher, Cherry & Flower, No.15 .... 24.00
Pitcher, Cherry, Advertising, No.15 .... 26.00
Pitcher, Cobalt Blue Tulips & Flowers, Small 25.00
Pitcher, Dropped Flower, No.69, Square 95.00
Pitcher, Leaf, Advertising 35.00
Pitcher, Milk, Apple 65.00
Pitcher, Red Apple, Iowa Falls, Iowa 28.00
Pitcher, Rooster, No.15 .... 40.00
Pitcher, Rooster, No.16 .... 50.00 To 60.00
Pitcher, Starflower, No.15 .... 30.00
Pitcher, Starflower, No.17 .... 55.00
Pitcher, Tulip, Stylized 65.00
Plate, Green Leaves, 8 In. 15.00
Salad Set, Bleeding Heart 175.00
Salt & Pepper, Apple .... 110.00 To 117.50
Salt & Pepper, Starflower, Advertising 85.00
Saltshaker, Apple, Hourglass 45.00
Saltshaker, Beaded Grape 15.00
Sugar, Apple 65.00

WAVE CREST WARE   Wave Crest glass is a white glassware manufactured by the Pairpoint Manufacturing Company of New Bedford, Massachusetts, and some French factories. It was decorated by the C. F. Monroe Company of Meriden, Connecticut. The glass was painted in pastel colors and decorated with flowers. The name "Wave Crest" was used after 1898.

WAVE CREST, Biscuit Jar, Painted Flowers, Silver Plated Fittings, 7 In. 650.00
Biscuit Jar, Pink & Coral Flowers, Cream Ground 325.00
Biscuit Jar, Pink Panels, Blue Floral & Leaf Transfer 215.00
Biscuit Jar, Yellow, Rose–Pink Dogwood, Green Leaves, 6 In. 350.00
Bowl, Porringer Style, Swirled, Pansies, Signed, 7 1/2 In. 250.00
Box, Baroque Shell, Pink Clover On Beige, 7 In. 525.00
Box, Baroque Shell, White, Blue, Pink Dogwood Blossom, 7 X 4 In. 510.00
Box, Bishop's Hat, Woman Picking Flowers, Footed 295.00
Box, Blue, Bridge Scene, Brass, Tan Lining, Black Mark, 3 X 2 In. 295.00
Box, Blue, Footed, Signed, 9 1/2 X 6 X 5 1/2 In. 895.00

Box, Collars & Cuffs, Flowers In Hinged Cover, Signed, 7 1/2 In. 1200.00
Box, Collars & Cuffs, Flowers, Gold–Plated Ormolu Mountings 1350.00
Box, Cream, Green, Bridge Scene, Cover, Black Mark, 3 X 2 In. 250.00
Box, Daisy On Cover, Scrolls & Curliques, Dotted Flowers, Square 165.00
Box, Dresser, Shell Design, Flowers, Hinged Lid, Signed, 4 In. 125.00
Box, Dresser, Violets, Gilded Mounts, Signed 100.00
Box, Embossed Design, Pink Flowers, Cupid Feet, 6 1/2 X 7 In. 1400.00
Box, Embossed White Panel, Hand Painted Flowers, Marked, 6 In. 1100.00
Box, Enameled Flower, Blue Ground, Lined, 3 X 2 1/2 In. 185.00
Box, Hinged Cover, Double Shell, Florals, White Dots, 3 In. 235.00
Box, Hinged Cover, Egg Crate, Beading, Flowers, Marked, 6 1/2 In. 500.00
Box, Hinged Cover, Jewelry, Puffy Egg Crate, Lined, 5 1/2 In. 395.00
Box, Hinged Cover, Rococo, Cherubs, Flowers, 5 1/2 X 4 In. 395.00
Box, Hinged Cover, Shell Design, 3 In. 185.00
Box, Jewel, Royal Blue, Yellow Roses, Aqua Leaves, 6 X 9 In. 1800.00
Box, Jewelry, Blue Flowers, White Dotting On Cover, 4 In. 495.00
Box, Pink, Blue, Green, Rust Florals, Lining, Black Mark, 3 X 3 In. 300.00
Box, Puffy, Cover, Hand Painted Mums, Red Banner, 6 1/2 In. 525.00
Box, Trees, Road & Lake, Signed, 4 In. 225.00
Box, Trinket, Floral, Scallop Shell Cover, Brass, 4 X 2 3/4 In. 138.00
Box, White, Forest Scene, Cover, Black Mark, 3 X 2 In. 245.00
Box, Words Collars & Cuffs, Puffy, 6 X 7 In. 675.00
Cigar Jar, Blue Florals, White Dotting 325.00
Cookie Jar, Petticoat Pattern, 8 1/2 In. 495.00
Cracker Jar, Blue Flower, Silver Plate Fittings 275.00
Cracker Jar, Ferns, Yellow, Silver Plated Cover & Bail 200.00
Cracker Jar, Pink Flowers Front & Back, Silver–Plated Frame 225.00
Cracker Jar, Swelling Shoulders, Carnations, Enameled Dots 175.00
Dish, Dresser, Gilded Rim, Swirl Ribbing, Flowers, 4 1/2 In. 115.00
Dish, Dresser, Ormolu Engraved Rim, Forget-Me-Nots, 4 1/4 In. 110.00
Dish, Dresser, Swirled Ribbing, Leaves, Flowers, Marked, 4 In. 110.00
Dish, Porringer Shape, Swirled, Floral, Signed, 3 1/4 In. 130.00
Dish, Puffed Sides, Flowers In Medallions, Brass Handles, 5 In. 100.00
Ewer, Buffalo Bill Cody Transfer, 14 In., Pair 395.00
Ewer, Pink Outlined Roses, Daisies, Brass Base, Handle & Spout 395.00
Fernery, Apple Blossoms, White Raised Dots, Pink, 4 X 8 In. 125.00
Fernery, Blue Floral, Black Mark, 7 X 7 In. 225.00
Fernery, Cream, Pink, Green, Daisies, Leaves, 7 X 4 In. 375.00
Fernery, Cream, Yellow, Blue Daisies, Leaves, Red Mark, 3 X 6 In. 395.00
Flower Form, White, Cream, Brown Leaves, Black Mark, 7 In. 475.00
Hair Receiver, Brass Lid, Floral Base, Black Mark, 5 3/4 In. 235.00
Hair Receiver, Florals, Blown-Out Design 195.00
Hair Receiver, Flowers, Brass Cover, Black Mark, 5 3/4 In. 215.00
Hair Receiver, Ormolu Collar, Floral & Raised Scrolls 75.00
Holder, Comb & Brush, Pink Flowers, Blue Edges 1000.00
Humidor, Cigar .... 500.00 To 650.00
Humidor, Cigarette 495.00
Humidor, Tobacco, Egg Crate, Yellow Daisies On Blue, 4 X 5 In. 425.00
Jardiniere, Band of Cherubs, Roses, White Dotting, Signed, 8 In. 450.00
Jardiniere, Flowers, Cupid Feet, Pink Ground, 8 1/2 In. 700.00
Mustard, Floral Design, 3 1/2 In. 295.00
Paperweight, Cream, Blue Floral Enamel Dots 375.00
Perfume Bottle, Pink To Deep Rose Open Roses, Egg Shape 265.00
Perfume Bottle, Square, Hand Painted Design 395.00
Perfume Bottle, Winged Cherub, Ribbons, Butterfly 345.00
Pomade Jar, Cover, Florals, White Dotting 375.00
Powder Box, Attached Swivel Mirror, Beveled Glass 495.00
Powder Box, Raised Flowers On Hinged Lid, Brass Rim, 4 1/2 In. 195.00
Salt & Pepper, Barrel Shape, Floral 40.00
Salt & Pepper, Tulip .... 45.00 To 75.00
Salt & Pepper, Tulip, Yellow Floral Design 95.00
Saltshaker, Helmschmied Swirl, Hand Painted, Pewter Top 175.00
Sugar Shaker, Blue Forget-Me-Nots, Silver Plated Fittings 125.00
Syrup, Swirl, Hand Painted Florals, 4 In. 285.00

Toothpick, Cat Design, Wreath of Florals & Leaves, Dotted Rim 245.00
Tray, Jewel, White, Blue, Pink Flower, Green Leaves, 3 X 3 In. 225.00
Tray, Pin, Square Puffy, Lavender Floral, 3 1/4 In. 95.00
Tray, Pin, Swirled, Pink Flowers, White Ground, Marked, 4 1/4 In. 85.00
Urn, Boy & Girl Playing, Melon Ribbed, Ornolu Spout, 17 In., Pair 395.00
Vase, Embossed Design, Enameled Flowers, Green Ground, 17 In. 1900.00
Vase, Enameled Flowers & Leaves, Pink Ground, Marked, 9 In. 425.00
Vase, Painted Flowers, Brass Holder, Marked, 11 In. 425.00
Vase, Petaled Chrysanthemum, Rust Ground, 12 In. 985.00
Vase, Poppies, Ornate Handles, Dolphin Feet, Marked, 14 1/2 In. 750.00
Vase, Wild Roses, Brass Plated Metal Stand, 6 3/8 In. 150.00

Weapons are listed here except those in their own categories. See also
Gun, Rifle, Sword, etc.

WEAPON, Spear, Mesopotamian Area, Luristan Bronze, 1200–800 B.C., 5 1/4 In. 85.00
Spear, Mesopotamian Area, Luristan Bronze, 5 5/8 In. 42.00

The earliest American weather vanes were used in seventeenth–
century Boston. The direction of the wind was an indication of
coming weather, important to the seafaring and farming
communities. By the mid–ninteenth century, commercial weather
vanes were made of metal. Today's collectors often consider weather
vanes to be examples of folk art, even though they may not have
been handmade.

WEATHER VANE, Angel Gabriel, Painted, Carved Pine & Copper, 13 X 22 In. 6325.00
Arrow & Windmill, Painted Wood, 20th Century, American, 37 In. 250.00
Arrow, Copper, Worn Gilding, 26 In. 450.00
Arrow, Pennsylvania, 5 Ft. 3500.00
Bannerette, Gilded Sheet Copper, C.1880, 10 X 18 In. 1430.00
Black Duck, Flying, Crowell 4125.00
Bull, Full-Bodied, Standing, Copper, 19th Century, 18 1/2 In. 750.00
Center Spindle, Directional Arrow, Wooden, 39 1/2 In. 150.00
Crowing Rooster, Arrow & Directionals, Sheet Iron, 22 In. 100.00
Dove, Full-Bodied, Raised Wings, Molded Zinc, 14 1/2 In. 1320.00
Eagle, Copper, 43-In.Wingspread, Late 19th Century 100.00
Eagle, Full-Bodied, On Ball, Copper, C.1870, 15 1/2 In. 350.00
Eagle, Raised Wings, Cast Head, Talons On Ball, Copper, 18 In. 1700.00
Eagle, Standing, On Large V, 15-In.Wingspan 1850.00
Fish, Wood & Copper 250.00
Goose, Full-Bodied, Crowell 6000.00
Hen, Wooden, Tin Wings, On Stand 250.00
Horse & Rider, Zinc, Traces of Gilding 5000.00
Horse, Jumping Through Hoop, Full-Bodied, Copper, 18 X 28 In. 2750.00
Horse, Running, Copper, Mid–19th Century, 29 1/2 In. 775.00
Horse, Running, Full-Bodied, Zinc Head, Molded Copper, 17 In. 1300.00
Horse, Running, Gilded, Yellow Paint, Copper, 74 In. 3000.00
Horse, Running, On Banner Dated 1901, Sheet Iron, 42 In. 650.00
Horse, Running, Open Mouth, Spelter, Tubular Base, 26 X 45 In. 2500.00
Horse, Sheet Metal Silhouette, White Paint, 56 In. 25.00
Horse, Standing, Gilded Copper, Zinc, Gilded, 14 In. 3410.00
Locomotive & Tender, Billowing Smoke, Sheet Iron, 22 In. 650.00
Rooster, Copper, 26 1/2 X 29 In. 5500.00
Rooster, Sheet Iron, On Rectangular Vase, C.1920, 20 X 23 In. 595.00
Rooster, Standing On Arrow, Copper, 19th Century, 25 In. 1100.00
Rooster, Zinc & Copper, J.Howard & Co., 29 X 25 In. 7425.00
Silhouette of Cannon On Mount, Balls, Sheet Copper, 24 In. 750.00
Sperm Whale, Copper, Brass Wind Letters, 3 Ft. 40.00

Webb glass was made by Thomas Webb & Sons of Stourbridge,
England. Many types of art and cameo glass were made by them
during the Victorian era. The factory is still producing glass. Webb
Burmese and Webb Peachblow are special colored glasswares of the
Victorian period.

WEBB BURMESE, Bowl, Floral Design, Applied Glass At Rim, Marked, 6 1/4 In. 1100.00

Bowl, Fluted Top, Ivy Leaves On Vine, 2 3/4 X 3 3/4 In. 325.00
Bowl, Piecrust Edge, Signed, 2 1/4 X 2 3/4 In. 210.00
Creamer, Fluted, Flower, Green Leaves, 2 5/8 In. 550.00
Fairy Lamp, Domed Shade, Ruffled Base, Clarke Cup, 5 5/8 In. 550.00
Fairy Lamp, Ribbed Clarke Base, 4 3/4 X 3 3/4 In. 210.00
Fairy Lamp, Squared Base, Clarke Insert & Cup, 6 1/8 In. 550.00
Fairy Lamp, Yellow Applied Leaf Holds Menu Card, 5 1/2 In. 475.00
Jam Jar, Silver Plated Frame, Lid & Spoon, 5 X 5 3/4 In. 265.00
Jar, Sweetmeat, Berries, Silver Plated Fittings, 3 1/2 In. 695.00
Perfume Bottle, Gold Leaves & Berries, Silver Cap, 3 1/2 In. 695.00
Perfume Bottle, Purple Flowers, Sterling Top, 3 1/2 In. 690.00
Perfume Bottle, Silver Cap, Gold Branches, Berries, 4 3/4 In. 695.00
Rose Bowl, 5–Petal Flowers, 8–Crimp Top, 2 7/8 X 3 In. 375.00
Rose Bowl, 5–Petal Lavender Flower, 3 X 3 In. 325.00
Rose Bowl, Flowers, Leaves, 8–Crimp, 2 3/8 In. 300.00
Sugar & Creamer, 6–Sided Tops, Grapes, Leaves, Plated Holder 795.00
Sugar & Creamer, Berries, Leaves, Silver Plated Holder 950.00
Toothpick, 5–Petal Flower, 6–Sided Collared Top, 2 5/8 In. 275.00
Vase, 4–Petal Top, Coral Buds, Green Leaves, 4 1/4 X 2 1/2 In. 365.00
Vase, 5–Petal Flower Design, Yellow Handles, Signed, 5 In. 675.00
Vase, 6–Sided Top, Grapes & Leaves, 3 1/2 X 3 5/8 In. 335.00
Vase, 6–Sided Top, Lavender Flowers, Leaves, 3 3/4 In. 335.00
Vase, Acorns & Oak Leaves, 4 X 3 1/8 In. 325.00
Vase, Blue & Yellow Flowers, Leaves & Stems, 3 1/4 In. 225.00
Vase, Brown Pine Cones, Hexagon Top, 3 1/4 In. 325.00
Vase, Flared Ruffled Top, Lavender Flowers, Leaves, 4 1/4 In. 325.00
Vase, Flower Petal Top, Red Berries, Leaves, Signed, 3 In. 350.00
Vase, Flower Petal Top, Red Berries, Signed, 2 3/4 In. 410.00
Vase, Fluted Scalloped Top, Ivy Leaves, 4 1/2 In. 325.00
Vase, Fluted, Yellow Feet, 3 1/4 In. 245.00
Vase, Folded Over Star Shaped Top, Signed, 3 3/8 In. 200.00
Vase, Gold Dragons Inside & Out, Flowers, 3 1/2 X 3 In. 295.00
Vase, Green Leaves, Coral Flower Buds,, 8 1/4 In. 695.00
Vase, Hexagon Top, Red Berries, Green Leaves, 3 1/4 In. 325.00
Vase, Melon, Salmon Shaded To Yellow, Ivy Leaves, 3 3/4 In. 395.00
Vase, Mums, Leaves, Bottle Shape, Signed, 10 In. 995.00
Vase, Petal Top, Squatty, Signed, 2 3/4 In. 225.00
Vase, Red Berries, Green Leaves, 3 1/4 In. 325.00
Vase, Ruffled Top, Orange Pods, Green Leaves, 4 In. 230.00
Vase, Ruffled, Floral Design, Paper Label, 4 1/8 In. 325.00
Vase, Star–Shaped Top, Enameled Flowers, 3 3/8 In. 295.00
Vase, Striped, Scalloped Top, 3 1/2 In. 225.00
Vase, Yellow & Rust Mums, Gold Trim, 10 In. 998.00
Vase, Yellow & Rust Mums, Leaves, Bottle Shape, Signed, 10 In. 998.00
WEBB PEACHBLOW, Biscuit Jar, Gold Prunus, Pine Needles, Butterfly, 6 In. 895.00
Dish, Mother–of–Pearl, Diamond–Quilted, 3–Footed, 8 In. 125.00
Dish, Shell Shape, Ruffled, Gold Prunus Blossoms, 7 1/8 In. 295.00
Gold Designs, Flowers, Butterfly, 7 1/2 In. 750.00
Rose Bowl, 8–Crimp Top, Cream Lining, 3 X 3 1/4 In. 225.00
Rose Bowl, Cherub, Signed, 4 1/2 In. 70.00
Rose Bowl, Gold Flowers, 4 3/8 In. 350.00
Sugar & Creamer, Blue Flowers, Gorham Base 485.00
Vase, 2 Birds & Flowers, Encrusted Gold, 6 3/4 X 15 In. 1150.00
Vase, Bottle Shape, Gold Leaves & Flowers, 9 7/8 In. 395.00
Vase, Branches, Gold Prunus Blossoms, Marked, 5 In., Pair 495.00
Vase, Coralene Seaweed, 5 3/4 In. 325.00
Vase, Crystal Flowers & Leaves, Footed, 5 In. 475.00
Vase, Embossed Swirls, Clear Berries, Loop Feet, 5 3/4 In. 550.00
Vase, Enameled Flowers, Blue Interior, Ruffled, 6 In., Pair 220.00
Vase, Enameled Flowers, Yellow Centers, Gold Trim, 5 1/4 In. 175.00
Vase, Gold & Silver Flowers, Gold Bug, 5 1/4 In. 295.00
Vase, Gold Birds & Flowers, Rose Shaded To Pink, 15 X 7 In. 1150.00
Vase, Gold Blossoms & Leaves On Branches, 8 1/2 In. 395.00
Vase, Gold Branches, Prunus Blossoms, Butterfly, 10 1/2 In. 1250.00

Vase, Gold Floral, Butterfly, Rose To Pink, 7 5/8 In. 850.00
Vase, Gold Florals, Bands & Butterfly, 7 1/2 In. 850.00
Vase, Gold Flowers & Leaves, Gold Dragonfly, Signed, 7 In. 650.00
Vase, Gold Flowers, Silver Centers, 4 1/2 In., Pair 450.00
Vase, Gold Leaves, Flower Pods, Dragonfly, 3 In. 230.00
Vase, Gold Leaves, Prunus Blossoms, Marked, 3 1/4 In. 285.00
Vase, Gold Prunus, Bee, Cream Lining, 7 3/4 In. 650.00
Vase, Horizontal Ribbing, White Interior, 8 1/4 In. 145.00
Vase, Silver Flowers, Gold Centers, Leaves, 6 5/8 In. 265.00
WEBB, Bowl, Intaglio Cut Flowers & Branches, Pink, White Lining, 5 3/4 In. 750.00
Bowl, Prunus Design, Cream Lining, 6–Crimp Top, Gold Feet, 4 In. 550.00
Bowl, Quilted Mother–of–Pearl, 6–Crimp, Flower Pontil, 4 7/8 In. 550.00
Bowl, Ruffled Rim, Enameled Flowers, Butterfly, Signed, 3 1/2 In. 300.00
Centerpiece, Blue Overlay, Ruffled, Enameled Floral, 7 X 12 1/2 In. 325.00
Cordial, Engraved Floral Pattern, English, Signed, 8 Piece 480.00
Epergne, Center Trumpet, 3 Hanging Baskets, Cranberry, Vaseline, 21 In. 850.00
Fairy Lamp, Burmese Dome Shade, Clarke Insert, 6 1/8 In. 550.00
Jar, Potpourri, Aqua, Gold Fringe, Brass Bottom, Hinged Lid, 5 1/2 In. 610.00
Jar, Sweetmeat, Herringbone, Mother–of–Pearl, Flowers, Rose To Pink 525.00
Jug, Claret, Tropical Foliage, Silver Plated Flip–Top Lid 185.00
Knob, Walking Stick, Cameo, Black, 2 1/4 In. ....*Illus*   300.00
Loving Cup, 3 Applied Handles, 2 Color Gold, Cameo, 7 1/2 In. 275.00
Perfume Bottle, Lay–Down, Sterling Embossed Top, White Flowers 775.00
Perfume Bottle, Red Shaded To Yellow To Deep Amber, Silver Top, 6 In. 250.00
Perfume Bottle, Russet & Green Leaves, Gold Leaves Allover, 4 In. 210.00
Pitcher, Bamboo Plant In Bloom, Loop Handles, Ivory, Signed, 6 1/2 In. 1475.00
Plate, Diamond–Quilted, Ruffled, Butterscotch, 6 1/2 In. 75.00
Rose Bowl, Amberina, Mother–of–Pearl, Diamond–Quilted, 7 1/4 In. 1200.00
Salt, Butterfly, Signed 45.00
Shade, Bees, Floral, Cranberry, Intaglio, Brass Holder 850.00
Sugar Shaker, Herringbone, Pink Mother–of–Pearl, Signed 270.00
Tumbler, Butterflies, Floral Cover, Frosted Over Clear 350.00
Vase, 3–Color, Foliated Branches, Blossoms, Converted Into Lamp, 12 In. 1250.00
Vase, Baluster Form, Butterflies & Flowers, 9 In., Pair 325.00
Vase, Cameo, Blue, Opalescent White, 11 3/4 In. ....*Illus*   3500.00
Vase, Cameo, Floral Branch, Red, Baluster, 9 1/4 In. ....*Illus*   1700.00
Vase, Cameo, Floral, Rigaree Handle, Marked, 6 1/2 In. 660.00
Vase, Cameo, Pinwheel, Handles, Woodall, 5 1/2 In. ....*Illus*   6000.00
Vase, Coin Spot, Signed, Amber, 7 1/2 X 8 In. 35.00
Vase, Diamond–Quilted, Satin Glass, Ruffled Top, Signed, 6 In. 310.00
Vase, Engraved 3 Japanese Scenes, Waisted Form, C.1880, 7 5/8 In. 1650.00
Vase, Flower Petal Top, Simulated Ivory, Leaves, Signed, 2 3/4 In. 650.00
Vase, Gold Flowers & Butterfly, Pink Lining, 5 In. 575.00
Vase, Gold Hydrangea Blossoms, Gold Leaves, Green, 4 1/2 In. 335.00
Vase, Gold Prunus Blossoms, Gold Butterfly, White Inside, 6 1/2 In. 325.00
Vase, Gold Prunus Design, Sprays of Blossoms, Gold Bee, 8 1/4 In. 295.00
Vase, Gold Prunus, Butterfly In Flight, Blue Ground, 7 3/4 In., Pair 425.00
Vase, Gourd Shape, Stick, Gold Flowers, Shaded Brown Ground, 6 In. 175.00
Vase, Gourd Shape, White Floral, Blue Ground, 10 1/2 In. 2850.00
Vase, Ivory, Carved Leaves, Brown Stain, 8–Crimp Top, 5 In. 850.00
Vase, Lavender Body, Internal Multicolors & Aventurine, 10 1/2 In. 475.00
Vase, Patchwork Design, Bottle Shape, Signed, 9 1/2 In. 225.00
Vase, Raindrop Pattern, Morning Glories, Gold Vines, Ruffled, 10 In. 475.00
Vase, Ruffled Leaves, Cream Lining, Coral, 11 7/8 In. 395.00
Vase, Simulated Ivory, Birds & Flowers, Scalloped, Signed, 5 1/4 In. 850.00
Vase, Simulated Ivory, Flower Petal Top, Signed, 2 3/4 X 3 1/4 In. 650.00
Vase, Stick, Gold Prunus & Butterfly, Cream Lining, 7 1/8 In. 350.00
Vase, Teal Green To Salmon, Gold Branches, Dimpled, 10 7/8 In. 495.00
Vase, Urn Type, Greek, Iridescent, Ribbed, Applied Handles, 7 In. 1500.00
Vase, White Flowers, Black & Gold Leaves, Red Ground, 7 1/2 In. 155.00
Vase, White On Citron, Cameo, Signed, 6 In. 1750.00
Vase, White On Red, Signed, 6 In. 1250.00
Wine, Alexandrite Honeycomb, Stem, 4 1/2 In. 750.00

WEDGWOOD

Josiah Wedgwood, although considered a cripple by his brother and forbidden to work at the family business, founded one of the world's most successful potteries. The pottery was founded in England in 1759. A large variety of wares has been made, including the well–known jasperware, basalt, creamware, and even a limited amount of porcelain. There are two kinds of jasperware. One is made from two colors of clay, the other is made from one color clay with a color dip to create the contrast in design. The firm is still in business.

WEDGWOOD, Ashtray Set, Jasperware, Classical Figures, Oak Leaf, Acorns, 4 Pc.	55.00
Ashtray, Jasperware, Apollo, Grapes & Vine, Black	15.00
Ashtray, Jasperware, Pegasus & Maidens, Blue–Gray	16.00
Ashtray, Scenic, Dow Library, Columbia University	45.00
Basket, Twig, Queenswear, 3 Letter Mark, 9 X 14 In.	90.00
Biscuit Barrel, Black & White, 1860, 8 1/2 In.	590.00
Biscuit Barrel, Lilac, C.1860, 8 1/2 In.	590.00
Biscuit Jar, Allegory To Love	185.00
Biscuit Jar, Dark & Light, Silver Plated Mountings, Marked, 1910	375.00
Biscuit Jar, Grecian Figures, Trees, Blue & White, Plated Frame	475.00
Biscuit Jar, Jasperware, Classical Women, Cupids, Tricolor, 6 In.	595.00
Biscuit Jar, Jasperware, Classical, Cherubs, Sage Green, 6 In.	175.00
Biscuit Jar, Jasperware, Floral Garlands, Tricolor, 6 5/8 In.	895.00
Biscuit Jar, Jasperware, Lavender Bands, Silver Plate Fittings	1000.00
Biscuit Jar, Jasperware, Women, Cupid, Acorn Finial, Tricolor, 6 In.	695.00
Biscuit Jar, Raised Gold Blackberries, Marked, 6 3/8 In.	135.00
Biscuit Jar, Yellow Bands Top & Bottom, White Figures, 9 1/2 In.	810.00
Bowl, Basalt, Herringbone & Bands, 11 X 4 1/2 In.	450.00
Bowl, Blue Lining, Gold Dragons Inside & Out, Marked, 8 1/2 In.	450.00
Bowl, Butterfly Luster, Green, Gold & Blue Interior, Signed, 8 In.	450.00
Bowl, Cover, Bramble, Pink, Handles, 5 In.	65.00
Bowl, Dragon Luster, 13 In. ....750.00 To 1100.00
Bowl, Dragon Luster, Oriental Design, Marked, 2 1/2 In.	175.00
Bowl, Fairyland Luster, Kang Hsi, Dragon, 3 1/2 X 8 1/2 In.	525.00
Bowl, Fairyland Luster, Leapfrogging Elves, 2 X 4 In.	495.00
Bowl, Fairyland Luster, Leapfrogging Elves, 3 1/8 X 4 3/4 In.	695.00
Bowl, Fairyland Luster, Leapfrogging Elves, Pedestal, 3 X 5 In.	695.00
Bowl, Fairyland Luster, Moorish Exterior, 4 X 8 1/2 In.	2700.00
Bowl, Fairyland Luster, Scene, Orange Ground, Inverted Foot, 10 In.	1600.00
Bowl, Fairyland Luster, Thumbelina & Frogs, Gold Trim, 6 3/8 In.	950.00
Bowl, Flying Hummingbirds, Red–Orange Inside, Gold Trim, 5 In.	245.00
Bowl, Garden of Paradise, 8 In.	2000.00
Bowl, Hummingbird Luster, 5 In.	150.00
Bowl, Hummingbird Luster, Flame Interior, Gold Outlined, 10 In.	475.00
Bowl, Jasperware, Dancing Figures, Grape Leaf Swag, 4 1/2 In.	65.00
Bowl, Jasperware, Dancing Hour, White On Black	450.00
Bowl, Vegetable, Kynance, Oval, 10 In.	18.00
Box, Cover, Black Basalt, Gilt Design, C.1880, 7 7/8 In.	550.00
Box, Cover, Dragon Luster, Marked, Rectangular, 2 5/8 X 4 X 7 In.	395.00
Box, Cover, Jasperware, Apollo, Chariot, Heart Shape, 3 X 2 In.	48.00
Box, Cover, Jasperware, Classical Figure, Berry & Laurel Rim, 4 In.	48.00
Box, Dragon Luster, Cover, Widow Finial, Marked, 5 1/4 X 5 5/8 In.	395.00
Bust, Black Basalt, Horace, Dated 1877, 14 3/4 In.	935.00
Bust, Black Basalt, Marcus Aurelius, 1774–80, 15 1/2 In. ....Illus	3575.00
Bust, Black Basalt, Prior, 11 1/2 In.	750.00
Bust, Black Basalt, Thomas Moore, Geoffry Chaucer, 12 7/8 In., Pr.	1045.00
Bust, Bobby Burden, C.1860, 8 3/4 In.	725.00
Butter, Cover, Underplate, Jasperware, Blue & White, 4 In.	225.00
Cache Pot, Lion Mask Design, Band of Roses, C.1810, 3 1/2 X 4 In.	450.00
Cheese Dish, Cover, Jasperware, Blue, C.1860, 11 1/8 In.	750.00
Chocolate Set, Gargoyles, White, Cobalt Blue Bands, 7 Piece	245.00
Compote, Edme, Ramshead Handles, Cover, Footed	75.00
Cracker Jar, Green, White Figures, Silver Base, Bail & Handle	110.00
Cream Cooler, Cover & Ladle, Endsleigh Dairy, C.1822, 15 In.	660.00
Creamer, Apollo & Flora Medallions, Handle, C.1790, 2 1/2 In.	650.00

Wedgwood, Urn, Jasperware, Cover, Green, Lavender, 14 In., Pair

Wedgwood, Bust, Black Basalt, Marcus Aurelius, 1774–80, 15 1/2 In.

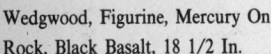

Wedgwood, Figurine, Mercury On Rock, Black Basalt, 18 1/2 In.

Creamer, Jasperware, Classical Scene	40.00
Cup & Saucer, Harvard Tercentenary, 1636–1936, Demitasse	20.00
Dinner Service, St.Austell Pattern, 97 Piece	2400.00
Dish, Pin, Blue, Cover	15.00
Dish, Potpourri, Black Basalt, Figures, Trees, 12 Holes In Lid, 1810	495.00
Figurine, Elephant, Glass Eyes, Jasper Tusks, C.1919, 3 1/2 In.	425.00
Figurine, Mercury On Rock, Black Basalt, 18 1/2 In. ....*Illus*	495.00
Flowerpot, Lilac & White	40.00
Flowerpot, Underplate, Tracery & Floral, C.1795, 3 X 3 7/8 In.	595.00
Hair Receiver, Classical Figures, Hearts, White, Marked, 3 1/2 In.	145.00
Hair Receiver, Jasperware, Heart Shape, Blue	50.00
Hair Receiver, Jasperware, Lacy Hearts, Flowers, Marked, 3 1/4 In.	145.00
Jam Jar, Ladies Around Sides, Silver Plated Fittings, 5 In.	110.00
Jam Jar, White Figures, Silver Plated Cover, 5 1/4 In.	118.00
Jar, Cover, Figures, Lacy Design, Blue & White, Marked, 3 In.	95.00
Jar, Sweetmeat, Classical Ladies, Silver Plated Fittings, Green	165.00
Jardiniere, Applied Classical Design, Marked, 4 3/8 In.	40.00
Jardiniere, Jasperware, 5 Mythological Medallions, 4 1/4 In.	55.00
Jardiniere, Jasperware, Washington, Lafayette, Franklin, 6 In.	295.00
Jug, Crimson, 8 In.	495.00
Melba Cup, Fairyland Luster, Leapfrogging Elves, 3 X 4 1/4 In.	750.00
Mug, Child's, Peter Rabbit	12.50
Mug, Ladies & Cupid, Medallion of Soldiers, Silver Rim, 5 In.	125.00
Pendant, Heart, Jasperware, 14K Gold Chain	28.00
Pitcher, Bird & Fan, Majolica, Large	485.00
Pitcher, Cobalt Blue Ships & Castles, White Ground, 6 1/2 In.	165.00
Pitcher, Gothic Figures, Brown, Blue Lining, 7 1/2 In.	125.00
Pitcher, Jasperware, Classical Scene, 4 1/2 In.	80.00
Pitcher, Jasperware, Classical Women, Dark Blue, 5 1/8 In.	135.00
Pitcher, Jasperware, Classical Women, Dark Blue, Tankard, 4 In.	110.00
Pitcher, Jasperware, Rope Handle, Dark Blue & White, 4 In.	55.00
Pitcher, Jasperware, White Figures, Blue, 6 In.	95.00

Pitcher, Jasperware, Yellow & White, Rope Handle, 4 In.	325.00
Pitcher, Ladies & Cherubs, Blue & White, Marked, 5 1/2 In.	165.00
Pitcher, Medallions, Franklin & Hamilton, Olive Green, 7 1/2 In.	350.00
Pitcher, Milk, Cauliflower, Marked	125.00
Pitcher, Pearlware, Mid–Eastern Scene, Guards, Marked, 5 1/2 In.	275.00
Pitcher, Tankard Shape, Dark Blue & White, Marked, 5 3/8 In.	95.00
Plaque, Birth & Dipping of Achilles, White On Black, 15 In.	350.00
Plaque, Cherubs, Dog Tree In White Relief, 3 X 2 In.	70.00
Plaque, Cupid, Psyche, White On Green, 8 X 9 In.	300.00
Plaque, Jasperware, Blindman's Bluff, Blue, Flaxman, 7 1/2 X 13 In.	450.00
Plaque, Jasperware, King Tut, Black, 8 X 8 1/2 In.	300.00
Plaque, Jasperware, Tricolor, Classical Women, Signed, 4 X 10 In.	525.00
Plate, Abraham Lincoln, Etruria, Blue, 9 1/4 In.	85.00
Plate, American Independence Victory At Yorktown	40.00
Plate, Annual, 1969	150.00
Plate, Annual, 1971	25.00
Plate, Apollo, 8 In.	35.00
Plate, Bicentennial, American Independence, Victory, Yorktown, Box	40.00
Plate, Capitol, 1907	37.50
Plate, Columbia University Scenes, 1932, 11 In., 12 Piece	375.00
Plate, Delaware Water Gap, 8 1/2 In.	33.00
Plate, Fallowdeer, Copper Luster, 9 In.	75.00
Plate, Hermitage, Nashville	20.00
Plate, Ivanhoe, Rebecca Repelling Templar, Marked, 10 1/4 In.	65.00
Plate, Lady With Hat, 9 3/4 In.	90.00
Plate, Morning Glory, 6 1/2 In.	8.50
Plate, Old Windmill, Florals On Rim, Mulberry, 1940, 10 In.	40.00
Plate, Pimpernel, Signed, 9 In.	10.00
Plate, Trophy, Commemorating American Bicentennial, 5 Colors	550.00
Plate, Valentine, 1982	20.00
Plate, Venice Scene, Blue & White, C.1885, 9 In.	45.00
Plate, West Point Academy, 10 1/2 In.	25.00
Plate, Windmill, Nantucket Island, Mauve, 10 In.	35.00
Plate, Yale University, Scenic, 10 In.	18.00
Platter, Pink Devonshire Sprays, Buff, Incised, 12 X 15 1/2 In.	85.00
Platter, Polychromed Cornucopia Shapes, Fruit, Flowers, 13 In.	65.00
Powder Box, Light Blue, Elizabeth Arden Puff, 3 1/2 In.	60.00
Punch Bowl, Commemorative, Harvard Tercentenary, 12 In.	275.00
Ring Tree, Jasperware, Classical, Dark Blue, 2 3/4 X 3 1/8 In.	165.00
Ring Tree, Jasperware, White Figures, Deep Blue, 2 2/3 In.	115.00
Salad Bowl, Jasperware, Green & White, Silver Plated Rim, 8 In.	125.00
Smoke Set, Jasperware, Green, Jar, Lighter, 3 Ashtrays	55.00
Stickpin Holder, Blue Forget–Me–Nots	75.00
Sugar & Creamer, Figures, Blue & White, Marked, 6 1/2 In.	225.00
Syrup, Hinged Pewter Top, Figures, Grapes, Blue & White, 5 1/4 In.	145.00
Syrup, Ladies, Cupid At Sides, Pewter Hinged Lid, 5 1/2 In.	135.00
Tea Set, Basalt, 3 Piece	150.00
Tea Set, Jasperware, Medium Blue, 1930s, 3 Piece	325.00
Tea Set, Jasperware, White On Royal Blue, 3 Piece	275.00
Tea Set, Personages Pattern, 35 Piece	100.00
Tea Set, White On Terra–Cotta, 4 Piece	350.00
Teapot, Black Basalt, 7 In.	20.00
Teapot, Black Basalt, Colored Enameled Flowers, 4 1/2 X 6 In.	335.00
Teapot, Black Basalt, Colored Enameled Flowers, Gold Trim, Marked	325.00
Teapot, Figural, Mr.Pickwick	55.00
Teapot, Jasperware, Classical Scenes, 4 X 8 In.	110.00
Teapot, Jasperware, Sage Green & White, Ladies, 4 1/4 X 4 3/4 In.	145.00
Teapot, Laurel	175.00
Tile, 1895	55.00
Tile, 1911	45.00
Tile, Hunting Dog Scene, Marked	100.00
Urn, Black Basalt, Bronze & Gold Finish, Relief Children, 16 In.	1540.00
Urn, Cover, Jasperware, Mythological, Tricolor, 14 In., Pair	1300.00
Urn, Cover, Jasperware, White Figurine, Lavender, 9 1/4 In.	1190.00

Urn, Jasperware, Apollo, 9 Muses, White On Lilac, 9 In. 350.00
Urn, Jasperware, Cover, Green, Lavender, 14 In., Pair ....*Illus* 1300.00
Urn, Jasperware, Dancing Maidens, Satyr Mask Handles, 8 In. 325.00
Vase, Black Basalt, Anthemia & Grape Border, Swags, 10 5/8 In. 675.00
Vase, Black Basalt, Cover, Satyr's Mask, 11 5/8 In. ....*Illus* 495.00
Vase, Black Basalt, Encaustic, Orange & White, 9 In. ....*Illus* 495.00
Vase, Blue Luster, Dragon & Cricket, 5 1/4 In. 305.00
Vase, Bud, Jasperware, Cupids, Light Blue, Pear Shape, 5 1/4 In. 30.00
Vase, Butterfly Luster, Gold Outlining, Gold Trim, 8 3/8 In. 375.00
Vase, Candlemas Scene, 9 In. 1200.00
Vase, Cover, Black Basalt, Fluted Neck & Foot, 13 7/8 In. 2475.00
Vase, Cover, Black Basalt, Satyr's Mask, Snake Handles, 14 1/8 In. 2750.00
Vase, Cover, Sacrifice Scene, Laurel Branches, Tricolor, 11 3/4 In. 665.00
Vase, Cover, Variegated, Creamware Body, Marked, 15 3/4 In. 6650.00
Vase, Cylinder, White Figures Around Sides, Marked, 3 In. 85.00
Vase, Dragon Luster, Blue Outside, Maroon & Gold Inside, 8 3/4 In. 475.00
Vase, Dragon Luster, Mother-of-Pearl Interior, 8 3/4 In. 475.00
Vase, Fairyland Luster, Goblins, Fairies, Orange Wings, 8 1/2 In. 1600.00
Vase, Flowers Over Band of Carved Leaves, Gold Trim, 12 1/2 In. 910.00
Vase, Frieze of Pelus & Thetis, Blue & White, 10 In. 1450.00
Vase, Jasperware, Black & White, Woman Playing Lyre, 6 1/2 In. 175.00
Vase, Jasperware, Dark Blue, Ram's Heads, Flowers, 6 3/4 In. 150.00
Vase, Jasperware, Portland, Black & White, 10 3/4 In. ....*Illus* 1430.00
Vase, White Pegasus & Ladies, Dark Green, 4 In. 65.00

LOUWELSA
WELLER
Weller pottery was first made in 1873 in Fultonham, Ohio. The firm moved to Zanesville, Ohio, in 1882. Art wares were first made in 1893. Hundreds of lines of pottery were made, including Louwelsa, Eocean, Dickens, and Sicardo, before the pottery closed in 1948.

WELLER, Basket, Cameo, Blue, 7 1/2 In. .... 30.00 To 45.00
Basket, Cameo, Green, Footed, 7 1/2 In. 30.00
Basket, Cameo, Peach, 7 1/2 In. 22.00
Basket, Florenzo, Inverted Umbrella Shape, Handles, 7 In. 55.00
Basket, Hanging, Cameo, Blue, White 25.00
Basket, Malvern, 8 X 6 In. 48.00
Bookends, Roma, Flower Basket 250.00
Bowl, Atlas, Blue, 4 In. 32.00
Bowl, Blossom, Green, 8 In. 20.00
Bowl, Blue Drapery, 5 1/2 X 3 In. 35.00
Bowl, Bouquet, Green, 3-Footed 25.00
Bowl, Burntwood, Flared, 4 3/4 X 3 3/4 In. 26.00
Bowl, Claywood, Fish, 3 3/8 X 2 1/4 In. 32.00

Wedgwood, Vases

Bowl, Fruitone, Green, Brown, 5 3/4 X 2 7/8 In. 27.00
Bowl, Luster, Blue, 8 X 2 1/4 In. 55.00
Bowl, Luster, Cinnamon, 7 X 3 In. 58.00
Bowl, Monochrome, Blue, 10 In. 22.00
Bowl, Orris, Green, 4–Footed, 7 X 3 In. 42.00
Bowl, Orris, Green, 6 X 2 1/2 In. 30.00
Bowl, Panella, Blue, 12 3/8 X 3 In. 34.00
Bowl, Roma, 5 In. 22.00
Bowl, Sabrinian, Oval, Paper Label, Marked, 6 X 8 In. 60.00
Bowl, Wild Rose, Triangular, Green, 3 X 7 In. 30.00
Bowl, Woodcraft, 8 1/4 In. 48.00
Candleholder, Woodcraft, 1928 .... 75.00
Candlestick, Bonito, 1 1/2 In., Pair 53.00
Candlestick, Cameo, Creamware, Handle, 5 X 7 In. 80.00
Candlestick, Floral, Tan, 5 3/8 X 3 In., Pair 22.00
Candlestick, Lavonia, Bulbous, 4 1/2 In., Pair 100.00
Candlestick, Noval, 9 1/2 In. 52.00
Candlestick, Wild Rose, Green, Pair 25.00
Casserole, Cover, Pierre, Turquoise, 7 1/2 In. 20.00
Clock, Louwelsa, 12 In. 900.00
Console Set, Ivoris, 7–In.Double Candlesticks, 14–In.Bowl, 3 Piece 48.00
Console, Candis, Green, 13 In. 25.00
Console, Coppertone, Lily Pad & Frog On Handle, 10 1/2 In. 170.00
Console, Floral, Tan, 10 1/2 X 6 X 5 In. 30.00
Cornucopia, Blossom, Blue, 8 1/2 In. 28.00
Cornucopia, Lido, Turquoise, Footed, 7 1/4 X 4 3/4 In., Pair 50.00
Creamer, Mammy .... 195.00 To 205.00
Cup & Saucer, Zona, Red Apple, Ivory Ground 9.50
Dachshund, Small 75.00
Dish, Child's, Feeding, Chickens 60.00
Dish, Child's, Feeding, Raised Bunny, Signed, 7 In. 58.00
Ewer, Dickens Ware, Ducks, 2nd Line 425.00
Ewer, Louwelsa, Carnations, 3 Spouts, 4 X 5 1/4 In. 155.00
Ewer, Louwelsa, Squat Base, 3 Spouts, 4 X 5 1/4 In. 155.00
Figurine, Black Crow, Life Size 350.00
Figurine, Frog, Coppertone, 2 In. 75.00
Figurine, Frog, Coppertone, 4 1/2 X 5 1/2 In. 135.00
Figurine, Kingfisher, 9 In. 150.00
Figurine, Pup, Bug–Eyed, Hand Painted, White With Black, Pink, 4 In. 260.00
Figurine, Squirrel, Woodcraft, Sitting On Bowl Edge, 6 In. 135.00
Flagon, Louwelsa, Corn Design, 17 In. 250.00
Flask, Figural, Eagle, F.O.E. 65.00
Flower Frog, Coppertone, 4 In. ....70.00 To 125.00
Flower Frog, Double Geese 225.00
Flower Frog, Green, 8 Holes, High Gloss 6.50
Flower Frog, Kingfisher ....225.00 To 265.00
Flower Frog, Muskota, Crab 42.00
Flower Frog, Salamander 45.00
Flower Frog, Scrub Woman 98.00
Flower Pot, Claywood, 3 In. 15.00
Jardiniere, Blue Ware, 3–Footed, 8 1/2 X 7 In. .... 140.00 To 150.00
Jardiniere, Burntwood, Winged Lions, Stylized Waves, 7 1/2 In. 110.00
Jardiniere, Cameo, Blue, White, 9 1/2 In. 20.00
Jardiniere, Drapery, Blue 125.00
Jardiniere, Forest, 9 X 11 In. 125.00
Jardiniere, Ivory, 9 1/2 X 8 In. 50.00
Jardiniere, Ivory, Pedestal, 13 X 10 In. 300.00
Jardiniere, Ivory, Women, Stylized Trees, C.1915, 35 In., Pair 2900.00
Jardiniere, Jewell, Etna–Gray, Maroon Jewels 70.00
Jardiniere, Louwelsa, Brown, Poppies, 8 In. 275.00
Jardiniere, MiFlo, Ivory, 4 X 6 1/2 In. 26.00
Jardiniere, Roma, Large ....95.00 To 98.00
Jardiniere, Rosemont, Black, Octagonal, 4 1/2 X 5 3/4 In. 150.00
Jug, Barcelona, Bright Colors, Marked, 9 In. 150.00

Jug, Louwelsa, Corn	85.00
Lamp, Dickens Ware I, Black, Pansies, 3-Footed, 8 1/4 In.	350.00
Mixing Bowl, Pierre, Green, 10 1/2 X 5 1/2 In.	30.00
Mug, Dickens Ware, Fish	275.00
Mug, Etna, 6 In.	85.00
Mug, Louwelsa, Blue	550.00
Pedestal, Zona, Brown, High Gloss, 18 3/4 In.	85.00
Pitcher, Kitchen Gem, Half Kiln Mark	27.00
Pitcher, Lido, Yellow, Cream, 6 In.	26.00
Pitcher, Louwelsa, Squat, Flowers	115.00
Pitcher, Silvertone, Lavender & Green, 5 3/4 In.	100.00
Pitcher, Zona, Cobalt Blue, Apple Design	100.00
Pitcher, Zona, Kingfisher, 8 In.	110.00
Pitcher, Zona, Pink, 7 In.	65.00
Planter, Cactus, Duck, Yellow, 5 In.	60.00
Planter, Florenzo, Cream, Square, 5 1/4 In.	18.00
Planter, Lido, Turquoise, 9 1/2 X 3 1/2 In.	25.00
Planter, Roma, Lion Head Corner, Square, 6 1/2 In.	34.00
Planter, Softone, Blue, 10 In.	20.00
Planter, Softone, Yellow, 7 1/2 X 4 1/2 X 3 1/2 In.	20.00
Planter, Woodcraft, Log	30.00
Plaque, Abraham Lincoln, 1904	98.00
Plaque, General Grant, 1904	58.00
Platter, Barcelona, 13 1/2 In.	90.00
Strawberry Pot, Coppertone, 8 1/2 In.	125.00
Strawberry Pot, Greenbriar, Greens & Browns, 8 1/2 In.	125.00
Sugar, Pierre, Beige	20.00
Tankard, Dickens Ware, Deer, Tree, 6 1/2 In.	400.00
Tankard, Etna, 10 In.	200.00
Tankard, Louwelsa, Signed, 18 In.	1000.00
Tankard, Woodcraft, Three Foxes	695.00
Teapot, Forest, High Glaze, Signed	135.00
Tobacco Jar, Dickens Ware, Turk	395.00 To 600.00
Umbrella Stand, 6 Women, Lavender Gowns, Floral, 20 In. ....*Illus*	358.00
Umbrella Stand, Flemish, Brown, 21 1/2 In.	225.00
Umbrella Stand, Flemish, Ivory, 22 In.	190.00
Umbrella Stand, Green Drip Glaze, Molded Flowers	235.00
Umbrella Stand, Orris, Green, 19 X 10 In.	180.00
Urn, Chengtu, 4 In.	35.00
Urn, Louwelsa, 2 Handles, 2 In.	95.00
Vase, Ardsley, 10 1/2 In.	40.00

Weller, Umbrella Stand, 6 Women,
Lavender Gowns, Floral, 20 In.

If you have to pack or store an oddly shaped antique, a footed bowl, or an unsteady figurine, get a damp polyurethane sponge, preferably the two-layer type with a stiffer bottom layer. Put the piece on the wet sponge. It will make the proper shaped indentation, and when the sponge dries the piece will be held safely in one position.

Vase, Baldin, 5 Fingers, Bud, 10 1/2 In.	48.00
Vase, Bonito, Floral, Signed, 10 In.	125.00
Vase, Bonito, Green, Side Handles, 7 3/4 X 5 In.	48.00
Vase, Bouquet, Brown, White Flowers, Twig Handles, 3–Footed, 7 In. ...	55.00
Vase, Bouquet, Handles, 5 1/2 In.	30.00
Vase, Bouquet, Twig Handles, White Flowers, Brown, 7 1/2 In.	55.00
Vase, Bud, Luxor, 1910	25.00
Vase, Bud, Silvertone, Twisted Body, Pink Matte Interior, 6 3/4 In.	45.00
Vase, Bud, Triple, Roma, 8 1/4 In.	65.00
Vase, Bud, Warwick, 8 1/2 In.	50.00
Vase, Bud, Woodcraft, 10 In. .... 25.00 To 40.00
Vase, Burntwood, 11 3/4 X 5 1/2 In.	115.00
Vase, Burntwood, 3 Wise Men, Museum Papers	475.00
Vase, Burntwood, 6 Sides, Etched Cherry Clusters, 8 1/4 In.	75.00
Vase, Burntwood, Birds, 8 1/2 In. .... 65.00 To 90.00
Vase, Burntwood, Cylinder, 9 3/4 X 4 1/4 In.	95.00
Vase, Cameo, Blue, 6 1/2 In.	15.00
Vase, Cameo, Blue, 14 1/2 In.	52.00
Vase, Cameo, Tan, Footed, 11 1/4 In.	38.00
Vase, Chase, Fan, 4 Holes, Blue, White, 8 In.	140.00
Vase, Chengtu, 8 1/2 In.	20.00
Vase, Clarmont, Looped Handles, 8 In.	75.00
Vase, Claywood, 10 1/4 X 4 1/2 In.	85.00
Vase, Cloudburst, Orange, 10 In.	48.00
Vase, Cloudburst, Yellow, 10 In.	80.00
Vase, Clown, 9 1/2 In.	500.00
Vase, Coppertone, Green, 15 In.	160.00
Vase, Darsie, Ivory, 7 X 6 1/2 In.	26.00
Vase, Dickens Ware, Golfer Design, 9 1/4 In.	550.00
Vase, Dickens Ware, Portrait of Black Girl, White Hat, 5 In.	800.00
Vase, Eocean, Pansies, Gray Ground, 4 X 5 1/2 In.	125.00
Vase, Etna, Cherries, 9 1/2 In.	70.00
Vase, Etna, Pink Florals, Gray, Signed, 8 1/2 In.	45.00
Vase, Etna, Relief Molded Florals On Gray, 8 1/2 In.	95.00
Vase, Evergreen, 3–Footed, Scalloped, 5 In.	18.00
Vase, Evergreen, Footed, Art Deco Shape, 9 X 4 1/2 In.	28.00
Vase, Fan, Florenzo, 5 In.	48.00
Vase, Flemish, 10 In. .... 65.00 To 85.00
Vase, Floral, 4 1/2 In.	10.00
Vase, Floretta, Brown, Art Nouveau, 12 3/4 In.	75.00
Vase, Floretta, Brown, Grapes, 6 In.	60.00
Vase, Forest, 8 In. .... 55.00 To 65.00
Vase, Forest, 10 1/2 In.	135.00
Vase, Frosted Matt, Green, Brown, 9 3/4 X 3 1/2 In.	90.00
Vase, Fruitone, Green, Brown, Shoulder Handles, 4 1/2 In.	27.00
Vase, Glendale, 3 Yellow Chicks On Branch, 9 In.	295.00
Vase, Horse & Rider Jumping Fence, Dog, Blue, 8 In.	125.00
Vase, Hudson Perfecto, Red Poppies, Yellow & Green, Marked, 6 In. ...	125.00
Vase, Hudson, Blue Floral, 7 In.	75.00
Vase, Hudson, Blue, Rose, Pillsbury, 8 X 4 1/2 In.	175.00
Vase, Hudson, Colored Flowers On White, Green Interior, Marked, 4 In. ...	95.00
Vase, Hudson, Dogwood Flowers, 9 1/2 In.	125.00
Vase, Hudson, Floral Design, Cream Colors, Signed, 13 In.	300.00
Vase, Hudson, Jonquils, 9 1/2 In.	165.00
Vase, Hudson, White Tulips, 12 X 6 1/4 In.	180.00
Vase, Ivoris, Cuspidor Shape, Shoulder Handles, 5 3/4 X 3 3/4 In. ...	18.00
Vase, Kenova, Roses In Relief, Green, 8 In.	65.00
Vase, Knifewood, Cylindrical, 7 1/2 In., Pair	85.00
Vase, Knifewood, Swans, 5 In.	65.00
Vase, LaMar, 8 In.	70.00
Vase, LaSa, 8 In.	375.00
Vase, LaSa, Trees, Sun, 11 1/8 In.	200.00
Vase, Louwelsa, 9 1/2 In.	110.00
Vase, Louwelsa, Clematis, High Shoulders, L.McGrath, 15 1/2 In. ...	300.00

Vase, Louwelsa, Floral, Signed Levi Burgess, 12 In. 175.00
Vase, Louwelsa, Poppies, Pinched, 8 In. 129.00
Vase, Louwelsa, Signed Bloomer, 4 1/2 In. 150.00
Vase, Louwelsa, Yellow Jonquil Floral, 15 1/2 In. 325.00
Vase, Luxor, 9 In. 25.00
Vase, Malvern, Shoulder Handles, 7 In. 42.00
Vase, Marvo, Brown, 7 1/2 In. 38.00
Vase, Marvo, Fan, 5 Holes 36.00
Vase, Orris, Flared, Sculptured Flowers, 12 X 7 In. 80.00
Vase, Orris, Leaves, Flowers, Flared, 7 X 4 3/4 In. 43.00
Vase, Paragon, Blue, 5 X 7 In. 105.00
Vase, Parian, 8 1/2 In. 40.00
Vase, Patricia, Duck Handles, 4 In. 42.00
Vase, Pearl, 6 In. 50.00
Vase, Pillow, Louwelsa, St.Bernard Portrait, 7 In. 425.00
Vase, Roma, 2 Bands of Leaves, Flowers, Cylinder, 7 5/8 In. 46.00
Vase, Roma, 3 Vertical Ribs, 9 X 3 In. 50.00
Vase, Rudlor, Green, Footed, Side Handle, 11 In. 30.00
Vase, Sabrinian, 11 In. 90.00
Vase, Scandia, Tan, Black, Straight Sides, 9 In. 53.00
Vase, Sicard, 5 In. .... 225.00 To 325.00
Vase, Sicard, 15 In. 795.00
Vase, Silvertone, Handle, Marked, 6 1/2 In. 63.50
Vase, Silvertone, Molded Floral, 7 1/2 In. 115.00
Vase, Souevo, 4 1/2 In. 65.00
Vase, Voile, Fan, 8 In. 70.00
Vase, Wild Rose, 2 Handles, Peach, 9 3/4 In. 45.00
Vase, Wild Rose, Double, Green, Basket Handle, 6 1/4 X 8 1/2 In. 20.00
Vase, Wild Rose, Peach To Green, 9 3/4 In. 45.00
Vase, Wild Rose, Pink, Tab Handles, Footed, 6 1/2 In. 20.00
Vase, Woodcraft, Plums, 12 In. .... 110.00 To 125.00
Vase, Woodcraft, Tree Trunk, 8 1/2 In. 35.00
Wall Pocket, Ivory, Cosmos Design, 9 1/2 In. 55.00
Wall Pocket, Tutone, 10 1/2 In. 85.00
Wall Pocket, Woodcraft, Owl & Squirrel 350.00
Water Bottle Set, Ollas, Red 45.00

Whieldon was a potter in England who worked alone and with Josiah Wedgwood in eighteenth-century England. Whieldon made many pieces in natural shapes, like cauliflowers or cabbages. The tortoiseshell glazed pieces are known as "clouded ware."

WHIELDON, Coffeepot, Tortoise Glaze, Embossed Leaf, 9 1/2 In. 1300.00
Dish, Leaf Shape, Bird, Trees, 8 In. 800.00
Plate, Tortoise Glaze, Blue, Green, Scalloped Rim, 9 7/8 In. 350.00
Teapot, Cauliflower Design, 4 In. 1200.00
Toby, Brown, Green, 9 1/2 In. 1400.00

Willets Manufacturing Company of Trenton, New Jersey, worked from 1879. The company made belleek in the late 1880s and 1890s in shapes similar to those used by the Irish Belleek factory. They stopped working about 1912. Pieces were marked with a variety of marks, all including the name Willets.

WILLETS, Cup & Saucer, Embossed Veining, Gold Tracery, Demitasse 50.00
Cup & Saucer, Gold, Yellow Flowers 110.00
Hatpin Holder, Violet Flowers, Green 125.00
Pitcher, Nautilus-Shell, Gold Coral Handle, Marked, 8 In. 495.00
Sugar, Cover, Dragon Handles, Enameled Flowers, Pink Mark 75.00
Vase, Hollyhock, Signed, 15 In. 425.00
Vase, Orange, 16 Blackbirds, 11 1/2 In. 295.00
    WILLOW, see Blue Willow

Stained glass and beveled glass windows were popular additions to houses during the late nineteenth and early twentieth centuries. The old windows became popular with collectors in the 1970s; today, old and new examples are seen.

WINDOW, Leaded, Geometric, 2 Slag Glass Strips, Oak Frame, 27 X 16 In., 4 Pc.	450.00
Leaded, Geometric, Slag Triangles, Oak Frame, 47 X 19 In., Pr.	400.00
Leaded, Ice Cream, From Drugstore, 1900s, 19 1/2 X 29 In.	425.00
Leaded, Rectilinear, C.1910, 4 Ft.9 X 21 1/2 In.	4510.00
Stained Glass, Frank Lloyd Wright Design, Squares, 26 X 14 In.	1320.00
Stained Glass, Geometric Field, C.1910, 31 X 9 3/4 In., 4 Panels	5500.00
Stained Glass, Turquoise & Ocher Fans, C.1910, 42 X 12 In., Pair	3300.00

Wood carvings and wooden pieces are listed separately in this book. There are also wooden pieces found in other sections, such as Kitchen.

WOOD CARVING, Bird, Stylized, Brown & Gray, Gold Traces, 7 In.	185.00
Blackamoor, Holding Tray, 1870s	2600.00
Bluejay, Mantel, Oak Leaf & Acorn Base, A.E.Crowell, Life Size	2200.00
Boy, Portuguese, Standing, Left Arm Uplifted, 29 In.	375.00
Bust, Bishop, Lacquer, 17–18th Century, England, 25 In.	650.00
Bust, Woman, Stylized, Hair Drawn Back, American, 6 In.	600.00
Cake Board, Eagle, Flag, Chariot, American, C.1800, 27 1/2 In.	8800.00
Cat, Black Paint, Polychrome Detail, 7 1/2 In.	55.00
Christ, Oval Wreath, Holding Orb With Cross, Oak, 18 In.	550.00
Crow, From Tree Knot, Driftwood Base, 9 1/2 In.	50.00
Dancer, Male & Female, Polychrome, 22 1/2 In., Pair	325.00
Dish, Soap, Lollipop–Shaped Tab Handle, Pine, 18th Century	200.00
Dragon, Polychrome, 6 In.	10.00
Eagle, Painted & Gesso, Wilhelm Schimmel, C.1880, 3 1/2 In.	2750.00
Eagle, Painted Flag, Don't Give Up The Ship, Bellamy–Type	700.00
Eagle, Wings Down, 42 X 30 In.	400.00
Elephant Head, Ivory Tusks, 18 1/2 In.	675.00
Female Dancer, Walnut, J.J.Adnet, France, 13 1/4 In.	2420.00
Frog & Young, Squatting, 2 Young Seated On Back	522.00
Griffin, Removable Wings, European, 36 In.	800.00
Horse, Horsehair Mane & Tail, C.1880, 13 3/4 X 14 3/4 In.	500.00
Indian Club, Inscribed G.T.Lyons, Black & Gold Bands, Pair	495.00
Man, In Swallowtail Coat, Arms To Body, Painted, 12 1/2 In.	1750.00
Man, Standing, Articulated Arms, Overalls, Painted, 1920, 31 In.	2500.00
Mask, Theater, 1 Demon, 1 Human, Japanese, 7 3/4 In., Pair	200.00
Mold, Fish, Handle, Mid–19th Century	120.00
Ornament, Fruit, Side Grapes, 16 X 17 In.	235.00
Owl, Carved & Painted, Leather Feet, 19th Century, 8 1/2 In.	1750.00
Peregrin Falcon, Wall Mount, Full–Bodied, C.1900, 10 1/2 In.	225.00
Plaque, American Eagle, Banner, J.H.Bellamy, 9 1/2 X 24 In.	7700.00
Puffin, 14 In.	105.00
Revolutionary War Soldier, 3–Dimensional, 68 In.	250.00
Shepherd Boy, Lamb, Tree Stumps, Walnut, Continental, 18 In.	550.00
Shoe, Pop–Out Snake, Sliding Lid, Primitive, Black Paint, 3 In.	125.00
Shoes, Ornate, Holland, 1928	79.00
Snake, Glass Eyes, Painted, American, 20th Century, 38 In.	400.00
St.Peter, Standing, White Paint, 61 In.	225.00
Trout, Diving Stance, Waves, Signed Moeller, 1739, 16 X 22 In.	400.00
Umbrella, Holder, Bear, Standing, 41 In.	1600.00
Woman, Hinged Front Skirt, Pornographic, 3 1/2 In.	825.00

Wood was used for many containers and tools used in the early home. Small wooden pieces are called "treenware" in England, but the term "woodenware" is more common in the United States.

WOODEN, see also Kitchen; Advertising; Tool

WOODEN, Berry Box, Cover, Bentwood, 2 1/2 X 6 In.	22.00
Bowl, Ash Burl, 2 1/4 X 6 3/4 In.	300.00
Bowl, Black Grained Exterior, Almond Shape, 12 X 20 1/2 In.	225.00

Bowl, Burl, 19th Century, Oval, 18 1/2 In. 675.00
Bowl, Burl, Cutout Handles, Raised Rim, 14 X 15 X 7 In. 900.00
Bowl, Burl, Grained, Molded Rim, American, 18th Century, 15 1/2 In. 800.00
Bowl, Burl, Handle Extensions, Oval, 14 3/8 X 10 1/2 In. 2750.00
Bowl, Burl, Oval, 3 3/4 X 11 X 9 1/2 In. 140.00
Bowl, Burl, Wild Ash Grain, 5 1/2 X 12 In. 150.00
Bowl, Oblong, 11 1/4 X 22 3/4 In. 85.00
Bowl, Oblong, 13 3/4 X 32 1/2 In. 145.00
Bowl, Red, Black & Gold Design, Russian, 10 1/4 In. 15.00
Bowl, Rounded Corners, Red, Rectangular, 15 1/2 X 22 1/2 In. 135.00
Bowl, Tiger Maple, Incised Lines At Rim, American, 21 1/2 In. 1000.00
Bowl, Turned From 1 Piece of Wood, Green Outside, 20 1/2 In. 115.00
Bowl, Walnut, 36 In. 635.00
Bowl, Wire Braces, Cutout Handles, 15 1/2 X 44 In. 85.00
Bucket, Grease, Conestoga Wagon 65.00
Bucket, Peat, Brass Bands, Liner & Lifting Handle, Mahogany, 13 In. 1300.00
Bucket, Peat, Brass Bands, Liner & Lifting Handle, Mahogany, 21 In. 1200.00
Bucket, Sap, 3 Wooden Hoops, 11 X 11 3/4 In. 33.00
Bucket, Sap, White Paint, 9 1/4 X 11 1/2 In. 16.50
Bucket, Sugar, 4 Wooden Hoops, Finger Lap Joints, Cover, 12 In. 62.00
Bucket, Tar, Connestoga Wagon, Leather Handle, 10 In. 65.00
Charger, Birch, Round Turned, C.1800, 19 1/2 X 20 In. 495.00
Doghouse, Scalloped Shingled Roof, Wire Mesh Door, French, C.1830 .... 2900.00
Dough Bowl, 19th Century, 22 1/2 In. 90.00
Firkin, Brown, Staved, Cover, Wooden Bail, Copper Fasteners, 9 3/4 In. 95.00
Foot Warmer, Wire Bail, Pierced, Square 250.00
Hat Rack, Maple, Folding, 7 Pegs 6.50
Hat Rack, Walnut, Folding, White Porcelain Tips 18.00
Mallet, Burl, Turned Handle, 18th Century, 13 In. 60.00
Measure, Dry, Tin Band Around Top, Date 1894 Stamped, 14 In.Diam. 18.50
Measure, Iron Bands, Old Red Paint, M.S.Baltimore, 10 1/2 In. 175.00
Mortar & Pestle, Tiger Maple, Double Ended Pestle, 7 In. & 9 In. 215.00
Mug, Drinking, Tavern Piece, 1800s, 3 1/2 X 6 In. 140.00
Panel, Dragon & Foliage, Relief Carved, Glass–Eyed Dragon, 78 In. 350.00
Pestle, Oak, Thick Handle, 2 1/2 X 5 1/2 X 13 1/4 In. 6.25
Piggin, Bucket Shape, Used For Butter, Primitive, 4 Piece 180.00
Pipe Holder, Oak Framed, 2 Monks, 16 X 20 In. 140.00
Rack, Fruit Drying, Wall, Amish 275.00
Scoop, Cranberry, Galvanized Bottom, G.N.Sampson's Shop, 21 In. 105.00
Scoop, Cranberry, Steel Teeth, Pine & Plywood, 11 X 19 In. 45.00
Smoothing Board, Chip–Carved Designs, Horse Handle 1050.00
Smoothing Board, Chip–Carved Pinwheels, Stars, Date 1803, 26 In. 250.00
Spoon, Child's, Curved Handle, With Hook 220.00
Stand, Betty Lamp, Stool Shape, Oak, Varnish Finish, 7 1/8 In. 175.00
Stirrer, Apple Butter, Handle, 3 In. 23.50
Tray, Knife, Cherry, Slant, 2 Sections, Carrying Handle, 8 X 13 In. 65.00
Tray, Knife, Slant Sides, Center Handle, C.1840, 7 1/2 X 13 1/2 In. 150.00
Tub, Stave Construction, 2 Staves Rim Handles, Dark Finish, 16 In. 60.00
Wall Pocket, Walnut, Openwork Back, 8 X 4 1/2 In. 14.50
Wheelbarrow, Iron Wheel, Gray Paint 110.00

 Worcester porcelains were made in Worcester, England, from 1751. The firm went through many name changes and eventually, in 1862, became The Royal Worcester Porcelain Company Ltd. Collectors often refer to Dr. Wall, Barr, Flight, and other names that indicate time periods and artists at the factory. It became part of Royal Worcester Spode Ltd. in 1976.

WORCESTER, see also Royal Worcester
WORCESTER, Basket, Chestnut, Reticulated Cover & Stand, 1770–75, 10 1/8 In. 1100.00
Basket, Chestnut, Reticulated Cover, C.1775, 11 In. 2090.00
Beaker, Mythological, Zeus Drinking, C.1800, 3 3/8 In. 1320.00
Beaker, Topographical, Gilt–Edged Panel, C.1800, 3 5/8 In. 1430.00
Bowl, Jabberwocky, Flowering Shrubs, C.1775, 7 3/8 In. 660.00
Bowl, Old Japan Fan, Gilt Floral, 1768–72, 8 1/8 In. 1870.00

Worcester, Jug, Milk, 2 Quail, Pear Shape, 3 7/8 In.

Teabowls & Saucers, Eloping Bride & Arcade
Patterns

Worcester, Cup, Imari Pattern, Red, Orange, 2 1/2 In.

Bowl, Red Bull, Chinese Cowherd, Maiden, C.1758, 4 1/4 In.	550.00
Bowl, Waste, Gilt–Edged Rim, Gilt Scrollwork, C.1770, 6 1/2 In.	550.00
Bowl, Waste, Hop Sprays, C.1775, 6 11/16 In.	1200.00
Bowl, Waste, Royal Marriage, C.1772, 6 9/16 In.	665.00
Butter Tub, Pavilion, Stylized Clouds, C.1770, 4 1/2 In.	825.00
Creamer, Cream Boat Sprays, Hexagonal, 1757–60, 4 1/8 In.	715.00
Creamer, Molded Palmette On Spout, Painted Cartouche, C.1758	2420.00
Cup & Saucer, Bird Cartouches, Panels of Insects, 1770, 5 1/4 In.	445.00
Cup & Saucer, Blue & White, Demitasse	110.00
Cup & Saucer, Claret & Turquoise Striped, Fluted, C.1774	2200.00
Cup & Saucer, Feuille De Choux, C.1770, 5 3/8 In.	550.00
Cup & Saucer, Garlands of Peaches, Red Berries, Leaves, C.1770	1450.00
Cup & Saucer, Gilt Scroll Rim, Blue, 1770–75	495.00
Cup & Saucer, Hop Trellis Pattern, C.1770, 5 1/4 In.	660.00
Cup & Saucer, Jabberwocky, C.1770, 2 1/8 In.	445.00
Cup, Imari Pattern, Red, Orange, 2 1/2 In. ....*Illus*	60.00
Dish, Brocade Pattern, Lozenge Shape, 1772–75, 10 7/8 In.	1450.00
Dish, Hop Swags, Gilt C–Scrolls, C.1775, 9 1/4 In.	1450.00
Dish, Junket, Basketwork Center, Floral Garlands, C.1765, 9 In.	6875.00
Dish, Leaf Shape, Bouquet, C.1770, 13 3/4 In., Pair	1210.00
Dish, Old Japan Fan, Lozenge Shape, 1768–72, 9 1/4 In.	1320.00
Dish, Rose Plums & Green Leaves Center, C.1775, 8 1/2 In.	2090.00
Dish, Sprays & Sprigs of Flowers, Scalloped, C.1770, 7 7/8 In.	1200.00
Dish, Sweetmeat, Blind Earl, Gilt–Edged Rim, C.1770, 6 1/4 In.	1650.00
Dish, Sweetmeat, Blind Earl, Twig Handle, C.1765, 6 3/16 In.	1650.00
Dish, Sweetmeat, Parrot, C.1768, 6 7/16 In.	990.00
Dish, Sweetmeat, Queen Charlotte, C.1770, 6 1/8 In.	1550.00
Dish, Valentine, Lettuce Leaf, C.1760, 10 3/8 In.	1650.00
Jug, Cabbage Leaf Mold, Ribbon–Tied Bouquets, C.1775, 11 3/4 In.	600.00
Jug, Milk, 2 Quail, Pear Shape, 3 7/8 In. ....*Illus*	1650.00
Jug, Monk, Pear Shape, 3 Orange Panels, C.1775, 4 1/4 In.	450.00
Mug, Gardener, Handle, Chinese Figures, 1765, 4 7/8 In.	385.00
Mug, Topographical, River View of Worcester, C.1805, 3 1/8 In.	900.00
Pitcher, Flying Butterflies & Bees, C.1880, 13 1/2 In.	725.00
Plate, Blind Earl, Green Twig, 2 Green Rosebuds, 1765, 7 5/8 In.	2200.00
Plate, Blind Earl, Molded Twig In Brown, 1765–70, 7 5/8 In.	1320.00
Plate, Blue & Gold Central Flowerhead, C.1775, 8 5/16 In.	1200.00
Plate, Blue Center, Floral Spray, Gold Garlands, 1775, 9 In.	1045.00
Plate, Design On Outside, Central Scene, Woman, Walking, 8 1/4 In.	2300.00
Plate, Exotic Birds, River Landscape, 1770–72, 8 3/8 In.	550.00
Plate, Floral Center, Shell Feet, Reticulated Edge, 10 1/2 In.	750.00
Plate, Hop Swags Pendant From Gilt C–Scrolls, C.1775, 8 1/2 In.	3200.00

Plate, Kakiemon, 3 Panels, 1770–75, 7 11/16 In., Pair 1650.00
Plate, Painted Center Cluster of Hops, S–Scolls Rim, 7 1/2 In. 775.00
Plate, Quail, Octagonal, C.1765, 8 9/16 In. 1210.00
Plate, Reticulated Rim, Floral Center, Grainger, 10 1/2 In. 750.00
Plate, Sir Joshua Reynolds' Pattern, C.1770, 8 7/8 In. 1760.00
Sauceboat, Basket Mold, Molded Cartouche, 1760–65, 8 1/8 In. 600.00
Sauceboat, Leaf Mold, Curled Stem Handle, 1758–62, 7 1/4 In. 1100.00
Sauceboat, Sinking Boat, Fisherman, C.1754, 5 7/8 In. 4125.00
Sauceboat, Strap Flute, Floral Sprays, C.1760, 5 In. 715.00
Sugar & Creamer, Open, Relief Design, White & Gold, C.1810 .... 110.00
Teabowl & Saucer, Arcade Pattern, 1762–68, 2 1/2 In. ....*Illus* 1760.00
Teabowl & Saucer, Eloping Bride, 1762–68, 2 1/2 In. ....*Illus* 3025.00
Teabowl & Saucer, Floral Garlands, Foliate Sprigs, C.1770 .... 1200.00
Teapot, Old Japan Fan Pattern, Sprig Knop, 1768–92, 6 1/4 In. 1750.00
Tray, Spoon, Fluted, Center Reserve, Gilt Scalloped Rim, 6 In. 605.00
Tray, Spoon, Interior Molded Flowering Vine, C.1765, 6 3/16 In. 1200.00
Tray, Spoon, Jabberwocky, Hexagonal, C.1770, 6 1/8 In. 1450.00
Tureen, Sauce, Cover, Whorl Panels, Ring Handles, BFB, C.1810 .... 770.00
Urn, Insect Design, Gilt, Fenestrated, Handles, Grainger, 12 In. 445.00
Urn, Topographical, Beadwork Band, Marked BFB, C.1810, 5 In. 1875.00
Vase, Dragonflies, Yellow Iris, 9 1/2 In. 295.00
Vase, Panel Painted In Kakiemon Palette, C.1770, 7 1/4 In. 550.00
Vase, Yellow Iris & Dragonflies, 9 In. 275.00
Wall Pocket, Cornucopia Daisy, C.1760, 11 3/4 In., Pair 2200.00

Souvenirs of World War I and World War II are collected today. Be careful not to store anything that includes live ammunition. Your local police station will tell you how to dispose of the explosives.

WORLD WAR I, Badge, Observer, Germany 425.00
Badge, Pilot, Bavarian 395.00
Badge, Pilot, Germany 375.00
Bayonet, Ersatz Kaiser, Metal Sheath 35.00
Bayonet, German, Solingen 65.00
Box, Naval Officer's, With Hat & Epaulettes, Metal, 18 X 8 In. 250.00
Bugle, Brass 47.00
Button, Liberty Bond, Statue of Liberty, 1918, 5/8 In. 3.00
Button, Liberty V Loan, Blue & White, Celluloid, 5/8 In. 5.00
Card, Liggett & Myers Tobacco, Doughboys Overseas, 6 X 3 In. 7.50
Card, Playing, Victory World War I, Statue of Liberty, 1917, Box 48.00
Compass 35.00
Dallas Wings, Silver With Gold, United States 1200.00
Handkerchief, Silk, With World Leaders 9.00
Hat, Field, Domed, Wool, Swedish 16.00
Helmet, Air Force, Leather 30.00
Knife, Trench, Field Made, Brass Guard, 6 3/4-In. Blade 42.50
Knife, Trench, Leather Sheath 20.00
Leggings, Brass Eyes & Hooks 10.00
Menu, Armistice Day, Poe & Heros, Hotel Oakland, Ca., 1929, 7 In. 5.00
Postcard Set, Photograph, 43 Different Scenes 75.00
Poster, 4 Marines, Flag Bearers, Riflemen, Island, 40 X 30 In. 200.00
Poster, Every Fighter, A Woman Worker, 40 X 28 In. 90.00
Poster, Gee I Wish I Were A Man I'd Join The Navy, 40 X 28 In 90.00
Poster, Hey Fellows, Your Money Brings The Book We Need 125.00
Poster, Hip Hip Another Ship–Another Victory, Framed, 61 In. 300.00
Poster, His Home Over There, 40 X 28 In. 75.00
Poster, Liberty Loan, Submarine & Naval Ship, L.A. Shafer 75.00
Poster, Sure We'll Finish The Job, G. Beneker, 40 X 26 In. 65.00
Poster, Tell That To The Marines, Flagg, 1918, 49 X 30 In. 200.00
Poster, The Navy Is Calling Enlist Now, L. Button, 40 X 28 In. 85.00
Poster, They Said We Couldn't Fight, 41 X 30 In. 65.00
Poster, U.S. Marines–Soldiers, Leyendecker, 1918, 40 X 30 In. 250.00
Songbook, Navy, 1919 .... 7.00
Stereo Card, Army Calisthenics 12.00
Stereo Card, Over The Top, Troops Charge Out of Trenches 12.00

Sword, NCO, Brass Hilt, Wire Sharkskin Grip, Monogram, Germany 145.00
Toy, Naval Warship, Wooden, Japan, 25 Piece 119.00
Vase, Shell Art, Argonne, 1918, Brass 60.00
Water Bucket, Canvas, Collapsible 20.00
WORLD WAR II, Arm Band, Civilian Defense 5.00
Arm Band, Military Police 6.00
Arm Band, Swastika 30.00
Army Overcoat 70.00
Ashtray, Child Urinating On Swastika, Brass 20.00
Banner, Large Star, Says Over There 5.00
Bayonet, Scabbard, Nazi Dress, 8–In. Blade, Diced Grip Hilt 35.00
Belt, Canteen, Pocket, Army, 1944 .... 10.00
Bombadier Wings, Sterling Silver 35.00
Book, Air Transport At War, Harper & Bros., 1946 .... 8.00
Broadside, Instructions, Japanese Ancestry, San Fran., 22 In. 605.00
Card, Playing, Plane Spotters II, Silhouettes, USPCC, 1942, Box 67.00
Card, We Are Proud To Be Americans, 3 1/2 X 3 1/2 In. 3.50
Dagger, Dress, Luftwaffe Officer, No.1 .... 225.00
Dagger, Dress, Luftwaffe Officer, No.2 .... 125.00
Dagger, Hitler Youth 30.00
Dagger, Nazi, Eagle & Swastika 215.00
Flag, Battle, Nazi, Iron Cross In Corner, 3 X 5 Ft. 100.00
Game, Shooting Marble, You're In The Army Now, 1942 .... 45.00
Helmet, German, M–35, Decal 88.00
Helmet, Japanese, With Net 95.00
Helmet, Knapsack Kit, Civil Defense, 1940s 20.00
ID Badge, Factory 6.00
Jacket, Ike 85.00
Knife, Nazi 150.00
Letter Poster, MacArthur Photos, 11 X 14 In. 3.00
Map, Issued By War Dept., Wall, 6 Piece 50.00
Maptalk, Military Publication, 1945, 12 Issues 20.00
Mitts, Leather 40.00
Pants, Bomber, Leather, Fleece 85.00
Photograph, Adolph Hitler, Polish Campaign, October, 1939 .... 5.00
Pigeon Timer, With Swastika, Germany 45.00
Pin, Hitler, Mechanical, Let's Pull Together 30.00
Pin, Kilroy Was Here, Pictoral, 1943 .... 15.00
Pin, Relief Fund, Multicolor, Austro–Hungarian, 1 1/4 In. 8.00
Pin, To Hell With Hitler, Celluloid, Yellow, Blue, 1 1/2 In. 10.00
Pin, Uncle Sam, I Am Proud He Is My Uncle, 1940, 1 1/4 In. 12.00
Pincushion, Hitler, Plaster, 1941, 5 In. 85.00
Plate, Luftwaffe Presentation, Swastika, Meissen, 8 In. 265.00
Postcard, Nazi Emblem, Photos, Wine Festival, Speyer, 45 Cards 40.00
Postcard, SS, Views, Unused, 7 Piece 10.00
Postcard, Queen Elizabeth Ship, Troop Carrier, Unused 3.00
Poster, Be A U.S. Marine, Recruiting, 49 X 29 In. 295.00
Poster, Beast of Budapest, Movie, Nazi Soldier Beating Girl 25.00
Poster, Care Is Costly, Buy War Bonds & Stamps 75.00
Poster, Marine Recruiting, Join U.S. Marines 80.00
Poster, Marines, On Beach, Browning Machine Gun, 49 X 30 In. 244.00
Poster, Nazi Propaganda, 1940–44, 9 1/2 X 14 In., 12 Piece 212.00
Poster, O.P.A., Ration Free–Children's Shoes, 28 X 11 In. 20.00
Poster, Save Freedom, Speech, War Bonds, Rockwell, 20 X 24 In. 42.50
Poster, Soldier's Life, Tom Woodburn, 38 X 25 In. 125.00
Poster, U.S. Marines Active Service, Land & Sea, 40 X 28 In. 85.00
Ration Book, No.1 .... 3.50
Razor Kit, Made For Armed Forces 10.00
Sextant, Air Force, Case 85.00
Shovel, Foxhole 8.00
Stationery, V–Mail, Red, White & Blue, Unused 3.00
Sticker, 5th War Loan, 1 In. Diam. 3.00
Sticker, Shield Shape, Victory & Good Business, Red, White 5.00
Sword, Nazi, Brass, Bronze Hilt, Wire Grip, 29 1/2–In. Blade 115.00

Sword, United States Officer .... 325.00 To 375.00
Telephone, Field 30.00
Token, Ration, Celluloid Container, Marked OPA, 32 Piece 7.50
Toy, Adolf Hitler, Hand Carved Wood 125.00
Tunic, Flight, Luftwaffe 200.00
Valentine, Paper Doll Design W.A.A.C., 1943, 5 X 5 1/4 In. 17.50
Valentine, Smiling G.I., Mechanical, Walk A Million Miles 5.00

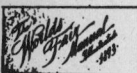

Souvenirs of all world's fairs are collected. The first fair was the Great Exhibition of 1851 in London. Other important exhibitions and fairs include Philadelphia, 1876 (Centennial); Chicago, 1893 (World's Columbian); Buffalo, 1901 (Pan–American); St. Louis, 1904 (Louisiana Purchase); San Francisco, 1915 (Panama–Pacific); Philadelphia, 1926 (Sesquicentennial); Chicago, 1933 (Century of Progress); Cleveland, 1936 (Great Lakes); San Francisco, 1939 (Golden Gate International); New York, 1939 (World of Tomorrow); Seattle, 1962 (Century 21); New York, 1964 (World's Fair); Montreal, 1967 (Man and His World); and Knoxville, 1982 (Energy Expo). Memorabilia of fairs include directories, pictures, fabrics, ceramics, etc.

WORLD'S FAIR, Ashtray, 1933, Chrysler 12.00
Ashtray, 1933, Enamel & Porcelain 20.00
Ashtray, 1939, Brass, New York 18.00
Ashtray, 1939, Logo In Center, Brass, 3 1/4 In. 20.00
Ashtray, 1939, New York, Bakelite 7.00
Bank, 1940, Underwood Typewriter, Figural 40.00
Blotter, 1939, New York, Hotel Martinique, Unused 28.00
Blotter, 1939, New York, Hotel Martinique 28.00
Book, 1893, Columbian Gallery of Photographs 35.00
Book, 1893, Piano Music Collection, Oliver Ditson Co., 145 Pg. 10.00
Book, 1962, Official Guide, Illustrations, 192 Pages 8.00
Booklet, 1939, New York 18.00
Booklet, 1939, New York World's Fair Views 20.00
Booklet, 1939, New York, Borden's, Elsie 18.00
Bowl, 1939, Logo In Center, Paden City Pottery, 10 In. 50.00
Box, 1939, New York, Green, Logo, Lenox, 5 X 3 1/2 In. 278.00
Cake Plate, 1904, St.Louis, U.S.Government Building, 9 1/2 In. 40.00
Calendar, 1962, Seattle, Northern Pacific R.R. 20.00
Cane & Folding Seat, 1939, New York, Decal, Wooden 45.00
Cap, 1939, Garrison–Style, New York, Logo 38.00
Card, Trade, 1893, Chicago, King's Dining & Lunch Room 7.50
Cards, Playing, 1933, Chicago, Century of Progress, Box 29.00
Charm, 1939, Swiss Premium Ham, Ham Shape, Plastic, Hook, 1 In. 4.50
Cigarette Case, 1933, Metal 20.00
Clip, 1964, Ford Building, New York, Glows In Dark, Plastic 5.00
Coaster Set, 1964, New York, Unisphere, Graniteware, 4 Piece 13.00
Coffeepot, 1939, Drip, Porcelier China 120.00
Coin, 1939, Chrysler, Brass, Commemorative, 1924 Model, 1 In. 139.00
Cup, 1904, Enameled 95.00
Cup, 1904, St. Louis, Enameled 60.00
Fan, 1904, Gold Dust Twins, St. Louis 100.00
Flyer, 1933, Century of Progress, United Airlines, 10 X 6 In. 18.00
Frisbee, 1982 .... 5.00
Guide, 1939, Official 10.00
Handkerchief, 1876, Centennial Exhibition, Philadelphia 275.00
Handkerchief, 1904, Multicolored 20.00
Hatchet, 1893, Columbian, George Washington & Legend, Glass 20.00
Ice Bucket, 1939, Glass 50.00
Jacket, Police, 1939, Orange & Blue Piping, Gold Buttons 95.00
Jewelry Box, 1893, View of Fair On Cover, Columbian, 7 X 4 In. 45.00
Lamp, Oil, 1893, Chicago, Milk Glass 185.00
Letter Opener, 1939 .... 15.00
Letter, 1904, To Traveling U.S.Men, Pres.Louisiana Purc.Expo. 35.00
Lighter, Cigarette, 1939, Fireball, Chase Brass Co. 80.00

Locket, 1939, New York, Logo, Metal 36.00
Mirror, 1904, St. Louis, Missouri State Building, Pocket 35.00
Mirror, 1933, Buildings 20.00
Money Clip, 1904, St. Louis, Bronze, Embossed Eagle, Tiffany 65.00
Needle Book, 1939 .... 7.00
Newspaper, 1939, N.Y. Herald Tribune, April 30, Fair Edition 16.00
Paper Doll, 1964, New York, Book, Uncut 20.00
Paperweight, 1904, Cascades, St. Louis 15.00
Pencil Sharpener, 1939, New York, Bakelite, Red, Yellow, 4 In. 32.00
Pencil, 1939, Westinghouse, 4 In. 2.50
Pennant, 1933, Chicago, Felt 9.00
Pin, 1933, Chicago, Reliance Shirt Co., 1 In. 15.00
Pin, 1939, Heinz, Green Pickles 4.00
Pin, 1939, New York, Logo, Original Card 34.00
Pin, 1939, New York, Orange, Blue & Orange Ribbon, 1 1/4 In. 20.00
Pin, Zepplin, 1933, Chicago, Tag 20.00
Pitcher, 1964, George Washington 15.00
Plate, 1893, Chicago, Machinery Hall, Satin Glass, White, 11 In. 350.00
Plate, 1904, St. Louis, Glass, Lattice Edge 15.00
Plate, 1933, Pewter, Box 18.00
Plate, 1939, Potters, New York, Turquoise 45.00
Plate, 1939, Swedish Pavilion, New York, Painted Girl, 7 In. 45.00
Pocket Knife, 1933, Chicago 18.00
Postcard, 1904, St. Louis, Administration Bldg., Hold To Light 20.00
Postcard, 1933, 3 Railroads, Century of Progress, 10 Cards 12.40
Postcard, 1933, Chicago, Souvenir Packet 20.00
Postcard, 1964, New York City 10.00
Poster Stamp Set, 1939, New York, 18 Piece 10.00
Program, 1964, Dick Button's Ice–Travaganza, New York 7.00
Purse, Evening, 1937, Tapestry, Administration Building 48.00
Quilt, 1893, Crazy, Chicago, Insert Dated 1893, 64 X 56 In. 190.00
Saltshaker, 1933, Chicago, Metal, 4 3/4 In. 12.00
Saltshaker, 1933, Chicago, Travel Bldg., Carillon Tower, Metal 20.00
Sharpener, Pencil, 1939, New York, Bakelite, Red, Yellow, 4 In. 32.00
Sheet Music, 1939, Yours For A Song 15.00
Spoon, 1893, Columbian Expo, Sterling Silver 22.50
Spoon, 1901, Pan–Am Expo, Sterling Silver 15.00
Spoon, 1904, St. Louis, Sterling Silver 14.00
Spoon, 1915, Pan–Pacific, Silver Plated 15.00
Spoon, 1933, Chicago, Silver Plate 45.00
Spoon, 1933, Sterling Silver 12.00
Spoon, 1939, New York, Textile Building, Silver Plate 14.00
Spoon, Pacific Exposition, Sterling, Calif., Perfume Co. 70.00
St. Louis, 1904, Plate, Open Edge, Glass, 7 1/4 In. 35.00
Stereo Card, 1904, St. Louis, Gondolas On Basin, Festival Hall 15.00
Sugar & Creamer, 1933, Art Institute & Chicago Court House 150.00
Thermometer, 1939, New York, Composition, Scene 45.00
Token, 1904, St. Louis, Brass, Majestic Ranges, 1 1/4 In. 6.00
Toothpick, 1893, Scalloped, Red 45.00
Toothpick, 1904, St. Louis, Milk Glass, Red Lettering, 2 In. 30.00
Toy, 1939, Bus, Greyhound, Cast Iron, Arcade 200.00
Toy, 1964, Mechanical Ferris Wheel, Tire Shape, New York 65.00
Tray, 1964, New York, Unisphere, 12 In. Diam. 10.00
Tray, 1967, Montreal Expo, Smoke Glass, Gold, White, Expo Scene 5.00
Tumbler, 1893, Columbian, Etched Glass 23.00
Tumbler, 1904, Machinery Hall, Etched 18.00
Tumbler, 1964, New York, Unisphere 3.00
Umbrella, 1933 .... 20.00 To 40.00
Watch Fob, 1893 .... 20.00
Watch Fob, 1939 .... 22.00

 Yellowware is a heavy earthenware made of a yellowish clay. It varies in color from light yellow to orange–yellow. Many nineteenth– and twentieth–century kitchen bowls and jugs were

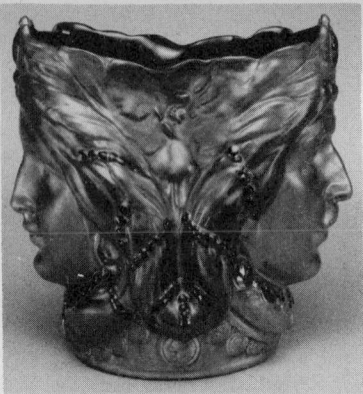

Yellowware, Trinket Box, Sleeping Baby Cover,   Zsolnay, Vase, King & Queen, Double Face,
C. 1830, 4 In.   1900, 19 3/4 In.

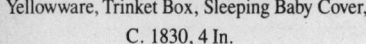

made of yellowware. It was made in England and in the United States. Another form of pottery that is sometimes classed as yellowware is listed in this book under Mocha.

YELLOWWARE, Bank, Piggy, Brown Sponging	145.00
Bedpan	20.00
Bottle, Pig Form, Brown Sponged Glaze, 4 5/8 In.	70.00
Bottle, Pig, Brown Sponging, 8 In.	275.00
Bowl, 5 Brown Bands, 9 In.	55.00
Bowl, Blue Band, 11 In.	35.00
Bowl, Blue Bands, White Pin Stripes, 4 3/4 In.	36.00
Bowl, Blue Sponging, 9 In.	60.00
Bowl, Brown Stripes, 12 In.	35.00
Bowl, Brown Stripes, Blue Seaweed, Cover, E. Liverpool, 9 1/2 In.	575.00
Bowl, England, Top Rim, C.1910, 8 In.	45.00
Bowl, Medorlia Potteries, Medicine Hat, Canada, C.1910, 9 In.	35.00
Bowl, Mixing, 3 Blue Bands, 7 In.	44.00
Bowl, Mixing, Beige, Brown & White Stripes, 9 In.	14.00
Bowl, Mixing, Beige, Brown & White Stripes, 11 3/4 In.	20.00
Bowl, Mixing, Beige, White & Aqua Stripes, Gold–N–Bake, 12 In.	25.00
Bowl, Mixing, Embossed Sides, England, 1920, 10 In.	65.00
Bowl, Mixing, Pink & Blue Stripes, McCoy, 14 X 6 1/2 In.	35.00
Bowl, Newhall, Iowa, Embossed Fruit, 9 In.	35.00
Bowl, Slip Design, American, 1880, 7 In.	135.00
Bowl, Spinach Leaves, Green Rim, 5 In.	28.00
Bowl, Tan & Blue Bands, 9 In.	55.00
Bowl, Weller, 9 In.	30.00
Bowl, White Band, 5 3/4 X 13 1/2 In.	45.00
Box, Trinket, Sleeping Baby Cover, C.1830, 4 In.	45.00
Chamber Pot, Child's	68.00
Chamber Pot, Handle, White Band	37.00
Chamber Pot, White Band, Brown Stripes, Miniature	85.00
Collander, Embossed Leaf, White Interior Glaze, Hole, 9 X 5 In.	250.00
Cookie Jar, 2 Handles, Cover, 9 1/2 In.	65.00
Cookie Jar, Cover, Rope Handles	45.00
Crock, Sailboats In Relief, 14 X 10 In.	150.00
Crock, White Center Band, Word Butter, 4 1/2 X 6 1/2 In.	110.00
Cup, Applied Handle, 5 X 9 In.	50.00
Cup, Stirrup, Dog's Head, Brown Glaze, 4 1/4 In.	185.00
Custard Cup, 3 1/2 X 2 1/2 In.	30.00
Figurine, Cat, 4 In.	39.00
Figurine, Dog, Blue Glaze, 9 1/2 In.	160.00

Figurine, Dog, Seated, Blue Mottled Glaze, Ohio, 10 1/4 In. 1150.00
Figurine, Lion, Dark Blue Mottled Glaze, Ohio, 9 3/4 In. 825.00
Flowerpot, Attached Saucer, Blue Sponge Spatter, 8 In. 150.00
Mold, Corn Pudding 45.00
Mold, Food, Rabbit Inside, 4 1/2 X 6 In. 65.00
Mold, Parrot & Basket of Fruit 425.00
Mold, Rabbit 95.00
Mug, Blue Bands, Buckeye 55.00
Mug, Blue Bands, Marked 45.00
Mug, Cobalt Blue Stripes 25.00
Nested Bowls, Storybook, Graduated, Set of 3 .... 145.00
Paperweight, Woman, Hat, Glaze, 4 In. 90.00
Pie Plate, Rockingham Glaze 395.00
Pitcher, Advertising, Spencer Cement Blocks, 5 In. 25.00
Pitcher, Embossed Hunt Scene, Miss Miria Handy, Mass., 9 In. 65.00
Pitcher, Flower Pattern 30.00
Pitcher, Hahn's Advertising 110.00
Rolling Pin, Wooden Handles, 3 X 8 In. 250.00
Salt, Hinged Lid, Hanging 37.50
Salt, White Band, Blue Seaweed Design, 2 1/4 In. 125.00
Spittoon, Brown Sponging 90.00
Trinket Box, Sleeping Baby Cover, c. 1830, 4 In. ....*Illus* 45.00
Vase, Embossed Foliage, White Glaze, Blue Stripes, 7 3/4 In. 125.00

ZANE WARE Zane Pottery was founded in 1921 by Adam Reed and Harry McClelland in South Zanesville, Ohio, at the old Peters and Reed Building. Zane pottery is very similar to Peters and Reed pottery, but it is usually marked. The factory was sold in 1941 to Lawton Gonder.

ZANE, Bowl, Bulb, Blue Mottled, Flat, 8 X 2 1/2 In. 22.00
Flower Frog, Tortoiseshell Color, 8 Hole 10.00
Tankard Set, Lomora, Matte, 7 Piece 250.00

LA MORO The Zanesville Art Pottery was founded in 1900 by David Schmidt in Zanesville, Ohio. The firm made faience umbrella stands, jardinieres, and pedestals. The company closed in 1962. Many pieces are marked with just the words "La Moro."

ZANESVILLE, Ashtray, Bird, Perched, Yellow, Green, Small 4.00
Pitcher, Sgrafito, Albany Slip Glaze 190.00

Zsolnay pottery was made in Hungary after 1862 and was characterized by Persian, Art Nouveau, or Hungarian motifs. A series of new Zsolnay figurines with green–gold luster finish is available in many shops today. Early Zsolnay was not marked; but by 1878, the tower trademark was used.

ZSOLNAY, Dish, Pink & Gold Flowers, Reticulated Side Borders, 8 1/2 In. 160.00
Figurine, Dog, Sitting, Green, Gold Iridescent, 4 3/4 In. 65.00
Figurine, Frog, Green Gold 35.00
Figurine, Puli, Hungarian Sheep Dog, 4 1/4 X 5 1/4 In. 95.00
Group, Mother, Child On Knee, Cubistically Modeled, 1922, 8 1/2 In. 2750.00
Jug, Gilded, 7 1/4 In. 95.00
Pitcher, Duck, Double Wall 165.00
Plate, Center Flowers, Reticulated Border, Gold Trim, 12 In. 220.00
Tray, Footed, Faience Pottery, Round, 13 X 1 5/8 In. 143.00
Vase, Art Pottery, Purple, 4 Pierced Sides & Griffin Handles, 5 In. 90.00
Vase, Beading On Arabesque Design, Gold Mark, 8 In. 160.00
Vase, Figural, Coiled Cobra, Head Forms Handle, C.1920, 9 In. 3575.00
Vase, Flowers & Leaves, 2 Upright Handles, Claw Feet, 9 1/4 In. 495.00
Vase, Grecian Figures, Iridescent Green, Gold Trim, Marked, 6 In. 175.00
Vase, King & Queen, Double Face, 1900, 19 3/4 In. ....*Illus* 3850.00
Vase, River Scene, Village In Background, Marked, C.1920, 12 1/4 In. 6600.00

THE KOVELS' LIBRARY

Kovels' 365 Collectibles Calendar 1990

America's collecting passion! From Arts & Crafts to Art Moderne, Majolica to memorabilia, cookie jars, penny banks, and Pez. A new-old treasure is pictured everyday in a Page-A-Day™ calendar with all the right pieces.

Available wherever calendars are sold.

Workman Publishing
708 Broadway
New York, New York 10003

Page-A-Day is a trademark of Workman Publishing.

American Country Furniture 1780–1875

Over 700 close-up photographs identify styles, construction, woods, finishes, hardware, and other details. All the information you need to be an expert on American country furniture. Special sections on Pennsylvania, Shaker furniture, spool furniture and furniture construction, plus an illustrated glossary of accessories and terms.
54668X $14.95 paper

Dictionary of Marks—Pottery and Porcelain (1580–1880)

A classic in the field, the *Dictionary of Marks* is a comprehensive guide to more than 5,000 American and European pottery and porcelain marks. It shows at a glance the geographical location of the factory, family name or manufacturer's name, type of ware, color of mark, and the date the mark was used.

001411 $10.95 hardcover

Kovels' New Dictionary of Marks—Pottery and Porcelain
1850 TO THE PRESENT

Kovels' New Dictionary of Marks provides the quickest and easiest way to identify more than 3,500 American, European, and Oriental marks. The perfect companion to the Kovels' original best seller, *The Dictionary of Marks—Pottery and Porcelain,* this is the most comprehensive reference for nineteenth- and twentieth-century marks. Together, the two volumes are an indispensable guide to the porcelain and pottery marks of the last four centuries.

559145 $17.95 hardcover

Kovels' Advertising Collectibles Price List
FIRST EDITION

Over 6,000 prices for advertising signs, labels, premium giveaways, wrappers, stickers, bookmarks, trade cards, lithographed tins, fans, bottle tops, T-shirts, paper bags, toys, trays, and much more. Over 300 illustrations in color and black and white. This is a comprehensive index with extensive cross-references. Includes hundreds of trademarks, logos, and fascinating histories of manufacturers.
558718 $11.95 paper

Kovels' American Silver Marks

Almost everyone owns an old piece of silver. Few know the complete history of that piece. This is a simple-to-use guide to identifying marks and monograms that appear on silver. Collectors and professional dealers can quickly determine the maker of a piece of silver. Each listing includes working dates, location, mark (if known), and bibliographic references to more than 200 books and articles. Makers working from 1650 to the present are included, and over 10,000 silversmiths are listed in alphabetical order, with a cross-indexing system for monograms and pictorial marks.
568829 $40.00 hardcover

Kovels' Bottles Price List
EIGHTH EDITION

Over 10,000 current prices for hundreds of types of bottles — more than any other bottle price list on the market. More than 500 illustrations in full color and black and white. Includes old and new bottles, bitters, figurals, flasks, Avons, Beams, and a host of others. Notes on styles and manufacturers, lists of bottle magazines and clubs, and an extensive bibliography. The most definitive listing of current prices available.
566133 $12.95 paper

Kovels' Depression Glass & American Dinnerware Price List
THIRD EDITION

The inexpensive pastel-colored glassware that became popular from 1925 on and the ceramic dinnerware produced during the same period are now attracting collectors in great numbers. Here are the latest and most accurate prices, based on a comprehensive survey of actual sales, shows, catalogs, auctions, and other reliable sources.
568659 $12.95 paper